Black Writers

Black Writers

A Selection of Sketches from *Contemporary Authors*

Contains more than four hundred entries on twentieth-century black writers, all updated or originally written for this volume.

Linda Metzger
Senior Editor

Hal May
Deborah A. Straub
Susan M. Trosky
Editors

Gale Research Inc. · DETROIT · LONDON

The paper used in this publication meets the minimum requirements
of American National Standard for Information Sciences—Permanence
Paper for Printed Library Materials, ANSI Z39.48-1984.

Copyright © 1989
Gale Research Inc.
835 Penobscot Bldg.
Detroit, MI 48226-4094

Library of Congress Catalog Card Number 89-114835
ISBN 0-8103-2772-4

Published simultaneously in the United Kingdom
by Gale Research International Limited
(An affiliated company of Gale Research Inc.)

Contents

Introduction xxiii

Peter Abrahams 1919-
A South African-born writer of mixed black and white descent, Abrahams writes about the problems of non-white groups in his country. 1

Chinua Achebe 1930-
Widely considered to be the finest Nigerian novelist, Achebe was the first African to gain an international following with his classic work, *Things Fall Apart*. 3

Ama Ata Aidoo 1942-
Aidoo is the Ghanaian author of *Our Sister Killjoy; or, Reflections From a Black-Eyed Squint*. 8

Jamil Abdullah Al-Amin 1943-
Al-Amin, who changed his name from H. Rap Brown when he converted to Islam, was an outspoken black civil rights activist of the 1960s. 8

Robert L. Allen 1942-
Allen's writings, such as *Black Awakening in Capitalist America*, concern the affect of social change on accepted beliefs. 10

Samuel W. Allen 1917-
Allen is best known for his essays and lectures on African and Afro-American literature. 10

T. M. Aluko 1918(?)-
Aluko, Nigerian author of *State of Our Own*, has been interviewed on Voice of America's radio program "Conversations With African Writers." 11

Elechi Amadi 1934-
Amadi is the author of *Sunset in Biafra*, a diary about life during the 1960s civil war in his native Nigeria. 12

Johari M. Amini
See **Johari M. Amini Kunjufu**

Raymond Andrews 1934-
Andrews won the 1978 James Baldwin Prize for fiction for his first novel, *Appalachee Red*. 12

Maya Angelou 1928-
Angelou, an author and performer, is well known for her poetry and her series of autobiographies, including *I Know Why the Caged Bird Sings*. 13

Michael Anthony 1932-
Caribbean author who writes novels and short stories, often told from a child's viewpoint, about life on the island of Trinidad. 15

Ayi Kwei Armah 1939-
A novelist born in what is now called Ghana, Armah is known for his vivid prose style and realistic portrayals of postindependent African society. 16

Russell Atkins 1926-
Atkins's avant-garde music and concrete poetry—emphasizing the actual appearance of the poems—are extolled for their experimental qualities. 18

Alvin Aubert 1930-
Poet whose writings are influenced by his native Louisiana. 19

Kofi Awoonor 1935-
Ghanaian-born Awoonor explores in his poetry traditional African culture and ritual. 20

Pearl Bailey 1918-
Bailey, an acclaimed singer and entertainer, earned fame and a special Tony Award for her starring role in the Broadway musical "Hello Dolly." 22

Augusta Baker 1911-
Baker, the editor of books on children's literature, is best known as a children's storyteller. 23

Houston A. Baker, Jr. 1943-
English professor and critic who specializes in twentieth-century black American literature. . . . 23

Bakr el-Toure
See **Askia Muhammad Abu Bakr el Toure**

James Baldwin 1924-1987
Author of *Go Tell It on the Mountain* and numerous other works, Baldwin is considered an eloquent and impassioned literary witness to American race relations. 24

Toni Cade Bambara 1939-
Bambara is as recognized for her civil rights activities as for her writings, which include short stories, novels, screenplays, and essays. 31

Amiri Baraka   1934-
Formerly known as LeRoi Jones, Baraka is a prolific critic of American civilization and was a major figure in the 1960s black arts movement. 33

Gerald William Barrax   1933-
Barrax wrote two volumes of poetry and contributed verse to periodicals and anthologies. 42

Francis Bebey   1929-
Bebey, the author of *African Music: A People's Art,* is an internationally renowned West African guitarist and composer. 42

Barry Beckham   1944-
Beckham's novels are acclaimed for their innovative depiction of the psychological impact of racism. . 44

James Madison Bell   1826-1902
Poet and political activist who supported the abolition of slavery during the Civil War. 45

George Harold Bennett   1930-
Author, under the name Hal Bennett, of novels depicting blacks who imitate white codes of race discrimination. 45

Gwendolyn B. Bennett   1902-1981
Bennett's poems, published mainly in periodicals during the Harlem Renaissance, are represented in numerous anthologies. 46

Lerone Bennett, Jr.   1928-
Bennett is senior editor of *Ebony* magazine and the author of historical works noted for their accuracy, readability, and emotional impact. 47

Mary Frances Berry   1938-
A former assistant secretary in the Department of Health, Education, and Welfare, Berry wrote about racial and sexual discrimination and the U.S. Constitution. 48

Mongo Beti
See **Alexandre Biyidi**

Maurice Bishop   1944-1983
Bishop was prime minister of Grenada from 1979 to 1983, when he was executed by supporters of a rival political faction. 49

Alexandre Biyidi   1932-
Cameroonian author who, under the name Mongo Beti, explores in his novels the encroachment of Western ways upon African civilization. 49

John W. Blassingame   1940-
Blassingame, a history professor at Yale University, specializes in nineteenth-century black American history. 52

Julian Bond   1940-
Bond was a leading civil rights activist of the 1960s and a founder of the Student Nonviolent Coordinating Committee. 52

Arna Bontemps   1902-1973
Bontemps was a prolific author of fiction, biographies for children, and literary criticism. 53

David Bradley   1950-
Bradley won the 1982 PEN/Faulkner Award and other honors for *The Chaneysville Incident,* a blend of historical fact and fiction. 55

Ed Bradley   1941-
A television journalist who began working for CBS in 1971 and ten years later became a correspondent for its "Sixty Minutes" news program. 57

E. R. Braithwaite   1920-
Guyanese diplomat who wrote autobiographies, including *To Sir, with Love,* which later became an acclaimed movie. 58

William Stanley Braithwaite   1878-1962
Though he never addressed racial issues in his own writings, Braithwaite included many black writers among the poets in his anthologies. 59

William Branch   1927-
Award-winning producer, writer, and director of plays, films, and news documentaries, who strives to overcome racial barriers in entertainment and news media. 61

Edward Brathwaite   1930-
A prolific West Indian poet, Brathwaite explores his identity as a black person living in the Caribbean. 62

Benjamin Brawley   1882-1939
Brawley, whose books are often considered standard classroom texts, is best known for his literary and social histories. 63

Gwendolyn Brooks   1917-
With her 1949 poetry collection *Annie Allen,* Brooks became the first black writer to win the Pulitzer Prize. 64

Cecil M. Brown   1943-
A novelist and playwright, Brown is probably best known for his first work, *The Life and Loves of Mr. Jiveass Nigger.* 69

Claude Brown   1937-
With the publication of his autobiographical *Manchild in the Promised Land,* Brown became one of the first to express the plight of the urban black. 70

H. Rap Brown
See **Jamil Abdullah Al-Amin**

Margery Brown
Author and illustrator of children's books, including *That Ruby* and *Yesterday I Climbed a Mountain.* 71

Sterling Allen Brown   1901-
An author of poetry and nonfiction and one of the first writers to identify folklore as an important component of the black aesthetic. 71

Wesley Brown   1945-
Brown's novel *Tragic Magic* was praised for its originality and lifelike evocation of urban black America. 75

William Anthony Brown   1933-
Producer and host of award-winning television newsmagazine "Tony Brown's Journal," originally known as "Black Journal.". 75

Dennis Brutus   1924-
Brutus, a South African-born poet who was imprisoned for his anti-apartheid activities, is best known for his poems about imprisonment and exile. 76

Ashley F. Bryan   1923-
Award-winning author and illustrator of children's books who works to preserve African traditions in America. 79

Ed Bullins   1935-
A principal figure in the black arts movement of the 1960s, Bullins examines in his plays the disillusionment and frustration of ghetto life. . . . 80

Ralph J. Bunche   1904-1971
Former American official in the United Nations who won the 1950 Nobel Peace Prize, the first black to do so, for mediating the Palestine conflict. 83

Margaret Taylor Burroughs   1917-
Burroughs founded Chicago's DuSable Museum of African-American History and won critical acclaim for her own artwork. 85

Octavia E. Butler   1947-
Award-winning science fiction writer whose novels examine such concepts as genetic engineering in terms of racial and sexual awareness. 86

Ben Caldwell   1937-
Caldwell's satirical plays comment on the situation of black people in white-dominated America. 88

Stokely Carmichael   1941-
A former leader of the Student Nonviolent Coordinating Committee and of the Black Panthers, Carmichael is credited with originating the slogan "Black Power.". 89

Vinnette Carroll
An award-winning performer and director of productions celebrating black culture, Carroll created and led New York City's Urban Arts Theatre. . . 90

Wilfred Cartey   1931-
Cartey is a West Indian scholar and critic of African, American, and Caribbean literature. 93

Xam Wilson Cartier   1949(?)-
In her novel *Be-Bop, Re-Bop,* Cartier describes the liberating presence of jazz in the main character's life. 93

Aime Cesaire   1913-
Prominent Caribbean poet and playwright who is best known for his book-length poem *Return to My Native Land.* 94

Barbara Chase-Riboud   1939-
Chase-Riboud, an internationally known sculptress, has also produced works of poetry and fiction.   . 97

Charles W. Chesnutt   1858-1932
An important figure in early black American literature, Chesnutt wrote serious fiction, such as *The Conjure Woman.* 98

Alice Childress   1920-
Author of plays and novels, including *A Hero Ain't Nothin' but a Sandwich,* that are noted for their frank treatment of racial issues. 100

Shirley Chisolm   1924-
Chisolm was the first black female member of Congress and the first black woman to run a serious campaign for the U.S. presidency. 103

Barbara T. Christian   1943-
Christian, who was born in the Virgin Islands, de-scribes in her books the evolution of black feminist literature. 105

John Pepper Clark   1935-
Nigerian author of *The Anarchist Movement: Reflections on Culture, Nature, and Power,* as well as plays, poetry, and literary criticism. 105

Kenneth B. Clark   1914-
Clark, a professor of psychology, studied the psychological effects of racism in educational settings. 106

Austin C. Clarke   1934-
West Indian novelist whose works, including the autobiographical *Growing Up Stupid Under the Union Jack,* describe blacks' struggle for success in white society. 107

John Henrik Clarke   1915-
Editor, essayist, and lecturer on black history in the United States and West Africa. 108

Eldridge Cleaver   1935-
An outspoken leader of the Black Panthers who became the Peace and Freedom Party's U.S. presidential candidate in 1968. 109

Michelle Cliff   1946-
Cliff, a Jamaican journalist, poet, and novelist, challenges colonialism and racism through her writings. 110

Lucille Clifton 1936-
Poet and children's writer who is most often recognized for her "Everett Anderson" series for children. 111

Wanda Coleman 1946-
Coleman is well known in her native Los Angeles as a compelling composer and reader of poetry. . . . 115

Cyrus Colter 1910-
Colter's fiction about American blacks, though not overtly political, is praised for its eschewal of racial stereotype. 116

Mercer Cook 1903-1987
Cook, a scholar of black literature, served during the 1960s as U.S. ambassador to Niger, Senegal, and Gambia. 116

Orde M. Coombs 1939(?)-1984
In *Do You See My Love for You Growing?* West Indian author Coombs discusses the need for blacks to unite and support one another. 117

J. California Cooper
Author of short stories and the novels *Homemade Love* and *Some Soul to Keep.* 118

Sam Cornish 1935-
Cornish gained an audience for his simple, direct poetry during the black arts movement of the 1960s. 118

Jayne Cortez 1936-
Cortez, who intends her poems to be read orally, has made recordings of her work read aloud to the accompaniment of jazz music. 119

William Henry Cosby, Jr. 1937-
Bill Cosby, a popular comedian since the early 1960s, most recently created the 1980s family comedy "The Cosby Show." 119

Joseph Seamon Cotter, Sr. 1861-1949
Proficient in many verse styles, Cotter is remembered for his ballad "The Tragedy of Pete" and his blank verse drama "Caleb, the Degenerate." 122

Joseph Mason Andrew Cox 1930-
Cox, president of Cox & Hopewell Publishers, is the author of works of poetry, drama, and fiction. . . . 123

Victor Hernandez Cruz 1949-
Puerto Rican poet whose work is a creative blend of Spanish and English. 123

Countee Cullen 1903-1946
One of the best known of the Harlem Renaissance writers, Cullen believed that art transcends race and strove for a color-blind artistic freedom. 124

William Waring Cuney 1906-1976
Cuney, whose verse reflects the language of the ghetto-dweller, is remembered for his widely anthologized poem "No Images." 129

David Dabydeen 1955-
Guyanese author whose poetry collection *Slave Song* is lauded for its lyrical use of Creole and its portrayal of life on Guyanese sugar plantations. 130

Bernard Binlin Dadie 1916-
A government official in his native Ivory Coast, Dadie is a prolific writer of French-language fiction, poetry, plays, and essays. 131

Leon-Gontran Damas 1912-1978
Damas, who was born in French Guiana, was a founder of the French literary movement known as Negritude. 132

Raymond Garfield Dandridge 1882-1930
Harlem Renaissance poet best known for his verse written in black dialect. 133

Margaret Danner 1915-
Danner celebrates in her poetry the African heritage of black Americans. 134

O. R. Dathorne 1934-
Guyanese poet, editor, and educator who has taught English, black studies, and literature in West Africa and the United States. 135

Allison Davis 1902-1983
A respected psychologist and social anthropologist, Davis challenged the objectivity and validity of standard intelligence tests. 135

Angela Davis 1944-
Davis is best known as a political activist dedicated to eradicating black poverty and oppression. 136

Arthur P. Davis 1904-
Davis, professor emeritus at Howard University, devoted most of his studies and teachings to black American literature. .139

Charles T. Davis 1918-1981
Professor at Yale University and influential scholar of both black and white American literature. 139

Frank Marshall Davis 1905-1987
Davis, who was executive editor of the Associated Negro Press and the *Chicago Star,* produced five volumes of poems. 140

George B. Davis 1939-
Davis examines relations between black and white business managers in his co-authored study *Black Life in Corporate America.* 142

Nolan Davis 1942-
Press and broadcast journalist whose novel *Six Black Horses* was praised as a witty and realistic portrait of black life. 142

Ossie Davis   1917-
Recognized for his stage and screen performances, Davis won critical acclaim for his 1961 play "Purlie Victorious," later adapted as a musical and motion picture. 143

Ruby Dee
See **Ruby Ann Wallace**

Samuel R. Delany   1942-
Acclaimed science fiction writer whose works explore such contemporary issues as the black experience in America, women's rights, and gay rights. 145

William Demby   1922-
Demby's novels, including *Beetlecreek, Love Story Black,* and *Blueboy,* are praised for their universality. 149

Thomas C. Dent   1932-
Tom Dent, who co-published the poetry magazine Umbra and co-founded the literary journal *Callaloo,* also helped establish cultural workshops and collectives. 150

Alexis De Veaux   1948-
In her writings and illustrations De Veaux hopes to challenge racial, economic, and sexual inequalities. 151

Birago Diop   1906-
Senegalese veterinarian and writer best known for his short stories inspired by West African folktales. 152

Cheikh Anta Diop   1923-1986
In his native Senegal, Diop established Africa's first carbon-14 dating laboratory, and he also wrote several books on African history. 153

Owen Dodson   1914-1983
An influential drama instructor at Howard University for twenty-three years, Dodson made a significant impact on black theater. 154

Rita Dove   1952-
Dove is best known for her Pulitzer Prize-winning work *Thomas and Beulah,* a collection of poems loosely based on her grandparents' lives. 155

William Joe Drummond   1944-
Drummond, professor at Berkeley and former writer for the *Los Angeles Times,* served as associate press secretary during President Jimmy Carter's administration. 156

David G. Du Bois   1925-
Du Bois served as official spokesperson for the Black Panther Party and editor in chief of the Black Panther Intercommunal News Service. 156

Shirley Graham Du Bois   1906-1977
A longtime civil rights supporter, Du Bois wrote several biographies of famous minority leaders. . .157

W. E. B. Du Bois   1868-1963
A prolific scholar and committed civil rights defender, Du Bois is remembered for his essay collection *The Souls of Black Folk.* 157

Henry L. Dumas   1934-1968
Dumas, who wrote the well-received *Poetry for My People* and other volumes of poetry and short stories, died before seeing his work published. 161

Alice Moore Dunbar
See **Alice Ruth Moore Dunbar Nelson**

Paul Laurence Dunbar   1872-1906
Regarded as America's first great black poet, Dunbar was most appreciated for poems he wrote in black dialect. 162

Katherine Dunham   1910-
An accomplished anthropologist and writer, Dunham is best known for her contributions to the world of dance. 165

Alice Allison Dunnigan   1906-1983
Dunnigan was the first black journalist to work in the Senate, House of Representatives, and the White House. 167

Marian Wright Edelman   1939-
The first black female member of the Mississippi bar, Edelman now serves in Washington as an advocate for American children. .169

Randolph Edmonds   1900-1983
This playwright and educator was a driving force behind dramatics in Afro-American universities for more than forty years. 170

Cyprian Ekwensi   1921-
A Nigerian writer of novels, short stories, and books for young readers that describe life in Lagos. . . .172

Lonne Elder III   1931-
A poet, short story writer, and actor, Elder won awards for the play "Ceremonies in Dark Old Men" and the screenplay "Sounder." 173

Ralph Ellison   1914-
A fiction writer and essayist, Ellison is best known for his novel *Invisible Man,* the story of a black man's search for personal and cultural identity. 176

El Muhajir   1944-
This poet, playwright, and editor has also founded two San Francisco theatres, the political-cultural center Black House, and the Al Kitab Sudan Publishing Company. 183

James A. Emanuel   1921-
Emanuel is a poet, educator, writer of essays on black literature, and co-editor of the important anthology *Dark Symphony.* 184

Buchi Emecheta   1944-
Nigeria's best known female writer, Emecheta crafts fiction about being female and about the clash between cultures. 185

Mari Evans   1923-
A children's author, award-winning poet, and respected critic, Evans has filled a gap in literary criticism on black women writers. 188

Sarah Webster Fabio   1928-1979
Fabio is a poet, teacher, and the author of *Black Talk: Soul, Shield, and Sword.* 192

Ronald L. Fair   1932-
Fair's experimental fiction and poetry have won awards from the National Institute of Arts and Letters and the American Library Association. 192

Frantz Fanon   1925-1961
Anti-colonialist hero of the Algerian National Liberation Front who inspired liberation movements in Canada, the United States, and throughout Africa. 193

Jessie Redmon Fauset   1884(?)-1961
A novelist, poet, short story writer, and essayist, Fauset was literary editor of *Crisis,* which first published many black writers. 195

Muriel Feelings   1938-
Feelings is a children's author of books about African culture and language inspired by her years as a teacher and traveler in Africa. 196

Thomas Feelings   1933-
A storyteller whose craft is rooted in African traditions, Feelings is a children's book author and illustrator. 196

Julia Fields   1938-
Poet, short story writer, and playwright whose books include *A Summoning, A Shining* and *The Green Lion of Zion Street.* 197

John J. Figuero   1920-
West Indian poet and scholar who has supported the rich diversity of Caribbean literature in his verse, criticism, and several anthologies. 197

Rudolph Fisher   1897-1934
The Conjure-Man Dies, a novel by this Harlem Renaissance writer and physician, was the first to include only black characters. 198

Ray Fleming   1945-
Fleming is a poet and educator whose books are informed by his travels and training in comparative literature. 201

Calvin Forbes   1945-
Forbes's poems are shaped by his years as a hitchhiker, studies of John Donne, Gwendolyn Brooks, and Philip Larkin, and the artistic climate of the 1970s. 201

Nick Aaron Ford   1904-1982
Poet and author of *American Culture in Literature,* Ford was an educator who studied and worked to improve literacy standards in American schools. . . . 202

Leon Forrest   1937-
Forrest's award-winning novels about racially-mixed descendants of a slaveowner have been compared to the works of Faulkner. 202

Charlotte Forten
See **Charlotte L. Forten Grimke**

J. E. Franklin   1937-
This playwright's two-act work "Black Girl" enjoyed a successful run Off-Broadway and was adapted into a motion picture. 203

John Hope Franklin   1915-
The author of a critically acclaimed biography *George Washington Williams,* Franklin is known as a pioneering and distinguished black historian. 204

Charles Fuller   1939-
The writer of stage, screen, and television plays that expose racism and question integration, Fuller won the Pulitzer Prize for "A Soldier's Play." 206

Hoyt Fuller   1927-1981
Journalist and magazine editor Fuller's dedication to black literature earned the Doctor of Determination Award from the University of Michigan Center for Afro-American Studies. 208

Ernest J. Gaines   1933-
In such works as *The Autobiography of Miss Jane Pittman* and *A Gathering of Old Men,* Gaines recalls the storytelling traditions of his native Louisiana. 209

Marcus Garvey   1887-1940
Perhaps the most prominent black rights activist of his era, Garvey led a movement that numbered eight million at its peak. 212

Henry Louis Gates, Jr.   1950-
Gates is a literary scholar and critic whose essays on black literature in the twentieth century are considered indispensible. 215

Addison Gayle, Jr.   1932-
Gayle is a Southern writer and educator whose emergence from self-loathing to black pride finds parallels in his best-known work of criticism *The Black Aesthetic.* 216

Donald B. Gibson   1933-
An educator, Gibson has edited collections of literary criticism on black writers, including *The Politics of Literary Expression.* 217

Paula Giddings   1948-
Giddings wrote *When and Where I Enter,* a study of activism among black women that identifies their contributions to racial and sexual equality in America. 217

Christopher Gilbert   1949-
Gilbert, who has a dual career in psychology and poetry, won the Walt Whitman Award for his first volume, *Across the Mutual Landscape.* 218

Nikki Giovanni   1943-
An internationally known poet, essayist, and lecturer, Giovanni was a leading figure in the black literary renaissance of the 1960s. 219

Donald Goines   1937(?)-1974
Goines wrote sixteen popular books about ghetto crime that were informed by his own heroin addiction and seven prison terms. 222

Marita Golden   1950-
Trained as a journalist, this educator has written poetry, fiction, and an autobiography to help her make sense of her experiences in America and Africa. 224

Charles Gordone   1925-
A playwright, Gordone received rave reviews and comparison to Edward Albee for his Broadway success, "No Place to Be Somebody." 224

Lorenz Graham   1902-
Graham is a former teacher and missionary known for writing children's books that recast Biblical tales in black English. 226

William Greaves   1926-
An innovative filmmaker whose documentaries about Afro-American history and black life in America have won ten major awards. 227

Eloise Greenfield   1929-
The author of more than a dozen prize-winning books for children, Greenfield also writes novels and poetry for adults. 229

Sam Greenlee   1930-
A former foreign service officer for the United States Information Agency and author of an award-winning science fiction novel *The Spook Who Sat by the Door.* 230

Dick Gregory   1932-
Black comedian and activist who was the first to break the "color barrier" and win a white audience with humor aimed at social issues. 231

Angelina Weld Grimke   1880-1958
A teacher, playwright, and poet popular during the Harlem Renaissance whose love poems have been widely anthologized. 233

Charlotte L. Forten Grimke   1837(?)-1914
Grimke's books are based on her experiences in the Civil War abolitionist movement and the Port Royal Experiment in Education. 234

Verta Mae Grosvenor   1938-
The author of columns in *Amsterdam News* and *Chicago Courier,* Grosvenor has published an autobiography and *Plain Brown Rapper,* a book of poems. 235

Nicolas Guillen   1902-
A former journalist, Guillen is one of Cuba's best known poets and a master of the "Afro-Cuban" style. 235

William Harrison Gunn   1934-
The author of two novels, Bill Gunn is best known for plays and screenplays that pit the serious artists against a materialist society. 238

Rosa Guy   1928-
Readers of all ages enjoy books about black teens written by this Trinidadian novelist. 239

Alex Haley   1921-
Author of the Afro-American epic *Roots,* described as a "literary-television phenomenon" and a "sociological event." 241

Warren J. Halliburton   1924-
Educator, free-lance writer and editor Halliburton is the author of several book on black history, including *The Fighting Redtails: America's First Black Airmen.* 242

Virginia Hamilton   1936-
One of the most prolific and influential authors of books about black children. 243

Lorraine Hansberry   1930-1965
The first black woman to have a Broadway production and the first and youngest black playwright to win the New York Drama Critics Circle Award. 245

Nathan Hare   1934-
A prominent leader of the black studies movement, Hare is also known as "an unorthodox academician." 247

Francis Ellen Watkins Harper   1825-1911
One of the first black protest poets, now recognized as an early feminist, Harper addressed social ills in her poetry and speeches. 249

Michael S. Harper   1938-
Author of *History Is Your Own Heartbeat,* and an award-winning poet who draws from folk traditions and history to chronicle black life in America. . . 251

Wilson Harris   1921-
In highly symbolic novels, Harris introduces the little-known interior of Guyana, his native land. 253

Paul Carter Harrison   1936-
A playwright best known for integrating elements of traditional African culture with contemporary American thought in plays that have a ceremonial impact on their audience. 255

James S. Haskins   1941-
Haskins has written more than eighty books—many of them biographies of black people—for young readers. 257

Robert C. Hayden, Jr.   1937-
This educator's books provide young readers with information about black American scientists, inventors, and doctors. 260

Robert E. Hayden   1913-1980
Known for his formal poetry about the black experience in history, Hayden was a poetry consultant for the Library of Congress from 1976 to 1978. . . . 260

Bessie Head   1937-1986
The daughter of a racially-mixed South African couple, Head wrote fiction that explores racial discrimination and oppression. 262

Nathan C. Heard   1936-
Heard's semi-autobiographical novels *Howard Street* and *House of Slammers* bring the frustration and violence of ghetto and prison life to the reader's attention. 265

John Hearne   1926-
A West Indian writer whose novels and nonfiction works focus on the cultural and political aspects of Caribbean life. 266

David Henderson   1942-
A Harlem-born black nationalist poet and author of the biography *Jimi Hendrix: Voodoo Child of the Aquarian Age.* 267

George Wylie Henderson   1904-
An Alabama author who began his literary career with a highly praised novel and ended it after his second novel was negatively received. 268

Stephen E. Henderson   1925-
Howard University professor whose studies of black literature center on the political concerns and the rich musical heritage of black writers. 269

A. Doris Banks Henries   1913(?)-1981
An American educator who adopted Liberia as her homeland and became one of its most prolific writers. 269

Frank Hercules   1917-
Author of three novels, a history of black revolution in America, and "To Live in Harlem," an article that received national attention. 270

Calvin C. Hernton   1934-
Essays about the relation of sexism to racism have made this sociologist, poet, and novelist well known. 270

Errol Gaston Hill   1921-
A West Indian playwright and anthologist, Hill wrote the unique *Shakespeare in Sable: A History of Black Shakespearean Actors.* 271

Leslie Pinckney Hill   1880-1960
A dedicated educator and poet, Hill wrote *Wings of Oppression* and *Toussaint L'Ouverture,* two works that encourage endurance and non-violent means of social change. 272

Chester Himes   1909-1984
Expatriate American writer who treated the subject of racism in successful novels of social protest, autobiographies, and popular crime thrillers. 273

Everett Hoagland   1942-
Poet, fiction writer, and educator whose works stress the importance of racial pride. 276

Julius W. Hobson   1922(?)-1977
Civil rights activist who led reform movements in Washington, D.C., that improved conditions for black school children and urban blacks. 277

Frank Horne   1899-1974
A Harlem Renaissance poet who followed the publication of his prize-winning poems with a career in public service to improve housing opportunities for blacks. 277

Nathan Irvin Huggins   1927-
Historian whose books, including *Harlem Renaissance* and *Black Odyssey: The Afro-American Ordeal in Slavery,* shed light on important areas of black history. 279

Langston Hughes   1902-1967
Prolific and versatile poet, novelist, playwright, and essayist who enjoyed an enthusiastic critical and popular reception to his work. 280

Gloria T. Hull   1944-
Feminist poet, critic, and educator who compiled the collection *All the Women Are White, All the Blacks Are Men, but Some of Us Are Brave.* 284

Kristin Hunter   1931-
Hunter's novels, stories, and prize-winning books for young adults show young urban blacks overcoming individual and social problems. 285

Zora Neale Hurston   1891-1960
A Harlem Renaissance writer and folklorist who influenced Ralph Ellison, Toni Morrison, Toni Cade Bambara, and other black novelists. 287

George Jackson   1941-1971
Prisoner and political activist who wrote *Soledad Brother* and *Blood in My Eye* from Soledad and San Quentin prisons. 289

Jesse Jackson   1908-1983
The first children's author to openly discuss racial prejudice in his fiction and nonfiction for young readers. 290

C. L. R. James   1901-
A leading figure in Trinidadian politics and literature, James was influenced by Pan-African and Marxist ideas, which he promoted in three countries. . . 291

Lance Jeffers   1919-1985
A poet who also wrote short fiction and a novel, Jeffers was motivated by the struggle against racial prejudice. 294

Roland S. Jefferson   1939-
Writer, psychiatrist, and filmmaker who wrote his first novel to combat a perceived threat against America's black population. 295

Ted Joans   1928-
An expatriate writer who contributed his knowledge of African art and jazz idioms to the Black Arts movement of the 1970s. 295

Charles Johnson   1948-
A cartoonist and fiction writer who studied with John Gardner, Johnson has been called one of America's "most interesting and inventive young writers." 296

Charles S. Johnson   1893-1956
The chief black sociologist of his period, this Fisk University president helped generate the Harlem Renaissance by founding *Opportunity* magazine. 298

Fenton Johnson   1888-1958
A poet of the early twentieth century who actively sought a place in American literature but died in literary obscurity. 300

Georgia Douglas Johnson   1886-1966
A poet and playwright who was among the first black women writers to achieve prominence in America and is considered among the best writers of her time. 302

James Weldon Johnson   1871-1938
This civil rights leader, distinguished man of letters, lawyer, diplomat, and secretary of the National Association for the Advancement of Colored People, wrote novels, poems, and nonfiction. 303

Gayl Jones   1949-
Jones is a fiction writer and poet whose works show the impact of sexual and racial exploitation on black women. 307

Jacqueline Jones   1948-
A historian whose books about the roles of black men and women during Reconstruction are considered valuable contributions to scholarship. 309

LeRoi Jones
See **Amiri Baraka**

Barbara Jordan   1936-
Politician and gifted orator who was a member of the Texas Senate, U.S. House of Representatives, and the House Judiciary Committee that found Richard Nixon impeachable. 310

June Jordan   1936-
Jordan writes poetry, novels, essays, and children's books that suggest optimism for the survival of the individual against social pressure. 312

Bob Kaufman   1925-1986
Published through the efforts of his friends, this poet of the Beat Generation improvised jazz-like poems and influenced many San Francisco writers. . . .315

Legson Kayira   1942-
African novelist whose first book was an account of his journey to become the first of his countrymen to earn a college degree in the United States. 316

William Melvin Kelley   1937-
Kelley's fiction views the civil rights movement of the 1960s from a black perspective. 317

Adrienne Kennedy   1931-
A playwright whose unique combination of poetry with drama brought her play "Funnyhouse of a Negro" an Obie Award. 320

Jomo Kenyatta   1891(?)-1978
Kenyatta, the first president of Kenya, expressed his political beliefs in *Facing Mount Kenya, Kenya: Land of Conflict,* and other writings. 321

Keorapetse Kgositsile   1938-
A South African poet now living in America who calls for militancy in his writings. 323

John Oliver Killens   1916-1987
Books by this novelist, playwright, and essayist earned several awards and an international audience. . . . 324

Jamaica Kincaid   1949-
A Jamaican author of short stories set in her native Antigua, Kincaid has gained a position of prominence in American literature. 326

Coretta Scott King   1927-
The wife of slain civil rights activist Martin Luther King, Jr., she continues in her late husband's work. 328

Martin Luther King, Jr.   1929-1968
Civil rights leader who was given the Nobel Peace Prize in 1964 for encouraging non-violent social action in the fight for racial justice. 329

Martin Luther King, Sr.   1899-1984
A minister, King explains his own role in the civil rights movement in his book *Daddy King*. 334

Woodie King, Jr.   1937-
Called "the renaissance man of black theatre," this playwright and writer of short stories is best known for his support of black theatre in America. 336

Etheridge Knight   1931-
Encouraged to develop his writing talents while in prison, Knight has become a major poet who believes he must sing of black "deeds and misdeeds." . . 337

S.A. Konadu   1932-
A novelist who writes under several pseudonyms and a world traveler who went with the president of Ghana, his homeland, to visit the Soviet Union. 339

Mazisi Kunene   1930-
Born in South Africa, Kunene writes African epic poetry about Zulu history, culture, and religion. 339

Johari M. Amini Kunjufu   1935-
An American poet who writes under the name Johari M. Amini. 340

Joyce A. Ladner   1943-
A sociologist whose twenty years of study on the lives of black women and the social forces that shape them is found in her writings. 341

Alex La Guma   1925-1985
A South African political activist and novelist who declaimed apartheid while a political prisoner and later during his exile in England. 342

George Lamming   1927-
A West Indian poet and novelist, Lamming is known for *In the Cast of My Skin* and other novels that depict life in the Caribbean islands. 343

Pinkie Gordon Lane   1923-
Lane's poems have been compared to those of Phyllis Wheatley, and her volume *The Mystic Female* was nominated for the Pulitzer Prize. 345

Nella Larsen   1891-1964
This nurse wrote two novels, including the award-winning *Quicksand*. 346

Camara Laye   1928-1980
A Guinean novelist whose prize-winning autobiography *The Dark Child* and highly acclaimed novel *The Radiance of the King* set the standard for French African narrative prose. 348

Andrea Lee   1953-
This noteworthy journalist has won critical acclaim for *Russian Journal*, based on her visit to the Soviet Union, and for *Sarah Phillips*, her first novel. . . . 350

Don L. Lee
See **Haki R. Madhubuti**

George W. Lee   1894-1976
An insurance executive who wrote the popular *Beale Street: Where the Blues Began* to promote pride in black business. 351

Shelton Jackson Lee   1957(?)-
A self-styled "instigator," Lee confirmed his status as an important filmmaker with the comic films "She's Gotta Have It" and "School Daze." 352

Spike Lee
See **Shelton Jackson Lee**

Julius Lester   1939-
Poet, novelist, and folklorist considered foremost among authors of his generation that preserve and build on black cultural history. 355

Theophilus Lewis   1891-1974
A self-educated and respected drama critic who wrote for numerous black periodicals and Catholic journals. 356

Claude M. Lightfoot   1910-
Lightfoot is a political activist and former vice-chairman of the American Communist Party. . . . 357

C. Eric Lincoln   1924-
Sociologist Lincoln explores various aspects of black life in his writings. .357

Malcolm Little   1925-1965
Prominent civil rights activist better known as Malcolm X who was an influential leader of the black nationalist movement. 358

Taban lo Liyong   1938-
Liyong is a Ugandan novelist, essayist, and poet 361

Alain Locke   1886-1954
In 1925, Locke edited *The New Negro: An Interpretation*, a pioneering anthology that helped initiate the Harlem Renaissance. 361

Rayford W. Logan   1897-1982
Logan is a historian who co-edited the landmark *Dictionary of American Literary Biography*. . . .362

Louis E. Lomax   1922-1970
A journalist, Lomax wrote books on racial issues, including *The Reluctant African*. 363

Richard A. Long   1927-
Long is a scholar of Afro-American studies who also writes poetry and plays. 363

Audre Lorde   1934-
Lorde writes poems that often focus on her triumphs and setbacks as a black woman in America. . . . 364

W. F. Lucas   1927-
A playwright, Lucas is the founding director of Carpetbag Theatre in Knoxville, Tennessee. . . . 366

William Wellington Mackey   1937-
Mackey's plays portray the effects of political struggle on the American black family. 368

Naomi Long Madgett   1923-
Madgett's books of poetry include *Pink Ladies in the Afternoon* and *Phantom Nightingale*. 369

Haki R. Madhubiti   1942-
Formerly Don L. Lee, this poet, publisher, editor, and critic reflects his commitment to fostering black culture in his work. 370

Roger Mais   1905-1955
Influential among other West Indian writers, Mais wrote novels of social protest which focused on the urban oppressed of his native Jamaica. 372

Clarence Major   1936-
A noted experimental novelist and poet, Major draws heavily on his experience as a black in America's South to create new modes of literary expression. 373

Miriam Makeba   1922-
Grammy Award-winning South African folk singer, Makeba penned her 1987 autobiography *Makeba: My Story*. 376

Malcolm X
See **Malcolm Little**

Nelson R. Mandela   1918-
Jailed South African founder of the African National Congress, Mandela has become a focal point in the struggle against apartheid. 378

Winnie Mandela   1936-
South African political activist and wife of the imprisoned Nelson Mandela, she is a leader of the anti-apartheid movement. 382

Rene Maran   1887-1960
Maran's novel *Batoula* is considered the first authentic record of African tribal life under colonial French rule. 383

Paule Marshall   1929-
Marshall has been praised for her skillful use of West-Indian/Afro-American dialogue and colorful Barbadian expressions. 384

Herbert Woodward Martin   1933-
Martin's books of poetry include *The Persistence of the Flesh* and *The Forms of Silence*. 386

Tony Martin   1942-
Martin is a Trinidadian-born American educator and author of works on early twentieth-century black nationalist Marcus Garvey. 386

Marvin X
See **El Muhajir**

Mark Mathabane   1960-
South African Mathabane's autobiographical first work, *Kaffir Boy*, portrays life in the poverty-stricken black township of Alexandria. 387

John F. Matheus   1887-1983
Matheus wrote popular short stories that advocated Christian principles in countering the influences of evil. 388

Sharon Bell Mathis   1937-
Mathis is a children's author noted for her starkly realistic portrayals of people and events. 389

Julian Mayfield   1928-1984
Best known for his novels *The Hit* and *The Long Night*, Mayfield enjoyed a diverse career as an author, educator, actor, and political advisor. 390

Benjamin E. Mays   1894-1984
An influential civil rights leader, Mays served from 1940 through 1967 as president of Morehouse College. 392

James A. Mays   1939-
Cardiologist whose 1975 novel, *Mercy Is King*, portrays the interactions of black and white working professionals. 394

John S. Mbiti   1931-
Kenyan-born Anglican priest living in Switzerland, Mbiti has authored theological studies of African religions and Christianity. 395

George Marion McClellan   1860-1934
A poet and short story writer who wrote in a conservative style reflecting much of black thought at the turn of the century. 395

John McCluskey, Jr.   1944-
McCluskey is a fiction writer best known for his novels *Look What They Done to My Song* and *Mr. America's Last Season Blues*. 396

Colleen J. McElroy   1935-
McElroy is a poet whose books include *Queen of the Ebony Isles* and *Bone Flames*. 397

Claude McKay
See **Festius Claudius McKay**

Festius Claudius McKay   1889-1948
Jamaican-born American writer, McKay was the author of the commercially successful novel *Home to Harlem*. 398

James Alan McPherson 1943-
Author of the Pulitzer Prize-winning *Elbow Room,* McPherson writes of the problems facing working-class blacks. 401

Louise Meriwether 1923-
Meriwether's first novel, *Daddy Was a Number Runner,* is the authentic narrative of a young black girl recounting her family's economic collapse. 402

Arthenia Jackson Bates Millican 1920-
Millican is a fiction writer whose works include the novel *The Deity Nodded* and the short story collection *Seeds beneath the Snow.* 403

Ron Milner 1938-
Milner is a playwright whose works offer spirited glimpses into the triumphs and problems of contemporary America's urban blacks. 404

Loften Mitchell 1919-
A playwright and theatre historian, Mitchell wrote the musical "Bubbling Brown Sugar" and *Black Drama,* a study of black theatre. 406

Edgar Austin Mittelhoelzer 1909-1965
A novelist born in what was then British Guiana, Mittelhoelzer was considered an influential voice in the establishment of modern West Indian literature. 408

Barbara Jean Molette 1940-
Molette is a playwright whose works include "Rosalee Pritchett," co-authored with husband Carlton W. Molette. 409

Carlton W. Molette II 1939-
Playwright Molette's works include "Rosalee Pritchett," which he wrote with wife Barbara Jean Molette. 410

Anne Moody 1940-
Author of the autobiographical *Coming of Age in Mississippi,* Moody began writing after ending her involvement with the civil rights movement. . . . 410

Toni Morrison 1931-
Morrison is the critically-acclaimed and bestselling author of such novels as *Song of Solomon,* which won the National Book Critics Circle Award, and *Beloved,* winner of the Pulitzer Prize. 411

E. Frederic Morrow 1909-
Appointed in 1955 by President Eisenhower as an administrative assistant, Morrow was the first black man to serve as a White House aide. 417

Willard Motley 1912-1965
After years of traveling across the United States, Motley wrote novels that contained realistic, often grim, portrayals of people and events. 417

Ezekiel Mphahlele 1919-
A South African author of autobiographies, short stories, and essays, Mphahlele explores race relationship and ghetto life in his country. 418

Albert L. Murray 1916-
Murray is a fiction writer, essayist, and author of books on blues music. 420

Pauli Murray 1910-1985
A pioneer for both the civil rights and feminist movements, Murray was a lawyer, educator, and the first black woman to be ordained an Episcopal priest. 421

Walter Dean Myers 1937-
Regarded as one of the foremost authors of fiction for young blacks, Myers is best known for his novels that portray the youth of Harlem. 423

Gloria Naylor 1950-
Winner of an American Book Award for her first novel, *The Women of Brewster Place,* Naylor is respected for her imaginative use of language. . .426

Lawrence P. Neal 1937-1981
Larry Neal was an essayist and playwright who was a staunch advocate of a separate black literary movement. 428

Alice Ruth Moore Dunbar Nelson 1875-1935
One of the first black women to distinguish herself in American literature, Nelson wrote short stories, poetry, and criticism. .429

Ngugi wa Thiong'o 1938-
Kenyan-born novelist, dramatist, essayist, and literary critic who is East Africa's most prominent writer. 430

Charles H. Nichols 1919-
Nichols is a scholar of black literature and edited *Arna Bontemps and Langston Hughes Letters, 1925-1967.* 433

Davidson Nicol 1924-
A foreign diplomat and doctor in his native Sierra Leone, Nicol has been critically recognized for his short stories. 433

Lewis Nkosi 1936-
South African writer living in England, Nkosi has been called "one of the architects of the contemporary black consciousness in South Africa." 435

Richard Bruce Nugent 1906(?)-
Important for his connections to many of the prominent literary figures of the Harlem Renaissance, Nugent is himself a writer and illustrator. 436

Julius K. Nyerere 1922-
The first prime minister of Tanganyika and the former president of Tanzania, Nyerere is one of Africa's foremost statesmen. 437

Asenath Odaga   1937-
A Kenyan author of stories for both children and adults, Odaga often writes about the common experiences of daily life. 439

Therman B. O'Daniel   1908-
O'Daniel is a scholar of Afro-American literature and has written critical studies of Langston Hughes and James Baldwin. 440

Gabriel Okara   1921-
Okara's 1964 novel *The Voice* was written in protest of the Nigerian government's perpetuation of colonial practices. 440

Christopher Okigbo   1932-1967
Nigerian poet who fused ancient tribal beliefs with modern political consciousness in his work. . . . 441

Joseph Okpaku   1943(?)-
Nigerian-born playwright, author of nonfiction, and professor who abandoned engineering to write and founded *Journal of the New African Literature and the Arts.* 442

Dillibe Onyeama   1951-
Onyeama is Nigerian-born novelist living in England whose writings address the political issues of his homeland. 442

Sembene Ousmane   1923-
Sengalese novelist and filmmaker Ousmane is best known for the novel *O Pays, mon beau peuple!* and the film "Mandabi." 443

Nell Irvin Painter   1942-
Painter is a historian who specializes in the Reconstruction and Progressive eras of black American history. 446

C. Everard Palmer   1930-
Jamaican-born Palmer is an educator and writer of children's literature who resides in Canada. . . . 447

Gordon Parks   1912-
Parks was the first black photographer for *Life* magazine before directing such feature films as "Shaft" and "Leadbelly." 447

Lindsay Patterson   1942-
Patterson has written and edited numerous books that illuminate the accomplishments of black Americans in the arts. 449

Orlando Patterson   1940-
Novelist and author of sociological studies, Jamaican writer Patterson explores ethnicity and slavery in West Indian societies. 449

Okot p'Bitek   1931-1982
Ugandan poet and theatre director, p'Bitek sought to preserve the customs of his native Acholi culture. 450

Margaret Perry   1933-
Perry is a literary critic and scholar who specializes in the Harlem Renaissance period. 452

Richard Perry   1944-
Perry's works include the novels *Changes* and *Montgomery's Children.* 453

Lenrie Peters   1932-
The work of this Gambian-born surgeon, novelist, and poet reflects both his career as a physician and his dual heritage as an African raised in Europe. 453

Ann Petry   1908-
In her landmark 1946 novel, *The Street,* Petry portrayed the problems of lower-class black women. 454

Robert Deane Pharr   1916-
Offering authentic accounts of black American life, Pharr's novels often focus on denial of access to the "American dream." .456

Sterling D. Plumpp   1927-
Plumpp's poetry, for which he is best known, stems from his experiences as a youth in Mississippi. . .457

Sidney Poitier   1927-
The first black male to receive an Academy Award for acting, Poitier is also a film director and has written screenplays. 458

Carlene Hatcher Polite   1932-
Polite's novels, *The Flagellants* and *Sister X and the Victims of Foul Play,* have been noted for their characters' sharp rhetoric. 461

**Theodore Roosevelt Augustus Major Poston
1906-1974**
A *New York Post* reporter from the late 1930s until 1972, Poston was one of the first black journalists to work for a white-owned newspaper. 462

Adam Clayton Powell, Jr.   1908-1972
Powell was New York City's first black council member and Harlem's first black congressman. .462

Benjamin Quarles   1904-
Quarles is a historian who specializes in the period from the Revolutionary War to the Civil War. . .466

Dudley Randall   1914-
Founder of the influential black publishing house Broadside Press, Randall is himself an accomplished poet. 468

A. Philip Randolph   1889-1979
Organizer of the first all-black labor union chartered by the AFL, Randolph fought discrimination in government jobs. 470

William J. Raspberry   1935-
Raspberry is a nationally syndicated columnist for the *Washington Post.* 472

H. Cordelia Ray   1849(?)-1916
A poet, Ray was one of the few nineteenth-century black women to earn critical recognition for her writing. 473

Saunders Redding   1906-1988
Historian Redding wrote *To Make a Poet Black,* the first comprehensive study of black literature before the Harlem Renaissance. 474

Eugene B. Redmond   1937-
A poet, playwright, critic, and editor, Redmond advocated the separatist black literary movement of the 1960s. 476

Ishmael Reed   1938-
Novelist and poet Reed draws on black folk culture to produce provocative works that indict universal evils, especially racism. 478

Vic Reid   1913-
Reid is a Jamaican journalist and novelist whose works include *New Day* and *The Jamaicans.* . . 484

Trevor D. Rhone   1940-
This Jamaican playwright and screenwriter is perhaps best known for his cult film classic, "The Harder They Come." 484

Nola Richardson   1936-
Richardson's poetic works include *When One Loves: The Black Experience in America* and *Even in a Maze.* 485

Willis Richardson   1889-1977
Richardson was the first black playwright to have a nonmusical play produced on Broadway. 485

Richard Rive   1931-
South African fiction writer Rive often employs humor and irony to illuminate the injustices of apartheid. 487

Conrad Kent Rivers   1933-1968
Rivers was a poet whose books included *The Black Bodies* and *This Sunburnt Face* and *The Still Voice of Harlem.* 488

Paul Robeson   1898-1976
This prominent actor and singer enjoyed an enormously successful theatrical career that was ended by reaction to his controversial political views. . . . 488

Max Robinson   1939-
Robinson was the first black journalist to anchor a prime-time network program, "ABC World News Tonight." 490

William H. Robinson   1922-
A black literature scholar, Robinson has extensively studied the work of poet Phillis Wheatley. 491

Carolyn M. Rodgers   1945-
Rodgers is one of the better-known poets to have emerged in the 1960s from Chicago's Organization of Black Culture. 491

Charlemae Hill Rollins   1897-1979
Rollins was a librarian and educator who wrote books for young people on famous black Americans. . . .494

Ola Rotimi   1938(?)-
One of Nigeria's foremost English language playwrights, Rotimi addresses his country's historical and political problems. 494

Jacques Roumain   1907-1944
Haitian political activist and writer, Roumain was a proponent of the Haitian nationalist movement of the 1920s and 1930s. .495

Carl Thomas Rowan   1925-
A prominent journalist and former U.S. ambassador, Rowan writes a column for the Field Newspaper Syndicate and is a frequent television commentator. 498

Bayard Rustin   1910(?)-1987
A leading civil rights activist and promoter, Rustin promoted non-violent, yet radical, alteration of American society. 498

Primus St. John   1939-
St. John is a poet whose books include *Skins on the Earth* and *Love Is Not a Consolation: It Is a Light.* 501

Andrew Salkey   1928-
This Panamanian-born author is best known for his adult novels and his stories for young people. . .501

Sonia Sanchez   1934-
A poet involved in the black nationalist literary movement of the 1960s, Sanchez emphasizes the performance aspects of poetry as a link to African oral traditions. 502

George S. Schuyler   1895-1977
Popular satirist of the 1930s and 1940s, Schuyler lost favor with leaders of the 1960s civil rights movement. 506

Philippa Schuyler   1934-1967
A noted composer and concert pianist, Schuyler was also a foreign news correspondent. 507

Nathan A. Scott, Jr.   1925-
Scott is a theologian and literary scholar who often examines the treatment of religion in literature. .508

Gil Scott-Heron   1949-
Best known as a recording artist, Scott-Heron is also a novelist and poet. 509

Robert George Seale 1936-
A political activist and member of the "Chicago Eight," Bobby Seale co-founded the Black Panther Party. 510

Francis Selormey 1927-
Selormey is a Ghanian author whose autobiography is entitled *The Narrow Path: An African Childhood.* 511

Leopold Sedar Senghor 1906-
Former president of the Republic of Senegal, Senghor is often regarded as Africa's premier statesman and intellectual. 511

John H. Sengstacke 1912-
A publisher and journalist, Sengstacke founded the Negro Newspaper Publishers Association (now National Newspaper Publishers Association) in 1940. 517

Ntozake Shange 1948-
Shange is the author of the internationally-acclaimed "For Colored Girls Who Have Considered Suicide When the Rainbow is Enuf." 518

Saundra Sharp 1942-
Sharp is a poet, scriptwriter, and actress whose books include the poetry collections *In the Midst of Change* and *Soft Song.* 523

Bernard Shaw 1940-
Shaw is an anchor for the nationally-distributed Cable News Network. 523

Ted Shine 1931-
Playwright Shine often employs humor in his portrayals of serious subject matter. 524

Ann Allen Shockley 1927-
Shockley is a librarian and author of such novels as *Loving Her* and *Say Jesus and Come to Me.* . . 524

Herbert A. Simmons 1930-
Simmons's novels *Corner Boy* and *Man Walking on Eggshells* recreate his native St. Louis as it was in the 1940s and 1950s. 525

William Gardner Smith 1927(?)-1974
Smith was the news editor for Agence France-Presse and wrote several novels, including *Anger at Innocence* and *The Stone Face.* 526

Ellease Southerland 1943-
Southerland's poetry and novels show influences of the Bible, ancient Egyptian mythology, and African history and traditions. 526

Thomas Sowell 1930-
Economist Sowell argues in his books and newspaper column that government intervention hampers blacks from achieving true economic independence. . . 527

Wole Soyinka 1934-
This Nobel Prize-winning Nigerian novelist, play-wright, and poet is often compared to Shakespeare and the Greek dramatists because of his powerful portrayal of universal issues. 529

A. B. Spellman 1935(?)-
A poet and leading jazz critic, Spellman is one of a group of black poets who emerged in the 1960s and were concerned with the universal plight of black Americans. 534

Robert B. Stepto 1945-
Stepto is an English and Afro-American studies professor at Yale University and a noted critic and editor of black American literature. 534

John Steptoe 1950-
Author and illustrator of children's books who won a Caldecott Honor Book Award for his 1988 work *Mufaro's Beautiful Daughters.* 535

Efua Sutherland 1924-
The plays of this Ghanaian playwright and poet are often based on traditional African folklore and emphasize rhyme, rhythm, music, dance, and spectator response. 536

Ellen Tarry 1906-
Influenced by her involvement in the civil rights movement, Tarry was one of the first authors to use blacks as main characters in books for children. .538

Margaret Taylor
See **Margaret Taylor Burroughs**

Mildred D. Taylor
Winner of numerous awards for her books, including the Newbery Medal, a *New York Times* Outstanding Book of the Year citation, and a Christopher Award. 538

Philippe Thoby-Marcelin 1904-1975
A Haitian novelist and former poet, Thoby-Marcelin is best remembered for critically-acclaimed novels depicting peasant life. 539

Joyce Carol Thomas 1938-
Playwright, poet, and author of novels for young adults, including the award-winning *Marked by Fire* and *Bright Shadow.* 540

Lorenzo Thomas 1944-
Panamanian-born poet known for his surrealistic verse that identifies strongly with Africa while questing for individual identity. 541

Howard Thurman 1900-1981
A teacher and administrator at several universities, including Boston University, where he was the first black full-time faculty member. 543

Wallace Thurman   1902-1934
An editor, playwright, and novelist, whose work
includes the novel *The Blacker the Berry.* 545

Melvin B. Tolson   1898(?)-1966
Known for his complex, challenging poetry, including
Libretto for the Republic of Liberia and *Harlem
Gallery,* Tolson was appointed poet laureate of Li-
beria in 1947. 547

Jean Toomer   1894-1967
Toomer wrote the novel *Cain,* a three-part work
comprised of prose and poetry. 548

Askia Muhammad Abu Bakr el Toure   1938-
A leader of the black aesthetics movement, Toure is an
American poet best known for such works as *Songhai!*
and *Juju.* 550

Quincy Troupe   1943-
Troupe is an American poet whose collection
Snakeback Solos: Selected Poems, 1969-1977 won an
Amer-ican Book Award in 1980. 551

Darwin T. Turner   1931-
A noted English professor, critic of black literature,
editor, and poet. 553

Waters Edward Turpin   1910-1968
Turpin has been labelled the progenitor of the
Afro-American saga for his novels *These Low
Grounds* and *O Canaan!* 554

Desmond M. Tutu   1931-
A South African Anglican bishop, archbishop of
Capetown, and one of the world's foremost black
critics of South Africa's apartheid government. 555

Amos Tutuola   1920-
Tutuola became the first internationally recognized
Nigerian writer with the publication of his 1952 novel
*The Palm-Wine Drunkard and His Dead Palm-Wine
Tapster in the Dead's Town.* 560

Henry Van Dyke   1928-
Van Dyke writes novels that critics often describe as
offbeat, comical, and sometimes macabre. 563

Melvin Van Peebles   1932-
Novelist, playwright, and actor who may be best
known for his screenplays "Sweet Sweetback's
Baadasssss Song" and "Greased Lightning." . . . 563

Mary Elizabeth Vroman   1923-1967
Best known for her short story "See How They Run,"
which portrayed her teaching experiences in the
segregated, rural South. 566

Derek Walcott   1930-
A West Indian poet and playwright of mixed racial
and ethnic heritage, Walcott won an Obie Award for
his play "Dream on Monkey Mountain" and a *Los
Angeles Times* Book Prize for his *Collected
Poems.* 567

Alice Walker   1944-
American novelist, poet, and short story writer whose
novel *The Color Purple* won the Pulitzer Prize and
American Book Award in 1983 and was made into a
popular motion picture. 571

Joseph A. Walker   1935-
An actor, director, producer, and playwright who
penned "The River Niger," which garnered a Tony
Award and Drama Desk Award amid other
prizes. 573

Margaret Abigail Walker   1915-
Author of *Jubilee,* which was the first novel by a black
author to speak out for the liberation of black
women. 575

Ruby Ann Wallace   1923(?)-
Known as Ruby Dee, she is one of America's most
prominent black actresses appearing in productions
from Shakespeare to television series. 578

Eric Walrond   1898-1966
Born in British Guiana, Walrond migrated to New
York City at the age of twenty and established himself
as one of the more important young writers of the
Harlem Renaissance. 579

Douglas Turner Ward   1930-
A playwright who co-founded the Negro Ensemble
Co. in New York City and serves as its artistic director,
Ward is also an Obie Award-winning actor. 579

Theodore Ward   1902-1983
Once regarded as "the dean of black dramatists,"
Ward contributed to the advancement of black theatre
in the United States. 581

Booker T. Washington   1856-1915
Co-founder of Alabama's Tuskegee Normal and
Industrial Institute, Washington believed economic
strength would provide blacks with political and social
equality. 582

Mary Helen Washington   1941-
An editor and critic, Washington has introduced the
work of a number of talented black women writers in
her anthologies. .585

Tom Weatherly   1942-
A poet and educator, Weatherly "interpret[s] the
human condition by particularizing the black experience," according to the *Dictionary of Literary
Biography.* 586

Ron Welburn   1944-
Welburn attributes the oral tradition of Pennsylvania
and his love of nature and music as important to his
development as a poet. 586

Richard Wesley   1945-
Award-winning playwright and screenwriter whose
work includes the screenplays "Uptown Saturday
Night" and "Native Son." 587

Edgar White   1947-
A West Indian-born novelist, playwright, and musician whose writing is noted for its irony, literary allusions, and wit. 589

Walter F. White   1893-1955
Executive secretary of the National Association for the Advancement of Colored People for more than twenty years and author of six books. 590

John Edgar Wideman   1941-
An educator and novelist, Wideman wrote *Sent for You Yesterday,* which won the 1984 P.E.N./Faulkner Award for fiction. 591

Roger Wilkins   1932-
An award-winning journalist, Wilkins is also the author of a critically-acclaimed autobiography, *A Man's Life.* 593

Roy Wilkins   1901-1981
Wilkins served as executive director of the National Association for the Advancement of Colored People for more than twenty years. 595

Brenda Wilkinson   1946-
Wilkinson is a novelist whose "Ludell" trilogy has been praised for its accurate portrayal of rural black life. 596

Eric Williams   1911-1981
A Trinidadian educator, historian, and author, Williams was the first prime minister of Trinidad and Tobago. 597

John A. Williams   1925-
Williams won an American Book Award in 1983 for his novel *!Click Song.* 598

Samuel Arthur Williams   1946-
Best known under the name Samm-Art Williams, this actor and playwright wrote the award-winning comedy-drama "Home." 601

Sherley Anne Williams   1944-
An award-winning novelist and poet, Williams is considered an insightful critic of black literature. 602

August Wilson   1945-
Wilson's play "Ma Rainey's Black Bottom" won the New York Drama Critics Circle Award in 1985; "Fences" won a Pulitzer Prize, a Tony Award, and the Outer Critics Circle Award in 1987. 604

Charles Stevenson Wright   1932-
Wright has written such satiric novels as *The Messenger* and *Absolutely Nothing to Get Alarmed About.* 606

Richard Wright   1908-1960
One of the most influential black writers of the twentieth century, Wright wrote such works as the novel *Native Son* and an autobiography, *Black Boy.* 607

Sarah E. Wright   1928-
A poet and novelist who wrote *This Child's Gonna Live,* which was praised for its ambitious techniques and compelling drama. 612

Camille Yarbrough   1938-
Dancer, poet and actress, Yarbrough has appeared in such plays as "To Be Young, Gifted, and Black," "Trumpets of the Lord," and "Sambo." 613

Frank G. Yerby   1916-
Yerby is a prolific novelist whose work has not received the critical attention that many feel such best sellers as *The Foxes of Harrow* and *Pride's Castle* merit. 613

Al Young   1939-
An award-winning novelist, poet, and music critic, Young is considered a gifted stylist and a keen observer of the human comedy. 616

Whitney M. Young, Jr.   1921-1971
As director of the National Urban League and member of several Presidential Commissions, Young worked for civil rights through traditional channels. 618

INTRODUCTION

Black Writers provides complete and accurate biographical and bibliographical information on more than four hundred black authors active during the twentieth century. Entries in this volume were selected from Gale's acclaimed *Contemporary Authors* series and completely updated for the publication of *Black Writers*. More than one hundred sketches were written especially for this volume, to furnish the most comprehensive coverage possible, and will appear in future volumes of *Contemporary Authors*.

Scope

Before preparing this volume, the editors of *Contemporary Authors* conducted a telephone survey of librarians, mailed a print survey to more than four thousand libraries, and met with an advisory board comprised of librarians from university, high school, and public libraries around the country.

Our librarian advisors told us that they indeed felt a need for an information source that specifically covered black writers of the twentieth century. They wanted this source to contain the type of in-depth primary information not found in other works on black writers as well as critical material and sources when available. These librarians also told us that our inclusion criteria for this volume should be broad, rather than narrow, in terms of the types of writers we listed and their predominant period of activity.

Following their advice, we have not only included entries for the pre-eminent black novelists, poets, short story writers, dramatists, and journalists writing today but have also sketched those individuals active in the earlier portion of the century, particularly writers prominent during the Harlem Renaissance. Also included in *Black Writers* are individuals who have written books but are better known for their work in the political or social arena, such as Booker T. Washington, Ralph J. Bunche, Malcolm X, and Desmond Tutu. And, because our advisors thought this volume should have an international scope, we have included important African and Caribbean black writers who are of interest to an American audience (and, of course, who have written in English or had their works translated into English).

Format

Both the newly-written and the completely-updated entries in *Black Writers* provide in-depth information that is unavailable in any other single reference source. The format is designed for ease of use—for students, teachers, scholars, and librarians. Individual paragraphs, labelled with descriptive rubrics, ensure that a reader seeking specific information can quickly focus on the pertinent portion of an entry.

A typical entry in *Black Writers* contains the following, clearly-labelled information sections:

Personal: dates and places of birth and death; parents' names and occupations; name of spouse(s), date(s) of marriage(s); names of children; colleges attended and degrees earned; political and religious affiliation when known.

Addresses: complete home, office, and agent's addresses.

Career: name of employer, position, and dates for each career post; resumé of other vocational achievements; military service.

Member: memberships, and offices held, in professional and civic organizations.

Awards, honors: literary and professional awards received and dates.

Writings: title-by-title chronological bibliography of books written and edited, listed by genre when known; list of other notable publications, such as plays, screenplays, and periodical contributions.

Work in Progress: description of projects in progress.

Sidelights: a biographical portrait of the author's development; information about the critical reception of the author's works; revealing comments, often by the authors themselves, on their personal interests, aspirations, motivations, and thoughts on writing.

Biographical/Critical Sources: books, feature articles, and reviews in which the writer's work has been treated.

Acknowledgments

The editors wish to gratefully acknowledge the contributions of the many librarians who assisted us in the compilation of this volume with their responses to our telephone and mail survey or by participating on our advisory board. We especially wish to thank the following individuals for their help: Nancy Bellaire, Monroe County Library System; Jean Curtis, Detroit Public Library; Dawn Heller, Riverside-Brookfield High School Library; Neil Jordahl, Enoch Pratt Free Library; Tim LaBorie, Drexel University Library; Jane Lawless, Darien High School Library; Lucille C. Thomas, library consultant and researcher; and Emmy-Lou Wilson, Detroit Public Library.

Comments Are Appreciated

We hope that you find *Black Writers* a useful reference tool and welcome your comments about this work. Send comments to: The Editors, *Black Writers,* Gale Research Inc., Book Tower, Detroit, MI 48226-1822; or call toll-free at 1-800-521-0707.

Black Writers

ABRAHAMS, Peter (Henry) 1919-

PERSONAL: Born March 19, 1919, at Vrededorp, near Johannesburg, South Africa; son of James Henry and Angelina (DuPlessis) Abrahams; married Dorothy Pennington, 1942 (marriage dissolved, 1948); married Daphne Elizabeth Miller (an artist), June 1, 1948; children: (second marriage) Anne, Aron, Naomi. *Education:* Attended St. Peter's College and Teacher's Training College.

ADDRESSES: Home—Red Hills, St. Andrew, Jamaica, West Indies. *Agent*—Faber & Faber Ltd.; 3 Queen Sq., London WC1N 3AU, England; and 50 Cross St., Winchester, Mass.

CAREER: Began working, as a tinsmith's helper, at the age of nine; attended schools between periods of working at jobs such as kitchen helper, dishwasher, porter, and clerk; failed in his attempt to start a school near Capetown for poor Africans; for a short time worked as an editor in Durban; in 1939, to reach England, he took work as a stoker, and spent two years at sea; correspondent in Kenya and South Africa for the London *Observer* and the *New York Herald Tribune* (New York and Paris), 1952-54; commissioned by British Government in 1955 to write a book on Jamaica; emigrated to Jamaica in 1956; regular radio news commentator in Jamaica, 1957—; editor of the *West Indian Economist*, Jamaica, 1958-62, and radio commentator and controller for the "West Indian News" Program, 1958-62; full-time writer, 1964—. Radio Jamaica chairman, set up a new ownership structure, making major interest groups into shareholders, 1978-80.

MEMBER: International PEN, Society of Authors, Authors League.

WRITINGS:

NOVELS

Song of the City, Dorothy Crisp, 1945.
Mine Boy, Dorothy Crisp, 1946, Knopf, 1955, Collier Books, 1970.
The Path of Thunder, Harper, 1948, Chatham Bookseller, 1975.
Wild Conquest (historical fiction), Harper, 1950, Anchor Books, 1970.
A Wreath for Udomo, Knopf, 1956, Collier Books, 1971.
A Night of Their Own, Knopf, 1965.
This Island Now, Faber, 1966, Knopf, 1967, revised edition, Faber & Faber, 1985.

The View from Coyaba (historical fiction), Faber & Faber, 1985.

OTHER

A Blackman Speaks of Freedom (poetry), Universal Printing Works (Durban, South Africa), 1941.
Dark Testament (short stories), Allen and Unwin, 1942, Kraus Reprint, 1970.
Return to Goli (autobiography), Faber & Faber, 1953.
Tell Freedom (autobiography), Knopf, 1954, published as *Tell Freedom: Memories of Africa,* Knopf, 1969, abridged edition, Macmillan, 1970.
Jamaica: An Island Mosaic (travel), H.M.S.O., 1957.
(And editor) *Souvenir Pictorial Review of the West Indies Federation, 1947-57,* Edna Manley (Kingston, Jamaica), c. 1958.
(With the staff of *Holiday* magazine and others) *The World of Mankind,* Golden Press, 1962.
(With others) *History of the Pan-African Congress,* Hammersmith Bookshop, 1963.

Contributor to *Modern African Prose,* edited by Richard Rive and to *Schwarze Ballade,* edited by Janheinz Jahn. Also author of radio scripts for British Broadcasting Corp. during the 1950s. Contributor to *Holiday* and *Cape Standard.*

MEDIA ADAPTATIONS: Abrahams' novel *Mine Boy* was adapted as a play; the novel *Path of Thunder* was made into a movie and a ballet in the Soviet Union.

SIDELIGHTS: Peter Abrahams, the son of an Ethiopian father and a mother of mixed French and African ancestry, published his first book at a time when nearly all the novelists in South Africa were white. Abrahams himself was considered Colored, a legal designation referring to the descendents from blacks and early white settlers. The Colored people had traditionally remained aloof from blacks, but Abrahams took a unique step by siding with black South Africans. Abrahams also stood apart by being one of South Africa's first non-whites to make a living as a writer. And whether using fiction or autobiography, his focus has remained on the non-whites' struggle for respect and political power. In the book *Peter Abrahams,* Michael Wade writes that "Peter Abrahams is a novelist of ideas. He writes about the machinery of politics and power, but he uses his considerable grasp of this area of activity to serve his central interest, which is the problem of individual freedom in contemporary affairs.''

Abrahams grew up in the slums of Johannesburg, where illiteracy was common. He didn't learn to read until he was nine, but thereafter immersed himself in books. He sought out British classics, including Shakespeare, and found works by black American authors in the local library. At the age of eleven, he started writing short stories. Abrahams left school early and tried to support himself as a journalist, but jobs were hard to find for a non-white; almost every door seemed closed to him. While he considered himself a Marxist, editors sharing his political beliefs found him too restrained, while black editors thought him too left-wing to hire for black newspapers. At twenty, Abrahams decided he had to leave South Africa. In his autobiographical *Return to Goli,* he explains, ''I had to escape or slip into that negative destructiveness that is the offspring of bitterness and frustration.'' He worked his way to England as a ship's stoker, later moving to France, and then to Jamaica, which became his permanent home. After emigrating, he only returned to South Africa as a visitor.

While Abrahams has always felt strongly about the problems of non-whites in Africa, when writing his early works he restrained his anger toward the government. In *Return to Goli,* he explains that he had ''purged himself of hatred,'' since ''art and beauty come of love, not hate.'' Believing that love was necessary to overcome racial prejudice, Abrahams frequently incorporated mixed-race love affairs in his early novels. These relationships and their resulting children represented a new order, where the individual would not be judged by his color. In *An African Treasury,* Abrahams claims that this perception comes from tribal Africa, where ''the attitude to colour is healthy and normal. Colour does not matter. Colour is an act of God that neither confers privileges nor imposes handicaps on a man. . . . What does matter to the tribal African, what is important, is the complex pattern of his position within his own group and his relations with the other members of the group. . . . The important things in his life are anything but race and colour—until they are forced on him.''

And yet at the same time, Abrahams felt that the great influence of African tribalism on contemporary blacks was a handicap. He embraced Western culture, because, as he wrote in an issue of *International Affairs,* ''The true motive forces of Western culture are to be found in the first place in the teachings of the Christ who taught a new concept of men's relations with their God and with each other, a concept that cuts across tribal gods and tribal loyalties and embraces all men in all lands offering them a common brotherhood.'' In his novel, *A Night of Their Own,* Abrahams emphasizes the common goals of South African Indians and blacks. Both groups work together to change their tyrannical government. While the setting is fictional, Abrahams tied it to contemporary issues by dedicating the book to imprisoned South African activists Walter Sisulu and Nelson Mandela.

Although critics praise Abrahams' handling of political issues, they often fault his characterization. In the *New York Times Book Review,* Martin Levin says, ''What is rich in this novel is the complexity of its political climate,'' but adds that ''what snarls matters is the author's tendency to spell out his characters' thinking.'' In *The Writing of Peter Abrahams,* Kolawole Ogungbesan voices a similar concern: ''The tone of [*A Night of Their Own*] is uncompromisingly noble and determinedly serious, making the characters' gestures as stagey as their dialogues. But the cumulative effect is powerful.''

In *This Island Now,* Abrahams turns from his early call for a pluralistic society to insisting that blacks first establish their own identity, socially and politically, as free men. He also stops looking to Western civilization for solutions. The plot concerns a left-wing black leader who rises to power on a fictional island. But according to Ogungbesan ''There is no doubt that the physical terrain of *This Island Now* is largely that of Jamaica as described in [Abrahams'] essay, *The Real Jamaica,* . . . [with] the political terrain of Haiti.'' *New York Times Book Review* contributor Peter Buitenhuis comments, ''As an analysis of this kind of political process, [*This Island Now*] throws light on the motivations of black leaders who have risen to power in recent years in the Caribbean and elsewhere. Unfortunately [Abrahams'] attempt to make this material into a novel has not been too successful. He has tried to embody each interest—political, journalistic, financial, etc.—in a different character, and as a result, the book is overpopulated and over-schematic.'' But Ogungbesan feels the book's strengths and weaknesses are inseparable, and that it must be regarded as a purely political work. He remarks, ''The book is a serious political novel precisely because it avoids the easy banalities that its theme . . . might provoke. . . . Abrahams is so preoccupied with the political conflict that everything else recedes to the background.''

The View from Coyaba is the work that reflects Abrahams' thorough disenchantment with what he calls ''destructive Westernism.'' Some critics, however, find Abrahams' work closer to a tract or treatise than a novel. While *Times Literary Supplement* contributor David Wright considers the book ''high-minded, sincere, committed,'' he thinks that ''as a philosophic and humane survey of the history of black emancipation since the British abolition of slavery, his book may be recommended; as a novel, not.'' Judith Wilson, writing in the *New York Times Book Review,* agrees in finding *The View from Coyaba* ''unmistakably didactic fiction.'' However, she finds that ''the originality of Mr. Abrahams' message, its global sweep and political urgency exert their own force. . . . Peter Abrahams challenges us to rethink a large chunk of modern history and to question many of our current ideological assumptions.'' But Andrew Salkey in *World Literature Today* never questions whether the work is a true novel, as Abrahams has produced, he states, ''the most dramatically resonant writing I have read in many years. . . . It is not only a composite novelistic picture, but also a reverberating metaphor.''

While Abrahams' books may not point to any definite means of eliminating racism, they contain hope that conditions will improve. Ogungbesan affirms, ''Himself such an incurable optimist, all his books are open to the future, based on his belief that change is inevitable, a natural process. This is why the image of the day assumes such symbolic significance in his novels. The implication is that although the black people in South Africa are passing through a long night, their ordeal will not last for ever: after the night inevitably comes the dawn. Abrahams thinks that it will be a glorious dawn if the whites and the blacks can co-operate peacefully to work towards that day.''

AVOCATIONAL INTERESTS: Gardening, tennis, walking, conversation, reading, travel.

BIOGRAPHICAL/CRITICAL SOURCES:

BOOKS

Abrahams, Peter, *Return to Goli,* Faber, 1953.

Barnett, Ursula A., *A Vision of Order: A Study of Black South African Literature in English (1914-1980),* University of Massachusetts Press, 1983.
Contemporary Literary Criticism, Volume 4, Gale, 1975.
Hughes, Langston, editor, *An African Treasury,* Gollancz, 1961.
Lindfors, Bernth, *Early Nigerian Literature,* Africana Publishing, 1982.
Ogungbesan, Kolawole, *The Writing of Peter Abrahams,* Africana Publishing, 1979.
Tucker, Martin, *Africa in Modern Literature: A Survey of Contemporary Writing in English,* Ungar, 1967.
Wade, Michael, *Peter Abrahams,* Evans Brothers, 1971.

PERIODICALS

Critique, Volume XI, number 1, 1968.
Los Angeles Times Book Review, July 14, 1985.
New Statesman, February 22, 1985.
New Yorker, September 25, 1965.
New York Times Book Review, April 11, 1965, September 24, 1967, April 2, 1972, May 26, 1985.
Observer, February 17, 1985.
Times Literary Supplement, March 25, 1965, October 20, 1966, March 22, 1985.
World Literature Today, fall, 1985.

—*Sketch by Jani Prescott*

*   *   *

ACHEBE, (Albert) Chinua(lumogu)   1930-

PERSONAL: Born November 16, 1930, in Ogidi, Nigeria; son of Isaiah Okafo (a Christian churchman) and Janet N. (Iloegbunam) Achebe; married Christie Chinwe Okoli, September 10, 1961; children: Chinelo (daughter), Ikechukwu (son), Chidi (son), Nwando (daughter). *Education:* Attended Government College, Umuahia, 1944-47; attended University College, Ibadan, 1948-53; London University, B.A., 1953; studied broadcasting at the British Broadcasting Corp., London, 1956.

ADDRESSES: Home—33 Umunkanka St., Nsukka, Anambra State, Nigeria. *Office*—Institute of African Studies, University of Nigeria, Nsukka, Anambra State, Nigeria; and University of Massachusetts, Amherst, Mass. 01003.

CAREER: Writer. Nigerian Broadcasting Corp., Lagos, Nigeria, talks producer, 1954-57, controller of Eastern Region in Enugu, 1958-61, founder, and director of Voice of Nigeria, 1961-66; University of Nigeria, Nsukka, senior research fellow, 1967-72, professor of English, 1976-81, professor emeritus, 1985—; Anambra State University of Technology, Enugu, pro-chancellor and chairman of council, 1986—; University of Massachusetts—Amherst, professor, 1987-88. Served on diplomatic missions for Biafra during the Nigerian Civil War, 1967-69. Visiting professor of English at University of Massachusetts—Amherst, 1972-75, and University of Connecticut, 1975-76. Lecturer at University of California, Los Angeles, and at universities in Nigeria and the United States; speaker at events in numerous countries throughout the world. Chairman, Citadel Books Ltd., Enugu, Nigeria, 1967; director, Heinemann Educational Books Ltd., Ibadan, Nigeria, 1970—; director, Nwamife Publishers Ltd., Enugu, Nigeria, 1970—. Founder, and publisher, *Uwa Ndi Igbo: A Bilingual Journal of Igbo Life and Arts,* 1984—. Governor, Newsconcern International Foundation, 1983. Member, University of Lagos Council, 1966, East Central State Library Board, 1971-72, Anambra State Arts Council, 1977-79, and National Festival Committee, 1983; director, Okike Arts Centre, Nsukka,

1984—. Deputy national president of People's Redemption Party, 1983; president of town union, Ogidi, Nigeria, 1986—.

MEMBER: International Social Prospects Academy (Geneva), Writers and Scholars International (London), Writers and Scholars Educational Trust (London), Commonwealth Arts Organization (member of executive committee, 1981—), Association of Nigerian Authors (founder; president, 1981-86), Ghana Association of Writers (fellow), Royal Society of Literature (London), Modern Language Association of America (honorary fellow), American Academy and Institute of Arts and Letters (honorary member).

AWARDS, HONORS: Margaret Wrong Memorial Prize, 1959, for *Things Fall Apart;* Rockefeller travel fellowship to East and Central Africa, 1960; Nigerian National Trophy, 1961, for *No Longer at Ease;* UNESCO fellowship for creative artists for travel to United States and Brazil, 1963; Jock Campbell/*New Statesman* Award, 1965, for *Arrow of God;* D.Litt., Dartmouth College, 1972, University of Southampton, 1975, University of Ife, 1978, University of Nigeria, Nsukka, 1981 University of Kent, 1982, Mount Allison University, 1984, University of Guelph, 1984, and Franklin Pierce College, 1985; Commonwealth Poetry Prize, 1972, for *Beware, Soul-Brother, and Other Poems;* D.Univ., University of Stirling, 1975; Neil Gunn international fellow, Scottish Arts Council, 1975; Lotus Award for Afro-Asian Writers, 1975; LL.D., University of Prince Edward Island, 1976; D.H.L., University of Massachusetts—Amherst, 1977; Nigerian National Merit Award, 1979; named to the Order of the Federal Republic of Nigeria, 1979; Commonwealth Foundation senior visiting practitioner award, 1984; *A Man of the People* was cited in Anthony Burgess's 1984 book *Ninety-nine Novels: The Best in England since 1939;* Booker Prize nomination, 1987, for *Anthills of the Savannah.*

WRITINGS:

Things Fall Apart (novel), Heinemann, 1958, McDowell Obolensky, 1959, reprinted, Fawcett, 1988.
No Longer at Ease (novel), Heinemann, 1960, Obolensky, 1961, 2nd edition, Fawcett, 1988.
The Sacrificial Egg, and Other Stories, Etudo (Onitsha, Nigeria), 1962.
Arrow of God (novel), Heinemann, 1964, John Day, 1967.
A Man of the People (novel), John Day, 1966, published with an introduction by K.W.J. Post, Doubleday, 1967.
Chike and the River (juvenile), Cambridge University Press, 1966.
Beware, Soul-Brother, and Other Poems, Nwankwo-Ifejika (Enugu, Nigeria), 1971, Doubleday, 1972, revised edition, Heinemann, 1972.
(With John Iroaganachi) *How the Leopard Got His Claws* (juvenile), Nwankwo-Ifejika, 1972, (bound with *Lament of the Deer,* by Christopher Okigbo), Third Press, 1973.
Girls at War (short stories), Heinemann, 1973, reprinted, Fawcett, 1988.
Christmas in Biafra, and Other Poems, Doubleday, 1973.
Morning Yet on Creation Day (essays), Doubleday, 1975.
The Flute (juvenile), Fourth Dimension Publishers (Enugu), 1978.
The Drum (juvenile), Fourth Dimension Publishers, 1978.
(Editor with Dubem Okafor) *Don't Let Him Die: An Anthology of Memorial Poems for Christopher Okigbo,* Fourth Dimension Publishers, 1978.
(Co-editor) *Aka Weta: An Anthology of Igbo Poetry,* Okike (Nsukka, Nigeria), 1982.

The Trouble with Nigeria (essays), Fourth Dimension Publishers, 1983, Heinemann, 1984.

(Editor with C. L. Innes) *African Short Stories,* Heinemann, 1984.

Anthills of the Savannah (novel), Anchor Books, 1988.

Hopes and Impediments (essays), Heinemann, 1988.

CONTRIBUTOR

Ellis Ayitey Komey and Ezekiel Mphahlele, editors, *Modern African Stories,* Faber, 1964.

Neville Denny, compiler, *Pan African Stories,* Nelson, 1966.

Paul Edwards, compiler, *Through African Eyes,* two volumes, Cambridge University Press, 1966.

Mphahlele, editor, *African Writing Today,* Penguin Books (Baltimore), 1967.

Barbara Nolen, editor, *Africa and Its People: Firsthand Accounts from Contemporary Africa,* Dutton, 1967.

Ime Ikiddeh, compiler, *Drum Beats: An Anthology of African Writing,* E. J. Arnold, 1968.

Ulli Beier, editor, *Political Spider: An Anthology of Stories from "Black Orpheus,"* Africana Publishing, 1969.

John P. Berry, editor, *Africa Speaks: A Prose Anthology with Comprehension and Summary Passages,* Evans, 1970.

Joseph Conrad, *Heart of Darkness,* edited by Robert Kimbrough, 3rd edition, Norton, 1987.

OTHER

Founding editor, "African Writers Series," Heinemann, 1962-72. Editor, *Okike: A Nigerian Journal of New Writing,* 1971—; editor, *Nsukkascope,* a campus magazine. *Things Fall Apart* has been translated into forty-five languages.

SIDELIGHTS: Since the 1950s, Nigeria has witnessed "the flourishing of a new literature which has drawn sustenance both from traditional oral literature and from the present and rapidly changing society," writes Margaret Laurence in her book *Long Drums and Cannons: Nigerian Dramatists and Novelists.* Thirty years ago, Chinua Achebe was among the founders of this new literature and over the years many critics have come to consider him the finest of the Nigerian novelists. His achievement has not been limited to his native country or continent, however. As Laurence maintains in her 1968 study of his novels, "Chinua Achebe's careful and confident craftsmanship, his firm grasp of his material and his ability to create memorable and living characters place him among the best novelists now writing in any country in the English language."

Unlike some African writers struggling for acceptance among contemporary English-language novelists, Achebe has been able to avoid imitating the trends in English literature. Rejecting the European notion "that art should be accountable to no one, and [needs] to justify itself to nobody," as he puts it in his book of essays, *Morning Yet on Creation Day,* Achebe has embraced instead the idea at the heart of the African oral tradition: that "art is, and always was, at the service of man. Our ancestors created their myths and legends and told their stories for a human purpose." For this reason, Achebe believes that "any good story, any good novel, should have a message, should have a purpose."

Achebe's feel for the African context has influenced his aesthetic of the novel as well as the technical aspects of his works. As Bruce King comments in *Introduction to Nigerian Literature:* "Achebe was the first Nigerian writer to successfully transmute the conventions of the novel, a European art form, into African literature." In an Achebe novel, King notes, "European character study is subordinated to the portrayal of communal life; European economy of form is replaced by an aesthetic appropriate to the rhythms of traditional tribal life." Kofi Awoonor writes in *The Breast of the Earth* that in wrapping this borrowed literary form in African garb "he created a new novel that possesses its own autonomy and transcends the limits set by both his African and European teachers."

On the level of ideas, Achebe's "prose writing reflects three essential and related concerns," observes G. D. Killam in his book *The Novels of Chinua Achebe,* "first, with the legacy of colonialism at both the individual and societal level; secondly, with the *fact* of English as a language of national and international exchange; thirdly, with the obligations and responsibilities of the writer both to the society in which he lives and to his art." Over the past century, Africa has been caught in a war for its identity between the forces of tradition, colonialism, and independence. This war has prevented many nations from raising themselves above political and social chaos to achieve true independence. "Most of the problems we see in our politics derive from the moment when we lost our initiative to other people, to colonizers," Achebe observes in his book of essays. He goes on to explain: "What I think is the basic problem of a new African country like Nigeria is really what you might call a 'crisis in the soul.' We have been subjected—we have subjected ourselves too—to this period during which we have accepted everything alien as good and practically everything local or native as inferior."

In order to reestablish the virtues of precolonial Nigeria, chronicle the impact of colonialism on native cultures, expose present day corruption, and communicate these to his fellow countrymen and to those outside his country, Achebe must make use of English, the language of colonialism. The ways in which he transforms language to achieve his particular ends distinguishes his writing from the writing of other English-language novelists. To convey the flavor of traditional Nigeria, Achebe translates Ibo proverbs into English and weaves them into his stories. "Among the Ibo the art of conversation is regarded very highly," he writes in his novel *Things Fall Apart,* "and proverbs are the palm-oil with which words are eaten." "Proverbs are cherished by Achebe's people as tribal heirlooms, the treasure boxes of their cultural heritage," explains Adrian A. Roscoe in his book *Mother Is Gold: A Study of West African Literature.* "Through them traditions are received and handed on; and when they disappear or fall into disuse . . . it is a sign that a particular tradition, or indeed a whole way of life, is passing away." Achebe's use of proverbs also has an artistic aim, as Bernth Lindfors suggests in *Folklore in Nigerian Literature.* "Achebe's proverbs can serve as keys to an understanding of his novels," comments the critic, "because he uses them not merely to add touches of local color but to sound and reiterate themes, to sharpen characterization, to clarify conflict, and to focus on the values of the society he is portraying."

To engender an appreciation for African culture in those unfamiliar with it, Achebe alters English to reflect native Nigerian languages in use. "Without seriously distorting the nature of the English," observes Eustace Palmer in *The Growth of the African Novel,* "Achebe deliberately introduces the rhythms, speech patterns, idioms and other verbal nuances of Ibo. . . . The effect of this is that while everyone who knows English will be able to understand the work and find few signs of awkwardness, the reader also has a sense, not just of black men using English, but of black Africans speaking and living in a genuinely black African rural situation." In the opinion of *Busara* contributor R. Angogo, this "ability to shape and mould English to suit character and event and yet still give the impression of an African story is one of the greatest of Achebe's achievements.'' The reason, adds the reviewer, is that ''it puts into the reader a kind of emotive effect, an interest, and a thirst which so to say awakens the reader.''

Finally, Achebe uses language, which he sees as a writer's best resource, to expose and combat the propaganda generated by African politicians to manipulate their own people. ''Language is our tool,'' he told Anthony Appiah in a *Times Literary Supplement* interview, ''and language is the tool of the politicians. We are like two sides in a very hostile game. And I think that the attempt to deceive with words is countered by the efforts of the writer to go behind the words, to show the meaning.''

Faced with his people's growing inferiority complex and his leaders' disregard for the truth, the African writer cannot turn his back on his culture, Achebe believes. ''A writer has a responsibility to try and stop [these damaging trends] because unless our culture begins to take itself seriously it will never . . . get off the ground.'' He states his mission in his essay ''The Novelist as Teacher'': ''Here then is an adequate revolution for me to espouse—to help my society regain belief in itself and to put away the complexes of the years of denigration and self-abasement. And it is essentially a question of education, in the best sense of that word. Here, I think, my aims and the deepest aspirations of society meet.''

Although he has also written poetry, short stories, and essays—both literary and political—Achebe is best known for his novels: *Things Fall Apart, No Longer at Ease, Arrow of God, A Man of the People,* and *Anthills of the Savannah.* Considering Achebe's novels, Anthony Daniels writes in the *Spectator,* ''In spare prose of great elegance, without any technical distraction, he has been able to illuminate two emotionally irreconcilable facets of modern African life: the humiliations visited on Africans by colonialism, and the utter moral worthlessness of what replaced colonial rule.'' Set in this historical context, Achebe's novels develop the theme of ''tradition verses change,'' and offer, as Palmer observes, ''a powerful presentation of the beauty, strength and validity of traditional life and values and the disruptiveness of change.'' Even so, the author does not appeal for a return to the ways of the past. Palmer notes that ''while deploring the imperialists' brutality and condescension, [Achebe] seems to suggest that change is inevitable and wise men . . . reconcile themselves to accommodating change. It is the diehards . . . who resist and are destroyed in the process.''

Two of Achebe's novels—*Things Fall Apart* and *Arrow of God*—focus on Nigeria's early experience with colonialism, from first contact with the British to widespread British administration. ''With remarkable unity of the word with the deed, the character, the time and the place, Chinua Achebe creates in these two novels a coherent picture of coherence being lost, of the tragic consequences of the African-European collision,'' offers Robert McDowell in a special issue of *Studies in Black Literature* dedicated to Achebe's work. ''There is an artistic unity of all things in these books which is rare anywhere in modern English fiction.''

Things Fall Apart, Achebe's first novel, was published in 1958 in the midst of the Nigerian renaissance. Achebe explained his motivation to begin writing at this time in an interview with Lewis Nkosi published in *African Writers Talking: A Collection of Radio Interviews:* ''One of the things that set me thinking [about writing] was Joyce Cary's novel set in Nigeria, *Mr*

Johnson, which was praised so much, and it was clear to me that this was a most superficial picture . . . not only of the country, but even of the Nigerian character. . . . I thought if this was famous, then perhaps someone ought to try and look at this from the inside.'' Charles R. Larson, in his book *The Emergence of African Fiction,* details the success of Achebe's effort, both in investing his novel of Africa with an African sensibility and in making this view available to African readers. ''In 1964, . . . *Things Fall Apart* became the first novel by an African writer to be included in the required syllabus for African secondary school students throughout the English-speaking portions of the continent.'' Later in that decade, it ''became recognized by African and non-African literary critics as the first 'classic' in English from tropical Africa,'' adds Larson.

The novel tells the story of an Ibo village of the late 1800s and one of its great men, Okonkwo. Although the son of a ne'er-do-well, Okonkwo has achieved much in his life. He is a champion wrestler, a wealthy farmer, a husband to three wives, a title-holder among his people, and a member of the select *egwugwu* whose members impersonate ancestral spirits at tribal rituals. ''The most impressive achievement of *Things Fall Apart . . .,*'' maintains David Carroll in his book *Chinua Achebe,* ''is the vivid picture it provides of Ibo society at the end of the nineteenth century.'' He explains: ''Here is a clan in the full vigor of its traditional way of life, unperplexed by the present and without nostalgia for the past.Through its rituals the life of the community and the life of the individual are merged into significance and order.''

This order is disrupted, however, with the appearance of the white man in Africa and with the introduction of his religion. ''The conflict in the novel, vested in Okonkwo, derives from the series of crushing blows which are levelled at traditional values by an alien and more powerful culture causing, in the end, the traditional society to fall apart,'' observes Killam. Okonkwo is unable to adapt to the changes that accompany colonialism. In the end, in frustration, he kills an African employed by the British, and then commits suicide, a sin against the tradition to which he had long clung. The novel thus presents ''two main, closely intertwined tragedies,'' writes Arthur Ravenscroft in his study *Chinua Achebe,* ''the personal tragedy of Okonkwo . . . and the public tragedy of the eclipse of one culture by another.''

Although the author emphasizes the message in his novels, he still receives praise for his artistic achievement. As Palmer comments, ''Chinua Achebe's *Things Fall Apart* . . . demonstrates a mastery of plot and structure, strength of characterization, competence in the manipulation of language and consistency and depth of thematic exploration which is rarely found in a first novel.'' Achebe also achieves balance in re-creating the tragic consequences of the clash of two cultures. Killam notes that ''in showing Ibo society before and after the coming of the white man he avoids the temptation to present the past as idealized and the present as ugly and unsatisfactory.'' And, as Killam concludes, Achebe's ''success proceeds from his ability to create a sense of real life and real issues in the book and to see his subject from the point of view which is neither idealistic nor dishonest.''

Arrow of God, the second of Achebe's novels of colonialism, takes place in the 1920s after the British have established a presence in Nigeria. The ''arrow of god'' mentioned in the title is Ezeulu, the chief priest of the god Ulu who is the patron deity of an Ibo village. As chief priest, Ezeulu is responsible for initiating the rituals that structure village life, a position vested with a great deal of power. In fact, the central theme of this novel, as Laurence points out, is power: "Ezeulu's testing of his own power and the power of his god, and his effort to maintain his own and his god's authority in the face of village factions and of the [Christian] mission and the British administration." "This, then, is a political novel in which different systems of power are examined and their dependence upon myth and ritual compared," writes Carroll. "Of necessity it is also a study in the psychology of power."

In Ezeulu, Achebe presents a study of the loss of power. After his village rejects his advice to avoid war with a neighboring village, Ezeulu finds himself at odds with his own people and praised by the British administrators. The British, seeking a candidate to install as village chieftain, make him an offer, which he refuses. Caught in the middle with no allies, Ezeulu slowly loses his grip on reality and slips into senility. "As in Achebe's other novels," observes Gerald Moore in *Seven African Writers*, "it is the strong-willed man of tradition who cannot adapt, and who is crushed by his virtues in the war between the new, more worldly order, and the old, conservative values of an isolated society."

The artistry displayed in *Arrow of God*, Achebe's second portrait of cultures in collision, has drawn a great deal of attention, adding to the esteem in which the writer is held. Charles Miller comments in a *Saturday Review* article that Achebe's "approach to the written word is completely unencumbered with verbiage. He never strives for the exalted phrase, he never once raises his voice; even in the most emotion-charged passages the tone is absolutely unruffled, the control impeccable." Concludes this reviewer, "It is a measure of Achebe's creative gift that he has no need whatever for prose fireworks to light the flame of his intense drama."

Killam recognizes this novel as more than a vehicle for Achebe's commentary on colonialism. He suggests in his study that "Achebe's overall intention is to explore the depths of the human condition and in this other more important sense *Arrow of God* transcends its setting and shows us characters whose values, motivations, actions and qualities are permanent in human kind." Laurence offers this evaluation in her 1968 book: "*Arrow of God*, in which [Achebe] comes into full maturity as a novelist, . . . is probably one of the best novels written anywhere in the past decade."

Achebe's three other novels—*No Longer at Ease, A Man of the People*, and *Anthills of the Savannah*—examine Africa in the era of independence. This is an Africa less and less under direct European administration, yet still deeply affected by it, an Africa struggling to regain its footing in order to stand on its own two feet. Standing in the way of realizing its goal of true independence is the corruption pervasive in modern Africa, an obstacle Achebe scrutinizes in each of these novels.

In *No Longer at Ease*, set in Nigeria just prior to independence, Achebe extends his history of the Okonkwo family. Here the central character is Obi Okonkwo, grandson of the tragic hero of *Things Fall Apart*. This Okonkwo has been raised a Christian and educated at the university in England. Like many of his peers, he has left the bush behind for a position as a civil servant in Lagos, Nigeria's largest city. "*No Longer at Ease* deals with the plight of [this] new generation of Nigerians," observes Palmer, "who, having been exposed to education in the western world and therefore largely cut off from their roots in traditional society, discover, on their return,

that the demands of tradition are still strong, and are hopelessly caught in the clash between the old and the new."

Many, faced with this internal conflict, succumb to corruption. Obi is no exception. "The novel opens with Obi on trial for accepting bribes when a civil servant," notes Killam, "and the book takes the form of a long flashback." "In a world which is the result of the intermingling of Europe and Africa . . . Achebe traces the decline of his hero from brilliant student to civil servant convicted of bribery and corruption," writes Carroll. "It reads like a postscript to the earlier novel [*Things Fall Apart*] because the same forces are at work but in a confused, diluted, and blurred form." In *This Africa: Novels by West Africans in English and French*, Judith Illsley Gleason points out how the imagery of each book depicts the changes in the Okonkwo family and the Nigeria they represent. As she points out, "The career of the grandson Okonkwo ends not with a machet's swing but with a gavel's tap."

Here again in this novel Achebe carefully shapes language, to inform, but also to transport the reader to Africa. "It is through [his characters'] use of language that we are able to enter their world and to share their experiences," writes Shatto Arthur Gakwandi in *The Novel and Contemporary Experience in Africa*. Gakwandi adds: "Through [Achebe's] keen sensitivity to the way people express themselves and his delicate choice of idiom the author illuminates for us the thoughts and attitudes of the whole range of Nigerian social strata." The impact of Achebe's style is such that, as John Coleman observes in the *Spectator*, his "novel moves towards its inevitable catastrophe with classic directness. Nothing is wasted and it is only after the sad, understated close that one realises, once again how much of the Nigerian context has been touched in, from the prejudice and corruption of Lagos to the warm, homiletic simplicities of life."

A Man of the People is "the story of the yokel who visits the sinful city and emerges from it scathed but victorious," writes Martin Tucker in *Africa in Modern Literature*, "while the so-called 'sophisticates' and 'sinners' suffer their just desserts." In this novel, Achebe casts his eye on African politics, taking on, as Moore notes, "the corruption of Nigerians in high places in the central government." The author's eyepiece is the book's narrator Odili, a schoolteacher; the object of his scrutiny is Chief the Honorable M. A. Nanga, Member of Parliament, Odili's former teacher and a popular bush politician who has risen to the post of Minister of Culture in his West African homeland.

At first, Odili is charmed by the politician; but eventually he recognizes the extent of Nanga's abuses and decides to oppose the minister in an election. Odili is beaten, both physically and politically, his appeal to the people heard but ignored. The novel demonstrates, according to Gakwandi, that "the society has been invaded by a wide range of values which have destroyed the traditional balance between the material and the spiritual spheres of life, which has led inevitably to the hypocrisy of double standards." Odili is a victim of these double standards.

Despite his political victory, Nanga, along with the rest of the government, is ousted by a coup. "The novel is a carefully plotted and unified piece of writing," writes Killam. "Achebe achieves balance and proportion in the treatment of his theme of political corruption by evoking both the absurdity of the behavior of the principal characters while at the same time suggesting the serious and destructive consequences of their behavior to the commonwealth." The seriousness of the fictional situation portrayed in *A Man of the People* became real very soon after the novel was first published in 1966 when Nigeria itself was racked by a coup.

Two decades passed between the publications of *A Man of the People* and Achebe's most recent novel, *Anthills of the Savannah*. During this period, the novelist wrote poetry, short stories, and essays. He also became involved in Nigeria's political struggle, a struggle marked by five coups, a civil war, elections marred by violence, and a number of attempts to return to civilian rule. *Anthills of the Savannah* represents Achebe's return to the novel, and as Nadine Gordimer comments in the *New York Times Book Review,* "it is a work in which 22 years of harsh experience, intellectual growth, self-criticism, deepening understanding and mustered discipline of skill open wide a subject to which Mr. Achebe is now magnificently equal." It also represents a return to the themes informing Achebe's earlier novels of independent Africa. "This is a study of how power corrupts itself and by doing so begins to die," writes *Observer* contributor Ben Okri. "It is also about dissent, and love."

Three former schoolmates have risen to positions of power in an imaginary West African nation, Kangan. Ikem is editor of the state-owned newspaper; Chris is the country's minister of information; Sam is a military man become head of state. Sam's quest to have himself voted president for life sends the lives of these three and the lives of all Kangan citizens into turmoil. "In this new novel . . . Chinua Achebe says, with implacable honesty, that Africa itself is to blame," notes Neal Ascherson in the *New York Review of Books,* "and that there is no safety in excuses that place the fault in the colonial past or in the commercial and political manipulations of the First World." Ascherson continues that the novel becomes "a tale about responsibility, and the ways in which men who should know better betray and evade that responsibility."

The turmoil comes to a head in the novel's final pages. All three of the central characters are dead. Ikem, who spoke out against the abuses of the government, is murdered by Sam's secret police. Chris, who flees into the bush to begin a journey of transformation among the people, is shot attempting to stop a rape. Sam is kidnapped and murdered in a coup. "The three murders, senseless as they are, represent the departure of a generation that compromised its own enlightenment for the sake of power," writes Ascherson. And, as Okri observes, "The novel closes with the suggestion that power should reside not within an elite but within the awakened spirit of the people." Here is the hope offered in the novel, hope that is also suggested in its title, as Charles Trueheart relates in the *Washington Post:* "When the brush fires sweep across the savanna, scorching the earth, they leave behind only anthills, and inside the anthills, the surviving memories of the fires and all that came before."

Anthills of the Savannah has been well received and has earned for Achebe a nomination for the Booker Prize. In Larson's estimation, printed in the Chicago *Tribune Books,* "No other novel in many years has bitten to the core, swallowed and regurgitated contemporary Africa's miseries and expectations as profoundly as 'Anthills of the Savannah.'" It has also enhanced Achebe's reputation as an artist; as *New Statesman* contributor Margaret Busby writes, "Reading [this novel] is like watching a master carver skilfully chiselling away from every angle at a solid block of wood: at first there is simply fascination at the sureness with which he works, according to a plan apparent to himself. But the point of all this activity

gradually begins to emerge—until at last it is possible to step back and admire the image created."

In his novels, Achebe offers a close and balanced examination of contemporary Africa and the historical forces that have shaped it. "His distinction is to have [looked back] without any trace either of chauvinistic idealism or of neurotic rejection, those twin poles of so much African mythologizing," maintains Moore. "Instead, he has recreated for us a way of life which has almost disappeared, and has done so with understanding, with justice and with realism." And Busby commends the author's achievement in "charting the socio-political development of contemporary Nigeria." However, Achebe's writing reverberates beyond the borders of Nigeria and beyond the arenas of anthropology, sociology, and political science. As literature, it deals with universal qualities. And, as Killam writes in his study: "Achebe's novels offer a vision of life which is essentially tragic, compounded of success and failure, informed by knowledge and understanding, relieved by humour and tempered by sympathy, embued with an awareness of human suffering and the human capacity to endure." Concludes the critic, "Sometimes his characters meet with success, more often with defeat and despair. Through it all the spirit of man and the belief in the possibility of triumph endures."

MEDIA ADAPTATIONS: Things Fall Apart was adapted for the stage and produced by Eldred Fiberesima in Lagos, Nigeria; it was also adapted for radio and produced by the British Broadcasting Corp. in 1983, and for television in English and Igbo and produced by the Nigerian Television Authority in 1985.

AVOCATIONAL INTERESTS: Music.

BIOGRAPHICAL/CRITICAL SOURCES:

BOOKS

Achebe, Chinua, *A Man of the People,* introduction by K.W.J. Post, Doubleday, 1967.
Achebe, Chinua, *Morning Yet on Creation Day,* Doubleday, 1975.
Achebe, Chinua, *Things Fall Apart,* Fawcett, 1977.
Awoonor, Kofi, *The Breast of the Earth,* Doubleday, 1975.
Baldwin, Claudia, *Nigerian Literature: A Bibliography of Criticism,* G. K. Hall, 1980.
Carroll, David, *Chinua Achebe,* Twayne, 1970.
Contemporary Literary Criticism, Gale, Volume 1, 1973, Volume 3, 1975, Volume 5, 1976, Volume 7, 1977, Volume 11, 1979, Volume 26, 1983, Volume 51, 1988.
Duerden, Dennis and Cosmo Pieterse, editors, *African Writers Talking: A Collection of Radio Interviews,* Africana Publishing, 1972.
Gakwandi, Shatto Arthur, *The Novel and Contemporary Experience in Africa,* Africana Publishing, 1977.
Gleason, Judith Illsley, *This Africa: Novels by West Africans in English and French,* Northwestern University Press, 1965.
Killam, G. D., *The Novels of Chinua Achebe,* Africana Publishing, 1969.
King, Bruce, *Introduction to Nigerian Literature,* Africana Publishing, 1972.
King, Bruce, *The New English Literatures: Cultural Nationalism in a Changing World,* Macmillan, 1980.
Larson, Charles R., *The Emergence of African Fiction,* Indiana University Press, 1972.

Laurence, Margaret, *Long Drums and Cannons: Nigerian Dramatists and Novelists,* Praeger, 1968.

Lindfors, Bernth, *Folklore in Nigerian Literature,* Africana Publishing, 1973.

McEwan, Neil, *Africa and the Novel,* Humanities Press, 1983.

Moore, Gerald, *Seven African Writers,* Oxford University Press, 1962.

Njoku, Benedict Chiaka, *The Four Novels of Chinua Achebe: A Critical Study,* Peter Lang, 1984.

Palmer, Eustace, *The Growth of the African Novel,* Heinemann, 1979.

Ravenscroft, Arthur, *Chinua Achebe,* Longmans, Green, for the British Council, 1969.

Roscoe, Adrian A., *Mother Is Gold: A Study of West African Literature,* Cambridge University Press, 1971.

Tucker, Martin, *Africa in Modern Literature,* Ungar, 1967.

Wren, Robert M., *Achebe's World: The Historical and Cultural Context of the Novels,* Three Continents, 1980.

PERIODICALS

Boston Globe, March 9, 1988.
Busara, Volume VII, number 2, 1975.
Commonweal, December 1, 1967.
Economist, October 24, 1987.
English Studies in Africa, September, 1971.
Listener, October 15, 1987.
Lively Arts and Book Review, April 30, 1961.
London Review of Books, August 7, 1986, October 15, 1987.
Los Angeles Times Book Review, February 28, 1988.
Michigan Quarterly Review, fall, 1970.
Nation, October 11, 1965, April 16, 1988.
New Statesman, January 4, 1985, September 25, 1987.
New York Review of Books, March 3, 1988.
New York Times, August 10, 1966, February 16, 1988.
New York Times Book Review, December 17, 1967, May 13, 1973, August 11, 1985, February 21, 1988.
Observer, September 20, 1987.
Saturday Review, January 6, 1968.
Spectator, October 21, 1960, September 26, 1987.
Studies in Black Literature: Special Issue; Chinua Achebe, spring, 1971.
Times Educational Supplement, January 25, 1985.
Times Literary Supplement, February 3, 1966, March 3, 1972, May 4, 1973, February 26, 1982, October 12, 1984, October 9, 1987.
Tribune Books (Chicago), February 21, 1988.
Village Voice, March 15, 1988.
Wall Street Journal, February 23, 1988.
Washington Post, February 16, 1988.
Washington Post Book World, February 7, 1988.
World Literature Today, summer, 1985.
World Literature Written in English, November, 1978.

—*Sketch by Bryan Ryan*

* * *

AFTON, Effie
See HARPER, Frances Ellen Watkins

* * *

AIDOO, (Christina) Ama Ata 1942-

PERSONAL: Born in 1942, in Abeadzi Kyiakor, Ghana. *Education:* University of Ghana, B.A. (with honors), 1964; attended Stanford University.

ADDRESSES: Office—Department of English, University of Ghana, Cape Coast Branch, Cape Coast, Ghana.

CAREER: University of Ghana, Cape Coast, professor of English; writer.

AWARDS, HONORS: Short story prize from Mbari Press competition; prize from *Black Orpheus* for story, "No Sweetness Here"; research fellowship, Institute of African Studies, University of Ghana.

WRITINGS:

Dilemma of a Ghost (play; first produced in Legon, Ghana, at Open Air Theatre, March, 1964), Longmans, Green, 1965, Macmillan, 1971.
Anowa (play), Humanities, 1970.
No Sweetness Here (stories), Longmans, Green, 1970, Doubleday, 1971.
Our Sister Killjoy; or, Reflections from a Black-Eyed Squint (novel), NOK Publishing, 1976.
Someone Talking to Sometime, College Press (Harare, Zimbabwe), 1985.

CONTRIBUTOR TO ANTHOLOGIES

Ellis A. Komey and Ezekiel Mphahlele, editors, *Modern African Stories,* Faber, 1964.
Ulli Beier, editor, *Black Orpheus: An Anthology of New African and Afro-American Stories,* Longmans, 1964, McGraw-Hill, 1965.
Neville Denny, compiler, *Pan African Short Stories,* Thomas Nelson, 1966.
New Sum of Poetry from the Negro World, Presence Africaine, 1966.
Mphahlele, editor, *African Writing Today,* Penguin, 1967.
Charles Angoff and John Povey, editors, *African Writing Today,* Manyland Books, 1969.
Beier, editor, *Political Spider: An Anthology of Stories from 'Black Orpheus,'* Africana Publishing, 1969.
Joseph Okpaku, editor, *African Literature and the Arts,* Volume I, Crowell, 1970.

OTHER

Contributor of stories and poems to magazines, including *Okyeame, Black Orpheus, Presence Africaine, Journal of African Literature,* and *New African.*

BIOGRAPHICAL/CRITICAL SOURCES:

BOOKS

Pieterse, Cosmo and Dennis Duerdon, editors, *African Writers Talking,* Africana Publishing, 1972.

* * *

Al-AMIN, Jamil Abdullah 1943-
(H. Rap Brown)

PERSONAL: Name originally Hubert Gerold Brown; became known as H. Rap Brown; assumed present name during 1970s; born October 4, 1943, in Baton Rouge, La.; son of a worker for an oil company; married Lynne Doswell (a schoolteacher), May 3, 1968. *Education:* Attended Southern University, 1960-64.

CAREER: U.S. Department of Agriculture, Washington, D.C., librarian, 1964-65; Nonviolent Action Group, Washington, D.C., chairman, beginning in 1964; neighborhood worker in government poverty program in Washington, D.C., beginning in 1965; Student Nonviolent Coordinating Committee (SNCC; renamed Student National Coordinating Committee, 1969), organizer in Greene County, Ala., beginning in 1966, Alabama state project director, beginning in 1966, chairman, beginning in 1967; imprisoned for robbery in state of New York, 1971-76; operator of a small grocery in Atlanta, Ga., c. 1976—.

WRITINGS:

(Under name H. Rap Brown) *Die Nigger Die!* (autobiography), Dial, 1969.

SIDELIGHTS: Jamil Abdullah Al-Amin was an outspoken young black leader who came to prominence in the late 1960s, when he was widely known as H. Rap Brown. In the aftermath of the struggle by Martin Luther King, Jr., to win black civil rights through nonviolent protest, some in Brown's generation believed that a more direct confrontation with white racism was necessary. Brown became known for his belief that black people should be prepared to use guns to assert their rights, and many charged that he was an advocate of violence. Brown countered that his views were necessitated by the virulence of racism. "I preach a response to violence," he wrote in his 1969 autobiography, *Die Nigger Die!*—"Meet violence with violence." If someone deprives you of your human rights, Brown contended, he is being violent. "It's your responsibility to jump back" at your oppressor, because "if you don't, he knows that you're scared and that he can control you." The reactions to Brown varied widely. *Newsweek* magazine accused him of "hate-mongering," for instance, while Kiarri Cheatwood in *Black World* called him "a young man of deep sensibilities."

In his autobiography Brown recounted some of the experiences that led him to such controversial views. During the early 1960s he studied sociology at Southern University, a black college in his hometown of Baton Rouge, Louisiana. He concluded, however, that the school's administration was unwilling to stand up to racial injustice. He worked briefly in a government antipoverty program in Washington, D.C., but sensed that blacks were being co-opted there. "The poverty program," he wrote, "was designed to take those people whom the government considered threatening to the structure and buy them off. It didn't address itself to the causes of poverty but to the effects of poverty."

Brown increasingly looked outside of traditional American institutions to change society. While chairman of the Washington, D.C., Nonviolent Action Group in 1965, he joined several black leaders at a meeting with U.S. President Lyndon Johnson. He gained notoriety for berating the strong-willed president. "I'm not happy to be here," he remembered telling Johnson, "and I think it's unnecessary that we have to be here protesting against the brutality that Black people are subjected to." The next year Brown went to Greene County, Alabama, as an organizer for the Student Nonviolent Coordinating Committee (SNCC), facing the hostility of white citizens and police as he encouraged local black people to exercise their rights to vote and to hold public office. He became the SNCC's Alabama project director a few months later and in 1967 was elected chairman of the entire organization.

Brown's post brought him national attention. He made repeated statements about the need for a violent confrontation with racism, becoming widely known for such remarks as "violence is as American as cherry pie." He suggested that the riots sweeping America's poor black neighborhoods heralded a political insurrection, and riots broke out in the cities

of Dayton, Ohio, East St. Louis, Illinois, and Cambridge, Maryland, shortly after he spoke there. Authorities in Maryland indicted Brown for inciting the Cambridge riot and engaging in arson, and for the next few years he was mired in a succession of highly publicized legal battles involving such charges as illegally possessing a gun and violating the terms of his bail. Supporters of Brown argued that he was being harassed for his political beliefs.

At the height of his fame Brown wrote *Die Nigger Die!*, and the book garnered mixed reactions, as had its author. John Leonard of the *New York Times* found the work unsatisfactory both as autobiography and as political commentary, charging that Brown was "so busy proving his *machismo* that his material never comes into focus." But in the *New York Times Book Review,* Shane Stevens asserted that *Die Nigger Die!* expressed the author's "essential humanism . . . , cloaked though it may be in fear and hate." Citing Brown's ability to combine his outrage with an irreverent sense of humor, Stevens wrote that "the cutting edge of deep pain is there. But so is the raucous, sometimes slightly hysterical, laughter of life." Cheatwood stressed Brown's political analyses, lauding his "depth," "historically-shaped consciousness," and "mature thought." As an example, Cheatwood observed that "perhaps better than anyone before him," the author outlined "the responsibilities of Black students to their people."

In 1970 Brown went into hiding, delaying the start of his riot trial in Maryland. The Federal Bureau of Investigation (FBI) promptly placed him on its list of most-wanted criminals. The next year New York City police took him into custody near the scene of a barroom robbery. He remained imprisoned while he was tried and convicted of taking part in the holdup and was sentenced to further time in jail. When he pleaded guilty to eluding his Maryland trial, authorities in that state dropped their riot and arson charges.

During his incarceration Brown converted to Islam and adopted his current name. Paroled in 1976, he moved to Atlanta, Georgia, where he operates a small grocery. Though no longer in the national headlines, he has given occasional interviews to journalists. In 1985 he met with *Washington Post* columnist George F. Will, who found him "enveloped in a strange serenity." Brown's life, Will suggested, was now centered on his Muslim faith, and the onetime political activist was working with neighbors on plans for a religious school. "Many people reckon time from the '60s," Brown observed, because "time stopped for them then." He added, "I don't miss the '60s."

BIOGRAPHICAL/CRITICAL SOURCES:

BOOKS

Brown, H. Rap, *Die Nigger Die!*, Dial, 1969.

PERIODICALS

Black World, October, 1975.
Chicago Tribune Book World, May 11, 1969.
New Republic, June 14, 1969.
Newsweek, August 7, 1967, June 3, 1968, February 12, 1973.
New York Times, August 13, 1967, April 30, 1969, November 7, 1973, September 25, 1976.
New York Times Book Review, June 15, 1969.
Saturday Review, May 3, 1969.
Village Voice, November 2, 1967.
Washington Post, June 15, 1978, September 19, 1985.

—Sketch by Thomas Kozikowski

ALEXANDER, Ric
See LONG, Richard A(lexander)

*   *   *

ALLEN, Robert L(ee)   1942-
(Benjamin Peterson)

PERSONAL: Born May 29, 1942, in Atlanta, Ga.; son of Robert Lee and Sadie (Sims) Allen; married Pamela Parker, August 28, 1965 (separated January 1, 1978); children: Casey Douglass. *Education:* Attended University of Vienna, 1961-62; Morehouse College, B.S., 1963; graduate study at Columbia University, 1963-64; New School for Social Research, M.A., 1967; University of California, San Francisco, Ph.D., 1983.

ADDRESSES: Office—Ethnic Studies Department, Mills College, Oakland, Calif. 94613. *Agent*—Wendy Weil, Julian Bach Literary Agency, Inc., 747 Third Ave., New York, N.Y.

CAREER: Department of Welfare, New York, N.Y., caseworker, 1964-65; reporter for *National Guardian,* 1967-69; San Jose State College (now University), San Jose, Calif., began as instructor, became assistant professor of black studies, 1969-72; Mills College, Oakland, Calif., began as lecturer, became assistant professor of ethnic studies, 1973—. Active in civil rights and anti-war movements.

MEMBER: American Sociological Association, African-American Historical and Cultural Society, Association of Black Sociologists, Black World Foundation (vice president), Pacific Sociological Association, Council for Black Studies, Bay Area Black Journalists.

AWARDS, HONORS: Merrill grant for Austria, 1961-62; Woodrow Wilson fellowship, 1963-64; Guggenheim fellowship, 1978.

WRITINGS:

Black Awakening in Capitalist America, Doubleday, 1969.
Reluctant Reformers: The Impact of Racism on American Social Reform Movements, Howard University Press, 1974.
The Port Chicago Disaster and Its Aftermath, University of California, San Francisco, 1983.

Contributor to magazines, sometimes under the pseudonym Benjamin Peterson. Associate editor of *Black Scholar,* 1972-75, editor, 1975—.

SIDELIGHTS: Robert L. Allen commented: "A recurrent theme in my work is a concern with the role of beliefs and ideologies in the process of social change. I consider myself a materialist sociologist, but I also think that human action is shaped by the subjective understandings that people have of their situations; hence, getting inside the heads of actors is as important as measuring the social forces that impinge upon them."

For his book on the Port Chicago disaster Allen drew upon documents and oral histories he had collected from survivors to describe the events that, according to Allen, "followed the disastrous explosion at the Port Chicago (California) Naval Ammunition Magazine in July, 1944. After the explosion fifty black sailors were accused of mutiny when, as part of a larger group, they refused to return to work loading ammunition on ships. (More than three hundred men had been killed in the blast.) The fifty men were court-martialed amid great public-ity, convicted, and jailed. A national campaign was organized by the Legal Defense Fund of the National Association for the Advancement of Colored People (NAACP), under the leadership of Thurgood Marshall, to free the men. Eventually the sentences were set aside and the men released. The Port Chicago explosion was the worst home front disaster of World War II, and the trial of the fifty men was the largest mass mutiny trial in U.S. Navy history."

*   *   *

ALLEN, Samuel W(ashington)   1917-
(Paul Vesey)

PERSONAL: Born December 9, 1917, in Columbus, Ohio; son of Alexander Joseph (a clergyman) and Jewett (Washington) Allen; divorced; children: Marie-Christine. *Education:* Fisk University, A.B. (magna cum laude), 1938; Harvard University, J.D., 1941; graduate study at New School for Social Research, 1947-48, and Sorbonne, University of Paris, 1949-50. *Politics:* Democrat. *Religion:* African Methodist Episcopal.

ADDRESSES: Home—145 Cliff Ave., Winthrop, Mass. 02152.

CAREER: Office of District Attorney, Manhattan, N.Y., deputy assistant district attorney, 1946-47; civilian attorney with U.S. Armed Forces in Europe, 1951-55; private practice of law, New York, N.Y., 1956-58; Texas Southern University, Houston, Tex., associate professor of law, 1958-60; U.S. Information Agency, Washington, D.C., assistant general counsel, 1961-64; U.S. Departments of Justice and Commerce, Community Relations Service, Washington, D.C., chief counsel, 1965-68; Tuskegee Institute, Tuskegee Institute, Ala., Avalon Professor of Humanities, 1968-70; Boston University, Boston, Mass., professor of English and Afro-American literature, 1971-81. Visiting professor at Wesleyan University, 1970-71, Duke University, 1972-74, and Rutgers University, 1981; writer in residence at Tuskegee Institute. Member of board of directors, Southern Education Foundation, 1969-76, and New England Museum of Afro-American History; volunteer and member of board of directors, School Volunteers for Boston. *Military service:* U.S. Army, Adjutant Generals Corps, 1942-46; became first lieutenant.

MEMBER: African Studies Association, African Heritage Studies Association, New York Bar Association, New England Poetry Club (member, board of directors).

AWARDS, HONORS: National Endowment for the Arts literature fellow, 1979; Wurlitzer Foundation fellow, 1979, 1980-81; grant from Rockefeller Foundation, 1981.

WRITINGS:

(Under pseudonym Paul Vesey) *Elfenbein Zahne* (title means "Ivory Tusks"; a bilingual edition of poems), translated into German by Janheinz Jahn, Wolfgang Rothe, 1956.
(Translator) Jean Paul Sartre, *Black Orpheus* (translation first published in *Presence Africaine,* 1951), Presence Africaine, 1960.
(Author of introduction) *Pan-Africanism Reconsidered,* University of California Press, 1962.
Ivory Tusks and Other Poems, Poets Press, 1968.
(Author of introduction) Naseer Aruri and Edmund Ghareeb, editors, *Enemy of the Sun: Poetry of the Palestinian Resistance,* Drum & Spear Press, 1970.
(Editor and author of introduction) *Poems from Africa,* Crowell, 1973.
Paul Vesey's Ledger (poetry), Paul Breman, 1975.

Every Round and Other Poems, Lotus Press, 1987.

CONTRIBUTOR

Jacob Drachler, editor, *African Heritage,* Crowell, 1959.
The American Negro Writer and His Roots, American Society of African Culture, 1960.
Africa Seen by American Negro Scholars, American Society of African Culture, 1963.
Arna Bontemps, editor, *American Negro Poetry,* Hill & Wang, 1963.
Langston Hughes, editor, *New Negro Poets: USA,* Indiana University Press, 1964.
Arthur P. Davis and Saunders Redding, editors, *Cavalcade,* Houghton, 1970.
Nathan Wright, Jr., editor, *What Black Educators Are Saying,* Hawthorn, 1970.
Raymond F. Betts, editor, *The Ideology of Blackness,* Heath, 1971.
Ruth Miller, editor, *Background to Black American Literature,* Glencoe Press, 1971.
Stephen Henderson, editor, *Understanding the New Black Poetry: Black Speech and Black Music as Poetic Reference,* Morrow, 1973.
Woodie King, Jr., editor, *The Forerunners: Black Poets in America,* Howard University Press, 1981.

Contributor of poems and essays to numerous other anthologies.

OTHER

Contributor of poems, essays, book reviews, and translations to journals, including *Presence Africaine, Negro Digest, Journal of Afro-American Studies, Black World, Benin Review* (Nigeria), and *Massachusetts Review.*

SIDELIGHTS: Samuel W. Allen "has played a significant role in African and Afro-American criticism as a scholar, reviewer, translator, editor, and lecturer," comments Ruth L. Brittin in a *Dictionary of Literary Biography* essay. While working as a lawyer in France and Germany after World War II, Allen became involved with the negritude movement of poets and from their example was "inspired to write a poetry grounded in the fusion of African and Afro-American culture," describes Brittin. Allen articulates his idea of the role of the black American poet in *The Forerunners: Black Poets in America:* "Black poets are continuing with an increasingly sharpened sense of direction both to define and to vivify the black experience, drawing up and utilizing a more profoundly explored heritage. They listen with new awareness . . . and conjure up from the wellsprings of the creative consciousness an identity both old and new, a vision whole and sufficient."

MEDIA ADAPTATIONS: A reading by Allen of his own poetry was recorded at the Library of Congress in 1972.

BIOGRAPHICAL/CRITICAL SOURCES:

BOOKS

Cooke, M. G., editor, *Modern Black Novelists,* Prentice-Hall, 1971.
Dictionary of Literary Biography, Volume 41: *Afro-American Poets Since 1955,* Gale, 1985.
King, Woodie, Jr., editor, *The Forerunners: Black Poets in America,* Howard University Press, 1981.
Mphahlele, Ezekiel, editor, *Voices in the Whirlwind,* Hill & Wang, 1972.
Redmond, Eugene, editor, *Drumvoices: The Mission of Afro-American Poetry, A Critical History,* Anchor Books, 1976.

PERIODICALS

Black Orpheus, October, 1958.
Rheinische Post, September 14, 1957.

*   *   *

ALUKO, T(imothy) M(ofolorunso)   1918(?)-

PERSONAL: Born June 14, 1918 (one source says 1920), in Ilesha, West Nigeria; married Janet Adebisi Fajemisin, 1950; children: six. *Education:* Attended Government College, Ibadan, Nigeria, 1933-38, and Yaba Higher College, Lagos, Nigeria, 1939-42; University of London, England, B.Sc., 1948, Diploma in Town Planning, 1950; University of Newcastle upon Tyne, England, M.Sc., 1969; University of Lagos, Ph.D., 1976.

ADDRESSES: Home—53 Ladipo Oluwole Rd., Apapa, P.O. Box 1854, Lagos, Nigeria. *Office*—Scott Wilson Kirkpatrick & Partners, P.O. Box 1854, Lagos, Nigeria.

CAREER: Public works department, Lagos, Nigeria, junior engineer, 1943-46; public works departments of Ibadan, Oyo, Oshogbo, and Lagos, all Nigeria, executive engineer, 1950-56; Lagos Town Council, Lagos, town engineer, 1956-60; Ministry of Works and Transport, Western Nigeria, director and permanent secretary, 1960-66; University of Ibadan, Ibadan, Nigeria, senior lecturer, 1966; University of Lagos, Lagos, senior research fellow in municipal engineering, 1966-78, associate professor of public health engineering, 1978; Scott Wilson Kirkpatrick & Partners (consulting engineers), partner, 1978—. Commissioner for finance, Government of Western Nigeria, 1971-73.

MEMBER: Institution of Civil Engineers (fellow), Institution of Municipal Engineers (fellow), Institution of Public Health Engineers (fellow), Institution of Nigerian Society of Engineers (fellow), Nigerian Institute of Town Planners (fellow), Royal Town Planning Institute.

AWARDS, HONORS: Officer, Order of the British Empire, 1963; Officer, Order of the Niger, 1964.

WRITINGS:

NOVELS

One Man, One Wife, Nigerian Printing and Publishing Co., 1959, Humanities Press, 1968.
One Man, One Matchet, Heinemann, 1964, Verrey, 1965.
Kinsman and Foreman, Heinemann, 1966.
Chief, the Honourable Minister, Humanities Press, 1970.
His Worshipful Majesty, Heinemann, 1972.
Wrong Ones in the Dock, Heinemann, 1982.
State of Our Own, Macmillan, 1986.

Work included in *African New Writing,* Lutterworth Press, 1947. Contributor of short stories to *West African Review.* Interviewee with Lee Nichols on radio program "Conversations With African Writers," Voice of America, Washington, D.C., 1978.

SIDELIGHTS: T. M. Aluko commented: "For me, fiction writing has continued to be a most pleasurable hobby. I have discovered that, more and more, I need this medium of expression for keeping my sanity in the mad, mad world, and for making satirical comments on the activities of those charged with the responsibility for the administration of the affairs of their fellow men. I have watched with sadness through the over forty years of my writing career a steady decline in the standard of morality of these leaders. Whereas before the country became independent they made their followers believe that all their woes were attributable to their colonial masters and that once these masters were driven away the country would be transformed to paradise here on earth. Now, near three decades after independence, these followers have learnt that in addition to the colonial masters they have to drive away ignorance, superstition, illiteracy and massive corruption. And more than these, they have discovered the bitter truth that the rule of the African by the African is sometimes more oppressive than rule by any colonial master.''

BIOGRAPHICAL/CRITICAL SOURCES:

BOOKS

Laurence, Margaret, *Long Drums and Cannons,* Macmillan, 1968.

* * *

AMADI, Elechi (Emmanuel)   1934-

PERSONAL: Born May 12, 1934, in Aluu, Nigeria; son of Daniel Wonuchuku and Enwere (Weke) Amadi; married Dorah Nwonne Ohale, December, 1957; children: Eberechi, Chinyere, Ejimole, Nyege, Okachi, Aleru (all daughters). *Education:* University College of Ibadan (now University of Ibadan), B.Sc., 1959. *Politics:* Independent. *Religion:* Protestant.

ADDRESSES: Home—Mbodo, Aluu, Rivers State, Nigeria. *Office*—Box 331, Port Harcourt, Nigeria.

CAREER: Surveyor in Enugu, Nigeria, 1959-60; science teacher in Nigerian schools, 1960-63, and headmaster, 1966-67; Government of the Rivers State of Nigeria, Ahoada and Port Harcourt, 1968—, began as government divisional officer and senior assistant secretary, became an administrative officer (permanent secretary). *Military service:* Nigerian Army, 1963-66; became captain; rejoined in 1968 and served with Marine Commandos during the civil war.

WRITINGS:

The Concubine (novel), Humanities, 1966.
The Great Ponds (novel), Humanities, 1969.
Okpukpe (prayerbook in Ikwerre), C.S.S. Printers (Port Harcourt), 1969.
(With Obiajunwo Wali and Greensille Enyinda) *Okwukwo Eri* (hymnbook in Ikwerre), C.S.S. Printers, 1969.
Isiburu (play; produced in Ibadan, Port Harcourt, and Aiyetoro), Heinemann, 1973.
Sunset in Biafra (Civil War diary), Humanities, 1973.
Peppersoup [and] *Ibadan* (plays), Onibonoje, 1977.
The Slave (novel), Humanities, 1979.
Ethics in Nigerian Culture (philosophy), Heinemann, 1982.
Estrangement (novel), Humanities, 1985.

Also author of twenty-two poems.

WORK IN PROGRESS: Short stories; translating the entire Protestant prayerbook into Ikwerre; an expanded edition of the hymnal *Okwukwo Eri.*

SIDELIGHTS: Elechi Amadi is ''preoccupied with matter, space, life's purpose (if any), and man.'' His novels, plays, and poems are set in his own country. He has traveled to Britain, West Germany, and the United States.

AVOCATIONAL INTERESTS: Music, lawn tennis, table tennis, hockey.

BIOGRAPHICAL/CRITICAL SOURCES:

PERIODICALS

Spectator, September 20, 1969.
West Africa, March 14, 1970.

* * *

AMINI, Johari M.
See KUNJUFU, Johari M. Amini

* * *

ANDREWS, Raymond   1934-

PERSONAL: Born June 6, 1934, in Madison, Ga.; son of George Cleveland (a sharecropper) and Viola (Perryman) Andrews; married Adelheid Wenger (an airline sales agent), December 28, 1966 (divorced June 2, 1980). *Education:* Attended Michigan State University, 1956-57. *Politics:* None. *Religion:* None.

ADDRESSES: Home—2013 Morton Rd., Athens, Ga. 30605. *Agent*—Susan Ann Protter, 110 West 40th St., Suite 1408, New York, N.Y. 10018.

CAREER: Writer. Worked variously as sharecropper, 1943-49, hospital orderly, 1949-51, bartender, busboy, dishwasher, and stockroom worker, 1951-52, postal mail sorter, 1956, and stockroom clerk, 1957; KLM Royal Dutch Airlines, New York City, airline employee, 1958-66; photograph librarian, 1967-72; Archer Courier, New York City, messenger, telephone operator, night dispatcher, and bookkeeper, 1972-84. *Military service:* U.S. Air Force, 1952-56.

AWARDS, HONORS: James Baldwin Prize for Fiction, 1978, for *Appalachee Red.*

WRITINGS:

Appalachee Red (novel), illustrations by brother, Benny Andrews, Dial, 1978.
Rosiebelle Lee Wildcat Tennessee (novel), illustrations by B. Andrews, Dial, 1979.
Baby Sweet's (novel), illustrations by B. Andrews, Dial, 1983.

Contributor to *Sports Illustrated* and *Ataraxia.*

WORK IN PROGRESS: A novel, *99 Years and a Dark Day.*

SIDELIGHTS: Raymond Andrews commented: ''As children, my brother and I drew, with him continuing on and becoming an artist, while I stopped drawing and became more interested in reading. To me, there was nothing better than a *good* story. But in the farming—sharecropping—community I came from, most people couldn't read. This, along with a poor school system, did not encourage budding authors. Yet in the back of my head a writer was what I wanted to be most of all, and I couldn't help but feel that someday, *somehow,* I would write.

''It wasn't until the day of my thirty-second birthday that I finally got around to doing something about this nagging in the back of my head which down through the years had absolutely refused to shut up. At the time I was working for an airline and was being given what I felt was an uncalled-for hard time over the telephone by a client. I told him to wait and put the call on hold. At precisely 12:36, after eight years, two months, two weeks, and three days, I walked out, never to return. I went home and had my telephone disconnected. The next morning upon rising at my usual early hour, I told myself, 'you *are* going to write.' And I've been at it ever since.''

In his writing, Andrews draws upon his personal experience as a youth in a small sharecropping community in the South. He has set each of his novels in the town of Appalachee, the county seat of the fictional Muskhogean county in northern Georgia. The close connection between Andrews's stories and their setting is part of their appeal. ''Andrews has a deep and intricate understanding of the small southern town,'' writes David Guy in the *Washington Post Book World,* ''and displays this understanding not only in passages of exposition but also in the hearts of his narratives.'' The author's choice of a small southern town with its population of blacks and whites living in close proximity also allows him to examine, as Janet Boyarin Blundell notes in *Library Journal,* the ''complex interracial relationships'' that occur.

Andrews's first novel, *Appalachee Red,* won for its author the first James Baldwin Prize for Fiction. It is the story of a young black woman who, while her husband is in jail, has the child of one of the town's most influential white men. The child, Appalachee Red, is sent north to be raised. Years later he returns to take revenge upon his father and the town. Although *Best Sellers* contributor Russ Williams finds that ''the thin line between sociological trauma and stark fiction is not drawn,'' he does admit, ''Raymond Andrews has an especial gift and skill of narrative, one which enables him to compel the reader through even the most unlikely passages.'' A *Publishers Weekly* reviewer also comments upon the author's ability: ''Andrews is an extremely gifted storyteller in the best Southern revivalist tradition.'' Concludes Blundell, ''This is a pungent, witty, and powerful first novel, deserving winner of the first James Baldwin Prize for Fiction.''

The title of the author's second novel, *Rosiebelle Lee Wildcat Tennessee,* is also the name of its main character, a part American Indian, part black woman who comes to Appalachee, goes to work for the town's richest man, becomes first the mistress of the man's son, and much later the matriarch to the town's black population. ''Andrews has skillfully created a portrait of an aggressive, life-hungry black woman, her four children, and the surrounding community,'' comments Blundell. Once again, reviewers note the author's capacity to fashion a good tale. A reviewer for the *New Yorker* writes, ''Mr. Andrews is well versed in the rights and duties of the traditional storyteller, and he knows just how far to stretch his audience's memory and credulity as he spins and weaves his colorful yarns.'' And a *Publishers Weekly* contributor adds, ''Raymond Andrews is an extraordinary writer—a true and absolutely original American voice.''

In *Baby Sweet's* ''the characters are larger than life and often seem to represent phenomena as much as they do flesh and blood human beings,'' observes David Guy in the *Washington Post Book World.* Baby Sweet's is the name given to the brothel opened by the eccentric son of Appalachee's leading citizen to provide black prostitutes for the white population. Once again, Andrews examines how the intermingling of the races affects the entire community. Reviewers also note the folksy style evident in *Baby Sweet's.* ''Andrews' writing stems from a black oral tradition and could effectively be read aloud,'' notes Guy. In the *New York Times Book Review* Frederick Busch writes that *Baby Sweet's* ''is a novel chanted to achieve the feeling of blues . . . [and] it is the music of Mr. Andrews's narrative that makes this book a pleasure to read.'' Finally, Guy commends Andrews ''for his raucous and robust humor,

his really profound knowledge of the South, his ultimately accepting and benign vision . . . and most of all for the entertaining voice that tells the stories.''

BIOGRAPHICAL/CRITICAL SOURCES:

PERIODICALS

Best Sellers, February, 1979.
Chicago Tribune Book World, February 8, 1981.
Ebony, September, 1980.
Essence, December, 1980.
Library Journal, October 1, 1978, May 15, 1980.
Madisonian, June 8, 1978.
New Yorker, August 11, 1980.
New York Times Book Review, August 17, 1980, July 24, 1983.
Publishers Weekly, July 24, 1978, May 2, 1980.
Synergos, spring, 1981.
Washington Post Book World, July 31, 1983.

*   *   *

ANGELOU, Maya   1928-

PERSONAL: Name originally Marguerita Johnson; surname is pronounced ''*An*-ge-lo''; born April 4, 1928, in St. Louis, Mo.; daughter of Bailey (a naval dietician) and Vivian (Baxter) Johnson; married Tosh Angelos (divorced); married Paul Du Feu, December, 1973 (divorced); children: Guy. *Education:* Attended public schools in Arkansas and California; studied music privately; studied dance with Martha Graham, Pearl Primus, and Ann Halprin; studied drama with Frank Silvera and Gene Frankel.

ADDRESSES: Home—Sonoma, Calif. *Agent*—Gerald W. Purcell Associates Ltd., 133 Fifth Ave., New York, N.Y. 10003.

CAREER: Author, poet, playwright, professional stage and screen producer, director, and performer, and singer. Appeared in ''Porgy and Bess'' on twenty-two-nation tour sponsored by the U.S. Department of State, 1954-55; appeared in Off-Broadway plays ''Calypso Heatwave,'' 1957, and ''The Blacks,'' 1960; produced and performed in ''Cabaret for Freedom,'' with Godfrey Cambridge, Off-Broadway, 1960; University of Ghana, Institute of African Studies, Legon-Accra, Ghana, assistant administrator of School of Music and Drama, 1963-66; appeared in ''Mother Courage'' at University of Ghana, 1964, and in ''Meda'' in Hollywood, 1966; made Broadway debut in ''Look Away,'' 1973; directed film ''All Day Long,'' 1974; directed her play ''And Still I Rise'' in California, 1976; appeared in film ''Roots,'' 1977. Television narrator, interviewer, and host for Afro-American specials and theatre series, 1972—. Lecturer at University of California, Los Angeles, 1966; writer in residence at University of Kansas, 1970; distinguished visiting professor at Wake Forest University, 1974, Wichita State University, 1974, and California State University, Sacramento, 1974. Northern coordinator of Southern Christian Leadership Conference, 1959-60; appointed member of American Revolution Bicentennial Council by President Gerald R. Ford, 1975-76; member of National Commission on the Observance of International Women's Year.

MEMBER: American Federation of Television and Radio Artists, American Film Institute (member of board of trustees, 1975—), Directors Guild, Equity, Women's Prison Association (member of advisory board).

AWARDS, HONORS: Nominated for National Book Award, 1970, for *I Know Why the Caged Bird Sings;* Yale University fellowship, 1970; Pulitzer Prize nomination, 1972, for *Just Give Me a Cool Drink of Water 'fore I Diiie;* Antoinette Perry (''Tony'') Award nomination from League of New York Theatres and Producers, 1973, for performance in ''Look Away''; Rockefeller Foundation scholar in Italy, 1975; named Woman of the Year in Communications by *Ladies' Home Journal,* 1976; Tony Award nomination for best supporting actress, 1977, for ''Roots''; honorary degrees from Smith College, 1975, Mills College, 1975, and Lawrence University, 1976.

WRITINGS:

I Know Why the Caged Bird Sings (autobiography; Book-of-the-Month Club selection), Random House, 1970.
Just Give Me a Cool Drink of Water 'fore I Diiie (poetry), Random House, 1971.
Gather Together in My Name (autobiography; Book-of-the-Month Club selection), Random House, 1974.
Oh Pray My Wings Are Gonna Fit Me Well (poetry), Random House, 1975.
Singin' and Swingin' and Gettin' Merry Like Christmas (autobiography; Book-of-the-Month Club selection), Random House, 1976.
And Still I Rise (poetry; also see below), Random House, 1978.
The Heart of a Woman (autobiography), Random House, 1981.
Shaker, Why Don't You Sing? (poetry), Random House, 1983.
All God's Children Need Traveling Shoes (autobiography), Random House, 1986.
Mrs. Flowers: A Moment of Friendship (fiction), illustrations by Etienne Delessert, Redpath Press, 1986.
Poems: Maya Angelou, four volumes, Bantam, 1986.
Now Sheba Sings the Song, illustrations by Tom Feelings, Dial Books; 1987.

PLAYS

(With Godfrey Cambridge) ''Cabaret for Freedom'' (musical revue), first produced in New York at Village Gate Theatre, 1960.
''The Least of These'' (two-act drama), first produced in Los Angeles, 1966.
(Adapter) Sophocles, ''Ajax'' (two-act drama), first produced in Los Angeles at Mark Taper Forum, 1974.
''And Still I Rise'' (one-act musical), first produced in Oakland, Calif., at Ensemble Theatre, 1976.

Also author of two-act drama ''The Clawing Within,'' 1966, and of two-act musical ''Adjoa Amissah,'' 1967, both as yet unproduced.

SCREENPLAYS

''Georgia, Georgia,'' Independent-Cinerama, 1972.
''All Day Long,'' American Film Institute, 1974.

TELEVISION PLAYS

''Blacks, Blues, Black'' (ten one-hour programs), National Educational Television (NET-TV), 1968.
''Sister, Sister'' (drama), National Broadcasting Co. (NBC-TV), 1982.

Also author of ''Assignment America'' series, 1975, and two Afro-American specials ''The Legacy'' and ''The Inheritors,'' 1976.

RECORDINGS

Miss Calypso (songs), Liberty Records, 1957.
The Poetry of Maya Angelou, GWP Records, 1969.
Women in Business, University of Wisconsin, 1981.

OTHER

Composer of songs, including two songs for movie ''For Love of Ivy,'' and composer of musical scores for both her screenplays. Contributor to Ghanaian Broadcasting Corp., 1963-65. Contributor of articles, short stories, and poems to periodicals, including *Harper's, Ebony, Ghanaian Times, Mademoiselle, Redbook,* and *Black Scholar.* Associate editor, *Arab Observer* (English-language news weekly in Cairo, Egypt), 1961-62; feature editor, *African Review* (Accra, Ghana), 1964-66.

SIDELIGHTS: By the time she was in her early twenties, Maya Angelou had been a Creole cook, a streetcar conductor, a cocktail waitress, a dancer, a madam, and an unwed mother. The following decades saw her emerge as a successful singer, actress, and playwright, an editor for an English-language magazine in Egypt, a lecturer and civil rights activist, and a popular author of four collections of poetry and five autobiographies.

Angelou is hailed as one of the great voices of contemporary black literature and as a remarkable Renaissance woman. She began producing books after some notable friends, including author James Baldwin, heard Angelou's stories of her childhood spent shuttling between rural, segregated Stamps, Arkansas, where her devout grandmother ran a general store, and St. Louis, Missouri, where her worldly, glamorous mother lived. *I Know Why the Caged Bird Sings,* a chronicle of her life up to age sixteen (and ending with the birth of her son, Guy) was published in 1970 with great critical and commercial success. Although many of the stories in the book are grim—as in the author's revelation that she was raped at age eight by her mother's boyfriend—the volume also recounts the self-awakening of the young Angelou. ''Her genius as a writer is her ability to recapture the texture of the way of life in the texture of its idioms, its idiosyncratic vocabulary and especially in its process of image-making,'' reports Sidonie Ann Smith in *Southern Humanities Review.* ''The imagery holds the reality, giving it immediacy. That [the author] chooses to recreate the past in its own sounds suggests to the reader that she accepts the past and recognizes its beauty and its ugliness, its assets and its liabilities, its strength and its weakness. Here we witness a return to the final acceptance of the past in the return to and full acceptance of its language, the language a symbolic construct of a way of life. Ultimately Maya Angelou's style testifies to her reaffirmation of self-acceptance, [which] she achieves within the pattern of the autobiography.''

Her next two volumes of autobiography, *Gather Together in My Name* and *Singin' and Swingin' and Gettin' Merry Like Christmas,* take Angelou from her late adolescence, when she flirted briefly with prostitution and drug addiction, to her early adulthood as she established a reputation as a performer among the avant-garde of the early 1950s. Not as commercially successful as *I Know Why the Caged Bird Sings,* the two books were guardedly praised by some critics. Lynn Sukenick, for example, remarks in *Village Voice* that *Gather Together in My Name* is ''sculpted, concise, rich with flavor and surprises, exuding a natural confidence and command.'' Sukenick adds, however, that one fault lies ''in the tone of the book. . . . [The author's] refusal to let her earlier self get off easy, and the self-mockery which is her means to honesty, finally becomes in itself a glossing over; although her laughter at herself is witty, intelligent, and a good preventative against maudlin confession, . . . it eventually becomes a tic and a substitute for a deeper look.''

Annie Gottlieb has another view of *Gather Together in My Name*. In her *New York Times Book Review* article, Gottlieb states that Angelou "writes like a song, and like the truth. The wisdom, rue and humor of her storytelling are borne on a lilting rhythm completely her own, the product of a born writer's senses nourished on black church singing and preaching, soft mother talk and salty street talk, and on literature."

The year 1981 brought the publication of *The Heart of a Woman*, a book that "covers one of the most exciting periods in recent African and Afro-American history," according to Adam David Miller in *Black Scholar*. Miller refers to the era of civil rights marches, the emergence of Dr. Martin Luther King, Jr., and Malcolm X, and the upheaval in Africa following the assassination of the Congolese statesman Patrice Lumumba. The 1960s see Angelou active in civil rights both in America and abroad; at the same time she enters into a romance with African activist Vusumzi Make, which dissolves when he cannot accept her independence or even promise fidelity. In a *Dictionary of Literary Biography* piece on Angelou, Lynn Z. Bloom considers *The Heart of a Woman* the author's best work since *I Know Why the Caged Bird Sings*: "Her enlarged focus and clear vision transcend the particulars and give this book a fascinating universality of perspective and psychological depth that almost matches the quality of [Angelou's first volume]. . . . Its motifs are commitment and betrayal."

Washington Post Book World critic David Levering Lewis also sees a universal message in *The Heart of a Woman*. "Angelou has rearranged, edited, and pointed up her coming of age and going abroad in the world with such just-rightness of timing and inner truthfulness that each of her books is a continuing autobiography of Afro-America. Her ability to shatter the opaque prisms of race and class between reader and subject is her special gift," he says. To Bloom, "it is clear from [this series of autobiographies] that Angelou is in the process of becoming a self-created Everywoman. In a literature and a culture where there are many fewer exemplary lives of women than of men, black or white, Angelou's autobiographical self, as it matures through successive volumes, is gradually assuming that exemplary stature."

In her fifth autobiographical work, *All God's Children Need Traveling Shoes*, Angelou describes her four-year stay in Ghana, "just as that African country had won its independence from European colonials," according to Barbara T. Christian in the *Chicago Tribune Book World*. Christian indicates that Angelou's "sojourn in Africa strengthens her bonds to her ancestral home even as she concretely experiences her distinctiveness as an Afro-American."

This book has also received praise from reviewers. Wanda Coleman in the *Los Angeles Times Book Review* calls it "a thoroughly enjoyable segment from the life of a celebrity," while Christian describes it as "a thoughtful yet spirited account of one Afro-American woman's journey into the land of her ancestors." In Coleman's opinion, *All God's Children Need Traveling Shoes* is "an important document drawing more much needed attention to the hidden history of a people both African and American."

MEDIA ADAPTATIONS: I Know Why the Caged Bird Sings has been adapted into a television movie.

BIOGRAPHICAL/CRITICAL SOURCES:

BOOKS

Angelou, Maya, *I Know Why the Caged Bird Sings*, Random House, 1970.

Angelou, Maya, *Gather Together in My Name*, Random House, 1974.
Angelou, Maya, *Singin' and Swingin' and Gettin' Merry Like Christmas*, Random House, 1976.
Angelou, Maya, *The Heart of a Woman*, Random House, 1981.
Angelou, Maya, *All God's Children Need Traveling Shoes*, Random House, 1986.
Contemporary Literary Criticism, Gale, Volume 12, 1980, Volume 35, 1985.
Dictionary of Literary Biography, Volume 38: *Afro-American Writers After 1955: Dramatists and Prose Writers*, Gale, 1985.

PERIODICALS

Black Scholar, summer, 1982.
Black World, July, 1975.
Chicago Tribune, November 1, 1981.
Chicago Tribune Book World, March 23, 1986.
Detroit Free Press, May 9, 1986.
Harper's, November, 1972.
Harvard Educational Review, November, 1970.
Ladies' Home Journal, May, 1976.
Los Angeles Times, May 29, 1983.
Los Angeles Times Book Review, April 13, 1986, August 9, 1987.
Ms., January, 1977.
New Republic, July 6, 1974.
Newsweek, March 2, 1970.
New York Times, February 25, 1970.
New York Times Book Review, June 16, 1974.
Observer (London), April 1, 1984.
Parnassus: Poetry in Review, fall-winter, 1979.
Poetry, August, 1976.
Southern Humanities Review, fall, 1973.
Time, March 31, 1986.
Times (London), September 29, 1986.
Times Literary Supplement, February 17, 1974, June 14, 1985, January 24, 1986.
Village Voice, July 11, 1974, October 28, 1981.
Washington Post, October 13, 1981.
Washington Post Book World, October 4, 1981, June 26, 1983, May 11, 1986.

*   *   *

ANTHONY, Michael 1932-

PERSONAL: Born February 10, 1932, in Mayaro, Trinidad and Tobago; son of Nathaniel (a farmer) and Eva (Jones) Anthony; married Yvette (a typist), February 8, 1958; children: two sons, two daughters. *Education:* "No institution of note attended and no degrees or awards gained." *Politics:* "Uncategorized."

ADDRESSES: Home—99 Long Circular Rd., St. James, Port-of-Spain, Trinidad and Tobago.

CAREER: Held a number of factory jobs after immigrating to England; Reuter News Agency, London, England, sub-editor, 1964-68; lived in Brazil, 1968-70; Texaco Trinidad, Pointe-a-Pierre, Trinidad and Tobago, assistant editor, 1970-72; Ministry of Culture, Port-of-Spain, Trinidad and Tobago, researcher, 1972—.

WRITINGS:

The Games Were Coming (novel), Deutsch, 1963, expanded edition with introduction by Kenneth Ramchand, Heinemann and Deutsch, 1977.

The Year in San Fernando (novel), Deutsch, 1965, revised
edition with introduction by Paul Edwards and Kenneth
Ramchand, Heinemann, 1970.
Michael Anthony's Tales for Young and Old, Stockwell, 1967.
Green Days by the River (novel), Houghton, 1967.
Cricket in the Road (short stories), Heinemann Educational,
1973.
Sandra Street and Other Stories, Heinemann Educational, 1973.
*Glimpses of Trinidad and Tobago with a Glance at the West
Indies,* Columbus (Trinidad), 1974.
King of the Masquerade, Thomas Nelson, 1974.
*Profile Trinidad: A Historical Survey from the Discovery to
1900,* Macmillan, 1975.
(Editor with Andrew Carr) *David Frost Introduces Trinidad
and Tobago,* Deutsch, 1975.
Folk Tales and Fantasies (short stories), illustrations by Pat
Chu Foon, Columbus, 1976.
Streets of Conflict (novel), Deutsch, 1976.
The Making of Port-of-Spain, 1757-1939, Key Caribbean, 1978.
All that Glitters (novel), Deutsch, 1981.
Handbook of Small Business Advertisiing, Addison-Wesley,
1981.
Bright Road to El Dorado (novel), Nelson Caribbean, 1982.
First in Trinidad, Circle Press, 1985.

SIDELIGHTS: Michael Anthony writes apparently simple tales
of life on the island of Trinidad that convey deep insights on
human relationships. Often told from the viewpoint of a child,
these tales also give the reader a taste of Caribbean life. *New
York Times* contributor Martin Levin claims, "Mr. Anthony
has perfect pitch and an artist's eye for the finer shadings of
the native scene he knows so intimately." Writing of Anthony's short story collection *Cricket in the Road* in *Books and
Bookmen,* James Brockway finds "an evocative power I have
rarely come across, a power drawn not merely from observation, but from observing *the things that matter,* and conveying them in exactly the right words and not a word too
many." Discussing Anthony's book *Green Days by the River,*
Levin reports that the author "makes his characters appealing
without overly romanticizing them, and his ear for dialogue is
magnificently accurate." Brockway concludes, "Mr. Anthony
reminds us that there are simpler, more essential things in life
than getting and spending and he writes about them with a
serenity that can only come from strength."

Anthony once said, "I am essentially a novelist and since I
hold that the novel tells a story I feel strongly that I should
not use the medium to air my philosophies. However, I feel
very strongly about the brotherhood of mankind and as a consequence abominate war. One of my main hopes is that human
beings will find a way to live together without friction, and
my feeling is that the most distressing thing in this world is
the inhumanity of man to man on the grounds of race. I feel
that if the racial problem is solved man will have found the
key to peace on this planet. Although I am not hopeful about
any immediate change in the Southern African situation, I
think the thousands of people who are trying to solve the problem in the United States must make a great difference to the
basic situation there. Yet, though I feel this way, the books I
write have nothing (on the surface) to do with race or war."

Anthony also writes that he is extremely interested in space
exploration "as I sometimes find the mystery of the Universe
too much to bear. I often wonder if space exploration will one
day explode our present theories about God, and about the
origin and formation of the matter about us. I do consider
man's quest for knowledge vital and, in fact, inevitable." He

also commented that he would "like to see this world of rich
and poor nations, powerful and weak nations, superseded by
a world of one strong nation formed out of all. In other words
I am advocating World Government. I sometimes think that I
am merely being idealistic, but being an optimist I am not
surprised."

BIOGRAPHICAL/CRITICAL SOURCES:

BOOKS

Ramchand, Kenneth, *The West Indian Novel and its Background,* Faber, 1970.

PERIODICALS

Books and Bookmen, February, 1974.
London Magazine, April, 1967.
New York Times Book Review, August 6, 1967, April 14,
1968.
Observer, July 26, 1981.
Punch, February 22, 1967.
Spectator, February 21, 1976.
Times Literary Supplement, March 4, 1965, April 13, 1967.
World Literature Today, spring, 1984.

*   *   *

ARMAH, Ayi Kwei   1939-

PERSONAL: Born in 1939, in Takoradi, Gold Coast (now
Ghana). *Education:* Harvard University, B.A. (cum laude);
attended Achimota College, University of Ghana, and Columbia University.

ADDRESSES: c/o Third World Press, 7524 South Cottage Grove
Rd., Chicago, Ill. 60019.

CAREER: Worked in Algiers as translator for the magazine
Revolution Africaine, as a scriptwriter in Ghana for Ghana
Television, and as a teacher of English at Navrongo School in
Ghana, 1966; *Jeune Afrique* (news magazine), Paris, France,
editor and translator, 1967-68; writer, 1968—. Visiting pro-
fessor at Teacher's College, Dar es Salaam University, Uni-
versity of Massachusetts, Amherst University, University of
Lesotho, and University of Wisconsin—Madison.

AWARDS, HONORS: Farfield Foundation grant.

WRITINGS:

NOVELS

The Beautyful Ones Are Not Yet Born, Houghton, 1968, re-
printed with an introduction by Christina Ama Ata Aidoo,
Collier Books, 1969.
Fragments, Houghton, 1970.
Why Are We So Blest? Doubleday, 1971.
Two Thousand Seasons, East African Publishing House (Nai-
robi), 1973, Third World Press, 1980.
The Healers, East African Publishing House, 1978, Heine-
mann, 1979.

OTHER

Poetry included in anthology *Messages: Poems from Ghana,*
edited by K. Awoonor and G. Adali-Mortty, Heinemann, 1970.
Contributor of short stories and articles to periodicals, including *Atlantic, Harper's, New African, New York Review of Books,
Okyeame,* and *Presence Africaine.*

SIDELIGHTS: With the publication of *The Beautyful Ones Are
Not Yet Born* in 1968, Ghanaian author Ayi Kwei Armah es-

tablished prominence among younger African novelists writing in English. Armah is often cited for his vivid prose as well as for his realistic portrayals of the legacy of colonialism in postindependent African society. In *The Emergence of African Fiction*, Charles R. Larson states that Armah "is the most skilled prose stylist in Anglophone Africa today, a painter whose medium happens to be prose." Armah's longer fiction falls into two categories. His first three novels, *The Beautyful Ones Are Not Yet Born, Fragments,* and *Why Are We So Blest?*, depict "an African wasteland, where corruption in the government [is] rampant and where the African intellectual, educated abroad, [feels] totally out of place, frustrated to the point of rage or despair by his inability to make any change in the system," according to Larson in the *Saturday Review.* More recently, Armah's *Two Thousand Seasons* and *The Healers* explore Africa's rich cultural heritage through fictional characters placed in historical contexts. *New Statesman* contributor S. Nyamfukudza sees these works as part of Armah's spiritual quest "to recapture as well as create a saving vision of a time when black people were one and their relationship was one of 'reciprocity' between individuals." In *African Literature Today*, Bernth Lindfors contends that the body of Armah's work presents "Africa as a victim of outside forces that it resists but cannot contain," but that through his historical fiction, "instead of merely cursing various symptoms of the colonial disease, . . . Armah now wants to work towards effecting a cure."

In his essay in *The Emergence of African Fiction*, Larson suggests that Armah's early protagonists "become alienated men—lonely, isolated individuals confronting a thoroughly dehumanized society in which everyone else seems insane, although it is usually Armah's insular protagonists who, because of their determination to dance to a different drummer, become the accused criminals or madmen." Larson finds *The Beautyful Ones Are Not Yet Born* "a richly evocative work" and "a deeply disturbing picture of the foibles of all decadent political systems—a decadence which has nothing to do with age—of all late bourgeois worlds where morals and values have been lost and even the man of good intentions begins to doubt his sanity, begins to feel that he is the guilty one for not being corrupt." Martin Tucker, reviewing *Fragments* for *New Republic*, notes that the work, "while a powerful moral indictment of the present state of [Armah's] country makes its force felt through symbolism, not direct propagandistic means. . . . The result is a wonderfully sensuous appreciation of the dissociation of life, the inward nature of each individual, the ultimate unknowingness of things."

Armah relies upon metaphor and symbolism in his early works as a means to relate individual actions to wider human and social behavior patterns. According to Gareth Griffiths in *Studies in Black Literature*, *The Beautyful Ones Are Not Yet Born* "operates through a series of remarkable metaphorical links which institute a set of correspondences between the body of man, his society and his landscape; between, too, the inner processes of feeding and reproduction and their social equivalents, inheritance and consumption; and, finally, between the personal rot of conscience and ideals and the physical decay and putrescence of the world in which this rot occurs." Griffiths concludes: "The man struggling in the squalor of compromise and disillusion is a vision of Ghana itself, and its whole people. . . . The novel pictures vividly the process by which in the colonial period the envy and aggression of the colonised people finds expression in a self-destructive process in which each turns upon his fellow." *Journal of Common-*

wealth Literature contributor James Booth writes: "In my view Armah is attempting . . . by careful simplification and dazzling symbolism to shock his readers into accepting a crude and subjective deduction from the dubiousness and relativity of real individual experience. Armah's work gains much of its distinctive power from such emotive symbolism. He sees life instinctively in terms of brilliant, resonant images, which usually express a moral or spiritual attitude in shocking physical terms. . . . Such images are compulsive and unforgettable." Although Armah's symbolism sometimes merely reveals his particular subjective emotions, the critic nonetheless notes: "Armah asserts against the European 'I think therefore I am,' an 'African' 'I feel therefore I am.' The protagonists of his first three novels are all desperately, wincingly sensitive beings."

Critics praise Armah's first three works for their mature artistry. In *The Emergence of African Fiction*, Larson calls *The Beautyful Ones Are Not Yet Born* "a novel which burns with passion and tension, with a fire so strongly kindled that in every word and every sentence one can almost hear and smell the sizzling of the author's own branded flesh." "*Fragments* is a caustic exposure of the sickness of modern African urban life," writes M. M. Mahood in *Saturday Review*. Mahood further comments: "Essentially it is a novel, of high and consistent artistry. . . . *Fragments* lets us see many things in the mind of thoughtful West Africans today; one takes away from the book the recollection of filmlike sequences of incompetence, callousness, cynicism, concern with status. . . . *Fragments* is a novel of genuine engagement." Tucker feels that *Fragments* succeeds best as "a tone poem of powerful allegorical force." According to Booth, *Why Are We So Blest?* is "the most powerful work of a novelist of genius. . . . The disturbing power of Armah's novel is that it confronts this individual/communal dichotomy in racism and ruthlessly insists that there is *no* personal or individual escape."

As Nyamfukudza notes, *Two Thousand Seasons* "presents a considerable departure from what [Armah] has done before. . . . The collective racial memory of the black people is given voice through their pilgrimage of self-assertion in received versions of the long years of collision, destruction and enslavement by . . . 'the destroyers,' both Arab and Caucasian, who have colonised and plundered Africa." This historical theme continues in *The Healers*, a fictional chronicle based on the history of the Ashanti people. In his work *The Novels of Ayi Kwei Armah: A Study in Polemical Fiction*, Robert Fraser claims that *The Healers* "is thus not merely a reinstatement of a neglected and misunderstood phase of the colonial past, but part of the total reclamation of history on behalf of those whose contribution received opinion has traditionally slighted or abused. . . . Armah, in pursuit of his ideal of spiritual health, has used history as a medicine for rankling sores, and hence acted as a healer of his own people." In *International Fiction Review*, Eustace Palmer comments that Armah's exercise in racial retrieval "is part of the strategy for the transformation of modern society. It is much more therefore than a complacent, self-regarding idealization of blackness and black culture. The values thus retrieved must be actively used as the leaven for humanizing contemporary society."

Critical reception of *Two Thousand Seasons* and *The Healers* reflects continuing respect for Armah's accomplishments. A study group for *Black Books Bulletin* writes of *Two Thousand Seasons*: "The sheer beauty of Armah's prose is almost enough to make this novel outstanding, but the power of his ideas is what brings this book into the realm of the extraordinary. . . . We commend [Armah] for this monumental task." Lindfors calls *The Healers* "a major attempt by a major African writer to reinterpret a major event in African history." The critic concludes: "I think it will have its major impact on young people, and this is as it should be in any remythologizing of Africa. One must aim at winning the hearts and minds of the young, imbuing them with the highest ideals and making them proud and happy to be Africans. This *The Healers* does better than any other novel Armah has written. And this is why it is potentially his most important book and certainly his healthiest."

Armah, who was educated in the United States as well as in Ghana, has been compared to fiction writers of the Western literary tradition. Larson states: "In his depiction of the stifled artist in contemporary Africa, and specifically of the writer, Armah has turned to a theme almost as old as Western fiction itself." Joyce Johnson feels, nevertheless, that as an artist, Armah evinces a sense of his responsibility to show "the extent to which the masses are responsible for perpetuating their own servile condition. . . . The Ghanaian masses, Armah suggests, . . . need to be rescued not only from the abuses of those with power but also from the destructive tendencies within themselves." Larson, in his *Saturday Review* article, contends that though Armah's criticism seems aimed at life in his native country, "indirectly it [points] away from Africa—especially at Western commercialism and neo-colonialism." Larson expresses the opinion that Armah, "this most talented of the younger African novelists," writes books that "will make people talk . . . for a long time to come."

BIOGRAPHICAL/CRITICAL SOURCES:

BOOKS

Achebe, Chinua, *Morning Yet on Creation Day: Essays,* Doubleday, 1975.
Armah, Ayi Kwei, *The Beautyful Ones Are Not Yet Born,* with an introduction by Christina Ama Ata Aidoo, Collier Books, 1969.
Fraser, Robert, *The Novels of Ayi Kwei Armah: A Study in Polemical Fiction,* Heinemann, 1979.
Larson, Charles R., *The Emergence of African Fiction,* revised edition, Indiana University Press, 1972.

PERIODICALS

African Literature Today, Number 11, 1980.
America, April 22, 1972.
Black Books Bulletin, winter, 1976.
Black World, March, 1974.
International Fiction Review, winter, 1981.
Journal of Commonwealth Literature, August, 1980.
National Review, November 5, 1968.
New Republic, January 31, 1970.
New Statesman, March 7, 1980.
New York Times, January 16, 1970.
New York Times Book Review, April 2, 1972.
Saturday Review, August 31, 1968, January 17, 1970, March 18, 1972.
Studies in Black Literature, summer, 1971.
Times Literary Supplement, March 27, 1969.
Washington Post Book World, April 2, 1972.
World Literature Today, spring, 1970.
World Literature Written in English, autumn, 1982.

*   *   *

ASARE, Bediako
  See KONADU, S(amuel) A(sare)

ATKINS, Russell   1926-

PERSONAL: Born February 25, 1926, in Cleveland, Ohio; son of Perry Kelly and Mamie (Harris) Atkins. *Education:* Attended Cleveland School of Art (now Cleveland Institute of Art), 1943-44, and Cleveland Institute of Music, 1944-45; private music study, 1950-54. *Politics:* "Nothing particular." *Religion:* None.

ADDRESSES: Home—6005 Grand Ave., Cleveland, Ohio 44104.

CAREER: Editor, writer and composer; founder and editor of *Free Lance* magazine, 1950-1979. Publicity manager and assistant to director, Sutphen School of Music (of National Guild of Community Music Schools), Cleveland, Ohio, 1957-60; lecturer, Poets and Lecturers Alliance, 1963-65; writing instructor, Karamu House, 1972-86; writer-in-residence, Cuyahoga Community College, summer, 1973; instructor, Ohio Program in the Humanities, 1978. Affiliated with Iowa Workshop, University of Iowa, 1953-54. Member, Artists-in-Schools Program of Ohio Arts Council and National Endowment for the Arts, 1973—. Participant, Bread Loaf Writers' Conference, 1956; member of literary advisory panel, Ohio Arts Council, 1973-76; member, Cleveland State University Poetry Forum; member, Coordinating Council of Literary Magazines of National Endowment for the Arts. Consultant to Karamu Writers Conference, 1971, and to other writers conferences and workshops; consultant, WVIZ-TV, 1969-72, and to Cleveland Board of Education, 1972-73.

MEMBER: Committee of Small Magazine Editors and Publishers, Poets League of Greater Cleveland (member of board of trustees).

AWARDS, HONORS: Honorary Ph.D., Cleveland State University, 1976; individual artist grant, Ohio Arts Council, 1978.

WRITINGS:

POETRY

A Podium Presentation, Poetry Seminar Press, 1960.
Phenomena, Free Lance Poets and Prose Workshop, Wilberforce University, 1961.
Objects, Hearse Press, 1963.
Objects 2, Renegade Press, 1963.
Heretofore, Paul Breman, 1968.
Presentations, Podium Press, 1969.
Here in The, Cleveland State University Poetry Center, 1976.
Whichever, Free Lance Press, 1978.

MUSICAL COMPOSITIONS

(With Langston Hughes and Hale Smith) *Elegy* (poetry set to music), Highgate Press, 1968.
Objects (for piano), Free Lance Press, 1969.

Also composer of unpublished musical works.

CONTRIBUTOR TO ANTHOLOGIES

Paul Breman, editor, *Sixes and Sevens,* Paul Breman (London), 1962.
Adelaide Simon, editor, *Silver Cesspool,* Renegade Press, 1964.
D. A. Levy, editor, *Four, Five, Six,* Seven Flowers Press, 1966.
Richard E. Peck, editor, *Sounds and Silences: Poetry for Now,* Delacorte, 1969.

June Jordan, editor, *Soulscript: Afro-American Poetry*, Doubleday, 1970.
Jeanne Hollyfield, editor, *Yearbook of Modern Poetry*, Young Publications, 1972.
Anthologies in Braille, Bell Telephone Laboratories, 1970.
Lewis Turco, editor, *Poetry: An Introduction through Writing*, Prentice-Hall, 1972.
Robert McGovern and Richard Snyder, editors, *The Strong Voice Two*, Ashland Poetry, 1972.
Willemien Vroom, editor, *Penguin Book of Verse*, Penguin (England), 1973.
Woodie King, Jr., editor, *The Forerunners*, Howard University Press, 1975.
Arnold Adoff, editor, *Celebrations*, Follett, 1977.
Peter Hargitai and Lolette Kuby, editors, *Forum*, Mentor Press, 1978.
Citino, Turner, and Bennett, editors, *Seventy-three Ohio Poets*, Ohio State University, 1978.
Robert Fox, editor, *Poems, 1978-1983*, Ohio Arts Council, 1983.

OTHER

Psychovisual Perspective for 'Musical' Composition (chapbook; musical theory), Free Lance Press, 1958.
Two by Atkins: The Abortionist and The Corpse: Two Poetic Dramas to Be Set to Music, Free Lance Press, 1963.
The Nail, to Be Set to Music (poetic libretto), Free Lance Press, 1970.
Maleficium (short stories), Free Lance Press, 1971.
"By Yearning and by Beautiful" (poem set to music by Hale Smith), first performed at Lincoln Center for the Performing Arts, New York, N.Y., 1986.

Contributor of poems and articles to *New York Times Book Review, Beloit Poetry Journal, Western Review, Minnesota Quarterly, Poetry Now*, and numerous other journals.

WORK IN PROGRESS: Revising and adding to "Spyrytuals," for piano; developing a theory for avant-garde poetic drama.

SIDELIGHTS: Russell Atkins' work, says Ronald Henry High in the *Dictionary of Literary Biography*, distinguishes him as "one of the leading experimental figures of the past three decades." His works in music and poetic drama, according to High, place him firmly in the avant-garde. An early exponent of concrete poetry—in which the arrangement or design of the words takes precedence over the words themselves—Atkins' "starkly dramatic handling of such subjects in poetry as dope addiction, sexual aberration, necrophilia, and abortion went beyond the academic reserve of the early 1950s," High continues. His theory of psychovisualism, the critic states, is based on Gestalt hypotheses which study the formation of patterns, and "explains how we perceive the nonverbal 'high and low' in music," by recognizing the function of the brain in understanding music.

Atkins commented: "My work seeks to go beyond the mere distributing of a few good images throughout an argumentative poetic context of 'insights' and 'observations.' To me, a poet's task is to use the imagination to exploit range, to create a body of effect, event, colors, characteristics, moods, verbal stresses pushed to a maximum."

Atkins's poems were read over the radio by poets Langston Hughes in 1950, and Marianne Moore in 1951. *Elegy* was

recorded as "In Memoriam" in 1964 by the Kulas Chorus conducted by Robert Shaw with the Cleveland Orchestra. Karamu House presented an evening called "A Tribute to Russell Atkins" in 1971.

BIOGRAPHICAL/CRITICAL SOURCES:

BOOKS

Breman, Paul, *You Better Believe It*, Penguin, 1973.
Dictionary of Literary Biography, Volume 41: *Afro-American Poets since 1955*, Gale, 1985.
Redmond, Eugene B., *Drum Voices*, Doubleday, 1976.
Stuckenschmidt, H. H., *20th Century Music*, McGraw, 1969.

PERIODICALS

Free Lance (special Russell Atkins issue), number 14, 1970-71.

*   *   *

AUBERT, Alvin (Bernard)   1930-

PERSONAL: Born March 12, 1930, in Lutcher, La.; son of Albert (a laborer) and Lucille (Roussel) Aubert; married second wife, Bernadine Tenant (a teacher and librarian), October 29, 1960; children: (first marriage) Stephenie; (second marriage) Miriam, Deborah. *Education:* Southern University, B.A., 1959; University of Michigan, A.M., 1960; further graduate study at University of Illinois, 1963-64, 1966-67.

ADDRESSES: Home—18234 Parkside Ave., Detroit, Mich. 48221. *Office*—Department of English, Wayne State University, Detroit, Mich. 48202.

CAREER: Southern University, Baton Rouge, La., instructor, 1960-62, assistant professor, 1962-65, associate professor of English, 1965-70; State University of New York College at Fredonia, associate professor, 1970-74, professor of English, 1974-79; Wayne State University, Detroit, Mich., professor of English, 1979—. Visiting professor at University of Oregon, summer, 1970. Member of board of directors, Coordinating Council of Literary Magazines, 1982-86. Has given readings of his poems at educational institutions.

MEMBER: Modern Language Association of America, National Council of Teachers of English, African Heritage Studies Association, National Council for Black Studies.

AWARDS, HONORS: Woodrow Wilson fellow, 1959; National Endowment for the Arts grant, 1973, 1981; scholarship for Bread Loaf Writers' Conference, Middlebury, Vt., 1978; Coordinating Council of Literary Magazines Editors fellow, 1979.

WRITINGS:

Against the Blues (poems), Broadside Press, 1972.
Feeling Through (poems), Greenfield Review Press, 1976.
A Noisesome Music (poems), Blackenergy South Press, 1979.
South Louisiana: New and Selected Poems, Lunchroom Press, 1985.
"Home from Harlem" (play; adapted from *The Sport of the Gods* by Paul Laurence Dunbar), first produced in Detroit at the Bonstelle Theatre, January 24, 1986.

CONTRIBUTOR TO ANTHOLOGIES

J. W. Corrington and Miller Williams, editors, *Southern Writing in the Sixties: Poetry, Volumes I and II, Louisiana State University Press, 1966.

Williams, editor, Contemporary Poetry in America, Random House, 1973.

Arnold Adoff, editor, Celebrations: An Anthology of Black Poetry, Follett, 1979.

Edward Field, editor, A Geography of Poets: An Anthology of the New Poetry, Bantam, 1979.

Guy Owen and Mary C. Williams, editors, Contemporary Southern Poetry, Louisiana State University Press, 1979.

Williams, editor, Patterns of Poetry: An Encyclopedia of Forms, Louisiana State University Press, 1986.

Leon Stokesburg, editor, The Made Thing: An Anthology of Contemporary Southern Poetry, University of Arkansas Press, 1987.

OTHER

Contributor to Contemporary Novelists, 1972, and Writers of the English Language, 1979. Contributor of poems, articles, and reviews to literary journals, including Nimrod, Black American Literature Forum, American Poetry Review, Black World, Prairie Schooner, Black Scholar, Iowa Review, Journal of Black Poetry, American Book Review, and Epoch. Book reviewer, Library Journal, 1972-74. Advisory editor of Drama and Theatre, 1973-75, Black Box, 1974—, Gumbo, 1976-78, and Callaloo, 1977—; founding editor of Obsidian: Black Literature in Review, 1975-85.

WORK IN PROGRESS: Poems; a novel, "Port Hudson," set in South Louisiana; a play, "Family Reunion"; several short stories.

SIDELIGHTS: Alvin Aubert wrote: "I grew up in a small Mississippi River town about midway between New Orleans and Baton Rouge, and this locale—particularly the river—and the people, but especially the people, continue to motivate me; not to the extent of my finding out exactly who and what they were (if that were possible), but of initiating and maintaining a spiritual connection. Most representative of this influence are poems of mine such as 'Baptism,' 'Remembrance,' 'Feeling Through,' 'Spring 1937,' 'Father, There,' 'South Louisiana,' 'The Housemovers,' 'All Singing in a Pie,' and 'Fall of '43.' I like to think that all of my writings explore various aspects of the human situation and celebrate human existence at a particular and consequently universal level."

BIOGRAPHICAL/CRITICAL SOURCES:

BOOKS

Dictionary of Literary Biography, Volume 41: Afro-American Poets since 1955, Gale, 1985.

PERIODICALS

American Book Review, March, 1987.
Black American Literature Forum, fall, 1987.
Buffalo Courier Express, June 8, 1973.
Kliatt, November, 1972.

                    *   *   *

AWOONOR, Kofi (Nyidevu) 1935-
(George Awoonor-Williams)

PERSONAL: Name originally George Awoonor-Williams; born March 13, 1935, in Wheta, Ghana; son of Atsu E. and Kosiwo (Nyidevu) Awoonor; married; children: three sons, one daughter, including Sika, Dunyo, Kalepe. Education: University College of Ghana, B.A., 1960; University College, London, M.A., 1970; State University of New York at Stony Brook, Ph.D., 1972. Religion: Ancestralist.

ADDRESSES: Home and office—Embassy of Ghana, SQS 111 Bloco B, Apt. 603, Brasilia, Brazil 70466. Agent—Harold Ober Associates, Inc., 40 East 49th St., New York, N.Y. 10017.

CAREER: University of Ghana, Accra, lecturer and research fellow, 1960-64; Ghana Ministry of Information, Accra, director of films, 1964-67; State University of New York at Stony Brook, assistant professor of English, 1968-75; arrested for suspected subversion, charged with harboring a subversionist, served one year in prison in Ghana, 1975-76; University of Cape Coast, Cape Coast, Ghana, professor of English, beginning in 1976; Ghana ambassador to Brazil in Brasilia, with accreditation to Argentina, Uruguay, Venezuela, Surinam, and Guyana, 1983—.

MEMBER: African Studies Association of America.

AWARDS, HONORS: Longmans fellow at University of London, 1967-68; Fairfield fellow; Gurrey Prize and National Book Council award, both 1979, for poetry.

WRITINGS:

(Under name George Awoonor-Williams) Rediscovery, and Other Poems, Northwestern University Press, 1964.

(Editor with G. Adali-Mortty) Messages: Poems from Ghana, Heinemann, 1970, Humanities, 1971.

Ancestral Power and Lament, Heinemann, 1970.

This Earth, My Brother: An Allegorical Tale of Africa, Doubleday, 1971.

Night of My Blood (poetry), Doubleday, 1971.

Ride Me, Memory (poetry), Greenfield Review Press, 1973.

Guardians of the Sacred Word, NOK Publishers, 1974.

The Breast of the Earth: A Survey of the History, Culture, and Literature of Africa South of the Sahara, Doubleday, 1975.

The House by the Sea (poetry), Greenfield Review Press, 1978.

(Translator) When Sorrow-Song Descends on You (chapbook), edited by Stanley H. Barkan, Cross-Cultural Communications, 1981.

Fire in the Valley, NOK Publishers, 1983.

The Breast of the Earth: A Survey of the History, Culture, and Literature of Africa South of the Sahara, NOK Publishers, 1983.

The Ghana Revolution: Background Account From a Personal Perspective, Oases Publishers, 1984.

Until the Morning After: Selected Poems, 1963-1985, Greenfield Review Press, 1987.

Alien Corn (novel), Oases Publishers, in press.

Contributor to Africa Report and Books Abroad. Associate editor of Transition, 1967-68, World View, and Okike.

WORK IN PROGRESS: Notes from Prison, a personal account; "The Zambezi Flows Here," a screenplay.

SIDELIGHTS: Kofi Awoonor wrote: "The written word came almost as if it had no forebears. So my poetry assays to restate the oral beginnings, to articulate the mysterious relation between the WORD and the magical dimensions of our cognitive world. I work with forces that are beyond me, ancestral and ritualized entities who dictate and determine all my literary endeavors. Simply put, my work takes off from the world of all our aboriginal instincts. It is for this reason that I have translated poetry from my own society, the Ewes, and sat at the feet of ancient poets whose medium is the voice and whose forum is the village square and the market place.''

AVOCATIONAL INTERESTS: Politics, jazz, tennis, herbal medicine (African).

BIOGRAPHICAL/CRITICAL SOURCES:

PERIODICALS

Ariel, January, 1975.

*   *   *

AWOONOR-WILLIAMS, George
    See AWOONOR, Kofi (Nyidevu)

B

BAILEY, Pearl (Mae) 1918-

PERSONAL: Born March 29, 1918, in Newport News, Va.; daughter of Joseph James (a minister) and Ella Mae Bailey; married John Randolph Pinkett, Jr., August 31, 1948 (divorced, March, 1952); married Louis Bellson, Jr. (a jazz drummer), November 19, 1952; children: Tony Bellson, DeeDee Bellson. *Education:* Attended public schools in Philadelphia, Pa.

ADDRESSES: P.O. Box 52, Northridge, Calif. 91324. *Agent*—William Morris Agency, 1350 Avenue of the Americas, New York, N.Y. 10019.

CAREER: Singer and entertainer, 1933—; vocalist with various popular bands, including Count Basie and Cootie Williams bands; made Broadway stage debut in "St. Louis Woman," 1946, followed by "Arms in the Girl," 1950, "Bless You All," 1950, "House of Flowers," 1954, and "Hello, Dolly," 1967-69; motion pictures include "Variety Girl," 1947, "Isn't It Romantic," 1948, "Carmen Jones," 1954, "That Certain Feeling," 1955, "St. Louis Blues," 1957, "Porgy and Bess," 1959, "All the Fine Young Cannibals," 1960, "The Landlord," 1970, "Norman, Is That You?," 1976, and "Lost Generation"; television work includes the "Pearl Bailey Show," a musical variety program on American Broadcasting Co. (ABC-TV), 1970-71, "Pearl's Kitchen," a cooking show, and guest appearances on several variety programs; night club entertainer in New York, Boston, Hollywood, Las Vegas, Chicago, London; contract recording artist for Coral Records, Decca Records, and Columbia Records. Special representative, United States delegation to United Nations.

AWARDS, HONORS: Donaldson Award for most promising new performer, 1946, for performance in "St. Louis Woman"; Entertainer of the Year Award from *Cue* magazine and special Tony Award, both 1967, both for "Hello, Dolly"; March of Dimes Woman of the Year, 1968; U.S.O. Woman of the Year, 1969; citation from Mayor John Lindsay of New York City, 1969; Coretta Scott King Award, American Library Association, 1976, for *Duey's Tale*.

WRITINGS:

The Raw Pearl (autobiography), Harcourt, 1968.
Talking To Myself (autobiography), Harcourt, 1971.
Pearl's Kitchen: An Extraordinary Cookbook, Harcourt, 1973.

Duey's Tale (juvenile), Harcourt, 1975.
Hurry Up, America, and Spit, Harcourt, 1976.

SIDELIGHTS: Pearl Bailey's entertainment career began in 1933 when she won first prize in an amateur night contest at the Pearl Theatre in Philadelphia. She continued in vaudeville, then moved into cabarets, eventually appearing on the stage, in movies, on television, and as one of the most popular nightclub performers in the United States. Her starring role in the long-running Broadway musical "Hello Dolly" earned her a special Tony Award and widespread critical acclaim. "For Miss Bailey this was a Broadway triumph for the history books," writes Clive Barnes in the *New York Times*. "She took the whole musical in her hands and swung it around her neck as easily as if it were a feather boa. Her timing was exquisite, with asides tossed away as languidly as one might tap ash from a cigarette, and her singing had that deep throaty rumble that. . .is always so oddly stirring."

In 1968, Bailey published an autobiographical account of her life entitled *The Raw Pearl*. Although she expresses reservations about her skill with language in the book's foreword, writing that "this is new to me. I don't always have the kind of words I want to express myself," many reviewers have praised the book. "Pearl Bailey writes about her life the way she sings," observes a *Saturday Review* critic, "with gusto and warmth and honesty."

Following the success of *The Raw Pearl*, Bailey penned a second autobiographical account, *Talking to Myself*. According to *Publishers Weekly*, it offers "affectionate homilies laced with recollections of her life and travels during recent years." Jo Hudson acknowledges in *Black World* that the book "may be criticized from a literary standpoint as being very loosely constructed, a little off-beat, and repetitive in its message. However, if we accept Pearl as being distinctive and truly possessing a style of her own, we will accept *Talking to Myself* in like manner."

BIOGRAPHICAL/CRITICAL SOURCES:

BOOKS

Bailey, Pearl, *The Raw Pearl*, Harcourt, 1968.
Bailey, Pearl, *Talking to Myself*, Harcourt, 1971.

PERIODICALS

Black World, March, 1972.

Cue, January 6, 1968.
Ebony, January, 1968.
Newsweek, December 4, 1967.
New York Times, November 13, 1967, November 26, 1967.
Publishers Weekly, August 23, 1971.
Saturday Review, February 22, 1969.
Time, November 24, 1967.

* * *

BAKER, Augusta 1911-

PERSONAL: Born April 1, 1911, in Baltimore, Md.; daughter of Winfort J. and Mabel (Gough) Braxston; married second husband, Gordon Alexander, November 23, 1944; children: (first marriage) James Henry Baker III. *Education:* New York College for Teachers (now State University of New York at Albany), A.B., 1933, B.S., 1934. *Religion:* Presbyterian.

ADDRESSES: Home—830 Armour St., Columbia, S.C. 29203.

CAREER: New York Public Library, New York, N.Y., children's librarian, 1937-53, assistant coordinator and storytelling specialist, 1953-61, coordinator of children's services, 1961-74; University of South Carolina, College of Library and Information Sciences, Columbia, storyteller in residence, 1980—. Visiting lecturer, Columbia University, 1955-79. Organized children's library service for Trinidad Public Library, Port of Spain, 1953. Founded James Weldon Johnson Memorial Collection at the Countee Cullen Regional Branch of the New York Public Library. Broadcaster of weekly series "The World of Children's Literature" for WNYC-Radio, beginning 1971. Has served as consultant to various organizations.

MEMBER: International Reading Association, American Library Association (member of board of directors, 1958-61 and 1966-69; councillor, 1965-72; president of child services division, 1967-68; member of executive board, 1968-72), Newbery-Caldecott Committee (chairman, 1966), Association of Early Childhood Education, Private Libraries Association, Southeastern Library Association, New York Library Association (member of executive board, 1960), South Carolina Library Association, Friends of Children's Services of the New York Public Library.

AWARDS, HONORS: Dutton-Macrae Award, 1953, for advanced study in field of library work with children; *Parents' Magazine* Medal Award, 1966, for "outstanding service to the nation's children"; Grolier Award from American Library Association, 1968, for "outstanding achievement in guiding and stimulating the reading of children and young people"; Constance Lindsay Skinner Award from Women's National Book Association, 1971; Distinguished Alumni Award from State University of New York at Albany, 1974; Harold Jackson Memorial Award, 1974; honorary doctorate of letters, St. John's University, Jamaica, N.Y., 1978; Regina Medal from Catholic Library Association, 1981.

WRITINGS:

(Editor) *Talking Tree,* Lippincott, 1955.
(Editor) *Golden Lynx,* Lippincott, 1960.
(Editor with Eugenia Garson) *Young Years: Best Loved Stories and Poems for Little Children,* Parents' Magazine Press, 1960.
(Editor) *Once Upon a Time,* 2nd edition, New York Library Association, 1964.
(Contributor) *Come Hither! Papers on Children's Literature and Librarianship,* Yeasayers Press, 1966.

(Editor) *The Black Experience in Children's Books,* New York Public Library, 1971.
Storytelling (sound recording), Children's Book Council, 1975.
(With Ellin Greene) *Storytelling: Art and Technique,* Bowker, 1977, 2nd edition, 1987.

Contributor of introductions to books. Compiler of numerous reading lists and pamphlets.

AVOCATIONAL INTERESTS: Gardening, civic work.

BIOGRAPHICAL/CRITICAL SOURCES:

BOOKS

Flynn, James J., *Negroes' Achievement in Modern America,* Dodd, 1970.
Josey, E. J., editor, *The Black Librarian in America,* Scarecrow, 1970.

PERIODICALS

Bookwoman, November, 1971.
Horn Book, August, 1971.

* * *

BAKER, Houston A., Jr. 1943-

PERSONAL: Born March 22, 1943, in Louisville, Ky.; married Charlotte Pierce; children: Mark Frederick. *Education:* Howard University, B.A. (magna cum laude), 1965; University of California, Los Angeles, M.A., 1966, Ph.D., 1968; graduate study at University of Edinburgh, 1967-68.

ADDRESSES: Office—Department of English, University of Pennsylvania, Philadelphia, Pa. 19104.

CAREER: Howard University, Washington, D.C., instructor in English, summer, 1966; Yale University, New Haven, Conn., instructor, 1968-69, assistant professor of English, 1969-70; University of Virginia, Charlottesville, associate professor, 1970-73, professor of English, 1973-74, member of Center for Advanced Studies, 1970-73; University of Pennsylvania, Philadelphia, professor of English, 1974—, director of Afro-American Studies Program, 1974-77, Albert M. Greenfield Professor of Human Relations, 1982—. Distinguished visiting professor at Cornell University, 1977; visiting professor at Haverford College, 1983-85. Member of Fulbright-Hays literature screening committee, 1973-74; member of committee on scholarly worth, Howard University Press, 1973—.

MEMBER: Modern Language Association of America, College Language Association, Phi Beta Kappa, Kappa Delta Pi.

AWARDS, HONORS: Alfred Longueil Poetry Award from University of California, Los Angeles, 1966; National Phi Beta Kappa visiting scholar, 1975-76; Center for Advanced Study in the Behavioral Sciences fellow, 1977-78; Guggenheim fellow, 1978-79; National Humanities Center fellow, 1982-83; Rockefeller Minority Group fellow, 1982-83.

WRITINGS:

(Contributor) John Morton Blum, general editor, *Key Issues in the Afro-American Experience,* Harcourt, 1971.
(Editor) *Black Literature in America,* McGraw, 1971.
Long Black Song: Essays in Black American Literature and Culture, University Press of Virginia, 1972.
(Editor) *Twentieth-Century Interpretations of Native Son,* Prentice-Hall, 1972.
Singers of Daybreak: Studies in Black American Literature, Howard University Press, 1974.

A Many-Colored Coat of Dreams: The Poetry of Countee Cul-len, Broadside Press, 1974.

(Contributor) *Contemporary Poets*, St. Martin's, 1975.

(Editor) *Reading Black: Essays in the Criticism of African, Caribbean, and Black American Literature*, Africana Studies and Research Center, Cornell University, 1976.

(Editor with wife, Charlotte Pierce-Baker) *Renewal: A Volume of Black Poems*, Afro-American Studies Program, University of Pennsylvania, 1977.

(Editor) *A Dark and Sudden Beauty: Two Essays in Black American Poetry by George Kent and Stephen Henderson*, Afro-American Studies Program, University of Pennsylvania, 1977.

No Matter Where You Travel, You Still Be Black (poems), Lotus Press, 1979.

The Journey Back: Issues in Black Literature and Criticism, University of Chicago Press, 1980.

Spirit Run, Lotus Press, 1981.

(Editor with Leslie Fiedler) *English Literature: Opening Up the Canon, Selected Papers from the English Institute, 1979*, English Institute, Johns Hopkins University, 1981.

(Editor) *Three American Literatures: Essays in Chicano, Native American, and Asian-American Literature for Teachers of "American" Literature*, Modern Language Association of America, 1982.

(Editor and author of introduction) *Narrative of the Life of Frederick Douglass, an American Slave, Written by Himself*, Penguin Books, 1982.

Blues, Ideology, and Afro-American Literature: A Vernacular Theory, University of Chicago Press, 1984.

Blues Journeys Home, Lotus, 1985.

(Editor with Joe Weixlmann) *Belief versus Theory in Black American Literary Criticism*, Penkevill, 1985.

Modernism and the Harlem Renaissance, University of Chicago Press, 1987.

Also author of *Long Black Song: Essays in Black American Literature and Culture*, UMI Publications. Contributor of about twenty articles and reviews to literature and black studies journals, including *Victorian Poetry, Phylon, Black World, Obsidian, Yale Review*, and *Journal of African-Afro-American Affairs*. Advisory editor of *Columbia Literary History of the United States*, Columbia University Press. Member of advisory boards of *Maji*, 1974-76, *Black American Literature Forum*, 1976—, and *Minority Voices*, 1977—.

WORK IN PROGRESS: Contributing to *Research in African Literatures*, edited by Marion Berghahn.

BIOGRAPHICAL/CRITICAL SOURCES:

PERIODICALS

Los Angeles Times Book Review, December 16, 1984.
New York Times Book Review, January 24, 1988.
Washington Post Book World, January 3, 1988.

*   *   *

BAKR el TOURE, Askia Muhammad Abu
    See TOURE, Askia Muhammad Abu Bakr el

*   *   *

BALDWIN, James (Arthur)   1924-1987

PERSONAL: Born August 2, 1924, in New York, N.Y.; died of stomach cancer December 1 (some sources say November 30), 1987, in St. Paul de Vence, France; son of David (a clergyman and factory worker) and Berdis (Jones) Baldwin. *Education:* Graduate of De Witt Clinton High School, New York, N.Y., 1942.

ADDRESSES: Home—St. Paul de Vence, France. *Agent*—Edward Acton, Inc., 17 Grove St., New York, N.Y. 10014.

CAREER: Writer, 1944-87. Youth minister at Fireside Pentecostal Assembly, New York, N.Y., 1938-42; variously employed as handyman, dishwasher, waiter, and office boy in New York City, and in defense work in Belle Meade, N.J., 1942-46. Lecturer on racial issues at universities in the United States and Europe, 1957-87. Director of play, "Fortune and Men's Eyes," in Istanbul, Turkey, 1970, and film, "The Inheritance," 1973.

MEMBER: Congress on Racial Equality (member of national advisory board), American Academy and Institute of Arts and Letters, Authors League, International PEN, Dramatists Guild, Actors' Studio, National Committee for a Sane Nuclear Policy.

AWARDS, HONORS: Eugene F. Saxton fellowship, 1945; Rosenwald fellowship, 1948; Guggenheim fellowship, 1954; National Institute of Arts and Letters grant for literature, 1956; Ford Foundation grant, 1959; National Conference of Christians and Jews Brotherhood Award, 1962, for *Nobody Knows My Name: More Notes of a Native Son;* George Polk Memorial Award, 1963, for magazine articles; Foreign Drama Critics Award, 1964, for *Blues for Mister Charlie;* D.Litt. from the University of British Columbia, Vancouver, 1964; National Association of Independent Schools Award, 1964, for *The Fire Next Time;* American Book Award nomination, 1980, for *Just above My Head;* named Commander of the Legion of Honor (France), 1986.

WRITINGS:

FICTION

Go Tell It on the Mountain (novel), Knopf, 1953.
Giovanni's Room (novel; also see below), Dial, 1956, reprinted, Transworld, 1977.
Another Country (novel), Dial, 1962.
Going to Meet the Man (short stories), Dial, 1965.
(Contributor) *American Negro Short Stories*, Hill & Wang, 1966.
Tell Me How Long the Train's Been Gone (novel), Dial, 1968.
If Beale Street Could Talk (novel), Dial, 1974.
Little Man, Little Man: A Story of Childhood (juvenile), M. Joseph, 1976, Dial, 1977.
Just above My Head (novel), Dial, 1979.

Also author of *Harlem Quartet* (novel), 1987.

NONFICTION

Autobiographical Notes, Knopf, 1953.
Notes of a Native Son (essays), Beacon Press, 1955.
Nobody Knows My Name: More Notes of a Native Son (essays), Dial, 1961.
The Fire Next Time, Dial, 1963.
(Author of text) Richard Avedon, *Nothing Pesonal* (photographic portraits), Atheneum, 1964.
(With others) *Black Anti-Semitism and Jewish Racism*, R. W. Baron, 1969.
(With Kenneth Kaunda) Carl Ordung, editor, *Menschenwuerde und Gerechtigkeit* (essays delivered at the fourth assembly of the World Council of Churches), Union-Verlag, 1969.

(With Margaret Mead) *A Rap on Race* (transcripted conversation), Lippincott, 1971.

No Name in the Street (essays), Dial, 1972.

(With Francoise Giroud) *Cesar: Compressions d'or,* Hachette, 1973.

(With Nikki Giovanni) *A Dialogue* (transcripted conversation), Lippincott, 1973.

The Devil Finds Work (essays), Dial, 1976.

(With others) John Henrik Clarke, editor, *Harlem, U.S.A.: The Story of a City within a City,* Seven Seas [Berlin], 1976.

The Evidence of Things Not Seen, Holt, 1985.

The Price of the Ticket: Collected Nonfiction 1948-1985, St. Martin's, 1985.

(With others) Michael J. Weber, editor, *Perspectives: Angles on African Art,* Center for African Art, 1987.

PLAYS

The Amen Corner (first produced in Washington, D.C. at Howard University, 1955; produced on Broadway at Ethel Barrymore Theatre, April 15, 1965), Dial, 1968.

''Giovanni's Room'' (based on novel of same title), first produced in New York City at Actors' Studio, 1957.

Blues for Mister Charlie (first produced on Broadway at ANTA Theatre, April 23, 1964), Dial, 1964.

One Day, When I Was Lost: A Scenario (screenplay; based on *The Autobiography of Malcolm X,* by Alex Haley), M. Joseph, 1972, Dial, 1973.

''A Deed for the King of Spain,'' first produced in New York City at American Center for Stanislavski Theatre Art, January 24, 1974.

Also author of ''The Welcome Table,'' 1987.

OTHER

Jimmy's Blues: Selected Poems, M. Joseph, 1983, St. Martin's, 1985.

Contributor of book reviews and essays to numerous periodicals in the United States and abroad, including *Harper's, Nation, Esquire, Playboy, Partisan Review, Mademoiselle,* and *New Yorker.*

WORK IN PROGRESS: A study of the life of Martin Luther King, Jr.

SIDELIGHTS: A novelist and essayist of considerable renown, James Baldwin bore articulate witness to the unhappy consequences of American racial strife. Baldwin's writing career began in the last years of legislated segregation; his fame as a social observer grew in tandem with the civil rights movement as he mirrored blacks' aspirations, disappointments, and coping strategies in a hostile society. *Tri-Quarterly* contributor Robert A. Bone declared that Baldwin's publications ''have had a stunning impact on our cultural life'' because the author ''. . . succeeded in transposing the entire discussion of American race relations to the interior plane; it is a major breakthrough for the American imagination.'' In his novels, plays, and essays alike, Baldwin explored the psychological implications of racism for both the oppressed and the oppressor. Bestsellers such as *Nobody Knows My Name: More Notes of a Native Son* and *The Fire Next Time* acquainted wide audiences with his highly personal observations and his sense of urgency in the face of rising black bitterness. As Juan Williams noted in the *Washington Post,* long before Baldwin's death, his writings ''became a standard of literary realism. . . . Given the messy nature of racial hatred, of the half-truths, blasphem-

ies and lies that make up American life, Baldwin's accuracy in reproducing that world stands as a remarkable achievement. . . . Black people reading Baldwin knew he wrote the truth. White people reading Baldwin sensed his truth about the lives of black people and the sins of a racist nation.''

Critics accorded Baldwin high praise for both his style and his themes. ''Baldwin has carved a literary niche through his exploration of 'the mystery of the human being' in his art,'' observed Louis H. Pratt in *James Baldwin.* ''His short stories, novels, and plays shed the light of reality upon the darkness of our illusions, while the essays bring a boldness, courage, and cool logic to bear on the most crucial questions of humanity with which this country has yet to be faced.'' In the *College Language Association Journal,* Therman B. O'Daniel called Baldwin ''the gifted professor of that primary element, genuine talent. . . . Secondly he is a very intelligent and deeply perceptive observer of our multifarious contemporary society. . . . In the third place, Baldwin is a bold and courageous writer who is not afraid to search into the dark corners of our social consciences, and to force out into public view many of the hidden, sordid skeletons of our society. . . . Then, of course, there is Baldwin's literary style which is a fourth major reason for his success as a writer. His prose . . . possesses a crystal clearness and a passionately poetic rhythm that makes it most appealing.'' *Saturday Review* correspondent Benjamin De Mott concluded that Baldwin ''retains a place in an extremely select group: That composed of the few genuinely indispensible American writers. He owes his rank partly to the qualities of responsiveness that have marked his work from the beginning. . . . Time and time over in fiction as in reportage, Baldwin tears himself free of his rhetorical fastenings and stands forth on the page utterly absorbed in the reality of the person before him, strung with his nerves, riveted to his feelings, breathing his breath.''

Baldwin's central preoccupation as a writer lay in ''his insistence on removing, layer by layer, the hardened skin with which Americans shield themselves from their country,'' according to Orde Coombs in the *New York Times Book Review.* The author saw himself as a ''disturber of the peace''—one who revealed uncomfortable truths to a society mired in complacency. Pratt found Baldwin ''engaged in a perpetual battle to overrule our objections and continue his probe into the very depths of our past. His constant concern is the catastrophic failure of the American Dream and the devastating inability of the American people to deal with that calamity.'' Pratt uncovered a further assumption in Baldwin's work; namely, that all of mankind is united by virtue of common humanity. ''Consequently,'' Pratt stated, ''the ultimate purpose of the writer, from Baldwin's perspective, is to discover that sphere of commonality where, although differences exist, those dissimilarities are stripped of their power to block communication and stifle human intercourse.'' The major impediment in this search for commonality, according to Baldwin, is white society's entrenched moral cowardice, a condition that through longstanding tradition equates blackness with dark impulses, carnality and chaos. By denying blacks' essential humanity so simplistically, the author argued, whites inflict psychic damage on blacks and suffer self-estrangement—a ''fatal bewilderment,'' to quote Bone. Baldwin's essays exposed the dangerous implications of this destructive way of thinking; his fictional characters occasionally achieve interracial harmony after having made the bold leap of understanding he advocated. In the *British Journal of Sociology,* Beau Fly Jones claimed that Baldwin was one of the first black writers ''to discuss with such insight the psychological handicaps that most Negroes must face; and to realize the complexities of Negro-white relations in so many different contexts. In redefining what has been called the Negro problem as white, he has forced the majority race to look at the damage it has done, and its own role in that destruction.''

Dictionary of Literary Biography essayist John W. Roberts felt that Baldwin's ''evolution as a writer of the first order constitutes a narrative as dramatic and compelling as his best story.'' Baldwin was born and raised in Harlem under very trying circumstances. His stepfather, an evangelical preacher, struggled to support a large family and demanded the most rigorous religious behavior from his nine children. Roberts wrote: ''Baldwin's ambivalent relationship with his stepfather served as a constant source of tension during his formative years and informs some of his best mature writings. . . . The demands of caring for younger siblings and his stepfather's religious convictions in large part shielded the boy from the harsh realities of Harlem street life during the 1930s.'' As a youth Baldwin read constantly and even tried writing; he was an excellent student who sought escape from his environment through literature, movies, and theatre. During the summer of his fourteenth birthday he underwent a dramatic religious conversion, partly in response to his nascent sexuality and partly as a further buffer against the ever-present temptations of drugs and crime. He served as a junior minister for three years at the Fireside Pentecostal Assembly, but gradually he lost his desire to preach as he began to question blacks' acceptance of Christian tenets that had, in essence, been used to enslave them.

Shortly after he graduated from high school in 1942, Baldwin was compelled to find work in order to help support his brothers and sisters; mental instability had incapacitated his stepfather. Baldwin took a job in the defense industry in Belle Meade, New Jersey, and there, not for the first time, he was confronted with racism, discrimination, and the debilitating regulations of segregation. The experiences in New Jersey were closely followed by his stepfather's death, after which Baldwin determined to make writing his sole profession. He moved to Greenwich Village and began to write a novel, supporting himself by performing a variety of odd jobs. In 1944 he met author Richard Wright, who helped him to land the 1945 Eugene F. Saxton fellowship. Despite the financial freedom the fellowship provided, Baldwin was unable to complete his novel that year. He found the social tenor of the United States increasingly stifling even though such prestigious periodicals as the *Nation, New Leader,* and *Commentary* began to accept his essays and short stories for publication. Eventually, in 1948, he moved to Paris, using funds from a Rosenwald Foundation fellowship to pay his passage. Most critics feel that this journey abroad was fundamental to Baldwin's development as an author.

''Once I found myself on the other side of the ocean,'' Baldwin told the *New York Times,* ''I could see where I came from very clearly, and I could see that I carried myself, which is my home, with me. You can never escape that. I am the grandson of a slave, and I am a writer. I must deal with both.'' Through some difficult financial and emotional periods, Baldwin undertook a process of self-realization that included both an acceptance of his heritage and an admittance of his bisexuality. Bone noted that Europe gave the young author many things: ''It gave him a world perspective from which to approach the question of his own identity. It gave him a tender love affair which would dominate the pages of his later fiction.

But above all, Europe gave him back himself. The immediate fruit of self-recovery was a great creative outburst. First came two [works] of reconciliation with his racial heritage. *Go Tell It on the Mountain* and *The Amen Corner* represent a search for roots, a surrender to tradition, an acceptance of the Negro past. Then came a series of essays which probe, deeper than anyone has dared, the psychic history of this nation. They are a moving record of a man's struggle to define the forces that have shaped him, in order that he may accept himself.''

Many critics view Baldwin's essays as his most significant contribution to American literature. Works such as *Notes of a Native Son, Nobody Knows My Name, The Fire Next Time, No Name in the Street* and *The Evidence of Things Not Seen* ''serve to illuminate the condition of the black man in twentieth-century America,'' according to Pratt. Highly personal and analytical, the essays probe deeper than the mere provincial problems of white versus black to uncover the essential issues of self-determination, identity, and reality. ''An artist is a sort of emotional or spiritual historian,'' Baldwin told *Life* magazine. ''His role is to make you realize the doom and glory of knowing who you are and what you are. He has to tell, because nobody else *can* tell, what it is like to be alive.'' *South Atlantic Quarterly* contributor Fred L. Standley asserted that this quest for personal identity ''is indispensible in Baldwin's opinion and the failure to experience such is indicative of a fatal weakness in human life.'' C. W. E. Bigsby elaborated in *The Fifties: Fiction, Poetry, Drama:* ''Baldwin's central theme is the need to accept reality as a necessary foundation for individual identity and thus a logical prerequisite for the kind of saving love in which he places his whole faith. For some this reality is one's racial or sexual nature, for others it is the ineluctable fact of death. . . . Baldwin sees this simple progression as an urgent formula not only for the redemption of individual men but for the survival of mankind. In this at least black and white are as one and the Negro's much-vaunted search for identity can be seen as part and parcel of the American's long-standing need for self-definition.''

Inevitably, however, Baldwin's assessments of the ''sweet'' and ''bitter'' experiences in his own life led him to describe ''the exact place where private chaos and social outrage meet,'' according to Alfred Kazin in *Contemporaries.* Eugenia Collier described this confrontation in *Black World:* ''On all levels, personal and political . . . life is a wild chaos of paradox, hidden meanings, and dilemmas. This chaos arises from man's inability—or reluctance to face the truth about his own nature. As a result of this self-imposed blindness, men erect an elaborate facade of myth, tradition, and ritual behind which crouch, invisible, their true selves. It is this blindness on the part of Euro-Americans which has created and perpetuated the vicious racism which threatens to destroy this nation.'' In his essays on the 1950s and early 1960s, Baldwin sought to explain black experiences to a white readership as he warned whites about the potential destruction their psychic blindness might wreak. *Massachusetts Review* contributor David Levin noted that the author came to represent ''for 'white' Americans, the eloquent, indignant prophet of an oppressed people, a voice speaking . . . in an all but desperate, final effort to bring us out of what he calls our innocence before it is (if it is not already) too late. This voice calls us to our immediate duty for the sake of our own humanity as well as our own safety. It demands that we stop regarding the Negro as an abstraction, an invisible man; that we begin to recognize each Negro in his 'full weight and complexity' as a human being; that we face the horrible reality of our past and present treatment of Negroes—a reality we do not know and do not want to know.'' In *Ebony* magazine, Allan Morrison observed that Baldwin evinced an awareness ''that the audience for most of his non-fictional writings is white and he uses every forum at his disposal to drive home the basic truths of Negro-white relations in America as he sees them. His function here is to interpret whites to themselves and at the same time voice the Negro's protest against his role in a Jim Crow society.''

Because Baldwin sought to inform and confront whites, and because his fiction contains interracial love affairs—both homosexual and heterosexual—he came under attack from the writers of the Black Arts Movement, who called for a literature exclusively by and for blacks. Baldwin refused to align himself with the movement; he continued to call himself an ''American writer'' as opposed to a ''black writer'' and continued to confront the issues facing a multi-racial society. Eldridge Cleaver, in his book *Soul on Ice,* accused Baldwin of a hatred of blacks and ''a shameful, fanatical fawning'' love of whites. What Cleaver saw as complicity with whites, Baldwin saw rather as an attempt to alter the real daily environment with which American blacks have been faced all their lives. Pratt noted, however, that Baldwin's efforts to ''shake up'' his white readers put him ''at odds with current white literary trends'' as well as with the Black Arts Movement. Pratt explained that Baldwin labored under the belief ''that mainstream art is directed toward a complacent and apathetic audience, and it is designed to confirm and reinforce that sense of well-being. . . . Baldwin's writings are, by their very nature, iconoclastic. While Black Arts focuses on a black-oriented artistry, Baldwin is concerned with the destruction of the fantasies and delusions of a contented audience which is determined to avoid reality.'' As the civil rights movement gained momentum, Baldwin escalated his attacks on white complacency from the speaking platform as well as from the pages of books and magazines. *Nobody Knows My Name* and *The Fire Next Time* both sold more than a million copies; both were cited for their predictions of black violence in desperate response to white oppression. In *Encounter,* Colin MacInnes concluded that the reason ''why Baldwin speaks to us of another race is that he still believes us worthy of a warning: he has not yet despaired of making us *feel* the dilemma we all chat about so glibly, . . . and of trying to save us from the agonies that we too will suffer if the Negro people are driven beyond the ultimate point of desperation.''

Retrospective analyses of Baldwin's essays highlight the characteristic prose style that gives his works literary merit beyond the mere dissemination of ideas. In *A World More Attractive: A View of Modern Literature and Politics,* Irving Howe placed the author among ''the two or three greatest essayists this country has ever produced.'' Howe claimed that Baldwin ''has brought a new luster to the essay as an art form, a form with possibilities for discursive reflection and concrete drama. . . . The style of these essays is a remarkable instance of the way in which a grave and sustained eloquence—the rhythm of oratory, . . . held firm and hard—can be employed in an age deeply suspicious of rhetorical prowess.'' ''Baldwin has shown more concern for the painful exactness of prose style than any other modern American writer,'' noted David Littlejohn in *Black on White: A Critical Survey of Writing by American Negroes.* ''He picks up words with heavy care, then sets them, one by one, with a cool and loving precision that one can feel in the reading. . . . The exhilarating exhaustion of reading his best essays—which in itself may be a proof of their honesty

and value—demands that the reader measure up, and forces him to learn.''

Baldwin's fiction expanded his exploration of the ''full weight and complexity'' of the individual in a society prone to callousness and categorization. His loosely autobiographical works probed the milieus with which he was most familiar—black evangelical churches, jazz clubs, stifling Southern towns, and the Harlem ghetto. In *The Black American Writer: Fiction,* Brian Lee maintained that Baldwin's ''essays explore the ambiguities and ironies of a life lived on two levels—that of the Negro and that of the man—and they have spoken eloquently to and for a whole generation. But Baldwin's feelings about the condition—alternating moods of sadness and bitterness—are best expressed in the paradoxes confronting the haunted heroes of his novels and stories. The possible modes of existence for anyone seeking refuge from a society which refuses to acknowledge one's humanity are necessarily limited, and Baldwin has explored with some thoroughness the various emotional and spiritual alternatives available to his retreating protagonists.'' Pratt felt that Baldwin's fictive artistry ''not only documents the dilemma of the black man in American society, but it also bears witness to the struggle of the artist against the overwhelming forces of oppression. Almost invariably, his protagonists are artists. . . . Each character is engaged in the pursuit of artistic fulfillment which, for Baldwin, becomes symbolic of the quest for identity.''

Love, both sexual and spiritual, was an essential component of Baldwin's characters' quests for self-realization. John W. Aldridge observed in the *Saturday Review* that sexual love ''emerges in his novels as a kind of universal anodyne for the disease of racial separatism, as a means not only of achieving personal identity but also of transcending false categories of color and gender.'' Homosexual encounters emerged as the principal means to achieve important revelations; as Bigsby explained, Baldwin felt that ''it is the homosexual, virtually alone, who can offer a selfless and genuine love because he alone has a real sense of himself, having accepted his own nature.'' Baldwin did not see love as a ''saving grace,'' however; his vision, given the circumstances of the lives he encountered, was more cynical than optimistic. In his introduction to *James Baldwin: A Collection of Critical Essays,* Kenneth Kinnamon wrote: ''If the search for love has its origin in the desire of a child for emotional security, its arena is an adult world which involves it in struggle and pain. Stasis must yield to motion, innocence to experience, security to risk. This is the lesson that . . . saves Baldwin's central fictional theme from sentimentality. . . . Similarly, love as an agent of racial reconciliation and national survival is not for Baldwin a vague yearning for an innocuous brotherhood, but an agonized confrontation with reality, leading to the struggle to transform it. It is a quest for truth through a recognition of the primacy of suffering and injustice in the American past.'' Pratt also concluded that in Baldwin's novels, ''love is often extended, frequently denied, seldom fulfilled. As reflections of our contemporary American society, the novels stand as forthright indictments of the intolerable conditions that we have accepted unquestioningly as a way of life.''

Black family life—the charged emotional atmosphere between parents and children, brothers and sisters—provided another major theme in Baldwin's fiction. This was especially apparent in his first and best-known novel, *Go Tell It on the Mountain,* the story of a Harlem teenager's struggles with a repressive father and with religious conversion. According to Roberts, *Go Tell It on the Mountain* ''proved that James Baldwin had become a writer of enormous power and skill. [It] was an essential book for Baldwin. Although clearly a fictional work, it chronicles two of the most problematic aspects of his existence as a young man: a son's relationship to his stepfather and the impact of fundamentalist religion on the consciousness of a young boy.'' In her work entitled *James Baldwin,* Carolyn Wedin Sylvander praised Baldwin's family chronicle particularly because the author ''is dealing comprehensively and emotionally with the hot issue of race relations in the United States at a time . . . when neither white ignorance and prejudice nor black powerlessness is conducive to holistic depictions of black experience.'' Indeed, the overt confrontation between the races that characterizes Baldwin's later work was here portrayed as a peripheral threat, a danger greater than, but less immediate than, the potential damage inflicted by parents on children. Sylvander wrote: ''It is painfully, dramatically, structurally clear throughout *Go Tell It on the Mountain* that the struggles every individual faces—with sexuality, with guilt, with pain, with love—are passed on, generation to generation.'' Littlejohn described Baldwin's treatment of this essential American theme as ''autobiography-as-exorcism, . . .a lyrical, painful, ritual exercise whose necessity and intensity the reader feels.'' Pratt likewise stated that *Go Tell It on the Mountain* ''stands as an honest, intensive, self-analysis, functioning simultaneously to illuminate self, society, and mankind as a whole.''

In addition to his numerous books, Baldwin was one of the few black authors to have had more than one of his plays produced on Broadway. Both *The Amen Corner,* another treatment of storefront pentecostal religion, and *Blues for Mister Charlie,* a drama based on the racially-motivated murder of Emmett Till in 1955, had successful Broadway runs and numerous revivals. Standley commented in the *Dictionary of Literary Biography* that in both plays, ''as in his other literary works, Baldwin explores a variety of thematic concerns: the historical significance and the potential explosiveness in black-white relations; the necessity for developing a sexual and psychological consciousness and identity; the intertwining of love and power in the universal scheme of existence as well as in the structures of society; the misplaced priorities in the value systems in America; and the responsibility of the artist to promote the evolution of the individual and the society.'' In *The Black American Writer: Poetry and Drama,* Walter Meserve offered remarks on Baldwin's abilities as a playwright. ''Baldwin tries to use the theatre as a pulpit for his ideas,'' Meserve stated. ''Mainly his plays are thesis plays—talky, over-written, and cliche dialogue and some stereotypes, preachy, and argumentative. Essentially, Baldwin is not particularly dramatic, but he can be extremely eloquent, compelling, and sometimes irritating as a playwright committed to his approach to life.'' Meserve added, however, that although the author was criticized for creating stereotypes, ''his major characters are the most successful and memorable aspects of his plays. People are important to Baldwin, and their problems, generally embedded in their agonizing souls, stimulate him to write. . . . A humanitarian, sensitive to the needs and struggles of man, he writes of inner turmoil, spiritual disruption, the consequence upon people of the burdens of the world, both White and Black.''

Baldwin's oratorical prowess—honed in the pulpit as a youth—brought him into great demand as a speaker during the civil rights era. Sylvander observed that national attention ''began to turn toward him as a spokesperson for blacks, not as much because of his novels as his essays, debates, interviews, panel discussions.'' Baldwin embraced his role as ra-

cial spokesman reluctantly and grew increasingly disillusioned as the American public ''disarmed him with celebrity, [fell] in love with his eccentricities, and institutionalized his outrage . . . into prime-time entertainment,'' to quote Aldridge. Nor was Baldwin able to feel that his speeches and essays were producing social change—the assassinations of three of his associates, Medgar Evers, Martin Luther King, Jr., and Malcolm X, shattered his remaining hopes for racial reconciliation. Kinnamon remarked that by 1972, the year Baldwin published *No Name in the Street,* ''the redemptive possibilities of love seemed exhausted in that terrible decade of assassination, riot, and repression. . . . Social love had now become for Baldwin more a rueful memory than an alternative to disaster.'' *London Magazine* contributor James Campbell also noted that by 1972 ''Baldwin the saviour had turned into Baldwin the soldier. What [observers] failed to notice was that he was still the preacher and the prophet, that his passion and rage were mingled with detachment, and that his gloomy prognostications were based on powerful observation and an understanding of the past which compelled their pessimism.''

Many critics took Baldwin to task for the stridency and gloom that overtook his writings. ''To function as a voice of outrage month after month for a decade and more strains heart and mind, and rhetoric as well,'' declared Benjamin DeMott in the *Saturday Review*. ''The consequence is a writing style ever on the edge of being winded by too many summonses to intensity.'' *New Republic* correspondent Nathan Glazer likewise stated that Baldwin had become ''an accusing voice, but the accusation is so broad, so general, so all-embracing, that the rhetoric disappears into the wind.'' Stephen Donadio offered a similar opinion in the *Partisan Review:* ''As his notoriety increased, his personality was oversimplified, appropriated, and consumed. . . . Mr. Baldwin created a situation in which the eye of the audience was fixed on the author as a performer, and the urgency of the race problem in America became a backdrop for elaborate rhetorical assaults which could be dutifully acknowledged but forgotten with a sigh.''

Baldwin's passionate detractors were offset by equally passionate defenders, however. Sylvander wrote: ''Wading through vehement and sometimes shallow reactions to the deep water of the statements and works themselves, one is struck repeatedly by the power of Baldwin's prose, and by our continuing need, as readers and as citizens, for his steadying apocalyptic vision. Finally, in his fantastic, experientially various, wide-ranging, searching, and committed life, one can find a vigorous model for venturing beyond charted areas.'' Charles Newman made two points in *James Baldwin: A Collection of Critical Essays*. First, Newman noted that Baldwin's experience is ''unique among our artists in that his artistic achievements mesh so precisely with his historical circumstances. He is that nostaglic type—an artist speaking for a genuinely visible revolution.'' Second, Newman maintained that as an observer of this painful revolution, ''almost alone [Baldwin] . . . continued to confront the unmanageable questions of modern society, rather than creating a nuclear family in which semantic fantasies may be enacted with no reference to the larger world except that it stinks.'' Kinnamon concluded: ''James Baldwin has always been concerned with the most personal and intimate areas of experience and also with the broadest questions of national and global destiny—and with the intricate interrelationships between the two. Whatever the final assessment of his literary achievement, it is clear that his voice—simultaneously that of victim, witness, and prophet—has been among the most urgent of our time.''

At the time of his death from cancer late in 1987, Baldwin was still working on two projects—a play, "The Welcome Table," and a biography of Martin Luther King, Jr. Although he lived primarily in France, he had never relinquished his United States citizenship and preferred to think of himself as a "commuter" rather than as an expatriate. The publication of his collected essays, *The Price of the Ticket: Collected Nonfiction 1948-1985*, and his subsequent death sparked reassessments of his career and comments on the quality of his lasting legacy. "Mr. Baldwin has become a kind of prophet, a man who has been able to give a public issue all its deeper moral, historical, and personal significance," remarked Robert F. Sayre in *Contemporary American Novelists*. ". . . Certainly one mark of his achievement, . . . is that whatever deeper comprehension of the race issue Americans now possess has been in some way shaped by him. And this is to have shaped their comprehension of themselves as well." Sylvander asserted that what emerges from the whole of Baldwin's work is "a kind of absolute conviction and passion and honesty that is nothing less than courageous. . . . Baldwin has shared his struggle with his readers for a purpose—to demonstrate that our suffering is our bridge to one another."

Perhaps the most telling demonstration of the results of Baldwin's achievement came from other black writers. Orde Coombs, for instance, concluded: "Because he existed we felt that the racial miasma that swirled around us would not consume us, and it is not too much to say that this man saved our lives, or at least, gave us the necessary ammunition to face what we knew would continue to be a hostile and condescending world." Playwright Amiri Baraka phrased a similar assessment even more eloquently in his funeral eulogy to Baldwin. "This man traveled the earth like its history and its biographer," Baraka said. "He reported, criticized, made beautiful, analyzed, cajoled, lyricized, attacked, sang, made us think, made us better, made us consciously human. . . . He made us feel . . . that we could defend ourselves or define ourselves, that we were in the world not merely as animate slaves, but as terrifyingly sensitive measurers of what is good or evil, beautiful or ugly. This is the power of his spirit. This is the bond which created our love for him." In a posthumous profile for the *Washington Post*, Juan Williams wrote: "The success of Baldwin's effort as the witness is evidenced time and again by the people, black and white, gay and straight, famous and anonymous, whose humanity he unveiled in his writings. America and the literary world are far richer for his witness. The proof of a shared humanity across the divides of race, class and more is the testament that the preacher's son, James Arthur Baldwin, has left us."

MEDIA ADAPTATIONS: The Amen Corner was adapted as a musical stage play, "Amen Corner," by Garry Sherman, Peter Udell and Philip Rose, and produced on Broadway at the Nederlander Theater, November 10, 1983. *Go Tell It on the Mountain* was dramatized under the same title for the Public Broadcasting System's "American Playhouse" series, January 14, 1985.

BIOGRAPHICAL/CRITICAL SOURCES:

BOOKS

Balakian, Nona, and Charles Simmons, editors, *The Creative Present: Notes on Contemporary Fiction*, Doubleday, 1963.

Bigsby, C.W.E., *Confrontation and Commitment: A Study of Contemporary American Drama*, University of Missouri Press, 1967.

Bigsby, C.W.E., editor, *The Black American Writer*, Volume I: *Fiction*, Volume II: *Poetry and Drama*, Everett/Edwards, 1969.

Bone, Robert, *The Negro Novel in America*, Yale University Press, 1965.

Brustein, Robert, *Seasons of Discontent: Dramatic Opinions 1959-1965*, Simon & Schuster, 1965.

Burgess, Anthony, *The Novel Now: A Guide to Contemporary Fiction*, Norton, 1967.

Chapman, Abraham, editor, *Black Voices: An Anthology of Afro-American Literature*, New American Library, 1968.

Cleaver, Eldridge, *Soul on Ice*, McGraw-Hill, 1968.

Cohn, Ruby, *Dialogue in American Drama*, Indiana University Press, 1971.

Concise Dictionary of American Literary Biography: The New Consciousness 1941-1968, Gale, 1987.

Contemporary Authors Bibliographical Series, Volume I: *American Novelists*, Gale, 1986.

Contemporary Literary Criticism, Gale, Volume I, 1973, Volume II, 1974, Volume III, 1975, Volume IV, 1975, Volume V, 1976, Volume VIII, 1978, Volume XIII, 1980, Volume XV, 1980, Volume XVII, 1981, Volume XLII, 1987.

Cook, M. G., editor, *Modern Black Novelists: A Collection of Critical Essays*, Prentice-Hall, 1971.

Culture for the Millions, Van Nostrand, 1959.

Dance, Daryl, *Black American Writers: Bibliographical Essays*, St. Martin's, 1978.

Dictionary of Literary Biography, Gale, Volume II: *American Novelists since World War II*, 1978, Volume VIII: *Twentieth-Century American Dramatists*, 1981, Volume XXXIII: *Afro-American Fiction Writers after 1955*, 1984.

Eckman, Fern Marja, *The Furious Passage of James Baldwin*, M. Evans, 1966.

French, Warren, editor, *The Fifties: Fiction, Poetry, Drama*, Everett/Edwards, 1970.

Frost, David, *The Americans*, Stein & Day, 1970.

Gayle, Addison, Jr., *The Way of the World: The Black Novel in America*, Anchor Press, 1975.

Gibson, Donald B., editor, *Five Black Writers: Essays on Wright, Ellison, Baldwin, Hughes, and LeRoi Jones*, New York University Press, 1970.

Hesse, H. Ober, editor, *The Nature of a Humane Society*, Fortress, 1976.

Hill, Herbert, editor, *Anger and Beyond*, Harper, 1966.

Howe, Irving, *A World More Attractive: A View of Modern Literature and Politics*, Horizon Press, 1963.

Hyman, Stanley Edgar, *Standards: A Chronicle of Books for Our Time*, Horizon Press, 1966.

Kazin, Alfred, *Bright Book of Life: American Novelists & Storytellers from Hemingway to Mailer*, Little, Brown, 1973.

Kazin, Alfred, *Contemporaries*, Little, Brown, 1962.

King, Malcolm, *Baldwin: Three Interviews*, Wesleyan University Press, 1985.

Kinnamon, Kenneth, editor, *James Baldwin: A Collection of Critical Essays*, Prentice-Hall, 1974.

Klein, Marcus, *After Alienation: American Novels in Mid-Century*, World Publishing, 1964.

Littlejohn, David, *Black on White: A Critical Survey of Writing by American Negroes*, Viking, 1966.

Lumley, Frederick, *New Trends in 20th Century Drama: A Survey since Ibsen and Shaw*, Oxford University Press, 1967.

Macebuh, Stanley, *James Baldwin: A Critical Study,* Joseph Okpaku, 1973.

Major, Clarence, *The Dark and Feeling: Black American Writers and Their Work,* Joseph Okpaku, 1974.

Moeller, Karin, *The Theme of Identity in the Essays of James Baldwin,* Acta Universitatis Gotoburgensis, 1975.

Moore, Harry T., editor, *Contemporary American Novelists,* Southern Illinois University Press, 1964.

O'Daniel, Therman B., *James Baldwin: A Critical Evaluation,* Howard University Press, 1977.

Panichas, George A., *The Politics of Twentieth-Century Novelists,* Hawthorn, 1971.

Podhoretz, Norman, *Doings and Undoings,* Farrar, Straus, 1964.

Pratt, Louis Hill, *James Baldwin,* Twayne, 1978.

Rosenblatt, Roger, *Black Fiction,* Harvard University Press, 1974.

Sheed, Wilfrid, *The Morning After,* Farrar, Straus, 1971.

Simon, John, *Uneasy Stages: Chronicle of the New York Theatre,* Random House, 1975.

Sontag, Susan, *Against Interpretation and Other Essays,* Farrar, Straus, 1966.

Standley, Fred and Nancy Standley, *James Baldwin: A Reference Guide,* G. K. Hall, 1980.

Standley, Fred and Nancy Standley, editors, *Critical Essays on James Baldwin,* G. K. Hall, 1981.

Sylvander, Carolyn Wedin, *James Baldwin,* Frederick Ungar, 1980.

Turner, Darwin T., *Afro-American Writers,* Appleton, 1970.

Weatherby, William J., *Squaring Off: Mailer vs. Baldwin,* Mason/Charter, 1977.

Williams, John A. and Charles F. Harris, editors, *Amistad I: Writings on Black History and Culture,* Random House, 1970.

Williams, Sherley Anne, *Give Birth to Brightness: A Thematic Study in Neo-Black Literature,* Dial, 1972.

PERIODICALS

America, March 16, 1963.

Atlanta Constitution, May 19, 1976.

Atlantic, July, 1961, July, 1962, March, 1963, July, 1968, June, 1972.

Atlas, March, 1967.

Black Scholar, December, 1973-January, 1974.

Black World, June, 1972, December, 1974.

Books and Bookmen, August, 1968, September, 1972, December, 1979.

Book Week, May 31, 1964, September 26, 1965.

British Journal of Sociology, June, 1966.

Bulletin of Bibliography, January-April, 1965, May-August, 1968.

Chicago Tribune, September 16, 1979, October 10, 1979, November 15, 1985, December 16, 1987.

Christian Science Monitor, July 19, 1962.

College Language Association Journal, Number 7, 1964, Number 10, 1966, March, 1967.

Commentary, November, 1953, January, 1957, December, 1961, June, 1968, December, 1979, December, 1985.

Commonweal, May 22, 1953, December 8, 1961, October 26, 1962, December 7, 1962, October 12, 1973, June 24, 1977.

Critical Quarterly, summer, 1964.

Critique, winter, 1964-65.

Cross Currents, summer, 1961.

Ebony, October, 1961.

Ecumenical Review, October, 1968.

Encounter, August, 1963, July, 1965.

English Journal, May, 1973.

Esquire, July, 1968.

Freedomways, summer, 1963.

Globe & Mail (Toronto), January 11, 1986.

Harper's, March, 1963, September, 1968.

Hollins Critic, December, 1965.

Hudson Review, autumn, 1964, autumn, 1968.

Intellectual Digest, July, 1972.

Life, May 24, 1963, June 7, 1968, June 4, 1971, July 30, 1971.

Listener, July 25, 1974.

London Magazine, December, 1979-January, 1980.

Lone Star Book Review, January-February, 1980.

Look, July 23, 1968.

Los Angeles Times Book Review, December 1, 1985.

Mademoiselle, May, 1963.

Massachusetts Review, winter, 1964.

Midcontinent American Studies Journal, fall, 1963.

Muhammad Speaks, September 8, 1973, September 15, 1973, September 29, 1973, October 6, 1973.

Nation, July 14, 1962, November 17, 1962, March 2, 1963, December 13, 1965, April 10, 1972, June 10, 1968, July 3, 1976, November 3, 1979.

National Observer, March 6, 1967, June 3, 1968.

National Review, May 21, 1963, July 7, 1972.

Negro American Literature Forum, spring, 1969, winter, 1972.

Negro Digest, June, 1963, October, 1966, April, 1967.

New Leader, June 3, 1968, May 27, 1974, May 24, 1976.

New Republic, December 17, 1956, August 7, 1961, August 27, 1962, November 27, 1965, August 17, 1968, June 15, 1974, November 24, 1979, December 30, 1985.

New Statesman, July 13, 1962, July 19, 1963, December 4, 1964, November 3, 1972, June 28, 1974, February 25, 1977, November 29, 1985.

Newsweek, February 4, 1963, June 3, 1969, May 27, 1974.

New Yorker, June 20, 1953, November 25, 1961, August 4, 1962, July 8, 1974, November 26, 1979.

New York Herald Tribune Book Review, June 17, 1962.

New York Review of Books, May 28, 1964, December 17, 1964, December 9, 1965, June 29, 1972, June 13, 1974, December 6, 1979, January 21, 1988.

New York Times, May 3, 1964, April 16, 1965, May 31, 1968, February 2, 1969, May 21, 1971, May 17, 1974, June 4, 1976, September 4, 1977, September 21, 1979, September 23, 1979, November 11, 1983, January 10, 1985, January 14, 1985.

New York Times Book Review, February 26, 1956, July 2, 1961, June 24, 1962, December 12, 1965, June 2, 1968, June 23, 1968, May 28, 1972, May 19, 1974, May 2, 1976, September 23, 1979, May 24, 1984.

New York Times Magazine, March 7, 1965.

Nickel Review, February 27, 1970.

Observer, November 24, 1985, April 6, 1986.

Partisan Review, summer, 1963, winter, 1966.

People, January 7, 1980.

Progressive, August, 1972.

Queen's Quarterly, summer, 1965.

San Francisco Chronicle, June 28, 1962.

Saturday Review, December 1, 1956, July 1, 1961, July 7, 1962, February 2, 1963, February 8, 1964, May 2, 1964, November 6, 1965, June 1, 1968, May 27, 1972, June 15, 1974, January 5, 1980.

Sight and Sound, autumn, 1976.

South Atlantic Quarterly, summer, 1966.

Southern Humanities Review, winter, 1970.
Southern Review, summer, 1985.
Spectator, July 12, 1968, July 6, 1974, January 11, 1986, April 26, 1986.
Studies in Short Fiction, summer, 1975, fall, 1977.
Time, June 30, 1961, June 29, 1962, November 6, 1964, June 7, 1968, June 10, 1974.
Times (London), May 15, 1986, January 19, 1987, January 22, 1987.
Times Educational Supplement, December 27, 1985.
Times Literary Supplement, July 26, 1963, December 10, 1964, October 28, 1965, July 4, 1968, April 28, 1972, November 17, 1972, June 21, 1974, December 21, 1979, August 2, 1984, January 24, 1986, September 19, 1986.
Tri-Quarterly, winter, 1965.
Twentieth-Century Literature, April, 1967.
Village Voice, October 29, 1979, January 12, 1988.
Vogue, July, 1964.
Washington Post, September 23, 1979, October 15, 1979, September 9, 1983, September 25, 1983.
Washington Post Book World, September 11, 1977, September 23, 1979, October 27, 1985, December 9, 1987.
Western Humanities Review, spring, 1968.
World Literature Today, spring, 1980.
Yale Review, October, 1966.

OBITUARIES:

PERIODICALS

Chicago Tribune, December 2, 1987.
Detroit Free Press, December 2, 1987, December 8, 1987.
Los Angeles Times, December 2, 1987.
New York Times, December 2, 1987, December 9, 1987.
Philadelphia Inquirer, December 2, 1987, December 9, 1987, December 14, 1987.
Times (London), December 2, 1987.
Washington Post, December 2, 1987.

—Sketch by Anne Janette Johnson

*   *   *

BAMBARA, Toni Cade   1939-
(Toni Cade)

PERSONAL: Surname originally Cade, name legally changed in 1970; born March 25, 1939, in New York, N.Y.; daughter of Helen Brent Henderson Cade. *Education:* Queens College (now Queens College of the City University of New York), B.A., 1959; University of Florence, studied Commedia dell'Arte, 1961; student at Ecole de Mime Etienne Decroux in Paris, 1961, New York, 1963; City College of the City University of New York, M.A., 1964; additional study in linguistics at New York University and New School for Social Research. Also attended Katherine Dunham Dance Studio, Syvilla Fort School of Dance, Clark Center of Performing Arts, 1958-69, and Studio Museum of Harlem Film Institute, 1970.

ADDRESSES: Home—5720 Wissahickon Ave., Apt. E12, Philadelphia, Pa. 19144.

CAREER: Free-lance writer and lecturer. Social investigator, New York State Department of Welfare, 1959-61; director of recreation in psychiatry department, Metropolitan Hospital, New York City, 1961-62; program director, Colony House Community Center, New York City, 1962-65; English instructor in SEEK Program, City College of the City University of New York, New York City, 1965-69, and in New Careers

Program of Newark, N.J., 1969; assistant professor, Livingston College, Rutgers University, New Brunswick, N.J., 1969-74; visiting professor of African American studies, Stephens College, Columbia, Mo., 1975; Atlanta University, visiting professor, 1977, research mentor and instructor, School of Social Work, 1977, 1979. Founder and director of Pamoja Writers Collective, 1976-85. Production artist-in-residence for Neighborhood Arts Center, 1975-79, Stephens College, 1976, and Spelman College, 1978-79. Production consultant, WHYY-TV, Philadelphia, Pa. Has conducted numerous workshops on writing, self-publishing, and community organizing for community centers, museums, prisons, libraries, and universities. Has lectured and conducted literary readings at many institutions, including the Library of Congress, Smithsonian Institute, Afro-American Museum of History and Culture and for numerous other organizations and universities. Humanities consultant to New Jersey Department of Corrections, 1974, Institute of Language Arts, Emory University, 1980, and New York Institute for Human Services Training, 1978. Art consultant to New York State Arts Council, 1974, Georgia State Arts Council, 1976, 1981, National Endowment for the Arts, 1980, and the Black Arts South Conference, 1981.

MEMBER: National Association of Third World Writers, Screen Writers Guild of America, African American Film Society, Sisters in Support of South African Sisterhood.

AWARDS, HONORS: Peter Pauper Press Award, 1958; John Golden Award for Fiction from Queens College (now Queens College of the City University of New York), 1959; Theatre of Black Experience award, 1969; Rutgers University research fellowship, 1972; Black Child Development Institute service award, 1973; Black Rose Award from *Encore,* 1973; Black Community Award from Livingston College, Rutgers University, 1974; award from the National Association of Negro Business and Professional Women's Club League; George Washington Carver Distinguished African American Lecturer Award from Simpson College; *Ebony*'s Achievement in the Arts Award; Black Arts Award from University of Missouri; American Book Award, 1981, for *The Salt Eaters;* Best Documentary of 1986 Award from Pennsylvania Association of Broadcasters and Documentary Award from National Black Programming Consortium, both 1986, for ''The Bombing of Osage.''

WRITINGS:

Gorilla, My Love (short stories), Random House, 1972.
The Sea Birds Are Still Alive (short stories), Random House, 1977.
The Salt Eaters (novel), Random House, 1980.
(Author of preface) Cecelia Smith, *Cracks,* Select Press, 1980.
(Author of foreword) Cherrie Moraga and Gloria Anzaldua, editors, *This Bridge Called My Back: Radical Women of Color,* Persephone Press, 1981.
(Author of foreword) *The Sanctified Church: Collected Essays by Zora Neale Hurston,* Turtle Island, 1982.
If Blessing Comes (novel), Random House, 1987.

SCREENPLAYS

''Zora,'' produced by WGBH-TV, 1971.
''The Johnson Girls,'' produced by National Educational Television, 1972.
''Transactions,'' produced by School of Social Work, Atlanta University, 1979.
''The Long Night,'' produced by American Broadcasting Co., 1981.

"Epitaph for Willie," produced by K. Heran Productions, Inc., 1982.

"Tar Baby" (based on Toni Morrison's novel), produced by Sanger/Brooks Film Productions, 1984.

"Raymond's Run," produced by Public Broadcasting System, 1985.

"The Bombing of Osage," produced by WHYY-TV, 1986.

"Cecil B. Moore: Master Tatician of Direct Action," produced by WHYY-TV, 1987.

EDITOR

(And contributor, under name Toni Cade) *The Black Woman*, New American Library, 1970.

(And contributor) *Tales and Stories for Black Folks*, Doubleday, 1971.

(With Leah Wise) *Southern Black Utterances Today*, Institute for Southern Studies, 1975.

CONTRIBUTOR

Addison Gayle, Jr., editor, *Black Expression: Essays by and about Black Americans in the Creative Arts*, Weybright, 1969.

Jules Chametsky, editor, *Black and White in American Culture*, University of Massachusetts Press, 1970.

Ruth Miller, *Backgrounds to Blackamerican Literature*, Chandler Publishing, 1971.

Janet Sternburg, editor, *The Writer on Her Work*, Norton, 1980.

Paul H. Connolly, editor, *On Essays: A Reader for Writers*, Harper, 1981.

Howe, editor, *Women Working*, Feminist Press, 1982.

Mari Evans, editor, *Black Women Writers (1950-1980): A Critical Evaluation*, Doubleday, 1984.

Baraka and Baraka, editors, *Confirmations*, Morrow, 1984.

Claudia Tate, editor, *The Black Writer at Work*, Howard University Press, 1984.

OTHER

Contributor to *What's Happnin, Somethin Else*, and *Another Eye*, all readers published by Scott, Foresman, 1969-70. Contributor of articles and book and film reviews to *Massachusetts Review, Negro Digest, Liberator, Prairie Schooner, Redbook, Audience, Black Works, Umbra, Onyx*, and other periodicals. Guest editor of special issue of *Southern Exposure*, summer, 1976, devoted to new southern black writers and visual artists.

SIDELIGHTS: Toni Cade Bambara is a well known and respected civil rights activist, professor of English and of African American studies, editor of two anthologies of black literature, and author of short stories and a novel. According to Alice A. Deck in the *Dictionary of Literary Biography*, "in many ways Toni Cade Bambara is one of the best representatives of the group of Afro-American writers who, during the 1960s, became directly involved in the cultural and sociopolitical activities in urban communities across the country." However, Deck points out that "Bambara is one of the few who continued to work within the black urban communties (filming, lecturing, organizing, and reading from her works at rallies and conferences), producing imaginative reenactments of these experiences in her fiction. In addition, Bambara established herself over the years as an educator, teaching in colleges and independent community schools in various cities on the East Coast."

Bambara's first two books of fiction, *Gorilla, My Love* and *The Sea Birds Are Still Alive*, are collections of her short sto-

ries. Susan Lardner remarks in the *New Yorker* that the stories in these two works, "describing the lives of black people in the North and the South, could be more exactly typed as vignettes and significant anecdotes, although a few of them are fairly long. . . . All are notable for their purposefulness, a more or less explicit inspirational angle, and a distinctive motion of the prose, which swings from colloquial narrative to precarious metaphorical heights and over to street talk, at which Bambara is unbeatable."

In a review of *Gorilla, My Love,* for example, a writer remarks in the *Saturday Review* that the stories "are among the best portraits of black life to have appeared in some time. [They are] written in a breezy, engaging style that owes a good deal to street dialect." A critic writing in *Newsweek* makes a similar observation, describing Bambara's second collection of short stories, *The Sea Birds Are Still Alive*, in this manner: "Bambara directs her vigorous sense and sensibility to black neighborhoods in big cities, with occasional trips to small Southern towns. . . . The stories start and stop like rapid-fire conversations conducted in a rhythmic, black-inflected, sweet-and-sour language." In fact, according to Anne Tyler in the *Washington Post Book World*, Bambara's particular style of narration is one of the most distinctive qualities of her writing. "What pulls us along is the language of [her] characters, which is startlingly beautiful without once striking a false note," notes Tyler. "Everything these people say, you feel, ordinary, real-life people are saying right now on any street corner. It's only that the rest of us didn't realize it was sheer poetry they were speaking."

In terms of plot, Bambara tends to avoid linear development in favor of presenting "situations that build like improvisations of a melody," as a *Newsweek* reviewer explains. Commenting on *Gorilla, My Love*, Bell Gale Chevigny observes in the *Village Voice* that despite the "often sketchy" plots, the stories are always "lavish in their strokes—there are elaborate illustrations, soaring asides, aggressive sub-plots. They are never didactic, but they abound in far-out common sense, exotic home truths."

Numerous reviewers have also remarked on Bambara's sensitive portrayals of her characters and the handling of their situations, portrayals that are marked by an affectionate warmth and pride. Laura Marcus writes in the *Times Literary Supplement* that Bambara "presents black culture as embattled but unbowed. . . . Bambara depicts black communities in which ties of blood and friendship are fiercely defended." Deck expands on this idea, remarking that "the basic implication of all of Toni Cade Bambara's stories is that there is an undercurrent of caring for one's neighbors that sustains black Americans. In her view the presence of those individuals who intend to do harm to people is counterbalanced by as many if not more persons who have a genuine concern for other people."

C. D. B. Bryan admires this expression of the author's concern for other people, declaring in the *New York Times Book Review* that "Bambara tells me more about being black through her quiet, proud, silly, tender, hip, acute, loving stories than any amount of literary polemicizing could hope to do. She writes about love: a love for one's family, one's friends, one's race, one's neighborhood and it is the sort of love that comes with maturity and inner peace." According to Bryan, "all of [Bambara's] stories share the affection that their narrator feels for the subject, an affection that is sometimes terribly painful, at other times fiercely proud. But at all times it is an affection that is so genuinely *genus homo sapiens* that her stories are not only *black* stories.''

In 1980, Bambara published her first novel, a generally well-received work entitled *The Salt Eaters.* Written in an almost dream-like style, *The Salt Eaters* explores the relationship between two women with totally different backgrounds and lifestyles brought together by a suicide attempt by one of the women. John Leonard, who describes the book as ''extraordinary,'' writes in the *New York Times* that *The Salt Eaters* ''is almost an incantation, poem-drunk, myth-happy, mud-caked, jazz-ridden, prodigal in meanings, a kite and a mask. It astonishes because Toni Cade Bambara is so adept at switching from politics to legend, from particularities of character to prehistorical song, from LaSalle Street to voodoo. It is as if she jived the very stones to groan.''

In a *Times Literary Supplement* review, Carol Rumens states that *The Salt Eaters* ''is a hymn to individual courage, a sombre message of hope that has confronted the late twentieth-century pathology of racist violence and is still able to articulate its faith in 'the dream'.'' And John Wideman notes in the *New York Times Book Review:* ''In her highly acclaimed fiction and in lectures, [Bambara] emphasizes the necessity for black people to maintain their best traditions, to remain healthy and whole as they struggle for political power. *The Salt Eaters,* her first novel, eloquently summarizes and extends the abiding concerns of her previous work.''

MEDIA ADAPTATIONS: Three of Bambara's short stories ''Gorilla, My Love,'' ''Medley,'' and ''Witchbird'' have been adapted for film.

BIOGRAPHICAL/CRITICAL SOURCES:

BOOKS

Contemporary Literary Criticism, Volume XXIX, Gale, 1984.
Dictionary of Literary Biography, Volume XXXVIII: *Afro-American Writers after 1955: Dramatists and Prose Writers,* Gale, 1985.
Parker, Bell and Beverly Guy-Sheftall, *Sturdy Black Bridges: Visions of Black Women in Literature,* Doubleday, 1979.
Prenshaw, Peggy Whitman, editor, *Women Writers of the Contemporary South,* University Press of Mississippi, 1984.
Tate, Claudia, editor, *Black Women Writers at Work,* Continuum, 1983.

PERIODICALS

Black World, July, 1973.
Books of the Times, June, 1980.
Chicago Tribune Book World, March 23, 1980.
Drum, spring, 1982.
First World, Volume II, number 4, 1980.
Los Angeles Times Book Review, May 4, 1980.
Ms., July, 1977, July, 1980.
National Observer, May 9, 1977.
Newsweek, May 2, 1977.
New Yorker, May 5, 1980.
New York Times, October 11, 1972, October 15, 1972, April 4, 1980.
New York Times Book Review, February 21, 1971, May 2, 1971, November 7, 1971, October 15, 1972, December 3, 1972, March 27, 1977, June 1, 1980, November 1, 1981.
Saturday Review, November 18, 1972, December 2, 1972, April 12, 1980.
Sewanee Review, November 18, 1972, December 2, 1972.

Times Literary Supplement, June 18, 1982, September 27, 1985.
Village Voice, April 12, 1973.
Washington Post Book World, November 18, 1973, March 30, 1980.

—*Sketch by Margaret Mazurkiewicz*

*   *   *

BARAKA, Amiri   1934-
(LeRoi Jones)

PERSONAL: Born October 7, 1934, in Newark, N.J.; original name Everett LeRoi Jones; name changed to Bantuized Muslim appelation Imamu (''spiritual leader'') Ameer ('blessed'') Baraka (''prince''); later modified to Amiri Baraka; son of Coyette Leroy (a postman and elevator operator) and Anna Lois (Russ) Jones; married (divorced, August, 1965); married Sylvia Robinson (Bibi Amina Baraka), 1966; children: (first marriage) Kellie Elisabeth, Lisa Victoria Chapman; (second marriage) Obalaji Malik Ali, Ras Jua Al Aziz, Shani Isis, Amiri Seku, Ahi Mwenge. *Education:* Attended Rutgers University for one year; also attended Howard University, Columbia University and New School for Social Research.

ADDRESSES: Office—Department of Africana Studies, State University of New York, Long Island, N.Y. 11794-4340.

CAREER: Founded *Yugen* magazine and Totem Press, 1958; New School for Social Research, New York, N.Y., instructor, 1961-64; State University of New York at Stony Brook, associate professor, 1983-85, professor of Afro-American studies, 1985—. Visiting professor, University of Buffalo, summer, 1964, Columbia University, fall, 1964, and 1966-67, Yale University, 1977-78, George Washington University, 1978-79, and San Francisco State University. Founder, April, 1964, and director, 1964-66, of Black Arts Repertory Theatre, disbanded, 1966; currently director of Spirit House (also known as Heckalu Community Center), Newark, a black community theatre, and head of advisory group at Treat Elementary School, Newark. Member, Political Prisoners Relief Fund, and African Liberation Day Commission. In 1968 Jones ran for a seat on a Newark community council which would oversee slum rehabilitation, but lost the election. *Military service:* U.S. Air Force, 1954-57; weather-gunner; stationed for two and a half years in Puerto Rico with intervening trips to Europe, Africa, and the Middle East.

MEMBER: Black Academy of Arts and Letters, National Black Political Assembly (secretary general; co-governor), Congress of African People (chairman), United Brothers; All African Games; Pan African Federation.

AWARDS, HONORS: Longview Best Essay of the Year award, 1961, for ''Cuba Libre''; John Whitney Foundation fellowship for poetry and fiction, 1962; Obie Award, 1964, for *Dutchman*; Guggenheim fellowship, 1965-66; Yoruba Academy fellow, 1965; second prize, International Art Festival, Dakar, 1966, for ''The Slave''; National Endowment for the Arts grant, 1966; Doctorate of Humane Letters, Malcolm X College, Chicago, Ill., 1972; Rockefeller Foundation fellow, 1981; Poetry Award, National Endowment for the Arts, 1981; New Jersey Council for the Arts award, 1982; American Book Award, Before Columbus Foundation, 1984, for *Confirmation: An Anthology of African-American Women*; Drama Award, 1985.

WRITINGS—Under name LeRoi Jones until 1967:

PLAY PRODUCTIONS

"A Good Girl Is Hard to Find," first produced in Montclair, N.J., at Sterington House, August 28, 1958.

"Dante" (an excerpt from the novel *The System of Dante's Hell*; also see below), first produced in New York, at Off-Bowery Theatre, October, 1961; produced again as "The Eighth Ditch," at the New Bowery Theatre, 1964.

"Dutchman" (also see below), first produced Off-Broadway at Village South Theatre, January 12, 1964; produced Off-Broadway at Cherry Lane Theater, March 24, 1964; produced in London, 1967.

"The Baptism" (also see below), first produced Off-Broadway at Writers' Stage Theatre, May 1, 1964, produced in London, 1971.

"The Slave" [and] "The Toilet" (also see below), first produced Off-Broadway at St. Mark's Playhouse, December 16, 1964.

"Jello" (also see below), first produced in New York by Black Arts Repertory Theatre, 1965.

"Experimental Death Unit #1" (also see below), first produced Off-Broadway at St. Mark's Playhouse, March 1, 1965.

"A Black Mass" (also see below), first produced in Newark, at Proctor's Theatre, May, 1966.

"Slave Ship: A Historical Pageant" (also see below), produced in Newark, at Spirit House, March, 1967; first produced in New York City, November 19, 1969.

"Madheart" (also see below), first produced in San Francisco, Calif., at San Francisco State College, May, 1967.

"Arm Yourself, or Harm Yourself!" (also see below), first produced in Newark, at Spirit House, 1967.

"Great Goodness of Life (A Coon Show)" (also see below), first produced in Newark, at Spirit House, November, 1967.

"Home on the Range" (also see below), first produced in Newark, at Spirit House, March, 1968; produced in New York City at a Town Hall rally, March, 1968.

"Resurrection in Life," first produced in Harlem, N.Y., August 24, 1969.

"Junkies Are Full of SHHH. . ." and "Bloodrites" (also see below), produced Off-Broadway at Henry Street Playhouse, November 21, 1970.

"A Recent Killing," first produced Off-Broadway at the New Federal Theatre, January 26, 1973.

"Columbia the Gem of the Ocean," first produced in Washington, D.C., by Howard University Spirit House Movers, 1973.

"The New Ark's A-Moverin," first produced in Newark, February, 1974.

"Sidnee Poet Heroical, or If in Danger of Suit, The Kid Poet Heroical" (also see below), first produced Off-Broadway at the New Federal Theatre, May 15, 1975.

"S-1" (also see below), first produced in New York at Afro-American Studios, July 23, 1976.

'The Motion of History" (also see below), first produced in New York at New York City Theatre Ensemble, May 27, 1977.

"What Was the Relationship of the Lone Ranger to the Means of Production?" (also see below), first produced in New York at Ladies Fort, May, 1979.

"Dim Cracker Party Convention," first produced in New York at Columbia University, July 1980.

"Boy and Tarzan Appear in a Clearing," first produced Off-Broadway at New Federal Theatre, October, 1981.

"Money," first produced Off-Broadway at La Mama Experimental Theatre Club, January, 1982.

Also author of "Board of Education," "The Kid Poeta Tragical," "The Coronation of the Black Queen," "Insurrection," and "Vomit and the Jungle Bunnies," all unpublished.

PUBLISHED PLAYS

Dutchman [and] *The Slave*, Morrow, 1964.

The Toilet (also see below), Sterling Lord, 1964.

The Baptism: A Comedy in One Act (also see below), Sterling Lord, 1966.

The System of Dante's Hell (contains "Dante"), Grove, 1965.

Dutchman, Faber & Faber, 1967.

Slave Ship, Jihad, 1967.

The Baptism [and] *The Toilet*, Grove, 1967.

Arm Yourself, or Harm Yourself! A One-Act Play, Jihad, 1967.

Four Black Revolutionary Plays: All Praises to the Black Man (contains "Experimental Death Unit # One," "A Black Mass," "Great Goodness of Life," and "Madheart"), Bobbs-Merrill, 1969.

(Contributor) Ed Bullins, editor, *New Plays from the Black Theatre* (contains "The Death of Malcolm X"), Bantam, 1969.

J-E-L-L-O, Third World Press, 1970.

(Contributor) Woodie King and Ron Milner, editors, *Black Drama Anthology* (contains "Bloodrites" and "Junkies Are Full of SHHH. . ."), New American Library, 1971.

(Contributor) Rochelle Owens, editor, *Spontaneous Combustion: Eight New American Plays* (contains "Ba-Ra-Ka"), Winter House, 1972.

What Was the Relationship of the Lone Ranger to the Means of Production?: A Play in One Act, Anti-Imperialist Cultural Union, 1978.

The Motion of History and Other Plays (contains "Slave Ship" and "S-1"), Morrow, 1978.

The Sidnee Poet Heroical, in Twenty-Nine Scenes, Reed & Cannon, 1979.

Selected Plays and Prose of LeRoi Jones/Amiri Baraka, Morrow, 1979.

Also author of the plays "Home on the Range" and "Police," published in *Drama Review*, summer, 1968, "Rockgroup," published in *Cricket*, December, 1969, and "Black Power Chant," published in *Drama Review*, December, 1972.

SCREENPLAYS

"Dutchman," Gene Persson Enterprises, Ltd., 1967.

"Black Spring," Black Arts Alliance (San Francisco), 1968.

"A Fable" (based on "The Slave"), MFR Productions, 1971.

"Supercoon," Gene Persson Enterprises, Ltd., 1971.

POETRY

April 13 (broadside), Number 133, Penny Poems (New Haven), 1959.

Spring & So Forth (broadside), Number 111, Penny Poems, 1960.

Preface to a Twenty Volume Suicide Note, Totem/Corinth, 1961.

The Dead Lecturer (also see below), Grove, 1964.

Black Art (also see below), Jihad, 1966.

Black Magic (also see below), Morrow, 1967.

A Poem for Black Hearts, Broadside Press, 1967.

Black Magic: Sabotage; Target Study; Black Art; Collected Poetry, 1961-1967, Bobbs-Merrill, 1969.
It's Nation Time, Third World Press, 1970.
Spirit Reach, Jihad, 1972.
Afrikan Revolution: A Poem, Jihad, 1973.
Hard Facts: Excerpts, People's War, 1975, 2nd edition, Revolutionary Communist League, 1975.
Spring Song, Baraka, 1979.
AM/TRAK, Phoenix Bookship, 1979.
Selected Poetry of Amiri Baraka/Leroi Jones (contains "Poetry for the Advanced"), Morrow, 1979.
In the Tradition: For Black Arthur Blythe, Jihad, 1980.
Reggae or Not! Poems, Contact Two, 1982.

ESSAYS

Blues People: Negro Music in White America, Morrow, 1963, published in England as *Negro Music in White America*, MacGibbon & Kee, 1965, reprinted under original title, Greenwood Press, 1980.
Home: Social Essays (contains "Cuba Libre," "The Myth of a 'Negro Literature,'" "Expressive Language," "the legacy of malcolm x, and the coming of the black nation," and "state/meant"), Morrow, 1966.
Black Music, Morrow, 1968, Greenwood Press, 1980.
Raise, Race, Rays, Raze: Essays since 1965, Random House, 1971.
Strategy and Tactics of a Pan-African Nationalist Party, Jihad, 1971.
Kawaida Studies: The New Nationalism, Third World Press, 1972.
Crisis in Boston!, Vita Wa Watu—People's War, 1974.
Daggers and Javelins: Essays, 1974-1979, Morrow, 1984.
(With wife, Amina Baraka) *The Music: Reflections on Jazz and Blues*, Morrow, 1987.

EDITOR

January 1st 1959: Fidel Castro, Totem, 1959.
Four Young Lady Poets, Corinth, 1962.
(And author of introduction) *The Moderns: An Anthology of New Writing in America*, 1963, published as *The Moderns: New Fiction in America*, 1964.
(And co-author) *In-formation*, Totem, 1965.
Gilbert Sorrentino, *Black & White*, Corinth, 1965.
Edward Dorn, *Hands Up!*, Corinth, 1965.
(And contributor) *Afro-American Festival of the Arts Magazine*, Jihad, 1966, published as *Anthology of Our Black Selves*, 1969.
(With Larry Neal and A. B. Spellman) *The Cricket: Black Music in Evolution*, Jihad, 1968, published as *Trippin': A Need for Change*, New Ark, 1969.
(And contributor, with Larry Neal) *Black Fire: An Anthology of Afro-American Writing*, Morrow, 1968.
A Black Value System, Jihad, 1970.
(With Billy Abernathy under pseudonym Fundi) *In Our Terribleness (Some Elements of Meaning in Black Style)*, Bobbs-Merrill, 1970.
(And author of introduction) *African Congress: A Documentary of the First Modern Pan-African Congress*, Morrow, 1972.
(With Diane DiPrima) *The Floating Bear, A Newsletter, No. 1-37, 1961-1969*, McGilvery, 1974.
(Co-editor with Amina Baraka) *Confirmation: An Anthology of Afro-American Women*, Morrow, 1983.

OTHER

The Disguise (broadside), [New Haven], 1961.

Cuba Libre, Fair Play for Cuba Committee (New York City), 1961.
(Contributor) Herbert Hill, editor, *Soon, One Morning*, Knopf, 1963.
The System of Dante's Hell (novel), Grove, 1965.
(Author of introduction) David Henderson, *Felix of the Silent Forest*, Poets Press, 1967.
Striptease, Parallax, 1967.
Tales (short stories), Grove, 1967.
(Author of preface), *Black Boogaloo (Notes on Black Liberation)*, Journal of Black Poetry Press, 1969.
"Focus on Amiri Baraka: Playwright LeRoi Jones Analyzes the 1st National Black Political Convention" (sound recording), Center for Cassette Studies, 1973.
Three Books by Imamu Amiri Baraka (LeRoi Jones), (contains *The System of Dante's Hell*, *Tales*, and *The Dead Lecturer*), Grove, 1975.
The Autobiography of LeRoi Jones/Amiri Baraka, Freundlich, 1983.

Works represented in more than seventy-five anthologies, including *A Broadside Treasury*, *For Malcolm*, *The New Black Poetry*, *Nommo*, and *The Trembling Lamb*. *Blues People*, *The System of Dante's Hell*, and *Tales* have been translated into German; *Blues People* and *The Slave* have been translated into French; *Blues People*, *The Dead Lecturer*, and *Home: Social Essays*, have been translated into Spanish. Editor with Diane Di Prima, *The Floating Bear*, 1961-1963. Contributor to *Evergreen Review*, *Poetry*, *Downbeat*, *Metronome*, *Nation*, *Negro Digest*, *Saturday Review*, and other periodicals.

WORK IN PROGRESS: "Why's/Wise," an epic poem.

SIDELIGHTS: Amiri Baraka (formerly LeRoi Jones) is a major and controversial author. He is one of those mavericks, such as Allen Ginsberg and Norman Mailer, who have produced large bodies of work that are highly critical of American civilization. Perhaps more than Ginsberg or Mailer, Baraka continues to be an irritant to the American literary establishment. Baraka may be the most difficult American author to evaluate dispassionately since the modernist poet Ezra Pound, another important writer whose work still evokes volatile critical response. Like Pound, Baraka has dared to bring radical politics into the world of literature and to deliver his explosive ideas in an inflammatory style.

It is not surprising, then, that critical opinion about Baraka is highly divided. For example, Stanley Kauffmann says in *Dissent* that Baraka is "the luckiest man of our times, a writer who . . . would be less than lightly held if he did not happen to be a Negro at this moment in American history." Kimberly Benston, on the other hand, asserts in *Baraka: The Renegade and the Mask*, "Imamu Amiri Baraka is one of the foremost American artists of our century." Baraka is an author who demands that his audience accept his Afro-American identity as central to his art. Furthermore, he is an avant-garde writer whose variety of forms, including poetry, drama, music criticism, fiction, autobiography, and the essay, makes him difficult to categorize. Moreover, Baraka's stormy history clouds critical objectivity. No armchair artist, he has gone through a series of dramatic stages, from wild Beatnik ranting against the square world in the late 1950s through early 1960s, to black cultural nationalist renouncing the white world in the mid 1960s through mid 1970s, to Marxist-Leninist rejecting monopoly capitalism since the mid 1970s. Beyond Baraka's multifarious talents as a creative writer, his ideas and art—especially, as the primary architect of the Black Arts

Movement of the 1960s—have had a profound influence on the direction of subsequent black literature. therefore, when Arnold Rampersad claims in *American Book Review* that Baraka "stands with [Phillis] Wheatley, [Frederick] Douglass, [Paul Laurence] Dunbar, [Langston] Hughes, [Zora Neale] Hurston, [Richard] Wright and [Ralph] Ellison as one of the eight figures . . . who have significantly affected the course of African-American literary culture," he does not overstate the case.

During his Beat period, when he was known as LeRoi Jones, Baraka lived in New York's Greenwich Village and Lower East Side, where he published important little magazines such as *Yugen* and *Floating Bear* and socialized with such Bohemian figures as Ginsberg, Frank O'Hara, and Gilbert Sorrentino. He was greatly influenced by the white avant-garde: Charles Olson, O'Hara, and Ginsberg, in particular, shaped his conception of a poem as being exploratory and open in form. Donald Allen records in *The New American Poetry: 1945-1960* Baraka's Beat-period views on form: "There must not be any preconceived notion or design for what a poem ought to be. 'Who knows what a poem ought to sound like? Until it's thar' says Charles Olson . . . & I follow closely with that. I'm not interested in writing sonnets, sestina or anything . . . only poems."

Baraka's first book, *Preface to a Twenty Volume Suicide Note*, has met with general critical approval. In *The New Poets: American and British Poetry since World War II*, M. L. Rosenthal says that the early Jones/Baraka "has a natural gift for quick, vivid imagery and spontaneous humor, and his poems are filled with sardonic or sensuous or slangily knowledgeable passages." Theodore Hudson, in *From Leroi Jones to Amiri Baraka: The Literary Works*, observes: "All things considered, *Preface* was an auspicious beginning for LeRoi Jones the poet." However, sometimes the positive critical response to the early work comes at the expense of the later poetry. Lloyd Brown represents such a position when he announces in *Amiri Baraka*: "The scurrilities and general lack of control are a major drawback in the later collections, especially the black nationalist and socialist verse. But, despite the monotony that plagues the style of the first two volumes they remain Baraka's most consistently successful collections of poetry."

At first glance *Preface* looks like a typical product of integrated Bohemia; in fact, it ends: "You are / as any other sad man here / american." Yet there is a "blues feeling" throughout, that is, an infusion of black culture and reference. The reader can hear the "moaning . . . [of] Bessie Smith" in the book's lines, although blackness is not its principal focus. As David Ossman reports in *The Sullen Art: Interviews with Modern American Poets*, Baraka remarked in early 1960: "I'm fully conscious all the time that I am an American Negro, because it's part of my life. But I know also that if I want to say, 'I see a bus full of people,' I don't have to say, 'I am a Negro seeing a bus full of people.' I would deal with it when it has to do directly with the poem, and not as a kind of broad generalization that doesn't have much to do with a lot of young writers today who are Negroes." This view proved to be transitory. With the Civil Rights movement, Martin Luther King, and the black political upsurge of the late 1960s, Baraka's attitude toward race and art changed; he found that being a Negro wasn't some abstract and generalized stance but was integral to his art. Furthermore, with the coming of ethnic consciousness came political consciousness and the slow and painful rejection of Bohemia.

In July 1960 Baraka visited Castro's Cuba. In *The Autobiography of LeRoi Jones/Amiri Baraka*, Baraka refers to this visit as "a turning point in my life." While in Cuba he met forceful and politically committed Third World artists and intellectuals who forced him to reconsider his art and his apolitical stance. They attacked him for being an American; he tried to defend himself in "Cuba Libre," an essay reprinted in *Home: Social Essays*, by saying: "Look, why jump on me? . . . I'm in complete agreement with you. I'm a poet . . . what can I do? I write, that's all, I'm not even interested in politics." The Mexican poet, Jaime Shelley, answered him: "You want to cultivate your soul? In that ugliness you live in, you want to cultivate your soul? Well, we've got millions of starving people to feed, and that moves me enough to make poems out of." Finally, the Cuban revolution impressed Baraka as an alternative to the unanchored rebellion of his Bohemian friends at home. In Cuba the young intellectuals seemed to be doing something concrete to create a better and more humane world. Baraka felt that the Cuban government, unlike that of the United States, was actually being run by young intellectuals and idealists. This trip was the beginning of Baraka's radical political art and his identification with Third World artists.

Although Baraka started publishing in the early 1960s, he did not achieve fame until the 1964 publication of his play *Dutchman*, which won the *Village Voice*'s Obie Award. Werner Sollors notes in *Amiri Baraka/LeRoi Jones: The Quest for a "Populist Modernism"* that Norman Mailer called it "the best play in America." Baraka's most famous work, it has often been reprinted and performed, including a British film version by Anthony Harvey. (The play also provides scenes for Jean-Luc Godard's movie *Masculine-Feminine*.) In *Dutchman* Baraka no longer presents the melancholy hipster world where, as he declared in *Preface*, "Nobody sings anymore," but instead a realm where an angry young man fights for his ethnic identity and his manhood. Lula, the symbolic agent of the white state, sent out to find the latent murderer in the assimilated middle-class Negro Clay, locates and kills him. The play is highly stylized, reflecting the 1960s movement to propel black literature away from naturalism, the principal mode from the 1940s to 1960s, to a more experimental avant-garde art. Moreover, Baraka believed what a character in his play *The Slave* says: "the worst thing that ever happened to the West was the psychological novel." In a 1979 *New York Times Book Review* Darryl Pinckley commends Baraka's skill as a playwright: "He is a highly gifted dramatist. Much of the black protest literature of the 60's now seems diminished in power, even sentimental. But 'Dutchman' immediately seizes the imagination. It is radically economical in structure, striking in the vivacity of its language and rapid shifts of mood."

The Dead Lecturer, Baraka's second book of poetry, is the work of a black man who wants to leave white music and the white world behind. As civil rights activities intensified, Baraka became more and more disappointed with his white friends; in fact, the word "friends" becomes ironic in this second volume. In "Black Dada Nihilismus," for example, he realizes that he must "Choke my friends / in their bedrooms" to escape their influence and vision. To elude Western metaphysical domination Baraka must call up the dark gods of the black soul; he demands violence in himself and his people to escape the white consciousness. He no longer wants to be the Dead Lecturer; he wants life. In this book of poetry he attempts to reject the "quiet verse" of the Beat Generation and claim the black chant of political commitment.

This blackening and politicalization of Baraka's art is formal as well as thematic. The poetic line becomes longer as the verse imitate the chant. In the poem "Rhythm and Blues,"Baraka reveals that he does not want to become a martyr for Western art. Richard Howard, writing in the *Nation,* finds the Baraka of *The Dead Lecturer* "much surer of his own voice.... These are the agonized poems of a man writing to save his skin, or at least to settle in it, and so urgent is his purpose that not one of them can trouble to be perfect." Howard understands Baraka's pain. In a negative review of *The Dead Lecturer* in *Salmagundi,* Rosenthal makes an important statement which anticipates the far more political art of Baraka's Black Arts and Marxist periods: "No American poet since Pound has come closer to making poetry and politics reciprocal forms of action." Rosenthal perceives that Baraka wants his poems to act on the world; as Baraka wrote to his friend, Black Mountain poet Edward Dorn, in a 1961 letter: "'Moral earnestness'... ought [to] be transformed into action.... I know we think that to write a poem, and be Aristotle's God is sufficient. But I can't sleep.... There is a right and a wrong. And it's up to me, you, all of the so called minds, to find out. It is only knowledge of things that will bring this 'moral earnestness'."

Baraka had joined the Beat Generation because he regarded its members as spiritual outsiders who were against white middle-class America. Yet over the years he became disillusioned with this apolitical avant-garde that refused to take action in the world. Disengagement was no longer enough for Baraka who notes in the essay "Cuba Libre": "The rebels among us have become merely people like myself who grow beards and will not participate in politics. Drugs, juvenile delinquency, complete isolation from the vapid mores of the country, a few current ways out. But name an alternative here." Baraka wanted an alternative to Bohemianism.

During this transitional period Baraka produced two fine works, his only serious efforts in fiction: *The System of Dante's Hell,* a novel, and *Tales,* a collection of short stories. As Sollors points out, the sections of the novel parallel the themes and even passages found in *Preface, Dead Lecturer,* and the early uncollected poems. Although *System* was published in 1965 it was mostly written in the early 1960s. Baraka commented on the book and the times to Kimberly Benston in an interview published in *Boundary 2:* "I was really writing defensively. I was trying to get away from the influence of people like Creeley and Olson. I was living in New York then and the whole Creeley-Olson influence was beginning to beat me up. I was in a very closed circle—that was about the time I went to Cuba—and I felt the need to break out of the type of form that I was using them. I guess this was not only because of the form itself but because of the content which was not my politics."

Tales, published in 1967, treats the years 1963 through 1967, a time of radical change in Baraka's life, and reflects the themes of the poetry in *Black Magic,* which also appeared in 1967. Both works try to convey a sense of the ethnic self away from the world of white culture. In *Conscientious Sorcerers: The Black Postmodernist Fiction of LeRoi Jones/Baraka, Ishmael Reed and Samuel R. Delany,* Robert Elliot Fox remarks on Baraka's fiction: "However, the essential energy linking these two works—which recount and reevaluate his life up to that time—is a relentless momentum deeper into blackness. These fugitive narratives describe the harried flight of an intensely self-conscious Afro-American artist/intellectual from neo-slavery of blinding, neutralizing whiteness, where the arena of

struggle is basically within the mind. In *Tales* Baraka describes the posture and course he wishes to adopt: that of "The straight ahead people, who think when that's what's called for, who don't when they don't have to. Not the Hamlet burden, which is white bullshit, to always be weighing and analyzing, and reflecting." Baraka wants action, and the story "Screamers" casts action in musical terms. For Baraka dance and music are associated with vitality and political action. In this tale blacks riot in the streets because of the wild music of Lynn Hope, a jazz saxophonist: "We screamed at the clear image of ourselves as we should always be. Ecstatic, completed, involved in a secret communal expression. It would be the sweetest revolution, to hucklebuck into the fallen capital, and let the oppressors lindy hop out." In the 1960s Baraka was the pioneer of black experimental fiction, probably the most important since Jean Toomer who had written during the Harlem Renaissance of the 1920s. In the 1970s and 1980s Baraka has been joined by a band of younger experimental black writers, including Ishmael Reed, Clarence Major, and Charles Johnson.

During the early 1960s Baraka composed his major social-aesthetic study of black music in America, *Blues People: Negro Music in White America.* A history, it begins in slavery and ends with contemporary avant-garde jazz (John Coltrane, Ornette Coleman, and Cecil Taylor). Baraka argues that since Emancipation the blues have been an essential feature of black American music and that this form was born from the union of the American and the African experience; as Baraka says, "Undoubtedly, none of the African prisoners broke out into 'St. James Infirmary' the minute the first of them was herded off the ship." *Blues People* gave Baraka an opportunity to meditate on a profound and sophisticated art form created by blacks and to do so during a time when he was trying to find a model for his own art that was not white avant-garde. Although he later retracted his evaluation, he had temporarily rejected black literature as mediocre and middle-brow. In his *Home* essay "The Myth of a 'Negro Literature,'" he declares: "Only in music, and most notably in blues, jazz, and spirituals, *i.e.,* 'Negro Music,' has there been a significantly profound contribution by American Negroes." In the *New York Times Book Review,* Jason Berry calls Baraka "an eloquent jazz critic; his 1963 study, *Blues People: Negro Music in White America* is a classic." Furthermore, Clyde Taylor maintains in James B. Gwynne's *Amiri Baraka: The Kaleidoscopic Torch,* "The connection he nailed down between the many faces of black music, the sociological sets that nurtured them, and their symbiotic evolutions through socio-economic changes, in *Blues People,* is his most durable conception, as well as probably the one most indispensable thing said about black music."

Although *Blues People* is his only sustained study of Afro-American music, Baraka has published two other collections containing important essays on the subject: *Black Music,* written from a cultural nationalist perspective, and *The Music: Reflections on Jazz and Blues,* written from a Marxist one. In *Black Music* Baraka crystallizes the idea of John Coltrane as the prime model for the new black art: "Trane is a mature swan whose wing span was a whole world. But he also shows us how to murder the popular song. To do away with weak Western forms. He is a beautiful philosopher." Brown asserts: "As an essayist Baraka's performance is decidedly uneven. The writings on music are always an exception. As historian, musicological analyst, or as a journalist covering a particular performance Baraka always commands attention because of his obvious knowledge of the subject and because of a style that is engaging and persuasive even when the sentiments are questionable and controversial.'' In *The Kaleidoscopic Torch* Joe Weixlmann states: ''Baraka's expertise as an interpreter of Afro-American music is, of course, well-known. Had he never done any belletristic writing or political organizing, he would be remembered as the author of *Blues People . . .* and *Black Music*.''

In 1965, following the assassination of Black Muslim leader Malcolm X, Baraka left Greenwich Village and the Bohemian world and moved uptown to Harlem and a new life as a cultural nationalist. He argued in ''the legacy of malcolm x, and the coming of the black nation'' (collected in *Home*) that ''black People are a race, a culture, a Nation.'' Turning his back on the white world, he established the Black Arts Repertory Theatre/School in Harlem, an influential model that inspired black theaters throughout the country. In 1967, he published his black nationalist collection of poetry, *Black Magic*, which traces his painful exit from the white world and his entry into blackness. Unfortunately, his exorcism of white consciousness and values included a ten-year period of intense hatred of whites and most especially Jews; in ''A POEM SOME PEOPLE WILL HAVE TO UNDERSTAND,'' Baraka expresses his impatience with liberals and Bohemians, and he requests: ''Will the machinegunners please step forward?'' Espousing political action and political art, he declares, ''We want poems that kill.'' After a year in Harlem, he returned home to his birthplace, Newark, New Jersey, where he continued his cultural nationalist activities. In 1967 he changed his name from LeRoi Jones to the Bantuized Muslim appellation Imamu (''spiritual leader,'' later dropped) Ameer (later Amiri, ''blessed'') Baraka ('prince''), as confirmation of his pride in his blackness.

While in Harlem Baraka had become the main theorist of the Black Aesthetic, defined by Houston Baker in *Black American Literature Forum* as ''a distinctive code for the creation and evaluation of black art.'' The aesthetician felt that the black artist must express his American experience in forms that spring from his own unique culture and that his art must be evaluated by standards that grow out of his own culture. Baraka writes in ''Expressive Language,'' an essay in *Home:* ''Words' meanings, but also the rhythm and syntax that frame and propel their concatenation, seek their culture as the final reference for what they are describing of the world.'' In ''And Shine Swam On,'' an essay in *Black Fire: An Anthology of Afro-American Writing,* Larry Neal provides one of the central statements of the Black Aesthetic: ''The artist and the political activist are one. They are both shapers of the future reality. Both understand and manipulate the collective myths of the race. Both are warriors, priests, lovers and destroyers.'' In his *Home* essay, ''state/meant'' Baraka declares fiercely: ''The Black Artist's role in America is to aid in the destruction of America as he knows it. His role is to report and reflect so precisely the nature of the society, and of himself in that society, that other men will be moved by the exactness of his rendering and, if they are black men, grow strong through this moving, having seen their own strength, and weakness; and if they are white men, tremble, curse, and go mad, because they will be drenched with the filth of their evil.'' In a less rhetorical fashion, Fox presents the goals of the contemporary black artist: ''The radical inversion of Western systems of belief and order [that black artists] engage in can be termed 'mythoclasm,' the drastic demystification of ideological signs that have been turned into false universals. . . . Their praxis as artists involves countering the hegemonic [authoritarian] code inscribed by the master culture with alternatives of discourse and desire (transformational longings).'' Or, as Baraka writes

in his essay ''the legacy of malcolm x,'' ''The song title 'A White Man's Heaven Is a Black Man's Hell' describes how complete an image reversal is necessary in the West.''

In *Understanding the New Black Poetry: Black Speech and Black Music as Poetic References,* Stephen Henderson observes, ''[Baraka] is the central figure of the new black poetry awakening''; in an essay collected in *Modern Black Poets,* Arthur P. Davis calls him ''the high priest of this new Black literary renaissance and one who has done most to shape its course.'' Baraka dominated the Black Arts Period of the late 1960s both as a theorist and artist. He was the main artist-intellectual responsible for shifting the emphasis of contemporary black literature from an integrationist art conveying a raceless and classless vision to a literature rooted in the black experience. The Black Arts Era, both in terms of creative and theoretical writing, is the most important one in black literature since the Harlem Renaissance. No post-Black Arts artist thinks of himself or herself as simply being a human being who happens to be black; blackness is central to his or her experience and art. Furthermore, Black Arts had its impact on other ethnic groups and primarily through the person of Baraka. The Native American author Maurice Kenny writes of Baraka in *The Kaleidoscopic Torch:* ''He opened tightly guarded doors for not only Blacks but poor whites as well and, of course, Native Americans, Latinos and Asian-Americans. We'd all still be waiting the invitation from the *New Yorker* without him. He taught us all how to claim it and take it.'' In *The Kaleidoscopic Torch* Clyde Taylor says of Baraka's poems of the Black Arts period: ''There are enough brilliant poems of such variety in *Black Magic* and *In Our Terribleness* to establish the unique identity and claim for respect of several poets. But it is beside the point that Baraka is probably the finest poet, black or white, writing in this country these days.'' However, the response to the poetry was not all favorable. In *With Eye and Ear,* the avant-garde critic and poet Kenneth Rexroth contended: ''In recent years he [Baraka] has succumbed to the temptation to become a professional Race Man of the most irresponsible sort. . . . His loss to literature is more serious than any literary casualty of the Second War.''

The play ''Madheart'' epitomizes Baraka's writings of the Black Arts period. It is a morality play in which Black Man ritualistically tries to kill White Woman, who symbolizes the power of white consciousness and influences the consciousness of blacks. Until such influence is destroyed, the play contends, the black mind cannot be free. Baraka insists in ''the legacy of malcolm x'' that ''the Black artist . . . is desperately needed to change the images his people identify with, by asserting Black feeling, Black mind, Black judgment.'' Implicitly, Black Man is a black cultural nationalist artist.

In 1966 Baraka published *Home,* an important book of essays, in which the reader sees Baraka becoming ''blacker'' and more radical in each essay. The collection includes the famous ''Cuba Libre,'' which documents his trip to Cuba and his awakening to Third-World conceptions of art and political activism. A spiritual autobiography written at its author's fullest powers, *Home* assumes the same importance in Baraka's career as *Advertisements for Myself* does in Mailer's. The poet Sterling D. Plumpp observes in *The Kaleidoscopic Torch* that he regards *Home* as a major work ''for its forthrightness and daring courage to call for 'revolutionary changes,' [and moreover it] . . . is unsurpassed for its seminal ideas regarding black art which is excellent and people-centered.''

Baraka's years in Greenwich Village had made him a master of avant-garde technique that he utilized in his own work and passed on to younger black artists such as Nikki Giovanni and Don L. Lee. Ironically, avant-garde ideas of form cohered perfectly with the new black artist's need to express his or her own oral traditions; the free verse and the eccentric typography of the white avant-garde were ideal vehicles for black oral expression and experience. Unlike Harlem Renaissance poets—such as Claude McKay, who constantly battled the rigid, archaic form of the English sonnet replete with nineteenth-century diction and conventions to express 1920s black American language and life—the Black Arts poet had the flexibility of contemporary forms, forms committed to orality and polyrhythms. In a 1971 issue of *Black World* Dudley Randall observes: "The younger poets have a teacher of great talent, and while they think they are rejecting white standards, they are learning from LeRoi Jones, a man versed in German philosophy, conscious of literary traditions . . . who uses the structure of Dante's *Divine Comedy* in his *The System of Dante's Hell* and the punctuation, spelling and line divisions of sophisticated contemporary poets." Arnold Rampersad maintains in *American Book Review:* "Among all the major writers who helped to wean younger black writers away from imitation and compulsive traditionalism and toward modernism, Baraka has been almost certainly the most influential. . . . In speaking of his modernizing influence on younger black poets, one does not mean that Baraka taught them to imitate or even to admire the verse of Pound and Eliot, Stevens and Williams, Ginsberg and Kerouac, all of whose poetry he himself attempted to absorb. More than any other black poet, however, he taught younger black poets of the generation past how to respond poetically to their lived experience, rather than to depend as artists on embalmed reputations and outmoded rhetorical strategies derived from a culture often substantially different from their own."

In 1974, dramatically reversing himself, Baraka rejected black nationalism as racist and became a Third World Socialist. He declared, in *The New York Times:* "It is a narrow nationalism that says the white man is the enemy. . . . Nationalism, so-called, when it says 'all non-blacks are our enemies,' is sickness or criminality, in fact, a form of fascism." Since 1974 he has produced a number of Marxist poetry collections and plays, including *Hard Facts,* "Poetry for the Advanced," and "What Was the Relationship of the Lone Ranger to the Means of Production?" He has also published a book of Marxist essays, *Daggers and Javelins.* The goal of his socialist art is the destruction of the capitalist state and the creation of a socialist community. In *The Poetry and Poetics of Amiri Baraka: The Jazz Aesthetic,* William J. Harris records Baraka's assessment of his goals as a Third World Socialist: "I think fundamentally my intentions are similar to those I had when I was a Nationalist. That might seem contradictory, but they were similar in the sense I see art as a weapon, and a weapon of revolution. It's just now that I define revolution in Marxist terms. I once defined revolution in Nationalist terms. But I came to my Marxist view as a result of having struggled as a Nationalist and found certain dead ends theoretically and ideologically, as far as Nationalism was concerned and had to reach out for a communist ideology." His socialist art is addressed to the black community, which has, he believes, the greatest revolutionary potential in America.

Baraka's socialist works have not fared well in the establishment press. In the *New York Times Book Review* Darryl Pinckney comments that Baraka has "sacrificed artistic vitality on the altar of his political faith. . . . his early work is far better than his recent efforts: he now seems content to express his Marxism in the most reductive, shrill propaganda." Henry C. Lacey in his 1981 book on Baraka, *To Raise, Destroy, and Create: The Poetry, Drama, and Fiction of Imamu Amiri Baraka (LeRoi Jones),* ignores the Marxist work entirely; Fox, in his 1987 study, says, "The Marxist work is intellectually determined, whereas the cultural-nationalist pieces are emotionally felt." On the other hand, E. San Juan, an exiled Filipino leftist intellectual, writes in *The Kaleidoscopic Torch* that he finds the "Lone Ranger" "the most significant theatrical achievement of 1978 in the Western hemisphere." Weixlmann sensitively responds in *The Kaleidoscopic Torch* to the tendency to categorize the radical Baraka instead of analyze him: "At the very least, dismissing someone with a label does not make for very satisfactory scholarship. Initially, Baraka's reputation as a writer and thinker derived from a recognition of the talents with which he is so obviously endowed. The assaults on that reputation have, too frequently, derived from concerns which should be extrinsic to informed criticism."

As the critical climate cools, critics will find merit in the recent poetry, especially the long *In the Tradition: For Black Arthur Blythe,* and the epic-in-progress, "Why's/Wise," both accomplished works. Also with the 1984 publication of *The Autobiography* Baraka has joined the great tradition of the black autobiography, which runs from Frederick Douglass to W. E. B. DuBois to Richard Wright to Malcolm X. Like other authors in this tradition, in the act of making sense of his life, Baraka makes sense of American culture. Arnold Rampersad comments on Baraka and his autobiography in *The Kaleidoscopic Torch:* "His change of heart and head is testimony to his honesty, energy, and relentless search for meaning, as demonstrated recently once again with the publication of his brilliant *The Autobiography of LeRoi Jones.*"

In a piece on Miles Davis in *The Music: Reflections on Jazz and Blues,* Baraka quotes the contemporary trombonist, Craig Harris: "Miles is gonna do what Miles wants to do. And everybody else can follow, if they feel like it." Like Davis, Baraka is going his own way; he is an original, and others can follow if they like. He is a black writer who has taken the techniques and notions of the white avant-garde and made them his own; like the great bop musicians before him, he has united avant-garde art with the black voice, creating a singular expressive mode. Baraka has created a major art, not by trying to blend into Western tradition but by trying to be true to himself and his culture. He speaks out of a web of personal and communal experience, minimizing the so-called universal features he shared with the white world and focusing on the black cultural difference—what has made the black experience unique in the West. Out of this experience Baraka fashions his art, his style, his distinctive vision of the world.

Papers by and about Amiri Baraka/LeRoi Jones are housed in the Dr. Martin Sukov Collection at Yale University's Beinecke Rare Book and Manuscript Library; numerous letters to and from the author, and several of Baraka's manuscripts are collected at Indiana University's Lilly Library; the author's letters to Charles Olson are housed at the University of Connecticut's Special Collections Library; other manuscripts and materials are collected at Syracuse University's George Arents Research Library.

BIOGRAPHICAL/CRITICAL SOURCES:

BOOKS

Abramson, Doris E., *Negro Playwrights in the American Theatre: 1925-1959,* Columbia University Press, 1969.

Allen, Donald M., *The New American Poetry: 1945-1960,* Grove, 1960.

Allen, Donald M., and Warren Tallman, editors, *Poetics of the New American Poetry,* Grove, 1973.

Allen, Robert L., *Black Awakening in Capitalist America,* Doubleday, 1970.

Archer, Leonard C., *Black Images in the American Theatre,* Pageant-Poseidon, 1973.

Baraka, Amiri, *Tales,* Grove, 1967.

Baraka, Amiri and Larry Neal, editors, *Black Fire: An Anthology of Afro-American Writing,* Morrow, 1968.

Baraka, Amiri, *Black Magic: Sabotage; Target Study; Black Art; Collected Poetry, 1961-1967,* Bobbs-Merrill, 1969.

Baraka, Amiri, *The Autobiography of LeRoi Jones/Amiri Baraka,* Freundlich Books, 1984.

Benston, Kimberly A., editor, *Baraka: The Renegade and the Mask,* Yale University Press, 1976.

Benston, Kimberly A., *Imamu Amiri Baraka (LeRoi Jones): A Collection of Critical Essays,* Prentice-Hall, 1978.

Bigsby, C. W. E., *Confrontation and Commitment: A Study of Contemporary American Drama, 1959-66,* University of Missouri Press, 1968.

Bigsby, C. W. E., editor, *The Black American Writer, Volume II: Poetry and Drama,* Everett/Edwards, 1970, Penguin, 1971.

Bigsby, C. W. E., *The Second Black Renaissance: Essays in Black Literature,* Greenwood Press, 1980.

Birnebaum, William M., *Something for Everybody Is Not Enough,* Random House, 1972.

Brown, Lloyd W., *Amiri Baraka,* Twayne, 1980.

Cohn, Ruby, *Dialogue in American Drama,* Indiana University Press, 1971.

Concise Dictionary of American Literary Biography, Volume 1: *The New Consciousness,* Gale, 1987.

Contemporary Literary Criticism, Gale, Volume 1, 1973, Volume 2, 1974, Volume 3, 1975, Volume 5, 1976, Volume 10, 1979, Volume 14, 1980, Volume 33, 1985.

Cook, Bruce, *The Beat Generation,* Scribner, 1971.

Cruse, Harold, *The Crisis of the Negro Intellectual,* Morrow, 1967.

Dace, Letitia, *LeRoi Jones (Imamu Amiri Baraka): A Checklist of Works by and about Him,* Nether Press, 1971.

Dace, Letitia and Wallace Dace, *The Theatre Student: Modern Theatre and Drama,* Richards Rosen Press, 1973.

Dictionary of Literary Biography, Gale, Volume 5: *American Poets since World War II,* 1980, Volume 7: *Twentieth-Century American Dramatists,* 1981, Volume 16: *The Beats: Literary Bohemians in Postwar America,* 1983, Volume 38: *Afro-American Writers after 1955: Dramatists and Prose Writers,* 1985.

Dukore, Bernard F., *Drama and Revolution,* Holt, 1971.

Ellison, Ralph, *Shadow and Act,* New American Library, 1966.

Emanuel, James A., and Theodore L. Gross, editors, *Dark Symphony: Negro Literature in America,* Free Press, 1968.

Fox, Robert Elliot, *Conscientious Sorcerers: The Black Postmodernist Fiction of LeRoi Jones/Baraka, Ishmael Reed and Samual R. Delany,* Greenwood Press, 1987.

Frost, David, *The Americans,* Stein & Day, 1970.

Gayle, Addison, editor, *Black Expression: Essays by and about Black Americans in the Creative Arts,* Weybright & Talley, 1969.

Gayle, Addison, *The Way of the New World: The Black Novel in America,* Anchor/Doubleday, 1975.

Gibson, Donald B., *Five Black Writers: Essays on Wright, Ellison, Baldwin, Hughes, LeRoi Jones,* New York University Press, 1970.

Gibson, Donald B., editor, *Modern Black Poets: A Collection of Critical Essays,* Prentice-Hall, 1973.

Gilman, Richard, *Common and Uncommon Masks: Writings on the Theatre 1961-1970,* Random House, 1971.

Gwynne, James B., editor, *Amiri Baraka: The Kaleidoscopic Torch,* Steppingstones Prress, 1985.

Hall, Veronica, *Chicorel Theater Index to Plays in Anthologies, Periodicals, Discs and Tapes,* Chicorel Library Publishing, 1970.

Harris, William J., *The Poetry and Poetics of Amiri Baraka: The Jazz Aesthetic,* University of Missouri Press, 1985.

Haskins, James, *Black Theater in America,* Crowell, 1982.

Hatch, James V., *Black Image on the American Stage: A Bibliography of Plays and Musicals, 1770-1970,* Drama Book Specialists, 1970.

Hatch, James V., editor, *Black Theatre, U.S.A.,* Free Press, 1974.

Henderson, Stephen E., *Understanding the New Black Poetry: Black Speech and Black Music as Poetic References,* Morrow, 1973.

Hill, Herbert, *Soon, One Morning,* Knopf, 1963.

Hill, Herbert, editor, *Anger, and Beyond: The Negro Writer in the United States,* Harper, 1966.

Hudson, Theodore, *From LeRoi Jones to Amiri Baraka: The Literary Works,* Duke University Press, 1973.

Hughes, Langston, and Milton Meltzer, *Black Magic: A Pictorial History of the Negro in American Entertainment,* Prentice-Hall, 1967.

Jones, LeRoi, *Preface to a Twenty Volume Suicide Note,* Totem Press/Corinth Books, 1961.

Jones, LeRoi, *The Dead Lecturer,* Grove, 1964.

Jones, LeRoi, *Blues People: Negro Music in White America,* Morrow, 1963.

Jones, LeRoi, *Home: Social Essays,* Morrow, 1966.

Keil, Charles, *Urban Blues,* University of Chicago Press, 1966.

King, Woodie, and Ron Milner, editors, *Black Drama Anthology,* New American Library, 1971.

Klinkowitz, Jerome, *Literary Disruptions: The Making of a Post-Contemporary American Fiction,* 2nd edition, University of Illinois, 1980.

Knight, Arthur and Kit Knight, editors, *The Beat Vision,* Paragon House, 1987.

Kofsky, Frank, *Black Nationalism and the Revolution in Music,* Pathfinder, 1970.

Lacey, Henry C., *To Raise, Destroy, and Create: The Poetry, Drama, and Fiction of Imamu Amiri Baraka (LeRoi Jones),* The Whitson Publishing Company, 1981.

Lewis, Allan, *American Plays and Playwrights,* Crown, 1965.

Littlejohn, David, *Black on White: A Critical Survey of Writing by American Negroes,* Viking, 1966.

Lumley, Frederick, *New Trends in Twentieth Century Drama,* Oxford University Press, 1967.

Mezu, Okechukwu, editor, *Modern Black Literature,* Black Academy Press, 1971.

O'Brien, John, *Interviews with Black Writers,* Liveright, 1973.

Ossman, David, *The Sullen Art: Interviews with Modern American Poets,* Corinth, 1963.

Pool, Rosy E., editor, *Beyond the Blues,* Hand & Flower Press, 1962.

Popkin, Michael, editor, *Modern Black Writers,* Ungar, 1978.

Rexroth, Kenneth, *With Eye and Ear,* Herder and Herder, 1970.

Ricard, Alain, *Theatre et Nationalisme: Wole Soyinka et LeRoi Jones,* Presence Africaine, 1972.

Rosenthal, M. L., *The New Poets: American and British Poetry since World War II*, Oxford University Press, 1967.
Sollors, Werner, *Amiri Baraka/LeRoi Jones: The Quest for a "Populist Modernism,"* Columbia University Press, 1978.
Stepanchev, Stephen, *American Poetry since 1945*, Harper, 1965.
Weales, Gerald, *The Jumping-Off Place: American Drama in the 1960s*, Macmillan, 1969.
Whitlow, Roger, *Black American Literature: A Critical History*, Nelson Hall, 1973.
Williams, Martin, *The Jazz Tradition*, New American Library, 1971.
Williams, Sherley Anne, *Give Birth to Brightness: A Thematic Study in Neo-Black Literature*, Dial, 1972.

PERIODICALS

America, May 26, 1984.
American Book Review, February, 1980, May-June, 1985.
American Dialog, spring, 1968.
American Imago, Volume 28, summer, 1972.
Antioch Review, fall, 1967.
Atlantic, January, 1966, May, 1966.
Avant Garde, September, 1968.
Best Sellers, August, 1971.
Black American Literature Forum, spring, 1980, spring, 1981, fall, 1982, spring, 1983, winter, 1985.
Black Collegian, March 3, 1973.
Black Dialogue, July-August, 1965.
Black Lines, winter, 1970.
Black Scholar, March, 1971.
Black Theatre, 1968.
Black Times, October, 1974.
Black World, volume 29, number 6, April, 1971, December, 1971, November, 1974, July, 1975.
Book Week, December 24, 1967.
Book World, October 28, 1979.
Boundary, Volume 2, number 6, 1978.
Chicago Defender, January 11, 1965.
Chicago Tribune, October 4, 1968.
Christian Science Monitor, June 21, 1966.
CLA Journal, March, 1971, September, 1971, September, 1972, September, 1973, December, 1977.
Commentary, February, 1965.
Commonweal, June 28, 1968, June 13, 1969.
Comparative Drama, summer, 1984.
Contemporary Literature, Volume 12, 1971.
Cue, June 6, 1964.
Der Spiegel, August 18, 1969.
Detroit Free Press, January 31, 1965.
Detroit News, January 15, 1984, August 12, 1984.
Dissent, spring, 1965.
Downbeat, January 2, 1964, August, 1987.
Drama Review, summer, 1968, winter, 1970.
Ebony, August, 1967, August, 1969, February, 1971.
Educational Theatre Journal, March, 1968, March, 1970, March, 1976.
Esquire, June, 1966.
Essence, September, 1970, May, 1984, September, 1984, May, 1985.
Evergreen Review, November, 1965, December, 1967, June, 1968, February, 1970.
Freedomways, winter, 1968.
Globe & Mail (Toronto), September 19, 1987.
Greenfield Review, fall, 1980.
Guardian, March 23, 1968, March 30, 1968.

Hudson Review, winter, 1964.
International Times, February 2-15, 1968.
Jazz, April, 1966-July, 1967.
Jazz Review, June, 1959.
Jet, January 16, 1975, July 23, 1984.
Journal of Black Poetry, fall, 1968, spring, 1969, summer, 1969, fall, 1969.
Journal of Black Studies, December, 1973.
Journal of Ethnic Studies, spring, 1974.
Journal of Popular Culture, fall, 1969.
Kenyon Review, Volume XXX, number 5, 1968.
Liberator, February, 1965, February, 1966.
Life, August 4, 1967.
Listener, March 14, 1968, September 25, 1969.
Literary Times, May-June, 1967.
Los Angeles Free Press, Volume 5, number 18, May 3-May 9, 1968.
Los Angeles Times Book Review, May 15, 1983, March 29, 1987.
Massachusetts Review, spring, 1973.
Metronome, September, 1961.
Midwest Quarterly, volume 12, July, 1971.
Minnesota Review, spring, 1978.
Minority Voices, spring, 1977.
Modern Drama, February, 1971, summer, 1972, September, 1972, June, 1974.
Ms., September, 1983.
Nation, October 14, 1961, November 14, 1961, March 13, 1964, April 13, 1964, January 4, 1965, March 15, 1965, January 22, 1968, February 2, 1970.
National Guardian, July 4, 1964.
National Observer, June 29, 1964.
National Review, March 23, 1965, December 23, 1983.
Negro American Literature Forum, March, 1966, winter, 1973.
Negro Digest, December, 1963, February, 1964, Volume 13, number 19, August, 1964, March, 1965, April, 1965, March, 1966, April, 1966, June, 1966, April, 1967, April, 1968, January, 1969, April, 1969.
New Leader, March 13, 1967.
New Republic, January 23, 1965, May 28, 1966.
Newsday, August 20, 1969.
New Statesman, July 16, 1965, September 5, 1969.
Newsweek, March 13, 1964, April 13, 1964, November 22, 1965, May 2, 1966, March 6, 1967, December 4, 1967, December 1, 1969, February 19, 1973.
New York, November 5, 1979.
New Yorker, April 4, 1964, December 26, 1964, March 4, 1967, December 30, 1972.
New York Herald Tribune, March 25, 1964, April 2, 1964, December 13, 1964, October 27, 1965.
New York Post, March 16, 1964, March 24, 1964, January 15, 1965, March 18, 1965.
New York Review of Books, January 20, 1966, May 22, 1964, July 2, 1970, October 17, 1974, June 11, 1984, June 14, 1984.
New York Times, April 28, 1966, May 8, 1966, August 10, 1966, September 14, 1966, October 5, 1966, January 20, 1967, February 28, 1967, July 15, 1967, January 5, 1968, January 6, 1968, January 9, 1968, January 10, 1968, February 7, 1968, April 14, 1968, August 16, 1968, November 27, 1968, December 24, 1968, August 26, 1969, November 23, 1969, February 6, 1970, May 11, 1972, June 11, 1972, November 11, 1972, November 14, 1972, November 23, 1972, December 5, 1972, December 27, 1974,

December 29, 1974, November 19, 1979, October 15, 1981, January 23, 1984.

New York Times Book Review, January 31, 1965, November 28, 1965, May 8, 1966, February 4, 1968, March 17, 1968, February 14, 1971, June 6, 1971, June 27, 1971, December 5, 1971, March 12, 1972, December 16, 1979, March 11, 1984, July 5, 1987, December 20, 1987.

New York Times Magazine, February 5, 1984.

Observer, May 14, 1967, February 25, 1968, August 31, 1969, December 1, 1985.

Obsidian, spring, 1975.

Partisan Review, Volume 31, summer, 1964.

Poetry, March, 1965, February, 1967.

Progressive Leader, November-December, 1964.

Publishers Weekly, August 8, 1966, January 15, 1968, September 10, 1979.

Ramparts, June 29, 1968.

Realist, May, 1965.

Salmagundi, spring-summer, 1973.

San Francisco Chronicle, August 23, 1964.

San Francisco Review of Books, November, 1984.

Saturday Evening Post, July 13, 1968.

Saturday Review, April 20, 1963, January 11, 1964, January 9, 1965, December 11, 1965, December 9, 1967, October 2, 1971, July 12, 1975.

Southwestern Review, spring, 1982.

Spectator, September 16, 1966, February 16, 1968.

Studies in Black Literature, spring, 1970, Volume 1, number 2, 1970, Volume 3, number 2, 1972, Volume 3, number 3, 1972, Volume 4, number 1, 1973.

Sunday News (New York), January 21, 1973.

Theatre Journal, May, 1982.

Time, December 25, 1964, November 19, 1965, May 6, 1966, January 12, 1968, April 26, 1968, June 28, 1968, June 28, 1971.

Times Literary Supplement, November 25, 1965, September 1, 1966, September 11, 1969, October 9, 1969.

Trace, summer, 1967.

Tribune Books, March 29, 1987.

Village Voice, December 17, 1964, May 6, 1965, May 19, 1965, August 30, 1976, August 1, 1977, December 17-23, 1980, October 2, 1984.

Virginia Quarterly Review, August, 1966.

Washington Post, August 15, 1968, September 12, 1968, November 27, 1968, December 5, 1980, January 23, 1981, June 29, 1987.

Washington Post Book World, December 24, 1967, May 22, 1983.

Woman's Review of Books, summer, 1983.

World Literature Today, spring, 1979, winter, 1981, summer, 1984.

—*Sidelights by William J. Harris*

*   *   *

BARRAX, Gerald William 1933-

PERSONAL: Born June 21, 1933, in Attalla, Ala.; son of Aaron (a custodian) and Dorthera (Hedrick) Barrax; married Geneva Catherine Lucy, 1954 (divorced, 1971); married Joan Dellimore; children: (first marriage) Dennis Scott, Gerald William, Joshua Cameron; (second marriage) Shani Averyl, Dara Hilary. *Education:* Duquesne University, B.A., 1963; University of Pittsburgh, M.A., 1969.

ADDRESSES: Home—808 Cooper Rd., Raleigh, N.C. 27610. *Office*—Department of English, North Carolina State University, Raleigh, N.C. 27607.

CAREER: U.S. Post Office, Pittsburgh, Pa., clerk and carrier, 1958-67; North Carolina Central University, Durham, instructor, 1969-70; North Carolina State University, Raleigh, special instructor in English department, 1970—. *Military service:* U.S. Air Force, 1953-57; became airman first class.

AWARDS, HONORS: Gold Medal Award, Catholic Poetry Society of America.

WRITINGS:

Another Kind of Rain (poetry), University of Pittsburgh Press, 1970.

An Audience of One (poetry), University of Georgia Press, 1980.

The Deaths of Animals and Lesser Gods, edited by Charles H. Rowell, University of Kentucky, 1984.

CONTRIBUTOR TO ANTHOLOGIES

Robert Hayden, editor, *Kaleidoscope: Poems by American Negro Poets,* Harcourt, 1968.

Understanding the New Black Poetry: Black Speech and Black Music as Poetic References, Morrow, 1973.

The Poetry of Black America: Anthology of the 20th Century, Harper, 1973.

Contemporary Poetry of North Carolina, John F. Blair, 1977.

OTHER

Contributor of poetry to periodicals, including *Poetry, Four Quarters, Spirit, Southern Poetry Review, World Order, Black World, Poetry Northwest, Hyperion, Nimrod, Georgia Review, Obsidian, Callahoo,* and *Pembroke.*

*   *   *

BARROW, William
See FULLER, Hoyt (William)

*   *   *

BASS, Kingsley B., Jr.
See BULLINS, Ed

*   *   *

BATES, Arthenia J.
See MILLICAN, Arthenia Jackson Bates

*   *   *

BEBEY, Francis 1929-

PERSONAL: Born July 15, 1929, in Douala, Cameroon; son of Fritz N'Dedi (a pastor) and Maria N'Gobo Eyidi; married Jacqueline Edinguele, August 14, 1956; children: Eyidi, Christiane, Fanta, Francis, Jr., Patrick. *Education:* Attended Sorbonne, University of Paris, and New York University. *Religion:* Protestant.

ADDRESSES: c/o Lawrence Hill & Co., 520 Riverside Ave., Westport, Conn. 06880.

CAREER: Radiodiffusion Outre-mer, Paris, France, radio producer and journalist, 1957-61; UNESCO, Paris, France, program specialist, 1961-74; free-lance writer, musicologist, concert guitarist, and composer, 1974—. Has worked for Radio Ghana and Radio Cameroon.

MEMBER: Cercle Renaissance, Association des Escrivains de Langue Francaise, Societe des Auteurs, Compositeurs et Editeurs de Musique.

AWARDS, HONORS: Grand Prix Litteraire de l'Afrique Noire, Association des Ecrivains de Langue Francaise, 1968, for the novel *Le Fils d'Agatha Moudio;* prix jeune chanson from S.A.C.E.M., Paris, 1977, for recording "La Condition Masculine."

WRITINGS:

La radiodiffusion en Afrique noire (title means "Broadcasting in Black Africa"), Editions Saint-Paul, 1963.
(Contributor) Clive Wake, editor, *An Anthology of African and Malagasy Poetry in French*, Three Crowns Press, 1965.
Le ·Fils d'Agatha Moudio (novel), Editions CLE, 1967, 3rd edition, 1971, translation by Joyce A. Hutchinson published as *Agatha Moudio's Son,* Heinemann, 1971, Lawrence Hill, 1973.
Embarras et cie: Nouvelles et poemes (stories and poems; title means "Embarrassment and So On"), Editions CLE, 1968.
Musique de l'Afrique, with recording, Horizons de France, 1969, translation by Josephine Bennett published as *African Music: A People's Art*, Lawrence Hill, 1975.
Trois petits cireurs (novel; title means "Three Little Shoeblacks"), Editions CLE, 1972.
La poupee ashanti (novel), Editions CLE, 1973, translation by Joyce A. Hutchinson published as *The Ashanti Doll*, Lawrence Hill.
Le Roi Albert d'Effidi (novel; title means "King Albert of Effidi"), Editions CLE, 1974, translation by Hutchinson published as *King Albert*, Lawrence Hill, 1981.
La Musique africaine moderne (title means "Modern African Music"), Editions Presence Africaine, 1975.
Le Petit Fumeur (story; title means "The Little Smoker"), Editions Rencontres, 1976.
Concert pour un vieux masque: Poeme, L'Harmattan (Paris), 1980.
Nouvelle saison des fruits, Nouvelles Editions Africaines (Dakar), 1980.

Author of script for film "Sonate en bien majeur."

WORK IN PROGRESS: Two novels; "Musique africaine," a film on African music.

SIDELIGHTS: Born in Cameroon, West Africa, Francis Bebey began his career as a radio journalist and broadcaster, and currently enjoys an international reputation not only as an author, but as an accomplished musician as well. As a guitarist and composer, Bebey has recorded several of his own compositions and has performed in concert throughout the world. As a writer, Bebey has explored several genres, including poetry, and has written extensively about the subject of music for both a popular and academic audience. Some of his work appears in English, Dutch, German, Polish, and Russian translation.

Bebey's *Musique de l'Afrique*, translated into English by Josephine Bennett as *African Music: A People's Art*, concerns the music of his native West Africa especially. John Blacking writes in the *Times Literary Supplement* that the book could serve as a "useful record guide for those who can afford a collection of West African music or persuade their libraries to assemble one." A contributor to *Choice* praises the book for

its practical aids, stating that "the text, photographs, and discography represent a kind of home-study course in African music." Although Blacking thinks that the book neglects the music of eastern, central and southern Africa, Gary Giddins concludes in the *New York Times Book Review* that "Bebey eloquently pleads for a broad dissemination of unmodernized tribal music while hinting only tenuously at the impact it has already had on world-wide music."

Although Bebey has written in many genres, he is perhaps best known for his novel *Le Fils d'Agatha Moudio*, which was translated into English by Joyce A. Hutchinson as *Agatha Moudio's Son* and awarded the Grand Prix Litteraire de l'Afrique Noire. The novel, which has also been translated into German, Italian, and Dutch, is about the "matrimonial misfortunes" of a young man from a Cameroon fishing village. Says a *Times Literary Supplement* contributor: "His first wife, an adolescent imposed upon him by parental and chiefly wishes, presents him with a baby before he has even brought himself to touch her. When he follows his own long-standing choice and marries the beautiful, notorious Agatha Moudio, against the united opposition of the village, she presents him with a son of such unmistakable European paternity as to make him a laughing stock." Stating that Bebey "writes with a shrewdness and alert humor which constantly recall the traditional raconteur," the *Times Literary Supplement* contributor adds that "Bebey writes of this life with a real sense of its grandeur, isolation and spectacular beauty, praising 'the absolute horizon of days which dawn and die.'" And John Updike, who finds that "the novel brims with the village's most precious gift—its bestowal of value upon every life within it," observes in the *New Yorker* that "Bebey writes with the lightness and irreverence and affectionate thoughtfulness that the patterns of acculturation have bestowed upon the literature of Francophone Africa."

A contributor to *A New Reader's Guide to African Literature*, edited by Hans M. Zell, Carol Bundy, and Virginia Coulon, indicates that Bebey sometimes turns to music when the "literary vision" fails to materialize, and that his recent *Concert pour un vieux masque: Poeme* exemplifies his efforts to "integrate his activities as musician and creative writer more closely than he has in the past." Bebey commented: "As a performing guitarist (classical, African, and my own music), I travel very much, through which as an author I discover how wonderful the world is, and how similar human beings are wherever I meet them."

MEDIA ADAPTATIONS: A film adaptation of *Le Fils d'Agatha Moudio* is planned.

BIOGRAPHICAL/CRITICAL SOURCES:

BOOKS

Zell, Hans M., Carol Bendy, and Virginia Coulton, editors, *A New Reader's Guide to African Literature,* 2nd completely revised and expanded edition, Africana Publishing Company, 1983.

PERIODICALS

Africa Today, Volume 29, number 3, 1982.
New Yorker, January 21, 1974, August 15, 1977.
New York Times Book Review, September 14, 1975, July 17, 1977.
Times Literary Supplement, March 3, 1972, August 15, 1975.
World Literature Today, autumn, 1977, summer, 1982.

BECKHAM, Barry (Earl)   1944-

PERSONAL: Born March 19, 1944, in Philadelphia, Pa.; son of Clarence and Mildred (Williams) Beckham; married Betty Louise Hope, February 19, 1966 (divorced, 1977); married Geraldine Lynne Palmer, 1979; children: (first marriage) Brian Elliott, Bonnie Lorine. *Education:* Brown University, A.B., 1966; attended law school at Columbia University. *Religion:* Episcopalian.

ADDRESSES: Home—140 Lancaster St., Providence, R.I. 02906. *Office*—Department of English, Brown University, Brown Station, Providence, R.I. 02912. *Agent*—William Morris Agency, 1350 Ave. of the Americas, New York, N.Y. 10019.

CAREER: Chase Manhattan Bank, New York City, public relations consultant, 1966-67, urban affairs associate, 1969-70; National Council of Young Men's Christian Associations, New York City, public relations associate, 1967-68; Western Electric Co., New York City, public relations associate, 1968-69; Brown University, Providence, R.I., visiting lecturer, 1970-72, assistant professor, 1972-78, associate professor of English, 1979—, director of graduate creative writing program, 1980—. Visiting professor, University of Wyoming, 1972. Member of literature panel, Rhode Island Council on the Arts, 1980—. President, Beckham House Publishers, Inc.

MEMBER: Authors Guild, PEN (member of executive board, American Center, 1970-71).

WRITINGS:

My Main Mother (novel), Walker & Co., 1969 (published in England as *Blues in the Night*, Tandem, 1974).
Runner Mack (novel), Morrow, 1972.
"Garvey Lives!" (play), produced in Providence, R.I., 1972.
Double Dunk (fictionalized biography of Earl Manigault), Holloway House, 1981.
(Editor and contributor) *The Black Student's Guide to College* (nonfiction), Dutton, 1982.

Contributor to *Black Review, Brown Alumni Monthly, Esquire, Intellectual Digest, New York, New York Times, Novel.*

WORK IN PROGRESS: A portrait of Chase Manhattan Bank; another novel.

SIDELIGHTS: Barry Beckham's first novel, *My Main Mother,* won praise as the probing account of a young black man and the events that lead him to the murder of his mother. Narrated by its protagonist, Mitchell Mibbs, the novel is "basically . . . a psychological study of the ruinous effect on a child who is either ignored or tormented by a parent," writes Peter Rowley in the *New York Times Book Review.* Mitchell's beautiful and self-centered mother (Pearl), in delusions of becoming a rich and famous singer, shuns and abandons the already fatherless boy. Mitchell's lone source of support and companionship comes from a kindly uncle, whose death "and the horror of a sordid squabble over his money spur Mitchell into matricide," notes Rowley. A *Times Literary Supplement* contributor observes that "the single act of violence towards which the book works appropriately underlines the particular, personal anxieties which made it, for Mitchell, an inevitability." Less prominently featured, yet as influential as the psychological devastation of Mitchell's upbringing, are the forces of racism in a white dominant society. The *Times Literary Supplement* contributor notes that "the manifestations of racial inequality, when they do appear, have a potency which lies precisely in understatement." Rowley particularly praises the second half of *My Main Mother:* "The scenes of Harlem, of how it feels to be an aged

black from Maine getting a flat tire on Times Square, of encountering a homosexual in the Village, of street gangs and boarding houses, of the ironies of racism . . . are fantastically vivid and compelling." Rowley continues: "If Barry Beckham's second book is as brilliant as the second half of his first, he may well become one of the best American novelists of the decade."

In *Runner Mack,* Beckham "move[s] far beyond the boundaries of his first novel," writes Mel Watkins in the *New York Times Book Review.* The story of a naive Southern black man (Henry Adams) who moves to the North to find fortune as a professional baseball player, *Runner Mack* is more directly critical of an American society embedded in racism. "Loosely connected," according to Watkins, by a series of "satirical and burlesque episodes . . . held together by a matter-of-fact prose that belies their nightmarish qualities," the novel takes on a surrealistic quality as Henry is stymied in his attempts to achieve personal fulfillment and identity. En route to a job interview, Henry is hit by a Mack truck and stumbles, bleeding, into the interviewer's office—only to be questioned about his teeth, whether he's had smallpox, or whether he'll "run away" if he "doesn't like the work." He later fails to win a spot on a local professional baseball team, despite outplaying everyone at the tryout. After finding the space and time to have a meaningful conversation with his wife, Henry receives a draft notice saying he must immediately report for military service. He ends up being sent to the front lines of the "Alaskan War," where he meets up with a revolutionary named Runner Mack, who involves Henry in a plot to blow up the White House.

"Its humor and burlesque notwithstanding," writes Watkins, *Runner Mack* ". . . is an unsettling book." Phyllis Rauch Klotman writes in *Another Man Gone: The Black Runner in Contemporary Afro-American Literature* that "each experience in the novel is a kind of education," and notes a disturbing continuity in that "Henry moves from one mad, dehumanizing way of life to another." Watkins views *Runner Mack* as an allegory of Afro-American history, "parallel[ing] black history from slave ship to . . . militant revolutionaries." He continues: "By creating an ironic verbal world, [Beckham] has produced an allegory that both illuminates the despair and recurring frustration that has characterized blacks' struggle for freedom and brilliantly satirizes the social conditions that perpetuate that frustration." As such, *Runner Mack* has far-reaching implications. "By the novel's midpoint, Beckham has utterly leveled the American Dream of success," notes Joe Weixlmann in *Dictionary of Literary Biography.* "Beckham causes the reader of *Runner Mack* to contemplate what he or she might do to ameliorate the deplorable condition of current-day America. . . . *Runner Mack* is a tightly wrought masterpiece which probes deeply into the American psyche."

MEDIA ADAPTATIONS: The film rights to *My Main Mother* have been acquired by William Castle.

AVOCATIONAL INTERESTS: Photography, chess, film production.

BIOGRAPHICAL/CRITICAL SOURCES:

BOOKS

Beckham, Barry, *Runner Mack,* Morrow, 1972.
Dictionary of Literary Biography, Volume 33: *Afro-American Fiction Writers after 1955,* Gale, 1984.

Klotman, Phyllis Rauch, *Another Man Gone: The Black Runner in Contemporary Afro-American Literature*, Kennikat Press, 1977.

PERIODICALS

Black Images, autumn, 1974.
MELUS, winter, 1981.
Modern Fiction Studies, spring, 1987.
New York Times, October 10, 1982.
New York Times Book Review, November 30, 1969, September 17, 1972.
Studies in Black Literature, winter, 1974.
Times Literary Supplement, February 12, 1971.
Variety, January 14, 1970.

* * *

BEDIAKO, Kwabena Asare
See KONADU, S(amuel) A(sare)

* * *

BELL, James Madison 1826-1902

PERSONAL: Born April 3, 1826, in Gallipolis, Ohio; died in 1902; married Louisiana Sanderline in 1847 (some sources say 1848); children: seven. *Education:* Attended schools in Cincinnati and Cleveland, Ohio.

CAREER: Plasterer, social activist, poet, and orator.

WRITINGS:

A Poem: Delivered August 1st, 1862 . . . at the Grand Festival to Commemorate the Emancipation of the Slaves in the British West Indian Isles, B. F. Sterett, 1862.
A Poem Entitled "The Day and the War," Delivered January 1, 1864, at Platt's Hall at the Celebration of the First Anniversary of President Lincoln's Emancipation Proclamation, Agnew & Deffebach, 1864.
An Anniversary Poem Entitled "The Progress of Liberty," Delivered January 1st, 1866 . . . at the Celebration of the Third Anniversary of President Lincoln's Proclamation, Agnew & Deffebach, 1866.
A Poem, Entitled "The Triumph of Liberty," Delivered April 7, 1870, at Detroit Opera House on the Occasion of the Fifteenth Amendment to the Constitution of the United States, Tunis Steam Printing, 1870.
The Poetical Works of James Madison Bell, introduction by B. W. Arnett, Wynkoop, Hallenbeck, Crawford, 1901.
"Modern Moses, or 'My Policy' Man" (poem), published in *Early Black Poets,* edited by William H. Robinson, W. C. Brown, 1969.

Also author of "Emancipation in the District of Columbia" and the poem "Andrew Jackson Swinging Around in a Circle." Poetry represented in anthologies, including *An Anthology of Verse by American Negroes,* edited by N. I. White and W. C. Jackson, 1924.

SIDELIGHTS: James Madison Bell was a poet known primarily for his writings and activism in support of the abolition of slavery during the American Civil War. A friend of abolitionist John Brown, Bell wrote and read poetry for antislavery rallies and took part in the oganization of Brown's 1859 raid on the arsenal at Harpers Ferry, West Virginia. Regarded as somewhat conventional, his writings are nonetheless respected for their inspirational qualities and their moral and political stands.

A plasterer throughout his life, Bell "mastered the literary traditions and poetic conventions of his day" despite receiving only a limited education, reported Keith E. Byerman in the *Dictionary of Literary Biography.* Observed Byerman, "Such mastery of convention was itself an argument for equality at a time when most whites, including many abolitionists, assumed that blacks were inherently incapable of acquiring even the rudiments of culture." Bell regularly used iambic tetrameter and both alternating rhyme and couplets in his poetry, and while his imagery and phrasing were considered conventional, his intent was often political rather than aesthetic. "It must be recognized that Bell was not as interested in the craftsmanship of his poetry as he was in the moral and political arguments that could be made through verse," asserted Byerman.

In addition to working as a plasterer and poet, Bell was involved in politics. During the 1870s he served as a county delegate of the Republican party, and in 1872 he was elected a delegate to the Republican National Convention. He gave speeches, read his poetry at commemorative gatherings, and supported various party candidates for many years. A number of his poems, in fact, were written to celebrate anniversaries of U.S. President Abraham Lincoln's Emancipation Proclamation or the freeing of slaves in the British West Indies. Concluded Byerman, Bell "adopted whatever techniques would facilitate his goal as a spokesman against slavery and for black rights." While the bulk of his work featured political themes, in later years Bell also used his poetry to promote Christianity, addressing subjects such as immortality, the nature of evil, and Protestant doctrine.

BIOGRAPHICAL/CRITICAL SOURCES:

BOOKS

Dictionary of Literary Biography, Volume 50: *Afro-American Writers Before the Harlem Renaissance,* Gale, 1986.

* * *

BENNETT, George Harold 1930-
(Hal Bennett)

PERSONAL: Born April 21, 1930, in Buckingham, Va. *Education:* Attended Mexico City College. *Addresses:* 170 South Park St., No. 1, Hackensack, N.J. 07601. *Agent*— Owen Laster, William Morris Agency, Inc., 1350 Avenue of the Americas, New York, N.Y. 10019.

CAREER: Writer. Feature writer for the *Newark Herald News,* 1946; fiction editor of Afro-American newspaper, 1953-55. Worked as a dancer, iguana hunter, and bartender. *Military service:* U.S. Air Force; served as writer for Public Information Division and editor of newspaper in Korea.

AWARDS, HONORS: Fellow of Centro Mexicano de Escritores; Bread Loaf Writer's Conference fiction fellowship for *A Wilderness of Vines,* 1966; named most promising young writer of the year by *Playboy* magazine for the short story "Dotson Gerber Resurrected," 1970; P.E.N./Faulkner Award for fiction, 1973.

WRITINGS—Under name Hal Bennett:

The Mexico City Poems [and] *House on Hay* (latter a play in verse), Obsidian Press, 1961.
A Wilderness of Vines (novel), Doubleday, 1966.
The Black Wine (novel), Doubleday, 1969.
Lord of the Dark Places (novel), Norton, 1970.

(With Michael Samuels) *The Well Body Book*, Random House, 1973.

(With Samuels) *Spirit Guides: Access to Secret Worlds*, Random House, 1974.

Wait Until the Evening (novel), Doubleday, 1974.

Seventh Heaven, Doubleday, 1976.

Insanity Runs in Our Family (collection of short stories containing "Black Wings," "Insanity Runs in Our Family," "Where Are the White People?" "The Ghost of Martin Luther King," "Dotson Gerber Resurrected," "Whatever Happened to Henry Oates?" "Million Dollar Baby," "The Abominable Snow Man," "The Woman Who Loved Cockroaches," "The Mountain to Mohammed," "The Judgement of Father Anselmo," "The Day My Sister Hid the Ham," "Second Sunday," "Also Known as Cassius," and "Sightless")), Doubleday, 1977.

SIDELIGHTS: With the advent of *A Wilderness of Vines* on the literary scene, many critics agreed that Hal Bennett was a writer of talent, albeit undeveloped talent. His first novel, which took ten years to complete, describes the town of Burnside, Virginia, in which the black inhabitants imitate white codes of discrimination by color. Ronald Walcott in *Black World* declared *A Wilderness of Vines* "a flawed, awkward, at times ineptly written, but insightful and occasionally provocative work, written by an author "in search of a style.""

The author's second novel, *The Black Wine*, continues the story of Burnside and depicts the migration of eight-year-old David Hunter and his family to Newark, New Jersey. Critics again stressed Bennett's artistic inconsistencies. Irving Howe remarked in *Harper's* that the author's "books are wildly uneven and sometimes atrocious, but there are sections that lead one to think he might do for Burnside something like what Faulkner did for Yoknapatawpha." Howe further claimed that Bennett, in *A Wilderness of Vines* and *The Black Wine*, "sometimes brilliantly, sometimes clumsily, . . . has begun to provision an imagined world of American blacks." Walcott concurred: "What Bennett gives us here is the stuff of racial stereotype at the point where stereotype is transformed into archetype . . . and fiction myth."

Walcott praised Bennett's next novel as an affirmation of the author's growing maturity as a writer. "*Lord of the Dark Places* is where Bennett's fiction has been heading all along, and it arrives in this powerful, aesthetically satisfying, tightly controlled novel possessed of a plot that fairly explodes with incident and invention. It covers territory Bennett has traveled before, but this time, he owns it."

Wait Until the Evening also received favorable reviews. *New York Times Book Review* critic Jonathan Yardley declared that when Bennett "is good he is very, very good. . . . His feel for rural Virginia is as strong and accurate as William Styron's. . . . Bennett reveals himself to have a deep understanding of the complexity and difficulty of interracial communication."

BIOGRAPHICAL/CRITICAL SOURCES:

BOOKS

Contemporary Literary Criticism, Volume 5, Gale, 1976.
Dictionary of Literary Biography, Volume 33, Gale, 1984.

PERIODICALS

Black World, June, 1974, July, 1974.
Harper's, December, 1969.

New York Times Book Review, May 5, 1968, September 22, 1974.

*   *   *

BENNETT, Gwendolyn B.   1902-1981

PERSONAL: Born July 8, 1902, in Giddings, Tex.; died May 30, 1981; daughter of Joshua (a teacher) and Maime (a teacher) Bennett; married Alfred Jackson (a physician) in 1927 (died in early 1930s); married Richard Crosscup (an antiques collector and dealer; died c. 1980). *Education:* Graduated from Pratt Institute in 1924; attended Columbia University, 1921-24; studied at Academie Julian and Ecole du Pantheon, Paris, 1925.

ADDRESSES: Home—Kutztown, Pa.

CAREER: Howard University, Washington, D.C., instructor in watercolor and design, 1924 and 1926; taught art education and English at Tennessee State College in 1927; Works Progress Administration (W.P.A.; U.S. Government agency), associated with Federal Works Project during 1930s and with Federal Art Project's Harlem Community Art Center in New York, N.Y., as assistant director, 1937, and director, 1938-41; teacher and member of administrative staff of Jefferson School for Democracy, beginning in 1941; director of George Washington Carver School, beginning in 1943; worked as secretary for Consumer's Union during the mid-1940s; became antiques dealer in Kutztown, Pa. Cover illustrator for *Crisis* and *Opportunity* magazines, 1923-31.

AWARDS, HONORS: Received Alfred C. Barnes Foundation fellowship, 1926.

WRITINGS:

CONTRIBUTOR

James Weldon Johnson, editor, *The Book of American Negro Poetry*, Harcourt, 1922, revised edition, 1931.

Alain LeRoy Locke, editor, *The New Negro: An Interpretation*, Boni, 1925.

William Stanley Braithwaite, editor, *Anthology of Magazine Verse for 1925 and Yearbook of American Poetry*, B. J. Brimmer, 1926.

Braithwaite, editor, *Anthology of Magazine Verse for 1926 and Yearbook of American Poetry*, B. J. Brimmer, 1927.

Countee Cullen, editor, *Caroling Dusk: An Anthology of Verse by Negro Poets*, Harper, 1927.

Charles S. Johnson, editor, *Ebony and Topaz: A Collectanea*, National Urban League, 1927.

Victor Francis Calverton, editor, *Anthology of American Negro Literature*, Modern Library, 1929.

Robert Burns Eleazer, editor, *Singers in the Dawn: A Brief Supplement to the Study of American Literature*, Conference on Education and Race Relations, 1934, published as *Singers in the Dawn: A Brief Anthology of American Negro Poetry*, Commission on Interracial Cooperation, 1942.

Rosey E. Pool and Eric Walrond, editors, *Black and Unknown Bards: A Collection of Negro Poetry*, Hand and Flower Press, 1958.

Arna Wendell Bontemps, editor, *American Negro Poetry*, Hill & Wang, 1963.

Lindsay Patterson, editor, *An Introduction to Black Literature in America From 1746 to the Present*, Volume 10 of "The International Library of Negro Life and History," Association for the Study of Negro Life, 1969.

Bontemps and Langston Hughes, editors, *The Poetry of the Negro, 1946-1970: An Anthology,* revised edition (Bennett was not associated with earlier edition), Doubleday, 1970.

Arnold Adoff, editor, *The Poetry of Black America: Anthology of the Twentieth Century,* Harper, 1973.

Contributor to *Afro-American Literature,* 1979. Also contributor of poetry, short stories, and articles to periodicals, including *Crisis, Fire!!, Gypsy, Howard University Record, Messenger, Opportunity, Palms,* and *Southern Workman.*

OTHER

Author of monthly column "The Ebony Flute" for *Opportunity,* 1926-28, assistant editor, 1926-28.

SIDELIGHTS: A minor literary figure and artist associated with the Afro-American artistic movement known as the Harlem Renaissance, Gwendolyn B. Bennett was considered a promising young writer by her peers. Her poetry received favorable reviews from critics, though only a few of the poems appeared in print and no collection was ever compiled. The majority of Bennett's published writings appeared in "The Ebony Flute," her literary and fine arts column written for *Opportunity* magazine. The monthly column offered news and commentary about contemporary black artists and their works and eventually proved to be an important chronicle of Afro-American cultural history. In addition, Bennett was a graphic artist and illustrated several magazine covers for *Crisis* and *Opportunity;* she worked in a variety of media, principally pen and ink, watercolor, oil, batik, and woodcuts.

BIOGRAPHICAL/CRITICAL SOURCES:

BOOKS

Dictionary of Literary Biography, Volume 51: *Afro-American Writers From the Harlem Renaissance to 1940,* Gale, 1987.

Fax, Elton C., *Seventeen Black Artists,* Dodd, 1971.

Perry, Margaret, *Silence to the Drums: A Survey of the Literature of the Harlem Renaissance,* Greenwood Press, 1976.

*   *   *

BENNETT, Hal
    See BENNETT, George Harold

*   *   *

BENNETT, Lerone, Jr.   1928-

PERSONAL: Born October 17, 1928, in Clarksdale, Miss.; son of Lerone and Alma (Reed) Bennett; married Gloria Sylvester, July 21, 1956; children: Joy, Constance and Courtney (twins), Lerone III. *Education:* Morehouse College, A.B., 1949; Atlanta University, graduate study, 1949.

ADDRESSES: Home—1308 East 89th St., Chicago, Ill. 60619. *Office*—*Ebony* Magazine, 820 South Michigan Ave., Chicago, Ill. 60616.

CAREER: Atlanta Daily World, Atlanta, Ga., reporter, 1949-52, city editor, 1952-53; *Jet* (magazine), Chicago, Ill., associate editor, 1953; *Ebony* (magazine), Chicago, associate editor, 1954-57, senior editor, 1958—. Visiting professor of history, Northwestern University, 1968-69; Institute of the Black World, senior fellow, 1969, currently member of board of directors; member of board of directors, Chicago Public Li-

brary; member of board of trustees, Martin Luther King Memorial Center.

MEMBER: Black Academy of Arts and Letters (fellow), Phi Beta Kappa, Kappa Alpha Psi, Sigma Delta Chi.

AWARDS, HONORS: Book of the Year Award from Capital Press Club, 1963; D.L., Morehouse College, 1965; Patron Saints Award from Society of Midland Authors, for *What Manner of Man,* 1965; D.Hum., Wilberforce University, 1977; Academy Institute literary award, American Academy of Arts and Letters, 1978; D.Litt., Marquette University, 1979, Voorhees College, 1981, Morgan State University, 1981; L.H.D., University of Illinois, Lincoln College, and Dillard University, all 1980.

WRITINGS:

Before the Mayflower: A History of the Negro in America, 1619-1966, Johnson Publishing Co. (Chicago), 1962, 5th edition, 1982.

The Negro Mood, and Other Essays, Johnson Publishing Co., 1964.

What Manner of Man: A Biography of Martin Luther King, Jr., Johnson Publishing Co., 1964, 3rd revised edition, 1968, 4th revised edition, 1976.

Confrontation: Black and White, Johnson Publishing Co., 1965.

Black Power U.S.A.: The Human Side of Reconstruction, 1867-1877, Johnson Publishing Co., 1967.

Pioneers in Protest, Johnson Publishing Co., 1968.

(Editor with others) *Ebony Pictorial History of Black America,* four volumes, Johnson Publishing Co., 1971.

The Challenge of Blackness, Johnson Publishing Co., 1972.

The Shaping of Black America, Johnson Publishing Co., 1975.

Wade in the Water: Great Moments in Black History, Johnson Publishing Co., 1979.

CONTRIBUTOR TO ANTHOLOGIES

Doris Sanders, editor, *The Day They Marched,* Johnson Publishing Co., 1963.

Langston Hughes, editor, *New Negro Poets: U.S.A.,* Indiana University Press, 1964.

Ebony magazine staff, editors, *The White Problem in America,* Johnson Publishing Co., 1966.

Also contributor to *Contemporary American Negro Short Stories.*

OTHER

Contributor of articles, short stories, and poems to popular magazines.

SIDELIGHTS: "Lerone Bennett, Jr., senior editor of *Ebony* magazine, has pioneered and excelled in the writing of popular black history," reports A. C. Gulliver in the *Christian Science Monitor.* From *Before the Mayflower: A History of the Negro in America, 1619-1966* to *The Shaping of Black America,* a study of black Americans in the worlds of slavery, emancipation, work and business, Bennett has produced interesting texts known for their factual accuracy and readability. Critics especially recommend *Before the Mayflower, Confrontation: Black and White,* and *Black Power, U.S.A.: The Human Side of Reconstruction.*

Pointing to the author's background in journalism (Bennett worked as a reporter for the *Atlanta Daily World* before becoming a magazine editor), Kyle Haselden of the *Christian Century* comments that in *Before the Mayflower,* Bennett "employs a reporter's sense of what is significant and arresting. . . . In the main he lets the facts speak for themselves, but he selects those facts which have an emotional as well as an intellectual impact.'' To represent the valor of black Americans, for example, he records the victories of pre-Civil War insurrectionists and the accomplishments of black soldiers in major conflicts since then, always in the face of humiliation and opposition from their white compatriots. The highest ranking black officer at the beginning of World War I was not allowed to fight due ''to high blood pressure'' although his health was sound; the black commander of the all-black 369th regiment was excluded from the Rainbow Division that served in France because ''he was told, he said, that black was not one of the colors of the rainbow.'' Nonetheless, adds Bennett, that regiment ''was the first Allied unit to reach the Rhine. The regiment, which was under fire for 191 days, never lost a foot of ground, a trench or a soldier through capture.'' And to represent the many lynchings that took place in 1918 and 1919, Bennett writes, ''More disturbing than the number [147] was the increasing sadism of the mobs. . . . Though pregnant, [Mary Turner] was lynched in Valdosta, Georgia. She was hanged to a tree, doused with gasoline and motor oil and burned. As she dangled from the rope, a man stepped forward with a pocketknife and ripped open her abdomen in a crude cesarean operation. 'Out tumbled the prematurely born child,' wrote Walter White. 'Two feeble cries it gave—and received for answer the heel of a stalwart man, as life was ground out of the tiny form.''' Benjamin Quarles, writing in *American History Review,* suggests that some of these materials may ''seem incredible because [they are] unfamiliar. . . . But whether or not one is familiar with the book's content, he may well be moved by its unusual ability to evoke the tragedy and the glory of the Negro's role in the American past.''

Hailed by reviewers as an objective analysis of social problems touching black Americans in the 1960s, *Confrontation* calls for better communication not only between blacks and ill-informed white Americans, but also between black leaders and the masses, which Bennett says have grown apart and need to work more closely toward meaningful change. As *New York Times Book Review* contributor Nat Hentoff sees it, the ''need to stimulate masses of black Americans into cohesive action'' is the book's major theme. Kenneth B. Clark, writing in the *Saturday Review,* deems the book ''a valuable contribution to the understanding of America's perennial number-one domestic problem.'' In addition to its usefulness for civil rights leaders, writes Clark, ''*Confrontation* also has much to say to the serious student of American society.''

Black Power, U.S.A.: The Human Side of Reconstruction, 1867-1877 shows Bennett's mastery ''of exposition, for he makes sense out of the amazingly complex, conglomerate, and contradictory situations'' found in southern cities following the Civil War, says Harry Hansen. Earlier in the *Saturday Review* article, Hansen comments, ''In his remarkable assessment of the constitutional conventions, Mr. Bennett describes the black man as entering a 'desperate and bloody struggle for political survival, flanked by two white allies, one Southern-born, the other Northern-born. To remain in power the black man had to preserve the coalition. But to preserve the coalition he had to make fatal concessions on radical reform.''' Consequently, Bennett presents the growth ''of black power during Reconstruction as a dream unfulfilled,'' Hansen relates. A. K. Randall points out in a *Library Journal* review that one need not agree with Bennett to appreciate the book's ''readable synthesis of historical research'' and ''lively narrative.''

BIOGRAPHICAL/CRITICAL SOURCES:

BOOKS

Bennett, Lerone, Jr., *Before the Mayflower: A History of the Negro in America, 1619-1966,* Johnson Publishing Co., 1962, 5th edition, 1982.
Bennett, Lerone, Jr., *Black Power, U.S.A.: The Human Side of Reconstruction, 1867-1877,* Johnson Publishing Co., 1967.
Newquist, Roy, editor, *Conversations,* Rand McNally, 1967.

PERIODICALS

American History Review, July, 1963.
Best Sellers, April, 1975.
Freedomways, fall, 1965.
Journal of American History, June, 1965.
Negro Digest, May, 1965.
New York Times Book Review, February 27, 1966.
Phylon, June, 1977.
Saturday Review, January 16, 1965, October 16, 1965, April 23, 1966, March 23, 1968.
Times Literary Supplement, May 5, 1966.

*   *   *

BERRY, Mary Frances   1938-

PERSONAL: Born February 17, 1938, in Nashville, Tenn.; daughter of George F. and Frances (Southall) Berry. *Education:* Howard University, B.A., 1961, M.A., 1962; University of Michigan, Ph.D., 1966, J.D., 1970.

ADDRESSES: Office—Howard University Law School, 2400 Sixth St. N.W., Washington, D.C. 20001.

CAREER: Central Michigan University, Mount Pleasant, assistant professor of history, 1966-68; Eastern Michigan University, Ypsilanti, assistant professor, 1968-70, associate professor of history, 1970; University of Maryland, College Park, associate professor of history, 1969; University of Colorado, Boulder, faculty member, 1976-80; Howard University, Washington, D.C., professor of history and law, 1980—. Adjunct associate professor, University of Michigan, 1970-71. Former chancellor, University of Colorado; former provost, University of Maryland. Former Assistant Secretary for Education, Department of Health, Education, and Welfare.

MEMBER: American Historical Association, Organization of American Historians, American Society for the Study of Legal History.

WRITINGS:

Black Resistance/White Law: A History of Constitutional Racism in America, Appleton, 1971.
Military Necessity and Civil Rights Policy: Black Citizenship and the Constitution, 1861-1868, Kennikat, 1977.
Stability, Security, and Continuity: Mr. Justice Burton and Decision-Making in the Supreme Court, 1945-1958, Greenwood Press, 1978.
(With John W. Blassingame) *Long Memory: The Black Experience in America,* Oxford University Press, 1982.
Why ERA Failed: Women's Rights, and the Amending Process of the Constitution, Indiana University Press, 1986.

Contributor of articles and reviews to history and law journals.

BETI, Mongo
  See BIYIDI, Alexandre

*   *   *

BINLIN-DADIE, Bernard
  See DADIE, Bernard Binlin

*   *   *

BISHOP, Maurice 1944-1983

PERSONAL: Born May 29, 1944, in Aruba; executed, October 19, 1983, in St. George, Grenada. *Education:* Attended Presentation College in Grenada; studied law in London, England.

CAREER: Called to the Bar at Gray's Inn, 1969; founder of Movement for Assemblies of the People, Grenada, 1972; founder of New Jewel (Joint Endeavor for Welfare, Education, and Liberation) Movement, Grenada, 1973; Grenada Government, opposition leader in Parliament, beginning in 1976, minister for foreign and home affairs, information, and culture, and for national security and Carriacou affairs, 1979-81, prime minister, 1979-83, minister for defense, the interior, and health, beginning in 1981. Former minister for Petit Martinique affairs.

WRITINGS:

Forward Ever! Pathfinder Press, 1982.
Maurice Bishop Speaks: The Grenada Revolution, 1979-1983, edited by Bruce Marcus and Michael Taber, Pathfinder Press, 1984.
In Nobody's Backyard: Maurice Bishop's Speeches, 1979-1983, a Memorial Volume, Humanities, 1984.

SIDELIGHTS: Maurice Bishop, a lawyer and political activist in the Caribbean island nation Grenada, was the leader of the leftist New Jewel Movement, which peacefully overthrew Prime Minister Eric Gairy in 1979 while Gairy was out of the country. As the new prime minister of Grenada, Bishop promoted moderate socialism, accepting aid from Communist countries, including Cuba and the Soviet Union, while allowing private business to continue with little government interference. He was credited with increasing the country's exports, stabilizing its economy, improving health and education, and undertaking public works such as the construction of new roads. His Communist contacts, however, unsettled U.S. authorities, who especially questioned Bishop's motives in building (with Cuban assistance) an airport judged larger than Grenada's tourism required—large enough to accommodate state-of-the-art Soviet fighter planes.

Bishop's administration encountered internal difficulties also. Headed by Deputy Prime Minister Bernard Coard, a stricter Marxist faction challenged Bishop for power, and the escalating turmoil ended when Coard's military supporters arrested and executed Bishop in October, 1983. The takeover—the first violent one in the eastern Caribbean—spurred a U.S. invasion of Grenada by nearly two thousand Marines, ostensibly to protect the one thousand Americans on the island. Some observers later asserted that the United States, in fact, wished to prevent another revolutionary government from forming.

In 1982 Bishop published *Forward Ever!,* and after his death a volume of his speeches appeared. *Maurice Bishop Speaks: The Grenada Revolution, 1979-1983* documents the New Jewel Movement revolution and includes Bishop's final speech, given four months before his death.

BIOGRAPHICAL/CRITICAL SOURCES:

PERIODICALS

Business Week, December 27, 1982, January 3, 1983.
Encore, May 9, 1980.
Newsweek, March 31, 1980.
Time, October 31, 1983.
Times (London), October 21, 1983.
Washington Post, March 17, 1979.

*   *   *

BIYIDI, Alexandre 1932-
  (Mongo Beti, Eza Boto)

PERSONAL: Professionally known as Mongo Beti; born June 30, 1932, in M'Balmayo (one source says Akometam), Cameroon; married; children: three. *Education:* Attended University of Aix-Marseille; received B.A. (with honors) from Sorbonne, University of Paris, M.A., 1966. *Politics:* Marxist.

ADDRESSES: Agent—Helena Strassova, Paris, France.

CAREER: Educator in Lamballe, France; secondary education instructor in classical Greek, Latin, and French literature in Rouen, France. Writer, 1953—.

AWARDS, HONORS: Sainte-Beuve Prize, 1948, for *Mission Accomplished,* and 1957, for *King Lazarus.*

WRITINGS:

NOVELS; UNDER PSEUDONYM MONGO BETI, EXCEPT AS NOTED:

(Under pseudonym Eza Boto) *Ville cruelle* (title means "Cruel City"), Editions Africaines, 1954.
Le Pauvre Christ de Bomba, Laffont, 1956, translation by Gerald Moore published as *The Poor Christ of Bomba,* Heinemann Educational [London], African Writers Series, 1971.
Mission terminee, Buchet Chastel/Correa, 1957, translation by Peter Green published as *Mission Accomplished,* Macmillan, 1958 (published in England as *Mission to Kala,* Muller, 1958), rewritten by John Davey and published as *Mission to Kala* (illustrated by Peter Edwards), Heinemann Educational, African Writers Series, 1964.
Le Roi miracule: Chronique des Essazam, Buchet Chastel/Correa, 1958, English translation published as *King Lazarus,* Muller [London], 1960, published as *King Lazarus: A Novel* (introduction by O. R. Dathorne), Macmillan/Collier, 1971.
Main basse sur le Cameroun: Autopsie d'une decolonisation (political essay; title means "The Plundering of Cameroon"), F. Maspero, 1972.
Remember Ruben (title in pidgin English), Buchet Chastel, 1973, translation by Gerald Moore published under the same title, Three Continents Press, 1980.
Perpetue et l'habitude du malheur, Buchet Chastel, 1974, translation by John Reed and Clive Wake published as *Perpetua and the Habit of Unhappiness,* Heinemann Educational, African Writers Series, 1978.
La Ruine presque cocasse d'un polichinelle: Remember Ruben deux, Harmattan, 1979, translation by Richard Bjornson published as *Lament for an African Pol,* Three Continents Press, 1985.
Les Deux Meres de Guillaume Ismael Dzewatama: Futur Camionneur, Buchet Chastel, 1982.
La Revanche de Guillaume Ismael Dzewatama, Buchet Chastel, 1984.

Founder in 1978 and editor of *Peuples noirs Peuples africains* (tribune of French-speaking black radicals). Contributor during the early 1960s to the anti-colonial journals *Tumultueux Cameroun* and *Revue camerounaise*.

SIDELIGHTS: Born in the Cameroon town of M'Balmayo and educated in French missionary schools and universities, Mongo Beti, as he prefers to be known, centers his novels on the encroachment of Western ideals, education, and religion upon African civilization. In particular, he laments the inability of European administrators and missionaries during the early twentieth century colonial rule to recognize the inherent value of existing African religions and beliefs, as well as the Africans' own inability to withstand European influence. Calling Beti "one of the most elegant and sophisticated of African writers," Eustace Palmer reflected in his book *The Growth of the African Novel* that "taken as a whole [Beti's work] probably gives the most thoroughgoing exposure to the stupidity of the imperialist attempt to devalue traditional education and religion and replace them by an inadequate western educational system and a hypocritical Christian religion."

In his first four novels, written from 1954 to 1958, Beti couches his disdain for European imperialist advances and his own countrymen's gullibility in episodic tales combining comic farce and bitter satire. Thomas Cassirer pointed out in a *L'Esprit Createur* review that each of Beti's anti-imperialist novels features an "African village . . . situated at the meeting point between traditional communal life and a new awareness of imminent change." When European administrators and missionaries—sometimes well-meaning and sometimes corrupt, but always ignorant—arrive in an untouched African village, misunderstanding and chaos inevitably ensue. Beti emphasizes the absurdity of the misunderstandings, suggesting through satire the harm that befalls both the modern and traditional societies when their people attempt to impose conflicting values on one another.

While a student at Aix, Beti penned his first novel, *Ville cruelle*—which means "Cruel City"—under the pseudonym Eza Boto. He has since repudiated both the name and the novel, which is generally considered weak and melodramatic. Critics have noted, however, that this early effort displays much of the perceptive wit found in his later writings. Set in Tanga, the site of lumber mills and rail yards, the novel details the bewilderment and anger of African workers and their families at this unsolicited imposition of Western industrialization.

In *The Poor Christ of Bomba,* set in the colonial 1930s, comic irony arises when the well-meaning Reverend Father Superior Drumont sets out to convert the inhabitants of a bush village and save them from the greed and temptation that had corrupted Europeans, later to discover that the Africans had only embraced his religion hoping to learn the Europeans' secrets of material success. He also learns that the "sixa," a missionary house where African girls live for several months to learn the duties of a Christian wife, has become an agent not of Christian piety but of venereal disease. "Faced with this horrendous proof that he has unknowingly [perpetrated] the very corruption from which he tried to protect the Africans," Cassirer related, "Father Drumont returns to Europe in despair."

Father Drumont represents the type of missionary Beti treats sympathetically in his novels, according to Cassirer. "They are . . . the only ones who explicitly believe in a universal humanity that transcends barriers of race and culture," he explained. "Yet the missionaries' faith in universal humanity remains purely abstract because their primitivist view of the African leads them to treat him as a pure child of nature with no cultural identity of his own." A. C. Brench further described Beti's missionaries in *The Novelists' Inheritance in French Africa* as "the kind who want to do good for the Africans but, unfortunately for them, start from the premise that all Africans are unable to organize their lives unless helped by Europeans." This well-meaning denial of an inherent African culture and intellect is not only insulting to Africans, Brench suggested, but is harmful to both cultures, as the character Father Drumont learns. "The change that takes place in the Father is one of the most interesting features of the novel," Palmer found. Although not all missionaries are so enlightened during the course of their work, Palmer explained, with each discovery of a failed good intention "the Father seems to be gradually groping his way towards a realization of the validity of traditional life and culture."

The missionary in *King Lazarus,* Father Le Guen, is somewhat more zealous and uncompromising than Father Drumont of *The Poor Christ of Bomba.* Palmer noted, "Thematically, [*King Lazarus*] is similar to the earlier novels since it is also concerned with the exposure of the pretentiousness of an alien cultural and imperialist system which shows little respect for the traditional life and dignity of the people." In the novel, Father Le Guen persuades the polygamous tribal chief of the Essazam to convert to Christianity and give up all but one of his wives. The twenty-two former wives and their families, outraged at the breach of tribal custom as well as at the rudeness of turning the women out of their home, protest to the French colonial authorities. In the confrontation between the civil administration, the missionary, and the tribal chief, Beti exposes the vices of each party. The authorities, attempting to stop Father Le Guen from converting the chief, do not do so out of any respect for the tribal culture but for reasons of political expediency, Palmer pointed out. Father Le Guen believes his firm stand on Christianity and monogamy are for the best, but he ignores such thoughtful and practical considerations as where the now-homeless ex-wives will live. "His zeal might have been partly excused if the conversion to Christianity had made the chief a better man," Palmer maintained. "On the contrary, it seems to liberate the most repulsive impulses in him." Irony and comedy pervade in *King Lazarus* as in Beti's other works, but, according to Palmer, "its prevailing cynicism suggests the bitterness of a man who is probably fed up with most things."

Like *The Poor Christ of Bomba* and *King Lazarus,* Beti's *Mission Accomplished* "is a farce but, at the same time, there is bitterness and sorrow," judged Brench. Set in the 1950s—the last decade of colonial rule in Cameroon—the novel details the shortcomings of the colonial educational system. No whites appear in the novel, but European influence is introduced by the protagonist, Jean-Marie Medza, who returns to his village home after failing his exams at a French secondary school. He is immediately sent to Kala, a bush village, to retrieve the runaway wife of a distant relative. "Initially, he looks upon this mission as a means of parading his superior knowledge," Brench related, and the villagers reward him with food, animals, and the chief's daughter in marriage for the wisdom they believe he is teaching them. "Only later does he realize how inadequate his education and understanding of life really are," Brench remarked. "Jean-Marie appreciates more and more, as his stay lengthens, the positive qualities they have and which he has never been able to acquire."

Summarizing Beti's thesis in the novel, Palmer explained that "the formal classical education to which young francophones were exposed was ultimately valueless, since it alienated them from their roots in traditional society, taught them to consider the values of that society inferior to French ones and gave them little preparation for the life they were to lead.''

An opponent of the French government in control of his country and, later, of the Yaounde regime in power, Beti left Cameroon before it achieved its independence in 1960. After settling in France, Beti became a teacher and for more than a decade gave up writing. In 1972, however, he composed a lengthy essay entitled *Main basse sur le Cameroun: Autopsie d'une decolonisation* (the title means ''The Plundering of Cameroon''), criticizing the Yaounde regime for remaining under the control of the French after the country's formal liberation.

A series of novels soon followed, focusing more on the problems of modern, decolonized Cameroon than on the country during its colonization. Still containing elements of satire, the books assume a documentary-style narrative and approach cynicism more closely than Beti's previous works. In *Remember Ruben, Perpetua and the Habit of Unhappiness*, and *Lament for an African Pol*, Beti depicts the harsh aspects of life under the rule of Baba Toura, a tyrannical president of the United Republic of Cameroon after the country's independence. Wrote Robert P. Smith, Jr., in *World Literature Today*, ''Toura's administration, which fosters famine, misery, persecution and corruption in the wake of African independence, is perpetuated by evil characters in the novels against whom heroic protagonists struggle constantly.'' Heroic inspiration arises from the memory of patriot Ruben Um Nyobe, leader of political opposition in Cameroon before its independence. Although Ruben himself never appears in the novels, tales of his valiant deeds and lofty ideals motivate oppressed villagers into revolutionary action.

Remember Ruben follows the life of a solitary, young boy renamed Mor-Zamba by the villagers who take him in, and a friend he makes, Abena. When Mor-Zamba is older his neighbors send him to a labor camp to prevent his marriage to the daughter of a prominent villager, and Abena goes after him. The men reunite eighteen years later, Abena having become a revolutionary and a hero, and Mor-Zamba having learned his true origin. Ben Okri of *New Statesman* praised the author's handling of ''the relationship between individuals and a complex, clouded situation of emerging national politics,'' adding that ''Beti's depiction of a colony's traumas, confusions and corruptions is vivid and masterly.''

Again emphasizing the corruption of national politics through glimpses of the harshness of individual lives, Beti laments the slave-like conditions of the modern woman in contemporary Africa in his *Perpetua and the Habit of Unhappiness*. The novel focuses on the miserable marriage of the main character, Perpetua, to her husband, Edouard; the tender but doomed affair between Perpetua and her lover, Zeyang; and the true friendship between Perpetua and her companion, Anna-Marie. Robert P. Smith, Jr., writing in the *College Language Association Journal*, called the novel ''a dramatic indictment of the ill-fated independence in [Beti's] native land dominated by corrupt dictatorial power, as well as a forceful denunciation of the disgraceful status of African women in such regimes.'' Smith praised Beti's treatment of modern-day Africa, saying the author wrote *Perpetua* ''not to criticize the colonial past as was his custom, but to accuse the present period of independence and self-government, and to pave the way to a better future for Africa and Africans.''

A novel that ''no serious reader of African literature can afford to neglect,'' advised *Choice*'s N. F. Lazarus, Beti's *Lament for an African Pol* chronicles the activities of Mor-Zamba, who reappears from the novel *Remember Ruben* with two revolutionary friends to organize a resistance ''against the despotic rule of a colonially sanctioned chief.'' According to Smith in *World Literature Today*, ''the novel takes on a 'Robin Hood' atmosphere when the three resolute Rubenists set out on their long journey, robbing the rich and giving to the poor, outwitting the oppressors and conveying courage to the oppressed.'' Affirming that Beti's ''storytelling technique remains vibrant and captivating,'' Smith noted that, as in *Perpetua*, ''of particular interest is the author's sympathetic treatment of African women.''

Again ''studying marriage patterns and the evolving roles of women,'' Beti's 1982 novel, *Les Deux Meres de Guillaume Ismael Dzewatama: Futur Camionneur*, recounts ''a curious love story, full of drama, harmonizing the political and literary,'' assessed Hal Wylie in a review of the book in *World Literature Today*. Wylie explained that, similar to Beti's other writings, *Les Deux Meres* ''focuses on a unique family which nevertheless dramatizes the sad plight of a corrupt, dictatorial country like Beti's own Cameroon.'' The family in the novel consists of young Guillaume Ismael, his father, and Guillaume's two mothers—the father's first wife and his French mistress, whom he married to resolve a difficult situation. The double marriage solves nothing; instead, it prompts more confusion. Reflected Wylie, ''Seeing the tensions from the point of view of the African boy and his good-hearted, idealistic but naive white mother throws into relief the melodrama and pathos of modern Africa and all its ironies.''

Commenting on Beti's range of political and social statements and his episodic, satirical method of conveying them, Brench remarked: ''Nothing is sacred: prejudices, passions, ideals, purity are all corrupted by Beti's unrelenting laughter and insistence on the physical nature of things. . . . Yet, behind all this there is this inexpressible sadness, as if a great deception had made life bitter and cynical humour was the only relief.'' Several critics have pointed to a statement about Cameroon made by the character Jean-Marie at the end of *Mission Accomplished*, calling it Beti's lament for the plight of the African people: ''The tragedy which our nation is suffering today is that of a man left to his own devices in a world which does not belong to him, which he has not made and does not understand.''

MEDIA ADAPTATIONS: Perpetua and the Habit of Unhappiness was adapted by Michael Etherton as a play by the same title; it was first produced in Zaria, Nigeria, in 1981.

BIOGRAPHICAL/CRITICAL SOURCES:

BOOKS

Brench, A. C., *The Novelists' Inheritance in French Africa: Writers From Senegal to Cameroon*, Oxford University Press, 1967.
Contemporary Literary Criticism, Volume 27, Gale, 1984.
Moore, Gerald, *Seven African Writers*, Oxford University Press, 1962.
Palmer, Eustace, *The Growth of the African Novel*, Heinemann Educational, 1979.
The Penguin Companion to Classical, Oriental, and African Literature, McGraw, 1969.

PERIODICALS

Choice, October, 1975, January, 1986.

College Language Association Journal, March, 1976.
Journal of Black Studies, December, 1976.
L'Esprit Createur, autumn, 1970.
Nation, October 11, 1965.
New Statesman, January 30, 1981.
Times Literary Supplement, May 15, 1969, October 29, 1971.
World Literature Today, winter, 1982, winter, 1984.

—*Sketch by Christa Brelin*

* * *

BLASSINGAME, John W(esley) 1940-

PERSONAL: Born March 23, 1940, in Covington, Ga. *Education:* Fort Valley State College, B.A., 1960; Howard University, M.A., 1961; Yale University, M.Phil., 1968, Ph.D., 1971.

ADDRESSES: Office—Department of Afro-American Studies, Yale University, New Haven, Conn. 06520.

CAREER: Howard University, Washington, D.C., instructor in social science, 1961-65; Carnegie-Mellon University, Pittsburgh, Pa., associate of curriculum project in American history, 1965-70; Yale University, New Haven, Conn., lecturer, 1970-71, assistant professor, 1971-72, associate professor of history, 1972-73, professor, 1974—, acting chairman of Afro-American studies, 1971-72. Lecturer at University of Maryland and assistant editor of Booker T. Washington papers, 1968-69. Member of advisory board of Afro-American Bicentennial Corp., 1971—; member of board of directors of Centre Internationale de Recherches Africaines, 1971—.

MEMBER: American Historical Association (member of review board, 1972-73; member of executive council, 1974), Organization of American Historians (chairman of progressive committee, 1974), Association for the Study of Afro-American Life and History (member of executive council, 1973—), Association of Behavioral and Social Sciences, Southern Historical Association, Phi Alpha Theta.

AWARDS, HONORS: Fellowship from National Endowment for the Humanities, 1972-73.

WRITINGS:

(Editor) *New Perspectives on Black Studies*, University of Illinois Press, 1971.
(Editor with David Fowler, Eugene Levy, and Jacqueline Haywood) *In Search of America*, Holt, 1972.
(Editor with Louis Harlan) *The Booker T. Washington Papers*, Volume I: *The Autobiographical Writings*, University of Illinois Press, 1972.
The Slave Community: Plantation Life in the Antebellum South, Oxford University Press, 1972, revised and enlarged edition, 1979.
Black New Orleans: 1860-1880, University of Chicago Press, 1973.
(Contributor) William H. Cartwright and Richard L. Watson, editors, *The Reinterpretation of American History*, National Council for the Social Studies, 1973.
(Editor) *Slave Testimony: Two Centuries of Letters, Speeches, Interviews, and Autobiographies*, Louisiana State University Press, 1977.
(Contributor) Al-Tony Gilmore, editor, *Revisiting Blassingame's "The Slave Community,"* Greenwood Press, 1978.
(Editor with others) *The Frederick Douglass Papers; Series 1: Speeches, Debates, and Interviews*, Yale University Press,

Volume 1: *1841-1846*, 1979, Volume 2: *1847-1854*, 1982, Volume 3: *1855-1863*, 1985.
(Editor) *Antislavery Newspapers and Periodicals*, G. K. Hall, Volumes I-III (with Mae G. Henderson), 1980-81, Volumes IV-V (with Henderson and Jessica M. Dunn), 1984.
(With Mary F. Berry) *Long Memory: The Black Experience in America*, Oxford University Press, 1982.

Contributor to *Encyclopedia of Black America*. Contributor of more than twenty articles and reviews to history journals, including *Journal of Southern History*, *Black Scholar*, *Journal of Social History*, *Journal of Negro History*, *Caribbean Studies*, and *Journal of Negro Education*. Contributing editor of *Black Scholar*, 1971—; member of editorial boards of *Reviews in American History*, 1973-76, *Journal of Negro History*, 1973-77, *Southern Studies*, and *Integrated Education*. Editor of Frederick Douglass papers, jointly sponsored by National Endowment for the Humanities and National Historical Publications Commission, 1973—.

BIOGRAPHICAL/CRITICAL SOURCES:

BOOKS

Contemporary Issues Criticism, Volume 1, Gale, 1982.

* * *

BOMKAUF
See KAUFMAN, Bob (Garnell)

* * *

BOND, Julian 1940-

PERSONAL: Born January 14, 1940, in Nashville, Tenn.; son of Horace Mann (a dean of education and former college president) and Julia Agnes (a college librarian; maiden name, Washington) Bond; married Alice Louise Clopton, July 28, 1961; children: Phyllis Jane, Horace Mann, Michael Julian, Jeffrey, Julia. *Education:* Morehouse College, B.A., 1971.

ADDRESSES: Home—361 Westview Dr. S.W., Atlanta, Ga. 30310. *Office*—State Senate, Georgia General Assembly, Atlanta, Ga. 30334.

CAREER: Atlanta Inquirer, Atlanta, Ga., reporter and feature writer, 1960-61, managing editor, 1963; Student Nonviolent Coordinating Committee (SNCC), Atlanta, co-founder, 1960, communications director, 1961-66; representative from Atlanta's 111th District, Georgia House of Representatives, 1967-74; senator, Georgia State Senate, 1974—; candidate for U.S. Congress, 1986.

Lecturer; visiting fellow, Metropolitan Applied Research Center of New York City, 1967. Co-chairman of Georgia Loyal National Convention. President, Institute for Southern Studies. Research associate of Voter Education Project, 1968; honorary trustee, Institute of Applied Politics. Member of board of numerous organizations, including Delta Ministry Project of National Council of Churches, Robert F. Kennedy Memorial Fund, Martin Luther King, Jr., Center for Social Change, Center for Community Change, Highlander Research and Education Center, National Sharecroppers' Fund, Southern Regional Council, New Democratic Coalition, Voter Education Project, and Southern Elections Fund.

MEMBER: Southern Correspondents Reporting Racial Equality Wars, National Association for the Advancement of Colored People (president of Atlanta branch; member of board), IPFU, Phi Kappa.

AWARDS, HONORS: LL.D. from Dalhousie University, University of Bridgeport, Wesleyan University, and University of Oregon, all 1969, Syracuse University, 1970, and Eastern Michigan University, Tuskegee Institute, Howard University, Morgan State University, and Wilberforce University, all 1971; D.C.L. from Lincoln University, 1970.

WRITINGS:

(With Kenneth B. Clark and Richard G. Hatcher) *The Black Man in American Politics: Three Views,* Metropolitan Applied Research Center for the Institute for Black Elected Officials, 1969.

(Author of foreword) Angela Davis, *If They Come in the Morning,* Third Press, 1971.

A Time to Speak, A Time to Act: The Movement in Politics, Simon & Schuster, 1972.

Black Candidates, Voter Education Project, in press.

CONTRIBUTOR

Arna Bontemps, editor, *American Negro Poetry,* Hill & Wang, 1963.

Langston Hughes, editor, *New Negro Poets U.S.A.,* Indiana University Press, 1964.

Hughes, editor, *The Book of Negro Humor,* Dodd, 1965.

James Finn, editor, *Pacifism and Politics: Some Passionate Views on War and Nonviolence,* Random House, 1968.

OTHER

Contributor of poems and articles to periodicals, including *Negro Digest, motive, Rights and Reviews, Life, Freedomways,* and *Ramparts.*

SIDELIGHTS: Julian Bond first became known during the 1960s as a leading civil rights activist. One of the founders of the Student Nonviolent Coordinating Committee, a prominent civil rights group active on college campuses, Bond became a national figure when he was elected to a seat in the Georgia House of Representatives in 1965, but was prevented from taking office by members of the legislature who objected to his statements about the war in Viet Nam. After winning a second election in 1966, a special House Committee again voted to bar him from membership in the legislature. Bond won a third election in November, 1966; in December, 1966, the U.S. Supreme Court ruled unanimously that the Georgia House had erred in refusing him his seat. He officially became a member of the Georgia House of Representatives on January 7, 1967. In 1974, he was elected to the Georgia State Senate.

At the Democratic National Convention in 1968, Bond led an unrecognized, rival delegation from Georgia, charging that the local party leadership had deliberately kept blacks from participating in the nomination process. He argued that the officially-sanctioned state delegation should not be seated. After a heated battle, his group was granted half the votes normally given to the Georgia delegation.

It was at this same convention that Bond made history, becoming the first black man to have his name entered for the nomination for the vice-presidential spot on the Democratic Party ticket. "Young and good-looking," as a writer for *Newsweek* puts it, "[Bond] became a media darling and was hailed as heir to the legacy of Martin Luther King." As Nicholas von Hoffman remarked in the *Washington Post* in 1972,

"Julian Bond is the only person since King to command a national constituency of blacks, whites and young people."

During the 1970s and 1980s, Bond served as a Georgia state senator. This was in keeping with his belief that blacks can best advance their position in American society by actively working in the political arena. His book *A Time to Speak, A Time to Act: The Movement in Politics* outlines Bond's political strategy. G. L. Chamberlain of *America* explains that the book is "a call and a brief blueprint for the election of black people through black solidarity and a vision for black-white coalitions." Norman Lederer of the *Library Journal* states Bond's message as "the necessity for blacks to form pragmatic, workable coalitions with various non-black dissenting groups in the U.S. to effect meaningful social change."

In 1986, Bond attempted to win a seat in the U.S. Congress but was defeated for the Democratic nomination. The congressional campaign was marred by a challenge from Bond's opponent, John Lewis, that Bond submit to a drug test. He refused. In 1987, the question of his possible drug use resurfaced when Bond's estranged wife told police that her husband was a cocaine addict. She later recanted her accusation.

Despite these recent trials, Bond retains what Walter Isaacson of *Time* calls "the boyish smile and laid-back cool that made him a celebrity in the '60s." And von Hoffman notes that Bond "can lay claim to his own personality, with its own kind of suave and charm and power to get his people up and cheering."

BIOGRAPHICAL/CRITICAL SOURCES:

PERIODICALS

America, August 19, 1972.
Detroit Free Press, May 31, 1980.
Ebony, May, 1969.
Encore, January 16, 1978.
Essence, November, 1983.
Harper's Bazaar, January, 1972.
Library Journal, June 15, 1972.
Newsweek, August 16, 1976, April 27, 1987.
Time, October 25, 1976, August 4, 1986.
Virginia Quarterly Review, autumn, 1972.
Washington Post, October 1, 1968, February 23, 1972.

*   *   *

BONTEMPS, Arna(ud Wendell)   1902-1973

PERSONAL: Born October 13, 1902, in Alexandria, La.; died of a heart attack, June 4, 1973, in Nashville, Tenn.; son of Paul Bismark (a brick mason) and Maria Caroline (a teacher; maiden name, Pembrooke) Bontemps; married Alberta Johnson, August 26, 1926; children: Joan Marie Bontemps Williams, Paul Bismark, Poppy Alberta Bontemps Booker, Camille Ruby Bontemps Graves, Constance Rebecca Bontemps Thomas, Arna Alex. *Education:* Pacific Union College, B.A., 1923; University of Chicago, M.A., 1943.

ADDRESSES: Home—3506 Geneva Cir., Nashville, Tenn. 37209. *Office*—Fisk University, Nashville, Tenn. 37203.

CAREER: Teacher in New York, N.Y., Huntsville, Ala., and Chicago, Ill., 1923-38; Fisk University, Nashville, librarian, 1943-65; University of Illinois at Chicago Circle, professor, 1966-69; Yale University, New Haven, Conn., visiting professor and curator of James Weldon Johnson Collection, 1969;

Fisk University, writer in residence, 1970-73. Member of Metropolitan Nashville Board of Education.

MEMBER: National Association for the Advancement of Colored People, P.E.N., American Library Association, Dramatists Guild, Sigma Pi Phi, Omega Psi Phi.

AWARDS, HONORS: Poetry prize from *Crisis* magazine, 1926; Alexander Pushkin poetry prizes, 1926 and 1927; short story prize from *Opportunity*, 1932; Julius Rosenwald fellowship, 1938-39 and 1942-43; Guggenheim fellowship for creative writing, 1949-50; Jane Addams Children's Book Award, 1956, for *Story of the Negro;* Dow Award from Society of Midland Authors, 1967, for *Anyplace But Here;* L.H.D. from Morgan State College, 1969.

WRITINGS:

God Sends Sunday (novel), Harcourt, 1931, reprinted, AMS Press, 1972.

(With Langston Hughes) *Popo and Fifina: Children of Haiti* (juvenile), Macmillan, 1932.

You Can't Pet a Possum, Morrow, 1934.

Black Thunder (historical novel), Macmillan, 1936, reprinted with new introduction by author, Beacon Press, 1968.

Sad Faced Boy (juvenile), Houghton, 1937.

Drums at Dusk (novel), Macmillan, 1939.

(Compiler) *Golden Slippers: An Anthology of Negro Poetry for Young Readers,* Harper, 1941.

(Editor) W. C. Handy, *Father of the Blues: An Autobiography,* Macmillan, 1941, reprinted, Collier, 1970, reprinted, Da Capo Press, 1985.

(With Jack Conroy) *The Fast Sooner Hound* (juvenile), Houghton, 1942.

(With Conroy) *They Seek a City* (history), Doubleday, 1945, revised edition published as *Anyplace But Here,* Hill & Wang, 1966.

We Have Tomorrow (history), Houghton, 1945.

(With Conroy) *Slappy Hooper, the Wonderful Sign Painter* (juvenile), Houghton, 1946.

(With Countee Cullen) "St. Louis Woman" (play; adapted from Bontemps's novel *God Sends Sunday*), first produced on Broadway at Martin Beck Theatre, March 30, 1946; published in *Black Theatre,* edited by Lindsay Patterson, Dodd, 1971.

Story of the Negro, Knopf, 1948, 5th edition, 1969.

(Editor with Hughes) *The Poetry of the Negro: 1746-1949,* Doubleday, 1949, revised edition published as *The Poetry of the Negro: 1746-1970,* 1970.

"Free and Easy" (play), first produced in Amsterdam at Theatre Carre, December 15, 1949.

George Washington Carver, Row, Peterson, 1950.

(With Conroy) *Sam Patch, the High, Wide and Handsome Jumper* (juvenile), Houghton, 1951.

Chariot in the Sky: A Story of the Jubilee Singers (juvenile), Winston, 1951, new edition, Holt, 1971.

The Story of George Washington Carver (juvenile biography), Grosset, 1954.

Lonesome Boy (juvenile), Houghton, 1955.

(Editor with Hughes) *The Book of Negro Folklore,* Dodd, 1958, 2nd edition, 1983.

Frederick Douglass: Slave, Fighter, Freeman, Knopf, 1958.

(Author of introduction) James Weldon Johnson, *The Autobiography of an Ex-Colored Man,* Hill & Wang, 1960.

One Hundred Years of Negro Freedom (history), Dodd, 1961, reprinted, Greenwood Press, 1980.

(Editor) *American Negro Poetry,* Hill & Wang, 1963, revised edition, 1974.

Personals, Paul Bremen, 1963, 2nd edition, 1973.

Famous Negro Athletes (juvenile), Dodd, 1964.

(With Hughes) *I Too Sing America,* Verlag Lamber Lensing, 1964.

(Editor with others) *American Negro Heritage,* Century Schoolbooks Press, 1965.

(Contributor) Herbert Hill, editor, *Anger, and Beyond,* Harper, 1966.

(Compiler and author of introduction) *Great Slave Narratives,* Beacon Press, 1969.

(Author of introduction) Langston Hughes, *Don't You Turn Back: Poems,* Knopf, 1969.

(Compiler) *Hold Fast to Dreams: Poems Old and New,* Follett, 1969.

Mr. Kelso's Lion, Lippincott, 1970.

Free at Last: The Life of Frederick Douglass, Dodd, 1971.

(Editor with others) *Five Black Lives: The Autobiographies of Venture Smith, James Mars, William Grimes, G. W. Offley, and James L. Smith,* Wesleyan University Press, 1971.

Young Booker: Booker T. Washington's Early Days, Dodd, 1972.

(Editor and author of commentary) *The Harlem Renaissance Remembered: Essays,* Dodd, 1972.

The Old South: "A Summer Tragedy" and Other Stories of the Thirties, Dodd, 1973.

Arna Bontemps-Langston Hughes Letters, 1925-1967, edited by Charles H. Nichols, Dodd, 1980.

Author of plays "Creole" and "Careless Love." Fiction represented in numerous anthologies, including *Grandma Moses' Story Book,* Random House, 1961. Contributor to periodicals, including *Crisis, Ebony, Harper's,* and *Saturday Review.*

SIDELIGHTS: Arna Bontemps, who was born in Louisiana and raised in California, returned to the South to take the post of librarian at Fisk University and "to write something about the changes I have seen in my lifetime, and about the Negro's awakening and regeneration. That is my theme, and this is where the main action is." For Bontemps, the resolution of American racism should not result in the superimposition of black people on white culture; rather, the "shedding of . . . Negroness is not only impossible but unthinkable. . . . The Southern Negro's link with his past seems to me worth preserving. His greater pride in being himself, I would say, is all to the good, and I think I detect a growing nostalgia for these virtues."

Jonathan Yardley found this nostalgia in Bontemps's book *The Old South.* He commented that the fourteen stories in this book "occupy a territory somewhere between fiction and personal reminiscence. They are low-key, informal and chatty, but possessed of more depth than one initially realizes. Most of them are set in the Depression which was an especially bad time for Southern blacks, yet their mood is neither despairing nor bitter. Rather, Bontemps writes nostalgically about boyhood in the rural South. . . . There are, to be sure, depictions of the terror that could strike the lives of smalltown blacks in the 1930s, but overall the stories convey a genuine love for the South, its people and its land."

In a memorial essay, Virginia Lacy Jones commented on Bontemps's role in American literature. She wrote that his death "marked the end of a brilliant career of an editor, writer, librarian, literary critic, and teacher. He began writing in the early 1920s during the epoch in black literary production known as the Harlem Renaissance, at which time he was closely associated with black poets Langston Hughes, Countee Cullen, James Weldon Johnson, Claude McKay, Sterling Brown, and others, as well as with Charles Johnson, the sociologist, Alain Locke, the prominent cultural historian of the period, and Arthur Schomburg, the famous collector of Negro literature and history. As one of the last survivors of this august group of black writers and artists, he was in constant demand to write and speak. . . . After having produced more than 25 books, . . . Arna Bontemps became a literary critic of considerable stature. His critical insights have been and will continue to be invaluable in the development of understanding and appreciation of black literature and history.''

AVOCATIONAL INTERESTS: Literature, theatre, and sports.

BIOGRAPHICAL/CRITICAL SOURCES:

BOOKS

Baker, Houston A., Jr., *Black Literature in America*, McGraw, 1971.
Bone, Robert A., *The Negro Novel in America*, Yale University Press, 1965.
Contemporary Literary Criticism, Gale, Volume 1, 1973, Volume 18, 1981.
Dictionary of Literary Biography, Gale, Volume 48: *American Poets, 1880-1945*, Second Series, 1986, Volume 51: *Afro-American Writers From the Harlem Renaissance to 1940*, 1987.
Nichols, Charles H., editor, *Arna Bontemps-Langston Hughes Letters, 1925-1967*, Dodd, 1980.

PERIODICALS

Black World, September, 1973.
Harper's, April, 1965.
Library Journal, July, 1973.
National Review, September 15, 1972.
Negro Digest, September, 1963, August, 1967.
New Republic, November 4, 1972, January 14, 1974.
New York Times Book Review, December 23, 1973.
Washington Post Book World, September 7, 1969.

*   *   *

BOTO, Eza
    See BIYIDI, Alexandre

*   *   *

BRADLEY, David (Henry, Jr.)   1950-

PERSONAL: Born September 7, 1950, in Bedford, Pa.; son of David Henry (a minister and historian) and Harriette M. (maiden name, Jackson) Bradley. *Education:* University of Pennsylvania, B.A. (summa cum laude), 1972; attended Institute for United States Studies, London; King's College, London, M.A., 1974.

ADDRESSES: Home—433270 Viamarin, La Jolla, Calif. 92024. *Office*—Department of English, Temple University, Philadelphia, Pa. 19122. *Agent*—Wendy Weil Literary Agency, Inc., 747 Third Ave., New York, N.Y. 10017.

CAREER: Educational Testing Service, Princeton, N.J., research assistant with Office of Data Analysis and Research, 1971; J. B. Lippincott Co. (publisher), Philadelphia, Pa., assistant editor in Philadelphia and New York, N.Y., 1974-76;

Temple University, Philadelphia, visiting instructor, 1976-77, assistant professor, 1977-81, associate professor of English, 1981—. Guest lecturer at University of Warwick, University of Nottingham, and University of Edinburgh, 1972-73; visiting lecturer at University of Pennsylvania, 1975, and San Diego State University, 1980-81. Member of board of directors of Bradley, Burr & Sherman, 1977-79.

MEMBER: Authors Guild, Authors League of America, PEN, National Book Critics Circle.

AWARDS, HONORS: PEN/Faulkner Award, American Academy and Institute of Arts and Letters award for literature, and *New York Times Book Review* ''Editors' Choice'' citation, all 1982, all for *The Chaneysville Incident*.

WRITINGS:

South Street (novel), Viking, 1975, reprinted, Scribner's, 1986.
The Chaneysville Incident (novel; Book-of-the-Month Club alternate selection), Harper, 1981.

Contributor of articles, stories, and reviews to magazines and newspapers, including *Signature, Savvy, Tracks, Quest, New York Arts Journal, Esquire, New York Times Magazine, Philadelphia Magazine, Southern Review, New York Times Book Review, Los Angeles Times Book Review, Washington Post Book World*, and *Philadelphia Inquirer Magazine*.

WORK IN PROGRESS: A nonfiction book on race in America.

SIDELIGHTS: David Bradley has reaped considerable critical acclaim for his novels *South Street* and *The Chaneysville Incident*, both published before he turned thirty-five. *Dictionary of Literary Biography* contributor Valerie Smith ranks Bradley ''among the most sophisticated literary stylists of his generation,'' a fiction writer whose works ''present subtle and original perspectives on issues that traditionally have concerned significant Afro-American writers: the meaning of community, the effects of racism, the shape and substance of history.'' Indeed, *The Chaneysville Incident*, winner of the 1982 PEN/Faulkner Award, blends historical fact and fiction in its representation of a rural Pennsylvania community through which the Underground Railroad once ran. Acclaimed ''by fiction writers and by popular and scholarly writers alike,'' notes Smith, the work has ''placed Bradley in the vanguard of contemporary novelists.'' A professor of English at Philadelphia's Temple University, Bradley is a self-styled perfectionist who can work many years crafting a novel. He also writes nonfiction articles for magazines and newspapers, including *Esquire* and the *New York Times Book Review*, and is a member of the National Book Critics Circle.

Geographically, the city of Philadelphia is less than three hundred miles from Bradley's home town of Bedford, Pennsylvania. As Bradley notes in a *New York Times Book Review* profile, however, the region that formed his authorial sensibility was starkly different from the urban area in which he now lives. ''The town of Bedford is perilously close to the Mason-Dixon line,'' he said. ''. . . It was not that hospitable for blacks—or that comfortable.'' Bradley grew up among a community of about one hundred blacks in a county with a scattered population of 30,000; his experiences in that environment imbued him with skepticism toward the Black Power movement that was gaining momentum as he entered college. ''I had grown up in a rural white society,'' he said, ''and I knew damn well we [blacks] had no power.'' Although an honors student at the University of Pennsylvania, Bradley felt alienated from his peers because of his rural background; as an undergraduate he discovered a group of compatriots in an unlikely setting—a bar on Philadelphia's South Street. "I really enjoyed that place," he recollected. ". . . My experiences there confirmed my impression that the things I saw in the blacks at the university, my contemporaries, were as artificial as everything else. The people on South Street were totally without power. Their lives were terrible—they just lived with the situation and made the best of it."

Bradley's first novel—written while he was still an undergraduate—was inspired by his visits to the South Street bar. The book, *South Street*, "is not simply another grim, naturalistic litany of the anguish of the downtrodden," notes Mel Watkins in the *New York Times*. "Without blunting the pathos of this tale, Mr. Bradley has infused what could have been a standard story and stock characters with new vigor. Probing beneath the sociological stereotypes, he portrays his characters with a fullness that amplifies much of the lusty irony of ghetto life. . . . It is Bradley's unerring depiction of the vitality that rears itself even within this despairing setting that distinguishes this novel." The work centers on Adlai Stevenson Brown, a young poet who begins to frequent Lightnin' Ed's Bar. There he talks to patrons and listens to their stories; this plot structure provides for vignettes recounted by other characters. "The novel is really about the street itself, as Bradley's energetic and shifting narrative makes clear," Smith writes. ". . . These frequent changes in perspective illustrate various ways in which individuals confront the turbulence of ghetto life. Furthermore, the shifts imitate the vibrancy and the multifariousness of the world the author explores."

Bradley began to conceive *The Chaneysville Incident* while he was in college, too, but he spent nearly a decade reworking four different drafts of the story before arriving at the final manuscript. The author had grown up hearing stories about the Underground Railroad in Bedford County. But in 1969, Bradley's mother told him a story he had not heard before, about thirteen runaway slaves who, upon the point of recapture in Bedford County, had chosen death over a return to slavery. The slaves were buried in thirteen unmarked graves in a family burial plot on a nearby farm. Bradley told the *New York Times Book Review:* "I knew my second novel would be about those 13 runaway slaves. And in writing about them I wanted to use material that had been glossed over, material that had been mined for descriptions of the horror of slavery without bringing along any understanding of how the system came about."

The Chaneysville Incident is the story of a young man's confrontation with his personal past, his family history, and the living legacies of racism and slavery. The protagonist, a history professor, returns to his hometown in western Pennsylvania to visit the deathbed of a man who helped to raise him. With the aid of his dying mentor, the professor begins to explore his father's mysterious death in the mountains outside Bedford—and this exploration leads, in time, to a reconstruction of one telling moment in the history of American blacks. Smith contends that the novel "is somewhat reminiscent of a musical composition in which the different movements represent variations on a common theme." Smith also notes that the varieties of narrative—the protagonist's pedantic lectures and increasingly emotional flashbacks, his old friend's tales of bootlegging and lynchings—"all exemplify the kinds of physical and emotional cruelty that are commonplace within a racist culture."

In addition to the prestigious PEN/Faulkner Award, *The Chaneysville Incident* won an American Academy and Institute of Arts and Letters grant for literature, and it was cited by the editors of the *New York Times Book Review* as one of the best novels of 1981. *Los Angeles Times* book editor Art Seidenbaum calls the book "the most significant work by a new male black author since James Baldwin," and *Christian Science Monitor* contributor Bruce Allen finds it "the best novel about the black experience in America since Ellison's 'Invisible Man' nearly 30 years ago." Vance Bourjaily offers similar praise in the *New York Times Book Review*. "Whatever else may be said," Bourjaily claims, ". . . [Bradley's] a writer. What he can do, at a pretty high level of energy, is synchronize five different kinds of rhetoric, control a complicated plot, manage a good-sized cast of characters, convey a lot of information, handle an intricate time scheme, pull off a couple of final tricks that dramatize provocative ideas, and generally keep things going for 200,000 words." The critic concludes that *The Chaneysville Incident* "deserves what it seems pretty sure to get: a lot of interested and challenged readers."

Bradley commented: "I think of myself as an 'old-fashioned' writer, primarily because my fictional models are 'old-fashioned.' Like the Victorians, I am interested in the basics of plot and character, less concerned with abstract ideas. It is my belief that writers of novels should have no belief, that the idea of what is true is something that emerges from the writing, rather than being placed into it. Ultimately, I believe that if I cannot create a character who holds an idea, write a conversation (as opposed to a speech) that expresses it, or work out a plot that exemplifies it, there is something wrong either with my understanding of the idea or with the idea itself. In either case it has no place in my writing.

"I must frankly say that I do not love many 'contemporary' novels. For the most part they seem to me self-absorbed, self-indulgent, derivative, and basically lacking truth. Our technique has become an end rather than a means, primarily, I think, because we writers have been led to believe that truth does not sell. If we would write well, we are told, we will be obscure. Obscurity, then, becomes the measure of writing well. I do not believe this. I have faith in the ability of people to respond to a story that treats them with kindness, honesty, dignity, and understanding. I put my faith not in publishers, and certainly not in reviewers and/or critics, but in those who read."

BIOGRAPHICAL/CRITICAL SOURCES:

BOOKS

Contemporary Literary Criticism, Volume 23, Gale, 1983.
Dictionary of Literary Biography, Volume 33: *Afro-American Fiction Writers after 1955,* Gale, 1984.

PERIODICALS

America, May 30, 1981.
Atlantic, May, 1981.
Christian Science Monitor, May 20, 1981.
Los Angeles Times, April 8, 1981.
New York Times, October 4, 1975, May 12, 1981.
New York Times Book Review, September 28, 1975, April 19, 1981.
Publishers Weekly, April 10, 1981.
Saturday Review, July, 1981.
Times Literary Supplement, January 16, 1987.
Washington Post, April 12, 1982.
Washington Post Book World, April 12, 1981.

BRADLEY, Ed(ward R.) 1941-

PERSONAL: Born June 22, 1941, in Philadelphia, Pa.; son of Ed R. (in business) and Gladys Bradley; divorced; married second wife, Priscilla Coolidge (a singer), 1981 (divorced, 1984). *Education:* Cheyney State College, B.A., 1964.

ADDRESSES: Home—Manhattan, N.Y. *Office*—CBS-News, 524 West 57th St., New York, N.Y. 10019.

CAREER/WRITINGS: Elementary school teacher in Philadelphia, Pa.; WDAS-Radio, Philadelphia, news reporter, 1963-67; WCBS-Radio, New York City, news reporter, 1967-71; Columbia Broadcasting System, Inc. (CBS-TV), New York City, stringer, 1971-73, principal correspondent reporting from Southeast Asia, beginning in 1973, White House correspondent, 1976, anchorperson of "CBS Sunday Night News," 1976-78, principal correspondent for "CBS Reports," 1978-81, correspondent for news program "60 Minutes," 1981—.

AWARDS, HONORS: Overseas Press Club of America Award for best radio spot news from abroad and Distinguished Commentator Award from New York Chapter of National Association of Media Women, both 1975; Association of Black Journalists award, 1977; Emmy Award from National Academy of Television Arts and Sciences, Edward R. Murrow Award from Overseas Press Club of America, and Alfred I. DuPont-Columbia University Award in Broadcast Journalism, all 1979, all for television documentary "The Boat People"; Emmy Award, George Foster Peabody Broadcasting Award from University of Georgia, and Ohio State Award, all 1979, all for television documentary "Blacks in America: With All Deliberate Speed"; American Black Achievement Award from *Ebony* magazine for "the most significant and enduring achievement in communications," and George Polk Award for Foreign Television Reporting, both 1979; Alfred I. DuPont-Columbia University Award for "Blacks in America: With All Deliberate Speed," Emmy Awards for television documentaries "Too Little Too Late" and "Miami: The Trial That Sparked the Riots," and Capital Press Club National Media Award, all 1980.

SIDELIGHTS: "Ed Bradley is the preeminent black correspondent today," declared Richard M. Levine in a *TV Guide* article. And with his 1981 appointment as a co-host and correspondent for CBS-TV's news magazine program "60 Minutes," "the only non-entertainment series," according to the *New Yorker,* "consistently to attract a vast and seemingly unflagging following," Bradley is considered by many in his field to have television reporting's "plum job."

Bradley became one of the "60 Minutes" tigers, as executive producer Don Hewitt likes to call the program's four correspondents, following ten years of service at CBS. He began as a stringer in 1971, and by 1973 he had become a principal correspondent. Recognized for his reporting in Southeast Asia, Bradley covered the fall of Cambodia and Vietnam and earned a reputation as a humane reporter. Bradley has "a feel for what's going on," attested former CBS cameraman Norman Lloyd in *TV Guide.* "It's really humanity, I think, and he's got a hell of a lot of it."

During the 1970's Bradley advanced swiftly, becoming anchorperson of the "CBS Sunday Night News" in 1976 and a principal correspondent for "CBS Reports" in 1978. In the latter capacity he made several award-winning documentaries. One resulted from a 1978 assignment to Malaysia, where he prepared a highly acclaimed report on the Indochinese political refugees known as the "boat people." "Those who have seen it," reported Ron Townley in *TV Guide,* "will not forget the image of Bradley carrying refugees ashore through the breaking surf." Another success for Bradley came in 1979 when he put together a two-part edition of "CBS Reports" entitled "Blacks in America: With All Deliberate Speed." In that examination of the progress black Americans have made in both the northern and southern United States since the U.S. Supreme Court outlawed segregation in public schools, Bradley was able to use "his color with stunning effect," wrote Richard M. Levine in *TV Guide. Newsweek*'s Dennis A. Williams recounted that at the beginning of the report Bradley describes Mississippi as a place where "I could never have gone 25 years ago, as a reporter who is black, even if CBS hired me." And after speaking with a member of the Ku Klux Klan, Bradley observed that in the past, "I would have been beaten or possibly killed instead of getting answers to my questions." He was commended by Williams for bringing "sensitivity and a certain historical perspective to the subject."

Being a correspondent who is black has not always worked to Bradley's advantage, however. Levine pointed out that blacks have been excluded from top television management and consequently have no power in news departments. "Their on-air gains could be threatened at any time for lack of what [newswoman] Charlayne Hunter-Gault calls a 'support network,'" explained Levine, and "this situation contributes to the widespread feeling among black network correspondents that their numbers and influence have peaked." In fact, as anchor of the "CBS Sunday Night News" in 1979, Bradley numbered as one of only three black network anchors in the nation. He also informed Levine that he worries about "getting typecast as the urban and Third World correspondent on '60 Minutes'" and admitted postponing what he called a "perfectly good" profile of a black public figure for that very reason. Bradley would simply like to be known, he said, as "a reporter who happens to be black."

Bradley is a reporter who also happens to be more pragmatic than his peers, according to Laurence Bergreen in *TV Guide.* Unlike many news people, who deny that being in the right place at the right time has played an important role in their careers, Bradley admits that "a story can make you or break you." Observed Bradley, "You can be the best reporter in the world, but if what you're covering doesn't get on the air, what good does it do?"

As a "60 Minutes" correspondent, however, Bradley sees plenty of air time. In fact, the kind of exposure enjoyed by the "60 Minutes" reports allows colleagues and media experts ample opportunity to analyze individual appeal. According to journalist Kristin McMurran in *People,* Bradley's peers "regard him as a dogged, well-prepared reporter," with executive producer Hewitt declaring, "Bradley is one-fourth of why we are what we are." He also has an "ability to establish rapport [which] is 'something elemental' and one of his greatest strengths," assessed former "CBS Reports" senior executive producer Howard Stringer. Townley remarked that that "something elemental" might be Bradley's most significant contribution to "60 Minutes" and asked him to define his reporting style. But Bradley replied, "I'd rather not think about it and just go out and *do* it, and it will come naturally." And that, suggested Townley, might be what Bradley's style is all about: "spontaneous, down-to-earth, natural, the approach of a man with his options and his mind still open."

BIOGRAPHICAL/CRITICAL SOURCES:

PERIODICALS

Ebony, January, 1979.

Fortune, July 14, 1980, May 4, 1981.
Jet, April 2, 1981.
Nation, July 25, 1981.
Newsweek, July 30, 1979, March 16, 1981.
New Yorker, July 19, 1982, July 26, 1982.
People, November 14, 1983.
Time, August 25, 1980, February 21, 1983.
TV Guide, October 18, 1980, July 25, 1981, February 20, 1982, January 22, 1983.
Variety, September 9, 1981.
Vogue, December, 1981.

* * *

BRAITHWAITE, (Eustace) E(dward) R(icardo) 1920-

PERSONAL: Born June 27, 1920 (some sources cite 1912), in Georgetown, British Guiana (now Guyana); son of Charles Edwardo and Elizabeth Martha (Greene) Braithwaite. *Education:* Attended Queen's College, British Guiana; City College (now of the City University of New York), B.Sc., 1940; Gonville and Caius College, Cambridge, M.Sc., 1949; further study at Institute of Education, London.

CAREER: Writer. Schoolmaster in London, England, 1950-57; London County Council, Department of Child Welfare, London, welfare officer and consultant on affairs of blacks, 1958-60; World Veterans' Foundation, Paris, France, human rights officer, 1960-63; UNESCO, Paris, educational consultant and lecturer, 1963-66; United Nations, New York, N.Y., permanent representative from Guyana, 1967-68; Guyanan ambassador to Venezuela, 1968-69. Professor of English at New York University. *Military service:* Royal Air Force, 1941-45, served as fighter pilot.

MEMBER: International P.E.N. Club.

AWARDS, HONORS: Anisfield-Wolf Award from *Saturday Review*, 1960, for *To Sir, with Love.*

WRITINGS:

To Sir, with Love (autobiography), Bodley Head, 1959, Prentice-Hall, 1960, new edition in large print, Chivers, 1980.
A Kind of Homecoming, Prentice-Hall, 1962.
Paid Servant (autobiography), Bodley Head, 1962, McGraw, 1968.
Choice of Straws (novel), Bodley Head, 1965, Bobbs-Merrill, 1967.
Reluctant Neighbors (autobiography), McGraw, 1972.
"Honorary White": A Visit to South Africa, McGraw, 1975.

Contributor of articles to *Time.*

SIDELIGHTS: "E. R. Braithwaite is a perceptive and sensitive writer who can convey his impressions most effectively . . . from within a situation of extreme ambivalence," writes Trevor Huddlestone in *Books and Bookmen.* Braithwaite, who has worked as a teacher, social worker, and diplomat, wrote his first and best-known book, *To Sir, with Love,* on the difficulties and rewards of teaching in the East End working-class district of London. While his other books vary between autobiography, journalism, and fiction, the tension of a black man's experiences in an often hostile world is always present.

Braithwaite did not originally plan to teach. But despite his background as a Royal Air Force pilot during World War II and a master's degree in physics, he received a stream of refusals from potential employers. He relates in his 1972 au-

tobiographical work, *Reluctant Neighbors,* that racial discrimination was responsible for the endless job search. In desperation, he finally took a job as a schoolmaster. As a Cambridge-educated black from British Guiana (now Guyana), Braithwaite experienced many frustrations in leading a class of forty-six undisciplined white students. However, the job provided him with the material to write *To Sir, with Love,* which eventually became a movie starring Sidney Poitier. It also provided a springboard into his next position as a London welfare officer. *Paid Servant* relates his experiences as a specialist in finding homes for nonwhite children. The title refers to Braithwaite's conception of his work, that of a true "public servant." While Braithwaite's color was considered by his superiors as an asset in relating to nonwhite children, the author feels that his empathy with his clients went beyond racial similarities or differences. He writes in *Paid Servant* that "'My people' were not only the black ones; they were all the unfortunates temporarily down on their luck, needing a helping hand; and they were . . . all those who did not limit their love and kindliness by the unprobable barriers of color or caste, or creed." Paul Showers in the *New York Times Book Review* calls the book "a kind of social-worker's journal, offering intimate glimpses into troubled lives but without jargon or tortured psychoanalytic interpretations." While the book covers a variety of situations, the story of a mixed-race four-year-old who needs a permanent home is a major theme. A *Booklist* reviewer says that the child's story "provides a warm but never sentimental unifying narrative throughout the book."

Braithwaite's next book, *Choice of Straws,* returns to the working-class world of *To Sir, with Love.* On a grimmer note, however, the novel concerns a young white factory worker and his brother who accost black passersby in deserted areas at night, "just for a giggle." Their plans go astray when they lose control and kill one of their victims. According to Martin Levin in the *New York Times Book Review,* Braithwaite "shows his mettle as a novelist by telling his story from the viewpoint of the white hooligan." Still, a *Times Literary Supplement* reviewer who applauds Braithwaite's effort believes that the author has not completely succeeded: "He has made heavy demands on himself: in the end he is all but defeated by the complexity of his themes and the complexity of his own responses to them. . . . The crux of the novel is Mr. Braithwaite's attitude towards his narrator, and it is by no means clear what it is. He appears to be at odds with himself, divided into three parts as novelist, welfare worker, and human being."

Reluctant Neighbors is "an autobiographical essay about an author-diplomat-educator who wants the world to know that his talent has not put him at a safe distance from the arrogance of white people," writes Orde Coombs in the *New York Times Book Review.* Coombs adds, "He serves up his life to us through a feast of flashbacks while sitting near a public-relations man" who occupies the same train compartment. "The device does not work, for the white man—your prototype 40-year-old-smiling-liberal-child wallows in banalities and props himself up with . . . vapid assumptions." Braithwaite's anger toward racial prejudice is more fully expressed in *Reluctant Neighbors* than in his earlier books. Gonville Ffrench-Beytagh contends in *Books and Bookmen* that "it is true that he has a great deal to be angry about, but his rage and hatred sometimes override his judgment. . . . He has, or had at the time about which he writes, an almost paranoid bitterness in his reactions to what seem to be perfectly ordinary questions which one might ask of any stranger in a strange land, such as 'do you feel the cold much?'" Still, Ffrench-Beytagh adds, "Let me go on to say how much there is that is good about this book. It is honest. It has its origins in the guts of the black man and it is time that we came to recognise all that lies buried there of rage and hatred.''

In 1973, Braithwaite visited South Africa for six weeks. Due to his credentials as a writer and diplomat, the government granted him the position of ''Honorary White'' during his stay. This put him in the awkward position of enjoying such rights as the freedom of movement and the access to better hotels and restaurants that were usually denied to blacks. In *''Honorary White'': A Visit to South Africa,* Braithwaite portrays the relationships between South African blacks and whites. Claims Huddlestone, ''E. R. Braithwaite was given his status as 'Honorary White' in order that he might be able to see for himself the changes that have taken place in South African society and, as a distinguished black communicator, tell the world what he had seen. Unfortunately for South Africa that is exactly what he *has* done.'' But according to Ezekiel Mphahlele in the *New York Times Book Review,* ''It is rather Braithwaite the man who holds our attention—Braithwaite man of the world and black man, who is outraged by the squalor and the injustice staring him in the face, driven to search for answers to his own dilemma as an Honorary White who must speak to impoverished blacks from a position of luxury and freedom.'' A *Booklist* reviewer emphasizes the work's effect, writing that ''the impressions are conveyed with a bitter honesty . . . becoming a testimony of disturbing intensity.''

MEDIA ADAPTATIONS: The film ''To Sir, with Love,'' based on Braithwaite's novel of the same title, was produced by Columbia Pictures in 1966.

AVOCATIONAL INTERESTS: Tennis, dancing.

BIOGRAPHICAL/CRITICAL SOURCES:

BOOKS

Braithwaite, E. R., *Paid Servant,* Bodley Head, 1962, McGraw, 1968.
Braithwaite, E. R., *Choice of Straws,* Bodley Head, 1965, Bobbs-Merrill, 1967.

PERIODICALS

America, April 13, 1968.
Best Sellers, October 1, 1972.
Booklist, July 15, 1968, July 15, 1975.
Books and Bookmen, December, 1972, April, 1976.
Chicago Sunday Tribune, April 3, 1960, August 5, 1962.
Newsweek, April 1, 1968.
New York Herald Tribune Weekly Book Review, February 28, 1960, April 29, 1962.
New York Times Book Review, May 1, 1960, August 5, 1962, February 12, 1967, May 19, 1968, September 17, 1972, July 13, 1975.
Saturday Review, June 16, 1962, May 11, 1968.
Times Literary Supplement, November 4, 1965, May 19, 1968, October 13, 1972.

—*Sketch by Jani Prescott*

*   *   *

BRAITHWAITE, William Stanley (Beaumont) 1878-1962

PERSONAL: Born December 6, 1878, in Boston, Mass.; died following a brief illness, June 8, 1962; son of William Smith and Emma (DeWolfe) Braithwaite; married Emma Kelly, June 30, 1903; children: Fiona Lydia Rossetti (Mrs. Merrill Carter), Katherine Keats (Mrs. William J. Arnold), William Stanley Beaumont, Edith Carman, Paul Ledoux, Arnold DeWolfe, Francis Robinson. *Education:* Self-educated; apprenticed to a typesetter at Ginn and Company.

CAREER: Colored American Magazine, Boston, Mass., editor, 1901-02; *Boston Evening Transcript,* Boston, literary editor and columnist, beginning in 1905; Atlanta University, Atlanta, Ga., professor of creative literature, 1935-45. Publisher of *The Poetic Journal in Boston,* 1912-14; editor of *Poetry Review,* 1916-17; founder and editor of B. J. Brimmer Publishing Co., 1921-27; member of editorial board of *Phylon.*

MEMBER: Poetry Society of America, New England Poetry Society, Boston Authors' Club.

AWARDS, HONORS: Spingarn Medal from the National Association for the Advancement of Colored People for outstanding achievement by a member of the colored race, A.M. from Atlanta University, and Litt.D. from Talladega College, all 1918.

WRITINGS:

POETRY

Lyrics of Life and Love (collection), H. B. Turner, 1904, reprinted, University Microfilms, 1971.
(Editor) *The Book of Elizabethan Verse,* introduction by Thomas Wentworth Higginson, H. B. Turner, 1906, reprinted, Folcroft/Norwood, 1980.
The House of Falling Leaves (collection), J. W. Luce, 1908, reprinted, Mnemosyne Publishing, 1969.
(Editor) *The Book of Georgian Verse,* Brentano's, 1909, reprinted, Books for Libraries Press, two volumes, 1969.
(Editor) *The Book of Restoration Verse,* Brentano's, 1910.
(Editor) *Anthology of Magazine Verse and Yearbook of American Poetry,* seventeen volumes, G. Sully, 1913-29, reprinted, Books for Libraries Press, 1972—.
(Editor with Henry Thomas Schnittkind) *Representative American Poetry,* R. G. Badger, 1916.
(Editor) *The Poetic Year for 1916: A Critical Anthology,* Small, Maynard, 1917.
(Editor) *The Golden Treasury of Magazine Verse,* Small, Maynard, 1918.
(Author of introduction) Georgia Douglas Johnson, *The Heart of a Woman and Other Poems,* Cornhill, 1918.
(Editor) *The Book of Modern British Verse,* Small, Maynard, 1919.
(Editor) *Victory! Celebrated by Thirty-eight American Poets,* introduction by Theodore Roosevelt, Small, Maynard, 1919.
(Editor) *Anthology of Massachusetts Poets,* Small, Maynard, 1922.
(Editor) *Our Lady's Choir: A Contemporary Anthology of Verse by Catholic Sisters,* foreword by Hugh Francis Blunt, introduction by Ralph Adams Cram, B. Humphries, 1931.
Selected Poems (collection), Coward-McCann, 1948.
(Editor) *Anthology of Magazine Verse for 1958,* Pentelic, 1959.

Also author of the collection *Sandy Star,* 1926.

OTHER

The Canadian (novel), Small, Maynard, 1901.
The Story of the Great War (juvenile; essays), F. A. Stokes, 1919.

Going Over Tindal: A Fragment Wrenched From the Life of Titus Jabson (novel), B. J. Brimmer, 1924.

The Bewitched Parsonage: The Story of the Brontes, Coward-McCann, 1950.

The William Stanley Braithwaite Reader, edited by Philip Butcher, University of Michigan Press, 1972.

Also author of *Our Essayists and Critics of Today,* 1920, *Frost on the Green Tree* (stories), 1928, and *The Story of the Years Between, 1918-1939,* 1940.

Contributor of book reviews, verse, essays, and articles to periodicals, including *Alexander's Magazine, American Magazine, Atlantic Monthly, Bookman, Book News Monthly, Boston Courant, Century, Christian Endeavor Herald, Crisis, Forum, Independent, Lippincott's, National Magazine, New England Magazine, New Era, New Republic, Opportunity, Poet Lore, Scribner's,* and *Voice of the Negro.* Braithwaite's autobiography, "The House Under Arcturus," was serialized in *Phylon,* 1941-42.

SIDELIGHTS: A major force behind the American poetry revival of the first three decades of the twentieth century, William Stanley Braithwaite was a respected columnist at the *Boston Evening Transcript* and editor of annual poetry anthologies. For seventeen years he introduced many fine poets to the general reading public through his verse compilations and critical writings, and he attempted to widen his audience's understanding of poetry by prefacing his anthologies with educational, up-to-date information on literary trends. He was also a skillful poet in his own right. Introduced to literature while apprenticed to a typesetter, Braithwaite was so moved by English romantic poetry, especially John Keats's "Ode on a Grecian Urn," that he began studying the great writers and composing his own verse.

Braithwaite published his first collection of poetry, *Lyrics of Life and Love,* in 1904. In it he paid homage to his idol through the sonnets "Keats Was an Unbeliever" and "On a Pressed Flower in My Copy of Keats." Four years later Braithwaite published a second volume of poems, *House of Falling Leaves,* which celebrated New England nature and included a number of sonnet sequences. The volume also contained "White Magic: An Ode Read at the Centenary Celebration of the Birth of John Greenleaf Whittier at Faneuil Hall, December 17, 1907," in which the poet commends the abolitionist Whittier for giving up composing poetry to write about Negro emancipation in prose. "White Magic" offers an important clue to Braithwaite's poetical philosophy, indicating that he thought socio-political subject matter incompatible with aesthetics; that poetry, an art form, should be written only for its own sake.

Braithwaite's third collection, *Selected Poems,* was published in 1948, forty years after *The House of Falling Leaves.* Appearing in *Selected Poems* are works from his first two books of verse and others that were previously published in periodicals, as well as new poems. The later verse shows a continuing romantic influence on the author's themes and forms, and critics also cite a new obscurity—a dreamy, otherworldliness—in Braithwaite's work, especially in the poems "Ascension" and "Myths of the Circumference," that are reminiscent of the early romantic poet William Blake.

As a whole, Braithwaite's poetry explores typically romantic themes—life and death, nature, innocent love—through skillfully sounded rhyme schemes and traditional verse forms, especially the sonnet. Yet, unlike the romantic poets, Braithwaite never addressed social and political issues, which prompted

a number of his contemporaries, unaware of his aesthetic view of poetry, to claim that he was ashamed of being black. In fact, Braithwaite felt that race did not have to direct one's creativity. Even the poet Countee Cullen—whom Braithwaite respected but feared was mired in racial issues—concurred with Braithwaite on this point, writing in *Caroling Dusk: An Anthology of Verse by Negro Poets,* which he dedicated to Braithwaite, that American Negro poetry does not exist; only poetry written by American Negroes.

Braithwaite's talent as a poet and his unwillingness to address black issues elicited responses from critics such as Newman Ivey White, who, in *Anthology of Verse by American Negroes,* claimed that much of Braithwaite's verses in *Lyrics of Life and Love* possess "a technical finish well above average. Some are rather exquisite; many have a delicate beauty, but . . . there is no interest in racial questions at all, nor in much else that implies stress or conflict." This detachment was also evident in Braithwaite's second collection, *The House of Falling Leaves,* prompting the critic to observe that its poetry has "a somewhat pale and graceful estheticism with no feeling of 'mission' or racial self-consciousness." Black writer James Weldon Johnson agreed, stating in *The Book of American Negro Poetry:* "As an Afroamerican poet [Braithwaite] is unique; he has written no poetry motivated or colored by race. . . . It is simply that race has not impinged upon him as it has upon other Negro poets."

Braithwaite joined the staff of the *Boston Evening Transcript* in 1905, at the beginning of a poetic renaissance that would excite the country for the next twenty-five years. As literary editor he wrote a column on contemporary poetry, analyzing the genre that previously had been used only as filler in magazines. In 1913 he began culling through magazines and journals to gather works by various poets for an annual anthology, which would also feature his criticism on authors. Yearly, until 1929, the *Anthology of Magazine Verse and Yearbook of American Poetry* brought to the general reading public good verse before it was published in book form. Keeping abreast of the literary trends and focusing on the yet undiscovered poets, Braithwaite wrote in these anthologies prefaces on the art of poetry, in hopes of educating his audience. Today these prefaces and newspaper columns are considered invaluable tools for analyzing past American poetical works and movements.

Although Braithwaite favored the traditional and romantic in his own verse, he was extremely broad-minded and could recognize literary ability. He published works by experimental and avant-garde poets, even when he did not accept their philosophies. For example, Braithwaite included works by the imagist writers, although some of those poets were known for their outspoken prejudice against blacks. And though he was criticized for not mentioning his being black in his own poetry, Braithwaite did introduce many Negro writers to the nation, especially during the Harlem Renaissance of the 1920s. Indeed, he helped black literary criticism emerge by reviewing works by Negroes rather than just providing biographical information on them, as was done previously. Braithwaite included biographical indexes in his anthologies with statements on the authors' lives and influences, but he never mentioned nationality or race. Aware that black works were judged by lower standards than white works because critics at the time deemed literature by Negroes novel and exotic, Braithwaite attempted to evaluate literature strictly by merit and to teach his readers to do the same.

As Braithwaite's influence grew, to be included in one of his anthologies was to have gained acceptance in the literary world. An article in *Phylon* claimed the editor "Made American Writers Famous," yet he had his adversaries, including Conrad Aiken, who claimed in his *Scepticisms: Notes on Contemporary Poetry* that Braithwaite's poetic tastes tended toward the mundane and sentimental, or "marshmallows and tears." In his *Negro Poetry and Drama*, Sterling A. Brown disagreed with Aiken's description of Braithwaite as an editor, claiming that because of Braithwaite's numerous anthologies and objective eye, he "was one of the pioneers in the poetry revival in America."

BIOGRAPHICAL/CRITICAL SOURCES:

BOOKS

Aiken, Conrad, *Scepticisms: Notes on Contemporary Poetry,* Knopf, 1919.

Brown, Sterling A., *Negro Poetry and Drama,* Associates in Negro Folk Education, 1937, reprinted with *The Negro in American Fiction,* Atheneum, 1969.

Cullen, Countee, editor, *Caroling Dusk: An Anthology of Verse by Negro Poets,* Harper, 1927, reprinted, 1974.

Daniels, John, *In Freedom's Birthplace: A Study of the Boston Negroes,* Houghton, 1914.

Dictionary of Literary Biography, Gale, Volume 46: *American Literary Publishing Houses, 1900-1980: Trade and Paperback,* 1986, Volume 50: *Afro-American Writers Before the Harlem Renaissance,* 1986, Volume 54: *American Poets, 1880-1945, Third Series,* 1987.

Johnson, James Weldon, editor, *The Book of American Negro Poetry,* Harcourt, 1922, revised edition, 1931, reprinted, 1983.

Robinson, William H., *Black New England Letters,* Boston Public Library, 1977.

Wagner, Jean, *Black Poets of the United States,* translation by Kenneth Douglas, University of Illinois Press, 1973.

White, Newman Ivey, editor, *An Anthology of Verse by American Negroes,* Trinity College Press, 1924, reprinted, Folcroft, 1975.

Who's Who of the Colored Race, reprinted, Gale, 1976.

PERIODICALS

CLA Journal, December, 1971, September, 1973.
New England Magazine, December, 1905.
Poetry, January, 1917.
Southern Literary Journal, spring, 1971.

OBITUARIES:

PERIODICALS

Negro History Bulletin, January, 1963, April, 1963.
New York Times, June 9, 1962.
Phylon, summer, 1969.
Publishers Weekly, June 18, 1962.

—*Sketch by Carol Lynn DeKane*

*   *   *

BRANCH, William (Blackwell) 1927-

PERSONAL: Born September 11, 1927, in New Haven, Conn.; son of James Matthew (a minister) and Iola (Douglas) Branch; divorced; children: Rochelle Ellen. *Education:* Northwestern University, B.S., 1949; Columbia University, M.F.A., 1958, graduate study, 1958-60; Yale University, graduate study, 1965-66.

ADDRESSES: Home and office—53 Cortlandt Ave., New Rochelle, N.Y. 10801.

CAREER: Has worked as an actor in theatre, films, radio, and television; field representative for *Ebony*, 1949-60; free-lance producer, writer, and director of plays, films, and news documentaries, 1950—; president of William Branch Associates (development, production, and consulting firm), 1973—. Director of "The Jackie Robinson Show," NBC-Radio, 1959-60; staff producer, contributing writer, and director of documentary films for "The City" series, Educational Broadcasting Corp., 1962-64; writer and director of "The Alma John Show," 1963-65; writer and producer of television documentary programs for NBC-TV, 1972-73; executive producer of "Black Perspectives on the News," Public Broadcasting System, 1978-79.

Visiting professor at University of Ghana, 1963, and University of Maryland, Baltimore County, 1979-82; associate in film at Columbia University, 1968-69; visiting playwright at Smith College, summer, 1970, and North Carolina Central University, spring-summer, 1971; visiting Luce Fellow at Williams College, 1983; lecturer at colleges and universities, including Harvard University, Fisk University, and University of California, Los Angeles. Member of board of directors of American Society of African Culture, 1963-70, and National Citizens Committee for Broadcasting, 1969-71; member of national advisory board of Library of Congress Center for the Book, 1979-83. *Military service:* U.S. Army, 1951-53; served as educational instructor in Germany.

AWARDS, HONORS: Robert E. Sherwood Television Award and National Council of Christians and Jews citations, 1958, both for television drama "Light in the Southern Sky"; Hannah del Vecchio Award from Columbia University, 1958; Guggenheim fellowship for creative writing in drama, 1959-60; Yale University-American Broadcasting Company fellowship for creative writing in television drama, 1965-66; Emmy Award nomination from National Academy of Television Arts and Sciences and American Film Festival award, 1969, both for television documentary "Still a Brother: Inside the Negro Middle Class."

WRITINGS:

PLAYS

"A Medal for Willie," first produced in New York at Club Baron, 1951.
"In Splendid Error," first produced in New York at Greenwich Mews Playhouse, 1955.
"To Follow the Phoenix," first produced in Chicago at Civic Opera House, 1960.
"A Wreath for Udomo" (based on a novel by Peter Abrahams), first produced in London at Lyric Hammersmith Theater, 1961.
"Baccalaureate," first produced in Hamilton, Bermuda, at City Hall Theatre, 1975.

MOTION PICTURES

"Fifty Steps Toward Freedom" (documentary drama), National Association for the Advancement of Colored People (NAACP), 1959.
"The Man on Meeting Street" (documentary drama), Alpha Kappa Alpha Sorority, 1960.
"Benefit Performance," Universal, 1969.

"Judgement!" Belafonte Enterprises, 1969.
"Together for Days," Olas Corp., 1971.

TELEVISION DOCUMENTARIES AND DRAMAS

"The Way," American Broadcasting Co., 1955.
"What Is Conscience?" Columbia Broadcasting System, 1955.
"Let's Find Out" (series), National Council of Churches, 1956.
"Light in the Southern Sky," National Broadcasting Co. (NBC-TV), 1958.
"Legacy of a Prophet," Educational Broadcasting Corp., 1959.
"Still a Brother: Inside the Negro Middle Class," National Educational Television, 1968.
"The Case of the Non-Working Workers," NBC-TV, 1972.
"The 20 Billion Dollar Rip-Off," NBC-TV, 1972.
"No Room to Run, No Place to Hide," NBC-TV, 1972.
"The Black Church in New York," NBC-TV, 1973.
"Afro-American Perspectives" (series), Maryland Center for Public Broadcasting, 1973-80.

OTHER

(Contributor) John A. Davis, editor, *The American Negro Writer and His Roots,* American Society of African Culture, 1960.

Author of filmstrips, screenplay outlines, and radio scripts; author of syndicated newspaper column with Jackie Robinson, 1958-60. Work represented in anthologies, including *Black Scenes,* edited by Alice Childress, Doubleday, 1971; *Black Theater,* edited by Lindsay Patterson, Dodd, Mead, 1971; *Black Drama Anthology,* edited by Woodie King and Ron Milner, Columbia University Press, 1972; *Black Theatre U.S.A.,* edited by James V. Hatch and Ted Shine, Free Press, 1974; *Standing Room Only,* edited by Daigon and Bernier, Prentice-Hall, 1977; and *Meeting Challenges,* edited by J. Nelson, American Book, 1980. Contributor to periodicals.

WORK IN PROGRESS: A play and a screenplay.

SIDELIGHTS: William Branch wrote: "Though considerable progress, relatively, seems to have been made in the past quarter-century in mainstream utilization of black Americans as subject matter in the arts and the media, and of black American writers and other creative professionals in these fields, my concern continues to be focused upon how much further there is yet to go before racism no longer constitutes the unspoken barrier which must almost constantly be overcome before we can then move on to more basic and realistic curriculum vitae such as talent, craft, and creative vision."

BIOGRAPHICAL/CRITICAL SOURCES:

BOOKS

Abramson, Doris E., *Negro Playwrights in the American Theatre, 1925-1969,* Columbia University Press, 1969.
Aptheker, Herbert, *Toward Negro Freedom,* New Century, 1956.
Berry, Mary Frances and John W. Blassingame, *Long Memory,* Oxford University Press, 1982.
Emanuel, James and Theodore Gross, editors, *Dark Symphony,* Free Press, 1968.
Mitchell, Loften, *Black Drama: The Story of the American Negro in the Theatre,* Hawthorne, 1967.

PERIODICALS

Freedomways, summer, 1963.
Negro Digest, January, 1968.
New York Times, December 20, 1978.

BRATHWAITE, Edward (Kamau) 1930-

PERSONAL: Born May 11, 1930, in Bridgetown, Barbados; son of Hilton Edward and Beryl (Gill) Brathwaite; married Doris Monica Welcome (a teacher and librarian), March 26, 1960; children: Michael. *Education:* Attended Harrison College, Barbados; Pembroke College, Cambridge, B.A. (honors in history), 1953, Diploma of Education, 1954; University of Sussex, D.Phil., 1968.

ADDRESSES: Office—Department of History, University of the West Indies, Mona, Kingston 7, Jamaica.

CAREER: Writer, poet, playwright, and editor. Education officer with Ministry of Education of Ghana, 1955-62; University of the West Indies, Kingston, Jamaica, tutor in Department of Extra Mural Studies assigned to island of Saint Lucia, 1962-63, university lecturer, 1963-72, senior lecturer in history, 1972-76, reader, 1976-83, professor of social and cultural history, 1982—. Plebiscite Office for the United Nations in the Trans-Volta Togoland, 1956-57.

MEMBER: Caribbean Artists Movement (founding secretary, 1966—).

AWARDS, HONORS: Arts Council of Great Britain bursary, 1967; Camden Arts Festival prize, 1967; Cholmondeley Award, 1970, for *Islands;* Guggenheim fellowship, 1972; City of Nairobi fellowship, 1972; Bussa Award, 1973; Casa de las Americas Prize for Poetry, 1976; Fulbright fellow, 1982; Institute of Jamaica Musgrave Medal, 1983.

WRITINGS:

The People Who Came, three volumes, Longman, 1968-72.
Folk Culture of the Slaves in Jamaica, New Beacon, 1970, revised edition, 1981.
The Development of Creole Society in Jamaica, 1770-1820, Clarendon Press, 1971.
Caribbean Man in Space and Time, Savacou Publications, 1974.
Contradictory Omens: Cultural Diversity and Integration in the Caribbean, Savacou Publications, 1974.
Our Ancestral Heritage: A Bibliography of the Roots of Culture in the English-Speaking Caribbean, Literary Committee of Carifesta, 1976.
Wars of Respect: Nanny, Sam Sharpe, and the Struggle for People's Liberation, API, 1977.
The Colonial Encounter: Language, University of Mysore, 1984.
History of the Voice: The Development of Nation Language in Angolophone Caribbean Poetry, New Beacon, 1984.

POETRY

Rights of Passage (also see below), Oxford University Press, 1967.
Masks (also see below), Oxford University Press, 1968.
Islands (also see below), Oxford University Press, 1969.
Panda No. 349, Roy Institute for the Blind, 1969.
The Arrivants: A New World Trilogy (contains *Rights of Passage, Masks,* and *Islands*), Oxford University Press, 1973.
Days and Nights, Caldwell Press, 1975.
Other Exiles, Oxford University Press, 1975.
Black and Blues, Casa de las Americas, 1976.
Mother Poem, Oxford University Press, 1977.
Word Making Man: A Poem for Nicolas Guillen, Savacou Publications, 1979.
Sun Poem, Oxford University Press, 1982.
Third World Poems, Longman, 1983.

X/Self, Oxford University Press, 1987.

PLAYS

Four Plays for Primary Schools (first produced in Saltpond, Ghana, 1961), Longmans, Green, 1964.
Odale's Choice (first produced in Saltpond, Ghana, 1962), Evans Brothers, 1967.

EDITOR

Iouanaloa: Recent Writing from St. Lucia, Department of Extra Mural Studies, University of West Indies, 1963.
Barbados Poetry, 1661-1979, Savacou Publications, 1979.
New Poets from Jamaica (anthology), Savacou Publications, 1979.

RECORDINGS

The Poet Speaks 10, Argo, 1968.
Rights of Passage, Argo, 1969.
Masks, Argo, 1972.
Islands, Argo, 1973.
The Poetry of Edward Kamau Brathwaite, Casa de las Americas, 1976.
Poemas, Casa de las Americas, 1976.

OTHER

Contributor to *Bim* and other periodicals. Editor, *Savacou* (magazine), 1970—.

SIDELIGHTS: Edward Brathwaite is generally regarded as one of the West Indies' most prolific and talented writers. More well known for his poetry, most of Brathwaite's writings seek to explore his past and present self while examining his identity as a black person living in the Caribbean. Andrew Motion writes in the *Times Literary Supplement* that "throughout his career Brathwaite has been concerned to define his identity as a West Indian."

It was the publication of *Rights of Passage* in 1967, *Masks* in 1968, and *Islands* in 1969, that brought Brathwaite to the attention of a larger group of critics and readers. These three books of poetry constitute an autobiographical trilogy collectively entitled *The Arrivants: A New World Trilogy* that examines a Caribbean man's search for identity. The volumes trace Brathwaite's initial encounter with white culture, his journey to Africa in search of a racial self-image, and his eventual return to his Caribbean homeland. Laurence Lieberman writes in *Poetry:* "[Brathwaite] has been able to invent a hybrid prosody which, combining jazz/folk rhythms with English-speaking meters, captures the authenticity of primitive African rituals." "In general," writes Hayden Carruth in the *Hudson Review,* "[Brathwaite] has been remarkably successful in reproducing black speech patterns, both African and Caribbean, in English syntax, using the standard techniques of contemporary poetry, and he has been equally successful in suggesting to an international audience the cultural identities and attitudes of his own people."

In 1977 Brathwaite released *Mother Poem,* the first book in a proposed second trilogy. The second book of the trilogy, *Sun Poem,* was published in 1982. As in Brathwaite's first trilogy, *Mother Poem* and *Sun Poem* continue Brathwaite's exploration of his selfhood. As Andrew Motion explains in the *Times Literary Supplement:* "In *Mother Poem,* [Brathwaite] provides another detailed account of his home [in the West Indies]. But in addition to exploring his complex relationship with the place, he also recounts its own efforts to find an independent and homogeneous character." David Dorsey remarks in *World Lit-*

erature Today: "Brathwaite is particularly ingenious in achieving semantic complexity through his use of assonance, enjambment, word divisions, grammatical and lexical ambiguity, puns and neologisms. This *joie d'esprit* occurs within a rhythm always obedient to the emphases and feelings intended. The style paradoxically reveals the author's sober, passionate and lucid perception on the beauty and pain black Barbadians are heir to."

In a *World Literature Today* review of *Sun Poem* Andrew Salkey comments that "Brathwaite writes 'performance,' 'rituals' and 'illuminations' which result in conflated portraits of persons, places and events recalled through a filter of sequential evocative poems—no ordinary creative accomplishment."

BIOGRAPHICAL/CRITICAL SOURCES:

BOOKS

Authors and Areas of the West Indies, Steck-Vaughn, 1970.
Caribbean Writers, Three Continents, 1979.
Contemporary Literary Criticism, Volume 11, Gale, 1979.
West Indian Literature, Archon Books, 1979.

PERIODICALS

Books, January, 1970.
Books and Bookmen, May, 1967.
Book World, November 3, 1968.
Caribbean Quarterly, June, 1973.
Caribbean Studies, January, 1971.
Choice, June, 1976.
Critical Quarterly, summer, 1970.
Hudson Review, summer, 1974.
Library Journal, March 15, 1970.
New Statesman, April 7, 1967.
Poetry, April, 1969, May, 1971.
Saturday Review, October 14, 1967.
Times Literary Supplement, February 16, 1967, August 15, 1968, January 28, 1972, June 30, 1972, November 14, 1975, Janaury 20, 1978, February 18, 1983.
Virginia Quarterly Review, autumn, 1963, autumn, 1968, spring, 1970.
World Literature Today, winter, 1977, summer, 1978, summer, 1983.

*   *   *

BRAWLEY, Benjamin (Griffith)   1882-1939

PERSONAL: Born April 22, 1882, in Columbia, S. C.; died after a brief illness following a stroke, February 1, 1939, in Washington, D. C.; son of Edward MacKnight (a clergyman and an educator) and Margaret Sophronia (Dickerson) Brawley; married Hilda Damaris Prowd, July 20, 1912. *Education:* Atlanta Baptist College (now Morehouse College), B.A., 1901; University of Chicago, B.A., 1906; Harvard University, M.A., 1908.

ADDRESSES: Home—1201 Harvard St. N. W., Washington, D. C. 20009.

CAREER: Educator and author. Taught in a rural one-room school in Georgetown, Fla., 1901-02; Morehouse College, Atlanta, Ga., instructor in English, history, and Latin, 1902-10; Howard University, Washington, D. C., professor of English, 1910-12; Morehouse College, professor of English and dean, 1912-20; ordained to Baptist ministry, 1921; Messiah Baptist Church, Brockton, Mass., pastor, 1921-22; Shaw University, Raleigh, N. C., professor of English, 1923-31, dean, 1930-

31; Howard University, professor of English, 1931-39. President of Association of Colleges for Negro Youth, 1919-20. Conducted a study of educational and social conditions on the west coast of Africa in 1930; gave lectures to various colleges and universities.

AWARDS, HONORS: Recipient of honorary doctorates from Shaw University, 1927, and Morehouse College, 1937.

WRITINGS:

A Toast to Love and Death (poems), Atlanta Baptist College, 1902.
The Problem, and Other Poems (poems), Atlanta Baptist College, 1905.
A Short History of the American Negro, Macmillan, 1913, 4th revised edition, 1939.
History of Morehouse College, Morehouse College (Atlanta, Ga.), 1917, reprinted, McGrath Publishing, 1970.
The Negro in Literature and Art in the United States, Duffield, 1918, revised edition, 1921, reprinted, Scholarly Press, 1972.
Women of Achievement, Woman's American Home Baptist Mission Society, 1919, reprinted, University Microfilms (Ann Arbor, Mich.), 1978.
A Short History of the English Drama, Harcourt, 1921, reprinted, Books for Libraries, 1969.
A Social History of the American Negro, Macmillan, 1921, reprinted, AMS Press, 1971.
New Survey of English Literature: A Textbook for Colleges, Knopf, 1925, reprinted, 1930.
Doctor Dillard of the Jeanes Fund, with an introduction by Anson Phelps Stokes, Revell, 1930, reprinted, Books for Libraries, 1971.
History of the English Hymn, Abingdon, 1932.
(Editor) *Early Negro American Writers,* University of North Carolina Press, 1935, reprinted, Books for Libraries, 1968.
Paul Laurence Dunbar, Poet of His People, University of North Carolina Press, 1936, reprinted, Kennikat, 1967.
Negro Builders and Heroes, University of North Carolina Press, 1937, reprinted, 1965.
The Negro Genius: A New Appraisal of the Achievement of the American Negro in Literature and the Fine Arts, Dodd, 1937, reprinted, Biblo & Tannen, 1966.
The Seven Sleepers of Ephesys (poems), Foote & Davis (Atlanta, Ga.), 1971.

Also author of short stories and other poems and editor of *The Best Stories of Paul Laurence Dunbar,* 1938. Contributor of scholarly articles to the *Dictionary of American Biography* and of historical essays, social commentaries, poems, and book reviews to *Crisis, Dial, Lippincott's Magazine, Christian Advocate, Bookman, Southern Workman, Opportunity, Journal of Negro History, Harvard Monthly, Sewanee Review,* the *Springfield Republican,* and other publications. Editor of *Home Mission College Review* for several years.

SIDELIGHTS: Regarded as one of the most prolific writers of all Afro-American educators, Benjamin Brawley is best known for his works in literary and social history. Several of his books are considered standard texts in college and university curriculums. Among these are *The Negro in Literature and Art in the United States, New Survey of English Literature,* and Brawley's two biographical volumes, *The Negro Genius,* which focuses on black artists and literary figures, and *Negro Builders and Heroes,* which covers a wider field of black notables.

BIOGRAPHICAL/CRITICAL SOURCES:

BOOKS

Brown, Sterling A., Arthur P. Davis, and Ulysses Lee, editors, *The Negro Caravan,* Arno, 1969.
Hughes, Langston, and Arna Bontemps, editors, *Poetry of the Negro, 1746-1949,* Doubleday, 1949.
Thorpe, Earl Endris, *Black Historians,* Morrow, 1971.

PERIODICALS

Afro-American, February 11, 1939.
New York Times, February 7, 1939.
Phylon, Volume X, number 1, 1949.

*   *   *

BROOKS, Gwendolyn   1917-

PERSONAL: Born June 7, 1917, in Topeka, Kan.; daughter of David Anderson and Keziah Corinne (Wims) Brooks; married Henry Lowington Blakely, September 17, 1939; children: Henry Lowington, III, Nora. *Education:* Graduate of Wilson Junior College, 1936.

ADDRESSES: Home—7428 South Evans Ave., Chicago, Ill. 60619.

CAREER: Poet and novelist. Publicity director, NAACP Youth Council, Chicago, Ill., 1937-38. Taught poetry at numerous colleges and universities, including Columbia College, Elmhurst College, Northeastern Illinois State College (now Northwestern Illinois University), and University of Wisconsin—Madison, 1969; Distinguished Professor of the Arts, City College of the City University of New York, 1971. Member, Illinois Arts Council.

MEMBER: American Academy of Arts and Letters, National Institute of Arts and Letters, Society of Midland Authors (Chicago).

AWARDS, HONORS: Named one of ten women of the year, *Mademoiselle* magazine, 1945; National Institute of Arts and Letters grant in literature, 1946; American Academy of Arts and Letters award for creative writing, 1946; Guggenheim fellowships, 1946, 1947; Eunice Tietjens Memorial Prize, *Poetry* magazine, 1949; Pulitzer Prize in poetry, 1950, for *Annie Allen;* Robert F. Ferguson Memorial Award, Friends of Literature, 1964, for *Selected Poems;* Thormod Monsen Literature Award, 1964; Anisfield-Wolf Award, 1968, for *In the Mecca;* named Poet Laureate of Illinois, 1968—; Black Academy of Arts and Letters Award, 1971, for outstanding achievement in letters; Shelley Memorial Award, 1976; Poetry Consultant to the Library of Congress, 1985-86; forty-nine honorary degrees from universities and colleges, including Columbia College, 1964, Lake Forest College, 1965, and Brown University, 1974.

WRITINGS:

POETRY

A Street in Bronzeville (also see below), Harper, 1945.
Annie Allen (also see below), Harper, 1949, reprinted, Greenwood Press, 1972.
The Bean Eaters (also see below), Harper, 1960.
In the Time of Detachment, In the Time of Cold, Civil War Centennial Commission of Illinois, 1965.
In the Mecca (also see below), Harper, 1968.
For Illinois 1968: A Sesquicentennial Poem, Harper, 1968.
Riot (also see below), Broadside Press, 1969.

Family Pictures (also see below), Broadside Press, 1970.
Aloneness, Broadside Press, 1971.
Aurora, Broadside Press, 1972.
Beckonings, Broadside Press, 1975.
Primer for Blacks, Black Position Press, 1980.
To Disembark, Third World Press, 1981.
Black Love, Brooks Press, 1982.
Mayor Harold Washington [and] *Chicago, The I Will City,* Brooks Press, 1983.
The Near Johannesburg Boy, and Other Poems, The David Co., 1987.

Also author of *A Catch of Shy Fish,* 1963.

JUVENILE

Bronzeville Boys and Girls (poems), Harper, 1956.
The Tiger Who Wore White Gloves, Third World Press, 1974, reissued, 1987.

FICTION

Maud Martha (novel; also see below), Harper, 1953, reprinted, The David Co., 1987.
(Contributor) Herbert Hill, editor, *Soon One Morning: New Writing by American Negroes, 1940-1962* (contains the short story "The Life of Lincoln West"), Knopf, 1963, published in England as *Black Voices,* Elek, 1964.
(Contributor) Langston Hughes, editor, *The Best Short Stories by Negro Writers: An Anthology from 1899 to the Present,* Little, Brown, 1967.

COLLECTED WORKS

Selected Poems, Harper, 1963.
The World of Gwendolyn Brooks (contains *A Street in Bronzeville, Annie Allen, Maud Martha, The Bean Eaters, In the Mecca*), Harper, 1971.
Blacks (includes *A Street in Bronzeville, Annie Allen, The Bean Eaters, Maud Martha, A Catch of Shy Fish, Riot, In the Mecca,* and most of *Family Pictures*), The David Co., 1987.

OTHER

(Author of foreword) Langston Hughes, editor, *New Negro Poets USA,* Indiana University Press, 1964.
(With others) *A Portion of that Field: The Centennial of the Burial of Lincoln,* University of Illinois Press, 1967.
(Editor) *A Broadside Treasury,* (poems), Broadside Press, 1971.
(Editor) *Jump Bad: A New Chicago Anthology,* Broadside Press, 1971.
Report from Part One: An Autobiography, Broadside Press, 1972.
(Author of introduction) Arnold Adoff, editor, *The Poetry of Black America: Anthology of the Twentieth Century,* Harper, 1973.
(With Keorapetse Kgositsile, Haki R. Madhubuti, and Dudley Randall) *A Capsule Course in Black Poetry Writing,* Broadside Press, 1975.
Young Poet's Primer (writing manual), Brooks Press, 1981.
Very Young Poets (writing manual), Brooks Press, 1983.

Also author of broadsides *The Wall* and *We Real Cool,* for Broadside Press, and *I See Chicago,* 1964. Contributor of poems and articles to *Ebony, McCall's, Nation, Poetry,* and other periodicals. Contributor of reviews to *Chicago Sun-Times, Chicago Daily News,* and *New York Herald Tribune.*

WORK IN PROGRESS: A sequel to *Maud Martha; Winnie,* poems interpreting Winnie Mandela of South Africa.

SIDELIGHTS: In 1950, Gwendolyn Brooks, a highly regarded poet, became the first black author to win the Pulitzer Prize. Her poems from this period, specifically *A Street in Bronzeville* and *Annie Allen,* were "devoted to small, carefully cerebrated, terse portraits of the Black urban poor," Richard K. Barksdale comments in *Modern Black Poets: A Collection of Critical Essays.* Jeanne-Marie A. Miller calls this "city-folk poetry" and describes Brooks's characters as "unheroic black people who fled the land for the city—only to discover that there is little difference between the world of the North and the world of the South. One learns from them," Miller continues in the *Journal of Negro Education,* "their dismal joys and their human griefs and pain." Audiences in Chicago, inmates in prisons around the country, and students of all ages have found her poems accessible and relevant. Haki Madhubuti, cited in Jacqueline Trescott's *Washington Post* article on Brooks, points out that Brooks "has, more than any other nationally acclaimed writer, remained in touch with the community she writes about. She lives in the core of Chicago's black community.... She is her work." In addition, notes Toni Cade Bambara in the *New York Times Book Review,* Brooks "is known for her technical artistry, having worked her word sorcery in forms as disparate as Italian terza rima and the blues. She has been applauded for revelations of the African experience in America, particularly her sensitive portraits of black women."

Though best known for her poetry, in the 1950s, Brooks published her first novel. *Maud Martha* presents vignettes from a ghetto woman's life in short chapters, says Harry B. Shaw in *Gwendolyn Brooks.* It is "a story of a woman with doubts about herself and where and how she fits into the world. Maud's concern is not so much that she is inferior but that she is perceived as being ugly." Eventually, she takes a stand for her own dignity by turning her back on a patronising, racist store clerk. "The book is . . . about the triumph of the lowly," comments Shaw. "[Brooks] shows what they go through and exposes the shallowness of the popular, beautiful white people with 'good' hair. One way of looking at the book, then, is as a war with . . . people's concepts of beauty." Its other themes include "the importance of spiritual and physical death," disillusionment with a marriage that amounts to "a step down" in living conditions, and the discovery "that even through disillusionment and spiritual death life will prevail," Shaw maintains. Other reviewers feel that Brooks is more effective when treating the same themes in her poetry, but David Littlejohn, writing in *Black on White: A Critical Survey of Writing by American Negroes,* feels the novel 'is a striking human experiment, as exquisitely written . . . as any of Gwendolyn Brook's poetry in verse. . . . It is a powerful, beautiful dagger of a book, as generous as it can possibly be. It teaches more, more quickly, more lastingly, than a thousand pages of protest." In a *Black World* review, Annette Oliver Shands appreciates the way in which *Maud Martha* differs from the works of other early black writers: "Miss Brooks does not specify traits, niceties or assets for members of the Black community to acquire in order to attain their just rights. . . . So, this is not a novel to inspire social advancement on the part of fellow Blacks. Nor does it say *be poor, Black and happy.* The message is to accept the challenge of being human and to assert humanness with urgency."

Although, as Martha Liebrum notes in the *Houston Post,* Brooks "wrote about being black before being black was beautiful," in retrospect her poems have been described as sophisticated, intellectual, and European, or "conditioned" by the established literary tradition. Like her early favorites Emily Dickinson, John Keats, and Percy Bysshe Shelley, Brooks expresses in poetry her love of "the wonders language can achieve," as she told Claudia Tate in an interview for *Black Women Writers at Work*. Barksdale states that by not directly emphasizing any "rhetorical involvement with causes, racial or otherwise," Brooks was merely reflecting the "the literary mood of the late 1940's." He suggests that there was little reason for Brooks to confront the problems of racism on a large scale since, in her work, "each character, so neatly and precisely presented, is a racial protest in itself and a symbol of some sharply etched human dilemma."

However, Brooks' later poems show a marked change in tone and content. Just as her first poems reflected the mood of their era, her later works mirror their age by displaying what *National Observer* contributor Bruce Cook calls "an intense awareness of the problems of color and justice." Bambara comments that, at the age of fifty "something happened [to Brooks], a something most certainly in evidence in 'In the Mecca' (1968) and subsequent works—a new movement and energy, intensity, richness, power of statement and a new stripped lean, compressed style. A change of style prompted by a change of mind."

"Though some of her work in the early 1960s had a terse abbreviated style, her conversion to direct political expression happened rapidly after a gathering of black writers at Fisk University in 1967," Trescott reports. Brooks told Tate, "They seemed proud and so committed to their own people. . . . The poets among them felt that black poets should write as blacks, about blacks, and address themselves *to* blacks." If many of her earlier poems had fulfilled this aim, it was not due to conscious intent, she said; but from this time forward, Brooks has thought of herself as an African who has determined not to compromise social comment for the sake of technical proficiency.

Although *In the Mecca* and later works are characterized as tougher and possess what a reviewer for the *Virginia Quarterly Review* describes as "raw power and roughness," critics are quick to indicate that these poems are neither bitter nor vengeful. Instead, according to Cook, they are more "about bitterness" than bitter in themselves. *Dictionary of Literary Biography* essayist Charles Israel suggests that *In the Mecca*'s title poem, for example, shows "a deepening of Brooks's concern with social problems." A mother has lost a small daughter in the block-long ghetto tenement, the Mecca; the long poem traces her steps through the building, revealing her neighbors to be indifferent, or insulated by their own personal obsessions. The mother finds her little girl, who "never learned that black is not beloved," who "Was royalty when poised, / sly, at the A and P's fly-open door," under a Jamaican resident's cot, murdered. The *Virginia Quarterly Review* contributor compares the poem's impact to that of Richard Wright's fiction. R. Baxter Miller, writing in *Black American Poets Between Worlds, 1940-1960*, comments, "*In the Mecca* is a most complex and intriguing book; it seeks to balance the sordid realities of urban life with an imaginative process of reconciliation and redemption." Other poems in the book, occasioned by the death of Malcolm X, or the dedication of a mural of black heroes painted on a Chicago slum building, express the poet's commitment to her people's awareness of themselves as a political as well as a cultural entity.

Her interest in encouraging young blacks to assist and appreciate fledgling black publishing companies led her to leave Harper & Row. In the seventies, she chose Dudley Randall's Broadside Press to publish her poetry (*Riot, Family Pictures, Aloneness, Aurura*, and *Beckonings*) and *Report from Part One*, the first volume of her autobiography. She edited two collections of poetry—*A Broadside Treasury* and *Jump Bad: A New Chicago Anthology*—for the Detroit-based press. The Chicago-based Third World Press, run by Haki R. Madhubuti (formerly Don L. Lee, one of the young poets she had met during the sixties), has also brought two Brooks titles into print. She does not regret having given her support to small publishers who dedicated themselves to the needs of the black community. Brooks was the first writer to read in Broadside's Poet's Theatre Series when it began, and was also the first poet to read in the second opening of the series when the press revived under new ownership in 1988.

Riot, Family Pictures, Beckonings, and other books brought out by black publishers were given brief notice by critics of the literary establishment who "did not wish to encourage Black publishers," said Brooks. Some were disturbed by the political content of these poems. *Riot,* in particular, in which Brooks is the spokesman for the "HEALTHY REBELLION" going on then, as she calls it, was accused of "celebrating violence" by L. L. Shapiro in a *School Library Journal* review. Key poems from these books, later collected in *To Disembark,* call blacks to "work together toward their own REAL emancipation," Brooks indicated. Even so, "the strength here is not in declamation but in [the poet's] genius for psychological insight," claims J. A. Lipari in the *Library Journal*. Addison Gayle points out that the softer poems of this period—the ones asking for stronger interpersonal bonds among black Americans—are no less political: "To espouse and exult in a Black identity, outside the psychic boundaries of white Americans, was to threaten . . . . To advocate and demand love between one Black and another was to begin a new chapter in American history. Taken together, the acknowledgment of a common racial identity among Blacks throughout the world and the suggestion of a love based upon the brotherhood and sisterhood of the oppressed were meant to transform Blacks in America from a minority to a majority, from world victims to, to use Madhubuti's phrase, 'world makers.'"

In the same essay, printed in *Black Women Writers (1950-1980): A Critical Evaluation,* Gayle defends *Riot* and the later books, naming them an important source of inspiration to a rising generation: "It may well be . . . that the function of poetry is not so much to save us from oppression nor from Auschwitz, but to give us the strength to face them, to help us stare down the lynch mob, walk boldly in front of the firing squad. It is just such awareness that the poetry of Gwendolyn Brooks has given us, this that she and those whom she taught/ learned from have accomplished for us all. They have told us that for Black Americans there are no havens, that in the eyes of other Americans we are, each and every one of us, rioters. . . . These are dangerous times for Black people. The sensitive Black poet realizes that fact, but far from despairing, picks up his pen, . . . and echoes Gwendolyn Brooks: 'My aim . . . is to write poems that will somehow successfully "call" . . . all black people . . . in gutters, in schools, offices, factories, prisons, the consulate; I wish to teach black people in pulpits, black people in mines, on farms, on thrones." Brooks pointed out "a serious error" in this quote; she wants to "reach" people, not "teach" them. She added, "The times for Black people—when*ever* in the clutches of white *manipulation,* have ALWAYS been dangerous." She also advised young poets,

"Walking in front of a firing squad is *crazy*. Your effort should be in preventing the *formation* of a firing squad."

The poet's search "for an *expression* relevant to all manner of blacks," as she described her change in focus to Tate, did not alter her mastery of her craft. "While quoting approvingly Ron Karenga's observation that 'the fact that we are black is our ultimate reality,' blackness did not, to her, require simplification of language, symbol, or mural perception," notes C. W. E. Bigsby in *The Second Black Renaissance: Essays in Black Literature*. It did include "the possibility of communicating directly to those in the black community." In the bars and on the street corners were an audience not likely to "go into a bookstore" to buy poetry by anyone, she told George Stavros in a *Contemporary Literature* interview reprinted in *Report from Part One: An Autobiography*. And in the late sixties, Brooks reported, "some of those folks DID" enter bookstores to buy poetry and read it "standing up." To better reach the street audience, Brooks's later poems use more open, less traditional poetic forms and techniques. Penelope Moffet of the *Los Angeles Times* records the poet's statement that since 1967, she has been "successfully escaping from close rhyme, because it just isn't natural. . . . I've written hundreds . . . of sonnets, and I'll probably never write another one, because I don't feel that this is a sonnet time. It seems to me it's a wild, raw, ragged free verse time." She told Stavros, "I want to write poems that will be non-compromising. I don't want to stop a concern with words doing good jobs, which has always been a concern of mine, but I want to write poems that will be meaningful to those people I described a while ago, things that will touch them." Speaking of later works aimed for that audience, Robert F. Kiernan offers in *American Writing since 1945: A Critical Survey,* "She remains, however, a virtuoso of the lyric and an extraordinary portraitist—probably the finest black poet of the post-Harlem generation."

When *Report from Part One* came out in 1972, some reviewers complained that it did not provide the level of personal detail nor the insight into black literature that they had expected. "They wanted a list of domestic spats," remarked Brooks. Bambara notes that it "is not a sustained dramatic narrative for the nosey, being neither the confessions of a private woman/poet or the usual sort of mahogany-desk memoir public personages inflict upon the populace at the first sign of a cardiac. . . . It documents the growth of Gwen Brooks." Other reviewers value it for explaining the poet's new orientation toward her racial heritage and her role as a poet. In a passage she has presented again in later books as a definitive statement, she writes: "I—who have 'gone the gamut' from an almost angry rejection of my dark skin by some of my brainwashed brothers and sisters to a surprised queenhood in the new Black sun—am qualified to enter at least the kindergarten of new consciousness now. New consciousness and trudge-toward-progress. I have hopes for myself. . . . I know now that I am essentially an essential African, in occupancy here because of an indeed 'peculiar' institution. . . . I know that Black fellow-feeling must be the Black man's encyclopedic Primer. I know that the Black-and-white integration concept, which in the mind of some beaming early saint was a dainty spinning dream, has wound down to farce. . . . I know that the Black emphasis must be not *against white* but FOR *Black*. . . . In the Conference-That-Counts, whose date may be 1980 or 2080 (woe betide the Fabric of Man if it is 2080), there will be no looking up nor looking down." In the future, she envisions "the profound and frequent shaking of hands, which in Africa is so important. The shaking of hands in warmth and strength and union."

Brooks put some of the finishing touches on the second volume of her autobiography while serving as Poetry Consultant to the Library of Congress. Brooks was sixty-eight when she became the first black woman to be appointed to the post. Of her many duties there, the most important, in her view, were visits to local schools. "Poetry is life distilled," she told students in a Washington school, Schmich reports. "She urged them to keep journals. She read them a poem about teen suicide. She told them poetry exists where they might not recognize it," such as in John Lennon's song "Eleanor Rigby." Similar visits to colleges, universities, prisons, hospitals, and drug rehabilitation centers characterize her tenure as Poet Laureate of Illinois. In that role, she has sponsored and hosted annual literary awards ceremonies at which she presents prizes paid for "out of [her] own pocket, which, despite her modest means, is of legendary depth," Reginald Gibbons relates in *Tribune Books*. She has honored and encouraged many poets in her state through the Illinois Poets Laureate Awards and Significant Illinois Poets Awards programs. At one ceremony, says Gibbons, "poetry was, for a time, the vital center of people's lives."

Though her writing is "*to* Blacks," it is "*for* anyone who wants to open the book," she emphasized to Schmich. Brook's objectivity is perhaps the most widely acclaimed feature of her poetry. Janet Overmeyer notes in the *Christian Science Monitor* that Brooks' "particular, outstanding, genius is her unsentimental regard and respect for all human beings. . . . She neither foolishly pities nor condemns—she creates." Overmeyer continues, "From her poet's craft bursts a whole gallery of wholly alive persons, preening, squabbling, loving, weeping; many a novelist cannot do so well in ten times the space." Brooks achieves this effect through a high "degree of artistic control," claims Littlejohn. "The words, lines, and arrangements," he states, "have been worked and worked and worked again into poised exactness: the unexpected apt metaphor, the mock-colloquial asides amid jewelled phrases, the half-ironic repetitions—she knows it all." More importantly, Brooks' objective treatment of issues such as poverty and racism "produces genuine emotional tension," he writes.

This quality also provides her poems with universal appeal. Blyden Jackson states in *Black Poetry in America: Two Essays in Historical Interpretation* that Brooks "is one of those artists of whom it can truthfully be said that things like sex and race, important as they are,. . . appear in her work to be sublimated into insights and revelations of universal application." Although Brooks' characters are primarily black and poor, and live in Northern urban cities, she provides, according to Jackson, through "the close inspection of a limited domain,. . . a view of life in which one may see a microscopic portion of the universe intensely and yet, through that microscopic portion see all truth for the human condition wherever it is." And although the goals and adjustments of black nationalism have been her frequent topics, Houston A Baker, Jr., says of Brooks in the *CLA Journal,* "The critic (whether black or white) who comes to her work seeking only support for his ideology will be disappointed for, as Etheridge Knight pointed out, she has ever spoken the truth. And truth, one likes to feel, always lies beyond the boundaries of any one ideology. Perhaps Miss Brooks' most significant achievement is her endorsement of this point of view. From her hand and fertile imagination have come volumes that transcend the dogma on either side of the American veil." Baker feels that Brooks "represents a singular achievement. Beset by a double consciousness, she has kept herself from being torn asunder by crafting poems that equal the best in the black and white American literary traditions.''

Proving the breadth of Brooks's appeal, poets representing a wide variety of ''races and . . . poetic camps'' gathered at the University of Chicago to celebrate the poet's 70th birthday in 1987, reports Gibbons. Brooks brought them together, he says, ''in . . . a moment of good will and cheer.'' In recognition of her service and achievements, a junior high school in Harvey, Illinois has been named for her. She is also honored at Western Illinois University's Gwendolyn Brooks Center for African-American Literature.

Summing up the poet's accomplishments, Gibbons writes that, beginning with *A Street in Bronzeville*, Brooks has brought national attention to ''a part of life that had been grossly neglected by the literary establishment. . . . ''And because Brooks has been a deeply serious artist . . . , she has created works of special encouragement to black writers and of enduring importance to all readers.''

BIOGRAPHICAL/CRITICAL SOURCES:

BOOKS

Authors in the News, Volume 1, Gale, 1976.
Baker, Houston A., Jr., *Singers of Daybreak: Studies in Black American Literature*, Howard University Press, 1974.
Bigsby, C. W. E., editor, *The Black American Writer, Volume II: Poetry and Drama*, Deland, 1969.
Bigsby, C. W. E., *The Second Black Renaissance: Essays in Black Literature*, Greenwood Press, 1980.
Brooks, Gwendolyn, *In the Mecca*, Harper, 1968.
Brooks, Gwendolyn, *Report from Part One: An Anthology*, Broadside Press, 1972.
Brown, Patricia L., Don L. Lee, and Francis Ward, editors, *To Gwen with Love: An Anthology Dedicated to Gwendolyn Brooks*, Johnson Publishing, 1971.
Concise Dictionary of Literary Biography, 1941-1968, Gale, 1985.
Contemporary Literary Criticism, Gale, Volume 1, 1973, Volume 2, 1974, Volume 4, 1975, Volume 5, 1976, Volume 15, 1980.
Dictionary of Literary Biography, Volume 5: *American Poets since World War II*, Gale, 1980.
Dembo, L. S. and Pondrom, C. N., editors, *The Contemporary Writer: Interviews with Sixteen Novelists and Poets*, University of Wisconsin Press, 1972.
Drotning, Philip T. and Wesley W. Smith, editors, *Up from the Ghetto*, Cowles, 1970.
Emanuel and Gross, editors, *Dark Symphony: Negro Literature in America*, Free Press, 1968.
Evans, Mari, editor, *Black Women Writers (1950-1980): A Critical Evaluation*, Anchor/Doubleday, 1984.
Gates, Henry Louis, Jr., editor, *Black Literature and Literary Theory*, Methuen, 1984.
Gayle, Addison, editor, *Black Expression*, Weybright & Talley, 1969.
Gibson, Donald B., editor, *Modern Black Poets: A Collection of Critical Essays*, Prentice-Hall, 1973.
Gould, Jean, *Modern American Women Poets*, Dodd, Mead, 1985.
Jackson, Blyden and Louis D. Rubin, Jr., *Black Poetry in America: Two Essays in Historical Interpretation*, Louisiana State University Press, 1974.
Kent, George, *Gwendolyn Brooks: A Life*, University Press of Kentucky, 1988.

Kufrin, Joan, *Uncommon Women*, New Century Publications, 1981.
Littlejohn, David, *Black on White: A Critical Survey of Writing by American Negroes*, Viking, 1966.
Madhubuti, Haki R., *Say that the River Turns: The Impact of Gwendolyn Brooks*, Third World Press, 1987.
Melhem, D. H., *Gwendolyn Brooks: Poetry and the Heroic Voice*, University Press of Kentucky, 1987.
Miller, R. Baxter, *Langston Hughes and Gwendolyn Brooks: A Reference Guide*, Hall, 1978.
Miller, R. Baxter, *Black American Poets between Worlds, 1940-1960*, University of Tennessee Press, 1986.
Mootry, Maria K. and Gary Smith, editors, *A Life Distilled: Gwendolyn Brooks, Her Poetry and Fiction*, University of Illinois Press, 1987.
Newquist, Roy, *Conversations*, Rand McNally, 1967.
Redmond, Eugene B., *Drumvoices: The Mission of Afro-American Poetry*, Doubleday, 1976.
Shaw, Harry F., *Gwendolyn Brooks*, Twayne, 1980.
Tate, Claudia, *Black Women Writers at Work*, Continuum, 1983.

PERIODICALS

Atlantic Monthly, September, 1960.
Best Sellers, April 1, 1973.
Black American Literature Forum, spring, 1977, winter, 1984.
Black Enterprise, June, 1985.
Black Scholar, March, 1981, November, 1984.
Black World, August, 1970, January, 1971, July, 1971, September, 1971, October, 1971, January, 1972, March, 1973, June, 1973, December, 1975.
Book Week, October 27, 1963.
Chicago Tribune, January 14, 1986, June 7, 1987.
Christian Science Monitor, September 19, 1968.
CLA Journal, December, 1962, December, 1963, December, 1969, September, 1972, September, 1973, September, 1977, December, 1982.
Contemporary Literature, March 28, 1969, winter, 1970.
Critique, summer, 1984.
Discourse, spring, 1967.
Ebony, July, 1968.
Essence, April, 1971, September, 1984.
Explicator, Volume 58, April, 1976, Volume 36, number 4, summer, 1978.
Houston Post, February 11, 1974.
Journal of Negro Education, winter, 1970.
Library Journal, September 15, 1970.
Los Angeles Times, November 6, 1987.
Los Angeles Times Book Review, September 2, 1984.
Modern Fiction Studies, winter, 1985.
Nation, September, 1962, July 7, 1969.
National Observer, November 9, 1968.
Negro American Literature Forum, fall, 1967, summer, 1974.
Negro Digest, December, 1961, January, 1962, August, 1962, July, 1963, June, 1964, January, 1968.
New Statesman, May 3, 1985.
New Yorker, September 22, 1945, December 17, 1949, October 10, 1953, December 3, 1979.
New York Times, November 4, 1945, October 5, 1953, December 9, 1956, October 6, 1963, March 2, 1969.
New York Times Book Review, October 23, 1960, October 6, 1963, March 2, 1969, January 2, 1972, June 4, 1972, December 3, 1972, January 7, 1973, June 10, 1973, December 2, 1973, September 23, 1984, July 5, 1987.

Phylon, Volume XXII, summer, 1961, Volume XXXVII, number 1, March, 1976.

Poetry, Volume 67, December, 1945, Volume 126, 1950, Volume 103, March, 1964.

Publishers Weekly, June 6, 1970.

Ramparts, December, 1968.

Saturday Review, January 19, 1946, September 17, 1949, February 1, 1964.

Saturday Review of Literature, May 20, 1950.

Southern Review, spring, 1965.

Studies in Black Literature, autumn, 1973, spring, 1974, summer, 1974, spring, 1977.

Tribune Books, July 12, 1987.

Virginia Quarterly Review, winter, 1969, winter, 1971.

Washington Post, May 19, 1971, April 19, 1973, March 31, 1987.

Washington Post Book World, November 3, 1968, November 11, 1973.

Women's Review of Books, December, 1984.

World Literature Today, winter, 1985.

*   *   *

BROWN, Cecil M(orris)   1943-

PERSONAL: Born July 3, 1943, in Bolton, N.C.; son of Cecil (a tobacco sharecropper) and Dorothy Brown. *Education:* Attended Agricultural and Technical State University, Greensboro, N.C., 1961; Columbia University, B.A., 1966, University of Chicago, M.A., 1967.

ADDRESSES: Office—1856 Dwight Way, Berkeley, Calif. 94703.

CAREER: Writer. University of Illinois at Chicago Circle, lecturer in English, 1968-69; University of California, Berkeley, lecturer in English, 1969-70; lecturer in English and producer of plays, Merrit College, Oakland, Calif. Screenwriter, Warner Brothers, 1977-79, and Universal Studios.

AWARDS, HONORS: Before Columbus Foundation American Book Award, 1984, for *Days Without Weather.*

WRITINGS:

The Life and Loves of Mr. Jiveass Nigger (novel), Farrar, Straus, 1970.

(With Carl Gottlieb) "Which Way is Up?" (screenplay; adapted from *The Seduction of Mimi* by Lina Wertmuller), Universal, 1977.

Days Without Weather, Farrar, Straus, 1982.

Author of plays, including "The African Shades: A Comedy in One Act," "The Gila Monster," and "Our Sisters Are Pregnant." Contributor of articles to *Partisan Review, Black World, Kenyon Review, Yardbird Reader, Evergreen Review, Negro Digest,* and other periodicals.

SIDELIGHTS: The major themes of Cecil Brown's work include stories of "black survival in a corrupt society" and how "a culture victimizes all its minorities if it denies a voice to any one of them," describes Jean M. Bright in a *Dictionary of Literary Biography* essay. *The Life and Loves of Mr. Jiveass Nigger,* Brown's first and probably best-known work, relates the story of George Washington, a young black who leaves the United States "to find out if everyone in the world lies as much as he lies in his dedicated search for invisibility," summarizes Richard Rhodes in the *New York Times Book Review.* Living in Copenhagen and drifting through various relation-

ships with whites and blacks, Washington finally admits, as Bright relates it, "that he is a fool and a prodigal destroying himself by wallowing in a moral pigsty among swinish people."

Reception of Brown's novel was mixed, inviting comparisons to James Joyce on one hand and blunt criticism on the other. A *Times Literary Supplement* critic finds that woven into the story of Washington's "jiving" are subtleties which are "carefully placed. . . . Slowly but surely we pick up the idea that perhaps Jiveass is really on the losing side." Christopher Lehmann-Haupt writes in the *New York Times* that "at the beginning of 'The Life and Loves of Mr. Jiveass Nigger' we know that we are into good stuff. Mr. Brown has a hard, driving style that toys with the stereotypes of black verbal rhythms and punches when one isn't looking." Although Lehmann-Haupt admires the author's style, he faults the novel's plotting: "Gradually, as certain scenes (or the points of certain scenes) repeat themselves, the fictional illusion begins to wear thin . . . and one's attention wanders." An *Antioch Review* writer calls the work "crude," remarking that "neither is this soul novel very good reading, as a remembrance of *Invisible Man* could tell you." Rhodes draws a more favorable comparison, however, observing that the novel "recalls, in its form and language, other novels . . . [including] Joyce's 'Portrait of the Artist as a Young Man' and [Ralph] Ellison's 'Invisible Man.'" The critic continues: "The awareness of black invisibility and its uses (and its self-destructiveness) . . . creates a form reminiscent of Ellison's."

At the end of *Life and Loves,* Washington considers writing a novel upon his return to America; he says that "If you say something about sex and being a nigger then you got a best seller." Rhodes remarks that Washington's new vocation will still require him to work with lies and "jive"; in deciding to become an artist, Washington "knows that he must explain himself, must take on that ultimate jiving which is art." The *Times Literary Supplement* critic, however, finds a darker meaning in the novel's ending, one that reflects upon Brown's own career: "Mr. Brown's complaint, like that of Jiveass, is that his blackness forces him to attitudinize. He cannot be a writer, he has got to be a *black* writer, and this book, more than anything, is a bitter joke at its own expense."

It was thirteen years before Brown followed up *Life and Loves* with a second novel, *Days Without Weather.* In between these publications, Brown held a variety of positions, one of which was as a screenwriter for Warner Brothers and Universal. *Days Without Weather* draws upon Brown's own Hollywood experiences, relating the story of Jonah, a young black comedian whose attempts at bringing a friend's script about a historic slave revolt to the screen are corrupted by everyone involved. In the process of making the film, Jonah is betrayed by the producer, who breaks her promise to film the script intact, and his uncle Gadge, whose revisions transform the script into a work of exploitation. The worst corruption takes place when the playwright "visits the set, discovers the deception and protests, starting a riot between white actors and black actors," as David Bradley describes in the *New York Times Book Review.* The studio films the riot and releases the film, which is highly praised.

Days Without Weather is typical of the "Hollywood" novel, demonstrating the "classic quandary of the performing artist, whether to compromise his integrity to win applause," describes James Idema in the *Chicago Tribune Book World.* Art Seidenbaum, writing in the *Los Angeles Times Book Review,* sees the treatment of this subject as a flaw in the novel: "The trouble with Hollywood novels may be the way novelists moralize, setting up one pure soul sinking in a universal cesspool, alluding to fine art when frivolous amusement is more often the business at hand.'' David Bradley agrees with this assessment, noting in the *New York Times Book Review* that the hypocrisy of Jonah's own lies and betrayals are never fully explored. Both critics also believe that Jonah's comedic routines do not translate very well to written form. For Idema, however, Jonah's work on stage provides some of the best scenes in the book; ''white or black,'' the critic comments, ''you'll laugh at Jonah's raunchy routines.'' Bright believes that *Days Without Weather*, combined with Brown's *Life and Loves*, demonstrates that ''he can use his outrageous sense of humor as an effective form of social protest, earning the praise of comedian Richard Pryor while pleasing social critic James Baldwin as well.''

The Life and Loves of Mr. Jiveass Nigger has been translated into German.

BIOGRAPHICAL/CRITICAL SOURCES:

BOOKS

Dictionary of Literary Biography, Volume 33: *Afro-American Fiction Writers After 1955*, Gale, 1984.

PERIODICALS

Antioch Review, winter, 1970.
Atlantic Monthly, February, 1970.
Chicago Tribune Book World, January 23, 1983.
Los Angeles Times Book Review, January 16, 1983.
New Statesman, June 19, 1970.
New York Times, January 14, 1970.
New York Times Book Review, February 1, 1970, June 7, 1970, April 17, 1983.
Time, February 2, 1970.
Times Literary Supplement, July 31, 1970.

*   *   *

BROWN, Claude   1937-

PERSONAL: Born February 23, 1937, in New York, N.Y.; son of Henry Lee (a railroad worker) and Ossie (a domestic; maiden name, Brock) Brown; married Helen Jones (a telephone operator), September 9, 1961. *Education:* Howard University, B.A., 1965; further study at Stanford University and Rutgers University Law Schools.

ADDRESSES: Office—c/o Stein & Day Publishers, Scarborough House, Briarcliff Manor, N.Y. 10510.

CAREER: Worked as a busboy, watch crystal fitter, shipping clerk and jazz pianist in Greenwich Village, 1954-57; playwright for American Negro Theater Guild, 1960-61; writer, lecturer, and activist. Member of Harlem Improvement Project Group.

AWARDS, HONORS: Metropolitan Community Methodist Church grant, 1959; *Saturday Review* Ansfield-Wolf Award for furthering inter-group relations, 1965, for *Manchild in the Promised Land;* Family Life Book Award, Child Study Association of America/Wel-Met, 1966, for *Manchild in the Promised Land.*

WRITINGS:

Manchild in the Promised Land (autobiography), Macmillan, 1965.

The Children of Ham, Stein & Day, 1976.

Contributor of articles to *Dissent, Esquire,* and other periodicals.

SIDELIGHTS: Before the publication of Claude Brown's *Manchild in the Promised Land,* some social critics observed that there had not been anyone who effectively expressed the situation of the urban black. ''There is no doubt that Negroes have much to be angry about,'' writes *Antioch Review* contributor William Mathes, ''and I'm all for anger, righteous or otherwise. Not hate, but anger. There is room for dialogue in that emotion. It gets things moving; someone answers with shock; someone applauds; something happens.'' Tired of the ''high-pitched'' anger of James Baldwin and the ''too fraught-with-love'' anger of Roy Wilkins and James Farmer, Mathes calls for ''words that convey hurt and deprivation themselves, words that can permit many people—especially white people—to identify with the Negro. So far we have lacked words that impart the feelings of what it is to be a Negro in this country at this time.'' These words, Mathes and other social commentators agree, come with Brown's *Manchild in the Promised Land.*

Brown, a survivor of Harlem's ''Bebopping gang,'' the Buccaneers, recounts the story of his youth in *Manchild in the Promised Land.* He received his primary education from two reformatories and years of ''roaming the streets with junkies, whores, pimps, hustlers, the 'mean cats' and the numbers runners.'' By the time he was thirteen he had been struck by a bus, chain-whipped, tossed into a river, and shot in the stomach. Four years later, after two years of working confidence games and dealing drugs, he decided to resume his formal education and moved away from Harlem; a move, he writes, ''away from fear, toward challenges, towards the positive anger that I think every young man should have.''

Encouraged by Ernest Papanek, his former mentor at Wiltwyck School, Brown wrote an article on Harlem for *Dissent.* After its publication, Macmillan offered Brown an expense account to write a book about his life in Harlem. By 1963 he completed a 1,537 page manuscript of *Manchild in the Promised Land.*

Praised by critics for its deft realism and remarkable clarity, Brown's book became a harbinger of hope to the civil rights movement as it drew increasing interest and concern to the plight of urban blacks. ''I want to talk about the experiences of a misplaced generation,'' Brown begins, ''of a misplaced people in an extremely complex, confused society. This is a story of their searching, their dreams, their sorrows, their small and futile rebellions, and their endless battle to establish their own place in America's greatest metropolis—and in America itself.'' Romulus Linney writes in the *New York Times Book Review* that *Manchild in the Promised Land* ''is written with brutal and unvarnished honesty in the plain talk of the people, in language that is fierce, uproarious, obscene and tender, but always sensible and direct. And to its enormous credit,'' continues Linney, ''this youthful autobiography gives us its devastating portrait of life without one cry of self-pity, outrage or malice, with no caustic sermons or searing rhetoric. Claude Brown speaks for himself—and the Harlem people to whom his life is bound—with open dignity, and the effect is both shattering and deeply satisfying.'' More than a decade after its publication, George Davis in *New York Times Book Review* claims that *Manchild in the Promised Land* ''remains one of the great personal, nonideological views of life in the rawest parts of Harlem.''

For his second book, *The Children of Ham,* Brown returns to Harlem to document the story of a group of Harlem teenagers who band together and transform abandoned apartments into "spots" where they can "interact free of the 'monster' heroin that dominated their homes and the narrow Harlem side street out front," describes Davis. The group maintains little connection to anything except themselves, their religion is survival, and they encourage each other "to stay clean and stay in school, or to develop whatever latent talents each might have," summarizes the critic. Although some critics find the book less moving than Brown's first, *New Republic* contributor Arnold Rampersad writes that "it is alike in its power, if not in its art, to Stephen Crane's first novel, *Maggie, A Girl of the Streets;* as a book about those young people whose primary gift is a determination to live, it reminds one of the diary of another tenement prisoner struggling for the right of survival, Anne Frank."

"As a child," Brown writes in *Manchild in the Promised Land,* "I remember being morbidly afraid. It was a fear that was like a fever that never lets up. Sometimes it became so intense that it would just swallow you. At other times, it just kept you shaking. But it was always there. I suppose, in Harlem, even now, the fear is still there." If *Manchild in the Promised Land* "chronicled [Brown's] escape from disaster there," observes Rampersad, "*Children of Ham* is his testimony that no such escape is totally possible, that one *must* go home again or live and die a traitor. Brown brings the survivor's guilt to his reportage; this is the story of other menchildren and womenchildren left behind in his escape though born after his time."

BIOGRAPHICAL/CRITICAL SOURCES:

BOOKS

Brown, Claude, *Manchild in the Promised Land,* Macmillan, 1965.
Contemporary Literary Criticism, Volume 30, Gale, 1984.

PERIODICALS

Antioch Review, fall, 1965.
Detroit Free Press, March 12, 1967.
New Republic, September 25, 1965, May 8, 1976.
New Statesman, August 5, 1966.
New York Times, August 14, 1965, April 16, 1976.
New York Times Book Review, August 22, 1965, August 15, 1976.
Washington Post Book World, April 11, 1976.

*   *   *

BROWN, H. Rap
See Al-AMIN, Jamil Abdullah

*   *   *

BROWN, Margery (Wheeler)

PERSONAL: Born in Durham, N.C.; daughter of John Leonidas and Margaret (Hervey) Wheeler; married Richard E. Brown, December 22, 1936 (deceased); children: Janice (Mrs. Jan E. Carden). *Education:* Spelman College, B.A.; Ohio State University, art studies, 1932-34. *Religion:* Presbyterian.

ADDRESSES: Home—245 Reynolds Terrace, Orange, N.J. 07050.

CAREER: Art teacher in Newark, N.J., 1948-74; writer.

WRITINGS:

JUVENILES

That Ruby (self-illustrated), Reilly & Lee, 1969.
Animals Made by Me (self-illustrated), Putnam, 1970.
The Second Stone, Putnam, 1974.
Yesterday I Climbed a Mountain, Putnam, 1976.
No Jon, No Jon, No!, Houghton, 1981.

ILLUSTRATOR

G. Allred, *Old Crackfoot,* Obolensky, 1965.
I'm Glad I'm Me, Putnam, 1971.

OTHER

Contributor to *Life* and *School Arts.*

WORK IN PROGRESS: Stories for and about inner city children.

*   *   *

BROWN, Sterling Allen   1901-

PERSONAL: Born May 1, 1901, in Washington, D.C.; son of Sterling Nelson (a writer and professor of religion at Howard University) and Adelaide Allen Brown; married Daisy Turnbull, September, 1927; children: John L. Dennis. *Education:* Williams College, A.B., 1922; Harvard University, A.M., 1923, graduate study, 1930-31.

ADDRESSES: c/o John L. Dennis, 9704 Saxony Rd., Silver Spring, Md. 20910.

CAREER: Virginia Seminary and College, Lynchburg, Va., English teacher, 1923-26; also worked as a teacher at Lincoln University in Jefferson City, Mo., 1926-28, and at Fisk University, 1928-29; Howard University, Washington, D.C., professor of English, 1929-69. Visiting professor at University of Illinois, University of Minnesota, New York University, New School for Social Research, Sarah Lawrence College, and Vassar College. Editor on Negro Affairs, Federal Writers' Project, 1936-39, and staff member of Carnegie-Myrdal Study of the Negro, 1939.

MEMBER: Phi Beta Kappa.

AWARDS, HONORS: Guggenheim fellowship for creative writing, 1937; honorary doctorates from Howard University, 1971, University of Massachusetts, 1971, Northwestern University, 1973, Williams College and Boston University, both 1974, Brown University and Lewis and Clark College, both 1975, Harvard University, Yale University, University of Maryland, Baltimore County, Lincoln University (Pennsylvania), and University of Pennsylvania; Lenore Marshall Poetry Prize, 1982, for *The Collected Poems of Sterling A. Brown;* named poet laureate of District of Columbia, 1984.

WRITINGS:

POETRY

Southern Road, Harcourt, 1932, revised edition, Beacon Press, 1974.
The Last Ride of Wild Bill, and Eleven Narrative Poems, Broadside Press, 1975.
The Collected Poems of Sterling A. Brown, selected by Michael S. Harper, Harper, 1980.

NONFICTION

The Negro in American Fiction (also see below), Associates in Negro Folk Education, 1937, Argosy-Antiquarian, 1969.

Negro Poetry and Drama (also see below), Associates in Negro Folk Education, 1937, revised edition, Atheneum, 1969.

(Editor with Arthur P. Davis and Ulysses Lee, and contributor) *The Negro Caravan*, Dryden, 1941, revised edition, Arno, 1970.

Negro Poetry and Drama [and] *The Negro in American Fiction*, Ayer, 1969.

(With George E. Haynes) *The Negro Newcomers in Detroit* [and] *The Negro in Washington*, Arno, 1970.

CONTRIBUTOR

Benjamin A. Botkin, editor, *Folk-Say*, University of Oklahoma Press, 1930.

American Stuff: An Anthology of Prose and Verse by Members of the Federal Writers' Project, with Sixteen Prints by the Federal Arts Project, U.S. Government Printing Office, 1937.

Washington City and Capital, U.S. Government Printing Office, 1937.

The Integration of the Negro into American Society, Howard University Press, 1951.

Lillian D. Hornstein, G. D. Percy, and others, editors, *The Reader's Companion to World Literature*, New American Library, 1956.

Langston Hughes and Arna Bontemps, editors, *The Book of Negro Folklore*, Dodd, Mead, 1958.

John Henrik Clarke, editor, *American Negro Short Stories*, Hill & Wang, 1966.

OTHER

Sixteen Poems by Sterling Brown (sound recording), Folkway Records, 1973.

Also author of *Outline for the Study of the Poetry of American Negroes*, 1930, and contributor to *What the Negro Wants*, 1948. Contributor of poetry and articles to anthologies and journals, including *Crisis, Contempo, Nation, New Republic,* and *Journal of Negro Education*. Contributor of column, "The Literary Scene: Chronicle and Comment" to *Opportunity*, beginning 1931.

SIDELIGHTS: Sterling Allen Brown has devoted his life to the development of an authentic black folk literature. A poet, critic, and teacher at Howard University for 40 years, Brown was one of the first people to identify folklore as a vital component of the black aesthetic and to recognize its validity as a form of artistic expression. He has worked to legitimatize this genre in several ways. As a critic, he has exposed the shortcomings of white literature that stereotypes blacks and demonstrated why black authors are best suited to describe the negro experience. As a poet, he has mined the rich vein of black Southern culture, replacing primitive or sentimental caricatures with authentic folk heroes drawn from Afro-American sources. As a teacher, Brown has encouraged self-confidence among his students, urging them to find their own literary voices and to educate themselves to be an audience worthy of receiving the special gifts of black literature. Overall, Brown's influence in the field of Afro-American literature has been so great that scholar Darwin T. Turner told *Ebony* magazine: "I discovered that all trails led, at some point, to Sterling Brown. His *Negro Caravan* was *the* anthology of Afro-American literature. His unpublished study of Afro-American theater was *the* major work in the field. His study of images of Afro-Americans in American literature was a pioneer work. His essays on folk literature and folklore were preeminent. He was

not always the best critic . . . but Brown was and is the literary historian who wrote the Bible for the study of Afro-American literature.''

Brown's dedication to his field has been unflinching, but it was not until he was in his late sixties that the author received widespread public acclaim. Before then, he labored in obscurity on the campus of Howard University. His fortune improved in 1968 when the Black Consciousness movement revived an interest in his work. In 1969, two of his most important books of criticism, *Negro Poetry and Drama* and *The Negro in American Fiction*, were reprinted by Argosy; five years later, in 1974, Beacon Press reissued *Southern Road*, his first book of poems. These reprintings stimulated a reconsideration of the author, which culminated in the publication of *The Collected Poems of Sterling A. Brown* in 1980. More than any other single publication, it is this title, which won the 1982 Lenore Marshall Poetry prize, that has brought Brown the widespread recognition that he deserves.

Because he had largely stopped writing poetry by the end of the 1940s, most of *Collected Poems* is comprised of Brown's early verse. Yet the collection is not the work of an apprentice, but rather "reveals Brown as a master and presence indeed . . . ," in the view of a *Virginia Quarterly Review* critic. While acknowledging that "his effective range is narrow," the critic calls Brown "a first-rate narrative poet, an eloquent prophet of the folk, and certainly our finest author of Afro-American dialect." *New York Times Book Review* contributor Henry Louis Gates appreciates that in *Collected Poems* "Brown never lapses into bathos or sentimentality. His characters confront catastrophe with all of the irony and stoicism of the blues and of black folklore. What's more, he is able to realize such splendid results in a variety of forms, including the classic and standard blues, the ballad, the sonnet and free verse." Despite Brown's relatively small poetic output, *Washington Post* critic Joseph McClellen believes this collection "is enough to establish the poet as one of our best."

While the book will help insure that Brown is not forgotten, some believe it serves as a painful reminder of a great talent that was stunted because it was ignored. Brown encountered inexplicable resistance to his poetry in the mid-1930s. Even though *Southern Road* had been heralded by critics as the work of a major talent, Brown could not find a publisher for his second volume of poetry. (Titled *No Hiding Place* the work has yet to be published separately though it was included in *Collected Poems*.) Nor was resistance from his publishers the only source of Brown's obscurity. Another part stemmed from Brown's lifelong dedication to Howard University. Offered a full-time teaching position at Vassar College in 1945—an offer so extraordinary for a black man at the time that it made national news—Brown politely declined. "I am devoted to Howard," he explained to *Ebony* some twenty-four years later. "These are my people and if I had anything to give they would need it more.'

Brown's connection with the university dates back to his birth. He was born in a house that has since become part of the Howard campus. His father, a minister at the Lincoln Congregational Church, was a professor of religion at Howard and a one-time member of the District of Columbia Board of Education. Because of his father's position, young Brown came into contact with some of the most important black leaders of the day. Sociologist and writer W.E.B. DuBois, cultural philosopher and critic Alain Locke, and social historian Kelly Miller were but three of the important personages he came to know while growing up at Howard. Important as these figures were, however, "the person who most encouraged Brown's admiration for literature and the cultural heritage of black people was his mother," according to Joanne V. Gabbin in Volume 51 of the *Dictionary of Literary Biography*.

Adelaide Allen was valedictorian of her graduating class at Fisk University. A poetry lover who read verse aloud, Adelaide introduced her son to the works of Henry Wadsworth Longfellow, Robert Burns, and black poet and family friend Paul Laurence Dunbar. In a 1973 interview with Stephen Jones quoted in Gabbin's article, Brown recalled of his mother: "I remember even now her stopping her sweeping . . . now standing over that broom and reading poetry to me, and she was a good reader, great sense of rhythm." The high school Brown attended further developed his gifts. Dunbar High School (named to honor the poet) was then considered one of the best black schools in the country. Brown had history classes taught by Haley Douglass, Frederick Douglass's grandson, and Neville Thomas, president of the Washington Branch of the NAACP. Among his other teachers were Angelina Weld Grimke and Jessie Redmond Fauset, "artists in their own right," who "taught him a strict sense of academic discipline," according to Gabbin.

After high school, Brown won a scholarship to the predominantly white, ivy league institution, Williams College. There he first began writing poetry. While other young poets his age were imitating T. S. Eliot, Ezra Pound, and other high modernists, Brown was not impressed with their "puzzle poetry." Instead, he turned for his models to the narrative versifiers, poets such as Edward Arlington Robinson, who captured the tragic drama of ordinary lives, and Robert Frost, who used terse vernacular that sounded like real people talking. At Williams, Brown studied literature with George Dutton, a critical realist who would exert a lasting influence. "Dutton was teaching Joseph Conrad," Brown recalled, as reported in the *New Republic*. "He said Joseph Conrad was being lionized in England . . . [but] Conrad was sitting over in the corner, quiet, not participating. Dutton said he was brooding and probably thinking about his native Poland and the plight of his people. He looked straight at me. I don't know what he meant, but I think he meant, and this is symbolic to me, I think he meant don't get fooled by any lionizing, don't get fooled by being here at Williams with a selective clientele. There is business out there that you have to take care of. Your people, too, are in a plight. I've never forgotten it."

Brown came to believe that one way to help his people was through his writing. "When Carl Sandburg said 'yes' to the American people, I wanted to say 'yes' to my people," Brown recalled in *New Directions: The Howard University Magazine*. In 1923, after receiving his Masters degree from Harvard, Brown embarked on a series of teaching jobs that would help him determine what form that "yes" should assume. He moved south and began to teach among the common people. As an instructor, he gained a reputation as a "red ink man," because he covered his students' papers with corrections. But as a poet, he was learning important lessons from students about black Southern life. Attracted by his openness and easygoing manner, they invited him into their homes to hear worksongs, ballads, and the colorful tales of local lore. He met ex-coal-miner Calvin "Big Boy" Davis, who became the inspiration for Brown's "Odyssey of Big Boy" and "Long Gone," as well as singer Luke Johnson, whom he paid a quarter for each song Luke wrote down. As Brown began to amass his own folklore collection, "he realized that worksongs, ballads, blues,

and spirituals were, at their best, poetical expressions of Afro-American life," writes Robert O'Meally in the *New Republic*. "And he became increasingly aware of black language as often ironic, understated and double-edged."

At this time many black writers were moving away from using dialect in literature. White abuse of the black idiom had reduced it to a simplistic cliche, which writer James Weldon Johnson believed was capable of only two full stops: humor and pathos. His criticism was largely a reaction against white plantation literature that ridiculed black speech, nonetheless, it was a powerful incentive to negro poets to use traditional English. Against this backdrop, Brown made a decision to explore the potential of folk language. As O'Meally explains, Brown made a commitment "to render black experience as he knew it, using the speech of the people. He would not, because of white stereotyping, avoid phonetical spellings. . . . His goal was not to run from the stereotype, but to celebrate the human complexity behind the now grinning, now teary-eyed mask."

In 1929, the same year his father died, Brown returned to Howard University, where he would remain for the rest of his career. Three years later, Harcourt, Brace published *Southern Road*, a first book of poems, drawn primarily from material he had gathered during his travels south. The book was heralded as a breakthrough for black poetry. Alain Locke, one of the chief proponents of what was then called the New Negro Movement, acknowledged the importance of the work in an essay collected in *Negro Anthology*. After explaining that the primary objective of Negro poetry should be "the poetic portrayal of Negro folk-life . . . true in both letter and spirit to the idiom of the folk's own way of feeling and thinking," he declared that with the appearance of *Southern Road*, it could be said "that here for the first time is that much-desired and long-awaited acme attained or brought within actual reach."

James Weldon Johnson was so moved by the work that he provided a glowing introduction in which he reconsidered his earlier objections to black dialect: "Brown's work is not only fine, it is also unique. He began writing just after the Negro poets had generally discarded conventionalized dialect, with its minstrel traditions of Negro life. . . . He infused his poetry with genuine characteristic flavor by adopting as his medium the common, racy, living speech of the Negro in certain phases of *real* life. For his raw material he dug down into the deep mine of Negro folk poetry." As Sterling Stuckey observes in his introduction to the *Collected Poems*, "it was a remarkable achievement for a young poet: not one of the major reviewers hailed Brown as a poet of promise, as a talented young man awaiting creative maturity; on the contrary, he was regarded as a poet of uncommon sophistication, of demonstrated brilliance whose work had placed him in the front rank of working poets here and elsewhere."

The success of *Southern Road* did not insure Brown's future as a publishing poet. Not only did Harcourt, Brace reject *No Hiding Place* when Brown submitted the manuscript a few years later, they also declined to issue a second printing of *Southern Road*, because they did not think it would be profitable. These decisions had a devastating impact upon Brown's poetic reputation. Because no new poems appeared, many of his admirers assumed he had stopped writing. "That assumption," writes Sterling Stuckey, "together with sadly deficient criticism from some quarters, helped to fix his place in time—as a not very important poet of the past."

Discouraged over the reception of his poems, Brown shifted his energies to other arenas; he continued teaching, but also produced a steady stream of book reviews, essays, and sketches about black life. He argued critically for many of the same goals he had pursued in verse: recognition of a black aesthetic, accurate depiction of the black experience, and the development of a literature worthy of his people's past. One of his most influential forums for dissemination of his ideas was a regular column he wrote for *Opportunity* magazine. There "Brown argued for realism as a mode in literature and against such romantic interpretations of the South as the ones presented in *I'll Take My Stand* (1930), the manifesto of Southern agrarianism produced by contributors to the *Fugitive,* including John Crowe Ransom, Allen Tate, and Robert Penn Warren," writes R.V. Burnette in Volume 63 of the *Dictionary of Literary Biography.* "Although he praised the efforts of white writers like Howard Odum ('he is a poetic craftsman as well as a social observer'), he was relentless in his criticism of popular works that distorted black life and character."

Brown did not limit his writing to periodicals, but also produced several major books on Afro-American studies. His 1938 works, *Negro Poetry and Drama* and *The Negro in American Fiction,* are seminal studies of black literary history. The former shows the growth of black artists within the context of American literature and delineates a black aesthetic; the latter examines what has been written about the black man in American fiction since his first appearance in obscure novels of the 1700s. A pioneering work that depicts how the prejudice facing blacks in real life is duplicated in their stereotyped treatment in literature, *The Negro in American Fiction* differs "from the usual academic survey by giving a penetrating analysis of the social factors and attitudes behind the various schools and periods considered," Alain Locke believes, as quoted in Volume 63 of the *Dictionary of Literary Biography.*

In 1941, Brown and two colleagues Arthur P. Davis and Ulysses S. Lee edited *The Negro Caravan,* a book that "defined the field of Afro-American literature as a scholarly and academic discipline," according to *Ebony.* In this anthology, Brown demonstrates how black writers have been influenced by the same literary currents that have shaped the consciousness of all American writers—"puritan didacticism, sentimental humanitarianism, local color, regionalism, realism, naturalism, and experimentalism"—and thus are not exclusively bound by strictures of race. The work has timeless merit, according to Julius Lester, who writes in the introduction to the 1970 revised edition that "it comes as close today as it did in 1941 to being the most important single volume of black writing ever published."

As a writer, Brown's first twelve years at Howard were his most productive. By the mid-1940s, he had completed the major works on which his reputation as an essayist, critic, and poet rests. But even his national reputation as a writer did little to secure his stature in the English department at Howard, where colleagues scoffed at his "lowbrow" interest in jazz and the blues. For decades, Brown paid no mind to this lack of recognition and simply went about his work. When he wanted to give poetry readings, he gave them as a guest lecturer at other campuses. Ultimately his "nonconformity cost him more than he realized," reports Michael Winston in the *Dictionary of Literary Biography,* Volume 51. Shunned by many of Howard's more conservative professors, Brown (who never completed his doctoral degree) began to suffer long periods of depression, sometimes so severe that he required hospitalization. The situation was partially rectified in the late 1960s when students participating in the Black Arts movement de-

manded that he receive the attention he deserved. In 1971, he was awarded an honorary doctorate from Howard (the first of many he would eventually garner), and several of his most important books were reprinted in the mid-seventies.

In summing up his impact on black literature of the twentieth century, *New Republic* contributor John F. Callahan observes: "It is his achievement to have fulfilled the complex double purpose of writing poetry worthy of a great audience and of helping to shape that diverse, responsive, critical, and inclusive audience through his essays and criticism." Concludes Henry Louis Gates, Jr., in the *New York Times Book Review:* "Such a prolific output in a life that spans the era of Booker T. Washington and the era of Black Power makes him not only the bridge between 19th and 20th-century black literature, but also the last of the great 'race men,' the Afro-American men of letters, a tradition best epitomized by W.E.B. DuBois. A self-styled 'Old Negro,' Sterling Brown is not only the Afro-American Poet Laureate, he is a great poet."

BIOGRAPHICAL/CRITICAL SOURCES:

BOOKS

Brown, Sterling A., Arthur P. Davis and Ulysses Lee, *The Negro Caravan,* Dryden, 1941, revised editon, Arno, 1970.
Brown, Sterling A., *The Collected Poems of Sterling A. Brown,* selected by Michael S. Harper, Harper, 1980.
Contemporary Literary Criticism, Gale, Volume 1, 1973, Volume 23, 1983.
Cunard, Nancy, editor, *Negro Anthology,* Wishart Co., 1934.
Davis, Arthur P., *From the Dark Tower: Afro-American Writers, 1900-1960,* Howard University Press, 1974.
Dictionary of Literary Biography, Gale, Volume 48: *American Poets, 1880-1945,* Second Series, 1986, Volume 51: *Afro-American Writers from the Harlem Renaissance to 1940,* 1987, Volume 63: *Modern American Critics, 1920-1955,* 1988.
Gayle, Addison, Jr., editor, *Black Expression: Essays by and About Black Americans in the Creative Arts,* Weybright & Talley, 1969.
Mangione, Jerre, *The Dream and the Deal: The Federal Writers' Project, 1935-1943,* Little, Brown, 1972.
Wagner, Jean, *Black Poets of the United States: From Paul Laurence Dunbar to Langston Hughes,* translated by Kenneth Douglas, University of Illinois Press, 1973.

PERIODICALS

Black American Literature Forum, spring, 1980.
Callaloo: A Black South Journal of Arts and Letters, February-May, 1982.
Ebony, October, 1976.
Los Angeles Times Book Review, August 3, 1980.
New Directions: The Howard University Magazine, winter, 1974.
New Republic, February 11, 1978, December 20, 1982.
New York Times, May 15, 1932.
New York Times Book Review, November 30, 1969, January 11, 1981.
Studies in the Literary Imagination, fall, 1974.
Village Voice, January 14, 1981.
Virginia Quarterly Review, winter, 1981.
Washington Post, November 16, 1969, May 2, 1979, September 4, 1980, May 12, 1984.

—*Sketch by Donna Olendorf*

BROWN, Tony

See BROWN, William Anthony

*   *   *

BROWN, Wesley 1945-

PERSONAL: Born May 23, 1945, in New York, N.Y. *Education:* Oswego State University, B.A. in political science and history, 1968.

ADDRESSES: Home—103 West 141st St., New York, N.Y. 10030.

CAREER: Writer.

WRITINGS:

Tragic Magic (novel), Random House, 1978.

Work represented in anthologies, including *Poetry* and *We Be Word Sorcerers*. Contributor of poems and short stories to *Essence, Black Creation,* and other periodicals.

SIDELIGHTS: Wesley Brown's first novel, *Tragic Magic,* is the story of Melvin Ellington, a well-educated, young black man who returns to his Queens, New York, neighborhood after serving two years in prison as a conscientious objector to the Vietnam War. The narrative covers the events of Ellington's first day home, interspersed with recollections of prison life and college days. Trying to get all the pieces of his life back together, Melvin rejoins his family for dinner, and later in the evening he goes out with a high school friend on a nighttime excursion that turns catastrophic.

Tragic Magic won the attention and praise of many critics. They particularly admired Brown's ability to evoke urban black America and his sensitivity to man's search for meaning and identity in life. "Wesley Brown has a careful eye for the details and nuances of urban black existence," remarked a *Choice* contributor, who then hailed Brown as "a gifted writer, capable of exploring a wide range of human emotions" and judged *Tragic Magic* "an impressive first novel." Likewise, a reviewer of the novel for *New Yorker* assessed Brown's portrait of Ellington as "effective and original" and lauded the author's recording of "the provocative, singsong slang of the street and prison." *Village Voice* contributor Lin Rosechild Harris complimented Brown for creating "a wonderful addition to the pantheon of heroic young initiates" while also observing that "the book sings with images and rhythms of urban black America," and Alan Cheuse, writing in *New York Times Book Review,* described *Tragic Magic* as a "jaunty prose version of the urban blues" that "deserves an attentive audience."

BIOGRAPHICAL/CRITICAL SOURCES:

PERIODICALS

American Book Review, summer, 1979.
Choice, February, 1979.
Nation, December 29, 1979.
New Yorker, October 23, 1978.
New York Times Book Review, February 11, 1979.
Village Voice, November 20, 1978.

*   *   *

BROWN, William Anthony 1933-
(Tony Brown)

PERSONAL: Known professionally as Tony Brown; born April 11, 1933, in Charleston, W.Va.; son of Royal and Catherine (Davis) Brown; divorced; children: Byron Anthony. *Education:* Wayne State University, B.A., 1959, M.S.W., 1961.

CAREER/WRITINGS: Detroit Courier, began as drama critic, became city editor; WTVS-TV, Detroit, Mich., worked variously as producer, host, and writer of series, including "C. P. T.," "For Whites Only," and "Free Play"; WNET-TV, New York City, producer and host of series "Black Journal," 1970-77; Howard University, Washington, D.C., founder and dean of school of communications and chairman of board of WHUR-FM Radio, 1971-74, later became professor; Tony Brown Productions, president, and producer and host of "Tony Brown's Journal," 1977-81; WRC-TV, Washington, D.C., producer and host of "Tony Brown at Daybreak"; WNET-TV, New York City, producer and host of "Tony Brown's Journal," 1982—.

Owner of public relations and advertising firm; publisher and editor of periodicals. Visiting professor at Central Washington State University, 1971-72. Member of communications advisory committee of National Institute of Mental Health, beginning in 1972, Congressional Black Caucus Communications Brain Trust, beginning in 1977, advisory board of National Council for Black Studies, beginning in 1977; member of board of directors of National Center of Afro-American Artists, National Black United Fund. Author of a syndicated column; lecturer. Helped coordinate March to Freedom With Dr. Martin Luther King, Jr., in Detroit, 1963; associated with Project '80 Coalition for Black Colleges, and Black College Day in Washington, D.C., 1980. *Military service:* U.S. Army, 1953-55.

MEMBER: National Communications Council (member of board of governors), Alpha Phi Alpha.

AWARDS, HONORS: "Black Journal" series nominated for Emmy Award by National Academy of Television Arts and Sciences, 1972; Business Achievement Award from Black Retail Action Group, 1972; Media Workshop Award, 1972; Communicator for Freedom Award from OPERATION PUSH, 1973; national achievement award from Nebraska Urban League, 1973; named one of one hundred most influential black Americans by *Ebony* magazine, 1973; Frederick Douglass Liberation Award from Howard University, 1974; named Communicator of the Year by National Association of Market Developers, 1976; public service award from National Urban League, 1977; award from International Key Women of America, 1977. Honorary LL.D. from University of Michigan, 1975.

SIDELIGHTS: Praised by *Black Enterprise* for his "provocative interviewing and analytical wit," Tony Brown is producer and host of the long-running television series "Tony Brown's Journal" (known until 1977 as "Black Journal"). As Bettelou Peterson observed in the *Detroit Free Press,* the program has special importance to television because it is "produced by and for blacks with an uncompromisingly black point of view." Within a newsmagazine format Brown presents documentaries, commentaries, interviews, and discussions covering a wide range of subjects. Over the years his viewers have learned about black colleges, seen rare footage from the early days of blacks in film, and heard President Ronald Reagan defend his controversial economic policies.

Originally Brown studied psychology, sociology, and social work at Wayne State University in Detroit, but after earning a master's degree in 1961 he sought work in the communications industry. Hired by Detroit's public television station,

WTVS, Brown produced its first series for a black audience, "C. P. T." ("Colored People's Time"). He proceeded to both produce and host a community-oriented program for the station titled "Free Play."

Brown gained national attention in 1970 when he became the new producer-host of "Black Journal." The series, produced under the auspices of WNET-TV in New York City, had been broadcast on public television stations across the country since 1968 and had already received an Emmy award. Brown was outspoken about the goals he held for his new job. As he told Charlayne Hunter in the New York Times, he did not intend "to sit there and outline racism so that some white liberal can sit at home and understand it. They want me to produce a show so that they can sit up in their suburban hi-rises and see an addict up in Harlem laying out in the alley with a needle in his arm." Instead of "show[ing] white people how awful it is to be Black," Brown hoped to present a positive vision of black life to a black audience, publicizing accomplishments and showing viewers how to improve their lives. "In all our programs we want to show blacks how to work for themselves," he told Peterson. "To be respected we must have something to be respected for. We should have learned long ago, we can't depend on anyone but ourselves."

As part of such self-reliance Brown sought to increase the number of blacks in the communications field, where they had traditionally been underrepresented both as performers and technicians. He looked outside the membership of white-dominated trade unions for much of his New York City staff, and although he sometimes needed white production companies to do on-location filming for the "Journal," he insisted that they work with black apprentices and producers. In 1971 Howard University, a prominent black institution, hired Brown to establish its school of communications. For the next few years he worked simultaneously as television producer in New York and as dean of Howard's communications faculty in Washington, D.C. While at the university Brown instituted an annual Careers in Communications Conference, designed to alert young people to opportunities in his field.

Although "Black Journal" drew praise from blacks and whites alike—garnering a second Emmy nomination in 1972—it also prompted controversy. As James D. Williams quoted Brown in Black Enterprise, "because 'Black Journal' insists on first-class citizenship in television, we are a threat." Many public broadcasting stations in the South refused to carry the program, an action Brown considered racist. Near the end of 1972 the Corporation for Public Broadcasting (CPB), which allocated government money to public television programs, left the "Journal" off the list of shows it would fund for the upcoming season. Critics immediately accused the corporation of trying to please conservatives in the administration of President Richard Nixon. Organizations such as the Congressional Black Caucus, the Newspaper Publishers Association, the Urban League—even local groups styling themselves "Friends of Black Journal"—protested vehemently. The CPB relented, but at an open meeting of its board of directors in November of 1973, Brown joined Jesse Jackson and other prominent blacks in criticizing the corporation's treatment of minority programming.

In 1977, with assistance from corporate sponsor Pepsi-Cola, Brown took "Black Journal" off public television and into commercial syndication, renaming it "Tony Brown's Journal." (The program was subsequently produced by Brown's own company, Tony Brown Productions, Inc.) He hoped that commercial television would bring a wider audience to the series, which soon topped the A. C. Nielsen ratings for syndicated educational and talk shows. Brown grew frustrated, however, by the limited number of stations that carried the program and the odd hours they sometimes chose to broadcast it, and in 1982 he returned the "Journal" to public television.

After Brown's syndication venture he spoke with C. Gerald Fraser of the New York Times, acknowledging that he had lost some illusions about his work. "Producing is a business," he observed. "When I started, I saw it [as] more of a creative enterprise than a business. It is creative in the sense that money can be attracted if you posture what you're doing in some kind of innovative context." As a friend had warned him, "money makes things happen." And, Brown added, "money makes people give you things—if you don't need it."

But Brown remained confident about his future in television. Whites in the medium might "have run out of ideas," he said, but black culture "hasn't even been scratched. . . . Everything black in this country is just sitting there reserved for me because white people are not interested." He expected to keep digging "into this gold mine of black history—into this gold mine of black contributions."

BIOGRAPHICAL/CRITICAL SOURCES:

PERIODICALS

Black Enterprise, January, 1974, September, 1979.
Detroit Free Press, September 24, 1971.
Essence, October, 1980.
Jet, February 15, 1979.
New York Times, November 29, 1970, February 7, 1982.
Sepia, March, 1972.

—Sketch by Thomas Kozikowski

*　　*　　*

BRUCE, Richard
    See NUGENT, Richard Bruce

*　　*　　*

BRUIN, John
    See BRUTUS, Dennis

*　　*　　*

BRUTUS, Dennis   1924-
    (John Bruin)

PERSONAL: Born November 28, 1924, in Salisbury, Southern Rhodesia (now Harare, Zimbabwe Rhodesia), Africa; came to the United States, 1971, granted political asylum, 1983; son of Francis Henry (a teacher) and Margaret Winifred (teacher, maiden name Bloemetjie) Brutus; married May Jaggers, May 14, 1950; children: Jacinta, Marc, Julian, Antony, Justina, Cornelia, Gregory, Paula. Education: Fort Hare University, B.A. (with distinction), 1947; University of the Witwatersrand, study of law, 1963-64.

ADDRESSES: Office—Department of Black Community Education Research and Development, University of Pittsburgh, Pittsburgh, Pa. 15260.

CAREER: Poet and political activist. High school teacher of English and Afrikaans in Port Elizabeth, South Africa, 1948-61; journalist in South Africa, 1960-61; imprisoned for antiapartheid activities, Robben Island Prison, 1964-65; teacher and journalist in London, England, 1966-70; Northwestern University, Evanston, Ill., professor of English, 1971-85; Swarthmore College, Swarthmore, Pa., Cornell Professor of English Literature, 1985-86; University of Pittsburgh, Pittsburgh, Pa., professor of black studies and English, chairman of department of black community education research and development, 1986—. Visiting professor, University of Denver, 1970, University of Texas at Austin, 1974-75, Dartmouth College, 1983.

Secretary, South African Sports Association, 1959; president of South African Non-Racial Olympic Committee, 1963—; director, World Campaign for Release of South African Political Prisoners (London); United Nations representative, International Defense and Aid Fund (London), 1966-71; chairman of International Campaign Against Racism in Sport, 1972—; member of advisory board, ARENA: Institute for the Study of Sport and Social Analysis, 1975—; chairman, International Advisory Commission to End Apartheid in Sport, 1975—; member of board of directors, Black Arts Celebration (Chicago), 1975—; member, Emergency Committee for World government, 1978—; member of Working Committee for Action Against Apartheid (Evanston), 1978—; president of Third World Energy Resources Institute.

MEMBER: International Poetry Society (fellow), International Platform Association, Union of Writers of the African People (Ghana; vice-president, 1974—), Modern Language Association, African Literature Association (founding chairman, 1975—, member of executive committee, 1979—), United Nations Association of Illinois and Greater Chicago (member of board of directors, 1978).

AWARDS, HONORS: Chancellor's prize, University of South Africa, 1947; Mbari Award, CCF, 1962, for *Sirens, Knuckles, Boots;* Freedom Writers Award, Society of Writers and Editors, 1975; Kenneth Kaunda Humanism Award, 1979; awarded key to city of Sumter, S.C., 1979; L.H.D., Worcester State College and University of Massachusetts, 1984; Langston Hughes Award, City University of New York, 1987.

WRITINGS:

POETRY

Sirens, Knuckles, Boots, Mbari Publications, 1963.
Letters to Martha and Other Poems from a South African Prison, Heinemann, 1968.
Poems from Algiers, African and Afro-American Research Institute, University of Texas at Austin, 1970.
(Under pseudonym John Bruin) *Thoughts Abroad,* Troubadour Press, 1970.
A Simple Lust: Selected Poems Including "Sirens, Knuckles, Boots," "Letters to Martha," "Poems from Algiers," "Thoughts Abroad," Hill & Wang, 1973.
Strains, edited by Wayne Kamin and Chip Dameron, Troubadour Press, 1975, revised edition, 1982.
China Poems, translations by Ko Ching Po, African and Afro-American Studies and Research Center, University of Texas at Austin, 1975.
Stubborn Hope: New Poems and Selections from "China Poems" and "Strains," Three Continents Press, 1978.
Salutes and Censures, Fourth Dimension Publishers (Nigeria), 1984, Africa World Press, 1985.

WORK REPRESENTED IN ANTHOLOGIES

New Sum of Poetry from the Negro World, Presence Africaine (Paris), 1966.

Cosmo Pieterse, editor, *Seven South African Poets,* Heinemann, 1966, Humanities, 1973.
Gerald Moore and Ulli Beier, editors, *Modern Poetry from Africa,* Penguin, 1966.

OTHER

The American-South African Connection (sound recording), Iowa State University of Science and Technology, 1975.
Informal Discussion in Third World Culture Class (sound recording), Media Resources Center, Iowa State University of Science and Technology, 1975.

Contributor to journals. Member of editoral board, *Africa Today,* 1976—, and *South and West.* Guest editor, *The Gar,* 1978.

SIDELIGHTS: Describing Dennis Brutus as a "soft-spoken man of acerbic views," Kevin Klose suggests in the *Washington Post* that "he is one of English-speaking Africa's best-known poets, and also happens to be one of the most successful foes of the apartheid regime in South Africa." Born in Southern Rhodesia of racially mixed parentage, Brutus spent most of his early life in South Africa. Dismissed from his teaching post and forbidden to write by the South African government as a result of anti-apartheid activities, he was arrested in 1963 for attending a meeting in defiance of a ban on associating with any group. Seeking refuge in Swaziland following his release on bail, Brutus was apprehended in Mozambique by Portuguese secret police, who surrendered him to South African secret police. Fearing that he would be killed in Johannesburg, where he was subsequently taken, he again tried to escape. Pursued by police, Brutus was shot in the back, tortured, and finally sentenced to eighteen months of hard labor at Robben Island Prison—"the escape-proof concentration camp for political prisoners off the South African coast," remarks Klose in another *Washington Post* article. The time Brutus spent there, says Klose, "included five months in solitary confinement, which brought him to attempt suicide, slashing at his wrists with sharp stones."

After Brutus's release from prison, he was placed under house arrest and was prohibited from either leaving his home or receiving visitors. He was permitted to leave South Africa, however, "on the condition that he not return, according to court records, and he took his family to England," states William C. Rempel in the *Los Angeles Times.* Granted a conditional British passport because of Rhodesia's former colonial status, Brutus journeyed to the United States, where temporary visas allowed him to remain. Rempel notes, however, that Brutus's "passport became snarled in technical difficulties when Rhodesia's white supremacist government was overthrown and Zimbabwe was created." In the process of applying for a new passport, Brutus missed his application deadline for another visa; and the United States government began deportation proceedings immediately. Brutus was ultimately granted political asylum because a return to Zimbabwe, given its proximity to South Africa, would place his life in imminent danger. Klose indicates that Brutus's efforts to remain in the United States have been at the expense of his art, though: "He has written almost no poetry, which once sustained him through the years of repression and exile."

Suggesting that Brutus's "poetry draws its haunting strength from his own suffering and from the unequal struggle of 25 million blacks, 'coloreds,' Indians and Orientals to throw off the repressive rule by the 4.5 million South African whites," Klose remarks that "there is no doubt in Brutus' mind of the power and relevance of his poetry to the struggle.'' Brutus's works are officially banned in South Africa. When, for example, his *Thoughts Abroad,* a collection of poems concerned with exile and alienation, was published under the pseudonym of John Bruin, it was immediately successful and was even taught in South African colleges; but when the government discovered that Brutus was the author, all copies were confiscated. The effectiveness of the South African government's censorship policies is evidenced by the degree to which Brutus's writing is known there. Colin Gardner, who thinks that ''it seems likely that many well-read South Africans, even some of those with a distinct interest in South African poetry, are wholly or largely unacquainted with his writing,'' declares in *Research in African Literatures* that ''Brutus as a writer exists, as far as the Pretoria government is concerned, as a vacuum, an absence; in the firmament of South African literature, such as it is, Brutus could be described as a black hole. But it is necessary to find him and read him, to talk and write about him, to pick up the light which in fact he does emit, because he is at his best as important as any other South African who has written poetry in English.''

Deeming Brutus's poetry ''the reaction of one who is in mental agony whether he is at home or abroad,'' R. N. Egudu suggests in Christopher Heywood's *Aspects of South African Literature* that ''this agony is partly caused by harrassments, arrests, and imprisonment, and mainly by Brutus's concern for other suffering people.'' Brutus's first volume of poetry, *Sirens, Knuckles and Boots,* which earned him the Mbari Award, was published while he was incarcerated and includes a variety of verse, including love poems as well as poems of protest against South Africa's racial policies. Much of his subsequent poetry concerns imprisonment and exile. For example, *Letters to Martha and Other Poems from a South African Prison* was written under the guise of letters—the writing of which, unlike poetry, was not prohibited—and is composed of poems about his experiences as a political prisoner. His *A Simple Lust: Selected Poems Including ''Sirens, Knuckles, Boots,'' ''Letters to Martha,'' ''Poems from Algiers,'' ''Thoughts Abroad,''* represents ''a collection of all Brutus' poetry relating to his experience of jail and exile,'' notes Paul Kameen in *Best Sellers.* Similarly, *Stubborn Hope: New Poems and Selections from ''China Poems'' and ''Strains''* ''contains several poems which deal directly with the traumatic period of his life when he was imprisoned on the island,'' states Jane Grant in *Index on Censorship.* Discussing the ''interaction between the personal and political'' in Brutus's poetry, Gardner points out that ''the poet is aware that he has comrades in his political campaigns and struggles, but under intense government pressure, there is no real sense of mass movement. The fight for liberation will be a long one, and a sensitive participant cannot but feel rather isolated. This isolation is an important aspect of the poet's mode and mood.''

Chikwenye Okonjo Ogunyemi thinks that although Brutus's writing is inspired by his imprisonment, it is ''artistic rather than overtly propangandistic''; the critic observes in *Ariel* that ''he writes to connect his inner life with the outside world and those who love him. . . . That need to connect with posterity, a reason for the enduring, is a genuine artistic feeling.'' Perceiving an early ''inner conflict between Brutus, the activist against *apartheid,* and Brutus, the highly literate writer of difficult, complex and lyrical poetry,'' Grant suggests that ''the months in solitary confinement on Robben Island seem to have led him to a radical reassessment of his role as poet.'' Moving toward a less complex poetry, ''the trend culminates

in the extreme brevity and economy of the *China Poems* (the title refers both to where they were written and to the delicate nature of the poems). . .,'' says Grant. ''They are seldom more than a few lines long, and are influenced by the Japanese *haiku* and its Chinese ancestor, the *chueh chu*.'' These poems, according to Hans Zell's *A New Reader's Guide to South African Literature,* evolved from Brutus's trip to the Republic of China, and were composed ''in celebration of the people and the values he met there.'' Calling him ''learned, passionate, skeptical,'' Gessler Moses Nkondo says in *World Literature Today* that ''Brutus is a remarkable poet, one of the most distinguished South Africa has produced.'' Nkondo explains that ''the lucidity and precision which he is at pains to develop in his work are qualities he admires from artistic conviction, as a humanist opposed both to romantic haze and conventional trends. But they also testify to a profound cultivation of spirit, a certain wholeness and harmony of nature, as they do too to a fine independence of literary fashion.''

Influenced by the seventeenth-century metaphysical poets, Brutus employs traditional poetic forms and rich language in his work; Nkondo proposes that what ''Brutus fastens on is a composite sensibility made up of the passionate subtleties and the intellectual sensuousness of the metaphysical poets and the masculine, ironic force of [John] Donne.'' Noting that Brutus assumes the persona of a troubadour throughout his poetry, Tanure Ojaide writes in *Ariel* that while it serves to unify his work, the choice of ''the persona of the troubadour to express himself is particularly significant as the moving and fighting roles of the medieval errant, though romantic, tally with his struggle for justice in South Africa, a land he loves dearly as the knight his mistress. The movement contrasts with the stasis of despair and enacts the stubborn hope that despite the suffering, there shall be freedom and justice for those *now* unfree.'' And Gardner believes that ''Brutus's best poetry has a resonance which both articulates and generalizes his specific themes; he has found forms and formulations which dramatize an important part of the agony of South Africa and of contemporary humanity.''

Brutus ''has traveled widely and written and testified extensively against the Afrikaner-run government's policies,'' remarks Klose. ''In the world of activism, where talk can easily outweigh results, his is a record of achievement.'' For instance, Klose states that Brutus's voice against apartheid is largely responsible for South Africa's segregated sports teams having been ''barred from most international competitions, including the Olympics since 1964.'' Egudu observes that in Brutus's ''intellectual protest without malice, in his mental agony over the apartheid situation in South Africa, in his concern for the sufferings of the others, and in his hope which has defied all despair—all of which he has portrayed through images and diction that are imbued with freshness and vision—Brutus proves himself a capable poet fully committed to his social responsibility.'' And according to Klose, Brutus maintains: ''You have to make it a two-front fight. You have to struggle inside South Africa to unprop the regime, and struggle in the United States—to challenge the U.S. role, and if possible, inhibit it. Cut off the money, the flow of arms, the flow of political and military support. You have to educate the American people. And that is what I think I'm doing.''

BIOGRAPHICAL/CRITICAL SOURCES:

BOOKS

Beier, Ulli, editor, *Introduction to African Literature,* Northwestern University Press, 1967.

Contemporary Literary Criticism, Volume 43, Gale, 1987.

Heywood, Christopher, editor, *Aspects of South African Literature,* Africana Publishing, 1976.

A History of Africa, Horizon Press, 1971.

Legum, Colin, editor, *The Bitter Choice,* World Publishing, 1968.

Pieterse, Cosmo, and Dennis Duerden, editors, *African Writers Talking,* Africana Publishing, 1972.

Zell, Hans M., and others, *A New Reader's Guide to African Literature,* 2nd revised and expanded edition, Holmes & Meier, 1983.

PERIODICALS

Ariel, October, 1982, January, 1986.
Best Sellers, October 1, 1973.
Index on Censorship, July/August, 1979.
Los Angeles Times, September 7, 1983.
New York Times, January 29, 1986.
Research in African Literatures, fall, 1984.
Washington Post, August 13, 1983, September 7, 1983.
World Literature Today, spring, 1979, autumn, 1979, winter, 1981.

—*Sketch by Sharon Malinowski*

*   *   *

BRYAN, Ashley F.   1923-

PERSONAL: Born July 13, 1923, in New York, N.Y. *Education:* Attended Cooper Union and Columbia University.

ADDRESSES: Office—Department of Art, Dartmouth College, Hanover, N.H. 03755.

CAREER: Author and illustrator of books for children; professor emeritus of art and visual studies at Dartmouth College.

AWARDS, HONORS: American Library Association, Social Responsibilities Round Table, Coretta Scott King Award, 1980, for illustrating *Beat the Story-Drum, Pum-Pum,* 1986, for writing *Lion and the Ostrich Chicks and Other African Folk Tales,* and Coretta Scott King Honor Award, 1988, for illustrating *What a Morning! The Christmas Story in Black Spirituals.*

WRITINGS:

JUVENILES; SELF-ILLUSTRATED

The Ox of the Wonderful Horns and Other African Folktales, Atheneum, 1971.

The Adventures of Aku; or, How It Came about That We Shall Always See Okra the Cat Lying on a Velvet Cushion while Okraman the Dog Sleeps among the Ashes, Atheneum, 1976.

The Dancing Granny, Macmillan, 1977.

Beat the Story-Drum, Pum-Pum (Nigerian folk tales), Atheneum, 1980.

The Cat's Drum, Atheneum, 1985.

Lion and the Ostrich Chicks and Other African Folk Tales, Atheneum, 1986.

ILLUSTRATOR

Rabindranath Tagore, *Moon, for What Do You Wait?* (poems), edited by Richard Lewis, Atheneum, 1967.

Mari Evans, *Jim Flying High* (juvenile), Doubleday, 1979.

Susan Cooper, *Jethro and the Jumbie* (juvenile), Atheneum, 1979.

John Langstaff, editor, *What a Morning! The Christmas Story in Black Spirituals,* Macmillan, 1987.

OTHER

(Compiler) *Black American Spirituals,* Volume I: *Walk Together Children* (self-illustrated), Atheneum, 1974, Volume II: *I'm Going to Sing* (self-illustrated), Macmillan, 1982.

(Compiler and author of introduction) Paul Laurence Dunbar, *I Greet the Dawn: Poems,* Atheneum, 1978.

SIDELIGHTS: As a folklorist, Ashley Bryan works to preserve African traditions in America. For example, his collection of the spirituals of American slaves *Walk Together Children* records "the brave and lonely cries of men and women forced to trust in heaven because they had no hope on earth," remarks Neil Millar in the *Christian Science Monitor.* The subject of bondage set to native African rhythms produced songs such as "Go Down Moses," "Deep River," "Mary Had a Baby," "Go Tell It on the Mountain," "Nobody Knows the Trouble I Seen," "Walk Together Children," "O Freedom," "Little David," and "Swing Low, Sweet Chariot." "With Ashley Bryan's collection," writes Virginia Hamilton of the *New York Times Book Review,* "the tradition of preserving the spiritual through teaching the young is surely enriched."

Several of the folklorist's collections contain stories that explain why certain animals became natural enemies. In *The Adventures of Aku* Bryan recounts the day that the enmity between dogs and cats began. This "is a long involved magic tale that has echoes of Aladdin's lamp and Jack and the Beanstalk to mention just two familiar stories with similar motifs," says the *New York Times Book Review*'s Jane Yolen. It utilizes a magic ring, a stupid son, a heroic quest, and Ananse, the standard trickster figure in African folklore, to capsulize the Ashanti proverb stating, "No one knows the story of tomorrow's dawn."

The Nigerian folktales in *Beat the Story-Drum, Pum-Pum* also reveal the origins of hostilities between animals, such as that between the snake and the frog or the bush cow and the elephant. These "retellings make the stories unique, offering insight into the heart of a culture," notes M. M. Burns in *Horn Book.* Each story, the reviewer adds, "has a style and beat appropriate to the subject, the overall effect being one of musical composition with dexterously designed variations and movements."

Like *The Adventures of Aku,* *The Dancing Granny* continues the saga of the trickster Ananse. Originally titled "He Sings to Make the Old Woman Dance," this folktale recounts the day when a little old lady, who danced continually, foiled the Spider Ananse's plan to eat all of her food. While Granny worked, Ananse sang so that she might dance. Then, when she danced away, the spider would eat up her corn. This went on four times until Granny took Ananse to be her partner and danced him away, too.

For all of his work, Bryan creates block prints, paintings and drawings which, according to a *Horn Book* reviewer, "add flavor and authenticity" to the books.

MEDIA ADAPTATIONS: Ashley Bryan recorded *The Dancing Granny and Other African Tales* for Caedmon.

BIOGRAPHICAL/CRITICAL SOURCES:

PERIODICALS

Christian Science Monitor, November 6, 1974, November 3, 1976, August 2, 1985.

Commonweal, November 22, 1974.

Horn Book, February, 1977, April, 1981, February, 1983, May, 1985.

Language Arts, March, 1977, February, 1978, March, 1984, October, 1985.

Ms., December, 1974.

New York Times Book Review, November 3, 1974, October 10, 1976.

Scientific American, December, 1980.

Washington Post Book World, November 7, 1971, December 12, 1976.

Wilson Library Bulletin, February, 1986.

*   *   *

BULLINS, Ed   1935-
(Kingsley B. Bass, Jr.)

PERSONAL: Born July 2, 1935, in Philadelphia, Pa.; son of Edward and Bertha Marie (Queen) Bullins; married; wife's name, Trixie. *Education:* Attended Los Angeles City College and San Francisco State College (now University).

ADDRESSES: Home—2128A Fifth St., Berkeley, Calif. 94710. *Agent*—Helen Merrill, 435 West 23rd St., No. 1A, New York, N.Y. 10011.

CAREER: Left Philadelphia, Pa. for Los Angeles, Calif. in 1958, moved to San Francisco, Calif. in 1964; co-founder, Black Arts/West; co-founder of the Black Arts Alliance, Black House (Black Panther Party headquarters in San Francisco), cultural director until 1967, also serving briefly as Minister of Culture of the Party; joined The New Lafayette Theatre, New York, N.Y., in 1967, becoming playwright in residence, 1968, associate director, 1971-73; writers unit coordinator, New York Shakespeare Festival, 1975-82; People's School of Dramatic Arts, San Francisco, playwriting teacher, 1983; City College of San Francisco, instructor in dramatic performance, play directing, and playwriting, 1984—. Playwright in residence, American Place Theatre, beginning 1973; producing director, The Surviving Theatre, beginning 1974; public relations director, Berkeley Black Repertory, 1982; promotion director, Magic Theatre, 1982-83; group sales coordinator, Julian Theatre, 1983; playwriting teacher, Bay Area Playwrights Festival, summer, 1983. Also instructor in playwriting at numerous colleges and universities, including Hofstra University, New York University, Fordham University, Columbia University, Amherst College, Dartmouth College, Antioch University, and Sonoma State University. *Military service:* U.S. Navy, 1952-55.

MEMBER: Dramatists Guild.

AWARDS, HONORS: American Place Theatre grant, 1967; Vernon Rice Drama Desk Award, 1968, for plays performed at American Place Theatre; four Rockefeller Foundation grants, including 1968, 1970, and 1973; National Endowment for the Arts playwriting grant; Obie Award for distinguished playwriting, and Black Arts Alliance award, both 1971, for "The Fabulous Miss Marie" and "In New England Winter"; Guggenheim fellowship for playwriting, 1971 and 1976; grant from Creative Artists Public Service Program, 1973, in support of playwriting; Obie Award for distinguished playwriting and New York Drama Critics Circle Award, both 1975, for "The Taking of Miss Janie"; Litt.D., Columbia College, Chicago, 1976.

WRITINGS:

The Hungered One (collected short fiction), Morrow, 1971.
The Reluctant Rapist (novel), Harper, 1973.

PUBLISHED PLAYS

How Do You Do?: A Nonsense Drama (one-act; first produced as "How Do You Do" in San Francisco at Firehouse Repertory Theatre, August 5, 1965; produced Off-Broadway at La Mama Experimental Theatre Club, February, 1972), Illuminations Press, 1967.

(Editor and contributor) *New Plays from the Black Theatre* (includes "In New England Winter" [one-act; first produced Off-Broadway at New Federal Theatre of Henry Street Playhouse, January 26, 1971]), Bantam, 1969.

Five Plays (includes: "Goin' a Buffalo" [three-act; first produced in New York City at American Place Theatre, June 6, 1968], "In the Wine Time" [three-act; first produced at New Lafayette Theatre, December 10, 1968], "A Son Come Home" [one-act; first produced Off-Broadway at American Place Theatre, Feburary 21, 1968; originally published in *Negro Digest,* April, 1968], "The Electronic Nigger" [one-act; first produced at American Place Theatre, February 21, 1968], and "Clara's Ole Man" [one-act; first produced in San Francisco, August 5, 1965; produced at American Place Theatre, February 21, 1968]), Bobbs-Merrill, 1969 (published in England as *The Electronic Nigger, and Other Plays,* Faber, 1970).

"Ya Gonna Let Me Take You Out Tonight, Baby?" (first produced Off-Broadway at Public Theatre, May 17, 1972), published in *Black Arts,* Black Arts Publishing (Detroit), 1969.

"The Gentleman Caller" (one-act; first produced in Brooklyn, N.Y., with other plays as "A Black Quartet" by Chelsea Theatre Center at Brooklyn Academy of Music, April 25, 1969), published in *A Black Quartet,* New American Library, 1970.

The Duplex: A Black Love Fable in Four Movements (one-act; first produced at New Lafayette Theatre, May 22, 1970; produced at Forum Theatre of Lincoln Center, New York, N.Y., March 9, 1972), Morrow, 1971.

The Theme Is Blackness: The Corner, and Other Plays (includes: "The Theme Is Blackness" [first produced in San Francisco by San Francisco State College, 1966], "The Corner" [one-act; first produced in Boston by Theatre Company of Boston, 1968, produced Off-Broadway at Public Theatre, June 22, 1972], "Dialect Determinism" [one-act; first produced in San Francisco, August 5, 1965; produced at La Mama Experimental Theatre Club, February 25, 1972], "It Has No Choice" [one-act; first produced in San Francisco by Black Arts/West, spring, 1966, produced at La Mama Experimental Theatre Club, February 25, 1972], "The Helper" [first produced in New York by New Dramatists Workshop," June 1, 1970], "A Minor Scene" [first produced in San Francisco by Black Arts/West, spring, 1966; produced at La Mama Experimental Theatre Club, February 25, 1972], "The Man Who Dug Fish" [first produced by Theatre Company of Boston, June 1, 1970], "Black Commercial #2," "The American Flag Ritual," "State Office Bldg. Curse," "One Minute Commercial," "A Street Play," "Street Sounds" [first produced at La Mama Experimental Theatre Club, October 14, 1970], "A Short Play for a Small Theatre," and "The Play of the Play"), Morrow, 1972.

Four Dynamite Plays (includes: "It Bees Dat Way" [one-act; first produced in London, September 21, 1970; produced in New York at ICA, October, 1970], "Death List" [one-act; first produced in New York by Theatre Black at University of the Streets, October 3, 1970], "The Pig Pen" [one-act; first produced at American Place Theatre, May 20, 1970], and "Night of the Beast" [screenplay]), Morrow, 1972.

(Editor and contributor) *The New Lafayette Theatre Presents; Plays with Aesthetic Comments by Six Black Playwrights: Ed Bullins, J. E. Gaines, Clay Gross, Oyamo, Sonia Sanchez, Richard Wesley,* Anchor Press, 1974.

"The Taking of Miss Janie" (first produced in New York at New Federal Theatre, May 4, 1975) published in *Famous American Plays of the 1970s,* edited by Ted Hoffman, Dell, 1981.

Plays represented in anthologies, including *New American Plays,* Volume III, edited by William M. Hoffman, Hill & Wang, 1970. Also author of "Malcolm: '71 or Publishing Blackness," published in *Black Scholar,* June, 1975.

UNPUBLISHED PLAYS

(With Shirley Tarbell) "The Game of Adam and Eve," first produced in Los Angeles at Playwrights' Theatre, spring, 1966.

(Under pseudonym Kingsley B. Bass, Jr.) "We Righteous Brothers" (adapted from Albert Camus's *The Just Assassins*), first produced in New York at New Lafayette Theatre, April 1969.

"A Ritual to Raise the Dead and Foretell the Future," first produced in New York at New Lafayette Theatre, 1970.

"The Devil Catchers," first produced at New Lafayette Theatre, November 27, 1970.

"The Fabulous Miss Marie," first produced at New Lafayette Theatre, March 5, 1971; produced at Mitzi E. Newhouse Theatre of Lincoln Center, May, 1979.

"Next Time...," first produced in Bronx, N.Y. at Bronx Community College, May 8, 1972.

"The Psychic Pretenders (A Black Magic Show)," first produced at New Lafayette Theatre, December, 1972.

"House Party, a Soul Happening," first produced at American Place Theatre, fall 1973.

"The Mystery of Phillis Wheatley," first produced at New Federal Theatre, February 4, 1976.

"I Am Lucy Terry," first produced at American Place Theatre, February 11, 1976.

"Home Boy," first produced in New York at Perry Street Theatre, September 26, 1976.

"JoAnne!," first produced in New York at Theatre of the Riverside Church, October 7, 1976.

"Storyville," first produced in LaJolla at the Mandeville Theatre, University of California, May 1977.

"DADDY!," first produced at the New Federal Theatre, June 9, 1977.

"Sepia Star," first produced in New York at Stage 73, August 20, 1977.

"Michael," first produced in New York at New Heritage Repertory Theatre, May, 1978.

"C'mon Back to Heavenly House," first produced in Amherst, Mass. at Amherst College Theatre, 1978.

"Leavings," first produced in New York at Syncopation, August, 1980.

"Steve and Velma," first produced in Boston by New African Company, August, 1980.

OTHER

Editor of *Black Theatre,* 1968-73; editor of special black issue of *Drama Review,* summer, 1968. Contributor to *Negro Digest, New York Times,* and other periodicals.

SIDELIGHTS: Ed Bullins is one of the most powerful black voices in contemporary American theater. He began writing plays as a political activist in the mid-1960s and soon emerged as a principal figure in the black arts movement that surfaced in that decade. First as Minister of Culture for California's Black Panther Party and then as associate director of Harlem's New Lafayette Theatre, Bullins helped shape a revolutionary "theater of black experience" that took drama to the streets. In over fifty dramatic works, written expressly for and about blacks, Bullins probed the disillusionment and frustration of ghetto life. At the height of his militancy, he advocated cultural separatism between races and outspokenly dismissed white aesthetic standards. Asked by *Race Relations Reporter* contributor Bernard Garnett how he felt about white critics' evaluations of his work, Bullins replied: "It doesn't matter whether they appreciate it. It's not for them." Despite his disinterest, by the late 1960s establishment critics were tracking his work, more often than not praising its lyricism and depth and commending the playwright's ability to transcend narrow politics. As C. W. E. Bigsby points out in *The Second Black Renaissance: Essays in Black Literature,* Bullins "was one of the few black writers of the 1960s who kept a cautious distance from a black drama which defined itself solely in political terms." In the 1970s, Bullins won three Obie Awards for disinguished playwriting, a Drama Critics Circle Award, and several prestigious Guggenheim and Rockefeller playwriting grants.

Bullins's acceptance into the theatrical mainstream, which accelerated as the black arts movement lost momentum, presents some difficulty for critics trying to assess the current state of his art. The prolific output of his early years has been replaced by a curious silence. One possible explanation, according to *Black American Literature Forum* contributor Richard G. Scharine, is that Bullins is facing the same artistic dilemma that confronts Steve Benson, his most autobiographical protagonist: "As an artist he requires recognition. As a revolutionary he dare not be accepted. But Bullins has been accepted.... The real question is whether, severed from his roots and his hate, Bullins can continue to create effectively." In a written response published with the article, Bullins answered the charge: "I was a conscious artist before I was a conscious artist-revolutionary, which has been my salvation and disguise.... I do not feel that I am severed from my roots."

Whatever the reasons, productions of Bullins's work have been absent from the New York stage for a number of years. There is no indication, however, that the author has stopped writing. Bullins remains at work on his "Twentieth Century Cycle"—a projected series of twenty plays, six of which have been produced. This dramatic cycle, which features several recurring characters at different times and in different places, will portray various facets of black life. Bullins's hope, as he explained to Jervis Anderson in a 1973 *New Yorker* interview, is "that the stories will touch the audience in an individual way, with some fresh impressions and some fresh insights into their own lives [and] help them to consider the weight of their experience."

Bullins's desire to express the reality of ordinary black experience reflects the philosophy he developed during his six-year association with the New Lafayette Theatre, a community-based playhouse that was a showpiece of the black arts movement until it closed for lack of funds in 1973. During its halcyon days, the New Lafayette provided a sanctuary wherein the black identity could be assuaged and nurtured, a crucial goal of Bullins and all the members of that theatrical family. "Our job," former New Lafayette director Robert Macbeth told Anderson, "has always been to show black people who they are, where they are, and what condition they are in. . . . Our function, the healing function of theatre and art, is absolutely vital."

In order to reach his black audience, Bullins has consistently ignored many accepted playwrighting conventions. "Bullins has never paid much attention to the niceties of formal structure, choosing instead to concentrate on black life as it very likely really is—a continuing succession of encounters and dialogues, major events and non-events, small joys and ever-present sorrows," Catharine Hughes comments in *Plays and Players*. New York theatre critic Clive Barnes calls him "a playwright with his hand on the jugular vein of people. He writes with a conviction and sensitivity, and a wonderful awareness of the way the human animal behaves in his human jungle. . . . Bullins writes so easily and naturally that you watch his plays and you get the impression of overhearing them rather than seeing them."

Part of the authenticity Bullins brings to his dramas may stem from his use of characters drawn from real life. Steve Benson, Cliff Dawson, and Art Garrison are but three of the recurring protagonists who have been closely identified with the author himself. In the early 1970s Steve Benson, who appears in Bullins's novel *The Reluctant Rapist* as well as in "It Has No Choice," "In New England Winter" and other plays, became so closely associated with his creator that Bullins threatened to eliminate him. "Everybody's got him tagged as me," he told *New York Times* contributor Mel Gussow. "I'm going to kill him off." To a large extent, Steve Benson has disappeared from Bullins's recent dramas, but the link between his art and his life experiences remains a strong one. *Dictionary of Literary Biography* contributor Leslie Sanders explains: "While Bullins frequently warns against turning to his writing for factual details of his life and against identifying him with any single one of his characters, he has never denied the autobiographical quality of his writing. Thus, the tenor, if not the exact substance, of his early years emerges from several of his plays."

Bullins was born and raised in a North Philadelphia ghetto, but was given a middle-class orientation by his mother, a civil servant. He attended a largely white elementary school, where he was an excellent student, and spent his summers vacationing in Maryland farming country. As a junior high student, he was transferred to an inner-city school and joined a gang, the Jet Cobras. During a street fight, he was stabbed in the heart and momentarily lost his life (as does his fictional alter-ego Steve Benson in *The Reluctant Rapist*). The experience, as Bullins explained to *New York Times* contributor Charles M. Young, changed his attitude: "See, when I was young, I was stabbed in a fight. I died. My heart stopped. But I was brought back for a reason. I was gifted with these abilities and I was sent into the world to do what I do because that is the only thing I can do. I write."

Bullins did not immediately recognize his vocation, but spent several years at various jobs. After dropping out of high school, he served in the Navy from 1952-55, where he won a shipboard lightweight boxing championship and started a program of self-education through reading. Not much is known about the years he spent in North Philadelphia after his discharge, but Sanders says "his 1958 departure for Los Angeles quite literally saved his life. When he left Philadelphia, he left be-

hind an unsuccessful marriage and several children." In California, Bullins earned a GED high school equivalency degree and started writing. He turned to plays when he realized that the black audience he was trying to reach did not read much fiction and also that he was naturally suited to the dramatic form. But even after moving to San Francisco in 1964, Bullins found little encouragement for his talent. "Nobody would produce my work," he recalled of his early days in the *New Yorker*. "Some people said my language was too obscene, and others said the stuff I was writing was not theatre in the traditional sense." Bullins might have been discouraged had he not chanced upon a production of two plays by LeRoi Jones, "Dutchman" and "The Slave," that reminded him of his own. "I could see that an experienced playwright like Jones was dealing with the same qualities and conditions of black life that moved me," Bullins explained.

Inspired by Jones's example, Bullins and a group of black revolutionaries joined forces to create a militant cultural-political organization called Black House. Among those participating were Huey Newton and Bobby Seale, two young radicals whose politics of revolution would soon coalesce into the Black Panther Party. But the alliance between the violent "revolutionary nationalists," such as Seale and Newton, and the more moderate "cultural nationalists," such as Bullins, would be short-lived. As Anderson explains in the *New Yorker*: "The artists were interested solely in the idea of a cultural awakening while the revolutionaries thought, in Bullins' words, that 'culture was a gun.'" Disheartened by the experience, Bullins resigned the post he had been assigned as Black Panther Minister of Culture, severed his ties with the ill-fated Black House, and accepted Robert Macbeth's invitation to work at the New Lafayette Theater in New York.

To date, Bullins's six-year association with the New Lafayette Theatre has been one of the most productive creative periods in his life. Between 1967 and 1973 Bullins created and/or produced almost a dozen plays, some of which are still considered his finest work. He also edited the theatre magazine, *Black Theatre*, and compiled and edited an anthology of six New Lafayette plays. During this time, Bullins was active as a playwriting teacher and director as well. Despite Bullins's close ties to the New Lafayette, his plays were also produced Off-Broadway and at other community theaters, notably the American Place Theatre where he became playwright in residence after the New Lafayette's demise.

Bullins's plays of this period share common themes. "Clara's Ole Man," an early drama that established the playwright's reputation in New York during its 1968 production, introduces his concerns. Set in the mid-fifties, it tells the story of 20-year-old Jack, an upwardly mobile black who goes to the ghetto to visit Clara one afternoon when her "ole man" is at work. Not realizing that Clara's lover is actually Big Girl, a lesbian bully who is home when Jack calls, he gets brutally beaten as a result of his ignorance. Leslie Sanders believes that "in *Clara's Ole Man*, Bullins's greatest work is foreshadowed. Its characters, like those in many of his later plays, emerge from brutal life experiences with tenacity and grace. While their language is often crude, it eloquently expresses their pain and anger, as well as the humor that sustains them." C. W. E. Bigsby believes that "Clara's Ole Man," as well as "Goin' A Buffalo," "In the Wine Time," "In New England Winter," and other plays that Bullins wrote in the mid-to-late 1960s project the "sense of a brutalized world. . . . Love devolves into a violent sexuality in which communion becomes simple possession, a struggle for mental and physical dominance. Money is a dominating reality, and alcohol and drugs, like sexuality, the only relief. The tone of the plays is one of desperation and frustration. Individuals are locked together by need, trapped by their own material and biological necessities. Race is only one, and perhaps not even the dominant, reality.''

By and large, Bullins's plays of this period have fared well artistically while being criticized, by both black and white critics, for their ideology. Some blacks have objected to what Bigsby calls the ''reductive view of human nature'' presented in these dramas, along with ''their sense of the black ghetto as lacking in any redeeming sense of community or moral values.'' Other blacks, particularly those who have achieved material success, resent their exclusion from this art form. ''I am a young black from a middle-class family and well-educated,'' reads a letter printed in the *New York Times Magazine* in response to a black arts article. ''What sense of self will I ever have if I continue to go to the theatre and movies and never see blacks such as myself in performance?'' For the white theater-going community, Bullins's exclusively black drama has raised questions of cultural elitism that seems ''to reserve for black art an exclusive and, in some senses, a sacrosanct critical territory,'' Anderson believes.

Bullins some time ago distanced himself from the critical fray, saying that if he'd listened to what critics have told him, he would have stopped writing long ago. ''I don't bother too much what anyone thinks,'' he told Anderson. ''When I sit down in that room by myself, bringing in all that I ever saw, smelled, learned, or checked out, I am the chief determiner of the quality of my work. The only critic that I really trust is me.''

BIOGRAPHICAL/CRITICAL SOURCES:

BOOKS

Bigsby, C. W. E., *The Second Black Renaissance: Essays in Black Literature*, Greenwood Press, 1980.
Contemporary Literary Criticism, Gale, Volume I, 1973, Volume V, 1976, Volume VII, 1977.
Dictionary of Literary Biography, Volume VII: *Twentieth Century American Dramatists*, Gale, 1981.
Dictionary of Literary Biography, Volume XXXVIII: *Afro-American Writers after 1955—Dramatists and Prose Writers*, Gale, 1985.
Gayle, Addison, editor, *The Black Aesthetic*, Doubleday, 1971.

PERIODICALS

Black American Literature Forum, fall, 1979.
Black Creation, winter, 1973.
Black World, April, 1974.
CLA Journal, June, 1976.
Nation, November 12, 1973, April 5, 1975.
Negro Digest, April, 1969.
Newsweek, May 20, 1968.
New Yorker, June 16, 1973.
New York Times, September 22, 1971, May 18, 1975, June 17, 1977, May 31, 1979.
New York Times Book Review, June 20, 1971, September 30, 1973.
New York Times Magazine, September 10, 1972.
Plays and Players, May, 1972, March, 1973.
Race Relations Reporter, February 7, 1972.

—*Sketch by Donna Olendorf*

BUNCHE, Ralph J(ohnson)   1904-1971

PERSONAL: Born August 7, 1904, in Detroit, Mich.; died after a long series of illnesses, December 9, 1971, in New York, N.Y.; son of Fred (a barber) and Olive Agnes (a musician; maiden name Johnson) Bunche; married Ruth Ethel Harris, June 23, 1930; children: Ralph, Jr., Joan, Jane (Mrs. Burton Pierce; died in 1966). *Education:* University of California, Los Angeles, B.A. (summa cum laude), 1927; Harvard University, M.A., 1928, Ph.D., 1934; postdoctoral study at Northwestern University, 1936, London School of Economics and Political Science, London, 1937, and Capetown University, 1937. *Religion:* Nonsectarian. *Politics:* Independent.

ADDRESSES: Home—Kew Gardens, New York, N.Y.

CAREER: Howard University, Washington, D.C., instructor, 1928, assistant professor and department chairman, beginning in 1929, special assistant to the president of the university, 1931-32, professor of political science, 1937-42; staff member serving as chief aide to Swedish sociologist Gunnar Myrdal at Carnegie Corporation of New York, 1938-40; Office of the Coordinator of Information (later Office of Strategic Services), Washington, D.C., senior social science analyst, beginning in 1941, principal research analyst in the Africa and Far East section, 1942-43, chief of the Africa Section of the Research and Analysis Branch, 1943-44; U.S. State Department, Washington, D.C., divisional assistant for colonial problems in the Division of Political Studies and area specialist on Africa and dependent areas in the Division of Territorial Studies, both 1944, acting associate chief, 1945, and associate chief of the Division of Dependent Area Affairs (also serving some months as acting chief), 1945-47, assistant secretary to the U.S. delegation at Dumbarton Oaks conference, 1944, technical expert on trusteeship for the U.S. delegation at the conference on International Organization at San Francisco, 1945, appointed by President Truman to membership on Anglo-American Caribbean Commission, 1945, adviser to the U.S. delegation to the United Nations General Assembly in London, 1946, adviser to the U.S. delegation to International Labor conferences in Paris and Philadephia; United Nations Secretariat, Washington, D.C., director of the Trusteeship Division, 1947-55, undersecretary, 1955-57, undersecretary for special political affairs serving under Secretary-General Dag Hammarskjold, 1957-67, undersecretary-general serving under Secretary-General U Thant, 1967-71. Special assistant to the Secretary-General's Special Committee on Palestine, and appointed principal secretary of the Palestine Commission, both 1947, head of the Palestine Commission, 1948, directed peace-keeping operations in such areas as Suez, 1956, Congo, 1960, Yemen, 1962-64, Cyprus, 1964, and India and Pakistan, 1965. Founder of National Negro Congress, 1936. Co-director of Institute of Race Relations at Swarthmore College, 1936; member of faculty of Harvard University, 1950-52; became trustee of Oberlin College, 1950, and the Rockefeller Foundation, 1955; member of the Harvard University board of overseers, 1958-65.

MEMBER: American Political Science Association (member of executive council; president, 1953-54), National Association for the Advancement of Colored People (member of board of directors, c. 1949-71), William Allen White Committee, Phi Beta Kappa.

AWARDS, HONORS: New York's Town Hall Distinguished Service Award, 1949; awarded citation by the American Association for the United Nations, 1949, for ''distinguished and unselfish service in advancing the ideas of the United Nations''; Spingarn Award of the National Association for the Advancement of Colored People, 1949, and the Nobel Peace Prize, 1950, both for negotiating the 1949 armistice between Arab and Israeli states; One World Award; Franklin D. Roosevelt Four Freedoms Award from Four Freedoms Foundation, Inc.; Medal of Freedom, 1963; Ozias Goodwin fellowship from Harvard University, Rosenwald Field fellowship, and Social Science Research Council fellowship for anthropology and colonial policy; more than fifty honorary degrees from colleges and universities.

WRITINGS:

A World View of Race, Association in Negro Folk Education, 1936, reprinted, Kennikat, 1968.
Peace and the United Nations, Leeds University, 1952.
The Political Status of the Negro in the Age of FDR (collection of interviews), edited and with an introduction by Dewey W. Grantham, University of Chicago Press, 1973.

Contributor of articles on colonial policy, trusteeship, and race relations to periodicals, including *New Republic, National Municipal Review, Annals, Journal of Negro History,* and *Journal of Negro Education.* Also contributor to trusteeship sections of the United Nations Charter, 1945.

SIDELIGHTS: The highest ranking American official in the United Nations and the first black recipient of the Nobel Peace Prize, Ralph J. Bunche was ''an ideal international civil servant, a black man of learning and experience open to men and ideas of all shades,'' according to Robert D. McFadden of the *New York Times.* For his leading role in negotiating peace talks between Arab and Israeli states in 1949 and his direction of numerous peace-keeping forces around the world, Bunche is considered one of the most significant American diplomats of the twentieth century.

Born in Detroit in 1904, Bunch moved to Los Angeles at the age of thirteen upon the death of his parents. After graduating from the University of California at Los Angeles in 1927 and receiving his master's degree in government at Harvard University the following year, he began teaching at the all-black Howard University in Washington, D.C., soon becoming the head of the political science department there. He returned to Harvard where he obtained a doctorate in government and international relations in 1934. His later postdoctoral work in anthropology and colonial policy led to worldwide travel, field work in Africa, and completion of his 1937 book *A World View of Race.* Concerned with racial problems, Bunche went on to work with Swedish sociologist Gunnar Myrdal from 1938 to 1940 surveying the conditions of the Negro in America. Their interview work in the South—which caused them to be chased out of some Alabama towns and almost lynched by a mob of angry whites—led to the publication of Myrdal's widely acclaimed 1944 *An American Dilemma,* a massive study of race relations.

Bunche eventually became known as an expert on colonial affairs. During World War II he served as a specialist in African and Far Eastern affairs for the Office of Strategic Services before moving to the U.S. State Department, where he soon became associate chief of its Division of Dependent Area Affairs. He was the first black to hold a desk job in the department. For his expertise on trusteeship, Bunche was recommended by Secretary-General Trygve Lie to direct the Trusteeship Division at the United Nations in 1947. Later that year the diplomat was appointed special assistant to the Secretary-General's Special Committee on Palestine, and in 1948

he became head of the Palestine Commission when its original appointee, Count Folke Bernadotte of Sweden, was assassinated. Bunche consequently was faced with the great challenge of continuing cease-fire talks between the long-time fighting Arab and Israeli nations.

''As it turned out,'' commented Homer Metz of *New Review,* ''he was exactly suited for the difficult task of bringing Arabs and Jews together.'' Hailed for his endless patience, sensitivity, and optimism, Bunche, after eighty-one days of negotiations on the island of Rhodes, worked out the ''Four Armistice Agreements'' which resulted in an immediate cessation of the hostilities between the two combatants. ''The art of his compromise,'' lauded McFadden, ''lay in his seemingly boundless energy and the order and timing of his moves.'' A writer for *Time* further praised the diplomat: ''It required painstaking, brilliant diplomacy to bring the Arabs and Israelis together on the island of Rhodes; Bunche's forceful personality . . . helped to keep them there.'' Garnering worldwide praise for his successful peace-keeping efforts, Bunche won the 1950 Nobel Peace Prize, becoming the first black recipient of the coveted award.

Bunche did not consider his work on Rhodes, however, his most fulfilling mission. McFadden quoted Bunche from a 1969 interview: '''The Peace Prize attracted all the attention, but I've had more satisfaction in the work I've done since.''' For example, the statesman went on to conduct peace forces in the Congo, Yemen, Cyprus, India, and Pakistan, and he regarded his work in the Suez area of Egypt—where he organized and directed the deployment of a 6,000-man neutral force which maintained peace there from 1956 to 1967—as his most satisfying accomplishment. About that mission, Bunche was quoted in *Time:* '''For the first time . . . we have found a way to use military men for peace instead of war.'''

Bunche's peace-keeping efforts for the United Nations soon earned the diplomat the position of undersecretary in 1955, the highest post held by an American in the world organization. And by the time he became undersecretary-general in 1967 (the post he held until his retirement in 1971), Bunche's ''diplomatic skills—a masterwork in the practical application of psychology—[had] became legendary at the United Nations,'' noted McFadden. But the international civil servant was not only valuable to the United Nations; Bunche was considered an inspiration to millions of Americans and was what *Newsweek* called ''the foremost Negro of his generation—the distinguished symbol of how far a black man could rise in the Establishment.'' Furthermore, concluded *Time,* ''Bunche had achieved a unique status: a black without color and an American who belonged to all the nations.'' His book *Peace and the United Nations* appeared in 1952, and *The Political Status of the Negro in the Age of FDR*—a collection of more than five hundred interviews conducted in the American South—was published posthumously in 1973.

BIOGRAPHICAL/CRITICAL SOURCES:

BOOKS

Kugelmass, J. Alvin, *Ralph J. Bunche: Fighter for Peace,* Messner, 1962.
Mann, Peggy, *Ralph Bunche: UN Peacemaker,* Coward, McCann & Geoghegan, 1975.

PERIODICALS

American History Review, June, 1974.
Journal of American History, June, 1974.

New Review, May 30, 1949.

OBITUARIES:

PERIODICALS

Nation, December 27, 1971.
Newsweek, December 20, 1971.
New York Times, December 10, 1971.
Time, December 20, 1971.

—*Sketch by Janice E. Drane*

*   *   *

BURROUGHS, Margaret G.
  See BURROUGHS, Margaret Taylor (Goss)

*   *   *

BURROUGHS, Margaret Taylor (Goss)   1917-
(Margaret G. Burroughs, Margaret Taylor)

PERSONAL: Born November 1, 1917, in St. Rose, La.; daughter of Alexander (a laborer) and Octavia (Pierre) Taylor; married Bernard Goss, 1939 (divorced, 1947); married Charles Gordon Burroughs (a museum curator), December 23, 1949; children: (first marriage) Gayle Goss Toller; (second mariage; adopted) Paul. *Education:* Chicago Teachers College (now Chicago State University), graduate, 1937; Art Institute of Chicago, B.F.A., 1944, M.F.A., 1948; Teachers College, Columbia University, graduate study, summers, 1958, 1959, 1960; Esmerelda Art School, Mexico City, 1952-53.

ADDRESSES: Home—3806 South Michigan Ave., DuSable City, Ill. 60653. *Office*—DuSable Museum, 740 East 56th Pl., Chicago, Ill. 60657.

CAREER: DuSable High School, Chicago, Ill., teacher of art, 1946-69; Kennedy-King Community College, Chicago, professor of humanities, 1969-79. Instructor in African and African-American art history, Chicago Institute of Art, 1968. Officer and member of board of directors, South Side Art Community Center, Chicago, 1940—; director, DuSable Museum of African-American History, Chicago, 1961-84, director emeritus, 1984—. Exhibitions of artwork at American Negro Exhibition, Chicago, 1940, Atlanta Negro Art Exhibition, 1947, and 1955, San Francisco Civic Museum, 1949, Leipzig, East Germany, 1965, Friendship House, Moscow, U.S.S.R., 1967, "Two Centuries of Black American Artists" traveling exhibition, 1976, Evans-Tibbs Collection, Washington, D.C., 1982, Nicole Gallery, Chicago, 1986, South Side Community Art Center, Chicago, 1987, Museum of Fine Arts, Houston, Tex., 1988, and others. Member of board of directors, American Forum for International Studies, 1969-72; member, Chicago Council on Fine Arts, 1976-80, National Commission on Negro History and Culture, 1981—; founder, Burroughs Group.

MEMBER: National Conference of Negro Artists (founder, 1959), Phi Delta Kappa.

AWARDS, HONORS: Honorable mention in printmaking, Atlanta Negro Art Exhibition, Atlanta University, 1947; citation from South Side Community Art Center, Chicago, 1953; first prize in Watercolor Purchase Award, Atlanta Negro Art Exhibition, Atlanta University, and citation from Committee for the Negro in Arts, both 1955; Hallmark prize for best art work, Lincoln University, 1962; National Endowment for the Humanities grant and Field Museum of Natural History internship grant, both 1968, both for study of museum sciences; African

travel grant, American Forum for International Study, 1968; D.H.L., Lewis College, 1973; Y.W.C.A. leadership award, 1973, for excellence in art; citation as one of ten outstanding black artists from President Carter, 1980; senior citizen of the year choice, Chicago Park District, 1980; honorarium from Friends of the Anne Spencer Foundation, 1982; Excellence in Art Award, National Association of Negro Museums, 1982; D.H.L., Chicago State University, 1983; saluted by Illinois State Legislature, 1986; February 1, 1986 proclaimed "Dr. Margaret Burroughs Day in Chicago" by Mayor Harold Washington; cited for outstanding service in the arts and humanities, Chicago, DuSable, Fort Dearborn Historical Commission, Inc., 1986; certificate of appreciation, U.S. Postal Service—Chicago Branch, 1987; Progressive Black Woman's Award, Enverite Charity Club, Distinguished Woman Award, Women's Network to Re-elect Mayor Harold Washington, Paul Robeson High School Award, Recognition of Excellence Award, I'R Electrical Organization, Chicago Youth Center Award, and Community Service Award, Black Law Students Association of John Marshall Law School, all 1987; senior achievement in the arts citation and Woman's Caucus for Art Award, Houston Museum of Fine Art, both 1988.

WRITINGS:

Whip Me Whop Me Pudding and Other Stories of Riley Rabbit and His Fabulous Friends, Praga Press, 1966.
(Editor, under name Margaret G. Burroughs, with Dudley Randall) *For Malcolm: Poems on the Life and the Death of Malcolm X*, preface and eulogy by Ossie Davis, Broadside Press, 1967, 2nd edition under name Margaret Taylor Burroughs, 1969.
What Shall I Tell My Children Who Are Black? (also see below), M.A.A.H. Press, 1968.
Africa, My Africa, DuSable Museum, 1970.
What Shall I Tell My Children: An Addenda with a Letter from Ruwa Chiri (includes *What Shall I Tell My Children Who Are Black*), DuSable Museum, 1973.

UNDER NAME MARGARET TAYLOR

Jaspar, the Drummin' Boy (self-illustrated), Viking, 1947, revised edition under name Margaret Taylor Burroughs, illustrated by Ted Lewin, Follett, 1970.
(Compiler) *Did You Feed My Cow?: Rhymes and Games from City Streets and Country Lanes*, illustrated by Paul Galdone, Crowell, 1956, revised edition under name Margaret Taylor Burroughs published as *Did You Feed My Cow?: Street Games, Chants, and Rhymes*, illustrated by Joe E. De Valasco, Follett, 1969.
Landscapes: Etchings, forward, titles, and visions by Rochelle Holt, Ragnarok Press, 1974.
Sketchbook 1976, Tiamat Press, 1976.

OTHER

(Contributor under name Margaret Taylor) *Celebrating Negro History and Brotherhood: A Folio of Prints by Chicago Artists*, Seven Arts Workshop, 1956.
(Contributor) Woodie King, Jr., editor, *The Forerunners: Black Poets in America*, Howard University Press, 1981.
(Contributor) Erlene Stetson, editor, *Black Sister: Poetry by Black American Women, 1746-1980*, Indiana University Press, 1981.

Contributor to educational journals.

SIDELIGHTS: Margaret Taylor Burroughs "has carved out a place for herself as a poet whose work reflects a keen awareness of the multiple dimensions of Afro-American life and history,'' according to Mary Jane Dickerson in the *Dictionary of Literary Biography*. But the Chicago native is not only a poet; for many years Burroughs worked as an art teacher in Chicago schools, and her artwork has garnered much critical acclaim. Later, she founded the DuSable Museum, dedicating it to the preservation of African and African-American arts and letters. Her greatest contributions, continues Dickerson, lie in ''her dedication to an African identity and heritage which are visible not merely in her poetry but in her inspirational life's work, in her teaching the young, creating art, directing the DuSable Museum, and sustaining other artists and writers.''

BIOGRAPHICAL/CRITICAL SOURCES:

BOOKS

Dictionary of Literary Biography, Volume 41: *Afro-American Poets since 1955*, Gale, 1985.

PERIODICALS

Chicago Sun Book Week, May 11, 1947.
Chicago Sunday Tribune, November 11, 1956.
Christian Science Monitor, October 10, 1970.
New York Herald Tribune Weekly Book Review, April 13, 1947.
New York Times, May 4, 1947.

*   *   *

BUTLER, Octavia E(stelle)   1947-

PERSONAL: Born June 22, 1947, in Pasadena, Calif.; daughter of Laurice and Octavia M. (Guy) Butler. *Education:* Pasadena City College, A.A., 1968; attended California State University, Los Angeles, 1969.

ADDRESSES: Home—P.O. Box 6604, Los Angeles, Calif. 90055.

CAREER: Free-lance writer, 1970—.

MEMBER: Science Fiction Writers of America.

AWARDS, HONORS: Hugo Award, World Science Fiction Convention, 1984, for short story ''Speech Sounds''; Hugo Award, World Science Fiction Convention, Nebula Award, Science Fiction Writers of America, and Locus Award, *Locus* magazine, all 1985, all for novelette ''Bloodchild.''

WRITINGS:

SCIENCE FICTION NOVELS

Patternmaster, Doubleday, 1976.
Mind of My Mind, Doubleday, 1977.
Survivor, Doubleday, 1978.
Kindred, Doubleday, 1979.
Wild Seed, Doubleday, 1980.
Clay's Ark, St. Martin's, 1984.
Dawn: Xenogenesis, Warner Books, 1987.

CONTRIBUTOR

Robin Scott Wilson, editor, *Clarion*, New American Library, 1970.
Roy Torgeson, editor, *Chrysalis 4*, Zebra Books, 1979.

Contributor to *Isaac Asimov's Science Fiction Magazine*, *Future Life*, *Transmission*, and other publications.

SIDELIGHTS: Concerned with genetic engineering, psionic powers, advanced alien beings, and the nature and proper use of power, Octavia E. Butler's science fiction presents these themes in terms of racial and sexual awareness. ''Butler consciously explores the impact of race and sex upon future society,'' as Frances Smith Foster explains in *Extrapolation*. As one of the few black writers in the science fiction field, and the only black woman, Butler's racial and sexual perspective is unique. This perspective, however, does not limit her fiction or turn it into mere propaganda. ''Her stories,'' Sherley Anne Williams writes in *Ms.*, ''aren't overwhelmed by politics, nor are her characters overwhelmed by racism or sexism.'' Speaking of how Butler's early novels deal with racial questions in particular, John R. Pfeiffer of *Fantasy Review* maintains that ''nevertheless, and therefore more remarkably, these are the novels of character that critics so much want to find in science fiction—and which remain so rare. Finally, they are love stories that are mythic, bizarre, exotic and heroic and full of doom and transcendence.''

After attending the Clarion Science Fiction Writers' Workshop in 1970, where she studied under some of the field's top writers, Butler began to sell her short stories to science fiction magazines. But she had been writing for many years before Clarion. ''I began writing,'' she comments, ''when I was about ten years old for the same reason many people begin reading—to escape loneliness and boredom. I didn't realize then that writing was supposed to be work. It was too much fun. It still is.''

Butler's stories have been well received by science fiction fans. In 1985 she won three of the field's top honors—the Nebula Award, the Hugo Award, and the Locus Award—for her novella ''Bloodchild,'' the story of human males on another planet who bear the children of an alien race. ''Bloodchild,'' Williams maintains, ''explores the paradoxes of power and inequality, and starkly portrays the experience of a class who, like women throughout most of history, are valued chiefly for their reproductive capacities.''

It is through her novels, especially those set in the world of the ''Patternists,'' that Butler reaches her largest audience. These novels tell of a society dominated by an elite, specially-bred group of telepaths who are mentally linked together into a heirarchical pattern. Led by a four thousand-year-old alien who survives by killing and then taking over younger bodies, these telepaths seek to create a race of superhumans. The Patternist society is also wracked by an alien plague which genetically alters human beings. The novels range over vast reaches of time and space, tracing many hundreds of years of human history from the remote past to the space-faring future.

Among Butler's strengths as a writer is her creation of believable, independent female characters. ''Her major characters are black women,'' Foster explains, and through these characters Butler explores the possibilities for a society open to true sexual equality. In such a society Butler's female characters, ''powerful and purposeful in their own right, need not rely upon eroticism to gain their ends,'' Foster writes. Williams finds that Butler posits ''a multiracial society featuring strong women characters.''

Critics also praise Butler's controlled, economical prose style. Writing in the *Washington Post Book World*, Elizabeth A. Lynn calls Butler's prose ''spare and sure, and even in moments of great tension she never loses control over her pacing or over her sense of story.'' ''Butler,'' writes Dean R. Lambe of the *Science Fiction Review*, ''has a fine hand with lean, well-paced prose.''

Butler's only novel not set in the Patternist society is *Kindred*, a novel her publisher marketed as mainstream fiction despite its time-travel theme. It concerns Dana, a contemporary black woman who is pulled back in time by her great-great-grandfather, a white plantation owner in the antebellum American South. To insure that he will live to father her great-grandmother, and thus insure her own birth in the twentieth century, Dana is called upon to save the slaveowner's life on several occasions. "Butler makes new and eloquent use of a familiar science-fiction idea, protecting one's own past, to express the tangled interdependency of black and white in the United States," Joanna Russ writes in the *Magazine of Fantasy and Science Fiction*. Williams calls *Kindred* "a startling and engrossing commentary on the complex actuality and continuing heritage of American slavery."

"I began writing science fiction and fantasy," Butler explains, "because both inspire a high level of creativity and offer a great deal of freedom." But she soon found that few science fiction writers exercised this creative freedom. "I remember that when I began reading science fiction," she continues, "I was disappointed at how little this creativity and freedom was used to portray the many racial, ethnic, and class variations. Also, I could not help noticing how few significant women characters there were in science fiction. Fortunately, all of this has been changing over the past few years. I intend my writing to contribute to the change."

Butler enjoys a solid reputation among both readers and critics of science fiction. Although Williams notes that Butler has a "cult status among many black women readers," she also notes that "Butler's work has a scope that commands a wide audience." Speaking of *Kindred* and *Wild Seed*, Pfeiffer argues that with these books Butler "produced two novels of such special excellence that critical appreciation of them will take several years to assemble. To miss them will be to miss unique novels in modern fiction." Margaret Anne O'Connor of the *Dictionary of Literary Biography* simply calls Butler "one of the most promising new writers in America today."

BIOGRAPHICAL/CRITICAL SOURCES:

BOOKS

Contemporary Literary Criticism, XXXVIII, Gale, 1986.
Dictionary of Literary Biography, Volume XXXIII: *Afro-American Fiction Writers after 1955*, Gale, 1984.

PERIODICALS

Analog: Science Fiction/Science Fact, January 5, 1981, November, 1984.
Black American Literature Forum, summer, 1984.
Black Scholar, March/April, 1986.
Equal Opportunity Forum Magazine, Number 8, 1980.
Essence, April, 1979.
Extrapolation, spring, 1982.
Fantasy Review, July, 1984.
Janus, winter, 1978-79.
Los Angeles Times, January 30, 1981.
Magazine of Fantasy and Science Fiction, February, 1980, August, 1984.
Ms., March, 1986, June, 1987.
Salaga, 1981.
Science Fiction Review, May, 1984.
Thrust: Science Fiction in Review, summer, 1979.
Washington Post Book World, September 28, 1980, June 28, 1987.

—*Sketch by Thomas Wiloch*

C

CADE, Toni
See BAMBARA, Toni Cade

*　　*　　*

CALDWELL, Ben(jamin) 1937-

PERSONAL: Born September 24, 1937, in New York, N.Y.

ADDRESSES: Office—P.O. Box 656, Morningside Station, New York, N.Y. 10026.

CAREER: Writer.

AWARDS, HONORS: Guggenheim fellowship for playwriting, 1970.

WRITINGS:

PLAYS

The Job (one-act; first produced in 1966; also produced as part of "What Is Going On"; see below); published in *Drama Review,* summer, 1968, published in *Black Identity,* edited by Francis E. Kearns, Holt, 1970, published in *Nommo: An Anthology of Modern African and Black American Literature,* edited by William H. Robinson, Macmillan, 1972.

Riot Sale; or, Dollar Psyche Fake-Out (first produced in 1966), published in *Drama Review,* summer, 1968, published in *Black Culture: Reading and Writing Black,* edited by Gloria M. Simmons and Helene D. Hutchinson, Holt, 1972.

Mission Accomplished (first produced in 1967), published in *Drama Review,* summer, 1968.

Prayer Meeting; or, The First Militant Minister (one-act; first produced as "Militant Preacher" in Newark, N.J., at Spirit House Theatre, April, 1967), Jihad, 1968, published in *Black Fire: An Anthology of Afro-American Writing,* edited by Le Roi Jones and Larry Neal, Morrow, 1968; published in *A Black Quartet: Four New Black Plays* (anthology of works by four playwrights; first produced Off-Broadway by Chelsea Theatre Center at Brooklyn Academy of Music, April 25, 1969), introduction by Clayton Riley, New American Library, 1970.

The King of Soul; or, The Devil and Otis Redding: A One-Act Musical Tragedy (first produced in 1968), published in *New Plays From the Black Theatre,* edited by Ed Bullins, Bantam, 1969.

Family Portrait; or, My Son, the Black Nationalist (one-act; produced as part of "What Is Going On"; see below), published in *New Plays From the Black Theatre,* edited by Ed Bullins, Bantam, 1969.

Top Secret; or, A Few Million After B.C. (first produced in Los Angeles, Calif., by Performing Arts Society in 1969; produced as part of "What Is Going On"; see below), published in *Drama Review,* summer, 1968.

Hypnotism (one-act), published in *Afro-Arts Anthology,* Jihad, 1969, published in *Black Culture: Reading and Writing Black,* edited by Gloria M. Simmons and Helene D. Hutchinson, Holt, 1972.

"Run Around" (one-act), first produced in New York City at Third World House, June, 1970.

All White Caste; After the Separation: A Slow-Paced One-Act Play (produced as part of "What Is Going On"; see below), published in *Black Drama Anthology,* edited by Woodie King, Jr., and Ronald Milner, New American Library, 1971.

An Obscene Play (for Adults Only), published in *Alafia,* winter, 1971.

The Wall (one-act), published in *Scripts,* May, 1972.

"What Is Going On," (program of short plays; contains "All White Caste," "Family Portrait," "Rights and Reasons," "The Job," "Top Secret"), first produced in New York City at New Federal Theatre, November 23, 1973.

"The World of Ben Caldwell: A Dramatized Examination of the Absurdity of the American Dream and Subsequent Reality," first produced in New York City at New Federal Theatre, April, 1982.

"Moms," first produced Off-Broadway at Astor Palace Theater, August 4, 1987.

Also author of "The Fanatic; or, Testifying" (one-act), "The Interview," "Recognition" (one-act), "Reverend Mac; or, God and Company," "Right Attitude; or, Is You Is or Is You Ain't a Revolutionary," "Un-Presidented; or, What Needs to Be Done" (one-act), and "Uptight or . . ."

OTHER

(With Askia Muhammad Toure) *Juju: Magic Songs for the Black Nation* (collection of poetry and prose), Third World Press, 1970.

SIDELIGHTS: Born in New York City's Harlem neighborhood, Ben Caldwell is known for short satirical plays that comment on the situation of black people in white-dominated America. He first came to prominence in the 1960s as the result of his association with LeRoi Jones (now known as Imamu Amiri Baraka), a major black playwright whose Spirit House Theatre premiered one of Caldwell's best-known works, "Prayer Meeting; or, The First Militant Minister" (originally titled "Militant Preacher"). In "Prayer Meeting," Caldwell uses a comic premise to dramatize the political message that black people must be willing to struggle actively for their rights and that they should not expect an easy accommodation with white society. The play shows a black minister as he returns home and prays for God's help in avoiding an angry reaction by members of his congregation to the death of a black teenager at the hands of the police. The minister does not realize that his arrival has interrupted a burglary in his own house. Remaining unseen by the minister, the burglar disdainfully responds to the man's prayer by claiming to be the voice of God. Berated into action by "God," the minister abandons his philosophy of nonconfrontation and resolves to lead his parishioners on City Hall. "Prayer Meeting" was presented Off-Broadway as part of the production "A Black Quartet," which also includes plays by Jones and two other prominent black playwrights, Ed Bullins and Ronald Milner. Reviewing the "Quartet" for the *New York Times*, Clayton Riley praised Caldwell's play for its "beautifully delineated satiric focus."

In other plays Caldwell casts doubts on the motives of whites who claim to help black people. "Top Secret; or, A Few Million After B.C." shows white government leaders—silently attended by their black servants—trying to develop new ways to maintain their racial domination. The leaders decide that contraception, which promises blacks the freedom of an active sexual life without pregnancy, will actually aid the white power structure by limiting the size of the black population.

Two programs of Caldwell's short works have been presented at the New Federal Theatre in New York City. "What Is Going On" comprises five plays, including "Top Secret." "The World of Ben Caldwell" is a collection of skits and monologues, subtitled "A Dramatized Examination of the Absurdity of the American Dream and Subsequent Reality." Reviewing the latter show for the *Village Voice*, Stanley Crouch noted that "Caldwell's strong suit is a great ability to stitch together fabrics of rhetoric ranging from bureaucratic to black bottom barber shop."

BIOGRAPHICAL/CRITICAL SOURCES:

BOOKS

Dictionary of Literary Biography, Volume 38, *Afro-American Writers After 1955: Dramatists and Prose Writers*, Gale, 1985.

PERIODICALS

New York Times, August 3, 1969, November 28, 1973, April 10, 1982, August 9, 1987.
Players, February-March, 1976.
Village Voice, April 27, 1982.

*   *   *

CARMICHAEL, Stokely 1941-

PERSONAL: Born June 29, 1941, in Port-of-Spain, Trinidad and Tobago, British West Indies (now an independent republic); came to United States, 1952; self-exiled to Guinea, West Africa, May, 1969; son of Adolphus (a carpenter) and Mabel F. (also known as May Charles) Carmichael; married former wife, Miriam Makeba (a professional singer), April, 1968. *Education:* Howard University, B.A., 1964.

ADDRESSES: Home—Conakry, Guinea. *Office*—c/o Random House, Inc., 201 East 50th St., New York, N.Y. 10022.

CAREER: Civil Rights organizer and political activist. Student Nonviolent Coordinating Committee (SNCC; later renamed Student National Coordinating Committee; commonly called "Snick"), Atlanta, Ga., organizer, 1964-66, chairman, 1966-67; Black Panthers, Oakland, Calif., prime minister, 1967-69. Director of Civil Rights activities, Mississippi Summer Project, 1964; field organizer for voter registration, Lowndes County, Miss.; organizer for All-Black Lowndes County Freedom Organization; organizer for All Afrikan People's Revolutionary Party. Lecturer at numerous universities and colleges, 1966-67.

AWARDS, HONORS: LL.D., Shaw University.

WRITINGS:

(Contributor) Robert Penn Warren, *Who Speaks for the Negro?*, Random House, 1965.
(With Charles V. Hamilton) *Black Power: The Politics of Liberation in America*, Random House, 1967.
(Contributor) John Hope Franklin and Isidore Starr, editors, *The Negro in Twentieth Century America: A Reader on the Struggle for Civil Rights*, Vintage Books, 1967.
Stokely Speaks: Black Power Back to Pan-Africanism (speeches and essays), Random House, 1971.

OTHER

"Black Americans: Stokely Carmichael" (cassette recording of interview on "Face the Nation," Columbia Broadcasting System [CBS-TV], June 19, 1966), Holt Information Systems, c. 1973.
"Stokely Carmichael" (cassette recording of interview dated February, 1975), Pacifica Tape Library, 1975.

Contributor to *Black Scholar*, *Massachusetts Review*, and *New York Review of Books*.

SIDELIGHTS: Civil Rights activist Stokely Carmichael is credited with originating the slogan "Black Power," which became the watchword for numerous black liberation groups in the 1960s. A native of the British West Indies who moved to New York City's Harlem in 1952, Carmichael first became involved with the Civil Rights movement in the 1960s as a participant in the Freedom Rides. In 1964 he joined what was then the Student Nonviolent Coordinating Committee (SNCC), where he gained influence as the leader of a task force sent to increase black voter registration in Lowndes County, Mississippi. The task force helped raise the number of registered black voters in the predominantly black county to a number that surpassed the white populace. Carmichael later helped organize the Lowndes County Freedom organization, an all-black political party which adopted the panther as its symbol.

Carmichael assumed the chairmanship of SNCC in 1966 and began to draw controversy with the slogan "Black Power," which some groups criticized as embodying racism in reverse. Carmichael left SNCC in 1967 to join the more militant Black Panthers, the urban group whose political base was primarily found in the ghettos of northern American cities. Carmichael rose to the level of prime minister with the Black Panthers, yet took issue with the party's acquiescence towards white radicals, and in May of 1969 left the United States on a self-imposed exile to Guinea, West Africa. Carmichael resigned from the Black Panthers in July of the same year, stating in a publicly disclosed letter: "The party has become dogmatic in its newly acquired ideology and thinks that it has the only correct position. . . . [Furthermore,] the alliances being formed by the party are alliances which I cannot politically agree with, because the history of Africans living in the United States has shown that any premature alliance with white radicals has led to complete subversion of the blacks by the whites, through their direct or indirect control of the black organization." By the late 1960s, Carmichael's politics were Pan-Africanist in nature, advocating a homeland in Africa for oppressed black minorities throughout the Western world.

Carmichael's 1967 book *Black Power: The Politics of Liberation in America,* co-written with Charles V. Hamilton, examines the concept "Black Power" and its implications for the Civil Rights movement. The book advocates the need for blacks to reject the values of an American society fraught with racism, and to develop their own independent, self-supportive organizations. In the authors' words, Black Power "is a call for black people in this country to unite, to recognize their heritage, to build a sense of community. It is a call for black people to define their own goals, to lead their own organizations and to support those organizations. It is a call to reject the racist institutions and values of this society." Carmichael and Hamilton explain that the concept "rests on a fundamental premise: *Before a group can enter the open society, it must first close ranks.*" Bill Goode comments in the *Antioch Review* that "Carmichael and Hamilton have a revolutionary eschatology; they do not have a transitional program leading to the apocalypse.The final goal is a completely restructured society, the immediate goal is 'control of the turf.'" In the preface to *Black Power,* the authors state the urgency of their message: "This book presents a political framework and ideology which represents the last reasonable opportunity for this society to work out its racial problems short of prolonged destructive guerilla warfare."

Reception of *Black Power* was mixed, ranging from those who saw the book as a major document of revolution, to those who viewed Carmichael and Hamilton's proposals as non-revolutionary or in need of a more thorough analysis. Of the former view, Shane Stevens in the *Saturday Review* credits *Black Power* as "surely the most important document to have come forth from the whole black-white arena of public affairs. . . . Simply stated, the authors' thesis, is that in these United States power (which happens to be white) has been pitted all these years against powerlessness (which happens to be black). This white power is complete in the political, economic, and social sectors of our life. And if the black people in America are ever going to have full equality and social justice, they will have first to acquire an equal amount of political and economic power." Fred Powledge in the *New York Times Book Review,* on the other hand, writes that Carmichael and Hamilton's "suggestions sound sadly like those advanced for so long by the paper leaders—ideas that sound great, that are essentially democratic but that move editorial writers to use words like 'dramatic' or 'revolutionary' or 'radical,' depending on their source, but suggestions that have little behind them in the way of hard-thought-out strategies." Powledge praises the book for "an excellent description of the way in which American whites need not perform personal acts of discrimination against blacks, but rather allow the institutions of a sick society to do it for them," and calls "perceptive" the "authors" rejection of the idea that a coalition between whites and blacks is likely." He concludes, however, that "in the absence of more detailed

political frameworks and ideologies for black Americans, some students of the struggle are likely to conclude, after reading this book, that Black Power is not much more than an organizing vehicle and a scare phrase."

Critical opinion was also mixed on Carmichael's 1971 collection of speeches and essays, *Stokely Speaks: Black Power Back to Pan-Africanism.* Julius Lester writes in the *New York Times Book Review* that the collection presents "the thoughts of a civil-rights organizer, a black radical and a Pan-Africanist, but the relationship of the three voices is vague. . . . The speeches are replete with insights of brilliance, but insights alone do not make a political ideology." Lester also contends that the force of Carmichael's rhetoric is dependent on the "background" of racial violence that was occurring in the 1960s. He writes: "Carmichael is historically important, but this collection makes it clear that his importance comes from the fact that he happened to be saying certain things at the precise moment when poor blacks were lecturing America with Molotov cocktails." Other reviewers, however, note that the book stands on its own in documenting a major area of the 1960s Civil Rights movement. A *Publishers Weekly* contributor writes that "relatively sophisticated readers will be able to trace, through this collection, the direction that at least one segment of the Black Power movement has taken in recent years," adding that Carmichael's speeches emerge as "challenging, outspoken and lucid."

BIOGRAPHICAL/CRITICAL SOURCES:

BOOKS

Carmichael, Stokely, and Charles V. Hamilton, *Black Power: The Politics of Liberation in America,* Random House, 1967.

PERIODICALS

Antioch Review, spring, 1968.
New York Review of Books, February 29, 1968.
New York Times, January 18, 1969, July 4, 1969, July 25, 1969.
New York Times Book Review, December 10, 1967, May 16, 1971.
Publishers Weekly, August 28, 1967, March 1, 1971.
Saturday Review, November 11, 1967.
Times Literary Supplement, April 18, 1968.

—*Sketch by Michael E. Mueller*

*   *   *

CARROLL, Vinnette (Justine)

PERSONAL: Born in New York, N.Y.; daughter of Edgar Edgerton (a dentist) and Florence (a teacher; maiden name, Morris) Carroll; children: Clinton Derricks-Carroll. *Education:* Long Island University, B.A., 1944; New York University, M.A., 1946; graduate study at Columbia University, 1945-46, and New School for Social Research, 1948-50; studied acting under Erwin Piscator, Lee Strasberg, and Stella Adler.

ADDRESSES: Office—Vinnette Carroll Repertory Company, P.O. Box 030473, Fort Lauderdale, Fla. 33303.

CAREER: Psychologist with New York City Bureau of Child Guidance, New York City; High School for the Performing Arts, New York City, instructor in drama, 1953-64; Urban Arts Corps (now Theatre), New York City, founder and artistic director, beginning in 1967; Vinnette Carroll Repertory Company, Fort Lauderdale, Fla., producing artistic director, 1984—.

Director of Ghetto Arts Program for New York State Council on the Arts; associate director of Inner City Repertory Theatre, Los Angeles, Calif., beginning in 1967.

Actress in stage productions, including "Agamemnon," 1948, "The Little Foxes," 1948, "Deep Are the Roots," 1949, "Caesar and Cleopatra," 1950, "A Streetcar Named Desire," 1956, "The Grass Harp," 1956, "Small War on Murray Hill," 1957, "The Crucible," 1958, "Moon on a Rainbow Shawl," 1958, 1959, and 1962, "Jolly's Progress," 1959, "A Member of the Wedding," 1960, and "The Octoroon," 1961; actress in films, including "A Morning for Jimmy," 1960, "One Potato, Two Potato," 1964, "Up the Down Staircase," 1967, and "Alice's Restaurant," 1969; actress in television productions, including "A Member of the Wedding," 1960, "Black Nativity," 1962, "We the Women," 1974, "Sojourner," 1975, and episodes of "All in the Family," 1977-78; has appeared on numerous talk shows and documentaries.

Director of stage productions, including "Dark of the Moon," 1960, "Black Nativity," 1961, 1962, 1963, and 1964, "Ondine," 1961, "The Disenchanted," 1962, "The Prodigal Son," 1965, "The Flies," 1966, 1967, 1973, and 1974, "Slow Dance on the Killing Ground," 1967, "Old Judge Mose Is Dead," 1967, "The Lottery," 1967, "But Never Jam Today," 1969, 1978, and 1979 (also produced as "Alice," 1977), "Moon on a Rainbow Shawl," 1969, "Bury the Dead," 1971, "Don't Bother Me, I Can't Cope," 1971, 1972, and 1973, "Croesus and the Witch," 1971 and 1973, "Step Lively, Boy," 1973, "The Ups and Downs of Theophilus Maitland," 1974, 1976, and 1984, "An Evening of Black Folktales," 1974, "All the King's Men," 1974, "Desire Under the Elms," 1974 and 1982, "Your Arms Too Short to Box With God," 1975 and 1976, "I'm Laughin' But I Ain't Tickled," 1976, "Play Mas," 1976, "The Gingham Dog," 1977, "What You Gonna Name That Pretty Little Baby?" 1978, "When Hell Freezes Over I'll Skate," 1979 and 1984, "Lost in the Stars," 1980, "The Life and Times of Marilyn Monroe," 1982, "Medea," 1986, "Next Time I'll Rain Down Fire," 1987, "The Green Bay Tree," 1987, and "Ladies in Waiting"; director of television programs, including "Beyond the Blues," 1964, and "Jubilation," 1964.

MEMBER: American Federation of Television and Radio Artists, Actors' Equity Association, Actors Studio (Directors Unit), Screen Actors Guild.

AWARDS, HONORS: Grant from Ford Foundation, 1960-61; Obie Award for distinguished performance from *Village Voice,* 1962, for "Moon on a Rainbow Shawl"; Emmy awards for conception and direction from National Academy of Television Arts and Sciences, 1964, for "Beyond the Blues" and "Jubilation"; Image Award for distinguished director from National Association for the Advancement of Colored People, Los Angeles Drama Critics Circle Award for distinguished directing, and Drama Desk Award for best director, all 1972, all for "Don't Bother Me, I Can't Cope"; Harold Jackman Memorial Award from Harold Jackman Foundation, 1973, for outstanding contribution to black culture; Antoinette Perry ("Tony") Award nomination for directing from League of New York Theatres and Producers, 1973, for "Don't Bother Me, I Can't Cope"; Audelco Achievement Award, 1975, for outstanding contribution to black theatre; Frank Silvera Writers' Workshop Foundation Award, 1977; Tony Award nominations for best book of a musical and best director of a musical, 1977, for "Your Arms Too Short to Box With God";

Black Filmmakers Hall of Fame award, 1979; Golden Circle Award.

WRITINGS:

STAGE PRODUCTIONS

(Adapter) "Trumpets of the Lord" (two-act musical based on James Weldon Johnson's poetry volume *God's Trombone*), first produced Off-Broadway at Astor Place, December 21, 1963; produced on Broadway at Brooks Atkinson, April 29, 1969.

(Adapter) "But Never Jam Today" (one-act musical based on Lewis Carroll's novels *Alice's Adventures in Wonderland* and *Through the Looking Glass*), first produced in New York at New York City Center Black Expo, April 23, 1969; produced as "Alice" in 1977; produced in two acts under original title on Broadway at Longacre Theatre, July 31, 1979.

(Author of concept) Micki Grant, "Don't Bother Me, I Can't Cope" (two-act revue), first produced in New York at Urban Arts Corps Theatre, October 7, 1970; revised and expanded version produced on Broadway at Playhouse Theatre, April 19, 1972.

"Croesus and the Witch" (two-act musical; music and lyrics by Grant), first produced in New York at Urban Arts Corps Theatre, August 24, 1971.

"Step Lively, Boy" (two-act), first produced in New York at Urban Arts Corps Theatre, February 7, 1973.

"The Ups and Downs of Theophilus Maitland" (two-act musical; music by Grant), first produced in New York at Urban Arts Corps Theatre, November 13, 1974.

(Adapter) Robert Penn Warren, "All the King's Men" (two-act), first produced in New York at Urban Arts Corps Theatre, May 14, 1974.

(Author of concept) "Your Arms Too Short to Box With God" (two-act musical based on Gospel of St. Matthew; music and lyrics by Alex Bradford and Grant), first produced in Spoleto, Italy, at Festival of Two Worlds, 1975; produced in Washington, D.C., at Ford's Theatre, November 4, 1975; produced in New York at Urban Arts Corps Theatre, 1975; produced on Broadway at Lyceum, December 22, 1976.

"I'm Laughin' But I Ain't Tickled" (two-act), first produced in New York at Urban Arts Corps Theatre, May, 1976.

"What You Gonna Name That Pretty Little Baby?" (two-act), first produced in New York at Urban Arts Corps Theatre, December, 1978.

(Adapter) "When Hell Freezes Over I'll Skate" (two-act musical based on poetry by Paul Laurence Dunbar, linda-michellebaron, and Langston Hughes), first produced in New York at Urban Arts Corps Theatre, January, 1979.

OTHER

Contributor of articles and plays to periodicals.

SIDELIGHTS: Since the 1960s Vinnette Carroll has become known as a talented director and creator of exuberant theatre productions. Blending drama and gospel music, her work both celebrates and supports black culture—she created and led New York City's Urban Arts Theatre (formerly Corps), in which many black actors, singers, and writers have begun their careers. Several Tony Award nominations, the Los Angeles Drama Critics Circle Award, and the Drama Desk Award attest to her talents, and audiences throughout the United States have flocked to performances of her works.

Working as an actress for twelve years, Carroll experienced racial prejudice in several forms. She was sometimes prevented from entering the lobby of a theatre at which she was performing, she was refused lodging near the theatre, and she was denied the opportunity to perform roles she wanted. The role restrictions encouraged her to work independently, and in the early 1950s she created a one-woman show with selections from "Medea" and the writings of T. S. Eliot, Langston Hughes, and Margaret Walker. Between 1952 and 1957 she toured intermittently with the show in the United States and the West Indies.

In 1960 Carroll began to direct for the stage, and among her early projects was "Trumpets of the Lord," her first adaptation from another medium. Featuring six verse sermons from James Weldon Johnson's book *God's Trombone,* the 1963 production was "richly and beautifully embellished" with gospel music, observed Lewis Funke in the *New York Times.* Staged as a religious service, the show moves between sermons and hymns, using the actors as ministers and treating the theatre audience as a congregation. "Woven together out of the simple grace and feeling inherent in Mr. Johnson's poetry," Funke asserted, the play "stands on its own, possessed of its own beauty and strength and boasting in addition a swift conciseness." According to Funke, "It has a built-in impact that is stimulating, inspiring and contagiously exciting."

Like other plays Carroll directed in the early sixties, "Trumpets of the Lord" displayed the talents of black actors. In 1967 many of them became the nucleus of her repertory company, the Urban Arts Theatre, and funding from the New York State Council on the Arts and other benefactors helped Carroll acquire a small upstairs auditorium at which they were to perform. Comprising mostly blacks, the company was to provide "a place where [black actors] could work on material they wouldn't have an opportunity to work on otherwise," Carroll told Candice Russell in a *Miami Herald* article. Under her leadership the theatre began to produce, with primarily black casts, works by playwrights such as Jean-Paul Sartre, Eugene O'Neill, Anton Chekhov, and William Shakespeare in addition to those by black writers. Furthermore, in order to make professional theatre more accessible to audiences as well as actors, performances at the Urban Arts Theatre were sometimes offered free of charge, attracting a wide cross-section of the New York City population.

"But Never Jam Today," adapted by Carroll from Lewis Carroll's "Alice in Wonderland" books, was among the Urban Arts Theatre's productions in 1969. With the original material modernized and set to music, the play premiered with a racially-mixed cast at New York's Black Expo and garnered praise from critics such as Richard F. Shepard of the *New York Times,* who found it "fun." Shepard appreciated the problems of tinkering with "the antisemantic illogicalities of Lewis Carroll," and he commended Carroll for adopting them "delightfully and rhythmically." Although the critic admitted that the production harbored a few technical flaws, he judged them minor and concluded, "'But Never Jam Today' is something original and entertaining."

The 1970 revue "Don't Bother Me, I Can't Cope" was the first of Carroll's many collaborations with black composer and actress Micki Grant; Carroll provided the concept and direction and Grant wrote the music and lyrics. In the *New York Times* Clive Barnes described the work, which features songs in traditional black styles on subjects ranging from ghetto life to romantic love, as "a mixture of a block party and a revival meeting." Summing up what distinguishes "Cope" from other "black shows," *Nation* reviewer Harold Clurman assessed that "its defiance is confident and joyous." Barnes concurred, deeming it "a militant show, but not at all bitter." Many critics, among them Clurman and *New York Times* writers Barnes and Mel Gussow, lauded the show's exuberance and quality. Concluded Barnes, "Cope" is "a show that deserves a wide audience."

Based on the New Testament's Gospel of Matthew, "Your Arms Too Short to Box With God" was another collaboration between Carroll and Grant. Premiering in 1975, it included additional songs by Alex Bradford and was widely acclaimed. The play maintains a celebratory mood as it traces the scriptural events, in the context of a religious service, from the day Jesus Christ arrives in Jerusalem to the morning of the Resurrection. In a *New Yorker* review, Brendan Gill asserted: "The Psalms urge us . . . to make a joyful noise unto the Lord, and this is precisely what [the work] does. Indeed, on opening night the audience threatened never to leave the theatre." Theatregoers across the United States packed playhouses and extended the musical's planned six-month tour to nearly triple that time, during which the show grossed more than six million dollars. Critical reception was similarly positive—*Newsweek*'s Jack Kroll, for example, hailed it as "the best of the musical shows that the astonishingly vigorous Carroll has come up with."

In 1979 Carroll and the Urban Arts Theatre opened the Black Theatre Festival U.S.A. with "When Hell Freezes Over I'll Skate," prompting *New York Times* reviewer Thomas Lask to remark that the festival "could not have begun more auspiciously." In this stage production, which is made up of songs, poetry, comedy, Bible stories, and dance, "the parts are meshed so smoothly and delivered with such technical finish and honest feeling that the piece becomes something larger than the sum of its parts," according to Lask. The critic perceived in the segments a summary of the black experience in America, a "chronicle of suffering we can all share" presented along with scenes of love and laughter.

Carroll commented: "In southern Florida I am continuing my work as artistic director of the Vinnette Carroll Repertory Company. We are currently renovating a church in Fort Lauderdale, converting it into a beautiful theatre facility."

AVOCATIONAL INTERESTS: Sports cars, horseback riding, swimming.

BIOGRAPHICAL/CRITICAL SOURCES:

PERIODICALS

Christian Science Monitor, November 29, 1969.
Miami Herald, May 5, 1974.
Nation, May 8, 1972, January 15, 1977.
Newsweek, January 10, 1977.
New York, April 28, 1969.
New Yorker, January 4, 1964, May 31, 1976, January 3, 1977.
New York Times, December 12, 1961, December 23, 1963, May 21, 1965, April 24, 1969, April 30, 1969, August 29, 1969, October 8, 1970, December 18, 1970, June 27, 1971, August 27, 1971, April 20, 1972, December 19, 1976, May 10, 1978, May 3, 1979, August 2, 1979, May 9, 1980, June 3, 1980, September 10, 1982.
Saturday Review, March 22, 1975.
Time, January 24, 1977.

Washington Post, May 7, 1984.

—*Sketch by Polly A. Vedder*

*   *   *

CARTER-HARRISON, Paul
   See HARRISON, Paul Carter

*   *   *

CARTEY, Wilfred (George Onslow)   1931-

PERSONAL: Born July 19, 1931, in Port-of-Spain, Trinidad, British West Indies. *Education:* University of the West Indies, B.A., 1955; Columbia University, M.A., 1956, Ph.D., 1964.

ADDRESSES: Home—New York, N.Y. *Office*—City College of the City University of New York, 138th St. and Convent Ave., New York, N.Y. 10031.

CAREER: Columbia University, New York City, instructor in Spanish, 1957-62, associate professor of comparative literature, 1963-69, adjunct professor, 1969—; City College of the City University of New York, New York City, professor of comparative literature, 1969-72, distinguished professor, 1973-79, distinguished professor of black studies, 1979—. Brooklyn College of the City University of New York, Brooklyn, N.Y., Martin Luther King Distinguished Professor of Comparative Literature, 1972-73. Visiting scholar and lecturer at University of Puerto Rico, summer, 1959; visiting professor at University of Vermont, summer, 1964; visiting professor at University of the West Indies, summer, 1965, resident professor, summer, 1973; visiting professor at University of Ghana, 1967-68; visiting distinguished professor of Romance languages at Howard University, 1976; visiting distinguished professor of Afro-American studies at University of California, Berkeley, spring, 1979.

MEMBER: African Studies Association, African Heritage Studies Association, American Association of University Professors, American Friends Service Committee, Association of Black and Puerto Rican Faculty, Hispanic Institute in the U.S., African American Heritage Association, Institute of Caribbean Studies, Modern Language Association of America, PEN, Black Academy of Arts and Letters.

AWARDS, HONORS: Bernard Van Leer Foundation Fellow, 1955-56; Fulbright travel grant, 1955-59; urban center grant, 1970; City University of New York Research Foundation fellow, 1985-86.

WRITINGS:

Some Aspects of African Literature, University of Vermont, 1964.
The West Indies: Islands in the Sun, Thomas Nelson, 1967.
(Contributor) *The African Experience*, Northwestern University Press, 1968.
Whispers from a Continent: The Literature of Contemporary Black Africa, Random House, 1969, reprinted, Vintage, 1987.
(With J. G. Colmen and others) *The Human Uses of the University: Planning a Curriculum in Urban and Ethnic Affairs at Columbia University*, Praeger, 1970.
(Author of introduction) Norman Shapiro, editor and translator, *Negritude: French African and Caribbean Poets*, October House, 1970.
(Author of introduction) Cheikh Hamidou Kane, *Ambiguous Adventure*, Collier Books, 1970.

(Author of introduction) *Black African Voices*, Scott, Foresman, 1970.
(Author of introduction) Peter Abrahams, *Tell Freedom*, Collier Books, 1970.
(With Marlin Kilson) *The African Reader*, Volume I: *Colonial Africa*, Volume II: *Independent Africa*, Random House, 1970.
Palaver: Critical Anthology of African Literature, Thomas Nelson, 1970.
Black Images: The Evolution of the Image of the Black Man in the Poetry of Spanish-English-French-Speaking Caribbean, the United States, Latin America, and West Africa, Teachers College Hall, 1970.
The House of Blue Lightning (poems), Emerson Hall, 1973.
Red Rain, Emerson Hall, 1977.
Embryos, illustrated by Ademola Olugebefola, W. Cartey, 1982.

Also author of *Waters of My Soul*, 1975, *Suns and Shadows*, 1978, *Fires in the Wind*, 1980, *The Dawn, the Desert, the Sands, Kundiya*, 1982, *Black Velvet Time*, 1984, *Children of Lalibela*, 1985, and *Potentialities*, 1987. Co-editor of "Documents in Afro-American History" series, Random House, 1970—. Work represented in *Forum Anthology*, Columbia University Press, 1968. Contributor to *Grolier Encyclopedia, Encyclopedia Americana*, and *Standard Reference Encyclopedia*. Contributor of articles and reviews to professional journals and national magazines, including *Commonwealth, New Republic*, and *Negro Digest*. Literary editor of *African Forum*, 1967-68; member of executive board of *Pan African Journal*, 1970—; contributing editor of *Confrontation: A Journal of Third World Literature*, 1970—, and *SAVACOU*, 1970—.

WORK IN PROGRESS: Whispers from the Caribbean, a critique of the literature of the Caribbean world; a study of black autobiography.

BIOGRAPHICAL/CRITICAL SOURCES:

PERIODICALS

Best Sellers, October 1, 1970.
Black World, January, 1971.
Commonweal, October 10, 1969.
English Journal, May, 1969.
Journal of Black Studies, December, 1984.
Kenyon Review, Volume 31, number 3, 1969.
Saturday Review, April 17, 1971.
Times Literary Supplement, October 1, 1971.
Washington Post, June 23, 1978.

*   *   *

CARTIER, Xam Wilson   1949(?)-

PERSONAL: Born in St. Louis, Mo.

ADDRESSES: Home—San Francisco, Calif.

CAREER: Artist, pianist, dancer, and writer.

WRITINGS:

Be-Bop, Re-Bop (novel), Available Press/Ballantine, 1987.

SIDELIGHTS: The unnamed black woman who narrates Xam Wilson Cartier's first novel *Be-Bop, Re-Bop* recalls significant moments in her childhood and young adulthood and reflects on the liberating presence of jazz in her life. Like her father before her, the narrator finds that cares surrender—at least momentarily—to the lyrics and melodies of black music; "jazz seems to mirror key elements in black culture: spontaneity, improvisation,'' related Cartier, ''because your situation is always in flux.'' Discussing *Be-Bop, Re-Bop* in the *New York Times Book Review,* Valerie Smith wrote: ''Jazz informs the style as well as the subject of Ms. Cartier's novel. Metaphors and rhymes resonate off one another, off alliterative phrases with all the intensity of an inspired riff.'' While the critic did find ''minor difficulties'' in the novel's singular focus (''the easy way in which music alleviates grief and fear and anxiety at times seems simplistically upbeat''), she nevertheless decided that ''the power of the language . . . is so compelling one can overlook these minor shortcomings.'' Smith added, ''This marvelous first novel . . . demonstrate[s] the deep connections between music and narrative.''

BIOGRAPHICAL/CRITICAL SOURCES:

PERIODICALS

New York Times Book Review, December 13, 1987.

* * *

CASEY, Patrick
   See THURMAN, Wallace (Henry)

* * *

CESAIRE, Aime (Fernand) 1913-

PERSONAL: Born June 25, 1913, in Basse-Pointe, Martinique, West Indies; son of Fernand (a comptroller with the revenue service) and Marie (Hermine) Cesaire; married Suzanne Roussi (a teacher), July 10, 1937; children: Jacques, Jean-Paul, Francis, Ina, Marc, Michelle. *Education:* Attended Ecole Normale Superieure, Paris; Sorbonne, University of Paris, licencie es lettres.

ADDRESSES: Office—Assemblee Nationale, 75007 Paris, France; and La Mairie, 97200 Fort-de-France, Martinique, West Indies.

CAREER: Lycee of Fort-de-France, Martinique, teacher, 1940-45; member of the two French constituent assemblies, 1945-46; mayor of Fort-de-France, 1945—; deputy for Martinique in the French National Assembly, 1946—. Conseiller general for the fourth canton (district) of Fort-de-France; president of the Parti Progressiste Martiniquais.

AWARDS, HONORS: Aime Cesaire: The Collected Poetry was nominated for *Los Angeles Times* Book Award, 1984.

WRITINGS:

(With Gaston Monnerville and Leopold Sedar-Senghor) *Commemoration du centenaire de l'abolition de l'esclavage: Discours pronounces a la Sorbonne le 27 avril 1948* (title means ''Commemoration of the Centenary of the Abolition of Slavery: Speeches Given at the Sorbonne on April 27, 1948''), Presses Universitaires de France, 1948.
Discours sur le colonialisme, Reclame, 1950, 5th edition, Presence Africaine (Paris), 1970, translation by Joan Pinkham published as *Discourse on Colonialism,* Monthly Review Press, 1972.
Lettre a Maurice Thorez, 3rd edition, Presence Africaine, 1956, translation published as *Letter to Maurice Thorez,* Presence Africaine, 1957.
Toussaint L'Ouverture: la revolution francaise et le probleme coloniale (title means ''Toussaint L'Ouverture: The French Revolution and the Colonial Problem''), Club Francais du Livre, 1960, revised edition, Presence Africaine, 1962.

Ouvres completes (title means ''Complete Works''), three volumes, Editions Desormeaux, 1976.
(Contributor) *Studies in French,* William Marsh Rice University, 1977.
Culture and Colonization, University of Yaounde, 1978.

POEMS

Les armes miraculeuses (title means ''The Miracle Weapons''; also see below), Gallimard, 1946, reprinted, 1970.
Soleil Cou-Coupe (title means ''Solar Throat Slashed''), K (Paris), 1948, reprinted (bound with *Antilles a main armee* by Charles Calixte), Kraus, 1970.
Cahier d'un retour au pays natal, Presence Africaine, 1956, 2nd edition, 1960, translation by Emil Snyders published as *Return to My Native Land,* Presence Africaine, 1968, translation by John Berger and Anna Bostock published under same title, Penguin Books, 1969.
Ferrements (title means ''Shackles''; also see below), Editions du Seuil, 1960.
Cadastre (also see below), Editions de Seuil, 1961, translation by Gregson Davis published as *Cadastre,* Third Press, 1972, translation by Snyders and Sanford Upson published under same title, Third Press, 1973.
State of the Union, translation by Clayton Eshleman and Dennis Kelly of selections from *Les armes miraculeuses, Ferrements,* and *Cadastre,* [Bloomington, Ill.], 1966.
Aime Cesaire: The Collected Poetry, translation and with an introduction by Eshleman and Annette Smith, University of California Press, 1983.
Non-Vicious Circle: Twenty Poems, translation by Davis, Stanford University Press, 1985.

Also author of *Corps perdu* (title means ''Lost Body''), illustrations by Pablo Picasso, 1949, and of *Moi, laminaire.*

PLAYS

Et les chiens se taisaient: Tragedie (title means ''And the Dogs Were Silent: A Tragedy''), Presence Africaine, 1956.
La tragedie du roi Christophe, Presence Africaine, 1963, revised edition, 1973, translation by Ralph Manheim published as *The Tragedy of King Christophe,* Grove, 1970.
Une saison au Congo, Editions du Seuil, 1966, translation by Manheim published as *A Season in the Congo* (produced in New York at the Paperback Studio Theatre, July, 1970), Grove, 1969.
Une tempete: d'apres ''le tempete'' de Shakespeare. Adaptation pour un theatre negre (title means ''A Tempest: After 'The Tempest' by Shakespeare. Adaptation for the Negro Theatre''), Editions du Seuil, 1969.

OTHER

Editor of *Tropiques,* 1941-45, and of *L'Afrique.*

SIDELIGHTS: Because of his role in creating and promoting negritude, a cultural movement which calls for black people to renounce Western society and adopt the traditional values of black civilization, Aime Cesaire is a prominent figure among blacks in the Third World. A native of the Caribbean island of Martinique, where he has served as mayor of the city of Fort-de-France since 1945, Cesaire also enjoys an international literary reputation for his poems and plays. His 1,000-line poem *Return to My Native Land,* a powerful piece written in extravagant, surreal language and dealing with the reawakening of black racial awareness, is a major work in contemporary French-language literature. Cesaire is, Serge Gavronsky states in the *New York Times Book Review,* "one of the most powerful French poets of this century."

At the age of 18 Cesaire left his native Martinique, at that time a colony of France, to attend school in Paris. The city was the center for a number of political and cultural movements during the 1930s, several of which especially influenced the young Cesaire and his fellow black students. Marxism gave them a revolutionary perspective, while surrealism provided them with a modernist esthetic by which to express themselves. Together with Leon-Goutran Damas and Leopold Sedar Senghor, who later became president of Senegal, Cesaire founded the magazine *L'Etudiant Noir,* in which the ideology of negritude was first developed and explained. "Negritude... proclaimed a pride in black culture and, in turning their contemporaries' gaze away from the fascination of things French, these young students began a revolution in attitudes which was to make a profound impact after the war," Clive Wake explains in the *Times Literary Supplement.* The influence of the movement on black writers in Africa and the Caribbean was so pervasive that the term negritude has come to refer to "large areas of black African and Caribbean literature in French, roughly from the 1930s to the 1960s," Christopher Miller writes in the *Washington Post Book World.*

The first use of the word negritude occurred in Cesaire's poem *Return to My Native Land (Cahier d'un retour au pays natal),* first published in the magazine *Volontes* in 1939. In this poem, Cesaire combines an exuberant wordplay, an encyclopedic vocabulary, and daring surreal metaphors with bits of African and Caribbean black history to create an "exorcism... of the poet's 'civilized' instincts, his lingering shame at belonging to a country and a race so abject, servile, petty and repressed as is his," Marjorie Perloff writes in the *American Poetry Review.* Gavronsky explains that the poem "is a concerted effort to affirm [Cesaire's] stature in French letters by a sort of poetic one-upmanship but also a determination to create a new language capable of expressing his African heritage." *Return to My Native Land,* Perloff maintains, is "a paratactic catalogue poem that piles up phrase upon phrase, image upon image, in a complex network of repetitions, its thrust is to define the threshold between sleep and waking—the sleep of oppression, the blind acceptance of the status quo, that gives way to rebirth, to a new awareness of what is and may be."

Written as Cesaire himself was leaving Paris to return to Martinique, *Return to My Native Land* reverberates with both personal and racial significance. The poet's definition of his own negritude comes to symbolize the growing self-awareness of all blacks of their cultural heritage. Judith Gleason, writing in the *Negro Digest,* believes that Cesaire's poetry is "grounded in the historical sufferings of a chosen people" and so "his is an angry, authentic vision of the promised land." Jean Paul Sartre, in an article for *The Black American Writer: Poetry and Drama,* writes that "Cesaire's words do not describe negritude, they do not designate it, they do not copy it from the outside like a painter with a model: they *create* it; they compose it under our very eyes."

Several critics see Cesaire as a writer who embodies the larger struggles of his people in all of his poetry. Hilary Okam of *Yale French Studies,* for example, argues that "Cesaire's poetic idiosyncracies, especially his search for and use of uncommon vocabulary, are symptomatic of his own mental agony in the search for an exact definition of himself and, by extension, of his people and their common situation and destiny." Okam concludes that "it is clear from [Cesaire's] use

of symbols and imagery, that despite years of alienation and acculturation he has continued to live in the concrete reality of his Negro-subjectivity." Writing in the *CLA Journal,* Ruth J. S. Simmons notes that although Cesaire's poetry is personal, he speaks from a perspective shared by many other blacks. "Poetry has been for him," Simmons explains, "an important vehicle of personal growth and self-revelation, [but] it has also been an important expression of the will and personality of a people.... It is... impossible to consider the work of Cesaire outside of the context of the poet's personal vision and definition of his art. He defines his past as African, his present as Antillean and his condition as one of having been exploited.... To remove Cesaire from this context is to ignore what he was and still is as a man and as a poet."

The concerns found in *Return to My Native Land* ultimately transcend the personal or racial, addressing liberation and self-awareness in universal terms. Gleason calls *Return to My Native Land* "a masterpiece of cultural relevance, every bit as 'important' as 'The Wasteland,' its remarkable virtuosity will ensure its eloquence long after the struggle for human dignity has ceased to be viewed in racial terms." Andre Breton, writing in *What Is Surrealism?: Selected Writings,* also sees larger issues at stake in the poem. "What, in my eyes, renders this protest invaluable," Breton states, "is that it continually transcends the anguish which for a black man is inseparable from the lot of blacks in modern society, and unites with the protest of every poet, artist and thinker worthy of the name... to embrace the entire intolerable though amendable condition created for *man* by this society."

Cesaire's poetic language was strongly influenced by the French surrealists of the 1930s, but he uses familiar surrealist poetic techniques in a distinctive manner. Breton claims that Cesaire "is a black man who handles the French language as no white man can handle it today." Alfred Cismaru states in *Renascence* that Cesaire's "separation from Europe makes it possible for him to break with clarity and description, and to become intimate with the fundamental essence of things. Under his powerful, poetic eye, perception knows no limits and pierces appearances without pity. Words emerge and explode like firecrackers, catching the eye and the imagination of the reader. He makes use of the entire dictionary, of artificial and vulgar words, of elegant and forgotten ones, of technical and invented vocabulary, marrying it to Antillean and African syllables, and allowing it to play freely in a sort of flaming folly that is both a challenge and a tenacious attempt at mystification."

The energy of Cesaire's poetic language is seen by some critics as a form of literary violence, with the jarring images and forceful rhythms of the poetry assaulting the reader. Perloff finds that Cesaire's "is a language so violently charged with meaning that each word falls on the ear (or hits the eye) with resounding force." Gleason explains this violence as the expression of an entire race, not just of one man: "Cesaire's is the turbulent poetry of the spiritually dislocated, of the damned. His images strike through the net.... Cesaire's is the Black Power of the imagination."

This violent energy is what first drew Cesaire to surrealism. The surrealist artists and writers of the 1930s saw themselves as rebels against a stale and outmoded culture. Their works were meant to revive and express unconscious, suppressed, and forbidden desires. Politically, they aligned themselves with the revolutionary left. As Gavronsky explains, "Cesaire's efforts to forge a verbal medium that would identify him with the opposition to existing political conditions and literary conventions [led him to] the same camp as the Surrealists, who had combined a new poetics that liberated the image from classical restraints with revolutionary politics influenced by Marx and his followers." Cesaire was to remain a surrealist for many years, but he eventually decided that his political concerns would best be served by more realistic forms of writing. "For decades," Karl Keller notes in the *Los Angeles Times Book Review*, "[Cesaire] found the surreal aesthetically revolutionary, but in the face of the torture and the suffering, he has pretty well abandoned it as a luxury."

In the late 1950s Cesaire began to write realistic plays for the theatre, hoping in this way to attract a larger audience to his work. These plays are more explicitly political than his poetry and focus on historical black nationalist leaders of the Third World. *The Tragedy of King Christophe (La tragedie du roi Christophe)* is a biographical drama about King Henri Christophe of Haiti, a black leader of that island nation in the early nineteenth century. After fighting in a successful revolution against the French colonists, Christophe assumed power and made himself king. But his cruelty and arbitrary use of power led to a rebellion in turn against his own rule, and Christophe committed suicide. Writing in *Studies in Black Literature*, Henry Cohen calls *The Tragedy of King Christophe* "one of French America's finest literary expressions." *A Season in the Congo (Une saison au Congo)* follows the political career of Patrice Lumumba, first president of the Republic of the Congo in Africa. Lumumba's career was also tragic. With the independence of the Congo in 1960, Lumumba became president of the new nation. But the resulting power struggles among black leaders led in 1961 to Lumumba's assassination by his political opponents. The reviewer for *Prairie Schooner* calls *A Season in the Congo* "a passionate and poetic drama." Wake remarks that Cesaire's plays have "greatly widened [his] audience and perhaps tempted them to read the poetry." Gavronsky claims that "in the [1960s, Cesaire] was . . . the leading black dramatist writing in French."

Despite the international acclaim he has received for his poetry and plays, Cesaire is still best known on Martinique for his political career. Since 1945 he has served as mayor of Fort-de-France and as a member of the French National Assembly. For the first decade of his career Cesaire was affiliated with the Communist bloc of the assembly, then moved to the Parti du Regroupement Africain et des Federalistes for a short time, and is now president of the Parti Progressiste Martiniquais, a leftist political organization. Cesaire's often revolutionary rhetoric is in sharp contrast to his usually moderate political actions. He opposes independence for Martinique, for example, and was instrumental in having the island declared an oversea department of France—a status similar to that of Puerto Rico to the United States. And as a chief proponent of negritude, which calls for blacks to reject Western culture, Cesaire nonetheless writes his works in French, not in his native black language of creole.

But what may seem contradictory in Cesaire's life and work is usually seen by critics as the essential tension that makes his voice uniquely important. A. James Arnold, in his *Modernism and Negritude: The Poetry and Poetics of Aime Cesaire*, examines and accepts the tension between Cesaire's European literary sources and his black subject matter and between his modernist sensibility and his black nationalist concerns. Miller explains that "Arnold poses the riddle of Cesaire with admirable clarity" and "effectively defuses . . . either a wholly African or a wholly European Cesaire." This uniting of the European and African is also noted by Clayton Eshleman and

Annette Smith in their introduction to *Aime Cesaire: The Collected Poetry*. They describe Cesaire as "a bridge between the twain that, in principle, should never meet, Europe and Africa. . . . It was by borrowing European techniques that he succeeded in expressing his Africanism in its purest form." Similarly, Sartre argues that "in Cesaire, the great surrealist tradition is realized, it takes on its definitive meaning and is destroyed: surrealism—that European movement—is taken from the Europeans by a Black man who turns it against them and gives it vigorously defined function."

It is because of his poetry that Cesaire is primarily known worldwide, while in the Third World he is usually seen as an important black nationalist theoretician. Speaking of his poetry, Gavronsky explains that Cesaire is "among the major French poets of this century." Cismaru believes that Cesaire "is a poet's poet when he stays clear of political questions, a tenacious and violent propagandist when the theme requires it. His place in contemporary French letters . . . is assured in spite of the fact that not many agree with his views on Whites in general, nor with his opinions on Europe, in particular." *Return to My Native Land* has been his most influential work, particularly in the Third World where, Wake notes, "by the 1960s it was widely known and quoted because of its ideological and political significance." To European and American critics, *Return to My Native Land* is seen as a masterpiece of surrealist literature. Cesaire's coining of the term negritude and his continued promotion of a distinctly black culture separate from Western culture has made him especially respected in the emerging black nations. Eshleman and Smith report that "although Cesaire was by no means the sole exponent of negritude, the word is now inseparable from his name, and largely responsible for his prominent position in the Third World."

BIOGRAPHICAL/CRITICAL SOURCES:

BOOKS

Aime Cesaire: Ecrivain Martiniquais, Fernand Nathan, 1967.
Arnold, A. James, *Modernism and Negritude: The Poetry and Poetics of Aime Cesaire*, Harvard University Press, 1981.
Bigsby, C. W. E., editor, *The Black American Writer: Poetry and Drama*, Volume II, Penguin Books, 1971.
Breton, Andre, *What Is Surrealism?: Selected Writings*, edited by Franklin Rosemont, Monad Press, 1978.
Contemporary Literary Criticism, Gale, Volume XIX, 1981, Volume XXXII, 1985.
Kesteloot, Lilyan, *Aime Cesaire*, P. Seghers, 1962, new edition, 1970.
Leiner, Jacqueline, *Soleil eclate: Melanges offerts a Aime Cesaire a l'occasion de son soixante-dixieme anniversaire par une equipe internationale d'artiste et de chercheurs*, Gunter Narr Verlag (Tubingen), 1985.

PERIODICALS

American Poetry Review, January-February, 1984.
CLA Journal, March, 1976.
Comparative Literature Studies, summer, 1978.
Le Monde, December, 1981.
Los Angeles Times Book Review, December 4, 1983.
Negro Digest, January, 1970.
New York Times Book Review, February 19, 1984.
Prairie Schooner, spring, 1972.
Renascence, winter, 1974.
Studies in Black Literature, winter, 1974.
Times Literary Supplement, July 19, 1985.
Twentieth Century Literature, July, 1972.

Washington Post Book World, February 5, 1984.
Yale French Studies, Number 53, 1976.

—*Sketch by Thomas Wiloch*

*   *   *

CHASE-RIBOUD, Barbara (Dewayne Tosi)   1939-

PERSONAL: Surname is pronounced "Chase-Ri-boo"; born June 26, 1939, in Philadelphia, Pa.; daughter of Charles Edward (a building contractor) and Vivian May (a medical assistant; maiden name, West) Chase; married Marc Eugene Riboud (a photojournalist), December 25, 1961; married Sergio Tosi (an art expert, broker, and historian), 1981; children: (first marriage) David, Alexis. *Education:* Temple University, B.F.A., 1957; Yale University, M.F.A., 1960.

ADDRESSES: Home—3 rue Auguste Comte, 75006 Paris, France. *Agent*—Maggie Curren, International Creative Management, 40 West 57th St., New York, N.Y. 10019.

CAREER: Sculptor, poet, and novelist. One-woman shows include those at Cadran Solaire, Paris, France, 1966, Bertha Schaefer Gallery, New York City, February, 1970, Massachusetts Institute of Technology, Cambridge, April, 1970, Betty Parsons Gallery, New York City, March-April, 1972, University Museum, Berkeley, Calif., January, 1973, Leslie Rankrow Gallery, New York City, April, 1973, Detroit Institute of Art, Detroit, Mich., May, 1973, Indianapolis Art Museum, Indianapolis, Ind., August, 1973, Museum of Modern Art, Paris, April-June, 1974, Kunsthalle, Baden-Baden, West Germany, September, 1974, Kunstmuseum, Dusseldorf, West Germany, October, 1974, Merian Gallery, Krefeld, West Germany, November, 1974, United States Cultural Center, Tunis, Tunisia, March, 1975, United States Cultural Center, Dakar, Senegal, April, 1975, United States Cultural Center, Tehran, Iran, December, 1975, Kunstmuseum, Freiburg, West Germany, January, 1976, and Musee Reattu, Arles, France, July-September, 1976.

Work exhibited in group shows, including: "Festival of Two Worlds," Spoleto, Italy, 1957, "International Exhibition of Painting and Sculpture," Carnegie Institute, Pittsburgh, Pa., 1959, "New York Architectural League Selection," Commercial Museum, Philadelphia, Pa., 1965, "Premier Festival des Arts Negres," Dakar, Senegal, 1966, "Festival d'Avignon," Avignon, France, 1969, "Afro-American Artists," Boston Museum of Fine Arts, Boston, Mass., 1970, "Two Generations," Newark Museum of Art, Newark, N.J., 1971, "Contemporary Black Artists," Whitney Museum of Art, New York City, 1971, "Annual Exhibition of Sculpture," Whitney Museum of Art, New York City, 1971, Salon de Mai, Paris, 1971-72, Salon des Nouvelles Realities, Paris, 1971-72, "Gold," Metropolitan Museum of Art, New York City, 1973, "Sculpture as Jewelry as Sculpture," Institute of Contemporary Art, Boston, 1973, "Internationaler Markt fur Aktuelle Kunst," Dusseldorf, West Germany, 1973, "Women's Art: American Art 74," Philadelphia Civil Museum, Philadelphia, 1974, "Masterworks of the 70's: Jewelers and Weavers," Albright-Knox Art Gallery, Buffalo, N.Y., 1974, "Documenta 77," Kessel, West Germany, 1977, and those at the Museum of Contemporary Crafts, New York City, 1977, and Renwick Gallery, Smithsonian Institution, Washington, D.C., 1977.

Work represented in permanent collections including those at Centre Pompidou, Paris, Museum of Modern Art, New York City, Metropolitan Museum of Art, New York City, University Museum, Berkeley, Calif., Newark Museum, Newark,

N.J., Lannon Foundation, Palm Springs, Fla., Centre National des Arts Contemporains, Paris, Geigy Foundation, New York City, Philadelphia Art Alliance, Philadelphia, Pa., and Schoenburg Collection, New York Public Library, New York City. Has appeared in documentaries and interviews for film and television, including the television show "Sixty Minutes," Columbia Broadcasting System (CBS), May, 1979.

AWARDS, HONORS: John Hay Whitney Foundation fellowship, 1957-58, for study at the American Academy in Rome; National Endowment for the Arts fellowship, 1973; first prize in the New York City Subway Competition, 1973, for architecture; U.S. State Department traveling grant, 1975; named Academic of Italy with gold medal, 1978, for sculpture and drawing; Janet Heidinger Kafka Prize, 1979, for best novel by an American woman; honorary doctorate from Temple University, 1981.

WRITINGS:

From Memphis to Peking (poems), Random House, 1974.
Sally Hemings (novel), Viking, 1979.
Valide: A Novel of the Harem, Morrow, 1986.
Portrait of a Nude Woman as Cleopatra (poems), Morrow, 1987.

WORK IN PROGRESS: A book of poems titled *Love Perfecting.*

SIDELIGHTS: Fascinated by Fawn Brodie's biography *Thomas Jefferson: An Intimate History,* which touches on the relationship between the U.S. president and his alleged mistress Sally Hemings, a mulatto slave, internationally known sculptress Barbara Chase-Riboud decided to research the couple herself. The result of Chase-Riboud's efforts is her 1979 best-selling historical novel, *Sally Hemings.* Although Chase-Riboud uncovered few facts about Hemings's life and her relationship with Jefferson, the findings reaffirmed the suspicion that Jefferson was Hemings's lover and the father of her seven children. Chase-Riboud's research also allowed her to construct a rough outline of Hemings's life, beginning with the slave's employment in Jefferson's Paris household. To this, Chase-Riboud "added imagination," explained Jacqueline Trescott in the *Washington Post.* "She walked the same streets of Paris, scoured American and French libraries," trying to recreate the experiences and emotions of Hemings, continued Trescott, "and ended up with a tender story of a faithful, sometimes ambiguous woman."

In *Sally Hemings,* Chase-Riboud endeavored to present the Hemings-Jefferson relationship from various angles, exploring some of its sociological, political, and emotional implications for all races, both sexes, and the United States as a whole. Reviewers differed in their assessment of the result. Marcy Heidish of the *Washington Post,* for example, noted that *Sally Hemings*'s narrative thread is "uneven [and its] recurring changes in voice and chronology tend to blur the book's focus and power, disrupting the narrative flow and the reader's empathy with the characters." The *New York Times*'s John Russell, on the other hand, lauded Chase-Riboud's ability to portray life in Hemings's time from different points of view. "The slave world," Russell explained, "is made vivid to us in terms of physical and psychic hardship alike. The scenes of high life, whether in Monticello or in Paris, are as succinct as they are deft. . . . [Chase-Riboud] is everywhere on top of her material."

The Hemings-Jefferson story intrigued Chase-Riboud because of its complexity and because she saw in it a union of black and white American history. As Chase-Riboud explained to

Susan McHenry of *Ms.*, "What struck me were the very complicated and convoluted relationships between those two families—the 'black' Hemingses and the 'white' Jeffersons. That's typically American." Yet, according to Chase-Riboud, "America perceives itself as a white man's country, and this has nothing to do with reality.... There *has* to be a kind of synthesis between 'black' experience and 'white' experience in America, because they are the same."

Calling the United States a "mulatto country," the author explained in an *International Herald Tribune* article by Flora Lewis that racial "mixing began [in the United States] when the races collided in the 17th century." According to Lewis, Chase-Riboud believes that "white, as a racial word, was invented by the colonists who wanted to distinguish themselves from the natives they found in America and the Africans they brought." And interracial mixing remains "the last taboo, which has to be faced," concluded Chase-Riboud.

Chase-Riboud's concern with synthesis, with union, is found not only in the author's writing and political views, but in her artwork as well. For instance, in her drawing and her metal and textile sculpture, Chase-Riboud is attracted to what she calls the theme of the couple, the combination of opposites. She is drawn to it, she explained to McHenry, because it is "banal and impossible, the need to join opposing forces: male/female, negative/positive, black/white."

Despite the impossibility of merging these forces, Chase-Riboud feels there are harmonious ways for races, sexes, and individuals to influence each other, much as colors and materials influence one another in her art. As McHenry noted, what Chase-Riboud calls "'the metaphysics of color' gives the lie to the myth of race and to the destructive reality of racism through an essentially feminist and humanist acceptance of human diversity." "There are differences," Chase-Riboud commented to McHenry, concerning the races' experiences, "but there is no escape from the influence of one to the other, from their interrelation and interlocking," much as, in the prismatic scale, "one color relates to another, takes on its attributes as they touch." Indeed, Chase-Riboud remarked in the *International Herald Tribune* article, "white and black mean nothing by themselves, only in relation to each other."

BIOGRAPHICAL/CRITICAL SOURCES:

PERIODICALS

Chicago Tribune, July 3, 1979.
International Herald Tribune, October 26, 1979.
Ms., October, 1980.
National Review, December 21, 1979.
New Republic, July 7, 1979.
New York Times, September 5, 1979.
New York Times Book Review, October 28, 1979, August 10, 1986.
People, October 8, 1979.
Washington Post, June 15, 1979, July 8, 1986.

*   *   *

CHESNUTT, Charles W(addell)   1858-1932

PERSONAL: Born June 20, 1858, in Cleveland, Ohio; died November 15, 1932, in Cleveland, Ohio; son of Andrew Jackson (in grocery business) and Ann (one source says Anne) Maria (Sampson) Chesnutt; married Susan Utley Perry (a teacher), June 6, 1878; children: Ethel, Helen Maria, Edwin,

Dorothy. *Education:* Educated at schools in Cleveland, Ohio, and Fayetteville, N.C.

ADDRESSES: 9719 Lamont Ave., Cleveland, Ohio.

CAREER: Teacher, lawyer, businessman, and writer. Taught at public schools in Spartanburg, S.C., Charlotte, N.C., and Fayetteville, N.C., 1872-77; New State Normal School, Fayetteville, assistant principal, 1877-80, principal, 1880-83; worked as a reporter for Dow Jones & Co., 1883; *New York Mail and Express*, New York, N.Y., stenographer, reporter, and author of daily column "Wall Street Gossip," 1883; Nickel Plate Railroad Co., Cleveland, Ohio, 1884-89, began as clerk, became stenographer for the firm's legal counsel; admitted to the Bar of Ohio, 1887; private practice of court reporting, beginning in 1890. Active in community affairs and social causes; served on General Committee of National Association for the Advancement of Colored People (NAACP).

AWARDS, HONORS: Spingarn Medal from NAACP, 1928.

WRITINGS:

The Conjure Woman (short stories; contains "The Goophered Grapevine," "Po' Sandy," "Mars Jeems's Nightmare," "The Conjurer's Revenge," "Sis' Becky's Pickaninny," "The Gray Wolf's Ha'nt," and "Hot-Foot Hannibal"), Houghton, 1899, deluxe edition with a foreword by Joel Elias Spingarn, 1929, reprinted, Gregg, 1968, retold for young readers by Ray Anthony Shepard as *Conjure Tales*, with illustrations by John Ross and Clare Romano, Dutton, 1973.

The Wife of His Youth, and Other Stories of the Color Line (short stories; contains "The Wife of His Youth," "Her Virginia Mammy," "The Sheriff's Children," "A Matter of Principle," "Cicely's Dream," "The Passing of Grandison," "Uncle Wellington's Wives," "The Bouquet," and "The Web of Circumstance"), Houghton, 1899, reprinted with illustrations by Clyde O. DeLand, Gregg, 1967.

Frederick Douglass (biography), Small, Maynard, 1899, reprinted, Johnson Reprints, 1970.

The House Behind the Cedars (novel), Houghton, 1900, reprinted, Gregg, 1968, reprinted with an introduction by Darwin Turner, P. F. Collier, 1969.

The Marrow of Tradition (novel), Houghton, 1901, reprinted, Gregg, 1968.

The Colonel's Dream (novel), Doubleday, Page, 1905, reprinted, Gregg, 1968.

The Short Fiction of Charles W. Chesnutt, edited with an introduction by Sylvia Lyons Render, Howard University Press, 1974.

Work represented in anthologies.

Contributor to periodicals, including *Alexander's Magazine, Boston Evening Transcript, Family Fiction, Puck, Youth's Companion, Cleveland News and Herald, Atlantic Monthly, Crisis, Overland Monthly, Chicago Ledger, Century, New Haven Register, New York Independent, Outlook*, and *Southern Workman*.

SIDELIGHTS: In her biography, *Charles W. Chesnutt: Pioneer of the Color Line*, Helen M. Chesnutt describes her father as "a pioneer Negro author, the first to exploit in fiction the complex lives of men and women of mixed blood." Similarly, Sylvia Lyons Render writes admiringly in her introduction to *The Short Fiction of Charles W. Chesnutt* of his "extraordinary ability to blend his African and European heritages into distinctly American forms.'' Because of his fair complexion, Render pointed out, Chesnutt could have ''passed'' for white; instead ''he chose to remain identified as an Afro-American and sought to remove rather than to avoid various forms of discrimination.'' Chesnutt also merits recognition as one of the first black American fiction writers to receive serious critical attention and acclaim for portraying blacks realistically and sensitively, shunning condescending characterizations and nostalgia for antebellum days of slavery in the South.

Chesnutt was born in 1858 in Cleveland, Ohio, the son of free Negro parents who had moved from Fayetteville, North Carolina, before the Civil War in flight from increasingly severe restrictions imposed on the free colored population of North Carolina. In 1866 the family returned to Fayetteville, and Chesnutt's father started a grocery store there. When young Charles wasn't working in the store, he attended the Howard School for blacks, founded by the Freedman's Bureau in 1865. Pressed to help support his family, Chesnutt was forced to end his formal education when he was only fourteen. However, Robert Harris, the school's principal, prevailed upon Charles's father to let his son stay at the school as a pupil-teacher and turn his modest salary over to his father. At sixteen Chesnutt went to Charlotte as a full-time teacher, and in 1877 he returned to Fayetteville as assistant principal of Howard School, becoming upon Harris's death three years later its principal. Concomitantly Chesnutt commenced a vigorous program of reading and study that led to his proficiency in Latin, German, French, mathematics, and stenography. In 1883 Chesnutt resigned his school-administrator post and struck out alone in search of more lucrative employment in the North. He found a job in New York City as a stenographer and journalist on Wall Street, then later returned to Cleveland, where he was hired as a railway clerk and, in 1884, settled with his family.

Chesnutt eventually became a stenographer for the railway company's lawyer, Judge Samuel E. Williamson, in whose office he studied law, and in 1887 he passed the Ohio Bar at the top of his class. Judge Williamson offered to finance a law practice for Chesnutt in Europe, which was less racist than the United States, but Chesnutt declined the offer. He also turned down the invitation of George Washington Cable, a prominent American writer, to become his private secretary.

Instead, in 1890 Chesnutt chose to support his growing family by establishing a court reporting business and devoting his evenings to his longtime avocation, writing fiction. His first stories were generally light in tone and dealt with conventional subjects of appeal to lesser magazines ranging from *Puck* to *Youth's Companion* and to newspaper syndicates such as S. S. McClure's. These early efforts were crowned by *Atlantic Monthly*'s acceptance of his stories ''The Goophered Grapevine'' in 1887 and ''Po' Sandy'' in 1888. At Cable's urging he also contributed commentary to the *New York Independent* and other liberal publications, and by 1889 Chesnutt had completed his first novel, eventually published in 1900 as *The House Behind the Cedars*.

Most of the stories Chesnutt produced after 1890, according to Render, ''differ in form, tone, and focus from earlier works. The mood is more serious, the humor increasingly subtle and satirical, the irony more apparent, and the action [focused] largely upon Afro-Americans.'' Furthermore, instead of using contemporary settings, Chesnutt placed his characters in times of slavery or Reconstruction in the Cape Fear River area of North Carolina, where he had lived from age eight to age

twenty-five. In so doing, he displayed such fidelity to his settings and to the idiosyncrasies of the people of the area—including their folkways, dialects, and superstitions—as to prompt critics to compare his work to that of leading nineteenth-century local colorists Bret Harte and Mark Twain.

Chesnutt's first published volume, *The Conjure Woman*—issued in 1899 by Houghton Mifflin—was a collection of dialect stories told by an old Negro gardener, ''Uncle'' Julius McAdoo, to his Northern employer. Ostensibly simple tales of metamorphosis, voodoo, and conjuring, they nonetheless illuminate the dynamics of master-slave relationships and the injustices of slavery. One slave-owner, for instance, resorts to conjuring his grapevine to protect his grapes from thieving slaves. That idea misfires when a new slave mistakenly eats some of the ''goophered'' grapes. Even after he has tried a magic antidote, the unlucky slave has strange tendrils of grapes growing all over his head—grapes that appear every spring and die down in the winter along with his strength and youth, which also wax and wane with the seasons. Yet his owner profits from this, selling the slave in the spring, when he is young and vigorous, and buying him back cheaply in the fall, when he looks about to die. As several critics noted, these stories convey a very different picture of Southern society from those in the Uncle Remus stories of Joel Chandler Harris, in which happy slaves cheerfully tell animal fables about mischievous Brer Rabbit.

In *The Wife of His Youth, and Other Stories of the Color Line,* a second collection of short stories also published in 1899, Chesnutt portrays the dilemma of mulattoes who felt alien in the black community and excluded from the white. Chesnutt satirized the race-conscious Blue Veins of Cleveland—people of Negro descent with skin light enough to show the blueness of their veins—for snubbing their darker-skinned relatives and mimicking middle-class whites. A third 1899 Chesnutt publication was *Frederick Douglass,* a biography of the prominent abolitionist, for the series ''Beacon Biographies of Eminent Americans.''

In September, 1900, buoyed by the favorable initial reception given *The Conjure Woman, The Wife of His Youth,* and *Frederick Douglass,* Chesnutt closed down his stenography business so that he could write and lecture full time. Financial success, however, did not match critical acclaim and recognition. His first two novels, *The House Behind the Cedars* and *The Marrow of Tradition,* published in 1900 and 1901 respectively, attracted more controversy than sales. Reviewers who had applauded *The Conjure Woman* became disenchanted with Chesnutt when he began to treat taboo themes such as miscegenation and racial hatred. His sympathetic treatment of erotic love in *The House Behind the Cedars* and his pessimism toward the likelihood of racial harmony in *The Marrow of Tradition* outraged critics. Even William Dean Howells, the distinguished American novelist and critic who in 1900 had praised Chesnutt for ''sound[ing] a fresh note, boldly, not blatantly'' and placed him in the top rank of American short story writers, declared in a 1901 issue of *North American Review* that ''at his worst, [Chesnutt] is no worse than the higher average of the ordinary novelists, but he ought always to be very much better, for he began better.''

Chesnutt's earnings from the sales of his two novels and from his free-lance journalism and speaking engagements proved inadequate to the financial needs of his family. Consequently in 1902 he reopened the stenography firm he had closed two years earlier. Chesnutt continued writing, however, and in 1905 he published *The Colonel's Dream,* a novel examining the futility of amoral schemes for the economic regeneration of the South. *The Colonel's Dream* received less attention than *The Marrow of Tradition* and garnered even fewer sales. It was to be Chesnutt's last book-length work to appear during his lifetime.

In 1910, five years after the publication of *The Colonel's Dream,* Chesnutt collapsed in his Cleveland office, and he remained unconscious for several days. His recovery was slow, necessitating curtailment of his strenuous schedule of social, public, and professional engagements. In 1920 he suffered an attack of appendicitis followed by peritonitis that left his health permanently impaired.

The 1920s brought some belated recognition to Chesnutt for his literary labors at the turn of the century. In 1928 the NAACP awarded him its Spingarn Medal for his "pioneer work as a literary artist depicting the life and struggles of Americans of Negro descent, and for his long and useful career as scholar, worker, and freeman." And in 1929 Houghton Mifflin reprinted *The Conjure Woman* in a deluxe edition that restored Chesnutt to print thirty years after he had first become an author.

Chesnutt's last published work was an article titled "Post-Bellum—Pre-Harlem" that appeared in *Colophon* a year before his death in 1932. In the article Chesnutt reflected on his literary life and on the history of Afro-American writing in general. He summarized his various books and commented on the ambivalence of his publishers toward revealing his racial identity during the early years of his career. He accepted the fact that literary fashion had passed him by, but he proudly noted that Afro-American literature and the attitude of the white literary world had advanced considerably since the days of his earliest publications. Once possibly the only black American to write serious fiction about Negroes, Chesnutt had devoted his art to reorienting his readers toward what he considered the real issues of race in America.

History has at least partially restored Chesnutt's place as one of the most important figures in the early history of black literature in the United States. Critics now acknowledge that Chesnutt helped establish a truly Afro-American literary heritage in the short story and novel, and they credit him with making the broad range of black experience his artistic domain and considering practically everything within it worthy of treatment. Chesnutt is also remembered as a brilliant, gifted man endowed with an indefatigable capacity for hard work and self-discipline and as an ardent crusader for civil rights and equal opportunity. Among the tributes paid Chesnutt at the time of his death was that of American Negro civil rights leader W.E.B. DuBois, who wrote in the January, 1933, *Crisis:* "[Chesnutt] was not a Negro; he was a man. . . . If his white friends could not tolerate colored friends, they need not come to Mr. Chesnutt's home. If colored friends demanded racial segregation and hatred, he had no patience with them. Merit and friendship in his broad and tolerant mind knew no lines of color or race, and all men, good, bad, and indifferent, were simply men."

BIOGRAPHICAL/CRITICAL SOURCES:

BOOKS

Andrews, William L., *The Literary Career of Charles W. Chesnutt,* Louisiana State University Press, 1980.
Bigsby, E.W.E., editor, *The Black American Writer,* Everett/Edwards, 1969.
Bone, Robert A., *The Negro Novel in America,* Yale University Press, 1965.
Brown, Sterling, *The Negro in American Fiction,* Associates in Negro Folk Education, 1937.
Chesnutt, Helen M., *Charles Waddell Chesnutt: Pioneer of the Color Line,* University of North Carolina Press, 1952.
Dictionary of Literary Biography, Volume 12: *American Realists and Naturalists,* Gale, 1982, Volume 50: *Afro-American Writers Before the Harlem Renaissance,* Gale, 1986.
Ellison, Curtis W. and E. W. Metcalf, Jr., *Charles W. Chesnutt: A Reference Guide,* G. K. Hall, 1977.
Heermance, J. Noel, *Charles W. Chesnutt: America's First Great Black Novelist,* Shoe String, 1974.
Keller, Frances Richardson, *An American Crusade: The Life of Charles Waddell Chesnutt,* Brigham Young University Press, 1978.
Render, Sylvia Lyons, editor, *The Short Fiction of Charles W. Chesnutt,* Howard University Press, 1974.
Twentieth-Century Literary Criticism, Gale, Volume 5, 1981.

PERIODICALS

American Literature, May, 1975.
American Scholar, winter, 1972.
Atlantic Monthly, May, 1900.
Books and Bookmen, December, 1975.
CLA Journal, March, 1972, December, 1974.
Colophon, Volume II, number 5, 1931.
Crisis, January, 1933.
Growing Point, January, 1976.
Kirkus Reviews, September 15, 1973, December 15, 1973.
Kliatt, winter, 1979.
New Republic, March 1, 1975.
New York Times Book Review, November 4, 1973, January 17, 1974.
Observer, December 7, 1975.
Phylon, spring, 1971.
Saturday Review, June 21, 1969, October 25, 1969.
Southern Literary Journal, fall, 1982.
Spectator, March 21, 1969, August 16, 1979.
Times Literary Supplement, December 5, 1975.

—*Sketch by Joanne M. Peters*

*   *   *

CHILDRESS, Alice   1920-

PERSONAL: Surname is pronounced *Chil-*dress; born October 12, 1920, in Charleston, S.C.; married second husband, Nathan Woodard (a musician), July 17, 1957; children: (first marriage) Jean (Mrs. Richard Lee). *Education:* Attended public schools in New York, N.Y.

ADDRESSES: Home—New York, N.Y. *Agent*—Flora Roberts, Inc., 157 West 57th St., Penthouse A, New York, N.Y. 10019.

CAREER: Playwright, novelist, actress, and director. Began career in theatre as an actress, with her first appearance in "On Strivers Row," 1940; actress and director with American Negro Theatre, New York, N.Y., for eleven years; played in "Natural Man," 1941, "Anna Lucasta," 1944, and her own play "Florence" (which she also directed), 1949; has also performed on Broadway and television. Lecturer at universities and schools; member of panel discussions and conferences on Black American theatre at numerous institutions, including New School for Social Research, 1965, and Fisk University,

1966; visiting scholar at Radcliffe Institute for Independent Study (now Mary Ingraham Bunting Institute), Cambridge, Mass., 1966-68. Member of governing board of Frances Delafield Hospital.

MEMBER: PEN, Dramatists Guild (member of council), American Federation of Television and Radio Artists, Writers Guild of America East (member of council), Harlem Writers Guild.

AWARDS, HONORS: Obie Award for best original Off-Broadway play, *Village Voice,* 1956, for "Trouble in Mind"; John Golden Fund for Playwrights grant, 1957; Rockefeller grant, 1967; *A Hero Ain't Nothin' but a Sandwich* was named one of the Outstanding Books of the Year by *New York Times Book Review,* 1973, and a Best Young Adult Book of 1975 by American Library Association; Woodward School Book Award, 1974, Jane Addams Children's Book Honor Award for young adult novel, 1974, National Book Award nomination, 1974, and Lewis Carroll Shelf Award, University of Wisconsin, 1975, all for *A Hero Ain't Nothin' but a Sandwich*; named honorary citizen of Atlanta, Ga., 1975, for opening of "Wedding Band"; Sojourner Truth Award, National Association of Negro Business and Professional Women's Clubs, 1975; Virgin Islands film festival award for best screenplay, 1977, for "A Hero Ain't Nothin' but a Sandwich"; first Paul Robeson Award for Outstanding Contributions to the Performing Arts, Black Filmmakers Hall of Fame, 1977, for "A Hero Ain't Nothin' but a Sandwich"; "Alice Childress Week" officially observed in Charleston and Columbia, S.C., 1977, to celebrate opening of "Sea Island Song"; *Rainbow Jordan* was named one of the "Best Books" by *School Library Journal,* 1981, one of the Outstanding Books of the Year by *New York Times,* 1982, and a notable children's trade book in social studies by National Council for the Social Studies and Children's Book Council, 1982; honorable mention, Coretta Scott King Award, 1982, for *Rainbow Jordan.*

WRITINGS:

Like One of the Family: Conversations from a Domestic's Life, Independence Publishers, 1956, reprinted with an introduction by Trudier Harris, Beacon Press, 1986.
(Editor) *Black Scenes* (collection of scenes from plays written by Afro-Americans about the Black experience), Doubleday, 1971.
A Hero Ain't Nothin' but a Sandwich (novel; also see below), Coward, 1973.
A Short Walk (novel), Coward, 1979.
Rainbow Jordan (novel), Coward, 1981.
Many Closets, Coward, 1987.

PLAYS

"Florence" (one-act), first produced in New York City at American Negro Theatre, directed by and starring Childress, 1949.
"Just a Little Simple " (based on Langston Hughes's short story collection *Simple Speaks His Mind*), first produced in New York City at Club Baron Theatre, September, 1950.
"Gold through the Trees," first produced at Club Baron Theatre, 1952.
"Trouble in Mind," first produced Off-Broadway at Greenwich Mews Theatre, directed by Childress, November 3, 1955, revised version published in *Black Theatre: A Twentieth-Century Collection of the Work of Its Best Playwrights,* edited by Lindsay Patterson, Dodd, 1971.

Wedding Band: A Love/Hate Story in Black and White (first produced in Ann Arbor, Mich., at University of Michigan, December 7, 1966; produced Off-Broadway at New York Shakespeare Festival Theatre, directed by Childress and Joseph Papp, September 26, 1972; also see below), Samuel French, 1973.
"String" (one-act; based on Guy de Maupassant's story "A Piece of String"; also see below), first produced Off-Broadway at St. Mark's Playhouse, March 25, 1969.
"Mojo: A Black Love Story" (one-act; also see below), produced in New York City at New Heritage Theatre, November, 1970.
Mojo [and] *String,* Dramatists Play Service, 1971.
When the Rattlesnake Sounds: A Play (juvenile), illustrated by Charles Lilly, Coward, 1975.
Let's Hear It for the Queen: A Play (juvenile), Coward, 1976.
"Sea Island Song," produced in Charleston, S.C., 1977, produced as "Gullah" in Amherst, Mass., at University of Massachusetts—Amherst, 1984.
"Moms: A Praise Play for a Black Comedienne" (based on the life of Jackie "Moms" Mabley), music and lyrics by Childress and her husband, Nathan Woodard, first produced by Green Plays at Art Awareness, 1986, produced Off-Broadway at Hudson Guild Theatre, February 4, 1987.

Also author of "Martin Luther King at Montgomery, Alabama," music by Woodard, 1969, "A Man Bearing a Pitcher," 1969, "The African Garden," music by Woodard, 1971, and "Vashti's Magic Mirror"; author of "The Freedom Drum," music by Woodard, produced as "Young Martin Luther King" by Performing Arts Repertory Theatre (on tour), 1969-71.

SCREENPLAYS

Wine in the Wilderness: A Comedy-Drama (first produced in Boston by WGBH-TV, March 4, 1969), Dramatists Play Service, 1969.
"Wedding Band" (based on her play of the same title), American Broadcasting Companies (ABC-TV), 1973.
"A Hero Ain't Nothin' but a Sandwich" (based on her novel of the same title), New World Pictures, 1978.
"String" (based on her play of the same title), Public Broadcasting Service (PBS-TV), 1979.

CONTRIBUTOR

Langston Hughes, editor, *The Best Short Stories by Negro Writers: An Anthology from 1899 to the Present,* Little, Brown, 1967.
Plays to Remember (includes "The World on a Hill"), Macmillan, 1968.
Stanley Richards, editor, *The Best Short Plays of 1972,* Chilton, 1972.
The Young American Basic Reading Program, Lyons & Carnaham, 1972.
Success in Reading, Silver Burdette, 1972.
Richards, editor, *Best Short Plays of the World Theatre, 1968-1973,* Crown, 1973.
Patterson, editor, *Anthology of the Afro-American in the Theatre: A Critical Approach,* Publishers Agency, 1978.
R. Baxter Miller, editor, *Black American Literature and Humanism,* University of Kentucky Press, 1981.
Mari Evans, editor, *Black Women Writers (1950-1980): A Critical Evaluation,* Doubleday-Anchor, 1984.

Also contributor to *Keeping the Faith,* edited by Pat Exum.

OTHER

Author of "Here's Mildred" column in *Baltimore Afro-Amer-*

ican, 1956-58. Contributor of plays, articles, and reviews to *Masses and Mainstream, Black World, Freedomways, Essence, Negro Digest, New York Times*, and other publications.

SIDELIGHTS: Alice Childress's work is noted for its frank treatment of racial issues, its compassionate yet discerning characterizations, and its universal appeal. Because her books and plays often deal with such controversial subjects as miscegenation and teenage drug addiction, her work has been banned in certain locations. She recalls that some affiliate stations refused to carry the nationally televised broadcasts of "Wedding Band" and "Wine in the Wilderness," and in the case of the latter play, the entire state of Alabama banned the telecast. Childress notes in addition that as late as 1973 the novel *A Hero Ain't Nothin' but a Sandwich* "was the first book banned in a Savannah, Georgia school library since *Catcher in the Rye*, which the same school banned in the fifties." Despite such regional resistance, Childress has won praise and respect for writings that a *Variety* reviewer terms "powerful and poetic."

A talented writer and performer in several media, Childress began her career in the theater, initially as an actress and later as a director and playwright. Although "theater histories make only passing mention of her,... she was in the forefront of important developments in that medium," writes *Dictionary of Literary Biography* contributor Trudier Harris. Rosemary Curb points out in another *Dictionary of Literary Biography* article that Childress's 1952 drama "Gold Through the Trees" was "the first play by a black woman professionally produced on the American stage." Moreover, Curb adds, "As a result of successful performances of [her 1950 play 'Just a Little Simple' and 'Gold Through the Trees'], Childress initiated Harlem's first all-union Off-Broadway contracts recognizing the Actors Equity Association and the Harlem Stage Hand Local."

Partly because of her pioneering efforts, Childress is considered a crusader by many. But she is also known as "a writer who resists compromise," says Doris E. Abramson in *Negro Playwrights in the American Theatre: 1925-1959*. "She tries to write about [black] problems as honestly as she can." The problems Childress addresses most often are racism and its effects. Her "Trouble in Mind," for example, is a play within a play that focuses on the anger and frustration experienced by a troupe of black actors as they try to perform stereotyped roles in a play that has been written, produced, and directed by whites. As Sally R. Sommer explains in the *Village Voice*, "The plot is about an emerging rebellion begun as the heroine, Wiletta, refuses to enact a namby-Mammy, either in the play or for her director." In the *New York Times*, Arthur Gelb states that Childress "has some witty and penetrating things to say about the dearth of roles for [black] actors in the contemporary theatre, the cutthroat competition for these parts and the fact that [black] actors often find themselves playing stereotyped roles in which they cannot bring themselves to believe." And of "Wedding Band," a play about an interracial relationship that takes place in South Carolina during World War I, Clive Barnes writes in the *New York Times*, "Childress very carefully suggests the stirrings of black consciousness, as well as the strength of white bigotry."

Critics Sommer and the *New York Times*'s Richard Eder find that Childress's treatment of the themes and issues in "Trouble in Mind" and "Wedding Band" gives these plays a timeless quality. "Writing in 1955,... Alice Childress used the concentric circles of the play-within-the-play to examine the mul-

tiple roles blacks enact in order to survive," Sommer remarks. She finds that viewing "Trouble in Mind" years later enables one to see "its double cutting edge: It predicts not only the course of social history but the course of black playwriting." Eder states: "The question [in "Wedding Band"] is whether race is a category of humanity or a division of it. The question is old by now, and was in 1965, [when the play was written,] but it takes the freshness of new life in the marvelous characters that Miss Childress has created to ask it."

The strength and insight of Childress's characterizations have been widely commented upon; critics contend that the characters who populate her plays and novels are believable and memorable. Eder praises the "rich and lively characterization" of "Wedding Band." Similarly impressed, Harold Clurman writes in the *Nation* that "there is an honest pathos in the telling of this simple story, and some humorous and touching thumbnail sketches reveal knowledge and understanding of the people dealt with." In the novel *A Short Walk*, Childress chronicles the life of a fictitious black woman, Cora James, from her birth in 1900 to her death in the middle of the century, illustrating, as *Washington Post* critic Joseph McLellan describes it, "a transitional generation in black American society." McLellan notes that the story "wanders considerably" and that "the reader is left with no firm conclusion that can be put into a neat sentence or two." What is more important, he asserts, is that "the wandering has been through some interesting scenery, and instead of a conclusion the reader has come to know a human being—complex, struggling valiantly and totally believable." And of Childress's novel about teenage heroin addiction, *A Hero Ain't Nothin' but a Sandwich*, the *Lion and the Unicorn*'s Miguel Oritz states, "The portrait of whites is more realistic in this book, more compassionate, and at the same time, because it is believable, more scathing."

Some criticism has been leveled at what such reviewers as Abramson and Edith Oliver believe to be Childress's tendency to speechify, especially in her plays. "A reader of the script is very much aware of the author pulling strings, putting her own words into a number of mouths," Abramson says of "Trouble in Mind." According to Oliver in the *New Yorker*, "The first act [of 'Wedding Band'] is splendid, but after that we hit a few jarring notes, when the characters seem to be speaking as much for the benefit of us eavesdroppers out front ... as for the benefit of one another."

For the most part, however, Childress's work has been acclaimed for its honesty, insight, and compassion. In his review of *A Hero Ain't Nothin' but a Sandwich*, Oritz writes: "The book conveys very strongly the message that we are all human, even when we are acting in ways that we are somewhat ashamed of. The structure of the book grows out of the personalities of the characters, and the author makes us aware of how much the economic and social circumstances dictate a character's actions." Loften Mitchell concludes in *Crisis*: "Childress writes with a sharp, satiric touch. Character seems to interest her more than plot. Her characterizations are piercing, her observations devastating."

Alice Childress commented: "Books, plays, tele-plays, motion picture scenarios, etc., I seem caught up in a fragmentation of writing skills. But an idea comes to me in a certain form and, if it stays with me, must be written out or put in outline form before I can move on to the next event. I sometimes wonder about writing in different forms; could it be that women are used to dealing with the bits and pieces of life and do not feel as [compelled to specialize]? The play form is the one most familiar to me and so influences all of my writing—I think in scenes.

"My young years were very old in feeling, I was shut out of so much for so long. [I] soon began to embrace the low-profile as a way of life, which helped me to develop as a writer. Quiet living is restful when one's writing is labeled 'controversial.'

"Happily, I managed to save a bit of my youth for spending in these later years. Oh yes, there are other things to be saved [besides] money. If we hang on to that part within that was once childhood, I believe we enter into a new time dimension and every day becomes another lifetime in itself. This gift of understanding is often given to those who constantly battle against the negatives of life with determination."

BIOGRAPHICAL/CRITICAL SOURCES:

BOOKS

Abramson, Doris E., *Negro Playwrights in the American Theatre, 1925-1959,* Columbia University Press, 1969.
Betsko, Kathleen and Rachel Koenig, *Interviews with Contemporary Women Playwrights,* Beech Tree Books, 1987.
Children's Literature Review, Volume 14, Gale, 1988.
Contemporary Literary Criticism, Gale, Volume 12, 1980, Volume 15, 1980.
Dictionary of Literary Biography, Gale, Volume 7: *Twentieth-Century American Dramatists,* 1981, Volume 38: *Afro-American Writers after 1955: Dramatists and Prose Writers,* 1985.
Donelson, Kenneth L. and Alleen Pace Nilson, *Literature for Today's Young Adults,* Scott, Foresman, 1980, 2nd edition, 1985.
Evans, Mari, editor, *Black Women Writers (1950-1980): A Critical Evaluation,* Doubleday-Anchor, 1984.
Hatch, James V. *Black Theater, U.S.A.: Forty-five Plays by Black Americans,* Free Press, 1974.
Mitchell, Loften, editor, *Voices of the Black Theatre,* James White, 1975.
Street, Douglas, editor, *Children's Novels and the Movies,* Ungar, 1983.

PERIODICALS

Crisis, April, 1965.
Freedomways, Volume 14, number 1, 1974.
Interracial Books for Children Bulletin, Volume 12, numbers 7-8, 1981.
Lion and the Unicorn, fall, 1978.
Los Angeles Times, November 13, 1978, February 25, 1983.
Los Angeles Times Book Review, July 25, 1982.
Ms., December, 1979.
Nation, November 13, 1972.
Negro Digest, April, 1967, January, 1968.
Newsweek, August 31, 1987.
New Yorker, November 4, 1972, November 19, 1979.
New York Times, November 5, 1955, February 2, 1969, April 2, 1969, October 27, 1972, November 5, 1972, February 3, 1978, January 11, 1979, January 23, 1987, February 10, 1987, March 6, 1987, August 18, 1987, October 22, 1987.
New York Times Book Review, November 4, 1973, November 11, 1979, April 25, 1981.
Show Business, April 12, 1969.
Variety, December 20, 1972.
Village Voice, January 15, 1979.
Washington Post, May 18, 1971, December 28, 1979.

CHISHOLM, Shirley (Anita St. Hill)   1924-

PERSONAL: Born Nobember 30, 1924, in Brooklyn, N.Y.; brought to Barbados, 1927; brought to U.S., 1934; daughter of Charles Christopher and Ruby (Seale) St. Hill; married Conrad Q. Chisholm (a social service investigator), October 8, 1949 (divorced February, 1977); married Arthur Hardwick (a businessman), November 26, 1977. *Education:* Brooklyn College (now Brooklyn College of the City University of New York), B.A. (cum laude), 1946; Columbia University, M.A., 1952. *Politics:* Democrat. *Religion:* Methodist.

ADDRESSES: Home—48 Crestwood Lane, Williamsville, N.Y. 14221. *Office*—Department of Sociology and Anthropology, Mount Holyoke College, South Hadley, Mass. 01075.

CAREER: Mt. Calvary Child Care Center, Harlem, N.Y., 1946-53, began as teacher's aide, became teacher; Friend in Need Nursery, Brooklyn, N.Y., director, 1953; Hamilton-Madison Child Care Center, New York City, director, 1954-59; New York City Bureau of Child Welfare, Division of Day Care, New York City, education consultant, 1959-64; New York State Assembly, Albany, member, 1964-68; U. S. Congress, representative from 12th District, New York City, 1968-83; Mt. Holyoke College, Department of Sociology and Anthropology, South Hadley, Mass., Purington Professor, 1983—. Fellow of School of Social Work, Adelphi University of Social Work. Unsuccessful Democratic presidential primary candidate, 1972. Founding member, National Women's Political Caucus. Former member of board of directors, Brooklyn Home for Aged. Consultant to Central Brooklyn Coordinating Council.

MEMBER: National Association of College Women, League of Women Voters, Americans for Democratic Action, Democratic Women Workshop, National Association for the Advancement of Colored People, United Negro College Fund, Advertising Council, Key Women, Inc. (president, Brooklyn chapter), Bedford-Stuyvesant Political League, Brooklyn College Alumnae, Delta Sigma Theta.

AWARDS, HONORS: Award for Outstanding Work in Field of Child Welfare, Women's Council of Brooklyn, 1957; Key Woman of the Year Award, 1963; Woman of Achievement Award, Key Women, Inc., 1965; Committee to Friends plaque, 1965; Human Relations Award, Central Nassau Club of Business and Professional Women, 1965; citation for outstanding service in the field of early childhood education and welfare, Sisterhood of Concord Baptist Church (Brooklyn), 1965; "Outstanding Service in Good Government" plaque, Christian Women's Retreat, 1965; Louise Waterman Wise Award, National Women's Division of the American Jewish Congress, 1969, for distinguished service in the cause of human rights; Award of Honor, Brooklyn College, 1969; Distinguished Service medal, Teachers College, 1969; Youth in Action Humanitarian Award of family counselling, 1969; Albert Einstein College of Medicine achievement award, 1969; Deborah Gannett Award, National Media Women, 1969; Meritorious Achievement award, Essex County college, 1971; Clairol's "Woman of the Year" Award, 1973, for outstanding achievement in public affairs; Civic and Community Leadership award, Council of Churches of New York City (Brooklyn Division), 1977; Certificate of Appreciation, College of Buffalo, State University of New York, 1981.

Honorary degrees from numerous colleges and universities in United States, including: L.H.D., North Carolina Central University, 1969, and Hampton Institute, 1970; LL. D., from Talladega College, 1969, Wilmington College, 1970, LaSalle College, William Patterson College of New Jersey, University of Maine, Capitol University, and Coppin State College, all 1971, Pratt Institute, 1972, Kenyon College, 1973, Aquinas College and Reed College, both 1974, University of Cincinnati, and Smith College, both 1975, Simmons College, 1977, Metropolitan State College, 1980, Mount Holyoke College and Villa Maria College, both 1981, Western Michigan University, Spelman College, and Saint Francis College, all 1982.

WRITINGS:

AUTOBIOGRAPHY

Unbought and Unbossed, Houghton, 1970.
The Good Fight, Haper, 1973.

CONTRIBUTOR

Lester Thomsen, editor, *Representative American Speeches, 1968-69,* Wilson, 1969.
Waldo H. Braden, editor, *Representative American Speeches, 1971-72,* Wilson, 1972.
Waldo H. Braden, editor, *Representative American Speeches, 1972-73,* Wilson, 1973.

OTHER

Contributor of articles to newspapers and periodicals.

SIDELIGHTS: "Shirley Chisholm is true grit," Susan Brownmiller writes in *Shirley Chisholm.* "Her cometlike rise from clubhouse worker to Representative in the United States Congress was no accident of the political heavens. It was accomplished by the wiles of a steely politician with a belief in her own abilities which at times approaches an almost Messianic fervor."

The title of Chisholm's first book, *Unbought and Unbossed* (also the campaign slogal of her first Congressional campaign), exemplifies the intense individualism of Chisholm's private and public life. Reviewers of the book express admiration for what it reveals about its author. Like Brownmiller, they applaud Chisholm's unflagging spirit which carried her from poverty to the Congress of the United States where she was the first black female member.

In *Catholic World,* for example, Sr. Elizabeth Kolmer comments: "Chisholm's story is a lively one. She herself is a petite woman, intelligent and dedicated with a fire twice her size. There is a singleness of purpose in her book just as there is in her life." Similarly, Jeffrey M. Elliot writes in the *Negro History Bulletin:* "Chisholm's *Unbought and Unbossed* is an absorbing, literate, revealing and inspiring account of those circumstances which made it possible for an idealist, an independent, a fighter; a woman of deep conviction, rare courage, and unquestionable honesty to do battle with party bosses, influence peddlers, and political hacks, and win."

Although while in college Chisholm had decided to dedicate herself to becoming a teacher of young children, the decision wasn't entirely her own. In *Unbought and Unbossed* she explains, "There was no other road open to a young black woman. Law, medicine, even nursing were too expensive, and few schools would admit black men, much less a woman."

While pursuing her childcare career, Chisholm became active in local politics, holding positions of leadership in several community groups. After ten years of doing everything from decorating cigar boxes to helping voters get to the polls, Chis-

holm decided to do the one thing she hadn't done, run for office. Although she encountered much opposition to her candidacy—mainly because of her sex—she won her first campaign by a wide margin and became a member of the New York State Assembly.

During her four years in Albany she learned more about the intricacies of politics and her constituents learned more about her political priorities. In *Unbought and Unbossed,* Chisholm points with pride to the eight bills she saw passed of the fifty she introduced. "Two I was especially satisfied with," she writes. "One created a program called SEEK, to make it possible for young men and women from disadvantaged backgrounds to go to college, by seeking them out and assisting them while they go to school. . . . The other was a bill to set up the state's first unemployment insurance coverage for personal and domestic employees."

As these two bills reveal, among Chisholm's causes are better educational opportunities for minority groups, programs for the poor and disadvantaged, and a constant push for equality for ethnic minorities and for women. After her election to Congress in 1968, she introduced, co-sponsored, and ardently supported many important measures linked to these causes including proposals to create a study commission on Afro-American history and culture, to enlarge the powers of the Department of Housing and Urban Development, to establish a Department of Consumer Affairs at a full Cabinet level, and several anti-poverty and welfare programs.

While election to Congress was the realization of a dream for Chisholm, she soon focused on another goal, running for President of the United States. Her second book, *The Good Fight,* details her campaign for the Democratic presidential nomination in 1972.

Although Chisholm failed in her presidential bid, *Best Sellers* contributor Norman Lederer maintains that her candidacy was an important political event. "Chisholm's campaign was unusual," he observes, "in that it stressed real issues omitted from the platforms of the major candidates and obscured by dogma among minority candidates. . . . Chisholm's failure to obtain the nomination was a foregone conclusion but through her intrepid effort a new life and vitality was infused into the American political scene."

Chisholm also sees her candidacy in a positive light. In *The Good Fight* she notes, "The mere fact that a black woman dared to run for President, *seriously,* not expecting to win but sincerely trying to, is what it was all about. 'It can be done'; that was what I was trying to say, by doing it."

"We Americans," she adds, "have a chance to become someday a nation in which all racial stocks and classes can exist in their own selfhoods, but meet on a basis of respect and equality and live together, socially, economically, and politically. . . . I hope I did a little to make it happen. I am going to keep trying to make it happen as long as I am able. I will not run for President again, but in a broad sense my campaign will continue. In fact, it is just beginning."

BIOGRAPHICAL/CRITICAL SOURCES:

BOOKS

Brownmiller, Susan, *Shirley Chisholm,* Doubleday, 1970.
Chisholm, Shirley, *Unbought and Unbossed,* Houghton, 1970.
Chisholm, Shirley, *The Good Fight,* Harper, 1973.
Contemporary Issues Criticism, Volume 2, Gale, 1984.

PERIODICALS

Atlantic, November, 1970.
Best Sellers, October 15, 1970, July 15, 1973.
Catholic World, February, 1971.
Congressional Digest, January, 1971.
Ebony, February, 1969.
Freedomways, first quarter, 1974.
Los Angeles Times, December 18, 1983.
McCall's, August, 1970.
Nation, January 26, 1970.
Negro History Bulletin, May, 1972.
New York Times Book Review, November 1, 1970, October 21, 1973.
New York Times Magazine, April 13, 1969.
Time, November 2, 1970.
Washington Post, October 10, 1970.

—Sketch by Marian Gonsior

*   *   *

CHRISTIAN, Barbara T.   1943-

PERSONAL: Born December 12, 1943, in St. Thomas, U.S. Virgin Islands. *Education:* Marquette University, A.B. (cum laude), 1963; Columbia University, M.A., 1964, Ph.D. (with honors), 1970.

ADDRESSES: Home—2920 Benvenue, Berkeley, Calif. 94705. *Office*—Department of Afro-American Studies, University of California, 3335 Dwinelle, Berkeley, Calif. 94720.

CAREER: City College of the City University of New York, New York, N.Y., lecturer, 1965-70, assistant professor of English, 1971-72; University of California, Berkeley, lecturer, 1971-72, assistant professor, 1972-78, associate professor and chairperson of Afro-American studies, 1978—. Consultant to Far West Laboratories.

MEMBER: Modern Language Association of America, National Women's Studies Association, National Council for Black Studies.

AWARDS, HONORS: Before Columbus Foundation American Book Award, 1984, for *Black Women Novelists.*

WRITINGS:

(Contributor) Addison Gayle, editor, *Black Expression,* Weybright & Talley, 1969.
Black Women Novelists: Development of a Tradition, 1892-1976, Greenwood Press, 1980.
Black Feminist Criticism: Perspectives on Black Women Writers, Pergamon, 1985.

Also author of teaching guide for *Black Foremothers, Three Lives* by Dorothy Sterling, Feminist Press, 1980. Contributor to *Black Scholar* and *Journal of Ethnic Studies.*

*   *   *

CLARK, Al C.
See GOINES, Donald

*   *   *

CLARK, J. P.
See CLARK, John(son) Pepper

CLARK, John(son) Pepper   1935-
(J. P. Clark)

PERSONAL: Born April 6, 1935, in Kiagbodo, Nigeria; son of Clark Fuludu and Poro Clark Bakederemo. *Education:* University of Ibadan, B.A. (with honors), 1960.

ADDRESSES: Office—PEC Repertory Theatre, J. K. Randle Hall, King George V Rd., Onikan, Lagos, Nigeria. *Agent*—Curtis Brown Ltd., 162-168 Regent St., London W1R 5TA, England.

CAREER: Nigerian Federal Government, information officer, 1960-61; *Daily Express,* Lagos, Nigeria, head of features and editorial writer, 1961-62; University of Lagos, Lagos, research fellow, 1964-66, professor of African literature and instructor in English, beginning in 1966, professor of English, beginning in 1976; director of repertory theatre in Nigeria, 1980—. Poet, playwright, and filmmaker. Visiting distinguished fellow at Wesleyan University, Middletown, Conn., 1975-76.

MEMBER: Society of Nigerian Authors (founding member).

AWARDS, HONORS: Institute of African Studies research fellow, 1961-62 and 1963-64; Parvin fellow at Princeton University, 1962-63.

WRITINGS:

Song of a Goat (also see below; play; first produced at Ibadan University, 1961; produced in London at Commonwealth Festival of the Arts, 1965), Mbari Writers Club, 1961.
Poems, Mbari Press (Ibadan), 1962.
(Contributor) Gerald Moore, editor, *Seven African Writers,* Oxford University Press, 1962.
Three Plays: Song of a Goat, The Masquerade, The Raft, Oxford University Press, 1964.
(Contributor) John Reed and Clive Wake, editors, *A Book of African Verse,* Heinemann, 1964.
America, Their America (nonfiction), Deutsch, 1964, Africana Publishing, 1969.
A Reed in the Tide, Longmans, Green, 1965, 2nd edition published as *A Reed in the Tide: A Selection of Poems,* Humanities, 1970.
Ozidi: A Play, Oxford University Press, 1966.
(Contributor) *West African Verse: An Anthology,* Longmans, Green, 1967.
(Under name J. P. Clark) *Casualties: Poems, 1966-1968,* Africana Publishing, 1970.
The Example of Shakespeare: Critical Essays on African Literature, Northwestern University Press, 1970.
(Translator under name J. P. Clark) Okabou Ojobolo, *The Ozidi Saga,* Ibadan University Press, 1977.
The Philosophical Anarchism of William Godwin, Princeton University Press, 1977.
A Decade of Tongues: Selected Poems, 1958-1968, Longman, 1981.
The Anarchist Moment: Reflections on Culture, Nature, and Power, Black Rose Press, 1984.
The Bikaroa Plays: The Boat, The Return Home and Full Circle, Oxford University Press, 1985.

Also author of *Max Stirner's Egoism,* Left Bank. Author of plays "Dear Native Land" and "Return to Dear Native Land"; author of screenplays, director, and producer of two documentary films, "The Ozidi of Atazi" and "The Ghost Town." Founder and editor, *The Horn* (literary magazine; Ibadan); co-editor of *Black Orpheus,* 1968—. Contributor of literary criticism to periodicals, including *Presence Africaine, Nigeria, Transition, African Forum,* and *Black Orpheus.*

BIOGRAPHICAL/CRITICAL SOURCES:

PERIODICALS

New York Times, December 20, 1985.

*   *   *

CLARK, Kenneth B(ancroft) 1914-

PERSONAL: Born July 24, 1914, in Panama Canal Zone; son of Arthur Bancroft and Miriam (Hanson) Clark; married Mamie Phipps (a psychologist), April 14, 1938 (died, 1983); children: Kate Miriam (Mrs. Donald Harris), Hilton Bancroft. *Education:* Howard University, B.A., 1935, M.S., 1936; Columbia University, Ph.D., 1940. *Religion:* Episcopalian.

ADDRESSES: Home—17 Pinecrest Dr., Hastings-on-Hudson, N.Y. 10706. *Office*—Clark, Phipps, Clark & Harris, Inc., 60 East 86th St., New York, N.Y. 10028.

CAREER: Hampton Institute, Hampton, Va., assistant professor of psychology, 1940-41; U.S. Office of War Information, Washington, D.C., assistant social science analyst, 1941-42; City College of the City University of New York, New York, N.Y., instructor, 1942-49, assistant professor, beginning 1949, professor, 1960-70, distinguished professor of psychology, 1970-75, professor emeritus, 1975—; president and chairman of the board, Clark, Phipps, Clark & Harris, 1975—. Visiting professor at Columbia University, summer, 1955, University of California, Berkeley, summer, 1958, and Harvard University, summer, 1965. Founder and research director, Northside Center for Child Development, 1946-66; founder and chairman of board of directors, Harlem Youth Opportunities Unlimited (HARYOU), 1962-64; president, Metropolitan Applied Research Center, Inc. (MARC Corp.), 1967-75. Member of Committee on Foreign Affairs Personnel, U.S. Department of State, 1961-62. Member of board of directors of Harper & Row, Lincoln Savings Bank, Presidential Life Insurance, and Woodrow Wilson International Center for Scholars; former member of board of directors, New York State Urban Development Corp., and chairman of Affirmative Action Commission, 1971-75. Member, New York State Board of Regents, 1966—; trustee, University of Chicago. Social science consultant, Legal and Educational Division, National Association for the Advancement of Colored People, 1950—; consultant, Personnel Division, U.S. Department of State, 1961-68, 1976-77.

MEMBER: American Psychological Association (fellow; director, 1969; president, 1970-71), American Association for the Advancement of Science (president, 1970-71), Society for the Psychological Study of Social Issues (member of council, 1954—; president, 1959-60), Century Association, Phi Beta Kappa, Sigma Xi.

AWARDS, HONORS: Rosenwald fellow, 1940-41; Spingarn Medal, National Association for the Advancement of Colored People, 1961; Kurt Lewin Memorial Award, Society for the Psychological Study of Social Issues, 1965; Sidney Hillman Prize Book Award, Sidney Hillman Foundation, 1965, for *Dark Ghetto: Dilemmas of Social Power;* College Board medal for distinguished service to education, 1980; Franklin Delano Roosevelt Four Freedoms Award, Franklin and Eleanor Roosevelt Institute, 1985. Honorary degrees from Amherst College, Columbia University, Haverford College, Yeshiva Uni-

versity, Oberlin College, Johns Hopkins University, New York University, Princeton University, University of Massachusetts, Lincoln University, Morgan State University, Carnegie-Mellon University, and others.

WRITINGS:

Prejudice and Your Child, Beacon Press, 1955, 2nd enlarged edition, 1963, reprinted, Wesleyan University Press, 1986.
(With Lawrence Plotkin) *The Negro Student at Integrated Colleges,* National Scholarship Service and Fund for Negro Students, 1963.
The Negro Protest: James Baldwin, Malcolm X, Martin Luther King Talk with Kenneth B. Clark, Beacon Press, 1963, published as *King, Malcolm, Baldwin: Three Interviews,* Wesleyan University Press, 1985.
Dark Ghetto: Dilemmas of Social Power, foreword by Gunnar Myrdal, Harper, 1965.
Social and Economic Implications of Integration in the Public Schools (pamphlet condensed from seminar on manpower policy and program), U.S. Department of Labor, 1965.
(Editor with Talcott Parsons) *The Negro American,* foreword by President Lyndon B. Johnson, Houghton, 1966.
(With Jeannette Hopkins) *A Relevant War against Poverty: A Study of Community Action Programs and Observable Change,* Metropolitan Applied Research Center, 1968, Harper, 1969.
(With Harold Howe) *Racism and American Education: A Dialogue and Agenda for Action,* Harper, 1970.
(Editor with Meyer Weinberg) *W. E. B. Du Bois: A Reader,* Harper, 1970.
(Editor) Allen W. Trelease, *White Terror: The Ku Klux Klan Conspiracy and Southern Reconstruction,* Harper, 1971.
Pathos of Power, Harper, 1974.
"Problems of Freedom and Behavior Modification" (cassette), introduction by Mortimer Brown, American Psychological Association, 1976.

Also author of *Beyond the Ghetto.* Contributor to journals.

SIDELIGHTS: Kenneth B. Clark's studies on the psychological effects of racism were cited by the U.S. Supreme Court in *Brown v. Board of Education of Topeka,* its landmark school desegregation decision of 1954. As a founder of Harlem Youth Opportunities Unlimited (HARYOU), Clark developed several concepts which became important measures in the national anti-poverty program of the 1960s. His book *Dark Ghetto: Dilemmas of Social Power,* based on his experiences with HARYOU, is "an indispensable contribution to the Freedom movement," comments Michael Harrington in *Book Week.*

Dark Ghetto: Dilemmas of Social Power has been translated into German, Spanish, and Italian.

BIOGRAPHICAL/CRITICAL SOURCES:

PERIODICALS

Best Sellers, July 1, 1974.
Book Week, May 9, 1965.
Newsweek, July 29, 1974.
New York Times, September 28, 1974.
Virginia Quarterly Review, fall, 1974.
Wall Street Journal, July 11, 1974.

SOUND RECORDINGS

"An Interview with Kenneth Clark," Harper, 1975.

CLARKE, Austin C(hesterfield) 1934-

PERSONAL: Born July 26, 1934, in Barbados, West Indies; son of Kenneth Trothan (an artist) and Gladys Clarke; children: Janice, Loretta, Mphahlele. *Education:* Attended Harrison College, Barbados, West Indies; Oxford and Cambridge Higher Certificate, 1950; additional study at University of Toronto.

ADDRESSES: Agent—Harold Ober Associates, 40 East 49th St., New York, N.Y. 10017.

CAREER: Canadian Broadcasting Corp., Toronto, Ontario, producer and free-lance broadcaster, beginning in 1963; Brandeis University, Waltham, Mass., Jacob Ziskind Professor of Literature, 1968-69; Williams College, Williamstown, Mass., Margaret Bundy Scott Professor of Literature, 1971-72; Barbados Embassy, Washington, D.C., cultural and press attache, 1974-75; affiliated with Caribbean Broadcasting Corp., St. Michael, Barbados. Visiting professor of Afro-American literature and creative writing, Yale University, 1968-71. Member of board of trustees of Rhode Island School of Design, Providence, 1970-75.

MEMBER: Writers Guild, Canadian Union of Writers, Yale Club (New Haven).

AWARDS, HONORS: Canada Council senior arts fellowships, 1968, 1970, and 1974; University of Western Ontario President's Medal for best story, 1965; Belmont Short Story Award for "Four Stations in His Circle"; Casa de las Americas Literary Prize, 1980.

WRITINGS:

NOVELS, EXCEPT AS NOTED

The Survivors of the Crossing, McClelland & Stewart, 1964.
Amongst Thistles and Thorns, McClelland & Stewart, 1965.
The Meeting Point, Macmillan, 1967.
When He Was Free and Young and He Used to Wear Silks (short stories), Anansi, 1971, Little, Brown, 1974.
Storm of Fortune, Little, Brown, 1973.
The Bigger Light, Little, Brown, 1975.
The Prime Minister, General Publishing, 1977.
Growing Up Stupid Under the Union Jack (autobiographical novel), McClelland & Stewart, 1980.

Author of *Short Stories of Austin Clarke,* 1984; also author of "Myths and Memories," "African Literature," and other filmscripts for Educational Television (ETV), Toronto, 1968—.

WORK IN PROGRESS: A study of the symbolism in Richard Wright's story "The Man Who Lived Underground"; research concerning the position of black women in the Black American Revolution.

SIDELIGHTS: Austin C. Clarke's childhood in colonial Barbados and his experiences as a black immigrant to Canada have provided him with the background for most of his fiction. His writing is almost exclusively concerned with the cultural contradictions that arise when blacks struggle for success in a predominantly white society. Clarke's "one very great gift," in the words of a *New Yorker* critic, is the ability to see "unerringly into his characters' hearts," and this ability is what makes his stories memorable. Martin Levin writes in the *New York Times Book Review:* "Mr. Clarke is plugged into the fixations, hopes, loves and dreams of his characters. He converts them into stories that are charged with life."

Clarke's autobiographical novel, *Growing Up Stupid Under the Union Jack,* is an example of the author's typical theme and style. The narrator, Tom, is a young man from a poor Barbadan village. Everyone in the village is proud that Tom is able to attend the Combermere School, for it is run by a "real, true-true Englishman"—an ex-British Army officer who calls his students "boy" and "darky" and who flogs them publicly. The students eagerly imitate this headmaster's morals and manners, for to them, he represents "Mother England"; they are unaware that in England he would be looked down upon as a mere working-class soldier. The book is "a personal, captivating, provoking and often humorous record of ignorance, inhumanity and lowly existence under colonial imperialism in World War II Barbados. . . . With its major emphasis on education and childhood, *Growing Up Stupid Under the Union Jack* continues to draw attention to one of the chief preoccupations of the anti-colonial Anglo-Caribbean novel," writes Robert P. Smith in *World Literature Today.* The theme is well rendered in what Darryl Pinckney calls in the *New York Review of Books* Clarke's "tender, funny, unpolemical style."

Clarke's best-known work is a trilogy detailing the lives of Barbadan blacks who immigrate to Toronto hoping to better their lot. In these novels, *The Meeting Point, Storm of Fortune,* and *The Bigger Light,* "it is as if the flat characters of a Dickensian world have come into their own at last, playing their tragicomic roles in a manner which owes much to Clarke's extraordinary facility with the Barbadan dialect," writes Diane Bessai in *Canadian Literature.* Bessai also expresses eagerness for Clarke to "continue to create his Brueghel-like canvasses with their rich and contrasting detail and mood." "The sense of defeat among the poor islanders is enlivened by the humour of the characters and their glowing fantasies about the presumed wealth of relatives and friends who make it big in the fatlands of the United States or Canada," writes John Ayre in *Saturday Night.*

The first two novels dwell mostly on Bernice Leach, a live-in maid at a wealthy Toronto home, and her small circle of fellow immigrants. Martin Levin writes in the *New York Times Book Review:* "Mr. Clarke is masterful at delineating the oppressive insecurities of Bernice and her friends, and the claustrophobic atmosphere that envelops such a mini-minority" as the Caribbean blacks in Toronto. The third novel, *The Bigger Light,* explores the life of Boysie, the most successful of this immigrant group, and his wife, Dots. Boysie has at last realized the dream that compelled him to leave Barbados: he owns a prosperous business and his own home. However, in the process of realizing his goals, he has become alienated from his wife and his community. Now he searches for a greater meaning to his life—a "bigger light." "*The Bigger Light* is a painful book to read," writes David Rosenthal in *Nation.* It is "a story of two people with many things to say and no one to say them to, who hate themselves and bitterly resent the society around them. . . . Certain African novelists have also dealt with the isolation of self-made blacks, but none with Clarke's bleak intensity." A *New Yorker* writer praises the book further, citing Clarke's strong writing skill as the element that lifts the book beyond social comment: "The universal longings of ordinary human beings are depicted with a simplicity and power that make us grateful for all three volumes of this long and honest record."

BIOGRAPHICAL/CRITICAL SOURCES:

BOOKS

Contemporary Literary Criticism, Volume VIII, Gale, 1978.

PERIODICALS

Canadian Literature, summer, 1974.
Listener, June 15, 1978.
Nation, November 1, 1975.
New Yorker, February 24, 1975.
New York Review of Books, May 27, 1982.
New York Times Book Review, April 9, 1972, December 9, 1973, February 16, 1975.
Saturday Night, October, 1971, June, 1975.
Times Literary Supplement, October 24, 1986.
World Literature Today, winter, 1982.

*   *   *

CLARKE, John Henrik   1915-

PERSONAL: Born January 1, 1915, in Union Springs, Ala.; son of John (a farmer) and Willella (Mays) Clarke; married Eugenia Evans (a teacher), December 24, 1961; children: Nzingha Marie, Sonni Kojo. *Education:* Attended New York University, 1948-52, New School for Social Research, 1956-58, University of Ibadan (Nigeria), University of Ghana. *Politics:* Socialism. *Religion:* Nondenominational.

ADDRESSES: Home—223 West 137th St., New York, N.Y. 10030. *Agent*—Ronald Hobbs Literary Agency, 516 Fifth Ave., Suite 507, New York, N.Y. 10036.

CAREER: Pittsburgh Courier, Pittsburgh, Pa., feature writer, 1957-58; *Ghana Evening News,* Accra, Ghana, feature writer, 1958; New School for Social Research, New York City, occasional teacher of African and Afro-American history, 1956-58, developer of African Study Center, 1957-59, assistant to director, 1958-60; Hunter College of the City University of New York, New York City, associate professor of Black and Puerto Rican studies, 1970—. Director, Haryou-Act (teaching program), 1964-69; director of training program in Black history, Columbia University, summer, 1969; Carter G. Woodson distinguished visiting professor in African history, Cornell University, 1969—; visiting lecturer, New York University; teacher (by special license) at Malverne High School (People's College), Malverne, N.Y. Research director for African Heritage Exposition in New York City, 1959; coordinator and special consultant to Columbia Broadcasting System, Inc. (CBS-TV) television series, "Black Heritage," 1968; consultant to American Heritage Press and John Wiley & Sons (publishers). Member of board of directors of Langston Hughes Center for Child Development, 1967—; member of advisory board of Martin Luther King Library Center, 1969. *Military service:* U.S. Army Air Forces, 1941-45; became master sergeant.

MEMBER: International Society of African Culture, African Studies Association, American Society of African Culture, Black Academy of Arts and Letters (founding member), Association for Study of Negro Life and History (vice-president, 1949-55), American Historical Society, American Academy of Political and Social Science, African Heritage Studies Association (president, 1969-73), African Scholars Council (member of board of directors), Harlem Writers Guild (founding member).

AWARDS, HONORS: Carter G. Woodson Award, 1968, for creative contribution in editing, and 1971, for excellence in teaching; National Association for Television and Radio Announcers citation for meritorious achievement in educational television, 1969; L.H.D. from University of Denver, 1970.

WRITINGS:

Rebellion in Rhyme (poems), Dicker Press, 1948.

(Editor) *Harlem U.S.A.: The Story of a City within a City,* Seven Seas Books (Berlin), 1964, revised edition, Collier, 1970.

(Editor) *Harlem: A Community in Transition,* Citadel, 1965, 3rd edition, 1970.

(Editor) *American Negro Short Stories,* Hill & Wang, 1966.

(Editor) *William Styron's Nat Turner: Ten Black Writers Respond,* Beacon Press, 1968, reprinted, Greenwood Press, 1987.

Black Soldier, illustrated by Harold James, Doubleday, 1968.

(Editor and author of introduction) *Malcolm X: The Man and His Times,* Macmillan, 1969.

(Editor with Vincent Harding) *Slave Trade and Slavery,* Holt, 1970.

(Editor) *Harlem* (short stories), New American Library, 1970.

(Editor with others) *Black Titan: W. E. B. Du Bois,* Beacon Press, 1970.

(Editor) J. A. Rogers, *World's Great Men of Color,* two volumes, Macmillan, 1972.

(Editor with Amy Jacques Garvey, and author of introduction and commentaries) *Marcus Garvey and the Vision of Africa,* Random House, 1974.

(Guest editor) *Black Families in the American Economy,* Education-Community Counselors Association (Washington, D.C.), 1975.

(Editor) *Dimensions of the Struggle against Apartheid: A Tribute to Paul Robeson,* African Heritage Studies Association in cooperation with United Nations Centre against Apartheid, 1979.

Also author of "The Lives of Great African Chiefs" published serially in *Pittsburgh Courier,* 1957-58, and of syndicated column, "African World Bookshelf." Author of numerous papers on African studies presented at international conferences. Contributor to *Negro History Bulletin, Chicago Defender, Journal of Negro Education, Phylon, Presence Africaine,* and others. Book review editor, *Negro History Bulletin,* 1947-49; co-founder and associate editor, *Harlem Quarterly,* 1949-51; editor, *African Heritage,* 1959; associate editor, *Freedomways,* 1962—.

WORK IN PROGRESS: The Black Woman in History; an African curriculum for elementary school teachers.

SIDELIGHTS: As an editor, essayist, and educator, John Henrik Clarke has written and lectured extensively about African and Afro-American history both in the United States and West Africa. *Malcolm X: The Man and His Times,* a collection of essays about and writings by Malcolm X edited by Clarke, is described by the *New York Times*'s Christopher Lehmann-Haupt: "Malcolm is seen through different eyes at various stages of his career as Muslim, ex-Muslim, and founder of the Organization of Afro-American Unity. He is defined and redefined by friends and followers." And although Lehmann-Haupt considers the collection "overwhelmingly sympathetic," he thinks that Clarke has produced a "multifaceted picture that . . . traces his development from drifter to prophet, spells out his aims (and thereby dispels his distorted image as apostle of violent separatism) and explains why his stature among so many blacks today is heroic." Similarly, in the *New York Review of Books,* Charles V. Hamilton finds that "Clarke has done an excellent job of pulling together various stimulating sources to give the reader what the title promises, a look at the man and his time—a look at a genuine folk hero of black Americans and a master of the Politics of Sportsmanship."

BIOGRAPHICAL/CRITICAL SOURCES:

BOOKS

Authors in the News, Volume I, Gale, 1976.

PERIODICALS

Atlanta Journal, April 8, 1973.
Black World, February, 1971.
New York Review of Books, September 12, 1968.
New York Times, May 10, 1967, August 1-2, 1968, September 29, 1969.
New York Times Book Review, March 5, 1967, August 11, 1968, September 28, 1969.
Saturday Review, January 14, 1967, August 12, 1968.

*   *   *

CLEAVER, (Leroy) Eldridge   1935-

PERSONAL: Born August 31, 1935, in Wabbaseka, Ark.; son of Leroy (a dining car waiter) and Thelma (a janitor) Cleaver; married Kathleen Neal, December, 1967; children: Maceo (son), Joju (daughter). *Education:* Attended junior college; also educated in Soledad Prison.

CAREER: Prisoner at Soledad Prison, 1954-57 and 1958-66; *Ramparts* (magazine), San Francisco, Calif., assistant editor and contributing writer, 1966-68; Black Panther Party, Oakland, Calif., minister of information, 1967-71; U.S. presidential candidate, Peace and Freedom Party, 1968; in exile in Cuba, Algeria, and France, 1968-75; owner of boutique in Hollywood, Calif., 1978-79; founder of Eldridge Cleaver Crusades, 1979; independent candidate for U.S. Congress in 8th Congressional District, Calif., 1984. Lecturer at universities.

AWARDS, HONORS: Martin Luther King Memorial Prize, 1970, for *Soul on Ice.*

WRITINGS:

Soul on Ice, introduction by Maxwell Geismar, McGraw, 1968.
Eldridge Cleaver: Post-Prison Writings and Speeches, edited by Robert Scheer, Random House, 1969.
Eldridge Cleaver's Black Papers, McGraw, 1969.
(Author of introduction) Jerry Rubin, *Do It!* Simon & Schuster, 1970.
(Contributor) G. Louis Heath, editor, *The Black Panther Leaders Speak: Huey P. Newton, Bobby Seale, Eldridge Cleaver, and Company Speak Out Through the Black Panther Party's Official Newspaper,* Scarecrow, 1976.
Soul on Fire, Word Inc., 1978.

Also author, with others, of *War Within: Violence or Nonviolence in Black Revolution,* 1971, of *Education and Revolution,* Center for Educational Reform, and of pamphlets for the Black Panther Party and People's Communication Network. Work represented in anthologies, including *Prize Stories, 1971: The O. Henry Awards.* Contributor to periodicals, including *Ramparts, Commonweal,* and *National Review.*

SIDELIGHTS: Speaking of his days as a leader of the revolutionary Black Panther Party, Eldridge Cleaver told Lynne Baranski and Richard Lemon of *People* that at that time he felt "there was no hope of effecting real freedom within the capitalistic system. I was the guy who demanded we go down shooting." Cleaver's radical exhortations endeared him to the militant nationalists who made up the Black Panthers. During the Party's short and turbulent history, nineteen Panthers were killed in gun battles with the police. "It was exhilarat-

ing . . . ," Cleaver's wife Kathleen told Baranski and Lemon about that period. "But it was also terrible—people getting killed."

Cleaver joined the Black Panther Party shortly after his release from prison in 1966. He had served nine years for drug dealing and rape and was only released on parole after a number of literary figures petitioned the government on his behalf. *Soul on Ice,* a book Cleaver wrote while in prison, was the catalyst for the literary campaign. A collection of essays about the situation of black people in America and about Cleaver's own life, *Soul on Ice* is "an original and disturbing report on what a black man, reacting to a society he detests, reacting to life behind bars for nine years, finally becomes," as Gertrude Samuels writes in *Saturday Review.* Charlayne Hunter of the *New York Times Book Review* judges Cleaver to be "not a nihilist like so many of his contemporaries who share his revolutionary zeal more than his sense of history. He can tear the system apart, but, unlike them, he has a few ideas about how to put it back together again." In *Soul on Ice,* Jervis Anderson of *Commentary* believes, Cleaver expresses "the profound alienation from America which black nationalists feel and the extreme political and cultural view of its future which they take."

The inspiration for *Soul on Ice* comes from a number of writers Cleaver read while in prison, including Thomas Paine, Karl Marx, Nikolai Lenin, and James Baldwin. The most important influence, however, was Malcolm X, a leader of the Black Muslims. Cleaver joined the Muslims in the early 1960s and, when Malcolm X broke away from Elijah Muhammed's leadership of the group, Cleaver followed. Shortly after this break, Malcolm X was assassinated. "I have, so to speak," Cleaver writes in *Soul on Ice,* "washed my hands in the blood of the martyr, Malcolm X, whose retreat from the precipice of madness created new room for others to turn about in, and I am now caught up in that tiny space, attempting a maneuver of my own."

Shortly after his release from prison, Cleaver became the minister of information for the Black Panther Party. Calling for an armed insurrection to overthrow the United States government and establish a black socialist government in its place, the Panthers were described by Federal Bureau of Investigation (F.B.I.) director J. Edgar Hoover, *People* notes, as the nation's "greatest threat." The Panthers ran free lunch programs for poor children and operated other service-oriented programs in several cities. But they were also heavily armed for "self-defense" and had frequent problems with the police, including a number of gun battles. *Playboy* noted at the time that Cleaver "has been called the first black leader since Malcolm X with the potential to organize a militant mass movement of 'black liberation.' Whether he will succeed in forging it, whether he will remain free—or even alive—to lead it, and whether, if he does, it will be a force for racial reconciliation or division remains to be seen."

The extent of support Cleaver and the Panthers enjoyed in the white liberal and black communities became clear when Cleaver's parole was revoked in 1968 after he was involved in a gun battle with the police in Oakland, California. One Panther was killed and a police officer and Cleaver were wounded in the battle. He was charged with assault and attempted murder. Support for Cleaver came from throughout the world. A demonstration in New York City on his behalf included participants such as writer Susan Sontag and actor Gary Merrill. In Europe, French film director Jean-Luc Godard urged his audience to donate to Cleaver's defense fund. Later that same year, while he was still fighting these charges, his wide liberal support became even more clear when Cleaver was chosen as the presidential candidate of the Peace and Freedom Party, an organization of both black and white radicals. "I never exactly dreamed of waking up in the White House after the November election," Cleaver tells Nat Hentoff in a *Playboy* interview, "but I took part in that campaign because I think it's necessary to pull a lot of people together, black and white."

Rather than face charges over the gun battle with police, Cleaver fled the country in late 1968. Over the next seven years he lived in Cuba, Algeria, and France and was warmly welcomed on his visits to the Soviet Union, China, North Vietnam, and North Korea. During this time, writes Richard Gilman in the *New Republic,* "Cleaver played a complicated role from afar in the troubled internal politics of the Black Panthers, served as an unofficial emissary of American radicalism to various communist regimes . . . , fathered two children with his wife Kathleen and found himself growing more and more disenchanted with both his life as an expatriate and his former political beliefs."

This disenchantment stemmed from his realization, after actually visiting and living in many communist countries, that communism did not work as well as he had thought. "I had heard," Cleaver writes in *Soul on Fire,* "so much rhetoric about their glorious leaders and their incredible revolutionary spirit that even to this very angry and disgruntled American, it was absurd and unreal." Cleaver now "derides Cuba's system as 'voodoo socialism,'" Baranski and Lemon report, "and says North Korea and Algeria are 'even worse, because they have been doing it longer.'" Parallel to this political awakening was Cleaver's conversion to Christianity, the result of a mystical vision. Cleaver saw his own face on the moon, then the faces of "my former heroes . . . Fidel Castro, Mao Tsetung, Karl Marx, Friedrich Engels. . . . Finally, at the end of the procession, in dazzling, shimmering light, the image of Jesus Christ appeared. . . .'' Cleaver explains in *Soul on Fire.* "I fell to my knees."

In 1975, Cleaver returned to the United States and surrendered to the F.B.I. Although he faced up to seventy-two years in prison, Cleaver struck a deal with the government. By pleading guilty to the assault charge, he had the attempted murder charge dropped and was sentenced to 1,200 hours of community service. One reason for the lenient treatment was the feeling that Cleaver's religious conversion had changed him. Baranski and Lemon quote Earl Anthony, an ex-Panther, who believes: "Eldridge changed from one of the most vicious dudes against the system into a person who is reaching out. He's become a nice human being."

Cleaver has been involved in a number of ventures since returning to the United States. In 1978, he opened a boutique in Hollywood featuring men's trousers with a codpiece, his own design. The following year he founded the Eldridge Cleaver Crusades, an evangelical organization with plans to open a headquarters in the Nevada desert. Cleaver returned to politics in 1984 as an independent conservative candidate for Congress; his bid for election was unsuccessful. Denying charges that he has somehow mellowed since his return, Cleaver tells Baranski and Lemon: "That implies your ideas have changed because of age. I've changed because of new conclusions."

BIOGRAPHICAL/CRITICAL SOURCES:

BOOKS

Cleaver, Eldridge, *Soul on Ice,* McGraw, 1968.

Cleaver, Eldridge, *Soul on Fire,* Word Inc., 1978.
Contemporary Literary Criticism, Volume 30, Gale, 1984.
Cranston, Maurice, editor, *The New Left,* Library Press, 1971.
Hemenway, Robert, editor, *Black Novelist,* Merrill, 1970.
Lockwood, Lee, *Conversation with Eldridge Cleaver: Algiers,* McGraw, 1970.
Oliver, John A., *Eldridge Cleaver: Ice and Fire!* Bible Voice, 1977.
Parks, Gordon, *Born Black,* Lippincott, 1971.

PERIODICALS

Antioch Review, fall, 1968.
Atlantic, June, 1968.
Best Sellers, February, 1979.
Christianity Today, March 23, 1977, July 8, 1977, December 7, 1979, April 20, 1984.
Commentary, December, 1968.
Critic, June-July, 1969.
Detroit Free Press, August 30, 1976.
Dissent, July/August, 1969.
Economist, November 22, 1975.
Evergreen Review, October, 1968.
Humanist, September/October, 1976.
Jet, August 20, 1984, September 3, 1984.
Life, February 6, 1970.
Look, January, 1969.
Los Angeles Times, October 5, 1987.
Nation, May 13, 1968, January 20, 1969, August 11, 1969, December 6, 1975.
National Review, December 5, 1975, February 10, 1984.
Negro American Literature Forum, March, 1970.
Negro Digest, June, 1968, October, 1969.
New Leader, March 25, 1968.
New Letters, winter, 1971.
New Republic, March 9, 1968, March 13, 1968, November 30, 1968, January 20, 1979.
Newsweek, December 9, 1968, December 1, 1975, September 11, 1978, August 13, 1979, December 3, 1979.
New York Review of Books, December 19, 1968, May 8, 1969.
New York Times, March 13, 1968, November 27, 1968, December 1, 1968, October 7, 1969, November 1, 1970, September 9, 1972.
New York Times Book Review, March 24, 1968, April 27, 1969.
New York Times Magazine, September 7, 1969, January 16, 1977.
People, March 22, 1982.
Playboy, May, 1968, December, 1968.
Progressive, May, 1968, July, 1969.
Ramparts, May, 1968, June, 1968, December, 1968, September, 1969.
Reader's Digest, September, 1976.
Saturday Evening Post, November 16, 1968.
Saturday Review, March 9, 1968, March 1, 1969.
Spectator, February 2, 1969, September 13, 1969.
Time, April 5, 1968, September 20, 1968.
Times Literary Supplement, February 27, 1969.
Village Voice, April 11, 1968, March 6, 1969.
Washington Post, December 11, 1968.
Yale Review, October, 1968.

*   *   *

CLIFF, Michelle   1946-

PERSONAL: Born November 2, 1946, in Kingston, Jamaica;

American citizen born abroad. *Education:* Wagner College, A.B., 1969; Warburg Institute, London, M.Phil., 1974.

ADDRESSES: Home and office—418 Frederick St., Santa Cruz, Calif. 95062. *Agent*—Charlotte Sheedy Literary Agency, Inc., 145 West 86th St., New York, N.Y. 10024.

CAREER: Life, New York City, reporter and researcher, 1969-70; W. W. Norton & Co., Inc. (publisher), New York City, production supervisor of Norton Library, 1970-71, copy editor, 1974-75, manuscript and production editor, specializing in history, politics, and women's studies, 1975-79; *Sinister Wisdom,* Amherst, Mass., co-publisher and editor, 1981-83; Norwich University, Vermont College Campus, Montpelier, member of cycle faculty for adult degree program, 1983-84; Martin Luther King, Jr., Public Library, Oakland, Calif., teacher of creative writing and history, 1984—. Member of faculty at New School for Social Research, 1974-76, Hampshire College, 1980 and 1981, University of Massachusetts at Amherst, 1980, and Vista College, 1985; speaker at workshops and symposia in United States and abroad.

MEMBER: Authors Guild, Poets and Writers.

AWARDS, HONORS: MacDowell fellow at MacDowell Colony, 1982; fellow of National Endowment for the Arts, 1982, and Massachusetts Artists Foundation, 1984; Eli Kantor fellow at Yaddo, 1984.

WRITINGS:

(Editor) Lillian Smith, *The Winner Names the Age: A Collection of Writings,* Norton, 1978.
Claiming an Identity They Taught Me to Despise (poems), Persephone Press, 1980.
(Author of introduction) Audre Lorde and Adrienne Rich, *Macht und Sinnlichkeit,* Subrosa Frauenverlag, 1983.
Abeng: A Novel, Crossing Press, 1984.
(Contributor) Carol Asher, Louise De Salvo, and Sally Ruddick, editors, *Between Women,* Beacon Press, 1984.
The Land of Look Behind: Prose and Poetry, Firebrand Books, 1985.
No Telephone to Heaven (novel), Dutton, 1987.

Work represented in anthologies, including *Extended Outlooks,* Macmillan, 1983; and *Home Girls,* edited by Barbara Smith, Kitchen Table Press, 1983. Contributor of articles and reviews to magazines, including *Chrysalis, Conditions, Feminary, Sojourner, Heresies,* and *Feminist Review.* Member of editorial board of *Signs: A Journal of Women in Culture and Society,* 1980—.

WORK IN PROGRESS: A book on black women in the visual arts, "particularly the connection with African art and philosophy."

SIDELIGHTS: Michelle Cliff commented: "I received my education in the United States, Jamaica, and England. I have traveled widely in Europe and lived in London from 1971 through 1974. I am proficient in several languages, including French, Italian, and Spanish, and I have a reading knowledge of Latin. My interests, besides creative writing, are black history, especially the survival of African forms and ideas among Afro-American and Afro-Caribbean people, and visual art, particularly the art of the Italian Renaissance and the art of Afro-American women. Along with my present writing projects, I am engaged in preparing a writing course for young black writers in the Oakland, California, community.

"In my writing I am concerned most of all with social issues and political realities and how they affect the lives of people.

Because I am a Jamaican by birth, heritage, and indoctrination, born during the time the island was a British Crown Colony, I have experienced colonialism as a force firsthand. Thus colonialism and the racism upon which it is based are subjects I address in most of my writing.

"In my novel *Abeng* I try to show the evils of colonialism, including the brutalities of slavery, the erasure of the history of a colonized people, and the rifts which occur among colonized peoples. The primary relationship in my book, around which the plot pivots, is that between a light-skinned girl named Clare Savage and a darker girl named Zoe. They have between them a past in which lighter-skinned people become the oppressors of darker people—although both groups are comprised of people of color and both groups have their origins in slavery. Generally speaking, the Creoles of Jamaica, of mixed racial heritage—African and English for the most part, but also of other groups—were placed higher in the social and economic strata of the island by the colonial overlords. Zoe and Clare meet across this divide, sharing at first an idyllic friendship on the country property of Clare's grandmother, on which Zoe, her mother, and her sister are squatters. Gradually—then suddenly—through an incident of violence in which Clare's indoctrination as a member of the almost-ruling class is shown, the split between the two girls becomes obvious. The novel ends with Clare only barely aware of who she is in this society, but certain that something is wrong in her homeland and with her people.

"While most of the actual events of the book are fiction, emotionally the book is an autobiography. I was a girl similar to Clare and have spent most of my life and most of my work exploring my identity as a light-skinned Jamaican, the privilege and the damage that comes from that identity. For while identification with the status of oppressor can be seen as privilege and brings with it opportunities denied oppressed people, it also inflicts damage on the privileged person. In *No Telephone to Heaven,* my sequel to *Abeng,* I take Clare Savage into her thirties through a journey in which she rejects the privilege offered her and seeks both wholeness as a person of color and a recommitment to her country.

"I am also interested in black women as visual artists, particularly in the survival of African art forms and in African philosophical and religious principles among Afro-American artists. This reflects my continuing interest in history and my growing awareness of how much of history is submerged, how much written history is distorted. I see, for example, that the leadership positions held by many Afro-American women in the abolitionist movement, the civil rights movement, and the anti-lynching movement are similar to the roles that have been assumed by women in West African societies. The book I am writing on this subject will deal with visual art, but also with the larger questions of the historic role of black American women, the values they have conveyed, the social responsibility they have assumed."

BIOGRAPHICAL/CRITICAL SOURCES:

PERIODICALS

Los Angeles Times Book Review, September 6, 1987.
New York Times Book Review, July 15, 1987.
Washington Post Book World, August 2, 1987.

*   *   *

CLIFTON, (Thelma) Lucille   1936-

PERSONAL: Born June 27, 1936, in Depew, N.Y.; daughter

of Samuel Louis, Sr. (a laborer) and Thelma (a laborer; maiden name, Moore) Sayles; married Fred James Clifton (an educator, writer, and artist), May 10, 1958 (died November 10, 1984); children: Sidney, Fredrica, Channing, Gillian, Graham, Alexia. *Education:* Attended Howard University, 1953-55, and Fredonia State Teachers College (now State University of New York College at Fredonia), 1955.

ADDRESSES: Agent—Marilyn Marlow, Curtis Brown Ltd., 10 Astor Pl., New York, N.Y. 10003.

CAREER: New York State Division of Employment, Buffalo, claims clerk, 1958-60; U.S. Office of Education, Washington, D.C., literature assistant for CAREL (Central Atlantic Regional Educational Laboratory), 1969-71; Coppin State College, Baltimore, Md., poet in residence, 1971-74; writer. Visiting writer, Columbia University School of the Arts; Jerry Moore Visiting Writer, George Washington University, 1982-83; University of California, Santa Cruz, professor of literature and creative writing, 1985—. Trustee, Enoch Pratt Free Library, Baltimore.

MEMBER: International PEN, Authors Guild, Authors League of America.

AWARDS, HONORS: Discovery Award, New York YW-YMHA Poetry Center, 1969; *Good Times: Poems* cited as one of the year's ten best books by the *New York Times*, 1969; National Endowment for the Arts awards, 1970 and 1972; Poet Laureate of the State of Maryland, 1979-82; Juniper Prize, 1980; Coretta Scott King Award, 1984, for *Everett Anderson's Goodbye.* Honorary degrees from University of Maryland and Towson State University.

WRITINGS:

ADULTS

Good Times: Poems, Random House, 1969.
Good News about the Earth: New Poems, Random House, 1972.
An Ordinary Woman (poetry), Random House, 1974.
Generations: A Memoir (prose), Random House, 1976.
Two-Headed Woman (poetry), University of Massachusetts Press, 1980.
Good Woman: Poems and a Memoir, 1969-1980, Boa Editions, 1987.
Next: New Poems, Boa Editions, 1987.

JUVENILES

The Black BCs (alphabet poems), Dutton, 1970.
Good, Says Jerome, illustrations by Stephanie Douglas, Dutton, 1973.
All Us Come Cross the Water, pictures by John Steptoe, Holt, 1973.
Don't You Remember?, illustrations by Evaline Ness, Dutton, 1973.
The Boy Who Didn't Believe in Spring, pictures by Brinton Turkle, Dutton, 1973.
The Times They Used to Be, illustrations by Susan Jeschke, Holt, 1974.
My Brother Fine with Me, illustrations by Moneta Barnett, Holt, 1975.
Three Wishes, illustrations by Douglas, Viking, 1976.
Amifika, illustrations by Thomas DiGrazia, Dutton, 1977.
The Lucky Stone, illustrations by Dale Payson, Delacorte, 1979.
My Friend Jacob, illustrations by DiGrazia, Dutton, 1980.
Sonora Beautiful, illustrations by Michael Garland, Dutton, 1981.

"EVERETT ANDERSON" SERIES; JUVENILE

Some of the Days of Everett Anderson, Holt, 1970.
Everett Anderson's Christmas Coming, illustrations by Ness, Holt, 1971.
Everett Anderson's Year, illustrations by Ann Grifalconi, Holt, 1974.
Everett Anderson's Friend, illustrations by Grifalconi, Holt, 1976.
Everett Anderson's 1 2 3, illustrations by Grifalconi, Holt, 1977.
Everett Anderson's Nine Month Long, illustrations by Grifalconi, Holt, 1978.
Everett Anderson's Goodbye, illustrations by Grifalconi, Holt, 1983.

OTHER

(Contributor) Marlo Thomas and others, *Free to Be . . . You and Me,* McGraw-Hill, 1974.
(Contributor) Langston Hughes and Arna Bontemps, *Poetry of the Negro, 1746-1970,* Doubleday, 1970.

Also contributor to *Free to Be a Family,* 1987, *Norton Anthology of Literature by Women, Coming into the Light,* and *Stealing the Language.* Contributor of fiction to *Negro Digest, Redbook, House and Garden,* and *Atlantic.* Contributor of nonfiction to *Ms.* and *Essence.*

SIDELIGHTS: Lucille Clifton "began composing and writing stories at an early age and has been much encouraged by an ever-growing reading audience and a fine critical reputation," writes Wallace R. Peppers in a *Dictionary of Literary Biography* essay. "In many ways her themes are traditional: she writes of her family because she is greatly interested in making sense of their lives and relationships; she writes of adversity and success in the ghetto community; and she writes of her role as a poet." Clifton's work emphasizes endurance and strength through adversity. Ronald Baughman suggests in his *Dictionary of Literary Biography* essay that "Clifton's pride in being black and in being a woman helps her transform difficult circumstances into a qualified affirmation about the black urban world she portrays." Writing in Mari Evans's *Black Women Writers (1950-1980): A Critical Evaluation,* Haki Madhubuti (formerly Don L. Lee) states: "She is a writer of complexity, and she makes her readers work and think. Her poetry has a quiet force without being pushy or alien. Whether she is cutting through family relationships, surviving American racial attitudes, or just simply renewing love ties, she puts something heavy on your mind. The great majority of her published poetry is significant. At the base of her work is concern for the Black family, especially the destruction of its youth. Her eye is for the uniqueness of our people, always concentrating on the small strengths that have allowed us to survive the horrors of Western life."

Clifton's first volume of poetry, *Good Times: Poems,* which was cited by the *New York Times* as one of 1969's ten best books, is described by Peppers as a "varied collection of character sketches written with third person narrative voices." Baughman notes that "these poems attain power not only through their subject matter but also through their careful techniques; among Clifton's most successful poetic devices . . . are the precise evocative images that give substance to her rhetorical statements and a frequent duality of vision that lends complexity to her portraits of place and character." Calling the book's title "ironic," Baughman indicates, "Although the urban ghetto can, through its many hardships, create figures who are tough enough to survive and triumph, the overriding concern of this book is with the horrors of the location, with the human carnage that results from such problems as poverty, unemployment, substandard housing, and inadequate education.'' Baughman recognizes that although ''these portraits of human devastation reflect the trying circumstances of life in the ghetto . . . the writer also records some joy in her world, however strained and limited that joy might be.'' Madhubuti thinks that although this is her first book of poetry, it ''cannot be looked upon as simply a 'first effort.' The work is unusually compacted and memory-evoking.'' As Johari Amini (formerly Jewel C. Latimore) suggests in *Black World*, ''The poetry is filled with the sensations of coming up black with the kind of love that keeps you from dying in desperation.''

In Clifton's second volume of poetry, *Good News about the Earth: New Poems,* ''the elusive good times seem more attainable,'' remarks Baughman, who summarizes the three sections into which the book is divided: the first section ''focuses on the sterility and destruction of 'white ways,' newly perceived through the social upheavals of the early 1970s''; the second section ''presents a series of homages to black leaders of the late 1960s and early 1970s''; and the third section ''deals with biblical characters powerfully rendered in terms of the black experience.'' Harriet Jackson Scarupa notes in *Ms.* that after having read what Clifton says about blackness and black pride, some critics ''have concluded that Clifton hates whites. [Clifton] considers this a misreading. When she equates whiteness with death, blackness with life, she says: 'What I'm talking about is a certain kind of white arrogance—and not all white people have it—that is not good. I think airs of superiority are very dangerous. I believe in justice. I try not to be about hatred.''' Writing in *Poetry,* Ralph J. Mills, Jr. says that Clifton's poetic scope transcends the black experience ''to embrace the entire world, human and non-human, in the deep affirmation she makes in the teeth of negative evidence. She is a master of her style, with its spare, elliptical, idiomatic, rhythmical speech, and of prophetic warning in the same language.'' Angela Jackson, who thinks that it ''is a book written in wisdom,'' concludes in *Black World* that ''Clifton and *Good News about the Earth* will make you shake yo head. Ain't nothing else to say.''

An Ordinary Woman, Clifton's third collection of poems, ''abandons many of the broad racial issues examined in the two preceding books and focuses instead on the narrower but equally complex issues of the writer's roles as woman and poet,'' says Baughman. Peppers notes that ''the poems take as their theme a historical, social, and spiritual assessment of the current generation in the genealogical line'' of Clifton's great great-grandmother who had been taken from her home in Dahomey, West Africa, and brought to America in slavery in 1830. Peppers notes that by taking an ordinary experience and personalizing it, ''Clifton has elevated the experience into a public confession'' which may be shared, and ''it is this shared sense of situation, an easy identification between speaker and reader, that heightens the notion of ordinariness and gives. . . the collection an added dimension.'' Helen Vendler writes in the *New York Times Book Review* that ''Clifton recalls for us those bare places we have all waited as 'ordinary women,' with no choices but yes or no, no art, no grace, no words, no reprieve.'' ''Written in the same ironic, yet cautiously optimistic spirit as her earlier published work,'' observes Peppers, the book is ''lively, full of vigor, passion, and an all-consuming honesty.''

In *Generations: A Memoir,* ''it is as if [Clifton] were showing us a cherished family album and telling us the story about each person which seemed to sum him or her up best,'' says a *New Yorker* contributor. Calling the book an ''eloquent eulogy of [Clifton's] parents,'' Reynolds Price writes in the *New York Times Book Review* that ''as with most elegists, her purpose is perpetuation and celebration, not judgment. There is no attempt to see either parent whole; no attempt at the recovery of history not witnessed by or told to the author. There is no sustained chronological narrative. Instead, clusters of brief anecdote gather round two poles, the deaths of father and mother.'' Price, however, believes that *Generations* stands ''worthily'' among the other modern elegies which assert that ''we may survive, some lively few, if we've troubled to *be* alive and loved.'' However, a contributor to *Virginia Quarterly Review* thinks that the book is ''more than an elegy or a personal memoir. It is an attempt on the part of one woman to retrieve, and lyrically to celebrate, her Afro-American heritage.''

''Clifton is a poet of a literary tradition which includes such varied poets as Walt Whitman, Emily Dickinson, and Gwendolyn Brooks, who have inspired and informed her work,'' writes Audrey T. McCluskey in Evans's *Black Women Writers (1950-1980).* McCluskey finds that ''Clifton's belief in her ability (and ours) to make things better and her belief in the concept of personal responsibility pervade her work. These views are especially pronounced in her books for children.'' Clifton's books for children are characterized by a positive view of black heritage and an urban setting peopled by nontraditional families. Critics recognize that although her works speak directly to a specific audience, they reveal the concerns of all children. In a *Language Arts* interview with Rudine Sims, Clifton was asked where she gets her ideas for stories: ''Well, I had six kids in seven years, and when you have a lot of children, you tend to attract children, and you see so many kids, you get ideas from that. And I have such a good memory from my own childhood, my own time. I have great respect for young people; I like them enormously.''

Clifton's books for children are designed to help them understand their world. *My Friend Jacob,* for instance, is a story ''in which a black child speaks with affection and patience of his friendship with a white adolescent neighbor . . . who is retarded,'' writes Zena Sutherland in *Bulletin of the Center for Children's Books.* ''Jacob is Sam's 'very very best friend' and all of his best qualities are appreciated by Sam, just as all of his limitations are accepted . . . it is strong in the simplicity and warmth with which a handicapped person is loved rather than pitied, enjoyed rather than tolerated.'' Critics find that Clifton's characters and their relationships are accurately and positively drawn. Ismat Abdal-Haqq notes in *Interracial Books for Children Bulletin* that ''the two boys have a strong relationship filled with trust and affection. The author depicts this relationship and their everyday adventures in a way that is unmarred by the mawkish sentimentality that often characterizes tales of the mentally disabled.'' And a contributor to *Reading Teacher* states that ''in a matter-of-fact, low-keyed style, we discover how [Sam and Jacob] help one another grow and understand the world.''

Clifton's children's books also facilitate an understanding of black heritage specifically, which in turn fosters an important link with the past generally. Her *All Us Come Cross the Water,* for example, ''in a very straight-forward way . . . shows the relationship of Africa to Blacks in the U.S. without geting into a heavy rap about 'Pan-Africanism,''' states Judy Richardson in the *Journal of Negro Education,* adding that Clifton ''seems able to get inside a little boy's head, and knows how to represent that on paper.'' An awareness of one's origins figures also in *The Times They Used to Be*. Called a "short and impeccable vignette—laced with idiom and humor of rural Black folk,'' by Rosalind K. Goddard in *School Library Journal*, it is further described by Lee A. Daniels in the *Washington Post* as a "story in which a young girl catches her first glimpse of the new technological era in a hardware store window, and learns of death and life.'' "Most books that awaken adult nostalgia are not as appealing to young readers,'' says Sutherland in *Bulletin of the Center for Children's Books*, "but this brief story has enough warmth and vitality and humor for any reader.''

In addition to quickening an awareness of black heritage, Clifton's books for children frequently include an element of fantasy as well. Writing about *Three Wishes*, in which a young girl finds a lucky penny on New Year's Day and makes three wishes upon it, Christopher Lehmann-Haupt in the *New York Times Book Review* calls it "an urbanized version of the traditional tale in which the first wish reveals the power of the magic object . . . the second wish is a mistake, and the third undoes the second.'' Lehmann-Haupt adds that "too few children's books for blacks justify their ethnicity, but this one is a winning blend of black English and bright illustration.'' And *The Lucky Stone*, in which a lucky stone provides good fortune for all of its owners, is decribed by Ruth K. MacDonald in *School Library Journal* as: "Four short stories about four generations of Black women and their dealings with a lucky stone. . . . Clifton uses as a frame device a grandmother telling the history of the stone to her granddaughter; by the end, the granddaughter has inherited the stone herself.'' A contributor to *Interracial Books for Children Bulletin* states that "the concept of past and present is usually hard for children to grasp but this book puts the passing of time in a perspective that children can understand. . . . This book contains information on various aspects of Black culture—slavery, religion and extended family—all conveyed in a way that is both positive and accurate.'' Michele Slung writes in the *Washington Post Book World* that the book "is at once talisman and anthology: over the years it has gathered unto it story after story, episodes indicating its power, both as a charm and as a unit of oral tradition. Clifton has a knack for projecting strong positive values without seeming too goody-goody; her poet's ear is one fact in this, her sense of humor another.''

While Clifton's books for children emphasize an understanding of the past, they also focus on the present. Her series of books about Everett Anderson, for instance, explore the experiences of a young child's world in flux. Writing in *Language Arts* about *Everett Anderson's 1 2 3*, in which a young boy's mother considers remarriage, Ruth M. Stein notes that "previous books contained wistful references to Everett Anderson's absent daddy; the latest one tells how the worried little boy gradually became reconciled to the idea of a new father joining the family.'' And writing about *Everett Anderson's Nine Month Long*, which concerns the anticipated birth of the family's newest member, a contributor to *Interracial Books for Children Bulletin* considers that "this book, written in wonderful poetic style . . . projects a warm, loving, understanding and supportive family.'' Joan W. Blos, who feels that "the establishment of an active, effective, and supportive male figure is an important part of this story,'' adds in *School Library Journal*, "So is its tacit acknowledgment that, for the younger child, a mother's pregnancy means disturbing changes now as well as a sibling later.'' However, just as the

birth of a sibling can cause upheaval in a child's world, so, too, can death. In *Everett Anderson's Goodbye*, Everett has difficulty coping with the death of his father; he "misses his Daddy, as he moves through the five stages of grief: denial, anger, bargaining, depression and acceptance,'' writes a *Washington Post Book World* contributor.

Barbara Walker writes in *Interracial Books for Children Bulletin* that "Clifton is a gifted poet with the greater gift of being able to write poetry for children.'' Clifton indicates to Sims that she doesn't think of it as poetry especially for children, though. "It seems to me that if you write poetry for children, you have to keep too many things in mind other than the poem. So I'm just writing a poem.'' *Some of the Days of Everett Anderson* is a book of nine poems, about which Marjorie Lewis observes in *School Library Journal*, "Some of the days of six-year-old 'ebony Everett Anderson' are happy; some lonely—but all of them are special, reflecting the author's own pride in being black.'' In the *New York Times Book Review*, Hoyt W. Fuller thinks that Clifton has "a profoundly simple way of saying all that is important to say, and we know that the struggle is worth it, that the all-important battle of image is being won, and that the future of all those beautiful black children out there need not be twisted and broken.'' *Everett Anderson's Christmas Coming* concerns Christmas preparations in which "each of the five days before Everett's Christmas is decribed by a verse,'' says Anita Silvey in the *Horn Book*, observing that "the overall richness of Everett's experiences dominates the text.'' Jane O'Reilly suggests in the *New York Times Book Review* that "Everett Anderson, black and boyish, is glimpsed, rather than explained through poems about him.'' *Everett Anderson's Year* celebrates "a year in the life of a city child . . . in appealing verses,'' says Beryl Robinson in *Horn Book*, adding that "mischief, fun, gaiety, and poignancy are a part of his days as the year progresses. The portrayals of child and mother are lively and solid, executed with both strength and tenderness.''

Language is important in Clifton's writing. In answer to Sim's question about the presence of both black and white children in her work, Clifton responds specifically about *Sonora Beautiful*, which is about the insecurities and dissatisfaction of an adolescent girl and which has only white characters: "In this book, I *heard* the characters as white. I have a tendency to *hear* the language of the characters, and then I know something about who the people are.'' However, regarding objections to the black vernacular she often uses, Clifton tells Sims: "I do not write out of weakness. That is to say, I do not write the language I write because I don't know any other. . . . But I have a certain integrity about my art, and in *my* art you have to be honest and you have to have people talking the way they really talk. So all of my books are not in the same language.'' Asked by Sims whether or not she feels any special pressures or special opportunities as a black author, Clifton responds: "I do feel a responsibility. . . . First, I'm going to write books that tend to celebrate life. I'm about that. And I wish to have children see people like themselves in books. . . . I also take seriously the responsibility of not lying. . . . I'm not going to say that life is wretched if circumstance is wretched, because that's not true. So I take that responsibility, but it's a responsibility to the truth, and to my art as much as anything. I owe everybody that. . . . It's the truth as I see it, and that's what my responsibility is.''

"Browsing through a volume of Lucille Clifton's poems or reading one of her children's books to my son,'' says Scarupa, "always makes me feel good: good to be black, good to be a woman, good to be alive.'' ''I am excited about her work because she reflects me; she tells my story in a way and with an eloquence that is beyond my ability,'' concurs Madhubuti, who concludes: ''To be original, relevant, and revolutionary in the mouth of fire is the mark of a dangerous person. Lucille Clifton is a poet of *mean* talent who has not let her gifts separate her from the work at hand. She is a teacher and an example. To read her is to give birth to bright seasons.'' Clifton, herself, has commented on her role as a poet in *Black Women Writers (1950-1980)*: ''I am interested in trying to render big ideas in a simple way . . . in being understood not admired. I wish to celebrate and not be celebrated (though a little celebration is a lot of fun). I am a woman and I write from that experience. I am a Black woman and I write from that experience. I do not feel inhibited or bound by what I am.'' She adds: ''Sometimes I think that the most anger comes from ones who were late in discovering that when the world said nigger it meant them too. I grew up knowing that the world meant me too but that was the world's insanity and not mine. I have been treated in publishing very much like other poets are treated, that is, not really very well. I continue to write since my life as a human only includes my life as a poet, it doesn't depend on it.''

BIOGRAPHICAL/CRITICAL SOURCES:

BOOKS

Beckles, Frances N., *20 Black Women,* Gateway Press, 1978.
Children's Literature Review, Volume V, Gale, 1983.
Contemporary Literary Criticism, Volume IX, Gale, 1981.
Dictionary of Literary Biography, Gale, Volume V: *American Poets since World War II,* 1980, Volume XLI: *Afro-American Poets since 1955,* 1985.
Dreyer, Sharon Spredemann, *The Bookfinder: A Guide to Children's Literature about the Needs and Problems of Youth Aged 2-15,* Volume I, American Guidance Service, 1977.
Evans, Mari, editor, *Black Women Writers (1950-1980): A Critical Evaluation,* Doubleday-Anchor, 1984.

PERIODICALS

America, May 1, 1976.
Black Scholar, March, 1981.
Black World, July, 1970, February, 1973.
Book World, March 8, 1970, November 8, 1970, November 11, 1973, November 10, 1974, December 8, 1974, December 11, 1977, September 14, 1980, July 20, 1986, May 10, 1987.
Bulletin of the Center for Children's Books, March, 1971, November, 1974, March, 1976, September, 1980.
Horn Book, December, 1971, August, 1973, February, 1975, December, 1975, October, 1977.
Interracial Books for Children Bulletin, Volume V, numbers 7 and 8, 1975, Volume VII, number 1, 1976, Volume VIII, number 1, 1977, Volume X, number 5, 1979, Volume XI, numbers 1 and 2, 1980, Volume XII, number 2, 1981.
Journal of Negro Education, summer, 1974.
Journal of Reading, February, 1977, December, 1986.
Kirkus Reviews, April 15, 1970, October 1, 1970, December 15, 1974, April 15, 1976, February 15, 1982.
Language Arts, January, 1978, February 2, 1982.
Ms., October, 1976.
New Yorker, April 5, 1976.
New York Times, December 20, 1976.

New York Times Book Review, September 6, 1970, December 6, 1970, December 5, 1971, November 4, 1973, April 6, 1975, March 14, 1976, May 15, 1977.
Poetry, May, 1973.
Reading Teacher, October, 1978, March, 1981.
Redbook, November, 1969.
Saturday Review, December 11, 1971, August 12, 1972, December 4, 1973.
School Library Journal, May, 1970, December, 1970, September, 1974, December, 1977, February, 1979, March, 1980.
Tribune Books, August 30, 1987.
Virginia Quarterly Review, fall, 1976.
Voice of Youth Advocates, April, 1982.
Washington Post, November 10, 1974, August 9, 1979.
Washington Post Book World, February 10, 1980.
Western Humanities Review, summer, 1970.

—*Sketch by Sharon Malinowski*

*   *   *

COLEMAN, Emmett
See REED, Ishmael

*   *   *

COLEMAN, Wanda   1946-

PERSONAL: Born November 13, 1946, in Los Angeles, Calif.; daughter of George (in advertising) and Lewana (a seamstress; maiden name, Scott) Evans; children: Anthony, Tunisia, Ian Wayne Grant. *Education:* Attended California State College at Los Angeles (now California State University, Los Angeles), 1964, Los Angeles City College, 1967, and various workshops.

ADDRESSES: Home—P.O. Box 29154, Los Angeles, Calif. 90029.

CAREER: Writer and performer. Worked as production editor, proofreader, magazine editor, waitress, and assistant recruiter for Peace Corps/Vista, 1968-75; staff writer for ''Days of Our Lives,'' National Broadcasting Co. (NBC-TV), 1975-76; medical transcriber and insurance billing clerk, 1979-84. Writer in residence at Studio Watts, 1968-69; co-host of interview program for Pacific Radio, 1981—.

MEMBER: P.E.N.

AWARDS, HONORS: Named to Open Door Program Hall of Fame, 1975; Emmy Award for best writing in a daytime drama from Academy of Television Arts and Sciences, 1976, for ''Days of Our Lives''; fellowships from National Endowment for the Arts, 1981-82, and Guggenheim Foundation, 1984.

WRITINGS:

Art in the Court of the Blue Fag (chapbook), Black Sparrow Press, 1977.
Mad Dog Black Lady, Black Sparrow Press, 1979.
Imagoes, Black Sparrow Press, 1983.
Heavy Daughter Blues: Poems and Stories, 1968-1986, Black Sparrow Press, 1987.

Also author of ''The Time Is Now'' episode for ''The Name of the Game,'' NBC-TV, 1970.

SIDELIGHTS: Wanda Coleman is known in the Los Angeles area for her poetry and her poetry readings. ''As a poet,'' she related ''I have gained a reputation, locally, as an electrifying performer/reader, and have appeared at local rock clubs, reading the same poetry that has taken me into classrooms and community centers for over one hundred public readings since 1973.'' Critics seem to agree that Coleman is an exciting artist. Stephen Kessler wrote in *Bachy* that Coleman ''shows us scary and exciting realms of ourselves,'' and Holly Prado noted in the *Los Angeles Times* that Coleman's ''heated and economical language and head-on sensibility take her work beyond brutality to fierce dignity.''

Coleman also commented: ''Words seem inadequate in expressing the anger and outrage I feel at the persistent racism that permeates every aspect of black American life. Since words are what I am best at, I concern myself with this as an urban actuality as best I can.''

BIOGRAPHICAL/CRITICAL SOURCES:

PERIODICALS

Bachy, fall, 1979, spring, 1980.
Los Angeles, April, 1983.
Los Angeles Times, September 15, 1969, November 26, 1973, January 31, 1982, November 13, 1983.
Stern, May 16, 1974.

*   *   *

COLTER, Cyrus   1910-

PERSONAL: Born January 8, 1910, in Noblesville, Ind.; son of James Alexander and Ethel Marietta (Bassett) Colter; married Imogene MacKay, January 1, 1943. *Education:* Attended Youngstown and Ohio State Universities; Chicago-Kent College of Law, LL.B., 1940.

ADDRESSES: Home—1115 South Plymouth Court, Chicago, Ill. 6060ʒ.

CAREER: Deputy collector of internal revenue, Chicago, Ill., 1940-42; attorney in Chicago, 1946—; Northwestern University, Evanston, Ill., Chester D. Tripp Professor of Humanities, 1973-78, professor emeritus 1978—; writer. Associated with Young Men's Christian Association (YMCA) in Youngstown, Ohio, 1932-34, and in Chicago, 1934-40; consultant to American Telephone and Telegraph (AT&T), 1974—; chairman of Illinois Emergency Transport Board; member of Administrative Conference of the United States. Member of board of trustees, Chicago Symphony Orchestra, WTTW (public television station in Chicago), Great Books Foundation, and Illinois Humanities Council; vice-chairman of citizens committee of Chicago Public Library. *Military service:* U.S. Army, 1942-46; became captain.

MEMBER: National Association of Regulatory Utility Commissioners (member of Commission on Railroads), National Association for the Advancement of Colored People (NAACP), Chicago Urban League, Chicago Bar Association, Chicago Historical Society (member of board), Commercial Club, Cliff Dwellers Club, Kappa Alpha Psi.

AWARDS, HONORS: Fiction prize from University of Iowa School of Letters and Robert F. Ferguson Memorial Award from Friends of Literature, both 1971, both for *The Beach Umbrella;* D.Litt. from University of Illinois at Chicago Circle, 1977; Carl Sandburg Literary Arts Award from Friends of the Chicago Public Library, 1980, for *Night Studies.*

WRITINGS:

The Beach Umbrella (stories), University of Iowa Press, 1970.

The River of Eros (novel), Swallow Press, 1972.
The Hippodrome (novel), Swallow Press, 1973.
Night Studies (novel), Swallow Press, 1979.
A Chocolate Soldier (novel), Thunder's Mouth, 1988.

Contributor to anthologies; contributor of stories to magazines. Member of editorial board of *Chicago Reporter.*

SIDELIGHTS: Cyrus Colter's *Night Studies,* writes Walter Sublette in *Chicago Tribune Book World,* ''is mainly about the human side of blacks living in contemporary America. It is a realistic novel of characterization, not social or political ideology, with complex racial subjects interwoven as adjuncts in the lives of its people.'' In a *Times Literary Supplement* review, Sandra Salmans criticizes what she sees as the book's excessive length, commenting that the author operates ''on the theory that three words are thrice as good as one.'' Yet Salmans finds what ultimately redeems the novel is Colter's ''ambitiousness and obvious sincerity.'' Sublette concludes that *Night Studies* ''is a remarkable accomplishment, . . . refreshingly free of slanted rhetoric and racial stereotype, pleasantly absent of a dominating polemic.''

BIOGRAPHICAL/CRITICAL SOURCES:

PERIODICALS

Chicago Tribune, May 11, 1988.
Chicago Tribune Book World, January 13, 1980.
National Observer, July 8, 1972.
Negro Digest, January, 1968.
Times Literary Supplement, August 1, 1980.

*   *   *

COOK, (Will) Mercer   1903-1987

PERSONAL: Born March 30, 1903, in Washington, D.C.; died October 4, 1987, of pneumonia in Washington, D.C.; son of William Marion and Abbie (Mitchell) Cook; married Vashti Smith (a social worker), August 31, 1929 (died, 1969); children: Mercer, Jacques. *Education:* Amherst College, B.A., 1925; University of Paris, diploma, 1926; Brown University, M.A., 1931, Ph.D., 1936. *Religion:* Roman Catholic.

ADDRESSES: Home—4811 Blagden Ave. N.W., Washington, D.C. 20001. *Office*—Department of Romance Languages, Howard University, Washington, D.C.

CAREER: Howard University, Washington, D.C., assistant professor, 1927-36; Atlanta University, Atlanta, Ga., professor of French, 1936-43; University of Haiti, Port-au-Prince, professor of English, 1943-45; Howard University, professor of romance languages, 1945-60; U.S. ambassador to the Republic of Niger, 1961-64, and to Senegal and Gambia, 1964-66; Howard University, professor of romance languages and head of department, 1966-70, professor emeritus, 1970-87. Foreign representative, American Society for African Culture, 1958-60; director of African program, Congress for Cultural Freedom, 1960-61; alternate delegate to United Nations General Assembly, 1963; visiting professor, Harvard University, 1969-70.

MEMBER: Association for the Study of Negro Life and History, American Society of Composers, Authors and Publishers (ASCAP), American Association of Teachers of French, National Association for the Advancement of Colored People (NAACP), Phi Beta Kappa.

AWARDS, HONORS: Received decorations from the Government of Haiti, 1945, the Republic of Niger, 1964, and Senegal, 1966; awarded Palmes Academiques (France), LL.D. from Amherst College, 1965, and Brown University, 1970.

WRITINGS:

Five French Negro Authors (criticism), Associated Publishers, 1943.
Handbook for Haitian Teachers of English, H. Deschamps (Port-au-Prince), 1944.
Education in Haiti, Federal Security Agency, Office of Education, 1948.
(With Stephen Henderson) *The Militant Black Writer in Africa and the United States* (criticism), University of Wisconsin Press, 1969.

EDITOR

Le Noir: Morceaux choisis de vingt-neuf francais celebres, American Book Co., 1934.
Portraits americains, Heath, 1939.
The Haitian-American Anthology: Haitian Readings from American Authors, Imprimerie de l'Etat, 1944.
An Introduction to Haiti, Department of Cultural Affairs, Pan American Union, 1951.

TRANSLATOR

Leopold Senghor, *African Socialism,* American Society of African Culture, 1959.
Mamadou Dia, *The African Nations and World Solidarity,* Praeger, 1961, reprinted, 1987.
(And editor) Cheikh A. Diop, *The African Origin of Civilization: Myth or Reality?,* Lawrence Hill, 1974.

OTHER

Also author of *The Haitian Novel* (criticism), for Gordon. Contributor to *Journal of Negro History, Journal of Human Relations, Negro Digest, Opportunity, Phylon,* and *Crisis.*

SIDELIGHTS: Before his retirement from Howard University, Mercer Cook co-authored *The Militant Black Writer in Africa and the United States* with Stephen Henderson of Morehouse College. Hoyt Fuller in the *New York Times Book Review* noted that the book contains two excellent essays that are "expanded and edited versions of addresses delivered by the authors during the 1968 Conference on Afro-American Culture at the University of Wisconsin." Fuller further credited Cook with "drawing on his long experience as student and professor of African literature, as ambassador to two African nations, and as a personal friend to many of this century's African men of letters." *The Militant Black Writer in Africa and the United States* is, said Fuller, "all that those with a genuine interest in black literature, its past and its future need as an introduction to a rich and rewarding field of study."

BIOGRAPHICAL/CRITICAL SOURCES:

PERIODICALS

Crisis, April, 1957, December, 1963.
New York Times Book Review, October 19, 1969.

OBITUARIES:

PERIODICALS

New York Times, October 7, 1987.
Washington Post, October 6, 1987.

COOMBS, Orde M.   1939(?)-1984

PERSONAL: Born in St. Vincent, West Indies; died August 27, 1984 in New York, N.Y. *Education:* Yale University, B.A., 1965; graduate study at Clare College, Cambridge, 1965-66; New York University, M.A., 1971.

ADDRESSES: Office—755 Second Ave., New York, N.Y. 10016.

CAREER: Producer of documentaries dealing with West Indian culture, 1958-61; Doubleday & Co., New York City, associate editor, 1966-68; Western Electric Co., New York City, senior public relations specialist, 1968-69; McCall Publishing Co., New York City, senior editor, 1969-71. Adjunct lecturer, New York University, 1973. Co-host for "Black Conversations" (talk show), WPIX-TV, 1975.

AWARDS, HONORS: Alicia Patterson Award, 1974; media award for public service reporting, 1974.

WRITINGS:

NONFICTION

(With John H. Garabedian) *Eastern Religions in the Electric Age,* Grosset, 1968.
Do You See My Love for You Growing?, Dodd, 1972.
(With Chester Higgins, Jr.) *Drums of Life,* Doubleday, 1974.
Sleep Late with Your Dreams, Doubleday, 1977.
(With Chester Higgins, Jr.) *Some Time Ago; A Historical Portrait of Black Americans from 1850-1950,* Doubleday, 1980.

EDITOR

We Speak as Liberators: Young Black Poets, Dodd, 1970.
What We Must See: Young Black Storytellers, Dodd, 1971.
Is Massa Day Dead? Black Moods in the Caribbean, Doubleday, 1974.

OTHER

(Contributor) Mel Watkins, editor, *Black Review No. 2,* Morrow, 1971.

Contributor to periodicals, including *New York Times, Harper's,* and *Black World.* Contributing editor for *New York* magazine.

SIDELIGHTS: Liz Grant notes that Orde Coombs dealt with "some of the toughest and longest standing problems we [blacks] have" in the series of eleven essays which comprise *Do You See My Love for You Growing?* Gant praises Coombs for having "stirred up some things that never should have been allowed to lie still," such as the "inability to protect ourselves [and] . . . the inability to come together on common ground."

BIOGRAPHICAL/CRITICAL SOURCES:

PERIODICALS

Black World, February, 1973.
New York Times, February 6, 1981.
New York Times Book Review, June 20, 1971.

OBITUARIES:

PERIODICALS

September 1, 1984.

COOPER, J. California

PERSONAL: Born in Berkeley, Calif.; daughter of Joseph C. and Maxine Rosemary Cooper; children: Paris A. Williams. *Education:* Attended technical high school and various colleges. *Politics:* None. *Religion:* Christian.

CAREER: Writer.

WRITINGS:

A Piece of Mine (stories), Alice Walker, 1984.
Homemade Love, St. Martin's, 1986.
Some Soul to Keep, St. Martin's, 1987.

Also author of plays in anthology *Center Stage.*

WORK IN PROGRESS: A novel; a collection of short stories for children; a collection of stories for adults.

* * *

CORNISH, Sam(uel James) 1935-

PERSONAL: Born December 22, 1935, in Baltimore, Md.; son of Herman and Sarah Cornish; married Jean Faxon, September, 1967. *Education:* Attended schools in Baltimore, Md., Goddard College, Vt., and Northwestern University.

ADDRESSES: Home—50 Monastery Rd., Brighton, Mass. 02135. *Office*—Department of English, Emerson College, 100 Beacon St., Boston, Mass. 02116.

CAREER: Enoch Pratt Library, Baltimore, Md., writing specialist, 1965-66, 1968-69; bookseller, 1966-67; Central Atlantic Regional Educational Laboratories (CAREL), Washington, D.C., editorial consultant, 1967-68; Highland Park Free School, Roxbury, Mass., teacher of creative writing, 1969—; currently instructor in Afro-American Survey, Emerson College, Boston, Mass.; poet. Former editor of *Chicory* (magazine), for the Enoch Pratt Library, and of *Mimeo,* a poetry magazine. Education Development Center, Open Education Follow Through Project, Newton, Mass., staff adviser and consultant on children's writing, 1973-78; consultant in elementary school teaching, CAREL. *Military service:* U.S. Army Medical Corps, 1958-60.

AWARDS, HONORS: National Endowment for the Arts grant, 1968; poetry prize, Humanities Institute of Coppin State College, 1968.

WRITINGS:

JUVENILES

Your Hand in Mind, illustrated by Carl Owens, Harcourt, 1970.
Grandmother's Pictures, illustrated by Jeanne Johns, Bookstore Press, 1974.
My Daddy's People Were Very Black, illustrated by Johns, Open Education Follow Through Project, Education Development Center, 1976.
Walking the Streets with Mississippi John Hurt, Bradbury, 1978.

Also author of *Harriet Tubman,* published by Third World Press.

VERSE

In This Corner: Sam Cornish and Verses, Fleming-McCallister Press, 1964.
People beneath the Window, Sacco Publishers, 1962, reprinted, 1987.

Generations, and Other Poems, edited by Jean Faxon, Beanbag Press, 1964, enlarged edition with preface by Ruth Whitman published as *Generations: Poems,* Beacon Press, 1971.
Angles, Beanbag Press, 1965.
Winters, Sans Souci Press, 1968.
Short Beers, Beanbag Press, 1969.
A Reason for Intrusion: An Omnibus of Musings from the Files of Sam Cornish, Pamela Williams [and] *Paul D. McAllister,* Fleming-McAllister Publishers, 1969, reprinted, 1987.
Streets, Third World Press, 1973.
Sometimes: Ten Poems, Pym-Randall Press, 1973.
Sam's World: Poems, Decatur House, 1978.
Songs of Jubilee: New and Selected Poems, 1969-1983, Unicorn Press, 1986.

WORK REPRESENTED IN ANTHOLOGIES

LeRoi Jones and Larry Neal, editors, *Black Fire: An Anthology of Afro-American Writing,* Morrow, 1968.
Harry Smith, editor, *Smith Poets,* Horizon Press, 1969.
Clarence Major, editor, *New Black Poetry,* International Publishers, 1969.
George Plimpton and Peter Ardery, editors, *American Literary Anthology 3,* Viking, 1970.
Ted Wilentz and Tom Weatherly, editors, *Natural Process,* Hill & Wang, 1972.
Arnold Adoff, editor, *One Hundred Years of Black Poetry,* Harper, 1972.
A Penguin Anthology of Indian, African, and Afro-American Poetry, Penguin, 1973.
David Alan Evans, editor, *New Voices in American Poetry,* Winthrop, 1973.
Adoff, editor, *Celebrations: A New Anthology of Black American Poetry,* Follett, 1977.

OTHER

(Editor with Lucian W. Dixon) *Chicory: Young Voices from the Black Ghetto* (poetry and prose collection), Association Press, 1969.
(Editor with Hugh Fox, and contributor) *The Living Underground: An Anthology of Contemporary American Poetry,* Ghost Dance Press, 1969.

Contributor of poems and reviews to *Ann Arbor Review, Poetry Review, Journal of Black Poetry, Essence, Boston Review of the Arts,* and Boston newspapers.

SIDELIGHTS: "Sam Cornish emerged as one of the numerous Afro-American poets who gained an audience during the revolution in the arts that took place in the late 1960s," writes Jon Woodson in a *Dictionary of Literary Biography* essay. Calling his poems simple, direct, and honest, Woodson suggests that although he is "not as public a figure as several of the writers in the black arts movement, Cornish produced some of the most profound work to come out of that group. Though his work reflects the dictates of the black aesthetic, with its emphasis on popular speech, social protest, and the celebration of black culture, it is never at the expense of craft, insight, and individuality. Because of the intelligence and clarity of his poems, Cornish has won the interest of a wide reading audience and the admiration of poets of differing schools."

Cornish comments that he has been influenced by Robert Lowell, T. S. Eliot, and LeRoi Jones. He said: "Most of my major themes are of urban life, the Negro predicament here in the cities, and my own family. I try to use a minimum of words to express the intended thought or feeling, with the effect of being starkly frank at times. Main verse form is unrhymed, free.''

BIOGRAPHICAL/CRITICAL SOURCES:

BOOKS

Dictionary of Literary Biography, Volume XLI: *Afro-American Poets since 1955,* Gale, 1985.

PERIODICALS

Black World, July, 1970.
Choice, September, 1978, October, 1986.
Commonweal, May 22, 1970.

*   *   *

CORTEZ, Jayne   1936-

PERSONAL: Born May 10, 1936, in Arizona; children: Denardo Coleman.

ADDRESSES: c/o Bola Press, Box 96, Village Station, New York, N.Y. 10014.

CAREER: Poet. Has lectured and read her poetry alone and with music throughout the United States, Europe, Africa, and the Caribbean.

AWARDS, HONORS: Rockefeller Foundation grant, 1970; Creative Artists Program Service poetry award, New York State Council on the Arts, 1973, 1981; National Endowment for the Arts fellowship in creative writing, 1979-80.

WRITINGS:

POETRY

Pissstained Stairs and the Monkey Man's Wares, Phrase Text, 1969.
Festivals and Funerals, Bola Press, 1971.
Scarifications, Bola Press, 1973, 2nd edition, 1978.
Mouth on Paper, Bola Press, 1977.
Firespitter, Bola Press, 1982.
Coagulations: New and Selected Poems, Thunder's Mouth, 1984.

RECORDINGS

Celebrations and Solitudes: The Poetry of Jayne Cortez, Strata-East Records, 1975.
Unsubmissive Blues, Bola Press, 1980.
There It Is, Bola Press, 1982.

CONTRIBUTOR TO ANTHOLOGIES

Orde Coombs, editor, *We Speak as Liberators,* Dodd, 1970.
Arnold Adoff, editor, *The Poetry of Black America,* Harper, 1972.
Abraham Chapman, editor, *New Black Voices,* New American Library, 1972.
Lindsay Patterson, editor, *A Rock Against the Wind: Black Love Poems,* Dodd, 1973.
Quincy Troupe and Rainer Schulte, editors, *Giant Talk,* Random House, 1975.
Homage a Leon Gontran Damas, Presence Africaine, 1979.
Erlene Stedson, editor, *Black Sister,* Indiana University Press, 1981.
Ann Snitow, Christine Stansell, and Sharon Thompson, editors, *Powers of Desire,* Monthly Review Press, 1983.
Amina Baraka and Amiri Baraka, editors, *Confirmation,* Quill, 1983.

OTHER

Contributor to numerous periodicals, including *Free Spirits, Mother Jones, Unesco Courier, Black Scholar, Heresies,* and *Mundus Artium.*

SIDELIGHTS: Jayne Cortez follows the oral tradition of literature, writing poems intended to be read aloud, often with musical accompaniment. Nikki Giovanni, reviewing Cortez's *Pissstained Stairs and the Monkey Man's Wares* in *Negro Digest,* writes: ''We haven't had many jazz poets who got inside the music and the people who created it. We poet about them, but not of them. And this is Cortez's strength. She can wail from Theodore Navarro and Leadbelly to Ornette and never lose a beat and never make a mistake. She's a genius and all lovers of jazz will need this book—lovers of poetry will want it.''

About Cortez's *Unsubmissive Blues,* Warren Woessner asserts in *Small Press Review* that the record ''is the most accomplished collaboration between a poet and a jazz group that I've listened to in recent years.'' He continues: ''*Unsubmissive Blues* is an unqualified success. The sum of this collaboration is always greater than its individual pieces.''

BIOGRAPHICAL/CRITICAL SOURCES:

PERIODICALS

Detroit News, March 31, 1985.
Negro Digest, December, 1969.
Small Press Review, March, 1981.

*   *   *

COSBY, Bill
See COSBY, William Henry, Jr.

*   *   *

COSBY, William Henry, Jr.   1937-
(Bill Cosby)

PERSONAL: Born July 12, 1937, in Philadelphia, Pa.; son of William Henry (a U.S. Navy mess steward) and Anna Cosby (a domestic worker); married Camille Hanks, January 25, 1964; children: Erika Ranee, Erinn Chalene, Ennis William, Ensa Camille, Evin Harrah. *Education:* Attended Temple University, 1961-62; University of Massachusetts, M.A., 1972, Ed. D., 1977.

ADDRESSES: Agent—The Brokaw Co., 9255 Sunset Blvd., Los Angeles, Calif. 90069.

CAREER: Comedian, actor, and recording artist. Performer in nightclubs, including The Cellar, Philadelphia, Pa., Gaslight Cafe, New York City, Bitter End, New York City, and Hungry i, San Francisco, 1962—; performer in television series for National Broadcasting Co. (NBC-TV), including ''I Spy,'' 1965-68, ''The Bill Cosby Show,'' 1969-71, and ''The Cosby Show,'' 1984—, for Columbia Broadcasting System (CBS-TV), ''The New Bill Cosby Show,'' 1972-73, and American Broadcasting Co. (ABC-TV), ''Cos,'' 1976; actor in motion pictures, including ''Hickey and Boggs,'' 1972, ''Man and Boy,'' 1972, ''Uptown Saturday Night,'' 1974, ''Let's Do It Again,'' 1975, ''Mother, Jugs, and Speed,'' 1976, ''A Piece of the Action,'' 1977, ''California Suite,'' 1978, ''The Devil and Max Devlin,'' 1981, ''Bill Cosby Himself,'' 1985, and ''Leonard Part VI,'' 1987; creator of animated children's programs ''The Fat Albert Show'' and ''Fat Albert and the Cosby

Kids,'' CBS-TV, 1972-84. Performer on ''The Bill Cosby Radio Program,'' television specials ''The First Bill Cosby Special'' and ''The Second Bill Cosby Special,'' in animated feature ''Aesop's Fables,'' in ''An Evening with Bill Cosby'' at Radio City Music Hall, 1986, and in videocassette ''Bill Cosby: 49,'' sponsored by Kodak, 1987. Guest on Public Broadcasting Co. (PBS-TV) children's programs ''Sesame Street'' and ''The Electric Company,'' and NBC-TV's ''Children's Theatre''; host of Picture Pages segment of CBS-TV's ''Captain Kangaroo's Wake Up.'' Commercial spokesman for Jell-O Pudding (General Foods Inc.), Coca-Cola Co., Ford Motor Co., Texas Instruments, E.F. Hutton, and Kodak Film. President of Rhythm and Blues Hall of Fame, 1968. Member of Carnegie Commission for the Future of Public Broadcasting, board of directors of National Council on Crime and Delinquency, Mary Holmes College, and Ebony Showcase Theatre, board of trustees of Temple University, advisory board of Direction Sports, communications council at Howard University, and steering committee of American Sickle Cell foundation. *Military service:* U.S. Navy Medical Corps, 1956-60.

AWARDS, HONORS: Eight Grammy Awards for best comedy album from National Society of Recording Arts and Sciences, including 1964, for ''Bill Cosby Is a Very Funny Fellow . . . Right!,'' 1965, for ''I Started Out as a Child,'' 1966, for ''Why Is There Air?,'' 1967, for ''Revenge,'' and 1969, for ''To Russell, My Brother, Whom I Slept With''; Emmy Award for best actor in a dramatic series from Academy of Television Arts and Sciences, 1965-66, 1966-67, and 1967-68, for ''I Spy''; named ''most promising new male star'' by *Fame* magazine, 1966; Emmy Award, 1969, for ''The First Bill Cosby Special''; Seal of Excellence, Children's Theatre Association, 1973; Ohio State University award, 1975, for ''Fat Albert and the Cosby Kids''; NAACP Image Award, 1976; named ''Star Presenter of 1978'' by *Advertising Age*; Gold Award for Outstanding Children's Program, International Film and Television Festival, 1981, for ''Fat Albert and the Cosby Kids''; Emmy Award for best comedy series, 1985, for ''The Cosby Show''; honorary degree, Brown University; Golden Globe Award, Hollywood Foreign Press Association; four People's Choice Awards; voted ''most believable celebrity endorser'' three times in surveys by Video Storyboard Tests Inc.

WRITINGS—Under name Bill Cosby:

The Wit and Wisdom of Fat Albert, Windmill Books, 1973.
Bill Cosby's Personal Guide to Tennis Power; or, Don't Lower the Lob, Raise the Net, Random House, 1975.
(Contributor) Charlie Shedd, editor, *You Are Somebody Special,* McGraw, 1978, 2nd edition, 1982.
Fatherhood, Doubleday, 1986.
Time Flies, Doubleday, 1987.

Also author of *Fat Albert's Survival Kit.* Author of recordings, including ''Bill Cosby Is a Very Funny Fellow . . . Right!,'' 1964, ''I Started Out as a Child,'' 1965, ''Why Is There Air?,'' 1966, ''Wonderfulness,'' 1967, ''Revenge,'' 1967, ''To Russell, My Brother, Whom I Slept With,'' 1969, ''Bill Cosby Is Not Himself These Days, Rat Own, Rat Own, Rat Own,'' 1976, ''My Father Confused Me . . . What Must I Do? What Must I Do?,'' 1977, ''Disco Bill,'' 1977, ''Bill's Best Friend,'' 1978, and also ''It's True, It's True,'' ''Bill Cosby Himself,'' ''200 MPH,'' ''Silverthroat,'' ''Hooray for the Salvation Army Band,'' ''8:15, 12:15,'' ''For Adults Only,'' ''Bill Cosby Talks to Kids About Drugs,'' and ''Inside the Mind of Bill Cosby.''

WORK IN PROGRESS: A book on love and marriage.

SIDELIGHTS: ''When I was a kid I always used to pay attention to things that other people didn't even think about,'' claims William H. Cosby, Jr. ''I'd remember funny happenings, just little trivial things, and then tell stories about them later. I found I could make people laugh, and I enjoyed doing it because it gave me a sense of security. I thought that if people laughed at what you said, that meant they like you.'' As an adult, Bill Cosby has developed his childhood behavior into a comedic talent that earns him millions of dollars annually for his work in films, television, and commercials.

What Cosby calls his ''storytelling knack'' may have had its roots in his mother's nightly readings of Mark Twain and the Bible to her three sons. Their father, a Navy cook, was gone for long stretches of time, but Anna Cosby did her best to provide a strong moral foundation for the family she raised in Philadelphia's housing projects. Bill Cosby helped with the family's expenses by delivering groceries and shining shoes. His sixth-grade teacher described him as ''an alert boy who would rather clown than study''; nevertheless, he was placed in a class for gifted students when he reached high school. His activities as captain of the track and football teams and member of the baseball and basketball teams continued to distract him from academics, however, and when his tenth-grade year ended, Cosby was told he'd have to repeat the grade. Instead of doing so, he quit school to join the Navy. It was a decision he soon came to regret, and during his four-year hitch in the Navy, Cosby earned his high school diploma through a correspondence course. He then won an athletic scholarship to Temple University in Philadelphia, where he entered as a physical education major in 1961.

Cosby had continued to amuse his schoolmates and shipmates with his tales. He first showcased his humor professionally while a student at Temple, in a five-dollar-a-night job telling jokes and tending bar at ''The Cellar,'' a Philadelphia coffeehouse. More lucrative engagements soon followed; before long Cosby's budding career as an entertainer was conflicting with his school schedule. Forced to choose between the two, Cosby dropped out of Temple, although the university eventually awarded him a bachelor's degree on the basis of ''life experience.'' His reputation as a comic grew quickly as he worked in coffeehouses from San Francisco to New York City. Soon he was playing the biggest nightclubs in Las Vegas, and shortly after signing a recording contract in 1964, he became the best-selling comedian on records, with several of his recordings earning over one million dollars in sales.

His early performances consisted of about 35 percent racial jokes, but Cosby came to see this kind of humor as something that perpetuated racism rather than relieving tensions, and he dropped all such jokes from his act. ''Rather than trying to bring the races together by talking about the differences, let's try to bring them together by talking about the similarities,'' he urges. Accordingly, he developed a universal brand of humor that revolved around everyday occurrences. A long-time jazz devotee, the comedian credits the musical improvisations of Miles Davis, Charles Mingus and Charlie Parker with inspiring him to come up with continually fresh ways of restating a few basic themes. ''The situations I talk about people can find themselves in . . . it makes them glad to know they're not the only ones who have fallen victims of life's little ironies,'' states Cosby.

The comedian first displayed his skill as an actor when he landed the co-starring lead in ''I Spy,'' a popular NBC-TV program of the late 1960s that featured suspense, action, and sometimes humor. Cosby portrayed Alexander Scott, a multi-lingual Rhodes scholar working as part of a spy team for the United States. Scott and his partner (played by Robert Culp) travelled undercover in the guises of a tennis pro and his trainer. The Alexander Scott role had not been created especially for a black actor, and Cosby's casting in the part was hailed as an important breakthrough for blacks in television.

"The Bill Cosby Show" followed "I Spy." In this half-hour comedy, Cosby portrayed Chet Kincaid, a high-school gym teacher—a role closer to his real-life persona than that of Alexander Scott. In fact, at this time Cosby announced that he was considering quitting show business to become a teacher. Although he never followed through on that statement, Cosby did return to college and earned a doctorate in education in 1977. His doctoral thesis, "An Integration of the Visual Media via Fat Albert and the Cosby Kids into the Elementary School Curriculum as a Teaching Aid and Vehicle to Achieve Increased Learning," analyzed an animated Saturday-morning show that Cosby himself had created. "Fat Albert and the Cosby Kids" had its roots in the comedy routines about growing up in Philadelphia. It attempted to entertain children while encouraging them to confront moral and ethical issues, and it has been used as a teaching tool in schools.

During the 1970s, Cosby teamed with Sidney Poitier and several other black actors to make a highly successful series of comedies, including "Uptown Saturday Night," "Let's Do It Again," and "A Piece of the Action." These comedies stood out in a time when most of the films for black audiences were oriented to violence. Critics are generous in their praise of Cosby's acting; Tom Allen notes his "free-wheeling, jiving, put-down artistry," and Alvin H. Marritt writes that, in "Let's Do It Again," Cosby "breezes through the outrageous antics."

Concern over his family's television viewing habits led Cosby to return to prime-time in 1984. "I got tired of seeing TV shows that consist of a car crash, a gunman and a hooker talking to a black pimp," Jane Hall quotes him in *People*. "It was cheaper to do a series than to throw out my family's six TV sets." But Cosby found that network executives were resistant to his idea for a family-oriented comedy. He was turned down by both CBS and ABC on the grounds that a family comedy—particularly one featuring a black family—could never succeed on modern television. NBC accepted his proposal and "The Cosby Show" very quickly became the top-rated show on television, drawing an estimated 60 million weekly viewers.

Like most of Bill Cosby's material, "The Cosby Show" revolves around everyday occurrences and interactions between siblings and parents. Cosby plays obstetrician Cliff Huxtable, who with his lawyer wife Claire has four daughters and one son—just as Cosby and wife Camille do in real life. Besides entertaining audiences, Cosby aims to project a positive image of a family whose members love and respect one another. The program is hailed by some as a giant step forward in the portrayal of blacks on television. Writes Lynn Norment in *Ebony*, "This show pointedly avoids the stereotypical Blacks often seen on TV. There are no ghetto maids or butlers wisecracking about Black life. Also, there are no fast cars and helicopter chase scenes, no jokes about sex and boobs and butts. And, most unusual, both parents are present in the home, employed and are Black."

"The Cosby Show" has not been unanimously acclaimed, however. As Norment explains, "Despite its success, the show is criticized by a few for not being 'Black enough,' for not dealing with more controversial issues, such as poverty and racism and interracial dating, for focusing on a Black middle-class family when the vast majority of Black people survive on incomes far below that of the Huxtables." Cosby finds this type of criticism racist in itself. "Does it mean only white people have a lock on living together in a home where the father is a doctor and the mother is a lawyer and the children are constantly being told to study by their parents?" Hall quotes Cosby in *People*. "This is a black American family. If anybody has difficulty with that, it's their problem, not ours."

The paternal image of Cliff Huxtable led a publisher to ask Cosby for a humorous book to be called *Fatherhood*. Cosby obliged, making notes for the project with shorthand and tape recorder between his entertainment commitments. The finished book sold a record 2.6 million hardcover copies and was quite well-received by critics. *Newsweek* book reviewer Cathleen McGuigan states that it "is like a prose version of a Cosby comedy performance—informal, commiserative anecdotes delivered in a sardonic style that's as likely to prompt a smile of recognition as a belly laugh. . . . [But] it's not all played for laughs. There's a tough passage in which he describes the only time he hit his son, and a reference to a drinking-and-driving incident involving a daughter and her friends that calls upon him to both punish and forgive. Cosby's big strength, though, is his eye and ear for the everyday event—sibling squabbles, children's excuses." Jonathan Yardley concurs in the *Washington Post Book World*: "Cosby has an extraordinarily keen ear for everyday speech and everyday event, and knows how to put just enough of a comic spin on it so that even as we laugh we know we are getting a glimpse of the truth."

Following the huge success of *Fatherhood*, Doubleday published *Time Flies*, in which Cosby treats the subject of aging in the same style as his earlier book. Toronto *Globe & Mail* reviewer Leo Simpson comments, "Decay and the drift into entropy wouldn't get everyone's vote as a light-hearted theme, yet Time Flies is just as illuminating, witty and elegantly hilarious as . . . Fatherhood." Although Cosby complains in *Time Flies* that he is slowing down with age, his performing, directing, writing and devotion to charitable projects provide him with a very busy schedule. As he told the *Los Angeles Times*, "I think one of the most important things to understand is that my mother, as a domestic, worked 12 hours a day, and then she would do the laundry, and cook the meals and serve them and clean them up, and for this she got $7 a day. So 12 hours a day of whatever I do is as easy as eating a Jell-O Pudding Pop."

AVOCATIONAL INTERESTS: Tennis.

BIOGRAPHICAL/CRITICAL SOURCES:

BOOKS

Adams, Barbara Johnston, *The Picture Life of Bill Cosby*, F. Watts, 1986.

Johnson, Robert E., *Bill Cosby: In Words and Pictures*, Johnson Publishing (Chicago), 1987.

Smith, R. L., *Cosby*, St. Martin's, 1986.

Woods, H., *Billy Cosby, Making America Laugh and Learn*, Dillon, 1983.

PERIODICALS

Chicago Tribune, September 14, 1987.

Chicago Tribune Books, May 3, 1987.

Ebony, May, 1964, June, 1977, April, 1985, February, 1986, February, 1987.

Films in Review, November, 1975.
Globe & Mail (Toronto), July 5, 1986, October 24, 1987.
Jet, January 12, 1987, January 19, 1987, February 9, 1987, February 23, 1987, March 9, 1987.
Ladies Home Journal, June, 1985.
Los Angeles Times, September 25, 1987, December 20, 1987, January 24, 1988.
Los Angeles Times Book Review, June 15, 1986.
National Observer, January 6, 1964.
Newsweek, November 5, 1984, September 2, 1985, May 19, 1986, September 14, 1987.
New York Post, February 23, 1964.
New York Times Book Review, September 20, 1987.
New York Times Magazine, March 14, 1965.
People, December 10, 1984, September 14, 1987.
Playboy, December, 1985.
Saturday Evening Post, April, 1985, April, 1986.
Time, September 28, 1987.
Village Voice, November 3, 1975.
Washington Post, September 7, 1987.
Washington Post Book World, April 27, 1986.

—Sketch by Joan Goldsworthy

*   *   *

COTTER, Joseph Seamon, Sr.   1861-1949
(Joseph S. Cotter, Sr.)

PERSONAL: Born February 2, 1861, in Bardstown, Ky.; died March 14, 1949; son of Micheil J. and Martha (Vaughn) Cotter; married Maria F. Cox (a teacher and principal), July 22, 1891; children: Florence Olivia (died in 1914), Joseph Seamon (died in 1919), Leonidas (died in 1900). *Education:* Attended school through third grade; attended night school in Louisville, Ky.

ADDRESSES: Home—Louisville, Ky.

CAREER: Worked odd jobs throughout childhood and adolescence, including ragpicking, serving as a teamster on a levee, distillery work, tobacco stemming, and prizefighting; taught school in Kentucky, 1885-89; Louisville Public Schools, Louisville, Ky., teacher at Western Colored School, 1889-93, founder and principal of Paul L. Dunbar School, 1893-1911, principal of Samuel Coleridge-Taylor School, 1911-42; retired, 1942-49. Elected to the Louisville Board of Education, 1938.

MEMBER: Author's League of America, National Association for the Advancement of Colored People, Story Tellers League, Kentucky Negro Educational Association, Louisville Colored Orphan's Home Society (past director).

WRITINGS—UNDER NAME JOSEPH S. COTTER, SR., EXCEPT AS NOTED:

POETRY, EXCEPT AS NOTED

A Rhyming (includes "The Bachelor," "Man Does Not Know," and "Description of a Kentucky School House"), New South Publishing, 1895.
Links of Friendship (includes "Answer to Dunbar's 'After a Visit,'" "Answer to Dunbar's 'A Choice,'" "Six in Deportment," "The Devil and the Higher Critics," "A Just Reward," and "Sequel to 'The Pied Piper of Hamelin'"), Bradley & Gilbert, 1898.
Caleb, the Degenerate; A Play in Four Acts: A Study of the Types, Customs, and Needs of the American Negro (po-

etic drama), Bradley & Gilbert, 1903, recent edition, AMS Press, 1973.
A White Song and a Black One (includes "A White Song," "A Black Song," "Grant and Lee," "Reporting the Sermon," "The Loafing Negro," "The Don't Care Negro," and "The Vicious Negro"), Bradley & Gilbert, 1909, recent edition, AMS Press, 1975.
Negro Tales (short stories; includes "Caleb," "Rodney," "Tesney, the Deceived," "Regnan's Anniversary," "A Rustic Comedy," "Kotchin' De Nines," and "Observation"), Cosmopolitan Press, 1912, recent edition, Mnemosyne Publishing, 1969.
(Under name Joseph Seamon Cotter, Sr.) *Collected Poems of Joseph S. Cotter, Sr.* (includes "Style," "Babe on Babe," "The Negro Preacher," "The Negro Woman," and "The Negro Child"), Henry Harrison, 1938, recent edition, Books for Libraries Press, 1971.
Sequel to "The Pied Piper of Hamelin," and Other Poems (includes "Sequel to 'The Pied Piper of Hamelin,'" "A Poem," "The Door-Sill," "My Lad," "Mr. Goody's Goat," "Johnny's Dream of Santa Claus," "The Race Welcomes Dr. W. E. B. Du Bois as Its Leader," "The Tragedy of Pete," "The Wooded Path," and "Christmas Turkey"), Henry Harrison, 1939.
(Under name Joseph Seamon Cotter, Sr.) *Negroes and Others at Work and Play* (poems and prose; includes "A Town Sketch," "Another Cinderella," "One Strange Night," "The Chastisement," "Caesar Driftwood," "The True Negro," "Walnut Street," "Fourth Avenue of Yesteryear," "Psalm of the Zoot-Suit," and "The A-Bomb"), Paebar, 1947.

SIDELIGHTS: Joseph Seamon Cotter, Sr., overcame a childhood filled with odd jobs that staved off poverty and became a respected educator and author. Best remembered for his poem "The Tragedy of Pete," and for *Caleb, the Degenerate,* only the second play by a black American to be published, he is praised for his proficiency in different verse styles. Equally comfortable with black dialect poems influenced by his friendship with poet Paul Laurence Dunbar and with the rhyme and meter of Italian sonnets and traditional English ballads, Cotter produced several volumes of poems and short stories during his lengthy career as a teacher, principal, and member of the school board in Louisville, Kentucky.

When Cotter's art deals with the problems blacks faced in his times, it usually approaches the race issue in a conciliatory manner, according to A. Russell Brooks in the *Dictionary of Literary Biography.* In his blank verse drama *Caleb, the Degenerate,* Cotter, like famed black educator Booker T. Washington, argues that blacks are less likely to advance through political activism than through hard work in the fields of industry. Through contrasting Caleb and his corruptor, minister-politician Rahab, with the virtuous Bishop and his daughter Olivia, who run an industrial school for blacks, Cotter makes his case. Rahab, in Brooks's words, "instills in [Caleb] the notion that the ideal gentleman eats and wears only what he has picked up, borrowed, or stolen." He also leads Caleb to murder his own father and sell the corpse to a medical student. Another character, Dude, is also under Rahab's influence at the beginning of *Caleb,* but by the play's end he has been swayed to the side of good by Bishop and Olivia.

"It is not known if [*Caleb*] was ever produced," Brooks reported; the play was perceived as poor closet drama by many critics. Despite its unsuitability for the stage and some "stilted" dialogue, however, Brooks claimed that "pleasant surprises await the persevering reader: for example, several passages written in imitation of [English poet] John Milton's use of the epic simile.''

Cotter ''used dialect effectively in relating humorous incidents and situations,'' lauded Brooks. His dialect poems include ''Reporting the Sermon,'' which concerns a preacher who delivers a sermon on the evils of drink only to try and drain the last drops from a near-empty liquor bottle while its former possessors watch from behind some weeds. ''Christmas Turkey'' takes advantage of black dialect to add flair to the speaker's plot to bore his fellow diners with an account of the turkey's life so that they lose their appetites and leave the whole turkey to him. Cotter's famous ''The Tragedy of Pete,'' the story of a black man who kills the drunk driver responsible for the death of his girlfriend, takes the form of a folk ballad. Another of his poems in ballad form, ''The Bachelor,'' portrays a boy taunting an old man into telling the strange reason why he never married—while he was looking to see if an old abandoned cottage was truly inhabited by witches, a huge weight came down on his back, rendering him incapable of enjoying women. Cotter also wrote many poems for children, such as ''Sequel to 'The Pied Piper of Hamelin,''' which Robert T. Kerlin announced in the *South Atlantic Quarterly* ''surpasses the original—[English poet Robert] Browning's—that is, in rushing rhythms and ingenious rhymes.''

Cotter's fiction, often judged inferior to his better poems, includes the story ''Regnan's Anniversary.'' Depicting a man who is late for his wedding because he was chased into a pond by two rival gangs, ''Regnan's Anniversary'' and Cotter's ''Kotchin' De Nines,'' about a man whose dreams of riches lead him to poverty, were praised by Brooks for their ''natural dialogue and characters and unified plots.'' Though Cotter's own stories are not considered memorable, he ''was widely known and loved for his promotion of . . . the story-telling contests which he initiated in the Louisville public libraries,'' revealed Brooks.

BIOGRAPHICAL/CRITICAL SOURCES:

BOOKS

Dictionary of Literary Biography, Volume 50: *Afro-American Writers Before the Harlem Renaissance,* Gale, 1986.

PERIODICALS

South Atlantic Quarterly, July, 1921.

* * *

COX, Joseph Mason Andrew 1930-

PERSONAL: Born July 12, 1930, in Boston, Mass.; son of Hiram and Edith (a nurse; maiden name, Henderson) Cox. *Education:* Columbia University, B.A., 1945, LL.B., 1953; World University, Hong Kong, A.Ps.D., 1972. *Politics:* Democrat. *Religion:* Unitarian-Universalist.

ADDRESSES: Home and office—Tilden Towers II, 801 Tilden St., New York, N.Y. 10467.

CAREER: New York Post, New York City, reporter and feature writer, 1958-60; Afro-Asian Purchasing Commission, New York City, president, 1961-68; New York City Board of Education, Brooklyn, N.Y., consultant, 1969-71; Manhattan Community College of the City University of New York, New York City, lecturer, 1972-73; Medgar Evers College of the City University of New York, Brooklyn, assistant professor

of English, 1973-74; Cox & Hopewell Publishers, Inc., New York City, president, 1974—. Producer and moderator for television program ''Focus on Profound Thought.''

MEMBER: International Poetry Society (fellow), International Poets Shrine, United Poets Laureate International, World Literature Academy (fellow), Authors League, Poetry Society of America (member of executive board, 1971-72), Poetry Society of London, Centro Studi e Scambi Internazionali (Rome), Rosicrucian Order.

AWARDS, HONORS: International Essay Award from Daniel S. Mead Agency, 1964; ''Great Society'' writer's award from President Lyndon B. Johnson, 1965; Master Poets Award from American Poet Fellowship Society, 1970; World Poets Award from World Poetry Fellowship Society, 1971; PEN grant, 1972; Humanitarian Award and Gold Medal for poetry from International Poets Shrine, both 1974; American Book Award nomination, 1979, for *New and Selected Poems;* ''Statue of Victory'' World Culture Prize from Accademia Italia, 1985.

WRITINGS:

The Search (novel), Freedom Press, 1963.
Ode to Dr. Martin Luther King, Jr. (three-act play; first produced in Pittsburgh, Pa., at University of Pittsburgh's Creatadrama Theatre, 1970), J. Brook Dendy, 1970.
The Collected Poetry of Joseph Mason Andrew Cox, Golden Quill, 1970.
Shore Dimly Seen (poetry), Cox & Hopewell Publishers, 1974.
New and Selected Poems, Blue Diamond Press, 1979.
Great Black Men of Masonry: Qualitative Black Achievers Who Were Freemasons, Blue Diamond Press, 1982.

Also author of *Bouquet of Poems* and *Indestructible Monument* (novel), both 1974.

CONTRIBUTOR TO ANTHOLOGIES

Paul Scott Mowrer and Clarence E. Farrar, editors, *Golden Quill Anthology, 1968,* Golden Quill, 1968.
Frank Bensley, Lou Lu Toor, and Jerry McCarty, editors, *World Poets Anthology,* World of Poets Publishing, 1971.
Sue Scott Boyd, editor, *Poems by Blacks,* South and West Publishers, 1972.

OTHER

Columnist, *Caribbean Echo,* 1969-71. Contributor to periodicals, including *Poetry Review* and *South and West Review.*

WORK IN PROGRESS: Great Black Men of Masonry, Volumes 2 and 3; *Profound Reality and Fantasy Remembered,* a psychological novel.

* * *

CRUZ, Victor Hernandez 1949-

PERSONAL: Born February 6, 1949, in Aguas Buenas, P.R.; son of Severo and Rosa Cruz; children: Ajani. *Education:* Attended high school in New York, N.Y.

CAREER: Poet. Guest lecturer at University of California, Berkeley, 1969; San Francisco State University, San Francisco, Calif., instructor, 1973—.

AWARDS, HONORS: Creative Artists public service award, 1974, for *Tropicalization.*

WRITINGS:

Papo Got His Gun! and Other Poems, Calle Once Publications, 1966.

Doing Poetry, Other Ways, 1968.
Snaps (poems), Random House, 1969.
(Editor with Herbert Kohl) *Stuff: A Collection of Poems, Visions and Imaginative Happenings from Young Writers in Schools—Open and Closed,* Collins & World, 1970.
Mainland (poems), Random House, 1973.
Tropicalization (poems and prose), Reed, Cannon, 1976.
The Low Writings, Lee/Lucas Press, c. 1980.
By Lingual Wholes, Momo's, 1982.

Contributor to periodicals, including *Ramparts* and *Village Voice.* Work represented in anthologies, including *Black Out Loud,* Macmillan, 1970, and *Giant Talk: An Anthology of Third World Writings,* Random House, 1975. Editor, *Umbra.*

WORK IN PROGRESS: A novel, for Random House.

SIDELIGHTS: Victor Hernandez Cruz writes: "My family life was full of music, guitars and conga drums, maracas and songs. My mother sang songs. Even when it was five below zero in New York she sang warm tropical ballads." He adds: "My work is on the border of a new language, because I create out of a consciousness steeped in two of the important world languages, Spanish and English. A piece written totally in English could have a Spanish spirit. Another strong concern in my work is the difference between a tropical village, such as Aguas Buenas, Puerto Rico, where I was born, and an immensity such as New York City, where I was raised. I compare smells and sounds, I explore the differences, I write from the center of a culture which is not on its native soil, a culture in flight, living half the time on memories, becoming something totally new and unique, while at the same time it helps to shape and inform the new environment. I write about the city with an agonizing memory of a lush tropical silence. This contrast between landscape and languages creates an intensity in my work."

Nancy Sullivan writes in *Poetry* magazine: "Cruz allows the staccato crackle of English half-learned, so characteristic of his people, to enrich the poems through its touching dictional inadequacy. If poetry is arching toward the condition of silence as John Cage and Susan Sontag suggest, perhaps this mode of inarticulateness is a bend on that curve. . . . I think that Cruz is writing necessary poems in a period when many poems seem unnecessary."

BIOGRAPHICAL/CRITICAL SOURCES:

BOOKS

Dictionary of Literary Biography, Volume 41, *Afro-American Poets Since 1955,* Gale, 1985.

PERIODICALS

Bilingual Review, September-December, 1974.
Christian Science Monitor, August 7, 1969.
New Republic, November 21, 1970.
Poetry, May, 1970.

*   *   *

CULLEN, Countee   1903-1946

PERSONAL: Birth-given name Countee LeRoy Porter; first name pronounced "Coun-tay"; born May 30, 1903, in Louisville, Ky. (some sources say New York, N.Y., or Baltimore, Md.); died of uremic poisoning, January 9, 1946, in New York, N.Y.; buried in Woodlawn Cemetery, New York, N.Y.; married Nina Yolande DuBois, April 9, 1928 (divorced, 1930); married Ida Mae Roberson, September 27, 1940. *Education:* New York University, B.A., 1925; Harvard University, M.A., 1926.

CAREER: Poet, columnist, editor, novelist, playwright, children's writer, and educator. Assistant editor and author of monthly column "The Dark Tower" for *Opportunity: Journal of Negro Life,* 1926-28; traveled back and forth between France and the United States, 1928-34; Frederick Douglass Junior High School, New York, N.Y., teacher of English, French, and creative writing, 1934-45.

MEMBER: New York Civic Club, Phi Beta Kappa, Alpha Delta Phi.

AWARDS, HONORS: Witter Bynner Prize for poetry for "Poems," John Reed Memorial Prize from *Poetry* magazine for "Threnody for a Brown Girl," Amy Spingarn Award from *Crisis* magazine for "Two Moods of Love," and second prize winner in *Palm* Poetry Contest for "Wisdom Cometh With the Years," all 1925; second prize winner in *Crisis* Poetry Contest, 1926, for "Thoughts in a Zoo"; Harmon Foundation Literary Award from National Association for the Advancement of Colored People (NAACP), 1927, for "distinguished achievement in literature by a Negro"; Guggenheim Foundation fellowship, France, 1928-30.

WRITINGS:

POETRY

Color (includes "Heritage," "Atlantic City Waiter," "Near White," "To a Brown Boy," "For a Lady I Know," "Yet Do I Marvel," "Incident," "The Shroud of Color," "Oh, for a Little While Be Kind," "Brown Boy to Brown Girl," and "Pagan Prayer"), Harper, 1925, reprinted, Arno Press, 1969.
Copper Sun (includes "If Love Be Staunch," "The Love Tree," "Nocturne,'" "Threnody for a Brown Girl," and "To Lovers of Earth: Fair Warning"), decorations by Charles Cullen, Harper, 1927.
(Editor) *Caroling Dusk: An Anthology of Verse by Negro Poets,* decorations by Aaron Douglas, Harper, 1927, reprinted, 1974.
The Black Christ, and Other Poems (includes "The Black Christ," "Song of Praise," "Works to My Love," "In the Midst of Life," "Self Criticism," "To Certain Critics," and "The Wish"), decorations by Charles Cullen, Harper, 1929, reprinted, University Microfilms, 1973.
The Medea, and Some Poems (includes translation of Euripides' play *Medea,* "Scottsboro, Too, Is Worth Its Song," "Medusa," "The Cat," "Only the Polished Skeleton," "Sleep," "After a Visit," and "To France"), Harper, 1935.
On These I Stand: An Anthology of the Best Poems of Countee Cullen (includes "Dear Friends and Gentle Hearts," "Christus natus est," and some previously unpublished poems), Harper, 1947.

OTHER

The Ballad of the Brown Girl: An Old Ballad Retold, illustrations and decorations by Charles Cullen, Harper, 1927.
(Author of introduction) Frank Ankenbrand and Isaac Benjamin, *The House of Vanity,* Leibman Press, 1928.
One Way to Heaven (novel), Harper, 1932, reprinted, AMS Press, 1975 (also see below).
(Contributor) Fred J. Ringel, editor, *America as Americans See It,* Harcourt, 1932.

The Lost Zoo (a Rhyme for the Young, but Not Too Young), illustrations by Charles Sebree, Harper, 1940, new edition, with illustrations by Joseph Low, Follett, 1969.

My Lives and How I Lost Them (juvenile; autobiography of fictional character Christopher Cat), drawings by Robert Reid Macguire, Harper, 1942, new edition, with illustrations by Rainey Bennett, Follett, 1971.

(With Owen Dodson) "The Third Fourth of July" (one-act play), published in *Theatre Arts,* 1946.

(With Arna Bontemps) "St. Louis Woman" (musical adaptation of Bontemps's novel *God Sends Sunday;* first produced at Martin Beck Theater in New York City, March 30, 1946), published in *Black Theatre,* edited by Lindsay Patterson, Dodd, 1971.

Also author of unpublished plays, including "Let the Day Perish" (with Waters Turpin), "The Spirit of Peace," and "Heaven's My Home" (an adaptation, with Harry Hamilton, of Cullen's novel, *One Way to Heaven*), and of book reviews.

Contributor to *Crisis, Phylon, Bookman, Harper's, American Mercury, Century, Nation, Poetry,* and other periodicals.

SIDELIGHTS: Countee Cullen was perhaps the most representative voice of the Harlem Renaissance. His life story is essentially a tale of youthful exuberance and talent—of a star that flashed across the Afro-American firmament and then sank toward the horizon. When his paternal grandmother and guardian died in 1918, the fifteen-year-old Countee LeRoy Porter was taken into the home of the Reverend Frederick A. Cullen, the pastor of Salem Methodist Episcopal Church, Harlem's largest congregation. There the young Countee entered the approximate center of black politics and culture in the United States and acquired both the name and awareness of the influential clergyman who was later elected president of the Harlem chapter of the National Association for the Advancement of Colored People (NAACP).

In view of America's racial climate during the 1920s, Harlem was scarcely a serene place, but it was an enormously stimulating milieu for Afro-American intellectuals. The high hopes of the black community for acceptance and equality had turned to disillusionment at the end of World War I, when returning black soldiers all too often experienced unemployment and were otherwise mistreated. Resentment pulsated through black urban centers like Harlem, which had burgeoned during the war as black workers migrated there to fill jobs temporarily vacated by the diversion of white laborers into the military. For the first time in Afro-American history, a black urban consciousness—conducive to the flowering of the arts—was developing. From Harlem, the largest of the new, densely populated black urban communities—in which Cullen was listening and learning—burst forth an outpouring of Afro-American arts known as the Harlem Renaissance.

While Cullen's informal education was shaped by his exposure to black ideas and yearnings, his formal education derived from almost totally white influences. This dichotomy heavily influenced his creative work and his criticism, particularly because he did extremely well at the white-dominated institutions he attended and won the approbation of white academia. In high school Cullen earned academic honors that in turn garnered him the posts of vice-president of his class and editor of the school newspaper, as well as prizes for poetry and oratory. His glory continued at New York University, where he obtained first or second prizes in a number of poetry contests, including the national Witter Bynner Contests for undergraduate poetry and contests sponsored by *Poetry* magazine. Har-

vard University's Irving Babbitt publicly lauded Cullen's "The Ballad of the Brown Girl," and in 1925—which proved a bumper year for the young man's harvest of literary prizes—Cullen graduated from New York University, was accepted into Harvard's masters program, and published his first volume of poetry, *Color.*

During the next four years Cullen reached his zenith. A celebrated young man about Harlem, he had in print by 1929 four books of his own poems and a collection of poetry he edited, *Caroling Dusk,* written by other Afro-Americans. His letters from Harvard to his Harlem friend Harold Jackman exuded self-satisfaction and sometimes the snide intolerance of the *enfant terrible.* The climax of those heady years may have come in 1928. That year Cullen was awarded a Guggenheim fellowship to write poetry in France, and he married Nina Yolande DuBois—the daughter of W. E. B. DuBois, a man who for decades was the acknowledged leader of the Afro-American intellectual community. Few social events in Harlem rivaled the magnitude of the latter event, and much of Harlem joined in the festivities that marked the joining of the Cullen and DuBois lineages, two of its most notable families.

Because of Cullen's success in both black and white cultures, and because of his romantic temperament, he formulated an aesthetic that embraced both cultures. He came to believe that art transcended race and that it could be used as a vehicle to minimize the distance between black and white peoples. When he chose as his models poet John Keats and—to a lesser extent—A. E. Housman, he did so not consciously to curry favor with white America but for four logical reasons: First, though there had been Afro-American poets, there was not yet an Afro-American poetic tradition—in any meaningful sense of the term—to draw upon. Second, the English poetic tradition was the one that was available to him—the one that had been taught to him in schools he attended. Third, he felt challenged to demonstrate that a black poet could excel within that traditional framework. And fourth, he felt absolutely free to choose as exemplars any poets in the world with whom he sensed a temperamental affinity (and he certainly had that affinity with Housman and, especially, Keats). In addition, he shared their romantic self-involvement; he had an ego that was sensitive to the slightest tremors and that needed expression to remain whole, and—like Keats—he had to believe in human perfectibility.

In poems such as "Heritage" and "Atlantic City Waiter," Cullen reflects the urge to hearken back to African arts—a phenomenon called "Negritude" that was one of the motifs of the Harlem Renaissance. The cornerstone of his aesthetic, however, was the call for black-American poets to work conservatively, as he did, within English conventions. In his 1927 foreword to *Caroling Dusk,* Cullen observed that "since theirs is . . . the heritage of the English language, their work will not present any serious abberation from poetic tendencies of their times." Braving the wrath of less moderate peers, he further stated that "negro poets, dependent as they are on the English language, may have more to gain from the rich background of English and American poetry than from any nebulous atavistic yearnings toward an African inheritance." Even the subtitle of the collection, *An Anthology of Verse by Negro Poets,* reflects his belief in the essential oneness of art; it implies no distinction between white poetry and black poetry, and it assumes there is only poetry, which in the case of *Caroling Dusk* is simply composed by Afro-American writers.

His dedication to oneness led Cullen to be cautious of any black writer's work that threatened to erect rather than pull down barricades between the races. Thus, in a February, 1926, "Dark Tower" column in which Cullen reviewed Langston Hughes's *The Weary Blues,* Cullen pressed Hughes not to be a "racial artist" and to omit jazz rhythms from his poems. In a later column he prodded black writers to censor themselves by avoiding "some things, some truths of Negro life and thought . . . that all Negroes know, but take no pride in." For Cullen, showcasing unpleasant realities would "but strengthen the bitterness of our enemies" and thereby weaken the bridge of art between blacks and whites.

Such warnings, however, did not prevent the critic Cullen from praising black artists whenever he found their work meritorious, even when it was overtly racial. In another of his "Dark Tower" columns, he complimented Amy Spingarn's *Pride and Humility,* for example, even though he thought its "clearest notes" were to be heard "in those poems which have a racial framework." Since his primary criterion for judging a work was always aesthetic, Cullen applauded any poetry that appealed to him, without regard to the color of the writer. He had good things to say about Edna St. Vincent Millay, E. A. Robinson, and Robert Frost, but he was less favorable toward such avant garde poets as Amy Lowell, in whose work he found little "for the hungry heart to feed upon." Generally, three principles informed his criticism: First, he tended to be more attracted to romantic rather than unromantic poetry. Second, he was conservative in his tastes and therefore put off by experimentation such as that of Amy Lowell. Third, although he put special effort into trying to further the interests of black artists, he was governed by a keen sense of impartiality and a commitment to bringing the races into closer harmony.

A paradox exists, however, between Cullen's philosophy and writing. While he argued that racial poetry was a detriment to the color-blindness he craved, he was at the same time so affronted by the racial injustice in America that his own best verse—indeed most of his verse—gave voice to racial protest. In fact, the title of Cullen's 1925 collection, *Color,* was not chosen unintentionally, nor did Cullen include sections with that same title in later volumes by accident. Both early and late in his career he was, in spite of himself, largely a racial poet. This is evident throughout Cullen's works from the *Color* pieces and the introduction of racial violence into his 1927 *Ballad of a Brown Girl* to the poems that he selected for the posthumously published *On These I Stand,* of which substantially more than half are racial poems.

Of the six identifiable racial themes in Cullen's poetry, the first is Negritude, or Pan-African impulse, a pervasive element of the 1920s international black literary movement that scholar Arthur P. Davis in a 1953 *Phylon* essay called "the alien-and-exile theme." Specific examples of this motif in Cullen's poetry include his attribution of descent from African kings to the girl featured in his *Ballad of a Brown Girl* as well as the submerged pride exhibited by the waiter in the poem "Atlantic City Waiter" whose graceful movement resulted from "Ten thousand years on jungle clues." Probably the best-known illustration of the Pan-African impulse in Cullen's poetry is found in "Heritage," where the narrator realizes that although he must suppress his African heritage, he cannot ultimately surrender his black heart and mind to white civilization. "Heritage," like most of the Negritude poems of the Harlem Renaissance and like political expression such as Marcus Garvey's popular back-to-Africa movement, powerfully suggests the duality of the black psyche—the simultaneous allegiance to America and rage at her racial inequities.

Four similar themes recur in Cullen's poems, expressing other forms of racial bias. These include a kind of black chauvinism that prevailed at the time and that Cullen portrayed in both *Ballad of the Brown Girl* and *The Black Christ,* when in those works he judged that the passion of blacks was better than that of whites. Likewise, the poem "Near White" exemplifies the author's admonition against miscegenation, and in "To a Brown Boy" Cullen propounds a racially motivated affinity toward death as a preferred escape from racial frustration and outrage. Another poem, "For a Lady I Know," presents a satirical view of whites obliviously mistreating their black counterparts as it depicts blacks in heaven doing their "celestial chores" so that upper-class whites can remain in their heavenly beds.

Using a sixth motif, Cullen exhibits a direct expression of irrepressible anger at racial unfairness. His outcry is more muted than that of some other Harlem Renaissance poets—Hughes, for example, and Claude McKay—but that is a matter of Cullen's innate and learned gentility. Those who overlook his strong indictment of racism in American society miss the main thrust of Cullen's work. His poetry throbs with anger as in "Incident" when he recalls his personal response to being called "nigger" on a Baltimore bus, or in the selection "Yet Do I Marvel," in which Cullen identifies what he regards as God's most astonishing miscue—that he could "make a poet black, and bid him sing!" In addition to his own personal experiences, Cullen also focuses on public events. For instance, in "Scottsboro, Too, Is Worth Its Song," he upbraids American poets, who had championed the cause of white anarchists in the controversial Sacco-Vanzetti trials, for not defending the nine black youths indicted on charges of raping two white girls in a freight car passing through Scottsboro, Alabama, in 1931.

In *The Book of American Negro Poetry,* author James Weldon Johnson explained with acute sympathy Cullen's compulsion to write poetry that seems to fly in the face of his declarations against poetry of race. Johnson wrote: "Strangely, it is because Cullen revolts against . . . racial limitations—technical and spiritual—that the best of his poetry is motivated by race. He is always seeking to free himself and his art from these bonds. He never entirely escapes, but from the very fret and chafe he brings forth poetry that contains the quintessence of race consciousness."

Cullen, then, was a forceful but genteel protest poet; yet, he was much more. He was also consistent in his intention to write good traditional poetry for the social purpose of showing what common sense should have told white Americans but what they still demanded be proven to them—that blacks *could* write poetry and write it as well as anyone. To that end, much of Cullen's poetry deals with such universal subjects as faith and doubt, love, and mortality.

On the subject of religion, Cullen waywardly progressed from uncertainty to Christian acceptance. Early on he was given to irony and even defiance in moments of youthful skepticism. In "Heritage," for example, he observes that a black Christ could command his faith better than the white one. When he was twenty-four, he provided a third-person description of himself in which he commented that his "chief problem has been that of reconciling a Christian upbringing with a pagan inclination. His life so far has not convinced him that the problem is insoluble." But before very long, his grandmother Porter's influence and that of the Cullen rectory won out. Outrage over racial injustice notwithstanding, he had fairly well controlled the "pagan inclination" in favor of Christian orthodoxy by 1929, when he published *The Black Christ, and Other Poems*. In the opening of the book's narrative title poem, the protagonist sings of embracing Good in spite of certain earthly obstacles that he summarizes as "my country's shame." The speaker's brother has been beaten to death by a white lynch mob for an innocent relationship with a white woman; the narrator's resentment toward a savior who allows such evil to occur is overcome by his mother's proclamation of her unshakable faith, and any residue of doubt disappears when the murdered brother is resurrected. At the end the family is left to prosper in its piety. Furthermore, among the few previously unpublished poems that Cullen selected for inclusion in the posthumously published collection *On These I Stand* is one that confirms his continuing religious commitment as a way to cope with the injustices and disappointments of his life. Written during World War I, "Christus natus est" asserts that amid all the tragedy of war "The manger still / Outshines the throne" and that "Christ must and will / Come to his own."

To understand Cullen's treatment of love it is necessary first to examine the effete—weak or effeminate—quality of many of his love poems. David Levering Lewis, in *When Harlem Was in Vogue,* asserted that "impotence and death run through [Cullen's] poetry like dark threads, entangling his most affirmative lines." In general, Cullen's love poetry is clearly characterized not only by misgivings about women but also by a distrust of the emotion of heterosexual love. His "Medusa" and "The Cat," both contained in *The Medea, and Some Poems,* illustrate this vision of male-female relationships. In Cullen's version of the ancient myth, it is not the hideousness of Medusa that blinds the men who gaze upon her, but rather her beauty. So great is the destructive power of the attractive female that the narrator in "The Cat" imagines in the animal "A woman with thine eyes, satanic beast / Profound and cold as scythes to mow me down." Male lovers, on the other hand, are often portrayed as sickly with apprehension that a relationship is about to be ended either by a fickle partner or by death. In "If Love Be Staunch," for example, the speaker warns that love lasts no longer than "water stays in a sieve," and in "The Love Tree" Cullen portrays love as a crucifixion whereby future lovers may realize that " 'Twas break of heart that made the love tree grow." What Lewis identified in Cullen's love poems as a "corroding suspicion of life cursed from birth" may have resulted from Cullen's alleged homosexuality.

Cullen's treatment of death in his writing was shaped by his early encounters with the deaths of his parents, brother, and grandmother, as well as by a premonition of his own premature demise. Running through his poems are a sense of the brevity of life and a romantic craving for the surcease of death. In "Nocturne" and "Works to My Love," death is readily accepted as a natural element of life. "Threnody for a Brown Girl" and "In the Midst of Life" portray even warmer feelings towards death as a welcome escape. And in poems such as "Only the Polished Skeleton" death is gratefully anticipated to bring relief from racial oppression: A stripped skeleton has no race; it can but "measure the worth of all it so despised." Looking forward to death, Cullen meanwhile accepted sleep as an effective surrogate. In the poem "Sleep" he portrays slumber as "lovelier" and "kinder" than any alternative. It is both a feline killer and gentle nourisher that suckles the sleeper: "though the suck be short 'tis good." In April, 1943, less than three years before he died of uremic poisoning, Cul-

len related in "Dear Friends and Gentle Hearts" that "blessedly this breath departs."

After 1929 Cullen's production of verse dropped off dramatically. It was limited to his translation of Euripides' play *Medea,* which appeared along with some new poems in his 1935 *Medea and Some Poems* and later with half a dozen previously unpublished pieces that were included in his posthumously published collection, *On These I Stand.* A complexity of reasons contributed to the dimming of his poetic star. The Harlem Renaissance required a white audience to sustain it, and as whites became preoccupied with their own tenuous situation during the Great Depression, they lost interest in the Afro-American arts. Also, Cullen's idealism about building a bridge of poetry between the races had been sorely tested by the time the 1920s ended. Moreover, he seemed affected by legitimate doubts concerning his growth as a poet. In "Self Criticism" he reflected whether he would go on singing a "failing not still vainly clinging / To the throat of the stricken swan." While his supporters continued to defend him on racial rather than literary grounds, his detractors gradually increased in numbers with the publication of each successive collection of his poetry. Harry Alan Potamkin, in a 1927 *New Republic* review of *Copper Sun,* found that Cullen had not really progressed since *Color* and that the poet had "capitalized on the fact of race." The reviewer concluded, in fact, that Cullen's poetry "begins and ends with a epithet skill." With the appearance of *The Black Christ, and Other Poems* in 1929, *Nation*'s Granville Hicks joined the chorus of critics expressing reservations and remarked that "in general, Mr. Cullen's talents do not seem to be developing as one might wish."

For a combination of causes, then, beginning in the early 1930s Cullen largely curtailed his poetic output and channeled his creative energy into other genres. He wrote a novel, *One Way to Heaven,* published in 1932, but its poor critical reception made it his only novel. The book reveals a flair for satire in its secondary plot, which centers around the Harlem salon of the irrepressible hostess Constancia Brandon; one particularly effective episode features a white intellectual bigot who is invited to read his tract, "The Menace of the Negro to Our American Civilization," to an audience of mainly black intellectuals. The novel itself, however, suffers from a fatal structural flaw. Cullen never successfully integrated the secondary plot—a takeoff on his own experience in Harlem intellectual circles—with the major story line, a melodrama in which itinerant con man Sam Lucas undergoes a fake religious conversion to edge his way into a Harlem congregation; marries and then cheats on his sweet young wife; and finally, on his death bed undergoes a change of heart. The characters in the main plot are generally based on stereotypes common in black-American folklore—the fast-talking trickster and the sagacious saintly old aunt, for example. Although Cullen displays some compassion toward them and a good deal of good-natured wit in dealing with the satirical figures, the two plots never adequately come together. As Rudolph Fisher said in a *New York Herald Tribune* review of *One Way to Heaven,* it was as if Cullen were "exhibiting a lovely pastel and cartoon on the same frame."

When thirty-one-year-old Cullen turned to teaching in 1934, he was determined to find some way other than literature to contribute to social change, but he did not abandon writing entirely. In 1935 he published his version of *Medea* (with the speeches and choral passages curiously attenuated) and collaborated with Harry Hamilton on "Heaven's My Home," a dramatic adaptation of *One Way to Heaven.* The play, which was never published, is actually more contrived than Cullen's novel, but unlike the original work "Heaven's My Home" manages to integrate the two plots by introducing a sexual relationship between the protagonists Lucas and Brandon.

Toward the end of his life, in the 1940s, Cullen was relatively successsful as a dramatist. With another collaborator, Owen Dodson, he worked on several projects, including "The Third Fourth of July," a one-act play printed in *Theatre Arts* in August, 1946. During this period Cullen rejected a professorship at Fisk University and instead remained in New York to work with Arna Bontemps on a dramatic version of her novel *God Sends Sunday*. Cullen, who suggested the adaptation, made this endeavor the center of his life, but the enterprise caused him much grief. By 1945 the play had become the musical "St. Louis Woman," and celebrated performer Lena Horne was expected to star in its Broadway and Hollywood productions. Then disaster struck. Walter White of the National Association for the Advancement of Colored People (NAACP) argued that the play, set in the black ghetto of St. Louis and featuring lower-class and seedy characters, was demeaning to blacks. Cullen was blamed for revealing the seamy side of black life, the very thing he had warned other black writers not to do. Many of Cullen's friends refused to defend him; some joined the attack, which was patently unjust. Admittedly, greed and criminality figure in the play, which focuses on the struggle between overbearing salon keeper-gambler Bigelow Brown and diminutive jockey Lil Augie for the affections of Della Greene, a hard-nosed and soft-hearted beauty. But as Cullen argued, the play really deals with human virtues—honor, love, decency, and loyalty. The controversy surrounding it wore on, however, until 1946. In March of that year, "St. Louis Woman" finally premiered on Broadway, featuring songs by Johnny Mercer and Harold Arlen such as "Come Rain, Come Shine" and making singer Pearl Bailey a star. Unfortunately, Cullen had died almost three months earlier and was to be remembered primarily for the poems he had written in his twenties—when he was one of Harlem's brightest luminaries.

The limitations of Cullen's poetry—such as its archaic and imitative ring, its occasional verbosity, and its tendency to sacrifice sense for conventional prosody—restricted his literary status to that of a minor poet with a real lyrical gift. But he was not guilty of the obsequious acceptance of white values for which 1960s black power poets such as Don Lee were to dismiss him. Cullen never compromised his integrity as a black man to gain advantage for himself. His primary goal was to bring America closer to racial harmony through his own art and that of his peers and ultimately to achieve complete and colorblind artistic freedom. As he defiantly proclaimed in "To Certain Critics" (published in *The Black Christ*), though some might call him a traitor to blacks, his program was too universal to be contained: "Never shall the clan / Confine my singing to its ways / Beyond the ways of man."

Probably more than any other writer of the Harlem Renaissance, Cullen carried out the intentions of black American intellectual leaders such as W. E. B. DuBois and James Weldon Johnson. These men had nothing but the highest praise for Cullen, for he was brilliantly practicing what they advocated, and he came close to embodying Alain Locke's "New Negro." "In a time," DuBois wrote in a 1928 *Crisis* essay, "when it is the vogue to make much of the Negro's aptitude for clownishness or to depict him objectively as a serio-comic figure, it is a fine and praiseworthy act for Mr. Cullen to show through the interpretation of his own subjectivity the inner workings of the Negro soul and mind." Johnson was pleased with Cullen's decision not to recognize "any limitation to 'racial' themes and forms." In Cullen's wish not to be "a negro poet," Johnson insisted, the writer was "not only within his right; he is right." As these authorities attest, to read Countee Cullen's work is to hear a voice as representative of the Harlem Renaissance as it is possible to find.

BIOGRAPHICAL/CRITICAL SOURCES:

BOOKS

Baker, Houston A., Jr., *A Many-Colored Coat of Dreams: The Poetry of Countee Cullen*, Broadside Press, 1974.
Bone, Robert, *The Negro Novel in America*, Yale University Press, 1965.
Bronz, Stephen H., *Roots of Racial Consciousness: The 1920s: Three Harlem Renaissance Authors*, Libra, 1964.
Davis, Arthur P., *From the Dark Tower: Afro-American Writers, 1900-1960*, Howard University Press, 1974.
Ferguson, Blanche E., *Countee Cullen and the Negro Renaissance*, Dodd, 1966.
Huggins, Nathan Irvin, *Harlem Renaissance*, Oxford, 1971.
Johnson, James Weldon, *The Book of American Negro Poetry*, Harcourt, 1922, revised edition, 1931, Harbrace, 1959.
Johnson, James Weldon, *Black Manhattan*, Knopf, 1930.
Lee, Don L., *Dynamite Voices I: Black Voices of the 1960s*, Broadside Press, 1971.
Littlejohn, David, *Black on White: A Critical Survey of Writing by American Negroes*, Viking, 1966.
Lewis, David Levering, *When Harlem Was in Vogue*, Knopf, 1981.
Locke, Alain, *Four Negro Poets*, Albert & Charles Boni, 1925.
Locke, Alain, *The New Negro, An Interpretation*, Albert & Charles Boni, 1925.
Margolies, Edward, *Native Sons: A Critical Study of Twentieth-Century Negro American Authors*, Lippincott, 1968.
Perry, Margaret, *A Bio-Bibliography of Countee P. Cullen, 1903-1946*, Greenwood, 1971.
Redding, J. Saunders, *To Make a Poet Black*, University of North Carolina Press, 1939.
Rosenblatt, Roger, *Black Fiction*, Harvard University Press, 1974.
Shucard, Alan, *Countee Cullen*, Twayne, 1984.
Singh, Amritjit, *The Novels of the Harlem Renaissance: Twelve Black Authors, 1923-1933*, Pennsylvania State University Press, 1976.
Wagner, Jean, *Black Poets of the United States: From Paul Laurence Dunbar to Langston Hughes*, University of Illinois Press, 1973.

PERIODICALS

Atlantic Monthly, No. 79, March, 1947.
College Language Association Journal, No. 13, 1970.
Crisis, No. 35, June, 1928.
Critique, No. 11, 1969.
Nation, March 12, 1930.
New Republic, No. 52, 1927.
New York Herald Tribune of Books, February 28, 1932.
Phylon, No. 14, 1953.

—Sidelights by Alan Shucard

*　　　*　　　*

CUNEY, Waring
See CUNEY, William Waring

CUNEY, William Waring   1906-1976
(Waring Cuney)

PERSONAL: Born May 6, 1906, in Washington, D. C.; died June 30, 1976; son of Norris Cuney II and Madge Louise Baker. *Education:* Attended Howard University and Lincoln University; studied music at the New England Conservatory of Music in Boston and at the Conservatory in Rome.

CAREER: Writer. *Military service:* U. S. Army; served more than three years in the South Pacific as a technical sergeant during World War II; received Asiatic Pacific Theater Ribbon and three Bronze Stars.

AWARDS, HONORS: Poem ''No Images'' won first prize in *Opportunity* magazine contest in 1926.

WRITINGS:

POEMS

Chain Gang Chant, [Norman, Okla.], 1930.
Puzzles, selected and introduced by Paul Breman, woodcuts by Ru van Rossem, De Roos (Utrecht, Holland), 1960.
Storefront Church, P. Breman (London), 1973.

OTHER

(Editor under name Waring Cuney, with Langston Hughes and Bruce McM. Wright) *Lincoln University Poets: Centennial Anthology, 1854-1954,* foreword by Horace Mann Bond, introduction by J. Saunders Redding, Fine Editions, 1954.

Also author of several songs and broadsides, including *The Alley Cat Brushed His Whiskers, Two Poems: ''Darkness Hides His Throne''* [*and*] *''We Make Supplication,''* and *Women and Kitchens.*

Work represented in anthologies, including *American Negro Poetry, An Anthology of Magazine Verse for 1926, Negro Caravan, Caroling Dusk, Cavalcade, Book of American Negro Poetry, Negro Poets and Their Poems,* and *Beyond the Blues.* Contributor of poems and criticism to periodicals, including *Crisis, Harlem Quarterly, Negro Quarterly, Opportunity,* and *Black World.*

SIDELIGHTS: One of the poets of the Harlem Renaissance, a period of burgeoning black American literary activity during the 1920s and 1930s, Cuney is best known for his widely anthologized poem ''No Images.'' Though the rest of his work has been largely overlooked, a number of critics regard his poetry as both unprecedented and unsurpassed in its reflection of the language and tempo of the ghetto-dweller.

BIOGRAPHICAL/CRITICAL SOURCES:

BOOKS

Bontemps, Arna, *The Harlem Renaissance Remembered,* Dodd, 1972.
Dictionary of Literary Biography, Volume 51: *Afro-American Writers From the Harlem Renaissance to 1940,* Gale, 1987.

PERIODICALS

Black World, November, 1970, March, 1973.
Negro History Bulletin, February, 1948, March, 1948.

D

DABYDEEN, David 1955-

PERSONAL: Born December 9, 1955, in Guyana; immigrated to England, 1969; son of Krishna Prasad and Vera Dabydeen. *Education:* Cambridge University, B.A. (with honors), 1978; University of London, Ph.D., 1981; postdoctoral study at Oxford University, 1983-87.

ADDRESSES: Home—London, England. *Office*—Wolfson College, Oxford University, Oxford OX2 6UD, England.

CAREER: Community education officer in Wolverhampton, England, 1982-84; University of Warwick, Coventry, England, lecturer in Caribbean studies, 1984-86.

MEMBER: Association for the Teaching of Caribbean, African, and Asian Literature (president, 1985-87), Society for Caribbean Studies (executive member), Black Media Research Committee (honorary consultant).

AWARDS, HONORS: Quiller-Couch Prize from Cambridge University, 1978, for poetry; resident fellowship from Yale University's Centre for British Art, 1982, and postdoctoral research fellowship from Oxford University, 1983; Commonwealth Poetry Prize, 1984, for *Slave Song*.

WRITINGS:

Slave Song (poems), Dangaroo Press, 1984.
Hogarth's Blacks: Images of Blacks in Eighteenth Century English Art, Dangaroo Press, 1985, University of Georgia Press, 1987.
(Editor and contributor) *The Black Presence in English Literature,* Manchester University Press, 1985.
Caribbean Literature: A Teacher's Handbook, Heinemann, 1986.
Hogarth and Walpoleian England, Swan Publications, 1988.

Also author of television program "Britain and Its Empire," 1986.

WORK IN PROGRESS: A poem collection, *Coolie Odyssey.*

SIDELIGHTS: Marking David Dabydeen's debut as a poet and earning him the 1984 Commonwealth Poetry Prize, the poem collection *Slave Song* was critically acclaimed for its passionate and revealing portrayal of life on the sugar plantations in Guyana and, in particular, its author's lyrical use of Guyanese Creole—a language derived from African, English, East Indian, French, and Spanish dialects. Reviewers such as Faustin Charles of the *Caribbean Times* praised *Slave Song*'s language as "raw, earthly, controlled and spun," and lauding Dabydeen for his rhythmic verse, the critic asserted that the "intensity of speech-patterns" places the reader "within the action of things. The poet's capacity to feel is near miraculous." Charles declared that Dabydeen is "convincing by his music, and most of all, he has kept the people's language as it should always be, a strong, living, imaginative expression." In what the reviewer labeled "a powerful piece of Caribbean writing," the Guyanese-born poet displays a concern for the social and political oppression of his country's peasant workers while evoking both the fullness and the despair of Caribbean culture.

In his introduction to *Slave Song,* Dabydeen proclaims that "the poems . . . (a jumble of fact and myth, past and present) are largely concerned with an exploration of the erotic energies of the colonial experience, ranging from a corrosive to a lyrical sexuality." Depicting the experience of black Guyanese canecutters degraded in their servitude to colonial white rule, the poet explores the passion, toil, and brutality of their existence. He achieves this largely through his use of the Creole dialect, which the author describes as "angry, crude, energetic." Stressing that his poems are meant to be read aloud in order for their tone to come through, Dabydeen maintains that he has "retained the full vulgarity of the language for it is a profound element in Guyanese life." And in his "recognition and expression of the uniqueness of the people, the particularity of their being," the poet additionally notes in his introduction that he employed the Guyanese Creole in *Slave Song* to express "the full experience of its users which is a very deep one, deep in suffering, cruelty, drunken merriment and tenderness."

Dabydeen further extols the cultural importance and value of blacks in a subsequent work, *Hogarth's Blacks: Images of Blacks in Eighteenth-Century English Art.* In the study, which *Times Literary Supplement* reviewer Roy Porter called a "revelation," Dabydeen explains the significance of the recurring presence of blacks in British artist William Hogarth's paintings. Although the eighteenth-century painter seemed to stereotypically portray blacks in such figures as the kneeling Sambo-like servant, Dabydeen, according to Porter, argues that "[Hogarth's] blacks weren't just 'invisible men' or conventional symbols. He meant their presence as contrasts to provoke, threaten and subvert.'' Dabydeen, Porter continued, believes that Hogarth intentionally incorporated bestial or unnatural images of blacks in his works in order to challenge the viewer, for the figures ''hold up the mirror to the barbarity of polite society,'' serving as emblems of the dark side of humanity. The reviewer assessed the author's explorations in *Hogarth's Blacks* as ''invigorating, his interpretation powerful and his judgment secure.'' He concluded that Dabydeen ''shows what can be achieved with sound historical research and a sharp pair of eyes.''

Another study of the significance of blacks in history is Dabydeen's *The Black Presence in English Literature.* A compilation of essays originally delivered by various authors at a 1982 conference Dabydeen organized in Wolverhampton, England, the work addresses the often-ignored contributions by and existence of black people in famous works of literature. ''Polemical rather than scholarly, [Dabydeen's] contributors aim to provoke a reappraisal of the literature taught in British schools by pointing out some of the gaps and mistaken assumptions in English studies today,'' expressed *Times Literary Supplement* reviewer Dennis Walder. Including Dabydeen's own essay dealing with slavery and commerce in eighteenth-century poetry, the book embraces discussions of black characters in Renaissance drama, the ''Afro-Black'' in nineteenth-century Australian literature, and the manipulation of Africa in contemporary adventure fiction, among others. The work was hailed as rich and instructive, and Walder noted that *The Black Presence in English Literature* ''does some justice'' to a timely subject that has ''received disappointingly little attention outside specialist circles.''

BIOGRAPHICAL/CRITICAL SOURCES:

BOOKS

Contemporary Literary Criticism, Volume 34, Gale, 1985.
Dabydeen, David, *Slave Song,* Dangaroo Press, 1984.

PERIODICALS

Caribbean Times, May 10, 1984, November 30, 1984.
Times Literary Supplement, September 13, 1985, June 13, 1986.

*   *   *

DADIE, Bernard
See DADIE, Bernard Binlin

*   *   *

DADIE, Bernard B.
See DADIE, Bernard Binlin

*   *   *

DADIE, Bernard Binlin   1916-
(Bernard Binlin-Dadie, Bernard Dadie, Bernard B. Dadie)

PERSONAL: Born in 1916 in Assinie, Ivory Coast; son of Gabriel Binlin and Enouaye (Nongbou) Dadie; married Rosa Assamala Koutoua in 1950; children: Renee, Michele, Benjamin, Dominique, Claude, Claire, Andre, Paule, Pierre. *Education:* Ecole Primaire Superieure Bingerville (Ivory Coast), certificat etudes primaires superieures; Ecole Normale William Ponty (Senegal), diplome de sortie. *Politics:* Parti Democra-

tique de la Cote d'Ivoire-Rassemblement Democratique Africaine (PDCI-RDA). *Religion:* Roman Catholic.

ADDRESSES: Home—Abidjan, Ivory Coast. *Office*—Direction des Affaires Culturelles, BP V 39 Abidjan, Ivory Coast.

CAREER: University of Dakar, Institut Fondamental d'Afrique Noir, Dakar, Senegal, librarian and archivist, 1936-47; press secretary to the Committee Director of PDCI-RDA, Ivory Coast, 1947-53; Government of the Ivory Coast, head of Cabinet of Ministry of National Education, 1957-59, director of Information Services, 1959-61, director of Cultural Affairs for the Ministry of National Education, 1961—. Member and vice-president of Executive Council of UNESCO, 1964-72; director, Commission Nationale de la Fondation Felix Houphouet-Boigny (African Institute for Historical and Political Research); member of Conseil Economique et Social, 1976-77; president of Conference Generale de l'Agence de Cooperation Culturelle et Technique, 1977-79.

MEMBER: Association Internationale pour le Developpement de la Documentation des Bibliotheques et des Archives en Afrique (president), Societe Africaine de Culture (president of Ivory Coast chapter), P.E.N. (vice-president of Ivory Coast chapter), Association Generale des Arts et Lettres de Cote d'Ivoire (president), Association pour le Developpement de la Documentation, des Bibliotheques, des Archives, et des Musees de Cote d'Ivoire (president), L'Academie de l'Union Literaire et Artistique de France, Societe des Gens de Lettres de France, Association des Ecrivains de Langue Francaise (Mer et Outre Mer), Violetti Picards et Normands (honorary member), Academie des Sciences Sociales et Politiques du Bresil (corresponding member), Academie Hispano-Americaine des Belles Lettres (corresponding member), Academie bresilienne des Arts (corresponding member).

AWARDS, HONORS: L'Ordre National de la Cote d'Ivoire, Commandeur, Grand Officier; Commandeur de l'Ordre du Merite de l'Education Nationale; Officier du Merite National Francais; Chevalier des Arts et Lettres; Chevalier de l'Elite Francaise (bronze medal); Laureat du Grand Prix Litteraire de l'Afrique Noire, 1965, for *Patron de New York;* gold medal of l'Academie de Trevise; silver medal of la Ville de Paris; silver medal of la Ville de Bordeaux; Prix America ''Marciano Moreno'' d'Argentine; Ph.D. from l'Academie Internationale de Vancouver; Ph.D. and membre d'honneur of l'Academie des Sciences et Relations Humaines de Mexico; Ph.D. from University of Sheffield; diplome d'honneur et membre protecteur du Club de la Presse de la Republique Dominicaine.

Troubadour d'Honneur du College des Troubadours; gold medal from UNESCO; gold medal of l'Academie Populaire de Guyenne et Gascogne; gold medal (St. Francois) of the Haute Academie Internationale de Lutece; Edgar Allan Poe Poetry Prize, 1975; cross from l'Academie des Sciences d'Outre-Mer; cross of honor, first class for Science and Art (Austria); medal of Alfonso X El Sabio; Officier, Ordre National des Arts et Lettres (France); Commandeur de l'Ordre du Merite Francais d'Outre-Mer, 1964; Commandeur de Pleiade de l'Ordre de la Francophonie et du Dialogue des Cultures; Commandeur d'Ordre National de la Legion d'Honneur (France); Grand Officier de l'Ordre de Leopold (Belgium); Grand Officier de l'Ordre National du Merite (France); Grand Officier de l'Ordre du Merite de la Republique Federale d'Allemagne.

WRITINGS:

FICTION

(Under name Bernard B. Dadie) *Un Negre a Paris* (novel), Presence Africaine, 1939, reprinted, 1966.

Legendes africaines (stories; also see below), Seghers, 1954.

(Under name Bernard B. Dadie) *Le Pagne noir: Contes africaines* (stories), Presence Africaine, 1955, published under name Bernard Dadie with stories by Andre Terrisse as *Les Belles histoires de Kacou Ananze l'araignee*, F. Nathan, 1963, original version translated by Karen C. Hatch published under name Bernard Binlin Dadie as *The Black Cloth: A Collection of African Folktales*, foreword by Es'kia Mphahlele, University of Massachusetts Press, 1987.

(Under name Bernard B. Dadie) *Climbie* (novel; also see below), Seghers, 1956, translated by Karen C. Chapman under original title, Africana Publishing, 1971.

(Under name Bernard B. Dadie) *Patron de New York* (novel), Presence Africaine, 1964.

(Under name Bernard B. Dadie) *La Ville ou nul ne meurt* (chronicle), Presence Africaine, 1968, translated by Janis Mayes as *The City Where No One Dies*, Three Continents, 1986.

(Under name Bernard B. Dadie) *Commandant Taureault et ses negres*, CEDA (Abidjan), 1980.

(Under name Bernard B. Dadie) *Les Jambes du fils de Dieu* (novellas), CEDA, 1980.

(Under name Bernard B. Dadie) *Les Contes de Koutou-As-Samala* (stories), Presence Africaine, 1982.

POETRY

Afrique debout (also see below), Seghers, 1950.

(Under name Bernard B. Dadie) *La Ronde des jours* (also see below), Seghers, 1956, third edition, 1982.

Hommes de tous les continents, Presence Africaine, 1967, reprinted, 1985.

PLAYS

"Les Villes," 1933, produced at a festival in Ivory Coast, 1934.

(Under name Bernard Binlin-Dadie) *Assemien Dehyle, roi du Sanwi: Precede de Mon pays et son theatre*, Album officiel de la Mission Pontificale, 1936, 3rd edition, CEDA, 1979.

(Under name Bernard B. Dadie, with F. J. Amon d'Aby and G. Coffi Gadeau) *Le Theatre populaire en Republique de Cote d'Ivoire* (contains Dadie's "Min Adja-o [C'est mon heritage!]," first produced in 1960; and "Serment d'amour" and "Situation difficile," both produced at Theatre Populaire en Republique de Cote d'Ivoire, 1965), Cercle Culturel et Folklorique de Cote d'Ivoire (Abidjan), 1965.

(Under name Bernard B. Dadie) *Monsieur Thogo-gnini* (comedy; first produced in 1969), Presence Africaine, 1970, translated by Townsend Brewster under original title, Ubu Repertory Theater Publications, 1986.

(Under name Bernard Dadie) *Les Voix dans le vent* (tragedy; first produced in 1969), Editions Cle, 1970.

(Under name Bernard B. Dadie) *Beatrice du Congo: Piece en trois actes* (three-act; first produced in 1969), Presence Africaine, 1970.

(Under name Bernard B. Dadie) *Iles de Tempete: Piece en sept tableaux*, Presence Africaine, 1973.

(Under name Bernard B. Dadie) *Papassidi, maitre-escroc* (comedy; first produced in 1960), Nouvelles editions africaines, 1975.

Mhoi-Ceul: Comedie en 5 tableaux, Presence Africaine, 1979.

OTHER

(Under name Bernard B. Dadie) *Legendes et poemes: Afrique debout! Legendes africaines. Climbie. La Ronde des jours*, Seghers, 1966, published as *Legendes et poemes*, 1973, published as *Legendes africaines*, 1982.

(Under name Bernard Dadie) *Opinions d'un negre: Aphorismes, 1934-1946* (essays), Nouvelles Editions Africaines, 1979.

(Under name Bernard B. Dadie) *Carnet de prison* (biography), CEDA, 1981.

Also author of *Textes*, edited by R. Mercier and M. Battestini, French & European Publications, and of commentary for film "L'Italie vue par un africain," 1961.

WORK IN PROGRESS: *Les Ecrivains dans la lutte pour la liberte*, for CEDA.

BIOGRAPHICAL/CRITICAL SOURCES:

BOOKS

Banhma, M., editor, *African Theatre Today*, Pitman, 1976.

Battestini, Monique, *Bernard B. Dadie, ecrivain ivoirien*, F. Nathan, 1964.

Brench, A. C., *The Novelists' Inheritance in French Africa*, Oxford University Press, 1967.

Quillateau, C., *Bernard Binlin Dadie: L'Homme et l'oeuvre*, Presence Africaine, 1962.

PERIODICALS

Antioch Review, summer, 1967.

* * *

DAMAS, Leon-Gontran   1912-1978

PERSONAL: Born March 28, 1912, in Cayenne, French Guiana; died January 23 (some sources say January 22), 1978, in Washington, D.C.; married wife, Marieth. *Education:* Attended the Universite de Paris in the early 1930s.

CAREER: Poet, 1934-78. Worked in various positions, including editor for the overseas department of Editions Fasquelles, co-founder of *L'Etudiant noir*, and researcher on African culture in the Caribbean and Brazil. Represented French Guiana in the French National Assembly, beginning in 1948, and represented the Societie Africanine de Culture of the United Nations Educational, Scientific, and Cultural Organization (UNESCO). Taught modern and African literature at Federal City College and Howard University in Washington, D.C.

AWARDS, HONORS: Made Officer of National Orders of Honor and Merit by the Republic of Haiti.

WRITINGS:

POETRY; EXCEPT AS NOTED

Pigments (includes "The Black Man's Lament," "They Came That Night," "Sell Out," "Blues," "Reality," "If Often," "Whitewashed," "Shine," "Like the Legend," "Obsession," "There Are Nights," "Position," "*Et Cetera*," and "Hiccups"), [Paris], 1937, revised edition, Presence Africaine, 1962 (also see below).

Veillees noires (short stories), 2nd edition, Stock, 1943.

(Editor) *Poetes d'expression francaise d'Afrique Noire, Madagascar, Reunion, Guadeloupe, Martinique, Indochine, Guyane: 1900-1945*, Seuil, 1947.

Poems negres sur des airs africains, GLM, 1948.

Graffiti, Seghers, 1952.

Black-Label, Gallimard, 1956.

African Songs of Love, War, Grief, and Abuse, translation by Miriam Koshland and Ulli Beier, illustrations by Georgina Betts, Mbari Publications, 1961.

Nevralgies, Presence Africaine, c. 1965 (also see below).

(With Claude Souffrant, Roger Bastide, and Peter D. Thomas) *Hommage a Jean Price-Mars* [and] *A Touch of Negritude* (nonfiction; the former by Damas, Souffrant, and Bastide, the latter by Thomas) Presence Africaine, 1969.

Pigments [and] *Nevralgies*, Presence Africaine, 1972 (also see above).

Contributor of poems to French periodicals, including *Esprit*.

SIDELIGHTS: In the 1930s, Leon-Gontran Damas banded together with fellow French-speaking black writers Aime Cesaire and Leopold Sedar Senghor in Paris to form the literary movement that later became known as Negritude. They founded the journal *L'Etudiant noir* (title means, ''The Black Student'') as a forum for Negritude, which derived some of its ideals from the Harlem Renaissance in the United States but expressed its emphasis on black culture in French. Damas was the first of the movement's founders to publish a book of poems—his famous *Pigments*, which came out in 1937. In addition to producing several other volumes of poetry and a collection of short stories entitled *Veillees noires*, Damas represented his native French Guiana in the French National Assembly for a brief period before coming to the United States to teach literature at the college level in Washington, D.C.

''*Pigments* is an attack, a cry of pain, an anguished inventory of the personal loss of Africa, of Black identity, of discomfort and revolt at the inauthenticity of being 'whitewashed,''' asserted critic Ellen Conroy Kennedy in *Black World*. The poems in *Pigments* range from the very specific, such as ''*Et Cetera*,'' which urges the Senegalese soldiers fighting for the French army to turn on the French and fight for their own independence, to those, like ''The Black Man's Lament,'' ''Sell Out,'' and ''Shine,'' which Kennedy claimed ''could well have been written by a Black American today.'' Still other pieces, such as ''Obsession,'' ''There Are Nights,'' and ''Position,'' have more universal, non-racial themes—depression and despair. Kennedy praised the ''blunt, dry, vivid style'' of *Pigments*, concluding that ''marked by fresh images, unashamedly plain language, staccato rhythms and acridly witty puns, Damas'[s] short poems lay bare their author's often violent rejection of white European [civilization].''

BIOGRAPHICAL/CRITICAL SOURCES:

BOOKS

Racine, Daniel L., editor, *Leon-Gontran Damas, 1912-1978: Founder of Negritude; A Memorial Casebook*, University Press of America, 1979.

PERIODICALS

Black World, January, 1972.

                    *   *   *

DANDRIDGE, Ray G.
   See DANDRIDGE, Raymond Garfield

DANDRIDGE, Raymond Garfield   1882-1930
   (Ray G. Dandridge)

PERSONAL: Born in 1882 in Cincinnati, Ohio; died February 24, 1930; son of Ellen C. Dandridge. *Education:* Attended high school in Cincinnati, Ohio.

ADDRESSES: Home—Cincinnati, Ohio.

CAREER: Poet. House painter and decorator; solicited phone orders for Roger Kemper Rogan's coal company.

WRITINGS:

POETRY

(Under name Ray G. Dandridge) *Penciled Poems*, Powell & White, 1917.

The Poet and Other Poems, Powell & White, 1920, reprinted, AMS Press, 1975.

(Contributor) Robert T. Kerlin, *Negro Poets and Their Poems*, Associated Publishers, 1923.

(Contributor) Newman Ivey White and Walter Clinton Jackson, editors, *An Anthology of Verse by American Negroes*, Trinity College Press, 1924.

Zalka Peetruza and Other Poems, McDonald, 1928.

(Contributor) James Weldon Johnson, editor, *The Book of American Negro Poetry*, expanded edition, Harcourt, 1931.

(Contributor) Robert B. Eleazer, *Singers in the Dawn: A Brief Anthology of American Negro Poetry*, Conference on Education and Race Relations, 1934.

Poetry also represented in anthology *The Poetry of Black America* and in periodicals.

OTHER

Literary editor for *Cincinnati Journal*.

SIDELIGHTS: Most known for his poetry written in the black dialect tradition, Raymond Garfield Dandridge aligned himself with other Harlem Renaissance writers of the 1920s whose poetry expressed discovery, affirmation, achievement, and opportunity for their race. After suffering paralysis of both legs and his right arm from a stroke in 1912, Dandridge taught himself to write verse with his left hand while lying on his back. It is said that his poetry was, perhaps, born out of a courageous spirit to give his thoughts the movement his body had been denied. Optimistic in spirit, the poet was attracted to the charm, humor, and spontaneity of humble people, incorporating their situations and especially the rhythms of their speech into such poems as ''De Drum Majah,'' ''Sprin' Fevah,'' and ''Close Mouf.'' Although his dialect poetry was sometimes considered imitative and erratic, Dandridge's work was popular because of the poet's good-natured approach to life and avoidance of life's more difficult aspects. Dandridge was also able to exhibit the racial protest and militant vigor that marked the 1920s in such later poems as ''Time to Die,'' ''Supplication, Brother Mine,'' and ''Awake and Forward.'' Although he was never considered a great poet such as contemporaries Paul Laurence Dunbar or Alain Locke, his work is said to reflect the democratic, optimistic, and proud spirit characteristic of the black race of his era.

BIOGRAPHICAL/CRITICAL SOURCES:

BOOKS

Dictionary of Literary Biography, Volume 51: *Afro-American Writers From the Harlem Renaissance to 1940*, Gale, 1987.

DANNER, Margaret (Essie)   1915-

PERSONAL: Born January 12, 1915, in Chicago, Ill.; daughter of Caleb and Naomi Danner; married Cordell Strickland; married second husband, Otto Cunningham; children: (first marriage) Naomi (Mrs. Sterling Montrose Washington). *Education:* Attended YMCA College, Roosevelt University, and Loyola University, Chicago, Ill.; also studied under Karl Shapiro and Paul Engle. *Religion:* Baha'i.

ADDRESSES: Home—626 East 102nd Pl., Chicago, Ill. 60628.

CAREER: Poet. *Poetry* magazine, Chicago, Ill., editorial assistant, 1951-55, assistant editor, 1956-57; Wayne State University, Detroit, Mich., poet in residence, 1961-62; touring poet, Baha'i Teaching Committee, 1964-66; Whitney fellow in Senegal, Africa and Paris, France, 1966; Virginia Union University, Richmond, poet in residence, 1968-69. Poet in residence, LeMoyne-Owen College, Memphis, Tenn. Founder, Boone House (center for the arts), Detroit, Mich., and Nologonyu's, Chicago.

MEMBER: Writers, Inc. (president), Nologonya African Cultural Organization.

AWARDS, HONORS: Poetry Workshop Award, Midwestern Writers Conference, 1945; Women's Auxiliary of Afro-American Interests grant, 1950; African Studies Association grant, 1950; John Hay Whitney Foundation Award, 1951; Harriet Tubman Award, 1956; American Society of African Culture grant, 1960; awards from African Studies Association, 1961, and Poets in Concert, 1968.

WRITINGS:

POETRY

Impressions of African Art Forms, Broadside Press, 1960.
To Flower: Poems, Counterpoise Series, 1963.
(With Dudley Randall) *Poem Counterpoem*, Broadside Press, 1966, revised edition, 1969.
Iron Lace, Poets Press, 1968.
(Editor) *Brass Horses* (anthology), Virginia Union University, 1968.
(Editor) *Regroup* (anthology), Virginia Union University, 1969.
The Down of a Thistle: Selected Poems, Prose Poems, and Songs, Country Beautiful, 1976.

CONTRIBUTOR TO ANTHOLOGIES

Rosey E. Poole, editor, *Beyond the Blues: New Poems by American Negroes*, Hand and Flower Press, 1962.
Arna Bontemps, editor, *American Negro Poetry*, Hill & Wang, 1963.
Langston Hughes, editor, *La Poesie Negro-Americaine*, Editions Seghers, 1966.
Robert Hayden, editor, *Kaleidoscope*, Harcourt, 1967.
Randall and Margaret Burroughs, editors, *For Malcolm: Poems of the Life and Death of Malcolm X*, Broadside Press, 1967.
Patricia L. Brown Johnson and others, editors, *To Gwen With Love*, Johnson Publishing (Chicago), 1971.
Randall, editor, *The Black Poets*, Harcourt, 1971.
Richard Barksdale and Keneth Kinnamon, editors, *Black Writers of America: A Comprehensive Anthology*, Macmillan, 1972.
Arnold Adoff, editor, *The Poetry of Black America: Anthology of the 20th Century*, Harper, 1973.

Stephen Henderson, editor, *Understanding the New Black Poetry*, Morrow, 1973.
Erlene Stetson, editor, *Black Sister: Poetry by Black American Women, 1746-1980*, Indiana University Press, 1981.

OTHER

Also author, with Langston Hughes, of sound recording *Writers of the Revolution*, Black Forum. Contributor to *Negro Digest, Baha'i World Order, Poetry, Accent,* and *Chicago Review*.

SIDELIGHTS: Margaret Danner writes: "I have for many years been involved in the study of Africana, especially African Art, because I feel that man reveals a sensitivity through his creative work that is a clue to his present day reactions to problems and pleasures. . . ." In 1966, Danner finally visited Africa on a Whitney fellowship award that she had won in 1951. "It is evident from her poetry that Africa was very much a part of Danner's consciousness and poetry long before she visited there," writes *Dictionary of Literary Biography* contributor June M. Aldridge. "Her visit sharpened her aesthetic sensibility." Aldridge continues: "Several critics have praised Danner's African poems because they, more than any other category of her poems, form her strongest aesthetic and philosophical statements."

Danner has always been involved with the black literary community. During her years in Detroit, Danner helped establish Boone House, a community arts center directed primarily towards children. She also participated in the Phyllis Wheatley Poetry Festival in 1973, a gathering of leading black women poets. This concern for the black community surfaces in her work, especially in her collaboration with Dudley Randall entitled *Poem Counterpoem*. A book of alternating poems, the two poets "treat similar subjects, ranging from the civil rights movement, to old age, to black heritage," describes Aldridge. Nevertheless, Danner's work is not overtly topical; as Aldridge relates, "The few critics who have written about Danner's work praise her highly for her exotic and exact images, her subtle protest poems, and her message that black Americans should preserve, appreciate, and celebrate their African heritage." Responding to the question of black writers directing their output toward black audiences, Danner says: "A writer should write what he feels, and yet I believe that we should help each other. If our talent is writing, we can help in this way—by deliberately directing some of our work toward black audiences. Because of the predicament that the black man is in, and faces, those of us who are black should unite to extricate ourselves and each other."

BIOGRAPHICAL/CRITICAL SOURCES:

BOOKS

Bailey, Leonard Pack, editor, *Broadside Authors and Artists: An Illustrated Biographical Directory*, Broadside Press, 1974.
Dictionary of Literary Biography, Volume 41: *Afro-American Poets Since 1955*, Gale, 1985.
Madhubuti, Haki, *Dynamite Voices I: Black Poets of the 1960s*, Broadside Press, 1971.
Redmond, Eugene, *Drumvoices: The Mission of Afro-American Poetry*, Anchor Books, 1976.

PERIODICALS

Negro Digest, January, 1968.

DATHORNE, O(scar) R(onald)   1934-

PERSONAL: Born November 19, 1934, in Georgetown, British Guiana (now Guyana); son of Oscar Robertson and Rosalie Belona (Peazer) Dathorne; married Hildegard Ostermaier, 1959; children: Shade Cecily and Alexander Franz Keith. *Education:* University of Sheffield, B.A. (honors), 1958, M.A., 1960, Ph.D., 1966; University of London, Grad. Cert. in Ed., 1959, Diploma in Ed., 1967; University of Miami, M.B.A., M.P.A., 1984.

ADDRESSES: Home—8904 Friedberg bei Augsburg, Luberstrasse 2, Germany. *Office*—Department of English, University of Miami, Coral Gables, Fla. 33124.

CAREER: Ahmadu Bello University, Zaria, Nigeria, lecturer in English, 1959-63; University of Ibadan, Ibadan, Nigeria, lecturer in English, 1963-66; U.N.E.S.C.O., Paris, France, adviser to Government of Sierra Leone, 1967-68; University of Sierra Leone, Njala University College, Freetown, professor of English and chairman of department, 1968-70; professor of Afro-American studies at Howard University, Washington, D.C. and University of Wisconsin, Madison, 1970-71; Ohio State University, Columbus, professor of English and black studies, 1971-74, 1975-77; visiting professor of literature, Florida International University, 1974-75; University of Miami, Coral Gables, Fla., professor of English and director of American Studies, 1977—. Has given radio lectures and poetry readings for Nigerian Broadcasting Corp., B.B.C. (London), and several university-owned radio stations. Part-time teacher at Western Nigerian Training College, 1963-66, University of Sierra Leone, 1967-68; visiting professor at Yale University, 1970.

WRITINGS:

Dumplings in the Soup (novel), Cassell, 1963.
The Scholar-Man (novel), Cassell, 1964.
The Black Mind: A History of African Literature, University of Minnesota Press, 1974, abridged edition published as *African Literature in the Twentieth Century,* 1976.
Kelly Poems (verse), privately printed, 1977.
Dark Ancestor: The Literature of the Black Man in the Caribbean, Louisiana State University Press, 1981.
Dele's Child (novel), Three Continents, 1986.

EDITOR

(And author of introduction) *Caribbean Narrative: An Anthology of West Indian Writing,* Heinemann, 1966.
(And author of introduction) *Caribbean Verse: An Anthology,* Heinemann, 1967.
(With Willfried Feuser) *Africa in Prose,* Penguin, 1969.
(And author of introduction) *African Poetry for Schools and Colleges,* Macmillan, 1969.
Derek Walcott, *Selected Poems,* Heinemann, 1977.
Afro World: Adventures in Ideas, University of Wisconsin Press, 1984.
(With others) *Four Way Dictionary,* Cassell, in press.

CONTRIBUTOR

P. L. Brent, editor, *Young Commonwealth Poets '65,* Heinemann, 1965.
Andrew Salkey, editor, *Stories from the Caribbean,* Elek, 1965, published as *Island Voices,* Liveright, 1970.
Howard Sergeant, editor, *Commonwealth Poets of Today,* J. Murray, 1967.
Sergeant, editor, *New Voices of the Commonwealth,* Evans Brothers, 1968.

D. R. Dudley and D. M. Lang, editors, *Penguin Companion to Literature: Part IV,* Penguin, 1969.
Political Spider, Heinemann, 1969.
David Lowenthal and Lambros Comitas, editors, *West Indian Societies,* Doubleday, 1973.

OTHER

(Author of introduction) Donald St. John-Parsons, compiler, *Our Poets Speak,* University of London Press, 1966.
(Author of introduction) Mongo Beti, *King Lazarus,* Collier-Macmillan, 1971.

Editor, *Journal of Caribbean Studies.* Contributor of verse to *Black Orpheus, Transition, Outposts,* and *Presence Africaine;* contributor of stories to *Nigerian Radio Times,* Ibadan, 1967; contributor of critical articles to *Journal of Commonwealth Literature, Times Literary Supplement, New African, Phylon, London Magazine,* and others.

WORK IN PROGRESS: A-Z of African Literature; translating Aime-Cesaire's *Et les chiens se taissaient;* a novel, *Granman* (tentative title); and poetry, *Songs from a New World.*

BIOGRAPHICAL/CRITICAL SOURCES:

PERIODICALS

Choice, October, 1986.
New Yorker, February 28, 1970.
Times Literary Supplement, July 28, 1966, April 2, 1982.
World Literature Today, winter, 1965, autumn, 1965, spring, 1977, winter, 1987.

*   *   *

DAVIS, (William) Allison   1902-1983

PERSONAL: Born October 14 (some sources say October 10), 1902, in Washington, D.C.; died following heart surgery, November 21, 1983, in Chicago, Ill.; son of John Abraham and Gabrielle Dorothy (Beale) Davis; married Alice Elizabeth Stubbs, June 23, 1929 (died, 1966); married Lois L. Mason, January 7, 1969; children: (first marriage) Allison Stubbs, Gordon Jamison. *Education:* Williams College, A.B., 1924; Harvard University, M.A. (English), 1925, M.A. (anthropology), 1932; graduate study at London School of Economics and Political Science, London, 1932-33; University of Chicago, Ph.D., 1942.

CAREER: Harvard University, Cambridge, Mass., co-director of field research in social anthropology, 1933-35; Dillard University, New Orleans, La., professor of anthropology, 1935-38; Yale University Institute of Human Relations, New Haven, Conn., research associate in psychology, 1938-39; University of Chicago, Chicago, Ill., research associate and assistant professor of human development at Center on Child Development, 1939-42, assistant professor, 1942-47, associate professor, 1947-48, professor of education, 1948-70, John Dewey Distinguished Service Professor, 1970-78, retired as professor emeritus, 1978. Member of President's Commission on Civil Rights, 1966-67; vice-chairman for Commission on Manpower Retraining for U.S. Department of Labor, 1968-72; director of Great Books Foundation, beginning in 1970. Lecturer at Harvard University, Smith College, University of Pittsburgh, University of Wisconsin, and University of Rochester.

MEMBER: American Academy of Arts and Sciences (first fellow elected from the field of education), American Psychiatric

Association, Center for Advanced Study in the Behavioral Sciences (fellow, 1959-60), Phi Beta Kappa, Sigma Xi, Phi Delta Kappa.

AWARDS, HONORS: Elected George E. Miller Distinguished Professor at University of Illinois, 1965; elected Prentiss M. Brown Distinguished Service Professor at Albion College, 1970; elected John Dewey Distinguished Service Professor at University of Chicago, 1970; Teachers College Medal from Columbia University, 1977, for distinguished service in education; Solomon Carter Fuller award from American Psychiatric Association, 1977; grants from Spencer Foundation, 1978-80 and 1981-82.

WRITINGS:

(With John Dollard) *Children of Bondage: The Personality Development of Negro Youth in the Urban South,* American Council on Education, 1940, special educational edition, 1956.
(With Burleigh B. Gardner and Mary R. Gardner) *Deep South: A Social Anthropological Study of Caste and Class,* directed by W. Lloyd Warner, University of Chicago Press, 1941, abridged edition, with foreword by James W. Silver, 1965, reprinted, University of California Press, 1988.
(With Robert J. Havighurst) *Father of the Man: How Your Child Gets His Personality,* Houghton, 1947.
Social-Class Influences Upon Learning, Harvard University Press, 1948.
(With Kenneth Eells) *Davis-Eells Games,* World Book, 1953.
(With Eells) *Davis-Eells Test of General Intelligence or Problem-Solving Ability: Directions for Administering and Scoring,* World Book, 1953.
(With Eells) *Davis-Eells Test of General Intelligence or Problem-Solving Ability: Manual,* World Book, 1953.
Psychology of the Child in the Middle Class, University of Pittsburgh Press, 1960.
(With Benjamin S. Bloom and Robert Hess) *Compensatory Education for Cultural Deprivation,* Department of Education, University of Chicago, c. 1964.
(With Hess) *Relationships Between Achievement in High School, College, and Occupation: A Follow-up Study,* University of Chicago Press, 1965.
Leadership, Love, and Aggression, Harcourt, c. 1983.

Also author of *The Motivation of the Underprivileged Worker, The Relation Between Color Caste and Economic Stratification in Two "Black" Plantation Counties,* and, with J. J. G. St. Clair Drake, *The Negro Church and Associations in the Lower South: Research Memorandum* [and] *The Negro Church and Associations in Chicago.* Supervised production of *Intelligence and Cultural Differences: A Study of Cultural Learning and Problem-Solving,* by Kenneth Walter Eells and others. Contributor to newspapers, journals, and magazines.

SIDELIGHTS: Allison Davis was a respected psychologist, social anthropologist, and educator. As assistant professor at the University of Chicago beginning in 1939, Davis was one of the first blacks to hold a full-time teaching position at a major northern university. In 1970 he was named John Dewey Distinguished Service Professor by the University of Chicago, and eight years later he retired as professor emeritus. Many of his writings, including *Children of Bondage: The Personality Development of Negro Youth in the Urban South, Psychology of the Child in the Middle Class,* and *Compensatory Education for Cultural Deprivation,* reflect the author's interest in the psychological development and educational opportunities of children in various social and economic classes.

One of Davis's first works, co-authored by Burleigh B. Gardner and Mary R. Gardner, was the 1941 *Deep South: A Social Anthropological Study of Caste and Class.* The book details the authors' observations and conclusions about the lives of black and white residents in a small southern town. Social psychologist John Dollard determined in *American Anthropologist* that "there is no other single book which does such an excellent job of portraying the social and economic systems of a community," and renowned anthropologist Margaret Mead predicted in 1941 that *Deep South* would "prove an effective background for the kind of thinking which leads to social change." Although the analysis was limited to only one community, stated L. C. Copeland in *American Journal of Sociology,* "the series of studies represented by [*Deep South*] bids fair to extend our knowledge of culture as a whole and of society as a functioning system."

In his 1948 study *Social-Class Influences Upon Learning,* Davis challenged the validity of intelligence tests, asserting that children from lower-class families consistently scored lower than those from middle-class families not because of an intelligence difference, but because the tests were biased toward middle-class culture and educational methods. His findings prompted a re-evaluation of teaching and testing procedures and the development of learning programs such as Head Start for economically disadvantaged children.

In his last book, *Leadership, Love, and Aggression,* Davis analyzes the lives and accomplishments of four prominent black men: Frederick Douglass, W. E. B. Du Bois, Richard Wright, and Martin Luther King, Jr. Citing anger as a common motivating factor in the men's lives, Davis demonstrates how each transformed the negative emotion into positive action. Calling *Leadership, Love, and Aggression* "an extraordinary piece of research," a reviewer in *West Coast Review of Books* stated: "This work is more than a psychobiography of the four but is also a descriptive analysis of the suffering of the American Black at the hands of the government and the larger society."

BIOGRAPHICAL/CRITICAL SOURCES:

PERIODICALS

American Anthropologist, October, 1942.
American Journal of Sociology, November, 1942.
New York Herald Tribune Books, December 7, 1941.
West Coast Review of Books, November, 1983.

OBITUARIES:

PERIODICALS

Chicago Tribune, November 24, 1983.
Newsweek, December 5, 1983.
New York Times, November 22, 1983.
Washington Post, November 23, 1983.

*   *   *

DAVIS, Angela (Yvonne)   1944-

PERSONAL: Born January 26, 1944, in Birmingham, Ala.; daughter of B. Frank (a teacher and businessman) and Sallye E. (a teacher) Davis. *Education:* Attended Sorbonne, University of Paris, 1963-64; Brandeis University, B.A. (magna cum laude), 1965; graduate study at University of Frankfurt, 1965-67; University of California, San Diego, M.A., 1968, graduate study, 1968-69. *Politics:* Communist.

ADDRESSES: Office—3520 18th Street, No. 1, San Francisco, Calif. 94110.

CAREER: University of California, Los Angeles, assistant professor of philosophy, 1969-70; currently professor, teaching courses in philosophy, aesthetics, and women's studies, at San Francisco State University and San Francisco Art Institute. Communist Party candidate for vice-president of the United States, 1980, 1984.

MEMBER: Communist Party (member of Central Committee), National Alliance Against Racist and Political Repression (founder and co-chairperson), National Board of Directors of the National Political Congress of Black Women, National Black Women's Health Project (national board member), Che-Lumumba Club (Los Angeles), Black Panthers (Los Angeles), Phi Beta Kappa.

AWARDS, HONORS: Lenin Peace Prize conferred by the Union of Soviet Socialist Republics, 1979; Ph.D. from Lenin University.

WRITINGS:

(With Ruchell Magee, the Soldedad Brothers, and others) *If They Come in the Morning: Voices of Resistance,* foreword by Julian Bond, Third Press, 1971.
Angela Davis: An Autobiography, Random House, 1974, reprinted, Bantam, 1975.
Women, Race and Class, Random House, 1981.

Also author of sound recording "Angela Davis Speaks," Folkways, 1971. Contributor of articles to *Ebony* and other periodicals.

SIDELIGHTS: Long known as a political activist, Angela Davis has committed her life to the eradication of oppression and poverty, especially among blacks. As a child growing up in Birmingham, Alabama, in an area called "Dynamite Hill," she became painfully aware of the constant threat of racist reprisals faced by black families—a 1963 bombing by the Ku Klux Klan of a black church resulted in the deaths of four of her friends who had been attending Sunday school at the church. A controversial figure in the American public eye, Davis's political convictions propel her to fight for the rights of minority groups. Through her active involvement in the American Communist Party, she has worked ceaselessly and often militantly to guarantee political freedom for repressed peoples.

Although she didn't formally espouse communism until the age of twenty-four, Davis experienced exposure to multiple socio-economic systems throughout her youth. She participated in civil rights demonstrations and helped form interracial study groups as a teenager. Her family had numerous Communist friends; she joined a Communist youth group, Advance, while on a scholarship provided by the American Friends Service Committee at Elizabeth Irwin High School in New York. Additionally, in college she studied under political philosopher Herbert Marcuse, who considered her the best student he ever taught. At the University of California, San Diego, she participated in several activist organizations, including the San Diego Black Conference and the Student Nonviolent Coordinating Committee; she also helped found the Black Students Council. Elinor Langer of the *New York Times Book Review* asserts that Davis's later political philosophies reflect her early influences of socialism and communism: "Both the anticapitalist theory she studied and the interracial Communist community to which she was accustomed must have affected her negative analysis of the American black political scene."

Davis believes that blacks have traditionally lacked the same rights fundamentally available to whites in the United States. In *If They Come in the Morning: Voices of Resistance,* she states, "Needless to say, the history of the United States has been marred from its inception by an enormous quantity of unjust laws, far too many expressly bolstering the oppression of Black people." As a result, she believes, numerous minority members fall prey to the very political and economic conditions that support the upper classes. She explains in *If They Come in the Morning:* "Prisoners—especially Blacks, Chicanos, and Puerto Ricans—are increasingly advancing the proposition that they are political prisoners. They contend that they are political prisoners in the sense that they are largely the victims of an oppressive politico-economic order, swiftly becoming conscious of the causes underlying their victimization."

Davis further characterizes political prisoners as not merely "victims" but rather actual pioneers in the fight against repression. She argues that these prisoners' actions demonstrate a protest against the "oppressive politico-economic order" of which she speaks. She defines the political prisoner in *If They Come in the Morning:* "The offense of the political prisoner is his political boldness, his persistent challenging—legally or extra-legally—of fundamental social wrongs fostered and reinforced by the state. He has opposed unjust laws and exploitative, racist social conditions in general, with the ultimate aim of transforming these laws and this society into an order harmonious with the material and spiritual needs and interests of the vast majority of its members."

Davis views her work with political prisoners as an outgrowth of her personal devotion "to defend our embattled humanity," she states in *Angela Davis: An Autobiography.* She contends that she did not want to write her autobiography, but comments in it: "When I decided to write the book after all, it was because I had come to envision it as a *political* autobiography that emphasized the people, the events and forces in my life that propelled me to my present commitment." Her autobiography details how her aims to help oppressed individuals found expression in the political ideals of communism. About her early introduction to communism, she states in her autobiography: "The *Communist Manifesto* hit me like a bolt of lightning. I read it avidly, finding in it answers to many of the seemingly unanswerable dilemmas which had plagued me. . . . I began to see the problems of Black people within the context of a large working-class movement. My ideas about Black liberation were imprecise, and I could not find the right concepts to articulate them; still, I was acquiring some understanding about how capitalism could be abolished." She continues, explaining the connection between communism and minority liberation, "What struck me so emphatically was the idea that once the emancipation of the proletariat became a reality, the foundation was laid for the emancipation of all oppressed groups in society."

Within the Communist Party, U.S.A., Davis allied herself primarily with the Che-Lumumba Club, a black faction of the Los Angeles Party membership. The club had already declared as its goal the liberation of black peoples in the Los Angeles area through application of Marxist-Leninist philosophies when Davis officially joined the party in July, 1968. Her search for a revolutionary community with which to involve herself did not end with her membership in the Communist party, however. She actively initiated militant demonstrations and protests designed to focus public attention on the plight of minorities. Her radical views eventually interfered with her career as an educator. In 1969, the Board of Regents of the University of California dismissed her from the faculty; a court order reinstated her shortly thereafter. However, the University of California, Los Angeles, did not renew her contract in 1970, despite her rating as an "excellent" and reasonably unbiased teacher by the administration. The American Association of University Professors censured the institution for its decision, and a final attempt by the philosophy department to reinstate her in 1972 failed.

Concurrent with her professional difficulties, Davis's radical beliefs led to her involvement in a 1970 prison break. Political prisoner George Jackson and others attempted to escape from the Marin County, California, courthouse. The situation deteriorated into a shoot-out. In connection with the incident, Davis was charged with kidnapping, conspiracy, and murder. Her subsequent imprisonment and trial aroused international concern and interest; she was ultimately acquitted of all charges.

Davis's controversial behavior has not lessened since her prison and courtroom experiences. She adopts, however, more conventional methods for spreading her ideologies than perhaps she once did. She has immersed herself in the Communist Party, lecturing around the world. Even within the party, her activities have followed more traditional political avenues to effect change: in the 1980 and 1984 U.S. Presidential elections, Angela Davis was the Communist party's vice-presidential candidate.

About *If They Come in the Morning: Voices of Resistance,* Steven V. Roberts of *Commonweal* observes, "In essence, . . . this is a book written by revolutionaries, true believers, who can justify anything in the name of their cause." Although he finds that "the book bristles with contradictions," Roberts adds that "the best parts of [the collection] are several essays by Miss Davis."

Angela Davis: An Autobiography "is less an autobiography than a preliminary probe of her own fiber, her humble realization that she is made of stern stuff," according to the *New Republic*'s Ivan Webster. "She is eloquent, tough and stubborn in her moral integrity." Yet, Webster notes a failing: "It's when she moves away from hard, stark issues that the book falters." Julius Lester of the *Progressive* comments: "One is left with the impression of a woman who lives as she thinks it necessary to live and not as she would like to, if she allowed herself to have desires. She seems to be a woman of enormous self-discipline and control, who willed herself to a total political identity. Her will is so strong that, at times, it is frightening." Lester continues, "Davis has used her politics to eradicate everything in her which would interfere with her commitment to revolutionary change."

Paula Giddings, in *Black World*, shares Lester's view of Davis's intensity and autonomous vision: "[After] reading the last page, one's immediate reaction is, but what have we learned about Angela Davis? The answer is a great deal. . . . She has little desire to project herself as a singularly charismatic figure; . . . the primary purpose of her book is to illuminate the political causes and concerns central to her life." George E. Kent, writing in *PHYLON: The Atlanta University Review of Race and Culture,* also remarks upon Davis's devotion to her aims, noting that "despite its single-minded emphasis upon proper ideological response, the passion with which this political autobiography is written enhances its educational objective."

Davis's *Women, Race and Class* traces and documents the historical development of feminism. Carolly Erickson of the *Los Angeles Times Book Review* states that the book "is as useful an exposition of the current dilemmas of the women's movement as one could hope for." She adds, "*Women, Race and Class* offers a view from the underside of nineteenth-century feminism, and argues that the profound differences that estranged black and white women in the early days of the women's movement still estrange them today." Ann Jones of the *New York Times Book Review* explains further: "Against this intricate background of the separate and unequal histories of black and white women, Miss Davis sets in perspective some contemporary women's issues: rape, reproductive freedom, housework and child care." Jones continues: "I wish she had spoken to us here, as she has so movingly in the past, in a voice less tuned at times to the Communist Party, more insistently her own. But she is herself a woman of undeniable courage. She should be heard."

Angela Davis's political commitments keep her involved in an unending fight against oppression. Her communist beliefs alienate her from many American citizens—Ronald Reagan, while California State Governor, once declared Davis would never teach in the California university system due to her political beliefs and activities—yet she continues to lecture and write in support of her philosophies. Although Davis's ideologies garner much opposition in the United States, Jones remarks upon her tenacity, describing Davis as one "who has never shied from impossible tasks."

MEDIA ADAPTATIONS: Angela Davis may be seen in the documentary "Portrait of a Revolutionary," prepared by one of her students.

BIOGRAPHICAL/CRITICAL SOURCES:

BOOKS

Ashman, Charles R., *The People vs. Angela Davis,* Pinnacle Books, 1972.
Contemporary Issues Criticism, Volume I, Gale, 1982.
Davis, Angela, *Angela Davis: An Autobiography,* Random House, 1974.
Davis, Angela, Ruchell Magee, the Soldedad Brothers, and others, *If They Come in the Morning: Voices of Resistance,* Third Press, 1971.
Lund, Caroline, *The Czechoslovak Frame-Up Trials,* Pathfinder Press, 1973.
Smith, Nelda J., *From Where I Sat,* Vantage, 1973.

PERIODICALS

Black World, March, 1975.
Commonweal, March 24, 1972.
New Republic, November 16, 1974.
Los Angeles Times Book Review, April 4, 1982.
New York Times Book Review, October 27, 1974, January 10, 1982.
PHYLON: The Atlanta University Review of Race and Culture, March, 1976.
Progressive, February, 1975.
Voice Literary Supplement, June, 1982.

OTHER

The Angela Davis Trial (microfilm), Oceana, 1974.
Davis, Angela, "Angela Davis Speaks" (sound recording), Folkways, 1974.

DAVIS, Arthur P(aul) 1904-

PERSONAL: Born November 21, 1904, in Hampton, Va.; son of Andrew (a plasterer) and Frances (Nash) Davis; married Clarice Winn, October 6, 1928; children: Arthur Paul, Jr. *Education:* Columbia University, A.B., 1927, A.M., 1929, Ph.D., 1942. *Politics:* Independent. *Religion:* Episcopalian.

ADDRESSES: Home—3001 Veazey Ter. N.W., Washington, D.C. 20008. *Office*—Graduate School, Howard University, Washington, D.C. 20059.

CAREER: North Carolina College (now North Carolina Central University), Durham, professor of English, 1927-28; Virginia Union University, Richmond, professor of English, 1929-44; Howard University, Washington, D.C., professor of English, 1944-69, university professor, 1969-80, university professor emeritus, 1980—. Conducted series of talks, "Ebony Harvest," on Radio WAMU-FM, Washington-Baltimore, 1972-73.

MEMBER: Modern Language Association of America, College Language Association, Phi Beta Kappa.

AWARDS, HONORS: Proudfit fellow, Columbia University, 1937; National Hampton alumni award, 1947; Award from Howard University's Institute for the Arts and Humanities, 1973; award from College Language Association, 1975, for distinguished contribution to literary scholarship.

WRITINGS:

(Editor with Sterling A. Brown and Ulysses Lee) *The Negro Caravan*, Dryden, 1941, Arno, 1970.
Isaac Watts: His Life and Works, Dryden, 1943.
(Editor with Saunders Redding) *Cavalcade: Negro American Writers from 1760 to the Present*, Houghton, 1971.
From the Dark Tower: Afro-American Writers from 1900 to 1960, Howard University Press, 1974.
(Editor with Michael Peplow) *The New Negro Renaissance: An Anthology*, Holt, 1975.

Writer of column, "With a Grain of Salt," *Journal and Guide* newspaper, 1933-50.

WORK IN PROGRESS: The Life and Observations of Arthur P. Davis, Middle Class Negro (tentative title).

SIDELIGHTS: Arthur P. Davis writes: "In 1929, I taught my first course in Negro literature. Very, very few Negro and no white schools in those days had a course in this subject. Believing strongly in the importance of the Negro's contribution to American literature, I have devoted practically all of my adult working years to teaching and writing in the field of Negro letters. It has been gratifying to note the subject's growth in popularity since 1929."

BIOGRAPHICAL/CRITICAL SOURCES:

PERIODICALS

New York Times Book Review, December 30, 1969.
Saturday Review of Literature, February 21, 1942.
Times Literary Supplement, November 27, 1948.

*   *   *

DAVIS, Charles T(witchell) 1918-1981

PERSONAL: Born April 29, 1918, in Hampton, Va.; died in 1981; married; children: two. *Education:* Dartmouth College, A.B., 1939; University of Chicago, A.M., 1942; New York University, Ph.D., 1951.

CAREER: New York University, New York, N.Y., began as instructor, became assistant professor of English, 1948-55; Princeton University, Princeton, N.J., assistant professor, 1955-61; Pennsylvania State University, University Park, Pa., began as associate professor, became professor, 1961-70; University of Iowa, Iowa City, professor of English, 1970-76; Yale University, New Haven, Conn., professor of English and chairman of Afro-American studies, 1972-81, master of Calhoun College, 1973-81. Chairman of the Senate Committeee on Student Affairs at Pennsylvania State University during the 1960s; member of supervisory committee, English Institute, 1962-65; Fulbright professor at the University of Turin, 1966-67; fellow, Center for Advanced Study in Behavioral Science in Stanford, Calif., 1976-77; member of advisory council, Center of Independent Study in New Haven, 1977-81; member of board of trustees, National Humanities Center in Research Triangle Park, N.C., 1978-81; member of board, State of Connecticut's academic awards, 1979-81.

MEMBER: Modern Language Association of America, American Studies Association, Society for the Study of Southern Literature.

AWARDS, HONORS: Rockefeller Humanities Fellowship.

WRITINGS:

(With Gay Wilson Allen) *Walt Whitman's Poems: Selections With Critical Aids*, New York University Press, 1955.
(Editor) E. A. Robinson, *Selected Early Poems and Letters*, Holt, 1960.
(Editor) Lucy Larcom, *A New England Girlhood*, Corinth Books, 1961.
(Editor) *On Being Black: Writings by Afro-Americans From Frederick Douglass to the Present*, Fawcett, 1970.
(With Michel Fabre) *Richard Wright: A Primary Bibliography*, G. K. Hall, 1982.
Black Is the Color of the Cosmos: Essays on Afro-American Literature and Culture, 1942-1981, edited by Henry Louis Gates, Jr., foreword by A. Bartlett Giamatti, Garland Publishing, 1982.
(Editor with Gates) *The Slave's Narrative*, Oxford University Press, 1985.

WORK IN PROGRESS: The Shaping of the Afro-American Literary Tradition, a two-volume history, left unfinished at time of death.

SIDELIGHTS: Charles T. Davis, professor of English and chairman of the Afro-American studies department at Yale University for the last years of his life, had become one of the most influential scholars of black American literature by the time of his death in 1981. Also an expert on nineteenth-century white American authors such as poet Walt Whitman, Davis is now best known for his posthumously published works—his collection of writings on black literature and culture, *Black Is the Color of the Cosmos*, and a compilation of critical essays he edited with Henry Louis Gates, Jr., *The Slave's Narrative*. Lauded as "a fine critical mind" by reviewer Peter Nazareth in *World Literature Today*, Davis was mourned by Ishmael Reed in the *Yale Review* as "the critic of tomorrow," whose "biculturalism, which enabled him to move comfortably through both black and white American literary and cultural traditions," would be missed.

Black Is the Color of the Cosmos discusses many issues in the field of black literature with "original insight and clarity," according to Reed. Davis opines on the relation of the 1960s Black Arts Movement to nineteenth-century American romanticism, asserts the precedence of black lecturer and writer Frederick Douglass's *Narrative* over those published by most other former slaves, and declares that Charles Chestnutt—one of the first black novelists to be published in the United States—produced an "achievement in fiction . . . superior to that of any other Negro artist until the time of the Harlem Renaissance." Davis also explores the Harlem Renaissance itself, and holds forth on the work of later black authors Richard Wright, Ralph Ellison, and James Baldwin. To these and other writers, "he brings a superior intelligence and the perspectives of a sophisticated humanist," summed reviewer P. Butcher in *World Literature Today*. Davis's work was perceived by some, however, as too greatly influenced by white, Western cultural tradition. "When Davis suggests the appropriateness of reading [authors] Gwndolyn Brooks and Robert Hayden on Western grounds," complained critic R. Baxter Miller in *Black American Literature Forum*, "he hardly considers any other way of reading to be possible."

The Slave's Narrative, which Davis edited with Gates, was labeled "an impressive collection" by Frances Smith Foster in *The New York Times Book Review*, who upheld "the book's rightful claim as a contribution to the re-evaluation of slave narratives." The essays which Davis and Gates compiled address issues such as the literary and historical merits of autobiographical accounts by former slaves. The book also includes reviews published shortly after the narratives themselves, and moved critic William L. Andrews to conclude in *Black American Literature Forum*: "It is unlikely that any single collection of essays could do greater justice than *The Slave's Narrative* has to the breadth, vitality, and untapped potential of this topic and the discourse it has generated."

BIOGRAPHICAL/CRITICAL SOURCES:

BOOKS

Davis, Charles T., *Black Is the Color of the Cosmos: Essays on Afro-American Literature and Culture, 1942-1981*, Garland Publishing, 1982.

PERIODICALS

Black American Literature Forum, winter, 1984, spring, 1986.
New York Times Book Review, July 7, 1985.
World Literature Today, summer, 1983, autumn, 1983.
Yale Review, summer, 1983.

                              *   *   *

DAVIS, Frank Marshall   1905-1987

PERSONAL: Born December 31, 1905, in Arkansas City, Kan.; died July 26, 1987, in Honolulu, Hawaii; married; children: Lynn, Beth, Jeanne, Jill, Mark. *Education:* Attended Friends University, 1923; attended Kansas State Agricultural College (now Kansas State University of Agricultural and Applied Science), 1924-27, 1929.

CAREER: Worked for various newspapers in Illinois, including the *Chicago Evening Bulletin, Whip,* and *Gary American,* 1927-29; *Atlanta Daily World,* Atlanta, Ga., editor and cofounder, 1931-34; Associated Negro Press, Chicago, Ill., executive editor, 1935-47; *Chicago Star,* Chicago, executive editor, 1946-48; owned wholesale paper business in Honolulu, Hawaii, beginning c. 1948. Served as a jazz radio disc jockey in the early 1940s. Authored weekly column for *Honolulu Record*. Toured black colleges as a lecturer, 1973.

MEMBER: League of American Writers, Allied Arts Guild, Southside Chicago Writers Group.

AWARDS, HONORS: Julius Rosenwald Foundation grant, 1937.

WRITINGS:

Black Man's Verse (poems; includes "Giles Johnson, Ph.D.," "Lynched [Symphonic Interlude for Twenty-One Selected Instruments]," "Mojo Mike's Beer Garden," "Cabaret," and "Ebony Under Granite"), Black Cat, 1935.
I Am the American Negro (poems; includes "I Am the American Negro," "Flowers of Darkness," "To One Who Would Leave Me," "Awakening," "Come to Me," "Modern Man—The Superman: A Song of Praise for Hearst, Hitler, Mussolini, and the Munitions Makers," "'Mancipation Day," "Onward Christian Soldiers," "Christ Is a Dixie Nigger," "Note Left by a Suicide," "Ebony Under Granite," and "Frank Marshall Davis: Writer"), Black Cat, 1937.
Through Sepia Eyes (poems; includes "Chicago Skyscrapers," "To Those Who Sing America," "Life Is a Woman," and "Coincidence"), Black Cat, 1938.
47th Street: Poems (includes "47th Street," "Pattern for Conquest," "Egotistic Runt," "Tenement Room," "Black Weariness," "Snapshots of the Cotton South," "Peace Quiz for America," "For All Common People," "War Zone," "Nothing Can Stop the People," "Peace Is a Fragile Cup," and "Self-Portrait"), Decker, 1948.
Awakening, and Other Poems, Black Cat, 1978.

Also author of poem "Chicago's Congo" and of a volume of poetry entitled *Jazz Interlude*, 1985; author of the unpublished manuscript "That Incredible Waikiki Jungle." Poems published in anthologies, including *The Negro Caravan*, Dryden, 1942; *Kaleidoscope: Poems by American Negro Poets*, Harcourt, 1967; *Black Voices: An Anthology of Afro-American Literature*, New American Library, 1968; *The Poetry of the Negro, 1746-1970*, Anchor Books, 1970; *Black Insights*, Ginn, 1971; *Understanding the New Black Poetry*, Morrow, 1973; and *The New Negro Renaissance: An Anthology*, Holt, 1975. Contributor to periodicals, including *National, Light and Heebie Jeebies,* and *Voices*.

SIDELIGHTS: Frank Marshall Davis's poetry "not only questioned social ills in his own time but also inspired blacks in the politically charged 1960s," according to John Edgar Tidwell in the *Dictionary of Literary Biography*. Davis, who has been compared to poets such as Walt Whitman and Carl Sandburg, published his first volume, *Black Man's Verse*, in 1935. The book met with much applause from critics, including Harriet Monroe, who concluded in *Poetry* that its author was "a poet of authentic inspiration, who belongs not only among the best of his race, but who need not lean upon his race for recognition as an impassioned singer with something to say." Davis concerned himself with portraying black life, protesting racial inequalities, and promoting black pride. The poet described his work thus in the poem "Frank Marshall Davis: Writer" from his *I Am the American Negro:* "When I wrote / I dipped my pen / In the crazy heart / Of mad America."

Davis grew up in Arkansas City, Kansas, surrounded by racism. Tidwell reports that when the poet was five years old he was nearly killed by some older white children who had heard stories of lynchings and wanted to try one for themselves. The result of this incident and others was that Davis hated whites in his youth. He gained some relief, according to Tidwell, when he left the prejudiced, small-town atmosphere of Arkansas City in 1923 to attend Friends University in Wichita; he eventually transferred to Kansas State Agricultural College's school of journalism. There, because of a class assignment, Davis received his first introduction to writing free verse—his preferred poetic form. When he left Kansas State, he traveled to Chicago where he wrote free-lance articles for magazines and worked for several black newspapers while continuing to produce poems. After a brief return to Kansas State, Davis moved to Atlanta, Georgia, to take an editing post on a semiweekly paper. With the help of his leadership, the periodical became the *Atlanta Daily World,* the first successful black daily newspaper in America. Meanwhile, one of Davis's published poems, "Chicago's Congo," which concerns the underlying similarities between the blacks of Chicago and those still living the tribal life of the African Congo, attracted the attention of bohemian intellectual Frances Norton Manning. When Davis returned to Chicago, Manning introduced him to Norman Forgue, whose Black Cat Press subsequently published Davis's *Black Man's Verse.*

A critical success, *Black Man's Verse* "is experimental, cacophonous, yet sometimes harmonious," according to Tidwell. The volume includes poems such as "Giles Johnson, Ph.D.," in which the title character starves to death in spite of his four college degrees and knowledge of Latin and Greek because he did not wish to teach and was incapable of doing the manual labor that made up the majority of work available to blacks. Other pieces in *Black Man's Verse*—"Lynched," "Mojo Mike's Beer Garden," and "Cabaret," for example—make use of Davis's expertise on the subject of jazz to combine "the spirit of protest in jazz and free verse with . . . objections to racial oppression, producing a poetry that loudly declaims against injustice," explained Tidwell. Another well-known part of the volume is entitled "Ebony Under Granite." Likened to author Edgar Lee Masters's *Spoon River Anthology,* this section discusses the lives of various black people buried in a cemetery. Characters include Reverend Joseph Williams, who used to have sex with most of the women in his congregation; Goldie Blackwell, a two-dollar prostitute; George Brown, who served life in prison for voting more than once—in Mississippi he had seen white voters commit the same crime many times without punishment; and Roosevelt Smith, a black writer who was so frustrated by literary critics that he became a postman.

I Am the American Negro, Davis's second collection of poems, was published two years after his first. While drawing generally favorable reviews, it did not attract as much attention as *Black Man's Verse,* and some critics complained that it was too similar to the earlier book. For example, Tidwell quotes black critic Alain Locke's assertion that *I Am the American Negro* "has too many echoes of the author's first volume. . . . It is not a crescendo in the light of the achievement of [*Black Man's Verse*]." One of the obvious similarities between the two collections is that Davis also included an "Ebony Under Granite" section in the second. Members of this cast are people like the two Greeley sisters—the first's earlier promiscuous life-style did not prevent her from marrying respectably, while the second's lack of sexual experience caused her husband to be unfaithful; Nicodemus Perry, killed by loiterers for accidentally bumping into a white woman while, ironically, lost in memories of the sexual abuse his female relatives suffered at the hands of white men; and Mrs. Clifton Townsend, prejudiced against the darker-skinned members of her own race, who dies after giving birth to a baby much blacker than herself.

Other poems featured in *I Am the American Negro* are "Modern Man—The Superman," which laments the state of modern civilization and has mock musical notations in its margins such as "Eight airplane motors, each keyed to a different pitch, are turned on and off to furnish musical accompaniment within the range of an octave"; and the title poem, which is a diatribe against Southern laws treating blacks differently from whites. Davis also placed love poems such as "Flowers of Darkness" and "Come to Me" in this book.

The poems of Davis's limited-edition third volume, *Through Sepia Eyes,* were later published along with others in his 1948 collection, *47th Street.* Though Tidwell described *47th Street* as "the culmination of Davis's thought and poetic development," Davis himself remarked on the time span between *I Am the American Negro* and his fourth book in a 1973 interview for *Black World:* "I was going through a number of changes during that particular time and I had to wait for these changes to settle and jell before I produced other work which I thought would be suitable to appear in a volume. And, of course, some critics naturally have thought that I would have been better off had I just continued to jell indefinitely." *47th Street* is composed of poems such as "Coincidence," which narrates the life stories of Donald Woods, a white man, and Booker Scott, a black man, who shared their dates of birth and death—by the poem's end the reader discovers that they also shared the same white biological father. The title poem, "unlike [Davis's] previous descriptions of Southside Chicago as exclusively black," noted Tidwell, "presents a 'rainbow race' of people." Indeed, Tidwell saw the whole of *47th Street* as having more universal concerns than his earlier works. When questioned about this issue Davis declared: "I am a Black poet, definitely a Black poet, and I think that my way of seeing things is the result of the impact on our civilization upon what I like to think of as a sensitive Black man. . . . But I do not think the Black poet should confine himself exclusively to Black readership. I think poetry, if it is going to be any good, should move members of all groups, and that is what I hope for."

In the same year that *47th Street* was published, Davis left Chicago for Honolulu, Hawaii. What began as a vacation turned into permanent residency. Except for a few poems that appeared in *Voices* in 1950, Davis virtually disappeared from the literary world until going on a college lecture tour in 1973. He later published other volumes of poetry, and at the time of his death in 1987 he had been working on a manuscript called "That Incredible Waikiki Jungle," about his Hawaiian experiences. When asked why he decided to remain in Hawaii, Davis cited the relative lack of racial problems and added, "I think one of the reasons why was that this [was] the first time that I began to be treated as a man instead of a Black curiosity. That was important to me, for my feeling of dignity and self-respect."

BIOGRAPHICAL/CRITICAL SOURCES:

BOOKS

Davis, Frank Marshall, *I Am the American Negro,* Black Cat, 1978.
Dictionary of Literary Biography, Volume 51: *Afro-American Writers From the Harlem Renaissance to 1940,* Gale, 1987.

PERIODICALS

Black World, January, 1974.
Poetry, August, 1936.

OBITUARIES:

PERIODICALS

Chicago Tribune, August 9, 1987.

—*Sketch by Elizabeth Thomas*

*   *   *

DAVIS, George B.   1939-

PERSONAL: Born November 29, 1939, in Shepherdstown, W. Va.; son of Clarence (a clergyman) and Winnie Davis; married Mary Cornelius (a secretary), August 31, 1963; children: Pamela, George. *Education:* Colgate University, B.A., 1961; Columbia University, M.F.A., 1971.

ADDRESSES: Home—327 Claremont Ave., Mt. Vernon, N.Y. 10552. *Office*—Rutgers University, New Brunswick, N.J. 08903.

CAREER: U.S. Air Force, 1961-68, became captain; *Washington Post,* Washington, D.C., staff writer, 1968-69; *New York Times,* New York, N.Y., deskman, 1969-70; Bronx Community College of the City University of New York, Bronx, N.Y., assistant professor, 1974-78; Rutgers University, New Brunswick, N.J., assistant professor, 1978—. Teacher of writing workshops at Columbia University and Greenhaven Prison. Cofounder and president, Black Swan Communications; president of Contemporary Communications (marketing firm).

MEMBER: Authors Guild, Authors League of America.

AWARDS, HONORS: Military: Air Medal. Other: Awards from New York State Council on the Arts, America the Beautiful Fund, and National Endowment for the Humanities.

WRITINGS:

Coming Home (novel), Random House, 1971.
Love, Black Love (nonfiction), Doubleday, 1978.
(With Glegg Watson) *Black Life in Corporate America: Swimming in the Mainstream,* Doubleday, 1982.

Contributor of articles and short stories to numerous periodicals, including *Black World, Essence, National Observer, Smithsonian, New York Times Magazine, Black Enterprise,* and *Beauty Trade.*

SIDELIGHTS: George Davis's book *Black Life in Corporate America* explores the status of black people in management positions in business today. For three years Davis and his co-author Glegg Watson researched this project, interviewing well over 150 managers—both black and white—and talking with numerous experts in the field of blacks in the business world. Wente Bowen writes in the *Los Angeles Times* that after analyzing all of the data, Davis and Watson point out in their book that "on the surface, most blacks and whites get along quite well in most corporate settings, but many black managers find the corporate environment to be 'living hell' for them. Their suggestions are ignored, and they invariably end up being second in charge behind a white guy. 'Even if he's dumb, they will trust him more.' In short, racism holds back the progress of the black manager inside corporate America."

BIOGRAPHICAL/CRITICAL SOURCES:

PERIODICALS

Chicago Tribune Book World, May 19, 1985.
Los Angeles Times, September 9, 1982.

Newsweek, April 6, 1970.
New York Times Book Review, October 24, 1982.

*   *   *

DAVIS, Nolan   1942-

PERSONAL: Born July 23, 1942, in Kansas City, Mo.; son of William L. (a fireman) and Frances Ann (Davis) Davis; married Carol Lorraine Christian (an artist), July 27, 1963; children: Arian Valentinian, Pelia de Valoria. *Education:* Attended San Diego Evening College, 1964-65, and Stanford University, 1967-68. *Politics:* Democrat.

ADDRESSES: Home—3532 Sixth Ave., Los Angeles, Calif. 90018.

CAREER: San Diego Evening Tribune, San Diego, Calif., staff writer, 1963-66; Economic Opportunities Commission of San Diego County, San Diego, director of public relations, 1966-67; *Newsweek* (magazine), New York, N.Y., staff correspondent, 1967-70; KNXT-TV, Hollywood, Calif., producer and senior writer, 1970-71; KABC-TV, Hollywood, chief newswriter, 1971; SHARC Productions, Inc., Los Angeles, Calif., partner and vice-president, beginning 1971; novelist, screenwriter, and producer and director of televisions and films. *Military service:* U.S. Navy, journalist, 1960-63.

MEMBER: Authors League of America, Writers Guild, Sigma Delta Chi.

WRITINGS:

Six Black Horses (novel), Putnam, 1971.
(With John O'Grady) *O'Grady* (biography), Tarcher/Hawthorne, 1974.

TELEVISION SCRIPTS

"Grave Undertaking," episode of series "Sanford and Son," produced by National Broadcasting Co., 1970.
"Storyline," produced by American Broadcasting Co., 1971.
"The Jazz Show with Billy Eckstein," produced by NBC-TV, 1972.
"Further Than the Pulpit," produced by NBC-TV, 1972.

Also author of episode of "Ironsides," produced by Universal, 1974.

OTHER

Author of screenplays "The Stellar Story," produced by Stellar Industries Corp., 1970, and "Men (and Women) Managing Money," produced by Shareholders Management Co., 1971. Also author of screenplays, "Six Black Horses" and "The Fighting 99th." Recorded "The Good News Blues," released by Crossover Records, 1975. Contributor to *Newsweek, National Catholic Reporter, Reader's Digest,* and other periodicals.

SIDELIGHTS: Nolan Davis's novel, *Six Black Horses,* is the story of a young man, Lawrence Xavier Jordan, who gives up his aspirations of becoming an artist to study as an apprentice to the very successful and flamboyant mortician, Southwall Lovingood. Jordan eventually becomes the leading black mortician in Kansas City, Missouri, but has to pay the price for all his success. Bruce Allen writes in the *Library Journal* that *Six Black Horses* is "the realistic chronicle of black life, the Dreiser-like saga of flawed ambition's rise and fall, the folk tale of demonic possession."

"Davis's novel is an imaginative and often witty allegory about the death-traps which can ensare even the most vital of men," states Doren Arden in the *Detroit News.* Arthur Cooper remarks in *Newsweek:* "Davis has written a splendidly mordant funny first novel. . . . If Evelyn Waugh and Ralph Ellison had collaborated on a novel, the result might well have been something like *Six Black Horses.*" And a reviewer for *Booklist* comments that *Six Black Horses* "succeeds as a human comedy and is a uniquely detailed fictional account of the mortuary business." Finally, Zena Sutherland notes in *Saturday Review* that "not since *The Loved One* [by Evelyn Waugh] has there been such a funny, funny book about the business of death. . . . The writing has wit, humor, and vitality."

BIOGRAPHICAL/CRITICAL SOURCES:

PERIODICALS

Booklist, December 15, 1971.
Detroit News, December 26, 1971.
Library Journal, December 1, 1971.
Publishers Weekly, August 16, 1971.
Saturday Review, January 15, 1970.

* * *

DAVIS, Ossie 1917-

PERSONAL: Born December 18, 1917, in Cogdell, Ga.; son of Kince Charles (a railway construction worker) and Laura (Cooper) Davis; married Ruby Ann Wallace (an actress; professional name Ruby Dee), December 9, 1948; children: Nora, Guy, La Verne. *Education:* Attended Howard University, 1935-39, and Columbia University, 1948.

ADDRESSES: Agent—Artists Agency, 10000 Santa Monica Blvd., Suite 305, Los Angeles, Calif. 90067.

CAREER: Actor, playwright, screenwriter, and director and producer of stage productions and motion pictures. Worked as janitor, shipping clerk, and stock clerk in New York, N.Y, 1938-41. Actor in numerous stage productions, including "Joy Exceeding Glory," 1941, "Jeb," 1946, "No Time for Sergeants," 1957, and "A Raisin in the Sun," 1959. Actor in motion pictures and teleplays, including "The Joe Louis Story," 1953, "The Emperor Jones," 1955, "The Cardinal," 1963, "Man Called Adam," 1966, "Teacher, Teacher," 1969, and "Let's Do It Again," 1976. Director of motion pictures, including "Black Girl," 1972, and "Gordon's War," 1973. Co-host of radio program "Ossie Davis and Ruby Dee Story Hour," 1974-78, and of television series "With Ossie and Ruby," Public Broadcasting System (PBS-TV), 1981. Co-producer of stage production "Ballad for Bimshire," 1963. Founder, Institute of Cinema Artists, 1973. Performer on recordings for Caedmon and Folkways Records. Civil rights activist. *Military service:* U.S Army, 1942-45; served as surgical technician in Liberia, West Africa, and with Special Services Department.

AWARDS, HONORS: Emmy Award nomination for outstanding single performance by an actor in a leading role, Academy of Television Arts and Sciences, 1969, for "Teacher, Teacher"; with wife Ruby Dee, Frederick Douglass Award from New York Urban League, 1970.

WRITINGS:

PLAYS

(And director) "Goldbrickers of 1944," first produced in Liberia, West Africa, 1944.
"Alice in Wonder," one-act; first produced in New York at Elks Community Theatre, September 15, 1952; revised and expanded version produced as "The Big Deal" in New York at New Playwrights Theatre, March 7, 1953.

Purlie Victorious (first produced in New York at Cort Theatre, September 28, 1961; also see below), French, 1961.
Curtain Call, Mr. Aldridge, Sir (first produced in Santa Barbara at the University of California, summer, 1968), published in *The Black Teacher and the Dramatic Arts: A Dialogue, Bibliography, and Anthology,* edited by William R. Reardon and Thomas D. Pawley, Negro University sities Press, 1970.
(With Philip Rose, Peter Udell, and Gary Geld) *Purlie* (adaptation of *Purlie Victorious;* first produced on Broadway at Broadway Theatre, March 15, 1970), French, 1971.
Escape to Freedom: A Play about Young Frederick Douglass (first produced in New York at the Town Hall, March 8, 1976), Viking, 1978.
Langston: A Play, Delacorte, 1982.

Also author of "Last Dance for Sybil."

SCREENPLAYS AND TELEPLAYS

"Gone Are the Days" (adaptation of Davis's *Purlie Victorious;* also released as "Purlie Victorious" and "The Man from C.O.T.T.O.N."), Trans Lux, 1963.
(With Arnold Perl, and director) "Cotton Comes to Harlem," United Artists, 1970.
(And director) "Kongi's Harvest" (adapted from work by Wole Soyinka), Calpenny Films Nigeria Ltd., 1970.
"Today Is Ours," Columbia Broadcasting System (CBS-TV), 1974.

Also author of teleplay "Just Say the Word," 1969, and author and director of screenplay "Countdown at Krisni," 1976. Also author of scripts for television series, including "Bonanza" and "N.Y.P.D."

OTHER

(Contributor) Herbert Hill, editor, *Anger, and Beyond: The Negro Writer in the United States,* Harper, 1966.
(Contributor) Hill, editor, *Soon, One Morning: New Writing by American Negroes, 1940-1962,* Knopf, 1968.
(Contributor) Ruby Dee, editor, *Glowchild, and Other Poems,* Third Press, 1972.
(With others) "The Black Cinema: Foremost Representatives of the Black Film World Air Their Views" (sound recording), Center for Cassette Studies 30983, 1975.
(Author with Hy Gilbert of book, and director) "Bingo" (baseball musical based on novel *The Bingo Long Traveling All-Stars and Motor Kings* by William Brashler), first produced in New York at AMAS Repertory Theater, November, 1985.

Contributor to journals and periodicals, including *Negro History Bulletin, Negro Digest,* and *Freedomways.*

SIDELIGHTS: "Ossie Davis is best known as an actor, but his accomplishments extend well beyond the stage," writes Michael E. Green in the *Dictionary of Literary Biography.* "In the theater, in motion pictures, and in television he has won praise both for his individual performances and those he has given with his wife, Ruby Dee. He has, however, also been a writer, director, producer, social activist, and community leader."

He began his career after enrolling at Howard University, where Alain Locke, a drama critic and professor of philosophy, spurred Davis's budding interest in the theatre. On Locke's counseling, Davis became involved in several facets of stage life, including maintenance and set construction, while biding time as an actor. He first appeared on the stage as a member of

Harlem's Ross McClendon Players in a 1941 production of "Joy Exceeding Glory." Few offers followed, however, and Davis was reduced to sleeping in parks and scrounging for food.

In 1942 Davis was inducted into the army, where he served as a medical technician in Liberia, West Africa. After his transfer to Special Services, he began writing and producing stage works to entertain military personnel. Upon discharge, though, Davis returned to his native Georgia. There he was reached by McClendon director Richard Campbell, who encouraged Davis to return to New York City and audition for Robert Ardrey's "Jeb." Davis accepted Campbell's encouragement and eventually secured the title role in Ardrey's work. The play, which concerns a physically debilitated veteran's attempt to succeed as an adding machine operator in racist Louisiana, was poorly received, but Davis was exempted for his compelling performance.

Davis married fellow "Jeb" performer Ruby Dee in 1948 after they completed a stint with the touring company of "Anna Lucasta." The pace of his acting career then accelerated as Davis performed admirably in works such as "Stevedore," in which he played a servant who assumes a misplaced worldliness following a visit to Paris, and "The Green Pastures," in which he played one of several angels in a black-populated Heaven.

While acting, Davis also continued to devote attention to his writing. "As a playwright Davis was committed to creating works that would truthfully portray the black man's experience," says Jayne F. Mulvaney in a *Dictionary of Literary Biography* essay. In 1953, his play "Alice in Wonder," which re-created McCarthy-era action, was dimly received in Harlem; however, his 1961 opus *Purlie Victorious* generated a more favorable response. Mulvaney describes the play as a comedy about the schemes of an eloquent itinerant preacher who returns to his Georgia home with hopes of buying the old barn that once served as a black church, and establishing an integrated one. To realize his plan, he must secure the inheritance of his deceased aunt, a former slave, whose daughter has also died. Because Captain Cotchipee, the play's antagonist and holder of the inheritance, is unaware of the death of Purlie's cousin, Purlie plans to have a pretty young black girl impersonate his cousin so that he can claim the inheritance to finance the church of his dreams. "The action of the play involves the hilarious efforts of Purlie, his family, and the captain's liberal son, Charlie, to outwit the captain," says Mulvaney; and critics were especially pleased with Davis's humorous portrayal of the black preacher's efforts to swipe the five-hundred-dollar inheritance from the white plantation owner.

Greene calls *Purlie Victorious* a "Southern fable of right against wrong, with Purlie's faith in the cause of equality triumphing over the bigotry of Ol' Cap'n Cotchipee, the local redneck aristocrat." Considering the comedy's brilliance to derive "chiefly from how cliches and stereotypes are blown out of proportion," Mulvaney suggests that "*Purlie Victorious* is satire which proceeds toward reconciliation rather than bitterness. Its invective is not venomous." "Unfortunately, despite the reviews, the endorsement of the National Association for the Advancement of Colored People, and the play's seven-and-a-half month run, neither playwright nor producer made money," says Mulvaney. "The financial support of the black community was not enough; the white audiences did not come." Greene suggests that the play would have been considerably more successful had it been written either ten years before or after it was, "Davis himself recognized that his handling of stereotypes, black and white, would have been offensive had a white writer created them." Also, Greene writes that Davis "argues that one of his purposes in the play was to present justice as an ideal, as something that is not always the same as traditional law-and-order, which allows the Ol' Cap'ns of American society to win too often."

Purlie Victorious was adapted by Davis as the motion picture "Gone Are the Days." A. H. Weiler, writing in the *New York Times,* complained that the film rarely availed itself of cinematic techniques, but added that the work "is still speaking out against injustice in low, broad, comic fashion." Weiler praised the performances of Davis, who played the preacher Purlie Victorious, and Ruby Dee, Purlie's lover.

In 1970 Davis collaborated with the songwriting team of Peter Udell and Gary Geld on "Purlie," a musical adaptation of the play. The *New York Times*'s Clive Barnes called the new version "so strong, . . . so magnificent" that audiences would respond by shouting "Hallelujah!" in praise. He deemed it "by far the most successful and richest of all black musicals" and attributed its prominence to "the depth of the characterization and the salty wit of the dialogue." For Davis, "Purlie" was not just another success—it was an experience in self-discovery. "Purlie told me," he wrote, "I would never find my manhood by asking the white man to define it for me. That I would never become a man until I stopped measuring my black self by white standards."

The careers of Dee and Davis have been intertwined throughout the 1970s and 1980s. They have performed together in stage productions, films, and recordings and shared duties as hosts/performers on the brief PBS-TV series "With Ossie and Ruby." Dee and Davis have also been active in the civil rights movement, participating in marches and hearings and sponsoring showings before hospital, church, and prison groups. *Ebony* called their marriage "a living argument against the popular notion that the theater is bound to wreck the homes of those couples who choose it as a profession."

BIOGRAPHICAL/CRITICAL SOURCES:

BOOKS

Abramson, Doris E., *Negro Playwrights in the American Theatre, 1925-1959,* Columbia University Press, 1969.
Dictionary of Literary Biography, Gale, Volume 7: *Twentieth-Century American Dramatists,* 1981, Volume 38: *Afro-American Writers after 1955: Dramatists and Prose Writers,* 1985.
Funke, Lewis, *The Curtain Rises—The Story of Ossie Davis,* Grosset & Dunlap, 1971.
Patterson, Lindsay, editor, *Anthology of the American Negro in the Theatre,* Association for the Study of Life and History/Publishers Company, 1967.

PERIODICALS

Detroit Free Press, November 11, 1983.
Ebony, February, 1961, December, 1979.
Freedomways, spring, 1962, summer, 1965, summer, 1968.
Nation, April 6, 1970.
National Observer, March 22, 1970.
Negro Digest, February, 1966, April, 1966.
Negro History Bulletin, April, 1967.
Newsweek, March 30, 1970.
New York, April, 1970.

New Yorker, October 7, 1961.
New York Times, September 24, 1963, May 5, 1968, October 12, 1969, March 10, 1970, November 11, 1985.
Variety, March 5, 1969, January 28, 1970, March 28, 1970.

*   *   *

DEE, Ruby
See WALLACE, Ruby Ann

*   *   *

DELANY, Samuel R(ay, Jr.)   1942-

PERSONAL: Born April 1, 1942, in New York, N.Y.; son of Samuel R. (a funeral director) and Margaret Carey (a library clerk; maiden name, Boyd) Delany; married Marilyn Hacker (a poet), August 24, 1961 (divorced, 1980); children: Iva Alyxander. *Education:* Attended City College (now of the City University of New York), 1960 and 1962-63.

ADDRESSES: Agent—Henry Morrison, Inc., Box 235, Bedford Hills, N.Y. 10507.

CAREER: Writer. Butler Professor of English, State University of New York at Buffalo, 1975; senior fellow at the Center for Twentieth Century Studies, University of Wisconsin—Milwaukee, 1977; senior fellow at the Society for the Humanities, Cornell University, 1987; professor of comparative literature, University of Massachusetts—Amherst, 1988.

AWARDS, HONORS: Nebula Award, Science Fiction Writers of America, 1967, for best novel, *Babel-17*, 1968, for best short story, ''Aye and Gomorrah,'' and for best novel, *The Einstein Intersection*, and 1970, for best novelette, ''Time Considered as a Helix of Semi-Precious Stones''; Hugo Award, Science Fiction Convention, for ''Time Considered as a Helix of Semi-Precious Stones''; American Book Award nomination, 1980, for *Tales of Neveryon;* Pilgrim Award, Science Fiction Research Association, 1985.

WRITINGS:

SCIENCE FICTION

The Jewels of Aptor (abridged edition bound with *Second Ending* by James White), Ace Books, 1962, hardcover edition, Gollancz, 1968, complete edition published with an introduction by Don Hausdorff, Gregg Press, 1976.
Captives of the Flame (first novel in trilogy; bound with *The Psionic Menace* by Keith Woodcott), Ace Books, 1963, revised edition published under author's original title *Out of the Dead City* (also see below), Sphere Books, 1968.
The Towers of Toron (second novel in trilogy; also see below; bound with *The Lunar Eye* by Robert Moore Williams), Ace Books, 1964.
City of a Thousand Suns (third novel in trilogy; also see below), Ace Books, 1965.
The Ballad of Beta-2 (also see below; bound with *Alpha Yes, Terra No!* by Emil Petaja), Ace Books, 1965, hardcover edition published with an introduction by David G. Hartwell, Gregg Press, 1977.
Empire Star (also see below; bound with *The Three Lord of Imeten* by Tom Purdom), Ace Books, 1966, hardcover edition published with an introduction by Hartwell, Gregg Press, 1977.
Babel-17, Ace Books, 1966, hardcover edition, Gollancz, 1967, published with an introduction by Robert Scholes, 1976.

The Einstein Intersection, slightly abridged edition, Ace Books, 1967, hardcover edition, Gollancz, 1968, complete edition, Ace Books, 1972.
Nova, Doubleday, 1968.
The Fall of the Towers (trilogy; contains *Out of the Dead City, The Towers of Toron*, and *City of a Thousand Suns*), Ace Books, 1970, hardcover edition published with introduction by Joseph Milicia, Gregg Press, 1977.
Driftglass: Ten Tales of Speculative Fiction, Doubleday, 1971.
The Tides of Lust, Lancer Books, 1973.
Dhalgren, Bantam, 1975, hardcover edition published with introduction by Jean Mark Gawron, Gregg Press, 1978.
The Ballad of Beta-2 [and] *Empire Star*, Ace Books, 1975.
Triton, Bantam, 1976.
Empire: A Visual Novel, illustrations by Howard V. Chaykin, Berkley Books, 1978.
Distant Stars, Bantam, 1981.
Stars In My Pocket Like Grains of Sand, Bantam, 1984.
The Complete Nebula Award-Winning Fiction, Bantam, 1986.

''RETURN TO NEVERYON'' SERIES; SWORD AND SORCERY NOVELS

Tales of Neveryon, Bantam, 1979.
Neveryona; or, The Tale of Signs and Cities, Bantam, 1983.
Flight from Neveryon, Bantam, 1985.
The Bridge of Lost Desire, Arbor House, 1987.

OTHER

The Jewel-Hinged Jaw: Notes on the Language of Science Fiction, Dragon Press, 1977, revised edition, Berkley Publishing, 1978.
The American Shore: Meditations on a Tale of Science Fiction by Thomas M. Disch—''Angouleme'' (criticism), Dragon Press, 1978.
Heavenly Breakfast: An Essay on the Winter of Love (memoir), Bantam, 1979.
Starboard Wine: More Notes on the Language of Science Fiction, Dragon Press, 1984.
The Motion of Light in Water: Sex and Science Fiction Writing in the East Village, 1957-1965, Arbor House, 1988.
Wagner/Artaud: A Play of Nineteenth and Twentieth Century Critical Fictions, Ansatz Press, 1988.
Straits of Messina (essays), Serconia Press, 1988.

Also author of scripts, director, and editor for two short films, ''Tiresias,'' 1970, and ''The Orchid,'' 1971; author of two scripts for the ''Wonder Woman Comic Series,'' 1972, and of the radio play ''The Star Pit,'' based on his short story of the same title.

Editor, *Quark*, 1970-71.

SIDELIGHTS: ''Samuel R. Delany is one of today's most innovative and imaginative writers of science-fiction,'' comments Jane Branham Weedman in her study of the author, *Samuel R. Delany*. In his science fiction, which includes over fifteen novels and two collections of short stories, the author ''has explored what happens when alien world views intersect, collide, or mesh,'' writes Greg Tate in the *Voice Literary Supplement*. Delany first appeared on the science-fiction horizon in the early 1960s and in the decade that followed he established himself as one of the stars of the genre. Like many of his contemporaries who entered science fiction in the 1960s, he is less concerned with the conventions of the genre, more interested in science fiction as literature, literature which offers a wide range of artistic opportunities. As a result, maintains Weedman, ''Delany's works are excellent examples of modern science-fiction as it has developed from the earlier and more limited science-fiction tradition, especially because of his manipulation of cultural theories, his detailed futuristic or alternate settings, and his stylistic innovations.''

"One is drawn into Delany's stories because they have a complexity,'' observes Sandra Y. Govan in the *Black American Literature Forum,* ''an acute consciousness of language, structure, and form; a dextrous ability to weave together mythology and anthropology, linguistic theory and cultural history, gestalt psychology and sociology as well as philosophy, structuralism, and the adventure story.'' At the center of the complex web of personal, cultural, artistic, and intellectual concerns that provides the framework for all of his work is Delany's examination of how language and myth influence reality. ''According to [the author],'' writes Govan in the *Dictionary of Literary Biography,* ''language identifies or negates the self. It is self-reflective; it shapes perceptions.'' By shaping perceptions, language in turn has the capacity to shape reality. Myths can exercise much the same power. In his science fiction, Delany ''creates new myths, or inversions of old ones, by which his protagonists measure themselves and their societies against the traditional myths that Delany includes,'' Weedman observes. In this way, as Peter S. Alterman comments in the *Dictionary of Literary Biography,* the author confronts ''the question of the extent to which myths and archetypes create reality.''

In societies in which language and myth are recognized as determinants of reality, the artist—one who works in language and myth—plays a crucial part. For this reason, the protagonist of a Delany novel is often an artist of some sort. ''The role which Delany defines for the artist is to observe, record, transmit, and question paradigms in society,'' explains Weedman. But Delany's artists do more than chronicle and critique the societies of which they are a part. His artists are always among those at the margin of society; they are outcasts and often criminals. ''The criminal and the artist both operate outside the normal standards of society,'' observes Alterman, ''according to their own self-centered value systems.'' The artist/criminal goes beyond observation and commentary. His actions at the margin push society's values to their limits and beyond, providing the experimentation necessary to prepare for eventual change.

Delany entered the world of science fiction in 1962 with the publication of his novel, *The Jewels of Aptor.* Over the next six years, he published eight more, including *Babel-17, The Einstein Intersection,* and *Nova,* his first printed originally in hardcover. Douglas Barbour, writing in *Science Fiction Writers,* describes these early novels as ''colorful, exciting, entertaining, and intellectually provocative to a degree not found in most genre science fiction.'' Barbour adds that although they do adhere to science-fiction conventions, they ''begin the exploration of those literary obsessions that define [Delany's] oeuvre: problems of communication and community; new kinds of sexual/love/family relationships; the artist as social outsider . . . ; cultural interactions and the exploration of human social possibilities these allow; archetypal and mythic structures in the imagination.''

With the publication of *Babel-17* in 1966, Delany began to gain recognition in the science fiction world. The novel, which earned its author his first Nebula Award, is a story of galactic warfare between the forces of the Alliance, which includes the Earth, and the forces of the Invaders. The poet Rydra Wong is enlisted by Alliance intelligence to decipher communications intercepted from its enemy. When she discovers that

these dispatches contain not a code but rather an unknown language, her quest becomes one of learning this mysterious tongue labeled Babel-17. While leading an interstellar mission in search of clues, Rydra gains insights into the nature of language and, in the process, discovers the unique character of the enigmatic new language of the Invaders.

Babel-17 itself becomes an exploration of language and its ability to structure experience. A central image in the novel, as George Edgar Slusser points out in his study, *The Delany Intersection: Samuel R. Delany Considered as a Writer of Semi-Precious Words,* is that of ''the web and its weaver or breaker.'' The web, continues Slusser, ''stands, simultaneously, for unity and isolation, interconnectedness and entanglement.'' And, as Peter Alterman points out in *Science-Fiction Studies,* ''the web is an image of the effect of language on the mind and of the mind as shaper of reality.'' Weedman elaborates in her essay on the novel: ''The language one learns necessarily constrains and structures what it is that one says.'' In its ability to connect and constrain is the power of the language/web. ''Language . . . has a direct effect on how one thinks,'' explains Weedman, ''since the structure of the language influences the processes by which one formulates ideas.'' At the center of the language as web ''is one who joins and cuts—the artist-hero,'' comments Slusser. And, in *Babel-17,* the poet Rydra Wong demonstrates that only she is able to master this new language weapon and turn it against its creators.

Delany followed *Babel-17* with another Nebula winner, *The Einstein Intersection.* This novel represents a ''move from a consideration of the relationship among language, thought, action and time to an analytic and imaginative investigation of the patterns of myths and archetypes and their interaction with the conscious mind,'' writes Alterman. Slusser sees this development in themes as part of a logical progression: ''[Myths] too are seen essentially as language constructs: verbal scenarios for human action sanctioned by tradition or authority.'' Comparing this novel to *Babel-17,* he adds that ''Delany's sense of the language act, in this novel, has a broader social valence.''

The Einstein Intersection relates the story of a strange race of beings that occupies a post-apocalyptic Earth. This race assumes the traditions—economic, political, and religious—of the extinct humans in an attempt to make sense of the remnant world in which they find themselves. ''While they try to live by the myths of man,'' writes Barbour in *Foundation,* ''they cannot create a viable culture of their own. . . . Their more profound hope is to recognize that they do not have to live out the old myths at all, that the 'difference' they seek to hide or dissemble is the key to their cultural and racial salvation.''

''Difference is a key word in this novel,'' Weedman explains, ''for it designates the importance of the individual and his ability to make choices, on the basis of being different from others, which affect his life, thus enabling him to question the paradigms of his society.'' The artist is the embodiment of this difference and in *The Einstein Intersection* the artist is Lobey, a musician. The power of Lobey's music is its ability to create order, to destroy the old myths and usher in the new. At its core, then, ''*The Einstein Intersection* is . . . a novel about experiments in culture,'' Weedman comments.

Delany's next novel, *Nova,* ''stands as the summation of [his] career up to that time,'' writes Barbour in *Science Fiction Writers: Critical Studies of the Major Authors from the Early Nineteenth Century to the Present Day.* ''Packing his story full of color and incident, violent aciton and tender introspective moments, he has created one of the grandest space operas ever written.'' In this novel, Delany presents a galaxy divided into three camps, all embroiled in a bitter conflict caused by a shortage of the fuel illyrion on which they all depend. In chronicling one group's quest for a new source of the fuel, the author examines, according to Weedman, ''how technology changes the world and philosophies for world survival. Delany also explores conflicts between and within societies, as well as the problems created by people's different perceptions and different reality models.''

''In developing this tale,'' notes Slusser, ''Delany has inverted the traditional epic relationship, in which the human subject (the quest) dominates the 'form.' Here instead is a 'subjunctive epic.' Men do not struggle against an inhuman system so much as *inside* an unhuman one.'' The system inside which these societies struggle is economic; the goal of the quester, who is driven by selfishness, is a commodity. Whether the commodity is abundant or scarce, as Jeanne Murray Walker points out in *Extrapolation*, this ''is a world where groups are out of alignment, off balance, where some suffer while others prosper, where the object of exchange is used to divide rather than to unite.'' Walker concludes in her essay that ''by ordering the action of *Nova* in the quest pattern, but assuming a value system quite different from that assumed by medieval romance writers, Delany shows that neither pattern nor action operate as they once did. Both fail.'' Even so, as she continues, ''individuals must continue to quest. Through their quests they find meaning for themselves.''

After the publication of *Nova*, Delany turned his creative urges to forms other than the novel, writing a number of short stories, editing four quarterlies of speculative fiction, and dabbling in such diverse media as film and comic books. Also at this time, he engaged himself in conceiving, writing, and polishing what would become his longest, most complex, and most controversial novel, *Dhalgren*—a work that would earn him national recognition. On its shifting surface, this novel represents the experience of a nameless amnesiac, an artist/criminal, during the period of time he spends in a temporally and spatially isolated city scarred by destruction and decay. As Alterman relates in the *Dictionary of Literary Biography*, ''it begins with the genesis of a protagonist, one so unformed that he has no name, no identity, the quest for which is the novel's central theme.'' The critic goes on to explain that ''at the end Kid has a name and a life, both of which are the novel itself; he is a persona whose experience in *Dhalgren* defines him.''

Dhalgren's length and complexity provide a significant challenge to readers, but as Gerald Jones observes in the *New York Times Book Review*, ''the most important fact about Delany's novel . . . is that nothing in it is clear. Nothing is *meant* to be clear.'' He adds: ''An event may be described two or three times, and each recounting is slightly disconcertingly different from the one before.'' What is more, continues the reviewer, ''the nameless narrator experiences time discontinuously; whole days seem to be excised from his memory.'' According to Weedman, ''Delany creates disorientation in *Dhalgren* to explore the problems which occur when reality models differ from reality.'' And in Jonas's estimation, ''If the book can be said to be *about* anything, it is about nothing less than the nature of reality.''

''*Dhalgren* has drawn more widely divergent critical response than any other Delany novel,'' comments Govan in her *Dictionary of Literary Biography* essay. ''Some reviewers deny that it is science fiction, while others praise it for its daring and experimental form.'' For instance, the *Magazine of Fantasy and Science Fiction* book reviewer Algis Budrys contends that ''this book is not science fiction, or science fantasy, but allegorical quasi-fantasy on the [James Gould] Cozzens model. Thus, although it demonstrates the breadth of Delany's education, and many of its passages are excellent prose, it presents no new literary inventions.'' In his *Science Fiction Writers* essay, Barbour describes the same novel as ''the very stuff of science fiction but lacking the usual structural emblems of the genre.'' ''One thing is certain,'' offers Jonas, '''Dhalgren' is not a conventional novel, whether considered in terms of S.F. or the mainsream.''

Following the exhaustive involvement with Kid necessary to complete *Dhalgren*, Delany chose to do a novel in which he distanced himself from his protagonist, giving him a chance to look at the relationship between an individual and his society in a new light. ''I wanted to do a psychological analysis of someone with whom you're just not in sympathy, someone whom you watch making all the wrong choices, even though his plight itself is sympathetic,'' Delany explained in an interview with Larry McCaffery and Sinda Gregory published in their book *Alive and Writing: Interviews with American Authors of the 1980s*. The novel is *Triton;* its main character is Bron.

''*Triton* is set in a sort of sexual utopia, where every form of sexual behavior is accepted, and sex-change operations (not to mention 'refixations,' to alter sexual preference) are common,'' observes Michael Goodwin in *Mother Jones*. In this world of freedom lives Bron, who Govan describes in *Black American Literature Forum* as ''a narrow-minded, isolated man, so self-serving that he is incapable of reaching outside himself to love another or even understand another despite his best intentions.'' In an attempt to solve his problems, he undergoes a sex-change operation, but finds no happiness. ''Bron is finally trapped in total social and psychological stasis, lost in isolation beyond any help her society can offer its citizens,'' comments Barbour in *Science Fiction Writers*.

In this novel, once again Delany creates an exotic new world, having values and conventions that differ from ours. In exploring this fictional world, he can set up a critique of our present-day society. In *Triton*, he casts a critical eye, as Weedman points out, on ''sexual persecution against women, ambisexuals, and homosexuals.'' She concludes that the work is ''on the necessity of knowing one's self despite sexual identification, knowing one's sexual identity is not one's total identity.''

In the 1980s, Delany has continued to experiment in his fiction writing. In his ''Neveryon'' series, which includes *Tales of Neveryon, Neveryona; or, The Tale of Signs and Cities, Flight from Neveryon*, and *The Bridge of Lost Desire*, he chooses a different setting. ''Instead of being set in some imagined future, [they] are set in some magical, distant past, just as civilization is being created,'' observes McCaffery in a *Science-Fiction Studies* interview of Delany. Their focus, suggests Gregory in the same interview, is ''power—all kinds of power: sexual, economic, even racial power via the issue of slavery.''

Throughout these tales of a world of dragons, treasures, and fabulous cities, Delany weaves the story of Gorgik, a slave who rises to power and abolishes slavery. In one story, the novel-length ''Tale of Plagues and Carnivals,'' he shifts in time from his primitive world to present day New York and back to examine the devastating effects of a disease such as

AIDS. And, in the appendices that accompany each of these books, he reflects on the creative process itself. Of the four, it is *Neveryona*, the story of Pryn—a girl who flees her mountain home on a journey of discovery—that has received the most attention from reviewers. *Science Fiction and Fantasy Book Review* contributor Michael R. Collings calls it "a stirring fable of adventure and education, of heroic action and even more heroic normality in a world where survival itself is constantly threatened." Faren C. Miller finds the book groundbreaking; she writes in *Locus:* "Combining differing perspectives with extraordinary talent for the *details* of a world—its smells, its shadows, workaday furnishings, and playful frills—Delany has produced a sourcebook for a new generation of fantasy writers." The book also "presents a new manifestation of Delany's continuing concern for language and the magic of fiction, whereby words become symbols for other, larger things," Collings observes.

In *Stars in My Pocket Like Grains of Sand*, Delany returns to distant worlds of the future. The book is "a densely textured, intricately worked out novelistic structure which delights and astonishes even as it forces a confrontation with a wide range of thought-provoking issues," writes McCaffery in *Fantasy Review*. Included are "an examination of interstellar politics among thousands of far flung worlds, a love story, a meandering essay on the variety of human relationships and the inexplicability of sexual attractiveness, and a hypnotic crash-course on a fascinating body of literature which does not yet exist," notes H. J. Kirchhoff in the Toronto *Globe and Mail*.

Beneath the surface features, as Jonas suggests in the *New York Times Book Review,* the reader can discover the fullness of this Delany novel. The reviewer writes: "To unpack the layers of meaning in seemingly offhand remarks or exchanges of social pleasantries, the reader must be alert to small shifts in emphasis, repeated phrases or gestures that assume new significance in new contexts, patterns of behavior that only become apparent when the author supplies a crucial piece of information at just the proper moment." Here in the words and gestures of the characters and the subtle way in which the author fashions his work is the fundamental concern of the novel. "I take the most basic subject here to be the nature of information itself," McCaffery explains, "the way it is processed, stored and decoded symbolically, the way it is distorted by the present and the past, the way it has become a commodity . . . the way that the play of textualities defines our perception of the universe."

"This is an astonishing new Delany," according to Somtow Sucharitkul in the *Washington Post Book World,* "more richly textured, smoother, more colorful than ever before." Jonas commends the novel because of the interaction it encourages with the reader. "Sentence by sentence, phrase by phrase, it invites the reader to collaborate in the process of creation, in a way that few novels do," writes the reviewer. "The reader who accepts this invitation has an extraordinarily satisfying experience in store for him/her." "*Stars in My Pocket Like Grains of Sand . . .* confirms that [Delany] is American SF's most consistently brilliant and inventive writer," McCaffery claims.

Critics often comment on Delany's use of fiction as a forum to call for greater acceptance of women's rights and gay rights; yet, as Govan maintains in her *Dictionary of Literary Biography* contribution, "a recurring motif frequently overlooked in Delany's fiction is his subtle emphasis on race. Black and mixed-blood characters cross the spectrum of his speculative futures, both as a testimony to a future Delany believes will change to reflect human diversity honestly and as a commentary on the racial politics of the present."

In novels such as *Babel-17,* Delany demonstrates how language can be used to rob the black man of his identity. "White culture exerts a great influence because it can force stereotypic definitions on the black person," writes Weedman. She adds that "if the black person capitulates to the definition imposed on him by a force outside of his culture, then he is in danger of losing his identity." In his other novels, Govan points out, "Delany utilizes existing negative racial mythologies about blacks, but, in all his works, he twists the commonplace images and stereotypes to his own ends." In using his fiction to promote awareness of the race issue, he and other black writers like him "have mastered the dominant culture's language and turned it against its formulators in protest," writes Weedman.

"Delany is not only a gifted writer," claims Barbour in his *Foundation* article, "he is one of the most articulate theorists of sf to have emerged from the ranks of its writers." In such critical works as *The Jewel-Hinged Jaw, The American Shore,* and *Starboard Wine,* "he has done much to open up critical discussion of sf as a genre, forcefully arguing its great potential as art," adds the reviewer. In his nonfiction, Delany offers a functional description of science fiction and contrasts it with other genres such as naturalistic fiction and fantasy. He also attempts to expand "the domain of his chosen genre by claiming it the modern mode of fiction *par excellence,*" comments Slusser, "the one most suited to deal with the complexities of paradox and probability, chaos, irrationality, and the need for logic and order."

Samuel R. Delany is not a simple man: a black man in a white society, a writer who suffers from dyslexia, an artist who is also a critic. His race, lifestyle, chosen profession, and chosen genre keep him far from the mainstream. "His own term 'multiplex' probably best describes his work (attitudes, ideas, themes, craftsmanship, all their inter-relations, as well as his relation, as artist, to them all)," Barbour suggests. And, adds the reviewer, "His great perseverance in continually developing his craft and never resting on his past achievements is revealed in the steady growth in [his] artistry." In Weedman's estimation, "Few writers approach the lyricism, the command of language, the powerful combination of style and content that distinguishes Delany's works. More importantly," she concludes, "few writers, whether in science fiction or mundane fiction, so successfully create works which make us question ourselves, our actions, our beliefs, and our society as Delany has helped us do."

BIOGRAPHICAL/CRITICAL SOURCES:

BOOKS

Bleiler, E. F., editor, *Science Fiction Writers: Critical Studies of the Major Authors from the Early Nineteenth Century to the Present Day,* Scribner, 1982.
Contemporary Literary Criticism, Gale, Volume 8, 1978, Volume 14, 1980, Volume 38, 1986.
Delany, Samuel R., *The Jewel-Hinged Jaw: Notes on the Language of Science Fiction,* Dragon Press, 1977, revised edition, Berkley Publishing, 1978.
Delany, Samuel R., *Heavenly Breakfast: An Essay on the Winter of Love,* Bantam, 1979.
Delany, Samuel R., *The Motion of Light in Water: Sex and Science Fiction Writing in the East Village, 1957-1965,* Arbor House, 1988.

Dictionary of Literary Biography, Gale, Volume 8: *Twentieth-Century American Science Fiction Writers*, 1981, Volume 33: *Afro-American Fiction Writers after 1955*, 1984.

McCaffery, Larry, and Sinda Gregory, editors, *Alive and Writing: Interviews with American Authors of the 1980s*, University of Illinois Press, 1987.

Peplow, Michael W., and Robert S. Bravard, *Samuel R. Delany: A Primary and Secondary Bibliography, 1962-1979*, G. K. Hall, 1980.

Platt, Charles, editor, *Dream Makers: The Uncommon People Who Write Science Fiction*, Berkley Books, 1980.

Slusser, George Edgar, *The Delany Intersection: Samuel R. Delany Considered as a Writer of Semi-Precious Words*, Borgo, 1977.

Weedman, Jane Branham, *Samuel R. Delany*, Starmont House, 1982.

PERIODICALS

Analog Science Fiction/Science Fact, April, 1985.
Black American Literature Forum, summer, 1984.
Commonweal, December 5, 1975.
Extrapolation, fall, 1982.
Fantasy Review, December, 1984.
Foundation, March, 1975.
Globe and Mail (Toronto), February 9, 1985.
Locus, summer, 1983.
Los Angeles Times Book Review, March 13, 1988.
Magazine of Fantasy and Science Fiction, November, 1975, June, 1980.
Mother Jones, August, 1976.
New York Times Book Review, February 16, 1975, March 28, 1976, October 28, 1979, February 10, 1985.
Publishers Weekly, January 29, 1988.
Science Fiction and Fantasy Book Review, July/August, 1983.
Science Fiction Chronicle, November, 1987.
Science-Fiction Studies, Volume 4, number 11, Volume 14, number 2, 1987.
Voice Literary Supplement, February, 1985.
Washington Post Book World, January 27, 1985.

—*Sketch by Bryan Ryan*

*   *   *

DEMBY, William   1922-

PERSONAL: Born December 25, 1922, in Pittsburgh, Pa.; son of William and Gertrude (Hendricks) Demby; married Lucia Drudi (a novelist); children: James. *Education:* Attended West Virginia State College; Fisk University, B.A., 1947; additional study at University of Rome, Italy.

ADDRESSES: Home—New York, N.Y. *Office*—College of Staten Island of the City University of New York, Staten Island, N.Y. 10017.

CAREER: Has worked as jazz musician and screenwriter in Rome, Italy, and as advertising agent in New York, N.Y.; currently associate professor at College of Staten Island of the City University of New York. Novelist. *Military service:* Served in North Africa during World War II.

MEMBER: European Community of Writers, Alpha Phi Alpha.

WRITINGS:

NOVELS

Beetlecreek, Rinehart, 1950, reprinted, Chatham Bookseller, 1972.

The Catacombs, Pantheon, 1965.
Love Story Black, Reed, Cannon & Johnson, 1978.
Blueboy, Pantheon, 1979.

CONTRIBUTOR TO ANTHOLOGIES

Herbert Hill, editor, *Soon One Morning: New Writing by American Negroes, 1940-62*, Knopf, 1963.

Edward Margolies, editor, *A Native Son's Reader*, Lippincott, 1970.

Saunders Redding and Arthur P. Davis, editors, *Cavalcade: Negro American Writing From 1760 to the Present*, Houghton, 1971.

SIDELIGHTS: William Demby "has been separated from the tradition of black literature because his novels have a universality about them," states *Dictionary of Literary Biography* contributor Margaret Perry. "His work does not fit tidily into a niche reserved for black writers," she continues; "indeed, his writings reflect not only some aspects of black life but focus seriously upon the human conditions all people experience: Demby's literary lens focuses upon the myriad elements that illuminate character and situation in a world where moral choices create drama." In novels such as *Beetlecreek*, *The Catacombs*, and *Love Story Black*, she concludes, Demby explores existential themes in the context of modern life.

In an interview with John O'Brien in *Studies in Black Literature*, William Demby speaks of writing and the novelist's function: "It must be very, very difficult not to write because there's certainly plenty of things to write, but the whole context of the novel seems to have moved into another ball field. You can do almost anything you want . . . yet, you have to remain in contact with the consciousness of your reader, at the same time you are seeing things yourself. . . . How much can we feed back, how much should we feed back . . . ? The novelist must have this function of seeing connections." Demby assesses that the writer "also has the responsibility (and this may be true for all artists), to make some connection with the past. That is, to illustrate how much of the past is living in the present and how much of the present is only the future and the past. All these things he must bring to life, all the connections, or 'myths' if you will, by which people will imagine things to survive. I suppose that that may be the artist's function, as you say, to make all the connections," he concludes, "because if we disavow the chronological progression idea of history, then it must be something like that tapestry, it must be made up at the same moment of the past, present and future."

BIOGRAPHICAL/CRITICAL SOURCES:

BOOKS

Dictionary of Literary Biography, Volume 33: *Afro-American Fiction Writers after 1955*, Gale, 1984.

Margolies, Edward, *Native Sons: A Critical Study of Twentieth Century Negro American Authors*, Lippincott, 1968.

O'Brien, John, *Interviews With Black Writers*, Liveright, 1973.

Whitlow, Roger, *Black American Literature*, Nelson Hall, 1973.

PERIODICALS

New York Times Book Review, July 11, 1965.
Studies in Black Literature, Number 2, 1972, Number 3, 1972.
TriQuarterly, spring, 1969.
Washington Post Book World, December 1, 1986.

DENT, Thomas C(ovington) 1932-
(Tom Dent)

PERSONAL: Born March 20, 1932, in New Orleans, La.; son of Albert (a university president) and Jessie (a teacher and concert pianist; maiden name, Covington) Dent. *Education:* Morehouse College, B.A., 1952; Goddard College, M.A., 1974.

ADDRESSES: Home—Box 50584, New Orleans, La. 70150. *Agent*—Lawrence Jordan, 2067 Broadway, Suite 41, New York, N.Y. 10023.

CAREER: Houston Informer, Houston, Tex., reporter, 1950-52; *New York Age,* New York, N.Y., reporter, 1959; National Association for the Advancement of Colored People (NAACP), New York City, public information worker for Legal Defense Fund, 1961-63; Free Southern Theater, New Orleans, La., associate director, 1966-70; Total Community Action, New Orleans, public relations officer, 1971-73; public lecturer. Co-publisher of political newspaper *On Guard for Freedom,* 1960; co-founder of Umbra Workshop, New York City, 1962, and co-publisher of poetry magazine *Umbra;* co-founder of literary journal *Callaloo,* 1978; founder of Congo Square Writers Union, New Orleans, 1974; free-lance writer and poetry reader. Instructor at Mary Holmes College, 1968-70, University of New Orleans, 1979-81. Executive director of New Orleans Jazz and Heritage Foundation. *Military service:* U.S. Army, 1957-59.

MEMBER: Modern Language Association, African Literature Association.

AWARDS, HONORS: Whitney Young fellow, 1973-74.

WRITINGS:

(Editor with Richard Schechner and Gilbert Moses) *The Free Southern Theater, by the Free Southern Theater,* Bobbs-Merrill, 1969.
(Under name Tom Dent) *Magnolia Street* (poems), privately printed, 1976, reprinted, 1987.
(Under name Tom Dent) *Blue Lights and River Songs: Poems,* Lotus Press, 1982.

PLAYS

"Negro Study No. 34A" (one-act), first produced in New Orleans, La., at Free Southern Theater, 1970.
"Snapshot" (one-act), first produced in New Orleans at Free Southern Theater, 1970.
"Ritual Murder" (one-act), first produced in New Orleans at Ethiopian Theater, 1976.

Also author, with Val Ferdinand, of one-act play "Song of Survival."

OTHER

"The Ghetto of Desire" (prose narrative), Columbia Broadcasting System (CBS-TV), 1966.

Writings represented in anthologies, including *Anthology of the American Negro in the Theatre, Black Culture, An Introduction to Black Literature in America,* and *New Black Voices.* Contributor of poetry, short stories, and drama to *Callaloo, Nkombo, Umbra,* and *Pacific Moana Quarterly;* of articles and critical reviews to *Black American Literature Forum, Black Creation, Black River Journal, Crisis, Black World, Freedom-ways, Jackson Advocate, Negro Digest, Obsidian,* and others. Editor, *Black River Journal,* 1976; co-editor of *Nkombo,* 1968-74.

WORK IN PROGRESS: With Andrew Young, under name Tom Dent, an autobiography, for Bantam.

SIDELIGHTS: Born into a prominent, socially committed family, Tom Dent was educated in both public and private schools in New Orleans. He earned a degree in political science from Morehouse College, where he began his literary career as editor of the *Maroon Tiger;* during summer vacations he also worked as a cub reporter for the *Houston Informer.* "Certainly," Dent remembered, "I had no concept of what it meant to be a black writer.... We were taught and prepared to *belong....* We had been taught that race as a subject was limiting, something to escape from if possible, and the further one escaped the more successful one became."

Dent's move to New York City in 1959, however, brought a new race-consciousness as he lived and worked among other black writers. A reporter for the black paper *New York Age,* Dent became involved with the political publication *On Guard for Freedom* and—with Calvin Hernton and David Henderson—founded the influential Umbra Workshop. A collective of black artists, activists, and thinkers on the lower east side of New York City, the workshop explored the interface of politics, art, and social reality with black identity. Publishers of the poetry magazine *Umbra,* workshop writers gave public readings, "continuing a trend popularized by the 'beat generation' poets of the 1950s," commented Lorenzo Thomas in the *Dictionary of Literary Biography,* "challeng[ing] their audiences' cultural preconceptions." Recalling that theirs was the first group to use "the language black people speak," Dent wrote: "Umbra was my introduction to the Black Arts Movement; it turned me into viewing reality through a black lens."

Like the Umbra Workshop, New Orleans's Free Southern Theater was a cultural project conceived to challenge the status quo. Comprised of theater professionals and political activists, the organization assailed racism and segregation in the Deep South. When Dent returned to New Orleans in 1965 he joined the ranks of the Free Southern Theater, eventually becoming its associate director. Among his controversial projects was a program of poetry readings, "The Ghetto of Desire," for the CBS television show "Look Up and Live" in 1966. Objecting to the presentation's bleak portrayal of black life in New Orleans, the city's housing authority tried to prevent a national broadcast by pressuring the program's sponsor. Rejecting censorship, the National Council of Churches presented "The Ghetto of Desire" intact, although some southern stations refused to air it.

While earning considerable attention as a dramatist and poet, Dent has focused more on the organization and distribution of the works and ideas of other black artists. Seeing the office of the poet as essential to the life of a community—uncovering the "subliminal truth" that lies beyond "surface reality"—Dent believes that art can effect social change. Yet he also acknowledges that it is the individual, and not the community, who creates; in the arts collectives he has formed or directed (including New Orleans's Congo Square Writers Union) Dent has addressed the tension that exists between community consciousness and individual vision. Lorenzo Thomas reflected: "It is pertinent to view Tom Dent's first twenty years of literary activity as an attempt to design viable models of collective work.... Urging his community to attend the writer's personal vision, forcing artists' collectives to confront their members' individualism, Dent has attempted to solve philosophical and practical problems of organization."

It is to the community, however, that Dent looks for black survival. "He opposes the idea that economic and political advancement of the black American depends upon a middle class that can achieve integration into the larger society," Lorenzo Thomas related; "Dent's alternative depends upon race pride and a collective solidarity, in opposition to narrow self-interest." The poems collected in Dent's *Magnolia Street* and *Blue Lights and River Songs*, the *Dictionary of Literary Biography* writer continued, "affirm [that] . . . black people can only find their true identities within a community founded on recognition of their African heritage and common historical experience." Capturing the improvisational quality of jazz music, Dent's verse focuses on the struggle for racial and self-identity in contemporary urban America. Much of his drama explores the desperation that springs from a lack of identity; in the 1976 play "Ritual Murder," for example, the dramatist shows how young black men, denied a legitimate heritage and most common avenues of self-esteem, turn their rage inward and violently upon one another.

BIOGRAPHICAL/CRITICAL SOURCES:

BOOKS

Dictionary of Literary Biography, Volume 38: *Afro-American Writers After 1955: Dramatists and Prose Writers*, Gale, 1985.

PERIODICALS

Callaloo, November 4, 1978.
Drama Review, fall, 1987.
World Literature Today, autumn, 1982.
Xaiver Review, Volume 6, No. 1, 1986.

*   *   *

DENT, Tom
See DENT, Thomas C(ovington)

*   *   *

De VEAUX, Alexis   1948-

PERSONAL: Born September 24, 1948, in New York, N.Y.; daughter of Richard Hill and Mae De Veaux. *Education:* State University of New York Empire State College, B.A., 1976.

ADDRESSES: Home—135 Eastern Parkway, Suite 8K, Brooklyn, N.Y. 11238.

CAREER: Writer and illustrator. New York Urban League, New York, N.Y., assistant instructor in English for WIN Program, 1969-71; Frederick Douglass Creative Arts Center, New York City, instructor in creative writing, 1971-72; Bronx Office of Probations, New York City, community worker, 1972-73; Project Create, New York City, instructor in reading and creative writing, 1973-74. Intern for Roundabout Theatre/Stage One, 1974; cultural coordinator of Black Expo for the Black Coalition of Greater New Haven, 1975. Poetry editor, *Essence* magazine. Has given readings at colleges, churches, and theaters; has appeared on radio and television programs in New York City, Washington, D.C., and New Haven, Conn. Artist and co-founder of Coeur de l'Unicorne Gallery, 1975—.

MEMBER: Screen Writers Guild of America (East), Poets and Writers, Inc., American Theatre Association, Black Theatre Alliance, Afro-American Cultural Center (Yale University).

AWARDS, HONORS: First prize from Black Creation, 1972, for short story; best production award from Westchester Community College Drama Festival, 1973, for "Circles"; Art Books for Children awards from Brooklyn Museum, 1974 and 1975, for *Na-ni*; *Don't Explain: A Song of Billie Holiday* appeared on the American Library Association's Best Books for Young Adults list in 1981; Coretta Scott King Honor Award, 1988, for *An Enchanted Hair Tale*.

WRITINGS:

(And illustrator) *Na-ni* (juvenile), Harper, 1973.
(And illustrator) *Spirits in the Street* (novel), Doubleday, 1973.
Li Chen/Second Daughter First Son (prose poem), Ba Tone Press, 1975.
Don't Explain: A Song of Billie Holiday, Harper, 1980.
An Enchanted Hair Tale (juvenile), Harper, 1987.

Also author of *Blue Heat* and *Adventures of the Dread Sisters*.

PLAYS

"Circles" (one-act), first produced in New York, N.Y., at Frederick Douglass Creative Arts Center, March, 1973.
"The Tapestry," first broadcast on KCET-TV (PBS), March, 1976, produced in New York at Harlem Performance Center, May, 1976.
"A Season to Unravel," first produced Off-Broadway at St. Mark's Playhouse, January 27, 1979.

OTHER

Contributor of poems and stories to *Sunbury II, Encore, Black Creation,* and *New Haven Advocate*.

WORK IN PROGRESS: This Handed/That Handed (tentative title), for children; "Fox Street War" (tentative title), a play; research on the life of Lorraine Hansberry.

SIDELIGHTS: Writer and illustrator Alexis De Veaux believes that "art should confront head-on the racial and economic inequities in American life," writes *Dictionary of Literary Biography* contributor Priscilla R. Ramsey. In her self-illustrated children's story *Na-ni*, for example, De Veaux writes about a poor Harlem child, Na-ni, whose dream of a new bicycle goes unfulfilled when the family's welfare check is stolen. Reviews of *Na-ni* praised both the storyline and illustrations. "The style is spare, poetic—a performance startlingly personal and alive," Margaret F. O'Connell writes in the *New York Times Book Review*. A *Library Journal* contributor comments, "this is a unique, poignant, and poetic book, illustrated with line drawings of haunting power." Concludes a *Horn Book* reviewer: "Powerful and stark, the text itself has such a poetic quality that the reader is simultaneously aware of the tragedy and the beauty in Na-ni's life."

De Veaux also has a particular interest in addressing the image of the black woman in her work. Ramsey relates that De Veaux once stated: "In all of the work I've done, there is a certain and deliberate care I've taken with laying out the image of the black woman as I have seen or experienced her, which indicates that there is a clear and conscious desire to address myself to her." In *Don't Explain: A Song of Billie Holiday* De Veaux recreates, in lyric form, the life of the renowned jazz singer. *Ms.* contributor June Jordan writes: "De Veaux gives you the life of Billie Holiday fitted into its time, the music of Billie Holiday traced back to its source, the voice of Billie Holiday fathomed for its meaning." *Don't Explain* is written for young adults, and reviewers note that the book will enlighten this audience in several ways. A *Publishers Weekly* contributor believes that *Don't Explain* "can help young people understand inequity and iniquity and arm themselves against the deadly lure of drugs." Mary Laka Cannella concludes in *Best Sellers:* "[*Don't Explain*] is melodic, gripping and emotional. It could turn on some young readers to poetry."

AVOCATIONAL INTERESTS: Studying Egyptian mythology and ancient culture, astrology, art history, "development of a new language composed of musical sounds and derived from African, Haitian, American Black, and neo-sexual sources."

BIOGRAPHICAL/CRITICAL SOURCES:

BOOKS

Dictionary of Literary Biography, Volume 38: *Afro-American Writers after 1955: Dramatists and Prose Writers,* Gale, 1985.

PERIODICALS

Best Sellers, October, 1980.
Booklist, May 15, 1980.
Children's Literature in Education, winter, 1986.
Essence, June, 1981.
Horn Book, June, 1973.
Library Journal, May 15, 1973.
Ms., June, 1980.
New York Times, January 26, 1979.
New York Times Book Review, April 1, 1973.
Publishers Weekly, February 5, 1973, May 30, 1980.
School Library Journal, August, 1980.

*   *   *

DIAMANO, Silmang
  See SENGHOR, Leopold Sedar

*   *   *

DIOP, Birago (Ismael)   1906-
  (Max, d'Alain Provist)

PERSONAL: Some sources spell middle name "Ismail"; born December 11, 1906, in Ouakam (some sources say Dakar), Senegal; son of Ismael (a master mason) and Sokhna (Diawara) Diop; married Marie-Louise Pradere (an accountant), 1934 (deceased); children: Renee, Andree. *Education:* Received doctorate from Ecole Nationale Veterinaire de Toulouse, 1933; attended Institut de Medecine Veterinaire Exotique, c. 1934, and Ecole Francaise des Cuirs et Peaux.

ADDRESSES: B.P. No. 5018, Dakar, Senegal.

CAREER: Head of government cattle inspection service in Senegal and French Sudan (now Mali), c. 1934-42; employed at Institut de Medecine Veterinaire Exotique in Paris, France, 1942-44; interim head of zoological technical services in Ivory Coast, 1946; head of zoological technical services in Upper Volta (now Burkina Faso), 1947-50, in Mauritania, 1950-54, and in Senegal, 1955; administrator for Societe de la Radiodiffusion d'Outre-Mer (broadcasting company), 1957; ambassador from Senegal to Tunisia during early 1960s; veterinarian in private practice in Dakar, Senegal, c. 1964—. Vice-president of Confederation Internationale des Societes d'Auteurs et Compositeurs, 1982; president of reading board of Nouvelles Editions Africaines (publisher); official of Institut des Hautes Etudes de Defense Nationale (French national defense institute). *Military service:* Nurse in military hospital in St.-Louis, Senegal, 1928-29.

MEMBER: Association des Ecrivains du Senegal (president), Bureau Senegalais des Droits d'Auteur (president of admin-istrative council), Societe des Gens de Lettres de France, Pen-Club, Rotary-Club de Dakar, Anemon.

AWARDS, HONORS: Grand Prix Litteraire de l'Afrique-Occidentale Francaise, for *Les Contes d'Amadou Koumba;* Grand Prix Litteraire de l'Afrique Noire from Association des Ecrivains d'Expression Francaise de la Mer et de l'Outre Mer (now Association des Ecrivains de Langue Francaise), 1964, for *Contes et lavanes.* Officier de la Legion d'Honneur; commandeur des Palmes Academiques; chevalier de l'Etoile Noire; chevalier du Merite Agricole; chevalier des Arts et des Lettres; grand-croix de l'Ordre National Senegalais; grand officier de l'Ordre de la Republique Tunisienne; grand officier de l'Ordre National Ivoirien.

WRITINGS:

SHORT STORIES

Les Contes d'Amadou Koumba (includes "Maman-Caiman," "Les Mamelles," and "Sarzan"), Fasquelle, 1947, reprinted, Presence Africaine, 1978.
Les Nouveaux Contes d'Amadou Koumba (title means "The New Tales of Amadou Koumba"; includes "L'Os de Mor Lam"), preface by Leopold Sedar Senghor, Presence Africaine, 1958.
Contes et lavanes (title means "Tales and Commentaries"), Presence Africaine, 1963.
Tales of Amadou Koumba (collection; includes "A Judgment"), translation and introduction by Dorothy S. Blair, Oxford University Press, 1966.
Contes choisis (collection), edited with an introduction by Joyce A. Hutchinson, Cambridge University Press, 1967.
Contes d'Awa, illustrations by A. Diallo, Nouvelles Editions Africaines, 1977.
Mother Crocodile—Maman-Caiman, translation and adaptation by Rosa Guy, illustrations by John Steptoe, Delacorte Press, 1981.

PLAYS; ADAPTED FROM HIS SHORT STORIES

"Sarzan," performed in Dakar, Senegal, 1955.
L'Os de Mor Lam (performed at Theatre National Daniel Sorano, Senegal, 1967-68), Nouvelles Editions Africaines, 1977.

Also adapted "Maman-Caiman" and "Les Mamelles."

OTHER

Leurres et lueurs (poems; title means "Lures and Lights"; includes "Viatique"), Presence Africaine, 1960.
Birago Diop, ecrivain senegalais (collection), commentary by Roger Mercier and M. and S. Battestini, F. Nathan, 1964.
Memoires (autobiography), Presence Africaine, volume 1: *La Plume raboutee* (title means "The Piecemeal Pen"), 1978, volume 2: *A Rebrousse-temps* (title means "Against the Grain of Time"), 1982, volume 3: *A Rebrousse-gens: Epissures, entrelacs, et reliefs,* 1985.

Work represented in anthologies, including *Anthologie de la nouvelle poesie negre et malagache de langue francaise,* edited by Leopold Sedar Senghor, Presses Universitaires de France, 1948; *A Book of African Verse,* Heinemann, 1964; *An Anthology of African and Malagasy Poetry in French,* Oxford University Press, 1965.

Contributor to periodicals, including *L'Echo des etudiants* (sometimes under pseudonyms Max and d'Alain Provist), *L'Etudiant noir,* and *Presence africaine.*

SIDELIGHTS: Birago Diop is an author and poet best known for short stories inspired by the folktales of West Africa. Born and raised in Senegal, formerly a French colony, Diop writes in French, although some of his works have been translated into English and other languages. As a young man Diop left Senegal for France, where he studied veterinary science at the Ecole Nationale Veterinaire in Toulouse. After receiving his doctorate in 1933 he went to Paris, where he encountered a community of black writers from the French colonial empire that included Aime Cesaire of Martinique and Leopold Sedar Senghor of Senegal. Senghor and Cesaire led the Negritude movement, which rejected the assimilation of black colonial peoples into French culture, asserting instead the value of the black heritage. Inspired by the movement, Diop wrote poems such as "Viatique," a vivid portrayal of the initiation ceremony of an African tribe. His work appeared in two of Senghor's groundbreaking efforts at publishing Franco-African authors: the journal *L'Etudiant noir* and the book *Anthologie de la nouvelle poesie negre et malagache de langue francaise.*

Later in the 1930s Diop returned to French West Africa, and in his work as a government veterinarian he traveled widely throughout the region, sometimes into remote areas of the interior. He turned from poetry to the short story, "the most traditional form of African literature," as Joyce A. Hutchinson observed in her introduction to *Contes choisis.* For centuries African literature was primarily spoken, and storytellers such as the *griots* of West Africa found the short story a convenient form in which to provide moral lessons or to discuss the human condition. When Diop published his first collection of stories, *Les Contes d'Amadou Koumba,* he said they were drawn verbatim from a *griot* named Amadou whom he had met during his travels. In a later interview for *Le Soleil,* however, he acknowledged that Amadou was a composite of many storytellers he had encountered, including members of his own family.

In fact many commentators, including Senghor, have suggested that Diop's stories succeed on the printed page because they are a skillful combination of African oral tradition and the author's own considerable talent as a writer. Diop "uses tradition, of which he is proud," Hutchinson wrote, "but he does not insist in an unintelligent fashion on tradition for tradition's sake. He resuscitates the spirit and the style of the traditional *conte* [tale] in beautiful French, without losing all the qualities which were in the vernacular version."

Diop's tales have often been praised for their varied and skillful observations on human nature. In "L'Os de Mor Lam," for instance, a selfish man prefers to be buried alive rather than share his supper with a neighbor. The author often draws upon traditional animal tales, which put human foibles on display by endowing animals with exaggerated forms of human characteritics. In one African story cycle, which Diop uses extensively, a physically strong but foolish hyena is repeatedly bested by a hare who relies on intelligence rather than strength.

Reviewers generally note that Diop prefers laughter to melodrama in his stories, and in *The African Experience in Literature and Ideology* Abiola Irele stressed the "gentle" quality of Diop's humor. But other commentators agreed with Dorothy S. Blair, who in her foreword to *Tales of Amadou Koumba* held that some stories contain a sharper element of social satire. In "Sarzan," for example, Diop describes the comeuppance of an African villager who returns from service in the French Army and tries to impose French culture on his people. And in "A Judgment," according to John Field of *Books and Bookmen,* a couple with marital problems must endure first the "pompous legalism" of the village elders and then the "arbitrary and callous" judgment of a Muslim lord.

In adapting the oral folktale to a written form, Diop strives to maintain the spontaneity of human speech, and to do so he intersperses his prose with dialogue, songs, and poems—all part of the African storyteller's technique, as Hutchinson noted. "Diop's use of dialogue," she remarked, "is masterly. He uses the whole range of human emotional expression: shouts, cries, tears, so vividly that one can without difficulty imagine and supply the accompanying gestures and the intonation of the voice." Accordingly, Diop has adapted several of his stories for the stage, including "Sarzan" and "L'Os de Mor Lam." Writing in *World Literature Today,* Eileen Julien praised Diop's adaptation of "L'Os" for "depict[ing] in a warm and colorful style the manners of an African village," including "gatherings, prayers, communal rites and . . . ubiquitous, compelling chatter." "All of these," she averred, "are the matter of which theatre is made."

Diop's adaptations of the folktale have made him one of Africa's most widely read authors, and he has received numerous awards and distinctions. His first volume of tales promptly won the Grand Prix Litteraire de l'Afrique-Occidentale Francaise, and for his second volume Senghor, who had become one of Senegal's most prominent writers and political leaders, wrote a laudatory preface. After Senghor led Senegal to independence in 1960 he sought Diop as the country's first ambassador to Tunisia. Since 1978 Diop has produced three highly detailed volumes of memoirs, including his account of the early days of the Negritude movement in Paris. Summarizing Diop's literary achievement, Hutchinson praised the author for showing that short stories in the traditional African style are "not just children's tales, not just sociological or even historical material, but a work of art, part of Africa's cultural heritage."

BIOGRAPHICAL/CRITICAL SOURCES:

BOOKS

Diop, Birago, *Contes choisis,* edited with an introduction by Joyce A. Hutchinson, Cambridge University Press, 1967.
Diop, Birago, *Les Nouveaux Contes d'Amadou Koumba,* preface by Leopold Sedar Senghor, Presence Africaine, 1958.
Diop, Birago, *Tales of Amadou Koumba,* translation and introduction by Dorothy S. Blair, Oxford University Press, 1966.
Irele, Abiola, *The African Experience in Literature and Ideology,* Heinemann, 1981.

PERIODICALS

Books and Bookmen, October, 1986.
Le Soleil, December 11, 1976.
World Literature Today, winter, 1979, autumn, 1986.

—*Sketch by Thomas Kozikowski*

*   *   *

DIOP, Cheikh Anta   1923-1986

PERSONAL: Born in 1923 in Diourbel, Senegal; died February 7, 1986, in Dakar, Senegal. *Education:* Received a Litt.D. in France.

CAREER: Historian. Headed the carbon-14 dating laboratory for the Institut Fondamentale d'Afrique Noire in Senegal.

Founder of two political parties in the 1960s, the Bloc des Masses Senegalaises and the Front Nationale Senegalaise.

AWARDS, HONORS: Honored by the World Festival of Negro Arts in 1966 as the black intellectual who had exercised the most fruitful influence in the twentieth century.

WRITINGS:

Nations negres et culture, Editions Africaines, 1955, two-volume edition published as *Nations negres et culture: De l'antiquite negre egyptienne aux problemes culturels de l'Afrique noire d'aujourd'hui,* Presence Africaine, 1979, partial translation by Mercer Cook in *The African Origin of Civilization: Myth or Reality,* Lawrence Hill, 1974 (also see below).

L'Unite culturelle de l'Afrique noire: Domaines du patriarcat et du matriarcat dans l'antiquite classique, Presence Africaine, 1959, translation published as *The Cultural Unity of Negro Africa: The Domains of Patriarchy and of Matriarchy in Classical Antiquity,* Presence Africaine, 1962, translation with introduction by John Henrik Clarke and afterword by James G. Spady published as *The Cultural Unity of Black Africa: The Domains of Patriarchy and of Matriarchy in Classical Antiquity,* Third World Press, 1978.

Les Fondements culturels, techniques et industriels d'un futur etat federal d'Afrique noire, Presence Africaine, 1960, revised edition published as *Les Fondements economiques et culturels d'un etat federal d'Afrique noire,* Presence Africaine, 1974, translation by Harold Salemson published as *Black Africa: The Economic and Cultural Basis for a Federated State,* Lawrence Hill, 1978.

L'Afrique noire pre-coloniale: Etude comparee des systemes politiques et sociaux de l'Europe et de l'Afrique noire, de l'antiquite a la formation des etats modernes, Presence Africaine, 1960.

Anteriorite des civilisations negres: Myth ou verite historique? Presence Africaine, 1967, partial translation by Cook in *The African Origin of Civilization: Myth or Reality,* Lawrence Hill, 1974 (also see below).

Le Laboratoire de radiocarbone de l'IFAN, Institut Fondamentale d'Afrique Noire, 1968.

Physique nucleaire et chronologie absolue, Institut Fondamentale d'Afrique Noire, 1974.

The African Origin of Civilization: Myth or Reality (translation of portions of *Anteriorite des civilisations negres* and *Nations negres et culture* by Cook), Lawrence Hill, 1974 (also see above).

Parente genetique de l'egyptien pharaonique et des langues negro-africaines: Processus de semitisation, Nouvelles Editions Africaines, 1977.

SIDELIGHTS: Cheikh Anta Diop began the first carbon-14 dating laboratory in Africa and founded two political parties in his native Senegal that were later banned, but he is best remembered for his historical works about Africa. His books attempt to prove that blacks had a larger role in the beginnings of civilization than was previously accorded them. Diop argued that the ancient Egyptians, extremely advanced in science and culture, were black; he also held that the first steps toward civilization began south of the Sahara Desert.

OBITUARIES:

PERIODICALS

Publishers Weekly, March 7, 1986.

DODSON, Owen (Vincent) 1914-1983

PERSONAL: Born November 28, 1914, in Brooklyn, N.Y.; died June 21, 1983, of a heart attack in New York, N.Y.; son of Nathaniel (a journalist) and Sarah Elizabeth (Goode) Dodson. *Education:* Bates College, B.A., 1936; Yale University, M.F.A., 1939.

ADDRESSES: Home—New York, N.Y.

CAREER: Spelman College, Atlanta, Ga., drama director, 1938-41; Atlanta University, Atlanta, instructor and director of drama, 1938-42; Hampton Institute, Hampton, Va., instructor and director of drama, 1942-43; Howard University, Washington, D.C., faculty member, 1947-69, professor of drama and department chairman, 1960-69. Lecturer at Vassar College, Kenyon College, and Cornell University; poet in residence, Ruth Stephen Poetry Center, University of Arizona, 1969-70. Consultant to Community Theatre, Harlem School of Arts, 1970-71; director of Summer Theatre, Theatre Lobby, Washington, D.C.; director of theatre at Lincoln University. Conducted seminars in theatre and playwriting. *Military service:* U.S. Navy, 1942-43.

MEMBER: American Film Center (executive secretary; member of executive committee for mass education in race relations), American Negro Theatre (member of board of directors), Phi Beta Kappa.

AWARDS, HONORS: General Education Board fellowship, 1937; winner of Tuskegee Institute Playwriting Contest, 1939; winner of Maxwell Anderson Verse Play Contest, Stanford University, 1940; Rosenwald fellowship, 1945; Guggenheim fellowship, 1953; *Paris Review* short story prize, 1956; D.Litt. from Bates College, 1967; Rockefeller Foundation fellowship, 1968; Outstanding Pioneer Award from Audience Development Committee, 1975.

WRITINGS:

Powerful Long Ladder (poems), Farrar, Straus, 1946, reprinted, 1970.

Boy at the Window (novel), Farrar, Straus, 1951, reprinted, 1977, paperback edition published as *When Trees Were Green,* Popular Library, 1951.

The Confession Stone: A Song Cycle Sung by Mary about Jesus (poems), [Washington, D.C.], published as *The Confession Stone,* Broadside Press, 1970 (published in England as *The Confession Stone: Song Cycles,* P. Bremen, 1970, 2nd edition, 1971).

Come Home Early, Child (novel), Popular Library, 1977.

(With James Van Der Zee and Camille Billops) *The Harlem Book of the Dead* (foreword by Toni Morrison), Morgan & Morgan, 1978.

Also author of *Cages* (poems), 1953.

PLAYS

"Divine Comedy," 1938, produced in New York City at New Federal Theatre, January, 1977.

"New World A-Coming: An Original Pageant of Hope," first produced in New York City at Madison Square Garden, 1944.

Also author of "The Shining Town," 1937; "With This Darkness" (revised as "Garden of Time"), 1939; "Amistad," 1939; "Doomsday Tale," 1941; "Gonna Tear Them Pillars Down," 1942; "Heroes on Parade" (collection of short plays), 1943; (with Countee Cullen) "The Third Fourth of July," 1946;

"Bayou Legend," 1946; "The Decision" [and] "For the Riesers," 1947; (with Cullen) "Medea in Africa," 1963.

OTHER

"Long Look: Owen Dodson" (sound recording), Pacifica Tape Library, 1975.

Also author of operas, "A Christmas Miracle," 1955, and "Till Victory Is Won," 1967, both with music by Marx Fax; also author, with Gary Keyes, of *Sound of Soul,* 1978. Also contributor to anthologies. Contributor to periodicals.

WORK IN PROGRESS: A libretto entitled "The Morning Duke Ellington Praised the Lord and Seven Little Black Davids Tap Danced Unto."

SIDELIGHTS: In his twenty-three years in the drama department of Howard University, Owen Dodson was an important influence on black theater. Jeff Newman, chairman of the drama department at Howard, states in the *New York Times* that "there were not many professionals in the business who did not come through him." A diverse group of artists can be listed as former students of Dodson, including Debbie Allen, Roxie Roker, Amiri Baraka, Earle Hyman, and Ossie Davis. Dodson was especially noted for attracting leading drama professionals to speak to his classes, such as Sir John Gielgud, Sidney Poitier, and Vivien Leigh. In 1949, Dodson led the Howard Unviersity Players on a fourteen-city European tour—the first U.S. State Department-sponsored European tour by a black theater group—in which they presented over fifty performances of plays by Henrik Ibsen and DuBose Heyward.

In 1974, a collection of Dodson's writing was adapted by the Black Repertory Theatre of Washington, D.C., as a tribute in dramatic collage entitled "Owen's Song."

BIOGRAPHICAL/CRITICAL SOURCES:

PERIODICALS

Black World, October, 1971, May, 1972.
New York Times Book Review, February 13, 1977.

OBITUARIES:

PERIODICALS

Los Angeles Times, June 24, 1983.
New York Times, June 22, 1983.

* * *

DOMINI, Rey
   See LORDE, Audre (Geraldine)

* * *

DOVE, Rita (Frances) 1952-

PERSONAL: Born August 28, 1952, in Akron, Ohio; daughter of Ray (a chemist) and Elvira (Hord) Dove; married Fred Viebahn (a writer); children: Aviva Chantal Tamu Dove-Viebahn. *Education:* Miami University, Oxford, Ohio, B.A. (summa cum laude), 1973; attended Universitaet Tuebingen, West Germany, 1974-75; University of Iowa, M.F.A., 1977.

ADDRESSES: Office—Department of English, Arizona State University, Tempe, Ariz. 85287.

CAREER: Arizona State University, Tempe, assistant professor, 1981-84, associate professor, 1984-87, professor of English, 1987—. Writer-in-residence at Tuskegee Institute, 1982.

National Endowment for the Arts, member of literature panel, 1984-86, chair of poetry grants panel, 1985. Commissioner, Schomburg Center for the Preservation of Black Culture, New York Public Library, 1987—.

MEMBER: PEN, Associated Writing Programs (member of board of directors, 1985-88, president, 1986-87), Academy of American Poets, Poetry Society of America, Poets and Writers, Phi Beta Kappa, Phi Kappa Phi.

AWARDS, HONORS: Fulbright fellowship, 1974-75; grants from National Endowment for the Arts, 1978, and Ohio Arts Council, 1979; International Working Period for Authors fellowship for West Germany, 1980; Portia Pittman fellowship at Tuskegee Institute from National Endowment for the Humanities, 1982; John Simon Guggenheim fellowship, 1983; Peter I. B. Lavan Younger Poets Award, Academy of American Poets, 1986; Pulitzer Prize in poetry, 1987, for *Thomas and Beulah;* General Electric Foundation Award for Younger Writers, 1987; Honorary Doctor of Letters, Miami University, 1988; Bellagio (Italy) residency, Rockefeller Foundation, 1988; Mellon fellowship, National Humanities Center, North Carolina, 1988-89.

WRITINGS:

Ten Poems (chapbook), Penumbra Press, 1977.
The Only Dark Spot in the Sky (poetry chapbook), Porch Publications, 1980.
The Yellow House on the Corner (poems), Carnegie-Mellon University Press, 1980.
Mandolin (poetry chapbook), Ohio Review, 1982.
Museum (poems), Carnegie-Mellon University Press, 1983.
Fifth Sunday (short stories), Callaloo Fiction Series, 1985.
Thomas and Beulah (poems), Carnegie-Mellon University Press, 1986.
The Other Side of the House (poems), photographs by Tamarra Kaida, Pyracantha Press, 1988.

Work represented in anthologies. Contributor of poems, stories, and essays to magazines, including *Agni Review, Antaeus, Georgia Review, Nation,* and *Poetry.* Member of editorial board, *National Forum,* 1984—; poetry editor, *Callaloo,* 1986—; advisory editor, *Gettysburg Review,* 1987—, and *Tri-Quarterly,* 1988—.

SIDELIGHTS: Black American writer Rita Dove is best known for her book of poems *Thomas and Beulah,* which garnered her the 1987 Pulitzer Prize in poetry. Dove has been described as a quiet leader, a poet who does not avoid race issues, but does not make them her central focus. As Dove herself explains in the *Washington Post:* "Obviously, as a black woman, I am concerned with race. . . . But certainly not every poem of mine mentions the fact of being black. They are poems about humanity, and sometimes humanity happens to be black. I cannot run from, I *won't* run from any kind of truth."

The poems in *Thomas and Beulah* are loosely based on the lives of Dove's maternal grandparents, and are arranged in two sequences: one devoted to Thomas, born in 1900 in Wartrace, Tennessee, and the other to Beulah, born in 1904 in Rockmart, Georgia. *Thomas and Beulah* is viewed as a departure from Dove's earlier works in both its accessibility and its chronological sequence that has, to use Dove's words, "the kind of sweep of a novel." On the book's cover is a snapshot of the author's grandparents, and *New York Review of Books* contributor Helen Vendler observes that "though the photograph, and the chronology of the lives of Thomas and Beulah appended to the sequence, might lead one to suspect that Dove is a poet of simple realism, this is far from the case. Dove has learned . . . how to make a biographical fact the buried base of an imagined edifice.''

In the *Washington Post,* Dove describes the poems this way: ''The poems are about industrialization, discrimination sometimes—and sometimes not—love and babies—everything. It's not a dramatic story—nothing absolutely tragic happened in my grandparents' life. . . . But I think these are the people who often are ignored and lost.'' Peter Stitt expresses a similar view in the *Georgia Review:* ''The very absence of high drama may be what makes the poems so touching—these are ordinary people with ordinary struggles, successes, and failures.'' He concludes: ''There is a powerful sense of community, residing both in a family and in a place, lying at the heart of this book, and it is this that provides a locus to the poems. Rita Dove has taken a significant step forward in each of her three books of poems; she must be recognized as among the best young poets in the country today.''

AVOCATIONAL INTERESTS: Travel (Israel, southern Europe, West Germany).

BIOGRAPHICAL/CRITICAL SOURCES:

PERIODICALS

American Book Review, July, 1985.
American Poetry Review, January, 1982.
Callaloo, winter, 1986.
Georgia Review, summer, 1984, winter, 1986.
New York Review of Books, October 23, 1986.
North American Review, March, 1986.
Poetry, October, 1984.
Washington Post, April 17, 1987.

*   *   *

DRUMMOND, William Joe   1944-

PERSONAL: Born September 29, 1944, in Oakland, Calif.; son of Jack Martin (a carpenter) and Mary Louise (a machinist; maiden name, Tompkins) Drummond; married Faye Boykin (a teacher), June 22, 1962; children: Tammerlin, Sean. *Education:* University of California, Berkeley, B.A., 1965; Columbia University, M.S., 1966. *Politics:* Independent. *Religion:* Protestant.

ADDRESSES: Office—School of Journalism, University of California, Berkeley, Calif., 94720.

CAREER/WRITINGS: Los Angeles Times, Los Angeles, Calif., staff writer, 1967-71, bureau chief in New Delhi, India, 1971-74, in Jerusalem, Israel, 1974-76; U.S. Department of State, Washington, D.C., special assistant, 1976-77; Office of U.S. President, Washington, D.C., White House associate press secretary, 1977; *Los Angeles Times,* staff writer for Washington bureau, 1977-83; University of California, Berkeley, professor of journalism, 1983—, Chancellor's Distinguished Lecturer, 1983. Notable assignments include coverage of the west coast black power movement, 1967-71; Senator Robert F. Kennedy's assassination, 1968; the liberation of Bangladesh, December, 1971; India's first atomic explosion, May, 1974; Israeli rescue of hijacked airline passengers at Entebbe, July 4, 1976. National Public Radio, correspondent, 1979-83, special correspondent, 1983.

MEMBER: White House Fellows Association.

AWARDS, HONORS: Received journalism award for *Vision* magazine, 1966; National Press Club Foundation Award, 1980;

Edwin Hood Award, 1983, for distinguished foreign correspondence.

WORK IN PROGRESS: A book of essays on media criticism for Random House.

SIDELIGHTS: William Joe Drummond remarked: ''Every new reporter should serve some time as a news source (which I did for ten months as associate press secretary in the White House). Jimmy Carter's Presidency is the most specialized evolution, so far, of the White House care and feeding of mass media. One of the President's closest advisers is his press secretary, Jody Powell, who has a staff of more than forty persons, including a former television network producer and half a dozen former newsmen. Press play considerations are probably more frequently brought to bear in scheduling Carter than any previous president, because of Powell's unique role in the inner sanctum. Powell is both confidential adviser and press secretary. As a result, much of what Carter does and how and when he does it is determined by the requirements of the media, which are Powell's clientele.

''In helping to implement Powell's decisions on presidential choreography I couldn't help but conclude that accommodating the press does not necessarily result in better and more informative reporting of the presidency. Instead, the press often reacted with increasing cynicism and greater criticism. I couldn't help but feel that the public was left bewildered.''

*   *   *

Du BOIS, David G(raham)   1925-

PERSONAL: Born September, 1925, in Seattle, Wash.; son of William Edward Burghardt (stepfather; a writer and scholar) and Shirley (Graham) Du Bois; divorced. *Education:* Attended Oberlin Conservatory of Music, 1942-43, and New York School of Social Work, Columbia University, and Peking University; Hunter College (now of the City University of New York), B.A., 1950; New York University, M.A., 1972. *Politics:* Independent.

ADDRESSES: c/o Ramparts Press, P.O. Box 50128, Palo Alto, Calif. 94303.

CAREER: First National City Bank of New York, New York, N.Y., clerk-typist, 1950-59; *Arab Observer,* Cairo, Egypt, editor/reporter, 1960-72. News editor, *Egyptian Gazette;* reporter and editor, Middle East News and Features Agency; announcer and program writer, Radio Cairo. In public relations for Ghana government, Cairo, 1965-66; official spokesperson for Black Panther Party, and editor-in-chief of Black Panther Intercommunal News Service. Lecturer, School of Criminology, University of California, Berkeley, and Cairo University. *Military service:* U.S. Army Air Forces, Infantry, 1942-46; became second lieutenant.

WRITINGS:

And Bid Him Sing (novel), Ramparts, 1975.

Contributor to *Black Scholar.* Editor of *Black Panther,* 1973—.

SIDELIGHTS: David G. Du Bois wrote: ''I write to share ideas and feelings which move me to serve humankind. Thirteen years outside the U.S.A. (in China and Africa) opened up new worlds of experience. As a Black American and revolutionary Marxist-Leninist, I am committed to revolutionary suicide.''

Du BOIS, Shirley Graham 1906-1977
(Shirley Graham)

PERSONAL: Born November 11, 1906, in Indianapolis, Ind.; died March 27, 1977, in Peking, China; daughter of David Andrew (a Methodist minister) and Etta (Bell) Graham; married Shadrach T. McCanns; married second husband W. E. B. Du Bois (a writer, editor, and educator), February 14, 1951 (died, 1963); children: (first marriage) two sons. *Education:* Oberlin College, B.A., 1934, M.A., 1935; additional graduate study, New York University; also attended Yale University Drama School, 1939-1941, and Sorbonne, University of Paris, 1946-47.

CAREER: Author and dramatist. Taught music at Morgan College, Baltimore, 1930-32; supervisor of the Negro unit of the Chicago Federal Theater, 1936-39; USO director at Fort Hauchaca, Arizona, 1941-43; field secretary, NAACP, 1942-44; founding editor, *Freedomways*, 1960-63; organizing director, Ghana Television, 1964-66; English editor, Afro-Asian Writers Bureau, Peking, China, 1968.

MEMBER: P.E.N., Kappa Delta Pi, Sigma Delta Theta.

AWARDS, HONORS: Julius Messner Award, 1946, for *There Once Was a Slave;* Anisfield-Wolf Award, 1949, for *Your Most Humble Servant;* National Institute of Arts and Letters Award, 1950; L.H.D., University of Massachusetts, 1973.

WRITINGS:

(With George D. Lipscomb) *Dr. George Washington Carver, Scientist* (illustrated by Elton C. Fax), J. Messner, 1944, reprinted, Archway, 1967.
Paul Robeson: Citizen of the World, J. Messner, 1946, reprinted, 1971.
There Once Was a Slave: The Heroic Story of Frederick Douglass, J. Messner, 1947, reprinted, 1968.
Your Most Humble Servant, J. Messner, 1949, reprinted, 1965.
The Story of Phillis Wheatley (illustrated by Robert Burns), J. Messner, 1949, reprinted, Washington Square Press, 1970.
The Story of Pocahontas (illustrated by Mario Cooper), Grosset & Dunlap, 1953.
Jean Baptiste Pointe de Sable: Founder of Chicago, J. Messner, 1953.
Booker T. Washington: Educator of Hand, Head, and Heart, J. Messner, 1955.
His Day Is Marching On: A Memoir of W. E. B. Du Bois, Lippincott, 1971.
Gamal Abdel Nasser, Son of the Nile: A Biography, Third Press, 1972.
Zulu Heart, Third Press, 1974.
Julius K. Nyerere: Teacher of Africa, J. Messner, 1975.
A Pictorial History of W. E. B. Du Bois, Johnson, 1976.

Composer and librettist for "Tom-Tom" (an opera), produced by Cleveland Opera Co., 1932; designer, composer, and director of "Little Black Sambo" (a children's opera), 1938. Author of several plays, including "Track Thirteen," 1940; "Dust to Earth," 1941; "Elijah's Ravens," 1941; and "I Gotta Home," 1942. Contributor to periodicals, including *Black Scholar, Crisis, Etude, Freedomways,* and *Harlem Quarterly.*

SIDELIGHTS: The farm on which Shirley Graham Du Bois was born had been part of the underground railroad, and had served as a stopping point for runaway slaves en route to Canada. The farm belonged to Du Bois's grandfather, a former slave who had been freed prior to the Civil War.

Though Du Bois was a longtime supporter of civil rights and "leftist" causes, she was, in her later years, often "viewed in the shadow of her late husband, the black writer, co-founder of the National Association for the Advancement of Colored People and controversial civil rights crusader," a *New York Times* report stated. The *Times* article pointed out, however, that "Mrs. Du Bois won fame on her own many years before she married Mr. Du Bois, as a playwright, composer and stage director."

In 1961, the Du Boises moved to Ghana and at the invitation of then president, Kwane Nkrumah, became citizens. W. E. B. Du Bois died in 1963, and in 1967, when Nkrumah's regime was ousted by a military coup, Shirley Du Bois was forced to leave Ghana. She lived in Cairo for several years and attempted to come to New York in 1971. According to the *New York Times,* however, the Justice Department denied Du Bois a visa, maintaining that she "had been associated with more than thirty organizations on the Attorney General's list of subversive groups." But the department eventually relented and allowed Du Bois to visit the United States for two months. She returned to New York City again to be a guest speaker at a memorial tribute to Prime Minister Chou En-lai of China, held in the city's Chinatown.

On April 2, 1977, a memorial meeting for Du Bois was held at Papaoshan Cemetery for Revolutionaries, in China. Several Chinese political figures were present at the memorial, including Deputy Prime Minister Chen Yung-kuei. The president of the Association for Friendship with Foreign Countries, Wang Ping-nan, gave the eulogy calling Du Bois a "close friend" who "did a lot of work in enhancing the friendship and understanding between Chinese people and the people of the United States and the Third World."

OBITUARIES:

PERIODICALS

AB Bookman's Weekly, June 27, 1977.
New York Times, April 5, 1977.
Washington Post, April 5, 1977.

*   *   *

Du BOIS, W(illiam) E(dward) B(urghardt) 1868-1963

PERSONAL: Born February 23, 1868, in Great Barrington, Mass.; immigrated to Ghana, 1960, naturalized citizen, 1963; died August 27, 1963, in Accra, Ghana; buried in Accra; son of Alfred and Mary (Burghardt) Du Bois; married Nina Gomer, 1896 (died, 1950); married Shirley Graham (an author), 1951 (died, 1977); children: Burghardt (deceased), Yolande Du Bois Williams (deceased). *Education:* Fisk University, B.A., 1888; Harvard University, B.A. (cum laude), 1890, M.A., 1891, Ph.D., 1896; graduate study at University of Berlin, 1892-94. *Politics:* Joined Communist Party, 1961.

CAREER: Wilberforce University, Wilberforce, Ohio, professor of Greek and Latin, 1894-96; University of Pennsylvania, Philadelphia, assistant instructor in sociology, 1896-97; Atlanta University, Atlanta, Ga., professor of history and economics, 1897-1910; National Association for the Advancement of Colored People (NAACP), New York City, director of publicity and research and editor of *Crisis,* 1910-34; Atlanta University, professor and chairman of department of sociology, 1934-44; NAACP, director of special research, 1944-48; Peace Information Center, New York City, director, 1950. Co-founder and general secretary of Niagara Movement, 1905-09. Organizer of the Pan-African Congress, 1919. Vice-chairman of the Council of African Affairs, 1949. American Labor Party candidate for U.S. senator from New York, 1950.

AWARDS, HONORS: Spingarn Medal from NAACP, 1932; elected to the National Institute of Arts and Letters, 1943; Lenin International Peace Prize, 1958; Knight Commander of the Liberian Humane Order of African Redemption conferred by the Liberian Government; Minister Plenipotentiary and Envoy Extraordinary conferred by President Calvin Coolidge; LL.D. from Howard University, 1930, and Atlanta University, 1938; Litt.D., Fisk University, 1938; L.H.D., Wilberforce University, 1940; honorary degrees from Morgan State College, University of Berlin, and Charles University (Prague).

WRITINGS:

NOVELS

The Quest of the Silver Fleece, A. C. McClurg, 1911, reprinted, Kraus Reprint, 1974.
Dark Princess: A Romance, Harcourt, 1928, reprinted, Kraus Reprint, 1974.
The Ordeal of Mansart (first novel in trilogy; also see below), Mainstream Publishers, 1957.
Mansart Builds a School (second novel in trilogy; also see below), Mainstream Publishers, 1959.
Worlds of Color (third novel in trilogy; also see below), Mainstream Publishers, 1961.
The Black Flame (trilogy; includes *The Ordeal of Mansart, Mansart Builds a School,* and *Worlds of Color*), Kraus Reprint, 1976.

POETRY

Selected Poems, Ghana University Press, c. 1964, reprinted, Panther House, 1971.

PLAYS

"Haiti," included in *Federal Theatre Plays,* edited by Pierre De Rohan, Works Progress Administration, 1938.

Also author of pageants, "The Christ of the Andes," "George Washington and Black Folk: A Pageant for the Centenary, 1732-1932," and "The Star of Ethiopia."

WORKS EDITED IN CONJUNCTION WITH THE ANNUAL CONFERENCE FOR THE STUDY OF NEGRO PROBLEMS; ALL ORIGINALLY PUBLISHED BY ATLANTA UNIVERSITY PRESS

Mortality among Negroes in Cities, 1896, reprinted, Octagon, 1968.
Social and Physical Condition of Negroes in Cities, 1897, reprinted, Octagon, 1968.
Some Efforts of American Negroes for Their Own Social Benefit, 1898, reprinted, Octagon, 1968.
The Negro in Business, 1899, reprinted, AMS Press, 1971.
A Select Bibliography of the American Negro: For General Readers, 1901.
The Negro Common School, 1901, reprinted, Octagon, 1968.
The Negro Artisan, 1902, reprinted, Octagon, 1968.
The Negro Church, 1903, reprinted, Arno Press, 1968.
Some Notes on Negro Crime, Particularly in Georgia, 1904, reprinted, Octagon, 1968.
A Select Bibliography of the Negro American, 1905, reprinted, Octagon, 1968.
The Health and Physique of the Negro American, 1906, reprinted, Octagon, 1968.

Economic Co-operation among Negro Americans, 1907, reprinted, Russell & Russell, 1969.
The Negro American Family, 1908, reprinted, MIT Press, 1970.
Efforts for Social Betterment among Negro Americans, 1909, reprinted, Russell & Russell, 1969.
(With Augustus Granville Dill) *The College-Bred Negro American,* 1910, reprinted, Arno Press, 1968.
(With Dill) *The Common School and the Negro American,* 1911, reprinted, Russell & Russell, 1969.
(With Dill) *The Negro American Artisan,* 1912, reprinted, Russell & Russell, 1969.
(With Dill) *Morals and Manners among Negro Americans,* 1914, reprinted, Russell & Russell, 1969.
Atlanta University Publications, two volumes, Hippocrene, 1968.

OTHER

The Suppression of the African Slave-Trade to the United States of America, 1638-1870, Longmans, Green, 1896, reprinted, Kraus Reprint, 1973.
The Conservation of Races, American Negro Academy, 1897, reprinted, Arno Press, 1969.
The Philadelphia Negro: A Special Study (bound with *A Special Report on Domestic Service,* by Isobel Eaton), University of Pennsylvania, 1899, reprinted, Kraus Reprint, 1973.
The Souls of Black Folk: Essays and Sketches (young adult), A. C. McClurg, 1903, reprinted, Buccaneer, 1986.
(With Booker Taliaferro Washington) *The Negro in the South: His Economic Progress in Relation to His Moral and Religious Development* (lectures), G. W. Jacobs, 1907, reprinted, Metro Books, 1972.
John Brown (biography), G. W. Jacobs, 1909, reprinted, Kraus Reprint, 1973, 2nd revised edition, International Publishing, 1974.
The Negro, Holt, 1915, reprinted, Kraus Reprint, 1975.
Darkwater: Voices from Within the Veil (semi-autobiographical), Harcourt, 1920, reprinted, Kraus Reprint, 1975.
The Gift of Black Folk: The Negroes in the Making of America, Stratford Co., 1924, reprinted, Kraus Reprint, 1975.
Africa: Its Geography, People and Products (also see below), Haldeman-Julius Publications, 1930.
Africa: Its Place in Modern History, Haldeman-Julius Publications, 1930, reprinted in a single volume with *Africa: Its Geography, People and Products,* Unipub-Kraus International, 1977.
Black Reconstruction: An Essay Toward a History of the Part Which Black Folk Played in the Attempt to Reconstruct Democracy in America, 1860-1880, Harcourt, 1935, reprinted, Kraus Reprint, 1976, published as *Black Reconstruction in America, 1860-1880,* Atheneum, 1969.
Black Folk, Then and Now: An Essay in the History and Sociology of the Negro Race, Holt, 1939, reprinted, Kraus Reprint, 1975.
Dusk of Dawn: An Essay Toward an Autobiography of a Race Concept, Harcourt, 1940, reprinted, Kraus Reprint, 1975.
Color and Democracy: Colonies and Peace, Harcourt, 1945, reprinted, Kraus Reprint, 1975.
The World and Africa: An Inquiry into the Part Which Africa Has Played in World History, Viking, 1947, revised edition, 1965.
(Editor) *An Appeal to the World: A Statement on the Denial of Human Rights to Minorities in the Case of Citizens of Negro Descent in the United States of America and an*

Appeal to the United Nations for Redress, [New York], 1947.

In Battle for Peace: The Story of My 83rd Birthday (autobiography), Masses and Mainstream, 1952, reprinted, Kraus Reprint, 1976.

An ABC of Color: Selections From Over Half a Century of the Writings of W. E. B. Du Bois, Seven Seas Publishers (Berlin), 1963.

John H. Franklin, editor, *Three Negro Classics,* Avon, 1965.

Herbert Aptheker, editor, *The Autobiography of W. E. Burghardt Du Bois: A Soliloquy on Viewing My Life from the Last Decade of Its First Century,* International Publishers, 1968.

Philip S. Foner, editor, *W. E. B. Du Bois Speaks: Speeches and Addresses,* Pathfinder Press, 1970.

Walter Wilson, editor, *The Selected Writings of W. E. B. Du Bois,* New American Library, 1970.

Black North in 1901: A Social Study, Ayer, 1970.

Meyer Weinberg, editor, *W. E. B. Du Bois: A Reader,* Harper, 1970.

Julius Lester, editor, *The Seventh Son: The Thought and Writings of W. E. B. Du Bois,* Random House, 1971.

Andrew G. Paschal, editor, *A W. E. B. Du Bois Reader,* Macmillan, 1971.

Daniel Walden, editor, *W. E. B. Du Bois: The Crisis Writings,* Fawcett Publications, 1972.

Henry Lee Moon, editor, *The Emerging Thought of W. E. B. Du Bois: Essays and Editorials from "The Crisis,"* Simon & Schuster, 1972.

Aptheker, editor, *The Correspondence of W. E. B. Du Bois,* University of Massachusetts Press, Volume I: *1877-1934,* 1973, Volume II: *1934-1944,* 1976, Volume III: *1944-1963,* 1978.

Aptheker, editor, *The Education of Black People: Ten Critiques, 1906-1960,* University of Massachusetts Press, 1973.

Virginia Hamilton, editor, *The Writings of W. E. B. Du Bois,* Crowell, 1975.

Aptheker, editor, *Book Reviews,* KTO Press, 1977.

Aptheker, editor, *Prayers for Dark People,* University of Massachusetts Press, 1980.

(And editor) *Writings in Periodicals,* UNIPUB-Kraus International, 1985.

Creative Writings by W. E. B. Du Bois: A Pageant, Poems, Short Stories and Playlets, UNIPUB-Kraus International, 1985.

Pamphlets and Leaflets by W. E. B. Du Bois, UNIPUB-Kraus International, 1985.

Aptheker, editor, *Against Racism: Unpublished Essays, Papers, Addresses, 1887-1961,* University of Massachusetts Press, 1985.

Dan S. Greene and Edwin D. Driver, editors, *W. E. B. Du Bois on Sociology and the Black Community,* University of Chicago Press, 1987.

W. E. B. Du Bois Writings, Library of America, 1987.

Columnist for newspapers, including *Chicago Defender, Pittsburgh Courier, New York Amsterdam News,* and *San Francisco Chronicle.* Contributor to numerous periodicals, including *Atlantic Monthly* and *World's Work.* Founder and editor of numerous periodicals, including *Moon,* 1905-06, *Horizon,* 1908-10, *Brownies' Book,* 1920-21, and *Phylon Quarterly,* 1940. Editor in chief of *Encyclopedia of the Negro,* 1933-46. Director of *Encyclopaedia Africana.*

SIDELIGHTS: W. E. B. Du Bois was at the vanguard of the civil rights movement in America. Of French and African descent, Du Bois grew up in Massachusetts and did not begin to comprehend the problems of racial prejudice until he attended Fisk University in Tennessee. Later he was accepted at Harvard, but while he was at that institution he voluntarily segregated himself from white students. Trained as a sociologist, Du Bois began to document the oppression of black people and their strivings for equality in the 1890s. By 1903 he had learned enough to state in *The Souls of Black Folk* that "the problem of the twentieth century is the problem of the color line," and he spent the remainder of his long life trying to break down racial barriers.

The Souls of Black Folk was not well received when it first came out. Houston A. Baker, Jr. explained in his *Black Literature in America* that white Americans were not "ready to respond favorably to Du Bois's scrupulously accurate portrayal of the hypocrisy, hostility, and brutality of white America toward black America." Many blacks were also shocked by the book, for in it Du Bois announced his opposition to the conciliatory policy of Booker T. Washington and his followers, who argued for the gradual development of the Negro race through vocational training. Du Bois declared: "So far as Mr. Washington apologizes for injustice, North or South, does not rightly value the privilege and duty of voting, belittles the emasculating effects of caste distinctions, and opposes the higher training and ambition of our brighter minds—so far as he, the South, or the Nation, does this—we must unceasingly and firmly oppose him. By every civilized and peaceful method we must strive for the rights which the world accords to men." In retrospect, many scholars have pointed to *The Souls of Black Folk* as a prophetic work. Harold W. Cruse and Carolyn Gipson noted in the *New York Review of Books* that "nowhere else was Du Bois's description of the Negro's experience in American Society to be given more succinct expression. . . . *Souls* is probably his greatest achievement as a writer. Indeed, his reputation may largely rest on this remarkable document, which had a profound effect on the minds of black people."

A few years after *The Souls of Black Folk* was published, Du Bois banded with other black leaders and began the Niagara Movement, which sought to abolish all distinctions based on race. Although this movement disintegrated, it served as the forerunner of the National Association for the Advancement of Colored People (NAACP). Du Bois helped to establish the NAACP and worked as its director of publicity and research for many years. As the editor of *Crisis,* a journal put out by the NAACP, he became a well-known spokesman for the black cause. In 1973 Henry Lee Moon gathered a number of essays and articles written by Du Bois for *Crisis* and published them in a book, *The Emerging Thought of W. E. B. Du Bois.*

In addition to the articles and editorials he wrote for *Crisis,* Du Bois produced a number of books on the history of the Negro race and on the problems of racial prejudice. In *Black Reconstruction,* Du Bois wrote about the role that blacks played in the Reconstruction, a role that had been hitherto ignored by white historians. The history of the black race in Africa and America was outlined in *Black Folk: Then and Now.* H. J. Seligmann found the book impressive in the *Saturday Review of Literature:* "No one can leave it without a deepened sense of the part the Negro peoples have played and must play in world history." An even higher compliment was paid by Barrett Williams reviewing for the *Boston Transcript:* "Professor Du Bois has overlooked one of the strongest arguments against racial inferiority, namely, this book itself. In it, a man of color has proved himself, in the complex and exacting field of scholarship, the full equal of his white colleagues.''

Although Du Bois's novels did not attract as much notice as his scholarly works, they also were concerned with the plight of the black race. His first novel, *The Quest of the Silver Fleece,* dramatized the difficulties created by the low economic status of the Southern Negro. *Dark Princess* dealt with miscegenation. After reading *Dark Princess,* a reviewer for the *Springfield Republican* observed: ''The truth is, of course, that Du Bois is not a novelist at all, and that the book judged as a novel has only the slightest merit. As a document, as a program, as an exhortation, it has its interest and value.''

Du Bois gradually grew disillusioned with the moderate policies of the NAACP and with the capitalistic system in the United States. When he advocated black autonomy and ''nondiscriminatory segregation'' in 1934, he was forced to resign from his job at the NAACP. Later he returned to the NAACP and worked there until another rift developed between him and that organization's leaders in 1944. More serious conflicts arose between Du Bois and the U.S. government. Du Bois had become disenchanted with capitalism relatively early. In *Darkwater: Voices from Within the Veil,* he had depicted the majority of mankind as being subjugated by an imperialistic white race. In the 1940s he returned to this subject and examined it in more detail. *Color and Democracy: Colonies and Peace* presented a case against imperialism. ''This book by Dr. Du Bois is a small volume of 143 pages,'' critic H. A. Overstreet observed in the *Saturday Review of Literature,* ''but it contains enough dynamite to blow up the whole vicious system whereby we have comforted our white souls and lined the pockets of generations of free-booting capitalists.'' *The World and Africa* contained a further indictment of the treatment of colonials. Du Bois ''does not seek exaggeration of Africa's role, but he insists the role must not be forgotten,'' Saul Carson remarked in the *New York Times.* ''And his insistence is firm. It is persuasive, eloquent, moving. Considering the magnitude of the provocation, it is well-tempered, even gentle.''

Du Bois not only wrote about his political beliefs; he acted upon them. He belonged to the Socialist party for a brief time in the early 1900s. Later he conceived a program of Pan-Africanism, a movement that he called ''an organized protection of the Negro world led by American Negroes.'' In 1948 he campaigned for the Progressive Party in national elections, and in 1950 he ran for senator from New York on the American Labor Party ticket. Du Bois's radical political stance provoked some run-ins with the U.S. Government, the first of which occurred in 1949, when he accepted an honorary position as vice-chairman of the Council on African Affairs. This organization was labeled ''subversive'' by the Attorney General. His work with the Peace Information Center, a society devoted to banning nuclear weapons, also embroiled him in controversy. Along with four other officers from the Peace Information Center, Du Bois was indicted for ''failure to register as an agent of a foreign principal.'' The case was brought to trial in 1951 and the defendants were acquitted.

After the trial was over, Du Bois wanted to travel outside the United States, but he was denied a passport on the grounds that it was not in ''the best interests of the United States'' for him to journey abroad. Later the State Department refused to issue a passport to him unless he stated in writing that he was not a member of the Communist Party, a condition that Du Bois rejected. In 1958 the Supreme Court handed down a decision which declared that ''Congress had never given the

Department of State any authority to demand a political affidavit as prerequisite to issuing a passport.'' This decision enabled Du Bois and his wife to leave the country the same year. For several months they traveled in Europe, the U.S.S.R., and China.

Du Bois's travels abroad had a profound influence on his thinking. In 1961 he joined the Communist Party. He explained in his autobiography how he reached this decision: ''I have studied socialism and communism long and carefully in lands where they are practiced and in conversation with their adherents, and with wide reading. I now state my conclusion frankly and clearly: I believe in communism. . . . I believe that all men should be employed according to their ability and that wealth and services should be distributed according to need. Once I thought that these ends could be attained under capitalism, means of production privately owned, and used in accord with free individual initiative. After earnest observation I now believe that private ownership of capital and free enterprise are leading the world to disaster.''

After joining the Communist Party, Du Bois moved to Ghana at the invitation of President Nkrumah. While there he served as the director of the *Encyclopaedia Africana* project. In August, 1963, the ninety-five-year-old leader inspired a protest march on the U.S. embassy in Accra to show support for the historic ''March for Jobs and Freedom'' taking place in Washington, D.C. that same month. Shortly afterward, Du Bois died. Although Du Bois was a controversial figure in his lifetime, his reputation has grown in the past decade. A large number of books and scholarly studies about him have recently appeared. In a discussion of the revival of interest in Du Bois, Cruse and Gipson wrote: ''It is important to remember that he continued to plead for a truly pluralistic culture in a world where the superiority of whites is still an *a priori* assumption. In so far as he grasped the basic dilemma of Western blacks as being a people with 'two souls, two thoughts, two unreconciled strivings,' Du Bois's attitudes have been vindicated. He was, as we can now see, one of those unique men whose ideas are destined to be reviled and then revived, and then, no doubt, reviled again, haunting the popular mind long after his death.''

Some of Du Bois's books have been published in French and Russian.

BIOGRAPHICAL/CRITICAL SOURCES:

BOOKS

Baker, Houston A., Jr., *Black Literature in America,* McGraw, 1971.

Bone, Robert A., *The Negro Novel in America,* Yale University Press, revised edition, 1965.

Contemporary Literary Criticism, Gale, Volume I, 1973, Volume II, 1974.

Dictionary of Literary Biography, Gale, Volume XLVII: *American Historians, 1866-1912,* 1986, Volume L: *Afro-American Writers before the Harlem Renaissance,* 1986.

Du Bois, Shirley Graham, *His Day Is Marching On: A Memoir of W. E. B. Du Bois,* Lippincott, 1971.

Du Bois, W. E. B., *Darkwater: Voices from Within the Veil,* Harcourt, 1920, reprinted, Kraus Reprint, 1975.

Du Bois, W. E. B., *Dusk of Dawn: An Essay Toward an Autobiography of Race Concept,* Harcourt, 1940, reprinted, Kraus Reprint, 1975.

Du Bois, W. E. B., *In Battle for Peace: The Story of My 83rd Birthday,* Masses and Mainstream, 1952, reprinted, Kraus Reprint, 1976.

Du Bois, W. E. B., *The Autobiography of W. E. B. Du Bois: A Soliloquy on Viewing My Life from the Last Decade of Its First Century,* International Publishers, 1968.

Hawkins, Hugh, editor, *Booker T. Washington and His Critics: Black Leadership in Crisis,* Heath, 1974.

Logan, Rayford W., editor, *W. E. B. Du Bois: A Profile,* Hill & Wang, 1971.

Rampersad, Arnold, *Art and Imagination of W. E. B. Du Bois,* Harvard University Press, 1976.

Rudwick, Elliott M., *W. E. B. Du Bois: Propagandist of the Negro Protest,* Atheneum, 1968.

Something About the Author, Volume XLII, Gale, 1986.

Sterne, Emma Gelders, *His Was the Voice: The Life of W. E. B. Du Bois,* Crowell-Collier, 1971.

PERIODICALS

Boston Transcript, June 24, 1939.
Ebony, August, 1972, August, 1975.
Los Angeles Times Book Review, January 25, 1987.
New Republic, February 26, 1972.
Newsweek, August 23, 1971.
New York Review of Books, November 30, 1972.
New York Times, March 9, 1947, October 24, 1979.
New York Times Book Review, September 29, 1985.
Saturday Review of Literature, July 29, 1939, June 23, 1945.
Springfield Republican, May 28, 1928.
Times Literary Supplement, April 22, 1988.

*   *   *

DUMAS, Henry L.   1934-1968

PERSONAL: Born July 20, 1934, in Sweet Home, Ark.; died May 23, 1968, in New York, N.Y. *Education:* Attended City College (now of the City University of New York), and Rutgers University, 1958-61; studied in residence with the musician-philosopher Sun Ra.

CAREER: International Business Machines (IBM), New York City, operator of printing machines, 1963-64; social worker for the State of New York, New York City, 1965-66; Hiram College, Hiram, Ohio, assistant director of Upward Bound, 1967; Southern Illinois University, Carbondale, teacher-counselor and director of language workshops for the University's Experiment in Higher Education, 1967-68. Editor, publisher and distributor of little magazines, including *Anthologist, Untitled, Camel, Hiram Poetry Review,* and *Collection,* 1953-68. *Military Service:* U.S. Air Force, 1953-57.

AWARDS, HONORS: Several awards for creative writing published in Air Force newspapers and magazines, 1953-57; Editors Award for Creative Writing, for *Untitled,* 1963; creative writing award from *Anthologist.*

WRITINGS:

Poetry for My People, edited by Hale Chatfield and Eugene B. Redmond, Southern Illinois University Press, 1970, published as *Play Ebony, Play Ivory,* edited by Redmond, Random House, 1974.

Ark of Bones, and Other Stories, edited by Chatfield and Redmond, Southern Illinois University Press, 1970.

Jonoah and the Green Stone (novel), arranged by Redmond, Random House, 1976.

Rope of Wind and Other Stories, edited by Redmond, Random House, 1979.

Goodbye Sweetwater (anthology), edited by Redmond, Thunder's Mouth, 1988.

Black Tongue (tentative title; poems), Third World Press, in press.

Work represented in many anthologies, including *Black Fire,* edited by Imamu Amiri Baraka and Roy Neal, Morrow, 1968; *Black Out Loud,* edited by Arnold Adoff, Macmillan, 1970; *Brothers and Sisters,* edited by Adoff, Macmillan, 1970; *Open Poetry,* edited by Ronald Gross, Simon & Schuster, 1972; *The Poetry of Black America,* edited by Adoff, Harper, 1973; *Understanding the New Black Poetry,* edited by Stephen Henderson, Morrow, 1973; *Cutting Edges,* compiled by Jack Hicks, Holt, 1973.

Contributor to periodicals, including *Negro Digest, Freedom Ways, Umbra, Trace, Anthologist, Hiram Poetry Review,* and *American Weave.*

SIDELIGHTS: Henry Dumas did not live to see his poetry and fiction published in book form. On May 23, 1968, he was shot and killed by a policeman on the Harlem Station platform of the New York Central Railroad. The reasons and circumstances behind his death are uncertain, but critics agree that the bullet cut down a promising young writer. When *Poetry for My People* appeared in 1970, critic Jascha Kessler observed in the *Saturday Review:* "His work indicates that Dumas was an ambitious writer aware of the current obsessions of black poets. He seems to have been working his way through styles, dictions, and forms—trying to assemble the black heritage through its history and memories . . . and music, while maintaining a powerful ideological sweep." Julius Lester in the *New York Times Book Review* found *Play Ebony, Play Ivory* to be evidence that "Henry Dumas was the most original Afro-American poet of the sixties."

One quality of Dumas's work consistently praised by critics is the authenticity of his poetic voice. About *Play Ebony, Play Ivory,* a reviewer for *Choice* said, "His ear captures the language of black America of the fifties and sixties and in the best of these verses that language achieves considerable strength and grace." Lester pointed out that "Dumas's authentic voice is heard most clearly when he writes from within what seems to have been his subject: Africa and Nature. He is the first Afro-American poet to speak convincingly in the voice of an African."

Dumas's fiction has also attracted favorable notices. His collection of short stories, *Ark of Bones,* inspired John Deck to write in a *New York Times Book Review* critique, "Dumas had a rich and varied talent, and he was foremost an original." Angela Jackson, reviewing for *Black World,* lauded the characterizations in *Ark of Bones* and noted that "these stories are close to Biblical in their shape, though these myths are less leaden in tone and embrace. They sing with a humor that moves the way we normally do, not overdone. There is, too, a moral exactness that our tradition has cherished. There is spine and point." Describing *Ark of Bones* as a "collection of extraordinary short stories," a reviewer for *New Yorker* lamented: "Mr. Dumas was thirty-four when he died. One of the saddest things about his book is that it leaves no doubt in the reader's mind that there were even better books to come."

Now over twenty years since Dumas's death, a rekindling of interest in his work has begun. This renewed awareness is due, for the most part, to a number of new publishing projects:

Goodbye Sweetwater, an anthology of short stories acclaimed and promoted by novelist Toni Morrison and Eugene B. Redmond, a collection of poetry, and an issue of *Black American Literature Forum* focusing on his writings. That it took Dumas's writing two decades to attract this type of attention did not surprise Redmond, editor of much of Dumas's published work. "Dumas is not an easy person to read if you have a closed mind," Redmond told *Publishers Weekly* contributor Maureen J. O'Brien. "Henry wrote in a rhythmic kind of language that was both basic and very complex. His rhythms came from gospel music, mystification, the Deep South and the streets, and his words spoke pure truth." And in Redmond's opinion, "Up until very recently, people just had no basis for understanding him."

The *Hiram Poetry Review* sponsors an Annual Henry Dumas Memorial Poetry Contest, and Southern Illinois University's Experiment in Higher Education has a Henry Dumas Memorial Library.

BIOGRAPHICAL/CRITICAL SOURCES:

BOOKS

Contemporary Literary Criticism, Volume VI, Gale, 1976.
Dictionary of Literary Biography, Volume XLI: *Afro-American Poets Since 1955,* Gale, 1985.
Dumas, Henry L., *Goodbye Sweetwater,* edited by Eugene B. Redmond, Thunder's Mouth, 1988.

PERIODICALS

Black American Literature Forum, summer, 1988.
Black World, January, 1975.
Choice, March, 1975.
Commonweal, April 29, 1977.
New Yorker, January 6, 1975.
New York Times Book Review, October 20, 1974, January 19, 1975, July 22, 1979.
Publishers Weekly, April 15, 1988.
Saturday Review, October 2, 1971.

*   *   *

DUNBAR, Alice
  See NELSON, Alice Ruth Moore Dunbar

*   *   *

DUNBAR, Alice Moore
  See NELSON, Alice Ruth Moore Dunbar

*   *   *

DUNBAR, Paul Laurence   1872-1906

PERSONAL: Born June 27, 1872, in Dayton, Ohio; died of tuberculosis, February 9, 1906, in Dayton, Ohio; buried in Woodland Cemetery, Dayton, Ohio; son of Joshua (a former slave, soldier, and plasterer) and Matilda Glass (a former slave and laundress; maiden name, Burton) Dunbar; married Alice Ruth Moore (a writer and teacher), March 6, 1898 (separated, 1902). *Education:* Educated in Dayton, Ohio.

ADDRESSES: Home—219 North Summit St., Dayton, Ohio.

CAREER: Writer. Worked as elevator operator; editor of *Dayton Tattler* in Dayton, Ohio, 1890; court messenger, 1896; assistant clerk at Library of Congress in Washington, D.C., 1897-98.

WRITINGS:

POETRY

Oak and Ivy, Press of United Brethren Publishing House, 1893 (also see below).
Majors and Minors, Hadley & Hadley, 1896 (also see below).
Lyrics of Lowly Life (includes poems from *Oak and Ivy* and *Majors and Minors;* also see above), introduction by William Dean Howells, Dodd, 1896, reprinted, Arno, 1969.
Lyrics of the Hearthside, Dodd, 1899, reprinted, AMS Press, 1972.
Poems of Cabin and Field, Dodd, 1899, reprinted, AMS Press, 1972.
Candle-lightin' Time, Dodd, 1901, reprinted, AMS Press, 1972.
Lyrics of Love and Laughter, Dodd, 1903.
When Malindy Sings, Dodd, 1903, reprinted, AMS Press, 1972.
Li'l Gal, Dodd, 1904, reprinted, AMS Press, 1972.
Chris'mus Is a Comin', and Other Poems, Dodd, 1905.
Howdy, Honey, Howdy, Dodd, 1905, reprinted, AMS Press, 1972.
Lyrics of Sunshine and Shadow, Dodd, 1905, reprinted, AMS Press, 1972.
A Plantation Portrait, Dodd, 1905.
Joggin' erlong, Dodd, 1906, reprinted, Mnemosyne Publishing, 1969.
The Complete Poems of Paul Laurence Dunbar, Dodd, 1913, reprinted, 1980.
Speakin' o' Christmas, and Other Christmas and Special Poems, Dodd, 1914, reprinted, AMS Press, 1975.
Little Brown Baby: Poems for Young People, edited and with biographical sketch by Bertha Rodgers, illustrated by Erick Berry, Dodd, 1940, reprinted, 1966.
I Greet the Dawn: Poems, selected and with introduction by Ashley Bryan, Atheneum, 1978.

FICTION

The Uncalled (novel), Dodd, 1898, reprinted, AMS Press, 1972.
Folks From Dixie (short stories), Dodd, 1898, reprinted, Books for Libraries, 1969.
The Love of Landry (novel), Dodd, 1900, reprinted, Literature House, 1970.
The Strength of Gideon, and Other Stories, Dodd, 1900, reprinted, Arno, 1969.
The Fanatics (novel), Dodd, 1901, reprinted, Literature House, 1970.
The Sport of the Gods (novel), Dodd, 1902, reprinted, with introduction by Kenny J. Williams, 1981 (published in England as *The Jest of Fate: A Story of Negro Life,* Jarrold, 1902).
In Old Plantation Days (short stories), Dodd, 1903, reprinted, Negro Universities Press, 1969.
The Heart of the Happy Hollow (short stories), Dodd, 1904, reprinted, Books for Libraries, 1970.
The Best Stories of Paul Laurence Dunbar, edited and with introduction by Benjamin Brawley, Dodd, 1938.

PLAYS

"Uncle Eph's Christmas" (one-act musical), produced in 1900.

Also author of lyrics to songs in musical plays such as "In Dahomey."

OTHER

The Life and Works of Paul Laurence Dunbar, edited and with biography by Lida Keck Wiggins, J. L. Nichols, 1907, reprinted, Kraus Reprint, 1971.

The Letters of Paul and Alice Dunbar: A Private History (two volumes), edited by Eugene Wesley Metcalf, University Microfilms, 1974.
The Paul Laurence Dunbar Reader, edited by Jay Martin and Gossie H. Hudson, Dodd, 1975.

Author of lyrics to songs such as "Jes Lak White Folk," "Down De Lovers Lane: Plantation Croon," and "Who Knows."

Work represented in anthologies.

Contributor to periodicals, including *Bookman, Century, Detroit Free Press, Nation,* and *Saturday Evening Post.*

SIDELIGHTS: Paul Laurence Dunbar is widely acknowledged as the first important black poet in American literature. He enjoyed his greatest popularity in the early twentieth century following the publication of dialectic verse in collections such as *Majors and Minors* and *Lyrics of Lowly Life.* But the dialectic poems constitute only a small portion of Dunbar's canon, which is replete with novels, short stories, essays, and many poems in standard English. In its entirety, Dunbar's literary body has been acclaimed as an impressive representation of black life in turn-of-the-century America. As Dunbar's friend James Weldon Johnson noted in the preface to his *Book of American Poetry:* "Paul Laurence Dunbar stands out as the first poet from the Negro race in the United States to show a combined mastery over poetic material and poetic technique, to reveal innate literary distinction in what he wrote, and to maintain a high level of performance. He was the first to rise to a height from which he could take a perspective view of his own race. He was the first to see objectively its humor, its superstitions, its short-comings; the first to feel sympathetically its heart-wounds, its yearnings, its aspirations, and to voice them all in a purely literary form."

Dunbar began showing literary promise while still in high school in Dayton, Ohio, where he lived with his widowed mother. The only black in his class, he became class president and class poet. By 1889, two years before he graduated, he had already published poems in the *Dayton Herald* and worked as editor of the short-lived *Dayton Tattler,* a newspaper for blacks published by classmate Orville Wright, who later gained fame with brother Wilbur Wright as inventors of the airplane.

Dunbar aspired to a career in law, but his mother's meager financial situation precluded his university education. He consequently sought immediate employment with various Dayton businesses, including newspapers, only to be rejected because of his race. He finally settled for work as an elevator operator, a job that allowed him time to continue writing. At this time Dunbar produced articles, short stories, and poems, including several in the black-dialect style that later earned him fame.

In 1892 Dunbar was invited by one of his former teachers to address the Western Association of Writers then convening in Dayton. At the meeting Dunbar befriended James Newton Matthews, who subsequently praised Dunbar's work in a letter to an Illinois newspaper. Matthews's letter was eventually reprinted by newspapers throughout the country and thus brought Dunbar recognition outside Dayton. Among the readers of this letter was poet James Whitcomb Riley, who then familiarized himself with Dunbar's work and wrote him a commendatory letter. Bolstered by the support of both Matthews and Riley, Dunbar decided to publish a collection of his poems. He obtained additional assistance from Orville Wright and then solicited a Dayton firm, United Brethren Publishing, that eventually printed the work, entitled *Oak and Ivy,* for a modest sum.

In *Oak and Ivy* Dunbar included his earliest dialect poems and many works in standard English. Among the latter is one of his most popular poems, "Sympathy," in which he expresses, in somber tone, the dismal plight of blacks in American society. In another standard English poem, "Ode to Ethiopia," he records the many accomplishments of black Americans and exhorts his fellow blacks to maintain their pride despite racial abuse. The popularity of these and other poems inspired Dunbar to devote himself more fully to writing.

Shortly after the publication of *Oak and Ivy* Dunbar was approached by attorney Charles A. Thatcher, an admirer sympathetic to Dunbar's financial strife, who offered to help finance Dunbar's college education. Dunbar, however, was greatly encouraged by sales of *Oak and Ivy* and so rejected Thatcher to pursue a literary career. Thatcher then applied himself to promoting Dunbar in nearby Toledo, Ohio, and helped him obtain work there reading his poetry at libraries and literary gatherings. Dunbar also found unexpected support from psychiatrist Henry A. Tobey, who helped distribute *Oak and Ivy* in Toledo and occasionally sent Dunbar much needed financial aid.

Tobey eventually teamed with Thatcher in publishing Dunbar's second verse collection, *Majors and Minors.* In this book Dunbar produced poems on a variety of themes and in several styles. He grouped the more ambitious poems, those written in standard English, under the heading "Majors," and he gathered the more superficial, dialect works as "Minors." Although Dunbar invested himself most fully in his standard poetry—which bore the influences of such poets as the English romantics and Americans such as Riley—it was the dialect verse that found greater favor with his predominantly white readership, and it was by virtue of these dialect poems that Dunbar gained increasing fame throughout the country. Instrumental to Dunbar's growing popularity was a highly positive, though extremely patronizing, review by eminent novelist William Dean Howells. Writing in *Harper's Weekly,* Howells praised Dunbar as "the first man of his color to study his race objectively" and commended the dialect poems as faithful representations of the black race.

Through Thatcher and Tobey, Dunbar met an agent and secured more public readings and a publishing contract. He then published *Lyrics of Lowly Life,* a poetry collection derived primarily from verse already featured in *Oak and Ivy* and *Majors and Minors.* This new volume sold impressively across America and established Dunbar as the nation's foremost black poet. On the strength of his recent acclaim Dunbar commenced a six-month reading tour of England. There he found publishers for a British edition of *Lyrics of Lowly Life* and befriended musician Samuel Coleridge-Taylor, with whom he then collaborated on the operetta "Dream Lovers."

When Dunbar returned to the United States in 1897 he obtained a clerkship at the Library of Congress in Washington, D.C. Soon afterwards he married fellow writer Alice Ruth Moore. Although his health suffered during the two years he lived in Washington, the period nonetheless proved fruitful for Dunbar. In 1898 he published his first short story collection, *Folks From Dixie,* in which he delineated the situation of blacks in both pre- and post-emancipation America. Although these tales, unlike some of his dialect verse, were often harsh examinations of racial prejudice, *Folks From Dixie* was well received upon publication.

Not so Dunbar's first novel, *The Uncalled,* which recalled Nathaniel Hawthorne's *The Scarlet Letter* in probing the spiritual predicament of a minister. Critics largely rejected *The Uncalled* as dull and unconvincing in its portrait of Frederick Brent, a pastor who had, in childhood, been abandoned by an alcoholic father and then raised by a zealously devout spinster, Hester Prime (Hawthorne's protagonist in *The Scarlet Letter* was named Hester Prine). After securing a pastor's post, Brent alienates church-goers by refusing to reproach an unwed mother. He resigns from his pastorship and departs for Cincinnati. After further misadventure—he ends his marriage engagement and encounters his father, now a wandering preacher—Brent finds fulfillment and happiness as minister in another congregation.

At the end of 1898, his health degenerating still further, Dunbar left the Library of Congress and commenced another reading tour. He published another verse collection, *Lyrics of the Hearthside,* and recovered any status he may have jeopardized with *The Uncalled.* In the spring of 1899, however, his health lapsed sufficiently to threaten his life. Ill with pneumonia, the already tubercular Dunbar was advised to rest in the mountains. He therefore moved to the Catskills in New York State, but he continued to write while recovering from his ailments.

In 1900, after a brief stay in Colorado, Dunbar returned to Washington, D.C. Shortly before his return he published another collection of tales, *The Strength of Gideon,* in which he continued to recount black life both before and after slavery. Reviewers at the time favored his pre-emancipation stories full of humor and sentiment, while ignoring more volatile accounts of abuse and injustice. More recently these latter stories have gained greater recognition from critics eager to substantiate Dunbar's opposition to racism.

Dunbar followed *The Strength of Gideon* with his second novel, *The Love of Landry,* about an ailing woman who arrives in Colorado for convalescence and finds true happiness with a cowboy. Like the earlier *Uncalled, The Love of Landry* was deemed unconvincing in its presentation of white characters and was dismissed as inferior to Dunbar's tales of blacks. Dunbar suffered further critical setback with his next novel, *The Fanatics,* about America at the beginning of the Civil War. Its central characters are from white families who differ in their North-South sympathies and spark a dispute in their Ohio community. *The Fanatics* was a commercial failure upon publication, and in the ensuing years it has continued to be regarded as a superficial, largely uncompelling work. Among the novel's many detractors is Robert Bone, who wrote in *The Negro in America* that Dunbar resorted to "caricature in his treatment of minor Negro characters" and that his stereotypic portraits of black characters only served to reinforce prejudice.

The Sport of the Gods, Dunbar's final novel, presents a far more critical and disturbing portrait of black America. The work centers on butler Berry Hamilton and his family. After Berry is wrongly charged with theft by his white employers, he is sentenced to ten years of prison labor. His remaining family—wife, son, and daughter—consequently find themselves targets of abuse in their southern community, and after being robbed by the local police they head north to Harlem. There they encounter further hardship and strife: the son becomes embroiled in the city's seamy nightlife and succumbs to alcoholism and crime; the naive daughter is exploited by fellow blacks and begins a questionable dancing career; and the mother, convinced that her husband's prison sentence has negated their marriage, weds an abusive profligate. A happy resolution is achieved only after Berry's accuser confesses,

while dying, that his charge was fabricated, whereupon Berry is released from prison. He then travels north and finds his family in disarray. But the cruel second husband is then, conveniently, murdered, and the parental Hamiltons are reunited in matrimony.

Although its acclaim was hardly unanimous, *The Sport of the Gods* nonetheless earned substantial praise as a powerful novel of protest. By this time, however, Dunbar was experiencing considerable turmoil in his own life. Prior to writing *The Sport of the Gods* he had suffered another lapse of poor health, and he compounded his problems by resorting to alcohol. And after *The Sport of the Gods* appeared in 1902, Dunbar's marital situation—always troublesome—degenerated further due to his continued reliance on alcohol and to antagonism from his wife's parents.

Dunbar and his wife separated in 1902, but that separation only contributed to his continued physical and psychological decline. The next year, following a nervous breakdown and another bout of pneumonia, Dunbar managed to assemble another verse collection, *Lyrics of Love and Laughter,* and another short story collection, *In Old Plantation Days.* With *Lyrics of Love and Laughter* he confirmed his reputation as America's premier black poet. The volume contains both sentimental and somberly realistic expressions and depictions of black life, and it features both dialect and standard English verse. *In Old Plantation Days* is comprised of twenty-five stories set on a southern plantation during the days of slavery. Here Dunbar once again resorted to caricaturing his own race, portraying black slaves as faithful and obedient, slow-witted but good-natured workers appreciative of their benevolent white owners. Dunbar drew the ire of many critics for his stereotyped characters, and some of his detractors even alleged that he contributed to racist concepts while simultaneously disdaining such thinking.

If *In Old Plantation Days* was hardly a pioneering work, it was at least a lucrative publication and one that confirmed the preferences of much of Dunbar's public. With the short story collection *The Heart of Happy Hollow* he presented a greater variety of perspectives on aspects of black life in America, and he even included a tale on the moral folly of lynching. Dunbar followed *The Heart of Happy Hollow* with two more poetry collections, *Lyrics of Sunshine and Shadow* and *Howdy, Howdy, Howdy,* both of which featured works from previous volumes.

Dunbar's health continued to decline even as he persisted in producing poems. But his reliance on alcohol to temper his chronic coughing only exacerbated his illness, and by the winter of 1905 he was fatally ill. He died on February 9, 1906, at age thirty-three.

In the years immediately following his death, Dunbar's standing as America's foremost black poet seemed assured, and his dialect poems were prized as supreme achievements in black American literature. In the ensuing decades, however, his reputation was damaged by scholars questioning the validity of his often stereotypic characterizations and his apparent unwillingness to sustain an anti-racist stance. Among his most vehement detractors from this period was Victor Lawson, whose *Dunbar Critically Examined* remains a provocative, if overly aggressive, study.

More recently Dunbar's stature has increased markedly. He is once again regarded as America's first great black poet, and his standard English poems are now, perhaps surprisingly, prized as his greatest achievements in verse. Contemporary champions include Addison Gayle, Jr., whose *Oak and Ivy: A Biography of Paul Laurence Dunbar*, is considered a key contribution to Dunbar studies, and black poet Nikki Giovanni, whose prose contribution to *A Singer in the Dawn: Reinterpretations of Paul Laurence Dunbar*, edited by Jay Martin, hails Dunbar as "a natural resource of our people." For Giovanni, as for other Dunbar scholars, his work constitutes both a history and a celebration of black life. "There is no poet, black or nonblack, who measures his achievement," she declared. "Even today. He wanted to be a writer and he wrote."

MEDIA ADAPTATIONS: Portions of Dunbar's work were adapted by Pauline Myers for the stage production "The World of My America: A One Woman Dramatization," and by Vinnette Carroll for the stage production "When Hell Freezes Over, I'll Skate."

BIOOGRAPHICAL/CRITICAL SOURCES:

Bone, Robert, *Down Home: A History of Afro-American Short Fiction From Its Beginnings to the End of the Harlem Renaissance*, Putnam, 1975.
Brawley, Benjamin, *Paul Laurence Dunbar: Poet of His People*, University of North Carolina Press, 1936.
Brown, Sterling, *The Negro in American Fiction*, Associates in Negro Folk Education, 1937.
Cunningham, Virginia, *Paul Laurence Dunbar and His Song*, Dodd, 1947.
Dictionary of Literary Biography, Volume 51: *Afro-American Writers From the Harlem Renaissance to 1940*, Gale, 1987, Volume 54: *American Poets, 1880-1945, Third Series*, Gale, 1987.
DuBois, W. E. Burghardt, *The Gift of Black Folk: The Negro in the Making of America*, Stratford, 1924.
Gayle, Addison, Jr., *Oak and Ivy: A Biography of Paul Laurence Dunbar*, Anchor/Doubleday, 1971.
Gould, Jean, *That Dunbar Boy*, Dodd, 1958.
Johnson, James Weldon, editor, *The Book of American Negro Poetry*, Harcourt, 1922.
Lawson, Victor, *Dunbar Critically Examined*, Associated Publishers, 1941.
Loggins, Vernon, *The Negro Author: His Development in America to 1900*, Columbia University Press, 1931.
Martin, Jay, editor, *A Singer in the Dawn: Reinterpretations of Paul Laurence Dunbar*, Dodd, 1975.
Revell, Peter, *Paul Laurence Dunbar*, Twayne, 1979.
Twentieth-Century Literary Criticism, Gale, Volume 2, 1979, Volume 12, 1984.
Wagner, Jean, *Les Poetes negres des Etats-Unis*, Librairie Istra, 1963, translation by Kenneth Douglas published as *Black Poets of the United States: From Paul Laurence Dunbar to Langston Hughes*, University of Illinois Press, 1973.
Williams, Kenny J., *They Also Spoke: An Essay on Negro Literature in America*, Townsend Press, 1970.

PERIODICALS

American Literature, March, 1976.
American Scholar, spring, 1949.
CLA Journal, June, 1981.
Colored American Magazine, April, 1901, May, 1905.
Harper's Weekly, June 27, 1896.
Journal of Negro History, January, 1967.
Nation, June 23, 1926.
Ohio Historical Quarterly, April, 1958.
Phylon, March, 1959.

Poet Lore, spring, 1897.
Psychoanalytic Review, January, 1938.
Southern Workman, October, 1921.
Texas Quarterly, summer, 1971.

—*Sketch by Les Stone*

*   *   *

DUNBAR-NELSON, Alice
   See NELSON, Alice Ruth Moore Dunbar

*   *   *

DUNBAR-NELSON, Alice Moore
   See NELSON, Alice Ruth Moore Dunbar

*   *   *

DUNHAM, Katherine   1910-
   (Kaye Dunn)

PERSONAL: Born June 22, 1910, in Joliet, Ill.; daughter of Albert Millard (an operator of a cleaning and dyeing establishment, a musician, and a singer) and Annette (a teacher; maiden name, Poindexter) Dunham; married John Thomas Pratt (a theatre designer), July 10, 1941; children: Marie Christine. *Education:* University of Chicago, Ph.B.; Northwestern University, Ph.D.

ADDRESSES: Home—Residence Leclerc, Port au Prince, Haiti, West Indies. *Office*—Performing Arts Training Center, Southern Illinois University, East St. Louis, Ill. 62201.

CAREER: Director and teacher of own schools of dance, theatre, and cultural arts in Chicago, New York, Haiti, Stockholm, and Paris, beginning 1931; professional dancer, beginning 1934, with theatre experience beginning with performances in Chicago Opera, Chicago World's Fair, and eventually including world-wide tours; choreographer for theatre, opera, motion pictures, and television nationally and internationally. Lecturer nationally and internationally, beginning 1937; Southern Illinois University, artist in residence at Carbondale and Edwardsville campuses, 1967, cultural counselor and director of Performing Arts Training Center at East St. Louis campus, 1967—, university professor at Edwardsville campus, 1968—.

Member of Chicago Opera Co., 1935-36; supervisor of Chicago City Theater Project on cultural studies, 1939; dance director of Labor Stage, 1939-40; producer and director for Katherine Dunham Dance Co., 1945; established school in Port-au-Prince, Haiti, 1961. U.S. State Department adviser to First World Festival on Negro Art, 1966; artistic and technical adviser to president of Senegal, 1966-67. Productions for her own dance companies include "Bal Negre," 1946, "New Tropical Revue," 1948, "Caribbean Rhapsody," 1948, and "Bamboche," 1963. Appearances in motion pictures include "Star Spangled Rhythm," Paramount Pictures, 1943; "Stormy Weather," Twentieth Century-Fox, 1943; "Casbah," Universal-International, 1949; "Mambo," Paramount Pictures, 1966; and "The Bible," Twentieth Century-Fox, 1966.

President, Dunham Fund for Research and Development of Cultural Arts, Inc.; founder, Foundation for the Study of Arts and Sciences of the Vodun; vice-president, Foundation for the Development and Preservation of Cultural Arts, Inc.; board member, National Institute on Aging and Illinois Arts Council; member, Illinois committee of J. F. Kennedy Center-Alliance Arts Education, American Council on Arts in Education, and

Arts Worth/Intercultural Committee. Consultant, Interamerican Institute for Ethnomusicology and Folklore (Caracas, Venezuela), National Endowment for the Humanities review committee, and Organization of American States; advisory board member, Modern Organization for Dance Evolvement.

MEMBER: American Guild of Variety Artists, American Society of Composers, Authors, and Publishers (ASCAP), American Guild of Music Artists (member of board of governors, 1943-49), American Federation of Radio Artists, Screen Actors Guild, Writers Guild, Actors' Equity Association, Black Academy of Arts and Letters, Institute of the Black World (board member), Negro Actors Guild, Royal Anthropological Society, Lincoln Academy, Sigma Epsilon.

AWARDS, HONORS: Julius Rosenwald travel fellowship to West Indies, 1936-37; Haitian Legion of Honor and Merit Chevalier, 1950, Commander, 1958, Grand Officer, 1968; named honorary citizen of Port au Prince, Haiti, 1957; awarded key to East St. Louis, Ill., 1968; *Dance Magazine* award, 1969; Eight Lively Arts award, 1969; Southern Illinois University distinguished service award, 1969; St. Louis Argus Award, 1970; East St. Louis Monitor Award, 1970; International Who's Who in Poetry certificate of merit, 1970-71; American Association for Health, Physical Education, and Recreation dance division heritage award, 1972; National Center of Afro-American Artists award, 1972; Black Merit Academy award, 1972; Mather scholar, Case Western Reserve University, 1973; Black Filmmakers Hall of Fame, 1974; American Dance Guild Annual Award, 1975; Kennedy Center Board of Trustees sixth annual award, 1983; State Department of International Education Fulbright fellow; University of Chicago professional achievement award; L.H.D., MacMurray College, Jacksonville, Ill., 1972, and Ph.D.L., Atlanta University, 1977; Candace Award, National Coalition of One Hundred Black Women, 1987.

WRITINGS:

Katherine Dunham's Journey to Accompong, Holt, 1946, reprinted, Greenwood Press, 1972.
A Touch of Innocence (autobiography), Harcourt, 1959, reprinted, Books for Libraries, 1980.
Island Possessed, Doubleday, 1969.
(Author of foreword) Lynne F. Emery, *Black Dance in the United States from 1619 to 1970,* Mayfield, 1972.
Kasamance: A Fantasy, Third Press, 1974.
Dances of Haiti (revised version of doctoral thesis), Center for Afro-American Studies, 1983.

Also co-author of play, "Ode to Taylor Jones," 1967-68. Author of television scripts, produced in Mexico, Australia, France, England, and Italy. Contributor of short stories, sometimes under pseudonym Kaye Dunn, to popular magazines, including *Esquire, Mademoiselle, Show,* and *Realities,* and to anthropology, travel, and dance magazines. Consulting editor, *Dance Scope.*

SIDELIGHTS: Best known for her contributions to the world of dance, Katherine Dunham is also an accomplished anthropologist and writer. As an aspiring young student, she was equally attracted to the disciplines of science and art, and it wasn't until she abandoned her dream of classical ballet and embraced ethnic dance that she could reconcile her interests. Her investigation into the origins of Caribbean dance led to a 1936 Rosenwald travel fellowship to the West Indies. There, "she plunged into voodoo and became initiated as a way of finding herself and doing research," according to a writer for the *New York Times Book Review.* Her participation in and description of native rituals made a valuable contribution to anthropology, provided her with raw materials for original choreography, and furnished the subject matter for her doctoral thesis—later revised and published as *Dances of Haiti.* Commenting in the *Saturday Review,* dance critic Walter Terry sums up her achievements this way: "Dunham, who began dancing professionally in 1931, was among the first of her race to conceive of black dance as art as well as entertainment. Certainly she was the first to explore and use for dance the anthropological and ethnological origins of her race. With a Ph.D. in anthropology from the University of Chicago, she evolved not only a dance technique and style but a concept of black dance theatre."

Like many black artists, Dunham had to overcome racial prejudice in order to succeed, and she once suggested to an *Ebony* reporter that her greatest accomplishment had been "breaking through various social barriers." In the early 1930s, when Dunham was searching for a performing avenue, there were no black ballerinas and no Negro Ballet. Even if there had been, her acceptance would not have been assured. As her college mentor and dance instructor Mark Turbyfill explained in *Dance Magazine,* Dunham came to him untrained, "an ambitious Negro girl, who had never had a lesson in her life in the art, but who wanted to become a ballet dancer."

Together Dunham and Turbyfill—a white poet and dancer with an appetite for the untried—conceived the notion of a Negro Ballet. With encouragement from prominent black citizens and a few open-minded artists, they borrowed time in an existing studio and began to recruit students. Within months, there were problems, as Turbyfill recalls in his diary, which is excerpted in *Dance Magazine:* "The manager of the building is not pleased to see Negroes coming to class. I have to give up [this] place. I look for another studio, but everywhere I go I am indignantly refused. Finally, I go to the small dingy R—— studio and succeed in renting time. Pupils lose interest and drop off. We talk of taking a place of our own. Katherine and I are forced to stand on street corners and on El platforms while making plans for the Negro Ballet."

Though Turbyfill did finally finagle a studio of his own, the new locale did not solve many problems. He discovered that some of his black pupils had been attracted not to his classes per se, but to the access that attendance gave them to a Michigan Avenue studio. When he moved to the new location, classes became alarmingly small. To make matters worse, choreographer Agnes de Mille dropped by to visit one day and informed him "that the idea of a ballet for Negroes is all wrong. She reminds me that it has never been done, that it isn't physiologically in the picture. I tell her that I am not thinking of a physiological picture, but rather an abstract one."

Discouraged by such resistance, Dunham's interest waned, and just a year after its conception the project was abandoned. Out of the failure of a Negro Ballet, however, grew a splendid opportunity. After observing Dunham in class one day, choreographer/dancer Ruth Page noted her potential and, in 1933, recommended Dunham for a part in *La Guiablesse,* a new ballet based on a West Indian legend.

Dunham's participation in this performance marked a turning point in her life. "After *La Guiablesse,* she turned more of her attention to the dances and culture of the displaced Africans in the West Indies," Page reports in *Dance Magazine.* In 1936, she won the Rosenwald grant to travel to the Caribbean, and this in turn led to the development of a long and happy relationship between Dunham and the West Indies—particularly Haiti. She returned to the area—at first by herself and later with her husband and costume designer John Pratt—and eventually established a second residence in Port au Prince, Haiti.

Out of her experiences Dunham fashioned a new style of dance that "included anatomical bases of ballet and modern dance and emphasized the torso movements of the primitive ritual of Caribbean-African dance and jazz rhythms," according to *Dance Magazine*. Her innovative synthesis of old and new movement brought her international acclaim as a dancer/choreographer. She made her Off-Broadway debut in 1940 with *Tropics and Le Jazz Hot* and went on to star on Broadway and in several Hollywood films, including *Carnival of Rhythm*, a twenty-minute short, and *Stormy Weather*, a full-length feature.

Since her retirement from the stage in the 1960s, Dunham has devoted her energies to the Performing Arts Training Center in the predominantly black city of East St. Louis, Illinois, where she was invited to teach. "On the very day she arrived," reports *Ebony* contributor Lynn Norment, "she was arrested because she protested the random arrest of young Black men. University officials criticized her for being friendly with 'militant types' and suggested that she move to the Carbondale, Illinois, campus. 'I'm here now and this is where I'll stay!' the strong-willed Miss Dunham announced. 'There was something burning all the time in this city,' she recalls, 'and I decided to direct some of that energy into something useful.'"

Dunham was honored for her choreographic work in 1987 when New York City's Alvin Ailey American Dance Theater presented "The Magic of Katherine Dunham." The three-act production, which reconstructs several of Dunham's dances and dance styles, won high praise from critics. Anna Kisselgoff describes the tribute in her *New York Times* review as a "fantastically staged full-evening program of sassy, colorful and vibrant revivals," and she raves: "Miss Dunham's shrewd mix of show business, art and anthropology zings across the imaginary footlights like a thunderbolt."

In addition to her dance career, Dunham has published five well-received books, ranging from fantasy to autobiography to nonfiction. Most of this writing addresses some aspect of her art, but *A Touch of Innocence* is a third-person chronicle of her early life that scarcely alludes to dancing. "As a study in questing childhood and what she calls 'defeated adolescence' . . . this can be extremely touching," reports a *Times Literary Supplement* reviewer of her autobiography. "As writing," notes Arthur Todd in the *Saturday Review*, "it is honest, searing, graphic and touching, giving us a rather heart-breaking early view of the young American Negro who was later to make a name for herself. . . . Though it hardly has a word about dance in it, it is notable for the background it provides and what it foretells of her future." Writing in the *New York Times Book Review*, Elizabeth Janeway calls *A Touch of Innocence* "one of the most extraordinary life-stories I have ever read. . . . Not one breath of sentimentality or self-pity mars or falsifies the clear picture of her girlhood, her family and her surroundings. . . . The content of this book is so heartbreaking that only the strongest artistic skill could keep it from leaking out in sobbing self-pity, but Katherine Dunham's art contains it, understands it and refuses to be overwhelmed by its terrors." Katherine Dunham, concludes *Time* magazine, "writes with skill and taste."

With *Island Possessed*, her next book, Dunham "continues her autobiography which began with 'A Touch of Innocence,'" a *Publishers Weekly* writer reports. The book describes her experiences among the people of Haiti over a period of twenty-three years and touches on such disparate topics as Haitian politics and history, as well as her participation in ancient voodoo rites. "A rambling, often fascinating, thoroughly honest, highly personal and sometimes egocentric monologue," *Island Possessed* is "of great value," according to a critic for *America*. "In her double role as devout participant and trained observer, she gained access to—as well as an understanding of—those secret services and sacrifices that other researchers know only from a distance." *American Anthropologist* contributor Erika Bourguignon, on the other hand, concludes that "this book is of interest not as an ethnography, nor for what it may tell us about Haiti but as a personal document of an American Negro woman, an artist seeking identity and roots, her 'lares and penates,' as she puts it, while uprootedly traveling about the world in the exercise of her art."

AVOCATIONAL INTERESTS: Steam baths, horseback riding, cooking, painting (her work has been shown in Australia, Italy, and England), reading, walking after midnight.

BIOGRAPHICAL/CRITICAL SOURCES:

BOOKS

Adams, Russell L., *Great Negroes, Past and Present*, Afro-American Publishing, 3rd edition, 1969.
Biemiller, Ruth, *Dance: The Story of Katherine Dunham*, Doubleday, 1969.
Buckle, Richard, editor, *Katherine Dunham: Her Dancers, Singers, and Musicians*, Ballet Publications, 1949.
Cluzel, Madeleine E., *Glimpses of the Theatre and Dance*, Kamin, 1953.
Crosland, Margaret, *Ballet Carnival*, Arco, 1955.
Dunham, Katherine, *A Touch of Innocence*, Harcourt, 1959.
Dunham, Katherine, *Island Possessed*, Doubleday, 1969.
Hurok, Solomon and Ruth Goode, *Impresario: A Memoir*, Random House, 1946.
Hurok, Solomon, *Solomon Hurok Presents*, Hermitage, 1953.

PERIODICALS

America, December 27, 1969.
American Anthropologist, October, 1970.
Dance Magazine, December, 1983.
Ebony, January, 1985.
Newsweek, May 1, 1950.
New Yorker, April 29, 1950.
New York Times, November 22, 1987, December 4, 1987, December 22, 1987.
New York Times Book Review, November 8, 1959, September 28, 1969.
Opera News, December 7, 1963.
Publishers Weekly, July 14, 1969.
Saturday Review, December 5, 1959, May 26, 1979.
Time, December 7, 1959.
Times Literary Supplement, November 25, 1960.

*   *   *

DUNN, Kaye
   See DUNHAM, Katherine

*   *   *

DUNNIGAN, Alice Allison   1906-1983

PERSONAL: Born April 27, 1906, in Russellville, Ky.; died

of ischemic bowel disease, May 6, 1983, in Washington, D.C.; daughter of Willie and Lena Pittman; married Charles Dunnigan, January 8, 1932; children: Robert William. *Education:* Attended Western Kentucky Industrial College, 1930-32; Louisville Municipal College, 1935; Tennessee Agricultural and Industrial State College (now Tennessee State University), 1936-37; Howard University, 1943.

ADDRESSES: Home—1462 Ogden St., Washington, D.C. 20010. *Office*—801 19th St., Washington, D.C. 20006.

CAREER: Teacher in Kentucky public schools, 1924-42; federal government employee, 1942-46; Associated Negro Press, Washington, D.C., bureau chief and member of Senate and House of Representatives press galleries, 1947-61, White House correspondent, 1948-61; U.S. Department of Labor, Washington, D.C., information officer, 1965-67. Writer for several Kentucky newspapers, including the *Louisville Defender, Kentucky Reporter,* and *Hopkinsville Globe,* from 1920, and the *Atlanta Daily World.* Served on speaker's bureau of the Democratic National Committee during the 1948 presidential election campaign; member of the Inaugural Public Relations Committee, 1949. Educational consultant to the President's Commission on Equal Employment Opportunity, 1961-65; associate editor for the President's Council on Youth Opportunity, 1967-70; member of the Presidential Committee for "National Employ the Physically Handicapped Week."

MEMBER: National Council of Negro Women, Women's National Press Club, Writer's Association, Capital Press Club, White House Correspondent's Association, State Department Correspondent's Association, First Lady's Press Association, Sigma Gamma Rho.

AWARDS, HONORS: Elected to the University of Kentucky's Journalism Hall of Fame; recipient of more than fifty journalism awards.

WRITINGS:

A Black Woman's Experience: From Schoolhouse to White House, Dorrance, 1974.

The Fascinating Story of Black Kentuckians: Their Heritage and Traditions, Associated Publishers, 1982.

Contributor of articles to various magazines and newspapers.

SIDELIGHTS: Following an early career as a public school teacher and newspaper writer in Kentucky, Alice Allison Dunnigan moved to Washington, D.C., in 1942. While in the capital she worked for the federal government but maintained her interest in journalism by contributing articles, on a free-lance basis, to several Kentucky newspapers. Her appointment as chief of the Washington bureau of the Associated Negro Press, in 1947, signaled her full-time commitment to journalism as a career.

During her fourteen years with the bureau, Dunnigan had the distinction of becoming the first black female member of the Senate and House of Representatives press galleries, in 1947, the first black female White House correspondent in 1948, and the first black elected to the Women's National Press Club. Her reputation as a journalist grew steadily throughout the 1940s, reaching a peak with her reporting of President Harry S. Truman's election campaign of 1948 when, as one of only three black newspaper reporters with the Truman entourage, she became the only woman to accompany the president throughout his entire western campaign.

In addition to her career in journalism, Dunnigan was a committed member of several social policy advisory organizations, including the Presidential Committee on Equal Employment Opportunity between 1967 and 1970, lending her own accomplishments to the community as a fine example of minority achievement. After her retirement in 1970 Dunnigan continued to contribute articles to newspapers and completed two books: her autobiography, *A Black Woman's Experience,* and *The Fascinating Story of Black Kentuckians: Their Heritage and Traditions.*

OBITUARIES:

PERIODICALS

New York Times, May 9, 1983.
Washington Post, May 8, 1983.

E

EDELMAN, Marian Wright 1939-

PERSONAL: Born June 6, 1939, in Bennettsville, S.C.; daughter of Arthur J. and Maggie (Bowen) Wright; married Peter Benjamin Edelman, July 14, 1968; children: Joshua Robert, Jonah Martin, Ezra Benjamin. *Education:* Attended University of Paris and University of Geneva, 1958-59; Spelman College, B.A., 1960; Yale University, LL.B., 1963.

ADDRESSES: Office—Children's Defense Fund, 122 C St. N.W., Washington, D.C. 20001.

CAREER: National Association for the Advancement of Colored People (NAACP), Legal Defense and Education Fund, Inc., New York, N.Y., staff attorney, 1963-64; director of office in Jackson, Miss., 1964-68; partner of Washington Research Project of Southern Center for Public Policy, 1968-73; Children's Defense Fund, Washington, D.C., founder and president, 1973—. W. E. B. Du Bois Lecturer at Harvard University, 1986. Member of Lisle Fellowship's U.S.-U.S.S.R. Student Exchange, 1959; member of executive committee of Student Non-Violent Coordinating Committee (SNCC), 1961-63; member of Operation Crossroads Africa Project in Ivory Coast, 1962; congressional and federal agency liaison for Poor People's Campaign, summer, 1968; director of Harvard University's Center for Law and Education, 1971-73. Member of Presidential Commission on Americans Missing and Unaccounted for in Southeast Asia (Woodcock Commission), 1977, United States-South Africa Leadership Exchange Program, 1977, National Commission on the International Year of the Child, 1979, and President's Commission for a National Agenda for the Eighties, 1979; member of board of directors of Carnegie Council on Children, 1972-77, Aetna Life and Casualty Foundation, Citizens for Constitutional Concerns, U.S. Committee for UNICEF, and Legal Defense and Education Fund of the NAACP; member of board of trustees of Martin Luther King, Jr., Memorial Center, and Joint Center for Political Studies.

MEMBER: Council on Foreign Relations, Delta Sigma Theta (honorary member).

AWARDS, HONORS: Merrill scholar in Paris and Geneva, 1958-59; honorary fellow of Law School at University of Pennsylvania, 1969; Louise Waterman Wise Award, 1970; Presidential Citation from American Public Health Association, 1979; Outstanding Leadership Award from National Alliance of Black School Educators, 1979; Distinguished Service Award from National Association of Black Women Attorneys, 1979; National Award of Merit from National Council on Crime and Delinquency, 1979; named Washingtonian of the Year, 1979; Whitney M. Young Memorial Award from Washington Urban League, 1980; Professional Achievement Award from *Black Enterprise* magazine, 1980; Outstanding Leadership Achievement Award from National Women's Political Caucus and Black Caucus, 1980; Outstanding Community Service Award from National Hookup of Black Women, 1980; Woman of the Year Award from Big Sisters of America, 1980; Award of Recognition from American Academy of Pedodontics, 1981; Rockefeller Public Service Award, 1981; Gertrude Zimand Award from National Child Labor Committee, 1982; Florina Lasker Award from New York Civil Liberties Union, 1982; Anne Roe Award from Graduate School of Education at Harvard University, 1984; Roy Wilkins Civil Rights Award from National Association for the Advancement of Colored People, 1984; award from Women's Legal Defense Fund, 1985; Hubert H. Humphrey Award from Leadership Conference on Civil Rights, 1985; fellow of MacArthur Foundation, 1985; Grenville Clark Prize from Dartmouth College, 1986; Compostela Award of St. James Cathedral, 1987; more than thirty honorary degrees.

WRITINGS:

(Contributor) *Children Out of School in America,* Children's Defense, 1974.
(Contributor) Nathan B. Talbot, editor, *Raising Children in Modern America: Problems and Prospective Solutions,* Little, Brown, 1975.
(Contributor) David C. Warner, editor, *Toward New Human Rights: The Social Policies of the Kennedy and Johnson Administrations,* Lyndon B. Johnson School of Public Affairs, University of Texas at Austin, 1977.
Families in Peril: An Agenda for Social Change, Harvard University Press, 1987.

Principal author of *School Suspensions: Are They Helping Children?* 1975, and *Portrait of Inequality: Black and White Children in America,* 1980. Contributor to magazines.

SIDELIGHTS: Dubbed "the 101st Senator on children's issues" by Senator Edward Kennedy, Marian Wright Edelman left her law practice in 1968, just after the assassination of civil rights leader Martin Luther King, Jr., to work toward a better future for American children. She was the first black woman on the Mississippi bar and had been a civil rights lawyer with the National Association for the Advancement of Colored People. "Convinced she could achieve more as an advocate than as a litigant for the poor," wrote Nancy Traver in *Time,* Edelman moved to Washington, D.C., and began to apply her researching and rhetorical skills in Congress. She promotes her cause with facts about teen pregnancies, poverty, and infant mortality and—with her Children's Defense Fund—has managed to obtain budget increases for family and child health care and education programs. Her book, *Families in Peril: An Agenda for Social Change,* was judged "a powerful and necessary document" of the circumstances of children by *Washington Post* reviewer Jonathan Yardley, and it urges support for poor mothers and children of all races. In *Ms.* magazine Katherine Bouton described Edelman as "the nation's most effective lobbyist on behalf of children . . . an unparalleled strategist and pragmatist."

Edelman told *CA:* "I have been an advocate for disadvantaged Americans throughout my professional career. The Children's Defense Fund, which I have been privileged to direct, has become one of the nation's most active organizations concerned with a wide range of children's and family issues, especially those which most affect America's children: our poorest Americans.

"Founded in 1968 as the Washington Research Project, the Children's Defense Fund monitors and proposes improvements in federal, state, and local budgets, legislative and administrative policies in the areas of child and maternal health, education, child care, child welfare, adolescent pregnancy prevention, youth employment, and family support systems.

"In 1983 the Children's Defense Fund initiated a major long-term national campaign to prevent teenage pregnancy and provide positive life options for youth. Since then, we have launched a multimedia campaign that includes transit advertisements, posters, and television and radio public service announcements, a national prenatal care campaign, and Child Watch coalitions in more than seventy local communities in thirty states to combat teen pregnancy.

"The Children's Defense Fund also has been a leading advocate in Congress, state legislatures, and courts for children's rights. For example, our legal actions blocked out-of-state placement of hundreds of Louisiana children in Texas institutions, guaranteed access to special education programs for tens of thousands of Mississippi's children, and represented the interests of children and their families before numerous federal administrative agencies."

BIOGRAPHICAL/CRITICAL SOURCES:

PERIODICALS

Ebony, July, 1987.
Ms., July/August, 1987.
New York Times Book Review, June 7, 1987.
Time, March 23, 1987.
Washington Post, March 4, 1987.

*   *   *

EDMONDS, (Sheppard) Randolph   1900-1983

PERSONAL: Born April 30, 1900, in Lawrenceville, Va.; died March 28, 1983; son of George Washington (a tenant farmer and sharecropper) and Frances (Fisherman) Edmonds; married

Irene Colbert, 1931 (died, 1968); children: Henriette Highland Garnett, S. Randolph, Jr. *Education:* Oberlin College, B.A., 1926; Columbia University, M.A., 1932; further graduate study at Yale University, University of Dublin, and London School of Speech Training and Dramatic Art.

CAREER: Morgan State College, Baltimore, Md., instructor in English and drama, 1926-1935; Dillard University, New Orleans, La., chairman of speech and theatre department, 1935-47; Florida Agricultural and Mechanical University, Tallahassee, Fla., chairman of theatre arts department, 1947-70. Founder and president of Negro Intercollegiate Drama Association, 1930; organized Morgan College Dramatic Club, Southern Association of Drama and Speech Arts, 1936 (now National Association of Dramatic and Speech Arts; president, 1936-43), and Southeastern Theatre Conference. President of Crescent Concerts Company, New Orleans, 1942-43.

MEMBER: American Educational Theatre Association (fellow).

AWARDS, HONORS: Rockefeller Foundation scholarship, 1934-35; Rosenwald Fellowship, 1938; first prize in a contest from Foundation of Expressive Arts, 1941, for *The Land of Cotton;* Litt.D. from Bethune-Cookman College, 1947; special citation from the American Theatre Association, 1972.

WRITINGS:

PLAYS

"Rocky Roads" (three-act), first produced in Oberlin, Ohio, at Oberlin High School, May 15, 1926.
"Job Hunting" (one-act), first produced in Baltimore at Morgan College, February 18, 1928.
Shades and Shadows (contains "Shades and Shadows," "The Devil's Price," "Hewers of Wood," "Everyman's Land," "The Tribal Chief," and "The Phantom Treasure"), Meador, 1930, reprinted, University Microfilms, 1971.
"Shades and Shadows" (first produced in Baltimore at Douglass High School, April 24, 1931), published in *Shades and Shadows,* Meador, 1930 (also see above).
"Bad Man" (one-act; first produced in New York on NBC-Radio, February 26, 1932), published in *Six Plays for a Negro Theatre,* Walter H. Baker, 1934 (also see below).
Six Plays for a Negro Theatre (contains "Bad Man," "Old Man Pete," "Nat Turner," "Breeders," "Bleeding Hearts," and "The New Window"), foreword by Frederick H. Koch, Walter H. Baker, 1934, reprinted, University Microfilms, 1974.
"Nat Turner" (first produced in New Orleans at Dillard University Theatre, January 17, 1936), published in *Six Plays for a Negro Theatre,* Walter H. Baker, 1934 (also see above).
"The High Court of Historia" (first produced in New Orleans at Dillard University Workshop Theatre, February, 1939), published in *The Land of Cotton, and Other Plays,* Associated, 1942 (also see below).
"The Land of Cotton" (four-act; first produced in New Orleans at Longshoreman's Hall, March 20, 1941), published in *The Land of Cotton, and Other Plays,* Associated, 1942 (also see below).
The Land of Cotton, and Other Plays (contains "The Land of Cotton," "Gangsters Over Harlem," "Yellow Death," "Silas Brown," and "The High Court of Historia"), Associated, 1942, University Microfilms, 1974.
"Simon in Cyrene" (four-act), first produced in New Orleans at Dillard University Little Theatre, February 11, 1943.

"Earth and Stars" (first produced in New Orleans at Dillard University Little Theatre, February 13, 1946), revised version published in *Black Drama in America*, Fawcett, 1971.

"Whatever the Battle Be: A Symphonic Drama," first produced in Tallahassee at Lee Auditorium, November 3, 1950.

Also author of more than twenty-five unproduced and unpublished plays, including "A Merchant in Dixie," "For Fatherland," "Shadow Across the Path," "The Shape of Wars to Come," "The Trial and Banishment of Uncle Tom," and "Prometheus and the Atom."

Work represented in anthologies, including *Negro History in Thirteen Plays*, edited by Willis Richardson and May Miller, Associated, 1935; *The Negro Caravan*, edited by Sterling A. Brown, Arthur P. Davis, and Ulysses Lee, Dryden, 1941; and *The American Theatre: A Sum of Its Parts*, edited by Henry B. Williams, Samuel French, 1971. Contributor to periodicals, including *Arts Quarterly, Crisis, Florida A & M University Bulletin, Messenger, Opportunity, Pittsburgh Courier*, and *University of North Carolina Playbook*.

SIDELIGHTS: As a playwright, critic, teacher, and leader in theatre organizations, Randolph Edmonds was a driving force behind academic dramatics in Afro-American universities for more than four decades. He published many articles in journals to help foster an appreciation for collegiate and regional theatre, to educate its audience, and to urge others to take an active role in it. In his own popular plays Edmonds addressed issues ranging from civil rights to slavery, dramatized lives of prominent black historical figures, and looked to the daily experiences of blacks for subject matter.

Edmonds began writing plays while a student at Oberlin College during the 1920s. His first full-length work, "Rocky Roads," a farce about a medical student at Howard University, was produced in 1926 while he was a senior. Following graduation Edmonds taught English at Morgan State College in Baltimore, Maryland, and organized there the first drama department in any black university in the country. He also founded a student acting club that distinguished itself by being the first college players ever to appear on Broadway. After teaching at Morgan State for nine years Edmonds moved to Dillard University in New Orleans, Louisiana, where he established and directed its speech and theatre arts department. At Dillard he founded the Southern Association of Dramatic and Speech Arts and acted as its president for seven years.

Edmonds realized that a major drawback of the black American theatre was that it lacked skillful playwrights. To contend with this problem he compiled six plays that he had written while a student at Oberlin. The collection, *Shades and Shadows*, was published in 1930. Although a reviewer for the *Pittsburgh Post Gazette* wrote that the dialogue featured in the plays was "somewhat amateurish," he predicted that "with further experience [Edmonds] will be able to make important contributions to the literature of his race." The playwright's next collection, *Six Plays for a Negro Theatre*, proved the critic right, for reviewers held that the quality of Edmonds's writing was much improved. Writing in the preface the dramatist explained that his plays were meant to be staged at the "Negro Little Theatres, where there has been for many years a great need for plays of Negro life written by Negroes."

Intrigued by the folk plays that a professor at the University of North Carolina and his students were writing, Edmonds based the plays for his second collection on the experiences of Southern Negroes, who would also be the primary audience for them. The plays utilize incidents from the daily lives, legends, and language of the common people. By writing the plays in dialect, Edmonds intended to lend authenticity to the drama but was later condemned by critics who thought it degraded Negroes. The playwright defended his writing in the vernacular, however, believing that tragedy is grievous regardless of the language in which it is written. More important to Edmonds were universal themes to which the audience could relate, thought-provoking conflicts, dynamic characterization, and melodrama.

Critics praised the folk dramas of *Six Plays for a Negro Theatre* for their vivid imagery, exciting plots, and interesting characters. Most of the plays were melodramatic and sentimental, and some depicted blacks victimized by white society as well as by other members of the black community. In "Breeders," for example, Edmonds decries the practice of forcing slaves to mate so that they could produce able bodies to work the fields and in "Bad Man" he tells the tale of an innocent black man who was lynched by a mob of whites bent on avenging the murder of a white man. The playwright also explores the difficulties in adjusting to city life that many Southern Negroes and whites faced when migrating to the North during the first three decades of the twentieth century in "Old Man Pete," and the historical drama "Nat Turner" chronicles the life of the folk hero who led a slave revolt on a Virginia plantation in 1831.

In 1942 Redmond published a third collected book of dramas with socially relevant and historical subjects, *The Land of Cotton, and Other Plays*. The work "Simon in Cyrene" is a rendering of the life of the African who helped Jesus Christ carry his cross to Calvary. The title play, "The Land of Cotton," tells the story of two men attempting to unionize black tenant farmers in the South against the resistance of the racist Ku Klux Klan, while "The High Court of Historia" is a condemnation of historians who either are not proud of their African heritage or do not instruct their students in black history.

In honor of his outstanding contributions to the development of interest in the theatre and his organizing drama departments and associations in predominately black colleges of the southern United States, Edmonds was named by the National Association of Dramatic and Speech Arts "Dean of Black Academic Theatre" in 1970. In his nearly forty-five years as an active critic and teacher he not only inspired and educated audiences and playwrights alike, but also entertained playgoers who were moved by seeing their ancestors—or even themselves—on the stage in the characters Edmonds portrayed.

BIOGRAPHICAL/CRITICAL SOURCES:

BOOKS

Abramson, Doris, *Negro Playwrights in the American Theatre, 1925-1959*, Columbia University Press, 1969.

Bond, Frederick, *The Negro and the Drama*, Associated Press, 1940.

Brawley, Benjamin G., *Negro Genius*, Dodd, 1937.

Dictionary of Literary Biography, Volume 51: *Afro-American Writers From the Harlem Renaissance to 1940*, Gale, 1987.

Dreer, Herman, *American Literature by Negro Authors*, Macmillan, 1950.

Isaacs, Edith J. R., *The Negro in the American Theatre*, McGrath, 1947.

Turner, Darwin T., editor, *Black American Literature: Essays, Poetry, Fiction, Drama,* three volumes, Merrill, 1970.
Wallace, Karl R., editor, *The History of Speech Education in America,* Appleton-Century, 1954.

PERIODICALS

Freedomways, 3rd quarter, 1982.
Pittsburgh Post Gazette, May 2, 1931.
Washington Post, February 21, 1979.

—*Sketch by Carol Lynn DeKane*

*   *   *

EDWARDS, Eli
See McKAY, Festus Claudius

*   *   *

EKWENSI, C. O. D.
See EKWENSI, Cyprian (Odiatu Duaka)

*   *   *

EKWENSI, Cyprian (Odiatu Duaka)   1921-
(C. O. D. Ekwensi)

PERSONAL: Born September 26, 1921, in Minna, Nigeria; son of Ogbuefi David Duaka and Uso Agnes Ekwensi; married Eunice Anyiwo; children: five. *Education:* Attended Achimota College, Ghana, and Ibadan University; received B.A.; further study at Chelsea School of Pharmacy, London, and University of Iowa, Iowa City.

ADDRESSES: Home—12 Hillview, Independence Layout, P.O. Box 317, Enugu, Nigeria.

CAREER: Novelist and writer of short stories and stories for children. Igbodi College, Lagos, Nigeria, lecturer in biology, chemistry, and English, 1947-49; School of Pharmacy, Lagos, lecturer in pharmacognosy and pharmaceutics, 1949-56; pharmacist superintendent for Nigerian Medical Services, 1956-57; head of features, Nigerian Broadcasting Corp., 1957-61; Federal Ministry of Information, Lagos, director of information, 1961-66; chairman of Bureau for External Publicity during Biafran secession, 1967-69, and director of an independent Biafran radio station; chemist for a plastics firm in Enugu, Nigeria; managing director of Star Printing & Publishing Co. (publishers of *Daily Star*), 1975-79; managing director of Niger Eagle Publishing Company, 1980-81. Owner of East Niger Chemists and East Niger Trading Company. Chairman of East Central State Library Board, 1972-75. Newspaper consultant to *Weekly Trumpet* and *Daily News* of Anambra State and to *Weekly Eagle* of Imo State, 1980-83; consultant on information to the executive office of the president; consultant to Federal Ministry of Information; public relations consultant.

MEMBER: P.E.N., Society of Nigerian Authors, Pharmaceutical Society of Great Britain, Institute of Public Relations (London), Institute of Public Relations (Nigeria; fellow).

AWARDS, HONORS: Dag Hammarskjold International Prize for Literary Merit, 1969.

WRITINGS:

(Under name C. O. D. Ekwensi) *When Love Whispers* (novella), Tabansi Bookshop (Onitsha, Nigeria), 1947.

People of the City (novel), Andrew Dakers, 1954, Northwestern University Press, 1967, revised edition, Fawcett, 1969.
Jagua Nana (novel), Hutchinson, 1961, Fawcett, 1969.
Burning Grass (novel), Heinemann, 1962.
Beautiful Feathers (novel), Hutchinson, 1963.
The Rainmaker and Other Stories (short story collection), African Universities Press, 1965.
Lokotown and Other Stories (short story collection), Heinemann, 1966.
Iska, Hutchinson, 1966.
The Restless City and Christmas Gold, Heinemann, 1975.
Survive the Peace, Heinemann, 1976.
(Editor) *Festac Anthology of Nigerian Writing,* Festac, 1977.
Divided We Stand (novel), Fourth Dimension Publishers, 1980.
Motherless Baby (novella), Fourth Dimension Publishers, 1980.

FOR YOUNG PEOPLE

(Under name C. O. D. Ekwensi) *Ikolo the Wrestler and Other Ibo Tales,* Thomas Nelson, 1947.
(Under name C. O. D. Ekwensi) *The Leopard's Claw,* Thomas Nelson, 1950.
The Drummer Boy, Cambridge University Press, 1960.
The Passport of Mallam Ilia, Cambridge University Press, 1960.
An African Night's Entertainment (folklore), African Universities Press, 1962.
Yaba Roundabout Murder (short novel), Tortoise Series Books (Lagos, Nigeria), 1962.
The Great Elephant-Bird, Thomas Nelson, 1965.
Juju Rock, African Universities Press, 1966.
The Boa Suitor, Thomas Nelson, 1966.
Trouble in Form Six, Cambridge University Press, 1966.
Coal Camp Boy, Longman, 1971.
Samankwe in the Strange Forest, Longman, 1973.
The Rainbow Tinted Scarf and Other Stories (collection), Evans Africa Library, 1975.
Samankwe and the Highway Robbers, Evans Africa Library, 1975.

OTHER

Writer of plays and scripts for BBC radio and television, Radio Nigeria, and other communication outlets. Contributor of stories, articles, and reviews to magazines and newspapers in Nigeria and England, including *West African Review,* London *Times, Black Orpheus, Flamingo,* and *Sunday Post.*

SIDELIGHTS: Reviewing Cyprian Ekwensi's *Beautiful Feathers* in *Critique: Studies in Modern Fiction,* John F. Povey writes: "The very practice of writing, the developing professionalism of his work, makes us find in Ekwensi a new and perhaps important phenomenon in African writing. By constant productivity, his style is becoming purged of its derivative excess and his plots begin to take on a less picaresque structure. Ekwensi is interesting because he is concerned with the present, with the violence of the new Lagos slums, the dishonesty of the new native politicians. Other Nigerian novelists have sought their material from the past, the history of missionaries and British administration as in Chinua Achebe's books, the schoolboy memoirs of Onuora Nzekwu. Ekwensi faces the difficult task of catching the present tone of Africa, changing at a speed that frighteningly destroys the old certainties. In describing this world, Ekwensi has gradually become a significant writer."

Ekwensi states that his life in government and quasi-government organizations like the Nigerian Broadcasting Corporation has prevented him from expressing any strong political opinions, but adds, ''I am as much a nationalist as the heckler standing on the soap-box, with the added advantage of objectivity.'' During the late 1960s Biafran war, during which the eastern region of Biafra seceded temporarily from the rest of Nigeria, Ekwensi visited the United States more than once to help raise money for Biafra and to purchase radio equipment for the independent Biafran radio station of which he was director. He has also traveled in western Europe.

Several of Ekwensi's novels have been translated into other languages, including Russian, Italian, German, Serbo-Croatian, Danish, and French. His novellas have been used primarily in schools as supplementary readers.

AVOCATIONAL INTERESTS: Hunting game, swimming, photography, motoring, and weightlifting.

BIOGRAPHICAL/CRITICAL SOURCES:

BOOKS

Contemporary Literary Criticism, Volume IV, Gale, 1975.
Tucker, Martin, *Africa in Modern Literature: A Survey of Contemporary Writing in English,* Ungar, 1967.

PERIODICALS

Books Abroad, autumn, 1967.
Critique: Studies in Modern Fiction, October, 1965.
Times Literary Supplement, June 4, 1964.

*   *   *

ELDER, Lonne III   1931-

PERSONAL: Born December 26, 1931, in Americus, Ga.; son of Lonne, Jr., and Quincy Elder; married Betty Gross, 1963 (divorced, 1967); married Judith Ann Johnson (an actress), February 14, 1969; children: (first marriage) David DuBois; (second marriage) Christian, Loni. *Education:* Attended Yale University School of Drama, 1965-67. *Religion:* Episcopalian.

ADDRESSES: Home—Sherman Oaks, Calif. *Office*—c/o Avon Books, 959 Eighth Ave., New York, N.Y. 10019.

CAREER: Playwright, screenwriter, and free-lance writer. Has worked as a political activist, phone clerk, waiter, professional gambler, and dock worker; actor in ''A Raisin in the Sun'' in New York City, 1959, and on tour, 1960-61; actor in ''A Day of Absence'' in New York City, 1965; Negro Ensemble Company, New York City, director of playwrights division, 1967-69; Talent Associates, New York City, writer, 1968; Cinema Center Films, Hollywood, Calif., writer and producer, 1969-70; Universal Pictures, Hollywood, writer, 1970-71; Radnitz/Mattel Productions, Hollywood, writer, 1971; Talent Associates, Hollywood, writer and producer, 1971; Metro-Goldwyn-Mayer, Inc., Hollywood, writer, 1971; Columbia Pictures Industries, Inc., Hollywood, writer, 1972; American Broadcasting Co., New York City, scriptwriter. Co-founder, Banneker Productions (a filmmaking company), 1969; founder, Black Artists Alliance. *Military service:* Served in U.S. Army.

MEMBER: Black Academy of Arts and Letters, Writers Guild of America, West, New Dramatists, Harlem Writer's Guild.

AWARDS, HONORS: Stanley Drama Award in playwriting, 1965, Pulitzer Prize nomination, 1969, Outer Drama Critics Circle Award, 1970, Vernon Rice Drama Desk Award, 1970, Stella Holt Memorial Playwrights Award, 1970, Los Angeles Drama Critics Award, 1970, and Christopher Award, 1975, all for *Ceremonies in Dark Old Men;* John Hay Whitney fellowship, 1965-66; ABC fellowship in television writing, 1965-66; Hamilton K. Bishop Award in playwriting; American National Theatre Academy Award, 1967; Joseph E. Levine fellowship in filmmaking at Yale University School of Drama, 1966-67; John Golden fellowship, 1966-67; Award of Merit, University of Southern California Film Conference, 1971; Academy Award nomination for best screenplay based on material from another medium, from Academy of Motion Picture Arts and Sciences, Christopher Award, Atlanta Film Festival Silver Award, and Image Award, all 1972, all for ''Sounder,'' which was also nominated for an Academy Award for best picture; Award of Merit, California Association of Teachers of English, 1973.

WRITINGS:

PLAYS

Ceremonies in Dark Old Men (two-act; first produced in New York City at Wagner College, July, 1965; revised version produced in New York City at St. Mark's Playhouse, February 4, 1969; also see below), Farrar, Straus, 1969.
''Charades on East Fourth Street'' (one-act; commissioned by New York City Mobilization for Youth, Inc.), first produced at Expo-67 in Montreal, Quebec, 1967, published in *Black Drama Anthology,* edited by Woodie King and Ron Milner, New American Library, 1971.
''Splendid Mummer'' (mono-drama), first produced Off-Broadway at American Place Theater, April 24, 1988.

Also author of plays: ''A Hysterical Turtle in a Rabbit Race,'' 1961; ''Kissing Rattlesnakes Can Be Fun'' (one-act), 1966; and ''Seven Comes Up, Seven Comes Down'' (one-act), 1966.

SCREENPLAYS AND TELEVISION DRAMAS

''The Terrible Veil,'' National Broadcasting Corporation (NBC-TV), 1964.
''Sounder'' (adaptation of novel of same title by William H. Armstrong), Twentieth Century-Fox, 1972.
''Melinda,'' Metro-Golwyn-Mayer, 1972.
''Ceremonies in Dark Old Men'' (based on his play of same title), American Broadcasting Co. (ABC-TV), 1975.
''Sounder, Part 2,'' ABC-TV, 1976.
''A Woman Called Moses,'' NBC-TV, 1978.
''Bustin' Loose'' (adaptation of story by Richard Pryor), Universal Pictures, 1981.

Also author of screenplay about the life of Ethel Waters for World Wide Pictures, and of television drama, ''Deadly Circle of Violence.'' Author of scripts for ''Number One with a Bullet,'' an expose on the recording industry, for a film version of Richard Wright's novel, *Native Son,* and for television series, ''Camera Three,'' CBS-TV, 1963, ''N.Y.P.D.,'' ABC-TV, 1967-68, and ''McCloud,'' NBC-TV, 1970-71.

OTHER

(Contributor) Lindsay Patterson, editor, *Black Theater: A 20th-Century Collection of the Works of the Best Playwrights,* Dodd, 1971.
(Contributor) Clive Barnes, editor, *Best American Plays, Seventh Series, 1967-1973,* Crown, 1974.
''The Responsibilities of the Black Writer'' (sound recording), Center for Cassette Studies, 1975.

WORK IN PROGRESS: A play, ''After the Band Goes Home.''

SIDELIGHTS: "Lonne Elder III is a talented and creative actor, playwright, and screenwriter whose career has evolved from acting and writing for the stage to acting and writing for the screen," states Joseph Millichap in a *Dictionary of Literary Biography* essay. "Elder has remained committed to a program of raising audience consciousness of racial tensions through his analysis of the black identity in modern America. In particular, his vision has stressed the personal dedication necessary for Afro-Americans to overcome the handicaps imposed by generations of white prejudice and black fear. He has also used his writing to help change the portrayal of blacks in films and on television."

In an interview with Liz Gant in *Black World,* Elder indicates that although he began writing and "reading hungrily" at the early age of six or seven, he had no particular inclination to make writing his career. Elder recalls: "I don't think I even knew what a writer was. I just liked the idea of writing to myself; it was a way of expressing feelings that I didn't know how to express in other ways, like talking. There was no one to whom I could convey those kinds of thoughts and emotions in the environment I grew up in." Soon after Elder's birth in Georgia, his family moved to New Jersey and, orphaned in adolescence, Elder was raised by an aunt and uncle. Although Elder's formal education was not extensive, he indicates to Gant that the education he did receive was "good and well-balanced." And while he was stationed with the Army near Fisk University, he was introduced to the poet and teacher Robert Hayden, with whom he spent much time. "I gave him my work to read and he was very, very encouraging," recalls Elder in his interview with Gant, adding that Hayden helped him to "handle and structure" what he was trying to write. "He really made a tremendous impact on my life that has lasted up to this day."

"Elder's encounters with dramatist and actor Douglas Turner Ward moved him away from short stories and poetry and in the direction of playwriting," says Wilsonia E. D. Cherry in a *Dictionary of Literary Biography* essay. Elder and Ward shared an apartment during the 1950s; and it was during this time that Ward wrote his first play, to which Elder reacted with both wonder and determination. "It was a gigantic thing, one of the longest plays I'd ever seen," Elder tells Gant. "I read it and all I could do was shake my head. Damn! I thought. He wrote this whole thing! And he was one of my peers. . . . The most I'd ever written was maybe a 15-page short story or a one-page poem. So I said, well, I can do that too! And that's when I started writing plays." Explaining that it was "the immediacy of expressing a feeling or an emotion" that most excited him about drama, Elder also tells Gant, "I started going to the theater and I was impressed with playwrights who were being produced in small theaters. . . . There was something about it that just got to me. And no matter what I saw, I thought I could do better."

"Like other black dramatists of the last three decades—a period marked by an upsurge of plays by, about, and for black people—Lonne Elder articulates the sorrows, angers, and joys that characterize black life in America," states Cherry; and although Elder's dramatic canon is small, "the plays that he has written strongly emphasize his belief in the survival of a people traumatized both from without and from within." In a *Dictionary of Literary Biography* essay, William Bryan Hart notes that Elder weaves his "multifaceted" personal life into his plays, "For a number of years the struggling playwright supported himself as a professional political activist, dock worker, waiter, phone clerk, professional poker dealer, and

actor." Elder gained valuable insights into the theater through his experience as an actor, which "reinforced his positive feelings about writing for the stage," notes Cherry. And when his award-winning play *Ceremonies in Dark Old Men* was first produced, says Megan Rosenfeld in the *Washington Post,* "Lonne Elder III immediately entered the ranks of young black playwrights who sounded a new voice in the theater." The play was warmly received by critics such as the *New York Post*'s Richard Watts, who praised it as the "best American play of the season." Echoing the assessment that it was "one of the more notable plays to come out of the eruption of black theater in the late 1960s," David Richards adds in the *Washington Post* that it has weathered the years well, "Its compassion for the dispossessed and its insights into the souls of the misguided remain undimmed by time."

In the *New York Times,* Richard F. Shepard calls *Ceremonies in Dark Old Men* "a tragedy gleefully shrouded in comedy." And in the *Washington Post,* Joe Brown describes the cast of various Parker family members. The father "is an unemployed barber, a charming dreamer and yarn-spinner who spends his days playing ritual checker games and telling stories so well he even deceives himself." One of Parker's sons is "a restless schemer" while the other is "a lightfingered loafer," Brown continues; and the daughter "is full of righteous resentment about supporting three grown men, as her mother did before her." The family tries to "escape the poverty-stricken treadmill of their Harlem home by selling illegally made corn liquor . . . and by stealing from white Harlem store owners," says Cherry. According to Hart, Elder emphasizes that the greatest adversity threatening the Parker family extends to black Americans generally—"individual weakness compounded by the frustration of being incapable of prospering in a white-oriented society." Cherry suggests, however, that the play also "points toward the resilience of the American black family." Interviewed by C. W. E. Bigsby in his *The Black American Writer,* Elder indicates that he did not specifically aim the play at a black audience, "If I do that I think I'm crippling myself in terms of what I am and what I can do with the material before me. I write out of the black frame of reference, which is different from saying that I am writing for all black people."

Affirming the "overwhelmingly positive" critical response to *Ceremonies in Dark Old Men,* Cherry continues: "Although a few critics saw the play as inept, formulaic, and dated, the majority found it well wrought, rich, powerful, and meritorious. And rewarded it was." Having placed second in the voting for the Pulitzer Prize, the work was honored with several other dramatic awards, including a Christopher for the teleplay. Disagreeing with the assessment of some critics that the play was "naturalistic in the traditional or conventional sense of the word," Elder explains to Bigsby that it is only naturalistic "out of necessity in areas where it had to be. I would call it more akin to exalted realism." Elder tells Bigsby that "it's naturalism to [the critics] mainly because they're unacquainted with the flow and the various colours of life in the black ghetto." *Ceremonies in Dark Old Men,* Elder continues, "really is based on the daily ritual of survival in the black community, which does not necessarily have anything to do with black/white confrontation or any clenched fist anger." Writing in the *New York Times* about the play's recent revival, Mel Gussow feels that it "is marked by the breadth of its vision of interdependent, mutually harmful lives, and it is written with humor and a depth of understanding," and concludes that Elder's "absence has been a loss for the theater."

Despite his success with both theater and television, Elder journeyed west to launch a career as a screenwriter. Explaining to Gant that he decided to leave New York City because it "just became a mentally unbearable place to live in," Elder adds: "I'm just not made of the stuff to walk around with daggers in my eyes and a clenched fist. I just can't live like that." In his interview with Gant, Elder also speaks about the sense of closure that he experienced with *Ceremonies in Dark Old Men,* recalling: "It was well received in New York and I felt that, in terms of what I had set out to do, I'd accomplished that out of my own experiences and I didn't have to do it anymore. I said I wasn't going to write any more Black 'kitchen sink' dramas. From that point on, it was not exactly my choice." Nevertheless, Dan Sullivan points out in the *New York Times* that "as a black writer, [Elder] has had to deal with the particular temptations of the 'blaxploitation' film and the neo-Amos 'n' Andy TV comedy series, two genres that he has little respect for but that do offer good money and, what is almost as important in Hollywood, highly visible credits."

Regarding "Melinda," Elder's screenwriting debut and the only "blaxploitation" film with which he has been associated, Elder told Sullivan: "I went in under the delusion that I could write a crime melodrama that wouldn't just titillate. I wasn't able to do it. No, I wouldn't say I'm proud of that picture. But I'm not ashamed of it either." The film is a mystery about a disc jockey who is wrongly accused of killing his girlfriend and pursues the actual murderer himself. Elder acknowledges to Gant that, although he was not "anxious" to get involved with the film, he was prompted by commercial rather than artistic reasons; and Millichap recognizes in the film a "blending of Elder's commercial efforts for television and his more serious efforts at probing the effects of deprivation on black personality."

Released coincidentally at the same time as his critically deplored "Melinda" was Elder's award-winning "Sounder," a film about the difficulties endured by a black sharecropping family during the Depression, starring Cicely Tyson and Paul Winfield. Millichap believes that "Elder created a moving film which received much critical acclaim and provided an artistic counterpoint to the exploitation trend." "About 95 percent of what I wrote was represented on screen—a miracle by Hollywood standards," Elder relates to Gant. A *Chicago Sun-Times* contributor, who calls it "one of the most compassionate and truthful of movies," suggests that "the story is so simple because it involved, not so much what people do, but how they change and grow." Elder's other film work includes a sequel to "Sounder" and an adaptation of Richard Pryor's screen story "Bustin' Loose." Most of Elder's writing, however, has been for television and includes the well-received mini-series, "A Woman Called Moses," based on the life of Harriet Tubman.

"Elder has had to adjust to what he calls 'the whore mentality' that smogs the film-TV industry, the assumption that one's talent is on call to an inscrutable client who will drop you the minute you fail to give pleasure," comments Sullivan. Admitting to Gant that he is a "perfectionist," Elder adds that "contrary to what a lot of Black artists say, I don't think you have to create new standards and values. They're already there, on anybody's terms. But structure and craftsmanship are all-important. And this is something that I've thought about and taken myself to. I intend for whatever I write to be excellent. I'm not going to just shove things out." Perceiving an obligation to correct the industry's stereotyped depictions of black life, "Elder maintains that he is willing to play the Hollywood charade if it means changing the way black people are portrayed on television and film," Hart writes. "Elder says that these media have become rigid and resistant to authentic characterizations of black American life." Expressing his belief that "no one wants to really believe that black people are human," Elder remarks to Sullivan that "if the black man did emerge as a human entity, it would mean that he should participate in the culture, that he should own a part of it. That still bothers people."

Elder's "Splendid Mummer" signals his return to the theater. Calling the monodrama "an act of homage to his theatrical past and the little-known cultural history of his race," Steven Erlanger explains in the *New York Times* that the play is about Ira Frederick Aldridge, a black actor who left America in the 1820s for the "more racially tolerant England, Europe and Russia" to become a Shakespearean actor. Believed to have been the first black actor to perform the role of Othello, Aldridge headed his own touring company and was recognized as "one of the foremost interpreters of Shakespeare," notes Erlanger. According to Gussow in the *New York Times,* "he had an astonishing career in the English theater, one that has not been equaled by any other American classical actor." Describing Elder as "more at ease with himself than in the interviews of 20 years ago, when 'Ceremonies in Dark Old Men' became a sudden hit, thrusting him forward into the capricious world of New York theater," Erlanger relates Elder's response to a question concerning "his sense of responsibility to the black theater: "My responsibility basically starts with me, in terms of what I do and how I carry out whatever mission I take on."

Transcripts of Elder's one-act plays are housed in the Hatch-Billops Archives in New York and a collection of his manuscripts is maintained by Boston University. However, despite a canon that includes other plays and significant contributions to film and television, Hart notes that Elder's "reputation as a dramatist rests primarily upon this single, major work [*Ceremonies in Dark Old Men*]." Assessing the entirety of his writing, though, Millichap considers Elder "a committed, intelligent writer whose work is shaped by a responsible vision of black experience as an important part of modern American life." Similarly, Hart believes that Elder "celebrates the humanity of blacks and does not conveniently avoid the ironies and difficulties that are a part of his life." As Elder relates to Shepard: "I think I have a lot of respect for people, especially black people. I know there has always been an adventure in being black in America, a glorious and adventurous thing constantly unfolding in every day life in its beauty, speech, walk, dance and even in its anger."

BIOGRAPHICAL/CRITICAL SOURCES:

BOOKS

Arata, Esther Spring, and Nicholas John Rotoli, *Black American Playwrights: 1800 to the Present; A Bibliography,* Scarecrow, 1976.

Arata, Esther Spring, *More Black American Playwrights: A Bibliography,* Scarecrow, 1979.

Bigsby, C. W. E., editor, *The Black American Writer,* Volume 2: *Poetry and Drama,* Penguin Books, 1969.

Dictionary of Literary Biography, Gale, Volume 7: *Twentieth-Century American Dramatists,* 1981, Volume 38: *Afro-American Writers after 1955: Dramatists and Prose Writers,* 1985, Volume 44: *American Screenwriters,* 1986.

PERIODICALS

Arts in Society, summer, 1971.
Black Creation, summer, 1973, winter, 1973.
Black World, April, 1973.
Chicago Sun-Times, December 18, 1972.
CLA Journal, September, 1971, September, 1972, December, 1972, December, 1976.
Dialog on Film, May, 1973.
Dissent, winter, 1973, summer, 1976.
English Journal, April, 1970.
Freedomways, Volume 19, 1979.
MELUS, spring, 1980.
Negro History Bulletin, January, 1973.
New York Daily News, February 6, 1969.
New York Post, February 6, 1969.
New York Times, February 8, 1969, February 16, 1969, January 5, 1975, May 16, 1985, April 24, 1988, April 25, 1988.
Partisan Review, Volume 36, 1969.
Village Voice, November 12, 1972.
Wall Street Journal, February 19, 1969.
Washington Post, September 23, 1972, February 8, 1985, February 11, 1985.

—*Sketch by Sharon Malinowski*

*   *   *

ELLISON, Ralph (Waldo) 1914-

PERSONAL: Born March 1, 1914, in Oklahoma City, Okla.; son of Lewis Alfred (a construction worker and tradesman) and Ida (Millsap) Ellison; married Fanny McConnell, July, 1946. *Education:* Attended Tuskegee Institute, 1933-36.

ADDRESSES: Home and office—730 Riverside Dr., New York, N.Y. 10031, and Plainfield, Mass. *Agent*—Owen Laster, William Morris Agency, 1350 Ave. of the Americas, New York, N.Y. 10019.

CAREER: Writer, 1937—; worked as a researcher and writer on Federal Writers' Project in New York City, 1938-42; edited *Negro Quarterly,* 1942; lecture tour in Germany, 1954; lecturer at Salzburg Seminar, Austria, fall, 1954; U.S. Information Agency, tour of Italian cities, 1956; Bard College, Annandale-on-Hudson, N.Y., instructor in Russian and American literature, 1958-61; New York University, New York City, Albert Schweitzer Professor in Humanities, 1970-79, professor emeritus, 1979—. Alexander White Visiting Professor, University of Chicago, 1961; visiting professor of writing, Rutgers University, 1962-64; visiting fellow in American studies, Yale University, 1966. Gertrude Whittall Lecturer, Library of Congress, January, 1964; delivered Ewing Lectures at University of California, Los Angeles, April, 1964. Lecturer in American Negro culture, folklore, and creative writing at other colleges and universities throughout the United States, including Columbia University, Fisk University, Princeton University, Antioch University, and Bennington College.

Member of Carnegie Commission on Educational Television, 1966-67; honorary consultant in American letters, Library of Congress, 1966-72. Trustee, Colonial Williamsburg Foundation, John F. Kennedy Center for the Performing Arts, 1967-77, Educational Broadcasting Corp., 1968-69, New School for Social Research, 1969-83, Bennington College, 1970-75, and Museum of the City of New York, 1970-86. Charter member of National Council of the Arts, 1965-67, and of National Advisory Council, Hampshire College. *Military service:* U.S. Merchant Marine, World War II.

MEMBER: PEN (vice-president, 1964), Authors Guild, Authors League of America, American Academy and Institute of Arts and Letters, Institute of Jazz Studies (member of board of advisors), Century Association (resident member).

AWARDS, HONORS: Rosenwald grant, 1945; National Book Award and National Newspaper Publishers' Russwurm Award, both 1953, both for *Invisible Man;* Certificate of Award, *Chicago Defender,* 1953; Rockefeller Foundation award, 1954; Prix de Rome fellowships, American Academy of Arts and Letters, 1955 and 1956; *Invisible Man* selected as the most distinguished postwar American novel and Ellison as the sixth most influential novelist by *New York Herald Tribune Book Week* poll of two hundred authors, editors, and critics, 1965; recipient of award honoring well-known Oklahomans in the arts from governor of Oklahoma, 1966; Medal of Freedom, 1969; Chevalier de l'Ordre des Arts et Lettres (France), 1970; Ralph Ellison Public Library, Oklahoma City, named in his honor, 1975; National Medal of Arts, 1985, for *Invisible Man* and for his teaching at numerous universities. Honorary doctorates from Tuskegee Institute, 1963, Rutgers University, 1966, Grinnell College, 1967, University of Michigan, 1967, Williams College, 1970, Long Island University, 1971, Adelphi University, 1971, College of William and Mary, 1972, Harvard University, 1974, Wake Forest College, 1974, University of Maryland, 1974, Bard College, 1978, Wesleyan University, 1980, and Brown University, 1980.

WRITINGS:

Invisible Man (novel), Random House, 1952, published as a limited edition with illustrations by Steven H. Stroud, Franklin Library, 1980, original edition reprinted with new introduction by author as special thirtieth-anniversary edition, Random House, 1982.
(Contributor) Granville Hicks, editor, *The Living Novel: A Symposium,* Macmillan, 1957.
(Author of introduction) Stephen Crane, *The Red Badge of Courage and Four Great Stories,* Dell, 1960.
Shadow and Act (essays), Random House, 1964.
(With Karl Shapiro) *The Writer's Experience* (lectures; includes "Hidden Names and Complex Fate: A Writer's Experience in the U.S.," by Ellison, and "American Poet?," by Shapiro), Gertrude Clarke Whittall Poetry and Literature Fund for Library of Congress, 1964.
(Contributor) *Education of the Deprived and Segregated* (report of seminar on education for culturally-different youth, Dedham, Mass., September 3-15, 1963), Bank Street College of Education, 1965.
(Contributor) Robert Penn Warren, *Who Speaks for the Negro?,* Random House, 1965.
(With Whitney M. Young and Herbert Gnas) *The City in Crisis,* introduction by Bayard Rustin, A. Philip Randolph Educational Fund, 1968.
(Author of introduction) Romare Bearden, *Paintings and Projections* (catalogue of exhibition, November 25-December 22, 1968), State University of New York at Albany, 1968.
(Contributor) James MacGregor Burns, editor, *To Heal and to Build: The Programs of Lyndon B. Johnson,* prologue by Howard K. Smith, epilogue by Eric Hoffer, McGraw, 1968.
(Author of foreword) Leon Forrest, *There Is a Tree More Ancient than Eden,* Random House, 1973.

(Contributor) Bernard Schwartz, editor, *American Law: The Third Century, the Law Bicentennial Volume*, F. B. Rothman for New York University School of Law, 1976.

Going to the Territory (essays), Random House, 1986.

WORK REPRESENTED IN ANTHOLOGIES

Hans Otto Storm and others, editors, *American Writing*, J. A. Decker, 1940.

Edwin J. O'Brien, editor, *The Best Short Stories, 1941*, Houghton, 1941.

Edwin Seaver, editor, *Cross Section: A Collection of New American Writing, 1944*, L. B. Fischer, 1944.

New World Writing, 5, New American Library, 1954.

New World Writing, 9, New American Library, 1956.

Charles A. Fenton, editor, *Best Short Stories of World War II*, Viking, 1957.

Robert Penn Warren and Albert Erskine, editors, *A New Southern Harvest: An Anthology*, Bantam, 1957.

Langston Hughes and Arna Bontemps, editors, *The Book of Negro Folklore*, Dodd, 1958.

Dorothy Sterling, editor, *I Have Seen War: Twenty-five Stories from World War II*, Hill & Wang, 1960.

Herbert Gold and David L. Stevenson, editors, *Stories of Modern America*, St. Martin's, 1961.

John Alfred Williams, editor, *The Angry Black*, Lancer Books, 1962, 2nd edition published as *Beyond the Angry Black*, Cooper Square, 1966.

Herbert Hill, editor, *Soon, One Morning: New Writing by American Negroes, 1940-1962* (includes previously unpublished section from original manuscript of *Invisible Man*), Knopf, 1963 (published in England as *Black Voices*, Elek Books, 1964).

L. Hughes, editor, *The Best Short Stories by Negro Writers: An Anthology from 1899 to the Present*, Little, Brown, 1967.

Douglas Angus and Sylvia Angus, editors, *Contemporary American Short Stories*, Fawcett, 1967.

Don Gold, editor, *The Human Commitment: An Anthology of Contemporary Short Fiction*, Chilton, 1967.

Marcus Klein and Robert Pack, editors, *Short Stories: Classic, Modern, Contemporary*, Little, Brown, 1967.

James A. Emanuel and Theodore L. Gross, editors, *Dark Symphony: Negro American Literature in America*, Free Press, 1968.

Arnold Adoff, editor, *Brothers and Sisters: Modern Stories by Black Americans*, Macmillan, 1970.

Theodore Solotaroff, editor, *American Review 16: The Magazine of New Writing*, Bantam, 1973.

James H. Pickering, editor, *Fiction 100: An Anthology of Short Stories*, Macmillan, 1974.

Michael Timko, *Twenty-nine Short Stories: An Introductory Anthology*, Knopf, 1975.

John L. Kimmey, editor, *Experience and Expression: Reading and Responding to Short Fiction*, Scott, Foresman, 1976.

Joseph Maiolo and Jill N. Brantley, editors, *From Three Sides: Reading for Writers*, Prentice-Hall, 1976.

David Thorburn, editor, *Initiation: Stories and Short Novels on Three Themes*, 2nd edition, Harcourt, 1976.

Max Apple, editor, *Southwest Fiction*, Bantam, 1980.

Nancy Sullivan, compiler, *The Treasury of American Short Stories*, Doubleday, 1981.

OTHER

"Ralph Ellison: An Interview with the Author of Invisible Man" (sound recording), Center for Cassette Studies, 1974.

(With William Styron and James Baldwin) "Is the Novel Dead?: Ellison, Styron and Baldwin on Contemporary Fiction" (sound recording), Center for Cassette Studies, 1974.

Contributor to *Proceedings, American Academy of Arts and Letters and the National Institute of Arts and Letters*, second series, 1965 and 1967. Also contributor of short fiction, critical essays, articles, and reviews to numerous journals and periodicals, including *American Scholar, Contemporary Literature, Iowa Review, New York Review of Books, New York Times Book Review, Noble Savage, Partisan Review, Quarterly Review of Literature, Reporter, Time*, and *Washington Post Book World*. Contributing editor, *Noble Savage*, 1960, and member of editorial board of *American Scholar*, 1966-69.

WORK IN PROGRESS: A second novel, as yet untitled, to be published by Random House, portions of which have been published under various titles, including "And Hickman Arrives" in *Noble Savage*, March, 1960, "The Roof, the Steeple, and the People" in *Quarterly Review of Literature*, Number 3, 1960, "It Always Breaks Out" in *Partisan Review*, spring, 1963, "Juneteenth" in *Quarterly Review of Literature*, Volume 13, numbers 3-4, 1969, "Song of Innocence" in *Iowa Review*, spring, 1970, and "Cadillac Flambe" in *American Review 16: The Magazine of New Writing*, edited by Theodore Solotaroff, Bantam, 1973.

SIDELIGHTS: Growing up in Oklahoma, a "frontier" state that "had no tradition of slavery" and where "relationships between the races were more fluid and thus more human than in the old slave states," Ralph Ellison became conscious of his obligation "to explore the full range of American Negro humanity and to affirm those qualities which are of value beyond any question of segregation, economics or previous condition of servitude." This sense of obligation, articulated in his 1964 collection of critical and biographical essays, *Shadow and Act*, led to his staunch refusal to limit his artistic vision to the "uneasy sanctuary of race" and committed him instead to a literature that explores and affirms the complex, often contradictory frontier of an identity at once black and American and universally human. For Ellison, whom John F. Callahan in a *Chant of Saints: A Gathering of Afro-American Literature, Art, and Scholarship* essay calls a "moral historian," the act of writing is fraught with both great possibility and grave responsibility; as Ellison asserts, writing "offers me the possibility of contributing not only to the growth of the literature but to the shaping of the culture as I should like it to be. The American novel is in this sense a conquest of the frontier; as it describes our experience, it creates it."

For Ellison, then, the task of the novelist is a moral and political one. In his preface to the thirtieth anniversary edition of *Invisible Man*, Ellison argues that the serious novel, like the best politics, "is a thrust toward a human ideal." Even when the ideal is not realized in the actual, he declares, "there is still available that fictional *vision* of an ideal democracy in which the actual combines with the ideal and gives us representations of a state of things in which the highly placed and the lowly, the black and the white, the Northerner and the Southerner, the native-born and the immigrant are combined to tell us of transcendent truths and possibilities such as those discovered when Mark Twain set Huck and Jim afloat on the raft." Ellison sees the novel as a "raft of hope" that may help readers stay above water as they try "to negotiate the snags and whirlpools that mark our nation's vacillating course toward and away from the democratic ideal."

This vision of pluralism and possibility as the basic definition of self and serious fiction has its roots in Ellison's personal history, a history marked by vacillations between the ideal and the real. He recalls in *Shadow and Act* that, as teenagers, he and his friends saw themselves as "Renaissance Men" unlimited by any sense of racial inferiority and determined to be recipients of the American Dream, to witness the ideal become the real. Ellison recounts two "accidents" that contributed to his sense of self as something beyond the external definition of race. The first occurred while he lived in a white, middle-class neighborhood where his mother worked as a building custodian. He became friends with a young white boy, a friendship based not on the "race question as such" but rather on their mutual loneliness and interest in radios. The other contact with "that world beyond the Negro community" came as his mother brought home discarded copies of magazines such as *Vanity Fair* and *Literary Digest* and old recordings of operas. Ellison remembers that these books and music "spoke to me of a life which was broader" and which "I could some day make my own."

This sense of a world beyond his but to which he would ultimately belong translated itself into his sense of the world that *was* his and to which he *did* belong. He was profoundly aware of the richness, vitality, and variety in his black community; he was aware, also, that the affirmative reality of black life was something he never found in the books he read, was never taught in the schools he attended. Ellison had experienced the nonverbal articulation of these qualities in the jazz and blues that were so much a part of his upbringing. In particular he recalls, in *Shadow and Act,* Jimmy Rushing, the blues singer who "represented, gave voice to, something which was very affirming of Negro life, feelings which you couldn't really put into words." But recording and preserving the value of black life only in this medium did not satisfy Ellison; he was haunted, he admits, by a need "for other forms of transcendence and identification which I could only associate with classical music." As he explains, "I was taken very early with a passion to link together all I loved within the Negro community and all those things I felt in the world which lay beyond." This passion to join separate worlds and disparate selves into a unity of being infuses the content and style of *Invisible Man* and lies at the heart of Ellison's theory of fiction.

Early in his career, however, Ellison conceived of his vocation as a musician, as a composer of symphonies. When he entered Alabama's Tuskegee Institute in 1933 he enrolled as a music major; he wonders in *Shadow and Act* if he did so because, given his background, it was the only art "that seemed to offer some possibility for self-definition." The act of writing soon presented itself as an art through which he could link the disparate worlds he cherished, could verbally record and create the "affirmation of Negro life" he knew was so intrinsic a part of the universally human. To move beyond the old definitions that separated jazz from classical music, vernacular from literary language, the folk from the mythic, he would have to discover a prose style that could equal the integrative imagination of the "Renaissance Man."

Shadow and Act records that during 1935, his second year at Tuskegee, Ellison began his "conscious education in literature." Reading Emily Bronte's *Wuthering Heights* and Thomas Hardy's *Jude the Obscure* produced in him "an agony of unexpressible emotion," but T. S. Eliot's *The Waste Land* absolutely seized his imagination. He admits: "I was intrigued by its power to move me while eluding my understanding. Somehow its rhythms were often closer to those of jazz than were those of the Negro poets, and even though I could not understand then, its range of allusion was as mixed and varied as that of Louis Armstrong." Determined to understand the "hidden system of organization" that eluded him, Ellison began to explore the sources that Eliot had identified in the footnotes to the poem. This reading in ancient mythology, history, literature, and folklore led, in turn, to his reading of such twentieth-century writers as Ezra Pound, Ernest Hemingway, and Gertrude Stein, who led him back to the nineteenth-century authors Herman Melville and Mark Twain. The more Ellison read in literature and the sources of literature, the more he found that the details of his own history were "transformed." Local customs took on a "more universal meaning"; he became aware of the universal in the specific. His experience with *The Waste Land,* which forced him to wonder why he "had never read anything of equal intensity and sensibility by an American Negro writer," was his introduction to the universal power of the folk tradition as the foundation of literature.

During this same year, Ellison took a sociology course, an experience he describes in *Shadow and Act* as "humiliating." Presenting a reductive, unrealistic portrait of the American black as the "lady of the races," this sociological view denied the complex richness of black life that Ellison had so often experienced. In *The Craft of Ralph Ellison* Robert G. O'Meally argues that this encounter with a limited and limiting definition of blacks created in Ellison "an accelerated sense of urgency" to learn more about black culture and to find an artistic form to capture the vital reality of the black community that he had heard in the blues sessions, in the barbershops, and in the stories and jokes he had heard from some classmates as they returned from seasonal work in the cotton fields. Ironically, an accident intervened that propelled him on this course. Because of a mix-up about his scholarship, Ellison found himself without the money to return to Tuskegee. He went instead to New York, enacting the prototypical journey North, confident that he would return to Tuskegee after he had earned enough money.

Because Ellison did not get a job that paid him enough to save money for tuition, he stayed in New York, working and studying composition until his mother died in Dayton, Ohio. After his return to Dayton, he and his brother supported themselves by hunting. Though Ellison had hunted for years, he did not know how to wing-shoot; it was from Hemingway's fiction that he learned this process. Ellison studied Hemingway to learn writing techniques; from the older writer he also learned a lesson in descriptive accuracy and power, in the close relationship between fiction and reality. Like his narrator in *Invisible Man,* Ellison did not return to college; instead he began his long apprenticeship as a writer, his long and often difficult journey toward self-definition.

Ellison's early days in New York, before his return to Dayton, provided him with experiences that would later translate themselves into his theory of fiction. Two days after his arrival in "deceptively 'free' Harlem," he met black poet Langston Hughes who introduced him to the works of Andre Malraux, a French writer defined as Marxist. Though attracted to Marxism, Ellison sensed in Malraux something beyond a simplistic political sense of the human condition. Says Ellison: Malraux "was the artist-revolutionary rather than a politician when he wrote *Man's Fate,* and the book lives not because of a political position embraced at the time, but because of its larger concern with the tragic struggle of humanity." Ellison began to form his definition of the artist as a revolutionary concerned less with local injustice than with the timelessly tragic.

Ellison's view of art was furthered after he met black novelist Richard Wright. Wright urged him to read Joseph Conrad, Henry James, James Joyce, and Feodor Dostoevsky and invited Ellison to contribute a review essay and then a short story to the magazine he was editing. Wright was then in the process of writing *Native Son,* much of which Ellison read, he declares in *Shadow and Act,* "as it came out of the typewriter." Though awed by the process of writing and aware of the achievement of the novel, Ellison, who had just read Malraux, began to form his objections to the "sociological," deterministic ideology which informed the portrait of the work's protagonist, Bigger Thomas. In *Shadow and Act,* which Arthur P. Davis in *From the Dark Tower: Afro-American Writers, 1900 to 1960* accurately describes as partly an *apologia pro vita sua* (a defense of his life), Ellison articulates the basis of his objection: "I, for instance, found it disturbing that Bigger Thomas had none of the finer qualities of Richard Wright, none of the imagination, none of the sense of poetry, none of the gaiety." Ellison thus refutes the depiction of the black individual as an inarticulate victim whose life is one only of despair, anger, and pain. He insists that art must capture instead the complex reality, the pain and the pleasure of black existence, thereby challenging the definition of the black person as something less than fully human. Such a vision of art, which is at the heart of *Invisible Man,* became the focal point of an extended debate between Ellison and Irving Howe, who in a 1963 *Dissent* article accused Ellison of disloyalty to Wright in particular and to "protest fiction" in general.

From 1938 to 1944, Ellison published a number of short stories and contributed essays to journals such as *New Masses.* As with most of Ellison's work, these stories have provoked disparate readings. In an essay in *Black World,* Ernest Kaiser calls the earliest stories and the essays in *New Masses* "the healthiest" of Ellison's career. The critic praises the economic theories that inform the early fiction, and he finds Ellison's language pure, emotional, and effective. Lamenting a change he attributes to Ellison's concern with literary technique, Kaiser charges the later stories, essays, and novel with being no longer concerned with people's problems and with being "unemotional."

Other critics, like Marcus Klein in *After Alienation: American Novels in Mid-Century,* see the early work as a progressive preparation for Ellison's mature fiction and theory. In the earliest of these stories, "Slick Gonna Learn," Ellison draws a character shaped largely by an ideological, naturalistic conception of existence, the very type of character he later repudiated. From this imitation of proletarian fiction, Ellison's work moves towards psychological and finally metaphysical explorations of the human condition. His characters thus are freed from restrictive definitions as Ellison develops a voice that is his own, Klein maintains.

In the two latest stories of the 1938-1944 period, "Flying Home" and "King of the Bingo Game," Ellison creates characters congruent with his sense of pluralism and possibility and does so in a narrative style that begins to approach the complexity of *Invisible Man.* As Arthur P. Davis notes, in "Flying Home" Ellison combines realism, folk story, symbolism, and a touch of surrealism to present his protagonist, Todd. In a fictional world composed of myriad levels of the mythic and the folk, the classical and the modern, Todd fights to free himself of imposed definitions. However, it is in "King of the Bingo Game," published just before he began *Invisible Man,* that Ellison's growth is most evident.

As in "Flying Home," the writer experiments in "King of the Bingo Game" with integrating sources and techniques. As in all of Ellison's early stories, the protagonist is a young black man fighting for his freedom against forces and people that attempt to deny it. In "King of the Bingo Game," O'Meally argues, "the struggle is seen in its most abstracted form." This abstraction results from the "dreamlike shifts of time and levels of consciousness" that dominate the surrealistic story and also from the fact that "the King is Ellison's first character to sense the frightening absurdity of everyday American life." In an epiphany which frees him from illusion and which places him, even if for only a moment, in control, the King realizes "that his battle for freedom and identity must be waged not against individuals or even groups, but against no less than history and fate," O'Meally declares. The parameters of the fight for freedom and identity have been broadened. Ellison sees his black hero as one who wages the oldest and most universal battle in human history: the fight for freedom to be timelessly human, to engage in the "tragic struggle of humanity," as the writer asserts in *Shadow and Act.* The King achieves awareness for a moment; the Invisible Man not only becomes aware but is able to articulate fully the struggle. As Ellison notes in his preface to the anniversary edition of the novel, too often characters have been "figures caught up in the most intense forms of social struggle, subject to the most extreme forms of the human predicament but yet seldom able to articulate the issues which tortured them." The Invisible Man is endowed with eloquence; he is Ellison's radical experiment with a fiction that insists upon the full range and humanity of the black character.

Ellison began *Invisible Man* in 1945. Although he was at work on a never-completed war novel at the time, Ellison recalls in his 1982 preface that he could not ignore the "taunting, disembodied voice" he heard beckoning him to write *Invisible Man.* Published in 1952 after a seven-year creative struggle, and awarded the National Book Award in 1953, *Invisible Man* received critical acclaim. Although some early reviewers were puzzled or disappointed by the experimental narrative techniques, most now agree that these techniques give the work its lasting force and account for Ellison's influence on later fiction. The novel is a veritable fugue of cultural fragments, blended and counterpointed in a uniquely Ellisonian composition. Echoes of Homer, Joyce, Eliot, and Hemingway join forces with the sounds of spirituals, blues, jazz, and nursery rhymes. The Invisible Man is as haunted by Louis Armstrong's "What did I do / To be so black / And blue?" as he is by Hemingway's bullfight scenes and his matadors' grace under pressure. The linking together of these disparate cultural elements is what allows the Invisible Man to draw the portrait of his inner face that is the way out of his wasteland.

In the work, Ellison clearly employs the traditional motif of the *Bildungsroman,* or novel of education: the Invisible Man moves from innocence to experience, from darkness to light, from blindness to sight. Complicating this linear journey, however, is the narrative frame provided by the Prologue and Epilogue which the narrator composes after the completion of his above-ground educational journey. Yet readers begin with the Prologue, written in his underground chamber on the "border area" of Harlem where he is waging a guerrilla war against the Monopolated Light & Power Company by invisibly draining their power. At first denied the story of his discovery, readers must be initiated through the act of re-experiencing the events that led them and the narrator to this hole. Armed with some suggestive hints and symbols, readers then start the journey toward a revisioning of the Invisible Man, America, and themselves.

The journey is a deliberate baptism by fire. From the Battle Royal where the Invisible Man swallows his own blood in the name of opportunity; to the madness of The Golden Day; to the protagonist's anguished expulsion from the College; to the horror of his lobotomy; to his dehumanization by the Brotherhood; to his jubilant discovery of the unseen people of Harlem; to the nightmare that is Ras and the riots; and finally to the descent underground and the ritualistic burning of the contents of his briefcase, readers are made to participate in the plot because they, finally, are a part of it. The novel is about plots: the plots against the Invisible Man by Bledsoe and the Brotherhood; the conspiracy against himself that is the inevitable result of his illusions; the plot of the American ideal that keeps him dodging the forces of the actual; the plot of the reader against the writer; and the plot, ultimately, against every human being by life itself. The multiplicity of plot is part of the brilliance of the novel. Like the Invisible Man, readers are duped, time and time again, resisting the reality before them. And like him, they undergo a series of deaths and rebirths in their narrative journey. They are cast out of the realism of the college scenes into the surrealistic void of the riots, wondering what they did to be, if not always black, at least so blue. They are made to feel, in the words of the novel, every "itch, taunt, laugh, cry, scar, ache, rage or pain of it." And readers come to know that they—and the Invisible Man—share the responsibility for all of it.

In the Prologue and Epilogue the Invisible Man is the conscious, reflexive artist, recording his perceptions of self and other as he articulates the meaning of the journey and the descent. In the Epilogue he lets readers understand more clearly the preparatory hints and symbols he offered in the Prologue. He articulates his understanding of the old woman's words when she told him that freedom lay not in hating but in loving and in "knowing how to say" what is in one's head. Here too he unveils his insight into his grandfather, an ex-slave who "never had any doubts about his humanity" and who accepted the principle of America "in all its human and absurd diversity." As the Invisible Man records his journey through the underground America, he asserts a vision of America as it should be. He becomes the nation's moral conscience, embodying its greatest failure and its highest possibility. He reclaims his full humanity and freedom by accepting the world as a "concrete, ornery, vile and sublimely wonderful" reflection of the perceptive self.

The act of writing, of ordering and defining the self, is what gives the Invisible Man freedom and what allows him to manage the absurdity and chaos of everyday life. Writing frees the self from imposed definitions, from the straitjacket of all that would limit the productive possibilities of the self. Echoing the pluralism of the novel's form, the Invisible Man insists on the freedom to be ambivalent, to love and to hate, to denounce and to defend the America he inherits. Ellison himself is well-acquainted with the ambivalence of his American heritage; nowhere is it more evident than in his name. Named after the nineteenth-century essayist and poet Ralph Waldo Emerson, whom Ellison's father admired, the name has created for Ellison embarrassment, confusion, and a desire to be the American writer his namesake called for. And Ellison places such emphasis on his unnamed yet self-named narrator's breaking the shackles of restrictive definitions, of what others call reality or right, he also frees himself, as Robert B. Stepto in *From Behind the Veil: A Study of Afro-American Narrative* argues,

from the strictures of the traditional slave narratives of Frederick Douglas and W. E. B. DuBois. By consciously invoking this form but then not bringing the motif of "ascent and immersion" to its traditional completion, Ellison revoices the form, makes it his own, and steps outside it.

This stepping outside of traditional form, however, can be a dangerous act. In *Invisible Man,* Tod Clifton steps outside the historically powerful Brotherhood and is shot for "resisting reality." At the other extreme, Rinehart steps outside all definitions and becomes the embodiment of chaos. In *City of Words: American Fiction, 1950-1970* Tony Tanner notes that Ellison presents an overriding preoccupation of postmodern fiction: the fear of a rigid pattern that would limit all freedom of self, coupled with the fear of no pattern, of a chaotic void that would render illusory all sense of self. The Invisible Man is well aware of form and formlessness. As he says, "Without light I am not only invisible but formless as well; and to be unaware of one's form is to live a death." But step outside, or underneath, the Invisible Man does, although he would be the first to admit that he has had to be hit over the head to do it. Ellison, too, steps outside in his creation of the form of *Invisible Man;* he also steps inside the history of great literature that refuses to diminish the complexity of human identity and the search for the self.

The search for identity, which Ellison says in *Shadow and Act* is "*the* American theme," is the heart of the novel and the center of many critical debates over it. At novel's end, the journey is not complete; the Invisible Man must emerge from his hole and test the sense of self formed in hibernation. As he journeys toward this goal, toward the emergence of a sense of self that is at once black and American and universally human, questions recur: In his quest for pluralism, does he sacrifice his blackness? In his devotion to an imaginative rendering of self, does he lose his socially active self?

In her 1979 *PMLA* essay, Susan Blake argues that Ellison's insistence that black experience be ritualized as part of the larger human experience results in a denial of the unique social reality of black life. Because Ellison so thoroughly adapts black folklore into the Western tradition, Blake finds that the definition of black life becomes "not black but white"; it "exchanges the self-definition of the folk for the definition of the masters." Thorpe Butler, in a 1984 *College Language Association Journal* essay, defends Ellison against Blake's criticism. He declares that Ellison's depiction of specific black experience as part of the universal does not "diminish the unique richness and anguish" of that experience and does not "diminish the force of Ellison's protest against the blind, cruel dehumanization of black Americans by white society." This debate extends arguments that have appeared since the publication of the novel. Underlying these controversies is the old, uneasy argument about the relationship of art and politics, of literary practice and social commitment.

Ellison's sensitivity to this issue is painfully clear. He repeatedly defends his view, here voiced in *Shadow and Act,* that "protest is an element of all art, though it does not necessarily take the form of speaking for a political or social program." In a 1970 *Time* essay, Ellison defines further his particular definition of protest, of the "soul" of his art and his people: "An expression of American diversity within unity, of blackness with whiteness, soul announces the presence of a creative struggle against the realities of existence." Insisting in *Shadow and Act* that the novelist is a "manipulator and depictor of moral problems," Ellison claims that as novelist he does not try to escape the reality of black pain. He frequently reminds readers that he knows well the pain and anger that come with being black; his mother was arrested for violating Jim Crow housing laws, and in Alabama he was subjected daily to the outrageous policies of segregation. But for Ellison there needs to be more than even an eloquent depiction of this part of reality; he needs, as he says in *Shadow and Act,* "to transform these elements into art . . . to transcend, as the blues transcend the painful conditions with which they deal." In *Invisible Man* he declares that Louis Armstrong "made poetry out of being invisible." Social reality may place the creator in the underground, render him invisible, but his art leads him out of the hole, eloquent, visible, and empowered by the very people who put him there.

Although the search for identity is the major theme of *Invisible Man,* other aspects of the novel receive a great deal of critical attention. Among them, as Joanne Giza notes in her essay in *Black American Writers: Bibliographical Essays,* are literary debts and analogies; comic elements; the metaphor of vision; use of the blues; and folkloric elements. Although all of these concerns are part of the larger issue of identity, Ellison's use of blues and folklore has been singled out as a major contribution to contemporary literature and culture. Since the publication of *Invisible Man,* scores of articles have appeared on these two topics, a fact which in turn has led to a rediscovery, a revisioning of the importance of blues and folklore to American literature and culture in general.

Much of Ellison's groundbreaking work is presented in *Shadow and Act.* Published in 1964, this collection of essays, says Ellison, is "concerned with three general themes: with literature and folklore, with Negro musical expression—especially jazz and the blues—and with the complex relationship between the Negro American subculture and North American culture as a whole." This volume has been hailed as one of the most profound pieces of cultural criticism of the century. Writing in *Commentary,* Robert Penn Warren praises the astuteness of Ellison's perceptions; in *New Leader,* Stanley Edgar Hyman proclaims Ellison "the profoundest cultural critic we have." In the *New York Review of Books,* R. W. B. Lewis explores Ellison's study of black music as a form of power and finds that "Ellison is not only a self-identifier but the source of self-definition in others."

Published in 1986, *Going to the Territory* is a second collection of essays reprising many of the subjects and concerns treated in *Shadow and Act*—literature, art, music, the relationships of black and white cultures, fragments of autobiography, tributes to such noted black Americans as Richard Wright, Duke Ellington, and painter Romare Beardon. With the exception of "An Extravagance of Laughter," a lengthy examination of Ellison's response to Jack Kirkland's dramatization of Erskine Caldwell's novel *Tobacco Road,* the essays in *Going to the Territory* are reprints of previously published articles or speeches, most of them dating from the 1960s. While it conveniently gathers this material, the volume provides few new insights into the direction Ellison's work may take.

Ellison's influence as both novelist and critic, as artist and cultural historian, is enormous. Whether in agreement with or reaction against, writers respond passionately to his work. In special issues of *Black World* and *College Language Association Journal* devoted to Ellison, strident attacks appear alongside equally spirited accolades. Perhaps another measure of Ellison's stature and achievement is his readers' vigil for his long-awaited second novel. Although Ellison often refuses to answer questions about the work-in-progress, there is enough evidence to suggest that the manuscript is very large, that all or part of it was destroyed in a fire and is being rewritten, and that its creation has been a long and painful task. Most readers wait expectantly, believing that Ellison, who has said in *Shadow and Act* that he "failed of eloquence" in *Invisible Man,* is waiting until his second novel equals his imaginative vision of the American novel as conquerer of the frontier, equals the Emersonian call for a literature to release all people from the bonds of oppression.

Eight excerpts from this novel-in-progress have been published in journals such as *Quarterly Review of Literature, Massachusetts Review,* and *Noble Savage.* Set in the South in the years spanning the Jazz Age to the Civil Rights movement, these fragments seem an attempt to recreate modern American history and identity. The major characters are the Reverend Hickman, a one-time jazz musician, and Bliss, the light-skinned boy whom he adopts and who later passes into white society and becomes Senator Sunraider, an advocate of white supremacy. As O'Meally notes in *The Craft of Ralph Ellison,* the major difference between Bliss and Ellison's earlier young protagonists is that despite some harsh collisions with reality, Bliss refuses to divest himself of his illusions and accept his personal history. Says O'Meally: "Moreover, it is a renunciation of the blackness of American experience and culture, a refusal to accept the American past in all its complexity."

Like *Invisible Man,* this novel promises to be a broad and searching inquiry into identity, ideologies, culture, and history. The narrative form is similar as well; here, too, is the blending of popular and classical myth, of contradictory cultural memories, of an intricate pattern of images of birth, death, and rebirth. In *Shadow and Act* Ellison describes the novel's form as "a realism extended beyond realism" in which he explores again the multifaceted meanings of the folk as the basis of all literature and culture. What the ultimate form of the novel will be—if, indeed, these excerpts are to be part of one novel—remains hidden. But the pieces seize the reader's imagination even if they deny systematic analysis.

One thing does seem certain about these stories. In them Bliss becomes a traitor to his own race, loses his hold on those things of transforming, affirmative value. Hickman, on the other hand, accepts and celebrates his heritage, his belief in the timeless value of his history. As O'Meally writes in his book-length study of Ellison, Hickman "holds fast to personal and political goals and values." Ellison, too, holds fast to his values in the often chaotic and chameleon world of art and politics. The tone of these excerpts is primarily tragicomic, a mode well-suited to Ellison's definition of life. As he says in *Shadow and Act,* "I think that the mixture of the marvelous and the terrible is a basic condition of human life and that the persistence of human ideals represents the marvelous pulling itself up out of the chaos of the universe." Elsewhere in the book, Ellison argues that "true novels, even when most pessimistic and bitter, arise out of an impulse to celebrate human life." As *Invisible Man* before and the Hickman novel yet to come, they celebrate the "human and absurd" commixture of American life.

AVOCATIONAL INTERESTS: Jazz and classical music, photography, electronics, furniture-making, bird-watching, gardening.

BIOGRAPHICAL/CRITICAL SOURCES:

BOOKS

Allen, Walter Ernest, *The Modern Novel in Britain and the United States,* Dutton, 1964.

Alvarez, A., editor, *Under Pressure: The Writer in Society; Eastern Europe and the U.S.A.*, Penguin, 1965.

Baker, Houston, A., Jr., *Long Black Song: Essays in Black American Literature and Culture*, University Press of Virginia, 1972.

Baumbach, Jonathan, *The Landscape of Nightmare: Studies in the Contemporary American Novel*, New York University Press, 1965.

Benston, Kimberly W., editor, *Speaking for You: The Vision of Ralph Ellison*, Howard University Press, 1987.

Bigsby, C. W. E., editor, *The Black American Writer*, Volume I, Everett Edwards, 1969.

Bloom, Harold, editor, *Ralph Ellison: Modern Critical Views*, Chelsea Publishing, 1986.

Bone, Robert, *The Negro Novel in America*, Yale University Press, revised edition, 1965.

Breit, Harvey, *The Writer Observed*, World Publishing, 1956.

Callahan, John F., *In the African-American Grain: The Pursuit of Voice in Twentieth-Century Black Fiction*, University of Illinois Press, 1988.

Concise Dictionary of American Literary Biography: The New Consciousness, 1941-1948, Gale, 1987.

Contemporary Fiction in America and England, 1950-1970, Gale, 1976.

Contemporary Literary Criticism, Gale, Volume 1, 1973, Volume 3, 1975, Volume 11, 1979.

Cooke, Michael, *Afro-American Literature in the Twentieth Century: The Achievement of Intimacy*, Yale University Press, 1984.

Covo, Jacqueline, *The Blinking Eye: Ralph Waldo Ellison and His American, French, German, and Italian Critics, 1952-1971: Bibliographic Essays and a Checklist*, Scarecrow, 1974.

Davis, Arthur P., *From the Dark Tower: Afro-American Writers (1900 to 1960)*, Howard University Press, 1974.

Davis, Charles T., *Black Is the Color of the Cosmos: Essays on Afro-American Literature and Culture, 1942-1981*, edited by Henry Louis Gates, Jr., Garland, 1982.

Dictionary of Literary Biography, Volume 2: *American Novelists since World War II*, Gale, 1978.

Dietze, Rudolf F., *Ralph Ellison: The Genius of an Artist*, Carl (Nuremburg), 1982.

Ellison, Ralph, *Shadow and Act*, Random House, 1964.

Fabre, Michael, editor, *Delta Number 18: Ralph Ellison*, University Paul Valery (Paris), 1984.

Fischer-Hornung, Dorothea, *Folklore and Myth in Ralph Ellison's Early Works*, Hochschul (Stuttgart), 1979.

Fisher, Dexter, and Robert B. Stepto, editors, *Afro-American Literature: The Reconstruction of Instruction*, Modern Language Association of America, 1979.

Gayle, Addison, Jr., editor, *Black Expression: Essays by and about Americans in the Creative Arts*, Weybright & Talley, 1969.

Gayle, Addison, Jr., compiler, *The Black Aesthetic*, Doubleday, 1971.

Gayle, Addison, Jr., *The Way of the New World: The Black Novel in America*, Anchor Press, 1975.

Gibson, Donald B., compiler, *Five Black Writers: Essays on Wright, Ellison, Baldwin, Hughes, and Le Roi Jones*, New York University Press, 1970.

Gottesman, Ronald, editor, *Studies in Invisible Man*, Merrill, 1971.

Graham, John, *The Writer's Voice: Conversations with Contemporary Writers*, edited by George Garrett, Morrow, 1973.

Gross, Seymour L., and John Edward Hardy, editors, *Images of the Negro in American Literature*, University of Chicago Press, 1966.

Harper, Michael S., and R. B. Stepto, editors, *Chant of Saints: A Gathering of Afro-American Literature, Art, and Scholarship*, University of Illinois Press, 1979.

Henderson, Bill, editor, *The Pushcart Prize, III: Best of the Small Presses*, Avon, 1979.

Hersey, John, editor, *Ralph Ellison: A Collection of Critical Essays*, Prentice-Hall, 1974.

Hill, Herbert, editor, *Anger and Beyond: The Negro Writer in the United States*, Harper, 1966.

Inge, M. Thomas, and others, editors, *Black American Writers: Bibliographical Essays*, Volume II: *Richard Wright, Ralph Ellison, James Baldwin, and Amiri Baraka*, St. Martin's, 1978.

Kazin, Alfred, *Bright Book of Life: American Novelists and Storytellers from Hemingway to Mailer*, Atlantic-Little, Brown, 1973.

Klein, Marcus, *After Alienation: American Novels in Mid-Century*, World Publishing, 1964.

Kostelanetz, R., *On Contemporary Literature: An Anthology of Critical Essays on the Major Movements and Writers of Contemporary Literature*, Avon, 1964.

Margolies, Edward, *Native Sons: A Critical Study of Twentieth-Century Negro American Authors*, Lippincott, 1968.

O'Brien, John, *Interviews with Black Writers*, Liveright, 1973.

O'Meally, Robert G., *The Craft of Ralph Ellison*, Harvard University Press, 1980.

Ottley, Roi, William J. Weatherby, and others, editors, *The Negro in New York: An Informal Social History*, New York Public Library, 1967.

Plimpton, George, editor, *Writers at Work: The Paris Review Interviews*, second series, Viking, 1963.

Reilly, John M., editor, *Twentieth-Century Interpretations of Invisible Man: A Collection of Critical Essays*, Prentice-Hall, 1970.

Stepto, R. B., *From Behind the Veil: A Study of Afro-American Narrative*, University of Illinois Press, 1979.

Tanner, Tony, *City of Words: American Fiction, 1950-1970*, Harper, 1971.

Trimmer, Joseph F., editor, *A Casebook on Ralph Ellison's Invisible Man*, Crowell, 1972.

Waldmeir, Joseph J., editor, *Recent American Fiction: Some Critical Views*, Houghton, 1963.

Warren, Robert Penn, *Who Speaks for the Negro?*, Random House, 1965.

The Writer as Independent Spirit, [New York], 1968.

PERIODICALS

American Quarterly, March, 1972.

American Scholar, autumn, 1955.

Atlantic, July, 1952, December, 1970, August, 1986.

Barat Review, January, 1968.

Black Academy Review, winter, 1970.

Black American Literature Forum, summer, 1978.

Black Books Bulletin, winter, 1972.

Black Creation, summer, 1970.

Black World, December, 1970 (special Ellison issue).

Book Week, October 25, 1964.

Boundary 2, winter, 1978.

Brown Alumni Monthly, November, 1979.

Carleton Miscellany, winter, 1980 (special Ellison issue).

Chicago Review, Volume 19, number 2, 1967.

Chicago Tribune Book World, August 10, 1986.

College Language Association Journal, December, 1963, June, 1967, March, 1970 (special Ellison issue), September, 1971, December, 1971, December, 1972, June, 1973, March, 1974, September, 1976, September, 1977, Number 25, 1982, Number 27, 1984.

Commentary, November, 1953, Number 39, 1965.

Commonweal, May 2, 1952.

Crisis, March, 1953, March, 1970.

Critique, Number 2, 1968.

Daedalus, winter, 1968.

Daily Oklahoman, August 23, 1953.

December, winter, 1961.

English Journal, September, 1969, May, 1973, November, 1984.

'48 Magazine of the Year, May, 1948.

Grackle, Volume 4, 1977-78.

Harper's, October, 1959, March, 1967, July, 1967.

Journal of Black Studies, Number 7, 1976.

Los Angeles Times, August 8, 1986.

Massachusetts Review, autumn, 1967, autumn, 1977.

Modern Fiction Studies, winter, 1969-70.

Motive, April, 1966.

Muhammad Speaks, September, 1972, December, 1972.

Nation, May 10, 1952, September 9, 1964, November 9, 1964, September 20, 1965.

Negro American Literature Forum, July, 1970, summer, 1973, Number 9, 1975, spring, 1977.

Negro Digest, May, 1964, August, 1967.

Negro History Bulletin, May, 1953, October, 1953.

New Criterion, September, 1983.

New Leader, October 26, 1964.

New Republic, November 14, 1964, August 4, 1986.

Newsday, October, 1967.

Newsweek, August 12, 1963, October 26, 1964.

New Yorker, May 31, 1952, November 22, 1976.

New York Herald Tribune Book Review, April 13, 1952.

New York Review of Books, January 28, 1964, January 28, 1965.

New York Times, April 13, 1952, April 24, 1985.

New York Times Book Review, April 13, 1952, May 4, 1952, October 25, 1964, January 24, 1982, August 3, 1986.

New York Times Magazine, November 20, 1966.

Paris Review, spring, 1955, spring/summer, 1957.

Partisan Review, Number 25, 1958.

Phoenix, fall, 1961.

Phylon, winter, 1960, spring, 1970, spring, 1973, summer, 1973, summer, 1977.

PMLA, January, 1979.

Renascence, spring, 1974, winter, 1978.

Saturday Review, April 12, 1952, March 14, 1953, December 11, 1954, January 1, 1955, April 26, 1958, May 17, 1958, July 12, 1958, September 27, 1958, July 28, 1962, October 24, 1964.

Shenandoah, summer, 1969.

Smith Alumni Quarterly, July, 1964.

Southern Humanities Review, winter, 1970.

Southern Literary Journal, spring, 1969.

Southern Review, fall, 1974, summer, 1985.

Studies in American Fiction, spring, 1973.

Studies in Black Literature, autumn, 1971, autumn, 1972, spring, 1973, spring, 1975, spring, 1976, winter, 1976.

Tamarack Review, October, 1963, summer, 1964.

Time, April 14, 1952, February 9, 1959, February 1, 1963, April 6, 1970.

Times Literary Supplement, January 18, 1968.

Village Voice, November 19, 1964.

Washington Post, August 19-21, 1973, April 21, 1982, February 9, 1983, March 30, 1983, July 23, 1986.

Washington Post Book World, May 17, 1987.

Wisconsin Studies in Literature, winter, 1960, summer, 1966.

Y-Bird Reader, autumn, 1977.

—Sidelights by Judy R. Smith

* * *

El MUHAJIR 1944-
(Marvin X, Nazzam Al Fitnah Muhajir)

PERSONAL: Original name, Marvin Ellis Jackmon; born May 29, 1944, in Fowler, Calif.; son of Owendell and Marian Jackmon; married; five children. *Education:* Oakland City College (now Merritt College), A.A., 1964; additional study at San Francisco State College (now University), 1964-66, 1974.

CAREER: Poet, playwright, editor, and lecturer. Founder with Ed Bullins of Black Arts/West Theatre, San Francisco, Calif., 1966, and with Bullins and Eldridge Cleaver of Black House (political-cultural center), San Francisco, 1967; founder of Al Kitab Sudan Publishing Co., San Francisco, 1967; founder and director of Your Black Educational Theatre, Inc., San Francisco, beginning 1971. Teacher of black studies courses at California State University at Fresno, 1969, University of California, Berkeley, 1972, and Mills College, 1973; has given lectures or poetry readings at numerous universities and colleges, including Stanford University, Cornell University, Loyola University of Chicago, University of Toronto, University of California, Davis, University of California, Los Angeles, and University of Oklahoma.

AWARDS, HONORS: Writing grants totaling $8,000 from Columbia University, 1969, and National Endowment for the Arts, 1972; on-the-job training grant of $36,000 for Your Black Educational Theatre, 1971-72.

WRITINGS:

Sudan Rajuli Samia (poems), Al Kitab Sudan Publishing, 1967.

Black Dialectic (proverbs), Al Kitab Sudan Publishing, 1967.

(Under name Marvin X) *Fly to Allah: Poems,* Al Kitab Sudan Publishing, 1969.

(Under name Marvin X) *The Son of Man,* Al Kitab Sudan Publishing, 1969.

(Under name Marvin X) *Black Man Listen: Poems and Proverbs,* Broadside Press, 1969.

Black Bird (parable), Al Kitab Sudan Publishing, 1972.

Woman—Man's Best Friend (also see below), Al Kitab Sudan Publishing, 1973.

Selected Poems, Al Kitab Sudan Publishing, 1979.

(Under name Marvin X) *Confession of a Wife Beater and Other Poems,* Al Kitab Sudan Publishing, 1981.

Liberation Poems for North American Africans, Al Kitab Sudan Publishing, 1982.

PLAYS

"Flowers for the Trashman" (one-act), first produced in San Francisco at San Francisco State College, 1965, musical version produced as "Take Care of Business," in Fresno, Calif. at Your Black Educational Theatre, 1971.

"Come Next Summer," first produced in San Francisco at Black Arts/West Theatre, 1966.

"The Trial," first produced in New York City at Afro-American Studio for Acting and Speech, 1970.

"Resurrection of the Dead" (ritual dance drama), first produced in San Francisco at Your Black Educational Theatre, 1972.

"Woman—Man's Best Friend" (musical dance drama; based on author's book of same title), first produced in Oakland, Calif. at Mills College, 1973.

"In the Name of Love," first produced in Oakland at Laney College Theatre, 1981.

CONTRIBUTOR TO ANTHOLOGIES

Black Fire: An Anthology of Afro-American Writing, edited by Amiri Baraka and Larry Neal, Morrow, 1968.

New Plays from the Black Theatre, edited by Ed Bullins, Bantam, 1969.

Black Arts: An Anthology of Black Creations, edited by Ahmed Alhamisi and Haroun Kofi Wangara, Black Arts Publications, 1969.

Vietnam and Black America, edited by Clyde Taylor, Doubleday, 1973.

You Better Believe It, edited by Paul Breman, Penguin, 1973.

OTHER

Contributor to *Soul Book, Encore, Black World, Black Scholar,* and other magazines and newspapers. Fiction editor, *Black Dialogue,* 1965—; contributing editor, *Journal of Black Poetry,* 1965—; associate editor, *Black Theatre,* 1968; foreign editor, *Muhammad Speaks,* 1970.

WORK IN PROGRESS: An elementary Arabic textbook; *Black Man in the Americas,* a series of conversations with black writers, artists, historians, musicians, and politicians; *Handbook of Black Theatre,* a world guide; *Bibliography for the Proper Understanding of Black People.*

BIOGRAPHICAL/CRITICAL SOURCES:

BOOKS

Dictionary of Literary Biography, Volume 38: *Afro-American Writers after 1955,* Gale, 1985.

*   *   *

El-SHABAZZ, El-Hajj Malik
    See LITTLE, Malcolm

*   *   *

el-TOURE, Askia Muhammad Abu Bakr
    See TOURE, Askia Muhammad Abu Bakr el

*   *   *

EMANUEL, James A(ndrew)   1921-

PERSONAL: Born June 15, 1921, in Alliance, Neb.; son of Alfred A. (a farmer and railroad worker) and Cora Ann (Mance) Emanuel; married Mattie Etha Johnson, 1950 (divorced, 1974); children: James A., Jr. (deceased). *Education:* Howard University, A.B. (summa cum laude), 1950; Northwestern University, M.A., 1953; Columbia University, Ph.D., 1962. *Politics:* Democrat.

ADDRESSES: Home—340 East 90th St., 3B, New York, N.Y. 10028. *Office*—Department of English, City College of the City University of New York, Convent Ave. at 138th St., New York, N.Y. 10031.

CAREER: Canteen steward in Civilian Conservation Corps, Wellington, Kan., 1939-40; weighmaster with an iron company, Rock Island, Ill., 1941-42; U.S. War Department, Office of the Inspector General, Washington, D.C., confidential secretary to assistant inspector general of the Army, 1942-44; Army and Air Force Induction Station, Chicago, Ill., chief of pre-induction section (as civilian), 1950-53; YWCA Business and Secretarial School, New York City, teacher of English and commercial subjects, 1954-56; City College of the City University of New York, New York City, instructor, 1957-62, assistant professor, 1962-70, associate professor, 1970-73, professor of English, 1973—. Fulbright professor, University of Grenoble, France, 1968-69, and University of Warsaw, Poland, 1975-76. Visiting professor, University of Toulouse, France, 1971-73 and 1979-81. Sole U.S. representative at invitational Sarajevo "Days of Poetry" Festival, 1982. Has given readings of his poetry in universities, schools, and before civic groups in America and Europe. Consultant on Black literature with New York State Education Department and boards of education, 1970. *Military service:* U.S. Army, Infantry, 1944-46; served in Netherlands, East Indies, and the Philippines; became staff sergeant; received Army Commendation Ribbon.

MEMBER: Fulbright Alumni Association.

AWARDS, HONORS: John Hay Whitney Foundation Opportunity fellowship, 1952-54; Eugene F. Saxton Memorial Trust fellowship, 1964-65.

WRITINGS:

Langston Hughes (essays), Twayne, 1967.
The Treehouse and Other Poems, Broadside Press, 1968.
(Editor with Theodore Gross) *Dark Symphony: Negro Literature in America,* Free Press, 1968.
At Bay, Broadside Press, 1968.
Panther Man, Broadside Press, 1970.
(Contributor) Don L. Lee, general editor, *Dynamite Voices I: Black Poets of the 1960's,* Broadside Press, 1971.
(With McKinley Kantor and Lawrence Osgood) *How I Write/2,* Harcourt, 1972, new edition, 1975.
Black Man Abroad: The Toulouse Poems, Lotus Press, 1978.
A Chisel in the Dark: Poems, Selected and New, Lotus Press, 1980.
A Poet's Mind, Regents Publishing, 1983.
The Broken Bowl: New and Uncollected Poems, Lotus Press, 1983.

Also author of *Snowflakes and Steel: My Life as a Poet, 1971-80,* a manuscript autobiography written at the request of the Jay B. Hubbell Center for American Literary Historiography at Duke University and deposited there in 1981.

CONTRIBUTOR OF ESSAYS

Addison Gayle, editor, *Black Expression,* Weybright & Talley, 1969.
Richard Abcarian, editor, *Native Son: A Critical Handbook,* Wadsworth, 1970.
Gayle, editor, *The Black Aesthetic,* Doubleday, 1971.
Therman B. O'Daniel, editor, *Langston Hughes, Black Genius,* Morrow, 1971.
James Vinson, editor, *Contemporary Novelists,* St. James Press, 1972.
Lloyd W. Brown, editor, *The Black Writer in Africa and the Americas,* Hennessey & Ingalls, 1973.
Donald B. Gibson, editor, *Modern Black Poets,* Prentice-Hall, 1973.
Jay Martin, editor, *A Singer in the Dawn: Reinterpretations of Paul Laurence Dunbar,* Dodd, 1975.

Sy M. Kahn and Martha Raetz, editors, *Interculture: A Collection of Essays and Creative Writing . . .* , Wilhelm Braumueller, 1975.

Rayford Logan and Michael Winston, editors, *Dictionary of American Negro Biography,* Norton, 1982.

Poems anthologized in *Sixes and Sevens* (London), 1962, *American Negro Poetry,* 1963, *New Negro Poets: U.S.A.,* 1964, *Anthologie de la Poesie Negro-Americaine: 1770-1965* (Paris), and about one hundred other volumes. General editor, "Broadside Critics" series on Black poetry. About ninety poems have been published in periodicals, including *Phylon, Negro Digest, Renaissance,* and *Imprints Quarterly;* also contributor of book reviews to *Books Abroad* and *New York Times Book Review,* and of articles to scholarly journals.

WORK IN PROGRESS: A seventh volume of poems, tentatively entitled *Black Tender.*

SIDELIGHTS: James A. Emanuel remarks: "I compose poems at the typewriter whenever possible. . . . I like to break new ground in Black American literature: *Snowflakes and Steel, A Poet's Mind,* and *The Broken Bowl* are innovative in format; I hope that they will encourage readers to study Black literature more closely than ever." He adds that *Dark Symphony: Negro Literature in America* "was meant to overcome almost thirty years of neglect of Black literature by American publishers of anthologies and literary histories."

According to *Black American Poetry: A Critical Commentary,* Emanuel seems "destined to become one of the major Black poets." His poems have been read on a British Broadcasting Corporation program in England and on the Voice of America program "The Whole World is Listening." They have also been used in the Broadway show "A Hand Is on the Gate" and included in dramatic presentations on the college circuit. His greatest satisfaction, though, came from writing *Langston Hughes,* "a book evolving from my racial pride."

Emanuel's own readings have taken him to Africa, England, France, Austria, Poland, Hungary, Rumania, and elsewhere in Europe, where much of his poetry and prose since 1970 has been written. "My European experiences," he says, "have confirmed my faith in literary art and in Blackness as one of its deepest sources."

Langston Hughes has been translated into French.

BIOGRAPHICAL/CRITICAL SOURCES:

BOOKS

Black American Poetry: A Critical Commentary, Monarch, 1977.
The Crowell Handbook of Contemporary Poetry, Crowell, 1973.

PERIODICALS

Black American Literature Forum, Volume XIII, number 3, 1979.
Nation, December 4, 1967.
Negro American Literature Forum, Volume I, number 1, fall, 1967.
Negro Digest, April, 1965, June, 1966, January, 1968, January, 1969.
New York Times Book Review, November 26, 1968.
The Paperback, University of Warsaw, June, 1976.
Pregled 219, [Belgrade, Yugoslavia], 1982.

Ramparts, October, 1969.
Road Apple Review, winter, 1971-72.

*   *   *

EMECHETA, (Florence Onye) Buchi   1944-

PERSONAL: Born July 21, 1944, in Yaba, Lagos, Nigeria; daughter of Jeremy Nwabudike (a railway worker and molder) and Alice Ogbanje (Okwuekwu) Emecheta; married Sylvester Onwordi, 1960 (separated, 1966); children: Florence, Sylvester, Jake, Christy, Alice. *Education:* University of London, B.Sc. (with honors), 1972. *Religion:* Anglican.

ADDRESSES: Home—144 Craney Gardens, Muswell Hill, London N10 3AH, England.

CAREER: British Museum, London, England, library officer, 1965-69; Inner London Education Authority, London, youth worker and sociologist, 1969-76; community worker, Camden, N.J., 1976-78. Writer and lecturer, 1972—. Visiting professor at several universities throughout the United States, including Pennsylvania State University, University of California, Los Angeles, and University of Illinois at Urbana-Champaign, 1979; senior resident fellow and visiting professor of English, University of Calabar, Nigeria, 1980-81; lecturer, Yale University, 1982, London University, 1982—. Fellow, London University, 1986. Proprietor, Ogwugwu Afor Publishing Company, 1982-83. Member of Home Secretary's Advisory Council on Race, 1979—, and of Arts Council of Great Britain, 1982-83.

AWARDS, HONORS: Jock Campbell Award for literature by new or unregarded talent from Africa or the Caribbean, *New Statesman,* 1978; selected as the Best Black British Writer, 1978, and one of the Best British Young Writers, 1983.

WRITINGS:

In the Ditch, Barrie and Jenkins, 1972.
Second-Class Citizen (novel), Allison & Busby, 1974, Braziller, 1975.
The Bride Price: A Novel (paperback published as *The Bride Price: Young Ibo Girl's Love; Conflict of Family and Tradition*), Braziller, 1976.
The Slave Girl: A Novel, Braziller, 1977.
The Joys of Motherhood: A Novel, Braziller, 1979.
Destination Biafra: A Novel, Schocken, 1982.
Naira Power (novelette directed principally to Nigerian readers), Macmillan (London), 1982.
Double Yoke (novel), Schocken, 1982.
The Rape of Shavi (novel), Ogwugwu Afor, 1983, Braziller, 1985.
Adah's Story: A Novel, Allison & Busby, 1983.
Head above Water (autobiography), Ogwugwu Afor, 1984, Collins, 1986.
A Kind of Marriage (novelette), Macmillan, 1987.

JUVENILE

Titch the Cat (based on story by daughter Alice Emecheta), illustrated by Thomas Joseph, Allison & Busby, 1979.
Nowhere to Play (based on story by daughter Christy Emecheta), illustrations by Peter Archer, Schocken, 1980.
The Moonlight Bride, Oxford Univesity Press in association with University Press, 1981.
The Wrestling Match, Oxford University Press in association with University Press, 1981, Braziller, 1983.
Family Bargain (publication for schools), British Broadcasting Corp., 1987.

OTHER

(Author of introduction and commentary) Maggie Murray, *Our Own Freedom* (book of photographs), Sheba Feminist (London), 1981.

A Kind of Marriage (teleplay; produced by BBC-TV), Macmillan (London), 1987.

Also author of teleplays "Tanya, a Black Woman," produced by BBC-TV, and "The Juju Landlord." Contributor to journals, including *New Statesman, Times Literary Supplement,* and the *Guardian.*

SIDELIGHTS: Although Buchi Emecheta has resided in London since 1962, she is "Nigeria's best-known female writer," comments John Updike in the *New Yorker.* "Indeed, few writers of her sex . . . have arisen in any part of tropical Africa." Emecheta enjoys much popularity in Great Britain, and she has gathered an appreciative audience on this side of the Atlantic as well. Although Emecheta has written children's books and teleplays, she is best known for her historical novels set in Nigeria, both before and after independence. Concerned with the clash of cultures and the impact of Western values upon agrarian traditions and customs, Emecheta's work is strongly autobiographical; and, as Updike observes, much of it is especially concerned with "the situation of women in a society where their role, though crucial, was firmly subordinate and where the forces of potential liberation have arrived with bewildering speed."

Born to Ibo parents in Yaba, a small village near Lagos, Nigeria, Emecheta indicates that the Ibos "don't want you to lose contact with your culture," writes Rosemary Bray in the *Voice Literary Supplement.* Bray explains that the oldest woman in the house plays an important role in that she is the "big mother" to the entire family. In Emecheta's family, her father's sister assumed this role, says Bray: "'She was very old and almost blind,' Buchi recalls, 'And she would gather the young children around her after dinner and tell stories to us.'" The stories the children heard were about their origins and ancestors; and, according to Bray, Emecheta recalls: "I thought to myself 'No life could be more important than this.' So when people asked me what I wanted to do when I grew up I told them I wanted to be a storyteller—which is what I'm doing now."

Orphaned as a young child, Emecheta lived with foster parents who mistreated her. She attended a missionary high school for girls on a scholarship until she was sixteen, and then wed a man to whom she had been betrothed since the age of eleven. A mother at seventeen, she had two sons and three daughters by the time she was twenty-two. After the birth of her second child, Emecheta followed her husband to London, where she endured poor living conditions, including one-room apartments without heat or hot water, to help finance his education. "The culture shock of London was great," notes Bray, "but even more distressing was her husband's physical abuse and his constant resistance to her attempts at independence." The marriage ended when he read and then burned the manuscript of her first book. Supporting herself and five children on public assistance and by scrubbing floors, Emecheta continued to write in the mornings before her children arose, and also managed to earn an honors degree in sociology. *In the Ditch,* her first book, originally appeared as a series of columns in the *New Statesman.* Written in the form of a diary, it "is based on her own failed marriage and her experiences on the dole in London trying to rear alone her many children," state Charlotte and David Bruner in *World Literature Today.* Called a

"sad, sonorous, occasionally hilarious . . . extraordinary first novel," by Adrianne Blue in the *Washington Post Book World,* it details her impoverished existence in a foreign land, as well as her experience with racism, and "illuminates the similarities and differences between cultures and attitudes," remarks a *Times Literary Supplement* contributor, who thinks it merits "special attention."

Similarly autobiographical, Emecheta's second novel, *Second-Class Citizen,* "recounts her early marriage years, when she was trying to support her student-husband—a man indifferent to his own studies and later indifferent to her job searches, her childbearing, and her resistance to poverty," observe the Bruners. The novel is about a young, resolute and resourceful Nigerian girl who, despite traditional tribal domination of females, manages to continue her own education; she marries a student and follows him to London, where he becomes abusive toward her. "Emecheta said people find it hard to believe that she has not exaggerated the truth in this autobiographical novel," reports Nancy Topping Bazin in *Black Scholar.* "The grimness of what is described does indeed make it painful to read." Called a "brave and angry book" by Marigold Johnson in the *Times Literary Supplement,* Emecheta's story, however, "is not accompanied by a misanthropic whine," notes Martin Levin in the *New York Times Book Review.* Alice Walker, who thinks it is "one of the most informative books about contemporary African life" that she has read, observes in *Ms.* that "it raises fundamental questions about how creative and prosaic life is to be lived and to what purpose."

"Emecheta's women do not simply lie down and die," observes Bray. "Always there is resistance, a challenge to fate, a need to renegotiate the terms of the uneasy peace that exists between them and accepted traditions." Bray adds that "Emecheta's women know, too, that between the rock of African traditions and the hard place of encroaching Western values, it is the women who will be caught." Concerned with the clash of cultures, in *The Bride Price: A Novel,* Emecheta tells the story of a young Nigerian girl "whose life is complicated by traditional attitudes toward women," writes Richard Cima in the *Library Journal.* The young girl's father dies when she is thirteen; and, with her brother and mother, she becomes the property of her father's ambitious brother. She is permitted to remain in school only because it will increase her value as a potential wife. However, she falls in love with her teacher, a descendant of slaves; and because of familial objections, they elope, thereby depriving her uncle of the "bride price." When she dies in childbirth, she fulfills the superstition that a woman would not survive the birth of her first child if her bride price had not been paid; and Susannah Clapp maintains in the *Times Literary Supplement,* that the quality of the novel "depends less on plot or characterization than on the information conveyed about a set of customs and the ideas which underlay them." Calling it "a captivating Nigerian novel lovingly but unsentimentally written, about the survival of ancient marriage customs in modern Nigeria," Valerie Cunningham adds in *New Statesman* that this book "proves Buchi Emecheta to be a considerable writer."

Emecheta's *Slave Girl: A Novel* is about "a poor, gently raised Ibo girl who is sold into slavery to a rich African market-woman by a feckless brother at the turn of the century," writes a *New Yorker* contributor. Educated by missionaries, she joins the new church where she meets the man she eventually marries. In the *Library Journal,* Cima thinks that it provides an "interesting picture of Christianity's impact on traditional Ibo society." Perceiving parallels between marriage and slavery,

Emecheta explores the issue of "freedom within marriage in a society where slavery is supposed to have been abolished," writes Cunningham in the *New Statesman,* adding that the book indicts both "pagan and Christian inhumanity to women." And although a contributor to *World Literature Today* suggests that the "historical and anthropological background" in the novel tends to destroy its "emotional complex," another contributor to the same journal believes that the sociological detail has been "unobtrusively woven into" it and that *The Slave Girl* represents Emecheta's "most accomplished work so far. It is coherent, compact and convincing."

"Emecheta's voice has been welcomed by many as helping to redress the somewhat one-sided picture of African women that has been delineated by male writers," according to *A New Reader's Guide to African Literature.* Writing in *African Literature Today,* Eustace Palmer indicates that "the African novel has until recently been remarkable for the absense of what might be called the feminine point of view." Because of the relatively few female African novelists, "the presentation of women in the African novel has been left almost entirely to male voices . . . and their interest in African womanhood . . . has had to take second place to numerous other concerns," continues Palmer. "These male novelists, who have presented the African woman largely within the traditional milieu, have generally communicated a picture of a male-dominated and male-oriented society, and the satisfaction of the women with this state of things has been . . . completely taken for granted." Palmer adds that the emergence of Emecheta and other "accomplished female African novelists . . . seriously challenges all these cosy assumptions. The picture of the cheerful contented female complacently accepting her lot is replaced by that of a woman who is powerfully aware of the unfairness of the system and who longs to be fulfilled in her self, to be a full human being, not merely somebody else's appendage." For instance, Palmer notes that *The Joys of Motherhood: A Novel* "presents essentially the same picture of traditional society . . . but the difference lies in the prominence in Emecheta's novel of the female point of view registering its disgust at male chauvinism and its dissatisfaction with what it considers an unfair and oppressive system."

The Joys of Motherhood is about a woman "who marries but is sent home in disgrace because she fails to bear a child quickly enough," writes Bazin. "She then is sent to the city by her father to marry a man she has never seen. She is horrified when she meets this second husband because she finds him ugly, but she sees no alternative to staying with him. Poverty and repeated pregnancies wear her down; the pressure to bear male children forces her to bear child after child since the girls she has do not count." Palmer observes that "clearly, the man is the standard and the point of reference in this society. It is significant that the chorus of countrymen say, not that a woman without a child is a failed woman, but that a woman without a child *for her husband* is a failed woman." Bazin observes that in Emecheta's novels, "a woman must accept the double standard of sexual freedom: it permits polygamy and infidelity for both Christian and non-Christian men but only monogamy for women. These books reveal the extent to which the African woman's oppression is engrained in the African mores."

Acknowledging that "the issue of polygamy in Africa remains a controversial one," Palmer states that what Emecheta stresses in *The Joys of Motherhood* is "the resulting dominance, especially sexual, of the male, and the relegation of the female into subservience, domesticity and motherhood." Nonethe-

less, despite Emecheta's "angry glare," says Palmer, one can "glean from the novel the economic and social reasons that must have given rise to polygamy. . . . But the author concentrates on the misery and deprivation polygamy can bring." Palmer praises Emecheta's insightful psychological probing of her characters's thoughts: "Scarcely any other African novelist has succeeded in probing the female mind and displaying the female personality with such precision." In the *Washington Post Book World,* Adrianne Blue suggests that Emecheta "tells this story in a plain style, denuding it of exoticism, displaying an impressive, embracing compassion." Calling it a "graceful, touching, ironically titled tale that bears a plain feminist message," Updike adds in the *New Yorker* that "in this compassionate but slightly distanced and stylized story of a life that comes to seem wasted, she sings a dirge for more than African pieties. The lives within 'The Joys of Motherhood' might be, transposed into a different cultural key, those of our own rural ancestors."

Emecheta's "works reveal a great deal about the lives of African women and about the development of feminist perspectives," observes Bazin, explaining that one moves beyond an initial perspective of "personal experience," to perceive "social or communal" oppression. This second perspective "demands an analysis of the causes of oppression within the social mores and the patriarchal power structure," adds Bazin. Finding both perspectives in Emecheta's work, Bazin thinks that through her descriptions of "what it is like to be female in patriarchal African cultures," she provides a voice for "millions of black African women." Although her feminist perspective is anchored in her own personal life, says Bazin, she "grew to understand how son preference, bride price, polygamy, menstrual taboos, . . . wife beating, early marriages, early and unlimited pregnancies, arranged marriages, and male dominance in the home functioned to keep women powerless." The Bruners write that "obviously Emecheta is concerned about the plight of women, today and yesterday, in both technological and traditional societies, though she rejects a feminist label." Emecheta told the Bruners: "The main themes of my novels are African society and family; the historical social, and political life in Africa as seen by a woman through events. I always try to show that the African male is oppressed and he too oppresses the African women . . . I have not committed myself to the cause of African women only. I write about Africa as a whole."

Emecheta's *Destination Biafra: A Novel* is a story of the "history of Nigeria from the eve of independence to the collapse of the Biafran secessionist movement," writes Robert L. Berner in *World Literature Today.* The novel has generated a mixed critical response, though. In the *Times Literary Supplement,* Chinweizu feels that it "does not convey the feel of the experience that was Biafra. All it does is leave one wondering why it falls so devastatingly below the quality of Buchi Emecheta's previous works." Noting, however, that Emecheta's publisher reduced the manuscript by half, Berner suggests that "this may account for what often seems a rather elliptical narrative and for the frequently clumsy prose which too often blunts the novel's satiric edge." Finding the novel "different from any of her others . . . larger and more substantive," the Bruners state: "Here she presents neither the life story of a single character nor the delineation of one facet of a culture, but the whole perplexing canvas of people from diverse ethnic groups, belief systems, levels of society—all caught in a disastrous civil war." Moreover, the Bruners feel that the "very objectivity of her reporting and her impartiality in recounting atrocities committed by all sides, military and civilian, have even greater impact because her motivation is not sadistic.''

The Rape of Shavi represents somewhat of a departure in that ''Emecheta attempts one of the most difficult of tasks: that of integrating the requirements of contemporary, realistic fiction with the narrative traditions of myth and folklore,'' writes Somtow Sucharitkul in the *Washington Post Book World*. Roy Kerridge describes the novel's plot in the *Times Literary Supplement:* ''A plane crashes among strange tribespeople, white aviators are made welcome by the local king, they find precious stones, repair their plane and escape just as they are going to be forcibly married to native girls. The king's son and heir stows away and has adventures of his own in England.'' Called a ''wise and haunting tale'' by a *New Yorker* contributor, *The Rape of Shavi* ''recounts the ruination of this small African society by voracious white interlopers,'' says Richard Eder in the *Los Angeles Times*. A few critics suggest that in *The Rape of Shavi*, Emecheta's masterful portrayal of her Shavian community is not matched by her depiction of the foreigners. Eder, for instance, calls it a ''lopsided fable,'' and declares: ''It is not that the Shavians are noble and the whites monstrous; that is what fables are for. It is that the Shavians are finely drawn and the Westerners very clumsily. It is a duet between a flute and a kitchen drain.'' However, Sucharitkul thinks that portraying the Shavians as ''complex individuals'' and the Westerners as ''two dimensional, mythic types'' presents a refreshing, seldom expressed, and ''particularly welcome'' point of view.

Although in the *New York Times* Michiko Kakutani calls *The Rape of Shavi* ''an allegorical tale, filled with ponderous morals about the evils of imperialism and tired aphorisms about nature and civilization,'' Sucharitkul believes that ''the central thesis of [the novel] is brilliantly, relentlessly argued, and Emecheta's characters and societies are depicted with a bittersweet, sometimes painful honesty.'' Sucharitkul also praises Emecheta's ''persuasive'' prose: ''It is prose that appears unusually simple at first, for it is full of the kind of rhythms and sentence structures more often found in folk tales than in contemporary novels. Indeed, in electing to tell her multilayered and often very contemporary story within a highly mythic narrative framework, the author walks a fine line between the pitfalls of preciosity and pretentiousness. By and large, the tightrope act is a success.''

''Emecheta has reaffirmed her dedication to be a full-time writer,'' say the Bruners. ''Her culture and her education at first were obstacles to her literary inclination. She had to struggle against precedent, against reluctant publishers, and later against male-dominated audiences and readership.'' Her fiction is intensely autobiographical, drawing on the difficulties she has both witnessed and experienced as a woman, and most especially as a Nigerian woman. Indicating that in Nigeria, however, ''Emecheta is a prophet without honor,'' Bray adds that ''she is frustrated at not being able to reach women—the audience she desires most. She feels a sense of isolation as she attempts to stake out the middle ground between the old and the new.'' Remarking that ''in her art as well as in her life, Buchi Emecheta offers another alternative,'' Bray continues: ''What I am trying to do is get our profession back,'' Emecheta told Bray. ''Women are born storytellers. We keep the history. We are the true conservatives—we conserve things and we never forget. What I do is not clever or unusual. It is what my aunt and my grandmother did, and their mothers before them.''

AVOCATIONAL INTERESTS: Gardening, attending the theatre, listening to music, reading.

BIOGRAPHICAL/CRITICAL SOURCES:

BOOKS

Contemporary Literary Criticism, Volume 14, Gale, 1980.
Zell, Hans M., and others, *A New Reader's Guide to African Literature,* 2nd revised and expanded edition, Holmes & Meier, 1983.

PERIODICALS

African Literature Today, Number 3, 1983.
Atlantic, May, 1976.
Black Scholar, November/December, 1985, March/April, 1986.
Library Journal, September 1, 1975, April 1, 1976, January 15, 1978, May 1, 1979.
Listener, July 19, 1979.
Los Angeles Times, October 16, 1983, March 6, 1985.
Ms., January, 1976, July, 1984, March, 1985.
New Statesman, June 25, 1976, October 14, 1977, June 2, 1978, April 27, 1979.
New Yorker, May 17, 1976, January 9, 1978, July 2, 1979, April 23, 1984, April 22, 1985.
New York Times, February 23, 1985.
New York Times Book Review, September 14, 1975, November 11, 1979, January 27, 1980, February 27, 1983, May 5, 1985.
Times Literary Supplement, August 11, 1972, January 31, 1975, June 11, 1976, February 26, 1982, February 3, 1984, February 27, 1987.
Voice Literary Supplement, June, 1982.
Washington Post Book World, May 13, 1979, April 12, 1981, September 5, 1982, September 25, 1983, March 30, 1985.
World Literature Today, spring, 1977, summer, 1977, spring, 1978, winter, 1979, spring, 1980, winter, 1983, autumn, 1984, winter, 1985.

—*Sketch by Sharon Malinowski*

*　　*　　*

ESEKI, Bruno
See MPHAHLELE, Ezekiel

*　　*　　*

EVANS, Mari 1923-
(E. Reed)

PERSONAL: Born July 16, 1923, in Toledo, Ohio; divorced; children: two sons. *Education:* Attended University of Toledo.

ADDRESSES: Home—P.O. Box 483, Indianapolis, Ind. 46206. *Office*—Department of English, State University of New York—Albany, Albany, N.Y. 12203.

CAREER: Worked as an editor for a chain manufacturing company. Indiana University—Purdue University at Indianapolis, instructor in black literature and writer-in-residence, 1969-70; Indiana University at Bloomington, assistant professor of black literature and writer-in-residence, 1970-78; State University of New York—Albany, associate professor, 1985—. Visiting assistant professor, Northwestern University, 1972-73, Purdue University, West Lafayette, Ind., 1978-80, Washington University, St. Louis, 1980, Cornell University, 1981-84. Producer, director, writer for television program, ''The Black Experience,'' WTTV, Indianapolis, 1968-73; has lectured and read at numerous colleges and universities. Consultant to Discovery Grant Program, National Endowment for the Arts, 1969-70; consultant in ethnic studies, Bobbs-Merrill Co., 1970-73. Member of literary advisory panel, Indiana State Arts Commission, chairperson, 1976-77; chairman, Statewide Committee for Penal Reform; member of board of management, Fall Creek Parkway YMCA, 1975-80; member, Indiana Corrections Code Commission, 1978-79; member of board of directors, 1st World Foundation.

MEMBER: Authors Guild, Authors League of America, African Heritage Studies Association.

AWARDS, HONORS: John Hay Whitney fellow, 1965-66; Woodrow Wilson Foundation grant, 1968; Indiana University Writers' Conference award, and Black Academy of Arts and Letters first annual poetry award, both 1970, for *I Am a Black Woman;* L.H.D., Marian College, 1975; MacDowell fellow, 1975; Builders Award, Third World Press, Chicago, 1977; Indiana Committee for the Humanities grant, 1977; Black Liberation Award, Kuumba Theatre Workshop, Chicago, 1978; Copeland Fellow, Amherst College, 1980; Black Arts Celebration Poetry Award, Chicago, 1981; National Endowment for the Arts Creative Writing Award, 1981; Yaddo Writers Colony fellow, 1984.

WRITINGS:

Where Is All the Music? (poems), P. Breman, 1968.
I Am a Black Woman (poems), Morrow, 1970.
J. D. (juvenile), Doubleday, 1973, Avon, 1982.
I Look at Me (juvenile), Third World Press, 1974.
Rap Stories (juvenile), Third World Press, 1974.
Singing Black (juvenile), Reed Visuals, 1976.
"River of My Song" (play), first produced in Indianapolis, Ind., at Lilly Theatre, May, 1977, produced in Chicago, Ill., at Northeastern Illinois University, Center for Inner City Studies, 1977.
Jim Flying High (juvenile), Doubleday, 1979.
Night Star: 1973-1978 (poems), Center for African American Studies, University of California, Berkeley, 1980.
"Eyes" (a musical; adapted from Zora Neale Hurston's *Their Eyes Were Watching God*), first produced in New York at the Richard Allen Cultural Center, 1979, produced in Cleveland at Karamu Theatre of the Performing Arts, March, 1982.
(Editor and contributor) *Black Women Writers (1950-1980): A Critical Evaluation*, Doubleday-Anchor, 1984, published in England as *Black Women Writers, 1950-1980: Arguments and Interviews*, Pluto, 1985.

Also author of *Portrait of a Man*, 1979, "Boochie" (a play), 1979, "The Way They Made Beriani," and "Glide and Sons" (a musical).

CONTRIBUTOR TO ANTHOLOGIES

James A. Emanuel and Theodore L. Gross, editors, *Dark Symphony: Negro Literature in America*, Free Press, 1968.
Abraham Chapman, editor, *Black Voices: An Anthology of Afro-American Literature*, American Library, 1968.
Anita Dore, editor, *The Premier Book of Major Poets: An Anthology*, Fawcett, 1970.
Edna Johnson, editor, *Anthology of Children's Literature*, 4th edition, Houghton, 1970.
Alan Lomax and Raoul Abdul, editors, *3000 Years of Black Poetry: An Anthology*, Dodd, Mead, 1970.

Richard A. Long and Eugenia Collier, editors, *Afro-American Writing: An Anthology of Prose and Poetry*, New York University Press, 1972.
Chapman, editor, *New Black Voices: An Anthology of Contemporary Afro-American Literature*, New American Library, 1972.
Raoul Abdul, editor, *The Magic of Black Poetry*, Dodd, Mead, 1972.
Stephen Henderson, *Understanding the New Black Poetry: Black Speech and Black Music as Poetic References*, Morrow, 1973.
Arnold Adoff, editor, *Black Out Loud: An Anthology of Modern Poems by Black Americans*, Dell, 1975.

Poetry is represented in more than two hundred anthologies and textbooks.

OTHER

Writer for television program, "The Black Experience." Contributor to *Phylon, Black World* (formerly *Negro Digest*), *Dialog, Black Enterprise* (under the pseudonym E. Reed), *First World*, and other periodicals.

SIDELIGHTS: When a story Mari Evans wrote in the fourth grade was accepted for publication in her school paper, her father expressed his pride by marking the occasion as an important event in their family history. Just a few years later, the young Evans read *Weary Blues* by Langston Hughes and identified with the black literature that was to become her vocation. These two influences, she says in *Black Women Writers (1950-1980): A Critical Evaluation*, gave her the confidence she needed to become a professional writer despite the racism that plagued her apprenticeship as an editor for a chain manufacturing plant. Inspired by their early faith in her abilities, Evans has also endured frequent rejection from publishers who take issue with the strong social comment that characterizes her works. These obstacles, she relates, have taught her the importance of discipline in the writer's life. And they have not prevented her from becoming an award-winning writer who is a well-known advocate of the growth of black pride and the construction of the black community in America. As Wallace R. Peppers notes about Evans in the *Dictionary of Literary Biography*, "Her volumes of poetry, her books for adolescents, her work for television and other media, and her . . . volume on black women writers between 1950 and 1980 ensure her a lasting place among those who have made significant contributions to Afro-American life and culture."

The author's first book of poems, *Where Is All the Music?*, came out in 1968, the same year that Evans began to write, direct, and produce "The Black Experience," a program for WTTV in Indianapolis. While the program met with critical acclaim, the book received little notice from critics. Pepper feels it is significant, nonetheless, because of its "well-crafted first-person personae, effective linguistic devices, apt diction, and strong characterizations." The poet's ambition, he observes, is "to record the emotional vicissitudes of the individual soul; and to document the difficult, but necessary struggle to form meaningful human relationships." The book "barely suggests Evans's eventual concern for social relevancy," he comments, noting that only three of its poems treat "activist" themes.

Evans's focus on social issues becoms sharper in later volumes. *I Am a Black Woman*, her second book, "heralded the arrival of a poet who took her subject matter from the black community, and who celebrated its triumphs, . . . and who would mourn its losses, especially the deaths of Martin Luther King, Jr. and Malcolm X,'' Peppers relates. David Dorsey's essay on Evans's work in *Black Women Writers* comments on the obvious political intent of poems that declare ''i / will not sit / in Grateful meetings,'' and others that address the need for social change in ''more strident terms.'' But the last poem, notes Dorsey, emphasizes the positive foundation of her political stance when it asks, ''Who can be born black and not exult!'' *I Am a Black Woman* won Indiana University's Writers' Conference award and the Black Academy of Arts and Letters first annual poetry award in 1970.

The poet's commitment to the concerns of Black Americans grows stronger in *Nightstar,* say the critics, in poems that also show an improvement in poetic technique. Dorsey comments that his analysis of *Nightstar* ''cannot suggest the humane grace that pervades this book.'' Yet he means for the reader to see ''that mechanical means, poetic design, and didactic import are so interconnected [in it] that to separate them is to dismember an organism.'' A *Virginia Quarterly Review* writer has similar praise for Evans: ''Mari Evans is a powerful poet. Her craftsmanship does not interfere with the subject she treats with a fullness born of deep caring. She subtly interweaves private and public Black frustration and dignity with an infectious perception. Sparseness of speech belies a command of the language and knowledge of the Black experience. . . . We need to hear this authentic voice again and again, for there is strength in exquisitely revealing expressions of ghetto dynamics.''

Evans's command of Black idioms is one reason why her works should be valued, suggests Dorsey: ''There are several reasons why the corpus of Evans's published works to date [1984] are extremely illuminating for anyone interested in considering the nature of art in the Black American tradition. The first is that her creative works are of unquestionable artistic excellence. . . . Similarly, her adaptation of Black idiom in children's stories, in poetry, and in drama shows how the writer must manipulate idiom to achieve reader identification with the speaker, rather than aesthetic (and ideological) alienation.'' In her statement for *Black Women Writers,* Evans explains the role of idiom in her works: ''Idiom is larger than geography; it is the hot breath of a people—singing, slashing, explorative. Imagery becomes the magic denominator, the language of a passage, saying the ancient unchanging particulars, the connective currents that nod Black heads from Maine to Mississippi to Montana. No there ain't nothin universal about it. So when I write, I write reaching for all that. Reaching for what will nod Black heads over common denominators. . . . If there are those outside the Black experience who hear the music and can catch the beat, that is serendipity; I have no objections. But when I write, I write according to the title of poet Margaret Walker's classic: 'for my people.'''

Evans ''celebrates the known and the unsung among us,'' says *Black Women Writers* contributor Solomon Edwards. ''She writes of Wes Montgomery and Yusef Lateef, jazz titans. She asserts that Black education should begin in a loving Black home where concern for learning can mature in a friendly atmosphere of belonging rather than in a threatening often alien environ. Hence, the highly personalized preprimer, *I Look at Me,* was created.'' Using only forty-six vocabulary words, *I Look at Me* presents the black citizens of America in a variety of professions as ''a Beautiful nation.'' Evans has written other children's books helpful in the education of young readers to Black cultural values, he notes. ''*Singing Black* provides alternative nursery rhymes for the Black child's first encounter

with the music of Black values. In . . . *Jim Flying High,* [a West Indian dialect] underscores a humorous tale of problem identification, and interdependence that requires unselfish participation in order to strengthen the Black community.''

In essays and in plays as well, ''Evans maintains her unequivocal stride for Black autonomy,'' observes Edwards. ''She has tenderly sorted out the sweet, sour, salt, and bitter experiences of Black people and dramatized the suffering and shouts of Black strength.'' Earlier, he comments that Evans ''has a passion for the dramatic,'' seen in the fact that her poems generally focus specifically on well-drawn characters, and more so in the plays and musicals she has written. ''There is an intimate relation between Evans's poetry and her theater works,'' namely, their didactic intent, states Dorsey. ''River of My Song,'' produced in Indianapolis, and later in Chicago in 1977, is written for four musicians, three dancers, and four actresses. ''The use of poetry and music, the choice of instruments, the coordination of . . . 'movement, text, music' . . . all reflect adherence to traditional and genuine Black theatrical ritual,'' the essayist adds. ''Portrait of a Man'' and ''Boochie'' are more conventional but not less ritualistic. ''Portrait'' allows the audience to develop ''determination, pride, courage, and comprehension'' in the face of white indifference to human suffering, says Dorsey; and through the monologue of the one character in ''Boochie,'' the audience is ''led to a very specific and incisive recognition of the effects of social forces (unemployment, alcohol, welfare) on the Black woman, the Black man, the Black child.''

Observing that information on black women writers was scarce though their ranks held many accomplished poets, novelists, and two Pulitzer prize winners since the 1940s, Evans compiled new critical articles and personal statements from fifteen authors to make *Black Women Writers (1950-1980)*. The book, according to *World Literature Today* contributor Bettina L. Knapp, ''not only fills a vacuum, but it also makes for exciting and provocative reading.'' Zhana especially values each ''author's own writings, which were done in response to a questionnaire. . . . It is useful and informative to me, as a Black woman writer, to read of the joys, pains, blood, ecstasy of writers plying their craft,'' she says in the *New Statesman*. Writing in the *New York Times Book Review,* Rosellen Brown appreciates the opening essay by Stephen E. Henderson, which ''puts this exposition of talent into historical perspective.'' Brown also applauds ''a biography and bibliography so detailed that it . . . names the nine cities that have given their keys to Nikki Giovanni.'' For the first time, notes Brown, Margaret Walker, Alice Childress, and the other women in *Black Women Writers* are given the scholarly attention that is their due. Furthermore, the collection makes an important amendment to the literary canon, which she hopes will no longer exclude the black woman writer: ''[Evans's] book is a cause for delight to anyone who wants to share or, from a distance, to discover the world of black women writers, with the knowledge that there are many more waiting their turns. Partly by their efforts, the map of significance has been irrevocably changed.''

Translated versions of Evans's poetry have been published in Swedish, French, Russian, German, Italian, and Dutch textbooks and anthologies.

MEDIA ADAPTATIONS: Evans's poetry has been choreographed and used on record albums, filmstrips, television specials, and in two Off-Broadway productions, ''A Hand Is on the Gate'' and ''Walk Together Children.''

BIOGRAPHICAL/CRITICAL SOURCES:

BOOKS

Dictionary of Literary Biography, Volume 41: *Afro-American Poets since 1955,* Gale, 1985.
Evans, Mari, *I Am a Black Woman,* Morrow, 1970.
Evans, Mari, *I Look at Me,* Third World Press, 1974.
Evans, Mari, editor and contributor, *Black Women Writers (1950-1980): A Critical Evaluation,* Doubleday/Anchor, 1984.

PERIODICALS

Black American Literature Forum, winter, 1984.
Black Scholar, March, 1981.
Black World, January, 1971, July, 1971.
Book World, November 11, 1973, September 14, 1975.
Ebony, March, 1974.
Essence, September, 1984.
Freedomways, Volume XXIV, number 4, 1984.
Los Angeles Times Book Review, September 2, 1984.
Modern Fiction Studies, winter, 1985.
New Statesman, May 3, 1985.
New Yorker, September 3, 1979.
New York Times Book Review, September 23, 1984.
Publishers Weekly, July 6, 1970.
Virginia Quarterly Review, winter, 1971.
World Literature Today, winter, 1985.

—Sketch by Marilyn K. Basel

F

FABIO, Sarah Webster   1928-1979

PERSONAL: Born January 20, 1928, in Nashville, Tenn.; died November 7, 1979; married Cyril L. Fabio (divorced); children: Cheryl, Ronnie, Renee Angela, Leslie, Thomas. *Education:* Fisk University, B.A., 1946; San Francisco State College (now University), M.A.

ADDRESSES: Home—5255 Cole St., Oakland, Calif. 94601.

CAREER: Poet and teacher. Member of faculty at Merritt Junior College, Oakland, Calif., University of California, Berkeley, and Oberlin College, Oberlin, Ohio. Participated in First World Festival of Negro Art (Dakar, Senegal), 1966.

WRITINGS:

Saga of a Black Man, Turn Over Book Stores, 1968.
A Mirror [and] *A Soul* (two-part volume of poems), Julian Richardson, 1969.
Black Talk: Soul, Shield, and Sword, Doubleday, 1973.

Also author of *Race Results: U.S.A.,* 1966, and *Black Is a Panther Caged.* Contributor to magazines. Editor of *Journal of Black Arts Renaissance* and *Phase II.*

MEDIA ADAPTATIONS: Sarah Webster Fabio made two sound recordings, ''Boss Soul,'' and ''Soul Ain't, Soul Is,'' for Folkways Records, 1972.

*   *   *

FAIR, Ronald L.   1932-

PERSONAL: Born October 27, 1932, in Chicago, Ill.; son of Herbert and Beulah (Hunt) Fair; married Lucy Margaret Jones, November 10, 1952 (divorced); married Neva June Keres, June 19, 1968; children: (first marriage) Rodney D., Glen A.; (second marriage) Nile. *Education:* Attended Stenotype School of Chicago, 1953-55.

ADDRESSES: c/o Lotus Press, P.O. Box 21607, Detroit, Mich. 48221.

CAREER: City of Chicago, Ill., court reporter, 1955-67; writer, 1967—. Teacher of literature, Columbia College, Chicago; teacher of literature and fiction, Northwestern University, fall, 1968; Wesleyan University, Middletown, Conn., visiting fellow at Center for Advanced Studies, 1969, visiting professor, 1970-71. *Military service:* U.S. Naval Reserve, 1950-53.

AWARDS, HONORS: Arts and Letters Award, National Institute of Arts and Letters, 1970, for *World of Nothing;* Best Book Award, American Library Association, 1972, for *We Can't Breathe;* National Education Association fellow, 1974; Guggenheim Foundation fellow, 1975.

WRITINGS:

Many Thousand Gone: An American Fable, Harcourt, 1965.
Hog Butcher (novel), Harcourt, 1966, published as *Cornbread, Earl and Me,* Bantam, 1975.
World of Nothing: Two Novellas (contains ''World of Nothing'' and ''Jerome''), Harper, 1970.
We Can't Breathe (autobiographical novel), Harper, 1972.
Excerpts (poems), Paul Breman, 1975.
Rufus (poems), P. Schlack (Stuttgart), 1977, 2nd edition, Lotus Press, 1980.

Contributor to periodicals, including *Chicago Daily Defender* and *Chat Noir Review.*

SIDELIGHTS: ''Ronald L. Fair, novelist and poet, is known for his experimental and versatile literary forms,'' writes R. Baxter Miller in a *Dictionary of Literary Biography* essay. ''Although he sustains the naturalistic tradition of Richard Wright by clarifying the impersonal forces that both limit and determine human life, Fair also draws upon African proverb, medieval allegory, and classical epic.'' Noting that Fair's prose frequently ''transcends naturalism into surrealism,'' Miller suggests that Fair relies upon ''both fable and melodrama in order to shape the political novel, as well as the urban one, into absurdist fiction.'' While converting ''racial history into revealing metaphor,'' says Miller, Fair ''illuminates the ritual of the rural and urban blacks who survive.''

Fair's first novel, *Many Thousand Gone: An American Fable,* is, as the title suggests, ''a metaphorical tale rather than a realistic depiction of life,'' writes Robert E. Fleming in *College Language Association Journal.* Miller observes that it ''symbolically renders the historical and rural past through the story of one town . . . where blacks remain in slavery until 1938 . . . [and] encompasses every element of oppression existing in the South from the 1830s to the 1960s.'' Miller suggests that ''most reviewers of *Many Thousand Gone* translate politics into aesthetic judgments'' while ''other reviewers praised Fair's skill.'' Noting that ''the novel presents a southern microcosm,'' Fleming believes that it ''is an effective satire of the modern South and of the weakness of the nation as a whole in dealing with the treatment of southern black people.'' Discussing Fair's later novel *We Can't Breathe* in the *New York Times Book Review*, George Davis calls *Many Thousand Gone* ''one of the most beautifully written books of the last decade. Nowhere in our language is there a more tightly controlled and bitterly humorous treatment of brutal scenes such as rapes and lynchings and racist murders.''

Fair's second novel, *Hog Butcher*, is about a young boy who witnesses the murder of his hero ''by two policemen who mistake the innocent teenager for a burglary suspect,'' writes Fleming. ''Most of the novel deals with the attempts of the Chicago power structure to whitewash the incident.'' The boy must testify at a coroner's inquest and, ''sickened by the senseless butchery, seeks truth as a weapon of revenge,'' says John R. Greenya in the *Saturday Review*. ''His reaction to the inevitable pressure, inevitable because the police will not admit the possibility of having killed the wrong man, is so well handled by the author that even the cynical will find the ending plausible.'' Davis calls the novel ''a masterful tale of human determination,'' and critics laud the believability of Fair's depiction of ghetto life. Fleming believes that Fair's ''success in drawing a thorough, believable picture of the ghetto and its inhabitants suggests that naturalism is still a useful literary technique for dealing with the city and its problems.'' Although finding Fair's insight into ghetto life ''perceptive,'' a *Library Journal* contributor feels that the novel is ''marred by a one-sided, oversimplified indictment of the white power structure.'' Similarly, while observing that ''Fair is extremely honest in his presentation of his black characters,'' Fleming suggests that his ''greatest fault in *Hog Butcher* is his failure to treat white characters as effectively as their black counterparts.'' However, Greenya finds that despite its weakness of dialogue and cliche, the novel has ''moments of indisputable artistry.''

In *World of Nothing: Two Novellas*, Fair ''exposes religious hypocrisy,'' says Miller. The first book, ''Jerome,'' is described by Shane Stevens in the *New York Times Book Review* as ''a tale of sin and damnation amid the hypocrisy of modern religion.'' Fleming observes that ''Fair attacks the type of church that thrives on self-righteousness and a hypocritical observance of white middle-class values.'' The title novella, ''World of Nothing,'' is about the seamier side of Chicago life and relates the story of a young black man sharing an apartment with another man, whose ''lives are bounded by the bottle and the street,'' states Stevens. ''The derelict, the whore, the petty thieves, the outcasts and miscasts are all part of their nothing world.'' Fleming discusses the ''deceptively light'' tone of the novella: ''The narrator is relaxed in his environment; seeing no way out, he hedonistically enjoys the pleasures that are available to him.'' Depicting more than just the sordid side of ghetto life, Fair reveals that tragedy can also beget happiness or beauty, says Fleming, who believes that Fair ''has successfully conveyed this unseen side of ghetto life.''

Fair's fourth novel, *We Can't Breathe*, relates the story of a young boy growing up in the southern poverty of the 1930s and migrating to the north's urban violence. The novel opens with the protagonist ''and his gang roaming the streets scavenging, killing rats, smashing wine bottles, finding games in the filth,'' writes Jerry H. Bryant in the *Nation*, but it ends with the boy becoming a writer. ''It is problematical whether *We Can't Breathe* is elliptical autobiography or obsessive fiction,'' says Michael Cooke in the *Yale Review*, ''but its pres-

ence seizes, and wrenches, the mind.'' ''We witness families destroyed, lives wasted, justice denied,'' comments Leonard Fleischer in *Saturday Review*, who deems the novel most successful in the tone of ''compassion and regret'' that it conveys. Davis, who calls *We Can't Breathe* ''an honest book, full of brilliant revelations,'' suggests: ''It should be placed on the shelf beside those stories that tell us how often black people have lost the struggle in America. For this book, along with Ronald Fair's other novels, tells how nobly black people have survived. Not that either story is more valid than the other. They are, simply 'different shades of black.'''

''Fair is one of those American writers who keep producing fine work and getting little recognition,'' says Bryant. ''I associate him with writers like Wright Morris, Nelson Algren and Warren Miller, who have enjoyed considerable critical praise but have failed ever to win the profitable attention of the establishment.'' Speaking about Fair's self-exile in Finland, Miller indicates that since 1975, ''Fair has sometimes written anachronistically, but he has enhanced his skill as a writer, having turned his attention to poetry'' and reworking most of the thematic concerns of his fiction. ''Fair's achievement endures,'' writes Miller. ''In the same tradition as that of Richard Wright and Gwendolyn Brooks, his life and work merit critical examination because Fair has courageously sustained exceptional literary experimentation.''

AVOCATIONAL INTERESTS: Football, reading, sports cars.

MEDIA ADAPTATIONS: Hog Butcher has been made into a feature film.

BIOGRAPHICAL/CRITICAL SOURCES:

BOOKS

Contemporary Literary Criticism, Volume 18, Gale, 1981.
Dictionary of Literary Biography, Volume 33: *Afro-American Fiction Writers after 1955*, Gale, 1984.

PERIODICALS

American Book Review, summer, 1979.
College Language Association Journal, June, 1972.
Library Journal, November 15, 1966.
Nation, February 21, 1972.
Newsweek, September 5, 1966.
New York Times Book Review, August 23, 1970, February 6, 1972.
Saturday Review, September 3, 1966, February 19, 1972.
Studies in Black Literature, autumn, 1972.
Yale Review, summer, 1972.

—*Sketch by Sharon Malinowski*

*   *   *

FANON, Frantz   1925-1961

PERSONAL: Born July 20, 1925, in Fort-de-France, Martinique, French Antilles; died of leukemia, December 6, 1961, in Bethesda, Md.; married Josie Duble, 1952; children: Oliver. *Education:* Educated in Martinique and France.

CAREER: Blida-Joinville Hospital, Blida, Algeria, *chef de service*, 1953-56; Manouba Clinic and Centre Neuropsychiatrique de Jour de Tunis, Tunis, Tunisia, psychiatrist, 1957-59; writer. Teacher at University of Tunis in mid-1950s; participant at the First Congress of Black Writers and Artists in Paris in 1956 and at the All African People's Conference in Accra in 1958; ambassador to Ghana for the Algerian Provisional

Government in 1960. *Military service:* French Army, 1944; served with Free French forces fighting in North Africa and in Europe, 1944.

WRITINGS:

Peau noire, masques blancs, preface by Francis Jeanson, Editions du Seuil, 1952, translation by Charles Lam Markmann published as *Black Skin, White Masks,* Grove, 1967.

L'An V de la revolution algerienne, F. Maspero, 1959, enlarged edition, 1960, 4th edition published as *Sociologie d'une revolution,* F. Maspero, 1966, translation by Haakon Chevalier published as *Studies in a Dying Colonialism,* with introduction by Adolfo Gilly, Monthly Review Press, 1965, published as *A Dying Colonialism,* Grove, 1967.

Les Damnes de la terre, preface by Jean-Paul Sartre, F. Maspero, 1961, 2nd edition, 1962, translation by Constance Farrington published as *The Damned,* Presence Africaine, 1963, published as *The Wretched of the Earth,* Grove, 1965.

Pour la revolution africaine: Ecrits politiques, F. Maspero, 1964, translation by Chevalier published as *Toward the African Revolution: Political Essays,* Monthly Review Press, 1967.

Contributor of articles to professional journals. Editorial writer for *El Moudjahid* and *Resistance algerienne,* 1957-62.

SIDELIGHTS: According to *Phylon* contributor Dennis Forsythe, Frantz Fanon "stands as a great symbolic hero" whose "messianic and prophetic image . . . energizes contemporary liberation movements from French Canadian nationalism, Women's Liberation movements, to the Civil Rights movements stretching from Harlem to Africa." Moreover, continued Forsythe, "although [Fanon's] work was concerned essentially with the liberation of the 'colonised' people, his obvious 'humanism' is there for all the 'dispossessed' earnestly engaged in a fight against a historically oppressive system."

Born of middle-class parents on the Caribbean island of Martinique, a French overseas protectorate, Fanon learned at an early age that the power structure directing his education in the refinements of French language and culture also discriminated against him because he was black. It was a lesson reinforced by his experience with the Free French forces fighting in North Africa and Europe during World War II, when, according to *Saturday Review* critic Horace Sutton, Fanon "was to perceive . . . disparity between white and colonial troops and the broad caste lines between the French settlers of North Africa and the Arab natives." Following the war Fanon went to France to pursue studies in medicine, became a psychiatrist, and was accepted for the post of *chef de service* in Blida, just outside French-controlled Algiers. When armed rebellion broke out a year later, Fanon found himself treating the mental disorders of both the French and the Algerians. At the same time he became increasingly involved with the Algerian National Liberation Front, and his writings and work for the nationalists led to his expulsion in 1957 from the Blida hospital.

Aided by the French Left sympathetic to the resistance forces, Fanon was reassigned to the newly independent nation of Tunisia. Upon his arrival in Tunis, he intensified his commitment to the Algerian cause. He not only wrote for *El Moudjahid* and *Resistance algerienne,* the underground press publications of the National Liberation Front and National Liberation Army, respectively, but also worked closely with the Algerian nationalists. Falling ill with leukemia in 1961, Fanon went first to the Soviet Union for treatment and then to the National Institute of Health, outside Washington, D.C., where he spent his last days completing what biographer Irene L. Gendzier called "his political testament," *The Wretched of the Earth.* When he died in December, 1961, just a year before Algeria won its independence from France, his body was flown back to Tunis and his coffin escorted by members of the National Liberation Front to its burial place inside rebel-held Algeria.

In his brief lifetime Fanon wrote four books that chronicle the psychological and material costs of colonization and propose a different future for colonial peoples. In the first of those books, *Black Skin, White Masks,* according to *New York Times Book Review* writer Robert Coles, Fanon draws on his experiences with racism and on his background in philosophy and literature, particularly the works of Nietzsche, Marx, and Sartre, to examine black life in a white-dominated world and the black man's futile attempt to hide his blackness under a "white mask." Coles assessed, "Fanon leaves nothing undone to make his point that the black man, no matter how ingenious, adaptive or even deluded he becomes, cannot escape the history of his people."

According to *New York Times* writer Albert Memmi, the three books that followed *Black Skin, White Masks* reflect Fanon's Algerian experiences and his ambitions to "aid in the construction of a unified Africa, where the frontiers of skin color and cultural prejudice would no longer exist and even a black West Indian would find his place." Two of them, *A Dying Colonialism* and *Toward the African Revolution,* are collections of essays tracing the development of Fanon's thought on racism and colonialism from the time he left France to his death in 1961. The third, *The Wretched of the Earth,* represents the maturation of his philosophy and, in the opinion of *Saturday Review* contributor Emile Capouya, had the impact of "an explosion." In this work Fanon proposed political independence as the precursor to genuine economic and social change. Convinced that Western countries had infiltrated the underdeveloped areas of the world in order to exploit both the natural resources and the population, Fanon deemed social revolution the only feasible path to liberation. Moreover, he argued, this revolution would be accomplished not by the intelligentsia or the laboring class but by the Third World poor themselves, the "wretched of the earth," for they alone were uncorrupted by materialism.

It was also in *The Wretched of the Earth* that Fanon developed his much-publicized concept of the inevitability of violence during social revolution. Fanon viewed violence directed against an oppressor as both purifying and restorative for the one oppressed and recommended its use. This admittedly disquieting proposal nevertheless had its defenders. Capouya, for instance, called it that part of Fanon's philosophy that "administers the most salutary shock," pointing out that "violence is the essential feature of colonialism at all times; Fanon did not invent it." Sutton, too, reminded Fanon's critics that the violence advocated was only a means to overthrow oppression and then to invite the regeneration of men and society. "It is . . . important to understand that as a revolutionist and a practitioner of violence," wrote Sutton, "Fanon was not preaching a religion of nihilism. He was a builder, and . . . a voice of inspirational constructivism."

There are critics, however, who continue to consider Fanon's philosophy of revolution untenable. Memmi, for instance, questioned both its validity and its practicality. Fanon, explained Memmi, "overestimated the role of the peasants," suffered from a ''largely illusory'' concept of African unity, and subscribed to a theory of violence that was ''excessive, difficult to generalize, disturbing and surprising for a psychiatrist.'' Memmi wondered what Fanon would substitute for the political leadership and economic systems he rejected. Concluding that Fanon would probably propose what biographer David Caute called ''a very utopian alliance between the honest intellectuals and the peasantry,'' Memmi then asked: ''How does such a totally new man in such a totally new world function? Are we still in the domain of politics or already in a dream world?''

Coles, however, reflected that Fanon's impact lies not only in his message but also in his sheer determination to deliver it, observing that ''since he is writing to awaken people, to inform them so that they will act, he makes no effort to be systematic, comprehensive, or even orderly. Quite the contrary, one feels a brilliant, vivid and hurt mind, walking the thin line that separates effective outrage from despair.'' According to Coles, Fanon's ''ideas and feelings fairly pour out, and often he makes no effort to tone down his language, to sound like a detached *raisonneur*, the image so many American psychiatrists cultivate.'' Memmi likewise acknowledged the power of Fanon's messianism and concluded that ''death froze [Fanon] in the image of prophet of the Third World, of romantic hero of decolonization. . . . It is not an accident that he has become patron saint of the Black Panthers; for them, too, the fundamental problem is probably that of a confusion of identity and the difficulty of reconstructing a past and a culture with which they can identify.''

BIOGRAPHICAL/CRITICAL SOURCES:

BOOKS

Bouvier, Pierre, *Fanon*, Editions Universitaires, 1971.
Caute, David, *Fanon*, Viking, 1970.
Cranston, Maurice, editor, *The New Left*, Library Press, 1971.
Geismar, Peter, *Fanon*, Dial, 1971.
Gendzier, Irene L., *Frantz Fanon: A Critical Study*, Pantheon, 1973.

PERIODICALS

Horizon, winter, 1972.
Massachusetts Review, winter, 1973.
New York Times, March 14, 1971.
New York Times Book Review, April 30, 1967.
Phylon, June, 1973.
Saturday Review, April 24, 1965, July 17, 1971.
Time, April 2, 1973.

*   *   *

FAUSET, Jessie Redmon   1884(?)-1961

PERSONAL: Born April 27, 1884 (some sources say 1882 or 1886), in Snow Hill, N.J.; died April 30, 1961, in Philadelphia, Pa.; daughter of Redmon (a minister) and Annie (Seamon) Fauset; married Herbert Harris, 1929. *Education:* Cornell University, B.A., 1905; University of Pennsylvania, M.A.; attended Sorbonne, University of Paris.

CAREER: Teacher of French at high schools in Washington, D.C., and New York, N.Y.; literary editor of *Crisis*, New York City, 1919-26, and *Brownie's Book*, 1920-21; novelist, critic, and poet.

MEMBER: Phi Beta Kappa.

WRITINGS:

There is Confusion (novel), Boni & Liveright, 1924, AMS Press, 1974.
Plum Bun: A Novel Without a Moral, Mathews & Marrot (London), 1928, Frederick A. Stokes, 1929, Methuen, 1985.
The Chinaberry Tree: A Novel of American Life, Frederick A. Stokes, 1931, AMS Press, 1969.
Comedy, American Style (novel), Frederick A. Stokes, 1933, AMS Press, 1969.

Contributor of poems, short stories, and essays to periodicals, including *Crisis* and *Brownie's Book*.

SIDELIGHTS: The first black female to graduate from Cornell University, Fauset taught French at an all-black high school in Washington, D.C., until 1919 when sociologist W. E. B. Du Bois asked her to move to New York City to work for *Crisis* magazine, of which he was editor. As literary editor, Fauset published the works of many Harlem Renaissance writers, such as Countee Cullen, Langston Hughes, and Jean Toomer, as well as her own writings. Fauset also edited and was the primary writer for *Brownie's Book,* a magazine for black children.

Fauset wrote poetry, essays, short stories, and novels, most of which portrayed black life in a prejudice-wrought world. Her last novel, *Comedy, American Style,* is considered her most direct statement about the various effects of racial discrimination. The main character, Olivia Carey, is a woman who, because of the prejudice she encounters, hates being black and vainly desires to be white. Her passionate and futile desires threaten to destroy her, while at the same time her husband and son are proud of their heritage and exemplify the richness of black culture.

Fauset's novels received largely mixed reviews, some critics feeling the author unrealistically characterized her subjects. In *Black Writers of the Thirties,* for example, James O. Young commented: ''The black middle class was not an invalid subject for fiction, but Miss Fauset's idealized treatment of it had little redeeming value. . . . [Instead] of presenting a serious, realistic interpretation of middle-class black life, as she professed to do, Miss Fauset concocted a highly idealized romance. Her characters are not real human beings, they are idealizations of what the negro middle class conceived itself to be.'' And Gerald Sykes, reviewing *The Chinaberry Tree,* wrote in *Nation:* ''[It] attempts to idealize [the] polite colored world in terms of the white standards that it has adopted. . . . When she parades the possessions of her upper classes and when she puts her lovers through their Fauntleroy courtesies, she is not only stressing the white standards that they have adopted; she is definitely minimizing the colored blood in them. This is a decided weakness, for it steals truth and life from the book. Is not the most precious part of a Negro work of art that which is specifically Negroid, which none but a Negro could contribute?''

Despite her ''artistic errors,'' however, Sykes found ''Fauset has a rare understanding of people and their motives. . . . Inspired by the religious motive which so many Negro writers seem to feel, she has simply been trying to justify her world to the world at large. Her mistake has consisted in trying to do this in terms of the white standard.''

On the other hand, in a review of Fauset's *Comedy, American Style,* Hugh M. Gloster hailed Fauset's ''description of the lives and difficulties of Philadelphia's colored elite'' as ''one of the major achievements of American Negro fiction.'' And Joseph J. Feeney defended Fauset's portrayal of blacks, claiming in his *CLA Journal* article that critics ''who speak of her middle-class respectability and her 'genteel lace-curtain romances' miss the dark world of prejudice, sadness, and frustration just below the surface of her novels. There are two worlds in Jessie Fauset: the first is sunlit, a place of pride, talent, family love, and contentment; the other world is shadowed by prejudice, lost opportunities, a forced choice between color and country.'' Feeney continued: ''Miss Fauset, through structure and content has offered a far more complex and harrowing portrait of American black life than the critics have recognized. She is far more than a conventional writer of middle-class romances, and her reputation must be revised accordingly.... She was not a major writer. But she cannot be dismissed as 'vapidly genteel' or 'sophomoric.' In the construction of her novels and in her vision of the Negro world, she displayed a sensibility which comprehended tragedy, sardonic comedy, disillusioned hopes, slavery, prejudice, confusion, and bitterness against America.''

BIOGRAPHICAL/CRITICAL SOURCES:

BOOKS

Bone, Robert, *The Negro Novel in America*, Yale University Press, 1965.
Gloster, Hugh M., *Negro Voices in American Fiction*, University of North Carolina Press, 1948.
Young, James O., *Black Writers of the Thirties*, Louisiana State University Press, 1973.

PERIODICALS

CLA Journal, December, 1974, June, 1979.
Ebony, February, 1949, August, 1966.
Nation, July 27, 1932.
New Republic, July 9, 1924, April 10, 1929.
New York Times Book Review, November 19, 1933.
Saturday Review of Literature, April 6, 1929.

*   *   *

FEELINGS, Muriel (Grey)   1938-

PERSONAL: Born July 31, 1938, in Philadelphia, Pa.; married Thomas Feelings (an author and illustrator), February 18, 1969 (divorced, 1974); children: Zamani, Kamili. *Education:* Attended Philadelphia Museum School of Art, 1957-60; Los Angeles State College (now California State University, Los Angeles), B.A., 1963.

ADDRESSES: c/o Dial Books, 2 Park Ave., New York, N.Y. 10016.

CAREER: Writer. Teacher of Spanish and art in elementary and secondary schools in Philadelphia, Pa., and New York, N.Y.; teacher of art at a boys' secondary school in Kampala, Uganda.

MEMBER: Columbian Design Society.

AWARDS, HONORS: Moja Means One: Swahili Counting Book and *Jambo Means Hello: Swahili Alphabet Book* were American Library Association Notable Books; *Moja Means One* was a runner-up for the Caldecott Medal, 1972, and was cited by the Brooklyn Art Books for Children, 1973; *Jambo Means Hello* was also nominated for the American Book Award, 1982.

WRITINGS:

JUVENILES

Zamani Goes to Market (illustrated by husband, Thomas Feelings), Seabury, 1970.
Moja Means One: Swahili Counting Book (illustrated by T. Feelings), Dial, 1971.
Jambo Means Hello: Swahili Alphabet Book (illustrated by T. Feelings), 1974.

SIDELIGHTS: Muriel Feelings spent two years in Africa. During her stay there, she taught at a boys' secondary school in Kampala and traveled extensively in Uganda, Kenya, Tanzania, and Central Africa. Her experiences in Africa served as the inspiration for her three books, all of which are about African culture and language.

BIOGRAPHICAL/CRITICAL SOURCES:

PERIODICALS

Saturday Review, January 15, 1972.
Washington Post Book World, May 10, 1987.

*   *   *

FEELINGS, Thomas   1933-
(Tom Feelings)

PERSONAL: Born May 19, 1933, in Brooklyn, N.Y.; son of Samuel (a taxicab driver) and Anna (Nash) Feelings; married Muriel Grey (a school teacher), February 18, 1968 (divorced, 1974); children: Zamani, Kamili. *Education:* Attended School of Visual Art, 1951-53, 1957-60.

ADDRESSES: c/o Anna Morris, 21 St. James Pl., Brooklyn, N.Y. 11205.

CAREER: Writer and illustrator. Ghana Publishing Company, Ghana, West Africa, illustrator for *African Review*, 1964-66; Government of Guyana, Guyana, South America, teacher of illustrators for Ministry of Education, 1971-74. Has worked as free-lance illustrator for Ghana television programs and for newspapers and other businesses in Ghana. *Military service:* U.S. Air Force, illustrator in Graphics Division in London, England, 1953-57.

AWARDS, HONORS: Caldecott Honor Book runner-up for best illustrated children's book, 1972, for *Mojo Means One*, and 1974, for *Jambo Means Hello; Black Pilgrimage* was runner-up for Coretta Scott King Award, received Woodward School annual book award, and Brooklyn Museum citation, all 1973, and received an ALA notable book citation and appeared on the *Horn Book* honor list; *Boston Globe-Horn Book* Award, 1973, for *Jambo Means Hello;* School of Visual Art outstanding alumni achievement award, 1974; American Book Award nomination, 1981, for *Jambo Means Hello;* National Endowment for the Arts Visual Arts grant, 1982.

WRITINGS:

CHILDREN'S BOOKS

Black Pilgrimage (autobiography), Lothrop, 1972.
(With Eloise Greenfield) *Daydreamers*, Dial, 1981.

ILLUSTRATOR

Letta Schatz, *Bola and the Oba's Drummers*, McGraw, 1967.
Eleanor Heady, compiler, *When the Stones Were Soft: East African Folktales*, Funk, 1968.
Julius Lester, editor, *To Be a Slave*, Dial, 1968.

Osmond Molarsky, *Song of the Empty Bottles*, Walck, 1968.
Robin McKown, *The Congo: River of Mystery*, McGraw, 1968.
Nancy Garfield, *The Tuesday Elephant*, Crowell, 1968.
Kathleen Arnot, *Tales of Temba: Traditional African Stories*, Walck, 1969.
Ruskin Bond, *Panther's Moon*, Random House, 1969.
Rose Blue, *A Quiet Place*, F. Watts, 1969.
Lester, compiler, *Black Folktales*, Baron, 1969.
Muriel Feelings, *Zamani Goes to Market*, Seabury, 1970.
Jane Kerina, *African Crafts*, Lion Press, 1970.
Muriel Feelings, *Mojo Means One*, Dial, 1971.
Muriel Feelings, *Jambo Means Hello*, Dial, 1974.
Nikki Grimes, *Something on My Mind*, Dial, 1978.
Joyce Carol Thomas, *Black Child*, Zamani Productions, 1981.
Maya Angelou, *Now Sheba Sings the Song*, Dial, 1987.

WORK IN PROGRESS: An extensive illustrated book dealing with the history of slavery of the black man in North America.

SIDELIGHTS: Thomas Feelings commented: "My essential interest (and talent) in art, I believe, is that of a story-teller—telling the black story, one that is rooted in Africa and expanded in America. And I have chosen to direct my artistic skills towards this end using illustration/writing as a functional form, therefore [creating] a possible way of projecting our truth and reaffirming the beauty of the human spirit. [I am] always trying to balance this joy and pain of life, to balance a sense of the beauty magnified and a sense of the reality intensified, hoping to equal the sense of hope embedded in the souls of black folk that has helped us survive, to this day."

BIOGRAPHICAL/CRITICAL SOURCES:

BOOKS

Feelings, Thomas, *Black Pilgrimage*, Lothrop, 1972.

PERIODICALS

Black World, November, 1972.
Book World, May 7, 1972.
Negro Digest, September, 1967, August, 1971.
New York Times Book Review, May 7, 1972.
Sepia, September, 1969.

*   *   *

FEELINGS, Tom
  See FEELINGS, Thomas

*   *   *

FIELDS, Julia   1938-

PERSONAL: Born January, 1938, in Perry County, Ala.; daughter of Winston and Maggie Fields. *Education:* Knoxville College, B.S., 1961; Bread Loaf School of English, M.A., 1972; further study at University of Edinburgh, 1963.

ADDRESSES: Home—Box 209, Scotland Neck, N.C. 27874.

CAREER: Poet and author of short stories. Has worked as a high school teacher in Birmingham, Ala., and as poet-in-residence, lecturer, or instructor at several universities and colleges, including Miles College, Hampton Institute, St. Augustine College, East Carolina University, Howard University, North Carolina State University, and University of the District of Columbia. Founder and consultant to the Learning School of the American Language, 1979.

AWARDS, HONORS: National Endowment for the Arts grant, 1967; Seventh Conrad Kent Rivers Memorial Fund Award, 1973.

WRITINGS:

I Heard A Young Man Saying, Broadside Press, 1967.
Poems, Poets Press, 1968.
East of Moonlight, Red Clay Books, 1973.
A Summoning, A Shining, Scotland Neck, 1976.
Slow Coins, Three Continents Press, 1981.
The Green Lion of Zion Street, Macmillan, 1988.

PLAYS

"All Day Tomorrow," produced in Knoxville, Tenn. at the Knoxville College Drama Workshop, 1966.

CONTRIBUTOR TO ANTHOLOGIES

New Negro Poets: U.S.A., edited by Langston Hughes, Indiana University Press, 1964.
Kaleidoscope, edited by Robert Hayden, Harcourt, 1967.
Black Fire, edited by LeRoi Jones and Larry Neal, Morrow, 1968.
Nine Black Poets, edited by R. Baird Shuman, Moore, 1968.
The Poetry of the Negro, 1746-1970, edited by Hughes and Arna Bontemps, Doubleday, 1970.
The Poetry of Black America, edited by Arnold Adoff, Harper, 1972.

OTHER

Contributor of poetry and short stories to *Massachusetts Review*, *Black World*, *Callaloo*, *First World*, *Essence*, *Negro Digest*, and other periodicals.

SIDELIGHTS: In a biographical entry published in *Dictionary of Literary Biography* Mary Williams Burger writes that Julia Fields "is an important representative of the cultural and artistic renaissance that gave birth to her writings, not only because her poems and short stories probe the political, social, and moral status of black people, but because they are saturated with their authentic language, sensibilities, values, rituals, and myths." Burger continues to state that "against a background of surging and resurging black consciousness and aesthetics, her works capture and reflect the folk spirit in black life, shatter the illusions of history, and demystify sacred areas of Southern life and black experience; she liberates, therefore, the feelings, mind, and spirit of her readers and audiences."

BIOGRAPHICAL/CRITICAL SOURCES:

BOOKS

Dictionary of Literary Biography, Volume 41: *Afro-American Poets Since 1955*, Gale, 1985.

PERIODICALS

Los Angeles Times Book Review, May 22, 1988.

*   *   *

FIGUEROA, John
  See FIGUEROA, John J(oseph Maria)

*   *   *

FIGUEROA, John J(oseph Maria)   1920-
(John Figueroa)

PERSONAL: Born August 4, 1920, in Kingston, Jamaica; immigrated to England, 1979, dual British and Jamaican citizenship; son of Rupert Aston (an insurance salesman) and Isclena (a teacher; maiden name, Palomino) Figueroa; married Dorothy Grace Murray Alexander (a teacher and author), August 3, 1944; children: Dorothy Anna Jarvis, Catherine, J. Peter, Robert P. D., Mark F. E., Esther M., Thomas Theodore (deceased). *Education:* College of the Holy Cross, A.B. (cum laude), 1942; University of London, teachers diploma, 1947, M.A., 1950; graduate study at University of Indiana—Bloomington, 1964. *Religion:* Catholic.

ADDRESSES: Home—77 Station Rd., Woburn Sands, Buckinghamshire MK17 8SH, England.

CAREER: Water Commission, Kingston, Jamaica, clerk, 1937-38; teacher at secondary schools in Jamaica, 1942-46, and London, England, 1946-48; University of London, Institute of Education, London, lecturer in English and philosophy, 1948-53; University College of the West Indies, Kingston, senior lecturer, 1953-57, professor of education, 1957-73, dean of faculty of education, 1966-69; University of Puerto Rico, Rio Piedras and Cayey, professor of English and consultant to the president, 1971-73; El Centro Caribeno de Estudios Postgraduados, Carolina, Puerto Rico, professor of humanities and consultant in community education, 1973-76; University of Jos, Jos, Nigeria, professor of education and acting dean, 1976-80; Bradford College, Yorkshire, England, visiting professor of humanities and consultant in multicultural education, 1980; Open University, Milton Keynes, England, member of Third World Studies Course Team, 1980-83; Manchester Education Authority, Manchester, England, adviser on multicultural studies, West Indian language and literature, and Caribbean heritage students, 1983-85; fellow at Warwick University's Center of Caribbean studies, 1988. British Broadcasting Corporation, London, sports reporter and general broadcaster for programs including "Reflections" and poetry readings, 1946-60. Consultant to Ford and Carnegie foundations; consultant to Organization of American States and to West Indian governments. External examiner, Africa and West Indies. Has lectured and read his poetry in Africa, Canada, Europe, South America, the United Kingdom, and the United States.

MEMBER: Linguistic Society of America, Caribbean Studies Association, Society for the Study of Caribbean Affairs, Athenaeum Club.

AWARDS, HONORS: British Council fellowship, 1946-47; L.H.D. from College of the Holy Cross, 1960; Carnegie fellowship, 1960; Guggenheim fellowship, 1964; Lilly Foundation grant, 1973; Institute of Jamaica Medal, 1980.

WRITINGS:

Blue Mountain Peak (poetry and prose), Gleaner, 1944.
Love Leaps Here (poetry), privately printed, 1962.
Staffing and Examinations in British Caribbean Secondary Schools: A Report of the Conference of the Caribbean Heads, Evans, c. 1964.
(Editor under name John Figueroa) *Caribbean Voices: An Anthology of West Indian Poetry,* Evans, Volume I: *Dreams and Visions,* 1966, second edition, 1982, Volume II: *The Blue Horizons,* 1970; published in one volume, Evans, 1971, Luce, 1973.
Society, Schools, and Progress in the West Indies, Pergamon, 1971.
(Author of introduction) Edgar Mittelhoelzer, *A Morning at the Office,* Heinemann, 1974.

(Under name John Figueroa) *Ignoring Hurts: Poems* (includes "Cosmopolitan Pig" and "The Grave Digger"), introduction by Frank Getlein, Three Continents Press, 1976.
(Editor and author of introduction under name John Figueroa) Sonny Oti, *Dreams and Realities: Six One-Act Comedies,* J. West, 1978.
(Editor with Donald E. Herdeck and others) *Caribbean Writers,* Three Continents, 1979.
(Editor) *An Anthology of African and Caribbean Writing in English,* Heinemann, 1982.
(Editor under name John Figueroa) *Third World Studies: Caribbean Sampler,* Open University Press, 1983.

Screenwriter with Ed Milner of film, "St. Lucia: Peoples and Celebrations," for British Broadcasting Corporation. Translator of works by Horace. Contributor to *Whose Language?* 1985, and *The Caribbean in Europe,* Cass, 1986; contributor to periodicals, including *Commonweal, Dorenkamp, London Magazine, Universities Quarterly, Caribbean Studies, Cross Currents,* and *Caribbean Quarterly.* General editor of "Caribbean Writers" series for Heinemann. Editor of recording *Poets of the West Indies Reading Their Own Works,* Caedmon, 1972.

WORK IN PROGRESS: Articles on the role of London as a magnet for West Indian and other colonial writers in the 1940s and 1950s and on the attitude toward slavery expressed in *Tom Cringle's Log;* memoirs.

SIDELIGHTS: West Indian poet and scholar John J. Figueroa is known for his original verse, the anthologies he has edited, and his critical and academic writings. He draws on classical literature, such as the poetry of Virgil and Horace, as well as on the rhythms of Jamaican speech and calypso music for his poems, which at their best are regarded as sensual, spiritual, and unusually well crafted. His nonfiction writings reflect more than forty years of commitment to the academic field.

Figueroa commented: "It has been good to have grown up with and to have been part of the development and flowering of Caribbean literature, painting, and music. But it is a pity that there is so little appreciation of the *variety* as well as the achievement in these fields. People are much too quick to look for something they call identity, and to disown anyone who does not abjectly follow the tribe on the grounds that right or wrong doesn't matter—all that matters is whether it's 'one of us' who is involved.

"I have also been very lucky to have traveled and lived among various peoples in Africa, Europe, and the Americas, and to have seen the kinds of space explorations which have not, alas, made it clearer to dwellers on the Earth that caring for one's neighbor is not 'other worldly' but an imperative for life, and for living more abundantly."

AVOCATIONAL INTERESTS: Travel, Creole linguistics, cricket, Caribbean studies, music, painting, and lay theology and liturgy.

BIOGRAPHICAL/CRITICAL SOURCES:

PERIODICALS

Times Literary Supplement, January 28, 1972.
World Literature Today, spring, 1977.

*   *   *

FISHER, Rudolph 1897-1934

PERSONAL: Born May 9, 1897, in Washington, D.C.; died

of a chronic intestinal ailment, December 26, 1934. *Education:* Brown University, B.A. (with honors), 1919, M.A., 1920; Howard University, earned degree (summa cum laude); further study at Columbia University.

ADDRESSES: Home—New York, N.Y.

CAREER: Physician and writer. Roentgenologist with Department of Health in New York, N.Y.; teacher.

MEMBER: Phi Beta Kappa, Sigma Psi, Delta Sigma Rho.

AWARDS, HONORS: Spingarn Prize, 1925, for "High Yaller."

WRITINGS:

NOVELS

The Walls of Jericho, Knopf, 1928, reprinted with preface by William Robinson, Jr., Arno Press/New York Times, 1969.
The Conjure-Man Dies: A Mystery Tale of Dark Harlem, Covici, Friede, 1932, reprinted with introduction by Stanley Ellin, Arno Press/New York Times, 1971 (also see below).

SHORT STORIES

"The City of Refuge" in *Atlantic Monthly,* February, 1925; anthologized in *American Negro Short Stories,* edited by John Henrik Clark, Hill & Wang, 1966; and in *Black Literature in America,* edited by Houston A. Baker, Jr., McGraw, 1971.
"Ringtail" in *Atlantic Monthly,* May, 1925.
"High Yaller" in two parts in *Crisis,* October, 1925, November, 1925; anthologized in *Cavalcade: Negro American Writing From 1760 to the Present,* edited by Arthur P. Davis and Saunders Redding, Houghton, 1971.
"The Promised Land" in *Atlantic Monthly,* January, 1927.
"The Backslider" in *McClure's,* August, 1927.
"Blades of Steel" in *Atlantic Monthly,* August, 1927; anthologized in *Anthology of American Negro Literature,* edited by Victor F. Calverton, Modern Library, 1929.
"Fire by Night" in *McClure's,* December, 1927.
"Common Meter" in *Baltimore Afro-American,* February, 1930; anthologized in *Best Short Stories by Afro-American Writers,* edited by Nick Aaron Ford and H. L. Faggett, Meador Publishing, 1950; and in *Black Voices: An Anthology of Afro-American Literature,* edited by Abraham Chapman, Mentor Books, 1968.
"Dust" in *Opportunity,* February, 1931.
"Ezekiel" in *Junior Red Cross News,* March, 1932.
"Ezekiel Learns" in *Junior Red Cross News,* February, 1933.
"Guardian of the Law" in *Opportunity,* March, 1933.
"Miss Cynthie" in *Story,* June, 1933; anthologized in *The Best Short Stories by Negro Writers,* edited by Langston Hughes, Little, Brown, 1967; in *Dark Symphony: Negro Literature in America,* edited by James A. Emanuel and Theodore L. Gross, Free Press, 1968; and in *On Being Black: Writings by Afro-Americans From Frederick Douglass to the Present,* edited by Charles T. Davis and Daniel Walden, Fawcett, 1970.
"John Archer's Nose" in *Metropolitan,* January, 1935.

Also author of unpublished stories "Across the Airshaft" and "The Lindy Hop" held at Brown University Archives.

OTHER

"Conjur Man Dies" (play; adapted by Fisher from his novel *The Conjure-Man Dies: A Mystery Tale of Dark Harlem;* also see above), first produced c. 1936.

Contributor of nonfiction to periodicals, including *American Mercury, Survey Graphic Number,* and—with Earl B. McKinley—*Journal of Infectious Diseases.* Contributor of book reviews to *Book League Monthly* and *New York Herald Tribune Books.*

SIDELIGHTS: Rudolph Fisher was among the writers who sparked interest in black literature during the Harlem Renaissance of the 1920s. Within that group, he was notable for addressing the conditions of Harlem blacks and for adopting an incisively satiric approach in depicting that community. For these reasons, Fisher is widely regarded as one of the first writers to provide significant insights into the urban black society, and he is respected for both the realistic and humorous aspects of his short stories and novels. As Leonard J. Deutsch wrote in a 1979 issue of *Phylon:* "Fisher was an insider who scratched deeply. The stories reveal his love for the people of Harlem and the diversity of talents they represent. They also help us to understand the quality of life of Harlem during the Renaissance period."

Unlike the blacks that frequently populated his fiction, Fisher was sophisticated and extensively educated. He was born in Washington, D.C., and received his early education in New York and Rhode Island. He earned both undergraduate and graduate degrees from Brown University, where he distinguished himself for his academic prowess. He subsequently pursued a medical education at Howard University, from which he graduated with further honors, and at Columbia University.

It was during his time in medical school that Fisher published his first story, "The City of Refuge," in the *Atlantic Monthly.* Abjuring the stereotypical portraiture that fellow blacks Claude McKay and Jean Toomer had appropriated from leading white writers, Fisher presented fully developed, sympathetic black characters. In "The City of Refuge" he recounted the experiences of King Solomon Gillis, a naive out-of-towner who arrives enthusiastically in Harlem only to find himself exploited by his fellow blacks. This story, which Edward J. O'Brien selected for inclusion in the volume *Best Short Stories of 1925,* readily established Fisher as an iconoclast within the budding Harlem Renaissance.

Fisher quickly followed "The City of Refuge" with three more tales: "High Yaller," "Ringtail," and "The South Lingers On." In "High Yaller" he continued exploring exploitation and antagonism within the black community by focusing on a light-skinned black's predicament among abusive peers. As Arthur P. Davis noted in his volume *From the Dark Tower,* prejudice among blacks was a prevalent theme in Fisher's work. "Fisher . . . does not overplay the issue," Davis observed, "but he does not ignore or sidestep it." In "Ringtail" Fisher mined the same theme, only this time focusing on the abuses endured by a West Indian from Native Americans. A more humorous approach was taken by Fisher in "The South Lingers On," where he depicts Harlem as an extension of the South. Notable among the tale's five vignettes is the concluding portion, in which a transplanted Southern black regresses while attending a tent revival. As Davis noted in *From the Dark Tower,* the character "has not lost as much of his Southern upbringing as he had thought."

The more violent aspects of Harlem life are addressed by Fisher in tales such as "Blades of Steel" and "The Promised Land," both published in 1927. In "Blades of Steel" a gambler named Eight-Ball undoes the unsavory Dirty Cozzens by means of a clever, and grisly, trick with a razor. "The Promised Land," like other Fisher stories, deals with the plight of Southern blacks in the unfamiliar and unfriendly Harlem environs. Here a grandmother vainly attempts to reconcile two grandsons. Her efforts are futile, though, and one fellow eventually kills the other. Writing of "The Promised Land" in his book *Down Home*, Robert A. Bone noted Harlem's destructive effect on the unity of Southern blacks in Fisher's works. "Divisiveness," Bone wrote, "is the price the black community must pay to enter in the promised land."

Fisher's next important work is probably *The Walls of Jericho*, his satiric novel about a wealthy black's shattering experiences in a white portion of New York City. The novel's protagonist is Fred Merrit, a prosperous lawyer who moves into a strictly white neighborhood and consequently finds himself ostracized by both whites and blacks. Merrit, however, delights in distressing whites, and is only distressed by his own fellow blacks' reactions to his move. Unfortunately for Merrit, it is the antagonism he has generated within the black community that eventually undermines his life when a fellow black, hostile to Merrit's actions, torches his home.

The tone of *The Walls of Jericho* is largely satirical, with Fisher mocking aspiring blacks, out-of-towners, and—of course—righteous whites. When *The Walls of Jericho* was first published in 1928, reviewers focused on the work's humorous perspective. A critic for *Crisis* declared that Fisher's novel was "finely worked out with a delicate knowledge of human reactions." The critic added, however, that secondary characters were only "moderately funny" and speculated that Fisher's humor might mask his cynicism. "Perhaps he really laughs at all life and believes nothing," the reviewer considered. More impressed was a critic for the *Times Literary Supplement* who reported that *The Walls of Jericho* was "a sympathetic and extraordinarily impressive account" of black life. The reviewer added that Fisher "holds the reader's attention from the first to last" and that the tale is told "with unfailing and pungent humor."

Fisher followed *The Walls of Jericho* with "Common Meter," which appeared in the *Baltimore Afro-American* in 1930. "Common Meter" tells of two jazz musicians—drumming bandleader Bus Williams, who celebrates his music's strong ties to black culture; and light-skinned trumpeter Fess Baxter, who merely uses jazz as a forum for self-promotion and social climbing. The two musicians are rivals for the affections of a young woman, Jean. At a ballroom show, where the musicians' respective bands are engaged in a contest for "the jazz championship of the world," the loathsome Fess attempts to sabotage Bus's performance by slashing his drums. Jean then realizes that Bus possesses greater integrity and self-awareness, and she rescues his band by leading everyone—musicians and audience—in a foot stomping session that sustains the music's rhythm. Afterwards she rewards Bus with her love and the championship trophy.

In *Down Home*, Bone found "Common Meter" to be Fisher's reminder to fellow blacks of their heritage and rightful pride of achievement. "At bottom," wrote Bone, "Fisher is warning the black community to guard itself against a certain kind of spiritual loss. Don't abandon your ancestral ways when you move to the big city; don't discard the authentic blues idiom for the shallow, trivial, flashy, meretricious values of the urban world." Similarly, Thomas Friedman wrote in *Studies in Black Literature* that "Common Meter" was a superb example of black positivism. He declared: "By fully fifty years, Fisher anticipates the notion of 'Black is beautiful,' and uses the blackness of a man's skin to indicate his goodness. . . . As

such, "Common Meter" is a valuable source for those who look for early indications of the change in Black consciousness and for those who search literature for positive uses of the color black."

In 1932 Fisher published his second novel, *The Conjure-Man Dies*. This quasi-supernatural mystery concerns the efforts of two sleuths—police sergeant Perry Dart and physician John Archer—to fathom the possible demise of N'Gana Frimbo, an African king who indulges in fortune-telling in his capacity as a Harlem psychiatrist. *The Conjure-Man Dies* is remarkable in that it is probably the first American mystery novel entirely populated by black characters. In the *New York Times Book Review*, Isaac Anderson described Fisher's novel as an entertaining and enlightening volume. Anderson cited the work's "lively picture of Harlem" and praised Fisher's skills as a comedic writer. Hugh M. Gloster, in his 1948 volume *Negro Voices in American Fiction*, also noted the novel's humor as well as its strengths as a mystery. He called *The Conjure-Man Dies* "a refreshing creation."

Fisher apparently found great pleasure in recording the antics of sleuths Dart and Archer, and he had intentions of writing at least two more novels featuring the characters. Unfortunately he was able to write the pair in only one more work, the short story "John Archer's Nose," before his untimely death in 1934. The story, appraised by Deutsch in his *Phylon* essay, amusingly details the devastating effect of superstition in the black community. Deutsch deemed the tale "supremely clever and witty."

Of Fisher's last works, the most important is probably "Miss Cynthie," his often-anthologized tale of a grandmother's initial disappointment, and eventual pride, in her grandson's success as a musician. Like many of Fisher's previous tales, "Miss Cynthie" contrasts the values of Southern traditionalists and Northern blacks. Also consistent with Fisher's prior writings, "Miss Cynthie" uses music as a device for exploring these different values. In *Down Home*, Bone called "Miss Cynthie" "the best of Fisher's stories," and he noted that the story constituted an artistic breakthrough for Fisher. "Having given us a gallery of static characters," Bone contended, "he suddenly discovers how to *interiorize* his dramatic conflicts, so that his characters have an opportunity to grow."

"Miss Cynthie" and "John Archer's Nose" proved to be Fisher's last published works. His final writing was an adaptation, for the stage, of *The Conjure-Man Dies*. The play was produced in 1936, four years after Fisher's death. In the ensuing decades, his stature as a key black writer waned. In the early 1960s, however, critical interest in his work was revived, and today he is recognized as a unique and innovative artist.

BIOGRAPHICAL/CRITICAL SOURCES:

BOOKS

Abrahamson, Doris E., *Negro Playwrights in the American Theatre, 1925-1959,* Columbia University Press, 1969.

Bone, Robert A., *Down Home: A History of Afro-American Short Fiction From Its Beginnings to the End of the Harlem Renaissance,* Putnam, 1975.

Bone, Robert A., *The Negro Novel in America,* Yale University Press, 1965.

Bontemps, Arna, editor, *The Harlem Renaissance Remembered,* Dodd, 1972.

Brawley, Benjamin, *The Negro Genius: A New Appraisal of the Achievement of the American Negro in Literature and the Fine Arts,* Biblo & Tannen, 1937.

Brown, Sterling, *The Negro in American Fiction: Negro Poetry and Drama,* Arno Press, 1969.
Dictionary of Literary Biography, Volume 52: *Afro-American Writers From the Harlem Renaissance to 1940,* Gale, 1987.
Emanuel, James A. and Theodore L. Gross, editors, *Dark Symphony: Negro Literature in America,* Free Press, 1968.
Gayle, Addison, Jr., *The Way of the New World: The Black Novel in America,* Anchor Press/Doubleday, 1975.
Gross, Theodore L., *The Heroic Ideal in American Literature,* Free Press, 1971.
Hill, Herbert, editor, *Anger and Beyond,* Harper, 1966.
Huggins, Nathan Irvin, *Harlem Renaissance,* Oxford University Press, 1971.
Littlejohn, David, *Black on White: A Critical Survey of the Writings by Negroes,* Viking, 1966.
Twentieth-Century Literary Criticism, Volume 11, Gale, 1983.

PERIODICALS

Afro-American, August 11, 1928.
Amsterdam News, August 10, 1932.
Cleveland Open Shelf, December, 1928.
Crisis, November, 1928, September, 1932, July 1971.
New York Evening Post, July 30, 1932.
New York Herald Tribune, August 26, 1928, August 14, 1932.
New York Times, March 12, 1936.
New York Times Book Review, July 31, 1932.
Philadelphia Tribune, September 29, 1932.
Phylon, June, 1979.
Pittsburgh Courier, September 24, 1932.
Saturday Review of Literature, September 8, 1928, August 13, 1932.
Spectator, August 25, 1928.
Studies in Black Literature, spring, 1976.
Times Literary Supplement, September 6, 1928.

—*Sketch by Les Stone*

*   *   *

FLEMING, Ray(mond Richard)   1945-

PERSONAL: Born February 27, 1945, in Cleveland, Ohio; son of Theodore Robert and Ethel (Dorsey) Fleming; married Nancy Lu Runge, November 15, 1969; children: John Kenneth, Peter Carlton, Stephen Robert. *Education:* University of Notre Dame, B.A., 1967; attended University of Florence, 1967-68; Harvard University, Ph.D., 1976.

ADDRESSES: Home—710 South Oak, Oxford, Ohio 45056. *Office*—102 Roudebush Hall, Miami University, Oxford, Ohio 45056.

CAREER: U.S. Department of State, Washington, D.C., assistant officer at political desk for Ecuadorean Affairs, summer, 1966; University of Notre Dame, Notre Dame, Ind., instructor in Italian, 1969-72, chairman of Black Studies Committee, 1970; University of California, San Diego, La Jolla, assistant professor of comparative literature, 1973-80; Miami University, Oxford, Ohio, associate professor of Italian and assistant dean of Graduate School, 1980—. Assistant director, Upward Bound program, St. Mary's College, 1968. Consultant to U.S. Foreign Service. Visiting professor of literary theory at Centre Universitaire (Luxembourg), spring, 1984. Member of scholarship committee, American-Scandinavian Society.

MEMBER: Dante Society of America.

AWARDS, HONORS: Fulbright scholar in Italy, 1967-68; Woodrow Wilson fellow in comparative literature, Harvard University, 1968-69; poetry award from Ingram-Merrill Foundation, 1971; Ford Foundation fellowship for black Americans, 1972-73; American Council of Learned Studies fellowship, spring/summer, 1978; Alexander von Humboldt fellow in Germany, 1978-79; fellowship from Northwestern University's School of Criticism and Theory, 1981.

WRITINGS:

Ice and Honey (poems), Dorrance, 1979.
Diplomatic Relations (poems), Lotus Press, 1982.
Keats, Leopardi, and Holderlin: The Poet as Priest of the Absolute, Garland Publishing, 1987.
(Contributor) Spiro Peterson, editor, *International Bibliography of Daniel Defoe Scholarship,* G.K. Hall, in press.

WORK IN PROGRESS: Talking Back to the Moon, poems.

SIDELIGHTS: Ray Fleming remarked: "Much like Tennyson's Ulysses I would like to think that I am apart of all that I have met. My travels to other countries gave me a necessary and liberating exposure that I could never have received in America. The opportunity to live with people in different cultures has made my poetry more global in its settings (thereby revealing the communality of human experience) and more aware of the many voices that a poet must hear if that poetry is to speak to a wide audience.

"My training as a comparatist has enabled me to be at home within the contexts of both European and Afro-American poetry, and my reference seeks to combine those traditions when possible and to point out the contradictory assumptions of these cultures with humor and compassion."

*   *   *

FORBES, Calvin   1945-

PERSONAL: Born May 6, 1945, in Newark, N.J.; son of Jacob and Mary (Short) Forbes. *Education:* Attended New School for Social Research and Rutgers University; Brown University, M.F.A., 1978.

ADDRESSES: Home—Washington, D.C. *Office*—73 Arsdale Terrace, East Orange, N.J. 07018.

CAREER: Emerson College, Boston, Mass., assistant professor of English, 1969-73; Tufts University, Medford, Mass., assistant professor of English, 1973-74, 1975-77; Howard University, Washington, D.C., writer in residence; Washington College, Chestertown, Md., assistant professor of creative writing, 1988-89. Fulbright lecturer in Denmark, France, and England, 1974-75; guest lecturer at University of the West Indies, 1982-83.

MEMBER: Modern Language Association, College Language Association.

AWARDS, HONORS: Breadloaf Writers Conference fellowship in poetry, summer, 1973; summer residency at Yaddo, 1976-77; National Endowment for the Arts fellowship, 1982-83; D.C. Commission on the Arts fellowship, 1984; New Jersey State Council on the Arts fellowship.

WRITINGS:

POETRY

Blue Monday, Wesleyan University Press, 1974.
From the Book of Shine, Burning Deck Press, 1979.

CONTRIBUTOR

Arnold Adoff, editor, *The Poetry of Black America: Anthology of the Twentieth Century,* Harper, 1972.

Abraham Chapman, editor, *New Black Voices,* New American Library, 1972.

X. J. Kennedy, editor, *Messages: A Thematic Anthology of Poetry,* Little, Brown, 1973.

Daryl Hine and Joseph Parisi, editors, *The Poetry Anthology, 1912-1977,* Houghton, 1978.

Frank Stewart and John Unterecker, editors, *Poetry Hawaii: A Contemporary Anthology,* University Press of Hawaii, 1979.

Keith Waldrop and Rosemarie Waldrop, editors, *A Century in Two Decades: A Burning Deck Anthology, 1961-1981,* Burning Deck Press, 1982.

Also contributor to *The Morrow Anthology of Younger American Poets,* 1985.

WORK IN PROGRESS: A novel.

SIDELIGHTS: Poet Calvin Forbes is "one of the prominent black voices to develop out of the 1970s. . . . He communicates a . . . highly moral philosophy as well as the thoughts and emotions of a writer whose artistic ability and vision are still expanding," states *Dictionary of Literary Biography* essayist Robert A. Coles. An important part of the poet's development as a writer were the years he spent hitchhiking around the United States, notes Coles. The poet's early education also included an association with poet Jose Garcia Villa at the New School for Social Research, and intense study of John Donne, Gwendolyn Brooks, and Philip Larkin. Like these poets, Forbes writes in a complex, controlled style.

His subjects vary from the lives of street people to the origin of the artistic impulse, but in all his work, observes Coles, "Forbes is skillful in the way he suggests double, and sometimes, triple layered meanings through tight control over simile and metaphor, both of which spark clear, powerful phrases and images." For an example, writes Joseph Parisi in *Poetry* magazine, one only has to consider the title of Forbes's first volume, *Blue Monday:* "Both in subjects and style the analogy to the bittersweet blues is particularly apt in describing these poems, whose plangent phrases wander as digressive variations sprung out from, around, and back again to their central themes. The pains of, for the most part, love mingle with despair over the dreadful past and for the doubtful future; yet the burnt-out if not consuming feelings following failure aren't vented in rage but released in the tenderness of a sensuous lyrical mode."

BIOGRAPHICAL/CRITICAL SOURCES:

BOOKS

Dictionary of Literary Biography, Volume 41: *Afro-American Poets since 1955,* Gale, 1985.

PERIODICALS

Poetry, July, 1975.

* * *

FORD, Nick Aaron 1904-1982

PERSONAL: Born August 4, 1904, in Ridgeway, S.C.; died July 17, 1982, in Baltimore, Md.; son of Nick A. and Carrie Ford; married Janie Etheridge, September 8, 1927; married Ola Scroggins Tatum (a college teacher), June 4, 1968; chil-dren: (first marriage) Leonard Aaron. *Education:* Benedict College, A.B., 1926; University of Iowa, M.A., 1934, Ph.D., 1945. *Politics:* Democrat. *Religion:* Protestant.

ADDRESSES: Home—919 East 43rd St., Baltimore, Md. 21212. *Office*—Coppin State College, Baltimore, Md. 21216; and Brookings Institution, 1755 Massachusetts Ave., Washington, D.C.

CAREER: Schofield Normal School, Aiken, S.C., principal, 1926-28; Florida Normal and Industrial Institute (now Florida Memorial College), Miami, instructor in English, 1929-36; St. Philips Junior College, San Antonio, Tex., dean of faculty, 1936; Langston University, Langston, Okla., associate professor of English, 1937-44; Morgan State College, Baltimore, Md., professor of English and chairman of department, 1945-73, Alain Locke Professor of Black Studies, 1973-74; Coppin State College, Union Graduate School, Baltimore, professor and director of Center for Minority Students, 1974-82. Member of conference on college composition and communication. Consultant, U.S. Office of Education, 1964-66.

MEMBER: National Council of Teachers of English (member of board of directors, 1964-67), Modern Language Association of America, Association of Departments of English, College English Association (president, 1960-62), Langston Hughes Society, Middle Atlantic Writers Association.

AWARDS, HONORS: Research grant, United States Office of Education, 1964, for studies on improvement of literacy skills of disadvantaged college students; National Endowment for the Humanities grant, 1970-72; Outstanding Service Award, Maryland Council of Teachers of English, 1971, for raising professional standards and improving Language Arts instruction in Maryland; Community Service Award, African Association of Black Studies, 1974; Alumni Award, Benedict College, 1975, for distinguished service; Paul L. Dunbar Memorial Award, 1978; award from National Association for Equal Opportunity in Higher Education, 1981; Distinguished Literary Critics Award, Middle Atlantic Writers Association, 1982.

WRITINGS:

The Contemporary Negro Novel: A Study in Race Relations, Meador Press, 1936.

Songs From the Dark: Original Poems, Meador Press, 1940.

(Editor with H. L. Faggett) *Best Short Stories by Afro-American Writers,* Meador Press, 1950, published as *Baltimore Afro-American: Best Short Stories by Afro-American Writers, 1925-1950,* Kraus Reprint Co., 1977.

(With Waters E. Turpin) *Basic Skills for Better Writing,* Putnam, 1959, 2nd edition, 1962.

(Editor) *Language in Uniform: A Reader on Propaganda,* Odyssey, 1967.

American Culture in Literature, Rand McNally, 1967.

(With Turpin) *Extending Horizons: Selected Readings for Cultural Enrichment,* Random House, 1969.

(Editor) *Black Insights: Significant Literature by Black Americans—1760 to the Present,* Ginn, 1971.

Black Studies: Threat or Challenge?, Kennikat, 1973.

Seeking a Newer World: Memoirs of a Black American Teacher, Todd & Honeywell, 1982.

Contributor to professional journals.

* * *

FORREST, Leon 1937-

PERSONAL: Born January 8, 1937 in Chicago, Ill.; married

Marianne Duncan. *Education:* Attended Wilson Junior College, 1955-56, Roosevelt University, 1957-58, and University of Chicago, 1958-60, 1962-54.

ADDRESSES: Office—Department of African-American Studies, Northwestern University, 633 Clark, Evanston, Ill. 60201.

CAREER: Novelist and playwright. Managing editor, *Woodlawn Observer*, 1967-69; *Muhammed Speaks*, associate director, 1969-71, managing editor, 1971-73; Northwestern University, Evanston, Ill., professor of African-American studies, 1973—. Lecturer at Yale University, Rochester Institute of Technology, and Wesleyan University, 1974-79. *Military service:* United States Army, 1960-62.

MEMBER: Authors Guild, Authors League of America, Society of Midland Authors (president, 1981).

AWARDS, HONORS: Grant from Northwestern University, 1975; Sandburg Medallion, Chicago Public Library, 1978; Friends of the Chicago Public Library Carl Sandburg Award, 1985, and Society of Midland Authors Award, 1986, both for *Two Wings to Veil My Face.*

WRITINGS:

There Is a Tree More Ancient Than Eden (novel), introduction by Ralph Ellison, Random House, 1973.
The Bloodworth Orphans (novel), Random House, 1977.
Two Wings to Veil My Face (novel), Random House, 1983.

Also author of an opera libretto commissioned by the Indiana University School of Music, 1980, and a play.

SIDELIGHTS: Leon Forrest's novels reveal his debts to the oral traditions of storytellers and songwriters and the literary traditions of writers such as James Joyce, William Faulkner, and Ralph Ellison. "Like Joyce, like Faulkner, like Ellison, Forrest focuses on a particular people in a particular time and place, and in telling their story, touches universal themes that speak to us all," writes Bernard Rodgers in the *Chicago Tribune Book World.* Like these authors too, Forrest employs a stream of consciousness style, and all three of his novels are interrelated through reappearing characters and structural and stylistic similarities. Of the three, *There Is a Tree More Ancient Than Eden* and *Two Wings to Veil My Face* received the most critical attention.

There Is a Tree More Ancient Than Eden is about the complex relationships between the illegitimate children of an old family who once owned slaves. The book "represents an awe-inspiring fusion of American cultural myth, Black American history, Black fundamentalist religion, the doctrine and dogma of Catholicism (stations of the Cross and the Precious Blood Cathedral), and an autobiographical recall of days of anxiety and confusion in the city," writes Houston A. Baker, Jr., in *Black World.* Another *Black World* reviewer, Jack Gilbert, notes that "Forrest has woven an hypnotic fabric with words that are part jazz, part blues, part gospel," and likening the work to Ralph Ellison's *Invisible Man,* describes it as equally "moving and forceful in its poetic flow."

Other critics, noting the novel's stream of consciousness style and impending sense of doom, compare the work to Faulkner's writing. *Harvard Advocate* contributor Joel Motley calls the book "a powerful work of literature," and adds that while Forrest does use a Faulknerian style, he makes it into his own to express the "urban black experience." Baker concludes that *A Tree More Ancient Than Eden* "contains insight, streaks of

brilliance, and a finely-formed intelligence that promises further revelations."

In *Two Wings to Veil My Face* Nathaniel Witherspoon, a character from Forrest's first novel, records the life story of Momma Sweetie Reed, a former slave. "As she tells her story, Nathaniel is forced to redefine his own identity, to translate as well as transcribe the meaning of her memories," writes Rodgers. "In the end, the secrets Great-Momma Sweetie reveals to Nathaniel . . . radically alter both their lives."

New York Times Book Review contributor Benjamin DeMott observes that while the novel is at times overwritten and poorly structured, these "defects somehow fail to sink it." He explains: "The reason lies in the quality and complication of the feelings breathing in Sweetie Reed as she labors to teach young black generations the uses of the souls of black folk." Rodgers concludes: "It is a novel . . . that's not for everyone. Just for those who love the excitement of watching a truly unique writer practice his art; for those who can recognize the magic beneath the mundane, as Forrest does; for those who are willing to accept the challenge of a novel that really is extraordinary and unforgettable."

BIOGRAPHICAL/CRITICAL SOURCES:

BOOKS

Contemporary Literary Criticism, Volume 4, Gale, 1975.
Dictionary of Literary Biography, Volume 33: *Afro-American Fiction Writers after 1955*, Gale, 1984.
Lee, A. Robert, *Black Fiction: New Studies in the Afro-American Novel since 1945*, Barnes & Noble, 1980.

PERIODICALS

Black World, January, 1974.
Chicago Tribune Book World, February 5, 1984.
College Language Association Journal, December, 1978.
Harvard Advocate, Volume CVII, number 4, 1974.
Massachusetts Review, winter, 1977.
New Leader, July 9, 1973.
New York Times, June 8, 1973.
New York Times Book Review, May 1, 1977, February 26, 1984.

*   *   *

FORTEN, Charlotte
    See GRIMKE, Charlotte L(ottie) Forten

*   *   *

FRANKLIN, J(ennie) E(lizabeth)   1937-

PERSONAL: Born August 10, 1937, in Houston, Tex.; daughter of Robert (a cook) and Mathie (a maid; maiden name, Randle) Franklin; married Lawrence Siegel, November 12, 1964 (deceased); children: Malika N'zinga. *Education:* University of Texas, B.A., 1964.

ADDRESSES: Home—New York, N.Y. *Agent*—Victoria Lucas Associates, 888 Seventh Ave., Suite 400, New York, N.Y. 10019.

CAREER: Writer; Freedom School, Carthage, Miss., primary school teacher, summer, 1964; Neighborhood House Association, Buffalo, N.Y., youth director, 1964-65; U.S. Office of Economic Opportunity, New York, N.Y., analyst, 1967-68; Herbert H. Lehman College of the City University of New York, New York City, lecturer in education, 1969-75.

MEMBER: Authors League of America, Dramatists Guild, Professional Staff Congress.

AWARDS, HONORS: Media Women Award, 1971; New York Drama Desk Most Promising Playwright Award, 1971, for "Black Girl"; CAPS Award, 1972; Institute for the Arts and Humanities dramatic arts award from Howard University, 1974; Ajabu Children's Theater Annual Award, 1978; Better Boys Foundation Playwrighting Award, 1978; National Endowment on the Arts Creative Writing Fellowship, 1979; Rockefeller Grant, 1980.

WRITINGS:

Black Girl: From Genesis to Revelations (non-fiction; includes playscript), Howard University Press, 1976.

PLAYS

"A First Step to Freedom" (one-act), produced in Harmony, Miss., at Sharon Waite Community Center, 1964.
"The Mau Mau Room" (three-act), produced in New York at Negro Ensemble Company, 1969.
"Black Girl" (two-act), produced Off-Broadway at Theater de Lys, 1971; Dramatists Play Service, 1972.
"The Prodigal Sister" (two-act), produced Off-Broadway at Theatre de Lys, 1976.

Author of unpublished and unproduced plays, including "Another Morning Rising," "The Broussard Bunch," "Christchild," "The Creation," "Cut Out the Lights and Call the Law" (three-act), "The Enemy" (two-act), "Four Women" (one-act), "Fritz Was Here," "Guess What's Coming to Dinner," "The Hand-Me Downs," "The In-Crowd" (one-act), "Liars Die," "MacPilate" (one-act), "Things Our Way" (one-act), "Throw Thunder at This House," "Till the Well Run Dry" (three-act), and "Will the Real South Please Rise"; author of screenplays, "Black Girl," adapted from play of same title, and "If He Has Gun." Also contributor of articles to periodicals.

WORK IN PROGRESS: Split the Adam: Theological Roots of Ontological Engineering, a research on the effects of meta-biological engineering on the human species; Artcentric Education: A Unitive Approach to Learning.

SIDELIGHTS: J. E. Franklin's "Black Girl" ran for an entire season in New York and was the only Off-Broadway production of the 1971-72 season to have a film sale. The story involves the title character Billie Jean, a high-school dropout, who, in spite of being suppressed by both society and her matriarchal family, aspires to become a ballet dancer. Making choices is the underlying theme, which the playwright believes should be at the core of black theatre and the arts. Commented Franklin: "The character of art forms in our culture leaves a strong suggestion of a fundamental theocentric ingredient undergirding American socio-political thought. I would like to pursue an insight that the forces and systems which are at work in our culture spring from theological rather than economic ingredients."

BIOGRAPHICAL/CRITICAL SOURCES:

PERIODICALS

Black Creation, Fall, 1972.
Black World, April, 1972.
New York, August 2, 1971.
New York Times, July 13, 1971.
Time, December 4, 1972.

FRANKLIN, John Hope 1915-

PERSONAL: Born January 2, 1915, in Rentiesville, Okla.; son of Buck Colbert (an attorney; also the first Negro judge to sit in chancery in Oklahoma district court) and Mollie (Parker) Franklin; married Aurelia E. Whittington, June 11, 1940; children: John Whittington. Education: Fisk University, A.B., 1935; Harvard University, A.M., 1936, Ph.D., 1941.

ADDRESSES: Home—208 Pineview Rd., Durham, N.C. 27707. Office—Department of History, Duke University, Durham, N.C. 27708.

CAREER: Fisk University, Nashville, Tenn., instructor in history, 1936-37; St. Augustine's College, Raleigh, N.C., instructor in history, 1938-43; North Carolina College (now North Carolina Central University), Durham, instructor in history, 1943-47; Howard University, Washington, D.C., professor of history, 1947-56; Brooklyn College of the City University of New York, Brooklyn, professor of history and chairman of department, 1956-64; University of Chicago, Chicago, Ill., professor of history, 1964-82, John Matthews Manly Distinguished Service Professor, 1969-82, chairman of history department, 1967-70; Duke University, Durham, James B. Duke Professor of History, 1982-85, professor emeritus, 1985—. Visiting professor at University of California, Harvard University, University of Wisconsin, Cornell University, University of Hawaii, Australia National University, Salzburg (Austria) Seminar, and other institutions; Pitt Professor of American History and Institutions, Cambridge University, 1962-63. Board of Foreign Scholarships, member, 1962-69, chairman, 1966-69. Member of board of trustees, Fisk University, 1947-84, and De Sable Museum, Chicago.

MEMBER: American Historical Association (member of executive council, 1959-62; president, 1979), Organization of American Historians (president, 1975), Association for Study of Negro Life and History, NAACP (member of board of directors, Legal Defense and Education Fund), American Association of University Professors, American Philosophical Society, American Studies Association, Southern Historical Association (life member; president, 1970), Phi Beta Kappa (president, 1973-76), Phi Alpha Theta.

AWARDS, HONORS: Guggenheim fellowships, 1950-51, 1973-74; LL.D. from Morgan State University, 1960, Lincoln University, 1961, Virginia State College, 1961, Hamline University, 1965, Lincoln College, 1965, Fisk University, 1965, Columbia University, 1969, University of Notre Dame, 1970, and Harvard University, 1981; A.M., Cambridge University, 1962; L.H.D., Long Island University, 1964, University of Massachusetts, 1964, and Yale University, 1977; Litt.D., Princeton University, 1972; Clarence L. Holte Literary Award, 1986, for George Washington Williams: A Biography.

WRITINGS:

The Free Negro in North Carolina, 1790-1860, University of North Carolina Press, 1943, reprinted, Russell, 1969.
From Slavery to Freedom: A History of Negro Americans, Knopf, 1947, 6th edition (with Alfred A. Moss, Jr.), 1987.
The Militant South, 1800-1860, Belknap Press, 1956, revised edition, 1970.
Reconstruction after the Civil War, University of Chicago Press, 1961.
The Emancipation Proclamation, Doubleday, 1963.

(With John W. Caughey and Ernest R. May) *Land of the Free: A History of the United States,* Benziger, 1965, teacher's edition, 1971.

(With the editors of Time-Life Books) *Illustrated History of Black Americans,* Time-Life, 1970.

Racial Equality in America, University of Chicago Press, 1976.

A Southern Odyssey: Travelers in the Antebellum North, Louisiana State University Press, 1976.

George Washington Williams: The Massachusetts Years, American Antiquarian, 1983.

George Washington Williams: A Biography, University of Chicago Press, 1985.

EDITOR

The Civil War Diary of J. T. Ayers, Illinois State Historical Society, 1947.

Albion Tourgee, *A Fool's Errand,* Belknap Press, 1961.

T. W. Higginson, *Army Life in a Black Regiment,* Beacon Press, 1962.

Three Negro Classics, Avon, 1965.

(With Isadore Starr) *The Negro in Twentieth Century America: A Reader on the Struggle for Civil Rights,* Vintage Books, 1967.

Color and Race, Houghton, 1968.

W.E.B. Du Bois, *The Suppression of the African Slave Trade,* Louisiana State University Press, 1969.

John R. Lynch, *Reminiscences of an Active Life: The Autobiography of John R. Lynch,* University of Chicago Press, 1970.

Eugene Levy, *James Weldon Johnson: Black Leader, Black Voice,* University of Chicago Press, 1973.

(With August Meier) *Black Leaders of the Twentieth Century,* University of Illinois Press, 1982.

CONTRIBUTOR

Arthur S. Link and Richard Leopold, editors, *Problems in American History,* Prentice-Hall, 1952, 2nd revised edition, 1966.

Rayford W. Logan, editor, *The Negro Thirty Years Afterward,* Howard University Press, 1955.

The Americans: Ways of Life and Thought, Cohen & West, 1956.

Charles Frankel, editor, *Issues in University Education,* Harper, 1959.

Ralph Newman, editor, *Lincoln for the Ages,* Doubleday, 1960.

Charles G. Sellars, Jr., editor, *The Southerner as American,* University of North Carolina Press, 1960.

Abraham Seldin Eisenstadt, editor, *American History: Recent Interpretations,* Crowell, 1962.

Herbert Hill, editor, *Soon One Morning,* Knopf, 1963.

H. V. Hodson, editor, *The Atlantic Future,* Longmans, Green, 1964.

John C. McKinney and Edgar T. Thompson, editors, *The South in Continuity and Change,* Duke University Press, 1965.

John P. Davis, editor, *The American Negro Reference Book,* Prentice-Hall, 1966.

Harold Hyman, editor, *New Frontiers of the American Reconstruction,* University of Illinois Press, 1966.

Kenneth Clark and Talcott Parsons, editors, *The Negro American,* Houghton, 1966.

Daniel J. Boorstin, editor, *The American Primer,* University of Chicago Press, 1966.

C. Vann Woodward, editor, *The Comparative Approach to American History,* Basic Books, 1968.

William Edward Farrison, editor, *William Wells Brown: Author and Reformer,* University of Chicago Press, 1969.

Marcia M. Mathews, *Henry Ossawa Tanner, American Artist,* University of Chicago Press, 1969.

Also contributor to *Crusade for Justice: The Autobiography of Ida B.Wells,* edited by Alfreda M. Duster, 1970.

OTHER

Also author of pamphlets for U.S. Information Service. Contributor of articles to numerous journals and periodicals. Co-editor of series in American history for Crowell and AHM Publishing, 1964—; general editor of "Zenith Book" series on secondary education, Doubleday, 1965—; general editor of "Negro American Biographies and Autobiographies" series, Univeristy of Chicago Press, 1969; editor, with Eisenstadt, of "American History Series," Harlan Davidson, Inc., 1985—. Contributor of articles to numerous journals and periodicals.

WORK IN PROGRESS: A book on runaway slaves; a collection of essays; editing the autobiography of his father, Buck Colbert Franklin.

SIDELIGHTS: Author of the critically acclaimed *George Washington Williams: A Biography,* John Hope Franklin "has long been a leader in the study of Afro-American life," writes Ira Berlin in the *New York Times Book Review.* For over four decades, the distinguished Franklin has pioneered a number of historical studies; included among his books are *Reconstruction after the Civil War, The Emancipation Proclamation,* and *Racial Equality in America,* an examination of the egalitarian principles of America's founding fathers. Furthermore, his general history entitled *From Slavery to Freedom: A History of Negro Americans*—its sixth edition published in 1987—is considered by many to be the standard text on Afro-American history. Franklin's overall contributions to the field of Afro-American history prompted Roy Wilkins in the *New Republic* to remark: "John Hope Franklin is an uncommon historian who has consistently corrected in eloquent language the misrecording of this country's rich heritage."

In 1985, Franklin won recognition for *George Washington Williams: A Biography,* which represents forty years of Franklin's research into the life and achievements of the nineteenth century black historian. "Beginning in 1945 with less than a dozen letters and a hasty reading of Williams' African diary, which has since disappeared," remarks Louis R. Harlan in the *Washington Post Book World,* "Franklin has painstakingly gathered the pieces of evidence from three continents and, like an archaeologist, reconstructed a mosaic that is astonishingly life-like." Soldier, journalist, public speaker, historian—among other roles—the multi-faceted Williams was the author in 1883 of *History of the Negro Race in America from 1619 to 1880,* a two-volume history which represents one of the first scholarly treatments of the black experience in America. "Williams's sources and methods qualify him as a pioneer in the transformation of American historical scholarship from panegyrics to professionalism," Berlin states. "One of the most significant achievements of Mr. Franklin's biography is that it restores Williams to his proper place in the development of an American historiography." Robert A. Hill likewise praises Franklin's illuminating assessment of Williams's achievements: "On the basis of the evidence here presented, it becomes clear that Williams is entitled, by his virtuosity, erudition, and contribution to the fields of history and African protest, to a place among the most notable public figures of

America's Gilded Age, and this in an era truly rich in its profusion of outstanding personalities.''

An aspect of *George Washington Williams* that reviewers found particularly interesting was the insight offered into Franklin's own life as an Afro-American historian. ''Stalking George Washington Williams,'' the title of the book's opening chapter, ''offers a unique view of the historian as detective as well as scholar,'' notes Berlin: ''Beginning in 1945 when the author—who had never taken a course in Afro-American history—first considered writing a general history of black Americans, he sensed the connection between his own pioneering work and that of Williams. Through the next four decades he stalked his subject from Williams's origins in a small Pennsylvania town, across North America, to Mexico, to Europe, to central Africa, to Egypt and finally to England where Williams died. 'George Washington Williams' is thus part autobiography and part general history—a mixture that makes for fascinating and engaging reading.'' James Olney similarly comments in the *Southern Review:* ''The major interest of the book is that the life of John Hope Franklin is fully present in the (re)creation of the life of George Washington Williams, his predcecessor, his forefather, perhaps his alter ego.''

In 1975, thirty years into his study of Williams, Franklin discovered that the historian's burial place was an unmarked grave in a cemetery near the center of Blackpool, England. Accompanied by his wife, two reporters, and a photographer, Franklin laid a wreath at the site—now marked by a tablet that reads, ''George Washington Williams, Afro-American Historian, 1849-1891.''Olney draws a comparison to author Alice Walker's discovery of the unmarked grave of author Zora Neale Hurston, commenting on the particular importance of Franklin's work in Afro-American history: ''Just as Afro-American literary history is a matter of recovering predecessors, of reviving and revising, of crossing and combining ancestral figures, so also Afro-American history, in the person and present moment of John Hope Franklin, devotes itself to recovering and resuscitating the ancestral past and to rescuing its own particular progenitors and predecessors from the obscurity that has been so often their fate in this country.''

AVOCATIONAL INTERESTS: Fishing, growing orchids.

BIOGRAPHICAL/CRITICAL SOURCES:

BOOKS

Franklin, John Hope, *George Washington Williams: A Biography*, University of Chicago Press, 1985.

PERIODICALS

American Historical Review, April, 1962.
Chicago Tribune Book World, November 24, 1985.
Christian Science Monitor, September 22, 1947.
Commonweal, July 16, 1943, October 31, 1947, March 8, 1963.
Journal of American History, September, 1986.
New Republic, January 22, 1977.
New York Herald Tribune Book Review, December 14, 1947, September 23, 1956.
New York Times, October 12, 1947, September 23, 1956.
New York Times Book Review, April 7, 1963, December 10, 1967, November 17, 1985.
Saturday Review, December 22, 1956.
Saturday Review of Literature, June 19, 1943, November 8, 1947.
Southern Review, spring, 1986.

Times Literary Supplement, July 19, 1963.
Washington Post Book World, January 11, 1986, May 25, 1986.
Yale Review, winter, 1957.

*   *   *

FULLER, Charles (H., Jr.)   1939-

PERSONAL: Born March 5, 1939, in Philadelphia, Pa.; son of Charles H. (a printer) and Lillian (Anderson) Fuller. *Education:* Attended Villanova University, 1956-58, and La Salle College, 1965-68.

ADDRESSES: Home—Philadelphia, Pa. *Agent*—Esther Sherman, William Morris Agency, 1350 Avenue of the Americas, New York, N.Y. 10019.

CAREER: Playwright. Co-founder and co-director of Afro-American Arts Theatre, Philadelphia, Pa., 1967-71; writer and director of ''The Black Experience,'' WIP-Radio, Philadelphia, 1970-71.

MEMBER: Dramatists Guild, P.E.N., Writers Guild East.

AWARDS, HONORS: Creative Artist Public Service Award, 1974; Rockefeller Foundation fellow, 1975; National Endowment for the Arts fellow, 1976; Guggenheim fellow, 1977-78; Obie Award from the *Village Voice,* 1981, for ''Zooman and the Sign''; Audelco Award for best writing, 1981, for ''Zooman and the Sign''; Pulitzer Prize in drama, New York Drama Critics award for best American play, Audelco Award for best play, Theatre Club Award for best play, and Outer Circle Critics award for best off-Broadway play, all 1982, all for ''A Soldier's Play''; D.F.A. from La Salle College, 1982, and Villanova University, 1983; Hazelitt Award from Pennsylvania State Council on the Arts, 1984.

WRITINGS:

STAGEPLAYS

''The Village: A Party'' (two-act), first produced in Princeton, N.J., at McCarter Theatre, October, 1968, produced as ''The Perfect Party,'' in New York City at Tambellini's Gate Theatre, March 20, 1969.
''In My Many Names and Days'' (six one-acts), first produced in New York City at Henry Street Settlement, September, 1972.
''The Candidate'' (three-act), first produced in New York City at Henry Street Settlement, April, 1974.
''In the Deepest Part of Sleep'' (two-act), first produced in New York City at St. Marks Playhouse, June 4, 1974.
''First Love'' (one-act), first produced in New York City at Billie Holiday Theatre, June 1974.
''The Lay Out Letter'' (one-act), first produced in Philadelphia, Pa., at Freedom Theatre, spring, 1975.
''The Brownsville Raid'' (three-act), first produced in New York City at the Negro Ensemble Company, December 5, 1976.
''Sparrow in Flight'' (two-act), first produced in New York City at the AMAS Repertory Theatre, November 2, 1978.
Zooman and the Sign (two-act; first produced in New York City at the Negro Ensemble Company, November, 1979), Samuel French, 1981.
A Soldier's Play (two-act; first produced in New York City at the Negro Ensemble Company, November 20, 1981), Samuel French, 1982.

SCREENPLAYS

"A Soldier's Story" (adapted from the stageplay "A Soldier's Play"), Columbia Pictures, 1984.

TELEPLAYS

"Roots, Resistance, and Renaissance" (twelve-week series), WHYY-TV (Philadelphia), 1967.
"The Sky is Gray" ("American Short Story Series"), New York, 1980.

OTHER

Contributor of short stories to anthologies and periodicals, including *Black Dialogue* and *Liberator*. Also contributor of nonfiction to periodicals, including *Liberator*, *Negro Digest*, and *Philly Talk*.

WORK IN PROGRESS: A new play.

SIDELIGHTS: Charles Fuller is, according to Walter Kerr in the *New York Times,* "one of the contemporary American theater's most forceful and original voices." In his plays Fuller explores human relationships, particularly between blacks and whites, in what many critics find realistic, unbiased, and poignant terms. "He's not tendentious; the work isn't agitprop or anything near it," Kerr continued. "Mr. Fuller isn't really interested in special pleading, but in simply and directly—and cuttingly—observing what really does go on in this world of ours after you've brushed the stereotypes away."

Fuller first gained notice as a playwright with Princeton's McCarter Theatre production of "The Village: A Party." The "village" is a community comprised of racially-mixed couples. Life is peaceful in the protective society until its black leader falls in love with a black woman. Fearing their image will suffer from their leader's action, the other couples murder the defector and insist that his white widow marry a black man, thus perpetuating their tradition. Fuller examines integration through his play and intimates that integration often magnifies racial tension.

"Mr. Fuller has written a not-too-fanciful fantasy about racial integration that somberly concludes that it will not at present solve anybody's racial problems," wrote Dan Sullivan in a *New York Times* review of "The Village." "The play's originality and urgency are unquestionable and so is the talent of the playwright." A later production of "The Village," presented as "The Perfect Party," moved critic Lawrence Van Gelder, also writing in the *New York Times,* to applaud Fuller's "smooth, natural dialogue and deft characterization."

Another of Fuller's plays, "The Brownsville Raid," was based on a true incident that occurred in 1906 when an entire U.S. Army regiment was dishonorably discharged because none of the 167 black soldiers comprising the unit would confess to inciting a riot in Brownsville, Texas. Witnsses of the attack gave conflicting accounts of what happened, and no evidence was supplied to indict the men, but nevertheless they were released from service. Sixty-six years later the Army cleared the men's records, calling their discharge "a gross injustice." "Though it is Fuller's intention to condemn this incident for the disgrace it was," noted Martin Gottfried in the *New York Post,* "his play is no mere tract. His white characters are not caricatures, his black soldiers are not made to be aware ahead of their times." Gottfried found the play "engrossing, unusual, and strong," while *Village Voice* critic Julius Novick thought the story "a bit dull," but nevertheless deemed "The Brownsville Raid" "scrupulous dramatically as well as ideologically," and "clear" and "methodical."

With his play "Zooman and the Sign", Fuller won an Obie and proved to critic Gerald Weales, writing in the *Georgia Review,* that he is "an obviously talented playwright, ambitious in his attempt to deal with difficult and complex themes." "Zooman" is set in a decaying neighborhood in Philadelphia where a young girl was shot to death while playing jacks on her front porch. The child is dead when the play opens, but the grief of her family, the ambivalence of her neighbors, and the cocky, self-justifying attitude of her teen-aged murderer are demonstrated as the play progresses. "The play never quite succeeds in the ambitious terms in which it is conceived," Weales opined, "but its aspirations and its incidental strengths make it far more fascinating than many a neater, smaller play." In the *Los Angeles Times,* critic Don Shirley deemed "Zooman" "a rarity. Its story is simply but not simplistically told, and it examines vital urban issues with urgency but without hysteria."

In 1982 Fuller became the second black playwright to win the Pulitzer Prize for drama. His prizewinner, "A Soldier's Play," is set at an army base in Louisiana during World War II. The drama opens with the murder of black Technical Sergeant Vernon Waters, a tough and wrathful man who may have been killed by any one of several people or groups. For instance, Waters refused to play Uncle Tom to his white military superiors or to the white Southern community and the Ku Klux Klan surrounding the base, thus an angry Caucasian individual or group may have been responsible. But Waters was also viewed with disdain by some members of his own race; he often degraded his recruits, calling them "shiftless, lazy niggers" and other derogatory names, and chastised them for making their race look like "fools" to whites; therefore the murderer might be one of his black subordinates. Following Water's murder, the army sends an officer to investigate, an act that is more intended to appease the other black military men than to bring about justice.

To the surprise of the white officers at Fort Neal, the investigating official who arrives is Captain Richard Davenport, the first black officer they have ever seen. As Davenport questions possible suspects, Water's psychotic self-hatred and the damaging effects of racism on his life are revealed, as well as new episodes of racism as a result of Davenport's presence. "Here, as before," wrote Frank Rich in the *New York Times,* "the playwright has a compassion for blacks who might be driven to murder their brothers—because he sees them as victims of a world they haven't made." "Yet he doesn't let anyone off the hook," Rich continued. "Mr. Fuller demands that his black characters find the courage to break out of their suicidal, fratricidal cycle—just as he demands that whites end the injustices that have locked his black characters into the nightmare." In another *New York Times* piece on the drama, Rich wrote: "'A Soldier's Play' seems to me a rock-solid piece of architecture, briskly and economically peopled by dimensional blacks, whites and psychological misfits caught between. The work is tough, taut and fully realized." Walter Kerr suggested in the *New York Times:* "You should make Mr. Fuller's acquaintance. Now."

BIOGRAPHICAL/CRITICAL SOURCES:

BOOKS

Contemporary Literary Criticism, Volume 25, Gale, 1983.

PERIODICALS

Georgia Review, fall, 1981.
Los Angeles Times, August 15, 1982, July 23, 1983, November 6, 1983.
Nation, January 23, 1982.
New Leader, July 12-26, 1982.
Newsweek, December 21, 1981.
New Yorker, December 20, 1976.
New York Post, December 6, 1976.
New York Times, November 13, 1968, March 21, 1969, June 5, 1974, November 8, 1978, November 17, 1981, November 27, 1981, December 6, 1981, December 27, 1981, January 10, 1982, January 11, 1982, March 24, 1982, April 13, 1982.
Time, January 18, 1982.
Village Voice, December 20, 1976.
Washington Post, October 26, 1983, October 28, 1983.

*   *   *

FULLER, Hoyt (William)   1927-1981
(William Barrow)

PERSONAL: Born September 10, 1927, in Atlanta, Ga.; died of a heart attack, May 11, 1981, in Atlanta; son of Thomas and Lillie Beatrice Ellafair (a housewife; maiden name, Thomas) Fuller; married; children: James Harold, Robert, Hoyt William. *Education:* Wayne State University, B.A., 1950, graduate study, 1950-51. *Politics:* Independent.

ADDRESSES: Home—Atlanta, Ga. *Agent*—Bertha Klausner, 71 Park Ave., New York, N.Y. 10016.

CAREER: Detroit Tribune, Detroit, reporter, 1949-51; *Michigan Chronicle,* Detroit, feature editor, 1951-54; *Ebony,* Chicago, associate editor, 1954-57; *Haagse Post,* Amsterdam, Holland, West African correspondent, 1957-60; *Collier's Encyclopedia,* New York, N.Y., assistant editor, 1960-61; *Black World* (formerly *Negro Digest),* Chicago, executive editor, 1961-76; editor of *First World,* c. 1976-81. Teacher of Afro-American literature at Northwestern University, 1969-70, Indiana University, 1970-71, and Wayne State University, 1974. North American zone vice-chairman of World Black and African Festival of Arts and Culture, 1972-77. *Military service:* U.S. Army; private first class.

MEMBER: Organization of Black American Culture (founder, 1967).

AWARDS, HONORS: John Hay Whitney Opportunity fellowship, 1965-66; Kuumba Liberation Award, 1972; African Heritage Studies Association Award, 1975; Broadside Press Award, 1975; Doctor of Determination Award, University of Michigan Center for Afro-American and African Studies, 1976.

WRITINGS:

Journey to Africa, Third World Press, 1971.

Work represented in anthologies, including *American Negro Short Stories,* edited by John Henrik Clarke, Hill & Wang, 1966; *Beyond the Angry Black,* edited by John A. Williams, Cooper Square, 1966; *Black Expression: Essays in the Creative Arts by and about Black Americans,* edited by Addison Gayle, Jr., Weybright & Talley, 1969; *The Black Aesthetic,* edited by Gayle, Doubleday, 1971; *Black Literature in America,* edited by Houston Baker, McGraw, 1971; *Points of Departure,* edited by Ernece Kelly, Wiley, 1972; *The Black American Writer,* edited by C. W. E. Bigsby, New York University Press, 1972; and *Afro-American Writing,* edited by Richard Long and Eugenia Collier.

Contributor to *Collier's Encyclopedia Yearbook* and to magazines and newspapers, sometimes under pseudonym William Barrow, including *New Yorker, North American Review, New Republic, Christian Science Monitor, New York Times Book Review.*

WORK IN PROGRESS: At the time of his death Fuller was working on a novel, *An Hour of Breath,* and nonfiction works, *History and Analysis of Black Aesthetic Movement,* and *The New Black Renaissance,* about the black literacy movement of the 1960s and 1970s.

OBITUARIES:

PERIODICALS

Newsweek, May 25, 1981.
New York Times, May 13, 1981.
Time, May 25, 1981.

G

GAINES, Ernest J(ames) 1933-

PERSONAL: Born January 15, 1933, in Oscar, La. (some sources cite River Lake Plantation, near New Roads, Pointe Coupee Parish, La.); son of Manuel (a laborer) and Adrienne J. (Colar) Gaines. *Education:* Attended Vallejo Junior College; San Francisco State College (now University), B.A., 1957; graduate study at Stanford University, 1958-59.

ADDRESSES: Office—Department of English, University of Southwestern Louisiana, East University Ave., Lafayette, La. 70504. *Agent*—JCA Literary Agency, Inc., 242 West 27th St., New York, N.Y. 10001.

CAREER: "Writing, five hours a day, five days a week." Denison University, Granville, Ohio, writer in residence, 1971; Stanford University, Stanford, Calif., writer in residence, 1981; University of Southwestern Louisiana, Lafayette, professor of English and writer in residence, 1983—. Whittier College, visiting professor, 1983, and writer in residence, 1986. *Military service:* U.S. Army, 1953-55.

AWARDS, HONORS: Wallace Stegner Fellow, Stanford University, 1957; Joseph Henry Jackson Award, San Francisco Foundation, 1959, for "Comeback" (short story); award from National Endowment for the Arts, 1967; Rockefeller grant, 1970; Guggenheim fellowship, 1971; award from Black Academy of Arts and Letters, 1972; fiction gold medal, Commonwealth Club of California, 1972, for *The Autobiography of Miss Jane Pittman,* and 1984, for *A Gathering of Old Men;* award from Louisiana Library Association, 1972; honorary doctorate of letters, Denison University, 1980, Brown University, 1985, Bard College, 1985, and Louisiana State University, 1987; award for excellence of achievement in literature, San Francisco Arts Commission, 1983; D.H.L., Whittier College, 1986; literary award from American Academy and Institute of Arts and Letters, 1987.

WRITINGS:

FICTION

Catherine Carmier (novel), Atheneum, 1964.
Of Love and Dust (novel), Dial, 1967.
Bloodline (short stories; also see below), Dial, 1968.
A Long Day in November (story originally published in *Bloodline*), Dial, 1971.
The Autobiography of Miss Jane Pittman (novel), Dial, 1971.

In My Father's House (novel), Knopf, 1978.
A Gathering of Old Men (novel), Knopf, 1983.

Contributor of stories to anthologies and periodicals.

SIDELIGHTS: The fiction of Ernest J. Gaines, including his 1971 novel *The Autobiography of Miss Jane Pittman,* is deeply rooted in the black culture and storytelling traditions of rural Louisiana where the author was born and raised. His stories have been noted for their convincing characters and powerful themes presented within authentic—often folk-like—narratives that tap into the complex world of Southern rural life. Gaines depicts the strength and dignity of his black characters in the face of numerous struggles: the dehumanizing and destructive effects of racism; the breakdown in personal relationships as a result of social pressures; the choice between secured traditions and the sometimes radical measures necessary to bring about social change. Although the issues presented in Gaines's fiction are serious and often disturbing, "this is not hot-and-breathless, burn-baby-burn writing," Melvin Maddocks points out in *Time;* rather, it is the work of "a patient artist, a patient man." Expounding on Gaines's rural heritage, Maddocks continues: "[Gaines] sets down a story as if he were planting, spreading the roots deep, wide and firm. His stories grow organically, at their own rhythm. When they ripen at last, they do so inevitably, arriving at a climax with the absolute rightness of a folk tale." Larry McMurtry in the *New York Times Book Review* adds that as "a swimmer cannot influence the flow of a river, . . . the characters of Ernest Gaines . . . are propelled by a prose that is serene, considered and unexcited." Jerry H. Bryant in the *Iowa Review* writes that Gaines's fiction "contains the austere dignity and simplicity of ancient epic, a concern with man's most powerful emotions and the actions that arise from those emotions, and an artistic intuition that carefully keeps such passions and behavior under fictive control. Gaines may be one of our most naturally gifted story-tellers."

Gaines's boyhood experiences growing up on a Louisiana plantation provide many of the impressions upon which his stories are based. Particularly important, he told Paul Disruisseaux in the *New York Times Book Review,* were "working in the fields, going fishing in the swamps with the older people, and, especially, listening to the people who came to my aunt's house, the aunt who raised me." Although Gaines moved to California at the age of fifteen and subsequently went to college there, his fiction has been based in an imaginary Louisiana plantation region named Bayonne, which a number of critics have compared to William Faulkner's Yoknapatawpha County. Gaines has acknowledged looking to Faulkner, in addition to Ernest Hemingway, for language and to French writers such as Gustave Flaubert and Guy de Maupassant for style. A perhaps greater influence, however, has been 19th-century Russian authors. In a profile by Beverly Beyette for the *Los Angeles Times,* Gaines explains that reading the works of authors such as Nikolai Gogol, Ivan Turgenev, and Anton Chekhov helped unlock the significance of his rural past. ''I found something that I had not truly found in American writers,'' he told Beyette. ''They [the Russian writers] dealt with peasantry differently. . . . I did not particularly find what I was looking for in the Southern writers. When they came to describing my own people, they did not do it the way that I knew my people to be. The Russians were not talking about my people, but about a peasantry for which they seemed to show such feeling. Reading them, I could find a way to write about my own people.'' That Gaines knew a different South from the one he read about in books also provided an incentive to write. ''If the book you want doesn't exist, you try to make it exist,'' he told Joseph McLellan in the *Washington Post.* Gaines later told Beyette: ''That's the book that influenced me most. . . . I tried to put it there on that shelf, and I'm still trying to do that.''

Gaines's first novel, *Catherine Carmier,* is ''an apprentice work more interesting for what it anticipates than for its accomplishments,'' notes William E. Grant in the *Dictionary of Literary Biography.* The novel chronicles the story of a young black man, Jackson Bradley, who returns to Bayonne after completing his education in California. Jackson falls in love with Catherine, the daughter of a Creole sharecropper who refuses to let members of his family associate with anyone darker than themselves, believing Creoles racially and socially superior. The novel portrays numerous clashes of loyalty: Catherine torn between her love for Jackson and love for her father; Jackson caught between a bond to the community he grew up in and the experience and knowledge he has gained in the outside world. ''Both Catherine and Jackson are immobilized by the pressures of [the] rural community,'' writes Keith E. Byermann in the *Dictionary of Literary Biography,* which produces ''twin themes of isolation and paralysis [that] give the novel an existential quality. Characters must face an unfriendly world without guidance and must make crucial choices about their lives.'' The characters in *Catherine Carmier*—as in much of Gaines's fiction—are faced with struggles that test the conviction of personal beliefs. Winifred L. Stoelting in *CLA Journal* explains that Gaines is concerned more ''with how they [his characters] handle their decisions than with the rightness of their decisions—more often than not predetermined by social changes over which the single individual has little control.''

Gaines sets *Catherine Carmier* in the time of the Civil Rights movement, yet avoids making it a primary force in the novel. Grant comments on this aspect: ''In divorcing his tale from contemporary events, Gaines declares his independence from the political and social purposes of much contemporary black writing. Instead, he elects to concentrate upon those fundamental human passions and conflicts which transcend the merely social level of human existence.'' Grant finds Gaines ''admirable'' for doing this, yet also believes Jackson's credibility marred because he remains aloof from contemporary events. For Grant, the novel ''seems to float outside time and place

rather than being solidly anchored in the real world of the modern South.'' Byerman concurs, stating that the novel ''is not entirely successful in presenting its major characters and their motivations.'' Nonetheless, he points out that in *Catherine Carmier,* ''Gaines does begin to create a sense of the black community and its perceptions of the world around it. Shared ways of speaking, thinking, and relating to the dominant white society are shown through a number of minor characters.''

Gaines's next novel, *Of Love and Dust,* is also a story of forbidden romance, and, as in *Catherine Carmier,* a ''new world of expanding human relationships erodes the old world of love for the land and the acceptance of social and economic stratification,'' writes Stoelting. *Of Love and Dust* is the story of Marcus Payne, a young black man bonded out of prison by a white landowner and placed under the supervision of a Cajun overseer, Sidney Bonbon. Possessed of a rebellious and hostile nature, Marcus is a threat to Bonbon, who in turn does all that he can to break the young man's spirit. In an effort to strike back, Marcus pays special attention to the overseer's wife; the two fall in love and plot to run away. The novel ends with a violent confrontation between the two men, in which Marcus is killed. After the killing, Bonbon claims that to spare Marcus would have meant his own death at the hands of other Cajuns. Grant notes a similarity between *Of Love and Dust* and *Catherine Carmier* in that the characters are ''caught up in a decadent social and economic system that determines their every action and limits their possibilities.'' Similarly, the two novels are marked by a ''social determinism [which] shapes the lives of all the characters, making them pawns in a mechanistic world order rather than free agents.''

Of Love and Dust demonstrates Gaines's development as a novelist, offering a clearer view of the themes and characters that dominate his later work. Stoelting writes that ''in a more contemporary setting, the novel . . . continues Gaines's search for human dignity, and when that is lacking, acknowledges the salvation of pride,'' adding that ''the characters themselves grow into a deeper awareness than those of [his] first novel. More sharply drawn . . . [they] are more decisive in their actions.'' Byerman writes that the novel ''more clearly condemns the economic, social, and racial system of the South for the problems faced by its characters.'' Likewise, the first-person narrator in the novel—a co-worker of Marcus—''both speaks in the idiom of the place and time and instinctively asserts the values of the black community.''

Gaines turns to a first-person narrator again in his next novel *The Autobiography of Miss Jane Pittman,* which many consider to be his masterwork. Miss Jane Pittman—well over one hundred years old—relates a personal history that spans the time from the Civil War and slavery up through the Civil Rights movement of the 1960s. ''To travel with Miss Pittman from adolescence to old age is to embark upon a historic journey, one staked out in the format of the novel,'' writes Addison Gayle, Jr., in *The Way of the World: The Black Novel in America.* ''Never mind that Miss Jane Pittman is fictitious, and that her 'autobiography,' offered up in the form of taped reminiscences, is artifice,'' adds Josh Greenfield in *Life,* ''the effect is stunning.'' Gaines's gift for drawing convincing characters reaches a peak in *The Autobiography of Miss Jane Pittman.* ''His is not . . . an 'art' narrative, but an authentic narrative by an authentic ex-slave, authentic even though both are Gaines's inventions,'' Bryant comments. ''So successful is he in *becoming* Miss Jane Pittman, that when we talk about her story, we do not think of Gaines as her creator, but as her recording editor."

The character of Jane Pittman could be called an embodiment of the black experience in America. "Though Jane is the dominant personality of the narrative—observer and commentator upon history, as well as participant—in her odyssey is symbolized the odyssey of a race of people; through her eyes is revealed the grandeur of a people's journey through history," writes Gayle. "The central metaphor of the novel concerns this journey: Jane and her people, as they come together in the historic march toward dignity and freedom in Sampson, symbolize a people's march through history, breaking old patterns, though sometimes slowly, as they do." The important historical backdrop to Jane's narrative—slavery, Reconstruction, the Civil Rights movement, segregation—does not compromise, however, the detailed account of an individual. "Jane captures the experiences of those millions of illiterate blacks who never had a chance to tell their own stories," Byerman explains. "By focusing on the particular yet typical events of a small part of Louisiana, those lives are given a concreteness and specificity not possible in more general histories."

In his fourth novel, *In My Father's House*, Gaines focuses on a theme which appears in varying degrees throughout his fiction: the alienation between fathers and sons. As the author told Desruisseaux: "In my books there always seems to be fathers and sons searching for each other. That's a theme I've worked with since I started writing. Even when the father was not in the story. I've dealt with his absence and its effects on his children. And that is the theme of this book." *In My Father's House* tells of a prominent civil rights leader and reverend (Phillip Martin) who, at the peak of his career, is confronted with a troubled young man named Robert X. Although Robert's identity is initially a mystery, eventually he is revealed to be one of three offspring from a love affair the reverend had in an earlier, wilder life. Martin hasn't seen or attempted to locate his family for more than twenty years. Robert arrives to confront and kill the father whose neglect he sees as responsible for the family's disintegration: his sister has been raped, his brother imprisoned for the murder of her attacker, and his mother reduced to poverty, living alone. Although the son's intent to kill his father is never carried out, the reverend is forced "to undergo a long and painful odyssey through his own past and the labyrinthine streets of Baton Rouge to learn what really happened to his first family," writes William Burke in the *Dictionary of Literary Biography Yearbook*. McMurtry notes that as the book traces the lost family, "we have revealed to us an individual, a marriage, a community and a region, but with such an unobtrusive marshaling of detail that we never lose sight of the book's central thematic concern: the profoundly destructive consequences of the breakdown of parentage, of a father's abandonment of his children and the terrible and irrevocable consequences of such an abandonment."

Burke writes that *In My Father's House* presents the particular problem of manhood for the black male, which he notes as a recurring theme in Gaines's fiction: "Phillip Martin's failure to keep his first family whole, to honor his and [his companion's] love by marriage, and the dissipation of the first half of his adult life—these unfortunate events are clearly a consequence of Martin's fear of accepting the responsibilities of black manhood." Burke highlights the accumulated effects of racism on black males, and cites Gaines's comments to Desruisseaux: "You must understand that the blacks who were brought here as slaves were prevented from becoming the men

that they could be. . . . A *man* can speak up, he can do things to protect himself, his home and his family, but the slaves could never do that. If the white said the slave was wrong, he was wrong. . . . So eventually the blacks started stepping over the line, [saying] 'Damn what *you* think I'm supposed to be— I will be what I ought to be. And if I must die to do it, I'll die'. . . . Quite a few of my characters step over that line."

A Gathering of Old Men, Gaines's most recent novel, presents a cast of aging Southern black men who, after a life of subordination and intimidation, make a defiant stand against injustice. Seventeen of them, together with the 30-year-old white heiress of a deteriorating Louisiana plantation, plead guilty to murdering a hostile member (Beau Boutan) of a violent Cajun clan. While a confounded sheriff and vengeful family wait to lynch the black they've decided is guilty, the group members—toting recently fired shotguns—surround the dead man and "confess" their motives. "Each man tells of the accumulated frustrations of his life—raped daughters, jailed sons, public insults, economic exploitation—that serve as sufficient motive for murder," writes Byerman. "Though Beau Boutan is seldom the immediate cause of their anger, he clearly represents the entire white world that has deprived them of their dignity and manhood. The confessions serve as ritual purgings of all the hostility and self-hatred built up over the years." Fifteen or so characters—white, black, and Cajun—advance the story through individual narrations, creating "thereby a range of social values as well as different perspectives on the action," notes Byerman. Reynolds Price writes in the *New York Times Book Review* that the black narrators "are nicely distinguished from one another in rhythm and idiom, in the nature of what they see and report, especially in their specific laments for past passivity in the face of suffering." The accumulated effect, observes Elaine Kendall in the *Los Angeles Times Book Review,* is that the "individual stories coalesce into a single powerful tale of subjugation, exploitation and humiliation at the hands of landowners." Price comments that although "some of them, especially at the beginning, are a little long-winded and repetitive, in the manner of country preachers[,] . . . a patient reader will sense the power of their stories through their dead-level voices, which speak not from the heart of a present fear but from lifetimes of humiliation and social impotence. They are choosing now to take a stand, on ground where they've yielded for centuries—ground that is valuable chiefly through their incessant labor."

Another theme of *A Gathering of Old Men,* according to Ben Forkner in *America,* is "the simple, natural dispossession of old age, of the traditional and well-loved values of the past, the old trades and the old manners, forced to give way to modern times." Sam Cornish writes in the *Christian Science Monitor* that the novel's "characters—both black and white— understand that, before the close of the novel, the new South must confront the old, and all will be irrevocably changed. Gaines portrays a society that will be altered by the deaths of its 'old men,' and so presents an allegory about the passing of the old and birth of the new."

Alice Walker writes in the *New York Times Book Review* that Gaines "claims and revels in the rich heritage of Southern Black people and their customs; the community he feels with them is unmistakable and goes deeper even than pride. . . . Gaines is mellow with historical reflection, supple with wit, relaxed and expansive because he does not equate his people with failure." Gaines has been criticized by some, however, who feel his writing does not more directly focus on problems facing blacks. Gaines responds to Desruissaux that he feels "too many blacks have been writing to tell whites all about 'the problems,' instead of writing something that all people, including their own, could find interesting, could enjoy." Gaines has also remarked that more can be achieved than strictly writing novels of protest. In an interview for *San Francisco*, the author states: "So many of our writers have not read any farther back than [Richard Wright's] *Native Son*. So many of our novels deal only with the great city ghettos; that's all we write about, as if there's nothing else." Gaines continues: "We've only been living in these ghettos for 75 years or so, but the other 300 years—I think this is worth writing about."

MEDIA ADAPTATIONS: "The Autobiography of Miss Jane Pittman," adapted from Gaines's novel, aired on the Columbia Broadcasting System (CBS-TV), January 31, 1974, starring Cicely Tyson in the title role; the special won nine Emmy Awards. "The Sky is Gray," a short story originally published in *Bloodline*, was adapted for public television in 1980. "A Gathering of Old Men," adapted from Gaines's novel, aired on CBS-TV, May 10, 1987, starring Lou Gossett, Jr., and Richard Widmark.

BIOGRAPHICAL/CRITICAL SOURCES:

BOOKS

Authors in the News, Volume I, Gale, 1976.
Bruck, Peter, editor, *The Black American Short Story in the Twentieth Century: A Collection of Critical Essays*, B. R. Gruner (Amsterdam), 1977.
Contemporary Literary Criticism, Gale, Volume 3, 1975, Volume 11, 1979, Volume 18, 1981.
Dictionary of Literary Biography, Gale, Volume 2: *American Novelists since World War II*, 1978, Volume 33: *Afro-American Fiction Writers after 1955*, 1984.
Dictionary of Literary Biography Yearbook: 1980, Gale, 1981.
Gayle, Addison, Jr., *The Way of the New World: The Black Novel in America*, Doubleday, 1975.
Hicks, Jack, *In the Singer's Temple: Prose Fictions of Barthelme, Gaines, Brautigan, Piercy, Kesey, and Kosinski*, University of North Carolina Press, 1981.
O'Brien, John, editor, *Interview with Black Writers*, Liveright, 1973.

PERIODICALS

America, June 2, 1984.
Black American Literature Forum, Volume XI, 1977
Chicago Tribune Book World, October 30, 1983.
Christian Science Monitor, December 2, 1983.
CLA Journal, March, 1971, December, 1975.
Iowa Review, winter, 1972.
Life, April 30, 1971.
Los Angeles Times, March 2, 1983.
Los Angeles Times Book Review, January 1, 1984.
Nation, February 5, 1968, April 5, 1971, January 14, 1984.
Negro Digest, November, 1967, January, 1968, January, 1969.
New Orleans Review, Volume I, 1969, Volume III, 1972.
New Republic, December 26, 1983.
New Statesman, September 2, 1973, February 10, 1984.
Newsweek, June 16, 1969, May 3, 1971.
New Yorker, October 24, 1983.
New York Times, July 20, 1978.
New York Times Book Review, November 19, 1967, May 23, 1971, June 11, 1978, October 30, 1983.
Observer, February 5, 1984.
San Francisco, July, 1974.
Southern Review, Volume X, 1974.

Studies in Short Fiction, summer, 1975.
Time, May 10, 1971, December 27, 1971.
Times Literary Supplement, February 10, 1966, March 16, 1973, April 6, 1984.
Voice Literary Supplement, October, 1983.
Washington Post, January 13, 1976.
Washington Post Book World, June 18, 1978, September 21, 1983.

—*Sketch by Michael E. Mueller*

*   *   *

GARVEY, Marcus (Moziah, Jr.)   1887-1940

PERSONAL: Middle name cited in some sources as Mosiah; born August 17, 1887, in St. Anne's Bay, Jamaica; died after two strokes, June 10, 1940, in London, England; buried at St. Mary's Cemetery, Kensal Green, London, England; son of Marcus Moziah (a stone mason) and Sarah Jane (Richardson) Garvey; married Amy Ashwood (a secretary), December, 1919 (divorced, June 15, 1922); married Amy Jacques (a secretary), July, 1922; children: Marcus Jacques, Julius Winston. *Education:* Attended Birkbeck College (London), 1912.

ADDRESSES: Home—London, England.

CAREER: Activist. Worked as printer's apprentice in Jamaica, c. 1901; foreman at printing company in Kingston, Jamaica, c. 1904; employee at Jamaican government printing office, c. 1910; worked on banana plantations in Costa Rica, c. 1912; printer for *African Times and Orient Review*, c. 1913; lecturer in United States and England; political candidate in Jamaica in 1930s. Founded Universal Negro Improvement Association and African Communities League, both 1914; Black Star Line and Negro Factories Corporation, both 1919; African Orthodox Church, Negro Political Union, and Black Cross Navigation and Trading Company, all 1924. Publisher of *Negro World* in New York, N.Y., 1918-33, and *Black Man* in London, England, 1934.

WRITINGS:

The Philosophy and Opinions of Marcus Garvey; or, Africa for the Africans, edited by wife, Amy Jacques Garvey, Universal Publishing House, Volume 1, 1923, Volume 2, 1925; reprinted, Cass, 1967; with preface by William Loren Katz, Arno Press, Volume 1, 1968, Volume 2, 1969.
The Tragedy of White Injustice (poetry), privately printed, 1927, reprinted, Haskell House, 1972.
Garvey and Garveyism, edited by wife, Amy Jacques Garvey, [Kingston, Jamaica], 1963.
Marcus Garvey and the Vision of Africa, edited by wife, Amy Jacques Garvey, and John H. Clarke, Random House, 1974.
Collected Papers and Documents, edited by E.U. Essien-Udom, Africana Modern Libraries Series, 1974.
(With Lumumba and Malcolm X) *The Black Handbook: 100 and More Quotes by Garvey, Lumumba, and Malcolm X*, edited by Shawna Maglangbayan, Third World Press, 1975.
More Philosophy and Opinions of Marcus Garvey, edited by wife, Amy Jacques Garvey, and E.U. Essien-Udom, Africana Modern Libraries Series, 1977.
The Poetical Works of Marcus Garvey, Majority Press, 1983.
The Marcus Garvey and Universal Negro Improvement Association Papers, edited by Robert A. Hill, University of California Press, Volume 1: *1826-August 1919*, 1983, Volume 2: *August 27, 1919-August 31, 1920*, 1983, Volume 3: *September 1920-August 1921*, 1984, Volume 4:

September 1, 1921-September 2, 1922, 1985, Volume 5: *September 1922-August 1924,* 1987.
Message to the People: The Course of African Philosophy, edited by Tony Martin, Majority Press, 1986.

Also author of *Black Power in America,* edited by wife, Amy Jacques Garvey, 1968.

Contributor to periodicals, including *Africa Times and Orient Review, Black Man, Current History,* and *Negro World.*

SIDELIGHTS: Marcus Garvey was probably the most prominent black-rights champion of his era. As founder of the Universal Negro Improvement Association (UNIA) he led a movement promoting greater unity for blacks throughout the world. This movement, which counted more than eight million followers at its zenith, was the key force in the back-to-Africa cause that influenced black politics and social activism in the second and third decades of the twentieth century. In addition, Garvey promoted black-oriented businesses, notably the Black Star Line of ships for transporting blacks desiring a return to Africa. He also established *Negro World* and *Black Man,* two periodicals for black readers, and he devoted much of his energies to furthering the political union of blacks from all parts of the world. These various ambitions and enterprises rendered Garvey one of the most influential and, in some quarters, notorious blacks, one tirelessly dedicated to sparking greater achievements in black culture.

Garvey was born in 1887 in British-ruled Jamaica. In his youth he read voraciously, but his family's impoverished living circumstances compelled him to end his formal studies and begin working as a printer's apprentice. After moving to the Jamaican capital, Kingston, Garvey became foreman of a printing company. But his employment there ended after he organized a workers' strike for increased wages. He subsequently worked at another printing office, then moved to Costa Rica and briefly labored on a banana plantation. During this period—around 1912—Garvey grew increasingly incensed at the abuse of Jamaicans working abroad. Formal complaint proved futile, and Garvey, who had earlier experienced similar prejudice while leading the failed printers' strike, began doubting the workability of black-white relations.

After leaving Costa Rica, Garvey traveled to London, England, where he made his initial acquaintance with Africans. Among the many blacks he befriended in London was Egyptian nationalist Duse Mohammed Ali, a staunch advocate of African independence. Duse published *African Times and Orient Review,* and he enlisted Garvey's services as a printer for the periodical. While working for Duse's publication Garvey read extensively on African history. He was particularly impressed with J. E. Casely Hayford's *Ethiopia Unbound,* which called for African unity, and with Booker T. Washington's autobiography *Up From Slavery,* in which Washington articulated his rise from slavery to an esteemed rank in American letters. It was the latter work that exerted the most notable influence on Garvey, and after reading it he pledged himself to Ali's cause of African unity.

In 1914 Garvey returned to Jamaica and, with the aid of several friends, formed UNIA and its coordinating body, the African Communities League. The UNIA, which consumed much of Garvey's energies for the next several years, was designed to promote black unity through education and commerce. Garvey's first project with UNIA was the founding of a trades school in Jamaica. But the project, modeled after Booker T. Washington's Tuskegee Institute in Alabama, failed to develop, whereupon Garvey decided to meet with Washington in America and study the institute there.

Unfortunately, Garvey's projected trades school was further set back when Washington died before Garvey could meet him. Garvey thus found himself an outsider without contacts when he finally arrived in New York City in 1916. Undaunted, Garvey eventually befriended American blacks through three years of traveling and speaking before church congregations and community organizations. In 1918 he gained greater access to America's black populace through his weekly newspaper *Negro World,* which regularly featured his own appeals and justifications for a united African state. The following year, encouraged by the sizable readership of *Negro World,* Garvey established UNIA offices in New York City, where UNIA world headquarters quickly gained recognition as the center of the back-to-Africa movement. In addition, UNIA branches were established in several other metropolitan areas with substantial black populations.

By 1920 the UNIA counted impressive membership from around the world. At its first convention, held in New York City's Harlem district at the UNIA's Liberty Hall, approximately 25,000 delegates convened to address black issues. In his speeches Garvey called for greater emphasis on the black perspective in all areas of life. He implied the existence of a black deity and fostered the notion of black—specifically African—aesthetic standards. He also presented a revisionist historical outlook, one recognizing the innumerable, and previously ignored, accomplishments of blacks throughout time. In his most ambitious proposal, Garvey championed the creation of a united black nation. To facilitate the formation of such a state, Garvey had already established the Black Star Line for transporting blacks from the United States. This shipping business was, in turn, only one of several ventures—including a grocery-store chain, a publishing house, and restaurants—intended by Garvey to further black economic independence by serving blacks exclusively.

Garvey's then daring business plans, together with his more ambitious concept of a united black nation, powerfully impressed delegates at the UNIA convention. These delegates eventually founded a quasi-exile government, the Empire of Africa, and declared Garvey its provisional president. Garvey, in turn, appeared in public sporting colorful military regalia while accompanied by the renegade government's other officers—bearing titles such as the Knights of the Nile and the Dukes of the Niger—in similar garb. To further the creation of his exiled state, Garvey negotiated with Liberia's leaders in a vain effort to obtain land for colonization. He also appealed to the League of Nations in a similarly futile attempt to win control of Germany's former colonies in Africa.

But as Garvey's popularity and influence rose among like-minded blacks, so his notoriety grew among individuals, including resentful blacks, who disagreed with him. By 1919 he had already been the target of one assassination attempt, and by 1920 his publication *Negro World* was outlawed in Britain and France. He also met with increasing opposition from some American blacks, notably leaders of the comparably conservative National Association for the Advancement of Colored People (NAACP), which Garvey had rejected as elitist and unsympathetic to the plight of blacks outside the United States. In addition, Garvey outraged many black artists by dismissing the Harlem Renaissance of black arts as a mediocre cultural movement.

By 1921, one year after the UNIA convention, American opposition to Garvey and his organization had grown further. When Garvey attempted to return to the United States after touring Central America, his reentry visa was withheld for four months by the U.S. State Department. When he finally arrived back in the United States, Garvey applied for U.S. citizenship and began modifying his philosophy. But his new proposals only succeeded in further alienating American blacks, many of whom were particularly outraged by his distinctions of racial purity and his bizarre contention that American blacks provoked persecution because of their supposedly mediocre achievements. At this time the UNIA began losing supporters worldwide.

As Garvey's stature suffered, so did the economic stability of his organization. The Black Star Line, which had been sustained by stock sales, had obtained outmoded and unsuitable steamships and was absorbing a disastrous portion of the UNIA's funds. Garvey attempted to avert financial catastrophe by soliciting investors through the U.S. mail. This maneuver caused the demise of Garvey's organization, for American law enforcers, acting on information received from the NAACP, charged Garvey with mail fraud. Serving as his own legal counsel, Garvey attempted to refute the charges in court. An investigation of the UNIA's records, however, disclosed that Garvey had long been financially exploited by his own followers within the organization and by those brokers with whom he had worked on the Black Star Line. Unable to establish his economic credibility, Garvey nonetheless fought the legal charge, seizing his trial as a forum for proclaiming his radical beliefs.

As a result of his unorthodox legal defense, Garvey was unable to refute the mail fraud charge, although testimony and records established that he was an honest, though incompetent, businessman. In addition, his courtroom behavior offended jurors, and he consequently received a fine and a five-year prison sentence, though his codefendants were acquitted. Almost immediately after being sentenced Garvey was free on bail, and the UNIA raised further funds by selling stocks for a second shipping line, the Black Cross Navigation and Trading Company. But adversity continued to plague Garvey. The new shipping line proved another economic liability, and hopes for the back-to-Africa action fell when Liberia withdrew from negotiations with UNIA and arrested the organization's delegates.

In 1925, after the Supreme Court rejected an appeal, Garvey began serving his prison term. His wife and other UNIA officials tried to sustain the organization, and they found continued support from blacks convinced that Garvey was unjustly tried. The organization prospered further when American authorities commuted Garvey's remaining sentence and deported him to Jamaica. There he organized another impressive convention and founded the radical Jamaican Peoples Party, which called for independence from Britain and proposed several pro-black reforms. The world economic Depression, however, was already damaging the Jamaican economy and compelling Jamaican blacks to devote themselves to considerations more immediate than Garvey's ambitious designs. After his political candidacy failed, Garvey left Jamaica in 1935 and resettled in England. He subsequently commenced publication of a modest periodical, *Black Man,* and founded the School of African Philosophy, a mail-correspondence institution. In the late 1930s he organized a series of annual UNIA conventions in Canada. These conventions were only modest gatherings compared to earlier UNIA events, and they served as further indication of Garvey's lessening influence.

Garvey's health also declined at this time. By the late 1930s the asthmatic Garvey had twice endured pneumonia, and in 1940 he became partially paralyzed after a stroke. A second stroke proved fatal that June.

After Garvey's death the UNIA disbanded. Garvey, however, continues to be remembered as an inspirational force in black culture. In the 1960s, with the civil-rights movement and radical black organizations, his thoughts on black aesthetics and black nationalism held considerable relevance, and in a broader context he is respected as a galvanizing leader whose actions prompted greater international awareness of black culture in the first half of the twentieth century.

As a writer, Garvey is represented by several volumes containing works for the periodicals *Negro World* and *Black Man* and for the UNIA. *The Philosophy of Marcus Garvey,* his most prominent publication in his own lifetime, was reprinted in the late 1960s, and his writings for the UNIA have been published in several volumes by the University of California Press since 1983. Of the first two volumes in this series, *New York Times Book Review* critic Eric Foner found much to recommend. He called *The Marcus Garvey and Universal Negro Improvement Association Papers* "important records of the Afro-American experience." The series, Foner concluded, "lays the groundwork for a long overdue reassessment of Marcus Garvey and the legacy of racial pride, nationalism and concern with Africa he bequeathed to today's black community."

BIOGRAPHICAL/CRITICAL SOURCES:

BOOKS

Burkett, Randall K., *Black Redemption: Churchmen Speak for the Garvey Movement,* Temple University Press, 1978.

Cronon, Edmund David, *Black Moses: The Story of Marcus Garvey and the Universal Negro Improvement Association,* foreword by John Hope, University of Wisconsin Press, 1955.

Edwards, Adolph, *Marcus Garvey,* New Beacon, 1967.

Fax, Elton C., *Garvey: The Story of a Pioneer Black Nationalist,* foreword by John Henrik Clarke, Haskell House, 1969.

James, Cyril Lionel Robert, *A History of Pan-African Nationalism,* Dodd, 1972.

Martin, Tony, *Marcus Garvey, Hero,* Majority Press, 1984.

Martin, Tony, *Race First: The Ideological and Organizational Struggles of Marcus Garvey and the Universal Negro Improvement Association,* Greenwood Press, 1976.

Stein, Judith, *The World of Marcus Garvey: Race and Classism in Modern Society,* Louisiana State University Press, 1986.

Vincent, Theodore G., *Black Power and the Garvey Movement,* Ramparts, 1971.

PERIODICALS

Black Scholar, December, 1973.
Current History, September, 1923.
Essence, November, 1986.
Los Angeles Times Book Review, March 25, 1984.
Negro History Bulletin, October, 1962, November, 1974.
New Republic, October 29, 1984.
New York Times Book Review, February 5, 1984.

—*Sketch by Les Stone*

*   *   *

GATES, Henry Louis, Jr.   1950-

PERSONAL: Born September 16, 1950, in Keyser, W.Va.; son of Henry Louis and Pauline Augusta (Coleman) Gates; married Sharon Adams (a potter), September 1, 1979; children: Maude, Elizabeth. *Education:* Yale University, B.A. (summa cum laude), 1973; Clare College, Cambridge, M.A., 1974, Ph.D., 1979.

ADDRESSES: Home—3041 Yale Station, New Haven, Conn. 06520. *Office*—Department of English, Cornell University, Rockefeller Hall, Ithaca, N.Y. 14853. *Agent*—Carl Brandt, Brandt & Brandt Literary Agents, Inc., 1501 Broadway, New York, N.Y. 10036.

CAREER: Anglican Mission Hospital, Kilimatinde, Tanzania, general anesthetist, 1970-71; John D. Rockefeller Gubernatorial Campaign, Charleston, W.Va., director of student affairs, 1971, director of research, 1972; *Time,* London Bureau, London, England, staff correspondent, 1973-75; American Cyanamid Co., Wayne, N.J., public relations representative, 1975; Yale University, New Haven, Conn., lecturer, 1976-79, assistant professor, 1979-84, associate professor of English, 1984-85, director of undergraduate Afro-American studies, beginning 1979; Cornell University, Ithaca, N.Y., professor of English, 1985—, W. E. B. Du Bois Professor of Literature, 1988—. Created television series "The Image of the Black in the Western Imagination" for Public Broadcasting Service, 1982. Consultant to Menil Foundation.

MEMBER: Afro-American Academy (president), African Literature Association, Modern Language Association of America, Union of African Writers, College Language Association, Phi Beta Kappa.

AWARDS, HONORS: Carnegie Foundation fellowship for Africa, 1970-71; Phelps fellowship from Yale University, 1970-71; Mellon fellowship from Yale University, 1973-75, and 1983—; A. Whitney Griswold fellowship, 1980; grants from National Endowment for the Humanities, 1980-84, 1981-82; Rockefeller Foundation fellowship, 1981; MacArthur Prize fellowship from MacArthur Foundation, 1981-86; award from Whitney Humanities Center, 1982-84; Afro-American teaching prize, 1983; Ford Foundation grant, 1984-85; Zora Neale Hurston Society Award for Creative Scholarship, 1986.

WRITINGS:

(Editor and contributor) *Black Is the Color of the Cosmos: Charles T. Davis's Essays on Black Literature and Culture, 1942-1981,* Garland Publishing, 1982.

(Editor with Davis) *The Slave's Narrative: Texts and Contexts,* Oxford University Press, 1983.

(Editor) Harriet E. Wilson, *Our Nig; or, Sketches From the Life of a Free Black,* Random House, 1983.

(Editor) *Black Literature and Literary Theory,* Methuen, 1984.

(Compiler with James Gibb and Ketu H. Katrak) *Wole Soyinka: A Bibliography of Primary and Secondary Sources,* Greenwood Press, 1986.

(Editor) *"Race," Writing, and Difference,* University of Chicago Press, 1986.

Figures in Black: Words, Signs, and the Racial Self, Oxford University Press, 1987.

(Editor) *The Classic Slave Narratives,* New American Library, 1987.

(Editor) *The Schomburg Library of Nineteenth-Century Black Women Writers,* thirty volumes, Oxford University Press, 1987.

(Editor) *In the House of Oshugbo: A Collection of Essays on Wole Soyinka,* Oxford University Press, 1988.

The Signifying Monkey: Towards a Theory of Afro-American Literary Criticism, Oxford University Press, 1988.

(Editor) *Critical Essays on Jean Toomer,* Methuen, in press.

(Editor) *Frederick Douglass: The Author,* Methuen, in press.

CONTRIBUTOR

Herbert Sacks, editor, *The Book of Hurdles,* Atheneum, 1978.

Robert Stepto and Dexter Fisher, editors, *Afro-American Literature: The Reconstruction of Instruction,* Modern Language Association of America, 1979.

William H. Robinson, editor, *Critical Essays on Phyllis Wheatley,* G. K. Hall, 1982.

OTHER

Contributor of articles and reviews to periodicals and journals, including *Critical Inquiry, Black World, Black American Literature Forum, Yale Review, Black World, Antioch Review,* and *New York Times Book Review.* Member of board of editors of *Cultural Critique, American Quarterly, Black American Literature Forum, Studies in American Fiction,* and *Proteus;* member of board of directors of *Diacritics* and *Critical Inquiry.* Advisory editor, *Contributions to African and Afro-American Studies,* and *Studies on Black Life and Culture.*

SIDELIGHTS: Henry Louis Gates, Jr.'s *Black Literature and Literary Theory* is considered by many reviewers to be an important contribution to the study of black literature. According to Reed Way Dasenbrock in *World Literature Today:* "*Black Literature and Literary Theory* is an exciting, important volume. It is a collection of essays . . . that attempts to explore the relevance of contemporary literary theory, especially structuralism and poststructuralism, to African and Afro-American literature. . . . Anyone seriously interested in contemporary critical theory, in Afro-American and African literature, and in black and African studies generally will need to read and absorb this book."

R. G. O'Meally writes in *Choice* that in *Black Literature and Literary Theory* Gates "brings together thirteen superb essays in which the most modern literary theory is applied to black literature of Africa and the U.S. . . . For those interested in [the] crucial issues—and for those interested in fresh and challenging readings of key texts in black literature—this book is indispensable." Finally, Terry Eagleton remarks in the *New York Times Book Review* that "the most thought-provoking contributions to [this] collection are those that not only enrich our understanding of black literary works but in doing so implicitly question the authoritarianism of a literary 'canon.'"

BIOGRAPHICAL/CRITICAL SOURCES:

BOOKS

Dictionary of Literary Biography, Volume 67: *Modern American Critics since 1955,* Gale, 1988.

PERIODICALS

Choice, May, 1985.
New York Times Book Review, December 9, 1984.

Times Literary Supplement, May 17, 1985.
Voice Literary Supplement, June, 1985.
Washington Post Book World, July 3, 1983.
World Literature Today, summer, 1985.

*   *   *

GAYLE, Addison, Jr.   1932-

PERSONAL: Born June 2, 1932, in Newport News, Va.; son of Addison and Carrie (Holloman) Gayle; married Rosalie Norwood (a lecturer), September 12, 1965. *Education:* City College of the City University of New York, B.A., 1964; University of California, Los Angeles, M.A., 1965.

ADDRESSES: Office—Department of English, Bernard M. Baruch College of the City University of New York, 17 Lexington Ave., New York, N.Y. 10010.

CAREER: Porter, Brooklyn Army Base, 1959-60; University of California, Los Angeles, reader for department of English and research assistant, training laboratory animals, 1965-66; City College of the City University of New York, New York City, lecturer in English, 1966-69; Bernard M. Baruch College of the City University of New York, New York City, professor of English, 1969-82, distinguished professor of English, 1982—. Visiting professor of American and Afro-American literature, University of Washington, summer, 1971; assistant professor of creative writing, Rutgers University, 1971-72. Lecturer on black heritage and other subjects for various institutions, including Oberlin College, University of Virginia, Yale University, and University of California, Irvine. Annual donor of Richard Wright-Amiri Baraka Award for best critical essay published in *Black World* magazine; sponsor of the Richard Wright Award for SEEK student with the highest grade point average each semester. Member of presidential committee on student unrest, 1970, Baruch College affirmative action committee, chancellor's committee on prisons and the university, graduate center committee on programs in English, and Black Arts and Cultural Festival committee. Consultant to Minority Writers, Doubleday and Random House.

MEMBER: PEN, Authors Guild, Authors League of America.

WRITINGS:

(Editor) *Black Expression: Essays by and about Black Americans in the Creative Arts,* Weybright & Talley, 1969.
(Editor) *Bondage, Freedom and Beyond: The Prose of Black America,* Doubleday, 1970.
The Black Situation, Horizon, 1970.
(Editor) *The Black Aesthetic,* Doubleday, 1971.
Oak and Ivy: A Biography of Paul Lawrence Dunbar, Doubleday, 1971.
Claude McKay: The Black Poet at War, Broadside Press, 1972.
The Way of the New World: The Black Novel in America, Doubleday, 1975.
Wayward Child: A Personal Odyssey, Anchor Press/Doubleday, 1977.
Richard Wright: Ordeal of a Native Son, Doubleday, 1980.

Contributor of articles and reviews to numerous anthologies, journals, and magazines. Member of editorial staff, *Amistad* magazine, Third World Press, and *Black Lines* magazine; contributing book reviewer, *New York Times,* 1968-70.

SIDELIGHTS: A Southern black who grew up wishing he had "been born mulatto—with light skin, small lips, good hair," Addison Gayle, Jr., learned to overcome his self-loathing,

eventually rejecting the cultural mainstream of American life and embracing his African heritage. He describes this transition in *Wayward Child: A Personal Odyssey.* This autobiography traces Gayle's evolution from negro to black, illuminating the path he followed to his current position in the literary world where he is an outspoken and militant advocate of the Black Aesthetic. He has written in a variety of genres, including literary history, biography, and the personal essay, approaching them all from a black point of view. But his best-known work remains *The Black Aesthetic*—Gayle's diagnosis of white literary criticism and his controversial prescription for a cure.

A novel approach to the study of Afro-American literature, *The Black Aesthetic* is actually a collection of essays by prominent black artists that was compiled, contributed to, and edited by Gayle. While he makes no claim to speak for all the contributors, Gayle sets a combative tone for the book in his introduction, which proclaims that "the serious black artist of today is at war with the American society." Citing quotes by white critics that suggest black artists fall back on anger and rhetoric to mask literary deficiencies, Gayle refutes these assertions by negating the very premise on which they rest—that white aesthetics are a valid basis for judging black art.

Because aesthetics have traditionally been the domain of white poets, philosophers, and critics, Gayle argues that literary standards reflect Caucasian biases. Thus since the time of the ancient Greeks white has been associated with beauty and goodness, black with evil and ugliness. Today, many critics assert that there is no such thing as a white aesthetic and that, as Americans, black writers share with their fellow citizens a common cultural heredity. But, in a scathing indictment of American values, Gayle denies any association with the mainstream culture. "To be an American writer is to be an American," he writes in his introduction, "and, for black people, there should no longer be honor attached to either position." In fact, he maintains that the standards set by white society are irrelevant to black works of art. "A critical methodology has no relevance to the black community unless it aids men in becoming better than they are," he points out. Not only have such elements been lacking in the critical canons handed down by white aestheticians, but, consciously or unconsciously, critics have promoted works that "keep the nigger in his place."

"The question for the black critic today is not how beautiful is a melody, a play, a poem, or a novel," Gayle continues, "but how much more beautiful has the poem, melody, play, or novel made the life of a single black man? How far has the work gone in transforming an American Negro into an African-American or a black man? The Black Aesthetic then . . . is a corrective—a means of helping black people out of the polluted mainstream of Americanism, and offering logical, reasoned arguments as to why he should not desire to join the ranks of a Norman Mailer or a William Styron."

Breaking with the tradition that encouraged black writers to address a white audience, Gayle urges black writers to address their own people, making no attempt to disguise the hostility they feel. A frequent target is the liberal intellectual whose actions reveal his true bigotry. The purpose of such literature, however, is not to convert the liberal, but as Gayle puts it, "to point out to black people the true extent of the control exercised upon them by the American society, in the hope that a process of de-Americanization will occur in every black community in the nation."

The political and sociological implications of Gayle's philosophy have not escaped reviewers. "What these essays show is that the core of the Black Aesthetic is political," writes Jerry H. Bryant in the *Nation*. "And some of its most unequivocal spokesmen are not shy in saying so. In its most extreme form it implies black nationalism and separatism.... The Black Aesthetic is the means by which art accomplishes the political purpose of strengthening the unity between blacks as a people."

While most reviewers endorse the concept of black unity achieved through black literature, several object to Gayle's vision of separatism in art. "A good deal of this irritates me," writes Bryant. "No white man, any more than a black man, likes to be told that the color of his skin automatically disqualifies his insight, his sensibility, his intelligence from rendering valid judgments about a whole art.... Many of the Black Aesthetic proponents in this volume seem to be fighting the clubbiness of the white man with a clubbiness of their own.... Furthermore, there is no specific criticism of any black art in this book demonstrating that reliance on the Black Aesthetic or one's blackness discloses interpretations that can't be got at by honesty, intelligence and earnest and sincere effort." Asks the *New York Times'* Thomas Lask: "Why is not the black experience, repellent, inhuman and destructive as it was, part of the American experience that we all share?" And critic Carolyn F. Gerald raises a similar point in her *Black World* review: "Because we begin to realize that contact with white culture has been tantamount to self-annihilation, it is normal that we would try to withdraw ... or ... refuse to adapt any forms from white culture to our own world view. The problem remains that neither position will lead us toward a more mature aesthetic realization, nor comes to grips with the enormous borrowings that have already taken place back and forth."

Despite their objections, these reviewers recognize the significance of Gayle's contribution. Gerald points out that "without critical forums, such as *The Black Aesthetic,* we will become hopelessly lost in the maze. So we must credit Addison Gayle with a sense of the needs of the time and a talent for doing something about it." Bryant applauds the sense of purpose and set of values that black writers are bringing to American literature at a time when white writers seem aimless and exhausted. And Lask concludes that "in spite of its rancor and scorn and in spite of its attempted putdown, reading it is a buoyant experience. The sense of engagement, of passionate caring runs like fire through the book. It has the feel of life itself."

BIOGRAPHICAL/CRITICAL SOURCES:

BOOKS

Gayle, Addison, Jr., *Wayward Child: A Personal Odyssey,* Anchor Press/Doubleday, 1977.

PERIODICALS

Black World, October, 1971.
Nation, April 24, 1972, April 26, 1975.
New Republic, July 26, 1980.
New York Times, January 23, 1971, September 24, 1977.
New York Times Book Review, September 13, 1970, February 28, 1971, August 3, 1980.
Village Voice, October 29, 1980.
Washington Post Book World, March 30, 1975, August 3, 1980.

GIBSON, Donald B.   1933-

PERSONAL: Born July 2, 1933, in Kansas City, Mo.; son of Oscar J. Gibson (a tailor); married Jo Anne Ivory, December 14, 1963; children: David, Douglas. *Education:* University of Kansas City (now University of Missouri at Kansas City), B.A., 1955, M.A., 1957; Brown University, Ph.D., 1962.

ADDRESSES: Home—Princeton, N.J. *Office*—Department of English, Rutgers University, New Brunswick, N.J.

CAREER: Brown University, Providence, R.I., instructor in English, 1960-61; Wayne State University, Detroit, Mich., assistant professor of English, 1961-67; University of Connecticut, Storrs, associate professor, 1967-69, professor of English, 1969-74; Rutgers University, New Brunswick, N.J., professor of English, 1974—. Member of faculty, Jagiellonian University, Krakow, Poland, 1964-66.

MEMBER: Modern Language Association of America, College English Association.

AWARDS, HONORS: National Endowment for the Humanities award, 1970-71; American Philosophical Society award, 1970.

WRITINGS:

The Fiction of Stephen Crane, Southern Illinois University Press, 1968.
(Editor) *Five Black Writers: Essays on Wright, Ellison, Baldwin, Hughes, and LeRoi Jones,* New York University Press, 1970.
(Editor) *Black and White: Stories of American Life,* Washington Square Press, 1971.
(Editor) *Modern Black Poets: A Collection of Critical Essays,* Prentice-Hall, 1973.
(Editor) *The Politics of Literary Expression: A Study of Major Black Writers* (essays), Greenwood Press, 1981.

Contributor to literary journals.

WORK IN PROGRESS: Individualism and Community in Black History and Fiction.

*   *   *

GIDDINGS, Paula   1948-

PERSONAL: Born in 1948; daughter of a teacher and a school administrator. *Education:* Attended Howard University.

ADDRESSES: Office—Department of Social Science, Spelman College, 350 Spelman Lane, Atlanta, Ga. 30314.

CAREER: Free-lance writer. Served as Paris bureau chief for Encore America and Worldwide News; affiliated with Random House, New York, N.Y.; affiliated with Howard University Press, Washington, D.C.

WRITINGS:

(Contributor) John A. Williams and Charles F. Harris, editors, *Amistad Two,* Howard University Press, 1971.
When and Where I Enter: The Impact of Black Women on Race and Sex in America, Morrow, 1984.

Work represented in anthologies, including *We Speak As Liberators: Young Black Poets,* edited by Orde Coombs, Dodd, 1970, and *A Rock Against the Wind.* Contributor to *Black World.* Editor of *Afro-American Review.*

SIDELIGHTS: When and Where I Enter: The Impact of Black Women on Race and Sex in America is journalist Paula Giddings's detailed history of black women's contributions to racial and sexual equality. Arguing that the assertiveness and organization of black women furthered the cause of all women as well as all blacks, Giddings traces the development of black women's clubs, suffrage associations, and civil rights groups from the early 1890s to the 1940s. The book is "a jarringly fresh and challenging interpretation," judged *New York Times Book Review* contributor Gloria Naylor, who commended Giddings's realistic view of current women's and black rights and her account of gains made.

Giddings shows how black women's activism began before the Civil War, when slave women used contraceptives and abortions to avoid bearing children who would be slaves, and continued after the war with formation of the National Association of Colored Women. She explains how the Victorian ideal of womanhood—which insisted that women be submissive and confined to domestic life—conflicted with black women's need to work to help support their families, since jobs for black men were scarce. Such conflicts resulted in the redefinition of womanhood by blacks: as Jacqueline Trescott remarked in the *Washington Post*, "These women became the models for modern womanhood." Black women fought racism from whites both male and female, even where women's rights in general were at stake, and struggled against the sexism of black men who shared with whites the belief that women should remain at home. "Inherent in the Black women's defense of their integrity was a challenge to the Victorian ideas that kept all women oppressed," asserts Giddings. The author opens "our eyes to the relationship of racism and sexism in America," commented Wendy Kaminer in *Village Voice; Ms.* reviewer Margo Jefferson deemed the book "a readable, generally clear-sighted overview."

BIOGRAPHICAL/CRITICAL SOURCES:

PERIODICALS

Ms., May, 1984.
New York Times Book Review, July 8, 1984.
Village Voice, August 28, 1984.
Washington Post, February 28, 1985.

                    *   *   *

GILBERT, Christopher   1949-

PERSONAL: Born August 1, 1949, in Birmingham, Ala.; son of Floyd and Rosie (Walker) Gilbert. *Education:* University of Michigan, B.A., 1972; Clark University, M.A., 1975, Ph.D., 1986.

ADDRESSES: P.O. Box 371, West Side Station, Worcester, Mass. 01602.

CAREER: Judge Baker Guidance Center, Boston, Mass., staff psychologist, 1978-84; Cambridge Family and Children's Services, Cambridge, Mass., staff psychologist, 1984-85; poet, 1986—. Consultant psychologist at University of Massachusetts Medical School, 1979-84; visiting poet at University of Pittsburgh, 1986; poet in residence at Robert Frost Center, Franconia, N.H., 1986.

AWARDS, HONORS: Fellow of Massachusetts Artists Foundation, 1981, and National Endowment for the Arts, 1986; Walt Whitman Award from Academy of American Poets, 1983, for *Across the Mutual Landscape*.

WRITINGS:

Across the Mutual Landscape (poetry), Graywolf, 1984.
Life and Work of Thomas Chippendale, two volumes, Seven Hills Books, 1986.

Also author of *World,* a collection of poems, 1987. Work represented in anthologies, including *The Morrow Anthology of Younger Poets* and *Fifty Years of American Poetry, 1934-1984.*

WORK IN PROGRESS: A novel.

SIDELIGHTS: The poems in psychologist Christopher Gilbert's award-winning first collection, *Across the Mutual Landscape,* are, according to Alan Williamson writing in the *New York Times Book Review,* influenced by black music. The poetry's "subtle, syncopated rhythms" remind one of jazz, remarked Williamson, who pointed out that this music affects Gilbert's sense of the avenues for change, struggle, and outlet afforded by art. "It is a feeling often encountered in black American literature," explained Williamson, in which people living at the urban Midwest's poverty line seek "dignity and marginally steady work, but long for the sun and culture of the black South." This theme, Williamson determined, keeps Gilbert from overindulging in protest poetry or "too simple warmth and domesticity." The reviewer concluded that *Across the Mutual Landscape* is a "very fine, very promising first book."

Gilbert wrote: "I work at both poetry and psychology. Until 1986 I had always written poems while being employed in psychology. The poems got finished at home at night, after I had finished my daytime work doing psychotherapy, or research, or teaching psychology. Sometimes I would write poetry in the early morning. Sometimes I used the weekend for writing. Sometimes I wrote between breaths. This went on for about eight years; always the poems got finished. This year is the first that I have fully given over to writing poems. After April, 1987, I do plan to return to some kind of daytime job that involves my psychology background. Actually, I feel that my own ability to write poetry wants this; it wants its experience to be grounded in the firsthand world gained through contact with lives and people, with me—as subject—as an empathy, with a reflection toward one's deeper and longer life, with goals, with a concept of use. It is my way of making a living.

"I see the poem itself as a situation. Its formation is thought which must be musically stated. The situation is charged. The situation is sensuous. The situation is moving forward. The situation is music. Jazz pianist and composer Thelonious Monk, placing himself in the exact center of things, finding himself naked in his whole world except for his desire and his skill, could be listened to for a chart of the coming into newness that is the poem's formation.

"What I try to do is find the field in writing where I am honest, where I am determined to have a future in front of me. Once this nakedness is reached, after one has truly touched the features of 'his situation,' once one has made those parts of the usual—the regular denoted world—contextual, then there is the language that does not reach for things but poetry."

BIOGRAPHICAL/CRITICAL SOURCES:

PERIODICALS

Boston Globe, December 14, 1984.
New York Times Book Review, June 23, 1985.

Philadelphia Inquirer, December 2, 1984.
Virginia Quarterly Review, spring, 1985.

*   *   *

GIOVANNI, Nikki   1943-

PERSONAL: Birth-given name, Yolande Cornelia Giovanni, Jr.; born June 7, 1943, in Knoxville, Tenn.; daughter of Jones (a probation officer) and Yolande Cornelia (a social worker; maiden name, Watson) Giovanni; children: Thomas Watson. *Education:* Fisk University, B.A. (with honors), 1967; also attended University of Pennsylvania, Social Work School, and Columbia University, School of the Arts.

CAREER: Poet, writer, lecturer; Queens College of the City University of New York, Flushing, N.Y., assistant professor of black studies, 1968; Rutgers University, Livingston College, New Brunswick, N.J., associate professor of English, 1968-72. Visiting professor of English at Ohio State University, 1984; professor of creative writing at Mount St. Joseph on the Ohio, 1985—. Founder of publishing firm, Niktom Ltd., 1970. Has given numerous poetry readings and lectures at universities in the United States and Europe, including the University of Warsaw, Poland; has made television appearances on numerous talk shows; participated in "Soul at the Center," Lincoln Center for the Performing Arts, 1972. Cochairperson of Literary Arts Festival for State of Tennessee Homecoming, 1986.

MEMBER: National Council of Negro Women, Society of Magazine Writers, National Black Heroines for PUSH, Winnie Mandela Children's Fund Committee, Delta Sigma Theta.

AWARDS, HONORS: Grants from Ford Foundation, 1967, National Endowment for the Arts, 1968, and Harlem Cultural Council, 1969; named one of ten most admired black women, *Amsterdam News,* 1969; *Mademoiselle* award for outstanding achievement, 1971; Omega Psi Phi Fraternity award for outstanding contribution to arts and letters, 1971; Meritorious Plaque for Service, Cook County Jail, 1971; Prince Matchabelli Sun Shower Award, 1971; life membership and scroll, National Council of Negro Women, 1972; National Association of Radio and Television Announcers award for best spoken word album, 1972, for *Truth Is on Its Way;* Woman of the Year—Youth Leadership Award, *Ladies Home Journal,* 1972; Doctorate of Humanities, Wilberforce University, 1972; National Book Award nomination, 1973, for *Gemini;* American Library Association commendation for one of the best books for young adults, 1973, for *My House;* Doctorate of Literature, University of Maryland, Princess Anne Campus, 1974, Ripon University, 1974, Smith College, 1975, and Mount St. Joseph on the Ohio, 1983; Cincinnati Chapter YWCA Woman of the Year, 1983; elected to Ohio Women's Hall of Fame, 1985; named Outstanding Woman of Tennessee, 1985; keys to numerous cities, including Lincoln Heights, Ohio, Dallas, Tex., and Gary, Ind., all 1972, New York, N.Y., 1975, Buffalo, N.Y., and Cincinnati, Ohio, both 1979, Savannah, Ga., and Clarksdale, Miss., both 1981, Miami, Fla., 1982, New Orleans, La., Monroe, La., Fort Lauderdale, Fla., and Los Angeles, Calif., all 1984.

WRITINGS:

POETRY

Black Feeling, Black Talk (also see below), Broadside Press, 1968, 3rd edition, 1970.
Black Judgement (also see below), Broadside Press, 1968.

Black Feeling, Black Talk/Black Judgement (contains *Black Feeling, Black Talk* and *Black Judgement*), Morrow, 1970.
Re: Creation, Broadside Press, 1970.
Poem of Angela Yvonne Davis, Afro Arts, 1970.
Spin a Soft Black Song: Poems for Children, illustrated by Charles Bible, Hill & Wang, 1971, reprinted with illustrations by George Martin, Lawrence Hill, 1985, revised edition, Farrar, Straus, 1987..
My House, foreword by Ida Lewis, Morrow, 1972.
Ego Tripping and Other Poems for Young People, illustrated by George Ford, Lawrence Hill, 1973.
The Women and the Men, Morrow, 1975.
Cotton Candy on a Rainy Day, introduction by Paula Giddings, Morrow, 1978.
Vacation Time: Poems for Children, illustrated by Marisabina Russo, Morrow, 1980.
Those Who Ride the Night Winds, Morrow, 1983.
Sacred Cows . . . and Other Edibles, Morrow, 1988.

NONFICTION

Gemini: An Extended Autobiographical Statement on My First Twenty-five Years of Being a Black Poet, Bobbs-Merrill, 1971, reprinted, Penguin Books, 1980.
(With James Baldwin) *A Dialogue: James Baldwin and Nikki Giovanni,* Lippincott, 1973.
(With Margaret Walker) *A Poetic Equation: Conversations Between Nikki Giovanni and Margaret Walker,* Howard University Press, 1974.

EDITOR

Night Comes Softly: An Anthology of Black Female Voices, Medic Press, 1970.

SOUND RECORDINGS

Truth Is on Its Way, Right-On Records, 1971.
Like A Ripple on a Pond, Niktom, 1973.
The Way I Feel, Atlantic Records, 1974.
Legacies: The Poetry of Nikki Giovanni, Folkways Records, 1976.
The Reason I Like Chocolate, Folkways Records, 1976.
Cotton Candy on a Rainy Day, Folkways Records, 1978.

OTHER

Contributor to numerous anthologies. Author of columns, "One Woman's Voice," for Anderson-Moberg Syndicate of the *New York Times,* and "The Root of the Matter," in *Encore American and Worldwide News.* Contributor to magazines, including *Black Creation, Black World, Ebony, Essence, Freedom Ways, Journal of Black Poetry, Negro Digest,* and *Umbra.* Editorial consultant, *Encore American and Worldwide News.*

A selection of Giovanni's public papers are at Mugar Memorial Library of Boston University, Boston, Massachusetts.

SIDELIGHTS: Since establishing herself as one of the preeminent figures in the 1960s black literary renaissance, Nikki Giovanni has achieved international prominence as a poet, essayist, and lecturer. Her speaking tours of the United States and Europe have earned her the nickname "Princess of Black Poetry," as she often attracts sizeable and enthusiastic crowds to her readings. Best known for her books of poems on the themes of self-discovery and black consciousness, Giovanni has also received critical acclaim for her several volumes of children's verse as well as for her albums of poetry read to music, including the best-selling *Truth Is on Its Way.*

In the course of twenty years, Giovanni's work has evolved from the "open, aggressive, and explosive revolutionary tendencies that characterized her early verses" to "expressions of universal sensitivity, artistic beauty, tenderness, warmth, and depth," according to Mozella G. Mitchell in the *Dictionary of Literary Biography*. A central theme remains constant in Giovanni's poetry, however. Mitchell notes that Giovanni has a deep concern "about her own identity as a person . . . and what her purpose in life should be." This introspection often blends quite naturally with social and political activism, as Giovanni herself explains in *Ebony* magazine: "I write out of my own experiences—which also happen to be the experiences of my people. But if I had to choose between my people's experiences and mine, I'd choose mine because that's what I know best. That way I don't have to trap the people into some kind of *dreams* that I have about what they should be into. An artist's job is to show what he sees."

Giovanni was born Yolande Cornelia Giovanni, Jr., in Knoxville, Tennessee, the younger of two daughters in a close-knit family. She was particularly devoted to her sister Gary and to her maternal grandmother, Louvenia Terrell Watson, who was, Mitchell states, "assertive, militant, and terribly intolerant of white people." Mitchell feels that Louvenia Watson was instrumental in teaching Giovanni responsibility to her own race. When Giovanni was still young, her family moved to Cincinnati, Ohio, the city she still considers home, but she remained very close to her grandmother and spent several of her teen years in Knoxville. In her poetry, essays, and speeches, Giovanni celebrates the warmth of her formative years in Cincinnati and Knoxville. She told *Ebony:* "I had a really groovy childhood and I'm really pleased with my family. . . . Essentially everything was groovy." Mitchell characterizes Giovanni's poetry about her youth as "a return to the source, to the beginning, to the mother's womb, so to speak, from which a glorious rebirth is to be expected."

Giovanni entered Fisk University in 1960, at the age of seventeen. Mitchell describes the poet's ideology at that stage in her life: "Coming from a middle-class family residing in a suburb of Cincinnati, Ohio, she was then a Goldwater supporter who had read much of, among other books, Ayn Rand, cheap novels, and fairy tales. Yet, she was in a state of growth." The independent-minded Giovanni came into conflict with Fisk's dean of women and was released from the school because her "attitudes did not fit those of a Fisk woman." After a hiatus of several years, Giovanni returned to Fisk and became a serious student as well as a budding black rights activist. One of her first achievements on campus was her organization of a successful demonstration to restore the Fisk chapter of the Student Nonviolent Coordinating Committee that had lost its charter.

The 1960s saw a great expansion of the American civil rights movement, as blacks and other minority groups began to call more stridently for recognitiion, equality, and respect. Soon after her graduation with honors from Fisk University, and following the death of her beloved grandmother, Giovanni began to find a place in the ranks of the black literary movement that sought to raise black consciousness through poetry and prose. In a passage from *Gemini: An Extended Autobiographical Statement on My First Twenty-five Years of Being a Black Poet*, Giovanni credits a roommate named Bertha with bringing about her conversion to revolutionary ideals: "Before I met [Bertha] I was Ayn Rand-Barry Goldwater all the way. Bertha kept asking, how could Black people be conservative? What have they got to conserve? And after awhile (realizing that I had absolutely nothing, period) I came around." Though this passage suggests levity, Giovanni embraced the Black Power movement with great seriousness. According to Mitchell, "Her encounters in the Southern environment and her close observations of the progressive developments in the nation of the civil rights demonstrations, especially in the South, along with the great popularity of Malcolm X and the Nation of Islam around the country, among other things, captured the imagination and enthusiasm of this sensitive young woman."

Giovanni's first three books of poetry, *Black Feeling, Black Talk, Black Judgement*, and *Re: Creation*, were published between 1968 and 1970. The poems in these volumes cover many aspects of Giovanni's life at the time: her commitment to the revolution and anger over society's reaction to the revolutionary leaders, her lovers and the romantic feelings she experiences for them, and her family and emotionally secure childhood. Mitchell describes the poems in these books as "a kind of ritualistic exorcism of former nonblack ways of thinking and an immersion in blackness. Not only are they directed at other black people whom she wanted to awaken to the beauty of blackness, but also at herself as a means of saturating her own consciousness." This poetic "immersion in blackness" becomes evident, Mitchell feels, in the "daring questions, interspersed with ironic allusions to violent actions blacks have committed for the nation against their own color across the world." Giovanni's vision, however, "goes beyond . . . violent change to a vision of rebuilding." According to Alex Batman in the *Dictionary of Literary Biography*, Giovanni is "not so much urging violence for itself [in this poetry] as she is demanding black assertiveness, although one finds it hard to acknowledge that she may be willing to accept violence, even if she is not enthusiastic about it."

Critical reaction to Giovanni's early volumes centers upon her more revolutionary poems. In *Dynamite Voices I: Black Poets of the 1960s*, Don L. Lee observes that "Nikki writes about the familiar: what she knows, sees, experiences. It is clear why she conveys such urgency in expressing the need for Black awareness, unity, solidarity. . . . What is perhaps more important is that when the Black poet chooses to serve as political seer, he must display a keen sophistication. Sometimes Nikki oversimplifies and therefore sounds rather naive politically." Mitchell has a related criticism: "In this early stage of her commitment of her talent to the service of the black revolution, her creativity is bound by a great deal of narrowness and partiality from which her later work is freed." Batman is also one of several critics who find in Giovanni's early books an indebtedness to an oral, rather than a literary, tradition. "The poems . . . reflect elements of black culture, particularly the lyrics of rhythm-and-blues music," writes Batman. "Indeed, the rhythms of her verse correspond so directly to the syncopations of black music that her poems begin to show a potential for becoming songs without accompaniment." Lee comments: "Nikki is at her best in the short, personal poem. . . . Her effectiveness is in the area of the 'fast rap.' She says the right thing at the right time. Orally this is cool, but it doesn't come across as printed poetry." Batman concludes similarly that in reaching to create "a blues without music," Giovanni "repeats the worst mistake of the songwriter—the use of language that has little appeal of its own in order to meet the demands of the rhythm."

Despite the difficulties Batman and Lee note in the poet's early work, they both praise her as an artist of great potential. Lee writes: "She is definitely growing as a poet," and Batman claims that a careful reading of her verse "shows that the talent is indeed there.'' Critical reservations notwithstanding, Giovanni's earliest works were enormously successful, given the relatively low public demand for modern poetry. In an article for *Mademoiselle* magazine, Sheila Weller notes that *Black Judgement* sold six thousand copies in three months, making that volume five to six times more sellable than the average. Mitchell suggests that Giovanni's poems of the period brought her prominence ''as one of the three leading figures of the new black poetry between 1968 and 1971,'' and speaking engagements began to fill much of her time.

In 1969 Giovanni took a teaching position at Rutgers University. During the summer of that year, her son Thomas was born. Describing in *Ebony* magazine her choice to have a baby out of wedlock, she said: ''Tommy is what is fashionably known as 'an illegitimate baby' and there's no reason for my going on any other trip. I had a baby at 25 because I *wanted* to have a baby and I could *afford* to have a baby. I did not get married because I didn't *want* to get married and I could *afford* not to get married.'' She also told *Harper's Bazaar* that Tommy's birth caused her to reevaluate her priorities. ''To protect Tommy there is no question I would give my life,'' she said. ''I just cannot imagine living without him. But I can live without the revolution.''

Giovanni's work through the mid-1970s reflects this change in focus. In addition to her collection of autobiographical essays, *Gemini*, she published two books of poetry for children and two books of adult poetry, *My House* and *The Women and the Men*. Mitchell writes of this period in Giovanni's career: ''We see evidence of a more developed individualism and greater introspection, and a sharpening of her creative and moral powers, as well as of her social and political focus and understanding.'' Reflecting on *The Women and the Men*, published in 1975, Batman notes: ''The revolution is fading from the new poems, and in its place is a growing sense of frustration and a greater concern with the nature of poetry itself. Throughout these poems is a feeling of energy reaching out toward an object that remains perpetually beyond the grasp.''

The themes of family love, loneliness, frustration, and introspection explored in Giovanni's earlier works find further expression in *My House* and *The Women and the Men*. In the foreword to *My House*, Ida Lewis describes the key to understanding the poet's conviction: ''The central core [of Giovanni's work] is always associated with her family: the family that produced her and the family she is producing. She has reached a simple philosophy more or less to the effect that a good family spirit is what produces healthy communities, which is what should produce a strong (Black) nation.'' Mitchell discusses *The Women and the Men* with emphasis upon Giovanni's heightened sense of self: ''In this collection of poems,... she has permitted to flower fully portions of herself and her perception which have been evident only in subdued form or in incompletely worked-through fragments. Ideas concerning women and men, universal human relatedness, and the art of poetry are seen here as being in the process of fuller realization in the psyche of the author.'' Noting the aspects of personal discovery in *My House*, critic John W. Connor suggests in the *English Journal* that Giovanni ''sees her world as an extension of herself ... sees problems in the world as an extension of her problems, and ... sees herself existing amidst tensions, heartache, and marvelous expressions of love.... When a reader enters *My House*, he is invited to savor the poet's ideas about a meaningful existence in today's world.'' ''*My House* is not just poems,'' writes Kalumu Ya Salaam in *Black World*. ''*My House* is how it is, what it is to be a young, single,

intelligent Black woman with a son and no man. Is what it is to be a woman who has failed and is now sentimental about some things, bitter about some things, and generally always frustrated, always feeling frustrated on one of various levels or another.''

Concurrent with her poetry for adults, Giovanni has published three volumes of poetry for children, *Spin a Soft Black Song, Ego-Tripping and Other Poems for Young People,* and *Vacation Time*. According to Mitchell, the children's poems have ''essentially the same impulse'' as Giovanni's adult poetry; namely, ''the creation of racial pride and the communication of individual love. These are the goals of all of Giovanni's poetry, here directed toward a younger and more impressionable audience.'' In a *New York Times Book Review* article on *Spin a Soft Black Song*, Nancy Klein writes: ''Nikki Giovanni's poems for children, like her adult works, exhibit a combination of casual energy and sudden wit. No cheek-pinching auntie, she explores the contours of childhood with honest affection, sidestepping both nostalgia and condescension.'' A *Booklist* reviewer, commenting on *Ego-Tripping*, claims: ''When [Giovanni] grabs hold ... it's a rare kid, certainly a rare black kid, who could resist being picked right up.'' Critics of *Vacation Time* suggest that some of the rhyme is forced or guilty of ''an occasional contrivance to achieve scansion,'' in the words of Zena Sutherland for the *Bulletin of the Center for Children's Books*, but praise is still forthcoming for the theme of Giovanni's verses. ''In her singing lines, Giovanni shows she hadn't forgotten childhood adventures in ... exploring the world with a small person's sense of discovery,'' writes a *Publishers Weekly* reviewer. Mitchell, too, claims: ''One may be dazzled by the smooth way [Giovanni] drops all political and personal concerns [in *Vacation Time*] and completely enters the world of the child and brings to it all the fanciful beauty, wonder, and lollipopping.''

As early as 1971, Giovanni began to experiment with another medium for presenting her poetry—sound recording. Recalling how her first album, *Truth Is on Its Way*, came to be made, Giovanni told *Ebony:* ''Friends had been bugging me about doing a tape but I am not too fond of the spoken word or of my voice, so I hesitated. Finally I decided to try it with gospel music, since I really dig the music.'' Giovanni also told *Ebony* that she chose gospel music as background for her poetry because she wanted to make something her grandmother would listen to. *Truth Is on Its Way* was the best selling spoken-word album of 1971, contributing greatly to Giovanni's fame nationwide. ''I have really been gratified with the response [to the album] of older people, who usually feel that black poets hate them and everything they stood for,'' Giovanni told *Ebony*. The popularity of *Truth Is on Its Way* encouraged Giovanni to make subsequent recordings of her poetry as well as audio- and videotapes of discussions about poetry and black issues with other prominent poets.

In 1978 Giovanni published *Cotton Candy on a Rainy Day*, which Mitchell describes as ''perhaps her most sobering book of verse.... It contains thoughtful and insightful lyrics on the emotions, fears, insecurities, realities, and responsibilities of living.'' Mitchell detects a sense of loneliness, boredom, and futility in the work, caused in part by the incompleteness of the black liberation movement. Batman, too, senses a feeling of despair in the poems: ''What distinguishes *Cotton Candy on a Rainy Day* is its poignancy. One feels throughout that here is a child of the 1960s mourning the passing of a decade of conflict, of violence, but most of all, of hope.'' In her introduction to the volume, Paula Giddings suggests that the emotional complacency of the 1970s is responsible for Giovanni's apparent sense of despondency: ''Inevitably, the shining innocence that comes from feeling the ideal is possible is also gone, and one must learn to live with less. . . . The loneliness carries no blame, no bitterness, just the realization of a void. . . . Taken in the context of Nikki's work [*Cotton Candy on a Rainy Day*] completes the circle: of dealing with society, others, and finally oneself.''

Those Who Ride the Night Winds, Giovanni's 1983 publication, represents a stylistic departure from her previous works. ''In this book Giovanni has adopted a new and innovative form; and the poetry reflects her heightened self-knowledge and imagination, writes Mitchell. The subject matter of *Those Who Ride the Night Winds* tends once more to drift toward a subdued but persistent political activism, as Giovanni dedicates various pieces to Phillis Wheatley, Martin Luther King, Jr., Rosa Parks, and the children of Atlanta, Georgia, who were at the time living in fear of a serial murderer. Mitchell suggests that the paragraphs punctuated with ellipses characteristic of the volume make the poems ''appear to be hot off the mind of the author. . . . In most cases the poems are meditation pieces that begin with some special quality in the life of the subject, and with thoughtful, clever, eloquent and delightful words amplify and reconstruct salient features of her or his character.''

In addition to citing Giovanni's thoughtfulness and creativity throughout the body of her published material, Mitchell praises the poet's capacity for growth as ''a singular quality exhibited in her works as a whole. A steady progression toward excellence in craftsmanship is one of the key elements in her development.'' As Paula Giddings notes in the introduction to *Cotton Candy on a Rainy Day,* ''Nikki Giovanni is a witness. Her intelligent eye has caught the experience of a generation and dutifully recorded it. She has seen enough heroes, broken spirits, ironies, heartless minds and mindless hearts to fill several lifetimes.'' Later in the essay, Giddings concludes: ''I have never known anyone who cares so much and so intensely about the things she sees around her as Nikki. That speaks to her humanity and to her writing. Through the passion and the cynicism of the last two decades she has cared too much to have either a heartless mind or, just as importantly, a mindless heart.''

MEDIA ADAPTATIONS: A television film entitled ''Spirit to Spirit: The Poetry of Nikki Giovanni,'' featuring the poet reading from her published works, was produced by the Public Broadcasting Corporation, the Corporation for Public Broadcasting, and the Ohio Council on the Arts. It first aired in 1986 on public television stations.

BIOGRAPHICAL/CRITICAL SOURCES:

BOOKS

Authors in the News, Volume I, Gale, 1976.
Children's Literature Review, Volume VI, Gale, 1984.
Contemporary Literary Criticism, Gale, Volume II, 1974, Volume IV, 1975, Volume XIX, 1981.
A Dialogue: James Baldwin and Nikki Giovanni, Lippincott, 1972.
Dictionary of Literary Biography, Gale, Volume V: *American Poets Since World War II,* 1980, Volume XLI: *Afro-American Poets Since 1955,* 1985.
Evans, Mari, editor, *Black Women Writers, 1950-1980: A Critical Evaluation,* Doubleday, 1984.

Gibson, Donald B., editor, *Modern Black Poets: A Collection of Critical Essays,* Prentice-Hall, 1973.
Giovanni, Nikki, *Black Judgement,* Broadside Press, 1968.
Giovanni, Nikki, *Gemini: An Extended Autobiographical Statement on My First Twenty-five Years of Being a Black Poet,* Bobbs-Merrill, 1971.
Giovanni, Nikki, *My House,* foreword by Ida Lewis, Morrow, 1972.
Giovanni, Nikki, *Cotton Candy on a Rainy Day,* introduction by Paula Giddings, Morrow, 1978.
Henderson, Stephen, *Understanding the New Black Poetry: Black Speech and Black Music as Poetic References,* Morrow, 1973.
Lee, Don L., *Dynamite Voices I: Black Poets of the 1960s,* Broadside Press, 1971.
Noble, Jeanne, *Beautiful, Also, Are the Souls of My Black Sisters: A History of the Black Woman in America,* Prentice-Hall, 1978.
Tate, Claudia, *Black Women Writers at Work,* Crossroad Publishing, 1983.

PERIODICALS

Best Sellers, September 1, 1973, January, 1976.
Black World, December, 1970, January, 1971, February, 1971, April, 1971, August, 1971, August, 1972, July, 1974.
Bulletin of the Center for Children's Books, October, 1980.
Choice, May, 1972, March, 1973, September, 1974, January, 1976.
Christian Science Monitor, June 4, 1970, June 19, 1974.
CLA Journal, September, 1971.
Ebony, February, 1972, August, 1972.
Encore, spring, 1972.
English Journal, April, 1973, January, 1974.
Essence, August, 1981.
Harper's Bazaar, July, 1972.
Ingenue, February, 1973.
Jet, May 25, 1972.
Los Angeles Times, December 4, 1985.
Los Angeles Times Book Review, April 17, 1983.
Mademoiselle, May, 1973, December, 1973, September, 1975.
Milwaukee Journal, November 20, 1974.
New York Times, April 25, 1969, July 26, 1972.
New York Times Book Review, November 7, 1971, November 28, 1971, February 13, 1972, May 5, 1974.
Partisan Review, spring, 1972.
Publishers Weekly, November 13, 1972, May 23, 1980.
Saturday Review, January 15, 1972.
Time, April 6, 1970, January 17, 1972.
Washington Post, January 30, 1987.
Washington Post Book World, May 19, 1974, March 8, 1981, February 14, 1988.

OTHER

The Poet Today (sound recording), The Christophers, 1979.

*   *   *

GOINES, Donald   1937(?)-1974
(Al C. Clark)

PERSONAL: Born December 15, 1937 (some sources indicate 1935 or 1936), in Detroit, Mich.; died of gunshot wounds, October 21, 1974, in Highland Park, Mich.; married (common law) Shirley Sailor; children: nine, including Donna and Camille from common-law marriage. *Education:* Educated in Detroit, Mich.

ADDRESSES: Home—Highland Park, Mich.

CAREER: Writer and convicted criminal. *Military service:* U.S. Air Force, 1951-54; served in Japan during Korean War.

WRITINGS—NOVELS; PUBLISHED BY HOLLOWAY HOUSE:

Dopefiend: The Story of a Black Junkie, 1971.
Whoreson: The Story of a Ghetto Pimp, 1972.
Black Gangster, 1972.
Street Players, 1973.
White Man's Justice, Black Man's Grief, 1973.
Black Girl Lost, 1973.
(Under pseudonym Al C. Clark) *Cry Revenge!* 1974.
Eldorado Red, 1974.
Swamp Man, 1974.
Never Die Alone, 1974.
Daddy Cool, 1974.
Inner City Hoodlum, 1975.

UNDER PSEUDONYM AL C. CLARK; "KENYATTA" SERIES

Crime Partners, 1974.
Death List, 1974.
Kenyatta's Escape, 1974.
Kenyatta's Last Hit, 1975.

SIDELIGHTS: Donald Goines was known for his grim novels about drug users and prostitutes in Detroit, Michigan. He was born in Detroit in 1937 and attended Catholic schools there, proving himself an earnest and cooperative student. In his mid-teens, however, he abruptly left school and joined the Air Force. In joining the service he lied about his age, an act that may account for the later discrepancy regarding his actual birthdate. During the Korean War, Goines was stationed in Japan. There became a frequent drug user, and when he returned home in 1955 he was a heroin addict.

For the next fifteen years Goines supported his drug habit by pimping, robbing, and smuggling. For his crimes he was arrested fifteen times, and he served seven prison terms. While in jail—where he apparently remained free of heroin addiction—he was introduced to the writings of Robert "Iceberg Slim" Beck, a pimp-novelist who enjoyed substantial popularity among inmate readers. Inspired by Slim's *Trick Baby,* Goines—who had earlier attempted to write westerns—produced *Whoreson: The Story of a Ghetto Pimp,* a semiautobiographical novel about a pimp and his clashes with other seedy criminals. The world of *Whoreson* is an unsparing one where weakness or error inevitably leads to death. It is, perhaps, the raw, unyielding vision of *Whoreson* that made it popular with inmates whose opinions Goines solicited. Upon the advice of one particularly enthusiastic convict, Goines sent *Whoreson* to Iceberg Slim's publisher, the California-based Holloway House. The company, which specialized in black literature, readily accepted Goines's manuscript and requested additional works.

Though still in prison, Goines quickly produced *Dopefiend: The Story of a Black Junkie,* which became his first published work. In *Dopefiend* he presented a graphic account of the drug addict's sordid life, tracing the degeneration of two middle-class blacks. In a *Village Voice* assessment of Goines's writings, Michael Covino described *Dopefiend* as a "relentless" depiction of loathsome and disgusting individuals. Particularly memorable is Porky, a vicious drug dealer first presented examining a pornographic magazine amid bloody squalor while a desperate addict jabs a syringe into her groin. *Dopefiend* abounds in such repellent situations: In one episode a pimp

taunts a syphilitic prostitute, threatening to incorporate her into a sex show featuring animals; another passage details Porky's plan for killing two addicts who had robbed him. For Covino, the unsettling *Dopefiend* was "Goines's best book."

With advances from Holloway House for both *Dopefiend* and *Whoreson,* Goines could afford to concentrate on writing after he left prison in 1970. But by 1971 he had resumed drug use, and he consequently wrote only in the mornings, then spent the rest of each day indulging his heroin habit. In 1972 he nonetheless published a third novel, *Black Gangster,* about a cynical hoodlum who establishes a civil-rights organization as a front for prostitution and extortion. After publishing this novel, Goines moved to Los Angeles for greater access to Holloway House and to the nearby film industry, which he hoped to interest in his works.

In 1973 Goines published three more novels, including *White Man's Justice, Black Man's Grief,* an indictment of the American judicial system he termed racist. The novel tells of two inmates who conspire to commit a burglary after leaving prison. When one inmate is freed, he attempts the crime unassisted and kills a witness. Upon apprehension the killer names his black co-conspirator as the mastermind of the robbery and thus his accomplice in murder. The black convict is then tried and sentenced for murder even though he was in prison when the crime transpired.

Goines wrote eight more novels in 1974, including several works under the name of his friend Al C. Clark. Four of Goines's novels as Clark feature the ambitious militant Kenyatta, who rises from small-time hoodlum to leader of a two-thousand-member organization. With his mighty gang, Kenyatta hopes to eliminate all white police officers and rid the black ghetto of drugs and prostitution. Through considerable violence, he nearly succeeds. But in *Kenyatta's Last Hit*—the final work in a series that also features *Crime Partners, Death List,* and *Kenyatta's Escape*—he is killed while plotting the murder of a wealthy Los Angeles businessman dealing drugs.

Before writing *Kenyatta's Last Hit,* Goines returned to Detroit, having apparently disliked vast, unfamiliar Los Angeles. He settled with his common-law wife in nearby Highland Park. They were murdered there in October, 1974. Police suspected that robbery was the motive behind the slayings, though there were indications that Goines had once again involved himself in drug use.

In the years following his death Goines's novels continued to prove profitable for Holloway House, which reprinted his entire canon and reported total sales surpassing five million copies. Critical recognition, however, has been minimal. Mainstream publications ignore Goines's work, and more offbeat periodicals and literary journals rarely acknowledge his achievements. Covino's article in the *Village Voice* may promote greater recognition of Goines's talents as "a writer of unmediated raw realism, a chronicler of the black ghetto."

BIOGRAPHICAL/CRITICAL SOURCES:

BOOKS

Authors in the News, Volume 1, Gale, 1976.
Dictionary of Literary Biography, Volume 33: *Afro-American Fiction Writers After 1955,* Gale, 1984.
Stone, Eddie, *Donald Writes No More: A Biography of Donald Goines,* Holloway House, 1974.

PERIODICALS

Detroit Free Press, November 28, 1974.

Detroit News, November 15, 1974.
MELUS, summer, 1984.
Village Voice, August 4, 1987.

—*Sketch by Les Stone*

*   *   *

GOLDEN, Marita   1950-

PERSONAL: Born April 28, 1950, in Washington, D.C.; daughter of Francis (a taxi driver) and Beatrice (a landlord; maiden name, Reid) Golden; divorced; children: one son. *Education:* American University, B.A., 1972; Columbia University, M.Sc., 1973.

ADDRESSES: Home—Boston, Mass. *Agent*—Carol Mann, 168 Pacific Street, Brooklyn, N.Y. 11201.

CAREER: WNET-Channel 13, New York, N.Y., associate producer, 1974-75; University of Lagos, Lagos, Nigeria, assistant professor of mass communication, 1976-79; Roxbury Community College, Roxbury, Mass., assistant professor of English, 1979-81; Emerson College, Boston, Mass., professor of journalism, 1981-83. Member of nominating committee for the George K. Polk Awards.

MEMBER: Afro-American Writer's Guild (president).

WRITINGS:

(Contributor) Beatrice Murphy, editor, *Today's Negro Voices*, Messner, 1970.
(Contributor) *Keeping the Faith: Writings by Contemporary Black American Women*, Fawcett, 1974.
Migrations of the Heart (autobiography), Doubleday, 1983.
A Woman's Place, Doubleday, 1986.

Contributor of poetry to several anthologies, and contributor to periodicals, including *Essence, Daily Times* (Nigeria), *National Observer, Black World*, and *Amsterdam News*.

SIDELIGHTS: Marita Golden began writing her autobiography, *Migrations of the Heart*, when she was only twenty-nine years old. When asked about her motivation for the book, Golden told *Washington Post* reporter Jacqueline Trescott that she "stumbled into" it, adding: "I wanted to meditate on what it meant to grow in the '60's, what it meant to go to Africa the first time, what it meant to be a modern black woman living in that milieu. I had to bring order to the chaos of memory.... What I wanted to do was write a book that would take my life and shape it into an artifact that could inform and possibly inspire."

The book met with generally favorable reviews and was described by Diane McWhorter in the *New York Times Book Review* as "interesting" and "told in a prose that often seems possessed by some perverse genius." Reviewer Elayne B. Byman Bass commended Golden in the *Washington Post Book World* for her account of how "the love of a girl for her father evolves through several migrations into a woman's love for her man, her child and finally herself," while in *Ms.* magazine, critic Carole Bovoso suggested that Golden has earned a place among those black women writers who share a "greater and greater commitment . . . to understand self, multiplied in terms of the community, the community multiplied in terms of the nation, and the nation multiplied in terms of the world."

Golden's novel *A Woman's Place*—a "truncated *herstory*," according to Wanda Coleman in the *Los Angeles Times Book Review*—follows the lives of three black women who meet and become friends at an elite Boston university. Each of them confronts problems facing black women in today's society. One cannot adjust to the pressures her possessive Islamic husband puts on her, another suffers from guilt related to her love of a white man, and the third tries to lose herself working in a developing African nation. "By refusing to offer easy answers to the predicaments of women, and black women in particular," says *Washington Post Book World* contributor Susan Wood, "Golden makes us believe in her characters and care about them."

Golden remarked: "I was trained to be a journalist at Columbia's graduate school of journalism, but I was born, I feel, to simply write, using whatever medium best expresses my obsession at a particular time. I have written poetry and have been included in several anthologies and want in the future to write more. I use and need journalism to explore the external world, to make sense of it. I use and need fiction to give significance to and to come to terms with the internal world of my own particular fears, fantasies, and dreams, and to weave all of that into the texture of the outer, tangible world. I write essentially to complete myself and to give my vision a significance that the world generally seeks to deny."

BIOGRAPHICAL/CRITICAL SOURCES:

PERIODICALS

Antioch Review, winter, 1984.
Los Angeles Times Book Review, April 17, 1983, September 7, 1986.
Ms., June, 1983.
New Yorker, February 21, 1983.
New York Times Book Review, May 1, 1983, September 14, 1986.
Voice Literary Supplement, June, 1983.
Washington Post, May 22, 1983, December 13, 1987.
Washington Post Book World, June 4, 1983, July 30, 1986, December 13, 1987.

*   *   *

GORDONE, Charles   1925-

PERSONAL: Born October 12, 1925, in Cleveland, Ohio; son of William and Camille (Morgan) Gordon; married Jeanne Warner (a stage and film producer), 1959; children: Stephen, Judy, Leah Carla, David. *Education:* Los Angeles State College of Applied Arts and Sciences (now California State University, Los Angeles), B.A., 1952; also attended University of California, Los Angeles.

ADDRESSES: Home—17 West 100 St., New York, N.Y. 10025. *Office*—c/o Springer-Warner Productions, 365 West End Ave., New York, N.Y. 10024. *Agent*—Rosenstone/Wender, 3 East 48th St., New York, N.Y. 10017.

CAREER: Playwright, actor, and director. As actor, has appeared in plays, including "Of Mice and Men," 1953, "The Blacks," 1961-65, and "The Trials of Brother Jero," 1967. Director of about twenty-five plays, including "Rebels and Bugs," 1958, "Peer Gynt," 1959, "Tobacco Road," 1960, "Detective Story," 1960, "No Place to Be Somebody," 1967, "Cures," 1978, and "Under the Boardwalk," 1979. Co-founder of Committee for the Employment of Negro Performers, 1962, and chairman; member of Commission on Civil Disorders, 1967; instructor at Cell Block Theatre, Yardville and Bordontown Detention Centers, New Jersey, 1977-78; judge, Missouri Arts Council Playwriting Competition, 1978; instructor at New School for Social Research, 1978-79; member of Ensemble Studio Theatre and Actors Studio. *Military service:* U.S. Air Force.

AWARDS, HONORS: Obie Award for best actor, 1953, for performance in "Of Mice and Men"; Pulitzer Prize for Drama, Los Angeles Critics Circle Award, and Drama Desk Award, all 1970, all for "No Place to Be Somebody"; grant from the National Institute of Arts and Letters, 1971.

WRITINGS:

PLAYS

(With Sidney Easton) "Little More Light around the Place," first produced in New York City at Sheridan Square Playhouse, 1964.

No Place to Be Somebody: A Black-Black Comedy (first produced in New York City at Sheridan Square Playhouse, November, 1967; produced Off-Broadway at New York Shakespeare Festival Public Theatre, May, 1969; produced on Broadway at American National Theatre and Academy (ANTA) Theatre, December 30, 1969; produced in Los Angeles at the Matrix, July, 1987), introduction by Joseph Papp, Bobbs-Merrill, 1969.

"Willy Bignigga" [and] "Chumpanzee," first produced together in New York City at Henry Street Settlement New Federal Theatre, July, 1970.

"Gordone Is a Muthah" (collection of monologues; first produced in New York City at Carnegie Recital Hall, May, 1970), published in *The Best Short Plays of 1973*, edited by Stanley Richards, Chilton, 1973.

"Baba-Chops," first produced in New York City at Wilshire Ebel Theatre, 1975.

"The Last Chord," first produced in New York City at Billie Holiday Theatre, 1977.

Also author of an unproduced musical, "The Block," and of screenplays "No Place to Be Somebody" (adapted from the play), "The W.A.S.P.," (adapted from the novel by Julius Horwitz), "From These Ashes," "Under the Boardwalk," and "Liliom."

WORK IN PROGRESS: A play, "Anabiosis"; lyrics for a musical adaptation of "No Place to Be Somebody"; stage adaptation of "Under the Boardwalk."

SIDELIGHTS: Charles Gordone's "No Place to Be Somebody," a production of Joseph Papp's Public Theatre, opened on Broadway to rave reviews. Walter Kerr, reviewing the play in the *New York Times,* hailed Gordone as "the most astonishing new American playwright since Edward Albee," while other critics compared him to Eugene O'Neill. Like O'Neill, they posited, Gordone finds his truths in bars, where pretending is too troublesome. Set in a tawdry bar in Greenwich Village, "No Place" belongs in the category of American saloon dramas and follows in the tradition of such plays as "The Iceman Cometh" and "The Time of Your Life." But, as a *Time* critic pointed out, "'Johnny's Bar' is no oasis for gentle day-dreamers. It is a foxhole of the color war—full of venomous nightmares, thwarted aspirations and trigger-quick tempers."

The owner of the bar, Johnny Williams, is also a pimp who takes on the syndicate in an effort to obtain control of the local rackets. His ambition is to organize his own black mafia, and he uses the affections of a white female student to further his aims. Although he has "learned early to hate white society and not to trust anybody," Johnny supports an out-of-work

actor and retains an incompetent white employee. Other characters include a bartender who has "drug-induced daydreams of having once been a jazz musician," Johnny's two whores, a disillusioned ex-dancer and short-order cook, and Gabe Gabriel, an unemployed, light-skinned black actor who is too white for black roles. Gabe is Gordone's spokesman, introducing the acts of the play, and reciting monologues that "use humor and candor to express the absurdity and tragedy of racism." He is also an observer rather than a participant. At the end of the play, however, he shoots Johnny, at the request of Machine Dog, a black militant who exists only in Gabe's mind.

Although many critics noted that the play had some flaws, all praised Gordone's ability for characterization and dialogue. Some indicated that the play's only problem came from Gordone's ambition of trying to say too much in one work. As Edith Oliver noted in the *New Yorker:* "There are several plots . . . and subplots running through the script, but what is more important is the sense of life and intimacy of people in a place, and of the diversity of their moods—the sudden, sometime inexplicable, spurts of anger and wildness and fooling—and their understanding of one another." Kerr highlighted Gordone's "excellent habit" of pressing "his confrontations until they become reversals, until the roles are changed."

"Written with a mixture of white heat and intellectual clarity," wrote *Newsweek* contributor Jack Kroll, "it is necessarily and brilliantly grounded in realism but takes off from there with high courage and imagination; it is funny and sad and stoical, revolutionary and conciliatory." In a review for the *New Yorker,* Brendon Gill concurred: "Mr. Gordone is as fearless as he is ambitious, and such is the speed and energy with which he causes his characters to assault each other— every encounter is, in fact, a collision—that we have neither the time nor the will to catch our breath and disbelieve. The language is exceptionally rough and exceptionally eloquent; it is a proof of Mr. Gordone's immense talent that the excrementitious gutterances of his large cast of whores, gangsters, jailbirds, and beat-up drifters stamp themselves on the memory as beautiful."

Criticism from black reviewers was not, however, totally favorable. Along with Clayton Riley and Peter Bailey, some black critics found evidence of self-hate—"a hint of contempt for black people"—in Gordone's play. But most critics were quick to stress Gordone's concern with all people—black and white alike—who feel despair but continue to hope.

BIOGRAPHICAL/CRITICAL SOURCES:

BOOKS

Dictionary of Literary Biography, Volume 7: *Twentieth-Century American Dramatists,* Gale, 1981.

PERIODICALS

Black World, December, 1972.
Christian Science Monitor, September 21, 1970.
Critic's Choice, September, 1969.
Journal of Negro Education, spring, 1971.
Los Angeles Times, July 17, 1987, July 24, 1987.
Negro Digest, April, 1970.
Newsweek, June 2, 1969.
New York, June 9, 1969.
New Yorker, May 17, 1969, January 10, 1970.
New York Times, May 18, 1969, December 31, 1969, May 17, 1970.

Saturday Review, May 31, 1969.
Time, May 16, 1969.
Variety, May 28, 1969, June 10, 1970, August 26, 1970, January 14, 1970, September 15, 1971.
Village Voice, May 8, 1969, May 22, 1969.

*   *   *

GRAHAM, Lorenz (Bell) 1902-

PERSONAL: Born January 27, 1902, in New Orleans, La.; son of David Andrew (a minister) and Etta (Bell) Graham; married Ruth Morris, August 20, 1929; children: Lorenz, Jr., Jean (deceased), Joyce (Mrs. Campbell C. Johnson), Ruth (Mrs. Herbert R. May), Charles. *Education:* Attended University of Washington, Seattle, 1921, University of California, Los Angeles, 1923-24; Virginia Union University, A.B., 1936; Columbia University, M.S.W., 1954; also studied at New York School of Social Work for two years, and at New York University. *Politics:* "Liberal, Democratic, sometimes called Left." *Religion:* Disciples of Christ.

ADDRESSES: Home—1400 Niagara Ave., Claremont, Calif. 91711.

CAREER: Monrovia College, Liberia, West Africa, teacher and missionary, 1924-28; lecturer and fund raiser in United States for Foreign Mission Board, National Baptist Convention, 1929-32; teacher in Richmond, Va., 1933-35; U.S. Civilian Conservation Corps, camp educational adviser in Virginia and Pennsylvania, 1936-42; manager of public housing, Newport News, Va., 1943-45; free-lance writer, real estate salesman, and building contractor, Long Island, N.Y., 1946-49; Queens Federation of Churches, New York, N.Y., social worker, 1950-57; Los Angeles County (Calif.) probation officer, 1958-66. Lecturer, California State Polytechnic College (now University), Pomona, 1970-77.

MEMBER: P.E.N. International, Authors League of America, National Association for the Advancement of Colored People, U.S./China Peoples Friendship Association, U.S.A./Soviet Friendship Society.

AWARDS, HONORS: Thomas Alva Edison Foundation special citation for *The Ten Commandments;* Follett Award, 1958, and Child Study Association of America Award, 1959, both for *South Town;* Association for Study of Negro Life and History award, 1959; Los Angeles City Council award, 1966; Vassie D. Wright award, 1967; Southern California Council on Literature for Children and Young People award, 1968; first prize, *Book World*, 1969, for *Whose Town?;* California Association of Teachers of English citation, 1973; Martin Luther King Award, Southern California region of Christian Church, 1975; honorary D.H.L., Virginia University, 1983.

WRITINGS:

JUVENILES

How God Fix Jonah (collection of biblical tales told in Liberian dialect; also see below), illustrated by Letterio Calapai, Reynal & Hitchcock, 1946.
Tales of Momolu (also see below), illustrated by Calapai, Reynal & Hitchcock, 1946.
(Adapter) *The Story of Jesus*, Gilberton, 1955.
(Adapter) *The Ten Commandments*, Gilberton, 1956.
I, Momolu, illustrated by John Biggers, Crowell, 1966.
Every Man Heart Lay Down (originally published in *How God Fix Jonah*), illustrated by Colleen Browning, Crowell, 1970.

A Road Down in the Sea (originally published in *How God Fix Jonah*), illustrated by Gregorio Prestopino, Crowell, 1970.
God Wash the World and Start Again (originally published in *How God Fix Jonah*), illustrated by Clare Romano Ross, Crowell, 1971.
John Brown's Raid: A Picture History of the Attack on Harpers Ferry, Virginia, Scholastic Magazines, 1971.
David He No Fear (originally published in *How God Fix Jonah*), illustrated by Ann Grifalconi, Crowell, 1971.
(Compiler with John Durham and Elsa Graser) *Directions 3-4* (anthology), 2 volumes, Houghton, 1972.
Carolina Cracker (novelette), Houghton, 1972.
Detention Center (novelette), Houghton, 1972.
Stolen Car (novelette), Houghton, 1972.
Runaway (novelette), Houghton, 1972.
Hongry Catch the Foolish Boy (originally published in *How God Fix Jonah*), illustrated by James Brown, Crowell, 1973.
Song of the Boat (originally published in *Tales of Momolu*), illustrated by Leo and Diane Dillon, Crowell, 1975.
John Brown: A Cry for Freedom, Crowell, 1980.

"TOWN" SERIES; JUVENILES

South Town, Follett, 1958.
North Town, Crowell, 1965.
Whose Town?, Crowell, 1969.
Return to South Town, Crowell, 1976.

OTHER

Also author of plays for amateur groups, schools, and colleges. Contributor of articles to agency and department publications.

SIDELIGHTS: A former missionary and teacher, and the brother of writer Shirley Graham Du Bois, Lorenz Graham brings "realistic black characters to young adult literature," say Kenneth L. Donelson and Alleen Pace Nilsen in *Literature for Today's Young Adults*. Graham's adaptions of biblical tales rendered in Pidgin English are "told in a distinctly African way, yet the words retain the strength and timelessness of the language of the Bible," in the opinion of Sidney D. Long of *Horn Book* magazine. Similarly, states *New York Times Book Review* contributor Elizabeth Hodges, his stories of the young Liberian Momolu present "problems of growing up [which] are essentially the same, whether one lives in an American community or at the edge of the jungle."

Graham is also noted for his "Town" series, the account of David William's struggles to overcome prejudice and racism and become a doctor. "As a group," says Rudine Sims in *Shadow and Substance: Afro-American Experience in Contemporary Children's Fiction*, "these books tend to celebrate the courage and determination of Afro-American families and individuals who are faced with racism, oppression, or violence." "*Whose Town?*," she continues, "affirm[s] the idea that while Blacks must take responsibility for their own lives, Blacks and whites can learn to coexist—that people must be judged as individuals." She concludes that the struggle presented in the books "is not Black against white, but people against evil and hate."

Lorenz Graham remarked, "As a Negro I grew up with fears and hatreds for white people and came to understanding of these destructive emotions only after being outside the United States and separated from the 'race problem.' I concluded that people, all people, should be brought to better understanding of other people.

"For this I work and write. . . . My personal problem with publishers has been the difference between my images and theirs. Publishers have told me that my characters, African and American black people, are 'too much like white people.' And I say, 'If you look closely you will see that people are people.'"

BIOGRAPHICAL/CRITICAL SOURCES:

BOOKS

Books for Children, 1960-1965, American Library Association, 1966.
Children's Bookshelf, Child Study Association of America, Bantam, 1965.
Children's Literature Review, Volume X, Gale, 1985.
Donelson, Kenneth L., and Alleen Pace Nilsen, *Literature for Today's Young Adults,* Scott, Foresman, 1980.
Huck, Charlotte S., and D. A. Young, *Children's Literature in the Elementary School,* Holt, 1961.
Larrick, Nancy, *A Parent's Guide to Children's Reading,* 3rd edition, Doubleday, 1969.
Sims, Rudine, *Shadow and Substance: Afro-American Experience in Contemporary Children's Fiction,* National Council of Teachers of English, 1982.
Something about the Author Autobiography Series, Volume 5, Gale, 1988.

PERIODICALS

Chicago Tribune Book World, December 20, 1970.
Christian Science Monitor, May 6, 1965, May 6, 1971.
Commonweal, November 20, 1970, May 21, 1971.
Horn Book, February, 1967, August, 1969, December, 1970, April, 1971, December, 1971, December, 1975.
New York Times Book Review, December 8, 1946, February 2, 1947, April 4, 1965, November 29, 1970, August 22, 1971.
Saturday Review, May 10, 1969, March 20, 1971.
Washington Post Book World, May 4, 1969.
Young Readers' Review, May, 1969.

*   *   *

GRAHAM, Shirley
See Du BOIS, Shirley Graham

*   *   *

GREAVES, William 1926-

PERSONAL: Born October 8, 1926, in New York, N.Y.; son of Garfield (a cab driver and minister) and Emily (Muir) Greaves; married Louise Archambault, August 23, 1959; children: David, Taiyi, Maiya. *Education:* Attended New School of Social Research and New York Actors Studio, 1948, City College of New York (now City College of City University of New York), 1949-51, and New Institute for Film and Television, 1950.

ADDRESSES: Office—William Greaves Productions, Inc., 80 Eighth Ave., Suite 1703, New York, New York 10011.

CAREER: Performer, songwriter, producer, director, scriptwriter, and independent filmmaker. Began theatrical career with Sierra Leonian Asadata Dafora Dance Company as an African dancer, joined Pearl Primus Dance Troupe, then worked as an actor on stage, radio, television, and screen from 1943

to 1952. Actor in stage productions, including "Three's a Family," 1943, "Henri Christophe," 1945, "A Young American," 1946, "Finian's Rainbow," 1946, "John Loves Mary," (black cast), 1948, "Lost in the Stars," 1949, and "Arsenic and Old Lace," (black cast); actor in films, including "Miracle in Harlem," 1948, and "Lost Boundaries," 1949.

National Film Board of Canada, Ottawa, Ontario, film production staff, 1952-60; United Nations International Civil Aviation Organization (ICAO), Montreal, Quebec, public information officer, 1962-63, writer and producer, 1965-66; United Nations Television, New York, N.Y., producer and director, 1963-68; National Educational Television, New York City, executive producer, scriptwriter, and host of "Black Journal" television series, 1968-71; associated with "Black News" television series, 1975; William Greaves Productions, Inc., New York City, founder and president, producer, director, and scriptwriter, 1964—. Director and/or producer of documentary and feature films, c. 1952-81, including "Roads in the Sky" for International Civil Aviation Organization; "Emergency Ward" with Wolf Koening and "Four Religions, Part 2: Islam and Christianity" with James Beveridge for National Film Board of Canada; "The Life and Legacy of Booker T. Washington" for National Parks Service; "Cleared for Takeoff" with Alistair Cooke for United Nations Television; "Still a Brother: Inside the Negro Middle Class" and "Wealth of a Nation" for United States Information Agency; "Family Dream," for Universal Pictures; and "Choice of Destinies," "Deathgrip," "Liberty: On Being Black," and "Putting It Straight."

Founder and director, Canadian Drama Studio, Montreal, Quebec, and Toronto and Ottawa, Ontario, 1952-63; drama teacher, Lee Strasberg Theatre Institute, New York City, beginning in 1973; teacher, New York Actors Studio, New York City; visiting professor of film, Boston University, Boston, Mass.; lecturer at numerous institutions, including Boston, Brandeis, Columbia, Harvard, and Howard universities, City College of City University of New York, universities of Buffalo, Michigan, and Vermont, and Williams College. Member of Emmy Award panel, National Academy of Television Arts and Sciences; media panel judge for National Endowment for the Arts and National Endowment for the Humanitites, both beginning in 1979; member of media committee, Indo-American sub-commission on education and culture; chairman of film committee and council member, Massachusetts Foundation for the Humanities and Public Policy; film panelist, American Film Institute; vice-president of AMAS Repertory Theatre, Inc.

MEMBER: American Federation of Television and Radio Artists, American Guild of Authors and Composers, Directors Guild of America, National Association of Black Media Producers (co-founder, 1970), Writers Guild of America, Equity Association, New York Actors Studio (member of auditioning committee), Screen Actors Guild, National Urban League (member of communications committee).

AWARDS, HONORS: Won membership in New York Actors Studio, 1948; American Film Festival Award, c. 1964, for documentary "Still a Brother: Inside the Negro Middle Class"; Emmy Award nomination, c. 1964, for "Still a Brother: Inside the Negro Middle Class," Emmy Award, 1970, as executive producer of "Black Journal" television series, and three Emmy Award nominations, 1973, for documentary film "Voice of La Raza," all from National Academy of Television Arts and Sciences; Silver Medal, International Film and Television Festival, 1969; Atlanta International Film Festival Award, Chicago International Film Festival Award, and Randy Award from Job Film Fair Competition, all in 1969 for documentary "In the Company of Men"; John Russwurm Award from National Newspaper Publishers Association of America, 1970, for "Black Journal"; Special Gold Medal Award from Atlanta International Film Festival, Blue Ribbon American Festival Award, and San Francisco International Film Festival Award, all in 1970 for "In the Company of Men"; Oscar Michaud Award, 1980, for induction into the Black Filmmakers Hall of Fame; Hommage award, Festival of Black Independent American Cinema 1920-1980 (Paris, France), 1980; Dusa Award from New York Actors Studio, 1980; Doctor of Humane Letters from King Memorial College; recipient of more than sixty awards from International Film Festival for documentary and feature films.

WRITINGS:

FILM SCRIPTS

(And director) "First World Festival of Negro Arts," National Film Board of Canada for United States Information Agency, 1966.

(And director) "In the Company of Men" (documentary), William Greaves Productions for *Newsweek* magazine, 1969.

(And director) "Ali, the Fighter" (feature), William Greaves Productions, 1971.

(And director) "The Fighters" (documentary), William Greaves Productions, 1971.

(With Jose Garcia) "Voice of La Raza" (documentary), William Greaves Productions for Equal Employment Opportunity Commission, 1971.

"From These Roots" (documentary), William Greaves Productions, 1974.

(With Woody Robinson) "The Marijuana Affair" (feature documentary), 1975.

"Space for Women," National Aeronautics and Space Administration, 1981.

Also author of film scripts "The Magic Mineral," "Smoke and Weather," and "Symbiopsychotaxiplasm: Take One." Also composed more than one hundred popular songs, including "African Lullaby" with lyrics in both English and Swahili, recorded by Eartha Kitt in 1952.

SIDELIGHTS: In an autobiographical essay written in 1969 for *Sightlines* magazine, independent filmmaker William Greaves stated: "My interest in film stems from three basic sources. First, I have always had a deep interest in Africa and Afro-American history . . . [and I decided] to enter the mass media as a producer in order to disseminate information on the black experience. Secondly, I became infuriated by the racially degrading sterotypes of black people that white film producers threw up on American screens. . . . It became quite clear to me that unless we black people . . . began to produce information for screen and television, there would probably always be a distortion of the 'black image.' My third reason for entering the production side of films was . . . [the] need to channel my diverse interests. It occurred to me that film was a medium where many different talents could be employed while feigning to be a specialist. Somehow, these three reasons have become inextricably intertwined and I'm now simply a filmmaker with rambling interests, committed only to the expression of consciousness: mine and others."

Considered one of America's finest independent film producers during the 1960s and 1970s, Greaves actually learned his craft in Canada. Facing what he considered insurmountable racial barriers during the early 1950s, Greaves was forced to leave the United States in order to acquire the skills and experience necessary to pursue his career in documentary filmmaking. He worked ten years for Canada's National Film Board as a writer, editor, and director of more than seventy films, and during that time he helped introduce cinema verite—the art or technique of filmmaking that conveys candid realism—to the North American continent. Greaves returned to the United States in 1963. Explaining his reasons in *Sightlines*, Greaves stated: "What made me come back to America? I don't know. . . . Perhaps I felt that I had reached the limits of what Canada had to offer a creative artist. Maybe it was a decision to contribute to the redesign of the American psyche through the social engineering agency of film and television. Maybe it was Martin Luther King and the march on Washington and the hope that it held for America. . . . Maybe I was just plain homesick."

Whatever the reason, Greaves quickly established himself as a first-rate filmmaker, focusing primarily on the many facets of black experience. He made several feature and documentary films for the United Nations and the United States Information Agency, including the award-winning "Still a Brother: Inside the Negro Middle Class." In 1964 he set up his own company, William Greaves Productions, and over the next several years produced dozens of films and won numerous awards. In 1970 alone, as James P. Murray noted in *To Find an Image*, "he won ten major awards for film and television productions about the black man's problems, ambitions, and future in America." Greaves became increasingly well known and highly regarded for his innovation and independence as a filmmaker.

In 1968 William Greaves began a three-year period as scriptwriter and co-host of the original "Black Journal," National Educational Television's news show that, according to *Ebony,* "claims to be 'of, by, about and primarily for the black community.'" The program's basic purpose was to improve consciousness and pride within the Afro-American population—it aired for one hour once a month. Shortly after he began Greaves was asked to take over as executive producer, while remaining the program's co-host and writer. Consequently, "Black Journal" became the only black controlled network show in television and under Greaves's leadership earned a reputation for its exceptional quality as well as for its radical and militant approach. In 1970 the National Academy of Television Arts and Sciences paid tribute to the show's excellence and presented Greaves an Emmy Award as best executive producer.

Discussing the success of black filmmakers in an interview for Murray's *To Find an Image,* Greaves commented, "As far as I'm concerned, all the films we've done . . . have been successful, and I don't think we've had any difficulty in communicating our intentions to either the black community or the white community." He believes, moreover, that the future for black films and black film producers is a promising one. He told Murray: "I think it will be something like the same thing that has happened with black music. Our music, our speech, our behavior, and general life styles have been unique, but accepted and absorbed into society. Just like there is a steady growth and acceptance of new black publications, I feel the same will happen with black films."

AVOCATIONAL INTERESTS: Afro-American history and culture.

BIOGRAPHICAL/CRITICAL SOURCES:

BOOKS

Murray, James P., *To Find an Image: Black Films From Uncle Tom to Super Fly*, Bobbs-Merrill, 1973.

PERIODICALS

Ebony, September, 1969.
Film News, fall, 1980.
Jet, December 31, 1970.
Sightlines, September-October, 1969.

*   *   *

GREENFIELD, Eloise   1929-

PERSONAL: Born May 17, 1929, in Parmele, N.C.; daughter of Weston W. and Lessie (Jones) Little; married Robert J. Greenfield (a procurement specialist), April 29, 1950; children: Steven, Monica. *Education:* Attended Miner Teachers College, 1946-49.

ADDRESSES: Office—Honey Productions, Inc., P.O. Box 29077, Washington, D.C. 20017. *Agent*—Marie Brown, Marie Brown Associates, 412 West 154th St., New York, N.Y. 10032.

CAREER: U.S. Patent Office, Washington, D.C., clerk-typist, 1949-56, supervisory patent assistant, 1956-60; worked as a secretary, case-control technician, and an administrative assistant in Washington, D.C. from 1964-68. District of Columbia Black Writers' Workshop, co-director of adult fiction, 1971-73, director of children's literature, 1973-74; District of Columbia Commission on the Arts and Humanities, writer-in-residence, 1973, 1985-86. Participant in numerous school and library programs and workshops for children and adults.

AWARDS, HONORS: Carter G. Woodson Book Award, National Council for the Social Studies, 1974, for *Rosa Parks;* Irma Simonton Black Award, Bank Street College of Education, 1974, for *She Come Bringing Me That Little Baby Girl; New York Times* Outstanding Book of the Year citation, 1974, for *Sister;* Jane Addams Children's Book Award, Women's International League for Peace and Freedom, 1976, for *Paul Robeson;* American Library Association Notable Book citations, 1976, for *Me and Neesie*, 1979, for *Honey, I Love, and Other Love Poems*, 1982, for *Daydreamers;* Council on Interracial Books for Children award, 1977, for body of work; Coretta Scott King Award, 1978, for *Africa Dream;* Classroom Choice Book citation, 1978, for *Honey, I Love, and Other Love Poems;* Childen's Book of the Year citation, Child Study Book Committee, 1979, for *I Can Do It by Myself;* Notable Trade Book in the Field of Social Studies citations, 1980, for *Childtimes: A Three-Generation Memoir*, 1982, for *Alesia;* New York Public Library recommended list, 1981, for *Alesia;* National Black Child Development Institute award, 1981, for body of work; Mills College award, 1983, for body of work; Washington, D.C. Mayor's Art Award in Literature, 1983.

WRITINGS:

Sister (novel), illustrated by Moneta Barnett, Crowell, 1974.
Honey, I Love, and Other Love Poems, illustrated by Diane and Leo Dillon, Crowell, 1978.
Talk about a Family (novel), illustrated by James Calvin, Lippincott, 1978.

Nathaniel Talking (poems), Crowell, in press.

PICTURE BOOKS

Bubbles, illustrated by Eric Marlow, Drum & Spear, 1972, published with illustrations by Pat Cummings as *Good News*, Coward, 1977.
She Come Bringing Me That Little Baby Girl, illustrated by John Steptoe, Lippincott, 1974.
Me and Neesie, illustrated by Barnett, Crowell, 1975.
First Pink Light, illustrated by Barnett, Crowell, 1976.
Africa Dream, illustrated by Carole Byard, John Day, 1977.
(With mother, Lessie Jones Little) *I Can Do It by Myself*, illustrated by Byard, Crowell, 1978.
Darlene, illustrated by George Ford, Methuen, 1980.
Grandmama's Joy, illustrated by Byard, Collins, 1980.
Daydreamers, with pictures by Tom Feelings, Dial, 1981.

BIOGRAPHIES

Rosa Parks, illustrated by Marlow, Crowell, 1973.
Paul Robeson, illustrated by Ford, Crowell, 1975.
Mary McLeod Bethune, illustrated by Jerry Pinkney, Crowell, 1977.
(With Little) *Childtimes: A Three-Generation Memoir* (autobiography), illustrated by Pinkney, Crowell, 1979.
(With Alesia Revis) *Alesia*, illustrated by Ford, with photographs by Sandra Turner Bond, Philomel Books, 1981.

CONTRIBUTOR TO ANTHOLOGIES

Alma Murray and Robert Thomas, editors, *The Journey: Scholastic Black Literature*, Scholastic Book Services, 1970.
Karen S. Kleiman and Mel Cebulash, editors, *Double Action Short Stories*, Scholastic Book Services, 1973.
Love, Scholastic Book Services, 1975.
Encore (textbook), Houghton, 1978.
Daystreaming, Economy Company, 1978.
Forerunners, Economy Company, 1978.
Burning Bright, Open Court, 1979.
Friends Are Like That, Crowell, 1979.
Language Activity Kit: Teachers' Edition, Harcourt, 1979.
Building Reading Skills, McDougal, Littell, 1980.
New Routes to English: Book 5, Collier Books, 1980.
New Routes to English: Advanced Skills One, Collier Books, 1980.
Jumping Up, Lippincott, 1981.
Emblems, Houghton, 1981.
Listen, Children, Bantam, 1982.
Bonus Book, Gateways, Level K, Houghton, 1983.
New Treasury of Children's Poetry, Doubleday, 1984.
Scott, Foresman Anthology of Children's Literature, Scott, Foresman, 1984.

OTHER

Contributor to *World Book Encyclopedia;* author of 1979 bookmark poem for Children's Book Council. Also contributor to magazines and newspapers, including *Black World, Cricket, Ebony, Jr.!, Horn Book, Interracial Books for Children Bulletin, Ms., Negro History Bulletin, Scholastic Scope*, and *Washington Post*.

SIDELIGHTS: Eloise Greenfield stated that her goal in writing is "to give children words to love, to grow on." The author of more than a dozen prize-winning books for children, Greenfield admits that, since her own childhood, she has loved the sounds and rhythms of words. In her stories and poetry she tries to produce what she calls "word-madness," a creative, joyous response brought on by reading. As she explains in

Horn Book: "I want to be one of those who can choose and order words that children will want to celebrate. I want to make them shout and laugh and blink back tears and care about themselves."

Greenfield also lists as a priority of her writing the communication of "a true knowledge of Black heritage, including both the African and American experiences." Through her easy-to-read biographies of famous black Americans, such as *Rosa Parks, Paul Robeson,* and *Mary McLeod Bethune,* she seeks to inform young readers about the historical contributions of blacks in this nation. "A true history must be the concern of every Black writer," she states in *Horn Book.* "It is necessary for Black children to have a true knowledge of their past and present, in order that they may develop an informed sense of direction for their future."

This concern for a personal past as well as a public one has prompted Greenfield to team with her mother for *Childtimes: A Three-Generation Memoir.* The autobiographical work describes the childhood memories of Greenfield, her mother, and her maternal grandmother. According to Rosalie Black Kiah in *Language Arts,* each experience in *Childtimes,* "though set in a different time, is rich in human feeling and strong family love." *Washington Post Book World* contributor Mary Helen Washington writes: "I recognize the significance of *Childtimes* as a document of black life because . . . it unlocked personal recollections of my own past, which I do not want to lose." In the *Interracial Books for Children Bulletin,* Geraldine L. Wilson calls the book "carefully considered and thoughtful, . . . moving deliberately, constructed with loving care." M. R. Singer concludes in the *School Library Journal:* "The intimate details of loving and growing up and the honesty with which they are told . . . will involve all readers . . . and broaden their understanding of this country's recent past."

Much of Greenfield's fiction concerns family bonding, a subject the author finds as important as black history. Noting in *Horn Book* that "love is a staple in most Black families," she writes repeatedly of the changing patterns of parental and sibling involvement, stressing the child's ability to cope with novelties both positive and negative. In her Irma Simonton Black Award-winning picture book, *She Come Bringing Me That Little Baby Girl,* for instance, a young character named Kevin must learn to share his parents' love with his new sister. A novel entitled *Sister,* which received a *New York Times* Outstanding Book of the Year citation, concerns a girl caught in the family stress following a parent's death. Greenfield explains the point of *Sister* in *Horn Book:* "Sister . . . discovers that she can use her good times as stepping stones, as bridges, to get over the hard times. . . . My hope is that children in trouble will not view themselves as blades of wheat caught in countervailing winds but will seek solutions, even partial or temporary solutions, to their problems."

Unsatisfied with network television's portrayal of black families, which she calls "a funhouse mirror, reflecting misshapen images" in *Horn Book,* Greenfield seeks to reinforce positive and realistic aspects of black family life. While she tells *Language Arts* that she looks back on her own childhood with pleasure, she remains aware of the modern dynamics of family structure. She states: "Families come in various shapes. There is no one shape that carries with it more legitimacy than any other. . . . In the case of divorce and separation—the problems that parents have—the children can go on and build their own lives regardless of the problems of the parents. Children *have* to go on and build their own lives." Kiah notes that Greenfield

does not construct her fiction from personal incidents but rather looks for themes from a more universal background. "She draws from those things she has experienced, observed, heard about, and read about. Then she combines them, changes them and finally develops them into her stories." The resulting work has a wide appeal, according to Betty Valdes in the *Interracial Books for Children Bulletin.* Valdes feels that Greenfield "consistently . . . illuminates key aspects of the Black experience in a way that underlines both its uniqueness and its universality."

Greenfield has resided in Washington, D.C. since childhood and has participated in numerous writing workshops and conferences on literature there. She explains in *Language Arts* that her work with the District of Columbia Black Writers' Workshop convinced her of the need to build a collection of "good black books" for children. "It has been inspiring to me to be a part of this struggle," she affirms. "I would like to have time to write an occasional short story, . . . but I don't feel any urgency about them. It seems that I am always being pushed from inside to do children's books, those are more important." Stating another aim of hers in *Horn Book,* Greenfield claims: "Through the written word I want to give children a love for the arts that will provoke creative thought and activity. . . . A strong love for the arts can enhance and direct their creativity as well as provide satisfying moments throughout their lives."

MEDIA ADAPTATIONS: Daydreamers was dramatized for the Public Broadcasting System (PBS) Reading Rainbow Television Series.

BIOGRAPHICAL/CRITICAL SOURCES:

BOOKS

Children's Literature Review, Volume IV, Gale, 1982.
Greenfield, Eloise, and Lessie Jones Little, *Childtimes: A Three-Generation Memoir,* illustrated by Jerry Pinkney, Crowell, 1979.
Sims, Rudine, *Shadow and Substance: Afro-American Experience in Contemporary Children's Literature,* National Council of Teachers of English, 1982.

PERIODICALS

Africa Woman, March-April, 1980.
Encore, December 6, 1976.
Freedomways, Volume XXI, number 1, 1981, Volume XXII, number 2, 1982.
HCA Companion, first quarter, 1984.
Horn Book, December, 1975, April, 1977.
Interracial Books for Children Bulletin, Volume XI, number 5, 1980, Volume XI, number 8, 1980.
Language Arts, September, 1980.
Metropolitan Washington, August, 1982.
Negro History Bulletin, April-May, 1975, September-October, 1978.
New York Times Book Review, May 5, 1974, November 3, 1974.
School Library Journal, December, 1979.
Top of the News, winter, 1980.
Washington Post Book World, May 1, 1977, January 13, 1980, May 10, 1981.

*   *   *

GREENLEE, Sam 1930-

PERSONAL: Born July 13, 1930, in Chicago, Ill.; married;

wife's name Nienke. *Education:* University of Wisconsin, B.S., 1952; graduate study at University of Chicago, 1954-57, and University of Thessaloniki, Greece, 1963-64.

ADDRESSES: Home—6240 South Champlain Ave., Chicago, Ill. 60637.

CAREER: United States Information Agency, Washington, D.C., foreign service officer in Iraq, Pakistan, Indonesia, and Greece, 1957-65; L.M.O.C., deputy director, 1965-69. *Military service:* U.S. Army, Infantry, 1952-54; became first lieutenant.

AWARDS, HONORS: Meritorious service award from U.S. Information Agency; *The Spook Who Sat by the Door* was co-winner of London *Sunday Times* book of the year award, 1969.

WRITINGS:

The Spook Who Sat by the Door (science fiction), Baron, 1969, Schocken, 1985.
Blues for an African Princess (poems), Third World Press, 1971.
Baghdad Blues (novel), Bantam, 1976.

Author of *Ammunition!: Poetry and Other Raps,* 1975. Contributor of articles and stories to magazines and newspapers.

SIDELIGHTS: The Spook Who Sat by the Door has been made into a stage play.

*   *   *

GREGORY, Dick   1932-
(Richard Claxton Gregory)

PERSONAL: Born October 12, 1932, in St. Louis, Mo.; son of Presley and Lucille Gregory; married Lillian Smith, February 2, 1959; children: Michele, Lynne, Paula, Pamela, Stephanie, Gregory, Christian, Ayanna, Missy, Yohance. *Education:* Attended Southern Illinois University, 1951-53, 1955-56.

ADDRESSES: Home—Long Pond Rd., Plymouth, Mass. 02360. *Office*—Dick Gregory Health Enterprises, 39 South LaSalle, Chicago, Ill. 60603.

CAREER: Roberts Show Club, Chicago, Ill., master of ceremonies, 1959-60; entertainer and commentator, 1961—; Dick Gregory Health Enterprises, Chicago, chairman, 1984—. Lecturer at numerous universities in the United States. Candidate for mayor of Chicago, 1966; presidential candidate of Freedom and Peace Party, 1968. *Military service:* U.S. Army, 1953-55.

AWARDS, HONORS: Winner of Missouri mile championship, 1951, 1952; named outstanding athlete, Southern Illinois University, 1953; has received more than one hundred civil rights awards; presented with the key to the city of St. Louis.

WRITINGS:

From the Back of the Bus, edited by Bob Orben with an introduction by Hugh M. Hefner, Dutton, 1962.
(With Robert Lipsyte) *Nigger: An Autobiography,* Dutton, 1964, new edition with Bronson Dudley, McGraw, 1970.
What's Happening?, Dutton, 1965.
The Shadow That Scares Me, edited by James R. McGraw, Doubleday, 1968.
Write Me In!, edited by McGraw, Bantam, 1968.

(Under name Richard Claxton Gregory) *No More Lies: The Myth and Reality of American History,* edited by McGraw, Harper, 1972.
Dick Gregory's Political Primer, edited by McGraw, Harper, 1972.
Dick Gregory's Natural Diet for Folks Who Eat: Cookin' with Mother Nature, Harper, 1973.
Dick Gregory's Bible Tales, edited by McGraw, Stein & Day, 1974.
(With McGraw) *Up from Nigger* (autobiography), Stein & Day, 1976.
(With Mark Lane) *Code Name "Zorro: The Murder of Martin Luther King, Jr.,"* Prentice-Hall, 1977.

Also creator of comedy routines featured on a number of recordings, including "In Living Black and White," Colpix, 1961, "The Light Side, The Dark Side," Poppy, 1969, "Caught in the Act," Poppy, 1973, "Dick Gregory East and West", and "Dick Gregory at Kent State."

SIDELIGHTS: On January 13, 1961, black comedian Dick Gregory appeared at the Playboy Club in Chicago. His socially-conscious racial humor was so popular with the white audience at the club that his original one-night engagement (he was filling in for another comedian) was extended to a two-month engagement. Gregory's career took off: *Time* magazine featured him in a two-page article, Jack Paar invited him to appear on his television program, and Gregory was soon one of the hottest acts on the nightclub circuit. He took his sudden success with characteristic good humor. "Where else in the world but America," he says, "could I have lived in the worst neighborhoods, attended the worst schools, rode in the back of the bus, and got paid $5,000 a week just for talking about it?"

Gregory was the first black comedian to break the "color barrier" and perform for white audiences. The popularity of his comedy lay in its satirical approach to race relations and his introduction of the non-derogatory racial joke. Describing his attitude on stage at that time, Gregory writes in *Nigger: An Autobiography:* "I've got to go up there as an individual first, a Negro second. I've got to be a colored funny man, not a funny colored man." He would begin his routine with several jokes poking fun at himself, then switch to a topical joke, like: "They asked me to buy a lifetime membership in the NAACP, but I told them I'd pay a week at a time. Hell of a thing to buy a lifetime membership, wake up one morning and find the country's been integrated." As Gregory explains, "That makes fun of the whole situation." Then he would directly address the race issue with a line like: "Wouldn't it be a hell of a thing if all this was burnt cork and all you folks were being tolerant for nothing?"

Gregory's success as a comedian came only after years of hard work trying to break into the entertainment field. After a childhood of poverty in St. Louis, Gregory attended college on a track scholarship and later served two years in the army. In the middle 1950s he concentrated on finding work as a comedian, always having had, as he says, "a good rap." He spent several years working occasional gigs as master of ceremonies at Chicago area black night clubs, alternating his work with periods as a car washer and post office employee. In 1958, he opened his own nightclub, the Apex Club, in Robbins, Illinois, but the club soon failed, leaving Gregory in debt. A turning point came in late 1959 when he rented the Roberts Show Club in Chicago and organized a party for the Pan American Games teams. The success of the party and of

Gregory's role as its master of ceremonies convinced the owner of the club to hire Gregory as the regular master of ceremonies. But when the job ended a year later, Gregory was unemployed and broke once again. It was then that he got the one-night job at the Playboy Club that changed his life.

From the first, Gregory chose poverty, segregation, and racial injustice as targets for his satirical routines, reflecting his concern with social and political issues. As he became better established as a comedian, Gregory put his convictions into practice by devoting much of his time to the civil rights movement of the 1960s. On behalf of the Southern Christian Leadership Conference, the Congress on Racial Equality, and other prominent civil rights organizations, Gregory made appearances at demonstrations, marches, and rallies throughout the country. He performed in many fund-raising shows for the movement and participated in nonviolent civil disobedience actions. While marching for black voting rights by day, Gregory spent his evenings satirizing racism and social injustice in his nightclub appearances. At one point he commuted daily from San Francisco to Chicago so he could fulfill a nightclub engagement while participating in a series of civil rights demonstrations. On several occasions Gregory was arrested and jailed and once, while under arrest in Chicago, he was severely beaten by the police. "I wouldn't mind paying my income tax," Gregory said during this period, "if I knew it was going to a friendly country."

When his concern for America's social problems demanded a greater level of involvement, Gregory entered electoral politics. In 1966 he was a candidate for mayor of Chicago and, in 1968, the presidential candidate of the Freedom and Peace Party, a splinter group of the Peace and Freedom Party. Gregory's campaigns were closely associated with the New Left and Black Power movements of the late 1960s and called for civil rights, peace in Vietnam, and racial and social justice. Although neither of his electoral campaigns were successful, they did draw attention to issues that Gregory felt should be better known. His presidential bid, a write-in effort in most states, garnered some two hundred thousand votes and substantial media attention. Despite his loss of the presidential election, Gregory was sworn in as "President-in-Exile" by some of his supporters at a ceremony in Washington, D.C. At his "inauguration," Gregory pledged to continue his fight against "the insane, stinking, rotten racist system in the United States."

In such books as *The Shadow That Scares Me, No More Lies,* and *Dick Gregory's Political Primer,* Gregory has presented his political and social beliefs. In a review of *The Shadow That Scares Me,* Charles Dollen of *Best Sellers* finds that Gregory "preaches freedom; he teaches it; he satirizes over it, and no one is safe from his keen wit or his common sense." Speaking of the same book, *Library Journal*'s C. M. Weisenberg writes: "Most of [Gregory's] writing is reasonable and quite clear. . . . His view of America's urban problems is essentially economical, not racial. He maintains a sincere devotion to the principles of American democracy. He is, above all, a thoughtful individual concerned about the future of his country."

In the late 1960s Gregory came to believe that his personal life must be changed in order to bring it into harmony with his political beliefs. Accordingly, he became a vegetarian because of his commitment to nonviolence. "I didn't get into [vegetarianism] for health reasons," Gregory explains in *East West Journal.* "I got into it for moral reasons." When his

sinus trouble and ulcers left him after a few months as a vegetarian, however, Gregory studied his diet more closely. His research into diet and health led him to outspoken positions on the benefits of a vegetarian lifestyle and the ill effects of the normal American diet. Soon after, he quit the nightclub circuit in favor of speaking engagements at colleges, churches, and schools. When asked by Lawrence Levy of the *Detroit News* why he quit the nightclubs, Gregory responded: "They take time away from serving humanity." More importantly, they promoted a lifestyle that Gregory could no longer support. "How can I get up there," he has said, "and tell those students that drugs and alcohol and cigarets and even meat is bad for them, then afterwards say 'come on down and catch my act at the club and have a drink.'"

Encouraged by the benefits of his vegetarian lifestyle, Gregory began in the 1970s to explore other areas of health care and nutrition. He soon became interested in fasting and marathon running, activities he now practices as a personal witness to call attention to social issues. He has fasted a number of times to publicize the world hunger problem, to draw attention to the nation's drug abuse epidemic, and to emphasize the plight of the American Indians. Gregory has engaged in marathon runs for similiar reasons, running from Chicago to Washington, D.C., for example, to urge that action be taken by the government to ease world famine.

Gregory's unique career as entertainer and activist has garnered him substantial attention and admiration. "Gregory's name," writes Peter Barry Chowka of *East West Journal,* "is synonymous with progressive social and political causes. . . . He is that rare combination (like Gandhi) of activist and healer, one whose own life illustrates how real change first must come from within oneself."

BIOGRAPHICAL/CRITICAL SOURCES:

BOOKS

Gemme, Leila B., *New Breed of Performer,* Washington Square Press, 1976.
Gregory, Dick and Robert Lipsyte, *Nigger: An Autobiography,* Dutton, 1965, new edition with Bronson Dudley, McGraw, 1970.
Gregory, Dick and James R. McGraw, *Up from Nigger,* Stein & Day, 1976.

PERIODICALS

Best Sellers, February 1, 1968, May 15, 1972.
Booklist, November 15, 1976.
Book Week, November 1, 1964.
Book World, July 21, 1968, September 23, 1973, February 19, 1978.
Christian Century, November 27, 1974.
Christian Science Monitor, January 14, 1977.
Detroit News, April 7, 1974.
East West Journal, July, 1981.
Ebony, November, 1974.
Esquire, November, 1961.
Essence, August, 1979.
Library Journal, January 15, 1968.
National Observer, March 17, 1969.
New York Times, September 14, 1961.
New York Times Book Review, February 6, 1972, May 13, 1973, December 26, 1976, January 15, 1978.
New York Times Magazine, April 30, 1961.
Progressive, June, 1973.

Ramparts, August, 1975.
Time, February 17, 1961.

*   *   *

GREGORY, J. Dennis
   See WILLIAMS, John A(lfred)

*   *   *

GREGORY, Richard Claxton
   See GREGORY, Dick

*   *   *

GRIMKE, Angelina (Emily) Weld   1880-1958

PERSONAL: Born February 27, 1880, in Boston, Mass.; died after a long illness, June 10, 1958, in New York, N.Y.; daughter of Archibald Henry (a lawyer, diplomat, publisher, and writer) and Sarah Eliza (a writer; maiden name, Stanley) Grimke. *Education:* Boston Normal School of Gymnastics, earned degree, 1902; attended Harvard University, 1904-10.

ADDRESSES: Home—New York, N.Y.

CAREER: Writer. Taught at schools in Washington, D.C., beginning in 1902.

WRITINGS:

Rachel (three-act play; first produced in Washington, D.C., at the Myrtilla Miner Normal School, March 3, 1916; produced in New York City at the Neighborhood Playhouse, April 26, 1917), Cornhill, 1920, reprinted, McGrath, 1969.

Poetry represented in anthologies such as *Negro Poets and Their Poems* (includes Grimke's "Dawn," "A Winter Twilight," "The Puppet-Player," "The Want of You," "El Belso," "At the Spring Dawn," and "To Keep the Memory of Charlotte Forten Grimke"), edited by Robert T. Kerlin, Associated Publishers, 1923; and *Caroling Dusk* (includes Grimke's "Hushed By the Hands of Sleep," "Greenness," "The Eyes of My Regret," "Grass Fingers," "Surrender," "The Ways O' Men," "Tenebris," "When the Green Lies Over the Earth," "A Mona Lisa," "Paradox," "Your Hands," "I Weep," "For the Candle Light," "Dusk," and "A Winter Twilight"), edited by Countee Cullen, Harper, 1927.

Other anthologies featuring Grimke's verse include *Black and White: An Anthology of Washington Verse,* edited by J. C. Byars, Jr., Crane Press, 1927; *The Negro Caravan,* edited by Sterling A. Brown and others, Dryden Press, 1941; *The Poetry of the Negro, 1746-1949,* edited by Langston Hughes and Arna Bontemps, Doubleday, 1949; *American Negro Poetry,* edited by Arna Bontemps, Hill & Wang, 1963; *Black Writers of America,* edited by Richard K. Barksdale and Keneth Kinnamon, Macmillan, 1972; *The New Negro Renaissance: An Anthology,* co-edited by Michael W. Peplow, Holt, 1975; and *Black Sister: Poetry by Black American Women, 1746-1980,* Indiana University Press, 1981.

Contributor to periodicals, including *Birth Control Review, Boston Globe, Boston Pilot, Boston Transcript, Carolina, Crisis, Norfolk County Gazette,* and *Opportunity.*

SIDELIGHTS: Angelina Weld Grimke was a playwright and poet who produced her finest work—personal lyrics—during the Harlem Renaissance of the 1920s. Unlike many of her literary peers, Grimke came from an intellectual background. Her father was Archibald Grimke, a lawyer, writer, and pub-

lisher who championed black rights and served as vice-president of the National Association for the Advancement of Colored People (NAACP). Her mother was also a writer, but her influence was limited, for she abandoned the family in the late 1880s and never returned. Grimke was close to her father, though, and with his encouragement she attended prestigious liberal schools such as the Cushing Academy in Massachusetts. She graduated from the Boston Normal School of Gymnastics in 1902 and then moved to Washington, D.C., where she spent much of her career teaching high-school English.

By the time Grimke arrived in Washington, D.C., she had already published poems in both the *Norfolk County Gazette* and the *Boston Transcript.* Among these early works was a salutation to a nonagenarian relative. More daring was "Beware Les He Awakes!," her 1902 publication in which she warned of the revenge that might be sought eventually by persecuted blacks.

In 1909, seven years after she moved to Washington, D.C., Grimke produced her first extensively anthologized poem, "El Beso," which lyrically reflects on aspects of love. Throughout the next several years she wrote her greatest poems and gained recognition for her sensitive approach to subjects ranging from the social to the romantic. Unlike many Harlem Renaissance writers, however, Grimke avoided sensationalizing the plight of American blacks, and her social perspective is inevitably poignant. In her popular poem "The Black Finger" she stressed hope for the future of blacks by writing of a cypress tree that extends like a black finger into the air, and in "Written for the Fiftieth Anniversary Celebration at Dunbar High School" she assured slavery's descendants that a more promising world lay ahead. Other poems on race, however, offer a gloomier view. "Trees," for instance, describes a nature scene replete with dangling lynching victim, and "At April" notes the additional disappointment that will someday beset black children when they reach adulthood.

Although Grimke wrote compellingly about blacks, her preferred theme was love. Notable works on this theme include "When the Green Lies Over the Earth," "Greenness," "Grass Fingers," and "To Clarissa Scott Delany," poems in which love and the memory of love are elucidated through often pastoral imagery. In "When the Green Lies Over the Earth" springtime and the budding flowers and trees remind the poet of a former loved one, and in the elegiac "To Clarissa Scott Delany" Grimke mourns a dead woman whose finer qualities are perceived to endure even as nature endures.

In these and other poems Grimke also displays remarkable skill as an imagist. Works such as "Dawn" and "A Winter Twilight" reflect her melancholy state through brief descriptions of dim evenings, bleak fields, and pale stars. The four-line "Dawn," with its compact rendering of a gray world and a distant hermit-thrush, is notably compelling in this regard. And in "At the Spring Dawn" Grimke portrays a vividly colored field in which silence is broken by a single bird darting against the sun.

Aside from poetry, Grimke wrote "Rachel," a play sponsored by the NAACP in 1916. "Rachel" is about a young woman living with her brother and her mother in a New York City tenement. Early in the play Rachel and her brother are informed by their mother that their father had been killed years earlier by a lynching mob. Rachel's brother, Tom, responds with anger, but Rachel reacts by considering the bleak future she envisions for black children who will someday face cruel, and often violent, persecution. In the second act, set four years later, Tom tries to find work as a menial laborer and expresses bitter resentment toward America's racially prejudiced society. Rachel, meanwhile, learns of abuses endured by a withdrawn neighborhood girl and by a little boy, Jimmy, whom Rachel adopted after his parents died from chicken pox. The third, and final, act features Rachel distressed by her failure to soothe Jimmy, who has recurring nightmares. Rachel eventually receives a marriage proposal, but she rejects it, choosing to care for already existing black children rather than bring her own into an unfair world. Rarely performed in the ensuing decades, "Rachel" is nonetheless remembered as one of the first American plays written by and for blacks.

Another of Grimke's few non-verse works, the short story "The Closing Door," shares with "Rachel" a bleak perspective on the bearing of black children in a racist society. In "The Closing Door" a woman learns that her brother has been killed by a lynching mob. She is consequently devastated, and after giving birth she becomes insane and kills the child. This story, oddly enough, was first published in *Birth Control Review*.

In her lifetime Grimke was a prominent poet, and her work was included in many key anthologies, including Countee Cullen's *Caroling Dusk* and Langston Hughes and Arna Bontemps's *Poetry of the Negro, 1746-1949*. But in the years since her death in 1958 she has been ignored by most literary critics, though the few that do consider her writings have valued her as a substantial and surprisingly sophisticated artist from a key time in the history of black American literature.

BIOGRAPHICAL/CRITICAL SOURCES:

BOOKS

Dictionary of Literary Biography, Gale, Volume 50: *Afro-American Writers Before the Harlem Renaissance*, 1986, Volume 54: *American Poets, 1880-1945, Third Series*, 1987.

PERIODICALS

Black World, April, 1976.
CLA Journal, June, 1977.
Conditions: Five, 1979.
Drama Critique, spring, 1964.

—*Sketch by Les Stone*

*   *   *

GRIMKE, Charlotte L(ottie) Forten   1837(?)-1914
(Charlotte Forten; Miss C. L. F., Lottie, pseudonyms)

PERSONAL: Born August 17, 1837 (some sources say 1838), in Philadelphia, Pa.; died of a cerebral embolism, July 23, 1914, in Washington, D.C.; buried in Harmony Cemetery, Washington, D.C.; daughter of Robert Bridges (a sailmaker and abolitionist) and Mary Virginia (Wood) Forten; married Francis James Grimke (a Presbyterian minister and abolitionist), December 19, 1878; children: Theodora Cornelia (died in infancy). *Education:* State Normal School at Salem, teaching certificate, 1856.

CAREER: Epes Grammar School, Salem, Mass., teacher, 1856-58, 1860-61; Port Royal Relief Association and Freedman's Aid Society, St. Helena Island, S.C., teacher, 1862; Sumner High School, Washington, D.C., assistant to principal, 1871-72. Clerk for the Federal Treasury Department.

MEMBER: Salem Female Anti-Slavery Society.

WRITINGS:

(Translator, under pseudonym Miss C. L. F.) Emilie Erckmann and Alexander Chatrian, *Madame Therese; or, The Volunteers of '92*, Scribner, 1869.
Journal, edited with introduction and notes by Ray Allen Billington, Dryden Press, 1953, published as *A Free Negro in the Slave Era: The Journal of Charlotte L. Forten*, Collier, 1961 (published in England as *The Journal of Charlotte Forten: A Free Negro in the Slave Era*, Collier-Macmillan, 1967).
(Under name Charlotte Forten) *Life on the Sea Islands* (first published in *Atlantic Monthly*, May-June, 1864), reprinted in *Two Black Teachers During the Civil War: Mary S. Peake, the Colored Teacher at Fortress Monroe, by Lewis C. Lockenwood* [and] *Life on the Sea Islands by Charlotte Forten*, edited by W. L. Katz, Arno Press, 1969.

Poems represented in anthologies, including *The Rising Sun*, A. G. Brown, *Negro Poets and Their Poems*, Associated Publishing, 1935, *Life and Writings of the Grimke Family*, privately printed, 1951, *An Anthology of American Negro Literature*, and *Cavalcade*, Houghton, 1971.

Contributor of poems and essays to periodicals, sometimes under the pseudonyms Lottie or Miss C. L. F., including *Atlantic Monthly, New England Magazine, Liberator, National Anti-Slavery Standard, The Dunbar Speaker and Entertainer*, and *Christian Register*.

SIDELIGHTS: Charlotte L. Forten Grimke is known for her *Journal*, written between 1854 and 1864, that provided details of the abolitionist movement prior to and during the American Civil War. Grimke was born into a well-to-do Philadelphia, Pennsylvania, family. Her grandfather, James Forten, was a second generation freedman and the owner of a prosperous sailmaking business. He was also a nationally known advocate of the abolition of slavery. After Grimke's mother's death Grimke lived at his home and later with her uncle, Robert Purvis, whose estate offered a forum for abolitionist thinkers of the day and a haven for runaway slaves. Grimke was privately tutored while living in Philadelphia so she would not have to attend the segregated schools; but in 1854, when she moved to Salem, Massachusetts, to live with abolitionist Charles Lenox Remond and his wife, she enrolled in the integrated Salem Grammar School. She began her journal at the Remond home and often wrote of the progress of the Negroes' fight for liberation and of her contact with the leading reformers of the day, including John Greenleaf Whittier, Wendell Phillips, and William Lloyd Garrison.

Racial awareness and the abolitionist movement were foremost in Grimke's mind. She wrote in her diary about the injustice of discrimination and how it affected her world view. She wrote of runaway slaves being hounded by mobs and captured slaves dragged through streets, and preferred Salem to Philadelphia because of the indignities blacks suffered in Pennsylvania. There, for example, she and her family were barred from restaurants, museums, theaters, and lectures and were forced to occupy segregated sections on public transportation. Neither was Grimke accepted wholeheartedly in Salem. She writes of one of her schoolmates: "There is one young girl and only one—Miss [Sarah] B[rown] who I believe thoroughly and heartily appreciates anti-slavery,—*radical* anti-slavery, and has no prejudice against color. I wonder that every colored person is not a misanthrope. Surely we have everything to make us hate mankind." She continued to relate an incident where she was snubbed on the street by white girls who were friendly to her in the classroom. "These are but trifles, certainly, to the great, public wrongs which we as a people are obliged to endure. . . . 'How long oh! how long must we continue to suffer—to endure?' Conscience answers it is wrong, it is ignoble to despair; let us labor earnestly and faithfully to acquire knowledge, to break down the barriers of prejudice and oppression.''

Grimke's resentment prompted her driving ambition to prove herself as intelligent and as capable of improvement as whites. She was determined to study and learn all that she could in order to be a living example of the capabilities of black people. She was an outstanding student who taught herself French, German, and Latin and attended literary and political lectures. During a single year her diary shows that she read over one hundred books, ranging from the classics to contemporary poetry, that included works by Charles Dickens and Ralph Waldo Emerson.

Yet she was never satisfied with her progress. On Tuesday, June 15, 1858, Grimke wrote: "Have been under-going a thorough self-examination. The result is a mingled feeling of sorrow, shame and self-contempt. Have realized more deeply and bitterly than ever in my life my own ignorance and folly. Not only am I without the gifts of Nature,—wit, beauty and talent; without the accomplishments which nearly every one of my age, whom I know, possesses; but I am not even *intelligent*. And for *this* there is not the *shadow* of an excuse. Have had many advantages of late years; and it is entirely owning to my own want of energy, perseverance and application, that I have not improved them.''

Upon graduation from the Salem Normal School, Grimke took a teaching position at Epes Grammar School in Salem and became the first Negro in Massachusetts to instruct whites. She was accepted by her students, their parents, her colleagues, and the school board, but poor health forced her to resign in March, 1858. She fought recurring tuberculosis for the next three years then returned to teaching. With a letter of reference from John Greenleaf Whittier, Grimke petitioned the Boston Educational Commission in August 1862 to send her as a volunteer for the Port Royal Experiment, an educational endeavor taking place on a group of Confederate islands off the coast of South Carolina that the Union forces occupied in 1861. The influx of the Northern army prompted the slave-holding plantation owners of the islands to flee and leave behind rich cotton fields and eight thousand illiterate slaves. To Northern liberals this evacuation provided the opportunity to prove the worth of the black man: that he could be educated, trained as a soldier, and be a useful citizen. Under Northern supervision an extensive program of educational, medical, and material aid was inaugurated.

Grimke arrived at St. Helena Island in October 1862 to teach at a small school, determined to show her race was capable of great accomplishments. There she wrote: "Let our motto . . . be 'Excelsior' and we cannot fail to make some improvement." Additionally, she sought to inspire her students of the Port Royal Experiment "with courage and ambition (of a noble sort,) and a high purpose." She was fascinated by their musical abilities, their religious services, and the language that the newly freed blacks spoke—Gullah, a combination of African languages. She was also as interested in the soldiers' progress as her students'. She was elated that field workers became soldiers to defend their freedom against the Confederate army: "They say the black soldiers fought the rebels bravely;— . . . I can think of nothing but this reg[iment]. How

proud of it I am!'' Grimke sent Whittier an essay on the project, "Life on the Sea Islands," and he had it published in two parts in the *Atlantic Monthly* in May and June of 1864. The challenge of the experiment gave her great satisfaction, especially when her students progressed in their studies, but the work and the environment were physically and emotionally draining. She endured warfare, ill health, heat, and flea infestation but returned to Philadelphia in May of 1864.

For the next decade Grimke wrote poetry and prose and taught. In 1877 she met Francis Grimke, the son of a slave and a plantation owner and the nephew of the well known feminists and abolitionists Sarah and Angelina Grimke. Enslaved as a youth, he went on to graduate as valedictorian of his class from Lincoln College and earned a degree in theology from Princeton University after he was freed. They married in 1878 and settled in Washington, D.C, where they led socially and culturally active lives.

BIOGRAPHICAL/CRITICAL SOURCES:

BOOKS

Cooper, Anna Julia, *Life and Writings of the Grimke Family*, privately printed, 1951, New York Public Library, 1974.
Douty, Esther M., *Charlotte Forten, Free Black Teacher*, Garrard, 1971.
Forten, Charlotte L., *Journal*, edited with notes, by Ray Allen Billington, Dryden Press, 1953.
Longsworth, Polly, *Charlotte Forten, Black and Free*, Crowell, 1970.
Twentieth-Century Literary Criticism, Volume 16, Gale, 1985.

PERIODICALS

Negro History Bulletin, January, 1947.
New York Times Book Review, April 12, 1953.

*   *   *

GROSVENOR, Verta Mae   1938-

PERSONAL: Born April 4, 1938, in Fairfax, S.C.; married; children: Kali, Chandra. *Education:* Received high school education in Philadelphia, Pa.

ADDRESSES: c/o Penn Center, P.O. Box 126, Frogmore, S. C. 29920.

CAREER: Writer.

MEMBER: People United to Save Humanity (PUSH).

WRITINGS:

Vibration Cooking; or, The Traveling Notes of a Geechee Girl (autobiography), Doubleday, 1970.
Thursday and Every Other Sunday Off: A Domestic Rap, Doubleday, 1972.
Plain Brown Rapper (poems), Doubleday, 1975.

Work is represented in several anthologies. Author of food column in *Amsterdam News* and of column in *Chicago Courier*. Contributor of articles and stories to magazines and newspapers.

*   *   *

GUILLEN (y BATISTA), Nicolas (Cristobal)   1902-

PERSONAL: Surname pronounced "gee-*yane*," with a hard *g* as in geese; born July 10, 1902, in Camaguey, Cuba; son of Nicolas (a silversmith, newspaper editor, and politician) and

Argelia (Batista) Guillen. *Education:* Graduated from Camaguey Institute (high school), 1920; attended University of Havana, 1920-21.

ADDRESSES: Home—Calle O, No. 2, Edificio Someillan, Vedado, Havana, Cuba. *Office*—Union Nacional de Escritores y Artistas Cubanos, Calle 17, No. 351, Vedado, Havana, Cuba.

CAREER: Poet, 1922—. Founder and editor of *Lis* literary magazine in the early 1920s; contributor to Cuban newspapers and magazines, including *Diario de la marina,* c. 1922-37; correspondent in Spain for *Mediodia* magazine, 1937-38; candidate for political offices in Cuba on Popular Socialist (later Communist) ticket in the 1940s; lecturer and correspondent in Latin America and Europe in the 1940s and 1950s; president of Cuban National Union of Writers and Artists (UNEAC), 1961—; served as editor in chief of *La Gaceta de Cuba* (official cultural publication of UNEAC) and as Cuban ambassador.

AWARDS, HONORS: Lenin Peace Prize from the Soviet Union, 1954; Cuban Order of Jose Marti from the Republic of Cuba, 1981; Order of Merit from the Republic of Haiti; Order of Cyril and Methodius (first class) from the People's Republic of Bulgaria.

WRITINGS:

POETRY

Motivos de son (title means "Motifs of Sound"), 1930, special fiftieth anniversary edition, with music by Amadeo Roldan, Editorial Letras Cubanas, 1980.
Songoro cosongo, 1931, published as *Songoro cosongo: Poemas mulatos,* Presencia Latinoamericana, 1981.
West Indies Ltd.: Poemas, Imprenta Ucar, Garcia, 1934.
Cantos para soldados y sones para turistas (title means "Songs for Soldiers and Sones for Tourists"), Editorial Masas, 1937, published as *El son entero: Cantos para soldados y sones para turistas,* Editorial Losada, 1952.
Espana: Poema en cuatro angustias y una esperanza (title means "Spain: A Poem in Four Anguishes and a Hope"), Editorial Mexico Nuevo, 1937.
El son entero: Suma poetica, 1929-1946 (title means "The Entire Son"; with a letter by Miguel de Unamuno and musical notation by various composers), Editorial Pleamar, 1947, Premia Editora, 1982.
La paloma de vuelo popular (title means "The Dove of Popular Flight"), 1958, also published, in a single volume, with *Elegias* (title means "Elegies"), Editorial Losada, 1959.
Puedes? (title means "Can You?"; with drawings by the author), Libreria La Tertulia, 1961.
Elegia a Jesus Menendez, Imprenta Nacional de Cuba, 1962.
La rueda dentada (title means "The Serrated Wheel"), UNEAC, 1962.
Tengo (title means "I Have"), prologue by Jose Antonio Portuondo, Editora del Consejo Nacional de Universidades, 1964, translation by Richard J. Carr published as *Tengo,* Broadside Press, 1974.
Poemas de amor (title means "Love Poems"), Ediciones La Tertulia, 1964.
Nadie (title means "Nobody"), Sol y Piedra, 1966.
El gran zoo, Instituto del Libro, 1967, translation by Robert Marquez published as *Patria o muerte! The Great Zoo and Other Poems,* Monthly Review Press, 1972.
El diario que a diario, UNEAC, 1972.
Poemas Manuables, UNEAC, 1975.

El corazon con que vivo (title means "The Heart With Which I Live"), UNEAC, 1975.
Por que imperialismo?: Poemas (title means "Why Imperialism?: Poems"), Ediciones Calarca, 1976.
Elegias, edited by Jose Martinez Matos, illustrations by Dario Mora, UNEAC, 1977.
Coplas de Juan Descalzo (title means "The Ballad of John Barefoot"), Editorial Letras Cubanas, 1979.
Musica de camara (title means "Chamber Music"), UNEAC, 1979.
Sputnik 57, [Cuba], 1980.

Also author of *Poemas para el Che* (title means "Poems for Che"), *Buenos Dias, Fidel,* for Grafica Horizonte, and *Por el Mar de las Antillas anda un barco de papel: Poemas para ninos mayores de edad* (title means "Going Through the Antilles Sea in a Boat of Paper: Poems for Older Children"), with illustrations by Rapi Diego, for UNEAC.

POETRY COLLECTIONS

Cuba Libre, translated from the Spanish by Langston Hughes and Ben Frederic Carruthers, Anderson & Ritchie, 1948.
Songoro cosongo, Motivos de Son, West Indies Ltd., Espana: Poema en cuatro angustias y una esperanza, Editorial Losada, 1952.
Nicolas Guillen: Sus mejores poemas, Organizacion de los Festivales del Libro, 1959.
Los mejores versos de Nicolas Guillen, Editorial Nuestra America, 1961.
Antologia mayor: El son entero y otros poemas, UNEAC, 1964.
Antologia mayor, Instituto del Libro, 1969.
Antologia clave, prologue by Luis Inigo Madrigal, Editorial Nascimento, 1971.
Man-Making Words: Selected Poems of Nicolas Guillen, translated from the Spanish by Robert Marquez and David Arthur McMurray, University of Massachusetts Press, 1972.
Cuba, amor y revolucion: Poemas, Editorial Causachun, 1972.
Obra poetica, 1920-1972 (two volumes), edited by Angel Augier with illustrations by the author, Editorial de Arte y Literatura, 1974.
Latinamericason, Quatro Editores, 1974.
Nueva antologia mayor, edited by Augier, Editorial Letras Cubanas, 1979.
Paginas vueltas: Seleccion de poemas y apuntes autobiograficos (title means "Turned Pages: Selected Poems and Autobiographical Notes"), Grupo Editor de Buenos Aires, 1980.
Paginas vueltas: Memorias, UNEAC, 1982.

OTHER

Claudio Jose Domingo Brindis de Salas, el rey de las octavas (title means "Claudio Jose Domingo Brindis de Salas, King of the Octaves"; prose), Municipio de La Habana, 1935.
Prosa de prisa, cronicas (title means "Hasty Prose, Chronicles"; selection of journalistic articles published from 1938 to 1961), Universidad Central de las Villas, 1962, expanded edition published as *Prosa de prisa, 1929-1972* (three volumes), edited with introduction by Augier, Editorial Arte y Literatura, 1975.
El libro de las decimas, UNEAC, 1980.
El libro de los sones, Editorial Letras Cubanas, 1982.
Sol de domingo, UNEAC, 1982.

Cronista en tres epocas (title means "Journalist in Three Epochs"; selection of journalistic articles edited by Maria Julia Guerra Avila and Pedro Rodriguez Gutierrez), Editorial Politica, 1984.

Tengo was made into a sound recording in the 1970s and released by Consejo Nacional de Cultura.

Works represented in anthologies, including *Some Modern Cuban Poems by Nicolas Guillen and Others,* translated from the Spanish by Manish Nandy, Satyabrata Pal, 1968.

SIDELIGHTS: Nicolas Guillen, considered a master of the so-called "Afro-Cuban" style, is one of Cuba's best known and most respected poets. A mulatto from the provincial middle class, Guillen began his career as a newspaper journalist while writing poetry in his spare time. A 1930 visit to Cuba by the black American poet Langston Hughes, a leading figure in the black cultural movement known as the Harlem Renaissance, inspired Guillen to write and publish his first verse collection the same year, *Motivos de son* ("Motifs of Sound"). A group of eight poems structured rhythmically like the *son,* a popular Cuban song-and-dance arrangement with strong African elements, this work drew on a new international interest in primitive art and African culture and became identified with the Afro-Caribbean movement in Hispanic poetry that began in the mid-1920s. Like earlier white Afro-Caribbean poets in Cuba and Puerto Rico, Guillen treated local lower-class black life as his major theme and combined onomatopoeia—the use of words whose sounds imply their sense—and African rhythms as major stylistic devices, but he went further in both style and substance than his predecessors, who tended toward somewhat stereotypical depictions of a joyful, sensual, happy-go-lucky folk. Guillen instead wrote "from within"—as G. R. Coulthard noted in *Race and Colour in Caribbean Literature*—and subtly gave poetic voice to the lives of poverty and pathos behind the picturesque facade of Havana's black slum dwellers. Guillen was also credited with capturing the genuine dialect and speech patterns of Cuban blacks, which he blended with Yoruba African words to create a unique language that relied as much on sound and rhythm as on word sense for its meaning.

Guillen further refined his Afro-Cuban poetry in *Songoro cosongo,* a 1931 verse collection that quickly earned him a worldwide reputation and became widely regarded as the poet's masterwork. Published with Guillen's lottery winnings that year, this work evinces a deeper social consciousness and still bolder style in seeking to express the tragedy, passion, and vigor of black life in Cuba. The poet moves from an implicit criticism of slum life to direct denunciations of racism and an affirmation of the roles of black men and women in building Cuban and American culture and society. According to Guillen, he sought to create a "mulatto poetry" that would reflect Cuba's true history and racial composition.

Stylistically, Guillen's occasional use of the ballad form and reliance on naive, "nonsensical" imagery in *Songoro cosongo* shows the influence of the internationally acclaimed Spanish poet Federico Garcia Lorca, whom Guillen met in Cuba as Garcia Lorca was returning to Europe from the United States. The Cuban poet's extraordinary synthesis of traditional Spanish metric forms with Afro-Cuban words, rhythms, and folkloric symbols uniquely captures the cultural flavor of the Spanish-speaking Caribbean, critics have noted. Other poems in *Songoro cosongo* rely almost entirely on onomatopoeic effects and rhythm, becoming, in a sense, abstract word-paintings with no direct representational value at all—the title itself has

no meaning other than its rhythmic and symbolic suggestions. Though seemingly spontaneous, these verses are in fact carefully crafted, with rigorous attention to rhyme, meter, and tonal nuances. Often recited publicly to a drum accompaniment, Guillen's Afro-Cuban verse has also been set to music by the Spanish composer Xavier Montsalvatge and sung by the American mezzo-soprano Marilyn Horne, among others.

The current of social protest running through *Songoro cosongo* turns deeper and swifter in *West Indies Ltd.,* published just after the 1933 revolution that deposed Cuban dictator Antonio Machado. In verse that is by turns satirical and bitter, Guillen depicts the often cruel and exploitative history of slavery, colonialism, and imperialism (particularly in its contemporary American form) in the Antilles islands of the West Indies. The poet's commitment to social change grew when he traveled to Spain in 1937 to cover the civil war for *Mediodia* magazine and participate in the anti-fascist Second International Congress of Writers for the Defense of Culture. That year he joined the Cuban Communist party (then called Popular Socialist) and wrote a long, elegiac ode to the Spanish Republic titled *Espana: Poema en cuatro angustias y una esperanza* ("Spain: A Poem in Four Anguishes and a Hope") that voiced his hope for humanity's communist future. Guillen also devoted most of his 1937 verse collection, *Cantos para soldados y sones para turistas* ("Songs for Soldiers and Sones for Tourists"), to social and political themes.

Guillen spent much of the next two decades outside of Cuba, traveling around Europe and Latin America as a lecturer and correspondent for several Cuban journals. In 1962 he published a selection of these articles under the title *Prosa de prisa* ("Hasty Prose"). Guillen's poetic output during these years was somewhat reduced, although he published a major collection titled *El son entero* ("The Entire Son") in 1947 and his first English-language selection, *Cuba-Libre* (co-edited and translated by Langston Hughes), that following year. Denied permission to return to Cuba by the Fulgencio Batista dictatorship in the 1950s, Guillen spent several years in unhappy exile in Paris, France, where he wrote *La paloma de vuelo popular* ("The Dove of Popular Flight") and *Elegias* ("Elegies"), published together in one volume in 1958. These two works complement each other thematically and stylistically. The first consists mainly of broadly political—and often witty and ironical—protest poems against the Cuban dictatorship and American imperialism, while *Elegias* mourns the loss of friends and other victims of political repression in somber, lyrical tones.

The triumph of the Cuban revolution in early 1959 immediately brought Guillen back to his homeland, where he enthusiastically embraced the revolutionary cause. Already recognized as the country's greatest living poet, Guillen readily took on the role of poet laureate of the revolution. His 1964 verse collection *Tengo* ("I Have") is a joyful celebration of the revolutionary victory that reads somewhat like a historical epic, praising the insurgent heroes and depicting major battles against Batista, the dictator's flight, and the Cuban victory over the American-backed invasion at the Bay of Pigs. As the title suggests, Guillen also explores the new feelings of empowerment, possession, and comradeship that the revolution inspired in many poor Cubans.

The theme of social liberation is present as well in Guillen's 1967 collection, *El gran zoo.* Hailed as one of Guillen's outstanding later works, *El gran zoo* marked a major stylistic shift for a poet usually identified with the Afro-Cuban style. While still showing a crystalline attention to craft, these poems rely less on rhyme and strict meter than Guillen's past work and approach free verse with spare wording and fractured images. The volume is structured thematically as a visit to a metaphorical zoo, where some of the world's curious and beautiful social, natural, and metaphysical phenomena are catalogued in individual poems. Guillen's usually direct language is more allusive and enigmatic here, and his subjects range from critical jabs at imperialism to taut musings on love, the forces of nature, and the ineffable mystery of being.

Both *Tengo* and *El gran zoo*, along with another collection published in 1972, *Man-Making Words: Selected Poems of Nicolas Guillen*, are available in English translation. Guillen's poems have also been translated into many other languages, including French, German, Russian, and Hebrew. Awarded the Cuban Order of Jose Marti, the country's highest honor, in 1981, Guillen has served for many years as president of the National Union of Cuban Writers and Artists.

BIOGRAPHICAL/CRITICAL SOURCES:

BOOKS

Augier, Angel, *Nicolas Guillen: Notas para un estudio biografico-critico* (two volumes), Universidad de las Villas, 1963-64.
Coulthard, R. G., *Race and Colour in Caribbean Literature*, Oxford University Press, 1962.
Ellis, Keith, *Cuba's Nicolas Guillen: Poetry and Ideology*, University of Toronto Press, 1983.
Guillen, Nicolas, *Paginas vueltas: Memorias*, UNEAC, 1982.
Martinez Estrada, Ezequiel, *La Poesia de Nicolas Guillen*, Calicanto Editorial, c. 1977.
Sardinha, Dennis, *The Poetry of Nicolas Guillen: An Introduction*, New Beacon, 1976.

PERIODICALS

Black Scholar, July/August, 1985.
Hispania, October 25, 1942.
Latin America Research Review, Volume 17, number 1, 1982.
Opportunity, January, 1946.

—Sketch by Curtis Skinner

*   *   *

GUNN, Bill
  See GUNN, William Harrison

*   *   *

GUNN, William Harrison   1934-
  (Bill Gunn)

PERSONAL: Born July 15, 1934, in Philadelphia, Pa.; son of William Harrison and Louise (Alexander) Gunn. *Education:* Attended public schools in Philadelphia, Pa. *Politics:* Democrat.

ADDRESSES: Home—New York, N.Y. *Agent*—William Morris Agency, 1350 Avenue of the Americas, New York, N.Y. 10019.

CAREER: Actor on stage, television, and films, 1955—; writer. *Military service:* U.S. Navy.

AWARDS, HONORS: Emmy Award, National Academy of Television Arts and Sciences, 1972, for "Johnnas"; "Ganga and Hess" chosen one of ten best American films of the decade, Cannes Film Festival, 1973; Audelco Recognition Award, Audience Development Committee, and Best Play of the Year

award, both 1975, both for "Black Picture Show"; Guggenheim Foundation fellowship in filmmaking, 1980.

WRITINGS:

UNDER NAME BILL GUNN; NOVELS

All the Rest Have Died, Delacorte, 1964.
Rhinestone Sharecropping (also see below), Reed, Cannon, 1981.

UNDER NAME BILL GUNN; STAGE PLAYS

"Marcus in the High Grass," produced in New York by Theatre Guild, 1959.
"Johnnas," produced in New York at Chelsea Theatre, 1968.
Black Picture Show (produced in New York at Vivian Beaumont Theatre), Reed, Cannon, 1975.
"Rhinestone" (musical; based on novel *Rhinestone Sharecropping*), produced in New York at Richard Allen Center, 1982.
"Family Employment," produced in New York at Public Theatre, 1985.

Also author of "Celebration," produced in Los Angeles at Mark Taper Forum.

UNDER NAME BILL GUNN; SCREENPLAYS

"Fame Game," Columbia Pictures, 1968.
"Friends," Universal Studios, 1968.
"Stop" (never released), Warner, 1969.
(With Ronald Ribman) "The Angel Levine" (adaptation of novel by Bernard Malamud), United Artists, 1970.
"Don't the Moon Look Lonesome" (adaptation of novel by Don Asher), Chuck Barris Productions, 1970.
"The Landlord" (adaptation of novel by Kristin Hunter), United Artists, 1970.
"Ganja and Hess," Kelly-Jordan Enterprises, 1973, re-edited and released under title "Blood Couple," Heritage Enterprises, 1973.
"The Greatest: The Muhammed Ali Story," Columbia, 1976.

UNDER NAME BILL GUNN; TELEVISION SCREENPLAYS

"Johnnas," National Broadcasting Company, Washington, D.C., 1972.
"The Alberta Hunter Story," Southern Pictures/British Broadcasting Corporation, London, 1982.

WORK IN PROGRESS: A novel, *The Death Game;* plays.

SIDELIGHTS: Bill Gunn, an actor and director, is the author of several plays and novels which detail the "role of the artist in a materialistic and pitiless world," according to Ilona Leki in the *Dictionary of Literary Biography*. An early example,"Black Picture Show," is described by Jack Kroll of *Newsweek* as being "about a black artist who has to sell out to the devilish white culture in order to survive." But, Kroll adds, "there's more to the play than that. . . . The leading character is Alexander, a poet and writer whose sanity appears to have snapped in his lifelong attempt to make it as a black artist in a white, anti-art society. Beginning in a mental institution [where Alexander has been confined], the play breaks back into time to show how the pressure built up."

Critics Ted E. Kalem and Brendan Gill take issue with Gunn's depiction of a writer's compromise with the Hollywood system. Kalem, writing in *Time*, does not understand Gunn's purpose in depicting Alexander as a victim of exploitation: "No artist has ever been corrupted or humiliated by the quest for cash unless he was a willing accomplice." And Gill, while calling the author an ''obviously gifted'' playwright, wonders in the *New Yorker:* ''Why is it worse for a black to sell out to a white than for a white to sell out to a white, or, for that matter, for a black to sell out to a black? Except on grounds of racial snobbery, with its implication that all blacks ought to be counted on to behave more honorably than all whites, why should the question of color arise?'' Other critics, says Leki, ''commented in particular upon Gunn's brilliant depiction of the British director and his wife.'' The Audelco Award selection committee, a group that recognizes outstanding contributions to black theater, named Gunn the Best Playwright, and ''Black Picture Show'' the Best Play of the Year in 1975.

''Rhinestone,'' a stage musical Gunn adapted from his novel *Rhinestone Sharecropping,* is ''apparently inspired by [the author's] involvement with the 1976 Hollywood film biography of Muhammed Ali, 'The Greatest,' '' according to Frank Rich's *New York Times* review. The critic differs with Gunn's characterization in this production: ''The hero and the other black characters are vaguely written martyrs or naifs; the moguls are absurdly caricatured racist villains. By Act III, there's little left for the two sides to do but scream at one another in a simplistically polarized debate that strains credibility to the breaking point.'' Even so, states Rich, ''one finds patches of good writing [in ''Rhinestone,''] starting with a haunting opening monologue in which [the protagonist's] father . . . recounts how the producer David Belasco once exploited a Harlem vaudeville troupe during an earlier show-business era.'' ''The main problem is that Gunn is consumed with hate for not only Hollywood . . . but also, it seems, the whole white race,'' *New York* contributor John Simon writes. ''What, then, is left? The odd line flashing with honest anger, the occasional bit of searing sarcasm redolent of pain.''

Reception for Gunn's film ''Ganja and Hess'' was also mixed. Developed from a script about a black ''vampire'' who slakes his thirst at blood banks, the film actually treats the subject of addiction in general, Leki relates. He cites comments from critics who called it ''the most introspective of Black films'' and ''the most complicated, intriguing, subtle, sophisticated, and passionate Black film of the seventies.'' It was, he reports, ''the only one of three hundred American film entrants selected for showing during Critics' Week at the Cannes Film Festival in 1973,'' and it moved the usually quiet festival audience to loud applause. ''It was later chosen as one of the ten best films of the 1970s,'' he adds. However, New York theaters ran the film ''for a mere week.'' Despite this misfortune, Leki notes, the film was given a ''landmark'' showing at the Museum of Modern Art and has gained ''an excellent reputation and a small but enthusiastic following in the world of the underground film.''

BIOGRAPHICAL/CRITICAL SOURCES:

BOOKS

Authors in the News, Volume 1, Gale, 1976.
Contemporary Literary Criticism, Volume 5, Gale, 1976.
Dictionary of Literary Biography, Volume 38: *Afro-American Writers after 1955: Dramatists and Prose Writers,* Gale, 1985.
Monaco, James, *American Film Now,* Oxford University Press, 1979.
Schraufnagel, Noel, *From Apology to Protest: The Black American Novel,* Everett/Edwards, 1973.

PERIODICALS

Essence, October, 1973.

Los Angeles Times Book Review, May 9, 1982.
Newsweek, January 20, 1975.
New York, January 27, 1975, December 6, 1982.
New Yorker, January 20, 1975.
New York Times, December 23, 1982.
Philadelphia Bulletin, December 1, 1974.
Time, January 20, 1975.

*   *   *

GUY, Rosa (Cuthbert)   1928-

PERSONAL: Born September 1, 1928, in Trinidad and Tobago; came to United States in 1932; daughter of Henry and Audrey (Gonzales) Cuthbert; married Warner Guy (deceased); children: Warner.

ADDRESSES: Agent—Ellen Levine Literary Agency, Inc., 432 Park Ave. S., Suite 1205, New York, N.Y. 10016.

CAREER: Writer.

MEMBER: Harlem Writer's Guild (president).

AWARDS, HONORS: The Disappearance was named to the ''Best Books for Young Adults 1979'' list, by the Young Adult Services Division of the American Library Association.

WRITINGS:

NOVELS; EXCEPT AS INDICATED

Bird at My Window, Lippincott, 1966, reprinted, Schocken, 1985.
(Editor) *Children of Longing* (anthology), Holt, 1971.
The Friends (young adult), Holt, 1973.
Ruby: A Novel, Viking, 1976.
Edith Jackson, Viking, 1978.
The Disappearance (young adult), Delacorte, 1979.
Mirror of Her Own, Delacorte, 1981.
(Translator and adaptor) Birago Diop, *Mother Crocodile: An Uncle Amadou Tale from Senegal* (story), Delacorte, 1981.
A Measure of Time, Holt, 1983.
New Guys around the Block (young adult), Delacorte, 1983.
Paris, Pee Wee and Big Dog (juvenile), Gollancz, 1984, Delacorte, 1985.
My Love, My Love, or, the Peasant Girl, Holt, 1985.
And I Heard a Bird Sing (young adult), Delacorte, 1986.

OTHER

Also author of one-act play, ''Venetian Blinds,'' 1954. Contributor to *Cosmopolitan* and *Freedomways.*

WORK IN PROGRESS: A book, *Alexander Hamilton: The Enigma; Benidine,* a novel dealing with a Trinidadian family in New York; research in African languages.

SIDELIGHTS: Rosa Guy often writes about black teenagers, but her themes appeal to readers of all ages. And, although one of Guy's publishers once indicated that her '''literary themes stem from the fact that she is a black and a woman,''' Katherine Paterson asserts in *Washington Post Book World,* ''a great strength of Guy's work is her ability to peel back society's labels and reveal beneath them highly individual men and women.'' Her novel *Edith Jackson* is described by Brian Baumfield in the *Times Literary Supplement* as ''a vigorous, uncompromising'' book, with characters who ''live and breathe and are totally credible. The West Indian speech may prove difficult for some, but it is a raw novel of urgency and power, which readers of sixteen and older will find a moving experience.'' *New York Times Book Review* critic Selma G. Lanes comments that, in reading *New Guys around the Block*, ''the reader cannot resist rooting for'' the author's main character, ''with his intelligence and growing self-awareness, as he negotiates the booby traps of a difficult life.'' Alice Walker points out in the *New York Times Book Review* that, at ''the heart of'' Guy's novel *The Friends* is ''the fight to gain perception of one's own real character; the grim struggle for self-knowledge and the almost killing internal upheaval that brings the necessary growth of compassion and humility *and courage,* so that friendship (of any kind, but especially between those of notable economic and social differences) can exist.''

A Measure of Time is a departure from Guy's fiction for youths. In the opinion of Stuart Schoffman in the *Los Angeles Times,* it ''is a black *Bildungsroman* in the tradition of Claude McKay, Ralph Ellison and James Baldwin, a sharp and well-written meld of storytelling and sociology. Which is to say it is hardly an Alger tale, or if anything a bitter parody.'' The heroine of the novel, Dorine, born poor in Alabama, begins working as a maid when she is eight. Molested by her boss, she runs to Cleveland as a teenager with the money she has saved. There, she becomes a prostitute, and later, in Harlem during its 1920s renaissance, she takes up a career as a high-class shoplifter, a profession that sees her through the depression in style but eventually sends her to prison. She is released and regains a

modest success as a small businesswoman. Susan Isaacs describes her in the *New York Times Book Review* as ''a brash and intelligent guide; her observations about people and places are funny, pointed and often moving,'' although ''the other characters in this novel do not come to life. . . . Only Dorine stands on her own—she and the Harlem setting are vividly described, filled with life and a pleasure to read about.''

BIOGRAPHICAL/CRITICAL SOURCES:

BOOKS

Contemporary Literary Criticism, Volume XXVI, Gale, 1983.
Dictionary of Literary Biography, Volume XXXIII: *Afro-American Fiction Writers after 1955,* Gale, 1984.

PERIODICALS

Los Angeles Times, August 24, 1983.
New York Times Book Review, November 4, 1973, July 2, 1978, December 2, 1979, October 4, 1981, August 28, 1983, October 9, 1983, November 11, 1985.
Times Educational Supplement, June 6, 1980.
Times Literary Supplement, September 20, 1974, December 14, 1979, July 18, 1980, August 3, 1984.
Washington Post, January 9, 1966.
Washington Post Book World, November 11, 1979.

H

HALEY, Alex (Palmer) 1921-

PERSONAL: Born August 11, 1921, in Ithaca, N.Y.; son of Simon Alexander (a professor) and Bertha George (a teacher; maiden name, Palmer) Haley; married Nannie Branch, 1941 (divorced, 1964); married Juliette Collins, 1964 (divorced); children: Lydia Ann, William Alexander, Cynthia Gertrude. *Education:* Attended Elizabeth City Teachers College, 1937-39.

ADDRESSES: Office—Kinte Corporation, P. O. Box 3338, Beverly Hills, Calif. 90212.

CAREER: U.S. Coast Guard, 1939-59, retiring as chief journalist; free-lance writer, 1959—. Founder and president of Kinte Corporation, Los Angeles, Calif., 1972—. Script consultant for limited television series "Roots," "Roots: The Next Generation," and "Palmerstown, U. S. A."; has lectured extensively and appeared frequently on radio and television; adviser to African American Heritage Association, Detroit, Mich.

MEMBER: Authors Guild, Society of Magazine Writers.

AWARDS, HONORS: Litt. D. from Simpson College, 1971, Howard University, 1974, Williams College, 1975, and Capitol University, 1975; special citation from National Book Award committee, 1977, for *Roots;* special citation from Pulitzer Prize committee, 1977, for *Roots;* Spingarn Medal from NAACP, 1977; nominated to Black Filmmakers Hall of Fame, 1981, for producing "Palmerstown, U. S. A.," 1981.

WRITINGS:

(With Malcolm X) *The Autobiography of Malcolm X,* Grove, 1965.
Roots: The Saga of an American Family, Doubleday, 1976.

Initiated "Playboy Interviews" feature for *Playboy,* 1962. Contributor to periodicals, including *Reader's Digest, New York Times Magazine, Harper's,* and *Atlantic.*

WORK IN PROGRESS: My Search for Roots, an account of how *Roots* was researched and written; a study of Henning, Tenn., where Haley was raised.

SIDELIGHTS: Haley's book *Roots* is seldom mentioned without the word "phenomenon" tacked on. Combined with the impact of the televised "mini-series," *Roots* has become a "literary-television phenomenon" and a "sociological event,"

according to *Time.* By April, 1977, almost two million people had seen all or part of the eight-episode television series.

Although critics generally lauded Haley for his accomplishment, they seemed unsure whether to treat *Roots* as a novel or as a historical account. While it is based on factual events, the dialogue, thoughts, and emotions of the characters are fictionalized. Haley himself described the book as "faction," a mixture of fact and fiction. Most critics concurred and evaluated *Roots* as a blend of history and entertainment. And despite the fictional characterizations, Willie Lee Rose suggested in the *New York Review of Books,* Kunte Kinte's parents Omoro and Binte "could possibly become the African proto-parents of millions of Americans who are going to admire their dignity and grace." *Newsweek* found that Haley's decision to fictionalize was the right approach: "Instead of writing a scholarly monograph of little social impact, Haley has written a blockbuster in the best sense—a book that is bold in concept and ardent in execution, one that will reach millions of people and alter the way we see ourselves."

Some concern was voiced, especially at the time of the television series, that racial tension in America would be aggravated by *Roots.* But while *Time* reported several incidents of racial violence following the telecast, it commented that "most observers thought that in the long term, *Roots* would improve race relations, particularly because of the televised version's profound impact on whites. . . . A broad consensus seemed to be emerging that *Roots* would spur black identity, and hence black pride, and eventually pay important dividends." Some black leaders viewed *Roots* "as the most important civil rights event since the 1965 march on Selma," according to *Time.* Vernon Jordan, executive director of the National Urban League, called it "the single most spectacular educational experience in race relations in America."

Haley has heard only positive comments from both blacks and whites. He told William Marmon in a *Time* interview: "The blacks who are buying books are not buying them to go out and fight someone, but because they want to know who they are. *Roots* is all of our stories. It's the same for me or any black. It's just a matter of filling in the blanks—which person, living in which village, going on what ship across the same ocean, slavery, emancipation, the struggle for freedom. . . . The white response is more complicated. But when you start talking about family, about lineage and ancestry, you are talk-

241

ing about every person on earth. We all have it; it's a great equalizer. . . . I think the book has touched a strong, subliminal cord.''

But there was also concern, according to *Time*, that ''breast-beating about the past may turn into a kind of escapism, distracting attention from the present. Only if *Roots* turns the anger at yesterday's slavery into anger at today's ghetto will it really matter.'' And James Baldwin wrote in the *New York Times Book Review:* ''*Roots* is a study of continuities, of consequences, of how a people perpetuate themselves, how each generation helps to doom, or helps to liberate, the coming one—the action of love, or the effect of the absence of love, in time. It suggests, with great power, how each of us, however unconsciously, can't but be the vehicle of the history which has produced us. Well, we can perish in this vehicle, children, or we can move on up the road.''

For months after the publication of *Roots* in October, 1976, Haley signed at least five hundred books daily, spoke to an average of six thousand people a day, and traveled round trip coast-to-coast at least once a week, according to *People*. Stardom took its toll on Haley. *New Times* reported that on a trip to his ancestral village in Africa, Haley complained: ''You'll find that people who celebrate you will kill you. They forget you are blood and flesh and bone. I have had days and weeks and months of schedules where everything from my breakfast to my last waking moment was planned for me. . . . Someone has you by the arm and is moving you from room to room. Then people *grab* at you. You're actually pummeled—hit with books—and you ask yourself, 'My God, what *is* this?' ''

Although Haley now wishes that he were famous ''one day a month,'' stardom was not always a problem. Upon retiring from the Coast Guard in 1959, he decided to become a freelance writer and headed for Greenwich Village, rented a basement apartment, and ''prepared to starve,'' as he told John F. Baker in a *Publishers Weekly* interview. Unwilling to take a job because he wanted to devote his full energies to writing, he came close to starving. ''One day,'' he related to Baker, ''I was down to 18 cents and a couple of cans of sardines, and that was *it*.'' The next day a check came for an article he had written and he struggled on. Today the 18 cents and cans of sardines are framed and hang in the library of his home as symbols of his ''determination to be independent.''

BIOGRAPHICAL/CRITICAL SOURCES:

BOOKS

Contemporary Literary Criticism, Volume 8, Gale, 1978.
Dictionary of Literary Biography, Volume 38: *Afro-American Writers After 1955: Dramatists and Prose Writers*, Gale, 1985.

PERIODICALS

Ebony, April, 1977.
Forbes, February 15, 1977.
Ms., February, 1977.
National Review, March 4, 1977.
New Republic, March 12, 1977.
Newsweek, September 27, 1976, February 14, 1977.
New Yorker, February 14, 1977.
New York Review of Books, November 11, 1976.
New York Times, October 14, 1976.
New York Times Book Review, September 26, 1976, January 2, 1977, February 27, 1977.
People, March 28, 1977.

Publishers Weekly, September 6, 1976.
Saturday Review, September 18, 1976.
Time, October 18, 1976, February 14, 1977.

*   *   *

HALLIBURTON, Warren J.   1924-

PERSONAL: Born August 2, 1924, in New York, N.Y.; son of Richard H. (a book shipping manager) and Blanche (Watson) Halliburton; married Marion Jones, December 20, 1947; married second wife, Frances Fletcher (a teacher), February 11, 1971; children: (first marriage) Cheryl, Stephanie, Warren, Jr., Jena. *Education:* New York University, B.S., 1949; Columbia University, M.Ed., 1975, D.Ed., 1977.

ADDRESSES: Home—22 Scribner Hill Rd., Wilton, Conn. 06897.

CAREER: Prairie View Agricultural and Mechanical College (now Prairie View A & M University), Prairie View, Tex., instructor in English, 1949; Bishop College, Dallas, Tex., instructor in English, 1951; associate, Institute of International Education, 1952; *Recorder* (newspaper), New York City, reporter and columnist, 1953; teacher and dean in Brooklyn, N.Y. high school, 1958-60; coordinator for New York City Board of Education, and associate of New York State Department of Education, 1960-65; McGraw Hill, Inc., New York City, editor, 1967; Hamilton-Kirkland Colleges, Clinton, N.Y., visiting professor of English, 1971-72; Columbia University, Teachers College, New York City, editor, research associate, and director of scholarly journal, government program, and Ethnic Studies Center, 1972-77; currently editor and writer, *Reader's Digest*, New York City. Free-lance editor and writer. *Military service:* U.S. Army Air Forces, 1943-46.

WRITINGS:

(Editor with Mauri E. Pelkonen) *New Worlds of Literature*, Harcourt, 1966.
The Heist (novel), McGraw, 1969.
Cry, Baby! (novel), McGraw, 1969.
Some Things that Glitter (novel), illustrated by Elzia Moon, McGraw, 1969.
(With William L. Katz) *American Majorities and Minorities: A Syllabus of United States History for Secondary Schools*, Arno, 1970.
(With Laurence Swinburne and Steve Broudy) *They Had a Dream*, Pyramid Publications, 1970.
(Editor and contributor) *America's Color Caravan*, four volumes, Singer Graflex, 1971.
The Picture Life of Jesse Jackson, F. Watts, 1972, 2nd edition, 1984.
(Editor) *Short Story Scene*, Globe, 1973.
The History of Black Americans, Harcourt, 1973.
(With Agnes A. Postva) *Composing with Sentences*, Cambridge Books, 1974.
(With Ernest Kaiser) *Harlem: A History of Broken Dreams*, Doubleday, 1974.
Pathways to the World of English, Globe, 1974.
The Fighting Redtails: America's First Black Airmen, illustrated by John Gampert, Contemporary Perspectives, 1978.
Flight to the Stars: The Life of Daniel James, Jr., Contemporary Perspectives, 1979.
The People of Connecticut: A History Textbook on Connecticut, Connecticut Yankee, 1984.
The Picture Life of Michael Jackson, F. Watts, 1984.

Also adapter of text editions of Jack London's *Call of the Wild,* Douglas Wallop's *The Year the Yankees Lost the Pennant,* and Paddy Chayefsky's *Marty* and *Printer's Measure,* all McGraw, 1968.

Contributor of about one hundred short stories, adaptations, and articles to periodicals; writer of fifteen filmstrips and a motion picture, "Dig!"

SIDELIGHTS: Warren J. Halliburton comments: "Writing is a sanctuary of self-realization, affording me the opportunity for adventure and discovery of my relation with the world. This is a rare if not unique privilege in today's pigeon-holing society."

AVOCATIONAL INTERESTS: Jogging, a follow-through of his days in track and field competition.

BIOGRAPHICAL/CRITICAL SOURCES:

PERIODICALS

New Republic, March 1, 1985.

*   *   *

HAMILTON, Virginia 1936-

PERSONAL: Born March 12, 1936, in Yellow Springs, Ohio; daughter of Kenneth James (a musician) and Etta Belle (Perry) Hamilton; married Arnold Adoff (an anthologist and author), March 19, 1960; children: Leigh Hamilton (daughter), Jaime Levi (son). *Education:* Studied at Antioch College, 1952-55, Ohio State University, 1957-58, and at New School for Social Research.

ADDRESSES: Home—Yellow Springs, Ohio. *Agent*—Dorothy Markinko, McIntosh & Otis, Inc., 475 Fifth Ave., New York, N.Y. 10017.

CAREER: "Every source of occupation imaginable, from singer to bookkeeper."

AWARDS, HONORS: Zeely appeared on the American Library Association's list of notable children's books of 1967 and received Nancy Block Memorial Award of Downtown Community School Awards Committee, New York; Edgar Allan Poe Award for best juvenile mystery, 1969, for *The House of Dies Drear;* Ohioana Literary Award, 1969; John Newbery Honor Book Award, 1971, for *The Planet of Junior Brown;* Lewis Carroll Shelf Award, *Boston Globe-Horn Book* Award, 1974, John Newbery Medal and National Book Award, both 1975, all for *M. C. Higgins, the Great;* John Newbery Honor Book Award, Coretta Scott King Award, *Boston Globe-Horn Book* Award, and American Book Award nomination, all 1983, all for *Sweet Whispers, Brother Rush; Horn Book* Fanfare Award in fiction, 1985, for *A Little Love;* Coretta Scott King Award, *New York Times* Best Illustrated Children's Book Award, and *Horn Book* Honor List selection, all 1986, all for *The People Could Fly; American Black Folktales.*

WRITINGS:

(Editor) *The Writings of W. E. B. Du Bois,* Crowell, 1975.
The People Could Fly: American Black Folktales, Knopf, 1985, published with cassette, 1987.

JUVENILE BIOGRAPHIES

W. E. B. Du Bois: A Biography, Crowell, 1972.
Paul Robeson: The Life and Times of a Free Black Man, Harper, 1974.

JUVENILE NOVELS

Zeely, Macmillan, 1967, reprinted, 1986.
The House of Dies Drear, Macmillan, 1968, reprinted, 1985.
The Time-Ago Tales of Jahdu, Macmillan, 1969.
The Planet of Junior Brown, Macmillan, 1971, reprinted, 1986.
Time-Ago Lost: More Tales of Jahdu, illustrated by Ray Prather, Macmillan, 1973.
M. C. Higgins, the Great, Macmillan, 1974, published with teacher's guide by Lou Stanek, Dell, 1986.
Arilla Sun Down, Greenwillow, 1976.
Jahdu, pictures by Jerry Pinkney, Greenwillow, 1980.
Hugo Black: The Alabama Years, University of Alabama Press, 1982.
Sweet Whispers, Brother Rush, Philomel, 1982.
The Magical Adventures of Pretty Pearl, Harper, 1983.
Willie Bea and the Time the Martians Landed, Greenwillow, 1983.
A Little Love, Philomel, 1984.
Junius Over Far, Harper, 1985.
The Mystery of Drear House, Greenwillow, 1987.
A White Romance, Philomel, 1987.

"JUSTICE" TRILOGY

Justice and Her Brothers, Greenwillow, 1978.
Dustland, Greenwillow, 1980.
The Gathering, Greenwillow, 1981.

SIDELIGHTS: Virginia Hamilton is one of the most prolific and influential authors of books about black children. In an essay published in *Children's Literature Review,* Rudine Sims names Hamilton, along with four other respected black authors, as one of today's foremost image-makers for black Americans. Hamilton is also recognized as a gifted and demanding storyteller. Ethel L. Heins, for example, writes in *Horn Book:* "Few writers of fiction for young people are as daring, inventive, and challenging to read—or to review—as Virginia Hamilton. Frankly making demands on her readers, she nevertheless expresses herself in a style essentially simple and concise."

Throughout her writing career, Hamilton has struggled "to find a certain form and content to express black literature as American literature and perpetuate a pedigree of American black literature for the young," she told Wendy Smith in the *Chicago Tribune Book World.* Her struggle has resulted in the creation of stories woven of elements of history, myth, and folklore. Although these elements are a reflection of her black heritage, Hamilton believes that they are also an essential part of American culture and should, therefore, be important to all Americans. In a *Horn Book* essay, Hamilton explains her subject matter this way: "What I am compelled to write can best be described as some essence of the dreams, lies, myths, and disasters befallen a clan of my blood relatives whose troubled footfall is first discernible on this North American continent some one hundred fifty years ago. . . . I claim the right (and an accompanying responsibility) by dint of genealogy to 'plumb the line' of soul and ancestry."

Hamilton's vision has been deeply influenced by her background. "Time, place, the hometown become almost mythical for me," she told the Children's Literature Association Conference, as reported by Marilyn Apseloff in *Children's Literature in Education.* Hamilton grew up in southern Ohio, where her family has lived for generations. As a result, "I see that locale through my eyes, my mother's eyes, and my grandmother's eyes," she commented to Apseloff. Hamilton absorbed the history and folklore of her people from reading books and magazines and listening to the stories told by her kin. She continues to celebrate this heritage in her own writing in an effort to counteract the ''feeling that anything having to do with black history or culture is somehow humiliating, as if it were all part of slavery, and we don't want to deal with it,'' she told Smith.

In *Sweet Whispers, Brother Rush,* Hamilton uses the supernatural to illustrate how important an awareness of the past is in understanding the present. The book centers on Tree (short for Teresa), a teenager isolated from friends and school activities because she is responsible for caring for her brother Dab, who is stricken with a painful, debilitating illness. Tree and Dab have never known their father or any extended family; their mother Viola is a live-in nurse who comes home only occasionally to buy groceries and leave the children money. So when the ghost of Viola's brother appears, Tree, who has known ''quiet for years, the way other children knew noise and lots of laughter,'' welcomes both his company and the opportunity to learn about her family's unfortunate past.

Interracial Books for Children Bulletin contributor Geraldine Wilson compares *Sweet Whispers, Brother Rush* to ''a thoughtfully designed African American quilt.'' She elaborates: ''It is finely stitched, tightly constructed and rooted in cultural authenticity. Hamilton uses humor that is sometimes finely wrought into a sharp pathos. She clips the fabric of tragedy, turning it into an arresting applique that makes her handling and revelation of human error, of human inability to cope, of tragedy, memorable.''

Sweet Whispers, Brother Rush is written in dialect, and although several reviewers state that they had difficulty understanding the language, *New York Times Book Review* contributor Katherine Paterson believes it is one of Hamilton's more accessible books. She writes: ''To the more timid reader, young or old, who may feel inadequate to Miss Hamilton's always demanding fiction, I say: Just read the first page, just the first paragraph, of 'Sweet Whispers, Brother Rush.' Then stop—if you can.''

One of Hamilton's most notable books is *M. C. Higgins, the Great,* recipient of several awards, including the National Book Award and the John Newbery Medal. The story portrays the Higginses, a close-knit family who reside on Sarah's Mountain in southern Ohio. The mountain has special significance to the Higginses, for it has belonged to their family since M. C.'s great-grandmother Sarah, an escaped slave, settled there. The conflict in the story arises when a hugh spoil heap, created by strip mining, threatens to engulf their home. M. C. is torn between his love for his home and his concern for his family's safety, and he searches diligently for a solution that will allow him to preserve both.

M. C. Higgins, the Great was highly praised by critics, including poet Nikki Giovanni, who writes in the *New York Times Book Review:* ''Once again Virginia Hamilton creates a world and invites us in. 'M. C. Higgins, the Great' is not an adorable book, not a lived-happily-ever-after kind of story. It is warm, humane and hopeful and does what every book should do—creates characters with whom we can identify and for whom we care.'' Carol Vassallo expresses a similar opinion in *Children's Literature: Annual of the Modern Language Association Seminar on Children's Literature and the Children's Literature Association:* ''The beauty of the writing, the poetic imagery, the characters, each unique yet completely believable, and the original themes all make the reading of

this book an unforgettable experience, and mark Virginia Hamilton as one of the most important of today's writers for children.''

Although black folklore and myth play important roles in all of Hamilton's books, *The People Could Fly: American Black Folktales* is devoted entirely to restoring this literary heritage. The book is comprised of animal fables, supernatural tales, and slave narratives—stories that ''belong to all of us,'' Hamilton remarked to Wendy Smith in the *Chicago Tribune Book World.* The subtitle itself, Hamilton told Smith, is ''a political statement.'' Her editor wanted to call the stories black American folktales; Hamilton, however, maintains that they are ''American first and black second.''

To give *The People Could Fly* a universal appeal, Hamilton tells the stories in simple dialect, and she uses ''multiple voices . . . to give American children, black and white, a sense of the richness and complexity of black culture,'' writes Smith. *The People Could Fly* was welcomed by critics because, as Ishmael Reed observes in the *New York Times Book Review,* it ''makes these tales available to another generation of readers.'' Kristiana Gregory comments in the *Los Angeles Times Book Review:* ''Told in easy-to-understand dialect, the stories echo the voices of fugitives and slaves, some of whom were the authors' ancestors. We are reminded of the deep sorrow and fears of an oppressed people, but also that the human spirit, however enslaved, still feels love and hope. It is this spirit Hamilton celebrates.''

Since she began her writing career, Hamilton has had her books published consistently, but Rudine Sims believes that on the whole, publication of literature about black children is declining. In a guest essay for *Children's Literature Review* entitled ''Children's Books about Blacks: A Mid-Eighties Status Report,'' Sims writes: ''The heyday of publishing children's books about blacks is past. Since the mid-seventies, the number of available children's books dealing with black life has declined steadily.'' The conservatism of the eighties, maintains Sims in the *Christian Science Monitor,* has slowed publication of these books ''to a trickle, and the list of black authors remains small.''

Hamilton alludes to Sims's statement in the *Chicago Tribune Book World* interview with Smith, but she emphasizes what is, from her point of view, a more critical issue: distribution. Although Hamilton's books are written about black children, her books are more easily distributed, and thus sold, in white communities. Her solution, she told Smith, is to travel. ''So I go out all over the country all the time; that's what you have to do. They may say black books are dead, but we keep proving they aren't by winning awards and doing whatever else we have to. That's what I'm committed to.''

MEDIA ADAPTATIONS: The House of Dies Drear was adapted for the Public Broadcasting Service series ''Wonderworks'' in 1984.

BIOGRAPHICAL/CRITICAL SOURCES:

BOOKS

Authors in the News, Volume I, Gale, 1976.

Butler, Francelia, editor, *Children's Literature: Annual of the Modern Language Association Seminar on Children's Literature and the Children's Literature Association,* Volume IV, Temple University Press, 1975.

Children's Literature Review, Gale, Volume I, 1976, Volume VIII, 1985, Volume XI, 1986.

Contemporary Literary Criticism, Volume XXVI, Gale, 1983.
Dictionary of Literary Biography, Gale, Volume XXXIII: *Afro-American Fiction Writers after 1955,* 1984, Volume LII: *American Writers for Children Since 1960: Fiction,* 1986.
Hamilton, Virginia, *Sweet Whispers, Brother Rush,* Philomel, 1982.

PERIODICALS

Best Sellers, January, 1983.
Chicago Tribune Book World, November 10, 1985.
Childen's Literature in Education, winter, 1983.
Christian Science Monitor, May 12, 1980, August 3, 1984.
Cincinnati Enquirer, January 5, 1975.
Horn Book, February, 1970, February, 1972, June, 1973, April, 1975, August, 1975, October, 1982, June, 1983.
Interracial Books for Children Bulletin, Numbers 1 and 2, 1983, Number 5, 1984.
Kirkus Review, July 1, 1974, April 1, 1983, October 1, 1985.
Library Journal, September 15, 1971.
Listener, November 6, 1975.
Los Angeles Times Book Review, March 23, 1986.
New York Times Book Review, October 13, 1968, September 22, 1974, December 22, 1974, December 17, 1978, May 4, 1980, September 27, 1981, November 14, 1982, September 4, 1983, November 10, 1985, November 8, 1987.
School Library Journal, April, 1983.
Times (London), November 20, 1986.
Times Literary Supplement, May 23, 1975, September 19, 1980, November 20, 1981, February 28, 1986, October 30-November 5, 1987, November 20-26, 1987.
Village Voice, December 14, 1975.
Washington Post Book World, November 10, 1974, November 11, 1979, September 14, 1980, November 7, 1982, November 10, 1985.

*   *   *

HANSBERRY, Lorraine (Vivian)   1930-1965

PERSONAL: Born May 19, 1930, in Chicago, Ill.; died of cancer, January 12, 1965, in New York, N.Y.; buried in Beth-El Cemetery, Croton-on-Hudson, N.Y.; daughter of Carl Augustus (a realtor and banker) and Nannie (Perry) Hansberry; married Robert B. Nemiroff (a music publisher and songwriter), June 20, 1953 (divorced March, 1964). *Education:* Attended University of Wisconsin, Art Institute of Chicago, Roosevelt College, New School for Social Research, and studied in Guadalajara, Mexico, 1948-50.

ADDRESSES: Home—New York, N.Y. *Agent*—c/o Vivian Productions, 137 West 52nd St., New York, N.Y. 10019.

CAREER: Playwright. Worked variously as clerk in a department store, tag girl in a fur shop, aide to a theatrical producer, and as waitress, hostess, and cashier in a restaurant in Greenwich Village run by the family of Robert Nemiroff; worked on monthly magazine, *Freedom,* for two years.

MEMBER: Dramatists Guild, Ira Aldrich Society, Institute for Advanced Study in the Theatre Arts.

AWARDS, HONORS: New York Drama Critics Circle Award for Best American play, 1959, for "A Raisin in the Sun"; Cannes Film Festival special award and Screen Writers Guild nomination, both 1961, both for screenplay "A Raisin in the Sun."

WRITINGS:

(Author of text) *The Movement: Documentary of a Struggle for Equality* (collection of photographs) Simon & Schuster, 1964 (published in England as *A Matter of Colour: Documentary of the Struggle for Racial Equality in the U.S.A.,* introduction by Ronald Segal, Penguin, 1965).
(Contributor) Horst Frenz, editor, *American Playwrights on Drama,* Hill & Wang, 1965.
To Be Young, Gifted and Black: Lorraine Hansberry in Her Own Words, self-illustrated, adapted by Robert Nemiroff, introduction by James Baldwin, Prentice-Hall, 1969, acting edition published as *To Be Young, Gifted and Black: A Portrait of Lorraine Hansberry in Her Own Words,* Samuel French, 1971.

PLAYS

A Raisin in the Sun: A Drama in Three Acts (first produced in New York City at Ethel Barrymore Theatre, March 11, 1959; also see below), Random House, 1959.
"A Raisin in the Sun" (screenplay), released by Columbia, 1960.
The Sign in Sidney Brustein's Window: A Drama in Three Acts (first produced in New York City at Longacre Theatre, October 15, 1964; also see below), Random House, 1965.
Les Blancs (two-act; first produced in New York City at Longacre Theatre, November 15, 1970; also see below), Hart Stenographic Bureau, 1966, published as *Lorraine Hansberry's "Les Blancs": A Drama in Two Acts,* adapted by Nemiroff, Samuel French, 1972.
A Raisin in the Sun, The Sign in Sidney Brustein's Window, [and] *The 101 Final Performances of "Sidney Brustein": Portrait of a Play and Its Author,* by Robert Nemiroff, New American Library, 1966.
Nemiroff, editor, *Les Blancs: The Collected Last Plays of Lorraine Hansberry* (contains "The Drinking Gourd" [three-act television drama], "What Use Are Flowers?" [one-act fable], and "Les Blancs"), introduction by Julius Lester, Random House, 1972, published as *Lorraine Hansberry: The Collected Last Plays,* New American Library, 1983.
A Raisin in the Sun (expanded twenty-fifth anniversary edition) [and] *The Sign in Sidney Brustein's Window,* New American Library, 1987.

RECORDINGS

A Raisin in the Sun, three cassettes, Caedmon, 1972.
Lorraine Hansberry Speaks Out: Art and the Black Revolution, Caedmon, 1972.

OTHER

Work is represented in anthologies, including *Three Negro Plays,* Penguin, 1969. Also contributor to *Black Titan: W. E. B. Du Bois.* Contributor to periodicals, including *Negro Digest, Freedomways, Village Voice,* and *Theatre Arts.*

SIDELIGHTS: Lorraine Hansberry was born into a middle-class black family on Chicago's south side in 1930. She recalled that her childhood was basically a happy one; "the insulation of life within the Southside ghetto, of what must have easily been half a million people, protected me from some of the harsher and more bestial aspects of white-supremacist culture," the playwright stated in *Portraits in Color.* At the age of seven or eight, Hansberry and her upwardly-mobile family deliberately attempted to move into a restricted white neighborhood. Her father fought the civil-rights case all the way to the U.S. Supreme Court, eventually winning his claim to a home within the restricted area. "The Hansberrys determination to continue to live in this home in spite of intimidation and threats from their angry, rock-throwing white neighbors is a study in courage and strength," Porter Kirkwood assessed in *Freedomways*. "Lorraine's character and personality were forged in this atmosphere of resistence to injustice." "Both of my parents were strong-minded, civic-minded, exceptionally race-minded people who made enormous sacrifices in behalf of the struggle for civil rights throughout their lifetimes," Hansberry remembered.

While in high school, Hansberry first became interested in the theatre. "Mine was the same old story—" she recollected, "sort of hanging around little acting groups, and developing the feeling that the theatre embraces everything I liked all at one time." When Lorraine attended the University of Wisconsin she became further acquainted with great theatre, including the works of August Strindberg, Henrik Ibsen, and Sean O'Casey. She was particularly taken with the Irish dramatist's ability to express in his plays the complex and transcendant nature of man, to achieve "the emotional transformation of people on stage."

After studying painting in Chicago and abroad, Hansberry eschewed her artistic plans and moved to New York City in 1950 to begin her career as a writer. Politically active in New York, Hansberry wrote for Paul Robeson's *Freedom* magazine and participated in various liberal crusades. During one protest concerning practices of discrimination at New York University, Lorraine met Robert Nemiroff, himself a writer and pursuer of liberal politics. Although Nemiroff was white, a romance developed between the two, and in 1953 they married.

Nemiroff encouraged Hansberry in her writing efforts, going so far as to salvage her discarded pages from the wastebasket. One night in 1957, while the couple was entertaining a group of friends, they read a scene from Hansberry's play in progress, "A Raisin in the Sun." The impact left by the reading prompted Hansberry, Nemiroff, and friends to push for the completion, financing, and production of the drama within the next several months.

Enjoying solid success at tryout performances on the road, "A Raisin in the Sun" made its New York debut March 11, 1959, at the Ethel Barrymore Theatre. It was the first play written by a black woman to be produced on Broadway; it was the first to be directed by a black director in more than fifty years. When "A Raisin in the Sun" won the New York Drama Critics Circle Award, Hansberry became the youngest writer and the first black artist ever to receive the honor, competing that year with such theatre luminaries as Tennessee Williams, Eugene O'Neill, and Archibald MacLeish. In June, 1959, Hansberry was named the "most promising playwright" of the season by *Variety*'s poll of New York drama critics.

"A Raisin in the Sun" tells the story of a black family attempting to escape the poverty of the Chicago projects by buying a house in the suburbs with the money left from the insurance policy of their dead father. Conflict erupts when the son, Walter Lee, fights to use the money instead to buy his own business—a life's ambition. Yet when a white representative from the neighborhood that the family plans to integrate attempts to thwart their move, the young man submerges his materialistic aspirations—for a time, at least—and rallies to support the family's dream. Still Hansberry wonders, as expressed in the lines of poet Langston Hughes from which she takes her title, what will become of Walter Lee's frustrated desires: "What happens to a dream deferred? / Does it dry up like a raisin in the sun? / Or fester like a sore—and then run?"

Because the play explored a universal theme—the search for freedom and a better life—the majority of its audience loved it. According to Gerald Weales in *Commentary*, it reflected neither the traditional Negro show, folksy and exotic, or the reactionary protest play, with black characters spouting about the injustices of white oppression. Rather, "A Raisin in the Sun" was a play about a family that just happened to be Negro. "The thing I tried to show," Hansberry told Ted Poston in the *New York Post*, "was the many gradations in even one Negro family, the clash of the old and the new."

New York Times critic Brooks Atkinson admired "A Raisin in the Sun" because it explored serious problems without becoming academic or ponderous. "[Hansberry] has told the inner as well as outer truth about a Negro family in Chicago," the critic observed. "The play has vigor as well as veracity and is likely to destroy the complacency of anyone who sees it." Weales labeled "Raisin" "a good play" whose "basic strength lies in the character and the problem of Walter Lee, which transcends his being a Negro. If the play were only the Negro-white conflict that crops up when the family's proposed move is about to take place, it would be editorial, momentarily effective, and nothing more. Walter Lee's difficulty, however, is that he has accepted the American myth of success at its face value, that he is trapped, as Willy Loman was trapped, by a false dream. In planting so indigenous an American image at the center of her play, Miss Hansberry has come as close as possible to what she intended—a play about Negroes which is not simply a Negro play." The reviewer also found the play "genuinely funny and touching," with the dialogue between family members believable.

"A Raisin in the Sun" ran for 530 performances. Shortly thereafter a film version of the drama was released; Hansberry won a special award at the Cannes Film Festival and was nominated for an award from the Screen Writers Guild for her screenplay. She then began working on a second play about a Jewish intellectual who vacillates between social commitment and paralyzing disillusionment. Entitled "The Sign in Sidney Brustein's Window," the play ran on Broadway for 101 performances despite mixed reviews and poor sales. "Its tenure on Broadway parallels the playwright's own failing health," Kirkwood noted. The play closed on January 12, 1965, the day Hansberry died of cancer at the age of thirty-five.

Although Hansberry and her husband divorced in 1964, Nemiroff remained dedicated to the playwright and her work. Appointed her literary executor, he collected his ex-wife's writings and words after her death and presented them in the autobiographical *To Be Young, Gifted and Black*. He also edited and published her three unfinished plays, which were subsequently produced: "Les Blancs," a psychological and social drama of a European-educated African who returns home to join the fight against Colonialism; "The Drinking Gourd," a drama on slavery and emancipation expressed through the story of a black woman; and "What Use Are Flowers?," a fable about an aging hermit who, in a ravaged world, tries to impart to children his remembrances of the past civilization he had once renounced. "It's true that there's a great deal of pain for me in this," Nemiroff told Arlynn Nellhaus of the *Denver Post* about his custodianship, "but there's also a great deal of satisfaction. There is first-class writing and the joy of seeing [Lorraine's] ideas become a contemporary force again . . . [is] rewarding. . . . She was proud of black culture, the black experience and struggle. . . . But she was also in love with all cultures, and she related to the struggles of other people. . . . She was tremendously affected by the struggle of ordinary people—the heroism of ordinary people and the ability of people to laugh and transcend.''

To Be Young, Gifted and Black was made into a play that ran Off-Broadway in 1969, keeping the memory of Hansberry and critical examination of her small body of work alive. Martin Goffried, in *Women's Wear Daily,* hypothesized that ''Miss Hansberry's tragically brief playwrighting career charted the postwar steps in the racial movement, from working within the system ('A Raisin in the Sun') to a burgeoning distrust of white liberals ('The Sign in Sidney Brustein's Window') to the association with Africa in 'Les Blancs' that would evolve, after her death, from the ashes of passive resistance into the energy and danger of militant activism.'' Writing in *Beautiful, Also, Are the Souls of My Black Sisters,* Jeanne L. Noble examined the author in a similar sociological light, wondering where, in today's political continuum, Hansberry would stand in comparison with the new breed of black writers. Yet she concluded: ''Certainly for [Hansberry's] works to leave a continuing legacy—though she died at age 35, just before the fiercest testing period of the black revolution—is itself monumental. And we will always ponder these among her last words: 'I think when I get my health back I shall go into the South to find out what kind of revolutionary I am.'''

But most critics did not perceive of Hansberry as a particularly political or ''black'' writer, but rather as one who dealt more with human universals. Gerald Weales speculated in *Commonweal* that ''it is impossible to guess how she might have grown as a writer, but her two [finished] plays indicate that she had wit and intelligence, a strong sense of social and political possibility and a respect for the contradictions in all men; that she could create a milieu (the family in *Raisin,* the Greenwich Village circle in *Sign*) with both bite and affection; that she was a playwright—like Odets, like Miller—with easily definable flaws but an inescapable talent that one cannot help admiring.'' And *Life* magazine's Cyclops concluded that Hansberry's gentle and intelligent sensibilities could best be read in these lines from ''The Sign in Sidney Brustein's Window,'' when Sidney describes himself: ''A fool who believes that death is a waste and love is sweet and that the earth turns and men change every day and that rivers run and that people wanna be better than they are and that flowers smell good and that I hurt terribly today, and that hurt is desperation and desperation is energy and energy can *move* things.''

MEDIA ADAPTATIONS: A film version of ''A Raisin in the Sun,'' starring Sidney Poitier and Claudia McNeil, was released by Columbia in 1961; *To Be Young, Gifted and Black* was adapted into a play, first produced Off-Broadway at Cherry Lane Theatre, January 2, 1969; a musical version of ''The Sign in Sidney Brustein's Window'' was first produced on Broadway at Longacre Theatre, January 26, 1972; a musical version of ''A Raisin in the Sun,'' entitled ''Raisin,'' was first produced on Broadway at Forty-Sixth Street Theatre, October 18, 1973.

AVOCATIONAL INTERESTS: Ping-pong, skiing, walking in the woods, reading biographies, conversation.

BIOGRAPHICAL/CRITICAL SOURCES:

BOOKS

Authors in the News, Volume II, Gale, 1976.

Bigsby, C. W. E., and others, *Confrontation and Commitment: A Study of Contemporary American Drama,* MacGibbon & Kee, 1967.
Bigsby, C. W. E., editor, *The Black American Writer,* Volume 2, Penguin, 1969.
Cherry, Gwendolyn, and others, *Portraits in Color,* Pageant Press, 1962.
Contemporary Literary Criticism, Volume XVII, Gale, 1981.
Noble, Jeanne L., *Beautiful, Also, Are the Souls of My Black Sisters: A History of the Black Women in America,* Prentice-Hall, 1978.
Scheader, Catherine, *They Found a Way: Lorraine Hansberry,* Children's Press, 1978.

PERIODICALS

Commentary, June, 1959.
Commonweal, September 5, 1969, January 22, 1971.
Denver Post, March 14, 1976.
Esquire, November, 1969.
Freedomways, winter, 1963, summer, 1965, fourth quarter, 1978.
Life, January 14, 1972.
New Yorker, May 9, 1959.
New York Post, March 22, 1959.
New York Times, March 8, 1959, March 12, 1959, April 9, 1959, November 9, 1983, August 15, 1986.
Washington Post, November 16, 1986, December 2, 1986.
Women's Wear Daily, November 16, 1970.

OBITUARIES:

PERIODICALS

Antiquarian Bookman, January 25, 1965.
Books Abroad, spring, 1966.
Current Biography, February, 1965.
Newsweek, January 25, 1965.
New York Times, January 13, 1965.
Publishers Weekly, February 8, 1965.
Time, January 22, 1965.

*   *   *

HARE, Nathan 1934-

PERSONAL: Born April 9, 1934, in Slick, Okla.; son of Seddie Henry (a farmer) and Tishia (Davis) Hare; married Julie Reed (a public relations specialist), December 27, 1956. *Education:* Langston University, A.B., 1954; University of Chicago, M.A., 1957, Ph.D. (sociology), 1962; California School of Professional Psychology, Ph.D., 1975; also studied at Northwestern University, 1959.

ADDRESSES: Office—1801 Bush St., San Francisco, Calif. 94109.

CAREER: Briefly, a professional boxer; Virginia State College, Petersburg, instructor in sociology, 1957-58; National Opinion Research Center, Chicago, Ill., interviewer, 1959-61; Howard University, Washington, D.C., instructor, 1961-63, assistant professor of sociology, 1964-67; San Francisco State College (now University), director of Black Studies Curriculum, 1968, chairman of department of Black Studies, 1968-69, director, Center for Educational Innovation, summer, 1968; *Black Scholar,* Sausalito, Calif., founding publisher, 1969-75; Child Development Services, Oakland, Calif., clinical psychologist, 1975-76; psychologist in private practice, 1977—; San Francisco State University, lecturer, 1984—. Part-time visiting professor, Lone Mountain College, 1972-73; chairman of task force on demographic and communal characteristics, Teachers College, Columbia University, 1966-67. Chairman of workshop on education, National Conference on Black Power, 1968; founding president, Black World Foundation, 1970. Member of board of advisors, San Francisco Black Exposition, 1972; member of board of directors, North American Committee, Second World Black and African Festival of Arts and Culture, Lagos, Nigeria, 1974, and San Francisco Local Development Corporation; affiliated with Complete Help and Assistance Necessary for College Education (CHANCE) project, 1976. President and chairman of the board, Black Think Tank, 1982—. *Military service:* U.S. Army Reserve, 1958-64, active duty, 1958.

MEMBER: American Sociological Association, Association of Behavioral and Social Sciences, American Psychological Association, Association of Orthopsychiatry, American Association of University Professors, Eastern Sociological Association, New York Academy of Sciences, Sigma Gamma Rho.

AWARDS, HONORS: Danforth fellow, 1954-57; "Black Is Beautiful" citation from United Black Artists, 1968; Distinguished Alumni Award, Langston University, 1975; community-clinical psychology award, Southern Regional Education Board, Atlanta, 1978; Professional Person of the Year, San Francisco chapter of the National Association of Negro Business and Professional Women's Clubs, 1980; presidential citation, National Association for Equal Opportunity in Higher Education, 1982; national award, National Council on Black Studies, 1983.

WRITINGS:

The Black Anglo-Saxons, Marzani & Munsell, 1965.
(Author of introduction) W. E. B. DuBois, *The Souls of Black Folk,* Signet, 1969.
(Author of introduction) Lenneal Henderson, editor, *Black Political Life in the United States,* Chandler Publishing, 1972.
(Editor with Robert Chrisman) *Contemporary Black Thought: The Best from the Black Scholar,* Bobbs-Merrill, 1973.
(Editor with Chrisman) *Pan-Africanism,* Bobbs-Merrill, 1974.
(Contributor) David W. Swift, editor, *American Education: A Sociological View,* Houghton, 1976.
(With wife, Julia Hare) *The Endangered Black Family: Coping with the Unisexualization and Coming Extinction of the Black Race,* Black Think Tank, 1984.

Contributor of about sixty articles to sociology and black studies journals and to national periodicals, including *Newsweek, Ramparts, Saturday Review,* and *U.S. News and World Report.* Contributing editor, *Journal of Black Studies, Ebony, Black Scholar, Journal of Black Education,* and *Black Law Journal.*

SIDELIGHTS: Nathan Hare is "a major leader of the Black Studies movement," write Richard Barksdale and Keneth Kinnamon in *Black Writers of America: A Comprehensive Anthology.* Characterized by them as "an unorthodox academician," Hare sparked controversy while serving on the faculty of Howard University in the 1960s through his opposition to the war in Vietnam and the draft, his advocacy of Black power, his stint as a professional boxer, and his criticism of the university administration. In 1968 he launched a Black Studies program at San Francisco State College, and in 1969 began publication of the *Black Scholar,* in Barksdale's and Kinnamon's words, an "important 'Journal of Black Studies and Research.'"

Hare's work centers on the necessity for blacks everywhere to recognize the power of traditional black mores and ideas. For instance, in Hare's opinion, the mission of the black scholar is to rethink European modes of thought, replacing them with new insights and solutions to old problems. In an article published in Barksdale's and Kinnamon's *Black Writers of America,* he states, "[The black scholar must] de-colonize his mind so that he may effectively guide other intellectuals and students in their search for liberation." Because of the legacy of mis-education and abuse of learning, he continues, white society is "increasingly corrupt and bloody with no clear future. The air is filled with pollution and the land and forests are being destroyed as human alienation and conflict remain on the rise." The cure for this problem, according to Hare, lies in the removal of "icons of objectivity, amoral knowledge and its methodology, and the total demolition of the anti-social attitudes of Ivory-Towerism."

Similar views are expressed in Hare's book *The Black Anglo-Saxons* and the volume which he co-edited with Robert Chrisman called *Pan-Africanism. The Black Anglo-Saxons* is a critique of the black middle class, a group which Hare perceives as having shed black values and mores in favor of assimilated ethics and standards from a white culture. *Pan-Africanism* is a collection of essays by both Africans and Afro-Americans which promotes traditional black political concepts of communalism, as opposed to European socialism, in an attempt to chart Africa's future. Both works encourage a return to pre-colonial black ideals as a solution to problems in modern life.

Hare continues to advance ideals and mores drawn from black tradition. He says, in an article in *Ebony* magazine, "The Black middle class could begin now to solve the problems of juvenile delinquency, of in-group violence, school drop-outs, low academic performance, and many another ailment—maybe even racism—if we could come together, return to our own people, live with them, love them, learn from the wisdom of a long-suffering and creative race. But it will first be necessary to abandon the unbridled pursuit of materialism and the all-engulfing frenzy for White approval and acceptance."

BIOGRAPHICAL/CRITICAL SOURCES:

BOOKS

Barksdale, Richard and Keneth Kinnamon, editors, *Black Writers of America: A Comprehensive Anthology,* Macmillan, 1972.

PERIODICALS

American Sociological Review, December, 1965.
Annals of the American Academy, November, 1965.
Choice, June, 1974.
Ebony, August, 1987.
New York Times Book Review, February 21, 1971.

*   *   *

HARPER, F. E. W.
  See HARPER, Frances Ellen Watkins

*   *   *

HARPER, Frances E. W.
  See HARPER, Frances Ellen Watkins

HARPER, Frances E. Watkins
    See HARPER, Frances Ellen Watkins

*   *   *

HARPER, Frances Ellen
    See HARPER, Frances Ellen Watkins

*   *   *

HARPER, Frances Ellen Watkins   1825-1911
    (F. E. W. Harper, Frances Ellen Harper, Frances
    E. W. Harper, Frances E. Watkins Harper, Mrs.
    F. E. W. Harper, Frances Ellen Watkins; Effie
    Afton, a pseudonym)

PERSONAL: Born September 24, 1825, in Baltimore, Md.; died of heart failure, February 22, 1911, in Philadelphia, Pa.; buried at Eden Cemetery in Philadelphia; married Fenton Harper (a farmer), November 22, 1860 (died, May, 1864); children: Mary. *Education:* Educated in Baltimore, Md., and in Pennsylvania and Ohio. *Religion:* Unitarian.

CAREER: Writer, social reformer, and public lecturer. Worked as a nursemaid and domestic; Union Seminary, Columbus, Ohio, sewing teacher, 1850-52; elementary school teacher in Little York, Pa., 1852-53; Underground Railroad worker in Little York, 1853-54; lecturer for Maine Anti-Slavery Society, 1854-56, and other organizations, 1856-60, and reader of antislavery verse; lecturer and poetry reader advocating freedmen's rights, Christian temperance, and women's suffrage, 1864-1911. Organizer and assistant superintendent of Young Men's Christian Association (YMCA) Sabbath School, 1872; director of American Association of Education of Colored Youth, 1894. Associated with American Woman Suffrage Association conventions, 1875 and 1887; speaker at International Council of Women in Washington, 1888, National Council of Women, 1891, and World Congress of Representative Women at Columbian Exposition in Chicago, 1893.

MEMBER: National Council of Women in the United States, National Association of Colored Women (founding member, 1886; vice-president, 1897), National Women's Christian Temperance Union (executive committee member; superintendent of Philadelphia and Pennsylvania chapters of Colored Branch, 1875-82; head of northern U.S. division, 1883-93), American Equal Rights Association.

WRITINGS:

(Under name Frances Ellen Watkins) *Forest Leaves* (also referred to as *Autumn Leaves;* poems and prose), privately printed (Baltimore, Md.), c. 1845.
(Under name Frances Ellen Watkins) *Poems on Miscellaneous Subjects* (poems and essays), preface by William Lloyd Garrison, J. B. Yerrinton & Son (Boston, Mass.), 1854, reprinted, Kraus, 1971, enlarged edition, [Philadelphia, Pa.], 1855, 2nd enlarged edition, Merrihew & Thompson (Philadelphia), 1857, reprinted with new introduction by Maxwell Whiteman, Rhistoric Publications, 1969, 20th edition, enlarged, Merrihew & Son (Philadelphia), 1871.
(Under pseudonym Effie Afton) *Eventide* (poems and tales), Ferridge & Co. (Boston), 1854.

(Under name Mrs. F. E. W. Harper) *Moses: A Story of the Nile* (poems and essay), 2nd edition, Merrihew, 1869, 3rd edition, 1870, enlarged edition, privately printed (Philadelphia), 1889.
(Under name Frances E. Watkins Harper) *Poems,* Merrihew & Son, 1871, reprinted, AMS Press, 1975.
(Under name Frances E. Watkins Harper) *Sketches of Southern Life* (poems), George S. Ferguson (Philadelphia), 1891.
(Under name Frances E. W. Harper) *Iola Leroy; or, Shadows Uplifted* (novel), Garrigues Bros. (Philadelphia), 1892, 2nd edition, with introduction by William Still, James H. Earle, 1893, McGrath, 1969, AMS Press, 1971.
(Under name Frances Ellen Harper) *Atlanta Offering: Poems* (contains *The Sparrow's Fall and Other Poems* and *The Martyr of Alabama and Other Poems*), George S. Ferguson, 1895, reprinted, Mnemosyne, 1969.
(Under name Frances E. Watkins Harper) *Poems,* George S. Ferguson, 1895, Books for Libraries, 1970, enlarged edition, privately printed (Philadelphia), 1898, 2nd enlarged edition, privately printed (Philadelphia), 1900.
(Under name F. E. W. Harper) *Idylls of the Bible* (contains *Moses*), privately printed (Philadelphia), 1901, reprinted, AMS Press, 1975.
(Annotator) John Bartram, *Diary of a Journey Through the Carolina, Georgia, and Florida, July 1, 1775—April 10, 1776,* Philosophical Society (Philadelphia), 1942.
The Poems of Frances E. W. Harper, Books for Libraries, 1970.

Also author of poem collections *The Sparrow's Fall and Other Poems,* c. 1890, *The Martyr of Alabama and Other Poems,* c. 1894, and *Light Beyond Darkness,* Donohue & Henneberry (Chicago, Ill.). Poems and essays represented in anthologies and sociological/historical studies, including *The Black Man: His Antecedents, His Genius, and His Achievements,* edited by William Wells Brown, Hamilton/Wallcut, 1863; *The Negro Caravan,* edited by Sterling A. Brown, Arthur Davis, and Ulysses Lee, Dryden, 1941; *In Their Own Words: A History of the American Negro, 1619-1865,* edited by Milton Meltzer, Crowell, 1964; and *Kaleidoscope: Poems by American Negro Poets,* edited by Robert Hayden, Harcourt, 1967. Contributor to periodicals, including *African Methodist Episcopal Church Review, Anglo-African Magazine, Crisis, Englishwoman's Review, Frederick Douglass's Paper, Liberator,* and *National Anti-Slavery Standard.*

SIDELIGHTS: Afro-American Frances Ellen Watkins Harper captivated black and white audiences alike with dramatic recitations of her antislavery and social reform verse. Conventional lyric poetry with familiar themes and imagery, Harper's verse gained much—according to a contemporary, Phebe A. Hanaford in her *Daughters of America; or, Women of the Century*—from the orator/poet's "clear, plaintive, melodious voice" and "the flow of her musical speech." A social lecturer whose long life was devoted to abolition, freedmen's rights, Christian temperance, and women's suffrage, Harper used prose and poetry to enhance her message and stir audience emotions. "Mrs. Harper's verse is frankly propagandist, a metrical extension of her life dedicated to the welfare of others," Joan R. Sherman decided in *Invisible Poets: Afro-Americans of the Nineteenth Century.* "She believed in art for humanity's sake."

Born of free parents in the slave state of Maryland, Harper was raised by an aunt and uncle after her parents' early deaths and educated at her uncle's school for free blacks. Her first job at thirteen was caring for the children of a bookseller; there she began writing, composing poems, and reading the popular literature of the period. Intent on living in a free state, Harper moved to Ohio, where she worked as a teacher. A subsequent move to Little York, Pennsylvania, acquainted her with the workings of the Underground Railroad and she decided to become actively involved in the antislavery movement. Her first abolitionist speech was a marked success; preaching social and political reform and moral betterment, Harper spent the next several years lecturing for antislavery societies throughout the North and included readings from her *Poems on Miscellaneous Subjects.* The poet's most popular book, the collection sold several thousand copies and saw at least twenty editions. Containing her most-acclaimed abolitionist poem, "Bury Me in a Free Land," it firmly established Harper's literary reputation.

Thought to resemble the poetry of Henry Wadsworth Longfellow, John Greenleaf Whittier, and Felicia Dorothea Hemans, Harper's largely narrative verse uses rhymed tetrameter and the ballad stanza, both "well suited to some of her material" and creating "an excellent elocutionary pattern," commented J. Saunders Redding in *To Make a Poet Black.* Emotionally charged and frequently didactic (with authorial intrusions), the poems mirrored the conventions of the day and were tailored to Harper's social intent and to audience expectations. Varying little in form, language, or technique, the verse is simple, direct, and lyrical. Writing in *Drumvoices: The Mission of Afro-American Poetry,* Eugene B. Redmond observed: "Up until the Civil War, Mrs. Harper's favorite themes were slavery, its harshness, and the hypocrisies of America. She is careful to place graphic details where they will get the greatest result, especially when the poems are read aloud." He continued: "Critics generally agree that Mrs. Harper's poetry is not original or brilliant. But she is exciting and comes through with powerful flashes of imagery and statement."

Married to a farmer when she was thirty-five, Harper retired from public life and bore a child but soon returned to lecturing when she was widowed. Following the Civil War she traveled south for the first time and was appalled by the unfair treatment of freed blacks; she saw flagrant voting rights violations, meager educational opportunities, and overt physical abuse. Particularly stirred by the plight of black women—whose subjugation had not only continued, but had grown worse with emancipation—the poet determined that "a free people could be a moral people only when the women were respected," according to Larsen Scruggs, quoted in an article in *Black American Literature Forum,* and Harper appealed to sisters of all colors to work towards social equality. For the remaining decades of her life, Harper spoke and wrote for social and reform organizations that supported her ideals of racial justice, women's rights, and Christian humanism; her notable posts included director of the American Association of Education of Colored Youth, executive member of the National Women's Christian Temperance Union, and founding member and vice-president of the National Association of Colored Women.

Redding maintained that by addressing a spectrum of social ills in her writings Harper broke free of the "willful (and perhaps necessary) monopticism" that had confined other black authors. "If our talents are to be recognized we must write less of issues that are particular and more of feelings that are general," the poet once acknowledged to an editor acquaintance, Redding related. "We are blessed with hearts and brains that compass more than ourselves in our present plight." Sherman, too, saw Harper as an innovator who combined race issues with national and universal concerns, inspiring succeeding black writers. Like the majority of critics, Sherman

also proclaimed Harper's post-Civil War verse "more objective and intellectual" and informed with a strong optimism.

The poet breaks with conventional meter and sentiment, creating a correspondence between subject and technique, in *Moses: A Story of the Nile,* considered her best work. This volume is an extended blank-verse biblical allegory without overt racial references; recounting the life of the Hebrew patriarch and focusing on his leadership and self-sacrifice, Harper urges similar leadership and sacrifice among blacks. "The poem's elevated diction, concrete imagery, and formal meter harmoniously blend to magnify the noble adventure of Moses' life and the mysterious grandeur of his death," related Sherman, discussing the work's artistic merits. "Mrs. Harper maintains the pace of her long narrative and its tone of reverent admiration with scarcely a pause for moralizing. *Moses* is Mrs. Harper's most original poem and one of considerable power."

Referring to a second critically praised Harper work, Sherman added that the poet "shows a similar talent for matching technique and subject in the charming series of poems which make up most of *Sketches of Southern Life.*" Narrated by politically aware ex-slaves Aunt Chloe and Uncle Jacob, the poems provide a commentary on the concerns of southern blacks: family, education, religion, slavery, and Reconstruction. Admired for their wit and irony, the narratives are written in Afro-American vernacular speech—"a new idiom in black poetry," Sherman elaborated, "which ripens into the dialect verse of [James Edwin] Campbell, [Daniel Webster] Davis, and [Paul Laurence] Dunbar in the last decades of the century." "Serious issues sketched with a light touch are rare in Mrs. Harper's work," the critic added, "and it is unfortunate that Aunt Chloe's fresh and lively observations were not enlarged."

A writer of prose as well as poetry, Harper produced essays, articles, short stories, and a novel. "Her prose is frankly propagandic," remarked Redding, joining the consensus that the writer's prose is "less commendable" than her poetry. Harper's reform essays and articles appeared frequently in journals and periodicals, however, and her short story "The Two Offers" was the first to be published by a black American. In addition, her novel *Iola Leroy; or, Shadows Uplifted* pleased contemporary readers and critics, although current assessments consider it a contrived and sentimental piece unable to transcend the conventions of its age. The story of light-skinned Negroes who reject "passing" as whites in order to work and live among their people, *Iola Leroy* expresses its author's belief that sacrifice is essential to black progress. Considered a transitional novel because it treats both antebellum and postbellum periods, the story is particularly significant for featuring educated, socially committed black characters. Redding concluded that "as a writer of prose [Harper] is to be remembered rather for what she attempted than for what she accomplished."

A figure of more historic than artistic importance, Harper has sparked renewed interest among latter twentieth-century scholars. Described variously as an early feminist, one of the first Afro-American protest poets, and—in the words of *Black American Literature Forum* writer Patricia Liggins Hill—"a major healer and race-builder of nineteenth-century America," Harper nonetheless made aesthetic contributions of pioneer significance. In a *Crisis* editorial following the poet's death, W.E.B. Du Bois reflected: "It is, however, for her attempts to forward literature among colored people that Frances Harper deserves most to be remembered. She was not a great singer, but she had some sense of song; she was not a great writer, but she wrote much worth reading. She was, above all, sincere. She took her writing soberly and earnestly; she gave her life to it.''

BIOGRAPHICAL/CRITICAL SOURCES:

BOOKS

Barksdale, Richard and Keneth Kinnamon, *Black Writers of America: A Comprehensive Anthology,* Macmillan, 1972.

Bell, Roseann P. and others, editors, *Sturdy Black Bridges: Visions of Black Women in Literature,* Anchor Books, 1979.

Bone, Robert, *The Negro Novel in America,* revised edition, Yale University Press, 1965.

Brawley, Benjamin, *The Negro in Literature and Art in the United States,* Duffield, 1929.

Brown, Hallie Q., *Homespun Heroines and Other Women of Distinction,* Aldine, 1926, reprinted, Books for Libraries, 1971.

Christian, Barbara, *Black Women Novelists: The Development of a Tradition, 1892-1976,* Greenwood Press, 1980.

Christian, Barbara, *Black Feminist Criticism: Perspectives of Black Women Writers,* Pergamon, 1985.

Dannett, Sylvia G.L., *Profiles of Negro Womanhood:* Volume I: *1619-1900,* M. W. Lads, 1964.

Dictionary of Literary Biography, Volume 50: *Afro-American Writers Before the Harlem Renaissance,* Gale, 1986.

Giddings, Paula, *When and Where I Enter: The Impact of Black Women on Race and Sex in America,* Morrow, 1984.

Gloster, Hugh M., *Negro Voices in American Fiction,* University of North Carolina Press, 1948, Russell, 1968.

Goldstein, Rhoda L., *Black Life and Culture in the United States,* Crowell, 1971.

Hanaford, Phebe A., *Daughters of America; or, Women of the Century,* B. B. Russell, 1882.

Kerlin, Robert T., *Negro Poets and Their Poems,* Associated Publishers, 1923, revised third edition, 1935.

Loewenberg, Bert James and Ruth Bogin, *Black Women in Nineteenth-Century American Life: Their Words, Their Thoughts, Their Feelings,* Pennsylvania State University Press, 1976.

Loggins, Vernon, *The Negro Author: His Development in America,* Columbia University Press, 1931, reprinted, Kennikat, 1969.

Majors, M. A., *Noted Negro Women: Their Triumphs and Activities,* Donohue & Henneberry, 1893.

Montgomery, Janey Weinhold, *A Comparative Analysis of the Rhetoric of Two Negro Women Orators: Sojourner Truth and Frances E. Watkins Harper,* Fort Hays Kansas State College, 1968.

O'Connor, Lillian, *Pioneer Women Orators,* Columbia University Press, 1954.

Redding, J. Saunders, *To Make a Poet Black,* University of North Carolina Press, 1939, McGrath, 1968.

Redmond, Eugene B., *Drumvoices: The Mission of Afro-American Poetry, A Critical History,* Anchor/Doubleday, 1976.

Richings, G. F., *Evidences of Progress Among Colored People,* George S. Ferguson, 1896, AFRO-AM Press, 1969.

Robinson, William H., Jr., editor, *Early Black American Poets: Selections With Biographical and Critical Introductions,* W. C. Brown, 1969.

Sherman, Joan R., *Invisible Poets: Afro-Americans of the Nineteenth Century,* University of Illinois Press, 1974.

Sillen, Samuel, *Women Against Slavery,* Masses & Mainstream, 1955.

Still, William Grant, *The Underground Railroad,* Porter & Coates, 1872, reprinted, Arno/New York Times, 1968.

Twentieth-Century Literary Criticism, Volume 14, Gale, 1984.

Wagner, Jean, *Black Poets of the United States From Paul Laurence Dunbar to Langston Hughes,* translation by Kenneth Douglas, University of Illinois Press, 1973.

Whiteman, Maxwell, *A Century of Fiction by American Negroes, 1853-1952: A Descriptive Bibliography,* Albert Saifer, 1955.

Williams, Kenny J., *They Also Spoke: An Essay on Negro Literature in America, 1787-1930,* Townsend, 1970.

Woodson, Carter G. and Charles H. Wesley, *The Negro in Our History,* Associated Publishers, 1922.

PERIODICALS

African Methodist Episcopal Church Review, April, 1892.

Anglo-Saxon Magazine, May, 1859.

Black American Literature Forum, summer, 1981.

Black World, December, 1972.

Crisis, April, 1911.

Jet, February 23, 1961, February 24, 1966.

Journal of Negro History, October, 1917.

Massachusetts Review, winter/spring, 1972.

Messenger, February, 1927.

Nation, February, 1893.

Negro History Bulletin, December, 1938, January, 1942.

OTHER

Daniel, Theodora Williams, ''The Poems of Frances E.W. Harper'' (masters thesis), Howard University, 1937.

Graham, Maryemma, ''The Threefold Cord: Blackness, Womanness, and Art; A Study of the Life and Work of Frances Ellen Watkins Harper'' (masters thesis), Cornell University, 1973.

—Sketch by Nancy Pear

*   *   *

HARPER, Michael S(teven) 1938-

PERSONAL: Born March 18, 1938, in Brooklyn, N.Y.; son of Walter Warren and Katherine (Johnson) Harper; married Shirley Ann Buffington, December 24, 1965; children: Roland Warren, Patrice Cuchulain, Rachel Maria. *Education:* Los Angeles City College, A.A., 1959; Los Angeles State College of Applied Arts and Sciences (now California State University, Los Angeles), B.A., 1961, M.A., 1963; University of Iowa, M.F.A., 1963; additional study, University of Illinois, 1970-71.

ADDRESSES: Home—26 First St., Barrington, R.I. 02806. *Office*—Department of English, Box 1852, Brown University, Providence, R.I. 02912.

CAREER: Contra Costa College, San Pablo, Calif., instructor in English, 1964-68; Lewis and Clark College, Portland, Ore., poet in residence, 1968-69; California State College (now University), Hayward, associate professor of English, 1970; Brown University, Providence, R.I., associate professor, 1971-73, professor, 1973—, I. J. Kapstein Professor of English, 1983—, director of writing program. Visiting professor at Reed College, 1968-69, Harvard University, 1974, and Yale University, 1977; Benedict Distinguished Professor of English, Carleton College, 1979; Elliston poet, University of Cincinnati, 1979; National Humanities Distinguished Professor, Colgate University, 1985. Bicentennial poet, Bicentennary Exchange: Britain/USA, 1976. American specialist, International Congress of Africanists (ICA) State Department tour of Africa, 1977; lecturer, German University ICA tour of nine universities, 1978. Council member, Massachusetts Council on the Arts and Humanities, 1977-80; board member, Yaddo Artists Colony, Sarasota Springs, N.Y.; original founding member, African Continuum, St. Louis, Mo. Judge, National Book Awards in poetry, 1978.

MEMBER: American Academy of Arts and Letters.

AWARDS, HONORS: Fellow, Center for Advanced Study, University of Illinois, 1970-71; Black Academy of Arts and Letters award, 1972, for *History Is Your Own Heartbeat;* National Institute of Arts and Letters award and American Academy award in literature, both 1972; Guggenheim fellowship, 1976; National Endowment for the Arts creative writing award, 1977; nomination for National Book Award for poetry and Melville-Cane Award, both 1978, both for *Images of Kin: New and Selected Poems.*

WRITINGS:

POEMS

Dear John, Dear Coltrane, University of Pittsburgh Press, 1970.
History Is Your Own Hearbeat, University of Illinois Press, 1971.
Photographs, Negatives: History as Apple Tree (also see below), Scarab Press, 1972.
Song: I Want a Witness (includes *Photographs, Negatives: History as Apple Tree*), University of Pittsburgh Press, 1972.
Debridement, Doubleday, 1973.
Nightmare Begins Responsibility, University of Illinois Press, 1974.
Images of Kin: New and Selected Poems, University of Illinois Press, 1977.
Rhode Island: Eight Poems, Pym-Randall, 1981.
Healing Song for the Inner Ear, University of Illinois Press, 1985.

OTHER

(Compiler) Ralph Dickey, *Leaving Eden: Poems,* Bonewhistle Press, 1974.
(Editor with Robert B. Stepto, and contributor) *Chant of Saints: A Gathering of Afro-American Literature, Art, and Scholarship,* University of Illinois Press, 1979.
(Compiler) Sterling Allen Brown, *The Collected Poems of Sterling A. Brown,* Harper, 1980.
(Contributor) R. Baxter Miller, editor, *Black American Literature and Humanism,* University Press of Kentucky, 1981.

Also contributor to poetry anthologies, including *The Poetry of Black America, To Gwen with Love, Starting with Poetry, Understanding the New Black Poetry, The Black Poets,* and *Natural Process.* Contributor to periodicals, including *Black Scholar, Black World, Chicago Review, Negro American Literature Forum, Negro Digest,* and *Poetry.* Guest editor, *Iowa Review, Massachusetts Review,* and *American Poetry Review.* Editor with John Wright of special issue of *Carleton Miscellany* on Ralph Ellison, winter, 1980. Member of editorial boards of *TriQuarterly,* the *Georgia Review,* and *Obsidian.*

SIDELIGHTS: "Michael Harper is a deeply complex poet whose mission is to unite the fractured, inhumane technologies of our time with the abiding deep well of Negro folk traditions," says John Callahan in the *New Republic.* Harper does this,

notes *Poetry* reviewer Paul Breslin, by drawing "upon black history, literature, and myth," as do many other black writers. However, "what distinguishes Harper as a unique poet," states Norris B. Clark in the *Dictionary of Literary Biography,* "is a distinctive voice that captures the colors, mood, and realities of the personal, the racial, and the historical past, and a philosophy that bridges the traditional schism between black America and white America."

Harper himself supports Clark's statements, telling *CA* that his voice evolved from travels made in the late 1960s "to Mexico and Europe where those landscapes broadened my scope and interest in poetry and culture of other countries while I searched my own family and racial history for folklore, history and myth for themes that would give my writing the tradition and context where I could find my own voice. My travels made me look closely at the wealth of human materials in my own life, its ethnic richness, complexity of language and stylization, the tension between stated moral idealism and brutal historical realities, and I investigated the inner reality of those struggles to find the lyrical expression of their secrets in my own voice."

Harper's interest in history pervades his poetry, and his thesis in much of his work is directly related to this interest; in the words of David Lehman in *Poetry* magazine, his efforts are "attempts of a more historical nature to illuminate the black experience in America." He uses stories from both his family's past and from events in black history in general to illustrate his points: Harper's grandfather facing a mob threatening to burn his home; John Henry Louis, a Vietnam veteran and Congressional Medal of Honor winner, shot in the streets of Detroit by a shopkeeper who owed him money; a slave who, told to saw a limb off a tree, sat on the limb itself while working. Harper's poems also incorporate jazz and blues rhythms to "revive the past through the readers' inner feelings, by creating a new sense of time and by arranging a historical awareness," says Clark. His success in this is marked by a sense of "history automatically yielding up its metaphor, as the facts are salvaged by the careful eye and ear informed by a remarkable imagination which balances the American present and past," according to Laurence Lieberman in the *Yale Review.*

However, Harper's concentration on the past is not what makes his work unique. Robert B. Stepto, writing in the *Hollins Critic,* relates Harper's work to a primary tradition in Afro-American letters: "the honoring of kin," a tradition that Harper shares with writers such as Ralph Ellison and Robert Hayden. Although Harper's earlier work included many poems about his wife's family, his wife, and their children, it was not until the publication of *Nightmare Begins Responsibility* that Harper began to write about his own past. In that collection, Harper wrote poems for both his grandfathers and his mother's mother, poems whose "matter-of-fact, stoic lines," in Callahan's opinion, "enlarge the scale" of their lives. Callahan calls these poems "masterful and unforgettable"; he notes that "in [his work] Harper evokes for his children the lives of people whose legacy is a strength and integrity that crossed over the turf of survival."

Besides personal family figures Harper also uses, in Lieberman's words, the lives of key figures "in the black man's struggle to achieve an American identity" in collections such as *Debridement* and *Dear John, Dear Coltrane.* Figures such as the baseball player Jackie Robinson, the novelist Richard Wright, the poet Sterling Brown, and the jazz musician John

Coltrane are akin to Harper; they are"kin who share the goal of artistic excellence in whatever may be their craft or endeavor," says Stepto. Michael G. Cooke points out in *Afro-American Literature in the Twentieth Century: The Achievement of Intimacy* that Harper's honoring is not limited to ties of blood or race; he says, "*kinship* means social bonding, a recognition of likeness in context, concern, need, liability value. It is humanistic, a cross between consanguinuity and technical organization." "While [Harper] invokes blood relations in several inspired cases," he continues, "his approach to kinship is a radiant one, reaching out across time, across space, even across race" to include white men such as the Puritan dissident and founder of Rhode Island, Roger Williams, and the farmer-turned-abolitionist, John Brown.

Harper's acceptance of both black and white historical figures as kin is recognized by critics as an original factor in his poetry. Clark indicates that Harper "is neither a black poet nor a white poet; as he freely acknowledges, he uses both traditions and heritages rightfully his and America's to create images of power and beauty." He points out that Harper has stated that he reads white authors "to see how they make use of form, as well as to evaluate black character and motivation." Yet, although Harper criticizes white poets who, in his opinion, use the black idiom inconsistantly, he does not reject them. Clark concludes, "[Harper] is comfortable in not denying a dual tradition as many white American writers and black American writers have done. [He] continues to be a poet of harmony—accepting unity and diversity—rather than discord."

BIOGRAPHICAL/CRITICAL SOURCES:

BOOKS

Contemporary Literary Criticism, Gale, Volume VII, 1977, Volume XXII, 1982.
Cooke, Michael G., *Afro-American Literature in the Twentieth Century: The Achievement of Intimacy,* Yale University Press, 1984.
Dictionary of Literary Biography, Volume XLI: *Afro-American Poets since 1955,* Gale, 1985.
Harper, Michael S., and Robert B. Stepto, editors, *Chant of Saints: A Gathering of Afro-American Literature, Art, and Scholarship,* University of Illinois Press, 1979.
O'Brian, John, editor, *Interviews with Black Writers,* Liveright, 1973.

PERIODICALS

Hollins Critic, June, 1976.
Los Angeles Times, January 21, 1987.
Nation, June 21, 1980.
New Republic, May 17, 1985.
New York Times Book Review, March 5, 1978, October 13, 1985.
Parnassus: Poetry in Review, fall/winter, 1975.
Poetry, December, 1973.
Saturday Review, August 8, 1970.
Times Literary Supplement, May 30, 1980.
Virginia Quarterly Review, autumn, 1970.
World Literature Today, winter, 1981, winter, 1986.
Yale Review, October, 1973.

—*Sketch by Kenneth R. Shepherd*

*   *   *

HARPER, Mrs. F. E. W.
    See HARPER, Frances Ellen Watkins

HARRIS, (Theodore) Wilson   1921-
    (Kona Waruk)

PERSONAL: Born March 24, 1921, in New Amsterdam, British Guiana (now Guyana); immigrated to England, 1959; son of Theodore Wilson (an insurer and underwriter) and Millicent Josephine (Glasford) Harris; married Cecily Carew, 1945; married second wife, Margaret Nimmo Burns (a writer), April 2, 1959. *Education:* Queen's College, Georgetown, British Guiana, 1934-39; studied land surveying and geomorphology under government auspices, 1939-42.

ADDRESSES: Home—London, England. *Office*—c/o Faber and Faber, 3 Queen Square, London WC1N 3AU, England.

CAREER: British Guiana Government, government surveyor, 1942-54, senior surveyor, 1955-58; full-time writer in London, England, 1959—. Visiting lecturer, State University of New York at Buffalo, 1970, Yale University, 1979; guest lecturer, Mysore University (India), 1978; regents' lecturer, University of California, 1983; writer-in-residence, University of West Indies, 1970, University of Toronto, 1970, Newcastle University, Australia, 1979, University of Queensland, Australia, 1986; visiting professor, University of Texas at Austin, 1972, 1981-82, 1983, University of Aarhus, Denmark, 1973, and in Cuba. Delegate, UNESCO Symposium on Caribbean Literature in Cuba, 1968, National Identity Conference in Brisbane, Australia, 1968.

AWARDS, HONORS: English Arts Council grants, 1968 and 1970; Commonwealth fellow at University of Leeds, 1971; Guggenheim fellow, 1972-73; Henfield writing fellow at University of East Anglia, 1974; Southern Arts fellow, Salisbury, 1976; D.Lit., University of West Indies, 1984.

WRITINGS:

NOVELS

Palace of the Peacock (Book I of the "Guiana Quartet"; also see below), Faber, 1960.
The Far Journey of Oudin (Book II of the "Guiana Quartet"; also see below), Faber, 1961.
The Whole Armour (Book III of the "Guiana Quartet"; also see below), Faber, 1962.
The Secret Ladder (Book IV of the "Guiana Quartet"; also see below), Faber, 1963.
The Whole Armour [and] *The Secret Ladder,* Faber, 1963.
Heartland, Faber, 1964.
The Eye of the Scarecrow, Faber, 1965.
The Waiting Room, Faber, 1967.
Tamatumari, Faber, 1968.
Ascent to Omai, Faber, 1970.
Black Marsden: A Tabula Rasa Comedy, Faber, 1972.
Companions of the Day and Night, Faber, 1975.
Da Silva da Silva's Cultivated Wilderness [and] *Genesis of the Clowns* (also see below), Faber, 1977.
Genesis of the Clowns, Faber, 1978.
The Tree of the Sun, Faber, 1978.
The Angel at the Gate, Faber, 1982.
Carnival, Faber, 1985.
The Guyana Quartet (contains *Palace of the Peacock, The Far Journey of Oudin, The Whole Armour,* and *The Secret Ladder;* issued as a boxed set), Faber, 1985.

SHORT STORIES

The Sleepers of Roraima, Faber, 1970.

The Age of the Rainmakers, Faber, 1971.

POETRY

(Under pseudonym Kona Waruk) *Fetish,* privately printed (Georgetown, Guyana), 1951.
The Well and the Land, British Guiana, 1952.
Eternity to Season, privately printed (Georgetown), 1954, 2nd edition, New Beacon Books, 1978.

NONFICTION

Tradition and the West Indian Novel (lecture), introduction by C.L.R. James, New Beacon, 1965.
Tradition, the Writer and Society: Critical Essays, New Beacon, 1967.
History, Fable and Myth in the Caribbean and Guianas (booklet), National History and Arts Council, (Georgetown), 1970.
Fossil and Psyche (criticism), African and American Studies and Research Center, University of Texas, 1974.
(Contributor) J. T. Livingston, editor, *Caribbean Rhythms: The Emerging English Literature of the West Indies,* Washington Square Press, 1974.
(Contributor) Anna Rutherford and Kirsten Holst Petersen, editors, *Enigma of Values: An Introduction,* Dangaroo Press, 1975.
(Contributor) Edward Baugh, editor, *Critics on Caribbean Literature: Readings in Literary Criticism,* St. Martin's, 1978.
Explorations: A Series of Talks and Articles, 1966-1981, Hena Maes-Jelinek, editor and author of introduction, Dangaroo Press, 1981.
The Womb of Space: The Cross-Cultural Imagination, Greenwood Press, 1983.
The Infinite Rehearsal, Faber, 1987.

Also contributor to *Literary Half-Yearly, Kyk-over-al,* and *New Letters.*

SIDELIGHTS: Novelist Wilson Harris blends philosophy, poetic imagery, symbolism and myth to create new visions of reality. His fiction shows the reader a world where the borders between physical and spiritual reality, life and death have become indistinguishable. In *World Literature Today,* Richard Sander states that Harris has "realized a new, original form of the novel that in almost all respects constitutes a radical departure from the conventional novel." Reed Way Dasenbrock, also writing in *World Literature Today,* claims that Harris "has always operated at a very high level of abstraction, higher than any of his fellow West Indian novelists, higher perhaps than any other contemporary novelist in English. . . . And whether one regards Harris's evolution as a rich and exciting development or a one-way trip down an abstractionist cul-de-sac, there is no denying his unique vision or dedication to that vision." The constant use of abstraction has brought Harris both praise and criticism; while some find his work rewarding and challenging, others think his unorthodox methods alienate the reader.

Harris is perhaps best known to the general public for *The Guyana Quartet.* Important to all four works of the quartet is the landscape of the Guyanese interior, which Harris came to know well during his years as a government surveyor. "Two major elements seem to have shaped Harris's approach to art and his philosophy of existence: the impressive contrasts of the Guyanese landscapes, . . . and the successive waves of conquest which gave Guyana its heterogeneous population po-

larised for centuries into oppressors and their victims. The two, landscape and history, merge in his work into single metaphors symbolising man's inner space saturated with the effects of historical—that is, temporal—experiences," writes Hena Maes-Jelinek in *West Indian Literature.*

Harris's works are frequently difficult for critics to summarize because they move so far from the accepted definition of a novel. Harris uses dream, hallucination, psychic experiences, and various historical times without clearcut divisions, and critics often find it necessary to invent a genre for Harris's works in order to discuss them. Michael Thorpe in *World Literature Today* calls the author's more recent books "psychical 'expeditions.'" A *Times Literary Supplement* contributor terms *Palace of the Peacock,* the first volume of the "Guyana Quartet," "a 150-page definition of mystical experience given in the guise of a novel." And an *Encounter* contributor describes Harris's work as "a metaphysical shorthand on the surface of a narrative whose point cannot readily be grasped by any but those thoroughly versed in his previous work and able at once to recognise the recurrent complex metaphors."

Reviewers frequently mention that to fully grasp Harris's work it is necessary to be familiar with his metaphors, since the elaborately written passages and complex symbolism can make the writing nearly impenetrable for readers used to more traditional fiction. A *Times Literary Supplement* contributor warns, "no reader should attempt Mr. Harris's novels unless he is willing to work at them." Reviewing *Palace of the Peacock,* another *Times Literary Supplement* contributor says it is "a difficult book to read, yet it is the very concreteness of Mr. Harris's imagery that makes its denseness so hard to penetrate." Thorpe agrees, writing, "The uninitiated reader may become discouraged, wrestling with opaque ideas attached to tantalizing shadows of what he seeks in fiction: engagement with deeply apprehended lives and moving action." But according to J. P. Durix, also a *Times Literary Supplement* contributor, the reader who stays with Harris is rewarded by his "dense style and meticulous construction, his attention to visual and rhythmic effects, [which] are matched by an inventiveness which few contemporary novelists can equal."

Harris also writes literary criticism; in *The Womb of Space,* he expands upon many of the ideas contained in his novels. But in his general theory as well as in his fictional works, Harris's points can be hard to understand. Steven G. Kellman writes in *Modern Fiction Studies,* "I take it that Wilson Harris' theme is the ability of consciousness to transcend a particular culture. But his articulation of that theme is so turgid, so beset by mixed and obscure metaphors and by syntactical convolutions that much of the book simply remains unintelligible even to a sympathetic reader." Harris's goal in the work is to establish parallels between writers of various cultural backgrounds. He observes in *The Womb of Space* that "literature is still constrained by regional and other conventional but suffocating categories." His vision is of a new world community, based on cultural heterogeneity, not homogeneity, which, "as a cultural model, exercised by a ruling ethnic group, tends to become an organ of conquest and division because of *imposed* unity that actually subsists on the suppression of others." Sander believes that *The Womb of Space* is "an attack on the traditional critical establishment." A *Choice* contributor agrees, claiming, "*The Womb of Space* issues a direct challenge to the intellectual provincialism that often characterises literary study in the US."

But critics who applaud Harris's work believe he has contributed greatly to the understanding of art and consciousness.

John Hearne writes in *The Islands in Between,* "No other British Caribbean novelist has made quite such an explicit and conscious effort as Harris to reduce the material reckonings of everyday life to the significance of myth." And speaking of the breadth of Harris' work, Louis James states in the *Times Literary Supplement,* "The novels of Wilson Harris . . . form one ongoing whole. Each work is individual; yet the whole sequence can be seen as a continuous, ever-widening exploration of civilization and creative art."

BIOGRAPHICAL/CRITICAL SOURCES:

BOOKS

Baugh, Edward, editor, *Critics on Caribbean Literature: Readings in Literary Criticism,* St. Martin's, 1978.
Contemporary Literary Criticism, Volume 25, Gale, 1983.
Dance, Daryl Cumber, editor, *Fifty Caribbean Writers: A Bio-Bibliographical Critical Sourcebook,* Greenwood Press, 1986.
Drake, Sandra E., *Wilson Harris and the Modern Tradition: A New Architecture of the World,* Greenwood Press, 1986.
Fletcher, John, *Commonwealth Literature and the Modern World,* Didier (Brussels), 1975.
Gilkes, Michael, *The West Indian Novel,* Twayne Publishers, 1981.
Gilkes, Michael, *Wilson Harris and the Caribbean Novel,* Longman, 1975.
Harris, Wilson, *The Tree of the Sun,* Faber, 1978.
Harris, Wilson, *The Womb of Space: The Cross-Cultural Imagination,* Greenwood Press, 1983.
James, Louis, editor, *The Islands In Between,* Oxford University Press, 1968.
King, Bruce, editor, *West Indian Literature,* Archon Books, 1979.
Maes-Jelinek, Hena, *The Naked Design,* Dangaroo Press, 1976.
Maes-Jelinek, Hena, *Wilson Harris,* Twayne, 1982.
Moore, Gerald, *Chosen Tongue,* Longman, 1969.
Munro, Ian and Reinhard Sander, editors, *Kas-Kas: Interviews with Three Caribbean Writers in Texas,* African and Afro-American Research Institute, The University of Texas at Austin, 1972.
Ramchand, Kenneth, *An Introduction to the Study of West Indian Literature,* Nelson Caribbean, 1976.
Van Sertima, Ivan, *Enigma of Values,* Dangaroo Press, 1975.

PERIODICALS

Choice, March, 1984.
Encounter, May, 1987.
Journal of Commonwealth Literature, July, 1969, June, 1971, April, 1975.
Language and Literature, autumn, 1971.
Literary Half-Yearly, January, 1972.
Modern Fiction Studies, summer, 1984.
Observer, July 7, 1985.
Quill and Quire, October, 1985.
Spectator, March 25, 1978.
Times Educational Supplement, July 19, 1985.
Times Literary Supplement, December 9, 1965, July 4, 1968, May 21, 1970, October 10, 1975, May 25, 1977, May 19, 1978, October 15, 1982, July 12, 1985, September 25-October 1, 1987.
World Literature Today, winter, 1984, summer, 1985, spring, 1986.

—*Sketch by Jani Prescott*

HARRISON, Paul Carter 1936-
(Paul Carter-Harrison)

PERSONAL: Born March 1, 1936, in New York, N.Y. *Education:* Attended New York University, 1953; Indiana University, B.A., 1957; graduate study at Ohio University, summers, 1959 and 1960; New School for Social Research, M.A., 1962.

ADDRESSES: Home—P.O. Box 143, Leeds, Mass. 01053. *Office*—Department of Theater/Music, Columbia College, 600 South Michigan Ave., Chicago, Ill. 60605.

CAREER: Howard University, Washington, D.C., assistant professor of theater arts, 1968-70; Kent State University, Kent, Ohio, associate professor of Afro-American literature, 1969; California State University, Sacramento, professor of theater arts, 1970-72; University of Massachusetts at Amherst, professor of theater arts and Afro-American studies, 1972-76; Columbia College, Chicago, Ill., artistic producer and chairman of theater/music department, 1976-80, writer in residence, 1980—. Visiting artist in residence at State University of New York at Buffalo, summer, 1965; Institute of Pan-African Culture, resident fellow at the University of Massachusetts at Amherst, consultant to the New England Regional Committee in Lagos, Nigeria, 1973-74; adjunct professor of theater communications at University of Illinois at Chicago Circle, 1978-82; visiting professor of Afro-American studies at Smith College and Wesleyan University, spring, 1984. Dramaturgical consultant to the Mickery Theater, Loenesloat, Netherlands; resource adviser to Colloquium on Black Education, Pajaro Dunes, Calif., 1970-71; touring symposium member of the African Continuum Forum, 1970-72; literary adviser to Lincoln Center Repertory Company, 1972-73; consultant to Theater Communications Group, 1972-74; theater panelist of Illinois Arts Council, 1976-79. Associate producer of the Association for the Advancement of Creative Musicians concert series, Columbia College, 1983-85.

Director of plays, including "Junebug Graduates Tonight," 1967, "Tabernacle," 1969, "Ain't Supposed to Die a Natural Death," 1970, "Tophat," 1971, "Homecookin'," 1971, "Lady Day: A Musical Tragedy," 1972, "Ceremonies in Dark Old Men," 1979, "The Owl Answers," 1980, "In an Upstate Motel," 1981, "My Sister, My Sister," 1981, "No Place to Be Somebody," 1983, "The River Niger," 1987, and "Anchorman," 1988. Producer of plays, including "Black Recollections," 1972; artistic producer of new American plays at Columbia College Performance Company, 1976-80. Developer and associate producer of television film "Leave 'Em Laughin'," Columbia Broadcasting System (CBS-TV), 1981.

MEMBER: American Theater Association, Dramatists Guild, Society for Directors and Choreographers, Actors Studio (playwrights and directors units).

AWARDS, HONORS: National Science Foundation fellowship; Obie Award for Best Play from the *Village Voice,* 1974, for "The Great MacDaddy"; Audelco (Audience Development Committee) Recognition Award for outstanding musical creator, 1981, for "Tabernacle"; Humanitas Prize from the Human Family Educational and Cultural Institute, 1981, for 'Leave 'Em Laughin'"; Illinois Art Council grant for playwriting, 1984; Rockefeller Foundation fellowship for American playwriting, 1985-86.

WRITINGS:

(Editor, under name Paul Carter-Harrison) *Voetnoten bij mo-*

dern toneel (essays; title means "The Modern Drama Footnote"), Bezige, 1965.

Dialog van het verzet (essays; title means "Dialogue From the Opposition"), Bezige, 1966.

(Under name Paul Carter-Harrison) *The Drama of Nommo: Black Theater in the African Continuum* (essays), Grove, 1972.

(Editor, contributor, and author of introduction) *Kuntu Drama: Plays of the African Continuum,* preface by Oliver Jackson, Grove, 1974 (also see PLAYS).

(With Charles Stewart) *Chuck Stewart's Jazz Files* (photo documentary), New York Graphic Society/Little, Brown, 1985.

(Editor, contributor, and author of introduction) *Totem Voices* (plays), Grove, 1988.

PLAYS

"The Postclerks" (one-act), first produced in New York at Actor's Studio, 1963.

"Pavane for a Dead-Pan Minstrel" (one-act; first produced in New York at Actor's Studio, 1964), published in *Podium* (Amsterdam), November, 1965.

"Tophat" (one-act), first produced at Buffalo University Summer Theater, 1965; produced in New York by Negro Ensemble Co., 1972.

"Pawns" (one-act), first produced in New York by 2nd Story Players, 1966.

"The Experimental Leader" (one-act; first produced in New York by Dore Co., 1968), published in *Podium,* 1965.

"Folly for Two" (one-act; first produced in New York at Actor's Studio, 1968), published in *Podium,* 1967, revised as "Interface."

"Tabernacle" (first produced in Washington, D.C., at Howard University, 1969; produced in New York at Afro-American Studio, 1976), published in *New Black Playwrights,* Avon, 1970.

"Ain't Supposed to Die a Natural Death" (adapted from Melvin Van Peebles's *Ain't Supposed to Die a Natural Death;* first produced at University of California, Sacramento, 1970).

"The Great MacDaddy" (first produced at University of California, Sacramento, 1972; produced in New York at St. Mark's Playhouse, February 12, 1974), published in *Kuntu Drama: Plays of the African Continuum,* Grove, 1974.

"Dr. Jazz" (two-act), first produced on Broadway, 1975.

"The Death of Boogie Woogie" (two-act; first produced in Northampton, Mass., at Smith Collge, 1976; produced in New York at Richard Allen Center, 1979), published in *Callaloo,* 1985.

"Ameri/cain Gothic" (two-act), first produced in Chicago at Columbia College, 1980; produced in New York at New Federal Theater, 1985.

"Abercrombie Apocalypse" (two-act), first produced in Chicago at Columbia College, 1981; produced Off-Broadway at Westside Arts Theater, June 22, 1982.

Also author of "Adding Machine" and adapter of Van Peebles's "Brer Soul."

SCREENPLAYS

"Impressions of American Negro Society," VPRO-TV (Hilversum, Netherlands), c. 1963.

"Stranger on a Square," VPRO-TV, 1964.

"Intrusion," [Belgium], 1965.

"Lord Shango," Bryanstone Pictures, 1974.

"Youngblood," Aion, 1978.

"Gettin' to Know Me," Children's Television International, 1980.

OTHER

(With Julius Hemphill) "Anchorman" (two-act operetta; with music by Hemphill), first produced in Chicago at Columbia College, 1982; produced in New York at Theater Four, 1988.

Contributor to American and Dutch periodicals, including *American Rag, Black Review, Black World, Choice, Nummo,* and *Players.* Critical consultant to *Choice,* 1973—; theater and contributing editor to *Elan,* 1981-83.

WORK IN PROGRESS: "Kanaan," a folk opera; "Happy Hour," a play.

SIDELIGHTS: The playwright Paul Carter Harrison, best known for integrating modern American thought and African tradition in his works, sums up his theories on drama and the philosophy behind his play writing in his 1972 collection of critical essays, *The Drama of Nommo.* In this book, as in his plays, Harrison stresses the importance of combining traditional African values, rituals, and philosophy—including the belief in a holistic universe, where all elements are connected—with contemporary American points of view to reflect the total black experience on stage. The author feels that the theater should attempt to free blacks' spiritual energy by providing virtually ceremonial interaction between the actors and audience. Furthermore, Harrison maintains, a play should utilize black linguistic idiom, character, music, literature, and folklore, which show the audience the traditional mythologies at work in contemporary black experience. Critics deemed *The Drama of Nommo* valuable and thought-provoking, praising Harrison for stimulating African culture, for advancing black dramatic criticism, and for establishing black drama as an entity separate from the conventional body of writing for the theater.

Harrison graduated from Indiana University and then the New School for Social Research before setting out for Europe in 1961. He eventually settled in Amsterdam, Netherlands, and lived there for seven years, staging readings by black poets and writing and producing television programs and plays for the theater. He began composing one-act plays during this period, with characters ranging from blue-collar workers unhappy with their lives to a Jew living in Nazi Germany unsure of his future. Harrison also experimented with reversing traditional roles based on gender or race. For example, "Tophat" features a female dominating a submissive male, and in "Pavane for a Dead-Pan Minstrel" a white man and black man switch identities by marking their faces with clown-white and minstrel cork and assuming the other's behavior.

While visiting the United States in 1964 Harrison witnessed the Harlem riots. When he returned to Europe he began writing his first full-length play, "Tabernacle," about the events leading up to the racial unrest. The main character, the Reverend, has been compared to an African ceremonial leader as he conducts his congregation (the audience) in a church service commemorating the victimization of black youths by the police. Throughout the play Harrison mixes jazz and African music—thereby symbolically integrating American innovation with African tradition—and uses a number of devices to remove the barrier between actor and audience, such as giving the audience an active role in the drama. Although Harrison completed the play in 1965, he felt that because of its content

"Tabernacle" should be performed only by Afro-Americans, so it was not presented until 1969 at Howard University in Washington, D.C., where he directed the production.

Harrison also utilized techniques to lessen the distance between actor and audience in his adaptation of work by Melvin Van Peebles. He saw Van Peebles's work as an exploration of city life, so he created an urban atmosphere in the theater, filling it—on stage and in the audience—with actors playing derelicts, drunks, prostitutes, and other lowlife, who interacted with the theatergoers. Because the productions of "Ain't Supposed to Die" were improvisational, with Van Peebles's works acting only as the tying thread, each of the performances presented at California State University in Sacramento in November, 1970, provoked a unique audience response.

Four years later Harrison won an Obie Award for the Off-Broadway production of his play "The Great MacDaddy." In a review for the New York Times Clayton Riley declared the play a "brilliant ritual drama" and admired its "metaphorical richness and visual imagery." "The Great MacDaddy" features mythic figures from black American folklore, all of whom MacDaddy encounters on his spiritual trek across Depression-era America in search of, according to Riley, "the knowledge needed for blacks to retain their soul in the soulless technology of America." This play, in which many of Harrison's dramatic principles are winningly combined, is considered his masterpiece. In it the playwright introduced African cultural elements in an American setting, placed emphasis on the Afro-American's spirituality and place in society, and utilized black street slang and dialect and African rhythmic music in the drama. Harrison published "The Great MacDaddy" in a collection of critically acclaimed works that he edited, Kuntu Drama: Plays of the African Continuum. The anthology contains plays by black writers—including Aime Cesaire, Amiri Baraka, Adrienne Kennedy, and Lennox Brown—who agreed with Harrison's dramatic tenets and drew extensively on African speech rhythms, rituals, traditions, values, and myths in their works featured.

Harrison has also written on black themes for television and film. During the early 1960s he penned and produced two films for television in the Netherlands, "Impressions of American Negro Poetry" and "Stranger on a Square." His writing for American television includes four segments of a children's folklore series produced in 1980, "Gettin' to Know Me." In addition, Harrison wrote the screenplays for an Americn short feature filmed in Belgium and for the motion picture "Youngblood," an American commercial release about a teenager who joins a ghetto street gang.

BIOGRAPHICAL/CRITICAL SOURCES:

BOOKS

Arata, Esther Spring, More Black American Playwrights, Scarecrow Press, 1978.
Dictionary of Literary Biography, Volume 38: Afro-American Writers After 1955: Dramatists and Prose Writers, Gale, 1985.
Fabre, Genevieve, Drumbeats, Masks, and Metaphors: Contemporary Afro-American Theater, translated by Melvin Dixon, Harvard University Press, 1983.
Hill, Errol, editor, The Theater of Black Americans, two volumes, Prentice-Hall, 1980.

PERIODICALS

Los Angeles Times Book Review, January 5, 1986.

New York Times, March 3, 1974, May 25, 1978, June 27, 1982.

—Sketch by Carol Lynn DeKane

*   *   *

HASKINS, James S. 1941-
(Jim Haskins)

PERSONAL: Born September 19, 1941, in Montgomery, Ala., son of Henry and Julia (Brown) Haskins. Education: Georgetown University, B.A., 1960; Alabama State University, B.S., 1962; University of New Mexico, M.A., 1963; graduate study at New School for Social Research, 1965-67, and Queens College of the City University of New York, 1967-68.

ADDRESSES: Home—325 West End Ave., Apt. 7D, New York, N.Y., 10013. Office—Department of English, University of Florida, Gainesville, Fla., 32611.

CAREER: Smith Barney & Co., New York City, stock trader, 1963-65; New York City Board of Education, teacher, 1966-68; New School for Social Research, New York City, visiting lecturer, 1970-72; Staten Island Community College of the City University of New York, Staten Island, N.Y., associate professor, 1970-77; University of Florida, Gainesville, professor of English, 1977—. Reporter, New York Daily News, New York City, 1963-64. Visiting lecturer, Elisabeth Irwin High School, New York City, 1971-73; visiting professor, Indiana University/Purdue University—Indianapolis, 1973-76; visiting professor, College of New Rochelle, New York City campus, 1977. Director, Union Mutual Life, Health, and Accident Insurance Co., Philadelphia, Penn., 1970-73; member of board of advisers, Psi Systems, 1971-72; member of board of directors, Speedwell Services for Children, 1974-76. Member, Manhattan Community Board No. 9, 1972-73, and New York Urban League Manhattan Advisory Board, 1973-75; member, academic council for the State University of New York, 1972-74. Consultant, Education Development Center, Newton, Mass., 1975—, Department of Health, Education, and Welfare, 1977-79, National Research Council, 1979-80, and Grolier, Inc., 1979-82. Member of National Education Advisory Committee and vice-director of Southeast Region of Statue of Liberty—Ellis Island Foundation, 1986. Member of National Education Advisory Committee, Commission on the Bicentennial of the Constitution.

MEMBER: National Book Critics Circle, Authors League of America, Authors Guild, 100 Black Men, Phi Beta Kappa, Kappa Alpha Psi.

AWARDS, HONORS: Notable children's book in the field of social studies citations from Social Education, 1971, for Revolutionaries: Agents of Change, from Social Studies, 1972, for Resistance: Profiles in Nonviolence, The War and the Protest: Viet Nam, and Profiles in Black Power, and 1973, for A Piece of the Power: Four Black Mayors, from National Council for the Social Studies-Children's Book Council Book Review Committee, 1975, for Fighting Shirley Chisholm, and 1976, for The Creoles of Color of New Orleans and The Picture Life of Malcolm X, from Children's Book Council, 1978, for The Life and Death of Martin Luther King, Jr.; World Book Year Book literature for children citation, 1973, for From Lew Alcindor to Kareem Abdul-Jabbar; Books of the Year citations, Child Study Association of America, 1974, for Adam Clayton Powell: Portrait of a Marching Black and Street Gangs: Yesterday and Today; Books for Brotherhood bibliography citation, National Council of Christians and Jews book review committee, 1975, for *Adam Clayton Powell: Portrait of a Marching Black;* Spur Award finalist, Western Writers of America, 1975, for *The Creoles of Color of New Orleans;* Eighth Annual Coretta Scott King Award, and Books Chosen by Children citation, Children's Book Council, both 1977, both for *The Story of Stevie Wonder;* Merit Award, National Council for Social Studies, 1980, for *James Van DerZee: The Picture Takin' Man;* American Society of Composers, Authors, and Publishers-Deems Taylor Award, 1980, for *Scott Joplin: The Man Who Made Ragtime;* Ambassador of Honor book, English-Speaking Union Books-Across-the-Sea, 1983, for *Bricktop;* American Library Association best book for young adults citation, 1987, for *Black Music in America;* Alabama Library Association best juvenile work citation, 1987, for "Count Your Way" series; "Bicentennial Reading, Viewing, Listening for Young Americans" citations, American Library Association and National Endowment for the Humanities, for *Street Gangs: Yesterday and Today, Ralph Bunche: A Most Reluctant Hero,* and *A Piece of the Power: Four Black Mayors;* certificate of appreciation, Joseph P. Kennedy Foundation, for work with the Special Olympics program.

WRITINGS:

Pinckney Benton Stewart Pitchback: A Biography, Macmillan, 1973.

A New King of Joy: The Story of the Special Olympics, Doubleday, 1976.

(With Kathleen Benson) *Scott Joplin: The Man Who Made Ragtime,* Doubleday, 1978.

(With Bricktop) *Bricktop,* Atheneum, 1983.

(With Benson) *Lena: A Personal and Professional Biography,* Stein & Day, 1984.

(With Benson) *Nat King Cole,* Stein & Day, 1984.

Mabel Mercer: A Life, Atheneum, 1988.

JUVENILES

Resistance: Profiles in Nonviolence, Doubleday, 1970.

Revolutionaries: Agents of Change, Lippincott, 1971.

The War and the Protest: Viet Nam, Doubleday, 1971.

Religions, Lippincott, 1973.

Witchcraft, Mysticism and Magic in the Black World, Doubleday, 1974.

Street Gangs: Yesterday and Today, Hastings House, 1974.

Jobs in Business and Office, Lothrop, 1974.

The Creoles of Color of New Orleans, Crowell, 1975.

The Consumer Movement, F. Watts, 1975.

Who Are the Handicapped?, Doubleday, 1978.

(With J. M. Stifle) *The Quiet Revolution: The Struggle for the Rights of Disabled Americans,* Crowell, 1979.

The New Americans: Vietnamese Boat People, Enslow, 1980.

Black Theater in American, Crowell, 1982.

The New Americans: Cuban Boat People, Enslow, 1982.

The Guardian Angels, Enslow, 1983.

(With David A. Walker) *Double Dutch,* Enslow, 1986.

Black Music in America: A History through Its People, Crowell, 1987.

(With Benson) *A Sixties Reader,* Viking, 1988.

JUVENILE BIOGRAPHIES

From Lew Alcindor to Kareem Abdul Jabbar, Lothrop, 1972, 2nd edition, 1978.

A Piece of the Power: Four Black Mayors, Dial, 1972.

Profiles in Black Power, Doubleday, 1972.

Deep like the Rivers: A Biography of Langston Hughes, 1902-1967, Holt, 1973.

Adam Clayton Powell: Portrait of a Marching Black, Dial, 1974.

Babe Ruth and Hank Aaron: The Home Run Kings, Lothrop, 1974.

Fighting Shirley Chisholm, Dial, 1975.

The Picture Life of Malcolm X, F. Watts, 1975.

Dr. J: A Biography of Julius Erving, Doubleday, 1975.

Pele: A Biography, Doubleday, 1976.

The Story of Stevie Wonder, Doubleday, 1976.

Always Movin' On: The Life of Langston Hughes, F. Watts, 1976.

Barbara Jordan, Dial, 1977.

The Life and Death of Martin Luther King, Jr., Lothrop, 1977.

George McGinnis: Basketball Superstar, Hastings, 1978.

Bob McAdoo: Superstar, Lothrop, 1978.

Andrew Young: Man with a Mission, Lothrop, 1979.

I'm Gonna Make You Love Me: The Story of Diana Ross, Dial, 1980.

"Magic": A Biography of Earvin Johnson, Enslow, 1981.

Katherine Dunham, Coward-McCann, 1982.

Donna Summer, Atlantic Monthly Press, 1983.

Lena Horne, Coward-McCann, 1983.

About Michael Jackson, Enslow, 1985.

Diana Ross: Star Supreme, Viking, 1985.

Leaders of the Middle East, Enslow, 1985.

Corazon Aquino, Enslow, 1988.

The Magic Johnson Story, Enslow, 1988.

UNDER NAME JIM HASKINS

Diary of a Harlem Schoolteacher, Grove, 1969, 2nd edition, Stein & Day, 1979.

(Editor) *Black Manifesto for Education,* Morrow, 1973.

(With Hugh F. Butts) *The Psychology of Black Language,* Barnes & Noble, 1973.

Snow Sculpture and Ice Carving, Macmillan, 1974.

The Cotton Club, Random House, 1977, 2nd edition, New American Library, 1984.

(With Benson and Ellen Inkelis) *The Great American Crazies,* Condor, 1977.

Voodoo and Hoodoo: Their Tradition and Craft as Revealed by Actual Practitioners, Stein & Day, 1978.

(With Benson) *The Stevie Wonder Scrapbook,* Grosset & Dunlap, 1978.

Richard Pryor, a Man and His Madness: A Biography, Beaufort Books, 1984.

Queen of the Blues: A Biography of Dinah Washington, Morrow, 1987.

UNDER NAME JIM HASKINS; JUVENILES

Jokes from Black Folks, Doubleday, 1973.

Ralph Bunche: A Most Reluctant Hero, Hawthorne, 1974.

Your Rights, Past and Present: A Guide for Young People, Hawthorne, 1975.

Teen-age Alcoholism, Hawthorne, 1976.

The Long Struggle: The Story of American Labor, Westminster, 1976.

Real Estate Careers, F. Watts, 1978.

Gambling—Who Really Wins?, F. Watts, 1978.

James Van DerZee: The Picture Takin' Man, Dodd, Mead, 1979.

(With Pat Connolly) *The Child Abuse Help Book,* Addison Wesley, 1981.

Werewolves, Lothrop, 1982.

Sugar Ray Leonard, Lothrop, 1982.

(With Stifle) *Donna Summer: An Unauthorized Biography,* Little, Brown, 1983.
(With Benson) *Space Challenge: The Story of Guion Bluford, an Authorized Biography,* Carolrhoda Books, 1984.
Break Dancing, Lerner, 1985.
The Statue of Liberty: America's Proud Lady, Lerner, 1986.

UNDER NAME JIM HASKINS; JUVENILES; "COUNT YOUR WAY" SERIES

Count Your Way through China, Carolrhoda Books, 1987.
... through Japan, Carolrhoda Books, 1987.
... through Russia, Carolrhoda Books, 1987.
... through the Arab World, Carolrhoda Books, 1987.

OTHER

(Contributor) Emily Mumford, *Understanding Human Behavior in Health and Illness,* Williams & Wilkins, 1977.
(Contributor) *New York Kid's Catalog,* Doubleday, 1979.
(Contributor) *Notable American Women Supplement,* Radcliffe College, 1979.
(Contributor) Jerry Brown, *Clearings in the Thicket: An Alabama Humanities Reader,* Mercer University Press, 1985.

Also contributor to *Author in the Kitchen* and to *Children and Books,* 4th edition, 1976. General editor, under name Jim Haskins, of *The Filipino Nation,* three volumes, Grolier International, 1982. Contributor of articles and reviews to periodicals, including *American Visions, Now, Arizona English Bulletin, Rolling Stone, Children's Book Review Service, Western Journal of Black Studies, Elementary English, Amsterdam News, New York Times Book Review, Afro-Hawaii News,* and *Gainesville Sun.*

SIDELIGHTS: James Haskins says in *Something about the Author Autobiography Series:* "It has always seemed to me that truth is not just 'stranger than fiction,' but also more interesting. Also, it seems to me that the more you know about the real world the better off you are, and since there is so much in the real world to learn about, you are better off concentrating on fact rather than fiction." Haskins supports this idea in his many biographies of important black people, many of them politicians, performers or sports figures, as well as in his other writings, ranging from discussions of ice sculpture to forms of rope jumping to histories of gang violence and the Harlem night life of the Cotton Club.

Haskins' first book grew out of his experiences teaching a Special Education class at Public School 92 in New York. A social worker, he relates, "gave me a diary and suggested that I write down my thoughts about my students and teaching disadvantaged children in Harlem. *Diary of a Harlem Schoolteacher* was the result." Ronald Gross of the *New York Times Book Review* describes the book as "plain, concrete, unemotional and unliterary. . . . By its truthfulness alone does it command our concern." The episodes Haskins relates are not about "education with a big E," the critic continues; "Rather, the entries catalog the unremitting series of catastrophes, irritations and frustrations which make teaching and learning virtually impossible in most ghetto schools."

Once the *Diary* was published, Haskins continues, "major publishing companies actually approached me about writing books for young people. I knew exactly the kinds of books I wanted to do—books about current events and books about important black people so that students could understand the larger world around them through books written on a level that they could understand." Soon he produced volumes on the nonviolent civil rights movement, the Black Power movement, and the war in Vietnam—attempting to put these events in historical perspective—and biographies of important black people in politics and international affairs: Barbara Jordan, Adam Clayton Powell, Ralph Bunche, and Shirley Chisholm. Haskins originally steered away from sports figures, he says, because "it seemed to me that young blacks should have other role models besides successful athletes," but gradually "I realized that it doesn't matter so much *what* kids read as it does *that* they read. You can use new words and put sentences together properly just as easily when you are writing about a sports hero as when you are writing about a politician. The same goes for show-business stars like Stevie Wonder." Biographies of people ranging from black astronaut Guion Bluford to superstar Michael Jackson followed.

While many of Haskins' biographies are intended for a young audience, others are meant for adults. Some of his biographies of famous black performers and artists, such as Nat King Cole, Dinah Washington, Richard Pryor and Scott Joplin, have attracted critical attention because of their illumination of the stars' black experience. For instance, *Scott Joplin: The Man Who Made Ragtime,* states Joseph McLellan in the *Washington Post Book World,* focuses "special attention on his origins and plac[es] his life and his music in the black-American context without which it can be only incompletely understood." A biography of Nat King Cole "really points out the racial contradictions in American society [and] reveals the conflicts that exist between upper-class and lower-class African-Americans," according to Norman Richmond in the Toronto *Globe and Mail.* Another *Globe and Mail* contributor, Paul Washington, declares that *Queen of the Blues: A Biography of Dinah Washington* "ties Washington's story to the history of black Americans."

"Most of my books and articles are about black subjects—black history, black people," Haskins states. The reasons for this are partly due to "a certain segregation in the publishing industry," but also "because I remember being a child and not having many books about black people to read. I want children today, black and white, to be able to find books about black people and black history in case they want to read them."

MEDIA APAPTATIONS: Diary of a Harlem Schoolteacher has been recorded by Recordings for the Blind. *The Cotton Club* was the inspiration for the 1984 film of the same title.

BIOGRAPHICAL/CRITICAL SOURCES:

BOOKS

Brown, Jerry, *Clearings in the Thicket: An Alabama Humanities Reader,* Mercer University Press, 1985.
Children's Literature Review, Volume 3, Gale, 1978.
Something about the Author Autobiography Series, Volume 4, Gale, 1987.

PERIODICALS

Book World, November 10, 1974, September 11, 1977, February 5, 1978.
Chicago Tribune Book World, April 13, 1986.
Christian Science Monitor, March 12, 1970.
Globe and Mail (Toronto), July 6, 1985, September 12, 1987.
Los Angeles Times Book Review, July 24, 1983, March 11, 1984, January 20, 1985.
Manhattan Tribune, March 7, 1970.
New Leader, April 16, 1970.
New York Post, February 7, 1970.

New York Times Book Review, December 6, 1970, February 8, 1970, May 7, 1972, May 5, 1974, August 4, 1974, November 20, 1977, September 23, 1979, October 7, 1979, January 20, 1980, March 4, 1984, May 17, 1987, September 13, 1987.
Times Literary Supplement, May 24, 1985.
Washington Post, November 15, 1973.
Washington Post Book World, July 24, 1978, August 17, 1983, January 16, 1985, May 10, 1987.

*   *   *

HASKINS, Jim
    See HASKINS, James S.

*   *   *

HAYDEN, Robert C(arter), Jr.   1937-

PERSONAL: Born August 21, 1937, in New Bedford, Mass.; son of Robert C. (deceased) and Josephine (Hughes) Hayden; children: Deborah, Kevin, Karen. *Education:* Boston University, B.A., 1959, Ed.M., 1961, doctoral candidate, 1973—; Harvard University, certificate, 1966.

ADDRESSES: Home—P.O. Box 5453, Boston, Mass. 02102. *Office*—MassPEP, 553 Huntington Ave., Boston, Mass. 02115.

CAREER: Junior high school teacher of science in Newton, Mass.,1961-65; American Education Publications, Xerox Education Division, Middletown, Conn., editor and writer, 1966-68; Ginn & Co., Xerox Education Division, Boston, Mass., editor, 1968-69; Metropolitan Council for Educational Opportunity, Boston, Mass., executive director, 1970-73; Education Development Center, Newton, Mass., director of ethnic studies for Career Opportunities Program, 1973-74, managing director of Project Torque, 1974-76; Northeastern University, Boston, lecturer in African-American studies, 1978—; Boston Public Schools, Boston, special assistant and executive assistant to superintendent, 1982-85, director of project development, 1985-86; executive director of Massachusetts Pre-Engineering Program, 1987—. Instructor at State University of New York at Buffalo, summers, 1964, 1966, and Boston College, 1974-75; guest lecturer at Boston University, Harvard University, Boston State College, Tufts University, Simmons College, and University of Suffolk. Massachusetts Institute of Technology, community fellow, 1976—, director of secondary technical education project, 1980-82. Member of corporation of Museum of Afro-American History; member of board of directors of Roxbury Federation of Neighborhood Centers; member of advisory board of Child's World Day Care Centers, Inc.

MEMBER: Association for the Study of Afro-American Life and History (executive council member), National Alliance of Black School Educators, National Association of Science Writers, National Association for the Advancement of Colored People, Kappa Alpha Psi.

AWARDS, HONORS: All-American Award from Educational Press Association of America, 1968; local National Association for the Advancement of Colored People award, 1972; outstanding book award from National Science Teachers-Association and Children's Book Council, 1976, for *Nine Black American Doctors.*

WRITINGS:

Why You Are You: The Science of Heredity, Sex, and Development, American Education Publications, 1968.

Black in America: Episodes in U.S. History, Xerox Education Publications, 1969.
Seven Black American Scientists, Addison-Wesley, 1970.
Eight Black American Inventors, Addison-Wesley, 1972.
(With Jacqueline Harris) *Nine Black American Doctors,* Addison-Wesley, 1976.
Faith, Culture, and Leadership: A History of the Black Church in Boston (booklet), National Association for the Advancement of Colored People (Boston), 1983.

Contributor to *Dictionary of American Negro Biography, Boston's NAACP History: 1910-82,* and *A History of the Metropolitan Council for Educational Opportunity.* Author of "Boston's Black History," a weekly column in *Bay State Banner,* 1974-82. Book review editor of *Science Activities,* 1969-73; regional editor, *Western Journal of Black Studies,* 1976-83.

WORK IN PROGRESS: A biography of Roland Hayes.

SIDELIGHTS: Robert C. Hayden, Jr. comments that he "writes to provide youth of all ethnic and racial groups with accurate, useful information on the work of black Americans in science, invention, and medicine." In his work Hayden makes extensive use of oral history.

BIOGRAPHICAL/CRITICAL SOURCES:

BOOKS

Selected Black American Authors: An Illustrated Bio-Bibliography, G. K. Hall, 1977.

PERIODICALS

Horn Book, March, 1985.
New York Amsterdam News, April 9, 1977.

*   *   *

HAYDEN, Robert E(arl)   1913-1980

PERSONAL: Name originally Asa Bundy Sheffey; name legally changed by foster parents; born August 4, 1913, in Detroit, Mich.; died February 25, 1980, in Ann Arbor, Mich.; son of Asa and Gladys Ruth (Finn) Sheffey; foster son of William and Sue Ellen (Westerfield) Hayden; married Erma I. Morris, June 15, 1940; children: Maia. *Education:* Detroit City College (now Wayne State University), B.A., 1936; University of Michigan, M.A., 1944. *Religion:* Baha'i.

CAREER: Federal Writers' Project, Detroit, Mich., researcher, 1936-40; University of Michigan, Ann Arbor, teaching fellow, 1944-46; Fisk University, Nashville, Tenn., 1946-69, began as assistant professor, became professor of English; University of Michigan, professor of English, 1969-80. Bingham Professor, University of Louisville, 1969; visiting poet, University of Washington, 1969, University of Connecticut, 1971, and Denison University, 1972. Member, Michigan Arts Council, 1975-76; Consultant in Poetry, Library of Congress, 1976-78.

MEMBER: American Academy and Institute of Arts and Letters, Academy of American Poets, PEN, American Poetry Society, Authors Guild, Authors League of America, Phi Kappa Phi.

AWARDS, HONORS: Jules and Avery Hopwood Poetry Award, University of Michigan, 1938 and 1942; Julius Rosenwald fellow, 1947; Ford Foundation fellow in Mexico, 1954-55; World Festival of Negro Arts grand prize, 1966, for *A Ballad of Remembrance;* Russell Loines Award, National Institute of

Arts and Letters, 1970; National Book Award nomination, 1971, for *Words in the Mourning Time;* Litt.D., Brown University, 1976, Grand Valley State College, 1976, Fisk University, 1976, Wayne State University, 1977, and Benedict College, 1977; Academy of American Poets fellow, 1977; Michigan Arts Foundation Award, 1977; National Book Award nomination, 1979, for *American Journal.*

WRITINGS:

(Editor and author of introduction) *Kaleidoscope: Poems by American Negro Poets* (juvenile), Harcourt, 1967.
(Author of preface) Alain LeRoy Locke, editor, *The New Negro,* Atheneum, 1968.
(Editor with David J. Burrows and Frederick R. Lapides) *Afro-American Literature: An Introduction,* Harcourt, 1971.
(Editor with James Edwin Miller and Robert O'Neal) *The United States in Literature,* Scott, Foresman, 1973, abridged edition published as *The American Literary Tradition, 1607-1899,* 1973.
Collected Prose, edited by Frederick Glaysher, University of Michigan Press, 1984.

POEMS

Heart-Shape in the Dust, Falcon Press (Detroit), 1940.
(With Myron O'Higgins) *The Lion and the Archer,* Hemphill Press (Nashville), 1948.
Figure of Time: Poems, Hemphill Press, 1955.
A Ballad of Remembrance, Paul Breman (London), 1962.
Selected Poems, October House, 1966.
Words in the Mourning Time, October House, 1970.
The Night-Blooming Cereus, Paul Breman, 1972.
Angle of Ascent: New and Selected Poems, Liveright, 1975.
American Journal, limited edition, Effendi Press, 1978, enlarged edition, Liveright, 1982.
Robert Hayden: Collected Poems, edited by Glaysher, Liveright, 1985.

RECORDINGS

(With others) "Today's Poets," Folkways, 1967.

CONTRIBUTOR

The Legend of John Brown, Detroit Institute of Arts, 1978.

Contributor to periodicals, including *Atlantic, Negro Digest,* and *Midwest Journal.* Drama and music critic, *Michigan Chronicle,* late 1930s.

SIDELIGHTS: Robert E. Hayden was the first black poet to be chosen as Consultant in Poetry to the Library of Congress, a position described by Thomas W. Ennis of the *New York Times* as "the American equivalent of the British poet laureate designation." Hayden's formal, elegant poems about the black historical experience earned him a number of other major awards as well. "Robert Hayden is now generally accepted," Frederick Glaysher stated in Hayden's *Collected Prose,* "as the most outstanding craftsman of Afro-American poetry."

The historical basis for much of Hayden's poetry stemmed from his extensive study of American and black history. Beginning in the 1930s, when he researched black history for the Federal Writers' Project in his native Detroit, Hayden studied the story of his people from their roots in Africa to their present condition in the United States. "History," Charles T. Davis wrote in *Modern Black Poets: A Collection of Critical Essays,* "has haunted Robert Hayden from the beginning of his career as a poet." As he once explained to Glenford E. Mitchell of

World Order, Hayden saw history "as a long, tortuous, and often bloody process of becoming, of psychic evolution."

Other early influences on Hayden's development as a poet were W. H. Auden, under whom Hayden studied at the University of Michigan, and Stephen Vincent Benet, particularly Benet's poem "John Brown's Body." That poem describes the black reaction to General Sherman's march through Georgia during the Civil War and inspired Hayden to also write of that period of history, creating a series of poems on black slavery and the Civil War that won him a Hopwood Award in 1942.

After graduating from college in 1944, Hayden embarked on an academic career. He spent some twenty-three years at Fisk University, where he rose to become a professor of English, and ended his career with an eleven-year stint at the University of Michigan. Hayden told Mitchell that he considered himself to be "a poet who teaches in order to earn a living so that he can write a poem or two now and then."

Although history plays a large role in Hayden's poetry, many of his works are also inspired by the poet's adherence to the Baha'i faith, an Eastern religion which believes in a coming world civilization. Hayden served for many years as the poetry editor of the group's *World Order* magazine. The universal outlook of the Baha'is also moved Hayden to reject any narrow racial classification for his work. James Mann of the *Dictionary of Literary Biography* claimed that Hayden "stands out among poets of his race for his staunch avowal that the work of black writers must be judged wholly in the context of the literary tradition in English, rather than within the confines of the ethnocentrism that is common in contemporary literature written by blacks." As Lewis Turco explained in the *Michigan Quarterly Review,* "Hayden has always wished to be judged as a poet among poets, not one to whom special rules of criticism ought to be applied in order to make his work acceptable in more than a sociological sense."

This stance earned Hayden harsh criticism from other blacks during the polarized 1960s. He was accused of abandoning his racial heritage to conform to the standards of a white, European literary establishment. "In the 1960s," William Meredith wrote in his foreword to *Collected Prose,* "Hayden declared himself, at considerable cost in popularity, an American poet rather than a black poet, when for a time there was posited an unreconcilable difference between the two roles. . . . He would not relinquish the title of American writer for any narrower identity."

Ironically, much of Hayden's best poetry is concerned with black history and the black experience. "The gift of Robert Hayden's poetry," Vilma Raskin Potter remarked in *MELUS,* "is his coherent vision of the black experience in this country as a continuing journey both communal and private." Hayden wrote of such black historical figures as Nat Turner, Frederick Douglass, Malcolm X, Harriet Tubman, and Cinquez. He also wrote of the Underground Railroad, the Civil War, and the American slave trade. Edward Hirsch, writing in the *Nation,* called Hayden "an American poet, deeply engaged by the topography of American myth in his efforts to illuminate the American black experience."

Though Hayden wrote in formal poetic forms, his range of voices and techniques gave his work a rich variety. "Hayden," Robert G. O'Meally wrote in the *Washington Post Book World,* "is a poet of many voices, using varieties of ironic black folk speech, and a spare, ebullient poetic diction, to grip and chill his readers. He draws characters of stark vividness as he transmutes cardinal points and commonplaces of history into dramatic action and symbol.'' ''His work,'' Turco wrote, ''is unfettered in many ways, not the least of which is in the range of techniques available to him. It gives his imagination wings, allows him to travel throughout human nature.'' Speaking of Hayden's use of formal verse forms, Mann explained that Hayden's poems were ''formal in a nontraditional, original way, strict but not straight-jacketed'' and found that they also possessed ''a hard-edged precision of line that molds what the imagination wants to release in visually fine-chiseled fragmental stanzas that fit flush together with the rightness of a picture puzzle.''

It wasn't until 1966, with the publication of *Selected Poems,* that Hayden first enjoyed widespread attention from the nation's literary critics. As the *Choice* critic remarked at the time, *Selected Poems* showed Hayden to be ''the surest poetic talent of any Negro poet in America; more importantly, it demonstrated a major talent and poetic coming-of-age without regard to race or creed.'' With each succeeding volume of poems his reputation was further enhanced until, in 1976 and his appointment as Consultant in Poetry to the Library of Congress, Hayden was generally recognized as one of the country's leading black poets.

Critics often point to Hayden's unique ability to combine the historical and the personal when speaking of his own life and the lives of his people. Writing in *Obsidian: Black Literature in Review,* Gary Zebrun argued that ''the voice of the speaker in Hayden's best work twists and squirms its way out of anguish in order to tell, or sing, stories of American history— in particular the courageous and plaintive record of Afro-American history—and to chart the thoughts and feelings of the poet's own private space. . . . Hayden is ceaselessly trying to achieve . . . transcendence, which must not be an escape from the horror of history or from the loneliness of individual mortality, but an ascent that somehow transforms the horror and creates a blessed permanence.''

BIOGRAPHICAL/CRITICAL SOURCES:

BOOKS

Concise Dictionary of Literary Biography, Volume I: *The New Consciousness, 1941-1968,* Gale, 1987.
Contemporary Authors Bibliographical Series, Volume II, Gale, 1986.
Contemporary Literary Criticism, Gale, Volume V, 1976, Volume IX,1978, Volume XIV, 1980, Volume XXXVII, 1986.
Conversations with Writers, Volume I, Gale, 1977.
Davis, Arthur P., editor, *From the Dark Tower: Afro-American Writers, 1900-1960,* Howard University Press, 1974.
Dictionary of Literary Biography, Volume V: *American Poets since World War II,* Gale, 1980.
Fetrow, Fred M., *Robert Hayden,* Twayne, 1984.
Gayle, Addison, Jr., editor, *The Black Aesthetic,* Doubleday, 1971.
Gibson, Donald B., editor, *Modern Black Poets: A Collection of Critical Essays,* Prentice-Hall, 1973.
Harper, Michael S. and Robert B. Stepto, editors, *Chant of Saints: A Gathering of Afro-American Literature, Art, and Scholarship,* University of Illinois Press, 1979.
Hatcher, John, *From the Auroral Darkness: The Life and Poetry of Robert Hayden,* George Ronald, 1984.
How I Write/1, Harcourt, 1972.

Jackson, Blyden and Louis D. Rubin, Jr., *Black Poetry in America: Two Essays in Historical Interpretation,* Louisiana State University Press, 1974.
Littlejohn, David, *Black on White: A Critical Survey of Writing by American Negroes,* Grossman, 1966.
Litz, Walton, editor, *American Writers: A Collection of Literary Biographies,* Scribner, 1981.
O'Brien, John, *Interviews with Black Writers,* Liveright, 1973.
Rush, Theresa Gunnels, Carol Fairbanks Myers, and Esther Spring Arata, editors, *Black American Writers Past and Present,* Scarecrow, 1975.
Whitlow, Roger, *Black American Literature,* Nelson Hall, 1973.
Young, James O., *Black Writers of the Thirties,* Louisiana State University Press, 1973.

PERIODICALS

America, February 7, 1975.
Booklist, July, 1985.
Bulletin of Bibliography, September, 1985.
Carleton Miscellany, winter, 1980.
Choice, May, 1967, December, 1984.
College Language Association Journal, number 17, 1973, number 20, 1976, number 21, 1978, number 22, 1979.
Commentary, September, 1980.
Georgia Review, winter, 1984.
Hudson Review, spring, 1986.
Massachusetts Review, winter, 1977.
MELUS, spring, 1980, spring, 1982.
Michigan Quarterly Review, spring, 1977, winter, 1982, fall, 1983.
Midwest Quarterly, spring, 1974.
Nation, December 21, 1985.
Negro American Literature Forum, spring, 1975.
Negro Digest, June, 1966, January, 1968.
New York Times Book Review, January 17, 1971, February 22, 1976, October 21, 1979.
Obsidian: Black Literature in Review, spring, 1981.
Ontario Review, spring-summer, 1979.
Poetry, July, 1967, July, 1977.
Research Studies, September, 1979.
Virginia Quarterly Review, autumn, 1982.
Washington Post Book World, June 25, 1978.
World Order, spring, 1971, summer, 1975, winter, 1976, fall, 1981.

OBITUARIES:

PERIODICALS

AB Bookman's Weekly, April 21, 1980.
Black Scholar, March/April, 1980.
Chicago Tribune, February 27, 1980.
Encore, April, 1980.
Los Angeles Times, March 3, 1980.
New York Times, February 27, 1980.
Time, March 10, 1980.
Washington Post, February 27, 1980.

—*Sketch by Thomas Wiloch*

*   *   *

HEAD, Bessie   1937-1986

PERSONAL: Original name Bessie Amelia Emery; born July 6, 1937, in Pietermaritzburg, South Africa; died in Botswana of hepatitis, April 17, 1986; married Harold Head (a journalist), September 1, 1961 (divorced); children: Howard. *Ed-*

ucation: Educated in South Africa as a primary teacher. *Politics:* None ("dislike politics"). *Religion:* None ("dislike formal religion").

ADDRESSES: Home—P.O. Box 15, Serowe, Botswana, Africa. *Agent*—John Johnson, Clerkenwell House, 45/47 Clerkenwell Green, London EC1R 0HT, England.

CAREER: Teacher in primary schools in South Africa and Botswana for four years; journalist at Drum Publications in Johannesburg for two years; writer. Represented Botswana at international writers conference at University of Iowa, 1977-78, and in Denmark, 1980.

AWARDS, HONORS: The Collector of Treasures and Other Botswana Village Tales was nominated for the Jock Campbell Award for literature by new or unregarded talent from Africa or the Caribbean, *New Statesman,* 1978.

WRITINGS:

When Rain Clouds Gather (novel), Simon & Schuster, 1969.
Maru (novel), McCall, 1971.
A Question of Power (novel), Davis Poynter, 1973, Pantheon, 1974.
The Collector of Treasures and Other Botswana Village Tales (short stories), Heinemann, 1977.
Serowe: Village of the Rain Wind (historical chronicle), Heinemann, 1981.
A Bewitched Crossroad: An African Saga (historical chronicle), Donker (Craighall), 1984, Paragon House, 1986.

Contributor to periodicals, including the London *Times, Presence Africane, New African* and *Transition.*

SIDELIGHTS: "Unlike many exiled South African writers," said a London *Times* contributor, "[Bessie Head] was able to root her life and her work anew in a country close to her tormented motherland." Born of racially-mixed parentage in South Africa, Head lived and died in her adopted Botswana, the subject of much of her writing; in 1979, after fifteen years as part of a refugee community located at Bamangwato Development Farm, she was granted Botswanan citizenship. In *World Literature Written in English,* Betty McGinnis Fradkin described Head's meagre existence after a particularly lean year: "There is no electricity yet. At night Bessie types by the light of six candles. Fruit trees and vegetables surround the house. Bessie makes guava jam to sell, and will sell vegetables when the garden is enlarged." Despite her impoverished circumstances, Head acknowledged to Fradkin that the regularity of her life in the refugee community brought her the peace of mind she sought: "In South Africa, all my life I lived in shattered little bits. All those shattered bits began to grow together here. . . . I have a peace against which all the turmoil is worked out!"

"Her novels strike a special chord for the South African diaspora, though this does not imply that it is the only level at which they work or produce an impact as novels," observed Arthur Ravenscroft in *Aspects of South African Literature.* "They are strange, ambiguous, deeply personal books which initially do not seem to be 'political' in any ordinary sense of the word." Head's racially-mixed heritage profoundly influenced both her work and her life, for an element of exile as well as an abiding concern with discrimination, whatever its guise, permeate her writing. Noting in *Black Scholar* that Head has "probably received more acclaim than any other black African woman novelist writing in English," Nancy Topping Bazin added that Head's works "reveal a great deal about the lives of African women and about the development of feminist perspectives." According to Bazin, Head's analysis of Africa's "patriarchal system and attitudes" enabled her to make connections between the discrimination she experienced personally from racism and sexism, and the root of oppression generally in the insecurity that compels one to feel superior to another.

Head is "especially moving on the position of women, emerging painfully from the chrysalis of tribalist attitudes into a new evaluation of their relationship to men and their position in society," stated Mary Borg in a *New Statesman* review of Head's first novel, *When Rain Clouds Gather.* Considered "intelligent and moving" by one *Times Literary Supplement* contributor, it is described by another as combining "a vivid account of village life in Botswana with the relationship between an Englishman and an embittered black South African who try to change the traditional farming methods of the community." The black male flees South African apartheid only to experience discrimination from other blacks as a refugee in Botswana. For this novel, Head drew upon her own experience as part of a refugee community, which she indicated in *World Literature Written in English* had been "initially, extremely brutal and harsh." Head explained that she had not experienced oppression by the Botswanan government itself in any way, but because South African blacks had been "stripped bare of every human right," she was unaccustomed to witnessing "human ambition and greed . . . in a black form." Calling *When Rain Clouds Gather* "a tale of innocence and experience," Ravenscroft acknowledged that "there are moments of melodrama and excessive romanticism, but the real life of the novel is of creativity, resilience, reconstruction, fulfilment." Most of the major characters "are in one sense or another handicapped exiles, learning how to mend their lives," said Ravenscroft, adding that "it is the vision behind their effortful embracing of exile that gives Bessie Head's first novel an unusual maturity."

Ravenscroft found that in addition to the collective, cooperative enterprise that the village itself represents in *When Rain Clouds Gather,* it speaks to an essential concern of Head's writing by offering a solution for personal fulfillment: "Against a political background of self-indulgent, self-owning traditional chiefs and self-seeking, new politicians more interested in power than people, the village of Golema Mmidi is offered as a difficult alternative: not so much a rural utopia for the Africa of the future to aim at, as a means of personal and economic independence and interdependence, where the qualities that count are benign austerity, reverence for the lives of ordinary people (whether university-educated experts or illiterate villagers), and, above all, the ability to break out of the prison of selfhood without destroying individual privacy and integrity."

Head's second novel, *Maru,* is also set in a Botswanan village. According to Ravenscroft, though, in this book, "workaday affairs form the framework for the real novel, which is a drama about inner conflict and peace of mind and soul." *Maru* is about the problems that accompany the arrival of the well-educated new teacher with whom two young chiefs fall in love. It is "about interior experience, about thinking, feeling, sensing, about control over rebellious lusts of the spirit," said Ravenscroft, who questioned whether or not "the two chief male characters . . . who are close, intimate friends until they become bitter antagonists, are indeed two separate fictional characters, or . . . symbolic extensions of contending character-traits within the same man?" Although the new teacher has been raised and educated by a missionary's wife, she belongs to the "lowliest and most despised group in Botswana, the bushmen," explained the London *Times* contributor. "Problems of caste and identity among black Africans are explored with sensitivity," remarked Martin Levin in the *New York Times Book Review*. Ravenscroft suggested that while the novel is a more personal one than Head's first, it is also a more political one, and he was "much impressed and moved by the power . . . in the vitality of the enterprise, which projects the personal and the political implications in such vivid, authentic parallels that one feels they are being closely held together."

Head's critically well-received third novel, *A Question of Power,* relates the story of a young wman who experiences a mental breakdown. In a *Listener* review, Elaine Feinstein observed that "the girl moves through a world dominated by strange figures of supernatural good and evil, in which she suffers torment and enchantment in turn: at last she reaches the point where she can reject the clamorous visions which beset her and assert that there is 'only one God and his name is Man.'" According to Bazin, Head acknowledged in an interview with Lee Nichols in her *Conversations with African Writers: Interviews with Twenty-six African Authors* that *A Question of Power* is largely autobiographical. "Like Elizabeth, the protagonist in *A Question of Power,* Bessie Head was born in a South African mental hospital," explained Bazin. "Her mother, a wealthy, upperclass, white woman, was to spend the rest of her life there, because in an apartheid society, she had allowed herself to be made pregnant by a black stableman. Until age thirteen, Bessie Head, like Elizabeth, was raised by foster parents and then put in a mission orphange." Paddy Kitchen pointed out in the *New Statesman,* though, that the novel merely "contains parallels and winnowings from life, not journalist records," adding that "the incredible part is the clarity of the terror that has been rescued from such private, muddled nightmares." Similarly, Ravenscroft discerned no "confusion of identity" between the character and her creator: "Head makes one realize often how close is the similarity between the most fevered creations of a deranged mind and the insanities of deranged societies."

Lauded for the skill with which she recreated the hellish world of madness, Head was also credited by critics such as Jean Marquard in *London Magazine* with having written "the first metaphysical novel on the subject of nation and a national identity to come out of Southern Africa." In his *The Novel in the Third World,* Charles R. Larson credits the importance of *A Question of Power* not just to the introspection of its author, but to her exploration of subjects hitherto "foreign to African fiction as a sub-division of the novel in the Third World: madness, sexuality, guilt." Noting that the protagonist's "Coloured classification, her orphan status at the mission, and her short-lived marriage" represent the origin of most of her guilt, Larson attributed these factors directly to "the South African policy of apartheid which treats people as something other than human beings." Further, Larson felt that Head intended the reader to consider all the "variations of power as the evils that thwart each individual's desire to be part of the human race, part of the brotherhood of man."

A Question of Power, wrote Roberta Rubenstein in the *New Republic,* "succeeds as an intense, even mythic, dramatization of the mind's struggle for autonomy and as a symbolic protest against the political realities of South Africa." And in *Books Abroad,* Robert L. Berner considered it "a remarkable attempt to escape from the limitations of mere 'protest' literature in which Black South African writers so often find themselves."

Berner recognized that Head could have "written an attack on the indignities of apartheid which have driven her into exile in Botswana," but instead chose to write a novel about the "response to injustice—first in madness and finally in a heroic struggle out of that madness into wholeness and wisdom." Ravenscroft perceived in *A Question of Power* "an intimate relationship between an individual character's private odyssey of the soul and public convulsions that range across the world and from one civilization to another," and deemed the novel "a work of striking virtuosity—an artistically shaped descent into the linked hells of madness and oppression, and a resolution that provides the hope of both internal and external reconciliation."

Critics have analyzed Head's first three novels, *When Rain Clouds Gather, Maru,* and *A Question of Power,* collectively in terms of their thematic concerns and progression. Suggesting that the three novels "deal in different ways with exile and oppression," Marquard noted that "the protagonists are outsiders, new arrivals who try to forge a life for themselves in a poor, under-populated third world country, where traditional and modern attitudes to soil and society are in conflict." Unlike other African writers who are also concerned with such familiar themes, said Marquard, Head "does not idealize the African past and . . . she resists facile polarities, emphasizing personal rather than political motives for tensions between victim and oppressor." Ravenscroft recognized "a steady progression from the first novel to the third into ever murkier depths of alienation from the currents of South African, and African, matters of politics and power." Similarly, Marquard detected an inward movement "from a social to a metaphysical treatment of human insecurities and in the last novel the problem of adaptation to a new world, or new schemes of values, is located in the mind of a single character." Ravenscroft posited that "it is precisely this journeying into the various characters' most secret interior recesses of mind and (we must not fight shy of the word) of soul, that gives the three novels a quite remarkable cohesion and makes them a sort of trilogy."

Considering *When Rain Clouds Gather, Maru,* and *A Question of Power* to be "progressive in their philosophical conclusion about the nature and source of racism," Cecil A. Abrahams suggested in *World Literature Written in English* that "ultimately, Head examines . . . sources of evil and, conversely, of potential goodness. The most obvious source is the sphere of political power and authority; it is clear that if the political institutions which decree and regulate the lives of the society are reformed or abolished a better or new society can be established." According to Ravenscroft, the elements of imprisonment and control provide thematic unity among the novels. Pointing to the "loneliness and despair of exile" in each of them, Ravenscroft found the resilience of their characters "even more remarkable," and concluded that "what the three novels do say very clearly is that whoever exercises political power, however laudable his aims, will trample upon the faces and limbs of ordinary people, and will lust in that trampling. That horrible obscenity mankind must recognize in its collective interior soul." And Head, said Ravenscroft, "refuses to look for the deceiving gleam that draws one to expect the dawn of liberation in the South, but accepts what the meagre, even parched, present offers."

Head's collection of short stories, *The Collector of Treasures and Other Botswana Village Tales,* which was considered for the *New Statesman*'s Jock Campbell Award, explores several aspects of African life, especially the position of women. Linking Head to the "village storyteller of the oral tradition," Michael

Thorpe noted in *World Literature Today* that her stories are "rooted, folkloristic tales woven from the fabric of village life and intended to entertain and enlighten, not to engage the modern close critic." In the *Listener,* John Mellors related Head's statement that "she has 'romanticised and fictionalized' data provided by old men of the tribe whose memories are unreliable." In its yoking of present to past, the collection also reveals the inevitable friction between old ways and new. The world of Head's work "is not a simply modernizing world but one that seeks, come what may, to keep women in traditionally imprisoning holes and corners," said Valerie Cunningham in the *New Statesman.* "It's a world where whites not only force all blacks into an exile apart from humanity but where women are pushed further still into sexist exile." In *The Collector of Treasures and Other Botswana Village Tales,* added Cunningham, "Head puts a woman's as well as a black case in tales that both reach back into tribal legend and cut deep into modern Africa."

Head's last two books, *Serowe: Village of the Rain Wind* and *A Bewitched Crossroad: An African Saga,* are categorized as historical chronicles and combine historical accounts with the folklore of the region. The collected interviews in *Serowe* focus on a time frame that spans the eras of Khama the Great (1875-1923) and Tshekedi Khama (1926-1959) through the Swaneng Project beginning in 1963 under Patrick Van Rensburg, "a South African exile who, like Head herself, has devoted his life in a present-day Botswana to make some restitution for white rapacity," wrote Thorpe. Larson, who considers "reading any book by Bessie Head . . . always a pleasure," added that *Serowe* "falls in a special category." Calling it a "quasi-sociological account," Larson described it as "part history, part anthology and folklore." "Its citizens give their testimonies, both personal and practical, in an unselfconscious way," said Paddy Kitchen in the *Listener,* "and Bessie Head— in true African style—orders the information so that, above all, it tells a story." *Serowe* is "a vivid portrait of a remarkable place . . . one wishes there were many more studies of its kind," remarked a *British Book News* contributor. Kitchen believed it to be "a story which readers will find themselves using as a text from which to meditate on many aspects of society." And discussing her last book, *A Bewitched Crossroad,* which examines on a broader scope the African tribal wars in the early nineteenth century, Thorpe found that "in her moral history humane ideals displace ancestor-worship, and peace-loving strength displaces naked force."

Questioned by Fradkin about the manner in which she worked, Head explained: "Every story or book starts with something just for myself. Then from that small me it becomes a panorama—the big view that has something for everyone." Head "stresses in her novels the ideals of humility, love, truthfulness, freedom, and, of course, equality," wrote Bazin. At the time of her death, she had achieved an international reputation and had begun to write her autobiography. Head obviously endured much difficulty during her life; despite her rejection of and by South Africa as well as the hardships of her exiled existence, however, she emerged from the racist and sexist discrimination that she both witnessed and experienced, to the affirmation she told Fradkin represented the only two themes present in her writing—"that love is really good . . . and . . . that it is important to be an ordinary person." She added, "More than anything I want to be noble." According to Kitchen, "a great deal has been written about black writers, but Bessie Head is surely one of the pioneers of brown literature—a literature that includes everybody."

BIOGRAPHICAL/CRITICAL SOURCES:

BOOKS

Contemporary Literary Criticism, Volume 25, Gale, 1983.
Heywood, Christopher, editor, *Aspects of South African Literature,* Heinemann, 1976.
Larson, Charles R., *The Novel in the Third World,* Inscape Publishers, 1976.
Nichols, Lee, editor, *Conversations with African Writers: Interviews with Twenty-six African Writers,* Voice of America (Washington, D.C.), 1981.
Zell, Hans M., and others, *A New Reader's Guide to African Literature,* Holmes & Meier, 2nd edition, 1983.

PERIODICALS

Best Sellers, March 15, 1969.
Black Scholar, March/April, 1986.
Books Abroad, winter, 1975.
British Book News, November, 1981.
Listener, February 4, 1971, November 22, 1973, April 20, 1978, July 2, 1981.
London Magazine, December/January, 1978-79.
New Republic, April 27, 1974.
New Statesman, May 16, 1969, November 2, 1973, June 2, 1978.
New York Times Book Review, September 26, 1971.
Times Literary Supplement, May 2, 1969, February 5, 1971.
World Literature Today, winter, 1982, summer, 1983, winter, 1983, winter, 1986.
World Literature Written in English, Volume 17, number 1, 1978, Volume 17, number 2, 1978, Volume 18, number 1, 1979.

OBITUARIES:

PERIODICALS

Journal of Commonwealth Literature, Volume 21, number 1, 1986.
Ms., January, 1987.
Times (London), May 1, 1986.

—*Sketch by Sharon Malinowski*

*   *   *

HEARD, Nathan C(liff)   1936-

PERSONAL: Born November 7, 1936, in Newark, N.J.; son of Nathan E. (a laborer) and Gladys (a blues singer; maiden name, Pruitt) Heard; children: Melvin, Cliff, Natalie. *Education:* Educated in public schools in Newark, N.J. *Politics:* None. *Religion:* None.

ADDRESSES: c/o Macmillan Publishers, Publicity Dept., 866 3rd Ave., New York, N.Y. 10022.

CAREER: Writer. Fresno State College (now California State University, Fresno), Fresno, Calif., guest lecturer in creative writing, 1969-70; Rutgers University, New Brunswick, N.J., assistant professor of English, 1970-72. *Military service:* U.S. Air Force, 1952-53.

MEMBER: National Society of Literature and the Arts.

AWARDS, HONORS: Author's awards from New Jersey Association of Teachers of English, 1969, and Newark College of Engineering, 1973.

WRITINGS:

NOVELS

Howard Street, Dial, 1968.
To Reach a Dream, Dial, 1972.
A Cold Fire Burning, Simon & Schuster, 1974.
When Shadows Fall, Playboy Paperbacks, 1977.
The House of Slammers, Macmillan, 1983.

OTHER

(Contributor) Sonia Sanchez, editor, We Be Word Sorcerers: Twenty-five Stories by Black Americans, Bantam, 1973.

Also contributor to Essence.

WORK IN PROGRESS: A Time of Desperation, a novel.

SIDELIGHTS: Writer Nathan C. Heard "[depicts] with stark and brutal frankness the violence, frustrations, thwarted dreams, and tragedies of black ghetto experience," writes Richard Yarborough in the Dictionary of Literary Biography. Primarily a novelist, Heard is best known for his semiautobiographical works Howard Street and House of Slammers. Raised in a New Jersey ghetto similar to the one he depicts in Howard Street, Heard has been jailed twice during his lifetime, once for armed robbery, and again for violation of parole. His literary awakening occurred in prison, where he began to write and to read the works of James Baldwin, Langston Hughes, Jean Genet, and Samuel Beckett.

Heard's novel Howard Street describes the inhabitants of that street, focusing in particular on the love triangle between Lonnie, a hustler, Franchot, his hard-working brother, and Gypsy Pearl, a prostitute they both love. Howard Street is also peopled with pimps, drug pushers, addicts, gang members, and policemen—"all individually and most perceptively portrayed," according to Library Journal contributor J. McRee Elrod. Yarborough comments that Howard Street "is rich with many sharply etched portraits of people out to survive on the best available terms, and Heard's sensitivity to the pain and hardship which shape all of his characters' lives is the source of much of the novel's power." A Publishers Weekly critic concludes: "With no trace of condescension, without irony or sentimentality, with honesty and objectivity, he spins a raw and powerful story of ghetto life."

Heard's most widely reviewed novel is House of Slammers, an account of prison life. "As in his previous work," writes Mel Watkins in the New York Times Book Review, "Heard etches the gritty setting, the look, feel and corrosive tenor of life behind bars." The story's protagonist is Beans Butler, a black inmate who becomes an organizer in a work stoppage effort even though he is jeopardizing his upcoming parole by doing so. With the encouragement of the administration, the strike escalates into a full-scale prison riot, and several inmates are killed. Meanwhile, the prison warden and the chief deputy engage in lengthy penological debates.

These debates are viewed by several reviewers to be a flaw in Heard's novel. A Kirkus Reviews contributor calls the novel "excessively didactic," and a Publishers Weekly contributor believes that the dialogues between the two men "[become] a platform for opposing philosophies, and then the story bogs down." Yarborough offers this view: "What Heard holds up for the reader in House of Slammers is the violent, desperate, spirit-crushing life of the men in this country's penal institutions; and to the extent that it is meant to bring about change, this novel is his most didactic."

Washington Post Book World contributor John Edgar Wideman, however, maintains that "like the philosophical debates of medieval poetry, these set pieces are less an attempt to resolve conflicting points of view than to dramatize their irresolvability." He concludes: "House of Slammers both enlightens and entertains. Heard's work recalls Richard Wright's in style, intensity, acuity of insight, dogged determination to illuminate the larger forces controlling an individual's fate. And like Wright, Heard is not content to titillate his readers with horrific glimpses of life underground. . . . The implicit message of House of Slammers is that we must act upon the truth the artist brings us."

AVOCATIONAL INTERESTS: Competitive sports, singing, playing drums, band leading.

BIOGRAPHICAL/CRITICAL SOURCES:

BOOKS

Dictionary of Literary Biography, Volume 33: Afro-American Fiction Writers after 1955, Gale, 1984.
Schraufnagel, Noel, From Apology to Protest, Everett/Edwards, 1973.

PERIODICALS

Best Sellers, December, 1983.
Kirkus Reviews, August 1, 1983.
Library Journal, November 15, 1968.
New York Times, December 13, 1968, July 14, 1972.
New York Times Book Review, January 19, 1969, December 11, 1983.
Publishers Weekly, September 16, 1968, August 5, 1983.
Washington Post Book World, November 13, 1983.

*   *   *

HEARNE, John (Edgar Caulwell)   1926-
   (John Morris, a joint pseudonym)

PERSONAL: Born February 4, 1926, in Montreal, Quebec, Canada; son of Maurice Vincent and Doris (May) Hearne; married Joyce Veitch, September 3, 1947 (divorced); married Leeta Mary Hopkinson (a teacher), April 12, 1955; children: two. Education: Attended Jamaica College; Edinburgh University, M.A., 1950; University of London, teaching diploma, 1950. Religion: Christian.

ADDRESSES: Home—P.O. Box 335, Kingston 8, Jamaica. Office—Creative Arts Centre, University of the West Indies, Kingston 7, Jamaica. Agent—Claire Smith, Harold Ober Associates, Inc., 40 East 49th St., New York, N.Y. 10017.

CAREER: Teacher at schools in London, England, and in Jamaica, 1950-59; information officer, Government of Jamaica, 1962; University of the West Indies, Kingston, Jamaica, resident tutor in extramural studies, 1962-67, head of Creative Arts Centre, 1968—. Visiting Gregory Fellow in Commonwealth Literature at University of Leeds, England, 1967; Colgate University, New York, visiting O'Connor Professor in Literature, 1969-70, and visiting professor in literature, 1973. Military service: Royal Air Force, air gunner, 1943-46.

MEMBER: International P.E.N.

AWARDS, HONORS: John Llewelyn Rhys Memorial Prize, 1956, for Voices Under the Window; Silver Musgrave Medal from Institute of Jamaica, 1964.

WRITINGS:

NOVELS

Voices Under the Window, Faber, 1955, reprinted, 1985.
Stranger at the Gate, Faber, 1956.
The Faces of Love, Faber, 1957, published as *The Eye of the Storm,* Little, Brown, 1958.
The Autumn Equinox, Faber, 1959, Vanguard Press, 1961.
Land of the Living, Faber, 1961, Harper, 1962.
(With Morris Cargill, under joint pseudonym John Morris) *Fever Grass,* Putnam, 1969.
(With Cargill, under joint pseudonym John Morris) *The Candywine Development,* Collins, 1970, Lyle Stuart, 1971.
The Sure Salvation, Faber, 1981, St. Martin's, 1982.

SHORT STORIES

"The Wind in This Corner" and "At the Stelling" appear in *West Indian Stories,* edited by Andrew Salkey, Faber, 1960; "A Village Tragedy" and "The Lost Country" appear in *Stories From the Caribbean,* edited by Salkey, Elek, 1965, published as *Island Voices: Stories From the West Indies,* Liveright, 1970.

OTHER

(With Rex Nettleford) *Our Heritage,* University of the West Indies, 1963.
(Editor and author of introduction) *Carifesta Forum: An Anthology of Twenty Caribbean Voices,* Carifesta 76 (Kingston, Jamaica), 1976.
(Editor and author of introduction) *The Search for Solutions: Selections From the Speeches and Writings of Michael Manley,* Maple House Publishing Co., 1976.
(With Lawrence Coote and Lynden Facey) *Testing Democracy Through Elections: A Tale of Five Elections,* edited by Marie Gregory, Bustamante Institute of Public and International Affairs (Kingston, Jamaica), 1985.

Also author of teleplays, including "Soldiers in the Snow," with James Mitchell, 1960, and "A World Inside," 1962; author of stage play "The Golden Savage," 1965. Work represented in anthologies, including O. R. Dathorne's *Caribbean Narrative: An Anthology of West Indian Writing,* Heinemann, 1966, and Barbara Howes's *From the Green Antilles: Writings of the Caribbean,* Macmillan, 1966.

Contributor of short stories and articles to periodicals, including *Atlantic Monthly, New Statesman,* and the *Trinidad Guardian.*

SIDELIGHTS: A West Indian writer who sometimes collaborates with Morris Cargill as the pseudonymous John Morris, John Hearne is known for his vivid depictions of life among the West Indies and their people. In particular, several of his writings focus on Jamaica—the native land of his parents—and address complex social and moral issues affecting both individual relationships and, to a lesser extent, the cultural and political aspects of the island. Much of Hearne's fiction—including the novels *Stranger at the Gate, The Faces of Love, The Autumn Equinox,* and *Land of the Living*—also takes place on Cayuna, a mythical counterpart of Jamaica. More generally, his work relates a broad, first-hand account of the Caribbean experience and features elements of racial and social inequities as well as recurrent themes of betrayal and disenchantment. Especially noteworthy are Hearne's acclaimed narrative skill and descriptive style, which distinguish his fiction as characteristically evocative and lifelike.

Hearne's 1981 novel, *The Sure Salvation,* takes place in the southern Atlantic Ocean aboard a sailing ship of the same name. Set in the year 1860, the story chronicles the illegal buying and selling of negroes more than fifty years after England first enacted laws prohibiting the practice commonly known as slave trade. Through a "series of deft flashbacks," observed *Times Literary Supplement* critic T. O. Treadwell, Hearne recounts individual circumstances that led to his characters' unlawful fraternity on board the *Sure Salvation.* Risking constant danger and the death penalty if they are caught, the captain and crew hope to amend their ill-fated lives with monies paid for the vessel's charge of five hundred Africans. While the "beastliness isn't played down," Treadwell noted, we come "to understand, and even sympathize with" these men and their despicable dealings due to Hearne's successful literary craftsmanship and execution. Treadwell further announced that the "author's gift for irony . . . that the slavers are no freer than" their shackled cargo, provides this "absorbing" tale with its utmost pleasures, and he concluded that *The Sure Salvation* proves the "power of the sea story . . . as potent as ever."

Hearne commented that his writing is influenced by his growing up in an island society large enough to be interesting but small enough for "characters" to be known intimately. He added: "I have been much concerned with politics (as a commentator) as Jamaica has tried to fashion itself into a newly independent society since the early 1960s."

BIOGRAPHICAL/CRITICAL SOURCES:

BOOKS

James, Louis, editor, *The Islands In Between: Essays on West Indian Literature,* Oxford University Press, 1968.
Ramchand, Kenneth, *The West Indian Novel and Its Background,* Barnes & Noble, 1970.

PERIODICALS

Times Literary Supplement, June 19, 1981.

*   *   *

HENDERSON, David 1942-

PERSONAL: Born 1942, in New York, N.Y. *Education:* Attended Bronx Community College, 1960, Hunter College of the City University of New York, 1961, New School for Social Research, 1962, East West Institute, Cambridge, Mass., 1964, University Without Walls, Berkeley, Calif., 1972.

ADDRESSES: Office—Box 4358, Sathergate Station, Berkeley, Calif. 94704.

CAREER: Poet and editor. One of founders of *East Village Other* and Underground Press Service, New York City; *Umbra* (a racially- and socially-oriented magazine), New York City, 1962—, began as associate editor, became editor. Poet-in-residence at City College of New York, 1969-70, and Free Southern Theatre. Lecturer, City College of New York SEEK program, 1967-69, University of California, Berkeley, 1970-72, and University of California, San Diego, 1979-80, Manopa Institute, Colorado, 1981. As member of "Umbra Poets" group, has participated in more than one hundred poetry readings, including programs at Vassar College, Princeton University, Columbia University, American University, Carnegie Hall, and San Francisco State University; also has read his poetry over radio stations in New York City, Boston, Atlanta, and San Francisco. Consultant to National Endowment for the

Arts, 1967-68, 1980, Berkeley Public Schools, 1968, and New York Public Schools, 1969.

MEMBER: International PEN, Afro-American and Third World Writers Union.

AWARDS, HONORS: Great Lakes Colleges Award, Great Lakes Colleges Association, 1971, Great Lakes New Writers Award, 1971.

WRITINGS:

(Editor) *Umbra Anthology 1967-1968,* Society of Umbra, 1967.
(Editor) *Umbra/Latin Soul 1974-1975,* Society of Umbra, 1975.
Jimi Hendrix: Voodoo Child of the Aquarian Age (biography), Doubleday, 1978, condensed and revised edition published as *'Scuse Me while I Kiss the Sky: The Life of Jimi Hendrix,* Bantam, 1981.

POETRY

(Contributor) *New Negro Poets: USA,* edited by Langston Hughes, Indiana University Press, 1964.
(Contributor) *Poems Now,* Kulchur Press, 1965.
(Contributor) *Where Is Vietnam?: American Poets Respond,* Doubleday, 1967.
Felix of the Silent Forest, introduction by LeRoi Jones, Poets Press, 1967.
De Mayor of Harlem, Dutton, 1970, North Atlantic, 1985.
(Contributor) *Poetry of the Negro, 1746-1970,* edited by Hughes and Arna Bontemps, Doubleday, 1970.
The Low East, North Atlantic Books, 1980.

OTHER

(Author of introduction) *Joe Overstreet,* Institute for the Arts, Rice University, 1972.
"Ghetto Follies" (play), first produced in San Francisco, 1978.

Work represented in numerous other anthologies. Also editor of *Umbra Blackworks,* 1970-1971. Contributor to periodicals, including *Black World, Essence, Freedomways, Journal of Black Poetry, Negro Digest, Nickel Review, Paris Review, New American Review, Evergreen Review, New York Times, East Village Other,* and *National Guardian.*

WORK IN PROGRESS: A new collection of poetry, titled *Berkeley Trees*; a book on reggae.

SIDELIGHTS: "I grew up in Harlem as a black nationalist," recounts David Henderson in a *Saturday Review of the Arts* interview with Diane Middlebrook. "In the *Umbra* workshop on the Lower East Side in the early '60s, we established a basic ideal of black consciousness—though no one person's ideal dominated. But I don't think we should stop with nationalism. There is such a powerful spectrum in black art and thought that I don't think it should be tied down by racial ideology and politics. The avant-garde element in black art is an outgrowth of nationalism and involves poets as different as Cecil Brown, Ted Joans, Calvin Hernton, Quincy Troupe, Lennox Raphael, Steve Cannon, Ishmael Reed, Al Young, Mike Harper, N. H. Pritchard, Clarence Major, Larry Neal, Imamu Baraka [i.e., LeRoi Jones]; Joe Overstreet, the late William White, or Bob Thompson in painting; Ornette Coleman, Archie Shepp, and Sun-Ra in the new jazz, and many others. We're talking here about a diversity: a reliance on intuitions and personal mythologies, as opposed to scriptures and ideologies. . . . I believe black artists can display a sense of unity, of participation in the multiculture, that can serve as an example to others in the community."

David Henderson's poetry is in the Permanent Archives Library of Congress.

BIOGRAPHICAL/CRITICAL SOURCES:

BOOKS

Dictionary of Literary Biography, Volume 41: *Afro-American Poets since 1955,* Gale, 1985.

PERIODICALS

Saturday Review, April 3, 1971, September, 1982.
Saturday Review of the Arts, September 9, 1972.
Solid Ground: A New World Journal, winter, 1984.

* * *

HENDERSON, George Wylie 1904-

PERSONAL: Born June 14, 1904, in Warrior's Stand, Ala. *Education:* Attended Tuskegee Institute.

CAREER: Novelist and short story writer. Printing apprentice for New York *Daily News.*

WRITINGS:

NOVELS

Ollie Miss, Stokes, 1935, University of Alabama Press, 1988.
Jule, Creative Age, 1946.

Contributor of short stories to periodicals, including New York *Daily News* and *Redbook.*

SIDELIGHTS: In the history of Afro-American literature, George Wylie Henderson's writing places the novelist between the Harlem Renaissance, a period of heightened literary activity in the 1920s, and the social protest movement of the 1940s led by author Richard Wright. Most noted for his realistic and straightforward novels portraying the poor, the ordinary, and the forgotten with humanity and dignity, Henderson derived his works both from black tradition as well as the newly intensified social consciousness of his time. His first and more successful novel, the 1935 *Ollie Miss,* outlines the struggles of an alienated eighteen-year-old girl, Ollie, in a small southern town. Finding herself pregnant and rejected by her love Jule, the heroine perseveres with strength and independence. The novel was well received by critics, who praised the work for its pastoral elegance, stunning realism, careful characterization, and, especially, Henderson's authentic use of black dialect.

His second novel, *Jule*—a sequel to *Ollie Miss*—relates the growth and social struggle of Jule, the illegitimate son of Ollie and the elder Jule. Henderson traces the boy's passage from innocence to experience, as the southerner ventures north, only to be met with racial conflict. Unlike *Ollie Miss, Jule* addresses the issues of social protest and attempts to make a statement on racism. Despite its bold efforts, the book was negatively received. Reviewers criticized Henderson for failing to deal with the complex, internal states of his characters, as well as for his one-dimensional portrayals of blacks and whites. After this unsuccessful second work, Henderson never wrote another novel.

BIOGRAPHICAL/CRITICAL SOURCES:

BOOKS

Bone, Robert, *The Negro Novel in America,* Yale University Press, 1965.

Dictionary of Literary Biography, Volume 51: *Afro-American Writers Before the Harlem Renaissance to 1940,* Gale, 1987.

PERIODICALS

New York Herald Tribune, February 23, 1935.
New York Times, February 24, 1935, October 13, 1946.
Weekly Book Review, October 20, 1946.

*   *   *

HENDERSON, Stephen E.   1925-

PERSONAL: Born October 13, 1925, in Key West, Fla.; son of James and Leonora (Sands) Henderson; married Jeanne Holman, June 14, 1958; children: Stephen E., Jr., Timothy A., Philip L., Alvin Malcolm. *Education:* Morehouse College, A.B., 1949; University of Wisconsin, M.A., 1950, Ph.D., 1959.

ADDRESSES: Home—1703 Lebanon St., Langley Park, Md. 20783. *Office*—Institute for the Arts and the Humanities, 2400 Sixth St., Howard University, Washington, D.C. 20059.

CAREER: Taught at Virginia Union University, Richmond, 1950-62; Morehouse College, Atlanta, Ga., professor of English and chairman of department, 1962-71; Howard University, Washington, D.C., professor of Afro-American studies, 1971—, director of Institute for the Arts and the Humanities, 1973—. *Military service:* U.S. Army, 1944-45.

MEMBER: National Council of Teachers of English, American Association of University Professors, College Language Association, South Atlantic Modern Language Association, Phi Beta Kappa.

AWARDS, HONORS: Danforth research grant; Southern Fellowships Fund grant; American Council of Learned Societies, General Education Board grant.

WRITINGS:

(With Mercer Cook) *The Militant Black Writer in Africa and the United States,* University of Wisconsin Press, 1969.
Understanding the New Black Poetry: Black Speech and Black Music as Poetic References, Morrow, 1973.

Contributor of articles to *Ebony, Black World, New Directions.*

WORK IN PROGRESS: Long essay on contemporary black poetry; critical anthology of blues poetry.

AVOCATIONAL INTERESTS: Art (paints in water colors), folk and classical music, following current scientific developments.

*   *   *

HENRIES, A. Doris Banks   1913(?)-1981
(Doris Henries)

PERSONAL: Born February 11, 1913 (some sources say 1919 or 1930), in Live Oak, Fla. (some sources say Middletown, Conn., or Liberia); immigrated to Liberia, c. 1940; died of cancer, February 16, 1981, in Middletown (one source says Middleton), Conn.; married Richard Abrom Henries (a politician) in 1942 (died in April, 1980); children: two sons. *Education:* Received B.Sc. from Willimantic Normal School (now Eastern Connecticut State University); attended Connecticut State Teachers' College, Yale University, Hartford Seminary Foundation (now Hartford Seminary), and University of Be-

sancon in France; received M.A. and Ph.D. from Columbia University. *Politics:* True Whig. *Religion:* Methodist.

ADDRESSES: Home—Middletown, Conn.

CAREER: Principal of Fuller Normal School, 1934-39; United Methodist Church of the United States, missionary in Liberia, c. 1939; director of education in Maryland County, Liberia, 1940-42; Liberia College (became University of Liberia, 1951), Monrovia, professor, 1942-59, dean of William V. S. Tubman Teachers College, 1951-55, dean, 1955-59, acting president, 1956-57 and 1958-59; government of Liberia, director of higher education and textbook research, 1959-78, acting assistant minister of education, 1978. Served in Liberia as regional director for Africa and member of executive committee of World Council for Curriculum and Instruction, chairman of Methodist board of education, president of National YMCA (Young Men's Christian Association), and vice-chairman of Opportunities Industrial Centre.

MEMBER: African Studies Association, American Academy of Social Sciences, Liberian National Teachers Organization (former president), International Alliance of Women, Zonta International, Federation of Women's Organizations (former vice-president of Liberian chapter), Liberia Authors Association (former president).

AWARDS, HONORS: Methodist Trust Fund Grant from United Methodist Church of the United States, c. 1939; honorary D.Ed. from Liberia College, 1949; Knight Official, Star of Africa, 1950, Grand Band, Humane Order of African Redemption, 1955, Dame Grand Commander, Order of Knighthood of Pioneers of Liberia, 1959, all from Liberia; Ordre des Arts et des Lettres (France), 1958; Order of the Grand Cross and Order of Merit, both from Germany in 1962.

WRITINGS:

(Under name Doris Henries; with husband, Richard Henries) *Liberia, the West African Republic,* F. R. Bruns, 1950.
Civics for Liberian Schools, Collier-Macmillan, 1953, revised edition, 1966.
The Liberian Nation: A Short History, Collier-Macmillan, 1953, revised edition, 1966.
Heroes and Heroines of Liberia (juvenile), Macmillan, 1962.
More About Heroes and Heroines of Liberia, Book II (juvenile), illustrations by Ceasar W. Harris, Liberian Information Service, 1962.
Development of Unification in Liberia, Department of Education, Monrovia, Liberia, 1963.
(Editor) *Poems of Liberia, 1836-1961,* Macmillan (London), 1963.
Presidents of the First African Republic, Macmillan (London), 1963.
The Life of Joseph Jenkins Roberts, 1809-1876, and His Inaugural Addresses, illustrations by Geoffrey Whittman, Macmillan (London), 1964.
(Editor) *Liberian Folklore: A Compilation of Ninety-nine Folktales With Some Proverbs,* Macmillan (London), 1966, St. Martin's, 1968.
(Contributor) *New Sum of Poetry From the Negro World,* Volume 57, Presence Africaine, 1966.
A Biography of President William V. S. Tubman, Macmillan (London), 1967.
Africa: Our History, Collier-Macmillan, 1969.
(Editor) *Liberia's Fulfillment: Achievements of the Republic of Liberia During Twenty-five Years Under the Adminis-*

tration of President William V. S. Tubman, 1944-1969, Monrovia, 1969.
(Editor) *Liberian Literature, Grade 8,* Ministry of Education, Monrovia, 1976.
(Editor) *Liberian Literature, Grade 9,* Ministry of Education, Monrovia, 1976.

Also author of *Living Together in City and Country, Maryland Melodies,* and children's book *Liberians at Work;* co-author of *Education in Liberia* and *Fatu's Experiences.* Editor of *Education Laws of Liberia, 1926-1974.* Contributor to anthology *Liberian Writing.*

SIDELIGHTS: A. Doris Banks Henries grew up in America, but shortly after finishing her graduate education at Columbia University she immigrated to the African republic of Liberia. She became a leading educator of her adopted country, eventually serving as acting assistant minister of education, and was also one of Liberia's most prolific writers. Henries's works range from poetry, biography, and history to critical essays, anthologies, and textbooks. In April of 1980, the government of Liberia was overthrown in a coup and her husband, Richard A. Henries, who was the speaker of the House of Representatives of Liberia, was executed—one of thirteen Liberian officials killed by firing squad. One month later Henries returned to the United States.

AVOCATIONAL INTERESTS: Bridge, drama, traveling, writing.

OBITUARIES:

PERIODICALS

New York Times, February 18, 1981.

*   *   *

HENRIES, Doris
    See HENRIES, A. Doris Banks

*   *   *

HERCULES, Frank (E. M.)

PERSONAL: Born February 12, 1917, in Port-of-Spain, Trinidad, West Indies; son of Felix Eugene Michael and Millicent (Dottin) Hercules (an educator and school administrator); married Dellora C. Howard, 1946; children: John, Eric. *Education:* Attended University Tutorial College, 1934-35, and Honorable Society of the Middle Temple of Inns of Court, 1935-39, 1950-51.

ADDRESSES: Home—505 Main St., Apt. 1308, Roosevelt Island, New York, N.Y. 10044. *Office*—c/o Trade Publications, Harcourt, Brace & Jovanovich, 111 Fifth Ave., New York, N.Y. 10003.

CAREER: Writer. Visiting scholar, Loyola University, New Orleans, La.; writer-in-residence, Xavier University, New Orleans, La. Member of final review panel, National Endowment for the Humanities.

AWARDS, HONORS: Fletcher Pratt Memorial Fellowship in Prose, Bread Loaf Writers' Conference, Middlebury College, 1961, for *Where the Hummingbird Flies;* Rockefeller fellow, Institute for Humanistic Studies, 1977.

WRITINGS:

(Contributor of untitled essay) *Voices for Life: Reflections on the Human Condition* (anthology), edited by Dom Moraes, Praeger, 1975.

NOVELS

Where the Hummingbird Flies, Harcourt, 1961.
I Want a Black Doll, Simon & Schuster, 1967.
On Leaving Paradise, Harcourt, 1980.

HISTORY

American Society and Black Revolution, Harcourt, 1972.

OTHER

Contributor to magazines in the United States and abroad, including *Reader's Digest, Opportunity, New York Herald Tribune Sunday Magazine, National Geographic, Die Zeit, Geo* (Hamburg, West Germany), *Harper's Bazaar* (German edition), and the *International Herald Tribune* (Paris).

WORK IN PROGRESS: A novel, *Return to Paradise.*

SIDELIGHTS: One of Frank Hercules's articles for *National Geographic,* "To Live in Harlem," was read into the Congressional Record by Senator Jacob K. Javits of New York and was translated and circulated abroad by the United States Information Agency.

BIOGRAPHICAL/CRITICAL SOURCES:

BOOKS

Dictionary of Literary Biography, Volume 33: *Afro-American Fiction Writers after 1955,* Gale, 1984.

PERIODICALS

Books and Bookmen, June, 1967.
Crisis, October, 1961.
Los Angeles Times Book Review, May 11, 1980.
Newsweek, July 17, 1967.
New York Times, July 14, 1975.

*   *   *

HERNTON, Calvin C(oolidge)   1934-

PERSONAL: Born April 28, 1934, in Chattanooga, Tenn.; son of Magnolia Jackson; married Mildred Webster, May 28, 1958; children: Antone. *Education:* Talladega College, B.A., 1954; Fisk University, M.A., 1956; attended Columbia University, 1961.

ADDRESSES: Office—Department of Black Studies, Oberlin College, Rice Hall, Oberlin, Ohio 44074. *Agent*—Marie Brown Associates, 412 West 154 St., New York, N.Y. 10032.

CAREER: Writer. Benedict College, Columbia, S.C., instructor in history and sociology, 1957-58; Alabama Agricultural and Mechanical College (now University), Normal, instructor in social sciences, 1958-59; Edward Waters College, Jacksonville, Fla., instructor in sociology, 1959-60; Southern University and Agricultural and Mechanical College, Baton Rouge, La., instructor in sociology, 1960-61; New York State Department of Welfare, New York City, social worker, 1961-62; *Umbra* (magazine), New York City, co-founder, 1963; London Institute of Phenomenological Studies, London, England, research fellow, 1965-69; Oberlin College, Oberlin, Ohio, writer in residence, 1970-72, professor of black studies and creative writing, 1973—. Poet in residence, Central State University, Wilberforce, Ohio, 1970.

WRITINGS:

(Contributor) Rosey E. Pool, editor, *Beyond the Blues: New Poems by American Negroes,* Hand & Flower Press, 1962.

The Coming of Chronos to the House of Nightsong: An Epical Narrative of the South (poetry), Interim, 1963.
Sex and Racism in America, Doubleday, 1965 (revised edition published in England as *Sex and Racism,* Deutsch, 1969).
White Papers for White Americans, Doubleday, 1966, reprinted, Greenwood Press, 1982.
(Contributor) LeRoi Jones and Larry Neal, editors, *Black Fire: An Anthology of Afro-American Writing,* Morrow, 1969.
Coming Together: Black Power, White Hatred, and Sexual Hangups, Random House, 1971.
(Contributor) D. L. Grummon and A. M. Barclay, editors, *Sexuality: A Search for Perspective,* Van Nostrand, 1971.
Scarecrow (novel), Doubleday, 1974.
(With Joseph Berke) *The Cannabis Experience: The Study of the Effects of Marijuana and Hashish,* Humanities, 1974.
Medicine Man (poetry), Reed, Cannon, & Johnson, 1976.
Sexual Mountains and Black Women Writers: Adventure in Sex, Literature, and Real Life, Doubleday, 1987.

Also author of plays "Glad to Be Dead," 1958, "Flame," 1958, and "The Place," 1972. Contributor to *Negro Digest, Freedomways,* and other periodicals.

SIDELIGHTS: A poet, scholar, and novelist, Calvin C. Hernton utilizes various literary forms to express his theories concerning sexism and racism. Hernton believes that "racism is inextricably related to sex and that the two have served to polarize America for centuries," relates Anthony S. Magistrale in a *Dictionary of Literary Biography* essay. Magistrale believes that this theme can be found throughout all of Hernton's work: "it remains the ascendant concept unifying his literary and scholarly activities."

Because of his familiarity with both verse and prose forms, Hernton's writing contains an interesting blend of the two. Speaking of *Coming Together: Social Struggle and Sexual Crisis,* Carol Eckberg Wadsworth in *Library Journal* says that Hernton is "more a poet than a theorist . . . [and] he seems to delve deeper than many writers on race and/or sex." Hernton's "style of writing is seldom jargonistic or academic sounding; instead, it is often passionate and highly personal," comments Magistrale. "Hernton's fiction and nonfiction thus represent an interesting blend of his roles as poet and social scientist."

White Papers for White Americans, for example, a series of essays on American culture and racism, "represent the best study on America's race problem that has come out in years," says Edward Margolies in a 1966 *Library Journal* review. "It is virtually impossible to bring something new to the area of race," writes Brooks Johnson in *Negro Digest,* "but, infrequently, the very gifted see and are able to express the centuried problems with something that approaches creativity because of the sensitivity and forcefulness with which they relate the old truths. Calvin C. Hernton's work is an example of such a process." Johnson believes that in *White Papers* Hernton demonstrates "the ability to tell, narrate, and explain, which he does at varying tempos and moods—in the manner of a good, highly polished jazz group. I don't mean to imply that his technique is slick—it isn't. Mr. Hernton is smooth because he is a man who knows his subject matter and has mastered the delicate balance between what observation and honesty dictate and what natural talent makes possible." The critic concludes that the result "is a book that knows no time."

Hernton's book *Sex and Racism in America* has been translated into Spanish, Japanese, Swedish, and French.

BIOGRAPHICAL/CRITICAL SOURCES:

BOOKS

Dictionary of Literary Biography, Volume 38: *Afro-American Writers after 1955: Dramatists and Prose Writers,* Gale, 1985.

PERIODICALS

Library Journal, March 1, 1966, May 15, 1971.
Negro Digest, May, 1967.
Publishers Weekly, January 10, 1966.
Saturday Review, February 12, 1966.

*   *   *

HILL, Errol Gaston 1921-

PERSONAL: Born August 5, 1921, in Trinidad, West Indies; son of Thomas David (an accountant) and Lydia (Gibson) Hill; married Grace Hope (a teacher), August 12, 1956; children: Da'aga, Claudia, Melina, Aaron. *Education:* Royal Academy of Dramatic Art (England), graduate diploma, 1951; University of London, diploma in drama, 1951; Yale University, B.A., 1962, M.F.A., 1962, D.F.A., 1966.

ADDRESSES: Office—Department of Drama, Dartmouth College, Hanover, N.H. 03755. *Agent*—Lucy Kroll Agency, 390 West End Ave., New York, N.Y. 10024.

CAREER: British Broadcasting Corp., London, England, announcer and actor, 1951-52; University of the West Indies, Kingston, Jamaica, and Port-of-Spain, Trinidad, creative arts tutor, 1953-58, 1962-65; University of Ibadan, Ibadan, Nigeria, teaching fellow in drama, 1965-67; City University of New York, College of Staten Island, associate professor of drama, 1967-68; Dartmouth College, Hanover, N.H., professor of drama, 1968—, John D. Willard Professor of Drama and Oratory, 1976, head of department, 1970-73, 1976-79. Evaluator, National Association of Schools Theatre; consultant, National Humanities Faculty, 1971-80. *Military service:* U.S. military engineer, Trinidad, 1941-43.

MEMBER: American Society for Theatre Research, Association for Commonwealth Language and Literature Studies.

AWARDS, HONORS: British Council Scholar, 1949-51; Rockefeller Foundation fellow, 1958-60; Theatre Guild of America playwriting fellow, 1961-62; Hummingbird Gold Medal, governments of Trinidad and Tobago, 1973; Guggenheim fellow, 1985-86; Barnard Hewitt Award for theatre history research, and Bertram Joseph Award for Shakespeare studies, both 1985; Fulbright fellow, 1988.

WRITINGS:

(Editor) *Caribbean Plays,* Extramural Department, University of West Indies, Volume I, 1958, Volume II, 1965.
(Editor and contributor) *The Artist in West Indian Society,* Extramural Department, University of West Indies, 1964.
The Trinidad Carnival: Mandate for a National Theatre, University of Texas Press, 1972.
(Contributor) *Resource Development in the Caribbean,* McGill University, 1972.
(With Peter Greer) *Why Pretend?* (a dialogue on the arts in education), Chandler, 1973.
(Editor) *A Time . . . and a Season: Eight Caribbean Plays,* Extramural Department, University of the West Indies, 1976.

(Editor) *Three Caribbean Plays for Secondary Schools,* Longman, 1979.

(Editor) *The Theatre of Black Americans: A Collection of Critical Essays,* two volumes, Prentice-Hall, 1980.

Shakespeare in Sable: A History of Black Shakespearean Actors, foreword by John Houseman, University of Massachusetts Press, 1984.

(Editor) *Plays for Today,* Longman, 1985.

PLAYS

The Ping-Pong (one-act), Extramural Department, University of the West Indies, 1958.

"Man Better Man" (three-act folk musical; first produced on Broadway at St. Mark's Playhouse, July 2, 1969), in John Gassner, editor, *Three Plays from the Yale School of Drama,* Dutton, 1964.

Dance Bongo (one-act), Extramural Department, University of the West Indies, 1965.

Oily Portraits (one-act), Extramural Department, University of the West Indies, 1966.

Square Peg (one-act), Extramural Department, University of the West Indies, 1966.

Dilemma (one-act), Extramural Department, University of the West Indies, 1966.

Strictly Matrimony (one-act), Extramural Deparment, University of the West Indies, 1966.

Wey-Wey (one-act), Extramural Department, University of the West Indies, 1966.

Also author of "Broken Melody," 1954. Plays anthologized in *Caribbean Literature,* edited by G. R. Coulthard, University of London Press, 1966, and *Black Drama Anthology,* edited by Woody King and Ron Milner, Signet, 1971.

OTHER

Contributor to *West Indian Review, Caribbean, Trinidad Guardian, Ethnomusicology, Cutures, Caribbean Quarterly,* and other West Indian periodicals, and to *Theatre Survey, Black American Literature Forum,* and *Theatre Journal.* Editor, *Bulletin of Black Theatre* (of the American Theatre Association), 1971-78.

WORK IN PROGRESS: Thespis in Jamaica: Profile of a Colonial Theatre; History of the Afro-American Drama and Theatre.

SIDELIGHTS: Errol Gaston Hill's book *Shakespeare in Sable: A History of Black Shakespearean Actors* "[documents] a long and often distinguished history of black actors who, while struggling against great adversity, made their mark on classical theatre," writes Robin Breon in the Toronto *Globe and Mail.* Covering the years from the 1820s through the 1970s, *Shakespeare in Sable* is the first book to describe how difficult it was, and sometimes still is, for even the most highly skilled black actors and actresses to secure roles in Shakespearean productions. *Shakespeare in Sable* is, therefore, "a story of courage to the point of heroism, persistence on to madness, and dreaming without hope," concludes James V. Hatch in *Black American Literature Forum.*

BIOGRAPHICAL/CRITICAL SOURCES:

PERIODICALS

American Anthropologist, August, 1973.
American Historical Review, June, 1985.
Black American Literature Forum, summer, 1985.
Comparative Drama, spring, 1986.
Globe and Mail (Toronto), February 9, 1985.

Journal of American Folklore, April, 1975.
Shakespeare Quarterly, summer, 1986.
Spotlight (Jamaica), October, 1958.
Theatre Journal, October, 1985.
Urbanite, March, 1961.

*   *   *

HILL, Leslie Pinckney   1880-1960

PERSONAL: Born May 14, 1880, in Lynchburg, Va.; died of a stroke, February 16 (one source says February 15), 1960, in Philadelphia, Pa.; buried in Kennett Square, Philadelphia, Pa.; son of Samuel Henry (a stationary engine operator) and Sarah Elizabeth (a laundress; maiden name, Brown) Hill; married Jane Ethel Clark, June 29, 1907; children: Eleanor Taylor (Mrs. Clifford Valentine), Hermione Clark (Mrs. Thomas S. Logan), Elaine Serena (Mrs. Frank Snowden), Natalie Dubois (Mrs. Rosamond Nelson), Mary Dorothea (Mrs. Herbert Tucker). *Education:* Harvard University, B.A. (cum laude), 1903, M.A., 1904. *Politics:* Republican.

ADDRESSES: Home—46 Lincoln Ave., Yeadon, Pa.

CAREER: Tuskegee Normal and Industrial Institute (now Tuskegee Institute), Tuskegee, Ala., English teacher and director of department of education, 1904-07; Manassas Industrial Institute, Manassas, Va., principal, 1907-13; Institute for Colored Youth (now Cheyney State College), Cheyney, Pa., principal, 1913-30, president, 1931-51, president emeritus, 1951-60; Mercy-Douglass Hospital, Philadelphia, Pa., administrator, 1953-56. Lecturing professor of general education at institutions, including University of California, Los Angeles. Member of Board of Presidents of Pennsylvania State Teachers Colleges, Pennsylvania Department of Welfare, Delaware County Board of Assistance, and Philadelphia Citizens Commission on City Policy; president of board of trustees of Manassas Industrial Institute; founder and president of Camp Hope; director of Armstrong Association of Philadelphia, Interracial Committee of Philadelphia, Delaware County Tuberculosis and Health Association, and Delaware County Health and Welfare Council.

MEMBER: National Education Association Committee on the Defense of Democracy Through Education, National Council Student Christian Associations, American Teachers Association, American Association of School Administrators, American Academy of Political and Social Science, United Service Organization, Peace Section of the American Friends Service Committee, Association of Negro Secondary and Industrial Schools (secretary-treasurer), Hoover Commission on Reorganization of Federal Government, Eastern States Association of Teachers Colleges and Professional Schools for Teachers, State Commission on Study of Urban Colored Population, Pennsylvania Education Association, Pennsylvania Association of Teachers of Colored Children (co-founder), Pennsylvania Teachers Association (founder), Pennsylvania State Negro Council (founder and president), Citizens Council of Delaware County, Visitation of Delaware County (member of board), West Chester Community Center (founder and president of board of directors), Phi Beta Kappa, Kappa Alpha Psi.

AWARDS, HONORS: Received LL.D. from Morgan State College, 1939, and Haverford College, 1951; Ed.D., Rhode Island College of Education, 1956; and Litt.D. from Lincoln University. Seltzer Award for distinguished service.

WRITINGS:

The Wings of Oppression (poems), Stratford, 1921, reprinted, Books for Libraries Press, 1971.
(Contributor) James Weldon Johnson, editor, *The Book of American Negro Poetry,* Harcourt, 1922.
(Contributor) Robert T. Kerlin, *Negro Poets and Their Poems,* Associated Publishers, 1923.
Toussaint L'Ouverture: A Dramatic History, Christopher, 1928.
(Contributor) Sterling A. Brown, Arthur P. Davis, and Ulysses Lee, editors, *The Negro Caravan,* Dryden, 1941.
(Contributor) Rayford W. Logan, editor, *What the Negro Wants,* University of North Carolina Press, 1944.
(Contributor) Langston Hughes and Arna Bontemps, editors, *The Poetry of the Negro,* Doubleday, 1949.

Also author of *Jethro,* a biblical drama, first published in 1931. Poetry represented in anthologies and in such periodicals as *Crisis, Life, Opportunity, Outlook, Phylon,* and *Teacher-Education Journal.*

SIDELIGHTS: Leslie Pinckney Hill is most known as a dedicated educator and activist poet who devoted his career and writings to the highest standards of education and equal race relations. After earning both his bachelor's and master's degrees from Harvard University, he began his teaching career at institutions in the South. Hill went on to serve at the Institute for Colored Youth in Pennsylvania (now Cheyney State College) for nearly forty years, guiding the school toward becoming a fully recognized and state-supported teachers college. Though primarily an educator and active participant in civic organizations, the poet Hill sought to lend hope to members of his race through his writings, emphasizing the value of blacks and their contributions to America.

In his collection of sixty-nine poems, *Wings of Oppression,* Hill characterizes the black race as a group specifically chosen by God to endure suffering and as a vehicle through which God would eventually establish universal brotherhood. Additionally, the author stresses patience and calm endurance, believing that a small victory is better than none. Hill furthered his philosophy of peaceful triumphs in the 1928 five-part, blank-verse drama *Toussaint L'Ouverture,* which portrays the famed Haitian leader. In depicting L'Ouverture's successful rule, Hill praises both the Haitian's advocation of racial harmony and freedom for all as well as his condemnation of massacre and violence as a means of revolution.

Hill's views of racial relations differed markedly from the protest and black-pride writers of his time, and it is not certain whether Hill's philosophy was widely shared by American blacks. Not all of the author's writing, though, contained racial overtones; some of his educational writings and lectures promoted industry, stressed the importance of knowledge, and urged general goodwill toward all of humanity.

BIOGRAPHICAL/CRITICAL SOURCES:

BOOKS

Dictionary of Literary Biography, Volume 51: *Afro-American Writers From the Harlem Renaissance to 1940,* Gale, 1987.
Mays, Benjamin E., *The Negro's God,* Atheneum, 1969.

OBITUARIES:

PERIODICALS

Journal of Negro History, April, 1960.
New York Times, February 16, 1960.

HIMES, Chester (Bomar)   1909-1984

PERSONAL: Born July 29, 1909, in Jefferson City, Mo.; died November 12, 1984, of Parkinson's disease, in Moraira, Spain; son of Joseph Sandy (a teacher) and Estelle (a teacher; maiden name, Bomar) Himes; married Jean Lucinda Johnson, August 13, 1937 (divorced); married second wife, Lesley. *Education:* Attended Ohio State University, 1926-28.

ADDRESSES: Home—Casa Griot, Pla del Mar 123, Moraira, Alicante, Spain. *Agent*—Rosalyn Targ, 250 West 57th St., New York, N.Y. 10019.

CAREER: Writer. Convicted of armed robbery of $53,000 at the age of nineteen and sentenced to twenty years in Ohio State Penitentiary; while in prison, began to write and contributed prison stories to magazines; released from prison about 1935, after serving six years; worked for Federal Writer's Project, subsequently completing a history of Cleveland (never published); worked briefly as a journalist for the Cleveland *Daily News,* as a writer for the labor movement and the Communist Party, and at odd jobs; during World War II, worked in shipyards and for aircraft companies in Los Angeles and San Francisco; left the United States to travel and live abroad in 1953; lived in Paris for many years; suffered a stroke in Mexico, 1965, and was temporarily inactive; made a film in Harlem for French television, 1967; lived in Spain for the last fifteen years of his life.

AWARDS, HONORS: Julius Rosenwald fellowship in creative writing, 1944-45; Yaddo fellowship, 1948; Grand Prix Policier, 1958, for *La Reine des Pommes.*

WRITINGS:

NOVELS

If He Hollers, Let Him Go, Doubleday, 1945, new edition, Berkley Publishing, 1964, reprinted, Thunder's Mouth, 1986.
The Lonely Crusade, Knopf, 1947, reprinted, Thunder's Mouth, 1987.
Cast the First Stone, Coward, 1952, reprinted, New American Library, 1975.
The Third Generation, World Publishing, 1954, reprinted, Chatham Bookseller, 1973.
The Primitive, New American Library, 1955, reprinted, New American Library, 1971.
Pinktoes, Olympia Press (Paris), 1961, Putnam, 1965.
Ne nous enervons pas! (title means "Be Calm"), translation by J. Fillion, Gallimard, 1961.
Mamie Mason; ou, Un Exercise de la bonne volonte, translation by Andre Mathieu, Editions Les Yeux Ouverts, 1963.
Une Affaire de viol, translation by Mathieu, Editions Les Yeux Ouverts, 1963, published in the original English as *A Case of Rape,* Howard University Press, 1984.

"SERIE NOIR"/"HARLEM DOMESTIC" SERIES; TRANSLATED INTO FRENCH FROM ORIGINAL ENGLISH MANUSCRIPTS

For Love of Imabelle, Fawcett, 1957, translation by Minnie Danzas published as *La Reine des Pommes,* Gallimard, 1958, revised English edition published as *A Rage in Harlem,* Avon, 1965, reprinted, Schocken, 1985.
Il pleut des coups durs, translation by C. Wourgaft, Gallimard, 1958, published as *The Real Cool Killers,* Avon, 1959, reprinted, Schocken, 1985.

The Crazy Kill (originally published in French by Gallimard, 1958), Avon, 1959, reprinted, Schocken, 1984.

Couche dans le pain (title means "A Jealous Man Can't Win"), translation by J. Herisson and H. Robillot, Gallimard, 1959.

Tout pour plaire, translation by Yves Malartic, Gallimard, 1959, published as *The Big Gold Dream*, Avon, 1960.

Dare-dare, translation by Pierre Verrier, Gallimard, 1959, published as *Run Man, Run*, Putnam, 1966.

Imbroglio negro, translation by Fillon, Gallimard, 1960, published as *All Shot Up*, Avon, 1960.

Retour en Afrique, translation by Pierre Sergent, Plon, 1964, published as *Cotton Comes to Harlem*, Putnam, 1965, translation published as *La Casse de l'Oncle Tom*, Plon, 1971, original English edition reprinted, Schocken, 1984.

The Heat's On (originally published in French by Gallimard, 1960), Putnam, 1966, published as *Come Back, Charleston Blue*, Dell, 1967, original English edition reprinted, Schocken, 1986 .

Blind Man With a Pistol, Morrow, 1969, published as *Hot Day Hot Night*, Dell, 1970, translation by Henri Robillot published as *L'Aveugle au pistolet*, Gallimard, 1970, original English edition reprinted, Schocken, 1986.

OTHER

The Autobiography of Chester Himes, Doubleday, Volume I: *The Quality of Hurt*, 1972, Volume II: *My Life of Absurdity*, 1977.

Black on Black: Baby Sister and Selected Writings (stories), Doubleday, 1973.

Work represented in many anthologies, including *Black Writers of America, Negro Caravan, Right On!, American Negro Short Stories,* and *The Best Short Stories by Negro Writers.* Contributor to periodicals, including *Atlanta Daily World, Coronet, Esquire,* and *Pittsburgh Courier.*

SIDELIGHTS: Chester Himes wrote successfully in many genres, including novels of social protest, autobiographies, and popular crime thrillers. But whatever form his writing took, it was always dedicated to one subject—"racism, the hurt it inflicts, and all the tangled hates," according to Stephen F. Milliken's book *Chester Himes: A Critical Appraisal.* Himes wrote about racial oppression with a bitter, unrelenting anger that earned him comparisons to Richard Wright and James Baldwin. "He writes with the same intense ferocity with which he might knock a man down," declared *Virginia Quarterly Review* writer Raymond Nelson. This sense of rage and the unforgiving strokes with which Himes painted both black and white characters alienated many readers of both races; as a result, Himes was for years almost unknown in this country, though he was highly respected in Europe even during his lifetime.

Himes was born to socially successful parents, but his early life was troubled due to the constant fighting between his light-skinned mother and his dark-skinned father. The racial tension between the couple was to form one of the recurring themes in Himes's fiction, that of discrimination by light-skinned blacks against those of darker color. He attended Ohio State University for two years before being expelled for leading his fraternity on a romp through Columbus's red light district that ended in a speakeasy brawl. Drifting into a life of petty crime, he was arrested for armed robbery in less than a year and sentenced to twenty years in Ohio State Penitentiary. There, Himes witnessed beatings, killings, riots, and a fire that took the lives of over three hundred convicts. He began to write short stories based on these experiences; they were soon accepted for publication in *Esquire* magazine, where they appeared signed with Himes's name and prison identification number.

Released from prison after serving six years of his sentence, Himes worked variously for the Federal Writers Project, the labor movement, the Communist Party and the Cleveland *Daily News* over the next few years. In 1941 he set out for California, lured by the prospect of profitable work in wartime industry. The government shipyards had a reputation for fair hiring and employment practices, but Himes found discriminatory "Jim Crow" policies as prevalent there as anywhere else. He later wrote in his autobiography that the hypocrisy of Los Angeles sickened him more than the outright hostility of the South. He expressed his bitter reaction to his Los Angeles experiences in *If He Hollers, Let Him Go,* his first novel.

In this work, the author used a naturalistic style to describe five days of steadily mounting tension in the life of Bob Jones, a black foreman in a wartime shipyard. Each day Bob awakes with his nerves taut, "struggling to keep from lashing back violently against a hateful environment," as *Dictionary of Literary Biography* essayist Frank Campenni described it. Various characters illustrate different attitudes adopted by blacks to get along in the white world. For example, Bob's light-skinned girlfriend, Alcie, sometimes passes as white; his co-worker, Smitty, adopts an "Uncle Tom"-like demeanor; and UCLA graduate Ben strives for equal achievements in a separate black community. Unable to accept any of these compromises, Bob feels completely at odds with himself and the world.

Taunted with a racial slur from one of his workers, Bob responds in kind. The incident results in a demotion for Bob, while Madge, his antagonist, goes unreprimanded. Madge is a bigoted Texan who pretends to fear Bob while secretly desiring him. Bob finds his hatred and disgust for her tinged with an inexplicable sexual attraction. Tension mounts between the two, culminating in Madge's attempted seduction of Bob; when he rejects her advances, she cries rape and he is nearly lynched. Himes convincingly depicted Bob's defeat as unavoidable, "the product not only of his environment but of the tortured desires and twisted fears of his damaged psyche," wrote Campenni. "The organization of the novel lends its stereotyped situation unexpected power. Each night during the five days encompassed, Jones has violent nightmares in which he is trapped or endangered, so that the actual events are not merely foreshadowed, but given an internalized inevitability. The surrealistic quality of these nightmares underscores vividly . . . the doom which hangs over Jones."

Himes followed *If He Hollers, Let Him Go* with *Lonely Crusade,* a novel similar in plot and theme to his first. *Lonely Crusade* is less powerful than its predecessor, however, due to "Himes's tendency toward melodrama and overstatement," in Campenni's opinion. Next came a trio of novels that were largely autobiographical: *Cast the First Stone, The Third Generation,* and *The Primitive. Cast the First Stone* is regarded by many critics to be the classic prison novel. It relates the harrowing events of Himes's term in Ohio State Penitentiary. In *The Third Generation,* the author skillfully reduced "the traumas generated within the black American Community itself by the pressures of racism to the story of a single black family, rent by the conflict between a black-hating mother and a black-accepting father, and the sons caught in between—Himes's own story," explained Milliken.

Himes regarded *The Primitive* as his favorite work. Like *If He Hollers, Let Him Go, The Primitive* used disturbing nightmares to foreshadow the violent and tragic end of the relationship between Jesse Robinson, the writer-protagonist, and Kriss, his white mistress. Based on Himes's real-life love affair with Vandi Haywood, this painful story blended "surrealistic and obsessive patterns quite successfully into what may well be the author's most profound novel," wrote Michel Fabre in *Black World*. Milliken reserved particular praise for Himes's compassionate portrait of Kriss, writing that her characterization represented "the most complete exposition [Himes] gave in his writing of his conviction that the hurts of the white woman are at least comparable to those of the black man, and that she endures a roughly similar, and equally pitiable, minority status."

Today these early novels are ranked among the classics of black American protest literature. At the time of their publication, however, they received scant critical attention and sold very few copies. Unable to support himself by writing, Himes was also barred from all but the most menial jobs because of his prison record. Completely disillusioned with what American society had to offer him, Himes left the country permanently in 1953. For many years he lived in Paris in the company of other black American expatriates, including Himes's literary model, Richard Wright. But while Wright lived as something of a Parisian celebrity, Himes was penniless and unknown when he arrived in France.

In his autobiography, Himes states that he was leading a "desperate" life in "a little crummy hotel" when he was contacted by French publisher Marcel Duhamel in 1956. Duhamel was familiar with Himes's work and wanted the author to produce a novel set in Harlem for his popular series of crime thrillers, "Serie Noir." Himes responded by locking himself in his room with two or three bottles of wine each day and within three weeks handed Duhamel a finished manuscript entitled *For Love of Imabelle*. Translated into French and published as *La Reine des Pommes,* the book was a tremendous success, winning the Grand Prix Policier in 1958. Himes went on to produce a total of ten novels for "Serie Noir"; he called the books his "Harlem Domestic" series.

All ten novels followed the same formula: a violent and inexplicable crime, enacted in private, touches off a wave of equally violent reactions in anarchy-ridden Harlem. Black detectives "Coffin" Ed Jones and "Grave Digger" Johnson try to bring order to the scene, usually by methods as illegal and deadly as those of the criminals. More often than not, they are only partially successful. French readers loved the irony and mordant humor which marked these fast-paced novels. Several of the books were eventually published in English under such titles as *A Rage in Harlem, The Real Cool Killers,* and *The Heat's On.* American critics at first voiced many objections to the graphic excesses of Himes's stories, but the books sold well, and it was through the "Harlem Domestic" series that the author first received some measure of recognition in the United States.

Himes found it quite ironic that he achieved his greatest success with the "Harlem Domestic" series, for he wrote each of the novels within a matter of weeks, motivated strictly by his need for cash. But while the author "may have thought he cut his own forebrain out when he began to write genre novels, . . . these works complement, rather than contradict, the agonized nostalgia of his other novels," asserted a *Voice Literary Supplement* contributor. Today, many critics feel that

almost in spite of himself, Himes produced some of his strongest work in his detective fiction. While the "Harlem Domestic" series contained no overt social messages, as Himes's other books had, their grim portrayal of ghetto life was itself a powerful statement on the failure of America's promises for blacks. Campenni commented that Himes's work was strengthened when he eliminated the obvious preaching that occasionally marred his earlier novels, for "by objectifying and externalizing his rage against racism, [he] seems paradoxically to have liberated his imagination and his exuberant sense of life."

An additional strength of the Harlem detective stories is their absurdist humor, believed Edward Margolies, contributor to *Studies in Black Literature.* "It is humor—resigned, bitter, earthy, slapstick, macabre—that protects author, readers and detectives from the gloom of omnipresent evil." Margolies added that Himes's humor was perfectly appropriate to the setting of his novels, for it is "the hard cynical wit of the urban poor who know how to cheat and lie to the white world to survive physically, and cheat and lie to themselves to survive psychologically." A *Times Literary Supplement* reviewer added: "Even in a book like [*Cotton Comes to Harlem*]—with a laugh on nearly every page—it is evident [Himes] is concerned with the Negro's plight in Harlem, aware of every corruption from whores and dope-addiction to mere urine-stained walls, aware of the unkillable hope in the minds of many of these people and of the hopelessness of their situation as it is now. . . . It is his value as a writer, and it makes this book a novel, that he can jest at all of it, make stiletto social comments, and keep his story running."

The "Harlem Domestic" novels have been criticized for perpetrating negative images of blacks, but a *Voice Literary Supplement* writer stressed that Himes's "women dressed in red, his jazzmen, pimps, and scam artists partying on barbecue and weed are saved from being reverse stereotypes because of the bitter density of the rage and humor from which they spring." In all his fiction Himes "drove deeper into the subject [of racism] than anyone ever had before," affirmed Milliken. "He recorded what happens to a man when his humanity is questioned, the rage that explodes within him, the doubts that follow, and the fears, and the awful temptation to yield, to embrace degradation. . . . [He] has produced . . . the most complete and perfect statement of the nature of native American racism to be found in American literature, and one of the most profound statements about the nature of social oppression, and the rage and fear it generates in individuals, in all of modern literature."

Yale University has a major collection of Himes's literary manuscripts and letters. His works have been published in France, Germany, Denmark, Sweden, Italy, Holland, Portugal, Norway, and Japan.

MEDIA ADAPTATIONS: Cotton Comes to Harlem was produced as a film, starring Godfrey Cambridge and Raymond St. Jacques, by United Artists, 1970; *The Heat's On* was produced as "Come Back, Charleston Blue," starring the same actors, by Warner Brothers, 1972.

BIOGRAPHICAL/CRITICAL SOURCES:

BOOKS

Amistad I, Knopf, 1970.
Contemporary Literary Criticism, Gale, Volume II, 1974, Volume IV, 1975, Volume VII, 1977, Volume XVIII, 1981.

Dictionary of Literary Biography, Volume II: *American Novelists Since World War II,* Gale, 1978.

Himes, Chester, *The Autobiography of Chester Himes,* Doubleday, Volume I: *The Quality of Hurt,* 1972, Volume II: *My Life of Absurdity,* 1977.

Hughes, Carl Milton, *The Negro Novelist, 1940-1950,* Citadel, 1970.

Littlejohn, David, *Black on White: A Critical Survey of Writing by American Negroes,* Viking, 1966.

Lundquist, James, *Chester Himes,* Ungar, 1976.

Margolies, Edward, *Native Sons,* Lippincott, 1968.

Milliken, Stephen, *Chester Himes: A Critical Appraisal,* University of Missouri Press, 1976.

Symons, Julian, *Mortal Consequences: A History—From the Detective Story to the Crime Novel,* Harper, 1972.

PERIODICALS

America, April 15, 1972, July 21, 1973.

American Libraries, October, 1972.

Best Sellers, July 15, 1965, December 1, 1966, March 15, 1969.

Black World, July, 1970, March, 1972, July, 1972.

Booklist, July 15, 1972.

Books and Bookmen, September, 1967, August, 1968, October, 1971.

Book Week, March 28, 1965, August 8, 1965.

Book World, February 22, 1970, March 26, 1972.

Chicago Review, Volume XXV, number 3, 1973.

College Language Association Journal, Number 15, 1972.

Commonweal, December 1, 1972.

Critique: Studies in Modern Fiction, Volume XVI, number 1, 1974.

Esquire, May, 1972.

Journal of American Studies, April, 1978.

Journal of Popular Culture, spring, 1976.

L'Express, April 5-11, 1971.

Nation, December 20, 1971.

Negro Digest, July, 1967.

New Statesman, April 11, 1975.

New York Times, March 6, 1972, March 8, 1972.

New York Times Book Review, February 7, 1965, August 15, 1965, November 27, 1966, February 23, 1969, March 12, 1972, April 30, 1972, June 4, 1972, February 13, 1977.

Observer Review, June 18, 1967, June 29, 1969.

Prairie Schooner, winter, 1974-75.

Publishers Weekly, January 17, 1972, January 31, 1972, April 3, 1972, June 23, 1975.

Punch, July 23, 1969.

Saturday Review, March 22, 1969, April 15, 1972.

Spectator, July 12, 1969.

Studies in Black Literature, summer, 1970.

Studies in Short Fiction, summer, 1975.

Times (London), June 28, 1969, August 11, 1985.

Times Literary Supplement, April 25, 1975.

Variety, April 9, 1969, March 15, 1972, July 5, 1972.

Virginia Quarterly Review, spring, 1972, summer, 1972, summer, 1973.

OBITUARIES:

PERIODICALS

Detroit Free Press, November 14, 1984.

Los Angeles Times, November 15, 1984.

Newsweek, November 16, 1984.

New York Times, November 14, 1984.

Publishers Weekly, November 30, 1984.

Times (London), November 14, 1984.

Washington Post, November 16, 1984.

*   *   *

HOAGLAND, Everett (III)   1942-

PERSONAL: Born December 18, 1942, in Philadelphia, Pa.; son of Everett, Jr. and Estelle (Johnson) Hoagland; children: Kamal (son), Nia, Ayan-Estelle, Reza Eve (daughters). *Education:* Lincoln University, Lincoln University, Pa., A.B., 1964; Brown University, M.A., 1973.

ADDRESSES: Office—Room 323, Group I Building, Department of English, Southeastern Massachusetts University, Old Westport Rd., North Dartmouth, Mass. 02747.

CAREER: Teacher of English in public schools of Philadelphia, Pa., 1964-67; Lincoln University, Lincoln University, Pa., assistant director of admissions, 1967-69; Claremont College, Claremont, Calif., administrative assistant and teacher of Black poetry at Black Studies Center, 1969-70, poet in residence, 1970-71; Swarthmore College, Swarthmore, Penn., instructor in humanities, 1972; Southeastern Massachusetts University, North Dartmouth, staff position in department of English, 1973-76, associate professor of English, 1976—. Coordinator and teacher of Afro Culture and Society, Chino Institute for Men; instructor in English at Mount San Antonio College and for Upward Bound program, Claremont College. Clerk of corporation and board member, New Bedford Foster Grandparents Program, 1976-82.

AWARDS, HONORS: Fellowship in creative writing, Brown University, 1971-73; Gwendolyn Brooks Award for Fiction, *Black World* (magazine), 1974; Creative Artists Fellowship, Massachusetts Arts & Humanities Foundation, 1975; fellowships from National Endowment for the Humanities, 1984, and Artists Foundation Statewide Poetry Competition, 1986.

WRITINGS:

Ten Poems: A Collection, American Studies Institute, 1968.

Black Velvet (poetry), Broadside Press, 1970.

Scrimshaw (poetry), Patmos Press, 1976.

CONTRIBUTOR

The New Black Poetry, edited by Clarence Major, International, 1969.

Patterns, edited by H. N. Rosenberg, Idlewild, 1970.

The Black Poets, edited by Dudley Randall, Bantam, 1971.

A Broadside Treasury, edited by Gwendolyn Brooks, Broadside Press, 1971.

New Black Voices: An Anthology of Contemporary American Literature, edited by Abraham Chapman, Mentor Books, 1972.

Dues: An Anthology of New Earth Writings, edited by Ron Welburn, Emerson-Hall, 1973.

Giant Talk: An Anthology of Third World Writings, edited by Quincy Troupe and Rainer Schulte, Vintage Book, 1975.

Also author of ''. . . HERE . . . ,'' a volume of poetry. Contributor to anthologies, including *Significance: The Struggle We Share.* Weekly editorial page columnist for the *Standard-Times* (New Bedford), 1979-82. Contributor of poetry and fiction to periodicals, including *American Poetry Review, Black World, Negro Digest, Essence, First World, Nimrod, Massachusetts Review, Iowa Review,* and *Beloit Poetry Journal.* Contributing editor, *American Poetry Review,* 1984—.

WORK IN PROGRESS: Two novels, *King Dust* and *Bedrock Mass.*

SIDELIGHTS: Poet Everett Hoagland's work has changed both thematically and structurally with time, but it has always stressed the importance of racial pride. His more recent collections dwell on contemporary blacks' African roots, and on the links connecting American and African blacks. Linda E. Scott writes in the *Dictionary of Literary Biography* that ''Everett Hoagland's concern for humanity has grown through the years. Accompanying it is an outrage at all that has thwarted the development of human beauty. The result is a poetry which seeks to teach as well as to entertain. As it is informed by Afro-American history and culture, his poetic style has become an eclectic fusion of agit-prop, historical narrative, and bebop.'' While not much criticism exists on Hoagland, his frequent appearance in anthologies ''indicates a reader appreciation for his work,'' writes Scott. Hoagland says he was influenced by the eloquent epic poetry of Sterling Brown and Robert Hayden and by the linguistic inventiveness of Jayne Cortez and Ntozake Shange, whose language is ''both ironic and infused with a joyful appreciation of the sounds and senses of black life and culture,'' describes Scott. She concludes, ''For Hoagland, black art is black life.''

BIOGRAPHICAL/CRITICAL SOURCES:

BOOKS

Dictionary of Literary Biography, Volume XLI: *Afro-American Poets since 1955,* Gale, 1985.
Lee, Don L., *Dynamite Voices: Black Poets of the 1960s,* Broadside Press, 1971.

* * *

HOBSON, Julius W(ilson) 1922(?)-1977

PERSONAL: Born c. 1922, in Birmingham, Ala.; died of cancer, March 23, 1977, in Washington, D.C.; married first wife, 1947 (divorced, 1966); married Tina Lower, 1969; children: (first marriage) one son, one daughter; (second marriage) two stepsons. *Education:* Attended Tuskegee Institute and Howard University. *Politics:* Marxist.

ADDRESSES: Home—Washington, D.C.

CAREER: Civil rights activist and writer. Social Security Administration, Washington, D.C., economist and statistician, c. 1950-1970. Member of Washington, D.C., school board, 1968; head of Washington Institute for Quality Education until 1971; political candidate, 1971 and 1972; member of District of Columbia City Council, 1974-77. Founder of District of Columbia Association Community Teams.

MEMBER: ACT (chairman).

WRITINGS:

(With Janet Harris) *Black Pride: A People's Struggle,* Mc-Graw, 1969.
The Damned Children: A Layman's Guide to Forcing Change in Public Education, Washington Institute for Quality Education, 1970.
The Damned Information: Acquiring and Using Public Information to Force Social Change, Washington Institute for Quality Education, 1971.

SIDELIGHTS: Julius W. Hobson was a civil-rights activist who spearheaded a number of successful reform movements in Washington, D.C., including some with nationwide impli-

cations. He sponsored litigation that led to reforms in the District of Columbia's school system and improved conditions for urban blacks. In the mid-1960's, he amassed collections of data proving that the school system was still operating under segregative guidelines more than a decade after the Supreme Court had ruled against such practices. Hobson also won the 1967 *Hobson v. Hansen* case in which a U.S. Court of Appeals decision invalidated the school district's student tracking program, a system that channeled students into certain types and levels of classes based on overall performances. The court ruled that the system perpetuated the segregation of blacks. Another of Hobson's victories came in 1970 when U.S. District Judge J. Skelly Wright upheld Hobson's complaint that the District of Columbia was spending more money per capita at predominantly white schools than at black schools.

Hobson is also credited with winning employment and promotion opportunities for blacks. He sued the Washington, D.C., police department to end discriminatory practices and to secure promotions for blacks on the force. He also organized picketers to demonstrate against merchants who had refused to hire blacks. And a threatened boycott engineered by Hobson resulted in the city's prompt hiring of black bus drivers.

Hobson also served on the Washington, D.C., school board and city council. His 1974 campaign was conducted from a wheelchair because he was suffering from cancer. Nonetheless, he was a strident supporter of reform measures, including the adoption of a citizen's initiation and referendum ordinance that allowed the public to draft legislation and place it on the ballot for popular vote.

In *Black Pride: A People's Struggle,* Hobson and co-author Janet Harris recount the black individual's struggle for freedom and equality from the days of slavery to the 1960's militancy. Focusing on the development of pride in black culture and achievement, the book includes studies of black leaders such as Marcus Garvey, W. E. B. DuBois, Malcolm X, and Martin Luther King, Jr.

BIOGRAPHICAL/CRITICAL SOURCES:

BOOKS

Wormley, Stanton L. and Lewis Fenderson, editors, *Many Shades of Black,* Morrow, 1969.

PERIODICALS

Ebony, May, 1965, November, 1973.
Jet, December 14, 1972.
New York Times Book Review, May 4, 1969.
Saturday Evening Post, April 20, 1968.
Time, December 4, 1972.
Washington Post, October 21, 1969, October 22, 1974, October 27, 1974.

OBITUARIES:

PERIODICALS

Jet, April 14, 1977.
New York Times, March 25, 1977.
Newsweek, April 4, 1977.

* * *

HORNE, Frank (Smith) 1899-1974 (Xavier I)

PERSONAL: Born August 18, 1899, in Brooklyn, N.Y.; died

of arteriosclerosis, September 7, 1974, in New York, N.Y.; son of Edwin Fletcher and Cora (Calhoun) Horne; married Frankye Priestly (one source says Frankie Bunn), August 19, 1930 (died c. 1940); married Mercedes Christopher Rector, August 15, 1950; children: two stepchildren. *Education:* College of the City of New York (now City College of the City University of New York), B.S. (one source says B.A.), 1921; received degree from Northern Illinois College of Optometry (now Illinois College of Optometry), c. 1922; University of Southern California, A.M., c. 1932.

CAREER: Private practice of optometry in Chicago, Ill., and New York, N.Y., 1922-26; Fort Valley High and Industrial School (renamed Fort Valley Normal and Industrial School, 1932-39; now Fort Valley State College), Fort Valley, Ga., c. 1926-36, began as teacher, became dean and acting president; National Youth Administration, Washington, D.C., assistant director of Negro Affairs division c. 1936-38; worked in various administrative capacities for agencies of U.S. Housing Authority, including Housing and Home Finance Agency and Office of Race Relations, Washington, D.C., and later New York City c. 1938-55; New York City Commission on Intergroup Relations, New York City, executive director c. 1956-62; New York City Housing Redevelopment Board, New York City, consultant on human relations c. 1962-74; poet. Founder of National Committee Against Discrimination in Housing.

MEMBER: American Civil Liberties Union (past board member), National Association for the Advancement of Colored People (NAACP), National Association of Housing Officials, National Association of Intergroup Relations Officials, National Housing Conference, Phelps-Stokes Fund (past secretary), Hudson Guild (past board member), Omega Psi Phi.

AWARDS, HONORS: Received second prize for poetry in *Crisis* Amy Spingarn Contest, 1925, for composite poem "Letters Found Near a Suicide"; recipient of James J. and Jane Hoey Award for Inter-Racial Justice from Catholic Inter-Racial Council of New York, Inc.

WRITINGS:

POETRY

Haverstraw (collection; contains "Haverstraw," "Walk," "Mamma!," "Patience," "Hubbard Tank," "Communion," "Symphony," and composite "Letters Found Near a Suicide" [also see below]), Breman, 1963.

Also author of "On Seeing Two Brown Boys in a Catholic Church," "To a Persistent Phantom," "Kid Stuff," "Toast," "More Letters Found Near a Suicide," "'Balm in Gilead': A Christmas Jingle," "He Won't Stay Put: A Carol for All Seasons," "Nigger, A Chant for Children," and others.

"Letters Found Near a Suicide" was originally published in *Crisis,* under the pseudonym Xavier I.

Work represented in numerous anthologies, including *Caroling Dusk: An Anthology of Verse by Negro Poets,* edited by Countee Cullen, Harper, 1927; *The Poetry of the Negro, 1746-1949,* edited by Langston Hughes and Arna Bontemps, Doubleday, 1949; and *American Negro Poetry,* edited by Bontemps, Hill & Wang, 1963.

OTHER

Author of pamphlet *I Never Saw Him Before: A Mississippi Folk Song,* published by Breman in 1962.

Contributor of poetry, short stories, essays, and articles—such as "Black Verse," "I Am Initiated Into the Negro Race," "Harlem," "The Man Who Wanted To Be Red: A Story," "The Epic of Fort Valley," "Running Fools: Athletics in a Colored School," "Concerning White People," "Providing New Housing for Negroes," and "Dog House Education"— to periodicals, including *Crisis* and *Opportunity.*

SIDELIGHTS: As a poet and public administrator on race relations who wrote about prevailing prejudices and oppression experienced by blacks, Frank Horne qualifies as "an important minor voice of the Harlem Renaissance," according to Sarah M. Washington in *Dictionary of Literary Biography.* He especially took issue with inequitable housing practices and with discrimination on the basis of color. To a greater extent, however, Horne's poetry focuses on personal concerns rather than on emerging issues of the "New Negro" espoused by younger writers of the period. Much of his work features such somber themes as death and infirmity as well as "a crisis of faith" that Washington further observed as prevalent among many early twentieth-century writers.

Horne's literary reputation derives mainly from his award-winning 1925 "Letters Found Near a Suicide," published in *Crisis.* A composite work that was pseudonymously submitted under the name Xavier I, it contains eleven poems individually addressing people who had an impact on the speaker's life. With the exception of "To Chick," which recalls a rewarding friendship with a fellow football player, the letters express mainly negative feelings and a general disappointment with life and the world. By 1929 Horne added seven new poems that were also published in *Crisis* as "More Letters Found Near a Suicide." These subsequently appeared along with the original eleven letters as the first section of Horne's 1963 collection, *Haverstraw.*

A portion of Horne's poetry also reflects a preoccupation with ill health. Reportedly the victim of a disease that impaired his ability to walk and required him to move to a warmer climate, he imbued his poems with frequent references to dysfunctional legs and the accompanying physical pain. In particular, the tone of "To James" (contained in "More Letters Found Near a Suicide") suggests Horne's lamentation over his handicap and envy for those more physically fit, as the poem's speaker encourages a boy to *run* to victory.

Other writings prove variously influenced by political and religious themes, and some Horne intended as a means of instruction. His poem "Nigger, A Chant for Children," for instance, serves as a history lesson that teaches black children to be proud of their race and heritage. Through repeated emphasis on the term "nigger" and an effective "juxtaposition of children's songs and shouts of the bigot," explained Washington, Horne manages to transcend the negative connotation traditionally attributed to the word. In a similar fashion, the story "The Man Who Wanted To Be Red" illustrates what Horne perceived as the absurdities of discrimination purely on the basis of skin color.

In 1936 Horne embarked upon a career in public service, specializing in problems of public housing. His administrative involvement precipitated various related publications, including "Providing New Housing for Negroes," and virtually eclipsed his creative output. Nonetheless, Horne continued producing a sporadic number of poems, and this—coupled with his earlier poetry—seems to validate further discussion and reading of his work.

BIOGRAPHICAL/CRITICAL SOURCES:

BOOKS

Bontemps, Arna, editor, *The Harlem Renaissance Remembered,* Dodd, 1972.
Brown, Sterling, *Negro Poetry and Drama,* Associates in Negro Folk Education, 1937.
Dictionary of Literary Biography, Volume 51: *Afro-American Writers From the Harlem Renaissance to 1940,* Gale, 1987.
Kerlin, Robert T., *Negro Poets and Their Poems,* 2nd edition, Associated Publishers, 1935.

OBITUARIES:

PERIODICALS

New York Times, September 8, 1974.

*   *   *

HUGGINS, Nathan Irvin   1927-

PERSONAL: Born January 14, 1927, in Chicago, Ill.; son of Winston John (a waiter) and Marie (Warsaw) Huggins; married Brenda Carlita Smith (an actress and writer), July 18, 1971. *Education:* University of California, Berkeley, A.B., 1954, M.A., 1955; Harvard University, A.M., 1959, Ph.D., 1962.

ADDRESSES: Office—Department of History, Harvard University, Cambridge, Mass. 02138.

CAREER: Long Beach State College (now California State University, Long Beach), assistant professor of history, 1962-64; Lake Forest College, Lake Forest, Ill., assistant professor of history, 1964-66; University of Massachusetts at Boston, assistant professor, 1966-69, associate professor of history, 1969-70; Columbia University, New York, N.Y., professor of history, 1970-80; Harvard University, Cambridge, Mass., professor of history, 1980—. Visiting associate professor, University of California, Berkeley, 1969-70; Fulbright senior lecturer in Grenoble, France, 1974-75. Founding president, American Museum of Negro History, Boston, 1966-69; Howard Thurman Educational Trust, trustee, 1966—, vice-president, 1969—; council member, Smithsonian Institution, 1974—; board of directors member, New York Council on the Humanities, 1978—; director, Library of America, 1978—; director, American Council of Learned Societies, 1980—. Consultant to various organizations, including Danforth Foundation, Educational Testing Service, Anti-Defamation League, and Brooklyn Educational and Cultural Alliance. Juror for awards and prizes, including Francis Parkman Prize, Dunning Prize, and National Endowment for the Humanities Awards. *Military service:* U.S. Army, 1945-46.

MEMBER: American Historical Association, Association of American Historians (program committee member, 1971-72), Association for the Study of Afro-American Life and History (executive council member, 1972—), Organization of American Historians (executive council member, 1972—).

AWARDS, HONORS: Guggenheim fellow, 1971-72; Ford Foundation research and travel grant, 1971-72; American Specialist Award, U.S. State Department, 1976; Center for Advanced Studies fellow, 1979-80.

WRITINGS:

Protestants against Poverty: Boston's Charities, 1870-1900, foreword by Oscar Handlin, Greenwood Press, 1971.

(Editor with Martin Kilson and Daniel Fox; also contributor) *Key Issues in the Afro-American Experience,* two volumes, Harcourt, 1971.
Harlem Renaissance, Oxford University Press, 1971.
(Author of foreword) Marina Wikramanayake, *A World in Shadow: The Free Black in Antebellum South Carolina,* University of South Carolina Press, 1973.
(Editor) *Voices from the Harlem Renaissance,* Oxford University Press, 1976.
Black Odyssey: The Afro-American Ordeal in Slavery, Pantheon, 1977.
(Contributor) John Higham, editor, *Studies of Ethnic Leadership,* Johns Hopkins University Press, 1978.
Slave and Citizen: The Life of Frederick Douglass, edited by Handlin, Little, Brown, 1980.
Afro-American Studies: A Report to the Ford Foundation, Ford Foundation, 1985.
(Editor) W. E. B. Du Bois, *Writings* (annotated), Library of America, 1986.
(Editor) Du Bois, *The Suppression of the African Slave-Trade, the Souls of Black Folk and Dusk of Dawn: An Essay toward an Autobiography of a Race Concept,* Library of America, 1986.

Contributor of articles to periodicals, including *New York Times* and *Center Magazine.* Editor, *Journal of Ethnic Studies,* 1979—; member of board of editors, *American Historical Review;* consulting editor, "Foundations in Social Sciences" textbook series, Harcourt. Consultant to a number of broadcast productions, including "On Being Black," WGBH-TV, 1968-69; "Sesame Street," 1970—, and "The Best of Families," 1975-77, both Children's Television Workshop; "20th Century Humanists," National Public Radio, 1976—; "Look Away: The Old South," South Carolina Educational Television, 1977—; "Chance or Destiny?," WNET-TV, 1977—.

SIDELIGHTS: Nathan Irvin Huggins is the author of several noted works that illuminate important areas in black American history. His 1971 book *Harlem Renaissance* examines the 1920s period—centered in New York City's Harlem—that saw a flourishing of the arts among blacks, and out of which arose such famous artists as Langston Hughes, Arna Bontemps, Claude McKay, Jean Toomer, Countee Cullen, and Aaron Douglas. George E. Kent notes in the *New York Times Book Review* that "Huggins's particular contribution, as cultural historian, is his placement and analysis of the Renaissance within the context of America's general cultural history. His thesis is that, given the crude stage of an American provincialism and innocence and the resulting unknowing dependency of black men and white men upon each other in their scrambles for identity, the failures of the Renaissance were inevitable." Charles R. Larson in *Nation* writes that Huggins's historical approach towards understanding the Harlem Renaissance "has resulted in a book that is immensely readable, never pedantic, always fresh in its evaluation of the materials he has so carefully studied." Kent concludes that Huggins's book is "provocative and often brilliant."

Black Odyssey: The Afro-American Ordeal in Slavery is a historical narrative that has been noted for its attempt to communicate the personal impact of slavery on slaves. David Herbert Donald writes in the *New York Times Book Review* that "Huggins wants his readers to feel what it was like to live in an African village raided by slavers, to sense how infamous the 'middle passage' across the ocean really was, to understand what it meant to be owned by another human being." Al-Tony Gilmore in the *Washington Post Book World* points out that

Black Odyssey represents "a major departure from the conventional descriptive and analytical exposition of standard historical works." Huggins's account "seeks to grasp and recapture the range of emotions, fears, insecurities and frustrations of the slave based on his African heritage, his enslavement in Africa and America, and his efforts to deal pragmatically with his incredible condition." It is this aspect of *Black Odyssey* that Huggins ultimately stresses. "Research has enlightened us to see [slaves] not only as victims but also as builders of the world they lived in," comments Theodore Rosengarten in *New Republic*. "The lesson of slavery is not the destruction of the personality but rather what Nathan Huggins, and others, call the 'triumph of the human spirit over adversity.'" A reviewer in the *New Yorker* adds that *Black Odyssey* "appears to be the classic on the subject for a long time to come. Specialists in many fields (music, ethnology, religion) will be aware of how much information is tucked in; the general reader, for whom the work is written, will simply be enthralled."

Huggins's 1980 *Slave and Citizen: The Life of Frederick Douglass* appeared as a volume in historian Oscar Handlin's "Library of American Biography" series. A number of reviewers have praised Huggins's portrayal of Douglass the public figure. Marc Pachter writes in the *Washington Post Book World* that Huggins's "brief, elegant study of the great abolitionist stops us in the middle of our lazy genuflection. We encounter a life whose central drama is not an escape from slavery but patronage, whose heroism comes from struggle not only with oppression but success." A reviewer for the *Atlantic* comments on the book's objectivity: "Nathan Huggins's succinct and thoughtful biography . . . does not gloss over Douglass's faults—the arrogance, the inflexibility, the occasional personal insensitivity," adding that Huggins "emphasizes as well the courage and foresight that characterized so much of Douglass's life." Similarly, Robert Kirsch in the *Los Angeles Times* praises the accurate portrayal of Douglass: "Huggins has not mythologized Douglass. There is a credible and real Douglass, trying to mediate between the demands of his ideology and the practice of its preachments."

BIOGRAPHICAL/CRITICAL SOURCES:

PERIODICALS

Atlantic, July, 1980.
Los Angeles Times, March 17, 1980.
Los Angeles Times Book Review, January 25, 1987.
Nation, November 15, 1971.
New Republic, November 5, 1977, March 15, 1980.
New Yorker, March 20, 1978.
New York Review of Books, January 26, 1978.
New York Times Book Review, January 2, 1972, December 11, 1977.
Times Literary Supplement, June 9, 1972.
Washington Post, February 22, 1987.
Washington Post Book World, December 18, 1977, March 30, 1980.
Yale Review, summer, 1981.

*   *   *

HUGHES, (James) Langston   1902-1967

PERSONAL: Born February 1, 1902, in Joplin, Mo.; died May 22, 1967 of congestive heart failure in New York, N.Y.; son of James Nathaniel (a businessman, lawyer, and rancher) and Carrie Mercer (a teacher; maiden name, Langston) Hughes.

Education: Attended Columbia University, 1921-22; Lincoln University, A.B., 1929.

ADDRESSES: Home—20 East 127th St., New York, N.Y. *Agent*—Harold Ober Associates, Inc., 40 East 49th St., New York, N.Y. 10017.

CAREER: Poet, novelist, short story writer, playwright, song lyricist, radio writer, translator, author of juvenile books, and lecturer. In early years worked as assistant cook, launderer, busboy, and at other odd jobs; worked as seaman on voyages to Africa and Europe. Lived at various times in Mexico, France, Italy, Spain, and the Soviet Union. Madrid correspondent for *Baltimore Afro-American* 1937; visiting professor in creative writing, Atlanta University, 1947; poet-in-residence, Laboratory School, University of Chicago, 1949.

MEMBER: Authors Guild, Dramatists Guild, American Society of Composers, Authors, and Publishers, P.E.N., National Institute of Arts and Letters, Omega Psi Phi.

AWARDS, HONORS: Opportunity magazine literary contest, first prize in poetry, 1925; Witter Bynner undergraduate poetry prize contests, first prize, 1926; *Palms* magazine Intercollegiate Poetry Award, 1927; Harmon Gold Medal for Literature, 1931; Guggenheim fellowship for creative work, 1935; Rosenwald fellowship, 1941; Litt.D., Lincoln University, 1943; American Academy of Arts and Letters grant, 1947; Anisfield-Wolf Award for best book on racial relations, 1954; Spingarn Medal, National Association for the Advancement of Colored People, 1960.

WRITINGS:

POETRY; PUBLISHED BY KNOPF, EXCEPT AS INDICATED

The Weary Blues, 1926.
Fine Clothes to the Jew, 1927.
The Negro Mother and Other Dramatic Recitations, Golden Stair Press, 1931.
Dear Lovely Death, Troutbeck Press, 1931.
The Dream Keeper and Other Poems, 1932.
Scottsboro Limited: Four Poems and a Play, Golden Stair Press, 1932.
A New Song, International Workers Order, 1938.
(With Robert Glenn) *Shakespeare in Harlem*, 1942.
Jim Crow's Last Stand, Negro Publication Society of America, 1943.
Freedom's Plow, Musette Publishers, 1943.
Lament for Dark Peoples and Other Poems, Holland, 1944.
Fields of Wonder, 1947.
One-Way Ticket, 1949.
Montage of a Dream Deferred, Holt, 1951.
Ask Your Mama: 12 Moods for Jazz, 1961.
The Panther and the Lash: Poems of Our Times, 1967.

NOVELS

Not Without Laughter, Knopf, 1930, reprinted, Macmillan, 1986.
Tambourines to Glory, John Day, 1958, reprinted, Hill & Wang, 1970.

SHORT STORIES

The Ways of White Folks, Knopf, 1934, reprinted, Random House, 1971.
Simple Speaks His Mind, Simon & Schuster, 1950.
Laughing to Keep from Crying, Holt, 1952.
Simple Takes a Wife, Simon & Schuster, 1953.
Simple Stakes a Claim, Rinehart, 1957.

Something in Common and Other Stories, Hill & Wang, 1963.

Simple's Uncle Sam, Hill & Wang, 1965.

AUTOBIOGRAPHY

The Big Sea: An Autobiography, Knopf, 1940, reprinted, Thunder's Mouth, 1986.

I Wonder as I Wander: An Autobiographical Journey, Rinehart, 1956, reprinted, Thunder's Mouth, 1986.

NONFICTION

A Negro Looks at Soviet Central Asia, Co-operative Publishing Society of Foreign Workers in the U.S.S.R., 1934.

(With Roy De Carava) *The Sweet Flypaper of Life,* Simon & Schuster, 1955, reprinted, Howard University Press, 1985.

(With Milton Meltzer) *A Pictorial History of the Negro in America,* Crown, 1956, 4th edition published as *A Pictorial History of Blackamericans,* 1973.

Fight for Freedom: The Story of the NAACP, Norton, 1962.

(With Meltzer) *Black Magic: A Pictorial History of the Negro in American Entertainment,* Prentice-Hall, 1967.

Black Misery, Paul S. Erickson, 1969.

JUVENILE

(With Arna Bontemps) *Popo and Fifina: Children of Haiti,* Macmillan, 1932.

The First Book of Negroes, F. Watts, 1952.

The First Book of Rhythms, F. Watts, 1954.

Famous American Negroes, Dodd, 1954.

Famous Negro Music Makers, Dodd, 1955.

The First Book of Jazz, F. Watts, 1955, revised edition, 1976.

The First Book of the West Indies, F. Watts, 1956 (published in England as *The First Book of the Caribbean,* E. Ward, 1965).

Famous Negro Heroes of America, Dodd, 1958.

The First Book of Africa, F. Watts, 1960, revised edition, 1964.

EDITOR

Four Lincoln University Poets, Lincoln University, 1930.

(With Bontemps) *The Poetry of the Negro, 1746-1949,* Doubleday, 1949, revised edition published as *The Poetry of the Negro, 1746-1970,* 1970.

(With Waring Cuney and Bruce M. Wright) *Lincoln University Poets,* Fine Editions, 1954.

(With Bontemps) *The Book of Negro Folklore,* Dodd, 1958, reprinted, 1983.

An African Treasury: Articles, Essays, Stories, Poems by Black Africans, Crown, 1960.

Poems from Black Africa, Indiana University Press, 1963.

New Negro Poets: U.S., foreword by Gwendolyn Brooks, Indiana University Press, 1964.

The Book of Negro Humor, Dodd, 1966.

The Best Short Stories by Negro Writers: An Anthology from 1899 to the Present, Little, Brown, 1967.

TRANSLATOR

(With Mercer Cook) Jacques Roumain, *Masters of Dew,* Reynal & Hitchcock, 1947, second edition, Liberty Book Club, 1957.

(With Frederic Carruthers) Nicolas Guillen, *Cuba Libre,* Ward Ritchie, 1948.

Selected Poems of Gabriela Mistral, Indiana University Press, 1957.

OMNIBUS VOLUMES

Selected Poems, Knopf, 1959, reprinted, Vintage Books, 1974.

The Best of Simple, Hill & Wang, 1961.

Five Plays by Langston Hughes, edited by Webster Smalley, Indiana University Press, 1963.

The Langston Hughes Reader, Braziller, 1968.

Don't You Turn Back (poems), edited by Lee Bennett Hopkins, Knopf, 1969.

Good Morning Revolution: The Uncollected Social Protest Writing of Langston Hughes, edited by Faith Berry, Lawrence Hill, 1973.

OTHER

(With Bontemps) *Arna Bontemps-Langston Hughes Letters: 1925-1967,* edited by Charles H. Nichols, Dodd, 1980.

Author of numerous plays (most have been produced), including "Little Ham," 1935, "Mulatto," 1935, "Emperor of Haiti," 1936, "Troubled Island," 1936, "When the Jack Hollers," 1936, "Front Porch," 1937, "Joy to My Soul," 1937, "Soul Gone Home," 1937, "Little Eva's End," 1938, "Limitations of Life," 1938, "The Em-Fuehrer Jones," 1938, "Don't You Want to Be Free," 1938, "The Organizer," 1939, "The Sun Do Move," 1942, "For This We Fight," 1943, "The Barrier," 1950, "The Glory Round His Head," 1953, "Simply Heavenly," 1957, "Esther," 1957, "The Ballad of the Brown King," 1960, "Black Nativity," 1961, "Gospel Glow," 1962, "Jericho-Jim Crow," 1963, "Tambourines to Glory," 1963, "The Prodigal Son," 1965, "Soul Yesterday and Today," "Angelo Herndon Jones," "Mother and Child," "Trouble with the Angels," and "Outshines the Sun."

Also author of screenplay, "Way Down South," 1942. Author of libretto for operas, "The Barrier," 1950, and "Troubled Island." Lyricist for "Just Around the Corner," and for Kurt Weill's "Street Scene," 1948. Columnist for *Chicago Defender* and *New York Post.* Poetry, short stories, criticism, and plays have been included in numerous anthologies. Contributor to periodicals, including *Nation, African Forum, Black Drama, Players Magazine, Negro Digest, Black World, Freedomways, Harlem Quarterly, Phylon, Challenge, Negro Quarterly,* and *Negro Story.*

SIDELIGHTS: Langston Hughes was first recognized as an important literary figure during the 1920s, a period known as the "Harlem Renaissance" because of the number of emerging black writers. Du Bose Heyward wrote in the *New York Herald Tribune* in 1926: "Langston Hughes, although only twenty-four years old, is already conspicuous in the group of Negro intellectuals who are dignifying Harlem with a genuine art life. . . . It is, however, as an individual poet, not as a member of a new and interesting literary group, or as a spokesman for a race that Langston Hughes must stand or fall. . . . Always intensely subjective, passionate, keenly sensitive to beauty and possessed of an unfaltering musical sense, Langston Hughes has given us a 'first book' that marks the opening of a career well worth watching."

Despite Heyward's statement, much of Hughes' early work was roundly criticized by many black intellectuals for portraying what they thought to be an unattractive view of black life. In his autobiographical *The Big Sea,* Hughes commented: "*Fine Clothes to the Jew* was well received by the literary magazines and the white press, but the Negro critics did not like it at all. The Pittsburgh *Courier* ran a big headline across the top of the page, *LANGSTON HUGHES' BOOK OF POEMS TRASH.* The headline in the New York *Amsterdam News* was *LANGSTON HUGHES—THE SEWER DWELLER.* The Chicago *Whip* characterized me as 'the poet low-rate of Harlem.' Others called the book a disgrace to the race, a return to the dialect tradition, and a parading of all our racial defects before the public.... The Negro critics and many of the intellectuals were very sensitive about their race in books. (And still are.) In anything that white people were likely to read, they wanted to put their best foot forward, their politely polished and cultural foot—and only that foot.''

An example of the type of criticism of which Hughes was writing is Estace Gay's comments on *Fine Clothes to the Jew*. ''It does not matter to me whether every poem in the book is true to life,'' Gay wrote. ''Why should it be paraded before the American public by a Negro author as being typical or representative of the Negro? Bad enough to have white authors holding up our imperfections to public gaze. Our aim ought to be [to] present to the general public, already mis-informed both by well meaning and malicious writers, our higher aims and aspirations, and our better selves.''

Commenting on reviewers like Gay, Hughes wrote: ''I sympathized deeply with those critics and those intellectuals, and I saw clearly the need for some of the kinds of books they wanted. But I did not see how they could expect every Negro author to write such books. Certainly, I personally knew very few people anywhere who were wholly beautiful and wholly good. Besides I felt that the masses of our people had as much in their lives to put into books as did those more fortunate ones who had been born with some means and the ability to work up to a master's degree at a Northern college. Anyway, I didn't know the upper class Negroes well enough to write much about them. I knew only the people I had grown up with, and they weren't people whose shoes were always shined, who had been to Harvard, or who had heard of Bach. But they seemed to me good people, too.''

Hoyt W. Fuller commented that Hughes ''chose to identify with plain black people—not because it required less effort and sophistication, but precisely because he saw more truth and profound significance in doing so. Perhaps in this he was inversely influenced by his father—who, frustrated by being the object of scorn in his native land, rejected his own people. Perhaps the poet's reaction to his father's flight from the American racial reality drove him to embrace it with extra fervor.'' (Langston Hughes' parents separated shortly after his birth and his father moved to Mexico. The elder Hughes came to feel a deep dislike and revulsion for other American blacks.)

In Hughes' own words, his poetry is about ''workers, roustabouts, and singers, and job hunters on Lenox Avenue in New York, or Seventh Street in Washington or South State in Chicago—people up today and down tomorrow, working this week and fired the next, beaten and baffled, but determined not to be wholly beaten, buying furniture on the installment plan, filling the house with roomers to help pay the rent, hoping to get a new suit for Easter—and pawning that suit before the Fourth of July.'' In fact, the title *Fine Clothes to the Jew*, which was misunderstood and disliked by many people, was derived from the Harlemites Hughes saw pawning their own clothing; most of the pawn shops and other stores in Harlem at that time were owned by Jewish people.

Lindsay Patterson, a novelist who served as Hughes' assistant, believed that Hughes was ''critically, the most abused poet in America.... Serious white critics ignored him, less serious ones compared his poetry to Cassius Clay doggerel, and most black critics only grudgingly admired him. Some, like James Baldwin, were downright malicious about his poetic achievement. But long after Baldwin and the rest of us are gone, I suspect Hughes' poetry will be blatantly around growing in stature until it is recognized for its genius. Hughes' tragedy was double-edged: he was unashamedly black at a time when blackness was demode, and he didn't go much beyond one of his earliest themes, black *is* beautiful. He had the wit and intelligence to explore the black human condition in a variety of depths, but his tastes and selectivity were not always accurate, and pressures to survive as a black writer in a white society (and it was a miracle that he did for so long) extracted an enormous creative toll. Nevertheless, Hughes, more than any other black poet or writer, recorded faithfully the nuances of black life and its frustrations.''

Although Hughes had trouble with both black and white critics, he was the first black American to earn his living solely from his writing and public lectures. Part of the reason he was able to do this was the phenomenal acceptance and love he received from average black people. A reviewer for *Black World* noted in 1970: ''Those whose prerogative it is to determine the rank of writers have never rated him highly, but if the weight of public response is any gauge then Langston Hughes stands at the apex of literary relevance among Black people. The poet occupies such a position in the memory of his people precisely because he recognized that 'we possess within ourselves a great reservoir of physical and spiritual strength,' and because he used his artistry to reflect this back to the people. He used his poetry and prose to illustrate that 'there is no lack within the Negro people of beauty, strength and power,' and he chose to do so on their own level, on their own terms.''

Hughes brought a varied and colorful background to his writing. Before he was twelve years old he had lived in six different American cities. When his first book was published, he had already been a truck farmer, cook, waiter, college graduate, sailor, and doorman at a nightclub in Paris, and had visited Mexico, West Africa, the Azores, the Canary Islands, Holland, France, and Italy. As David Littlejohn observed in his *Black on White: A Critical Survey of Writing by American Negroes:* ''On the whole, Hughes' creative life [was] as full, as varied, and as original as Picasso's, a joyful, honest monument of a career. There [was] no noticeable sham in it, no pretension, no self-deceit; but a great, great deal of delight and smiling irresistible wit. If he seems for the moment upstaged by angrier men, by more complex artists, if 'different views engage' us, necessarily, at this trying stage of the race war, he may well outlive them all, and still be there when it's over.... Hughes' [greatness] seems to derive from his anonymous unity with his people. He *seems* to speak for millions, which is a tricky thing to do.''

Hughes reached many people through his popular fictional character, Jesse B. Semple (shortened to Simple). Simple is a poor man who lives in Harlem, a kind of comic no-good, a stereotype Hughes turned to advantage. He tells his stories to Boyd, the foil in the stories who is a writer much like Hughes, in return for a drink. His tales of his troubles with work, women, money, and life in general often reveal, through their very simplicity, the problems of being a poor black man in a racist society. ''White folks,'' Simple once commented, ''is the cause of a lot of inconvenience in my life.''

Donald C. Dickinson wrote in his *Bio-Bibliography of Langston Hughes* that the ''charm of Simple lies in his uninhibited pursuit of those two universal goals, understanding and security. As with most other humans, he usually fails to achieve either of these goals and sometimes once achieved they disappoint him. . . . Simple has a tough resilience, however, that won't allow him to brood over a failure very long. . . . Simple is a well-developed character, both believable and lovable. The situations he meets and discusses are so true to life everyone may enter the fun. This does not mean that Simple is in any way dull. He injects the ordinary with his own special insights. . . . Simple is a natural, unsophisticated man who never abandons his hope in tomorrow.''

A reviewer for *Black World* commented on the popularity of Simple: ''The people responded. Simple lived in a world they knew, suffered their pangs, experienced their joys, reasoned in their way, talked their talk, dreamed their dreams, laughed their laughs, voiced their fears—and all the while underneath, he affirmed the wisdom which anchored at the base of their lives. It was not that ideas and events and places and people beyond the limits of Harlem—all of the Harlems—did not concern him; these things, indeed, were a part of his consciousness; but Simple's rock-solid commonsense enabled him to deal with them with balance and intelligence. . . . Simple knows *who* he is and *what* he is, and he knows that the status of expatriate offers no solution, no balm. The struggle is here, and it can only be won here, and no constructive end is served through fantasies and illusions and false efforts at disguising a basic sense of inadequacy. Simple also knows that the strength, the tenacity, the commitment which are necessary to win the struggle also exist within the Black community.''

Hoyt W. Fuller believed that, like Simple, ''the key to Langston Hughes . . . was the poet's deceptive and *profound* simplicity. Profound because it was both willed and ineffable, because some intuitive sense even at the beginning of his adulthood taught him that humanity was of the essence and that it existed undiminished in all shapes, sizes, colors and conditions. Violations of that humanity offended his unshakable conviction that mankind is possessed of the divinity of God.''

It was Hughes' belief in humanity and his hope for a world in which people could sanely and with understanding live together that led to his decline in popularity in the racially turbulent latter years of his life. Unlike younger and more militant writers, Hughes never lost his conviction that ''*most people are generally good*, in every race and in every country where I have been.'' Reviewing *The Panther and the Lash: Poems of Our Times* in *Poetry*, Laurence Lieberman recognized that Hughes' ''sensibility [had] kept pace with the times,'' but he critized his lack of a personal political stance. ''Regrettably, in different poems, he is fatally prone to sympathize with starkly antithetical politics of race,'' Lieberman commented. ''A reader can appreciate his catholicity, his tolerance of all the rival—and mutually hostile—views of his outspoken compatriots, from Martin Luther King to Stokely Carmichael, but we are tempted to ask, what are Hughes' politics? And if he has none, why not? The age demands intellectual commitment from its spokesmen. A poetry whose chief claim on our attention is moral, rather than aesthetic, must take sides politically.''

Despite some recent criticism, Langston Hughes' position in the American literary scene seems to be secure. David Littlejohn wrote that Hughes is ''the one sure Negro classic, more certain of permanence than even Baldwin or Ellison or Wright. . . . His voice is as sure, his manner as original, his position as secure as, say Edwin Arlington Robinson's or Robinson Jeffers'. . . . By molding his verse always on the sounds of Negro talk, the rhythms of Negro music, by retaining his own keen honesty and directness, his poetic sense and ironic intelligence, he maintained through four decades a readable newness distinctly his own.''

Hughes' poems have been translated into German, French, Spanish, Russian, Yiddish, and Czech; many of them have been set to music. Donald B. Gibson noted in the introduction to *Modern Black Poets: A Collection of Critical Essays* that Hughes ''has perhaps the greatest reputation (worldwide) that any black writer has ever had. Hughes differed from most of his predecessors among black poets, and (until recently) from those who followed him as well, in that he addressed his poetry to the people, specifically to black people. During the twenties when most American poets were turning inward, writing obscure and esoteric poetry to an ever decreasing audience of readers, Hughes was turning outward, using language and themes, attitudes and ideas familiar to anyone who had the ability simply to read. He has been, unlike most nonblack poets other than Walt Whitman, Vachel Lindsay, and Carl Sandburg, a poet of the people. . . . Until the time of his death, he spread his message humorously—though always seriously—to audiences throughout the country, having read his poetry to more people (possibly) than any other American poet.''

BIOGRAPHICAL/CRITICAL SOURCES:

BOOKS

Baker, Houston A., Jr., *Black Literature in America*, McGraw, 1971.

Bone, Robert A., *The Negro Novel in America*, Yale University Press, 1965.

Contemporary Literary Criticism, Gale, Volume I, 1973, Volume V, 1976, Volume X, 1979, Volume XXXV, 1985.

Davis, Arthur P. and Saunders Redding, editors, *Cavalcade*, Houghton, 1971.

Dekle, Bernard, *Profiles of Modern American Authors*, Charles E. Tuttle, 1969.

Dickinson, Donald C., *A Bio-Bibliography of Langston Hughes, 1902-1967*, Archon Books, 1967.

Dictionary of Literary Biography, Gale, Volume IV: *American Writers in Paris, 1920-1939*, 1980, Volume VII: *Twentieth-Century American Dramatists*, 1981, Volume XLVIII: *American Poets, 1880-1945, Second Series*, 1986, Volume LI: *Afro-American Writers from the Harlem Renaissance to 1940*, 1987.

Emanuel, James, *Langston Hughes*, Twayne, 1967.

Gibson, Donald B., editor, *Five Black Writers*, New York University Press, 1970.

Gibson, Donald B., editor and author of introduction, *Modern Black Poets: A Collection of Critical Essays*, Prentice-Hall, 1973.

Hart, W., editor, *American Writers' Congress*, International, 1935.

Hughes, Langston, *The Big Sea: An Autobiography*, Knopf, 1950.

Hughes, Langston, *I Wonder as I Wander: An Autobiographical Journey*, Rinehart, 1956.

Jackson, Blyden and Louis D. Rubin, Jr., *Black Poetry in America: Two Essays in Historical Interpretation*, Louisiana State University, 1974.

Jahn, Janheinz, *A Bibliography of Neo-African Literature from Africa, America and the Caribbean*, Praeger, 1965.

Littlejohn, David, *Black on White: A Critical Survey of Writing by American Negroes*, Viking, 1966.

Meltzer, Milton, *Langston Hughes: A Biography*, Crowell, 1968.

Myers, Elizabeth P., *Langston Hughes: Poet of His People*, Garrard, 1970.

O'Daniel, Thermon B., editor, *Langston Hughes: Black Genius, a Critical Evaluation*, Morrow, 1971.

Rollins, Charlamae H., *Black Troubador: Langston Hughes*, Rand McNally, 1970.

Something About the Author, Volume XXXIII, Gale, 1983.

PERIODICALS

American Mercury, January, 1959.
Black Scholar, June, 1971, July, 1976.
Black World, June, 1970, September, 1972, September, 1973.
Booklist, November 15, 1976.
CLA Journal, June, 1972.
Chicago Tribune Book World, April 13, 1980.
Crisis, August-September, 1960, June, 1967, February, 1969.
Ebony, October, 1946.
English Journal, March, 1977.
Life, February 4, 1966.
Nation, December 4, 1967.
Negro American Literature Forum, winter, 1971.
Negro Digest, September, 1967, November, 1967, April, 1969.
New Leader, April 10, 1967.
New Republic, January 14, 1974.
New Yorker, December 30, 1967.
New York Herald Tribune, August 1, 1926.
New York Herald Tribune Books, November 26, 1961.
New York Times, May 24, 1967, June 1, 1968, June 29, 1969, December 13, 1970.
New York Times Book Review, November 3, 1968.
Philadelphia Tribune, February 5, 1927.
Poetry, August, 1968.
San Francisco Chronicle, April 5, 1959.
Saturday Review, November 22, 1958, September 29, 1962.
Washington Post, November 13, 1978.
Washington Post Book World, February 2, 1969, December 8, 1985.

*   *   *

HULL, Gloria T(heresa Thompson)   1944-

PERSONAL: Born December 6, 1944, in Shreveport, La.; daughter of Robert T. (a laborer) and Jimmie (a domestic worker; maiden name, Williams) Thompson; married Prentice R. Hull, June 12, 1966 (divorced, 1983); children: Adrian Prentice. *Education:* Southern University, B.A. (summa cum laude), 1966; graduate study at University of Illinois, 1966; Purdue University, M.A., 1968, Ph.D., 1972.

ADDRESSES: Home—1111 West 9th St., Wilmington, Del. 19806. *Office*—Department of English, University of Delaware, Newark, Del. 19716.

CAREER: University of Delaware, Newark, instructor, 1971, assistant professor, 1972-77, associate professor, 1977-86, professor of English, 1986—. Visiting scholar, Stanford University, 1987-88. Has given poetry readings, conducted poetry workshops, and guest lectured at various institutions nationwide, including Lincoln University, 1974, Wilmington College, 1977, Yale University, 1977, and University of Alabama, 1979.

MEMBER: College Language Association, Modern Language Association of America, National Association for the Advancement of Colored People, Alpha Kappa Alpha.

AWARDS, HONORS: Outstanding Service Award from University of Delaware Black Student Union, 1975-76; research grant from University of Delaware, summer, 1976; stipend from National Endowment for the Humanities, summer, 1979; Rockefeller Foundation fellowship, 1979-80; Outstanding Contribution and Service to University of Delaware Minority Students Award, 1980-81; National Institute of Women of Color Award, 1982, for *All the Women Are White, All the Blacks Are Men, but Some of Us Are Brave: Black Women's Studies;* Mellon National fellowship from Wellesley College, 1983; Fulbright fellowship to University of West Indies, Jamaica, 1984-86; Ford Foundation fellowship, 1987-88.

WRITINGS:

(Editor with Patricia Bell Scott and Barbara Smith, and contributor) *All the Women Are White, All the Blacks Are Men, but Some of Us Are Brave: Black Women's Studies,* Feminist Press, 1982.

(Editor and author of introduction) *Give Us Each Day: The Diary of Alice Dunbar-Nelson,* Norton, 1984.

Color, Sex, and Poetry: Three Women Writers of the Harlem Renaissance, Indiana University Press, 1987.

(Editor and author of introduction) *The Works of Alice Dunbar-Nelson),* three volumes, Oxford University Press, 1988.

CONTRIBUTOR

Alex Preminger, editor, *The Princeton Encyclopedia of Poetry and Poetics,* Princeton University Press, 1974.

In a Walled Garden: First State Writers Anthology, Lenape, 1974.

Lucille Clifton, Amma Khalil, and Audre Lorde, editors, *Hoo-Doo,* Volume V, Energy Blacksouth Press, 1976.

Roseann Bell, Parker, and Sheftall, editors, *Sturdy Black Bridges: Visions of Black Women in Literature,* Doubleday, 1979.

Sandra Gilbert and Susan Gubar, editors, *Shakespeare's Sisters: Feminist Essays on Women Poets,* Indiana University Press, 1979.

Deborah Rosenfelt and Leonore Hoffmann, editors, *Teaching Women's Literature from a Regional Perspective,* Modern Language Association of America, 1982.

Smith, editor, *Home Girls: A Black Feminist Anthology,* Kitchen Table Press, 1983.

Crider, editor, *African American Writing in the United States,* Institute for the Preservation and Study of African American Writing, 1983.

Charlotte Bunch and Sandra Pollack, editors, *Learning Our Way: Essays on Feminist Education,* Crossing Press, 1984.

Carol Ascher, Louise DeSalvo, and Sara Ruddick, editors, *Between Women: Biographers, Novelists, Critics, Teachers and Artists Write about Their Work on Women,* Beacon Press, 1984.

Marjorie Pryse and Hortense Spillers, editors, *Conjuring: Black Women, Literary Tradition, and Fiction,* Indiana University Press, 1985.

OTHER

''A Day with Alice Dunbar-Nelson'' (videotape), Instructional Resource Center, University of Delaware, 1976.

Contributor of articles, reviews, and poetry to periodicals, including *Black American Literature Forum, Radical Teacher, Ariel: A Review of International English Literature, Obsidian: Black Literature in Review, Feminist Studies, Black Scholar, Ms.,* and *Mississippi Quarterly.* Advisory editor, *Black Amer-*

ican Literature Forum, 1978-86; editorial consultant, *Feminist Studies,* 1981—.

WORK IN PROGRESS: A book of essays on black women writing.

SIDELIGHTS: In her work entitled *All the Women Are White, All the Blacks Are Men, but Some of Us Are Brave: Black Women's Studies,* Gloria T. Hull wrote: "Everything that I have been saying . . . illustrates the Black feminist critical approach which I used in researching [Alice] Dunbar-Nelson. . . .

"It goes without saying that I approached her as an important writer and her work as genuine literature. Probably as an (over?)reaction to the condescending, witty but empty, British urbanity of tone which is the hallmark of traditional white male literary scholarship (and which I dislike intensely), I usually discuss Dunbar-Nelson with level high seriousness—and always with caring. Related to this are my slowly-evolving attempts at being so far unfettered by conventional style as to write creatively, even poetically, if that is the way the feeling flows. Here, the question of audience is key. Having painfully developed these convictions and a modicum of courage to buttress them, I now include, visualize everybody (my department chair, the promotion and tenure committee, my mother and brother, my Black feminist sisters, the chair of Afro-American Studies, lovers, colleagues, friends) for each organic article, rather than write sneaky, schizophrenic essays from under two or three different hats.''

Hull commented: "*But Some of Us Are Brave* is the first published interdisciplinary work on Afro-American women compiled/written from a conscious and avowed anti-racist, anti-sexist perspective. It was sorely needed because the black studies and women's studies movements were not adequately incorporating the untapped wealth of material on the lives and experiences of black women—despite the fact that an audience of students, teachers, and general readers was eager for this information.''

Hull later added: "I am still urged by my need to heal, to communicate through and around deceptive splits (within myself, in critical language-practice, between 'politics' and writing, etc.) in order to produce ever more transformative work which will change consciousness and reverberate in manifest ways.''

BIOGRAPHICAL/CRITICAL SOURCES:

PERIODICALS

Compass, April 2, 1981.
Evening Journal (Wilmington, Delaware), June 6, 1977.
Ms., January, 1982.
New York Times Book Review, April 14, 1985.
off our backs: a women's newsjournal, May, 1985.
University of Delaware Review, October 8, 1976.
Washington Post, March 15, 1982.

*   *   *

HUNTER, Kristin (Eggleston) 1931-

PERSONAL: Born September 12, 1931, in Philadelphia, Pa.; daughter of George Lorenzo (a principal and U.S. Army colonel) and Mabel (a pharmacist and teacher; maiden name, Manigault) Eggleston; married John I. Lattany, June 22, 1968. *Education:* University of Pennsylvania, B.S. in Ed., 1951.

ADDRESSES: Office—Department of English, University of Pennsylvania, Philadelphia, Pa, 19104.

CAREER: Writer. Columnist and feature writer for Philadelphia, Pa., edition of *Pittsburgh Courier,* 1946-52; copywriter, Lavenson Bureau of Advertising, Philadelphia, 1952-59, and Werman & Schorr, Inc., Philadelphia, 1962-63; research assistant, School of Social Work, University of Pennsylvania, 1961-62; information officer, City of Philadelphia, 1963-64, 1965-66; Temple University, Philadelphia, director of comprehensive health services, 1971-72; University of Pennsylvania, Philadelphia, lecturer in English, 1972-79, adjunct professor of English, 1981-83, senior lecturer in English, 1983—. Writer-in-residence, Emory University, 1979.

MEMBER: Authors League of America, Authors Guild, Modern Language Association, PEN, National Council of Teachers of English, University of Pennsylvania Alumnae Association (director, 1970-73).

AWARDS, HONORS: Fund for the Republic Prize, 1955, for television documentary, "Minority of One"; John Hay Whitney fellowship, 1959-60; Philadelphia Athenaeum Award, 1964; National Council on Interracial Books for Children award, 1968, for *The Soul Brothers and Sister Lou;* Sigma Delta Chi reporting award, 1968; Mass Media Brotherhood Award from National Conference of Christians and Jews, 1969, for *The Soul Brothers and Sister Lou;* Lewis Carroll Shelf Award, 1971, for *The Soul Brothers and Sister Lou;* Book World Festival Award, 1973; Christopher Award, 1974, for *Guests in the Promised Land;* Drexel Children's Literature Citation, 1981; New Jersey State Council on the Arts prose fellowship, 1981-82; Pennsylvania State Council on the Arts literature fellowship, 1983-84.

WRITINGS:

"Minority of One" (television play), Columbia Broadcasting System, 1955.
God Bless the Child, Scribner, 1964, Howard University Press, 1986.
"The Double Edge (play)," first produced in Philadelphia, 1965.
The Landlord, Scribner, 1966.
(Contributor) Langston Hughes, editor, *The Best Short Stories by Negro Writers,* Little, Brown, 1967.
"The Landlord," (screenplay), United Artists, 1970.
The Survivors, Scribner, 1975.
The Lakestown Rebellion, Scribner, 1978.

YOUNG ADULT BOOKS

The Soul Brothers and Sister Lou, Scribner, 1968.
The Pool Table War, Houghton, 1972.
Uncle Daniel and the Raccoon, Houghton, 1972.
Guests in the Promised Land (story collection), 1973.
Lou in the Limelight, Scribner, 1981.

JUVENILE

Boss Cat, Avon, 1971.

OTHER

Contributor to *Nation, Essence, Black World, Good Housekeeping,* and other publications.

SIDELIGHTS: Noted for their depictions of black ghetto life, Kristin Hunter's writings have won critical praise for their realism and sense of optimism. Paul Heins, writing in *Horn Book,* calls the short stories in *Guests in the Promised Land* "superb for their exploration of black experience as well as for their art.''

God Bless the Child, Hunter's first novel, introduces the themes explored in Hunter's later works, telling the story of a young black girl who works desperately to rise from poverty, but eventually finds herself working in the illegal gambling underworld. Hunter's evocation of Harlem life, J. G. Murray writes in *America,* is the novel's strongest feature. "The sights, sounds, smells, and struggles for survival in Harlem [are] real and moving, the writing convincing and the narrative vigorous," Murray states. In her review of the book for the *Christian Science Monitor,* Henrietta Buckmaster echoes this opinion. "Hunter," she writes, "does not miss a sight or a sound of humor, pain, or vulgarity. Her eye is sharp, her ear true." Although she believes the novel "too long" and "too frantic," Buckmaster concludes that "the explosive vitality does not obscure its humanity nor lessen Miss Hunter's cool and relentless irony."

In her next novel, *The Landlord,* Hunter again deals with the black poor. Told in an amusing manner, the novel relates the consequences of a wealthy young man buying a ghetto apartment building so he can prove himself to his father. It is "an elaborate spoof," writes Abraham Chapman in *Saturday Review,* "that somehow manages to combine touches of the absurd and intimations of the surreal, strokes of caricature, slapstick, and the grotesque with an inherent, down-to-earth sanity and realism." Although she finds several items which "may occasion some tightening of Negro lips," Gwendolyn Brooks writes in *Book Week* that "the characters [in *The Landlord*] are not lovable or loathable.... They are lookable—due to the inventiveness and earnestly exercised power of Miss Hunter's talent."

Perhaps Hunter's best-known novel is *The Soul Brothers and Sister Lou,* a book about a black girl named Louretta ("Sister Lou") who joins a local street gang. When one of the gang members is killed by a white policeman, who mistakes an epileptic seizure for an attempted assault, Lou reacts with racial hatred. But when other gang members urge a violent revenge, it is Lou who stops them. "Hunter doesn't mince words: whites expecting gratitude, older Negroes awaiting the next world, militants welcoming a martyr—all get a going over," writes the *Kirkus Reviews* critic. It is, according to Susan O'Neal in *Library Journal,* "one of the few juvenile books attempting to present the culture of the ghetto rather than merely its economic impoverishment." Because of its successful recreation of black life, Nedra Stimpfle of *English Journal* recommends *The Soul Brothers and Sister Lou* "for the teacher who is attempting to introduce aspects of black culture to students who have limited racial experiences." Some critics find the novel's ending—Lou and three of the gang members form their own singing group and are immediately successful—to be highly unlikely and the book's major flaw. To Zena Sutherland of *Saturday Review,* it is "a too-pat ending for a book that is honest, convincing, and incisive." John Neufield writes in the *New York Times Book Review:* "Hunter writes too well—of revivalism, of revolt, of despairing blacks hanging onto the church, or a crowbar, with equal determination—to have settled for a false solution, when honest ones exist."

Speaking in *Publishers Weekly* about the novel, Hunter explains that in *The Soul Brothers and Sister Lou,* "I have tried to show some of the positive values existing in the so-called ghetto—the closeness and warmth of family life, the willingness to extend help to strangers in trouble, . . . the natural acceptance of life's problems and joys—and there is a great deal of joy in the ghetto—and the strong tradition of religious

faith. All of these attitudes have combined to create the quality called 'soul,' which is the central theme of the book."

In *Lou in the Limelight,* Hunter continues the story of Lou and her singing group, showing the pitfalls that can accompany sudden success. The young band members succumb to several vices, including drugs and gambling, in what Marilyn Kaye in the *New York Times Book Review* calls an "ambitious indictment of the entertainment industry." With the help of Lou's Aunt Jerutha, the band members pay off their gambling debts and get back on their feet again, ready to begin a new tour. Despite a few problems, including characters who are sometimes "two-dimensional," Becky Johnson of the *Voice of Youth Advocates* finds *Lou in the Limelight* "a highly readable depiction of talented young performers and the difficulty of their rise from ghetto poverty."

Hunter offers another portrait of black people overcoming problems in *The Lakestown Rebellion.* When an interstate highway is scheduled to go through their town, tearing up their neighborhood, the black residents resist with a series of comical acts of sabotage. The uniting of the diverse community—everyone from prostitutes to ministers—forms the core of the story. "It is less a tale of black militancy," writes Gregory B. Witcher in the *Washington Post,* "than of courage and endurance—and of humor as well, as the rebellion develops imaginative and funny tactics to defend the town's proud history and remaining rural charm." Some of these tactics include spiking the drinks of the construction crew and filling in holes that have been dug. "This could have been just a series of whimsical skits," writes the *New Yorker* reviewer, "but Kristin Hunter adds several ugly accidents that darken and deepen the story and keep it from becoming sheer fantasy, and she endows her characters with a variety of voices, which all ring true." Witcher, too, sees something deeper in *The Lakestown Rebellion:* "Today, when Americans seem overly concerned with individual gratification, 'The Lakestown Rebellion' reminds us of the greater rewards that can be had when we work together."

BIOGRAPHICAL/CRITICAL SOURCES:

BOOKS

Children's Literature Review, Volume III, Gale, 1978.
Dictionary of Literary Biography, Volume 33: *Afro-American Fiction Writers after 1955,* Gale, 1984.
Tate, Claudia, *Black Women Writers at Work,* Crossroad Publishing, 1983.

PERIODICALS

America, September 12, 1964.
Black World, September, 1974.
Book Week, May 8, 1966.
Book World, November 3, 1968.
Christian Science Monitor, September 10, 1964.
Commonweal, November 22, 1968.
English Journal, March, 1977.
Horn Book Magazine, August, 1973.
Kirkus Reviews, July 15, 1968.
Library Journal, November 15, 1968.
New Yorker, July 10, 1978.
New York Times Book Review, April 24, 1966, January 26, 1969, February 21, 1982.
Philadelphia Inquirer, November 24, 1974.
Philadelphia Magazine, October, 1978.
Publishers Weekly, May 27, 1968.
Saturday Review, May 14, 1966, October 19, 1968.

School Library Journal, September, 1972.
Times Literary Supplement, June 12, 1987.
Top of the News, January, 1970.
Voice of Youth Advocates, February, 1982.
Washington Post, June 29, 1978.

* * *

HURSTON, Zora Neale   1891-1960

PERSONAL: Born January 7, 1891, in Eatonville, Fla.; died January 28, 1960, in Fort Pierce, Fla.; daughter of John (a preacher and carpenter) and Lucy (a seamstress; maiden name, Potts) Hurston; married Herbert Sheen, May 19, 1927 (divorced, 1931); married Albert Price III, June 27, 1939 (divorced). *Education:* Attended Howard University, 1923-24; Barnard College, B.A., 1928; graduate study at Columbia University.

ADDRESSES: Home—Fort Pierce, Fla.

CAREER: Writer and folklorist. Collected folklore in the South, 1927-31; Bethune-Cookman College, Daytona, Fla., instructor in drama, 1933-34; collected folklore in Jamaica, Haiti, and Bermuda, 1937-38; collected folklore in Florida for the Works Progress Administration, 1938-39; Paramount Studios, Hollywood, Calif., staff writer, 1941; collected folklore in Honduras, 1946-48; worked as a maid in Florida, 1950; freelance writer, 1950-56; Patrick Air Force Base, Fla., librarian, 1956-57; writer for *Fort Pierce Chronicle* and part-time teacher at Lincoln Park Academy, both in Fort Pierce, Fla., 1958-59. Was a librarian at the Library of Congress, Washington, D.C.; was professor of drama at North Carolina College for Negroes (now North Carolina Central University), Durham; was assistant to writer Fannie Hurst.

MEMBER: American Folklore Society, American Anthropological Society, American Ethnological Society, Zeta Phi Beta.

AWARDS, HONORS: Guggenheim fellowship, 1936, 1938; Litt.D. from Morgan College, 1939; Anisfield Award, 1943, for *Dust Tracks on a Road.*

WRITINGS:

(With Clinton Fletcher and Time Moore) "Fast and Furious" (musical play), published in *Best Plays of 1931-32,* edited by Burns Mantle and Garrison Sherwood, 1931.
Jonah's Gourd Vine (novel), with an introduction by Fanny Hurst, Lippincott, 1934, reprinted with a new introduction by Larry Neal, 1971.
Mules and Men (folklore), with an introduction by Franz Boas, Lippincott, 1935, reprinted, Indiana University Press, 1978.
Their Eyes Were Watching God (novel), Lippincott, 1937, reprinted, University of Illinois Press, 1978.
Tell My Horse (nonfiction), Lippincott, 1938, reprinted, Turtle Island Foundation, 1981, published as *Voodoo Gods: An Inquiry into Native Myths and Magic in Jamaica and Haiti,* Dent, 1939.
Moses, Man of the Mountain (novel), Lippincott, 1939, reprinted, University of Illinois Press, 1984.
Dust Tracks on a Road (autobiography), Lippincott, 1942, reprinted with an introduction by Neal, 1971.
(With Dorothy Waring) *Stephen Kelen-d'Oxylion Presents Polk County: A Comedy of Negro Life on a Sawmill Camp with Authentic Negro Music* (three acts), [New York], c. 1944.
Seraph on the Suwanee (novel), Scribner, 1948, reprinted, AMS Press, 1974.

I Love Myself When I Am Laughing. . . and Then Again When I Am Looking Mean and Impressive, edited by Alice Walker, Feminist Press, 1979.
The Sanctified Church, Turtle Island Foundation, 1983.
Spunk: The Selected Stories of Zora Neale Hurston, Turtle Island Foundation, 1985.
The Gilded Six-Bits, Redpath Press, 1986.

Also author of play with Langston Hughes, "Mule Bone: A Comedy of Negro Life in Three Acts," 1931; author of "The First One" (one-act play), published in *Ebony and Topaz,* edited by Johnson, and of "Great Day" (play). Work represented in anthologies, including *Black Writers in America,* edited by Barksdale and Kinnamon; *Story in America,* edited by E. W. Burnett and Martha Foley, Vanguard, 1934; *American Negro Short Stories,* edited by Clarke; *The Best Short Stories by Negro Writers,* edited by Hughes; *From the Roots,* edited by James; *Anthology of American Negro Literature,* edited by Watkins. Contributor of stories and articles to periodicals, including *American Mercury, Negro Digest, Journal of American Folklore, Saturday Evening Post,* and *Journal of Negro History.*

SIDELIGHTS: Although Hurston was closely associated with the Harlem Renaissance and has influenced such writers as Ralph Ellison, Toni Morrison, Gayl Jones, and Toni Cade Bambara, interest in her has only recently been revived after decades of neglect. Hurston's four novels and two books of folklore are important sources of black myth and legend. Through her writings, Robert Hemenway wrote in *The Harlem Renaissance Remembered,* Hurston "helped to remind the Renaissance—especially its more bourgeois members—of the richness in the racial heritage; she also added new dimensions to the interest in exotic primitivism that was one of the most ambiguous products of the age."

Hurston was born and raised in the first incorporated all-black town in America, and was advised by her mother to "jump at de sun." At the age of thirteen she was taken out of school to care for her brother's children. At sixteen, she joined a traveling theatrical troupe and worked as a maid for a white woman who arranged for her to attend high school in Baltimore. Hurston later studied anthropology at Barnard College and Columbia University with the anthropologist Franz Boas, which profoundly influenced her work. After graduation she returned to her hometown for anthropological study: The data she collected would be used both in her collections of folklore and her fictional works.

"I was glad when somebody told me: 'You may go and collect Negro folklore,'" Hurston related in the introduction to *Mules and Men.* "In a way it would not be a new experience for me. When I pitched headforemost into the world I landed in the crib of Negroism. From the earliest rocking of my cradle, I had known about the capers Br'er Rabbit is apt to cut and what the Squinch Owl says from the housetop. But it was fitting me like a tight chemise. I couldn't see it for wearing it. It was only when I was off in college, away from my native surroundings, that I could see myself like somebody else and stand off and look at my garment. Then I had to have the spyglass of anthropology to look through at that."

Hurston was an ambiguous and complex figure. She embodied seemingly antipodal traits, and Hemenway described her in his *Zora Neale Hurston: A Literary Biography* as being "flamboyant yet vulnerable, self-centered yet kind, a Republican conservative and an early black nationalist." Hurston was never bitter and never felt disadvantaged because she was black.

Henry Louis Gates, Jr., explained in the *New York Times Book Review:* "Part of Miss Hurston's received heritage—and perhaps the traditional notion that links the novel of manners in the Harlem Renaissance, the social realism of the 30s, and the cultural nationalism of the Black Arts movement—was the idea that racism had reduced black people to mere ciphers, to beings who react only to an omnipresent racial oppression, whose culture is 'deprived' where different, and whose psyches are in the main 'pathological'.... Miss Hurston thought this idea degrading, its propagation a trap. It was against this that she railed, at times brilliantly and systematically, at times vapidly and eclectically."

Older black writers criticized Hurston for the frequent crudeness and bawdiness of the tales she told. The younger generation criticized her propensity to gloss over the injustices her people were dealt. According to Judith Wilson, Hurston's greatest contribution was "to all black Americans' psychic health. The consistent note in her fieldwork and the bulk of her fiction is one of celebration of a black cultural heritage whose complexity and originality refutes all efforts to enforce either a myth of inferiority or a lie of assimilation." Wilson continued, "Zora Neale Hurston had figured out something that no other black author of her time seems to have known or appreciated so well—that our home-spun vernacular and street-corner cosmology is as valuable as the grammar and philosophy of white, Western culture."

Hurston herself wrote in 1928: "I am not tragically colored. There is no great sorrow dammed up in my soul, nor lurking behind my eyes. I do not mind at all. I do not belong to the sobbing school of Negrohood who hold that nature somehow has given them a lowdown dirty deal and whose feelings are all hurt about it.... No, I do not weep at the world—I am too busy sharpening my oyster knife."

Their Eyes Were Watching God is generally acknowledged to be Hurston's finest work of fiction. Still, it was controversial. Richard Wright found the book to be "counter-revolutionary" in a *New Masses* article. June Jordan praised the novel for its positiveness. She declared in a *Black World* review: "Unquestionably, *Their Eyes Were Watching God* is the prototypical Black novel of affirmation; it is the most successful, convincing, and exemplary novel of Blacklove that we have. Period. But the book gives us more: the story unrolls a fabulous, written-film of Blacklife freed from the constraints of oppression; here we may learn Black possibilities of ourselves if we could ever escape the hateful and alien context that has so deeply disturbed and mutilated our rightly effloresence—*as people.* Consequently, this novel centers itself on Blacklove—even as *Native Son* rivets itself upon white hatred."

"She was full of sidesplitting anecdotes, humorous tales, and tragicomic stories," Langston Hughes wrote of Hurston, "remembered out of her life in the South as a daughter of a traveling minister of God. She could make you laugh one minute and cry the next...."

"But Miss Hurston was clever, too—a student who didn't let college give her a broad 'a' and who had great scorn for all pretensions, academic or otherwise. That is why she was such a fine folklore collector, able to go among the people and never act as if she had been to school at all. Almost nobody else could stop the average Harlemite on Lenox Avenue and measure his head with a strange-looking, anthropological device and not get bawled out for the attempt, except Zora, who used to stop anyone whose head looked interesting, and measure it."

BIOGRAPHICAL/CRITICAL SOURCES:

BOOKS

Bone, Robert, *Down Home: A History of Afro-American Short Fiction from Its Beginnings to the End of the Harlem Renaissance*, Putnam, 1975.
Contemporary Literary Criticism, Gale, Volume 7, 1977, Volume 30, 1984.
Davis, Arthur P., *From the Dark Tower*, Howard University Press, 1974.
Dictionary of Literary Biography, Volume 51: *Afro-American Writers from the Harlem Renaissance to 1940*, Gale, 1987.
Hemenway, Robert E., *Zora Neale Hurston: A Literary Biography*, University of Illinois Press, 1977.
Hughes, Langston, *The Big Sea*, Knopf, 1940.
Hughes and Arna Bontemps, editors, *The Harlem Renaissance Remembered*, Dodd, 1972.
Hurston, Zora Neale, *Dust Tracks on a Road* (autobiography), Lippincott, 1942.
Turner, Darwin T., *In a Minor Chord: Three Afro-American Writers and Their Search for Identity*, Southern Illinois University Press, 1971.

PERIODICALS

Black World, August, 1972, August, 1974.
Ms., March, 1975, June, 1978.
Negro American Literature Forum, spring, 1972.
Negro Digest, February, 1962.
New Masses, October 5, 1937.
New Republic, February 11, 1978.
New York Times Book Review, February 19, 1978, April 21, 1985.
Village Voice, August 17, 1972.
Washington Post Book World, July 23, 1978.

OBITUARIES:

BOOKS

Britannica Book of the Year, 1961-1962, Volume 1, Encyclopaedia Britannica, 1961.

PERIODICALS

Current Biography, April, 1960.
Newsweek, February 15, 1960.
New York Times, February 5, 1960.
Publishers Weekly, February 15, 1960.
Time, February 15, 1960.
Wilson Library Bulletin, April, 1960.

J

JACKSON, George (Lester) 1941-1971

PERSONAL: Born September 23, 1941, in Chicago, Ill.; shot to death, August 21, 1971, in San Quentin, Calif.; son of Robert Lester and Georgia Jackson. *Education:* Completed the tenth grade at the Paso Robles School for Boys.

CAREER: Writer. Worked as laborer in Bakersfield, Calif., 1958; prisoner and political activist at Soledad and San Quentin prisons in California, 1961-71.

AWARDS, HONORS: Nonfiction book award from the Black Academy of Arts and Sciences, 1971, for *Soledad Brother: The Prison Letters of George Jackson.*

WRITINGS:

Soledad Brother: The Prison Letters of George Jackson, introduction by Jean Genet, Coward McCann, 1970.
Blood in My Eye (collected letters and essays), Random House, 1972.

SIDELIGHTS: As a high-ranking leader in the Black Panther Party, George Jackson was a well-known political radical when he died in San Quentin prison in August, 1971, a month before his thirtieth birthday. At the time, Jackson was serving a one-year-to-life prison sentence for robbing a gasoline station of seventy-one dollars eleven years earlier. With two convictions for robberies as a juvenile, Jackson faced the indefinite sentence subject to annual parole review, under the state of California's "three-time loser" rule for repeat felons. A number of times he failed to win parole for what prison officials said were disciplinary infractions, but Jackson claimed he was singled out for punishment because of his refusal to submit to the racist attitudes and degrading conditions of prison life and because of his growing political activism.

Introduced to Marxist literature by an older black prisoner when he arrived at the Soledad correctional facility at age nineteen, Jackson went on to intensively study classic works on political economy, revolutionary theory, and the American black experience. He emerged from this self-education program—much of it undertaken during the eight years he spent in solitary confinement—a declared communist and black power militant who posited the need for black-led urban guerrilla warfare to overthrow U.S. capitalism and imperialism. Jackson concluded that some of the best potential revolutionaries were to be found in prisons, and he led organizing efforts at the Soledad and San Quentin institutions for the radical Black Panther Party in the late 1960s.

In January, 1970, Soledad prison made headlines when a white guard, shooting from a watchtower, killed three black prisoners during an inmate scuffle in the exercise yard. Three days later a different white guard at the prison was found beaten to death. On the basis of inmate interrogations, authorities charged Jackson and two other black prisoners, Fleeta Drumgo and John Clutchette, with the crime. Counter-charging that the accused were the victims of a political frame-up, the Black Panthers organized a political and legal defense for the trio, who became known as the Soledad Brothers. If convicted of the guard's murder, Jackson faced a mandatory death sentence under California law as an inmate already serving a life sentence. Many well-known leftists, liberals, and civil libertarians rallied to the Soledad Brothers' defense, including Angela Davis, a black militant and, at the time, a University of California philosophy instructor.

When the case attracted national attention, Coward McCann published a collection of Jackson's prison letters from the years 1964 to 1970 under the title *Soledad Brother.* An autobiographical record and a revolutionary manifesto, the book evoked comparisons to the writings of black militants Malcolm X and Eldridge Cleaver and became a national best-seller. In letters to his family members, lawyers, political supporters, and others, Jackson wrote vividly of the brutalization of prison life, described his own personal and political development, and discussed revolutionary strategy in the Third World and the United States. A *Times Literary Supplement* reviewer judged the book most revealing "as the record of a human personality developing under conditions of extreme stress" and noted that Jackson communicates "with unusual force the tensions and contradictions as well as the strengths of Black radicalism."

George Jackson's letters had a powerful effect on his teenage brother Jonathan, who also became a political radical. On August 7, 1970, Jonathan Jackson led a desperate armed takeover of the Marin County, California, courthouse in an attempt to free three militant San Quentin convicts on trial there and to force the release of the Soledad Brothers. The escape bid got no farther than the building's parking lot, where Jonathan Jackson was stopped by police bullets. Presiding Judge Harold J. Haley, whom Jackson had taken as a hostage, also died, as did two of the San Quentin inmates. Angela Davis was later tried and acquitted on charges of supplying the younger Jackson with the weapons he used in the assault.

George Jackson quoted extensively from Jonathan's correspondence with him in his second book, *Blood in My Eye*. Completed just a week before the author met his own death, the manuscript became, in effect, his ''last will and testament,'' as David Lewis observed in the *New York Times Book Review*. The essays and letters chosen for *Blood in My Eye* are more abstractly political and less personal than those in *Soledad Brother*, and they include a theoretical discourse on fascism, Jackson's prediction of an imminent civil war, and a call to revolutionary action. In the book Jackson also prophesied his own murder in prison. Though *Blood in My Eye* ''suffers from both slapdash urgency and from Jackson's certainty that he is doomed,'' remarked Lewis, the book ''must be read—not so much for what it says, but for its tragic-heroic reflection of the apocalyptic state of mind of millions of black Americans whose hopelessness it will encourage.''

On August 21, 1971, Jackson was shot to death in San Quentin prison. The circumstances surrounding his violent end are still disputed. According to the official prison version, a prison guard escorting Jackson back to his maximum security cell after the convict had met with his lawyer, Stephen Bingham, noticed that Jackson was wearing an Afro-style wig. When he ordered Jackson to remove it, the convict pulled out an automatic pistol hidden beneath the wig and shot the guard. Jackson then entered his cellblock and released a number of his fellow inmates who went on a rampage, killing three guards and two other convicts. Several minutes later, Jackson burst out of the cellblock and began running for the prison wall in an apparent escape attempt, exchanging fire with tower guards who shot and killed him.

Jackson's family and political supports publicly disputed that explanation and suggested instead that prison authorities conspired to set up and murder Jackson to silence a potent prison critic and to prevent him from testifying at the upcoming Soledad Brothers trial. Introducing little direct evidence for the supposed plot, these critics pointed instead to inconsistencies and improbabilities in the state's account. They asserted that it would have been extremely difficult for Jackson to balance a large automatic pistol and two clips of ammunition on his head and then walk for many yards and up stairs before being detected, and suicidal for him to try to escape by rushing a twenty-five-foot wall in broad daylight. Adversaries of the prison's investigation also cited a revised autopsy report, which initially found that Jackson had been shot in the head, but was amended to read that the head wound had been caused by a bullet entering the back and deflected up Jackson's spine—a path that seemed unlikely if the convict was shot by tower guards above him. In June, 1986, almost fifteen years after Jackson's death, a Marin County, California, jury found former fugitive Stephen Bingham not guilty of smuggling the pistol to Jackson, but the trial yielded no further answers as to what really happened at San Quentin that bloody Saturday afternoon.

BIOGRAPHICAL/CRITICAL SOURCES:

PERIODICALS

Ebony, November, 1971.
New York Times, August 1, 1971, September 20, 1971, June 16, 1986, July 3, 1986.
New York Times Book Review, April 16, 1972.
Times Literary Supplement, May 28, 1971, July 7, 1972.

JACKSON, Jesse 1908-1983

PERSONAL: Born January 1, 1908, in Columbus, Ohio; died April 14, 1983, in Boone, N.C.; son of Jesse (a trucker) and Mable (Rogers) Jackson; married Ann Newman (a social worker), September 19, 1938; children: Judith Ann. *Education:* Attended Ohio State University, 1927-29. *Politics:* Independent. *Religion:* Baptist.

ADDRESSES: Home—80 La Salle St., New York, N.Y. 10027. *Office*—Duncan Hall, Appalachian State University, Boone, N.C. 28608. *Agent*—Anita Diamant, Writers' Workshop, Inc., 51 East 42nd St., New York, N.Y. 10017.

CAREER: Writer. Worked as juvenile probation officer, in Columbus, Ohio, beginning 1936; worked for the U.S. Postal Service in Columbus; worked for H. Wolfe Book Manufacturing Company; worked as a reader for National Bureau of Economic Research, 1951-68; Appalachian State University, Boone, N.C., 1974-83, instructor, lecturer, and writer in residence.

MEMBER: Authors Guild, Authors League of America, Kiwanis Club.

AWARDS, HONORS: Award from Child Study Association for *Call Me Charley;* commendation from Council of Christians and Jews for *Anchor Man;* MacDowell Colony fellowship; Carter G. Woodson Book Award, National Council for the Social Studies, 1975, for *Make a Joyful Noise unto the Lord!: The Life of Mahalia Jackson, Queen of Gospel Singers;* LL.D., Appalachian State University, 1982.

WRITINGS:

YOUNG ADULT NOVELS

Call Me Charley, illustrated by Doris Spiegel, Harper, 1945, Dell, 1968.
Anchor Man, illustrated by Spiegel, Harper, 1947, Dell, 1968.
Room for Randy, Friendship Press, 1957.
Charley Starts from Scratch, illustrated by Frank C. Nicholas, Harper, 1958.
Tessie, illustrated by Harold James, Harper, 1968.
Tessie Keeps Her Cool, Harper, 1970.
The Sickest Don't Always Die the Quickest, Doubleday, 1971.
The Fourteenth Cadillac, Doubleday, 1972.

YOUNG ADULT NONFICTION

I Sing Because I'm Happy (biography of Mahalia Jackson), Rutledge Books, 1972.
(With Elaine Landau) *Black in America: A Fight for Freedom*, Messner, 1973.
Make a Joyful Noise unto the Lord!: The Life of Mahalia Jackson, Queen of Gospel Singers, Crowell, 1974.

OTHER

Contributor of articles and reviews to periodicals, including *Crisis*.

SIDELIGHTS: For more than three decades, Jesse Jackson wrote books directed towards black adolescents growing up in America. His landmark novel *Call Me Charley*, first published in 1945, stands as one of the first books for young adults that openly dealt with racial prejudice. The story of Charles Moss, a young black boy who lives in an all-white neighborhood and attends an all-white school, *Call Me Charley* ''was the first book to present anything resembling a genuine black-white confrontation,'' notes Dorothy M. Broderick in *Image of the Black in Children's Fiction*. In a memorable scene from the book, Charles responds to a white boy's calling him ''Sambo'' by answering, ''My name is Charles. Charles Moss.'' The novel charts the young boy's experiences and struggles as he sets out to gain respect and acceptance from the whites he lives among.

Call Me Charley was praised as a sincere account of a young black boy's experiences in a racially discriminatory world. ''The hurt and bewilderment of a boy who is treated differently because of the color of his skin gets across to the reader with an impact he is not likely to forget,'' wrote a reviewer for *Book Week*. May Hill Arbuthnot and Zena Sutherland commented in *Children and Books* that ''Jesse Jackson has given a full and moving account of the kind of discriminations a black child may encounter. . . . It is a touching story made more poignant by Charley's quiet, patient acceptance of his lot. . . . The author has too realistic an approach to suggest a complete solution, but he tells a good story of a brave, likeable boy in a difficult world.'' Calling the novel ''a contribution to understanding,'' May Lamberton Becker in the *New York Herald Tribune Book World* added that ''the young author, whose ear is uncommonly sensitive, reproduces the staccato touch and distinctive turn of Negro speech without attributing dialect to educated Northern negroes.''

In a 1977 profile by Ruby J. Lanier for *Language Arts,* Jackson commented on how he decided to write books for young people. While working as a juvenile probation officer in the 1930s, Jackson encountered the case of three Ohio boys who had been convicted of the robbery and murder of a restaurant owner. ''Investigation of their case brought out that all three boys had dropped out of school because they were ashamed to tell their teachers they could not read. Their ages ran from fourteen to sixteen when this occurred. How to write something non-readers would want to read became an obsession of mine and still is.'' In the same profile, Jackson discussed the origins of *Call Me Charley* and the objectives he set for his first novel: ''Prior to this time most blacks were lost like peas in a pod under such titles as George, Sam, Sambo, Coon, Nigger. . . . So with this *Call Me Charley* it was my aim to single out one black boy, to have him fight for at least the respect of being called Charles Moss. Charley had a game plan and the game plan began with recognize me as an individual and then we will go on from there and I'll try to get into the boys' club and try to win admission to the swimming pool and try to get a part in the school play.''

Call Me Charley remains a popular book among adolescents, yet some recent criticism has pointed out that the story now appears dated. In *Written for Children: An Outline of English-Language Children's Literature*, John Rowe Townsend remarks that ''the black characters bear injustice with a patience which now appears Uncle Tommish. . . . There is some resemblance to the treatment of the poor in books by well-meaning Victorians. Just as the poor were expected to rely on and be grateful for the beneficence of the rich, so the black must rely on and be grateful for the beneficence of the white.'' Townsend concedes, however, that in its time, *Call Me Charley* was a step in the right direction; he states, ''We have no right to sneer from our vantage-point in the 1970s at advice which was sensible when it was given.'' In his later novel *Tessie,* Jackson again presents a character trying to live between two worlds. *Tessie* is the story of a young girl from Harlem who wins a scholarship to an all-white private school. In her new situation,

Tessie ''encounters an entirely different city and an entirely different world,'' notes Jane H. Clarke in *Book World*, adding that Jackson ''writes compassionately of a girl's struggle to face a strange world and be true to herself.''

Jackson's young adult writings hold special relevance for black adolescents, yet both his fiction and nonfiction display a simplicity, honesty, and readability that can appeal to a wide range of readers. Regarding Jackson's novel *The Fourteenth Cadillac*, John W. Conner writes in *English Journal:* ''Jesse Jackson has a talent for combining description and fast-paced narrative. . . . *The Fourteenth Cadillac* is great fun to read. It will touch many adolescents where their weaknesses in familial relationships occur.'' Jackson's 1974 biography of Mahalia Jackson, *Make a Joyful Noise unto the Lord!,* prompted the following comments from Lorain Alterman in the *New York Times Book Review:* ''Jesse Jackson tells the story well—explaining vividly why Miss Jackson stuck with gospel rather than singing the blues. . . . On the whole [the book] will induce young readers to listen to some of Mahalia Jackson's recordings and to discover for themselves what made her gift so special.''

BIOGRAPHICAL/CRITICAL SOURCES:

BOOKS

Arbuthnot, May Hill, and Zena Sutherland, *Children and Books,* Scott, Foresman, 1947, 4th edition, 1972.
Broderick, Dorothy M., *Image of the Black in Children's Fiction,* Bowker, 1973.
Contemporary Literary Criticism, Volume 12, Gale, 1980.
Jackson, Jesse, *Call Me Charley,* Harper, 1945, Dell, 1968.
Townsend, John Rowe, *Written for Children: An Outline of English-Language Children's Literature,* Lippincott, 1965, revised edition, 1974.

PERIODICALS

Book Week, November 11, 1945.
Book World, May 5, 1968.
Bulletin of the Center for Children's Books, April, 1974.
English Journal, May, 1971, Febraury, 1973.
Language Arts, March, 1977.
Library Journal, October 15, 1968.
New York Herald Tribune Book Review, November 11, 1945.
New York Times, December 23, 1945.
New York Times Book Review, May 26, 1968, February 14, 1971, June 16, 1974.
Saturday Review, June 15, 1968.
School Library Journal, October, 1968, January, 1975.
Washington Post Book World, May 19, 1974.

OBITUARIES

PERIODICALS

Publishers Weekly, June 3, 1983.
School Library Journal, September, 1983.

*   *   *

JAMES, C(yril) L(ionel) R(obert) 1901- (J. R. Johnson)

PERSONAL: Born January 4, 1901, in Chaguanas, Trinidad; son of a schoolteacher; married first wife (divorced); married Selma Weinstein, 1955; children (first marriage): one. *Education:* Queen's Royal College secondary school (Port of Spain), graduated, 1918.

ADDRESSES: c/o Allison & Busby, 6-A Noel St., London WIV 3RB, England. *Home*—Brixton, London, England.

CAREER: Writer, c. 1920—; member of the Maple cricket team, Port of Spain, Trinidad; *Trinidad* (literary magazine), Port of Spain, editor, 1929-30; teacher at Queen's Royal College, Port of Spain, until 1932; *Manchester Guardian,* London, England, correspondent, 1932-38; editor of *Fight* (later *Workers' Fight;* Marxist publication), London, until 1938; trade union organizer and political activist in the United States, 1938-53; West Indian Federal Labor Party, Port of Spain, secretary, 1958-60; *The Nation,* Port of Spain, editor, 1958-60. Lecturer at colleges and universities, including Federal City College, Washington, D.C.; commentator for the British Broadcasting Company (BBC); cricket columnist for *Race Today.*

WRITINGS:

The Life of Captain Cipriani: An Account of British Government in the West Indies, Nelson, Lancashire, Coulton, 1932, abridged edition published as *The Case for West-Indian Self-Government,* Hogarth, 1933, University Place Book Shop, 1967.

(With L. R. Constantine) *Cricket and I,* Allan, 1933.

Minty Alley (novel), Secker & Warburg, 1936, New Beacon, 1971.

Toussaint L'Ouverture (play; first produced in London, 1936; revised version titled *The Black Jacobins* and produced in Ibadan, Nigeria, 1967), published in *A Time and a Season: Eight Caribbean Plays,* edited by Errol Hill, University of the West Indies (Port of Spain), 1976.

World Revolution 1917-1936: The Rise and Fall of the Communist International, Pioneer, 1937, Hyperion Press, 1973.

A History of Negro Revolt, Fact, 1938, Haskell House, 1967, revised and expanded edition published as *A History of Pan-African Revolt,* Drum and Spear Press, 1969.

The Black Jacobins: Toussaint L'Ouverture and the San Domingo Revolution, Dial, 1938, Random House, 1963.

(Translator from the French) Boris Souvarine, *Stalin: A Critical Survey of Socialism,* Longman, 1939.

State Capitalism and World Revolution (published anonymously), privately printed, 1950, Facing Reality, 1969.

Mariners, Renegades, and Castaways: The Story of Herman Melville and the World We Live In, privately printed, 1953, Bewick Editions, 1978.

Modern Politics (lectures), PNM (Port of Spain), 1960.

Beyond a Boundary, Hutchinson, 1963, Pantheon, 1984.

The Hegelian Dialectic and Modern Politics, Facing Reality, 1970, revised edition published as *Notes on Dialectics: Hegel, Marx, Lenin,* Lawrence Hill, 1980.

Nkrumah and the Ghana Revolution, Lawrence Hill, 1977, revised edition, Allison & Busby, 1982.

The Future in the Present: Selected Writings of C. L. R. James, Lawrence Hill, 1977.

(With Tony Bogues and Kim Gordon) *Black Nationalism and Socialism,* Socialists Unlimited, 1979.

(With George Breitman, Edgar Keemer, and others) *Fighting Racism in World War II,* Monad, 1980.

Spheres of Existence: Selected Writings, Lawrence Hill, 1981.

Eightieth Birthday Lectures, Race Today, 1983.

At the Rendezvous of Victory: Selected Writings, Lawrence Hill, 1985.

Cricket, Allison & Busby, 1986.

Contributor of short stories to the collections *The Best Short Stories of 1928,* Cape, 1928, and *Island Voices,* Liveright, 1970; author, sometimes under pseudonym J. R. Johnson, of numerous political pamphlets; contributor of articles to newspapers and magazines.

WORK IN PROGRESS: An autobiography.

SIDELIGHTS: C. L. R. James is a leading Trinidadian political and literary figure whose interests and values were profoundly shaped by his experience growing up in the British West Indian colony at the beginning of the century. The son of a schoolteacher father, James was raised in the capital of Port of Spain in a highly respectable—indeed, rather puritanical—middle-class black family suffused in British manners and culture. The James family home faced the back of a cricket field, and young Cyril developed a lifelong passion for the baseball-like sport watching matches from his living room window. The boy also grew up with an intense love for English literature—at age ten he had memorized long passages of William Makepeace Thackeray's *Vanity Fair*—and both his reading and his cricket-playing often distracted him from his studies at the elite Queen's Royal College in Port of Spain. Dashing his parents' hopes that he would pursue a political career with the colonial administration, James chose instead to play professional cricket and teach at the Queen's Royal College in the 1920s. At the same time, he set about chronicling the lives of the Trinidadian lower class in a series of naturalistic short stories that shocked his peers and foreshadowed his future Marxism. James's first-hand study of the Port of Spain slums also furnished background for his only novel, *Minty Alley,* an affecting but unsentimental look at the complex personal relationships and humble aspirations of the denizens of a rundown boarding house.

In 1932, chafing under the placid routines of a life in a colonial backwater, James accepted an invitation to go to London to help the great black Trinidadian cricketer Learie Constantine write his autobiography. With Constantine's help, James secured a job as a cricket correspondent with the *Manchester Guardian* and published his first nonfiction book, *The Life of Captain Cipriani: An Account of British Government in the West Indies* (later abridged and published as *The Case for West-Indian Self-Government*). This influential treatise—one of the first to urge full self-determination for West Indians—introduced James to leading figures in the two political movements that were to profoundly shape his thinking in the years to come: Pan Africanism and Marxism.

James first developed his Pan Africanist ideas in Trinidadian leftist activist George Padmore's London-based African Bureau, where he joined future African independence leaders Jomo Kenyatta and Kwame Nkrumah as a political propogandist in the mid-1930s. James emphasized the importance of West Indians' coming to terms with their African heritage in order to help forge a sense of national identity in their racially and culturally polyglot society. He also came to regard the struggle to liberate and politically unify colonial Africa as a way of inspiring and mobilizing oppressed people of color around the world to seize control of their destinies. James later examined Pan Africanist theory and practice in two historical works, *A History of Negro Revolt* (later revised and published as *History of Pan-African Revolt*), which surveys nearly two centuries of the black liberation struggle against European colonialism, and *Nkrumah and the Ghana Revolution,* an analysis of the first successful independence movement in modern Africa.

While participating in the vanguard of the African liberation movement, James also became a committed Marxist during his sojourn in London in the 1930s. He took the Trotskyist position in the great dispute over Stalinism that split the world communist movement during those years and wrote a history from that perspective in 1937 titled *World Revolution, 1917-1936: The Rise and Fall of the Communist International*. James's Marxism also informed his 1938 historical study *The Black Jacobins: Toussaint L'Ouverture and the San Domingo Revolution*. In this book, generally regarded as his masterwork, James analyzes the socioeconomic roots and leading personalities of the Haitian revolution of 1791 to 1804, the first and only slave revolt to achieve political independence in world history.

At the center of the revolution and the book stands Toussaint L'Ouverture. The self-taught black slave turned charismatic political leader and redoubtable military commander organized and led a disciplined army of former slaves, who defeated crack French and British expeditionary forces mustered to crush the insurgency. Of particular interest in *The Black Jacobins*, critics noted, is the author's success in relating the Haitian events to the course of the French Revolution, whose ideals inspired Toussaint even as he fought first Maximilien Robespierre and then Napoleon Bonaparte to free France's most important Caribbean sugar colony, then known as Saint Domingue. The democratic ideals of the Haitian revolution, which culminated in full political independence a year after Toussaint's death in 1803, touched off a wave of slave revolts throughout the Caribbean and helped inspire anti-slavery forces in the southern United States. *New York Herald Tribune Books* reviewer Clara Gruening Stillman judged *The Black Jacobins* as gripping as the events it recounted: "Brilliantly conceived and executed, throwing upon the historical screen a mass of dramatic figures, lurid scenes, fantastic happenings, the absorbing narrative never departs from its rigid faithfulness to method and documentation."

Shortly after publishing *The Black Jacobins* James moved to the United States, where he joined the Trotskyist Socialist Workers Party (SWP) and became a full-time political activist, organizing auto workers in Detroit, Michigan, and tenant farmers in the South. He broke with the SWP in the late 1940s over the question of the nature of the Soviet Union, which he dubbed "state capitalist," and co-founded a new Detroit-based Trotskyist political organization with Leon Trotsky's former secretary Raya Dunayevskaya. James's political activities eventually provoked the wrath of the McCarthy-era U.S. government, which denied him American citizenship and deported him to Great Britain in 1953. While awaiting his expulsion on Ellis Island, the ever-resourceful James managed to write a short study of Herman Melville titled *Mariners, Renegades, and Castaways* that drew a parallel between Ahab's pursuit of the great white whale in Melville's classic, *Moby Dick*, and left-wing intellectuals' infatuation with Soviet political leader Joseph Stalin.

After five years in London, James returned to Trinidad in 1958 to join the movement for political independence there. In Port of Spain he edited *The Nation* magazine and served as secretary of the West Indian Federal Labor Party, whose leader, Dr. Eric Williams, became Trinidad's first premier in 1960. Like the United States authorities, however, Williams found James's outspoken Marxism politically threatening and soon compelled James, who had once been Williams's schoolmaster, to go back to England. James left Trinidad aggrieved that the emerging Caribbean nations had failed to achieve a lasting formula for political federation, which he believed necessary to further their social and economic development.

Back in London, James returned to political writing and lecturing, particularly on the Pan Africanist movement, West Indian politics, and the black question in the United States. He also rekindled his passion for cricket after leading a successful campaign to have the Trinidadian Frank Worrell named the first black captain of the West Indian international cricket team. Worrell's spectacular playing at the Australian championship competition in 1961 galvanized a sense of national pride and identity among the emerging West Indian nations and partly inspired James to write *Beyond a Boundary,* his much-praised 1963 survey of cricket's social and cultural significance in Great Britain and the Caribbean. The book's title refers both to the game's objective of driving a ball beyond a marked boundary and James's novel thesis that this gentlemen's sport can help overcome certain false cultural, racial, and political boundaries within society. On a purely aesthetic level, James argues, cricket has "the perfect flow of motion" that defines the essence of all great art; he holds that a good cricket match is the visual and dramatic equivalent of so-called "high art" and that the sport should be recognized as a genuinely democratic art form. Cricket's high standards of fairness and sportsmanship, on the other hand, illustrate "all the decencies required for a culture" and even played a historic role by showing West Indian blacks that they could excel in a forum where the rules were equal for everyone. The integrated Caribbean cricket teams, James believes, helped forge a new black self-confidence that carried the West Indian colonies to independence. The author renders these observations in a lively, anecdotal style that includes both biographical sketches of great cricketers and personal reminiscences from his own lifelong love affair with the sport. "*Beyond a Boundary* is one of the finest and most finished books to come out of the West Indies," remarked Trinidadian novelist V. S. Naipaul in *Encounter*. "There is no more eloquent brief for the cultural and artistic importance of sport," added *Newsweek*'s Jim Miller.

In recent years, James has published two well-received collections of essays and articles that display his broad literary, cultural, and political interests. *The Future in the Present* contains that author's short story "Triumph," about women tenants in a Port of Spain slum, along with essays ranging from critical interpretations of Pablo Picasso's painting "Guernica" and Melville's *Moby Dick* to a political analysis of workers' councils in Hungary and a personal account of organizing a sharecroppers' strike in Missouri in 1942. "The writings are profound, sometimes; cranky, occasionally; stimulating, always," remarked *Village Voice* critic Paul Berman, and *Times Literary Supplement* reviewer Thomas Hodgkin found the book "a mine of richness and variety." *At the Rendezvous of Victory,* whose title James took from a verse by the great West Indian poet Aime Cesaire, includes an essay on the Solidarity union movement in Poland and critical discussions of the work of black American novelists Toni Morrison and Alice Walker. The more than eighty-year-old James "shows no diminution of his intellectual energies," wrote Alastair Niven in his review of the collection for *British Books News*. "Throughout this book James's elegant but unmannered style, witty and relaxed when lecturing, reflective and analytical when writing for publication, always conveys a sense of his own robust, humane, and giving personality. Was there ever a less polemical or more persuasive radical?"

BIOGRAPHICAL/CRITICAL SOURCES:

BOOKS

James, C. L. R., *Beyond a Boundary*, Pantheon, 1984.

James, C. L. R., *The Future in the Present: Selected Writings of C. L. R. James,* Lawrence Hill, 1977.

Mackenzie, Alan, and Paul Gilroy, *Visions of History,* Pantheon, 1983.

PERIODICALS

American Scholar, summer, 1985.
British Book News, May, 1984.
CLA Journal, December, 1977.
Encounter, September, 1963.
Nation, May 4, 1985.
Newsweek, March 26, 1984.
New Yorker, June 25, 1984.
New York Herald Tribune Books, November 27, 1938.
New York Times Book Review, March 25, 1984.
Radical America, May, 1970.
Times Literary Supplement, December 2, 1977, January 20, 1978, September 25, 1987.
Village Voice, February 11, 1981, July 10, 1984.
Washington Post Book World, April 22, 1984.

—*Sketch by Curtis Skinner*

*   *   *

JEFFERS, Lance   1919-1985

PERSONAL: Born November 28, 1919, in Fremont, Neb.; died 1985; son of Henry Nelson (a messenger) and Dorothy Jeffers; married Camille Jones (a social worker), May, 1946 (divorced); married Trellie Lee James (a college professor), May 22, 1958; children: Lance, Valjeanne, Sidonie Colette, Honoree. *Education:* Columbia University, B.A. (cum laude), 1951, M.A.; graduate study at University of Toronto. *Politics:* Democrat. *Religion:* African Methodist Episcopal.

ADDRESSES: Home—2608 East Weaver St., Durham, N.C. 27707.

CAREER: Florida A&M University, Tallahassee, assistant professor of English, 1964-65; Indiana University, Kokomo, instructor in English, 1966-68; California State University, Long Beach, assistant professor of English, 1968-73; North Carolina State University, Raleigh, started as associate professor of English in 1973, became professor; Bowie State College, Bowie, Md., chairman of English department. Visiting professor, Duke University, 1976-77. Has lectured at Shaw University, Federal City College, Bowie State College, and Tuskegee Institute. *Military service:* U.S. Army, 1942-46.

MEMBER: International P.E.N., College Language Association.

AWARDS, HONORS: Franklin T. Baker Citation from Columbia University.

WRITINGS:

My Blackness Is the Beauty of This Land (poems), Broadside Press, 1970.
When I Know the Power of My Black Hand (poems), Broadside Press, 1974.
O Africa, Where I Baked My Bread (poems), illustrations by Beverly Rose Enright, Lotus Press, 1977.
Grandsire (poems), Lotus Press, 1979.
Witherspoon (novel), Flippin Press, 1983.

Also author of *Let My Last Breath,* edited by Trellie Jeffers, to be published posthumously.

CONTRIBUTOR

The Best American Short Stories—1948, edited by Martha Foley, Houghton, 1948.
Burning Spear, edited by Percy Johnston, Jupiter Hammon, 1963.
Nine Black Poets, edited by R. Baird Shuman, Moore, 1968.
The Black Seventies, edited by Floyd Barbour, Porter-Sargent, 1970.
A Galaxy of Black Writing, edited by Shuman, Moore, 1970.
New Black Voices, edited by Abraham Chapman, New American Library, 1971.
A Broadside Treasury, edited by Gwendolyn Brooks, Broadside Press, 1971.
You Better Believe It: The Penguin Book of Black Verse, edited by Paul Bremen, Penguin, 1973.
Vietnam and Black America, edited by Clyde Taylor, Doubleday, 1973.
Quilt 1, edited by Al Young and Ishmael Reed, [Berkeley, Calif.], 1981.

Also contributor of about thirty-five poems, articles, and stories to literary magazines, including *Confrontation, Mainstream, Black Scholar, College Language Association Journal, Blackstage, Hyperion, Southern Poetry Review,* and *Negro Digest.*

WORK IN PROGRESS: Two books of poetry, tentatively titled *Whales* and *The Janitor's Wife,* both for Dark Harbingers Press.

SIDELIGHTS: Although primarily known as a poet, Lance Jeffers also wrote several short stories and a novel. According to David F. Dorsey, Jr. in the *Dictionary of Literary Biography,* ''Lance Jeffers's poetry is an important and striking expression of black contemporary poetics. Yet, because it is so unique, it offers interesting evidence for the flexibility and potentials of a communal aesthetic. It is even more important, however, as a unique and passionate reflection of black life in the United States.'' In his poetry, Jeffers's themes and metaphors reach back to slavery and beyond to life in Africa. His novel, *Witherspoon,* however, deals with a contemporary minister and the convict he wants to save from execution. As Jeffers told Jerry M. Ward, Jr. in *Black Literature Forum, Witherspoon*'s purpose is to make readers aware ''of what black people are. There still are . . . strong working-class black people. And there are heroes still among us, strong heroes. . . . I feel strongly, and I try to say this, that the black working-class will have the final voice, the final influence on our getting our freedom.'' The struggle against racial prejudice motivated Jeffers to write. He told Ward, ''I feel that my deepest feeling goes to the matter of white oppression of black people. Either in poetry or in fiction, I have to align what I'm doing with my feelings. It is true to say that a black writer should have the deepest grasp of human affairs. This is true. Nevertheless . . . *I* find my deepest passion engaged by the conflict between blacks and whites. This is symbolic of the worldwide struggle between oppressor and oppressed. But I can't be parochial about this, and I can't imitate neurotic American elitism either. . . . I simultaneously have to be as broad as humanity, and as intense and angry as the black man successfully fighting for his life against a pack of lynchers.''

Jeffers once wrote: ''I look at the unrealized potentialities of humanity—not in technological development, but in tenderness, empathy, and wisdom—and I write, in essence, of the potential grandeur that lies undeveloped in the genes of man, of the obstacles that frequently defeat him, of his tenacity and vision. This is the motive force behind my writing: the passion to help create an environment that will allow humanity to move into an unlived-in region of its personality. I dredge up from my own personal seabed everything that I can and move it into poetry, for what is in me and innumerable others is what is most basic in human experience and character: the defeat, the oppression, the sorrow, the strength, the struggle, the movement forward, the vision forged from empathy, and the empathy wrenched, in my own personal experience, from the oppression as a Black person in America, which is, simultaneously the experience of a people.''

BIOGRAPHICAL/CRITICAL SOURCES:

BOOKS

Dictionary of Literary Biography, Volume 41: *Afro-American Poets since 1955,* Gale, 1985.

PERIODICALS

Black American Literature Forum, winter, 1984.

* * *

JEFFERSON, Roland S(pratlin) 1939-

PERSONAL: Born May 16, 1939, in Washington, D.C.; son of Bernard S. (a judge) and Devonia (Spratlin) Jefferson; married Melanie L. Moore (a teacher), 1966; children: Roland, Jr., Rodney, Shannon, Royce. *Education:* University of Southern California, B.A., 1961; Howard University, M.D., 1965.

ADDRESSES: Office—3870 Crenshaw Blvd., No. 215, Los Angeles, Calif. 90008.

CAREER: Physician in Los Angeles, Calif., 1965—; writer and filmmaker. Films include ''Disco 9000,'' ''Pacific Inferno,'' and ''Angel Dust: The Wack Attack.'' *Military service:* U.S. Air Force, 1969-71; became captain.

MEMBER: Writers Guild of America, Association of Black Motion Picture and Television Producers, National Medical Association.

AWARDS, HONORS: Admitted to Black Filmmakers Hall of Fame, 1979; NAACP Image Award, 1980.

WRITINGS:

The School on 103rd Street (novel), Vantage Press, 1976, published as *The Secret Below 103rd Street,* Holloway, 1983.
A Card for the Players (novel), edited by Saul Burnstein, New Bedford, 1978.
Time of the Jihad (novel), New Bedford, 1984.
Five Fifty-Nine to Damascus, Exposition Press, 1985.
Five Hundred Fifty-Nine to Damascus, edited by David Weiss, New Bedford, 1986.

SIDELIGHTS: Roland S. Jefferson commented: ''Most of my writing (with the exception of *A Card for the Players*) covers subject matter that I consider to be socially relevant. I particularly like political background conflicts against the development of my characters. *The School on 103rd Street* was conceived because of the prevailing belief at the time by black America that it was not inconceivable to feel threatened by government attempts to incarcerate the entire population. Certainly I was influenced by Sam Greenlee's *The Spook Who Sat By the Door* and John William's *The Man Who Cried,* as well as Sam Yette's *The Choice*—all novels of the sixties and seventies that reflected a similar viewpoint.

''My views and feelings come from the people I've known in life. As a psychiatrist, I have the unique opportunity to observe and to listen to people express themselves, so I borrow a little from this person and a little from that person, add my own interpretation to the mixture, and thus my characters are born.

''I became involved in filmmaking quite by accident. I had always wanted to be a writer of sorts. In college I was frustrated in this pursuit because my family was very traditional and felt that writers could not support themselves; thus, I had to study medicine. I have no regrets except that I waited longer than I would have liked to begin writing again. So, while in the Air Force, I became a film critic. This evolved into writing fiction in the form of novels, and eventually this moved me into film.

''Film is the most creative and the most expensive art form there is, but its influence is unfathomable. I discovered that what I really wanted was to be able to move or to touch, if you will, masses of people in some capacity. But the film industry is a closed shop, and breaking in is very difficult. To do so you must find one who thinks, feels, and is willing to gamble as much as you will on a project. I've been lucky on three occasions. 'Disco 9000' was my first film and preceded 'Saturday Night Fever' by over a year. 'Pacific Inferno,' my second film, is a World War II adventure set in the Phillipines and has racial overtones not normally found in films of the genre. 'Angel Dust: The Wack Attack,' my last, was made for television and was a powerful drama about the evils of drug abuse. All of the films had subtle, unconscious meanings attached to them that, in some respects, made them quite controversial for their times.

''I practice medicine now as infrequently as I can manage. Some of my writing in the past has been for academic journals, but my real interest is in writing fiction with universal themes that people can all identify with. My aspirations are much like those of Michael Crichton, Somerset Maugham, and George Miller (director of the film 'Road Warrior'); they were all physicians who gave up medicine because they discovered the beauty and satisfaction that lay within the arts.''

* * *

JOANS, Ted 1928-

PERSONAL: Born July 4, 1928, in Cairo, Ill.; married then divorced; married a Norwegian, 1961; children: ten. *Education:* Indiana University, B.F.A., 1951. *Politics:* ''Human Liberation.''

ADDRESSES: Home—Timbuktu, Republic of Mali, Africa (winter); c/o Rare Book Room, 125 Greenwich Ave., New York, N.Y. 10014.

CAREER: Painter, jazz musician, poet, and travel writer. Investigator for Afro-American Ancestral Art Association; journalist for Organization of African Unity, 1969—.

WRITINGS:

Beat Poems, Deretchin, 1957.
Funky Jazz Poems, Deretchin, 1959.
All of Ted Joans and No More: Poems and Collages, Excelsior Press, 1960.
(Contributor) Elias Wilentz, editor, *The Beat Scene,* Corinth Books, 1960.
(Contributor) Arna Bontemps, editor, *American Negro Poetry,* Hill & Wang, 1963.

The Hipsters, Corinth Books, 1967.

Black Pow Wow: Jazz Poems, Hill & Wang, 1969.

Une Proposition pour un manifeste, pouvoir noir, [Paris], 1969.

Mijn Scwartze Gedacht, Van Geneep, 1970.

A Black Manifesto in Jazz Poetry and Prose, Calder & Boyars, 1971.

(And illustrator) *Afrodisia: New Poems*, Hill & Wang, 1971, Calder & Boyars, 1976.

Spetrophilia: Poems, Collages, Amsterdamsch Litterair Cafe de Engelbewaarder (Amsterdam), 1973.

(Contributor) Paul Breman, editor, *You Better Believe It: Black Verse in English*, Penguin, 1973.

(With Joyce Mansour) *Flying Piranha*, with illustrative collages by M. Sila Errus, Bola Press, 1978.

Vergriffen: Oder, Blitzlieb Poems, Loose Blaetter Presse, 1979.

The Aardvark-Watcher: Der Erdferkelforscher (bilingual edition), Literarisches Colloquium Berlin, 1980.

Sure, Really I Is, Transformation, 1982.

Merveilleux Coup de Foudre Poetry of Jayne Cortez and Ted Joans, Handshake Editions (France), 1982.

Also author of *A Few Poems*, 1981. Contributor to *Black World*, *Coda Jazz Magazine* (Toronto), *Jazz* (Paris), and *Presence Africaine*. Editor, *Dies Und Das* (first surrealist magazine published in Germany), 1984.

WORK IN PROGRESS: A Black Man Guides You to Africa; "Travelin'," a poem; *Spadework: The Autobiography of a Hipster; Niggers from Outer Space: A Black Power Novel;* and *I Black Surrealist; or, Well Shut My Mouth Wide Open.*

SIDELIGHTS: American poet, world traveler, and former jazz musician Ted Joans is also known as the only Afro-American surrealist painter, James A. Miller reports in the *Dictionary of Literary Biography: The Beats, Literary Bohemians in Postwar America.* The poet's "irreverent writings," says Jon Woodson in *Dictionary of Literary Biography: Afro-American Poets since 1955*, are characterized by "celebrations of sexuality, jazz music, African culture, and social revolution. His poetry is equally a vehicle for social protest; his favorite targets are racism, sexual repression, and injustice."

Woodson also observes that Joans's "poetry has kept pace with his personal development." Joans inherited music and travel as an occupation from his father, a riverboat musician who gave the twelve-year-old Joans a trumpet just before dropping him off in Memphis, Tennessee, to fend for himself. "A wanderer and free spirit since then, Joans remained settled long enough to receive a Bachelor of Fine Arts degree from Indiana University in 1951," Miller writes. Then Joans moved to New York's Greenwich Village where he became a popular poet associated with Jack Kerouac, Allen Ginsberg, Bob Kaufman, and other members of the Beat generation during the 1950s.

In the next decade, Joans became an expatriate. As he explains in the introduction to *All of Ted Joans and No More*, "Like man, I came to the Village scene after doing the school bit . . . came here to paint and I did . . . after four years, divorce, blues, beat bread, then split for Europe, Middle East Africa, fell in love with Tangiers and the European people and the African people. . . . I hate cold weather and they will not let me live democratically in the warm states of the United States, so I'm splitting and letting America perish." Woodson relates that Joans "established a pattern of moving to European cities such as Paris, Copenhagen, and Amsterdam in the summer months and moving back to Africa in the winter months. . . . While continuing to write poems, Joans also painted, but he supported himself largely by selling African masks and sculptures which he collected on his travels through Africa." He also gained membership in some of Africa's secret societies. Joans read poems inspired by these experiences, largely collected in *Afrodisia: New Poems*, to American audiences as his contribution to the growing black arts movement of the 1970s.

Concludes Woodson, "Because Ted Joans is a black poet who began his career as a Beat and became an expatriate, he has been able to provide American readers of poetry with a unique perspective of their culture; Joans writes as a trebly alienated insider." Speaking of his impact on the world of literature, Woodson adds, "Joans has not been widely acknowledged critically, but his influence on Afro-American writers has been great. His style of coloquial, jazz poetry is the common ground of black poetry as it has been written and defined since the mid 1960s. . . . Like his mentor Langston Hughes, Ted Joans is a poet of the people who has used the jazz idiom to create a style of poetry that has gained wide popular acceptance because of its fluidity, honesty, and vitality."

BIOGRAPHICAL/CRITICAL SOURCES:

BOOKS

Dictionary of Literary Biography, Gale, Volume 16: *The Beats, Literary Bohemians in Postwar America*, 1983, Volume 41: *Afro-American Poets since 1955*, 1985.

Joans, Ted, *All of Ted Joans and No More: Poems and Collages*, Excelsior Press, 1960.

Wilentz, Elias, editor, *The Beat Scene*, Corinth Books, 1960.

PERIODICALS

Cultural Correspondence, Numbers 2-4, summer, 1981.

Hudson Review, spring, 1970.

Passion (Paris), January, 1986.

Times Literary Supplement, August 6, 1971.

Transition, Number 48, April/June, 1975.

Western Humanities Review, autumn, 1971.

* * *

JOHNSON, Charles (Richard) 1948-

PERSONAL: Born April 23, 1948, in Evanston, Ill.; son of Benjamin Lee and Ruby Elizabeth (Jackson) Johnson; married Joan New (an elementary school teacher), June, 1970; children: Malik, Elizabeth. *Education:* Southern Illinois University, B.A., 1971, M.A., 1973; post-graduate work at State University of New York at Stony Brook, 1973-76.

ADDRESSES: Office—Department of English, University of Washington, Seattle, Wash. 98105.

CAREER: Chicago Tribune, Chicago, Ill., cartoonist and reporter, 1969-70; *St. Louis Proud*, St. Louis, Mo., member of art staff, 1971-72; University of Washington, Seattle, assistant professor, 1976-79, associate professor, 1979-82, professor of English, 1982—. Writer and cartoonist. Fiction editor of *Seattle Review*, 1978—. Director of Associated Writing Programs Awards Series in Short Fiction, 1979-81, member of board of directors, 1983—.

AWARDS, HONORS: Named journalism alumnus of the year by Southern Illinois University, 1981; Governors Award for Literature from State of Washington, 1983, for *Oxherding Tale;* Callaloo Creative Writing Award, 1983, for short story "Popper's Disease"; citation in *Pushcart Prize's* Outstanding Writers section, 1984, for story "China"; Writers Guild Award for best children's show, 1986, for "Booker"; nomination for the PEN/Faulkner Award from the PEN American Center, 1987, for *The Sorcerer's Apprentice*.

WRITINGS:

NOVELS

Faith and the Good Thing, Viking, 1974.
Oxherding Tale, Indiana University Press, 1982.

CARTOON COLLECTIONS

Black Humor (self-illustrated), Johnson Publishing, 1970.
Half-Past Nation Time (self-illustrated), Aware Press, 1972.

Contributor of cartoons to periodicals, including *Ebony, Chicago Tribune, Jet, Black World*, and *Players*.

TELEVISION SCRIPTS

"Charlie's Pad" (fifty-two-part series on cartooning), PBS, 1970.
"Charlie Smith and the Fritter Tree," PBS "Visions" series, 1978.
(With John Alman) "Booker," PBS, 1983.

Contributor of scripts to numerous television series, including "Up and Coming," PBS, 1981, and "Y.E.S., Inc.," PBS, 1983.

OTHER

The Sorcerer's Apprentice (short stories), Atheneum, 1986.
(Contributor) Jeff Henderson, editor, *Thor's Hammer: Essays on John Gardner*, Arkansas Philological Association, 1986.
Being and Race: Black Writing Since 1970, Indiana University Press, 1988.

Work represented in anthologies, including *Best American Short Stories, 1982*, edited by John Gardner and Shannon Ravenel, Houghton, 1982. Contributor of short stories and essays to periodicals, including *Mother Jones, Callaloo, Choice, Indiana Review, Nimrod, Intro 10, Obsidian*, and *North American Review*.

WORK IN PROGRESS: Rutherford's Travels, a novel; "Dragonslayer," a tribute to the late author and medievalist John Gardner, for WGBH-TV in Boston.

SIDELIGHTS: "Charles Johnson has enriched contemporary American fiction as few young writers can," observed *Village Voice* critic Stanley Crouch, adding that "it is difficult to imagine that such a talented artist will forever miss the big time." A graduate of Southern Illinois University, Johnson studied with the late author John Gardner, under whose direction he wrote *Faith and the Good Thing*. Though Johnson had written six "apprentice" novels prior to his association with Gardner, *Faith* was the first to be accepted for publication. Johnson professes to "share Gardner's concern with 'moral fiction'" and believes in the "necessity of young (and old) writers working toward becoming technicians of language and literary form."

Faith and the Good Thing met with an enthusiastic response from critics such as Garrett Epps of *Washington Post Book World*, who judged it "a brilliant first novel" and commended its author as "one of this country's most interesting and inventive younger writers." Roger Sale, writing in the *Sewanee Review*, had similar praise for the novel. He commented: "Johnson, it is clear, is a writer, and if he works too hard at it at times, or if he seems a little too pleased with it at other times, he is twenty-six, and with prose and confidence like his, he can do anything."

The book is a complex, often humorous, folktale account of Faith Cross, a Southern black girl traveling to Chicago in search of life's "Good Thing," which she has learned of from her dying mother. In her quest, noted *Time*'s John Skrow, Faith "seeks guidance from a swamp witch, a withered and warty old necromancer with one green and one yellow eye," who nonetheless "spouts philosophy as if she were Hegel." Skrow deemed the work a "wry comment on the tension felt by a black intellectual," and Annie Gottlieb of *New York Times Book Review* called *Faith and the Good Thing* a "strange and often wonderful hybrid—an ebullient philosophical novel in the form of a folktale-cum-black-girl's odyssey." She noted that the novel's "magic falls flat" on occasion, "when the mix . . . is too thick with academic in-jokes and erudite references," but she added that "fortunately, such moments are overwhelmed by the poetry and wisdom of the book." In conclusion, Gottlieb found the novel "flawed yet still fabulous."

Johnson described his second novel, *Oxherding Tale*, as "a modern, comic, philosophical slave narrative—a kind of dramatization of the famous 'Ten Oxherding Pictures' of Zen artist Kakuan-Shien," which represent the progressive search of a young herdsman for his rebellious ox, a symbol for his self. The author added that the novel's style "blends the eighteenth-century English novel with the Eastern parable."

Like his first novel, Johnson's *Oxherding Tale* received widespread critical acclaim. It details the coming of age of Andrew Hawkins, a young mulatto slave in the pre-Civil War South. Andrew is conceived when, after much drinking, plantation owner Jonathan Polkinghorne convinces his black servant, George Hawkins, to swap wives with him for the evening. Unaware that the man sharing her bed is not her husband, Anna Polkinghorne makes love with George and consequentially becomes pregnant with Andrew. After the child is born Anna rejects him as a constant reminder of her humiliation, and he is taken in by George's wife, Mattie. Though he is raised in slave quarters Andrew receives many privileges, including an education from an eccentric tutor who teaches him about Eastern mysticism, socialism, and the philosophies of Plato, Schopenhauer, and Hegel.

Writing in *Literature, Fiction, and the Arts Review*, Florella Orowan called Andrew "a man with no social place, caught between the slave world and free white society but, like the hapless hero Tom Jones, he gains from his ambiguous existence the timeless advantage of the Outsider's omniscience and chimerism: he can assume whatever identity is appropriate to the situation." *Oxherding Tale* accompanies its hero on a series of adventures that include an exotic sexual initiation, an encounter with the pleasures of opium, escape from the plantation, "passing" as white, and eluding a telepathic bounty hunter called the Soulcatcher. As Michael S. Weaver observed in *Gargoyle*, Andrew "lives his way to freedom through a succession of sudden enlightenments. . . . Each experience is another layer of insight into human nature" that has "a touch of Johnson's ripe capacity for laughter." The book's climax, noted Crouch, is "remarkable for its brutality and humble tenderness; Andrew must dive into the briar patch of his identity and risk destruction in order to express his humanity."

Weaver admitted that "at times *Oxherding Tale* reads like a philosophical tract, and may have been more adequately billed as Thus Spake Andrew Hawkins." But he concluded that the novel "is nonetheless an entertaining display of Johnson's working knowledge of the opportunities for wisdom afforded by the interplay between West and East, Black and White, man and woman, feeling and knowing—all of them seeming contradictions.'' According to Crouch, the novel is successful ''because Johnson skillfully avoids melodramatic platitudes while creating suspense and comedy, pathos and nostalgia. In the process, he invents a fresh set of variations on questions about race, sex, and freedom.''

The Sorcerer's Apprentice, Johnson's collection of short stories, met with highly favorable reviews and garnered him a nomination for the PEN/Faulkner Award for fiction. ''These tales,'' reported Michael Ventura in the *New York Times Book Review,* ''are realistic without strictly adhering to realism, fantastic without getting lost in fantasy.'' The title story concerns a young black man, Allan, who is the son of a former slave and wishes to become a sorcerer. He is taken under wing by Rubin, an African-born member of the Allmuseri, a tribe of wizards, and must accept his heritage before winning the ability to make true magic. The book also contains ''Alethia,'' about a black professor, seemingly well-assimilated to academia, who must deal with his past in the slums of Chicago. ''The Education of Mingo'' again focuses attention on the Allmuseri, and ''Popper's Disease'' discusses the issues of assimilation and alienation through an encounter between a black doctor and the sick extraterrestrial he is called in to treat. ''It is one of the achievements of these stories,'' lauded Michiko Kakutani of the *New York Times,* ''that, while concerned at heart with questions of prejudice and cultural assimilation, they are never parochial and only rarely didactic. Rather, Mr. Johnson has used his generous storytelling gifts and his easy familiarity with a variety of literary genres to conjure up eight moral fables that limn the fabulous even as they remain grounded in the language and social idioms of black American communities.'' Kakutani did not, however, extend this praise to the volume's ''Moving Pictures,'' calling it ''a tired one-liner about escapism and the movies.'' Ventura concurred, lamenting that Johnson's ''magic wears thin'' in the case of ''Moving Pictures,'' but he asserted that ''there's no risk in predicting that 'The Education of Mingo,'... 'Alethia' and 'The Sorcerer's Apprentice' will be anthologized for a very long time.''

Johnson commented: ''As a writer I am committed to the development of what one might call a genuinely systematic philosophical black American literature, a body of work that explores classical problems and metaphysical questions against the background of black American life. Specifically, my philosophical style is phenomenology, the discipline of Edmund Husserl, but I also have a deep personal interest in the entire continuum of Asian philosophy from the Vedas to Zen, and this perspective inevitably colors my fiction to some degree.

''I have been a martial artist since the age of nineteen and a practicing Buddhist since about 1980. So one might also say that in fiction I attempt to interface Eastern and Western philosophical traditions, always with the hope that some new perception of experience—especially 'black experience'—will emerge from these meditations.''

Johnson and two fellow writers, Frank Chin and Colleen McElroy, are the subjects of a documentary film profile titled ''Spirit of Place.'' Written by filmmaker Jean Walkinshaw, the film was first broadcast by KCTS-TV in Seattle, Washington, and has been submitted for national broadcast by the Public Broadcasting Service.

BIOGRAPHICAL/CRITICAL SOURCES:

BOOKS

Contemporary Literary Criticism, Volume 7, Gale, 1977.
Dictionary of Literary Biography, Volume 33: *Afro-American Fiction Writers After 1955,* Gale, 1984.

PERIODICALS

Callaloo, October, 1978.
CLA Journal, June, 1978.
Gargoyle, June, 1978.
Literature, Fiction, and the Arts Review, June 30, 1983.
Los Angeles Times Book Review, November 21, 1982.
New Yorker, December 20, 1982.
New York Times, February 5, 1986.
New York Times Book Review, January 12, 1975, January 9, 1983, March 30, 1986.
Sewanee Review, January, 1975.
Time, January 6, 1975.
Times Literary Supplement, January 6, 1984.
Village Voice, July 19, 1983.
Washington Post Book World, December 15, 1982.

*   *   *

JOHNSON, Charles S(purgeon)   1893-1956

PERSONAL: Born July 24, 1893, in Bristol, Va.; died following a heart attack, October 27, 1956, in Louisville, Ky.; son of Charles Henry (a minister) and Winifred (Branch) Johnson; married Marie Antoinette Burgette, November 6, 1920; children: Charles, Jr., Robert Burgette, Jeh Vincent, Patricia Marie Clifford. *Education:* Virginia Union University, B.A., 1916; University of Chicago, Ph.B., 1918. *Politics:* Democrat. *Religion:* Congregationalist.

ADDRESSES: Home—1611 Meharry Blvd., Nashville, Tenn. *Office*—c/o Fisk University, Nashville, Tenn.

CAREER: Director of Department of Research and Investigations for Chicago Urban League, 1917-19; associate executive secretary for Chicago Commission on Race Relations, 1919-21; National Urban League, New York, N. Y., director of Department of Research and Investigations, 1921-28; Fisk University, Nashville, Tenn., professor of sociology and chairman of department of social sciences, beginning in 1928, president of the university, 1946-56. Delegate to United Nations Educational, Scientific, and Cultural Organization (UNESCO) conferences in Paris in 1946 and in Mexico City in 1947. Delegate to World Council of Churches in Amsterdam in 1948 and to Conference on Indian-American Relations in New Delhi in 1949. Member of numerous government committees on sociological matters, including the commission appointed by the League of Nations to investigate forced labor in Liberia in 1930, the commission sent to Japan in 1946 by the State Department to organize the Japanese educational system, and the commission established by the Eisenhower administration in 1952 to study the health needs of the nation. Participant in several private organizations, including director in 1933 and co-director from 1934 to 1938 of the Institute of Race Relations at Swarthmore College, co-director of the race relations program and a member of the board of trustees from 1943 to 1948 of the Julius Rosenwald Fund, and a director from 1944 to 1950 of the Race Relations Division of the American Missionary Association of the Congregational and Christian Churches of America. *Military service:* U. S. Army, 1918-19, served as a sergeant with the 893d Pioneer Infantry.

AWARDS, HONORS: Recipient of many awards and honors, including the William E. Harmon Gold Medal from the Harmon Foundation, 1930, for his achievements in the field of social science, the Anisfield-Wolf Award from *Saturday Review*, 1938, for his book *The Negro College Graduate*, the Russwurm Award for Public Service from the Negro Newspaper Publishers' Association, and the Social Action Churchmanship Award of the General Council of the Congregational Christian Churches. Honorary Litt.D. degrees conferred by Virginia Union University in 1938 and Columbia University in 1947, an honorary L.H.D. degree by Howard University in 1941, and honorary LL.D. degrees by Harvard University in 1948, the University of Glasgow, Scotland, in 1952, Lincoln University in 1955, and Central State College, Xenia, Ohio, in 1956.

WRITINGS:

(Editor) *Ebony and Topaz: A Collectanea*, Urban League, 1927, reprinted, Books for Libraries, 1971.

The Negro in American Civilization: A Study of Negro Life and Race Relations in the Light of Social Research, Holt, 1930, reprinted, Johnson, 1970.

Negro Housing: Report of the Committee on Negro Housing, edited by John M. Gries and James Ford, President's Conference on Home Building and Home Ownership (Washington, D. C.), 1932, reprinted, Negro Universities Press, 1969.

The Economic Status of Negroes: Summary and Analysis of the Materials Presented at the Conference on the Economic Status of the Negro, Held in Washington, D.C., May 11-13, 1933, Under the Sponsorship of the Julius Rosenwald Fund, Fisk University Press, 1933, reprinted, New York Public Library, 1974.

Shadow of the Plantation, University of Chicago Press, 1934, reprinted, 1966.

(With Willis Duke Weatherford) *Race Relations: Adjustment of Whites and Negroes in the United States*, Heath, 1934, reprinted, Negro Universities Press, 1969.

(With Edwin R. Embree and W.W. Alexander) *The Collapse of Cotton Tenancy: Summary of Field Studies and Statistical Surveys, 1933-1935*, University of North Carolina Press, 1935, reprinted, Books for Libraries, 1972.

A Preface to Racial Understanding, Friendship, 1936.

The Negro College Graduate, University of North Carolina Press, 1938, reprinted, Negro Universities Press, 1969.

Growing Up in the Black Belt: Negro Youth in the Rural South, with an introduction by St. Clair Drake, American Council on Education, 1941, reprinted, Schocken, 1967.

(Co-author) *Statistical Atlas of Southern Counties: Listing and Analysis of Socio-Economic Indices of 1,104 Southern Counties*, University of North Carolina Press, 1941.

Patterns of Negro Segregation, Harper, 1943, reprinted as *Backgrounds to Patterns of Negro Segregation*, Crowell, 1970.

(Co-author) *To Stem This Tide: A Survey of Racial Tension Areas in the United States*, Pilgrim Press, 1943, reprinted, AMS Press, 1969.

(Editor) *Education and the Cultural Process: Papers Presented at Symposium Commemorating the Seventy-fifth Anniversary of the Founding of Fisk University, April 29-May 4, 1941*, University of Chicago Press, 1943, reprinted, Negro Universities Press, 1970.

(With Herman H. Long) *People Versus Property: Race Restrictive Covenants in Housing*, Fisk University Press, 1947.

(Co-author) *Into the Main Stream: A Survey of Best Practices in Race Relations in the South*, University of North Carolina Press, 1947, reprinted, 1967.

Bitter Canaan: The Story of the Negro Republic, with an introduction by John Stanfield, Transaction Books, 1987.

Contributor to *Recent Gains in American Civilization*, edited by Kirby Page, Harcourt, 1928. Contributor of articles to periodicals, including *Opportunity*, *Journal of Negro History*, and *New York Times*.

SIDELIGHTS: For four decades Charles S. Johnson worked quietly but steadfastly in his efforts to improve race relations between blacks and whites in the United States. As the chief black sociologist of his period Johnson wrote the scholarly books that documented the causes of race riots, the effects of racism on the personalities of black youths, and the necessity for blacks to become a part of the mainstream of American life. As the first black president of Fisk University Johnson was the driving force behind the establishment of Fisk as a first-rate institution the rival of Booker T. Washington's Tuskegee Institute. And, most of all, as founder and editor of the National Urban League's *Opportunity: A Journal of Negro Life*, Johnson helped generate one of the most impressive cultural movements in American history, the Harlem Renaissance of the 1920s.

It was in 1923 that, in addition to his duties as director of the National Urban League's Department of Research and Investigations, Johnson assumed the task of editing the league's new magazine, *Opportunity*. Eugene Kinckle Jones, executive secretary of the league, set the tone of *Opportunity* when in the first issue he wrote that it would "depict Negro life as it is with no exaggerations. We shall try to set down interestingly but without sugar-coating or generalization the findings of careful scientific surveys and the facts gathered from research." Johnson, while supporting Jones's position, noted an additional dimension that *Opportunity* would report, when in the next issue he wrote: "There are aspects of the cultural side of Negro life that have been long neglected." Very quickly *Opportunity* became more than a house organ of the Urban League.

Like W.E.B. Du Bois's *Crisis* magazine, *Opportunity* provided an outlet for publication to young black writers and scholars whose work was not acceptable to other established media. Although *Crisis* was older and had a larger circulation than *Opportunity*, the orientation of its editor, W.E.B. Du Bois, was more political than Johnson's. *Opportunity* did not neglect political issues: it too reported on scientific surveys of discrimination and conditions in the black community in housing, health, employment, and other economical and sociological areas. *Opportunity*, however, made its most enduring contribution in reporting black culture in the United States and the world at large. In the May, 1924, issue, for instance, black scholars Alain Locke, Albert C. Barnes, and Paul Guillaume all contributed articles to a special issue on African art. And in the November, 1926, issue, *Opportunity* presented a special "Caribbean issue." Among other features it included poems by Claude McKay, an article on West Indian composers and musicians, and W.A. Domingo's "The West Indies."

It was in the popular *Opportunity* dinners and contests, however, that Johnson was most successful in promoting the new awakening of black culture. An early observer of the creative genius of the many black artists of the 1920s, Johnson, along with the Urban League administration, moved deliberately to bring the white publishers and the black writers together. The dinners, which gathered together white editors and black artists, served to showcase black literary and artistic talent and to secure patronage for the Renaissance movement from white publishers. The contests, which awarded first, second, and third prizes for short stories, poems, plays, and essays as well as a guarantee of publication, were open not only to black contributors but also to nonblacks on topics about blacks. Many of the contest winners, for the most part unknown to white publishers, were well known within black literary circles. Among them were short-story writers John F. Matheus, Zora Neale Hurston, and Eric D. Walrond, poets Langston Hughes and Countee Cullen, essayists E. Franklin Frazier, Sterling A. Brown, and Laura D. Wheatley, and playwright Warren A. MacDonald.

The first *Opportunity* dinners and contests were the most successful. In subsequent years there were more contestants, but the submissions were of a lesser quality, causing Johnson's enthusiasm to wane. In 1927, the year before he left the Urban League, Johnson gathered what he judged to be the best of the work published in *Opportunity* and collected it in *Ebony and Topaz, A Collectanea*. A diverse sampling of Johnson's conception of Afro-American artistic pursuits in the 1920s, the volume contained poetry, short fiction, drama, essays, translations, paintings, and drawings. Represented are the best known artists and writers of the Harlem Renaissance, including Gwendolyn Bennett, Arna Bontemps, Sterling A. Brown, Countee Cullen, Langston Hughes, Zora Neale Hurston, and Helene Johnson.

Years later Johnson had occasion in "The Negro Renaissance and Its Significance," a speech given at Howard University and later assembled by Fisk University Library into a special collection, to look back at the Harlem Renaissance. Even though more than a quarter of a century had passed since its heyday, Johnson seemed more convinced than ever of its success. He said of the 1920s: "It was a period, not only of the quivering search for freedom but of a cultural, if not a social and racial emancipation. It was unabashedly self-conscious and race conscious. But it was race consciousness with an extraordinary facet in that it had virtues that could be incorporated into the cultural bloodstream of the nation."

BIOGRAPHICAL/CRITICAL SOURCES:

BOOKS

Anderson, Jervis, *This Was Harlem: A Cultural Portrait, 1900-1950,* Farrar, Straus, 1981.
Blackwell, James E. and Morris Janowitz, editors, *Black Sociologists: Historical and Contemporary Perspectives,* University of Chicago Press, 1974.
Bone, Robert A., *The Negro Novel in America,* Yale University Press, 1958.
Bontemps, Arna, editor, *The Harlem Renaissance Remembered,* Dodd, 1972.
Clarke, John Henrik, editor, *Harlem: A Community in Transition,* Citadel, 1964.
Cruse, Harold, *The Crisis of the Negro Intellectual,* Apollo, 1968.
Current Biography, H.W. Wilson, 1946, January, 1957.
Dictionary of Literary Biography, Volume 51: *Afro-American Writers From the Harlem Renaissance to 1940,* Gale, 1987.
Embree, Edwin R., *Thirteen Against the Odds,* Viking, 1945.
Huggins, Nathan I., *Harlem Renaissance,* Oxford University Press, 1971.
Lewis, David Levering, *When Harlem Was in Vogue,* Knopf, 1981.
Locke, Alain, *The New Negro,* Atheneum, 1969.

Meier, August, *Negro Thought in America, 1880-1915,* University of Michigan Press, 1963.
Richardson, Joe M., *A History of Fisk University, 1865-1946,* University of Alabama Press, 1980.

PERIODICALS

Black World, November, 1970.
Ebony, February, 1957.
Massachusetts Review, autumn, 1979.
Negro History Bulletin, April, 1968.
Opportunity, Volume I, number 1, January, 1923; Volume I, number 2, February, 1923.
Phylon, Volume 17, fourth quarter, 1956.

OBITUARIES:

PERIODICALS

New York Times, October 28, 1956.

—*Sketch by Joanne M. Peters*

*   *   *

JOHNSON, Fenton   1888-1958

PERSONAL: Born May 7, 1888, in Chicago, Ill.; died September 17, 1958; son of Elijah H. and Jesse (Taylor) Johnson; married. *Education:* Attended University of Chicago, Northwestern University, and Columbia University, c. 1913.

CAREER: State University, Louisville, Ky., English teacher, c. 1912; writer for Eastern Press Association in New York City; acting dramatic editor of *New York News; Champion* (magazine), Chicago, Ill., editor, 1916-17; *Favorite Magazine,* Chicago, founder, 1918, editor, 1918-20; worked for Federal Writers' Project (Works Progress Administration) in Chicago during the 1930s. Founder of Reconciliation Movement (for racial cooperation), New York City, 1919-20.

MEMBER: Authors' League of America, Alpha Phi Alpha.

WRITINGS:

A Little Dreaming (poems), Peterson Linotyping Co. (Chicago), 1913, reprint, McGrath, 1969.
Visions of the Dusk (poems), privately printed (New York), 1915, facsimile edition, Books for Libraries, 1971.
Songs of the Soil (poems), privately printed (New York), 1916, reprint, AMS press, 1975.
For the Highest Good (essays), Favorite Magazine (Chicago), 1920, reprint, McGrath, 1969.
Tales of Darkest America (short stories), Favorite Magazine, 1920, facsimile edition, Books for Libraries, 1971.

Also author of unpublished poem collections "African Nights" and "The Daily Grind: 42 WPA Poems"; author of plays produced at Pekin Theater in Chicago, Ill., c. 1907. Work represented in anthologies, including *The New Poetry: An Anthology of Twentieth-Century Verse in English,* edited by Harriet Monroe and Alice Corbin Henderson, Macmillan, 1923; *An Anthology of American Poetry: Lyric America, 1630-1930,* edited by Alfred Kreymborg, Tudor, 1930; *The Book of American Negro Poetry,* edited by James Weldon Johnson, Harcourt, 1922, enlarged edition, 1931; *The Poetry of the Negro, 1746-1949,* edited by Langston Hughes and Arna Bontemps, Doubleday, 1949; *American Negro Poetry,* edited by Bontemps, Hill & Wang, 1963, revised edition, 1974; and *Black-american Literature, 1760-Present,* edited by Ruth Miller, Glencoe Press, 1971. Contributor to periodicals, including *Po-*

etry: A Magazine of Verse, Others, Crisis, Favorite Magazine, and *Liberator.*

SIDELIGHTS: In her *Dictionary of Literary Biography* entry for early twentieth-century poet Fenton Johnson, Shirley Lumpkin described Johnson's literary career as "a downward spiral." The only child in a middle-class black family living in Chicago, Johnson was able to indulge his interest in drama and poetry; some of his plays were produced at the Pekin Theater when he was nineteen and his first poetry collection was published soon after. The privately-printed volume was well received, its generous patrons financing two more collections of poems as well as Johnson's matriculation at the Pulitzer School of Journalism at Columbia University. But while Johnson wrote for the Eastern Press Association for a time, his real ambitions lay in exploring the boundaries of literature. He founded several literary publications, the most notable being *Favorite Magazine;* it folded after two years, however, typifying Johnson's lifelong struggle "to obtain a foothold in literature." Widespread recognition continued to elude the writer and his self-published final two books—essay and short story collections—added little to his reputation. After 1920 Johnson's work appeared in print largely through the interest of others, finding its way into an occasional anthology or literary magazine. He spent the remaining three decades of his life in literary obscurity.

Scholars agree that Johnson's failure to capture the literary imagination of his time was due, in part, to the age of transition in which he lived. Rural blacks were migrating to American cities, igniting an era of intense racism; "serious literary men of color," wrote J. Saunders Redding in *To Make a Poet Black,* "found it hard to go beyond the limits of popular concept and to destroy the picture of themselves as it had been purposefully created in the mind of white America." Johnson's active literary years followed the reign of popular Negro dialect poet Paul Laurence Dunbar and presaged new black writers Claude McKay, Jean Toomer, Langston Hughes, and Countee Cullen. Ironically, the dozen or so poems through which Johnson's reputation survives were written after the poet's youthful successes, when poverty and obscurity prompted him to abandon his celebratory lyric and dialect styles for free verse depictions of urban despair and racial hopelessness.

According to Lumpkin, Johnson's first book of verse—*A Little Dreaming*—is marked by "Victorian/romantic diction, which was characteristic of the popular public 'cultivated' Anglo-American poetry of the early twentieth century." James P. Hutchinson judged the volume artificial and imitative in a *Studies in Black Literature* article, writing, "It is evident . . . that . . . Johnson sacrifices his own experience and tradition for that line of disembodied, sentimental and lyric verse written in a style which deservedly became outmoded." But while exploring the traditional poetic subjects of love, birth, death, grief, and gladness in *A Little Dreaming,* informed Lumpkin, Johnson also praises "the beauty of Afro-Americans"; "conceiving of himself and his poetry in such archaic, cliched, pseudoromantic terms in 1913 did not . . . mean that Johnson saw himself as separate from other black people." And the atypical theme of one poem in the collection, "The Plaint of the Factory Child," anticipates the writer's later, more powerful verse.

In his second poetry volume, *Visions of the Dusk,* "Johnson exchanges the lyric tradition for the Negro dialect tradition," observed Hutchinson, with "the subject matter . . . largely the portrayal of Negro life in America." Using the popular plantation-dialect style—with its gross misspellings and naive misuses of English representing black speech—for much of his verse, Johnson also experimented with poetic versions of Negro spirituals. "Neither dialect nor transcriptions of folk spirituals, Johnson's poetic imitations use rhythmical arrangements, imagery, and repetition to catch the patterns of the spirituals successfully enough to interest many future anthologists and editors," Lumpkin reported. "Fenton Johnson's spiritual poems . . . were the first genuinely powerful attempts to communicate some of the essence of spirituals in purely literary form."

The poetry collection *Songs of the Soil* contains more of the same; judging Johnson's nondialect verse superior, Lumpkin explained that the poet "did not discover the limitations of plantation dialect until later in his career." Still, "Johnson never used it to maintain plantation stereotypes," the critic stated. "It [was] never an evocation of the 'good old days of slavery'. . . . Nor were his speakers ever the foolish, sentimental, or undignified caricatures associated with minstrel characterizations of blacks." Lumpkin continued: "[Johnson's] linguistic styles might be imitative and reflective of the tastes of his age, but his attitudes and ideas are not sentimental nor are they molded by the stereotypical expectation of a white audience."

While the six short stories that comprise Johnson's *Tales of Darkest America* are largely dismissed as undistinguished, the collection does introduce the new theme of the Negro in the city. "The most memorable sketch, 'A Woman of Good Cheer,' succeeds because it treats the discrepancy between the uncomplicated life of the rural Negro and the destruction apparent in the urban experience of Blacks," wrote Hutchinson. "This latter theme is, fortunately, the subject of most of Johnson's [later] poems." Beset by professional failures and financial ruin, the writer expressed his weariness and despair in free verse that employed the stylistic innovations pioneered by Chicago "golden era" poets Vachel Lindsay, Edgar Lee Masters, and Carl Sandburg; Redding noted that "it is probably through Fenton Johnson that the influence of [these] midwestern poets . . . first touched Negro writers." Conveying a nihilistic view of life rarely encountered before in Afro-American verse (as in his best-known poem "Tired"), Johnson is regarded by some as one of the first black revolutionary poets. But to label his as such "is to engage in critical distortion," declared Hutchinson, maintaining that a survey of Johnson's literary output reveals a sentimental lyricist whose bleak free verse is atypical. Calling the writer "a minor poet . . . who responded, somewhat tardily, to the spirit of the times among the black urban poor," Lumpkin agreed, but added: "Considering the times during which he tried to make his way as a poet who sang of his people, times which included the most virulent expression of racial hatred and the Great Depression, and considering his own reversal of fortune, it seems remarkable that Johnson was able to write even a handful of living poems, poems that continue to strike the hearts of poets and readers."

BIOGRAPHICAL/CRITICAL SOURCES:

BOOKS

Brown, Sterling A., *Negro Poetry and Drama,* Associates in Negro Folk Education (Washington, D.C.), 1937.

Brown, Sterling A., Arthur Davis, and Ulysses Lee, editors, *The Negro Caravan,* Dryden, 1941.

Chapman, Abraham, editor, *Black Voices,* New American Library, 1968.

Cullen, Countee, editor, *Caroling Dusk: An Anthology of Verse by Negro Poets*, Harper, 1927.

Dictionary of Literary Biography, Volume 45: *American Poets, 1880-1945*, Gale, 1986.

Gibson, Donald B., editor, *Modern Black Poets: A Collection of Critical Essays*, Prentice-Hall, 1973.

Gloster, Hugh, *Negro Voices in American Fiction*, University of North Carolina Press, 1948, Russell, 1968.

Hayden, Robert, editor and author of introduction, *Kaleidoscope: Poems by American Negro Poets*, Harcourt, 1967.

Johnson, James Weldon, *The Book of American Negro Poetry*, Harcourt, 1922, reprint, 1969.

Kerlin, Robert T., *Negro Poets and Their Poems*, Associated Publishers, 1923, revised third edition, 1935.

Redding, J. Saunders, *To Make A Poet Black*, University of North Carolina Press, 1939, McGrath, 1968.

Redmond, Eugene B., *Drumvoices: The Mission of Afro-American Poetry, A Critical History*, Anchor/Doubleday, 1976.

Wagner, Jean, *Black Poets of the United States From Paul Laurence Dunbar to Langston Hughes*, translated by Kenneth Douglas, University of Illinois Press, 1973.

White, Newman Ivey and Walter Clinton Jackson, editors, *An Anthology of Verse by American Negroes*, Trinity College Press, 1924, Moore, 1968.

PERIODICALS

American Review of Reviews, January, 1914.
Crisis, volume 7, 1914, volume 12, 1916.
Literary World (London), April 2, 1914.
Poetry: A Magazine of Verse, volume 12, 1918.
Studies in Black Literature, autumn, 1976.

—*Sketch by Nancy Pear*

* * *

JOHNSON, Georgia Douglas (Camp) 1886-1966

PERSONAL: Born September 10, 1886, in Atlanta, Ga.; died May 14, 1966, in Washington, D.C.; daughter of George and Laura (Jackson) Camp; married Henry Lincoln Johnson (a lawyer and politician) in 1903 (husband died, 1925); children: Henry Lincoln, Jr., Peter Douglas. *Education:* Attended Atlanta University, Howard University, and Oberlin College. *Politics:* Republican.

CAREER: Writer. Taught school in Alabama. Served various U.S. government agencies in Washington, D.C., including as commissioner of conciliation in Department of Labor, 1925-34.

MEMBER: League of Neighbors, League for Abolition of Capital Punishment.

AWARDS, HONORS: First prize in drama contest sponsored by *Opportunity* magazine, 1927, for *Plumes;* received honorary doctorate in literature from Atlanta University, 1965.

WRITINGS:

POETRY

The Heart of a Woman, and Other Poems, introduction by William Stanley Braithwaite, Cornhill, 1918, AMS Press, 1975.

Bronze: A Book of Verse, introduction by W. E. B. DuBois, B. J. Brimmer, 1922, AMS Press, 1975.

An Autumn Love Cycle, introduction by Alain Locke, H. Vinal, 1928, Books for Libraries Press, 1971.

Share My World: A Book of Poems, privately printed in Washington, D.C., 1962.

Poetry represented in anthologies, including *An Anthology of Revolutionary Poetry*, edited by Graham Marcus; *Black and White: An Anthology of Washington Verse*, edited by Joseph Cloyd Byars; *The Book of American Negro Poetry*, edited by James Weldon Johnson; *The Poetry of Black America*, edited by Arnold Adoff; *The Poetry of the Negro, 1746-1970*, edited by Langston Hughes and Arna Wendell Bontemps; and *Voice of the Negro, 1919*, edited by Robert T. Kerlin.

PLAYS

Blue Blood (first produced in New York City in 1927), Appleton, 1927.

Plumes: A Play in One Act (first produced in Brooklyn at Central YMCA, February 28, 1928), Samuel French, 1927.

"Frederick Douglass Leaves for Freedom," first produced in Los Angeles at the New Negro Theatre, 1940, published in *Negro History in Thirteen Plays*, edited by Willis Richardson and May Miller, Associated (Washington, D.C.), 1935.

Also author of "William and Ellen Craft," "A Sunday Morning in the South: A One-Act Play," "Blue-Eyed Black Boy," and "Safe."

Plays represented in anthologies, including *An Anthology of American Negro Literature*, edited by Victor Francis Calverton; *Black Theatre, U.S.A.: Forty-five Plays by Black American Playwrights, 1847-1974*, edited by James V. Hatch and Ted Shine; *Fifty More Contemporary One-Act Plays*, edited by Frank Shay; and *Plays of Negro Life*, edited by Alain Locke and Montgomery Gregory.

OTHER

Also author of songs and short stories.

Contributor to periodicals, including *Crisis, Journal of Negro History, Liberator, Opportunity, Phylon, Voice of the Negro*, and *Worker's Monthly*.

WORK IN PROGRESS: Rainbow Silhouettes, a collection of short stories; *The Life and Times of Henry Lincoln Johnson*, a book about Georgia Douglas Johnson's husband; *The Torch*, a collection of works by various authors.

SIDELIGHTS: Georgia Douglas Johnson was one of the first black female poets to achieve prominence in America and is considered one of the finest writers of her time. Her four volumes of verse, published between 1918 and 1962, contain more that two hundred poems, and her poems and plays have been published in numerous anthologies of black literature. A resident of Washington, D.C., since 1909, Johnson took part in literary activities there and hosted regular meetings with Harlem Renaissance writers and other artists, including Countee Cullen, Langston Hughes, Alain Locke, May Miller, and Jean Toomer. In addition to writing, Johnson worked for U.S. government agencies and actively supported women's and minorities' rights.

Johnson's first volume of poetry, *The Heart of a Woman, and Other Poems*, contains short, introspective verses describing emotions—such as "Sympathy," "Isolation," and "Despair"—that the author felt dwell within "the heart of a woman." The poet's second collection, *Bronze*, addresses the issue of race as well as that of gender; in contrast to the subtle, placid tone of Johnson's first work, observed Winona Fletcher

302

in *Dictionary of Literary Biography*, *Bronze* "gives evidence of a new strength in Johnson's feelings of protest against injustice and racism." Through her verse, Fletcher noted, Johnson "reached out to the people who had blazed the trail from slavery through Reconstruction to the modern world of segregation and racism."

An Autumn Love Cycle, Johnson's third collection of poetry, expresses mature acceptance of life's conditions instead of impetuous outrage at civil inequality. "It [reflects] more of the earlier, romantic poet" depicted in *The Heart of a Woman,* ventured Fletcher, "and less of the voice of social protest" in *Bronze*. Divided into five sections, "*An Autumn Love Cycle* focuses upon the various states of love, from enraptured initial engagement to disillusionment with the loss of love," the reviewer explained. Johnson's final collection of verse, *Share My World,* was printed privately in 1962.

In addition to her poetry, Johnson wrote several plays. Two were published in 1927: *Blue Blood* and *Plumes,* which was named best play by *Opportunity* magazine in its 1927 drama contest. Through many of her plays, Johnson expressed the moral outrage she withheld from her poetry. "A Sunday Morning in the South," "Blue-Eyed Black Boy," and "Safe," for example, protested the brutal and unreasonable lynchings of blacks by white mobs. Despite the respect the plays have gained since their publication in various anthologies, producers during Johnson's lifetime refused to stage the plays because, as Fletcher explained, "they were all aghast at [Johnson's] notion that a lynching could take place for no obvious 'good reason' and impugned the playwright for suggesting this in her drama."

In 1965 the poet and playwright accepted an honorary doctorate in literature from Atlanta University. At the time of her death the following year, Johnson left uncompleted three manuscripts: *The Torch,* a collection of works by various authors; *The Life and Times of Henry Lincoln Johnson,* about the author's husband; and *Rainbow Silhouettes,* a collection of Johnson's short stories.

BIOGRAPHICAL/CRITICAL SOURCES:

BOOKS

Dictionary of Literary Biography, Volume 51: *Afro-American Writers From the Harlem Renaissance to 1940,* Gale, 1987.

PERIODICALS

Atlanta University Bulletin, July, 1953, July, 1963.
Crisis, number 25, 1923, number 36, 1929, December, 1952.
Ebony, February, 1949.
Opportunity, December, 1923, April, 1929.

*   *   *

JOHNSON, J. R.
See JAMES, C(yril) L(ionel) R(obert)

*   *   *

JOHNSON, James Weldon   1871-1938

PERSONAL: Born June 17, 1871, in Jacksonville, Fla.; died following an automobile accident, June 26, 1938, in Wiscasset, Me.; buried in Brooklyn, N.Y.; son of James (a restaurant headwaiter) and Helen Louise (a musician and schoolteacher; maiden name, Dillette) Johnson; married Grace Nail, February 3, 1910. *Education:* Atlanta University, A.B., 1894, A.M., 1904; graduate study at Columbia University, c. 1902-05.

ADDRESSES: Home—Nashville, Tenn.

CAREER: Poet, novelist, songwriter, editor, historian, civil rights leader, diplomat, lawyer, and educator. Stanton Central Grammar School for Negroes, Jacksonville, Fla., teacher, later principal, 1894-1901; *Daily American* (newspaper), Jacksonville, founder and co-editor, 1895-96; admitted to the Bar of the State of Florida, 1898; private law practice, Jacksonville, 1898-1901; songwriter for the musical theater in partnership with brother, J. Rosamond Johnson, and Bob Cole, New York City, 1901-06; United States Consul to Puerto Cabello, Venezuela, 1906-09, and to Corinto, Nicaragua, 1909-13; *New York Age* (newspaper), New York City, editorial writer, 1914-24; National Association for the Advancement of Colored People (NAACP), New York City, field secretary, 1916-20, executive secretary, 1920-30; Fisk University, Nashville, Tenn., professor of creative literature and writing, 1931-38.

Elected treasurer of the Colored Republican Club, New York City, and participated in Theodore Roosevelt's presidential campaign, both in 1904; lectured on literature and black culture at numerous colleges and universities during the 1930s, including New York, Northwestern, and Yale universities, Oberlin and Swarthmore colleges, and the universities of North Carolina and Chicago. Served as director of the American Fund for Public Service and as trustee of Atlanta University.

MEMBER: American Society of Composers, Authors, and Publishers (charter member), Academy of Political Science, Ethical Society, Civic Club (New York City).

AWARDS, HONORS: Spingarn Medal from NAACP, 1925, for outstanding achievement by an American Negro; Harmon Gold Award for *God's Trombones;* Julius Rosenwald Fund grant, 1929; W.E.B. Du Bois Prize for Negro Literature, 1933; named first incumbent of Spence Chair of Creative Literature at Fisk University; honorary doctorates from Talladega College and Howard University.

WRITINGS:

The Autobiography of an Ex-Coloured Man (novel), Sherman, French, 1912, Arden Library, 1978.
(Translator) Fernando Periquet, *Goyescas; or, The Rival Lovers* (opera libretto), G. Schirmer, 1915.
Fifty Years and Other Poems, Cornhill, 1917, AMS Press, 1975.
(Editor) *The Book of American Negro Poetry,* Harcourt, 1922, revised edition (publisher unknown), 1969.
(Editor) *The Book of American Negro Spirituals,* Viking, 1925.
(Editor) *The Second Book of Negro Spirituals,* Viking, 1926.
(Editor) *The Books of American Negro Spirituals* (contains *The Book of American Negro Spirituals* and *The Second Book of Negro Spirituals*), Viking, 1940, reprinted, 1964.
God's Trombones: Seven Negro Sermons in Verse (poetry), illustrations by Aaron Douglas, Viking, 1927, Penguin, 1976.
Black Manhattan (nonfiction), Knopf, 1930, Arno, 1968.
Along This Way: The Autobiography of James Weldon Johnson, Viking, 1933, Da Capo, 1973.
Negro Americans, What Now? (nonfiction), Viking, 1934, Da Capo, 1973.
Saint Peter Relates an Incident: Selected Poems, Viking, 1935, AMS Press, 1974.
The Great Awakening, Revell, 1938.

Also author of *Selected Poems*, 1936.

Contributor of articles and poems to numerous newspapers and magazines, including the *Chicago Defender*, *Times-Union* (Jacksonville, Fla.), *New York Age*, *New York Times*, *Pittsburgh Courier*, *Savannah Tribune*, *The Century*, *The Crisis*, *The Nation*, *The Independent*, *Harper's*, *The Bookman*, *Forum*, and *Scholastic;* poetry represented in many anthologies; songs published by Joseph W. Stern & Co., Edward B. Marks Music Corp., and others; author of numerous pamphlets on current events published by the NAACP, *The Nation*, *The Century*, and others.

SIDELIGHTS: James Weldon Johnson distinguished himself equally as a man of letters and as a civil rights leader in the early decades of the twentieth century. A talented poet and novelist, Johnson is credited with bringing a new standard of artistry and realism to black literature in such works as *The Autobiography of an Ex-Coloured Man* and *God's Trombones*. His pioneering studies of black poetry, music, and theater in the 1920s also helped introduce many white Americans to the genuine Afro-American creative spirit, hithterto known mainly through the distortions of the minstrel show and dialect poetry. Meanwhile, as head of the National Association for the Advancement of Colored People (NAACP) during the 1920s, Johnson led determined civil rights campaigns in an effort to remove the legal, political, and social obstacles hindering black achievement. Johnson's multi-faceted career, which also included stints as a diplomat in Latin America and a successful Tin Pan Alley songwriter, testified to his intellectual breadth, self-confidence, and deep-rooted belief that the future held unlimited new opportunities for black Americans.

Johnson was born in Jacksonville, Florida, in 1871, and his upbringing in this relatively tolerant Southern town may help explain his later political moderation. Both his father, a resort hotel headwaiter, and his mother, a schoolteacher, had lived in the North and had never been enslaved, and James and his brother John Rosamond grew up in broadly cultured and economically secure surroundings that were unusual among Southern black families at the time. Johnson's mother stimulated his early interests in reading, drawing, and music, and he attended the segregated Stanton School, where she taught, until the eighth grade. Since high schools were closed to blacks in Jacksonville, Johnson left home to attend both secondary school and college at Atlanta University, where he took his bachelor's degree in 1894. It was during his college years, as Johnson recalled in his autobiography, *Along This Way*, that he first became aware of the depth of the racial problem in the United States. Race questions were vigorously debated on campus, and Johnson's experience teaching black schoolchildren in a poor district of rural Georgia during two summers deeply impressed him with the need to improve the lives of his people. The struggles and aspirations of American blacks form a central theme in the thirty or so poems that Johnson wrote as a student.

Returning to Jacksonville in 1894, Johnson was appointed a teacher and principal of the Stanton School and managed to expand the curriculum to include high school-level classes. He also became an active local spokesman on black social and political issues and in 1895 founded the *Daily American*, the first black-oriented daily newspaper in the United States. During its brief life, the newspaper became a voice against racial injustice and served to encourage black advancement through individual effort—a "self-help" position that echoed the more conservative civil rights leadership of the day. Although the

newspaper folded for lack of readership the following year, Johnson's ambitious publishing effort attracted the attention of such prominent black leaders as W.E.B. Du Bois and Booker T. Washington.

Meanwhile Johnson read law with the help of a local white lawyer, and in 1898 he became the first black lawyer admitted to the Florida Bar since Reconstruction. Johnson practiced law in Jacksonville for several years in partnership with a former Atlanta University classmate while continuing to serve as the Stanton School's principal. He also continued to write poetry and discovered his gift for songwriting in collaboration with his brother Rosamond, a talented composer. Among other songs in a spiritual-influenced popular idiom, Johnson penned the lyrics to "Lift Every Voice and Sing," a tribute to black endurance, hope, and religious faith that was later adopted by the NAACP and dubbed "the Negro National Anthem."

In 1901, bored by Jacksonville's provincialism and disturbed by mounting incidents of racism there, the Johnson brothers set out for New York City to seek their fortune writing songs for the musical theater. In partnership with Bob Cole they secured a publishing contract paying a monthly stipend and over the next five years composed some two hundred songs for Broadway and other musical productions, including such hit numbers as "Under the Bamboo Tree," "The Old Flag Never Touched the Ground," and "Didn't He Ramble." The trio, who soon became known as "Those Ebony Offenbachs," avoided writing for racially exploitative minstrel shows but often found themselves obliged to present simplified and stereotyped images of rural black life to suit white audiences. But the Johnsons and Cole also produced works like the six-song suite titled "The Evolution of Ragtime" that helped document and expose important black musical idioms.

During this time James Weldon Johnson also studied creative literature formally for three years at Columbia University and became active in Republican party politics. He served as treasurer of New York's Colored Republican Club in 1904 and helped write two songs for Republican candidate Theodore Roosevelt's successful presidential campaign that year. When the national black civil rights leadership split into conservative and radical factions—headed by Booker T. Washington and W.E.B. Du Bois, respectively—Johnson backed Washington, who in turn played an important role in getting the Roosevelt Administration to appoint Johnson as United States consul in Puerto Cabello, Venezuela, in 1906. With few official duties, Johnson was able to devote much of his time in that sleepy tropical port to writing poetry, including the acclaimed sonnet "Mother Night" that was published in *The Century* magazine and later included in Johnson's verse collection *Fifty Years and Other Poems*.

The consul also completed his only novel, *The Autobiography of an Ex-Coloured Man*, during his three years in Venezuela. Published anonymously in 1912, the novel attracted little attention until it was reissued under Johnson's own name more than a decade later. Even then, the book tended to draw more comment as a sociological document than as a work of fiction. (So many readers believed it to be truly autobiographical that Johnson eventually wrote his real life story, *Along This Way*, to avoid confusion.)

The Autobiography of an Ex-Coloured Man bears a superficial resemblance to other "tragic mulatto" narratives of the day that depicted, often in sentimental terms, the travails of mixed-race protagonists unable to fit into either racial culture. In Johnson's novel, the unnamed narrator is light-skinned enough to pass for white but identifies emotionally with his beloved mother's black race. In his youth, he aspires to become a great black American musical composer, but he fearfully renounces that ambition after watching a mob of whites set fire to a black man in the rural South. Though horrified and repulsed by the whites' attack, the narrator feels an even deeper shame and humiliation for himself as a black man and he subsequently allows circumstances to guide him along the easier path of "passing" as a middle-class white businessman. The protagonist finds success in this role but ends up a failure in his own terms, plagued with ambivalence over his true identity, moral values, and emotional loyalties.

Early criticism of *The Autobiography of an Ex-Coloured Man* tended to emphasize Johnson's frank and realistic look at black society and race relations more than his skill as a novelist. Carl Van Vechten, for example, found the novel "an invaluable source-book for the study of Negro psychology," and the *New Republic*'s Edmund Wilson judged the book "an excellent, honest piece of work" as "a human and sociological document" but flawed as a work of literature. In the 1950s and 1960s, however, something of a critical reappraisal of the *Autobiography* occurred that led to a new appreciation of Johnson as a crafter of fiction. In his critical study *The Negro Novel in America*, Robert A. Bone called Johnson "the only true artist among the early Negro novelists," who succeeded in "subordinating racial protest to artistic considerations." Johnson's subtle theme of moral cowardice, Bone noted, set the novel far above "the typical propaganda tract of the day." In a 1971 essay, Robert E. Fleming drew attention to Johnson's deliberate use of an unreliable narrative voice, remarking that *The Autobiography of an Ex-Coloured Man* "is not so much a panoramic novel presenting race relations throughout America as it is a deeply ironic character study of a marginal man." Johnson's psychological depth and concern with aesthetic coherence anticipated the great black literary movement of the 1920s known as the Harlem School, according to these and other critics.

In 1909, before the *Autobiography* had been published, Johnson was promoted to the consular post in Corinto, Nicaragua, a position that proved considerably more demanding than his Venezuelan job and left him little time for writing. His three-year term of service occurred during a period of intense political turmoil in Nicaragua, which culminated in the landing of U.S. troops at Corinto in 1912. In 1913, seeing little future for himself under President Woodrow Wilson's Democratic administration, Johnson resigned from the foreign service and returned to New York to become an editorial writer for the *New York Age*, the city's oldest and most distinguished black newspaper. The articles Johnson produced over the next ten years tended toward the conservative side, combining a strong sense of racial pride with a deep-rooted belief that blacks could individually improve their lot by means of self-education and hard work even before discriminatory barriers had been removed. This stress on individual effort and economic independence put Johnson closer to the position of black educator Booker T. Washington than that of the politically militant writer and scholar W.E.B. Du Bois in the great leadership dispute on how to improve the status of black Americans, but Johnson generally avoided criticizing either man by name and managed to maintain good relations with both leaders.

During this period Johnson continued to indulge his literary love. Having mastered the Spanish language in the diplomatic service, he translated Fernando Periquet's grand opera *Goyescas* into English and the Metropolitan Opera produced his libretto version in 1915. In 1917, Johnson published his first verse collection, *Fifty Years and Other Poems*, a selection from twenty years' work that drew mixed reviews. "Fifty Years," a sonorous poem commemorating the half-century since the Emancipation Proclamation, was generally singled out for praise, but critics differed on the merits of Johnson's dialect verse written after the manner of the great black dialect poet Paul Laurence Dunbar. The dialect style was highly popular at the time, but has since been criticized for pandering to sentimental white stereotypes of rural black life. In addition to his dialect work, Johnson's collection also included such powerful racial protest poems as "Brothers," about a lynching, and delicate lyrical verse on non-racial topics in the traditional style.

In 1916, at the urging of W.E.B. Du Bois, Johnson accepted the newly created post of national field secretary for the NAACP, which had grown to become the country's premier black rights advocacy and defense organization since its founding in 1910. Johnson's duties included investigating racial incidents and organizing new NAACP branches around the country, and he succeeded in significantly raising the organization's visibility and membership through the years following World War I. In 1917, Johnson organized and led a well-publicized silent march through the streets of New York City to protest lynchings, and his on-site investigation of abuses committed by American marines against black citizens of Haiti during the U.S. occupation of that Caribbean nation in 1920 captured healines and helped launch a congressional probe into the matter. Johnson's in-depth report, which was published by the *Nation* magazine in a four-part series titled "Self-Determining Haiti," also had an impact on the presidential race that year, helping to shift public sentiment from the interventionist policies associated with the Wilson Democrats toward the more isolationist position of the Republican victor, Warren Harding.

Johnson's successes as field secretary led to his appointment as NAACP executive secretary in 1920, a position he was to hold for the next ten years. This decade marked a critical turning point for the black rights movement as the NAACP and other civil rights organizations sought to defend and expand the social and economic gains blacks had achieved during the war years, when large numbers of blacks migrated to the northern cities and found industrial and manufacturing jobs. These black gains triggered a racist backlash in the early years of the decade that found virulent expression in a sharp rise in lynchings and the rapid growth of the white supremacist Ku Klux Klan terror organization in the North as well as the South. Despite this violent reaction, Johnson was credited with substantially increasing the NAACP's membership strength and political influence during this period, although his strenuous efforts to get a federal anti-lynching bill passed proved unsuccessful.

Johnson's personal politics also underwent change during the postwar years of heightened black expectations. Disappointed with the neglectful minority rights policies of Republican presidents Harding and Calvin Coolidge, Johnson broke with the Republican party in the early 1920s and briefly supported Robert LaFollette's Progressive party. LaFollette also lost the NAACP leader's backing, however, when he refused to include black demands in the Progressives' 1924 campaign platform. Though frustrated in his political objectives, Johnson opposed Marcus Garvey's separatist "Back to Africa" movement and instead urged the new black communities in the northern cities to use their potentially powerful voting strength to force racial concessions from the country's political establishment.

Even with the heavy demands of his NAACP office, the 1920s were a period of great literary productivity for Johnson. He earned critical acclaim in 1922 for editing a seminal collection of black verse, titled *The Book of American Negro Poetry*. Johnson's critical introduction to this volume provided new insights into an often ignored or denigrated genre and is now considered a classic analysis of early black contributions to American literature. Johnson went on to compile and interpret outstanding examples of the black religious song form known as the spiritual in his pioneering *The Book of American Negro Spirituals* and *The Second Book of Negro Spirituals*. These renditions of black voices formed the background for *God's Trombones*, a set of verse versions of rural black folk sermons that many critics regard as Johnson's finest poetic work. Based on the poet's recollections of the fiery preachers he had heard while growing up in Florida and Georgia, Johnson's seven sermon-poems about life and death and good and evil were deemed a triumph in overcoming the thematic and technical limitations of the dialect style while capturing, according to critics, a full resonant timbre. In *The Book of American Negro Poetry*, Johnson had compared the traditional Dunbar-style dialect verse to an organ having only two stops, one of humor and one of pathos, and he sought with *God's Trombones* to create a more flexible and dignified medium for expressing the black religious spirit. Casting out rhyme and the dialect style's buffoonish misspellings and mispronunciations, Johnson's clear and simple verses succeeded in rendering the musical rhythms, word structure, and vocabulary of the unschooled black orator in standard English. Critics also credited the poet with capturing the oratorical tricks and flourishes that a skilled preacher would use to sway his congregation, including hyperbole, repetition, abrupt mood juxtapositions, an expert sense of timing, and the ability to translate biblical imagery into the colorful, concrete terms of everyday life. "The sensitive reader cannot fail to hear the rantings of the fire-and-brimstone preacher; the extremely sensitive reader may even hear the unwritten 'Amens' of the congregation," declared Eugenia W. Collier in a 1960 essay for *Phylon*.

Johnson's efforts to preserve and win recognition for black cultural traditions drew praise from such prominent literary figures as H. L. Mencken and Mark Van Doren and contributed to the spirit of racial pride and self-confidence that marked the efflorescence of black music, art, and literature in the 1920s known as the Harlem Renaissance. This period of intense creative innovation forms the central subject of *Black Manhattan*, Johnson's informal survey of black contributions to New York's cultural life beginning as far back as the seventeenth century. The critically well-received volume focuses especially on blacks in the theater but also surveys the development of the ragtime and jazz musical idioms and discusses the earthy writings of Harlem Renaissance poets Langston Hughes, Countee Cullen, and Claude McKay. "*Black Manhattan* is a document of the 1920's—a celebration, with reservations, of both the artistic renaissance of the era and the dream of a black metropolis," noted critic Allan H. Spear in his preface to the 1968 edition of Johnson's book.

In December 1930, fatigued by the demands of his job and wanting more time to write, Johnson resigned from the NAACP and accepted a part-time teaching post in creative literature at Fisk University in Nashville, Tennessee. In 1933, he published his much-admired autobiography *Along This Way*, which discusses his personal career in the context of the larger social,

political, and cultural movements of the times. Johnson remained active in the civil rights movement while teaching at Fisk, and in 1934 he published a book-length argument in favor of racial integration titled *Negro Americans, What Now?* The civil rights struggle also figures in the title poem of Johnson's last major verse collection, *Saint Peter Relates an Incident: Selected Poems*. Inspired by an outrageous act of public discrimination by the federal government against the mothers of black soldiers killed in action, Johnson's satirical narrative poem describes a gathering of veterans' groups to witness the Resurrection Day opening of the Tomb of the Unknown Soldier. When this famous war casualty is finally revealed, he turns out to be black, a circumstance that provokes bewilderment and consternation among the assembled patriots. Despite this original conceit, the poem is generally regarded as one of Johnson's lesser efforts, hampered by structural flaws and somewhat bland writing.

Johnson died tragically in June 1938 after a train struck the car he was riding in at an unguarded rail crossing in Wiscasset, Maine. The poet and civil rights leader was widely eulogized and more than two thousand mourners attended his Harlem funeral. Known throughout his career as a generous and invariably courteous man, Johnson once summed up his personal credo as a black American in a pamphlet published by the NAACP: "I will not allow one prejudiced person or one million or one hundred million to blight my life. I will not let prejudice or any of its attendant humilitations and injustices bear me down to spiritual defeat. My inner life is mine, and I shall defend and maintain its integrity against all the powers of hell." Johnson was buried in Brooklyn's Greenwood Cemetery dressed in his favorite lounging robe and holding a copy of *God's Trombones* in his hand.

MEDIA ADAPTATIONS:

"God's Trombones" (sound recording with biographical notes by Walter White, and texts of the poems), read by Bryce Bond, music by William Martin, Folkways Records, 1965.

"Reading Poetry: The Creation" (motion picture with study guide), read by Raymond St. Jacques and Margaret O'Brien, Oxford Films, 1972.

"James Weldon Johnson" (motion picture), includes an adaptation of "The Creation" read by Raymond St. Jacques, Oxford Films, 1972.

BIOGRAPHICAL/CRITICAL SOURCES:

BOOKS

Bone, Robert A., *The Negro Novel in America*, Yale University Press, 1958.

Fleming, Robert E., *James Weldon Johnson and Arna Wendell Bontemps: A Reference Guide*, G. K. Hall, 1978.

Johnson, James Weldon, *Along This Way: The Autobiography of James Weldon Johnson*, Viking, 1933, Da Capo, 1973.

Levy, Eugene, *James Weldon Johnson: Black Leader, Black Voice*, Chicago University Press, 1973.

Twentieth-Century Literary Criticism, Volume 19, Gale, 1986.

Wagner, Jean, *Les Poetes negres des Etats Unis*, Librairie Istra, 1962, translation by Kenneth Doublas published as *Black Poets of the United States: From Paul Laurence Dunbar to Langston Hughes*, University of Illinois Press, 1973.

PERIODICALS

American Literature, March, 1971.

Crisis, June, 1971.

Journal of Popular Culture, Spring, 1968.
Nation, July 2, 1938.
New Republic, February 1, 1928, February 21, 1934.
Newsweek, July 4, 1938.
Phylon, December, 1960, Winter, 1971.
Time, July 4, 1938.

—*Sketch by Curtis Skinner*

*   *   *

JONES, Gayl 1949-

PERSONAL: Born November 23, 1949, in Lexington, Ky.; daughter of Franklin (a cook) and Lucille (Wilson) Jones. *Education:* Connecticut College, B.A., 1971; Brown University, M.A., 1973, D.A., 1975.

ADDRESSES: Office—c/o Beacon Press, 25 Beacon St., Boston, Mass. 02108.

CAREER: University of Michigan, Ann Arbor, 1975-83, began as assistant professor, became professor of English.

MEMBER: Authors Guild, Authors League of America.

AWARDS, HONORS: Award for best original production in the New England region, American College Theatre Festival, 1973, for "Chile Woman"; playwriting grant from Shubert Foundation, 1973-74; grant from Southern Fellowship Foundation, 1973-75; fellowship from Yaddo, 1974; grant from Rhode Island Council on the Arts, 1974-75; award from Howard Foundation, 1975; fiction award from *Mademoiselle*, 1975; fellowship from National Endowment of the Arts, 1976; fellowship from Michigan Society of Fellows, 1977-79; Henry Russell Award from University of Michigan, 1981.

WRITINGS:

FICTION

Corregidora (novel), Random House, 1975.
Eva's Man (novel), Random House, 1976.
White Rat (short stories), Random House, 1977.

POETRY

Song for Anninho, Lotus Press, 1981.
The Hermit-Woman, Lotus Press, 1983.
Xarque and Other Poems, Lotus Press, 1985.

OTHER

Chile Woman (play), Shubert Foundation, 1974.
(Contributor) Amiri Baraka and Amina Baraka, editors, *Confirmation*, Morrow, 1983.

Also contributor to *Chants of Saints; Keeping the Faith; Midnight Birds; Norton Anthology;* and *Soulscript.* Contributor to *Massachusetts Review.*

WORK IN PROGRESS: Research on sixteenth- and seventeenth-century Brazil and on settlements of escaped slaves, such as Palmares.

SIDELIGHTS: "Though not one of the best-known of contemporary black writers, Gayl Jones can claim distinction as the teller of the most intense tales," Keith E. Byerman writes in *Dictionary of Literary Biography.* Jones's novels *Corregidora* and *Eva's Man*, in addition to many of the stories in her collection *White Rat*, offer stark, often brutal accounts of black women whose psyches reflect the ravages of accumulated sexual and racial exploitation. In *Corregidora*, Jones reveals the tormented life of a woman whose female forebears—at the hands of one man—endured a cycle of slavery, prostitution, and incest over three generations. *Eva's Man* explores the deranged mind of a woman institutionalized for poisoning and sexually mutilating (by dental castration) a male acquaintance. And in "Asylum," a story from *White Rat*, a young woman is confined to a mental hospital for a series of bizarre behaviors that protest a society she sees bent on personal violation. "The abuse of women and its psychological results fascinate Gayl Jones, who uses these recurring themes to magnify the absurdity and the obscenity of racism and sexism in everyday life," comments Jerry W. Ward, Jr., in *Black Women Writers (1950-1980): A Critical Evaluation.* "Her novels and short fictions invite readers to explore the interior of caged personalities, men and women driven to extremes." Byerman elaborates: "Jones creates worlds radically different from those of 'normal' experience and of storytelling convention. Her tales are gothic in the sense of dealing with madness, sexuality, and violence, but they do not follow in the Edgar Allan Poe tradition of focusing of private obsession and irrationality. Though her narrators are close to if not over the boundaries of sanity, the experiences they record reveal clearly that society acts out its own obsessions often violently."

Corregidora, Jones's first novel, explores the psychological effects of slavery and sexual abuse on a modern black woman. Ursa Corregidora, a blues singer from Kentucky, descends from a line of women who are the progeny, by incest, of a Portuguese slaveholder named Corregidora—the father of both Ursa's mother and grandmother. "All of the women, including the great-granddaughter Ursa, keep the name Corregidora as a reminder of the depredations of the slave system and of the rapacious natures of men," explains Byerman. "The story is passed from generation to generation of women, along with the admonition to 'produce generations' to keep alive the tale of evil." Partly as a result of this history, Ursa becomes involved in abusive relationships with men. The novel itself spawns from an incident of violence; after being thrown down a flight of stairs by her first husband and physically injured so that she cannot bear children, Ursa "discharges her obligation to the memory of Corregidora by speaking [the] book," notes John Updike in the *New Yorker.* The novel emerges as Ursa's struggle to reconcile her heritage with her present life. *Corregidora* "persuasively fuses black history, or the mythic consciousness that must do for black history, with the emotional nuances of contemporary black life," Updike continues. "The book's innermost action . . . is Ursa's attempt to transcend a nightmare black consciousness and waken to her own female, maimed humanity."

Corregidora was acclaimed as a novel of unusual power and impact. "No black American novel since Richard Wright's *Native Son* (1940)," writes Ivan Webster in *Time*, "has so skillfully traced psychic wounds to a sexual source." Darryl Pinckney in *New Republic* calls *Corregidora* "a small, fiercely concentrated story, harsh and perfectly told. . . . Original, superbly imagined, nothing about the book was simple or easily digested. Out of the worn themes of miscegenation and diminishment, Gayl Jones *excavated* the disturbingly buried damage of racism." Critics particularly praised Jones's treatment of sexual detail and its illumination of the central character. "One of the book's merits," according to Updike, "is the ease with which it assumes the writer's right to sexual specifics, and its willingness to explore exactly how our sexual and emotional behavior is warped within the matrix of family and race." In the book's final scene, Ursa comes to a reconciliation with her first husband Mutt by envisioning an ambivalent sexual relationship between her great-grandmother and the slavemaster Corregidora. *Corregidora* is a novel "filled with sexual and spiritual pain," writes Margo Jefferson in *Newsweek:* "hatred, love and desire wear the same face, and humor is blues-bitter.... Jones's language is subtle and sinewy, and her imagination sure."

Jones's second novel, *Eva's Man,* continues her exploration into the psychological effects of brutality, yet presents a character who suffers greater devastation. Eva Medina Canada, incarcerated for the murder and dental castration of a male acquaintance, narrates a personal history which depicts the damaging influences of a society that is sexually aggressive and hostile. Updike describes the exploitative world that has shaped the mentally deranged Eva: "Evil permeates the erotic education of Eva Canada, as it progresses from Popsicle-stick violations to the witnessing of her mother's adultery and a growing awareness of the whores and 'queen bees' in the slum world around her, and on to her own reluctant initiation through encounters in buses and in bars,where a man with no thumb monotonously propositions her. The evil that emanates from men becomes hers." In a narrative that is fragmented and disjointed, Eva gives no concrete motive for the crime committed; furthermore, she neither shows remorse nor any signs of rehabilitation. More experimental than *Corregidora, Eva's Man* displays "a sharpened starkness, a power of ellipsis that leaves ever darker gaps between its flashes of rhythmic, sensuously exact dialogue and visible symbol," according to Updike. John Leonard adds in the *New York Times* that "not a word is wasted" in Eva's narrative. "It seems, in fact, as if Eva doesn't have enough words, as if she were trying to use the words she has to make a poem, a semblance of order, and fails of insufficiency." Leonard concludes: "'Eva's Man' may be one of the most unpleasant novels of the season. It is also one of the most accomplished."

Eva's Man was praised for its emotional impact, yet some reviewers found the character of Eva extreme or inaccessible. June Jordan in the *New York Times Book Review* calls *Eva's Man* "the blues that lost control. This is the rhythmic, monotone lamentation of one woman, Eva Medina, who is nobody I have ever known." Jordan explains: "Miss Jones delivers her story in a strictly controlled, circular form that is wrapped, around and around, with ambivalence. Unerringly, her writing creates the tension of a problem unresolved." In the end, however, Jordan finds that the fragmented details of Eva's story, "do not mesh into illumination." On the other hand, some reviewers regard the gaps in *Eva's Man* as appropriate and integral to its meaning. Pinckney calls the novel "a tale of madness; one exacerbated if not caused by frustration, accumulated grievances" and comments on aspects that contribute to this effect: "Structurally unsettled, more scattered than *Corregidora, Eva's Man* is extremely remote, more troubling in its hallucinations.... The personal exploitation that causes Eva's desperation is hard to appreciate. Her rage seems never to find its proper object, except, possibly, in her last extreme act." Updike likewise holds that the novel accurately portrays Eva's deranged state, yet points out that Jones's characterization skills are not at their peak: "Miss Jones apparently wishes to show us a female heart frozen into rage by deprivation, but the worry arises, as it did not in 'Corregidora,' that the characters are dehumanized as much by her artistic vision as by their circumstances."

Jordan raises a concern that the inconclusiveness of *Eva's Man* harbors a potentially damaging feature. "There is the very real, upsetting accomplishment of Gayl Jones in this, her second novel: sinister misinformation about women—about women, in general, about black women in particular." Jones comments in *Black Women Writers (1950-1980)* on the predicament faced in portraying negative characters: "To deal with such a character as Eva becomes problematic in the way that 'Trueblood' becomes problematic in [Ralph Ellison's] *Invisible Man.* It raises the questions of possibility. Should a Black writer ignore such characters, refuse to enter 'such territory' because of the 'negative image' and because such characters can be misused politically by others, or should one try to reclaim such complex, contradictory characters as well as try to reclaim the idea of the 'heroic image'?" In an interview with Claudia Tate for *Black Women Writers at Work,* Jones elaborates: "'Positive race images' are fine as long as they're very complex and interesting personalities. Right now I'm not sure how to reconcile the various things that interest me with 'positive race images.' It's important to be able to work with a range of personalities, as well as with a range within one personality. For instance, how would one reconcile an interest in neurosis or insanity with positive race image?"

Although Jones's subject matter is often charged and intense, a number of critics have praised a particular restraint she manages in her narratives. Regarding *Corregidora,* Updike remarks: "Our retrospective impression of 'Corregidora' is of a big territory—the Afro-American psyche—rather thinly and stabbingly populated by ideas, personae, hints. Yet that such a small book could seem so big speaks well for the generous spirit of the author, unpolemical where there has been much polemic, exploratory where rhetoric and outrage tend to block the path." Similarly, Jones maintains an authorial distance in her fiction which, in turn, makes for believable and gripping characters. Byerman comments: "The authority of [Jones's] depictions of the world is enhanced by [her] refusal to intrude upon or judge her narrators. She remains outside the story, leaving the reader with none of the usual markers of a narrator's reliability. She gives these characters the speech of their religion, which, by locating them in time and space, makes it even more difficult to easily dismiss them; the way they speak has authenticity, which carries over to what they tell. The results are profoundly disturbing tales of repression, manipulation, and suffering."

Reviewers have also noted Jones's ability to innovatively incorporate Afro-American speech patterns into her work. In *Black Women Writers (1950-1980),* Melvin Dixon contends that "Gayl Jones has figured among the best of contemporary Afro-American writers who have used Black speech as a major aesthetic device in their works. Like Alice Walker, Toni Morrison, Sherley Williams, Toni Cade Bambara, and such male writers as Ernest Gaines and Ishmael Reed, Jones uses the rhythm and structure of spoken language to develop authentic characters and to establish new possibilities for dramatic conflict within the text and between readers and the text itself." In her interview with Tate, Jones remarks on the importance of storytelling traditions to her work: "At the time I was writing *Corregidora* and *Eva's Man* I was particularly interested— and continue to be interested—in oral traditions of storytelling—Afro-American and others, in which there is always the consciousness and importance of the hearer, even in the interior monologues where the storyteller becomes her own hearer. That consciousness or self-consciousness actually determines my selection of significant events."

Jones's 1977 collection of short stories, *White Rat,* received mixed reviews. A number of critics noted the presence of

Jones's typical thematic concerns, yet also felt that her shorter fiction did not allow enough room for character development. Diane Johnson comments in the *New York Review of Books* that the stories in *White Rat* "were written in some cases earlier than her novels, so they confirm one's sense of her direction and preoccupations: sex is violation, and violence is the principal dynamic of human relationships." Mel Watkins remarks in the *New York Times,* however, on a drawback to Jones's short fictions: "The focus throughout is on desolate, forsaken characters struggling to exact some snippet of gratification from their lives.... Although her prose here is as starkly arresting and indelible as in her novels, except for the longer stories such as 'Jeveta' and 'The Women,' these tales are simply doleful vignettes—slices of life so beveled that they seem distorted."

While Jones's writing often emphasizes a tormented side of life—especially with regards to male-female relationships—it also raises the possibility for more positive interactions. Jones points out in the Tate interview that "there seems to be a growing understanding—working itself out especially in *Corregidora*—of what is required in order to be genuinely tender. Perhaps brutality enables one to recognize what tenderness is." Some critics have found ambivalence to be at the core of Jones's fiction. Dixon remarks: "Redemption... is most likely to occur when the resolution of conflict is forged in the same vocabulary as the tensions which precipitated it. This dual nature of language makes it appear brutally indifferent, for it contains the source and the resolution of conflicts.... What Jones is after is the words and deeds that finally break the sexual bondage men and women impose upon each other."

BIOGRAPHICAL/CRITICAL SOURCES:

BOOKS

Contemporary Literary Criticism, Gale, Volume 6, 1976, Volume 9, 1978.
Dictionary of Literary Biography, Volume 33: *Afro-American Fiction Writers after 1955,* Gale, 1984.
Evans, Mari, editor, *Black Women Writers (1950-1980): A Critical Evaluation,* Anchor Books, 1984.
Tate, Claudia, editor, *Black Women Writers at Work,* Continuum, 1986.

PERIODICALS

Black World, February, 1976.
Esquire, December, 1976.
Kliatt, spring, 1986.
Literary Quarterly, May 15, 1975.
Massachusetts Review, winter, 1977.
National Review, April 14, 1978.
New Republic, June 28, 1975, June 19, 1976.
Newsweek, May 19, 1975, April 12, 1976.
New Yorker, August 18, 1975, August 9, 1976.
New York Review of Books, November 10, 1977.
New York Times, April 30, 1976, December 28, 1977.
New York Times Book Review, May 25, 1975, May 16, 1976.
Time, June 16, 1975.
Washington Post, October 21, 1977.
Yale Review, autumn, 1976.

—*Sketch by Michael E. Mueller*

*   *   *

JONES, Jacqueline   1948-

PERSONAL: Born June 17, 1948, in Wilmington, Del.; daughter of Albert H. (an accountant) and Sylvia (a teacher; maiden name, Phelps) Jones; married Jeffrey B. Abramson (a professor and lawyer), May 18, 1980; children: Sarah Jones Abramson, Anna Jones Abramson. *Education:* University of Delaware, B.A., 1970; University of Wisconsin—Madison, M.A., 1972, Ph.D., 1976.

ADDRESSES: Office—Department of History, Wellesley College, Wellesley, Mass. 02181.

CAREER: Wellesley College, Wellesley, Mass., associate professor of American history, 1981—, chair of history department, 1985—.

MEMBER: Organization of American Historians, National Women's Studies Association.

AWARDS, HONORS: ACLS grant-in-aid, 1977; National Endowment for Humanities research fellowship, 1979-80; Bancroft Prize from Columbia University, 1986, for *Labor of Love, Labor of Sorrow: Black Women, Work, and the Family From Slavery to the Present.*

WRITINGS:

Soldiers of Light and Love: Northern Teachers and Georgia Blacks, 1865-1873, University of North Carolina Press, 1980.
Labor of Love, Labor of Sorrow: Black Women, Work, and the Family From Slavery to the Present, Basic Books, 1985.

WORK IN PROGRESS: A history of East Coast seasonal and migratory laborers with a special emphasis on the roles of women, 1860 to the present.

SIDELIGHTS: In *Soldiers of Light and Love: Northern Teachers and Georgia Blacks, 1865-1873,* Jacqueline Jones narrates the experiences of a small group of Yankee teachers who went to Georgia following the Civil War to provide recently freed blacks with their first formal education in the Reconstruction South. Jones tells of blacks' efforts to develop their own schools, chronicles the daily interaction between white schoolteachers and their black pupils, analyzes the teachers' educational theories and ideological motivations, and describes the relationships that developed among the teachers and with their supervisors from the national missionary organizations.

One of her findings, noted by William L. Stanley, Jr., in his review for the *Journal of Negro Education,* was that "black leaders made every effort to maintain their cultural independence and not to become 'black Yankees'" and that their resistance to white benevolence "had a debilitating effect on the structured educational program being presented." Stanley underscored the point made by Jones that "the northern teachers never understood the freedmen's character; therefore their efforts represented 'the institutionalization of antebellum abolitionist ideology' a by-product of middle-class northern culture." Reviewers for *Choice* and *Virginia Quarterly Review* judged *Soldiers of Light and Love* fascinating, well written, and carefully organized. Stanley echoed their opinions, calling the book "a scholarly and definitive job" and recommending it as "an invaluable reference for black historians and students of education."

In a second book, *Labor of Love, Labor of Sorrow: Black Women, Work, and the Family From Slavery to the Present,* Jones surveys black women's roles as workers and as family and community members. She focuses on slaves and rural working-class women in the South from 1830 to 1915 and

309

depicts the broad transition from rural South to urban North, from farm and domestic labor to industrial work, from servile to politically active status. She examines the nature of employment and home life for the black woman through the eras of bondage in the South and the so-called freedom that came with Reconstruction, to the years between emancipation and the large-scale migration to the North, to the northern flight itself, the Depression, and the civil rights and feminist movements. She draws upon demographic studies and analyses of government labor statistics, as well as the stories of individual black women as told in letters, interviews, and magazine articles. She shows how black women have confronted the racially and sexually segmented labor market and tried—despite low pay, long hours, and often humiliating working conditions—to maintain self-respect and provide for their families.

Jones begins her chronicle with a detailed account of the work of black women as field hands and domestic servants during slavery, pointing out that most black women preferred work in the fields to domestic assignments because the former gave them more time with their families and spared them the capricious demands of white supervisors. She then takes up each ensuing period of occupational change for black Americans and documents the ways in which black women were driven into a low-wage work force. As contributing factors, Jones cites the lack of employment opportunities for black women, the chronic unemployment and underemployment of black men, and the subsequent necessity for black women to serve as heads of household.

Nevertheless, avers Jones, it was this need to sustain family life that shaped the work habits of blacks in general and black women in particular. Fully half of Jones's book, noted black novelist Toni Morrison, writing in the New York Times Book Review, is "devoted to strategies slaves and newly freed women used to balance labor with family." Morrison added, "Examining black women as laborers is one thing; examining this labor force in the context of its life-and-death struggle to save the family is quite another." It is "a singular idea," advanced the reviewer, "for which we owe the author gratitude."

Morrison praised Jones's work on several other counts as well. Declaring that Labor of Love, Labor of Sorrow "exorcises several malignant stereotypes and stubborn myths, . . . is free of the sexism and racism it describes, and interprets old data in new ways," Morrison pronounced the book "a valuable contribution to scholarship about blacks." Fellow Afro-American novelist Charles Johnson concurred. In his review for the Los Angeles Times Book Review, Johnson called Jones's study "brilliant, bedrock scholarship crucial to our understanding of the crisis of the black family in the 1980s." According to Johnson, Jones "ever so slightly shifts our perspectives . . . so that we see, beyond all doubt, that from the beginning of slavery, freedom has always meant family preservation for black Americans, and that . . . the weight of this centuries-old struggle rested literally on the backs of black women." Moreover, this preeminence of the family is the means by which, in Johnson's opinion, Jones not only explains black survival but "debunks, once and for all, the damaging 'black matriarchy thesis' held by some sociologists who portray black men as worthless or lazy compared to their women, and . . . black mothers as emasculators of their male children."

Other reviewers declared Labor of Love, Labor of Sorrow bold, important, compelling, inspiring, comprehensive, and remarkable. Women's Review of Books contributor Rosalyn Terborg-Penn, who called the book "illuminating" and "innovative,"

complimented Jones's "pioneering effort to bring a feminist perspective to black women's history through a narrative survey that utilizes sound historical methods."

Not all reviewers, however, were as complimentary to Jones's work. Critiquing Labor of Love, Labor of Sorrow for Ms. magazine, for example, Paula Giddings, author of the widely praised When and Where I Enter: The Impact of Black Women on Race and Sex in America, dubbed Jones "arrogant and incorrect" in her analyses of contemporary black women. Giddings faulted particularly Jones's accusation that black women are more concerned with racist than with feminist issues and took exception to Jones's assertions that black women are reluctant to join predominantly white feminist organizations and that they vote along strictly racial lines. "Jones' logic fails when it comes to analyzing contemporary black women," posited Giddings. "Our whole history reveals a dual concern with racial and feminist issues." Writing in review in the Black Scholar, Julianne Malveaux described Jones's book as "really two books": the first, "a history of black women and work from slavery to 1940" and "a welcome addition to our knowledge . . . about black women's history"; and the second, "a poorly developed discussion of the status of contemporary black women."

Similarly, Morrison deemed the portions of Jones's book that deal with earlier history more informative than those that chronicle events of the 1970s and 1980s, observing that the latter sections "merely track events without offering insights into them." Nevertheless, Morrison pronounced Jones's tome "a perceptive, well-written study," an evaluation shared by Signs contributor Bonnie Thorton Dill, who contended that Jones's Labor of Love, Labor of Sorrow—read together with Gidding's When and Where I Enter—provides "an analysis of black women in American society that is unequaled in depth and conviction."

BIOGRAPHICAL/CRITICAL SOURCES:

PERIODICALS

Best Sellers, June, 1985.
Black Scholar, March/April, 1986.
Booklist, March 1, 1985.
Choice, April, 1981.
Journal of Negro Education, winter, 1982.
Kirkus Reviews, January 1, 1985.
Los Angeles Times Book Review, May 5, 1985.
Ms., October, 1985.
New York Times Book Review, April 14, 1985.
Signs, summer, 1986.
Virginia Quarterly Review, spring, 1981.
Women's Review of Books, July, 1985.

*   *   *

JONES, LeRoi
See BARAKA, Amiri

*   *   *

JORDAN, Barbara (Charline) 1936-

PERSONAL: Born February 21, 1936, in Houston, Tex.; daughter of Benjamin M. (a clergyman and warehouse clerk) and Arlyne (a housewife; maiden name, Patten) Jordan. Education: Texas Southern University, B.A. (magna cum laude), 1956; Boston University, LL.B., 1959. Politics: Democrat. Religion: Baptist.

ADDRESSES: Office—Lyndon B. Johnson School of Public Affairs, University of Texas at Austin, Drawer Y, University Station, Austin, Tex. 78713.

CAREER: Admitted to the Bar of the Commonwealth of Massachusetts and the State Bar of Texas, both in 1959, and the District of Columbia Bar, 1979; engaged in practice of law in Houston, Tex., 1959-66; administrative assistant to county judge in Harris County, Tex., 1964-66; member of Texas Senate, Austin, Tex., 1966-72, president pro tempore, 1972, and member of Labor and Management Relations Committee and Urban Affairs Study Committee; U.S. House of Representatives, Washington, D.C., representative from Eighteenth Congressional District of Texas, 1973-78, member of Judiciary Committee, Committee on Government Operations, special task force on Ninety-fourth Congress, and steering and policy committee of House Democratic Caucus; Lyndon B. Johnson School of Public Affairs, University of Texas at Austin, professor, 1979-82, Lyndon B. Johnson Centennial Professor of National Policy, 1982—.

Member of President's Commission on Income Maintenance Programs, 1968, environmental health committee of Council of State Governments, 1968, environmental health committee of Council of State Governments, 1968, Presidential Advisory Board on Ambassadorial Appointments, 1979-81, Trilateral Commission, 1984, and United Nations panel on multinational corporations in South Africa and Namibia, 1985. Hearings officer for National Institute of Education hearings on minimum testing, 1981; member of executive committee of National Democratic Policy Council, 1981, and for Julia C. Hester House Foundation; chairman of advisory commission of Texas Public Service Career Program. Hostess of PBS series "Crisis to Crisis with Barbara Jordan," 1982. Member of boards of directors of Mead Corp., 1979-, Texas Commerce Bankshares, Inc., 1979—, *Washington Star*, 1980, and Public Broadcasting System, 1985.

MEMBER: American Bar Association, American Bar Foundation (fellow), Texas Bar Association, Texas Trial Lawyers Association, Houston Bar Association, Democratic National Committee, American Management Associations, National Association for the Advancement of Colored People, Southern Regional Council, Delta Sigma Theta.

AWARDS, HONORS: Named outstanding freshman senator of Texas Senate, 1966, elected Democratic woman of the year by Women's National Democratic Club and received Faith in Humanity Award from National Council of Jewish Women, both 1975; named one of *Good Housekeeping* magazine's ten most admired women, 1977 and 1978, and to lists of most influential women by *World Almanac, Ladies Home Journal,* and *Harper's Bazaar;* rated first in performance of congressional women by *Redbook,* 1978; Eleanor Roosevelt Humanities Award, Distinguished Alumnus Award from American Association of State Colleges and Universities, and inducted into the Orators Hall of Fame by the International Platform Association, all 1984; Barbara Jordan Fund for Gifted Students established in her honor at Lyndon B. Johnson School for Public Affairs; received more than twenty honorary doctorates from institutions such as Harvard and Princeton Universities and the University of Cincinnati.

WRITINGS:

(With Shelby Hearon) *Barbara Jordan: A Self-Portrait,* Doubleday, 1979.

(With Terrell Blodgett) *Local Government Election Systems,* Lyndon B. Johnson School of Public Affairs, 1984.

SIDELIGHTS: "The story of Barbara Jordan begins like those of most black Americans of her generation—in a poverty-stricken, all-black ghetto in Houston, Texas, but unlike many others, it did not lead to perpetual poverty, degradation, and obscurity but to national fame," said Alton Hornsby, Jr., in the *Journal of Southern History.* Elected to the U.S. House of Representatives in 1972, Jordan gained widespread attention two years later while serving as a member of the House Judiciary Committee. That body was then meeting to determine whether president Richard M. Nixon had committed impeachable offenses in connection with the notorious break-in of the Democratic National Committee headquarters in the Watergate office complex. In a speech delivered during the nationally televised proceedings Jordan declared her dedication to the principles of the Constitution of the United States in what *Newsweek* called "the most memorable indictment of Richard Nixon to emerge from the House impeachment hearings." The passionate eloquence of her remarks favorably impressed television viewers and established the congresswoman as one of the nation's most powerful orators.

Jordan began her political career during the national election campaign of 1960 when she helped direct local efforts in support of presidential candidate John F. Kennedy. During the early 1960s Jordan campaigned twice on her own behalf for a seat in the Texas House of Representatives, but she lost both times. In 1966, however, she received 80 percent of the votes cast in her successful bid for election to the Texas Senate, where she both initiated and supported much social reform legislation. Social issues continued to interest Jordan after her election to the U.S. Congress, and she backed proposals to increase the minimum wage, to extend social security benefits to housewives, to provide free legal services for the indigent, and to expand existing programs to benefit the aged and ill. Though the Texas lawmaker also supported civil rights legislation in Congress, she resisted attempts by black colleagues and others to induce her to become a spokesperson for the civil rights movement. "Jordan," observed Hornsby, "did not view national affairs from an as narrowly black perspective as some of her fellow blacks." In addition, according to *Los Angeles Times* writer Beverley Beyette, Jordan "always said she was into not black power, but 'brain power.'" But some observers regarded Jordan's efforts to disassociate herself from black as well as other liberal constituencies as a means of ensuring good relations with the congressional establishment. "She's . . . a consummate politician," explained Kaye Northcott in her *New York Times Book Review* critique of *Barbara Jordan,* "who knows better than to ruffle the dominant economic interests in this country."

Jordan's reputation for inspired oratory was confirmed in 1976 with her keynote address to the Democratic National Convention. "We cannot improve on the system of government handed down to us by the founders of the Republic," Jordan insisted to conventioneers in her widely quoted remarks, "but we can find new ways to implement that system and realize our destiny." In its call for "a national community" with everyone sharing in "the American dream," the speech made clear the implications of Jordan's own rise from a Houston ghetto to the halls of Congress and seemed especially relevant in light of her role as the first woman and the first black to serve as Party keynoter. Jordan had also been the first black since the Reconstruction era to be elected to the Texas Senate as well as the first woman to be chosen president pro tempore of that body. In addition, she was the first black woman from the South to serve in the U.S. Congress. "She was," wrote Joseph Nocera in *Washington Monthly,* "a symbol, in the most uplifting sort of way, of how far blacks and women had come in this country." But, according to Beyette, Jordan felt too much emphasis had been placed on her race and gender. "I didn't get where I am by being black or a woman," she insisted. "I got there by working hard."

Political pundits began speculating about Jordan becoming the Democrats' first woman candidate for vice-president. But Jordan refused to pursue that office, announcing in a widely quoted statement, "It's not my turn. When it's my turn, you'll know it." Indications were that she hoped to be named attorney general if her Party's nominee, Jimmy Carter, waged a successful campaign for the presidency in the 1976 national election. Though Carter defeated incumbent Gerald Ford, the president-elect offered the post of attorney general to Georgia lawyer Griffin Bell. Jordan was reelected to the House and continued to serve her constituents from the Eighteenth District in Texas through 1978, when she retired from Congress after serving three terms as a representative. She explained her decision to leave politics in her autobiography, *Barbara Jordan: A Self-Portrait:* "I felt more of a responsibility to the country as a whole, as contrasted with the duty of representing the half-million people in the Eighteenth Congressional District. I felt some necessity to address national issues. I thought that my role now was to be one of the voices in the country defining where we were, where we were going, what the policies were that were being pursued, and where the holes in those policies were. I felt that I was more in an instructive role than a legislative role." She, therefore, accepted a teaching post at the Lyndon B. Johnson School of Public Affairs at the University of Texas at Austin.

Regarding her new career as an educator, Jordan told Liz Carpenter in an interview published in *Ms.* in 1985: "Now that I am teaching I think my future is in seeing to it that the next generation is ready to take over." Similarly, she was quoted in *Newsweek:* "I want [my students] to be premier public servants who have a core of principles to guide them. They are my future, and the future of this country."

BIOGRAPHICAL/CRITICAL SOURCES:

BOOKS

Bryant, Ira Babington, *Barbara Charline Jordan: From the Ghetto to the Capitol,* D. Armstrong, 1977.
Contemporary Issues Criticism, Volume 2, Gale, 1984.
Crawford, Ann Fears and Crystal Sasse Ragsdale, *Women in Texas,* Eakin Publications, 1982.
Jordan, Barbara and Shelby Hearon, *Barbara Jordan: A Self-Portrait,* Doubleday, 1979.
Stineman, Esther F., *American Political Women: Contemporary and Historical Profiles,* Libraries Unlimited, 1980.

PERIODICALS

Jet, July 30, 1984, December 24, 1984.
Journal of Southern History, February, 1980.
Los Angeles Times, March 22, 1979.
Ms., February, 1979, April, 1985.
Newsweek, November 4, 1974, July 4, 1976, November 15, 1976, December 19, 1983.
New York Times Book Review, February 18, 1979.
Washington Monthly, March, 1979.

—*Sketch by Susan M. Trosky*

JORDAN, June   1936-
(June Meyer)

PERSONAL: Born July 9, 1936, in Harlem, New York, N.Y.; daughter of Granville Ivanhoe (a postal clerk) and Mildred Maude (Fisher) Jordan; married Michael Meyer, 1955 (divorced, 1965); children: Christopher David. *Education:* Attended Barnard College, 1953-55, 1956-57, and University of Chicago, 1955-65. *Politics:* "Politics of survival and change." *Religion:* "Humanitarian."

ADDRESSES: Home—New York, N.Y. *Office*—Department of English, State University of New York at Stony Brook, Stony Brook, N.Y. 11794. *Agent*—Joan Daves, 59 East 54th St., New York, N.Y. 10022.

CAREER: Poet, novelist, essayist, and writer of children's books. Assistant to producer for motion picture "The Cool World," New York City, 1963-64; Mobilization for Youth, Inc., New York City, associate research writer in technical housing department, 1965-66; City College of the City University of New York, New York City, instructor in English and literature, 1966-68; Connecticut College, New London, teacher of English and director of Search for Education, Elevation and Knowledge (SEEK Program), 1967-69; Sarah Lawrence College, Bronxville, N.Y., instructor in literature, 1969-74; City College of the City University of New York, assistant professor of English, 1975-76; State University of New York at Stony Brook, professor of English, 1982—.

Visiting poet-in-residence at MacAlester College, 1980; writer-in-residence at City College of the City University of New York. Visiting lecturer in English and Afro-American studies, Yale University, 1974-75; chancellor's distinguished lecturer, University of California, Berkeley, 1986. Has given poetry readings in schools and colleges around the country and at the Guggenheim Museum. Founder and co-director, Voice of the Children, Inc.; co-founder, Afro-Americans against the Famine, 1973—. Director of Poetry Center, 1986—, and Poets and Writers, Inc. Member of board of directors, Teachers and Writers Collaborative, Inc., 1978—, and Center for Constitutional Rights, 1984—.

MEMBER: American Writers Congress (member of executive board), PEN.

AWARDS, HONORS: Rockefeller grant for creative writing, 1969-70; Prix de Rome in Environmental Design, 1970-71; Nancy Bloch Award, 1971, for *The Voice of the Children;* New York Times selection as one of the year's outstanding young adult novels, 1971, and nomination for National Book Award, 1971, for *His Own Where;* New York Council of the Humanities award, 1977; Creative Artists Public Service Program poetry grant, 1978; Yaddo fellowship, 1979; National Endowment for the Arts fellowship, 1982; achievement award for international reporting from National Association of Black Journalists, 1984; New York Foundation for the Arts fellow in poetry, 1985.

WRITINGS:

Who Look at Me, Crowell, 1969.
(Editor) *Soulscript: Afro-American Poetry,* Doubleday, 1970.
(Editor with Terri Bush) *The Voice of the Children* (a reader), Holt, 1970.
Some Changes (poems), Dutton, 1971.
His Own Where (young adult novel), Crowell, 1971.

Dry Victories (juvenile and young adult), Holt, 1972.
Fannie Lou Hamer (biography), Crowell, 1972.
New Days: Poems of Exile and Return, Emerson Hall, 1973.
New Room: New Life (juvenile), Crowell, 1975.
Things That I Do in the Dark: Selected Poetry, Random House, 1977.
Okay Now, Simon & Schuster, 1977.
Passion: New Poems, 1977-1980, Beacon Press, 1980.
Civil Wars (essays, articles, and lectures), Beacon Press, 1981.
Kimako's Story (juvenile), illustrated by Kay Burford, Houghton, 1981.
Living Room: New Poems, 1980-84, Thunder's Mouth Press, 1985.
On Call: New Political Essays, 1981-1985, South End Press, 1985.
High Tide—Marea Alta, Curbstone, 1987.

PLAYS

"In the Spirit of Sojourner Truth," produced in New York City at the Public Theatre, May, 1979.
"For the Arrow that Flies by Day" (staged reading), produced in New York City at the Shakespeare Festival, April, 1981.

OTHER

Composer of lyrics and libretto, "Bang Bang Ueber Alles," 1985. Contributor of stories and poems, prior to 1969 under name June Meyer, to national periodicals, including *Esquire, Nation, Evergreen, Partisan Review, Black World, Black Creation, Essence, Village Voice, New York Times,* and *New York Times Magazine.*

SIDELIGHTS: June Jordan is considered to be one of the more significant black women writers publishing today. Although better known for her poetry, Jordan writes for a variety of audiences from young children to adults and in a number of genres from essays to plays. However, in all of her writings, Jordan powerfully and skillfully explores the black experience in America. "The reader coming to June Jordan's work for the first time can be overwhelmed by the breadth and diversity of her concern, and by the wide variety of literary forms in which she expresses them," writes Peter B. Erickson in the *Dictionary of Literary Biography.* "But the unifying element in all her activities is her fervent dedication to the survival of black people."

Chad Walsh writes of Jordan in *Washington Post Book World,* "exploring and expressing black consciousness, [Jordan] speaks to everyman, for in his heart of hearts every man is at times an outsider in whatever society he inhabits." Susan Mernit writes in the *Library Journal* that "Jordan is a poet for many people, speaking in a voice they cannot fail to understand about things they will want to know." In a *Publishers Weekly* interview with Stella Dong, Jordan explains: "I write for as many different people as I can, acknowledging that in any problem situation you have at least two viewpoints to be reached. I'm also interested in telling the truth as I know it, and in telling people, 'Here's something new that I've just found out about.' I want to share discoveries because other people might never know the thing, and also to get feedback. That's critical."

Reviewers have generally praised Jordan for uniquely and effectively uniting in poetic form the personal everyday struggle and the political oppression of blacks. For example, Mernit believes that Jordan "elucidates those moments when personal life and political struggle, two discrete elements, suddenly entwine.... [Jordan] produces intelligent, warm poetry that is exciting as literature." Honor Moore comments in *Ms.* that Jordan "writes ragalike pieces of word-music that serve her politics, both personal and public." And Peter B. Erickson remarks: "Given her total commitment to writing about a life beset on all sides, Jordan is forced to address the whole of experience in all its facets and can afford to settle for nothing less. Jordan accepts, rises to, the challenge."

Jordan sees poetry as a valid and useful vehicle to express her personal and political ideas while at the same time masterfully creating art. "Jordan is an accomplished poet, who knows how to express her political views while at the same time practicing her art; hence these poems make for engaging reading by virtue of their rhythm and poignant imagery." And Moore states in *Ms.* that Jordan "never sacrifices poetry for politics. In fact, her craft, the patterning of sound, rhythm, and image, make her art inseparable from political statement, form inseparable from content. [She] uses images contrapuntally to interweave disparate emotions."

Jordan is also noted for the intense passion with which she writes about the struggles against racism. Susan McHenry remarks in *Nation* that "Jordan's characteristic stance is combative. She is exhilarated by a good fight, by taking on her antagonists against the odds.... However, Jordan [succeeds] in effectively uniting her impulse to fight with her need and desire to love." Jascha Kessler comments in *Poetry* that Jordan's literary "expression is developed out of, or through, a fine irony that manages to control her bitterness, even to dominate her rage against the intolerable, so that she can laugh and cry, be melancholic and scornful and so on, presenting always the familiar faces of human personality, integral personality." Kessler adds that Jordan "adapts her poems to the occasions that they are properly, using different voices, and levels of thought and diction that are humanly germane and not disembodied rages or vengeful shadows; thus she can create her world, that is, people it for us, for she has the singer's sense of the dramatic and projects herself into a poem to express its special subject, its individuality. Of course it's always her voice, because she has the skill to use it so variously: but the imagination it needs to run through all her changes is her talent."

Faith and optimism are perhaps the two common threads that weave through all of Jordan's work, whether it be prose or poetry, for juvenile readers or for a more mature audience. For example, in a *Ms.* review of Jordan's *Civil Wars,* Toni Cade Bambara writes that Jordan has written a "chilling but profoundly hopeful vision of living in the USA. Jordan's vibrant spirit manifests itself throughout this collection of articles, letters, journal entries, and essays. What is fundamental to that spirit is caring, commitment, a deep-rooted belief in the sanctity of life.... 'We are not powerless,' she reminds us. 'We are indispensable despite all atrocities of state and corporate power to the contrary.' " And as Patricia Jones points out in *Village Voice:* "Whether speaking on the lives of children, or the victory in Nicaragua, or the development of her poetry, or the consequences of racism in film Jordan brings her faithfulness to bear; faith in her ability to make change.... You respect June Jordan's quest and her faith. She is a knowing woman."

BIOGRAPHICAL/CRITICAL SOURCES:

BOOKS

Children's Literature Review, Volume 10, Gale, 1986.

Contemporary Literary Criticism, Gale, Volume 5, 1976, Volume 11, 1979, Volume 23, 1983.

Dictionary of Literary Biography, Volume 38: *Afro-American Writers after 1955: Dramatists and Prose Writers,* Gale, 1985.

PERIODICALS

Black Scholar, January-February, 1981.
Choice, October, 1985.
Christian Science Monitor, November 11, 1971.
Library Journal, December 1, 1980.
Ms., April, 1975, April, 1981.
Nation, April 11, 1981.
Negro Digest, February, 1970.
New York Times, April 25, 1969.
New York Times Book Review, November 7, 1971.
Poetry, February, 1973.
San Francisco Examiner, December 7, 1977.
Saturday Review, April 17, 1971.
Washington Post, October 13, 1977.
Washington Post Book World, July 4, 1971.

—Sketch by Margaret Mazurkiewicz

K

KAUFMAN, Bob (Garnell)   1925-1986
(Bomkauf)

PERSONAL: Born April 18, 1925, in New Orleans, La.; died of emphysema, January 12, 1986, in San Francisco, Calif.; married second wife, Eileen (a writer and literary agent), June 23, 1958 (separated); children: Tony (daughter), Parker (son). *Education:* Attended public schools in New Orleans, La. *Religion:* Buddhist.

CAREER: Poet. Worked as a merchant seaman. Read poetry at colleges and universities, including Harvard University, and on the Public Broadcasting System (PBS) television program "Images," 1982.

AWARDS, HONORS: Nominated for Guinness Poetry Award, 1960-61; National Endowment for the Arts creative writing grant, 1981.

WRITINGS:

POETRY

Does the Secret Mind Whisper (also see below), City Lights, 1959.
Second April (also see below), City Lights, 1959.
Abomunist Manifesto (also see below), City Lights, 1959.
Solitudes Crowded With Loneliness (contains *Does the Secret Mind Whisper, Second April,* and *Abomunist Manifesto*), New Directions, 1965.
Golden Sardine, City Lights, 1966.
Watch My Tracks, Knopf, 1971.
The Ancient Rain: Poems, 1956-1978, New Directions, 1981.

Also author of *Bastard Angel,* 1972.

CONTRIBUTOR

Clarence Major, editor, *The New Black Poetry,* International, 1969.
Arnold Adoff, editor, *City in All Directions,* Macmillan, 1969.
Langston Hughes and Arna Bontemps, editors, *The Poetry of the Negro, 1746-1970,* Doubleday, 1970.
Alan Lomax and Raoul Abdul, editors, *Three Thousand Years of Black Poetry,* Dodd, 1970.
Nick Harvey, editor, *Mark in Time: Portraits and Poetry— San Francisco,* Glide, 1971.
William M. Chace and JoAn E. Chace, editors, *Making It New: American Poems and Songs,* Canfield, 1972.

Adoff, editor, *The Poetry of Black America,* Harper, 1972.

Also contributor to *Points of Light,* 1971, *Understanding the New Black Poetry,* 1972, and *Visions of America,* 1973.

OTHER

Prepared the program "Coming from Bob Kaufman, Poet," which appeared on "Soul," a national hour-long broadcast by National Education Television, 1972, starring Ossie Davis and Ruby Dee. Founder and editor, with Allen Ginsberg, William Margolis, and John Kelly, of the poetry magazine *Beatitude.*

SIDELIGHTS: Viewed by some to have been the great unsung poet of the Beat Generation, Bob Kaufman was a major influence on better known contemporaries such as Jack Kerouac, Lawrence Ferlinghetti, and Gregory Corso. Kaufman was born in New Orleans in 1925. His father was a German Orthodox Jew who ran a pool hall; his mother was a black Catholic from Martinique. During his childhood, Kaufman participated in both Catholic and Jewish religious services and was also exposed to the voodoo beliefs of his grandmother. At the age of thirteen he ran away to sea. For twenty years Kaufman sailed with the Merchant Marine, circumnavigating the globe nine times and surviving four shipwrecks during his term of service.

A shipmate in the Merchant Marine served as Kaufman's informal tutor, urging him to read the classics and loaning him many books. When Kaufman gave up his seagoing career in the early 1940s, he went to study literature at New York City's New School for Social Research. There he became acquainted with William S. Burroughs and Allen Ginsberg, who would become two of the most famous writers of the Beat Generation. Together with Burroughs and Ginsberg, Kaufman traveled to San Francisco where Ferlinghetti, Kerouac, and Corso were then living.

San Francisco's North Beach jazz bars were favorite gathering places for the emerging Beat writers. Kaufman was particularly inspired by the long improvised solos and complex rhythms of bebop jazz. He began to create poetry based on those foundations. In bars and coffeehouses as well as on the streets Kaufman recited his spontaneous compositions, using a style that quickly earned him the nickname "The Original Be-Bop Man." Jon Woodson noted in the *Dictionary of Literary Biography* that many San Francisco writers, including Kenneth Rexroth, LeRoi Jones, Ginsberg, Corso, and Ferlinghetti, "enthusiastically took their cues from Kaufman's innovations." But as Woodson also noted in his essay, "they have not been as quick in recognizing his influence."

Kaufman was so dedicated to his ideal of spontaneous composition that he rarely bothered to write down any of his poems—a fact that certainly helped keep his work relatively obscure. Most of his publications were transcriptions of his oral performances, submitted to publishers by his friends. Three poetry broadsides—*Abomunist Manifesto, Second April,* and *Does the Secret Mind Whisper?*—came out under his name in 1959. Woodson remarked of the *Abomunist Manifesto:* "Since the Beats were dedicated to a program of disaffiliation, they never produced a serious document that was a collective Beat manifesto; a Beat manifesto would have been entirely contradictory. In one sense, [however, the *Abomunist Manifesto*] is the closest thing to a manifesto that a member of the Beat generation could produce. In actuality the *Abomunist Manifesto* is an antimanifesto that ridicules the entire enterprise of formulating a system of beliefs."

Kaufman's first three broadsides were collected in book form as *Solitudes Crowded With Loneliness.* The book provoked little excitement in the United States except among those already familiar with Kaufman's work. It caused a sensation when translated and published overseas, however, with major French critics calling Kaufman "the American Rimbaud." Translated into German, Italian, Polish, Russian, Spanish, Arabic, and Danish as well as French, *Solitudes Crowded With Loneliness* proved to be influential in spreading Beat philosophies and attitudes throughout Europe. Kaufman himself continued to be indifferent to his fame or lack of it. In 1959 he founded *Beatitude* magazine along with Allen Ginsberg, John Kelley, and William Margolis. The four poets dedicated their magazine to the publication of work by talented unknowns. Through his work on *Beatitude,* Kaufman furthered the careers of many aspiring poets.

In 1960 Kaufman returned to the East Coast after being invited to Harvard University to read his poetry. The following year he was nominated for Great Britain's prestigious Guinness Poetry Award, which was won that year by T. S. Eliot. But even as his work was beginning to gain recognition from the poetry establishment, Kaufman's personal life was disintegrating. His next few years were marked by poverty, methedrine addiction, and imprisonment. In 1963, the poet reacted to the assassination of John F. Kennedy by taking a Buddhist vow of silence and withdrawing from society.

Kaufman did not speak for the next twelve years. *Golden Sardine* was published under his name in 1967; it consisted of poetry collected by a friend, Mary Beach, from Kaufman's scattered bits of manuscript. The title phrase was found among his belongings, scrawled across a sheet of brown wrapping paper. Woodson praised *Golden Sardine* as "a collection of poems that range from the energetically surreal filmscript of 'a horror movie to be shot with the eyes' to an eloquent, restrained Buddhist prayer." In 1975, on the day the Vietnam war ended, Kaufman stunned those around him by breaking into a dramatic speech at a local gathering. With the gesture he entered a three-year period of intense activity, producing what Woodson termed "some of his most provocative and challenging poems," which were collected in *The Ancient Rain: Poems, 1956-1978.* In 1978, however, Kaufman once again withdrew abruptly into silence.

Until his death from emphysema in 1986, Kaufman emerged only occasionally from his self-imposed exile from society.

Woodson noted that "just prior to resuming his vow of silence, Kaufman told Raymond Foye, the editor of *The Ancient Rain,* 'I want to be anonymous . . . my ambition is to be completely forgotten.'" *Dictionary of Literary Biography* essayist A. D. Winans expressed his doubt that Kaufman could ever achieve this wish, however, for his work "still rings true today, even after two decades have passed—a clear indicator of his power as a poet."

BIOGRAPHICAL/CRITICAL SOURCES:

BOOKS

Dictionary of Literary Biography, Gale, Volume XVI: *The Beats: Literary Bohemians in Postwar America,* 1983, Volume XLI: *Afro-American Poets Since 1955,* 1985.
Emanuel, James A. and Theodore L. Gross, editors, *Dark Symphony: Negro Literature in America,* Free Press, 1968.
Jordan, June, editor, *Soulscript: Afro-American Poetry,* Doubleday, 1970.
Knight, Arthur, and Kit Knight, editors, *Beat Angels,* the unspeakable visions of the individual, 1982.
Redmond, Eugene, *Drumvoices: The Mission of Afro-American Poetry, A Critical History,* Anchor, 1976.

OBITUARIES:

PERIODICALS

Chicago Tribune, January 15, 1986.
Detroit Free Press, January 14, 1986.
Los Angeles Times, January 14, 1986.
Washington Post, January 15, 1986.

*   *   *

KAYIRA, Legson (Didimu) 1942-

PERSONAL: Surname is pronounced Kaw-*yee*-ra; born May 10, 1942, in Karonga, Nyasaland (now Malawi), Africa; son of Timothy and Ziya (Nakawonga) Kayira; married Carol Lawson. *Education:* Skagit Valley College, A.A., 1963; University of Washington, B.A., 1965; Cambridge University, graduate study, 1965-66. *Religion:* Presbyterian.

ADDRESSES: c/o Three Continents Press, 1346 Connecticut Ave., Suite 224, Washington, D. C. 20036.

CAREER: Writer.

AWARDS, HONORS: Northwest Non-Fiction Prize for autobiography, *I Will Try.*

WRITINGS:

I Will Try (autobiography), Doubleday, 1965.
The Looming Shadow (novel), Doubleday, 1967.
Jingala (novel), Doubleday, 1969.
Things Black and Beautiful (novel), Doubleday, 1970.
The Civil Servant (novel), Longman, 1971.
The Detainee (novel), Heinemann, 1974.

SIDELIGHTS: Soon after Kayira's birth, his mother threw him into the Didimu River because she felt she could not feed and care for him. After he was rescued and returned to her, he was given his middle name, Didimu. While he was in school, he decided to add an English-sounding name and coined Legson. According to *Time,* after attending school in Nyasaland for eleven years, Kayira decided: "We have 3,000,000 people in Nyasaland and only 22 university graduates. Nobody has ever earned a degree from an American college. I want to be the first." In 1958 he began a journey, on foot, to the United

States. Subsisting on a diet of bananas, which he bought with money earned doing chores for a few cents a day, reported *Reader's Digest,* "he traveled in dry season and wet, in blinding dust and miasmic jungle, through friendly villages and hostile. He tried to learn three words in each tongue: *food, water, job.*"

In January, 1960, he reached Kampala, Uganda. At the United States Information Service (USIS) free library there, he stumbled on a directory of American colleges and universities. The first entry he saw was Skagit Valley Junior College at Mount Vernon, Washington. He wrote to Skagit Valley and received a letter informing him that his application had been favorably received, that he might apply for a scholarship, and that the school would find a job for him. While Kayira studied algebra at the USIS library in Khartoum, the students at Skagit Valley raised seventeen thousand dollars to bring him to the United States.

On December 16, 1960, Kayira arrived at Skagit Valley to a standing ovation from students. He had completed a journey of two years and twelve thousand miles; twenty-five hundred miles had been accomplished on foot. Of his future plans, Kayira told *Time:* "When I go back to Nyasaland, I will be a teacher. Then I enter politics. When I get defeated, I go back to teaching. You can always trust education."

AVOCATIONAL INTERESTS: Travel, reading, bicycling, classical music, photography.

BIOGRAPHICAL/CRITICAL SOURCES:

BOOKS

Kayira, Legson, *I Will Try,* Doubleday, 1965.

PERIODICALS

Guideposts, April, 1964.
Reader's Digest, February, 1962.
Time, December 19, 1960.

*   *   *

KAYMOR, Patrice Maguilene
   See SENGHOR, Leopold Sedar

*   *   *

KELLEY, William Melvin   1937-

PERSONAL: Born November 1, 1937, in New York, N.Y.; son of William (an editor) and Narcissa Agatha (Garcia) Kelley; married Karen Isabelle Gibson (a designer), December, 1962; children: Jessica, Ciratikaiji. *Education:* Attended Harvard University, 1957-61.

ADDRESSES: Office—P.O. Box 2658, New York, N.Y. 10027.

CAREER: Free-lance writer and photographer. Writer in residence, State University of New York at Geneseo, spring, 1965; instructor, New School for Social Research, 1965-67; guest lecturer in American literature, University of Paris, Nanterre, 1968; guest instructor, University of West Indies, Mona, 1969-70.

AWARDS, HONORS: Dana Reed Prize from Harvard University, 1960; Bread Loaf Scholar, 1962; John Hay Whitney Foundation Award and Rosenthal Foundation Award, 1963, both for *A Different Drummer; Transatlantic Review* Award, 1964, for *Dancers on the Shore;* fiction award from Black

Academy of Arts and Letters, 1970, for *Dunfords Travels Everywheres.*

WRITINGS:

FICTION

A Different Drummer (novel), Doubleday, 1962.
Dancers on the Shore (short stories), Doubleday, 1964, reprinted (introduction by Mel Watkins), Howard University Press, 1984.
A Drop of Patience (novel), Doubleday, 1965.
dem (novel), Doubleday, 1967, reprinted (introduction by Willie E. Abraham), Collier Books, 1969.
Dunfords Travels Everywheres (novel), Doubleday, 1970.

CONTRIBUTOR TO ANTHOLOGIES

Langston Hughes, editor, *The Best Short Stories by Negro Writers: An Anthology from 1899 to the Present,* Little, Brown, 1967.
Richard Kostelanetz, editor, *The Young American Writers,* Funk, 1967.
James A. Emanuel and Theodore Gross, editors, *Dark Symphony: Negro Literature in America,* Free Press, 1968.
Edward Margolies, editor, *Native Sons: A Critical Study of Twentieth-Century Negro American Authors,* Lippincott, 1968.
Arnold Adoff, editor, *Brothers and Sisters: Modern Stories by Black Americans,* Macmillan, 1970.
Lettie J. Austin, Lewis W. Fenderson, and Sophia P. Nelson, editors, *The Black Man and the Promise of America,* Scott, Foresman, 1970.
Bradford Chambers and Rebecca Moon, editors, *Right On!: Anthology of Black Literature,* New American Library, 1970.
John Henrik Clarke, editor, *Harlem: Voices from the Soul of Black America,* New American Library, 1970.
Charles L. James, editor, *From the Roots: Short Stories by Black Americans,* Dodd, 1970.
Francis E. Kearns, editor, *Black Experience: An Anthology of American Literature for the 1970's,* Viking, 1970.
Darwin T. Turner, editor, *Black American Literature: Essays, Poetry, Fiction, Drama,* Merrill, 1970.
Houston A. Baker, Jr., editor, *Black Literature in America,* McGraw-Hill, 1971.
Arthur P. Davis and J. Saunders Reddings, editors, *Cavalcade: Negro American Writing from 1760 to the Present,* Houghton, 1971.
Nick Aaron Ford, editor, *Black Insights: Significant Literature by Black Americans, 1760 to the Present,* Ginn, 1971.
Richard K. Barksdale and Kenneth Kinnamon, editors, *Black Writers of America: A Comprehensive Anthology,* Macmillan, 1972.
Abraham Chapman, editor, *New Black Voices,* New American Library, 1972.
Richard A. Long and Eugenia W. Collier, editors, *Afro-American Writing: An Anthology of Prose and Poetry,* New York University Press, 1972.
William Smart, editor, *Women and Men, Men and Women,* St. Martin's, 1975.

OTHER

"Excavating Harlem" (video), produced by Manhattan Cable/Channel D, 1988.

Contributor to periodicals, including *Accent, Canto, Jazz and Pop, Mademoiselle, Negro Digest, New York Times Maga-*

zine, *Partisan Review, Playboy, Quilt, River Styx, Urbanite,* and *Works in Progress.*

WORK IN PROGRESS: Days of Our Lives.

SIDELIGHTS: The fiction of William Melvin Kelley published between 1962 and 1970—spanning the most tumultuous years of the civil rights movement—displays the author's evolving perceptions of black and white in American society. Kelley's fiction undergoes noticeable transformations from his first novel, *A Different Drummer,* supportive of nonviolence as a means to affect social change, to his later works which become increasingly experimental in structure and more vehemently critical of social injustice. Kelley begins with "a vision of racial coexistence," explains Valerie M. Babb in *Dictionary of Literary Biography,* yet as he "became more aware of the systematic degradation of blacks throughout American history, the themes and concerns of his writing took on a more radical stance. He shifted from characters making quiet protests to regain their lost dignity to characters angrily avenging past wrongs." This progression in Kelley's fiction offers a paradigm to changes within the 1960s civil rights movement itself. "In his personal development, we can see a chapter of our nation's history," contends Babb, "and in his literary development, we can note some of the clearest articulations of American culture at the time."

Kelley's four novels, along with his short story collection *Dancers on the Shore,* are often collectively examined as a saga of contemporary Afro-American experience. Robert Bone notes in the *New York Times Book Review* that Kelley's "books are unified in over-all design," comparing the effect to a "reverse" variation on William Faulkner's Yoknapatawpha County legend: "an epic treatment of American history from a Negro point of view." Jill Weyant similarly comments in *CLA Journal:* "The purpose of writing a serious saga . . . is to depict impressionistically a large, crowded portrait, each individual novel presenting enlarged details of the whole, each complete in itself, yet evoking a more universal picture than is possible in a single volume." Weyant elaborates that the "Kelley saga is an attempt to redefine the Complete Man and to overturn inaccurate racial stereotypes that, in Kelley's opinion, have too long held sway." Kelley himself has commented on a goal of interrelatedness in his fiction, telling Roy Newquist in *Conversations:* "Perhaps I'm trying to follow the Faulknerian pattern—although I guess it's really Balzacian when you connect everything. I'd like to be eighty years old and look up at the shelf and see that all of my books are really one big book."

Throughout his fiction, Kelley emphasizes the worth and intrinsic rights of humans as individuals. Babb comments on the early stages of Kelley's outlook: "In the beginning stages of his writing career, Kelley saw that to be black in America was an amalgam of many experiences, yet many white and even black leaders sought to view black consciousness as a single entity. The individual has an obligation, Kelley believed, to focus more on 'what we really are: human beings, not simply members of a race.'" This belief exists behind the title of Kelley's first novel, *A Different Drummer,* recalling the famous lines of Henry David Thoreau: "If a man does not keep pace with his companions, perhaps it is because he hears a different drummer. Let him step to the music which he hears, however measured or far away." Hugh J. Ingrasci comments on the resilience of Kelley's concept of individuality: "The world Kelley portrays . . . projects a life of possibilities, one wherein the struggle to eliminate racial inequities is viable, but only for the individual who hammers away at exploitation

with one irresistible conviction: that each human person has too great a value to allow others to regard him as a mere social commodity." It matters little, Ingrasci continues, if one "wins his battle with the society he finds. . . . It is his belief that he is humanly equal to anyone else that has set him free, and not the prospect of attaining social justice."

In the preface to his short story collection *Dancers on the Shore,* Kelley likewise emphasizes an approach to writing that focuses on the individual. He criticizes those who would lump all black authors into a single category, the "Negro literary ghetto," as he describes it. "An American writer who happens to have brown skin faces this unique problem," Kelley explains: "Solutions and answers to the Negro Problem are very often read into his work. At the instant they open his book, the readers begin to search fervently, and often with honest concern, for some key or answer to what is happening today between black and white people in America." Kelley likewise applies an emphasis on individuality to his own characters: "At this time, let me say for the record that I am not a sociologist or a politician or a spokesman. Such people try to give answers. A writer, I think, should ask questions. He should depict people, not symbols or ideas disguised as people."

Critical response to Kelley's individual books has been divided. He is often noted for maintaining a controlled and calculated distance from his subject matter, yet at times is criticized for writing too facilely, or—in seeming contradiction to his stated intentions—from too ideological a perspective. Regarding *Dancers on the Shore,* Louis Rubin, Jr., comments in the *New York Herald Tribune Book Week* that Kelley's stories "bear all the earmarks of having been written while the author was still searching for his true subject" and that they suffer in two main areas: "Either they are underdeveloped, with the author having worked only at the surface of his material, or else (and sometimes at the same time) they are content with presenting aspects of what Mr. Kelley said he wasn't going to try to solve, The Negro Problem." Michele Murray in *Commonweal,* on the other hand, praises Kelley's perspective in *Dancers on the Shore,* writing that the stories benefit from "a fineness that comes from the *tone* of the telling—very spare, very quiet, very honest." Kelley's third book, *A Drop of Patience,* similarly received mixed comments. The story of a black jazz musician who is blind, *A Drop of Patience* "is a moving, painful and stinging experience," writes David Boroff in the *New York Times Book Review:* "Kelley's prose is tight and spare, the novel's anger and bitterness straining against the stripped-down language." He concludes, however, that Kelley's main character is "in the end . . . too simple a figure, a slice of folklore rather than a convincing human being." Likewise, Whitney Balliett in the *New Yorker,* although in praise of Kelley's going "about his work calmly" while working with subject matter that can "turn well-meaning novelists into polemicists," comments on over-ideologized characters: "Kelley's characters . . . tend to spring from his ideas, rather than the other way around. If he were to press deeper into the ordinary hearts he writes of, instead of forcing them to grow on intellectual trellises, he would help us to know our own hearts."

Kelley's fourth book, the novel *dem,* takes a distinctly radical approach in communicating the destructive influences of racism in America. An "overt satire of the ways of white people," according to Bone, Kelley's novel is the story of a white couple who, through a rare fertilization process, become the parents of twin boys, one white and one black. Calling the book "a jarring surprise," Henry S. Resnik in the *Saturday Review* describes *dem*'s major characters: "The protagonist, Mitchell Pierce, is upper-middle-class white, an advertising copy-writer, emotionally and sexually impotent, a travesty of a man. His wife, Tam, is a domineering bitch whose principal characteristics are her penchant for ridicule and her preoccupation with her hairdo." Resnick adds: "The book is an angry, if not always original, portrait of American society. . . . Kelley is not only angry at savagery, racism, emasculation, and matriarchy; he takes a good hard crack at our slim hold on reality."

As with Kelley's previous fiction, some reviewers objected to a level of superficiality in the novel. Dan Jaffe remarks in *Prairie Schooner:* "The texture of the language, the settings, and the dialogue, give the reader a sense of life, of the alienation of a confused white man who suspects he is on the periphery of a life-rhythm more natural and substantial than his own. Unfortunately, the rest of the novel is slick and stagey by comparison." Frank C. Shapiro comments in *Book World* that the main character of *dem* is not quite believable: "There are good scenes in this unsatisfying book, and good writing, too, but on the whole, reading *dem* is like watching a basketball player, in perfect form, fake out a guard, arch for a pivot shot, and miss." Bone, however, praises Kelley's use of satire to effectively communicate his message: "[Kelley's] present mood is bitter, disillusioned, alienated to the point of secession from American society. The expatriate impulse, however, has found in satire a controlling form. Kelley's images are able to encompass his negative emotions. The result is a sharp increase in perception for the victims of his satire." Babb commends Kelley's innovative approach in that it "represents a reordering of the social history of America. Rather than having blacks as the victims, in [*dem*] it is the whites who suffer as Kelley parodies their traditions and their values. . . . Kelley suggests that white America is sterile in the values it pursues and is consciously, deliberately cruel."

Kelley's next novel, *Dunfords Travels Everywheres,* is his most experimental. "Inspired by *Finnegans Wake* and the problem [James] Joyce faced as an Irish writer within a larger English context," notes Babb, "*Dunfords Travels Everywheres* is constructed from a language derived from Bantu, Pidgin English, and Harlem argot, among other forms of black speech." In the novel, Kelley combines this experimental, collective language ("Langleash") with that of standard English prose to relate the internal exploration of Chig Dunford, a contemporary Harvard-educated black. In his self-exploration, Dunford comes upon an aspect of himself embodied in a character named Carlyle Bedlow, a Harlem-raised black; these twin aspects of the same person converge along common bonds that are understood through their secret language. Michael Wood explains in the *New York Review of Books:* "In the half-gibberish of their dreams, represented in the novel by Joycean metalanguage, . . . they know the truth which escapes them in waking life—shown here by Kelley in more conventional prose, as a place of assassinations and deceit, where slaves are suddenly encountered on a lower deck of a modern liner, where vast competing conspiracies, secret societies of whites against blacks and vice versa, are glimpsed beneath the surfaces of an innocent-looking world." Dunford emerges as a far-reaching representative of the Afro-American, according to David Galloway in *The Black American Short Story in the Twentieth Century: A Collection of Critical Essays:* "Just as Joyce's hero, H. C. E., metamorphoses into 'Here comes Everybody,' so Dunford is a kind of 'everybody' traveling everywhere—Harlem spade, Ivy League Negro, crook and cowboy and lover and artist and pilgrim."

Regarding *Dunfords Travels Everywheres* critical opinion was again divided on Kelley. Wood comments that like Joyce, Kelley "as a black American and a writer, is caught in the language and culture of an enemy country, and his use of *Finnegans Wake* reflects a legitimate distress: it is a mockery both of 'good English' and of black manglings of it." Wood concludes, however, that "the effort looks in the wrong direction. The experimental idiom is ingenious, but it is, also, thin and obscure." On the other hand, Christopher Lehmann-Haupt notes in the *New York Times* that the "black form of the dream language of James Joyce's *Finnegans Wake* . . . has released in Kelley a creative exuberance that was being choked with bitterness in his last book." Although Lehmann-Haupt agrees that some aspects of the novel "seem curiously cryptic and incomplete," he commends Kelley for "the way the 'real' surface is undermined, so that finally it threatens to splinter into hallucination at every moment. Chief among the myriad themes . . . is that the way to the black man's roots is not over Harlem and out, but back to the streets of the ghetto and in through its language."

Regarding possible political statements in his fiction, Kelley remarked in his 1967 *Conversations* interview: "I simply want to try to write good books. It isn't that I'm naive, that I'm trying to divorce myself from the racial struggle, but I don't think it should enter into my art in such a way that my writing becomes propagandistic. If my novels are so strongly tied to the times the book would have no reason to live once the present struggles are over—if indeed, they ever will be over. I want my books to have reason to exist." Galloway comments that, as enduring literature, Kelley's novels and short stories "manage to carve a reasonably secure niche for themselves within the American system; the trials to which they are submitted have as much to do with being human as they do, specifically, with being black." Galloway notes a particular relevance of Kelley's fiction: "The dilemma he frequently underscores is that the black's destiny is in many ways indistinguishable from the destiny of the entire post-modern American society, but that participation in such a destiny must not be allowed to submerge entirely the ethnic, cultural, and personal identity of the black."

BIOGRAPHICAL/CRITICAL SOURCES:

BOOKS

Bruck, Peter, editor, *The Black American Short Story in the Twentieth Century: A Collection of Critical Essays,* Gruener, 1977.
Contemporary Literary Criticism, Volume 22, Gale, 1982.
Dictionary of Literary Biography, Volume 33: *Afro-American Fiction Writers after 1955,* Gale, 1984.
Kelley, William Melvin, *Dancers on the Shore,* Doubleday, 1964.
Kelley, William Melvin, *dem,* Doubleday, 1967.
Kelley, William Melvin, *Dunfords Travels Everywheres,* Doubleday, 1970.
Littlejohn, David, *Black on White,* Grossman, 1966.
Newquist, Roy, editor, *Conversations,* Rand McNally, 1967.
Whitlow, Roger, *Black American Literature: A Critical History,* Nelson Hall, 1973.
Williams, Sherley Anne, *Give Birth to Brightness,* Dial, 1972.

PERIODICALS

America, April 17, 1965.
American Literature, January, 1973.
Best Sellers, April 15, 1964, April 15, 1965, October 1, 1970.

Booklist, July 1, 1962.
Book World, October 22, 1967.
CLA Journal, December, 1975.
Commonweal, July 3, 1964.
Critique: Studies in Modern Fiction, fall, 1984.
Esquire, August, 1963.
Harper's, December, 1969.
Negro Digest, October, 1962, January, 1967, March, 1967,
    May, 1968, November, 1969.
Newsweek, April 12, 1965.
New Yorker, May 22, 1965.
New York Herald Tribune Books, June 17, 1962.
New York Herald Tribune Book Week, March 22, 1964.
New York Review of Books, March 11, 1971.
New York Times, April 9, 1965, September 7, 1970.
New York Times Book Review, June 17, 1962, May 2, 1965,
    September 24, 1967, November 8, 1970.
Partisan Review, spring, 1968.
Prairie Schooner, spring, 1968.
Reporter, May 21, 1964.
Saturday Review, April 17, 1965, October 28, 1967.
Studies in Black Literature, summer, 1971, fall, 1972, winter,
    1974, fall, 1975.
Times Literary Supplement, March 17, 1966.

—*Sketch by Michael E. Mueller*

*   *   *

KENNEDY, Adrienne (Lita)   1931-

PERSONAL: Born September 13, 1931, in Pittsburgh, Pa.;
daughter of Cornell Wallace and Etta (Haugabook) Hawkins;
married Joseph C. Kennedy, May 15, 1953; children: Joseph
C., Adam. *Education:* Ohio State University, B.A.,1952;
graduate study at Columbia University, 1954-56; also studied
at New School for Social Research, American Theatre Wing,
Circle in the Square Theatre School, and Edward Albee's
workshop.

ADDRESSES: Office—Department of Afro-American Studies,
Princeton University, Princeton, N.J. 08544. *Agent*—Bridget
Aschenberg, 40 West 57th St., New York, N.Y. 10019.

CAREER: Playwright. Lecturer, Yale University, 1972-74,
Princeton University, 1977; visiting associate professor, Brown
University, 1979-80. International Theatre Institute represen-
tative, Budapest, 1978. Member of playwriting unit, Actors
Studio, New York, N.Y. 1962-65.

MEMBER: PEN (member of board of directors, 1976-77).

AWARDS, HONORS: Obie Award from *Village Voice,* 1964,
for "Funnyhouse of a Negro"; Guggenheim memorial fellowship, 1967; Rockefeller grants, 1967-69, 1974, 1976; National
Endowment for the Arts grant, 1973; CBS fellow, School of
Drama, 1973; Creative Artists Public Service grant, 1974; Yale
fellow, 1974-75; Stanley award for play writing; New England
Theatre Conference grant.

WRITINGS:

People Who Led to My Plays (memoir), Knopf, 1987.

PLAYS

Funnyhouse of a Negro (one-act; first produced Off-Broadway
    at Circle in the Square Theatre, 1962), Samuel French,
    1969.

"The Owl Answers" (one-act; also see below), first produced
    in Westport, Conn., at White Barn Theatre, 1963, pro-
    duced Off-Broadway at Public Theatre, January 12, 1969.
"A Lesson in a Dead Language" (also see below), first pro-
    duced in 1964.
"A Rat's Mass" (also see below), first produced in Boston,
    Mass., by the Theatre Company, April, 1966, produced
    Off-Broadway at La Mama Experimental Theatre Club,
    November, 1969.
"A Beast's Story" (one-act; also see below), first produced
    in 1966, produced Off-Broadway at Public Theatre, Jan-
    uary 12, 1969.
(With John Lennon and Victor Spinetti) *The Lennon Play: In
    His Own Write* (adapted from Lennon's books *In His Own
    Write* and *A Spaniard in the Works;* first produced in
    London by National Theatre, 1967; produced in Albany,
    N.Y., at Arena Summer Theatre, August, 1969), Simon
    & Schuster, 1969.
"Sun: A Poem for Malcolm X Inspired by His Murder" (also
    see below), first produced on the West End, London, at
    Royal Court Theatre, 1968, produced in New York at La
    Mama Experimental Theatre Club, 1970.
Cities in Bezique (contains "The Owl Answers" and "A Beast
    Story"; first produced in New York at Shakespeare Fes-
    tival, 1969), Samuel French, 1969.
"Boats," first produced in Los Angeles at the Forum, 1969.
"An Evening With Dead Essex," first produced in New York
    by American Place Theatre Workshop, 1973.
"A Movie Star Has to Star in Black and White" (also see
    below), first produced in New York by Public Theatre
    Workshop, 1976.
"A Lancashire Lad" (for children), first produced in Albany,
    N.Y., at Governor Nelson A. Rockefeller Empire State
    Plaza Performing Arts Center, May, 1980.
"Orestes and Electra," first produced in New York at Julliard
    School of Music, 1980.
"Black Children's Day," first produced in Providence, R.I.,
    at Brown University, November, 1980.
"Solo Voyages" (contains excerpts from "The Owl An-
    swers," "A Rat's Mass," and "A Movie Star Has to
    Star in Black and White"), first produced in New York
    at Interart Center, 1985.

CONTRIBUTOR

William M. Hoffman, editor, *New American Plays,* Hill &
    Wang, 1968.
Edward Parone, editor, *Collision Course* (includes "A Lesson
    in a Dead Language"), Random House, 1968.
William Couch, Jr., editor, *New Black Playwrights* (includes
    "A Rat's Mass"), Louisiana State University Press, 1968.
Rochelle Owens, editor, *Spontaneous Combustion* (includes
    "Sun: A Poem for Malcolm X Inspired by His Murder"),
    Winter House, 1972.
Paul C. Harrison, editor, *Kuntu Drama* (includes "A Beast's
    Story" and "The Owl Answers"), Grove Press, 1974.
Wordplay 3 (includes "A Movie Star Has to Star in Black and
    White"), Performing Arts Journal Publications, 1984.

OTHER

Contributor of plays to periodicals, including *Scripts 1.*

SIDELIGHTS: "While almost every black playwright in the
country is fundamentally concerned with realism . . . Miss
[Adrienne] Kennedy is weaving some kind of dramatic fabric
of poetry," Clive Barnes comments in the *New York Times.*
"What she writes is a mosaic of feeling, with each tiny stone

stained with the blood of the gray experience. Of all our black writers, Miss Kennedy is most concerned with white, with white relationship, with white blood. She thinks black, but she remembers white. It gives her work an eddying ambiguity.''

In her complex and introspective plays, Martin Duberman remarks in *Partisan Review*, Kennedy is ''absorbed by her private fantasies, her interior world. She disdains narrative, 'everyday' language and human interaction; the dream, the myth, the poem are her domain.'' James Hatch and Ted Shine also note that ''in a tradition in which the major style has long been realism, Adrienne Kennedy has done what few black playwrights have attempted: used form to project an interior reality and thereby created a rich and demanding theatrical style.''

Kennedy's first play, ''Funnyhouse of a Negro,'' examines the psychological problems of Sarah, a young mulatto woman who lives with a Jewish poet in a boarding house run by a white landlady. Dealing with the last moments before Sarah's suicide, the play consists of scenes of the young woman's struggle with herself. Tortured by an identity crisis, Sarah is ''lost in a nightmare world where black is evil and white is good, where various personages, including Queen Victoria, Patrice Lumumba, and Jesus Himself, materialize to mock her,'' says *New Yorker*'s Edith Oliver. ''Funnyhouse of a Negro'' earned Kennedy an Obie award, and, notes a *Variety* reviewer, a reputation as ''a gifted writer with a distinctive dramatic imagination.''

Oliver described ''The Owl Answers'' as another fantasy of ''a forbidden and glorious white world, viewed with a passion and frustration that shred the spirit and nerves and mind of the dispossessed heroine.'' The illegitimate child of a black cook and the wealthiest white man in Georgia, the heroine is riding on a New York subway. The subway doors become the doors to the chapel of the Tower of London through which appear masked historical characters, including Chaucer, Shakespeare, Anne Boleyn, and the Virgin Mary, who at times unmask to become other characters, such as the heroine's mother and father.

''A Beast's Story,'' produced with ''The Owl Answers'' under the title ''Cities in Bezique,'' was described as more elaborate, hallucinatory and obscure than the first play. It draws analogies, says Steve Tennen in *Show Business*, ''between inhuman beings and man's bestial tendencies.'' Kennedy's later play, ''A Rat's Mass,'' staged as a parody mass, is also abstract, centering around the relationship between a black brother and sister and their childhood involvement with the white girl next door.

In all of these plays, Kennedy's writing is poetic and symbolic; plot and dialogue are secondary to effect. Her reliance on such devices as masks, characters who become other characters, characters played by more than one actor, and Christian symbolism makes her work difficult to understand, and her plays have been seen as both nightmarish rituals and poetic dances. Marilyn Stasio explains in *Cue*: ''Kennedy is a poet, working with disjointed time sequences, evocative images, internalized half-thoughts, and incantatory language to create a netherworld of submerged emotions surfacing only in fragments. Events are crucial only for the articulated feelings they evoke.''

During 1971, Kennedy joined five other women playwrights to found the Women's Theatre Council, a theatre cooperative devoted to producing the works of women playwrights and providing opportunities for women in other aspects of the theatre, such as directing and acting. Mel Gussow of the *New York Times* notes that the council's ''founding sisters all come from Off Off Broadway, are exceeding prolific, have had their plays staged throughout the United States and in many foreign countries and feel neglected by the New York commercial theater. Each has a distinctive voice, but their work is related in being largely non-realistic and experimental. The women feel unified as innovators and by their artistic consciousness.''

Kennedy branched out into juvenile theatre in 1980 after being commissioned by the Empire State Youth Theatre Institute. ''A Lancashire Lad,'' her first play for children, is a fictionalized version of Charles Chaplin's childhood. Narrated by the hero, the play traces his life growing up in Dickensian England and beginning his career in the British music halls. Although an entertaining musical, the show confronts the poverty and pain of Chaplin's youth. Praising Kennedy's language for achieving ''powerful emotional effects with the sparest of means,'' *New York Times* reviewer Frank Rich concludes: ''The difference between 'The Lancashire Lad' and an adult play is, perhaps, the intellectual simplicity of its ambitions. Yet that simplicity can also be theater magic in its purest and most eloquent form.''

BIOGRAPHICAL/CRITICAL SOURCES:

BOOKS

Abramson, Doris E., *Negro Playwrights in the American Theatre, 1925-1959*, Columbia University Press, 1969.
Betsko, Kathleen, and Rachel Koenig, *Interviews with Contemporary Women Playwrights*, Beech Tree Books, 1987.
Cohn, Ruby, *New American Dramatists: 1960-1980*, Grove Press, 1982.
Dictionary of Literary Biography, Volume XXXVIII: *Afro-American Writers after 1955; Dramatists and Prose Writers*, Gale, 1985.
Harrison, Paul Carter, *The Drama of Nommo*, Grove Press, 1972.
Hatch, James V., and Ted Shine, editors, *Black Theater U.S.A.*, Free Press, 1974.
Mitchell, Loften, *Black Drama*, Hawthorne Books, 1967.
Oliver, Clinton, and Stephanie Sills, *Contemporary Black Drama*, Scribners, 1971.

PERIODICALS

City Arts Monthly, February, 1982.
CLA Journal, December, 1976.
Cue, January 18, 1969, October 4, 1969.
Drama Review, December, 1977.
International Times, September 22, 1968.
Los Angeles Times Book Review, July 12, 1987.
Ms., June, 1987.
New Yorker, January 25, 1964, January 25, 1969.
New York Times, January 15, 1964, June 20, 1968, July 9, 1968, January 13, 1969, January 19, 1969, November 1, 1969, February 22, 1972, May 21, 1980, February 15, 1981, September 11, 1985, September 20, 1985.
Observer Review, June 23, 1968.
Partisan Review, Number 3, 1969.
Show Business, January 25, 1969, October 4, 1969.
Studies in Black Literature, summer, 1975.
Variety, January 29, 1969.
Village Voice, August 14, 1969, September 25, 1969.

*   *   *

KENYATTA, Jomo   1891(?)-1978

PERSONAL: Name originally Kamau wa Ngengi; baptized as

Johnstone Kamau, 1914; known subsequently as Johnstone Kenyatta and Jomo Kenyatta; born c. October 20 in 1891 (some sources say 1889, 1890, 1893, 1897, or 1898), in Ichaweri (some sources say Ngenda), British East Africa Protectorate (now Kenya); died August 21 (some sources say August 22), 1978, in Mombasa, Kenya; son of Muigai (a small farmer and herdsman) and Wambui; married Grace Wahu, November 28, 1922; married Edna Grace Clarke (a schoolteacher and governess), May 11, 1942; married third wife, Grace; married fourth wife, Ngina; children: (first marriage) Peter Mugai, Margaret Wambui; (second marriage) Peter Magana; (third marriage) Jane Wambui; (fourth marriage) Uhuru, Muhoho, Nyokabi (some sources say a total of four sons and four daughters). *Education:* Attended Woodbroke College, 1931-32; studied in Moscow, U.S.S.R., c. 1932; attended London School of Economics and Political Science, c. 1936.

CAREER: Courier for sisal company in Nairobi, British East Africa Protectorate (became Kenya, 1920), c. 1915; interpreter for Supreme Court in Nairobi, 1919; stores clerk and water meter reader for city of Nairobi, 1922-28; Kikuyu Central Association, general secretary beginning in 1928, envoy in London, England, beginning in 1929; University of London, London, England, assistant in phonetics at School of Oriental and African Studies, beginning in 1933; farm worker in England and lecturer for British Army and Workers' Educational Association, c. 1939-45; Independent Teachers' College, Githunguri, Kenya, vice-principal, 1946-47, principal, beginning in 1947; president of Kenya African Union (political party), beginning in 1947; imprisoned at Lokitaung, Kenya, 1953-59; detained in Lodwar, Kenya, 1959-61, and Marlal, Kenya, 1961; president of Kenya African National Union (political party), beginning in 1961; Government of Kenya, Nairobi, member of Legislative Council representing Fort Hall, beginning in 1962, minister of state for constitutional affairs and economic planning, 1962-63, prime minister and minister for internal security and defense, 1963-64, president, 1964-78. Helped organize fifth Pan-African Congress in Manchester, England, 1945; co-founder of Organization of African Unity. Actor in film "Sanders of the River," 1935.

MEMBER: International African Friends of Abyssinia (co-founder and honorary secretary), International African Service Bureau.

AWARDS, HONORS: Knight of Grace in Order of St. John of Jerusalem, 1972; Order of Golden Ark from World Wildlife Fund, 1974. Honorary fellow of London School of Economics and Political Science; honorary doctorates from Victoria University of Manchester and University of East Africa.

WRITINGS:

(Contributor) Nancy Cunard, editor, *Negro Anthology,* privately printed, 1934.
Facing Mount Kenya: The Tribal Life of the Gikuyu, introduction by Bronislaw Malinowski, Secker & Warburg, 1938, Vintage, 1962, AMS Press, 1978.
(With Lilias E. Armstrong) *The Phonetic and Tonal Structure of Kikuyu,* Oxford University Press, 1940.
My People of Kikuyu and the Life of Chief Wangombe, United Society for Christian Literature, 1942, Oxford University Press, 1966.
Kenya: The Land of Conflict, Panaf Service, 1945, International African Service Bureau, 1971.
Harambee! The Prime Minister of Kenya's Speeches, 1963-1964, From the Attainment of Internal Self-Government to the Threshold of the Kenya Republic, foreword by Mal-

colm MacDonald, edited by Anthony Cullen, Oxford University Press, 1964.
Suffering Without Bitterness: The Founding of the Kenya Nation, East African Publishing House, 1968.
The Challenge of Uhuru: The Progress of Kenya, 1968 to 1970; Selected and Prefaced Extracts From the Public Speeches of Jomo Kenyatta, President of the Republic of Kenya, East African Publishing House, 1971.

Founder and editor of *Muigwithania,* 1928-30. Contributor to periodicals, including *Daily Worker, Labour Monthly, Manchester Guardian, Negro Worker,* and *Sunday Worker.*

SIDELIGHTS: Jomo Kenyatta led the newly independent African nation of Kenya from 1964 until his death in 1978. He grew up in a traditional African culture as a member of Kenya's largest ethnic group, the Kikuyu. (His exact age is a matter of conjecture because the Kikuyu classified themselves by age-group, ignoring an individual's birthday.) Son of a small farmer and herdsman, Kenyatta saw firsthand how black Africans suffered when white settlers took over their land. As a young man Kenyatta moved to the capital city of Nairobi, where he held a succession of minor jobs. In 1928 he became general secretary of the Kikuyu Central Association (KCA), which sought to improve the living conditions of the Kikuyu under British rule, and as part of his job he traveled widely among his people. The periodical he edited for the association, *Muigwithania,* is believed to be the first black journal in Kenya. The next year Kenyatta went to England as a KCA representative, lobbying successfully for independent Kikuyu schools and unsuccessfully for land reform.

Kenyatta spent most of the next seventeen years in England, promoting the cause of black Kenyans in a wide variety of forums. He wrote letters to the Colonial Office and articles for British periodicals, joined Pan-African groups such as the International African Service Bureau, and lobbied influential guests at London cocktail parties. He commiserated with black activists such as Paul Robeson, famous American singer and actor; W. E. B. Du Bois, a leader of America's National Association for the Advancement of Colored People; and Kwame Nkrumah, future president of Ghana. Traveling widely in Europe, Kenyatta studied for several months at an institute in Moscow that hoped to inspire Communist revolutionaries. (When he later became president of Kenya, however, he declared his country unsuitable for communism.) Some of Kenyatta's political concerns are summarized in the short work *Kenya: Land of Conflict.*

Although Kenyatta never earned a bachelor's degree, he became a graduate student in anthropology at the London School of Economics and Political Science in the mid-1930s, turning a series of papers he wrote about Kikuyu culture into the book *Facing Mount Kenya.* The work uses the format and terminology of a Western scholarly study, devoting chapters to religion, education, sexual practices, and land ownership. But *Facing Mount Kenya* is also a defense of Kenyatta's African background, for it suggests that European influence had harmed the Kikuyu, whose culture at its most untouched was as worthy of respect as that of Europe. In the *New York Times Book Review,* John Barkham said that Kenyatta's eagerness to defend his people had compromised his work, but the *Times Literary Supplement* praised the book as "very readable and highly instructive," noting that Kenyatta had maintained professional standards and had stated his opinions with "due restraint." *Facing Mount Kenya* has been reprinted several times since it first appeared, and in 1953 *Christian Science*

Monitor reviewer Marian Sorenson suggested that the book remained a useful background source for understanding black complaints against colonial rule.

Kenyatta returned to Kenya in 1946 and was elected president of a prominent political party, the Kenya African Union. He championed a reform program that included voting rights for blacks, an end to racial discrimination, and a more equitable distribution of land. At the same time, however, a black clandestine movement known as the Mau Mau began efforts to force the British from Kenya, murdering a small number of white settlers and many blacks suspected of collaborating with the white regime. British authorities, already concerned by Kenyatta's political prominence, became convinced that he was involved with the Mau Mau despite his public repudiation of its violence. Arrested in 1952, Kenyatta was tried and sentenced to prison as a Mau Mau organizer. Many sources cast doubt on the state's case against him.

As opposition to the colonial regime continued, the British resigned themselves to Kenya's eventual independence. Kenyatta, who remained highly popular while in prison and detention, was released from exile in a remote province in 1961. He was soon elected president of Kenya's largest political party, the Kenya African National Union, and led his country to independence in 1964. Kenyatta's national agenda, which included giving blacks a more balanced share of the Kenyan economy and creating a sense of social unity, is reflected in *Harambee,* a collection of his speeches. The book was named for Kenyatta's political rallying cry—Swahili for "let us all pull together!"

Although Kenyatta insisted that Kenya become a one-party state and suppressed rivals to his personal rule, his political philosophy was notably pragmatic. Certain speeches in *Suffering Without Bitterness* outline Kenyatta's doctrine of "African socialism"—an eclectic mixture of individual initiative and concern for the common good. Assessing Kenyatta's career in *New Times,* Charles Mohr wrote that the Kenyan leader's "admirers and critics alike had come to see him as perhaps the leading exponent in Africa of moderate politics [and] laissez-faire economics." Kenyatta allowed nonblacks to remain and contribute their skills to the new country. The economy prospered, and with government encouragement blacks increasingly entered the fields of business and large-scale farming, helping to create Africa's largest black middle class. The press was "nearly free," as Kenneth Labich and James Pringle wrote in *Newsweek.* Kenyatta remained interested in Pan-Africanism, helping to found the Organization of African Unity and a short-lived common market with the neighboring states of Uganda and Tanzania.

Although Kenyatta faced recurrent political discontent—including complaints that he countenanced nepotism and official corruption—when he died in 1978 commentators generally held that he was a great asset to his country and would be difficult to replace. "The Kenya he governed," Mohr asserted, "is today one of the most . . . free societies on the continent."

BIOGRAPHICAL/CRITICAL SOURCES:

BOOKS

Arnold, Guy, *Kenyatta and the Politics of Kenya,* Dent, 1974.
Murray-Brown, Jeremy, *Kenyatta,* Allen & Unwin, 1972, Dutton, 1973, 2nd edition, Allen & Unwin, 1979.

PERIODICALS

Christian Science Monitor, August 27, 1953.

New York Times, August 22, 1978.
New York Times Book Review, September 6, 1953.
Times Literary Supplement, March 11, 1939.

OBITUARIES:

PERIODICALS

Newsweek, September 4, 1978.
New Times, September 18, 1978.
New York Times, November 6, 1978.
Time, September 4, 1978.

—*Sketch by Thomas Kozikowski*

*   *   *

KGOSITSILE, Keorapetse (William) 1938-

PERSONAL: Born September 19, 1938, in Johannesburg, South Africa; came to United States in 1961; married wife, Melba. *Education:* Educated in Africa; additional study at Lincoln University, University of New Hampshire, New School for Social Research, and Columbia University.

ADDRESSES: Office—Department of Literature, University of Nairobi, P.O. Box 30197, Nairobi, Kenya.

CAREER: Poet, essayist, and critic. North Carolina Agricultural and Technical State University, Greensboro, poet-in-residence, beginning 1971; lecturer in literature, University of Nairobi. Visiting professor at Sarah Lawrence College, Queens College of the City University of New York, Bennett College, North Carolina Central University, and University of Denver. Member of staff, *Black Dialogue* and *Spearhead.*

AWARDS, HONORS: Conrad Kent Rivers Memorial Award, 1969; National Endowment for the Arts grant, 1970.

WRITINGS:

Spirits Unchained (poems), Broadside Press, 1969.
For Melba (poems), Third World Press, 1970.
My Name Is Afrika (poems), introduction by Gwendolyn Brooks, Doubleday, 1971.
(Editor) *The Word Is Here: Poetry from Modern Africa,* Doubleday, 1973.
(Author of introduction) Sterling Plumpp, *Steps to Break the Circle,* Third World Press, 1974.
The Present Is a Dangerous Place to Live, Third World Press, 1974.
(With others) *A Capsule Course in Black Poetry Writing,* Broadside Press, 1975.
Places and Bloodstains: Notes for Ipelang, Achebe Publications, 1975.

Contributor of poetry to anthologies and to periodicals, including *Transition* and *Guerrilla.* African editor-at-large, *Black Dialogue.*

SIDELIGHTS: Although Keorapetse Kgositsile lived in the United States for several years, his poetry has always been considered "African" in its treatment of the themes of black unification and liberation. In *My Name Is Afrika,* according to *Booklist,* "passionate poems of the horror of black slavery in Africa and America symbolize universal suffering of the oppressed. Rhythmic and rhetorical calls to action, contemplations on black leaders, and acute observations couched in authentic dialogue are preceded by a characteristically penetrating and artistic introduction by Gwendolyn Brooks." Diane Ackerman writes in the *Library Journal* that in *My Name Is Afrika*

"Kgositsile demands militancy—if he ignites his reader, his poems are successful. [However,] when the furor subsides, Kgositsile can be passionate, perceptive, even delicate, producing an articulate record of black protest."

In *For Melba*, writes Christopher Scott in *Books Abroad*, "Kgositsile employs the medium of his love for his wife Melba to make a rather political statement. Revolutionary nationalism, as the poet sees it, has its foundation in the (concrete of) the family unit, both nuclear and extended. It would seem that for revolutionary nationalism the health of the personal and familial building blocks of society is causally related to the health of the nation. Kgositsile's message to his black brothers and sisters is, finally, 'Let us stop playing games.'" The poems of *For Melba*, Scott adds, trace the "physical and spiritual movement of the poet (and, by extension, all black people) in his personal and consequently political struggle for dignity."

A *Choice* reviewer calls Kgositsile's *The Word Is Here: Poetry from Modern Africa* an "attractive, original, and highly recommended collection of recent poetry from Africa."

BIOGRAPHICAL/CRITICAL SOURCES:

PERIODICALS

Booklist, September 1, 1971.
Books Abroad, spring, 1971.
Choice, October, 1973.
Christian Century, March 14, 1973.
Library Journal, March 15, 1971.

*   *   *

KILLENS, John Oliver   1916-1987

PERSONAL: Born January 14, 1916, in Macon, Ga.; died of cancer, October 27, 1987, in Brooklyn, N.Y.; son of Charles Myles, Sr., and Willie Lee (Coleman) Killens; married Grace Ward Jones; children: Jon Charles, Barbara Ellen Rivera. *Education:* Attended Edward Waters College, Morris Brown College, Atlanta University, Howard University, Robert H. Terrell Law School, Columbia University, and New York University.

ADDRESSES: Home—1392 Union St., Brooklyn, N.Y. 11212.

CAREER: Member of staff, National Labor Relations Board, 1936-42, and 1946; free-lance writer, 1954-87. Writer in residence, Fisk University, 1965-68, Columbia University, 1970-73, Howard University, 1971-72, Bronx Community College, 1979-81, and Medgar Evers College of the City University of New York, 1981-87. Former lecturer and teacher of creative writing at New School for Social Research, and lecturer at several other colleges and universities, including Southern University, Cornell University, Rutgers University, University of California, Los Angeles, Tufts University, Brandeis College (now Brandeis University), Springfield College, Western Michigan University, Savannah State College, and Trinity College. Co-founder and past chairperson, Harlem Writers Guild, 1952. *Military service:* U.S. Army, Pacific Amphibian Forces, 1942-45.

MEMBER: PEN, American Poets, Playwrights, Editors, Essayists, and Novelists (former member of executive board), Black Academy of Arts and Letters (former vice-president), National Center of Afro-American Artists (former member of executive board).

AWARDS, HONORS: Afro Art Theatre Cultural Award, 1955; Literary Arts Award, National Association for the Advance-

ment of Colored People (Brooklyn), 1957; Culture, Human Relations Award, Climbers Business Club; citation from Empire State Federation of Women; cultural award, New York State Fraternal Order of Elks; Charles Chesnut Award, Brooklyn Association for the Study of Negro Life and History; *And Then We Heard the Thunder* was nominated for a Pulitzer Prize, 1962; Rabinowitz Foundation grant, 1964; *The Cotillion; or, One Good Bull Is Half the Herd* was nominated for a Pulitzer Prize, 1971; Harlem Writers Guild award, 1978; National Endowment for the Arts fellowship, 1980; Lifetime Achievement Award, Before Columbus Foundation, 1986; elected to Black Filmmaker's Hall of Fame.

WRITINGS:

FICTION

Youngblood, Dial, 1954, published with foreword by Addison Gayle, University of Georgia Press, 1982.
And Then We Heard the Thunder, Knopf, 1962, reprinted, Howard University Press, 1983.
'Sippi, Trident Press, 1967, reprinted, Thunder's Mouth Press, 1988.
Slaves, Pyramid, 1969.
The Cotillion; or, One Good Bull Is Half the Herd (also see below), Trident Press, 1971, reprinted, Ballantine, 1988.
Great Gittin' Up Morning: A Biography of Denmark Vesey (young adult), Doubleday, 1972.
A Man Ain't Nothin' but a Man: The Adventures of John Henry (young adult), Little, Brown, 1975.
The Great Black Russian: A Novel on the Life and Times of Alexander Pushkin, Wayne State University Press, 1988.

Also author of *The Minister Primarily*.

PLAYS

(With Loften Mitchell) "Ballad of the Winter Soldier," first produced in Washington, D.C., at Philharmonic Hall, Lincoln Center, September 28, 1964.
"Lower Than the Angels," first produced in New York City, at American Place Theatre, January, 1965.
"Cotillion" (based on Killens's novel of same title, with music by Smokey Robinson and Willie Hutch), first produced in New York City at New Federal Theatre, July, 1975.

SCREENPLAYS

(With Nelson Gidding) "Odds Against Tomorrow," Belafonte Productions/United Artists, 1959.
(With Herbert J. Biberman and Alida Sherman) "Slaves," Theatre Guild-Walter Reade/Continental, 1969.

WORK REPRESENTED IN ANTHOLOGIES

David Boroff, *The State of the Nation*, Prentice-Hall, 1966.
John Henrik Clarke, editor, *American Negro Short Stories*, Hill & Wang, 1966.
Langston Hughes, editor, *The Best Short Stories by Negro Writers: An Anthology from 1899 to the Present*, Little, Brown, 1967.
Harlem, New American Library, 1970.
Raman K. Singh and Peter Fellowes, editors, *Voices from the Soul of Black America*, Crowell, 1970.
Nick Aaron, editor, *Black Insights: Significant Literature by Black Americans, 1760 to the Present*, Ginn, 1971.
Patricia L. Brown, Don L. Lee, and Francis Ward, editors, *To Gwen with Love: An Anthology Dedicated to Gwendolyn Brooks*, Johnson, 1971.

Addison Gayle, Jr., editor, *The Black Aesthetic*, Doubleday, 1971.

John A. Williams and Charles F. Harris, editors, *Amistad 2*, Vintage Books, 1971.

William H. Robinson, editor, *Nommo: An Anthology of Modern African and Black American Literature*, Macmillan, 1972.

OTHER

Black Man's Burden (essays), Trident Press, 1965.

(Author of prologue) Fred Halstead, *Harlem Stirs*, photographs by Don Hogan Charles and Anthony Aviles, Marzani & Munsell, 1966.

(Contributor) John Henrik Clarke, editor, *William Styron's Nat Turner: Ten Black Writers Respond*, Beacon, 1968.

(Editor and author of foreword) *Trial Record of Denmark Vesey*, Beacon, 1970.

(Author of introduction) Woodie King, editor, *Black Short Story Anthology*, Columbia University Press, 1972.

"John O. Killens on Alexander Pushkin" (audio cassette), Institute of Afro-American Affaris (New York), 1976.

"John Oliver Killens" (audio cassette), Tapes for Readers (Washington, D.C.), 1978.

Also author of *Write On!: Notes from a Writers Workshop*. Contributor to periodicals, including *Ebony, Black World, Black Aesthetic, African Forum, Library Journal, Nation, Saturday Evening Post, Black Scholar, Freedomways, Redbook*, and *Arts in Society*.

SIDELIGHTS: "Ever since I can remember, I have always been a sucker for a well-told tale, and the more outlandish and outrageous, the better, as far as I was concerned," John Oliver Killens wrote in his autobiographical essay in *Contemporary Authors Autobiography Series*, "The Half Ain't Never Been Told." Killens credited his beloved paternal great-grandmother for his decision to become a writer. Seven years old when slavery was abolished, she had regaled Killens in his youth with memorable stories about those days: "Puffing on her corncob pipe, speaking in the mellifluous voice, enriched by age. . . . She seemed to encompass within herself all the wisdom of the ages. Sometimes at the end of each tale, she would shake her head, all white with age, the skin of her face unwrinkled and tight as a newborn baby's backside, stretchd tautly over high cheekbones. And she'd say, 'Aaah Lord, Honey, THE HALF AIN'T NEVER BEEN TOLD!'" And challenged to tell at least part of that untold half, Killens remarked, "I felt I owed that much to Granny."

Killens also indicated in his autobiographical essay that he had been a voracious reader as a child, taking his cherished library books to bed with him to read by flashlight. During his teenage years, his early dreams of becoming a physician, though, were replaced with those of becoming a lawyer. And despite years of studying law by night and working by day at the Negro Labor Relations Board, he decided during a stint with the U.S. Army in the South Pacific that he would not return to law school, but would become a writer instead. "One evening in the early fifties or late forties, I gathered with seven others up above a store front on 125th Street in Harlem and, in a very trembly voice, read the first chapter of *Youngblood*," wrote Killens in his autobiographical essay. This early group of young, black, and soon-to-be prominent writers, formed the nucleus of the distinguished and prolific Harlem Writers Guild; and Killens's first book, *Youngblood*, was the first novel to be published from it.

Youngblood is about a Southern black family's struggle for survival. Through the characters of the parents and their two children, Killens "exposes his readers to what life was like for Afro-Americans living in the American South during the first third of this century," wrote William H. Wiggins, Jr. in the *Dictionary of Literary Biography*. "The novel demonstrates how these four characters band together to overcome the economic, educational, social, and religious manifestations of Jim Crow life in their hometown of Crossroads, Georgia." Called a "fine novel, vivid, readable," by Ann Petry in the *New York Herald Tribune Book Review*, *Youngblood* is described by Granville Hicks in the *New York Times* as "a record of petty, mean-spirited, wanton discrimination." And although Hicks found it "didactic" at times, he also found it to have "the power of the author's passion" and declared that "the novel of social protest, which survives precariously today, justifies itself when it is as moving as 'Youngblood' and deals with so gross an evil."

Killens's second novel, *And Then We Heard the Thunder*, is based on his own experience with segregation and racism in the military during the Second World War. According to Martin Levin in the *New York Times Book Review*, the novel's black protagonist, who wishes only to be "the best damn soldier," is forced instead "to make common cause with his race rather than with his army." Although critics tended to fault the style of the novel, they nonetheless responded well to its message. While Nelson Algren suggested in the *New York Herald Tribune Book Review* that the book "lacked the passion of men at war," J. H. Griffin in the *Saturday Review* found the battle scenes in particular filled with "hallucinatory power," and declared that the reader who has not experienced racial discrimination, "living all the indignities of the Negro soldier, sees clearly how it looked from the other side of the color line." Griffin concludes that "this novel magnificently illumines the reasons why" the wounds remain despite discrimination having been eliminated from the armed forces.

Killens's *'Sippi* "reflects his new militancy," wrote Wiggins, indicating that the title originates from a "civil rights protest joke" in which a black man informs his white landlord that he will no longer include mister or miss when addressing others, including the state of Mississippi, "It's just plan 'Sippi from now on!'" The novel concerns the struggles over voting rights during the 1960s and Wiggins added that Killens "recounts in vivid detail the bombings, shootings, and other acts of terror and intimidation endured by the courageous students and local blacks who dare stand up and push for voter registration." Wiggins reported that there was a lack of a critical middle ground regarding the novel—critics either did or did not like it. Acknowledging in his autobiographical essay that the novel "was a critical bust," Killens added, "I heartily disagreed with the critics, naturally. Or else why would I have written it?"

Killens's *The Cotillion; or One Good Bull Is Half the Herd* is a satire about an annual ball held by an exclusive black women's club in Brooklyn. "Through hyperbole and cutting social and political commentary, Killens's novel becomes a biting didactic piece of Afro-American literature, written in the tradition of verbal contests known as the dozens to many Afro-Americans," explained Wiggins. "The object of the game is to unsettle one's verbal opponent with exaggerated statements of personal insults." Noting that "this is precisely the plot" of *The Cotillion*, Wiggins wrote that by the end of the novel, "Killens has reduced this sedate group of society matrons to a confused and disorganized group of babbling black women who have been verbally stripped of their veneer of white middle-class values and exposed for what they truly are: comically tragic Afro-Americans who are out of touch with their cultural heritage.'' Calling its language ''Afro-Americanese,'' George Davis commented in *Black World* that *The Cotillion* ''signifies and lies and intrudes on itself whenever it sees fit. It dances around while it is talking and comes all out of itself to make sure you get the point that it is making. It starts to exaggerate and keeps on exaggerating even though it knows that you know that the truth is being stretched out of shape.'' Leonard Fleischer observed in *Saturday Review* that ''in a prose often buoyantly evocative and musical, Killens caricatures some of the more egregious foibles of black and white society.'' Moreover, continued Fleischer, while making use of stereotyped blacks to satirically reveal a ''willing acceptance of the standards of white culture,'' Killens is simultaneously ''mocking the rage for instant blackness.''

''Killens's major themes evolve around social protest and cultural affirmation,'' wrote Wiggins, who felt that Killens ''fashioned his career in the protest mold of Richard Wright. For both of these writers the primary purpose of art is to attack and ultimately change society for the better.'' Although recognized and praised for his novels, Killens also achieved distinction for his essays on the quality of black life in America. Wiggins wrote that Killens's collection of political essays, *Black Man's Burden*, ''demonstrates the shift in Killens's philosophy'' away from the nonviolence espoused by Martin Luther King, Jr., and toward the more militant views of his friend, Malcolm X: ''In the series of essays on such subjects as white paternalism, black manhood, unions, sit-ins, boycotts, religion, black nationalism, Africa, nonviolence, and the right of self-defense, Killens argued that passive acceptance of racial oppression only encourages more racial violence. Killens believed that the only way blacks could break the vicious cycle of racial violence would be to respond to white violence with black violence.'' In an *America* review of the collection, John Hattman stated that ''Killens writes in rough strong language, but it is a language well suited to carry the author's harsh message.'' And in the *Saturday Review*, Frank M. Cordasco observed that Killens had assembled ''a pastiche of perceptive, sharply delineated vignettes animated by the twin engines of hate and despair.''

Killens's work is internationally known, having been translated into more than a dozen languages. In his autobiographical essay, he wrote that when he travelled to Africa in 1961 to do research for a British Broadcasting Corp. script, he viewed a screening of his own motion picture, ''Odds Against Tomorrow,'' with French subtitles. And when the author journeyed to China in 1973 with a group of writers and teachers, he learned that he and Ernest Hemingway were ''two of the most widely read writers there.'' Killens's travels also took him to the Soviet Union. In 1968 and 1970, he attended a festival in the Soviet Union where ''writers and artists are invited . . . from all over the world to celebrate the life of Alexander Sergeievich Pushkin,'' the subject of a novel on which he had worked since the middle 1960s. Killens indicated in his autobiographical essay that he had also completed a comedic novel entitled *The Minister Primarily*, and a book about the art and craft of creative writing entitled *Write On!: Notes from a Writers Workshop*. As a prominent novelist, playwright, essayist, and teacher, Killens ''strove in all his work to distill and express the black experience in this country,'' wrote Richard Pearson in the *Washington Post*. ''In doing so he reached an audience that transcended boundaries of race or color to express common denominators in human nature.''

BIOGRAPHICAL/CRITICAL SOURCES:

BOOKS

Contemporary Authors Autobiography Series, Volume 2, Gale, 1985.
Contemporary Literary Criticism, Volume 10, Gale, 1979.
Dictionary of Literary Biography, Volume 33: *Afro-American Fiction Writers after 1955*, Gale, 1984.
Gayle, Addison, Jr., *The Way of the World: The Black Novel in America*, Anchor Press/Doubleday, 1975.
Littlejohn, David, *Black on White: A Critical Survey of Writing by American Negroes*, Viking Penguin, 1966.
Williams, John A., and Charles F. Harris, editors, *Amistad 2*, Random House, 1971.

PERIODICALS

Atlantic, February, 1971.
Best Sellers, February 1, 1963, October 1, 1965, March 15, 1972.
Black Scholar, November, 1971.
Black World, June, 1971.
Christian Science Monitor, May 4, 1972.
Crisis, October, 1954, April, 1965.
Freedomways, 1971.
Keystone Folklore Quarterly, fall, 1972.
Midwest Journal, summer, 1954.
Nation, August 21, 1954.
National Observer, July 15, 1968.
Negro Digest, November, 1967.
Newsweek, May 26, 1969.
New York Herald Tribune Book Review, July 11, 1954, April 14, 1963.
New York Review of Books, April 20, 1972.
New York Times, June 6, 1954, March 2, 1969, March 28, 1969, March 27, 1970, May 29, 1972.
New York Times Book Review, February 27, 1966, January 17, 1971, April 30, 1972, August 10, 1975.
Saturday Review, January 26, 1963, March 12, 1966, March 6, 1971.
Time, October 26, 1959.
Washington Post Book World, May 29, 1988.

OBITUARIES:

PERIODICALS

Jet, November 16, 1987.
Los Angeles Times, October 31, 1987.
New York Times, October 30, 1987.
Washington Post, November 3, 1987.

—*Sketch by Sharon Malinowski*

*			*			*

KINCAID, Jamaica   1949-

PERSONAL: Born May 25, 1949, in St. John's, Antigua, West Indies; immigrated to United States; naturalized U.S. citizen; daughter of a carpenter and Annie Richardson; married Allen Shawn (a composer); children: one daughter. *Religion:* Methodist.

ADDRESSES: Home—284 Hudson, New York, N.Y. *Office*—*New Yorker*, 25 West 43rd St., New York, N.Y. 10036.

CAREER: Writer. Staff writer for *New Yorker* in New York, N.Y., 1976—.

AWARDS, HONORS: Morton Dauwen Zabel Award from American Academy and Institute of Arts and Letters, 1983, for *At the Bottom of the River.*

WRITINGS:

At the Bottom of the River (short stories), Farrar, Straus, 1983.
Annie John (short story cycle), Farrar, Straus, 1985.
A Small Place, Farrar, Straus, 1988.

Contributor to periodicals, including *New Yorker.*

SIDELIGHTS: Jamaica Kincaid is the acclaimed author of *At the Bottom of the River* and *Annie John.* In these books about life on the Caribbean island Antigua, where she was born, Kincaid employs a highly poetic literary style, one celebrated for its rhythms and imagery, and shows herself a master of characterization and elliptic narration. As Ike Onwordi wrote in *Times Literary Supplement:* "Jamaica Kincaid uses language that is poetic without affectation. She has a deft eye for salient detail while avoiding heavy symbolism and diverting exotica. The result captures powerfully the essence of vulnerability."

In her first book, *At the Bottom of the River,* Kincaid showed an imposing capacity for detailing life's mundane aspects. This characteristic of her writing is readily evident in the often cited tale "Girl," which consists almost entirely of a mother's orders to her daughter: "Wash the white clothes on Monday and put them on the stone heap; wash the color clothes on Tuesday and put them on the clothesline to dry; don't walk barehead in the hot sun; cook pumpkin fritters in very hot sweet oil . . . ; on Sundays try to walk like a lady, and not like the slut you are so bent on becoming." Anne Tyler, in her review for *New Republic,* declared that this passage provides "the clearest idea of the book's general tone; for Jamaica Kincaid scrutinizes various particles of our world so closely and so solemnly that they begin to take on a nearly mystical importance."

"The Letter From Home," another story from *At the Bottom of the River,* serves as further illustration of Kincaid's style of repetition and her penchant for the mundane. In this tale a character recounts her daily chores in such a manner that the entire tale resembles an incantation: "I milked the cows, I churned the butter, I stored the cheese, I baked the bread, I brewed the tea," the tale begins, and it continues in this manner for several pages before ending as one long sentence. In *Ms.,* Suzanne Freeman cited this tale as evidence that Kincaid's style "is . . . akin to hymn-singing or maybe even chanting." Freeman added that Kincaid's "singsong style" produces "images that are as sweet and mysterious as the secrets that children whisper in your ear."

Upon publication in 1983, *At the Bottom of the River* marked Kincaid's arrival as an important new voice in American fiction. Edith Milton wrote in the *New York Times Book Review* that Kincaid's tales "have all the force of illumination, and even prophetic power," and David Leavitt noted in the *Village Voice* that they move "with grace and ease from the mundane to the enormous." Leavitt also stated that "Kincaid's particular skill lies in her ability to articulate the internal workings of a potent imagination without sacrificing the rich details of the external world on which that imagination thrives." Doris Grumbach expressed similar praise in her review for the *Washington Post Book World.* She declared that the world of Kincaid's narrators "hovers between fantasy and reality" and as-

serted that Kincaid's prose "results not so much in stories as in states of consciousness." Grumbach also wrote that Kincaid's style, particularly its emphasis on repetition, intensifies "the feelings of poetic jubilation Kincaid has . . . for all life."

That exuberance for life is also evident in Kincaid's second book, *Annie John,* which contains interrelated stories about a girl's maturation in Antigua. In *Annie John,* the title character evolves from young girl to aspiring nurse and from innocent to realist: she experiences her first menstruation, buries a friend, gradually establishes a life independent of her mother, and overcomes a serious illness. After recovering her health Annie John decides to depart from Antigua to become a nurse in England, though this decision results in a painful, and necessary, separation from her mother. "No, I am not you," Annie John eventually informs her mother in one tale; "I am not what you made me." By book's end Annie John has left her mother to pursue a nursing career. She is ultimately torn by her pursuit of a career outside her life in Antigua, and Kincaid renders that feeling so incisively that, as Elaine Kendall noted in her review for the *Los Angeles Times,* "you can almost believe Kincaid invented ambivalence."

Like *At the Bottom of the River,* Kincaid's *Annie John* earned widespread acclaim. Susan Kenney, writing in the *New York Times Book Review,* observed that "Kincaid . . . has packed a lot of valuable insight about the complex relationship between mothers and daughters into this slender novel." Kenney noted Annie John's ambivalence about leaving behind her life in Antigua and declared that such ambivalence was "an inevitable and unavoidable result of growing up." Furthermore, Kenney stated that she couldn't "remember reading a book that illustrates this [ambivalence] more poignantly than" *Annie John.* Kendall, who called *Annie John* a "fully fledged novel," seconded Kenney's assessment and confirmed Kincaid's status as a major writer. According to Kendall, *Annie John* possessed "a timeless quality, adding substance and weight to the smallest incident and detail."

Many critics focused particular praise on Kincaid's poetic style and artistic sensitivity. An *Atlantic* reviewer noted the "cool, precise style" of *Annie John,* and *Nation* reviewer Barbara Fisher Williamson noted that the volume's first-person narrative—Annie John's "tone flat, her language modest"—"works best when it is undercut by ironic detachment or overburdened by intense feeling." Comparing *Annie John* favorably to the earlier *At the Bottom of the River,* *Washington Post* critic Susan Wood noted that the later work "retains the shimmering, strange beauty of the earlier stories, but its poetry is grounded in detail, in the lovingly rendered life of its adolescent heroine." And Kendall wrote in the *Los Angeles Times* that "Kincaid's imagery is so neon-bright that the traditional story of a young girl's passage into adolescence takes on a shimmering strangeness, the familiar outlines continually forming surprising patterns."

With only two books, Kincaid has become a prominent figure in American literature, and even though her books are set in a foreign land, the West Indies, she credits the United States as the place where "I did find myself and did find my voice." In the *New York Times Book Review,* where she made the aforementioned comment, she added: "What I really feel about America is that it's given me a place to be myself—but myself as I was formed somewhere else."

BIOGRAPHICAL/CRITICAL SOURCES:

BOOKS

Contemporary Literary Criticism, Volume 43, Gale, 1987.

PERIODICALS

Atlantic, May, 1985.
Boston Herald, March 31, 1985.
Christian Science Monitor, April 5, 1985.
Listener, January 10, 1985.
Los Angeles Times, April 25, 1985.
Maclean's, May 20, 1985.
Ms., January, 1984.
Nation, June 15, 1985.
New Republic, December 31, 1983.
New Statesman, September 7, 1984.
New York Times Book Review, January 15, 1984.
Times Literary Supplement, November 29, 1985.
Village Voice, January 17, 1984.
Virginia Quarterly Review, summer, 1985.
Voice Literary Supplement, April, 1985.
Washington Post, April 2, 1985.
Washington Post Book World, February 5, 1984.
World Literature Today, autumn, 1985.

—Sketch by Les Stone

* * *

KING, Coretta Scott   1927-

PERSONAL: Born April 27, 1927, in Marion, Ala.; daughter of Obidiah (a pulpwood dealer) and Bernice (McMurry) Scott; married Martin Luther King, Jr. (Baptist minister and civil rights activist), June 18, 1953 (died April 4, 1968); children: Yolanda Denise, Martin Luther III, Dexter Scott, Bernice Albertine. *Education:* Antioch College, B.A., New England Conservatory of Music, Mus.B., 1954, Mus.D., 1971. *Religion:* Baptist.

ADDRESSES: Office—Martin Luther King, Jr. Center for Nonviolent Social Change, Inc., 449 Auburn Ave., N.E., Atlanta, Ga. 30312; Press Relations, Cable News Network, 1050 Techwood Dr., N.W., Atlanta, Ga. 30318.

CAREER: Affiliated with Martin Luther King, Jr. Foundation and Martin Luther King, Jr. Memorial Center for Nonviolent Social Change, Atlanta, Ga., 1968—; Cable News Network, Atlanta, Ga., news commentator, 1980—. Singer, beginning 1948; Morris Brown College, Atlanta, voice instructor, 1962; presenter of "freedom concerts" in which she sings, recites poetry and lectures, beginning 1964; narrator of Aaron Copeland's "A Lincoln Portrait" with Washington National Symphony Orchestra in Washington, D.C., and New York City, 1968, and with San Francisco Symphony, in San Francisco, Calif., 1970. Lecturer, writer and delegate to White House Conference on Children and Youth, 1960. Sponsor, Sane Nuclear Policy, Committee on Responsibility, Inc., and Mobilization to End the War in Viet Nam, 1966-67, and Margaret Sanger Memorial Foundation. Member of board of directors, Southern Christian Leadership Conference, National Organization of Women, and Martin Luther King, Jr. Foundation—Great Britain; member of executive board, National Health Insurance Commission. Trustee, Robert F. Kennedy Memorial Center.

MEMBER: Women's International League for Peace and Freedom, National Council of Negro Women, Women's Strike for Peace, United Church Women (member of board of managers), Alpha Kappa Alpha.

AWARDS, HONORS: Annual Brotherhood Award, National Council of Negro Women, 1957; Outstanding Citizenship Award, Montgomery (Ala.) Improvement Association, 1959; Merit Award, St. Louis *Argus*, 1960; Woman of the Year Award, Utility Club (New York City), 1962; Distinguished Achievement Award, National Organization of Colored Women's Clubs, 1962; citation for work in peace and freedom, Women's Strike for Peace, 1963; Louise Waterman Wise Award, American Jewish Congress Women's Auxiliary, 1963; Human Dignity and Human Rights Award, Norfolk Chapter of Links, Inc., 1964; Myrtle Wreath Award, Cleveland Hadassah, 1965; Wateler Peace Prize, 1968; named "Woman of the Year," National Association of Radio and TV Announcers, 1968; Women of Conscience Award, National Council of Women, 1968; selected in national college student poll as most admired woman, 1968, 1969; Pacem in Terris Award, International Overseas Service Foundation, 1969; Dag Hammarskjoeld Award and diploma as academicien, World Organization of the Diplomatic Press-Academie Diplomatique de la Paix, 1969; Candace Award, National Coalition of 100 Black Women, 1987; Human Relations Award, Academia Nazionale Del Lincei (Italy). Honorary doctorates from Boston University, Marymount Manhattan College, and Brandeis University, all 1969, Morehouse College, Wilberforce University, University of Bridgeport, Morgan State College, Bethune-Cookman College, Keuka College, and Princeton University, all 1970, Northeastern University and Bates College, both 1971.

WRITINGS:

AUTOBIOGRAPHY

My Life with Martin Luther King, Jr. (Book-of-the-Month Club selection), Holt, 1969.

AUTHOR OF INTRODUCTION OR FOREWORD

Martin Luther King, Jr., *Where Do We Go From Here: Chaos or Community?*, memorial edition, Bantam, 1968 (published in England as *Chaos or Community?*, Hodder & Stoughton, 1968).
Martin Luther King, Jr., *Trumpet of Conscience*, Harper, 1968.
Schulke, Flip, editor, *Martin Luther King, Jr.: A Documentary . . . : Montgomery to Memphis*, Norton, 1976.
(And editor) Martin Luther King, Jr., *The Words of Martin Luther King, Jr.*, Newmarket Press, 1983.
Dorothy S. Strickland, *Listen Children: An Anthology of Black Literature*, Bantam, 1986.

OTHER

Contributor of articles to magazines, including *Good Housekeeping*, *New Lady*, *McCall's*, *Theology Today*, and *Ebony*.

SIDELIGHTS: "My husband," writes Coretta Scott King in her introduction to *The Words of Martin Luther King, Jr.*, "was a man who hoped to be a Baptist preacher to a large, Southern, urban congregation. Instead, by the time he died in 1968, he had led millions of people into shattering forever the Southern system of segregation of the races."

Like her husband's life, Coretta Scott King's own life took a dramatically different turn than the one she had planned. As she relates in her autobiography, *My Life with Martin Luther King, Jr.*, when Coretta Scott first met the young preacher, she was studying music at the New England Conservatory in Boston and had already begun a career as a concert singer. Although she had thought that she would never consider being a preacher's wife, she found her future husband to be different than the stereotyped man of God she had imagined. As she observes in her introduction to *The Words of Martin Luther King, Jr.*, "Martin was an unusual person. . . . He was so alive and so much fun to be with. He had strength that he imparted to me and others that he met.''

Coretta Scott married Martin Luther King, Jr., giving up her personal career plans to join him as a civil rights activist. Side by side with her husband she led marches and gave speeches, but as the spouse of a popular public figure, she also endured many hours alone. In *My Life with Martin Luther King, Jr.* she notes that ''in spite of Martin's being away so much, he was wonderful with his children, and they adored him. When Daddy was home it was something special.''

While the book is filled with many such personal glimpses of the civil rights leader, reviewers find it flawed by its portrayal of Dr. King as a man without human weaknesses. ''Understandably enough,'' Patricia Canham writes in the *Christian Science Monitor,* ''it is the public image, the 'noble servant of humanity' that Mrs. King wishes to perpetuate.'' A *Time* critic, however, notes that ''dispassionate reportage is not her real purpose. Rather, she has undertaken to bear witness to his life, and she has done so with great warmth and skill.'' A *Publishers Weekly* contributor deems the autobiography ''one of the noblest and most moving human documents of this or any season.''

The success of *My Life with Martin Luther King, Jr.* added to Coretta King's prominence as a public figure in her own right but her fame had spread even before the book's publication as she led a silent memorial march of more than 50,000 people through the streets of Memphis on April 8, 1968, just four days after her husband's death. The following day, at Dr. King's funeral, she shared her grief with an estimated 120 million people who watched on television and crowds of mourners who filled the streets of Atlanta.

In *King Remembered,* Flip Shulke and Penelope O. McPhee praise Coretta King's ability to continue her husband's work so soon after his death. ''As she would prove many times in the future,'' they write, ''she was prepared to take up her late husband's cause. . . . But it came as no surprise to her friends or to her husband's associates. They knew she had always lent a quiet support and calming spirit to everything Martin had undertaken.''

Her leadership capabilities were further tested soon thereafter as King strove to preserve her husband's memory with the foundation in 1968 of both the Martin Luther King, Jr. Memorial Center for Nonviolent Social Change and the Martin Luther King, Jr. Federal Holiday Commission. As chairperson of both organizations King made hundreds of speeches, logged thousands of miles traveling around the world, and met with countless national and local leaders proclaiming her husband's message of nonviolence. Her energies became focused on two goals: the opening of a scholarly center dedicated to her husband where nonviolence could be taught and studied and the celebration of his birthday as a national holiday.

The first of these two projects to be realized, the Martin Luther King, Jr. Center for Nonviolent Social Change, became a reality in 1981 when the $8.4 million center was dedicated in Atlanta, Georgia. The complex includes exhibit areas, a 250-seat auditorium, a 90-seat theater, administrative offices, a library, archives and the Martin Luther King, Jr. gravesite.

In an *Ebony* article, King explains some of the Center's activities. ''Since it was founded,'' she writes, ''the King Center has trained thousands of future leaders in the spirit and tradition of its namesake through a series of wide-ranging programs and workshops in the philosophy and strategy of nonviolence.

The Center has also emerged as a catalyst for massive social change coalitions, including the National Committee for Full Employment and the 1983 mobilization of the 20th Anniversary March on Washington, which brought more than a half-million demonstrators to the nation's capitol.''

King also observes that the Center's library and archives contain over one million documents related to the civil rights movement, including a vast collection of personal King items, which are examined by nearly 5,000 scholars annually.

The Center has been instrumental in the achievement of Coretta King's second goal, the establishment of a Martin Luther King, Jr. national holiday. The Center led a campaign that collected six million signatures to present to Congress in support of the proposed holiday and sponsored annual national programs celebrating the holiday during the years between Martin Luther King, Jr.'s death and the first official celebration of the day in January, 1986.

Talking about her work in an *Ebony* interview, Coretta King notes, ''I will always be out here doing the things I do, and I'm not going to stop talking about Martin and promoting what I think is important in terms of teaching other people, particularly young people, his meaning so they can live in such a way to make a contribution to our advancement and progress.''

BIOGRAPHICAL/CRITICAL SOURCES:

BOOKS

King, Coretta Scott, *My Life with Martin Luther King, Jr.,* Holt, 1969.
King, Martin Luther, Jr., *The Words of Martin Luther King, Jr.,* edited by and with an introduction by Coretta Scott King, Newmarket Press, 1983.
Schulke, Flip, and Penelope O. McPhee, *King Remembered,* Norton, 1986.

PERIODICALS

American Visions, January/February, 1986.
Book World, September 28, 1969.
Christian Science Monitor, September 25, 1969.
Ebony, September, 1968, January, 1986, January, 1987.
Good Housekeeping, June, 1964.
Jet, January 20, 1986.
Ladies Home Journal, January, 1987.
New Statesman, January 23, 1970.
Newsweek, April 22, 1968.
New York Times, September 29, 1969.
Publishers Weekly, August 18, 1969.
Saturday Review, October 11, 1969.
Time, October 3, 1969, September 22, 1986.
Times Literary Supplement, June 11, 1970.

—*Sketch by Marian Gonsior*

*   *   *

KING, Martin Luther, Jr.   1929-1968

PERSONAL: Given name, Michael, changed to Martin; born January 15, 1929, in Atlanta, Ga.; assassinated April 4, 1968, in Memphis, Tenn.; originally buried in South View Cemetery, Atlanta; reinterred at Martin Luther King, Jr. Center for Nonviolent Social Change, Atlanta; son of Martin Luther (a minister) and Alberta Christine (a teacher; maiden name, Williams) King; married Coretta Scott (a concert singer), June 18, 1953; children: Yolanda Denise, Martin Luther III, Dexter Scott, Bernice Albertine. *Education:* Morehouse College, B.A.,

1948; Crozer Theological Seminary, B.D., 1951; Boston University, Ph.D., 1955, D.D., 1959; Chicago Theological Seminary, D.D., 1957; attended classes at University of Pennsylvania and Harvard University.

CAREER: Ordained Baptist minister, 1948; Dexter Avenue Baptist Church, Montgomery, Ala., pastor, 1954-60; Southern Christian Leadership Conference (S.C.L.C.), Atlanta, founder, 1957, and president, 1957-68; Ebenezer Baptist Church, Atlanta, co-pastor with his father, 1960-68. Vice-president, National Sunday School and Baptist Teaching Union Congress of National Baptist Convention; president, Montgomery Improvement Association.

MEMBER: National Association for the Advancement of Colored People (NAACP), Alpha Phi Alpha, Sigma Pi Phi, Elks.

AWARDS, HONORS: Selected one of ten outstanding personalities of 1956 by *Time*, 1957; Spingarn Medal, National Association for the Advancement of Colored People, 1957; L.H.D., Morehouse College, 1957, and Central State College, 1958; L.L.D., Howard University, 1957, and Morgan State College, 1958; Anisfield-Wolf Award, 1958, *Stride toward Freedom; Time* Man of the Year, 1963; Nobel Prize for Peace, 1964; Judaism and World Peace Award, Synagogue Council of America, 1965; Brotherhood Award, 1967, for *Where Do We Go from Here: Chaos or Community?;* Nehru Award for International Understanding, 1968; Presidential Medal of Freedom, 1977; received numerous awards for leadership of Montgomery Movement; two literary prizes were named in his honor by National Book Committee and Harper & Row.

WRITINGS:

Stride Toward Freedom: The Montgomery Story, Harper, 1958, reprinted, 1987.
The Measure of a Man, Christian Education Press (Philadelphia), 1959, memorial edition, Pilgrim Press, 1968, reprinted, Fortress, 1988.
Letter from Birmingham City Jail, American Friends Service Committee, 1963, published as *Letter from Birmingham Jail* (also see below), Overbrook Press, 1968.
Why We Can't Wait (includes "Letter from Birmingham Jail"), Harper, 1964, reprinted, New American Library, 1987.
Where Do We Go from Here: Chaos or Community?, Harper, 1967, memorial edition with an introduction by wife, Coretta Scott King, Bantam, 1968 (published in England as *Chaos or Community?*, Hodder & Stoughton, 1968).
(Author of introduction) William Bradford Huie, *Three Lives for Mississippi*, New American Library, 1968.
(Contributor) John Henrik Clarke and others, editors, *Black Titan: W.E.B. Du Bois*, Beacon Press, 1970.

OMNIBUS VOLUMES

"Unwise and Untimely?" (letters; originally appeared in *Liberation*, June, 1963), Fellowship of Reconciliation, 1963.
Strength to Love (sermons), Harper, 1963, reprinted, Walker, 1985.
A Martin Luther King Treasury, Educational Heritage (New York), 1964.
The Wisdom of Martin Luther King in His Own Words, edited by staff of Bill Alder Books, Lancer Books, 1968.
"*I Have a Dream*": *The Quotations of Martin Luther King, Jr.*, edited and compiled by Lotte Hoskins, Grosset, 1968.
The Trumpet of Conscience (transcripts of radio broadcasts), introduction by C. S. King, Harper, 1968.
We Shall Live in Peace: The Teachings of Martin Luther King, Jr., edited by Deloris Harrison, Hawthorn, 1968.

Speeches about Vietnam, Clergy and Laymen Concerned about Vietnam (New York), 1969.
A Martin Luther King Reader, edited by Nissim Ezekiel, Popular Prakashan (Bombay), 1969.
Words and Wisdom of Martin Luther King, Taurus Press, 1970.
Speeches of Martin Luther King, Jr., commemorative edition, Martin Luther King, Jr. Memorial Center (Atlanta), 1972.
Loving Your Enemies, Letter from Birmingham Jail [and] *Declaration of Independence from the War in Vietnam* (also see below), A. J. Muste Memorial Institute, 1981.
The Words of Martin Luther King, Jr., edited and with an introduction by C. S. King, Newmarket Press, 1983.
A Testament of Hope: The Essential Writings of Martin Luther King, Jr., edited by James Melvin Washington, Harper, 1986.

SPEECHES

The Montgomery Story, [San Francisco, Calif.], 1956.
I Have a Dream, John Henry and Mary Louise Dunn Bryant Foundation (Los Angeles), 1963.
Nobel Lecture, Harper, 1965.
Address at Valedictory Service, University of the West Indies (Mona, Jamaica), 1965.
The Ware Lecture, Unitarian Universalist Association (Boston), 1966.
Conscience for Change, Canadian Broadcasting Co., 1967.
Beyond Vietnam, Altoan Press, 1967.
Declaration of Independence from the War in Vietnam, [New York], 1967.
A Drum Major for Justice, Taurus Press, 1969.
A Testament of Hope (originally appeared in *Playboy*, January, 1969), Fellowship of Reconciliation, 1969.

CONTRIBUTOR TO ANTHOLOGIES

H. John Heinz III, editor, *Crisis in Modern America*, Yale University, 1959.
Robert A. Goldwin, editor, *Civil Disobedience: Five Essays*, Public Affairs Conference Center, Kenyon College, 1968.
William B. Thomas, editor, *Shall Not Perish: Nine Speeches by Three Great Americans*, Gyldendalske Boghandel, 1969.
William M. Chace and Peter Collier, editors, *Justice Denied: The Black Man in White America*, Harcourt, 1970.
Leslie H. Fishel, Jr., and Benjamin Quarles, editors, *The Black American: A Documentary History*, Morrow, 1970.
Richard K. Barksdale and Kenneth Kinnamon, editors, *Black Writers of America: A Comprehensive Anthology*, Macmillan, 1972.

Also contributor to many other anthologies.

OTHER

Pilgrimage to Nonviolence (monograph; originally appeared in *Christian Century*), Fellowship of Reconciliation, 1960.

Contributor to periodicals, including *Harper's*, *Nation*, and *Christian Century*.

WORK IN PROGRESS: King's papers are being edited by Clayborn Carson to be published in a twelve-volume set over a fifteen-year period.

SIDELIGHTS: "We've got some difficult days ahead," civil rights activist Martin Luther King, Jr., told a crowd gathered at Memphis's Clayborn Temple on April 3, 1968, in a speech now collected in *The Words of Martin Luther King, Jr.* "But it really doesn't matter to me now," he continued, "because I've been to the mountaintop. . . . And I've seen the promised land. I may not get there with you. But I want you to know tonight that we as a people will get to the promised land.'' Uttered the day before his tragic assassination, King's words were prophetic of his death. They were also a challenge to those he left behind to see that his ''promised land'' of racial equality became a reality; a reality to which King devoted the last twelve years of his life.

Just as important as King's dream was the way he chose to achieve it: nonviolent resistance. He embraced nonviolence as a method for social reform after being introduced to the non-violent philosophy of Mahatma Gandhi while doing graduate work at Pennsylvania's Crozer Seminary. Gandhi had led a bloodless revolution against British colonial rule in India. According to Stephen B. Oates in *Let the Trumpet Sound: The Life of Martin Luther King, Jr.,* King became ''convinced that Gandhi's was the only moral and practical way for oppressed people to struggle against social injustice.''

What King achieved during the little over a decade that he worked in civil rights was remarkable. ''Rarely has one individual,'' noted Flip Shulke and Penelope O. McPhee in *King Remembered,* ''espousing so difficult a philosophy, served as a catalyst for so much significant social change. . . . There are few men of whom it can be said their lives changed the world. But at his death the American South hardly resembled the land where King was born. In the twelve years between the Montgomery bus boycott and King's assassination, Jim Crow was legally eradicated in the South.''

The first public test of King's adherence to the nonviolent philosophy came in December, 1955, when he was elected president of the Montgomery [Alabama] Improvement Association (M.I.A.), a group formed to protest the arrest of Rosa Parks, a black woman who refused to give up her bus seat to a white. Planning to end the humiliating treatment of blacks on city bus lines, King organized a bus boycott that was to last more than a year. Despite receiving numerous threatening phone calls, being arrested, and having his home bombed, King and his boycott prevailed. Eventually, the U.S. Supreme Court declared Montgomery's bus segregation laws illegal and, in December, 1956, King rode on Montgomery's first integrated bus.

''Montgomery was the soil,'' wrote King's widow in her autobiography, *My Life with Martin Luther King, Jr.,* ''in which the seed of a new theory of social action took root. Black people found in nonviolent, direct action a militant method that avoided violence but achieved dramatic confrontation which electrified and educated the whole nation.''

King was soon selected to be president of an organization of much wider scope than the M.I.A., the Southern Christian Leadership Conference (S.C.L.C.). The members of this group were black leaders from throughout the South, many of them ministers like King, himself. Their immediate goal was for increased black voter registration in the South with an eventual elimination of segregation.

1957 found King drawn more and more into the role of national and even international spokesman for civil rights. In February a *Time* cover story on King called him ''a scholarly . . . Baptist minister . . . who in little more than a year has risen from nowhere to become one of the nation's remarkable leaders of men.'' In March, he was invited to speak at the ceremonies marking the independence from Great Britain of the new African republic of Ghana.

The following year, King's first book, *Stride Toward Freedom: The Montgomery Story,* which told the history of the boycott, was published. *New York Times* contributor Abel Plenn called the work ''a document of far-reaching importance for present and future chroniclings of the struggle for civil rights in this country.'' A *Times Literary Supplement* writer quoted U.S. Episcopalian Bishop James Pike's reaction to the book: *Stride Toward Freedom* ''may well become a Christian classic. It is a rare combination: sound theology and ethics, and the autobiography of one of the greatest men of our time.''

In 1959, two important events happened. First, King and his wife were able to make their long-awaited trip to India where they visited the sites of Gandhi's struggle against the British and met face-to-face with people who had been acquainted with the Indian leader. Second, King resigned as pastor of Dexter Avenue Baptist Church in Montgomery so he could be closer to S.C.L.C.'s headquarters in Atlanta and devote more of his time to the civil rights effort.

King's trip to India seemed to help make up his mind to move to Atlanta. The trip greatly inspired King as Oates observed: ''He came home with a deeper understanding of nonviolence and a deep commitment as well. For him, nonviolence was no longer just a philosophy and a technique of social change; it was now a whole way of life.''

Despite his adherence to the nonviolent philosophy, King was unable to avoid the bloodshed that was to follow. Near the end of 1962, he decided to focus his energies on the desegregation of Birmingham, Alabama. Alabama's capital was at that time what King called in his book *Why We Can't Wait,* ''the most segregated city in America,'' but that was precisely why he had chosen it as his target.

In *Why We Can't Wait* King detailed the advance planning that was the key to the success of the Birmingham campaign. Most important was the training in nonviolent techniques given by the S.C.L.C.'s Leadership Training Committee to those who volunteered to participate in the demonstrations. ''The focus of these training sessions,'' King noted in his book, ''was the socio-dramas designed to prepare the demonstrators for some of the challenges they could expect to face. The harsh language and physical abuse of the police and self-appointed guardians of the law were frankly presented, along with the non-violent creed in action: to resist without bitterness; to be cursed and not reply; to be beaten and not hit back.''

One of the unusual aspects of the Birmingham campaign was King's decision to use children in the demonstrations. When the protests came to a head on May 3, 1963, it was after nearly one thousand young people had been arrested the previous day. As another wave of protestors, mostly children and teenagers, took to the streets, they were suddenly hit with jets of water from powerful fire hoses. Police dogs were then released on the youngsters.

The photographs circulated by the media of children being beaten down by jets of water and being bitten by dogs brought cries of outrage from throughout the country and the world. President Kennedy sent a Justice Department representative to Birmingham to work for a peaceful solution to the problem. Within a week negotiators produced an agreement that met King's major demands, including desegregation of lunch counters, restrooms, fitting rooms and drinking fountains in the city and hiring of blacks in positions previously closed to them.

Although the Birmingham campaign ended in triumph for King, at the outset he was criticized for his efforts. Imprisoned at the beginning of the protest for disobeying a court injunction forbidding him from leading any demonstrations in Birmingham, King spent some of his time in jail composing an open letter answering his critics. This document, called "Letter from Birmingham Jail," appeared later in his book *Why We Can't Wait*. Oates viewed the letter as "a classic in protest literature, the most elegant and learned expression of the goals and philosophy of the nonviolent movement ever written."

In the letter King addressed those who said that as an outsider he had no business in Birmingham. King reasoned: "I am in Birmingham because injustice is here. . . . I cannot sit idly by in Atlanta and not be concerned about what happens in Birmingham. Injustice anywhere is a threat to justice everywhere. We are caught in an inescapable network of mutuality, tied in a single garment of destiny."

Another important event of 1963 was a massive march on Washington, D.C., which King planned together with leaders of other civil rights organizations. When the day of the march came, an estimated two hundred and fifty thousand people were on hand to hear King and other dignitaries speak at the march's end point, the Lincoln Memorial.

While King's biographers noted that the young minister struggled all night writing words to inspire his people on this historic occasion, when his turn came to speak, he deviated from his prepared text and gave a speech that Schulke and McPhee called "the most eloquent of his career." In the speech, which contained the rhythmic repetition of the phrase "I have a dream," King painted a vision of the "promised land" of racial equality and justice for all that he would return to often in speeches and sermons in the years to come, including his final speech in Memphis. Schulke and McPhee explained the impact of the day: "The orderly conduct of the massive march was an active tribute to [King's] philosophy of non-violence. Equally significant, his speech made his voice familiar to the world and lives today as one of the most moving orations of our time."

On January 3, 1964, King was proclaimed "Man of the Year" by *Time*, the first black to be so honored. Later that same year, King's book, *Why We Can't Wait*, was published. In the book King gave his explanation of why 1963 was such a critical year for the civil rights movement. He believed that celebrations commemorating the one-hundredth anniversary of Lincoln's Emancipation Proclamation reminded American blacks of the irony that while Lincoln made the slaves free in the nineteenth century, their twentieth-century grandchildren still did not feel free.

Reviewers generally hailed the work as an important document in the history of the civil rights movement. In *Book Week*, J. B. Donovan called it "a basic handbook on non-violent direct action." *Critic* contributor C. S. Stone praised the book's "logic and eloquence" and observed that it aimed a death blow "at two American dogmas—racial discrimination, and the even more insidious doctrine that nourishes it, gradualism."

In December of 1964, King received the Nobel Peace Prize, becoming the twelfth American, the third black, and the youngest—he was thirty-five—person ever to receive the award. He donated the $54,600 prize to the S.C.L.C. and other civil rights groups. The Nobel Prize gave King even wider recognition as a world leader. "Overnight," commented Shulke and McPhee, "King became . . . a symbol of world peace. He

knew that if the Nobel Prize was to mean anything, he must commit himself more than ever to attaining the goals of the black movement through peace."

The next two years were marked by both triumph and despair. First came King's campaign for voting rights, concentrating on a voters registration drive in Selma, Alabama. Selma would be, according to Oates, "King's finest hour."

Voting rights had been a major concern of King's since as early as 1957 but, unfortunately, little progress had been made. In the country surrounding Selma, for example, only 335 of 32,700 blacks were registered voters. Various impediments to black registration, including poll taxes and complicated literacy tests, were common throughout the South.

Demonstrations continued through February and on into early March, 1965, in Selma. One day nearly five hundred school children were arrested and charged with juvenile delinquency after they cut classes to show their support for King. In another incident, over a hundred adults were arrested when they picketed the county courthouse. On March 7, state troopers beat nonviolent demonstrators who were trying to march from Selma to Montgomery to present their demands to Governor Wallace.

Angered by such confrontations, King sent telegrams to religious leaders throughout the nation calling for them to meet in Selma for a "ministers' march" to Montgomery. Although some 1500 marchers assembled, they were again turned back by a line of state troopers, but this time violence was avoided.

King was elated by the show of support he received from the religious leaders from around the country who joined him in the march, but his joy soon turned to sorrow when he learned later that same day that several of the white ministers who had marched with him had been beaten by club-wielding whites. One of them died two days later.

The brutal murder of a clergyman seemed to focus the attention of the nation on Selma. Within a few days, President Johnson made a televised appearance before a joint session of Congress in which he demanded passage of a voting rights bill. In the speech Johnson compared the sites of revolutionary war battles such as Concord and Lexington with their modern-day counterpart, Selma, Alabama.

Although Johnson had invited King to be his special guest in the Senate gallery during the address, King declined the honor, staying instead in Selma to complete plans to again march on Montgomery. A federal judge had given his approval to the proposed Selma-to-Montgomery march and had ordered Alabama officials not to interfere. The five-day march finally took place as hundreds of federal troops stood by overseeing the safety of the marchers.

Later that year, President Johnson signed the 1965 Voting Rights Act into law, this time with King looking on. The act made literacy tests as a requirement for voting illegal, gave the Attorney General the power to supervise federal elections in seven southern states, and urged the Attorney General to challenge the legality of poll taxes in state and local elections in four Southern states. "Political analysts," Oates observed, "almost unanimously attributed the voting act to King's Selma campaign. . . . Now, thanks to his own political sagacity, his understanding of how nonviolent, direct-action protest could stimulate corrective federal legislation, King's long crusade to gain southern Negroes the right to vote . . . was about to be realized."

By this time, King was ready to embark on his next project, moving his nonviolent campaign to the black ghettoes of the North. Chicago was chosen as his first target, but the campaign did not go the way King had planned. Rioting broke out in the city just two days after King initiated his program. He did sign an open-housing agreement with Chicago Mayor Daley but, according to Oates, many blacks felt it accomplished little.

Discord was beginning to be felt within the civil rights movement. King was afraid that advocates of "black power" would doom his dream of a nonviolent black revolution. In his next book, *Where Do We Go from Here: Chaos or Community?*, published in 1967, he explored his differences with those using the "black power" slogan.

According to *New York Times Book Review* contributor Gene Roberts, while King admitted in the volume that black power leaders "foster[ed] racial pride and self-help programs," he also expressed regret that the slogan itself produced "fear among whites and [made] it more difficult to fashion a meaningful interracial political coalition. But above all, he [deplored] . . . an acceptance of violence by many in the movement."

In *Saturday Review* Milton R. Knovitz noted other criticisms of the movement which King voiced in the book. King saw black power as "negative, even nihilistic in its direction," "rooted in hopelessness and pessimism" and "committed to racial—and ethical—separatism." In *America,* R. F. Drinan wrote, "Dr. King's analysis of the implications of the black power movement is possibly the most reasoned rejection of the concept by any major civil rights leader in the country."

Where Do We Go from Here touched on several issues that became King's major concerns during the last two years of his life. He expressed the desire to continue nonviolent demonstrations in the North, to stop the war in Vietnam, and to join underprivileged persons of all races in a coalition against poverty.

His first wish never materialized. Instead of nonviolent protest, riots broke out in Boston, Detroit, Milwaukee and more than thirty other U.S. cities between the time King finished the manuscript for the book and when it was published in the late summer.

By that time, King had already spoken out several times on Vietnam. His first speech to be entirely devoted to the topic was given on April 15, 1967, at a huge anti-war rally held at the United Nations Building in New York City. Even though some of King's followers begged him not to participate in anti-war activities, fearful that King's actions would antagonize the Johnson administration which had been so supportive in civil rights matters, King could not be dissuaded.

In *The Trumpet of Conscience,* a collection of radio addresses published posthumously, King explained why speaking out on Vietnam was so important to him. He wrote: "I cannot forget that the Nobel Prize for Peace was also a commission—a commission to work harder than I ever worked before for the 'brotherhood of man.' This is a calling which takes me beyond national allegiances."

Commenting on King's opposition to the war, Coretta King observed that her husband's "peace activity marked incontestably a major turning point in the thinking of the nation. . . . I think history will mark his boldness in speaking out so early and eloquently—despite singularly virulent opposition—as one of his major contributions."

When King was assassinated in Memphis on April 4, 1968, he was in the midst of planning his Poor People's Campaign.

Plans called for recruitment and training in nonviolent techniques of 3,000 poor people from each of fifteen different parts of the country. The campaign would culminate when they were brought to Washington, D.C., to disrupt government operations until effective anti-poverty legislation was enacted.

On hearing of King's death, angry blacks in one hundred and twenty-five cities across the nation rioted. As a result, thirty people died, hundreds suffered injuries, and more than thirty million dollars worth of property damage was incurred. But, fortunately, rioting was not the only response to his death. Accolades came from around the world as one by one world leaders paid their respects to the martyred man of peace. Eventually, King's widow and other close associates saw to it that a permanent memorial—the establishment of Martin Luther King, Jr.'s birthday as a national holiday in the United States—would assure that his memory would live on forever.

In her introduction to *The Trumpet of Conscience,* Coretta King quoted from one of Martin Luther King, Jr.'s most famous speeches as she gave her thoughts on how she hoped future generations would remember her husband. "Remember him," she wrote, "as a man who tried to be 'a drum major for justice, a drum major for peace, a drum major for righteousness.' Remember him as a man who refused to lose faith in the ultimate redemption of mankind."

BIOGRAPHICAL/CRITICAL SOURCES:

BOOKS

Bennett, Lerone, Jr., *What Manner of Man*, Johnson Publishing (Chicago, Ill.), 1964.

Bishop, Jim, *The Days of Martin Luther King, Jr.*, Putnam, 1971.

Bleiweiss, Robert M., editor, *Marching to Freedom: The Life of Martin Luther King, Jr.*, New American Library, 1971.

Clayton, Edward T., *Martin Luther King, Jr.: The Peaceful Warrior*, Prentice-Hall, 1968.

Collins, David R., *Not Only Dreamers: The Story of Martin Luther King, Sr. and Martin Luther King, Jr.*, Brethren Press, 1986.

Davis, Lenwood G., *I Have a Dream: The Life and Times of Martin Luther King, Jr.*, Adams Book Co., 1969.

Frank, Gerold, *An American Death: The True Story of the Assassination of Dr. Martin Luther King, Jr. and the Greatest Manhunt of Our Time*, Doubleday, 1972.

Garrow, David J., *Bearing the Cross: Martin Luther King, Jr. and the Southern Christian Leadership Conference*, Morrow, 1986.

Harrison, Deloris, editor, *We Shall Live in Peace: The Teachings of Martin Luther King, Jr.*, Hawthorn, 1968.

King, Coretta Scott, *My Life with Martin Luther King, Jr.*, Holt, 1969.

King, Martin Luther, Jr., *The Trumpet of Conscience*, with an introduction by Coretta Scott King, Harper, 1968.

King, Martin Luther, Jr., *The Words of Martin Luther King, Jr.*, edited and with an introduction by Coretta Scott King, Newmarket Press, 1983.

Lewis, David, L., *King: A Critical Biography*, Praeger, 1970.

Lincoln, Eric C., editor, *Martin Luther King, Jr.: A Profile*, Hill & Wang, 1970, revised edition, 1984.

Lokos, Lionel, *House Divided: The Life and Legacy of Martin Luther King*, Arlington House, 1968.

Lomax, Louis E., *To Kill a Black Man*, Holloway, 1968.

Martin Luther King, Jr.: The Journey of a Martyr, Universal Publishing & Distributing, 1968.

Martin Luther King, Jr., 1929-1968, Johnson Publishing (Chicago, Ill.), 1968.

Martin Luther King, Jr., Norton, 1976.

Miller, William Robert, *Martin Luther King, Jr.: His Life, Martyrdom, and Meaning for the World,* Weybright, 1968.

Oates, Stephen B., *Let the Trumpet Sound: The Life of Martin Luther King, Jr.,* Harper, 1982.

Paulsen, Gary and Dan Theis, *The Man Who Climbed the Mountain: Martin Luther King,* Raintree, 1976.

Playboy Interviews, Playboy Press, 1967.

Schulke, Flip, editor, *Martin Luther King, Jr.: A Documentary . . . Montgomery to Memphis,* with an introduction by Coretta Scott King, Norton, 1976.

Schulke, Flip and Penelope O. McPhee, *King Remembered,* with a foreword by Jesse Jackson, Norton, 1986.

Small, Mary Luins, *Creative Encounters with "Dear Dr. King": A Handbook of Discussions, Activities, and Engagements on Racial Injustice, Poverty, and War,* edited by Saunders Redding, Buckingham Enterprises, 1969.

Smith, Kenneth L. and Ira G. Zepp, Jr., *Search for the Beloved Community: The Thinking of Martin Luther King, Jr.,* Judson, 1974.

Westin, Alan, and Barry Mahoney, *The Trial of Martin Luther King,* Crowell, 1975.

Witherspoon, William Roger, *Martin Luther King, Jr.: To the Mountaintop,* Doubleday, 1985.

PERIODICALS

A B Bookman's Weekly, April 22, 1968.

America, August 17, 1963, October 31, 1964, July 22, 1967, April 20, 1968.

American Vision, January/February, 1986.

Antioch Review, spring, 1968.

Books Abroad, autumn, 1970.

Book World, July 9, 1967, September 28, 1969.

Choice, February, 1968.

Christian Century, August 23, 1967, January 14, 1970, August 26, 1970.

Christian Science Monitor, July 6, 1967.

Commonweal, November 17, 1967, May 3, 1968.

Critic, August, 1964.

Ebony, April, 1961, May, 1968, July, 1968, April, 1984, January, 1986, January, 1987, April, 1988.

Economist, April 6, 1968.

Esquire, August, 1968.

Harper's, February, 1961.

Life, April 19, 1968, January 10, 1969, September 12, 1969, September 19, 1969.

Listener, April 11, 1968, April 25, 1968.

Los Angeles Times Book Review, December 11, 1983.

National Review, February 13, 1987, February 27, 1987.

Negro Digest, August, 1968.

Negro History Bulletin, October, 1956, November, 1956, May, 1968.

New Republic, February 3, 1986, January 5, 1987.

New Statesman, March 22, 1968.

Newsweek, January 27, 1986.

New Yorker, June 22, 1967, July 22, 1967, April 13, 1968, February 24, 1986, April 6, 1987.

New York Herald Tribune, October 16, 1964.

New York Post, October 15, 1964.

New York Review of Books, August 24, 1967, January 15, 1987.

New York Times, October 12, 1958, October 15, 1964, July 12, 1967, April 12, 1968, April 13, 1968.

New York Times Book Review, September 3, 1967, February 16, 1969, February 16, 1986, November 30, 1986.

Punch, April 3, 1968.

Ramparts, May, 1968.

Saturday Review, July 8, 1967, April 20, 1968.

Time, February 18, 1957, January 3, 1964, February 5, 1965, February 12, 1965, April 19, 1968, October 3, 1969, January 27, 1986, January 19, 1987.

(London) *Times,* April 6, 1968.

Times Literary Supplement, April 18, 1968.

Virginia Quarterly Review, autumn, 1968.

Washington Post, January 14, 1970.

Washington Post Book World, January 19, 1986, January 18, 1987.

OBITUARIES:

PERIODICALS

New York Times, April 5, 1968.

Time, April 12, 1968.

(London) *Times,* April 5, 1968.

—*Sketch by Marian Gonsior*

*   *   *

KING, Martin Luther, Sr.   1899-1984

PERSONAL: Born December 19, 1899, in Stockbridge, Ga.; died of heart disease, November 11, 1984, in Atlanta, Ga.; son of James (a sharecropper) and Delia King; married Alberta Christine (a schoolteacher; maiden name, Williams), 1926 (murdered, 1974); children: Christine, Martin Luther, Jr. (assassinated, 1968), Alfred Daniel Williams (died, 1969), James (died, some sources say in infancy), Delia (died, some sources say in infancy). *Education:* Morehouse College, B.Theol., 1930 (some sources say 1931).

ADDRESSES: Office—Ebenezer Baptist Church, 407-413 Auburn Ave. N.E., Atlanta, Ga. 30312.

CAREER: Ordained as lay preacher, 1914; Second Baptist Church of College Park, Atlanta, Ga., founder, 1920; Ebenezer Baptist Church, Atlanta, pastor, became pastor emeritus, 1931-75 (some sources say 1932-75). Moderator, became moderator emeritus, of Atlanta Missionary Baptist Association. Board member of the Social Action Committee of the National Association for the Advancement of Colored People (NAACP). Board member emeritus of the Southern Christian Leadership Conference, Atlanta University, Citizen's Trust Co., and Carrie-Steele-Pitts Children's Home, Atlanta. Also served on the board of trustees of Morehouse College School of Religion at the Interdenominational Theological Center, Atlanta.

MEMBER: National Baptist Convention, Atlanta Negro Voters League, Inter-racial Council of Atlanta.

AWARDS, HONORS: Voted Clergyman of the Year by Georgia region of National Conference of Christians and Jews, 1972, and Council of Christians and Jews, 1973; Order of the Lion from Republic of Senegal, West Africa, 1975; named National Father of the Year in Religion, 1978; named honorary president of Martin Luther King, Jr., Center for Social Change; recipient of Distinguished Ministers Fellowship award; holder of ten honorary doctoral degrees, including D.D. from Morris Brown College, 1945, D.Letters from University of Haiti, 1968, D.D. from Morehouse College, 1969, and D.Th. from Lutheran Academy, Hungary, 1978.

WRITINGS:

(With Clayton Riley) *Daddy King: An Autobiography,* Morrow, 1980.

SIDELIGHTS: "To many, perhaps most Americans, both black and white, the civil rights movement is a part of history, embracing the years following 1954 (with the landmark Supreme Court decision of Brown vs. Board of Education) and ending in 1968 on a motel balcony in Memphis with the assassination of Martin Luther King Jr.," Valerie Shaw commented in the *Los Angeles Times Book Review.* But in the book Shaw reviewed, *Daddy King: An Autobiography,* the Reverend Martin Luther King, Sr., states that the roots of the civil rights movement extended beyond just the years of his son's brief career to form part of a powerful political movement towards racial equality that is a central part of America's evolving social history. What the autobiography does, Shaw contended, is to reveal the powerful, if not always prominent, role the elder King played in the civil rights movement for over half a century.

In many ways, the story of King's rise from a poor background in rural Georgia to his becoming a key civic leader first in Atlanta, and later throughout the country as a whole, epitomizes the very struggle for respect the thousands of black Americans he represented faced in the United States during the early twentieth century. The second of ten children born into a poor sharecropper's family in Stockbridge, Georgia, in 1899, King learned early the harsh realities of being poor and black in the southern United States. In his early teens he was beaten by a white mill owner for refusing to hand over a bucket of water he had fetched for his mother, and he witnessed the hanging of a black man by a drunken white mob. Incidents like these, compounded by a repressive social environment, at first embittered the young King. Harris Wofford recalled King's thoughts in a review of *Daddy King* for the *Washington Post Book World.* A difficult thing "to get through his head was the idea of loving his enemies. At his mother's death bed, he 'cursed whites' who had brought so much pain to her and swore he would 'hate every white face [he] saw.'" However, the lesson he learned from his mother's response stayed with him the rest of his life. "Hatred," she told him, "makes nothin' but more hatred. . . . Don't you do it." In his autobiography King frequently stresses the importance to his later life of such lessons learned from the advice of family members.

At the age of sixteen, and already an ordained lay preacher in the Stockbridge area, the young Martin Luther King left home and moved to Atlanta, where he believed he would have a better opportunity to complete his education. As Wofford noted, King greatly valued education, and "credits his elder sister for getting through his 'stubborn head' that there was nothing you could do without [it]." So, by working on the railroads by day, and attending night school, he gained his high school diploma in 1925, and that same year persuaded the president of Morehouse College, despite the objections of the registrar, to admit him to the School of Theology, passionately predicting that "I can go further, if I work at it, and I will," Charles Kaiser in *Newsweek* cited King's autobiography.

The year of his acceptance to Morehouse, King married Alberta Hunter, the daughter of the Reverend A. D. Williams, pastor of Ebenezer Baptist, a leading black church in Atlanta. The marriage was significant not only for the couple's happiness, but it enabled King to eventually extend his reputation as a preacher. When he arrived in Atlanta, he had already been ordained and quickly established himself as pastor of two small community churches. Aware of his son-in-law's energetic and

popular public speaking, Williams asked King to undertake some of the preaching duties at Ebenezer Baptist. Faced with a large congregation for the first time, King was presented with an opportunity to consolidate his oratorical and clerical skills. Over a five-year period he did just that, gaining the respect and trust of the local community while building a reputation as a gifted clergyman. When Williams died in 1931, King was chosen as his successor. The move to Ebenezer Baptist proved to be critically influential to the future direction of King's career. Gradually, over a period of months, his preaching style and popularity drew more people to the church. Membership of a few hundred under Williams's leadership swelled to several thousand. The larger congregation for King's sermons became the trial audience for his messages which he directed increasingly to the needs and concerns of the black community of Atlanta. As a reviewer for *Newsweek* wrote, it was "from the Ebenezer Baptist pulpit, where he preached for 44 years, [that] 'Daddy King' helped shape the destiny of a nation."

Throughout the 1930s, King began to find many answers to the racism and civil rights issues that plagued the southern states in the messages he preached from the Bible. With the problems clear for many, especially blacks, to see, and with solutions apparently at hand, it seemed an inevitable progression for an idealistic, driven man such as King to seek to implement change through social action. Where he found support for his ideas was in the ranks of like-minded thinkers and activists who had begun rallying around the banner of civil rights. During the 1930s, King joined organizations intent on confronting social injustice such as the National Association for the Advancement of Colored People (NAACP), the Atlanta Negro Voters League, and the Inter-racial Council of Atlanta and, more and more, the leadership he displayed in his official position of pastor to a community church was carried over into a broader, civic context. In 1936, for instance, he led a black voting rights march, the first in Atlanta's history, to the city hall, later campaigned against the discriminatory hiring policy of the Ford Motor Company and for the desegregation of elevators in the Atlanta court house, and, in 1960, played a critical role in the success of John Kennedy's presidential campaign by mobilizing black support for the Kennedy cause. As King's commitment to the civil rights movement grew, so did his reputation and influence in the black community. But perhaps his greatest influence was still to be felt—that which he exerted on his family and, in particular, on his son, Martin Luther King, Jr.

Authors and critics have only speculated as to the role the elder King played in shaping his son, but what seems clear is the strength of support "Daddy King" gave him. When Martin Luther King, Jr., then on the verge of assuming a leading role in the civil rights movement, decided to return to Montgomery, Alabama, to face almost certain imprisonment for incitement during the height of that city's race riots in 1956, it was his father who, despite pleading with his son not to go, finally acceded and drove him and his wife, Coretta, from Atlanta to Montgomery, stopping in that city to pray with his son. Seven years later, King, Sr., welcomed his son on his triumphant return to Atlanta following the famous oration the younger King gave in Washington, D.C., and was even with his son, campaigning on behalf of low-paid public service workers, when Martin Luther King, Jr., was assassinated in Memphis, Tennessee, in 1968.

The death of King, Jr., began a tragic six-year period in the elder King's life that also saw his younger son, the Reverend

A. D. King, mysteriously drown in a swimming pool accident in 1969, and Alberta, his wife of forty-seven years, murdered by a crazed gunman while she played the organ during a Sunday morning service at Ebenezer Baptist. The gunman later confessed that he had been aiming for King. But even in the face of such extreme personal tragedy, King's belief in nonviolence and understanding did not waiver. Wofford related that in his autobiography King described a three-hour family meeting following his wife's murder in which the younger relatives asked, "Why did God let that crazy man kill Big Mama? Why do all these terrible things happen to our family?" To which he replied that although it was difficult to understand, "God wants us to love one another. . . . Now get out of here, and remember: Don't ever stoop so low that you let anybody make you hate."

In the years following the deaths of his wife and sons, King's continued adherence to the doctrine of nonviolence and equality earned him great respect. He could regularly be heard preaching the dual messages of love and equality at Ebenezer Baptist, and it seemed natural that, in the realm of public speaking, he should assume the mantle of his assassinated son, King, Jr. Giving speeches and addresses to organizations where his son's efforts and influence had already been felt, King's own stature as a civic leader grew to a point where, in 1976, he played a critical role in the presidential campaign of former Georgia governor Jimmy Carter. Carter had made a remark about "ethnic purity" in regards to his housing policy which, if construed as racist, could have cost him the majority of the black vote—a critical portion of the total electorate. King leapt to the candidate's defense, according to an article in *The Annual Obituary 1984*, proclaiming at a rally in Atlanta that "It is wrong to jump on a man for a slip of the tongue that everyone knows does not represent his thinking," and embraced Carter in a powerful public exoneration. Carter went on to win the 1976 presidential election with an estimated 90 percent of the black vote. Acknowledging his gratitude at King's funeral, Carter announced that "the turning-point in my 1976 campaign came . . . when Daddy King held up my hand for the world to see."

In many ways, the public celebrity of the elder King came through the greater visibility afforded him by an expanding mass media in the latter portion of this century, and by his son's tragic death. Yet he became a powerful spokesman for almost four generations of Americans during an era of massive social upheaval. In his autobiography, King offers two reasons for the South's failure to solve its racial problems, as Kaiser noted: "The long-time refusal of any white Southern minister to embrace the civil-rights movement, and the perception among whites—which endured until the 1960s—that integration would mean their own public humiliation." Nevertheless King still managed to offer an optimistic message for the future. Kaiser reported that King once remarked, "How many people thought, when I was a boy, that segregation would be gone before my life was over?"

When King died, nearly three thousand mourners listened to the tributes paid him by such figures as former President Carter, Vice-President George Bush, and Jesse Jackson, who—quoted in *The Annual Obituary*—said: "This man grew from obscurity to become king in a royal household. . . . When you hear the name Judas you think of betrayal. When you hear the name Rockefeller you think of money. When you hear the name Martin Luther King you think of justice, human rights, morality, love and character."

BIOGRAPHICAL/CRITICAL SOURCES:

BOOKS

Collins, David R., *Not Only Dreamers: The Story of Martin Luther King, Sr., and Martin Luther King, Jr.*, Brethren Press, 1986.

King, Martin Luther, Sr., and Clayton Riley, *Daddy King: An Autobiography*, Morrow, 1980.

PERIODICALS

Los Angeles Times Book Review, January 4, 1981.
Newsweek, July 4, 1976, September 15, 1980.
New York Times Book Review, February 8, 1981.
Washington Post Book World, September 21, 1980.

OBITUARIES:

BOOKS

The Annual Obituary 1984, St. James Press, 1985.

PERIODICALS

Newsweek, November 26, 1984.
New York Times, November 12, 1984.
Time, November 26, 1984.

—Sketch by Jeremy Kane

*   *   *

KING, Woodie, Jr. 1937-

PERSONAL: Born July 27, 1937, in Mobile, Ala.; son of Woodie and Ruby (Johnson) King; married Willie Mae Washington; children: Michelle, Woodie Geoffrey, Michael. *Education:* Attended Will-o-Way School of Theatre, 1958-62, Wayne State University, 1961, and Detroit School of Arts and Crafts.

ADDRESSES: Office—Woodie King Associates, Inc., 417 Convent Ave., New York, N.Y. 10031.

CAREER: Professional model, 1955-68; Mobilization for Youth, New York City, cultural arts director, 1965-70; New Federal Theatre, New York City, founder and artistic director, 1970—. Co-founder and manager of Concept East Theatre, Detroit, Mich., 1960-63; president of Woodie King Associates; founder, National Black Touring Circuit, 1980. Actor in touring production of "Study in Color" at Union Theological Seminary in New York City, 1964; actor, "Serpico" and "Together for Days." Directed five plays at American Place Theatre, 1965. Associate producer at Lincoln Center; producer of plays, including "A Black Quartet," 1969, "Black Girl," 1971, "Prodigal Sister," 1974, "Medal of Honor Rag," 1976, "Slaveship," "In New England Winters," "What the Wine Sellers Buy," and "For Colored Girls Who Have Considered Suicide/When the Rainbow Is Enuf"; executive producer of Broadway musical "Reggae," 1980. Producer of films, including "Right On!," 1970, and of short films with Mobilization for Youth; producer and director, "The Long Night," 1975, "The Black Theatre Movement: 'A Raisin in the Sun' to the Present," 1978, and "The Torture of Mothers," 1980. Producer of record albums "New Black Poets in America" and "Nation Time" for Motown, 1972. Arts and humanities consultant to Rockefeller Foundation, 1968-70.

AWARDS, HONORS: John Hay Whitney fellowship, American Place Theatre, 1965-66; award from Venice Festival, 1968, for "The Game"; Oberhausen Award, 1968, for "The Game";

International Film Critics Award, 1970, for ''Right On!''; A. Phillip Randolph Award from New York Film Festival, 1971, for ''Epitaph.''

WRITINGS:

(Contributor) *The Best Short Stories by Negro Writers*, edited by Langston Hughes, Little, Brown, 1967.

(Editor with Ron Milner) *Black Drama Anthology*, Columbia University Press, 1971, New American Library, 1986.

(Editor) *A Black Quartet: Four One-Act Plays*, New American Library, 1971.

(Editor) *Black Spirits: A Festival of New Black Poets in America*, Random House, 1972.

(Editor with Earl Anthony, and contributor) *Black Poets and Prophets: The Theory, Practice, and Esthetics of the Pan-Africanist Revolution*, New American Library, 1972.

(Editor and contributor) *Black Short Story Anthology*, Columbia University Press, 1972.

(Contributor) *We Be Word Sorcerers*, edited by Sonia Sanchez, Bantam, 1973.

(Editor) *The Forerunners: Black Poets in America*, preface by Dudley Randall, Howard University Press, 1975.

Black Theatre, Present Condition, Publishing Center for Cultural Resources, 1981.

SCRIPTS

''The Weary Blues'' (two-act play; adaptation of work by Langston Hughes), first produced in New York City at Lincoln Center Library, October 31, 1966.

''Simple Blues'' (one-act play; adaptation of work by Hughes), first produced in New York City at Clark Center of Performing Arts, 1967.

(Co-author) ''The Long Night,'' a film released by Mahler Films of New York, 1976.

OTHER

Also author of screenplays, including ''The Black Theatre Movement: 'A Raisin in the Sun' to the Present,'' 1978, ''The Torture of Mothers,'' 1980, and ''Death of a Prophet,'' 1982. Writer for television series, including ''Sanford and Son'' and ''Hot 1 Baltimore.'' Work represented in anthologies, including *Black Theatre Anthology: City Street*. Drama critic for *Detroit Tribune*, 1959-62. Contributor of stories and reviews to magazines, including *Black Creation, Black Scholar, Black American Literature Forum, Drama Review, Liberator, Negro Digest*, and *Negro History Bulletin*, and to newspapers.

SIDELIGHTS: ''Woodie King, Jr., has been called the renaissance man of black theater,'' comments Stephen M. Vallillo in the *Dictionary of Literary Biography*. He continues that while King has adapted plays and written short stories, ''his real importance to black literature is his support for black theater. Through his essays and his productions, he has tried to bring about a vital theater for black audiences.'' From his experience as an actor and director, King found that popular productions contained little to spark a black audience. Vallillo relates that King ''was not interested in continuing the traditions that he saw in the white educational and commercial theaters of the time, but wanted blacks to address their theater to their needs.'' While King had been arguing for such a change through essays and articles, in 1970 he was able to pursue it concretely by taking the position of artistic director of Henry Street Settlement's New Federal Theatre, located on the lower east side of New York City. According to Mel Gussow in the *New York Times*, ''Under Mr. King's leadership, Henry Street has become a prime generator of new black plays. In common,

many of these plays have been naturalistic and socially conscious (though not polemical). A number of them have dealt with, as Mr. King describes it, 'split black families.' Occasionally the plays are roughhewn and unpolished, but they are charged with energy, conviction and passion.''

The plays King selects must match his audience. He told Gussow, ''I stay away from plays that have a European setting. I turn down plays dealing with senseless black-white conflict, plays that make fun of people just for the sake of making fun, or plays where the writer has not yet made a commitment to be a writer.'' Ticket costs at the New Federal Theatre are low and audiences tend to represent the community, instead of an artistic elite. ''It takes away the image of the man in the suit-and-tie watching some heavy intellectual thing on stage,'' King remarked to Gussow. ''We give the audience a lot of fun—and let the message sneak up on them.''

BIOGRAPHICAL/CRITICAL SOURCES:

BOOKS

Dictionary of Literary Biography, Volume 38, *Afro-American Writers after 1955: Dramatists and Prose Writers*, Gale, 1985.

PERIODICALS

Negro Digest, January, 1968.
New York Times, October 31, 1976, October 16, 1981.

*   *   *

KITUOMBA
See ODAGA, Asenath (Bole)

*   *   *

KNIGHT, Etheridge   1931-

PERSONAL: Born April 19, 1931, in Corinth, Miss.; son of Bushie and Belzora (Cozart) Knight; married Sonia Sanchez (divorced); married Mary Ann McAnally, June 11, 1973 (divorced); married Charlene Blackburn; children: (second marriage) Mary Tandiwe, Etheridge Bambata; (third marriage) Isaac Bushie. *Education:* Attended high school for two years; self-educated at ''various prisons, jails.'' *Politics:* ''Freedom.'' *Religion:* ''Freedom.''

ADDRESSES: *Home*—2126 North Dexter St., Indianapolis, Ind. 46202.

CAREER: Poet. Writer-in-residence, University of Pittsburgh, Pittsburgh, Pa., 1968-69, and University of Hartford, Hartford, Conn., 1969-70; Lincoln University, Jefferson City, Mo., poet-in-residence, 1972. Inmate at Indiana State Prison, Michigan City, 1960-68. *Military service:* U.S. Army, 1947-51.

AWARDS, HONORS: National Endowment for the Arts grants, 1972 and 1980;

National Book Award and Pulitzer Prize nominations, both 1973, for *Belly Song and Other Poems;* Self Development through the Arts grant, for local workshops, 1974; Guggenheim fellowship, 1974.

WRITINGS:

(Contributor) *For Malcolm*, Broadside Press, 1967.
Poems from Prison, preface by Gwendolyn Brooks, Broadside Press, 1968.
(With others) *Voce Negre dal Carcere* (anthology), [Laterza, Italy], 1968, original English edition published as *Black*

Voices from Prison, introduction by Robert Giammanco, Pathfinder Press, 1970.

A Poem for Brother/Man (after His Recovery from an O.D.), Broadside Press, 1972.

Belly Song and Other Poems, Broadside Press, 1973.

Born of a Woman: New and Selected Poems, Houghton, 1980.

The Essential Etheridge Knight, University of Pittsburgh Press, 1986.

Work represented in many anthologies, including *Norton Anthology of American Poets, Black Poets, A Broadside Treasury, Broadside Poet, Dices and Black Bones,* and *A Comprehensive Anthology of Black Poets.* Contributor of poems and articles to many magazines and journals, including *Black Digest, Essence, Motive, American Report,* and *American Poetry.* Poetry editor, *Motive,* 1969-71; contributing editor, *New Letters,* 1974.

WORK IN PROGRESS: A historical novel on the life of Dermark Vesey.

SIDELIGHTS: Etheridge Knight began writing poetry while an inmate at the Indiana State prison and published his first collection, *Poems from Prison,* in 1968. "His work was hailed by black writers and critics as another excellent example of the powerful truth of blackness in art," writes Shirley Lumpkin in the *Dictionary of Literary Biography.* "His work became important in Afro-American poetry and poetics and in the strain of Anglo-American poetry descended from Walt Whitman." Since then, Knight has attained recognition as a major poet, earning both Pulitzer Prize and National Book Award nominations for *Belly Song and Other Poems,* as well as the acclaim of such fellow practitioners as Gwendolyn Brooks, Robert Bly, and Galway Kinnell.

When Knight entered prison, he was already an accomplished reciter of "toasts—long, memorized, narrative poems, often in rhymed couplets, in which "sexual exploits, drug activities, and violent aggressive conflicts involving a cast of familiar folk . . . are related . . . using street slang, drug and other specialized argot, and often obscenities," explains Lumpkin. Toast-reciting at Indiana State Prison not only refined Knight's expertise in this traditional Afro-American art form but also, according to Lumpkin, gave him a sense of identity and an understanding of the possibilities of poetry. "Since toast-telling brought him into genuine communion with others, he felt that poetry could simultaneously show him who he was and connect him with other people." In an article for the *Detroit Free Press* about Dudley Randall, the founder of Broadside Press, Suzanne Dolezal indicates that Randall was impressed with Knight and visited him frequently at the prison: "In a small room reserved for consultations with death row inmates, with iron doors slamming and prisoners shouting in the background, Randall convinced a hesitant Knight of his talent." And says Dolezal, Randall feels that because Knight was from the streets, "he may be a deeper poet than many of the others because he has felt more anguish."

Much of Knight's prison poetry, according to Patricia Liggins Hill in *Black American Literature Forum,* focuses on imprisonment as a form of contemporary enslavement and looks for ways in which one can be free despite incarceration. Time and space are significant in the concept of imprisonment, and Hill indicates that "specifically, what Knight relies on for his prison poetry are various temporal/spatial elements which allow him to merge his personal consciousness with the consciousness of Black people." Hill believes that this merging of consciousness "sets him apart from the other new Black poets . . . [who]

see themselves as poets/priests. . . . Knight sees himself as being one with Black people." Randall observes in *Broadside Memories: Poets I Have Known* that "Knight does not objure rime like many contemporary poets. He says the average Black man in the streets defines poetry as something that rimes, and Knight appeals to the folk by riming." Randall notes that while Knight's poetry is "influenced by the folk," it is also "prized by other poets."

Knight's *Born of a Woman: New and Selected Poems* includes work from *Poems from Prison, Black Voices from Prison,* and *Belly Song and Other Poems.* Although David Pinckney states in *Parnassus: Poetry in Review* that the "new poems do not indicate much artistic growth," a *Virginia Quarterly Review* contributor writes that Knight "has distinguished his voice and craftsmanship among contemporary poets, and he deserves a large, serious audience for his work." Moreover, H. Bruce Franklin suggests in the *Village Voice* that with *Born of a Woman,* "Knight has finally attained recognition as a major poet." Further, Franklin credits Knight's leadership "in developing a powerful literary mode based on the rhythms of black street talk, blues, ballads, and 'toasts.'"

Reviewing *Born of a Woman* for *Black American Literature Forum,* Hill describes Knight as a "masterful blues singer, a singer whose life has been 'full of trouble' and thus whose songs resound a variety of blues moods, feelings, and experiences and later take on the specific form of a blues musical composition." Lumpkin suggests that an "awareness of the significance of form governed Knight's arrangement of the poems in the volume as as his revisions. . . . He put them in clusters or groupings under titles which are musical variations on the book's essential theme—life inside and outside prison." Calling this structure a "jazz composition mode," Lumpkin also notes that it was once used by Langston Hughes in an arrangement of his poetry. Craig Werner observes in *Obsidian: Black Literature in Review:* "Technically, Knight merges musical rhythms with traditional metrical devices, reflecting the assertion of an Afro-American cultural identity within a Euro-American context. Thematically, he denies that the figures of the singer . . . and the warrior . . . are or can be separate." Lumpkin finds that "despite the pain and evil described and attacked, a celebration and an affirmation of life run through the volume." And in the *Los Angeles Times Book Review,* Peter Clothier considers the poems to be "tools for self-discovery and discovery of the world—a loud announcement of the truths they pry loose."

Lumpkin points out that "some critics find Knight's use of . . . [language] objectionable and unpoetic and think he does not use verse forms well," and some believe that he "maintains an outmoded, strident black power rhetoric from the 1960s." However, Lumpkin concludes: "Those with reservations and those who admire his work all agree . . . upon his vital language and the range of his subject matter. They all agree that he brings a needed freshness to poetry, particularly in his extraordinary ability to move an audience. . . . A number of poets, Gwendolyn Brooks, Robert Bly, and Galway Kinnell among them . . . consider him a major Afro-American poet because of his human subject matter, his combination of traditional techniques with an expertise in using rhythmic and oral speech patterns, and his ability to feel and to project his feelings into a poetic structure that moves others."

Knight commented that he believes a definition of art and aesthetics assumes that "every man is the master of his own destiny and comes to grips with the society by his own efforts.

The 'true' artist is supposed to examine his own experience of this process as a reflection of his self, his ego.'' Knight feels ''white society denies art, because art unifies rather than separates; it brings people together instead of alienating them.'' The western/European aesthetic dictates that ''the artist speak only of the beautiful (himself and what *he* sees); his task is to edify the listener, to make him see *beauty* of the world.'' Black artists must stay away from this because ''the red of this aesthetic rose got its color from the blood of black slaves, exterminated Indians, napalmed Vietnamese children.'' According to Knight, the black artist must ''perceive and conceptualize the collective aspirations, the collective vision of black people, and through his art form give back to the people the truth that he has gotten from them. He must sing to them of their own deeds, and misdeeds.''

BIOGRAPHICAL/CRITICAL SOURCES:

BOOKS

Contemporary Literary Criticism, Volume XL, Gale, 1986.
Dictionary of Literary Biography, Volume XLI: *Afro-American Poets Since 1955,* Gale, 1985.
Knight, Etheridge, *Poems from Prison,* Broadside Press, 1968.
Randall, Dudley, *Broadside Memories: Poets I Have Known,* Broadside Press, 1975.

PERIODICALS

Black American Literature Forum, fall, 1980, summer, 1981.
Black World, September, 1970, September, 1974.
Detroit Free Press, April 11, 1982.
Hollins Critic, December, 1981.
Los Angeles Times Book Review, August 10, 1980.
Negro Digest, January, 1968, July 1968.
Obsidian: Black Literature in Review, summer and winter, 1981.
Parnassus: Poetry in Review, spring-summer, 1981.
Village Voice, July 27, 1982
Virginia Quarterly Review, winter, 1981.

—*Sketch by Sharon Malinowski*

*　　　*　　　*

KONADU, Asare
See KONADU, S(amuel) A(sare)

*　　　*　　　*

KONADU, S(amuel) A(sare)　　1932-
(Asare Konadu; pseudonyms: Bediako Asare, Kwabena Asare Bediako)

PERSONAL: Born January 18, 1932, in Asamang, Ghana; son of Kofi (a farmer) and Abena (Anowuo) Konadu; married Alice Dede, February 26, 1958; children: Samuel Asare, Jr., Cecilia, Lucy, Frederick, Birago, Yamoah. *Education:* Attended Abuakwa State College, Kibi, Ghana, 1948-51, Polytechnic, London, England, 1956-58, and University of Strasbourg, 1958. *Religion:* Seventh-day Adventist.

ADDRESSES: Home—100 Aburaso St., Asamang, Ashanti, Ghana. *Office*—2R McCarthy Hill, Box 3918, Accra, Ghana.

CAREER: Ghana Information Services, Accra, junior reporter, 1952-56, journalist, 1956-58; Ghana News Agency, Accra, editor, 1958-60, chief editor, 1961-63; full-time writer, 1963—. Publisher and director, Anowuo Educational Publishers.

MEMBER: Ghana Writers Club, Ghana Journalists Association.

AWARDS, HONORS: University of Strasbourg fellowship for research in history of the Ghanaian press, 1959.

WRITINGS:

Wizard of Asamang, Waterville Publishing, 1962.
The Lawyer Who Bungled His Life, Waterville Publishing, 1965.
Night Watchers of Korlebu, Anowuo Educational Publishers, 1967, Humanities Press, 1969.
Come Back Dora, Humanities Press, 1969.

UNDER NAME ASARE KONADU

Shadow of Wealth, Anowuo Educational Publishers, 1966.
A Woman in Her Prime, Heinemann, 1967, Humanities Press, 1969.
Ordained by the Oracle, Heinemann, 1968, Humanities Press, 1969.
Vanishing Shadows, Anowuo Educational Publishers, 1987.
Reconciliation, Anowuo Educational Publishers, 1988.

UNDER PSEUDONYM BEDIAKO ASARE

Rebel, Heinemann Educational, 1969.
Majuto, East African Literature Bureau, 1975.
The Stubborn, East African Literature Bureau, 1976.

UNDER PSEUDONYM KWABENA ASARE BEDIAKO

Don't Leave Me Mercy, Anowuo Educational Publishers, 1966.
A Husband for Esi Ellua, Anowuo Educational Publishers, 1967, Humanities Press, 1969.
Return of Mercy, Anowuo Educational Publishers, 1987.
The Koala Called Too Late, Anowuo Educational Publishers, 1988.

WORK IN PROGRESS: Research into traditional healing and Ghanaian customs.

SIDELIGHTS: In 1961 S. A. Konadu toured the Soviet Union with Kwame Nkrumah, ex-president of Ghana, visiting all of its states. He traveled in Europe in 1958 and 1962, and in the Congo, Rwanda, and Burundi, 1963. In 1968 Konadu was the guest of the U.S. State Department and spent ninety days on a publishing tour of eleven states.

*　　　*　　　*

KUNENE, Mazisi (Raymond)　　1930-

PERSONAL: Born in 1930 in Durban, South Africa. *Education:* Received M.A. from Natal University; attended School of Oriental and African Studies, London, 1959.

ADDRESSES: Office—Department of African Literature and Language, University of California, Los Angeles, 405 Hilgard, Los Angeles, Calif. 90024.

CAREER: Head of department of African studies at University College at Rome, Lesotho; director of education for South African United Front; African National Congress in Europe and United States, chief representative, 1962, director of finance, 1972; visiting professor of African literature at Stanford University, Palo Alto, Calif.; began as associate professor, became professor of African literature and language at University of California, Los Angeles.

AWARDS, HONORS: Winner of Bantu Literary Competition, 1956.

WRITINGS:

(And translator from the Zulu) *Zulu Poems,* Africana, 1970.

(And translator from the Zulu) *Emperor Shaka the Great: A Zulu Epic,* Heinemann, 1979.

(And translator from the Zulu) *Anthem of the Decades: A Zulu Epic,* Heinemann, 1981.

The Ancestors and the Sacred Mountain: Poems, Heinemann, 1982.

Work represented in anthologies, including *Modern Poetry From Africa,* edited by Gerald Moore and Ulli Beier, Penguin, 1963; *African Writing Today,* edited by Ezekiel Mphahlele, Penguin, 1967. Contributor of short stories to *Drum.*

SIDELIGHTS: Drawing on the oral tradition of Zulu literature, Mazisi Kunene writes poetry expressing Zulu culture, religion, and history. He has translated much of his work, originally written in Zulu, into English. *Emperor Shaka the Great* is Kunene's verse narrative about the life and achievements of the nineteenth-century Zulu leader who unified various Zulu fiefdoms and attempted to deal diplomatically with English settlers. Deeming it ''an African epic equal to *The Iliad* and *The Odyssey,*'' *World Literature Today* contributor Charles R. Larson judged the poem ''a monumental undertaking and achievement by any standards.'' *Anthem of the Decades* details the Zulu account of how death came to mankind, and Kunene's collection *The Ancestors and the Sacred Mountain,* containing more than one hundred poems, promotes humanity, appreciation of nature, ancestral wisdom, and social action.

BIOGRAPHICAL/CRITICAL SOURCES:

PERIODICALS

Times Educational Supplement, January 28, 1983.
Times Literary Supplement, May 14, 1982.
World Literature Today, summer, 1981, summer, 1983.

*   *   *

KUNJUFU, Johari M. Amini   1935-
(Johari M. Amini)

PERSONAL: Name legally changed; born February 13, 1935, in Philadelphia, Pa.; daughter of Vol William (a clergyman) and Alma Irene (Bazel) McLawler; married Jawanza Kunjufu; children: Marciana, Kim Allan (son), Shikamana (son). *Education:* Chicago City College, A.A., 1968; Chicago State College (now University), B.A., 1970; University of Chicago, M.A., 1972.

ADDRESSES: Office—University of Illinois—Chicago Circle, Black Studies Department, Box 4348, Chicago, Ill. 60680.

CAREER: Worked as secretary, 1956-66; Chicago City College, Chicago, Ill., instructor in psychology, 1970-72; University of Illinois at Chicago Circle, lecturer in black literature, 1972-76. Co-founder, with Haki Madhubuti, of Third World Press, Chicago. Board member, Institute of Positive Education.

MEMBER: Institute of Positive Education, African Heritage Studies Association, Organization of Black American Culture (treasurer, 1967-75).

WRITINGS:

UNDER NAME JOHARI M. AMINI

Common-sense Approach to Eating, Institute of Positive Education, 1972.

UNDER NAME JOHARI M. AMINI; POEMS

Images in Black, Third World Press, 1967.
Black Essence, Third World Press, 1968.
A Folk Fable for My People, Third World Press, 1969.
Let's Go Some Where, Third World Press, 1970.
A Hip Tale in the Death Style, Broadside Press, 1972.
An African Frame of Reference, Institute of Positive Education, 1972.

OTHER

Also author of *Re-Definition: Concept as Being.* Work appears in thirteen anthologies. Contributor to *Black World* and *Negro Digest.* Assistant editor of *Black Books Bulletin,* 1970—.

SIDELIGHTS: Some of Johari Kunjufu's poetry is included on the recordings ''Black Spirits,'' Motown/Black Forum Records, 1972, and ''Spectrum in Black,'' Scott, Foresman, 1971.

L

LADNER, Joyce A(nn) 1943-

PERSONAL: Born October 12, 1943, in Waynesboro, Miss.; married Walter Carrington. *Education:* Tougaloo College, B.A., 1964; Washington University, 1966, Ph.D., 1968; postdoctoral research at University of Dar es Salaam, Tanzania.

ADDRESSES: Office—Department of Sociology, Hunter College of the City University of New York, 695 Park Ave., New York, N.Y. 10021.

CAREER: Southern Illinois University, Edwardsville, assistant professor and curriculum specialist, 1968-69; affiliated with Wesleyan University, Middletown, Conn., 1969-70; University of Dar es Salaam, Dar es Salaam, Tanzania, research associate, 1970-71; Howard University, Washington, D.C., associate professor of sociology, 1971-76; Hunter College of the City University of New York, New York City, member of faculty of sociology, beginning in 1976.

MEMBER: American Sociological Association (member of board of directors), National Institute of Mental Health (review committee member of Minority Center), Social Science Research Council (fellow), Society for the Study of Social Problems, Caucus of Black Sociologists (member of board of directors), Association for the Study of Afro-American Life and History, Institute of the Black World (senior research fellow, 1969-71), Twenty-first Century Foundation (member of board of directors).

AWARDS, HONORS: Recipient of first fellowship from Black Women's Community Development Foundation, 1970-71, for study "Involvement of Tanzanian Women in Nation Building"; Russell Sage Foundation grant, 1972-73; Cummins Engine Foundation grant, 1972-73.

WRITINGS:

Tomorrow's Tomorrow: The Black Woman, Doubleday, 1971.
(Editor) *The Death of White Sociology* (collection of essays), Random House, 1973.
Mixed Families: Adopting Across Racial Boundaries, Doubleday, 1977.

Contributor to anthologies and to newspapers and periodicals. Contributing editor to *Black Scholar* and *Journal of Black Studies and Research.*

SIDELIGHTS: Sociologist Joyce A. Ladner has centered her twenty years of research and teachings on intergroup relations and minority issues in America. In her first work, *Tomorrow's Tomorrow: The Black Woman,* Ladner examines the lives of black women and the forces that mold their self-perceptions. Her findings are the result of interviews with more than thirty black adolescent girls from a St. Louis, Missouri, ghetto. The girls, in the words of Toni Cade Bambara in *Black World,* "speak on and live out what it means to grow up Black and female in a country that regards neither with any special fondness."

Analyzing her observations in the context of the black people's troubled history in America—"a society infamous for the lack of understanding and sympathy between the races," commented Susan E. Burke in *Best Sellers*—Ladner found the girls' aspirations refreshingly optimistic and their self-images surprisingly positive. Consequently, stated Bambara, *Tomorrow's Tomorrow* focuses not on "the weakness of the Black community . . . or on the crippling effects of racism . . . but rather on the intricate network of influences (familial, peer, societal, etc.) that bombard the young girl [and on] the counters and strategems she devises to get over from day to day—her inner strength." Dispelling the popular notion of low self-esteem among poor black women, noted Burke, Ladner found that "most of the girls [she interviewed] have the determination to 'make something' of themselves, and self-hatred is practically non-existent."

Ladner relates the inner strength of black women to their position in a society that holds different values from those of the white middle class. Because of differing cultural views of sexual morality, for example, an unmarried, pregnant black woman is less likely to be shunned or chastised than is an unmarried, pregnant white woman. Carol L. Adams, writing in the *American Journal of Sociology,* cited illegitimacy as a "concept viewed as inappropriate when studying the black community." Adams explained Ladner's perception "that the low-income black community holds an inherent value that no child can be 'illegal.' The child is seen as having the right to exist and [as] representing the fulfillment of womanhood, thus neither the mother nor the child is degraded and stigmatized."

Adams praised Ladner's "notion that black women are now serving as role models for white women who are beginning to question such things as the institution of marriage, the concept of illegitimacy, and the general moral code traditionally associated with this society." Although some critics accused Ladner's survey as being unscientific and thus inconclusive, Burke affirmed that "her observations are both valid and important," and Bambara called the study "a solid piece of scholarship . . . moving and vital and eminently sensible."

Ladner's 1977 *Mixed Families: Adopting Across Racial Boundaries* is "an interesting, well-balanced study" of transracial adoption, according to Diane A. Parente in *Best Sellers*. Transracial adoption became a popular trend in America during the late 1960s when white couples, eager to adopt but discouraged by a shortage of white infants available, were strongly encouraged by adoption agencies to take in "hard to place" minority children. During an era of civil rights activity, such an undertaking was also considered an important step in promoting interracial harmony. In the early 1970s, however, the trend slowed when an opposing philosophy arose, strongly supported by the National Association of Black Social Workers, maintaining that black children needed to grow up in black families to develop a positive self-image and a strong sense of identity.

Attempting to resolve the debate, Ladner interviewed 136 adoptive families to find out how they were coping with the personal and societal pressures they encountered. "Both sides of the controversy are objectively presented" in *Mixed Families*, determined Parente, adding that the "truth, apparently, lies somewhere in the middle." Some black adoptees—children and adults alike—and their white parents agree that it would have been better to have placed the black children with black parents, while other families maintain that the adoption helped them gain an irreplaceable understanding of racial differences and similarities. The author herself concludes that although efforts should be made to avoid unnecessary trauma by placing children with families of their own ancestry, transracial adoptions are preferable to institutional or foster care.

Ladner emphasizes the importance of parental understanding and patience, whatever the race of the adoptive parents and their adopted children. As David C. Anderson concluded in *New York Times Book Review:* "Relations between parent and child aren't supposed to be perfect; instead, they are richly complicated, molded by imponderable forces great and small. Our task, as parents, is only to manage the complexity as best we can." For mixed families, Ladner points out in her book this involves maintaining "a balanced view and not [erring] too much in either direction"—neither denying the child's blackness nor attempting, as a white parent, to become black by rejecting whiteness.

Marti Wilson of *Black Scholar* remarked that "the strength of *Mixed Families* is in the fact that it approaches the question of integration from a new perspective, and heightens the level of dialogue on the subject of cross racial adoptions." And Parente asserted that in *Mixed Families* "the author provides a realistic glimpse of American racial attitudes and their day-to-day effects on all concerned."

BIOGRAPHICAL/CRITICAL SOURCES:

BOOKS

Contemporary Issues Criticism, Volume 1, Gale, 1982.
Ladner, Joyce A., *Mixed Families: Adopting Across Racial Boundaries,* Doubleday, 1977.

PERIODICALS

American Journal of Sociology, September, 1972.

Best Sellers, August, 1971, October, 1977.
Black World, October, 1971.
Black Scholar, November/December, 1979.
New York Times Book Review, August 14, 1977.

—*Sketch by Christa Brelin*

*   *   *

La GUMA, (Justin) Alex(ander)   1925-1985

PERSONAL: Born February 20, 1925, in Cape Town, South Africa; immigrated to London, England, 1966; died October 11, 1985, in Havana, Cuba; son of Jimmy and Wilhelmina (Alexander) La Guma; married Blanche Valerie Herman (an office manager and former midwife), November 13, 1954; children: Eugene, Bartholomew. *Education:* Cape Technical College, student, 1941-42, correspondence student, 1965; London School of Journalism, correspondence student, 1964.

ADDRESSES: Agent—Hope Leresche & Sale, 11 Jubilee Pl., London SW3 3TE, England.

CAREER: New Age (weekly newspaper), Cape Town, South Africa, staff journalist, 1955-62; free-lance writer and journalist, 1962-85. Member of African National Congress, 1955-85. Member of editorial board, Afro-Asian Writers Bureau, 1965-85.

MEMBER: Afro-Asian Writers Association (deputy secretary-general, 1973-85).

AWARDS, HONORS: Afro-Asian Lotus Award for literature, 1969.

WRITINGS:

NOVELS

And a Threefold Cord, Seven Seas Publishers (East Berlin), 1964.
The Stone Country, Seven Seas Publishers (East Berlin), 1967, Heinemann, 1974.
In the Fog of the Season's End, Heinemann, 1972, Third Press, 1973.
Time of the Butcherbird, Heinemann, 1979.

CONTRIBUTOR

Richard Rive, editor, *Quartet: New Voices from South Africa,* Crown, 1963, new edition, Heinemann, 1968.
Ellis Ayitey Komey and Ezekiel Mphahlele, editors, *Modern African Stories,* Faber, 1964.
Mphahlele, editor, *African Writing Today,* Penguin, 1967.
O. R. Dathorne and Willfried Feuser, editors, *Africa in Prose,* Penguin, 1969.
Charles R. Larson, editor, *Modern African Stories,* Collins, 1971.

OTHER

A Walk in the Night (novelette), Mbari Publications (Ibadan, Nigeria), 1962, published with additional material as *A Walk in the Night and Other Stories,* Northwestern University Press, 1967.
(Editor) *Apartheid: A Collection of Writings on South African Racism by South Africans,* International Publishers, 1971.
A Soviet Journey (travel), Progress Publishers (Moscow), 1978.

Contributor of short stories to magazines, including *Black Orpheus* and *Africa South.*

SIDELIGHTS: Alex La Guma's active opposition to the South African government's racist policies permeates his fiction as it did his life. A member of the Cape Town district Communist party until it was banned in 1950, La Guma worked for a time on the staff of the leftist newspaper *New Age*. He came to the government's notice in 1955, when he helped draw up the Freedom Charter, a declaration of rights; in 1956, he was accused of treason, and in 1961 he was arrested for helping to organize a strike.

Various acts passed by the South African government kept La Guma either in prison or under twenty-four-hour house arrest for some years, including time in solitary confinement. La Guma spent this time writing; he composed the novel *And a Threefold Cord* while he was under house arrest in the early 1960s. He left South Africa in 1966, moving to London, where he remained until 1979, writing and working as a journalist. At the time of his death, he was serving as the African National Congress representative to Cuba.

Much of La Guma's work treats the situations and problems he saw in his native Cape Town. *A Walk in the Night* tells the story of Michael Adonis, a factory worker who has just lost his job because he talked back to his white supervisor. Frustrated, Michael commits a senseless crime; he kills the decrepit old ex-actor Doughty. Intertwined with Michael's fate are the lives of Raalt, a white constable on duty in the district where the murder is committed, and Willieboy, a malingerer and occasional criminal. The noveiette, says Shatto Arthur Gakwandi in his *The Novel and Contemporary Experience in Africa*, avoids "being a sermon of despair [while also evading] advocating sentimental solutions to the problems that it portrays. Without pathos, it creates a powerful impression of that rhythm of violence which characterizes South African life." He concludes, "All these characters are victims of a system that denies them the facility of living in harmony with fellow human beings and their frustrations find release in acts of violence against weaker members of their society." The power of La Guma's writing leads John Updike, writing for the *New Yorker*, to say of *In the Fog of the Season's End* that it "delivers, through its portrait of a few hunted blacks attempting to subvert the brutal regime of apartheid, a social protest reminiscent, in its closely detailed texture and level indignation, of Dreiser and Zola."

Several of Alex La Guma's books have been translated into Russian; his work is banned in South Africa.

BIOGRAPHICAL/CRITICAL SOURCES:

BOOKS

Contemporary Literary Criticism, Volume 19, Gale, 1981.
Duerden, Dennis, and Cosmo Pieterse, editors, *African Writers Talking: A Collection of Interviews*, Heinemann, 1972.
Encyclopedia of World Literature in the Twentieth Century, Volume 3, revised edition, Ungar, 1983.
Gakwandi, Shatto Arthur, *The Novel and Contemporary Experience in Africa*, Africana Publishing, 1977.
Mphahlele, Ezekiel, *African Image*, Praeger, 1962, reissued, 1974.
Wanjala, C. L., *Standpoints on African Literature*, East African Literature Bureau, Nairobi, Kenya, 1973.
Zell, Hans M., and others, *A New Reader's Guide to African Literature*, 2nd revised and expanded edition, Holmes & Meier, 1983.

PERIODICALS

Black Scholar, July/August, 1986.
Busara, Volume 8, number 1, 1976.

Journal of Commonwealth Literature, June, 1973.
New Statesman, January 29, 1965, November 3, 1972.
New Yorker, January 21, 1974.
PHYLON, March, 1978.
Sechaba (London), February, 1971.
Times Literary Supplement, January 21, 1965, October 20, 1972.
World Literature Today, winter, 1980.

OBITUARIES:

PERIODICALS

Freedomways, Volume 25, number 3, 1985.
Times (London), November 23, 1985.

*   *   *

LAMMING, George (William)   1927-

PERSONAL: Born June 8, 1927, in Barbados; emigrated to England, 1950. *Education:* Attended Combermere High School in Barbados.

ADDRESSES: Home—14-A Highbury Place, London N 5, England.

CAREER: Writer. Worked as schoolmaster in Trinidad, 1946-50; factory worker in England, 1950; broadcaster for British Broadcasting Corp. (BBC) Colonial Service, 1951. Writer-in-residence and lecturer in Creative Arts Centre and Department of Education, University of West Indies, Mona, Jamaica, 1967-68; visiting professor at University of Texas at Austin, 1977, and at University of Pennsylvania. Lecturer in Denmark, Tanzania, and Australia.

AWARDS, HONORS: Kenyon Review fellowship, 1954; Guggenheim Fellowship, 1955; Somerset Maugham Award, 1957; Canada Council fellowship, 1962; Commonwealth Foundation grant, 1976; Association of Commonwealth Literature Writers Award; D.Litt., University of West Indies.

WRITINGS:

NOVELS

In the Castle of My Skin, with introduction by Richard Wright, McGraw, 1953, with a new introduction by the author, Schocken, 1983.
The Emigrants, M. Joseph, 1954, McGraw, 1955, reprinted, Allison & Busby, 1980.
Of Age and Innocence, M. Joseph, 1958, reprinted, Allison & Busby, 1981.
Season of Adventure, M. Joseph, 1960, reprinted, Allison & Busby, 1979.
Water With Berries, Holt, 1972.
Natives of My Person, Holt, 1972.

CONTRIBUTOR OF POETRY TO ANTHOLOGIES

Peter Brent, editor, *Young Commonwealth Poets '65*, Heinemann, 1965.
John Figueroa, editor, *Caribbean Voices*, two volumes, Evans, 1966.
O. R. Dathorne, editor, *Caribbean Verse*, Heinemann, 1968.

CONTRIBUTOR OF SHORT FICTION TO ANTHOLOGIES

Andrew Salkey, editor, *West Indian Stories*, Faber, 1960.
Salkey, editor, *Stories from the Caribbean*, Dufour, 1965, published as *Island Voices*, Liveright, 1970.
O. R. Dathorne, editor, *Caribbean Narrative*, Heinemann, 1966.

Barbara Howes, editor, *From the Green Antilles,* Macmillan, 1966.
Salkey, editor, *Caribbean Prose,* Evans, 1967.
James T. Livingston, editor, *Caribbean Rhythms,* Pocket Books, 1974.

OTHER

The Pleasures of Exile (essays and autobiographical observations), M. Joseph, 1960, reprinted, Allison & Busby, 1984.
(With Henry Bangou and Rene Depestre) *Influencia del Africa en las literaturas antillanas* (title means "The Influence of Africa on the Antillian Literatures"), I. L. A. C. (Montevideo, Uruguay), 1972.
(Editor) *Cannon Shot and Glass Beads: Modern Black Writing,* Pan Books, 1974.

Co-editor of Barbados and Guyana independence issues of *New World Quarterly* (Kingston), 1965 and 1967. Contributor to journals, including *Bim* (Barbados), *Savacou, New World Quarterly, Caribbean Quarterly,* and *Casa de las Americas* (Cuba).

SIDELIGHTS: Barbadian writer "George Lamming is not so much a novelist," asserts *New York Times Book Review* contributor Jan Carew, "as a chronicler of secret journeys to the innermost regions of the West Indian psyche." George Davis, however, believes Carew's assessment does not go far enough. Davis notes in his own *New York Times Book Review* critique, "I can think of very few writers who make better use of the fictional moments of their stories to explore the souls of any of us—West Indian or not."

In Lamming's essay, "The Negro Writer in His World," the West Indian explains the universality on which Davis comments. In the essay Lamming maintains that black writers are the same as all other writers who use writing as a method of self-discovery. According to Carolyn T. Brown in *World Literature Today,* in Lamming's opinion, "the contemporary human condition . . . involves a 'universal sense of separation and abandonment, frustration and loss, and above all, of man's direct inner experience of something missing."

In Lamming's work the "something missing" is a true cultural identity for the West Indian. This lack of identity is, according to Lamming, a direct result of the long history of colonial rule in the region. Caribbean-born writer V. S. Naipaul explains the importance of this idea in his *New Statesman* review of Lamming's novel, *Of Age and Innocence:* "Unless one understands the West Indian's search for identity, [the novel] is almost meaningless. It is not fully realised how completely the West Indian Negro identifies himself with England. . . . For the West Indian intellectual, speaking no language but English, educated in an English way, the experience of England is really traumatic. The foundations of his life are removed."

James Ngugi makes a similar observation in his *Pan-Africanist* review of the same novel. "For Lamming," Ngugi writes, "a sense of exile must lead to action and through action to identity. The West Indian's alienation springs . . . from his colonial relationship to England."

Lamming's first four novels explore the West Indian search for identity, a search which often leads to a flight to England followed by, for some, a return to their Caribbean roots. His first novel, *In the Castle of My Skin,* which is nearly universally acclaimed by critics, is a quasi-autobiographical look at childhood and adolescence on Lamming's fictional Caribbean island, San Cristobal. The book "is generally regarded," notes Michael Gilkes in *The West Indian Novel,* "as a 'classic' of West Indian fiction. It is one of the earliest novels of any substance to convey, with real assurance, the life of ordinary village folk within a genuinely realized, native landscape: a 'peasant novel' . . . written with deep insight and considerable technical skill."

Several reviewers compare Lamming's prose style in the book to poetry. In *New Statesman and Nation* Pritchett describes Lamming's prose as "something between garrulous realism and popular poetry, and . . . quite delightful"; while in the *San Francisco Chronicle* J. H. Jackson says Lamming "is a poet and a human being who approaches a question vital to him, humanly and poetically." A *Time* contributor finds the book "a curious mixture of autobiography and a poetic evocation of a native life. . . . It is one of the few authentically rich and constantly readable books produced [thus far] by a West Indian."

Lamming's next novel, *The Emigrants,* follows a group of West Indians who—like Lamming, himself—leave their native islands for exile in England, while the two novels that follow, *Of Age and Innocence* and *Season of Adventure,* feature a return to San Cristobal. According to Carew, these last two novels also have a bit of autobiography in them because through their action it seems "as though Lamming [is] attempting to rediscover a history of himself by himself."

In Lamming's novels, as critics note, self-discovery is often achieved through an inquiry into his characters' pasts. For example, while *Yale Review* contributor Michael Cook quotes Lamming's *Of Age and Innocence* description of San Cristobal—"an old land inhabiting new forms of men who can never resurrect their roots and do not know their nature," the reviewer comments that "it is obvious" that in "*Season of Adventure* . . . [Lamming] is committed to his characters' at least trying to discover their roots and their natures." Details of the plot seem to verify Cook's assessment for the novel traces Fola Piggott's quest to discover whether her father was European or African.

According to Kenneth Ramchand in *The West Indian Novel and Its Background,* "*Season of Adventure* is the most significant of the West Indian novels invoking Africa." In the novel, Ramchand maintains, Lamming invokes "the African heritage not to make statements about Africa but to explore the troubled components of West Indian culture and nationhood." Lamming accomplishes "this without preventing us from seeing that Fola's special circumstances . . . are only a manifestation . . . of every man's need to take the past into account with humility, fearlessness, and receptivity."

After a silence of over a decade Lamming published two new novels almost simultaneously: *Water with Berries* and *Natives of My Person.* Again, his fiction focuses on the effects of history on the present. In both books Lamming uses symbolism to tell his story. In *Water with Berries* Lamming uses a theme previously dealt with in his nonfiction work *The Pleasures of Exile.* A *Times Literary Supplement* reviewer quotes from Lamming's collection of essays: "My subject is the migration of the West Indian writer, as colonial and exile, from his native kingdom, once inhabited by Caliban, to the tempestuous island of Prospero's and his language." Caliban and Prospero are both characters from Shakespeare's *The Tempest,* Caliban being the deformed slave of Prospero, ruler of an enchanted island. According to the *Times Literary Supplement* contributor, Lamming also refers to himself in the same book as an "exiled descendent of Caliban."

In *Water with Berries* Lamming uses the plot of *The Tempest* to symbolize the various ills of West Indian society, but critics are divided on the success of the novel. In *World Literature in English* Anthony Boxill notes that Lamming uses *The Tempest* to "help put across his points about disintegration of personality . . . , especially in people who are products of a colonial past. . . . However, the *Tempest* pattern which might have been the strength of this novel proves its undoing. . . . In his unrelenting faithfulness to this . . . pattern Lamming loses touch with the characters he is creating; they cease to be credible." A *Times Literary Supplement* contributor similarly states, "Lamming writes very well, but *Water with Berries* does not entirely convince either as a study of the pains of exile, or as an allegory of colonialism. . . . [And,] as for the melodrama of . . . Lamming's *Tempest* myth, it tells us nothing new."

Other critics praise Lamming's novel and disregard its connections to *The Tempest*. Paul Theroux and George Davis, for instance, find the work a very compelling statement on the effects of colonialism. In *Encounter* Theroux claims, "the poetic prose of the narrative has a perfect dazzle. . . . When expatriation is defined and dramatised . . . *Water with Berries* takes on a life of its own, for . . . Lamming is meticulous in diagnosing the condition of estrangement." *New York Times Book Review* contributor Davis writes: "This is an effectively written fictional work. Lamming brings his characters . . . into the same nightmare of arson, perversity, suicide and murder, which, we are forced to feel, is the legacy of the colonial experience."

Natives of My Person, according to Gilkes, "is an exceedingly complex work, full of allegorical and historical meanings and echoes. It is an embodiment of all [Lamming's] themes: a kind of *reviewing* process in which he appears to take stock of things." Boxill notes that the novel "provides richly complex insights into human personality and the history of colonialism." It tells the story of the sixteenth-century voyage of the ship *Reconnaissance* from Europe to America by way of Africa. The chief goal of the ship's Commandant is the establishment of a slave-free settlement on the island of San Cristobal, but he is killed by two of the ship's officers before he can accomplish his mission.

Some critics find that Lamming's prose detracts from the novel. In *Book World* Theroux calls Lamming "a marvelously skillful writer" but also refers to the novel's "shadowy action and vaguely poetical momentousness." A *Times Literary Supplement* reviewer complains that Lamming writes "a prose of discovery which is effortful, uncolloquial, and almost always mannered."

While Thomas R. Edwards and Carew also regret the complexity of Lamming's prose they are able to find redeeming qualities in the novel. "Lamming's prose is portentous," Edwards notes in the *New York Review of Books*, "hooked on simile, and anxious to suggest more than it says, inviting questions thestory never answers. . . . Yet if reading *Natives of My Person* is a voyage into frustration and annoyance, Lamming's story survives and grows in the mind afterward. . . . This imagined history reveals itself as a version of significances that 'real' history is itself only a version of."

Carew similarly comments on the book's difficult prose but calls the work "undoubtedly . . . Lamming's finest novel." In the book, according to Carew's assessment, Lamming ex-

presses better than in any of his other novels his concerns about the effects of colonization on the West Indies and its people. In *Natives of My Person*, Carew maintains, Lamming "succeeds in illuminating new areas of darkness in the colonial past that the colonizer has so far not dealt with; and in this sense it is a profoundly revolutionary and original work."

BIOGRAPHICAL/CRITICAL SOURCES:

BOOKS

Baugh, Edward, editor, *Homecoming: Essays on African and Caribbean Literature, Culture and Politics*, Laurence Hill, 1972.
Contemporary Literary Criticism, Gale, Volume 2, 1974, Volume 4, 1975.
Cooke, Michael G., editor, *Modern Black Novelists: A Collection of Critical Essays*, Prentice-Hall, 1971.
Gilkes, Michael, *The West Indian Novel*, Twayne, 1981.
Lamming, George, *In the Castle of My Skin*, McGraw, 1954.
Lamming, George, *Of Age and Innocence*, M. Joseph, 1958.
Lamming, George, *The Pleasures of Exile*, M. Joseph, 1960.
Massa, Daniel, editor, *Individual and Community in Commonwealth Literature*, University Press (Malta), 1979.
Paquet, Sandra Pouchet, *The Novels of George Lamming*, Heinemann, 1982.
Ramchand, Kenneth, *The West Indian Novel and Its Background*, Faber, 1970.

PERIODICALS

Book World, January 23, 1972.
Canadian Literature, winter, 1982.
Caribbean Quarterly, February, 1958.
Encounter, May, 1972.
New Statesman, December 6, 1958, January 28, 1972, December 19, 1980.
New Statesman and Nation, April 18, 1953.
New Yorker, December 5, 1953, May 28, 1955, April 29, 1972.
New York Herald Tribune Book Review, July 17, 1955.
New York Review of Books, March 9, 1972.
New York Times, November 1, 1953, July 24, 1955, January 15, 1972.
New York Times Book Review, February 27, 1972, June 4, 1972, October 15, 1972, December 3, 1972.
Observer, October 8, 1972.
Pan-Africanist, March, 1971.
Punch, August 19, 1981.
San Francisco Chronicle, November 17, 1953, June 24, 1955.
Saturday Review, December 5, 1953, May 28, 1955.
Studies in Black Literature, spring, 1973.
Time, November 9, 1953, April 25, 1955.
Times Literary Supplement, March 27, 1953, February 11, 1972, December 15, 1972, September 4, 1981, October 24, 1986.
World Literature Today, winter, 1983, spring, 1985.
World Literature Written in English, November, 1971, April, 1973, November, 1979.
Yale Review, autumn, 1953, summer, 1973.

—*Sketch by Marian Gonsior*

*   *   *

LANE, Pinkie Gordon   1923-

PERSONAL: Born January 13, 1923, in Philadelphia, Pa.; married Ulysses S. Lane (deceased); children: Gordon Edward. *Education:* Spelman College, B.A. (magna cum laude), 1949; Atlanta University, M.A., 1956; Louisiana State University, Ph.D., 1967.

ADDRESSES: Home—2738 77th Ave., Baton Rouge, La. 70807. *Office*—Department of English, Southern University, Baton Rouge, La. 70813.

CAREER: High school English teacher in Georgia, 1949-55; Southern University, Baton Rouge, La., instructor, 1959-60, assistant professor, 1960-62, associate professor, 1963-67, professor of English, 1967-86, professor emeritus, 1986—, chairperson of the department, 1974-86. Charter member, Mayor—President's Commission on the Needs of Women. Member of editorial board, South & West, Inc. Has given readings from her works in Arkansas, Tennessee, Oklahoma, New York, Mississippi, and Louisiana.

MEMBER: Modern Language Association of America, National Council of Teachers of English, Poetry Society of America, National Organization for Women, Louisiana Art and Artists' Guild, Delta Sigma Theta.

AWARDS, HONORS: Awards from National Writer's Club, 1970, and Tulsa Poets, 1970; nominated for Pulitzer Prize, 1978, for *Mystic Female;* national award from Washington chapter of Spelman College Alumnae Association, 1983, for outstanding achievement in the arts and humanities; Woman of Achievement award from Baton Rouge YWCA, 1984; honored as one of fifty-eight outstanding women in Louisiana, 1984.

WRITINGS:

Wind Thoughts (poems), South & West, 1972.
(Editor and contributor) *Discourses on Poetry* (an anthology of prose and poetry by black authors), South & West, 1972.
(Editor and contributor) *Poems by Blacks,* Volume 3, South & West, 1973.
Mystic Female (poems), introduction by Jerry W. Ward, South & West, 1978.
I Never Scream: New and Selected Poems, Lotus Press, 1985.

CONTRIBUTOR

Patricia L. Brown, Don L. Lee, and Francis Ward, editors, *To Gwen with Love,* Johnson Publishing Co., 1971.
Sue Abbott Boyd, editor, *Poems by Blacks,* Volumes 1-2, South & West, 1972.
Eugene B. Redmond, editor, *Griefs of Joy,* Black River Writers, 1977.

OTHER

Also contributor to literary journals, including *Phylon, Negro American Literary Forum, Journal of Black Poetry, Bardic Echoes, Personalist, South and West, Voices International, Energy West, Pembroke Magazine, Jeopardy, Poet: India, The Louisiana Review, The Last Cookie,* and *Hoo Doo.* Advisory editor, *Black Box,* 1976-79; editor-in-chief, *South and West: An International Literary Quarterly,* 1979-81; contributing and advisory editor, *Callaloo,* 1979-84, and *Black Scholar,* 1979-86.

Lane's works are included in the Beinecke Rare Book and Manuscript Library at Yale University in the James Weldon Johnson Collection of Negro Arts and Letters.

SIDELIGHTS: Pinkie Gordon Lane frequently writes poems to mark important events in her life and in the lives of family and friends. In this respect, her poetry has been favorably compared to that of Phillis Wheatley, one of the first black American poets published in modern times. Lane's most acclaimed book of poetry, *The Mystic Female,* was nominated for a Pulitzer Prize in 1979. Alluding to Lane's title, *Black Scholar* contributor S. Diane Bogus comments: "That [Lane] is great ripples through the low tide of her poetry like a moccasin through its Bayou waters—natural, deadly on contact, to be regarded with respect. Is this not mystic and female?" In a review of Lane's 1985 book *I Never Scream: New and Selected Poems,* which contains several poems from *The Mystic Female,* Lillian D. Roland writes in *Black American Literature Forum,* "Lane's poetic presence and power, arising from a great sub-conscious reservoir of knowledge, communicate, soul to soul, the deepest impulses of the human heart and mind."

AVOCATIONAL INTERESTS: Oil painting.

BIOGRAPHICAL/CRITICAL SOURCES:

BOOKS

Dictionary of Literary Biography, Volume 41: *Afro-American Poets since 1955,* Gale, 1985.

PERIODICALS

Black American Literature Forum, fall, 1986.
Black Scholar, May/June, 1980.
Callaloo, February, 1979.

*   *   *

LARSEN, Nella   1891-1964

PERSONAL: Born April 13, 1891, in Chicago, Ill.; died March 30, 1964, in New York, N.Y.; daughter of a Danish mother and a West Indian father; married Elmer S. Imes (a physicist), May 3, 1919 (divorced, 1933). *Education:* Attended Fisk University, Nashville, Tenn., 1909-10, and University of Copenhagen, 1910-12; studied nursing at Lincoln Hospital, New York, N.Y., 1912-15.

CAREER: Tuskegee Institute, Tuskegee, Ala., assistant superintendent of nurses, 1915-16; Lincoln Hospital, New York City, nurse, 1916-18; Department of Health, New York City, nurse, 1918-21; New York Public Library, Harlem branch, assistant librarian, 1922-23, children's librarian, 1924-26; worked as a night nurse and supervising nurse at hospitals on the lower east side of Manhattan, beginning in 1941; writer.

AWARDS, HONORS: Bronze medal from the Harmon Foundation, 1928, for *Quicksand;* first black woman to receive a Guggenheim fellowship, 1930.

WRITINGS:

Quicksand (novel), Knopf, 1928, reprinted, Negro Universities Press, 1969, also published with *Passing* (also see below).
Passing (novel), Knopf, 1929, reprinted, Negro Universities Press, 1969, also published with *Quicksand* (also see below).

OMNIBUS VOLUMES

Quicksand; and, Passing, edited with an introduction by Deborah E. McDowell, Rutgers University Press, 1986.

OTHER

Contributor of short stories to various periodicals.

SIDELIGHTS: Nella Larsen was a member of the coterie of black writers associated with the Harlem Renaissance, an era of outstanding achievement in black American art and literature during the 1920s and 1930s. Though not as well known as many of her contemporaries, Larsen nonetheless won recognition for her two published novels, *Quicksand* and *Passing.*

Quicksand, which appeared in 1928, is the largely autobiographical story of Helga Crane, the daughter of a black man and a Scandinavian woman, who searches in vain for sexual and racial identity. Her quest takes her from a teaching position at a small college in the South to the elite social circles of Copenhagen and New York City to a backwoods Atlanta community pastored by the illiterate preacher she marries. The marriage fulfills Helga's longing for an uncomplicated existence and for sexual gratification, but it leaves her mired in a life of rural poverty and continual pregnancies.

Quicksand won a Harmon Foundation prize and was greeted with generally enthusiastic reviews in contemporary periodicals. Some critics faulted Larsen's characterizations as shallow and underdeveloped, but most praised the novel's complexity, sophistication, and artistry. A writer for the *New York Times,* for example, called *Quicksand* "an articulate, sympathetic first novel, which tells its story and projects its heroine in a lucid, exaggerated manner." Similarly, writing in *Crisis,* W. E. B. Du Bois deemed it "the best piece of fiction that Negro America has produced since the heyday of [Charles] Chesnutt."

More than fifty years after its initial publication *Quicksand* continues to generate critical acclaim. In his volume *From the Dark Tower: Afro-American Writers, 1900 to 1960,* Arthur P. Davis described *Quicksand* as "a fascinating case study of an unhappy and unfortunate woman," calling Helga Crane a victim not so much of a racial situation as of "her own inability to make the right decisions." She is, pronounced Davis, intriguing and complex, "a superb creation," and he assessed Larsen's book "one of the better novels of the Harlem Renaissance." Margaret Perry, author of *Silence to the Drums: A Survey of the Literature of the Harlem Renaissance,* lauded Larsen for her "awareness of female sexuality," and Addison Gayle, Jr., in his *The Way of the New World: The Black Novel in America,* called *Quicksand* "almost modern in its plot and conflicts. . . . It seeks to broach the wider question of identity, not the loss of it, but the search for it, and to suggest that this search in a world, race mad, must produce serious psychological problems of the spirit and soul."

Passing, like *Quicksand,* examines what *Ms.* contributor Mary Helen Washington labeled "the marginal black woman of the middle class, who was both unwilling to conform to a circumscribed existence in the black world and unable to move freely in the white world." *Passing* is the story of Clare Kendry, a beautiful fair-skinned black woman who escapes likely impoverishment by passing for white. She marries a wealthy white man, who assumes that she is also white. Her passage across the color line is completely successful until "a longing for her own kind led her to take fatal risks," posited Margaret Cheney Dawson in her review of the novel for the *New York Herald Tribune.* Clare renews ties with childhood friend Irene Redfield, who has married a black physician and is living in the upper circles of Harlem. Clare finds herself attracted to Irene's husband and he to her. Perceiving Clare as a threat to her own marriage and security, Irene wills Clare's disappearance, a wish that comes true when Clare falls, jumps, or is pushed from an open window at a Harlem apartment party just

as her husband appears to confront her with his discovery of her black roots.

Critics were divided in their reaction to *Passing.* Most found it less good than *Quicksand,* flawed by what a reviewer for the *New York Times Book Review* called "its sudden and utterly unconvincing close, a close that solves most of the problems . . . by simply sweeping them out of existence through the engineered death of Clare Kendry, the girl who is passing." Those critics who defended the novel averred that its strengths outweighed its weaknesses. Among these was Addison Gayle, Jr., who judged *Passing* "superior" to *Quicksand* "in terms of character development, organization, and fidelity to language." Similarly, *Saturday Review of Literature* contributor W. B. Seabrook lauded the novel as "classically pure in outline, single in theme and in impression, and . . . powerful in its catastrophe." It was, added Seabrook, "a work so fine, sensitive, and distinguished that it rises above race categories and becomes that rare object, a good novel." Furthermore, Robert Bone wrote in his *The Negro Novel in America* that "despite a false and shoddy denouement," *Passing* was "probably the best treatment of the subject in Negro fiction." Claudia Tate, contributor to *Black American Literature Forum,* concurred, describing *Passing* as "a skillfully executed and enduring work of art that did not receive the critical attention it deserved."

At the height of her popularity in 1930, Larsen was accused of plagiarism in a dispute over a short story published in *Forum* magazine. Although later exonerated, she seemed stifled by the accusation and the scandal. At the same time she experienced marital problems that led to a crudely sensationalized 1933 divorce from her physicist husband. Consequently, during the next several years Larsen gradually withdrew from her circle of literary friends on the lower east side of New York City until she broke all ties with them. She spent the last twenty years of her life working as a nurse in Manhattan hospitals.

Larsen's work is now generally viewed both as a reflection of a black world now past and as a delineation of a particular female perspective that has endured. Larsen's two novels, according to Washington, reveal a writer "who is legally black but internally identifies with both blacks and whites, who is supposed to be content as a member of the black elite, but feels suffocated by its narrowness, who is emotionally rooted in the black experience and yet wants to live in the whole world."

Several critics expressed regret that Larsen's literary career was so brief. Among them were Washington, who averred that Larsen's "perceptive inquiries speak clearly to the predicament of the middle-class black woman of our generation," and Davis, who called Larsen "a sensitive writer, with great skill in narration." Similarly, George Kent, writing in *Blackness and the Adventure of Western Culture,* mused, "Certainly one regrets that she did not write more novels and senses that she had a complexity of awareness that might have produced great works."

BIOGRAPHICAL/CRITICAL SOURCES:

BOOKS

Bone, Robert, *The Negro Novel in America,* revised edition, Yale University Press, 1965.
Bontemps, Arna, editor, *The Harlem Renaissance Remembered,* Dodd, 1972.

Brown, Sterling, *The Negro in American Fiction*, Atheneum, 1965.

Contemporary Literary Criticism, Volume 37, Gale, 1986.

Davis, Arthur P., *From the Dark Tower: Afro-American Writers, 1900 to 1960*, Howard University Press, 1974.

Dictionary of Literary Biography, Volume 51: *Afro-American Writers From the Harlem Renaissance to 1940*, Gale, 1987.

Gayle, Addison, Jr., *The Way of the New World: The Black Novel in America*, Anchor Press, 1975.

Kent, George, *Blackness and the Adventure of Western Culture*, Third World Press, 1972.

Lewis, David Levering, *When Harlem Was in Vogue*, Knopf, 1981.

Perry, Margaret, *Silence to the Drums: A Survey of the Literature of the Harlem Renaissance*, Greenwood Press, 1976.

Singh, Amritjii, *The Novels of the Harlem Renaissance: Twelve Black Writers, 1923-1933*, Pennsylvania State University, 1976.

PERIODICALS

American Literature, December, 1986.
Black American Literature Forum, winter, 1980.
Bookman, June, 1929.
CLA Journal, March, 1973, December, 1974.
Crisis, June, 1928.
Ms., December, 1980.
New York Herald Tribune Books, May 13, 1928, April 28, 1929.
New York Times Book Review, April 8, 1928, April 28, 1929.
Opportunity, August, 1929.
Resources for American Literary Study, fall, 1978.
Saturday Review of Literature, May 19, 1928, May 18, 1929.
Voice Literary Supplement, March, 1987.
Women's Review of Books, October, 1986.

—*Sketch by Joanne M. Peters*

*   *   *

LAYE, Camara   1928-1980

PERSONAL: Family name, Kamara; personal name, Laye; born January 1, 1928, in Kouroussa, French Guinea (now Guinea), West Africa; died February 4, 1980, in Senegal; son of Kamara Komady (a goldsmith) and Daman Sadan; married; wife's name, Marie; children: four. *Education:* Attended Central School of Automobile Engineering, Ecole Ampere, Conservatoire des Arts et Metiers, and Technical College for Aeronautics and Automobile Construction, all near Paris, France.

CAREER: Worked in a market and at various other jobs in Paris, France, before becoming a motor mechanic for Simca Corp. in a Paris suburb, c. 1953; served as attache at ministry of youth in Paris; returned to Guinea, 1956; worked as engineer for the French colonial regime in Guinea, 1956-58; Government of Guinea, Conakry, diplomat in Liberia, Ghana, and other African countries, beginning 1958; became director of Centre de Recherche et d'Etudes in Conakry; self-exiled from Guinea, 1966; lived for a time in the Ivory Coast; research fellow in Islamic Studies at Dakar University, Senegal, c. 1971; associated with the Institut Francais d'Afrique Noire in Dakar; became a university teacher in Senegal.

AWARDS, HONORS: Prix Charles Veillon, 1954, for *L'Enfant noir.*

WRITINGS:

L'Enfant noir (autobiography), Plon, 1953, translation by James Kirkup, Ernest Jones, and Elaine Gottlieb published as *The Dark Child*, Noonday Press, 1954 (published in England as *The African Child*, Collins, 1959).

Le Regard du roi (novel), Plon, 1954, translation by Kirkup published as *The Radiance of the King*, Collins, 1956, Collier, 1971.

Dramouss (novel), Plon, 1966, translation by Kirkup published as *A Dream of Africa*, Collins, 1968, Collier, 1971.

Le Maitre de la parole: Kuoma Lafolo Kuoma, Plon, 1978, translation by Kirkup published as *The Guardian of the Word*, Random House, 1984.

Contributor of articles and short stories to *African Arts, Black Orpheus, Presence Africaine,* and *Paris-Dakar.*

SIDELIGHTS: Although the author of only four books, Camara Laye was "regarded by many critics of African literature as the continent's major Francophone novelist," according to Charles R. Larson in the *Times Literary Supplement.* Laye's autobiographical book *The Dark Child*, originally published as *L'Enfant noir*, was of historical importance in the development of modern West African literature. It is "the work that can with justice be regarded as having brought French African narrative prose finally into its own," as Abiola Irele explained in *The African Experience in Literature and Ideology.*

Born in Guinea and raised a Moslem in that nation's countryside, Laye first encountered the outside world when he left his family's village to attend high school in Conakry, the capitol of Guinea. In Laye's native village his father, because of his work as a goldsmith, was widely assumed to possess magical powers. Other ancient African superstitions were also commonly held. But in Conakry, society was modern; twentieth century technology was everywhere. The contrast between the two societies startled Laye and made his life in the capital difficult.

But when, after graduating from high school, Laye accepted a scholarship to study engineering in Paris, he found the differences between African and European cultures to be overwhelming. To ease the tension and loneliness of his student life, Laye began to write down remembrances of his childhood in the Guinean countryside. These writings became his first book, *The Dark Child*, published in 1953. Tracing Laye's development from his tribal childhood, through his schooling in Guinea's capital, to his college life in Paris, *The Dark Child* poses questions about the preservation of traditional ways of life in the face of technological progress. As Irele noted in an article for *West Africa*, Laye's autobiography presented "an image of a coherence and dignity which went with social arrangements and human intercourse in the self-contained African universe of his childhood."

Some black critics of the time faulted Laye for not speaking out against colonialism. They saw his concern with traditional African society as an irrelevancy in an age of struggle for African independence. But Gerald Moore pointed out in *Twelve African Writers* that the world of Laye's childhood was largely untouched by colonialism. "Though conquered and administered by France," Moore wrote, "a city like [Laye's native village] was complex and self-sufficient enough to go very much on its own immemorial way. Its people... were not constantly obsessed with the alien presence of Europe in their midst." In contrast to this view, Irele believed that because *The Dark Child* celebrated the traditional African ways of life, it was ''in fact a form of denial of the assumptions and explicit ideological outgrowth of the French colonial enterprise.''

Whatever the final judgement regarding the book's stance on colonialism, *The Dark Child* has been widely praised for the quiet restraint of its prose. Moore explained that *The Dark Child* ''is a unique book in many ways, written with a singular and gentle sincerity, yet with very conscious artistic skill. Laye does not proclaim his negritude or announce the coming dawn; he records what his childhood was, what was the quality and the depth of the life from which he sprang.'' In her study *The Writings of Camara Laye*, Adele King called *The Dark Child* ''a carefully controlled story . . . presented with economy and restraint. . . . A particular moment in Laye's life and in the history of Africa has been transformed into a minor classic, in which the autobiographical form has been raised to the level of art.'' The book, Eric Sellin noted in *World Literature Today*, won Laye ''instant acclaim and lasting respect as a limpid stylist.''

The book's success lifted Laye from the poverty of his student life and enabled him to devote his full time to writing. A year of intensive effort resulted in his second book, the 1954 novel *The Radiance of the King*, originally published as *Le Regard du roi*. The story takes a white European named Clarence into the African countryside where he is forced to adapt to the traditional culture to survive. He has no means to earn a living unless he can find his way to the king's court and gain a position there. His search for the king forms the basis of the plot. ''Clarence's search for the king with whom he hopes to hold an audience,'' Jeannette Macauley wrote in *Modern Black Novelists: A Collection of Critical Essays*, ''becomes an obsession. It's the mirage which lures him on through dark forests with people he doesn't feel anything for, with people who do not understand him.''

''Attempts have been made,'' Neil McEwan reported in his *Africa and the Novel*, ''to prove Kafka's 'influence' on the novel: 'an African Kafka' can be praise from some European critics, disparagement from some Africans.'' But McEwan believed that *The Radiance of the King* ultimately suggests ''innumerable European writers'' and proposed that ''symbolist, allegorical, mythic, archetypal, psychological, and comparative-cultural studies seem called for; indeed there are passages . . . in which one suspects that the author has deliberately provoked and mystified critical attention. . . . It mocks analysis.''

Several critics found a religious symbolism in the novel, with David Cook in *Perspectives on African Literature* noting that ''the book is, of course, cast in the form of a quest—a spiritual quest; though there is nothing pompous, ponderous or moralistic about it.'' Likewise, Janheinz Jahn in *Introduction to African Literature: An Anthology of Critical Writings from ''Black Orpheus,''* explained that *The Radiance of the King* ''is usually considered as an ingenious allegory about man's search for God. But I think that the book cannot be seen in this sense only; it is ambivalent, even multivalent.''

Because of the ambiguous nature of Clarence's quest, the novel is not restricted to a single interpretation. As Larson stated in *The Emergence of African Fiction*, ''Clarence, who is archetypal of Western man in particular, is symbolic of everyman and his difficulties in adjusting not only to a different culture, but to life itself.'' King explained that ''the novel deals with the theme of any man trying to adjust to a strange society, of every man's homelessness in the world. . . . Making this ordinary European a symbol for Everyman is a way of countering

'black racism,' a way of showing that the essential human experiences go beyond colour.''

Critical regard for *The Radiance of the King* has been very favorable, with some commentators placing it among the very best of contemporary African literature. The book's ''clever reversals, dreamlike evocations, surreal efforts and implementation in prose of techniques proper to film . . . ,'' Sellin remarked, ''have caused some admirers to deem it the finest African novel.'' Larson, writing in the *Times Literary Supplement*, called the novel Laye's ''masterpiece'' and explained that it ''has long been hailed as the great African novel.''

Laye's third book resulted in his forced exile from his native Guinea in 1966. *A Dream of Africa*, originally published as *Dramouss*, commented openly on the dictatorial policies of Guinean leader Sekou Toure, who forced Laye into fleeing the country with his family. He was to live in neighboring Senegal, under the protection of Senegal's president Leopold Senghor, for the remainder of his life.

The novel begins with the narrator, Fatoman, returning to Guinea from Paris, where he has been living in exile for six years. Although he is happy to be back in his homeland again, he soon discovers that his country has serious problems. The independence which it will soon be granted by France is accompanied by political violence and murder. Fatoman warns his people that this will only lead to a new, dictatorial government. ''Someone,'' Fatoman proclaims, ''must say that though colonialism . . . was an evil thing for our country, the regime you are now introducing will be a catastrophe whose evil consequences will be felt for decades. Someone must speak out and say that a regime built on spilt blood through the activities of indendiaries of huts and houses is nothing but a regime of anarchy and dictatorship, a regime based on violence.''

In 1970, during a visit back to Guinea to see her ailing mother, Laye's wife was arrested and imprisoned as an enemy of the state. Because he feared for her safety, Laye was to publish no more overtly political work. His next book did not appear until 1978 when, after teaching in Senegal for many years, he completed *The Guardian of the Word*, originally published as *Le Maitre de la parole: Kuoma Lafolo Kuoma*. A marked departure from his earlier works, *The Guardian of the Word* is an epic novel set in thirteenth century West Africa and following the life of the ''first Emperor of the ancient Malian empire,'' as Larson explained in the *Times Literary Supplement*. The novel is based on an oral account of the period popular among Guinean storytellers, or griots; Laye first heard the story from Babu Conde, one of the best known of Guinea's griots. Because the novel focuses in part on the conduct of Mali's first emperor and the standards of behavior which he set, it indirectly comments on the proper conduct of all governments, something Laye could not afford to do openly.

The Guardian of the Word, Alan Cheuse of the *Los Angeles Times Book Review* stated, is ''one of those books that transmit from one generation to the next elemental visions on which society is founded—on the laws and customs and manners by which it remains stable.'' In doing so, the novel recreates a historical period in full detail. ''There are fascinating passages,'' Larson noted in the *Times Literary Supplement*, ''devoted to almost all of the important stages of traditional life.'' Martin Tucker of the *New York Times Book Review* argued that in *The Guardian of the Word*, African history and culture is blended with a European literary sensibility. ''Although Laye's last work is filled with surrealistic shades and European psychological insight,'' he wrote, ''it is invigorated by the traditional African vision of the spiritual and historic.''

All of Laye's books are written according to predominantly European literary modes, yet they paradoxically affirm traditional African life and culture. He succeeds in combining these discordant elements into a satisfying whole which expresses his individual vision. Speaking of *The Radiance of the King* in particular, McEwan explained that ''Laye is an artist in whom sources are entirely absorbed and the question whether this novel is French literature or African seems pointless; it is Camara Laye's.'' King noted that Laye transcended his cultural background, concluding that his work ''belongs within the tradition of classic world literature, describing a personal and cultural dilemma in accents that speak to all mankind.''

BIOGRAPHICAL/CRITICAL SOURCES:

BOOKS

Beier, Ulli, editor, *Introduction to African Literature: An Anthology of Critical Writings from ''Black Orpheus,''* Northwestern University Press, 1967.
Contemporary Literary Criticism, Gale, Volume 4, 1975, Volume 38, 1986.
Cooke, Michael G., editor, *Modern Black Novelists: A Collection of Critical Essays*, Prentice-Hall, 1971.
Heywood, Christopher, editor, *Perspectives on African Literature*, Africana Publishing, 1971.
Irele, Abiola, *The African Experience in Literature and Ideology*, Heinemann, 1981.
King, Adele, *The Writings of Camara Laye*, Heinemann Educational Books, 1980.
Larson, Charles R., *The Emergence of African Fiction*, Indiana University Press, 1971.
Laye, Camara, *The Dark Child*, Noonday Press, 1954.
Laye, Camara, *A Dream of Africa*, Collier, 1971.
McEwan, Neil, *Africa and the Novel*, Humanities Press, 1983.
Moore, Gerald, *Twelve African Writers*, Indiana University Press, 1980.

PERIODICALS

African Literature Today, January, 1969.
Black Orpheus, November, 1959.
Books Abroad, spring, 1969, spring, 1971.
Los Angeles Times Book Review, September 2, 1984.
New York Times, September 16, 1969.
New York Times Book Review, June 24, 1984.
Observer Review, February 4, 1968.
Times Literary Supplement, May 4, 1967, July 17, 1981.
West Africa, April 7, 1980.
World Literature Today, summer, 1980.

OBITUARIES:

PERIODICALS

AB Bookman's Weekly, May 5, 1980.
Publishers Weekly, March 28, 1980.

—Sketch by Thomas Wiloch

*   *   *

LEE, Andrea   1953-

PERSONAL: Born in 1953 in Philadelphia, Pa.; married. *Education:* Received M.A. from Harvard University.

ADDRESSES—Office: New Yorker, 25 West 43rd St., New York, N.Y. 10036.

CAREER: Writer. Staff writer for *New Yorker* magazine in New York, N.Y.

AWARDS, HONORS: Nomination for American Book Award for general nonfiction, 1981, for *Russian Journal;* Jean Stein Award from American Academy and Institute of Arts and Letters, 1984.

WRITINGS:

Russian Journal (nonfiction), Random House, 1981.
Sarah Phillips (novel), Random House, 1984.

Contributor to periodicals, including *New Yorker, New York Times,* and *Vogue.*

SIDELIGHTS: Andrea Lee has distinguished herself as a noteworthy journalist and novelist. In her nonfiction work, *Russian Journal*, she provides an insightful perspective on contemporary Soviet life, and in her novel, *Sarah Phillips*, she recounts the reckless past of a middle-class black woman. These writings, while embracing different themes, have earned Lee praise as a keen observer and a consummate technician, one whose probing insights are inevitably rendered with concision and grace. As Susan Richards Shreve noted in the *New York Times Book Review*, ''Andrea Lee's authority as a writer comes of an unstinting honesty and a style at once simple and yet luminous.''

Lee's first book, *Russian Journal*, derives from a diary she kept in 1978 while in the Soviet Union, where her husband was studying for ten months on a fellowship. Relying on public transportation and a rudimentary grasp of the Russian language, Lee visited a wide variety of Soviet places, including public baths, college campuses, farmers' markets, and nightclubs. She met bureaucrats, dissidents, and even contraband sellers; encountered many cynics and youthful materialists; observed a disturbing number of public drunks; and became acquainted with some of the country's more unsettling aspects, notably surveillance. In her journal Lee wrote that, due to their circumstances, she and her husband ''got a view of life in Moscow and Leningrad that was very different from that of the diplomats and journalists we knew.''

Following the 1981 publication of *Russian Journal*, critics cited the book as a refreshing, if narrow, perspective on Soviet life. Susan Jacoby, writing in the *New York Times Book Review*, called Lee's book ''a subtly crafted reflection of both the bleak and golden shadings of Russian life'' and added: ''The subject matter of this journal is highly idiosyncratic. . . . What Miss Lee offers are the people, places and experiences that touched her most deeply.'' Like Jacoby, *Washington Post Book World* reviewer Peter Osnos cited the book's worth for ''conveying a feeling of place and atmosphere'' and declared: ''Lee writes very well. There is a warmth and freshness about her style that makes reading [*Russian Journal*] effortless.'' Osnos was especially impressed with Lee's depiction of the Soviet people, particularly its younger citizens. ''What is best about the book—what distinguishes it from other books about the Soviet Union published in recent years—is her accounts of friendships with young people,'' he contended. Similarly, *Newsweek*'s Walter Clemons praised Lee's ''unassuming delicacy and exactness'' asserting that ''her most winning quality is her capacity for friendship.'' Michael Irwin, who discussed *Russian Journal* in the *London Review of Books*, also found Lee an engaging reporter. He praised her ''astuteness'' and called *Russian Journal* ''a considerable exercise in observation, empathy and personal and literary tact.''

Lee's refusal to write about being a black person in the Soviet Union caused a few reservations among critics reviewing *Russian Journal*. Susan Jacoby called this omission "regrettable" and contended that Lee's race "must have affected [her Russian friends'] perceptions (and Miss Lee's) in some way." Jacoby added, "Miss Lee's responses would surely have been as interesting as the rest of her observations, and I wish she had included them." Peter Osnos also noted Lee's reluctance to write about race. He described the omission as "slightly awkward" and observed: "Apparently, she feels that her blackness has nothing to do with her time in the Soviet Union. That is her business. But she never even says as much."

As if responding to charges that she avoided racial subjects, Lee followed *Russian Journal* with *Sarah Phillips*, an episodic novel explicitly concerned with a contemporary black woman. The work's title character is introduced as a woman grown disgusted with her boorish, racist acquaintances—and lovers—in Paris, where she has been living in self-exile. At the end of the first chapter Sarah decides to leave Paris, and in the ensuing sections she recalls events—principally from childhood and adolescence—contributing to her present circumstances. Unlike most black characters in American fiction, Sarah is an assimilated elitist whose background is middle class, and her goal is to scandalize her bourgeois parents. She even accepts tokenism when she becomes the first black student at an exclusive girls' school. Her father is a minister involved in the civil rights movement, an involvement that actually leads to her embarrassment when he is briefly imprisoned for civil disobedience. Bored with America, Sarah leaves the country after her father's death and her graduation from college. She settles in Paris, where she indulges in various interracial sexual shenanigans, including a *menage-a-quatre*. By novel's end, however, Sarah realizes the emptiness of her assimilation into white society—both European and American—and reaches a greater understanding of herself and her heritage.

With *Sarah Phillips* Lee earned further literary acclaim. In *Saturday Review*, Bruce Van Wyngarden described the novel as a "coming-of-age remembrance in which detail and insight are delightfully, and sometimes poignantly, blended." He also deemed it "an engaging and promising" first novel. Likewise, *Best Sellers* reviewer Francis Goskowski called *Sarah Phillips* an "engaging, witty" work and asserted that with it Lee emerged as a "major novelistic talent." Patricia Vigderam was one of several critics who noted the novel's breakthrough perspective on race, particularly the characterization of Sarah as an assimilated black. Critiquing the work for the *Boston Review*, Vigderman conceded that "this novel does not fit easily into the Afro-American tradition, and may even meet with some disapproval," but she nonetheless considered it "a very gracefully written book about black identity."

With *Russian Journal* and *Sarah Phillips* Lee has gained recognition as a talented writer of immense promise, and her forthcoming works are greatly anticipated. "Without a doubt," stated Francis Goskowski, "Ms. Lee will be heard from again, and she will command our attention."

BIOGRAPHICAL/CRITICAL SOURCES:

BOOKS

Contemporary Literary Criticism, Volume 36, Gale, 1986.

PERIODICALS

Best Sellers, February, 1985.

Boston Review, February, 1985.
Economist, May 29, 1982.
London Review of Books, October 6, 1982.
National Review, September 3, 1982.
New Leader, December 10, 1984.
New Republic, February 24, 1982, November 19, 1984.
Newsweek, October 19, 1981.
New York Review of Books, November 5, 1981.
New York Times, December 6, 1984.
New York Times Book Review, October 25, 1981, November 18, 1984.
People, November 23, 1981.
Spectator, June 12, 1982.
Times Literary Supplement, August 13, 1982, April 5, 1985.
Washington Post Book World, October 25, 1981.

—*Sketch by Les Stone*

*   *   *

LEE, Don L.
See MADHUBUTI, Haki R.

*   *   *

LEE, George W(ashington)   1894-1976

PERSONAL: Born January 4, 1894, in Indianola, Miss.; died August 1, 1976; son of George (a minister) and Hattie Lee. *Education:* Alcorn Agricultural and Mechanical College (now Alcorn State University), B.S. *Politics:* Republican.

CAREER: Worked odd jobs as an adolescent, including cotton planter and picker, grocery boy, houseboy, dray driver, and bellhop; vice-president of the Mississippi Life Insurance Co., 1922-24; affiliated with the Atlanta Life Insurance Co., beginning as district manager, 1927-76. Edited *Vision*, a journal for the Atlanta Life Insurance Co. Active in the Republican party. *Military service:* U.S. Army, 1917-19, served in France; became lieutenant.

MEMBER: National Association for the Advancement of Colored People, National Insurance Association, American Legion, Urban League, West Tennessee Civic and Political League, Omega Psi Phi, Elks.

WRITINGS:

Beale Street: Where the Blues Began (history), R. O. Ballou, 1934.
River George (novel), Macaulay, 1937, AMS Press, 1975.
Beale Street Sundown (short stories; includes "Beale Street Anyhow," "A Beale Street Treasure Hunt," "The First Blues Singer," "King of the Rousters," "She Made a Preacher Lay His Bible Down," "Passing," and "The Beale Street Blues I'm Singing"), House of Field, 1942.

Contributor of short stories and articles to periodicals, including *Negro Digest*, *World's Digest*, *Southern Literary Messenger*, *Vision*, *Tri-State Defender*, *Memphis Press Scimitar*, and *Memphis World*.

SIDELIGHTS: George W. Lee's writings immortalized the Beale Street neighborhood of Memphis, Tennessee. As a leader in business and in his community, Lee was concerned with promoting pride in black business and decided in the early 1930s to write a factual book extolling black success in the Beale Street area. The result, 1934's *Beale Street: Where the Blues Began*, "gained wide critical acclaim," according to Edward D. Clark in *Dictionary of Literary Biography*. In spite of the fact that the book was extremely profitable for him due to its appeal to both black and white readers, Lee might have ended his career as an author to concentrate on the insurance business and politics if he had not been piqued by comments that it was *Beale Street*'s subject matter and not Lee's own writing ability that made it so popular. To put doubts concerning his literary ability to rest, Lee produced a novel, *River George*, in 1937. Later, he crowned his achievements with the short story collection *Beale Street Sundown*.

Beale Street: Where the Blues Began is divided into chapters about black individuals who contributed to the history of the neighborhood. These include Robert R. Church, Sr., who after the Civil War built up a multimillion dollar estate and helped turn Beale Street into a commercial center for the black community, and other "bankers, ministers, lawyers, realtors, doctors, businesswomen, and insurance executives, all people Lee knew," reported Clark. Lee described the yellow fever epidemic of 1878 and contrasted the numerous heroic blacks who stayed in Memphis to help save the city with the many whites who escaped in fear of the disease; he also discussed Julia A. Hooks, who started an integrated music school that produced many gifted students, and composer W. C. Handy, whom he credits with "distinguished orchestral work." Though Lee's purpose in *Beale Street* was to instill pride in black accomplishment, he balanced the work by revealing the negative aspects of the community. Pimps, prostitutes, drug dealers, and the destitute who sift through garbage piles for food share pages with Lee's objects of admiration.

Lee also intended his *River George* to promote black pride. Taking the man he wrote about in *Beale Street*'s third chapter and fictionalizing his past by adding some of his own experiences to it, Lee built a novel around the character of Aaron George. George goes to Lee's alma mater, Alcorn Agricultural and Mechanical College, in order to become a lawyer, but his education is interrupted by the death of his father. He returns home and becomes a sharecropper on Beaver Dam Plantation to help support his mother. Falling in love with a woman, Ada Green, who is also involved with the white postmaster, Fred Smith, George eventually has to leave the plantation because of a confrontation with Smith over the injustices suffered by the tenant farmers; this confrontation ends in Smith's death by his own gun. George runs to Memphis for safety and takes up lodgings with a Beale Street madame. Like the author, he enters the U.S. Army and becomes a lieutenant serving in Europe. When he returns to the United States, he tries to contact his mother and Ada, but he runs into trouble in Vicksburg, Mississippi from whites who resent his officer's uniform. Temporarily turned aside, George becomes a deckhand on the Mississippi river and wins fame for his fighting prowess. Eventually, however, he returns to the plantation only to be lynched for the postmaster's murder upon his arrival.

Though *River George* ends with George's death, its focus is on his struggles to succeed in a world of prejudice. By the time Lee published the short story collection *Beale Street Sundown*, however, his involvement with the Republican party had led him to place less importance on inspiring blacks toward achievement of their goals. Thus, in Clark's opinion, the emphasis of *Sundown* is on folklore. Lack of didactic purpose apparently gave Lee more artistic freedom; Clark declared that *Sundown* "is evidence of tremendous literary growth." The volume's stories include "Beale Street Anyhow," which concerns uproar over a possible name change to Beale Avenue, and "A Beale Street Treasure Hunt," involving an old man's plot to make money from a fraudulent treasure hunt. Also in

Sundown are "She Made a Preacher Lay His Bible Down," about an ex-prostitute who joins a church choir to win the love of a minister, and "Passing," about a black woman passing for white in a bordello.

BIOGRAPHICAL/CRITICAL SOURCES:

BOOKS

Dictionary of Literary Biography, Volume 51: *Afro-American Writers From the Harlem Renaissance to 1940*, Gale, 1987.
Lee, George W., *Beale Street: Where the Blues Began*, R. O. Ballou, 1934.

*   *   *

LEE, Shelton Jackson   1957(?)-
(Spike Lee)

PERSONAL: Born c. 1957 in Atlanta, Ga.; son of William (a musician and composer) and Jacqueline (a teacher; maiden name, Shelton) Lee. *Education:* Morehouse College, B.A., 1979; graduate study at New York University, 1982.

ADDRESSES: Home—Brooklyn, N.Y. *Office*—Forty Acres and a Mule Filmworks, 124 DeKalb Ave., Brooklyn, N.Y. 11217.

CAREER: Screenwriter and director of motion pictures and music videos.

AWARDS, HONORS: Student director's award from Academy of Motion Picture Arts and Sciences, 1982, for "Joe's Bed-Stuy Barber Shop: We Cut Heads"; Prix de Jeunesse from Cannes Film Festival, 1986, for "She's Gotta Have It."

WRITINGS:

UNDER NAME SPIKE LEE

(And director) "She's Gotta Have It" (screenplay), Island, 1986.
Spike Lee's Gotta Have It: Inside Guerilla Filmmaking (includes interviews and a journal), foreword by Nelson George, photographs by brother, David Lee, Simon & Schuster, 1987.
(And director) "School Daze" (screenplay), Columbia, 1988.
(With Lisa Jones) *Uplift the Race: The Construction of School Daze*, Simon & Schuster, 1988.

Also writer and director of short films, including "The Answer," 1980, and "Joe's Bed-Stuy Barbershop: We Cut Heads," 1982. Contributor of short films to "Saturday Night Live" and to Music Television (MTV) network.

WORK IN PROGRESS: Writing and directing the motion picture "Do the Right Thing," release by Universal expected in 1989.

SIDELIGHTS: Spike Lee has become one of the film world's most promising comedic talents to appear in the late 1980s, and he is among the few commercial filmmakers of his generation to address issues and themes specific to the black community. As writer and director of the critically and commercially successful "She's Gotta Have It" and the controversial "School Daze," Lee has exploited such subjects as sexism and elitism for their comedic worth while simultaneously exploring their ramifications and manifestations within black society. "My role in film, for the most part, is as an instigator," he has claimed. But that instigation, he believes, must extend beyond the black community and entertain and enrich a broader spectrum. "It has been my contention all along that an all-black film directed by a black person can still be universal, just as . . . in the other arts," he told the *New York Times*. "I mean, nobody stopped coming to see Duke Ellington's music because he had an all-black band."

Lee began his filmmaking career while a graduate student at New York University, where he wrote and directed the short film "Joe's Bed-Stuy Barbershop: We Cut Heads." That film, which concerned a Brooklyn barbershop fronting a gambling operation, fared well at a 1983 New Directors series in New York City and was subsequently featured at international film festivals. On the strength of "Joe's Bed-Stuy Barbershop" Lee met representatives of various theatrical agencies, but those representatives, as Lee later observed in the *New York Times*, "were unable to generate me any work, not even an after-school special." For Lee, the failure of the agencies confirmed his suspicion that he could only sustain a film career by creating his own projects: "I would have to go out alone and do it alone, not rely on anyone else."

In mid-1984 Lee tried to begin a film about bicycle messengers, and he eventually obtained grants from both the American Film Institute and the New York State Council on the Arts. But after eight weeks of pre-production Lee dissolved the project, claiming to *Film Comment* that "it just never really came together with all the money and stuff." Lee and his collaborators—including cinematographer Ernest Dickerson and production supervisor Monty Ross, both former classmates—then decided to film "She's Gotta Have It," a comedy he wrote about a woman and her three lovers. The American Film Institute consequently withdrew their $20,000 grant, leaving Lee with only $18,000 from the New York arts council. Still he persevered, and while Ross tirelessly solicited additional funds, Lee assembled a small cast and crew, including family members, and directed the entire work in only twelve days.

With "She's Gotta Have It," Lee managed to create an entertaining and provocative work despite formidable limitations of time and money. The film's protagonist is Nola Darling, a fun-loving, sensitive artist with a seemingly insatiable sexual appetite. Consequently, she has three lovers, and each one perceives her differently: Jamie Overstreet is an earnest romantic who sees Nola as his future wife; Greer Childs is a narcissistic pseudo-intellectual for whom Nola is an object to be shaped and molded to his liking; and Mars Blackmon (played by Lee) is a fast-talking, diminutive joker who considers the sex-addict Nola a "freak." Much of the humor in "She's Gotta Have It" derives from the various suitors' rivalries and their efforts to convince Nola to reject the others. Particularly funny are Mars's deadpan remarks and his monotonous plea, "Please baby please baby please baby baby baby please," when he begs for Nola's company. Nola's Thanksgiving dinner for all three lovers also provides opportunity for humor as the men berate each other. Greer calls Mars a "chain snatcher," and Mars replies that Greer is a "pseudo black man" and, even worse, a fan of the predominantly white Boston Celtics basketball team. When Jamie intercedes to diffuse hostilities, Greer asks, "What are you? Henry Kissinger?" Eventually, Nola senses that each of her lovers is trying to dominate her, whereupon she leaves all of them. "It's about control," she explains. "My body. My mind. Whose gonna own it, them or me?"

Upon release in 1986, "She's Gotta Have It" received substantial praise from critics. *Washington Post* reviewer Paul Attanasio deemed it an "impressive first feature" and added

that it was "discursive, jazzy, vibrant with sex and funny as heck." Similarly, Michael Wilmington wrote in the *Los Angeles Times* that Lee's film was "a joyfully idiosyncratic little jazz-burst of a film, full of sensuous melody, witty chops and hot licks." Wilmington was particularly impressed with the film's unstereotypic perspective and characters, declaring: "'She's Gotta Have It' gives you as non-standard a peek at black American life as you'll get: engaging, seductive and happily off-kilter. There's no overlay of sentiment or cynicism here. These characters aren't the radiant winners or sad victims you usually see, and there's not a normal citizen . . . in the bunch." Furthermore, Wilmington praised Lee as a refreshing figure in American film comedy and deemed him "an impudent original with a great eye and a flair for humor and eroticism."

"She's Gotta Have It," with its depiction of Nola as forthright and independent, also earned Lee recognition as a feminist filmmaker. Jeffrey Yorke, for instance, wrote in the *Washington Post* that Lee "managed to write a feminist story through a man's eye." Lee conceded to a *New York Times* writer that the opportunity to provide a woman's perspective on promiscuity proved his major motivation in making the film: "I decided it would be a good idea to do a film about a young black woman who's really leading her life like a man, in control, with three men dangling at her fingertips." And to *Film Comment* writer Marlaine Glicksman he confided that his film was also a response to the film world's stereotype of black men as crude and brutal. He charged the film industry with conspiring to portray black men as "one-dimensional animals," and asserted that his male characters were "full-bodied" and thus a rare exception to the stereotype.

As an independently produced, low-budget film, "She's Gotta Have It" proved a surprising success with the public as well as with critics, earning more than two million dollars at American box offices within weeks of its release—and more than seven million dollars by 1987. Lee, who seemed unsurprised by the public response to "She's Gotta Have It," credited the film's success to its unique approach and its avoidance of stereotypes. "I think that there are a lot of things in 'She's Gotta Have It' we've never seen before," he told a writer for the *Chicago Tribune*, adding that his movie was a "refreshing breath of air." And in the *New York Times* Lee noted that his film served as an indication that realistic films about blacks could be commercially viable. "The whole point is that you can take an unknown, all-black cast and put them in a story that comes from a black experience, and all kinds of people will come to see it if it's a good film," he observed. "I wish Hollywood would get that message."

The industry apparently understood, for soon after the success of "She's Gotta Have It" Lee secured approximately six million dollars from Columbia Pictures to film "School Daze," a musical comedy about rival factions at a black college. Making that film, however, proved somewhat trying despite its budget. He commenced filming in 1987 at Morehouse College, where he studied as an undergraduate, but university officials abruptly ceased cooperation, fearing adverse publicity from the film's uncompromising perspective and its inclusion of profanity. "They booted us out in the middle of shooting there," Lee declared. "The president of the school was upset because he heard we use [obscenity] in the film—and if parents heard that word they wouldn't let their sons be Morehouse men." Lee contended that his artistic intentions were legitimate and that he was not besmirching the school's integrity. "I loved going to that school," he later told an audience following a preview. "But you can still criticize the things that aren't right, can't you?"

Lee found much to criticize about black school life, but in "School Daze" he rendered that criticism within a comedic context. Set during homecoming weekend, "School Daze" concerns the rivalry between two major campus factions: the dark-skinned Jigaboos and the politically accomodating, lighter-skinned Wannabees (as in "want to be white"), many of whom belong to the elite fraternity Gamma Phi Gamma. Among the leading Jigaboos is Dap, the key figure in a campus campaign to force university divestiture from racist South Africa. Dap's rival is Gamma Phi Gamma leader Julian, an arrogant Wannabee who loathes the Jigaboos and defends the university's business practices. Other campus factions include the Gamma Rays, a band of women Wannabees devoted to pursuing the ideal of white feminine beauty—some of them even dye their hair blonde and sport blue contact lenses; the student government, apparently comprised of one ineffectual peacemaker; and the faculty, which seems more interested in the school's failing football team than in the divestiture controversy. Still another group are the non-student blacks living in the community, and one of the film's most provocative scenes is an encounter between Dap, who fancies himself sincerely pro-black, and the non-students, who sneer at his artistic posturing and remind him that when he finishes school he will become one of them. Contrasts between these and other factions afford Lee ample opportunity to explore such themes as bigotry, elitism, and sexism, thus making "School Daze" an ambitious and provocative, as well as entertaining, work.

As with "She's Gotta Have It," much of the humor in "School Daze" derives from the antics of Lee's character. Here he plays Half Pint, a Gamma Phi Gamma hopeful preoccupied with losing his virginity. Like others aspiring to the Gamma Phi Gamma fraternity, Half Pint sports a shaved scalp and a scrawled letter G on his forehead. Although he is Dap's cousin, Half Pint is a Wannabee, and he consequently courts the influential Julian's favor. This results in a particularly funny episode in which Half Pint tirelessly tours the campus trying to procure a sexual partner for the arrogant fraternity leader. Ultimately, Lee's character complicates the otherwise clear division between the Jigaboos and the Wannabees, and his behavior and values serve to indicate the negative repercussions of such schisms.

After finishing "School Daze" away from Morehouse College, Lee clashed with his Columbia producers, whose plans for distribution and promotion he found objectionable. He accused Columbia of "ghettoizing" "School Days" by suggesting that its release day be postponed because "Action Jackson," a crime drama featuring black characters, would be opening the same day and also be drawing black audiences. Incensed, Lee claimed that his fairly challenging "School Daze" would hardly appeal to the same audience as "Action Jackson," and he charged Columbia with ignoring the diverse interests and tastes of the black public. Film studios perceive blacks as "some monolithic . . . group out there," he declared, adding: "I don't see any studio worrying about having a Woody Allen movie coming out the same week as a Chuck Norris movie. It's the same blind mentality."

Released in early 1988, "School Daze" was perceived by many critics as a thematically and stylistically daring venture. *Village Voice* writer J. Hoberman called Lee's film "a spectacle of abundance" and declared that it was "so pumped up, preening, and packed with stuff that it's almost muscle-bound." Similarly, Michael Wilmington wrote in the *Los Angeles Times* that the work was "packed with breezy musical numbers and a brawling gang of characters, streaming through the movie in continuous eruptions of overlapping dialogue and dizzying badinage." For Wilmington, the movie's range of wildly ambitious themes and characterizations somewhat compromised its continuity and resulted in both an unsettling narrative rhythm and some unresolved themes. But he added that even with its shortcomings Lee's second film proved accomplished and admirable. "'School Daze' tries too many targets to hit them all," Wilmington observed. "The important thing is that it hits its share, with a view of black college life that's impudent, juicy and fresh."

"School Daze" earned commendations from many critics, but it also brought Lee notoriety as a provocateur within the black community. Prominent blacks protested that Lee had produced an unfavorable depiction of blacks, and others, while conceding that he offered a valid perspective, nonetheless argued that his perception of black campus life was one best withheld from a white society. Lee, however, had anticipated such criticism. "I wasn't afraid," he told students at Howard University following a preview. "I knew it would make people squirm." He acknowledged that his depiction of sexism and elitism was troubling and unsettling, but he contended that it was nonetheless valid and even invigorating. "These things are terrible," he declared, "and I think by putting this stuff on film we can view it for what it is."

With "School Daze" Lee confirmed his status as an important, provocative new filmmaker. And though he seems unimpressed with much of his acclaim, he is confident of his talent and his continuing development as an artist. He told Stuart Mieher in the *New York Times,* "I'm a very good filmmaker. . . . I think I will be making films for the rest of my life. And I'm just going to get better."

AVOCATIONAL INTERESTS: Basketball.

BIOGRAPHICAL/CRITICAL SOURCES:

BOOKS

Lee, Spike, *Spike Lee's Gotta Have It: Inside Guerilla Film-making,* foreword by Nelson George, photographs by brother, David Lee, Simon & Schuster, 1987.
Lee, Spike and Lisa Jones, *Uplift the Race: The Construction of School Daze,* Simon & Schuster, 1988.

PERIODICALS

American Film, September, 1986.
Chicago Tribune, August 13, 1986, August 20, 1986, October 5, 1986, February 25, 1988, March 3, 1988.
Ebony, January, 1987.
Essence, September, 1986.
Film Comment, October, 1986.
Film Quarterly, winter, 1986-87.
Los Angeles Times, August 21, 1986, February 11, 1988, February 12, 1988.
Newsweek, September 8, 1986.
New York Times, March 27, 1983, August 8, 1986, August 10, 1986, September 7, 1986, November 14, 1986, August 9, 1987.
People, October 13, 1986.
Time, October 6, 1986.
Village Voice, February 16, 1988, March 22, 1988.

Washington Post, August 22, 1986, August 24, 1986, August 29, 1986, March 20, 1987, February 19, 1988.

—*Sketch by Les Stone*

*   *   *

LEE, Spike
  See LEE, Shelton Jackson

*   *   *

LESTER, Julius (Bernard) 1939-

PERSONAL: Born January 27, 1939, in St. Louis, Mo.; son of W. D. (a minister) and Julia (Smith) Lester; married Joan Steinau (a researcher), 1962 (divorced, 1970); married Alida Carolyn Fechner, March 21, 1979; children: (first marriage) Jody Simone, Malcolm Coltrane; (second marriage) Elena Milad (stepdaughter), David Julius. *Education:* Fisk University, B.A., 1960.

ADDRESSES: Office—University of Massachusetts—Amherst, Amherst, Mass. 01002.

CAREER: Professional musician and singer, recorded with Vanguard Records; Newport Folk Festival, Newport, R.I., director, 1966-68; WBAI-FM, New York City, producer and host of live radio show, 1968-75; University of Massachusetts—Amherst, professor of Afro-American studies, 1971—, professor of Near Eastern and Judaic Studies, 1982—, acting director and associate director of Institute for Advanced Studies in Humanities, 1982-84. Lecturer at New School for Social Research, New York City, 1968-70; writer-in-residence, Vanderbilt University, 1985. Host of live television show, "Free Time," WNET-TV, New York City, 1971-73.

AWARDS, HONORS: Distinguished Teacher's Award, 1983-84; Faculty Fellowship Award for Distinguished Research and Scholarship, 1985; National Professor of the Year Silver Medal Award, from Council for Advancement and Support of Education, 1985; Massachusetts State Professor of the Year and Gold Medal Award for National Professor of the Year, both from Council for Advancement and Support of Education, both 1986; chosen distinguished faculty lecturer, 1986-87; *To Be a Slave* was nominated for the Newberry Award; *The Long Journey Home: Stories From Black History* was a National Book Award finalist.

WRITINGS:

(With Pete Seeger) *The 12-String Guitar as Played by Leadbelly,* Oak, 1965.
Look Out Whitey! Black Power's Gon' Get Your Mama!, Dial, 1968.
To Be a Slave, Dial, 1969, reprinted, Scholastic, Inc., 1986.
Black Folktales, Baron, 1969.
Search for the New Land: History as Subjective Experience, Dial, 1969.
Revolutionary Notes, Baron, 1969.
(Editor) *The Seventh Son: The Thoughts and Writings of W. E. B. Du Bois,* two volumes, Random House, 1971.
(Compiler with Rae Pace Alexander) *Young and Black in America,* Random House, 1971.
The Long Journey Home: Stories from Black History, Dial, 1972, reprinted, Scholastic, Inc., 1988.
The Knee-High Man and Other Tales, Dial, 1972.
Two Love Stories, Dial, 1972.
(Editor) Stanley Couch, *Ain't No Ambulances for No Nigguhs Tonight* (poems), Baron, 1972.

Who I Am (poems), Dial, 1974.
All Is Well: An Autobiography, Morrow, 1976.
This Strange New Feeling, Dial, 1982.
Do Lord Remember Me (novel), Holt, 1984.
The Tales of Uncle Remus: The Adventures of Brer Rabbit, Dial, 1987.
More Tales of Uncle Remus: The Further Adventures of Brer Rabbit, His Friends, Enemies, and Others, Dial, 1988.
Lovesong: Becoming a Jew (autobiographical), Holt, 1988.

Contributor of essays and reviews to numerous magazines and newspapers, including *New York Times Book Review, New York Times, Nation, Katallagete, Democracy,* and *Village Voice.* Associate editor, *Sing Out,* 1964-70; contributing editor, *Broadside of New York,* 1964-70.

SIDELIGHTS: Julius Lester is "foremost among young black writers who produce their work from a position of historical strength," writes critic John A. Williams in the *New York Times Book Review.* Drawing on old documents and folktales, Lester fashions stories that proclaim the heritage of black Americans and "attempt to recreate the social life of the past," note Eric and Naomi Foner in the *New York Review of Books.* Though historically accurate, Lester's tales are more than simple reportage. Their purpose, as the Foners point out, is "not merely to impart historical information, but to teach moral and political lessons." Because he feels that the history of minority groups has been largely ignored, Lester intends to furnish his young readers with what he calls "a usable past" and with what the Foners call "a sense of history which will help shape their lives and politics."

Lester's characters fall into two categories: those drawn from Afro-American folklore and those drawn from black history. The former are imaginary creatures, or sometimes animals, such as *The Knee-High Man's* Mr. Bear and Mr. Rabbit; the latter are real people, "ordinary men and women who might appear only in . . . a neglected manuscript at the Library of Congress," according to William Loren Katz in the *Washington Post Book World.* Critics find that Lester uses both types of characters to reveal the black individual's struggle against slavery.

Black Folktales, Lester's first collection of folk stories, features larger-than-life heroes (including a cigar-smoking black God), shrewd animals, and cunning human beings. While some of the characters are taken from African legends and others from American slave tales, they all demonstrate that "black resistance to white oppression is as old as the confrontation between the two groups," says Williams. Most reviewers applaud Lester's view of Afro-American folklore and praise his storytelling skills, but a few object to what they perceive as the anti-white tone of the book. Zena Sutherland, writing in *Bulletin of the Center for Children's Books,* calls *Black Folktales* "a vehicle for hostility. . . . There is no story that concerns white people in which they are not pictured as venal or stupid or both."

Lester also deals with white oppression in his second collection of folktales, *The Knee-High Man and Other Tales.* Although these six animal stories are funny, *New York Times Book Review* critic Ethel Richards suggests that "powerfully important lessons ride the humor. In 'The Farmer and the Snake,' the lesson is that kindness will not change the nature of a thing—in this case, the nature of a poisonous snake to bite." A *Junior Bookshelf* reviewer points out that this story—as well as others in the book—reflects the relationship between owner and slave. While pursuing the same theme, Lester moves into the realm of nonfiction with *The Long Journey Home: Stories from Black History,* a documentary collection of slave narratives, and *To Be a Slave,* a collection of six stories based on historical fact. Both books showcase ordinary people in adverse circumstances and provide the reader with a look at what Lester calls "history from the bottom up." *Black Like Me* author John Howard Griffin, writing in the *New York Times Book Review,* commends Lester's approach, saying that the stories "help destroy the delusion that black men did not suffer as another man would in similar circumstances," and the Foners applaud the fact that "Lester does not feel it is necessary to make every black man and woman a super-hero." *New York Times Book Review* contributor Rosalind K. Goddard recommends Lester's writing as both lesson and entertainment: "These stories point the way for young blacks to find their roots, so important to the realization of their identities, as well as offer a stimulating and informative experience for all."

Lester's books have been translated into seven languages. His photographs of the 1960s civil rights movement have been exhibited at the Smithsonian Institution and are on permanent display at Howard University.

BIOGRAPHICAL/CRITICAL SOURCES:

BOOKS

Children's Literature Review, Volume 2, Gale, 1976.
Krim, Seymour, *You and Me,* Holt, 1972.
Lester, Julius, *All Is Well: An Autobiography,* Morrow, 1976.

PERIODICALS

Bulletin of the Center for Children's Books, February, 1970.
Junior Bookshelf, February, 1975.
Los Angeles Times Book Review, January 31, 1988.
Nation, June 22, 1970.
New York Review of Books, April 20, 1972.
New York Times Book Review, November 3, 1968, November 9, 1969, July 23, 1972, February 4, 1973, September 5, 1982, February 17, 1985.
Publishers Weekly, February 12, 1988.
Times Literary Supplement, April 3, 1987.
Washington Post, March 12, 1985.
Washington Post Book World, September 3, 1972, February 14, 1988.

*   *   *

LEWIS, Theophilus   1891-1974

PERSONAL: Born March 4, 1891, in Baltimore, Md.; died September 3, 1974; son of Thomas and Anne Lewis; married, January 17, 1933; children: Selma Marie, Alfred Charles, Lowell Francis. *Education:* Attended public schools in Baltimore, Md., and New York, N.Y.

CAREER/WRITINGS: Manual laborer before World War I; worked for post office in New York, N.Y., beginning c. 1922. *Messenger* (periodical), drama critic, 1923-27, contributor of short stories, and co-author with George S. Schuyler of column "Shafts and Darts"; contributor of articles and drama and book reviews to numerous periodicals, including *America, Catholic World, Commonweal, Ebony and Topaz, Interracial Review, Inter-State Tattler, New York Amsterdam Star-News, Ohio Express, Opportunity, People's Voice, Pittsburgh Courier,* and *Sign.* Founding member of New York City Commission on Human Rights during 1950s. *Military service:* Served in American Expeditionary Force during World War I.

SIDELIGHTS: Theophilus Lewis wrote for numerous black and Catholic periodicals over the course of about fifty years. With no more than a high school education, he taught himself about the theater and became a well-regarded drama critic during the Harlem Renaissance, a period of heightened literary activity during the 1920s. As Theodore Kornweibel, Jr., observed in an article for *The Harlem Renaissance Remembered,* Lewis felt that theater served a vital social purpose—in Kornweibel's words, that "serious drama was the repository of a society's (or race's) collective spiritual life, culture, and character." As a drama critic for the periodical *Messenger* from 1923 to 1927, Lewis tried to encourage theater in New York City that would embody the values of black culture and eventually result in drama that would attract black audiences nationwide.

In his column for the *Messenger* Lewis repeatedly expressed disappointment with the black theater of his day, which relied heavily on comedy skits and lines of attractive female dancers to please its audience. While acknowledging the liveliness and entertainment value of such spectacles, he felt that they detracted from the higher goals of serious drama. Lewis saw black actors of great talent wasted in minor productions because they lacked substantial works to perform, and he laid part of the blame on black audiences and playwrights, both of whom, he felt, were given to low standards. But he also blasted the owners of major "black" theaters—often whites—whose background, he charged, was in circuses and carnivals rather than in culture. Such entrepreneurs were unwilling to use the profits of their light entertainment to offset the financial losses involved in promoting serious drama.

Accordingly, Lewis generally looked beyond the most popular and commercial black productions to find fit subjects for his praise. Surprisingly, some of the "black" dramas he liked were written by whites—including Eugene O'Neill's *The Emperor Jones* and *All God's Chillun Got Wings.* Lewis valued a play, regardless of its source, if it offered a realistic portrayal of black life and solid dramatic roles with which black actors could develop their talents. Furthermore, Lewis had high hopes for small, independent, nonprofit companies—often called "little theaters"—made up of black actors and playwrights. Such companies, he believed, if supported by small but appreciative audiences, could provide the basis for a dramatic community of the future that would be welcomed by black people throughout the country. As Kornweibel observed, Lewis accented the positive in his reviews of little-theater productions, overlooking technical flaws out of respect for the company's aspirations.

Lewis's dedication to his work brought him the respect of his fellow writers of the Harlem Renaissance. "Other 'critics' rarely displayed any discrimination and did little more than promote any show that promised to be successful," Kornweibel wrote. "The word was circulated among young artists and writers that Lewis was the only drama critic they could take seriously."

Lewis was unable to earn a living as a writer, however, remaining a post office worker from the 1920s until he reached retirement age years later. He continued to be published in periodicals throughout his life, and he explored other genres besides the drama review—for the *Messenger,* for instance, he wrote several short stories and collaborated with satirist George S. Schuyler on the column "Shafts and Darts." A convert to Catholicism in 1939, Lewis contributed to a number of Catholic magazines, including *Catholic World, Commonweal,* and *America,* in which his drama reviews appeared until a few years before he died.

BIOGRAPHICAL/CRITICAL SOURCES:

BOOKS

Bontemps, Arna, editor, *The Harlem Renaissance Remembered*, Dodd, 1972.

Scally, Sister Mary Anthony, *Negro Catholic Writers, 1900-1943*, Walter Romig, 1945.

(Date of death provided by Brother Frank Turnbull, S.J., of the office of the editor in chief of *America* magazine.)

*   *   *

LIGHTFOOT, Claude M.   1910-

PERSONAL: Born January 19, 1910, in Lake Village, Ark. *Education:* Attended Virginia Union University; received Ph.D. from Rostock University.

CAREER: Activist and writer. Elected to National Committee of American Communist Party, vice-chairman of party, 1959. Founder and business agent of Chicago Young Men's Democratic Organization, 1930; member of League of Struggle for Negro Rights, 1931; business agent for Consolidated Trade Council of Negro Skilled Workers, 1933.

AWARDS, HONORS: Outstanding Scholarship Achievement Award from Dr. W. E. B. Du Bois Communist Center, 1973; plaque from Government of Bulgaria, 1973; Salute to Black History Award, 1979.

WRITINGS:

Ghetto Rebellion to Black Liberation, International Publishers, 1968.
Black America and the World Revolution, New Outlook, 1970.
Racism and Human Survival: Lessons of Nazi Germany for Today's World, International Publishers, 1972.
Human Rights U.S. Style: From Colonial Times Through the New Deal, International Publishers, 1977.

*   *   *

LINCOLN, C(harles) Eric   1924-

PERSONAL: Born June 23, 1924, in Athens, Ala.; son of Less and Mattie (Sowell) Lincoln; married second wife, Lucy Cook (a teacher), July 1, 1961; children: (first marriage) Cecil Eric, Joyce Elaine; (second marriage) Hilary Anne, Less Charles II. *Education:* LeMoyne College, A.B., 1947; Fisk University, M.A., 1954; University of Chicago Divinity School, B.D., 1956; Boston University, M.Ed., 1960, Ph.D., 1960.

ADDRESSES: Office—Department of Religion, Duke University, Durham, N.C. 27706.

CAREER: LeMoyne College, Memphis, Tenn., director of public relations, 1950-51; Fisk University, Nashville, Tenn., associate personnel dean, 1953-54; Clark College, Atlanta, Ga., assistant professor of religion and philosophy, 1954-57, associate professor of social philosophy, 1960-61, professor of social relations, 1961-64, administrative assistant to president, 1961-63, director of Institute for Social Relations, 1963-65, assistant personnel dean; Portland State College (now University), Portland, Ore., professor of sociology, 1965-73; Union Theological Seminary, New York, N.Y., professor of sociology of religion, 1973-76; Fisk University, professor of religion and sociology and chairman of department of religious and philosophical studies, 1973-76; Duke University, Durham, N.C., professor of religion and culture, 1976—. Boston University, Human Relations Center, director of Panel of Americans, 1958-60, adjunct professor, 1963-65; Dartmouth College, lecturer-in-residence, 1962, visiting professor, 1962-63; visiting professor, Spelman College, 1966; adjunct professor, Vassar College, 1969-70; visiting professor at State University of New York at Albany, 1970-72, and Queens College of the City University of New York, 1972; adjunct professor of ethics and society, Vanderbilt University, 1973-76. Lecturer; has made numerous appearances on local and national television and on radio. Member of boards of directors or boards of trustees of several institutions, including Boston University, Jewish Theological Seminary, Institute for Religious and Social Studies, Clark Atlanta University, and Association of Theological Schools. Consultant in human relations. *Military service:* U.S. Navy, 1944-45.

MEMBER: American Academy of Arts and Sciences (fellow), American Sociological Association, Society for the Psychological Study of Social Issues, American Academy of Political and Social Science, Society for the Scientific Study of Religion, National Association of University Professors, National Education Association, Association for the Study of Negro Life and History, Black Academy of Arts and Letters (founding president; member of board of directors), American Association of Intergroup Relations Officials, Authors Guild, Authors League of America, National Geographic Society, Southern Sociological Society, New York Academy of Arts and Sciences, New York Academy of Sciences, Kappa Alpha Psi, Free and Accepted Masons, International Frontiers Club.

AWARDS, HONORS: John Hay Whitney fellow, 1957; Crusade fellow, Methodist Church, 1958; Lilly Endowment fellow, 1959; human relations fellow, Boston University, 1959-60; L.L.D. from Carleton College, 1968, Lane College, 1982, and Clark College, 1983; Creative Communications Award, Art Institute of Boston, 1970; L.H.D. from St. Michael's College, 1972; research grants from Society for the Psychological Study of Social Issues, Anti-Defamation League of B'nai B'rith, Fund for the Advancement of Education, Lilly Endowment, and Ford Foundation.

WRITINGS:

The Black Muslims in America, Beacon Press, 1961, 2nd revised edition, 1982.
My Face Is Black, Beacon Press, 1964.
Sounds of the Struggle, Morrow, 1967.
The Negro Pilgrimage in America: The Coming of Age of the Blackamericans, Bantam, 1967.
Is Anybody Listening?, Seabury, 1968.
(With Langston Hughes and Milton Meltzer) *A Pictorial History of the Negro in America*, Crown, 1968, 5th revised edition, 1983.
A Profile of Martin Luther King, Jr., Hill & Wang, 1969, revised edition, 1984.
The Blackamericans, Bantam, 1969.
The Black Church since Frazier, Schocken, 1974.
(Editor) *The Black Experience in Religion: A Book of Readings*, Doubleday, 1974.
Race, Religion, and the Continuing American Dilemma, Hill & Wang, 1984.
The Avenue: Clayton City, Morrow, 1988.

EDITOR; "C. ERIC LINCOLN SERIES IN BLACK RELIGION"

James H. Cone, *A Theology of Black Liberation*, Lippincott, 1970.
Henry Mitchell, *Black Preaching*, Lippincott, 1970.

Gayraud Wilmore, *Black Religion and Black Radicalism*, Doubleday, 1972.

Joseph R. Washington, Jr., *Black Sects and Cults*, Doubleday, 1972.

William R. Jones, *Is God a White Racist?*, Doubleday, 1973.

Leonard E. Barrett, *Soul-Force*, Doubleday, 1973.

CONTRIBUTOR

Alice Horowitz, editor, *The Outlook for Youth*, H. W.Wilson, 1962.

Earl Raab, editor, *New Frontiers in Race Relations*, Doubleday, 1962.

Mulford Sibley, editor, *The Quiet Battle*, Doubleday, 1963.

Louis Lomax, editor, *When the Word Is Given*, New American Library,1963.

Arnold Rose, editor, *Assuring Freedom to the Free*, Wayne State University Press, 1963.

Rolf Italiaander, editor, *Die Herasforderung des Islam*, Muster-Schmidt-Verlag (Gottingen), 1965.

Arnold Rose and Caroline Rose, editors, *Minority Problems*, Harper, 1965.

Gerald H. Anderson, editor, *Sermons to Men of Other Faiths*, Abingdon, 1966.

John P. Davis, editor, *The American Negro Reference Book*, Prentice-Hall, 1966.

Nils Petter Gleditsch, editor, *Kamp Uten Vapen*, Eides Boktrykkeri (Bergen), 1966.

Edgar A. Shuler and others, editors, *Readings in Sociology*, Crowell, 1967.

William C. Kvaraceus and others, editors, *Poverty, Education and Race Relations*, Allen & Bacon, 1967.

Milgon L. Barron, editor, *Minorities in a Changing World*, Knopf, 1967.

Bradford Chambers, editor, *Chronicles of Negro Protest*, New American Library, 1968.

Peter T. Rose, editor, *Old Memories, New Moods*, Atherton Press, 1970.

David Reimers, editor, *The Black Man in America since Reconstruction*, Crowell, 1970.

Benjamin Brawley, editor, *A Social History of the American Negro*, Macmillan, 1970.

George Ducas, editor, *Great Documents in Black American History*, Praeger, 1970.

Robert Weisbard and Arthur Stein, editors, *The Bittersweet Encounter*, Negro Universities Press, 1970.

Scott G. McNall, editor, *The Sociological Perspective*, Little, Brown, 1971.

Michael V. Namorato, editor, *Have We Overcome?: Race Relations since Brown*, University Press of Mississippi, 1979.

OTHER

Contributor to *Encyclopaedia Britannica, Encyclopedia Americana, Encyclopedia of Southern Religion, World Book Encyclopedia,* and *Encyclopdia of World Biography.* Contributor of articles, poetry, and reviews to numerous journals and popular periodicals.

SIDELIGHTS: C. Eric Lincoln has long been considered an important and respected sociologist studying such topics as race relations in the United States, the historical development of black protest and black nationalism, the growth and importance of the Black church, the Black Muslim movement, and the backgrounds and influence of Black leaders on the civil rights cause. Many reviewers feel that through his lectures, his appearances on national television and radio programs, and his writings, Lincoln has examined the various

elements of black life in America in an intelligent, insightful, and thorough manner. As Herbert Mitgang remarks in the *Saturday Review*, "[Lincoln] writes dispassionately and from the inside about where the Negro stands and what he hopes for today."

The publication of his first book, *The Black Muslims in America*, gained Lincoln and his work national attention. As one of the first sociological accounts of the Black Muslim movement in the United States, this book explores the movement's beginnings, doctrines, goals, strengths, leaders, and the powerful influence the group has had on the black American. P. J. Gleason writes in the *San Francisco Chronicle* that "Lincoln's study of the pseudo-Islamic sect of Black Muslims is timely, fascinating . . . to read." Gleason continues to note that "the story of the rise of this sect is logically and deftly told by Dr. Lincoln. . . . This is the first survey in depth on one of the most important, as well as one of the most significant, movements in contemporary America and it is well done."

"As an objective study of a social phenomenon [*The Black Muslims in America*] is outstanding," remarks K. B. Clark in the *Saturday Review*. "The author is at his best when he is describing the ideas, manner, ambiguities—intentional or unintentional—of the leaders and the appeals to and techniques of control of their followers. . . . [Lincoln] writes with clarity, with compassion, and with some evidence of deep personal conflict." And M. E. Burgess states in *Social Forces* that "whatever course the Movement takes in years ahead, it bears close watching. Dr. Lincoln's insightful analysis of the rationale, the appeal, and the implications of such a movement is a valuable contribution to the literature."

BIOGRAPHICAL/CRITICAL SOURCES:

PERIODICALS

Atlanta Journal/Constitution, March 13, 1988.
Best Sellers, February 15, 1970.
Commonweal, August 9, 1985.
Fayetteville Observer, April 3, 1988.
Greensboro News and Record, April 22, 1988.
Library Journal, January 15, 1970.
New York Review of Books, February 11, 1965.
New York Times Book Review, April 23, 1961.
San Francisco Chronicle, May 7, 1961.
Saturday Review, May 13, 1961, January 16, 1965, January 27, 1968, February 14, 1970.
Social Forces, December, 1961.

*   *   *

LITTLE, Malcolm   1925-1965
(El-Hajj Malik El-Shabazz, Malcolm X)

PERSONAL: Born May 19, 1925, in Omaha, Neb.; assassinated February 21, 1965, in New York, N.Y.; son of Earl (a minister and activist) and Louise Little; married wife, Betty (a student nurse), 1958; children: six daughters. *Religion:* Muslim.

CAREER: Activist. Worker in Lost-Found Nation of Islam (Black Muslims) religious sect, 1952-64, began as assistant minister of mosque in Detroit, Mich., then organized mosque in Philadelphia, Pa., became national minister, 1963; established Muslim Mosque, Inc., 1964; lecturer and writer. Founded Organization of Afro-American Unity in New York City, 1964.

WRITINGS:

UNDER NAME MALCOLM X

(With Alex Haley) *The Autobiography of Malcolm X*, introduction by M. S. Handler, epilogue by Haley, Grove, 1965.

Malcolm X Speaks: Selected Speeches and Statements, edited and with prefatory notes by George Breitman, Merit Publishers, 1965.

Malcolm X on Afro-American History, Merit Pubilshers, 1967, expanded edition, Pathfinder Press, 1970.

The Speeches of Malcolm X at Harvard, edited and with an introductory essay by Archie Epps, Morrow, 1968.

Malcolm X Talks to Young People, Young Socialist Alliance, 1969.

Malcolm X and the Negro Revolution: The Speeches of Malcolm X, edited and with an introductory essay by Archie Epps, Owen, 1969.

Two Speeches by Malcolm X, Merit Publishers, 1969.

By Any Means Necessary: Speeches, Interviews, and a Letter by Malcolm X, edited by George Breitman, Pathfinder Press, 1970.

The End of White World Supremacy: Four Speeches, edited and with an introduction by Benjamin Goodman, Merlin House, 1971.

Work represented in anthologies, including *100 and More Quotes by Garvey, Lumumba, and Malcolm X*, compiled by Shawna Maglangbayan, Third World Press, 1975.

Also speaker, with Bayard Rustin, on recording *A Choice of Two Roads*, Pacifica Archives.

SIDELIGHTS: Malcolm Little was a religious and sociopolitical activist who rose to prominence, and notoriety, in the mid-1950s under the name Malcolm X. A staunch, outspoken advocate of black separatism, he inspired many with his efforts on behalf of Elijah Muhammad's Black Muslim religion, which characterizes the black race as superior and the white race as inherently evil. For Malcolm X, the Western black's sole response to racism was total withdrawal from Western culture and society. These radical contentions, while uniting a portion of the American black community, alienated other members, including civil rights activists and pacifists. Eventually Malcolm X became disillusioned with Elijah Muhammad's antagonistic religion and left to start his own Muslim organization. This action, in turn, offended Elijah Muhammad and his followers, and in early 1965, while preparing to speak in a Harlem ballroom, Malcolm X was gunned down by men believed sympathetic to the Black Muslims.

As I. F. Stone noted in the *New York Review of Books*, "Malcolm X was born into Black Nationalism." Earl Little, Malcolm's father, was a Baptist minister who strongly supported separatist Marcus Garvey's back-to-Africa movement in the 1920s. For his actions on behalf of Garvey, Earl Little soon found himself the target of hostility while living in Omaha, Nebraska, where members of the racist Ku Klux Klan organization threatened his family because he was sparking dissension among the normally cooperative blacks. The Littles consequently left Omaha, but during the next few years they failed to find a hospitable community and thus moved often. In his autobiography, Malcolm X recalled a particularly harrowing experience in Lansing, Michigan, where his family home was torched by members of the Black Legion, an oddly named band of white supremacists. Shortly afterwards the corpse of Earl Little was found horribly butchered.

Following Earl Little's death, Louise Little and her eight children subsisted on welfare. Eventually, however, the severe strain overwhelmed her and she succumbed to mental illness. Louise Little was then placed in a mental institution and her children were sent separately to various foster homes. Despite this continued adversity and emotional hardship, Malcolm still held aspirations of assimilation in America's predominantly white society. But even those hopes faded after he confided to his high-school English teacher that he hoped to someday become a lawyer, whereupon the teacher urged him towards a vocation instead of a profession and told him to be "realistic about being a nigger."

A distinguished student, Malcolm was shattered by his teacher's racist counseling, and soon afterward he quit high school. Living with a sister in Boston, Malcolm found menial work and began associating with low-lifes and criminals. He became involved with illegal gambling, managed his own prostitution ring, and consorted with drug dealers. Eventually he also sold narcotics, to which he swiftly became addicted, and turned to robbery to sustain his drug habit. He developed a formidable reputation as an enterprising, quick-thinking hustler, becoming notorious in the Boston ghetto as "Detroit Red." With that notoriety, however, came increasing attention from the police, and in early 1946 Malcolm was arrested and charged with robbery. That February—three months before his twenty-first birthday—he was sentenced to ten years imprisonment.

In the penitentiary Malcolm continued his reckless ways, using drugs and presenting such an unsavory demeanor that his fellow inmates referred to him as "Satan." Because of his vicious behavior he was often held in solitary confinement. But he did manage to befriend another convicted burglar, Bimbi, who introduced him to the prison's extensive library. Through the library Malcolm broadened his education and familiarized himself with subjects ranging from philosophy to politics. He also began studying the tenets of the Black Muslims' Lost-Found Nation of Islam, a religion that extolled the superiority of the black race and denounced the white as evil and doomed to destruction. The Black Muslims' founder and leader, Elijah Muhammad, proclaimed himself divine messenger of the Muslim deity, Allah, and—like Marcus Garvey—he counseled his followers to abjure white America in favor of an autonomous black society. Elijah Muhammad's doctrine of black pride exerted considerable appeal to Malcolm, who denounced his allegedly enslaving Christian surname and adopted the name Malcolm X.

While still in prison Malcolm X corresponded with Elijah Muhammad, who lived comfortably at Black Muslim headquarters in Chicago, and after obtaining freedom in 1952 he traveled there and commenced a brief tutelage under the Muslim leader. He then served briefly as an assistant minister at a Detroit mosque before becoming minister at Harlem's Mosque Number Seven. It was in Harlem that Malcolm X achieved impressive status as an articulate, mercurial spokesperson for the radical black perspective. From street corners, church pulpits, and college podiums he railed against racism and championed separatism and faith in Allah as the salvation of blacks. He claimed that civil rights, equal opportunity, and integration were all futile within a society that was determinedly racist. Even Christianity was reviled as a method of enslavement and was denounced as a historical distortion—Christ having been, according to Malcolm X, a black. He advised blacks to reject white society and unite under Elijah Muhammad and the Black Muslim faith, which held the true way to dignity for blacks.

Malcolm X proved an impressive representative for Elijah Muhammad, and as he enthusiastically proselytized for the Black Muslims their membership increased significantly. Elijah Muhammad, acknowledging the impressive effectiveness of his acolyte, named him the religion's first national minister. As Malcolm X rose in status, however, he became increasingly critical of Elijah Muhammad's materialism, particularly his many expensive cars and business suits and his lavishly furnished estate in Chicago. In addition, he was dismayed when former secretaries claimed that Elijah Muhammad had seduced them and sired their children, thus violating the sect's tenet on sexual promiscuity. Elijah Muhammad, in turn, reportedly grew resentful of Malcolm X's growing prominence across the nation and thus his formidable influence within the Black Muslim organization.

Rivalry between the two men peaked in 1963 when Malcolm X violated Elijah Muhammad's commandment of silence regarding the November 22nd assassination of President Kennedy and termed it a case of "the chicken coming home to roost." Malcolm X, who later explained that his comment was meant to indicate that "the hate in white men . . . finally had struck down the President," was reprimanded by Elijah Muhammad for the potentially incendiary remark. "That was a very bad statement," Elijah Muhammad told him. "The country loved this man." He ordered Malcolm X to refrain from public comment for ninety days, and Malcolm complied.

Within days, however, Malcolm X learned that members of his sect were plotting his demise. His dissatisfaction with the Black Muslims mounted, and he decided to tour Mecca, birthplace of the Muslim prophet Muhammad. Once there, Malcolm X experienced a powerful conversion, one which left him with greater compassion for people of all races and nationalities. He renamed himself El-Hajj Malik El-Shabazz and vowed to promote greater harmony among all blacks, including non-Muslims and civil rights activists he had alienated earlier with his uncompromising positions. Once back in the United States he founded his own Muslim association, the Organization of Afro-American Unity, and began actively working to unite blacks throughout the world.

Once he began operating outside the Black Muslim sect, Malcolm X was apparently perceived as a threat to the organization. "Now I'm out," he stated. "And there's the fear [that] if my image isn't shattered, the Muslims in the movement will leave." He was informed that members within the organization were plotting to end his life, and in mid-February he told the *New York Times* that he was a "marked man." Around that time his home was firebombed. But he was undaunted and continued to speak on behalf of black unity and harmony. On February 21, 1965, he stepped to the podium in a Harlem ballroom and greeted the audience of four hundred that had gathered to hear him speak. Within seconds at least three men rose from their seats and began firing at Malcolm X with shotguns and pistols. Seven shots slammed him backwards while spectators scrambled for cover. As gunfire continued—more than thirty shots were reportedly heard—daring witnesses attacked and subdued the assassins. Three men—Talmadge Hayer and Black Muslims Norman 3X Butler and Thomas 15X Johnson—were eventually convicted of the killing, and it is widely believed the assassins intended to intimidate Malcolm X's followers into remaining within the Black Muslim fold.

In the years since his death Malcolm X has come to be recognized as a leading figure in the black struggle for recognition and equality. *The Autobiography of Malcolm X*, published the same year as his death, is highly regarded as a moving account of his own experiences with racism, his criminal past, and his years as an activist for both the Black Muslims and his own Afro-American organization. During the remaining years of the 1960s Malcolm X's speeches and comments were collected and published in volumes such as *Malcolm X Speaks, Malcolm X on Afro-American History*, and *Malcolm X and the Negro Revolution*. Together with the autobiography, these books offer numerous insights into America's social climate from the mid-1950s to the mid-60s and articulate the concerns of a significant portion of the black community in those years. Additionally, they serve as an imposing indication of Malcolm X's beliefs, his achievements, and his potential, which—like that of President Kennedy, Reverend Martin Luther King, Jr., and Senator Robert Kennedy—were violently rendered unrealized. As I. F. Stone noted in his essay-review for the *New York Review of Books:* "There are few places on earth where whites have not grown rich robbing [blacks]. It was Malcolm's great contribution to help make us aware of this." Stone called Malcolm X's murder "a loss to the country as well as to his race."

MEDIA ADAPTATIONS: James Baldwin adapted portions of *The Autobiography of Malcolm X* as *One Day, When I Was Lost: A Scenario*, Dial, 1973.

BIOGRAPHICAL/CRITICAL SOURCES:

BOOKS

Alexander, Rae Pace, *Young and Black in America*, Random House, 1973.
Breitman, George, *The Last Year of Malcolm X: The Evolution of a Revolutionary*, Merit Publications, 1967.
Clarke, John Henrik, editor and author of introduction, *Malcolm X: The Man and His Times*, Macmillan, 1969.
Curtis, Richard, *Life of Malcolm X*, Macrae Smith, 1971.
Darling, Edward, *When Sparks Fly Upward*, Washburn, 1970.
Goldman, Peter Louis, *Death and Life of Malcolm X*, University of Illinois Press, 1979.
Haskins, James, *Revolutionaries*, Lippincott, 1971.
Jamal, Hakin A., *From the Dead Level: Malcolm X and Me*, Random House, 1972.
Lomax, Louise E., *To Kill a Black Man*, Holloway House, 1968.
McKinley, James, *Assassination in America*, Harper, 1977.
Miah, Malik, editor and author of introduction, *Assassination of Malcolm X*, Pathfinder Press, 1976.
Paris, Peter J., *Black Leaders in Conflict: Joseph H. Jackson, Martin Luther King, Jr., Malcolm X, Adam Clayton Powell, Jr.*, Pilgrim Press, 1978.
Parks, Gordon, *Born Black*, Lippincott, 1971.
Playboy Interviews, Playboy Press, 1967.
Wolfenstein, Eugene Victor, *Victims of Democracy: Malcolm X and the Black Revolution*, University of California Press, 1981.

PERIODICALS

Catholic World, September, 1967.
Christian Century, April 7, 1965.
Ebony, October, 1965, June, 1969.
Encounter, September, 1973.
Harper's, June, 1964.
Life, March 20, 1964.
Journal of Black Studies, December, 1981.
Nation, March 8, 1965, November 8, 1965.

Negro Education Review, January, 1979.
New Statesman, June 12, 1964.
Newsweek, December 16, 1963, November 15, 1965, March 3, 1969, January 8, 1973, May 7, 1979.
New York Review of Books, November 11, 1965.
New York Times Book Review, September 11, 1966, April 13, 1969, May 16, 1971.
Saturday Review, November 20, 1965, July 30, 1966.
Spectator, February 26, 1965.
Time, March 5, 1965, February 23, 1970, June 12, 1972.
Times Literary Supplement, June 9, 1966, May 28, 1971.
Yale Review, December, 1966.

OBITUARIES:

PERIODICALS

New York Times, February 22, 1965.

—*Sketch by Les Stone*

* * *

LIYONG, Taban lo 1938-

PERSONAL: Born in 1938 in Uganda. *Education:* Attended Government Teacher Training College, Kyambogo, Uganda, Knoxville College, University of North Carolina, and Georgetown University; National Teachers College, Kampala, Uganda, B.A.; Howard University, B.A., 1966; University of Iowa, M.F.A., 1968.

ADDRESSES: Office—Department of English, University of Nairobi, P.O. Box 30197, Nairobi, Kenya.

CAREER: University of Nairobi, Nairobi, Kenya, lecturer in English, 1968—, member of Institute for Development Studies Cultural Division, 1968—.

WRITINGS:

Fixions and Other Stories by a Ugandan Writer, Humanities, 1968 (published in England as *Fixions and Other Stories,* Heinemann, 1969).
The Last Word: Cultural Synthesism, East African Publishing House, 1969.
The Uniformed Man (short stories), East African Literature Bureau, 1971.
Popular Culture of East Africa: Oral Literature, Longman, 1972.
Thirteen Offensives Against Our Enemies, East African Literature Bureau, 1973.
(Editor of reprint) Ham Mukasa, *Sir Apolo Kagwa Discovers Britain,* Heinemann, 1975.
Meditations of Taban lo Liyong, Collings, 1978.

NOVELS

Meditations in Limbo, Equatorial Publishers, 1970, revised edition published as *Meditations,* 1977.

POEMS

(Editor) *Eating Chiefs: Lwo Culture From Lolwe to Malkal,* Humanities, 1970.
Frantz Fanon's Uneven Ribs, With Poems, More and More, Humanities, 1971.
Another Nigger Dead: Poems, Humanities, 1972.
Ballads of Underdevelopment: Poems and Thoughts, East African Literature Bureau, 1976.

Also author of *To Still a Passion* (poems), 1977. Editor of *Mila.*

WORK IN PROGRESS: A Calendar of Wisdom, proverbs in verse; *The African Tourist,* culture criticism; *The American Education of Taban lo Liyong; The Lubumbashi Lectures;* editing *East African Anthology: Literature from Zinjanthropus to Extelcom.*

* * *

LOCKE, Alain (Le Roy) 1886-1954

PERSONAL: Born September 13, 1886, in Philadelphia, Pa.; died following a long illness, June 9 (some sources say June 10), 1954, in New York, N.Y.; son of Pliny I. (a schoolteacher) and Mary (a schoolteacher; maiden name, Hawkins) Locke. *Education:* Harvard University, B.A. (with honors), 1907, Ph.D., 1918; Oxford University, B.Litt., 1910; graduate study at University of Berlin, 1910-11. *Religion:* Episcopalian.

ADDRESSES: Home—1326 R St. N.W., Washington, D.C.

CAREER: Howard University, Washington, D.C., assistant professor, 1912-17, professor of philosophy, 1917-53, chairman of philosophy department, 1918-53. Exchange professor at Fisk University, 1927-28; Inter-American Exchange Professor in Haiti, 1943; visiting professor at University of Wisconsin, 1945-46, and at The New School for Social Research, 1947.

MEMBER: International Institute of African Languages and Culture, American Negro Academy, American Philosophical Association, League of American Writers, Associates in Negro Folk Education (former secretary-editor), Conference on Science, Philosophy, and Religion (founding member), Society for Historical Research, Phi Beta Kappa, Phi Beta Sigma (honorary member), Theta Sigma, Sigma Pi Phi, Academie des Sciences Colonailes (corresponding member), Sociedad de Estudios Afro-Cubanos (honorary fellow), National Order of Honor and Merit (Haiti).

AWARDS, HONORS: Rhodes scholar, 1907-10; named to 1942 Honor Roll of Race Relations.

WRITINGS:

(Editor) *The New Negro: An Interpretation* (anthology), illustrations by Winold Reiss, A. & C. Boni, 1925, reprinted, with preface by Robert Hayden, Atheneum, 1970.
(Editor) *Four Negro Poets,* Simon & Schuster, 1927.
(Editor with Montgomery Gregory) *Plays of Negro Life: A Source-Book of Native American Drama,* illustrations by Aaron Douglas, Harper, 1927, Negro University Press, 1970.
The Negro in America (bibliography), American Library Association, 1933.
The Negro and His Music, Associates in Negro Folk Education, 1936, Kennikat, 1968, also published with *Negro Art: Past and Present,* Arno Press, 1969 (also see below).
Negro Art: Past and Present, Associates in Negro Folk Education, 1936, also published with *The Negro and His Music,* Arno Press, 1969 (also see below).
(Editor and annotator) *The Negro in Art: A Pictorial Record of the Negro Artist and of the Negro Theme in Art,* Associates in Negro Folk Education, 1940, Hacker Art Books, 1971.
(Editor with Bernhard J. Stern) *When Peoples Meet: A Study in Race and Culture Contacts,* Committee on Workshops, Progressive Education Association, 1942, revised edition, Hinds, Hayden & Eldredge, 1946.

Le Role du Negre dans la culture des Ameriques, Impr. de l'Etat, 1943.

The Negro and His Music [and] *Negro Art: Past and Present,* Arno Press, 1969.

Also author of *Race Contacts and Inter-Racial Relations,* 1916; *The Problem of Classification in Theory of Value,* 1918; *The Negro in American Literature,* 1929; and *Frederick Douglass: A Biography of Anti-Slavery,* 1935. Works represented in anthologies, including *The Black Aesthetic* and *Theatre: Essays on the Arts of the Theatre.*

Contributor to reference books and periodicals, including *Britannica Book of the Year, Harlem: A Forum of Negro Life, Phylon, Opportunity, Nation, Annals of the American Academy of Political and Social Science, Modern Quarterly, Theatre Arts, Carolina Magazine,* and *Crisis.* Edited a special Harlem issue of *Survey Graphic,* 1925, and the ''Bronze Booklet'' series of studies on Negro cultural achievements.

SIDELIGHTS: Alain Locke virtually brought about the Harlem Renaissance, a period of great literary and artistic activity originating in New York City during the 1920s, by compiling an anthology of the most outstanding Negro poetry and prose of the early twentieth century, *The New Negro: An Interpretation.* Because of the high literary merit of the works in the anthology, critics were forced to take black writing seriously. *The New Negro* also served as a unifying link for struggling black authors who previously thought that they were alone in their literary endeavors. Exposed to other writers' works and able to study different forms and themes, a generation of black authors were inspired by *The New Negro.*

Locke also urged Negroes to seek inspiration and take pride in their rich cultural heritage. In *The Negro in Art: A Pictorial Record of the Negro Artist and of the Negro Theme in Art* Locke stressed that the black man should look to the works of his African ancestors for subject matter, methods, and motifs to apply to modern painting and sculpture. The first section of the *Negro in Art* provides examples of seventeenth- to twentieth-century art works by Negroes, mostly American. The second section contains illustrations of black subjects in art; and the third part deals with the influence of African art on modern painting and sculpture.

Locke first became aware of the need to promote African culture while touring the American South for six months in 1911. He witnessed prejudice and discrimination, and realized that the black literati and artists could hold the key to easier race relations. He felt that by setting high standards for themselves and using their talents to gain the respect of the whites, blacks would cast aside their self-doubt, become more confident, and would think of themselves as equal to whites. Locke's 1916 social study, *Race Contacts and Inter-Racial Relations,* grew out of his experiences in the South. He was also interested in interactions between majority and minority groups on a national and international level. On that subject Locke edited, with Bernhard J. Stern, *When Peoples Meet: A Study in Race and Culture Contacts* and wrote, while an Inter-American Exchange Professor in Haiti, *Le Role du Negre dans la culture des Ameriques,* about blacks in American society.

BIOGRAPHICAL/CRITICAL SOURCES:

BOOKS

Butcher, Margaret J., *The Negro in American Culture: Based on Materials Left by Alain Locke,* Knopf, 1956.

Dictionary of Literary Biography, Volume 51: *Afro-American Writers From the Harlem Renaissance to 1940,* Gale, 1987.

*   *   *

LOGAN, Rayford W(hittingham)   1897-1982

PERSONAL: Born January 7, 1897, in Washington, D.C.; died November 4, 1982, of congestive heart failure in Washington, D.C.; buried in Fort Lincoln Cemetery, Washington, D.C.; son of Arthur C. and Martha (Whittingham) Logan; married Ruth Robinson, 1927 (died June 30, 1966). *Education:* Williams College, A.B., 1917; Harvard University, A.M., 1930, Ph.D., 1936.

ADDRESSES: Home—30001 Veazey Terrace N.W., Washington, D.C. 20008.

CAREER: Virginia Union University, Richmond, head of history department, 1925-30; Atlanta University, Atlanta, Ga., head of history department, 1933-38; Howard University, Washington, D.C., professor of history, 1938-69, 1971-74, distinguished professor emeritus, 1974-82, head of department, 1942-64, historian of the university. Chairman of federal committee on participation of blacks in national defense, 1940-45; member of U.S. national commission for UNESCO, 1947-50; participant in State Department's Bureau of Inter-American Affairs. *Military service:* U.S. Army, Infantry, 1917-19; became first lieutenant.

MEMBER: American Historical Association, Phi Beta Kappa, Alpha Phi Alpha, Epsilon Chapter, Sigma Pi Phi.

AWARDS, HONORS: Commander of the National Order of Honor and Merit, Republic of Haiti; L.H.D., Williams College, 1965; L.L.D., Howard University, 1972; Spingarn Medal, National Association for the Advancement of Colored People (NAACP), 1980.

WRITINGS:

Education in Haiti, [Washington, D.C.], 1930.

The Diplomatic Relations of the United States with Haiti, 1776-1891, University of North Carolina Press, 1941, reprinted, Kraus Reprint, 1969.

The Operation of the Mandate System in Africa, 1919-1927: With an Introduction on the Problem of the Mandates in the Post-War World, Foundation Publishers, 1942.

The Negro and the Post-War World: A Primer, Minorities Publishers, 1945.

The Senate and the Versailles Mandate System, Minorities Publishers, 1945, reprinted, Greenwood Press, 1975.

The African Mandates in World Politics, Public Affairs Press, 1949.

The Negro in American Life and Thought: The Nadir, 1877-1901, Dial Press, 1954, published as *The Betrayal of the Negro from Rutherford B. Hayes to Woodrow Wilson,* Collier Books, 1965.

The Negro in the United States: A Brief History (also see below), Van Nostrand, 1957.

(With Irving S. Cohen) *The American Negro: Old World Background and New World Experience,* Houghton, 1967.

(With Philip Sterling) *Four Took Freedom: The Lives of Harriet Tubman, Frederick Douglass, Robert Smalls, and Blanche K. Bruce,* illustrated by Charles White, Doubleday, 1967.

Haiti and the Dominican Republic, Oxford University Press, 1968.

Howard University: The First Hundred Years, 1867-1967, New York University Press, 1969.

The Negro in the United States, Van Nostrand, Volume 1: *A History to 1945: From Slavery to Second-Class Citizenship* (originally published as *The Negro in the United States: A Brief History*), 1970, Volume 2: (with Michael R. Winston) *The Ordeal of Democracy,* 1971.

EDITOR

The Attitude of the Southern White Press toward Negro Suffrage, 1932-1940, Foundation Publishers, 1940.

What the Negro Wants, University of North Carolina Press, 1944.

Memoirs of a Monticello Slave, as Dictated to Charles Campbell in the 1840's by Isaac, One of Thomas Jefferson's Slaves, University of Virginia Press, 1951.

The New Negro Thirty Years Afterward: Papers Contributed to the Sixteenth Annual Spring Conference of the Division of Social Science, Howard University Press, 1955.

W. E. B. Du Bois: A Profile, Hill & Wang, 1971.

(With Winston) *Dictionary of American Negro Biography,* Norton, 1982.

OTHER

Contributor of articles and reviews to professional journals. Editor, *Journal of Negro History.*

WORK IN PROGRESS: The Struggle for Human Rights, for Howard University Press; *Within and without the Veil,* an autobiography.

SIDELIGHTS: The late Rayford W. Logan was "one of the great Afro-American historians," according to Nathan Irvin Huggins in the *Washington Post Book World.* Shortly before his death Logan completed, with the assistance of co-editor Michael R. Winston, the massive *Dictionary of American Negro Biography,* "a volume as significant to the study of black Americans as the Dictionary of American Biography has been to American Studies," in the opinion of *New York Times Book Review* contributor Henry Louis Gates, Jr. Containing around 700 entries, the work includes people from all walks of life, chosen for their historical significance. "There are teachers, preachers, doctors, lawyers, politicians, poets, revolutionaries and so on," says Huggins. "But there are also mountain men, cowboys, hustlers (gamblers and outlaws of the West), rodeo performers too," he adds. Acclaiming the volume as "a model of balanced judgement, sober assessment, and scholarly codification," Gates concludes that "the standard of excellence . . . for any future black biographical dictionary will remain the Dictionary of American Negro Biography."

AVOCATIONAL INTERESTS: Travel.

BIOGRAPHICAL/CRITICAL SOURCES:

PERIODICALS

American Journal of Sociology, January, 1945.
Commonweal, December 7, 1945.
Los Angeles Times Book Review, March 13, 1983.
Nation, September 4, 1954.
New York Herald Tribune Book Review, March 14, 1954.
New York Review of Books, November 30, 1972.
New York Times, February 14, 1954.
New York Times Book Review, May 1, 1983.
Survey, March, 1945.
Washington Post Book World, August 7, 1983.
Yale Review, summer, 1954.

OBITUARIES:

PERIODICALS

AB Bookman, January 10, 1983.
New York Times, November 6, 1982.
Washington Post, November 7, 1982.

*   *   *

LOMAX, Louis E(manuel)   1922-1970

PERSONAL: Born August 16, 1922, in Valdosta, Ga.; died in an automobile accident, July 30, 1970, in Santa Rosa, N.M.; son of James (a teacher and clergyman) and Fannie (Hardon) Lomax; divorced from third wife, April, 1967; married fourth wife, Robinette G. Kirk, March 1, 1968. *Education:* Paine College, A.B., 1942; graduate study at American University and Yale University.

ADDRESSES: Home—Baldwin Harbor, N.Y.

CAREER: Newspaperman, 1941-58; free-lance writer, 1958-70. News commentator on WNTA-TV, New York, N.Y., 1958-60, and for Metromedia Broadcasting, 1964-68. News analyst for KTTV, Los Angeles, Calif.; news director for WNEW-TV, New York City; news writer for "Mike Wallace Show"; host of television program "Louis Lomax." Former assistant professor of philosophy at Georgia State University, and former professor of humanities and social sciences at Hofstra University.

AWARDS, HONORS: Anisfield-Wolf Award for best book concerned with racial problems, 1961, for *The Reluctant African;* awarded two honorary doctorates.

WRITINGS:

The Reluctant African, Harper, 1960.
The Negro Revolt, Harper, 1962.
When the Word is Given: A Report on Elijah Muhammad, Malcolm X, and the Black Muslim World, New American Library, 1963.
Thailand: The War That Is, The War That Will Be, Random House, 1966.
To Kill a Black Man, Holloway, 1968.

Contributor to *Life, Look, Saturday Evening Post,* and newspapers. Syndicated columnist for the North American Newspaper Alliance.

WORK IN PROGRESS: A three-volume history of the Negro.

BIOGRAPHICAL/CRITICAL SOURCES:

PERIODICALS

Virginia Quarterly Review, spring, 1968.

*   *   *

LONG, Naomi Cornelia
See MADGETT, Naomi Long

*   *   *

LONG, Richard A(lexander)   1927-
(Ric Alexander)

PERSONAL: Born February 9, 1927, in Philadelphia, Pa.; son of Thaddeus B. and Lela (Washington) Long. *Education:* Temple University, A.B., 1947, M.A., 1948; further study at

University of Pennsylvania and University of Paris; University of Poitiers, D.es L., 1965.

ADDRESSES: Office—Graduate Institute of the Liberal Arts, Emory University, Atlanta, Ga. 30322.

CAREER: West Virginia State College, Institute, instructor in English, 1949-50; Morgan State College (now University), Baltimore, Md., assistant professor, 1951-64, associate profesor of English, 1964-66; Hampton Institute, Hampton, Va., professor of English and French, 1966-68; Atlanta University, Atlanta, Ga., professor of English and Afro-American studies, 1968-87; currently faculty member of Graduate Institute of the Liberal Arts, Emory University, Atlanta. Visiting lecturer in Afro-American Studies, Harvard University, 1970-72. *Military service:* U.S. Army, 1944-45.

MEMBER: American Dialect Society, American Studies Association, South Atlantic Modern Language Association, Modern Language Association of America, College Language Association (president, 1971-72), Modern Humanities Research Association, Linguistics Society of America, Southeastern Conference on Linguistics.

AWARDS, HONORS: Fulbright scholar, University of Paris, 1957-58.

WRITINGS:

(Editor with Albert H. Berrian) *Negritude: Essays and Studies,* Hampton Institute Press, 1967, revised edition, 1987.
(Editor with Eugenia W. Collier) *Afro-American Writing: An Anthology of Prose and Poetry,* two volumes, New York University Press, 1972, 2nd and enlarged edition, Pennsylvania State University Press, 1985.
Ascending and Other Poems, Du Sable Museum, 1975.
Black America, Chartwell, 1985.
Black Writers and the American Civil War, Blue and Gray Press, 1988.

DRAMATIC WORKS UNDER NAME RIC ALEXANDER

"The Pilgrim's Pride" (sketches), 1963.
"Stairway to Heaven" (gospel opera), 1964.
"Joan of Arc" (folk opera), 1964.
"Reasons of State" (play), 1966.
"Black Is Many Hues" (play), 1969.

OTHER

Member of editorial boards, *Phylon* and *Bulletin of Research in the Humanities.* Former member of editorial board of *Black Books Bulletin.*

BIOGRAPHICAL/CRITICAL SOURCES:

PERIODICALS

Journal of American Studies, April, 1987.
Library Journal, February 1, 1973.

* * *

LORDE, Audre (Geraldine) 1934-
(Rey Domini)

PERSONAL: Born February 18, 1934, in New York, N.Y.; daughter of Frederic Byron (a real estate broker) and Linda (Belmar) Lorde; married Edwon Ashley Rollins (an attorney), March 31, 1962 (divorced, 1970); children: Elizabeth, Jonathan. *Education:* Attended National University of Mexico, 1954; Hunter College (now Hunter College of the City University of

New York), B.A., 1959; Columbia University, M.L.S., 1961. *Politics:* Radical. *Religion:* Quaker.

ADDRESSES: Home—AZ Judith's Fancy, Christiansted, St. Croix 00820, U.S. Virgin Islands. *Office*—Department of English, Hunter College of the City University of New York, 695 Park Ave., New York, N.Y. 10019.

CAREER: Mount Vernon Public Library, Mount Vernon, N.Y., librarian, 1961-63; Town School Library, New York City, head librarian, 1966-68; City University of New York, New York City, lecturer in creative writing at City College, 1968, lecturer in education department at Herbert H. Lehman College, 1969-70, associate professor of English at John Jay College of Criminal Justice, beginning 1970, professor of English at Hunter College, 1980—, Thomas Hunter Professor, 1987—. Distinguished visiting professor, Atlanta University, 1968; poet in residence, Tougaloo College, 1968. Lecturer throughout the United States.

MEMBER: American Association of University Professors, Harlem Writers Guild.

AWARDS, HONORS: National Endowment for the Arts grants, 1968 and 1981; Creative Artists Public Service grants, 1972 and 1976; National Book Award nominee for poetry, 1974, for *From a Land Where Other People Live;* Borough of Manhattan President's Award for literary excellence, 1987.

WRITINGS:

The Cancer Journals (nonfiction), Spinsters Ink, 1980.
Zami: A New Spelling of My Name (fiction), Crossing Press, 1982.
Sister Outsider (nonfiction), Crossing Press, 1984.
Burst of Light, Firebrand Books, 1988.

POETRY

The First Cities, introduction by Diane di Prima, Poets Press, 1968.
Cables to Rage, Broadside Press, 1970.
From a Land Where Other People Live, Broadside Press, 1973.
The New York Head Shop and Museum, Broadside Press, 1974.
Coal, Norton, 1976.
Between Our Selves, Eidolon, 1976.
The Black Unicorn, Norton, 1978.
Chosen Poems Old and New, Norton, 1982.
Our Dead Behind Us, Norton, 1986.

CONTRIBUTOR OF POETRY TO ANTHOLOGIES

Langston Hughes, editor, *New Negro Poets, USA,* University of Indiana Press, 1962.
P. Breman, editor, *Sixes and Sevens,* Breman Ltd. (London), 1963.
R. Pool, editor, *Beyond the Blues,* Hand & Flower Press (Amsterdam), 1964.
G. Menarini, editor, *I Negri: Poesie E Canti,* Edizioni Academia (Rome), 1969.
C. Major, editor, *New Black Poetry,* International Press, 1969.
T. Wilentz, editor, *Natural Process,* Hill & Wang, 1970.
T. Cade, editor, *The Black Woman,* American Library Publishing, 1970.

Contributor of poetry to other anthologies, including *Soul-Script,* edited by J. Meyer, Simon & Schuster.

OTHER

Contributor of poetry to periodicals, including *Iowa Review,*

Black Scholar, Chrysalis, Black World, Journal of Black Poetry, Transatlantic Review, Massachusetts Review, Pound, Harlem Writers' Quarterly, Freedomways, Seventeen, and *Women: A Journal of Liberation;* contributor of fiction, under pseudonym Rey Domini to *Venture* magazine. Editor, *Pound* magazine (Tougaloo, Miss.), 1968; poetry editor, *Chrysalis* and *Amazon Quarterly.*

WORK IN PROGRESS: Poetry and collected essays.

SIDELIGHTS: Audre Lorde's poetry and "indeed all of her writing," according to contributor Joan Martin in *Black Women Writers (1950-1980): A Critical Evaluation,* "rings with passion, sincerity, perception, and depth of feeling." Her first poem to be published was accepted by *Seventeen* magazine when she was still in high school. The poem had been rejected by her school paper, Lorde explains in *Black Women Writers,* because her "English teachers . . . said [it] was much too romantic." Her mature poetry, published in volumes including *New York Head Shop and Museum, Coal,* and *The Black Unicorn,* is sometimes romantic also.Often dealing with her lesbian relationships, her love poems have nevertheless been judged accessible to all by many critics. In Martin's words, "one doesn't have to profess heterosexuality, homosexuality, or asexuality to react to her poems. . . . Anyone who has ever been in love can respond to the straightforward passion and pain sometimes one and the same, in Lorde's poems."

As Jerome Brooks reports in *Black Women Writers (1950-1980): A Critical Evaluation,* however, "Lorde's poetry of anger is perhaps her best-known work." In her poem "The American Cancer Society Or There Is More Than One Way to Skin a Coon," she protests against white America thrusting its unnatural culture on blacks; in "The Brown Menace or Poem to the Survival of Roaches," she likens blacks to cockroaches, hated, feared, and poisoned by whites. *Poetry* critic Sandra M. Gilbert remarks that "it's not surprising that Lorde occasionally seems to be choking on her own anger . . . [and] when her fury vibrates through taut cables from head to heart to page, Lorde is capable of rare and, paradoxically, loving jeremiads." Her anger does not confine itself to racial injustice but extends to feminist issues as well, and occasionally she criticizes black men for their role in the perpetuating of sex discrimination: "As Black people, we cannot begin our dialogue by denying the oppressive nature of *male privilege,*" Lorde states in *Black Women Writers.* "And if Black males choose to assume that privilege, for whatever reason, raping, brutalizing, and killing women, then we cannot ignore Black male oppression. One oppression does not justify another."

Of her poetic beginnings Lorde comments in *Black Women Writers:* "I used to speak in poetry. I would read poems, and I would memorize them. People would say, well what do you think, Audre. What happened to you yesterday? And I would recite a poem and somewhere in that poem would be a line or a feeling I would be sharing. In other words, I literally communicated through poetry. And when I couldn't find the poems to express the things I was feeling, that's what started me writing poetry, and that was when I was twelve or thirteen." As an adult, her primary poetic goal is still communication. "I have a duty," she states later in the same publication, "to speak the truth as I see it and to share not just my triumphs, not just the things that felt good, but the pain, the intense, often unmitigating pain." As a mature poet, however, rather than relying solely on poetry as a means of self-expression Lorde often extracts poems from her personal journals. Explaining the genesis of "Power," a poem about the police

shooting of a ten-year-old black child, Lorde discusses her feelings when she learned that the officer involved had been acquitted: "A kind of fury rose up in me; the sky turned red. I felt so sick. I felt as if I would drive this car into a wall, into the next person I saw. So I pulled over. I took out my journal just to air some of my fury, to get it out of my fingertips. Those expressed feelings are that poem."

In addition to race problems and love affairs, another important theme that runs through many of Lorde's volumes of poetry is the parent-child relationship. Brooks sees a deep concern with the image of her deceased father in Lorde's "Father, Son, and Holy Ghost" which carries over to poems dealing with Africa in *The Black Unicorn.* According to Brooks, "the contact with Africa is the contact with the father who is revealed in a wealth of mythological symbols. . . . The fundamental image of the unicorn indicates that the poet is aware that Africa is for her a fatherland, a phallic terrain." Martin, however, takes a different view: "Audre Lorde is a rare creature. . . . She is the Black Unicorn: magical and mysterious bearer of fantasy draped in truth and beauty." Further, Martin finds the poet's feelings about her mother to be more vital to an understanding of her works. In many of Lorde's poems, the figure of her mother is one of a woman who resents her daughter, tries to repress her child's unique personality so that she conforms with the rest of the world, and withholds the emotional nourishment of parental love. For example, Lorde tells us in *Coal*'s "Story Books on a Kitchen Table": "Out of her womb of pain my mother spat me / into her ill-fitting harness of despair / into her deceits / where anger reconceived me." In *The Black Unicorn*'s "From the House of Yemanja," the mother's efforts to shape the speaker into something she is not do not quench the speaker's desire for the mother's love: "Mother I need / mother I need / . . . I am / the sun and moon and forever hungry." "Ballad From Childhood" in *The New York Head Shop and Museum* is Lorde's depiction of the ways in which a child's hopes and dreams are crushed by a restrictive mother. After the mother has made withering replies to her child's queries about planting a tree to give some beauty to their wasteland surroundings, the child gives up in defeat, saying: "Please mommy do not beat me so! / yes I will learn to love the snow! / yes I want neither seed nor tree! / yes ice is quite enough for me! / who knows what trouble-leaves might grow!"

As Martin notes, however, Lorde's ambivalent feelings about her mother "did not make [her] bitter against her own children when circumstances changed her role from that of child to mother." *Coal* includes the poem "Now That I Am Forever with Child," which discusses the birth of Lorde's daughter. "I bore you one morning just before spring," she recounts, "my legs were towers between which / A new world was passing. / Since then / I can only distinguish / one thread within runnings hours / You, flowing through selves / toward You."

Lorde is also famed for writing the courageous account of her agonizing struggle to overcome breast cancer and mastectomy, *The Cancer Journals.* Her first major prose work, the *Journals* discuss Lorde's feelings about facing the possibility of death. Beyond death, Martin asserts, Lorde feared "she should die without having said the things she as a woman and an artist needed to say in order that her pain and subsequent loss might not have occurred in vain." The book also explains Lorde's decision not to wear a prosthesis after her breast was removed. As Brooks points out, "she does not suggest [her decision] for others, but . . . she uses [it] to expose some of the hypocrisies of the medical profession." Lorde summarizes her attitude on the issue thus in the *Journals:* "Prosthesis offers the empty comfort of 'Nobody will know the difference.' But it is that very difference which I wish to affirm, because I have lived it, and survived it, and wish to share that strength with other women. If we are to translate the silence surrounding breast cancer into language and action against this scourge, then the first step is that women with mastectomies must become visible to each other." Martin concludes: "*The Cancer Journals* affords all women who wish to read it the opportunity to look at the life experience of one very brave woman who bared her wounds without shame, in order that we might gain some strength from sharing in her pain."

Lorde's 1982 novel, *Zami: A New Spelling of My Name,* is described by its publishers as a "biomythography, combining elements of history, biography and myth," and Rosemary Daniell, in the *New York Times Book Review,* considers the work "excellent and evocative.... Among the elements that make the book so good are its personal honesty and lack of pretentiousness, characteristics that shine through the writing, bespeaking the evolution of a strong and remarkable character." Daniell says that, throughout the book, Lorde's "experiences are painted with exquisite imagery. Indeed, her West Indian heritage shows through most clearly in her use of word pictures that are sensual, steamy, at times near-tropical, evoking the colors, smells—repeatedly, the smells—shapes, textures that are her life."

BIOGRAPHICAL/CRITICAL SOURCES:

BOOKS

Addison, Gayle, editor, *Black Expression,* Weybright & Talley, 1969.
Bigsby, C. W. E., editor, *The Black American Writer,* Penguin, 1969.
Christian, Barbara, editor, *Black Feminist Criticism: Perspectives on Black Women Writers,* Pergamon, 1985.
Contemporary Literary Criticism, Volume 18, Gale, 1981.
Evans, Mari, editor, *Black Women Writers (1950-1980): A Critical Evaluation,* Doubleday, 1984.
Lorde, Audre, *The New York Head Shop and Museum,* Broadside Press, 1974.
Lorde, Audre, *Coal,* Norton, 1976.
Lorde, Audre, *The Black Unicorn,* Norton, 1978.
Lorde, Audre, *The Cancer Journals,* Spinsters Ink, 1980.
Tate, Claudia, editor, *Black Women Writers at Work,* Continuum, 1984.

PERIODICALS

Callaloo, Volume 9, number 4, 1987.
Essence, January, 1988.
Ms., September, 1974.
Negro Digest, September, 1968.
New York Times Book Review, December 19, 1982.
Poetry, February, 1977.

—*Sketch by Elizabeth Thomas*

*   *   *

LOTTIE
See GRIMKE, Charlotte L(ottie) Forten

*   *   *

LUCAS, W(ilmer) F(rancis, Jr.)   1927-

PERSONAL: Born September 1, 1927, in Brooklyn, N.Y.; son of Wilmer Francis (a certified public accountant) and Inez (a teacher; maiden name, Williams) Lucas; married Cleo Melissa Martin (a professor of history), February 18, 1969 (died); children: Alain Francis. *Education:* Attended New York University, 1945-48. *Religion:* Episcopalian.

ADDRESSES: Home and office—1936 Prospect Pl., Knoxville, Tenn. 37915.

CAREER: New York Amsterdam News, New York City, United Nations correspondent, 1959-60; Howard News Syndicate, New York City, associate editor in United Nations Bureau, 1960-61; New School for Social Research, New York City, lecturer in comparative Afro-American literature, 1962-68; Knoxville College, Knoxville, Tenn., writer-in-residence, 1968-70; University of Tennessee, Knoxville, director of Black Experience Institute, 1970-71, lecturer at Educational Opportunities Planning Center, 1971-72, co-director of humanities summer program, 1972, instructor in humanities, 1971—. Playwright, 1965—; full-time writer, 1973—. Special guest lecturer for colleges, universities, and civic organizations. Visiting lecturer in English at Lincoln University, 1966-67; research consultant for Opportunities Industrial Center, 1967-68. Founder and executive director of Carpetbag Theatre, 1971—; producer-director of "The Carpetbag Theatre Presents," WUOT-FM, Knoxville, 1972—; past member of theater arts advisory council for Tennessee Arts Commission and Knoxville City Commission for the Arts. Chairman of Duke Ellington Society.

AWARDS, HONORS: Day Foundation grant for writer in residency, Knoxville College, 1968-70; National Endowment for the Arts award and grant, 1973, for perpetuation of the Carpetbag Theatre.

WRITINGS:

Bottom Fishing: A Novella and Other Stories, Carpetbag Press, 1974.

PLAYS

"Patent Leather Sunday" (one-act; first produced in Lincoln University, Pa., spring, 1967), published in *Patent Leather Sunday: And S'More One Act Plays* (also see below), Carpetbag Press, 1975.
"Fandangos for Miss X" (one-act), first produced in Philadelphia, 1969.
"Aunt Lotties's Wake" (one-act), first produced in Knoxville at Carpetbag Theatre, 1972.
"Africa Too Young" (one-act), first produced in Knoxville at Carpetbag Theatre, 1972
"Elevator Stomp" (one-act), first produced in Knoxville at Carpetbag Theatre, 1973.
Patent Leather Sunday: And S'More One Act Plays, Carpetbag Press, 1975.
"The Planet of President Pandora" (three-act), first produced in Knoxville at Carpetbag Theatre, May, 1977.

Also author of several one-act plays done in workshops.

OTHER

Contributor to magazines and local newspapers in Haiti and the United States. Associate editor of *African Heritage,* 1963-64; book review editor of Negro Book Club, 1964-65, and *East Village Other,* 1968-69; contributing editor of *News Illustrated,* 1965-66, and *Our Voice,* 1970-72; editor at large and author of column "At Last" in *Keyana-Spectrum,* 1974-

75. Affiliated with ''Afro-American Literature,'' a filmstrip, Educational Dimensions, 1969-70.

WORK IN PROGRESS: Tropical Philadelphia, an experimental novel; *An Okra Venue,* a novel of regional aperture; *Bottom Fishing Revisited* (or *BF II*), a further collection of short stories.

SIDELIGHTS: W. F. Lucas commented: ''Having lived in Appalachia for nearly ten years without direct recourse to the mainstream of the publishing industry (except via perfunctory correspondence), I am in pursuit of a more constant and responsible liaison with the industry which I hope will see fit to afford me greater publishing opportunities. Without the aid of both agent and publisher who are equally cogently empathetic and imaginative, the source of much material I am capable of is becoming a still-born legacy that will one day arise like Lazarus in my lifetime.

''The sense of being a New Yorker and Yankee to boot still is primary in my consciousness, and will be there till the end. As an avid reader of all media, I am not only a bibliophile, but also an activist is issues that relate to the projection of the Carpetbag Theatre that I founded in 1971 to bring responsible theatre to the community in which I live. Trying to bring the past and the future to the present is virtually literary social work that I now feel can stand on its own. In the beginning it was social concern (and equally economic), and now it reverts to its true original premise of aesthetics in the quality of its own genre and milieu.

''My work bears the indelibility of cultural pluralism in a world in which I have traveled in both fact and imagination. The two are indistinguishable but hopefully the sense of art survives. The sophisticated truth and the real truth is the bridge that is being built on which we can all stand. I live both in the attic as well as the cellar. In between I survive.

''My relationship to the South by exposure is no less than an exposure to my environment. I am by nature eternally curious and a voyeur of sorts whose previous apprenticeship to people, places, and problems of the arts is already history. I now concentrate on my family, my work, and my theatre.''

AVOCATIONAL INTERESTS: ''Gigging'' with other musicians with his vibraharp, fiction, literary criticism, creative living.

M

MACKEY, William Wellington   1937-

PERSONAL: Born May 28, 1937, in Miami, Fla.; son of Milton and Doris Louise (Baso) Mackey. *Education:* Southern University (now Southern University and Agricultural and Mechanical College System), B.A., 1959; University of Minnesota, M.Ed., 1964.

CAREER: Playwright. Worked variously as a high school teacher, physical therapist, waiter, and bellhop; writer-in-residence at La Mama Experimental Theatre Club, New York, N.Y., 1971-72, and at Clark Center, New York City, 1973; visiting professor and writer-in-residence at Southern University (now Southern University and Agricultural and Mechanical College System), Baton Rouge, La., 1972.

AWARDS, HONORS: Rockefeller Foundation Playwright's Grant, 1972, to begin work on play "Love Me, Love Me, Daddy, or I Swear I'm Gonna Kill You."

WRITINGS:

PLAYS

Behold! Cometh the Vanderkellans! (three-act; first produced in Denver at Eden Theatrical Workshop, November 12, 1965; produced Off-Broadway at Theatre De Lys, March 31, 1971), Azazel Books, 1966.
"A Requiem for Brother X," first produced in Chicago at Chicago Hull House Parkway Theatre, 1968; produced Off-Off Broadway at Players Workshop, January 5, 1973.
"Billy Noname," first produced Off-Broadway at Truck and Warehouse Theatre, March 2, 1970.
"Family Meeting," first produced Off-Broadway at La Mama Experimental Theatre Club, January 28, 1972.
"Saga" (five-act musical), first produced in Miami at Cultural Arts Center of the Model Cities Program, 1976.
"Love Me, Love Me, Daddy, or I Swear I'm Gonna Kill You," first produced in New York City at American Folk Theatre, 1982.

Also author of "Death of Charlie Blackman" and "Homeboys." Work represented in anthologies, including *New Black Playwrights,* edited by William Couch, Jr., Avon, 1970, and *Black Drama Anthology,* edited by Woodie King and Ron Milner, New American Library, 1972.

SIDELIGHTS: Playwright William Wellington Mackey has won acclaim for his ability to portray, within the turmoil of a single representative family, the political struggles of the black people in America. Mackey's first production, "Behold! Cometh the Vanderkellans!" equates the disintegration of a well-established black family with the social upheaval in 1960s America, when racial perspectives were changing radically. The drama takes place during a family reunion in the fine home of the president of a prestigious southern black college. One by one, family members expose one another's vices and their own previously hidden fears and prejudices, causing their hypocritical family structure to break down. "The children are revealed as a whore, a homosexual, and an Uncle Tom; the parents' marriage is a sham," recounted critic Michele Gerrig in *Show Business.* In addition, Gerrig continued, "as the conflicts within the home are heightened, they are paralleled by student unrest and rioting outside," demonstrating the exposure of vices and prejudices in the American community. In his "unsettling" and "tense drama," Gerrig ventured, "William Wellington Mackey shows us, in microcosm, the agony of a race in transition."

In "Family Meeting," which was first produced Off-Broadway in 1972, Mackey again portrays radical social transformations of values in the breakdown of a black middle-class family. The dialogue in "Family Meeting" is more surrealistic than in "Behold!" however, and is carried principally by the young male protagonist. In a violent monologue the young man questions traditional beliefs and opinions about his race, delving into perplexing areas such as madness and death, portrayed by his white self and black self. The boy's personal confusion, according to reviewers, represents the turmoil that results from white values being forced upon black people.

"A Requiem for Brother X" was inspired by the sudden death in 1965 of black American religious and political leader Malcolm X. As in his other plays, Mackey examines the black community by focusing on a family gathering, but this time the characters are ghetto residents. While in "Behold!" and "Family Meeting" Mackey portrays the black middle-class members as destroying themselves with their own hypocrisy and greed, in "Requiem" he shows the poorer blacks as being trapped and ruined by external forces.

BIOGRAPHICAL/CRITICAL SOURCES:

BOOKS

Dictionary of Literary Biography, Volume 38: *Afro-American*

Writers After 1955: Dramatists and Prose Writers, Gale, 1985.

PERIODICALS

Black World, April, 1975.
Negro Digest, April, 1967.
Show Business, April 8, 1971.
Variety, April 21, 1971.

*   *   *

MADGETT, Naomi Long   1923-
(Naomi Cornelia Long, Naomi Long Witherspoon)

PERSONAL: Born July 5, 1923, in Norfolk, Va.; daughter of Clarence Marcellus (a clergyman) and Maude Selena (a teacher; maiden name, Hilton) Long; married Julian F. Witherspoon, March 31, 1946 (divorced April 27, 1949); married William Harold Madgett, July 29, 1954 (divorced December 21, 1960); married Leonard Patton Andrews (an elementary school principal), March 31, 1972; children: (first marriage) Jill Witherspoon Boyer. *Education:* Virginia State College, B.A., 1945; Wayne State University, M.Ed., 1956; University of Detroit, graduate study; International Institute for Advanced Studies, Ph.D., 1980. *Politics:* Independent, but usually Democratic Party. *Religion:* Protestant (Congregational).

ADDRESSES: Home—16886 Inverness St., Detroit, Mich. 48221. *Office*—English Department, Eastern Michigan University, Ypsilanti, Mich. 48197.

CAREER: Michigan Chronicle, Detroit, Mich., reporter and copy reader, 1945-46; Michigan Bell Telephone Co., Detroit, service representative, 1948-54; English teacher in public high schools, Detroit, 1955-65, 1966-68; Oakland University, Rochester, Mich., research associate, 1965-66; Eastern Michigan University, Ypsilanti, Mich., associate professor, 1968-73, professor of English, 1973-84, professor emeritus, 1984—. Visiting lecturer in English, University of Michigan, 1970-71; lecturer on Afro-American literature at colleges and universities. Editor, Lotus Press, Detroit, 1974—. Michigan Council for the Arts, participant in Poetry Readings in the Classroom and member of minority advisory panel. Staff member, Writers' Workshop, Oakland University, 1968—.

MEMBER: College Language Association, National Council for Teachers of English, National Association for the Advancement of Colored People, Poetry Society of Michigan, Detroit Women Writers, Metropolitan Detroit Alliance of Black School Educators, Alpha Kappa Alpha, Alpha Rho Omega.

AWARDS, HONORS: Esther R. Beer poetry award, National Writers Club, 1957, for ''Native''; Mott fellowship in English, Oakland University, 1965-66; Distinguished English Teacher of the Year, Metropolitan Detroit English Club, 1967; Alpha Kappa Alpha Sorority award, 1969; Josephine Nevins Keal Development Fund Award, 1979; Distinguished Service Award, Chesapeake/Virginia Beach Links, Inc., 1981.

WRITINGS:

POEMS

(Under name Naomi Cornelia Long) *Songs to a Phantom Nightingale,* Fortuny's, 1941.
One and the Many, Exposition, 1956.
Star by Star, Harlo, 1965, revised edition, 1970.
Pink Ladies in the Afternoon, Lotus Press, 1972.
Exits and Entrances: New Poems, illustrations by Beverley Rose Enright, Lotus Press, 1978.

Phantom Nightingale: Juvenilia, Lotus Press, 1981.

CONTRIBUTOR

Langston Hughes and Arna Bontemps, editors, *The Poetry of the Negro, 1746-1949,* Doubleday, 1949.
Rosey E. Pool, editor, *Beyond the Blues,* Hand & Flower, 1962.
Robert Hayden, editor, *Kaleidoscope,* Harcourt, 1967.
June Meyer Jordan, editor, *Soulscript,* Doubleday, 1970.
Charlotte I. Lee, editor, *Oral Interpretation,* Houghton, 1971.
Abraham Chapman, editor, *New Black Voices,* New American Library, 1972.
Betsy Ryan, editor, *Within You, Without You,* Scholastic Book Services, 1973.
Lee Bennett Hopkins, editor, *On Our Way,* Knopf, 1974.
Judith Goren, Elinor K. Rose, Gay Rubin, and Elaine Watson, editors, *Echoes from the Moon,* Hot Apples Press, 1976.
Carol Koner and Dorothy Walters, editors, *I Hear My Sisters Saying,* Crowell, 1976.
Bo Andersson and Gunilla Jensen, editors, *Lat Vaerlden bli en svart Dikt* (in translation), Forum (Stockholm), 1978.
Ved Ivor Teigum, editor, *Svarte amerikanske Dikt* (in translation), Det Norske Samlaget (Oslo), 1979.
Dexter Fischer, editor, *The Third Woman,* Houghton, 1980.

Poetry represented in over eighty anthologies. Contributor of poetry to numerous periodicals, including *Negro Digest, Negro History Bulletin, Poetry Digest, Virginia Statesman, Journal of Black Poetry, Ebony,* and *Great Lakes Review.*

OTHER

(With Ethel Tincher and Henry B. Maloney) *Success in Language and Literature B* (high school textbook), Follett, 1967.
(Editor) *Deep Rivers, A Portfolio: Twenty Contemporary Black American Poets* (booklet), Lotus Press, 1978.
A Student's Guide to Creative Writing (textbook), Lotus Press, 1980.

SIDELIGHTS: Naomi Long Madgett once wrote, ''As a child I was motivated by my father's library and the interests and inspiration of literary parents. I discovered Alfred Lord Tennyson and Langston Hughes at about the same time, [while] sitting on the floor of my father's study when I was about seven or eight. I think my poetry represents something of the variety of interest and style that these two widely divergent poets represent. I would rather be a good poet than anything else I can imagine. It pleases me tremendously that my social-worker daughter is becoming a very good poet.''

Madgett's papers are housed in the Special Collections Library at Fisk University.

BIOGRAPHICAL/CRITICAL SOURCES:

PERIODICALS

Black American Literature Forum, summer, 1980.
Black Books Bulletin, spring, 1974.
Black Scholar, March-April, 1980.
Black World, September, 1974.
English Journal, April, 1957.
First World, Volume II, number 4, 1980.
Michigan Chronicle, January 15, 1966.
Negro Digest, September, 1966.
New Orleans Review, September, 1976.
Phylon, winter, 1956.
Richmond News Leader (Va.), March 28, 1979.

MADHUBUTI, Haki R.   1942-
(Don L. Lee)

PERSONAL: Born February 23, 1942, in Little Rock, Ark.; son of Jimmy L. and Maxine (Graves) Lee; married Johari Amini; children: two. *Education:* Attended Wilson Junior College, Roosevelt University, and University of Illinois, Chicago Circle; University of Iowa, M.F.A., 1984.

ADDRESSES: Office—Third World Press, 7524 South Cottage Grove Ave., Chicago, Ill. 60619; Department of English, Speech, and Theatre, Chicago State University, 95th St. at King Dr., Chicago, Ill. 60628.

CAREER: DuSable Museum of African American History, Chicago, Ill., apprentice curator, 1963-67; Montgomery Ward, Chicago, stock department clerk, 1963-64; post office clerk in Chicago, 1964-65; Spiegels, Chicago, junior executive, 1965-66; Cornell University, Ithaca, N.Y., writer-in-residence, 1968-69; Northeastern Illinois State College, Chicago, poet-in-residence, 1969-70; University of Illinois, Chicago, lecturer, 1969-71; Howard University, Washington, D.C., writer-in-residence, 1970-78; Morgan State College, Baltimore, Md., 1972-73; Chicago State University, Chicago, Ill., associate professor of English, 1984—. Publisher and editor, Third World Press, 1967—. Director of Institute of Positive Education, Chicago, 1969—. *Military service:* U.S. Army, 1960-63.

MEMBER: African Liberation Day Support Committee (vice-chairperson), Congress of African People (past member of executive council), Organization of Black American Culture, Writers Workshop (founding member, 1967-75).

WRITINGS:

UNDER NAME DON L. LEE

Think Black, Broadside Press, 1967, revised edition, 1968, enlarged edition, 1969.

Black Pride, Broadside Press, 1967.

For Black People (and Negroes Too), Third World Press, 1968.

Don't Cry, Scream (poems), Broadside Press, 1969.

We Walk the Way of the New World (poems), Broadside Press, 1970.

(Author of introduction) *To Blackness: A Definition in Thought,* Kansas City Black Writers Workshop, 1970.

Dynamite Voices I: Black Poets of the 1960s (essays), Broadside Press, 1971.

(Editor with P. L. Brown and F. Ward) *To Gwen with Love,* Johnson Publishing, 1971.

Directionscore: Selected and New Poems, Broadside Press, 1971.

(Author of introduction) Marion Nicholas, *Life Styles,* Broadside Press, 1971.

The Need for an African Education (pamphlet), Institute of Positive Education, 1972.

UNDER NAME HAKI R. MADHUBUTI

Book of Life (poems), Broadside Press, 1973.

From Plan to Planet—Life Studies: The Need for Afrikan Minds and Institutions, Broadside Press, 1973.

(With Jawanza Kunjufu) *Black People and the Coming Depression* (pamphlet), Institute of Positive Education, 1975.

(Contributor) *A Capsule Course in Black Poetry Writing,* Broadside Press, 1975.

Enemies: The Clash of Races (essays), Third World Press, 1978.

Earthquakes and Sunrise Missions: Poetry and Essays of Black Renewal, 1973-1983 (poems), Third World Press, 1984.

Killing Memory, Seeking Ancestors (poems), Lotus, 1987.

Say That the River Turns: The Impact of Gwendolyn Brooks (poetry and prose), Third World Press, 1987.

OTHER

Also author of *Back Again, Home,* 1968, and *One Sided Shootout,* 1968. Contributor to more than one hundred anthologies. Contributor to numerous magazines and literary journals, including *Black World, Negro Digest, Journal of Black Poetry, Essence, Journal of Black History,* and *Chicago Defender.* Founder and editor of *Black Books Bulletin,* 1972—; contributing editor, *Black Scholar* and *First World.*

WORK IN PROGRESS: Black Men: Obsolete, Single, Dangerous?, essays; *Gifted Genius: African-American Political Poets,* criticism; *Collected Poetry (1966-1989);* and *Collected Essays (1969-1989).*

SIDELIGHTS: "Poetry in my home was almost as strange as money," Don L. Lee, also known by his swahili name Haki R. Madhubuti, relates in *Dynamite Voices I: Black Poets of the 1960s.* Abandoned by his father, then bereaved of his mother at the age of sixteen, Madhubuti made his living by maintaining two paper routes and cleaning a nearby bar. Poetry was scarce in his early life, he explains in the same source, because "what wasn't taught, but was consciously learned, in our early educational experience was that writing of any kind was something that Black people just didn't do." Nonetheless, he has become one of the best known poets of the black arts movement of the 1960s, a respected and influential critic of Black poetry, and an activist dedicated to the cultural unity of his people. "In many ways," writes Catherine Daniels Hurst in the *Dictionary of Literary Biography,* Madhubuti "is one of the most representative voices of his time. Although most significant as a poet, his work as an essayist, critic, publisher, social activist, and educator has enabled him to go beyond the confines of poetry to the establishment of a black press and a school for black children."

The literature of the Harlem Renaissance—a literary movement of the 1920s and 1930s in which the works of many black artists became popular—was not deeply felt by the majority of America's black population, he writes. "In the Sixties, however, Black Art in all its various forms began to flourish as never before: music, theater, art (painting, sculpture), films, prose (novel[s], essays), and poetry. The new and powerful voices of the Sixties came to light mainly because of the temper of the times." The writers of this turbulent generation who worked to preserve a cultural heritage distinct from white culture did not look to previous literary traditions—black or white—for inspiration. Says Madhubuti, "The major influences on the new Black poets were/are Black music, Black life style, Black churches, and their own Black contemporaries."

An *Ebony* article on the poet by David Llorens hails him as "a lion of a poet who splits syllables, invents phrases, makes letters work as words, and gives rhythmic quality to verse that is never savage but often vicious and always reflecting a revolutionary black consciousness." As a result, his "lines rumble like a street gang on the page," remarks Liz Gant in a *Black World* review. Though Madhubuti believes, as he declares in *Don't Cry, Scream,* that "most, if not all blackpoetry will be *political,*" he explains in *Dynamite Voices I* that it must do more than protest, since "mere 'protest' writing is generally a weak reaction to persons or events and often lacks the substance necessary to motivate and move people." Black poetry will be powerful, he says, if it is "a genuine reflection of [the poet] and his people," presenting "the beauty and joy" of the black experience as well as outrage against social and economic oppression.

However, some critics hear only the voice of protest in Madhubuti's work. Paul Breman's piece in C. W. E. Bigsby's *The Black American Writer, Volume I: Poetry and Drama,* calls him a poet whose "all-out ranting . . . has become outdated more rapidly than one could have hoped." And Jascha Kessler, writing in a *Poetry* review, sees no poetry in Madhubuti's books. "Anger, bombast, raw hatred, strident, aggrieved, perhaps charismatically crude religious and political canting, propaganda and racist nonsense, yes. . . . [Madhubuti] is outside poetry somewhere, exhorting, hectoring, cursing, making a lot of noise." But the same elements that grate against the sensibilities of such critics stem from the poet's cultural objectives and are much better received by the poet's intended audience, say others. "He is not interested in modes of writing that aspire to elegance," writes Gwendolyn Brooks in the introduction of *Don't Cry, Scream.* Madhubuti writes for and to Blacks, and "the last thing these people crave is elegance. It is very hard to enchant, with elegant song, the ears of a fellow whose stomach is growling," she notes. Explains Hurst, "often he uses street language and the dialect of the uneducated Black community. . . . He uses unconventional abbreviations and strung-together words . . . in a visually rendered dialect designed to convey the stress, pitch, volume, texture, resonance, and the intensity of the black speaking voice. By these and other means, Madhubuti intends to engage the active participation of a black audience accustomed to the oral tradition of storytelling and song."

Poems in *Don't Cry, Scream* and *We Walk the Way of the New World* show the activist-poet's "increasing concern for incorporating jazz rhythms"; more and more, the poet styled the poems "for performance, the text lapsing into exultant screams and jazz scats," writes C. W. E. Bigsby in *The Second Renaissance: Essays in Black Literature.* The title poem of *Don't Cry, Scream,* believes Hurst, "should be dedicated to that consummate musician, John Coltrane, whose untimely death left many of his admirers in deep mourning. In this poem (which begs to be read out loud as only the poet himself can do it), Madhubuti strains to duplicate the virtuoso high notes of Coltrane's instrumental sound." Critic Sherley Anne Williams, speaking to interviewer Claudia Tate in *Black Women Writers at Work,* explains why this link to music is significant for the black writer. Whereas white Americans preserve themselves or their legacy through literature, black Americans have done so in music, in the blues form: "The blues records of each decade explain something about the philosophical basis of historical continuity for black people. It is a ritualized way of talking about ourselves and passing it on. This was true until the late sixties." Madhubuti elaborates in *Dynamite Voices I:* "Black music is our most advanced form of Black art. In spite of the debilitating conditions of slavery and its aftermath, Black music endured and grew as a communicative language, as a sustaining spiritual force, as entertainment, and as a creative extension of our African selves. It was one of the few mediums of expression open to Black people that was virtually free of interferences. . . . To understand . . . art . . . which is uniquely Black, we must start with the art form that has been least distorted, a form that has so far resisted being molded

into a *pure* product of European-American culture." Numerous references to Black musicians and lines that imitate the sounds of Black music connect Madhubuti's poetry to that tradition and extend its life as well.

Hurst claims that the poet's "unique delivery has given him a popular appeal which is tantamount to stardom." In 1969, reports Greene, the poet "averaged three appearances a week, reading his poetry and carrying on dialogs at schools, churches, and community centers all over the country." Phenomenal sales in excess of 100,000 by that time alerted reviewer Helen Vendler that "something [was] happening." Writing in the *New York Times Book Review,* she attributed the sales to Madhubuti's "nerve, stamina, and satire. In him the sardonic and savage turn-of-phrase long present in black speech as a survival tactic finds its best poet." Greene suggests that a general concern about black militance and possible urban rioting accounted for the sales, but went on to say that "people in the publishing industry are convinced that untold numbers of older and ill-educated Negroes, whose reading up till now might have been limited to comic and pulp fiction, are being lured to book shops and paperback stands by volumes exploring the 'black experience' in language they can understand."

Madhubuti's poetic voice softened somewhat during the 1970s, during which time he directed his energies to the writing of political essays (*From Plan to Planet—Life Studies: The Need for Afrikan Minds and Institutions* and *Enemies: The Clash of Races*). In addition, he contributed to the establishment of a black aesthetic for new writers through critical essays and reviews. *Dynamite Voices I,* for instance, "has become one of the major contemporary scholarly resources for black poetry," notes Hurst. Fulfilling the role of "cultural stabilizer," he also gave himself to the construction of institutions that promote the cultural independence and education of his people. In a fight against "brain mismanagement" in America, he founded the Third World Press in 1967 to encourage literacy and the Institute of Positive Education in 1969 "to provide educational and communication services to a community struggling to assert its identity amidst powerful, negative forces," he told Donnarae MacCann for an interview published in *Interracial Books for Children Bulletin.*

Students at the Institute in Chicago are schooled in the works of black writers because he feels black children need a better education than the one he received: "My education was . . . acculturation, that process in which one is brought into another's culture, regardless of the damage. For the most part, my generation did not question this acculturation process. . . . In school I read Hawthorne, Twain, Hemingway, Fitzgerald— the major Western writers. My generation learned from that Western tradition, but we were not given the tradition that spoke best to our insides." Black authors such as Langston Hughes, Margaret Walker, Gwendolyn Brooks and Richard Wright (discovered "by accident" when he was thirteen), helped him to become "complete."

In the same interview, he defines the publishing goals of the Third World Press: "We look for writers who continue to critically assess the ambivalence of being Black in America. . . . What we are trying to do is to service the great majority of Black people, those who do not have a voice, who have not made it. Black themes over the past years have moved from reaction and rage to contemplative assessments of today's problems to a kind of visionary look at the world," a vision that includes not only blacks, but all people. But the development of the black community remains its main focus, he told David Streitfield for a *Washington Post* article. "There's just so much negative material out there, and so little that helps. That's not to say we don't publish material that is critical, but it has to be constructive." As Streitfield reports, "Third World's greatest succes has been with . . . Chancellor Williams' *Destruction of Black Civilization*, which has gone through 16 printings." Other articles as well commended the press for breaking even for the first time in nineteen years in 1987.

Summing up Madhubuti's accomplishment as a writer, Williams comments that in *Give Birth to Brightness: A Thematic Study in Neo-Black Literature* that as one of "the vocal exponents of Neo-Black literature," he has "come to symbolize most of what is strong and beautiful and vital in Black Experience and Black Art." Hurst's summary states, "His books have sold more than a million copies, without benefit of a national distributor. Perhaps Madhubuti will even succeed in helping to establish some lasting institutions in education and in the publishing world. Whether he does or not, he has already secured a place for himself in American literature. He is among the foremost anthologized contemporary revolutionary poets, and he has played a significant role in stimulating other young black talent. As Stephen Henderson has observed, he is 'more widely imitated than any other Black poet with the exception of Imamu Baraka (LeRoi Jones). . . . His influence is enormous, and is still growing.'"

BIOGRAPHICAL/CRITICAL SOURCES:

BOOKS

Bigsby, C. W. E., *The Black American Writer, Volume I: Poetry & Drama*, Penguin, 1969.
Bigsby, C. W. E., *The Second Renaissance: Essays in Black Literature*, Greenwood Press, 1980.
Contemporary Literary Criticism, Gale, Volume II, 1974, Volume VI, 1976.
Dictionary of Literary Biography, Gale, Volume V: *American Poets since World War II*, 1980, Volume XLI: *Afro-American Poets since 1955*, 1985.
Gibson, Donald B., editor, *Modern Black Poets: A Collection of Critical Essays*, Prentice-Hall, 1973.
Henderson, Stephen, *Understanding the New Black Poetry: Black Speech and Black Music as Poetic References*, Morrow, 1973.
Lee, Don L., *Don't Cry, Scream*, Broadside Press, 1969.
Lee, Don L., *Dynamite Voices, I: Black Poets of the 1960s*, Broadside Press, 1971.
Mosher, Marlene, *New Directions from Don L. Lee*, Exposition, 1975.
Tate, Claudia, editor, *Black Women Writers at Work*, Continuum, 1983.
Vendler, Helen, *Part of Nature, Part of Us*, Howard University Press, 1980.
Williams, John A., and Charles F. Harris, editors, *Amistad 2*, Random House, 1971.
Williams, Sherley Anne, *Give Birth to Brightness: A Thematic Study in Neo-Black Literature*, Dial, 1972.

PERIODICALS

Black Collegian, February/March, 1971, September/October, 1974.
Black World, April, 1971, June, 1972, January, 1974.
Chicago Sun Times, December 11, 1987.
Chicago Sun Times Showcase, July 18, 1971.
Chicago Tribune, December 23, 1987.
College Literature Association Journal, September, 1971.
Ebony, March, 1969.
Interracial Books for Children Bulletin, Volume 17, number 2, 1986.
Jet, June 27, 1974.
Journal of Negro History, April, 1971.
National Observer, July 14, 1969.
Negro Digest, December, 1969.
New Lady, July/August, 1971.
New York Times, December 13, 1987.
New York Times Book Review, September 29, 1974.
Poetry, February, 1973.
Washington Post, June 6, 1971, January 17, 1988.

　　　　　　　　　　　　　　　—Sketch by Marilyn K. Basel

*　　　*　　　*

MAIS, Roger　1905-1955

PERSONAL: Born August 11, 1905, in Kingston, Jamaica; died of cancer, June 21, 1955, in Kingston, Jamaica. *Education:* Attended public schools in the Blue Mountains, Jamaica.

CAREER: Writer. Worked variously as a civil servant, painter, farmer, photographer, and journalist for the *Daily Gleaner* and *Public Opinion*.

WRITINGS:

And Most of All Man (short stories and verse), City Printery (Kingston, Jamaica), 1939.
Face and Other Stories (short stories and verse), Universal Printery, 1942.
"The Potter's Field" (play), first published in *Public Opinion*, December 23, 1950.
Atalanta at Calydon (play), J. Cape, 1950.
Come Love, Come Death, Hutchinson, 1951.
The Hills Were Joyful Together, J. Cape, 1953, reprinted, with introduction by Daphne Morris, Heinemann, 1981 (also see below).
(And illustrator) *Brother Man*, J. Cape, 1954, reprinted, with introduction by Edward Brathwaite, Heinemann, 1974 (also see below).
Black Lightning, J. Cape, 1955, reprinted, with introduction by Jean D'Costa, Heinemann, 1983 (also see below).
The Three Novels of Roger Mais (contains *The Hills Were Joyful Together*, *Brother Man*, and *Black Lightning*), introduction by Norman W. Manley, J. Cape, 1966 (also see above).
Listen, The Wind, and Other Stories, Longman, c. 1986.

Also author of other plays, such as "Hurricane," "Masks and Paper Hats," and "The First Sacrifice."

WORK IN PROGRESS: A fourth novel.

SIDELIGHTS: Roger Mais, "the spokesman of emergent Jamaica," according to Jean D'Costa in her 1978 critique on Mais, is known primarily for his three novels of social protest. Among the first Jamaican novels to realistically examine that country's squalid urban conditions, *The Hills Were Joyful Together*, *Brother Man*, and *Black Lightning* greatly influenced the development of West Indian literature. Despite his middle-class upbringing in Jamaica's Blue Mountains, Mais empathized with the less fortunate urban slum dwellers and, as a writer, remained "fiercely dedicated to the exposure of social ills in [mid-twentieth-century] Jamaica," wrote D'Costa.

Of the three novels, *The Hills* provides the most explicit portrait of Caribbean slum life. Set in a ghetto in Kingston, Jamaica, *The Hills* examines the lives of three groups of black lower-class people. "Violence and misery is their common lot," observed reviewer Karina Williamson in the *Journal of Commonwealth Literature. The Hills*'s subject matter disturbed many members of Jamaican society, according to Jean Creary, who explained in *The Islands in Between* that Mais's readers were "thrown straight into a world everyone in Jamaica knew existed, and yet which the middle classes were united in a conspiracy of silence to ignore and reject." She found, however, that "within and behind this human underworld lies beauty and pattern." In one particularly acclaimed passage, Williamson wrote, Mais describes the ghetto community's "common capacity for gaiety and goodwill" during a beach celebration. In other instances he depicts sympathy and loyalty between characters despite their misfortunes, indicating that personal integrity can withstand even the most hostile environment. "Mais's attitude . . . is ultimately neither cynical nor defeatist," Williamson explained, asserting that it is the author's balanced perspective that accounts for the novel's literary merit. "The book has its grave weaknesses," Creary admitted, citing wordiness and melodrama, but it succeeds because the author's "weaknesses come from the same source where lies his strength—from his innocent and yet potent awareness of himself and of his environment."

Mais's second novel, *Brother Man*, focuses on Rastafarianism, a Caribbean religious movement in which members seek a return of blacks to Africa. For some of their rituals, which include smoking marijuana—though shunning alcohol—and refusing to cut their hair, Rastafarians were "feared, despised, and rejected" during the 1940s and 1950s, explained Edward Brathwaite in his 1974 introduction to Mais's novel. The protagonist of *Brother Man* is a peaceful Rastafarian leader named John Power or "Bra Man," whose life resembles that of Jesus Christ. "In many ways," wrote Oscar R. Dathorne in *Studies in the Novel,* "the parallel between Christ and Bra Man is followed almost too carefully." Most critics agreed that the novel's credibility weakens whenever Bra Man becomes too Christ-like, healing the sick and teaching in parables, for example. Dathorne added, however, that "in spite of all this, Bra Man is convincing, not only as a messianic Christ-figure but as a person."

Reviewers praised Mais's refinement in *Brother Man* of a complex linguistic technique he had introduced in *The Hills.* Combining the figurative language of the King James Bible with the words and syntax of Jamaican Creole, Mais developed an elaborate writing style that enhanced his allegorical narratives. This style, according to Creary, is especially effective in descriptions of Bra Man, "Mais's vision of the reincarnate Christ. . . . This Gospel Presence fuses with Mais's writing in the rhythmical, Biblical prose." Dathorne agreed, explaining that "the language helps to identify Bra Man, and the rhythm of the Bible is reserved for him."

Black Lightning, Mais's third novel, is a biblical allegory like *Brother Man.* Unlike Mais's first two novels, however, *Black Lightning* skirts social issues, focusing instead on the solitary artist. Set in the Jamaican countryside, the novel follows the progress a sculptor, Jake, makes on a statue he is carving of the biblical hero Samson. "As it takes shape," Creary noted, "the figure of Samson becomes increasingly identified with Jake himself." Initially perceiving himself as strong and independent, the artist begins fashioning his work after his own self-image. After his wife leaves him, Jake becomes more aware of his dependence on her and begins molding his statue into the image of a weaker man. "The finished work Jake contemptuously reveals . . . is not Samson in his prime, but the blinded Samson, a figure of ruined strength leaning on a little boy," related Kenneth Ramchand in *The West Indian Novel and Its Background.* Like Samson, Jake is eventually blinded and, in despair, he kills himself.

Although Mais's first two novels received greater popular and critical acclaim upon their publication, Ramchand believes that the author's third book is his most powerful one. "The work has been virtually disregarded in the West Indies," the critic pointed out, "but I would like to contend that it is in *Black Lightning* that Mais's art and understanding are in greatest harmony, and that it is upon this . . . novel that his reputation must rest." Williamson also lauded *Black Lightning*'s artistic merit and its contribution to Caribbean literature: "*Black Lightning,* more than either of Mais's other novels, seems to me a landmark in the development of the West Indian novel."

A supporter of the Jamaican nationalist movement of the 1930s and 1940s, Mais was imprisoned in 1944 for an essay he wrote, titled "Now We Know," attacking English colonialism. Already the author of two short story collections, *And Most of All Man* and *Face and Other Stories,* Mais began writing his first novel during his six months in prison. Published nine years later, *The Hills Were Joyful Together* was quickly followed by *Brother Man* and *Black Lightning.* The author traveled to Europe in 1951 in search of a more accommodating artistic climate, but he returned to his homeland three years later, suffering from cancer. He died in Kingston in 1955, the year his third novel was published, leaving a fourth novel incomplete.

BIOGRAPHICAL/CRITICAL SOURCES:

BOOKS

D'Costa, Jean, *Roger Mais: "The Hills Were Joyful Together" and "Brother Man,"* Longman, 1978.
James, Louis, editor, *The Islands in Between: Essays on West Indian Literature,* Oxford University Press, 1968.
Mais, Roger, *Brother Man,* introduction by Edward Brathwaite, Heinemann, 1974.
Moore, Gerald, *The Chosen Tongue: English Writings in the Tropical World,* Harper, 1969.
Ramchand, Kenneth, *The West Indian Novel and Its Background,* Barnes & Noble, 1970.
Twentieth-Century Literary Criticism, Volume 8, Gale, 1982.

PERIODICALS

Black Images, summer, 1972.
Journal of Commonwealth Literature, December, 1966.
Studies in the Novel, summer, 1972.

—*Sketch by Christa Brelin*

*   *   *

MAJOR, Clarence 1936-

PERSONAL: Born December 31, 1936, in Atlanta, Ga.; son of Clarence and Inez (Huff) Major; married Joyce Sparrow, 1958 (divorced, 1964); married Pamela Jane Ritter. *Education:* Attended Art Institute of Chicago, 1953, Armed Forces Institute, 1956, and New School for Social Research, 1972; State University of New York at Albany, B.S.; Union for Experimenting Colleges and Universities, Ph.D.

ADDRESSES: Home—1751 Norwood Ave., Boulder, Colo. 80302. *Office*—Department of English, Box 226, University of Colorado, Boulder, Colo. 80309. *Agent*—Susan Bergholz, 340 W. 72nd St., New York, N.Y. 10023.

CAREER: Writer. Harlem Education Program, The New Lincoln School, New York City, director of creative writing program, 1967-68; Sarah Lawrence College, Bronxville, N.Y., lecturer, 1972-75; Howard University, Washington, D.C., assistant professor, 1974-76; University of Washington, Seattle, assistant professor, 1976-77; University of Colorado, Boulder, associate professor, 1977-81, professor of English, 1981—.

Visiting professor, University of Nice, France, 1981-82 and 1983; visiting assistant professor, University of Maryland at College Park and State University of New York at Buffalo, 1976. Writer-in-residence at colleges and universities. Research analyst for Simulmatics Corp., New York City, 1967; newspaper reporter, 1968. Lecturer and guest lecturer at colleges, universities, libraries, and other institutions in the United States, Europe, and Africa; has given readings of his work at various institutions around the world and has recorded his work on tapes, videotapes, and records; has been interviewed on radio and television. Judge, Creative Artists Public Service Program, 1972, Whiteside Poetry Contest, Brooklyn College, 1975, Massachusetts Foundation for the Arts and Humanities, 1976, Academy of American Poets, University of Washington, 1976, Ohio Arts Consortium, 1979, Consuelo Ford Award, Poetry Society of America, 1979, Arts Symposium, Colorado State University, 1981, Henfield Foundation Fiction Prize, 1983. Artist; has exhibited and published his photographs and paintings. Editorial consultant, University of Pittsburgh Press, 1974, Wesleyan University Press, 1984, and University of Georgia Press, 1987; consultant, Pennsylvania Advancement School, 1967-68, University of Colorado Writers Conference, 1977, and Liberian Association of Writers, 1982; member of advisory board, Reading Program, New York Public School District 5, 1970. *Military service:* U.S. Air Force, 1955-57; served as record specialist.

MEMBER: International Platform Association, Authors Guild, Authors League of America, Poetry Society of America, PEN, American Association of University Professors, Modern Language Association of America, Union for Experimenting Colleges and Universities, Society for the Study of Dictionaries and Lexicography, Dictionary Society of North America.

AWARDS, HONORS: Recipient of numerous grants; National Council on the Arts Award, Association of American University Presses, 1970; Pushcart Prize certificate, 1976, for poem "Funeral," from *The Syncopated Cakewalk;* Fulbright-Hays Inter-University Exchange Award, Franco-American Commission for Educational Exchange, Paris, France, 1981-83; Western States Book Award for fiction, 1986, for *My Amputations.*

WRITINGS:

Love Poems of a Black Man, Coercion, 1965.
Human Juices (poetry), Coercion, 1966.
(Editor) *Writers Workshop Anthology,* Harlem Education Program, 1967.
(Editor) *Man Is Like a Child: An Anthology of Creative Writing by Students,* Macomb Junior High School, 1968.
(Editor and author of introduction) *The New Black Poetry,* International Publications, 1969.
All-Night Visitors (novel), Olympia, 1969.
Dictionary of Afro-American Slang, International Publications, 1970 (published in England as *Black Slang: A Dictionary of Afro-American Talk,* Routledge & Kegan Paul, 1971).

Swallow the Lake (poetry), Wesleyan University Press, 1970.
Symptoms and Madness (poetry), Corinth Books, 1971.
Private Line (poetry), Paul Breman Ltd., 1971.
The Cotton Club: New Poems, Broadside Press, 1972.
No (novel), Emerson Hall, 1973.
The Dark and Feeling: Black American Writers and Their Work (essays), Third Press, 1974.
The Syncopated Cakewalk (poetry), Barlenmir, 1974.
(Editor) Jerry Bumpus, *Things in Place* (short stories), Fiction Collective, 1975.
Reflex and Bone Structure (novel), Fiction Collective, 1975.
Emergency Exit (novel), Fiction Collective, 1979.
Inside Diameter: The France Poems, Permanent Press, 1985.
My Amputations: A Novel, Fiction Collective, 1986.
Such Was the Season: A Novel (Literary Guild selection), Mercury House, 1987.
Surfaces and Masks (poetry), Coffee House Press, 1987.
Some Observations of a Stranger at Zuni in the Latter Part of the Century (poetry), Sun & Moon, 1988.
Painted Turtle: Woman with Guitar (novel), Sun & Moon, 1988.
Fun and Games (short stories), Holy Cow!, 1988.

Also author of *The Fires That Burn in Heaven,* 1954, and *On the Other Side of the Wall,* not yet published.

CONTRIBUTOR TO ANTHOLOGIES

19 Necromancers from Now (fiction), Doubleday, 1970.
Black on Black (fiction), Bantam, 1972.
Penguin Book of Black Verse, Penguin, 1972.
Black Spirits (poetry), Random House, 1972.
Studies in Black American Fiction, Larrimer, 1973.
From the Belly of the Shark (nonfiction), Random House, 1973.
The Pushcart Prize: The Best of the Small Presses, Pushcart Press, 1976.

Works also represented in *Ten Times Black, Writing under Fire: Stories of the Vietnam War,* and thirty more anthologies.

OTHER

Author of column, *American Poetry Review,* 1973-76. Distinguished Contributing Editor, *The Pushcart Prize: The Best of the Small Presses,* 1977—. Reviewer, *Essence,* 1970-73, and *Library Journal,* 1974-77. Author of television script, "Africa Speaks to New York," 1970. Contributor of fiction, nonfiction, and poetry to numerous periodicals in the United States, Mexico, Africa, India, Canada, Europe, Russia, and Australia; staff writer, *Proof,* 1960-61. Editor, *Coercion Review,* 1958-66; *American Book Review,* editor, 1977-78, associate editor, 1978—; associate editor, *Caw,* 1967-70, *Journal of Black Poetry,* 1967-70, *Bopp,* 1977-78, *Gumbo,* 1978, *Departures,* 1979, and *par rapport,* 1979—; contributing editor, *American Poetry Review,* 1976—, *Dark Waters,* 1977. Member of board of directors, *What's Happening* magazine, Columbia University, 1969; member of editorial board, *Umojo: A Scholarly Journal of Black Studies,* 1979; committee member, *Signes,* 1983—; fiction editor, *High Plains Literary Review,* 1986—.

WORK IN PROGRESS: The Boatman's Tenure, a novel.

SIDELIGHTS: American writer Clarence Major "has been in the forefront of experimental poetry and prose," states Eugene B. Redmond in *Parnassus.* "In prose he fits 'loosely' into a category with William Melvin Kelley and Ishmael Reed. But his influences and antecedents are not so easy to identify." Best known for his novels such as *All-Night Visitors, Reflex and Bone Structure, No,* and *Emergency Exit,* the author draws on his experience as a Southern Black American to "[defy] the white-imposed 'traditions' of black literature [and] to develop a brilliant lyricism in new forms of fiction," according to Jerome Klinkowitz in his book *The Life of Fiction*. But Major's art, continues Klinkowitz, "inevitably turns back to the basic social and personal concerns which must remain at the heart of any literary experience."

The fact that Major's prose often centers on scenes of violence prompts comment from *Black Creation* critic Jim Walker. In *No*, for instance, says Walker, "the novel, like so many Black novels before it, deals with a young boy growing up in the South. Major has filled *No* with the violence we expect of Southern life; violence of whites against Blacks, and more unfortunately, violence of Blacks against Blacks. . . . But the point Major is obviously trying to make with these kinds of scenes is that violence is an integral part of life for Southern Blacks and moreover, that it helps shape their lives and attitudes."

But it is the writer's innovative use of language that has brought him the most critical attention. As Klinkowitz notes, "by focusing on language, Major has found a way to treat a recognizable subject matter without having it turn into a stereotyped notion of the documentary world. He creates the flavor and tone of everyday black speech not by mimicking dialect, but by using his syntax to suggest the rhythm of the spoken word. He is less interested in external characters than in the imaginations he creates for them, which we are never allowed to forget are projections of the author's own mind. In his novels, the fictional experience is often suspended on images rather than dependent upon narrative drive."

In *Reflex and Bone Structure*, for example, "Major slips deliberately surreal images into otherwise realistic scenes (a rubber plant dries the dishes, the TV slushes back and forth), reminding the reader that for all the comfortable associations with reality this is still an artificially constructed work," Klinkowitz notes in *The Practice of Fiction in America: Writers from Hawthorne to the Present*. Similarly, Major's novel *Emergency Exit* presents a conventional story line, "But Major has found several ways to keep the story from turning into social realism," Klinkowitz observes. "As in *Reflex,* images are culled from American popular culture—movies, records, and folk mores. . . . A mood emerges from them quite independently of the narrative story line, and as a result that story line becomes less important to the reader. Attention has been focused on the writing and the words."

Critics again praise Major's unique use of language in *My Amputations: A Novel,* the winner of the Western States Book Award in 1986. On the narrative level, it shows how easily the well-read parolee Mason Ellis impersonates a black novelist named Clarence McKay, whom he has taken hostage. McKay's literary agent plays along, and almost no one who meets the imposter on his world-wide lecture tour can tell the difference between Mason and the author whose identity he has usurped. "Major has fashioned a parable of the black writer as the most invisible and misrepresented of us all," notes Greg Tate in a *Washington Post* review. *New York Times Book Review* contributor Richard Perry finds *My Amputations* "a book in which the question of identity throbs like an infected tooth, . . . a picaresque novel that comes wailing out of the blues tradition: it is ironic, irreverent, sexy, on a first-name basis with the human condition, and defined in part by exaggeration and laughter." In a *Nation* review, Stuart Klawans suggests, "Mere description cannot convey the wild hu-

mor and audacity to be found here, nor the anxiety and cunning. . . . The novel is supersaturated with names, allusions, quotations. . . . When a writer loads a book with so many references, the reader is entitled to ask whether he knows what he's doing. Believe me, Clarence Major knows. He has fashioned a novel that is simultaneously a deception and one great, roaring self-revelation." Comments Tate, "Major feels particular ardor for mixing the rhythms of American slang with those of historical, scientific, mythological, and occult texts. He turns these combinations into marvelously florid passages, creating a homemade mythos full of mirth and mystery. . . . The integration of such alchemical language into the mundane human affairs of its subjects is part of what makes 'My Amputations' such a provocative advance in contemporary American writing. This novel should do much to make the name of Clarence Major a byword among aficionados of adventurous fiction everywhere."

Such Was the Season is "more structured and accessible" than Major's earlier novels, notes David Nicholson of the *Washington Post Book World*. To Nicholson, it "seems rooted in Major's experience, and much of the book's success has to do with the warmth of the central character. . . . Annie Eliza . . . speaks to us for more than 200 pages of things past and present in a voice that is always uniquely hers." In this matriarch of a black middle-class Atlanta family who speaks an authentic vernacular, "Major has created a delightfully lifelike, story-telling woman whose candor is matched only by her devotion to truth and her down-to-earth yea-saying to life," Al Young suggests in the *New York Times Book Review*. He continues, "It is as if Clarence Major, the avid *avant-gardiste*, has himself come home to touch base with the blues and spirituals that continue to nourish and express the lives of those people he writes about so knowingly, and with contagious affection."

Such Was the Season, Young summarizes, is a "straight-ahead narrative crammed with action, a dramatic storyline and meaty characterization." In the one week described by Annie Eliza, several scandals touching family members erupt in the wake of her daughter-in-law's candidacy for the State Senate. Even so, "the book's pleasures have less to do with what happens and more with Annie Eliza and her tale," maintains Nicholson; details that belong more to fantasy than to reality, and the matriarch's frequent digressions from the story line draw attention to the storyteller's craft and away from the plot. Therefore, he says, "though at first glance Major seems to have abandoned his postmodern explorations, *Such Was the Season* actually has much in common with those earlier works."

"When he is at his best," Doug Bolling remarks in the *Black American Literature Forum*, "Major helps us to see that fiction created within an aesthetic of fluidity and denial of 'closure' and verbal freedom can generate an excitement and awareness of great value; that the rigidities of plot, characterization, and illusioned depth can be softened and, finally, dropped in favor of new and valid rhythms. Spaces and times need no longer conform to the abstract demands either of plot or symbolic urgency, for example, but can be free to float in their own energies." Commenting on the author's place in the history of fiction, Klinkowitz concludes in *The Practice of Fiction in America*, "Major's innovations have made a fully nonrepresentational fiction possible. Such a radical aesthetic makes for an entirely new kind of fiction, much as visual art was reinvented by the cubists in the first decade of this century." It also asks for more alert, more active readers, Bolling claims. "His way and that of other postmodern writers can help us realize all over again that the activity of 'reading' is a highly conditioned one, too often a matter of the learned response rather than an engagement of the free and open mind. Thus, time spent with the fictions can be both a trip into the richness and surprise of words and their relationships and a way of redefining the self. In place of the hermetic quality with its correlative webbing of internally sustained ironies and symbols that one associates with modernist writing, the reader of Major's fiction finds that he must himself take part in the creation of the work and that in doing so he experiences a pleasurable liberation quite removed from the kind of response elicited by older fiction.''

All-Night Visitors has been translated into Italian and German; *Reflex and Bone Structure* has been translated into French; *Such Was the Season* has been translated into German.

BIOGRAPHICAL/CRITICAL SOURCES:

BOOKS

Bell, Bernard W., *The Afro-American Novel and Its Tradition*, University of Massachusetts Press, 1987.
Blacks in America: Bibliographical Essays, Doubleday, 1971.
Byerman, Kieth E., *Fingering the Jogged Grain: Tradition and Form in Recent Black Fiction*, University of Georgia Press, 1985.
Chapman, A., editor, *New Black Voices: An Anthology of Contemporary Afro-American Literature*, New American Library, 1972.
Contemporary Authors Autobiography Series, Volume 6, Gale, 1988.
Contemporary Literary Criticism, Gale, Volume 3, 1975, Volume 19, 1981.
Critical Survey of Short Fiction: Current Writers, Salem Press, 1981.
Dictionary of Literary Biography, Volume 33: *Afro-American Writers since 1955*, Gale, 1984.
Dillard, J. L., *Lexicon of Black English*, Seabury Press, 1977.
Finding the Words: Conversations with Writers Who Teach, Ohio University Press, 1984.
Henderson, Bill, editor, *Pushcart Prize: The Best of the Small Presses, 1976-77*, Pushcart Press, 1976.
Hoffman, Daniel, editor, *The Harvard Guide to Contemporary American Writing*, Harvard University Press, 1979.
Johnson, Charles, *Being and Race*, Indiana University Press, 1988.
Kiernan, Robert F., *American Writing since 1945: A Critical Survey*, Ungar, 1983.
Klinkowitz, Jerome, *The Life of Fiction*, University of Illinois Press, 1977.
Klinkowitz, Jerome, *The Practice of Fiction in America: Writers from Hawthorne to the Present*, Iowa State University Press, 1980.
Klinkowitz, Jerome, *Literary Disruptions: The Making of a Post-Contemporary American Fiction*, revised edition, University of Illinois, 1980.
Major, Clarence, *The Dark and Feeling: Black American Writers and Their Work*, Third Press, 1974.
O'Brien, John, *Interviews with Black Writers*, Liveright, 1973.
Redmond, Eugene B., *Drumvoices: The Mission of Afro-American Poetry—A Critical History*, Anchor/Doubleday, 1976.
Shapiro, Nancy and Ron Padgett, editors, *The Point: Where Teaching and Writing Intersect*, Teachers and Writers, 1983.
Wepman, Dennis, and others, *The Life: The Lore and Folk Poetry of the Black Hustler*, University of Pennsylvania Press, 1976.

Williams, Sherley Anne, *Give Birth to Brightness: A Thematic Study in Neo-Black Literature*, Dial, 1972.
World Literature since 1945: Critical Surveys of the Contemporary Literatures of Europe and the Americas, Ungar, 1973.

PERIODICALS

American Anthropologist, June, 1975.
American Book Review, September/October, 1982, September, 1986.
Best Sellers, June 1, 1973.
Black American Literature Forum, Number 12, 1978, Volume 12, number 2, 1979, Volume 17, number 3, fall, 1983.
Black Creation, summer, 1973.
Black Scholar, January, 1971.
Chicago Sun-Times, April 28, 1974.
Chicago Tribune, October 6, 1986.
Cleveland Plain Dealer, December 3, 1987.
Essence, November, 1970.
Greenfield Review, winter, 1971.
Ms., July, 1977.
Nation, January 24, 1987.
Negro Digest, December, 1969.
Newsday, November 1, 1987.
New York Times, April 7, 1969.
New York Times Book Review, February 13, 1972, July 1, 1973, November 30, 1975, September 28, 1986, December 13, 1987.
Obsidian, Volume 4, number 2, 1978.
par rapport, Volume 2, number 1, 1979.
Parnassus, spring/summer, 1975.
Penthouse, February, 1971.
Phylon, winter, 1972.
Poetry, August, 1971.
Publishers Weekly, March 24, 1969, March 19, 1973, May 9, 1986, July 4, 1986, July 31, 1987.
Quarterly Journal of Speech, April, 1977.
San Francisco Review of Books, Volume 1, number 12, 1976, Volume 7, number 3, 1982.
Saturday Review, December 5, 1970, April 3, 1971.
Tribune Books (Chicago), October 6, 1986.
Virginia Quarterly Review, winter, 1971.
Voice Literary Supplement, February, 1987.
Washington Post Book World, September 13, 1986, January 10, 1988.

—*Sketch by Marilyn K. Basel*

*   *   *

MAKEBA, (Zensi) Miriam   1932-

PERSONAL: Born March 4, 1932, in Prospect, South Africa; came to United States, 1959; daughter of a teacher and a domestic worker; married Sonny Pillay (a singer; marriage ended); married Hugh Masekela (a musician; marriage ended); married Stokely Carmichael (a civil rights leader; marriage ended); married fifth husband Bageot Bah (an airline executive); children: Bongi (daughter). *Education:* Attended Kimerton Training Institute in Pretoria, South Africa.

ADDRESSES: Home—Guinea, West Africa. *Office*—Jazz Singer, 472 N. Woodlawn St., Englewood, N.J. 07631.

CAREER: Domestic worker in Johannesburg, South Africa; vocalist touring in South Africa, Rhodesia (now Zimbabwe), and the Belgian Congo with the Black Mountain Brothers, 1954-57; singer in concert halls and nightclubs in Africa, United

States, England, France, Denmark, and Italy, 1957—. United Nations delegate from Guinea, West Africa. Singer on "Graceland" tour with Paul Simon and Hugh Masekela in Africa, 1987; featured singer with Masekela on American tour, 1988. Recording artist featured on albums, including "The Voice of Africa," "Popular Songs and African Folk Songs," RCA, "Miriam Makeba Sings," RCA, "The World of Miriam Makeba," RCA, "Makeba Sings," RCA, "The Click Song," "Wimoweh," "Back of the Moon," Kapp, "Miriam Makeba in Concert," Reprise, and "Sangoma." Actress, including appearances in opera "King Kong" and film "Come Back Africa," both 1959; guest on television and radio programs, including "Steve Allen Show," "Soul," and "Like It Is." Member of delegation from Guinea to United States, 1975.

MEMBER: American Society of Composers, Authors, and Publishers.

AWARDS, HONORS: Grammy Award from National Academy of Recording Arts and Sciences, 1965, for best folk music for "An Evening with Belafonte/Makeba"; Dag Hammerskjoeld Peace Prize, 1986.

WRITINGS:

The World of African Song, edited by Jonas Gwangwa and E. John Miller, Jr., Times Books, 1971.
(With James Hall) *Makeba: My Story,* New American Library, 1987.

Author of musical compositions, including "Unhome," "Amampondo Dubala," "Pole Mze," "Boot Dance," and "Mangwene Mpulele."

SIDELIGHTS: Miriam Makeba is "known in this country as the prime representative of African folk song," writes Doris Grumbach in the *Chicago Tribune.* Makeba gained international renown after starring in the anti-apartheid, semidocumentary film "Come Back Africa," in 1959. A black South African, Makeba was a well-known singer and actress in her native country before making the motion picture. When "Come Back Africa" was to be shown at the Venice Film Festival, she left her home for the first time and traveled to the city to attend. After the festival, Makeba journeyed to London where she met singer and performer Harry Belafonte. Extremely impressed with her renditions of unusual native African songs, Belafonte proclaimed her "easily the most revolutionary new talent to appear in any medium in the last decade." He became Makeba's promoter and introduced her to American audiences. In November, 1959, she was a guest on "The Steve Allen Show." Her nightclub debut at the Village Vanguard in New York City followed soon afterward. She quickly began performing in larger clubs and concert halls.

But when Makeba married Black Panther Stokely Carmichael, her successful career took an abrupt turn. "My marriage to Stokely Carmichael didn't change my life—it just made my career disappear!" Makeba told Leigh Behrens in a *Chicago Tribune* interview. She continued, "I don't know why people did that to me. Because I just married a man I loved. I didn't calculate or think. When you want to marry somebody, you follow your feelings. I married him, and then all my contracts were cancelled." In order to keep working, Makeba left for Europe where she continued her career.

Much of Makeba's tumultuous life appears in her memoir written with James Hall, called *Makeba: My Story.* "Makeba's life has been one of high peaks and low valleys. Her auto-

biography documents her ups and downs in life," writes Norman Richmond in the *Globe and Mail.* Grumbach calls the work "fascinating," and says, "Makeba's life is a model of determination, almost unreasonable hope and irrepressible talent and accomplishment." Richmond, however, did add, "There are faults with Makeba's work. James Hall, who assisted her, seems to have rushed to get the book out. For example, many personalities in the book are only referred to by their last names."

Makeba was exiled from South Africa early in her adult life, and it has affected her music. She told Behrens, "Being a singer doesn't mean I don't feel or think. I can't afford that luxury of being a singer that just says, 'Baby, baby, I love you.' No. I have love, but I also have suffering. I am a South African. I left part of me there. I belong there. . . . I would be very presumptious to think my little voice or my songs can change apartheid. But what my songs do, and what all of us do is try to raise the consciousness of people, to join us in our cry for freedom and our cry against apartheid. I think the more voices we have, the better."

Makeba, who has been "trying for decades" to alert Americans to the oppression of blacks in South Africa, is encouraged "that people are *finally* listening," reports Dennis Hunt in the *Los Angeles Times.* The pain of exile still troubles Makeba even though "she has been quietly invited to return to her homeland," he says, "but she refuses to go back until the apartheid system is gone. 'After 29 years outside my country, why would I go back and let this racist government use me?,' she said. 'They're trying to make the world think they're changing. They would use me as an example that things are getting better. But things are still the same. My people are not free. I'll go back home but only when my people are free. . . . As long as my people aren't free I still have no country.'"

Although most popular for singing African tunes in her Xhosan tribe dialect, Makeba also sings many other types of music. Her recordings include Hebrew and Yiddish songs, Portuguese fados and bossa novas, Haitian chants, and English ballads.

BIOGRAPHICAL/CRITICAL SOURCES:

BOOKS

Crane, Louise, *Ms. Africa,* Lippincott, 1973.

PERIODICALS

Africa Report, January, 1977.
Chicago Tribune, March 20, 1988.
Ebony, April, 1963, July, 1968.
Globe and Mail (Toronto), April 2, 1988.
Los Angeles Times Book Review, February 7, 1988, April 14, 1988, April 16, 1988.
Newsweek, January 25, 1960.
New York Times, February 28, 1960.
Time, February 1, 1960.
Times Literary Supplement, March 11-17, 1988.
Tribune Books (Chicago), January 24, 1988.
Washington Post, April 19, 1988.

*   *   *

MALCOLM X
See LITTLE, Malcolm

MANDELA, Nelson R(olihlahla) 1918-

PERSONAL: Born 1918 in Umtata, Transkei, South Africa; son of Henry (a Tembu tribal chief) Mandela; married Edith Ntoko (a nurse; divorced); married Nomzamo Winnie Madikileza (a social worker and political activist), June 14, 1958; children: (first marriage) two sons (one deceased) and one daughter, Makaziwe Phumla Mandela; (second marriage) Zenani (married to Prince Thumbumuzi Dhlamini of Swaziland), Zindziswa. *Education:* Attended University College of Fort Hare and Witwatersrand University; University of South Africa, law degree, 1942.

ADDRESSES: Pollsmoor Prison, Cape Town, South Africa; c/o African National Congress of South Africa, 801 Second Avenue, New York, N.Y. 10017.

CAREER: Mandela and Tambo law firm, Johannesburg, South Africa, partner, 1952- c. 1960; political organizer and leader of the African National Congress (ANC), Johannesburg, South Africa, 1944—, held successive posts as secretary and president of the Congress Youth League, deputy national president of the ANC, and commander of the Umkonto we Sizwe ("Spear of the Nation") paramilitary organization; sentenced to five years in prison for inciting Africans to strike and for leaving South Africa without a valid travel document, 1962; sentenced to life imprisonment for sabotage and treason, 1964; incarcerated in various penal institutions, including Robben Island and Pollsmoor prisons, South Africa, 1962—.

AWARDS, HONORS: Honorary doctor of laws degrees from the National University of Lesotho, 1979, and City College of the City University of New York, 1983; Jawaharlal Nehru Award for International Understanding from the government of India, 1980; Bruno Kreisky Prize for Human Rights from the government of Austria, 1981; named honorary citizen of Glasgow, 1981, and Rome, 1983; Simon Bolivar International Prize from UNESCO, 1983; nominated for 1987 Nobel Peace Prize.

WRITINGS:

No Easy Walk to Freedom (nonfiction), Basic Books, 1965.
Nelson Mandela Speaks (nonfiction), African National Congress Publicity and Information Bureau (London), c. 1970.
The Struggle Is My Life (nonfiction), International Defence and Aid Fund (London), 1978, revised and updated edition published by Pathfinder Press, 1986.

Contributor of articles to the South African political journal *Liberation,* 1953-59.

SIDELIGHTS: Nelson and Winnie Mandela have been called "the first family of South Africa's freedom fight." Through their charismatic leadership and great personal sacrifices, the husband-and-wife team have come to symbolize the struggle against apartheid, the system of enforced racial inequality that denies political rights to the country's black majority. Nelson Mandela, a leader of the banned African National Congress (ANC) insurgent movement, has been jailed by white governments for the past quarter of a century for his efforts to enfranchise his fellow blacks. His incarceration has raised his political prestige to almost messianic proportions in the eyes of his oppressed countrymen, and public opinion polls show that he would easily be elected South Africa's first black prime minister if democratic elections were held today. Many political observers believe that the nationalist leader represents the

last hope for achieving a negotiated solution between blacks and whites in the current South African climate of rising violence and racial polarization, but the governing authorities have resisted a worldwide campaign to free him. During the course of her husband's long confinement, Winnie Mandela has carried his political torch with distinction, enduring repeated jailings, banishment, and house arrest to emerge as a redoubtable leader in her own right and the most visible and outspoken antagonist of white minority government in South Africa today.

Both Nelson and Winnie Mandela are descended from Xhosa-speaking tribal chieftains from the Transkei region of South Africa. Because of their eighteen-year age difference, Nelson Mandela had already become a well-known political figure while his future wife was still a schoolgirl. As Winnie was to do some years later, Nelson left his ancestral home at a young age to avoid an arranged marriage and pursue a professional career in the commercial capital of Johannesburg. He was soon drawn to the struggle for black social and political rights being waged by the ANC and decided to study law to prepare for a political career. Obtaining his law degree from the University of South Africa in 1942, Nelson Mandela joined the ANC two years later at the age of twenty-six and helped found the Congress Youth League (CYL) with Walter Sisulu, Oliver Tambo, and others. With Mandela as its secretary, the CYL urged its parent organization (the ANC) to abandon the strictly constitutional approach to reform that it had fruitlessly pursued with successive white minority governments since its founding in 1912 and to pursue a more militant and confrontational strategy. Under strong youth pressure, the ANC adopted a new program of action in 1949 that recognized such nonviolent but sometimes illegal tactics as electoral boycotts, "stay-at-homes" (general strikes), student demonstrations, and civil disobedience as legitimate weapons in the struggle to win black rights.

In June, 1952, Nelson Mandela mounted the first major test of the new ANC program by organizing the Defiance Against Unjust Laws campaign, a coordinated civil disobedience of six selected apartheid laws by a multiracial group of some eighty-six hundred volunteers. The legal and social code known as apartheid (meaning "apartness" in the Afrikaans language) denied South African blacks—who make up three-quarters of the country's population—the right to vote or run for national public office. It also restricted them to low-paying occupations, prevented them from choosing freely where to live, travel, and work, and kept them rigidly segregated from whites in all public facilities. The government's heavy-handed response of beatings and jailings to the Defiance Campaign generated a backlash of popular support for the ANC that helped thrust Nelson Mandela into national prominence. It also brought him a nine-month suspended jail sentence, a two-year government "banning" order that confined him to Johannesburg and prohibited him from attending public gatherings, and an order to resign his ANC leadership posts as deputy president of the national organization, president of the Transvaal branch, and president of the CYL. Mandela refused to do so, but he was obliged to conduct most of his political organizing work under the cover of his Johannesburg law partnership with Oliver Tambo and to limit his public profile to writing articles for the pro-ANC journal *Liberation.*

In December, 1956, following a year of ANC-led mass protests against the Nationalists' proposal to create seven tiny tribal "homelands" in which to segregate South Africa's black population, the government brought charges against Nelson Mandela and 155 other antiapartheid leaders under anti-Communist and treason statutes. During most of the four-and-one-half years that the so-called Treason Trial lasted, Mandela remained free on bail and continued to work at his law office during the evenings and discreetly engage in political activities within the limitations of a new five-year banning order leveled on him in February, 1956. In early 1960, however, the ANC and a more militantly black nationalist offshoot, the Pan-Africanist Congress (PAC), began organizing street demonstrations against the so-called pass laws that required black South Africans to carry government identification documents showing their assigned residence and employment at all times. In a notorious action that marked a historical watershed in the peaceful struggle for black rights in South Africa, the police turned their weapons on a group of unarmed pass protesters in the Johannesburg suburb of Sharpeville in March of that year, killing sixty-nine people. The massacre sparked a wave of angry new protests and public pass-book burnings, to which the government responded by declaring a state of national emergency, banning the ANC and PAC, and detaining some eighteen hundred political activists without charges, including Nelson Mandela and the other Treason Trial defendants. This crackdown prompted the trial lawyers to withdraw from the case, declaring that the emergency restrictions prevented them from mounting an effective defense, and left Mandela, Duma Nokwe, Walter Sisulu, and several others to represent their sizable group of ANC leaders.

As an advocate, Nelson Mandela distinguished himself with his legal ability and eloquent statements of the ANC's political and social philosophy. He stoutly defended the 1949 Programme of Action and the Defiance Campaign as necessary disruptive tactics when the government was indifferent to legal pressure, and he sought to assuage white fears of a black political takeover by insisting that the ANC's form of nationalism recognized the right of all South African racial groups to enjoy political freedom and nondiscrimination together in the same country. In a unique legal victory for South African black activists, the trial judge acquitted all the defendants for insufficient evidence in March, 1961, finding that the ANC did not have a policy of violence. Nelson Mandela's impressive defense at the widely publicized Treason Trial brought him international recognition and the respect of many South Africans of all races.

Among those anxiously awaiting the verdict was Nomzamo Winnie Madikileza, who had married Nelson Mandela during the early stages of the trial in June, 1958. A graduate of the Jan Hofmeyr School of Social Work in Johannesburg, Winnie Mandela had taken a job as South Africa's first black medical social worker at Baragwaneth Hospital in the sprawling black satellite city of Soweto. Her political life as a leader of the ANC's Women's League and her status as the wife of Nelson Mandela soon overshadowed her professional career, however. In 1958, after taking part in an antipass protest, Winnie Mandela was jailed for two weeks and then fired from her hospital job, the first of many professional posts she was to lose in the years to come because of her antiapartheid activism. After much difficulty, she subsequently found a similar position with the privately run Child Welfare Society in Johannesburg that allowed her to continue with her political work.

The government's ban of the ANC meant an end to any normal home life for the Mandelas, however. Immediately after his release, Nelson Mandela went underground to avoid new government banning orders. He surfaced in late March to deliver the keynote speech at the All-In African Conference held in Pietermaritzburg, which had been organized by the ANC and other opposition political organizations to address the Nationalists' plan to declare a racialist South African republic in May of that year. The All-In Conference opposed this proposal with a demand that the government hold elections for a fully representative national convention empowered to draft a new and democratic constitution for all South Africans. Meeting no response to the assembly's demands from the H. F. Verwoerd government, Mandela helped organize a three-day general strike for the end of May to press for the convention. Verwoerd's security forces mobilized heavily against the strike by suspending civil liberties, making massive preemptive arrests, and deploying heavy military equipment, which succeeded in limiting public support for the action, although hundreds of thousands of Africans nationwide still stayed away from work.

Facing arrest, Nelson Mandela once again disappeared underground, this time for seventeen months, and assumed numerous disguises in a cat-and-mouse game with the police during which he became popularly known as the "Black Pimpernel." Remarkably, Winnie managed to elude near-constant police surveillance and meet with her fugitive husband on numerous occasions during this period. The ANC leader was finally captured disguised as a chauffeur in the province of Natal by police acting on an informer's tip in August, 1962. Brought to trial in October on charges of inciting Africans to strike and on leaving the country without a valid travel document, Mandela turned his defense into a ringing indictment of the apartheid system. In an eloquent statement to the presiding judge, the ANC leader rejected the right of the court to hear the case on the grounds that—as a black man—he could not be given a fair trial under a judicial system intended to enforce white domination, and furthermore, he considered himself neither legally nor morally bound to obey laws created by a parliament in which he had no representation. Mandela vigorously cross-examined prosecution witnesses on the inequities of apartheid and delivered a stirring pre-sentencing statement in which he described his personal career and political education, and explained why he felt justified in having taken "extra-legal" (as opposed to illegal) action. Despite his bravura courtroom performance, Mandela was convicted of both charges and sentenced to five years in prison.

Unknown to the authorities at the time of his trial, Nelson Mandela and other ANC leaders had also reluctantly decided to launch an underground paramilitary movement in 1961 for the first time in the ANC's history. Among the principal factors prompting this decision were the Sharpeville massacre and the government's repressive response to the May, 1961, general strike, which seemed to close the door on avenues for peaceful change. Mandela also believed that the black townships were about to explode into spontaneous violence, and that this violence would either be channeled into a conscious political movement or degenerate into anarchic terrorism and race war. Accordingly, in November of 1961, he helped organize and assumed command of the Umkonto we Sizwe ("Spear of the Nation") guerrilla organization and began planning a sabotage campaign directed against government installations, other symbols of apartheid, and economic infrastructure. Umkonto's first military action occurred on December 16, 1961, when the organization simultaneously attacked government buildings in Johannesburg, Port Elizabeth, and Durban. The group went on to engage in many more acts of sabotage over the next year while Mandela traveled surreptitiously to England, Ethiopia, Algeria, and other African countries to meet political leaders, seek arms for the movement, and undergo military training.

Mandela's role in leading Umkonto came to light in June, 1963, when police raided the ANC's underground headquarters in the Johannesburg suburb of Rivonia and discovered documents relating to the armed movement. Nine top ANC leaders were arrested, including Walter Sisulu, Govan Mbeki, and Dennis Goldberg, and brought to trial with Mandela in early 1964 on charges of committing sabotage and conspiring to overthrow the government by revolution and with the help of foreign troops. Mandela once again conducted his own vigorous defense, using the courtroom as a platform to explain and justify the ANC's turn to armed struggle and to condemn the apartheid regime. "Peace in our country must be considered already broken when a minority Government maintains its authority over the majority by force and violence," Mandela had earlier declared in a speech before the 1961 Pan-Africanist Conference in Ethiopia, and, he added at the trial, "it would be unrealistic and wrong for African leaders to continue preaching peace and non-violence at a time when the Government met our peaceful demands with force." He fully acknowledged helping to found Umkonto and planning acts of sabotage, but denied the government's contention that the ANC and Umkonto intended to subject the antiapartheid struggle to revolutionary control, either foreign or domestic.

Mandela specifically addressed at some length the government's often-stated claim that he, and the ANC as a whole, were manipulated and controlled by the South African Communist Party. The ANC leader acknowledged longstanding ties and significantly overlapping memberships between the two organizations, but insisted that their alliance was a practical one relating to their shared objective of ending apartheid and achieving black majority rule. Mandela counterposed the Communists' declared long-term objective of alleviating class struggle, overthrowing capitalism, and undertaking an economic revolution to the ANC's African nationalism, which sought to harmonize class distinctions under conditions of majority rule. While he acknowledged being strongly influenced by Marxist thought, Mandela denied ever having been a member of the Communist party, insisting rather that he held a deep and abiding admiration for Western legal and political institutions and wished to "borrow the best from both East and West" to reshape South African society. As elaborated in the ANC's Freedom Charter, a 1955 manifesto that Mandela helped to draft that remains the basic statement of the group's political purpose, the ANC looked forward to a democratic, pluralist society with certain mildly socialist reforms—including land redistribution, nationalization of the country's mines, and a progressive tax and incomes policy—intended to dilute the economic power of the white race and raise the country's majority out of poverty. In recent interviews, the ANC leader has reiterated that his basic political objectives remain a unified South Africa with no artificial homelands, black representation along with all other races in a central parliament, and one-man, one-vote democracy in a multi-party system. The ANC leader also asserted that his organization would be prepared to immediately suspend the armed struggle once the minority government agrees to legalize the ANC and other black political parties, to release all political prisoners, and to start negotiations to dismantle the apartheid system.

Nelson Mandela's trial ended in June, 1964, when he and eight other defendants were convicted of sabotage and treason and sentenced to life imprisonment. Confined to the notorious Robben Island fortress for political prisoners seven miles offshore from Cape Town, the ANC leaders were kept rigidly isolated from the outside world. They were denied access to radio, television, and newspapers and prohibited from publishing articles, giving public interviews, or even discussing politics with visitors. All Mandela's past speeches and published work were banned, and merely possessing his writings in South Africa was made a criminal offense. Despite these restrictions, two book-length collections of Mandela's best-known political statements were published abroad and have since circulated widely among South African antiapartheid activists. *No Easy Walk to Freedom,* published in 1965, includes Mandela's 1953 presidential address to the Transvaal province ANC, in which he discusses the Defiance Campaign, his speech at the 1961 All-In African Conference, and excerpts from his testimony at his three political trials. A second collection, *The Struggle Is My Life,* was published by Pathfinder Press in 1986 and contains material from 1944 to 1985, including four prison statements from Mandela.

Nelson Mandela's political views and leadership were also tirelessly promoted by his wife, Winnie, who endured near-constant government harassment in the 1960s and 1970s to emerge as a formidable black leader in her own right. Shortly after Nelson's 1962 conviction, Winnie Mandela received her first government banning order restricting her to Johannesburg and preventing her from attending public or private meetings of any kind. In 1965 the government forced her out of her job with the Child Welfare Society by further restricting her to her home township of Orlando West and preventing her from engaging in essential fieldwork elsewhere in the Soweto district. She was then fired from a succession of low-paying jobs in the white commercial district after the security police pressured her employers, and she finally found herself reduced to supporting her two young daughters on the charity of friends and political associates.

Despite this hardship, Winnie Mandela continued to work surreptitiously with the ANC in the 1960s by helping produce banned political pamphlets and newsletters in her home. The suspicious police ransacked the Mandela house repeatedly during this period, arresting Winnie so often that she began keeping a suitcase permanently packed with her prison necessities, but prosecutors could never find enough evidence to bring a court case against her. In May, 1969, however, Winnie Mandela was arrested with other suspected ANC sympathizers under a new law that allowed the government to detain "terrorist" suspects indefinitely without charges. Taken to Pretoria Prison, she was interrogated virtually nonstop for five days and nights about her supposed links to ANC saboteurs. She was then jailed without charges for seventeen months, spending the first two hundred days of this period incommunicado and in solitary confinement. Deprived of any reading, recreational, or work materials, she later described spending days taking apart and reweaving her blanket and scouring her cell for an ant or fly in her desperation to see another living creature. Her diet consisted mainly of gruel and she received a one-liter bottle of water per day to satisfy all of her drinking and bathing needs. Finally, under pressure from Nelson Mandela's lawyers, the authorities improved Winnie's confinement conditions and brought her to trial on twenty-one political charges in September, 1970. The trial judge dismissed the case against her and all but one of her co-defendants for insufficient evidence, and Winnie Mandela was released that month.

Though freed from prison, Winnie Mandela was still subjected to close police vigilance in the early 1970s as South Africa's white minority government reacted to new challenges from a growing world antiapartheid movement and the anticolonial wars in nearby Mozambique and Angola. Immediately upon her release, she was placed under a new five-year banning order that confined her to her home during the evenings and on weekends. She was subjected to frequent police home searches in ensuing years and was arrested and sentenced to six months in prison for talking to another banned person in 1974. Remarkably, though, the authorities allowed her banning order to expire in October, 1975, and over the next ten months she was able to enjoy the rights of free association and movement for the first time in many years.

This period of relative freedom for Winnie Mandela coincided with the birth of a militant "Black Consciousness" youth movement led by Stephen Biko and other students in Soweto. Inspired in part by the recent nationalist victories in Angola and Mozambique, the student revolt had as its immediate aim the annulment of the Bantu Education Act, which consigned blacks to inferior education and obliged them to learn Afrikaans, the language of South African whites of Dutch descent, instead of English. When police shot down a number of unarmed demonstrators in Soweto in June, 1976, however, the township's youth erupted in a fury of uncontrolled rioting and clashes with the security forces that left at least six hundred people dead. Many of those participants in the Soweto uprising who escaped being killed or imprisoned fled the country and made contact with ANC exile headquarters in Lusaka, Zambia. This militant young cadre helped to radicalize the Congress and substantially strengthen its military wing, allowing the ANC to reestablish both a political and military presence inside South Africa by the end of the decade.

As a leader of the Black Parents' Association in Soweto, Winnie Mandela had sought to mediate the conflict between the student leaders and the authorities and prevent the rebellion from degenerating into indiscriminate rioting. The security police, however, suspected her of having incited the uprising and detained her again for five months, along with the other Parents' Association leaders. She was released to house arrest in January, 1977, but in May of that year the police made yet another midnight raid on her home and informed her that she was being banished immediately to the remote town of Brandfort in conservative Orange Free State. As government trucks carted off their possessions, she and her daughter Zindziswa (nicknamed Zinzi) were taken that very night to their new home—a tiny, three-room house in the black ghetto, with no electricity, sewage, or running water. To further isolate her, the authorities kept Winnie Mandela under a banning order that confined her to her home during evenings and weekends, prevented her from meeting with more than one person at a time, and prohibited her from having her remarks published or quoted in South Africa. Despite these restrictions, she still managed to subvert the rigid rural segregation system during her seven years of exile in Brandfort by ignoring "whites only" signs in public places, which inspired other blacks to do the same. Winnie Mandela also put her social worker's skills to use improving conditions in the wretchedly impoverished ghetto and attempting to empower its meek and humble inhabitants. With outside donations, she managed to open a medical clinic and a soup kitchen in her home, and she trained groups of local women to start sewing and baking enterprises. Instead of isolating her as the regime had hoped, Winnie Mandela's exile only increased international interest in her as a symbol of the antiapartheid movement, and she received visits from a steady stream of journalists and diplomats who reported her views abroad.

The ebb in the popular struggle after the Soweto uprising lasted until 1984, when the townships exploded again over the adoption of a new South African constitution that year that gave parliamentary representation to "Coloureds" and Indians but none to blacks. The townships remained in a state of near-continuous political turmoil in succeeding years as antigovernment youth clashed violently with the security forces and other blacks accused of collaborating with the regime. But unlike the situation a decade earlier, when the township civilians stood unorganized and alone against the might of the apartheid state, a number of powerful social and political forces joined the fray in the mid-1980s to mount the greatest challenge to white minority rule in South African history. The United Democratic Front (UDF), a coalition of some 680 antiapartheid organizations that supports the political line of the ANC, organized large street demonstrations and protests by township squatters facing eviction that were harshly repressed by the government in 1985. Meanwhile, the ANC itself stepped up its guerrilla campaign in South Africa and began targeting white residential areas and causing civilian casualties for the first time. The Nationalist government of P. W. Botha also came under mounting attack from abroad as the United States and other Western countries imposed limited trade and investment sanctions on South Africa in a bid to force reform. Finally, the one-million-strong black trade union movement began to flex its powerful muscles in 1987 with strikes by workers in the strategic transport and mining sectors.

Winnie and Nelson Mandela continue to play central roles in this many-sided campaign against white minority rule. A common demand voiced by all the diverse forces seeking to change the apartheid system is that Nelson Mandela, South Africa's foremost black leader, be released immediately. In 1985, Winnie Mandela managed to break the government restrictions on her and return to Soweto to join the fight for her husband's freedom. This remarkable turn of events occurred after her Brandfort house was firebombed and burned to the ground in August of that year while she was in Johannesburg for medical treatment. Accusing the security police of the attack and saying that she feared for her life, Winnie Mandela insisted on moving back to her Soweto house, and amid much local and international publicity, the Botha government permitted her to do so. She subsequently turned down an offer of $10,000 from the U.S. Government to rebuild her Brandfort house in protest of the Reagan Administration's aquiescent policy of "constructive engagement" with the apartheid regime, but she later accepted a $100,000 donation from the United Nations diplomatic community. In succeeding months Winnie Mandela took advantage of the government's weakened position and openly flouted her banning orders by giving press interviews and speaking out militantly at public demonstrations and at the funerals of young township victims of government repression. Speaking at a funeral on a return visit to Brandfort in April, 1986, for example, Winnie Mandela denounced the authorities as "terrorists" and called on blacks to take "direct action" against the government to free the imprisoned nationalist leaders. "The time has come where we must show that we are disciplined and trained warriors," she added in what some observers interpreted as a call to insurrection. Astonishingly, the Botha regime chose not to prosecute her but instead lifted all banning restrictions on Winnie Mandela in July, 1986, in a bid to improve its international image and deflect criticism of a new state of emergency it had imposed the previous month. Among Winnie Mandela's first public actions once her right to free speech had been restored was to call for international economic sanctions against the apartheid government.

Winnie Mandela discusses her personal and political past and her hopes for the future in her 1985 autobiography, *Part of*

My Soul Went With Him. The book is based on a series of tape-recorded interviews that the black leader gave to South African journalist Anne Benjamin and also includes personal sketches of Winnie by friends and colleagues and copies of her recent correspondence with Nelson Mandela. In her political comments, Winnie Mandela affirms the multiracial goals of the ANC but rejects the idea of special minority rights in a transitional government, as proposed by some South African liberals, insisting rather that the only topic worthy of political discussion concerns the mechanics of handing over power directly to the country's black majority. She also describes in some detail the tribulations of her Brandfort exile and the happier time of her courtship and early years of marriage with Nelson. In a particularly poignant passage, the author recounts a visit to her imprisoned husband in May, 1984, when the couple was permitted to embrace for the first time in twenty-two years. *Part of My Soul Went With Him* "is both a moving personal story of courage and dignity and a powerful indictment of apartheid in South Africa," opined Toronto *Globe and Mail* reviewer Norman Richmond.

The future for the Mandelas and South Africa remains unsettled. Thus far, the Botha government has met the current crisis with a "divide and rule" strategy combining harsh repression and isolated reforms that do not fundamentally alter the structure of apartheid. While repealing such egregious symbols of apartheid as the pass laws and long-standing bans on interracial sex and marriage, the government has violently crushed the township uprisings and detained tens of thousands of antiapartheid protestors without trial under sweeping state-of-emergency powers. In late 1987 the Botha regime began hinting of the possibility that it might finally release Nelson Mandela unconditionally in an attempt to mollify domestic and international public opinion. The advisability of releasing the ANC leader in terms of domestic politics has reportedly stimulated a hot debate in the Botha cabinet, with those in favor of the move arguing that Mandela is now more conservative than much of the current ANC leadership and could effect a split in the organization. Detractors contend that freeing South Africa's best-known political prisoner could further alienate hard-line whites and possibly stimulate a black insurrection. Reform-minded South Africans, on the other hand, believe Mandela may now be the only political leader prestigious enough to win the confidence of both liberal whites and the increasingly alienated black township youth, thereby delivering the country from the specter of race war. Fearing the popular reaction if Mandela were to die in prison, previous South African governments had sought to find a face-saving way to free him at least as early as 1973, but the confined ANC leader had always rejected conditions that he accept exile abroad or in the Transkei "homeland" and that he renounce violence by the insurgent organization. In November, 1987, the authorities unconditionally freed Mandela's long-time comrade-in-arms Govan Mbeki, a top ANC and South African Communist party leader who was convicted at the Rivonia Trial and served twenty-four years on Robben Island, as a way of testing the political waters for Mandela's possible release.

While this debate goes on, Winnie Mandela has been allowed to continue her public political work with only occasional harassment. In January, 1987, she and Zinzi were detained by the police for several hours without explanation and in November the police raided her Soweto home and arrested several of her young bodyguards. Nelson Mandela endures his incarceration at Pollsmoor Prison near Cape Town, having been transferred to the more modern facility from Robben Island in 1982. The conditions of his confinement have improved markedly in recent years, and he is now allowed to receive weekly family visits and give occasional interviews for publication. Nelson Mandela shares a relatively spacious, sunlit cell with four other ANC leaders and spends his time studying (economics and history are favorite subjects) and tending a rooftop vegetable garden. Although he is still denied access to current news sources, visitors describe the black leader as remarkably well-informed about current affairs in South Africa and abroad.

The sixty-nine-year-old Mandela is said to be still the healthy, commanding, and charismatic leader of old, completely unbroken by his long years of confinement and possessed by the firm conviction that he will one day be free to help his people achieve their social and political emancipation. Winnie Mandela firmly shares this belief. "I am like a battery—I go down there to be recharged," she remarked to *New York Times* correspondent John F. Burns of her visits to her imprisoned husband. "You see, he is liberated already! With his attitude, he is already free!"

BIOGRAPHICAL/CRITICAL SOURCES:

BOOKS

Benson, Mary, *Nelson Mandela: The Man and the Movement,* Norton, 1986.
Harrison, Nancy, *Winnie Mandela* (biography), Braziller, 1986.
Mandela, Nelson R., *No Easy Walk to Freedom,* Basic Books, 1965.
Mandela, Nelson R., *The Struggle Is My Life,* Pathfinder Press, 1986.
Mandela, Winnie, *Part of My Soul Went With Him* (autobiography), edited by Anne Benjamin and Mary Benson, Norton, 1985.

PERIODICALS

Crisis, February, 1983.
Ebony, December, 1985, September, 1986.
Globe and Mail (Toronto), December 14, 1985.
Ms., November, 1985, January, 1987.
New Statesman, June 7, 1985.
Newsweek, September 9, 1985, February 24, 1986.
New York Review of Books, May 8, 1986.
New York Times, July 19, 1978, July 7, 1985, July 29, 1986.
New York Times Book Review, December 8, 1985.
Time, January 5, 1987.

—*Sketch by Curtis Skinner*

*   *   *

MANDELA, (Nomzamo) Winnie (Madikileza)   1936-

PERSONAL: Born September, 1936, in Pondoland, Transkei, South Africa; daughter of Columbus (a schoolteacher and Pondo tribal chief; later minister of agriculture and forestry in Transkei Bantustan) and Gertrude (a schoolteacher and homemaker) Madikileza; married Nelson Mandela (an attorney and political activist), June 15, 1958; children: Zenani (married to Prince Thumbumuzi Dhlamini of Swaziland), Zindziswa. *Education:* Jan Hofmeyr School of Social Work, diploma, 1956. *Religion:* Anglican.

ADDRESSES: 8115 Orlando West, Soweto, South Africa; c/o African National Congress of South Africa, 801 Second Avenue, New York, N.Y. 10017.

CAREER: Baragwaneth General Hospital, Soweto, South Africa, medical social worker, 1956-58; Child Welfare Society,

Johannesburg, South Africa, social worker, c. 1960-65; worked briefly in Johannesburg at a furniture store, correspondence college, shoe shop, dry cleaners, and office; employed at Frank and Hirsch, Johannesburg, 1975-78. Joined Women's League of the African National Congress in 1957, later became branch chairman; executive member of the Federation of South African Women; under government banning orders restricting her employment and civil liberties, 1962-86; incarcerated seventeen months in Pretoria Prison, 1969-70; leader of the Black Parents' Association in Soweto, 1976; banished to Brandfort, Orange Free State, 1977-85; returned to political activism in Soweto in 1986.

AWARDS, HONORS: Honorary doctor of laws degree from Haverford Quaker College; Freedom Prize from newspapers *Politiken* (Denmark) and *Dagens Nyheter* (Sweden); Robert F. Kennedy Human Rights Award from Georgetown University, 1985; first International Simone de Beauvoir Award from *Ms.*, 1986.

WRITINGS:

Part of My Soul Went With Him (autobiography), edited by Anne Benjamin and Mary Benson, Norton, 1985.

See also *MANDELA, Nelson R(olihlahla)*.

BIOGRAPHICAL/CRITICAL SOURCES:

BOOKS

Harrison, Nancy, *Winnie Mandela* (biography), Braziller, 1986.
Mandela, Winnie, *Part of My Soul Went With Him* (autobiography), edited by Anne Benjamin and Mary Benson, Norton, 1985.

PERIODICALS

Detroit Free Press, December 17, 1985.
Ebony, December, 1985.
Globe and Mail (Toronto), December 14, 1985.
Insight, February 24, 1986.
Ms., November, 1985, January, 1987.
New York Review of Books, May 8, 1986.
New York Times, December 6, 1985, January 14, 1986, April 6, 1986, July 8, 1986, January 26, 1987, January 27, 1987.
New York Times Book Review, December 8, 1985, April 27, 1986.
Time, January 25, 1982, January 5, 1987, May 4, 1987.

*   *   *

MANDRAKE, Ethel Belle
See THURMAN, Wallace (Henry)

*   *   *

MARAN, Rene   1887-1960

PERSONAL: Born November 5 (some sources say November 15), 1887, in Fort-de-France, Martinique, West Indies; immigrated to France, c. 1891; died May 8, 1960, in Paris, France. *Education:* Graduated from Lycee de Talance, in Bordeaux, France, 1909.

CAREER: Served as an officer for the colonial civil service in French Equatorial Africa, 1909-23; poet, novelist, biographer, and essayist.

AWARDS, HONORS: Goncourt Prize from Goncourt Academy, 1922, for *Batouala;* Grand Prix Broguette-Gonin from l'Academie francaise, 1942; Grand Prix de la Societe des Gens de lettres, 1949; Prix de la Mer et de l'Outre-Mer, 1950; Prix de Poesie from l'Academie francaise, 1959.

WRITINGS:

NOVELS

Batouala: Veritable Roman negre, Albin, 1921, translation by Adele Szold Seltzer published as *Batouala*, T. Seltzer, 1922 (published in England as *Batouala: A Negro Novel From the French*, Cape, 1922), reprinted, Kennikat, 1969, translation by Alvah C. Bessie published as *Batouala: A Novel*, illustrations by Miguel Covarrubias, Limited Editions Club, 1932, *Batouala: Veritable Roman negre*, author's definitive edition (contains *Youmba, la mangouste;* also see below), Albin, 1938, reprinted, 1982, translation from the author's definitive edition by Barbara Beck and Alexandre Mboukou published as *Batouala: A True Black Novel*, introduction by Donald Herdeck, Black Orpheus, 1972, published as *Batouala: An African Love Story*, Black Orpheus, 1973.
Djouma, chien de brousse, Albin, 1927.
Le Coeur serre, Albin, 1931.
Le Livre de la brousse, Albin, 1934.
Betes de la brousse, Albin, 1941.
Un Homme pareil aux autres, Arc-un-Ciel, 1947.
Bacouya, le cynocephale, Albin, 1953.

POETRY

Le Visage calme, 7th edition, Aux Editions du Monde Nouveau, 1922.
Les Belles Images, Delmas, 1935.
Le Livre du souvenir, Presence Africaine, 1958.

Also author of *La Maison du bonheur* and *La Vie interieure*.

OTHER

''Le Petit Roi de Chimerie'' (short story), preface by Leon Bocquet, Albin, 1924.
Livingston et l'exploration de l'Afrique, Gallimard, 1938.
Brazza et la fondation de l'A.E.F., Gallimard, 1941.
Mbala, l'elephant, illustrations by Andre Collot, Arc-en-Ciel, 1943.
Les Pionniers de l'empire, three volumes, Albin, 1943-55.
Savorgnan de Brazza, Dauphin, 1951.
Felix Eboue, grand commis et loyal serviteur, 1885-1944, Editions Parisiennes, 1957.
Bertrand du Guesclin, l'epee du roi, Albin, 1960.
Djogoni: Eaux-fortes, Presence Africaine, c. 1966.
Voyages de decouverte au Canada entre les annees 1534 et 1542, Anthropos, 1968.

Also author of *Le Tchad de sable et d'or*, 1931, and *Peines de coeur*, 1944. Contributor of novellas, including *Bokorro, Boum et Dog, Deux amis, L'Homme qui attend, Legendes et coutumes negres de l'Oubanqui-Chari: Choses vues*, and *Youmba, la mangouste*, to a monthly Paris periodical, *Les Oeuvres libres*, between 1921 and 1937. Also contributor of essays to periodicals, including *Le Monde illustre* and *Candide*.

SIDELIGHTS: Acclaimed by some critics for writing a ''masterpiece'' of black literature, Rene Maran gained recognition as the first black author to authentically record African tribal life under colonial French rule during World War I in his 1921 novel *Batouala: Veritable Roman negre* (translated as *Batouala: A True Black Novel*). For this work Maran received the prestigious Goncourt Prize in 1922; he was the first black writer to be so honored. The novel was subsequently translated into fifty languages.

Born in Martinique in 1887 and educated in Bordeaux, France, Maran, by the age of sixteen, had begun writing and already had some of his poetry published. In 1909 he joined the French colonial service in Africa, where he spent six years in the Congo. After writing *Batouala*, Maran returned permanently to France in 1923, where he was a prolific poet, biographer, essayist, and novelist. *Batouala*, however, is the only one of his works to have been translated from French. And its success, asserted *Nation*'s reviewer Charles R. Larson, is due to "Maran's genius" in rendering tribal life "so fully and objectively."

In *Batouala* Maran "presents us with the cycle of traditional African life from birth to death," observed Larson. The story is told mainly through the eyes of the aging African chief, Batouala, who finds his authority challenged by a younger man. Batouala and his small tribe of Bandas live under "oppressive French colonial rule," explained Michael Olmert of the *New York Times Book Review,* and are "resigned to the new lifestyle that clashes so stridently with the one that had done so well for their ancestors." But it is not so much the plot that makes *Batouala* impressive, but rather, stated Olmert, the fact that "the tale is a framework for what can almost be considered a compendium of Banda folklore and tribal life." The reader is able to experience the intimate aspects of Batouala's life as the book is, as Larson described, "alive with the sounds and smells of an African village." Olmert further praised the book: "Maran has done a perfect job of weaving the details of eating, shelter, rites of passage, lore, and art into his novel. Nothing escapes him."

Despite the novel's acclaim, *Batouala*, upon its first publication, met with controversy. Protest came from members of the French literary establishment who objected to *Batouala*'s preface, which is an attack on the French colonial service. With his novel, though, Maran only "wanted to be objective in his recording of African life as it was, as he knew it. 'It doesn't show indignation: it records,'" Larson quoted the author. But with this objective outlook—and contrary to the notion that this was a piece of black protest fiction—the novel's intimate and unromanticized portrayal of tribal rites and rituals paradoxically served to reinforce some readers' theories of black inferiority. Larson, nevertheless, deemed *Batouala* a "seminal piece of African literature," concluding that "Maran's novel deserves recognition as one of the most imaginative pieces of black writing of all times."

BIOGRAPHICAL/CRITICAL SOURCES:

PERIODICALS

Freeman, November 29, 1922.
Literary Review, September 9, 1922.
Nation, September 20, 1922, March 26, 1973.
New York Times, August 20, 1922.
New York Times Book Review, January 28, 1973.
Times Literary Supplement, January 8, 1922.

*   *   *

MARSHALL, Paule   1929-

PERSONAL: Born April 9, 1929, in Brooklyn, N.Y.; daughter of Samuel and Ada (Clement) Burke; married Kenneth E. Marshall, 1950 (divorced, 1963); married Nourry Menard, July 30, 1970; children (first marriage): Evan. *Education:* Brooklyn College (now of the City University of New York), B.A. (cum laude), 1953; attended Hunter College (now of the City University of New York), 1955.

ADDRESSES: Home—407 Central Park West, New York, N.Y. 10025.

CAREER: Free-lance writer. Worked as librarian in New York Public Libraries; *Our World* magazine, New York, N.Y., staff writer, 1953-56. Lecturer on creative writing at Yale University, 1970—; lecturer on Black literature at colleges and universities including Oxford University, Columbia University, Michigan State University, Lake Forrest College, and Cornell University.

MEMBER: Phi Beta Kappa.

AWARDS, HONORS: Guggenheim fellowship, 1960; Rosenthal Award from the National Institute of Arts and Letters, 1962, for *Soul Clap Hands and Sing;* Ford Foundation grant, 1964-65; National Endowment for the Arts grant, 1967-68; Before Columbus Foundation American Book Award, 1984, for *Praisesong for the Widow*.

WRITINGS:

Brown Girl, Brownstones (novel), Random House, 1959, reprinted with an afterword by Mary Helen Washington, Feminist Press, 1981.
Soul Clap Hands and Sing (short stories), Atheneum, 1961, reprinted, Howard University Press, 1987.
The Chosen Place, The Timeless People, Harcourt, 1969, reprinted, Vintage Books, 1984.
Praisesong for the Widow (novel), Putnam, 1983.
Reena and Other Stories (includes novella "Merle," and short stories "The Valley Between," "Brooklyn," "Barbados," and "To Da-duh, in Memoriam"), with commentary by the author, Feminist Press, 1983, reprinted as *Merle: A Novella and Other Stories,* Virago Press, 1985.

Also author of a teleplay based on *Brown Girl, Brownstones,* 1960.

Contributor of articles and short stories to periodicals.

SIDELIGHTS: "My work asks that you become involved, that you think," writer Paule Marshall once commented in the *Los Angeles Times.* "On the other hand, . . . I'm first trying to tell a story, because I'm always about telling a good story." Marshall received her first training in storytelling from her mother, a native of Barbados, and her mother's West Indian friends, all of whom gathered for daily talks in Marshall's home after a hard day of "scrubbing floor." Marshall pays tribute to these "poets in the kitchen" in a *New York Times Book Review* essay where she describes the women's gatherings as a form of inexpensive therapy and an outlet for their enormous creative energy. She writes: "They taught me my first lessons in the narrative art. They trained my ear. They set a standard of excellence. This is why the best of my work must be attributed to them; it stands as testimony to the rich legacy of language and culture they so freely passed on to me in the wordshop of the kitchen."

The standard of excellence set by these women has served Marshall well in her career as a writer. Her novels and stories have been lauded for their skillful rendering of West Indian-Afro-American dialogue and colorful Barbadian expressions. *Dictionary of Literary Biography* contributor Barbara T. Christian believes that Marshall's works "form a unique contribution to Afro-American literature because they capture in a lyrical, powerful language a culturally distinct and expansive world.'' This pursuit of excellence makes writing a time-consuming effort, according to Marshall. ''One of the reasons it takes me such a long time to get a book done,'' she explained in the *Los Angeles Times,* ''is that I'm not only struggling with my sense of reality, but I'm also struggling to find the style, the language, the tone that is in keeping with the material. It's in the process of writing that things get illuminated.''

Marshall indicates, however, that her first novel *Brown Girl, Brownstones* was written at a faster pace. ''I was so caught up in the need to get down on paper before it was lost the whole sense of a special kind of community, what I call Bajan (Barbardian) Brooklyn, because even as a child I sensed there was something special and powerful about it,'' she stated in the *Los Angeles Times.* When the novel was published in 1959 it was deemed an impressive literary debut, but because of the novel's frank depiction of a young black girl's search for identity and increasing sexual awareness, *Brown Girl, Brownstones* was largely ignored by readers. The novel was reprinted in 1981, and is now considered a classic in the female bildungsroman genre, along with Zora Neale Hurston's *Their Eyes Were Watching God* and Gwendolyn Brooks's *Maud Martha.*

The story has autobiographical overtones, for it concerns a young black Brooklyn girl, Selina, the daughter of Barbadian immigrants Silla and Deighton. Silla, her ambitious mother, desires most of all to save enough money to purchase the family's rented brownstone. Her father Deighton, on the other hand, is a charming spendthrift who'd like nothing better than to return to his homeland. When Deighton unexpectedly inherits some island land, he makes plans to return there and build a home. Silla meanwhile schemes to sell his inheritance and fulfill her own dream.

Selina is deeply affected by this marital conflict, but ''emerges from it self-assured, in spite of her scars,'' writes Susan McHenry in *Ms.* Selina eventually leaves Brooklyn to attend college; later, realizing her need to become acquainted with her parents' homeland, she resolves to go to Barbados. McHenry writes: ''*Brown Girl, Brownstones* is meticulously crafted and peopled with an array of characters, and the writing combines authority with grace. . . . Paule Marshall . . . should be more widely read and celebrated.'' Carol Field comments in the *New York Herald Tribune Book Review:* ''[*Brown Girl, Brownstones*] is an unforgettable novel written with pride and anger, with rebellion and tears. Rich in content and in cadences of the King's and 'Bajan' English, it is the work of a highly gifted writer.''

Marshall's most widely reviewed work to date is *Praisesong for the Widow,* winner of the Before Columbus American Book Award. The novel is thematically similar to *Brown Girl, Brownstones* in that it also involves a black woman's search for identity. This book, though, concerns an affluent widow in her sixties, Avatar (Avey) Johnson, who has lost touch with her West Indian-Afro-American roots. In the process of struggling to make their way in the white man's world, Avey and her husband Jerome (Jay) lost all of the qualities that made them unique. Novelist Anne Tyler remarks in the *New York Times Book Review,* ''Secure in her middle class life, her civil service job, her house full of crystal and silver, Avey has become sealed away from her true self.''

While on her annual luxury cruise through the West Indies, however, Avey has several disturbing dreams about her father's great aunt whom she visited every summer on a South Carolina island. She remembers the spot on the island where the Ibo slaves, upon landing in America, supposedly took one look around at their new life and walked across the water back to Africa. Avey decides to try to escape the uneasiness by flying back to the security of her home. While in her hotel on Grenada awaiting the next flight to New York, Avey reminisces about the early years of her and Jay's marriage, when they used to dance to jazz records in their living room, and on Sundays listen to gospel music and recite poetry. Gradually though, in their drive for success they lost ''the little private rituals and pleasures, the playfulness and wit of those early years, the host of feelings and passions that had defined them in a special way back then, and the music which had been their nourishment,'' writes Marshall in the novel.

In the morning, Avey becomes acquainted with a shopkeeper who urges her to accompany him and the other islanders on their annual excursion to Carriacou, the island of their ancestors. Still confused from the past day's events, she agrees. During the island celebration, Avey undergoes a spiritual rebirth and resolves to keep in close contact with the island and its people and to tell others about her experience.

Reviewers question if Avey's resolution is truly enough to compensate for all that she and Jay have lost, if ''the changes she envisions in the flush of conversion commensurate with the awesome message of the resisting Ibos,'' to use *Village Voice Literary Supplement* reviewer Carol Ascher's words. ''Her search for roots seems in a way the modern, acceptable equivalent of the straightened hair and white ways she is renouncing,'' writes *Times Literary Supplement* contributor Mary Kathleen Benet, who adds: ''On the other hand there is not much else she can do, just as there was not much else Jerome Johnson could do. Paule Marshall respects herself enough as a writer to keep from overplaying her hand; her strength is that she raises questions that have no answers.''

Los Angeles Times Book Review contributor Sharon Dirlam offers this view: ''[Avey] has learned to stay her anger and to swallow her grief, making her day of reckoning all the more poignant. She has already missed the chance to apply what she belatedly learns, except for the most important lesson: What matters is today and tomorrow, and, oh yes, yesterday—life, at age 30, age 60, the lesson is to live.'' Jonathan Yardley concludes in the *Washington Post Book World:* ''*Praisesong for the Widow* . . . is a work of quiet passion—a book all the more powerful precisely because it is so quiet. It is also a work of exceptional wisdom, maturity and generosity, one in which the palpable humanity of its characters transcends any considerations of race or sex; that Avey Johnson is black and a woman is certainly important, but Paule Marshall understands that what really counts is the universality of her predicament.''

BIOGRAPHICAL/CRITICAL SOURCES:

BOOKS

Bruck, Peter, and Wolfgang Karrer, editor, *The Afro-American Novel since 1960,* B. R. Gruener, 1982.

Christian, Barbara, *Black Women Novelists,* Greenwood Press, 1980.

Contemporary Literary Criticism, Volume 27, Gale, 1984.

Dictionary of Literary Biography, Volume 33: *Afro-American Fiction Writers after 1955,* Gale, 1984.

Evans, Mari, editor, *Black Women Writers, 1950-1980,* Anchor Press, 1984.

Marshall, Paule, *Brown Girl, Brownstones,* Random House, 1959, reprinted with an afterword by Mary Helen Washington, Feminist Press, 1981.

Marshall, Paule, *Praisesong for the Widow,* Putnam, 1983.

PERIODICALS

Black American Literature Forum, winter, 1986, spring/summer, 1987.

Black World, August, 1974.

Book World, December 28, 1969.

Callaloo, spring/summer, 1983.

Chicago Tribune Book World, May 15, 1983.

Christian Science Monitor, January 22, 1970, March 23, 1984.

CLA Journal, March, 1961, September, 1972.

Critical Quarterly, summer, 1971.

Essence, May, 1980.

Freedomways, 1970.

Journal of Black Studies, December, 1970.

London Review of Books, March 7, 1985.

Los Angeles Times, May 18, 1983.

Los Angeles Times Book Review, February 27, 1983.

Ms., November, 1981.

Nation, April 2, 1983.

Negro American Literature Forum, fall, 1975.

Negro Digest, January, 1970.

New Letters, autumn, 1973.

New Yorker, September 19, 1959.

New York Herald Tribune Book Review, August 16, 1959.

New York Review of Books, April 28, 1983.

New York Times, November 8, 1969, February 1, 1983.

New York Times Book Review, November 30, 1969, January 9, 1983, February 20, 1983.

Novel: A Forum on Fiction, winter, 1974.

Saturday Review, September 16, 1961.

Times Literary Supplement, September 16, 1983, April 5, 1985.

Village Voice, October 8, 1970, March 22, 1983, May 15, 1984.

Village Voice Literary Supplement, April, 1982.

Washington Post, February 17, 1984.

Washington Post Book World, January 30, 1983.

—*Sketch by Melissa Gaiownik*

*   *   *

MARTIN, Herbert Woodward 1933-

PERSONAL: Born October 4, 1933, in Birmingham, Ala.; son of David Nathaniel and Willie Mae (Woodward) Martin. *Education:* University of Toledo, B.A., 1964; State University of New York at Buffalo, M.A., 1967; Middlebury College, M.Litt., 1972; Carnegie-Mellon University, D.A., 1979. *Religion:* Lutheran.

ADDRESSES: Home—715 Turner St., Toledo, Ohio 43607. *Office*—Department of English, 300 College Park, Dayton, Ohio 45469-0001.

CAREER: State University of New York at Buffalo, instructor, summer, 1966; Aquinas College, Grand Rapids, Mich., 1967-70, began as instructor, became assistant professor and poet-in-residence; University of Dayton, Dayton, Ohio, 1970—, began as assistant professor, became professor of English and poet-in-residence. Visiting distinguished professor of poetry at Central Michigan University, fall, 1973. Consultant for contemporary black writers collection at University of Toledo, 1974—.

WRITINGS:

"Dialogue" (one-act play), produced in New York City at Hardware Poets Playhouse, 1963.

"Three Garbage Cans," first produced in Grand Rapids, Michigan, fall, 1968.

New York: The Nine Million and Other Poems, Abracadabra Press, 1969.

The Shit-Storm Poems, Pilot Press, 1972.

The Persistence of the Flesh (poems), Lotus Press, 1976.

Paul Laurence Dunbar: A Singer of Songs (booklet), State Library of Ohio, 1979.

The Forms of Silence, Lotus Press, 1980.

Also author of *Letters from the World.* Work represented in anthologies, including *The Poetry of Black America, Introduction to Black Literature, Urban Reader, 10 Michigan Poets,* and *Face the Whirlwind.* Contributor of poetry to journals, including *Obsidian, Poetry Australia, Nimrod, Nexus, Wisconsin Review, Images,* and *Beloit Poetry Journal.* Editor, *Great Lakes Review,* 1978—; guest editor, *University of Dayton Review,* 1988.

WORK IN PROGRESS: Revision of *The Shit-Storm Poems; Arias and Silences: Poems Edited for Ezra Pound; The Log of the Vigilante,* a long poem; *Chasing the Wind; Presiding; Private Poems; Public Portraits.*

SIDELIGHTS: When asked to comment on his work and other interests, Herbert Woodward Martin remarked, "I have said so many foolish things in the past, that I think I will sit this one out."

Martin has studied with John Ciardi, Karl Shapiro, W. D. Snodgrass, John Frederick Nims, Miller Williams, Judson Jerome, Donald Hall, John Logan, Robert Creely, and Edward Albee.

In addition to having given poetry readings at several universities, Martin has performed as narrator for orchestral presentations including Aaron Copeland's "A Lincoln Portrait," Sir William Walton's "Facade," Vincent Persichetti's "Second Lincoln Inaugural," and Robert Borneman's "Reformation 69/70." He has also collaborated with composer Joseph Fennimore on settings for song cycles.

*   *   *

MARTIN, Tony 1942-

PERSONAL: Born February 21, 1942, in Port-of-Spain, Trinidad and Tobago; son of Claude G. and Vida (Scope) Martin. *Education:* Honourable Society of Gray's Inn, Barrister-at-Law, 1965; University of Hull, B.Sc. (with honors), 1968; Michigan State University, M.A., 1970, Ph.D., 1973.

ADDRESSES: Office—Department of Black Studies, Wellesley College, Wellesley, Mass. 02181.

CAREER: Called to English Bar, 1966, and to Trinidad Bar, 1969; accounts clerk in Water Department, Trinidad Public Service, 1961; accounts clerk, Office of the Prime Minister, Federal Government of the West Indies, Trinidad and Tobago, 1961-62; master of Latin, French, Spanish, English, history, and geography, St. Mary's College, Trinidad and Tobago, 1962-63; lecturer in economics and politics, Cipriani Labour College, Trinidad and Tobago, 1968-69; Michigan State University, East Lansing, instructor in history, 1970-71; University of Michigan—Flint, assistant professor of history and coordinator of African-Afro-American studies program, 1971-

73; Wellesley College, Wellesley, Mass., associate professor, 1973-79, professor of black studies, 1979—, chairman of department, 1976-78, 1981-84, and 1985—. Visiting professor at Brandeis University, fall, 1974 and 1981, and at University of Minnesota, fall, 1975; visiting professor at Colorado College, 1985 and 1986.

MEMBER: Association for the Study of Afro-American Life and History, African Heritage Studies Association (member of executive board, 1982), Association of Caribbean Historians (member of executive board, 1985-86, 1986-87), National Council for Black Studies (vice-president of New England region, 1984-86), Organization of American Historians.

WRITINGS:

Race First: The Ideological and Organizational Struggles of Marcus Garvey and the Universal Negro Improvement Association, Greenwood Press, 1976.
(Co-author) *Rare Afro-Americana: A Reconstruction of the Adger Library,* G. K. Hall, 1981.
(Editor) *The Poetical Works of Marcus Garvey,* Majority Press, 1983.
Literary Garveyism: Garvey, Black Arts, and the Harlem Renaissance, Majority Press, 1983.
Marcus Garvey, Hero, Majority Press, 1983.
The Pan-African Connection: From Slavery to Garvey and Beyond, Majority Press, 1984.
(Editor) *In Nobody's Backyard: The Grenada Revolution in Its Own Words,* Majority Press, Volume I: *The Revolution at Home,* 1984, Volume II: *Facing the World,* 1985.
(Editor) Marcus Garvey, *Message to the People: The Course of African Philosophy,* Majority Press, 1986.
Amy Ashwood Garvey: Pan-Africanist, Feminist, and Wife Number One, Majority Press, 1988.
(Editor) *African Fundamentalism: A Literary Anthology of the Garvey Movement,* Majority Press, 1989.

Also author of pamphlets. Contributor of numerous articles and reviews to professional journals, including *Negro History Bulletin, American Historical Review, Journal of Modern African Studies, African Studies Review, Journal of Negro History, Mazungumzo, Race,* and *Journal of Human Relations.* Guest editor, *Pan-African Journal,* 1974.

WORK IN PROGRESS: African Fundamentalism; Audrey Jeffers, a biography; *Auntie Kay,* a biography.

*   *   *

MARVIN X
See El MUHAJIR

*   *   *

MATHABANE, Mark 1960-

PERSONAL: First name originally Johannes; name changed, 1976; born in Alexandra, South Africa; son of Jackson (a laborer) and Magdelene (a washerwoman; maiden name, Mabaso) Mathabane; married Gail Ernsberger (a writer), in 1987. *Education:* Attended Limestone College, 1978, St. Louis University, 1979, and Quincy College, 1981; Dowling College, B.A., 1983; attended Columbia University, 1984. *Religion:* "Believes in God."

ADDRESSES: Home—341 Barrington Park Ln., Kernersville, N.C. 27284.

CAREER: Free-lance lecturer and writer, 1985—.

MEMBER: Authors Guild.

AWARDS, HONORS: Christopher Award, 1986.

WRITINGS:

Kaffir Boy: The True Story of a Black Youth's Coming of Age in Apartheid South Africa, Macmillan, 1986, published as *Kaffir Boy: Growing out of Apartheid,* Bodley Head, 1987.

WORK IN PROGRESS: A sequel to *Kaffir Boy.*

SIDELIGHTS: "What television newscasts did to expose the horrors of the Vietnam War in the 1960s, books like 'Kaffir Boy' may well do for the horrors of apartheid in the '80s," Diane Manuel determined in a *Chicago Tribune Book World* review of Mark Mathabane's first novel. In his 1986 *Kaffir Boy: The True Story of a Black Youths' Coming of Age in Apartheid South Africa,* Mathabane recounts his life in the squalid black township of Alexandra, outside of Johannesburg, where he lived in dire poverty and constant fear until he seemingly miraculously received a scholarship to play tennis at an American college. *Washington Post Book World* critic Charles R. Larson called *Kaffir Boy* "violent and hard-hitting," while Peter Dreyer in the *Los Angeles Times Book Review* found Mathabane's autobiography "a book full of a young man's clumsy pride and sorrow, full of rage at the hideousness of circumstances, the unending destruction of human beings, [and] the systematic degradation of an entire society (and not only black South African society) in the name of a fantastic idea."

The Alexandra of *Kaffir Boy* is one of overwhelming poverty and deprivation, of incessant hunger, of horrific crimes committed by the government and citizen gangs, and of fear and humiliation. It is a township where one either spends hours at garbage dumps in search of scraps of food discarded by Johannesburg whites or prostitutes himself for a meal, and where "children grow up accepting violence and death as the norm," reflected Larson. One of Mathabane's childhood memories is of his being startled from sleep, terrified to find police breaking into his family's shanty in search of persons who emigrated illegally, as his parents had, from the "homelands," or tribal reserves. His father was imprisoned following one of these raids, and was repeatedly jailed after that. Mathabane recalls in *Kaffir Boy* that his parents "lived the lives of perpetual fugitives, fleeing by day and fleeing by night, making sure that they were never caught together under the same roof as husband and wife" because they lacked the paperwork that allowed them to live with their lawful spouses. His father was also imprisoned—at one time for more than a year with no contact with his family—for being unemployed, losing jobs as a laborer because he once again lacked the proper documents.

"Born and bred in a tribal reserve and nearly twice my mother's age," Mathabane wrote in his memoir, "my father existed under the illusion, formed as much by a strange innate pride as by a blindness to everything but his own will, that someday all white people would disappear from South Africa, and black people would revert to their old ways of living." Mathabane's father, who impressed upon his son tribal laws and customs, was constantly at odds with his wife, who was determined to see her son get an education. Mathabane's mother waited in lines at government offices for a year in order to obtain his birth certificate so that he could attend school, then worked as a washerwoman for a family of seventeen so that he could continue to study and, with luck, escape the hardships of life in Alexandra. The father burned his son's schoolbooks and ferociously beat his wife in response to her efforts, claiming that an education would only teach Mathabane to be subservient.

Yet those living in the urban ghettos near Johannesburg are more fortunate than people in the outlying "homelands," where black Africans are sent to resettle. "Nothing is more pathetic in this book than the author's description of a trip he takes with his father to the tribal reserve, ostensibly so that the boy will identify with the homelands," judged Larson. "The son, however, sees the land for what it really is—barren, burned out, empty of any meaning for his generation." In *Kaffir Boy* Mathabane depicts the desolation of the Venda tribal reserve as "mountainous, rugged and bone-dry, like a wasteland. . . . Everywhere I went nothing grew except near lavatories. . . . Occasionally I sighted a handful of scrawny cattle, goats and pigs grazing on the stubbles of dry brush. The scrawny animals, it turned out, were seldom slaughtered for food because they were being held as the people's wealth. Malnutrition was rampant, especially among the children." Larson continued to note that "the episode backfires. The boy is determined to give up his father's tribal ways and acquire the white man's education."

Although Mathabane had the opportunity to get at least a primary education, he still contemplated suicide when he was only ten years old. "I found the burden of living in a ghetto, poverty-stricken and without hope, too heavy to shoulder," he confesses in his memoir. "I was weary of being hungry all the time, weary of being beaten all the time: at school, at home and in the streets. . . . I felt that life could never, would never, change from how it was for me." But his first encounter with apartheid sparked his determination to overcome the adversities.

His grandmother was a gardener for an English-speaking liberal white family, the Smiths, in an affluent suburb of Johannesburg. One day she took her grandson to work, where he met Clyde Smith, an eleven-year-old schoolboy. "My teachers tell us that Kaffirs [blacks] can't read, speak or write English like white people because they have smaller brains, which are already full of tribal things," Smith told Mathabane, the author recalled in his autobiography. "My teachers say you're not people like us, because you belong to a jungle civilization. That's why you can't live or go to school with us, but can only be our servants." He resolved to excel in school, and even taught himself English—blacks were allowed to learn only tribal languages at the time—through the comic books that his grandmother brought home from the Smith household. "I had to believe in myself and not allow apartheid to define my humanity," Mathabane points out.

Mrs. Smith also gave Mathabane an old wooden tennis racket. He taught himself to play then obtained coaching. As he improved and fared well at tournaments he gained recognition as a promising young athlete. In 1973 Mathabane attended a tennis tournament in South Africa where the American tennis pro Arthur Ashe publicly condemned apartheid. Ashe became Mathabane's hero, "because he was the first free black man I had ever seen," the author later was cited in the *New York Times.* After watching the pro play, he strove to do as well as Ashe. Mathabane eventually became one of the best players in his country and made contacts with influential white tennis players who did not support apartheid. Stan Smith, another American tennis professional, befriended Mathabane, and urged him to apply for tennis scholarships to American schools. Mathabane won one, and *Kaffir Boy* ends with the author boarding a plane headed for South Carolina.

Lillian Thomas in the *New York Times Book Review* asserted that "it is evident that [Mathabane] wrestled with the decision whether to fight or flee the system" in South Africa. The author participated in the 1976 uprisings in Soweto, another black township near Johannesburg, after more than six hundred people were killed there when police opened fire on a peaceful student protest. Yet Mathabane continued to be friends with whites whom he had met at his athletic club. He also was the only black in a segregated tournament that was boycotted by the Black Tennis Association, but he participated believing that he would meet people who could help him leave South Africa. Afterward he was attacked by a gang of blacks who resented his association with whites and only escaped because he outran them.

David Papineau in the *Times Literary Supplement* does not find fault with Mathabane for leaving South Africa. The critic contended that Mathabane "does make clear the limited choices facing black youths in South Africa today. One option is political activity, with the attendant risk of detention or being forced underground. . . . Alternatively you can keep your head down and hope for a steady job. With luck and qualifications you might even end up as a white-collar supervisor with a half-way respectable salary."

"For me to deny my anger and bitterness would be to deny the reality of apartheid," Mathabane told David Grogan in *People.* The author resides in the United States and maintains that he would be jailed for speaking out against apartheid if he returned to South Africa. "If I can turn that anger into something positive, I really am in a very good position to go on with my life," he said to the *New York Times.* Now he lectures, taking the memoir of his early life "as a springboard to talk about apartheid in human terms." But he does want to return to South Africa, with the hopes of inspiring "other boys and girls into believing that you can still grow up to be as much of an individual as you have the capacity to be," Mathabane was quoted in another article in the *New York Times.* "That is my dream."

BIOGRAPHICAL/CRITICAL SOURCES:

BOOKS

Mathabane, Mark, *Kaffir Boy,* Macmillan, 1986.

PERIODICALS

Chicago Tribune Book World, April 13, 1986.
Christian Science Monitor, May 2, 1986.
Los Angeles Times Book Review, March 30, 1986.
New York Times, March 2, 1987, September 24, 1987.
New York Times Book Review, April 27, 1986.
People, July 7, 1986.
Times Literary Supplement, August 21, 1987.
Washington Post Book World, April 20, 1986.

—*Sketch by Carol Lynn DeKane*

*   *   *

MATHEUS, John F(rederick)   1887-1983

PERSONAL: Born September 10, 1887, in Keyser, W.Va.; died February 19, 1983; son of John William (a bank messenger and tannery worker) and Mary Susan (Brown) Matheus; married Maude A. Roberts, September 1, 1909 (died in 1965); married Ellen Turner Gordon, July 31, 1973. *Education:* Western Reserve University (now part of Case Western Reserve University), A.B. (cum laude), 1910; Columbia University, A.M., 1921; graduate study at the Sorbonne, Paris, summer 1925, and at University of Chicago, 1927.

ADDRESSES: Home—Charleston, W.Va.

CAREER: Florida Agricultural and Mechanical College (now University), Tallahassee, teacher of Latin, 1911-13, professor of modern languages, 1913-22; Department of Romance Languages at West Virginia State College (West Virginia Collegiate Institute from 1915 to 1929), Institute, professor and head of department, 1922-53, professor emeritus, beginning in 1953; professor of foreign languages at Maryland State College, 1953-54; Dilliard University, New Orleans, La., professor of Romance languages, 1954-57; Morris Brown College, Atlanta, Ga., associate professor of German and Spanish, 1958-59; Texas Southern University, Houston, assistant professor of foreign languages and literatures, 1959-61. Visiting professor at Hampton Institute, 1961-62, and at Kentucky State College (now University), 1962. Served U.S. League of Nations commission to investigate slavery in Liberia, c. 1930; director of teaching English in Haiti for Inter-American Educational Foundation, 1945-46; consultant to Lexicographic Board. Plays featured at a festival in Cleveland, Ohio.

MEMBER: American Association of University Professors, College Language Association (treasurer, beginning in 1942), American Association of Teachers of French (president of West Virginia chapter, 1949-50), Modern Language Teachers' Association (president of West Virginia chapter, 1952-53), American Association of Teachers of Spanish and Portuguese, American Academy of Language Research, West Virginia Association of Higher Education, Alpha Pi Alpha, Sigma Pi Phi, Sigma Delta Pi, among others.

AWARDS, HONORS: "Fog" received first prize in *Opportunity* short story contest, 1925; "Swamp Moccasin" received first prize in *Crisis* short story contest, 1926; award for best review of the year from *Journal of Negro History,* 1936; awarded "Officier de l'Ordre Nationale 'Honneur et Merite'" from Haitian Government.

WRITINGS:

SHORT STORIES

A Collection of Short Stories, edited by Leonard A. Slade, Jr., privately printed, 1974.

Author of "Fog," "Clay," "Swamp Moccasin," "Anthropoi," and twenty other stories.

DRAMA

"Tambour" (one-act play), first produced in Boston, 1929.
(Librettist) *Ouanga!* (opera in three acts; first produced in South Bend, Indiana, June, 1949), music by Clarence Cameron White, privately printed by White, 1939.

Also author of plays "'Cruiter," "Ti Yette," "Black Damp," and "Guitar."

OTHER

(Editor with W. Napoleon Rivers) *Dumas' Georges: An Intermediate French Reader* (based on novel by Alexandre Dumas pere), Associated Publishing, 1936.
(Contributor) Therman B. O'Daniel, editor, *Langston Hughes: Black Genius; A Critical Evaluation,* Morrow, 1971.

Work represented in numerous anthologies, including *Anthology of American Negro Literature,* 1929, *The New Negro: An Interpretation,* 1970, *Caroling Dusk: An Anthology of Verse by Negro Poets,* 1974, and *Plays and Pageants From the Life of the Negro,* 1979.

Contributor of poetry, short stories, articles, and book reviews to periodicals, including *Opportunity, Crisis, Journal of Negro History, Modern Language Journal, Carolina Magazine,* and *Negro Digest.*

Contributing editor to *Color.*

SIDELIGHTS: A professor of Romance languages, John F. Matheus wrote poetry, plays, and short stories. The latter genre, however, proved most successful for him critically and resulted in his privately printed volume of fiction, *A Collection of Short Stories.* Regarded as a humanist, Matheus infused most of his work with themes revealing the racial prejudices prevalent in the South and suggesting Christian understanding and reconciliation as an effective means of countering the evils of humanity. In his contest-winning 1925 "Fog," for example, he illustrates that "ignorance is thick and impenetrable, but, like a fog, it can be replaced by the clear light of understanding," according to a profile in *Dictionary of Literary Biography.* Similarly, other stories—and especially his plays—focus on the hardships, humiliation, and exploitation characteristic of Negro life during his day. Allegedly too reliant on cliches and exaggerated language, Matheus nonetheless conveyed the true spirit and history of his race and thus distinguished his writing as authentic Afro-American literature.

AVOCATIONAL INTERESTS: Travel (Europe, Cuba, Haiti, Africa, Mexico, Canada, and South America).

BIOGRAPHICAL/CRITICAL SOURCES:

BOOKS

Bardolph, Richard, *The Negro Vanguard,* Rinehart, 1959.
Bond, Frederick W., *The Negro and the Drama: The Direct and Indirect Contribution Which the American Negro Has Made to Drama and the Legitimate Stage,* McGrath, 1969.
Brawley, Benjamin Griffith, *The Negro Genius: A New Appraisal of the Achievement of the American Negro in Literature and the Fine Arts,* Biblo & Tannen, 1966.
Dictionary of Literary Biography, Volume 51: *Afro-American Writers From the Harlem Renaissance to 1940,* Gale, 1987.

*   *   *

MATHIS, Sharon Bell   1937-

PERSONAL: Born February 26, 1937, in Atlantic City, N.J.; daughter of John Willie and Alice Mary (Frazier) Bell; married Leroy Franklin Mathis, July 11, 1957 (divorced, Januray 24, 1979); children: Sherie, Stacy, Stephanie. *Education:* Morgan State College, B.A., 1958; Catholic University of America, M.S. in L.S., 1975. *Religion:* Roman Catholic.

ADDRESSES: Home—1274 Palmer Rd., Fort Washington, Md. 20744. *Agent*—Marilyn Marlow, Curtis Brown Ltd., 60 East 56th St., New York, N.Y. 10022.

CAREER: Children's Hospital of District of Columbia, Washington, interviewer, 1958-59; teacher in parochial elementary school in Washington, D.C., 1959-65; Stuart Junior High School, Washington, D.C., special education teacher, 1965-75; Benning Elementary School, Washington, D.C., librarian, 1965-76; Friendship Educational Center, Washington, D.C., librarian, 1976—. Writer-in-residence, Howard University, 1972—. Writer in charge of children's literature division, Washington, D.C. Black Writers Workshop, 1970-73. Member of board of advisers of lawyers committee of District of Columbia Commission on the Arts, 1972-76; member of Black Women's Community Development Foundation, 1973—.

AWARDS, HONORS: Award from Council on Interracial Books for Children, 1970, for *Sidewalk Story;* awards from *New York Times* and American Library Association, 1972, for *Teacup Full of Roses;* fellowship from Wesleyan University and Weekly Readers Book Club, awarded at Bread Loaf Writer's Conference, 1970; Coretta Scott King Award, 1974, for *The Hundred Penny Box;* Arts and Humanities award from Archdiocese of Washington Black Secretariat, 1978; fellowship, MacDowell Colony, 1978.

WRITINGS:

JUVENILE

Brooklyn Story, Hill & Wang, 1970.
Sidewalk Story, Viking, 1971, reprinted, Penguin, 1986.
Teacup Full of Roses, Viking, 1972, reprinted, Penguin, 1987.
Ray Charles, Crowell, 1973.
Listen for the Fig Tree, Viking, 1973.
The Hundred Penny Box, Viking, 1975.
Cartwheels, Scholastic Book Services, 1977.

Author of "Ebony Juniors Speak!," a monthly column in *Ebony, Jr!* and "Society and Youth," a bi-weekly column in the now defunct *Liteside.*

WORK IN PROGRESS: A novel for young adults.

SIDELIGHTS: With the publication of her books *Brooklyn Story, Sidewalk Story, Teacup Full of Roses, Listen for the Fig Tree,* and *The Hundred Penny Box,* Sharon Bell Mathis established herself as a leader of the trend in children's literature that advocates portraying people and events in a starkly realistic light. "There are people in [Mathis's books]," writes Eloise Greenfield in *Black World,* "real, live people that every black reader will recognize. With every word, [the author] reveals . . . a profound knowledge of people and an infinite love and respect for black children. . . . [However,] these books will not be a comfort to those escapist adults who refuse to acknowledge that our children do not live carefree, Dick and Jane lives."

The basis of the latter observation becomes clear after scanning the contents of the books, for the predominant themes include drug addiction, alcoholism, senility, and death. Nevertheless, continues Greenfield, "every young person trying to grow up and survive physically, emotionally, mentally and spiritually will recognize them as truth."

Carol T. Gallagher also applauds Mathis's willingness to break the "last taboo" in children's books by realistically discussing such subjects as aging, senility, and death (specifically in *The Hundred Penny Box*), but she questions the ability of young children to understand what they are reading in the way in which the author intended (at least without the benefit of adult guidance). In general, though, she praises Mathis for illustrating the strong bond of affection and respect that can exist between the very young and the very old, and also for her attempts to explore the "day-to-day effects of an older person living with a young family . . . very different from the 'holiday visit from grandma' syndrome."

Annie Gottlieb, writing in *New York Times Book Review,* disagrees with Gallagher's contention that young children could not understand the subtleties of such a book: "The story makes you think of whoever has been old and dear in your life. . . .

The experience is universal. . . . What is so fine about this book is that it does not set out in that kind, condescending, nervous way to acquaint its young readers with the concepts of Old Age and Death. . . . It is a quiet work of art, not an educational project."

Hazel Copeland, however, feels that *The Hundred Penny Box* successfully blends both artistic and educational elements. She explains in *Black Books Bulletin:* "[It] is an excellent story of the family life and love that transcends generations and paints a very warm picture of human interactions. . . . [It] is definitely a step in the right direction toward literature that entertains and provides some positive direction for our children."

However "negative" the theme, though, Mathis never allows it to overwhelm the reader. For at the base of each story is a wellspring of hope, pride, love, and a will to survive. Although she is speaking primarily of *Teacup Full of Roses,* Greenfield's observation holds true for Mathis's other books as well: "Black strength is what this book is all about. . . . The story is told in words and symbols that confirm, without slogans, the strength and beauty of Blackness. . . . [It is] a book to grow on."

BIOGRAPHICAL/CRITICAL SOURCES:

BOOKS

Children's Literature Review, Volume 3, Gale, 1978.
Dictionary of Literary Biography, Volume 33: *Afro-American Fiction Writers After 1955,* Gale, 1984.
Something About the Author Autobiography Series, Volume 3, Gale, 1987.

PERIODICALS

Black Books Bulletin, winter, 1975.
Black World, August, 1971, May, 1973, August, 1973, May, 1974.
Catholic Library World, October, 1977.
Ebony, December, 1972.
Essence, April, 1973.
Jet, April 23, 1970, May 2, 1974.
Journal of Negro Education, summer, 1974.
New York Times, March 27, 1970.
New York Times Book Review, September 10, 1972, May 4, 1975.
Redbook, August, 1972.
Washington Post, March 21, 1971.

*   *   *

MAX
See DIOP, Birago (Ismael)

*   *   *

MAYFIELD, Julian (Hudson) 1928-1984

PERSONAL: Born June 6, 1928, in Greer, S.C.; died of a heart ailment, October 20, 1984, in Tacoma Park, Md.; son of Hudson Peter and Annie Mae (Prince) Mayfield; married Ana Livia Cordero (a physician), 1954 (divorced); married Joan Cambridge, July 10, 1973; children: (first marriage) Rafael Ariel, Emiliano Kewsi. *Education:* Attended Lincoln University. *Politics:* Blackist-Marxist. *Religion:* Atheist.

ADDRESSES: Office—ObserVision Group, P.O. Box 63428, Washington, D.C. *Agent*—Ruth Aley, Maxwell Aley Associates, 145 East 35th St., New York, N.Y. 10016.

CAREER: Writer. Government of Ghana, communications aide to President Kwame Nkrumah, 1962-66; Government of Guyana, advisor to Prime Minister Forbes Burnbaum, 1971-75. Co-founder, editor and theatre reviewer, *World Journal*, Puerto Rico, 1954-58; founding editor, *African Review*, Accra, Ghana, 1964-66; editor, *New Nation International*, 1973. Cornell University, Ithaca, N.Y., Society for the Humanities Fellow, 1967-68, first W.E.B. DuBois Distinguished Visiting Fellow, 1970-71. Lecturer, Albert Schweitzer Program in the Humanities, New York University, New York City, 1969-70; Fulbright-Hays teaching fellow in West Germany, Austria, Denmark, Algeria, and Turkey, 1976-77; visiting professor of black culture and American literature, University of Maryland, 1977-78; writer in residence at Howard University, 1978-84. Participated in First Conference of Negro Writers, American Society for African Culture in New York, 1959. Former actor on and off Broadway, 1949-54, debuting in the Broadway production of the Maxwell Anderson-Kurt Weill musical, "Lost in the Stars," based on Alan Paton's *Cry, the Beloved Country;* actor in film "Uptight," 1969. Co-producer of Ossie Davis's first play, "Alice in Wonder," 1952. *Military service:* U.S. Army.

MEMBER: Actors Equity Association, Writers Guild of America East, Ghanian Association of Journalists and Writers, Harlem Writers Guild, Fulbright Alumni Association, Lincoln University Alumni Association.

WRITINGS:

NOVELS

The Hit (based on Mayfield's one-act play, "417"), Vanguard, 1957.
The Long Night, Vanguard, 1958.
The Grand Parade, Vanguard, 1961, published as *Nowhere Street,* Paperback Library, 1963.

PLAYS

"Fount of the Nation," first produced in Baltimore by Arena Players at Community Theatre, February 17, 1978.

Also author of one-act plays, "417," "The Other Foot," and "A World Full of Men," produced together with Ossie Davis's first play, "Alice in Wonder."

SCREENPLAYS

(With Ruby Dee and Jules Dassin) "Uptight," Paramount, 1968.
"Children of Anger," Irving Jacoby Associates, 1971.
(With Woodie King) "The Long Night" (based on Mayfield's novel of same title), Woodie King-St. Claire Bourne Production Company, 1976.

Also author of "The Hitch," 1969.

OTHER

(Contributor) *The American Negro Writer and His Roots,* American Society of African Culture (New York), 1960.
(Editor) *The World without the Bomb: The Papers of the Accra Assembly,* Ghana Government Press, 1963.
(Contributor) James A. Emanuel and Theodore L. Gross, editors, *Dark Symphony: Negro Literature in America,* Free Press, 1968.
"The History of the Black Man in the United States" (filmstrip), Educational Audio Visual, 1969.
"The Odyssey of W.E.B. DuBois" (filmstrip), Buckingham Enterprises, 1970.

(Contributor) Houston A. Baker, Jr., editor, *Black Literature in America,* McGraw-Hill, 1971.
(Editor and contributor) *Ten Times Black: Stories from the Black Experience,* Bantam, 1972.

Also contributor of political articles to *Nation, Commentary, New Republic,* and other periodicals.

SIDELIGHTS: Julian Mayfield's death in 1984 closed an extraordinarily varied career. His "life and career were themselves the stuff from which novels, plays, and films could conceivably be fashioned," wrote William B. Branch in the *Dictionary of Literary Biography Yearbook: 1984.* He was "a novelist, playwright, critical essayist, university teacher, Broadway and Hollywood actor, journalist, and adviser to the leaders of two Third-World governments," explained Estelle W. Taylor in a *Dictionary of Literary Biography* essay. The variety of Mayfield's experience allowed him to "articulate and interpret the black experience through an interesting array of media," said Taylor, indicating that despite the change in both "literary milieu and even the philosophical reach and direction that his first published works took," Mayfield's literary reputation still rests upon his first two novels, *The Hit* and *The Long Night.* "In these works he became a significant part of a literary tradition," wrote Taylor, "one of a long line of writers who used Harlem as the vantage point from which to write about the black condition and the black experience."

After much acting experience both on and off Broadway, Mayfield debuted as a playwright with "417," which he expanded into the novel *The Hit.* It is the story of an impoverished but hard-working family in the Harlem ghetto. The father, James Lee Cooley, whose only hope is that "God will redeem Himself by letting him hit the numbers big," explained Taylor, borrows from the household money to support his numbers habit. Eventually Cooley's chosen number, 417, "hits" but the numbers writer absconds with the winnings. Called "well-plotted" and "extremely perceptive" by a *Kirkus Reviews* contributor, Langston Hughes wrote in the *New York Herald Tribune Book Review* that "as a fictional exploration into a comparatively new field of subject matter—the numbers game—'The Hit' is a first novel of unusual interest, treating as it does one phase of 'that most solid and persistent of all American phenomena—the dream.'" And Saunders Redding remarked that although "his characters are like reflections in a darkened mirror," the book represents "an intelligent, energetic foray into a complex milieux."

The Long Night, Mayfield's second Harlem novel, "tells the story of a young boy's fateful search for his father," wrote Branch; and according to Taylor, "Mayfield's Harlem shows signs of decay." A struggling father leaves his family in the charge of his ten year old son, Steely. Sent by his mother to retrieve the winnings from a numbers bet, Steely encounters a gang and is robbed. Taylor observed that, as in *The Hit,* Mayfield depicts "the variety of ways in which working-class blacks and those dependent upon them are systematically victimized by poverty and oppression, but the Harlem of Steely is much uglier than the Harlem of James Lee Cooley." In the *New York Herald Tribune Book Review,* Langston Hughes stated that the novel "is gentler and more poetic than many other such novels in its unfolding of a story that has been told before, and each time in the telling is too grim for tears."

"It was as an essayist that Mayfield's fertile mind found perhaps its most fulfilling utilization, however, as he turned out articles, editorials, academic papers, reviews, and other periodical and anthology contributions from among his earliest writings until just before his death,'' wrote Branch. Taylor indicated that Mayfield ''had become deeply involved in and touched by not only the civil rights movement in the United States but also by movements for freedom from oppression throughout the world.'' Mayfield journeyed to Cuba after Castro's revolution, and expatriated to Ghana as a journalist, serving as as communications aide and speech writer for the Ghanian president, and later went to Guyana where he was advisor to the prime minister there. Taylor added that ''Mayfield called for a separation of the Negro writer from the so-called mainstream. Following it could lead only to oblivion for blacks since the mainstreamers had isolated themselves from the 'great questions facing the peoples of the world.''' A black nationalist, Mayfield ''prophetically cautioned black American writers—and, by implication, black Americans generally—to pause and reexamine the headlong push of the time for across-the-board integration into the mainstream of American life, literary or otherwise.'' In a tribute to Mayfield in the *Dictionary of Literary Biography Yearbook,* John Oliver Killens wrote that ''he was a highly sensitive human being, and his art was consistently committed to the cause of freedom and justice and therefore always found itself aligned on the side of the angels.''

''It will no doubt require time for the ultimate impact of Julian Mayfield's career and writings to be critically assessed,'' concluded Branch. ''Suffice it to say here, however, that he was both black and American; both untiring in assailing injustice and unstinting in defending the rights of those he felt were being wronged; perspicacious in analyzing the world he lived in and prophetic in foretelling certain perils as well as opportunities which lay ahead. In his youth, he went forth, as he once put it, to 'engage the world.' And over the course of an extraordinary lifetime, engage it he did.''

BIOGRAPHICAL/CRITICAL SOURCES:

BOOKS

Davis, Arthur P., *From the Dark Tower: Afro-American Writers, 1900-1960,* Howard University Press, 1981.
Dictionary of Literary Biography, Volume 33: *Afro-American Fiction Writers after 1955,* Gale, 1984.
Dictionary of Literary Biography Yearbook: 1984, Gale, 1984.

PERIODICALS

Ebony, November, 1968.
Freedomways, summer, 1961.
Interracial Review, May, 1962.
Kirkus Reviews, August 15, 1957, August 15, 1958.
New Directions, April, 1979.
New York Herald Tribune Book Review, October 20, 1957, October 26, 1958, July 9, 1961.
New York Times, December 29, 1957.
New York Times Book Review, June 18, 1961.
Saturday Review, October 19, 1957.
Time, October 20, 1958.
Times Literary Supplement, January 22, 1960.
Washington Post, July, 1975.

OBITUARIES:

PERIODICALS

Chicago Tribune, October 25, 1984.
Los Angeles Times, November 3, 1984.
New York Times, October 23, 1984.

Philadelphia Inquirer, October 24, 1984.
Washington Post, October 23, 1984.

—*Sketch by Sharon Malinowski*

*   *   *

MAYS, Benjamin E(lijah)   1894-1984

PERSONAL: Born August 1, 1894, in Epworth, S.C.; died March 28, 1984, in Atlanta, Ga.; son of Hezekiah (a farmer) and Louvenia (Carter) Mays; married Ellen Harvin (deceased); married Sadie Gray (a social worker), August 9, 1926 (died October 11, 1969). *Education:* Bates College, A.B. (with honors), 1920; University of Chicago, M.A., 1925, Ph.D., 1935. *Politics:* Democrat.

CAREER: Ordained Baptist minister, 1922; teacher of higher mathematics at Morehouse College, Atlanta, Ga., and pastor of Shiloh Baptist Church, Atlanta, 1921-24; South Carolina State College, Orangeburg, instructor in English, 1925-26; Tampa Urban League, Tampa, Fla., executive secretary, 1926-28; Young Men's Christian Associations, New York City, national student secretary, 1928-30; director of study of Negro churches in America, sponsored by Institute of Social and Religious Research, New York City, 1930-32; Howard University, Washington, D.C., dean of School of Religion, 1934-40; Morehouse College, Atlanta, Ga., president, 1940-67, president emeritus, 1967-84.

Visiting professor and advisor to president, Michigan State University, 1968-69; consultant to U.S. Office of Education, 1969, and to Ford Foundation, 1970. President, United Negro College Fund, Inc., 1958-61; member of Atlanta Board of Education, beginning 1969, chairman, 1970-81. Member of advisory council, U.S. Committee for the United Nations, 1959, and the Peace Corps, 1961; member of U.S. National Commission for UNESCO, 1962; former trustee of Danforth Foundation and National Fund for Medical Education. Delegate to World Council of Churches, Amsterdam, 1948, and member of central committee, 1949-53; leader in Baptist World Alliance Assembly, 1950. Speaker at more than two hundred universities, colleges, and other educational institutions.

MEMBER: Phi Beta Kappa, Delta Sigma Rho.

AWARDS, HONORS: Alumnus of the Year Award, University of Chicago Divinity School, 1949; Texas State Fair Negro Achievement Award, 1950; Christian Culture Award, Assumption College, Windsor, 1961; Amistad Award, American Missionary Association, 1968; Merrick-Moore-Spaulding Award, North Carolina Mutual Life Insurance Co., 1968; Man of the Year Award, Society for the Advancement of Management, 1968; Myrtle Wreath Award, Hadassah (Atlanta chapter), 1969; Black Educational Services achievement award, 1970; Religious Leaders Award, National Conference of Christians and Jews, 1970; Russwurm Award, National Newspaper Publishers, 1970; American Baptist Churches of the South citation, 1971; Dorie Miller Award, Dorie Miller Foundation, 1971; National Freedom Day Award, City of Philadelphia, 1972; James Bryant Conant Award, Education Commission of the States, 1977; Roy Wilkins Award, National Association for the Advancement of Colored People (N.A.A.C.P.), 1977; Top Hat Award, *Chicago Defender,* 1978; Distinguished American Educator Award, U.S. Office of Education, 1978; Hale Woodruff Award, United Negro College Fund, 1978; National Black Child Development Institute award, 1978; National Leadership Award, National Association for Equal Opportunity in Higher Education, 1978; Alumni Medal, University of Chicago, 1978; Humanitarian Award, International New Thought Alliance, 1978; named to South Carolina Hall of Fame, 1984.

Honorary degrees: LL.D., Denison University, 1945, Virginia Union University, 1945, University of Liberia, 1960, St. Augustine's College, 1963, Lincoln University, 1965, Harvard University, 1967, Morgan College, 1967, Michigan State University, 1968, Centre College, 1970, Alderson-Broaddus College, 1972, Dartmouth College, 1975, and Bishop College, 1977; D.D., Howard University, 1945, Bates College, 1947, Bucknell University, 1954, Berea College, 1955, Kalamazoo College, 1959, Morris College, 1966, Ricker College, 1966, and Interdenominational Theological Center, 1974; Litt.D., South Carolina State College, 1946, Grinnell College, 1967, and University of Ife (Nigeria), 1971; H.H.D., Boston University, 1950, Benedict College, 1970, Lander College, 1974, Talladega College, 1978, and University of Southern California, 1978; L.H.D., Keuka College, 1962, Shaw University, 1966, Morehouse College, 1967, New York University, 1968, Emory University, 1970, Brandeis University, 1970, Yeshiva University, 1971, Pratt Institute, 1971, Coe College, 1972, Edward Waters College, 1974, Duke University, 1975, Dillard University, 1975, Kean College, 1975, and Bethune Cookman College, 1976; Ed.D., St. Vincent College, 1964; D.C.L., Middlebury College, 1969, and Atlanta University, 1979; D.S.T., Olivet College, 1974.

WRITINGS:

(With Joseph William Nicholson) *The Negro's Church,* Institute of Social and Religious Research, 1933, reprinted, Russell, 1969.

The Negro's God as Reflected in His Literature, Chapman & Grimes, 1938, reprinted, Russell, 1969.

(Compiler) *A Gospel for the Social Awakening: Selections from the Writings of Walter Rauschenbusch,* Association Press, 1950.

Seeking to Be Christian in Race Relations, Friendship, 1957, revised edition, 1965.

Disturbed about Man (sermons), John Knox, 1969.

Born to Rebel: An Autobiography, Scribner, 1971, reprinted, University of Georgia Press, 1986.

Lord, the People Have Driven Me On, Vantage, 1981.

Quotable Quotes of Benjamin E. Mays, Vantage, 1983.

Weekly columnist, *Pittsburgh Courier,* beginning 1946. Contributing editor, *Journal of Negro Education.*

CONTRIBUTOR

Christus Victor, Conference of Christian Youth, 1939.

William Stuart Nelson, editor, *The Christian Way in Race Relations,* Harper, 1947.

Contemporary Civilization, Scott, Foresman, 1959.

Huston Smith and others, editors, *The Search for America,* Prentice-Hall, 1959.

The Christian Mission Today, Abingdon for Board of Missions, Methodist Church, 1960.

Roy L. Hill, editor, *Rhetoric of Racial Revolt,* Gordon Bell Press, 1964.

E. P. Booth, editor, *Religion Ponders Science,* Appleton, 1964.

J. S. Childers, editor, *A Way Home,* Holt, 1964.

Bradford Daniel, editor, *Black, White, and Gray: 21 Points of View on the Race Question,* Sheed, 1964.

Why I Believe There Is a God: 16 Essays by Negro Clergymen, Johnson Publishing (Chicago), 1965.

Also contributor to *Sketches of Negro Life and History,* 1929, *Representative American Speeches,* 1946, *Best Sermons,* 1946, and other books. Contributor to *Crisis, Christian Century, Missions, Negro Digest, Saturday Review, Atlantic, Ebony, Christian Science Monitor,* and other publications.

SIDELIGHTS: The son of a Southern sharecropper, Benjamin E. Mays rose to become the president of Morehouse College, one of the nation's leading black schools. The list of the college's alumni, Ishmael Reed remarked in the *New York Times Book Review,* reads "like a who's who of Afro-America's recent intellectual, cultural and political history." Among prominent black Americans who attended Morehouse during Mays's tenure are Martin Luther King, Jr., Andrew Young, and Julian Bond. King once referred to Mays, according to Frank J. Prial of the *New York Times,* as "my spiritual mentor and my intellectual father."

Mays was known as a vigorous civil rights activist who was also an advocate of compromise, calling upon both white segregationists and black revolutionaries to find common ground for peaceful resolution of their differences. "Mays was a voice of moderation in the critical years of the civil rights movement," Prial reported. "He attacked white liberals who paid only lip service to racial equality, but he criticized, too, black extremists such as the Black Panthers." Mays, the *Los Angeles Times* admitted, "proved troublesome for both blacks and whites during his life."

According to his *Born to Rebel: An Autobiography,* Mays was raised with his father's advice to "Stay out of trouble with white people." But Mays ignored the injunction, preferring instead to challenge white society. He left the family farm in South Carolina to go to college in Maine, working summers as a Pullman porter to pay his way. After earning his bachelor's degree, Mays was ordained a Baptist minister in 1922 and went on to receive his master's and doctorate degrees from the University of Chicago. His early career included positions with South Carolina State College, the Tampa Urban League, and the Young Men's Christian Associations. In 1934, Mays became dean of Howard University's School of Religion. In 1940, he became president of Morehouse College in Atlanta, a position he was to hold until 1967.

Mays's academic writings of the 1930s were among the first to record important aspects of black American religious life. As director of a study of black churches in America for the Institute of Social and Religious Research, Mays surveyed over 600 urban and nearly 200 rural churches across the country to identify their problems, achievements, and influence in the black community. Such subjects as the education and training of ministers, the financial resources of church organizations, and the variety of religious and social programs sponsored by black churches were examined and thoroughly documented. Walter White of *Books* called the resulting report, *The Negro's Church,* "one of the few examinations of this sort and it is an important achievement in its understanding of all the social, economic and other forces which have made [the black church] what it is." The reviewer for *Christian Century* described the book as "a picture of the Negro church of today—as scientifically exact as the nature of the material permits."

During Mays's long career as a college administrator he achieved a national reputation for academic excellence. As dean of Howard University's School of Religion, Mays brought the institution to Class A rating with the American Association of Theological Schools. During his term as president of Morehouse College, Mays was instrumental in having the school approved for a chapter of Phi Beta Kappa, only the fourth Georgia college to win such approval.

But Mays's reputation as a leading black educator was based especially on the students he taught, inspired, and advised over several decades. "In his 27 years as president of Morehouse College," the *Los Angeles Times* reported, "he met regularly with students." Prial noted that Mays considered "his greatest honor [to be] having taught and inspired Martin Luther King, Jr. at Morehouse," while the *Washington Post* reported that Mays "was instrumental in the development of King as a civil rights leader." Mays also urged Andrew Young, now the mayor of Atlanta, to first seek public office, while Julian Bond, another Mays student, is a Georgia state senator.

Mays was also a leader in the civil rights movement in Georgia. He played a pivotal role in the integration of Atlanta. In 1960, several young blacks began a series of sit-ins at local lunch counters. They came to Mays for help in planning the actions. The struggle they began soon spread to Atlanta schools, and after an eighteen-month-long fight, the school system was integrated. Prial reported that Mays "fought for the integration of all-white colleges and universities but remained a champion of predominantly black colleges such as Morehouse." He did, however, urge black colleges to recruit white students.

In speaking of the inspiration behind his successful career, Mays wrote in *Born to Rebel*: "I cannot and would not apologize for being a Negro. We have a great history; we have a greater future . . . we have a rendezvous with America." In her review of *Born to Rebel* for the *Christian Science Monitor*, Henrietta Buckmaster noted that Mays "never writes bitterly [about racial discrimination], but he does tell you what happened . . . and then leaves you to reach your own conclusions." She concluded that *Born to Rebel* is "a noble book, a pragmatic and useful one." J. B. Cullen of *Best Sellers* believed that the book was more than the story of one man. "It is a condemnation of the white treatment of the blacks in the United States," Cullen argued, "and a very compact history of the blacks in the U.S. . . . [Mays] has written a story that should be read by everyone."

Described by Reed as someone whose "life exemplifies a tradition of excellence," Mays was fondly remembered upon his death in 1984. Bond claimed at a memorial ceremony: "I am kneeling at the feet of a giant." Young said that he "will always remember Benjamin Elijah Mays as a strong, tall, brisk-walking intellectual giant." Then-president Jimmy Carter, who knews Mays from when he served as governor of Georgia, called him "a credit to the Southland, to America and the world." The book *Our Help in Ages Past: Sermons from Morehouse,* compiled by Fred C. Lofton, is dedicated to the memory of Mays.

BIOGRAPHICAL/CRITICAL SOURCES:

BOOKS

Mays, Benjamin E., *Born to Rebel: An Autobiography,* Scribner, 1971, reprinted, University of Georgia Press, 1986.

PERIODICALS

Best Sellers, April 15, 1971.
Books, March 26, 1933.
Boston Transcript, September 16, 1939.
Christian Century, February 15, 1933, February 1, 1939.
Christian Science Monitor, April 17, 1971.
Journal of Religion, July, 1933.
New York Times Book Review, April 25, 1971.

Washington Post Book World, November 29, 1987.

OBITUARIES:

PERIODICALS

Chicago Tribune, March 30, 1984.
Crisis, March, 1984.
Los Angeles Times, March 29, 1984.
Newsweek, April 9, 1984.
New York Times, March 29, 1984.
Time, April 9, 1984.
Washington Post, March 29, 1984.

—*Sketch by Thomas Wiloch*

*   *   *

MAYS, James A(rthur)   1939-

PERSONAL: Born May 1, 1939, in Pine Bluff, Ark.; son of Talmadge and Edna (Motley) Mays; married Lovella Geans (a Project Headstart teacher), July 15, 1962; children: James Arthur, Jr., James Anthony, James Ornet, James Eddie. *Education:* Agricultural, Mechanical & Normal College (now University of Arkansas at Pine Bluff), B.S., 1960; University of Arkansas for Medical Sciences, B.S. and M.D., 1965. *Politics:* None. *Religion:* Protestant.

ADDRESSES: Office—9214 South Broadway, Los Angeles, Calif. 90003; Martin Luther King, Jr., General Hospital, 12021 South Wilmington Ave., Los Angeles, Calif. 90059.

CAREER: Queen of Angels Hospital, Los Angeles, Calif., intern, 1965-66; Wadsworth Veterans Administration Hospital, Los Angeles, resident in internal medicine, 1968-70; fellow in cardiology, Long Beach Veterans Administration Hospital, Long Beach, Calif., and University of California at Irvine, 1970-72; University of Southern California, Charles R. Drew Medical School, Los Angeles, assistant professor of medicine, 1972—; Martin Luther King, Jr., General Hospital, Los Angeles, acting chief of cardiology, 1972—. Executive secretary, West Coast Medical Management, 1970; co-founder and medical director, United High Blood Pressure Foundation, 1974—; member of board of directors, Cherkey Stroke Program, 1974—; member of California State Council of Hypertension Control, 1975—; member of board of directors, Watt & Health Foundation. Chancellor, Technical Health Careers School. Chairman, P.U.S.H. Los Angeles, 1981; founder of Adopt-a-Family. Member of steering committee, President Reagan's Committee on Tax Reform. *Military service:* U.S. Army, Medical Corps, 1966-68; served in Vietnam; became captain.

MEMBER: American College of Physicians (fellow), American College of Chest Physicians, American Medical Society, American Heart Association (Los Angeles affiliate; chairman of board of South Central governors, 1974—; member of board of directors, 1974—), Charles R. Drew Medical Society, California Medical Association, Arkansas Medical Society, Los Angeles County Medical Society, Long Beach Medical Society, Urban League (Silver Circle member), National Association for the Advancement of Colored People, Philantropee Association, Compton Intercultural Society (executive secretary, 1970—).

AWARDS, HONORS: American Medical Association physicians recognition awards, 1973-76, 1974-77; National Association of Media Women Newsmaker Award, 1975; George Washington Medal, Freedom Foundation of Valley Forge.

WRITINGS:

Mercy Is King (novel), Crescent, 1975.

Also author of *Radian*, 1981, and *Circle of Five*, 1981. Contributor to professional journals. Associate editor, *Charles R. Drew Society Newsletter*, 1973-74.

WORK IN PROGRESS: *Methods to Make Ethnic Foods Safer;* a novel, *Douche;* medical papers on high blood pressure and heart resuscitation.

SIDELIGHTS: James A. Mays commented: "*Mercy Is King* represents a story of Black and white professionals in a manner that has not been expressed in writing, and especially has been neglected by the media. I wrote *Mercy Is King* especially for movie and television presentation for image purposes. I now wait to see if producers, particularly television, have courage to present Blacks in realism other than Super Fly and comedy."

* * *

MBITI, John S(amuel) 1931-

PERSONAL: Born November 30, 1931, in Kitui, Kenya; married Verena Siegenthaler (a social worker and teacher), May 15, 1965; children: Samuel Kyeni, Maria Mwende, Esther Mwikali, Anna Kavata. *Education:* Makerere University College, University of East Africa (now Makerere University), B.A., 1953; Barrington College, A.B., 1956, Th.B., 1957; Cambridge University, Ph.D., 1963.

ADDRESSES: *Home and office*—Einschlagweg 11, CH 3400 Burgdorf, Switzerland.

CAREER: Anglican priest. Teacher Training College, Kangundo, Kenya, teacher, 1957-59; Selly Oak Colleges, Birmingham, England, visiting William Paton Lecturer, 1959-60; St. Michael's Church, St. Albans, England, curate, 1963-64; Makerere University, Kampala, Uganda, 1964-74, began as lecturer in New Testament and African religions and philosophy, became professor of theology and comparative religion, and head of department; Ecumenical Institute, Bossey, Geneva, Switzerland, director and professor, 1974-80; parish minister in Burgdorf, Switzerland, 1981—. Visiting lecturer, University of Hamburg, 1966-67; Harry Emerson Fosdick Visiting Professor, Union Theological Seminary, New York, N.Y., 1972-73; part-time professor at University of Bern, 1983—.

MEMBER: Studiorum Novi Testamenti Societas.

AWARDS, HONORS: L.H.D., Barrington College, 1973.

WRITINGS:

Mutunga na Ngewa Yake, Thomas Nelson, 1954.
(Translator into Kikamba) Robert Louis Stevenson, *Treasure Island*, East African Literature Bureau, 1954.
English-Kamba Vocabulary, East African Literature Bureau, 1959.
(Editor) *Akamba Stories* (collection of folktales), Oxford University Press, 1966.
African Religions and Philosophy, Praeger, 1969.
Poems of Nature and Faith, East African Publishing House, 1969.
Concepts of God in Africa, Praeger, 1970.
New Testament Eschatology in an African Background: A Study of the Encounter between New Testament Theology and African Traditional Concepts, Oxford University Press, 1971.

The Crisis of Mission in Africa, Uganda Church Press (Kampala), 1971.
The Voice of Nine Bible Trees, Uganda Church Press, 1973.
Love and Marriage in Africa, Longman, 1973.
Death and the Hereafter in the Light of Christianity and African Religion, Makerere University Printery, 1974.
Introduction to African Religion, Praeger, 1975.
The Prayers of African Religion, S.P.C.K., 1975, Orbis, 1976.
(Editor) *Confessing Christ in Different Cultures*, Ecumenical Institute (Bossey, Switzerland), 1977.
(Editor) *African and Asian Contributions to Contemporary Theology*, Ecumenical Institute, 1977.

Also author of *Bible and Theology in African Christianity*, 1984; also editor of *Indigenous Theology and the Universal Church*, 1979, and *Christian and Jewish Dialogue on Man*, 1980; also co-editor of *Evangelische Kirchenlexikon*, five volumes, 1985-89. Contributor of poems and articles to anthologies and periodicals in Europe, Africa, India, Japan, and the United States.

SIDELIGHTS: John S. Mbiti speaks Kikamba, Swahili, Gikuyu, French, and German. He reads New Testament Greek and some Old Testament Hebrew.

* * *

McCLELLAN, George Marion 1860-1934

PERSONAL: Born September 29, 1860, in Belfast, Tenn.; died May 17, 1934; son of George Fielding and Eliza (Leonard) McClellan; married Mariah Augusta Rabb, October 4, 1988; children: Marion S. (one source says Lochiel), Theodore R. *Education:* Fisk University, B.A., 1885, M.A., 1890; Hartford Theological Seminary, B.D., 1891; attended University of California at Los Angeles. *Religion:* Congregationalist. *Politics:* Republican.

ADDRESSES: *Home*—1123 West Hill St., Louisville, Ky.

CAREER: Poet and short story writer. Congregationalist minister in Louisville, Ky., c. 1887-90; Fisk University, Nashville, Tenn., financial agent, 1892-94; State Normal School, Normal, Alabama, teacher and chaplain, 1894-96; pastor for Congregationalist church in Memphis, Tenn., 1897-99; Central Colored High School, Louisville, teacher of Latin and English, 1899-1911; Dunbar Public School, Louisville, principal, 1911-19. Solicited funds for an anti-tubercular sanatorium for black people in Los Angeles, Calif.

WRITINGS:

Poems, A.M.E. Church Sunday School Union, 1895, reprinted, Books for Libraries Press, 1970.
Songs of a Southerner (poems), Press of Rockwell & Churchill, 1896.
(Contributor) Daniel Wallace Culp, editor, *Twentieth Century Negro Literature; or, A Cyclopedia of Thought on the Vital Topics Relating to the American Negro*, J. L. Nichols, 1902.
Old Greenbottom Inn and Other Stories, privately printed, 1906, reprinted, AMS Press, 1975.
The Path of Dreams (poems), J. P. Morton, 1916, reprinted, Books for Libraries Press, 1970.

SIDELIGHTS: George Marion McClellan, who wrote poetry and short stories during the late nineteenth and early twentieth centuries, was known for his sentimental and conservative works. In the 1890s McClellan's poetry "was based mainly on the kinds of themes and images that were staples in the popular, genteel verse of the period," noted Dickson D. Bruce, Jr., in *Dictionary of Literary Biography*. This type of sentimentalism was characteristic among black writers of that decade who, in hopes of making race insignificant, used literature to portray a sophisticated, middle-class black world that could be readily assimilated into white mainstream society. But at the beginning of the century many black writers turned to the unique history and experience of blacks in the United States, demonstrating in their works a strong race-consciousness and concern for racial identity. McClellan, however, held fast to the conservative assimilationist philosophy during this time, hence distinguishing himself from other black writers. "The strength of his views indicates, above all," commented Bruce, "the depth of his commitment to the American literary and cultural mainstream, a commitment which, however unusual, would remain a constant in his literary career."

Exemplary of McClellan's conservative, mainstream style is his 1895 *Poems*, a collection of sentimental works about nature, love, and religion. The poetry shows no awareness of the rising concern for a distinctive black literature, and in the book's introduction McClellan, explained Bruce, "actually, if tacitly, denied the validity of these new directions in black literary thought." Departing slightly from his sentimentalist approach, McClellan gives a general overview of black literature in a 1902 essay, "The Negro as a Writer," appearing in *Twentieth Century Negro Literature*. The author shows an interest in ideas of racial pride but, tied to his conservative views of black literature, focuses only on black writers who had significant white readership and works focusing on genteel heroes and heroines.

By 1906, though, McClellan came to a point in his writing where he was prepared to produce literature based on the unique aspects of black life in America. Illustrating his view that the struggle of blacks against society in the South contains the elements of classic tragedy is McClellan's short story collection *Old Greenbottom Inn*. The stories relate such scenarios as interracial love, folk tradition, seduction, and violence. "Uniting all the stories in the volume," related Bruce, "is a sense that blacks were caught up in a world not of their making and powerfully out of control." Bruce qualified, however, that McClellan still clung to an essentially white literary tradition, for he modeled his characters not after figures exclusive to black culture and history but, rather, after literary figures drawn from a larger Western tradition, such as those found in the tragic dramas of Aeschylus and William Shakespeare. Furthermore, continued Bruce, McClellan never actually departed from his assimilationist ideals: "Viewing the black experience as, most profoundly, the stuff of tragedy, [the author] saw the origins of tragedy in racism's indifferent hostility to black aspirations, which he conceived of as, above all, making a place in the American mainstream."

All but one of the stories in *Old Greenbottom Inn*, along with poetry previously appearing in *Poems*, were reprinted in McClellan's 1916 *The Path of Dreams*, which featured an additional story also dealing with the tragic theme of race relations. Summing up the author's work, Bruce wrote: "As he focused his attention on the tragedies of black American life, he wrote in ways that presented a consistent vision of the emotional and psychological realities of racism, helping to illuminate the impact of prejudice on human lives." Placing the author in the context of black American literary figures, Bruce concluded that, although McClellan was not a major writer during his lifetime, his work is "significant . . . because

of its conservatism," while it provides "an important perspective on the development of black thought and culture at the turn of the century."

BIOGRAPHICAL/CRITICAL SOURCES:

BOOKS

Culp, Daniel Wallace, *American Negro: His History and Literature*, Arno Press, 1969.
Dictionary of Literary Biography, Volume 50: *Afro-American Writers Before the Harlem Renaissance*, Gale, 1986.
Kerlin, Robert T., *Negro Poets and Their Poems*, revised and enlarged edition, Associated Publishers, 1935.
Long, Richard A. and Eugenia W. Collier, *Afro-American Writing: An Anthology of Prose and Poetry*, Volume 1, New York University Press, 1972.
Sherman, Joan R., *Invisible Poets: Afro-Americans of the Nineteenth Century*, University of Illinois Press, 1974.
White, Newman Ivey and Walter Clinton Jackson, *An Anthology of Verse by American Negroes*, Trinity College Press, 1924.

*   *   *

McCLUSKEY, John (A.), Jr. 1944-

PERSONAL: Born October 25, 1944, in Middletown, Ohio; son of John A. (a truck driver) and Helen (Harris) McCluskey; married Audrey Louise Thomas (a college instructor), December 24, 1969; children: Malik Douglass, Jerome Patrice, John Toure. *Education:* Harvard University, B.A. (cum laude), 1966; Stanford University, M.A., 1972.

ADDRESSES: Home—3527 Roxbury Circle, Bloomington, Ind. 47401. *Office*—Department of Afro-American Studies, Indiana University, Bloomington, Ind. 47405.

CAREER: Miles College, Birmingham, Ala., instructor in English, 1967-68; Valparaiso University, Valparaiso, Ind., lecturer in humanities and writer in residence, 1968-69; Case Western Reserve University, Cleveland, Ohio, coordinator of Afro-American studies, 1969-70, lecturer in Afro-American studies, 1970-72, assistant professor of American studies, 1972-74, assistant professor of English, 1974-77; Indiana University—Bloomington, associate professor, 1977-84, professor of Afro-American studies, 1984—, adjunct professor of English, 1984—, associate dean of graduate school, 1984—. Director, C.I.C. Minorities Fellowships Program, Indiana University, 1983—. Consultant, black studies pilot project, East Cleveland elementary school district, 1971; member of board of directors, Independent School of East Cleveland, 1972. Member of executive board, Bell Neighborhood Center, 1972; member of board of trustees, Goodrich Social Settlement, 1972. Member of advisory council, Karamu House Writers Conference, 1970; member of Cleveland planning committee, World Festival of Black Arts (Nigeria), 1974; director of black drama troupes in Birmingham and Cleveland. Consultant and editor, New Day Press, 1973-77. Has presented papers at numerous universities and on WJMO-Radio, Cleveland.

MEMBER: Modern Language Association of America, American Association of University Professors, National Council for Black Studies, Midwest Modern Language Association.

AWARDS, HONORS: Citation from Outstanding Educators of America, 1976; faculty research grants from Indiana University, 1977 and 1978; Yaddo residence fellowships, 1984 and 1986.

WRITINGS:

Look What They Done to My Song (novel), Random House, 1974.

(Editor) *Blacks in History, Volume II* (McCluskey was not associated with first volume), New Day Press, 1975.

(Editor) *Stories from Black History: Nine Stories*, five volumes, New Day Press, 1975.

(Editor) Ebraska Ceasor and others, *Blacks in Ohio: Seven Portraits*, New Day Press, 1976.

(Author of introduction) Robert Southgate, *Black Plots and Black Characters*, Gaylord, 1979.

(Contributor) Mari Evans, editor, *Black Women Writers (1950-1980): A Critical Evaluation*, Doubleday, 1983.

Mr. America's Last Season Blues (novel), Louisiana State University Press, 1983.

(Editor) *City of Refuge: Collected Stories of Rudolph Fisher*, University of Missouri Press, 1987.

CONTRIBUTOR TO ANTHOLOGIES

Orde Coombs, editor, *What We Must See: Young Black Storytellers*, Dodd, 1974.

Katharine Newman, editor, *Ethnic American Short Stories*, Simon & Schuster, 1975.

Martha Foley, editor, *Best American Short Stories*, Houghton, 1976.

William O'Rourke, editor, *On the Job*, Vintage, 1977.

OTHER

Contributor of poetry and short stories to magazines, including *Negro Digest, Obsidian, Black Review, Iowa Review, Seattle Review*, and *Choice;* contributor of reviews and articles to magazines and newspapers, including *Juju, Cleveland Magazine, Plain Dealer, Louisville Courier-Journal*, and *Black American Literature Forum*. Editor of *Juju*, 1974-77.

WORK IN PROGRESS: *The River People* (a novel) and short stories.

SIDELIGHTS: The fiction of John McCluskey, Jr., "reveals a strong awareness of history and an equally strong feeling for black cultural traditions," writes Frank E. Moorer in the *Dictionary of Literary Biography*. McCluskey's first novel, *Look What They Done to My Song*, is the story of a young travelling black musician (Mack) who, Moorer writes, "wants to preach a message of love with his music, . . . an evangelist with a horn spreading a message of love and understanding." As Mack travels across the country—"his pilgrimage to self-understanding," according to Moorer—he encounters a diverse cast of characters, including an old Southern couple who treat him like a son, a frustrated hustler, and a young woman who denies her black heritage, claiming she is Portuguese. James C. Kilgore writes in *Black World* that these minor characters represent people "trying to make it in the America of the late Sixties," at the same time Mack himself is "seeking [and] running" in search of a "standing place." A reviewer in the *New Yorker* comments that McCluskey "illuminates brilliantly" his characters, adding that "youngish blacks who have lived through the anguish of the sixties rarely [have had] a better spokesman." Kilgore concludes that *Look What They Done to My Song* "is a novel whose vision reflects deep insight. . . . [It is] a lyrical novel which sings of justice, of love, of freedom, of survival."

"For McCluskey," writes Moorer, "the Afro-American cultural experience has been a heroic one—one that has nurtured the individual and the group." His 1983 novel, *Mr. America's*

Last Season Blues, tells the story of a middle-aged former star athlete (Roscoe) who seeks to regain the hero status he once assumed in the small black community of Union City, Ohio. A former professional football player whose brief career ended with injuries, Roscoe has "settle[d] into a life of vague dissatisfaction, plagued by his regret over the stardom he never achieved," writes Jim Haskins in the *New York Times Book Review*. Moorer adds that Roscoe is continually "haunted by the black community's constant reminders of what he used to be and by his father's ghost which asks Roscoe if he still has the 'fighting spirit'." To prove himself, Roscoe initially becomes involved in a series of irresponsible actions, including a brief stint with the local semiprofessional football team and an extramarital affair with a former lover. However, he eventually finds himself trying to determine the truth behind a crime that his lover's son has wrongfully been charged with. "In doing so," observes Haskins, "he recognizes the cowardice and lying endemic to the declining black community of Union City and begins to assume greater responsibility for reversing that direction." It is at this point that the true nature of Roscoe's drive emerges, which Moorer describes as "regaining for the blacks in Union City a sense of identity, unity, and purpose." Don Johnson praises McCluskey in *Southern Humanities Review* for depicting Roscoe's struggles not as vain glory-seeking, but "as a mature man's attempt to comprehend and deal with the suffering wrought by time, love, and death."

McCluskey once commented: "As a writer, my commitment is to that level of creative excellence so ably demonstrated by Afro-American artists as diverse as Ralph Ellison, Romare Bearden, and Miles Davis. Hoping to avoid any fashionable ambiguity and pedantry, I want my fiction and essays to heighten the appreciation of the complexities of Afro-American literature and life."

AVOCATIONAL INTERESTS: Playing saxophone and bass clarinet, photography, swimming, jogging, and sailing; (McCluskey also coaches Little League football and Boys Club soccer).

BIOGRAPHICAL/CRITICAL SOURCES:

BOOKS

Dictionary of Literary Biography, Volume XXXIII: *Afro-American Fiction Writers after 1955*, Gale, 1984.

PERIODICALS

Black World, July, 1975.
New Yorker, November 25, 1974.
New York Times Book Review, November 17, 1974, April 1, 1984, December 20, 1987.
Southern Humanities Review, fall, 1984.

*   *   *

McELROY, Colleen J(ohnson)   1935-

PERSONAL: Born October 30, 1935, in St. Louis, Mo.; daughter of Jesse O. (an army officer) and Ruth (Long) Johnson; married David F. McElroy (a writer), November 28, 1968 (divorced); children: Kevin D., Vanessa C. *Education:* Attended University of Maryland, 1953-55; Harris Teachers College, A.A., 1956; Kansas State University, B.S., 1958, M.S., 1963; graduate study at University of Pittsburgh, 1958-59, and Western Washington State College (now Western Washington University), 1970-71; University of Washington, Ph.D., 1973.

ADDRESSES: *Home*—2616 4th St. N., Apt. 406, Seattle, Wash.

98109. *Office*—Department of English, University of Washington, Seattle, Wash. 98105.

CAREER: Rehabilitation Institute, Kansas City, Mo., chief speech clinician, 1963-66; Western Washington State College (now Western Washington University), Bellingham, assistant professor of English, 1966-73; University of Washington, Seattle, 1973—, began as assistant professor, currently professor of English. Affiliate member of speech faculty, University of Missouri—Kansas City, 1965-66; summer instructor, Project Head Start and Project New Careers. Moderator of "Outlook," KVOS-TV, 1968-72. Watercolors and pen-ink sketches displayed at gallery exhibit, 1978. Member of board, Washington State Commission for the Humanities.

MEMBER: American Speech and Hearing Association, National Council of Teachers of English, Conference on College Composition and Communication, Writers Guild of America East, United Black Artists Guild (Seattle).

AWARDS, HONORS: Carnation teaching incentive award, 1973; Breadloaf scholarship for fiction, 1974; Best of Small Presses award for poetry, Pushcart Book Press, 1976; National Endowment for the Arts fellowship in creating writing, 1978; Matrix Women of Achievement Award, 1985; Before Columbus American Book Award, 1985, for *Queen of the Ebony Isles.*

WRITINGS:

Speech and Language Development of the Preschool Child: A Survey, C. C. Thomas, 1972.
The Mules Done Long Since Gone (poems), Harrison-Madronna Press, 1973.
Music From Home: Selected Poems, Southern Illinois University Press, 1976.
(Contributor) *Iron Country* (anthology), Copper Canyon Press, 1978.
(Contributor) Dexter Fisher, editor, *The Third Woman* (anthology), Houghton, 1980.
(Contributor) *Backbone 2* (anthology), Seal Press, 1980.
Winters without Snow (poems), I. Reed, 1980.
Looking for a Country under Its Original Name (poems), Blue Begonia Press, 1985.
Queen of the Ebony Isles (poems), Wesleyan University Press, 1985.
Jesus and Fat Tuesday and Other Short Stories, Creative Arts Book Company, 1987.
Bone Flames (poems), Wesleyan University Press, 1987.

Also author of *Lie and Say You Love Me* (poems), Circinatum Press and, with Virginia Chappell, *Continuity: Writing Effective Paragraphs,* Random House; author of stories and scripts for television and of educational film scripts, including "Tracy Gains Language" and "Introduction to Clinical Practicum," distributed by the Bureau of Faculty Research, Western Washington University. Also contributor to *Black Sister: Poems by Black American Women, 1946-1980,* 1981, and other anthologies. Contributor of poems and short fiction to numerous literary reviews and little magazines, including *Wormwood Review, Poetry Northwest, Choice, Seneca Review, Southern Poetry Review, Confrontation, Massachusetts Review, Georgia Review, Southern Poetry Review,* and *Black Warrior Review.*

WORK IN PROGRESS: A short fiction collection, *Ain't Nobody's Business;* a novel, *Long Way from St. Louie.*

*   *   *

McKAY, Claude
See McKAY, Festus Claudius

McKAY, Festus Claudius   1889-1948
(Claude McKay; Eli Edwards, pseudonym)

PERSONAL: Born September 15, 1889 (some sources say 1890), in Sunny Ville (some sources say Clarendon), Jamaica, British West Indies (now Jamaica); immigrated to United States, 1912; naturalized U.S. citizen, 1940; died of heart failure, May 22, 1948, in Chicago, Ill.; buried at Calvary Cemetery, Woodside, N.Y.; son of Thomas Francis (a farmer) and Anne Elizabeth (a farmer; maiden name, Edwards) McKay; married Eulalie Imelda Edwards, July 30, 1914 (divorced); children: Ruth Hope. *Education:* Attended Tuskegee Normal & Industrial Institute, 1912, and Kansas State College, 1912-14. *Religion:* Roman Catholic.

ADDRESSES: Home—Chicago, Ill.

CAREER: Writer. Worked as cabinetmaker's apprentice and wheelwright; constable at Jamaican Constabulary, Kingston, 1909; longshoreman, porter, bartender, and waiter, 1910-14; restaurateur, 1914; writer for *Pearsons Magazine,* 1918, and *Workers' Dreadnought* in London, England, 1919; associate editor of *Liberator,* 1921; American Workers representative at Third International in Moscow, U.S.S.R., 1922; artist's model in mid-1920s; worked for Rex Ingram's film studio in Nice, France, c. 1926; shipyard worker, c. 1941.

AWARDS, HONORS: Medal from Jamaican Institute of Arts and Sciences, c. 1912; Harmon Foundation Award for distinguished literary achievement from the National Association for the Advancement of Colored People (NAACP), 1929, for *Harlem Shadows* and *Home to Harlem;* award from James Weldon Johnson Literary Guild, 1937.

WRITINGS:

UNDER NAME CLAUDE McKAY, EXCEPT AS NOTED

Songs of Jamaica (poetry), introduction by Walter Jekyll, Gardner, 1912, reprinted, Mnemosyne Publications, 1969 (also see below).
Constab Ballads (poetry), Watts, 1912 (also see below).
Spring in New Hampshire, and Other Poems, Richards, 1920.
Harlem Shadows: The Poems of Claude McKay, introduction by Max Eastman, Harcourt, 1922.
Home to Harlem (novel), Harper, 1928, reprinted, Pocket Books, 1965.
Banjo, a Story Without a Plot (novel), Harper, 1929, reprinted, Harcourt, 1970.
Gingertown (short stories), Harper, 1932.
Banana Bottom (novel), Harper, 1933, reprinted, Chatham, 1970.
A Long Way From Home (autobiography), Furman, 1937, reprinted, Arno Press, 1969.
Harlem: Negro Metropolis (nonfiction), Dutton, 1940, reprinted, Harcourt, 1968.
Selected Poems, introduction by John Dewey, biographical note by Max Eastman, Bookman, 1953.
The Passion of Claude McKay: Selected Poetry and Prose, 1912-1948, edited by Wayne F. Cooper, Schocken, 1973.
The Dialectic Poetry of Claude McKay (contains *Songs of Jamaica* and *Constab Ballads;* also see above), edited by Wayne F. Cooper, Books for Libraries Press, 1972.
Trial by Lynching: Stories About Negro Life in North America, re-translated into English from Russian-language version by Robert Winter, edited by Alan L. McLeod, preface by H. H. Anniah Gowda, Centre for Commonwealth Literature and Research, University of Mysore, 1977.

The Negroes in America, re-translated into English from Russian-language version by Robert Winter, edited by Alan L. McLeod, Kennikat, 1977.

Work represented in anthologies.

Contributor to periodicals, including *Workers' Dreadnought, Negro World, Catholic Worker, Ebony, Epistle, Interracial Review, Jewish Frontier, Nation, Seven Arts* (under pseudonym Eli Edwards), *New York Herald Tribune Books,* and *Phylon.*

SIDELIGHTS: Claude McKay was a key figure in the Harlem Renaissance, a prominent literary movement of the 1920s. His work ranged from vernacular verse celebrating peasant life in Jamaica to fairly militant poems challenging white authority in America, and from generally straightforward tales of black life in both Jamaica and America to more philosophically ambitious fiction addressing instinctual/intellectual duality, which McKay found central to the black individual's efforts to cope in a racist society. Consistent in his various writings is his disdain for racism and the sense that bigotry's implicit stupidity renders its adherents pitiable as well as loathsome. As Arthur D. Drayton wrote in his essay "Claude McKay's Human Pity" (included by editor Ulli Beier in the volume *Introduction to African Literature*): "McKay does not seek to hide his bitterness. But having preserved his vision as poet and his status as a human being, he can transcend bitterness. In seeing . . . the significance of the Negro for mankind as a whole, he is at once protesting as a Negro and uttering a cry for the race of mankind as a member of that race. His human pity was the foundation that made all this possible."

McKay was born in Sunny Ville, Jamaica, in 1889. The son of peasant farmers, he was infused with racial pride and a great sense of black heritage. His early literary interests, though, were in English poetry. Under the tutelage of his brother, schoolteacher Uriah Theophilus McKay, and a neighboring Englishman, Walter Jekyll, McKay studied the British masters—including John Milton, Alexander Pope, and the later romantics—and European philosophers such as eminent pessimist Arthur Schopenhauer, whose works Jekyll was then translating from German into English. It was Jekyll who advised aspiring poet McKay to cease mimicking the English poets and begin producing verse in Jamaican dialect.

At age seventeen McKay departed from Sunny Ville to apprentice as a woodworker in Brown's Town. But he studied there only briefly before leaving to work as a constable in the Jamaican capital, Kingston. In Kingston he experienced and encountered extensive racism, probably for the first time in his life. His native Sunny Ville was predominantly populated by blacks, but in substantially white Kingston blacks were considered inferior and capable of only menial tasks. McKay quickly grew disgusted with the city's bigoted society, and within one year he returned home to Sunny Ville.

During his brief stays in Brown's Town and Kingston McKay continued writing poetry, and once back in Sunny Ville, with Jekyll's encouragement, he published the verse collections *Songs of Jamaica* and *Constab Ballads* in London in 1912. In these two volumes McKay portrays opposing aspects of black life in Jamaica. *Songs of Jamaica* presents an almost celebratory portrait of peasant life, with poems addressing subjects such as the peaceful death of McKay's mother and the black people's ties to the Jamaican land. *Constab Ballads,* however, presents a substantially bleaker perspective on the plight of Jamaican blacks and contains several poems explicitly critical of life in urban Kingston. Writing in *The Negro Novel in America,* Rob-

ert Bone noted the differing sentiments of the two collections, but he also contended that the volumes share a sense of directness and refreshing candor. He wrote: "These first two volumes are already marked by a sharpness of vision, an inborn realism, and a freshness which provides a pleasing contrast with the conventionality which, at this time, prevails among the black poets of the United States."

For *Songs of Jamaica* McKay received an award and stipend from the Jamaican Institute of Arts and Sciences. He used the money to finance a trip to America, and in 1912 he arrived in South Carolina. He then traveled to Alabama and enrolled at the Tuskegee Institute, where he studied for approximately two months before transferring to Kansas State College. In 1914 he left school entirely for New York City and worked various menial jobs. As in Kingston, McKay encountered racism in New York City, and that racism compelled him to continue writing poetry.

In 1917, under the pseudonym Eli Edwards, McKay published two poems in the periodical *Seven Arts.* His verses were discovered by critic Frank Harris, who then included some of McKay's other poems in *Pearson's Magazine.* Among McKay's most famous poems from this period is "To the White Fiends," a vitriolic challenge to white oppressors and bigots. A few years later McKay befriended Max Eastman, Communist sympathizer and editor of the magazine *Liberator.* McKay published more poems in Eastman's magazine, notably the inspirational "If We Must Die," which defended black rights and threatened retaliation for prejudice and abuse. "Like men we'll face the murderous, cowardly pack," McKay wrote, "Pressed to the wall, dying, but fighting back!" In *Black Poets of the United States,* Jean Wagner noted that "If We Must Die" transcends specifics of race and is widely prized as an inspiration to persecuted people throughout the world. "Along with the will to resistance of black Americans that it expresses," Wagner wrote, "it voices also the will of oppressed people of every age who, whatever their race and wherever their region, are fighting with their backs against the wall to win their freedom."

Upon publication of "If We Must Die" McKay commenced two years of travel and work abroad. He spent part of 1919 in Holland and Belgium, then moved to London and worked on the periodical *Workers' Dreadnought.* In 1920 he published his third verse collection, *Spring in New Hampshire,* which was notable for containing "Harlem Shadows," a poem about the plight of black prostitutes in the degrading urban environment. McKay used this poem, which symbolically presents the degradation of the entire black race, as the title for a subsequent collection.

McKay returned to the United States in 1921 and involved himself in various social causes. The next year he published *Harlem Shadows,* a collection from previous volumes and periodicals publications. This work contains many of his most acclaimed poems—including "If We Must Die"—and assured his stature as a leading member of the literary movement referred to as the Harlem Renaissance. He capitalized on his acclaim by redoubling his efforts on behalf of blacks and laborers: he became involved in the Universal Negro Improvement Association and produced several articles for its publication, *Negro World,* and he traveled to the Soviet Union, which he had previously visited with Eastman, and attended the Communist party's Fourth Congress.

Eventually McKay went to Paris, where he developed a severe respiratory infection and supported himself intermittently by working as an artist's model. His infection eventually necessitated his hospitalization, but after recovering he resumed traveling, and for the next eleven years he toured Europe and portions of northern Africa. During this period he also published three novels and a short story collection. The first novel, *Home to Harlem*, may be his most recognized title. Published in 1928, it concerns a black soldier—Jake—who abruptly abandons his military duties and returns home to Harlem. Jake represents, in rather overt fashion, the instinctual aspect of the individual, and his ability to remain true to his feelings enables him to find happiness with a former prostitute, Felice. Juxtaposed with Jake's behavior is that of Ray, an aspiring writer burdened with despair. His sense of bleakness derives largely from his intellectualized perspective, and it eventually compels him to leave alien, racist America for his homeland of Haiti.

In *The Negro Novel in America*, Robert Bone wrote that the predominantly instinctual Jake and the intellectual Ray "represent different ways of rebelling against Western civilization." Bone added, however, that McKay was not entirely successful in articulating his protagonists' relationships in white society. He declared that *Home to Harlem* was "unable to develop its primary conflict" and thus "bogs down in the secondary contrast between Jake and Ray."

Despite thematic flaws, *Home to Harlem*—with its sordid, occasionally harrowing scenes of ghetto life—proved extremely popular, and it gained recognition as the first commercially successful novel by a black writer. McKay quickly followed it with *Banjo*, a novel about a black vagabond living in the French port of Marseilles. Like Jake from *Home to Harlem*, protagonist Banjo embodies the largely instinctual way of living, though he is considerably more enterprising and quick-witted than the earlier character. Ray, the intellectual from *Home to Harlem*, also appears in *Banjo*. His plight is that of many struggling artists who are compelled by social circumstances to support themselves with conventional employment. Both Banjo and Ray are perpetually dissatisfied and disturbed by their limited roles in white society, and by the end of the novel the men are prepared to depart from Marseilles.

Banjo failed to match the acclaim and commercial success of *Home to Harlem*, but it confirmed McKay's reputation as a serious, provocative artist. In his third novel, *Banana Bottom*, he presented a more incisive exploration of his principal theme, the black individual's quest for cultural identity in a white society. *Banana Bottom* recounts the experiences of a Jamaican peasant girl, Bita, who is rescued by white missionaries after suffering a rape. Bita's new providers try to impose their cultural values on her by introducing her to organized Christianity and the British educational system. Their actions culminate in a horribly bungled attempt to arrange Bita's marriage to an aspiring minister. The prospective groom is exposed as a sexual aberrant, whereupon Bita flees white society. She eventually finds happiness and fulfillment among the black peasants.

Critics agree that *Banana Bottom* is McKay's most skillful delineation of the black individual's predicament in white society. Unfortunately, the novel's thematic worth was largely ignored when the book first appeared in 1933. Its positive reviews then were related to McKay's extraordinary evocation of the Jamaican tropics and his mastery of melodrama. In the ensuing years, though, *Banana Bottom* has gained increasing acknowledgement as McKay's finest fiction and the culmination of his efforts to articulate his own tension and unease through the novel.

McKay's other noteworthy publication during his final years abroad was *Gingertown*, a collection of twelve short stories. Six of the tales are devoted to Harlem life, and they reveal McKay's preoccupation with black exploitation and humiliation. Other tales are set in Jamaica and even in North Africa, McKay's last foreign home before he returned to the United States in the mid-1930s. Once back in Harlem he began an autobiographical work, *A Long Way From Home*, in which he related his own problems as a black individual in a white society.

By the late 1930s McKay had developed a keen interest in Catholicism. Through Ellen Tarry, who wrote children's books, he became active in Harlem's Friendship House. His newfound religious interest, together with his observations and experiences at the Friendship House, inspired his essay collection, *Harlem: Negro Metropolis*. Like *Banjo*, *Banana Bottom*, and *Gingertown*, *Harlem: Negro Metropolis* failed to spark much interest from a reading public that was already tiring of literature by and about blacks. With his reputation already waning, McKay moved to Chicago and worked as a teacher for a Catholic organization. By the mid-1940s his health had deteriorated. He endured several illnesses throughout his last years and eventually died of heart failure in May, 1948.

In the years immediately following his death McKay's reputation continued to decline as critics found him conventional and somewhat shallow. Recently, however, McKay has gained recognition for his intense commitment to expressing the predicament of his fellow blacks, and he is now admired for devoting his art and life to social protest. As Robert A. Smith wrote in his *Phylon* publication "Claude McKay: An Essay in Criticism": "Although he was frequently concerned with the race problem, his style is basically lucid. One feels disinclined to believe that the medium which he chose was too small, or too large for his message. He has been heard."

BIOGRAPHICAL/CRITICAL SOURCES:

BOOKS

Barton, Rebecca Chalmers, *Witnesses for Freedom: Negro Americans in Autobiography*, Harper, 1948.

Beier, Ulli, editor, *Introduction to African Literature: An Anthology of Critical Writing From "Black Orpheus,"* Longmans, 1967.

Bone, Robert, *The Negro Novel in America*, Yale University Press, 1958.

Brawley, Benjamin, *The Negro Genius: A New Appraisal of the Achievement of the American Negro in Literature and the Fine Arts*, Dodd, 1937.

Bronze, Stephen, *Roots of Negro Consciousness, the 1920's: Three Harlem Renaissance Authors*, Libra, 1964.

Dictionary of Literary Biography, Gale, Volume 4: *American Writers in Paris, 1920-1939*, 1980, Volume 45: *American Poets, 1880-1945, First Series*, 1986, Volume 51: *Afro-American Writers From the Harlem Renaissance to 1940*, 1987.

Emanuel, James A., and Theodore L. Gross, *Dark Symphony: Negro Literature in America*, Free Press, 1968.

Fullinwider, S. P., *The Mind and Mood of Black America: 20th Century Thought*, Dorsey, 1969.

Gayle, Addison, Jr., *Claude McKay: The Black Poet at War*, Broadside, 1972.

Giles, James R., *Claude McKay*, Hall, 1976.

Gloster, Hugh M., *Negro Voices in American Fiction*, University of North Carolina Press, 1948.

Huggins, Nathan, *Harlem Renaissance,* Oxford University Press, 1971.

Hughes, Carl Milton, *The Negro Novelist: 1940-1950,* Citadel, 1953.

Kent, George E., *Blackness and the Adventure of Western Culture,* Third World Press, 1972.

Ramchand, Kenneth, *The West Indian Novel and Its Background,* Barnes & Noble, 1970.

Twentieth-Century Literary Criticism, Volume 7, Gale, 1982.

Wagner, Jean, *Les Poetes negres des Etats-Unis,* Librairies Istra, 1962, translation by Kenneth Douglas published as *Black Poets of the United States: From Paul Laurence Dunbar to Langston Hughes,* University of Illinois Press, 1973.

PERIODICALS

America, July 3, 1943.
Black Orpheus, June, 1965.
Bookman, April, 1928, February, 1930.
CLA Journal, March, 1972, June, 1973, December, 1975, March, 1980.
Crisis, June, 1928.
Extension, September, 1946.
Phylon, fall, 1948, fall, 1964.
New York Post, May 22, 1937.
Race, July, 1967.
Studies in Black Literature, summer, 1972.

—*Sketch by Les Stone*

*   *   *

McPHERSON, James Alan   1943-

PERSONAL: Born September 16, 1943, in Savannah, Ga.; son of James Allen and Mable (Smalls) McPherson. *Education:* Attended Morgan State University, 1963-64; Morris Brown College, B.A., 1965; Harvard University, LL.B., 1968; University of Iowa, M.F.A., 1969.

ADDRESSES: Office—Department of English, University of Iowa, Iowa City, Iowa 52242.

CAREER: University of Iowa, Iowa City, instructor in writing at Law School, 1968-69, instructor in Afro-American literature, 1969; University of California, Santa Cruz, faculty member, 1969-70; Morgan State University, Baltimore, Md., faculty member, 1975-76; University of Virginia, Charlottesville, faculty member, 1976-81; University of Iowa, Writers Workshop, Iowa City, professor, 1981—.

MEMBER: Authors League of America.

AWARDS, HONORS: First prize, *Atlantic* short story contest, 1965, for "Gold Coast"; grant from Atlantic Monthly Press and Little, Brown, 1969; National Institute of Arts and Letters award in literature, 1970; Guggenheim fellow, 1972-73; Pulitzer Prize, 1978, for *Elbow Room: Stories;* MacArthur fellowship, 1981.

WRITINGS:

Hue and Cry: Short Stories, Atlantic-Little, Brown, 1969.

(Editor with Miller Williams) *Railroad: Trains and Train People in American Culture,* Random House, 1976.

Elbow Room: Stories, Atlantic-Little, Brown, 1977.

(Author of foreword) Breece D'J Pancake, *The Stories of Breece D'J Pancake,* Atlantic-Little, Brown, 1983.

CONTRIBUTOR

J. Hicks, editor, *Cutting Edges,* Holt, 1973.

Nick A. Ford, editor, *Black Insights: Significant Literature by Afro-Americans, 1760 to the Present,* Wiley, 1976.

Llewellyn Howland and Isabelle Storey, editors, *Book for Boston,* Godine, 1980.

Kimberly W. Benson, editor, *Speaking for You,* Howard University Press, 1987.

Alex Harris, *A World Unsuspected,* [Chapel Hill], 1987.

OTHER

Also contributor to *New Black Voices,* New American Library. Contributor to *Atlantic, Esquire, New York Times Magazine, Playboy, Reader's Digest,* and *Callaloo.* Contributing editor, *Atlantic,* 1969—; editor of special issue, *Iowa Review,* winter, 1984.

SIDELIGHTS: James Alan McPherson's stories of ordinary, working class people, though often concerning black characters, are noted for their ability to confront universal human problems. "His standpoint," Robie Macauley explains in the *New York Times Book Review,* "[is] that of a writer and a black, but not that of a black writer. [McPherson] refused to let his fiction fall into any color-code or ethnic code." Because of this stance, McPherson's characters are more fully rounded than are those of more racially-conscious writers. As Paul Bailey writes in the *Observer Review,* "the Negroes and whites [McPherson] describes always remain individual people—he never allows himself the luxury of turning them into Problems." Explaining his approach to the characters in his stories, McPherson is quoted by Patsy B. Perry of the *Dictionary of Literary Biography* as saying: "Certain of these people [his characters] happen to be black, and certain of them happen to be white; but I have tried to keep the color part of most of them far in the background, where these things should rightly be kept." McPherson has published two collections of short stories, *Hue and Cry: Short Stories* and *Elbow Room: Stories.* In 1978 he was awarded the Pulitzer Prize for fiction.

McPherson was born and raised in Savannah, Georgia, a city in which several cultures—including the French, Spanish, and Indian—have been uniquely blended. He cites this rich cultural heritage as a determining factor in his own ability to transcend racial barriers. The McPherson family also influenced his development of values. His father, at one time the only licensed black master electrician in Georgia, and his mother, a domestic in a white household, had important contacts in both the white and black communities. Through their efforts, McPherson obtained work as a grocery boy in a local supermarket and as a waiter on a train. These experiences have formed the basis for several later stories. McPherson's train employment also allowed him to travel across the country. Perry notes that McPherson "affirms the importance of both white and black communities in his development as an individual and as a writer of humanistic ideas."

McPherson's writing career began in the 1960s while he was still attending law school. His story "Gold Coast" won first prize in a contest sponsored by the *Atlantic* magazine and was later published in the magazine as well. The *Atlantic* was to play a pivotal role in McPherson's career. After earning a bachelor's degree, a law degree, and a master's degree in creative writing, McPherson became a contributing editor of the *Atlantic* in 1969. And the magazine, in conjunction with Little, Brown, also published his two collections of short stories.

McPherson's first collection, *Hue and Cry*, deals with characters whose lives are so desperate that they can only rage impotently against their situations. "The fact that these characters . . . ," writes Perry, "know nothing else to do except to sink slowly into madness, scream unintelligibly, or seek refuge . . . provides reason enough for McPherson's hue and cry." The *Times Literary Supplement* critic points to the book's "mostly desperate, mostly black, mostly lost figures in the urban nightmare of violence, rage and bewilderment that is currently America."

Despite the grim nature of his stories, McPherson manages to depict the lives of his characters with sympathy and grace. Bailey allows that McPherson's "powers of observation and character-drawing are remarkable, displaying a mature novelist's understanding of the vagaries and inconsistencies of human affairs." Writing in *Harper's*, Irving Howe maintains that McPherson "possesses an ability some writers take decades to acquire, the ability to keep the right distance from the creatures of his imagination, not to get murkily involved and blot out his figures with vanity and fuss." Granville Hicks of *Saturday Review* notes that McPherson "is acutely aware of the misery and injustice in the world, and he sympathizes deeply with the victims whether they are black or white."

Among the most prominent admirers of *Hue and Cry* is novelist Ralph Ellison. In a statement he contributed to the book's dust jacket, Ellison speaks of the difference between McPherson's writing and that of most other black writers. "McPherson," Ellison claims, "promises to move right past those talented but misguided writers . . . who take being black as a privilege for being obscenely second-rate and who regard their social predicament as Negroes as exempting them from the necessity of mastering the craft and forms of fiction. . . . McPherson will never, as a writer, be an embarrassment to such people of excellence as Willie Mays, Duke Ellington, Leontyne Price—or, for that matter, Stephen Crane or F. Scott Fitzgerald."

Elbow Room, McPherson's second collection, won even more critical praise than its predecessor. Again concerned with characters in desperate situations, the stories of *Elbow Room* are nonetheless more optimistic than McPherson's earlier works, the characters more willing to struggle for some measure of success. They "engage in life's battles with integrity of mind and spirit," as Perry explains. This optimism is noted by several critics. Robert Phillips of *Commonweal*, for example, finds the stories in *Elbow Room* to be "difficult struggles for survival, yet [McPherson's] sense of humor allows him to dwell on moments which otherwise might prove unbearable." Writing in *Newsweek*, Margo Jefferson calls McPherson "an astute realist who knows how to turn the conflicts between individual personalities and the surrounding culture into artful and highly serious comedies of manners."

McPherson's ability to create believable characters, and his focus on the underlying humanity of all his characters, is praised by such critics as Phillips. McPherson's stories, Phillips believes, "ultimately become not so much about the black condition as the human condition. . . . *Elbow Room* is a book of singular achievement." Macauley explains that McPherson has been able "to look beneath skin color and cliches of attitude into the hearts of his characters. . . . This is a fairly rare ability in American fiction." The *New Yorker* reviewer lists several other characteristics of McPherson's stories that are worthy of attention, calling him "one of those rare writers who can tell a story, describe shadings of character, and make sociological observations with equal subtlety."

Speaking of the obstacles and opportunities facing black writers, McPherson writes in the *Atlantic*: "It seems to me that much of our writing has been, and continues to be, sociological because black writers have been concerned with protesting black humanity and racial injustice to the larger society in those terms most easily understood by nonblack people. It also seems to me that we can correct this limitation either by defining and affirming the values and cultural institutions of our people for their education or by employing our own sense of reality and our own conception of what human life should be to explore, and perhaps help define, the cultural realities of contemporary American life."

BIOGRAPHICAL/CRITICAL SOURCES:

BOOKS

Contemporary Literary Criticism, Volume XIX, Gale, 1981.
Dictionary of Literary Biography, Volume XXXVIII: *Afro-American Writers after 1955: Dramatists and Prose Writers*, Gale, 1985.

PERIODICALS

Antioch Review, winter, 1978.
Atlantic, December, 1970, February, 1977.
Chicago Tribune Book World, May 25, 1969.
Christian Science Monitor, July 31, 1969.
CLA Journal, June, 1979.
Commonweal, September 19, 1969, September 15, 1978.
Ebony, December, 1981.
Harper's, December, 1969.
Iowa Journal of Literary Studies, 1983.
Nation, December 16, 1978.
Negro Digest, October, 1969, November, 1969.
Newsweek, June 16, 1969, October 17, 1977.
New Yorker, November 21, 1977.
New York Review of Books, November 10, 1977.
New York Times Book Review, June 1, 1969, September 25, 1977, September 2, 1979, February 13, 1983, May 13, 1984.
Observer Review, December 7, 1969.
Saturday Review, May 24, 1969.
Spectator, November 22, 1969.
Studies in American Fiction, autumn, 1973.
Times Literary Supplement, December 25, 1969.
Washington Post Book World, October 30, 1977, March 6, 1983.

—Sketch by Thomas Wiloch

*   *   *

MERIWETHER, Louise   1923-

PERSONAL: Born May 8, 1923, in Haverstraw, N.Y.; daughter of Marion Lloyd and Julia Jenkins; married Angelo Meriwether (divorced); married Earl Howe (divorced). *Education:* New York University, B.A.; University of California at Los Angeles, M.S., 1965.

ADDRESSES: Home—392 Central Park W., Apt. 1C, New York, N.Y. 10025. *Office*—Prentice-Hall, Englewood Cliffs, N.J. 07632.

CAREER: Worked as a legal secretary in New York and California, 1950-61; *Los Angeles Sentinal*, Los Angeles, Calif., reporter, 1961-64; Universal Studios, Universal City, Calif., story analyst, 1965-67; free-lance writer, 1967—; Sarah Lawrence College, Bronxville, N.Y., currently a writing instructor. Former fiction instructor at Frederick Douglass Creative Arts Center.

MEMBER: PEN, Authors Guild, Watts Writers Workshop, Harlem Writers Guild.

WRITINGS:

Daddy Was a Number Runner (novel), Prentice-Hall, 1970, reprinted, Feminist Press at City University of New York, 1986.
The Freedom Ship of Robert Small (juvenile), Prentice-Hall, 1971.
The Heart Man: The Story of Daniel Hale Williams (juvenile), Prentice-Hall, 1972.
(Contributor) Mel Watkins, editor, *Black Review No. 2,* Morrow, 1972.
Don't Ride the Bus on Monday: The Rosa Parks Story (juvenile), Prentice-Hall, 1973.
(Contributor) Mary Helen Washington, editor, *Black-Eyed Susans,* Anchor Press, 1975.
(Contributor) Amiri Baraka and Amina Baraka, editors, *Confirmation: An Anthology of African American Women,* Morrow, 1983.

Contributor to periodicals, including *Antioch Review, Bronze America, Essence, Frontier,* and *Negro Digest.*

SIDELIGHTS: Louise Meriwether's first novel, *Daddy Was a Number Runner,* won praise as the authentic story of a young girl in Depression-era Harlem who recounts the collapse of her family under economic and racial pressures. Paule Marshall comments in the *New York Times Book Review:* ''In her perceptive and moving first novel about the social death of one Harlem family, Meriwether reaches deeply into the lives of her characters to say something about the way black people relate to each other—the customs, traditions and manners that bind up together and sustain our underground life. It is her expression of this tribal or communal quality of black life, its group solidarity and sharing, that lends such strength and humanity to the novel.''

Meriwether's next three books were all biographies of important blacks in American history: Robert Small, a slave who piloted a Confederate ship into Yankee waters and earned a promotion in the Union Army; Daniel Hale Williams, a black heart surgeon who performed the first successful open-heart surgery; and Rosa Parks, who sparked the black revolt in the 1960s by refusing to give up her seat on a public bus. Meriwether comments in *Black-Eyed Susans* on writing about black historical figures: ''After the publication of . . . *Daddy Was a Number Runner,* I turned my attention to black history for the kindergarten set, recognizing that the deliberate omission of Blacks from American history has been damaging to the children of both races. It reinforces in one a feeling of inferiority and in the other a myth of superiority.''

BIOGRAPHICAL/CRITICAL SOURCES:

BOOKS

Dictionary of Literary Biography, Volume 33: *Afro-American Fiction Writers after 1955,* Gale, 1984.
Washington, Mary Helen, editor, *Black-Eyed Susans,* Anchor Press, 1975.

PERIODICALS

Kirkus Reviews, June 15, 1972, December 15, 1973.

New Yorker, July 11, 1970.
New York Times Book Review, June 28, 1970.
Saturday Review of Literature, May 23, 1970, December 11, 1971.

* * *

MEYER, June
   See JORDAN, June

* * *

MILLICAN, Arthenia Jackson Bates   1920-
   (Arthenia J. Bates)

PERSONAL: Born June 1, 1920, in Sumter, S.C.; daughter of Calvin Shepard (an educator) and Susan Emma (a craftswoman; maiden name, David) Jackson; married Noah Bates, June 11, 1950 (divorced, 1956); married Wilbert Millican, August 14, 1969 (died April 10, 1982). *Education:* Morris College, B.A. (magna cum laude), 1941; Atlanta University, M.A., 1948; Louisiana State University, Ph.D., 1972. *Politics:* Democrat. *Religion:* Roman Catholic.

ADDRESSES: Home and office—Route 3, Box 286 G, Baker, La. 70714.

CAREER: High school English teacher in Kershaw, S.C., 1942-45; high school teacher of English and civics in Hartsville, S.C., 1945-46; Morris College, Sumter, S.C., head of department of English, 1947-49; high school English teacher in Halifax, Va., 1949-55; Mississippi Valley State University, Itta Bena, instructor in English, 1955-56; Southern University, Baton Rouge, La., instructor, 1956-59, assistant professor, 1959-63, associate professor, 1963-72, professor of English, 1972-74; Norfolk State University, Norfolk, Va., professor of English, 1974-77; Southern University, professor of English and creative writing, 1977-80. Instructor at American Youth Foundation's Camp Miniwanca, 1962, 1963. Member of board of directors of Community Advancement Incorporation for East Baton Rouge Parish, 1967-70. Conducted research for the State of Louisiana's first ''Black Culture Registry'' project, 1985.

MEMBER: National Council of Teachers of English, Conference on College Composition and Communication, College Language Association (life member; chairman of creative writing committee, 1974-75), Society for the Study of Southern Literature, Conference on Black South Literature and the Arts, Louisiana Folklore Society, Gamma Sigma Sigma (chairman of advisory committee, 1959-64).

AWARDS, HONORS: First prize from College Language Association's creative writing contest, 1960, for ''The Entertainers''; award of merit from McKendree Writers Association, 1962, for poem ''Wishes''; certificate of merit from *Writers Digest,* 1963; bronze medal from American Youth Foundation, 1963; fiction award from National Endowment for the Arts, 1976, for story ''Where You Belong''; award and presidential citation from National Association for Equal Opportunity in Higher Education, 1981.

WRITINGS:

The Deity Nodded (novel), Harlo, 1973.
Seeds beneath the Snow (short stories), Greenwich Book Publishers, 1969, published as *Seeds beneath the Snow: Vignettes of the South,* Howard University Press, 1975.
(Contributor) Pinkie Gordan Lane, editor, *Poems by Blacks, South and West,* 1975.

Such Things from the Valley (short stories), H.C. Young Press, 1977.

(Contributor) Therman B. O'Daniel, editor, *James Baldwin: A Critical Evaluation,* Howard University Press, 1977.

(Contributor) Roseann Bell, Bettye J. Parker, and Beverly Sheftall, editors, *Sturdy Black Bridges: Visions of Black Women in Literature,* Anchor Press, 1979.

(Contributor) *Biographical Memoirs of the Old South,* Volume 1: *The Pioneers and Early Settlers,* Heritage Publishers Services, 1986.

Contributor to anthologies, including *Poetry Broadcast,* 1946, and *National Poetry Anthology,* 1958, 1962, 1963, and 1973. Contributor of more than thirty-five articles, poems, stories, and reviews to magazines and newspapers, including *Negro Digest, Black World, Le Monde, Essence, Scriptiana, Baptist Advocate of Baton Rouge, Obsidian: Black Literature in Review, Negro American Literature Forum,* and *Mahogany.*

Contributing editor to *Obsidian: Black Literature in Review,* 1974-76, and *Callaloo,* 1976-84.

WORK IN PROGRESS: Research for a sequel to *The Deity Nodded;* collecting humorous material "peculiar to a local area in southern Louisiana"; short stories on mother-daughter relationships in the South from 1900 to the present.

SIDELIGHTS: Arthenia Jackson Bates Millican commented: "One of the most difficult lessons for me to learn as a student of creative writing is the advice about slanting. An essay delivered as a speech eulogizing Langston Hughes soon after his death, entitled 'The Sun Legend: A Tribute to Langston Hughes,' seemed to me to be a masterpiece of slanting. It would be of interest to blacks because Hughes is the subject, and of interest to scholars because it is a research article with the rich allusions in Greek mythology, and of interest to everyone else because the theme is death.

"You know the audacity of young blacks during the sixties. A young black poet said, 'Your idea of finding what you call sun-sense in Hughes is alright. You try to explain his warmth in terms of the folk quality, the African ethos and the humane factor in general; but you messed it up by alluding to Greek mythology. Hughes would have appreciated your using Egyptian mythology.'

"What he did not understand, from my point of view, was that I was a student (anthology-read) of Greek literature. I had the right to allude to Phaeton, the son of Apollo, and the nymph Clymene. Had he asked me, 'What does Africa mean to you?,' I would have said 'nothing' because I had not come to know the joy of riding on the communal wave of the mother spirit that matured with the 'Roots' phenomenon.

"Almost twenty years have passed and I am just coming into the knowledge of what I hope he also understands.

"The oil rigs are being constructed here and there in the Baker community of East Baton Rouge Parish where I used to live. A court case of slant-drilling against a driller seeking to cash in on this Tuscaloose Trend opened my eyes. How rich are your unmined resources? Mine? How will you know unless you drill? Slant-drilling is illegally mining the resources of another. You may have the rig on your territory but the gold, that black splatter, comes from the other man's territory.

"I know what the young poet was trying to tell me about the tradition and the individual talent."

BIOGRAPHICAL/CRITICAL SOURCES:

BOOKS

Dictionary of Literary Biography, Volume 38: *Afro-American Writers after 1955,* Gale, 1985.

PERIODICALS

Baton Rouge Morning Advocate, March 13, 1970.
Baton Rouge News Leader, February 9, 1969, March 15, 1970, June 14, 1970, August 13, 1972, December 23, 1973, January 13, 1974, May 19, 1974.
Chantaqua Daily, July 24, 1962.
College Language Association Journal, June, 1970, December, 1973.
Delta, summer, 1970.
Essence, July, 1980.
Freedom Ways, November 11, 1975.
Norfolk Journal and Guide, November 9, 1974.
Norfolk-Portsmouth Ledger Star, November 18, 1974.
Obsidian: Black Literature in Review, spring, 1977.
Virginian Pilot, July 4, 1976.
Washington Afro-American, June 2, 1970.
Washington Post, June 11, 1970.

*   *   *

MILNER, Ron(ald)   1938-

PERSONAL: Born May 29, 1938, in Detroit, Mich. *Education:* Attended Columbia University.

ADDRESSES: c/o New American Library, 1301 Sixth Ave., New York, N.Y. 10019.

CAREER: Playwright. Writer in residence, Lincoln University, 1966-67; teacher, Michigan State University, 1971-72; founder and director, Spirit of Shango theater company; director, "Don't Get God Started," 1986; led playwriting workshop, Wayne State University.

AWARDS, HONORS: Rockefeller grant; John Hay Whitney fellowship.

WRITINGS:

PLAYS

"Who's Got His Own" (three-act; also see below), first produced Off-Broadway at American Place Theatre, October 12, 1966.
"The Warning—A Theme for Linda" (one-act; first produced in New York with other plays as "A Black Quartet" at Chelsea Theatre Center, Brooklyn Academy of Music, April 25, 1969), published in *A Black Quartet: Four New Black Plays,* edited by Ben Caldwell and others, New American Library, 1970.
"The Monster" (one-act; first produced in Chicago at Louis Theatre Center, October, 1969), published in *Drama Review,* summer, 1968.
"M(ego) and the Green Ball of Freedom" (one-act; first produced in Detroit at Shango Theatre, 1971), published in *Black World,* April, 1971.
(Editor, author of introduction with Woodie King, Jr., and contributor) *Black Drama Anthology* (includes "Who's Got His Own"), New American Library, 1971.
What the Wine Sellers Buy (first produced in New York at New Federal Theatre, May 17, 1973), Samuel French, 1974.

"These Three," first produced in Detroit at Concept East Theater, 1974.

"Season's Reasons," first produced in Detroit at Langston Hughes Theatre, 1976.

"Work," first produced for Detroit Public Schools, January, 1978.

"Jazz-set," first produced in Los Angeles at Mark Taper Forum, 1980.

"Crack Steppin'," first produced in Detroit at Music Hall, November, 1981.

"Checkmates," produced in Los Angeles at Westwood Playhouse, July 17, 1987.

"Don't Get God Started," first produced on Broadway at Longacre Theatre, October, 1987.

Also author of "Life Agony" (one-act), first produced in Detroit at the Unstable Theatre and "The Greatest Gift," produced by Detroit Public Schools.

CONTRIBUTOR

Langston Hughes, editor, *Best Short Stories by Negro Writers*, Little, Brown, 1967.

Ahmed Alhamisi and Harun Kofi Wangara, editors, *Black Arts: An Anthology of Black Creations*, Black Arts, 1969.

Donald B. Gibson, editor, *Five Black Writers*, New York University Press, 1970.

Addison Gayle, Jr., editor, *The Black Aesthetic*, Doubleday, 1971.

William R. Robinson, editor, *Nommo: An Anthology of Modern Black African and Black American Literature*, Macmillan, 1972.

King, editor, *Black Short Story Anthology*, Columbia University Press, 1972.

Also contributor to *Black Poets and Prophets*, edited by King and Earl Anthony, New American Library.

OTHER

Contributor to *Negro Digest, Drama Review, Black World*, and other periodicals.

SIDELIGHTS: Ron Milner is "a pioneering force in the contemporary Afro-American theater," writes Beunyce Rayford Cunningham in the *Dictionary of Literary Biography*. Much of his work has involved growing beyond the theatre of the 1960s, where, as Milner told *Detroit News* reporter Bill Gray, "There used to be a lot of screaming and hate. . . . It was reacting to white racism and the themes were defiant directives at the white community. . . ." He continued, "We're no longer dealing with 'I am somebody' but more of who that 'somebody' really is." While not rejecting the revolutionary movements in black theatre, Milner represents a change in approach: a shift from combative performances to quieter dramas that still make a point. Comments Geneva Smitherman in *Black World*, "Those of us who were patient with our writers—as they lingered for what seems like an eternity in the catharsis/ screaming stage—applaud this natural change in the course of theatrical events." Adds Cunningham, "Ron Milner's is essentially a theatre of intense, often lyrical, retrospection devoted primarily to illuminating the past events, personalities, and values which have shaped his struggling people."

Milner grew up in Detroit, on Hastings Street, also known as "'The Valley'—with the Muslims on one corner, hustlers and pimps on another, winos on one, and Aretha Franklin singing from her father's church on the other," reports Smitherman. It "was pretty infamous and supposedly criminal," Milner

told David Richards of the *Washington Star-News*. But, he continued, "The more I read in high school, the more I realized that some tremendous, phenomenal things were happening around me. What happened in a Faulkner novel happened four times a day on Hastings Street. I thought why should these crazy people Faulkner writes about seem more important than my mother or my father or the dude down the street. Only because they had someone to write about them. So I became a writer."

Milner's work contains the constant appeal for stronger black families and tighter communities. According to Larry Neal in *The Black American Writer*, "Milner's main thrust is directed toward unifying the family around basic moral principles, toward bridging the 'generation gap.'" This has led some critics to label him a "preacher" and his dramas "morality plays." Not daunted by criticism, Milner told Betty DeRamus in the *Detroit Free Press* that art "has to educate as well as entertain. When people call me a preacher, I consider it a compliment . . . when you get an emotional response it's easier to involve the mind."

One of Milner's "morality plays" was very successful, both with the critics and with black audiences. *What the Wine-Sellers Buy* centers on the tempting of seventeen-year-old Steve by Rico, a pimp. Rico suggests that turning Steve's girlfriend into a prostitute is the easy way to make money. While Steve resists, future trials lay ahead. According to Cunningham, the play contains "many of the elements of Milner's previous family dramas: a young, innocent person forced to make a conscious decision about the direction of his or her life; a mother who retreats into the church; the figure of a male savior—this time a man of the church who befriends the mother and is determined to save her son. What is new here is the Faustian framework in which the menace to be dealt with is the seductions of street life represented by the pimp."

"As in all morality plays, good and the power of love" triumph, DeRamus notes, but adds, "what makes 'Wine Sellers' different is that the villain, Rico, is no cardboard figure who is easily knocked down. He is, in fact, so persuasive and logical that he seduces audiences as well as Steve." DeRamus reports that Milner patterned Rico after "the typical American businessman," and quotes Milner's comment that when Rico "talks about everything for profit, trading everything for money, he's talking about society. What he says about society is correct, but he is wrong in what he decides to trade. If you trade life, what do you buy?" In Rico, Milner did not create "simply the stereo-typical Black pimp," writes Smitherman. "Rather, Rico is the devious Seducer in our lives, moving to and fro, enticing us to compromise our morality, our politics and even our very souls." Still, the play leaves critics with a positive impression, as it focuses on young Steve triumphing over Rico's corruption. Edwin Wilson in the *Wall Street Journal* applauds the play's outlook: "the emphasis is not on past grievances and injustices, but on the future—on the problems and perils young people face growing up in broken homes and a hostile environment, and their determination to overcome these forces. . . . The play gives further evidence that black playwrights today . . . are determined to find their own way."

Much of Milner's energy in the 1970s was directed to defining and establishing a unique black theatre. "American theater was (and still is) the nut that few blacks are able to crack," Milner and his co-editor, Woodie King, Jr., observe in the introduction to *Black Drama Anthology*. They continue that "Black theater is, in fact, about the destruction of tradition, the traditional role of Negroes in white theater. . . . We say that if this theater is to be, it must—psychically, mentally, aesthetically, and physically,—go home.'' By ''going home,'' Milner and King mean returning to the experiences that have given blacks their identity. Added Milner to Smitherman, '''Theater' and 'play' have always meant going to see somebody else's culture and seeing how you could translate it into your own terms. People always felt they were going to a foreign place for some foreign reason. But now there's a theater written to them, of them, for them and about them.''

Milner believes that a local theatre can also help to unify the community. ''Theater lifts a community in more ways than one,'' he said to Smitherman. ''The idea of seeing yourself magnified and dramatized on stage gives you a whole perspective on who you are and where you are. You can isolate your emotions and thoughts and bring them to a place and ritualize them in an audience of people who empathize with you.'' Milner stresses the need for local theatre to communicate something valuable to its audience; he disapproves of creating art only for aesthetic reasons. ''Theater for theater's sake is incest,'' he told Richards. ''It gets thinner and thinner each time and drifts off into abstraction. But when it's directly involved in life, even when its badly done, it can cause people to argue, discuss, grow, or at least clarify where they stand. It's true, the aesthetic side can do something for you spiritually. But you can't let that prevent you from communicating on a basic level.''

The play that ''could thrust [Milner] into the role of the theater's primary chronicler of the contemporary black middle class,'' is ''Checkmates,'' writes Don Shirley for the *Los Angeles Times*. ''Checkmates,'' produced in 1987, examines the lives of an upwardly mobile couple in their thirties, who are coping with the stresses of marriage, two careers, and urban life. The pair is complemented by their landlords, an older couple with simpler lives, who remember the days when blacks worked in the fields, not offices. The landlords, despite their lack of sophistication, possess a steadiness that the younger, financially successful couple lack. Milner told Shirley, ''It's dangerous to identify with [the younger couple], because you can't tell what they might say or do next. They aren't fixed. They can't say, 'These are the values I stand for.' The point of the older couple's lives was to build for the future. Now here is the future, and there are no rules left for the younger couple.'' Dan Sullivan, also writing for the *Los Angeles Times* enjoys the play's humor: Milner ''knows his people so well that an equally big laugh will come on a quite ordinary remark, revealing more about the speaker than he or she realizes.'' But he also notes the underlying message. '''Checkmates' gives us a specific sense of today's corporate jungle and its particular risks for blacks, however hip, however educated.''

While Milner finds the idea of the middle-class ''one-dimensional,'' he is not hostile to the idea of writing to such an audience. ''I was never a writer who said the middle class should be lined up against a wall and shot,'' he told Shirley. As different as it may seem from his previous work, ''Checkmates'' still falls in with Milner's basic philosophy toward black theatre, as he told Richards: ''For a long time, black writers dwelled on our negative history. They could never see any real victory. For them, the only victory lay in the ability to endure defeat. I was consciously trying to break that. I function a great deal on what I intuitively feel are the needs of the time. And the needs of the time are for the positive.''

BIOGRAPHICAL/CRITICAL SOURCES:

BOOKS

Alhamisi, Ahmed and Harun Kofi Wangara, editors, *Black Arts: An Anthology of Black Creations*, Black Arts, 1969.
Authors in the News, Volume I, Gale, 1976.
Bigsby, C. W. E., editor, *The Black American Writer*, Volume II: *Poetry and Drama*, Penguin Books, 1969.
Dictionary of Literary Biography, Volume XXXVIII: *Afro-American Writers after 1955: Dramatists and Prose Writers*, Gale, 1985.
Hill, Errol, editor, *The Theater of Black Americans*, Volume I: *Roots and Rituals: The Search for Identity* [and] *The Image Makers: Plays and Playwrights*, Prentice-Hall, 1980.
King, Woodie, Jr., editor, *Black Short Story Anthology*, Columbia University Press, 1972.
King, Woodie, Jr., and Ron Milner, editors, *Black Drama Anthology*, Columbia University Press, 1972.
Robinson, William R., editor, *Nommo: An Anthology of Black African and Black American Literature*, Macmillan, 1972.

PERIODICALS

Black World, April, 1971, April, 1976.
Detroit Free Press, January 5, 1975.
Detroit Free Press Magazine, June 24, 1979.
Detroit News, October 20, 1974.
Drama Review, summer, 1968.
Los Angeles Times, March 19, 1980, September 3, 1986, July 12, 1987, July 20, 1987.
New Yorker, November 9, 1987.
New York Times, July 21, 1982, October 31, 1987.
Wall Street Journal, February 21, 1974.
Washington Star-News, January 5, 1975.

—*Sketch by Jani Prescott*

*   *   *

Miss C. L. F.
See GRIMKE, Charlotte L(ottie) Forten

*   *   *

MITCHELL, Loften   1919-

PERSONAL: Born April 15, 1919, in Columbus, N.C.; married Helen March, 1948; children: two. *Education:* Attended City College (now as the City University of New York), 1937-38; Talladega College, B.A., 1943; Columbia University, M.A., 1951; additional study at Union Theological Seminary, and General Theological Seminary.

ADDRESSES: Home—88-45 163rd St., Jamaica, N.Y. 11432.

CAREER: Playwright, theatre historian, and novelist. Began as actor in New York City during the 1930s; social worker for City of New York Department of Welfare; publicity director for Jewish Federation of Welfare Services; assistant for special programs at Harlem Preparatory School; WNCY-Radio, New York City, writer of weekly program ''The Later Years,'' 1950-62; WWRL-Radio, New York City, writer of daily program ''Friendly Adviser,'' 1954; State University of New York at Binghamton, department of theatre and department of Afro-American studies, professor, 1971-85, professor emeritus, 1985—. Adjunct professor of English, Long Island University, 1969, and New York University, 1970. *Military service:* U.S. Navy; served during World War II.

AWARDS, HONORS: Guggenheim fellowship, 1958-59; Rockefeller Foundation grant, 1961; Harlem Cultural Council special award, 1969; playwriting award, Research Foundation, State University of New York, 1974; Outstanding Theatrical Pioneer Award, Audience Development Committee (AU-DELCO), 1979.

WRITINGS:

Black Drama: The Story of the American Negro in the Theatre (essays), Hawthorn, 1967.
The Stubborn Old Lady Who Resisted Change (novel), Emerson Hall, 1973.
(Compiler and contributor) *Voices of the Black Theatre* (oral history), James T. White, 1975.

PLAYS

"Shattered Dreams" (originally entitled "Cocktails"), first produced in New York City by Pioneer Drama Group, 1938.
"Blood in the Night," first produced in New York City, 1946.
"The Bancroft Dynasty," first produced in New York City at 115th Street Peoples Theatre, 1948.
"The Cellar," first produced in New York City at Harlem Showcase Theatre, 1952.
A Land beyond the River (also see below; first produced off-Broadway at Greenwich Mews Theatre, March 28, 1957), Pioneer Drama Service, 1963.
(With Irving Burgie) "Ballad for Bimshire" (musical), first produced on Broadway at Mayfair Theatre, October 15, 1963, revised version produced in Cleveland, Ohio, 1964.
(With John Oliver Killens) "Ballad of the Winter Soldiers," first produced in New York City at Lincoln Center, 1964.
Star of the Morning: Scenes in the Life of Bert Williams (also see below; musical; music by brother, Louis D. Mitchell, lyrics by Romare Bearden and Clyde Fox; first produced as "Star of the Morning" in Cleveland, 1965, produced in New York City at American Folk Theatre, 1985), Free Press, 1965.
Tell Pharaoh (also see below; concert drama; first produced in New York City at Colden Theatre, Queens College, February 19, 1967), Negro Universities Press, 1970, revised edition, Broadway Play, 1987.
"The Phonograph," first produced off-Broadway at Maidman Playhouse, 1969.
"The Final Solution to the Black Problem in the United States; or, The Fall of the American Empire," first produced in New York City, 1970.
Bubbling Brown Sugar (musical; adapted from a concept by Rosetta LeNoire; music and lyrics by various artists; first produced off-Broadway at AMAS Repertory Theatre, 1975, produced on Broadway at ATNA Theatre, March 2, 1976), Broadway Play, 1984.
(Author of libretto) "And the Walls Came Tumbling Down" (opera; music by Willard Roosevelt), first produced in New York City at Lincoln Center, 1976.
"Cartoons for a Lunch Hour" (musical), first produced in New York City at Perry Street Theatre, 1978.
"A Gypsy Girl" (musical), first produced in Pine Bluff, Ark., 1982.
"Miss Ethel Waters" (musical), first produced off-Broadway at AMAS Repertory Theatre, 1983.

Also author of "Cross Roads" (1938); "Sojourn to the South of the Wall"; "The World of a Harlem Playwright"; and "The Afro-Philadelphian." Also author of musical, "Prelude to the Blues" (music by Wallace Pritchett).

SCREENPLAYS

"Young Man of Williamsburg," YM & YMHA of Brooklyn, 1954.
"Integration—Report One," Andover Productions, 1960.
"I'm Sorry," Courtney Hafela Productions, 1962.
"The Vampires of Harlem" Vanguard Productions, 1972.

CONTRIBUTOR

The American Negro Writer and His Roots, American Society of African Culture, 1960.
C.W.E. Bigsby, editor, *The Black American Writer,* two volumes, Penguin, 1969.
William Adams, Peter Conn, and Barry Slepian, editors, *Afro-American Literature: Drama* (contains "A Land beyond the River"), Houghton, 1970.
William R. Reardon and Thomas D. Pawley, editors, *The Black Teacher in the Dramatic Arts* (contains "A Land beyond the River" and "Tell Pharaoh"), Negro Universities Press, 1970.
Addison Gayle, Jr., editor, *The Black Aesthetic,* Doubleday, 1971.
Alice Childress, editor, *Black Scenes,* Doubleday, 1971.
Woodie King, Jr., and Ron Milner, editors, *Black Dream Anthology,* New American Library, 1971.
James V. Hatch and Ted Shine, editors, *Black Theatre U.S.A.: 1874-1974* (contains "Star of the Morning"), Free Press, 1974.

OTHER

Also author of *Harlem, My Harlem* (essay collection); also author of radio scripts. Contributor to *Oxford Companion to the Theatre* and *Encyclopedia della spetta colo* (Rome). Contributor to periodicals, including *Amsterdam News, Crisis, Freedomways, Negro Digest, New York Times,* and *Theatre Arts Monthly.* Editor of *Freedom Journal,* NAACP, 1964.

SIDELIGHTS: The contributions of playwright and theatre historian Loften Mitchell "to the black American theater—his plays and his essays—show his recognition of the contributions of those who preceded him," writes Ja A. Jahannes in *Dictionary of Literary Biography.* "He acknowledges throughout his work the belief that the black theater in America is the result of black artists' collective contributions of genius, talent, pioneering efforts, denials, sacrifices, sensitivity to black culture, race consciousness, and their view of theater as art." In a theatre career that spans over fifty years, Mitchell stands as "one of the chief chroniclers of the history of black theater in America," notes Jahannes. He "projects a holistic view of black culture in his plays and essays, . . . present[ing] his subject in the contexts of American development and the social, political, and economic histories of black people in America."

Mitchell began his theatre career while still a high school student in Harlem, where he wrote sketches for the Progressive Dramatizers Group at Salem Church and then worked as an actor for the Rose McClendon Players. In Harlem, Mitchell had exposure to a wide range of up-and-coming black theatrical performers, such as Ethel Waters, Ralph Cooper, and George Wiltshire. It was also in Harlem that Mitchell had the formulative experiences that taught him how blacks were discriminated against in America. He writes of an early experience: ". . . At age 10, I sold newspapers on the streets of New York—and got into a fist fight with a white boy who told me: 'This place belongs to us more than it does to youse.' Along with other newsboys I was later arrested for selling newspapers without a license. We were kept overnight in the Children's

Society where we 'colored boys had to sleep on cots in the hallway.''' (Mitchell adds that "ironically, in 1983 the AMAS Repertory Theatre presented my musical 'Miss Ethel Waters' in this same building—and there was a standing ovation"). Mitchell also came to realize that racial discrimination carried over to theatre. According to Jahannes, "Mitchell also saw that black people had been maligned, misrepresented, and deliberately cast in negative stereotypes in American theater. He dedicated himself to shattering those negative images, to projecting real-life images of the noble people who had lived in his beloved Harlem, and to harnessing their history as the principal vehicle of his artistic campaign."

Finding opportunities for black actors limited and scarce in the 1930s, Mitchell decided to leave New York City and accepted a scholarship to Talladega College in Alabama. He recalls in a *Freedomways* interview, as Doris Abramson cites in *Negro Playwrights in the American Theatre, 1925-1959*, that although many blacks during the Depression were financially or academically ineligible to attend college, "Southern Negro colleges, offering athletic scholarships and grants-in-aid, rescued many from the despair into which they had been dumped." At Talladega, Mitchell wrote the paper which would later become the basis for his acclaimed essay collection, *Black Drama: The Story of the American Negro in the Theatre*.

The predominant themes in Mitchell's essays and plays, Jahannes notes, center on "the contributions and struggles of black people in America, the evils of racism, and the potential of black artists to enrich American theater and American life." In a 1965 article for *Crisis,* Mitchell spoke of inadequate black representation in the contemporary art scene. "Today—with the Negro making headlines in a great revolution—our widely acclaimed writers are not fully represented on Broadway, in Hollywood, nor on television," he is quoted by Abramson. "Since the artist must seek the truth, communicate, educate, and entertain, I know that art is being distorted in these times. I know, too, that unless there is a sharp reversal, modern history will not be recorded in our plays and movies." *Black Drama: The Story of the American Negro in the Theatre* can be seen as an attempt to correct this situation. Isaiah Sheffer notes in *Nation* that "in an anecdotal and argumentative style, [*Black Drama*] traces the history of black theatre in this country from the West Indian slave, Mungo, who appears as a clown in a 1769 comedy, *The Padlock*, to the blackface minstrel shows of the pre-Civil War era, the Harlem theatre movements of the 1920s, and the struggles and problems of the fifties and sixties on and off Broadway." Jahannes adds that "more than anything else, [*Black Drama*] establishes the fact that there *is* a history of blacks in the American theater."

In 1975 Mitchell published a second book of history, *Voices of the Black Theatre*, which brought together first-hand testaments of seven important figures in American black drama: Ruby Dee, Abram Hill, Eddie Hunter, Dick Campbell, Vinnette Carroll, Frederick O'Neal, and Regina M. Andrews. Jahannes notes that each contributor "tells his or her story of a proud people determined to offer the best of theater to America; each attests to the indomitable will of black Americans to see their people portrayed in noble and realistic terms." Mitchell serves as commentator of this oral history, offering personal and historical insights to references made by the contributors. A reviewer in *Choice* calls the collection "readable, informative, and inspirational," adding that Mitchell's "writing reveals a warm and personal admiration for the standards set by these 'voices of the black theatre.'"

Among Mitchell's best-known theatrical works are the drama "A Land beyond the River" and the musical "Bubbling Brown Sugar." "A Land beyond the River" premiered in March of 1957 for a ten-week engagement at New York City's Greenwich Mews Theatre and was popular enough to be held over for a year. "Heavy with message, unashamedly didactic in purpose," according to Abramson, the play parallels the real-life story of Rev. Joseph A. DeLaine, who led a group from Clarendon County, South Carolina, on a legal battle for desegregation in schools and buses. Mitchell's play was especially praised for its vivid characters. In a review of the Greenwich Mews Theatre production, Brooks Atkinson of the *New York Times* writes that "Mitchell's craftsmanship is rough and ready—rough with theme, but ready with humor," a quality he attributes to "characters [that] are explosively emotional, quick to take offense from one another and quick to subside once they have let go with their fists or their tongues." This aspect contributes to what Jahannes identifies as one of the play's major themes, "the conflict between violence and non-violence as a means to achieve full rights." Nearly twenty years later, Mitchell wrote the script for the popular Broadway musical "Bubbling Brown Sugar," a nostalgic tribute to the entertainers of Harlem from the early 1920s to the 1940s. In the musical, a modern black couple is transported back to "an earlier Harlem where they see the real sites, sounds, and dancing feet of that community's artistic side," notes Jahannes. The Broadway production was nominated for a Tony Award as best musical of 1976, while Mitchell's script won praise for providing illuminating historical background to the lively song and dance numbers. Jahannes writes that "Bubbling Brown Sugar" and "A Land beyond the River", in addition to the rest of Mitchell's plays, relate "the saga of black life in America."

Collections of Mitchell's papers are housed by the State University of New York at Binghamton, the New York City Library Schomberg Collection, Talladega College, and Boston University.

BIOGRAPHICAL/CRITICAL SOURCES:

BOOKS

Abramson, Doris E., *Negro Playwrights in the American Theatre, 1925-1959*, Columbia University Press, 1969.
Dictionary of Literary Biography, Volume 38: *Afro-American Writers after 1955: Dramatists and Prose Writers*, Gale, 1985.

PERIODICALS

Choice, January, 1976.
Contemporary Literature, winter, 1968.
Crisis, February, 1965.
Freedomways, summer, 1963, fall, 1964.
Nation, August 25, 1969.
Negro Digest, June, 1966.
New York Post, March 29, 1957.
New York Times, March 29, 1957.

—*Sketch by Michael E. Mueller*

*   *   *

MITTELHOELZER, Edgar Austin   1909-1965

PERSONAL: Surname is pronounced Mittel-holtser; born December 16, 1909, in New Amsterdam, British Guiana (now Guyana); committed suicide May 6, 1965, by setting himself on fire; son of William Austin (an assistant town clerk) and

Rosamond Mabel (Leblanc) Mittelhoelzer; married second wife, Jacqueline Pointer (a writer), April 27, 1960; children: (first marriage) Anna, Stefan, Griselda, Hermann; (second marriage) Leodegar. *Education:* Attended schools in British Guiana. *Politics:* Conservative. *Religion:* Personal beliefs.

ADDRESSES: Home—Loushall House Cottage, Dippenhall, Farnham, Surrey, England. *Agent*—Rosica Colin, 4 Hereford Sq., London S.W. 7, England (translation rights only).

CAREER: Worked as customs officer, agricultural assistant, meteorological observer, cinema inspector, free lance journalist, and hotel receptionist, until 1941. Came to England in 1948, worked in book department of British Council, 1948-52. Professional writer, 1952-65.

AWARDS, HONORS: Guggenheim fellowship, 1952.

WRITINGS:

NOVELS

Creole Chips, Lutheran Press (New Amsterdam, British Guiana), 1937.
Corentyne Thunder, Eyre & Spottiswoode, 1941, reprinted, Heinemann, 1970.
A Morning in Trinidad, Doubleday, 1950 (published in England as *A Morning at the Office,* Hogarth, 1950, reprinted, Heinemann, 1970).
Shadows Move among Them, Lippincott, 1951.
Children of Kaywana, Day, 1952.
The Weather in Middenshot, Day, 1952.
The Life and Death of Sylvia, Day, 1953.
The Adding Machine: A Fable for Capitalists and Commercialists, Pioneer Press (Kingston, Jamaica), 1954.
The Harrowing of Hubertus, Secker & Warburg, 1954, published as *Kaywana Stock,* Corgi Books, 1976.
My Bones and My Flute: A Ghost Story in the Old-Fashioned Manner, Secker & Warburg, 1956, reprinted, Longman, 1982.
A Tale of Three Places, Secker & Warburg, 1957.
The Old Blood, Doubleday, 1958, reprinted, Fawcett, 1977 (published in England as *Kaywana Blood,* Secker & Warburg, 1958, reprinted, Corgi Books, 1976).
The Weather Family, Secker & Warburg, 1958.
A Tinkling in the Twilight, Secker & Warburg, 1959.
Latticed Echoes: A Novel in the Leitmotiv Manner, Secker & Warburg, 1960.
Eltonsbrody, Secker & Warburg, 1961.
Thunder Returning: A Novel in the Leimotive, Secker & Warburg, 1961.
The Piling of Clouds, Putnam, 1961.
The Mad MacMullochs, Owen Press, 1961.
The Wounded and the Worried, Putnam, 1962.
Uncle Paul, Macdonald & Co., 1963.
The Aloneness of Mrs. Chatham, Gibbs & Phillips, 1965.
The Jilkington Drama, Abelard, 1965.

OTHER

With a Carib Eye (reminiscences), Secker & Warburg, 1955, reprinted, Longman, 1982.
A Swarthy Boy (autobiography), Putnam, 1963.

WORK IN PROGRESS: Two novels.

MEDIA ADAPTATIONS: Shadows Move among Them was produced by Moss Hart on Broadway as "Climate of Eden," 1953.

AVOCATIONAL INTERESTS: Oriental occultism and psychical research.

*   *   *

MITTELHOLZER, Edgar Austin
See MITTELHOELZER, Edgar Austin

*   *   *

MOLETTE, Barbara Jean   1940-

PERSONAL: Born January 31, 1940, in Los Angeles, Calif.; daughter of Baxter R. and Nora L. (Johnson) Roseburr; married Carlton W. Molette II (a college administrator and writer), June 15, 1960; children: Carla Evelyn, Andrea Rose. *Education:* Florida Agricultural and Mechanical University, B.A. (with highest honors), 1966; Florida State University, M.F.A., 1969.

ADDRESSES: Home—255 West Lanvale Park, Baltimore, Md. 21217.

CAREER: Spelman College, Atlanta, Ga., instructor in fine arts, 1969-72, instructor in drama, 1972-75; Texas Southern University, Houston, assistant professor in fine arts, 1975-87. Makeup artist and designer, costume designer, technical theatre worker at Tuskegee Institute, 1960-61, University of Iowa, 1961, Iowa City Community Theatre, 1962, Des Moines Community Playhouse, 1962-63, and Howard University, 1964; member of costume construction crew, designer, and wardrobe mistress, Asolo Theatre Festival, Sarasota, Fla., summer, 1968; drama coordinator for Upward Bound Program, Florida Agricultural and Mechanical University, summer, 1969; costumer, Morehouse-Spelman Players, 1969-75. Costumer for motion picture, "Together for Days," 1971.

MEMBER: Dramatists Guild, Authors League of America, National Association of Dramatic and Speech Arts, National Conference of African American Theatre.

AWARDS, HONORS: Faculty development grant, Spelman College, 1972; graduate fellowship, University of Missouri, 1986-87; 3rd place, WMAR-TV Drama Competition, 1987, for "Perfect Fifth."

WRITINGS:

WITH HUSBAND, CARLTON W. MOLETTE II

Rosalee Pritchett (also see below; play; first produced in Atlanta by Morehouse-Spelman Players, March 20, 1970; produced Off-Broadway at St. Mark's Playhouse, January 12, 1971), Dramatists Play Service, 1972.
"Booji Wooji" (also see below; play), first produced at Atlanta University Summer Theatre, July 8, 1971.
(Contributor) Richard Barksdale and Keneth Kinnamon, editors, *Black Writers of America: A Comprehensive Anthology* (contains "Rosalee Pritchett"), Macmillan, 1972.
(And with Charles Mann) "Doctor B. S. Black" (also see below; musical), first produced at Atlanta University Summer Theatre, July 20, 1972.
(Compilers) *Afro-American Theatre: A Bibliography,* privately printed, 1972.
(Contributor) Eileen J. Ostrow, editor, *Center Stage: An Anthology of Twenty-One Contemporary Black-American Plays* (contains "Noah's Ark"), Sea Urchin, 1983.
Black Theatre: Premise and Presentation, Wyndham Hall, 1986.

Also co-author of filmstrip, "Stage Makeup for Black Actors," Paramount Theatrical Supplies; screenplay adaptation of "Booji Wooji"; and non-musical version of "Dr. B. S. Black."

OTHER

"The Escape; or, A Leap to Freedom" (adapted from the play by William Wells Brown), first produced at Texas Southern University, 1976.

Also author of teleplay, "Perfect Fifth." Author of syndicated column, "Upstage/Downstage." Contributor to periodicals. Book review editor, *Encore*, 1970-72.

*   *   *

MOLETTE, Carlton W(oodard) II   1939-

PERSONAL: Born August 23, 1939, in Pine Bluff, Ark.; son of Carlton William (a professor) and Evelyn Adelle (a college dean of women; maiden name, Richardson) Molette; married Barbara Jean Roseburr (a professor, writer, and costumer), June 15, 1960; children: Carla Evelyn, Andrea Rose. *Education:* Morehouse College, B.A., 1959; University of Iowa, M.A., 1962; Florida State University, Ph.D., 1968.

ADDRESSES: Home—255 West Lanvale Park, Baltimore, Md. 21217. *Office*—Vice President for Academic Affairs, Coppin State College, 2500 West North Ave., Baltimore, Md. 21216.

CAREER: Howard University, Washington, D.C., assistant professor of drama, 1963-64; Florida Agricultural and Mechanical University, Tallahassee, assistant professor, 1964-66, associate professor of speech and drama, 1967-69; Spelman College, Atlanta, Ga., associate professor of drama, 1969-75, chairman of department, 1971-73; Texas Southern University, Houston, dean of school of communications, 1975-85; Lincoln University, Jefferson City, Mo., dean of arts and sciences, 1985-87; Coppin State College, Baltimore, Md., vice-president for academic affairs, 1987—. Assistant director, Little Theatre, Tuskegee Institute, 1960-61; technical director, Des Moines Community Playhouse, 1962-63; guest director, University of Michigan, 1974. Theatre consultant to colleges, festivals, and organizations. Member of board of directors, Atlanta Arts Festival; chairman of board of trustees, Neighborhood Arts Center.

MEMBER: International Council of Fine Arts Deans, Association for Communication Administration, Dramatists Guild, National Association of Dramatic and Speech Arts, United States Institute for Theatre Technology, Alpha Phi Alpha.

AWARDS, HONORS: Ford Foundation scholarship, 1955-59; Carnegie Foundation grant, 1966-68; Atlanta University Center faculty research grant, 1970-71.

WRITINGS:

WITH WIFE, BARBARA JEAN MOLETTE

Rosalee Pritchett (also see below; play; first produced in Atlanta by Morehouse-Spelman Players, March 20, 1970; produced Off-Broadway at St. Mark's Playhouse, January 12, 1971), Dramatists Play Service, 1972.
"Booji Wooji" (also see below; play), first produced at Atlanta University Summer Theatre, July 8, 1971.
(Contributor) Richard Barksdale and Kenneth Kinnamon, editors, *Black Writers of America: A Comprehensive Anthology* (contains "Rosalee Pritchett"), Macmillan, 1972.

(And with Charles Mann) "Doctor B. S. Black" (also see below; musical), first produced at Atlanta University Summer Theatre, July 20, 1972.
(Compilers) *Afro-American Theatre: A Bibliography*, self-published, 1972.
(Contributor) Eileen J. Ostrow, editor, *Center Stage: An Anthology of Twenty-one Contemporary Black-American Plays* (contains "Noah's Ark"), Sea Urchin, 1983.
Black Theatre: Premise and Presentation, Wyndham Hall, 1986.

Also co-author of filmstrip, "Stage Makeup for Black Actors," Paramount Theatrical Supplies; screenplay adaptation of "Booji Wooji"; and non-musical version of "Dr. B. S. Black."

OTHER

(Contributor) Therman B. O'Daniel, editor, *James Baldwin: A Critical Evaluation*, Howard University Press, 1977.

Contributor of articles and reviews to journals. Editor, *Encore*, 1965-71; editorial consultant, *Southern Speech Journal*, 1966-68; member of advisory board, *Journal of Black Studies*, 1970-73.

*   *   *

MOODY, Anne   1940-

PERSONAL: Born September 15, 1940, in Wilkerson County, Miss.; daughter of Fred and Elmire (Williams) Moody; married Austin Straus, March 9, 1967 (divorced); children: Sascha. *Education:* Attended Natchez Junior College; Tougaloo College, B.S., 1964.

ADDRESSES: Home—New York, N.Y. *Agent*—c/o Harper & Row, 10 East 53rd St., New York, N.Y. 10022.

CAREER: Congress of Racial Equality (CORE), Washington, D.C., organizer, 1961-63, fundraiser, 1964; Cornell University, Ithaca, N.Y., civil rights project coordinator, 1964-65; artist in residence in Berlin, Germany, 1972; writer. Counsel for New York City's poverty program, 1967.

MEMBER: International P.E.N..

AWARDS, HONORS: Brotherhood Award from National Council of Christians and Jews, and Best Book of the Year Award from the National Library Association, both 1969, both for *Coming of Age in Mississippi;* silver medal from *Mademoiselle*, 1970, for "New Hopes for the Seventies"; German Academic Exchange Service grant, 1972.

WRITINGS:

Coming of Age in Mississippi (autobiography), Dial, 1969.
Mr. Death: Four Stories, foreword by John Donovan, Harper, 1975.

Contributor to *Ms.* and *Mademoiselle*.

WORK IN PROGRESS: Variations on a Dream of Death, short stories; *Black Woman's Book; The Clay Gully*, a novel.

SIDELIGHTS: Anne Moody commented: "In the beginning I never really saw myself as a writer. I was first and foremost an activist in the Civil Rights Movement in Mississippi. When I could no longer see that anything was being accomplished by our work there, I left and went north. I came to see through my writing that no matter how hard we in the Movement worked, nothing seemed to change; that we made a few visible little gains, yet at the root, things always remained the same; and

410

that the Movement was not in control of its destiny—nor did we have any means of gaining control of it. We were like an angry dog on a leash that had turned on its master. It could bark and howl and snap, and sometimes even bite, but the master was always in control. I realized that the universal fight for human rights, dignity, justice, equality, and freedom is not and should not be just the fight of the American Negro or the Indians or the Chicanos, it's the fight of every ethnic and racial minority, every suppressed and exploited person, every one of the millions who daily suffer one or another of the indignities of the powerless and voiceless masses. And this trend of thinking is what finally brought about an end to my involvement in the Civil Rights Movement, especially as it began to splinter and get more narrowly nationalistic in its thinking.''

MEDIA ADAPTATIONS: A sound recording, ''Anne Moody Reads Her Mr. Death and Bobo,'' was produced by Caedmon in 1980.

BIOGRAPHICAL/CRITICAL SOURCES:

PERIODICALS

New York Times, December 13, 1968.
New York Times Book Review, January 5, 1969.
Saturday Review, January 11, 1969.
Washington Post Book World, December 1, 1968, January 27, 1969.

*   *   *

MOORE, Alice Ruth
   See NELSON, Alice Ruth Moore Dunbar

*   *   *

MORRIS, John
   See HEARNE, John (Edgar Caulwell)

*   *   *

MORRISON, Toni   1931-

PERSONAL: Born Chloe Anthony Wofford, February 18, 1931, in Lorain, Ohio; daughter of George and Ramah (Willis) Wofford; married Harold Morrison, 1958 (divorced, 1964); children: Harold Ford, Slade Kevin. *Education:* Howard University, B.A., 1953; Cornell University, M.A., 1955.

ADDRESSES: Office—Random House, 201 East 50th St., New York, N.Y. 10022. *Agent*—Lynn Nesbit, International Creative Management, 40 West 57th St., New York, N.Y. 10019.

CAREER: Texas Southern University, Houston, instructor in English, 1955-57; Howard University, Washington, D.C., instructor in English, 1957-64; Random House, New York, N.Y., senior editor, 1965—; State University of New York at Purchase, associate professor of English, 1971-72; State University of New York at Albany, Schweitzer Professor of the Humanities, 1984-89; Princeton University, Princeton, N.J., Robert F. Goheen Professor of the Humanities, 1989—. Visiting lecturer, Yale University, 1976-77, and Bard College, 1986-88.

MEMBER: American Academy and Institute of Arts and Letters, National Council on the Arts, Authors Guild (council), Authors League of America.

AWARDS, HONORS: National Book Award nomination and Ohioana Book Award, both 1975, both for *Sula;* National Book Critics Circle Award and American Academy and Institute of Arts and Letters Award, both 1977, both for *Song of Solomon;* New York State Governor's Art Award, 1986; National Book Award nomination and National Book Critics Circle Award nomination, both 1987, and Pulitzer Prize for fiction and Robert F. Kennedy Award, both 1988, all for *Beloved;* Elizabeth Cady Stanton Award from the National Organization of Women.

WRITINGS:

The Bluest Eye (novel), Holt, 1969.
Sula (novel), Knopf, 1973.
(Editor) *The Black Book* (anthology), Random House, 1974.
Song of Solomon (novel; Book-of-the-Month Club selection), Knopf, 1977.
Tar Baby (novel), Knopf, 1981.
''Dreaming Emmett'' (play), first produced in Albany, New York, January 4, 1986.
Beloved (novel), Knopf, 1987.

Contributor of essays and reviews to numerous periodicals, including *New York Times Magazine.*

WORK IN PROGRESS: A sequel to *Beloved.*

SIDELIGHTS: Toni Morrison might best be described as the high priestess of village literature. Her award-winning novels chronicle small-town black American life, employing ''an artistic vision that encompasses both a private and a national heritage,'' to quote *Time* magazine contributor Angela Wigan. Through works such as *The Bluest Eye, Song of Solomon* and *Beloved,* Morrison has earned a reputation as a gifted storyteller whose troubled characters seek to find themselves and their cultural riches in a society that warps or impedes such essential growth. According to Charles Larson in the *Chicago Tribune Book World,* each of Morrison's novels ''is as original as anything that has appeared in our ltierature in the last 20 years. The contemporaneity that unites them—the troubling persistence of racism in America—is infused with an urgency that only a black writer can have about our society.'' Morrison's artistry has attracted critical acclaim as well as commercial success; *Dictionary of Literary Biography* contributor Susan L. Blake calls the author ''an anomaly in two respects'' because ''she is a black writer who has achieved national prominence and popularity, and she is a popular writer who is taken seriously.'' Indeed, Morrison has won two of modern literature's most prestigious citations, the 1977 National Book Critics Circle Award for *Song of Solomon* and the 1988 Pulitzer Prize for *Beloved. Atlantic* correspondent Wilfrid Sheed notes: ''Most black writers are privy, like the rest of us, to bits and pieces of the secret, the dark side of their group experience, but Toni Morrison uniquely seems to have all the keys on her chain, like a house detective. . . . She [uses] the run of the whole place, from ghetto to small town to ramshackle farmhouse, to bring back a panorama of black myth and reality that [dazzles] the senses.''

''It seems somehow both constricting and inadequate to describe Toni Morrison as the country's preeminent black novelist, since in both gifts and accomplishments she transcends categorization,'' writes Jonathan Yardley in the *Washington Post Book World,* ''yet the characterization is inescapable not merely because it is true but because the very nature of Morrison's work dictates it. Not merely has black American life been the central preoccupation of her . . . novels . . . but as she has matured she has concentrated on distilling all of black experience into her books; quite purposefully, it seems, she is striving not for the particular but for the universal.'' In her work Morrison strives to lay bare the injustice inherent in the black condition and blacks' efforts, individually and collectively, to transcend society's unjust boundaries. Blake notes that Morrison's novels explore "the difference between black humanity and white cultural values. This opposition produces the negative theme of the seduction and betrayal of black people by white culture . . . and the positive theme of the quest for cultural identity." *Newsweek* contributor Jean Strouse observes: "Like all the best stories, [Morrison's] are driven by an abiding moral vision. Implicit in all her characters' grapplings with who they are is a large sense of human nature and love—and a reach for understanding of something larger than the moment."

Quest for self is a motivating and organizing device in Morrison's fiction, as is the role of family and community in nurturing or challenging the individual. In the *Times Literary Supplement*, Jennifer Uglow suggests that Morrison's novels "explore in particular the process of growing up black, female and poor. Avoiding generalities, Toni Morrison concentrates on the relation between the pressures of the community, patterns established within families, . . . and the developing sense of self." According to Dorothy H. Lee in *Black Women Writers (1950-1980): A Critical Evaluation*, Morrison is preoccupied "with the effect of the community on the individual's achievement and retention of an integrated, acceptable self. In treating this subject, she draws recurrently on myth and legend for story pattern and characters, returning repeatedly to the theory of *quest*. . . . The goals her characters seek to achieve are similar in their deepest implications, and yet the degree to which they attain them varies radically because each novel is cast in unique human terms." In Morrison's books, blacks must confront the notion that all understanding is accompanied by pain, just as all comprehension of national history must include the humiliations of slavery. She tempers this hard lesson by preserving "the richness of communal life against an outer world that denies its value" and by turning to "a heritage of folklore, not only to disclose patterns of living but also to close wounds," in the words of *Nation* contributor Brina Caplan.

Although Morrison herself told the *Chicago Tribune* that there is "epiphany and triumph" in every book she writes, some critics find her work nihilistic and her vision bleak. "The picture given by . . . Morrison of the plight of the decent, aspiring individual in the black family and community is more painful than the gloomiest impressions encouraged by either stereotype or sociology," observes Diane Johnson in the *New York Review of Books*. Johnson continues, "Undoubtedly white society is the ultimate oppressor, and not just of blacks, but, as Morrison [shows,] . . . the black person must first deal with the oppressor in the next room, or in the same bed, or no farther away than across the street." Morrison is a pioneer in the depiction of the hurt inflicted by blacks on blacks; for instance, her characters rarely achieve harmonious heterosexual relationships but are instead divided by futurelessness and the anguish of stifled existence. *Times Literary Supplement* reviewer Jennifer Uglow writes: "We have become attuned to novels . . . which locate oppression in the conflicts of blacks (usually men) trying to make it in a white world. By concentrating on the sense of violation experienced within black neighborhoods, even within families, Toni Morrison deprives us of stock responses and creates a more demanding and uncomfortable literature." *Village Voice* correspondent Vivian Gornick contends that the world Morrison creates "is thick with an atmosphere through which her characters move slowly, in pain, ignorance, and hunger. And to a very large degree Morrison has the compelling ability to make one believe that all of us (Morrison, the characters, the reader) are penetrating that dark and hurtful terrain—the feel of a human life—simultaneously." Uglow concludes that even the laughter of Morrison's characters "disguises pain, deprivation and violation. It is laughter at a series of bad, cruel jokes. . . . Nothing is what it seems; no appearance, no relationship can be trusted to endure."

Other critics detect a deeper undercurrent to Morrison's work that contains just the sort of epiphany for which she strives. "From book to book, Morrison's larger project grows clear," declares Ann Snitow in the *Voice Literary Supplement*. "First, she insists that every character bear the weight of responsibility for his or her own life. After she's measured out each one's private pain, she adds on to that the shared burden of what the whites did. Then, at last, she tries to find the place where her stories can lighten her readers' load, lift them up from their own and others' guilt, carry them to glory. . . . Her characters suffer—from their own limitations and the world's—but their inner life miraculously expands beyond the narrow law of cause and effect." *Harvard Advocate* essayist Faith Davis writes that despite the mundane boundaries of Morrison's characters' lives, the author "illuminates the complexity of their attitudes toward life. Having reached a quiet and extensive understanding of their situation, they can endure life's calamities. . . . Morrison never allows us to become indifferent to these people. . . . Her citizens . . . jump up from the pages vital and strong because she has made us care about the pain in their lives." In *Ms.*, Margo Jefferson concludes that Morrison's books "are filled with loss—lost friendship, lost love, lost customs, lost possibilities. And yet there is so much life in the smallest acts and gestures . . . that they are as much celebrations as elegies."

Morrison sees language as an expression of black experience, and her novels are characterized by vivid narration and dialogue. *Village Voice* essayist Susan Lydon observes that the author "works her magic charm above all with a love of language. Her soaring . . . style carries you like a river, . . . sweeping doubt and disbelief away, and it is only gradually that one realizes her deadly serious intent." In the *Spectator*, Caroline Moorehead likewise notes that Morrison "writes energetically and richly, using words in a way very much her own. The effect is one of exoticism, an exciting curiousness in the language, a balanced sense of the possible that stops, always, short of the absurd." Although Morrison does not like to be called a poetic writer, critics often comment on the lyrical quality of her prose. "Morrison's style has always moved fluidly between tough-minded realism and lyric descriptiveness," notes Margo Jefferson in *Newsweek*. "Vivid dialogue, capturing the drama and extravagance of black speech, gives way to an impressionistic evocation of physical pain or an ironic, essay-like analysis of the varieties of religious hypocrisy." Uglow writes: "The word 'elegant' is often applied to Toni Morrison's writing; it employs sophisticated narrative devices, shifting perspectives and resonant images and displays an obvious delight in the potential of language." *Nation* contributor Earl Frederick concludes that Morrison, "with an ear as sharp as glass . . . has listened to the music of black talk and deftly uses it as the palette knife to create black lives and to provide some of the best fictional dialogue around today."

According to Jean Strouse, Morrison "comes from a long line of people who did what they had to do to survive. It is their stories she tells in her novels—tales of the suffering and richness, the eloquence and tragedies of the black American experience." Morrison was born Chloe Anthony Wofford in Lorain, Ohio, a small town near the shores of Lake Erie. *New York Review of Books* correspondent Darryl Pinckney describes her particular community as "close enough to the Ohio River for the people who lived [there] to feel the torpor of the South, the nostalgia for its folkways, to sense the old Underground Railroad underfoot like a hidden stream." While never explicitly autobiographical, Morrison's fictions draw upon her youthful experiences in Ohio. In an essay for *Black Women Writers at Work* she claims: "I am from the Midwest so I have a special affection for it. My beginnings are always there. . . . No matter what I write, I begin there. . . . It's the matrix for me. . . . Ohio also offers an escape from stereotyped black settings. It is neither plantation nor ghetto."

Two important aspects of Chloe Wofford's childhood—community spirit and the supernatural—inform Toni Morrison's mature writing. In a *Publishers Weekly* interview, Morrison suggests ways in which her community influenced her. "There is this town which is both a support system and a hammer at the same time," she notes. ". . . Approval was not the acquisition of things; approval was given for the maturity and the dignity with which one handled oneself. Most black people in particular were, and still are, very fastidious about manners, very careful about behavior and the rules that operate within the community. The sense of organized activity, what I thought at that time was burdensome, turns out now to have within it a gift—which is, I never had to be taught how to hold a job, how to make it work, how to handle my time." On several levels the pariah—a unique and sometimes eccentric individual—figures in Morrison's fictional reconstruction of black community life. "There is always an elder there," she notes of her work in *Black Women Writers: A Critical Evaluation.* "And these ancestors are not just parents, they are sort of timeless people whose relationships to the characters are benevolent, instructive, and protective, and they provide a certain kind of wisdom." Sometimes this figure imparts his or her wisdom from beyond the grave; from an early age Morrison absorbed the folklore and beliefs of a culture for which the supernatural holds power and portent. Strouse notes that Morrison's world, both within and outside her fiction, is "filled with signs, visitations, ways of knowing that [reach] beyond the five senses."

Lorain, Ohio, is in fact the setting of *The Bluest Eye,* published in 1969. Morrison's first novel portrays "in poignant terms the tragic condition of blacks in a racist America," to quote Chikwenye Okonjo Ogunyemi in *Critique: Studies in Modern Fiction.* In *The Bluest Eye,* Morrison depicts the onset of black self-hatred as occasioned by white American ideals such as "Dick and Jane" primers and Shirley Temple movies. The principal character, Pecola Breedlove, is literally maddened by the disparity between her existence and the pictures of beauty and gentility disseminated by the dominant white culture. As Phyllis R. Klotman notes in the *Black American Literature Forum,* Morrison "uses the contrast between Shirley Temple and Pecola . . . to underscore the irony of black experience. Whether one learns acceptability from the formal educational experience or from cultural symbols, the effect is the same: self-hatred." Darwin T. Turner elaborates on the novel's intentions in *Black Women Writers: A Critical Evaluation.* Morrison's fictional milieu, writes Turner, is "a world of grotesques—individuals whose psyches have been deformed by their efforts to assume false identities, their failures to achieve meaningful identities, or simply their inability to retain and communicate love."

Blake characterizes *The Bluest Eye* as a novel of initiation, exploring that common theme in American literature from a minority viewpoint. Ogunyemi likewise contends that, in essence, Morrison presents "old problems in a fresh language and with a fresh perspective. A central force of the work derives from her power to draw vignettes and her ability to portray emotions, seeing the world through the eyes of adolescent girls." Klotman, who calls the book "a novel of growing up, of growing up young and black and female in America," concludes her review with the comment that the "rite of passage, initiating the young into womanhood at first tenuous and uncertain, is sensitively depicted. . . . *The Bluest Eye* is an extraordinarily passionate yet gentle work, the language lyrical yet precise—it is a novel for all seasons."

In *Sula,* Morrison's 1973 novel, the author once again presents a pair of black women who must come to terms with their lives. Set in a Midwestern black community called The Bottom, the story follows two friends, Sula and Nel, from childhood to old age and death. Snitow claims that through *Sula,* Morrison has discovered "a way to offer her people an insight and sense of recovered self so dignified and glowing that no worldly pain could dull the final light." Indeed, *Sula* is a tale of rebel and conformist in which the conformity is dictated by the solid inhabitants of The Bottom and even the rebellion gains strength from the community's disapproval. *New York Times Book Review* contributor Sara Blackburn contends, however, that the book is "too vital and rich" to be consigned to the category of allegory. Morrison's "extravagantly beautiful, doomed characters are locked in a world where hope for the future is a foreign commodity, yet they are enormously, achingly alive," writes Blackburn. "And this book about them—and about how their beauty is drained back and frozen—is a howl of love and rage, playful and funny as well as hard and bitter." In the words of *American Literature* essayist Jane S. Bakerman, Morrison "uses the maturation story of Sula and Nel as the core of a host of other stories, but it is the chief unification device for the novel and achieves its own unity, again, through the clever manipulation of the themes of sex, race, and love. Morrison has undertaken a . . . difficult task in *Sula.* Unquestionably, she has succeeded."

Other critics have echoed Bakerman's sentiments about *Sula.* Yardley declares: "What gives this terse, imaginative novel its genuine distinction is the quality of Toni Morrison's prose. *Sula* is admirable enough as a study of its title character, . . . but its real strength lies in Morrison's writing, which at times has the resonance of poetry and is precise, vivid and controlled throughout." Turner also claims that in *Sula* "Morrison evokes her verbal magic occasionally by lyric descriptions that carry the reader deep into the soul of the character. . . . Equally effective, however, is her art of narrating action in a lean prose that uses adjectives cautiously while creating memorable vivid images." In her review, Davis concludes that a "beautiful and haunting atmosphere emerges out of the wreck of these folks' lives, a quality that is absolutely convincing and absolutely precise." *Sula* was nominated for a National Book Award in 1974.

From the insular lives she depicted in her first two novels, Morrison moved in *Song of Solomon* to a national and historical perspective on black American life. "Here the depths of the younger work are still evident," contends Reynolds Price in the *New York Times Book Review,* "but now they thrust outward, into wider fields, for longer intervals, encompassing many more lives. The result is a long prose tale that surveys nearly a century of American history as it impinges upon a single family.'' With an intermixture of the fantastic and the realistic, *Song of Solomon* relates the journey of a character named Milkman Dead into an understanding of his family heritage and hence, himself. Lee writes: ''Figuratively, [Milkman] travels from innocence to awareness, i.e., from ignorance of origins, heritage, identity, and communal responsibility to knowledge and acceptance. He moves from selfish and materialistic dilettantism to an understanding of brotherhood. With his release of personal ego, he is able to find a place in the whole. There is, then, a universal—indeed mythic—pattern here. He journeys from spiritual death to rebirth, a direction symbolized by his discovery of the secret power of flight. Mythically, liberation and transcendence follow the discovery of self.'' Blake suggests that the connection Milkman discovers with his family's past helps him to connect meaningfully with his contemporaries; *Song of Solomon*, Blake notes, ''dramatizes dialectical approaches to the challenges of black life.'' According to Anne Z. Mickelson in *Reaching Out: Sensitivity and Order in Recent American Fiction by Women*, history itself ''becomes a choral symphony to Milkman, in which each individual voice has a chance to speak and contribute to his growing sense of well-being.''

Mickelson also observes that *Song of Solomon* represents for blacks ''a break out of the confining life into the realm of possibility.'' Charles Larson comments on this theme in a *Washington Post Book World* review. The novel's subject matter, Larson explains, is ''the origins of black consciousness in America, and the individual's relationship to that heritage.'' However, Larson adds, ''skilled writer that she is, Morrison has transcended this theme so that the reader rarely feels that this is simply another novel about ethnic identity. So marvelously orchestrated is Morrison's narrative that it not only excels on all of its respective levels, not only works for all of its interlocking components, but also—in the end—says something about life (and death) for all of us. Milkman's epic journey . . . is a profound examination of the individual's understanding of, and, perhaps, even transcendence of the inevitable fate of his life.'' Gornick concludes: ''There are so many individual moments of power and beauty in *Song of Solomon* that, ultimately, one closes the book warmed through by the richness of its sympathy, and by its breathtaking feel for the nature of sexual sorrow.''

Song of Solomon won the National Book Critics Circle Award in 1977. It was also the first novel by a black writer to become a Book-of-the-Month Club selection since Richard Wright's *Native Son* was published in 1940. *World Literature Today* reviewer Richard K. Barksdale calls the work ''a book that will not only withstand the test of time but endure a second and third reading by those conscientious readers who love a well-wrought piece of fiction.'' Describing the novel as ''a stunningly beautiful book'' in her *Washington Post Book World* piece, Anne Tyler adds: ''I would call the book poetry, but that would seem to be denying its considerable power as a story. Whatever name you give it, it's full of magnificent people, each of them complex and multilayered, even the narrowest of them narrow in extravagant ways.'' Price deems *Song of Solomon* ''a long story, . . . and better than good. Toni Morrison has earned attention and praise. Few Americans know, and can say, more than she has in this wise and spacious novel.''

Morrison's 1981 book *Tar Baby* remained on bestseller lists for four months. A novel of ideas, the work dramatizes the fact that complexion is a far more subtle issue than the simple polarization of black and white. Set on a lush Caribbean is-

land, *Tar Baby* explores the passionate love affair of Jadine, a Sorbonne-educated black model, and Son, a handsome knockabout with a strong aversion to white culture. According to Caplan, Morrison's concerns ''are race, class, culture and the effects of late capitalism—heavy freight for any narrative. . . . She is attempting to stabilize complex visions of society—that is, to examine competitive ideas. . . . Because the primary function of Morrison's characters is to voice representative opinions, they arrive on stage vocal and highly conscious, their histories symbolically indicated or merely sketched. Her brief sketches, however, are clearly the work of an artist who can, when she chooses, model the mind in depth and detail.'' In a *Dictionary of Literary Biography Yearbook* essay, Elizabeth B. House outlines *Tar Baby*'s major themes; namely, ''the difficulty of settling conflicting claims between one's past and present and the destruction which abuse of power can bring. As Morrison examines these problems in *Tar Baby*, she suggests no easy way to understand what one's link to a heritage should be, nor does she offer infallible methods for dealing with power. Rather, with an astonishing insight and grace, she demonstrates the pervasiveness of such dilemmas and the degree to which they affect human beings, both black and white.''

Tar Baby uncovers racial and sexual conflicts without offering solutions, but most critics agree that Morrison indicts all of her characters—black and white—for their thoughtless devaluations of others. *New York Times Book Review* correspondent John Irving claims: ''What's so powerful, and subtle, about Miss Morrison's presentation of the tension between blacks and whites is that she conveys it almost entirely through the suspicions and prejudices of her black characters. . . . Miss Morrison uncovers all the stereotypical racial fears felt by whites and blacks alike. Like any ambitious writer, she's unafraid to employ these stereotypes—she embraces the representative qualities of her characters without embarrassment, then proceeds to make them individuals too.'' *New Yorker* essayist Susan Lardner praises Morrison for her ''power to be absolutely persuasive against her own preferences, suspicions, and convictions, implied or plainly expressed,'' and Strouse likewise contends that the author ''has produced that rare commodity, a truly public novel about the condition of society, examining the relations between blacks and whites, men and women, civilization and nature. . . . It wraps its messages in a highly potent love story.'' Irving suggests that Morrison's greatest accomplishment ''is that she has raised her novel above the social realism that too many black novels and women's novels are trapped in. She has succeeded in writing about race and women symbolically.''

Reviewers have praised *Tar Baby* for its provocative themes and for its evocative narration. *Los Angeles Times* contributor Elaine Kendall calls the book ''an intricate and sophisticated novel, moving from a realistic and orderly beginning to a mystical and ambiguous end. Morrison has taken classically simple story elements and realigned them so artfully that we perceive the old pattern in a startlingly different way. Although this territory has been explored by dozens of novelists, Morrison depicts it with such vitality that it seems newly discovered.'' In the *Washington Post Book World*, Webster Schott claims: ''There is so much that is good, sometimes dazzling, about *Tar Baby*—poetic language, . . . arresting images, fierce intelligence—that . . . one becomes entranced by Toni Morrison's story. The settings are so vivid the characters must be alive. The emotions they feel are so intense they must be real people.'' Maureen Howard states in *New Republic* that the work "is as carefully patterned as a well-written poem. . . . *Tar Baby* is a good American novel in which we can discern a new lightness and brilliance in Toni Morrison's enchantment with language and in her curiously polyphonic stories that echo life." Schott concludes: "One of fiction's pleasures is to have your mind scratched and your intellectual habits challenged. While *Tar Baby* has shortcomings, lack of provocation isn't one of them. Morrison owns a powerful intelligence. It's run by courage. She calls to account conventional wisdom and accepted attitude at nearly every turn."

In addition to her own writing, Morrison has served as an editor at Random House and has helped to publish the work of other noted black Americans, including Toni Cade Bambara, Gayle Jones, Angela Davis, and Muhammed Ali. Discussing her aims as an editor in a quotation printed in the *Dictionary of Literary Biography*, Morrison said: "I look very hard for black fiction because I want to participate in developing a canon of black work. We've had the first rush of black entertainment, where blacks were writing for whites, and whites were encouraging this kind of self-flagellation. Now we can get down to the craft of writing, where black people are talking to black people." One of Morrison's important projects for Random House was *The Black Book*, an anthology of items that illustrate the history of black Americans. *Ms.* magazine correspondent Dorothy Eugenia Robinson describes the work: "*The Black Book* is the pain and pride of rediscovering the collective black experience. It is finding the essence of ourselves and holding on. *The Black Book* is a kind of scrapbook of patiently assembled samplings of black history and culture. What has evolved is a pictorial folk journey of black people, places, events, handcrafts, inventions, songs, and folklore. . . . *The Black Book* informs, disturbs, maybe even shocks. It unsettles complacency and demands confrontation with raw reality. It is by no means an easy book to experience, but it's a necessary one."

While preparing *The Black Book* for publication, Morrison uncovered the true and shocking story of a runaway slave who, at the point of recapture, murdered her infant child so it would not be doomed to a lifetime of slavery. For Morrison the story encapsulated the fierce psychic cruelty of an institutionalized system that sought to destroy the basic emotional bonds between men and women, and worse, between parent and child. "I certainly thought I knew as much about slavery as anybody," Morrison told the *Los Angeles Times*. "But it was the interior life I needed to find out about." It is this "interior life" in the throes of slavery that constitutes the theme of Morrison's Pulitzer Prize-winning novel *Beloved*. Set in Reconstruction-era Cincinnati, the book centers on characters who struggle fruitlessly to keep their painful recollections of the past at bay. They are haunted, both physically and spiritually, by the legacies slavery has bequeathed to them. According to Snitow, *Beloved* "staggers under the terror of its material—as so much holocaust writing does and must."

In *People* magazine, V. R. Peterson describes *Beloved* as "a brutally powerful, mesmerizing story about the inescapable, excruciating legacy of slavery. Behind each new event and each new character lies another event and another story until finally the reader meets a community of proud, daring people, inextricably bound by culture and experience." Through the lives of ex-slaves Sethe and her would-be lover Paul D., readers "experience American slavery as it was lived by those who were its objects of exchange, both at its best—which wasn't very good—and at its worst, which was as bad as can be imagined," writes Margaret Atwood in the *New York Times*

Book Review. "Above all, it is seen as one of the most viciously antifamily institutions human beings have ever devised. The slaves are motherless, fatherless, deprived of their mates, their children, their kin. It is a world in which people suddenly vanish and are never seen again, not through accident or covert operation or terrorism, but as a matter of everyday legal policy." *New York Times* columnist Michiko Kakutani contends that *Beloved* "possesses the heightened power and resonance of myth—its characters, like those in opera or Greek drama, seem larger than life and their actions, too, tend to strike us as enactments of ancient rituals and passions. To describe 'Beloved' only in these terms, however, is to diminish its immediacy, for the novel also remains precisely grounded in American reality—the reality of Black history as experienced in the wake of the Civil War."

Acclaim for *Beloved* has come from both sides of the Atlantic. In his *Chicago Tribune* piece, Larson claims that the work "is the context out of which all of Morrison's earlier novels were written. In her darkest and most probing novel, Toni Morrison has demonstrated once again the stunning powers that place her in the first ranks of our living novelists." *Los Angeles Times Book Review* contributor John Leonard likewise expresses the opinion that the novel "belongs on the highest shelf of American literature, even if half a dozen canonized white boys have to be elbowed off. . . . Without 'Beloved' our imagination of the nation's self has a hole in it big enough to die from." Atwood states: "Ms. Morrison's versatility and technical and emotional range appear to know no bounds. If there were any doubts about her stature as a pre-eminent American novelist, of her own or any other generation, 'Beloved' will put them to rest." London *Times* reviewer Nicholas Shakespeare concludes that *Beloved* "is a novel propelled by the cadences of . . . songs—the first singing of a people hardened by their suffering, people who have been hanged and whipped and mortgaged at the hands of whitepeople—the men without skin. From Toni Morrison's pen it is a sound that breaks the back of words, making *Beloved* a great novel."

Morrison is an author who labors contentedly under the labels bestowed by pigeonholing critics. She has no objection to being called a black woman writer, because, as she told the *New York Times*, "I really think the range of emotions and perceptions I have had access to as a black person and a female person are greater than those of people who are neither. . . . My world did not shrink because I was a black female writer. It just got bigger." Nor does she strive for that much-vaunted universality that purports to be a hallmark of fine fiction. "I never asked Tolstoy to write for me, a little colored girl in Lorain, Ohio," she told the *New Republic*. "I never asked Joyce not to mention Catholicism or the world of Dublin. Never. And I don't know why I should be asked to explain your life to you. We have splendid writers to do that, but I am not one of them. It is that business of being universal, a word hopelessly stripped of meaning for me. Faulkner wrote what I suppose could be called regional literature and had it published all over the world. That's what I wish to do. If I tried to write a universal novel, it would be water. Behind this question is the suggestion that to write for black people is somehow to diminish the writing. From my perspective there are only black people. When I say 'people,' that's what I mean."

Black woman writer or simply American novelist, Toni Morrison is a prominent and respected figure in modern letters. In the *Detroit News*, Larson suggests that hers has been "among the most exciting literary careers of the last decade" and that each of her books "has made a quantum jump forward." Ironically, Elizabeth House commends Morrison for the universal nature of her work. "Unquestionably," House writes, "Toni Morrison is an important novelist who continues to develop her talent. Part of her appeal, of course, lies in her extraordinary ability to create beautiful language and striking characters. However, Morrison's most important gift, the one which gives her a major author's universality, is the insight with which she writes of problems all humans face. . . . At the core of all her novels is a penetrating view of the unyielding, heartbreaking dilemmas which torment people of all races." Snitow notes that the author "wants to tend the imagination, search for an expansion of the possible, nurture a spiritual richness in the black tradition even after 300 years in the white desert." Dorothy Lee concludes of Morrison's accomplishments: "Though there are unifying aspects in her novels, there is not a dully repetitive sameness. Each casts the problems in specific, imaginative terms, and the exquisite, poetic language awakens our senses as she communicates an often ironic vision with moving imagery. Each novel reveals the acuity of her perception of psychological motivation—of the female especially, of the Black particularly, and of the human generally."

"The problem I face as a writer is to make my stories mean something," Morrison states in *Black Women Writers at Work.* "You can have wonderful, interesting people, a fascinating story, but it's not about anything. It has no real substance. . . . I want my books to always be about something that is important to me, and the subjects that are important in the world are the same ones that have always been important." In *Black Women Writers: A Critical Evaluation,* she elaborates on this idea. Fiction, she writes, "should be beautiful, and powerful, but it should also *work.* It should have something in it that enlightens; something in it that opens the door and points the way. Something in it that suggests what the conflicts are, what the problems are. But it need not solve those problems because it is not a case study, it is not a recipe." The author who has said that writing "is discovery; it's talking deep within myself" told the *New York Times Book Review* that the essential theme in her growing body of fiction is "how and why we learn to live this life intensely and well."

BIOGRAPHICAL/CRITICAL SOURCES:

BOOKS

Bell, Roseann P., editor, *Sturdy Black Bridges: Visions of Black Women in Literature,* Doubleday, 1979.
Christian, Barbara, *Black Women Novelists: The Development of a Tradition, 1892-1976,* Greenwood Press, 1980.
Contemporary Literary Criticism, Gale, Volume 4, 1975, Volume 10, 1979, Volume 22, 1982.
Cooper-Clark, Diana, *Interviews with Contemporary Novelists,* St. Martin's, 1986.
Dictionary of Literary Biography, Gale, Volume 6: *American Novelists since World War II,* 1980, Volume 33: *Afro-American Fiction Writers after 1955,* 1984.
Dictionary of Literary Biography Yearbook: 1981, Gale, 1982.
Evans, Mari, editor, *Black Women Writers (1950-1980): A Critical Evaluation,* Doubleday, 1984.
Mekkawi, Mod, *Toni Morrison: A Bibliography,* Howard University Library, 1986.
Mickelson, Anne Z., *Reaching Out: Sensitivity and Order in Recent American Fiction by Women,* Scarecrow Press, 1979.
Ruas, Charles, *Conversations with American Writers,* Knopf, 1985.

Tate, Claudia, editor, *Black Women Writers at Work,* Continuum, 1986.

PERIODICALS

American Literature, January, 1981.
Atlantic, April, 1981.
Black American Literature Forum, summer, 1978, winter, 1979.
Black Scholar, March, 1978.
Black World, June, 1974.
Callaloo, October-February, 1981.
Chicago Tribune, October 27, 1987.
Chicago Tribune Books, August 30, 1988.
Chicago Tribune Book World, March 8, 1981.
CLA Journal, June, 1979, June, 1981.
Commentary, August, 1981.
Contemporary Literature, winter, 1983.
Critique: Studies in Modern Fiction, Volume XIX, number 1, 1977.
Detroit News, March 29, 1981.
Essence, July, 1981, June, 1983, October, 1987.
First World, winter, 1977.
Harper's Bazaar, March, 1983.
Harvard Advocate, Volume CVII, number 4, 1974.
Hudson Review, spring, 1978.
Los Angeles Times, March 31, 1981, October 14, 1987.
Los Angeles Times Book Review, August 30, 1987.
Massachusetts Review, autumn, 1977.
MELUS, fall, 1980.
Ms., June, 1974, December, 1974, August, 1987.
Nation, July 6, 1974, November 19, 1977, May 2, 1981.
New Republic, December 3, 1977, March 21, 1981.
Newsweek, November 30, 1970, January 7, 1974, September 12, 1977, March 30, 1981.
New York, April 13, 1981.
New Yorker, November 7, 1977, June 15, 1981.
New York Post, January 26, 1974.
New York Review of Books, November 10, 1977, April 30, 1981.
New York Times, November 13, 1970, September 6, 1977, March 21, 1981, August 26, 1987, September 2, 1987.
New York Times Book Review, November 1, 1970, December 30, 1973, June 2, 1974, September 11, 1977, March 29, 1981, September 13, 1987.
New York Times Magazine, August 22, 1971, August 11, 1974, July 4, 1976, May 20, 1979.
Obsidian, spring/summer, 1979.
People, July 29, 1974, November 30, 1987.
Philadelphia Inquirer, April 1, 1988.
Publishers Weekly, August 21, 1987.
Saturday Review, September 17, 1977.
Spectator, December 9, 1978, February 2, 1980, December 19, 1981.
Studies in Black Literature, Volume VI, 1976.
Time, September 12, 1977, March 16, 1981, September 21, 1987.
Times (London), October 15, 1987.
Times Literary Supplement, October 4, 1974, November 24, 1978, February 8, 1980, December 19, 1980, October 30, 1981, October 16-22, 1987.
U.S. News and World Report, October 19, 1987.
Village Voice, August 29, 1977, July 1-7, 1981.
Vogue, April, 1981, January, 1986.
Voice Literary Supplement, September, 1987.
Washington Post, February 3, 1974, March 6, 1974, September 30, 1977, April 8, 1981, Februrary 9, 1983, October 5, 1987.

Washington Post Book World, February 3, 1974, September 4, 1977, December 4, 1977, March 22, 1981, September 6, 1987.
World Literature Today, summer, 1978.

—*Sketch by Anne Janette Johnson*

*   *   *

MORROW, E(verett) Frederic   1909-

PERSONAL: Born April 20, 1909, in Hackensack, N.J.; son of John Eugene (a minister) and Mary Anne (Hayes) Morrow; married Catherine Louise Gordon, September 18, 1957. *Education:* Bowdoin College, A.B., 1930; Rutgers University, LL.B., 1948, Dr. Juris, 1949. *Politics:* Republican. *Religion:* Methodist.

ADDRESSES: Home—1270 Fifth Avenue, New York, N.Y. 10029. *Office*—Bank of America, 41 Broad St., New York, N.Y. 10004.

CAREER: Business manager, *Opportunity* (magazine), 1934-36; National Association for the Advancement of Colored People (NAACP), New York City, field secretary, 1937-48; Columbia Broadcasting System, New York City, began in 1949, member of public affairs department, 1951-53; U.S. Government, Washington, D.C., business adviser to Department of Commerce, 1953-55, administrative officer, Special Projects Group, The White House, 1955-61; African-American Institute, New York City, vice-president, 1961-64; Bank of America, International, New York City, vice-president, 1964—. *Military service:* U.S. Army, Field Artillery, 1942-46; became major.

MEMBER: Alpha Phi Alpha.

AWARDS, HONORS: L.L.D., Bowdoin College, 1970.

WRITINGS:

Black Man in the White House: A Diary of the Eisenhower Years by the Administrative Officer for Special Projects, the White House, 1955-1961, Coward, 1963.
Way down South up North, United Church Press, 1975.
Forty Years a Guinea Pig: A Black Man's View from the Top, Pilgrim Press, 1980.

WORK IN PROGRESS: When the Morning Comes.

SIDELIGHTS: E. Frederic Morrow became the first black man to serve as a White House aide when President Dwight D. Eisenhower appointed him as an administrative assistant in 1955.

BIOGRAPHICAL/CRITICAL SOURCES:

PERIODICALS

Los Angeles Times, December 5, 1980.

*   *   *

MOTLEY, Willard (Francis)   1912-1965

PERSONAL: Born July 14, 1912, in Chicago, Ill.; died of gangrene, March 4, 1965, in Mexico City, Mexico; son of Archibald John and Mary Frederica (Huff) Motley; children: Sergio, Raul. *Education:* Educated in Chicago, Ill.

ADDRESSES: Home—Mexico City, Mexico.

CAREER: Writer. Worked as ranch hand, cook, shipping clerk, photographer, interviewer for Chicago Housing Authority, and writer for Office of Civil Defense.

WRITINGS:

NOVELS

Knock on Any Door, Appleton-Century, 1947.
We Fished All Night, Appleton-Century-Crofts, 1951.
Let No Man Write My Epitaph, Random House, 1958.
Let Noon Be Fair, Putnam, 1966.

OTHER

The Diaries of Willard Motley, edited by Jerome Kinkowitz, foreword by Clarence Majors, Iowa State University Press, 1979.

SIDELIGHTS: Willard Motley was an important black novelist. He began writing after years of traveling—including hitchhiking stints across America, living in flophouses, and working odd jobs. Upon deciding to write, Motley moved into Chicago's slums and, as he related, "discovered myself and the sort of things I wanted to put on paper." His first novel, *Knock on Any Door,* was a grim account in the naturalist—or ultra-realist—style. It told of a ghetto boy's degeneration from church helper to hardened killer and explicitly condemned the ghetto environment as largely responsible for his fate.

In his review of *Knock on Any Door* in the *New York Times,* Charles Lee hailed Motley as "an extraordinary and powerful new naturalistic talent" and declared that the novel would "challenge society to mend its body and soul." H. R. Cayton, writing in the *New Republic,* was similarly impressed, calling Motley's first novel "a monumental work" and noting his "great compassion for the human spirit."

Motley followed *Knock on Any Door* with *We Fished All Night,* a saga of three men and their experiences in the 1940s. This second novel was considered weak by many critics, including a *New Yorker* reviewer who complained of Motley's "heavy, wearisome irony" and a *Time* writer who lamented Motley's "political sermonizing."

In his third novel, *Let No Man Write My Epitaph,* Motley returned to the tale of *Knock on Any Door* by detailing the escapades of Nick Romano, son of the altar-boy-turned-killer who was executed in the earlier work. Living in the ghetto with his mother, Nick Romano is supported by his encouraging mother and a small coterie of friends who have a similar interest in his success. Eventually Nick's mother becomes a drug addict, and he finds understanding from the daughter of a writer investigating drug trafficking. Many reviewers found *Let No Man Write My Epitaph* sentimental and unconvincing, while others, including Granville Hicks in *Saturday Review,* considered it unfocused. Hicks deemed it "full of distractions" and added that the drama was compromised by intrusive documentation.

Motley's final novel, *Let Noon Be Fair,* was published posthumously in 1966, the year after he died from gangrene in Mexico City. In this work Motley chronicled the development of a Mexican fishing village from its initial inhabitation by savages to modern times and its invasion by American tourists. Nelson Algren, writing in *Book Week,* praised *Let Noon Be Fair* as Motley's "saddest and most skillful book" and added that the result of the village's inevitable corruption was "not so much one of horror as one of brutalized triviality."

Motley's other posthumous publication is *The Diaries of Willard Motley,* which he began writing at age sixteen and concluded in 1943 before completing *Knock on Any Door.* A *Nation* reviewer valued the book for its examples of Motley's ability to incorporate actual experiences into his fiction, and for offering an explanation of Motley's refusal to specifically write about blacks. "My race," Motley contended, "is the human race."

MEDIA ADAPTATIONS: Knock on Any Door was adapted for film in 1949; *Let No Man Write My Epitaph* was adapted for film in 1960.

BIOGRAPHICAL/CRITICAL SOURCES:

BOOKS

Contemporary Literary Criticism, Volume 18, Gale, 1981.

PERIODICALS

Book Week, March 6, 1966.
New Republic, May 12, 1947.
New Yorker, May 24, 1947, November 24, 1951, August 10, 1958.
New York Times, May 4, 1947, November 18, 1951.
New York Times Book Review, February 27, 1966.
Saturday Review, August 9, 1958.
Time, November 26, 1951, August 11, 1958.

*   *   *

MPHAHLELE, Es'kia
See MPHAHLELE, Ezekiel

*   *   *

MPHAHLELE, Ezekiel   1919-
(Es'kia Mphahlele; Bruno Eseki, a pseudonym)

PERSONAL: Born December 17, 1919, in Marabastad Township, Pretoria, South Africa; son of Moses (a messenger) and Eva (a domestic; maiden name, Mogale) Mphahlele; married Rebecca Mochadibane (a social worker), 1945; children: Anthony, Teresa Kefilwe, Motswiri, Chabi Robert, Puso. *Education:* Attended Adams Teachers Training College, Natal, 1939-40; University of South Africa, B.A. (with honors), 1949, M.A., 1956; University of Denver, Ph.D., 1968.

ADDRESSES: Office—African Studies Institute, University of the Witwatersrand, Johannesburg 2001, South Africa.

CAREER: Clerk for an institute for the blind, 1941-45; Orlando High School, Johannesburg, South Africa, teacher of English and Afrikaans, 1945-52; *Drum* magazine, Johannesburg, fiction editor, 1955-57; University of Ibadan, Ibadan, Nigeria, lecturer in English literature, 1957-61; International Association for Cultural Freedom, Paris, France, director of African programs, 1961-63; Chemchemi Creative Centre, Nairobi, Kenya, director, 1963-65; University College, Nairobi, lecturer, 1965-66; University of Denver, Denver, Colo., visiting lecturer, 1966-68, associate professor of English, 1970-74; University of Zambia, Lusaka, senior lecturer in English, 1968-70; University of Pennsylvania, Philadelphia, professor of English, 1974-77; University of Witwatersrand, Johannesburg, senior resident fellow, 1978—, professor of African literature, 1979—. Inspector of education, Lebowa, Transvaal, 1978-79.

AWARDS, HONORS: African Arts magazine prize, 1972, for *The Wanderers.*

WRITINGS:

Man Must Live and Other Stories, African Bookman, 1947.

(Contributor) Prudence Smith, editor, *Africa in Transition,* Reinhardt, 1958.
Down Second Avenue (autobiography), Faber, 1959, reprinted, 1985.
The Living and the Dead and Other Stories, Black Orpheus, 1961.
The African Image (essays), Faber, 1962, Praeger, 1964, revised edition, 1974.
(Editor with Ellis Ayitey Komey) *Modern African Stories,* Faber, 1964.
The Role of Education and Culture in Developing African Countries, Afro-Asian Institute for Labor Studies in Israel, 1965.
A Guide to Creative Writing, East African Literature Bureau, 1966.
In Corner B and Other Stories, Northwestern University Press, 1967.
(Editor and contributor) *African Writing Today,* Penguin, 1967.
The Wanderers (autobiographical novel), Macmillan, 1971.
Voices in the Whirlwind and Other Essays, Hill & Wang, 1972.
(Under name Es'kia Mphahlele) *Chirundu* (novel), Lawrence Hill, 1981.
(Under name Es'kia Mphahlele) *The Unbroken Song: Selected Writings of Es'kia Mphahlele,* Ravan Press, 1981.
(Under name Es'kia Mphahlele) *Afrika My Music: An Autobiography, 1957-83,* Ravan Press, 1984, Ohio University Press, 1986.
Father Come Home (juvenile), Ravan Press, 1984.
(Under name Es'kia Mphahlele) *Bury Me at the Marketplace: Selected Letters of Es'kia Mphahlele,* edited by N. Chabani Mangayani, Skotaville, 1984.
Let's Talk Writing: Prose, Skotaville, 1985.
Let's Talk Writing: Poetry, Skotaville, 1985.

CONTRIBUTOR TO ANTHOLOGIES

Langston Hughes, editor, *An African Treasury: Articles, Essays, Stories, Poems by Black Africans,* Crown, 1960.
Jacob Drachler, editor, *African Heritage: An Anthology of Black African Personality and Culture,* Crowell, 1962.
Leonard Sainville, editor, *Anthologie de la litterature negro-africaine: Romaciers et conteurs negro-africains,* Volume II, Presence Africaine, 1963.
Richard Rive, editor, *Modern African Prose,* Heinemann, 1964, reprinted, 1982.
Ulli Beier, editor, *Black Orpheus: An Anthology of New African and Afro-American Stories,* Longmans, 1964, McGraw-Hill, 1965.
W. H. Whiteley, compiler, *A Selection of African Prose,* Volume II, Oxford University Press, 1964.
Anne Tibble, editor, *African-English Literature: A Survey and Anthology,* October House, 1965.
Hughes, editor, *Poems from Black Africa,* Indiana University Press, 1966.
Denny Neville, editor, *Pan African Short Stories,* Humanities, 1966.
Paul Edwards, compiler, *Modern African Narrative: An Anthology,* Humanities, 1966.
Edwards, compiler, *Through African Eyes,* Volume I, Cambridge University Press, 1966.
Lilyan Kesteloot, editor, *Anthologie negro-africaine: Panorama critique des prosateurs, poetes et dramatourges noirs du XXeme siecle,* Gerard, 1967.
Nadine Gordimer and Lionel Abrahams, editors, *South African Writing Today,* Penguin, 1967.

Herbert I. Shore and Megchelina Shore-Bos, editors, *Come Back, Africa: Fourteen Stories from South Africa,* International Publishers, 1968.

Ime Ikiddeh, compiler, *Drum Beats: An Anthology of African Writing,* E. J. Arnold, 1968.

Oscar Ronald Dathorne and Willfried Feuser, editors, *Africa in Prose,* Penguin, 1969.

John P. Berry, editor, *Africa Speaks: A Prose Anthology with Comprehension and Summary Passages,* Evans, 1970.

Joseph O. Okpaku, editor, *New African Literature and the Arts,* Volumes I and II, Crowell, 1970.

Charles Larson, editor, *African Short Stories: A Collection of Contemporary African Writing,* Macmillan, 1970.

Bernth Lindfors, editor, *South African Voices,* African and Afro-American Studies Research Center, 1975.

OTHER

Contributor of essays, short stories and poems, sometimes under pseudonym Bruno Eseki, to *Drum, Africa South, Denver Quarterly, Journal of Modern African Studies, Black World, New Statesman,* and other periodicals. Editor, *Black Orpheus,* 1960-66; member of staff, *Presence Africaine,* 1961-63; member of editorial staff, *Journal of New African Literature and the Arts.*

WORK IN PROGRESS: A Critical Anthology of African Poetry.

SIDELIGHTS: "A writer who has been regarded as the most balanced literary critic of African literature," Ezekiel Mphahlele can also "be acknowledged as one of its most significant creators," writes Emile Snyder in the *Saturday Review.* Mphahlele's transition from life in the slums of South Africa to life as a professor of English at a large American university was an odyssey of struggle both intellectually and politically. He trained as a teacher in South Africa, but was banned from the classroom in 1952 as a result of his protest of the segregationist Bantu Education Act. Although he later returned to teaching, Mphahlele first turned to journalism, criticism, fiction, and essay writing.

During an exile that took him to France and the United States, Mphahlele was away from Africa for over a decade. Nevertheless, "no other author has ever earned the right to so much of Africa as has Ezekiel Mphahlele," says John Thompson in the *New York Review of Books.* "In the English language, he established the strength of African literature in our time." Some critics, however, feel that Mphahlele's absence from his homeland has harmed his work by separating him from its subject. Ursula Barnett, writing in the conclusion of her 1976 biography *Ezekiel Mphahlele,* asserts that Mphahlele's "creative talent can probably gain its full potential only if he returns to South Africa and resumes his function of teaching his discipline in his own setting, and of encouraging the different elements in South Africa to combine and interchange in producing a modern indigenous literature."

Mphahlele himself has agreed with this assessment, for after being officially silenced by the government of his homeland and living in self-imposed exile for twenty years, Mphahlele returned to South Africa in 1977. "I want to be part of the renaissance that is happening in the thinking of my people," he told *CA.* "I see education as playing a vital role in personal growth and in institutionalizing a way of life that a people chooses as its highest ideal. For the older people, it is a way of reestablishing the values they had to suspend along the way because of the force of political conditions. Another reason for returning, connected with the first, is that this is my an-

cestral home. An African cares very much where he dies and is buried. But I have not come to die. I want to reconnect with my ancestors while I am still active. I am also a captive of place, of setting. As long as I was abroad I continued to write on the South African scene. There is a force I call the tyranny of place; the kind of unrelenting hold a place has on a person that gives him the motivation to write and a style. The American setting in which I lived for nine years was too fragmented to give me these. I could only identify emotionally and intellectually with the African-American segment, which was not enough. Here I can feel the ancestral Presence. I know now what Vinoba Bhave of India meant when he said: 'Though action rages without, the heart can be tuned to produce unbroken music,' at this very hour when pain is raging and throbbing everywhere in African communities living in this country.''

Chirundu, Mphahlele's first novel since his return to South Africa, "tells with quiet assurance this story of a man divided," says Rose Moss in a *World Literature Today* review. The novel "is clearly this writer's major work of fiction and, I suppose, in one sense, an oblique commentary on his own years of exile," observes Charles R. Larson in *World Literature Today.* Moss finds that in his story of a man torn between African tradition and English law, "the timbre of Mphahlele's own vision is not always clear"; nevertheless, the critic admits that "in the main his story presents the confused and wordless heart of his character with unpretentious mastery." "*Chirundu* is that rare breed of fiction—a novel of ideas, and a moving one at that," says Larson. "It has the capacity to involve the reader both intellectually and emotionally." The critic concludes by calling the work "the most satisfying African novel of the past several years."

On the subject of writing, Mphahlele commented: "In Southern Africa, the black writer talks best about the ghetto life he knows; the white writer about his own ghetto life. We see each other, black and white, as it were through a keyhole. Race relations are a major experience and concern for the writer. They are his constant beat. It is unfortunate no one can ever think it is healthy both mentally and physically to keep hacking at the social structure in overcharged language. A language that burns and brands, scorches and scalds. Language that is as a machete with a double edge—the one sharp, the other blunt, the one cutting, the other breaking. And yet there are levels of specifically black drama in the ghettoes that I cannot afford to ignore. I have got to stay with it. I bleed inside. My people bleed. But I must stay with it."

BIOGRAPHICAL/CRITICAL SOURCES:

BOOKS

Barnett, Ursula A., *Ezekiel Mphahlele,* Twayne, 1976.

Contemporary Literary Criticism, Volume 25, Gale, 1983.

Durden, Dennis, editor, *African Writers Talking,* Heinemann, 1972.

Herdeck, Donald E., *African Writers: A Companion to Black African Writing, 1300-1973,* Black Orpheus, 1973.

Lindfors, Bernth, editor, *South African Voices,* African and Afro-American Studies Center, 1975.

Moore, Gerald, *Seven African Writers,* Oxford University Press, 1962.

Moore, Gerald, *The Chosen Tongue,* Longmans, Green, 1969.

Mphahlele, Es'kia, *Afrika My Music: An Autobiography, 1957-1983,* Ravan Press, 1984, Ohio University Press, 1986.

Mphahlele, Ezekiel, *Down Second Avenue,* Faber, 1959.

PERIODICALS

Modern African Studies, March, 1963.
Nation, March 20, 1972.
New Statesman, April 25, 1959.
New York Review of Books, September 23, 1971.
New York Times Book Review, October 22, 1972.
Saturday Review, June 19, 1971.
Times Literary Supplement, August 11, 1961, March 23, 1967, March 10, 1972.
World Literature Today, summer, 1983, winter, 1983, winter, 1987.

* * *

MUHAJIR, Nazzam Al Fitnah
 See El MUHAJIR

* * *

MURRAY, Albert L. 1916-

PERSONAL: Born June 12, 1916, in Nokomis, Ala.; son of John Lee and Sudie (Graham) Young; married Mozelle Menefee, May 31, 1941; children: Michele. *Education:* Tuskegee Institute, B.S., 1939; New York University, M.A., 1948; postgraduate work at University of Michigan, 1940, Northwestern University, 1941, and University of Paris, 1950.

ADDRESSES: Home and office—45 West 132nd St., New York, N.Y. 10037.

CAREER: U.S. Air Force, 1943-62, retired as major. Instructor, Tuskegee Institute, 1940-43, 1946-51, director of College Little Theatre; lecturer, Graduate School of Journalism, Columbia University, 1968; Colgate University, O'Connor Professor of Literature, 1970, O'Connor Lecturer, 1973, professor of humanities, 1982; visiting professor of literature, University of Massachusetts, Boston, 1971; Paul Anthony Brick lecturer, University of Missouri, 1972; writer in residence, Emory University, 1978; adjunct associate professor of creative writing, Barnard College, 1981-83; lecturer and participant in symposia.

MEMBER: PEN International, Authors League of America, Authors Guild, Alpha Phi Alpha.

AWARDS, HONORS: Lillian Smith Award for fiction, 1974, for *Train Whistle Guitar;* Litt.D., Colgate University, 1975; ASCAP Deems Taylor Award for music criticism, 1976, for *Stomping the Blues.*

WRITINGS:

The Omni-Americans: New Perspectives on Black Experience and American Culture (essays), Outerbridge & Dientsfrey, 1970, published as *The Omni-Americans: Some Alternatives to the Folklore of White Supremacy,* Vintage Books, 1983.
South to a Very Old Place, McGraw, 1972.
The Hero and the Blues, University of Missouri Press, 1973.
Train Whistle Guitar (novel), McGraw, 1974.
Stomping the Blues, McGraw, 1976.
(With Count Basie) *Good Morning Blues: The Autobiography of Count Basie,* Random House, 1985.

WORK IN PROGRESS: The Spyglass Tree, a novel.

SIDELIGHTS: "As a writer, [Albert L. Murray] implicitly perceives himself as proceeding in the same fashion as he maintains legendary heroes, early Americans, and black Americans have always proceeded: by conceptualizing their lives out of chaos and against hostile forces," states *Dictionary of Literary Biography* contributor Elizabeth Schultz. Schultz declares that the "abiding concern of [Murray's] writing is the triumph, of Afro-American people, who, despite and, indeed, in Murray's view, because of centuries of difficulties, created a courageous, complex, life-sustaining, and life-enhancing culture—apparent in their language, religion, sports, fashions, food, dance, and above all in their music." Murray articulates these views in his collection of essays *The Omni-Americans: New Perspectives on Black Experience and American Culture,* in which he argues that black Americans have a distinctive identity of their own, developing a unique culture "which allows them to see themselves 'not as the substandard, abnormal *non-white* people of American social science surveys and the news media, but rather as if they were, so to speak, fundamental *extensions* of contemporary possibilities,'" says Schultz. "Like jam session musicians and blues singers," she continues, "they have learned the skills of improvisation, not only translating white models of excellence into their own terms, but also transforming degrading conditions into culture."

Murray expresses an interest in jazz in other works, especially in *The Hero and the Blues* and *Stomping the Blues,* an attempt to redefine "the music and its connotations for American culture," according to Jason Berry of *Nation.* S. M. Fry, writing in *Library Journal,* points out that Murray "views the music not as a primitive musical expression of black suffering but as an antidote to the bad times—active good-time music, music to be danced to, music that because of its substance and talented exponents, has emerged the most significant American music." Murray, the reviewer says, also emphasizes the importance of the performance, "the performing style and the music itself over the lyrics and social or political connotations of the blues as significant factors in its expression as an art." These books have made him "one of the foremost literary interpreters of blues, jazz and improvisation," states Brent Staples in the *New York Times Book Review.*

AVOCATIONAL INTERESTS: Recordings, photography, cookbooks, and gourmet cooking.

BIOGRAPHICAL/CRITICAL SOURCES:

BOOKS

Dictionary of Literary Biography, Volume 38: *Afro-American Writers since 1955: Dramatists and Prose Writers,* Gale, 1985.

PERIODICALS

Chicago Tribune Book World, January 19, 1986.
Library Journal, February 1, 1977.
Los Angeles Times Book Review, March 26, 1986.
Nation, Janaury 15, 1977.
Newsweek, March 23, 1970, January 31, 1972, December 20, 1976.
New Yorker, October 17, 1970, January 8, 1972, July 22, 1974.
New York Review of Books, February 24, 1972, June 18, 1974, January 16, 1986.
New York Times, April 4, 1972, December 11, 1976.
New York Times Book Review, May 3, 1970, January 2, 1972, June 4, 1972, December 3, 1972, May 12, 1974, December 1, 1974, December 26, 1976, December 26, 1982, February 2, 1986.
Rolling Stone, January 13, 1977.

Saturday Review, January 22, 1972.
Time, January 10, 1972, March 10, 1986.
Times Literary Supplement, July 28, 1978, July 11, 1986.
Voice Literary Supplement, February, 1982.
Washington Post Book World, March 22, 1970, December 26, 1971, December 8, 1974, January 8, 1986.

* * *

MURRAY, (Anna) Pauli(ne) 1910-1985

PERSONAL: Born November 20, 1910, in Baltimore, Md. (one source says Durham, N.C.); died of cancer, July 1, 1985, in Pittsburgh, Pa.; daughter of William Henry (a school principal) and Agnes Georgianna (a nurse; maiden name, Fitzgerald) Murray; divorced. *Education:* Hunter College (now of the City University of New York), A.B., 1933; Howard University, LL.B. (cum laude), 1944; University of California (now University of California, Berkeley), LL.M., 1945; Yale University, J.S.D., 1965; General Theological Seminary, M.Div. (cum laude), 1976.

ADDRESSES: Home—Pittsburgh, Pa.

CAREER: Worked at a number of odd jobs, including four years in U.S. Government work relief program Work Projects Administration. Admitted to the Bar of California State, 1945, the Bar of New York State, 1948, and the Bar of the U.S. Supreme Court, 1960; deputy attorney general of California, 1946; American Jewish Congress, New York, N.Y., attorney for commission on law and social action, 1946-47; worked for a time at private practice of law in New York City; Paul, Weiss, Rifkind, Wharton & Garrison (law firm), New York City, associate attorney in litigation department, 1956-60. University of Ghana, near Accra, senior lecturer, 1960-61; Benedict College, Columbia, S.C., vice-president, 1967-68, also served as professor of political science; Brandeis University, Waltham, Mass., professor of American studies, 1968-73, Louis Stulberg Professor of Law and Politics, 1972-73; Boston University, Boston, Mass., lecturer at school of law, 1972. Ordained Episcopal priest, 1977, served churches in Washington, D.C., Baltimore, Md., and Pittsburgh, Pa., retired in 1984.

Co-founder and member of National Organization for Women, 1970-84; director of Beacon Press, 1968-69. Consultant to fourth assembly of World Council of Churches in Uppsala, Sweden, 1968; member of Commission on Ordained and Licensed Ministries, 1969-70. Affiliated with a number of government agencies and civil rights groups, including Presidential Commission on the Status of Women, 1962-63; American Civil Liberties Union, 1965-73; Equal Employment Opportunity Commission, 1966-67; and Martin Luther King, Jr., Center for Non-Violent Social Change, 1970-84.

MEMBER: National Bar Association, American Bar Association (vice-chairperson of committee on women's rights, 1971-73), National Association for the Advancement of Colored People (NAACP; life member), National Association of Women Lawyers, National Council of Negro Women, New York County Bar Association, Hunter College Alumni Association.

AWARDS, HONORS: Recipient of honorary degrees, including LL.D. from Dartmouth College, 1976, D.H.L. from Radcliffe College, 1978, and D.D. from Yale University, 1979; named Woman of the Year by National Council of Negro Women, 1946, and by *Mademoiselle* magazine, 1947; alumni award for distinguished postgraduate achievement in law and

public service from Howard University, 1970; Eleanor Roosevelt award from Professional Women's Caucus, 1971; recipient of first Whitney M. Young, Jr., Memorial Award, 1972; named to Hunter College Hall of Fame, 1973; award for "Exemplary Christian Ministry" from National Institute for Women of Color, 1982; Robert F. Kennedy Book Award and Christopher Award, both 1988, for *Song in a Weary Throat: An American Pilgrimage;* among others.

WRITINGS:

(Editor) *States' Laws on Race and Color,* Woman's Division of Christian Service, Board of Missions and Church Extension, Methodist Church, 1951, supplement (with Verge Lake), 1955.
Proud Shoes: The Story of an American Family (biography), Harper, 1956, new edition, 1978.
(With Leslie Rubin) *The Constitution and Government of Ghana,* Sweet & Maxwell, 1961, 2nd edition, 1964.
Human Rights U.S.A., 1948-1966, Service Center, Board of Missions, Methodist Church, 1967.
Dark Testament, and Other Poems (collection), Silvermine, 1970.
(Contributor) Mary Lou Thompson, editor, *Voices of the New Feminism,* Beacon Press, 1970.
Song in a Weary Throat: An American Pilgrimage (autobiography), Harper, 1987.

Also author of speeches and addresses, including *The Negro Woman in the Quest for Equality,* 1964.

Contributor to journals and other publications, including *Crisis* magazine.

Poetry represented in anthologies, including *The Poetry of Black America,* edited by Arnold Adoff, Macmillan, 1968; *The Poetry of the Negro, 1746-1970,* edited by Langston Hughes and Arna Bontemps, Doubleday, 1970; and *A Rock Against the Wind: Black Love Poems,* edited by Lindsay Patterson, Dodd, 1973.

SIDELIGHTS: For her pioneering efforts in a number of different areas, Pauli Murray is remembered as a woman ahead of her time. As an activist for the civil rights and feminist movements, beginning in the late 1930s, she became a forerunner in the subsequent struggle for racial and sexual equality in the United States. During a period when blacks and women were still restricted from certain educational and professional opportunities, she achieved consecutive goals as an attorney and educator, and in 1977 Murray became the first black woman to be ordained an Episcopal priest. An aspiring writer, she also published a number of books on law as well as a collection of poetry, *Dark Testament, and Other Poems,* and two critically acclaimed personal histories, *Proud Shoes* and *Song in a Weary Throat.* Described as a versatile and determined woman, Murray allegedly maintained that her successive careers followed a logical progression toward eliminating racial and sexist discrimination. Along the way, Murray earned a dual reputation as a "freedom fighter" and a "firebrand." Each of her prodigious achievements "represented a calculated attack on some boundary—of sex, of race—that society had placed in her way," remarked Pat Williams in the *New York Times Book Review.* Similarly, *Detroit News* writer Frances A. Koestler commented that Murray's diverse accomplishments "were dictated by a burning sense that social inequities had to be challenged and overcome."

To some extent Murray's childhood both shaped her character and influenced her ambitions as an adult. Orphaned at the age of three, when her mother died and her father subsequently entered a mental hospital, she grew up in the care of her mother's relatives in Durham, North Carolina. Though sources disagree on whether it was Murray's maternal grandparents or aunts who actually reared her, there is a general consensus of opinion attributing Murray's independent nature and strong sense of pride to that of her appointed guardians. From them she learned of her heterogeneous ancestry that included not only blacks and whites, slaves and slave owners, but Cherokee Indians as well. Like most black Americans of her day who descended from a blend of cultures and races, Murray experienced alienation—feelings of not belonging to any specific group of people. Her mulatto background both prevented her from identifying solely with her African heritage and excluded her from white society. Though proud of her individuality, Murray—who preferred the term "Negro" to the word "black"—sought to discover the origins of her being and thus establish her roots.

In an attempt to recreate her past, Murray wrote *Proud Shoes: The Story of an American Family*. Due to a general lack of interest in its subject matter, however, the book "sank with scarcely a trace" after its initial publication in 1956, reflected *Los Angeles Times* reviewer Robert Kirsch. But with the appearance of an expanded edition in 1978, Murray's biography captured public attention and critical acclaim, eliciting comparisons to Alex Haley's best-selling novel *Roots*. Despite some similarities between the two works, Kirsch observed that Murray's "marvelous and moving family memoir . . . is a very different story." Describing what he thought distinguished Murray's story from Haley's, Jack Hicks wrote in *Nation* that "*Proud Shoes* traps the beast of American slavery" while *Roots* "dwells on African continuations in the black American family." Essentially, Murray's book focuses on the multiple conflicts affecting the progeny of interracial unions, those "unwilling agents of love and animosity" who were trapped between black and white, Hicks commented. According to Nellie McKay in the *Dictionary of Literary Biography*, Murray's *Proud Shoes* represents more than an individual's search for identity; it "embodies the most important elements in the evolution of the contemporary black family" and serves as a microcosm of the total black experience in white America. As such, *Proud Shoes* also qualifies as a slice of U.S. history.

During the course of her personal search for identity, Murray was confronted by questions of equality on the basis of sex and skin color. In particular, she "was awakened to the universal dimensions of the struggle for human dignity by sustained contact with the labor movement," reported Sherley Anne Williams in the *Los Angeles Times Book Review*. With characteristic defiance she challenged various institutions of government, business, education, and finally religion, opposing practices of discrimination and segregation that historically excluded blacks and women. In 1938, for example, Murray "waged a highly publicized battle for admission to" the University of North Carolina at Chapel Hill, related Susan McHenry in *Ms.* Though school officials rejected her application, her efforts forged the path leading to a federal court ruling that ordered the school's integration in 1951. Similarly, Murray was jailed for refusing to sit in the back of a Virginia bus in 1940. She also organized and/or participated in a number of rallies and demonstrations, among them a series of sit-ins aimed at desegregating restaurants and other public places in Washington, D.C. Murray's activism recurrently led to confrontations with the law. In view of this fact, she chose to become

an attorney, convinced "that the law was the fastest route to racial equality," wrote Koestler.

Murray's ongoing crusade against racial and sexual barriers eventually took issue with the U.S. Supreme Court and later with the Episcopal church. Though she proved unsuccessful in her appeal to fill the traditionally male-occupied position of Supreme Court Justice, Murray's initiative again prepared the way for others of her sex. Amid controversy she resolved in 1974 to enter the priesthood, a station the Episcopal church hitherto reserved only for men. In an article for the *New York Times*, Eleanor Blau quoted Murray on her objective: "'I want to be a positive force for reconciliation both in terms of race and . . . sex.'" Three years later Murray became the first woman ordained an Episcopal priest.

Dark Testament, and Other Poems, Murray's 1970 collection, serves as a reflection of her personal and professional encounters. In the words of McKay, the volume is "a poetic mirror of Murray's life and career, and a testament to" the broad expanse of her personal interests. Utilizing her imagination and an array of intense emotion, Murray features a melange of topics that range from philosophic musings and the concerns of racial oppression to themes of love and friendship. Especially noteworthy is the title poem, in which Murray uses symbolism to address specific characteristics of the human mind and will.

Like her volume of poetry, Murray's posthumously published autobiography, *Song in a Weary Throat: An American Pilgrimage*, documents her multifaceted career and exists as a testament to her lifelong quest for personal identity. Even more, it "distinctively recounts the kind of sustained commitment and often unheralded effort that fed into the great civil rights victories," asserted McHenry. Generally, critics viewed Murray's highly acclaimed book as a unique, eloquent, and inspiring piece of work. Reviewing in *Washington Post Book World*, Jonathan Yardley added that *Song in a Weary Throat* is "a splendid book . . . smoothly written, good-humored, passionate, thoughtful. . . . One comes to its powerfully moving final pages utterly convinced that Murray was one of the great Americans of her time."

BIOGRAPHICAL/CRITICAL SOURCES:

BOOKS

Diamonstein, Barbaralee, *Open Secrets: Ninety-four Women in Touch With Our Time*, Viking, 1972.
Dictionary of Literary Biography, Volume 41, *Afro-American Poets Since 1955*, Gale, 1985.

PERIODICALS

Detroit News, April 26, 1987.
Los Angeles Times Book Review, October 6, 1978, May 24, 1987.
Ms., May, 1987.
Nation, December 16, 1978, May 23, 1987.
New York Times, February 11, 1974.
New York Times Book Review, March 29, 1987.
Washington Post Book World, April 5, 1987.

OBITUARIES:

PERIODICALS

New York Times, July 4, 1985.
Washington Post, July 4, 1985.

—*Sketch by Barbara A. Cicchetti*

MYERS, Walter Dean   1937-
(Walter M. Myers)

PERSONAL: Given name Walter Milton Myers; born August 12, 1937, in Martinsburg, W.Va.; son of George Ambrose and Mary (Green) Myers; raised from age three by Herbert Julius (a shipping clerk) and Florence (a factory worker) Dean; married second wife, Constance Brendel, June 19, 1973; children: (first marriage) Karen, Michael Dean; (second marriage) Christopher. *Education:* Attended State College of the City University of New York; Empire State College, B.A.

ADDRESSES: Home—2543 Kennedy Blvd., Jersey City, N.J. 07304.

CAREER: New York State Department of Labor, Brooklyn, employment supervisor, 1966-69; Bobbs-Merrill Co., Inc. (publisher), New York City, senior trade book editor, 1970-77; writer, 1977—. Has also taught creative writing and black history on a part-time basis in New York City, 1974-75. *Military service:* U.S. Army, 1954-57.

MEMBER: PEN, Harlem Writers Guild.

AWARDS, HONORS: Council on Interracial Books for Children Award, 1968, for the manuscript of *Where Does the Day Go?;* Woodward Park School Annual Book Award, 1976, for *Fast Sam, Cool Clyde, and Stuff;* American Library Association "Best Books for Young Adults" citations, 1978, for *It Ain't All for Nothin'*, 1979, for *The Young Landlords*, and 1982, for *Hoops;* Coretta Scott King Awards, 1980, for *The Young Landlords*, and 1984, for *Motown and Didi: A Love Story;* Notable Children's Trade Book in Social Studies citation, 1982, for *The Legend of Tarik.*

WRITINGS:

JUVENILES

(Under name Walter M. Myers) *Where Does the Day Go?*, illustrated by Leo Carty, Parents' Magazine Press, 1969.

The Dragon Takes a Wife, illustrated by Ann Grifalconi, Bobbs-Merrill, 1972.

The Dancers, illustrated by Anne Rockwell, Parents' Magazine Press, 1972.

Fly, Jimmy, Fly!, illustrated by Moneta Barnett, Putnam, 1974.

The World of Work: A Guide to Choosing a Career, Bobbs-Merrill, 1975.

Fast Sam, Cool Clyde, and Stuff, Viking, 1975.

Social Welfare, F. Watts, 1976.

Brainstorm, with photographs by Chuck Freedman, F. Watts, 1977.

Mojo and the Russians, Viking, 1977.

Victory for Jamie, Scholastic Book Services, 1977.

It Ain't All for Nothin', Viking, 1978.

The Young Landlords, Viking, 1979.

The Black Pearl and the Ghost; or, One Mystery after Another, illustrated by Robert Quackenbush, Viking, 1980.

The Golden Serpent, illustrated by Alice Provensen and Martin Provensen, Viking, 1980.

Hoops, Delacorte, 1981.

The Legend of Tarik, Viking, 1981.

Won't Know Till I Get There, Viking, 1982.

The Nicholas Factor, Viking, 1983.

Tales of a Dead King, Morrow, 1983.

Mr. Monkey and the Gotcha Bird, illustrated by Leslie Morrill, Delacorte, 1984.

Motown and Didi: A Love Story, Viking, 1984.

The Outside Shot, Delacorte, 1984.

Sweet Illusions, Teachers & Writers Collaborative, 1986.

Crystal, Viking, 1987.

Shadow of the Red Moon, Harper, 1987.

Fallen Angels, Scholastic, Inc., 1988.

Scorpions, Harper, 1988.

"THE ARROW" SERIES; JUVENILES

Adventure in Granada, Viking, 1985.

The Hidden Shrine, Viking, 1985.

Duel in the Desert, Viking, 1986.

Ambush in the Amazon, Viking, 1986.

CONTRIBUTOR TO ANTHOLOGIES

Orde Coombs, editor, *What We Must See: Young Black Storytellers*, Dodd, 1971.

Sonia Sanchez, editor, *We Be Word Sorcerers: Twenty-five Stories by Black Americans*, Bantam, 1973.

OTHER

Contributor of articles and fiction to periodicals, including *Black Creation, Black World, McCall's, Espionage, Alfred Hitchcock Mystery Magazine, Essence, Ebony Jr.!,* and *Boy's Life.*

SIDELIGHTS: Walter Dean Myers is commonly recognized as one of modern literature's premier authors of fiction for young black people. Two of his novels for teens, *The Young Landlords* and *Motown and Didi: A Love Story*, have won the prestigious Coretta Scott King Award, and his text for the picture book *Where Does the Day Go?* received the Council on Interracial Books for Children Award in 1969. As Carmen Subryan notes in the *Dictionary of Literary Biography*, "Whether he is writing about the ghettos of New York, the remote countries of Africa, or social institutions, Myers captures the essence of the developing experiences of youth."

While Myers is perhaps best known for his novels that explore the lives of young Harlem blacks, he is equally adept at producing modern fairy tales, ghost stories, and adventure sagas. Subryan finds a common theme throughout Myers's far-ranging works. "He is concerned with the development of youths," she writes, "and his message is always the same: young people must face the reality of growing up and must persevere, knowing that they can succeed despite any odds they face. . . . This positive message enables youths to discover what is important in life and to reject influences which could destroy them."

In the *Interracial Books for Children Bulletin*, Myers describes his priorities as an author. He tries, he says, to provide good literature for black children, "literature that includes them and the way they live" and that "celebrates their life and their person. It upholds and gives special place to their humanity." He elaborates on this point in an essay for *Something about the Author Autobiography Series:* "I realized how few resources are available for Black youngsters to open the world to them. I feel the need to show them the possibilities that exist for them that were never revealed to me as a youngster; possibilities that did not even exist for me then."

One possibility Myers never foresaw as a youth was that of supporting himself as a writer. He was born into an impoverished family in Martinsburg, West Virginia, and at age three was adopted by Herbert and Florence Dean, who settled in New York City's Harlem district. Although he wrote poems and stories from his early teens onward and won awards for them, his parents did not encourage his literary talents. "I was from a family of laborers," he remembers in his autobiographical essay, "and the idea of writing stories or essays was far removed from their experience. Writing had no practical value for a Black child. These minor victories [and prizes] did not bolster my ego. Instead, they convinced me that even though I was bright, even though I might have some talent, I was still defined by factors other than my ability." The dawning realization that his possibilities were limited by race and economic status embittered Myers as a teen. "A youngster is not trained to want to be a gasoline station attendant or a clerk in some obscure office," he states. "We are taught to want to be lawyers and doctors and accountants—these professions that are given value. When the compromise comes, as it does early in Harlem to many children, it comes hard."

Myers admits he was not ready to accept that compromise. Through high school and a three-year enlistment in the army, he read avidly and wrote short stories. After his discharge from the service, he worked in a variety of positions, including mail clerk at the post office, interoffice messenger, and interviewer in a factory. None of these tasks pleased him, and when he began to publish poetry, stories and articles in magazines, he cautiously started to consider a writing profession. "When I entered a contest for picture book writers," he claims, "it was more because I wanted to write *anything* than because I wanted to write a picture book."

Myers won the contest, sponsored by the Council on Interracial Books for Children, for his text of *Where Does the Day Go?* In that story, a group of children from several ethnic backgrounds discuss their ideas about night and day with a sensitive and wise black father during a long walk. Inspired by the success of his first attempt to write for young people, Myers turned his attention to producing more picture books. Between 1972 and 1975, he published three: *The Dancers, The Dragon Takes a Wife,* and *Fly, Jimmy, Fly!* Though in more recent years he has concentrated on longer works for older children, Myers continues to write texts for picture books occasionally. In 1980 he released a fable set in India, *The Golden Serpent,* and in 1984 an animal adventure, *Mr. Monkey and the Gotcha Bird.*

Myers accepted an editorial position with the Bobbs-Merrill publishing company in 1970 and worked there until 1977. His seven-year tenure taught him "the book business from another viewpoint," as he puts it in his autobiographical essay. "Publishing is a business," he writes. "It is not a cultural institution. . . . It is *talked* about as if it were a large cultural organization with several branches. One hears pronouncements like 'anything worthwhile will eventually be published.' Nonsense, of course. Books are published for many reasons, the chief of which is profit." In retrospect, however, Myers feels that he has benefitted from his experiences at Bobbs-Merrill, even though he was laid off during a restructuring program. "After the initial disillusionment about the artistic aspects of the job, I realized how foolish I had been in not learning, as a writer, more about the business aspects of my craft," he concludes. Armed with the pragmatic knowledge of how the publishing industry works, Myers has supported himself by his writing alone since 1977.

By the time he left Bobbs-Merrill, Myers had already established a reputation as an able author of fiction for black children, based largely upon his highly successful novels for teens such as *Fast Sam, Cool Clyde, and Stuff* and *Mojo and the Russians.* Both tales feature, in Subryan's words, adventures depicting "the learning experiences of most youths growing up in a big city where negative influences abound." Central to the stories is the concept of close friendships, portrayed as a positive, nurturing influence. Subryan states: "Because of the bonding which occurs among the members of the group, the reader realizes that each individual's potential for survival has increased." Myers followed the two upbeat novels with a serious one, *It Ain't All for Nothin',* that Subryan feels "reflects much of the pain and anguish of ghetto life." The account of a boy caught in a web of parental abuse, conflicting values, and solitary self-assessment, *It Ain't All for Nothin'* "pretties up nothing; not the language, not the circumstances, not the despair," according to Jane Pennington in the *Interracial Books for Children Bulletin.* The story has a positive resolution, however, based on the care and support the central character receives from fellow community members.

Myers strives to present characters for whom urban life is an uplifting experience despite the potentially dangerous influences. In his first Coretta Scott King Award-winner, *The Young Landlords,* several teens learn responsibility when they are given a ghetto apartment building to manage. Lonnie Jackson, the protagonist of *Hoops,* profits from the example of an older friend who has become involved with gamblers. Concerned with stereotyping of a sexual as well as a racial sort, Myers creates plausible female characters and features platonic friendships between the sexes in his works. "The love in *Fast Sam, Cool Clyde, and Stuff* is not between any one couple," writes Alleen Pace Nilsen in the *English Journal.* "Instead it is a sort of a general feeling of good will and concern that exists among a group of inner city kids." Nilsen, among others, also notes that Myers's fiction can appeal to readers of any race. She concludes that he "makes the reader feel so close to the characters that ethnic group identification is secondary." Subryan expresses a similar opinion: "By appealing to the consciousness of young adults, Myers is touching perhaps the most important element of our society. Myers's books demonstrate that writers can not only challenge the minds of black youths but also emphasize the black experience in a nonracist way that benefits all young readers."

Myers writes in the *Something about the Author Autobiography Series* that the reception of his novels gave him a new role as an author. "As my books for teenagers gained in popularity I sensed that my soul-searching for my place in the artistic world was taking on added dimension. As a Black writer I had not only the personal desire to find myself, but the obligation to use my abilities to fill a void." Children and adults, he suggests, "must have role models with which they can identify," and he feels he must "deliver images upon which [they] could build and expand their own worlds." Noting that in his own life he has "acquired the strengths to turn away from disaster," Myers concludes: "As a Black writer, I want to talk about my people. . . . The books come. They pour from me at a great rate. I can't see how any writer can ever stop. There is always one more story to tell, one more person whose life needs to be held up to the sun."

MEDIA ADAPTATIONS: The Young Landlords was filmed by Topol Productions.

BIOGRAPHICAL/CRITICAL SOURCES:

BOOKS

Children's Literature Review, Volume 4, Gale, 1982.
Contemporary Literary Criticism, Volume 35, Gale, 1985.

Dictionary of Literary Biography, Volume 33: *Afro-American Fiction Writers after 1955,* Gale, 1984.

Rush, Theressa G., editor, *Black American Writers: Past and Present,* Scarecrow Press, 1975.

Something about the Author Autobiography Series, Volume 2, Gale, 1986.

PERIODICALS

Ebony, September, 1975.

Interracial Books for Children Bulletin, Volume 10, number 4, 1979, Volume 10, number 6, 1979.

New York Times Book Review, April 9, 1972, May 4, 1975, January 6, 1980, November 9, 1980, July 12, 1981, June 13, 1982.

*   *   *

MYERS, Walter M.
   See MYERS, Walter Dean

N

NAYLOR, Gloria 1950-

PERSONAL: Born January 25, 1950, in New York, N.Y.; daughter of Roosevelt (a transit worker) and Alberta (a telephone operator; maiden name, McAlpin) Naylor. *Education:* Brooklyn College of the City University of New York, B.A., 1981; Yale University, M.A., 1983.

ADDRESSES: Office—c/o Ticknor & Fields, 52 Vanderbilt Ave., New York, N.Y. 10016. *Agent*—Sterling Lord, One Madison Ave., New York, N.Y. 10010.

CAREER: Missionary for Jehovah's Witnesses in New York, North Carolina, and Florida, 1968-75; worked for various hotels in New York, N.Y., including Sheraton City Squire, as telephone operator, 1975-81; writer, 1981—. Writer in residence, Cummington Community of the Arts, 1983; visiting lecturer, George Washington University, 1983-84, and Princeton University, 1986-87; cultural exchange lecturer, United States Information Agency, India, 1985; scholar in residence, University of Pennsylvania, 1986; visiting professor, New York University, 1986, and Boston University, 1987; Fannie Hurst Visiting Professor, Brandeis University, 1988. Senior fellow, Society for the Humanities, Cornell University, 1988.

AWARDS, HONORS: American Book Award for best first novel, 1983, for *The Women of Brewster Place;* Distinguished Writer Award, Mid-Atlantic Writers Association, 1983; National Endowment for the Arts fellowship, 1985; Candace Award, National Coalition of 100 Black Women, 1986; Guggenheim fellowship, 1988.

WRITINGS:

FICTION

The Women of Brewster Place, Viking, 1982.
Linden Hills, Ticknor & Fields, 1985.
Mama Day, Ticknor & Fields, 1988.

NONFICTION

Centennial, Pindar Press, 1986.

OTHER

Also author of unproduced screenplay adaptation of *The Women of Brewster Place,* for American Playhouse, 1984, and of an unproduced original screenplay for Public Broadcasting System's "In Our Own Words," 1985. Contributor of essays and articles to periodicals, including *Southern Review, Essence, Ms., Life, Ontario Review,* and *People.* Contributing editor, *Callaloo,* 1984—; "Hers" columnist for *New York Times,* 1986.

WORK IN PROGRESS: A novel dealing with "whores, language, and music"; a screenplay for Zenith Productions, London.

SIDELIGHTS: "I wanted to become a writer because I felt that my presence as a black woman and my perspective as a woman in general had been underrepresented in American literature," Gloria Naylor commented. Her first novel, *The Women of Brewster Place,* which features a cast of seven strong-willed black women, won the American Book Award for best first fiction in 1983. Naylor has continued her exploration of the black female experience in two subsequent novels that remain focused on women while also expanding her fictional realm. In *Linden Hills,* for example, Naylor uses the structure of Dante's *Inferno* to create a contemporary allegory about the perils of black materialism and the ways in which denying one's heritage can endanger the soul. Naylor's third novel, *Mama Day,* draws on another literary masterpiece—Shakespeare's *Tempest*—and artfully combines Shakespearean elements with black folkloric strains. By drawing on traditional western sources, Naylor places herself firmly in the literary mainstream, broadening her base from ethnic to American writing. Unhappy with what she calls the "historical tendency to look upon the output of black writers as not really American literature," Naylor told *Publishers Weekly* interviewer William Goldstein that her work attempts to "articulate experiences that want articulating—for those readers who reflect the subject matter, black readers, and for those who don't—basically white middle class readers."

Naylor's first novel grew out of a desire to reflect the diversity of the black experience—a diversity that she feels neither the black nor the white critical establishment has recognized. "There has been a tendency on the part of both," she commented, "to assume that a black writer's work should be 'definitive' of black experience. This type of critical stance denies the vast complexity of black existence, even if we were to limit that existence solely to America. While *The Women of Brewster Place* is about the black woman's condition in America, I had to deal with the fact that one composite picture couldn't do justice to the complexity of the black female experience. So I tried to solve this problem by creating a microcosm on a dead-end street and devoting each chapter to a different woman's life. These women vary in age, personal background, political consciousness, and sexual preference. What they do share is a common oppression and, more importantly, a spiritual strength and sense of female communion that I believe all women have employed historically for their psychic health and survival.''

Reviewing *The Women of Brewster Place* in the *Washington Post*, Deirdre Donahue writes: ''Naylor is not afraid to grapple with life's big subjects: sex, birth, love, death, grief. Her women feel deeply, and she unflinchingly transcribes their emotions.... Naylor's potency wells up from her language. With prose as rich as poetry, a passage will suddenly take off and sing like a spiritual.... Vibrating with undisguised emotion, 'The Women of Brewster Place' springs from the same roots that produced the blues. Like them, her book sings of sorrows proudly borne by black women in America.''

To date, Naylor has linked her novels by carrying over characters from one narrative to another. In *The Women of Brewster Place,* one of the young residents is a refugee from Linden Hills, an exclusive black suburb. Naylor's second novel spotlights that affluent community, revealing the material corruption and moral decay that would prompt an idealistic young woman to abandon her home for a derelict urban neighborhood. Though *Linden Hills,* as the book is called, approaches the Afro-American experience from the upper end of the socioeconomic spectrum, it is also a black microcosm. This book ''forms the second panel of that picture of contemporary urban black life which Naylor started with in *Women of Brewster Place,*'' writes *Times Literary Supplement* contributor Roz Kaveney. ''Where that book described the faults, passions, and culture of the good poor, this shows the nullity of black lives that are led in imitation of suburban whites.''

In addition to shifting her focus, Naylor has also raised her literary sights in her second novel. *Linden Hills,* which has been described as a contemporary allegory with gothic overtones, is an ambitious undertaking structurally modeled after Dante Alighiere's *Inferno.* Among its many accomplishments, Dante's Italian masterpiece describes the nine circles of hell, Satan's imprisonment in their depths, and the lost souls condemned to suffer with him. In Naylor's modern version, ''souls are damned not because they have offended God or have violated a religious system but because they have offended themselves. In their single-minded pursuit of upward mobility, the inhabitants of Linden Hill, a black, middle-class suburb, have turned away from their past and from their deepest sense of who they are,'' writes Catherine C. Ward in *Contemporary Literature.* To correspond to Dante's circles, Naylor uses a series of crescent-shaped drives that ring the suburban development. Her heroes are two young street poets—outsiders from a neighboring community who hire themselves out to do odd jobs so they can earn Christmas money. ''As they move down the hill, what they encounter are people who have 'moved up' in American society... until eventually they will hit the center of their community and the home of my equivalent of Satan,'' Naylor told Goldstein. Naylor's Satan is one Luther Needed, a combination mortician and real estate tycoon, who preys on the residents' baser ambitions to keep them in his sway.

Though *Women's Review of Books* contributor Jewelle Gomez argues that ''the Inferno motif... often feels like a literary exercise rather than a groundbreaking adaptation,'' most critics commend Naylor's bold experiment. *San Francisco Review*

of Books contributor Claudia Tate, for instance, praises ''Naylor's skill in linking together complicated stories in a highly structured but unobtrusive narrative form. In combining elements of realism and fantasy with a sequence of ironic reversals, she sets into motion a series of symbols which become interlinked, producing complex social commentary. For example, the single ambition for residents of Linden Hills is to advance economically, but in order to achieve this end they must sacrifice the possibility of emotional and personal fulfillment. When the goal is attained, they measure their success by reversing the expected movement in social climbing.''

Even those who find the execution flawed endorse Naylor's daring. Says *New York Times Book Review* contributor Mel Watkins: ''Although Miss Naylor has not been completely successful in adapting the 'Inferno' to the world of the black middle class, in 'Linden Hills' she has shown a willingness to expand her fictional realm and to take risks. Its flaws notwithstanding, the novel's ominous atmosphere and inspired set pieces... make it a fascinating departure for Miss Naylor, as well as a provocative, iconoclastic novel about a seldom-addressed subject.'' Concludes the *Ms.* reviewer, ''In this second novel, Naylor serves notice that she is a mature literary talent of formidable skill.''

Naylor's third novel, *Mama Day,* is named for its main character—a wise old woman with magical powers whose name is Miranda Day, but whom everyone refers to as Mama Day. This ninety-year-old conjurer made a walk-on appearance in *Linden Hills* as the illiterate, toothless aunt who hauls about cheap cardboard suitcases and leaky jars of preserves. But it is in *Mama Day* that this ''caster of hoodoo spells... comes into her own,'' according to *New York Times Book Review* contributor Bharati Mukherjee. ''The portrait of Mama Day is magnificent,'' she declares.

Mama Day lives on Willow Springs, a wondrous island off the coast of Georgia and South Carolina that has been owned by her family since before the Civil War. The fact that slaves are portrayed as property owners demonstrates one of the ways that Naylor turns the world upside down, according to Rita Mae Brown. Another, continues Brown in her *Los Angeles Times Book Review,* is ''that the women possess the real power, and are acknowledged as having it.'' When Mama Day's grand niece Cocoa brings George, her citified new husband, to Willow Springs, he learns the importance of accepting mystery. ''George is the linchpin of 'Mama Day,''' Brown says. ''His rational mind allows the reader to experience the island as George experiences it. Mama Day and Cocoa are of the island and therefore less immediately accessible to the reader. The turning point comes when George is asked not only to believe in Mama Day's power but to act on it. Cocoa is desperately ill. A hurricane has washed out the bridge so that no mainland doctor can be summoned.'' Only Mama Day has the power to help George save her life. She gives him a task, which he bungles because he is still limited by purely rational thinking. Ultimately, George is able to save Cocoa, but only by great personal sacrifice.

The plot twists and thematic concerns of *Mama Day* have led several reviewers to compare the work to Shakespeare. ''Whereas 'Linden Hills' was Dantesque, 'Mama Day' is Shakespearean, with allusions, however oblique and tangential, to 'Hamlet,' 'King Lear,' and, especially, 'The Tempest,''' writes Chicago *Tribune Books* critic John Blades. ''Like Shakespeare's fantasy, Naylor's book takes place on an enchanted island.... Naylor reinforces her Shakespearean connection by naming her heroine Miranda." Mukherjee also believes that *Mama Day* "has its roots in 'The Tempest.' The theme is reconciliation, the title character is Miranda (also the name of Prospero's daughter), and Willow Springs is an isolated island where, as on Prospero's isle, magical and mysterious events come to pass."

Naylor's ambitious attempt to elevate a modern love story to Shakespearean heights "is more bewildering than bewitching," according to Blades. "Naylor has populated her magic kingdom with some appealingly offbeat characters, Mama Day foremost among them. But she's failed to give them anything very original or interesting to do." Mukherjee also acknowledges the shortcomings of Naylor's mythical love story, but asserts "I'd rather dwell on *Mama Day*'s strengths. Gloria Naylor has written a big, strong, dense, admirable novel; spacious, sometimes a little drafty like all public monuments, designed to last and intended for many levels of use."

BIOGRAPHICAL/CRITICAL SOURCES:

BOOKS

Contemporary Literary Criticism, Volume 28, Gale, 1984.

PERIODICALS

Chicago Tribune Book World, February 23, 1983.
Christian Science Monitor, March 1, 1985.
Commonweal, May 3, 1985.
Contemporary Literature, Volume XXVIII, number 1, 1987.
Detroit News, March 3, 1985, February 21, 1988.
Los Angeles Times, December 2, 1982.
Los Angeles Times Book Review, February 24, 1985, March 6, 1988.
London Review of Books, August 1, 1985.
Ms., June, 1985.
New Republic, September 6, 1982.
New York Times, February 9, 1985.
New York Times Book Review, August 22, 1982, March 3, 1985, February 21, 1988.
Publishers Weekly, September 9, 1983.
San Francisco Review of Books, May, 1985.
Times (London), April 21, 1983.
Times Literary Supplement, May 24, 1985.
Tribune Books (Chicago), January 31, 1988.
Washington Post, October 21, 1983.
Washington Post Book World, March 24, 1985, February 28, 1988.
Women's Review of Books, August, 1985.

—*Sketch by Donna Olendorf*

*   *   *

NEAL, Larry
    See NEAL, Lawrence P.

*   *   *

NEAL, Lawrence P.   1937-1981
    (Larry Neal)

PERSONAL: Born September 5, 1937, in Atlanta, Ga.; died of a heart attack, January 6, 1981, in Hamilton, N.Y.; son of Woodie and Maggie Neal; married Evelyn Rodgers (a chemist) in 1965; children: Avatar. *Education:* Lincoln University, B.A., 1961; University of Pennsylvania, M.A., 1963. *Politics:* Black Nationalist. *Religion:* Yoruba.

ADDRESSES: Home—Manhattan, N.Y.

CAREER: Writer. City College (now of the City University of New York), New York, N.Y., instructor in English, 1968-69; Wesleyan University, Middleton, Conn., writer-in-residence, 1969-70; Yale University, New Haven, Conn., fellow, 1970-75. Executive director of the District of Columbia Commission on the Arts and Humanities, 1976-78; education director of Panther Party.

AWARDS, HONORS: Guggenheim fellowship, 1971; Before Columbus Book Award, 1982.

WRITINGS—Under name Larry Neal:

BOOKS

(Editor with LeRoi Jones) *Black Fire: An Anthology of Afro-American Writing*, Morrow, 1968.
Black Boogaloo: Notes on Black Liberation, Journal of Black Poetry Press, 1969.
(With Imamu Baraka and A. B. Spellman) *Trippin': A Need for Change*, New Ark, 1969.
Hoodoo Hollerin' Bebop Ghosts, Howard University Press, 1971.

Also author of *Analytical Study of Afro-American Culture*, 1977.

OTHER

"Lenox Avenue Sunday" (television script), for Columbia Broadcasting System, 1966.
"Deep River" (television script), for American Broadcasting Companies, 1967.
Holler S.O.S. (screenplay), Johns Hopkins University, 1971.
Moving On Up (screenplay), A. Philip Randolph Institute, 1973.
"The Glorious Monster in the Bell of the Horn" (play), first produced in New York City at Frank Silvera's Writers Workshop, 1976, produced Off-Broadway at New Federal Theater, July, 1979.
"In an Upstate Motel" (play), first produced in New York City at St. Mark's Playhouse, 1981.

Work represented in many anthologies, including *Soulscript: Afro-American Poetry*, edited by June Jordan, Doubleday, 1970; *The Black Poets*, edited by Dudley Randall, Bantam, 1971; and *New Black Voices*, edited by Abraham Chapman, New American Library, 1972.

Contributor to periodicals, including *Black Dialogue, Cheyney Review, Drama Review, Journal of Black Poetry, Pride, Ebony, Essence, Liberation, Negro Digest*, and *New York Times*. Art editor of *Liberator*, 1964-66; co-editor of *Cricket* and editor of *Pride*.

SIDELIGHTS: Larry Neal's writings reflect his concern and interest in the black arts movement, which he described as "primarily concerned with the cultural and spiritual liberation of Black America." Neal wrote that the literature of the movement was not "protest literature," which he said was "a plea to white America for . . . human dignity," but literature for the black community. "We must address each other," the author stated. "We must touch each other's beauty, wonder, and pain." Neal believed black writers "carry the past and future memory of the race, of the Nation. They represent our various identities. They link us to the dependent, more profound aspects of our ancestry." He declared: "We are black writers, . . . the bearers of the ancient tribal tradition."

Black Fire: An Anthology of Afro-American Writing was described by Peter Berek in *Saturday Review* as "a polemic anthology of essays, poems, stories, and plays by some seventy contemporary Afro-American writers, and the editors [Neal and LeRoi Jones], by implication, set for themselves and their authors an enormous and revolutionary task: both to define a black esthetic and to illustrate scope and vitality.''

''The Glorious Monster in the Bell of the Horn,'' which opened Off-Broadway in July of 1979, ''is complex and often obscure,'' judged Richard Eder in the *New York Times,* ''but a formidable beauty and wit come through it.'' Set in Philadelphia at the end of World War II, the play ''is a layered exploration of the conscious and subconscious development of several black people,'' Eder explained. The reviewer praised the dialogue between the members of different social classes as ''one of many samples of Mr. Neal's splendid writing.''

BIOGRAPHICAL/CRITICAL SOURCES:

BOOKS

Bigsby, C. W. E., editor, *The Black American Writer,* Volume II: *Poetry and Drama,* Everett/Edwards, 1969.
Dictionary of Literary Biography, Volume 38: *Afro-American Writers after 1955: Dramatists and Prose Writers,* Gale, 1985.
Neal, Larry and LeRoi Jones, editors, *Black Fire: An Anthology of Afro-American Writing,* Morrow, 1968.

PERIODICALS

Ebony, August, 1969.
Negro Digest (now *Black World*), January, 1968.
New York Times, July 11, 1979, April 16, 1981.
Saturday Review, November 30, 1968.

OBITUARIES:

PERIODICALS

AB Bookman's Weekly, January 26, 1981.
New York Times, January 9, 1981.
Washington Post, January 12, 1981.

*   *   *

NELSON, Alice Ruth Moore Dunbar   1875-1935
(Alice Dunbar, Alice Moore Dunbar, Alice Dunbar-Nelson, Alice Moore Dunbar-Nelson, Alice Ruth Moore)

PERSONAL: Born July 19, 1875, in New Orleans, La.; died September 18, 1935, in Philadelphia, Pa.; daughter of Joseph (a seaman) and Patricia (a seamstress; maiden name, Wright) Moore; married Paul Laurence Dunbar (a writer), March 8, 1898 (separated, 1902; died, 1906); married Henry Arthur Callis (a teacher), January, 1910 (divorced, 1911); married Robert J. Nelson (a journalist), April, 1916. *Education:* Attended Straight University, c. 1890; Cornell University, M.A.; postgraduate study at Pennsylvania School of Industrial Art and University of Pennsylvania.

CAREER: Writer. Worked as a teacher at schools in New Orleans, La., 1892-96, New York City, 1897, and Wilmington, Del., 1902-20, and at various black colleges. Co-founder of White Rose Mission (became White Rose House for Girls), in New York City, and of Industrial School for Colored Girls in Delaware; volunteer worker for Circle for Negro War Relief, 1918; member of field staff of Women's Committee on the Council of Defense; also member of Delaware's State Republican Committee, 1920; executive secretary for American Friends Interracial Peace Committee, 1928-31.

WRITINGS:

(Under name Alice Ruth Moore) *Violets, and Other Tales,* Monthly Review Press, 1895.
(Under name Alice Dunbar) *The Goodness of St. Rocque, and Other Stories,* Dodd, 1899.
(Editor, under name Alice Moore Dunbar) *Masterpieces of Negro Eloquence: The Best Speeches Delivered by the Negro From the Days of Slavery to the Present Time,* Douglass, 1914.
(Editor and contributor, under name Alice Moore Dunbar-Nelson) *The Dunbar Speaker and Entertainer,* J. L. Nichols, 1920.
(Under name Alice Dunbar-Nelson) *Give Us Each Day: The Diary of Alice Dunbar-Nelson,* edited and with introduction by Gloria T. Hull, Norton, 1984.

Work represented in anthologies, including *Negro Poets and Their Poems,* edited by Robert T. Kerlin, Associated Publishers, 1923, and *Caroling Dusk,* edited by Countee Cullen, Harper, 1927.

Author of unpublished novels ''This Lofty Oak'' and ''Confessions of a Lazy Woman.''

Author—probably under name Alice Moore Dunbar-Nelson— of column ''Une Femme dit'' in *Pittsburgh Courier,* 1926 and 1930, and of column ''As in a Looking Glass'' in *Washington Eagle,* 1926-30.

Contributor, often under name variations, to periodicals, including *A.M.E. Church Review, Crisis, Daily Crusader, Education,* Wilmington *Journal Every Evening, Journal of Negro History, Leslie's Weekly, Messenger, Saturday Evening Mail, Smart Set, Southern Workman,* and *Opportunity.* Founder and co-editor of *Wilmington Weekly,* 1920.

SIDELIGHTS: Alice Ruth Moore Dunbar Nelson was probably the first black woman to distinguish herself in American literature. She was a versatile writer who produced short stories, poems, and a wide range of criticism, and she was also a staunch supporter of black rights, devoting herself—both in public and private—to furthering the causes of racial equality and world peace. Nelson is thus considered an important figure not only for her literary achievements but for her work in sociopolitical forums. It is her impressive array of accomplishments and efforts that has prompted writers such as *Ms.* reviewer Carolyn Heilbrun to hail her as ''gifted and ambitious.''

Nelson was born Alice Ruth Moore in 1875. In New Orleans she readily distinguished herself scholastically, and by age fifteen she had enrolled at the city's Straight University. There she trained for a teaching career but also studied nursing and stenography. In addition she played in local music groups— classical and popular—and edited the women's page of a black fraternity publication. Many of her experiences and observations inspired her first work, *Violets, and Other Tales,* which she published in 1895 after commencing her teaching career in New Orleans.

Violets, and Other Tales, which contains poems and essays in addition to short stories, at times focuses on the melancholic aspects of life and love. In the title story, a young woman gives her beloved a bouquet of violets and dies soon afterward. Later her married sweetheart happens upon the flowers but is unable to recall how he obtained them, whereupon his unsympathetic wife pitches the withered flowers into the fireplace flames. Also notable, though less characteristic of the collection, is "The Woman," an engaging essay supporting female independence and women's careers.

Soon after the publication of *Violets, and Other Tales* Nelson moved to Massachusetts with her family. She then began corresponding with Paul Laurence Dunbar, an increasingly famous writer who had reportedly become infatuated with Nelson upon spotting her photograph in a Boston periodical. Nelson and Dunbar corresponded for two years before actually meeting in early 1897 as he prepared to undertake a reading tour of England. They became formally engaged during their brief encounter and secretly wed the next spring. In the interim Nelson taught in New York City and helped establish its White Rose Mission in Harlem.

While married to Dunbar, Nelson completed *The Goodness of St. Rocque, and Other Stories,* fourteen tales of Creole life in New Orleans. The collection is remembered for its vivid portraits of admirable individuals overcoming unfavorable circumstances. Among the noteworthy tales in the volume is the title work, in which a Creole woman resorts to both voodoo and Catholic ritual in an ultimately successful attempt to regain the love of a dashing fellow.

In 1902 Nelson and Dunbar separated. Nelson then traveled to Delaware and began teaching at both high school and college levels. For the next eighteen years Nelson lived and taught in Delaware. Dunbar died in 1906, and four years later Nelson married a fellow teacher. That marriage ended in 1911, however, and five years later she married again, this time to journalist Robert J. Nelson, with whom she remained for the rest of her life.

During this often turbulent period Nelson continued her literary career. She contributed short stories and poems to various periodicals and edited the volumes *Masterpieces of Negro Eloquence* and *The Dunbar Speaker and Entertainer,* which were principally intended for students. Included in the latter are some of her own writings, notably "I Sit and Sew," a poem in which she expressed her irritation at the general denigration of women's potential for contribution during the years of World War I. Dissatisfied with merely complaining, Nelson demonstrated her own usefulness by serving with the Circle of Negro War Relief in 1918 and then joining the Women's Commission on the Council of Defense, through which she organized relief efforts by black women in Southern states.

In the 1920s Nelson increased her involvement in social causes and politics. She supervised the activities of black women in Delaware's State Republican Committee in 1920 and executed similar responsibilities for the Democratic Party in New York City four years later. Toward the close of the decade she also served as executive secretary for the American Friends Interracial Peace Committee. But even during this period of political involvement she continued her writing career by appearing as a columnist in the *Pittsburgh Courier* and the *Washington Eagle* and by publishing poems and stories in periodicals such as the *Messenger* and *Crisis.* Her productivity remained steady until the end of the 1920s, when she published only one article in 1928 and another one in 1929. A 1932 article for Wilmington's *Journal Every Evening* became her only piece from that decade. She died three years later.

Although Nelson is sometimes considered merely a peripheral figure in the Harlem Renaissance of black literature, she is nonetheless esteemed for her daring advocacy of equal rights for women and blacks and for the consistently high quality of her poetry and prose. The distinguishing aspects—simplicity, precision, incisiveness—of her fiction and essays were also evident in her posthumously published *Give Us Each Day: The Diary of Alice Dunbar-Nelson.* Brent Staples, writing in the *New York Times Book Review,* recommended the diary for its insights into both the suffrage and black rights movements, observing that the work "lets us inside what was then a thriving national network of black women's social groups." Staples also contended that throughout the diary Nelson maintains "an entertaining haughtiness" that seemed essential to her self-esteem. He called the posthumous work "a valuable contribution to women's letters."

BIOGRAPHICAL/CRITICAL SOURCES:

BOOKS

Bone, Robert, *Down Home: A History of Afro-American Short Fiction From Its Beginnings to the End of the Harlem Renaissance,* Putnam, 1975.
Brawley, Benjamin, *Paul Laurence Dunbar: Poet of His People,* University of North Carolina Press, 1936.
Dictionary of Literary Biography, Volume 50: *Afro-American Writers From the Harlem Renaissance to 1940,* Gale, 1987.
Dunbar-Nelson, Alice, *Give Us Each Day: The Diary of Alice Dunbar-Nelson,* edited and with introduction by Gloria T. Hull, Norton, 1985.

PERIODICALS

CLA Journal, March, 1976.
Ms., June, 1985.
New York Times Book Review, April 14, 1985.

—Sketch by Les Stone

*   *   *

NGUGI, James T(hiong'o)
See NGUGI wa Thiong'o

*   *   *

NGUGI wa Thiong'o   1938-
(James T[hiong'o] Ngugi)

PERSONAL: Original name, James Thiong'o Ngugi; born January 5, 1938, in Limuru, Kenya; married; children: five. *Education:* Makerere University, B.A., 1963; University of Leeds, B.A., 1964.

ADDRESSES: c/o William Heinemann Ltd., 15 Queen St., London W1X 8BE, England.

CAREER: Teacher in East African schools, 1964-70; Northwestern University, Evanston, Ill., visiting lecturer, 1970-71; senior lecturer and chairman of department of literature at University of Nairobi, Kenya.

AWARDS, HONORS: Recipient of awards from the 1965 Dakar Festival of Negro Arts and the East African Literature Bureau, both for *Weep Not, Child.*

WRITINGS:

Homecoming: Essays on African and Caribbean Literature, Culture, and Politics, Heinemann, 1972, Lawrence Hill, 1973.
Secret Lives, and Other Stories, Heinemann Educational, 1974, Lawrence Hill, 1975.
Petals of Blood (novel), Heinemann Educational, 1977.

(With Micere Githae Mugo) *The Trial of Dedan Kimathi*, Heinemann Educational, 1977, Swahili translation by the authors published as *Mzalendo kimathi*, c. 1978.

Mtawa Mweusi, Heinemann, 1978.

Caitaani mutharaba-ini, Heinemann Educational, 1980, translation by the author published as *Devil on the Cross*, Zimbabwe Publishing, 1983.

Writers in Politics: Essays, Heinemann, 1981.

Detained: A Writer's Prison Diary, Heinemann, 1981.

Njamba Nene na mbaathi i mathagu, Heinemann Educational, 1982.

(Co-author and translator with Ngugi wa Mirii) *I Will Marry When I Want* (play), Heinemann, 1982.

Barrel of a Pen: Resistance to Repression in Neo-Colonial Kenya, New Beacon, 1983.

Decolonising the Mind: The Politics of Language in African Literature, Heinemann, 1986.

UNDER NAME JAMES T. NGUGI

The Black Hermit (play; first produced in Nairobi in 1962), Mekerere University Press, 1963, Humanities, 1968.

Weep Not, Child (novel), introduction and notes by Ime Ikeddeh, Heinemann, 1964, P. Collier, 1969.

The River Between (novel), Humanities, 1965.

A Grain of Wheat (novel), Heinemann, 1967, 2nd edition, Humanities, 1968.

This Time Tomorrow (play; includes "The Reels" and "The Wound in the Heart"; produced and broadcast in 1966), East African Literature Bureau, 1970.

CONTRIBUTOR TO ANTHOLOGIES

E. A. Komey and Ezekiel Mphahlele, editors, *Modern African Short Stories*, Faber, 1964.

W. H. Whiteley, editor, *A Selection of African Prose*, Oxford University Press, 1964.

Neville Denny, editor, *Pan African Short Stories*, Nelson, 1965.

Oscar Ronald Dathorne and Willfried Feuser, editors, *Africa in Prose*, Penguin, 1969.

OTHER

Contributor of stories to *Transition* and *Kenya Weekly News*. Editor of *Zuka* and *Sunday Nation* (Nairobi).

SIDELIGHTS: Novelist, dramatist, essayist, and literary critic Ngugi wa Thiong'o is East Africa's most prominent writer. Known to many simply as Ngugi, he has been described by Shatto Arthur Gakwandi in *The Novel and Contemporary Experience in Africa* as a "novelist of the people," for his works show his concern for the inhabitants of his native country, Kenya, who have been oppressed and exploited by colonialism, Christianity, and in recent years, by black politicians and businessmen. As *Africa Today* contributor D. Salituma Wamalwa observes: "Ngugi's approach to literature is one firmly rooted in the historical experience of the writer and his or her people, in an understanding of society as it is and a vision of society as it might be."

Throughout his career as a writer and professor, Ngugi has worked to free himself and his compatriots from the effects of colonialism, Christianity, and other non-African influences. In the late 1960s, for example, Ngugi and several colleagues at the University of Nairobi successfully convinced school officials to transform the English Department into the Department of African Languages and Literature. Shortly thereafter Ngugi renounced his Christian name, James, citing Christianity's ties to colonialism. He took in its place his name in Gikuyu (or

Kikuyu), the dominant language of Kenya. Ngugi strengthened his commitment to the Kenyan culture in 1977, when he declared his intention to write only in Gikuyu or Swahili, not English. In response to a query posed in an interview for *Journal of Commonwealth Literature* concerning this decision, Ngugi stated: "Language is a carrier of a people's culture, culture is a carrier of a people's values; values are the basis of a people's self-definition—the basis of their consciousness. And when you destroy a people's language, you are destroying that very important aspect of their heritage . . . you are in fact destroying that which helps them to define themselves . . . that which embodies their collective memory as a people."

Ngugi's determination to write in Gikuyu, combined with his outspoken criticisms of both British and Kenyan rule, have posed threats to his security. In 1977 Ngugi's home was searched by Kenyan police, who confiscated nearly one hundred books, then arrested and imprisoned Ngugi without a trial. At the time of his arrest, Ngugi's play *Ngaahika Ndena* ("I Will Marry When I Want"), co-authored with Ngugi wa Mirii, had recently been banned on the grounds of being "too provocative," according to *American Book Review* contributor Henry Indangasi; in addition, his novel *Petals of Blood*, a searing indictment of the Kenyan government, had just been published in England. Although Ngugi was released from prison a year later, his imprisonment cost him his professorship at the University of Nairobi. When his theatre group was banned by Kenyan officials in 1982, Ngugi, fearing further reprisals, left his country for a self-imposed exile in London.

Ngugi chronicles his prison experience in *Detained: A Writer's Prison Diary*, and expresses his political views in other nonfiction works such as *Barrel of a Pen: Resistance to Repression in Neo-Colonial Kenya*. He has received the most critical attention, however, for his fiction, particularly his novels. Ngugi's first novel *Weep Not, Child* deals with the Mau Mau rebellion against the British administration in the 1950s, and his third novel *A Grain of Wheat* concerns the aftermath of the war and its effects on Kenya's people. Although critics describe the first novel as somewhat stylistically immature, many comment favorably on the universality of its theme of the reactions of people to the stresses and horrors of war and to the inevitable changes brought to bear on their lives.

In contrast, several reviewers believe that *A Grain of Wheat* fulfills the promise of Ngugi's first novel. *A Grain of Wheat* portrays four characters who reflect upon the events of the Mau Mau rebellion and its consequences as they await the day of Kenyan independence, December 12, 1963. G. D. Killam explains in his book *An Introduction to the Writings of Ngugi*: "Uhuru Day, the day when independence from the colonial power is achieved, has been the dream of each of these figures from their schooldays. But there is little joyousness in their lives as they recall over the four days their experiences of the war and its aftermath."

In their book *Ngugi wa Thiong'o: An Exploration of His Writings*, David Cook and Michael Okenimkpe praise the "almost perfectly controlled form and texture" of *A Grain of Wheat*. Killam comments: "*A Grain of Wheat* is the work of a writer more mature than when he wrote his first two books. . . . In *A Grain of Wheat* [Ngugi] takes us into the minds of his characters, sensibilities resonant with ambiguities and contradictions, and causes us to feel what they feel, to share in significant measure their hopes and fears and pain." Shatto Arthur Gakwandi similarly observes in *The Novel and Contemporary Experience in Africa:* "The general tone of *A Grain of Wheat* is one of bitterness and anger. The painful memories of Mau Mau violence still overhang the Kikuyu villages as the attainment of independence fails to bring the cherished social dreams.'' Gakwandi adds: ''While the novel speaks against the harshness of colonial oppression, it is equally bitter against the new leaders of Kenya who are neglecting the interests of the peasant masses who were the people who made the greatest sacrifices during the war of liberation. Ngugi speaks on behalf of those who, in his view, have been neglected by the new government.''

Petals of Blood, Ngugi's fourth novel, is considered his most ambitious and representative work. Like *A Grain of Wheat*, *Petals of Blood* describes the disillusionment of the common people in post-independence Kenya. Killam notes, however, that in *Petals of Blood* Ngugi ''widens and deepens his treatment of themes which he has narrated and dramatized before— themes related to education, both formal and informal; religion, both Christian and customary; the alienation of the land viewed from the historical point of view and as a process which continues in the present; the struggle for independence and the price paid to achieve it.'' *Petals of Blood* is also described as Ngugi's most overtly political novel. A *West Africa* contributor notes an ideological shift in the novel ''from the earlier emphasis on nationalism and race questions to a class analysis of society.'' Critics cite in particular the influence of both Karl Marx and Frantz Fanon, the latter of whom, according to Killam, ''places the thinking of Marx in the African context.'' In *World Literature Written in English* Govind Narian Sharma comments: ''Whereas traditional religious and moral thought has attributed exploitation and injustice in the world to human wickedness and folly, Ngugi, analyzing the situation in Marxist terms, explains these as 'the effect of laws of social development which make it inevitable that at a certain stage of history one class, pursuing its interests with varying degrees of rationality, should dispossess and exploit another.' ''

Petals of Blood concerns four principle characters, all being held on suspicion of murder: Karega, a teacher and labor organizer; Munira, headmaster of a public school in the town of Ilmorog; Abdulla, a half-Indian shopkeeper who was once a guerrilla fighter during the war for independence; and Wanja, a barmaid and former prostitute. ''Through these four [characters],'' writes Civia Tamarkin in the *Chicago Tribune Book World*, ''Ngugi tells a haunting tale of lost hopes and soured dreams, raising the simple voice of humanity against the perversity of its condition.'' *American Book Review* contributor Henry Indangasi describes *Petals of Blood* this way: ''Through numerous flashbacks, and flashbacks within flashbacks, and lengthy confessions, a psychologically credible picture of the characters, and a vast canvas of Kenya's history is unfolded.''

Several reviewers note that Ngugi's emphasis on the economic and political conditions in Kenya at times overshadows his narrative. The *West Africa* contributor explains: ''*Petals of Blood* is not so much a novel as an attempt to think aloud about the problems of modern Kenya: the sharp contrast between the city and the countryside, between the 'ill-gotten' wealth of the new African middle-class and the worsening plight of the unemployed workers and peasants.'' Charles R. Larson expresses a like opinion in *World Literature Today*: ''*Petals of Blood* is not so much about these four characters (as fascinating and as skillfully drawn as they are) as it is about political unrest in post-independence Kenya, and what Ngugi considers the failures of the new black elite (politicians and businessmen) to live up to the pre-independence expectations.'' Foreshadowing Ngugi's 1977 arrest, Larson con-

cludes, ''In this sense *Petals of Blood* is a bold venture— perhaps a risky one—since it is obvious that the author's criticisms of his country's new ruling class will not go unnoticed.''

Critics also maintain that this emphasis lends a didactic tone to the novel. Larson, for instance, comments in the *New York Times Book Review*: ''The weakness of Ngugi's novel as a work of the creative imagination ultimately lies in the author's somewhat dated Marxism: revolt of the masses, elimination of the black bourgeois; capitalism to be replaced with African socialism. The author's didacticism weakens what would otherwise have been his finest work.'' *New Yorker* contributor John Updike similarly observes that ''the characters . . . stagger and sink under the politico-symbolical message they are made to carry.'' *World Literature Today* contributor Andrew Salkey, on the other hand, offers this view: ''It's a willfully diagrammatic and didactic novel which also succeeds artistically because of its resonant characterization and deadly irony. It satisfies both the novelist's political intent and the obligation I know he feels toward his art.''

Despite these reservations, the majority of critics concur that *Petals of Blood* is an important literary contribution. Sharma, for example, writes that ''Ngugi's *Petals of Blood* is a complex and powerful work. It is a statement of his social and political philosophy and an embodiment of his prophetic vision. Ngugi provides a masterly analysis of the social and economic situation in modern Kenya, a scene of unprincipled and ruthless exploitation of man by man, and gives us a picture of the social and moral consequences of this exploitation.'' Cook and Ikenimkpe state that *Petals of Blood* ''stands as a rare literary achievement: with all its faults upon it, [it is still] a skillfully articulated work which in no degree compromises the author's fully fledged radical political viewpoint.'' Indangasis concludes: ''In many senses, literary and nonliterary, *Petals of Blood* will remain a major but controversial contribution to African literature, and the literature of colonised peoples.''

BIOGRAPHICAL/CRITICAL SOURCES:

BOOKS

Bailey, Diana, *Ngugi wa Thiong'o: The River Between, a Critical View*, edited by Yolande Cantu, Collins, 1986.
Contemporary Literary Criticism, Gale, Volume 3, 1975, Volume 7, 1977, Volume 13, 1980, Volume 36, 1986.
Cook, David and Michael Okenimkpe, *Ngugi wa Thiong'o: An Exploration of His Writings*, Heinemann, 1983.
Gakwandi, Shatto Arthur, *The Novel and Contemporary Experience in Africa*, Africana Publishing, 1977.
Killam, G. D., *An Introduction to the Writings of Ngugi*, Heinemann, 1980.
Ngugi wa Thiong'o, *Detained: A Writer's Prison Diary*, Heinemann, 1981.
Larson, Charles R., *The Emergence of African Fiction*, Indiana University Press, 1972.
Palmer, Eustace, *An Introduction to the African Novel*, Africana Publishing, 1972.
Palmer, Eustace, *The Growth of the African Novel*, Heinemann, 1979.
Robson, Clifford B., *Ngugi wa Thiong'o*, Macmillan (London), 1979.
Roscoe, Adrian, *Uhuru's Fire: African Literature East to South*, Cambridge University Press, 1977.
Tibble, Ann, *African/English Literature*, Peter Owen (London), 1965.
Tucker, Martin, *Africa in Modern Literature: A Survey of Contemporary Writing in English*, Ungar, 1967.

PERIODICALS

African Literature Today, Number 5, 1971, Number 10, 1979.
Africa Today, Volume 33, number 1, 1986.
American Book Review, summer, 1979.
Books Abroad, autumn, 1967, spring, 1968.
Books in Canada, October, 1982.
Chicago Tribune Book World, October 22, 1978.
Christian Science Monitor, October 11, 1978, September 5, 1986.
Iowa Review, spring/summer, 1976.
Journal of Commonwealth Literature, September, 1965, Number 1, 1986.
Listener, August 26, 1982.
Michigan Quarterly Review, fall, 1970.
New Republic, January 20, 1979.
New Statesman, October 20, 1972, July 24, 1981, June 18, 1982, August 8, 1986.
New Yorker, July 2, 1979.
New York Times, May 10, 1978, November 9, 1986.
New York Times Book Review, February 19, 1978.
Observer, June 20, 1982.
Times Literary Supplement, January 28, 1965, November 3, 1972, August 12, 1977, October 16, 1981, June 18, 1982, May 8, 1987.
Washington Post, October 9, 1978.
West Africa, February 20, 1978.
World Literature Today, spring, 1978, fall, 1978, spring, 1981, autumn, 1982, summer, 1983, winter, 1984, fall, 1987.
World Literature Written in English, November, 1979, autumn, 1982.

—*Sketch by Melissa Gaiownik*

*   *   *

NICOL, Charles H(arold)   1919-

PERSONAL: Born July 6, 1919, Brooklyn, New York; son of Charles F. (a clergyman) and Julia (King) Nichols; married Mildred Thompson (a career counselor), August 19, 1950; children: David, Keith, Brian. *Education:* Brooklyn College (now Brooklyn College of the City University of New York), B.A. (with honors), 1942; Brown University, Ph.D., 1948. *Politics:* Independent. *Religion:* Society of Friends (Quakers).

ADDRESSES: Home—Providence, R.I. *Office*—Department of English, Brown University, Providence, R.I. 02912.

CAREER: Morgan State College, Baltimore, Md., associate professor of English, 1948-49; Hampton Institute, Hampton, Va., professor of English, 1949-59; Free University of Berlin, Berlin, Germany, professor of North American literature, 1959-69; Brown University, Providence, R.I., professor of English, 1969—, also chairman of Afro-American Studies Program. Guest professor of American literature, Aarhus University, 1954-55; visiting professor at Grinnell College, 1969, and Stanford University, 1973.

MEMBER: Modern Language Association of America, American Studies Association, American Association of University Professors.

AWARDS, HONORS: Fulbright lecturer at Aarhaus University, 1954-55; senior fellowship from National Endowment for the Humanities, 1973-74; Fulbright grant for research in Germany, 1973-74.

WRITINGS:

Many Thousand Gone: The Ex-Slaves' Account of Their Bondage and Freedom, E. J. Brill, 1963.
Instructor's Guide to Accompany "Cavalcade: Negro American Writing from 1760 to the Present," Houghton, 1970.
(Editor) *African Nights: Black Erotic Folk Tales,* Herder & Herder, 1971.
(Editor) *Black Men in Chains: An Anthology of Slave Narratives,* Lawrence Hill, 1972.
(Contributor) *Comic Relief,* University of Illinois Press, 1978.
(Editor and author of introduction) *Arna Bontemps and Langston Hughes Letters, 1925-1967,* Dodd, 1980.
(Contributor) *The Dilemma of the New Black Middle Class,* University of Pennsylvania Press, 1980.

Contributor of more than sixty articles and reviews to education, literature, and literary journals in the United States and abroad, including *William and Mary Quarterly, America in the Twentieth Century, Nation, Modern Language Journal, Phylon, American-Scandinavian Review, School and Society,* and *Jahrbuch fuer Amerikastudien.* Member of editorial boards of *Studies in Black Literature* and of *Novel: A Forum in Fiction.*

SIDELIGHTS: Los Angeles Times reviewer Robert Kirsch writes in his review of *Arna Bontemps and Langston Hughes Letters, 1925-1967* that "the letters here, admirably edited by Professor Charles H. Nichols, along with an introduction and epilogue . . . are above all professional. They are vocational in the sense of mutual assistance marketing ideas, shop talk, awards, itineraries, publication, criticism, job offers."

Kirsch continues to explain that the letters selected and edited by Nichols show Bontemps and Hughes as "artists each in their own right, they became deep good friends, collaborators on a few books, testers of each other's ideas, sharers of experiences when it was almost as arduous to be a black writer as a black baseball player in the South. They had dignity but it was hard to achieve, scuffling to make a living, doing a review here, an article there, lecture tours by running a Ford along potted highways to remote colleges, driving in their tuxedos, facing out the slings and barbs of restaurant waitresses and motel keepers."

BIOGRAPHICAL/CRITICAL SOURCES:

BOOKS

Dunbar, Ernest, *The Black Expatriates,* Dutton, 1968.

PERIODICALS

Chicago Tribune, April 13, 1980.
Los Angeles Times, June 2, 1980.
New York Times Book Review, February 17, 1980.
Times Literary Supplement, December 5, 1980.
Washington Post Book World, March 23, 1980.

*   *   *

NICOL, Abioseh
See NICOL, Davidson (Sylvester Hector Willoughby)

*   *   *

NICOL, Davidson (Sylvester Hector Willoughby) 1924-
(Abioseh Nicol)

PERSONAL: Born September 14, 1924, in Freetown, Sierra

Leone; married; children: three sons, two daughters. *Education:* Attended London University, 1943; Christ's College, Cambridge, B.A. (first class honors), 1946, M.D., 1958; also received M.A., Ph.D. *Religion:* Christian.

ADDRESSES: Office—World Federation of United Nations Associations, c/o Palais des Nations, CH-1211 Geneva 10, Switzerland. *Agent*—Phyllis Westberg, Harold Ober Associates, 40 East 49th St., New York, N.Y. 10017; and David Higham Associates Ltd., 5-8 Lower John St., Golden Square, London W1R 4HA, England.

CAREER: University of London, London Hospital Medical College, London, England, house physician and research assistant, 1950-52; The Medical School, Ibadan, Nigeria, university lecturer, 1952-54; Cambridge University, Cambridge, England, Beit Memorial Fellow, 1954, fellow and supervisor in natural sciences and medicine at Christ's College, 1957-59; Sierra Leone Government, senior pathologist, 1958-60; Fourah Bay College, Freetown, Sierra Leone, principal, 1960-67; University of Sierra Leone, Freetown, first vice-chancellor, 1966-68; ambassador from Sierra Leone to United Nations, 1968-71, member of Economic and Social Council, 1969-70, chairman of Committee of 24 (decolonization), 1970, Security Council, member 1970-71, president, 1970; high commissioner of the Republic of Sierra Leone to United Kingdom, and ambassador to Denmark, Norway, Sweden, and Finland, 1971-72; United Nations, New York, New York, under-secretary and executive director of United Nations Institute for Training and Research (UNITAR), 1973-82; World Federation of United Nations Associations, Geneva, Switzerland, president, 1983—.

Member of West African Council for Medical Research, 1959-62; member of public service commission, Sierra Leone, 1960-68. Conference delegate to World Health Organization Assembly, 1960, United Nations Educational, Scientific, and Cultural Organization (UNESCO) Higher Education Conference, 1963, and Commonwealth Prime Ministers' Conference, 1965, 1969, and 1971. Chairman, United Nations Mission to Angola, 1976.

Member of executive council, Association of Universities of the British Commonwealth, 1960, 1966; member of commission for proposed University of Ghana, 1960; chairman, University of East Africa Visiting Committee, 1962; chairman, West African Exams Council, 1964-69. Visiting lecturer, University of Toronto, University of California—Berkeley, and Mayo Clinic, 1958. Aggrey-Fraser-Guggisberg memorial lecturer, University of Ghana, 1963; Danforth Fellowship lecturer in African affairs, Association of American Colleges, 1968-71. Visiting fellow, Johns Hopkins School of Advanced International Studies, 1983; visiting scholar, Woodrow Wilson International Center, 1983, and Hoover Institution, Stanford University, 1984. Member, governing body, Kumasi University, Ghana; member of board of trustees, African-American Institute and Fund for Peace. Chairman of Sierra Leone National Library Board, 1959-65. Former director, Central Bank of Sierra Leone, Consolidated African Selection Trust Ltd., and Davesme Corporation. Fellow, Christ's College, Cambridge, Royal College of Pathologists (London), West African College of Physicians, and West African College of Surgeons. Honorary consultant pathologist, Sierra Leone Government. Consultant to Ford Foundation.

MEMBER: Sierra Leone Red Cross Society (president, 1962-66), West Africa Science Association (president, 1964-66); Ghana Academy of Sciences (honorary member), United Oxford and Cambridge University, Royal Commonwealth Society, Senior Dinner (Freetown).

AWARDS, HONORS: Margaret Wrong Prize and Medal for Literature in Africa, 1951; Independence Medal, Government of Sierra Leone, 1961; D.Sc. from University of Newcastle on Tyne, and Kalamazoo College, both 1964, and Laurentian (Ontario) College; named Companion of the Order of St. Michael and St. George, 1964; LL.D., University of Leeds, 1968, Barat College, 1980, University of the West Indies, 1981, and Tuskegee College, 1981; D.Litt., Davis-Elkins College, 1971; Grand Commander of the Order of Rokel, Sierra Leone, 1974; Star of Africa, Liberia, 1974; honorary special fellow, UNITAR, 1983.

WRITINGS:

Alienation: An Essay, MacGibbon & Kee, 1960.
(Contributor) *An African Treasury,* Crown, 1960.
(Contributor) *An Anthology of Commonwealth Verse,* Blackie, 1963.
(Contributor) Langston Hughes, editor, *Poems from Black Africa,* Indiana University Press, 1963.
Africa: A Subjective View, Longmans, Green, 1964.
(Contributor) *African Heritage,* Macmillan (London), 1964.
(Contributor) *A Book of African Verse,* Heinemann, 1964.
(Under pseudonym Abioseh Nicol) *The Truly Married Woman and Other Stories* (fiction), Oxford University Press, 1965.
(Under pseudonym Abioseh Nicol) *Two African Tales* (fiction), Cambridge University Press, 1965.
(Contributor) D. I. Nwoga, editor, *West African Verse,* Longmans, Green, 1967.
(Contributor) *African Writing Today,* Penguin, 1967.
(Contributor) *Commonwealth Poems of Today,* J. Murray, 1967.
(Contributor) *New Voices of the Commonwealth,* Evans Brothers, 1968.
(Editor and author of introduction) *Africanus Horton: The Dawn of Nationalism in Modern Africa,* Longmans, Green, 1969, published as *Black Nationalism in Africa, 1867,* Africana Publishing, 1969.
New and Modern Roles for the Empire and Commonwealth, Cambridge University Press, 1976.
(Editor) *Regionalism and the New International Economic Order,* Pergamon, 1981.
(Editor) *Paths to Peace: The U.N. Security Council and Its Presidency,* Pergamon, 1981.
(Editor with Luis Echeverria) *Regionalism and the New International Economic Order,* Pergamon, 1981.
(Editor with Pamela D'Onofrio) *Scientific-Technological Change and the Role of Women in Development,* Westview, 1981.
(With Margaret Crole and Babatunde Adeniran) *The United Nations Security Council: Towards Greater Effectiveness,* UNITAR, 1982.
(Editor with Torill Stokland and Mallica Vajrathon) *Creative Women in Changing Societies: A Quest for Alternatives,* Transnational, 1982.

Also author of *The United Nations and Decision-Making: The Role of Women,* 1978, and *Nigeria and the Future of Africa,* 1980. Contributor to *Malnutrition in African Mothers and Children,* 1954, *The Mechanism of the Action of Insulin,* 1960, *The Structure of Human Insulin,* 1960, *Conditions of World Order,* and *The Task of Universities in a Changing World.* Contributor to *Encyclopaedia Britannica,* 1974, and *International Encyclopedia of Higher Education,* 1976. Contributor of articles, short stories, and verse to anthologies and periodicals, including *Encounter, Blackwood's Magazine,* the London *Times, Guardian,* and *Economist.*

SIDELIGHTS: Although most of his career has been spent in the fields of medicine and diplomatic service, Davidson Nicol, writing as Abioseh Nicol, is "in the very forefront of African short story writers," comments Adrian A. Roscoe in *Mother Is Gold: A Study in West African Literature.* While critical attention to African literature has focused more on novels and novelists, Roscoe finds that "there is no novelist in Nigeria... whose creative flair and command of prose are superior to those of Abioseh Nicol." Roscoe also commends Nicol's consistency, observing that he is able to sustain quality writing in his stories where some novelists weaken after a strong beginning. Nicol's talent lies in his "taking a slice of real life and offering it to us in all its workaday detail, all its blending of the tragic and the absurd," says Roscoe. "The style that allows this effect must possess the translucence of crystal."

Nicol's fiction deals more with "workaday" African life, often setting Westernized middle-class characters against an African background. Seemingly in contrast to these everyday subjects is Nicol's poetry, which Martin Tucker in *Africa in Modern Literature* characterizes as dealing with "Africa as a symbolic entity related to a social cause." Nicol reconciles these apparent differences, writing that his fiction addresses social issues, not by using symbols but by presenting a different viewpoint. In a foreword to *Two African Tales,* the author writes that his stories of colonial Africa "owe something to European writers... who wrote about similar situations. However, being both black and African, I was then on the other side of the fence and perhaps saw things differently."

MEDIA ADAPTATIONS: Readings of Nicol's poetry have been broadcast by the British Broadcasting Corp. and the Voice of America.

AVOCATIONAL INTERESTS: Antiques, especially old maps and coins.

BIOGRAPHICAL/CRITICAL SOURCES:

BOOKS

Nicol, Abioseh, *Two African Tales,* Cambridge University Press, 1965.
Roscoe, Adrian A., *Mother Is Gold: A Study in West African Literature,* Cambridge University Press, 1971.
Tibble, Anne, *African-English Literature,* P. Owen, 1965.
Tucker, Martin, *Africa in Modern Literature,* Ungar, 1967.

*   *   *

NKOSI, Lewis   1936-

PERSONAL: Born December 5, 1936, in Natal, South Africa; son of Samson and Christine Margaret (Makathini) Nkosi; married Bronwyn Ollernshaw; children: Louise, Joy (twins). *Education:* Attended M. L. Sultan Technical College, 1954-55, and Harvard University, 1961-62; University of London, diploma in English literature, 1974; University of Sussex, 1977.

ADDRESSES: Home—Flat 4, Burgess Park Mansions, Fortune Green Rd., London NW6, England. *Agent*—Deborah Rogers Ltd., 29 Goodge St., London WC1, England.

CAREER: Ilanga lase Natal (title means "Natal Sun," Zulu-English weekly newspaper), staff member, 1955; *Drum* (magazine), chief reporter, Johannesburg, South Africa, 1956-60,

Golden City Post (*Drum* Sunday newspaper), chief reporter, 1956-60; *South African Information Bulletin,* staff member, 1962-68; *The New African,* London, England, literary editor, 1965-68. Editor of journal in Dar es Salaam, Tanzania, during 1960s. Correspondent in southern United States, *Observer* (London). Producer of British Broadcasting Company (BBC) radio series "Africa Abroad," 1962-65, interviewer of leading African writers for National Education Television (NET) series "African Writers of Today," 1963. Visiting Regents Professor of African Literature, University of California, Irvine, 1970.

AWARDS, HONORS: Nieman fellowship in journalism, Harvard University, 1961-62; Dakar World Festival of Negro Arts prize, 1966, for *Home and Exile and Other Selections.*

WRITINGS:

The Rhythm of Violence (also see below; play; first produced in London, 1963), Oxford University Press, 1964.
Home and Exile and Other Selections (essays), Longmans, Green, 1965, expanded edition, Longman, 1983.
(Contributor) *African Writing Today,* edited by Ezekiel Mphalele, Penguin, 1967.
(Contributor) *Plays from Black Africa* (includes "The Rhythm of Violence"), edited by Frederic N. Litto, Hill & Wang, 1968.
"We Can't All Be Martin Luther King" (radio play), BBC, 1971.
"The Chameleon and the Lizard" (libretto), first produced in London at Queen Elizabeth Hall, 1971.
"Malcolm" (play), first produced in London, 1972.
The Transplanted Heart: Essays on South Africa, Ethiope Publishing, 1975.
Tasks and Masks: Themes and Styles of African Literature, Longman (London), 1981, published as *Tasks and Masks: An Introduction to African Literature,* Longman, 1982.
Mating Birds, East African Publishing House, 1983, Harper, 1987.

Also author of screenplay, "Come Back Africa," 1959. Author of television play, "Malcolm," produced in England and Sweden in 1967. Author of radio play, "The Trial," 1969. Contributor to periodicals and journals, including *Guardian, New Statesman, Observer, Transition, Black Orpheus, Spectator, West Africa, African Report, African Today,* and *New Yorker.*

WORK IN PROGRESS: A libretto for the King's Singers.

SIDELIGHTS: Exiled after leaving South Africa to study at Harvard University, Lewis Nkosi has written short stories, plays, and criticism from his adopted home in England. Much of his work, however, deals with African literature and social concerns. "As a playwright and short-story writer, he is also the most subtly experimental of the black South African writers, many of whom are caught in the immediacy of the struggle against apartheid," comments Henry Louis Gates, Jr. in the *New York Times Book Review.* According to Alistair Niven in *British Book News* Nkosi is "one of the architects of the contemporary black consciousness in South Africa."

Mating Birds, Nkosi's first novel, brought him wide critical attention. The book focuses on South Africa's response to miscegenation through the story of a young man, Ndi Sibiya, a rural chief's son, who "meets" a white stripper named Veronica, on a segregated beach. Although the rules of apartheid keeps them from speaking to each other, a wordless flirtation commences. Sibiya becomes pulled into an obsessive relationship with Veronica and ends up following her everywhere.

Eventually, Veronica seems to invite her suitor back to her bungalow, where Sibiya believes he is seduced. Veronica, however, calls the police and accuses Sibiya of rape, for which he is arrested. According to South African law, if he is found guilty, he can be executed.

Many critics see the novel as a comment on apartheid. According to *Nation* contributor George Packer, "*Mating Birds* feels like the work of a superb critic. Heavy with symbolism, analytical rather than dramatic, it attempts nothing less than an allegory of colonialism and apartheid, one that dares to linger in complexity." Gates writes that *Mating Birds* "confronts boldly and imaginatively the strange interplay of bondage, desire and torture inherent in interracial sexual relationships within the South African prison house of apartheid."

Critics have also praised Nkosi's portrayal of Sibiya's feelings for Veronica. Margaret Walters claims in the *Observer*, "the most remarkable thing in this short novel is the account of the obsession that grips Sibiya." Gates says that summarzing the plot "does not capture the book's lyrical intensity or its compelling narrative power. Mr. Nkosi has managed to re-create for his readers all the tortures of an illicit obsession, especially the ambiguities and interdeterminacy of motivation and responsibility." And *Washington Post Book World* contributor Alan Ryan writes, "*Mating Birds* is very possibly the finest novel by a South African, black or white, about the terrible distortion of love in South Africa since Alan Paton's *Too Late the Phalarope*."

But some readers dislike even the possibility of rape to convey Sibiya's response to white society. "Nkosi's handling of the sexual themes complicates the distribution of our sympathies, which he means to be unequivocally with the accused man," points out Rob Nixon in the *Village Voice*. "For in rebutting the prevalent white South African fantasy of the black male as a sex-crazed rapist, Nkosi edges unnecessarily close to reinforcing the myth of the raped woman as someone who deep down was asking for it." For Gates, however, the question of whether Sibiya rapes Veronica remains unclear. This causes problems for the reader, as "we are never certain who did what to whom or why." He quotes Sibiya's reflections on his trial: "But how could I make the judges or anyone else believe me when I no longer *knew* what to believe myself? . . . Had I raped the girl or not?" Gates continues, "We cannot say. Accordingly, this novel's great literary achievement—its vivid depiction of obsession—leads inevitably to its great flaw." Sara Maitland in the *New Statesman* objects to Nkosi's portrayal of Veronica: "Surely there must be another way for Nkosi's commitment, passion and beautiful writing to describe the violence and injustice of how things are than this stock image of the pale evil seductress, the eternally corrupting female?"

Despite the novel's shortcomings, says Michiko Kakutani in the *New York Times, Mating Birds* "nonetheless attests to the emergence of . . . a writer whose vision of South Africa remains fiercely his own." *West Coast Review of Books* contributor Sherman W. Smith believes that "Lewis Nkosi certainly must be one of the best writers out of Africa in our time." And Ryan suggests that "Nkosi's quiet voice is likely to linger in the ear long after the shouts and cries have faded away."

BIOGRAPHICAL/CRITICAL SOURCES:

BOOKS

Contemporary Literary Criticism, Volume 45, Gale, 1987.

Nkosi, Lewis, *Mating Birds*, East African Publishing House, 1983, Harper, 1987.

PERIODICALS

Best Sellers, July, 1986.
Books and Bookmen, October, 1986.
British Book News, March, 1987.
Choice, June, 1982.
Listener, August 28, 1986.
London Review of Books, August 7, 1986.
Nation, November 22, 1986.
New Statesman, August 29, 1986.
New Yorker, May 26, 1986.
New York Times, March 22, 1986.
New York Times Book Review, May 18, 1986.
Observer, July 27, 1986.
Spectator, August 16, 1986.
Times Literary Supplement, February 3, 1966, August 27, 1982.
Village Voice, July 29, 1986.
West Coast Review of Books, September, 1986.
World Literature Today, spring, 1983, summer, 1984.

*   *   *

NUGENT, Bruce
   See NUGENT, Richard Bruce

*   *   *

NUGENT, Richard Bruce   1906(?)-
   (Richard Bruce, Bruce Nugent)

PERSONAL: Born July 2, 1906 (one source says 1905), in Washington, D.C.; son of Richard Henry and Pauline Minerva (Bruce) Nugent; married wife, Grace.

ADDRESSES: Home—Hoboken, N.J.

CAREER: Artist, writer, and actor. Associated with Work Projects Administration, Federal Arts Project, and Federal Theater. Founder of Harlem Cultural Council. Work exhibited in shows at the Harmon Foundation, 1931 and 1936; work exhibited in collections, including the National Archives. Appeared on stage in "Porgy," and in documentary film "Before Stonewall," 1984.

WRITINGS:

(Under pseudonym Richard Bruce) "Sadhji, an African Ballet" (one-act; first produced in Rochester, N.Y., at the Eastman School of Music, 1932), published in *Plays of Negro Life: A Source-Book of Native American Drama*, Harper, 1927.
Lighting Fire!!, Fire!! Press (Metuchen, N.J.), 1982.

Works represented in anthologies, sometimes under the name Richard Bruce or Bruce Nugent, including *The New Negro: An Interpretation*, edited by Alain Locke, A. & C. Boni, 1925, and *Caroling Dusk: An Anthology of Verse by Negro Poets*, edited by Countee Cullen, Harper, 1927. Contributor of illustrations, poetry, and short stories to periodicals, including *Challenge, Crisis, Dance, Ebony, Fire!!, Harlem: A Forum of Negro Life, New Challenge, Opportunity, Palms, Topaz,* and *Trend*. Contributor to the "Negroes of New York," Federal Writers' Project.

SIDELIGHTS: Described as the "ultimate bohemian" by Eric Garber in an article in the *Dictionary of Literary Biography*, Richard Bruce Nugent was the basis for the character of Paul

Arbian—a talented but undisciplined artist and author—in Wallace Thurman's 1932 novel *Infants of the Spring*. Although he was not a prolific illustrator and writer, Nugent secured his position as an integral figure in New York literary circles during the 1920s by his association with some of the outstanding authors of the Harlem Renaissance.

First introduced to the black literati of New York at a party in 1925, Nugent emerged as a regular on the Harlem social scene. He was notorious for his liberal sexual escapades and carousing—he took the pseudonym Richard Bruce at this time not to upset his mother—as well as for what Thurman labeled the "bizarre and erotic" subjects of the drawings and writings he was producing. Nugent penned a first-person narrative about a nineteen-year-old unemployed artist who was struggling with his sexuality, "Smoke, Lilies, and Jade," which critics contended was loosely autobiographical. This short piece and two of his brush-and-ink illustrations appeared in *Fire!!*, the literary periodical Thurman edited, and Nugent's first published story, "Sadhji," focusing on an ill-fated love triangle set in historic Africa, was anthologized by Alain Locke and Montgomery Gregory in *Plays of Negro Life: A Source-Book of Native American Drama* after Nugent had rewritten it as a drama.

Although Nugent publishes literary works in anthologies and periodicals, he is primarily an artist. According to Thomas H. Wirth in the *Black American Literature Forum*, through innovative use of color and technique Nugent's creations—whether on the walls of nightclubs or in popular journals—are "highly stylized and instantly recognizable." Eroticism permeates Nugent's drawings, oil paintings, and pastel works, prompting Thurman to describe Arbian/Nugent's illustrations as "nothing but highly colored phalli." Wirth saw more, however, maintaining that the artist's "unexpected juxtapositions of colors, strongly idiosyncratic stylistic elements, and unconventional composition emphasizing the borders rather than the center combine to stunning effect."

BIOGRAPHICAL/CRITICAL SOURCES:

BOOKS

Dictionary of Literary Biography, Volume 51: *Afro-American Writers From the Harlem Renaissance to 1940*, Gale, 1987.
Thurman, Wallace, *Infants of the Spring*, Macauley, 1932.

PERIODICALS

Black American Literature Forum, spring, 1985.

* * *

NYERERE, Julius K(ambarage) 1922-

PERSONAL: Born in March, 1922, in Butiama-Musoma, Tanganyika (now Tanzania); son of Mtemi Nyerere Burito and Mugaya Nyang'ombe; married Maria Magige (a shopkeeper), 1953; children: five sons, two daughters. *Education:* Makerere University, teacher's diploma, 1945; received M.A., Edinburgh University. *Religion:* Roman Catholic.

ADDRESSES: Office—P.O. Box 9120, Dar es Salaam, Tanzania.

CAREER: St. Mary's Roman Catholic School, Tabora, Tanganyika, teacher, 1946-49; St. Francis's Roman Catholic College, Pugu, Tanganyika, teacher, 1953-55; Tanganyika Government, member of legislative council, 1957, leader of Elected Members Organization, 1958-60, member for Easter Province,

1958, member for Dar es Salaam, 1960; Republic of Tanganyika (now Tanzania), Dar es Salaam, chief minister, 1960-61, prime minister, 1961-62, president, 1962-64, minister of external affairs, 1962-63; United Republic of Tanzania, Dar es Salaam, president, 1964-85, minister of external affairs, 1965-72, commander in chief of the armed forces, beginning in 1973, founder and chairman of Chama Cha Mapinduzi (Revolutionary Party), beginning in 1977, chairman of Defense and Security Committee of Tanzania. Chancellor of University of East Africa, 1963-70, and of University of Dar es Salaam, 1970-85. President of Pan-African Freedom Movement of Eastern and Central Africa.

MEMBER: Organization for African Unity (chairman, 1984-85), African Association of Dar es Salaam (president, 1953), Tanganyika African Association (now Tanganyika African National Union; president, 1953-77).

AWARDS, HONORS: Third World Award, 1981; LL.D. from Edinburgh University and Duquesne University.

WRITINGS:

(Translator into Swahili) William Shakespeare, *Julius Caesar*, Oxford University Press, 1963.
(With Joshua Nkomo) *Rhodesia: The Case for Majority Rule*, Indian Council for Africa, 1966.
Freedom and Unity—Uhuru na Umoja: A Selection From Writings and Speeches, 1952-1965, Oxford University Press, 1967.
Freedom and Socialism—Uhuru na Ujamaa: A Selection From Writings and Speeches, 1965-1967, Oxford University Press, 1968.
Ujamaa: Essays on Socialism, Oxford University Press, 1968.
Nyerere on Socialism, Oxford University Press, 1969.
(Translator into Swahili) Shakespeare, *A Merchant of Venice*, Oxford University Press, 1969.
Quotations From President Julius K. Nyerere, Collected From Speeches and Writings, edited and published by Morogoro College of National Education, 1970.
Tanzania Ten Years After Independence: Report, Ministry of Information and Broadcasting, 1971.
Freedom and Development—Uhuru na Maendeleo: A Selection From Writings and Speeches, 1968-1973, Oxford University Press, 1973.
Moyo kabla ya silaha, EAPH, 1973.
Man and Development—Binadamu na Maendeleo, Oxford University Press, 1974.
The Arusha Declaration Ten Years After, Government Printer, 1977.
Wafanyakazi na ujamaa Tanzania, Makao Makuu ya NUTA, 1977.
Crusade for Liberation, Oxford University Press, 1978.
(With Samir Amin and Daniel Perren) *Le Dialogue inegal: Ecueils du nouvel ordre economique international*, Centre Europe-Tiers Monde, 1979.

Also author of booklet "Barriers to Democracy."

SIDELIGHTS: When the African nation of Tanganyika became independent in 1961, after decades of foreign rule, Julius K. Nyerere was its first prime minister. After the 1964 union of Tanganyika and Zanzibar under the name Tanzania, Nyerere governed the new country as well. Rising out of a tribal background to become teacher, political leader, and writer, he is "the father of homespun African socialism" and "one of the Third World's most prominent statesmen," according to *Time* writer Hunter R. Clark. Assessed John Darnton in the *New*

York Times, "No other African head of state has set such high standards for his countrymen, for Africa or, for that matter, for all mankind as the intense, scholarly ... President of Tanzania."

Originally a teacher, Nyerere turned increasingly to politics in the early 1950s, ultimately giving up academia to lead his country to independence and improved socioeconomic conditions. As president he socialized farming and industry—although 85 percent of the farmers returned to subsistence farming as a result of inefficient pricing and distribution—and promoted national pride, a national language, and improved health care and education. Noted Clark, "Although he has failed ... to create the prosperous, egalitarian society that he once envisioned, his policies will continue to shape the country—and the continent—for decades." Several of his policies were at least partially successful: Tanzania has achieved 83 percent literacy and enjoys "perhaps the lowest level of tribal strife of any country on the continent," observed Clark, and it has demonstrated concern for civil and human rights—helping to overthrow neighboring Uganda's brutal dictator Idi Amin in 1979.

Nyerere's numerous speeches, essays, and other writings detail his policies and viewpoints, emphasizing central themes such as the importance of human beings and of allowing a country to develop in its own way, considering useful ideas from without and within. *Freedom and Socialism—Uhuru na Ujamaa: A Selection From Writings and Speeches, 1965-1967* "sets out guidelines for new policies which are among the most exciting, and encouraging, in Africa," judged a *Times Literary Supplement* reviewer, who considered Nyerere's prescription "entirely realistic and rational." The author highlights racial equality and African unity in *Freedom and Unity— Uhuru na Umoja: A Selection From Writings and Speeches, 1952-1965.*

Throughout his political career, asserted a *Times Literary Supplement* critic, "Tanzania's President has dwelt on the deep underlying principles of statecraft." He has earned a reputation for consistency and integrity, for supporting human rights and democratic institutions such as free elections and independent courts of law. In 1976 U.S. Secretary of State Henry Kissinger "made it clear that he regards Mr. Nyerere as the prime link to black Africa," remarked Darnton. Upon Nyerere's resignation in 1985 a political opponent, quoted in *Time,* characterized the former president as "a real man of the people."

AVOCATIONAL INTERESTS: Reading.

BIOGRAPHICAL/CRITICAL SOURCES:

BOOKS

Hatch, John, *Two African Statesmen: Kaunda of Zambia and Nyerere of Tanzania,* Regnery, 1976.

PERIODICALS

New York Times, September 16, 1976.
Time, November 4, 1985.
Times Literary Supplement, March 30, 1967, August 28, 1969.

O

ODAGA, Asenath (Bole) 1937-
(Kituomba)

PERSONAL: Born July 5, 1937, in Rarieda, Kenya; daughter of Blasto Akumu Aum (a farmer and catechist) and Patricia Abuya Abok (a farmer); married James Charles Odaga (a manager), January 27, 1957; children: Odhiambo Odongo, Akelo, Adhiambo, Awnor. *Education:* Attended Kikuyu Teacher Training College, 1955-56; University of Nairobi, B.A. (with honors), 1974, Dip.Ed., 1974, M.A., 1981. *Religion:* Protestant.

ADDRESSES: Home and office—P.O. Box 1743, Kisumu, Kenya.

CAREER: Church Missionary Society's Teacher Training College, Ngiya, Kenya, teacher, 1957-58; teacher at Kambare School, 1957-58; Butere Girls School, Kahamega, Kenya, teacher, 1959-60; Nyakach Girls School, Kisumu district, Kenya, headmistress, 1961-63; Kenya Railways, Nairobi, Kenya, assistant secretary, 1964; Kenya Dairy Board, Nairobi, assistant secretary, 1965-68; Kenya Library Services, Nairobi, secretary, 1968; *East African Standard,* Nairobi, advertising assistant, 1969-70; Kerr Downey and Selby Safaris, Nairobi, advertising and office manager, 1969-70; Christian Churches Educational Association, Nairobi, assistant director of curriculum and development program, 1974-75; Institute of African Studies, University of Nairobi, Nairobi, research fellow, 1976-81; free-lance researcher, writer, and editor, 1982—. Manager of Thu Tinda Bookshop, 1982—, and Lake Publishers and Enterprises, 1982—; affiliated with Odaga & Associates (consulting firm), 1984—. Chairman of the board of governors of Nyakach Girls High School; member of Museum Management Committee, Kisumu, 1984—, and vice-chairman, 1984—.

MEMBER: Writers' Association of Kenya (founding member and secretary, 1978-87), Kenya Association of University Women (chairman of Kisumu chapter, 1983-87), Kenya Business and Professional Women's Club (past chairman), Rarieda Women's Group, Akala Women's Group (patron).

AWARDS, HONORS: Best Story award from *Voice of Women* magazine, 1967, for a short story, "The Suitor," and an unpublished play, "Three Brides in an Hour."

WRITINGS:

JUVENILE

The Secret of Monkey the Rock, illustrated by William Agutu, Thomas Nelson, 1966.
Jande's Ambition, illustrated by Adrienne Moore, East African Publishing, 1966.
The Diamond Ring, illustrated by A. Moore, East African Publishing, 1967.
The Hare's Blanket and Other Tales, illustrated by A. Moore, East African Publishing, 1967.
The Angry Flames, illustrated by A. Moore, East African Publishing, 1968.
Sweets and Sugar Cane, illustrated by Beryl Moore, East African Publishing, 1969.
The Villager's Son, illustrated by Shyam Varma, Heinemann Educational (London), 1971.
Kip on the Farm, illustrated by B. Moore, East African Publishing, 1972.
(Editor, with David Kirui and David Crippen) *God, Myself, and Others,* Evangel, 1976.
Kip at the Coast, illustrated by Gay Galsworthy, Evans, 1977.
Kip Goes to the City, illustrated by Galsworthy, Evans, 1977.
Poko Nyar Mugumba (title means "Poko Mugumba's Daughter"), illustrated by Sophia Ojienda, Foundation, 1978.
Thu Tinda: Stories From Kenya, Uzima, 1980.
The Two Friends (folktales), illustrated by Barrack Omondi, Bookwise (Nairobi), 1981.
Kenyan Folk Tales, illustrated by Margaret Humphries, Humphries (Caithness, Scotland), 1981.
(With Kenneth Cripwell) *Look and Write Book One,* Thomas Nelson, 1982.
(With Crimpwell) *Look and Learn Book Two,* Thomas Nelson, 1982.
My Home Book One, Lake Publishers (Kisumu), 1983.
Odilo Nungo Piny Kirom (title means "Ogilo, the Arms Can't Embrace the Earth's Waist"), illustrated by H. Kiruikoske, Heinemann Educational (London), 1983.
Nyamgondho Whod Ombare (title means "'Nyamgondho, the Son of Ombare' and Other Stories"), illustrated by Joseph Odaga, Lake Publishers, 1986.
Munde and His Friends, illustrated by Peter Odaga, Lake Publishers, 1987.
The Rag Ball, illustrated by J. Odaga, Lake Publishers, 1987.

Munde Goes to the Market, illustrated by P. Odaga, Lake Publishers, 1987.
Weche Sigendi gi Timbe Luo Moko (title means ''Stories and Some Customs of the Luo''), Lake Publishers, 1987.
Story Time (folktales), Lake Publishers, 1987.

OTHER

Nyathini Koa e Nyuolne Nyaka Higni Adek (title means ''Your Child From Birth to Age Three''), Evangel, 1976.
''Miaha'' (five-act; title means ''The Bride''), first produced in Nairobi, 1981.
(With S. Kichamu Akivaga) *Oral Literature: A School Certificate Course,* Heinemann Educational (Nairobi), 1982.
Simbi Nyaima (four-act; title means ''The Sunken Village''; first produced in Kisumu, 1982), Lake Publishers, 1983.
Nyamgondho (four-act), first produced in Kisumu, 1983.
Yesterday's Today: The Study of Oral Literature, Lake Publishers, 1984.
The Shade Changes (fiction), Lake Publishers, 1984.
The Storm, Lake Publishers, 1985.
Literature for Children and Young People in Kenya, Kenya Literature Bureau (Nairobi), 1985.
Between the Years (fiction), Lake Publishers, 1987.
A Bridge in Time (fiction), Lake Publishers, 1987.
The Silver Cup (fiction), Lake Publishers, 1987.
Riana's Choice (short stories), Lake Publishers, 1987.
A Taste of Life, Lake Publishers, 1988.
Love Potion and Other Stories, Lake Publishers, 1988.
A Reed on the Roof, Block Ten, With Other Stories, Lake Publishers, 1988.

Member of editorial committee of Western Kenya branch of Wildlife Society. Contributor, sometimes under the name Kituomba, to periodicals, including *Women's Mirror* and *Viva.*

WORK IN PROGRESS: A Luo-English, English-Luo dictionary; a book on Juogi beliefs among the Abasuba of Rusinga Island; a book on Luo oral literature.

SIDELIGHTS: Asenath Odaga commented: ''I'm basically a storyteller to both children and adults. And like any other artist, I strive to attain perfection through deeper perception and clear insights into the experiences of life and daily events that go on around me, because it's from some of these common banalities that I draw and fashion some of my writing. I realize that together with all those who possess this creative ability, we have in a small way, in all humility, become co-creators with our gods. In the foregoing realization lies my sensitivity (akin to religion) and profound feelings against injustices meted on others through negation of some of the universal human values on account of race (as in the case in South Africa): creed, gender, and culture.

''What I'm driving at is that art (literature) has several functions apart from providing entertainment. At least this has always been the case in most African societies where art, including literature, was never indulged in just for art's sake, or purely for its aesthetic and entertainment values, but always had several other functions in society.''

AVOCATIONAL INTERESTS: Reading, photography, music, cooking, walking, painting, collecting traditional costumes and other artifacts of Kenyan people.

*   *   *

O'DANIEL, Therman B(enjamin)   1908-

PERSONAL: Born July 9, 1908, in Wilson, N.C.; son of John

Wesley (a landscape gardener) and Ernestine (Williams) O'Daniel; married Lillian Gertrude Davis (a teacher), June 4, 1935. *Education:* Lincoln University, Pa., B.A., 1930; University of Pennsylvania, M.A., 1932; graduate study at Harvard University, summer, 1934, University of Chicago, 1936-37, Pennsylvania State College (now University), summer, 1945, and University of Pennsylvania, 1946-47; University of Ottawa, Ph.D., 1956. *Religion:* Protestant.

ADDRESSES: Office—P.O. Box 480, Jefferson City, Mo. 65102.

CAREER: Allen University, Columbia, S.C., instructor, 1933-34, assistant professor, 1934-35, associate professor, 1935-36, professor of English and head of Division of Languages and Literature, 1936-37, dean of Liberal Arts College, 1937-40, acting president, 1939; Fort Valley State College, Fort Valley, Ga., associate professor, 1940-43, professor of English, 1944-45, acting administrative dean and registrar, 1945-46, head of English department, 1946-52, registrar and director of summer school, 1952-55; Dillard University, New Orleans, La., associate professor of English, 1955-56; Morgan State University, Baltimore, Md., assistant professor, 1956-63, associate professor, 1963-67, professor of English, 1967-78.

MEMBER: Modern Language Association of America (life member), National Council of Teachers of English, College English Association, College Language Association (life member; editor of special projects, 1978—), National Education Association (life member), Melville Society, National Association for the Advancement of Colored People (life member), Association for the Study of Negro Life and History, Society for the Study of Southern Literature, Maryland Council of English Teachers, Omega Psi Phi.

AWARDS, HONORS: Ford Foundation fellowship; Alice E. Johnson Memorial Fund Award, Black Academy of Arts and Letters, 1972, for co-founding and editing *College Language Association Journal.*

WRITINGS:

(Author of introduction) Wallace Thurman, *The Blacker the Berry,* Collier, 1970.
(Editor) *Langston Hughes, Black Genius: A Critical Evaluation,* Morrow, 1971.
James Baldwin: A Critical Evaluation, Howard University Press, 1977.

Contributor to *Allen University Bulletin, Atlanta University Review of Race and Culture, College Language Association Bulletin, College Language Association Journal,* and *Lincoln University Bulletin.* Editor of *Allen University Faculty Research Bulletin,* 1938-40, and *College Language Association Bulletin,* 1950-51; co-founding editor of *College Language Association Journal,* 1957-78; editor of special projects for College Language Association, 1978—.

*   *   *

OKARA, Gabriel (Imomotimi Gbaingbain)   1921-

PERSONAL: Some sources spell middle names Imomotime, Momotimi Gbaing-Bain, Obainbaing, and Obaingaing; born April 24 (one source says 21), 1921, in Bumoundi, Nigeria; son of Samson G. (in business) and Martha (Olodiama) Okara; married and divorced three times; children: Timi Okara-Schiller, Ebi Daniel. *Education:* Attended Government College, Umuahia, Nigeria, 1935-41, and Northwestern University. *Religion:* Christian Scientist.

ADDRESSES: Home—24 Nembe Rd., Port Harcourt, Rivers, Nigeria. *Office*—Council for Arts and Culture, 74/76 Bonny St., Port Harcourt, Rivers, Nigeria.

CAREER: Printer and bookbinder for Government Press, 1945-54; principal information officer for Eastern Nigerian Government Service, 1964-70; general manager of Rivers State Newspaper and Television Corps, Nigeria, 1971-75; currently associated with Council for Arts and Culture, Port Harcourt, Nigeria. Commissioner for information and broadcasting for government of state of Rivers, Nigeria, 1971-76.

MEMBER: Society of Nigerian Artists.

AWARDS, HONORS: "Best all-round" award from Nigerian Festival of Art, 1953, for poem "Call of the River Nun"; Commonwealth Joint Poetry Award, 1979, for *The Fisherman's Invocation.*

WRITINGS:

The Voice (novel), F. Watts, 1964.
The Fisherman's Invocation (poetry), Heinemann, 1978.

Works represented in anthologies, including *Pergamon Poets,* Oxford University Press, 1968. Author of a column in *Tide.* Contributor of poetry and short stories to journals, including *Black Orpheus* and *Transition.*

WORK IN PROGRESS: A series of supplementary reading textbooks for Rivers state schools.

SIDELIGHTS: Gabriel Okara commented: "I wrote *The Voice* because of the inconsistencies of our rulers after the British had left Nigeria. In the fight for independence our politicians denounced certain measures and attitudes of the colonial government, only to perpetrate the same ones when they took over. To protest openly was to invite political and economic suicide or ostracism by sycophants and camp followers, or even physical harassment. So *The Voice* was my counter oblique harassment!"

                              *   *   *

OKIGBO, Christopher (Ifenayichukwu) 1932-1967

PERSONAL: Born in 1932, in Ojoto, Nigeria; killed August, 1967, in military action near Nsukka, Biafra (now in Nigeria); son of James (a school teacher) Okigbo; married wife, Sefi, in 1963; children: Ibrahimat (daughter). *Education:* University of Ibadan, B.A., 1956.

CAREER: Nigerian Department of Research and Information, Lagos, Nigeria, private secretary to the Minister, 1955-56; affiliated with Nigerian Tobacco Company and United Africa Company; Fiditi Grammar School, Fiditi, Nigeria, Latin teacher, 1959-60; University of Nigeria, Nsukka, assistant librarian, 1960-62; Cambridge University Press, Ibadan, Nigeria, West African representative, 1962-66; founder of small publishing company with Chinua Achebe in Enugu, Nigeria, 1967. Member of editorial staff of Mbari Press. *Military service:* Biafran Defense Forces, 1967; became major; killed in action.

AWARDS, HONORS: Dakar Festival of Arts first prize, 1966 (refused); posthumously awarded Biafran National Order of Merit.

WRITINGS:

POEMS

Heavensgate, Mbari Press (Ibadan, Nigeria), 1962.
Limits, Mbari Press, 1964.
Labyrinths, with Path of Thunder, Africana, 1971.
Collected Poems, with a preface by Paul Theroux and introduction by Adewale Maja-Pearce, Heinemann, 1986.

Contributor of poetry to periodicals, including *Transition* and *Black Orpheus.* Co-editor of *Transition.*

SIDELIGHTS: "There wasn't a stage when I decided that I definitely wished to be a poet," Christopher Okigbo once commented, "there was a stage when I found that I couldn't be anything else."

According to Paul Theroux in *Introduction to Nigerian Literature,* Okigbo was "an obscure poet, possibly the most difficult poet in Africa." Theroux suggests two approaches to Okigbo's work. One is to examine the words he used, many springing from his wide knowledge of other writers, and all having a special meaning in the context of his own work. The other is to "listen to his music." According to Theroux, one can hear three separate melodies in it: "the music of youth, the clamour of passage (that is, growing up) and lastly, the sounds of thunder."

Part of the complexity of Okigbo's poetry, according to Sunday O. Anozie in *Christopher Okigbo: Creative Rhetoric,* lies in the fact that "he is constantly exploring two irregular dimensions of myth . . . myth as a privileged religious mode of cognition" and myth, with totem, as "affective and even evaluative in a given cultural context." Anozie also cites the derivative nature of the poet's work, the "wide range of references to and echoes of other poets."

In Theroux's opinion, *Heavensgate* and *Limits* express the "music of growth," a music which also suggests the danger inherent in growing up. The bird imagery running through both poems is related to the speaker, the poet who appears in all of Okigbo's work and would seem to represent Okigbo himself. *Silences* and *Distances* speak of the disillusionments which can follow maturation and the loss of innocence. "It is safe to say that very few poems achieve the music and harmony that *Silences* does," Theroux commented. *Distances,* however, is characterized by pain, shocking images such as that of the "horizontal stone" which represents a morgue slab holding a corpse, and the repetition of the line, "I was the sole witness to my homecoming," indicating solitude at the attainment of maturity.

Okigbo felt none of the conflict between old and new that often seems to pose a problem for educated Africans. He often went back to his village for festivals and major religious ceremonies, and his own religion combined Christian and pagan elements. Interviewed by Marjory Whitelaw in *Journal of Commonwealth Literature,* he described the family shrine which housed their ancestral gods, the male Ikenga and the female Udo, whom he considered different aspects of the same force represented by the Christian god. Unlike others in his family, he never made sacrifices to these deities, but he declared: "My creative activity is in fact one way of performing these functions in a different manner. Every time I write a poem, I am in fact offering a sacrifice." Okigbo's maternal grandfather, of whom he was believed to be a reincarnation, was the priest of a shrine to Idoto, the river goddess, and the poet's idea of his own priesthood is apparent in much of his writing.

In spite of this oneness with his background and the local themes and images which abound in his work, Okigbo did not adhere to the literary concept of negritude, which, he felt, emphasized racial differences. He told Whitelaw: "I think I am just a poet. A poet writes poetry and once a work is published it becomes public property. It's left to whoever reads it to decide whether it's African poetry or English. There isn't any such thing as a poet trying to express African-ness. Such a thing doesn't exist. A poet expresses himself."

His interest in social and political change in his own country, however, formed an inseparable part of his work. Okigbo told Whitelaw of his conviction that the poet in any society could not examine his own identity in isolation, but that "any writer who attempts a type of inward exploration will in fact be exploring his own society indirectly." Okigbo's concern for humanity was perhaps best expressed in his commitment to the Biafran secession. He lost his life in August, 1967, fighting as a volunteer for the Biafran forces.

Anozie wrote: "Nothing can be more tragic to the world of African poetry in English than the death of Christopher Okigbo, especially at a time when he was beginning to show maturity and coherence in his vision of art, life and society, and greater sophistication in poetic form and phraseology. Nevertheless his output, so rich and severe within so short a life, is sure to place him among the best and the greatest of our time."

BIOGRAPHICAL/CRITICAL SOURCES:

BOOKS

Anozie, Sunday O., *Christopher Okigbo: Creative Rhetoric,* Evans Brothers, 1972.
Bing, Bruce, editor, *Introduction to Nigerian Literature,* Evans Brothers, 1972.
Contemporary Literary Criticism, Volume 25, Gale, 1983.
Egudu, Romanus N., *Four Modern West African Poets,* NOK Publishers International, 1977.

PERIODICALS

Books Abroad, spring, 1971.
Comparative Literature Studies, June, 1971.
Journal of Commonwealth Literature, July, 1968, July, 1970, June, 1972.

*   *   *

OKPAKU, Joseph (Ohiomogben)   1943(?)-

PERSONAL: Surname is pronounced Or-pah-koo; born March 24, 1943 (some sources say 1935), in Lokoja, Nigeria; came to United States in 1962; son of Alfred (a postmaster) and Victoria Odakai (Johnson) Okpaku; married Sheila Rush (an attorney), July 18, 1971; children: Joseph Ohiomogben. *Education:* Northwestern University, B.A., 1965; Stanford University, M.S., 1966, and further graduate study; University of Warsaw, research fellow, 1969. *Politics:* None.

ADDRESSES: Home and office—Okpaku Communications, 444 Central Park W., New York, N.Y. 10025.

CAREER: Bemis Brothers, Inc., Minneapolis, Minn., efficiency analyst, 1965; Mobil International, New York, N.Y., engineering intern, 1966; *Journal of the New African Literature and the Arts,* New York City, founder, editor, and publisher, 1966—; Sarah Lawrence College, Bronxville, N.Y., associate professor of literature, 1970—. Instructor in African literature, Stanford University, 1969. President of Okpaku Communications (book publishing firm).

MEMBER: International P.E.N., African Studies Association (member of executive board, 1971), National Writers Club.

AWARDS, HONORS: BBC drama award, 1967, for "The Virtues of Adultery."

WRITINGS:

The Virtues of Adultery (play; first broadcast by British Broadcasting Corp., 1967), Stanford University Press, 1966.
The Presidents: The Frogs on Capitol Hill; A Ritual in Three Acts (play), Stanford University Press, 1967.
Under the Iroko Tree (novella), published in *Literary Review,* 1968.
"The Silhouette of God" (play), first produced in Berkeley, California, May 17, 1969.
(With Verna Sadock) *Four Months and Fifteen Days: The Chicago Trial,* Third Press, 1970.
(With Verna Sadock) *Verdict!: The Exclusive Picture Story of the Trial of the Chicago Eight,* illustrations by Sadock, commentary by Okpaku, Third Press, 1970.
(Editor) *New African Literature and the Arts* (selections from *Journal of the New African Literature and the Arts*), Third Press, Volume I, 1970, Volume II, 1970, Volume III, 1973.
(Editor) *Nigeria, Dilemma of Nationhood: An African Analysis of the Biafran Conflict,* Greenwood Press, 1971.
Superfight Number Two: The Story Behind the Fights Between Muhammad Ali and Joe Frazier, Okpaku, 1974.

Also author of plays, "The Two Faces of Anirejouritse," 1965, and "Born Astride the Grave," 1966, and of a narrative pantomime, "The Silhouette of God." Contributor to *World Development,* edited by Helene Castel. Contributor to *Chicago Sun-Times, Africa Report, Presence Africaine, UNESCO, Frankfurter Allgemeine Zeitung,* and other periodicals.

WORK IN PROGRESS: African Mythology; Anatomy of the White American Male.

SIDELIGHTS: According to a *Publisher's Weekly* article on small Black presses in the United States, "[Joseph] Okpaku's decision to abandon engineering in favor of writing was based on ideology, on the conviction that 'Africa is being led astray by Western "experts" who dominate African cultural life.'" The article continues to say that "Okpaku formulated plans for a book publishing arm of his *Journal* (now a highly respected quarterly on African humanities) while still a graduate student at Stanford. 'I thought there was a need for a book publishing dialog in the humanities that was controlled by an African, not by the Paris or London publishing houses that now dominate African publishing,'" Okpaku was quoted. Founder of The Third Press in 1968, he plans to publish ten to twelve new titles a year, including a series of children's books.

BIOGRAPHICAL/CRITICAL SOURCES:

PERIODICALS

Publishers Weekly, March 15, 1971.

*   *   *

ONYEAMA, (Charles) Dillibe   1951-

PERSONAL: Born January 6, 1951, in Enugu, Nigeria; immigrated to England, 1959; son of Charles Dadi (a judge) and Susannah (a homemaker; maiden name, Ogwudu) Onyeama; married Ethel Ekwueme (a teacher), December 18, 1982; children: three. *Education:* Attended schools in Nigeria and England. *Politics:* "Free enterprise."

ADDRESSES: Home—8B Byron Onyeama Close, P.O. Box 1172, Enugu, Anambra State, Nigeria. *Office*—Delta Publications (Nigeria) Ltd., 172 Ogui Rd., Enugu, Nigeria. *Agent*—Elspeth Cochrane Agency, 11/13 Orlando Rd., London SW4, England.

CAREER: Drum Publications, London, England, subeditor, 1974-75; *West Africa* magazine, London, journalist, 1979; Delta Publications (Nigeria) Ltd., Nigeria, managing director, 1988—; free-lance writer and author. Former editor for Satellite Books.

WRITINGS:

Nigger at Eton, Frewin Publishers, 1972, revised edition, Delta, 1982.
John Bull's Nigger, Frewin Publishers, 1974.
(Compiler) *The Book of Black Man's Humour,* Satellite Books, 1975.
(Compiler of text, with John Walters) *I'm the Greatest! The Wit and Humour of Muhammad Ali,* Frewin Publishers, 1975.
Sex Is a Nigger's Game (novel), Satellite Books, 1976.
Ju Ju: A Novel, Satellite Books, 1977, Archer Editions, 1980.
Secret Society: A Novel, Satellite Books, 1978.
The Return: Homecoming of a Negro From Eton, Satellite Books, 1978.
Female Target: A Novel, Satellite Books, 1979.
Revenge of the Medicine Man, Sphere, 1980.
Rules of the Game: Nigeria's Constitution, Foulsham, 1981.
Chief Onyeama: The Story of an African God (biography), Delta, 1982.
Night Demon, Sphere, 1982.
Modern Messiah: The Jim Nwobodo Story, foreword by Nnamdi Azikiwe, Delta, 1983.
Godfathers of Voodoo: A Novel, Delta, 1985.
African Legend: The Incredible Story of Francis Arthur Nzeribe (biography), Delta, 1985.
Correct English, Foulsham, 1986.
Notes of a So-Called Afro-Saxon, Delta, 1988.

SIDELIGHTS: A one-time subeditor for Drum Publications in England and full-time journalist and author, Dillibe Onyeama has written various biographies and a number of controversial novels. In particular, his writing addresses racial and political issues, ranging from his personal experiences to those of his native country of Nigeria.

Onyeama told *CA:* "Words hold for me the same beauty and fascination as well-arranged flowers."

AVOCATIONAL INTERESTS: Reading, occult matters.

BIOGRAPHICAL/CRITICAL SOURCES:

PERIODICALS

Spectator, August 17, 1974.
Times Literary Supplement, July 14, 1972, April 19, 1985.

*   *   *

OUSMANE, Sembene   1923-

PERSONAL: Name cited in some sources as Ousmane Sembene; born January 8, 1923, in Ziguinchor, Casamance, Senegal. *Education:* Attended technical school; studied at Gorki Film Studios in early 1960s.

ADDRESSES: Home—c/o P.O. Box 8087 YOFF, Dakar, Senegal.

CAREER: Worked as fisherman in Casamance, Senegal, and as plumber, mechanic's aid, and bricklayer in Dakar, Senegal, before World War II; worked as docker and stevedore in Marseilles, France, in late 1940s; became union leader. Writer and filmmaker. *Military service:* Served in French Army during World War II.

AWARDS, HONORS: Literature prize from Dakar Festival of Negro Arts, 1966, for *Vehi-Ciosane ou Blanche-genese, suivi du Mandat;* prize from Cannes Film Festival, 1967, for "Le Noire de . . ."; special prize from Venice Film Festival, 1968, and award for best foreign film from Atlanta Film Festival, 1970, both for "Mandabi."

WRITINGS:

Le Docker noir (novel; title means "The Black Docker"), Nouvelles Editions Debresse, 1956.
Oh Pays, mon beau peuple! (novel; title means "Oh My Country, My Beautiful People"), Le Livre Contemporain, 1957.
Les Bouts de bois de Dieu (novel), Amiot-Dumont, 1960, translation by Francis Price published as *God's Bits of Wood,* Doubleday, 1962.
Voltaieque (short stories), Presence Africaine, 1962, translation by Len Ortzen published as *Tribal Scars, and Other Stories,* INSCAPE, 1974.
Vehi-Ciosane; ou, Blanche-genese, suivi du Mandat (two novellas), Presence Africaine, 1965, translation by Clive Wake published as *The Money Order, With White Genesis,* Heinemann, 1971.
Xala (novel; title means "Impotence"), Presence Africaine, 1973, translation by Clive Wake published as *Xala,* Lawrence Hill, 1976.
Dernier de l'empire (novel), Harmattan, 1981, translation by Adrian Adams published as *The Last of the Empire,* Heinemann, 1983.

Also author of the novel *Fat Ndiay Diop,* 1976.

OTHER PUBLISHED FICTION

"La Noire de . . ." (short story), published in *Presence africaine* in 1961, translation by Ellen Conroy Kennedy published as "Black Girl" in *African Short Stories,* edited by Charles R. Larson, Macmillan, 1970.
Referendum (novel; first novel in *L'Harmattan* trilogy), published in *Presence africaine* in 1964.

SCREENPLAYS; AND DIRECTOR

"La Noire de . . ." (adapted from Ousmane's story; also see above), Actualities Francais/Films Domirev of Dakar, 1966 (released in the United States as "Black Girl," New Yorker Films, 1969).
"Mandabi" (adapted from Ousmane's novella *The Money Order;* also see above), Jean Maumy, 1968 (released in the United States by Grove Press, 1969).
"Emitai," Paulin Soumanou Vieya, 1971 (released in the United States by New Yorker Films, 1973).
"Xala" (title means "Impotence"), Societe Nationale Cinematographique/Films Domirev, 1974 (released in the United States by New Yorker Films, 1975).
"Ceddo," released in the United States by New Yorker Films, 1978 (first released in 1977).

Also screenwriter and director of "Borom Sarret," 1964; "Niaye," 1964; "Tauw," 1970; and the unreleased film "Songhays," 1963.

OTHER

Contributor to periodicals, including *Presence africaine*. Founding editor of periodical *Kaddu*.

SIDELIGHTS: Sembene Ousmane is a respected Senegalese artist who has distinguished himself in both literature and film. He was born in 1923 in the Casamance region and attended school only briefly before working as a fisherman. After moving to Senegal's capital, Dakar, Ousmane found various jobs in manual labor. He worked in Dakar during the late 1930s, but when World War II began he was drafted by the colonial French into their armed forces, and he eventually participated in the Allied invasion of Italy. When the war ended Ousmane returned home to the Casamance area and resumed his early life as a fisherman. After a short period, however, he traveled back to France, where he found work as a stevedore on the Marseilles docks.

Ousmane's experiences as a dockworker provided background for his first novel, *Le Docker noir* ("The Black Docker"). In this work Ousmane wrote of a black stevedore who writes a novel but is robbed of the manuscript by a white woman. Much of the novel delineates the ensuing consequences of that incident. Although *Le Docker noir* proved somewhat flawed, it nonetheless represented an alternative career for Ousmane after a back injury rendered him unfit for dock work.

With *Le Docker noir* Ousmane sought to express the plight of many minorities—including Spaniards and Arabs as well as blacks—exploited and abused at the French dockyards. But while he specified afterwards that his perspective was that of the minority, and thus contrary to that of whites, Ousmane was quick to add that he was not advocating *negritude*, a black-pride movement that he dismissed as sentimental and narrow-minded in its emphasis. He remained, however, a champion of black rights in Africa.

Ousmane's concern over conflicting philosophies within Africa's black community is evident in his second novel, *O Pays, mon beau peuple!* ("O My Country, My Beautiful People"), which concerns the failings of an ambitious Senegalese farmer returning home after a long absence. Accompanied by his white wife, the farmer alienates himself from both whites and blacks, for both groups resent his interracial marriage and his efforts to modernize the community's farming system. Eventually the farmer's behavior becomes intolerable to the villagers, and he is killed.

Like *Le Docker noir*, *O Pays, mon beau peuple!* was written in French, but unlike the earlier novel, Ousmane's second work fared well throughout much of Europe and was even published in Japan. After completing *O Pays, mon beau peuple!* Ousmane spent a few years traveling in many of the countries where the novel was earning acclaim. He eventually left Europe, however, and visited Cuba, China, and even the Soviet Union, where he studied filmmaking at a leading studio.

In 1960 Ousmane published his third novel, *Les Bouts de bois de Dieu* (*God's Bits of Wood*), which became his first work to gain significant attention from English readers. *God's Bits of Wood* is a fictionalized account of a railroad workers' strike that stalled transportation from Dakar to Niger in late 1947 and early 1948. Much more ambitious than Ousmane's previous works, the third novel is a sweeping, epic-style account featuring several characters and spanning Senegal's political and social extremes. In 1970, when the novel appeared in English translation, *Times Literary Supplement*'s reviewer T. M. Aluko wrote that Ousmane's work was a vivid rendering of the strike and the strikers. Aluko also cited Ousmane's particular skills as a novelist, declaring that he possessed "the ability to control a wide social panorama, without once losing sight of, or compassion for, the complexity and suffering of individuals."

Ousmane followed *God's Bits of Wood* with a short story collection, *Voltaieque* (*Tribal Scars*), and *Referendum*, the first part of a trilogy entitled *L'Harmattan* ("The Storm"). He then completed *Vehi-Ciosane; ou, Blanche-genese, suivi du Mandat* (*The Money Order, With White Genesis*), a volume comprised of two novellas. The book was an immense critical success, earning Ousmane the literature prize from the 1966 Dakar Festival of Negro Arts.

By the mid-1960s Ousmane was also working in film. In 1964 he completed his first notable work in that medium, the sociological study "Borom Sarret," and three years later he wrote and directed "Le Noire de . . ." ("Black Girl"), which detailed the degrading circumstances endured by an African servant in a French household. These films were shown together in New York City in 1969, and A. H. Weiler writing in the *New York Times* called both works insightful and provocative. Weiler also wrote that Ousmane's films derived from "the quiet distinctions of simplicity, sincerity and subdued anger toward the freed black man's new burdens." In addition, Weiler contended that the works "put a sharp, bright focus on an emerging, once dark African area."

Ousmane enjoyed even greater acclaim as a filmmaker with "Mandabi," his adaptation of his own novella *The Money Order*. "Mandabi" is a comedy about a middle-aged fool, Dieng, who receives a considerable financial sum from a nephew in Paris. Much of the humor in "Mandabi" derives from Dieng's vain, foolhardy efforts to secure identification papers necessary for cashing the money order. In the course of his efforts Dieng is swindled, robbed, thrashed, and publicly humiliated by his greedy family and fellow citizens. Adding further to the humor is the actual behavior of Dieng, an arrogant dimwit who smugly parades about his village oblivious of the animosity he provokes. In the *New York Times*, Roger Greenspun noted as much when he wrote that because Dieng "is such a pompous fool, so blithely superior to his two wives, so gluttonous with his food and confident in his walk, his troubles seem deserved and funny." Greenspun described Ousmane's directorial style as "spare, laconic, slightly ironic" and added that he "displays a reticence towards his characters that grants him freedom from explicit moral judgment."

Humor did not figure in Ousmane's next film, "Emitai," which he completed in 1971. In this work he chronicles a conflict between Senegalese natives and French colonialists at the beginning of World War II. The conflict centers on the natives' opposition to French troops sent into the Senegalese village to commandeer several tons of rice. Neither faction particularly cherishes the rice: For the villagers it is intended for use in religious ceremonies; for the French, it is rendered unnecessary by a change in military tactics. Nonetheless, neither side concedes to the other, and the conflict is resolved with futile violence. In his *New York Times* review, Roger Greenspun found "Emitai" a refreshing, if sobering, counterpoint to the Hollywood adventure films of the 1930s and 1940s, observing that "the absolute ineffectiveness of massed spears against a few well-placed rifles should lay to rest the memories of a good many delicious terrors during Saturday afternoons at the movies." Greenspun also commended Ousmane's directorial reserve and subtlety and declared that the filmmaker's relatively detached style resulted in a film "that keeps surprising you with its ironic sophistication."

Ousmane's next filmmaking venture, "Xala," marked his return to comedy. In "Xala" he lampoons the increasing Westernization of African politics and business. The protagonist of "Xala" is El Hadji, a corrupt bureaucrat who also serves his community as an importer of fairly exotic goods, including whiskey, yogurt, and perfume. Like his Western counterparts, El Hadji wears costly European business suits, totes a briefcase, and continually confers with advisers and fellow bureaucrats. His corrupt ways, while causing no good to his community, have contributed greatly to his considerable prosperity. That prosperity, however, is undermined when El Hadji takes a third wife and discovers that he is suddenly impotent. Apparently the victim of a curse, El Hadji consults witch doctors, including one fellow who sports an expensive business suit while squatting in his hut. That witch doctor fails to cure El Hadji, but for a substantial sum another doctor is able to restore the bureaucrat's sexuality. Unfortunately, troubles continue to plague El Hadji when he is implicated in a corrupt business action and is dismissed, by equally corrupt fellow bureaucrats, from the community's chamber of commerce. More marital problems then ensue, for El Hadji fails to pay his witch doctor and is thus once again impotent. Another cure is then attempted, one in which El Hadji must remove his clothing and allow several cripples to spit on him. He complies, but a much greater catastrophe awaits him.

"Xala" was released in 1974, only months after Ousmane had published his novel of the same name. When the film was shown in the United States in 1975, it was commended in the *New York Times* as "an instructive delight" and as "cutting, radiant and hilarious." *Time*'s reviewer, Richard Eder, added that Ousmane's film was George Orwell's novel *Animal Farm* "applied to African independence." Similarly, Ousmane's novel *Xala* was cited by *Nation* reviewer Eve Ottenberg as a witty portrait of "the destruction of tribal values." She wrote that the themes of *Xala* allowed Ousmane "to show people at their most flawed, eccentric, energetic and comic."

Ousmane continued to probe cultural discontinuity in "Ceddo," his 1977 film about religious conflict in an unspecified African kingdom. This conflict is triggered when a Catholic king converts to Islam and brings a Moslem teacher into his band of advisers. The king's associates then convert to Islam, too, leaving only the common villagers outside the Islamic faith. Resentful of the king's changing policies, the villagers kidnap the king's daughter and thus force him to negotiate. During meetings between factions, the opportunistic Islamic teacher

intercedes and precipitates the slaughter of all the non-Moslems. Vincent Canby, in his review for the *New York Times*, noted that the manner of "Ceddo" was "reserved, cool, almost stately." He confirmed that the obviously anti-Moslem film had been banned in Senegal, but Canby observed that the banning was prompted by a seemingly trivial aspect: Ousmane refused to render the spelling of the film's title to be consistent with his government's own spelling.

Ousmane's stature as an African artist has risen steadily since he published his first work in 1956. In the ensuing years he has used his art to protest injustice against blacks and to decry the increasing disintegration of black Africa's heritages. He has also established himself as a formidable filmmaker in a medium where commercial considerations are usually dominant over the artistic, and the critical acclaim accorded his films in the United States testifies to his wide appeal and considerable achievements. Ousmane's works thus transcend cultural specifics and assure him recognition as a leading artist of his time.

BIOGRAPHICAL/CRITICAL SOURCES:

BOOKS

Brench, A. C., *The Novelists' Inheritance in French Africa: Writing From Senegal to Cameroon*, Oxford University Press, 1967.
Dathorne, O. R., *African Literature in the Twentieth Century*, Heinemann Educational, 1976.
Silver, Helene and Hans M. Zell, editors, *A Reader's Guide to African Literature*, Africana Publishing, 1971.

PERIODICALS

Africa Report, February, 1963.
American Cinematographer, November, 1972.
Black Orpheus, November, 1959.
Cineaste, Volume 6, number 1, 1973.
Cinema Quebec, March/April, 1973.
Film Quarterly, spring, 1973.
Nation, April 9, 1977.
New Yorker, May 16, 1977.
New York Times, January 13, 1969, September 30, 1969, November 9, 1969, February 10, 1973, October 1, 1975, January 27, 1978.
New York Times Book Review, November 28, 1976.
Quarterly Review of Film Studies, spring, 1979.
Times Literary Supplement, October 16, 1970.
World Literature Today, winter, 1978.

—Sketch by Les Stone

P

PAINTER, Nell Irvin 1942-

PERSONAL: Born August 2, 1942, in Houston, Tex.; daughter of Frank Edward (a chemist) and Dona Lolita (a personnel officer; maiden name, McGruder) Irvin. *Education:* University of California, Berkeley, B.A., 1964; University of California, Los Angeles, M.A., 1967; Harvard University, Ph.D., 1974; also attended University of Bordeaux, 1962-63, and University of Ghana, 1965-66. *Politics:* Democrat. *Religion:* None.

ADDRESSES: Home—Rt. 9, Boothe Hill 15, Chapel Hill, N.C. 27514. *Office*—Department of History, University of North Carolina at Chapel Hill, Chapel Hill, N.C. 27514.

CAREER: University of Pennsylvania, Philadelphia, assistant professor, 1974-77, associate professor of American and Afro-American history, 1978-80; University of North Carolina at Chapel Hill, professor of history, 1980—. Resident associate of Afro-American studies at W. E. B. Du Bois Institute, Harvard University, 1977-78.

MEMBER: Organization of American Historians, Association for the Study of Afro-American Life and History, Berkshire Conference of Women Historians, Association of Black Women Historians.

AWARDS, HONORS: Coretta Scott King Award from American Association of University Women, 1969; American Council of Learned Societies fellowship, 1976-77; fellow of the Charles Warren Center for Studies in American History, Harvard University, 1976-77; Radcliffe Institute fellowship, 1976-77; fellow in American history, National Humanities Center, North Carolina, 1978-79.

WRITINGS:

Exodusters: Black Migration to Kansas after Reconstruction, Knopf, 1977.
The Narrative of Hosea Hudson: His Life as a Negro Communist in the South, Harvard University Press, 1979.
The Progressive Era, Knopf, 1984.
Standing at Armageddon: The United States, 1877-1919, Norton, 1987.

Also author of *Disquieting Portents: The United States 1886-1919,* Knopf. Contributor to periodicals, including *New England Quarterly* and *Nation.*

WORK IN PROGRESS: Mixed Blood and Pure Blood in the Minds of Americans, 1890-1920, an intellectual history.

SIDELIGHTS: Nell Irvin Painter, a historian of the Progressive and Reconstruction eras in the United States, has received critical acclaim for her books *Exodusters: Black Migration to Kansas after Reconstruction* and *The Narrative of Hosea Hudson: His Life as a Negro Communist in the South.* Both works reveal aspects of black American life in the late nineteenth and early twentieth centuries, but the historian's method of presentation in each book is decidedly different. *Exodusters* explores the relocation of Southern blacks to Kansas in the 1880s, primarily utilizing written sources, and *The Narrative of Hosea Hudson* is a compilation of oral memoirs of a black union organizer who allied himself with the Communist party. The works have led *New York Times Book Review* contributor Joe Klein to comment that Painter "seems to have a knack for finding the more curious nooks and crannies of the black experience in America."

Theodore Rosengarten, reviewing *Exodusters* for *New Republic,* writes of Painter: "She proves, succinctly and beyond a doubt, that the initiative among [some blacks] to leave the South [for Kansas] was rooted in everyday oppression. Many historians have worked with the same kind of evidence; yet, Painter's presentation of 'The Economics of Oppression' is startlingly fresh. She exposes the heart and sword of post-Reconstruction rural tyranny—the contract between landlord and farmer." Calling *Exodusters* an "eloquent and moving book" in the *Washington Post Book World,* David Brion Davis concludes: "Painter admirably succeeds in portraying the great exodus of 1879 as a collective black response to blasted hopes, not as the response of ignorant folk to unscrupulous speculators and agitators." In an article for the *New York Times Book Review,* David Herbert Donald expresses the opinion that Painter's book is "one of the first serious historical studies produced by a young black scholar influenced by the doctrines of black nationalism and black separatism that became current in the late 1960s. . . . 'Exodusters' certainly succeeds in its larger purpose of challenging students of the Afro-American experience to re-examine grass-roots black protest movements."

Critics have been equally enthusiastic about *The Narrative of Hosea Hudson.* In the *Nation,* Benita Eisler praises the book as "a modern epic, tracing a twentieth-century hero's road from bondage to freedom. . . . Moving, fearful and funny, Hudson and Painter's *Narrative* is as valuable an American life as has ever been wrested from anonymity.'' Though the work is ostensibly comprised of Hudson's oral memoirs, Painter faced the monumental task of organizing hundreds of hours of recorded tape into a coherent whole. Painter admitted to Sarah Crichton in *Publishers Weekly* that the project wore her out. ''I feel like I've added 50 years to my own,'' she said. ''I OD'd on sound.'' Her efforts have not gone unnoticed, however. Eisler writes: ''Painter is an ideal collaborator in this complex enterprise. Shaping several years of taped interviews into a coherent dramatic narrative is, first of all, an impressive literary achievement.'' In an essay for the *New York Review of Books,* Theodore Draper makes a similar observation: ''[Painter] coaxed a story out of Hudson that belongs with the best of black—or white—autobiographies.''

BIOGRAPHICAL/CRITICAL SOURCES:

PERIODICALS

Nation, January 5-12, 1980.
New Republic, February 12, 1977.
Newsweek, January 17, 1977.
New York Review of Books, May 9, 1985.
New York Times, January 29, 1977.
New York Times Book Review, January 30, 1977, November 18, 1979, October 4, 1987.
Publishers Weekly, November 5, 1979.
Washington Post, January 24, 1988.
Washington Post Book World, March 6, 1977, January 27, 1980, November 22, 1987.

*   *   *

PALMER, C(yril) Everard   1930-

PERSONAL: Born October 15, 1930, in Kendal, Jamaica; son of Cyril (a farmer) and Vida Palmer. *Education:* Mico Training College, teaching diploma, 1955; Lakehead University, B.A.

ADDRESSES: P.O. Box 31, Nipigon, Ontario POT 2JO, Canada.

CAREER: Teacher, 1956—; teacher in Red Rock, Ontario, beginning 1971.

WRITINGS:

JUVENILE FICTION

A Broken Vessel, Pioneer Press (Kingston, Jamaica), 1960.
The Adventures of Jimmy Maxwell, Jamaica Publications Branch of Ministry of Education, 1962.
The Cloud with the Silver Lining, Deutsch, 1966, Pantheon, 1967.
Big Doc Bitteroot, Deutsch, 1968, Bobbs-Merrill, 1971.
The Sun Salutes You, Deutsch, 1970, Bobbs-Merrill, 1971.
The Hummingbird People, Deutsch, 1971.
A Cow Called Boy, Bobbs-Merrill, 1971.
The Wooing of Beppo Tate, Deutsch, 1972.
Baba and Mr. Big, Bobbs-Merrill, 1972.
My Father Sun-Sun Johnson, Deutsch, 1974.
A Taste of Danger, Ministry of Education, 1976.
A Dog Called Houdini, Deutsch, 1978.
Houdini, Come Home, Deutsch, 1981.

BIOGRAPHICAL/CRITICAL SOURCES:

PERIODICALS

Books and Bookmen, May, 1970.
Times Literary Supplement, April 16, 1970.

*   *   *

PARKS, Gordon (Alexander Buchanan)   1912-

PERSONAL: Born November 30, 1912, in Fort Scott, Kan.; son of Andrew Jackson and Sarah (Ross) Parks; married Sally Alvis, 1933 (divorced, 1961); married Elizabeth Campbell, December, 1962 (divorced, 1973); married Genevieve Young (a book editor), August 26, 1973; children: (first marriage) Gordon, Jr. (deceased), Toni (Mrs. Jean-Luc Brouillaud), David; (second marriage) Leslie. *Education:* Attended high school in St. Paul, Minn. *Politics:* Democrat. *Religion:* Methodist.

ADDRESSES: Home—860 United Nations Plaza, New York, N.Y. 10017. *Agent*—(Film) Ben Benjamin, Creative Management Associates, 9255 Sunset Blvd., Los Angeles, Calif. 90069.

CAREER: Photographer, writer, film director, and composer. Worked at various jobs prior to 1937; free-lance fashion photographer in Minneapolis, 1937-42; photographer with Farm Security Administration, 1942-43, with Office of War Information, 1944, and with Standard Oil Co. of New Jersey, 1945-48; *Life,* New York City, photo-journalist, 1948-72; *Essence* (magazine), New York City, editorial director, 1970-73. President of Winger Corp. Film director, 1968—, directing motion pictures for Warner Brothers-Seven Arts, Metro-Goldwyn-Mayer (M.G.M.), and Paramount Pictures, including ''The Learning Tree,'' Warner Brothers, 1968, ''Shaft,'' M.G.M., 1972, ''Shaft's Big Score,'' M.G.M., 1972, ''The Super Cops,'' M.G.M., 1974, and ''Leadbelly,'' Paramount, 1975, as well as several documentaries. Composer of concertos and sonatas performed by symphony orchestras in the United States and Europe.

MEMBER: Authors Guild (member of council, 1973-74), Authors League of America, Black Academy of Arts and Letters (fellow), Directors Guild of America (member of national council, 1973-76), Newspaper Guild, American Society of Magazine Photographers, Association of Composers and Directors, American Society of Composers, Authors, and Publishers, American Federation of Television and Radio Artists, National Association for the Advancement of Colored People, Directors Guild of New York (member of council), Urban League, Players Club (New York), Kappa Alpha Mu.

AWARDS, HONORS: Rosenwald Foundation fellow, 1942; once chosen Photographer of the Year, Association of Magazine Photographers; Frederic W. Brehm award, 1962; Mass Media Award, National Conference of Christians and Jews, for outstanding contributions to better human relations, 1964; Carr Van Adna Journalism Award, University of Miami, 1964, Ohio University, 1970; named photographer-writer who had done the most to promote understanding among nations of the world in an international vote conducted by the makers of Nikon photographic equipment, 1967; A.F.D., Maryland Institute of Fine Arts, 1968; Litt.D., University of Connecticut, 1969, and Kansas State University, 1970; Spingarn Medal from National Association for the Advancement of Colored People, 1972; H.H.D., St. Olaf College, 1973, Rutgers University, 1980, and Pratt Institute, 1981; Christopher Award, 1980, for *Flavio;* President's Fellow award, Rhode Island School of Design, 1984; named Kansan of the Year, Native Sons and Daughters of Kansas, 1986; additional awards include honorary degrees from Fairfield University, 1969, Boston University, 1969, Macalaster College, 1974, Colby College, 1974, Lincoln University, 1975, and awards from Syracuse University School of Journalism, 1963, University of Miami, 1964, Philadelphia Museum of Art, 1964, and Art Directors Club, 1964, 1968.

WRITINGS:

Flash Photography, [New York], 1947.
Camera Portraits: The Techniques and Principles of Documentary Portraiture, F. Watts, 1948.
The Learning Tree (novel; also see below), Harper, 1963.
A Choice of Weapons (autobiography), Harper, 1966, reprinted, Minnesota Historical Society, 1986.
A Poet and His Camera, self-illustrated with photographs, Viking, 1968.
(And composer of musical score) "The Learning Tree" (screenplay; based on novel of same title), produced by Warner Brothers-Seven Arts, 1968.
Gordon Parks: Whispers of Intimate Things (poems), self-illustrated with photographs, Viking, 1971.
Born Black (essays), self-illustrated with photographs, Lippincott, 1971.
In Love (poems), self-illustrated with photographs, Lippincott, 1971.
Moments without Proper Names (poems), self-illustrated with photographs, Viking, 1975.
Flavio, Norton, 1978.
To Smile in Autumn: A Memoir, Norton, 1979.
Shannon (novel), Little, Brown, 1981.

Also author of several television documentaries produced by National Educational Television, including "Flavio" and "Mean Streets." Contributor to *Show, Vogue, Venture,* and other periodicals.

SIDELIGHTS: Gordon Parks's "life constitutes an American success story of almost mythic proportions," Andy Grundberg once commented in the *New York Times.* A high school dropout who had to fend for himself at the age of sixteen, Parks overcame the difficulties of being black, uneducated, and poor to become a *Life* magazine photographer; a writer of fiction, nonfiction, and poetry; a composer; and a film director and producer. The wide scope of Parks's expertise is all the more impressive when viewed in its historical context, for many of the fields he succeeded in formerly had been closed to blacks. Parks was the first black to work at *Life* magazine, *Vogue,* the Office of War Information, and the Federal Security Administration. He was also the first black to write, direct, produce, and score a film, "The Learning Tree," based on his 1963 novel. Parks maintains that his drive to succeed in such a variety of professions was motivated by fear. "I was so frightened I might fail that I figured if one thing didn't work out I could fall back on another," Parks stated in the *Detroit News.*

Parks's first professional endeavor was photography, a craft he practiced as a free-lance fashion photographer in Minneapolis and later as a Rosenwald Foundation fellow in 1942. In 1948 he was hired as a *Life* magazine photographer, and throughout his over twenty-year affiliation with that publication photographed world events, celebrities, musicians, artists, and politicians. In addition to his work for *Life,* Parks has exhibited his photography and illustrated his books with photos. In a *New York Times* review of one of Parks's photography exhibitions, Hilton Kramer notes that while Parks is a versatile photographer, "it is in the pictures where his 'black childhood of confusion and poverty' still makes itself felt that he moves us most deeply." Grundberg similarly notes that Parks's "most memorable pictures, and the most vividly felt sections of the exhibition, deal specifically with the conditions and social fabric of black Americans."

Parks found, however, that despite his love of and expertise in photography, he needed to express in words the intense feelings about his childhood. This need resulted in his first novel, *The Learning Tree,* which in some ways parallels Parks's youth. The novel concerns the Wingers, a black family living in a small town in Kansas during the 1920s, and focuses in particular on Newt, the Wingers' adolescent son. "On one level, it is the story of a particular Negro family who manages to maintain its dignity and self-respect as citizens and decent human beings in a border Southern town," writes *Dictionary of Literary Biography* contributor Jane Ball. "On another, it is a symbolic tale of the black man's struggle against social, economic, and natural forces, sometimes winning, sometimes losing." A *Time* reviewer comments: "[Parks's] unabashed nostalgia for what was good there, blended with sharp recollections of staggering violence and fear, makes an immensely readable, sometimes unsettling book."

Parks explores his life further in two autobiographical volumes, *A Choice of Weapons* and *To Smile in Autumn.* The first volume begins when Parks is sixteen and describes how, after his mother's death and an unsuccessful stint living with relatives in Minneapolis, Parks found himself out on the street. For a decade, Parks struggled to feed and clothe himself, all the while cultivating his ambition to be a photographer. The book's theme, according to *Washington Post* contributor Christopher Schemering, is that "one's choice of weapons must be dignity and hard work over the self-destructive, if perhaps understandable, emotions of hate and violence." Alluding to the unfortunate circumstances of his youth, Parks expressed a similar view in the *Detroit News.* "I have a right to be bitter, but I would not let bitterness destroy me. As I tell young black people, you can fight back, but do it in a way to help yourself and not destroy yourself."

Saturday Review contributor Edwin M. Yoder, Jr., writes: "[*A Choice of Weapons*] is an excellent introduction to what it must have been like to be black and ambitious—and poor—in the America of a generation ago, when nearly every door was sealed to Negroes as never before or since in American history." Observing that "what [Parks] has refused to accept is the popular definition of what being black is and the limitations that the definition automatically imposes," Saunders Redding concludes in the *New York Times Book Review:* "'A Choice of Weapons' is . . . a perceptive narrative of one man's struggle to realize the values (defined as democratic and especially American) he has been taught to respect."

To Smile in Autumn, Parks's second autobiographical volume, covers the years from 1943 to 1979. Here Parks celebrates "the triumph of achievement, the abundance and glamour of a productive life," writes *New York Times Book Review* contributor Mel Watkins. Parks also acknowledges, however, that his success was not without a price. Ralph Tyler comments in the *Chicago Tribune Book World:* "Although this third memoir doesn't have the drama inherent in a fight for survival, it has a drama of its own: the conflict confronting a black American who succeeds in the white world." As Parks writes in *To Smile in Autumn:* "In escaping the mire, I had lost friends along the way. . . . In one world I was a social oddity. In the other world I was almost a stranger."

Schemering notes that the book contains material "recast" from Parks's earlier work, *Born Black*, and is in this respect somewhat disappointing. He writes: "It's unfortunate to see a major talent and cultural force coast on former successes. Yet, even at half-mast, Parks manages a sporadic eloquence, as in the last few pages when he pays tribute to his son Gordon Parks Jr., who died in a plane crash." Watkins offers this view: "Gordon Parks emerges here as a Renaissance man who has resolutely pursued success in several fields. His memoir is sustained and enlivened by his urbanity and generosity."

BIOGRAPHICAL/CRITICAL SOURCES:

BOOKS

Authors in the News, Volume 2, Gale, 1976.
Contemporary Literary Criticism, Gale, Volume 1, 1973, Volume 16, 1981.
Dictionary of Literary Biography, Volume 33: *Afro-American Fiction Writers after 1955*, Gale, 1984.
Harnan, Terry, *Gordon Parks: Black Photographer and Film Maker*, Garrard, 1972.
Monaco, James, *American Film Now: The People, the Power, the Money, the Movies*, New American Library, 1979.
Parks, Gordon, *A Choice of Weapons*, Harper, 1966, reprinted, Minnesota Historical Society, 1986.
Parks, Gordon, *To Smile in Autumn: A Memoir*, Norton, 1979.
Rolansky, John D., editor, *Creativity*, North-Holland Publishing, 1970.
Turk, Midge, *Gordon Parks*, Crowell, 1971.

PERIODICALS

Best Sellers, April 1, 1971.
Black World, August, 1973.
Chicago Tribune Book World, December 30, 1979.
Commonweal, September 5, 1969.
Cue, August 9, 1969.
Detroit News, February 1, 1976.
Films in Review, October, 1972.
Horn Book, April, 1971, August, 1971.
Newsweek, April 29, 1968, August 11, 1969, April 19, 1976.
New York, June 14, 1976.
New Yorker, November 2, 1963, February 13, 1966.
New York Times, October 4, 1975, December 3, 1975, March 1, 1986.
New York Times Book Review, September 15, 1963, February 13, 1966, December 23, 1979.
Saturday Review, February 12, 1966, August 9, 1969.
Show Business, August 2, 1969.
Time, September 6, 1963, September 29, 1969, May 24, 1976.
Variety, November 6, 1968, June 25, 1969.
Vogue, October 1, 1968.
Washington Post, October 20, 1978, January 24, 1980.

—*Sketch by Melissa Gaiownik*

*   *   *

PATTERSON, Lindsay 1942-

PERSONAL: Born July 22, 1942, in Bastrop, La.; son of James Harrison (a physician and dentist) and Frances Adele (a teacher; maiden name, Lindsay) Patterson. *Education:* Received B.A. from Virginia State College.

CAREER: Writer. Worked as an account executive for Harrison Advertising Agency, and as a feature writer and columnist for Associated Negro Press; was an editorial assistant for writer Langston Hughes; visiting lecturer at Hunter College of the City University of New York, 1974-75; co-host of "Celebrity Hour" on WRVR-FM Radio and "Black Conversations" on WPIX-TV. *Military service:* U.S. Army, information specialist and correspondent for *Stars and Stripes* in Europe, feature writer and managing editor for *Patton Post*, served in Germany.

AWARDS, HONORS: Award from National Foundation on the Arts and Humanities; three MacDowell Colony fellowships; two Edward Albee Foundation fellowships.

WRITINGS:

(Editor and author of introduction) *The Negro in Music and Art*, Publishers Co., 1967.
(Editor and author of introduction) *Anthology of the American Negro in the Theatre: A Critical Approach*, Publishers Co., 1967, 2nd edition, revised, 1968.
(Editor) *An Introduction to Black Literature in America: From 1746 to the Present*, Publishers Co., 1968.
The Afro-American in Music and Art, Association for Study of Afro-American Life and History, 1970, revised edition, 1976.
(Editor and author of introduction) *Black Theater: A Twentieth-Century Collection of the Work and Its Best Playwrights*, Dodd, 1971.
(Editor and author of introduction) *A Rock Against the Wind: Black Love Poems; An Anthology*, Dodd, 1973.
(Editor and author of introduction) *Black Films and Film-Makers: A Comprehensive Anthology from Stereotype to Superhero*, Dodd, 1973.

Also editor of *Black Theater*, New American Library. Works represented in anthologies, including *The Best Short Stories by Negro Writers; Young Black Storytellers; The World of Language*. Contributor of more than thirty stories, articles, and reviews to popular magazines, including *New Leader, Saturday Review, Essence*, and *Freedomways*, and to newspapers.

WORK IN PROGRESS: The Plot, a novel; "Roper," a screenplay; "Rock Against the Wind," a play on black love; "Black Magazine" for television.

SIDELIGHTS: Lindsay Patterson commented: "My primary interest is fiction, and I feel that my career as a fiction writer is just beginning. My aim is to write high quality fiction about blacks, with popular appeal."

*   *   *

PATTERSON, (Horace) Orlando (Lloyd) 1940-

PERSONAL: Born June 5, 1940, in Jamaica, West Indies; came to the U.S., 1970, domiciled, 1972; son of Charles A. and Almina (Morris) Patterson; married Nerys Wyn Thomas, September 5, 1965; children: Rhiannon, Barbara. *Education:* University of the West Indies, B.Sc., 1962; London School of Economics, Ph.D., 1965.

ADDRESSES: Office—520 James Hall, Harvard University, Cambridge, Mass. 02138.

CAREER: University of London, London School of Economics and Political Science, London, England, assistant lecturer, 1965-67; University of the West Indies, Kingston, Jamaica, lecturer, 1967-70; Harvard University, Cambridge, Mass., visiting lecturer, 1970-71, Allston Burr senior tutor, 1971-73, professor of sociology, 1971—; Institute for Advanced Study, Princeton, N.J., visiting member, 1975-76. Member of technical advisory committee to prime minister and government of Jamaica, 1972-74, special adviser to prime minister for social policy and development, 1973-80. Visiting fellow, Wolfson College, Cambridge University, 1978-79; Phi Beta Kappa visiting scholar, 1988-89.

MEMBER: American Sociological Association.

AWARDS, HONORS: Jamaica Government Exhibition scholar, 1959-62; Commonwealth scholar, Great Britain, 1962-65; first prize, Dakar Festival of Negro Arts, 1966, for *Children of Sisyphus;* M.A., Harvard University, 1971; Guggenheim fellow, 1978-79; distinguished contribution to scholarship award, American Sociological Association, 1983, for *Slavery and Social Death: A Comparative Study;* Ralph Bunch Award, American Political Science Association, 1983.

WRITINGS:

The Children of Sisyphus (novel), Hutchinson, 1964, Houghton, 1965, reprinted, Longman, 1982, published as *Dinah,* Pyramid Books, 1968.

(Contributor) Andrew Salkey, editor, *Stories from the Caribbean,* Elek, 1965, published as *Island Voices,* Liveright, 1970.

The Sociology of Slavery: An Analysis of the Origins, Development, and Structure of Negro Slave Society in Jamaica, MacGibbon & Kee, 1967, Farleigh Dickinson University Press, 1969.

An Absence of Ruins (novel), Hutchinson, 1967.

Die the Long Day (novel), Morrow, 1972.

Ethnic Chauvinism: The Reactionary Impulse, Stein & Day, 1977.

Slavery and Social Death: A Comparative Study, Harvard University Press, 1982.

Contributor of articles and short fiction to periodicals. Member of editorial board, *New Left Review,* 1965-66.

WORK IN PROGRESS: The Dark Side of Freedom: An Historical Sociology of the Western Mind (working title), for Basic Books.

SIDELIGHTS: Orlando Patterson's novels and scholarly work both reflect his West Indian background. Born in Jamaica, Patterson brings new insights to his subjects, whether they be the slave societies of his sociological studies or the Caribbean characters of his novels. His first novel, *The Children of Sisyphus,* is recognized as "a Jamaican landmark" by Richard Deveson in the *Times Literary Supplement.* Another novel, *Die the Long Day,* "once again looks at West Indian society through the anguish of its indomitable women," describes Jan Carew in the *New York Times Book Review.* Set on a colonial Jamaican sugar plantation, the work focuses on the attempts of a slave, Quasheba, to save her daughter from the syphilitic advances of a plantation owner. By focusing his story on Quasheba's struggle with the plantation system, Patterson "throws new light on this unstable situation and on the subtleties of the master-slave relationship," observes Carew. "In so doing, he gives a better understanding on contemporary West Indian society."

Patterson's focus on slave societies in his fiction is reflected in his sociological studies of slavery and ethnic issues. Although Patterson is dealing with social issues in his scholarly works, he uses historical research and techniques as his basis. In *The Sociology of Slavery: An Analysis of the Origins, Development, and Structure of Negro Slave Society in Jamaica,* the author has used "the critical techniques of the historian in extracting information and deriving conclusions from his wide-ranging documentation," relates a *Times Literary Supplement*

writer. Although the critic remarks that some of Patterson's assumptions are questionable, overall he finds that "Dr. Patterson has asked new questions and elicited some new answers. . . . [He] has much to say that is comparatively new and stimulating."

Slavery and Social Death: A Comparative Study takes the historical emphasis of Patterson's earlier work on Jamaica and extends it through several centuries and cultures. Studying slave societies from Ancient Rome to Civil War America, *Slavery and Social Death* "seeks a definition of slavery which is independent of [property] idioms and which provides a basis for considering the relations between the slave and the society into which he has, somehow, to be incorporated," summarizes Michael Banton in the *Times Literary Supplement.* In order to redefine the concept of slavery, Patterson uses sources from various fields, including history and economics, to support his theory. Remarks David Brion Davis in the *New York Review of Books:* "No previous scholar I know of has gained such a mastery of secondary sources in all the Western European languages."

Because of the broad base for Patterson's study, some critics find discrepancies and errors in the work. Davis finds that several points are unclear, and criticizes the author's "inconsistency in portraying the fundamental contradiction of human bondage." Banton also notes several specific errors; he does admit, however, that for a specialist colleague in ancient history, "Patterson's analytical model allows him to grasp the nature of slavery in the ancient Mediterranean world more securely than many professional classicists."

For whatever shortcomings *Slavery and Social Death* may contain, its value lies in Patterson's ability "to offer a coherent theory that challenges deeply rooted assumptions and presents new points of departure for further research," comments Davis. "Patterson has helped to set out the direction for the next decades of interdisciplinary scholarship." Banton's assessment of the work reflects what other critics have said about Patterson's writing overall, his fiction included: "Because it deals with fundamental issues both of past human life and of our attempts to understand it, *Slavery and Social Death* throws a questioning ray upon the present as well."

BIOGRAPHICAL/CRITICAL SOURCES:

PERIODICALS

New Republic, February 11, 1978.
New York Review of Books, February 17, 1983.
New York Times Book Review, September 10, 1972.
Times Literary Supplement, April 13, 1967, July 13, 1967, September 9, 1983, October 24, 1986.
Voice Literary Supplement, December, 1982.

*   *   *

p'BITEK, Okot   1931-1982

PERSONAL: Born in 1931 in Gulu, Uganda; died July 19, 1982; son of a schoolteacher; married twice. *Education:* Attended King's College, Budo; Government Training College, Mbarara, teaching certificate; Bristol University, certificate of education; University College of Wales, LL.B.; Institute of Social Anthropology, Oxford, B.Litt., 1963.

CAREER: Taught school in the area of Gulu, Uganda, and played on the Ugandan national soccer team in the mid-1950s; Makerere University, Kampala, Uganda, lecturer in sociology,

1964; Uganda National Theater and Uganda National Cultural Center, Kampala, director, 1966-68; University of Iowa, Iowa City, fellow of international writing program, 1969-70, writer in residence, 1971; University of Nairobi, Nairobi, Kenya, senior research fellow at Institute of African Studies and lecturer in sociology and literature, 1971-78; University of Ife, Ife, Nigeria, professor, 1978-82; Makerere University, Kampala, professor of creative writing, 1982; writer. Visiting lecturer at University of Texas, 1969. Founder of the Gulu Arts Festival, 1966, and the Kisumu Arts Festival, 1968.

AWARDS, HONORS: Jomo Kenyatta Prize for Literature from the Kenya Publishers Association, for *Two Songs,* 1972.

WRITINGS:

POETIC NOVELS

Song of Lawino: A Lament, East African Publishing, 1966, Meridian Books, 1969 (also see below).
Song of Ocol, East African Publishing, 1970 (also see below).
Song of a Prisoner, introduction by Edward Blishen, illustrations by E. Okechukwu Odita, Third Press, 1971 (also see below).
Two Songs: Song of Prisoner [and] *Song of Malaya,* illustrations by Trixi Lerbs, East African Publishing, 1971 (also see above).
Song of Lawino and Song of Ocol, introduction by G. A. Heron, illustrations by Frank Horley, East African Publishing, 1972 (also see above).

OTHER

Lak tar miyo kinyero wi lobo? (novel; title means "Are Your Teeth White? Then Laugh!"), Eagle Press, 1953.
African Religions in Western Scholarship, East African Literature Bureau, 1970.
Religion of the Central Luo, East African Literature, 1971.
Africa's Cultural Revolution (essays), introduction by Ngugi wa Thiong'o, Macmillan Books for Africa, 1973.
(Compiler and translator) *The Horn of My Love* (folk songs), Heinemann Educational Books, 1974.
(Compiler and translator) *Hare and Hornbill* (folktales), Heinemann Educational Books, 1978.

Contributor to periodicals, including *Transition.*

SIDELIGHTS: Eulogized as "Uganda's best known poet" in his London *Times* obituary, Okot p'Bitek had a distinguished career in the fields of sport, education, and the arts. While serving as a teacher in his native Uganda during the 1950s he played on the country's national soccer team, going to the 1956 Summer Olympic Games in London, England. P'Bitek stayed in Great Britain to obtain degrees from several universities before returning to Uganda to teach at the college level. He published his first book, *Lak tar miyo kinyero wi lobo?* (title means "Are Your Teeth White? Then Laugh!"), in 1953 but it was the 1966 publication of his *Song of Lawino* that brought p'Bitek his first real acclaim. In the same year, p'Bitek was named director of the Uganda National Theater and Cultural Center. In this post he founded the successful Gulu Arts Festival, a celebration of the traditional oral history, dance, and other arts of his ancestral Acholi people. Due to political pressures, however, p'Bitek was forced from his directorship after two years. He moved to Kenya, where, with the exception of visits to universities in the United States, he remained throughout the reign of Ugandan dictator Idi Amin. After founding the Kisumu Arts Festival in Kenya and later serving as a professor in Nigeria, p'Bitek eventually returned to Ma-

kerere University in Kampala, Uganda. He was a professor of creative writing there when he died in 1982.

P'Bitek sought, in his role as cultural director and author, to prevent native African culture from being swallowed up by the influences of Western ideas and arts. He was particularly interested in preserving the customs of his native Acholi. While serving as director for the Uganda National Theater and Cultural Center, p'Bitek proclaimed in an interview with Robert Serumaga which appeared in *African Writers Talking:* "The major challenge I think is to find what might be Uganda's contribution to world culture. . . . [W]e should, I think, look into the village and see what the Ugandans—the proper Ugandans—not the people who have been to school, have read—and see what they do in the village, and see if we cannot find some root there, and build on this." He further explained to Serumago his feelings about the influence of Western culture on his own: "I am not against having plays from England, from other parts of the world, we should have this, but I'm very concerned that whatever we do should have a basic starting point, and this should be Uganda, and then, of course, Africa, and then we can expand afterwards."

Song of Lawino, p'Bitek's most famous work, takes as its central issue the defense of Acholi tradition against the encroachment of Western cultural influences. Originally composed by p'Bitek in the Acholi (sometimes known as Lwo or Luo) language, he translated *Song of Lawino* into English before its publication. He put the English words to traditional Acholi verse patterns, however, and the result was pleasing to many critics. A reviewer in the *Times Literary Supplement* lauded p'Bitek's creation thus: "In rewriting his poem in English he has chosen a strong, simple idiom which preserves the sharpness and frankness of [its] imagery, a structure of short, free verses which flow swiftly and easily, and an uncondescending offer of all that is local and specific in the original."

Categorized as a poetic novel, *Song of Lawino* is narrated by an Acholi woman named Lawino who tells an audience her life story in the form of an Acholi song. Her main complaint is against her husband Ocol, who neglects her because of her adherence to Acholi ways. Ocol, in contrast, tries to become as westernized as possible, rejecting his culture as backward and crude. His negative feelings toward his background are further symbolized by his preferring his mistress, Clementina, over Lawino. Clementina is thoroughly westernized, from her name to her high-heeled shoes. Lawino tells us that her rival straightens her hair, uses lipstick, and "dusts powder on her face / And it looks so pale; / She resembles the wizard / Getting ready for the midnight dance." Lawino speaks disdainfully of what she perceives as unnatural behavior on the part of her husband and his mistress; in favorable opposition to this she praises the life of her village. Most critics agree that Lawino's loving descriptions of the simple Acholi rural activities and rituals leave the reader with no doubt as to whose side the author takes. As reported in the *Times Literary Supplement,* "It is Lawino's voice that we need to hear, reminding us of the human reality behind glib rejections of the backward, the primitive, the 'bush people.' " P'Bitek later wrote *Song of Ocol,* which purports to offer Lawino's husband's defense, but most reviewers concurred in believing that Ocol's words merely confirm Lawino's condemnation of him. Another *Times Literary Supplement* critic judged that *Song of Ocol* "savo[rs] too much of a conscientious attempt to give a voice to an essentially dull, pompous, and vindictive husband."

P'Bitek's next poetic novels, published as *Two Songs: Song of Prisoner* [*and*] *Song of Malaya,* together won him the Kenya Publishers Association's Jomo Kenyatta Prize in 1972. *Song of Prisoner* relates the thoughts, both hopeful and despairing, of a political prisoner, and, according to the *Times Literary Supplement,* "its imagery has much of the freshness and inventive energy of Okot's best work." The narrator describes his cell as a cold, imprisoning woman and relates his feelings of betrayal, his fears of his lover's unfaithfulness, and his daydreams of merrymaking. *Song of Malaya* is written in the persona of a prostitute and tells of the abuses she suffers. Judged slightly sentimental by some critics, the prose poem discusses, among other things, the irony in the fact that prostitutes are often rounded up and jailed by men who were their patrons the previous evening.

In his later years, p'Bitek's literary efforts turned primarily to translation. He published *The Horn of My Love,* a collection of Acholi folksongs in both Acholi and English translation, in 1974, and *Hare and Hornbill,* a collection of African folktales, in 1978. In *The Horn of My Love,* declared reviewer Gerald Moore in the *Times Literary Supplement,* "p'Bitek argues the case for African poetry as poetry, as an art to be enjoyed, rather than as ethnographic material to be eviscerated." The book contains ceremonial songs about death, ancient Acholi chiefs, and love and courtship. *Hare and Hornbill,* according to Robert L. Berner critiquing in *World Literature Today,* is divided roughly in half between tales of humans and tales of animals, including one about a hare seducing his mother-in-law. "P'Bitek is particularly qualified to deal with these tales," Berner proclaimed, and "reveals a thorough understanding of African folk materials."

BIOGRAPHICAL/CRITICAL SOURCES:

BOOKS

p'Bitek, Okot, *Song of Lawino: A Lament,* East African Publishing, 1966.
Pieterse, Cosmo, and Dennis Duerden, editors, *African Writers Talking,* Africana Publishing, 1972.

PERIODICALS

Times Literary Supplement, February 16, 1967, November 5, 1971, February 21, 1975.
World Literature Today, summer, 1979.

OBITUARIES:

PERIODICALS

Times (London), July 23, 1982.

—*Sketch by Elizabeth Thomas*

*   *   *

PERRY, Margaret 1933-

PERSONAL: Born November 15, 1933, in Cincinnati, Ohio; daughter of R. Patterson (a college president and professor) and Elizabeth (Anthony) Perry. *Education:* Western Michigan University, A.B., 1954; University of Paris, certificate, 1956; further graduate study at City College (now of the City University of New York), 1957-58; Catholic University of America, M.S.L.S., 1959. *Politics:* Democrat. *Religion:* Roman Catholic.

ADDRESSES: Home—1200 Wood St., Valparaiso, Ind. 46383.

Office—Moellering Library, Valparaiso University, Valparaiso, Ind. 46383.

CAREER: New York Public Library, New York, N.Y., young adult and reference librarian, 1954-55, 1957-58; U.S. Army, civilian librarian in Metz, Nancy, Toul, and Verdun, France, 1959-63, Orleans, France, 1964-65, and Hanau, Germany, 1965-67; U.S. Military Academy, West Point, N.Y., reference librarian, 1967-68, chief of circulation, 1968-70; University of Rochester, Rochester, N.Y., head of education library, 1970-75, assistant professor, 1973-75, associate professor of English, 1975-82, assistant professor of education, 1974-82, head of library's Reader Services Division, 1975-78, assistant director of libraries for reader services, 1978-82, acting director of libraries, 1976-77; Valparaiso University, Valparaiso, Ind., director of libraries, 1982—. Speaker at professional meetings.

MEMBER: American Library Association (life member), College Language Association, Modern Language Association of America, Council for Basic Education, National Society of Literature and the Arts, American Civil Liberties Union, Urban League of Rochester (member of board of directors; second vice-president, 1978-80), Delta Kappa Gamma.

AWARDS, HONORS: Scholarships from Salzburg Seminar in American Studies, for Schloss Leopoldskron, 1956; first prize from Armed Forces Writers League short story contest, 1966, for "Black Apostle"; second place from Frances Steloff Fiction Prize, 1969, for "Lions, Kings, and Dragons."

WRITINGS:

A Bio-Bibliography of Countee P. Cullen, 1903-1946, Greenwood Press, 1971.
(Contributor) E. J. Josey, editor, *What Black Librarians Are Saying,* Scarecrow, 1973.
Silence to the Drums: A Survey of the Literature of the Harlem Renaissance, Greenwood Press, 1976.
The Harlem Renaissance: An Annotated Bibliography and Commentary, Garland Publishing, 1982.
(Editor) *The Short Fiction of Rudolph Fisher,* Greenwood Press, 1987.

Contributor of articles, stories, and reviews to history and library journals, and to literary journals, including *Panache* and *Phylon.* Associate editor of *University of Rochester Library Bulletin,* 1970-73; contributing editor of *Afro-Americans in New York Life and History.*

WORK IN PROGRESS: One "serious" novel; one "not-so-serious" novel; short stories.

SIDELIGHTS: Margaret Perry commented: "Although the major portion of my published work is about Afro-American literature, I plan to devote more time to writing short stories. They are the poetry of fiction, and it's about time for me to give more time to them.

"I was always lucky to have encouragement from teachers and support from my parents. I sometimes think I had too easy a life; harder times may have given some bite to the fiction I write. But I must be content with my style and subjects, and try to make my stories an authentic expression of my artistry, however meager it may be."

AVOCATIONAL INTERESTS: Travel in France ("poking among the ruins"), collecting bookmarks and stamps (especially art stamps), playing violin (chamber music).

PERRY, Richard 1944-

PERSONAL: Born January 13, 1944, in New York, N.Y.; son of Henry (a minister) and Bessie (a homemaker; maiden name, Draines) Perry; married Jeanne Gallo (a legal services administrator), September 14, 1968; children: Malcolm David, Alison Wright. *Education:* City College of the City University of New York, B.A., 1970; Columbia University, M.F.A., 1972.

ADDRESSES: Office—Department of English, Pratt Institute, 215 Ryerson St., Brooklyn, N.Y. 11205. *Agent*—Charlotte Sheedy Literary Agency, Inc., 145 West 86th St., New York, N.Y. 10024.

CAREER: Pratt Institute, Brooklyn, N.Y., associate professor of English, 1972—. *Military service:* U.S. Army, 1968-70.

MEMBER: PEN, Teachers and Writers Collaborative, National Writers Union, National Council of Teachers of English.

AWARDS, HONORS: New Jersey State Council on the Arts Award, 1980, for fiction; citation from New Jersey Writers Conference, 1985, for *Montgomery's Children.*

WRITINGS:

Changes (novel), Bobbs-Merrill, 1974.
Montgomery's Children (novel), Harcourt, 1984.

Contributor of articles and short stories to magazines, including *Essence, Black World, Southern Review, Black Creation,* and *Snakeroots.*

WORK IN PROGRESS: Carla's Book, a novel.

SIDELIGHTS: Richard Perry's first novel, *Changes,* casts a black university teacher, Bill Taylor, as the protagonist. Recognizing that the circumstances of his own life have made him a part of the white man's world, Taylor still feels the need to be more involved in the fight for black rights. He does nothing, however, to act on those feelings, and his inaction "plays a crucial part in his growing dissatisfaction," suggested a *New York Times Book Review* critic. Taylor's ambivalent loyalties serve to compound his dilemma when he falls under the hypnotic spell of a mad scientist scheming to eliminate the white race by using a serum to turn white skin black. The novel examines one man's "admirably unpretentious struggle for self-definition," commented the reviewer in the *New York Times Book Review,* and raises the questions "about black men like Bill Taylor who try to resist apocalyptic solutions." "What is best about the book," the critic contended, "is its depiction of a conscientious man who fears he is doing less than he can."

In his second novel, *Montgomery's Children,* Perry focuses on several black families, mostly southern transplants seeking a share of World War II prosperity, and the changes that they undergo in the fictitious central New York town of Montgomery. As the story progresses from its 1948 beginnings through the next three decades towards its 1980 climax, the idyllic life these families have known is shattered as one after another of the evils of modern civilization—overcrowding, drugs, and crime—affects them and their offspring. Of the various characters in *Montgomery's Children,* representing two generations of black residents, three dominate the story—Norman Fillis, a middle-aged janitor who becomes both madman and prophet, foretelling the corruption and violence that will visit the townspeople; young Gerald Fletcher, so emotionally crippled by the brutal treatment he received as a child from his father that he eventually withdraws completely from life; and Gerald's girlfriend, Josephine Moore, also a victim of paternal abuse, both physical and sexual, who suffers first imprisonment for the murder of her father and, later, self-imposed exile.

Perry gained praise for *Montgomery's Children,* particularly for his delineation of character and his choice of language. Charles R. Larson, in his review for the *Detroit News,* lauded the novel for its "rich panorama of eccentric personalities." Critic Whitney Balliett of the *New Yorker* opined that Perry's narrative "has many voices, all of them original and patient and unflinching," then complimented the author on "a good ear and a nice oral prose sense," and assessed *Montgomery's Children* as "a comic novel, a realistic novel, a light-handed fantasy, a vivid testament to what black people, kept low for so long, still suffer."

Additionally, critic John Kissell of the *Los Angeles Times Book Review* noted that "Perry draws his characters, even the less admirable, with compassion and insight," and Mel Watkins, reviewer for the *New York Times Book Review,* found the novel "studded with memorable characters . . . drawn in rich, evocative prose in which the comic and surreal are nicely balanced." Watkins capsulized *Montgomery's Children* as "an impressive novel about the evils of modernism and the redemptive powers of the spirit" and called Perry "an extremely talented writer whose work bears watching."

Perry commented: "Writing is for me as necessary as loving; in fact, I would argue that writing *is* an act of love. Writing grew out of reading; as a child I decided that I wanted to be able to provide for myself the pleasure that books gave to me. Ultimately, along with the strong urge to tell stories, the recognition that writing is a way of ordering experience is the primary reason that I write."

AVOCATIONAL INTERESTS: Tennis, golf.

BIOGRAPHICAL/CRITICAL SOURCES:

PERIODICALS

Bestsellers, April, 1984.
Detroit News, February 5, 1984.
Los Angeles Times Book Review, February 19, 1984.
New Yorker, February 6, 1984.
New York Times Book Review, September 15, 1974, August 5, 1984.
Village Voice, April 17, 1984.

*   *   *

PETERS, Lenrie (Wilfred Leopold) 1932-

PERSONAL: Born September 1, 1932, in Banjul, Gambia. *Education:* Trinity College, Cambridge University, B.A. (with honors), 1956; University College Hospital, London, M.D., 1959.

ADDRESSES: Office—Westfield Clinic, P.O. Box 142, Banjul, Gambia.

CAREER: Surgeon and writer. Northampton General Hospital, Northampton, England, surgical registrar, 1966-69; Victoria Hospital, Gambia, surgeon specialist, 1969-72; surgeon specialist in private practice, Gambia, 1972—. Free-lance broadcaster for British Broadcasting Corp. (BBC) African and World Service programs, including "African Forum" and "Calling West Africa," 1955-68. Trustee, West African Examinations

Council Endowment Fund. Royal College of Surgeons of England, fellow, 1967. Former chairman of Gambia Monuments and Relics Commission, National Library Board, and Board of Governors of Gambia College.

MEMBER: West African College of Surgeons (fellow).

AWARDS, HONORS: Officer of the Republic of the Gambia.

WRITINGS:

Poems (also see below), Mbari Press, 1964.
The Second Round (novel), Heinemann, 1965, reprinted, 1986.
Satellites (poetry; contains *Poems*), Heinemann, 1967.
Katchikali (poetry), Heinemann, 1971.
Selected Poetry, Heinemann, 1981.

Work represented in numerous anthologies. Contributor to professional journals and other periodicals, including *African Literature Association Magazine, Afro-Asian Magazine, Black Orpheus, Outposts, Presence Africaine, Prism, Transatlantic Review,* and *West Africa.*

SIDELIGHTS: The writings of Lenrie Peters reveal two strong autobiographical influences. One is his career as a physician; images and themes reflecting surgery abound in his work. The second is Peters's dual heritage. Although the writer was born in Gambia and spent his childhood there, the majority of his adult life has been spent in Europe. Concern over the fate of Africa and feelings of separation and alienation from his native culture are frequently encountered in Peters's literary creations.

Peters's novel *The Second Round* is, in fact, a semi-autobiographical story of a doctor who returns to his home in Freetown, West Africa, after studying and practicing medicine for several years in England. The physician finds that he is unable to "connect" with his native culture, unable to relate to his African friends and their rapidly changing society. Permanently changed by his Western experiences, the doctor never realizes his dream of a "spiritual homecoming."

In *Africa Report,* Lewis Nkosi calls the plot of *The Second Round* "trite" with its overworked "man of two cultures" theme; he also finds Peters's "gallery of afflicted zany characters . . . ghastly melodramatic." Yet Charles R. Larson in *The Emergence of African Fiction* disagrees, stating that perhaps Peters's novel was not well-received because it did not fit into the category of classic African writing: Peters employs neither oral literary materials nor anthropological background in his writings, nor does he explore the usual theme of colonial protest. *The Second Round* is a novel of self-examination—an African's indictment of himself and his country. "In his depiction of the alienated African," Larson notes, "Lenrie Peters has created a haunting story of one man's attempt to hide from the demands of the culture and the people around him, to ignore the basic foundation on which all society is based. It is a fine novel—and the fact that its appeal at the moment seems to be limited to a non-African audience does not weaken its power." The critic sees Peters's novel as a forerunner in a new direction for African literature—"a much more detailed concern with the individual in African society, as African society itself changes, for better or for worse, from a concern with the communal."

Peters has achieved greater critical success with his volumes of poetry. In *Satellites,* the poet explores such diverse subjects as "sex, war, homecoming, surgery, the death of Churchill, the OAU, the Chinese bomb, parachute jumps, autumn, the passing of youth, the elusiveness of God, the nature of creativity, and the role of the artist," Robert E. Morseberger cat-

alogues in *Books Abroad.* "His verses have remarkable range in both language and content. . . . The style varies from elliptical obscurity to lucid lyricism and slashing satire; witty, learned, allusive but not pedantic, it is a metaphysical verse made modern, a fusion of wit and passion."

Other critics remark that Peters's wide range of interests make him an unlocalized poet rather than an African one, with a universal voice speaking on the general human predicament. The alienation, frustration, and confusion that the poet feels in his own heart echoes Everyman's struggle in the wake of technology and its destruction of human values. Yet Peters's verse is not pessimistic. "In the face of disappointment and disillusion one keeps going with a kind of fatalism that amounts to faith," writes Eldred Jones in *African Forum* about the poet's verse. "[Peters's] poems start with a wide variety of physical stimuli and usually end with reflection, an assertion of hope."

"My writing is a quest for understanding the future and a search into the meaning of life," commented Peters. "The central reality of this is the tragic history of man, etcetera."

BIOGRAPHICAL/CRITICAL SOURCES:

BOOKS

Larson, Charles R., *The Emergence of African Fiction,* Indiana University Press, 1972.

PERIODICALS

African Forum, summer, 1967.
Africa Report, December, 1966.
Books Abroad, winter, 1969.

*   *   *

PETERSON, Benjamin
See ALLEN, Robert L(ee)

*   *   *

PETRY, Ann (Lane)   1908-

PERSONAL: Born October 12, 1908, in Old Saybrook, Conn.; daughter of Peter Clarke (a druggist) and Bertha (James) Lane; married George D. Petry, February 22, 1938; children: Elisabeth Ann. *Education:* University of Connecticut, Ph.D., 1931; attended Columbia University, 1943-44.

ADDRESSES: Home—Old Saybrook, Conn. *Agent*—Russell & Volkening, Inc., 551 Fifth Ave., New York, N.Y. 10017.

CAREER: James' Pharmacy, Old Saybrook and Old Lyme, Conn., pharmacist, 1931-38; *Amsterdam News,* New York City, writer and advertising saleswoman, 1938-41; *People's Voice,* New York City, reporter and editor of woman's page, 1941-44; writer.

MEMBER: PEN, Authors Guild, Authors League of America (secretary, 1960).

AWARDS, HONORS: Houghton Mifflin literary fellowship, 1946.

WRITINGS:

ADULT FICTION; PUBLISHED BY HOUGHTON, EXCEPT AS INDICATED

The Street (novel), 1946, reprinted, Beacon Press, 1985.

Country Place (novel), 1947, reprinted, Chatham Bookseller, 1971.
The Narrows (novel), 1953, reprinted, Beacon Press, 1988.
Miss Muriel and Other Stories, 1971.

JUVENILE; PUBLISHED BY CROWELL, EXCEPT AS INDICATED

The Drugstore Cat, 1949.
Harriet Tubman: Conductor on the Underground Railroad, 1955, reprinted, Archway, 1971, (published in England as *A Girl Called Moses: The Story of Harriet Tubman,* Methuen, 1960).
Tituba of Salem Village, 1964.
Legends of the Saints, 1970.

OTHER

Work is represented in anthologies. Contributor to magazines.

SIDELIGHTS: With the publication of *The Street* in 1946, Ann Petry became the first black female author to address the problems black women face as they struggle to cope with life in the slums. Following in what Arthur P. Davis calls "the tradition of hard-hitting social commentary which characterized the Richard Wright school of naturalistic protest writing," *The Street* tells the story of Lutie Johnson's attempts to shield herself and her young son from the world outside their tiny Harlem apartment. Though several critics, including those commenting in the *New Yorker* and the *Saturday Review of Literature,* felt that the novel was somewhat "overwritten," they agreed with the majority of their colleagues that it was well worth reading.

For instance, despite what he termed "a bad sag in the last third of the book which is almost fatal," the *New Republic's* Bucklin Moon was moved enough by Petry's unflinching portrayal of violence and degradation to remark: "Mrs. Petry knows what it is to live as a Negro in New York City and she also knows how to put it down on paper so that it is as scathing an indictment of our society as has ever appeared. . . . To this reviewer Mrs. Petry is the most exciting new Negro writer of the last decade."

In his *New York Times* review, Alfred Butterfield noted that "Ann Petry has chosen to tell a story about one aspect of Negro life in America, and she has created as vivid, as spiritually and emotionally effective a novel as that rich and important theme has yet produced. . . . It deals with its Negro characters without condescension, without special pleading, without distortion of any kind. . . . [It overflows] with the classic pity and terror of good imaginative writing."

After *The Street,* Petry wrote two more novels, *Country Place* in 1947 and *The Narrows* in 1953. Each one, though, takes place not in the slums of New York City, but in small, middle-class New England towns, a change in locale that critic Carl Milton Hughes describes as the author's "assertion of freedom as a creative artist with the whole of humanity in the American scene as her province." In short, declares Hughes in *The Negro Novelist: 1940-1950,* "Petry's departure from racial themes and the specialized Negro problem add[ed] to her maturity."

But the change in locale did not bring about a corresponding change in plot. As she did in *The Street,* Petry continued to build her stories around the same basic themes of adultery, cruelty, violence, and evil. *Country Place,* for example, examines the disillusion of a returned soldier, Johnnie Roane, who discovers in the midst of a terrible storm that the town gossip about his wife's infidelity is true; though shattered by the realization, Roane resists the impulse to kill her and her

lover and decides instead to make a new life for himself in New York. *The Narrows,* on the other hand, deals with the tragic affair between a young, well-educated black man and a rich white girl—an affair that is doomed as soon as the townspeople, both black and white, find out about it.

Some reviewers, such as the *New York Herald Tribune Weekly Book Review's* Rose Feld and Richard Sullivan of the *New York Times,* criticize *Country Place's* occasional plot improbabilities as well as Petry's technique of switching the identity of her narrator in mid-story, but most regard it as a worthy follow-up to *The Street.* Said J. C. Smith of the *Atlantic:* "Most of the characters are well done, but, curiously enough, Johnny Roane, the hero, is not. . . . Taken as a whole, though, *Country Place* is a good story. . . . It preaches no sermons, waves no flags. It tells a plausible narrative of . . . some very human people." Feld cited "the feel of a small town, the integrity of dialogue, [and] the portrayal of Johnnie, of Glory, [and] of Mrs. Gramby" as being among the "exceedingly good" parts of *Country Place,* while Sullivan noted that "despite the violence of its events, [it is] a rather quiet book, carefully and economically phrased" and "full of fresh, effective writing."

Bradford Smith of the *Saturday Review of Literature,* however, criticizes Petry for never really developing her basic premise. He writes: "The book seems to say (though not for the first time) that humanity is as degraded in [a small town] as in Studs Lonigan's Chicago. The trouble is that, while the reader is made to understand the social forces which produced Studs Lonigan, there is no comparable explanation for Mrs. Petry's characters. Her 'good' people . . . are shadowy, while her 'bad' people lack motivation or background."

Petry's third novel, *The Narrows,* prompts Arna Bontemps to comment in the *Saturday Review:* "A novel about Negroes by a Negro novelist and concerned, in the last analysis, with racial conflict, *The Narrows* somehow resists classification as a 'Negro novel,' as contradictory as that may sound. In this respect Ann Petry has achieved something as rare as it is commendable. Her book reads like a New England novel, and an unusually gripping one." Admitting that in less skilled hands the theme "might have been merely sensational," the *New York Herald Tribune Book Review's* Mary Ross concludes that Petry "builds a novel that has depth and dignity. There is power and insight and reach of imagination in her writing."

On the other hand, a *New Yorker* critic characterizes *The Narrows* as "an anguished book, written with an enormous amount of emotion and some thought, that does not quite succeed because there is far too much of it." A *Nation* reviewer seemingly agrees, stating that "one gets the impression of a hodge-podge of styles, structures, ideas."

Wright Morris, discussing *The Narrows* in a *New York Times* article, is critical of another aspect of the book. "[Petry's] canvas has depth and complexity," he began, "but the surface drama central to the tragedy is like a tissue of tabloid daydreams, projected by the characters." In his book *Black on White: A Critical Survey of Writing by American Negroes,* David Littlejohn agrees that Petry has always had "an uncomfortable tendency to contrive sordid plots (as opposed to merely writing of sordid events). She seems to require a 'shocking' chain of scandalous doings . . . on which to cast her creative imagination." Nevertheless, he states, "so wise is her writing, . . . so real are her characters, so total is her sympathy, that one can often accept the faintly cheap horrors and contrivances. . . . And if one allows himself to be overexcited by these intrigues . . . he misses, I think, the real treasures of Ann Petry's fiction.''

Among these treasures, Littlejohn says, can be found a ''solid, earned, tested intelligence,'' ''a prose that is rich and crisp,'' and ''characters of shape and dimension, people made out of love, with whole histories evoked in a page. . . . This, to me, the intelligence, the style, and above all the creative sympathy, is what sets Ann Petry . . . into a place almost as prominent and promising as that of [Richard Wright, James Baldwin, and Ralph Ellison]. She is not, of course, writing 'about' the race war. . . . But if an American Negro can, despite all, develop such an understanding of other people as Ann Petry's—and more prodigious still, *convey* that understanding—then let her write what *Peyton Place*-plots she will, she is working toward a genuine truce in the war.''

Critique: Studies in Modern Fiction reviewer Thelma J. Shinn also has words of praise for Petry's ability to understand and depict people—not just black people, but all people who are weakened and disillusioned by poverty and by racial and sexual stereotypes. Writes Shinn: ''Petry has penetrated the bias of black and white, even of male and female, to reveal a world in which the individual with the most integrity is not only destroyed but is often forced to become an expression of the very society against which he is rebelling. . . . Ann Petry does not ignore the particular problems of blacks; her portrayals . . . display potentiality enough for admiration and oppression enough for anger to satisfy any black militant. Her novels protest against the entire society which would contrive to make any individual less than human, or even less than he can be.''

AVOCATIONAL INTERESTS: Gardening, sewing, cooking, writing poetry.

BIOGRAPHICAL/CRITICAL SOURCES:

BOOKS

Bone, Robert A., *The Negro Novel in America*, revised edition, Yale University Press, 1965.
Children's Literature Review, Volume 12, Gale, 1987.
Contemporary Literary Criticism, Gale, Volume 1, 1973, Volume 7, 1977, Volume 18, 1981.
Davis, Arthur P., *From the Dark Tower: Afro-American Writers from 1900 to 1960*, Howard University Press, 1974.
Hughes, Carl Milton, *The Negro Novelist: 1940-1950*, Citadel Press, 1953, reprinted, 1970.
Littlejohn, David, *Black on White: A Critical Survey of Writing by American Negroes*, Viking, 1966.
O'Brien, John, editor, *Interviews with Black Writers*, Liveright, 1973.

PERIODICALS

Atlantic, November, 1947.
Christian Science Monitor, February 8, 1946, August 19, 1971.
Commonweal, February 22, 1946.
Critique: Studies in Modern Fiction, Volume 16, number 1, 1974.
Nation, August 29, 1953.
New Republic, February 11, 1946.
New Yorker, February 9, 1946, October 11, 1947, August 29, 1953.
New York Herald Tribune Book Review, August 16, 1953.
New York Herald Tribune Weekly Book Review, October 5, 1947.
New York Times, February 10, 1946, September 28, 1947, August 16, 1953.

Pharmacy in History, Volume 28, number 1, 1986.
San Francisco Chronicle, August 26, 1953.
Saturday Review, August 22, 1953, October 2, 1971.
Saturday Review of Literature, March 2, 1946, October 18, 1947.
Times Literary Supplement, May 2, 1986.

* * *

PHARR, Robert Deane   1916-

PERSONAL: Born July 5, 1916, in Richmond, Va.; son of John Benjamin (a minister) and Lucie (a teacher; maiden name, Deane) Pharr; married Nellie Ellis, February 14, 1937; children: Lorelle (Mrs. Donald Jones). *Education:* Attended St. Paul's Normal and Industrial School (now St. Paul's College), Lawrenceville, Va., 1933, and Lincoln University, Lincoln University, Pa., 1934; Virginia Union University, B.A., 1939; Fisk University, graduate study. *Politics:* None. *Religion:* None.

CAREER: Employed chiefly as a waiter at exclusive resort hotels and private clubs, including a period at Columbia University's faculty club; novelist.

MEMBER: Omega Psi Psi.

AWARDS, HONORS: Grants from the Rockefeller Foundation, the New York State Council on the Arts, and other funding agencies.

WRITINGS:

The Book of Numbers, Doubleday, 1969.
S.R.O., Doubleday, 1971.
(Contributor) Abraham Chapman, editor, *New Black Voices*, New American Library, 1972.
The Welfare Bitch, Doubleday, 1973.
The Soul Murder Case: A Confession of the Victim, Avon, 1975.
Giveadamn Brown, Doubleday, 1978.

SIDELIGHTS: ''Both a persistent social critic and a perceptive student of the human condition,'' Robert Dean Pharr ''is committed to depicting the inevitable and often unpredictable tragedies of life,'' observes Richard Yarborough in a *Dictionary of Literary Biography* essay. Inspired by the example of Sinclair Lewis's novel *Babbitt*, Pharr writes novels that provide realistic insights into the life of black Americans. According to Yarborough, Pharr's first novel, *The Book of Numbers*, ''confronts one of the most painful questions surrounding the Afro-American experience: How can ambitious, intelligent, energetic blacks . . . achieve the capitalist American Dream when the conventional roads to power and financial security are unjustly closed to them?''

The Book of Numbers relates the story of Dave Greene, a young black man who arrives in a small Southern town and begins making his fortune by running a numbers game. Many critics praise the novel for its lifelike portrayal of the community; a *Times Literary Supplement* critic writes that the novel has ''a convincing sense of engulfment in that time and place of being *properly* there, rather than there because it is a bit like here.'' *New York Times Book Review* contributor Martin Levin echoes this assessment, commenting that ''fortifying the novel's supple style is its inescapable vitality; it surges through The Block, bringing to life every major and minor invention.'' Pharr achieves this effect by creating ''vividly rendered characters who represent a large cross section of Afro-America in the 1930s," remarks Yarborough.

While Pharr's subsequent novels have not been as successful as *The Book of Numbers,* they still demonstrate the author's gift for creating realistic characters and places. *S.R.O.,* which takes place entirely within the walls of a Harlem single-room-occupancy hotel, follows the lives of various drunks, junkies, homosexuals, and prostitutes, both black and white, who live on the edge of society. "Pharr's writing at the beginning is flawless," observes Jan Carew in the *New York Times Book Review.* "His description of narrator Sid Bailey's alcoholic fantasies is so vivid that one is almost forced to look away from the page to avoid the smell of his putrid breath and the bite of his terror." Although Jerry Bryant thinks that Pharr romanticizes the ghetto and its inhabitants, "there is an outrageous irony and an effective good-humored bitterness in his best writing," the critic comments in *Nation.* "He has an acute eye for detail and an instinct for shaping a sentence." Because of the extreme length of the novel (almost 600 pages), however, Yarborough finds that the novel loses some of its impact as it proceeds. Nevertheless, he admits that "at its best, *S.R.O.* is an alternately humorous and harrowing picaresque novel about a man desperately in search of a foundation, a rock upon which he might rest as he confronts a lifetime of failure, frustration, and emptiness."

Pharr's next novels were passed over by most critics, but in his 1978 novel *Giveadamn Brown,* Pharr once again demonstrated his ability to create a "knowing, surrealistically honest vision of life in Harlem," describes Garrett Epps in *Washington Post Book World.* Although a *New Yorker* critic finds the plot, dealing with an underground narcotics operation, "contrived," the critic also remarks that "the tough, emotion-laden dialogue and the scores of scarred lives the author describes ring absolutely true." Reflecting this opinion, Epps writes that when the plot of the novel seems tailor-made for a movie adaptation, "no movie could capture the haunted, painful narrative voice which has always been Pharr's chief strength." "If only through the sheer, relentless energy of his language," says Yarborough, "his fiction consistently carries the existential message that while life is often a hell, it can not only be survived but lived to the fullest." The critic concludes: "Chapters in an ongoing tale of physical and psychological endurance, Pharr's novels testify to the strength and resilience of the human spirit."

MEDIA ADAPTATIONS: The Book of Numbers was made into a movie entitled "Book of Numbers," released by Avco Embassy in 1973.

BIOGRAPHICAL/CRITICAL SOURCES:

BOOKS

Dictionary of Literary Biography, Volume 33: *Afro-American Fiction Writers After 1955,* Gale, 1984.

PERIODICALS

Nation, November 22, 1971.
Newsweek, June 16, 1969.
New Yorker, April 24, 1978.
New York Times, April 4, 1969.
New York Times Book Review, April 27, 1969, October 31, 1971, September 28, 1975.
Time, June 6, 1969.
Times Literary Supplement, October 30, 1970.
Washington Post Book World, April 9, 1978.

PLUMPP, Sterling D(ominic)   1940-

PERSONAL: Born January 30, 1940, in Clinton, Miss.; son of Cyrus Hampton (a laborer) and Mary (Emmanuel) Plumpp; married Falvia Delgrazia Jackson (a registered nurse), December 21, 1968; children: Harriet Nzinga. *Education:* St. Benedict's College (now Benedictine College), student, 1960-62; Roosevelt University, B.A., 1968, graduate study, 1969-71.

ADDRESSES: Home—1212 S. Michigan Ave., Apt. 1210, Chicago, Ill. 60605. *Office*—Department of Black Studies, University of Illinois at Chicago Circle, P.O. Box 4348, Chicago, Ill. 60680.

CAREER: Main Post Office, Chicago, Ill., distribution clerk, 1962-64, 1966-69; North Park College, Chicago, Ill., counselor, 1969-71; University of Illinois at Chicago Circle, Chicago, instructor, 1971-84, associate professor in Black Studies, 1984—. Poet in residence, Evanston School, Ill., and Youth Black Heritage Theater Ensemble Studio. Director of Young Writer's Workshop for Urban Gateways. *Military service:* U.S. Army, 1964-66.

MEMBER: National Association for the Advancement of Colored People, Operation PUSH.

AWARDS, HONORS: Illinois Arts Council Literary Award, 1975, for an excerpt from *Clinton;* Broadside Press Publishers Award, 1975; Illinois Arts Council Award, 1981, and Carl Sandburg Literary Award for Poetry, Friends of the Chicago Public Library, 1983, both for *The Mojo Hands Call, I Must Go.*

WRITINGS:

Portable Soul, Third World Press, 1969, revised edition, 1974.
Half Black, Half Blacker, Third World Press, 1970.
(Contributor) Patricia L. Brown, Don L. Lee, and Francis Ward, editors, *To Gwen with Love,* Johnson, 1971.
Muslim Men, Broadside Press, 1972.
Black Rituals, Third World Press, 1972.
Steps to Break the Circle, Third World Press, 1974.
Clinton (poems), Broadside Press, 1976.
(Editor) *Somehow We Survive: An Anthology of South African Writing,* illustrations by Dumile Feni, Thunder's Mouth Press, 1981.
(Contributor) Joyce Jones, Mary McTaggart, and Maria Mootry, editors, *The Otherwise Room,* The Poetry Factory Press, 1981.
The Mojo Hands Call, I Must Go (poems), Thunder's Mouth Press, 1982.
Blues: The Story Always Untold (poems), Another Chicago Press, in press.

Also contributor to all four volumes of *Mississippi Writers: Reflections of Childhood and Youth,* edited by Dorothy Abbott. Contributor to *Black World, Another Chicago Magazine, Black American Literature Forum, Black Scholar, AFRO-DIASPORA,* and *Journal of Black Poetry.* Editor for Third World Press, 1970—, and Institute for Positive Education; managing editor, *Black Books Bulletin,* 1971-73; poetry editor, *Black American Literature Forum,* 1982—.

WORK IN PROGRESS: Superbad and the Hip Jesus; research on black critics and on the work of Ernest Gaines and Henry Dumas; *Mighty Long Time,* a novel about a blues singer.

SIDELIGHTS: The contrast between Sterling D. Plumpp's early years in rural Mississippi and the "psychological maiming" that he sustained as an ambitious young student, postal worker, and draftee after coming to Chicago in 1962 "has provided a rich source of both verbal and psychological tension for his art," observes *Dictionary of Literary Biography* contributor James Cunningham. *Clinton,* a book of poetry named after the poet's birthplace, shows this most clearly, writes Cunningham: "As readers follow the poet from one period, from one part of the country, from one area of experience to another, they witness a great deal of psychological maiming. With the exception of the black Southern church, the chief violators are seen to be the major institutions in the hero's life: the tenant farming system, the educational system, the federal government in the civilian and military guises of post office employer and army trainer. Their main violence against the protagonist is their concerted effort to have him trade his own vision for theirs." The forces of oppression, evident in this and other works, can in part account for Plumpp's movement toward writing as a defense, according to Cunningham. "For the business of becoming a writer, . . . and its appeal for the besieged hero, are equivalent to achieving two forms of mastery: a personal point of view and the skill to express and preserve this vision through the medium of words."

Plumpp, who had written four books of poetry and *Black Rituals* (a prose work of social psychology about behavior that supports oppression of the black community) by 1975, won the Illinois Arts Council Literary Award that year for *Clinton.* His next and most comprehensive work, *The Mojo Hands Call, I Must Go,* brought him even more acclaim, winning another Illinois Arts Council Award for Poetry and the Carl Sandburg Literary Award for Poetry from the Friends of the Chicago Public Library in 1983. The poem "Fractured Dreams," says Cunningham, "dramatizes the effort of a self-doubting and self-denouncing protagonist to keep faith with that reservoir of collective identity best articulated by the blues tradition," and, in the title poem, reports a *Choice* reviewer, the speaker returns "to his rural origins via a reconversion to the mystical belief in the life force, the Mojo hands, that had sustained his people in the past."

Regarding his role as a poet, Plumpp commented that although he has been working steadily on *Mighty Long Time,* a novel about a blues singer, he sees himself "principally as a poet," and is reconciled to the fact "that I was put here to recover, mold and discover the most private of public languages speaking to me from the Afro-American side of time. The novel is an extension of my quest for language in the blues; as my concept of poetry develops, the more urgent it becomes for me to devote time to its callings." Dorothy Abbott's profile on Plumpp for the *Southern Register* cites his statement that he speaks most often from his Mississippi experiences because it allows him to "maneuver into the reservoir of my being without first having to plod through attacks against whites; I [can] see the survival lines of my people concealed in the many ways they did things. . . . When my work is read I would like you to think of what's behind a good blues song, behind the sweat and jubilation of a church rocking, or what's behind the laughter of old black women."

While other poets of Plumpp's generation have spoken with a more militant urban tone, his writing does not rely heavily on the use of Black English vernacular, nor does he express his politics directly. "He is not a street poet, like Don L. Lee [now Haki R. Madhubuti] or Carolyn Rodgers. . . . Plumpp is more of a poet's poet. He is somewhat more difficult [to read], condensed, cryptic, elliptic, general," comments Dudley Randall in a *Negro Digest* review. About Plumpp's distinctive voice, Cunningham suggests that the poet's "work is remark-

ably free of the restrictions imposed by the black aesthetic movement on such matters as subject matter, diction, and aesthetic stance. In his poetry, for instance, and in his limited forays into fiction, the Southern rural experience is on an equal footing with that of the urban Midwest. . . . Indeed, the range and complexity of statement, so characteristic of his poetry, can be viewed as significant correctives to the arbitrary biases of the black arts writer of the 1960s and early 1970s."

If his politics are not highlighted in his poetics, they are evident in his activities as editor for the Third World Press and the Institute for Positive Education, two black cultural institutions run by the activist-poet Haki R. Madhubuti. Plumpp also makes an indirect attack on apartheid in his collection *Somehow We Survive: An Anthology of South African Writing.* Poems he gathered from three continents, some brought forward from obscure publications, "focus . . . on life's complexities, not on apartheid, which is merely the ugliest part," says David Dorsey in *World Literature Today.* Plumpp has also worked to develop the skills of other writers as an associate professor at the University of Illinois at Chicago Circle since the 1970s.

Pieces written by Plumpp for *Another Chicago Magazine* and *Black American Literature Forum* during the 1980s, notes Cunningham, reflect "an intensified preoccupation with improving the quality of life in America, especially for families." The essayist concludes, "Plumpp's most ambitious recent efforts . . . have revealed not only a writer at the height of his current powers of illumination and eloquence but one who is intent on stretching himself to the utmost as an artist."

The Sterling D. Plumpp Collection, containing works by African and Afro-American writers, resides at the University of Mississippi.

BIOGRAPHICAL/CRITICAL SOURCES:

BOOKS

Dictionary of Literary Biography, Volume XLI: *Afro-American Poets since 1955,* Gale, 1985.
Redmond, Eugene B., editor, *Drumvoices: The Mission of Afro-American Poetry, A Critical History,* Anchor/Doubleday, 1976.

PERIODICALS

American Book Review, January, 1983.
Black World, April, 1971.
Choice, March, 1983.
Negro Digest, February, 1970.
Reader (Chicago), October 17, 1986.
Southern Register, winter, 1984.
World Literature Today, winter, 1984.

—*Sketch by Marilyn K. Basel*

*   *   *

POITIER, Sidney   1927-

PERSONAL: Born February 20, 1927, in Miami, Fla.; son of Reginald James (a tomato farmer) and Evelyn (a tomato farmer; maiden name, Outten) Poitier; married Juanita Hardy (a dancer), April 29, 1950 (divorced, 1965); married Joanna Shimkus (an actress), January 23, 1976; children: (first marriage) Beverly Poitier Mould, Pamela, Sherri, Gina; (second marriage) Anika, Sydney (daughters). *Education:* Attended school in Nassau, British West Indies (now Commonwealth of the Bahamas).

ADDRESSES: *Home*—Beverly Hills, Calif. *Office*—9350 Wilshire Blvd., Suite 310, Beverly Hills, Calif. 90212. *Agent*—Martin Baum, 1888 Century Pk. W., #1400, Los Angeles, Calif. 90067.

CAREER: Actor, director, and author. Actor in stage productions, including "Days of Our Youth," "Lysistrata," 1946, "Anna Lucasta," 1948, "A Raisin in the Sun," 1959, and "Striver's Row," "You Can't Take It With You," "Rain," "Freight," "The Fisherman," "Hidden Horizon," "Sepia Cinderella," and "Riders to the Sea"; actor in television productions, including "Parole Chief," 1952, "A Man Is Ten Feet Tall," 1955, "Fascinating Stranger," 1955, "The New Bill Cosby Show," 1972.

Actor in films, including "From Whom Cometh My Help," 1949, "No Way Out," 1950, "Cry, the Beloved Country," 1952, "Red Ball Express," 1952, "Go, Man, Go," 1954, "The Blackboard Jungle," 1955, "Goodbye, My Lady," 1956, "Edge of the City" (film adaptation of teleplay "A Man Is Ten Feet Tall"), 1957, "Something of Value," 1957, "Band of Angels," 1958, "The Defiant Ones," 1958, "The Mark of the Hawk," 1958, "Porgy and Bess," 1959, "Virgin Islands," 1960, "All the Young Men," 1960, "A Raisin in the Sun," 1961, "Paris Blues," 1961, "Pressure Point," 1962, "Lilies of the Field," 1963, "The Long Ships," 1964, "The Bedford Incident," 1965, "The Greatest Story Ever Told," 1965, "A Patch of Blue," 1965, "The Slender Thread," 1965, "Duel at Diablo," 1966, "Guess Who's Coming to Dinner," 1967, "In the Heat of the Night," 1967, "To Sir, With Love," 1967, "For the Love of Ivy," 1968, "The Lost Man," 1969, "King: A Filmed Record . . . Montgomery to Memphis," 1970, "They Call Me Mister Tibbs," 1970, "Brother John," 1971, "The Organization," 1971, "Buck and the Preacher," 1972, "A Warm December," 1973, "Uptown Saturday Night," 1974, "The Wilby Conspiracy," 1975, "Let's Do It Again," 1976, "A Piece of the Action," 1977, "Shoot to Kill," 1988, and "Little Nikita," 1988.

Director of a play, "Carry Me Back to Morningside Heights," 1968, and films, including "Buck and the Preacher," 1972, "A Warm December," 1973, "Uptown Saturday Night," 1974, "Let's Do It Again," 1976, "A Piece of the Action," 1977, "Stir Crazy," 1980, "Traces," 1981, "Hanky Panky," 1982, and "Fast Forward," 1985.

MEMBER: American Federation of Television and Radio Artists, American Film Institute, Directors Guild of America, National Association for the Advancement of Colored People (life member), Writers Guild of America, Actors Equity Association, Screen Actors Guild, Martin Luther King, Jr., Center for Nonviolent Social Change.

AWARDS, HONORS: Academy Award nomination for best actor from Academy of Motion Picture Arts and Sciences, and Silver Berlin Bear Award for best actor from Berlin International Film Festival, both 1958, both for "The Defiant Ones"; Georgio Cini award from Venice Film Festival, 1958, for "Something of Value"; Academy Award for best actor, 1963, for "Lilies of the Field"; San Sebastian Prize for best actor from San Sebastian International Film Festival, 1968, for "For the Love of Ivy"; Knight Commander of the Order of the British Empire, 1974; Cecil B. De Mille Award from Hollywood Foreign Press Association, 1982.

WRITINGS:

(Author of original story) "For the Love of Ivy," Palomar Pictures International, 1968.

This Life (autobiography), Knopf, 1980.

SIDELIGHTS: Sidney Poitier is "a social symbol of a sort," wrote Patricia Bosworth in the *Washington Post Book World.* "Celebrated as the first black actor to break through the stereotyping and racism of Hollywood, he has individualized and humanized the black experience with [his] powerful performances." A suave, dignified actor often compared to film legends Cary Grant and Clark Gable, Poitier climbed from less than glamorous origins to superstardom in a career boasting forty films, an Academy Award nomination, and the first best actor Oscar ever awarded to a black.

The son of a tomato farmer, Poitier spent his youth fishing, swimming, and catching turtles on the West Indian island that was his home, and attended school for only four years. As a teenager he moved to his brother's home in Miami, Florida, and, after experiencing racial prejudice for the first time, soon left for New York City, where he subsisted on restaurant jobs until he spotted a newspaper ad seeking actors. Knowing nothing about acting, except that it would be a change from dishwashing, he decided to audition for the American Negro Theatre. His strong West Indian accent and his limited reading ability lost him the audition, but he overcame both obstacles, learning by mimicking radio broadcasters and reading the newspaper with the help of a friend. Although his second audition with the same troupe was also unsuccessful, he stayed on as a janitor in exchange for acting lessons. Soon he began earning bit parts, which eventually launched a groundbreaking forty-year stage and film career.

Poitier landed his first major screen role in the 1950 "message movie" titled "No Way Out." A token black doctor in an otherwise all-white hospital, Poitier's character was the prototype of many of his 1950s roles, a black man who could do—better—anything a white man could. For Poitier, the character was a step toward changing the stereotyped screen image of blacks. "I used to go to pictures," *Ebony* magazine quoted Poitier, "and when I saw a Negro on the screen I always left the theater embarrassed and uneasy." Blacks played parts "devoid of any dignity," continued Poitier, "good maids who laughed too loud, good butlers afraid of ghosts." In contrast, Poitier's Dr. Brooks—a dedicated physician accused of murdering one of his white patients—maintains a "calm dignity," wrote *New York Times* critic Thomas M. Pryor, even in the face of savage racist attacks by the brother of the dead patient. Observed Christopher Lehmann-Haupt of the *New York Times,* Poitier would refuse "scripts that failed to satisfy his image of black Americans."

Although Poitier felt that "Hollywood . . . wasn't interested in supplying blacks with a variety of positive images," he expanded his own repertoire by playing a priest, a trucker, and a basketball player in his next several films, achieving what David Zinman termed in his book *Fifty from the Fifties* a "mixed success." Then in 1955, noted Zinman, Poitier's "searing, sensitive performance in *Blackboard Jungle* established his credentials as a dramatic actor." Poitier portrayed an insubordinate youth in an undisciplined, dangerous city school who eventually sides with authority in a switchblade confrontation between the chief troublemaker and a teacher. After "The Blackboard Jungle," observed Zinman, "when a part called for a tense, brooding young black, first call went to Poitier."

In 1958 Poitier reached a landmark that few black actors had achieved—for his role in "The Defiant Ones" he earned an Academy Award nomination. As an escaped black convict who is chained at the wrists to a white convict, Poitier was "intensely dynamic," judged Bosley Crowther of the *New York Times,* with "a deep and powerful strain of underlying compassion." Crowther found the film "a remarkably apt and dramatic visualization of a social idea": the two convicts hate each other at first, yet through their shared hardships as fugitives they come to accept the intangible link of humanity that binds them together as strongly as the chain. The following year Poitier won acclaim for his performance on Broadway in "A Raisin in the Sun." The drama of a poor black family trying to improve their lives, the play and the subsequent film version starred Poitier as an ambitious young husband who wants to open a business with insurance benefits from his father's death. *New York Times* critic Brooks Atkinson deemed Poitier "a remarkable actor with enormous power that is always under control," and he commended Poitier's versatility: "[Poitier] is as eloquent when he has nothing to say as when he has a pungent line to speak. He can convey devious processes of thought as graphically as he can clown and dance."

In 1963, Poitier became the first black to win the best actor Oscar, honored over strong white competition for his role in "Lilies of the Field"; other nominees that year were Albert Finney, Richard Harris, Rex Harrison, and Paul Newman. Cast as a wandering handyman in southwestern America who is challenged by a group of nuns into building a chapel, Poitier brought out his character's need to prove himself not only as a man confronted by a strong-willed woman, personified by the mother superior, but as a black. "Racial pride" surrounds Poitier in the film, according to Crowther, and racial progress attended the Oscar victory. In his article on the Academy Awards Murray Schumach reported that the ovation given Poitier was "recognition not only of [Poitier's] talent, but also of the fact that Hollywood has felt guilty about color barriers of the past, some of which still exist here." Said Poitier as he accepted the award, "It has been a long journey to this moment."

By 1967 Poitier was "an accepted and bankable star," recounted Mel Watkins in the *New York Times Book Review.* Three of his best-known films were released that year, and all of them featured Poitier in dignified, refined roles. In "To Sir, With Love" he portrayed a teacher who tames a belligerent class; for "In the Heat of the Night," a sophisticated detective solving a mysterious murder; in "Guess Who's Coming to Dinner," an eminent scientist about to marry a white girl. Poitier's courtly image made him a "crossover," a black who commanded the interest of whites, asserted James Powers in the *Los Angeles Times Book Review.* "Like Cary Grant," remarked James Wolcott in *New Republic,* "Sidney Poitier is suave from sole to crown."

When blaxploitation films became popular in the early 1970s, however, promoting a black-power image at odds with Poitier's gentlemanly one, writers began to criticize Poitier's "bleached-out roles," recounted Patricia Bosworth, and Poitier's acting career suffered. The actor "took an inordinate amount of flack from both black and liberal white critics," said Thomas Cripps in *American Film,* because "his high visibility made him an easy target for critics in search of a heavy on whom to lay blame for the long history of Hollywood's contempt for blacks." Some detractors held that Poitier was merely "a pretty black face that Hollywood could exploit without having to acknowledge black culture," Christopher Lehmann-Haupt explained. Poitier recognized that "the few black faces passing across the silver screen were not anywhere near enough to assuage the frustrations our people felt," but "however inadequate my steps appeared, it was important that we

make it." For his own part, Poitier "maneuvered himself into a position to make the films he wanted to whether Hollywood likes it or not," observed Lehmann-Haupt. Poitier wanted "to work someday exclusively as a director to control the image of blacks on the screen," as he once told *Ebony* magazine, so he began to direct his own films.

Poitier's first venture as a director resulted from being in the right place at the right time and seizing opportunity. "Buck and the Preacher," a western in which the heroes are black and the bad guys are white, had begun filming under the direction of Joseph Sargent, but when Sargent was fired because of artistic differences, Poitier "stepped in on the spur of the moment," reported Lehmann-Haupt, "and proved that he could direct." Poitier also co-starred in the film, but critic Vincent Canby of the *New York Times* ventured that Poitier's acting was secondary: "With what I suspect is the complete cooperation of Poitier," Canby wrote, "the film is stolen almost immediately by Harry Belafonte as a bogus preacher." In *Rolling Stone* Joseph McBridge praised the film for its "creative use of the conventions it turns inside out" and noted that "it mocks [the conventions] at the same time it allows black audiences . . . the pleasure of usurping the mythology which the Western has long used to keep minorities in their place."

"Uptown Saturday Night," another film that Poitier directed and starred in, showcased a host of "exceptionally talented and funny" blacks, including Poitier, Belafonte, Bill Cosby, Flip Wilson, and Richard Pryor. An "exuberant black joke," in Canby's words, "Uptown" is a black parody of gangster movies, using stereotypical attitudes of fear or sham courage in the service of laughs. According to Penelope Gilliatt in *New Yorker,* "any white who had made [the film] would have been run out of town for prolonging Uncle Tom stereotypes." Canby remarked that the film "has the effect of liberating all of us from our hangups," and he asserted that it is "so full of good humor and . . . high spirits that it reduces movie criticism to the status of a most nonessential craft."

Poitier has since channeled most of his film energies into directing, scoring a box-office victory with Gene Wilder and Richard Pryor in "Stir Crazy" in 1980. Although critical of the film for appearing "improvised, badly," Vincent Canby nevertheless conceded that "Stir Crazy," which also became a short-lived television series, was "one of the biggest money-making films of all time." A *Newsweek* reviewer blamed the picture's faults on scriptwriter Bruce Jay Friedman, maintaining that "director Poitier serves his leading men well."

Poitier's long and varied career is chronicled in his 1980 autobiography, *This Life.* According to Poitier, the book was written in the hope of leaving "a truer accounting" of himself to the public and his children. As he told *People* interviewer Lois Armstrong, "My years had been so full I wanted to itemize them while I was still lucid." His efforts were met enthusiastically by many reviewers. James Wolcott remarked, "Sassed-up with obscenity and street slang, *This Life* has the smack, humor, and vigor of an all-night rap session"; Patricia Bosworth applauded it as a "large-spirited, informative autobiography, one of the best additions to the small library of books on the black artist in films"; and in *American Film,* Thomas Cripps praised its "smooth writing, honest detail, and clear story line." Mel Watkins of the *New York Times Book Review* summed up *This Life* with admiration: "Without pretentiousness and with considerable charm it relates the story of one man's gritty struggle to reach the top in his profession and thereby open doors that had previously been denied his race.''

AVOCATIONAL INTERESTS: Reading, music, golf, football, tennis, gardening, travel.

BIOGRAPHICAL/CRITICAL SOURCES:

BOOKS

Contemporary Literary Criticism, Volume 26, Gale, 1983.
Marill, Alvin H., *The Films of Sidney Poitier,* Citadel, 1978.
Poitier, Sidney, *This Life,* Knopf, 1980.
Zinman, David, *Fifty from the Fifties,* Arlington, 1979.

PERIODICALS

American Film, September, 1980.
Chicago Tribune, January 31, 1988.
Los Angeles Times Book Review, June 1, 1980.
New Republic, May 10, 1980.
Newsweek, June 24, 1974, December 15, 1980.
New Yorker, June 17, 1974, September 15, 1975, November 3, 1975.
New York Times, August 17, 1950, March 21, 1955, May 11, 1957, September 25, 1958, March 12, 1959, March 29, 1959, June 25, 1959, August 27, 1960, March 30, 1961, October 2, 1963, June 15, 1967, August 3, 1967, December 12, 1967, February 29, 1968, July 18, 1968, April 29, 1972, June 17, 1974, June 2, 1980, December 12, 1980, June 4, 1982, February 15, 1985.
New York Times Book Review, August 17, 1980, March 29, 1981.
People, August 4, 1980, July 5, 1982.
Time, October 6, 1975, October 27, 1975, June 7, 1982.
Washington Post Book World, May 25, 1980.

*   *   *

POLITE, Carlene Hatcher   1932-

PERSONAL: Born August 28, 1932, in Detroit, Mich.; daughter of John and Lillian (Cook) Hatcher (both international representatives of the UAW-CIO); divorced; children: Glynda, Lila. *Education:* Attended Sarah Lawrence College and Martha Graham School of Contemporary Dance.

ADDRESSES: Home—147 Linwood St., Buffalo, N.Y. 14209. *Office*—Department of English, 321 Clemens Hall, State University of New York, Buffalo, N.Y. 14206.

CAREER: Concert Dance Theatre, New York City, dancer, 1955-59; Vanguard Playhouse, Detroit, Mich., dancer, 1960-62; Michigan Democratic Party, Detroit, staff worker, elected to Michigan State Central Committee, 1962; Equity Theatre, Detroit, dancer and organizer, 1962-64; worked as writer in Paris, France, 1964-71; State University of New York at Buffalo, member of faculty beginning 1971, associate professor of English, 1980—, former chair of African Studies department. Guest instructor of modern dance in the Martha Graham technique, Detroit YWCA, 1960, and Wayne State University. Detroit Council for Human Rights, special assistant and coordinator for Walk to Freedom, 1963, organizer of Northern Negro Leadership Conference, 1963, special assistant to Rev. C. L. Franklin, 1963-64.

MEMBER: National Foundation on the Arts and Humanities, NAACP, Afro-American Historical Society.

AWARDS, HONORS: National Foundation on the Arts and Humanities fellowship, 1967; Rockefeller Foundation fellowship, 1968.

WRITINGS:

The Flagellants (novel), Farrar, Straus, 1967, reprinted, Beacon Press, 1987 (original French translation by Pierre Alien published as *Les Flagellents,* Christian Bourgois Editeur, 1966).
Sister X and the Victims of Foul Play (novel), Farrar, Straus, 1975.

Contributor to periodicals, including *Mademoiselle* and *Yardbird Reader.*

WORK IN PROGRESS: Two more books; literary and political articles for American periodicals.

SIDELIGHTS: Experimental novelist Carlene Hatcher Polite has been noted for fiction that goes beyond conventional methods of plot and character development and is held together by what Hammett Worthington-Smith in *Dictionary of Literary Biography* calls ''tough, hard-edged, poetic prose.'' Praised by a reviewer in the *New Yorker* as ''an energetic and fearless writer,'' Polite relies on the strength of character monologues and speeches—''marked by a mastery of language and a love of rhetoric, especially that of black cultural revolution,'' notes Worthington-Smith—to express and emphasize her thematic issues. Polite has two novels to her credit, *The Flagellants* and *Sister X and the Victims of Foul Play,* the former first published in Paris where the Detroit native lived from 1964 to 1971. Having worked as a dancer, both performing and instructing, and political activist, who was elected to the State Central Committee of the Michigan Democratic Party, the diverse Polite moved to Paris in 1964 knowing that writing was her real ambition. Impressed by a letter of Polite's, French publisher Dominique de Roux encouraged her to continue writing, and in 1966 *The Flagellants* was the first novel published by Christian Borgois Editeur, a subsidiary of the major French publishing group Presses de la Cite. A year later *The Flagellants* was published in the United States, following praise from a number of French reviewers who saw Polite as an important and innovative voice in American black fiction.

The Flagellants is the story of a young black couple, whose attempts to construct a meaningful life together are ''thwarted,'' according to Worthington-Smith, ''because neither can move beyond the limited roles granted to black men and women in a racially oppressive society.'' The novel progresses according to a series of internal monologues and exchanges, exposing the couple's individual ''internal realities which have been shaped by the condition of their black forbears,'' notes Worthington-Smith. The crux of their interaction is that ''each literally flagellates the other as they seek not only to experience and understand love but also to define an individual and cultural identity.'' Lottmann writes that the couple's ''flagellations are mutual tongue-lashings, a clash which might be compared to [Edward Albee's] 'Who's Afraid of Virginia Woolf?' . . . The result is 'Theater of Cruelty' in book form.'' Nora Sayre in the *Nation* points out that the significance of these verbal 'flagellations'' is twofold: ''First, the sensation of being Negro means feeling beaten. Second, these lovers try to numb their racial pains by lacerating each other. At moments, they seem to seek mutual destruction in order to be reborn. . . . It all has a hideous logic, as the furious lovers fail to fortify each other, and finally writhe apart.'' Sayre particularly praises *The Flagellants* for being an ''absorbing novel [which] can't be colored—or discolored—into racial tradition. . . . The novel's abrasive strength springs from the rotation of white and Negro problems, embodied in a pair who hurl their historical past at each other.''

Polite's next novel, *Sister X and the Victims of Foul Play*, "carries her tendency to develop characters and themes by means of extended monologues and speeches even farther than did *The Flagellants*," writes Worthington-Smith. The novel recounts the life of the dead Sister X, an exotic black dancer killed in a fall in a Parisian nightclub. Her story is retold through the novel's only speaking characters, Sister X's costume designer (Abyssinia) and her former lover (Black Will). "All of the characters," notes Worthington-Smith, "are expatriates from the United States living on the fringes of the chic artistic world in Paris." Abyssinia and Black Will, through dialogues and flashbacks, "render Sister X's story and in the process pass on their observations about life from their own black cultural perspective," continues Worthington-Smith. Frederick Busch in the *New York Times Book Review* comments that "the outstanding feature of this second novel is its sledge-hammer social protest," yet adds that it suffers some from what he calls "grim rhetoric" and "characters stripped of specific traits." Worthington-Smith explains, however, that the novel's focus is Sister X and her link "to Abyssinia and Black Will as a black victim of foul play, racial preconceptions, and discrimination." When a French medical officer pronounces Sister X's death as a result of cancer, "he misses the irony in his finding. Because of the narrative perspective on Sister X, the reader knows what the doctor does not: Sister X's death is the result of a cancerous society which victimizes individuals and groups, particularly blacks in this novel, and literally kills their aspirations and dreams." A reviewer in the *New Yorker* praises *Sister X and the Victims of Foul Play* as "short, sarcastic, jubilant, [and] scalding."

BIOGRAPHICAL/CRITICAL SOURCES:

BOOKS

Dictionary of Literary Biography, Volume 33: *Afro-American Fiction Writers after 1955*, Gale, 1984.
Schraufnagel, Noel, *From Apology to Protest: The Black American Novel*, Everett/Edwards, 1973.

PERIODICALS

American Scholar, autumn, 1967.
Nation, October 9, 1967.
New Yorker, December 8, 1975.
New York Times Book Review, June 11, 1967, November 23, 1975.
Publishers Weekly, June 12, 1967.

*   *   *

POSTON, Ted
   See POSTON, Theodore Roosevelt Augustus Major

*   *   *

POSTON, Theodore Roosevelt Augustus Major
   1906-1974
   (Ted Poston)

PERSONAL: Known professionally as Ted Poston; born July 4, 1906, in Hopkinsville, Ky.; died after a long illness, January 11, 1974, in Brooklyn, N.Y.; son of Ephraim (a newspaper publisher) and Mollie (Cox) Poston; married Miriam Rivers, 1935 (divorced); married Marie Byrd Jackson, 1941 (divorced, 1955); married Ersa Hines, August 21, 1957. *Education:* Tennessee Agricultural and Industrial College (now Tennessee State University), A.B., 1928; attended New York University.

ADDRESSES: Home—101 Chauncey St., Brooklyn, N.Y.

CAREER: Contender, Hopkinsville, Ky., copy clerk, beginning in 1922; writer for Alfred E. Smith presidential campaign, New York, N.Y., 1928; dining car waiter for Pennsylvania Railroad and columnist for *Pittsburgh Courier*, c. 1928-29; *Amsterdam News*, New York City, reporter, 1929-34, city editor, 1934-c. 1936; writer for Works Progress Administration, c. 1936; *New York Post*, New York City, reporter, c. 1937-72. Traveled to U.S.S.R. as extra for unproduced film "Black and White," 1932. *Wartime service:* Worked in Washington, D.C., from 1940 to 1945 as public relations consultant for National Advisory Defense Commission, Office of Production Management, War Production Board, and War Manpower Commission, and as chief of Negro News Desk in news bureau of Office of War Information.

MEMBER: Newspaper Guild (Washington chapter), Omega Psi Phi.

AWARDS, HONORS: Heywood Broun Memorial Award from American Newspaper Guild, 1950, for coverage of racial discrimination in a trial in Tavares, Fla.; George Polk Award from Long Island University, 1950, for coverage of racial discrimination in Florida; award from Irving Geist Foundation, 1950, for coverage of antiblack rioting in Groveland, Fla.; award from Newspaper Guild of New York, 1950, and Unity Award from Beta Delta Mu, 1951, both for promoting interracial tolerance; award from Black Perspective, 1972; distinguished service medal from City of New York; distinguished service plaques from boroughs of Brooklyn, Bronx, and Queens.

WRITINGS:

SHORT STORIES

"A Matter of Record," published in *New Republic*, February 26, 1940.
"You Go South," published in *New Republic*, September 9, 1940.
"Law and Order in Norfolk," published in *New Republic*, October 7, 1940.
"The Making of Mamma Harris," published in *New Republic*, November 4, 1940.
"The Revolt of the Evil Fairies," published in *New Republic*, April 6, 1942.

Contributor of additional stories to periodicals. Work represented in anthologies, including *The Negro Caravan*, edited by Sterling A. Brown, Arthur P. Davis, and Ulysses Lee, Arno, 1970; *Black Joy*, edited by Jay David, Cowles, 1971; and *The Best Short Stories by Negro Writers: An Anthology From 1899 to the Present*, edited by Langston Hughes, Little, Brown, 1967.

OTHER

(Contributor) Paul L. Fisher and Ralph Lowenstein, editors, *Race and the News Media*, Praeger, 1967.

Contributor of articles and reviews to periodicals, including *Ebony, Nation, Negro Digest, New Republic, Satuday Review, Survey*.

SIDELIGHTS: A reporter for the *New York Post* from the late 1930s until he retired in 1972, Ted Poston was one of the first black journalists to work full time for a white-owned daily newspaper. He grew up in Hopkinsville, Kentucky, and as a teenager he helped out at his family's weekly, the *Contender*, until the paper became so controversial that it was moved out of town. After earning a bachelor's degree at Tennessee Agricultural and Industrial College in 1928, Poston joined the staff of a prominent black weekly in New York City, the *Amsterdam News*. He advanced to city editor in 1934, but after he helped lead a strike to unionize the *News*, its owners fired him.

A few years later Poston applied for a job at the *Post*—a difficult move, since only two black journalists had ever worked for a white-owned daily in the city. He was promised work if he could find a front-page story for the next day's paper. Doubtful of his prospects Poston took the subway back toward his home in Harlem, and as he left the train he saw a white man pursued by a group of angry blacks. Curiosity aroused, Poston discovered that the white was trying to serve notice of a lawsuit on Father Divine, a charismatic black preacher whose followers often called him an incarnation of God. The angry crowd represented some of Divine's protectors, known as his "angels." Poston had his story and his reporter's job.

The *Post* assigned him to cover New York City Hall, and as he later told *Editor and Publisher,* journalists there "would look at me as if to say I had a hell of a nerve coming into that white man's province. Whenever there was a breaking story, [they] would go into another room to compare notes." Finally, Poston said, "I got tired of it and began to scoop them on stories. That broke the ice."

Poston stressed that his reporting was not limited to events involving race, and in addition to the city hall beat he was known for exclusive interviews with two of the best-known politicians of his day: Huey Long, controversial political boss of Louisiana, and Wendell Willkie, 1940 Republican nominee for president. But Poston's most dramatic—and dangerous— work often concerned race relations in the South.

While employed by the *News* he went to Alabama to cover the Scottsboro case, in which a group of young black men was falsely accused of raping two white women. Poston was afraid to appear openly as a black reporter from the North, so he dressed in shabby clothes and attended the trial as an itinerant preacher. When a group of suspicious whites caught him mailing a report to New York City, he calmed them down by producing some false identification that showed he was a minister. (He later recounted the incident in an article for *Negro Digest* titled "My Most Humiliating Jim Crow Experience.") After Poston attended a similar rape trial in Florida for the *Post* in 1949, a gang of whites chased him out of town; when he covered the 1955 bus boycotts in Montgomery, Alabama, his boss asked him to call New York every night to show he was still alive. Such assignments earned Poston several awards in the 1950s, including the Heywood Broun Award of the American Newspaper Guild.

Over the course of Poston's life at least twenty of his short stories appeared in magazines and anthologies, and in *New Republic* he gained a national audience for several narratives about the plight of black Americans. In "A Matter of Record," for example, a decrepit boxer clings to a press clipping of his past glory; in "The Making of Mamma Harris" a woman leads a strike to unionize a tobacco factory; and in "You Go South" a New Yorker prepares himself for the racial humiliations he will face when he travels to the South.

Many of Poston's short stories are autobiographical accounts of life in Hopkinsville at the Booker T. Washington Colored Grammar School. "Revolt of the Evil Fairies," which appeared in *New Republic* and a number of anthologies, illustrates racial barriers in the South by depicting a school play in which roles are assigned on the basis of skin color. According to the narrator, Good Fairies tend to be children "with straight hair and white folks' features," and Prince Charming and Sleeping Beauty are "*always* light-skinned." "And therein lay my personal tragedy," the narrator continues. "I made the best grades in my class, I was the leading debater, and the scion of a respected family in the community. But I could never be Prince Charming, because I was black." Humiliated by his role as leader of the Evil Fairies, the narrator rebels in the middle of a performance by punching Prince Charming, and the dark- and light-skinned children are soon in open combat. "They wouldn't let me appear in the grand dramatic offering at all next year," the narrator concludes. "But I didn't care. I couldn't have been Prince Charming anyway."

Poston knew that his job on a white-owned daily was an opportunity that few blacks had been allowed to share. He actively encouraged more minorities to follow his lead, and when the *Post* hired minority trainees he monitored their progress and lobbied the paper's publisher to keep them on the staff. When Poston retired in 1972, the journalistic organization Black Perspective honored him both for professional excellence and for his efforts on behalf of other blacks in his field. Poston said he hoped to return to Hopkinsville and write more short stories about his youth, but his health failed and he died in 1974.

Shortly after his death Poston was lauded in the *Washington Post* by Joel Dreyfuss, a younger black reporter who had worked with him in New York. Dreyfuss praised Poston's "flowing graceful prose" and skill as a rewrite man, and reminded readers of the inner strength Poston must have possessed to endure the "constant pressure," "isolation," and humiliation of his difficult role. The headline on Dreyfuss's story read: "The Loneliness of Being First."

BIOGRAPHICAL/CRITICAL SOURCES:

BOOKS

Dictionary of Literary Biography, Volume 51: *Afro-American Writers From the Harlem Renaissance to 1940,* Gale, 1987.

PERIODICALS

Black Perspective, spring, 1972.
Editor and Publisher, April 29, 1972.
Negro Digest, April, 1944, December, 1949.
Newsweek, April 11, 1949.

OBITUARIES:

PERIODICALS

New York Times, January 12, 1974.
Time, January 21, 1974.
Washington Post, January 19, 1974.

—*Sketch by Thomas Kozikowski*

*   *   *

POWELL, Adam Clayton, Jr.   1908-1972

PERSONAL: Born November 29, 1908, in New Haven, Conn.; died of cancer, April 4, 1972, in Miami, Fla.; son of Adam Clayton (a minister) and Mattie (Fletcher) Powell; married Isabel G. Washington (a dancer), March 8, 1933 (divorced, 1943); married Hazel Scott (a pianist and singer), August, 1945 (divorced, 1960); married Yvette Marjorie Flores Diago, 1960 (separated, 1965); children: Preston (adopted); (second marriage) Adam Clayton III; (third marriage) Adam Diago.

Education: Colgate University, B.A., 1930; Columbia University, M.A., 1932.

ADDRESSES: Home—Bimini, Bahamas.

CAREER: Abyssinian Baptist Church, New York City, manager and assistant pastor, 1930-36, pastor, 1936-71; New York City councilman, 1941-45; founder, editor in chief, co-publisher, *People's Voice,* 1942; United States congressman, 1945-67 and 1969-70, served as chairman of House Committee on Education and Labor, 1960-67. Delegate to the Parliamentary World Conference in London, 1951-52, and to the ILO Conference in Geneva, 1961.

AWARDS, HONORS: Doctor of Divinity degree, Shaw University, 1938; LL.D., Virginia Union University, 1947; Knight of the Golden Cross, Ethiopia, 1954, for relief work.

WRITINGS:

Marching Blacks: An Interpretive History of the Rise of the Black Common Man, Dial, 1945, revised edition, 1973.
The New Image in Education: A Prospectus for the Future by the Chairman of the Committee on Education and Labor, U.S. Government Printing Office, 1962.
Keep the Faith, Baby!, Trident, 1967.
Adam by Adam: The Autobiography of Adam Clayton Powell, Jr., Dial, 1971.

SIDELIGHTS: According to Thomas A. Johnson in the *New York Times,* Adam Clayton Powell, Jr. was a man of many roles. "He was at once the leader of the largest church congregation in the nation, a political demagogue, a Congressional rebel, a civil rights leader three decades before the Montgomery bus boycott, a wheeler-dealer, a rabble-rouser, a grandstander, a fugitive, a playboy and a most effective chairman of the House Committee on Education and Labor." *Newsweek's* David M. Alpern described Powell's legacy: "Before black power, before black pride, before the civil rights movement took its first steps in the dusty streets of Montgomery, Ala., before any of it, there was Adam. For 30 years, Adam Clayton Powell Jr. did more than any other man to dramatize the quest of Negro Americans and, by an outrageous larger-than-life style, give his people a vicarious piece of the white man's action. He was New York's first black city councilman, Harlem's first black congressman—and the most celebrated black politician in the nation."

Shortly after his birth, Powell's family moved to New York City where his father was made pastor of the Abyssinian Baptist Church. In 1923 the church and the Powells moved to Harlem where young Adam was exposed to the ideas of Marcus Garvey and attended sessions of the African Nationalist Pioneer Movement. "Marcus Garvey was one of the greatest mass leaders of all time," Powell later wrote. "He was misunderstood and maligned, but he brought to the Negro people for the first time a sense of pride in being black." During the Depression, Powell became a leader in his own right. He led a series of demonstrations against department stores, bus lines, hospitals, the telephone company, and other big businesses in Harlem, forcing them to hire blacks. He became chairman of the Coordinating Committee on Employment and organized picket lines outside the executive offices of the 1939-40 World's Fair, thereby gaining jobs at the fair for hundreds of black workers.

The activist also organized the social and welfare programs at the Abyssinian Baptist Church, including a vocational guidance clinic as well as a soup kitchen and relief operation that supplied food, clothing, and fuel for thousands of Harlem residents. He served as the leader of the militant Harlem People's Committee and quickly earned a reputation, *Ebony's* Simeon Booker noted, "for scrap, for agitation and for stinging rebuke." People began calling him "the Angry Young Man" and "Fighting Adam." Booker credited him with singlehandedly changing the course of national negro affairs. In 1941 Powell was elected to the New York City Council. After serving four years on the council, Powell turned a voteless community into a "ballot kingdom," Booker observed, and went to Congress as the representative of central Harlem. In Washington the new legislator continued his fight against racial discrimination. Although unwritten prejudicial rules excluded him from such public places as dining rooms, steam baths, and barber shops, Powell defiantly made use of these facilities, often with his entire staff in tow. In Congress he debated furiously with Southern segregationists, challenged discrimination in the armed forces, and authored the Powell Amendment—an attempt to deny federal funds to projects that tolerated discrimination. Booker disclosed that Powell "upset tradition on Capitol Hill—against the wishes and combined efforts of many of his colleagues. Like no other Negro, except possibly the late Malcolm X, Adam knew how to anger, to irritate and to cajole his white counterparts."

Powell tackled a variety of causes. He fought for the admission of black journalists to the Senate and House press galleries. He introduced legislation to ban racist transportation, and he brought to the attention of Congress the discriminatory practices of such groups as the Daughters of the American Revolution (DAR). As chairman of the House Committee on Education and Labor, a position that made him perhaps the most powerful black in America, Powell's record was extraordinary. Under his direction the committee passed forty-eight major pieces of social legislation, including the 1961 Minimum Wage Bill, the Manpower Development and Training Act, the Anti-Poverty Bill, the Juvenile Delinquency Act, the Vocational Educational Act, and the National Defense Educational Act.

Booker asserted, however, that as Powell "became influential, powerful and dominating . . . he frequently clashed with Democrats, government officials, labor and educational leaders, and even the President on segregation and discrimination policies. While Southern chairmen blocked civil rights legislation at will, Adam tried to bottle major legislation whenever he felt it needed some anti-bias safeguards. This tactic brought him into open conflict with the 'white power structure.'" The resulting tense situation and Powell's record of high absenteeism brought upon him severe censure from his fellow legislators. This criticism was exacerbated by his reputation as a playboy and the accusation that he misused public funds by keeping on his payroll a receptionist with whom he was personally involved. His colleagues also charged him with tax evasion and junketeering. In response, Powell asserted: "The things other Congressmen try to hide, I do right out in the open. I'm not a hypocrite."

Powell's desire for public attention, though, also brought him into conflict with other black leaders. "He credited himself with being more powerful than the leaders and probably he was," explained Booker, "but the shortcoming was that the black teamwork he stressed, he never carried out." Still it wasn't until a television interview in March, 1960, that his flamboyant and outspoken public image jeopardized his political effectiveness. A court case ensued after Powell had called a sixty-three-year-old Harlem widow, Ester James, a "bag woman'' (a collector of graft for corrupt police). Powell ignored the libel case, refusing to make an apology or a settlement. After Mrs. James won and was awarded damages the congressman still would not comply with the court ruling. Eventually, Powell was found guilty of civil contempt but avoided arrest by appearing in New York City only on Sundays when summonses could not be served. When the politician was convicted of criminal contempt in 1966, he took up residence on the Bahamian island of Bimini.

In response to this conviction and the other charges of misbehavior, a select committee of representatives investigated Powell and on March 1, 1967, the House voted 307 to 116 to exclude him from the ninetieth Congress. Powell thus became the first committee chairman to be expulsed from the House in 160 years. Nevertheless, in a special election to fill his vacant seat two months later, Powell was overwhelmingly voted to his former position by his constituents. Ultimately, he paid the damages to Mrs. James and was then reseated in Congress in January, 1969. Powell, however, was fined for misuse of funds and stripped of his seniority.

During this time, white liberals with whom Powell had worked abandoned him while black leaders rallied to his defense. The split marked a breach in the civil rights movement, which Francis E. Kearns analyzed in *Commonweal:* "The chief significance of Adam Clayton Powell's recent difficulties with Congress lies not in the state of the Congressman's personal fortunes or even in the constitutional question of whether the House may deny a district representation by its duly elected Congressman. . . . Clearly Powell's censurable behavior hardly approaches in gravity the misconduct of some other Congressmen who have escaped punitive action. . . . The unseating of one of the most powerful Negro politicians in American history at the very time when a battery of editorialists are urging the Negro to temper his militancy is hardly likely to demonstrate that legislative action offers a viable alternative to mob action in the streets.''

Six months after Powell's return to Congress, the Supreme Court ruled that the 1967 House decision to exclude the errant politician had been unconstitutional. He told reporters at the time: "From now on, America will know the Supreme Court is the place where you can get justice.'' But Powell's political career was coming to an end. In 1969 he was defeated by Charles B. Rangel in a Democratic primary after having been hospitalized for cancer.

Powell's writing was as controversial as his lifestyle. In the *New York Times Book Review*, Frank Adams dwelled on the author's ''intemperance'' and ''intransigence,'' calling the congressman's first book, *Marching Blacks: An Interpretive History of the Rise of the Black Common Man,* ''the battle cry of an embittered man who avows the hope that his cause will triumph without bloodshed, but warns that only the conscience of white America can prevent another civil war from being

fought with all the fury of the war that freed the slaves.'' H. A. Overstreet of the *Saturday Review,* however, appraised the volume as ''a nonviolent fighting book,'' and the ''story of Negro unification. . . . In few books is the ugliness of racial injustice so vividly and succinctly described; in few is the case so clearly stated for the fact that race prejudice is poison that kills dignity and decency in the souls of race haters.''

Keep the Faith, Baby! is a collection of Powell's sermons and speeches. *Saturday Review*'s David Poling maintained that Powell ''has to be considered above average in ability to relate scripture to the needs and problems of everyday life. There is a directness, an economy of words that eludes too many preachers.'' Powell's autobiography met with a mixed reception from reviewers. A *New Yorker* critic described *Adam by Adam: The Autobiography of Adam Clayton Powell, Jr.* as an ''impenitent apologia,'' while Martin Kilsen of the *New York Times Book Review* found the book ''deficient in serious self-analysis.'' Kilsen praised the author, at the same time, though, as ''a discerning observer of American politics, both at the city and national levels, as well as of the pattern of cruel defeats and illustrations that surround the life of the ghetto Negro.''

BIOGRAPHICAL/CRITICAL SOURCES:

PERIODICALS

Commonweal, January 27, 1967.
Ebony, June, 1963, March, 1967, January, 1971, June, 1972.
Life, March 24, 1967.
Nation, February 16, 1946.
Newsweek, April 1, 1968, December 2, 1968, January 13, 1969, June 30, 1969.
New Yorker, November 13, 1971.
New York Times Book Review, February 9, 1946, November 7, 1971.
Saturday Review, February 9, 1946, April 22, 1967.
Time, January 12, 1942, June 15, 1942, January 10, 1969, June 27, 1969.

OBITUARIES:

PERIODICALS

L'Express, April 10, 1972.
Los Angeles Times, April 5, 1972.
Newsweek, April 17, 1972.
New York Times, April 5, 1972.
Time, April 17, 1972.
Washington Post, April 6, 1972.

*   *   *

PROVIST, d'Alain
See DIOP, Birago (Ismael)

Q

QUARLES, Benjamin 1904-

PERSONAL: Born January 23, 1904, in Boston, Mass.; son of Arthur Benedict (a waiter) and Margaret (O'Brien) Quarles; married Ruth Brett, December 21, 1952; children: (first marriage) Roberta; (second marriage) Pamela. *Education:* Shaw University, B.A., 1931; University of Wisconsin, M.A., 1933, Ph.D., 1940.

ADDRESSES: Home—2205 Southern Ave., Baltimore, Md. 21214. *Office*—Morgan State University, Baltimore, Md. 21239.

CAREER: Shaw University, Raleigh, N.C., instructor in history, 1934-38; Dillard University, New Orleans, La., professor of history, 1938-46, dean, 1946-53; Morgan State University, Baltimore, Md., professor of history and chairman of department, 1953-69, professor emeritus, 1969—. Member of national council, Frederick Douglass Museum of African Art, Smithsonian Institution; Maryland State Commission on Negro History and Culture (now Maryland State Commission on Afro-American History and Culture), chairman, 1969-71, currently honorary chairman. Member of fellowship selection committee, American Council of Learned Societies, 1976-78; member of building committee, Amistad Research Center. Member of Project Advisory Committee on Black Congressmembers, Joint Center for Political Studies; member of committee of advisors, National Humanities Center; member of Department of the Army Historical Advisory Committee, 1977-80.

MEMBER: Association for the Study of Afro-American Life and History (member of executive council, 1948-84), Center for African and African-American Studies (fellow), American Antiquarian Society, Maryland Historical Society (member of committee on publications).

AWARDS, HONORS: Guggenheim fellow, 1958-59; honorary consultant in United States history, Library of Congress, 1970-71; recipient of sixteen honorary degrees from universities and colleges in the United States, including University of Maryland, Colby College, Kent State University, Rutgers University, Howard University, and University of Pennsylvania.

WRITINGS:

Frederick Douglass, Associated Publishers, 1948, reprinted, Atheneum, 1968.

The Negro in the Civil War, Little, Brown, 1953, reprinted, Russell, 1968.
The Negro in the American Revolution, University of North Carolina Press, 1961.
Lincoln and the Negro, Oxford University Press, 1962.
The Negro in the Making of America, Collier Books, 1964, revised edition, 1971, reprinted, Macmillan, 1987.
(With Dorothy Sterling) *Lift Every Voice: The Lives of Booker T. Washington, W. E. B. Du Bois, Mary Church Terrell, and James Weldon Johnson,* Doubleday, 1965.
Black Abolitionists, Oxford University Press, 1969.
Allies for Freedom: Blacks and John Brown, Oxford University Press, 1974.
Black Mosaic: Essays in Afro-American History, University of Massachusetts Press, 1988.

EDITOR

Narrative of the Life of Frederick Douglass, an American Slave, Written by Himself, Harvard University Press, 1960.
(With Leslie H. Fishel) *The Negro American: A Documentary History,* Scott, Foresman, 1967, hardcover edition, Morrow, 1968, 3rd edition published as *The Black American: A Documentary History,* Scott, Foresman, 1976.
Frederick Douglass, Prentice-Hall, 1968.
Blacks on John Brown, University of Illinois Press, 1974.

OTHER

Also contributor of chapters and forewords to books; contributor of forewords to government publications and microfilm collection. Editor of documentary sources. Contributor of chapters to encyclopedias. Contributor of articles and reviews to journals, including *Journal of Negro History* and *Daedalus.* Member of editorial board, Frederick Douglass Papers Project, Yale University; member of board of editors, *Maryland Historical Magazine.* Member of board of advisors, Black Abolitionist Papers; member of advisory board, *America: History and Life,* American Bibliographical Center.

SIDELIGHTS: "With the appearance of his biography of Frederick Douglass in 1948," Benjamin Quarles "became a major contributor to the history of the black experience from the Revolutionary War through the Civil War," states August Meier in a *Civil War History* article. "His leading works include the standard volumes on the role of Negroes in both of those conflicts, pioneering studies on black participation in the abolitionist movement, and [work] on the interrelation between blacks and major white anti-slavery figures.''

Quarles once stated in a lecture at Howard University, as reported by the *Washington Post*, that ''for the black rank-and-file, the man in the street, . . . black history's main objective is to create a sense of pride and personal worth.'' For the white reader, on the other hand, its purpose ''is to eradicate the American myth of liberty and justice for all and illustrate the centrality of blacks in this country's experience.''

Quarles has been accused of being overly optimistic in his accounts of recent black history. In reviews of *The Negro American: A Documentary History*, Howard N. Meyer in the *Nation* and Eliot Fremont-Smith in the *New York Times* criticize Quarles and co-editor Leslie H. Fishel for ignoring the frustrations of blacks evidenced by the riots and demonstrations of the late 1960s. As Meier explains, ''given Quarles' focus on the contribution Negroes have made to the mainstream of American history, his interest in black-white interaction and the Negroes' white allies, and the minimal attention he gives to such themes as black nationalism or the development of black culture and institutions, one can clearly distinguish his work from what can be called the new paradigm of black history.''

Yet, overall, Quarles's work has been consistently praised as an important contribution to black history. Meier concludes that ''no matter how much Quarles' view differs from the new paradigm, it is clear that all of us in the field are greatly in his debt. . . . He has served as a model to a whole generation of scholars in Afro-American history, white and black alike. His synthesis of Civil War and abolition, his authoritative book on the Revolution, his sensitive analysis of Lincoln and the blacks are all volumes that remain unequalled or unsurpassed.''

BIOGRAPHICAL/CRITICAL SOURCES:

BOOKS

McPherson, James M., *The Struggle for Equality*, Princeton University Press, 1964.

PERIODICALS

American Historical Review, January, 1963.
Civil War History, Volume 16, number 2, 1980.
Journal of American History, December, 1969, March, 1975.
Journal of Negro History, October, 1953.
Mississippi Valley Historical Review, December, 1953.
Nation, June 3, 1968.
New England Quarterly, September, 1962.
New York Herald Tribune Book Review, May 27, 1962.
New York Review of Books, December 3, 1970.
New York Times, February 27, 1968, December 12, 1968.
Times Literary Supplement, August 7, 1969.
Virginia Quarterly Review, spring, 1970.
Washington Post, May 5, 1971, June 18, 1976.

R

RANDALL, Dudley (Felker) 1914-

PERSONAL: Born January 14, 1914, in Washington, D.C.; son of Arthur George Clyde (a Congregational minister) and Ada Viola (a teacher; maiden name, Bradley) Randall; married Ruby Hands, May 27, 1935 (marriage dissolved); married Mildred Pinckney, December 20, 1942 (marriage dissolved); married Vivian Spencer (a psychiatric social worker), May 4, 1957; children: (first marriage) Phyllis Ada (Mrs. William Sherron III). *Education:* Wayne University (now Wayne State University), B.A., 1949; University of Michigan, M.A.L.S., 1951; graduate study, University of Ghana, 1970. *Politics:* Independent. *Religion:* Congregational.

ADDRESSES: Home and office—12651 Old Mill Pl., Detroit, Mich. 48238.

CAREER: Ford Motor Co., River Rouge, Mich., foundry worker, 1932-37; U.S. Post Office, Detroit, Mich., carrier and clerk, 1938-51; Lincoln University, Jefferson City, Mo., librarian, 1951-54; Morgan State College, Baltimore, Md., associate librarian, 1954-56; Wayne County Federated Library System, Wayne, Mich., 1956-69, began as assistant branch librarian, became branch librarian, 1956-63, head of reference-interloan department, 1963-69; University of Detroit, Detroit, reference librarian and poet-in-residence, 1969-75. Visiting lecturer, University of Michigan, 1969. Founder and general editor, Broadside Press, Detroit, 1965-1977, consultant, 1977—. Founder, Broadside Poets Theater and Broadside Poetry Workshop, 1980. Member, Advisory Panel on Literature, Michigan Council for the Arts, and New Detroit, Inc., both since 1970. Has participated in several poetry seminars and festivals, including the East-West Culture Learning Institute's Seminar on socio-literature at the University of Hawaii. *Military service:* U.S. Army, signal corps, 1942-46.

MEMBER: International Afro-American Museum, National Association for the Advancement of Colored People, American Library Association, Michigan Library Association, Michigan Poetry Society, Detroit Society for the Advancement of Culture and Education.

AWARDS, HONORS: Tompkins Award, Wayne State University, 1962, 1966; Kuumba Liberation Award, 1973; Arts Award in Literature, Michigan Foundation for the Arts, 1975; D.Litt., University of Detroit, 1978; Creative Artist Award in Literature, Michigan Council for the Arts, 1981; National Endowment for the Arts fellowship, 1981, senior fellowship, 1986; appointed First Poet Laureate of the City of Detroit by Mayor Coleman A. Young, 1981.

WRITINGS:

(Contributor) Rosey E. Pool, editor and author of introduction, *Beyond the Blues*, Hand and Flower Press, 1962.

(With Margaret Danner) *Poem Counterpoem*, Broadside Press, 1966.

(Editor and contributor with Margaret G. Burroughs) *For Malcolm: Poems on the Life and Death of Malcolm X*, Broadside Press, 1967, 2nd edition, 1969.

Cities Burning, Broadside Press, 1968.

(Editor) *Black Poetry: A Supplement to Anthologies Which Exclude Black Poets*, Broadside Press, 1969.

(Author of introduction) Sonia Sanchez, *We a BaddDDD People*, Broadside Press, 1970.

Love You, Paul Breman, 1970.

More to Remember: Poems of Four Decades, Third World Press, 1971.

(Editor and author of introduction) *The Black Poets*, Bantam, 1971.

(Contributor) Addison Gayle, Jr. editor, *The Black Aesthetic*, Doubleday, 1971.

After the Killing, Third World Press, 1973.

(With Gwendolyn Brooks, Keorapetse Kgositsile, and Haki R. Madhubuti) *A Capsule Course in Black Poetry Writing*, Broadside Press, 1975.

Broadside Memories: Poets I Have Known, Broadside Press, 1975.

A Litany of Friends: New and Selected Poems, Lotus Press, 1981, 2nd edition, 1983.

Homage to Hoyt Fuller, Broadside Press, 1984.

(Editor with Louis J. Cantoni) *Golden Song: The Fiftieth Anniversary Anthology of the Poetry Society of Michigan, 1935-1985*, Harlo, 1985.

Contributor of poems to anthologies, including *American Negro Poetry*, *New Negro Poets: USA*, *Ik Ben de Nieuwe Neger*, *La Poesie negro-americaine*, and *Kaleidoscope*. Contributor of poems, short stories, articles, and reviews to *Midwest Journal*, *Free Lance*, *Black World*, *Black Academy Review*, *Umbra*, *Negro Digest*, *Journal of Black Poetry*, *Beloit Review*, *Wayne Review*, and *New World Review*.

SIDELIGHTS: The influence of Dudley Randall, founder of Broadside Press and Detroit's first poet laureate, "has been one of the strongest—some say the strongest—in the black poetry movement of the last 15 years," writes Suzanne Dolezal. The 1982 article in *Detroit* magazine, a *Detroit Free Press* supplement, continues, "As publisher of Detroit's Broadside Press between 1965 and 1977, Randall provided a forum for just about every major black poet to come along during those years. And dozens of anthologies include his own rapid, emotional lyrics about Detroit's bag ladies, lonely old drunks, strapping foundry workers and young women with glistening, corn-rowed hair." R. Baxter Miller explains Randall's importance in the *Dictionary of Literary Biography: Afro-American Poets Since 1955:* "Beyond Randall's contributions as a poet, his roles as editor and publisher have proven invaluable to the Afro-American community."

Randall's interest in poetry has been life-long. Born in Washington, D.C., the son of a minister and a teacher, he wrote his first poem when he was four years old, moved to Detroit when he was nine, and saw his poems first published in the *Detroit Free Press* when he was thirteen. A bright student, Randall graduated early. After working in Ford's River Rouge foundry for five years and serving in the army, he extended his reputation for scholarship by earning a master's degree in library science from the University of Michigan and by studying the humanities. Randall, who became the reference librarian for Wayne County, also became fluent in Russian, visited Europe, Africa, and Russia, and later translated many Russian poems into English.

Randall's first books, however, did not display his range, Miller indicates. *Poem Counterpoem,* a unique volume in which "ten poems each by [Margaret] Danner and Randall . . . are alternated to form a kind of double commentary on the subjects they address in common," contains "only the verses appropriately matched with Danner's," the essayist relates; and while *Cities Burning,* Randall's second opus, presents the spirit of the poet's urban environment and the politics of his times, it gathers only those poems that treat "the theme of a disintegrating era." But the third and more inclusive collection *More to Remember: Poems of Four Decades* "displays [Randall's] artistic breadth" in poems that address universal themes and explore "contradictions in human psychology and the black arts movement," observes Miller. Miller also sees "Randall's aesthetic theory" in poems that depict "the artist as a modifier of both literary tradition and classical form." Randall defines this aesthetic himself in *Negro Digest:* "Precision and accuracy are necessary for both white and black writers. . . . 'A black aesthetic' should not be an excuse for sloppy writing." He believes that for writers who adhere to the "black aesthetic" there is a future, "as long as their rejection of 'white standards' rejects only what is false. . . . How else can a black writer write than out of his black experience? Yet what we tend to overlook is that our common humanity makes it possible to write a love poem, for instance, without a word of race, or to write a nationalistic poem that will be valid for all humanity."

Later collections of Randall's poems also show his careful craftsmanship. Reviewing *After the Killing* (1973), Frank Marshall Davis declares, "Dudley Randall again offers visual proof of why he should be ranked in the front echelon of Black poets." When the poet evades "cliches and hackneyed rhymes, he excels at his craft," says Miller, who also believes that verses in *A Litany of Friends: New and Selected Poems* (1981) "demonstrate Randall's technical skill." Brief notices about

Randall's books in library trade journals are generally complimentary, in keeping with Davis's comment in *Black World* magazine and Miller's assessment.

Reviewers recognize Randall's work as a bridge between earlier black writers and the generation that raised its voice of affirmation in the 1960s. "Exploring racial and historical themes, introspective and self-critical, his work combines ideas and forms from Western traditional poetry as well as from the Harlem Renaissance movement," Miller notes. In an essay on Randall in *Black American Poets between Worlds, 1940-1960,* Miller elaborates, "Although attracted to the poetry of antiquity, including classical conventions, he also gives his energetic support to modern originality. . . . Black American literary art has benefited from his great talent and love for fifty years." Writing in the *Negro Digest* in 1969, Ron Welburn concurs: "[Randall's] is a keen functional awareness of what black poetry has been and remains, and there is no hint of an alienation from the ethos being developed by the new stylists." Welburn foresaw that younger poets would be somewhat influenced by Randall's voice and perhaps more potently by his example: "he is contributing something to black literature that has a lasting value."

Broadside Press—Randall's other contribution to black poetry in America—began in 1963. Randall had composed the poem "Ballad of Birmingham" after a bomb exploded in an Alabama church, killing four children. "Folk singer Jerry Moore of New York had it set to music, and I wanted to protect the rights to the poem by getting it copyrighted," the publisher recalls in *Broadside Memories: Poets I Have Known.* Leaflets, he learned, could be copyrighted, so he published the poem as a broadside, a single sheet of paper that could be printed and sold for a minimal price. Randall's "Dressed All in Pink," composed after John F. Kennedy's assassination, also recorded by Moore, became number two of the Broadside series, which was to include close to one hundred titles by 1982.

Randall became a book publisher when poets at a Fisk University conference nominated him to collect and publish "the many poems being written about the slain black leader" Malcolm X, reports Dolezal. The printing was delayed so that *For Malcolm: Poems on the Life and Death of Malcolm X* was not the first Broadside book published, but when it came out in 1967, it was a success. By that time aware that major publishers were seldom accepting works by young black poets, Randall "became dedicated to giving the emerging black poetry the forum it needed," Dolezal notes. Indeed, Randall's encouragement was essential to the writing careers of several black poets. Etheridge Knight, for example, was in prison when he contributed three poems to the Broadside anthology *For Malcolm,* and Randall's visits "convinced a hesitant Knight of his talent," Dolezal reports. Randall published first books for Knight and for Haki R. Madhubuti (formerly Don L. Lee), two poets who now enjoy international acclaim.

Altogether, the press produced nearly sixty volumes of poetry and criticism under Randall's tenure, all showcasing black writers, who rewarded his dedication by remaining loyal to Broadside even when larger publishing houses with generous promotion budgets beckoned. Gwendolyn Brooks insisted that Randall, not Harper & Row, would publish her autobiography; Sonia Sanchez preferred Broadside to the Third World Press, the small press founded by Madhubuti. Poet Nikki Giovanni explained to Dolezal, "Broadside was neither mother nor father of the poetry movement, but it was certainly midwife. Dudley understood the thrust of the movement, which was essentially vernacular. He . . . allowed his poets to find their own voices. That was the charm of Broadside.''

By 1977, Randall's determination to supply low-priced books to stores already in debt to him brought the small press, also deeply in debt, to the crisis point. The Alexander Crummell Memorial Center, a church in Highland Park, Michigan, bought the press, retaining Randall as its consultant. Though the poets he once published have found other publishers since the sale, Randall continues to be concerned for new poets and anticipates the publication of more new works when the press revives. But Dolezal concludes that whether or not that hope materializes, ''Randall's achievement remains intact.'' Furthermore, as the poet laureate of a sprawling midwestern metropolis told *New York Times* contributor Harold Blum, there is always plenty to do: ''[A poet] can change the way people look and feel about things. And that's what I want to do in Detroit.''

BIOGRAPHICAL/CRITICAL SOURCES:

BOOKS

Barksdale, Richard K. and Keneth Kinnamon, editors, *Black Writers in America: A Comprehensive Anthology*, Macmillan, 1972.
Black Poets: The New Heroic Genre, Broadside Press, 1983.
Contemporary Literary Criticism, Volume 1, Gale, 1973.
Dictionary of Literary Biography, Volume 41: *Afro-American Poets Since 1955*, Gale, 1985.
Gayle, Addison, editor, *The Black Aesthetic*, Doubleday, 1971.
King, Woodie, Jr., editor, *The Forerunners: Black Poets in America*, Howard University Press, 1981.
Miller, R. Baxter, editor, *Black American Poets between Worlds, 1940-1960*, University of Tennessee Press, 1986.
Randall, Dudley, *Broadside Memories: Poets I Have Known*, Broadside Press, 1975.
Randall, Dudley, *A Litany of Friends: New and Selected Poems*, Lotus Press, 1981, new edition, 1983.

PERIODICALS

Black American Literature Forum, Volume 17, number 3, 1983, February, 1984.
Black World, September, 1974.
Callaloo, Volume 6, number 1, 1983.
Detroit Free Press, April 11, 1982.
Library Journal, February 15, 1971, March 15, 1972.
Negro Digest, February, 1965, September, 1965, January, 1968, December, 1969.
New York Times, January 30, 1984.
New York Times Book Review, part 2, February 13, 1972.
Obsidian, Volume 2, number 1, 1976.

—*Sketch by Marilyn K. Basel*

*   *   *

RANDOLPH, A(sa) Philip   1889-1979

PERSONAL: Born April 15, 1889, in Crescent City (one source says Jacksonville), Fla.; died May 16, 1979, in New York, N.Y.; son of James William (a minister) and Elizabeth (Robinson) Randolph; married wife, Lucille E. (a beauty parlor operator), 1914 (one source says 1915). *Education:* Attended College of the City of New York (now City College of the City University of New York). *Politics:* Socialist. *Religion:* Methodist.

ADDRESSES: Home—230 West 150th Street, New York, N.Y. *Office*—Brotherhood of Sleeping Car Porters, 217 West 125th Street, New York, N.Y.

CAREER: The Messenger, New York, N.Y., editor, 1917-25; instructor at Rand School of Social Science, c. 1920; founder and president of International Brotherhood of Sleeping Car Porters, 1925-68, and Negro American Labor Council; president of National Negro Congress; founder of League for Nonviolent Civil Disobedience Against Military Segregation, 1947; vice-president of the American Federation of Labor-Congress of Industrial Organizations (AFL-CIO). Member of New York Mayor Fiorello La Guardia's Commission on Race, 1935, and of New York Housing Authority, 1942.

MEMBER: Elks, Masons.

AWARDS, HONORS: LL.D. from Howard University, 1941; Spingarn Medal from the National Association for the Advancement of Colored People, 1942, for leadership in labor; David L. Clendenin award from Workers' Defense League, 1944, for distinguished service to labor's rights; named honorary vice-chairman of Liberal party, 1946; Presidential Medal of Freedom, 1964.

WRITINGS:

The Negro Freedom Movement, Lincoln University, American Studies Institute, 1968.

Contributor to periodicals, including *Opportunity* and *Survey Graphic*.

SIDELIGHTS: ''With a rich baritone voice that seemed destined to command, an imperturbability under fire, a refusal to bend with the times or the fashions, A. Philip Randolph overcame opposition simply by being himself,'' began a *Time* magazine tribute to one of the most successful black American labor organizers and civil rights activists. Courteous yet determined, Randolph attacked social and economic injustices in government and industry for more than six decades. He organized the first all-black union that was chartered by the American Federation of Labor (AFL); he campaigned for the desegregation of the defense industry, the military, and the civil service; and he was an early and highly visible leader of the civil rights movement of the 1960s. ''[Randolph] confronted the establishment [and was] prepared to shake it to its foundations,'' asserted Nathan Irvin Huggins in the *New York Times Book Review*, ''but always with the aplomb and dignity of a gentleman.''

''What was your class at Harvard, Phil?'' President Franklin D. Roosevelt jokingly asked Randolph, remarking on the union leader's eloquence and graceful manner. In fact, Randolph had dreamed of becoming a Shakespearean actor but his plan was vetoed by his more realistic parents. Instead he took night classes in economics and political science at the College of the City of New York after traveling north from his home in Florida. Through his studies he learned German philosopher Karl Marx's theory that forms of economic inequality are based on race, and from his father, a Jacksonville minister, he learned of the power of united blacks. Once when a Negro accused of a crime was taken to a county jail, Randolph's father called the men of his parish together to stand guard outside the prison to protect the man from a group of angry whites. Through seeing the organized parishioners save a man from lynching and his readings on racial injustice, Randolph realized that economic and political wrongs could be remedied by cooperation among laborers and unity within racial groups. ''From the beginning,'' stated Huggins, ''[Randolph] insisted that blacks would get only what they could take and keep only what they could hold. And the power to take and to keep awaited blacks' willingness to organize themselves with purpose and discipline, for group-interest over self-interest, toward the radical transformation of the American economic system.''

In 1917 Randolph and Chandler Owen established *The Messenger: The Only Radical Negro Magazine in America,* a black-oriented monthly. In his editorials he urged black men not to fight in the armed forces during World War I because they would be defending a country that denied them civil rights. In response to Randolph's call, the U.S. Justice Department named *The Messenger* one of the most subversive publications in the nation and Randolph ''the most dangerous Negro in America.'' Previously Randolph had been arrested in Cleveland, Ohio, because of his open opposition to blacks participating in World War I, but he was released after spending two days in the city jail. ''He contended,'' explained writer and poet Langston Hughes in *Famous American Negroes,* ''that he was simply agitating for fulfillment of Constitutional guarantees for *all* citizens and protection of law for everybody,'' not just for black equity.

Randolph stressed that workers, regardless of race, could advance economically and socially through unionizing. He helped organize motion picture operators and garment trade workers, and founded a union of elevator operators. Then in 1925 five members of the fledgling Brotherhood of Sleeping Car Porters (BSCP) asked Randolph to help them organize. Notoriously overworked and underpaid, ''the porter has always been poor and menial,'' observed Murray Kempton in a *New Republic* article. ''Segregation created his job; the Pullman Company hired Negroes as porters because Negroes were inexpensive.'' Although he was not a porter, Randolph was elected president of the union, whose members were earning only $67.50 for three hundred to four hundred hours of work a month. At first membership in the union grew slowly because Pullman Palace Car Company strongly opposed the Brotherhood and fired workers who were active in the union. Nonetheless, by 1928 more than one-half of the railroad maids and porters were members of the BSCP and ready to strike if the railroad company refused to consider their demands for higher pay and shorter working hours. The workers' boycott was canceled due to lack of support from other railroad unions, but the struggle between Pullman and the Brotherhood, which also received little support from the Negro religious community and newspapers, raged for ten years.

Finally in 1934 the amended Railway Labor Act created a national mediation board, composed of railroad management and union representatives, to hear grievances. The membership of the porter's union increased. Three years later Pullman signed a contract with the BSCP giving the employees two million dollars in pay increases and guaranteeing them shorter hours and pay for overtime. By September, 1950, due to union pressure, the eighteen thousand members of the BSCP worked a monthly average of 205 hours for which they were paid a minimum of nearly $240. Randolph used the Brotherhood as an example of what could be attained through cooperation among laborers, and as a stronghold against discrimination within the workers' movement. Yet Huggins maintained that ''the Union's ultimate victory was to make Randolph one of the most respected and influential black men since Booker T. Washington.''

Randolph emphasized that blacks must organize their own groups, choose their own leaders, and raise their own funds, because only with financial independence could an organization control its direction. With the BSCP he made money by sponsoring picnics, parties, and sporting events rather than accepting the financial patronage of well-intentioned white unions. In 1929, when the BSCP joined the American Federation of Labor (AFL), it was the first all-black union to receive an international charter by that organization. Randolph's critics claimed he compromised the position of the Brotherhood by joining the white-run AFL, but he countered by saying that united laborers would have more bargaining power with industries than an isolated union would. When the AFL merged with the Congress of Industrial Organizations (CIO) in 1955, Randolph was named its first vice-president and he undertook a campaign against prejudice in the unions. Demanding that all chapters—black and white—be desegregated, he insisted that blacks had no more right than whites to exclude a prospective member because of race. George Meany and Lane Kirkland, the former president and former secretary-treasurer of the AFL-CIO, commended Randolph for his even-handedness in the desegregation of the organization. They were quoted in the *New York Times:* ''Even in the darkest days, Phil never lost sight of the goals, the needs, the aspirations of workers—both white and black, male and female.''

Believing that organized labor was in a position to make economic demands on businesses that held government contracts, Randolph entered the political arena. With the approach of World War II Randolph took the opportunity to fight discrimination in the industries producing armaments. Defense companies were not hiring blacks to work in the factories, and after Randolph met with a number of government leaders to no avail, he threatened to lead 50,000 Negroes to Washington, D.C., in protest against the injustice. President Franklin D. Roosevelt called Randolph to the White House immediately. After a standoff with the union leader, the president signed Executive Order 8802 on June 25, 1941, which established the Fair Employment Practices Committee, banning discrimination in the government and defense industries.

As tensions increased between the United States and the Soviet Union in the late 1940s, President Harry S. Truman called for the first peace-time draft in American history. Randolph, again by threatening a massive protest and Negroes' resistence to military service, pressured Truman into desegregating the armed forces. Huggins related that Randolph told Truman on March 22, 1948: ''The mood among Negroes of this country is that they will never bear arms again until all forms of bias and discrimination are abolished.'' Truman uttered in response, ''I wish you hadn't said that, Mr. Randolph. I didn't like it at all.'' The following month Randolph testified before the Senate Armed Services Committee, maintaining, ''Negroes have reached the limit of their endurance when it comes to going into another Jim Crow Army to fight another war for democracy—a democracy they have never gotten.'' As with Roosevelt, Randolph pressured Truman into issuing an executive order, this one officially banning racial segregation in the armed services.

Randolph finally did march on Washington in August, 1963. Originally he announced that he would call 100,000 Negroes to the capital in October, 1963, to demonstrate against unemployment, but in the late spring of that year President John F. Kennedy introduced his civil rights bill in Congress. Randolph rescheduled the protest for August so that it would include demonstrating for personal liberties. ''There was suddenly the surprising prospect that Congress would debate these bills with thousands of Negroes standing outside,'' recounted Kempton.

Today Randolph's ''March on Washington for Jobs and Freedom in 1963'' is better remembered as the massive civil rights demonstration where Martin Luther King, Jr., gave his famous ''I Have a Dream'' speech before more than 200,000 people. Randolph's star has been eclipsed by more famous leaders of the civil rights movement, especially King. ''It's so sad because there are so many young people today for whom that name means very little,'' observed Benjamin L. Hooks, former director of the National Association for the Advancement of Colored People in the *New York Times*, upon hearing of Randolph's death in 1979. ''And yet, for more than forty years, he was a tower and beacon of strength and hope for the entire black community.'' Kempton concurred, commenting on Randolph's program of passive resistance: ''He is a pacifist in a native American tradition; before most members of King's non-violent army were born, he was reminding the Negro of Thoreau's prescription to cast the total vote with feet and voice along with the ballot.''

Even Malcolm X, a leader of the Lost-Found Nation of Islam, the Black Muslims, respected Randolph's accomplishments. Randolph invited the advocate of black separatism from white Western society to join a committee that the union leader was organizing on Harlem's financial problems. Kempton related that when Randolph met with Malcolm X he explained his disagreement with the militant's separatist viewpoint, claiming that blacks and whites had to work together for socioeconomic harmony. He commended the Black Muslims, however, for their fight against drugs and liquor, calling it ''the greatest contribution any of us have ever made.'' Later Malcolm X stated that although all leaders of black communities are muddled, Randolph is the least confused. In the spring of 1963 the Black Muslims put a picture of the pacifist Randolph on the cover of their weekly journal, *Muhammad Speaks*.

A. H. Raskin in *New Leader* also paid tribute to the union organizer and activist, maintaining that ''Randolph's triumph paralleled that of Mahatma M. K. Gandhi in India, and it stemmed from the same ability to prevail by dint of an unshakeable combination of gentleness and conviction over the entrenched forces of obstructionism.'' Randolph's strength came from his belief in the inevitability of a reformed society, where all laborers enjoyed equal rights. He often stressed that ''we never separated the liberation of the white workingman from the liberation of the black workingman,'' related a reporter for *Time*. Nonetheless, when Randolph died on the eve of the twenty-fifth anniversary of the Supreme Court's historic decision outlawing segregation in public schools, Americans remembered his role as an agitator for civil rights as well as for his labor organizing. ''As an elder statesman, he was a guiding light for a new generation of civil-rights advocates,'' Dennis A. Williams of *Newsweek* commented. Former U.S. President Jimmy Carter, quoted in the *New York Times*, spoke of Randolph: ''His dignity and integrity, his eloquence, his devotion to nonviolence and his unshakeable commitment to justice all helped shape the ideals and spirit of the civil rights movement.''

AVOCATIONAL INTERESTS: Reading (especially William Shakespeare and George Bernard Shaw), baseball, basketball, football, tennis.

BIOGRAPHICAL/CRITICAL SOURCES:

BOOKS

Adams, Russell L., *Great Negroes, Past and Present*, Afro-American Publishing, 1963.

Anderson, Jervis, *A. Philip Randolph: A Biographical Portrait*, Harcourt, 1973.
Bontemps, Arna Wendell, *One Hundred Years of Negro Freedom*, Dodd, 1961.
Cook, Roy, *Leaders of Labor*, Lippincott, 1966.
Davis, Daniel S., *Mr. Black Labor: The Story of A. Philip Randolph, Father of the Civil Rights Movement*, Dutton, 1972.
Flynn, James J., *Negroes of Achievement in Modern America*, Dodd, 1970.
Hughes, Langston, *Famous American Negroes*, Dodd, 1954.
Quarles, Benjamin, *Black Leaders of the Twentieth Century*, University of Illinois Press, 1982.
Redding, Jay Saunders, *The Lonesome Road: The Story of the Negro's Part in America*, Doubleday, 1958.
Richardson, Ben, *Great American Negroes*, Crowell, 1945, 2nd revised edition, with W. A. Fahey, published as *Great Black Americans*, Crowell, 1976.

PERIODICALS

Crisis, August/September, 1979.
Dissent, fall, 1979.
Ebony, May, 1969.
Journal of Negro History, fall, 1979.
Negro History Bulletin, December, 1964, December, 1971.
New Leader, June 4, 1979.
New Republic, July 6, 1963.
Newsweek, September 30, 1940, June 7, 1948, May 28, 1979.
New Yorker, December 2, 1972, December 9, 1972, December 16, 1972.
New York Times, April 29, 1940, September 15, 1940.
New York Times Book Review, May 27, 1973.
Time, September 20, 1937, May 28, 1979.

OBITUARIES:

PERIODICALS

New York Times, May 18, 1979.
Washington Post, May 18, 1979.

—*Sketch by Carol Lynn DeKane*

*   *   *

RASPBERRY, William J(ames) 1935-

PERSONAL: Born October 12, 1935, in Okolona, Miss.; son of James Lee (a teacher) and Willie Mae (a teacher; maiden name, Tucker) Raspberry; married Sondra Patricia Dodson, November 12, 1966; children: Patricia D., Angela D., Mark J. *Education:* Indiana Central College, B.S., 1958.

ADDRESSES: Home—1301 Iris St. N.W., Washington, D.C. 20012. *Office*—1150 15th St. N.W., Washington, D.C. 20017.

CAREER/WRITINGS: Indianapolis Recorder, Indianapolis, Ind., 1956-60, began as reporter, photographer, proofreader, and editorial writer, became associate managing editor; *Washington Post*, Washington, D.C., teletypist, 1962, reporter, 1962-64, assistant city editor, 1965, columnist, 1966—. Instructor in journalism at Howard University, 1971-73; commentator for WTTG-TV in Washington, D.C., 1973-75; discussion panelist for WRC-TV in Washington, D.C., 1974-75; former juror for Robert F. Kennedy Awards; member of Pulitzer Prize Board, 1979-86; lecturer on race relations and public education; contributor of articles to magazines. *Military service:* U.S. Army, 1960-62; served as public information officer.

MEMBER: National Association of Black Journalists, Capital Press Club, Gridiron Club, Kappa Alpha Psi.

AWARDS, HONORS: Named Journalist of the Year by Capital Press Club, 1965, for coverage of the Los Angeles Watts riot; several awards for interpretive writing from Washington-Baltimore Newspaper Guild; Liberty Bell Award from Federal Bar Association for "outstanding community service in promoting responsible citizenship"; honorary degrees from Georgetown University, University of Maryland, University of Indianapolis, and Virginia State University; Pulitzer Prize nomination, 1982.

SIDELIGHTS: Described in a *Time* magazine article as "the Lone Ranger of columnists," William Raspberry is known for taking an independent stance on national and international issues. His thrice-weekly column for the *Washington Post* is nationally syndicated twice a week and has earned him several awards. Once referred to by *Time* as "the most respected black voice on any white U.S. newspaper," Raspberry was still a college student when he began working as a reporter for the black weekly *Indianapolis Recorder* in 1956. During his four years with the newspaper, he worked in almost every journalistic capacity and was named associate managing editor shortly before being drafted into the U.S. Army in 1960. After completing his service as an army public information officer in Washington, D.C., Raspberry joined the staff of the *Washington Post* in 1962 as a teletypist. Within a few months he was promoted to writing obituaries and soon afterward became a reporter on the periodical's city desk.

Raspberry served one year as assistant city editor of the *Washington Post* before taking over in 1966 as columnist of "Potomac Watch," a column that dealt with local issues. He gradually shaped the column to fit his own interests, focusing on local topics once a week while treating broader themes in his two syndicated columns. Raspberry is noted for delving into topics that other columnists have avoided, such as drug abuse, criminal justice, and minority issues. Furthermore, he has developed a reputation, according to *Time*, as the "unofficial ombudsman for local underdogs," occasionally serving as troubleshooter for individuals grappling with government bureaucracy.

In addition to writing his weekly columns, Raspberry has taught journalism at Howard University and has served as commentator and discussion panelist for television stations in Washington, D.C. A member of the Pulitzer Prize Board for several years, Raspberry himself was nominated for a Pulitzer Prize in 1982. He has received numerous awards for his writing, including the Capital Press Club's Journalist of the Year award in 1965 for his coverage of the Los Angeles Watts riot.

BIOGRAPHICAL/CRITICAL SOURCES:

PERIODICALS

Time, September 16, 1974.
Washington Post, November 23, 1969, June 25, 1971, September 17, 1971.

*   *   *

RAY, H(enrietta) Cordelia   1849(?)-1916

PERSONAL: Born in 1849 (some sources say 1850); died January 5, 1916, in New York, N.Y.; daughter of Charles Bennett (an editor and clergyman) and Charlotte Augusta (Burrough) Ray; unmarried. *Education:* Studied Greek, Latin, French, and German at Sauveneur School of Languages; University of the City of New York (now New York University), M.A., 1891.

ADDRESSES: Home—Woodside, Long Island, N.Y.

CAREER: Educator, poet, and author. Taught in New York public school system for about thirty years, beginning around 1868 at the Colored American Grammar School in Manhattan. Private tutor in music, mathematics, and languages.

WRITINGS:

(With sister, Florence T. Ray) *Sketch of the Life of the Rev. Charles B. Ray* (biography; includes sonnet "To Our Father"), J. J. Little & Co., 1887.
Lincoln: Written for the Occasion of the Unveiling of the Freedmen's Monument in Memory of Abraham Lincoln, April 14, 1876, J. J. Little & Co., 1893.
Sonnets (poetry; includes "To My Mother," "Niobe," "Life," "Aspiration," "Incompleteness," "Self-Mastery," "Two Musicians," and "The Poet's Ministrants"), J. J. Little & Co., 1893.
Poems (collection), Grafton Press, 1910.

Contributor of verse to periodicals.

SIDELIGHTS: A New York schoolteacher by profession, H. Cordelia Ray distinguished herself as one of the few nineteenth-century black women to earn recognition for her literary achievements. In particular, she is best remembered for her poetry, in which she demonstrated her skill in poetic form and technique. Additionally, Ray found favor with critics who were impressed with the genteel quality, versatility, and idealism characteristic of her verse. Writing on familiar themes such as human emotions, nature, and the arts, as well as personal experiences of life and self, she published two volumes containing more than 150 of her poems.

Ray first attracted public attention for her poetry in 1876, when her lengthy poem "Lincoln: Written for the Occasion of the Unveiling of the Freedmen's Monument in Memory of Abraham Lincoln" was recited at a public celebration commemorating the anniversary of the former president's death. Though widely circulated the rhymed testimonial, which had been commissioned especially for the event, remained unpublished until 1893. Six years earlier *Sketch of the Life of the Rev. Charles B. Ray* appeared. A short biography written with her elder sister, Florence, the work served as a tribute to Ray's father and contained the sonnet "To Our Father," a solo effort by the younger daughter.

In addition to the poems she contributed to various periodicals, Ray produced two collections of her work. The first, *Sonnets,* debuted in 1893—the same year *Lincoln* was published. A much larger volume, *Poems,* appeared in 1910. It contains 145 pieces and is dedicated to Ray's sister and lifelong companion, Florence. The poems, like those in *Sonnets,* are for the most part variations on a modest range of themes. What distinguishes Ray's work, say critics, is the masterful execution of poetic form and technique for which she was best known. Especially noteworthy in the latter collection are some innovative ballads that elude the conventions of more traditional verse.

Nothing more of Ray's poetry was published after *Poems.* Described as a shy and reclusive woman, she gradually faded into obscurity following her death in 1916. According to a profile in *Dictionary of Literary Biography,* writer Hallie Quinn Brown observed: "Among a generation of brainy New York women, she was probably the most accomplished, yet outside her immediate circle the least known.''

BIOGRAPHICAL/CRITICAL SOURCES:

BOOKS

Brown, Hallie Quinn, editor, *Homespun Heroines and Other Women of Distinction*, Aldine, 1926.
Dictionary of Literary Biography, Volume 50: *Afro-American Writers Before the Harlem Renaissance*, Gale, 1986.
Sherman, Joan R., *Invisible Poets: Afro-Americans of the Nineteenth Century*, University of Illinois Press, 1974.

*   *   *

REDDING, (Jay) Saunders   1906-1988

PERSONAL: Born October 13, 1906, in Wilmington, Del.; died of heart failure, March 2, 1988, in Ithaca, N.Y.; son of Lewis Alfred (a post office employee) and Mary Ann (Holmes) Redding; married Esther Elizabeth James, August 19, 1929; children: Conway Holmes, Lewis Alfred II. *Education:* Attended Lincoln University, 1923-24; Brown University, Ph.B., 1928, M.A., 1932; Columbia University, graduate study, 1933-34. *Politics:* Independent Democrat. *Religion:* Episcopalian.

ADDRESSES: Home—310 Winthrop Dr., Ithaca, N.Y. 14850. *Office*—Department of English, Cornell University, Ithaca, N.Y. 14850. *Agent*—Harold Matson Co., Inc., 276 Fifth Ave., New York, N.Y. 10001.

CAREER: Morehouse College, Atlanta, Ga., instructor in English, 1928-31; Louisville Municipal College, Louisville, Ky., instructor in English, 1934-36; Southern University, Baton Rouge, La., head of English department, 1936-38; Hampton Institute, Hampton, Va., professor of English and American literature, 1943-55, Johnson Professor of Literature and Creative Writing, 1955-66; National Endowment for the Humanities, Washington, D.C., director of Division of Research and Publication, 1966-70, conservator, 1970-88; Cornell University, Ithaca, N.Y., Ernest I. White Professor of American Studies, 1970-75; professor emeritus, 1975-88. Visiting professor at Brown University, 1949-50; lecturer at several universities and colleges in India, Africa, and South America under auspices of U.S. Department of State, 1952, 1962, and 1977. Member of board of fellows, Brown University, 1969-81; member of board of directors, American Council of Learned Societies, 1976-88; trustee, Fund for Research and Education, American Civil Liberties Union. Consultant on graduate scholarships, U.S. Department of Health, Education, and Welfare, 1958-59; special consultant, National Endowment for the Humanities, 1970-88; member of advisory board, Center for Advanced Study, University of Virginia, 1977-88.

MEMBER: College English Association, Phi Beta Kappa, Sigma Pi Phi.

AWARDS, HONORS: Rockefeller Foundation fellow, 1939-40; Guggenheim fellow, 1944-45, 1959-60; Mayflower Award for distinguished writing, North Carolina Historical Society, 1944, for *No Day of Triumph;* New York Public Library citation for outstanding contribution to interracial understanding, 1945, 1946; National Urban League citation for outstanding achievement, 1950; Ford Foundation fellow at Duke University, 1964-65, and at University of North Carolina; honorary degrees from Virginia State College, 1963, Hobart College, 1964, University of Portland, 1970, and Wittinberg University, 1977, and from Dickinson College, Brown University,

and University of Delaware; honorary conservator of American culture, Library of Congress, 1973-77.

WRITINGS:

To Make a Poet Black (criticism), University of North Carolina Press, 1939, reprinted, Core Collection Books, 1978, new edition, Cornell University Press, 1986.
No Day of Triumph, Harper, 1942.
Stranger and Alone (novel), Harcourt, 1950.
They Came in Chains: Americans from Africa, Lippincott, 1950, revised edition, 1973.
On Being Negro in America, Bobbs-Merrill, 1951.
An American in India: A Personal Report on the Indian Dilemma and the Nature of Her Conflicts, Bobbs-Merrill, 1954.
The Lonesome Road: The Story of the Negro's Part in America, Doubleday, 1958, reprinted, 1973.
The Negro, Potomac, 1967.
Of Men and the Writing of Books, Vail Memorial Library, Lincoln University, 1969.
Negro Writing and the Political Climate, Vail Memorial Library, Lincoln University, 1970.

CONTRIBUTOR

The American Negro Writer and His Roots, American Society of African Culture, 1960.
Herbert Hill, editor, *Soon, One Morning: New Writing by American Negroes 1940-1962*, Knopf, 1964.
(With Hill, Horace Cayton, and Arna Bontemps) Hill, editor, *Anger and Beyond: The Negro Writer in the United States*, Harper, 1966.
John Henrik Clarke, Esther Jackson, Ernest Kaiser, and J. H. O'Dell, editors, *Black Titan: W. E. B. DuBois, An Anthology by the Editors of Freedomways*, Beacon Press, 1970.
Jay Martin, editor, *A Singer in the Dawn: Reinterpretations of Paul Laurence Dunbar*, Dodd, 1975.

OTHER

(Editor with Ivan E. Taylor) *Reading for Writing*, Ronald Press, 1952.
(Author of introduction) W. E. B. DuBois, *The Souls of Black Folk: Essays and Sketches*, Peter Smith, 1963.
(Editor with Arthur P. Davis) *Cavalcade: Negro American Writing from 1760 to the Present*, Houghton, 1971.
(Author of introduction) Faith Berry, editor, *Good Morning Revolution: The Uncollected Social Protest Writings by Langston Hughes*, Lawrence Hill, 1973.

Member of editorial board, *American Scholar*, 1950-62, 1968-74. Contributor of numerous articles to publications, including *North American Review*, *American Mercury*, *Atlantic Monthly*, *American Scholar*, *Saturday Review*, *Nation*, and *American Heritage*.

WORK IN PROGRESS: A monograph to be included in the book, *History in Our Time*.

SIDELIGHTS: Saunders Redding has been called an outstanding figure in an older generation of black American writers. His works are recognized as having been instrumental in the education of white America in the areas of race relations and the problems of black existence in a white society. Redding's first book, *To Make a Poet Black*, published in 1939, is a unique appraisal of black literature from the point of view of a black scholar and creative writer. E. V. Stonequist in the *American Sociological Review* calls the book ''an interpretation of the literary development of his race, marked by a very high degree of sympathetic understanding combined with intellectual honesty and fairness in criticism, and by pithy, original comments upon particular writers and their writings, situating them in their particular cultural backgrounds.'' In *Commonweal*, Theophilus Lewis writes: ''There is more than a slight probability that future literary archeologists will refer to this book as a landmark of Negro literature. Not that it is even remotely a work of monumental significance. But it does mark a new departure. The Negro author has already won acceptance in the field of creative writing. In this volume he breaks new ground, emerges as critic and appraiser of the works of his fellow craftsmen.''

Redding's second book, *No Day of Triumph*, was the result of a commission by the University of North Carolina in which he was told to report on black life in the South. The author added a good deal of autobiography and personal comment to his findings and the result was, according to Wallace Stegner in the *Atlantic*, ''an angry and honest and compassionate book; a better book than the University of North Carolina and the Rockefeller Foundation, who financed it, had any right to expect; perhaps the sanest and most eloquent study of the Negro American that has appeared.'' And *Springfield Republican* contributor S. R. Harlow suggests that ''Mr. Redding's book ought to be read by every Negro of the middle class in America and by all of 'the talented tenth.' They need not agree with all that the author says as he flays the pessimism and self-indulgence of some of their class, but it will prove a healthy stimulant against falling into similar habits of thought and action. Members of the white group who read the book need to be warned that this is not a complete picture of the Negro in America today, but it is a revelation of much that goes on in the shadow of democracy.''

Redding's novel *Stranger and Alone* is the story of Shelton Howden, who is the son of a white father and a black mother. He despises his black heritage and eventually betrays his black friends to the white politicians of his Southern town. In a *New York Times* review of the book, Ralph Ellison writes: ''If in his novel Mr. Redding has selected a protagonist too limited in personal appeal, and if his writing lacks the high quality that marked his autobiographical *No Day of Triumph*, he has done, nevertheless, a vastly important job of reporting the little known role of those Negro 'leaders' who by collaborating with the despoilers of the South do insidious damage to us all.'' The book was described as controversial at the time of its publication in 1950, and S. C. Watkins, writing in the *Chicago Sunday Tribune*, calls it ''a story that few can read without having rather strong feelings aroused. It can be strongly liked or just as strongly disliked.'' *New York Herald Tribune Book Review* contributor Coleman Rosenberger says: ''It is an angry book, but one in which the anger is controlled and made purposeful. It is written with both insight and skill. There is the ring of truth about it. It is as if the author were writing a biography of the man which he might easily have been, if he had yielded to the ever present pressures about him, some crude and massively direct, some very subtle.'' Finally, Paul Pickrel in the *Yale Review* concludes that ''this book adds more to our understanding of Negro life than many more sensational books; it is, in a sense, more shocking than the shockers, because it shows the critically weak points in those very institutions which most of us look to as the solution—in part, at least—of the problem of the Negro.''

With *They Came in Chains: Americans from Africa*, Redding took on the task of compiling a history of the black race in America, which a reviewer for the *Springfield Republican* called ''a project often attempted but rarely carried out in a fully satisfactory manner. The historian either is white and a trifle condescending or black and too emotional. *They Came in Chains* by a Negro educator, is as good an in-between job as could be asked.'' L. P. Stavisky of *Survey* notes that ''the paucity of footnote documentation, including the omission of periodical literature, is certain to elicit a hue and cry that some of the broad generalizations are based upon insufficient evidence. Yet the book has considerable merit. Seldom have the chroniclers of American Negro history possessed the literary talents which Mr. Redding demonstrates throughout the volume. This is no dry recital of events. In a fluid and imaginative style, the author has given us a vivid commentary on the story of the Negro people in America.''

In another book of history, *The Lonesome Road: The Story of the Negro's Part in America*, Redding uses biographical sketches of twelve famous black Americans to trace the struggle from slavery to equal rights. In a review of the book appearing in *Library Journal*, M. S. Byam writes: ''The history of the Negro has been well-covered both verbally and pictorially in both scholarly and colloquial language by Negroes and others. Here is another; yet it is so dynamic a presentation, so true to itself in both subject and technique that its addition must be recommended. This is no mere angry or shrieking picture of the poor Negro's plight but rather a documentation of his complete belongingness to America historically and culturally.'' *New Republic* reviewer Paula Snelling, however, finds that although Redding's subject is most important, ''his book is not. This is due to no lack of literary skill or erudition on the author's part, but to his unwillingness to engage himself here on a deeply creative or philosophic level.'' Snelling feels that not enough space is devoted to recent developments or to the impact that black artists have had on our culture. ''But the contribution Mr. Redding neglects most (and this, I think, reveals an unverbalized bias) is that of Negro leaders who have kept their home base in the South and sought ways of communicating with white Southerners without relinquishing personal dignity or the aspirations of their race.''

Saunders Redding once remarked: ''Things bothered me, and I set out to write them away—beginning with adolescent love, I suppose. And things still bother me—life, the quality and purpose of it; the myths that fail to explain it; the general and specifics of the American experience and particularly the black American experience; and I'm still trying to write them away.... My first obligation is to truth—factual and emotional truth. Since life is short, there is only so much truth that one can know and experience in the deeply personal and intimate way that is necessary to the writer, and even the little truth that one can know and experience in this way is often painful—and 'painful' is a term frequently used to define anger. I think I am what is called a realist, but some of my critics say that I am an idealist. All I really know is that I'm obliged to tell, to write about, the little truth I know.''

BIOGRAPHICAL/CRITICAL SOURCES:

BOOKS

Davis, Arthur P., *From the Dark Tower: Afro-American Writers, 1900-1960*, Howard University Press, 1974.

Dictionary of Literary Biography, Volume 63: *Modern American Critics, 1920-1955*, Gale, 1988.

Wagner, Jean, *Black Poets of the United States: From Paul Laurence Dunbar to Langston Hughes*, University of Illinois Press, 1973.

PERIODICALS

American Sociological Review, June, 1939.
Atlantic, December, 1942.
Booklist, April 15, 1939, December 15, 1942.
Books, October 11, 1942.
Chicago Sunday Tribune, February 19, 1950.
Choice, April, 1968.
Christian Science Monitor, February 17, 1950, September 18, 1950, May 7, 1958.
Commonweal, May 12, 1939.
Library Journal, March 1, 1958.
Nation, November 17, 1951.
Negro Digest, January, 1968.
New Republic, October 12, 1942, June 23, 1958.
New Yorker, February 18, 1950, November 3, 1951.
New York Herald Tribune Book Review, February 19, 1950, July 16, 1950, November 11, 1951, March 3, 1958.
New York Times, October 25, 1942, February 19, 1950, July 30, 1950, October 21, 1951, April 20, 1958.
Saturday Review, February 16, 1952, March 22, 1969.
Saturday Review of Literature, November 21, 1942, February 25, 1950.
Springfield Republican, November 8, 1942, July 23, 1950, June 15, 1958.
Social Forces, March, 1952.
Survey, March, 1950, November, 1950.
Yale Review, spring, 1950.

OBITUARIES:

PERIODICALS

New York Times, March 5, 1988.

*   *   *

REDMOND, Eugene B.   1937-

PERSONAL: Born December 1, 1937, in East St. Louis, Ill.; son of John Henry and Emma (Hutchinson) Redmond. *Education:* Southern Illinois University, B.A., 1964; Washington University, M.A., 1966.

ADDRESSES: Home—1925 Seventh Ave., No. 7L, New York, N.Y. 10026. *Office*—Department of English, California State University, Sacramento, Calif. 95819.

CAREER: East St. Louis Beacon, East St. Louis, Ill., associate editor, 1961-62; *Monitor,* East St. Louis, contributing editor, 1963-65, executive editor, 1965-67, editorial page and contributing editor, 1967—; Southern Illinois University at Edwardsville, East St. Louis branch, teacher-counselor in Experiment in Higher Education, 1967-68, poet-in-residence and director of language workshops, 1968-69; Oberlin College, Oberlin, Ohio, writer-in-residence and lecturer in Afro-American studies, 1969-70; California State University, Sacramento, professor of English and poet-in-residence in ethnic studies, 1970—.

Visiting writer-in-residence, Southern University and Agricultural and Mechanical College, 1971-72; instructor of Afro-American literature, Oak Park School of Afro-American Thought, Sacramento City College, 1971; visiting lecturer, University of Leiden, summer, 1978; visiting professor and writer, University of Wisconsin, 1978-79; visiting professor, University of Nigeria, 1980; lecturer and reader at other colleges and universities in the United States and Canada. Coordinator of Annual Third World Writers and Thinkers Symposium, 1972—; director of Henry Dumas Creative Writing

Workshop, 1974—, and of Interracial-Intercultural Communications through the Arts, East St. Louis School District, 1977. Founder-publisher, Black River Writers Press. Member of board of directors, Olatunji Counseling Educational Center, East St. Louis, and IMPACT. Member of board and chairman of publicity, Young Disciples Foundation. Senior consultant, Performing Arts Training Center, East St. Louis, 1967—; consultant, Ghetto Communications Workshop Planners. *Military service:* U.S. Marines, 1958-61.

MEMBER: Congress of Racial Equality, American Newspaper Guild, National Newspaper Publishers Association, National Association of African American Educators, California Association of Teachers of English, African Association of Black Studies, California Writers Club, Northern California Black English Teachers Association.

AWARDS, HONORS: First prize, Washington University Annual Festival of the Arts, 1965, for poem "Eye in the Ceiling"; first prize of *Free Lance* (magazine), 1966, for poem "Grandmother"; Literary Achievement Award, Sacramento Regional Arts Council, 1974; Best of the Small Press Award, Pushcart Press, 1976; Poet-Laureate, East St. Louis, Ill., 1976; faculty research award, California State University, Sacramento, 1976; California Arts Council grant, 1977; Illinois Arts Council grant, 1977; New York Council on the Arts grant, 1977-78; Naitonal Endowment for the Arts creative writing fellowship, 1978.

WRITINGS:

POETRY

A Tale of Two Toms, or Tom-Tom (Uncle Toms of East St. Louis & St. Louis), Monitor, 1968.
A Tale of Time and Toilet Tissue, Monitor, 1969.
Sentry of the Four Golden Pillars, Black River Writers, 1970.
River of Bones and Flesh and Blood, Black River Writers, 1971.
Songs from an Afro/Phone: New Poems, Black River Writers, 1972.
In a Time of Rain and Desire: New Love Poems, Black River Writers, 1973.
Consider Loneliness as These Things, Centro Studi E Scambi Internazionali, 1973.

EDITOR

(And contributor) *Sides of the River: A Mini-Anthology of Black Writings* (fiction and poems), Bethany Press, 1969.
(With Hale Chatfield) Henry Dumas, *Ark of Bones, and Other Stories* (fiction), Random House, 1970.
(With Chatfield) *Poetry for My People,* Southern Illinois University Press, 1970.
Dumas, *Play Ebony, Play Ivory,* Random House, 1974.
Dumas, *Jonoah and the Green Stone,* Random House, 1976.
Griefs of Joy: Selected Afro-American Poetry for Students, Black River Writers, 1977.
Dumas, *Rope of Wind, and Other Stories* (fiction), Random House, 1979.

PLAYS

(Contributor and performer) "The Ode to Taylor Jones," first produced in East St. Louis at Southern Illinois University Performing Arts Training Center, 1968.
"9 Poets with the Blues," first produced in Sacramento at California State University, 1971.
"The Face of the Deep," first produced in Sacramento at California State University, 1971.

"River of Bones," first produced in Sacramento at California State University, 1971.

"The Night John Henry Was Born," first produced in Baton Rouge, La., at Southern University, Little Theatre, 1972.

"Will I Still Be Here Tomorrow?," first produced in Sacramento at California State University, produced Off-Broadway at the Martinique Theatre, 1972.

"Kwaanza: A Ritual in 7 Movements," first produced in Sacramento at California State University, December 25, 1973.

"Music and I Have Come Home at Last!," first produced in Sacramento at California State University Outdoor Theatre, 1974.

"There's a Wiretap in My Soup," first produced in Sacramento at California State University, 1974.

Also author of play, "Shadows before the Mirror," performed live and on television in Sacramento.

FOR TELEVISION

"Cry-Cry, Wind, through the Throats of Horns and Drums: A Jazz Ballet," KXTV, 1977.

"If You Love Me Why Don't You Know It: A Blues Ballet," KXTV, 1977.

CONTRIBUTOR TO ANTHOLOGIES

Tambourine, Washington University Press, 1966.

Clarence Major, editor, *The New Black Poetry*, International Publishers, 1969.

Today's Negro Voices, Simon & Schuster, 1969.

A Galaxy of Black Writing, Moore Publishing, 1969.

Arnold Adoff, editor, *The Poetry of Black America*, Harper, 1972.

Abraham Chapman, editor, *New Black Voices*, New American Library, 1972.

Quincy Troupe and Rainer Schulte, editors, *Giant Talk: Anthology of Third World Writings*, Random House, 1974.

Theodore Gross, editor, *open poetry*, Random House, 1975.

A Documentary History of the Little Magazine since 1950, Pushcart, 1978.

Ishmael Reed, and others, editors, *Califia: The California Poetry*, Y'bird, 1979.

OTHER

Drumvoices: The Mission of Afro-American Poetry, A Critical History, Anchor, 1976.

(Advisor) Angela Lobo-Cobb, editor, *A Confluence of Colors: The First Anthology of Wisconsin Minority Poets*, Blue Reed Press, 1976.

Contributor of poetry and articles to numerous journals and newspapers, including *Focus/Midwest, Fine Arts, Nickel Review, Black Scholar*, and *Triquarterly*. Contributing editor, *Confrontation: A Journal of Third World Literature*.

WORK IN PROGRESS: Adapting his own work and that of other writers for television.

SIDELIGHTS: "A poet, critic, journalist, playwright, and educator, Eugene B. Redmond is counted among the number of significant black literary figures who shaped the black arts movement of the late 1960s," Joyce Pettis writes in *Dictionary of Literary Biography: Afro-American Poets since 1955*. The dominant feature of his poetry, she feels, may be "a marked historical and cultural perspective.... Redmond is very conscious of choosing his allusions, images, and symbols from the black cultural context.... His poetry abounds with direct allusions to spirituals, blues, jazz, soul music, and black musicians. His poetry also shows an indebtedness to folk songs and expressions, the great 'folkloristic trunk' from which Redmond believes black literature stems."

Also notable is Redmond's work as an editor. A friend of the late Henry Dumas (writer and cultural activist in East St. Louis, Illinois), Redmond co-founded Black River Writers Publishing Company and worked with Dumas to develop an audience for poetry in their community. Redmond, the executor of the senior poet's estate, has edited several books by Dumas. But a perhaps greater contribution to the appreciation of black literature is his own *Drumvoices: The Mission of Afro-American Poetry, A Critical History*, "the result of eight years of exhaustive research, travel, interviews, and writing," notes Pettis. "The volume, which surveys black American poetry from 1746 to 1976, is important for students and teachers of Afro-American poetry because it follows a historical perspective, and links the eclipsed African culture with the American culture of the earliest black writers.... Redmond also includes an extensive and helpful bibliography."

Redmond commented: "Motherless and fatherless at age eight, I was raised in part by a grandmother and a group of neighborhood fathers—friends of my older brother and members of the Seventh-Day Adventist Church I attended.... I try to make maximum use of formal training and general experience. At the very center of this writer's life and work is the desire and struggle for Black self-determination and respect for basic humanity." Redmond notes that he has been influenced by "Langston Hughes, Melvin Tolson, Theodore Roethke, Smokey Bill Robinson, Yevgeny Yevtushenko, blues, jazz lyrics, and the movement currently underway." He is "concerned with dynamics of Black Block Voting, Black Language, Third World politics and writings, [and feels] indebted to [Franz] Fanon.... I perform regularly, acting and reading poetry with the Performing Arts Training Center (directed by Katherine Dunham, friend and critic)..., [and am] involved with music and basic rhythms—the key to 'style' of Black writing. I also play the percussive instruments.... [I] acquired speaking knowledge of Japanese while in Far East with Marines. [I have also] spent some time in Laos."

MEDIA ADAPTATIONS: Redmond has recorded *Bloodlinks and Sacred Places*, readings of his poetry with musical accompaniment. A play version of *Drumvoices: The Mission of Afro-American Poetry* was produced in Sacramento at California State University Center Theatre in 1976.

BIOGRAPHICAL/CRITICAL SOURCES:

BOOKS

Dictionary of Literary Biography, Volume 41: *Afro-American Poets since 1955*, Gale, 1985.

PERIODICALS

Black Scholar, November 1, 1976, September, 1977, March, 1981.

Black World, September, 1984.

Village Voice, October 10, 1974.

*   *   *

REED, E.
See EVANS, Mari

REED, Ishmael 1938-
(Emmett Coleman)

PERSONAL: Born February 22, 1938, in Chattanooga, Tenn.; son of Henry Lenoir (a fundraiser for YMCA) and Thelma Coleman (a homemaker and salesperson); stepfather, Bennie Stephen Reed (an auto worker); married Priscilla Rose, September, 1960 (divorced, 1970); married Carla Blank (a modern dancer); children: (first marriage) Timothy, Brett (daughter); (second marriage) Tennessee Maria (daughter). *Education:* Attended State University of New York at Buffalo, 1956-60. *Politics:* Independent.

ADDRESSES: Agent—Ellis J. Freedman, 415 Madison Ave., New York, N.Y. 10017.

CAREER: Writer. Yardbird Publishing Co., Inc., Berkeley, Calif., co-founder, 1971, editorial director, 1971-75; Reed, Cannon & Johnson Communications Co. (a publisher and producer of video cassettes), Berkeley, co-founder, 1973—; Before Columbus Foundation (a producer and distributor of work of unknown ethnic writers), Berkeley, co-founder, 1976—; Ishmael Reed and Al Young's Quilt, Berkeley, co-founder, 1980—. Teacher at St. Mark's in the Bowery prose workshop, 1966; guest lecturer, University of California, Berkeley, 1968—, University of Washington, 1969-70, State University of New York at Buffalo, summer, 1975, and fall, 1979; Yale University, fall, 1979, Dartmouth College, summer, 1980-81, Sitka Community Association, summer, 1982, Columbia University, 1983, University of Arkansas at Fayetteville, 1982, Harvard University, 1987, and Regents lecturer, University of California, Santa Barbara, 1988. Judge of National Poetry Competition, 1980, King's County Literary Award, 1980, University of Michigan Hopwood Award, 1981. Chairperson of Berkeley Arts Commission, 1980 and 1981. Coordinating Council of Literary Magazines, chairman of board of directors, 1975-79, advisory board chairman, 1977-79.

AWARDS, HONORS: Certificate of Merit, California Association of English Teachers, 1972, for *19 Necromancers from Now;* nominations for National Book Award in fiction and poetry, 1973, for *Mumbo Jumbo* and *Conjure: Selected Poems, 1963-70;* nomination for Pulitzer Prize in poetry, 1973, for *Conjure;* Richard and Hinda Rosenthal Foundation Award, National Institute of Arts and Letters, 1975, for *The Last Days of Louisiana Red;* John Simon Guggenheim Memorial Foundation award for fiction, 1974; Poetry in Public Places winner (New York City), 1976, for poem "From the Files of Agent 22," and for a bicentennial mystery play, *The Lost State of Franklin,* written in collaboration with Carla Blank and Suzushi Hanayagi; Lewis Michaux Award, 1978; American Civil Liberties Award, 1978; Pushcart Prize for essay "American Poetry: Is There a Center?," 1979; Wisconsin Arts Board fellowship, 1982; associate fellow of Calhoun College, Yale University, 1982—; A.C.L.U. publishing fellowship; three New York State publishing grants for merit; three National Endowment for the Arts publishing grants for merit; California Arts Council grant; associate fellow, Harvard Signet Society, 1987—.

WRITINGS:

FICTION

The Free-Lance Pallbearers, Doubleday, 1967, Avon, 1985.
Yellow Back Radio Broke-Down, Doubleday, 1969, reprinted, Bantam, 1987.
Mumbo Jumbo, Doubleday, 1972, reprinted, Bantam, 1987.
The Last Days of Louisiana Red (Book-of-the-Month Club alternate selection), Random House, 1974.
Flight to Canada, Random House, 1976.
The Terrible Twos, St. Martin's/Marek, 1982.
Reckless Eyeballing, St. Martin's, 1986.

NONFICTION

(Contributor) John A. Williams and Charles F. Harris, editors, *Armistad I: Writings on Black History and Culture,* Vintage Books, 1970.
(Contributor) Addison Gayle, Jr., editor, *The Black Aesthetic,* Doubleday, 1971.
(Contributor) *Nommo: An Anthology of Modern Black African and Black American Literature,* Macmillan, 1972.
(Contributor) Jack Hicks, compiler, *Cutting Edges: Young American Fiction for the 70s,* Holt, 1973.
(Contributor) Joe David Bellamy, editor, *Superfiction or The American Story Transformed: An Anthology,* Vintage Books, 1975.
(Contributor) William Heyen, editor, *American Poets in 1976,* Bobbs Merrill, 1976.
Shrovetide in Old New Orleans (essays; original manuscript entitled *This One's on Me*), Doubleday, 1978.
God Made Alaska for the Indians: Selected Essays, Garland, 1982.

EDITOR

(Under pseudonym Emmett Coleman) *The Rise, Fall, and . . .? of Adam Clayton Powell,* Bee-Line Books, 1967.
(And author of introduction, and contributor) *19 Necromancers from Now,* Doubleday, 1970.
(With Al Young) *Yardbird Lives!,* Grove Press, 1978.
(And contributor) *Calafia: The California Poetry,* Y-Bird Books, 1979.
Writin' Is Fightin': Thirty-seven Years of Boxing on Paper, Atheneum, 1988.

POETRY

catechism of d neoamerican hoodoo church, Paul Breman (London), 1970, Broadside Press, 1971.
Conjure: Selected Poems, 1963-1970, University of Massachusetts Press, 1972.
Chattanooga: Poems, Random House, 1973.
A Secretary to the Spirits, illustrations by Betye Saar, NOK Publishers, 1978.
New and Collected Poetry, Atheneum, 1988.

POETRY REPRESENTED IN ANTHOLOGIES

Walter Lowenfels, editor, *Poets of Today: A New American Anthology,* International Publishing, 1964.
Lowenfels, editor, *Where Is Vietnam? American Poets Respond: An Anthology of Contemporary Poems,* Doubleday, 1967.
Lowenfels, editor, *In a Time of Revolution: Poems from Our Third World,* Random House, 1969.
Clarence Major, editor, *The New Black Poetry,* International Publishers, 1969.
Arthur M. Eastman and others, editors, *The Norton Anthology of Poetry,* Norton, 1970.
Langston Hughes and Arna Bontemps, editors, *The Poetry of the Negro, 1746-1970,* Doubleday, 1970.
June Jordan, editor, *Soulscript: Afro-American Poetry,* Doubleday, 1970.
Adam David Miller, editor, *Dices or Black Bones: Black Voices of the Seventies,* Houghton, 1970.

Nick Aaron Ford, editor, *Black Insights: Significant Literature by Black Americans—1760 to the Present,* Ginn & Co., 1971.

Nick Harvey, editor, *Mark in Time: Portraits and Poetry/San Francisco,* Glide Publications, 1971.

Robert Hayden and others, editors, *Afro-American Literature: An Introduction,* Harcourt, 1971.

Lowenfels, editor, *The Writing on the Wall: 108 American Poems of Protest,* Doubleday, 1971.

Alma Murray and Robert Thomas, editors, *Major Black Writers,* Scholastic Book Services, 1971.

Dudley Randall, editor, *The Black Poets,* Bantam, 1971.

Arnold Adoff, editor, *The Poetry of Black America: Anthology of the 20th Century,* Harper, 1972.

Richard G. Barnes, compiler, *Episodes in Five Poetic Traditions,* Chandler Publishing, 1972.

Abraham Chapman, editor, *New Black Voices: An Anthology of Contemporary Afro-American Literature,* New American Library, 1972.

Richard Kostelanetz, editor, *Seeing through Shuck,* Ballantine Books, 1972.

Paul Breman, editor, *You Better Believe It,* Penguin, 1973.

George Quasha and Jerome Rothenberg, editors, *America, a Prophecy: A New Reading of American Poetry from Pre-Columbian Times to the Present,* Random House, 1973.

Helen Hill and Agnes Perkins, compilers, *New Coasts and Strange Harbors: Discovering Poems,* Crowell, 1974.

X. J. Kennedy, editor, *An Introduction to Poetry,* Little, Brown, 1974.

John F. Nims, editor, *Western Wind: An Introduction to Poetry,* Random House, 1974.

Lowenfels, editor, *For Neruda, for Chile,* Beacon Press, 1975.

Janice Mirikitani and others, editors, *Time to Greez: Incantations from the Third World,* Glide Publications/Third World Communications, 1975.

Quincy Troupe, editor, *Giant Talk: An Anthology of Third World Writings,* Random House, 1975.

William Heyen, editor, *American Poets in 1976,* Bobbs Merrill, 1976.

Linda W. Wagner and C. David Mead, editors, *Introducing Poems,* Harper, 1976.

Arnold Adoff, editor, *Celebrations: A New Anthology of Black Poetry,* Follett, 1977.

Robert Callahan and others, editors, *Before Columbus Foundation Catalog One: Contemporary American Literature, 1978-1979,* Before Columbus Foundation, 1978.

OTHER

"Ishmael Reed Reading His Poetry" (cassette), Temple of Zeus, Cornell University, 1976.

"Ishmael Reed and Michael Harper Reading in the UCSD New Poetry Series" (reel), University of California, San Diego, 1977.

(Author of introduction) Elizabeth A. Settle and Thomas A. Settle, *Ishmael Reed: A Primary and Secondary Bibliography,* G. K. Hall, 1982.

Cab Calloway Stands In for the Moon, Bamberger, 1986.

Also author with wife, Carla Blank, and Suzushi Hanayagi of a bicentennial mystery play, *The Lost State of Franklin.* Executive producer of pilot episode of soap opera, *Personal Problems* and co-publisher of *The Steve Cannon Show: A Quarterly Audio-Cassette Radio Show Magazine. Mumbo Jumbo* was translated into French and Spanish, 1975.

Contributor of fiction to such periodicals as *Fiction, Iowa Review, Nimrod, Players, Ramparts, Seattle Review,* and *Spokane Natural;* contributor of articles and reviews to numerous periodicals, including *Black World, Confrontation: Journal of Third World Literature, Essence, Le Monde, Los Angeles Times, New York Times, Playgirl, Rolling Stone, Village Voice, Washington Post,* and *Yale Review;* and contributor of poetry to periodicals, including *American Poetry Review, Black Scholar, Black World, Essence, Liberator, Negro Digest, Noose, San Francisco Examiner, Oakland Tribune, Life, Connoisseur,* and *Umbra.* Co-founder of periodicals, *East Village Other* and *Advance* (Newark community newspaper), both 1965. Editor of *Yardbird Reader,* 1972-76, editor-in-chief, *Y'Bird* magazine, 1978-80, and co-editor of *Quilt* magazine, 1981—.

SIDELIGHTS: The novels of contemporary black American writer Ishmael Reed "are meant to provoke," writes *New York Times* contributor Darryl Pinckney. "Though variously described as a writer in whose work the black picaresque tradition has been extended, as a misogynist or an heir to both [Zora Neale] Hurston's folk lyricism and [Ralph] Ellison's irony, he is, perhaps because of this, one of the most underrated writers in America. Certainly no other contemporary black writer, male or female, has used the language and beliefs of folk culture so imaginatively, and few have been so stinging about the absurdity of American racism." Yet this novelist and poet is not simply a voice of black protest against racial and social injustices but instead a confronter of even more universal evils, a purveyor of even more universal truths.

Reed's first novel, *The Free-Lance Pallbearers,* introduces several thematic and stylistic devices that reappear throughout his canon. In this novel, as in his later works, Reed's first satirical jab is at the oppressive, stress-filled, Western/European/Christian tradition. But in *The Free-Lance Pallbearers,* the oppressor/oppressed, evil/good dichotomy is not as simple as it first appears. While Reed blames whites, called HARRY SAM in the novel, for present world conditions, he also viciously attacks culpable individuals from different strata in the black community and satirizes various kinds of black leaders in the twentieth century. Reed implies that many such leaders argue against white control by saying they want to improve conditions, to "help the people," but that in reality they are only waiting for the chance to betray and exploit poor blacks and to appropriate power.

Leaders of the black movement at the time of the novel's publication regarded as permissible the ridiculing of the white, Christian Bible, as in this grotesque caricature of St. John's vision and the Four Horsemen of the Apocalypse: "I saw an object atop the fragments of dead clippings. I waded up to my knees through grassy film and the phlegm-covered flags and picked up an ivory music box. On the cover done in mother-of-pearl was a picture of Lenore in her Bickford's uniform. I opened the music box and heard the tape of the familiar voice: ROGER YOUNG IN THE FIRST AT SARATOGA / ROGER YOUNG IN THE NINTH AT CHURCHILL DOWNS / ROGER YOUNG IN THE FOURTH AT BATAVIA / ROGER YOUNG IN THE FIFTH AT AQUEDUCT / ANNOUNCED BY RAPUNZEL." But the inclusion of negative black characters was thought by critics such as Houston Baker, Amiri Baraka, and Addison Gayle to be the wrong subject matter for the times. Reed, however, could never agree to rigid guidelines for including or excluding material from the novel form. As he would say later in *Shrovetide in Old New Orleans* concerning his battle with the critics, "The mainstream aspiration of Afro-Americans is for more freedom—and not slavery—including freedom of artistic expression.''

Among the black characters whom Reed puts into a negative light in *The Free-Lance Pallbearers* are Elijah Raven, the Muslim/Black Nationalist whose ideas of cultural and racial separation in the United States are exposed as lies; Eclair Pockchop, the minister fronting as an advocate of the people's causes, later discovered performing an unspeakable sex act on SAM; the black cop who protects white people from the blacks in the projects and who idiotically allows a cow-bell to be put around his neck for "meritorious service"; Doopeyduk's neighbors in the projects who, too stupid to remember their own names, answer to "M/Neighbor" and "F/Neighbor"; and finally Doopeyduk himself, whose pretentions of being a black intellectual render all his statements and actions absurd. Yet Reed reserves his most scathing satire for the black leaders who cater to SAM in his palace: "... who mounted the circuitous steps leading to SAM'S, assuring the boss dat: 'Wasn't us boss. 'Twas Stokely and Malcolm. Not us, boss. No indeed. We put dat ad in da *Times* repudiating dem, boss? Look, boss. We can prove it to you, dat we loves you. Would you like for us to cook up some strange recipes for ya, boss? Or tell some jokes? Did you hear the one about da nigger in the woodpile? Well, seems dere was this nigger, boss. . . .'''

The rhetoric of popular black literature in the 1960s is also satirized in *The Free-Lance Pallbearers*. The polemics of the time, characterized by colloquial diction, emotionalism, direct threats, automatic writing, and blueprints for a better society, are portrayed by Reed as representing the negative kind of literature required of blacks by the reading public. Reed's point is that, while literature by blacks might have been saying that blacks would no longer subscribe to white dictates, in fact the converse was true, manifested in the very literature that the publishing houses generally were printing at the time.

Furthermore, *The Free-Lance Pallbearers* fully exemplifies Reed's orthographic, stylistic, and rhetorical techniques. He prefers phonetic spellings to standard spellings, thus drawing special attention to subjects otherwise mundane. He also uses capitalization for emphasis, substitutes numerals for words (*1* for *one*) when including number references in the text, borrows Afro-American oral folklore as a source for his characters (as when Doopeyduk acts the part of "Shine" of the old crafty black tale), and utilizes newsflashes and radio voice-overs to comment on the book's action.

In his second novel, *Yellow Back Radio Broke-Down*, Reed begins to use at length Hoodoo (or Voodoo) methods and folklore as a basis for his work. Underlying all of the components of Hoodoo are two precepts: 1) the Hoodoo idea of syncretism, or the combination of beliefs and practices with divergent cultural origins, and 2) the Hoodoo concept of time. Even before the exportation of slaves to the Caribbean, Hoodoo was a syncretic religion, absorbing all that it considered useful from other West African religious practices. As a religion formed to combat degrading social conditions by dignifying and connecting man with helpful supernatural forces, Hoodoo thrives because of its syncretic flexibility, its ability to take even ostensibly negative influences and transfigure them into that which helps the "horse," or the one possessed by the attributes of a Hoodoo god. Hoodoo is bound by certain dogma or rites, but such rules are easily changed when they become oppressive, myopic, or no longer useful.

Reed turns this concept of syncretism into a literary method that combines aspects of "standard" English, including dialect, slang, argot, neologisms, or rhyme, with less "standard" language, whose principal rules of discourse are taken from the streets, popular music, and television. By purposely mixing language from different sources in popular culture, Reed employs expressions that both evoke interest and humor through seeming incongruities *and* create the illusion of real speech. In *Black American Literature Forum*, Michel Fabre draws a connection between Reed's use of language and his vision of the world, suggesting that "his so-called nonsense words raise disturbing questions . . . about the very nature of language." Often, "the semantic implications are disturbing because opposite meanings co-exist." Thus Reed emphasizes "the dangerous interchangeability of words and of the questionable identity of things and people" and "poses anguishing questions about self-identity, about the mechanism of meaning and about the nature of language and communication."

The historical sense of time in Reed's discourse, based on the African concept of time, is not linear; dates are not generally ascribed to the past, and past events overlap with those in the present. Berndt Ostendorf in *Black Literature in White America* notes that the African time sense is "telescoped," that it contains no concept of a future, only the certainty that man's existence will never end. Reed's version of this concept of *synchronicity* or simultaneity, incorporates a future by positing a time cycle of revolving and re-evolving events, but maintains an essentially African concept of the past/present relationship as characters treat past and present matters as though they were simultaneous.

Syncretism and synchronicity, along with other facets of Hoodoo as literary method, are central to *Yellow Back Radio Broke-Down*. The title is street-talk for the elucidation of a problem, in this case the racial and oligarchical difficulties of an Old West town, Yellow Back Radio; these difficulties are explained, or "broke down," for the reader. The novel opens with a description of the Hoodoo fetish, or mythical cult figure, Loop Garoo, whose name means "change into." Loop is a truly syncretic character who embodies diverse ethnic backgrounds and a history and power derived from several religions.

At least one of Reed's themes from *The Free-Lance Pallbearers* is reworked in *Yellow Back Radio Broke-Down*, as Christianity is again unmercifully attacked. Three Horsemen of the Apocalypse are represented by the Barber, Marshall, and Doctor, criminals, hypocrites, and upholders of the one-and-only-way-of-doing-things, that is, the way which materially benefits them; and the fourth Horseman is embodied in the Preacher Reverend Boyd, who will make a profit on guilt with the volume of poetry he is putting together, *Stomp Me O Lord*. Loop calls his own betrayal by other blacks, Alcibiades and Jeff, and his resurrection, a parody of "His Passion." The Pope, who appears in Yellow Back Radio in the 1880s, is revealed as a corrupt defender of the white tradition, concerned only with preventing Loop's magic from becoming stronger than his own.

The year 1972 saw the publication of Reed's first major volume of poetry, *Conjure: Selected Poems, 1963-1970*, followed in 1973 by his second collection, *Chattanooga: Poems*, and in 1977 by *A Secretary to the Spirits*. It is really in *Conjure* that Reed fully develops his literary method. Although the poem beginning "I am a cowboy in the boat of Ra" continues an earlier Reed interest in Egyptian symbolism, after this work he lyrically draws his symbols from Afro-American and Anglo-American historical and popular traditions—two distinct, but intertwined sources for the Afro-American aesthetic. "Black

Power Poem'' succinctly states the Hoodoo stance in the West: ''may the best church win. / shake hands now and come out conjuring''; a longer poem ''Neo-Hoodoo Manifesto'' defines all that Hoodoo is, and thus sheds light on the ways Reed uses its principles in writing, primarily through his absorption of material from every available source and his expansive originality in treating that material.

The theme of *Mumbo Jumbo,* Reed's 1972 novel, is the origin and composition of the ''true Afro-American aesthetic.'' Testifying to the novel's success in fulfilling this theme, Houston Baker in *Black World* calls *Mumbo Jumbo* ''the first black American novel of the last ten years that gives one a sense of the broader vision and the careful, painful, and laborious 'fundamental brainwork' that are needed if we are to define the eternal dilemma of the Black Arts and work fruitfully toward its melioration. . . . [The novel's] overall effect is that of amazing talent and flourishing genius.'' *Mumbo Jumbo*'s first chapter is crucial in that it presents the details of the highly complex plot in synopsis or news-flash form. Reed has a Hoodoo detective named Papa LaBas (representing the Hoodoo god Legba) search out and reconstruct a black aesthetic from remnants of literary and cultural history. To lend the narrative authenticity, Reed inserts favorite scholarly devices: facts from nonfictional, published works; photographs and historical drawings; and a bibliography. The unstated subtext throughout the book is ''My aesthetic is just as good as yours—maybe better—and certainly is founded on no more ridiculous a set of premises than yours.''

At the opening of the novel, set in New Orleans in the 1920s, white municipal officials are trying to respond to ''Jes Grew,'' an outbreak of behavior outside of socially conditioned roles; white people are ''acting black'' by dancing half-dressed in the streets to an intoxicating new loa (the spiritual essence of a fetish) called jazz. Speaking in tongues, people also abandon racist and other oppressive endeavors because it is more fun to ''shake that thing.'' One of the doctors assigned to treat the pandemic of Jes Grew comments, ''There are no isolated cases in this thing. It knows no class no race no consciousness. It is self-propagating and you can never tell when it will hit.'' No one knows where the germ has come from; it ''jes grew.'' In the synoptic first chapter, the omniscient narrator says Jes Grew is actually ''an anti-plague. Some plagues caused the body to waste away. Jes Grew enlivened the host. Other plagues were accompanied by bad air (malaria). Jes Grew victims said the air was as clear as they had ever seen it and that there was the aroma of roses and perfumes which had never before enticed their nostrils. Some plagues arise from decomposing animals, but Jes Grew is electric as life and is characterized by ebullience and ecstasy. Terrible plagues were due to the wrath of God; But Jes Grew is the delight of the gods.'' Jes Grew also is reflected in Reed's writing style, which may take on any number of guises, but is intended both to illuminate and enliven the reader.

In the novel, Christianity is called ''Atonism,'' a word with its origin in the worship of the sun-god, Aton, of ancient Egypt. Atonists are forever at war to stamp out Jes Grew, as it threatens their traditions and their power. The word *Atonism* is also a cognate of the word *atone*, with its connotations of guilt. The Atonists do not simply wage war against nonwhites and non-Christians. Anyone who opposes their beliefs is attacked. When a white member of a multi-ethnic gang, Thor Wintergreen, sides with nonwhites, he is first duped and then killed by Atonist Biff Musclewhite. Though Musclewhite is initially being held captive by Wintergreen, the prisoner persuades

Wintergreen to release him by giving the following explanation of the Atonist cause: ''Son, this is a nigger closing in our mysteries and soon he will be asking our civilization to 'come quietly.' This man is talking about Judeo-Christian culture, Christianity, Atonism, whatever you want to call it. . . . I've seen them, son, in Africa, China, they're not like us, son, the Herronvolk. Europe. This place. They are lagging behind, son, and you know in your heart this is true. Son, these niggers writing. Profaning our sacred words. Taking them from us and beating them on the anvil of BoogieWoogie, putting their black hands on them so that they shine like burnished amulets. Taking our words, son, these filthy niggers and using them. . . . Why 1 of them dared to interpret, critically mind you, the great Herman Melville's *Moby Dick*!!'' *Mumbo Jumbo* thus presents a battle for supremacy between powers that see the world in two distinct, opposed ways, with the separate visions endemic to the human types involved: one, expansive and syncretic; the other, impermeable and myopic.

Hoodoo time resurfaces in *Mumbo Jumbo* through a stylistic technique that produces a synchronic effect. Certain chapters which have detailed past events in the past tense are immediately followed by chapters that begin with present-tense verbs and present-day situations; this effect introduces simultaneity to the text, and elicits from the reader a response that mirrors the feeling of the Hoodoo/oral culture. That is, the reader feels that all of the actions are thematically and rhetorically related, because they all seem to be happening in the same narrative time frame. Commenting on his use both of time and of fiction-filled news-flashes, Reed says in *Shrovetide in Old New Orleans* that in writing *Mumbo Jumbo,* he ''wanted to write about a time like the present or to use the past to prophesy about the future—a process our ancestors called necromancy. I chose the twenties because they are very similar to what's happening right now. This is a valid method and has been used by writers from time immemorial. Nobody ever accused James Joyce of making up things. Using a past event of one's country or culture to comment on the present.''

The close of *Mumbo Jumbo* finds Jes Grew withering with the burning of its text, the Book of Thoth, which lists the sacred spells and dances of the Egyptian god Osiris. LaBas says Jes Grew will reappear some day to make its own text: ''A future generation of young artists will accomplish this,'' says LaBas, referring to the writers, painters, politicians, and musicians of the 1960s, ''the decade that screamed,'' as Reed termed it in *Chattanooga.*

In the course of the narrative, Reed constructs his history of the true Afro-American aesthetic and parallels the uniting of Afro-American oral tradition, folklore, art, and history, with a written code, a text, a literate recapitulation of history and practice. By calling for a unification of text and tradition, Reed equates the Text (the Afro-American aesthetic) with the Vedas, the Pentateuch, the Koran, the Latin Vulgate, the Book of Mormon, and all ''Holy'' codifications of faith. *Mumbo Jumbo,* which itself becomes the Text, appears as a direct, written response to the assertion that there is no ''black'' aesthetic, that black contributions to the world culture have been insignificant at best.

As seen in *Mumbo Jumbo,* Reed equates his own aesthetic with other systems based on different myths. Then he insists that his notion of an aesthetic is more humanistic than others, especially those based on Americanized, Christian dogma. Finding its spiritual corollary in Hoodoo, Reed's method achieves a manual of codification in *Mumbo Jumbo.* This code also is used in his next two novels, *The Last Days of Louisiana Red* and *Flight to Canada,* to reaffirm his belief that Hoodoo, now understood as a spiritual part of the Afro-American aesthetic, can be used as a basis for literary response.

The Last Days of Louisiana Red consists of three major story lines that coalesce toward the close of the novel to form its theme. The first and main plot is the tale of Ed Yellings, an industrious, middle-class black involved in "The Business," an insider's term for the propagation of Hoodoo. Through experimentation in his business, Solid Gumbo Works, Yellings discovers a cure for cancer and is hard at work to refine and market this remedy and other remedies for the various aspects of Louisiana Red, the Hoodoo name for all evil. When he is mysteriously murdered, Hoodoo detective Papa LaBas appears, and the stage is set for the major part of the action. This action involves participants in the novel's second and third story lines, the tale of the Chorus and the recounting of the mythical Antigone's decisions to oppose the dictates of the state. Antigone is clearly heroic in her actions, but the Chorus also fulfills a significant function by symbolizing black Americans who will not disappear, even though they are relegated by more powerful forces to minor roles. Never satisfied with this position, black Americans want to be placed where they believe they belong: in the forefront of the action, where they can succeed or fail depending upon their merits. Therein lies Reed's theme in *The Last Days of Louisiana Red.*

In *Flight to Canada* Reed most effectively explores Hoodoo as a force that gives his black protagonists the strength to be hopeful and courageous in the face of seemingly hopeless situations. Canada has, in this novel, at least two levels of meaning. It is, first of all, a literal, historical region where slaves might flee to freedom. Second, it becomes a metaphor for happiness; that is, anything that makes an individual character happy may be referred to as "Canada."

The major plot of *Flight to Canada* involves the escape of Raven Quickskill from his owner, Massa Arthur Swille, and Swille's efforts to return Quickskill to captivity. The historical Canada is the eventual destination where Quickskill and other slaves wish to arrive when they flee from Swille in Virginia, but this historical Canada is not the heaven slaves think, and pray, it will be. Yet in the face of the depressing stories about Canada from his friends Leechfield, Carpenter, Cato, and 40s, Quickskill will not relinquish his dream. For him, Canada is personified beyond the physical plane. Refuting those who would deny or degrade the existence of the Canada that his reading tours have allowed him to see as well as the Canada that he must invent to live in peace, Quickskill reflects: "He was so much against slavery that he had begun to include prose and poetry in the same book, so that there would be no arbitrary boundaries between them. He preferred Canada to slavery, whether Canada was exile, death, art, liberation, or a woman. Each man to his own Canada. There was much avian imagery in the poetry of slaves. Poetry about dreams and flight. They wanted to cross that Black Rock Ferry to freedom even though they had different notions as to what freedom was. They often disagreed about it, Leechfield, 40s. But it was his writing that got him to Canada. 'Flight to Canada' was responsible for getting him to Canada. And so for him, freedom was his writing. His writing was his Hoodoo. Others had their way of Hoodoo, but his was his writing. It fascinated him, it possessed him; his typewriter was his drum he danced to."

In *Flight to Canada* Hoodoo becomes a kind of faith that sustains and uplifts without necessarily degrading those to whom it is opposed. Unable to explain how he has attained success, Quickskill can only attribute his freedom to things unseen. Ultimately, all of the black characters turn to this transcendent vision as their shield against the harsher aspects of reality. As is true with Quickskill when he is confronted with the truth about Canada, the black characters' ability to rely upon the metaphysical saves their lives as well as their dreams.

In *The Terrible Twos,* Reed maintains the implicit notions of Hoodoo, while using his main story line to resurrect another apocryphal tale: the legend of Santa Claus and his assistant/boss, Black Peter. The time frame of the novel is roughly Christmas 1980 to Christmases of the 1990s, and the novel is clearly an allegory on Ronald Reagan's presidency and its consequences, as Reed sees them, in the 1990s. The evil of *The Terrible Twos* is the type that comes from selfishness fed by an exclusive monetary system, such as capitalism. Yet Reed does not endorse any other sort of government now in existence but criticizes any person or system that ignores what is humanly right in favor of what is economically profitable. Santa Claus (actually an out-of-work television personality) exemplifies the way Hoodoo fights this selfish evil: by putting those who were prosperous onto the level of those who have nothing and are abandoned. Santa characterizes American capitalists, those with material advantages, as infantile, selfish and exclusionary because their class station does not allow them to empathize with those who are different: "'Two years old, that's what we are, emotionally—Americans, always wanting someone to hand us some ice cream, always complaining, Santa didn't bring me this and why didn't Santa bring me that.' People in the crowd chuckle. 'Nobody can reason with us. Nobody can tell us anything. Millions of people staggering about passing out in the snow and we say that's tough. We say too bad to the children who don't have milk. I weep as I read these letters the poor children send me at my temporary home in Alaska.'"

In *The Terrible Twos* Reed leaves overt Hoodoo references as a subtext and focuses on the Rasta and Nicolaite myths, two conflicting quasi-religious cults revitalized by Black Power; he also concentrates on the myths of power and privilege created by "the vital people," those who are white and wealthy. However, the racist policies of the Nicolaites are eventually thwarted by inexplicable circumstances that stem from the supernatural powers of Hoodoo and from the Hoodoo notion that time is circular and that therefore the mighty will possibly—even probably—fall.

One device used in the novel is perhaps central in conveying Reed's vision. The first chapter is almost all factual reportage about Christmas and related matters, thus laying the foundation of belief for the fantastic Christmas Reed is about to construct. Yet, in comparison, the facts of Christmas seem as preposterous as the fiction of Christmas: Is it fact or fantasy that around Christmas of 1980 the *Buffalo Evening News* put under the headline "The Wild West is Back in the Saddle Again" the story of "First Actor" campaigning in cowboy attire in the West and a Confederate uniform in the South; is it fact or fantasy that a 6,000-pound ice sculpture of Santa and his reindeer carved by Andrew Young appears in a San Francisco Christmas parade? As John Leonard declares in his *New York Times* review of the book: "Mr. Reed is as close as we are likely to get to a Garcia Marquez, elaborating his own mythology even as he trashes ours. . . . *The Terrible Twos* tells many jokes before it kills, almost as if it had been written with barbed wire."

Reckless Eyeballing is a biting satiric allegory. Ian Ball, a black male writer, responds to the poor reception of his earlier play, *Suzanna,* by writing *Reckless Eyeballing,* a play sure to please those in power with its vicious attacks against black men. (''Reckless eyeballing'' was, after all, one of the accusations against Emmett Till, the young Chicago black who was murdered in Mississippi in 1953 for ''looking and whistling at a white woman.'') Tremonisha Smarts, a black female writer whose first name is drawn from a Scott Joplin opera of that title, is alternately popular and unpopular with the white women who are promoting her books. The battle for whose vision will dominate in the literary market and popular culture is fierce, and those critics who have seen in the portrait of Tremonisha a thinly veiled response to the current popularity of feminist writers are probably correct.

In Joplin's opera, the character Tremonisha represents the powers of assimilation into American culture in opposition to the ''powers of the Hoodoo men.'' Thus, not only does Reed's version of the Tremonisha character allude to the original Tremonisha's disagreement with early African-American currents, but she also becomes one of the critical forces that Reed has long opposed. More ironically, this allusive connection may be merely a feint, a trick leading critics to believe that Reed is covering the same, familiar Hoodoo ground covered before; actually, he moves in this novel toward unearthing the truly universal structures of Hoodoo, which are rooted in the apocryphal rites of other religions.

For example, the name of the character Abiahus in *Reckless Eyeballing* is a variant of the Hebrew ''Lilith,'' and the name helps to remind the reader of the legend of the amulet used when Hebrew women gave birth to ward off child-stealers. Reed found the connections between the shared traditions of Judaism and Hoodoo in *The Legends of Genesis* by Hermann Gunkel, in David Meltzer's magazine *TREE,* and in Mike Gold's *Jews without Money,* the latter of which includes a description of a Jewish woman similar to the Mambos and Conjure Women of Hoodoo origin. Reed thus reminds readers that Hoodoo is ever-changing by constantly absorbing materials from diverse cultures. He also warns his readers that he, too, is ever-changing and that a sure way to be misled is to believe that one has Hoodoo's concepts (and Reed's) pinned down as to their ''one true'' meaning.

Syncretic and synchronic in form, Reed's novels focus most often on social circumstances that inhibit the development of blacks in American society. As satire is usually based on real types, the writer draws in part from history and the news to satirize America's cultural arrogance and the terrible price paid by those who are not ''vital people,'' members of the dominant culture or the moneyed class. His assertion, in a *Review of Contemporary Fiction* interview with Reginald Martin, that Hoodoo is ''solidly in the American tradition'' is supported by his collation of myth, fact, and apocryphal data into a history; from that history, a method or aesthetic is drawn not only for formulating art and multi-ethnic cultural standards but also for developing a different and more humane way of experiencing and influencing the world.

MEDIA ADAPTATIONS: Some of Reed's poetry has been scored and recorded on *New Jazz Poets;* a dramatic episode from *The Last Days of Louisiana Red* appears on *The Steve Cannon Show: A Quarterly Audio-Cassette Radio Show Magazine,* produced by Reed, Cannon & Johnson Communications.

BIOGRAPHICAL/CRITICAL SOURCES:

BOOKS

Bellamy, Joe David, editor, *The New Fiction: Interviews with Innovative American Writers,* University of Illinois Press, 1974.

Bruck, Peter, and Wolfgang Karrer, editors, *The Afro-American Novel since 1960,* B. R. Bruener (Amsterdam), 1982.

Chesi, Gert, *Voodoo: Africa's Secret Power,* Perlinger-Verlag (Austria), 1979.

Contemporary Literary Criticism, Gale, Volume 2, 1974, Volume 3, 1975, Volume 5, 1976, Volume 6, 1976, Volume 8, 1980, Volume 32, 1985.

Conversations with Writers, Volume 2, Gale, 1978.

Dictionary of Literary Biography, Gale, Volume 2: *American Novelists since World War II,* 1978, Volume 5: *American Poets since World War II,* 1980, Volume 33: *Afro-American Fiction Writers after 1955,* 1984.

Klinkowitz, Jerome, *Literary Subversions: New American Fiction and the Practice of Criticism,* Southern Illinois University Press, 1985.

Martin, Reginald, *Ishmael Reed and the New Black Aesthetic Critics,* Macmillan (London), 1987.

O'Brien, John, *Interviews with Black Writers,* Liveright, 1973.

Ostendorf, Berndt, *Black Literature in White America,* Noble, 1982.

Reed, Ishmael, *The Free-Lance Pallbearers,* Doubleday, 1967.

Reed, Ishmael, *Yellow Back Radio Broke-Down,* Doubleday, 1969.

Reed, Ishmael, *Conjure: Selected Poems, 1963-1970,* University of Massachusetts Press, 1972.

Reed, Ishmael, *Mumbo, Jumbo,* Doubleday, 1972.

Reed, Ishmael, *Chattanooga: Poems,* Random House, 1973.

Reed, Ishmael, *The Last Days of Louisiana Red,* Random House, 1974.

Reed, Ishmael, *Flight to Canada,* Random Hosue, 1976.

Reed, Ishmael, *A Secretary to the Spirits,* NOK Publishers, 1978.

Reed, Ishmael, *Shrovetide in Old New Orleans,* Doubleday, 1978.

Reed, Ishmael, *The Terrible Twos,* St. Martin's/Marek, 1982.

Reed, Ishmael, *Reckless Eyeballing,* St. Martin's, 1986.

Rush, Theresa Gunnels, Carol Fairbanks Myers, and Ester Spring Arata, *Black American Writers Past and Present: A Biographical and Bibliographical Dictionary,* Scarecrow, 1975.

Settle, Elizabeth A., and Thomas A., *Ishmael Reed: A Primary and Secondary Bibliography,* G. K. Hall, 1982.

Stebich, Ute, *Haitian Art,* Abrams, 1978.

PERIODICALS

Afriscope, May, 1977.

American Book Review, May/June, 1983.

American Poetry Review, May/June, 1976, January/February, 1978.

Arizona Quarterly, autumn, 1979.

Arts Magazine, May, 1967.

Berkeley News, April 10, 1975.

Black American Literature Forum, Volume 12, 1978, spring, 1979, spring, 1980, fall, 1984.

Black Books Bulletin, winter, 1976.

Black Creation, fall, 1972, winter, 1973.

Black Enterprise, January, 1973, December, 1982, April, 1983.

Black History Museum Newsletter, Volume 4, number 3/4, 1975.

Black Scholar, March, 1981.
Black Times, September, 1975.
Black World, October, 1971, December, 1972, January, 1974, June, 1974, June, 1975, July, 1975.
Changes in the Arts, November, 1972, December/January, 1973.
Chicago Review, fall, 1976.
Chicago Tribune Book World, April 27, 1986.
Critical Inquiry, June, 1983.
Essence, July, 1986.
Fiction International, summer, 1973.
Harper's, December, 1969.
Journal of Black Poetry, summer/fall, 1969.
Journal of Black Studies, December, 1979.
Journal of Negro History, January, 1978.
Los Angeles Free Press, September 18, 1970.
Los Angeles Times, April 29, 1975.
Los Angeles Times Book Review, April 20, 1986.
MELUS, spring, 1984.
Modern Fiction Studies, summer, 1976.
Modern Poetry Studies, autumn, 1973, autumn, 1974.
Nation, September 18, 1976, May 22, 1982.
Negro American Literature Forum, winter, 1967, winter, 1972.
Negro Digest, February, 1969, December, 1969.
New Republic, November 23, 1974.
New Yorker, October 11, 1969.
New York Review of Books, October 5, 1972, December 12, 1974, August 12, 1982, January 29, 1987.
New York Times, August 1, 1969, August 9, 1972, June 17, 1982, April 5, 1986.
New York Times Book Review, August 6, 1972, November 10, 1974, September 19, 1976, July 18, 1982, March 23, 1986.
Nickel Review, August 28-September 10, 1968.
Obsidian: Black Literature in Review, spring/summer, 1979.
Parnassus: Poetry in Review, spring/summer, 1976.
Partisan Review, spring, 1975.
People, December 16, 1974.
PHYLON: The Atlanta University Review of Race and Culture, December, 1968, June, 1975.
Review of Contemporary Fiction, summer, 1984, spring, 1987.
San Francisco Review of Books, November, 1975, January/February, 1983.
Saturday Review, October 14, 1972, November 11, 1978.
Southern Review, July, 1985.
Studies in American Fiction, Volume 5, 1977.
Studies in the Novel, summer, 1971.
Twentieth Century Literature, April, 1974.
Village Voice, January 22, 1979.
Virginia Quarterly Review, winter, 1973.
Washington Post Book World, March 16, 1986.
World Literature Today, autumn, 1978, autumn, 1986.

—*Sidelights by Reginald Martin*

*   *   *

REID, Vic(tor Stafford)   1913-

PERSONAL: Born May 1, 1913, in Kingston, Jamaica; son of Alexander Burbridge (a businessman) and Margaret (Campbell) Reid; married Monica Jacobs, August 10, 1935; children: Shirley June (Mrs. Carlton Davis), Victor Stafford, Jr., Fran Elaine (Mrs. Giles Endicott), Peter Johnathan. *Education:* Educated in Jamaica.

ADDRESSES: Home—Valley Hill Farm, Rock Hall, Jamaica.

CAREER: Reporter, editor, and foreign correspondent for various newspapers; worked in advertising; currently managing director and chairman of a printing and publishing company in Kingston, Jamaica. Chairman, National Trust Commission of Jamaica, 1973—.

MEMBER: International P.E.N.

AWARDS, HONORS: Canada Council fellowship, 1958-60; Guggenheim fellowship, 1961; Mexican Writers fellowship.

WRITINGS:

Buildings in Jamaica, Jamaica Information Service, 1970.
The Sun and Juan de Bolas (juvenile), Institute of Jamaica, 1974.

NOVELS

New Day, Knopf, 1948.
The Leopard, Viking, 1958, reprinted, Heinemann Educational, 1980.
Sixty-Five (juvenile), Collins, 1963.
The Young Warriors (juvenile), Longmans Canada, 1968.
Peter of Mount Ephraim (juvenile), Jamaica Publishing House, 1970.
The Jamaicans, Institute of Jamaica, 1975.

CONTRIBUTOR

Andrew Salkey, editor, *West Indian Stories*, Faber & Faber, 1960.
Barbara Howes, editor, *From the Green Antilles*, Souvenir Press, 1967.

Contributor to periodical *Life and Letters*.

WORK IN PROGRESS: A biography of Norman Manley, former premier of Jamaica.

*   *   *

RHONE, Trevor D.   1940-

PERSONAL: Born in 1940; married; children: three. *Education:* Attended Rose Bruford College.

ADDRESSES: Home—1 Haining Mews, Kingston 5, Jamaica.

CAREER: Barn Theater, Kingston, Jamaica, playwright in residence, 1971-79; playwright.

WRITINGS:

''Smile Orange'' (play), first produced in Kingston, Jamaica, at Barn Theater, 1970; produced in London at Tricycle Theater, 1983; produced in New York at Billie Holiday Theater.
(With Perry Henzell) ''The Harder They Come'' (screenplay), New World, 1973.
Old Story Time and Other Plays, Longman, 1981.
Two Can Play (play; first produced in London at Arts Theater, October, 1983; produced in New York at Theater Four, April, 1984), KET, 1984.
Two Can Play [and] *School's Out* (plays), Longman, 1986.

Also author of screenplay ''Milk and Honey.''

SIDELIGHTS: Trevor D. Rhone, described by C. Gerald Fraser in the *New York Times* as ''one of Jamaica's foremost playwrights and screenwriters,'' is known for his emphasis on Jamaican characters and situations and his use of Jamaican dialect. His dramatic writings have earned praise in Jamaica and abroad for their humor, honesty, and treatment of universal issues. In a 1984 London *Times* article Irving Wardle observed, ''Sitting tight in Jamaica and writing for his own audience, Trevor Rhone is rapidly becoming London's favourite West Indian playwright. . . . We have few enough writers of any kind with his gifts for loving characterization and powers of story-telling.''

Among Rhone's best-known works is the screenplay for ''The Harder They Come,'' a 1973 Jamaican film he co-authored with director Perry Henzell. Combining a rags-to-riches story based on Jamaican reggae singer Jimmy Cliff's career with the seedy side of Jamaican life, including its marijuana trade, shanty towns, and mob, it seemed ''a more revolutionary black film than any number of American efforts'' to *New York Times* reviewer Vincent Canby. Showing how a promising young reggae singer becomes a drug trafficker and something of a folk hero after being swindled in the music business, it was the first Jamaican feature film made, and it relies extensively on local culture. The dialogue, subtitled for release, is in heavily accented Jamaican English, and reggae music permeates the score. Canby judged the movie ''a true original'' in his 1974 retrospective, noting that ''although it's a sometimes technically ragged movie, 'The Harder They Come' has more guts, wit, humor and sheer exuberance than most movies you'll see in any one year of movie-going.'' Moderately well received upon release in 1973, the film built a cult following and is numbered among the most remarkable films of the seventies.

Rhone has also received acclaim for his numerous stage writings, including the comedy ''Two Can Play,'' in which a Jamaican husband learns to deal with his wife's newfound independence in the aftermath of his scheme to immigrate to the United States. Fed up with the strife and poverty of life in Jamaica, Jim arranges to divorce his wife, Gloria, have her marry an American friend to become eligible for U.S. citizenship, and ultimately remarry her in the United States. Several weeks of freedom, however, render Gloria unwilling to resume her prior condition of servitude to Jim, who must learn how to live with a liberated wife. *New York Times* critic Mel Gussow characterized the play as ''a boisterous two-character farce guaranteed to make theatergoers cheer the awakening wife.'' As in his other writings, Rhone features Jamaican dialect in the play; Gussow attributed his only reservations about the work to the thick patois that he suggested could obscure the dialogue. The reviewer concluded, nonetheless, that ''Two Can Play'' is ''worth staying with; in this two-hander, there is a comic payoff.''

MEDIA ADAPTATIONS: ''Smile Orange'' was adapted for film in 1976.

BIOGRAPHICAL/CRITICAL SOURCES:

PERIODICALS

New York Times, February 9, 1973, July 14, 1974, April 16, 1985, August 7, 1985.
Times (London), July 27, 1983, October 28, 1983, September 19, 1984.

*   *   *

RICHARDSON, Nola (Mae)   1936-

PERSONAL: Born November 12, 1936, in Los Angeles, Calif.; daughter of Oscar and Jessie Mae (Anderson) Smith; divorced, 1969; children: Nolan, Virgil, Anthony, Julie, Dawn. *Education:* Compton Junior College, certificate in management, 1973.

ADDRESSES: Home—10426 Crenshaw Blvd., #1, Inglewood, Calif. 90303. *Office*—Drew Postgraduate Medical School, 12012 Compton Ave., Los Angeles, Calif. 90059.

CAREER: North American Rockwell, Downey, Calif., administrative secretary, 1954-70; Drew Postgraduate Medical School, Los Angeles, Calif., administrative assistant, 1970-73 and 1974—; Central Medical Group, Los Angeles, executive secretary and supervisor, 1973-74. Member of Poetry in the Schools program, 1974-75. Has given poetry readings in colleges and universities.

WRITINGS:

When One Loves: The Black Experience in America (poems), photographs by John H. Thompson, Ronald Phillips, and Roger Lubin, Celestial Arts, 1974.
Even in a Maze (poems), Crescent, 1975.

Also author of skit, ''Just a Teardrop.'' Contributor of poems and medical articles to magazines.

WORK IN PROGRESS: Poet Know Thyself; Of You, a poem in book form; *To Share and Care and Then Let Go*, love poems; *Especially in My Dreams*, in poem form.

SIDELIGHTS: Nola Richardson commented: ''Writing was stimulated from a need of verbal communication whereby I discovered it was also self-therapy—I tend to respond on a hyper-emotional level venting and creating through my writing. I therefore have written on quite a few subjects, such as life in general, sociology, economics, racial and childhood experiences—some relating from a self-therapy aspect in addition to my continued writings of love.''

BIOGRAPHICAL/CRITICAL SOURCES:

PERIODICALS

George Washington Surveyor, June 14, 1974.
The Grapevine, November, 1974.
Los Angeles Times, July 28, 1974, December 8, 1974.
Orange County Evening News, September 18, 1974.
Scoop, June 13, 1974.

*   *   *

RICHARDSON, Willis   1889-1977

PERSONAL: Born November 5, 1889, in Wilmington, North Carolina; died November 8, 1977; son of Willis Wilder and Agnes Ann (Harper) Richardson; married Mary Ellen Jones, September 1 (one source says September 3), 1914; children: Jean Paula, Shirley Antonella, Noel Justine. *Education:* Graduated from high school in Washington, D.C.

CAREER: U.S. Bureau of Engraving and Printing, Washington, D.C., clerk, 1911-54; playwright, 1920-77. Director, drama historian, teacher at institutions including Morgan College (now Morgan State University), director of Little Theatre group in Washington, D.C.

MEMBER: National Association for the Advancement of Colored People, Dramatists Guild, Harlem Cultural Council.

AWARDS, HONORS: First prize in *Crisis* Contest Awards, 1925, for ''The Broken Banjo,'' and 1926, for ''The Bootblack Lover''; honorable mention in *Opportunity* Contest Awards, 1925, for ''Fall of the Conjurer''; Amy Spingarn

Prize for drama, 1925 and 1926; Public School Prize, 1926, for "The King's Dilemma"; Edith Schwarb Cup from Yale University Theatre, 1928.

WRITINGS:

PLAYS

"The Deacon's Awakening: A Play in One Act" (first produced in St. Paul, Minn., in 1921), published in *Crisis,* November, 1920.

"The King's Dilemma" (one-act for children; first produced in Washington, D.C., May, 1926), published in *Brownies' Book,* December, 1920.

"The Gypsy's Finger Ring" (one-act for children), published in *Brownies' Book,* March, 1921.

"The Children's Treasure" (one-act for children), published in *Brownies' Book,* June, 1921.

"The Dragon's Tooth" (one-act for children), published in *Brownies' Book,* October, 1921.

"The Chip Woman's Fortune" (one-act), first produced in Chicago, January 29, 1923; produced on Broadway at Frazee Theatre, May 15, 1923.

"Mortgaged," first produced in Washington, D.C., at Howard University, March 29, 1924.

"Compromise" (one-act), first produced in Cleveland at Karamu House, February 26, 1925; produced in New York, May 3, 1926.

"The Broken Banjo" (first produced in New York, August 1, 1925), published in *Crisis,* February, 1926, and March, 1926.

"The Idle Head" (one-act), published in *Carolina,* April, 1927.

"The Flight of the Natives" (one-act; first produced in Washington, D.C., May 7, 1927), published in *Carolina,* April, 1927.

(Editor and contributor) *Plays and Pageants From the Life of the Negro* (twelve plays, including "The Black Horseman," "The House of Sham," and "The King's Dilemma" [all by Richardson]), Associated Publishers, 1930, reprinted, Roth Publishing, 1980.

"The Black Horseman," first produced in Baltimore, October 12, 1931.

(Editor with May Miller, and contributor) *Negro History in Thirteen Plays* (includes the one-acts "Antonio Maceo," "Attucks, the Martyr," "The Elder Dumas," "In Menelik's Court," and "Near Calvary" [all by Richardson]), Associated Publishers, 1935.

"Miss or Mrs.," first produced in Washington, D.C., May 5, 1941.

The King's Dilemma, and Other Plays for Children: Episodes of Hope and Dream (includes "The Dragon's Tooth," "The Gypsy's Finger Ring," "The King's Dilemma," "Man of Magic," "Near Calvary," and "The New Santa Claus"), Exposition Press, 1956.

Also author of one-act plays *Alimony Rastus,* Willis N. Bugbee, early 1920s, *A Ghost of the Past,* Paine Publishing, early 1920s, "Rooms for Rent," 1926, "Bold Lover," "The Brown Boy," "The Curse of the Shell Road Witch," and "The Dark Haven"; the three-act plays "Fall of the Conjurer," "The Bootblack Lover," and a version of "The Chip Woman's Fortune"; and of plays "The Peacock's Feather," 1928, "The Amateur Prostitute," "Chase," "The Danse Calinda," "Hope of the Lonely," "Imp of the Devil," "The Jail Bird," "Joy Rider," "The Man Who Married a Young Wife," "The New Generation," "The Nude Siren," "A Pillar of the Church," "The Rider of the Dream," and "The Visiting Lady."

OTHER

Echoes From the Negro Soul (poetry), Alamo Printing, 1926.

Contributor to periodicals, including *Carolina, Crisis,* and *Opportunity.*

Work represented in anthologies, including *The New Negro: An Interpretation,* edited by Alain Locke, Boni, 1925; *Plays of Negro Life: A Source-book of Native American Drama,* edited by Alain Locke and Montgomery Gregory, Harper, 1927; *Fifty More Contemporary One-Act Plays,* edited by Frank Shay, Appleton, 1928; *Readings From Negro Authors,* edited by Otelia Cromwell, Eva B. Dykes, and Lorenzo D. Turner, Harcourt, 1931; *American Literature by Negro Authors,* edited by Herman Dreer, Macmillan, 1950; *Anthology of the American Negro in the Theatre: A Critical Approach,* edited by Lindsay Patterson, Publishers Company, 1967; *Black Drama in America: An Anthology,* edited by Darwin T. Turner, Fawcett, 1971; *Black Writers of America,* edited by Richard Barksdale and Keneth Kinnamon, Macmillan, 1972; *Black Theatre, U.S.A.: Forty-five Plays by Black Americans,* edited by James V. Hatch with Ted Shine, Free Press, 1974; *The New Negro Renaissance,* edited by Arthur P. Davis and Michael Peplow, Holt, 1975.

SIDELIGHTS: Willis Richardson, the first black playwright to have a nonmusical play produced on Broadway, is remembered for his contributions to black theatre. Widely considered a pioneer, he dared to write serious plays about all levels of black life at a time when white playwrights wrote about stereotypical "darkies" and other black playwrights confined themselves to propaganda plays showing how blacks were victimized by whites. According to Bernard L. Peterson, Jr., writing in *Black World,* Richardson was "the first to make a significant contribution to both the quantity and the quality of serious Black American drama."

Among Richardson's first writings were his plays for children, which often dramatize lives of black heroes or use fairy-tale techniques to promote charity, equality, and brotherhood. Several were published in the monthly magazine *Brownies' Book* or later appeared in his collection *The King's Dilemma, and Other Plays for Children: Episodes of Hope and Dream.* "The King's Dilemma," a one-act play, traces the beginnings of democracy in a kingdom whose prince chooses to befriend a black boy, despite the king's opposition. Popular among schoolchildren, the play won the Public School Prize in 1926. "The Children's Treasure" takes a contemporary subject, a poor person facing eviction, and shows how five children help by contributing their own savings toward their neighbor's rent. In other plays Richardson tells of heroic and prominent blacks in history such as former slave Crispus Attucks, who was among the first to die in the American Revolution, Emperor Menelik of Abyssinia, and King Massinissa of East Numidia.

"The Chip Woman's Fortune," one of Richardson's best known works for adults, is famous as the first serious black play to appear on Broadway. Noted Peterson, "Black playwrights had previously been represented on The Great White Way by musical comedies and revues, but never before by a serious drama, albeit a one-act play." Presented on the same bill as Oscar Wilde's "Salome," Richardson's play portrays Aunt Nancy, an old woman who supports herself by tending a man's invalid wife and collecting chips of wood and coal for fuel. When the man, Silas, faces losing his job and the Victrola he has not yet paid off, he asks Nancy to use her money to help him, but she has saved it for her son, Jim. Claiming the money Nancy has saved, Jim ultimately gives some of it to Silas for having provided for his mother.

Observed Peterson, "Most of [Richardson's] plays were attempts at realistic treatment of Black life (both contemporary and historical) on such a variety of themes as manhood and bravery; suffering under white tyranny . . . ; the problems of the urban family; . . . the social strivings of the middle class; Black exploitation of other Blacks, and many other relevant subjects." The playwright worked to preserve for history an image of blacks more comprehensive than that portrayed by white writers, capturing the "richness, diversity, and beauty of his race," described Patsy B. Perry in the *Dictionary of Literary Biography*. Through his plays and critical writings, his advocacy of black theatre, and his conviction that black drama should excel on the same merits as any other drama, Richardson did much to bring black artistry forward and promote the best characteristics of his, and all, people. Concluded Peterson, "Willis Richardson has tried to show us 'the soul of a people, and the soul of this people is truly worth showing.'"

BIOGRAPHICAL/CRITICAL SOURCES:

BOOKS

Dictionary of Literary Biography, Volume 51: *Afro-American Writers From the Harlem Renaissance to 1940*, Gale, 1987.

PERIODICALS

Black World, April, 1975.

*   *   *

RIVE, Richard (Moore) 1931-

PERSONAL: Surname rhymes with "leave"; born March 1, 1931, in Cape Town, South Africa; son of Nancy (Ward) Rive. *Education:* Hewat Training College (now Hewat College of Education), Cape Town, Teacher's Diploma, 1951; University of Cape Town, B.A., 1962, B.Ed., 1968; Columbia University, M.A., 1966; Oxford University, D.Phil., 1974.

ADDRESSES: Home—31 Windsor Park Ave., Heathfield 7800, Cape Town, South Africa.

CAREER: Former teacher of English and Latin at South Peninsula High School, Cape Town, South Africa; affiliated with Harvard University, Cambridge, Mass., 1987; Hewat College of Education, Cape Town, formerly lecturer in English, head of Department of English, 1988—.

AWARDS, HONORS: Farfield Foundation fellowship to travel and study contemporary African literature in English and French, 1963; Fulbright scholar and Heft scholar, 1965-66; named Writer of the Year for South Africa, 1970, for "The Visits"; African Theatre Competition Prize, British Broadcasting Corp., 1972, for "Make Like Slaves."

WRITINGS:

African Songs (short stories), Seven Seas, 1963.
(Editor and contributor) *Quartet: New Voices from South Africa*, Crown, 1963.
Emergency (novel), introduction by Ezekiel Mphahlele, Faber, 1964, Collier Books, 1970.
(Compiler) *Modern African Prose*, Heinemann, 1964, reprinted, 1982.
Selected Writings: Stories, Essays, and Plays, Ad Donker (Johannesburg), 1977.
Writing Black (autobiography), D. Philip (Cape Town), 1982.

Advance, Retreat: Selected Short Stories, D. Philip, 1983.
"Buckingham Palace," *District Six*, D. Philip, 1986, Ballantine, 1987.

CONTRIBUTOR TO ANTHOLOGIES

Peggy Rutherford, editor, *Darkness and Light: An Anthology of African Writing*, Drum Publications (Johannesburg), 1958, published as *African Voices*, Grosset, 1959.
Langston Hughes, editor, *An African Treasury: Articles, Essays, Stories, Poems by Black Africans*, Crown, 1960.
Hughes, editor, *Poems from Black Africa*, Indiana University Press, 1963.
Ellis Ayitey and Mphahlele, editors, *Modern African Stories*, Faber, 1964.
Neville Denny, editor, *Pan African Short Stories*, Thomas Nelson, 1965.
Mphahlele, editor, *African Writing Today*, Penguin, 1967.
Leonard Sainville, editor, *Anthologie de la litterature negro-africaine: Romanciers et conteurs negro-africains*, Volume II, Presence Africaine, 1968.
Austin J. Shelton, Jr., editor, *The African Assertion: A Critical Anthology of African Literature*, Odyssey Press, 1968.

OTHER

Also author of "Make Like Slaves" (play), 1972. Contributor to periodicals in Africa, Europe, Asia, New Zealand, and the United States. Assistant editor, *Contrast* (literary quarterly).

WORK IN PROGRESS: A South African Abroad.

SIDELIGHTS: Raised in Cape Town, the son of a black American father and "colored" South African mother, Richard Rive often writes of the injustices of apartheid with "delightful humor where one would expect bitterness and anger," describes Kofi Anyidoho in *World Literature Today*. Although much of Rive's work can be characterized as "strong stuff," his specialty lies in "the ironies inherent in racial relationships," notes Robert L. Berner in a *World Literature Today* review of *Selected Writings: Stories, Essays, and Plays*. *Writing Black*, for example, an autobiographical series of sketches and essays, "is a stream of countless little episodes spiced with brief, often devastating sketches of unforgettable characters" says Anyidoho. "Rive's design rarely abandons us to the singular beauty or horror of the individual episode or sketch," comments the critic. Instead of focusing on the meaning of each separate instance, in *Writing Black* Rive demonstrates the "larger patterns of converging significance."

Rive also uses multiple images and themes to unify his fiction writing. In the *Journal of the New African Literature and the Arts*, Bernth Lindfors describes Rive's style as "characterized by strong rhythms, daring images, brisk dialogue, and leit-motifs (recurring words, phrases, images) which function as unifying devices." In *Emergency*, a novel describing the declaration of a state of emergency in Cape Town, Lindfors finds that this style "stumbles along in fits and starts and spurts," hampering the flow of the novel. The critic thinks that for Rive to "write a successful novel he must learn to use his talent in a new way."

Like *Emergency*, Rive's "Buckingham Palace," *District Six* dramatizes the oppressive actions of the apartheid government in Cape Town. In relating the story of the inhabitants of District Six, a "colored" slum slated for demolition by the government, Rive "brilliantly intensifies their tragedy by homing in on their humorous humanity rather than on their eventual dispersal," comments a *Publishers Weekly* reviewer. Rive's talent, according to William Walsh in the *Times Educational Supplement,* allows him to ''keep in productive balance irony bordering on despair'' and characters that demonstrate the humor and strangeness of the human condition. William Finnegan, in the *New York Times Book Review,* criticizes some of these characters and situations, remarking that those based on ''worn-smooth issues . . . sink nearly to the level of a television sitcom.'' Nevertheless, Finnegan finds that the novel ''gains sudden, almost headlong momentum and a genuine power'' when describing the ''war'' of the government against District Six. Like most of Rive's writing, *''Buckingham Palace,'' District Six* ''is not writing from the revolution's front lines,'' comments Finnegan. ''But it is good, affecting melodrama. And it does help explain'' the effects of apartheid in Cape Town. ''The novelist in the South African setting has to handle material that has become by now a huge cliche,'' comments Ezekiel Mphahlele in the introduction to Rive's *Emergency,* ''violence, its aftermath, and the response it elicits. In this he travels a path that has many pitfalls.'' By focusing on the humanity of his characters so they are neither ''tiny'' nor ''poetic,'' Mphahlele feels that Rive ''has avoided these pitfalls.''

Rive's work has been translated into twelve languages, including Russian.

AVOCATIONAL INTERESTS: Mountain climbing, coaching track athletics.

BIOGRAPHICAL/CRITICAL SOURCES:

BOOKS

Rive, Richard, *Emergency,* introduction by Ezekiel Mphahlele, Collier Books, 1970.
Rive, Richard, *Writing Black* (autobiography), D. Philip (Cape Town), 1982.

PERIODICALS

Journal of the New African Literature and the Arts, fall, 1966.
New York Times Book Review, October 4, 1987.
Publishers Weekly, June 12, 1987.
Times Educational Supplement, August 21, 1987.
Times Literary Supplement, April 1, 1965.
Transition, February, 1966.
World Literature Today, spring, 1978, summer, 1982.

*   *   *

RIVERS, Conrad Kent   1933-1968

PERSONAL: Born October 15, 1933, in Atlantic City, N.J.; died March 24, 1968; son of William Dixon and Cora (McIver) Rivers. *Education:* Wilberforce University, A.B., 1960; graduate study at Chicago Teachers College, Indiana University, and Temple University.

CAREER: Poet and writer. Teacher in high schools in Chicago, Ill., and Gary, Ind., 1961-67; founder of public relations firm, Kent Conrad Associates. Co-founder of Organization of Black American Culture (OBAC). *Military service:* U.S. Army, 1953-55.

MEMBER: American Society of Writers, Poetry Guild of America, Seven Arts Guild, Art Guild of Chicago.

AWARDS, HONORS: Annual Conrad Kent Rivers Poetry Award was established by *Black World* magazine.

WRITINGS:

Perchance to Dream, Othello (poems), Wilberforce University Press, 1959.

The Black Bodies and This Sunburnt Face (poems), Free Lance Press (Cleveland, Ohio), 1962.
Dusk at Selma (play), Free Lance Press, 1965.
The Still Voice of Harlem (poems), Paul Breman (London), 1968, 2nd edition, 1972.
The Wright Poems, introduction by Ronald L. Fair, Paul Breman, 1972.

Also author of short stories and a play, *To Make a Poet Black.* Work represented in numerous anthologies, including *For Malcolm: Poems on the Life and Death of Malcolm X,* edited by Dudley Randall and Margaret G. Burroughs, 2nd edition, Broadside Press, 1969; *Afro-American Literature: Poetry,* edited by William Adams, Houghton, 1970; *Black Literature in America,* edited by H. A. Baker, McGraw, 1971; *Black Writers of America: A Comprehensive Anthology,* edited by Richard Barksdale and Kenneth Kinnamon, Macmillan, 1972; *Understanding the New Black Poetry: Black Speech and Black Music as Poetic References,* edited by Stephen Henderson, Morrow, 1973. Contributor of articles, stories, and poems to periodicals, including *Negro Digest, Kenyon Review, Antioch Review,* and *Umbra.*

SIDELIGHTS: Writing in *Dynamite Voices: Black Poets of the 1960's,* Don L. Lee described Conrad Kent Rivers as ''not only a world traveler but a word-traveler too.'' In the book, published after Rivers' death, Lee eulogized: ''Bodies pass on but words endure. Even though Rivers didn't have a long runway, his plane was able to lift off and it will always be in flight, dropping a still voice in Harlem and on the Southside of Chicago.''

BIOGRAPHICAL/CRITICAL SOURCES:

BOOKS

Baker, H. A., editor, *Black Literature in America,* McGraw, 1971.
Contemporary Literary Criticism, Volume 1, Gale, 1973.
Dictionary of Literary Biography, Volume 41: *Afro-American Poets Since 1955,* Gale, 1985.
Hayden, Robert, *Kaleidoscope,* Harcourt, 1967.
Lee, Don L., *Dynamite Voices: Black Poets of the 1960's,* Broadside Press, 1971.

PERIODICALS

Negro Digest, August, 1968.

*   *   *

ROBESON, Paul (Leroy Bustill)   1898-1976

PERSONAL: Surname is pronounced ''*Robe*-son''; born April 9, 1898, in Princeton, N.J.; died after suffering a stroke, January 23, 1976, in Philadelphia, Pa.; son of William Drew (a clergyman) and Maria Louisa (a schoolteacher; maiden name, Bustill) Robeson; married Eslanda Cardozo Goode, August 17, 1921 (died, December, 1965); children: Paul Jr. *Education:* Rutgers College (now University), A.B., 1919; Columbia University, LL.B., 1923.

CAREER: Admitted to the Bar of New York; employed in a law firm, 1923; actor in plays, including ''Simon the Cyrenian,'' 1921, ''All God's Chillun Got Wings,'' 1924, ''Othello,'' 1930 and 1943, and ''Toussaint L'Ouverture,'' 1936; actor in films, including ''Body and Soul,'' 1924, ''The Emperor Jones,'' 1933, ''Sanders of the River,'' 1935, and ''Show Boat,'' 1936; singer in concert performances, for recordings, and in musical productions, including ''Show Boat,'' 1928.

MEMBER: National Maritime Union (honorary member), Council on African Affairs (co-founder), Joint Anti-Fascist Refugee Committee, Committee to Aid China, Phi Beta Kappa, Alpha Phi Alpha, Sigma Tau Delta.

AWARDS, HONORS: Badge of Veterans of Abraham Lincoln Brigade, 1939; Donaldson Award for outstanding lead performance, 1944, for "Othello"; medal from American Academy of Arts and Letters, 1944, for good diction on the stage; Spingarn Medal from National Association for the Advancement of Colored People, 1944; Champion of African Freedom Award from National Church of Nigeria, 1950; Afro-American Newspapers Award, 1950; Stalin Peace Prize from U.S.S.R., 1952; German Peace Medal from East Germany, 1960; Ira Aldridge Award from Association for the Study of Afro-American Life and History, 1970; Civil Liberties Award from American Civil Liberties Union, 1970; Duke Ellington Medal from Yale University, 1972; Whitney M. Young, Jr., National Memorial Award from Urban League of Greater New York, 1972. Honorary degrees from Rutgers University, 1932 and 1973, Hamilton College, 1940, Morehouse College, 1943, Howard University, 1945, Moscow State Conservatory, 1959, and Humboldt University, 1960.

WRITINGS:

Here I Stand (autobiography), Othello Associates (New York), 1958.

COLLECTIONS

(Contributor) *Paul Robeson: The Great Forerunner,* Freedomways, 1971, new edition, Dodd, 1978, enlarged, 1985.
Paul Robeson: Tributes, Selected Writings, compiled and edited by Roberta Yancy Dent with the assistance of Marilyn Robeson and Paul Robeson, Jr., The Archives (New York), 1976.
Paul Robeson Speaks: Writings, Speeches, Interviews, 1918-1974, edited with an introduction by Philip S. Foner, Brunner, 1978.

Columnist for *People's Voice* during 1940s; editor and columnist for *Freedom,* c. 1951-55. Contributor to periodicals, including *African Observer, Afro-American, American Dialog, American Scholar, Daily Worker, Freedomways, Jewish Life, Masses and Mainstream, Messenger, National Guardian, New Statesman and Nation, New World Review, New York Age, Opportunity, Spectator,* and *Worker.*

SIDELIGHTS: Paul Robeson was one of America's most prominent black performers before his career was destroyed as a result of his controversial political positions, which ranged from promotion of racial equality to admiration for the Soviet Union. Though he became famous for his singing and acting, Robeson displayed a remarkable range of talents from an early age. As the third black student to attend Rutgers College, he distinguished himself academically and athletically, becoming a member of the Phi Beta Kappa honors society and an all-American football player. Robeson subsequently earned a law degree from Columbia University but soon became dissatisfied with the opportunities available to blacks in the legal profession. He turned to the theater and, although he had never intended to become a professional actor, appeared successfully in productions in New York City and London. In 1924 he joined the Provincetown Players, which was associated with playwright Eugene O'Neill, and attracted widespread critical attention with lead roles in two O'Neill plays—"The Emperor Jones" and "All God's Chillun Got Wings," a groundbreaking, controversial work about interracial marriage.

By the 1930s Robeson was a prosperous actor and singer of international stature. His stage credits included the title role in William Shakespeare's tragedy "Othello" and Joe in the musical "Show Boat," for which he sang the highly popular melody "Ol' Man River." Acclaimed for his singing voice, Robeson made numerous recordings and gave concerts in America and Europe that ranged from black spirituals to opera. He also appeared in several feature films, including adaptations of "The Emperor Jones" and "Show Boat."

As Robeson visited Europe to give performances, he increasingly identified with its political left. In England he was exposed to socialism by playwright George Bernard Shaw and adherents of the country's Labour party. He met African nationalists Jomo Kenyatta and Kwame Nkrumah, and eventually co-founded the anticolonial Council on African Affairs. Robeson was deeply affected during a trip in 1934 when he was harassed by racist officials in Nazi Germany but was welcomed in the Communist Soviet Union. He became convinced that the Soviet Union, thanks to its political system, had conquered racism.

Robeson soon made his political concerns a part of his performing career. He lent his talents to a variety of political causes, singing to raise money for Jewish refugees from the Nazis and entertaining antifascist troops during the Spanish Civil War. Disillusioned with the limited roles available to blacks in film, Robeson announced in 1939 that he would curtail his movie acting. As Loften Mitchell later quoted him in the *New York Times:* "The industry was not prepared to permit me to portray the life or express the living interests, hopes and aspirations of the struggling people from whom I come. You bet they will never let me play a part in a film in which a Negro is on top."

During the 1930s and early 1940s, Robeson's political outspokenness was no impediment to his popularity. In 1943, for instance, he was received enthusiastically by theater audiences when he became the first black actor to play Othello on Broadway with a white supporting cast. The production's long run set a Broadway record for a Shakespeare play, and Robeson garnered a Donaldson Award for outstanding lead performance and a photo story in *Life* magazine. As Roger M. Williams observed in *American Heritage,* Robeson "was . . . being hailed as America's leading Negro."

But Robeson's fortunes changed with the end of World War II, when the wartime alliance of the United States and the Soviet Union deteriorated into mistrust and hostility. Many feared a war between the two former allies, and a resurgent political right wing in America often equated the advocacy of liberal or left-wing causes with disloyalty to the United States. Robeson continued to openly espouse the concerns of the political left, announcing in 1947 that he would take a two-year break from performing in order to fight racism in America and campaigning the next year for Progressive presidential candidate Henry Wallace. In a controversial 1949 speech at the World Peace Congress in Paris, quoted by Williams, Robeson said that it was "unthinkable that American Negroes could go to war on behalf of those who have oppressed us for generations against the Soviet Union, which in one generation has raised our people to full human dignity." Right-wing hostility to Robeson erupted into violence later that year when the singer gave two concerts in Peekskill, New York, and political opponents harassed and assaulted the audience.

In the next few years Robeson's career disintegrated. He found few opportunities to perform, saw his income plummet, and lost access to his European audience when the U.S. Government barred him from traveling abroad because he would not sign an anti-communist loyalty oath. During this period of ostracism Robeson wrote his autobiography, *Here I Stand,* which is not only an account of his life but a discussion of his political views and how they developed. He offers a social and political agenda for black people, urging them to become aware of their African heritage and contending that the civil rights struggle should be a mass movement of the black community, independent of white leadership. In the *New York Times Book Review* Sterling Stuckey wrote that *Here I Stand* "appears to be addressed primarily to ordinary black people and only secondarily to intellectuals. It is as though, while taking it up, one is listening more than reading, hearing Robeson's own words as his personality, unaffected, generous, full of humanity, comes forth from the pages."

In 1958, the year *Here I Stand* was published, Robeson was once again allowed to go abroad—on a related case the Supreme Court agreed with Robeson's contention that Americans cannot be denied the right to travel because of their political views. He soon became ill, however, and spent the rest of his life in virtual seclusion in the United States, an obscure figure to many younger Americans. In the 1970s Robeson repeatedly failed to attend the tributes organized in his honor, including a celebration of his seventy-fifth birthday at New York City's Carnegie Hall that included such prominent guests as Coretta Scott King, widow of slain civil rights leader Martin Luther King, Jr. As reported by Laurie Johnston in the *New York Times,* Mrs. King told the gathering that Robeson "had been 'buried alive' because, earlier than her husband, he had 'tapped the same wells of latent militancy' among blacks." Robeson died in 1976, a few weeks after suffering a stroke.

BIOGRAPHICAL/CRITICAL SOURCES:

BOOKS

Davis, Lenwood G., *A Paul Robeson Research Guide: A Selected, Annotated Bibliography,* Greenwood Press, 1982.
Editors of *Freedomways, Paul Robeson: The Great Forerunner,* enlarged edition, Dodd, 1985.
Gilliam, Dorothy Butler, *Paul Robeson: All-American,* New Republic Books, 1976.
Hoyt, Edwin P., *Paul Robeson: The American Othello,* World Publishing, 1967.
Robeson, Susan, *The Whole World in His Hands: A Pictorial Biography of Paul Robeson,* Citadel, 1981.

PERIODICALS

American Heritage, April, 1976.
Black World, July, 1972.
Life, November 22, 1943.
New York Times, August 6, 1972, April 16, 1973.
New York Times Book Review, October 21, 1973.
Times Literary Supplement, September 5, 1958.
West Coast Review of Books, January, 1979.

OBITUARIES:

PERIODICALS

Nation, February 7, 1976.
Newsweek, February 2, 1976.
New York Times, January 24, 1976.
Time, February 2, 1976.

—*Sketch by Thomas Kozikowski*

ROBINSON, Max (C.) 1939-

PERSONAL: Born May 1, 1939, in Richmond, Va.; son of Maxie Cleveland and Doris (Jones) Robinson; married Beverly Hamilton; children: Mark, Maureen, Michael, Malik. *Education:* Attended Oberlin College, 1957-58, and Indiana University, 1959-60.

ADDRESSES: Home—Chicago, Ill.

CAREER/WRITINGS: WTOV-TV, Norfolk, Va., news announcer, 1959; WTOP-TV, Washington, D.C., correspondent and cameraman, 1965, anchorman, 1969-78; WRC-TV, Washington, correspondent, 1965-69; American Broadcasting Co., New York, N.Y., anchorman of "ABC World News Tonight" in Chicago, Ill., 1978-83; associated with WMAQ-TV in Chicago, beginning in 1983. Associate professor of communicative arts at Federal City College, 1968-72; journalist in residence at College of William and Mary, 1981. *Military service:* U.S. Air Force, 1959-60.

AWARDS, HONORS: Journalist of the Year award from Capital Press Club, 1967; award from National Education Association, 1966; Regional Emmy awards from National Academy of Television Arts and Sciences, both 1967, both for documentary "The Other Washington"; award from Ohio State University, 1967; awarded Star of Africa by the president of Liberia, 1972; outstanding news reporting award from the District of Columbia Chamber of Commerce, 1978; communication and leadership awards from Toastmasters International, 1978, Chicago State University, 1979, and Congress of National Black Churches, 1979; named honorary citizen of Indianapolis, Ind., 1978, Houston, Tex., 1978, Cincinnati, Ohio, 1979, Atlanta, Ga., 1979, and Gary, Ind., 1979; Max Robinson Day decreed in Washington, D.C., 1978, Richmond, Va., 1978, and Atlanta, Ga., 1981; LL.D. from North Carolina Agricultural and Technical State University, 1979; National Media Award from Capital Press Club, 1979; Litt.D. from Atlanta University, 1980, and Virginia University, 1981; National Emmy Award, 1981, for 1980 election coverage; honorary degree in public service from Voorhees College, 1981; D.Litt. from Virginia State University, 1981; Excellence in Journalism award from College of William and Mary, 1981; Drum Major for Justice Award from Martin Luther King, Jr., Memorial, 1981; recognition awards from National Association of Black Journalists, National Association of Media Women, and Detroit, Michigan, City Council, all 1981.

MEMBER: Society of Collegiate Journalists (honorary), Sigma Delta Chi.

WORK IN PROGRESS: An autobiographical work.

SIDELIGHTS: In 1979 *Ebony* described award-winning black television journalist Max Robinson as a "booming baritone" with an "extraordinary ability to understand people, [and] to analyze the news." The plaudits were in response to Robinson's work as one of four anchors of "ABC World News Tonight," which he joined in 1978 to become the first black to anchor a prime-time national network news program.

Robinson took up a career in broadcast journalism around 1959—a time when few, if any, blacks held positions in the field. He began as a voice-over news announcer for WTOV-TV in Norfolk, Virginia, and soon after he went to Washington, D.C., where he worked for stations WRC-TV and WTOP-TV. He had been anchoring the latter's "Eyewitness News" since 1969 when ABC selected him as anchorman of their national news desk in Chicago, Illinois. Together with "ABC

World News Tonight'' desk anchors Frank Reynolds in Washington, Peter Jennings in London, and Barbara Walters in New York City, Robinson is credited with helping to bring the evening news program's ratings to parity with those of the other major networks. Following Reynolds's death in 1983 Robinson left ABC and joined Chicago station WMAQ-TV.

BIOGRAPHICAL/CRITICAL SOURCES:

PERIODICALS

Detroit Free Press, July 9, 1978.
Ebony, January, 1979, August, 1979, August, 1983.
Variety, February 22, 1984, July 10, 1985.
Washington Post, December 31, 1987.

*   *   *

ROBINSON, William H(enry)   1922-

PERSONAL: Born October 24, 1922, in Newport, R.I.; son of Julia W. S. Robinson; married Doris Carol Johnson (an administrative assistant), June 8, 1948. *Education:* New York University, B.A., 1951; Boston University, M.A., 1957; Harvard University, Ph.D., 1964.

ADDRESSES: Home—80 Connection St., Newport, R.I. 02840. *Office*—Department of English, Rhode Island College, Providence, R.I. 02908.

CAREER: Prairie View Agricultural and Mechanical College, Prairie View, Tex., instructor in English, 1951-53; Agricultural and Technical College of North Carolina (now North Carolina Agricultural and Technical State University), Greensboro, member of English faculty, 1956-61, 1964-66; Boston University, Boston, Mass., associate professor of English and humanities, 1966-68; Howard University, Washington, D.C., professor of English, 1968-70; Rhode Island College, Providence, professor of English and director of black studies, 1970-85. Visiting professor of American and English literature, Brown University, 1987—. Community lecturer on black studies. *Military service:* U.S. Army, 1942-45; received Bronze Star.

MEMBER: College Language Arts Association, Association for Study of Negro Life and Culture.

WRITINGS:

(Editor) *Early Black American Poets: Selections, with Biographical and Critical Introductions,* W. C. Brown, 1969.
(Editor) *Early Black American Prose,* W. C. Brown, 1970.
(Editor) *Nommo: An Anthology of Modern Black African and Black American Literature,* Macmillan, 1972.
Phillis Wheatley in the Black American Beginnings, Broadside, 1975.
(Editor) *The Proceedings of the Free African Union Society and the African Benevolent Society, Newport, Rhode Island, 1780-1824,* Rhode Island Urban League, 1976.
Black New England Letters: The Uses of Writing in Black New England (lectures), Trustees of the Public Library of the City of Boston, 1977.
Phillis Wheatley: A Bio-Bibliography, G. K. Hall, 1981.
(Editor) *Critical Essays on Phillis Wheatley,* G. K. Hall, 1982.
Phillis Wheatley and Her Writings, Garland Publishing, 1984.

Also author of several dozen scripts for educational radio, stage, and television productions. Contributor to literature journals.

WORK IN PROGRESS: The Literature of Black America: A Critical Study; Black and Yankee Me, an autobiography; research on the early black American novel.

SIDELIGHTS: William H. Robinson's collection *Critical Essays on Phillis Wheatley* ''will not settle any of the major controversies over the significance of her poetry or her racial awareness,'' writes Gene England in *Black American Literature Forum.* ''However,'' adds England, ''the book does provide scholars and students of Afro-American and Early American literature access to an abundance of materials on Wheatley and to the varied critical opinions which have been argued for more than two hundred years.''

BIOGRAPHICAL/CRITICAL SOURCES:

PERIODICALS

Black American Literature Forum, spring, 1984.
Black World, September, 1971.
Negro Digest, October, 1969.
Southern Humanities Review, spring, 1986.

*   *   *

RODGERS, Carolyn M(arie)   1945-

PERSONAL: Born December 14, 1945, in Chicago, Ill.; daughter of Clarence and Bazella (Colding) Rodgers. *Education:* Attended University of Illinois, 1960-61; Roosevelt University, B.A., 1965; University of Chicago, M.A., 1983. *Religion:* African Methodist Episcopal.

CAREER: Y.M.C.A., Chicago, Ill., social worker, 1963-68; Columbia College, Chicago, lecturer in Afro-American literature, 1968-69; University of Washington, Seattle, instructor in Afro-American literature, summer, 1970; Albany State College, Albany, Ga., writer in residence, 1972; Malcolm X College, Chicago, writer in residence, 1972; Indiana University, Bloomington, instructor in Afro-American literature, summer, 1973.

MEMBER: Organization of Black American Culture Writers Workshop, Gwendolyn Brooks Writers Workshop, Delta Sigma Theta.

AWARDS, HONORS: First Conrad Kent Rivers Memorial Fund Award, 1968; National Endowment for the Arts grant, 1970; Poet Laureate Award, Society of Midland Authors, 1970; National Book Award nomination, 1976, for *how i got ovah: New and Selected Poems;* Carnegie Award, 1979, PEN awards.

WRITINGS:

POETRY

Paper Soul, Third World Press, 1968.
Songs of a Blackbird, Third World Press, 1969.
2 Love Raps, Third World Press, 1969.
Now Ain't That Love, Broadside Press, 1970.
For H. W. Fuller, Broadside Press, 1970.
For Flip Wilson, Broadside Press, 1971.
Long Rap/Commonly Known as a Poetic Essay, Broadside Press, 1971.
how i got ovah: New and Selected Poems, Doubleday/Anchor, 1975.
The Heart as Ever Green: Poems, Doubleday/Anchor, 1978.
Translation: Poems, Eden Press, 1980.
Finite Forms: Poems, Eden Press, 1985.

CONTRIBUTOR TO ANTHOLOGIES

Ahmed Alhamsi and Harun K. Wangara, editors, *Black Arts,* Broadside Press, 1969.
Arnold Adoff, editor, *Brothers and Sisters,* Macmillan, 1970.

Orde Coombs, editor, *We Speak as Liberators,* Dodd, 1970.

Ted Wilentz and Tom Weatherley, editors, *Natural Process,* Hill & Wang, 1970.

Gwendolyn Brooks, editor, *Jump Bad,* Broadside Press, 1971.

Dudley Randall, editor, *The Black Poets,* Bantam, 1971.

Woodie King, editor, *Blackspirits,* Random House, 1972.

Richard A. Long and Eugenia W. Collier, editors, *Afro-American Writing,* New York University Press, 1972.

William R. Robinson, editor, *Nommo,* Macmillan, 1972.

Adoff, editor, *The Poetry of Black America,* Harper, 1973.

Stephen Henderson, editor, *Understanding the New Black Poetry,* Morrow, 1973.

Black Sister, Indiana University Press, 1983.

Amiri Baraka, editor, *Confirmation Anthology,* Morrow, 1984.

Mari Evans, editor, *Black Women Writers (1950-1980): A Critical Evaluation,* Doubleday/Anchor, 1984.

Also contributor to *No Crystal Stairs,* 1984.

OTHER

(Editor) *Roots* (anthology), Indiana University Press, 1973.

A Little Lower Than Angels (novel), Eden Press, 1984.

Former reviewer for *Chicago Daily News* and columnist for *Milwaukee Courier.*

WORK IN PROGRESS: Rain, short stories; *Arise,* a novel.

SIDELIGHTS: "Carolyn Marie Rodgers is best known as one of the new black poets to emerge from the Chicago Organization of Black American Culture during the 1960s," writes Jean Davis in a *Dictionary of Literary Biography* essay. Calling her "one of the most sensitive and complex poets to emerge from this movement and struggle with its contradictions," Bettye J. Parker-Smith suggests in Mari Evans's *Black Women Writers (1950-1980): A Critical Evaluation* that Rogers has been "instrumental in helping create, and give a new definition or receptive power to, poetry as a Black art form." Although Rodgers's poetry has always concerned the search for self, it has evolved from a militant, sociological perspective to a more introspective one. Davis indicates that while Rodgers has spent most of her career as a poet in her native Chicago, she has gained national recognition for "her thematic concerns with feminist issues, particularly those affecting the black woman in a changing society." Angelene Jamison asserts in her essay, also in *Black Women Writers (1950-1980),* that like "most of the Black women poets of the last twenty years [who] are casually referred to only as by-products of the New Black Arts Movement," Rodgers still awaits both the attention her work deserves, as well as her "appropriate place in literature."

Rodgers began writing "quasi seriously" as an outlet for the frustrations of her first year at college, as she recalls in an interview with Evans in her *Black Women Writers (1950-1980);* she later participated in the Organization of Black American Culture's Writers Workshop and soon became part of the prolific black arts movement of the 1960s. Rodgers's "theological and philosophical approach to the ills that plague Black people . . . and her attempts to master an appropriate language to comunicate with the masses of Black people" suggest to Parker-Smith that she is "an exemplar of the 'revolutionary poet.'" Rodgers, who considers her work both art as well as polemic, tells Evans that she has no distinctly defined political stance and that she feels literature "functions as a type of catharsis or amen arena" in the lives of people: "I think it speaks not only to the political sensiblity but to the heart, the mind, the spirit, and the soul of every man, woman, and child."

Noting that Rodgers's poetry voices varied concerns, including "revolution, love, Black male-female relationships, religion, and the complexities of Black womanhood," Jamison declares that "through a skilfully uncluttered use of several literary devices, she convincingly reinterprets the love, pain, longings, struggles, victories, the day-to-day routines of Black people from the point of view of the Black woman. Gracefully courageous enough to explore long-hidden truths, about Black women particularly, her poetry shows honesty, warmth, and love for Black people." Commenting about the "intensely personal" aspect of Rodger's poetry, Parker-Smith believes that this autobiographical element helps one to more easily comprehend her work. Rodgers "struggles to affirm her womanliness," but hasn't the strength to "move beyond those obstacles that threaten the full development of Black womanhood," Parker-Smith explains. "For her, there are three major dilemmas: the fear of assimilating the value system of her mother, which interferes with claiming an independent lifestyle of her own; the attempt to define her 'self' by the standards of the social system responsible for creating her own and her mother's condition; and the search for love (a man) that will simultaneously electrify and save her."

Rogers's first volume of poetry, *Paper Soul,* "reflects the duality of an individual struggling to reconcile complex realities, dilemmas, and contradictions," says Davis, who recognizes a thematic shift in her second volume of poetry, *Songs of a Blackbird.* Davis suggests that the former addresses "identity, religion, revolution, and love, or more accurately a woman's need for love," whereas the latter deals with "survival, street life, mother-daughter conflict, and love." Indicating that these poems are increasingly concerned with "the black woman poet as a major theme," Davis states that "questions of identity for the poet remain connected with relationships between black men and women but become more centrally located in the woman's ability to express herself."

While finding Rodgers's poetry from the late 1960s "vivid and forceful," Davis notes that these first two volumes were not unanimously praised: "Nor did the young poet win unqualified acceptance as a significant new voice among black poets." She states, for instance, that Dudley Randall and Haki Madhubuti had "reservations about her language and her rendering of black speech." Davis posits, however, that Rodgers's "use of speech patterns and of lengthened prose-like lines was an attempt at breaking away from the restrictions of conventional forms and modes, and most especially from those considered appropriate for women poets." Inasmuch as "theme and language" were the general hallmarks of the black art movement from this period, Parker-Smith believes that "the use of obscenities and Black speech patterns" was especially courageous for female artists. Although acknowledging a certain inconsistency in the language of her early poetry, Davis believes that "Rodgers nonetheless had an eye for the contradictions of black experience, particularly the revolutionary or militant experience of the 1960s." And, despite their initial objections to her work, says Davis, poets and critics such as Madhubuti, Randall, and Gwendolyn Brooks, "nonetheless . . . recognized her genuine talent and remarked her development."

In Rodgers's *how i got ovah: New and Selected Poems,* written in the mid-1970s, though, she exhibits "a clarity of expression and a respect for well-crafted language," states Davis, who perceives "humor, sincerity, and love" in the autobiographical poems about "black revolution, feminism, religion, God, the black church, and the black family, especially the mother."

Similarly, Hilda Njoki McElroy writes in *Black World:* "It is obvious that Carolyn Rodgers loves her craft and her people. *How I got Ovah* is a result of this love match. It is an important literary contribution containing many aspects of human frailty/achievement, love/hate, positive/negative, funny/sad, beautiful/ugly which makes it deeeeep, very deeeeeep." Suggesting that these poems "reveal Rodgers's transformation from a . . . militant Black woman to a woman intensely concerned with God, traditional values, and her private self," Davis adds that "although her messages often explore social conflict, they usually conclude with a sense of peace, hope, and a desire to search for life's real treasure—inner beauty."

Parker-Smith describes what she refers to as the "two distinct and clear baptisms" that Rodgers's work has experienced: "The first can be viewed as being rough-hewn, folk-spirited, and held 'down at the river' amid water moccasins in the face of a glaring midday sun; the climax of a 'swing-lo-sweet-chariot' revival." Parker-Smith indicates that Rodgers's early work, which is "characterized by a potpourri of themes," exemplifies this period and "demonstrates her impudence, through the use of her wit, obscenities, the argumentation in her love and revolution poems, and the pain and presence of her mother." Parker-Smith points out that Rodgers "questions the relevance of the Vietnam War, declares war on the cities, laments Malcolm X, and criticizes the contradictory life-style of Blacks. And she glances at God." Although this was a time when Rodgers "whipped with a lean switch, often bringing down her wrath with stinging, sharp, and sometimes excruciating pain," Parker-Smith suggests that "the ribald outcry, the incongruity and cynicism that characterize the first period are links in Rodgers' chain of personal judgments—her attempts to come to grips with 'self'—and with the Black Arts Movement as a whole."

"The second baptism takes place just before Carolyn Rodgers is able to shake herself dry from the first river," Parker-Smith continues: "This one can perhaps be classified as a sprinkling and is protected by the blessings of a very fine headcloth. It is more sophisticated. It is cooler; lacks the fire and brimstone of the first period. But it is nonetheless penetrating." During this time, Rodgers moved from Third World Press to a larger commercial publishing house; and, according to Parker-Smith, having broken with the Organization of Black American Culture as well, Rodgers "moved back inside her once lone and timid world." Considering *how i got ovah* and *The Heart as Ever Green: Poems* to exemplify this second phase, Parker-Smith finds that Rodgers closely examines "the revolution, its contradictions, and her relationship to it." Rodgers also "listens to her mother's whispers" and "embraces God," says Parker-Smith, who concludes that "it is impossible to separate the poet's new attitude toward religion from her attitude toward revolution (the one seems to have evoked the other), they have converged to assist her in her continuous search for 'self.'" And although Parker-Smith suggests Rodgers did not take her craft seriously enough in the early poetry, she believes that "a more developed talent" emerges in the second period, revealing "growth and strength and a higher level of clarity, with a new level of sophistication."

Identity and potentiality are central themes in Rodgers's work; and according to Davis, "the evolving feminism" in her poetry is but "a natural extension of her reflections on herself and her world." "I see myself as becoming," Rodgers calls Evans. "I am a has-been, would perhaps, going to be. Underneath, I'm a dot. With no i's." Davis suggests that "de-

termination to grow and to be is the most prevalent idea" in Rodgers's *The Heart As Ever Green*, where "the themes of human dignity, feminism, love, black consciousness, and Christianity are repeated throughout." Rodgers expresses to Evans that "honesty in vision and aspect" are most important to her in her work; and suggesting that the "level of honesty in her work [is] indicative of her own freedom," Jamison believes that "in a variety of idioms ranging from the street to the church, she writes about Black women with a kind of sensitivity and warmth that brings them out of the poems and into our own lives." Jamison adds that "clearly, her artistry brings these women to life, but it is her love for them that gives them their rightful place in literature. The love, the skill, indeed the vision, which she brings to her poetry must certainly help Black women rediscover and better understand themselves."

"It is impossible to assess the actual merit of Carolyn Rodgers' achievements at this point," says Parker-Smith. "And it is difficult to see where she will go from here. She has changed from a rebel to a religious loyalist, but a religious loyalist of a peculiarly different state was present from the start. . . . Her frantic search for love, the constant battle with her mother, the ambiguity about religion, are factors that run wild in her soul." Davis remarks that Rodgers has witnessed changes both in herself and her work: "In the beginning of her career, she reveals, 'I was just a writer out here just writing. Then I went to an orientation of Black (Negro) work and then I wrote with a message, a sociological orientation. Actually, I've come full circle to a certain extent. I don't write the same message.'" Although survival represents a dominant theme in her stories and poetry, Davis adds that Rodgers "interweaves the idea of adaptability and conveys the concomitant message of life's ever-changing avenues for black people whom she sees as her special audience." Davis relates Rodgers's statement about her writing being "for whoever wants to read it . . . one poem doesn't do that. But I try to put as many as I can in a book. A poem for somebody young, religious people, the church people. Just people. Specifically, Black people. I would like for them to like me." Rodgers acknowledges to Evans that the direction of her writing has "indeed" changed in the last decade: "My focus is on life, love, eternity, pain, and joy. These matters are cared about by Brown people, aren't they?"

BIOGRAPHICAL/CRITICAL SOURCES:

BOOK

Dictionary of Literary Biography, Volume 41: *Afro-American Poets since 1955*, Gale, 1985.
Evans, Mari, editor, *Black Women Writers (1950-1980): A Critical Evaluation*, Doubleday-Anchor, 1984.

PERIODICALS

Black Scholar, March, 1981.
Black World, August, 1970, February, 1976.
Chicago Tribune, November 19, 1978.
Negro Digest, September, 1968.
Washington Post Book World, May 18, 1975.

—*Sketch by Sharon Malinowski*

*   *   *

ROLLINS, Charlemae
See ROLLINS, Charlemae Hill

ROLLINS, Charlemae H.
  See ROLLINS, Charlemae Hill

*   *   *

ROLLINS, Charlemae Hill   1897-1979
  (Charlemae Rollins, Charlemae H. Rollins)

PERSONAL: Born June 20, 1897, in Yazoo City, Miss.; died February 3, 1979; daughter of Allen G. and Birdie (Tucker) Hill; married Joseph Walter Rollins, April 8, 1918; children: Joseph Walter, Jr. *Education:* Graduated from Western University, 1915; attended Columbia University, 1932, and University of Chicago, 1934-36. *Religion:* African Methodist-Episcopal.

ADDRESSES: Home—500 East 33rd St., Chicago, Ill. 60616.

CAREER: Chicago Public Library, Chicago, Ill., librarian, 1927-63, children's librarian at George C. Hall Branch, 1932-63. Roosevelt University, Chicago, instructor in children's literature, 1949-60; instructor at Fisk University, 1950, and Morgan State College, 1953-54.

MEMBER: American Library Association (member of Newbery-Caldecott award committee, 1949-50; president, children's services division, 1957-58), National Association for the Advancement of Colored People, National Council of Teachers of English, Illinois Library Association (chairman, children's section, 1954-55), Phi Delta Kappa (honorary).

AWARDS, HONORS: American Brotherhood Award from the National Conference of Christians and Jews, 1952; Library Letter Award from the American Library Association, 1953; Grolier Society Award, 1955; woman of the year of Zeta Phi Beta, 1956; Good American Award of the Chicago Committee of One Hundred, 1962; Negro Centennial Awards, 1963; Children's Reading Round Table Award, 1963; Constance Lindsay Skinner Award from the Women's National Book Association, 1970; Coretta Scott King Award, 1971.

WRITINGS:

(Editor) *We Build Together: A Reader's Guide to Negro Life and Literature for Elementary and High School Use,* National Council of Teachers of English, 1941, 3rd edition, 1967.
The Magic World of Books, Science Research Associates, 1954.
(Editor) *Call of Adventure,* Crowell Collier, 1962.
(Compiler) *Christmas Gif': An Anthology of Christmas Poems, Songs, and Stories, Written by and About Negroes* (juvenile), Follett, 1963.
They Showed the Way: Forty American Negro Leaders (juvenile), Crowell, 1964.
Famous American Negro Poets (juvenile), Dodd, 1965.
Great Negro Poets for Children, Dodd, 1965.
Famous Negro Entertainers of Stage, Screen, and TV (juvenile), Dodd, 1967.
Black Troubadour: Langston Hughes (juvenile), Rand McNally, 1970.

Contributor to *American Childhood, Illinois Libraries, Junior Libraries,* and other journals. Member of editorial board of *The World Book Encyclopedia* and of *American Educator.*

BIOGRAPHICAL/CRITICAL SOURCES:

PERIODICALS

New York Times Book Review, May 9, 1965.

ROTIMI, E. G. O.
  See ROTIMI, (Emmanuel Gladstone) Ola(wale)

*   *   *

ROTIMI, (Emmanuel Gladstone) Ola(wale)   1938(?)-
  (E. G. O. Rotimi, Olawale Rotimi)

PERSONAL: Born c. 1938 in Sapele, Nigeria; son of Samuel Enitan and Dorcas Oruene (Addo) Rotimi; married Hazel Mae Gaudreau in 1965; children: Enitan, Oruene, Biodun Ola, Jr., Bankole. *Education:* Boston University, B.F.A., 1963; Yale University, M.F.A., 1966.

ADDRESSES: Home—Lagos, Nigeria. *Office*—Department of Creative Arts, University of Port Harcourt, P.M.B. 5323, Port Harcourt, Rivers State, Nigeria.

CAREER: University of Ife, Ife, Oyo State, Nigeria, research fellow, 1966-75, acting head of Department of Dramatic Arts, 1975-77; University of Port Harcourt, Port Harcourt, Rivers State, Nigeria, head of Department of Creative Arts and arts director, 1977—; playwright. Director of plays, including his own "The Gods Are Not to Blame," 1968, "The Prodigal," 1969, and "Holding Talks," 1970, Adegoke Durojaiye's "Gbe-Ku-de," 1969, and Aime Cesaire's "La Tragedie d'Henri Christophe," 1971.

MEMBER: African Writers Association, Association of Nigerian Authors, Society of Nigerian Theatre Artists.

AWARDS, HONORS: "Our Husband Has Gone Mad Again" was selected by Yale University as the major play of the year, 1966; first prize in international playwriting competition sponsored by *African Arts* magazine, 1969, for "The Gods Are Not to Blame"; first prize in Oxford University Press playwriting competition, 1969, for "Our Husband Has Gone Mad Again"; first prize at fourth Nigerian National Festival of the Arts, 1974, for creation and direction of dance-drama "And Man Brought the First Woman."

WRITINGS:

PLAYS

"To Stir the God of Iron" (three-act), first produced in Boston at Boston University Drama School, 1963.
Our Husband Has Gone Mad Again: A Comedy (three-act), first produced in New Haven, Conn., at Yale University Drama School, 1966, Oxford University Press, 1976.
The Gods Are Not to Blame (three-act; based on Sophocles' *Oedipus Rex*), first produced in Ife, Nigeria, at Ori Olokun Cultural Centre of the Institute of African Studies, University of Ife, 1968, Oxford University Press, 1971.
Kurunmi: An Historical Tragedy (three-act), first produced in Ife at second Ife Festival of the Arts, 1969, Oxford University Press, 1971.
"The Prodigal" (dance-drama), first produced in Ife at second Ife Festival of the Arts, 1969.
Holding Talks: An Absurdist Drama, first produced at the University of Ife, 1970, Oxford University Press, 1977.
Ovonramwen Nogbaisi: An Historical Tragedy in English (three-act), first produced in Ife at fourth Ife Festival of the Arts, 1971, Oxford University Press and Ethiope Publishing, 1977.
If, first produced at the University of Port Harcourt, 1979, Heinemann Educational Books, 1983.

"Hopes of the Living Dead," first produced at the University of Port Harcourt, 1984.

"Everyone His/Her Own Problem," first broadcast on British Broadcasting Corporation (BBC) African Theatre, London, 1987.

OTHER

(Contributor) Bruce King, editor, *Introduction to Nigerian Literature,* Evans Publications (London), 1971.

(Contributor) S. O. Biobaku, editor, *The Living Culture of Nigeria,* Thomas Nelson, 1976.

WORK IN PROGRESS: A Dictionary of Nigerian Pidgin English; In Praise of Poverty, a collection of original short stories on the psycho-emotional resilience of the poor in an uncaring society.

SIDELIGHTS: One of the most successful Nigerian playwrights writing in English, Ola Rotimi effectively conveys to both Nigerian and foreign audiences the culture and concerns of the African peoples. He specifically addresses the historical and political problems of Nigeria in a bold, sweeping style that, critics say, engrosses audiences in his productions.

Set in Nigeria, Rotimi's first play, "To Stir the God of Iron," was performed in 1963 by the Afro-American Dramatic Society of Boston University while Rotimi was a student there. Rotimi's next play, "Our Husband Has Gone Mad Again"—a politico-domestic comedy—was performed in 1966 at Yale University, where it was named the major play of the year.

After earning his master's of fine arts degree in 1966 from Yale University, Rotimi returned to Nigeria to take up a research fellowship at the University of Ife. While there he composed his highly successful "The Gods Are Not to Blame," based on Greek philosopher Sophocles' "Oedipus Rex," which he directed first at the Ori Olokun Cultural Centre in Ife in 1968 and later at London's Drum Arts Centre in 1978. "The Gods Are Not to Blame" is considered remarkable in its use of broken verse and powerful African imagery.

At the second Ife Festival of the Arts in 1969, Rotimi presented "Kurunmi" and "The Prodigal." "Kurunmi," considered one of his best works, is an epic play about the nineteenth-century Ijaiye War and a biting commentary on the Nigerian Civil War. In "Holding Talks," a 1970 absurdist drama, Rotimi exposes the irrationality of man's obsession with "talking" in situations that clearly demand action. "Ovonramwen Nogbaisi," produced in 1971 at the fourth Ife Festival of the Arts, indicts British imperialism for its role in the downfall of the Benin Empire, a highly organized kingdom in West Africa overtaken by the British in 1897. Provoked by Nigeria's socio-political inequities, Rotimi composed "If," a 1979 play that concerns the predicament of ordinary contemporary Nigerians trying to cope with adverse social and political circumstances following the war. "Hopes of the Living Dead," which premiered in 1984 to widespread critical acclaim and has since been revived twice, uses the historic rebellion of lepers against the British colonial administration in Nigeria at the turn of the century as a metaphor to articulate the striving and aspirations of the ordinary peoples of present-day Nigeria. Rotimi's radio play, "Everyone His/Her Own Problem," broadcast over the British Broadcasting Corporation's overseas service in 1987, recounts the universal preoccupation of man grappling with personal problems of one kind or another.

Rotimi commented: "A play—for that matter, any work of art—must aim at transcending the purlieus of sheer aesthetics.

Ultimate fulfillment comes to the artist when he realizes his work is being seriously discussed, that references or lessons are being drawn, that interpretations are being argued over, that new meanings are being adduced and rationalized, that topical analogies are being discovered. This, to my mind, is the enduring value, the consummation of the artistic expression. My creative passion as a playwright is for an accessible people's theatre informed by that which also impels it—namely, the spasms of the socio-political tendons of Africa yesterday, today, and tomorrow. As a director, my pictorial trademark is a preference for a convoluting concourse of juxtaposed, variegated happenings: a conjuration of the rhythm and agitations of existence in these (African) parts of our universe."

BIOGRAPHICAL/CRITICAL SOURCES:

BOOKS

Jones, Eldred, editor, *African Literature Today,* Heinemann Educational Books, 1982.

Ogungbesan, Kola, editor, *New West African Literature,* Heinemann Educational Books, 1979.

PERIODICALS

Bulletin of Black Theatre, winter, 1972.

* * *

ROTIMI, Olawale
  See ROTIMI, (Emmanuel Gladstone) Ola(wale)

* * *

ROUMAIN, Jacques (Jean Baptiste) 1907-1944

PERSONAL: Born June 4, 1907, in Port-au-Prince, Haiti; died of a heart attack, August 18, 1944, in Port-au-Prince, Haiti; married; children: one son. *Education:* Attended schools in Haiti, Switzerland, Germany, Spain, Belgium, France, and the United States, including University of Paris, Musee de l'Homme, Paris, c. 1938, and Columbia University, c. 1939.

CAREER: Political leader, ethnologist, and writer. Co-founder of journals *La Trouee: Revue d'interet general* and *La Revue indigene: Les Arts et la vie,* 1927-28; co-founder and president of Ligue de la jeunesse patriote haitien; chief of Haitian Department of Interior, beginning in 1930; founder of Haitian Communist Party, 1934; journalist in Cuba, c. 1940; co-founder of Bureau d'Ethnologie, Haiti, 1941; Haitian charge d'affaires to Mexico, beginning in 1942.

WRITINGS:

La Proie et l'ombre (short stories; title means "The Prey and the Darkness"; contains "La Veste," "Fragment d'une confession," "Preface a la vie d'un bureaucrate," and "Propos sans suite"), preface by Antonio Vieux, Editions La Press, 1930, reprinted, Ateliers Fardin, 1977.

Les Fantoches (novel; title means "The Puppets"), Imprimerie de l'Etat, 1931.

La Montagne ensorcelee (novel; title means "The Enchanted Mountain"), preface by Jean Price-Mars, Imprimerie E. Chassaing, 1931, reprinted, Editions Fardin, 1976.

Gouveneurs de la rosee (novel), Imprimerie de l'Etat, 1944; translation by Langston Hughes and Mercer Cook published as *Masters of the Dew,* Reynal & Hitchcock, 1947, reprinted with introduction by J. Michael Dash, Heinemann Educational, 1978, 2nd edition, introduction by Cook, Collier Books, 1971.

Bois d'ebene (poems), Imprimerie Henri Deschamps, 1945; translation by Sidney Shapiro published as *Ebony Wood* (includes French text; contains "Ebony Wood," "Love and Death," "New Negro Sermon," and "Dirty Negroes"), Interworld Press, 1972.

Oeuvres choisies (title means "Selected Works"), preface by Jacques-Stephen Alexis, study by Eugenie Galperina, Editions du Progress (Moscow), 1964.

La Montagne ensorcelee (collection; contains *La Proie et l'ombre*, *La Montagne ensorcelee*, essay "Griefs de l'homme noir," and poems), preface by Jacques-Stephen Alexis, Editeurs Francais Reunis, 1972.

Also author of ethnological monographs. Poems represented in anthologies, including *An Anthology of Contemporary Latin-American Poetry*, edited by Dudley Fitts, New Directions, 1942; *The Poetry of the Negro, 1746-1949*, edited by Langston Hughes and Arna Bontemps, Doubleday, 1949; and *Black Poets in French*, edited by Marie Collins, Scribner, 1972. Contributor of essays, articles, and fiction to periodicals, including *Bulletin du Bureau d'Ethnologie*, *Haiti-Journal*, *Le Nouvelliste*, *Le Petit Impartial*, *La Press*, *La Revue indigene*, and *La Trouee*.

SIDELIGHTS: During the late 1920s and 1930s Jacques Roumain was the leader of young Haitian intellectuals seeking an end to America's military occupation of Haiti. Riding a wave of nationalistic fervor, the youths demanded a new aesthetic as well—one that stirred national pride by focusing on native Haitian culture. Responding with writings about the intricacies of class, politics, and religion in his native land, Roumain also explored Haiti's African roots and the similar pasts of blacks in other countries of the Caribbean, Latin America, and the United States. Disenchantment, however, with the ineffectual nationalist government that replaced U.S. occupational forces —and with the myopic excesses of Africanists—eventually turned the writer to Marxism, where color and class are viewed not in moral terms, but as resultant economic phenomena. Roumain came "to consider the Haitian situation in non-parochial terms . . . in the context of an international system of exploitation," wrote J. Michael Dash in his *Literature and Ideology in Haiti, 1915-1961*, pointing out the "shift from the exclusively personal or national concerns of [Roumain's] early work to the broader vision of his last works." Discussing *Masters of the Dew*, the writer's final and most acclaimed piece, *Renaissance of Haitian Poetry* author Naomi M. Garret made a similar comment: "Here, [Roumain] changes his perspective and alters the aim of his art. A Comitern inspired view of the uniting of the working classes of all nations into a revolutionary international force supersedes his desire for the joining together of the forces of all Haitians into a power for the progress of his country and his race." And in *Anthologie negro-africaine* editor Lilyan Kesteloot observed, "What constitutes Roumain's greatness . . . is precisely the fact that he was able to give breadth to his humanism."

Son of a wealthy mulatto landowner (and grandson of Haitian president Tancrede Auguste), Roumain received much of his education abroad. Familiar with the great literatures of Europe and the Americas and with the art and philosophy of the Near East (as well as engineering and agronomy), the cosmopolite returned to Haiti in 1927, drawn by pro-nationalism activities. With other young Haitian intellectuals he founded the journals *La Trouee* and *La Revue indigene*, designed to inform and rouse the Haitian populace; the latter proved most successful, publishing the poetry and fiction of Haitian contributors. Roumain also wrote for the leftist newspaper *Le Petit Impartial*

and, with George Petit, founded the Ligue de la jeunesse patriote haitien, a coalition of youths from Haiti's fractured social strata. An article in *La Petit Impartial* criticizing the French clergy led to a seven-month imprisonment for the pair; it was to be the first of several political arrests for Roumain during his lifetime.

Already recognized as a nationalist leader by the age of twenty-three, Roumain was among Haitian representatives who determined that country's new provisional president at a U.S.-Haitian conference in 1930. President Eugene Roy appointed Roumain head of the Department of the Interior, a post he held again under Haiti's first elected president, Stenio Vincent. By mid-decade, however, the writer was unhappy with the nationalist government's inability to improve the economic and social conditions besetting the peasants and laborers with whom he so strongly sympathized. Gleaning a solution in the teachings of Marx and Engels, Roumain founded the Haitian Communist Party in 1934, and leftist political activities—real and imagined—resulted in charges of conspiracy and a three-year prison sentence.

Because communism was banned in Haiti in 1936, Roumain fled to Europe with his wife and child following release from prison. During a five-year exile he wrote articles and fiction for European journals; for a short time he worked as a journalist in Cuba. Roumain also pursued his keen interest in ethnology, studying at Paris's Musee de l'Homme and attending anthropology classes at Columbia University in New York City. When a new Haitian government offered amnesty to political exiles the writer returned to his homeland, establishing the Bureau d'Ethnologie for the study and preservation of Haiti's indigenous culture. Appointed charge d'affaires to Mexico in 1942 ("a kind of honorary banishment that would at least keep him out of prison and provide leisure for writing," explained Langston Hughes and Mercer Cook in the introduction to their translation of *Masters of the Dew*), Roumain died two years later of a heart attack. While the quantity of his writings was limited by political activities, incarceration, and exile, the impact of his life and works was profound in his native country. *Saturday Review of Literature* critic Linton Wells related, "Jacques Roumain['s] . . . sympathy for the underdog and . . . death . . . at thirty-eight, after years of imprisonment and exile, are said to have inspired the revolution which succeeded in overthrowing the dictatorial Lescot regime."

Roumain began to write poetry in his student days, initially exhibiting the influence of the French romantics, using traditional themes, forms, and imagery. Elements of nature reflected the human psyche; for Roumain this internal landscape was often melancholic—the speaker/poet unable to apprehend the meaning of existence, despairing over futile attempts to know and shape his destiny. The writer's early prose expressed similar themes and motifs, with the short story collection *La Proie et l'ombre* and novel *Les Fantoches* showing the aimlessness and despair that paralyzed many of his generation. The works feature young bourgeois intellectuals haunted by the pettiness and monotony of existence who turn to sordid diversions in the shadows of Port-au-Prince after dark. "The hero now, in the early prose, becomes a spokesman for a kind of Lost Generation, unable to find fulfillment in the old values and unable to find any new ones, and so existing in a vacuum," noted Carolyn Fowler in her Roumain literary biography *A Knot in the Thread*. "It is not the vacuum which ultimately destroys these heroes, but their lucidity about their condition."

Fowler also commented that in *La Proie et l'ombre*, published in 1930, "the storyteller implicit in the novelist vies still with the impressionmaker implicit in the poet." A year later in *Les Fantoches*, however, "the storyteller comes more clearly into his own, creating more fully developed characters, who move in a better delineated environment and who exteriorize their feelings to a much greater extent through conversation." Still, this tale of three young men—their attempts at love, public success, meaningful existence—"is not yet a fully developed novel," decided Fowler, "due to the sparseness of plot." She added that Roumain's contemporaries nevertheless embraced his formative prose, finding in it "a kind of solace . . . an esthetization of an inner life which they could recognize as their own." Literary critic Edmund Wilson, unimpressed by Roumain's later peasant novels, expressed admiration for *Les Fantoches* in his *Red, Black, Blond and Olive: Studies in Four Civilizations:* "It is quite evident that Jacques Roumain did not know the black peasants well. But he did know the Mulatto bourgeoisie, to which he himself belonged, and . . . *Les Fantoches,* . . . which deals with the elite of Port-au-Prince, throws so much light on its subject that one regrets it should not have been projected on a more extensive scale."

A rural counterpoint to Roumain's urban studies, *La Montagne ensorcelee* also explores the tension between passivity and action, this time in a Haitian peasant community. Relating how village inhabitants respond to a series of calamities with voodoocraft, the novel neither condemns nor sensationalizes the traditional practice; the author sees the religion as an important part of Haitian culture, reflecting and reinforcing feelings of powerlessness springing from restrictive attitudes about color and class. Concerned with indigenous cultural detail, *La Montagne ensorcelee* evokes the idioms of Haiti, with subtle shifts from French to Creole to patois, or slang. Of particular significance to Haitian letters as that country's first peasant novel, it is the work of a more assured storyteller. "Jacques Roumain already seems in full possession of his artistic abilities," wrote Roger Gaillard, discussing *La Montagne ensorcelee* in *L'Univers romanesque de Jacques Roumain.* "What strikes one first in this tale is its extraordinary precision: a simple story, related without digressions, with a deliberate intention to be brief; a clear, spare language that only approaches lyricism by accident; the avoidance of any complicity with negative characters in the story or pity for the victims. Let me say the word that comes to my mind as a description of his novel—classical. Classical because of the clarity of its construction; classical because of the inflexible detachment that the author imposes upon himself; classical because of the moderation of its style."

Roumain sought to evoke Haitian idioms in his later poetry as well, looking to other black poets, like America's Langston Hughes, for ways to transform indigenous musical forms and folk material into verse. Thematic content, however, was the primary focus of these later poems; in the collection *Ebony Wood,* produced while Roumain was in exile and published after his death, the poet angrily speaks for the world's downtrodden (but particularly for Africa's displaced), decrying slavery, exile, forced labor, lynching, segregation, and colonial oppression. Written in free verse, "the poems are unified by their utopian impulse," according to Dash, "and the Marxist imprecations they convey."

Dash further remarked that during the last four years of Roumain's life the writer forsook "the early iconoclasm" and pronouncements for "idealistic revolt," becoming "more capable of compromise." *Masters of the Dew*—considered the best work of fiction to come out of Haiti—was written during that time; unlike earlier Roumain protagonists incapable of action, its hero, Manuel, rallies feuding villagers to work together and irrigate their drought-stricken land. Although eventually killed by a jealous rival, the leader refuses to name the murderer as he dies, safeguarding the peasants' fledgling unity. Touching on a number of themes important to Roumain (nationalism, communism, romantic love, effective leadership, agricultural reform, and true friendship), *Masters of the Dew* is admired for its masterful synthesis of indigenous Haitian language, music, and folklore. "The novel is a beautiful, exact and tender rendering of Haitian life, of the African heritage, of the simple, impulsive, gravely formal folk, of the poetry and homely bite of their speech, of Congo dances, tropical luxuriance, the love of a land and its people," stated B. D. Wolfe in a critique for the *New York Herald Tribune Weekly Review.*

While manifestly a communist novel ("You have the struggle against the bourgeoisie, the summons of the exploited to class solidarity, the martyr who dies for the cause," enumerated Wilson), *Masters of the Dew* transcends its political parameters. Writing in *L'Esprit createur,* Beverly Ormerod remarked that "strong elements of myth and ritual . . . underpin the novel. . . . Earth and *coumbite,* dew and water, dust and drought are the recurrent symbols through which the hero's adventure is invested with a legendary quality." Allusions to Manuel as a Christ-figure are frequent, and to pagan vegetation gods Tammuz, Attis, and Adonis. Roumain scholar Jacques-Stephen Alexis called such writing "symbolic realism." "In theme and outline 'Masters of the Dew' is a fairly conventional proletarian novel; in style, imagination, observed detail it is a work of unusual freshness and beauty," judged R. G. Davis in the *New York Times.* Calling the work "charming, vivid, and original," a *New Yorker* critic concurred that it is "a routine, almost commonplace story, . . . but one that is so freshly told and has so highly colored a background that it achieves the glowing effect of a tropical blossom."

BIOGRAPHICAL/CRITICAL SOURCES:

BOOKS

Cobb, Martha, *Harlem, Haiti, and Havana: A Comparative Critical Study of Langston Hughes, Jacques Roumain, Nicolas Guillen,* Three Continents Press, 1979.

Cook, Mercer, editor, *An Introduction to Haiti,* Pan American Union (Washington, D.C.), 1951.

Coulthard, George Robert, *Race and Colour in Caribbean Literature,* Oxford University Press, 1962.

Dash, J. Michael, *Literature and Ideology in Haiti, 1915-1961,* Barnes & Noble, 1981.

Fisher, Dexter, and Robert B. Stepto, editors, *Afro-American Literature: The Reconstruction of Instruction,* Modern Language Association of America, 1979.

Fowler, Carolyn, *A Knot in the Thread: The Life and Work of Jacques Roumain,* Howard University Press, 1980.

Galliard, Roger, *L'Univers romanesque de Jacques Roumain,* Henri Deschamps (Port-au-Prince, Haiti), 1965.

Garret, Naomi M., *The Renaissance of Haitian Poetry,* 1954, reprinted, Presence Africaine, 1963.

Janheinz, Jan, *Neo-African Literature,* translation by Oliver Coburn and Ursula Lehrburger, Grove, 1968.

Kesteloot, Lilyan, editor, *Anthologie negro-africaine,* Gerard (Verviers, Belgium), 1967.

Twentieth-Century Literary Criticism, Volume 19, Gale, 1986.

Wilson, Edmund, *Red, Black, Blond, and Olive: Studies in Four Civilizations, Zuni, Haiti, Soviet Russia, Israel,* Oxford University Press, 1956.

PERIODICALS

African Literature Today, number 9, 1978.
Black Images, spring, 1973.
College Language Association Journal, September, 1974, December, 1974.
Europe, January, 1971.
French Review, May, 1946.
Journal of Negro History, April, 1947.
Left Review, October, 1937.
L'Esprit Createur, summer, 1977.
Massachusetts Review, winter, 1977.
New Masses, May 22, 1945.
New Republic, March 27, 1937.
New Yorker, June 28, 1947.
New York Herald Tribune Weekly Review, August 3, 1947.
New York Times, June 15, 1947.
Opportunity, May, 1935.
Phylon, Volume XVII, number 3, 1956.
Saturday Review of Literature, July 5, 1947.
Virginia Quarterly Review, spring, 1973.

—Sketch by Nancy Pear

* * *

ROWAN, Carl Thomas 1925-

PERSONAL: Born August 11, 1925, in Ravenscroft, Tenn.; son of Thomas David (a lumber stacker) and Johnnie (Bradford) Rowan; married Vivien Louise Murphy, August 2, 1950; children: Barbara, Carl Thomas, Jeffrey. *Education:* Attended Tennessee State University, 1942-43, and Washburn University, 1943-44; Oberlin College, A.B., 1947; University of Minnesota, M.A., 1948.

ADDRESSES: Home—3116 Fessenden St. N.W., Washington, D.C. 20008. *Office*—1220 19th St. N.W., Washington, D.C. 20036.

CAREER: Minneapolis Tribune, Minneapolis, Minn., copywriter, 1948-50, staff writer, 1950-61; U.S. Department of State, Washington, D.C., deputy assistant secretary for public affairs, 1961-63; U.S. ambassador to Finland, based in Helsinki, 1963-64; director of United States Information Agency (USIA), 1964-65; *Chicago Sun-Times* (formerly *Chicago Daily News*), Chicago, Ill., columnist for Field Newspaper Syndicate (formerly Publishers Hall Syndicate), 1965—. National affairs commentator on "The Rowan Report," heard nationally on radio five days a week; political commentator for radio and television stations of Post-Newsweek Broadcasting Company; regular panelist on "Agronsky & Co.," a nationally syndicated public affairs television show; frequent panelist on "Meet the Press." Lecturer. Former member of U.S. delegation to the United Nations. *Military service:* Served in the U.S. Navy.

AWARDS, HONORS: Sidney Hillman Award for best newspaper reporting, 1952; Sigma Delta Chi Awards, 1953, for coverage of school desegregation cases before the U.S. Supreme Court, 1954, for foreign correspondence from India, and 1955, for coverage of the conference in Bandung, Indonesia; distinguished achievement award from regents of University of Minnesota, 1961; communications award in human relations from Anti-Defamation League of B'nai B'rith, 1964; Contributions to American Democracy Award from Roosevelt University, 1964; Liberty Bell Award from Howard University, 1965; named Washington journalist of the year by Capital Press Club, 1978; American Black Achievement Award from

Ebony magazine, 1978, for contributions to journalism and public communication. Recipient of twenty-nine honorary degrees from colleges and universities, including Oberlin College, Notre Dame University, Howard University, University of Massachusetts, Temple University, Atlanta University, and Clark University.

WRITINGS:

South of Freedom, Knopf, 1952.
The Pitiful and the Proud, Random House, 1956.
Go South to Sorrow, Random House, 1957.
Wait Till Next Year: The Life Story of Jackie Robinson, Random House, 1960.
Just Between Us Blacks, Random House, 1974.
Race War in Rhodesia, PTV Publications, 1978

Editor of *Reader's Digest*.

SIDELIGHTS: The Washington Post has called Carl Thomas Rowan "the most visible black journalist in the country." The author of a syndicated column appearing three-times weekly nationwide, as well as a frequent commentator on public affairs radio and television programs, Rowan is well known for his coverage of civil rights conflicts in the United States. His other accomplishments have included government appointments in the Kennedy and Johnson administrations.

BIOGRAPHICAL/CRITICAL SOURCES:

BOOKS

Contemporary Issues Criticism, Volume I, Gale, 1982.

PERIODICALS

Washington Post, October 28, 1978.

* * *

RUSTIN, Bayard 1910(?)-1987

PERSONAL: Born March 17, 1910(?) (some sources list as 1912), in West Chester, Pa.; died August 24, 1987, of a heart attack, in New York City; son of Janifer (a caterer) and Julia (a social worker; maiden name, Davis) Rustin. *Education:* Attended Wilberforce University, 1930-31, Cheyney State Normal School (now Cheyney State College), 1931-33, and City College (now City College of the City University of New York), 1933-35. *Politics:* Socialist. *Religion:* Society of Friends (Quaker).

CAREER: Organizer, Young Communist League, 1936-41; race relations director, Fellowship of Reconciliation, 1941-53; jailed as conscientious objector, 1943-45; executive secretary, War Resisters' League, 1953-64; special assistant to Martin Luther King, Jr., 1955-60; A. Philip Randolph Institute, New York, N.Y., president, 1966-79, chairman, 1979-87. Field secretary and co-founder, Congress for Racial Equality, 1941. Chairman of Leadership Conference on Civil Rights and Recruitment and Training Program; co-chairman, Social Democrats of the U.S.A.; chairman of executive committee, Freedom House. Ratner Lecturer, Columbia University, 1974. Founder, Organization for Black Americans to Support Israel, 1975. Member of boards of directors, Notre Dame University, Metropolitan Applied Research Center, and League for Industrial Democracy. International vice-president, International Rescue Committee.

AWARDS, HONORS: Man of the Year Award, National Association for the Advancement of Colored People (NAACP),

Pittsburgh branch, 1965; Eleanor Roosevelt Award, Trade Union Leadership Council, 1966; Liberty Bell Award, Howard University Law School, 1967; LL.D. from New School for Social Research, 1968, and Brown University, 1972; Litt.D. from Montclair State College, 1968; John Dewey Award, United Federation of Teachers, 1968; Family of Man Award, National Council of Churches, 1969; John F. Kennedy Award, National Council of Jewish Women, 1971; Lyndon Johnson Award, Urban League, 1974; Murray Green Award, American Federation of Labor-Congress of Industrial Organizations (AFL-CIO), 1980; Stephen Wise Award, Jewish Committee, 1981; John La Farge Memorial Award, Catholic Interracial Council of New York, 1981; Defender of Jerusalem Award, Jabotinsky Foundation, 1987; also received honorary degrees from Columbia University, Clark College, Harvard University, New York University, and Yale University.

WRITINGS:

Down the Line: The Collected Writings of Bayard Rustin, Quadrangle, 1971.
Strategies for Freedom: The Changing Patterns of Black Protest, Columbia University Press, 1976.

Also author of pamphlets and published speeches. Contributor to periodicals. Editor, *Liberation* (magazine).

SIDELIGHTS: The late Bayard Rustin enjoyed a long and distinguished career as a civil rights activist. Beginning in the 1930s as an organizer for the American Communist Party's youth group, continuing as head of the pacifist War Resisters' League and as special assistant to Dr. Martin Luther King, Jr., Rustin ended his career by serving as president and chairman of the A. Philip Randolph Institute, an organization promoting civil rights and a radical restructuring of the nation's economic and social life. Influenced by his Quaker upbringing and the radical politics of the 1930s, Rustin called for a peaceful, nonviolent alteration of society. Eric Pace of the *New York Times* quoted Rustin listing the principles behind his career: "1. nonviolent tactics; 2. constitutional means; 3. democratic procedures; 4. respect for human personality; 5. a belief that all people are one." J. Y. Smith of the *Washington Post* characterized Rustin as "one of the great theorists and practitioners of the civil rights movement."

Rustin began his career as an organizer for the Young Communist League, an organization he later said he joined because it seemed to be the only one dedicated to civil rights. His work organizing protest marches and demonstrations for the league during the 1930s served him well in later years with the civil rights protests of the 1960s. Rustin left the Young Communist League in 1941 when he decided that the group's politics were too intolerant. He was, however, to remain a non-Communist socialist for the rest of his life. After leaving the group, Rustin was a co-founder of the Congress for Racial Equality, one of the early civil rights organizations, and worked with the Fellowship of Reconciliation, a Quaker antiwar organization.

During the Second World War, Rustin was imprisoned as a conscientious objector. Following a twenty-eight-month stint in a federal penitentiary, he was released at war's end. He was active during the late 1940s in some of the first freedom rides in the South and was arrested in North Carolina in 1947 for participating in an antisegregation protest. He spent twenty-two days on a chain gang for the offense. His subsequent account of his experience, written for a Baltimore newspaper and reprinted nationwide, resulted two years later in the abolition of chain gangs in North Carolina.

Rustin's strong pacifism led in 1953 to his appointment as executive secretary of the War Resisters' League, one of the country's largest pacifist organizations. In this role he was instrumental in planning a series of antinuclear demonstrations in England and North Africa, including the first annual protest rally of the Campaign for Nuclear Disarmament. Rustin also played a key role in a San Francisco-to-Moscow Peace Walk in the late 1950s.

While actively engaged in pacifist actions during the late 1950s and early 1960s, Rustin also assisted civil rights activists in their growing struggle. In 1955 he helped Dr. Martin Luther King, Jr. organize a bus boycott in Montgomery, Alabama, and went on to serve as a special assistant to King. Rustin also organized civil rights demonstrations at both the Democratic and Republican conventions in 1960, hoping to pressure the two major parties into support for the movement's aims. In 1963 he played a pivotal role in organizing the massive March on Washington for Jobs and Freedom, a civil rights protest drawing some 250,000 demonstrators to the nation's capital. It was, Jacqueline Trescott recounted in the *Washington Post,* "the single largest civil rights demonstration America has ever seen." It was during the protest that King delivered his famous "I Have a Dream" speech. The London *Times* noted that the March on Washington is "regarded by historians of the civil rights movement as the watershed of its campaign in the 1960s, and the chief influence on the civil rights bills of 1964 and 1965."

Rustin was also a leader of other important civil rights actions. In 1964, he organized a boycott of the New York City school system in protest of the school board's reluctance to integrate classrooms. Over 400,000 students participated in the boycott. In 1968, he organized the Poor People's Campaign, which brought thousands of poor blacks and whites to Washington to set up a makeshift "Resurrection City" on the grounds of the Lincoln Memorial. When rioting broke out in the Harlem ghetto, Rustin walked the city streets in an effort to persuade people to stop the fighting, an effort that earned him the label "Uncle Tom" from some blacks. "I'm prepared," Rustin explained to the *New York Herald Tribune,* "to be a Tom if it's the only way I can save women and children from being shot down in the street."

His resistance to black political violence estranged him from more radical elements of the civil rights movement. And Rustin argued against some of the more radical demands of other black activists as well. When black students demanded that colleges adopt black studies programs, Rustin denounced the idea as "stupid." He called for black history to be taught as an integral part of American history, not as a separate discipline. In the 1970s Rustin came out against racial quotas in employment and education. "I have not run into a single young black who wants something because he is black," Smith quoted Rustin explaining. "He wants to pass the test and meet the standards." Rustin's later support for Jewish issues, his work with refugees from Southeast Asia, and his continued involvement with trade unions spurred criticism from some black leaders who felt Rustin had distanced himself from the civil rights struggle. But Rustin dismissed the criticism. "I can't call on other people continuously to help me and mine," Rustin explained to Trescott, "unless I give indication that I am willing to help other people in trouble."

Rustin's long career on behalf of those in trouble earned him accolades from many quarters. Upon his death in 1987, the *Chicago Tribune* claimed that "Rustin was committed to the causes in which he believed, but he also followed the path of his reason wherever it led. He did not let his allegiance to the labor movement blind him to the virtues of free trade. He did not let his love for peace blind him to the dangers of expansion-minded dictators. He did not let his love for his own race blind him to the sorrows felt by the rest of the human race. He would not let his skin color get in the way of his conscience.''

BIOGRAPHICAL/CRITICAL SOURCES:

BOOKS

Contemporary Issues Criticism, Volume 1, Gale, 1982.
Moorehead, Caroline, *Troublesome People: The Warriors of Pacifism,* Adler & Adler, 1987.

PERIODICALS

American Notes and Queries, March, 1977.
Chicago Tribune, August 27, 1987.
Commonweal, December 1, 1972.
Journal of Southern History, February, 1977.
New Leader, November 29, 1971.
New Perspectives, winter, 1985.
New Yorker, June 21, 1976.
New York Herald Tribune, July 28, 1964, August 9, 1964.
New York Post, January 8, 1964, June 23, 1967.
New York Times, February 4, 1964.
New York World-Telegram, May 18, 1964.
Political Studies, June, 1978.
Saturday Evening Post, July 11, 1964.
Washington Post, August 21, 1983.

OBITUARIES:

PERIODICALS

Black Enterprise, November, 1987.
Chicago Tribune, August 25, 1987.
Jet, October 19, 1987.
Los Angeles Times, August 25, 1987.
Newsweek, September 7, 1987.
New York Times, August 25, 1987.
Time, September 7, 1987.
Times (London), August 26, 1987.
Washington Post, August 25, 1987.

—Sketch by Thomas Wiloch

S

St. JOHN, Primus 1939-

PERSONAL: Born July 21, 1939, in New York, N.Y.; son of Marcus L. St. John (an actor and teacher) and Pearle E. (a government clerk; maiden name, St. Louis) Hall; divorced; children: Joy Pearle, May Ginger. *Education:* Attended University of Maryland and Lewis and Clark College. *Politics:* Independent.

ADDRESSES: Home—3275 Fairview Way, West Linn, Ore. 97068. *Office*—Department of English, Portland State University, Portland, Ore. 97207.

CAREER: Taught at public schools in Tacoma, Wash., at Mary Holmes Junior College in West Point, Miss., and at the University of Utah; Portland State University, Portland, Ore., associate professor of English, 1973—. Also worked as a waiter, bartender, factory worker, and construction worker. Member of Portland Arts Commission, 1979-81; educational consultant.

AWARDS, HONORS: National Endowment for the Arts fellow, 1970, 1974, and 1982.

WRITINGS:

POETRY

Skins on the Earth, Copper Canyon Press, 1976.
Love Is Not a Consolation; It Is a Light, Carnegie Press, 1982.

CONTRIBUTOR TO ANTHOLOGIES

Harold W. Helfrich, Jr., editor, *Agenda for Survival,* Yale University Press, 1970.
Robert H. Ross and William Stafford, editors, *Poems and Perspectives,* Scott, Foresman, 1971.
Arnold Adoff, editor, *The Poetry of Black America,* Harper, 1973.
Clinton F. Larson and Stafford, editors, *Modern Poetry of Western America,* Brigham Young University Press, 1975.
William Heyen, editor, *American Poets in 1976,* Bobbs-Merrill, 1976.

OTHER

(Editor with Edward Lueders) *Zero Makes Me Hungry: A Collection of Poems for Today* (young adult textbook), Scott, Foresman, 1976.

Contributor to periodicals, including *Concerning Poetry, Poet-Lore, Poetry Northwest, Southern Poetry Review,* and *Iowa Review.*

WORK IN PROGRESS: Two books of poems, *Dreamer* and *Pausing at the Top of Ambiguity for the Jumper;* essays on the poetry of Alice Walker and on Afro-American literature for Portland Public Schools.

SIDELIGHTS: Primus St. John commented: "For me the poem is a playful thing—rough-hewn, not suave. When I am writing a poem, I try to transcend the limits I usually live by and embrace subjects with a more reckless abandon. I enjoy the sudden insights—the impulses—that come from cocky independence and a dreamy but sure-footed irreverence. As I write, I'd much rather try to sneak through a locked window than walk in through an open door."

*   *   *

SALKEY, (Felix) Andrew (Alexander) 1928-

PERSONAL: Born January 30, 1928, in Colon, Panama; son of Andrew Alexander and Linda (Marshall) Salkey; married Patricia Verden, February 22, 1957; children: Eliot Andrew, Jason Alexander. *Education:* Attended St. George's College, Kingston, Jamaica, and Munro College, St. Elizabeth, Jamaica; University of London, B.A., 1955.

ADDRESSES: Home—8 Windsor Court, Moscow Rd., London W2, England. *Office*—School of Humanities and Arts, Hampshire College, Amherst, Mass.

CAREER: Writer and broadcast journalist. British Broadcasting Corp. (BBC-Radio), London, England, interviewer, scriptwriter, and editor of literary program, 1952-56; Comprehensive School, London, assistant master of English literature and language, 1957-59; free-lance writer and general reviewer of books and plays, 1956-76; Hampshire College, Amherst, Mass., professor of writing, 1976—. Narrator in film "Reggae," 1978.

AWARDS, HONORS: Thomas Helmore poetry prize, 1955, for long poem, "Jamaica Symphony"; Guggenheim fellowship, 1960, for novel *A Quality of Violence,* and for folklore project; Casa de las Americas Poetry Prize, 1979, for *In the Hills Where Her Dreams Live: Poems for Chile, 1973-1978.*

WRITINGS:

A Quality of Violence (novel), Hutchinson, 1959, reprinted, New Beacon Books, 1979.

Escape to an Autumn Pavement, Hutchinson, 1960.

(Editor) *West Indian Stories,* Faber, 1960.

Hurricane (juvenile), Oxford University Press, 1964, reprinted, Arden Library, 1986.

(Editor of Caribbean section) *Young Commonwealth Poets '65,* Heinemann, 1965.

(Editor and author of introduction) *Stories from the Caribbean,* Elek, 1965, published as *Island Voices: Stories from the West Indies,* Liveright, 1970.

Earthquake (juvenile), Oxford University Press, 1965, reprinted, 1980.

The Shark Hunters, Nelson, 1966.

Drought, Oxford University Press, 1966.

Riot (juvenile), Oxford University Press, 1967.

(Compiler) *Caribbean Prose: An Anthology for Secondary Schools,* Evans, 1967.

The Late Emancipation of Jerry Stover, Hutchinson, 1968, reprinted, Longman, 1983.

Jonah Simpson (juvenile), Oxford University Press, 1969.

The Adventures of Catullus Kelly, Hutchinson, 1969.

(Editor and author of introduction) *Breaklight: An Anthology of Caribbean Poetry,* Hamish Hamilton, 1971, published as *Breaklight: The Poetry of the Caribbean,* Doubleday, 1972.

Havana Journal, Penguin, 1971.

Anancy's Score (short stories), Bogle-L'Ouverture, 1973.

Caribbean Essays: An Anthology, Evans Brothers, 1973.

Georgetown Journal: A Caribbean Writer's Journey from London via Port of Spain to Georgetown, Guayana, 1970, New Beacon Books, 1973.

Jamaica (poetry), Hutchinson, 1973, 2nd edition, 1983.

Joey Tyson (juvenile), Bogle-L'Ouverture, 1974.

Come Home, Malcolm Heartland, Hutchinson, 1976.

(Editor and author of introduction) *Writing in Cuba since the Revolution: An Anthology of Poems, Short Stories, and Essays,* Bogle-L'Ouverture, 1977.

In the Hills Where Her Dreams Live: Poems for Chile, 1973-1978, Casa de las Americas (Havana), 1979, published as *In the Hills Where Her Dreams Live: Poems for Chile, 1973-1980,* Black Scholar Press, 1981.

The River That Disappeared (juvenile), Bogle-L'Ouverture, 1979.

Away (poetry), Allison & Busby, 1980.

(Editor) *Caribbean Folk Tales and Legends,* Bogle-L'Ouverture, 1983.

Danny Jones (juvenile), Bogle-L'Ouverture, 1983.

One: The Story of How the People of Guyana Avenge the Murder of Their Pasero with Help from Anancy and Sister Buxton (novel), Bogle L'Ouverture, 1985.

Contributor of over thirty radio plays and features to British Broadcasting Corp., over twelve radio plays and features to radio stations in Belgium, Germany, and Switzerland, and many short stories, essays, features, and articles for newspapers and magazines in England, Europe, and Africa.

SIDELIGHTS: Although Andrew Salkey has written a collection of short stories, several volumes of poetry, and has edited a number of anthologies, he is perhaps more known for his adult novels and books for young people. Described by Peter Nazareth in *World Literature Today* as a "Third World storyteller extraordinaire in the Afro-Caribbean mold," Andrew Salkey writes books that contain significant themes, vivid im-

agery, lively dialogue, and spirited characterization. A reviewer for the *Times Literary Supplement* notes that a reader can recognize Salkey's fiction "by the importance of the themes he treats and sometimes by the sheer exhilaration and inventiveness of his dialogue and the exuberance of his characterization."

Salkey once expressed his thoughts on writing fiction in this manner: "I tend to write in a fairly straight line, from beginning to middle to end, although in fits and starts, and I don't mind going back over certain parts of the composition, rewriting and re-casting them, again and again, until they fit toegether with the other parts and help the whole story to shape up nicely. I like my writing to entertain me, if I can manage it; I like it to turn me on to write more and more, and to write well. Finally, I suppose the most important feature of my work as a writer is the matter of the central place I always give to persons and personal relationships in my storytelling. I simply couldn't make a narrative move without them."

Salkey's success as a storyteller may be due to the fact that Salkey himself has always loved folktales, myths, and legends. He explained in his introduction to *Caribbean Folk Tales and Legends* that these types of books "often conceal more than they tell; it's our business, as either listeners or readers, to winkle out the hidden meanings, associations and suggestions."

AVOCATIONAL INTERESTS: Collecting contemporary paintings by unestablished painters and classical and contemporary editions of novels, books of poetry, and literary criticism.

BIOGRAPHICAL/CRITICAL SOURCES:

BOOKS

Salkey, Andrew, *Caribbean Folk Tale and Legends,* Bogle-L'Ouverture, 1983.

PERIODICALS

Library Journal, March 15, 1970.
Los Angeles Times, January 9, 1981.
Times Literary Supplement, February 20, 1969, October 16, 1969, July 20, 1973, January 9, 1981.
World Literature Today, summer, 1979, autumn, 1980, spring, 1981, summer, 1981, summer, 1983.

*   *   *

SANCHEZ, Sonia   1934-

PERSONAL: Born September 9, 1934, in Birmingham, Ala.; daughter of Wilson L. and Lena (Jones) Driver; children: Anita, Morani Neusi, Mungu Neusi. *Education:* Hunter College (now Hunter College of the City University of New York), B.A., 1955; post-graduate study, New York University. *Politics:* "Peace, freedom, and justice."

ADDRESSES: Home—407 W. Chelten Ave., Philadelphia, Pa. 19144. *Office*—Department of English/Women's Studies, Temple University, Broad and Montgomery, Philadelphia, Pa. 19122.

CAREER: Staff member, Downtown Community School, New York City, 1965-67; San Francisco State College (now University), San Francisco, instructor, 1966-68; University of Pittsburgh, Pittsburgh, Pa., assistant professor, 1969-79; Rutgers University, New Brunswick, N.J., assistant professor, 1970-71; Manhattan Community College of the City University of New York, New York City, assistant professor of Black literature and creative writing, 1971-73; City College of the City University of New York, New York City, teacher of creative writing, 1972; Amherst College, Amherst, Mass., associate professor, 1972-75; University of Pennsylvania, Philadelphia, Pa., 1976-77; Temple University, Philadelphia, associate professor, 1977, professor, 1979—, faculty fellow in provost's office, 1986-87, presidential fellow, 1987-88. Member, Literature Panel of the Pennsylvania Council on the Arts.

AWARDS, HONORS: PEN Writing Award, 1969; National Institute of Arts and Letters grant, 1970; Ph.D., Wilberforce University, 1972; National Endowment for the Arts Award, 1978-79; Honorary Citizen of Atlanta, 1982; Tribute to Black Women Award, Black Students of Smith College, 1982; Lucretia Mott Award, 1984; American Book Award, Before Columbus Foundation, 1985, for *homegirls & handgrenades*.

WRITINGS:

Homecoming (poetry), Broadside Press, 1969.
We a BaddDDD People (poetry), with foreword by Dudley Randall, Broadside Press, 1970.
It's a New Day: Poems for Young Brothas and Sistuhs (juvenile), Broadside Press, 1971.
(Editor) *Three Hundred and Sixty Degrees of Blackness Comin' at You* (poetry), 5X Publishing Co., 1971.
A Sun Lady for All Seasons Reads Her Poetry (record album), Folkways, 1971.
Ima Talken bout the Nation of Islam, TruthDel, 1972.
Love Poems, Third Press, 1973.
A Blues Book for Blue Black Magical Women (poetry), Broadside Press, 1973.
The Adventures of Fat Head, Small Head, and Square Head (juvenile), Third Press, 1973.
(Editor and contributor) *We Be Word Sorcerers: 25 Stories by Black Americans*, Bantam, 1973.
I've Been a Woman: New and Selected Poems, Black Scholar Press, 1978.
A Sound Investment and Other Stories (juvenile), Third World Press, 1979.
Crisis in Culture—Two Speeches by Sonia Sanchez, Black Liberation Press, 1983.
homegirls & handgrenades (poems), Thunder's Mouth Press, 1984.
(Contributor) Mari Evans, editor, *Black Women Writers (1950-1980): A Critical Evaluation*, introduction by Stephen Henderson, Doubleday-Anchor, 1984.

PLAYS

"The Bronx Is Next," first produced in New York at Theatre Black, October 3, 1970 (included in *Cavalcade: Negro American Writing from 1760 to the Present*, edited by Arthur Davis and Saunders Redding, Houghton, 1971).
"Sister Son/ji," first produced with "Cop and Blow" and "Players Inn" by Neil Harris and "Gettin' It Together" by Richard Wesley as "Black Visions," Off-Broadway at New York Shakespeare Festival Public Theatre, 1972 (included in *New Plays from the Black Theatre*, edited by Ed Bullins, Bantam, 1969).
"Uh Huh; But How Do It Free Us?", first produced in Chicago, at Northwestern University Theater, 1975 (included in *The New Lafayette Theatre Presents: Plays with Aesthetic Comments by Six Black Playwrights, Ed Bullins, J. E. Gaines, Clay Gross, Oyamo, Sonia Sanchez, Richard Wesley*, edited by Bullins, Anchor Press, 1974).
"Malcolm Man/Don't Live Here No More," first produced in Philadelphia at ASCOM Community Center, 1979.

"I'm Black When I'm Singing, I'm Blue When I Ain't," first produced in Atlanta, Georgia at OIC Theatre, April 23, 1982.

Also author of "Dirty Hearts," 1972.

CONTRIBUTOR TO ANTHOLOGIES

Robert Giammanco, editor, *Potero Negro* (title means "Black Power"), Giu. Laterza & Figli, 1968.
Le Roi Jones and Ray Neal, editors, *Black Fire: An Anthology of Afro-American Writing*, Morrow, 1968.
Dudley Randall and Margaret G. Burroughs, editors, *For Malcolm: Poems on the Life and Death of Malcolm X*, Broadside Press, 1968.
Walter Lowenfels, editor, *The Writing on the Wall: One Hundred Eight American Poems of Protest*, Doubleday, 1969.
Arnold Adoff, editor, *Black Out Loud: An Anthology of Modern Poems by Black Americans*, Macmillan, 1970.
Lowenfels, editor, *In a Time of Revolution: Poems from Our Third World*, Random House, 1970.
June M. Jordan, editor, *Soulscript*, Doubleday, 1970.
Gwendolyn Brooks, editor, *A Broadside Treasury*, Broadside Press, 1971.
Randall, editor, *Black Poets*, Bantam, 1971.
Orde Coombs, editor, *We Speak as Liberators: Young Black Poets*, Dodd, 1971.
Bernard W. Bell, editor, *Modern and Contemporary Afro-American Poetry*, Allyn & Bacon, 1972.
Adoff, editor, *The Poetry of Black America: An Anthology of the 20th Century*, Harper, 1973.
J. Chace and W. Chace, *Making It New*, Canfield Press, 1973.
Donald B. Gibson, editor, *Modern Black Poets*, Prentice-Hall, 1973.
Stephen Henderson, editor, *Understanding the New Black Poetry: Black Speech and Black Music as Poetic References*, Morrow, 1973.
J. Paul Hunter, editor, *Norton Introduction to Literature: Poetry*, Norton, 1973.
James Schevill, editor, *Breakout: In Search of New Theatrical Environments*, Swallow Press, 1973.
Lucille Iverson and Kathryn Ruby, editors, *We Become New: Poems by Contemporary Women*, Bantam, 1975.
Quincy Troupe and Rainer Schulte, editors, *Giant Talk: An Anthology of Third World Writings*, Random House, 1975.
Henry B. Chapin, editor, *Sports in Literature*, McKay, 1976.
Brooks and Warren, editors, *Understanding Poetry*, Holt, 1976.
Ann Reit, editor, *Alone amid All the Noise*, Four Winds/Scholastic, 1976.
Erlene Stetson, editor, *Black Sister: Poetry by Black American Women, 1746-1980*, Indiana University Press, 1981.
Amiri and Amina Baraka, editors, *Confirmation: An Anthology of African-American Women*, Morrow, 1983.
Burney Hollis, editor, *Swords upon this Hill*, Morgan State University Press, 1984.
Jerome Rothenberg, editor, *Technicians of the Sacred: A Range of Poetries from Africa, America, Asia, Europe and Oceana*, University of California Press, 1985.
Marge Piercy, editor, *Early Ripening: American Women's Poetry Now*, Pandora (London), 1987.

Poems also included in *Night Comes Softly, Black Arts, To Gwen With Love, New Black Voices, Blackspirits, The New Black Poetry, A Rock Against the Wind, America: A Prophecy, Nommo, Black Culture,* and *Natural Process.*

OTHER

Author of column for *American Poetry Review*, 1977-78, for *Philadelphia Daily News*, 1982-83. Contributor of poems to *Minnesota Review*, *Black World*, and other periodicals. Contributor of plays to *Scripts*, *Black Theatre*, *Drama Review*, and other theater journals. Contributor of articles to several journals, including *Journal of African Civilizations*.

WORK IN PROGRESS: Editing a book of critical essays on four women poets, Audre Lorde, Margaret Walker, Gwendolyn Brooks, and Sonia Sanchez; a play.

SIDELIGHTS: Sonia Sanchez is often named among the strongest voices of black nationalism, the cultural revolution of the 1960s in which many black Americans sought a new identity distinct from the values of the white establishment. C. W. E. Bigsby comments in *The Second Black Renaissance: Essays in Black Literature* that "the distinguishing characteristic of her work is a language which catches the nuance of the spoken word, the rhythms of the street, and of a music which is partly jazz and partly a lyricism which underlies ordinary conversation." Her emphasis on poetry as a spoken art, or performance, connects Sanchez to the traditions of her African ancestors, an oral tradition preserved in earlier slave narratives and forms of music indigenous to the black experience in America, as Bernard W. Bell demonstrates in *The Folk Roots of Contemporary Afro-American Poetry*. In addition to her poetry, for which she has won many prizes, Sanchez has contributed equally-well-known plays, short stories, and children's books to a body of literature called "The Second Renaissance," as Bigsby's title reflects.

Sanchez reached adulthood in Harlem, which only thirty years before had been the cradle of the first literary "renaissance" in the United States to celebrate the works of black writers. Political science and poetry were the subjects of her studies at Hunter College and New York University during the fifties. In the next decade Sanchez began to combine these interests into one activity, "the creat[ion] of social ideals," as she wrote for a section about her writings in *Black Women Writers (1950-1980): A Critical Evaluation*, edited by Mari Evans. For Sanchez, writing and performing poetry is a means of constructive political activism to the extent that it draws her people together to affirm pride in their heritage and build the confidence needed to accomplish political goals. Yet the terms of "black rhetoric," or words by themselves, are not enough, she says often in poems and interviews. Biographers cite her record of service as an educator, activist, and supporter of black institutions as proof of her commitment to this belief. Writing in the *Dictionary of Literary Biography*, Kalamu ya Salaam introduces Sanchez as "one of the few creative artists who have significantly influenced the course of black American literature and culture."

Before Sanchez became recognized as a part of the growing black arts movement of the 1960s, she worked in the Civil Rights movement as a supporter of the Congress of Racial Equality. At that time, she, like many educated black people who enjoyed economic stability, held integrationist ideals. But after hearing Malcolm X say that blacks would never be fully accepted as part of mainstream America despite their professional or economic achievements, she chose to base her identity on her racial heritage. David Williams reports that the title of her first book, *Homecoming*, announces this return to a sense of self grounded in the realities of her urban neighborhood after having viewed it for a time from the outside through the lens of white cultural values. In the title poem, "Sanchez

presents the act of returning home as a rejection of fantasy and an acceptance of involvement," notes Williams in *Black Women Writers (1950-1980)*. For the same reasons, Sanchez did not seek a major publisher for the book. She preferred Dudley Randall's Broadside Press, a publisher dedicated to the works of black authors, that was to see many of her books into print. Reacting to the poems in *Homecoming*, Johari Amini's review in *Black World* warns that they "hurt (but doesn't anything that cleans good) and [the] lines are blowgun dartsharp with a wisdom ancient as kilimanjaro." Haki Madhubuti's essay in *Black Women Writers (1950-1980)* comments on this same effect, first remarking that "Sanchez . . . is forever questioning Black people's commitment to struggle," saying again later that she is "forever disturbing the dust in our acculturated lives."

One aspect of her stand against acculturation is a poetic language that does not conform to the dictates of standard English. Madhubuti writes, "More than any other poet, [Sanchez] has been responsible for legitimizing the use of urban Black English in written form. . . . She has taken Black speech and put it in the context of world literature." Salaam elaborates, "In her work from the 1960s she restructured traditional English grammar to suit her interest in black speech patterns"—a technique most apparent, he feels, in *We a BaddDDD People*. In one poem cited by Madhubuti which he says is "concerned with Black-on-Black damage," Sanchez predicts that genuine "RE VO LU TION" might come about "if moth- as programmed / sistuhs to / good feelings bout they blk / men / and i / mean if blk / fathas proved / they man / hood by fighten the enemy. . . ." These reviewers explain that by inserting extra letters in some word and extra space between lines, words, and syllables within a poem, Sanchez provides dramatic accents and other clues that indicate how the poem is to be said aloud.

The sound of the poems when read aloud has always been important to Sanchez. Her first readings established her reputation as a poet whose energetic performances had a powerful effect on her listeners. She has visited Cuba, China, the West Indies, Europe, and more than five hundred campuses in the United States to give readings, for which she is still in demand. Of her popularity, Salaam relates, "Sanchez developed techniques for reading her poetry that were unique in their use of traditional chants and near-screams drawn out to an almost earsplitting level. The sound elements, which give a musical quality to the intellectual statements in the poetry, are akin to Western African languages; Sanchez has tried to recapture a style of delivery that she felt had been muted by the experience of slavery. In her successful experimentation with such techniques, she joined . . . others in being innovative enough to bring black poetry to black people at a level that was accessible to the masses as well as enjoyable for them."

Sanchez is also known as an innovator in the field of education. During the sixties, she taught in San Francisco's Downtown Community School and became a crusader and curriculum developer for black studies programs in American colleges and universities. Materials on black literature and history had been absent from the schools she had attended, and she has worked to see that other young people are not similarly disenfranchised. Opposition to this goal has often complicated her career, sometimes making it difficult for her to find or keep teaching positions; nevertheless, Sanchez has fought to remain in the academic arena to shape and encourage the next generation. She wrote two books for her children (*The Adventures of Fat Head, Small Head, and Square Head*, and *A Sound*

Investment and Other Stories) for reasons she expressed to interviewer Claudia Tate in *Black Women Writers at Work:* "I do think that it's important to leave a legacy of my books for my children to read and understand; to leave a legacy of the history of black people who have moved toward revolution and freedom; to leave a legacy of not being afraid to tell the truth. . . . We must pass this on to our children, rather than a legacy of fear and victimization."

Because she takes action against oppression wherever she sees it, she has had to contend with not only college administrators, but also the FBI, and sometimes fellow-members of political organizations. Reviewers note that while her early books speak more directly to widespread social oppression, the plays she wrote during the seventies give more attention to the poet's interpersonal battles. For example, "Uh Huh; But How Do It Free Us?" portrays a black woman involved in the movement against white oppression who also resists subjection to her abusive husband. This kind of resistance, writes Salaam, was not welcomed by the leaders of the black power movement at that time.

Sanchez resigned from the Nation of Islam after three years of membership. She had joined the Nation of Islam in 1972 because she wanted her children to see an "organization that was trying to deal with the concepts of nationhood, morality, small businesses, schools. . . . And these things were very important to me," she told Tate. As Sanchez sees it, her contribution to the Nation was her open fight against the inferior status it assigned to women in relation to men. Believing that cultural survival requires the work of women and children no less than the efforts of men, Sanchez felt compelled to speak up rather than to give up the influence she could exert through public readings of her poetry. "It especially was important for women in the Nation to see that," stated Sanchez, who also told Tate that she has had to battle the "so-called sexism" of many people outside the Nation as well.

Thus Sanchez became a voice in what Stephen E. Henderson calls "a 'revolution within the Revolution'" that grew as black women in general began to reassess their position as ". . . the vicitms not only of racial injustice but of a sexual arrogance tantamount to dual colonialism—one from without, the other from within, the Black community," he writes in his introduction to Evans's book. This consciousness surfaces in works that treat politics in the context of personal relationships. Sanchez told Tate, "If we're not careful, the animosity between black men and women will destroy us." To avoid this fate, she believes, women must refuse to adopt the posture of victims and "move on" out of damaging relationships with men, since, in her words recorded in the interview, "If you cannot remove yourself from the oppression of a man, how in the hell are you going to remove yourself from the oppression of a country?"

Consequently, *A Blues Book for Blue Black Magical Women,* written during her membership in the Nation, examines the experience of being female in a society that "does not prepare young black women, or women period, to be women," as she told Tate. Another section tells about her political involvements before and after she committed herself to the establishment of ethnic pride. In this book, as in her plays and stories, "Sanchez uses many of the particulars of her own life as illustrations of a general condition," writes Salaam. He offers that Sanchez "remains the fiery, poetic advocate of revolutionary change, but she also gives full voice to the individual human being struggling to survive sanely and to find joy and love in life." *Love Poems* contains many of the haiku Sanchez wrote during a particularly stressful period of her life. An interview she gave to *Black Collegian* disclosed that she had been beset by the problems of relocation, illness and poverty. Writing haiku allowed her to "compress a lot of emotion" into a few lines, which helped her to stay sane. Under the circumstances, she also felt that there was no guarantee she would have the time to finish longer works. The poems in these two books are no less political for their being more personal, say reviewers. "The haiku in her hands is the ultimate in activist poetry, as abrupt and as final as a fist," comments Williams. In Salaam's opinion, "No other poet of the 1960s and 1970s managed so masterfully to chronicle both their public and personal development with poetry of such thoroughgoing honesty and relevant and revelatory depth."

Madhubuti says of the poet, "Much of her work is autobiographical, but not in the limiting sense that it is only about Sonia Sanchez." For example, in her well-known story "After Saturday Night Comes Sunday," a woman on the verge of madness finds strength to break out of a painful liaison with a drug abuser without herself becoming trapped in self-pity or alcoholism. "It's not just a personal story," the poet, who has survived divorce, told Tate. "It might be a personal experience, but the whole world comes into it." Readers of all backgrounds can appreciate writings concerned with black identity and survival, she declares in *Black Women Writers at Work,* mentioning that her works have been translated into European languages and remarking that "you don't have to whitewash yourself to be universal." At another point in the interview, she explained why she deliberately pushes her writing beyond autobiography: "We must move past always focusing on the 'personal self' because there's a larger self. There's a 'self' of black people. And many of us will have to make a sacrifice in our lives to ensure that our bigger self continues." In her statement for *Black Women Writers (1950-1980),* she presents her own life as an example of the price that must be paid to contribute to social change: "I see myself helping to bring forth the truth about the world. I cannot tell the truth about anything unless I confess to being a student. . . . My first lesson was that one's ego always compromised how something was viewed. I had to wash my ego in the needs/aspiration of my people. Selflessness is key for conveying the need to end greed and oppression. I try to achieve this state as I write."

According to *Detroit News* contributor Carole Cook, the title of the American Book Award winner *homegirls & homegrenades* "underscores the creative tension between love and anger intrinsic to . . . young black women poets." Speaking in *Black Women Writers (1950-1980)* of the creative tension between protest and affirmation in her writing, Sanchez declared, "I still believe that the age for which we write is the age evolving out of the dregs of the twentieth century into a more humane age. Therefore I recognize that my writing must serve a dual purpose. It must be a clarion call to the values of change while it also speaks to the beauty of a nonexploitative age." Throughout her poems, Sanchez emphasizes the importance of strong family relationships, and exposes the dangers of substance abuse among people who hope to be the vital agents of change, relates Richard K. Barksdale in *Modern Black Poets: A Collection of Critical Essays.* Her message, as he notes, is that the desired revolution will not come about through "violence, anger, or rage;" rather, "political astuteness and moral power" among black people are needed to build the new world. Commenting on the content of the poems as it has broadened over the years, Madhubuti observes that Sanchez "remains an intense and meticulous poet who has not compromised craft or skill for message."

"Her work has matured; she's a much better writer now than she was ten years ago. She has continued to grow, but her will has not changed," states critic Sherley Anne Williams, who told Tate that black women writers as a group have kept their commitment to social revolution strong, while others seem to be letting it die out. In the same book, Sanchez attributes this waning, in part, to the rewards that have been given to black writers who focus on themes other than revolution. "The greatness of Sonia Sanchez," believes Salaam, "is that she is an inspiration." Madhubuti shares this view, concluding, "Sanchez has been an inspiration to a generation of young poets. . . . Her concreteness and consistency over these many years is noteworthy. She has not bought refuge for day-to-day struggles by becoming a writer in the Western tradition. . . . Somehow, one feels deep inside that in a real fight, this is the type of black woman you would want at your side."

BIOGRAPHICAL/CRITICAL SOURCES:

BOOKS

Bankier, Joanna, and Deirdre Lashgari, editors, *Women Poets of the World,* Macmillan, 1983.

Bell, Bernard W., *The Folk Roots of Contemporary Afro-American Poetry,* Broadside Press, 1974.

Bigsby, C. W. E., editor, *The Second Black Renaissance: Essays in Black Literature,* Greenwood Press, 1980.

Contemporary Literary Criticism, Volume V, Gale, 1976.

Dictionary of Literary Biography, Volume LXI: *Afro-American Poets since 1955,* Gale, 1985.

Evans, Mari, editor, *Black Women Writers (1950-1980): A Critical Evaluation,* with introduction by Stephen E. Henderson, Doubleday-Anchor, 1984.

Gibson, Donald B., editor, *Modern Black Poets: A Collection of Critical Essays,* Prentice-Hall, 1973.

Randall, Dudley, *Broadside Memories: Poets I Have Known,* Broadside Press, 1975.

Redmond, Eugene B., *Drumvoices: The Mission of Afro-American Poetry, A Critical History,* Anchor, 1976.

Sanchez, Sonia, *We a BaddDDD People,* Broadside Press, 1970.

Tate, Claudia, editor, *Black Women Writers At Work,* Continuum, 1983.

PERIODICALS

Black Creation, fall, 1973.
Black Scholar, May, 1979, January, 1980, March, 1981.
Black World, August, 1970, April, 1971, September, 1971, April, 1972, March, 1975.
Book World, January 27, 1974.
CLA Journal, September, 1971.
Ebony, March, 1974.
Essence, July, 1979.
Indian Journal of American Studies, July, 1983.
Negro Digest, December, 1969.
New Republic, February 22, 1975.
Newsweek, April 17, 1972.
Phylon, June, 1975.
Poetry, October, 1973.
Poetry Review, April, 1985.
Publishers Weekly, October 1, 1973, July 15, 1974.
Time, May 1, 1972.

—*Sketch by Marilyn K. Basel*

SCHUYLER, George S(amuel)   1895-1977

PERSONAL: Born February 25, 1895, in Providence, R.I.; died August 31, 1977, in New York, N.Y.; son of George (a chef) and Eliza Jane (Fischer) Schuyler; married Josephine E. Lewis (a painter), January 6, 1928 (wife died, 1969); children: Philippa (deceased). *Education:* Educated in Syracuse, N.Y.

ADDRESSES: Home—270 Convent Ave., New York, N.Y. 10031.

CAREER: Clerk for U.S. Civil Service, 1919-20; co-founder and associate editor, *Messenger* magazine, 1923-28; *Pittsburgh Courier,* Pittsburgh, Pa., columnist, chief editorial writer, and associate editor, 1924-66, special correspondent to South America and West Indies, 1948-49, to French West Africa and Dominican Republic, 1958; analysis editor, *Review of the News,* 1967-77. Special correspondent to Liberia, *New York Evening Post,* New York, N.Y., 1931; editor, *National News,* 1932; business manager, *Crisis* magazine, 1937-44; literary editor, *Manchester Union Leader,* Manchester, N.H. Special publicity assistant, National Association for the Advancement of Colored People (NAACP), 1934-35. Member of international committee of Congress for Cultural Freedom, and U.S. delegation to Berlin and Brussels meetings, 1950. President of Philippa Schuyler Memorial Foundation. *Military service:* U.S. Army, 1912-18; became first lieutenant.

MEMBER: American Writers Association (vice-president), American Asian Educational Exchange, American African Affairs Association, Author's Guild.

AWARDS, HONORS: Citation of Merit award from Lincoln University School of Journalism, 1952; American Legion award, 1968; Catholic War Veterans Citation, 1969; Freedoms Foundation at Valley Forge award, 1972.

WRITINGS:

Racial Intermarriage in the United States, Haldeman-Julius, 1929.

Black No More: Being an Account of the Strange and Wonderful Workings of Science in the Land of the Free, A.D. 1933-1940 (novel), Macaulay, 1931, reprinted, with introduction by Charles R. Larson, Collier Books, 1971.

Slaves Today: A Story of Liberia, Brewer, Warren & Putnam, 1931, reprinted, McGrath, 1969.

The Communist Conspiracy Against the Negroes, Catholic Information Society, 1947.

The Red Drive in the Colonies, Catholic Information Society, 1947.

Black and Conservative: The Autobiography of George S. Schuyler, Arlington House, 1966.

Also author of *A Negro Looks Ahead,* 1930; *Fifty Years of Progress in Negro Journalism,* 1950; *The Van Vechten Revolution,* 1951; and, with Langston Hughes, *The Negro-Art Hokum* [and] *The Negro Artist and the Racial Mountain,* the former by Schuyler, the latter by Hughes, Bobbs-Merrill.

Contributor to Spadeau Columns, Inc., 1953-62, and to North American Newspaper Alliance, 1965-77. Contributor to the annals of the American Academy of Political Science and to periodicals, including *Nation, Negro Digest, Reader's Digest, American Mercury, Common Ground, Freeman, Americans,* and *Christian Herald American.* Contributing editor to *American Opinion* and *Review of the News.*

SIDELIGHTS: George S. Schuyler was a satirist on race relations and was known for upholding the opposite stance from what was popularly held on the subject. His shifting views attacked Marcus Garvey's back-to-Africa movement and civil rights leader Martin Luther King, Jr.'s practice of nonviolence. Black historian John Henrik Clarke was quoted in Schuyler's *New York Times* obituary as saying: "I used to tell people that George got up in the morning, waited to see which way the world was turning then struck out in the opposite direction."

"He was a rebel who enjoyed playing that role," continued Clarke. Schuyler put his wit and sarcasm to work with the publication of *Black No More,* a satirical novel that gave a fictitious solution to the race problem. Through glandular treatments, blacks could take a cream that would eventually turn them white and they would disappear into white society.

This novel and other works by Schuyler were initially highly rated by various black leaders, despite the ridicule present in his works that was directed toward some of these spokesmen. Rayford W. Logan, chairman of the department of history at Howard University, stated that "he could cut deeply and sometimes unfairly, but he was interesting to read."

In the early 1960s, however, when the civil rights movement began to gain momentum, civil rights leaders became less enthusiastic about Schuyler, whose positions moved farther right and seemed reactionary to those of most blacks. This era of civil rights proved to be too powerful for Schuyler, and he was soon overtaken completely. "His outlets became more and more limited," remarked George Goodman, Jr., in the *New York Times,* though "he nonetheless continued to champion conservative issues such as the presence of U.S. troops in Southeast Asia."

BIOGRAPHICAL/CRITICAL SOURCES:

BOOKS

Dictionary of Literary Biography, Gale, Volume 29: *American Newspaper Journalists, 1926-1950,* 1984, Volume 51: *Afro-American Writers From the Harlem Renaissance to 1940,* 1987.
Peplow, Michael W., *George S. Schuyler,* Twayne, 1980.
Schuyler, George Samuel, *Black and Conservative: The Autobiography of George S. Schuyler,* Arlington House, 1966.

PERIODICALS

Black American Literature Forum, Volume 12, 1978.
Black World, Volume 21, 1971.
Books and Bookmen, Volume 16, 1971.

OBITUARIES:

PERIODICALS

AB Bookman's Weekly, November 21, 1977.
New York Times, September 7, 1977.
Washington Post, September 9, 1977.

*   *   *

SCHUYLER, Philippa (Duke)   1934-1967

PERSONAL: Born August 21, 1934, in New York, N.Y.; died May 7, 1967, in helicopter crash in Danang, South Vietnam; daughter of George Samuel and Josephine (Duke) Schuyler. *Education:* Attended Manhattanville Convent of Sacred Heart; studied piano and composition with Herman Wasserman, Otto Cesana, and Gaston Dethier. *Religion:* Catholic.

ADDRESSES: Home—270 Convent Ave., New York, N.Y.

CAREER: Concert pianist, composer, newspaper correspondent, and writer. Began touring as child prodigy and performed in more than eighty countries, including three tours abroad under auspices of U.S. Department of State and other appearances sponsored by foreign universities and governments. Formerly foreign correspondent for United Press Features, *New York Daily Mirror, Manchester Union-Leader,* and Spadea News Syndicate. Secretary for Afro-Asian Educational Exchange.

AWARDS, HONORS: Winner of New York Philharmonic Notebook Contest; recipient of twenty-seven music awards, including two from Wayne State University and one from Detroit Symphony for composition, and three decorations from foreign governments. A memorial foundation to restore peaceful village life for the South Vietnamese was named in her honor.

WRITINGS:

Adventures in Black and White (autobiography), foreword by Deems Taylor, Robert Speller, 1960.
Who Killed the Congo?, Devin Adair, 1962.
Jungle Saints: Africa's Heroic Catholic Missionaries, Herder & Herder, 1963.
(With mother, Josephine Schuyler) *Kingdom of Dreams,* Robert Speller, 1963.
Good Men Die, Twin Circle, 1969.

Composer of *Manhattan Nocturne,* a symphonic poem, and "Rumpelstiltskin," a scherzo for a planned *Fairy Tale Symphony.* Also creator of numerous other musical compositions, including "Rococo," a song, "Sanga," an Ethiopian hero dance, "Chisamharu the Nogomo," and "White Nile Suite." Published compositions include *Six Little Pieces* and *Eight Little Pieces.*

SIDELIGHTS: Philippa Schuyler, the only child of an interracial marriage, was a gifted concert pianist and composer who began playing the piano and composing while still a toddler. According to the *New York Times,* when Schuyler was only two and one-half years of age, she "could recite verses from 'The Rubaiyat of Omar Khayyam,' spell and write rhinoceros and find the Mississippi River on a globe." The child prodigy began touring at an early age and, at the age of six, played a program of her own compositions before an audience of thousands at the New York World's Fair. *Manhattan Nocturne* was her first symphonic composition and was performed at Carnegie Hall when she was twelve. When she was thirteen, her symphonic scherzo, "Rumpelstiltskin," was performed by Dean Dixon Youth Orchestra, Boston Pops, New Haven Symphony, and the New York Philharmonic. At the age of fourteen, she appeared as soloist with New York Philharmonic in a performance that included her "Rumpelstiltskin."

Although Schuyler performed internationally as a concert pianist, she was also a writer and newspaper correspondent. Her *Who Killed the Congo?* is a historical as well as political look at the secession of the Katangan province from the Congo, now Zaire. Although in the *New York Herald Tribune Book Review,* Gwendolyn Carter deemed the book "sensational, illsubstantiated and, indeed, highly inaccurate," Chesly Manly in the *Chicago Sunday Tribune* considered it "a highly readable book that demolishes most of the liberal mythology about the Congo tragedy." In 1967, while serving in Vietnam as a correspondent for the New Hampshire *Manchester-Union Leader,* in addition to performing in concert halls, schools, and hospitals, Schuyler was killed in a U.S. Army helicopter accident. Her account of the Vietnamese conflict, *Good Men Die*, was published posthumously. Noting that the book had been written in dispatches without the opportunity for revision, an *Antioch Review* contributor reported that ''her fragmentary intercultural adventures as a 'colored' woman in an Asian wartime world are without precedent.''

BIOGRAPHICAL/CRITICAL SOURCES:

BOOKS

Portraits in Color, Pageant Press, 1962.

PERIODICALS

Antioch Review, spring, 1969.
Chicago Sunday Tribune, July 29, 1962.
Ebony, March, 1946, July, 1958.
Library Journal, March 15, 1962.
Negro Digest, September, 1944, August, 1945, September, 1945, July, 1946.
New York Herald Tribune Book Review, June 17, 1962.
New York Times, July 16, 1967, September 25, 1967.

OBITUARIES:

PERIODICALS

New York Times, May 10, 1967, May 18, 1967, May 19, 1967.
Washington Post, May 10, 1967.

*   *   *

SCOTT, Nathan A(lexander), Jr.   1925-

PERSONAL: Born April 24, 1925, in Cleveland, Ohio; son of Nathan A. (a lawyer) and Maggie (Martin) Scott; married Charlotte Hanley (a professor of business administration), December 21, 1946; children: Nathan A. III, Leslie Kristin. *Education:* Attended Wayne State University, 1940-41; University of Michigan, B.A., 1944; Union Theological Seminary, New York, N.Y., B.D., 1946; Columbia University, Ph.D., 1949.

ADDRESSES: Home—1419 Hilltop Rd., Charlottesville, Va. 22903. *Office*—Department of Religious Studies, University of Virginia, Charlottesville, Va. 22903.

CAREER: Virginia Union University, Richmond, dean of chapel, 1946-47; Howard University, Washington, D.C., instructor, 1948-50, assistant professor, 1950-53, associate professor of humanities, 1953-55, director of general education program in humanities, 1953-55; University of Chicago, Divinity School, Chicago, Ill., assistant professor, 1955-58, associate professor, 1958-64, professor of theology and literature, 1964-72, Shailer Mathews Professor of Theology and Literature, 1972-77; University of Virginia, Charlottesville, professor of English, William R. Kenan, Jr., Professor of Religious Studies, 1976—, chairman of department of religious studies, 1980—. Ordained priest in Episcopal Church, 1960. Adjunct professor, University of Michigan, 1969. Visiting professor, Gustavus Adolphus College, 1954; Walter and Mary Tuohy Visiting Professor, John Carroll University, 1970. Canon theologian, Cathedral of St. James, Chicago, Ill., 1966-76. Trustee of Seabury-Western Theological Seminary, Episcopal Radio-TV Foundation, Society for the Arts, Religion, and Contemporary Culture, and Chicago Historical Society.

MEMBER: Society for Religion in Higher Education (Kent fellow), American Philosophical Association, Modern Language Association of America, American Academy of Religion, American Academy of Arts and Sciences (fellow), Society for Values in Higher Education.

AWARDS, HONORS: Litt.D., Ripon College, 1965, St. Mary's College, 1969, Denison University, 1976, Brown University, 1981, and Northwestern University, 1982; L.H.D., Wittenberg University, 1965, and University of the District of Columbia, 1976; D.D., Philadelphia Divinity School, 1967, and Virginia Theological Seminary, 1985; S.T.D., General Theological Seminary, 1968.

WRITINGS:

Rehearsals of Discomposure: Alienation and Reconciliation in Modern Literature, King's Crown Press, 1952.
(Editor) *The Tragic Vision and the Christian Faith,* Association Press, 1957.
Modern Literature and the Religious Frontier, Harper, 1958.
The Broken Center: A Definition of the Crisis of Values in Modern Literature (lecture), National Council of the Protestant Episcopal Church, 1959.
Albert Camus, Hillary, 1962, 2nd revised edition, Bowes, 1969.
Reinhold Niebuhr (pamphlet), University of Minnesota Press, 1963.
(Editor) *The New Orpheus: Essays Toward a Christian Poetic,* Sheed, 1964.
(Editor) *The Climate of Faith in Modern Literature,* Seabury, 1964.
Samuel Beckett, Hillary, 1965, 2nd revised edition, Bowes, 1969.
(Editor) *Forms of Extremity in the Modern Novel,* John Knox, 1965.
(Editor) *Four Ways of Modern Poetry,* John Knox, 1965.
(Editor) *Man in the Modern Theatre,* John Knox, 1965.
The Broken Center: Studies in the Theological Horizon of Modern Literature, Yale University Press, 1966.
Ernest Hemingway: A Critical Essay, Eerdmans, 1966.
(Editor) *The Modern Vision of Death,* John Knox, 1967.
Craters of the Spirit: Studies in the Modern Novel, Corpus Publications, 1968.
(Editor) *Adversity and Grace: Studies in Recent American Literature,* University of Chicago Press, 1968.
The Unquiet Vision: Mirrors of Man in Existentialism, World Publishing, 1969.
Negative Capability: Studies in the New Literature and the Religious Situation, Yale University Press, 1969.
The Wild Prayer of Longing: Poetry and the Sacred, Yale University Press, 1971.
Nathanael West, Eerdmans, 1971.
Three American Moralists: Mailer, Bellow, Trilling, University of Notre Dame Press, 1973.
The Legacy of Reinhold Niebuhr, University of Chicago Press, 1975.
(Editor) *The Poetry of Civic Virtue: Eliot, Malraux, Auden,* Fortress, 1976.
Mirrors of Man in Existentialism, Collins, 1978.
The Poetics of Belief: Studies in Coleridge, Arnold, Pater, Santayana, Stevens, and Heidegger, University of North Carolina Press, 1985.

CONTRIBUTOR

F. Ernest Johnson, editor, *Religious Symbolism,* Harper, 1955.
M. H. Abrams, editor, *Literature and Belief,* Columbia University Press, 1958.
Rollo May, editor, *Symbolism in Religion and Literature,* Braziller, 1960.

Bartlett H. Stoodley, *Society and Self*, Free Press, 1962.
Finley Eversole, editor, *Christian Faith and the Contemporary Arts*, Abingdon, 1962.
Robert O. Evans, editor, *Graham Greene: Some Critical Considerations*, University of Kentucky Press, 1963.
Philip Hefner, editor, *The Scope of Grace*, Fortress, 1964.
Roger Lincoln Shinn, editor, *The Search for Identity: Essays on the American Character*, Harper, 1964.
Robert W. Corrigan, editor, *Comedy: Meaning and Form*, Chandler, 1965.
Melvin J. Friedman and Lewis A. Lawson, editors, *The Added Dimension: The Mind and Art of Flannery O'Connor*, Fordham University Press, 1966.
William Nicholls, editor, *Conflicting Images of Man*, Seabury, 1966.
William V. Spanos, editor, *Existentialism*, Crowell, 1966.
W. R. Robinson, editor, *Man and the Movies*, Louisiana State University Press, 1967.
Edward Cell, editor, *Religion and Contemporary Western Culture*, Abingdon, 1967.
Harry J. Mooney and Thomas Staley, editors, *The Shapeless God*, University of Pittsburgh Press, 1968.
James A. Emanuel and Theodore L. Gross, editors, *Dark Symphony: Negro Literature in America*, Free Press, 1968.
Addison Gayle, Jr., editor, *Black Expression: Essays by and About Black Americans in the Creative Arts*, Weybright & Talley, 1969.
Conrad Hyers, editor, *Holy Laughter*, Seabury, 1969.
Donald B. Gibson, editor, *Five Black Writers: Essays on Wright, Ellison, Baldwin, Hughes, and LeRoi Jones*, New York University Press, 1970.
Robert Hemenway, editor, *The Black Novelist*, C. E. Merrill, 1970.
Friedman and John B. Vickery, editors, *The Shaken Realist: Essays in Modern Literature in Honor of Frederick J. Hoffman*, Louisiana State University Press, 1970.
Arthur P. Davis and Saunders Redding, editors, *Cavalcade: Negro American Writing from 1760 to the Present*, Houghton, 1971.
Giles B. Gunn, editor, *Literature and Religion*, Harper, 1971.
Howard Hunter, editor, *Humanities, Religion, and the Arts Tomorrow*, Holt, 1972.
Ralph Ross, editor, *Makers of American Thought*, University of Minnesota Press, 1974.
William Handy and Max Westbrook, editors, *Twentieth-Century Criticism*, Free Press, 1974.
Linda W. Wagner, editor, *Ernest Hemingway: Five Decades of Criticism*, Michigan State University Press, 1974.
George B. Tennyson and Edward Ericson, editors, *Religion and Modern Literature*, Eerdmans, 1974.
Craig Walton and John P. Anton, editors, *Philosophy and the Civilizing Arts: Essays Presented to Herbert W. Schneider on His Eightieth Birthday*, Ohio University Press, 1974.
W. Moelwyn Merchant, editor, *Essays and Studies: 1977*, Volume XXX, J. Murray, 1977.
Daniel Hoffman, editor, *Harvard Guide to Contemporary American Writing*, Harvard University Press, 1979.
William A. Beardslee, editor, *The Poetics of Faith: Essays Offered to Amos Niven Wilder*, Scholars Press, 1981.
James M. Wall, editor, *Theologians in Transition*, Crossroad Publishing, 1981.
Richard Kostelanetz, editor, *American Writing Today*, Volume I, Voice of America, 1982.
Victor A. Kramer, editor, *American Critics at Work: Examinations of Contemporary Literary Theories*, Whitston, 1984.

James Luther Adams, Wilhelm Pauck, and Shinn, editors, *The Thought of Paul Tillich*, Harper, 1985.

OTHER

Contributor of articles to numerous periodicals, including *Carleton Miscellany, Virginia Quarterly Review, Boundary 2, Journal of Religion*, and *Journal of the American Academy of Religion*. Advisory editor, *Modernist Studies: Literature and Culture, 1920-1940; Christian Scholar*, co-editor, 1959-67, book review editor, 1960—; *Journal of Religion*, co-editor, 1964-77, member of board of consultants, 1977—; member of advisory board, *Religion and Literature* (formerly *Notre Dame English Journal*) and *Virginia Quarterly Review*.

BIOGRAPHICAL/CRITICAL SOURCES:

PERIODICALS

Books Abroad, winter, 1970.
Christian Century, February 19, 1969, May 6, 1970.
Comparative Literature, spring, 1968.
Contemporary Literature, spring, 1968.
Georgia Review, summer, 1969.
Virginia Quarterly Review, autumn, 1968.

*   *   *

SCOTT-HERON, Gil 1949-

PERSONAL: Born April 1, 1949, in Chicago, Ill.; son of Bobbie Scott (mother). *Education:* Attended Fieldston School of Ethical Culture and Lincoln University; Johns Hopkins University, M.A., 1972.

ADDRESSES: Home—Alexandria, Va. *Office*—c/o Mister E?, P.O. Box 11639, Alexandria, Va. 22312.

CAREER: Writer and musician. Teacher of creative writing at Federal City College in Washington, D.C., 1972-76.

WRITINGS:

The Vulture (novel), World Publishing, 1970.
Small Talk at 125th and Lenox (poems; also see below), photographs by Steve Wilson, World Publishing, 1970.
The Nigger Factory (novel), Dial, 1972.

Also author of a book of poetry, *So Far, So Good*, 1988.

RECORDINGS

"Small Talk at 125th and Lenox," Flying Dutchman, 1970.
"Pieces of a Man," Flying Dutchman, 1971.
"Free Will," Flying Dutchman, 1972.
"Winter in America," Strata East, 1973.
"The Revolution Will Not Be Televised," Flying Dutchman, 1974.
"The First Minute of a New Day," Arista, 1975.
"From South Africa to South Carolina," Arista, 1975.
"It's Your World," Arista, 1976.
"Bridges," Arista, 1977.
"The Mind of Gil Scott-Heron," Arista, 1979.
"1980," Arista, 1980.
"Real Eyes," Arista, 1980.
"No Nukes," M. V. S. E., 1980.
"Reflections," Arista, 1981.
"Moving Target," Arista, 1982.
"Sun City," Artists Against Apartheid, 1985.

Also recorded "Secrets," 1978, and "The Best of Gil Scott-Heron," 1984.

SIDELIGHTS: Recording artist Gil Scott-Heron's sixteen record albums "[have] overshadowed his writings to such a degree that, in the main, his audience is not aware of his early literary creations," writes Jon Woodson in the *Dictionary of Literary Biography*. While a college student during the turbulent late sixties and early seventies, Scott-Heron published two novels and a volume of poetry where he advocated revolution as a cure to the ills of society. These works, according to Woodson, "have taken on importance simply by being the literary outpourings of a figure better known as a public voice speaking out against oppression in the world."

In his first novel *The Vulture*, Scott-Heron depicts the corruption of a black neighborhood and the efforts of a revolutionary group, BAMBU, to rehabilitate the area. Woodson comments that *The Vulture* "reveals a corruption so basic to American society that even revolutionary groups that attempt to wrest power from their oppressors are finally included in the same destructive and parasitical patterns that drive the majority culture." *The Nigger Factory*, Scott-Heron's second novel, is set in southern Virginia at a fictional black college and describes how students' demands for meaningful change escalate into a three-day crisis. A *Book World* contributor observes that the novel contains some stylistic problems, but nevertheless concludes: "This is a young man's novel that can be read as much for its message as for its promise. Scott-Heron's prose will take care of itself—he has seen into the human heart, and that is what real novels are all about."

In subsequent years, Scott-Heron has devoted himself almost entirely to composing, performing, and recording music. His music includes elements of jazz, blues, and Latin rhythms and employs what *New York Times* social critic Janet Maslin describes as "tough, concise lyrics." Like his novels and poetry, Scott-Heron's music is concerned with issues such as social injustice, alcoholism, drug abuse, and political corruption, but Woodson notes that his earlier militancy has "moderated to the point where 'Third World Revolution' anthems can be balanced by such optimistic statements as 'Better Days Ahead' and 'A Prayer for Everybody.'"

BIOGRAPHICAL/CRITICAL SOURCES:

BOOKS

Dictionary of Literary Biography, Volume XLI: *Afro-American Poets since 1955*, Gale, 1985.

PERIODICALS

Book World, March 12, 1972.
Down Beat, January 25, 1979.
Ebony, July, 1975.
Newsweek, February 10, 1975.
New York Times, January 12, 1983.

*   *   *

SEALE, Bobby
See SEALE, Robert George

*   *   *

SEALE, Robert George   1936-
(Bobby Seale)

PERSONAL: Born October 22, 1936, in Dallas, Tex.; married wife, Artie; children: Malik Kkrumah Stagolee (son). *Education:* Attended Merritt College.

ADDRESSES: Office—Youth Employment Strategies, 6117 Germantown, Philadelphia, Pa. 19144.

CAREER: Political activist; chairman and founder, with Huey P. Newton, of the Black Panther Party, 1966. Orator. *Military service:* Served three years in U.S. Air Force.

AWARDS, HONORS: Received Martin Luther King Memorial Prize, 1971, for *Seize the Time*.

WRITINGS:

(Under name Bobby Seale) *Seize the Time: The Story of the Black Panther Party and Huey P. Newton*, Random House, 1970.
(Contributor) G. Louis Heath, editor, *The Black Panther Leaders Speak*, Scarecrow, 1976.
A Lonely Rage: The Autobiography of Bobby Seale, foreword by James Baldwin, Times Books, c. 1978.

RECORDINGS

(With Eldridge Cleaver and Rap Brown) "Huey!," Folkways, 1972.
"Bobby Seale's Address at Georgetown University, February 12, 1974," Georgetown University Library, 1974.

SIDELIGHTS: After being dishonorably discharged from the U.S. Air Force for opposing a white colonel, Bobby Seale returned to his California home, where he began his studies at Merritt College. As a member of the school's Afro-American Association, Seale met activist Huey P. Newton, with whom he founded the Black Panther Party, a militant organization aimed at protecting ghetto residents from police brutality and securing equal rights for blacks. Although at first an entirely black organization, the Panthers in 1968 included some white radical groups and came to be known as the Peace and Freedom Party.

In 1968 Seale and seven others, all leaders of the anti-war effort, demonstrated at the Democratic National Convention in Chicago. Dubbed the "Chicago Eight," the group was charged with violating the anti-riot provision of the new Civil Rights Act, which declared it a crime to cross state lines for the purpose of inciting a riot. Their trial in March of 1969 found Seale at odds with Judge Julius Hoffmann. Seale often disrupted proceedings by shouting that Hoffmann was a "pig," a "liar," and a "fascist." When Seale demanded the right to defend himself (his attorney was ill), Hoffmann ordered Seale bound and gagged. Seale was found guilty of sixteen counts of contempt of court, sentenced to four years in prison, and scheduled to stand trial for the conspiracy charges in 1970.

During his prison term Seale was also indicted in the murder of former Panther Alex Rackley, whom the Panthers suspected of disloyalty to the Party, and the activist was brought to trial for ordering Rackley's torture and execution. On May 25, 1971, Seale's trial ended in a hung jury, and Judge Harold M. Mulvey ordered all charges dropped against Seale. In 1972 the U.S. Government suspended the contempt charges, for which Seale had already served two years, and Seale was freed. Also in 1972 Seale announced his candidacy for mayor of Oakland, California. In the 1973 election the democratic candidate Seale lost with 43,710 votes to incumbent John Reading's 77,476.

Since he retired to a private life, Seale issued an autobiography, *A Lonely Rage*, in 1978. Having covered the politics and dogma of the Black Panthers in his earlier book, *Seize the Time*, the author reflected on his emotional and psychological status during his life as an activist. Howell Raines of the *New*

York Times Book Review, however, wished Seale had been less introspective: "The effort of describing his psychological revolution strains Mr. Seale's abilities as a writer. . . . 'A Lonely Rage' is at its best when Mr. Seale's eye is on the world of issues and action instead of on his own psyche." On the other hand, Best Sellers reviewer O. A. Bouise found A Lonely Rage "intimate" and "clear." "The story is intriguing," Bouise wrote, and "may be a good historical or sociological document."

BIOGRAPHICAL/CRITICAL SOURCES:

BOOKS

Freed, Donald, *Agony in New Haven: The Trial of Bobby Seale, Ericka Huggins, and the Black Panther Party*, Simon & Schuster, 1973.
Seale, Bobby, *A Lonely Rage: The Autobiography of Bobby Seale*, foreword by James Baldwin, Times Books, c. 1978.
Seale, Bobby, *Seize the Time: The Story of the Black Panther Party and Huey P. Newton*, Random House, 1970.

PERIODICALS

Best Sellers, April, 1978.
Ebony, August, 1973.
Jet, June 5, 1975.
Life, October 29, 1971.
Los Angeles Times, May 30, 1971.
National Review, August 25, 1970, March 31, 1978.
New York Times, January 25, 1978.
New York Times Book Review, March 5, 1978, March 10, 1978.
Newsweek, November 10, 1969, April 6, 1970.
Time, November 7, 1969, November 14, 1969, April 6, 1970.
Washington Post, May 22, 1970, May 26, 1970, May 29, 1970.

* * *

SELORMEY, Francis 1927-

PERSONAL: Born April 15, 1927, in Dzelukofe, Ghana; son of Felix Nani (a teacher) and Patience (Kulewoshie) Selormey; married Cordelia Amegayibor (a teacher), April 25, 1953; children: Cyrilla Mabel, Gertrude Felicia, Caspar Felix, Melchior Christian, Frances Kathleen, Gilbert Kofi, Kwesi. *Education:* St. Augustine's College, Cape Coast, Ghana, Teachers' Certificate A, 1946; Achimota College, Physical Education Certificate, 1951; College of Technology, Kumasi, Physical Education Certificate, 1954. *Religion:* Roman Catholic.

ADDRESSES: Home—Accra, Ghana.

CAREER: Primary and middle school teacher in Ghana schools, 1947-50, 1951-53; Teacher Training College, Hohoe, Ghana, tutor in physical education and health science, 1955-60; Central Organisation of Sports, Ho, Cape Coast, Ghana, regional sports director, 1961-65; Ghana Film Industry Corp., Accra, script writer, 1965-68; Ghana Sports Council, director of sports, 1968-72; Loyalty Group of Companies (textile firm), Accra, deputy managing director, 1972—. Quiz master on weekly program, "Treble Chance," for Ghana Television, 1966—.

WRITINGS:

The Narrow Path: An African Childhood (autobiographical novel), Praeger, 1966.
African Writers Speak, Heinemann, 1967.

Author of scripts "Toward a United Africa" and "The Great Lake." Also author of short stories and news commentaries for Ghana Broadcasting.

WORK IN PROGRESS: The Path Widens, a sequel to his first book (the story of an African childhood); *The Wickedness of God*, with the theme that God is wicked to have allowed man to fall into sin and to suffer; a collection of free verse, tentatively entitled *The Voice of a Ghanaian*.

SIDELIGHTS: Francis Selormey once commented: "Books should be written perpetuating the good in the past, for use in the future, to contrast the deteriorating state of the present. . . . The carefree attitude of parents towards the growth of children today, particularly in Ghana, led me to write *The Narrow Path*."

* * *

SEMBENE, Ousmane
See OUSMANE, Sembene

* * *

SENGHOR, Leopold Sedar 1906-
(Silmang Diamano, Patrice Maguilene Kaymor)

PERSONAL: Born October 9 (one source says August 9), 1906, in Joal, Senegal (part of French West Africa; now Republic of Senegal); son of Basile Digoye (one source says Bigoye; a cattle breeder and groundnut planter and exporter) and Nyilane Senghor; married Ginette Eboue (divorced, 1956); married Collette Hubert, 1957; children: (first marriage) Francis Aphang, Guy-Waly (deceased); (second marriage) Philippe-Maguilene (deceased). *Education:* Baccalaureat degree from Lycee Louis-le-Grand (Paris, France), 1928; Sorbonne, University of Paris, agregation de grammaire, 1933, licence-es-lettres, 1934, diplome d'etudes superieures, 1935; studied African languages at Ecole des Hautes Etudes, Paris, mid-1930s.

ADDRESSES: Home—Corniche Ouest, Dakar, Senegal Republic; 1 square de Tocqueville, 75017 Paris, France. *Office*—c/o Presidence de la Republique, Dakar, Senegal Republic.

CAREER: Lycee Descartes, Tours, France, instructor in Greek and Latin classics, 1935-38; Lycee Marcelin Berthelot, St. Maur-des-Fosses, France, instructor in literature and African culture, 1938-40, 1943-44; Ecole Nationale de la France d'Outre Mer, professor, 1945; French National Assembly, Paris, France, and General Council of Senegal, Dakar, Senegal, elected representative, beginning 1946; Bloc Democratique Senegalais, Dakar, founder, 1948; French Government, Paris, delegate to United Nations General Assembly in New York, New York, 1950-51, Secretary of State for scientific research, and representative to UNESCO conferences, 1955-56, member of consultative assembly, 1958, minister-counsellor to Ministry of Cultural Affairs, Education, and Justice, 1959-60, advisory minister beginning 1960; City of Thies, Senegal, mayor, beginning 1956; Senegalese Territorial Assembly, elected representative, beginning 1957; head of Union Progressiste Senegalaise, beginning 1959; Mali Federation of Senegal and Sudan, president of Federal Assembly, 1959-60; Republic of Senegal, President of the Republic, 1960-80, Minister of Defense, 1968-69; Socialist Inter-African, chairman of executive bureau, 1981—; Haut Conseil de la Francophonie, vice-president, 1985—. Co-founder, with Lamine Gueye, of Bloc Africain, 1945; representative for Senegal to French Constituent Assemblies, 1945, 1946; official grammarian for writing of French Fourth Republic's new constitution, 1946; sponsor of First World Festival of Negro Arts, Dakar, 1966; chairman of Organisation Commune Africaine et Mauricienne, 1972-74;

established West African Economic Community, 1974; chairman of ECONAS, 1978-79. *Military service:* French Army, second-class soldier, served in infantry battalion of colonial troops, 1939; prisoner of war, 1940-42; participated in French Resistance, 1942-45; received serviceman's cross, 1939-45.

MEMBER: Comite National des Ecrivains, Societe des Gens de Lettres, Societe Linguistique de France.

AWARDS, HONORS: Numerous awards, including corresponding membership in Bavarian Academy, 1961; International French Friendship Prize, 1961; French Language Prize (gold medal), 1963; International Grand Prize for Poetry, 1963; Dag Hammarskjoeld International Prize—Gold Medal for Poetic Merit, 1963; Marie Noel Poetry Prize, 1965; Red and Green International Literature Grand Prix, 1966, German Book Trade's Peace Prize, 1968; associate membership in French Academy of Moral and Political Sciences, 1969; Knokke Biennial International Poetry Grand Prix, 1970; membership in Academy of Overseas Sciences, 1971; membership in Black Academy of Arts and Sciences, 1971; Grenoble Gold Medal, 1972; Haile Selassie African Research Prize, 1973; Cravat of Commander of Order of French Arts and Letters, 1973; Apollinaire Prize for Poetry, 1974; Prince of Monaco's Literature Prize, 1977; Prix Eurafrique, 1978; Alfred de Vigny Prize, 1981; Aasan World Prize, 1981; election to Academie Francaise, 1983; Jawaharlal Nehru Award, 1984; Athinai Prize, 1985; also Grand Cross of French Legion of Honor, Commander of Academic Palms, Franco-Allied Medal of Recognition, membership in Agegres de Grammaire and American Academy of Arts and Letters. Numerous honorary doctorates, including those from Fordham University, 1961; University of Paris, 1962; Catholic University of Louvain (Belgium), 1965; Lebanese University of Beirut, 1966; Howard University, 1966; Laval University (Quebec), 1966; Harvard University, 1971; Oxford University, 1973; and from the universities of Ibadan (Nigeria), 1964; Bahia (Brazil), 1965; Strasbourg (France), 1965; Al-Azan (Cairo, Egypt), 1967; Algiers (Algeria), 1967; Bordeaux-Talence (France), 1967; Vermont, 1971; California at Los Angeles, 1971; Ethiopia—Haile Selassie I, 1971; Abidjan (Ivory Coast), 1971; and Lagos (Nigeria), 1972.

WRITINGS:

POETRY

Chants d'ombre (title means "Songs of Shadow"; includes "Femme noire" and "Joal"), Seuil, 1945; also see below.
Hosties noires (title means "Black Sacrifices"; includes "Au Gouverneur Eboue," "Mediterranee," "Aux Soldats Negro-Americains," "Tyaroye," and "Priere de paix"), Seuil, 1948; also see below.
Chants pour Naeett (title means "Songs for Naeett"), Seghers, 1949; also see below.
Chants d'ombre [suivi de] *Hosties noires* (see above; title means "Songs of Shadow" [followed by] "Black Sacrifices"), Seuil, 1956.
Ethiopiques (includes "Chaka," poetic adaptation of Thomas Mofolo's historical novel *Chaka;* "A New York"; and "Congo"), Seuil, 1956, critical edition with commentary by Papa Gueye N'Diaye published as *Ethiopiques: Poemes,* Nouvelles Editions Africaines, 1974.
Nocturnes (includes *Chants pour Naeett* [see above], "Elegie de minuit," and "Elegie a Aynina Fall: Poeme dramatique a plusieurs voix" [title means "Elegy for Aynina Fall: Dramatic Poem for Many Voices"]), Seuil, 1961, translation by John Reed and Clive Wake published as

Nocturnes, Heinemann Educational, 1969, with introduction by Paulette J. Trout, Third Press, 1971.
Lettres d'hivernage, illustrations by Marc Chagall, Seuil, 1973.

Poems published in periodicals such as *Chantiers, Les Cahiers du Sud, Les Lettres Francaises, Les Temps Modernes, Le Temp de la Poesie, La Revue Socialiste, Presence Africaine,* and *Prevue.*

CRITICAL AND POLITICAL PROSE

(With Robert Lemaignen and Prince Sisowath Youtevong) *La Communaute imperiale francaise* (includes "Views on Africa; or, Assimilate, Don't Be Assimilated"), Editions Alsatia, 1945.
(With Gaston Monnerville and Aime Cesaire) *Commemoration du centenaire de l'abolition de l'esclavage,* introduction by Edouard Depreux, Presses Universitaires de France, 1948.
(Contributor) *La Nation en construction,* [Dakar], 1959.
Rapport sur la doctrine et le programme du parti, Presence Africaine, 1959, translation published as *Report on the Principles and Programme of the Party,* Presence Africaine, 1959, abridged edition edited and translated by Mercer Cook published as *African Socialism: A Report to the Constitutive Congress of the Party of African Federation,* American Society of African Culture, 1959.
Rapport sur la politique generale, [Senegal], 1960.
Nation et voie africaine du socialisme, Presence Africaine, 1961, new edition published as *Liberte II: Nation et voie africaine du socialisme,* Seuil, 1971, translation by Mercer Cook published as *Nationhood and the African Road to Socialism,* Presence Africaine, 1962, abridged as *On African Socialism,* translation and introduction by Cook, Praeger, 1964.
(Contributor) *Cultures de l'Afrique noire et de l'Occident,* Societe Europeenne de Culture, 1961.
Rapport sur la doctrine et la politique generale; ou, Socialisme, unite africaine, construction nationale, [Dakar], 1962.
(With Pierre Teilhard de Chardin) *Pierre Teilhard de Chardin et la politique africaine* [and] *Sauvons l'humanite* [and] *L'Art dans la ligne de l'energie humaine* (the first by Senghor, the latter two by Teilhard de Chardin), Seuil, 1962.
(With others) *Le Racisme dans le monde,* Julliard, 1964.
Theorie et pratique du socialisme senegalais, [Dakar], 1964.
Liberte I: Negritude et humanisme, Seuil, 1964, selections translated and introduced by Wendell A. Jeanpierre published as *Freedom I: Negritude and Humanism,* [Providence, R.I.], 1974.
(In Portuguese, French, and Spanish) *Latinite et negritude,* Centre de Hautes Etudes Afro-Ibero-Americaines de l'Universite de Dakar, 1966.
Negritude, arabisme, et francite: Reflexions sur le probleme de la culture (title means "Negritude, Arabism, and Frenchness: Reflections on the Problem of Culture"), preface by Jean Rous, Editions Dar al-Kitab Allubmani (Beirut), 1967, republished as *Les Fondements de l'Africanite; ou, Negritude et arabite,* Presence Africaine, 1967, translation by Mercer Cook published as *The Foundations of "Africanite"; or, "Negritude" and "Arabite,"* Presence Africaine, 1971.
Politique, nation, et developpement moderne: Rapport de politique generale, Imprimerie Nationale (Rufisque), 1968.

Le Plan du decollage economique; ou, La Participation responsable comme moteur de developpement, Grande Imprimerie Africaine (Dakar), 1970.

Pourquoi une ideologie negro-africaine? (lecture), Universite d'Abidjan, 1971.

La Parole chez Paul Claudel et chez les Negro-Africains, Nouvelles Editions Africaines, 1973.

(With others) *Litteratures ultramarines de langue francaise, genese et jeunesse: Actes du colloque de l'Universite du Vermont,* compiled by Thomas H. Geno and Roy Julow, Naaman (Quebec), 1974.

Paroles (addresses), Nouvelles Editions Africaines, 1975.

(Contributor) *La Senegal au Colloque sur le liberalisme planifie et les voies africaines vers le socialisme, Tunis, 1-6 juillet 1975* (includes *Pour une relecture africaine de Marx et d'Engels;* also see below), Grand Imprimerie Africaine (Dakar), 1975.

Pour une relecture africaine de Marx et d'Engels (see above; includes "Le socialisme africain et la voie senegalaise"), Nouvelles Editions Africaines, 1976.

Pour une societe senegalaise socialiste et democratique: Rapport sur la politique generale, Nouvelles Editions Africaines, 1976.

Liberte III: Negritude et civilisation de l'universel (title means "Freedom III: Negritude and the Civilization of the Universal"), Seuil, 1977.

(With Mohamed Aziza) *La Poesie de l'action: Conversations avec Mohamed Aziza* (interviews). Stock (Paris), 1980.

Ce que je crois: Negritude, francite, et la civilisation de l'universel, Grasset, 1988.

Also author of *L'Apport de la poesie negre,* 1953; *Langage et poesie negro-africaine,* 1954; *Esthetique negro-africain,* 1956; and *Liberte IV: Socialisme et planification,* 1983. Author of four technical works on Wolof grammar.

Author of lectures and addresses published in pamphlet or booklet form, including *The Mission of the Poet,* 1966; *Negritude et germanisme,* 1968; *Problemes de developpement dans les pays sous-developpes,* 1975; *Negritude et civilisations mediterraneennes,* 1976; and *Pour une lecture negro-africaine de Mallarme,* 1981.

Contributor, sometimes under the pseudonyms Silmang Diamano or Patrice Maguilene Kaymor, of critical, linguistic, sociological, and political writings to periodicals and journals.

OTHER

(Editor) *Anthologie de la nouvelle poesie negre et malgache de langue francaise* [precede de] *Orphee noir, par Jean-Paul Sartre* (poetry anthology; title means "Anthology of the New Negro and Malagasy Poetry in French [preceded by] *Black Orpheus,* by Jean-Paul Sartre"), introduction by Sartre, Presses Universitaires de France, 1948, 4th edition, 1977.

(With Abdoulaye Sadji) *La Belle Histoire de Leuk-le-Lievre* (elementary school text; title means "The Clever Story of Leuk-the-Hare"), Hachette, 1953, reprinted as *La Belle Histoire de Leuk-le-Lievre: Cours elementaire des ecoles d'Afrique noir,* illustrations by Marcel Jeanjean, Hachette, 1961, British edition (in French) edited by J. M. Winch, illustrations by Jeanjean, Harrap, 1965, adaptation published as *Les Aventures de Leuk-le-Lievre,* illustrations by G. Lorofi, Nouvelles Editions Africaines, 1975.

(Author of introductory essay) *Anthologie des poetes du seizieme siecle* (anthology), Editions de la Bibliotheque Mondiale, 1956.

(Contributor of selected texts) *Afrique Africaine* (photography), photographs by Michel Huet, Clairfontaine, 1963.

(Contributor) *Terre promise d'Afrique: Symphonie en noir et or* (poetry anthology), lithographs by Hans Erni, Andre et Pierre Gonin (Lausanne), 1966.

(Contributor of selected texts) *African Sojourn* (photography), photographs by Uwe Ommer, Arpel Graphics, 1987.

Author of prose tale "Mandabi" (title means "The Money Order").

Translator of poetry by Mariane N'Diaye.

Founder of journals, including *Condition Humaine;* with Aime Cesaire and Leon Gontran Damas, *L'Etudiant Noir;* and, with Alioune Diop, *Presence Africaine.*

OMNIBUS VOLUMES

Leopold Sedar Senghor (collection of prose and poems; with biographical-critical introduction and bibliography), edited by Armand Guibert, Seghers, 1961, reprinted as *Leopold Sedar Senghor: Une Etude d'Armand Guibert, avec un choix de poemes* [et] *une chronologie bibliographique, "Leopold Sedar Senghor et son temps,"* Seghers, 1969.

(In English translation) John Reed and Clive Wake, editors and translators, *Selected Poems,* introduction by Reed and Wake, Atheneum, 1964.

Poemes (includes *Chants d'ombre, Hosties noires, Ethiopiques, Nocturnes,* and "poemes divers"), Seuil, 1964, 4th edition, 1969, reprinted 1974, new edition, 1984.

L. S. Senghor: Poete senegalais, commentary by Roger Mercier, Monique Battestini, and Simon Battestini, F. Nathan, 1965, reprinted, 1978.

(In English translation) *Prose and Poetry,* selected and translated by Reed and Wake, Oxford University Press, 1965, Heinemann Educational, 1976.

(In French with English translations) *Selected Poems = Poesies choisies,* English-language introduction by Craig Williamson, Collings, 1976.

(In French) *Selected Poems of Leopold Sedar Senghor,* edited, with English-language preface and notes, by Abiola Irele, Cambridge University Press, 1977.

Elegies majeures [suivi de] *Dialogue sur la poesie francophone,* Seuil, 1979.

(In English translation) *Poems of a Black Orpheus,* translated by William Oxley, Menard, 1981.

SIDELIGHTS: President of the Republic of Senegal from the proclamation of that country's independence in 1960 until he stepped down in 1980, Leopold Sedar Senghor is considered, according to *Time,* "one of Africa's most respected elder statesmen." Yet until 1960 Senghor's political career was conducted primarily in France rather than in Africa. He is a product of the nineteenth-century French educational system, a scholar of Greek and Latin, and a member of the elite Academie Francaise, but he is best known for developing "negritude," a wide-ranging movement that influenced black culture worldwide. As the chief proponent of negritude, Senghor is credited with contributing to Africa's progress toward independence from colonial rule and, according to Jacques Louis Hymans in his *Leopold Sedar Senghor: An Intellectual Biography,* with "setting in motion a whole series of African ideological movements." Senghor first gained widespread recognition, however, when his first collection of poetry was published in 1945; he followed that volume with a highly esteemed body of verse that has accumulated numerous prestigious honors, most notably consideration for the Nobel Prize in Literature.

Senghor, thus, seems to be, as Hymans suggests, "the living symbol of the possible synthesis of what appears irreconcilable: he is as African as he is European, as much a poet as a politician, . . . as much a revolutionary as a traditionalist."

From the outset, disparate elements comprised Senghor's life. He was born in 1906 in Joal, a predominantly Moslem community established by Portuguese settlers on the Atlantic coast south of Dakar, a major Senegalese port and capital of what was then known as French West Africa. Senghor's mother was a Roman Catholic, and through maternal or paternal lines Senghor was related to the Fulani ethnic group, the Mandingo tribe, and the Serer ethnic group—said to provide a connection between Senghor and Serer royalty. His early childhood afforded contact with traditional customs and beliefs, with indigenous poetry, and with the surrounding natural setting. These contacts, critics note, strongly influenced Senghor's later life. As Sebastian Okechukwu Mezu explained in his 1973 study, *The Poetry of Leopold Sedar Senghor:* "This early childhood gave Senghor the material for his lyric poems. . . . Despite the splendours of political life, perhaps because of the excess of its paraphernalia, [Senghor] comes back to these memories of childhood . . . in his poems, events evoked several times in his public speeches and television interviews, images that have become a kind of obsession, romanticized during the years of his absence from Senegal, and because of this process of nostalgic remembrance, taken to be reality itself. Poetic life for Senghor as a result of this becomes a continual quest for the kingdom of childhood, a recovery, a recapture of this idyllic situation."

As a child Senghor demonstrated a lively intelligence and an early ambition to become a priest or a teacher, and was accordingly enrolled in a Catholic elementary school in 1913. The following year he began living in a boarding house four miles from Joal at N'Gasobil, where he attended the Catholic mission school operated by the Fathers of the Holy Spirit. There Senghor was encouraged to disparage his ancestral culture while he learned Latin and studied European civilization as part of a typical nineteenth-century French teaching program. In 1922 he entered Libermann Junior Seminary in Dakar. In his four years there Senghor acquired a sound knowledge of Greek and Latin classics. Obliged to leave the seminary when he was deemed ill-suited to the priesthood, Senghor, disappointed, entered public secondary school at a French-style lycee in Dakar. There he earned numerous scholastic prizes and distinction for having bested white pupils in academic performance. Senghor obtained his secondary school degree with honors in 1928 and was awarded a half scholarship for continued study in France.

In Paris Senghor boarded at the Lycee Louis-le-Grand, where top-ranking French students study for entrance exams to France's elite higher education programs. One of Senghor's classmates was Georges Pompidou, later prime minister and, eventually, president of France. Pompidou exposed Senghor to the works of French literary masters Marcel Proust, Andre Gide, and Charles Baudelaire. During this time Senghor was also influenced by the writings of Paul Claudel, Arthur Rimbaud, and Maurice Barres. Senghor's lycee education in Paris emphasized methodology for rigorous thought and instilled habits of intellectual discipline, skills that Senghor embraced. He meanwhile continued to observe Roman Catholicism and expressed support for a restoration of the French government to monarchy. According to Hymans, Senghor in his student days was considered fully assimilated into Paris's intellectual milieu, which began including political and social liberation movements such as socialism, rationalism, humanism, and Marxism.

Europe was also reassessing African cultural traditions. European writers, artists, and musicians were exploring Africa's cultural wealth and incorporating what they discovered into their own creations. Paris of the late 1920s was permeated with Europe's new cultural appreciation of Africa, and in this atmosphere an exciting period of discovery began for Senghor. He began meeting with black students from the United States, Africa, and the Caribbean, and soon a friendship grew between Senghor and Aime Cesaire, a writer from the French West Indian territory of Martinique. Another of Senghor's acquaintances was Paulette Nardal, a West Indian and the editor of a journal, *La Revue du Monde Noir*. Published in French and English, the journal was intended to provide a forum for black intellectuals writing literary and scientific works, to celebrate black civilization, and to increase unity among blacks worldwide. Through its editor Nardal, Senghor met West Indian writers Etienne Lero and Rene Maran and read the poetry of black Americans.

In *The New Negro,* an anthology published in 1925, Senghor encountered the works of prominent writers such as Paul Laurence Dunbar, W. E. B. Du Bois, Countee Cullen, Langston Hughes, Claude McKay, Zora Neale Hurston, James Weldon Johnson, and Jean Toomer. The anthology's editor, Alain Locke, was a professor of philosophy at Harvard University and a contributor to *La Revue du Monde Noir;* Senghor met him through Nardal as well. When Senghor, Cesaire, and Leon Gontran Damas, a student from French Guiana, sought a name for the growing Francophone interest in African culture, they borrowed from the title of Locke's anthology and dubbed the movement "neo-negre" or "negre-nouveau." These labels were later replaced by "negritude," a term coined by Cesaire. Senghor credits Jamaican poet and novelist Claude McKay with having supplied the values espoused by the new movement: to seek out the roots of black culture and build on its foundations, to draw upon the wealth of African history and anthropology, and to rehabilitate black culture in the eyes of the world. With Cesaire and Damas, Senghor launched *L'Etudiant Noir,* a cultural journal.

In exalting black culture and values, Senghor emphasized what he perceived as differences between the races. He portrayed blacks as artistic geniuses less gifted in the areas of scientific thought, attributing emotion to blacks and reason to whites. Europe was seen as alien, dehumanized, and dying, while Africa was considered vital, nourishing, and thriving. As racism and fascism swept through Europe in the 1930s, Senghor's attitudes were affected. For a brief period he became disillusioned with Europe in general and abandoned his religious faith. "By Senghor's own admission," Hymans revealed, "the same Romantic anti-rationalism that fathered racism among the Fascists of the 1930s underlay his early reaction against the West." But Senghor observed the increasing turmoil in Europe caused by Fascist regimes in Italy and Germany and understood the dangers of racism. Accordingly he modified his position.

Senghor nevertheless continued to cite what he considered to be differences between the races, such as an intuitive African way of understanding reality. But more importantly, as negritude evolved, he emphasized racial pride as a way of valuing black culture's role in a universal civilization. In this vein, he published an essay in 1939 titled "What the Negro Contributes." Themes that Senghor introduced to negritude at this time included a humanism based on the solidarity of all races, a moderate position that gave primacy to culture and maintained respect for other values. As Senghor told an audience he addressed in Dakar in 1937: "Assimilate, don't be assimilated." He later developed negritude further, however, by working to insure not only that African cultural identity became accessible to blacks worldwide, but that the unique aspects of African life were accorded status in the cultural community of society as a whole. Once African modes of thought and artistic expression are restored to their proper place among the world's cultures, Senghor proposed, then a sort of cultural cross-breeding can occur. This mixing of the races, according to Mezu, was conceived as "a symbiotic union where blacks will bring to the rendezvous of the races their special ... talents." Hymans examined this development of negritude since its inception in the 1930s and quoted Senghor's retrospective assessment of the movement: "Like life, the concept of negritude has become historical and dialectical. It has evolved."

Much of what later informed negritude had yet to be developed when in 1933 Senghor became the first African to obtain the coveted agregation degree. This distinction led to his first teaching position, at the Lycee Descartes in Tours, France. Senghor's new appreciation for Africa, coupled with his estrangement from his homeland, created an internal conflict that found resolution when he began writing poetry. Influenced by the works of Andre Breton and other surrealist writers, Senghor drew on surrealist techniques for his poetic style. Surrealism, with its emphasis on the irrational, depended on a creative process that tapped latent energies and subconscious sources of imagination without drawing a distinction between the fantastic and the real. Senghor found this process similar to traditional African modes of thought and employed it in his poetry. "By adopting the surrealist techniques," Mezu explained, "he was at the same time modern and African: educated and modernist from the white European viewpoint, traditional and faithful to the motherland from the African viewpoint. This dualism, or rather ambivalence, is ever present in Senghor's theories, poetry and actions." Nevertheless, Mezu noted, "there is a difference between the surrealist norm and the Senghorian philosophy. The difference is basically one of degree. For the surrealists, their effort, and an effort only, was to discover the point where reality and dream merge into one. For Senghor ... this principle is already possessed, already a part of the ancestral culture."

The poems Senghor wrote in the late 1930s were later published in the collection *Chants d'ombre.* For the most part, these poems express Senghor's nostalgia for Africa, his sense of exile, estrangement, and cultural alienation, and his attempt to recover an idealized past. In a style based on musical rhythms, the poet evokes the beauty of the African landscape and peoples, the richness of Africa's past and the protecting presence of the dead, and the innocence and dignity inherent in his native culture. These poems, critics note, celebrate an Africa Senghor knew as a child, one transformed by nostalgia into a paradise-like simplicity. In some of the volume's other poems Senghor laments the destruction of the continent's culture and the suffering of its people under colonial rule. One of the collection's frequently cited pieces, "Femme noir," employs sensual yet worshipful language intended to glorify all black women. In "Joal" Senghor returns to his native village, revisiting places and inhabitants he had once known very well; it is, according to Mezu, "easily one of the most beautiful poems created by Senghor." When *Chants d'ombre* was published in 1945 it was well received in Paris and brought Senghor to public at-

tention as a voice of black Africa. "In recreating the distant continent by verse," Hymans observed, "Senghor helped blaze the trail that led to the phenomenon of negritude."

World War II intervened between the writing of the poems collected in *Chants d'ombre* and their eventual publication. Germany invaded Poland in September, 1939, and Senghor was immediately called to active duty to protect France at the German border. While the holder of a high academic degree is usually made a commissioned officer, Senghor as a black man was made a second-class soldier in the Colonial Infantry. France fell to the German assault in June, 1940, the same month Senghor was captured and interned in a German prison camp. At the time of his capture he was almost shot along with some other Senegalese prisoners, but a French officer interceded on his behalf. While in prison Senghor met African peasants who had been recruited into the French Army, and began to identify with their plight. He wrote a number of poems that he sent by letter to his old classmate and friend Georges Pompidou; they were hand-delivered by a German guard who had been a professor of Chinese at the University of Vienna before the war. These poems later formed the core of Senghor's second published collection, *Hosties noires,* which appeared in 1948.

Hosties noires documents Senghor's realization that he was not alone in his exile from Africa, explores his increasing sense of unity with blacks as an exploited race, and elucidates the positive meaning Senghor finds in the sacrifices blacks have made. In poems such as "Au Gouveneur Eboue," which treats a black man's willingness to die for the salvation of the white world, Senghor memorializes blacks fighting for Europe. Elsewhere in *Hosties noires,* Senghor protests the exploitation of black soldiers and attacks western sources of power and violence. In other poems, such as "Mediterranee" and "Aux Soldats Negro-Americains," he rejoices in the common bonds formed with fellow soldiers and with American blacks. And with "Priere de paix" and "Tyaroye" Senghor hopes for unity and peace; while denouncing colonialism, he calls for an end to hatred and welcomes the new life that succeeds death. The collection, according to Mezu, is "the most homogeneous volume of Senghor's poetry, from the point of view not only of theme but also of language and sentiment."

Through the influence of West Indian colleagues Senghor was released from prison in June, 1942, and resumed teaching at the lycee in suburban Paris where he had earlier served as instructor of literature and African culture. He joined a Resistance group and also participated in activities involving colonial students. During the war, negritude had gained momentum, and when *Chants d'ombre* appeared in 1945, a new group of black intellectuals eagerly embraced Senghor's poetry and cultural theories. That year he published the influential essay "Views on Africa; or, Assimilate, Don't Be Assimilated." While in the 1930s Senghor concentrated on cultural rather than political issues, after the war he was encouraged by colonial reforms extended to French West Africans. He decided to run for election as one of Senegal's representatives in the French National Assembly. With Lamine Gueye, Senghor formed the Bloc Africain to involve Senegalese in their political fate. France was forming a new constitution, and in recognition of his linguistic expertise, France's provisional government appointed Senghor the document's official grammarian. Senghor founded the Bloc Democratique Senegalais (BDS) in 1948; throughout the 1950s the BDS dominated Senegalese politics.

Senghor's literary activities also continued. In 1947 he founded, with Alioune Diop, the cultural journal *Presence Africaine.* Along with a publishing house of the same name, *Presence Africaine* under Diop's direction became a powerful vehicle for black writing worldwide. As editor of *Anthologie de la nouvelle poesie noire et malgache de langue francaise,* published in 1948, Senghor brought together contemporary poetry written by francophone blacks. An essay titled "Orphee noir" ("Black Orpheus"), by French philosopher and writer Jean-Paul Sartre, introduced the anthology. Sartre's essay outlined the cultural aims of black peoples striving to recapture their heritage. In the process Sartre defined and gained notoriety for the philosophy of negritude, portraying negritude as a step toward a united society without racial distinction. Many consider "Black Orpheus" to be the most important document of the negritude movement.

After 1948 Senghor became increasingly active politically, serving as France's delegate to the 1949 Council of Europe and as a French delegate to the United Nations General Assembly in 1950 and 1951; he won resounding reelection to the French National Assembly in 1951 as well. In 1955 and 1956 Senghor served in the cabinet of French president Edgar Faure as secretary of state for scientific research and attended UNESCO conferences as a representative of France. While some French-held territories sought independence from colonial rule, often with accompanying violence, Senghor pushed for an arrangement giving French overseas territories equal status in a federation relationship facilitating economic development. He constantly modified his stance while avoiding violence and making small gains. In Dakar in 1953, according to Hymans, Senghor defined politics as "the art of using a method which, by approximations that are constantly corrected, would permit the greatest number to lead a more complete and happy life."

A collection of poems Senghor had been working on since 1948 was published as *Ethiopiques* in 1956. These poems reflect Senghor's growing political involvement and his struggle to reconcile European and African allegiances through cross-breeding, both figurative and literal. The year *Ethiopiques* was published Senghor divorced his African wife to marry one of her friends, a white Frenchwoman; critics have suggested that Senghor's views on cross-breeding represent an attempt to resolve his personal conflict by eliminating the divisive social elements that divided his loyalties. One of *Ethiopique*'s poems, "Chaka," is a dramatic adaptation of Thomas Mofolo's novel about a Zulu hero who forged and ruled a vast domain in the early nineteenth century. Mezu called "Chaka" Senghor's "most ambitious piece." Others have drawn parallels between Senghor's life and the poem's attempt to combine in the character of Chaka both the poet and politician. In "Chaka" Senghor applied his theories about the combination of music, dance, and poetry found in native African art forms. As Mezu noted, "Senghor aimed to illustrate what he considered an indigenous form of art where music, painting, theatre, poetry, religion, faith, love, and politics are all intertwined." In addition to musical and rhythmic elements, native plants and animals also figure prominently in *Ethiopiques,* whose other poems include "A New York," and "Congo."

When France's Fourth Republic collapsed in 1958 and France began to form a new constitution—along with new African policies—Senghor joined the advocates of independence for African territories. The French government, under Charles de Gaulle, appointed Senghor to the consultative assembly that would formulate the new constitution and policies. De Gaulle's proposed constitution, which was adopted in late 1958, ac-

corded French West African territories autonomy within the French Community. At the same time De Gaulle warned Senghor that complete independence for West Africa would mean a cessation of technical and financial aid. In 1959 Senghor countered with the Mali Federation, linking Senegal and the Sudan (now Mali). The Mali Federation proclaimed its independence in June, 1960, but two months later Senegal withdrew and reproclaimed its independence. A Senegalese constitution was drawn up in August, 1960, and the following month Senghor was elected to a seven-year term as president of the new Republic of Senegal. Almost twenty-five years later Senghor told *Time,* "The colonizing powers did not prepare us for independence."

Poems Senghor wrote during the tumultuous years leading up to his election as president of Senegal were published in the 1961 collection *Nocturnes,* which featured a group of love poems previously published as *Chants pour Naeett* in 1949. In *Nocturnes* Senghor ponders the nature of poetry and examines the poetic process. Critics have noted that in this volume, particularly in poems such as "Elegie de minuit," Senghor reveals his regret for time spent in the empty pomp of political power, his nostalgia for his youth, and his reconciliation with death. Mezu called "Elegie de minuit" the poet's "'last' poem."

After 1960, Senghor wrote mainly political and critical prose, tied closely to the goals, activities, and demands of his political life. During this time he survived an attempted coup d'etat staged in 1962 by Senegal's prime minister, Mamadou Dia. The following year Senghor authorized the Senegalese National Assembly to draw up a new constitution that gave more power to the president, elected to five-year terms. Known for his ability to hold factions together, he remained in power, reelected in 1968 and 1973, despite more coup attempts, an assassination plot in 1967, and civil unrest in the late 1960s. Much of Senghor's writing from this era outlines the course he feels Africa must hold to, despite upheavals. Commenting on the instability suffered after African nations achieved independence, Senghor told *Time:* "The frequency of coups in Africa is the result of the backwardness in civilization that colonization represented. . . . What we should all be fighting for is democratic socialism. And the first task of socialism is not to create social justice. It is to establish working democracies."

According to Hymans, Senghor's brand of socialism, often called the African Road to Socialism, maps out a middle position between individualism and collectivism, between capitalism and communism. Senghor sees socialism as a way of eliminating the exploitation of individuals that prevents universal humanism. Some of Senghor's writings on this topic were translated by Mercer Cook and published in 1964 as *On African Socialism.* Appraising *On African Socialism* for *Saturday Review,* Charles Miller called its selections "exquisitely intellectual tours de force." Senghor's important political writings include *Liberte I: Negritude et humanisme,* of which portions are available in translation; a work translated by Cook as *The Foundations of "Africanite": or, "Negritude" and "Arabite"; Politique, nation, et developpement moderne; Liberte III: Negritude et civilization de l'universel;* and *Liberte IV: Socialisme et planification.* In a collection of interviews with Mohamed Aziza published in 1980, Senghor discussed poetry and both his politics and his life. Senghor "comes across in these interviews as a brilliant, sincere, and steadfast leader who has yet managed to retain a sense of humility," wrote Eric Sellin, reviewing the collection for *World Literature To-*

day. Sellin continued: "His unswerving fidelity to personal and national programs is more readily understandable in light of his autobiographical introspections about his youth and education." Published as *La Poesie de l'action,* the volume, Sellin concluded, is "an important and interesting book." Later in 1980, Senghor stepped down from Senegal's presidency when his protege, Prime Minister Abdou Diouf, took office.

Senghor is revered throughout the world for his political and literary accomplishments and a life of achievement that spans nearly six decades. He was widely thought to have been under consideration in 1962 for the Nobel Prize in Literature in recognition of his poetic output. When a major English-translation volume devoted to Senghor's body of poetry appeared in 1964, *Saturday Review* likened Senghor to American poet Walt Whitman and determined that the poems represented were "written by a gifted, civilized man of good will celebrating the ordinary hopes and feelings of mankind." The *Times Literary Supplement* called Senghor "one of the best poets now writing in [French]" and marveled at his "astonishing achievement to have combined so creative a life with his vigorous and successful political activities." Senghor was elected to one of the world's most prestigious and elite intellectual groups, the Academie Francaise, in 1983.

When a new collected edition of Senghor's poetry appeared in 1984, Robert P. Smith, Jr., writing in *World Literature Today* identified Senghor as a "great poet of Africa and the universe." Praising the masterly imagery, symbolism, and versification of the poetry, Smith expressed particular admiration for Senghor's "constant creation of a poetry which builds up, makes inquiries, and expands into universal dimensions," and cited an elegy Senghor wrote for his deceased son as "one of the most beautiful in modern poetry." Critics characterize Senghor's poetic style as serenely and resonantly rhetorical. While some readers detect a lack of tension in his poetry, most admire its lush sensuality and uplifting attitude. Offered as a means of uniting African peoples in an appreciation of their cultural worth, Senghor's poetry, most agree, extends across the chasm that negritude, at least in its early form, seemed to have created in emphasizing the differences between races. "It is difficult to predict whether Senghor's poetry will excite the same approbation when the prestige of the President and that of the idealist no longer colour people's view of the man," Mezu acknowledged. "The Senegalese poet will certainly survive in the history of the Black Renaissance as the ideologist and theoretician of negritude."

Senghor's negritude in its more evolved form refuses to choose between Africa and Europe in its quest for worldwide national, cultural, and religious integration. Himself a synthesis of disparate elements, Senghor, in his role as reconciler of differences, holds to negritude as a median between nationalism and cultural assimilation. "Politically, philosophically, Senghor has been a middle-of-the-roader, a man of conciliation and mediation," Mezu declared, adding: "Negritude should . . . be seen as a stage in the evolution of the literature of the black man. . . . The contemporary trend in African poetry seems to be away from the negritude movement as the racism and colonialism that inspired this literature dies out or becomes less barefaced." Senghor's life, according to Hymans, "might be summarized as an effort to restore to Africa an equilibrium destroyed by the clash with Europe." For those who see contradictions in Senghor's effort over more than five decades, Hymans observed that "one constant in his thought appears to surmount the contradictions it contains: universal reconciliation is his only goal and Africa's only salvation."

MEDIA ADAPTATIONS: Senghor's prose tale "Mandabi" was adapted for film by Ousmane Sembene.

BIOGRAPHICAL/CRITICAL SOURCES:

BOOKS

Crowder, Michael, *Senegal: A Study in French Assimilation Policy,* Oxford University Press, 1962.
Guibert, Armand, *Leopold Sedar Senghor: L'Homme et l'oeuvre,* Presence Africaine, 1962.
Hymans, Jacques Louis, *Leopold Sedar Senghor: An Intellectual Biography,* Univeristy Press, Edinburgh, 1971.
Markovitz, Irving Leonard, *Leopold Sedar Senghor and the Politics of Negritude,* Atheneum, 1969.
Mezu, Sebastian Okechuwu, *The Poetry of Leopold Sedar Senghor,* Fairleigh Dickinson University Press, 1973.
Moore, Gerald, *Seven African Writers,* Oxford University Press, 1962.
Neikirk, Barend van Dyk Van, *The African Image (Negritude) in the Work of Leopold Sedar Senghor,* A. A. Balkema, 1970.
Rous, Jean, *Leopold Sedar Senghor,* J. Didier, 1968.

PERIODICALS

Black World, August 14, 1978.
Ebony, August, 1972.
Essence, September, 1987.
French Review, May, 1982.
Saturday Review, January 2, 1965.
Time, June 9, 1978, January 16, 1984.
Times Literary Supplement, June 11, 1964.
World Literature Today, Spring, 1965, Autumn, 1978, Summer, 1981, Winter, 1985.

—*Sketch by Diane L. Dupuis*

*   *   *

SENGSTACKE, John H(erman Henry)   1912-

PERSONAL: Born November 25, 1912, in Savannah, Ga.; son of Herman Alexander (a minister) and Rosa Mae (Davis) Sengstacke; married Myrtle Elizabeth Picou, July 9, 1939 (divorced); children: John Herman, Robert Abbott, Lewis Willis. *Education:* Hampton Institute, B.S., 1934; also attended Northwestern University and Ohio State University. *Religion:* Congregationalist.

ADDRESSES: Office—Sengstacke Newspapers, 2400 South Michigan Ave., Chicago, Ill. 60616.

CAREER/WRITINGS: Robert S. Abbott Publishing Co. (newspaper publisher), Chicago, Ill., assistant to president, 1933, vice-president and manager, 1934-40, president and general manager, 1940—, editor of *Chicago Defender,* 1940—. Chairman of board of directors, Amalgamated Publishing Inc., New Pittsburg Courier Publishing Co., Pittsburg, Pa., Florida Courier Publishing Co., Miami, Michigan Chronicle Publishing Co., Detroit, *Tri-State Defender,* Memphis, Tenn., and *Louisville Defender,* Louisville, Ky.; president and chairman of the board of Sengstacke Newspapers. Founder, Negro Newspaper Publishing Association, 1940.

Appointed member of advisory committee of U.S. Office of War Information, 1941; appointed member and secretary of Committee on Equality of Treatment and Opportunity in the Armed Forces, 1948; appointed member of board of directors of Virgin Island Corp., 1952; appointed member of President John F. Kennedy's New Advisory Committee on Equal Opportunity in the Armed Forces, 1962; appointed member of U.S. Assay Commission, 1964; member of board of governors of United Service Organizations (U.S.O.), 1965-71; appointed member of executive board of National Alliance of Businessmen, 1968. Co-chairman of United Negro College Fund Drive; Boy Scouts of America, vice-president of Chicago Council and member of national advisory board.

Member of Illinois Commission on Human Relations, 1955, Chicago National Political Conventions Committee, 1963, Illinois Sesquicentennial Commission, 1965-69, and Chicago Economic Council. Chairman of the board of Provident Hospital and Training School Association; chairman of selection committee of Health and Hospitals Governing Commission of Cook County; member of South Side Planning Board; vice-chairman and founding member of Illinois Federal Savings and Loan Association. Trustee of Hampton Institute and Bethune-Cookman College.

MEMBER: American Newspaper Publishers Association, American Society of Newspaper Editors (member of board of directors), Negro Newspaper Editors (member of board of directors), Negro Newspaper Publishers Association (now National Newspaper Publishers Association; founder, 1940, past director, and past president), Chicago Press Club, Rotary Club, Metropolitan Club, Royal Order of Snakes, Masons, Elks, Original Forty Club of Chicago.

AWARDS, HONORS: First recipient of mass media award from American Jewish Committee; doctor of law degree from Elmhurst College, Bethune-Cookman College, and Allen University; honored by president of Haiti, 1953; Two Friends Award, 1954; Freedom Fighters Award from Chicago Urban League; alumni award from Hampton Institute, 1954; Commander of Star of Africa (Liberia), 1958.

*　　*　　*

SHANGE, Ntozake 1948-

PERSONAL: Original name Paulette Williams; name changed in 1971; name pronounced En-to-zaki Shong-gay; born October 18, 1948, in Trenton, N.J.; daughter of Paul T. (a surgeon) and Eloise (a psychiatric social worker and educator) Williams; married second husband, David Murray (a musician), July, 1977 (divorced). *Education:* Barnard College, B.A. (with honors), 1970; University of Southern California, Los Angeles, M.A., 1973; graduate study, University of Southern California.

ADDRESSES: Office—Department of Drama, University of Houston—University Park, 4800 Calhoun Rd., Houston, Tex. 77004.

CAREER: Writer and performer. Faculty member in women's studies, California State College, Sonoma Mills College, and the University of California Extension, 1972-75; artist in residence, New Jersey State Council on the Arts; creative writing instructor, City College of New York; currently associate professor of drama, University of Houston. Lecturer at Douglass College, 1978, and at many other institutions, such as Yale University, Howard University, Detroit Art Institute, and New York University. Dancer with Third World Collective, Raymond Sawyer's Afro-American Dance Company, Sounds in Motion, West Coast Dance Works, and For Colored Girls Who Have Considered Suicide (her own dance company); has appeared in Broadway and Off-Broadway productions of her own plays, including "For Colored Girls Who Have Considered Suicide/When the Rainbow Is Enuf," and "Where the Mississippi Meets the Amazon." Director of several productions, including "The Mighty Gents," produced by the New York Shakespeare Festival's Mobile Theatre, 1979, "A Photograph: A Study in Cruelty," produced in Houston's Equinox Theatre, 1979, and June Jordan's "The Issue" and "The Spirit of Sojourner Truth," 1979. Has given poetry readings.

MEMBER: Actors Equity, National Academy of Television Arts and Sciences, Dramatists Guild, PEN American Center, Academy of American Poets, Poets & Writers, Inc., Women's Institute for Freedom of the Press, New York Feminist Arts Guild.

AWARDS, HONORS: Obie Award, Outer Critics Circle Award, Audelco Award, Mademoiselle Award, and Tony, Grammy, and Emmy award nominations, 1977, all for "For Colored Girls Who Have Considered Suicide/When the Rainbow Is Enuf"; Frank Silvera Writers' Workshop Award, 1978; *Los Angeles Times* Book Prize for Poetry, 1981, for *Three Pieces;* Guggenheim fellowship, 1981; Medal of Excellence, Columbia University, 1981; Obie Award, 1981, for "Mother Courage and Her Children"; Pushcart Prize.

WRITINGS:

For Colored Girls Who Have Considered Suicide/When the Rainbow Is Enuf: A Choreopoem (first produced in New York City at Studio Rivbea, July 7, 1975; produced Off-Broadway at Anspacher Public Theatre, 1976; produced on Broadway at Booth Theatre, September 15, 1976), Shameless Hussy Press (San Lorenzo, Calif.), 1975, revised version, Macmillan, 1976.

Sassafrass (novella), Shameless Hussy Press, 1976.

Melissa & Smith, Bookslinger Editions, 1976.

"A Photograph: A Study of Cruelty" (poem-play), first produced Off-Broadway at Public Theatre, December 21, 1977, revised version, "A Photograph: Lovers in Motion" (also see below), produced in Houston, Texas, at the Equinox Theatre, November, 1979.

(With Thulani Nkabinde and Jessica Hagedorn) "Where the Mississippi Meets the Amazon," first produced in New York City at Public Theatre Cabaret, December 18, 1977.

Natural Disasters and Other Festive Occasions (prose and poems), Heirs, 1977.

Nappy Edges (poems), St. Martin's, 1978.

Boogie Woogie Landscapes (play; also see below; first produced in New York City at Frank Silvera Writers' Workshop, June, 1979, produced on Broadway at the Symphony Space Theatre, produced in Washington D.C. at the Kennedy Center), St. Martin's, 1978.

"Spell #7: A Geechee Quick Magic Trance Manual" (play; also see below), produced on Broadway at Joseph Papp's New York Shakespeare Festival Public Theater, July 15, 1979.

"Black and White Two Dimensional Planes" (play), first produced in New York City at Sounds in Motion Studio Works, February, 1979.

"Mother Courage and Her Children" (an adapted version of Bertolt Brecht's play, *Mother Courage and Her Children*), first produced Off-Broadway at the Public Theatre, April, 1980.

Three Pieces: Spell #7; A Photograph: Lovers in Motion; Boogie Woogie Landscapes (plays), St. Martin's, 1981.

A Photograph: Lovers in Motion, Samuel French, 1981.

Spell #7: A Theatre Piece in Two Acts, Samuel French, 1981.

Sassafrass, Cypress & Indigo: A Novel, St. Martin's, 1982.

"Three for a Full Moon" and "Bocas," first produced in Los Angeles, Calif., at the Mark Taper Forum Lab, Center Theatre, April 28, 1982.

(Adapter) Willy Russell, "Educating Rita" (play), first produced in Atlanta, Georgia, by Alliance Theatre Company, 1982.

A Daughter's Geography (poems), St. Martin's, 1983.

See No Evil: Prefaces, Essays and Accounts, 1976-1983, Momo's Press, 1984.

From Okra to Greens: Poems, Coffee House Press, 1984.

From Okra to Greens: A Different Kinda Love Story; A Play with Music & Dance (first produced in New York City at Barnard College, November, 1978), Samuel French, 1985.

Betsey Brown: A Novel, St. Martin's, 1985.

"Three Views of Mt. Fuji" (play), first produced at the Lorraine Hansberry Theatre, June, 1987, produced in New York City at the New Dramatists, October, 1987.

Ridin' the Moon in Texas: Word Paintings (responses to art in prose and poetry), St. Martin's, 1987.

Also author of *Some Men* (poems in a pamphlet that resembles a dance card), 1981. Author of the play "Mouths" and the operetta "Carrie," both produced in 1981. Has also written for a television special starring Diana Ross, and appears in a documentary about her own work for WGBH TV. Contributor to periodicals, including *Black Scholar, Third World Women, Ms.,* and *Yardbird Reader.*

WORK IN PROGRESS: "In the Middle of a Flower," a play; a film adaptation of her novella, *Sassafrass;* a third novel.

SIDELIGHTS: Born to a surgeon and an educator, Ntozake Shange—originally named Paulette Williams—was raised with the advantages available to the black middle class. But one by one, the roles she chose for herself—war correspondent, and jazz musician, to name a few—were dismissed as "'no good for a woman,'" she told Stella Dong in a *Publishers Weekly* interview. She chose to become a writer because "there was nothing left." Frustrated and hurt after separating from her first husband, Shange attempted suicide several times before focusing her rage against the limitations society imposes on black women. While earning a master's degree in American Studies from the University of Southern California, she reaffirmed her personal strength based on a self-determined identity and took her African name, which means "she who comes with her own things" and she "who walks like a lion." Since then she has sustained a triple career as an educator, a performer/director in New York and Houston, and a writer whose works draw heavily on her experiences and the frustrations of being a black female in America. "I am a war correspondent after all," she told Dong, "because I'm involved in a war of cultural and esthetic aggression. The front lines aren't always what you think they are."

Though she is an accomplished poet and an acclaimed novelist, Shange became famous for her play, "For Colored Girls Who Have Considered Suicide/When the Rainbow Is Enuf." A unique blend of poetry, music, dance and drama called a "choreopoem," it is still being produced around the country more than ten years after it "took the theater world by storm" in 1975. Before it won international acclaim, "For Colored Girls," notes Jacqueline Trescott in the *Washington Post,* "became an electrifying Broadway hit and provoked heated exchanges about the relationships between black men and women. . . . When [it] debuted, [it] became the talk of literary circles. Its form—seven women on the stage dramatizing poetry—was a refreshing slap at the traditional, one-two-three-

act structures." Whereas plays combining poetry and dance had already been staged by Adrienne Kennedy, Mel Gussow of the *New York Times* states that "Miss Shange was a pioneer in terms of her subject matter: the fury of black women at their double subjugation in white male America."

Shange's anger wasn't always so evident. "I was always what you call a nice child," she told *Time* magazine contributor Jean Vallely. "I did everything nice. I was the nicest and most correct. I did my homework. I was always on time. I never got into fights. People now ask me, 'Where did all this rage come from?' And I just smile and say it's been there all the time, but I was just trying to be nice."

Shange's childhood was filled with music, literature, and art. Dizzy Gillespie, Miles Davis, Chuck Berry, and W.E.B. Du Bois were among the frequent guests at her parents' house. On Sunday afternoons Shange's family held variety shows. She recalled them in a self-interview published in *Ms.*: "my mama wd read from dunbar, shakespeare, countee cullen, t. s. eliot. my dad wd play congas & do magic tricks. my two sisters & my brother & i wd do a soft-shoe & then pick up the instruments for a quartet of some sort: a violin, a cello, flute & saxophone. we all read constantly. anything. anywhere. we also tore the prints outta art books to carry around with us. sounds/images, any explorations of personal visions waz the focus of my world."

However privileged her childhood might have seemed, Shange felt that she was "living a lie." As she explained to *Newsday* reviewer Allan Wallach: "[I was] living in a world that defied reality as most black people, or most white people, understood it—in other words, feeling that there was something that I could do, and then realizing that there nobody was expecting me to do anything because I was colored and I was also female, which was not very easy to deal with."

Writing dramatic poetry became a means of expressing her dissatisfaction with the role of black women in society. She and a group of friends, including various musicians and the choreographer-dancer Paula Moss, would create improvisational works comprised of poetry, music, and dance, and would frequently perform them in bars in San Francisco and New York. When Moss and Shange moved to New York City, they presented "For Colored Girls" at a Soho jazz loft, the Studio Rivbea. Director Oz Scott saw the show and helped develop the production as it was performed in bars on the Lower East Side. Impressed by one of these, black producer Woodie King, Jr., joined Scott to stage the choreopoem Off-Broadway at the New Federal Theatre, where it ran successfully from November, 1975 to the following June. Then Joseph Papp became the show's producer at the New York Shakespeare Festival's Anspacher Public Theatre. From there, it moved to the Booth Theatre uptown. "The final production at the Booth is as close to distilled as any of us in all our art forms can make it," Shange says of that production in the introduction to *For Colored Girls,* published in 1976. "The cast is enveloping almost 6,000 people a week in the words of a young black girl's growing up, her triumphs and errors, [her] struggle to be all that is forbidden by our environment, all that is forfeited by our gender, all that we have forgotten."

In "For Colored Girls," poems dramatized by the women dancers recall encounters with their classmates, lovers, rapists, abortionists, and latent killers. The women survive the abuses and disappointments put upon them by the men in their lives and come to recognize in each other, dressed in the colors of Shange's personal rainbow, the promise of a better future. As one voice, at the end, they declare, ''i found god in myself / / and i loved her / . . . fiercely.'' To say this, remarks Carol P. Christ in *Diving Deep and Surfacing: Women Writers on Spiritual Quest,* is ''to say . . . that it is all right to be a woman, that the Black woman does not have to imitate whiteness or depend on men for her power of being.'' ''The poetry,'' says Marilyn Stasio in *Cue,* ''touches some very tender nerve endings. Although roughly structured and stylistically unrefined, this fierce and passionate poetry has the power to move a body to tears, to rage, and to an ultimate rush of love.''

While some reviewers are enthusiastic in their praise for the play, others are emphatically negative. ''Some Black people, notably men, said that . . . Shange broke a taboo when her 'For Colored Girls . . .' took the theater world by storm,'' Connie Lauerman reports in the *Chicago Tribune.* ''[Shange] was accused of racism, of 'lynching' the black male.'' But the playwright does not feel that she was bringing any black family secrets to light. She told Lauerman, ''Half of what we discussed in 'For Colored Girls' about the dissipation of the family, rape, wife-battering and all that sort of thing, the U.S. Census Bureau already had. . . . We could have gone to the Library of Congress and read the Census reports and the crime statistics every month and we would know that more black women are raped than anyone else. We would know at this point that they think 48 per cent of our households are headed by single females. . . . My job as an artist is to say what I see.''

If these conditions are unknown to some, she feels it is all the more important to talk about them openly. Defending her portrayal of the acquaintance who turned out to be a rapist, she told interviewer Claudia Tate that men who deal with the issues by saying they have never raped anyone trouble her: ''Maybe we should have a Congressional hearing to find out if it's the UFOs who are raping women. . . . After all, that is a denial of reality. It does *not* matter if you did or did not do something. . . . When is someone going to take responsibility for what goes on where we live?'' In the same interview, printed in *Black Women Writers at Work,* Shange explained that she wrote about Beau Willie Brown, a war veteran who is on drugs when he drops two small children off a high-rise balcony, because she ''refuse[s] to be a part of this conspiracy of silence'' regarding crimes that hurt black women.

Some feminist responses to the play were negative, reports *Village Voice* critic Michele Wallace, who suspects ''that some black women are angry because 'For Colored Girls' exposes their fear of rejection as well as their anger at being rejected. They don't want to deal with that so they talk about how Shange is persecuting the black man.'' Sandra Hollin Flowers, author of the *Black American Literature Forum* article '' 'Colored Girls': Textbook for the Eighties,'' finds most inappropriate the charges that Shange portrays black men as stupidly crude and brutal. ''Quite the contrary, Shange demonstrates a compassionate vison of black men—compassionate because though the work is not without anger, it has a certain integrity which could not exist if the author lacked a perceptive understanding of the crisis between black men and women. And there is definitely a crisis. . . . This, then is what makes *Colored Girls* an important work which ranks with [Ralph] Ellison's *Invisible Man,* [Richard] Wright's *Native Son,* and the handful of other black classics—it is an artistically successful female perspective on a long-standing issue among black people.''

''Shange's poems aren't war cries,'' Jack Kroll writes in a *Newsweek* review of the Public Theatre production of ''For Colored Girls.'' ''They're outcries filled with a controlled passion against the brutality that blasts the lives of 'colored girls'— a phrase that in her hands vibrates with social irony and poetic beauty. These poems are political in the deepest sense, but there's no dogma, no sentimentality, no grinding of false mythic axes.'' Critic Edith Oliver of the *New Yorker* remarks: ''The evening grows in dramatic power, encompassing, it seems, every feeling and experience a woman has ever had; strong and funny, it is entirely free of the rasping earnestness of most projects of this sort. The verses and monologues that constitute the program have been very well chosen—contrasting in mood yet always subtly building.''

While Wallace was not completely satisfied with ''For Colored Girls,'' and complained of the occasional ''worn-out feminist cliches,'' she was still able to commend Shange. She wrote: ''There is so much about black women that needs retelling; one has to start somewhere, and Shange's exploration of this aspect of our experience, admittedly the most primitive (but we were all there at some time and, if the truth be told, most of us still are) is as good a place as any. All I'm saying is that Shange's 'For Colored Girls' should not be viewed as the definitive statement on black women, but as a very good beginning.'' She continued: ''Very few have written with such clarity and honesty about the black woman's vulnerability and no one has ever brought Shange's brand of tough humor and realism to it.''

Reviews of Shange's next production, ''A Photograph: A Study of Cruelty,'' are less positive, although critics are generally impressed with the poetic quality of her writing. ''Miss Shange is something besides a poet but she is not—at least not at this stage—a dramatist,'' Richard Eder declares in a *New York Times* review. ''More than anything else, she is a troubadour. She declares her fertile vision of the love and pain between black women and black men in outbursts full of old malice and young cheerfulness. They are short outbursts, song-length; her characters are perceived in flashes, in illuminating vignettes.''

Shange's next play, ''Spell #7: A Geechee Quick Magic Trance Manual,'' more like ''For Colored Girls'' in structure, elicits a higher recommendation from Eder. Its nine characters in a New York bar discuss the racism black artists contend with in the entertainment world. At one point, the all-black cast appears in overalls and minstrel-show blackface to address the pressure placed on the black artist to fit a stereotype in order to succeed. ''That's what happens to black people in the arts no matter how famous we become. . . . Black Theater is not moving forward the way people like to think it is. We're not free of our paint yet,'' Shange told Tate. ''On another level, Spell #7 deals with the image of the black woman as a neutered workhorse, who is unwanted, unloved, and unattended by anyone,'' notes Elizabeth Brown in the *Dictionary of Literary Biography.* ''The emphasis is still on the experiences of the black woman but it is broadened and deepened, and it ventures more boldly across the sexual divide,'' Eder writes in the *New York Times.* Don Nelson, writing in the *New York Daily News,* deems the show ''black magic. . . . The word that best describes Shange's works, which are not plays in the traditional sense, is power.''

To critics and producers who have complained that Shange's theater pieces do not present an easily marketable issue or point, Shange responds that a work's emotional impact should be enough. As she told Tate, "Our society allows people to be absolutely neurotic and totally out of touch with their feelings and everyone else's feelings, and yet be very respectable. This, to me, is a travesty. So I write to get at the part of people's emotional lives that they don't have control over, the part that can and will respond.... *For Colored Girls* for me is not an issue play.... There are just some people who are interesting. There's something there to make you feel intensely. Black writers have a right to do this," she said, although such works are not often rewarded with financial success. She names a number of successful plays that don't have a point except to celebrate being alive, and claims, "Black and Latin writers have to start demanding that the fact we're alive is point enough!" Furthermore, works which rely on emotional appeal reach a larger audience, she maintains in the same interview: "The kind of esteem that's given to brightness/smartness obliterates average people or slow learners from participating fully in human life.... But you cannot exclude any human being from emotional participation."

Shange writes to fulfill a number of deeply felt responsibilities. Describing the genesis of *For Colored Girls,* for instance, Shange told Tate that she wrote its poems because she wanted young black women "to have information that I did not have. I wanted them to know what it was truthfully like to be a grown woman.... I don't want them to grow up in a void of misogynist lies." It is her commitment to break the silence of mothers who know, but don't tell their daughters, that "it's a dreadful proposition to lose oneself in the process of tending and caring for others," she said. The play "calls attention to how male-oriented black women ... [and] women in general are," and how their self-esteem erodes when they allow themselves to be exploited, writes Tate. Says Shange, "When I die, I will not be guilty of having left a generation of girls behind thinking that anyone can tend to their emotional health other than themselves."

Speaking of her works in general, she said, "I think it was Adrienne Rich or Susan Griffin who said that one of our responsibilities as women writers is to discover the causes for our pain and to respect them. I think that much of the suffering that women and black people endure is not respected. I was also trained not to respect it. For instance, we're taught not to respect women who can't get their lives together by themselves. They have three children and a salary check for $200. The house is a mess; they're sort of hair-brained. We're taught not to respect their suffering. So I write about things that I know have never been given their full due.... I want people to at least understand or have the chance to see that *this* is a person whose life is not only valid but whose life is valiant. My responsibility is to be as honest as I can and to use whatever technical skills I may possess to make these experiences even clearer, or sharper, or more devastating or more beautiful." Women writers should also demand more respect for writing love poems, for seeing "the world in a way that allows us to care more about people than about military power. The power we see is the power to feed, the power to nourish and to educate.... It's part of our responsibility as writers to make these things important," Shange said.

Shange's poetry books, like her theater pieces, are distinctively original. *Nappy Edges,* containing fifty poems, is too long, says Harriet Gilbert in the *Washington Post Book World;* however, she claims, "nothing that Shange writes is ever entirely unreadable, springing, as it does, from such an intense honesty, from so fresh an awareness of the beauty of sound and of vision, from such mastery of words, from such com-

passion, humor and intelligence." Alice H. G. Phillips relates in the *Times Literary Supplement,* "Comparing herself to a jazzman 'takin a solo', she lets go with verbal runs and trills, mixes in syncopations, spins out evocative hanging phrases, variations on themes and refrains. Rarely does she come to a full stop, relying instead on line breaks, extra space breaking up a line, and/or oblique strokes.... She constantly tries to push things to their limit, and consequently risks seeming overenthusiastic, oversimplistic or merely undisciplined.... But at its best, her method can achieve both serious humour and deep seriousness."

In her poetry, Shange takes many liberties with the conventions of written English, using nonstandard spellings and punctuation. Some reviewers feel that these innovations present unnecessary obstacles to the interested readers of *Nappy Edges, A Daughter's Geography,* and *From Okra to Greens: Poems.* Explaining her "lower-case letters, slashes, and spelling" to Tate, she said that "poems where all the first letters are capitalized" bore her; "also, I like the idea that letters dance.... I need some visual stimulation, so that reading becomes not just a passive act and more than an intellectual activity, but demands rigorous participation." Her idiosyncraitc punctuation assures her "that the reader is not in control of the process." She wants her words in print to engage the reader in a kind of struggle, and not be "whatever you can just ignore." The spellings, she said, "reflect language as I hear it.... The structure is connected to the music I hear beneath the words."

Shange's rejection of standard English serves deeper emotional and political purposes as well. In a *Los Angeles Times Book Review* article on Shange's *See No Evil: Prefaces, Essays and Accounts, 1976-1983,* Karl Keller relates, "[Shange] feels that as a black female performer/playwright/poet, she has wanted 'to attack deform n maim the language that i was taught to hate myself in. I have to take it apart to the bone.'" Speaking to Tate, she declared, "We do not have to refer continually to European art as the standard. That's absolutely absurd and racist, and I won't participate in that utter lie. My work is one of the few ways I can preserve the elements of our culture that need to be remembered and absolutely revered."

Shange takes liberties with the conventions of fiction writing with her first full-length novel, *Sassafrass, Cypress & Indigo.* "The novel is unusual in its form—a tapestry of narrative, poetry, magic spells, recipes and letters. Lyrical yet real, it also celebrates female stuff—weaving, cooking, birthing babies," relates Lauerman. Its title characters are sisters who find different ways to cope with their love relationships. Sassafrass attaches herself to Mitch, a musician who uses hard drugs and beats her; she leaves him twice, but goes back to him for another try. To male readers who called Mitch a "weak" male character, she replied to Lauerman, "[He] had some faults, but there's no way in the world you can say [he wasn't] strong.... I think you should love people with their faults. That's what love's about." Cypress, a dancer in feminist productions, at first refuses to become romantically involved with any of her male friends. Indigo, the youngest sister, retreats into her imagination, befriending her childhood dolls, seeing only the poetry and magic of the world. The music she plays on her violin becomes a rejuvenating source for her mother and sisters. "Probably there is a little bit of all three sisters in Shange," Lauerman suggests, "though she says that her novel is not autobiographical but historical, culled from the experiences of blacks and from the 'information of my feelings.'"

Critics agree that Shange's poetry is more masterfully wrought than her fiction, yet they find much in the novel to applaud. Writes Doris Grumbach in the *Washington Post Book World*, "Shange is primarily a poet, with a blood-red sympathy for and love of her people, their folk as well as their sophisticated ways, their innocent, loving goodness as much as their lack of immunity to powerful evil. . . . But her voice in this novel is entirely her own, an original, spare and primary-colored sound that will remind readers of Jean Toomer's *Cane*." In Grumbach's opinion, "Whatever Shange turns her hand to she does well, even to potions and recipes. A white reader feels the exhilarating shock of discovery at being permitted entry into this world she couldn't have known'" apart from the novel.

"There is poetry in . . . *Sassafrass, Cypress & Indigo:* the poetry of rich lyrical language, of women you want to know because they're so original even their names conjure up visions," comments Joyce Howe in the *Village Voice*. *Betsey Brown: A Novel*, "lacks those fantastical qualities, yet perhaps because this semiautobiographical second novel is not as easy to love, it is the truer book." Betsey is thirteen, growing into young womanhood in St. Louis during the 1950s. "An awakening sense of racial responsibility is as important to Betsey as her first kiss," relates Patchy Wheatley, a *Times Literary Supplement* reviewer. As one of the first students to be bused to a hostile white school, Betsey learns about racism and how to overcome it with a sense of personal pride. Says the reviewer, "By interweaving Betsey's story with those of the various generations of her family and community, Shange has also produced something of wider significance: a skilful exploration of the Southern black community at a decisive moment in its history."

"Black life has always been more various than the literature has been at liberty to show," comments Sherley Anne Williams in a *Ms.* review. Though she is not impressed with *Betsey Brown* "as a literary achievement," she welcomes this important-because-rare look at the black middle class. In a *Washington Post* review, Tate concurs, and notes the differences between *Betsey Brown* and Shange's previous works: "Shange's style is distinctively lyrical; her monologues and dialogues provide a panorama of Afro-American diversity. Most of Shange's characteristic elliptical spelling, innovative syntax and punctuation is absent from 'Betsey Brown.' Missing also is the caustic social criticism about racial and sexual victimization. . . . 'Betsey Brown' seems also to mark Shange's movement from explicit to subtle expressions of rage, from repudiating her girlhood past to embracing it, and from flip candor to more serious commentary." Shange told Dong that she is as angry and subversive as ever, but doesn't feel as powerless, she said, "because I know where to put my anger, and I don't feel alone in it anymore."

MEDIA ADAPTATIONS: A musical-operetta version of Shange's novel *Betsey Brown* was produced by Joseph Papp's Public Theater in 1986.

AVOCATIONAL INTERESTS: Playing the violin.

BIOGRAPHICAL/CRITICAL SOURCES:

BOOKS

Betsko, Kathleen and Rachel Koenig, editors, *Interviews with Contemporary Women Playwrights*, Beech Tree Books, 1987.
Christ, Carol P., *Diving Deep and Surfacing: Women Writers on Spiritual Quest*, Beacon Press, 1980.

Contemporary Literary Criticism, Gale, Volume 8, 1978, Volume 25, 1983, Volume 38, 1986.
Dictionary of Literary Biography, Volume 38: Afro-American Writers after 1955: Dramatists and Prose Writers, Gale, 1985.
Shange, Ntozake, For Colored Girls Who Have Considered Suicide/When the Rainbow Is Enuf, Shameless Hussy Press, 1975, Macmillan, 1976.
Shange, Ntozake, See No Evil: Prefaces, Essays and Accounts, 1976-1983, Momo's Press, 1984.
Squier, Susan Merrill, editor, Women Writers and the City: Essays in Feminist Literary Criticism, University of Tennessee Press, 1984.
Tate, Claudia, editor, Black Women Writers at Work, Continuum, 1983.

PERIODICALS

American Book Review, September, 1983, March, 1986.
Black American Literature Forum, summer, 1981.
Black Scholar, March, 1979, March, 1981, December, 1982, July, 1985.
Chicago Tribune, October 21, 1982.
Chicago Tribune Book World, July 1, 1979, September 8, 1985.
Christian Science Monitor, September 9, 1976, October 8, 1982, May 2, 1986.
Cue, June 26, 1976.
Daily News, July 16, 1979.
Detroit Free Press, October 30, 1978.
Ebony, August, 1977.
Essence, November, 1976, May, 1985, June, 1985.
Freedomways, Third Quarter, 1976.
Horizon, September, 1977.
Los Angeles Times, October 20, 1982, June 11, 1985, July 28, 1987.
Los Angeles Times Book Review, August 22, 1982, October 20, 1982, January 8, 1984, July 29, 1984, June 11, 1985, July 19, 1987.
Mademoiselle, September, 1976.
Ms., September, 1976, December, 1977, June, 1985, June, 1987.
New Leader, July 5, 1976.
Newsday, August 22, 1976.
New Statesman, October 4, 1985.
Newsweek, June 14, 1976, July 30, 1979.
New York Amsterdam News, October 9, 1976.
New Yorker, June 14, 1976, August 2, 1976, January 2, 1978.
New York Post, June 12, 1976, September 16, 1976, July 16, 1979.
New York Theatre Critics' Reviews, Volume XXXVII, number 16, September 13, 1976.
New York Times, June 16, 1976, December 22, 1977, June 4, 1979, June 8, 1979, July 16, 1979, July 22, 1979, May 14, 1980, June 15, 1980.
New York Times Book Review, June 25, 1979, July 16, 1979, October 21, 1979, September 12, 1982, May 12, 1985, April 6, 1986.
New York Times Magazine, May 1, 1983.
Plays & Players, Volume 27, number 3, December, 1979.
Publishers Weekly, May 3, 1985.
Saturday Review, February 18, 1978, May/June, 1985.
Time, June 14, 1976, July 19, 1976, November 1, 1976.
Times (London), April 21, 1983.
Times Literary Supplement, December 6, 1985, April 15-21, 1988.

Washington Post, June 12, 1976, June 29, 1976, February 23, 1982, June 17, 1985.
Washington Post Book World, October 15, 1978, July 19, 1981, August 22, 1982, August 5, 1984.
Variety, July 25, 1979.
Village Voice, August 16, 1976, July 23, 1979, June 18, 1985.

*   *   *

SHARP, Saundra   1942-

PERSONAL: Born December 21, 1942, in Cleveland, Ohio; daughter of Clarence and Faythe M. (McIntyre) Sharp. *Education:* Bowling Green State University, B.S. and certificate in radio and television production, 1964.

ADDRESSES: Home—P.O. Box 75796, Sanford Station, Los Angeles, Calif. 90075.

CAREER: Actress for stage and television, and poet. Teacher in New York Public Schools, 1965-67, and Duchess Community College, 1970. Founder and director, Lorraine Hansberry Playwrights Workshop, 1976. Has given readings on television programs, including "Soul" and "Like It Is." Has appeared in feature film "The Learning Tree"; has performed in Off-Broadway productions, including "Black Girl," "Hello, Dolly!," "Black Quartet," "Five on the Black Hand Side," "Poetry Now," and "To be Young, Gifted and Black"; has appeared with Theatre for the Forgotton, Al Fann Theatrical Ensemble, and Poets and Performers; played role of Cathy Robinson in Public Broadcasting Service's dramatic television series "Our Street"; has performed as pop singer on television and in clubs in United States, Mexico, and West Indies; reads poetry (by others) on record albums for Scholastic Magazines and on "The Black Experience," a radio series for New York City Board of Education; has made television and radio commercial announcements. Head of Togetherness Productions, a theatrical company for young black creative artists; member of board of directors of Children's Art Carnival.

WRITINGS:

POETRY

From the Windows of My Mind, Togetherness Productions, 1970.
In the Midst of Change, photographs by Chester Higgins, Jr., Cornell Norris, and Ronald St. Clair, Togetherness Productions, 1972, 2nd edition, 1975.
Soft Song, Togetherness Productions, 1978.

CONTRIBUTOR TO ANTHOLOGIES

Orde Coombs, editor, *We Speak As Liberators,* Dodd, 1970.
Raoul Abdul, editor, *The Magic of Black Poetry,* Dodd, 1972.
Lindsay Patterson, editor, *A Rock Against the Wind,* Dodd, 1974.

OTHER

Also author of numerous television scripts, including "The Way It's Done" for series "Our Street," PBS-TV, 1973, and of play "The Sistuhs," 1976-77. Columnist for *Expansions,* newspaper of Collective Black Artists, Inc. Contributor of poems to *Black Creation* and *Black Digest.*

*   *   *

SHAW, Bernard   1940-

PERSONAL: Born May 22, 1940, in Chicago, Ill.; son of Edgar (a railroad man and house painter) and Camilla (a housekeeper; maiden name, Murphy) Shaw; married Linda Allston, March 30, 1974; children: Amar Edgar, Anil Louise. *Education:* Attended University of Illinois at Chicago Circle (now at Chicago), 1963.

ADDRESSES: Office—Cable News Network, Turner Broadcasting System, 111 Massachusetts Ave. N.W., 3rd Floor, Washington, D.C. 20001.

CAREER/WRITINGS: WYNR/WNUS-Radio, Chicago, Ill., reporter, 1964-66; Westinghouse Broadcasting Co., Chicago, reporter, 1966-68, correspondent in Washington, D.C., 1968-71; Columbia Broadcasting System (CBS), Washington, D.C., television reporter, 1971-74, correspondent, 1974-77; American Broadcasting Companies (ABC), Miami, Fla., correspondent and chief of Latin American Bureau, 1977-79; Cable News Network (CNN), Washington, D.C., television news anchor, 1980—. Worked as ABC-News senior correspondent on Capital Hill. *Military service:* U.S. Marine Corps, 1959-63.

MEMBER: National Press Club, Sigma Delta Chi.

AWARDS, HONORS: Received honorary doctorate from Marion College, 1985; distinguished service award from Congressional Black Caucus, 1985.

SIDELIGHTS: Bernard Shaw began his broadcasting career in the wire room of a Chicago rhythm and blues radio station. But when Martin Luther King, Jr., visited the city, Shaw managed to get himself assigned to the story. "I really hustled," he comments about that break. "I worked very hard; I slept very little. . . . But I did so well they put me on staff."

That kind of determination has helped Shaw to cover major news events around the world. When the Jonestown mass suicide story broke in the remote jungle of Guyana, Shaw was assigned the story for ABC. He scooped the other networks with the first aerial photographs of Jonestown. But the exclusive photographs were not easily obtained. "We did it by flying over the site in a stretch Lear jet," Shaw remembers. "We went down as low as we could, and we were flying as slowly as we could, and the plane almost stalled. We really pushed safety considerations to the limits to get these aerials."

Shaw comments on the dedication he has to do his job right: "Who knows what inspires you and drives you on, whether it's in this business or any other business. How many times have we done more than our share of work because we believed in what we were doing and just pressed on? You don't get awards for that kind of thing, but if it's your responsibility you're expected to carry through with it. It's a cliche to say it, but it goes with the territory."

Shaw's hard work has taken him from local radio station reporter to news anchor on the Cable News Network, a 24-hours-a-day all-news format. Because of the network's extensive news coverage, Shaw faces daily reporting challenges, something that strongly appeals to him. "When it's a breaking story," Shaw states, "and uncertain events and factors are tumbling in on you, and you've got to separate the certain from the uncertain and report those facts and new developments calmly, put them all in perspective,. . . . these things are maximum challenges to your ability as a newsman to discern facts, to organize them, to report them cogently, and to keep the story line flowing. That to me is the maximum challenge. I love that. That is what I love most about anchoring."

SHINE, Ted 1931-

PERSONAL: Born April 26, 1931, in Baton Rouge, La.; son of Theodis Wesley and Bessie (Herson) Shine. *Education:* Howard University, B.A., 1953; Iowa State University of Science and Technology (now University of Iowa), M.A., 1958; University of California, Santa Barbara, Ph.D, 1971. *Politics:* Democrat. *Religion:* Baptist.

ADDRESSES: Home—10717 Cox Lane, Dallas, Tex. 75229. *Office*—P.O. Box 2082, Prairie View, Tex. 77445. *Agent*—Flora Roberts, Inc., 157 West 57th St., New York, N.Y. 10019.

CAREER: Dillard University, New Orleans, La., instructor in drama and English, 1960-61; Howard University, Washington, D.C., assistant professor of drama, 1961-67; Prairie View A & M University, Prairie View, Tex., professor and head of department of drama, 1967—. Board member, Texas Non-Profit Theatres, Inc. *Military service:* U.S. Army, 1955-57.

MEMBER: American Theatre Association, Southwest Theatre Conference, Texas Educational Theatre Association.

AWARDS, HONORS: Brook-Hines Award for Playwriting, Howard University, 1970, for "Morning, Noon, and Night."

WRITINGS:

PLAYS

Sho Is Hot in the Cotton Patch (one-act; first produced in Washington, D.C. at Howard University, 1950; produced as "Miss Weaver" in New York City at St. Mark's Playhouse, 1968), Encore, 1966.
Shoes (also see below), Encore, 1967.
"Morning, Noon, and Night" (three-act; first produced in Washington, D.C. at Howard University, 1964), published in *The Black Teacher and the Dramatic Arts,* edited by William Reardon and Thomas D. Pawley, Negro Universities Press, 1970.
"Plantation" (one-act; also see below), first produced in 1970.
Contributions: Three Short Plays (contains "Plantation," "Shoes," and "Contribution"), Dramatists Play Service, 1970. *Contribution* (one-act; first produced in New York City, 1967), Chilton, 1972.
(Editor with James V. Hatch, and contributor) *Black Theatre, U.S.A.: Forty-five Plays by Black Americans, 1847-1974* (includes "Herbert III." [one-act], first produced in Wichita Falls, Tex., at Midwestern State University, October, 1975), Free Press, 1974.
The Woman Who Was Tampered with in Youth (one-act; first produced at Fisk University, 1983), Sea Urchin Press, 1980.
Good Old Soul (one-act; first produced at Fisk University, 1983), Tennessee State University Press, 1984.
Going Berserk (one-act), National Association for Dramatic and Speech Arts, 1984.

UNPUBLISHED PLAYS

"Cold Day in August" (one-act), 1950.
"Dry August," 1952.
"Bat's Out of Hell," 1955.
"Good News," 1956.
"Entourage Royale" (musical), 1958.
"Epitaph for a Bluebird," 1958.
"A Rat's Revolt," 1959.
"Miss Victoria" (one-act), 1965.
"Pontiac" (one-act), 1967.
"Revolution," 1968.

"Jeanne West" (musical), 1968.
"The Coca-Cola Boys" (one-act), 1969.
"Comeback after the Fire" (full-length sequel to "Morning, Noon, and Night"), 1969.
"Flora's Kisses" (one-act), 1969.
"Hamburgers at Hamburger Haven Are Impersonal" (one-act), 1969.
"Idabel's Fortune" (one-act), 1969.
"The Night of Baker's End," 1974.
"Baby Cakes" (two-act), first produced in Austin, Tex. at the University of Texas at Austin, 1981.
"Old Grass," 1983.
"Ancestors" (three-act), first produced in Dallas, Tex., 1986.
"Deep Ellum Blues" (two-act ballet), first produced in Dallas, 1986.

OTHER

Also author of more than sixty scripts for television series "Our Street."

WORK IN PROGRESS: "Death Row," a documentary work concerning prisoners who find love on death row.

SIDELIGHTS: "Ted Shine continues a tradition established in American black theater by Langston Hughes—the use of humor as an incisive weapon and as a defense against weeping," writes Winona L. Fletcher in a *Dictionary of Literary Biography* essay. Noting that Shine "possesses microscopic insight and a finely tuned ear for dialogue and dialect, particularly that spoken by the rural Southerner," Fletcher finds that "his dramas work on stage and screen; his audiences, black or white, cannot escape from a sense of verity and from the messages Shine drives home to them." Fletcher considers Shine unique in his treatment of the thematic concerns he shares with other contemporary black playwrights, such as "the black family struggles, religion, a generation/communication gap caused by the 'new' thinking of the black revolution, and the need for love and acceptance." Says Fletcher, "Always there is serious meaning behind the laughter, and the route to self-determinism is clearly marked for those who wish to pursue it."

Shine commented: "Motivation for my work stems from life itself—a sad face, a broken heart, a trembling voice, a cry in the night. The purpose of drama for me continues to be to teach and to please, and hopefully my work will emerge realistically—uplifting the dignity of mankind."

BIOGRAPHICAL/CRITICAL SOURCES:

BOOKS

Dictionary of Literary Biography, Volume XXXVIII: *Afro-American Writers after 1955: Dramatists and Prose Writers,* Gale, 1985.
Harris, Trudier, *From Mammies to Militants: Domestics in Black American Literature,* Temple University Press, 1982.

PERIODICALS

Black American Literature Forum, summer, 1980.
Encore, number 12, 1969.

*   *   *

SHOCKLEY, Ann Allen 1927-

PERSONAL: Born June 21, 1927, in Louisville, Ky.; daughter of Henry (a social worker) and Bessie (a social worker; maiden name, Lucas) Allen; divorced; children: William Leslie Shockley, Jr., Tamara Ann Shockley. *Education:* Fisk University,

B.A., 1948; Western Reserve University (now Case Western Reserve University), M.S.L.S., 1959. *Politics:* Independent.

ADDRESSES: Home—5975 Post Rd., Nashville, Tenn. 37205. *Office*—Fisk University Library, Nashville, Tenn. 37203.

CAREER: Delaware State College, Dover, assistant librarian, 1959-60; Maryland State College (now University of Maryland Eastern Shore), Princess Anne, assistant librarian, 1960-66, associate librarian, 1966-69; Fisk University, Nashville, Tenn., associate professor of library science, 1970—, librarian for public services, 1975—, associate librarian for special collections and university archivist, 1980—. Lecturer at University of Maryland, 1968, and at Vanderbilt University and Jackson State College, both 1973; free-lance writer.

MEMBER: Authors Guild, American Library Association, Black Caucus of the American Library Association, Association for Study of Afro-American Life and History, Oral History Association, Society of American Archivists, National Women's Studies Association, Association of Black Women Historians, Tennessee Archivists, Tennessee Literary Arts Association.

AWARDS, HONORS: American Association of University Women short story award, 1962; Fisk University faculty research grant, 1970; University of Maryland Library Administrators Development Institute fellowship, 1974; American Library Association Black Caucus Award, 1975, for editorship of Black Caucus newsletter; First Annual Hatshepsut Award for Literature, 1981; Martin Luther King Black Author's Award, 1982.

WRITINGS:

(Contributor) E. J. Josey, editor, *Black Librarian in America*, Scarecrow, 1970.
(Editor with Sue P. Chandler) *Living Black American Authors: A Bibliographical Directory*, Bowker, 1973.
Loving Her (novel), Bobbs-Merrill, 1974.
(Contributor) Bill Katz and Robert Burgess, editors, *Library Lit. 5*, Scarecrow, 1975.
(Editor with Josey, and contributor) *A Handbook on Black Librarianship*, Libraries Unlimited, 1977.
The Black and White of It (short stories), Naiad Press, 1980.
Say Jesus and Come to Me (novel), Avon, 1982.

Work represented in anthologies, including: *Impressions in Asphalt*, edited by Ruthe T. Sheffey and Eugnia Collier, Scribner, 1969; *Out of Our Lives: A Selection of Contemporary Black Fiction*, edited by Quandra Prettyman Stadler, Howard University Press, 1975; *Lesbian Fiction*, edited by Elly Bulkin, Persephone Press, 1981; *Women Identified Women*, edited by Sandee J. Potter and Trudy E. Darty, Mayfield Publishing, 1982; *Home Girls: A Black Feminist Anthology*, edited by Barbara Smith, Kitchen Table: Women of Color Press, 1983; and *Between Mothers and Daughters*, edited by Susan Koppelman, The Feminist Press, 1984.

Contributor of short stories and articles to magazines, newspapers, and professional journals, including *Negro Digest, Umbra, Freedomways, Negro History Bulletin, Essence, Feminary, Azalea,* and *Phylon.*

Editor of American Library Association Black Caucus newsletter, 1972-74.

WORK IN PROGRESS: Afro-American Women Writers.

BIOGRAPHICAL/CRITICAL SOURCES:

PERIODICALS

Los Angeles Times Book Review, July 4, 1982.

*   *   *

SIMMONS, Herbert A(lfred)   1930-

PERSONAL: Born March 29, 1930, in St. Louis, Mo.; son of Alex and Almeda (Henderson) Simmons. *Education:* Attended Lincoln University, 1949-50, 1951-52; Washington University, B.A., 1958; State University of Iowa, additional study, 1959.

CAREER: Novelist and newspaper reporter. Producer of "Portraits in Rhythm," a combination of original poetry and selected writings read to jazz accompaniment in coffee houses. *Military service:* U.S. Army, two years.

MEMBER: Writers Guild of America West, Alpha Phi Alpha.

AWARDS, HONORS: Houghton Mifflin literary fellowship, 1957, for *Corner Boy;* Fannie Cook fellowship from St. Louis Peoples Art Center.

WRITINGS:

Corner Boy, Houghton, 1957.
Man Walking on Eggshells, Houghton, 1962.

Former editor of *Spliv,* a now-defunct literary journal.

WORK IN PROGRESS: Some Jazz Called Life; Freedom Bound.

SIDELIGHTS: Herbert A. Simmons's two novels, *Corner Boy* and *Man Walking on Eggshells,* were written "not only to create memorable characters but also to recreate the St. Louis of his mind," states Australia Henderson in a *Dictionary of Literary Biography* essay. "The jazz, joy, nostalgia, and pain in these works are as much a part of the city as those who live in it." Henderson adds that "Simmons's literary photography provides graphic details of time and place: the dress, language, walk, music, and life-style of black youth of the 1940s and 1950s. Such details alternate with panoramic shots of the city within a city—the Afro-American microcosm which exists, tries to survive, and is controlled by an indifferent macrocosm of whites." Although the novels are set in the 1940s and 1950s, Henderson finds in them a certain "timelessness" and suggests that "Simmons's portrait of city life is both a celebration of and a dirge for the black urban experience."

AVOCATIONAL INTERESTS: Jazz and art.

BIOGRAPHICAL/CRITICAL SOURCES:

BOOKS

Dictionary of Literary Biography, Volume 33: *Afro-American Fiction Writers after 1955,* Gale, 1984.
Joyce, Michael C., and Ann C. Watts, editors, *Literature and the Urban Experience,* Rutgers University Press, 1981.
Schraufnagel, Noel, *From Apology to Protest: The Black American Novel,* Everett/Edwards, 1973.

PERIODICALS

Jet, February 25, 1960.
Negro Digest, January, 1962.

SMITH, William Gardner   1927(?)-1974

PERSONAL: Born February 6, 1927 (some sources say 1926), in Philadelphia, Pa.; immigrated to France, c. 1951; died November 5, 1974, in Paris, France; divorced; children: Michele, Claude. *Education:* Graduated from Temple University.

CAREER: Writer. Former reporter for *Afro-American* and *Pittsburgh Courier* newspapers; news editor of English Language Services, for Agence France-Presse, 1954-74. Director of Ghana Institute of Journalism during the 1960s. *Military service:* U.S. Army, served in Germany during World War II.

WRITINGS:

Last of the Conquerors (novel), Farrar, Straus, 1948, reprinted, Chatham Bookseller, 1973.
Anger at Innocence (novel), Farrar, Straus, 1950, reprinted, Chatham Bookseller, 1973.
South Street (novel), Farrar, Straus, 1954.
The Stone Face (novel), Pocket Books, 1963.
Return to Black America, Prentice-Hall, 1970.

Contributor to American magazines and newspapers.

BIOGRAPHICAL/CRITICAL SOURCES:

PERIODICALS

Best Sellers, July 1, 1970.

OBITUARIES:

PERIODICALS

Black World, February, 1975.
New York Times, November 8, 1974.
Publishers Weekly, November 25, 1974.
Washington Post, November 8, 1974.

*   *   *

SNELLINGS, Rolland
See TOURE, Askia Muhammad Abu Bakr el

*   *   *

SOUTHERLAND, Ellease   1943-

PERSONAL: Born June 18, 1943, in Brooklyn, N.Y.; daughter of Monroe Penrose (a minister and baker) and Ellease (Dozier) Southerland. *Education:* Queens College of the City University of New York, B.A., 1965; Columbia University, M.F.A., 1974.

ADDRESSES: Home—160-27 119th Dr., Jamaica, N.Y. 11434. *Office*—Department of English, Pace University, 1 Pace Plaza, New York, N.Y. 10038.

CAREER: Department of Social Services, New York, N.Y., caseworker, 1966-72; Columbia University, Community Educational Exchange Program, New York City, instructor in English, 1973-76; Borough of Manhattan Community College of the City University of New York, New York City, adjunct assistant professor of black literature, 1973—; Pace University, New York City, poet-in-residence in African literature, 1975—; writer.

AWARDS, HONORS: John Golden Award for Fiction from Queen's College of the City University of New York, 1964, for novella *White Shadows;* Gwendolyn Brooks Poetry Award from *Black World,* 1972, for "Warlock"; *Let the Lion Eat Straw* was named one of the "Best Books for Young Adults"

by Young Adult Services Divison of the American Library Association, 1979.

WRITINGS:

The Magic Sun Spins (poetry collection; includes "That Love Survives" and "Black Is"), Paul Breman, 1975.
Let the Lion Eat Straw (autobiographical novel; Book-of-the-Month Club alternate selection), Scribner, 1979.
(Contributor) Roseann P. Bell, Bettye J. Parker, and Beverly Guy Sheftell, editors, *Sturdy Black Bridges: Visions of Black Women in Literature,* Anchor Press, 1979.

Also author of novella *White Shadows,* 1964. Contributor of short stories, essays, reviews, and poems—such as "Soldiers," "Warlock," and "Beck-Junior and the Good Shepherd"—to magazines and literary journals, including *Black World, Presence Africaine, Encore,* and *Journal of Black Poetry.*

WORK IN PROGRESS: A Feast of Fools, a novel; *A Silver Hieroglyph,* a collection of poetry; *A Green and Yellow Basket,* short stories.

SIDELIGHTS: Inspired by her uncle's recitation of a poem, Ellease Southerland resolved at the age of ten to become a poet. The fact that she has not published a great deal since that time is offset by the "meticulously distilled" quality of her work, wrote Mary Hughes Brookhart in the *Dictionary of Literary Biography.* Featuring a wide range of topics that draw mainly from her personal experiences, Southerland informs her writing with her knowledge of the Bible, ancient Egyptian mythology, and various aspects of African history and culture. "Whatever the subject or the format," remarked Brookhart, "one can expect an excellent body of literature to emerge from this still young author whose skill and talent, whose passion for beauty and clarity and the honesty of emotions, and whose good humor and rich perceptions" distinguish her work.

Abeba Williams, a black woman born illegitimately in the rural South, is the protagonist of Southerland's critically acclaimed first novel, *Let the Lion Eat Straw.* Left throughout infancy in the care of the aged midwife who delivered her, Abeba is uprooted at the age of six and transported by her natural mother to an alien life-style in Brooklyn, New York. There she finds the love of a kindly stepfather and encouragement for her exceptional musical ability. The chronicle of Abeba's life—the death of her adored stepfather, repeated rapes by an uncle during her adolescence, abandonment of a promising career as a pianist in favor of an early marriage, a husband stricken with bouts of madness, the bearing and rearing of fifteen children, and finally, death from cancer at the age of forty-five—is the "celebration of a difficult life well lived," wrote Robert Towers in the *New York Review of Books.* Agreeing with that assessment in her review for *Critic,* Faith R. Julian called the book "a remarkable account of a black woman's struggle, determination and triumph . . . despite the many vicissitudes of life."

Five years in the writing, the novel draws heavily from the author's personal life and the lives of her parents. Abeba is a close replica of Southerland's own mother, a gifted musician who gave up a potential career to marry a lay preacher with whom she eventually bore fifteen children. "The framework of Southerland's life and the world of her heroine . . . are mirrors, only slightly out of focus," noted *Washington Post* critic Jacqueline Trescott, and "the author forced herself through a painful catharsis to tell the story, patterned after the emotionally explosive lives of her parents." "Southerland's ingredients are familiar. But what she makes of them is remarkable,'' opined Annalyn Swan in *Time*. "*Let the Lion Eat Straw* is a graceful hymn of love.'' "Miss Southerland pays homage,'' concurred reviewer John Leonard in the *New York Times*. "In these few pages, an entire history of desire and talent and frustration and triumph—from boiled peanuts to Nebuchadnezzar—is whittled to an arrow in the heart.''

Joining in praise of Southerland's compact style, Swan remarked: "She compresses a lifetime of births and deaths and suffering and love into just 181 pages.'' "'Let the Lion Eat Straw' has not one extra word,'' elaborated Anne Wittels in the *Los Angeles Times Book Review*. "So condensed, distilled, is the style—and the story—sometimes the effect is of a play seen through Venetian blinds. It is all there. We can see it, really, quite clearly. And yet half is not there; half is hidden by thin shadows; half is between the lines.'' Offering further elucidation, Towers suggested that Southerland "has constructed a kind of linguistic screening device through which the events of her story—events of sometimes complex implication—are made to seem as direct, highly colored, and startling as a painting by an unusually gifted child. . . . The complexities, psychological and sociological, are not so much ignored as filtered out.''

Critics also lauded *Let the Lion Eat Straw* as an insightful depiction of black life in white America. Especially noteworthy are Southerland's characterizations, which successfully illustrate both the joys and hardships particular to being black. Commenting on the book's "allegorical quality,'' *New York Times Book Review* critic Mel Watkins noted the symbolic nature of Abeba's personal experiences. According to Watkins, Abeba "emerges as a prototype for generations of black who fled the South in search of a better life in the North and who, confronted with different but no less formidable barriers, were forced to transfer their hopes to their children.'' In agreement, Swan wrote: "Ellease Southerland's fine first novel bears witness to the world of her fathers and mothers, a world centered on the family, the community, the Lord''; "Abeba's monuments are her fifteen children with African names and with African pride to carry on after she dies.''

Clearly recognizing Southerland's place as a rising black novelist, Wittels likened the author's first novel to the works of Maya Angelou, Anne Moody, and Toni Morrison. Carrying her praise even further, Wittels hailed *Let the Lion Eat Straw* as "a story that sticks and haunts the shadowy places of one's mind. . . . a story that transcends race and class. . . . a story that raises questions which affect all of us.''

AVOCATIONAL INTERESTS: Music (especially jazz), exercise, dance, theatre, cooking (especially baking), embroidery, travel, hieroglyphs.

BIOGRAPHICAL/CRITICAL SOURCES:

BOOKS

Dictionary of Literary Biography, Volume 33: *Afro-American Fiction Writers After 1955*, Gale, 1984.

PERIODICALS

Best Sellers, August, 1979.
Chicago Tribune Book World, May 13, 1979.
Choice, October, 1976.
Christian Science Monitor, July 11, 1979.
Commonweal, February 29, 1980.
Critic, September 15, 1979.
First World, December, 1979.
Los Angeles Times Book Review, July 15, 1979.

New York Review of Books, October 11, 1979.
New York Times, May 10, 1979.
New York Times Book Review, June 3, 1979.
Time, June 18, 1979.
Washington Post, August 6, 1979.

*   *   *

SOWELL, Thomas 1930-

PERSONAL: Born June 30, 1930, in Gastonia, N.C.; married Alma Jean Parr; children: two. *Education:* Harvard University, A.B. (magna cum laude), 1958; Columbia University, A.M., 1959; University of Chicago, Ph.D., 1968.

ADDRESSES: Office—Hoover Institution, Stanford, Calif. 94305.

CAREER: U.S. Department of Labor, Washington, D.C., economist, 1961-62; Rutgers University, Douglass College, New Brunswick, N.J., instructor in economics, 1962-63; Howard University, Washington, D.C., lecturer in economics, 1963-64; American Telephone & Telegraph Co., New York, N.Y., economic analyst, 1964-65; Cornell University, Ithaca, N.Y., assistant professor of economics, 1965-69; director of Summer Intensive Training Program in Economic Theory, 1968; Brandeis University, Waltham, Mass., associate professor of economics, 1969-70; University of California, Los Angeles, associate professor, 1970-74, professor of economics, 1974-80; Urban Institute, Washington, D.C., project director, 1972-74; Center for Advanced Study in the Behavioral Sciences, Stanford, Calif., fellow, 1976-77; Hoover Institution, Stanford, senior fellow, 1977, 1980—. Visiting professor, Amherst College, 1977. *Military service:* U.S. Marine Corps, 1951-53.

WRITINGS:

(Contributor) I. H. Rima, editor, *Readings in the History of Economic Thought*, Holt, 1970.
Economics: Analysis and Issues, Scott, Foresman, 1971.
Black Education: Myths and Tragedies, McKay, 1972.
Say's Law: An Historical Analysis, Princeton University Press, 1972.
Classical Economics Reconsidered, Princeton University Press, 1974.
Affirmative Action: Was It Necessary in Academia?, American Enterprise Institute for Public Policy Research, 1975.
Race and Economics, McKay, 1975.
Patterns of Black Excellence, Ethics and Public Policy Center, Georgetown University, 1977.
(Editor) *American Ethnic Groups*, Urban Institute, 1978.
(Editor) *Essays and Data on American Ethnic Groups*, Urban Institute, 1978.
Markets and Minorities, Basic Books, 1981.
(Editor with others) *The Fairmont Papers: Black Alternatives Conference, December, 1980*, ICS Press, 1981.
Pink and Brown People, and Other Controversial Essays, Hoover Institution, 1981.
(Contributor) W. E. Block and M. A. Walker, editors, *Discrimination, Affirmative Action and Equal Opportunity: An Economic and Social Perspective*, Fraser Institute, 1982.
Knowledge and Decision, Basic Books, 1982.
Ethnic America: A History, Basic Books, 1983.
The Economics and Politics of Race: An International Perspective, Morrow, 1983.
Marxism: Philosophy and Economics, Morrow, 1985.
Civil Rights: Rhetoric or Reality?, Morrow, 1985.

Education: Assumptions versus History, Hoover Institution, 1986.
Compassion versus Guilt, and Other Essays, Morrow, 1987.
A Conflict of Visions: Ideological Origins of Political Struggles, Morrow, 1987.

Contributor to numerous periodicals, including *New York Times Magazine, Ethics, American Economic Review, Social Research, Education Digest, Western Review, University of Chicago Magazine, Oxford Economic Papers*, and *Economica*.

SIDELIGHTS: Called "a free-market economist and perhaps the leading black scholar among conservatives" by Fred Barnes of the *New York Times Book Review*, Thomas Sowell has written a score of controversial books about economics, race, and ethnic groups. His support for a laissez-faire economic system with few government constraints and his vocal opposition to most of the social programs and judicial actions favored by most other black spokesmen have made him a target for much criticism. Yet, Steven E. Plaut of *Commentary* calls Sowell "one of America's most trenchant and perceptive commentators on the subject of race relations and ethnicity." Davis Holmstrom, writing in the *Los Angeles Times*, maintains that "in the writing of economist Thomas Sowell, scholarship, clarity and genuine information come together as nicely and perfectly as a timeless quote."

Sowell has done extensive research into the economic performance of racial and ethnic groups throughout the world, trying to determine the factors which make some groups more successful than others. He has presented his research findings and the conclusions he has drawn from it in such books as *Race and Economics, American Ethnic Groups, Markets and Minorities, Ethnic America: A History, The Economics and Politics of Race: An International Perspective*, and *Civil Rights: Rhetoric or Reality?* These books have disproven a number of popularly held beliefs while bringing new and potentially valuable information to light. As George M. Fredrickson notes in the *New York Times Book Review*, "Sowell is engaged in a continuing polemic against the basic assumptions of liberals, radicals and civil rights leaders. But the quality of his evidence and reasoning requires that he be taken seriously. His ideological opponents will have to meet his arguments squarely and incisively to justify the kind of policies currently identified with the pursuit of racial equality and social justice."

One of Sowell's most controversial contentions is that a racial or ethnic group's economic success is not seriously hindered by discrimination from society at large. In *The Economics and Politics of Race*, for instance, he gives several examples of minority groups who have fared well despite prejudice against them, and of other groups with little discrimination to overcome who have done poorly. The Chinese minorities in Southeast Asian countries, despite intense resistance from the native populations, have done very well economically. They often dominate their local economies. European Jews have also faced opposition from majority population groups. Yet they too have performed outstandingly well and enjoy a high level of economic success. On the other hand, Plaut gives an example of underachievement from Sowell's *The Economics and Politics of Race:* "In Brazil and other parts of South America blacks face less racism than do American blacks. . . . Yet for all this tolerance, Brazil shows a larger gap in black-white earnings, social position, and education than does the United States."

The key factor in an ethnic group's economic success, Sowell argues, is "something economists refer to as human capital—values, attitudes and skills embodied in a culture," as Stanley

O. Williford explains it in the *Los Angeles Times Book Review*. An ethnic or racial group which emphasizes hard work, saving money, and acquiring an education will generally do well whatever the political or social climate. *Newsweek*'s David Gelman notes that Sowell "has a conservative message to impart. Essentially, it is that diligence, discipline and entrepreneurial drive can overthrow the most formidable barriers of poverty and bigotry."

Because of this belief, Sowell argues against continued efforts by the federal government to end racial discrimination, a problem he believes was largely eliminated during the civil rights struggle, and calls instead for a greater emphasis on free market economics. A healthy, growing economy, Sowell believes, does the most good for minority groups who suffer from poverty. As Aaron Wildavsky writes in the *National Review*, "When labor is scarce and the markets for it are competitive, wages go up regardless of the prejudices of employers." Sowell points out in *Civil Rights: Rhetoric or Reality?* that "the economic rise of minorities preceded by many years passage of the Civil Rights Act . . . [and] that this trend was not accelerated either by that legislation or by the quotas introduced during the seventies," as Tony Eastland reports in the *American Spectator*. Sowell believes that minority groups, Chris Wall writes in the *Los Angeles Times Book Review*, are "crying racism at every turn to divert attention from the fact that their cultures or subcultures may be economically unproductive."

Sowell dismisses much of what black civil rights leaders believe necessary for the betterment of American blacks. He questions, for example, the value for black students of integrated public schools, called for by the Warren Court in the case Brown vs. Board of Education. Joseph Sobran of *National Review* reports that Sowell finds that the court's contention "that segregated schools produced inferior black education . . . expresses and justifies a destructively paternalistic attitude, according to which a black child can't learn anything except in close proximity to a white one. With forced busing, [Sowell] reflects ironically, the white man's burden has become 'the white *child's* burden—to go forth and civilize the heathen.'"

Other government programs, including affirmative action racial quotas and public welfare, are also attacked by Sowell. Sowell is convinced, Nathan Glazer writes in the *New Republic*, "that hardly anything government will do can help blacks and other minorities with high levels of poverty and low levels of educational and economic achievement, and that almost anything government will do will only make matters worse." In a *Choice* review of *Civil Rights*, R. J. Steamer admits that "Sowell's revolutionary view—that government programs such as affirmative action, forced busing, and food stamps will not bring the disadvantaged black minority into the economic and social mainstream and might better be abandoned—will anger many." One such angered critic is Gelman, who claims that Sowell "seems to fault blacks for resting on their grievances instead of climbing aboard the success wagon." But Sowell sees government programs and those who call for them as part of a self-destructive mind-set. The black civil rights establishment, Sowell believes, "represents a thin layer of privileged blacks who have risen socially by echoing liberal ideology, with its view of blacks in general as helpless victims who depend on political favors for whatever gains they can make," Sobran explains.

Sowell's own life story seems to illustrate many of the values he now expounds. Born in North Carolina, Sowell attended a segregated high school where he was at the top of his class. "We never wondered why there weren't any white kids there," he tells Sobran. "We never thought we'd be learning more if there *had* been white kids there. In fact, we never *thought* about white kids." A graduate of Harvard University, Columbia University, and the University of Chicago, Sowell went on to hold a number of positions in government and academia before joining the Hoover Institution in 1980. Through it all, Sobran remarks, Sowell has been "matter-of-fact about his race and its bearing on his intellectual life."

The consistent differences between Sowell's views and those of other black commentators, and the differences between those of the political left and right, moved Sowell to examine the underlying assumptions that create this dichotomy. In *A Conflict of Visions: Ideological Origins of Political Struggle,* he describes "two divergent views of man and society that he convincingly contends underlie many of the political, economic and social clashes of the last two centuries and remain very much with us today," as Walter Goodman of the *New York Times* explains. Sowell posits the unconstrained and the constrained views of man. "The unconstrained see human beings as perfectible," Otto Friedrich of *Time* writes, "the constrained as forever flawed." Sowell writes in the book that "the constrained vision is a tragic vision of the human condition. The unconstrained vision is a moral vision of human intentions."

These two visions are, Daniel Seligman writes in *Fortune,* "the mind-sets that originally made [intellectuals] gravitate to some ideas instead of others." Those with an unconstrained view of man, for example, tend to believe that social problems can be ultimately solved, and that man will usually act rationally. Such beliefs can lead to social engineering efforts to correct perceived societal ills. Those with a constrained view of man see him as imperfect and human nature as unchanging. They often call for a limited government, a strong defense, and strict criminal penalties.

Sowell admits that not all people hold to one or the other vision consistently. And such ideologies as Marxism and fascism are compounds of both the constrained and unconstrained visions. Yet, critics see much of value in Sowell's plan. "Right or wrong in his main thesis," Sobran states, "he is full of stunning insights." "The split between the constrained and the unconstrained," Barnes notes, "works as a framework for understanding social theories and politics." Goodman finds that *A Conflict of Visions* "does lay out styles of thinking that we can readily recognize today in the divisions between left and right." And Michael Harrington, who explains in his *Washington Post Book World* review that "I reject the basic assumptions and the very inellectual framework" of the book, nonetheless concludes that "its insights and *apercus* reveal a serious mind honestly and fairly . . . trying to grapple with those visionary premises on which our supposedly objective data are so often based and ordered."

During his career as a leading black economist, Sowell "has spoken out often, with considerable force and eloquence, against many of the assumptions about black life in the United States that are widely held by the black leadership and its white allies," Jonathan Yardley reports in the *Washington Post Book World.* His arguments are beginning to attract converts in the black community. As Glazer notes, "One has the impression that increasingly he is heeded, that this unbending analyst is having a greater influence on the discussion of matters of race and ethnicity than any other writer of the past ten years."

Harrington, a socialist who admits that he is "utterly at odds" with Sowell's political beliefs, still calls him "one of the few conservative thinkers in America today who is interesting as a theorist."

BIOGRAPHICAL/CRITICAL SOURCES:

BOOKS

Sowell, Thomas, *Civil Rights: Rhetoric or Reality?*, Morrow, 1985.
Sowell, Thomas, *A Conflict of Visions: Ideological Origins of Political Struggles*, Morrow, 1987.

PERIODICALS

American Spectator, July, 1984.
Choice, September, 1984.
Commentary, December, 1983.
Fortune, March 16, 1987.
Los Angeles Times, March 22, 1985.
Los Angeles Times Book Review, September 6, 1981, January 8, 1984.
National Review, October 16, 1981, February 13, 1987.
New Republic, November 21, 1983, June 11, 1984.
Newsweek, August 24, 1981.
New York Times, January 24, 1987.
New York Times Book Review, October 16, 1983, January 25, 1987.
Time, March 16, 1987.
Washington Post Book World, April 29, 1984, January 4, 1987.

—*Sketch by Thomas Wiloch*

*   *   *

SOYINKA, Wole   1934-

PERSONAL: First name is pronounced *woh*-leh; surname is pronounced shaw-*yin*-ka; given name, Akinwande Oluwole; born July 13, 1934, in Isara, Nigeria; son of Ayo (a headmaster) and Eniola Soyinka. *Education:* Attended University of Ibadan; University of Leeds, B.A. (with honors), 1959. *Religion:* "Human liberty."

ADDRESSES: Office—Department of Dramatic Arts, University of Ife, Ile-Ife, Oyo, Nigeria. *Agent*—Greenbaum, Wolff & Ernst, 437 Madison Ave., New York, N.Y. 10022.

CAREER: Playwright, poet, and novelist. University of Ibadan, Nigeria, research fellow in drama, 1960-61, chairman of department of theatre arts, 1967-71; University of Ife, professor of drama, 1972; Cambridge University, Cambridge, England, fellow of Churchill College, 1973-74; University of Ife, chairman of department of dramatic arts, 1975—. Director of own theatre groups, Orisun Players and 1960 Masks, in Lagos and Ibadan, Nigeria. Visiting professor at University of Sheffield, 1974, University of Ghana, 1975, and Cornell University, 1986.

MEMBER: International Theatre Institute (president), Union of Writers of the African Peoples (secretary-general).

AWARDS, HONORS: Rockefeller Foundation grant, 1960; John Whiting Drama Prize, 1966; Dakar Negro Arts Festival award, 1966; *New Statesman* Jock Campbell Award, 1968, for *The Interpreters;* Nobel Prize in Literature, 1986; named Commander of the Federal Republic of Nigeria by General Ibrahim Babangida, 1986; D.Litt., Yale University and University of Leeds; Prisoner of Conscience Prize, Amnesty International.

WRITINGS:

The Man Died: Prison Notes of Wole Soyinka, Harper, 1972, 2nd edition, Rex Collings, 1973.
Myth, Literature and the African World (essays), Cambridge University Press, 1976.
Ake: The Years of Childhood (autobiography), Random House, 1981.
Isara, Random House, 1988.

NOVELS

The Interpreters, Deutsch, 1965.
(Translator) D. O. Fagunwa, *The Forest of a Thousand Daemons: A Hunter's Saga,* Nelson, 1967, Humanities, 1969.
Season of Anomy, Rex Collings, 1973.

POETRY

Idanre and Other Poems, Methuen, 1967, Hill & Wang, 1969.
Poems from Prison, Rex Collings, 1969, expanded edition published as *A Shuttle in the Crypt,* Hill & Wang, 1972.
(Editor and author of introduction) *Poems of Black Africa,* Hill & Wang, 1975.
Ogun Abibiman, Rex Collings, 1976.

CONTRIBUTOR

D. W. Jefferson, editor, *The Morality of Art,* Routledge & Kegan Paul, 1969.
O. R. Dathorne and Wilfried Feuser, editors, *African Prose,* Penguin, 1969.

PLAYS

"The Invention," first produced in London at Royal Court Theatre, 1955.
A Dance of the Forests (also see below; first produced in London, 1960), Oxford University Press, 1962.
The Lion and the Jewel (also see below; first produced at Royal Court Theatre, 1966), Oxford University Press, 1962.
Three Plays (includes "The Trials of Brother Jero" [also see below], one-act, produced Off-Broadway at Greenwich Mews Playhouse, November 9, 1967; "The Strong Breed" [also see below], one-act, produced at Greenwich Mews Playhouse, November 9, 1967; and "The Swamp Dwellers" [also see below]), Mbari Publications, 1962, Northwestern University Press, 1963.
Five Plays (includes "The Lion and the Jewel," "The Swamp Dwellers," "The Trials of Brother Jero," "The Strong Breed" and "A Dance of the Forests"), Oxford University Press, 1964.
The Road (produced in Stratford, England, at Theatre Royal, 1965), Oxford University Press, 1965.
Kongi's Harvest (also see below; produced Off-Broadway at St. Mark's Playhouse, April 14, 1968), Oxford University Press, 1966.
Three Short Plays, Oxford University Press, 1969.
The Trials of Brother Jero, Oxford University Press, 1969, published with "The Strong Breed" as *The Trials of Brother Jero and The Strong Breed: Two Plays,* Dramatists Play Service, 1969.
"Kongi's Harvest" (screenplay), produced by Calpenny-Nigerian Films, 1970.
Madmen and Specialists (two-act; produced in Waterford, Conn. at Eugene O'Neill Memorial Theatre, August 1, 1970), Methuen, 1971, Hill & Wang, 1972.
(Contributor) *Palaver: Three Dramatic Discussion Starters* (includes "The Lion and the Jewel"), Friendship Press, 1971.

Before the Blackout (revue sketches; also see below), Orisun Acting Editions, 1971.
(Editor) *Plays from the Third World: An Anthology,* Doubleday, 1971.
The Jero Plays (includes "The Trials of Brother Jero" and "Jero's Metamorphosis"), Methuen, 1973.
(Contributor) *African Theatre: Eight Prize Winning Plays for Radio,* Heinemann, 1973.
Camwood on the Leaves, Methuen, 1973, published with "Before the Blackout" as *Camwood on the Leaves and Before the Blackout,* Third Press, 1974.
(Adapter) *The Bacchae of Euripides: A Communion Rite* (first produced in London at Old Vic Theatre, August 2, 1973), Methuen, 1973, Norton, 1974.
Collected Plays, Oxford University Press, Volume 1, 1973, Volume 2, 1974.
Death and the King's Horseman (produced at University of Ife, 1976; produced in Chicago at Goodman Theatre, 1979; produced in New York at Vivian Beaumont Theatre, March, 1987), Norton, 1975.
Opera Wonyosi (light opera), Indiana University Press, 1981.
A Play of Giants, Methuen, 1984.
Six Plays, Methuen, 1984.
Requiem for a Futurologist, Rex Collings, 1985.

Also author of television script, "Culture in Transition."

OTHER

Co-editor, *Black Orpheus,* 1961-64; editor, *Transition* (now *Ch'Indaba*), 1974-76.

SIDELIGHTS: Many critics consider Wole Soyinka as Africa's finest writer. The Nigerian playwright's unique style blends traditional Yoruban folk-drama with European dramatic form to provide both spectacle and penetrating satire. Soyinka told *New York Times Magazine* writer Jason Berry that in the African cultural tradition, the artist "has always functioned as the record of the mores and experience of his society." His plays, novels and poetry all reflect that philosophy, serving as a record of twentieth-century Africa's political turmoil and its struggle to reconcile tradition with modernization. Eldred Jones states in his book *Wole Soyinka* that the author's work touches on universal themes as well as addressing specifically African concerns: "The essential ideas which emerge from a reading of Soyinka's work are not specially African ideas, although his characters and their mannerisms are African. His concern is with man on earth. Man is dressed for the nonce in African dress and lives in the sun and tropical forest, but he represents the whole race."

As a young child, Soyinka was comfortable with the conflicting cultures in his world, but as he grew older he became increasingly aware of the pull between African tradition and Western modernization. Ake, his village, was mainly populated wth people from the Yoruba tribe, and was presided over by the *ogboni,* or trial elders. Soyinka's grandfather introduced him to the pantheon of Yoruba gods and to other tribal folklore. His parents were key representatives of colonial influences, however: his mother was a devout Christian convert and his father acted as headmaster for the village school established by the British. When Soyinka's father began urging Wole to leave Ake to attend the government school in Ibadan, the boy was spirited away by his grandfather, who administered a scarification rite of manhood. Soyinka was also consecrated to the god Ogun, ruler of metal, roads, and both the creative and destructive essence. Ogun is a recurring figure in Soyinka's work and has been named by the author as his muse.

Ake: The Years of Childhood is Soyinka's account of his first ten years, and stands as "a classic of childhood memoirs wherever and whenever produced," states *New York Times Book Review* contributor James Olney. Numerous critics have singled out Soyinka's ability to recapture the changing perspective of a child as the book's outstanding feature; it begins in a light tone but grows increasingly serious as the boy matures and becomes aware of the problems faced by the adults around him. The book concludes with an account of a tax revolt organized by Soyinka's mother, and the beginnings of Nigerian independence. "Most of 'Ake' charms; that was Mr. Soyinka's intention," writes John Leonard of the *New York Times*. "The last 50 pages, however, inspire and confound; they are transcendent." Olney agrees that "the lyricism, grace, humor and charm of 'Ake' . . . are in the service of a profoundly serious viewpoint that attempts to show us how things should be in the community of men and how they should not be. Mr. Soyinka, however, does this dramatically, not discursively. Through recollection, restoration and re-creation, he conveys a personal vision that was formed by the childhood world that he now returns to evoke and exalt in his autobiography. This is the ideal circle of autobiography at its best. It is what makes 'Ake,' in addition to its other great virtues, the best introduction available to the work of one of the liveliest, most exciting writers in the world today."

Soyinka published some poems and short stories in *Black Orpheus*, a highly-regarded Nigerian literary magazine, before leaving Africa to attend the University of Leeds in England. There his first play was produced. "The Invention" is a comic satire based on a sudden loss of pigment by South Africa's black population. Unable to distinguish blacks from whites and thus enforce its apartheid policies, the government is thrown into chaos. "The play is Soyinka's sole direct treatment of the political situation in Africa," notes Thomas Hayes in the *Dictionary of Literary Biography Yearbook: 1986*. Soyinka returned to Nigeria in 1960, shortly after independence from colonial rule had been declared. He began to research Yoruba folklore and drama in depth and incorporated elements of both into his play *A Dance of the Forests*.

A Dance of the Forests was commissioned as part of Nigeria's independence celebrations. In his play, Soyinka warned the newly independent Nigerians that the end of colonial rule did not mean an end to their country's problems. It shows a bickering group of mortals who summon up the *egungun* (spirits of the dead, revered by the Yoruba people) for a festival. They have presumed the *egungun* to be noble and wise, but they discover that their ancestors are as petty and spiteful as any living people. "The whole concept ridicules the African viewpoint that glorifies the past at the expense of the present," suggests John F. Povey in *Tri-Quarterly*. "The sentimentalized glamor of the past is exposed so that the same absurdities may not be reenacted in the future. This constitutes a bold assertion to an audience awaiting an easy appeal to racial heroics." Povey also praises Soyinka's skill in using dancing, drumming and singing to reinforce his theme: "The dramatic power of the surging forest dance [in the play] carries its own visual conviction. It is this that shows Soyinka to be a man of the theatre, not simply a writer."

After warning against living in nostalgia for Africa's past in *A Dance of the Forests*, Soyinka lampooned the indiscriminate embrace of Western modernization in *The Lion and the Jewel*. A *Times Literary Supplement* reviewer calls this play a "richly ribald comedy," which combines poetry and prose "with a marvellous lightness in the treatment of both." The plot re-volves around Sidi, the village beauty, and the rivalry between her two suitors. Baroka is the village chief, an old man with many wives; Lakunle is the enthusiastically Westernized schoolteacher who dreams of molding Sidi into a "civilized" woman. In *Introduction to Nigerian Literature,* Eldred Jones comments that *The Lion and the Jewel* is "a play which is so easily (and erroneously) interpreted as a clash between progress and reaction, with the play coming down surprisingly in favour of reaction. The real clash is not between old and new, or between real progress and reaction. It is a clash between the genuine and the false; between the well-done and the half-baked. Lakunle the school teacher would have been a poor symbol of any desirable kind of progress. . . . He is a man of totally confused values. [Baroka's worth lies in] the traditional values of which he is so confident and in which he so completely outmaneouvres Lakunle who really has no values at all." Bruce King, editor of *Introduction to Nigerian Literature,* names *The Lion and the Jewel* "the best literary work to come out of Africa."

Soyinka was well established as Nigeria's premier playwright when in 1965 he published his first novel, *The Interpreters.* The novel allowed him to expand on themes already expressed in his stage dramas, and to present a sweeping view of Nigerian life in the years immediately following independence. Essentially plotless, *The Interpreters* is loosely structured around the informal discussions between five young Nigerian intellectuals. Each has been educated in a foreign country and returned hoping to shape Nigeria's destiny. They are hampered by their own confused values, however, as well as the corruption they encounter everywhere. Some reviewers liken Soyinka's writing style in *The Interpreters* to that of James Joyce and William Faulkner. Others take exception to the formless quality of the novel, but Eustace Palmer asserts in *The Growth of the African Novel:* "If there are reservations about the novel's structure, there can be none about the thoroughness of the satire at society's expense. Soyinka's wide-ranging wit takes in all sections of a corrupt society—the brutal masses, the aimless intellecutals, the affected and hypocritical university dons, the vulgar and corrupt businessmen, the mediocre civil servants, the illiterate politicians and the incompetent journalists. [The five main characters are all] talented intellectuals who have retained their African consciousness although they were largely educated in the western world. Yet their western education enables them to look at their changing society with a certain amount of detachment. They are therefore uniquely qualified to be interpreters of this society. The reader is impressed by their honesty, sincerity, moral idealism, concern for truth and justice and aversion to corruption, snobbery and hypocrisy; but anyone who assumes that Soyinka presents all the interpreters as models of behaviour will be completely misreading the novel. He is careful to expose their selfishness, egoism, cynicism and aimlessness. Indeed the conduct of the intellectuals both in and out of the university is a major preoccupation of Soyinka's in this novel. The aimlessness and superficiality of the lives of most of the interpreters is patent."

Neil McEwan points out in *Africa and the Novel* that for all its seriousness, *The Interpreters* is also "among the liveliest of recent novels in English. It is bright satire full of good sense and good humour which are African and contemporary: the highest spirits of its author's early work. . . . Behind the jokes of his novel is a theme that he has developed angrily elsewhere: that whatever progress may mean for Africa it is not a lesson to be learned from outside, however much of 'modernity' Africans may share with others." McEwan further observes that although *The Interpreters* does not have a rigidly structured plot, ''there is unity in the warmth and sharpness of its comic vision. There are moments which sadden or anger; but they do not diminish the fun.'' Palmer notes that *The Interpreters* notably influenced the African fiction that followed it, shifting the focus ''from historical, cultural and sociological analysis to penetrating social comment and social satire.''

1965 also marked Soyinka's first arrest by the Nigerian police. He was accused of using a gun to force a radio announcer to broadcast incorrect election results. No evidence was ever produced, however, and the PEN writers' organization launched a protest campaign, headed by William Styron and Norman Mailer. Soyinka was released after three months. He was next arrested two years later, during Nigeria's civil war. Soyinka was completely opposed to the conflict, and especially to the Nigerian government's brutal policies toward the Ibo people who were attempting to form their own country, Biafra. He traveled to Biafra to establish a peace commission composed of leading intellectuals from both sides; when he returned, the Nigerian police accused him of helping the Biafrans to buy jet fighters. Once again he was imprisoned. This time Soyinka was held for more than two years, although he was never formally charged with any crime. Most of that time he was kept in solitary confinement. When all of his fellow prisoners were vaccinated against meningitis, Soyinka was passed by; when he developed serious vision problems, they were ignored by his jailers. He was denied reading and writing materials, but he manufactured his own ink and began to keep a prison diary, written on toilet paper, cigarette packages and in between the lines of the few books he secretly obtained. Each poem or fragment of journal he managed to smuggle to the outside world became a literary event and a reassurance to his supporters that Soyinka still lived, despite rumors to the contrary. He was released in 1969 and left Nigeria soon after, not returning until a change of power took place in 1975.

Published as *The Man Died: Prison Notes of Wole Soyinka,* the author's diary constitutes ''the most important work that has been written about the Biafran war,'' believes Charles R. Larson, contributor to *Nation.* '''The Man Died' is not so much the story of Wole Soyinka's own temporary death during the Nigerian Civil War but a personified account of Nigeria's fall from sanity, documented by one of the country's leading intellectuals.'' Gerald Weales's *New York Times Book Review* article suggests that the political content of *The Man Died* is less fascinating than ''the notes that deal with prison life, the observation of everything from a warder's catarrh to the predatory life of insects after a rain. Of course, these are not simply reportorial. They are vehicles to carry the author's shifting states of mind, to convey the real subject matter of the book; the author's attempt to survive as a man, and as a mind. The notes are both a means to that survival and a record to it.'' Larson underlines the book's political impact, however, noting that ironically, ''while other Nigerian writers were emotionally castrated by the war, Soyinka, who was placed in solitary confinement so that he wouldn't embarrass the government, was writing work after work, books that will no doubt embarrass the Nigerian Government more than anything the Ibo writers may ever publish.'' A *Times Literary Supplement* reviewer concurs, characterizing *The Man Died* as ''a damning indictment of what Mr. Soyinka sees as the iniquities of wartime Nigeria and the criminal tyranny of its administration in peacetime.''

Many literary commentators feel that Soyinka's work changed profoundly after his prison term, darkening in tone and focusing on the war and its aftermath. In the *Dictionary of Literary Biography Yearbook: 1986,* Thomas Hayes quotes Soyinka on his concerns after the war: ''I have one abiding religion—human liberty . . . conditioned to the truth that life is meaningless, insulting, without this fullest liberty, and in spite of the despairing knowledge that words alone seem unable to guarantee its possession, my writing grows more and more preoccupied with the theme of the oppressive boot, the irrelevance of the color of the foot that wears it and the struggle for individuality.''

In spite of its satire, most critics had found *The Interpreters* to be ultimately an optimistic book. In contrast, Soyinka's second novel expresses almost no hope for Africa's future, says John Mellors in *London Magazine:* ''Wole Soyinka appears to have written much of *Season of Anomy* in a blazing fury, angry beyond complete control of words at the abuses of power and the outbreaks of both considered and spontaneous violence. . . . The plot charges along, dragging the reader (not because he doesn't want to go, but because he finds it hard to keep up) through forest, mortuary and prison camp in nightmare visions of tyranny, torture, slaughter and putrefaction. The book reeks of pain. . . . Soyinka hammers at the point that the liberal has to deal with violence in the world however much he would wish he could ignore it; the scenes of murder and mutilation, while sickeningly explicit, are justifed by . . . the author's anger and compassion and insistence that bad will not become better by our refusal to examine it.''

Like *Season of Anomy,* Soyinka's postwar plays are considered more brooding than his earlier work. *Madmen and Specialist* is called ''grim'' by Martin Banham and Clive Wake in *African Theatre Today.* In the play, a doctor returns from the war trained as a specialist in torture and uses his new skills on his father. The play's major themes are ''the loss of faith and rituals'' and ''the break-up of the family unit which traditionally in Africa has been the foundation of society,'' according to Charles Larson in the *New York Times Book Review.* Names and events in the play are fictionalized to avoid censorship, but Soyinka has clearly ''leveled a wholesale criticism of life in Nigeria since the Civil War: a police state in which only madmen and spies can survive, in which the losers are mad and the winners are paranoid about the possibility of another rebellion. The prewar corruption and crime have returned, supported by the more sophisticated acts of terrorism and espionage introduced during the war.'' Larson summarizes: ''In large part 'Madmen and Specialists' is a product of those months Soyinka spent in prison, in solitary confinement, as a political prisoner. It is, not surprisingly, the most brutal piece of social criticism he has published.'' In a similar tone, *A Play of Giants* presents four African leaders—thinly disguised versions of Jean Bedel Bokassa, Sese Seko Mobutu, Macias Ngeuma, and Idi Amin—meeting at the United Nations building, where ''their conversation reflects the corruption and cruelty of their regimes and the casual, brutal flavor of their rule,'' discloses Hayes. In Hayes's opinion, *A Play of Giants* demonstrates that ''as Soyinka has matured he has hardened his criticism of all that restricts the individual's ability to choose, think, and act free from external oppression. . . . . [It is] his harshest attack against modern Africa, a blunt, venomous assault on . . . African leaders and the powers who support them.''

Soyinka's work is frequently described as demanding but rewarding reading. Although his plays are widely praised, they are seldom performed, especially outside of Africa. The dancing and choric speech often found in them are unfamiliar and difficult for non-African actors to master, a problem Holly Hill notes in her London *Times* review of the Lincoln Center Theatre production of *Death and the King's Horseman*. She awards high praise to the play, however, saying it "has the stateliness and mystery of Greek tragedy." When the Swedish Academy awarded Soyinka the Nobel Prize in Literature in 1986, its members singled out *Death and the King's Horseman* and *A Dance of the Forests* as "evidence that Soyinka is 'one of the finest poetical playwrights that have written in English,'" reports Stanley Meisler of the *Los Angeles Times*. Hayes summarizes Wole Soyinka's importance: "His drama and fiction have challenged the West to broaden its aesthetic and accept African standards of art and literature. His personal and political life have challenged Africa to embrace the truly democratic values of the African tribe and reject the tyranny of power practiced on the continent by its colonizers and by many of its modern rulers."

BIOGRAPHICAL/CRITICAL SOURCES:

BOOKS

Banham, Martin and Clive Wake, *African Theatre Today*, Pitman Publishing, 1976.

Banham, Martin, *Wole Soyinka's "The Lion and the Jewel,"* Rex Collings, 1981.

Contemporary Literary Criticism, Gale, Volume 3, 1975, Volume 5, 1976, Volume 14, 1980, Volume 36, 1986, Volume 44, 1987.

Dictionary of Literary Biography Yearbook: 1986, Gale, 1987.

Dunton, C. P., *Notes on "Three Short Plays,"* Longman, 1982.

Gakwandi, Shatto Arthur, *The Novel and Contemporary Experience in America*, Heinemann, 1977.

Gibbs, James, editor, *Study Aid to "Kongi's Harvest,"* Rex Collings, 1973.

Gibbs, James, editor, *Critical Perspectives on Wole Soyinka*, Three Continents, 1980.

Gibbs, James, editor, *Notes on "The Lion and the Jewel,"* Longman, 1982.

Gibbs, James, *Wole Soyinka*, Macmillan, 1986.

Gibbs, James, Ketu Katrak and Henry Gates, Jr., editors, *Wole Soyinka: A Bibliography of Primary and Secondary Sources*, Greenwood Press, 1986.

Goodwin, K. L., *Understanding African Poetry*, Heinemann, 1979.

Jones, Eldred, editor, *African Literature Today, Number 5: The Novel in Africa*, Heinemann, 1971.

Jones, Eldred, editor, *African Literature Today, Number 6: Poetry in Africa*, Heinemann, 1973.

Jones, Eldred, *Wole Soyinka*, Twayne, 1973 (published in England as *The Writings of Wole Soyinka*, Heinemann, 1973).

Katrak, Ketu, *Wole Soyinka and Modern Tragedy: A Study of Dramatic Theory and Practice*, Greenwood Press, 1986.

King, Bruce, editor, *Introduction to Nigerian Literature*, Africana Publishing, 1972.

Larson, Charles R., *The Emergence of African Fiction*, revised edition, Indiana University Press, 1972.

Laurence, Margaret, *Long Drums and Cannons: Nigerian Dramatists and Novelists*, Praeger, 1968.

McEwan, Neil, *Africa and the Novel*, Humanities Press, 1983.

Moore, Gerald, *Wole Soyinka*, Africana Publishing, 1971.

Morell, Karen L., editor, *In Person—Achebe, Awoonor, and Soyinka at the University of Washington*, African Studies Program, Institute for Comparative and Foreign Area Studies, University of Washington, 1975.

Ogunba, Oyin, *The Movement of Transition: A Study of the Plays of Wole Soyinka*, Ibadan University Press, 1975.

Ogunba, Oyin, and others, editors, *Theatre in Africa*, Ibadan University Press, 1978.

Palmer, Eustace, *The Growth of the African Novel*, Heinemann, 1979.

Parsons, E. M., editor, *Notes on Wole Soyinka's "The Jero Plays,"* Methuen, 1982.

Pieterse, Cosmo, and Dennis Duerden, editors, *African Writers Talking: A Collection of Radio Interviews*, Africana Publishing, 1972.

Probyn, editor, *Notes on "The Road,"* Longman, 1981.

Ricard, Alain, *Theatre et Nationalisme: Wole Soyinka et LeRoi Jones*, Presence Africaine, 1972.

Roscoe, Adrian A., *Mother Is Gold: A Study in West African Literature*, Cambridge University Press, 1971.

Soyinka, Wole, *The Man Died: Prison Notes of Wole Soyinka*, Harper, 1972.

Soyinka, Wole, *Myth, Literature and the African World*, Cambridge University Press, 1976.

Soyinka, Wole, *Ake: The Years of Childhood*, Random House, 1981.

Tucker, Martin, *Africa in Modern Literature: A Survey of Contemporary Writing in English*, Ungar, 1967.

PERIODICALS

America, February 12, 1983.

Ariel, July, 1981.

Black Orpheus, March, 1966.

Book Forum, Volume III, number 1, 1977.

Books Abroad, summer, 1972, spring, 1973.

British Book News, December, 1984, April, 1986.

Chicago Tribune Book World, October 7, 1979.

Christian Science Monitor, July 31, 1970, August 15, 1970.

Commonweal, February 8, 1985.

Detroit Free Press, March 20, 1983, October 17, 1986.

Detroit News, November 21, 1982.

Globe & Mail (Toronto), June 7, 1986.

London Magazine, April/May, 1974.

Los Angeles Times, October 17, 1986.

Nation, October 11, 1965, April 29, 1968, September 15, 1969, November 10, 1969, October 2, 1972, November 5, 1973.

New Republic, October 12, 1974, May 9, 1983.

New Statesman, December 20, 1968.

Newsweek, November 1, 1982.

New Yorker, May 16, 1977.

New York Review of Books, July 31, 1969, October 21, 1982.

New York Times, November 11, 1965, April 19, 1970, August 11, 1972, September 23, 1982, May 29, 1986, May 31, 1986, June 15, 1986, October 17, 1986, November 9, 1986, March 1, 1987, March 2, 1987.

New York Times Book Review, July 29, 1973, December 24, 1973, October 10, 1982, January 15, 1984.

New York Times Magazine, September 18, 1983.

Research in African Literatures, spring, 1983.

Saturday Review/World, October 19, 1974.

Spectator, November 6, 1959, December 15, 1973, November 24, 1981.

Time, October 27, 1986.

Times (London), October 17, 1986, April 6, 1987.

Times Literary Supplement, April 1, 1965, June 10, 1965, January 18, 1968, December 31, 1971, March 2, 1973,

December 14, 1973, February 8, 1974, March 1, 1974, October 17, 1975, August 5, 1977, February 26, 1982.
Tri-Quarterly, fall, 1966.
Village Voice, August 31, 1982.
Washington Post, October 30, 1979, October 17, 1986.
World, February 13, 1973.
World Literature Today, winter, 1977, autumn, 1981, summer, 1982.

—*Sketch by Joan Goldsworthy*

*   *   *

SPELLMAN, A(lfred) B.   1935(?)-

PERSONAL: Born August 7, 1935 (some sources say 1934), in Nixonton (one source says Elizabeth City), N.C.; son of Alfred (a teacher) and Rosa (a teacher; maiden name, Bailey) Spellman. *Education:* Attended Howard University, 1952-58, received B.A.

ADDRESSES: Office—c/o Morehouse College, 223 Chestnut St. S.W., Atlanta, Ga. 30314.

CAREER: Poet, music critic, and writer. Worked mainly in bookstores and spent one year as disc jockey of a morning program on WBAI-Radio, New York, N.Y., 1958-67; taught classes in poetry, writing, black literature, Afro-American culture, and jazz at a number of universities, including Rutgers University and Harvard University; writer-in-residence at Morehouse College and Emory University, both Atlanta, Ga.; founded the Atlanta Center for the Black Arts, 1969; worked for National Endowment for the Arts and Education and as a panel member for the Rockefeller Foundation.

WRITINGS:

The Beautiful Days (poems; includes "the beautiful day," "daniele's poem," "*after reading tu fu,*" "for white," and "a theft of wishes"), Poets Press, 1965.
Four Lives in the Bebop Business, Pantheon, 1966, Limelight Editions/Harper, 1985, published as *Black Music: Four Lives,* Schocken, 1970.
(With Imamu Amiri Baraka and Larry Neal) *Trippin': A Need for Change,* Cricket, 1969.

Also author of "the beautiful day #9," "in orangeburg my brothers did," "when black people are," "tomorrow the heroes," and "friends i am like you tied," among other poems, and of a booklet for the "Giants of Jazz" series of albums by Time-Life.

Poetry represented in anthologies, including *Beyond the Blues: New Poems by American Negroes,* 1962; *Black Fire: An Anthology of Afro-American Writers,* 1968; *The New Black Poetry,* 1969; and *The Poetry of Black America: Anthology of the Twentieth Century,* 1972.

Contributor of poetry, articles on jazz, and record reviews to periodicals, including *Ebony, Negro Digest, Nation, Jazz, Metronome,* and *Downbeat.* Editor of *Cricket;* music editor of *Kulchur;* and co-founder of *Umbra.*

SIDELIGHTS: A. B. Spellman belongs to the group of new black poets who emerged during the 1960s and who were increasingly concerned with the universal plight of black Americans. His interest in poetry developed at Howard University, where his writing gained critical support from peers such as dramatist Joseph Walker and poet-playwright Amiri Baraka. Addressing themes of love, sorrow, nature, and mu-

sic, Spellman published his collection, *The Beautiful Days,* in 1965. According to Carmen Subryan's profile in the *Dictionary of Literary Biography,* the volume's contents reflect the "intensely personal" nature of the author's work, a characteristic that poet Frank O'Hara claimed "cuts through a lot of contemporary nonsense to what is actually happening to" Spellman. The poems are especially noted for their effective imagery and symbolism. Subryan wrote: "His images, which are vivid, sensual, real, and believable, stimulate the imagination. . . . It is in Spellman's love poems, however, that the personal passions which move the artist erupt." Subsequent pieces such as "tomorrow the heroes," "when black people are," and "friends i am like you tied" prove less self-oriented with their universal themes on socio-political issues. It is in these later works, which "signal Spellman's maturing social conscience," declared Subryan, that the poet's "perfection as an artist is manifested."

Aside from his reputation as a poet, Spellman is regarded as one of the leading critics on jazz in the United States. His numerous articles and reviews on the subject appear in such popular magazines as *Ebony, Jazz,* and *Downbeat,* and in 1966 he published *Four Lives in the Bebop Business.* Alternately published as *Black Music: Four Lives* and reprinted under its original title in 1985, the critically acclaimed volume profiles jazz musicians Herbie Nichols, Jackie McLean, Ornette Coleman, and Cecil Taylor.

BIOGRAPHICAL/CRITICAL SOURCES:

BOOKS

Dictionary of Literary Biography, Volume 41: *Afro-American Poets Since 1955,* Gale, 1985.
Henderson, Stephen, editor, *Understanding the New Black Poetry,* Morrow, 1973.
Hughes, Langston, editor, *New Negro Poets: USA,* Indiana University Press, 1964.

PERIODICALS

Book Week, November 13, 1966.
Christian Science Monitor, December 19, 1966.
Commonweal, February 3, 1967.
Ebony, August, 1969.
Harper's Bazaar, December, 1968.
High Fidelity, March, 1977.
Nation, March 20, 1967.
New Republic, May 11, 1968, August 17, 1968, September 14, 1968.
New Statesman, September 1, 1967.
New York Review of Books, October 17, 1974.
New York Times Book Review, November 20, 1966.
Times Literary Supplement, October 19, 1967.

*   *   *

STEPTO, Robert B(urns)   1945-

PERSONAL: Born October 28, 1945, in Chicago, Ill.; son of Robert Charles (a professor of medicine) and Ann (a teacher; maiden name, Burns) Stepto; married Michele Leiss (a college teacher), June 21, 1967; children: Gabriel Burns, Rafael Hawkins. *Education:* Trinity College, Hartford, Conn., B.A. (cum laude), 1966; Stanford University, M.A., 1968, Ph.D., 1974.

ADDRESSES: Office—Department of English, Yale University, New Haven, Conn. 06520.

CAREER: Williams College, Williamstown, Mass., assistant professor of English, 1971-74; Yale University, New Haven, Conn., assistant professor, 1974-79, associate professor of English and Afro-American studies, 1979—, director of Afro-American graduate studies, 1978—, fellow of Timothy Dwight College, 1975—. Visiting assistant professor at Trinity College, Hartford, Conn., summer, 1969, member of board of fellows, 1980-83; visiting associate professor at Wesleyan University, Middletown, Conn., summer, 1980; lecturer at colleges and universities. Connecticut Humanities Council, board member, 1980-82. Seminar director; guest on radio programs.

MEMBER: Modern Language Association of America (chairman of Commission on the Literatures and Languages of America, 1977-78), American Studies Association.

AWARDS, HONORS: Woodrow Wilson fellow, 1966-67.

WRITINGS:

(Editor with Dexter Fisher, and contributor) *Afro-American Literature: The Reconstruction of Instruction,* Modern Language Association of America, 1978.
From Behind the Veil: A Study of Afro-American Narrative, University of Illinois Press, 1979.
(Editor with Michael Harper, and contributor) *Chant of Saints: A Gathering of Afro-American Literature, Art, and Scholarship,* University of Illinois Press, 1979.
(Contributor) Charles T. Davis, editor, *The Slave's Narrative: Text and Context,* Louisiana State University Press, 1981.
(Contributor) Robert Hemenway and Donald Ringe, editors, *Toward a New Century: American Literary Study in 1980,* University of Kentucky Press, 1981.
(Editor with John M. Reilly) *Afro-American Literature: The Reconstruction of a Literary History,* Modern Language Association of America, 1981.
(Editor with Robert O'Meally) *The Collected Papers of Sterling Brown,* Volume I, Garland, 1981.
(Editor) *Selected Poems by Jay Wright,* Princeton University Press, 1987.

Contributor to literature journals.

WORK IN PROGRESS: Editing *The Collected Papers of Sterling Brown,* with Robert O'Meally, for Garland; research on narrative and cultural geography.

SIDELIGHTS: Stepto commented: "Despite my work in many areas, I am fundamentally an English teacher dedicated to the ideal of helping college students achieve a certain high level of literacy—regardless of their field or major. So, when I write about the passion for literacy that one sees, for example, among former slaves, I am attempting to pursue scholarly interests and provide my students with models for their educational careers. A student who can write will go far; a student who can read both books and the world surrounding him or her will go even further."

BIOGRAPHICAL/CRITICAL SOURCES:

PERIODICALS

Times Literary Supplement, May 30, 1980.
Washington Post, June 3, 1980.

* * *

STEPTOE, John (Lewis) 1950-

PERSONAL: Born September 14, 1950, in Brooklyn, N.Y.; son of John Oliver (a transit worker) and Elesteen (Hill) Steptoe; children: Bweela (daughter), Javaka (son). *Education:* Attended New York School of Art and Design, 1964-67.

ADDRESSES: Home—840 Monroe St., Brooklyn, N.Y. 11221. *Agent*—Alice Bach, 222 East 75th St., New York, N.Y.

CAREER: Artist and author of children's books. Teacher at Brooklyn Music School, summer, 1970.

MEMBER: Amnesty International.

AWARDS, HONORS: John Steptoe Library dedicated in Brooklyn, New York, 1970; Gold Medal, Society of Illustrators, 1970, and Lewis Carrol Shelf Award, 1978, both for *Stevie,* which was also named an American Library Association notable children's book; *The Story of Jumping Mouse: A Native American Legend* was named a Caldecott Honor Book, and was named to *Horn Book* Fanfare List, both 1985; Coretta Scott King Award, 1988, for *Mufaro's Beautiful Daughters: An African Tale,* which was also named a Caldecott Honor Book, 1988.

WRITINGS:

SELF-ILLUSTRATED; FOR CHILDREN

Stevie, Harper, 1969, published with cassette and guide, Live Oak Media, 1987.
Uptown, Harper, 1970.
Train Ride, Harper, 1971.
Birthday, Holt, 1972.
My Special Best Words, Viking, 1974.
Marcia, Viking, 1976.
Daddy Is a Monster . . . Sometimes, Lippincott, 1980.
Jeffrey Bear Cleans Up His Act, Lothrop, 1983.
The Story of Jumping Mouse: A Native American Legend, Lothrop, 1984.
Mufaro's Beautiful Daughters: An African Tale, Lothrop, 1987.
Baby Says, Lothrop, 1988.

ILLUSTRATOR; FOR CHILDREN

Lucille B. Clifton, *All Us Come Cross the Water,* Holt, 1972.
Eloise Greenfield, *She Come Bringing Me That Little Baby Girl,* Lippincott, 1974.
Arnold Adoff, *OUTside INside Poems,* Lothrop, 1981.
Birago Diop, *Mother Crocodile = Maman-Caiman,* Delacorte, 1981.
Adoff, *All the Colors of the Race: Poems,* Lothrop, 1982.

SIDELIGHTS: John Steptoe once commented: "One of my incentives for getting into writing children's books was the great and disastrous need for books that black children could honestly relate to. I ignorantly created precedents by writing such a book. I was amazed to find that no one had successfully written a book in the dialogue which black children speak."

Written when the author was sixteen, Steptoe's widely acclaimed *Stevie* recounts a child's experience with overcoming peer jealousy. The book is called "an honest and touching story, with stunning illustrations" by a *Saturday Review* contributor, and critics generally consider *Stevie* somewhat of a landmark book, in that it represents a very early example of an author's treatment of black life using a ghetto setting with black characters and dialogue. "I wrote the book for black children," Steptoe tells a *New York Times Book Review* contributor, "therefore the language reflects it. I think black children need this. I wrote it this way because they are never spoken to. They always read about themselves as the 'Negro'—something outside, not included." Pointing out that the book's "modified black English" is really "more a transcription of pronunciation than a different grammatical system," Ellen Tremper adds in *Lion and the Unicorn* that "the non-black reader certainly does not feel he is in a different language system, and the story line has universal appeal as well." Similarly, Barbara Novak O'Doherty suggests in the *New York Times Book Review* that while the story "certainly stems from black culture," it speaks to a "common experience."

In his books for children, Steptoe explores the common experiences or concerns of children and young adults. *Uptown*, for instance, is a story of two boys who ponder their future, wondering what they will be when they become adults; *Train Ride* tells the story about a subway ride two boys take without parental permission and the punishment they both receive as a result; and *Daddy Is a Monster . . . Sometimes* explores the inherent tensions between parents and their children, showing how interrelated their behavior often is, with parents responding in kind to the "monster" behavior of their offspring.

Critics note that Steptoe also speaks to an issue that many books for and about children neglect—sex education. "Most books for young children concerned with sex education describe the birth process," writes Marsha Kabakow Rudman in her *Children's Literature: An Issues Approach*. "They rarely take into consideration the other aspects of sexuality in a child's life." Steptoe's *My Best Special Words*, however, depicts a young girl's attempts to toilet train her brother. "The two children romp together in the bathroom," says Rudman. "They are comfortable with their bodies. The illustrations help to convey the sense of joy and comfort with themselves and each other. As usual, Steptoe is educational at the same that that he is disturbing the complacency of some of the reading public." And *Marcia*, Steptoe's first young adult novel, explores the responsibilities involved in becoming sexually active; and "for urban Black teen-age girls, this book deals frankly with male 'machismo,' responsible sex, and contraception," says Joan Scherer Brewer in *School Library Journal*. Concurring that the story "is appealing, and its concerns are common ones for young people," Denise M. Wilms adds in *Booklist* that "Steptoe hasn't flinched from dealing with the issue head on."

More recently, though, Steptoe has departed from creating books that speak directly to the experiences of children in urban environments, and has reworked older tales or legends. *The Story of Jumping Mouse: A Native American Legend*, for example, which is described in *Kirkus Reviews* as a story about "a seeking, selfless mouse who turns into an eagle," retells an American Indian explanation of the origin of the eagle. Not only is the story itself a departure for Steptoe, the artwork has changed as well. Donnarae MacCann and Olga Richard note in *Wilson Library Bulletin* that Steptoe is "moving in an entirely new direction. He creates mixtures of black and white, and is able to animate the surfaces and depict a rich environment with more success than most artists can achieve with a full range of color. He also designs arrangements that are handsome, asymmetrical, and unusual in their intricate weaving of negative and positive spaces." Steptoe's illustrations in *Mufaro's Beautiful Daughters: An African Tale* are described by Paulette Childress White in the *New York Times Book Review* as having "a muted brilliance and luminosity." White adds that "Steptoe weaves tribal culture and history, magic and mystery in this version of the timeless moral lesson of pride going before a fall" in his retelling of the "fates of two very beautiful and very different daughters." Describing the illustrations, Tim Wynne-Jones suggests in the Toronto *Globe and Mail* that "the lavish form of the book perfectly reflects

the noble content of the story." And a *Los Angeles Times Book Review* contributor writes, "While this beautiful picture book is dedicated to the children of South Africa, its story will touch youngsters of any culture."

Critics respond favorably to the candor, optimism, and universality of themes in Steptoe's books for children. Although some may feel that at times the work is not as strongly constructed as it could be, they nonetheless praise the authenticity and innovation in its presentation; and they continue to appreciate Steptoe's development as an artist. From the "icon-like intensity" of Steptoe's bold and colorful illustrations in *Stevie*, as described by Barbara Bader in her *American Picture Books from Noah's Ark to the Beast Within*, and the renderings in "black, white, and shades of gray like a full palette, with subtle gradations and nuances" in *The Story of Jumping Mouse*, as described by Ethel L. Heins in *Horn Book*, to the lushness that several critics believe distinguishes *Mufaro's Beautiful Daughters*, Steptoe's illustrations have earned several honors.

BIOGRAPHICAL/CRITICAL SOURCES:

BOOKS

Bader, Barbara, *American Picture Books from Noah's Ark to the Beast Within*, Macmillan, 1976.
Children's Literature Review, Gale, Volume 2, 1976, Volume 12, 1987.
Rudman, Marsha Kabakow, *Children's Literature: An Issues Approach*, D. C. Heath, 1976.

PERIODICALS

Booklist, May 1, 1976, June 15, 1984.
Children's Book Review Service, September, 1976.
Globe and Mail (Toronto), May 30, 1987.
Horn Book, August, 1984.
Interracial Books for Children Bulletin, Volume 12, numbers 7 and 8, 1981.
Kirkus Reviews, April 15, 1976, April 1, 1980.
Life, August 29, 1969.
Lion and the Unicorn, winter, 1979/80.
Los Angeles Times Book Review, May 17, 1987.
New York Times Book Review, October 10, 1969, November 30, 1969, November 11, 1970, June 28, 1987.
Saturday Review, September 13, 1969.
School Library Journal, May, 1976, February, 1981.
Times Literary Supplement, July 2, 1970.
Washington Post, December 18, 1987.
Wilson Library Bulletin, September, 1984.

—*Sketch by Sharon Malinowski*

*   *   *

SUTHERLAND, Efua (Theodora Morgue)   1924-

PERSONAL: Born June 27, 1924, in Cape Coast, Ghana; married William Sutherland (an educator), 1954; children: three. *Education:* Earned B.A. from Homerton College, Cambridge; attended School of Oriental and African Studies, London, and University of Cape Coast, Ghana.

ADDRESSES: Home—Legon, Ghana. *Office*—c/o Institute of African Studies, University of Ghana, Legon. *Agent*—c/o Longman Group, Longman House, Burnt Mill, Harlow, Essex CM20 2JE, England.

CAREER: Playwright, producer, director, and writer of children's stories. Teacher in Ghana, 1951-54. Founding director of Experimental Theatre Players (now Ghana Drama Studio),

Accra, 1958—. Co-founder (with husband, William Sutherland) of school in Trans-Volta region of upper Ghana. Founder of Ghana Society of Writers (now University of Ghana Writers Workshop), Legon. Founding director of Kusum Agoromba (children's touring theatre group) at University of Ghana School of Drama, Legon.

WRITINGS:

PLAYS

Foriwa (three-act; produced in Accra at Ghana Drama Studio, 1962), Ghana State Publishing Corporation, 1962, Panther House, 1970.

Edufa (based on the play *Alcestis,* by Euripidies; produced in Accra at Ghana Drama Studio, 1962), Longsmans, Green, 1967, published in *Plays from Black Africa,* edited by Frederic M. Litto, Hill & Wang, 1968.

Vulture! Vulture! and Tahinta: Two Rhythm Plays (juvenile), Ghana Publishing House, 1968, Panther House, 1970.

"Anase and the Dwarf Brigade" (juvenile; based on *Alice in Wonderland*), first produced in Cleveland at Karamu House Theatre, February 5, 1971.

The Marriage of Anasewa: A Storytelling Drama (one-act; first produced in Accra, Ghana, September, 1971), Longman, 1975.

OTHER

Playtime in Africa (poems for children), photographs by Willis E. Bell, Brown, Knight, & Truscott, 1960, Atheneum, 1962.

The Roadmakers (travel), photographs by Bell, Ghana Information Services, 1961.

The Original Bob: The Story of Bob Johnson, Ghana's Ace Comedian, photographs by Bell, Educational Publications, 1970.

Also author of radio plays, including "Odasani" (based on *Everyman*), "The Pineapple Child" (a fantasy), "Nyamekye" (music and dance), and "Anansegoro: You Swore an Oath" (one-act).

Contributor of poems and plays to various periodicals. Cofounder of *Okyeame* magazine, Accra.

SIDELIGHTS: Brought up in the Ghanaian city of Cape Coast, Sutherland was isolated from the traditional folk culture of her country's rural areas. Her goal has since been to discover that which is uniquely Ghanaian and to convey these traditional elements through her writing, uniting them with modern themes and techniques. In addition, Sutherland has sought to unify Ghana through the preservation of national art forms. To this end, she has designed open-air theatres that are well suited for the performance of traditional story-telling and of contemporary drama as well. Sutherland's own writing helps to preserve national art forms by incorporating traditional Ghanaian dramatic techniques such as story-telling and audience participation into her poems and plays.

Sutherland's plays, often based on traditional African folklore, are heavily sight- and sound-oriented. They emphasize rhyme, rhythm, music, dance, and spectator response, and best achieve their effect in live or broadcast performance. Consequently, much of Sutherland's work is not represented in print.

Sutherland writes for children in both English and Akan, a native Ghanaian language, as part of her efforts to promote a bilingual society in Ghana. Fearing that the language problem in Ghana will eventually result in the adoption of English as the official national language, Sutherland urges bilingual education for all children in both elementary and secondary schools.

T

TARRY, Ellen 1906-

PERSONAL: Born in 1906 in Birmingham, Ala.; children: Elizabeth. *Education:* Attended Alabama State College for Negroes Bank Street College Writers' Laboratory.

ADDRESSES: *Home*—New York, N.Y.

CAREER: Worked as a newspaperwoman, teacher, and social worker; served as deputy assistant to the Regional Administrator for Equal Opportunity, Department of Housing and Urban Development; writer.

WRITINGS:

Janie Belle, illustrations by Myrtle Sheldon, Garden City Publishing, 1940.
Hezekiah Horton, illustrations by Oliver Harrington, Viking, 1942.
(With Marie Hall Ets) *My Dog Rinty,* illustrations by Alexander Alland and Alexandra Alland, Viking, 1946, new edition, 1964.
The Runaway Elephant, illustrations by Harrington, Viking, 1950.
The Third Door: The Autobiography of an American Negro Woman, McKay, 1955, reprinted, Negro Universities Press, 1971.
Katharine Drexel: Friend of the Neglected, illustrations by Donald Bolognese, Farrar, Straus, 1958.
Martin de Porres: Saint of the New World, illustrations by James Fox, Vision Books, 1963.
Young Jim: The Early Years of James Weldon Johnson, Dodd, 1967.
The Other Toussaint: A Modern Biography of Pierre Toussaint, a Post-Revolutionary Black, St. Paul Editions, 1981.

SIDELIGHTS: Tarry's writings were heavily influenced by her involvement in the civil rights movement. As a result, she became one of the first authors to use blacks as main characters in books for children. One of Tarry's earlier books, *Hezekiah Horton,* told the adventures of a small black child growing up in New York. The book was enthusiastically received by many book critics. "At last we have a realistic, honest book about a negro boy in Harlem," noted a critic for *Saturday Review of Literature.*

Tarry's *Runaway Elephant* was based on an actual news story. "We say that fact is stranger than fiction; nevertheless, it takes genius to find such a fact in the news as the escape of a bull elephant from the circus and turn it into a good story. That genius Ellen Tarry has," observed a reviewer for the *New York Herald Tribune.*

In *The Third Door: The Autobiography of an American Negro Woman,* the author describes her experiences in New York and Alabama. Her book *Young Jim: The Early Years of James Weldon Johnson* is a biography of a major black poet. A *New York Times* book reviewer noted that "besides offering an inspiring life story, the book gives some penetrating insights into Negro life and problems at the turn of the century."

BIOGRAPHICAL/CRITICAL SOURCES:

BOOKS

Tarry, Ellen, *The Third Door: The Autobiography of an American Negro Woman,* McKay, 1955, reprinted, Negro University Press, 1971.

PERIODICALS

New York Herald Tribune, October 8, 1950.
New York Times, January 21, 1968.
Saturday Review of Literature, November 14, 1942.

*   *   *

TAYLOR, Margaret
See BURROUGHS, Margaret Taylor (Goss)

*   *   *

TAYLOR, Mildred D.

PERSONAL: Born September 13, in Jackson, Miss.; daughter of Wilbert Lee and Deletha Marie (Davis) Taylor. *Education:* University of Toledo, B.Ed., 1965; University of Colorado, M.A., 1969.

ADDRESSES: c/o Dial Books, 2 Park Ave., New York, N.Y. 10016.

CAREER: U.S. Peace Corps, teacher of English and history in Tuba City, Ariz., 1965, and in Yirgalem, Ethiopia, 1965-67, recruiter, 1967-68, instructor in Maine, 1968; study skills coordinator at University of Colorado, 1969-71; temporary office worker in Los Angeles, Calif., 1971-73; writer, 1973—.

AWARDS, HONORS: First prize in African-American category, Council on Interracial Books for Children, 1973, and Outstanding Book of the Year citation, *New York Times,* 1975, both for *Song of the Trees;* American Library Association Notable Book citation, 1976, National Book Award finalist, *Boston Globe-Horn Book* Honor Book citation, and Newbery Medal, all 1977, and Buxtehuder Bulle Award, 1985, all for *Roll of Thunder, Hear My Cry;* American Book Award nomination, 1982, Coretta Scott King Award, 1982, and Outstanding Book of the Year citation, *New York Times,* all for *Let the Circle be Unbroken;* Coretta Scott King Award, 1988, for *The Friendship;* Christopher Award, 1988, for *The Gold Cadillac.*

WRITINGS:

Song of the Trees, illustrated by Jerry Pinkney, Dial, 1975.
Roll of Thunder, Hear My Cry, Dial, 1976.
Let the Circle Be Unbroken, Dial, 1981.
The Friendship, illustrated by Max Ginsburg, Dial, 1987.
The Gold Cadillac, illustrated by Michael Hays, Dial, 1987.

SIDELIGHTS: Many of Mildred Taylor's books reflect her experiences growing up in a racially biased America. A former Peace Corps worker, Taylor is best known for her Newbery Award-winning novel *Roll of Thunder, Hear My Cry.* That book tells the story of the Logans, a black family living in the South during the Depression. Narrated by Cassie, the only Logan daughter, the book shows how the Logans cope with racism and its related injustices and indignities, and remain together as a family. Other volumes, including *Song of the Trees, Let the Circle Be Unbroken,* and *The Friendship,* continue the Logan history.

Taylor comments, "From as far back as I can remember my father taught me a different history from the one I learned in school. By the fireside in our Ohio home and in Mississippi, where I was born and where my father's family had lived since the days of slavery, I had heard about our past. . . . It was a history of ordinary people, some brave, some not so brave, but basically people who had done nothing more spectacular than survive in a society designed for their destruction. Some of the stories my father had learned from his parents and grandparents, as they had learned them from theirs; others he told first-hand, having been involved in the incidents himself. There was often humor in his stories, sometimes pathos, and frequently tragedy; but always the people were graced with a simple dignity that elevated them from the ordinary to the heroic.

"In those intervening years spent studying, traveling, and living in Africa and working with the Black student movement, I would find myself turning again and again to the stories I had heard in my childhood. I was deeply drawn to the roots of that inner world which I knew so well. . . . In *Roll of Thunder, Hear My Cry* I included the teachings of my own childhood, the values and principles by which I and so many other Black children were reared, for I wanted to show a family united in love and self-respect, and parents, strong and sensitive, attempting to guide their children successfully, without harming their spirits, through the hazardous maze of living in a discriminatory society.

"I also wanted to show the Black person as heroic. In my own school days, a class devoted to the history of Black people in the United States always caused me painful embarrassment. This would not have been so if that history had been presented truly, showing the accomplishments of the Black race both in Africa and in this hemisphere. . . . It is my hope that to the children who read my books, the Logans will provide those heroes missing from the schoolbooks of my childhood, Black men, women, and children of whom they can be proud."

MEDIA ADAPTATIONS: A dramatization of *Roll of Thunder, Hear My Cry* was recorded by Newbery Awards Records in 1978; a television adaption of the same book was also made that year.

BIOGRAPHICAL/CRITICAL SOURCES:

BOOKS

Children's Literature Review, Volume 9, Gale, 1985.
Contemporary Literary Criticism, Volume 21, Gale, 1982.
Dictionary of Literary Biography, Volume 52: *American Writers for Children since 1960: Fiction,* Gale, 1986.
Rees, David, *The Marble on the Water: Essays on Contemporary Writers of Fiction for Children and Young Adults,* Horn Book, 1980.
Something about the Author Autobiography Series, Volume 5, Gale, 1988.

PERIODICALS

Best Sellers, February, 1982.
Christian Science Monitor, November 3, 1976, October 14, 1981, October 5, 1984.
Commonweal, November 19, 1976.
Horn Book, August 1975, December, 1976, August, 1977, April, 1982.
Language Arts, May, 1981.
Los Angeles Times Book Review, January 3, 1988.
New York Times, February 3, 1982.
New York Times Book Review, May 4, 1975, November 16, 1975, November 21, 1976, March 19, 1978, November 15, 1981, September 2, 1982, December 11, 1983, November 15, 1987, February 21, 1988.
School Library Journal, December, 1981.
Times Educational Supplement, November 18, 1977.
Times Literary Supplement, December 2, 1977, March 26, 1982.
Washington Post Book World, February 13, 1977, April 23, 1978, May 10, 1987.

*   *   *

THOBY-MARCELIN, (Emile) Philippe   1904-1975

PERSONAL: Born December 11, 1904, in Port-au-Prince, Haiti; immigrated to United States, c. 1949; died August 13, 1975, in Cazenovia (some sources indicate Syracuse or New York City), N.Y.; son of Emile (a politician, novelist, and literary critic) and Eva (Thoby) Marcelin; married Eva Ponticello. *Education:* Attended Petit Seminaire College Saint-Martial in Port-au-Prince; received law degree.

CAREER: Writer. Served as a public official in the Haitian Ministry of Public Works prior to 1949; Pan American Union, Washington, D.C., French translator, beginning in 1949.

AWARDS, HONORS: Second Latin-American Literary Prize Competition award, 1943, for *Canape-Vert;* Guggenheim fellowship, 1951.

WRITINGS:

POETRY

Lago-Lago, publisher unknown, 1930.
La Negresse adolescente (collection), preface by Leon La-Leau, Impr. La Presse (Haiti), 1932.

Dialogue avec la femme endormie, Editions "La Reserve" (Haiti), 1941.
A fonds perdu, P. Seghers (Paris), 1953.

Also author of *Le Jour et la nuit*.

NOVELS

(With brother, Pierre Marcelin) *Canape-Vert*, Editions de la Maison Francaise, 1944, English translation by Edward Larocque Tinker, Farrar & Rinehart, 1944.

(With P. Marcelin) *La Bete de Musseau*, Editions de la Maison Francaise, 1946, translation by Peter C. Rhodes published as *The Beast of the Haitian Hills*, Rinehart, 1946, new edition with introduction by Thoby-Marcelin, Time Inc., 1964, City Lights, 1986.

(With P. Marcelin) *Le Crayon de Dieu*, La Table Ronde (Paris), 1952, translation by Leonard Thomas from original French manuscript published as *The Pencil of God*, introduction by Edmund Wilson, Houghton, 1951.

(With P. Marcelin) *Tous les hommes sont fous*, publisher unknown, 1970, translation by Eva Thoby-Marcelin published as *All Men Are Mad*, introduction by Edmund Wilson, Farrar, Straus, 1970.

OTHER

Panorama de l'art haitien (art history), Impr. de l'Etat, 1956.
Haiti (art history), Pan American Union, 1959.
(With brother, Pierre Marcelin) *Contes et legendes d'Haiti* (juvenile collection), illustrations by Philippe Degrave, F. Nathan (Paris), 1967, translation by Eva Thoby-Marcelin published as *The Singing Turtle, and Other Tales From Haiti*, illustrations by George Ford, Farrar, Straus, 1971.

SIDELIGHTS: A popular Haitian writer and former poet, Philippe Thoby-Marcelin gained widespread recognition for the critically acclaimed novels he and his brother Pierre wrote depicting peasant life in their native country. Originally written in French, the books feature a descriptive look at the various customs practiced by Haiti's predominantly black population, especially the voodoo rituals inspired by their African ancestors. Generally, critics described these stories as both entertaining and informative, and most hailed the authors for the clarity and detail distinguishing their lively prose. The brothers' prize-winning *Canape-Vert* holds the distinction of being the first Haitian fiction translated into the English language; as such it served to introduce Western civilization to Haitian literature, and some consider it a classic among the works of Caribbean writers. Voicing similar praise for another of their successful collaborations, Arna Bontemps wrote in the *New York Times Book Review* that *The Beast of the Haitian Hills* is "a poetically conceived account" in which the "skill, grace, and spice of the storytelling are art from a distant and neglected world."

Aside from the international reputation that his writing afforded him, Thoby-Marcelin is credited with both shaping the literary and artistic development of Haiti and preserving its cultural heritage. Most notably, he assumed a major role in the country's renaissance of arts and letters during the 1920s and served as a leading exponent of the avant-garde literary movement in Haiti. As a member of an elite group of intellectuals, Thoby-Marcelin also helped found the *Revue Indigene* magazine, which advocated the exclusive use of the standard French language as opposed to such imitative derivatives as the Creole dialect adopted by most of his countrymen. In effect he nurtured a return to the original folkways of his native land, a concern that prompted his adherence to an old custom of prefixing his surname with his mother's maiden name. Perhaps Thoby-Marcelin's commitment and dedication to perpetuating the rich cultural history of his people contributed to his stature as one of Haiti's most popular and renowned writers.

BIOGRAPHICAL/CRITICAL SOURCES:

PERIODICALS

New York Times Book Review, November 24, 1946.
Village Voice, June 23, 1987.

OBITUARIES:

PERIODICALS

New York Times, August 17, 1975.

*　　*　　*

THOMAS, Joyce Carol   1938-

PERSONAL: Born May 25, 1938, in Ponca City, Okla.; daughter of Floyd Dave (a bricklayer) and Leona (a housekeeper; maiden name, Thompson) Haynes; married Gettis L. Withers (a chemist), May 31, 1959 (divorced, 1968); married Roy T. Thomas, Jr. (a professor), September 7, 1968 (divorced, 1979); children: Monica Pecot, Gregory Withers, Michael Withers, Roy T. Thomas III. *Education:* Attended San Francisco City College, 1957-58, and University of San Francisco, 1957-58; College of San Mateo, A.A., 1964; San Jose State College (now University), B.A., 1966; Stanford University, M.A., 1967.

ADDRESSES: *Home*—Berkeley, Calif. *Agent*—Mitch Douglas, International Creative Management, 40 West 57th St., New York, N.Y. 10019.

CAREER: Worked as a telephone operator in San Francisco, Calif., 1957-58; Ravenwood School District, East Palo Alto, Calif., teacher of French and Spanish, 1968-70; San Jose State College (now University), San Jose, Calif., assistant professor of black studies, 1969-72; Contra Costa College, San Pablo, Calif., teacher of drama and English, 1973-75; St. Mary's College, Moranga, Calif., professor of English, 1975-77; San Jose State University, San Jose, reading program director, 1979-82, professor of English, 1982-83; full-time writer, 1982—. Visiting associate professor of English at Purdue University, spring, 1983; member of Berkeley Civic Arts Commission.

MEMBER: International Reading Association, Authors Guild, Western Reading Association, Sigma Delta Pi, Spanish Honors Society.

AWARDS, HONORS: Danforth graduate fellow at University of California at Berkeley, 1973-75; Stanford University scholar, 1979-80, and Djerassi fellow, 1982 and 1983; *Marked by Fire* was named outstanding book of the year by *New York Times* and a best book by American Library Association, both in 1982; Before Columbus American Book Award from Before Columbus Foundation (Berkeley, Calif.), 1982, and the American Book Award for Children's fiction from the Association of American Publishers, 1983, both for *Marked by Fire;* Coretta Scott King Award from American Library Association, 1984, for *Bright Shadow*.

WRITINGS:

NOVELS

Marked by Fire (young adult), Avon, 1982.
Bright Shadow (young adult; sequel to *Marked by Fire*), Avon, 1983.

Water Girl, Avon, 1986.
The Golden Pasture (young adult), Scholastic, Inc., 1986.
Amber, Scholastic, Inc., in press.

POETRY

Bittersweet, Firesign Press, 1973.
Crystal Breezes, Firesign Press, 1974.
Blessing, Jocato Press, 1975.
Black Child, Zamani Productions, 1981.
Inside the Rainbow, Zikawana Press, 1982.

PLAYS

(And producer) "A Song in the Sky" (two-act), first produced in San Francisco at Montgomery Theatre, 1976.
"Look! What a Wonder!" (two-act), first produced in Berkeley at Berkeley Community Theatre, 1976.
(And producer) "Magnolia" (two-act), first produced in San Francisco at Old San Francisco Opera House, 1977.
(And producer) "Ambrosia" (two-act), first produced in San Francisco at Little Fox Theatre, 1978.
"Gospel Roots" (two-act), first produced in Carson, Calif., at California State University, 1981.

OTHER

Contributor to periodicals, including *American Poetry Review, Black Scholar, Calafia, Drum Voices, Giant Talk,* and *Yardbird Reader.* Editor of *Ambrosia* (women's newsletter), 1980.

WORK IN PROGRESS: *An Act of God*, a novel, for Scholastic, Inc.; *House of Light*, a novel.

SIDELIGHTS: Often favorably compared to such prominent black female writers as Maya Angelou, Alice Walker, and Toni Morrison, Joyce Carol Thomas first established her literary reputation as a poet and playwright in the San Francisco Bay area of California. Raised in Oklahoma during the 1940s as the fifth child in a family of nine, Thomas developed an early fascination for storytelling when, during harvest time, sharing anecdotes and exchanging bits of family lore were popular sources of entertainment. Her works reflect this ingrained talent for telling stories; her first book, the 1982 award-winning young adult novel *Marked by Fire*, earned the author critical acclaim for what *San Francisco Chronicle Book World* reviewer Patricia Holt called Thomas's "ear for language and dialect, her gift for simplicity in description and the absolute authenticity of her setting and characters."

Marked by Fire chronicles twenty years in the life of Abyssinia Jackson, beginning with her birth in a cotton field, where she is scarred by a spark from a brush fire. As such, she is "marked for unbearable pain and unspeakable joy," according to Mother Barker, the character who serves as the local healer, spiritual adviser, and, eventually, Abyssinia's mentor. Set in Ponca City, Oklahoma—Thomas's birthplace—the story depicts Abyssinia as an especially bright, happy child who is gifted with an extraordinarily beautiful singing voice. At age ten, however, she loses this gift when an elder member of her church brutally rapes her. The incident brings the prophesied "unbearable pain" and a bitter questioning of her faith in God, but with time—and the support of the women in the close-knit community—Abyssinia gradually recovers from the ordeal. The remainder of *Marked by Fire* traces the heroine's passage into young womanhood and concludes with her decision to follow in Mother Barker's footsteps, attending to the needs of the town's troubled and sick.

The novel met with enthusiastic reviews and became required reading in many high school and university classrooms

throughout the United States. "Thomas writes with admirable simplicity and finds a marvelous fairy tale quality in everyday happenings," wrote *New York Times Book Review* critic Alice Childress. Holt declared the book a "hauntingly and beautifully written novel" that "reads with the rhythm and beauty of poetry" and deemed *Marked by Fire* "the kind of novel that *no one* should miss." California's *Peninsula Times Tribune* writer Charles Beardsley praised Thomas's portrayal of the main character, describing Abyssinia as "drawn full scale, shining forth as an unforgettable individual who welcomes life and thereby experiences as much joy as sorrow, life's ignominy and the grandeur of its heritage." Beardsley added that *Marked by Fire* "is no 'made up' story, but the sensitive distillation of the black experience as seen through the eyes of a remarkable writer."

In *Bright Shadow*, the 1983 sequel to *Marked by Fire*, Abyssinia enters college to prepare for a medical career. She meets and falls in love with Carl Lee Jefferson and, despite initial disapproval from Abyssinia's father, their relationship thrives. Together they endure the painful aftermath of the gruesome murder of Abyssinia's favorite aunt as well as the death of Carl Lee's abusive father, an event that reveals the truth of Carl Lee's ancestry.

Critical reception of *Bright Shadow* did not match that of its predecessor, but the book was nevertheless recommended in library and publishing journals and won the Coretta Scott King Award offered by the American Library Association in 1984. Thomas plans additional novels for the "Abyssinia" series.

MEDIA ADAPTATIONS: *Marked by Fire* was adapted by James Racheff and Ted Kociolek for the stage musical "Abyssinia," first produced in New York City at the CSC Repertory Theater in 1987.

BIOGRAPHICAL/CRITICAL SOURCES:

BOOKS

Dictionary of Literary Biography, Volume 33: *Afro-American Fiction Writers After 1955*, Gale, 1984.
Yalom, Marilyn, editor, *Women Writers of the West Coast*, Capra Press, 1983.

PERIODICALS

New York Times, November 30, 1982.
New York Times Book Review, April 18, 1982, December 5, 1982, March 18, 1984.
Peninsula Times Tribune (California), March 20, 1982.
San Francisco Chronicle Book World, April 12, 1982.

* * *

THOMAS, Lorenzo 1944-

PERSONAL: Born August 31, 1944, in the Republic of Panama; brought to United States in 1948; son of Herbert Hamilton (a pharmacist and chemist) and Luzmilda (a community organizer; maiden name, Gilling) Thomas. *Education:* Queens College (now of the City University of New York), B.A., 1967; graduate study at Pratt Institute.

ADDRESSES: *Home*—P.O. Box 14645, Houston, Tex. 77021.

CAREER: Pratt Institute, New York, N.Y., assistant reference librarian, 1967-68; Texas Southern University, Houston, writer in residence, 1973; Black Arts Center, Houston, Ethnic Arts Program creative writing teacher, 1973-75; *Living Blues*, Chicago, Ill., correspondent, 1976—; poet. Has worked with the

Poetry-in-the-Schools program in New York, Texas, Oklahoma, Florida, Arkansas, and Georgia. Organizer of Juneteenth Blues Festivals in Houston and other Texas cities. Member of advisory board, KPFT-FM, Houston, 1973—; member of literature advisory panel, Texas Commission on the Arts and Humanities, 1975—. *Military service:* U.S. Naval Reserve, 1968-72; served in Vietnam.

MEMBER: Coordinating Council of Literary Magazines (member of board of directors, 1974—).

AWARDS, HONORS: Dwight Durling prize in poetry, 1963; Poets Foundation awards, 1966 and 1974; Committee on Poetry grant, 1973; Lucille Medwick Award, 1974; National Endowment for the Arts creative writing fellowship, 1983; Houston Festival Foundation Arts award, 1984.

WRITINGS:

POETRY

A Visible Island, Adlib Press, 1967.
Fit Music: California Songs, Angel Hair Books, 1972.
Dracula, Angel Hair Books, 1973.
(Editor) *ANKH: Getting It Together,* Hope Development, 1974.
(Contributor) Steve Cannon, editor, *Jambalaya,* Reed, Cannon & Johnson, 1975.
Framing the Sunrise, Sun Be/Am Associates, 1975.
Sound Science, Sun Be/Am Associates, 1978.
The Bathers: Selected Poems, Reed, Cannon, 1978.
Chances Are Few, Blue Wind Press, 1979.

CONTRIBUTOR TO ANTHOLOGIES

Black Fire: An Anthology of Black American Writing, Morrow, 1968.
Arnold Adoff, editor, *The Poetry of Black America,* Harper, 1972.
Abraham Chapman, editor, *New Black Voices,* New American Library, 1972.
Michael Lally, editor, *None of the Above,* Crossing Press, 1976.

OTHER

Also translator of *Tho Tu Viet-Nam* (poems). Contributor to *Yardbird, Yardbird Reader, Art & Literature, Angel Hair, C, Massachusetts Review, Umbra,* and other periodicals. Editor, *Roots,* 1974—; advisory editor, *Nimrod,* 1977—; contributing editor, *Black Focus,* 1977—.

WORK IN PROGRESS: A collection of short stories on rural life in the South; essays on Afro-American music and literature.

SIDELIGHTS: ''The life and literary interests of Lorenzo Thomas span vast distances, ranging from Central America to New York City to the American Southwest, underscoring his stature as one of the most broadly based and multifaceted writers of African descent in America today,'' writes Tom Dent in a *Dictionary of Literary Biography* essay. Dent considers Thomas's poetry to be ''noteworthy for its extraordinary, imaginative depiction of popular American culture and for his unique intermixture of apparently unrelated frames of reference.'' Likening Thomas's poetic style to ''the feel of a camera gliding through a maze of sensual impressions and memories,'' Dent suggests that ''all of Thomas's poems reflect an extraordinary sensitivity to contemporary American culture, particularly the suggestive and image-laden world of cinema. He uses cinematic imagery in an effort to come to terms with the African heritage, an identity framed first by his West In-

dian upbringing, and by his experience as a black youth in New York.''

Thomas once commented: ''I came to New York City speaking Spanish; got beat up on the way home from school because I 'talked funny.' Never forgot it. Went way way away out of my way to become extra-fluent in English.'' Dent indicates that this attempt ''to make himself more acceptable to his schoolmates . . . led to his early interest in creative writing. His strivings for literacy were abetted, he has said, by 'the whole business of being Black and from a home full of race-conscious people, and the idea that if you are Black you had to be more qualified than necessary.'''

''In the late 1950s and early 1960s,'' Thomas remarked, ''I participated in the various avant-garde poetry movements in Greenwich Village and Harlem and on the lower East Side: the Umbra Workshop, the Black Arts Theatre, Le Doux Megots, the Poetry Project at Saint Marks-in-the-Bouwerie, and the Metro.'' Thomas's earliest literary influences ''were shaped by all the salient and social and artistic forces'' of this period, observes Dent, especially the civil rights movement, the awakening of black pride, and the ''new, positive cultural identification with their African heritage by many members from the African diaspora.''

Dent describes Thomas's work by referring to what Thomas has acknowledged as an early influence by ''the great Martinican poet, Aime Cesaire, the first Afro-Caribbean surrealist and one of the leading proponents of the francophone Negritude movement.'' Recognizing several aspects of Cesaire's work reflected in Thomas's style and content, Dent cites Thomas's use of ''surrealism, or magic realism'' and says that, like Cesaire, Thomas identifies strongly with Africa and its past, a black folk culture, and the struggles of the oppressed, and exhibits an ''extreme skepticism toward the technological, scientific/rational overemphasis of contemporary Western society.'' Dent observes also that ''like Cesaire's work, Thomas's poems are composed of disparate and widely varied elements: song, criticism, erudite allusions, sharp description, memory—all flow along rather evenly in his versification.'' His poems reveal a similar ''quest for identity'' as a major theme, says Dent, and share ''a belief in the powers of imagination and spirituality to overcome the more tangible problems of powerlessness, along with a belief in poetry as a protector of truth that cannot be bought, sold, or tailored by commerce.''

The cinematic imagery of Thomas's work is exemplified by the title poem of his collection, *The Bathers: Selected Poems.* Dent refers to the poem, which concerns the civil rights struggles in the deep South of the 1960s, as ''a series of refractions off the indelible photographic image of black demonstrators being attacked with police fire hoses during the Birmingham demonstrations.'' And speaking about Thomas's *Framing the Sunrise,* which he feels represents ''Thomas's most accomplished and imaginative work,'' Dent finds that the work ''offers several fascinating comments on the influence of television in blurring images of reality.'' Dent explains that ''images of events and faces flow from the omnipresent screen, filtered through the poet's memory as they have penetrated the living room of our collective consciousness, at the same time deadening our consciousness and our capacity to feel.''

In Thomas's recent comprehensive collection, *Chances Are Few,* the poems explore ''the everyday of popular American culture: TV, radio, movies, beer, motels, advertisements, bars, music—both popular and rarified—and deejays,'' writes Dent in *Freedomways*. Fielding Dawson finds it "a little astonishing to see a first book like this," adding in the *American Book Review*, "Thomas comes straight in, 100% ready to continue what has been clear to him for so long. There is very little that is innocent." Finding in the work "none of the self-consciousness of first collections," Dawson maintains that "Lorenzo Thomas is a pro, and he is a very very good pro." Although Maurice Kenny indicates in *Library Journal* that the poems are "sharp, urbane, caustic social criticism," Dent "encounters poems that are intensely non-ideological whose 'voice' has the aspect of a moving presence commenting on the ironies and absurdities of the perceived world." Noting Thomas's use of both horizontal and vertical rhymes in *Chances Are Few,* Dawson praises his "commitment to painting, and color, these pages blaze with primaries as well as suggestive color, and it's dazzling, music becomes color in minimum six voices." Dawson considers the collection a "profound key to poetry and prose of the future," adding: "To think this writing is being done for black audiences and being written by black writers, is to live in an inverted hypocrisy. These poems are guidelines for us all."

"Thomas's knowledge of music is extremely catholic," states Dent, who indicates that Thomas's recent involvement in organizing blues festivals in Texas expresses "his broad interests in black and American indigenous musics." Dent discusses Thomas's understanding of the similarities between the poet and the blues singer: "In terms of poetic concept, he has observed: 'I write poems because I can't sing.' We assume he means even though his poems are not written in song form, or that his language is not the language of the blues, the poet should play an artistic role akin to that of blues singers. The poet is like a blues singer with the same migratory tendencies, the same qualities of street prophet and historian, and the same fate of being held in low esteem by the ruling classes."

"In recent years," Thomas said, "I've spent my time studying languages and revolutionary lifestyles of the Third World, and translating literary works by Vietnamese and Portuguese African poets. Currently I am studying the works of Panamanian poets Roberto MacKay and Chang Marin (Afro- and Asian-Panamanians respectively). Most of my livelihood comes from working in public schools devising programs that will facilitate our needs for bilingual or multicultural education. I've spent the last five years working in 'problem areas.' At the present time, my main interests (and most of the writing I produce) concern bilingual and multicultural education; I study Afro-American (that's the whole hemisphere as far as I'm concerned) folklore and try to produce instructional modules and programs that are effective. I call them poems, articles, and short stories."

"Lorenzo Thomas's sense of irony, absurdity, and his social awareness are very much a part of the shared concerns of contemporary black literature," says Dent, and reveal him to be not "a racial protest poet, but a critic of the Western world writing from the perspective of Afro-America." Further, Dent observes that "Thomas believes Afro-Americans, guided by the light of the star of African culture and life principles, have the potential to lead the way in freeing from the destructive, capitalistic, money-obsessed American value system, and such an act of liberation must be at its core cultural and spiritual. This is the pervasive logic behind the fascinating and challenging poems and essays of Lorenzo Thomas."

BIOGRAPHICAL/CRITICAL SOURCES:

BOOKS

Dictionary of Literary Biography, Volume 41: *Afro-American Poets since 1955*, Gale, 1985.

PERIODICALS

American Book Review, May, 1982.
Black Scholar, May, 1980, March, 1981.
Freedomways, Volume 20, 1980.
Library Journal, April 1, 1980.

—*Sketch by Sharon Malinowski*

*   *   *

THURMAN, Howard   1900-1981

PERSONAL: Born November 18, 1900, in Daytona Beach, Fla.; died April 10, 1981, in San Francisco, Calif.; son of Saul Solomon and Alice (Ambrose) Thurman; married Sue E. Bailey (a writer and social historian), June 12, 1932; children: Anne Thurman Chiarenza, Olive Thurman Wong. *Education:* Morehouse College, A.B., 1923; Colgate-Rochester Theological Seminary, B.D., 1926.

ADDRESSES: Home—2020 Stockton St., San Francisco, Calif. 94133. *Office*—Howard Thurman Educational Trust, 2018 Stockton St., San Francisco, Calif. 94133.

CAREER: Ordained Baptist minister, 1925; Mt. Zion Baptist Church, Oberlin, Ohio, pastor, 1926-28; Morehouse College, Atlanta, Ga., professor of religion and director of religious life, 1929-32; Howard University, Washington, D.C., professor of theology, 1932-44, dean of Rankin Chapel, 1932-44; Church for the Fellowship of All Peoples, San Francisco, Calif., co-founder and pastor, 1944-53; Boston University, Boston, Mass., professor of spiritual resources and disciplines, 1953-65, dean of Marsh Chapel, 1953-64, dean emeritus, 1965-81, minister-at-large, 1964-65. Professor and director of religious life at Spelman College, 1929-32; Ingersol Lecturer at Harvard University, 1947; guest professor at University of Iowa, 1948; Merrick Lecturer at Ohio Wesleyan University, 1953; Ratcliff Lecturer at Tufts University, 1957; Beach Lecturer at Bangor Theological Seminary, 1958; Earl Foundation Lecturer at Pacific School of Religion, 1959; Smith-Wilson Lecturer at Southwestern College, 1960; Willson Lectuer at Nebraska Wesleyan University, 1961; Mendenhall Lecturer at DePauw University, 1961; Quaker Lecturer at Earlham College, 1962; Theme Lecturer for United Church of Canada, 1962; visiting professor at University of Ibadan, autumn, 1963, Earlham College, 1966, and Louisville Presbyterian Theological Seminary, 1967; Billings Lecturer at University of Hawaii, 1964; Oswald McCall Memorial Lecturer at University of California, Berkeley, 1964; Lambright Lecturer at Forest City Hospital; lecturer to Saskatchewan Federation of Indian Chiefs; Rufus Jones Memorial Lecturer to Society of Friends (Quaker); Ware Lecturer for American Unitarian Association; lecturer at more than five hundred schools throughout the world. Chairman of Student Christian Movements of India and the United States' Pilgrimage of Friendship to India, Burma, and Ceylon, 1935; American-British Pulpit Exchange preacher in London, England. Founder of Howard Thurman Educational Trust. Conducted "Meditation of the Heart," on KNBR-Radio, and "We Believe," on television; narrator and guest conductor of San Francisco Symphony Orchestra and San Francisco Municipal Chorus. Member of advisory board of American Committee on Africa; member of board of directors of Meals for Millions,

Hampton Institute, Whitney M. Young Memorial Foundation, and King Memorial Center for Social Change; past member of board of directors of Pacific School of Religion.

MEMBER: American Academy of Arts and Sciences (fellow), National Council of Religion in Higher Education (fellow), National Association for the Advancement of Colored People (NAACP; life member), National Urban League (member of board of directors), Authors Guild, Authors League of America, Travelers Aid Society (member of board of directors), Fellowship of Reconciliation, Harold Brunn Society for Medical Research, Schoolmaster Club of New England (life member), California Writers Club, Book Club of California, Phi Beta Kappa, Federal City Club.

AWARDS, HONORS: Honorary degrees include D.D. from Morehouse College, 1935, Wesleyan University, Middletown, Conn., 1946, Lincoln University and Howard University, both 1955, Oberlin College, 1958, Boston University, 1967, Bethune-Cookman College, Bishop College, and University of Redlands, LL.D. from Allen University, 1954, and Washington University, St. Louis, Mo., 1955, H.H.D. from Ohio Wesleyan University, 1954, Litt.D. from Tuskegee Institute, 1956, L.H.D. from Virginia State College, 1959, and Florida Normal College, 1961, and D.H.L. from Dillard University. Named one of twelve great preachers of the twentieth century by Life, 1953; Gutenberg Award from Chicago Bible Society, 1958, for distinguished achievement in communicating the gospel; Mary McLeod Bethune Medallion from Bethune-Cookman College, 1958, for achievement as an educator; annual Black Church Award, 1972; named honorary canon of Cathedral of St. John the Divine, 1975; Charter Day Award from trustees of Howard University, 1975; fellow of trustees of Boston University; first annual award from San Francisco Council of Churches, 1977; Jefferson Award from San Francisco Examiner, 1977; honorary member of medical staff at Forest City Hospital; distinguished black scholars' award from Garrett Evangelical Theological Seminary, 1979; American Black Achievement Award in Religion from Ebony, 1979; Roy Wilkins Award from NAACP, 1979; Citation Award from Upper Room, 1980.

WRITINGS:

The Greatest of These, Eucalyptus Press, 1941.
Deep River: An Interpretation of Negro Spirituals (also see below), Eucalyptus Press, 1945, revised edition, Harper, 1955.
The Negro Spiritual Speaks of Life and Death (also see below), Harper, 1947.
Meditations for Apostles of Sensitiveness, Beacon Press, 1948.
Jesus and the Disinherited, Abingdon, 1949, reprinted, Friends United Press, 1981.
Deep Is the Hunger, Harper, 1950, reprinted, Friends United Press, 1973.
Meditation's of the Heart, Harper, 1953, reprinted, Friends United Press, 1976.
The Creative Encounter, Harper, 1954, reprinted, Friends United Press, 1972.
The Growing Edge, Harper, 1956, reprinted, Friends United Press, 1974.
Apostles of Sensitiveness, Beacon Press, 1956.
Footprints of a Dream: The Story of the Church for the Fellowship of All Peoples, Harper, 1959.
(Author of introduction) Why I Believe There Is a God, Johnson Publishing Co., 1960.
Mysticism and the Experience of Love, Pendle Hill, 1961.

The Inward Journey, Harper, 1961, reprinted, Friends United Press, 1973.
Temptations of Jesus, Lawton Kennedy, 1962, reprinted, Friends United Press, 1979.
Disciplines of the Spirit, Harper, 1963.
The Luminous Darkness, Harper, 1965.
The Centering Moment, Harper, 1969, reprinted, Friends United Press, 1984.
The Search for Common Ground: An Inquiry into the Basis of Man's Experience of Community, Harper, 1971, reprinted, Friends United Press, 1986.
The Mood of Christmas, Harper, 1973.
(Editor) Olive Schreiner, A Track to the Water's Edge: The Olive Schreiner Reader, Harper, 1973.
(With Alfred Fisk) The First Footprints: The Dawn of the Idea of the Church for the Fellowship of All Peoples; Letters between Alfred Fisk and Howard Thurman, Lawton Kennedy, 1975.
Deep River [and] The Negro Spiritual Speaks of Life and Death, Friends United Press, 1975.
With Head and Heart: The Autobiography of Howard Thurman, Harcourt, 1980.
For the Inward Journey: The Writings of Howard Thurman, selected by Anne Spencer Thurman, Harcourt, 1984.

Contributor to Interpreter's Bible. Member of editorial board of Fellowship of Reconciliation.

SIDELIGHTS: The Reverend Dr. Howard Thurman, brought up in Florida by his ex-slave grandmother, was a trained Baptist minister, and a teacher and administrator at several universities, including Boston University, where he was the first black full-time member of the faculty. On a tour through India, Ceylon (now Sri Lanka), and Burma in the 1930s, he met Mahatma Gandhi, whose views on nonviolent resistance he espoused. "An eclectic in matters of theology and a synthesizer of ideas," Dr. Thurman "developed from [Gandhi's] studies and experiences a view in which Christianity 'would live for the weak as well as the strong—for all peoples whatever their color, whatever their caste,'" states J. Y. Smith in the Washington Post. Thurman later expressed this view in his own interracial Church for the Fellowship of All Peoples, which he co-organized in San Francisco in the 1940s. He communicated his ideas through his preaching and writing, and, according to Smith, "helped provide a framework for the leadership of the civil rights movement of the 1950s and 1960s." His thinking influenced such civil rights leaders as Dr. Martin Luther King, Jr.

Thurman made a number of recordings, including "Meditations of the Heart," "In Favor with God," "The Third Component," "The Dilemma of Commitment," "The Single Mind," and "Deep River."

BIOGRAPHICAL/CRITICAL SOURCES:

BOOKS

With Head and Heart: The Autobiography of Howard Thurman, Harcourt, 1979.
Yates, Elizabeth, Howard Thurman: Portrait of a Practical Dreamer, John Day, 1964.

PERIODICALS

Atlantic Monthly, October, 1953.
Life, April 6, 1955.
Nation, January 5-12, 1980.
New York Times, March 22, 1953.

New York Times Book Review, January 6, 1980.
San Francisco Chronicle, August 28, 1949, March 25, 1951, January 10, 1954, January 22, 1956, September 30, 1959.
Time, August 27, 1956.
Yankee, November, 1953.

OTHER

"The Life and Thought of Howard Thurman" (film), released by British Broadcasting Corporation, 1976.

OBITUARIES:

PERIODICALS

Newsweek, April 27, 1981.
New York Times, April 14, 1981.
Time, April 27, 1981.
Washington Post, April 16, 1981.

* * *

THURMAN, Wallace (Henry) 1902-1934
(Patrick Casey, Ethel Belle Mandrake)

PERSONAL: Born August 16, 1902, in Salt Lake City, Utah; died of tuberculosis, December 22 (one source says December 21), 1934, in New York, N.Y.; buried in Silver Mount Cemetery, New York, N.Y.; son of Oscar and Beulah Thurman; married Louise Thompson (a schoolteacher), August 22, 1928 (separated). *Education:* Attended University of Utah, 1919-20, and University of Southern California, 1922-23.

CAREER: Reporter and editor for *The Looking Glass;* member of the editorial staff of *Messenger,* 1925-26; circulation manager of *World Tomorrow,* 1926; member of editorial staff of McFadden Publications; began as reader, became editor in chief of Macaulay Publishing Co.

WRITINGS:

(With William Jourdan Rapp) "Harlem: A Melodrama of Negro Life in Harlem" (three-act play), first produced on Broadway at Apollo Theater, February 20, 1929.
The Blacker the Berry: A Novel of Negro Life, Macaulay, 1929, AMS Press, 1972.
Infants of the Spring, Macaulay, 1932, reprinted, with afterword by John A. Williams, Southern Illinois University Press, 1979.
(With A. L. Furman) *The Interne,* Macaulay, 1932, University Microfilms, 1973.
"Tomorrow's Children" (screenplay), Bryan Foy Productions, 1934.
"High School Girl" (screenplay), Bryan Foy Productions, 1935.

Also author of unpublished plays, including "Jeremiah, the Magnificent," 1930, "Savage Rhythm," 1931, and "Singing the Blues," 1932; author of column, "Inklings." Founder and editor of *Outlet, Harlem: A Forum of Negro Life,* and *Fire!!* Worked as a ghostwriter, sometimes under the pseudonyms Patrick Casey or Ethel Belle Mandrake, for books and periodicals, including *True Story.*

Works represented in anthologies, including *The Negro Caravan, Anthology of American Negro Literature, The Black Writer of America, Black American Literature: Fiction.* Contributor to periodicals, including *New Republic, Independent, New York Times, Negro World, Opportunity,* and *Dance Magazine.*

SIDELIGHTS: Wallace Thurman settled in New York City at the beginning of the Harlem Renaissance, a period of heightened black literary activity during the mid-1920s. Because of his unconventional lifestyle and penchant for parties and alcohol, he became popular in Harlem social circles, but he was only considered a minor literary figure. His fame lay with his influence on and support of younger and talented writers of the era and with his realistic—although sensationalized—portrayals of the lower classes of black American society. Thurman was lauded as a satirist and often used satire to accuse blacks of prejudice against darker-skinned members of their race. He also rejected the belief that the Harlem Renaissance was a substantial literary movement, claiming that the 1920s produced no outstanding writers and that those who were famous exploited, and allowed themselves to be patronized by, whites. He claimed, as did a number of authors of the decade, that white critics judged black works by lower standards than they judged white efforts. Thurman maintained that black writers were held back from making any great contribution to the canon of Negro literature by their race-consciousness and decadent lifestyles.

Born and raised in the American West, Thurman attended the University of Utah for a year before transferring in 1922 to the University of Southern California in Los Angeles. While in Los Angeles Thurman wrote a column, "Inklings," for a black-oriented newspaper. He then founded a magazine, *Outlet,* hoping to initate on the West Coast a literary renaissance like the one happening in Harlem. *Outlet* lasted only six months, and in 1925 Thurman went east. In New York City he took a job as a reporter and editor at *The Looking Glass,* then became managing editor of the *Messenger,* where his editorial expertise earned him notoriety. He published short works by the poet and author Langston Hughes—not because Thurman thought them good but because they were the best available—and pieces by the writer Zora Neale Hurston. He left in the autumn of 1926 to join the staff of a white-owned periodical, *World Tomorrow.*

In the summer of 1926 Hughes asked Thurman to edit *Fire!!,* a magazine that Hughes and artist and writer Bruce Nugent were planning. Hurston, the author Gwendolyn Bennett, and another artist, Aaron Douglas, were members of the editorial board. The board intended *Fire!!* to "satisfy pagan thirst for beauty unadorned," as was stated in the foreword to the first issue. *Fire!!* would offer a forum for younger black writers who wanted to stand apart from the older, venerated black literati, and it would be strictly literary, with no focus on contemporary social issues. Thurman agreed to edit the magazine and advanced a good deal of the publication money. The first issue featured short stories by Thurman, Hurston, and Bennett, poetry by Hughes, Countee Cullen, and Arna Bontemps, a play by Hurston, illustrations by Douglas, and the first part of a novel by Nugent. But *Fire!!* folded after one issue; it was plagued by financial and distribution problems and received mediocre reviews. It was also ignored by a number of white critics and harshly criticized by some blacks who thought it irreverent.

Two years later Thurman published *Harlem: A Forum of Negro Life,* a more moderate, broader-focused magazine, also devoted to displaying works by younger writers. The new effort, unlike the avant-garde *Fire!!,* would appeal to all age groups and was "to be a general magazine . . . on current events and debates on racial and non racial issues," Thurman wrote to the critic Alain Locke. The first volume contained an essay by Locke, a book review by Thurman, poetry by Alice Dunbar Nelson and Hughes, fiction by Hughes and George Schuyler, a theater review by the editor Theophilus Lewis, and a directory of New York City churches and nightclubs. But *Harlem,* too, failed after its premier issue.

Thurman's first play was entitled "Harlem: A Melodrama of Negro Life in Harlem." It opened on Broadway February 20, 1929, at the Apollo Theater, bringing Thurman immediate success. He collaborated on the drama with William Jourdan Rapp, a white man who later became the editor of *True Story* and would remain Thurman's lifelong friend. "Harlem" centers on the Williams family, who relocate in New York City to escape economic difficulties at the time of the "great migration" of Southerners to the North during the first two decades of the twentieth century. But instead of finding the city a promised land, they encounter many of the problems that often plagued the families of the migration: unemployment and tensions between generations heightened by difficulties in adjusting to city life.

"Harlem" received mixed reviews—ranging from "exciting" to "vulgar"—but was generally considered interesting. It was criticized by blacks who did not care for its focus on the seedier elements of life, like illicit sex, liquor, wild parties thrown to collect rent money, and gambling. R. Dana Skinner stated in a 1929 *Commonweal* review of "Harlem" that he was especially upset by "the particular way in which this melodrama exploits the worst features of the Negro and depends for its effects solely on the explosions of lust and sensuality." Nevertheless, many critics felt it "captured the feel of life" and was "constantly entertaining." "Harlem" played for an impressive ninety-three performances in what was considered a poor theater season and was taken on tour to the West Coast, the Midwest, and Canada.

In 1930 Thurman again collaborated with Rapp on a three-act play, "Jeremiah, the Magnificent," based on black nationalist Marcus Garvey's "back to Africa" movement of the early 1900s. Garvey had called for an exodus of blacks to Africa so that there they could create their own country and attain personal freedoms in a society where they would be in the majority. Although Thurman portrayed Garvey as a vain and unwise man, the playwright thought Garvey did much to promote the black ideal in the hope of fostering Negro unity worldwide. The play remained unpublished and was only performed once, after Thurman had died. Thurman's other unproduced and unpublished plays include "Singing the Blues," written in 1931, and "Savage Rhythm," written the following year.

Thurman's first novel, *The Blacker the Berry,* was published in 1929. Taken from the folk-saying "the blacker the berry, the sweeter the juice," its title was ironic, for the novel was an attack on prejudice within the race. Emma Lou, the protagonist, is a dark-skinned girl from Boise who is looked down upon by her fairer family members and friends. When she attends school at the University of Southern California in Los Angeles she again is scorned, so she travels to Harlem, where she believes that she won't be snubbed because of her dark coloring. But like the Williamses in "Harlem" and Thurman in his own life, Emma Lou is disillusioned with the city. She becomes unhappy with her work, her love affairs, and the pronounced discrimination in the nightclubs, where lighter-skinned females starred in extravagant productions while darker-skinned performers were forced to sing off stage. She uses hair straighteners and skin bleachers, and takes on the appearance and attitudes of the fairer-skinned people who degrade her. She in turn snubs darker men, whom she thinks inferior, and takes up with Alva, a man who is light-skinned but cruel. After viewing Alva in a lovers' embrace with an-

other man, Emma Lou realizes how hypocritical she's become. Critics praised Thurman for devoting a novel to the plight of the dark-skinned black girl, but they faulted him for being too objective: he recounted Emma Lou's tale without handing down any judgment on the world in which she lived. They also criticized Thurman for trying to do too much with *The Blacker the Berry,* accusing him of crafting a choppy, and occasionally incoherent, narrative by touching on too many themes.

Thurman's next novel, *Infants of the Spring,* also is set in 1920s Harlem. The story revolves around Raymond Taylor, a young black author who is trying to write a weighty novel in a decadent, race-oriented atmosphere. Taylor resides in a boardinghouse, nicknamed "Niggeratti Manor," with a number of young blacks who pretend to be aspiring authors. Thurman makes these pretenders the major victims of his satire, suggesting that they have destroyed their creativity by leading such decadent lives. Critics contend that Thurman based his characters on well-known figures of the Harlem Renaissance, including Hughes, Locke, Hurston, Cullen, Nugent, and Douglas.

In *Infants of the Spring* Thurman suggests that all American artists and writers—black and white—are overrated. He vigorously attacks black writers patronized by whites, who praise everything black authors produce, regardless of quality, as novel and ingenious. *Infants* received criticism similar to that of *The Blacker the Berry.* Reviewers objected to Thurman's examining too many issues and not presenting them clearly, and his not making a universal statement about the lifestyles presented. But unlike Thurman's first novel, which was considered too objective, *Infants* was thought to be overly subjective and Thurman overly argumentative. Yet critics praised him for his frank discussion of black society. Assessed Martha Gruening in the *Saturday Review:* "No other Negro writer has so unflinchingly told the truth about color snobbery within the color line, the ins and outs of 'passing' and other vagaries of prejudice. . . . [*Infants of the Spring*'s] quota of truth is just that which Negro writers, under the stress of propaganda and counterpropaganda, have generally and quite understandably omitted from their picture." In addition, critics considered *Infants of the Spring* one of the first books written expressly for black audiences and not white critics.

Thurman's third and final novel, *The Interne,* was a collaboration with Abraham L. Furman, a white man Thurman met while working at Macaulay's Publishing Company. The novel portrays medical life at an urban hospital as seen through the eyes of a young white doctor, Carl Armstrong. In his first three months at the hospital, Armstrong's ideals are shattered, during which time he witnesses staff members' corrupt behavior and comes in contact with bureaucratic red tape. Armstrong himself participates in the vice but soon realizes his own loss of ethics and saves himself by taking up doctoring in the country. Critics could not agree whether Thurman's accounts of medical wrongdoing were based on fact; many claimed that the novel had no semblance of reality while others stressed that incidents were actual, if unusual.

In 1934 Thurman returned to the West Coast to write screenplays. While in California he continued to lead a decadent lifestyle, drank excessively, and wrote two screenplays for Bryan Foy Productions, "Tomorrow's Children," released in 1934, and "High School Girl," released the following year. "Tomorrow's Children" was a production about the Masons, a poor white family supported by the seventeen-year-old daughter. She takes care of her younger brothers and sisters, who are either mentally or physically impaired, her drunken father, and her constantly pregnant mother. Two social workers, sent by a compassionate doctor, declare that if they wish to receive welfare money, the mother, father, and daughter must be sterilized. "Tomorrow's Children" was based on circumstances rarely explored in Hollywood at that time, and was considered groundbreaking because it used the medical term "vasectomy" to explain the procedure of male sterilization. Because of its revolutionary subject matter, "Tomorrow's Children" was banned in New York when it was released.

In ill health, Thurman returned to New York City in May, 1934, and went on one last drinking binge with his Harlem friends. He collapsed in the middle of the reunion party and was taken, ironically, to City Hospital, on Welfare Island, New York, the institution he condemned in *The Interne*. After spending half a year in the ward for incurables diagnosed with tuberculosis, he died there on December 22, 1934. His funeral services were held in New York City on Christmas Eve.

BIOGRAPHICAL/CRITICAL SOURCES:

BOOKS

Abramson, Doris E., *Negro Playwrights in the American Theatre, 1929-1959*, Columbia University Press, 1969.
Bontemps, Arna, editor, *The Harlem Renaissance Remembered*, Dodd, Mead, 1972.
Dictionary of Literary Biography, Volume 51: *Afro-American Writers from the Harlem Renaissance to 1940*, Gale, 1987.
Twentieth-Century Literary Criticism, Volume 6, Gale, 1982.

PERIODICALS

Black World, November, 1970, February, 1976.
Commonweal, March 6, 1929.
Nation, February 10, 1932.
New Yorker, March 2, 1929.
New York Times, February 21, 1929, March 3, 1929, April 7, 1929, February 28, 1932, June 5, 1932.
Opportunity, April, 1929, October, 1930, January, 1935.
Saturday Review, March 12, 1932, June 22, 1940.
Western American Literature, spring, 1971.

—*Sketch by Carol Lynn DeKane*

*   *   *

TOLSON, M. B.
See TOLSON, Melvin B(eaunorus)

*   *   *

TOLSON, Melvin B(eaunorus)   1898(?)-1966
(M. B. Tolson)

PERSONAL: Born February 6, 1898 (some sources say 1900), in Moberly, Mo.; died August 29 (one source says 28), 1966; buried in Guthrie, Okla.; son of Alonzo A. (a minister and teacher) and Lera (one source says Leah; maiden name, Hurt) Tolson; married Ruth Southall, January 29, 1922; children: Melvin B., Jr., Arthur, Wiley Wilson, Ruth Marie. *Education:* Attended Fisk University, c. 1918-19; Lincoln University, Lincoln University, Pa., B.A. (with honors), 1923; Columbia University, M.A., 1940.

CAREER: Worked at meat-packing plant; Wiley College, Marshall, Tex., teacher of English and speech, 1924-47, tennis, football, and boxing coach, director of Log Cabin Theatre, organizer of Wiley Forensic Society; Langston University,

Langston, Okla., professor of creative literature and director of Dust Bowl Theatre, 1947-65; Tuskegee Institute, Tuskegee Institute, Ala., Avalon Professor of the Humanities, 1965-66. Mayor of Langston, Oklahoma, 1952-58.

AWARDS, HONORS: First place in American Negro Exposition National Poetry Contest, 1939, for "Dark Symphony"; Omega Psi Phi Award for creative writing, 1945; Poet Laureate of Liberia, 1947; Bess Hokin Prize from *Poetry* magazine, 1951, for "E. & O. E."; Knight of the Order of the Star of Africa, 1954; appointed permanent Bread Loaf Fellow in Poetry and Drama, 1954; District of Columbia Citation and Award for Cultural Achievement in Fine Arts, 1965; National Institute and American Academy of Arts and Letters Award in Literature, 1966; honorary doctorates from Lincoln University, 1954 and 1965; fellowships from Rockefeller Foundation and Omega Psi Phi.

WRITINGS:

Rendezvous With America (poetry; includes "Rendezvous With America," "Dark Symphony," "Of Men and Cities," "The Idols of the Tribe," "Ballad of the Rattlesnake," and "Tapestries of Time"), Dodd, 1944.
(And director) "The Fire in the Flint" (play; adapted from Walter White's novel of the same title), first produced in Oklahoma City, Okla., at National Convention of National Association for the Advancement of Colored People, June 28, 1952.
(Under name M. B. Tolson) *Libretto for the Republic of Liberia* (poetry), preface by Allen Tate, Twayne, 1953.
(Under name M. B. Tolson) *Harlem Gallery: Book One, The Curator* (poetry), introduction by Karl Shapiro, Twayne, 1965.
A Gallery of Harlem Portraits (poetry; includes "Harlem," "Hilmar Enick," and "Harold Lincoln"), edited with afterword by Robert M. Farnsworth, University of Missouri Press, 1979.
Caviar and Cabbage (articles), edited with introduction by Farnsworth, University of Missouri Press, 1982.

Author of novel *Beyond the Zaretto;* author of plays, including "Black No More" (adapted from George Schuyler's novel of the same title), 1952, "Black Boy," 1963, "The Moses of Beale Street," and "Southern Front."

Work represented in numerous anthologies, including *Golden Slippers,* fourth edition, edited by Arna Bontemps, Harper, 1941; *The Poetry of the Negro, 1746-1949,* edited by Langston Hughes and Bontemps, Doubleday, 1949; *Black Voices,* edited by Abraham Chapman, New American Library, 1968; *The Writing on the Wall,* edited by Walter Lowenfels, Doubleday, 1969; *Black Poetry,* edited by Dudley Randall, Broadside, 1969; *The Black Experience,* edited by Francis E. Kearns, Viking, 1970; *Black Literature in America,* edited by Houston A. Baker, Jr., McGraw, 1971; *The Black Poets,* edited by Randall, Bantam, 1971; *Afro-American Poetry,* edited by Bernard W. Bell, Allyn & Bacon, 1972; *Black Writers of America,* edited by Richard Barksdale and Keneth Kinnamon, Macmillan, 1972; *The Poetry of Black America,* edited by Arnold Adoff, Harper, 1973; and *Understanding the New Black Poetry,* edited by Stephen Henderson, Morrow, 1973.

Author of weekly column "Caviar and Cabbage" in *Washington Tribune,* 1937-44. Contributor to periodicals, including *American Poet, Arts Quarterly, Atlantic Monthly, Midwest Journal, Modern Monthly, Modern Quarterly, Negro Digest,* and *Pittsburgh Courier.*

SIDELIGHTS: Known for his complex, challenging poetry, Melvin B. Tolson earned little critical attention through most of his life but eventually won a place among America's leading black poets. He was, in the opinion of Allen Tate, author of the preface to Tolson's *Libretto for the Republic of Liberia*, the first black poet to assimilate "completely the full poetic language of his time and, by implication, the language of the Anglo-American tradition." More, according to Karl Shapiro in his introduction to Tolson's *Harlem Gallery: Book One, The Curator*, Tolson wrote and thought "in Negro," thus adding to the quality of his best work. His sonnets, free verse, and epic poems, which employ both standard English and black idiom, illuminate the lives of black Americans and consider the role of black artists in white society. Noted James R. Payne in *World Literature Today*, Tolson's work is "a rich body of American poetry . . . that will give a great deal of satisfaction to readers."

Publication of Tolson's first collection of poetry, *Rendezvous With America*, came five years after his poem "Dark Symphony" won first place in the American Negro Exposition National Poetry Contest in 1939. "Dark Symphony," included in the collection, "celebrates . . . the historic contribution of black Americans and their struggle to gain recognition for their achievements, ending with a proud and defiant prediction of black accomplishment and cultural realization," asserted Robert M. Farnsworth in *Dictionary of Literary Biography*. Other poems in the volume, written during World War II, address the war's destruction, human aspirations and corruption, and the possibility of achieving "a new democracy of nations," according to Farnsworth. Poet and journalist Frank Marshall Davis, quoted by Farnsworth, characterized Tolson's writing in the volume as mature and masterful but "yet too complex for the masses"; many critics attribute the neglect of much of Tolson's writing to his complexity and erudition.

Appointed poet laureate of Liberia in 1947, Tolson attracted increased attention with his *Libretto for the Republic of Liberia*, an epic poem commemorating the African nation's centennial. Observed poet and critic John Ciardi in *Nation*, Tolson creates "a vision of Africa past, present, and future" with abundant imagery and "prodigious eclecticism." Portraying Liberia as an offshoot of America, newer and smaller with hopes of achieving more, Tolson continues the allusiveness and vision displayed in his earlier work. Ciardi commended the poet's "force of language and . . . rhythm," concluding that Tolson "has established a new dimension for American Negro poetry."

Published in 1965, Tolson's *Harlem Gallery: Book One, The Curator* was the product of years of work and is widely considered a poetic masterpiece. Robert Donald Spector, reviewing the poem for *Saturday Review* the year it appeared, judged that it "marks [Tolson] as one of America's great poets." Originally a sonnet, in the early 1930s it became the book-length *Gallery of Harlem Portraits*, which remained unpublished during Tolson's life; in the 1950s Tolson conceived it as part of a five-book epic about Harlem and black America and revised it as *Harlem Gallery: Book One, The Curator*. A fictional gallery curator "provides the central point of view" in the poem's discussions of black art and life, remarked Farnsworth, "but three major characters, all practicing artists, dramatically amplify the reader's view of the black artist's dilemma and achievement." Stanzas in the style of blues music punctuate the portraits, reinforcing Tolson's points or offering ironic commentary. Payne found such stanzas "very effective, among the most effective elements of the book."

Still, while Tolson used black elements such as the blues, focusing on black characters and a black setting, he did not espouse separatism. According to Blyden Jackson's *New Review* critique, "The brotherhood of man and the universality of serious art . . . catalyze [the poem's] perceptions."

Tolson's skillful delineation of character, his ability to turn discussions of aesthetics into social commentary, his breadth of vision, and his deftness with language garnered critical acclaim. Reviewers compared *Harlem Gallery* to works by Walt Whitman, Edgar Lee Masters, Hart Crane, and T. S. Eliot and praised with Spector "the richness and variety of [Tolson's] characters" and the "allusiveness that absorbs classical, Biblical, oriental, and African references." Admitting that *Harlem Gallery* presents the same complexity and involved syntax that rendered Tolson's earlier works somewhat inaccessible, Jackson asserted that "nevertheless [it] is a fine product of the imagination. . . . [Tolson] achieved a memorable presentation of the human comedy and of human values." Responding to other critics' neglect of Tolson's work, Spector declared, "Here is a poet whose language, comprehensiveness, and values demand a critical sensitivity rarely found in any establishment. . . . Whatever his reputation in the present critical climate, Tolson stands firmly as a great American poet."

BIOGRAPHICAL/CRITICAL SOURCES:

BOOKS

Contemporary Literary Criticism, Volume 36, Gale, 1986.
Dictionary of Literary Biography, Volume 48: *American Poets, 1880-1945*, Second Series, Gale, 1986.
Farnsworth, Robert M., *Melvin B. Tolson, 1898-1966: Plain Talk and Poetic Prophecy*, University of Missouri Press, 1984.
Flasch, Joy, *Melvin B. Tolson*, Twayne, 1972.
Gibson, Donald B., editor, *Modern Black Poets: A Collection of Critical Essays*, Prentice-Hall, 1973.
Russell, Mariann, *Melvin B. Tolson's Harlem Gallery*, University of Missouri Press, 1980.
Tolson, M. B., *Harlem Gallery: Book One, The Curator*, introduction by Karl Shapiro, Twayne, 1965.

PERIODICALS

Nation, February 27, 1954.
New Republic, December 4, 1976.
Saturday Review, August 7, 1965.
World Literature Today, winter, 1983.

—*Sketch by Polly A. Vedder*

*   *   *

TOOMER, Jean   1894-1967

PERSONAL: Born December 26, 1894, in Washington, D.C.; died March 30, 1967, in Doylestown, Pa.; son of Nathan and Nina (Pinchback) Toomer; married Margery Latimer, October 20, 1931 (deceased); married Marjorie Content, September 1, 1934; children: Margery. *Education:* Attended University of Wisconsin—Madison, 1914, Massachusetts College of Agriculture, 1915, American College of Physical Training, 1916, University of Chicago, 1916, New York University, 1917, and City College of New York (now of the City University of New York), 1917; also attended Gurdjieff Institute (France). *Religion:* Quaker.

ADDRESSES: Home—Bucks County, Pa.

CAREER: Writer. Worked as teacher in Georgia, 1920-21; associated with Gurdjieff Institute in Harlem, N.Y., 1925, and Chicago, Ill., 1926-33.

WRITINGS:

Cane (novel comprised of poems and short stories), Boni & Liveright, 1923, reprinted, Norton, 1987.

(Contributor) Alain Locke and Montgomery Gregory, editors, *Plays of Negro Life: A Source-Book of Native American Drama,* Harper, 1927, Negro University Press, 1970.

(Contributor) *The New American Caravan,* Macaulay, 1929.

Essentials (aphorisms and apothegms), Lakeside Press, 1931, reprinted, Xerox University Microfilms (Ann Arbor, Mich.), 1975.

An Interpretation of Friends Worship, Committee on Religious Education of Friends General Conference, 1947.

The Flavor of Man (lecture), Young Friends Movement of the Philadelphia Yearly Meetings, 1949, reprinted, 1974.

Darwin Turner, editor, *The Wayward and the Seeking: A Miscellany of Writings,* Howard University Press, 1978.

Author of plays, including "Portage Potential," 1931, "Eight-Day World," 1932, and an autobiography, "Outline of Autobiography," 1934. Short stories and poetry included in numerous anthologies. Contributor of short stories, poetry, and criticism to periodicals, including *Broom, Crisis, Dial, Liberator, Little Review, Modern Review, Nomad, Prairie,* and *Adelphi.*

SIDELIGHTS: Toomer's major contribution to literature is *Cane,* a novel comprised of poetry and prose which Robert Bone in *The Negro Novel in America* hailed as the product of a "universal vision." Upon the publication of *Cane* in 1923, Toomer was ranked with Ralph Ellison and Richard Wright as a leading figure in the Harlem Renaissance. In his introduction to *Cane,* Waldo Frank wrote that "a poet has arisen among our American youth who has known how to turn the essences and material of his Southland into the essences and materials of literature."

Cane's structure is of three parts. The first third of the book is devoted to the black experience in the Southern farmland. As Bernard W. Bell noted in *Black World,* "Part One, with its focus on the Southern past and the libido, presents the rural thesis." In his book *Black Literature in America,* Houston A. Baker, Jr., called Toomer's style "Southern psychological realism." The characters inhabiting this portion of the book are faced with an inability to succeed. Citing the story "Fern" as an example, Baker wrote: "The temptations and promises presented by Fern's body are symbolic of the temptations and promises held out by the road of life . . . which stretches before the rural black American, and the frustration experienced by men in their affairs with Fern is symbolic of the frustration of the life journey. Men are willing to give their all, but the result is simply frustration, haunting memory, and hysteria." Toomer infused much of the first part with poetry. "In the sketches, the poet is uppermost," wrote *New Republic* contributor Robert Littell. "Many of them begin with three or four lines of verse, and end with the same lines, slightly changed. The construction here is musical."

The second part of *Cane* is more urban oriented and concerned with Northern life. The writing style throughout is much the same as the initial section with poetry interspersed with stories. Charles W. Scruggs noted in *American Literature* that Toomer revealed the importance of the second section in a letter to the author's brother shortly before the publication of *Cane.* "From three angles, Cane's design is a circle," Scruggs quoted Toomer as writing. "Aesthetically, from simple forms to complex ones, and back to simple forms. Regionally, from the South up into the North, and back into the South again." But Toomer, in the same letter, also cited the completion of the "circle" as the story "Harvest Song," which is contained in the second section. As Scruggs explained, "Toomer is describing *Cane* in organic terms, and therefore it never really ends." Scruggs noticed the acceleration of the narrative as the novel's focus moved from South to North. "The spiritual quest which gains momentum in the agrarian South 'swings upward' in the electric beehive of Washington," he declared. "The 'cane-fluted' world does not die in the North. It continues to haunt the dreams and lives of those who have strayed far from their roots to dwell in the cities."

The concluding third of the novel is a prose piece entitled "Kabnis." Bell called this final part "a synthesis of the earlier sections." The character of Kabnis, Bell claimed, represented "the Black writer whose difficulty in reconciling himself to the dilemma of being an Afro-American prevents him from tapping the creative reservoir of his soul." Littell, as opposed to seeing "Kabnis" as a "synthesis" of the earlier portions, called it a "strange contrast to the lyric expressionism of the shorter pieces." Of the three sections, he wrote, "Kabnis" was by "far the most direct and most living, perhaps because it seems to have grown so much more than been consciously made. There is no pattern in it, and very little effort at poetry."

Many critics have offered interpretations of the title *Cane.* "Toomer uses Cain as a symbol of the African in a hostile land," wrote Scruggs, "tilling the soil of the earth, a slave, without enjoying her fruits. Yet strangely enough, this Cain receives another kind of nourishment from the soil, spiritual nourishment, which the owners of it are denied." Bell owned a slightly different perspective regarding the title. He wrote: "Equally important as a symbol of the rural life is sugar cane itself. Purple in color, pungently sweet in odor, mysteriously musical in sound, and deep-rooted in growth, cane represents the beauty and pain of living close to nature. It also represents the Gothic qualities of the Black American's African and southern past, especially his ambivalent attitude toward this heritage." Baker acknowledged the validity of the *Cane* image in the Northern portion of the novel. He contended that "even when Toomer deals with the life of the urban black American . . . he still presents the rhythms and psychological factors that condition life in the land of sugar cane, a land populated by the 'sons of Cane.'"

Praise for Toomer's writing is extensive. Baker cited his "mysterious brand of Southern psychological realism that has been matched only in the best work of William Faulkner." Kenneth Rexroth, in his book *American Poetry in the Twentieth Century,* was no less impressed. "Toomer is the first poet to unite folk culture and the elite culture of the white avant-garde," he contended, "and he accomplishes this difficult task with considerable success. He is without doubt the most important Black poet." Critics such as Bell and Gorham Munson preferred to dwell on Toomer's use of language. "There can be no question of Jean Toomer's skill as a literary craftsman," asserted Munson. "Toomer has found his own speech, now swift and clipped for violent narrative action, now languorous and dragging for specific characterizing purposes, and now lean and sinuous for the exposition of ideas, but always cadenced to accord with an unusually sensitive ear.'' Bell attributed *Cane's* ''haunting, illusive beauty'' to ''Toomer's fascinating way with words.'' He wrote, ''The meaning of the book is implicit in the arabesque pattern of imagery, the subtle movement of symbolic actions and objects, the shifting rhythm of syntax and diction, and the infrastructure of a cosmic consciousness.''

After the publication of *Cane,* Toomer continued writing prodigiously. However, most of his work was rejected by publishers. He became increasingly interested in the teachings of George I. Gurdjieff, a Greek spiritual philosopher, and turned to teaching Gurdjieff's beliefs in America. Finally, Toomer embraced the Quaker religion and lived his last decade as a recluse. In an article for *Phylon,* S. P. Fullwinder summed up Toomer's life as ''a story of tragedy.'' He wrote: ''As long as he was searching he was a fine creative artist; when the search ended, so did his creative powers. So long as he was searching his work was the cry of one caught in the modern human condition; it expressed modern man's lostness, his isolation. Once Toomer found an identity-giving absolute, his voice ceased to be the cry of modern man and became the voice of the schoolmaster complacently pointing out the way—his way.''

BIOGRAPHICAL/CRITICAL SOURCES:

BOOKS

Baker, Houston A., Jr., *Black Literature in America,* McGraw, 1971.
Benson, Bryan Joseph, and Mabel Mayle Dillard, *Jean Toomer,* Twayne, 1980.
Bone, Robert A., *The Negro Novel in America,* Yale University Press, 1965.
Bontemps, Arna, editor, *The Harlem Renaissance Remembered,* Dodd, 1972.
Contemporary Literary Criticism, Gale, Volume 1, 1973, Volume 4, 1975.
Dictionary of Literary Biography, Gale, Volume 45: *American Poets, 1880-1945, First Series,* 1986, Volume 51: *Afro-American Writers From the Harlem Renaissance to 1940,* 1987.
McKay, Nellie Y., *Jean Toomer, Artist,* University of North Carolina Press, 1984.
Rexroth, Kenneth, *American Poetry in the Twentieth Century,* Herder, 1971.
Short Story Criticism, Volume 1, Gale, 1988.
Toomer, Jean, *Cane,* introduction by Waldo Frank, Boni & Liveright, 1923, University Place Press, 1967.
Turner, Darwin T., *In a Minor Chord: Three Afro-American Writers and Their Search for Identity,* Southern Illinois University Press, 1971.

PERIODICALS

American Literature, May, 1972.
Black World, September, 1974.
Crisis, February, 1924.
New Republic, December 26, 1923.
Opportunity, September, 1925.
Phylon, winter, 1966.

*   *   *

TOURE, Askia Muhammad
See TOURE, Askia Muhammad Abu Bakr el

TOURE, Askia Muhammad Abu Bakr el   1938-
(Askia Muhammad Abu Bakr el-Toure, Rolland Snellings, Askia Muhammad Toure)

PERSONAL: Name originally Rolland Snellings; name changed c. 1970; listed in many sources as Askia Muhammad Toure; born October 13, 1938, in Raleigh, N.C.; son of Clifford R. and Nancy (Bullock) Snellings; married Dona Humphrey in June, 1966 (divorced); married Helen Morton Hobbs (Muslim name, Halima; a writer and editor) in 1970 (divorced); married third wife, Agila; children: (first marriage) Tariq Abdullah bin Toure, (second marriage) Jamil Abdus-Salam bin Toure. *Education:* Attended Art Students League of New York, 1960-62. *Religion:* Muslim.

ADDRESSES: Home—50 West 90th St., New York, N.Y. 10025.

CAREER: Poet, essayist, artist, editor, educator. Lecturer in African history, black studies, and creative writing at colleges and universities, including Yale University, Cornell University, Pennsylvania State University, Columbia University, University of California (Berkeley), San Francisco State College (now University), Central State College, and Queens College. *Military service:* U.S. Air Force, 1956-59.

MEMBER: Rockefeller Foundation (literary fellow), Omega Psi Phi (literary fellow).

AWARDS, HONORS: Modern Poetry Association award, 1952; Columbia University Creative Writing Grant, 1969.

WRITINGS—UNDER NAME ASKIA MUHAMMAD ABU BAKR EL-TOURE, EXCEPT AS NOTED:

(Author of introduction under name Rolland Snellings) *Samory Toure* (illustrated biography), designed by Matthew Meade, illustrated by Tom Feelings, produced by William E. Day, privately printed in New York, 1963.
Earth: For Mrs. Mary Bethune and the African and Afro-American Women, Broadside Press, 1968.
(With Ben Caldwell) *JuJu: Magic Songs for the Black Nation* (collection of poetry and prose), Third World Press, 1970.
Songhai! (collection of poetry and sketches), introduction by John O. Killens, Songhai Press, 1972.
(Contributor, under name Askia Muhammad Abu Bakr el Toure) Joe Goncalves, editor, *Black Art, Black Culture* (collection of articles from *Journal of Black Poetry*), Journal of Black Poetry Press, 1972.

Also author of the record *Black Spirits,* released by Black Forum. Work represented in anthologies, including *Black Fire: An Anthology of Afro-American Writing,* Morrow, 1968; *Black Arts,* Black Arts, 1969, *Black Nationalism in America,* Bobbs-Merrill, 1970; *Natural Process,* Hill & Wang, 1970; *The Poetry of Black America,* Harper, 1973; and *Understanding the New Black Poetry,* Morrow, 1973. Contributor of poetry and articles to periodicals, including *Black Theatre, Black World, Essence, Freedomways, Journal of Black Poetry, Liberation Magazine, Negro Digest, Soulbook,* and *Umbra.*

Staff member of *Umbra* magazine, 1962-63; member of editorial board of *Black America,* 1963-65; co-founder of *Afro World* newspaper, 1965; staff member of *Liberator Magazine,* 1965-66; associate editor of *Black Dialogue;* editor-at-large of *Journal of Black Poetry* (now *Kitabu Cha Jua*).

WORK IN PROGRESS: A volume of poetry, *Sunrise: A New Afrikan Anthem.*

SIDELIGHTS: A historian of African culture and a visionary poet foreseeing a "coming Age of Light" for humanity, Askia Muhammad Abu Bakr el Toure has been a leader of the black aesthetic movement since the early 1960s. The movement, whose influence extends to diverse fields, including poetry, theatre, music, journalism, politics, and religion, seeks to separate the spirit of black people from Western influence and define it in terms of its African origin.

While studying at the Art Students League of New York in the early 1960s, Toure helped compose one of the first books celebrating African heroes and history, *Samory Toure.* Toure collaborated with illustrator Tom Feelings, artist Elombe Brath, and others to produce the illustrated biography of the prominent grandfather of Sekou Toure, who was instrumental in maintaining Guinea's resistance to French domination in the nineteenth century.

After publishing his first book, Toure helped promote numerous journals supporting black awareness, including *Black America,* the black nationalist journal of the Revolutionary Action Movement (RAM), *Liberator Magazine,* and *Black Dialogue.* He eventually became editor-at-large of the *Journal of Black Poetry* (now known as *Kitabu Cha Jua*) after its emergence from *Black Dialogue.* With the newspaper he and author Larry Neal founded in 1965, *Afro World,* Toure helped strengthen the black liberation movement through the documentation of oppression and the analysis of racial injustice in America.

That same year Toure and Neal organized a Harlem Uptown Youth Conference with artists from the Black Arts Repertoir Theatre School, soon after which the Black Arts Theatre opened in Harlem. Black artists, including playwright LeRoi Jones (also known as Amiri Baraka), musicians Sun Ra and Milford Graves, and poets Toure and Neal acted out plays, performed music, and recited poetry in blocked-off streets in New York. "We would serenade the people on the streets of Harlem," Toure recalled, "and it made the authorities nervous as hell. We went all over Harlem and brought to its neglected, colonized masses the messages of Black power, dignity, and beauty."

Just as the nation was changing under the influence of the black arts and black liberation movements, Toure's personal life changed in the course of his activities. After moving with his wife, Dona Humphrey, to San Francisco soon after their marriage in 1966, Toure came under the influence of the Nation of Islam. Converting to the Islamic faith, he changed his name from Rolland Snellings to Askia Muhammad Abu Bakr el Toure. In his poem "Extension," published in *JuJu: Magic Songs for the Black Nation* in 1970, Toure praises the Islamic faith as "The TRUTH" that can engender "one large community with open doors [and] open minds." Pressures from his religious, social, and political activities, however, contributed to the strain on his marriage, and Toure and his wife divorced after the birth of their son.

After returning to New York, Toure married Helen Morton Hobbs in 1970, who encouraged Toure in his poetry and his newly embraced religion. Called by her Muslim name, Halima, she is probably the inspirational "woman panther-lithe and tawny, a princess come back to haunt me" in Toure's poem "Al Fajr: The Daybreak," published in *Songhai!* in 1972. They, too, divorced, however, after the birth of a son, and Toure moved to Philadelphia in 1974.

Reviewers admired *JuJu* and *Songhai!,* both collections of the visionary poetry and prose Toure composed during the height of his activity with the black aesthetic movement. *JuJu,* which includes three poems and an essay by Toure and a poem by playwright Ben Caldwell, guides the reader through the black person's "quest for national destiny and [his] spiritual identification with the universe," explained Carolyn F. Gerald in *Black World.* In *JuJu*—the title is a West African word meaning "magic"—Toure's epic poetry links the modern black soul to its African heritage through vibrant imagery and long, polyrhythmic lines that imitate classical black music. Inspired by black instrumentalists like John Coltrane and Milford Graves, Toure equates black music with African magic, believing music to be the most authentic expression of the black soul. He explains his belief in an essay he wrote in the *Journal of Black Poetry* in 1968: "When they stripped us of our obvious African culture (robes, drums, language, religion, etc.), the 'abstract' . . . aspect of our culture—our music—was the only thing, in altered form, permitted to remain. . . . As time passed, the Black Musician became *and remains* the major philosopher, priest, myth-maker and cultural hero of the Black Nation."

Praising the intricate form and stirring content of Toure's poetry, Gerald declared that *JuJu* is a collection "well worth buying and reading by all Black people, who stand to gain, in the reading, a greater sense of self."

Reviewer Addison Gayle, Jr., proclaimed in *Black World* that *Songhai!,* like *JuJu,* tells an important "truth: that the strength of Black people lay in a culture outside that of the American, and that [its attainment] is possible only after a return to the values and ethics of our African forefathers." The poetry and prose in *Songhai!,* however, suggests more than simply returning to African origins. In "an imaginative work overflowing with symbols, images, and metaphors of the new African world to come," Gayle pointed out, Toure "envisions the world . . . peopled by strong Black men and women equipped with the grace and endurance to survive." Gayle found that in the "coming Age of Light" of which the poet writes in his "Hymn to the People," Toure predicts "a world, where poet and people feed into each other's creative ethos, where all men are poets, where love and fidelity to the human condition remain sacrosanct."

BIOGRAPHICAL/CRITICAL SOURCES:

BOOK

Dictionary of Literary Biography, Volume 41, *Afro-American Poets Since 1955,* Gale, 1985.

PERIODICALS

Black World, June, 1971, September, 1974.
Journal of Literary Biography, volume 8, 1968.

—*Sketch by Christa Brelin*

* * *

TROUPE, Quincy (Thomas, Jr.) 1943-

PERSONAL: Born July 23, 1943, in New York, N.Y.; son of Quincy, Sr., and Dorothy (Marshall Smith) Troupe; married Margaret Porter; children: Antoinette, Tymme, Quincy, Porter. *Education:* Grambling College (now Grambling State University), B.A., 1963; Los Angeles City College, A.A., 1967.

ADDRESSES: Home—1925 7th Ave. #7L, New York, N.Y. 10026. *Office*—Department of Performing and Creative Arts, City University of New York, 130 Stuyvesant Place, Staten Island, N.Y. 10301; and School of the Arts, Writing Division,

Columbia University, New York, N.Y. 10027. *Agent*—Marie Brown, 412 West 154th St., No. 2, New York, N.Y. 10032.

CAREER: Watts Writers' Movement, Los Angeles, Calif., creative writing teacher, 1966-68; *Shrewd* (magazine), Los Angeles, associate editor, beginning 1968; University of California, Los Angeles, instructor in creative writing and black literature, 1968; Ohio University, Athens, instructor in creative writing and third world literature, 1969-72; Richmond College, Staten Island, N.Y., instructor in third world literature, beginning in 1972; instructor at institutions including University of California at Berkeley, California State University at Sacramento, and University of Ghana at Legon; College of Staten Island, City University of New York, New York City, associate professor of American and third world literatures and director of poetry center; Columbia University, New York City, member of faculty of Graduate Writing Program, 1985—. Director of Malcolm X Center and the John Coltrane Summer Festivals in Los Angeles, summers of 1969 and 1970. Has given poetry readings at various institutions, including Harvard University, New York University, Howard University, Yale University, Princeton University, Louisiana State University, Dartmouth College, Oberlin College, Ohio State University, University of Michigan, and Michigan State University. Presenter of lecture and readings series "Life Forces: A Festival of Black Roots" at the Church of St. John the Divine in New York City.

MEMBER: Poetry Society of America.

AWARDS, HONORS: International Institute of Education grant for travel in Africa, 1972; National Endowment for the Arts Award in poetry, 1978; grant from New York State Council of the Arts, 1979; American Book Award from the Association of American Publishers, 1980, for *Snake-back Solos;* New York Foundation for the Arts fellowship in poetry, 1987.

WRITINGS:

(Editor) *Watts Poets: A Book of New Poetry and Essays,* House of Respect, 1968.
Embryo Poems, 1967-1971 (includes "South African Bloodstone—For Hugh Masekela," "Chicago—For Howlin Wolf," "Profilin, A Rap/Poem—For Leon Damas," "The Scag Ballet," "Midtown Traffic," "Woke Up Crying the Blues," "The Earthquake of Peru; 1970; In 49 Seconds—For Cesar Vallejo, Great Peruvian Poet," "In the Manner of Rabearivello," "Poem From the Third Eye—For Eugene Redmond," and "Black Star, Black Woman"), Barlenmir, 1972.
(Editor with Rainer Schulte) *Giant Talk: An Anthology of Third World Writings,* Random House, 1975.
(Author of foreword) Arnold Adoff, editor, *Celebrations: A New Anthology of Black American Poetry,* Follet, 1977.
(With David L. Wolper) *The Inside Story of TV's "Roots,"* Warner Books, 1978.
Snake-back Solos: Selected Poems, 1969-1977 (includes "Springtime Ritual," "The Day Duke Raised," "La Marqueta," "For Miles Davis," "Up Sun South of Alaska," "Today's Subway Ride," "New York Streetwalker," "Steel Poles Give Back No Sweat," "Ghanaian Song—Image," and "Memory"), I. Reed Books, 1978.
Skulls Along the River (poetry), I. Reed Books, 1984.

Also founding editor of *Confrontation: A Journal of Third World Literature* and *American Rag;* guest editor of black poetry and black fiction issues of *Mundus Artium* in 1973; senior editor of *River Styx,* 1983—. Work represented in an-

thologies, including *The New Black Poetry,* 1969; *We Speak as Liberators,* 1970; *New Black Voices,* 1972; *Black Spirits,* 1972; *Poetry of Black America,* 1973; and *A Rock Against the Wind,* 1973. Contributor to periodicals, including *New Directions, Mundus Artium, Iowa Review, Black World, Callaloo, Essence, Antioch Review, Black Creation, Negro American Literature Forum, Umbra, Mediterranean Review, Concerning Poetry, Sumac, Paris Match, Black Review, New York Quarterly,* and *Village Voice.*

WORK IN PROGRESS: An autobiography of Miles Davis, with Miles Davis, for Simon & Schuster; *The Footmans,* a novel; a fourth collection of poems.

SIDELIGHTS: Quincy Troupe is "a poet of great feeling and energy," according to Michael S. Harper, reviewing *Snake-back Solos* in the *New York Times Book Review.* Troupe has also founded and edited magazines such as *Confrontation: A Journal of Third World Literature* and *American Rag,* in addition to having a distinguished academic career. He began teaching creative writing for the Watts Writers' Movement in 1966; his other teaching responsibilities have included courses in black literature and third world literature. Troupe was already an established poet and his scholarly interests had led him to compile *Giant Talk: An Anthology of Third World Writings* with Rainer Schulte when, in 1978, he reached a wider audience with *The Inside Story of TV's "Roots."* The book, which Troupe wrote with David L. Wolper, chronicles the production of the highly successful television miniseries about slavery in America, "Roots," which was based on Alex Haley's book of the same title. Troupe's *Inside Story* has sold over one million copies.

Troupe's first poetic publication came in 1964 when *Paris Match* featured his "What Is a Black Man?" Since then he has contributed poetry to many periodicals in addition to having volumes of his poems published in book form. The first of these, *Embryo Poems,* includes poems which display Troupe's interests in the use of dialect, such as "Profilin, A Rap/Poem—For Leon Damas," and in the area of music, such as "The Scag Ballet." The latter poem depicts the actions of drug addicts as a strange form of dance; another piece likens traffic noises to "black jazz piano." Yet another, "Woke Up Crying the Blues," concerns the assassination of black civil rights leader Martin Luther King, Jr. The sadness the speaker of the poem feels at the loss of "the peaceful man from Atlanta" mingles with the happiness of the news that one of his poems has been accepted for publication, producing a mixture of emotion essential to the singing of a blues song.

Snake-back Solos, Troupe's second volume of poetry, takes its title from a local name—"Snakeback"—for the Mississippi River, recalled from the poet's childhood in St. Louis. Harper cited such poems as "Today's Subway Ride" in praising Troupe's descriptions of "the strange reality of familiar scenes." The subway is painted starkly, its unpleasant atmosphere displayed in "pee smells assaulting nostrils/blood breaking wine stains everywhere." Though Harper faulted the repetition of some of *Snake-back Solos,* including "Up Sun South of Alaska," he lauded "Ghanaian Song—Image" and "Memory" as "striking" and concluded that "the strength and economy" of the poet's "best insights . . . are about people and places he has internalized and often left behind."

Troupe's academic work has also garnered applause from critics. *Giant Talk* was declared "comprehensive" by Jack Slater in the *New York Times Book Review.* The book, which Troupe edited with Rainer Schulte, contains poems, folk talkes, short stories, and novel excerpts by black Americans, native Americans, Hispanic Americans, black Africans, and Central and South Americans. According to Slater, the editors define third world writers as ''those who identify with the historically exploited segment of mankind, and who confront the establishment on their behalf''; hence the inclusion of U.S.-born authors along with those native to areas more traditionally identified with the third world. Slater hailed the editors' decision to group the anthologized pieces by concept rather than by geographical area or genre. By using categories like ''Oppression and Protest'' and ''Ritual and Magic,'' Troupe and Schulte ''have managed to lessen the unwieldiness of *Giant Talk*'s scope. The uninitiated reader can, therefore, savor with as much ease as possible bits and pieces of longer works . . . as well as enjoy complete works by . . . short-story writers and poets.''

BIOGRAPHICAL/CRITICAL SOURCES:

BOOKS

Dictionary of Literary Biography, Volume 41: *Afro-American Poets Since 1955*, Gale, 1985.
Troupe, Quincy, *Embryo Poems, 1967-1971*, Barlenmir, 1972.
Troupe, Quincy, and Rainer Schulte, *Giant Talk: An Anthology of Third World Writings*, Random House, 1975.
Troupe, Quincy, *Snake-back Solos: Selected Poems, 1969-1977*, I. Reed Books, 1978.

PERIODICALS

Black Scholar, March/April, 1981.
Freedomways, Volume XX, Number 2, 1980.
New York Times Book Review, November 30, 1975, October 21, 1979.

*   *   *

TURNER, Darwin T(heodore) 1931-

PERSONAL: Born May 7, 1931, in Cincinnati, Ohio; son of Darwin Romanes (a pharmacist) and Laura (a teacher; maiden name, Knight) Turner; married Edna Bonner, June 1, 1949 (divorced August, 1961); married Maggie Jean Lewis (a teacher), February 29, 1968; children: Pamela (Mrs. Robert Welch), Darwin Keith, Rachon. *Education:* University of Cincinnati, B.A., 1947, M.A., 1949; University of Chicago, Ph.D., 1956.

ADDRESSES: Home—5 Washington Pl., Iowa City, Iowa 52240. *Office*—University of Iowa, 303 English-Philosophy Bldg., Iowa City, Iowa 55242.

CAREER: Clark College, Atlanta, Ga., instructor in English, 1949-51; Morgan State College (now Morgan State University), Baltimore, Md., assistant professor of English, 1952-57; Florida A & M University, Tallahassee, professor of English and chairman of department, 1957-59; North Carolina Agricultural and Technical State University, Greensboro, professor of English, 1959-70, chairman of English department, 1959-66, dean of Graduate School, 1966-70; University of Michigan, Ann Arbor, professor of English, 1970-71; University of Iowa, Iowa City, visiting professor, 1971-72, professor, 1972-81, University of Iowa Foundation Distinguished Professor of English, 1981—, chairman of Afro-American studies, 1972—. Workshop director, Institute for Teachers of English in Colleges, Indiana University, 1965; visiting professor at University of Wisconsin-Madison, 1969, and University of Hawaii, summer, 1971. State chair for Iowa, Second International Festival of Black and African Culture, 1975-77;

delegate to American Studies African Regional Conference, 1976, and to Second International Festival of Black and African Arts, 1977. Member of Wellesley Conference on Pre-College Programs for Southern Negro Students, 1964, advisory committee to U.S. Office of Education, 1965, Graduate Record Examination Board, 1970-73, board of directors, National Council of Black Studies, 1976-79, Rockefeller Commission on the Humanities Center, 1978—. Consultant to National Endowment for the Humanities programs in ethnic studies and humanities, 1973—, American Council of Learned Societies, 1979-81, and to Rockefeller Foundation, 1980-83.

MEMBER: Modern Language Association of America, National Council of Teachers of English (director, 1971—, director of commission on literature, 1982—), American Association for the Advancement of the Humanities, College Language Association (president, 1963-65), Conference on College Composition and Communication (member of executive committee, 1965-67), College English Association (member of board of directors, 1971-74), Association for the Study of Afro-American Life and History, National Association for the Advancement of Colored People, Midwest Modern Language Association, South Atlantic Modern Language Association, North Carolina-Virginia College English Association, North Carolina Teachers Association, Phi Beta Kappa, Alpha Phi Alpha, Theta Alpha Phi, Lambda Iota Tau.

AWARDS, HONORS: American Council of Learned Societies research grant, 1965; Duke University-University of North Carolina Cooperative Program in Humanities fellowship, 1965-66; Creative Scholarship Award, College Language Association, 1970; Rockefeller Foundation research grant, 1971; Professional Achievement Award, University of Chicago Alumni Association, 1972; Carter G. Woodson Award, 1974; National Endowment for the Humanities grants for work and research in Afro-American studies, 1974-78; Distinguished Alumnus Award, University of Cincinnati Alumni Association, 1982; Doctor of Letters, University of Cincinnati, 1983.

WRITINGS:

Katharsis, Wellesley Press, 1964.
Nathaniel Hawthorne's ''The Scarlet Letter,'' Dell, 1967.
In a Minor Chord: Three Afro-American Writers and Their Search for Identity, Southern Illinois University Press, 1971.
(Co-author) *The Teaching of Literature by Afro-American Writers: Theory and Practice*, National Council of Teachers of English, 1972.

EDITOR

(With Jean M. Bright) *Images of the Negro in America*, Heath, 1965.
Black American Literature: Essays, C. E. Merrill, 1969.
Black American Literature: Fiction, C. E. Merrill, 1969.
Black American Literature: Poetry, C. E. Merrill, 1969.
(And compiler) *Afro-American Writers*, Appleton, 1970.
Black American Literature: Essays, Poetry, Fiction, Drama, C. E. Merrill, 1970.
(And author of introduction) *Black Drama in America: An Anthology*, Fawcett, 1971.
Voices from the Black Experience: African and Afro-American Literature, Ginn, 1972.
Responding: Five, Ginn, 1973.
The Wayward and the Seeking: A Collection of Writings by Jean Toomer, Howard University Press, 1980.

(With John Sekora) *The Art of the Slave Narrative: Original Essays in Criticism and Theory,* Western Illionis University Press, 1982.

CONTRIBUTOR

Lindsay Patterson, editor, *Anthology of the American Negro in the Theatre,* Association for the Study of Negro Life and History, 1967.

Louis Rubin, editor, *A Biographical Guide to Southern Literature,* University of North Carolina Press, 1969.

R. Hemenway, editor, *The Black Novelist,* C. E. Merrill, 1970.

N. Wright, Jr., editor, *What Black Educators Are Saying,* Hawthorn, 1970.

(And author of introduction) William Brasmer and Dominick Consolo, editors, *Black Drama: An Anthology,* C. E. Merrill, 1970.

A. Gayle, editor, *The Black Aesthetic,* Doubleday, 1971.

John Blassingame, editor, *New Perspectives on Black Studies,* University of Illinois Press, 1971.

Ruth Miller, editor, *Backgrounds to Black American Literature,* Chandler, 1971.

Therman B. O'Daniel, editor, *Langston Hughes, Black Genius: A Critical Evaluation,* Morrow, 1971.

Jay Martin, editor, *A Singer in the Dawn: Reinterpretations of Paul Laurence Dunbar,* Dodd, 1975.

Roy Brown and others, editors, *Dimensions of Detective Fiction,* Bowling Green University Popular Press, 1976.

T. B. O'Daniel, editor, *James Baldwin: A Critical Evaluation,* Howard University Press, 1977.

Evans Harrington and Ann L. Abadie, editors, *The South and Faulkner's Yoknapatawpha: The Actual and the Apocryphal,* University Press of Mississippi, 1977.

James Nagel, editor, *American Fiction,* Twayne, 1977.

W. Zyla and W. Aycock, editors, *Ethnic Literatures Since 1776: The Many Voices of America,* Texas Tech University Press, 1978.

Louis Budd and others, editors, *Toward a New American Literary History,* Duke University Press, 1980.

Errol Hill, editor, *The Theater of Black Experience,* Volume I, Prentice Hall, 1980.

(Author of afterword) Haki R. Madhubuti, *Earthquakes and Sun Rise Missions,* Third World Press, 1982.

Joseph Harris, editor, *Global Perspectives,* Howard University Press, 1983.

Poetry represented in many anthologies, including *A Rock Against the Wind,* edited by Lindsay Patterson, Dodd, 1974, and *When the Mode of the Music Changes: A Short Course in Song Lyrics and Poems,* Ginn, 1975.

OTHER

Also author of introductions to editions of works by authors such as Paul Laurence Dunbar, Charles W. Chesnutt, Zora Neale Hurston, Countee Cullen, and Jean Toomer.

Contributor to *Encyclopaedia Britannica, Encyclopedia International, Dictionary of American Biography, Contemporary Dramatists,* and *Encyclopedia of World Literature in the Twentieth Century.* Also contributor of articles, book reviews, and poetry to English, history, and sociology journals. Advisory editor, College Language Association *Journal,* 1960—, *Bulletin of Black Books,* 1971—, *Obsidian,* 1974—, and *American Literature,* 1976-78.

SIDELIGHTS: Darwin T. Turner observed: "I write poetry to purge myself of particular emotions and ideas. I write articles because I've been asked or because I have something which I

believe other people should know or may want to know. No single writer has been a major influence."

AVOCATIONAL INTERESTS: Chess, bridge.

BIOGRAPHICAL/CRITICAL SOURCES:

PERIODICALS

Baltimore Afro-American, May 10, 1947.
Chicago Defender, May 24, 1947.
Cincinnati Post, June 6, 1944, September 25, 1944.
Cincinnati Post and Times Star, June 12, 1964.
Negro Digest, January, 1969.
New York Times Book Review, July 13, 1980.
Washington Post Book World, July 13, 1980.

*   *   *

TURPIN, Waters Edward 1910-1968

PERSONAL: Born April 9, 1910, in Oxford, Md.; died November 19, 1968; son of Mary Rebecca Henry (a household manager and cook); married Jean Fisher, 1936. *Education:* Morgan College (now Morgan State University), B.A.; Columbia University, M.A., Ph.D.

CAREER: Served as a welfare investigator for the Works Progress Administration in the early 1930s; Storer College, Harper's Ferry, W. Va., professor and football coach, beginning in 1935; Lincoln University, Lincoln University, Pa., professor of English, 1940-49; Morgan State College (now Morgan State University), Baltimore, Md., professor, 1949-68.

AWARDS, HONORS: Rosenwald Fellowship in creative writing, 1941.

WRITINGS:

These Low Grounds (novel), Harper, 1937, McGrath, 1969.
O Canaan! (novel), Doubleday, 1939, AMS Press, 1975.
"Let the Day Perish" (play), first produced in Baltimore, Md., at Morgan State College (now Morgan State University), March 21, 1950.
"Saint Michaels Dawn" (two-act play), first produced in Baltimore at the Little Theater, Morgan State College (now Morgan State University) Christian Center, May 2, 1956.
(Author of lyrics) "Li'l Joe" (opera), first produced in Baltimore at the Chick Webb Memorial Recreation Center, Dunbar High School, May 11, 1957.
The Rootless (novel), Vantage Press, 1957.
(With Nick Aaron Ford) *Basic Skills for Better Writing: A Guide and Practice Book for Those Who Intend to Master the Essentials of Good English,* Putnam, 1959.
(Editor with Ford) *Extending Horizons: Selected Readings for Cultural Enrichment,* Random House, 1969.

Also author of "Long Way Home," a novel left unfinished at time of death. Contributor of short stories and articles to periodicals, including *Morgan State College Bulletin* and *Negro History Bulletin.*

SIDELIGHTS: Waters Edward Turpin was labeled the "progenitor of the Afro-American saga" by Burney Hollis in the *Dictionary of Literary Biography.* Paving the way for authors such as Alex Haley, who chronicled the history of one black family from pre-slavery days in Africa in his best-selling *Roots,* Turpin is best remembered for two of his novels: *These Low Grounds,* praised by reviewer Augusta Tucker in the *New York Times* for its "remarkable and just and fair balance," and *O Canaan!,* lauded as "a realistic and revealing picture of the way of his people'' by F. T. March critiquing for the same periodical. Turpin was known to have envisioned a set of five novels concerning different generations of the same family, which would have explored the experience of black people in America from the time of the American Revolution to the 1930s, but his career as an educator and his involvement in other writing projects allowed him to complete only three of the books before his death in 1968.

Turpin's commitment to featuring black experience in his historical novels was formed at an early age, according to Hollis. As a boy growing up in Oxford, Maryland, he enjoyed listening to his maternal grandfather's stories of heroic local blacks ''who fought and died for their freedom—the stuff of which legends are made,'' in Hollis's words. When Turpin was older and was attending secondary school at Morgan Academy, his mother took a job as household manager and cook for novelist Edna Ferber, famed for books such as *Show Boat* and *Cimarron*. Visiting his mother in Ferber's home on weekends and holidays, Turpin became the author's protege. Ferber allowed him the use of her library, introduced him to her acquaintances in the publishing field, and discussed with him whatever writing she was doing at the time. Reported Hollis: ''Turpin detected the absence in her writing of black achievers whom he saw as equivalent to the American white frontier pioneers about whom she was writing. . . . [This] fueled his growing determination to tell the story of black pioneers, no less valiant, adventuresome, or successful than those whom Ferber had immortalized.''

Turpin showed his first effort towards this goal, *These Low Grounds,* to Ferber, who praised the manuscript and arranged to send it to its eventual publisher, Harper. Set primarily in eastern Maryland, the novel details four generations of the Prince family, beginning with Martha, whom the Civil War freed from slavery. Martha's descendants rise in social status from lifetime to lifetime, making transitions from bondage to domestic service, farming, and teaching. Though *These Low Grounds* was generally well received by both black and white critics, many objected to what Hollis described as ''the overly ambitious scope of [Turpin's] first novel—its having attempted to trace rather sketchily four generations of a family in the confines of 350 pages.''

O Canaan!, Turpin's second novel, focuses on the city of Chicago rather than eastern Maryland. Concerning the migration of many southern blacks to a Chicago seen as the biblical promised land of Canaan in the early twentieth century, the book recounts the trials and triumphs of both the Prince family from *These Low Grounds* and the Benson family. The prosperity experienced by blacks who built on the city's south side, the devastation brought by the Great Depression, and the determination of characters like Joe Benson to recover from the ensuing state of disadvantage are all chronicled by Turpin. Hollis declared that ''the heroes of *O Canaan* are of mythical and biblical stature, and, more than a family chronicle, the novel is a black odyssey with a hero whose fighting spirit is equal to that of Ulysses.'' Other critics, such as R. A. Chace in the *Boston Transcript,* found the characters' realism to be more important than their larger-than-life qualities. ''More than anything else,'' Chace argued, ''the reader will recognize the common humanity of these people.''

In his next effort towards his planned pentology, *The Rootless,* Turpin went backwards in chronology to the time of the American Revolution. The story revolves around the ancestor of the Prince family, a man born on a Maryland slave ship. He grows up and gradually realizes that he is willing to pay any price, even death, to gain his freedom. *The Rootless* also focuses on a family of Maryland slaveowners and, through the characters of Louisa and Mariah Shannon, ''debunks, without apology or maudlin sentimentality, the myth of the purity of the southern belle,'' according to Hollis. More condemnatory of the ways in which whites shaped the black experience than Turpin's previous novels, *The Rootless* was unable to find itself a publisher for many years. Unwilling to soften the content of his novel merely to see it in print, Turpin decided to publish it himself in 1957, about ten years after he finished it. Due to the limited circulation of vanity press publications, there was little critical reaction to *The Rootless.*

Turpin took time out from his projected five-novel set to begin another book to which he gave the tentative title ''Long Way Home.'' Dealing more directly with a theme that had been a strong undercurrent in the Prince family sagas, that of the black woman being forced into a matriarchal role, ''Long Way Home'' features a heroine named Ella Winters. Ella is pushed into a strange dual role—she becomes the leader of her own family while serving as a domestic laborer for a white family. Centered more firmly on one character than any of his previous books, ''Long Way Home'' has ''considerable thematic and technical integrity and shows promise of being Turpin's best novel,'' judged Hollis.

Due to shifting priorities and interests, Turpin completed only two sections of ''Long Way Home.'' In addition to collaborating with Nick Aaron Ford on the nonfiction works *Basic Skills for Better Writing* and *Extending Horizons,* Turpin also began to write plays. His first, ''Let the Day Perish,'' takes its title from the biblical story of Job and concerns the hardships of a black family living in Harlem during the Great Depression. Though, as Hollis points out, the play ends on a note of determination and survival, it does not emphasize achievement and success as do Turpin's novels. Another of Turpin's dramas, ''Saint Michaels Dawn,'' portrays the adolescence of famed black lecturer and writer Frederick Douglass.

BIOGRAPHICAL/CRITICAL SOURCES:

BOOKS

Dictionary of Literary Biography, Volume 51: *Afro-American Writers From the Harlem Renaissance to 1940,* Gale, 1987.

PERIODICALS

Boston Transcript, August 19, 1939.
New York Times, September 26, 1937, July 16, 1939.

—*Sketch by Elizabeth Thomas*

*   *   *

TUTU, Desmond M(pilo) 1931-

PERSONAL: Born October 7, 1931, in Klerksdorp, Witwatersrand, Transvaal, South Africa; son of Zachariah (a school teacher), and Aletta (a domestic servant; maiden name, Tutu); married Leah Nomalizo Shenxane, July 2, 1955; children: Trevor Thamsanqa, Theresa Thandeka, Naomi Nontombi, Mpho Andrea. *Education:* Bantu Normal College, Pretoria, South Africa, teacher's diploma, 1953; University of South Africa, Johannesburg, B.A., 1954; St. Peter's Theological College, Johannesburg, L.Th., 1960; King's College, London, B.D., 1965, M.Th., 1966.

ADDRESSES: Home—Bishopscourt, Claremont, Cape Province 7700, South Africa. *Office*—c/o Diocesan Office, P.O. Box 1131, Johannesburg 2000, South Africa.

CAREER: Teacher at high schools in Johannesburg, South Africa, 1954-55, and in Krugersdorp, South Africa, 1955-58; ordained as deacon, 1960, and Anglican priest, 1961; St. Alban's Church, Benoni, Johannesburg, curate, 1960-61; St. Mary's Cathedral, Johannesburg, priest, 1961; St. Philip's Church, Alberton, Transvaal, South Africa, curate, 1961-62; St. Alban's Church, Golders Green, London, England, part-time curate, 1962-65; St. Mary's Church, Bletchingley, Surrey, England, part-time curate, 1965-66; lecturer at Federal Theological Seminary, Alice, Cape Province, South Africa, 1967-69; lecturer in theology at University of Botswana, Lesotho, and Swaziland, 1970-72; World Council of Churches' Theological Education Fund, Bromley, Kent, England, associate director, 1972-75; St. Augustine's Church, Grove Park, Kent, England, curate, 1972-75; dean of Johannesburg, Johannesburg, 1975-76; bishop of Lesotho, South Africa, 1976-78; general secretary of South African Council of Churches, 1978-85; assistant Anglican bishop of Johannesburg, 1978-85, bishop, 1984-86; St. Augustine's Parish, Soweto, South Africa, rector, 1981-85; archbishop of Cape Town and Anglican primate of southern Africa, 1986—; social reformer and political activist.

Chaplain at University of Fort Hare, 1967-69; visiting professor at General Theological Seminary, New York, N.Y., 1984; Richard Feetham Academic Freedom Lecture, University of the Witwatersrand, Johannesburg, 1985. Participant at several international conferences, including the "Salvation Today" conference, Bangkok, Thailand, Anglican Consultative Council, Port of Spain, Trinidad, and the World Council of Churches' 6th Assembly, Vancouver, Canada, 1983. Trustee of Phelps Stoke Fund.

MEMBER: National Association for the Advancement of Colored People.

AWARDS, HONORS: Fellow of King's College, London, 1978; Prix d'Athene from Onassis Foundation, 1980; designated member of International Social Prospects Academy, 1983; Family of Man Gold Medal Award, 1983; Martin Luther King, Jr., Humanitarian Award, 1984; Nobel Peace Prize from Norwegian Nobel Committee, 1984, for "role as unifying leader . . . in the campaign to resolve the problem of apartheid in South Africa"; Sam Ervin Free Speech Award, 1985. Recipient of numerous honorary doctoral degrees, including LL.D. from Harvard University, 1979, D.Th. from Ruhr University, and D.D. from Aberdeen University, 1984.

WRITINGS:

Crying in the Wilderness, Eerdmans, 1982.
Hope and Suffering: Sermons and Speeches, [Johannesburg], 1983, revised edition, edited by William B. Eerdmans, Eerdmans, 1984.
(Author of foreword) Omar Badsha, editor, *South Africa: The Cordoned Heart,* Gallery Press, 1986.
(Contributor) Buti Tlhagale and Itumeleng Mosala, editors, *Hammering Swords Into Ploughshares: Essays in Honor of Archbishop Mpilo Desmond Tutu,* Eerdmans, 1987.

Also author of several articles and reviews.

SIDELIGHTS: As archbishop of Capetown, leader of the Anglican Church in southern Africa, and one of the world's foremost black critics of South Africa's apartheid government,

Desmond M. Tutu is "nothing if not impassioned," wrote Joshua Hammer in *People* magazine. "Like all great preachers, his every speech and press conference is a blaze of emotion, his every gesture a drop of oil fueling the oratorical fire. Waving his arms, punching the air like a boxer, the elfin . . . figure draws in his followers with a stream of whispers, shouts and sobs, punctuated with roars of laughter." Yet until he received the Nobel Peace Prize in 1984, Tutu was little known outside his native South Africa.

During the 1970s and into the 1980s, first as general secretary of the South African Council of Churches, then as bishop of Johannesburg, and later as archbishop of Capetown, Tutu has campaigned vigorously for the abolition of apartheid, South Africa's system of government that defines and allocates political power and privileges to different groups of people on the basis of skin color and ethnic background. The vast majority of non-South African political commentators see apartheid as a means of keeping political power in the hands of South African whites—some five million people who constitute fifteen percent of the country's total population. The system does this, critics say, by designating South African blacks as "citizens" of specified areas called independent homelands. The government keeps the black population within each homeland below the total number of whites in South Africa, thus establishing an arbitrarily defined white "majority." Since 1948, when apartheid became official policy of the newly elected National party, the South African government has forced more than four million blacks to relocate to the homelands. Those allowed to remain near white-designated areas live in run-down townships segregated from the whites, and the blacks wishing to work in white areas must apply for a government permit to do so. Incomes average one-sixth of those received by whites for the same job; these black workers are also required to live in single-sexed hostels during the week, leaving their families in the homelands. Despite policy changes made by the government of President Pieter W. Botha, which lifted the ban on interracial marriages and enfranchised people of Asian and mixed descent, black South Africans are still denied the right to vote. It is against these forms of discrimination—economic and racial—that Archbishop Tutu stands.

Tutu's first recollections of the apartheid system in operation came when he was growing up in the western Transvaal mining town of Klerksdorp. He told Marc Cooper and Greg Goldin of *Rolling Stone* that the constant racial taunts of the white boys were not "thought to be out of the ordinary," but as he got older he "began finding things eating away at [him]." Recalling one incident in which he heard his father referred to as "boy," Tutu remarked, "I knew there wasn't a great deal I could do, but it just left me churned. . . . What he must have been feeling . . . being humiliated in the presence of his son. Apartheid has always been the same systematic racial discrimination: it takes away your human dignity and rubs it in the dust and tramples it underfoot." Young Tutu also witnessed the harsh economic realities of the government's discriminatory policies while attending the local school. The white children, for whom the government had arranged free school meals, disliked the institutional food and threw it away, preferring to eat what their mothers packed for them. Many black school children of poor families, recalled Tutu, were reduced to scavenging in the cafeteria's rubbish bins for food during lunch periods.

In 1943 the Tutu family moved to Johannesburg where Desmond's father continued to teach and his mother worked as a cook at a missionary school for the blind. The new surroundings greatly affected young Tutu. Not only was he deeply moved by the dedication and service shown by staff members to the children in the school where his mother worked, but it was here that he first met Father Trevor Huddleston, who became his most influential mentor and friend. A leading British critic of South Africa's apartheid system, Huddleston served as the parish priest in Sophiatown, a black slum district of Johannesburg. In an interview with the *Observer,* Tutu recalled his first meeting with the priest: "I was standing with my mother one day, when this white man in a cassock walked past and doffed his big black hat to her. I couldn't believe it— a white man raising his hat to a simple black labouring woman." Huddleston, who was beginning to build an international reputation as an outspoken opponent of apartheid and whom the South African authorities recognized as one of their most controversial critics, became a close friend of Tutu. When the young African contracted tuberculosis as a teenager and was hospitalized for almost twenty months, Huddleston visited him nearly every day. "Like many people, I came under the spell of Trevor Huddleston. I will never forget his compassion, caring, love and deep spirituality," Tutu told *People* reporters Peter Hawthorne and Dawn Clayton. The impact of Huddleston's friendship on Tutu's later life was immense.

Following full recovery from tuberculosis, Tutu resumed his education, and entered the School of Medicine at Witwatersrand University with the intention of becoming a doctor. When his family could no longer afford the tuition fees, however, he was forced to drop out of medical school and begin training as a teacher instead. Tutu received his B.A. from the University of Johannesburg in 1954 and taught high school in Johannesburg and Krugersdorp until 1957. It was then that Tutu's previous experiences with apartheid and the compassion he felt for his fellow man combined to change and redirect what might otherwise have been an uneventful career. While teaching at Munsieville High School in Krugersdorp, the South African government announced plans to introduce a state-run system of education especially intended for students in black districts. Limiting both the quality and extent of education, the system was considered by many to be deliberately second-rate. Tutu, along with several of his colleagues, found the plan ubiquitous and resigned. As a young man newly married, without a job, and sensing a growing urge to serve his community and country, Tutu, in retrospect, said he felt as if God had grabbed him by the scruff of his neck and, whether it was convenient or not, had sent him off to spread God's word. That same year, inspired by the ideals of his mentor Trevor Huddleston, he began theological studies with the priests of the Community of the Resurrection, the Anglican order to which Huddleston belonged.

Following ordainment as a priest in 1961, Tutu began to establish his career in the Anglican church, working in small parishes in England and South Africa. Concurrently he continued his education and in 1966 received a master's degree in theology from King's College, London. In 1972 he accepted a position in England as associate director of the Theological Education Fund. Thoroughly enjoying his role, he traveled extensively throughout Asia and Africa and presided over the allocation of World Council of Churches scholarships. Thoughts of South Africa and the discrimination faced by his black countrymen seemed to surface continually, however, demanding his consideration. Throughout the early 1970s, tensions increased between an angry black community and a white-dominated government determined to maintain its political powers. Finally, in 1975, Tutu decided to return to his homeland and

"contribute what I could to the liberation struggle," he explained to Hawthorne and Clayton. Upon returning, his presence and commitment to the cause of black Africans was felt almost immediately.

As Tutu ascended the ecclesial ranks of the Anglican church— in 1976 he was consecrated bishop of Lesotho, one of the government-designated black homelands—his involvement in the antiapartheid cause assumed an importance concomitant with his position. Choosing always to live in his parish, he closely monitored the feelings of his congregation and the local community; during the 1970s, in an atmosphere of mounting racial tensions, Tutu attempted to pacify angry black youths, encouraging them to seek change through peaceful means. In 1976, he met with black activist Nhato Motlana in an effort to curb the potential violence of youths in the black township of Soweto on the outskirts of Johannesburg. He also wrote to the incumbent South African Prime Minister Balthazar J. Vorster, warning him of the dangerous situation in Soweto. Tutu later claimed that Vorster dismissed his letter as a ploy engineered by political opponents. On June 16, 1976, however, racial tensions exploded into racial violence as black demonstrators met untempered reprisal from white security forces. Six hundred blacks were shot to death in the confrontation.

The tragic consequences of the Soweto riots seemed to mark a watershed in the attention given to the antiapartheid struggle in South Africa. Thereafter the situation received more extensive coverage from the world's press, which supplied the West with explanations of the escalating racial conflict and attempted to expose the possible reasons for it. For Tutu the increasing number of violent confrontations between blacks and security forces marked a change in his perception of his own involvement. Until the Soweto riots, he made himself generally available to discuss the situation with any representative from any side; following the riots he began to use his growing influence and openly initiated peaceful negotiation. This was not done in deference to the government; Tutu had become a highly visible and vocal critic.

By 1978 Tutu had been appointed the first black secretary general of the South African Council of Churches, and his personal attitude toward apartheid had hardened. He felt he could no longer condone the system on either political or moral grounds, and he determinedly set out to promote peaceful change toward a truly democratic system of government in South Africa. As head of the Council Tutu became spokesman for its thirteen million members, thus gaining increased political strength; due to its racial composition—eighty percent black— the Council was an ideal vehicle for voicing political opposition to the apartheid system. Under Tutu's direction the Council not only became openly critical of the South African government, but it also supported a network of anti-government protest. Responsible for paying the legal fees of arrested black protesters, for supporting the families of imprisoned activists, and for financing anti-government demonstrations, the Council did not endear itself to the South African authorities. The South African government began to single out Council leaders—Tutu prominent among them—for criticism, with the help of press agencies that supported government views. In addition Tutu and his colleagues were constantly harrassed with accusations of minor misdemeanors and, through government legislation, were deprived of certain rights of free movement. But in 1979, on two occasions, Tutu openly challenged the government, seriously confronting its credibility in the eyes of the rest of the world.

The first challenge came after the passing of the Group Areas Act, a policy that gave the government the power to forcibly remove blacks from their homes in urban South Africa and relocate them in government designated tribal homelands. The act made it virtually impossible for blacks to continue working at the better-paying city jobs without enduring lengthy and uncomfortable journeys every day or paying to live in one of the government's single-sexed hostels located in the city suburbs. And for those blacks who stayed in the homelands to work, their only hope was to eke out a meager living from very poor farmland. Appalled by the situation and by conditions in the homelands, Tutu compared the South African government with that of Nazi Germany, denouncing the forced relocation of blacks as South Africa's "final solution" to the black "problem." Although he later retracted the wording of his outburst, he continued to protest the policy and chided the government in Pretoria for deliberately starving people in South Africa while it boasted about its grain exports to nearby Zambia.

Tutu voiced his second major condemnation of the South African government before an international audience in autumn of 1979, which probably marks the beginning of his visibility in the world's media. In an interview for a Danish television program, Tutu called on the government of Denmark to cease buying South African coal as a sign of support for the antiapartheid cause. The appeal moved people in Western countries to consider economic sanction as the ultimate weapon in the battle against apartheid. Concerned citizens, particularly in Europe, had voiced disapproval of South Africa's white minority government for years, but they had never found an effective means of critical expression that would force the white government to reconsider its policies. Tutu's proposal offered a method that has since become a principal part of the strategy in the worldwide fight against apartheid. It also successfully focused attention upon the real possibility of positive change in South Africa.

Tutu's actions brought him very close to serious government reprisals. Returning from Denmark in 1979, authorities seized his passport, a move generally seen as a warning of possible imprisonment—the fate of two previous government critics, Nelson R. Mandela and Victor Tambo—or expulsion from the country. Tutu ignored the signal, however, and continued his antiapartheid campaign. The South African government eventually returned his passport in January, 1981, but confiscated it again in April. Thereafter Tutu was allowed to travel outside South Africa only with the government's permission and special travel documents that listed his nationality as "undetermined." In August, 1982, the South African government denied Tutu permission to go to New York to receive an honorary doctorate from Columbia University. Since the university does not grant degrees in absentia, Columbia's president traveled to South Africa and personally presented Tutu his degree in a ceremony held in Johannesburg.

It was during a permitted stay in the United States, on October 16, 1984, that Desmond Tutu received word that he was the 1984 Nobel peace laureate. Part of the Nobel citation read: "It is the committee's wish that the Peace Prize now awarded to Desmond Tutu should be regarded not only as a gesture of support to him and to the South African Council of Churches of which he is leader, but also to all individuals and groups in South Africa who, with their concern for human dignity, fraternity and democracy, incite the admiration of the world." According to *Time,* "much of white South Africa reacted grumpily or indifferently to the news." Said Tutu, in response: "You feel humble, you feel proud, elated and you feel sad.

One of my greatest sadnesses is that there are many in this country who are not joining in celebrating something that is an honor for this country." Less than a month later, on November 3, 1984, Tutu was elected first Anglican bishop of Johannesburg; he subsequently resigned as secretary general of the South African Council of Churches.

Tutu immediately expanded his efforts to abolish apartheid. He called upon the international community to use diplomatic, political, and economic pressures to convince the South African government in Pretoria to rid itself of apartheid. Maintaining a strong belief in nonviolence, Tutu was positive such actions offered the only viable means of avoiding massive bloodshed. His request caused considerable reaction in the United States. In December, 1984, Tutu traveled to Washington, D.C., to meet with President Ronald Reagan. He tried to persuade the president to impose economic sanctions against South Africa, arguing that such a measure would help put an end to police violence and lead to the release of political prisoners. But Reagan preferred, instead, to remain on friendly terms with Pretoria, believing only diplomacy would produce positive change in South Africa, a policy he called "constructive engagement." The president's stance provoked a nationwide response as hundreds of antiapartheid demonstrators picketed South African consulates and embassies throughout the country. In a well-received speech before a bipartisan congressional committee, Tutu called on the United States to make a stand against racism. In response to the bishop's appeal, increasing numbers of state and local governments, educational institutions, and labor unions began plans to withdraw investments from companies doing business with South Africa. Pretoria viewed the American developments with growing concern.

Over the next several months civil unrest in South Africa escalated from boycotts, strikes, and stone-throwing clashes between township blacks and police to bloody riots symptomatic of civil war. By July, 1985, more than five hundred people had been killed, including four leaders of the largely black nationalist United Democratic Front (UDF) party. Many of the victims were black government employees and town councillors attacked by blacks loyal to UDF, some were blacks who had patronized white businesses, others were killed when police opened fire on rioters. The deteriorating situation prompted President Botha to declare a state of emergency in more than thirty districts throughout the country, including Johannesburg and most of the Transvaal provinces. Invoking the emergency powers of South Africa's 1953 Public Security Act, the government was allowed to impose curfews, arrest and detain suspects for fourteen days without a warrant, interrogate prisoners without the presence of lawyers, and tighten censorship on the press. International response to Botha's move was guarded, but antiapartheid leaders in South Africa were incensed. Asked in a *Newsweek* interview if the state of emergency changed South Africa's situation, Bishop Tutu replied: "Declaring a state of emergency is a typical reaction. It doesn't really change much: it just removes the last vestiges of our rights, and it means that whatever they do to us now, they can do with more impunity."

The government outlawed funeral marches, for example, sensing that the traditionally communal affairs represented subversion and civil disorder. Funeral services, however, were permitted. During one instance in the black township of Daveyton, reported *Time,* police and military units surrounded the tent where family, friends, and community members gathered for the burial service of a young black woman shot and killed during a demonstration. Army troops held guns ready, police dogs were positioned atop armored cars, and helicopters surveyed the area from above. It was the largest display of government force since Botha's declaration of emergency began. The tension mounted as the government forces waited to see if the crowd would, in defiance, march to the cemetery located several blocks away. Just when violence seemed likely to erupt, Bishop Tutu arrived and the atmosphere relaxed immediately. The coffin of the slain girl was brought into the tent and set before the clergyman, who calmly performed the religious service. According to *Time*, "Tutu told the gathering that he had asked the government, 'Please allow us to mourn, to bury our dead with dignity, to share the burden of our sorrow. Do not rub salt in our wounds . . . I appeal to you because we are already hurt, already down. We are humans, not animals. When we have a death, we cry.'" In warning to the authorities, reported *Time*, "the bishop declared, 'I have been a minister for 24 years, and I am not going to start now being told what to preach. I do not want to defy the government. But Scripture says that when there is a conflict between the law of God and the law of man, we must obey the law of God. I will continue to preach as instructed.'" After the completion of the religious service, the police ordered the crowd to disperse, allowing people in vehicles only to go to the cemetery. Tutu pleaded with the police commandant to provide buses, warning that violence could otherwise erupt. After an hour of tense waiting, buses finally arrived and transported the mourners to the cemetery. A potentially bloody confrontation was avoided, order had been maintained, and peace prevailed. Recalling for a *Time* reporter the confrontation with the police commandant, Tutu chuckled and said, "He saluted me. Twice."

During the weeks following the Daveyton incident, international condemnation of Pretoria's declared state of emergency increased. Canada prepared to toughen its limited ecomonic sanctions, the U.S. House of Representatives approved the first imposition of broad economic sanctions against South Africa, and more than a dozen European nations recalled their diplomats in a gesture of disapproval. By the end of 1985, the rand (South Africa's monetary unit) lost fifty percent of its value. President Botha, however, was determined not to succumb to external pressure and his declaration of emergency held firm. Tutu also held firm to his own declaration to rid South Africa of apartheid, and he continued his outspoken appeal for international support of the antiapartheid cause. "We face a catastrophe in this land," warned Tutu, according to *Newsweek*. "Only the action of the international community, by applying pressure, can save us." Speaking in Wales some time later, reported *New Statesman*, Tutu declared, "It is still possible for us to move back from the edge of a precipice if the international community is prepared to intervene decisively." But international action was slow to develop, especially in the United States where President Reagan insisted on maintaining his current policy of deploring the apartheid system while opposing punitive sanctions. Angry with the Reagan administration's attitude, Tutu, according to *Newsweek*, observed: "President Reagan has [imposed sanctions on] Poland, Nicaragua and Libya. He is not opposed to sanctions per se. He is opposed to them when blacks are involved." Tutu also asserted, "In my view, the Reagan administration's support and collaboration with [the South African government] is immoral, evil and totally unchristian. You are either for or against apartheid, and not by rhetoric. You are either on the side of the oppressed or on the side of the oppressor. You can't be neutral."

Over the next several months antiapartheid forces did gain support in the United States when the House of Representatives approved a bill that would impose a trade embargo on South Africa. President Reagan still refused to approve sanctions, however, and promised to veto such a bill. In a speech made in July, 1986, Reagan stated that current U.S. policy toward South Africa would remain unchanged. Tutu's reaction, as disclosed in *Newsweek*, was unusually blunt: "[Tutu] called the speech 'nauseating,' likened Reagan to the 'great white chief of old' and said, 'The West, for my part, can go to hell.'" Pretoria seemed pleased with Reagan's message. Meanwhile the situation in South Africa worsened and Tutu's speeches began to take on fatalistic undertones. Speaking with *Time*, Tutu said: "I think the white ruling class is quite ready to do a Samson on us. That is, they will pull down the pillars, even if it means they perish in the process. They are really scared that we are going to treat them as they treated us."

In early September, 1986, Tutu was elected archbishop of Cape Town and the primate of the Anglican Church for all of southern Africa. Conducting his final service in Johannesburg before his enthronement as archbishop, according to *Time*, Tutu assured his congregation: "Despite all that the powers of the world may do, we are going to be free." But in a British Broadcasting Corporation interview reported by *Time* in April, 1987, President Botha declared, "I am not prepared to sacrifice my rights so that the other man can dominate me with his greater numbers. . . . I never read in the Bible that to be a good Christian means I must commit suicide to please the other man." Shortly thereafter, Pretoria toughened its policies against antiapartheid demonstrators even more. According to *Time* the South African government "announced a new emergency regulation banning South Africans from doing or saying anything to bring about the release of people who have been detained without trial"—an estimated eight thousand, including two thousand minors. The government also declared it "illegal to participate in 'any campaign, project or action aimed at accomplishing the release' of detainees. Among the forbidden acts . . . are the signing of petitions, the sending of telegrams and even the wearing of political stickers or shirts bearing anti-detention slogans."

Time reported that Tutu and other critics in South Africa "said they would ignore the restrictions and continue to speak their minds." Holding a prayer service to protest Pretoria's action, the archbishop warned: "Beware when you take on the Church of God. Others have tried and have come a cropper." He then added, "The government has gone crazy. I want to tell them that I am not going to stop calling for the release of detainees in or out of church." Governments worldwide, including the United States, also expressed official disapproval. Faced with such widespread opposition, Pretoria retreated somewhat, but they had once again fueled the fires of civil unrest and the antiapartheid cause. Tutu, adhering to his conviction that democracy and freedom can exist in South Africa, continued his campaign for the peaceful liberation of his countrymen.

Many of Tutu's orations have been collected in *Hope and Suffering: Sermons and Speeches*, described as "vintage Tutu" by Huston Horn in the *Los Angeles Times Book Review*. "Tutu's gaze rarely wanders from a benign, visionary South Africa ruled together by blacks and whites," explained Horn, and "the bishop's preachments [still] have contemporary relevance and ring." Colman McCarthy of *Washington Post Book World* called the book "stunning" and concluded that Bishop Tutu, even without his Nobel, "would still have been a force that no regime could stop or silence."

AVOCATIONAL INTERESTS: Music, reading, jogging.

BIOGRAPHICAL/CRITICAL SOURCES:

BOOKS

Tlhagale, Buti and Itumeleng Mosala, editors, *Hammering Swords into Ploughshares: Essays in Honor of Archbishop Mpilo Desmond Tutu*, Eerdmans, 1987.

PERIODICALS

Chicago Tribune, July 7, 1980.
Christian Science Monitor, April 26, 1979, March 28, 1984.
Economist, March 28, 1987, April 18, 1987.
Maclean's, August 12, 1985, April 14, 1986.
Manchester Guardian Weekly, October 28, 1984.
Newsday, October 17, 1984.
New Statesman, May 30, 1986.
Newsweek, October 29, 1984, December 17, 1984, July 29, 1985, August 4, 1986.
New York Times, October 17, 1984.
New York Times Magazine, March 14, 1982.
Observer (London), August 8, 1982, May 8, 1983.
People, December 17, 1984.
Rolling Stone, November 21, 1985.
Time, October 29, 1984, January 14, 1985, August 19, 1985, August 4, 1986, September 15, 1986, April 13, 1987, April 27, 1987.
Washington Post, October 17, 1984, October 19, 1984.

—*Sketch by Jeremy Kane and Linda S. Smouse*

*   *   *

TUTUOLA, Amos   1920-

PERSONAL: Born 1920, in Abeokuta, Nigeria; son of Charles (a cocoa farmer) and Esther (Aina) Tutuola; married Alake Victoria, 1947; children: Olubunmi, Oluyinka, Erinola. *Education:* Attended schools in Nigeria. *Religion:* Christian.

ADDRESSES: P.O. Box 2251, Ibadan, Nigeria. *Home*—Ago-Odo, West Nigeria. *Office*—Nigerian Broadcasting Corp., Ibadan, Nigeria, West Africa.

CAREER: Worked on father's farm; trained as a coppersmith; employed by Nigerian Government Labor Department, Lagos, and by Nigerian Broadcasting Corp., Ibadan, Nigeria. Freelance writer. Visiting research fellow, University of Ife, 1979; associate, international writing program at University of Iowa, 1983. *Military service:* Royal Air Force, 1943-45; served as metal worker in Nigeria.

MEMBER: Mbari Club (Nigerian authors; founder).

AWARDS, HONORS: Named honorary citizen of New Orleans, 1983; *The Palm-Wine Drinkard and His Dead Palm-Wine Tapster in the Dead's Town* and *My Life in the Bush of Ghosts* received second place awards in a contest held in Turin, Italy, 1985.

WRITINGS:

The Palm-Wine Drinkard and His Dead Palm-Wine Tapster in the Dead's Town, Faber, 1952, Grove, 1953.
My Life in the Bush of Ghosts, Grove, 1954, reprinted, Faber, 1978.
Simbi and the Satyr of the Dark Jungle, Faber, 1955.

The Brave African Huntress, illustrated by Ben Enwonwu, Grove, 1958.
The Feather Woman of the Jungle, Faber, 1962.
Ajaiyi and His Inherited Poverty, Faber, 1967.
(Contributor) *Winds of Change: Modern Short Stories from Black Africa*, Longman, 1977.
The Witch-Herbalist of the Remote Town, Faber, 1981.
The Wild Hunter in the Bush of the Ghosts (facsimile of manuscript), edited with an introduction and a postscript by Bernth Lindfors, Three Continents Press, 1982.
Pauper, Brawler, and Slanderer, Faber, 1987.

WORK REPRESENTED IN ANTHOLOGIES

Rutherford, Peggy, editor, *Darkness and Light: An Anthology of African Writing*, Drum Publications, 1958.
Hughes, Langston, editor, *An African Treasury: Articles, Essays, Stories, Poems by Black Africans*, Crown, 1960.
Hughes, Langston, and Christiane Reynault, editors, *Anthologie africaine et malgache*, Seghers, 1962.
Ademola, Frances, editor, *Reflections*, African Universities Press, 1962, new edition, 1965.
Sainville, Leonard, editor, *Anthologie de la litterature negro-africaine: Romanciers et conteurs negro africains*, two volumes, Presence Africaine, 1963.
Whiteley, W. H., compiler, *A Selection of African Prose*, two volumes, Oxford University Press, 1964.
Rive, Richard, editor, *Modern African Prose*, Heinemann Educational, 1964.
Komey, Ellis Ayitey and Ezekiel Mphahlele, editors, *Modern African Stories*, Faber, 1964.
Tibble, Anne, editor, *African-English Literature: A Survey and Anthology*, Peter Owen, 1965.
Edwards, Paul, compiler, *Through African Eyes*, two volumes, Cambridge University Press, 1966.
Mphahlele, Ezekiel, editor, *African Writing Today*, Penguin, 1967.
Beier, Ulli, editor, *Political Spider: An Anthology of Stories from "Black Orpheus,"* Heinemann Educational, 1969.
Larson, Charles, editor, *African Short Stories: A Collection of Contemporary African Writing*, Macmillan, 1970.

SIDELIGHTS: With the publication of his novel *The Palm-Wine Drinkard and His Dead Palm-Wine Tapster in the Dead's Town* in 1952, Amos Tutuola became the first internationally recognized Nigerian writer. Since that time, Tutuola's works, in particular *The Palm-Wine Drinkard*, have been the subject of much critical debate. *The Palm-Wine Drinkard* was praised by critics outside of Nigeria for its unconventional use of the English language, its adherence to the oral tradition, and its unique, fantastical characters and plot. Nigerian critics, on the other hand, described the work as ungrammatical and unoriginal. Discussing the first criticism in his book *The Growth of the African Novel*, Eustace Palmer writes: "Tutuola's English is demonstrably poor; this is due partly to his ignorance of the more complicated rules of English syntax and partly to interference from Yoruba." The second criticism, concerning Tutuola's lack of originality, is based on similarities between Tutuola's works and those of his predecessor, O. B. Fagunwa, who writes in the Yoruba language.

The influence of Fagunwa's writings on Tutuola's work has been noted by several critics, including Abiola Irele, who writes in *The African Experience in Literature and Ideology:* "It is clear that much of the praise and acclaim that have been lavished upon Tutuola belong more properly to Fagunwa who provided not only the original inspiration but indeed a good measure of material for Tutuola's novels. The echoes of Fagunwa in Tutuola's works are numerous enough to indicate that the latter was consciously creating from a model provided by the former.'' Irele adds, however, ''that despite its derivation from the work of Fagunwa, Tutuola's work achieves an independent status that it owes essentially to the force of his individual genius.''

Tutuola's genius is described by reviewers as an ability to refashion the traditional Yoruba myths and folktales that are the foundation of his work. Eustace Palmer notes, for instance, in *The Growth of the African Novel:* ''Taking his stories direct from his people's traditional lore, he uses his inexhaustible imagination and inventive power to embellish them, to add to them or alter them, and generally transform them into his own stories conveying his own message.'' O. R. Dathorne comments in an essay published in *Introduction to Nigerian Literature:* ''Tutuola is a literary paradox; he is completely part of the folklore traditions of the Yorubas and yet he is able to modernize these traditions in an imaginative way. It is on this level that his books can best be approached.... Tutuola deserves to be considered seriously because his work represents an intentional attempt to fuse folklore with modern life.''

In *The Palm-Wine Drinkard,* for example, the Drinkard's quest for his tapster leads him into many perilous situations, including an encounter with the Red Fish, a monster Tutuola describes as having thirty horns ''spread out as an umbrella,'' and numerous eyes that ''were closing and opening at the same time as if a man was pressing a switch on and off.'' Tutuola also amends a traditional tale concerning a Skull who borrows appendages belonging to other persons in order to look like a ''complete gentleman'' to include referencesto modern warfare. Tutuola writes: ''If this gentleman went to the battle field, surely, enemy would not kill him or capture him and if bombers saw him in a town which was to be bombed, they would not throw bombs on his presence, and if they did throw it, the bomb itself would not explode until this gentleman would leave that town, because of his beauty.'' Gerald Moore observes in *Seven African Writers* that these descriptions are evidence ''of Tutuola's easy use of the paraphernalia of modern life to give sharpness and immediacy to his imagery.''

The Palm-Wine Drinkard was hailed by critics such as V. S. Pritchett and Dylan Thomas, the latter of whom describes the work in the *Observer* as a ''brief, thronged, grisly and bewitching story.'' Thomas concludes: ''The writing is nearly always terse and direct, strong, wry, flat and savoury.... Nothing is too prodigious or too trivial put down in this tall, devilish story.'' The work also has been favorably compared to such classics as *The Odyssey, Pilgrim's Progress,* and *Gulliver's Travels.* Some critics, however, expressed reservations about Tutuola's ability to repeat his success. According to Charles R. Larson's *The Emergence of African Fiction,* critic Anthony West stated, ''*The Palm-Wine Drinkard* must be valued for its own freakish sake, and as an unrepeatable happy hit.''

Despite the reservations of critics like West, Tutuola went on to publish seven additional works, and while critics are, as Larson observes in *The Emergence of African Fiction,* ''a little less awed now than they were in the early 1950's,'' Tutuola's works continue to merit critical attention. Among the more widely reviewed of these books is *The Witch-Herbalist of the Remote Town.* Published thirty years after *The Palm-Wine*

Drinkard, this book involves a quest initiated by the protagonist, a hunter, to find a cure for his wife's barrenness. The journey to the Remote Town takes six years; along the way the hunter encounters bizarre and sometimes frightening places and people, including the Town of the Born-and-Die Baby and the Abnormal Squatting Man of the Jungle, who can paralyze opponents with a gust of frigid air by piercing his abdomen. The hunter eventually reaches the Remote Town, and the witch-herbalist gives him a broth guaranteed to make his wife fertile. The plot is complicated though, when the hunter, weak from hunger, sips some of the broth.

As with *The Palm-Wine Drinkard,* critical commentary of *The Witch-Herbalist of the Remote Town* focuses in particular on Tutuola's use of the English language. Edward Blishen, for instance, comments in the *Times Educational Supplement:* ''The language is wonderfully stirring and odd: a mixture of straight translation from Yoruba, and everyday modern Nigerian idiom, and grand epical English. The imagination at work is always astonishing.... And this, not the bargain, is folklore not resurrected, but being created fresh and true in the white heat of a tradition still undestroyed.'' *Voice Literary Supplement* critic Jon Parales writes: ''His direct, apparently simple language creates an anything-can-happen universe, more whacky and amoral than the most determinedly modern lit.'' *Washington Post Book World* contributor Judith Chettle offers this view: ''Tutuola writes with an appealing vigor and his idiosyncratic use of the English idiom gives the story a fresh and African perspective, though at times the clumsiness of some phrasing does detract from the thrust of the narrative. No eye-dabbing sentimentalist, Tutuola's commentary is clear-eyed if not acerbic, but underlying the tale is a quiet and persistent lament for the simpler, unsophisticated and happier past of his people.''

An *Africa Today* contributor, Nancy J. Schmidt, observes that Tutuola's language has become increasingly more like that of standard English over the years. She cites other differences between this work and earlier ones as well. ''Tutuola's presence is very evident in *Witch-Herbalist,* but the strength of his presence and his imagination are not as strong as they once were,'' writes Schmidt, who adds that ''neither Tutuola nor his hero seem to be able to take a consistent moral stand, a characteristic that is distinctly different from Tutuola's other narratives.'' Commenting on the reasons for these differences, Schmidt writes: ''They may reflect contemporary Yoruba culture, Tutuola's changing attitude toward Yoruba and Nigerian cultures as well as his changing position in Yoruba and Nigerian cultures, the difficulties of writing an oral narrative for an audience to whom oral narratives are becoming less familiar and less related to daily behavior, and the editorial policies for publishing African fictional narratives in the 1980s.''

In the *New York Times Book Review* Charles Larson likewise notes Tutuola's use of standard English, but maintains that ''the outstanding quality of Mr. Tutuola's work—the brilliance of the oral tradition—still remains.'' Larson concludes: ''*The Witch-Herbalist of the Remote Town'* is Mr. Tutuola at his imaginative best. Every incident in the narrative breathes with the life of the oral tradition; every episode in the journey startles with a kind of indigenous surrealism. Amos Tutuola is still his continent's most fantastic storyteller.''

MEDIA ADAPTATIONS: Kola Ogunmola has written a play

in Yoruba entitled *Omuti*, based on *The Palm-Wine Drinkard*, published by West African Book Publishers.

BIOGRAPHICAL/CRITICAL SOURCES:

BOOKS

Collins, Harold R., *Amos Tutuola*, Twayne, 1969.

Contemporary Literary Criticism, Gale, Volume 5, 1976, Volume 14, 1980, Volume 29, 1984.

Herskovits, Melville J. and Francis S. Herskovits, *Dahomean Narrative: A Cross-Cultural Analysis*, Northwestern University Press, 1958.

Irele, Abiola, *The African Experience in Literature and Ideology*, Heinemann, 1981.

King, Bruce, editor, *Introduction to Nigerian Literature*, Evans Brothers, 1971.

Larson, Charles R., *The Emergence of African Fiction*, revised edition, Indiana University Press, 1972.

Laurence, Margaret, *Long Drums and Cannons: Nigerian Dramatists*, Praeger, 1969.

Lindfors, Bernth, editor, *Critical Perspectives on Amos Tutuola*, Three Continents Press, 1975.

Lindfors, Bernth, *Early Nigerian Literature*, Africana Publishing, 1982.

Moore, Gerald, *Seven African Writers*, Oxford University Press, 1962.

Palmer, Eustace, *The Growth of the African Novel*, Heinemann, 1979.

Tucker, Martin, *Africa in Modern Literature: A Survey of Contemporary Writing in English*, Ungar, 1967.

Tutuola, Amos, *The Palm-Wine Drinkard and His Dead Palm-Wine Tapster in the Dead's Town*, Faber, 1952, Grove, 1953.

PERIODICALS

Africa Today, Volume 29, number 3, 1982.

Ariel, April, 1977.

Books Abroad, summer, 1968.

Critique, fall/winter, 1960-61, fall/winter, 1967-68.

Journal of Canandian Fiction, Volume 3, number 4, 1975.

Journal of Commonwealth Literature, August, 1974, August, 1981, Volume 17, number 1, 1982.

Listener, December 14, 1967.

London Review of Books, April 2, 1987.

Los Angeles Times Book Review, August 15, 1982.

Nation, September 25, 1954.

New Statesman, December 8, 1967.

New Yorker, April 23, 1984.

New York Times Book Review, July 4, 1982.

Observer, July 6, 1952, November 22, 1981.

Okikie, September, 1978.

Presence Africaine, 3rd trimestre, 1967.

Spectator, October 24, 1981.

Times Educational Supplement, February 26, 1982.

Times Literary Supplement, January 18, 1968, February 26, 1982, August 28, 1987.

Voice Literary Supplement, June, 1982.

Washington Post, July 13, 1987.

Washington Post Book World, August 15, 1982.

—Sketch by Melissa Gaiownik

V

Van DYKE, Henry   1928-

PERSONAL: Born October 3, 1928, in Allegan, Mich.; son of Henry Lewis (a professor) and Bessie (Chandler) Van Dyke. *Education:* University of Michigan, A.B., 1953, M.A., 1955.

ADDRESSES: Home—40 Waterside Plaza, New York, N.Y. 10010. *Agent*—Maia Gregory Associates, 311 East 72nd St., New York, N.Y.10021.

CAREER: University of Michigan, Ann Arbor, associate editor, University Engineering Research Institute, 1956-58; Crowell Collier & Macmillan, Inc., New York, N.Y., correspondent for book clubs, 1959-67; full-time writer, 1967—. Writer-in-residence, Kent State University, fall terms, 1969—. *Military service:* U.S. Army, 1948-50.

AWARDS, HONORS: Jule and Avery Hopwood Award for fiction, 1954; Guggenheim fellowship, 1971; American Academy of Arts and Letters award, 1974.

WRITINGS:

NOVELS

Ladies of the Rachmaninoff Eyes, Farrar, Straus, 1965.
Blood of Strawberries, Farrar, Straus, 1969.
Dead Piano, Farrar, Straus, 1971.
Lunacy and Caprice, Ballantine, 1987.

OTHER

Contributor to *The O. Henry Prize Stories, 1979.* Also contributor to *Transatlantic Review, Generation,* and *Antioch Review.*

WORK IN PROGRESS: Another novel.

SIDELIGHTS: Henry Van Dyke's novels are frequently described by critics as offbeat, comical, and sometimes macabre. Upon the publication of his novel *Dead Piano* in 1971, Van Dyke was hailed by Alfred Kazin in the *Saturday Review* as "one of the most brilliant and unpredictable of the younger black novelists." *Dead Piano* describes how black revolutionaries invade the home of the Blakes, an upper-middle-class black family, and attempt to extort money from them, "ostensibly for a revolutionary cause, actually as a criminal shakedown," as a *Library Journal* contributor observes.

Dead Piano, writes Newgate Callendar in the *New York Times Book Review,* suggests that "well-to-do blacks . . . have as little to communciate to black revolutionists as middle-class whites. Even less." Kazin, however, believes that "[Van Dyke's] mind is too independent, ironic, and even humorous for messages." The *Library Journal* contributor concludes that *Dead Piano* "[stresses] psychological change, with a chilling opening, a philosophical conclusion—and [Van Dyke's] usual stylistic dash."

BIOGRAPHICAL/CRITICAL SOURCES:

BOOKS

Dictionary of Literary Biography, Volume 33: *Afro-American Fiction Writers after 1955,* Gale, 1984.

PERIODICALS

Black World, June, 1972.
Library Journal, August, 1971.
New York Times, January 4, 1969.
New York Times Book Review, May 23, 1965, January 5, 1969, October 31, 1971.
Pembroke, spring, 1973.
Publishers Weekly, June 28, 1971.
Saturday Review, June 12, 1965, January 4, 1969, October 2, 1971.
Times Literary Supplement, November 4, 1965.

* * *

Van PEEBLES, Melvin   1932-

PERSONAL: Born August 21, 1932, in Chicago, Ill.; children: Mario, Meggan, Melvin. *Education:* Graduated from Ohio Wesleyan University.

CAREER: Writer, actor, producer of plays, director, and composer. Worked as operator of cable cars in San Francisco, Calif., and as a floor trader for the American Stock Exchange. Director of motion pictures, including "Watermelon Man," 1970. *Military service:* U.S. Air Force; served as navigator-bombardier.

MEMBER: Directors Guild of America, French Directors Guild.

AWARDS, HONORS: First Prize from Belgian Festival for "Don't Play Us Cheap."

WRITINGS:

Un ours pour le F.B.I. (novel), Buchet-Chastel, 1964, translation published as *A Bear for the F.B.I.*, Trident, 1968.

Un Americain en enfer (novel), Editions Denoel, 1965, translation published as *The True American: A Folk Fable*, Doubleday, 1976.

Le Chinois du XIV (short stories), Le Gadenet, 1966.

La Fete a Harlem [and] *La Permission* (two novels; former adapted from the play by Van Peebles, ''Harlem Party''; also see below), J. Martineau, 1967, translation of *La Fete a Harlem* published as *Don't Play Us Cheap: A Harlem Party*, Bantam, 1973.

Sweet Sweetback's Baadasssss Song (adapted from the screenplay by Van Peebles; also see below), Lancer Books, 1971.

The Making of Sweet Sweetback's Baadasssss Song (nonfiction), Lancer Books, 1972.

Aint Supposed to Die a Natural Death (play; directed by the author and produced in New York City at the Ethel Barrymore Theatre, 1971; adapted from the recordings by Van Peebles, ''Brer Soul'' and ''Ain't Supposed to Die a Natural Death''), Bantam, 1973.

Just an Old Sweet Song, Ballantine, 1976.

(With Kenneth Vose, Leon Capetanos, and Lawrence Du Kose) *Greased Lightning* (screenplay; produced by Warner Bros., 1977), Yeah, 1976.

Bold Money: A New Way to Play the Options Market, Warner Books, 1986.

Bold Money: How to Get Rich in the Options Market, Warner Books, 1987.

OTHER

''Harlem Party'' (play), produced in Belgium, 1964, produced as ''Don't Play Us Cheap,'' directed by the author and produced in New York City at the Ethel Barrymore Theatre, 1972.

(And director) ''The Story of a Three Day Pass'' (screenplay), Sigma III, 1968.

(And director) ''Sweet Sweetback's Baadasssss Song'' (screenplay), Cinemation Industries, 1971.

''Sophisticated Gents'' (television screenplay; adapted from *The Junior Bachelor Society* by John A. Williams), produced as a four hour miniseries and broadcast on NBC-TV, September, 1981.

''Waltz of the Stork'' (play), directed by author and produced in New York City at the Century Theatre, 1982.

''Champeeen!'' (play), directed by author and produced in New York City at the New Federal Theatre, 1983.

Also author and director of ''Don't Play Us Cheap'' (adapted from the play by Van Peebles). Also creator of short films, including ''Sunlight,'' Cinema 16, and ''Three Pick Up Men for Herrick,'' Cinema 16.

Composer for recordings, including ''Brer Soul,'' ''Aint Supposed to Die a Natural Death,'' ''Watermelon Man'' (soundtrack for the motion picture), ''Serious as a Heart Attack,'' ''Sweet Sweetback's Baadasssss Song'' (soundtrack for the motion picture), and ''Don't Play Us Cheap'' (soundtrack for the motion picture).

SIDELIGHTS: Melvin Van Peebles began his career as an artist by creating short films. He had hoped that his first film efforts would lead to a filmmaking opportunity in Hollywood but moguls there were unimpressed. Instead of obtaining a position as a director or even assistant director, he was offered a job as an elevator operator. Seemingly at a dead end, Van Peebles suddenly received word from Henri Langlois, an associate of the French Cinematheque film depository who'd been impressed with Van Peebles's films. Langlois invited Van Peebles to come to Paris. There, Van Peebles enjoyed brief celebrity as an avant-garde filmmaker. But he had no opportunities to pursue filmmaking.

Van Peebles worked for some time as an entertainer in cafes until he discovered a means by which he could once again take up filmmaking. In France, one could gain entry into the Directors Guild if he wished to adapt his own French writings. So Van Peebles, in self-taught French, began writing novels. His first work, *A Bear for the F.B.I.*, concerned events in the life of an American middle-class black. Critical response was favorable, with Martin Levin remarking in the *New York Times Book Review* that ''Van Peebles crystallizes the racial problem with rare subtlety.'' However, Van Peebles noted that the subtlety of the novel hindered his chances of being published in the United States. ''I wrote the first work and my 'calling card,' to establish my reputation so I could get my 'black' novels published,'' Van Peebles claimed. ''But the publishers aren't interested unless you either lacerate whites or apologize to them.''

American publishers displayed a similar lack of interest toward Van Peebles's next novel, *The True American*, which was written in 1965 but not published in the United States until 1976. It is the story of George Abraham Carver, a black prisoner who is accidentally killed by falling rocks. Carver arrives in Hell and learns that blacks are treated well there. This is because the majority of Hell's residents are white and, supposedly, the preferential attention the blacks receive causes the white residents more grief. Despite the ''promising'' premise, the novel was reviewed unfavorably in *New Yorker*. ''Unfortunately,'' wrote the critic, ''the book never really lives up to its promise, largely because of its pasteboard characters, its meandering plot, and its author's tendency to use a two-ton sledgehammer to drive home every point he makes about racist America.''

Van Peebles continued to write, though, and produced in rapid succession a collection of short stories, *Le Chinois du XIV*, and two short novels, *La Fete a Harlem* and *La Permission*. At the same time, he was also arranging another film project. With the financial assistance of the French Ministry of Cultural Affairs and a private citizen, Van Peebles made ''The Story of a Three Day Pass,'' a film about a black soldier's encounter with a French woman. ''The Story of a Three Day Pass'' attracted substantial audiences in France and, upon its release in the United States, Van Peebles was in demand in Hollywood.

In 1969, after returning to the United States, Van Peebles agreed to direct a film written by Herman Raucher entitled ''Watermelon Man.'' This film deals with a white insurance agent who awakens one morning to discover that he's turned into a black man. ''It's authentic stuff,'' related Van Peebles, ''that laughs *with*, not at people.'' Later, he insisted, ''I thought I had to make 'Watermelon Man' in order to do the films I really wanted to do.

Van Peebles's next film, ''Sweet Sweetback's Baadasssss Song,'' is probably his best known work to date. He made the film in three weeks, using nonunion crews while keeping union officials disinterested by spreading rumors that he was making a pornographic film, something unworthy of their attention. Hollywood had refused to finance the film after a reading of the screenplay failed to impress studio officials. Fortunately,

Van Peebles received a sizeable loan from Bill Cosby which enabled him to complete the film. There was also difficulty promoting the film. Distributors declined to present it, theatres refused to book it, and talk shows refused to host Van Peebles. Eventually, he resorted to promoting it himself by passing out leaflets on street corners. Such determination ultimately paid off for Van Peebles. As a writer for *Time* noted, Van Peebles's "fast talk, plus audience word of mouth, made it a limited success. But that was enough." After the initial success of the film, it was mass-released to more than one hundred theatres and enjoyed brief status as the top money-makng film in *Variety*.

The film elicited a variety of critical responses. The story of a black sex-show performer who avenges a youth's beating at the hands of two policemen by murdering them and eventually escapes to Mexico enraged some reviewers. Robert Hatch accused him in *Nation* of relying "on rather irreponsible contemporary emotionalism to revitalize stock films he must have seen in his childhood." In the *New York Times* Vincent Canby claimed, "instead of dramatizing injustice, Van Peebles merchandizes it." He also declared that "the militancy of 'Sweet Sweetback' is of a dull order, seemingly designed only to reinforce the prejudices of black audiences without in any way disturbing those prejudices." Clayton Riley conceded in the *New York Times*, "The film is an outrage," but then observed that it was "designed to blow minds." He wrote, "Through the lens of the Van Peebles camera comes a very basic Black America, unadorned by faith, and seething with an eternal violence." In the same review, Riley contended, "It is a terrifying vision, the Blood's nightmare journey through Watts, and it is a vision Black people alone will really understand in all of its profane and abrasive substance." In his study of black filmmakers published in the 1979 book, *American Film Now: The People, the Power, the Money, the Movies*, James Monaco takes a new look at Van Peebles's 1971 screenplay. "['Sweet Sweetback's Baadasssss Song'] situates itself squarely in a long and important tradition in Black American narrative art," Monaco writes. "The Sweetback character has been mimicked and repeated a number of times since, but never with such purity of purpose and such *elan*. Van Peebles bent the medium of film to his will. No one else has bent it so far or so well since."

Van Peebles told a *Time* reporter that the film was not just for black audiences. "If films are good," he expressed, "the universality of the human experience will transcend the race and creed and crap frontiers." But he also noted that the film does have some specific messages for blacks. "Of all the ways we've been exploited by the Man, the most damaging is the way he destroyed our self-image," he asserted. "The message of 'Sweetback' is that if you can get it together and stand up to the Man, you can win." In a *New York Times* interview, Van Peebles asked a writer, "When's the last time you saw a film in which the black man won in the end?" He then declared, "In my film, the black audience finally gets a chance to see some of their own fantasies acted out—about rising out of the mud and kicking ass."

After the success of "Sweet Sweetback," Van Peebles was inundated with filmmaking offers from Hollywood studios. However, he insisted that he maintain his independence. "I'll only work with them on my terms," he stated. "I've whipped the man's ass on his own turf. I'm number one at the box office—which is the way America measures things—and I did it on my own. Now they want me, but I'm in no hurry."

Much of Van Peebles's most recent work has been as a playwright. "Aint Supposed to Die a Natural Death," his first play to be produced in the United States, proved to be a popular one with Broadway audiences. In *Cue* Marilyn Stasio called it a "tremendously vital musical with a dynamic new form all its own." She also wrote, "The show is an electrifying piece of theatre without having songs, a book, a story line, choreography, or even standard production numbers— and yet all these elements are on the stage, skillfully integrated into a jolting new experience." And Peter Bailey commented in *Black World* that "Aint Supposed to Die a Natural Death" "presented us with an effective and meaningful evening in the theater. Broadway has never seen anything like it. Van Peebles' characters come alive and make us deal with them on their own terms."

A writer for *Variety* was impressed with the U.S. production of another Van Peebles play, "Don't Play Us Cheap." The reviewer noted that "this new show does not seem to be infused with hate, and it offers what appears to [be] a racial attitude without foul language, deliberate squalor or snarling ugliness." The same critic observed that "points are made with humor rather than rage and are probably more palatable for general audiences." "'Don't Play Us Cheap' is a somewhat special show," concluded the writer for *Variety*, "probably with greater meaning and appeal for black audiences than for whites." Van Peebles later adapted the play for film.

In 1986, Van Peebles published *Bold Money: A New Way to Play the Options Market* adding another twist to his variety of writing talents. As a result of losing an interesting wager with a friend, Van Peebles was obliged to take the examination to become an options trader. After failing the exam, Van Peebles became a clerk on the floor of the American Stock Exchange in order to learn enough to pass the exam. As Van Peebles told Laurie Cohen and Fred Marc Biddle in the *Chicago Tribune*, "If I had to find one characteristic that is most symbolic of me, I think I am tenacious."

After trading options for three years and passing the examination, Van Peebles was asked by Warner Books to write a how-to-book on making money in the options market. A critic for *Kirkus Reviews* writes of *Bold Money: A New Way to Play the Options Market* that Van Peebles's "often impudent but prudent text is an excellent choice for rookies seeking a like-it-is introduction to a fast game." A year after his first money book was published he wrote *Bold Money: How to Get Rich in the Option Market*.

BIOGRAPHICAL/CRITICAL SOURCES:

BOOKS

Contemporary Literary Criticism, Gale, Volume 2, 1974, Volume 20, 1982.
Monaco, James, *American Films Now: The People, the Power, the Money, the Movies*, Oxford University Press, 1979.

PERIODICALS

Best Sellers, October 15, 1968.
Black World, April, 1972.
Chicago Tribune, March 24, 1986.
Cue, October 30, 1971, May 27, 1972.
Kirkus Reviews, December 1, 1985.
Nation, May 24, 1971.
Newsweek, June 6, 1969, June 21, 1971.
New Yorker, March 1, 1976.

New York Times, May 18, 1969, April 24, 1971, May 9, 1971, September 29, 1981, January 6, 1982.
New York Times Book Review, October 6, 1968.
Saturday Review, August 3, 1968.
Time, August 16, 1971.
Variety, May 24, 1971.

*   *   *

VESEY, Paul
See ALLEN, Samuel W(ashington)

*   *   *

VROMAN, Mary Elizabeth (Gibson)   1923-1967

PERSONAL: Born in 1923 in Buffalo, N.Y.; died from complications following surgery, April 29, 1967, in New York, N.Y.; married Oliver M. Harper (a dentist). *Education:* Received B.A. from Alabama State Teachers College (now Alabama State University).

ADDRESSES: Home—892 Eastern Parkway, Brooklyn, N.Y.

CAREER: Teacher at Camden Academy, Camden, Ala., and other public schools in Alabama, Chicago, and New York for twenty years. Music and art coordinator for New York board of education "Higher Horizons" program.

MEMBER: Screen Writers Guild, Delta Sigma Theta.

AWARDS, HONORS: Christopher Award for inspirational magazine writing, 1952, for "See How They Run."

WRITINGS:

(And technical advisor) "Bright Road" (screenplay; based on Vroman's short story "See How They Run"), Metro-Goldwyn-Mayer, 1953.
Esther: A Novel, Bantam, 1963.
Shaped to Its Purpose: Delta Sigma Theta, The First Fifty Years, Random House, 1965.
Harlem Summer (young adult novel), illustrations by John Martinez, Putnam, 1967.

Work represented in anthology *Best Short Stories by Negro Writers.* Contributor of nonfiction, short stories, and poetry to *National Education Association Journal, Freedomways,* and *Ladies' Home Journal.*

SIDELIGHTS: During her tragically abridged literary career (she died of post-surgical complications while in her early forties), Mary Elizabeth Vroman portrayed the hard realities of black life without becoming strident. A writer whose race consciousness expressed itself in humanistic terms, Vroman explored how black people, confronted with adversity, managed to "retain their sense of humanity," described Edith Blicksilver in the *Dictionary of Literary Biography,* "and . . . find joy in their lives." Best known for the acclaimed short story "See How They Run" about her teaching experiences in the segregated, rural South, Vroman questioned the effectiveness of "angry stories by angry writers." "I just thought about how much I loved [the children] and tried to put it down on paper," she stated.

Like Vroman, the protagonist of "See How They Run" is an idealistic teacher from the North who is unprepared for the inadequacies of the segregated school system. In charge of forty-three poor black students, Jane Richards shows how caring and perseverance can gradually weaken poverty's powerful grasp. Like the blind mice of the nursery rhyme from which the story's title is taken, the students are urged to flee the privations of their environment through education. First published in the *Ladies' Home Journal,* "See How They Run" won a Christopher Award for its "humanitarian quality." It was later made into the motion picture "Bright Road," and Vroman became the fist black female member of the Screen Writers Guild with her screen adaptation.

Esther, Vroman's first novel, illustrates how breaking free of one's environment is particularly hard for the southern black woman. Lydia Jones, a black midwife bent on providing granddaughter Esther with a nursing education, acknowledges: "a colored woman . . . got to fight for it all the way"; her assertion is borne out by Esther's long, toilsome struggle to join that profession. Yet the younger woman eventually does reach her goal, achieving substantial career success. "The story ends on a note of optimistic brotherhood as both black and white medical personnel cooperate together to aid the victims of ptomaine [poisoning]," Blicksilver related.

In Vroman's young-adult novel, *Harlem Summer,* sixteen-year-old John Brown leaves his Montgomery, Alabama, home to spend the summer living and working in New York's Harlem. Encountering a variety of unfamiliar experiences, the youth discovers "that being a Negro is not as simple as it seemed in the safety of a loving home environment," wrote Dorothy M. Broderick in the *New York Times Book Review;* through new acquaintances John sees how anger, complacency, withdrawal, and pride are used to cope with poverty and degradation. "The novel provides a good range of attitudes and associations within an urban Negro community," one *Saturday Review* critic decided. While noting the novel's sparse plot and melodramatic climax, Broderick agreed, calling *Harlem Summer* "an exciting, provocative story [that] . . . explores the complexities of Negro ghetto life." The reviewer added: "It is in this honest portrayal, without descending to cynicism, that the book lays the groundwork for the reader to move on to 'Go Tell It on the Mountain,' something no other young people's novel has done."

BIOGRAPHICAL/CRITICAL SOURCES:

BOOKS

Dictionary of Literary Biography, Volume 33: *Afro-American Fiction Writers After 1955,* Gale, 1984.
The Ethnic American Woman: Problems, Protests, Lifestyle, Kendall/Hunt, 1978.

PERIODICALS

Ebony, July, 1952.
Negro American Literature Forum, spring, 1973.
New York Times Book Review, May 7, 1967, May 4, 1969.
Saturday Review, May 13, 1967.

OBITUARIES:

PERIODICALS

New York Times, April 30, 1967.
Publishers Weekly, June 19, 1967.

W

WALCOTT, Derek (Alton) 1930-

PERSONAL: Born January 23, 1930, in Castries, St. Lucia, West Indies; son of Warwick (a civil servant) and Alix (a teacher) Walcott; married Fay Moston, 1954 (divorced, 1959); married Margaret Ruth Maillard, 1962 (divorced); married Norline Metivier (actress and dancer); children: one son (first marriage), two daughters (second marriage). *Education:* St. Mary's College, St. Lucia, B.A., 1953; attended University of the West Indies, Kingston, Jamaica.

ADDRESSES: Home—165 Duke of Edinburgh Ave., Diego Martin, Trinidad and Tobago, (summers); 71 St. Mary's, Brookline, Mass. 02146 (winters). *Office*—Creative Writing Department, Boston University, 236 Bay State Rd., Boston, Mass. 02215. *Agent*—Bridget Aschenberg, International Famous Agency, 1301 Avenue of the Americas, New York, N.Y. 10019.

CAREER: Poet and playwright. Teacher at St. Mary's College, St. Lucia, at Boys' Secondary School, Grenada, and at Kingston College, Jamaica. Founding director of Trinidad Theatre Workshop, 1959—. Visiting professor at Columbia University, 1981, and Harvard University, 1982; visiting professor in Creative Writing Department of Boston University, 1985—. Also lecturer at Rutgers and Yale Universities.

AWARDS, HONORS: Rockefeller fellowship, 1957; Jamaica Drama Festival prize, 1958, for "Drums and Colours"; Guinness Award, 1961; Heinemann Award, Royal Society of Literature, 1966, for *The Castaway,* and, 1983, for *The Fortunate Traveller;* Cholmondeley Award, 1969, for *The Gulf;* Eugene O'Neill Foundation-Wesleyan University fellowship, 1969; Order of the Humming Bird, Trinidad and Tobago, 1969; Obie Award, 1971, for "Dream On Monkey Mountain"; honorary doctorate of letters, University of the West Indies, 1972; Jock Campbell/*New Statesman* Prize, 1974, for *Another Life;* John D. and Catherine T. MacArthur Foundation grant, 1981; *Los Angeles Times Book Review* Prize in poetry, 1986, for *Collected Poems, 1948-1984;* National Writer's Council Prize, Welsh Arts Council.

WRITINGS:

POETRY

Twenty-Five Poems, Guardian Commercial Printery, 1948.

Epitaph for the Young: A Poem in XII Cantos, Advocate (Bridgetown, Barbados), 1949.
Poems, Kingston City Printery (Jamaica), 1953.
In a Green Night: Poems, 1948-1960 (also see below), J. Cape, 1962.
Selected Poems (includes poems from *In a Green Night: Poems, 1948-1960),* Farrar, Straus, 1964.
The Castaway and Other Poems (also see below), J. Cape, 1965.
The Gulf and Other Poems, J. Cape, 1969, published with selections from *The Castaway and Other Poems* as *The Gulf: Poems,* Farrar, Straus, 1970.
Another Life (long poem), Farrar, Straus, 1973, 2nd edition published with introduction, chronology and selected bibliography by Robert D. Hammer, Three Continents Press, 1982.
Sea Grapes, J. Cape, 1976, slightly revised edition, Farrar, Straus, 1976.
Selected Verse, Heinemann, 1976.
The Star-Apple Kingdom, Farrar, Straus, 1979.
The Fortunate Traveller, Farrar, Straus, 1981.
Selected Poetry, selected, annotated and introduced by Wayne Brown, Heinemann, 1981.
The Caribbean Poetry of Derek Walcott, and the Art of Romare Beardon, Limited Editions Club (New York), 1983.
Midsummer, Farrar, Straus, 1984.
Collected Poems, 1948-1984, Farrar, Straus, 1986.
The Arkansas Testament, Farrar, Straus, 1987.

PLAYS

Henri Christophe: A Chronicle in Seven Scenes (first produced in Castries, St. Lucia, West Indies, 1950, produced in London, England, 1951), Advocate (Bridgetown, Barbados), 1950.
Harry Dernier: A Play for Radio Production, Advocate, 1951.
Wine of the Country, University College of the West Indies (Mona, Jamaica), 1953.
The Sea at Dauphin: A Play in One Act (first produced in Mona, Jamaica, 1953, produced in London, 1960; also see below), Extra-Mural Department, University College of the West Indies, 1954.
Ione: A Play with Music (first produced in Port of Spain, Trinidad, 1957), Extra-Mural Department, University College of the West Indies, 1957.

"Drums and Colours: An Epic Drama" (published in *Caribbean Quarterly,* March-June, 1961), first produced in Kingston, Trinidad, April 23, 1958.

"In a Fine Castle," first produced in Jamaica, 1970, produced in Los Angeles, Calif., 1972.

"Ti-Jean and His Brothers" (also see below), first produced in Port of Spain, Trinidad, 1958, produced Off-Broadway at Delacorte Theatre, July 20, 1972.

Malcochon; or, Six in the Rain (one-act; first produced as "Malcochon" in Castries, St. Lucia, 1959, produced in London under title "Six in the Rain," 1960, produced Off-Broadway at St. Mark's Playhouse, March 25, 1969; also see below), Extra-Mural Department, University of West Indies, 1966.

"Dream on Monkey Mountain" (also see below), first produced in Toronto, Ontario, Canada, 1967, produced Off-Broadway at St. Mark's Playhouse, March 9, 1971.

Dream on Monkey Mountain and Other Plays (contains "Dream on Monkey Mountain," "Sea at Dauphin," "Malcochon; or, Six in the Rain," "Ti-Jean and His Brothers," and the essay "What the Twilight Says: An Overture"; also see below), Farrar, Straus, 1970.

"The Joker of Seville" (musical; also see below), first produced in Port of Spain, Trinidad, 1974.

"The Charlatan," first produced in Los Angeles, 1974.

"O Babylon!" (also see below), first produced in Port of Spain, Trinidad, 1976.

"Remembrance" (three-act; also see below), first produced in St. Croix, Virgin Islands, December, 1977, produced Off-Broadway at The Other Stage, May 9, 1979.

"Pantomime" (also see below), first produced in Port of Spain, Trinidad, 1978, produced at the Hudson Guild Theater, 1986.

The Joker of Seville & O Babylon!: Two Plays, Farrar, Straus, 1978.

Remembrance & Pantomime: Two Plays, Farrar, Straus, 1980.

"The Isle Is Full of Noises," first produced at the John W. Huntington Theater, in Hartford, Conn., April, 1982.

Three Plays (contains "The Last Carnival," "Beef, No Chicken," and "A Branch of the Blue Nile"), Farrar, Straus, 1986.

Also author of "Franklin, a Tale of the Islands," "Jourmard," and "To Die for Grenada."

CONTRIBUTOR

John Figueroa, editor, *Caribbean Voices,* Evans, 1966.

Barbara Howes, editor, *From the Green Antilles,* Macmillan, 1966.

Howard Sergeant, editor, *Commonwealth Poems of Today,* Murray, 1967.

O. R. Dathorne, editor, *Caribbean Verse,* Heinemann, 1968.

Anne Walmsley, compiler, *The Sun's Eye: West Indian Writing for Young Readers,* Longmans, 1968.

Orde Coombs, editor, *Is Massa Day Dead?,* Doubleday, 1974.

D. J. Enright, editor, *Oxford Book of Contemporary Verse, 1945-80,* Oxford University Press, 1980.

Errol Hill, editor, *Plays for Today,* Longman, 1985.

Also contributor to *Caribbean Literature,* edited by George Robert Coulthard; *New Voices of the Commonwealth,* edited by Sergeant; and, *Young Commonwealth Poetry,* edited by Peter Ludwig Brent.

OTHER

Art and literature critic for *Trinidad Guardian;* feature writer for *Public Opinion* (Jamaica). Contributor of poems to numerous periodicals, including *New Statesman, London Magazine, Encounter, Evergreen Review, Caribbean Quarterly, Tamarack Review,* and *Bim.*

SIDELIGHTS: Although born of mixed racial and ethnic heritage on St. Lucia, a West Indian island where a French/English patois is spoken, poet and playwright Derek Walcott was educated as a British subject. Taught to speak English as a second language, he grew to be a skilled craftsman in his adopted tongue. His use of the language has drawn praise from critics including British poet and novelist Robert Graves who, according to *Times Literary Supplement* contributor Vicki Feaver, "has gone as far to state that [Walcott] handles English with a closer understanding of its inner magic than most (if not all) of his English-born contemporaries."

Walcott's major theme is the dichotomy between black and white, subject and ruler, Caribbean and Western civilization present in his culture and ancestry. In "What the Twilight Says," the introduction to *Dream on Monkey Mountain and Other Plays,* Walcott refers to his "schizophrenic boyhood" in which he led "two lives: the interior life of poetry [and] the outward life of action and dialect." In *Derek Walcott* Robert D. Hamner notes that this schizophrenia is common among West Indians and comments further that "since [Walcott] is descended from a white grandfather and a black grandmother on both paternal and maternal sides, he is a living example of the divided loyalties and hatreds that keep his society suspended between two worlds."

"As a West Indian . . . writing in English, with Africa and England in his blood," Alan Shapiro writes in the *Chicago Tribune Book World,* "Walcott is inescapably the victim and beneficiary of the colonial society in which he was reared. He is a kind of a Caribbean Orestes . . . unable to satisfy his allegiance to one side of his nature without at the same time betraying the other." Caryl Phillips describes Walcott's work in much the same way in her *Los Angeles Times Book Review* essay. The critic notes that Walcott's poetry is "steeped in an ambivalence toward the outside world and its relationship to his own native land of St. Lucia."

One often-quoted poem, "A Far Cry from Africa," from *In a Green Night,* deals directly with Walcott's sense of cultural confusion. "Where shall I turn, divided to the vein? / I who have cursed / the drunken officer of British rule, how choose / Between this Africa and the English tongue I love? / Betray them both, or give back what they give?"

In another poem, "The Schooner *Flight,*" from his second collection, *The Star-Apple Kingdom,* the poet uses a Trinidadian sailor named Shabine to appraise his own place as a person of mixed blood in a world divided into whites and blacks. According to the mariner: "The first chain my hands and apologise, 'History'; / the next said I wasn't black enough for their pride." Not white enough for whites, not black enough for blacks, Shabine sums up the complexity of his situation near the beginning of the poem saying: "I had a sound colonial education, / I have Dutch, nigger and English in me, / and either I'm nobody or I'm a nation."

It is Walcott, of course, who is speaking, and *New York Review of Books* contributor Thomas R. Edwards notes how the poet suffers the same fate as his poetic alter-ego, Shabine. Edwards writes, "Walcott is a cultivated cosmopolitan poet who is black, and as such he risks irrelevant praise as well as blame, whites finding it clever of him to be able to sound so much like other sophisticated poets, blacks feeling that he's sold his soul by practicing white arts.''

Although pained by the contrasts in his background, Walcott has chosen to embrace both his island and colonial heritage. His love of both sides of his psyche is apparent in an analysis of his work. As Hamner notes: ''Nurtured on oral tales of gods, devils, and cunning tricksters passed down by generations of slaves, Walcott should retell folk stories; and he does. On the other hand, since he has an affinity for and is educated in Western classics, he should retell the traditional themes of European experience; and he does. As inheritor of two vitally rich cultures, he utilizes one, then the other, and finally creates out of the two his own personalized style.''

Walcott seems closest to his island roots in his plays. For the most part, he has reserved his native language—patois or creole—to them. They also feature Caribbean settings and themes. According to *Literary Review* contributor David Mason, through Walcott's plays he hopes to create a ''catalytic theater responsible for social change or at least social identity.''

Although a volume of poems was his first published work, Walcott originally concentrated his efforts on the theater. In the fifties, he wrote a series of plays in verse, including *Henri Christophe: A Chronicle, The Sea at Dauphin,* and *Ione.* The first play deals with an episode in Caribbean history: ex-slave Henri Christophe's rise to kingship of Haiti in the early 1800s. The second marks Walcott's first use of the mixed French/English language of his native island in a play.

In *Dictionary of Literary Biography Yearbook: 1981* Dennis Jones notes that while Walcott uses the folk idiom of the islands in the play, the speech of the characters is not strictly imitative. It is instead ''made eloquent, as the common folk represented in the work are made noble, by the magic of the artist.''

In ''What the Twilight Says'' Walcott describes his use of language in his plays. In particular, he expresses the desire to mold ''a language that went beyond mimicry, . . . one which finally settled on its own mode of inflection, and which begins to create an oral culture, of chants, jokes, folk-songs, and fables.''

The presence of ''chants, jokes, and fables'' in Walcott's plays causes critics such as Jones and the *Los Angeles Times*'s Juana Duty Kennedy to call the playwright's best pieces for theater folk dramas. In *Books and Bookmen* Romilly Cavan observes the numerous folk elements in Walcott's plays: ''The laments of superstitious fishermen, charcoal-burners and prisoners are quickly counter-pointed by talking crickets, frogs, and birds. Demons are raised, dreams take actual shape, [and] supernatural voices mingle with the natural lilting elliptical speech rhythms of downtrodden natives.'' Animals who speak and a folk-representation of the devil are characters, for example, in the play, ''Ti-Jean and His Brothers.''

Walcott's most highly praised play, *Dream on Monkey Mountain,* is also a folk drama. It was awarded a 1971 Obie Award and deemed ''a poem in dramatic form'' by Edith Oliver in the *New Yorker.* The play's title is itself enough to immediately transport the viewer into the superstitious legend-filled world of the Caribbean backcountry.

In the play, Walcott draws a parallel between the hallucinations of an old charcoal vendor and the colonial reality of the Caribbean. Islanders subjected to the imposition of a colonial culture over their own eventually question the validity of both cultures. Ultimately, they may determine that their island culture—because it has no official status other than as an enticement for tourists—is nothing but a sterile hallucination. Or, as Jones notes, they may reach the conclusion at which Walcott wishes his audience to arrive: the charcoal vendor's ''dreams connect to the past, and that it is in that past kept alive in the dreams of the folk that an element of freedom is maintained in the colonized world.''

Perhaps because of critics' unfamiliarity with the Caribbean reality which Walcott describes in his plays, the author's work for theater has received only mixed reviews in this country. For example, while Walter Goodman writes in the *New York Times* that Walcott's ''Pantomime'' ''stays with you as a fresh and funny work filled with thoughtful insights and illuminated by bright performances,'' the *New York Times*'s Frank Rich's comments on the same play are not as favorable. ''Walcott's best writing has always been as a poet . . . ,'' Rich observes, ''and that judgment remains unaltered by 'Pantomime.' For some reason, [he] refuses to bring the same esthetic rigor to his playwriting that he does to his powerfully dense verse.''

In James Atlas's *New York Times Magazine* biographical/critical essay on Walcott, the critic confronts Rich's remarks head on, asserting that the poet would respond to Rich by commenting ''that he doesn't conceive of his plays as finished works but as provisional effects to address his own people. 'The great challenge to me,' he says, 'was to write as powerfully as I could without writing down to the audience, so that the large emotions could be taken in by a fisherman or a guy on the street, even if he didn't understand every line.'''

If Walcott's plays reveal what is most Caribbean about him, his poetry reveals what is most English. If he hopes to reach the common man in his plays, the same cannot be said of his poetry. His poems are based on the traditional forms of English poetry, filled with classical allusions, elaborate metaphors, complex rhyme schemes, and other poetic devices.

In the *New York Times Book Review,* Selden Rodman calls Walcott's poems ''almost Elizabethan in their richness.'' The *New York Times*'s Michiko Kakutani agrees, noting that ''from England, [Walcott] appropriated an old-fashioned love of eloquence, an Elizabethan richness of words and a penchant for complicated, formal rhymes. In fact, in a day when more and more poets have adopted a grudging, minimalist style, [his] verse remains dense and elaborate, filled with dazzling complexities of style.''

Some critics object that Walcott's attention to style sometimes detracts from his poetry, either by being unsuitable for his Caribbean themes or by becoming more important than the poems' content. Denis Donoghue, for example, remarks in the *New York Times Book Review,* ''It is my impression that his standard English style [is] dangerously high for nearly every purpose except that of Jacobean tragedy.'' In Steve Ratiner's *Christian Science Monitor* review of *Midsummer,* the critic observes that ''after a time, we are so awash in sparkling language and intricate metaphor, the subject of the poem is all but obscured.'' In her *New York Review of Books* essay, Helen Vendler finds an ''unhappy disjunction between [Walcott's] explosive subject . . . and his harmonious pentameters, his lyrical allusions, his stately rhymes, [and] his Yeatsian meditations.''

More criticism comes from those who maintain that the influence of other poets on Walcott's work have drowned out his authentic voice. While Vendler, for instance, describes Walcott as a "man of great sensibility and talent," she dismisses much of his poetry as "ventriloquism" and maintains that in Walcott's 1982 collection of poems, *The Fortunate Traveller,* he seems "at the mercy of influence, this time the influence of Robert Lowell."

Poet J. D. McClatchy also notices Lowell's influence in *The Fortunate Traveller* as well as two other Walcott poetry collections: *The Star-Apple Kingdom* and *Midsummer.* In his *New Republic* review McClatchy not only finds similarities in the two men's styles but also a similar pattern of development in their poetry. "Like Lowell," the critic notes, "Walcott's mode has . . . shifted from the mythological to the historical, from fictions to facts, and his voice has gotten more clipped and severe. There are times when the influence is almost too direct, as in 'Old New England,' [a poem from *The Fortunate Traveller,*] where he paces off Lowell's own territory."

Both major criticisms of Walcott's poetry are answered in Sven Birkerts's *New Republic* essay. Birkerts observes: "Walcott writes a strongly accented, densely packed line that seldom slackens and yet never loses conversational intimacy. He works in form, but he is not formal. His agitated phonetic surfaces can at times recall Lowell's, but the two are quite different. In Lowell, one feels the torque of mind; in Walcott, the senses predominate. And Walcott's lines ring with a spontaneity that Lowell's often lack."

Other critics defend the integrity of Walcott's poems. Poet James Dickey notes in the *New York Times Book Review,* "Fortunately, for him and for us, . . . Walcott has the energy and the exuberant strength to break through his literary influences into a highly colored, pulsating realm of his own." In his *Poetry* review of *Midsummer* Paul Breslin writes: "For the most part, . . . Walcott's voice remains as distinctive as ever, and the occasional echoes of Lowell register as homage rather than unwitting imitation."

Hamner maintains that when dealing with Walcott's poetry the term assimilation rather than imitation should be used. The critic observes: "Walcott passed through his youthful apprenticeship phase wherein he consciously traced the models of established masters. He was humble enough to learn from example and honest enough to disclose his intention to appropriate whatever stores he found useful in the canon of world literature. . . . But Walcott does not stop with imitation. Assimilation means to ingest into the mind and thoroughly comprehend; it also means to merge into or become one with a cultural tradition."

The uniqueness of Walcott's work stems from his ability to interweave British and island influences, to express what McClatchy calls "his mixed state" and do so "without indulging in either ethnic chic or imperial drag." His plays offer pictures of the common Caribbean folk and comment on the ills bred by colonialism. His poetry combines native patois and English rhetorical devices in a constant struggle to force an allegiance between the two halves of his split heritage.

According to *Los Angeles Times Book Review* contributor Arthur Vogelsang, "These continuing polarities shoot an electricity to each other which is questioning and beautiful and which helps form a vision all together Caribbean and international, personal (him to you, you to him), independent, and essential for readers of contemporary literature on all the continents."

BIOGRAPHICAL/CRITICAL SOURCES:

BOOKS

Contemporary Literary Criticism, Gale, Volume 2, 1974, Volume 4, 1975, Volume 9, 1978, Volume 42, 1987.
Dictionary of Literary Biography Yearbook: 1981, Gale, 1982.
Goldstraw, Irma, *Derek Walcott: An Annotated Bibliography of His Works,* Garland Publishing, 1984.
Hamner, Robert D., *Derek Walcott,* Twayne, 1981.
Walcott, Derek, *Collected Poems, 1948-1984,* Farrar, Straus, 1986.
Walcott, Derek, *Dream on Monkey Mountain and Other Plays,* Farrar, Straus, 1970.

PERIODICALS

Books and Bookmen, April, 1972.
Book World, December 13, 1970.
Chicago Tribune Book World, May 2, 1982, September 9, 1984, March 9, 1986.
Christian Science Monitor, March 19, 1982, April 6, 1984.
Georgia Review, summer, 1984.
Hudson Review, summer, 1984.
Literary Review, spring, 1986.
London Magazine, December, 1973-January, 1974, February-March, 1977.
Los Angeles Times, November 12, 1986.
Los Angeles Times Book Review, April 4, 1982, May 21, 1985, April 6, 1986, October 26, 1986, September 6, 1987.
Nation, February 12, 1977, May 19, 1979, February 27, 1982.
National Review, November 3, 1970, June 20, 1986.
New Republic, November 20, 1976, March 17, 1982, January 23, 1984, March 24, 1986.
New Statesman, March 19, 1982.
New Yorker, March 27, 1971, June 26, 1971.
New York Magazine, August 14, 1972.
New York Review of Books, December 31, 1964, May 6, 1971, June 13, 1974, October 14, 1976, May 31, 1979, March 4, 1982.
New York Times, March 21, 1979, August 21, 1979, May 30, 1981, May 2, 1982, January 15, 1986, December 17, 1986.
New York Times Book Review, September 13, 1964, October 11, 1970, May 6, 1973, October 31, 1976, May 13, 1979, January 3, 1982, April 8, 1984, February 2, 1986, December 20, 1987.
New York Times Magazine, May 23, 1982.
Poetry, February, 1972, December, 1973, July, 1977, December, 1984, June, 1986.
Review, winter, 1974.
Spectator, May 10, 1980.
Time, March 15, 1982.
Times Literary Supplement, December 25, 1969, August 3, 1973, July 23, 1976, August 8, 1980, September 8, 1980, September 24, 1982, November 9, 1984, October 24, 1986.
Tribune Books (Chicago), November 8, 1987.
TriQuarterly, winter, 1986.
Village Voice, April 11, 1974.
Virginia Quarterly Review, winter, 1974, summer, 1984.
Washington Post Book World, February 21, 1982, April 13, 1986.
Western Humanities Review, spring, 1977.
World Literature Today, spring, 1977, summer, 1979, sum-

mer, 1981, winter, 1985, summer, 1986, winter, 1987. *Yale Review,* October, 1973.

—*Sketch by Marian Gonsior*

*   *   *

WALKER, Alice (Malsenior)   1944-

PERSONAL: Born February 9, 1944, in Eatonton, Ga.; daughter of Willie Lee and Minnie Tallulah (Grant) Walker; married Melvyn Rosenman Leventhal (a civil rights lawyer), March 17, 1967 (divorced, 1976); children: Rebecca Grant. *Education:* Attended Spelman College, 1961-63; Sarah Lawrence College, B.A., 1965.

ADDRESSES: Home—San Francisco, Calif. *Office*—Wild Trees Press, P.O. Box 378, Navarro, Calif. 95463. *Agent*—Wendy Weil, Julian Bach Literary Agency, 747 Third Ave., New York, N.Y. 10017.

CAREER: Writer. Wild Trees Press, Navarro, Calif., co-founder and publisher, 1984—. Has been a voter registration worker in Georgia, a worker in Head Start program in Mississippi, and on staff of New York City welfare department. Writer-in-residence and teacher of black studies at Jackson State College, 1968-69, and Tougaloo College, 1970-71; lecturer in literature, Wellesley College and University of Massachusetts—Boston, both 1972-73; distinguished writer in Afro-American studies department, University of California, Berkeley, spring, 1982; Fannie Hurst Professor of Literature, Brandeis University, Waltham, Mass., fall, 1982. Lecturer and reader of own poetry at universities and conferences. Member of board of trustees of Sarah Lawrence College. Consultant on black history to Friends of the Children of Mississippi, 1967.

AWARDS, HONORS: Bread Loaf Writer's Conference, scholar, 1966; first prize, *American Scholar* essay contest, 1967; Merrill writing fellowship, 1967; McDowell Colony fellowship, 1967, 1977-78; National Endowment for the Arts grant, 1969, 1977; Radcliffe Institute fellowship, 1971-73; Ph.D., Russell Sage College, 1972; National Book Award nomination, 1973, for *Revolutionary Petunias and Other Poems;* Lillian Smith Award, Southern Regional Council, 1973, for *Revolutionary Petunias;* Richard and Hinda Rosenthal Foundation Award, American Academy and Institute of Arts and Letters, 1974, for *In Love and Trouble;* Guggenheim Award, 1977-78; National Book Critics Circle Award nomination, 1982, Pulitzer Prize, 1983, and American Book Award, 1983, all for *The Color Purple;* D.H.L., University of Massachusetts, 1983; O. Henry Award, 1986, for "Kindred Spirits."

WRITINGS:

POETRY

Once: Poems (also see below), Harcourt, 1968, reprinted, Women's Press, 1988.
Five Poems, Broadside Press, 1972.
Revolutionary Petunias and Other Poems (also see below), Harcourt, 1973.
Goodnight, Willie Lee, I'll See You in the Morning (also see below), Dial, 1979.
Horses Make a Landscape Look More Beautiful, Harcourt, 1984.
Alice Walker Boxed Set—Poetry: Good Night, Willie Lee, I'll See You in the Morning; Revolutionary Petunias and Other Poems; Once, Poems, Harcourt, 1985.

FICTION

The Third Life of Grange Copeland (novel; also see below), Harcourt, 1970.
In Love and Trouble: Stories of Black Women (also see below), Harcourt, 1973.
Meridian (novel), Harcourt, 1976.
You Can't Keep a Good Woman Down (short stories; also see below), Harcourt, 1981.
The Color Purple (novel), Harcourt, 1982.
Alice Walker Boxed Set—Fiction: The Third Life of Grange Copeland, You Can't Keep a Good Woman Down, and In Love and Trouble, Harcourt, 1985.
To Hell with Dying (juvenile), illustrations by Catherine Deeter, Harcourt, 1988.

CONTRIBUTOR TO ANTHOLOGIES

Helen Haynes, editor, *Voices of the Revolution,* E. & J. Kaplan (Philadelphia), 1967.
Langston Hughes, editor, *The Best Short Stories by Negro Writers from 1899 to the Present: An Anthology,* Little, Brown, 1967.
Robert Hayden, David J. Burrows, and Frederick R. Lapides, compilers, *Afro-American Literature: An Introduction,* Harcourt, 1971.
Toni Cade Bambara, compiler, *Tales and Stories for Black Folks,* Zenith Books, 1971.
Woodie King, compiler, *Black Short Story Anthology,* New American Library, 1972.
Arnold Adoff, compiler, *The Poetry of Black America: An Anthology of the Twentieth Century,* Harper, 1973.
Lindsay Patterson, editor, *A Rock against the Wind: Black Love Poems,* Dodd, 1973.
Sonia Sanchez, editor, *We Be Word Sorcerers: Twenty-five Stories by Black Americans,* Bantam, 1973.
Mary Anne Ferguson, compiler, *Images of Women in Literature,* Houghton, 1973.
Margaret Foley, editor, *Best American Short Stories: 1973,* Hart-Davis, 1973.
Foley, editor, *Best American Short Stories, 1974,* Houghton, 1974.
Michael S. Harper and Robert B. Stepto, editors, *Chants of Saints: A Gathering of Afro-American Literature, Art and Scholarship,* University of Illinois Press, 1980.
Mary Helen Washington, editor, *Midnight Birds: Stories of Contemporary Black Women Authors,* Anchor Press, 1980.
Dexter Fisher, editor, *The Third Woman: Minority Women Writers of the United States,* 1980.

OTHER

Langston Hughes: American Poet (children's biography), Crowell, 1973.
(Editor) *I Love Myself When I'm Laughing . . . and Then Again When I Am Looking Mean and Impressive: A Zora Neale Hurston Reader,* introduction by Mary Helen Washington, Feminist Press, 1979.
In Search of Our Mothers' Gardens: Womanist Prose, Harcourt, 1983.
Living by the Word: Selected Writings, 1973-1987, Harcourt, 1988.

Contributor to periodicals, including *Negro Digest, Denver Quarterly, Harper's, Black World,* and *Essence.* Contributing editor, *Southern Voices, Freedomways,* and *Ms.*

WORK IN PROGRESS: Finding the Green Stone, "a fable," with Catherine Deeter; another novel.

SIDELIGHTS: "*The Color Purple,* Alice Walker's third [novel,] could be the kind of popular and literary event that transforms an intense reputation into a national one," according to Gloria Steinem of *Ms.* Judging from the critical enthusiasm for *The Color Purple,* Steinem's words have proved prophetic. "Walker . . . has succeeded," as Andrea Ford notes in the *Detroit Free Press,* "in creating a jewel of a novel." Peter S. Prescott presents a similar opinion in a *Newsweek* review. "I want to say," he comments, "that *The Color Purple* is an American novel of permanent importance, that rare sort of book which (in Norman Mailer's felicitous phrase) amounts to 'a diversion in the fields of dread.'"

Although Walker's other books—novels, volumes of short stories, and poems—have not been completely ignored, they have not received the amount of attention that many critics feel they deserve. For example, William Peden, writing about *In Love and Trouble: Stories of Black Women* in *The American Short Story: Continuity and Change, 1940-75,* calls the collection of stories "a remarkable book that deserves to be much better known and more widely read." And while Steinem points out that *Meridian,* Walker's second novel, "is often cited as the best novel of the civil rights movement, and is taught as part of some American history as well as literature courses," Steinem maintains that Walker's "visibility as a major American talent has been obscured by a familiar bias that assumes white male writers, and the literature they create, to be the norm. That puts black women (and all women of color) at a double remove."

Jeanne Fox-Alston and Mel Watkins both feel that the appeal of *The Color Purple* is that the novel, as a synthesis of characters and themes found in Walker's earlier works, brings together the best of the author's literary production in one volume. Fox-Alston, in the *Chicago Tribune Book World,* remarks: "Celie, the main character in Walker's third . . . novel, *The Color Purple,* is an amalgam of all those women [characters in Walker's previous books]; she embodies both their desperation and, later, their faith." Watkins states in the *New York Times Book Review:* "Her previous books . . . have elicited praise for Miss Walker as a lavishly gifted writer. *The Color Purple,* while easily satisfying that claim, brings into sharper focus many of the diverse themes that threaded their way through her past work."

Walker's central characters are almost always black women; the themes of sexism and racism are predominant in her work, but her impact is felt across both racial and sexual boundaries. Walker, according to Steinem, "comes at universality through the path of an American black woman's experience. . . . She speaks the female experience more powerfully for being able to pursue it across boundaries of race and class." This universality is also noted by Fox-Alston, who remarks that Walker has a "reputation as a provocative writer who writes about blacks in particular, but all humanity in general."

However, many critics see a definite black and female focus in Walker's writings. For example, in her review of *The Color Purple,* Ford suggests that the novel transcends "culture and gender" lines but also refers to Walker's "unabashedly feminist viewpoint" and the novel's "black . . . texture." Walker does not deny this dual bias; the task of revealing the condition of the black woman is particularly important to her. Thadious M. Davis, in his *Dictionary of Literary Biography* essay, comments: "Walker writes best of the social and personal drama in the lives of familiar people who struggle for survival of self in hostile environments. She has expressed a special concern

with 'exploring the oppressions, the insanities, the loyalties and the triumph of black women.'" Walker explains in a *Publishers Weekly* interview: "The black woman is one of America's greatest heroes. . . . Not enough credit has been given to the black woman who has been oppressed beyond recognition."

Critics reviewing Walker's first collection of short stories, *In Love and Trouble: Stories of Black Women,* respond favorably to the author's rendering of the black experience. In *Ms.* Barbara Smith observes: "This collection would be an extraordinary literary work, if its only virtue were the fact that the author sets out consciously to explore with honesty the textures and terror of black women's lives. Attempts to penetrate the myths surrounding black women's experiences are so pitifully rare in black, feminist, or American writing that each shred of truth about these experiences constitutes a breakthrough. The fact that Walker's perceptions, style, and artistry are also consistently high makes her work a treasure." Mary Helen Washington remarks in a *Black World* review: "The stories in *In Love and Trouble* . . . constitute a painfully honest, searching examination of the experiences of thirteen Black women. . . . The broad range of these characters is indication of the depth and complexity with which Alice Walker treats a much-abused subject: the Black woman."

Walker bases her description of black women on what Washington refers to as her "unique vision and philosophy of the Black woman." According to Barbara A. Bannon of *Publishers Weekly,* this philosophy stems from the "theme of the poor black man's oppression of his family and the unconscious reasons for it." Walker, in her interview with the same magazine, asserts: "The cruelty of the black man to his wife and family is one of the greatest [American] tragedies. It has mutilated the spirit and body of the black family and of most black mothers." Through her fiction, Walker describes this tragedy. For instance, Smith notes: "Even as a black woman, I found the cumulative impact of these stories [contained *In Love and Trouble*] devastating. . . . Women love their men, but are neither loved nor understood in return. The affective relationships are [only] between mother and child or between black woman and black woman." David Guy's commentary on *The Color Purple* in the *Washington Post Book World* includes this evaluation: "Accepting themselves for what they are, the women [in the novel] are able to extricate themselves from oppression; they leave their men, find useful work to support themselves." Watkins further explains: "In *The Color Purple* the role of male domination in the frustration of black women's struggle for independence is clearly the focus."

Some reviewers criticize Walker's fiction for portraying an overly negative view of black men. Katha Pollitt, for example, in the *New York Times Book Review,* calls the stories in *You Can't Keep a Good Woman Down* "too partisan." The critic adds: "The black woman is *always* the most sympathetic character." Guy notes: "Some readers . . . will object to her overall perspective. Men in [*The Color Purple*] are generally pathetic, weak and stupid, when they are not heartlessly cruel, and the white race is universally bumbling and inept." Charles Larson, in his *Detroit News* review of *The Color Purple,* points out: "I wouldn't go as far as to say that all the male characters [in the novel] are villains, but the truth is fairly close to that." However, neither Guy nor Larson feel that this emphasis on women is a major fault in the novel. Guy, for example, while conceding that "white men . . . are invisible in Celie's world," observes: "This really is Celie's perspective, however—it is psychologically accurate to her—and Alice Walker might argue that it is only a neat inversion of the view that has prevailed in western culture for centuries.'' Larson also notes that by the end of the novel, ''several of [Walker's] masculine characters have reformed.''

This idea of reformation, this sense of hope even in despair, is at the core of Walker's vision, even though, as John F. Callahan states in *New Republic,* ''There is often nothing but pain, violence, and death for black women [in her fiction].'' In spite of the brutal effects of sexism and racism suffered by the characters of her short stories and novels, critics note what Art Seidenbaum of the *Los Angeles Times* calls Walker's sense of ''affirmation . . . [that] overcomes her anger.'' This is particularly evident in *The Color Purple,* according to reviewers. Ford, for example, asserts that the author's ''polemics on . . . political and economic issues finally give way to what can only be described as a joyful celebration of human spirit— exulting, uplifting and eminently universal.'' Prescott discovers a similar progression in the novel. He writes: ''[Walker's] story begins at about the point that most Greek tragedies reserve for the climax, then . . . by immeasurable small steps . . . works its way toward acceptance, serenity and joy.'' Walker, according to Ray Anello, who quotes the author in *Newsweek,* agrees with this evaluation. Questioned about the novel's importance, Walker explains: ''Let's hope people can hear Celie's voice. There are so many people like Celie who make it, who come out of nothing. People who triumph.''

Davis refers to this idea as Walker's ''vision of survival'' and offers a summary of its significance in Walker's work. ''At whatever cost, human beings have the capacity to live in spiritual health and beauty; they may be poor, black, and uneducated, but their inner selves can blossom.'' Steinem adds: ''What . . . matters is the knowledge that everybody, no matter how poor or passive on the outside, has . . . possibilities inside.''

MEDIA ADAPTATIONS: The Color Purple was made into a feature film by Warner Brothers in 1985; the film was directed by Steven Spielberg, and received several Academy Award nominations.

BIOGRAPHICAL/CRITICAL SOURCES:

BOOKS

Contemporary Literary Criticism, Gale, Volume 5, 1976, Volume 6, 1976, Volume 9, 1978, Volume 19, 1981, Volume 27, 1984, Volume 46, 1988.
Dictionary of Literary Biography, Gale, Volume 6: *American Novelists since World War II,* 2nd series, 1980, Volume 33: *Afro-American Fiction Writers after 1955,* 1984.
Evans, Mari, editor, *Black Women Writers (1950-1980): A Critical Evaluation,* Anchor, 1984.
O'Brien, John, *Interviews with Black Writers,* Liveright, 1973.
Peden, William, *The American Short Story: Continuity and Change, 1940-1975,* 2nd edition, revised and enlarged, Houghton, 1975.
Prenshaw, Peggy W., editor, *Women Writers of the Contemporary South,* University Press of Mississippi, 1984.

PERIODICALS

American Scholar, winter, 1970-71, summer, 1973.
Ann Arbor News, October 3, 1982.
Atlantic, June, 1976.
Black Scholar, April, 1976.
Black World, September, 1973, October, 1974.
Chicago Tribune, December 20, 1985.
Chicago Tribune Book World, August 1, 1982, September 15, 1985.
Commonweal, April 29, 1977.

Detroit Free Press, August 8, 1982, July 10, 1988.
Detroit News, September 15, 1982, October 23, 1983, March 31, 1985.
Freedomways, winter, 1973.
Globe and Mail (Toronto), December 21, 1985.
Jet, February 10, 1986.
Los Angeles Times, April 29, 1981, June 8, 1983.
Los Angeles Times Book Review, August 8, 1982.
Ms., February, 1974, July, 1977, July, 1978, June, 1982, September, 1986.
Nation, November 12, 1973, December 17, 1983.
Negro Digest, September-October, 1968.
New Leader, January 25, 1971.
New Republic, September 14, 1974, December 21, 1974.
Newsweek, June 21, 1982.
New Yorker, February 27, 1971, June 7, 1976.
New York Review of Books, January 29, 1987.
New York Times, December 18, 1985, January 5, 1986.
New York Times Book Review, March 17, 1974, May 23, 1976, May 29, 1977, December 30, 1979, May 24, 1981, July 25, 1982, April 7, 1985, June 5, 1988.
New York Times Magazine, January 8, 1984.
Oakland Tribune, November 11, 1984.
Parnassus: Poetry in Review, spring-summer, 1976.
Poetry, February, 1971, March, 1980.
Publishers Weekly, August 31, 1970, February 26, 1988.
Saturday Review, August 22, 1970.
Southern Review, spring, 1973.
Times Literary Supplement, August 19, 1977, June 18, 1982, July 20, 1984, September 27, 1985, April 15, 1988.
Washington Post, October 15, 1982, April 15, 1983, October 17, 1983.
Washington Post Book World, November 18, 1973, October 30, 1979, December 30, 1979, May 31, 1981, July 25, 1982, December 30, 1984.
World Literature Today, winter, 1985, winter, 1986.
Yale Review, autumn, 1976.

*   *   *

WALKER, Joseph A. 1935-

PERSONAL: Born February 23, 1935, in Washington, D.C.; son of Joseph (a house painter) and Florine Walker; married Barbara Brown (divorced, 1965); married Dorothy A. Dinroe, 1970. *Education:* Howard University, B.A., 1956; Catholic University of America, M.F.A., 1970; New York University, Ph.D.

ADDRESSES: Home—New York, N.Y. *Office*—Department of Speech and Theatre, City College of the City University of New York, New York, N.Y. 10031.

CAREER: Educator, actor, director, playwright, choreographer, producer. Worked as taxi driver, shoe and cosmetics salesman, and postal clerk; English teacher at junior high and high schools in Washington, D.C., and New York City; actor, set designer, and playwright in New York City, beginning 1967; Negro Ensemble Co., New York City, playwright, director and choreographer, beginning 1969; Yale University, New Haven, Conn., playwright-in-residence, 1970-71; City College of the City University of New York, New York City, currently instructor; Howard University, Washington, D.C., currently instructor of advanced acting and playwrighting. Actor in stage productions, including ''The Believers,'' 1967, ''Cities of Beziques,'' 1969, ''Once in a Lifetime,'' ''A Raisin in the Sun,'' and ''Purlie Victorious,'' in motion pictures, including "April Fools," 1969, and "Bananas," 1971, and in television program "N.Y.P.D." (ABC-TV); narrator of "In Black America" (CBS-TV). Co-founder and artistic director of The Demi-Gods (dance-music theatre repertory company). *Military service:* U.S. Air Force; became second lieutenant.

AWARDS, HONORS: Guggenheim fellowship, 1973; Obie Award, 1971, Antoinette Perry (Tony) Award, 1973, Elizabeth Hull-Kate Award from Dramatist Guild, First Annual Audelco Award, John Gassner Award from Outer Circle, Drama Desk Award, Black Rose, all for "The River Niger"; Rockefeller Foundation grant, 1979.

WRITINGS:

PLAYS

(With Josephine Jackson) *The Believers* (first produced Off-Broadway at the Garrick Theatre, May 9, 1968), published in *The Best Plays of 1967-1968,* edited by Otis L. Guernsey, Dodd, 1968.
"The Harangues" (two one-act plays), first produced Off-Broadway at St. Mark's Playhouse, December 30, 1969.
Ododo (title means "The Truth"; first produced Off-Broadway at St. Mark's Playhouse, November 24, 1970), published in *Black Drama Anthology,* edited by Woodie King and Ron Milner, Columbia University Press, 1972.
"Yin Yang," first produced Off-Off-Broadway at the Afro-American Studio, June 30, 1972, produced Off-Broadway at St. Mark's Playhouse, May 30, 1973.
The River Niger (three-act; first produced Off-Broadway at St. Mark's Playhouse, December 5, 1972; also see below), Hill & Wang, 1973.
"Antigone Africanus," first produced in New York, 1975.
"The Lion Is a Soul Brother," first produced in New York, 1976.
"District Line," first produced Off-Broadway at Theatre Four, December, 1984.

Also author of "Themes of the Black Struggle" and "The Hiss."

OTHER

"The River Niger" (screenplay; based on play of the same title), Cine Artists, 1976.

Contributor to periodicals, including the *New York Times.*

SIDELIGHTS: When Joseph A. Walker's first solo effort, "The Harangues," was produced by the Negro Ensemble Company in 1970, Walter Kerr wrote in the *New York Times:* "The company has come upon a playwright whose theatrical instincts are strong even when he is letting them gallop along a little bit ahead of him; that is better than playing it shy, or tentative, or safe."

Certainly, Walker does not play it safe. Alan Bunce of the *Christian Science Monitor* describes "The Harangues" as "an unabashed polemic whose impact on the stage is ultimately stirring." The play consists of two main segments sandwiched between a tribal prologue and interlude. In the first main act, a black man, engaged to a pregnant white woman, intends to murder his fiancee's millionaire father; the other of the two long segments concerns another pregnant white woman, her "liberal" brother, and her black fiance, all of whom are confronted by a gun-wielding black intruder who talks them into confessing their true racial attitudes. Likening the entire performance to the films of Luis Bunuel, Martin Washburn writes in the *Village Voice:* "Walker's play is strong because he has

the courage to speak directly from his tradition instead of disguising it."

After seeing "Ododo," *New York Times* contributor Clive Barnes was prompted to observe that the Negro Ensemble Company seemed to have become more "separatist, militant and black" than it had previously been. The play is a musical, tracing the background and history of the North American black from the African jungle through slave ships, American slavery, Lincoln, and reconstruction to the ghetto and contemporary black consciousness. While John Simon of *New York* magazine dismisses "Ododo" as "a black supremist, racist show," Barnes concedes that, though propaganda, it is "beautifully-written propaganda" nevertheless.

With *The River Niger* Walker achieved his first true critical success. Grace Cooper in the *Dictionary of Literary Biography* claims the play "shows [Walker's] full growth as a playwright." She continues, "While it expresses many of the same strong feelings of the earlier plays, *The River Niger* is more subtle, therefore allowing him to make his points acceptable to a larger audience. The play has been widely recognized as a realistic depiction of black life." Mel Gussow says in *Time* that Walker "has a distinct voice and his own sensitive awareness of what makes people different. The play is rich with character, atmosphere, and nuance." In the *New York Times,* Kerr describes the dialogue as "exemplary, knife sharp when adrenalin is meant to flow and gently rhetorical whenever the father of a Harlem family remembers that he meant to be a poet." Dedicated "to my mother and father and to highly underrated Black daddies everywhere," the play is semi-autobiographical and centers on the father's struggle and sacrifice for his family amidst the violent world they live in. Reviewing the play in the *Washington Post,* Anthony Astrachan says, "It is unquestionably black theater: Its characters could only be black. But it is also universal theater: It speaks to audiences of all colors." Barnes also believes *The River Niger* can speak to a multi-racial audience. "This strong family drama eludes simple labels such as black," he affirms in the *New York Times.* "Broadway audiences, whether they be black, white, or sky-blue pink, will assuredly react to the strength of its melodrama and the pulse of its language. . . . It is a testimony to man's unending fight for survival."

MEDIA ADAPTATIONS:

The River Niger was made into a film starring Cicely Tyson and James Earl Jones.

BIOGRAPHICAL/CRITICAL SOURCES:

BOOKS

Contemporary Literary Criticism, Volume 19, Gale, 1981.
Dictionary of Literary Biography, Volume 38: *Afro-American Writers after 1955: Dramatists and Prose Writers,* Gale, 1985.

PERIODICALS

Black World, April, 1971.
Christian Science Monitor, January 23, 1970.
Cue, December 5, 1970.
Modern Drama, December, 1976.
Nation, February 2, 1970, December 25, 1972.
New Republic, September 29, 1973.
New York, December 14, 1970.
New Yorker, January 24, 1970, December 16, 1972.
New York Times, May 10, 1968, January 14, 1970, January 25, 1970, November 25, 1970, December 6, 1970, De-

cember 14, 1970, December 6, 1972, December 17, 1972, March 28, 1973, May 31, 1973, December 5, 1984.
Saturday Review, February 14, 1970.
Show Business, November 28, 1970.
Time, January 1, 1973.
Variety, December 9, 1970.
Village Voice, January 22, 1970.
Washington Post, April 13, 1973.

*   *   *

WALKER, Margaret Abigail   1915-

PERSONAL: Born July 7, 1915, in Birmingham, Ala.; daughter of Sigismund C. (a Methodist minister) and Marion (Dozier) Walker (a music teacher); married Firnist James Alexander, June 13, 1943 (deceased); children: Marion Elizabeth, Firnist James, Sigismund Walker, Margaret Elvira. *Education:* Northwestern University, A.B., 1935; University of Iowa, M.A., 1940, Ph.D., 1965. *Religion:* Methodist.

ADDRESSES: Home—2205 Guynes St., Jackson, Miss. 39213. *Office*—Department of English, Jackson State College, Jackson, Miss. 39217.

CAREER: Worked as a social worker, newspaper reporter, and magazine editor; Livingstone College, Salisbury, N.C., member of faculty, 1941-42; West Virginia State College, Institute, W.Va., instructor in English, 1942-43; Livingstone College, professor of English, 1945-46; Jackson State College, Jackson, Miss., professor of English, 1949—, director of Institute for the Study of the History, Life, and Culture of Black Peoples, 1968—. Lecturer, National Concert and Artists Corp. Lecture Bureau, 1943-48. Visiting professor in creative writing, Northwestern University, spring, 1969. Staff member, Cape Cod Writers Conference, Craigville, Mass., 1967 and 1969. Participant, Library of Congress Conference on the Teaching of Creative Writing, 1973.

MEMBER: National Council of Teachers of English, Modern Language Association, Poetry Society of America, American Association of University Professors, National Education Association, Alpha Kappa Alpha.

AWARDS, HONORS: Yale Series of Younger Poets Award, 1942, for *For My People;* named to Honor Roll of Race Relations, a national poll conducted by the New York Public Library, 1942; Rosenthal fellowship, 1944; Ford fellowship for study at Yale University, 1954; Houghton Mifflin Literary Fellowship, 1966; Fulbright fellowship, 1971; National Endowment for the Humanities, 1972; Doctor of Literature, Northwestern University, 1974; Doctor of Letters, Rust College, 1974; Doctor of Fine Arts, Dennison University, 1974; Doctor of Humane Letters, Morgan State University, 1976.

WRITINGS:

POETRY

For My People, Yale University Press, 1942, reprinted, Ayer Co., 1969.
Ballad of the Free, Broadside Press, 1966.
Prophets for a New Day, Broadside Press, 1970.
October Journey, Broadside Press, 1973.

Also author of *This Is My Century*.

PROSE

Jubilee (novel), Houghton, 1965, Bantam, 1981.
How I Wrote "Jubilee," Third World Press, 1972.

(With Nikki Giovanni) *A Poetic Equation: Conversations between Nikki Giovanni and Margaret Walker*, Howard University Press, 1974, reprinted with new postscript, 1983.
Richard Wright: Daemonic Genius, Dodd, 1987.

CONTRIBUTOR

Addison Gayle, editor, *Black Expression*, Weybright & Tally, 1969.
Stanton L. Wormley and Lewis H. Fenderson, editors, *Many Shades of Black*, Morrow, 1969.
Henderson, Stephen, *Understanding the New Black Poetry: Black Speech and Black Music as Poetic References*, Morrow, 1973.

Also contributor to numerous anthologies, including Adoff's *Black Out Loud*, Weisman and Wright's *Black Poetry for All Americans*, and Williams's *Beyond the Angry Black*.

OTHER

Contributor to *Yale Review, Negro Digest, Poetry, Opportunity, Phylon, Saturday Review,* and *Virginia Quarterly*.

WORK IN PROGRESS: Minna and Jim, a sequel to *Jubilee; Mother Broyer,* a novel; an autobiography, for Howard University Press.

SIDELIGHTS: When *For My People* by Margaret Walker won the Yale Younger Poets Series Award in 1942, "she became one of the youngest Black writers ever to have published a volume of poetry in this century," as well as "the first Black woman in American literary history to be so honored in a prestigious national competition," notes Richard K. Barksdale in *Black American Poets between Worlds, 1940-1960.* Walker's first novel, *Jubilee,* is notable for being "the first truly historical black American novel," according to University of Maryland professor Joyce Anne Joyce, reports *Washington Post* contributor Crispin Y. Campbell. It was also the first work by a black writer to speak out for the liberation of the black woman. The cornerstones of a literature that affirms the African folk roots of black American life, these two books have also been called visionary for looking toward a new cultural unity for black Americans that will be built on that foundation.

The title of Walker's first book, *For My People,* denotes the subject matter of "poems in which the body and spirit of a great group of people are revealed with vigor and undeviating integrity," says Louis Untermeyer in the *Yale Review.* Here, in long ballads, Walker draws sympathetic portraits of characters such as the New Orleans sorceress Molly Means; Kissie Lee, a tough young woman who dies "with her boots on switching blades;" and Poppa Chicken, an urban drug dealer and pimp. Other ballads give a new dignity to John Henry, killed by a ten-pound hammer, and Stagolee, who kills a white officer but eludes a lynch mob. In an essay for *Black Women Writers (1950-1980): A Critical Evaluation,* Eugenia Collier notes, "Using . . . the language of the grass-roots people, Walker spins yarns of folk heroes and heroines: those who, faced with the terrible obstacles which haunt Black people's very existence, not only survive but prevail—with style." Soon after it appeared, the book of ballads, sonnets and free verse found a surprisingly large number of readers, requiring publishers to authorize three printings to satisfy popular demand.

Some critics found fault with the sonnets in the book, but others deemed it generally impressive, R. Baxter Miller summarizes in *Black American Poets between Worlds.* "The title poem is itself a singular and unique literary achievement," Barksdale claims. In *Black American Literature: A Critical*

History, Roger Whitlow elaborates, ''The poem, written in free verse, rhythmically catalogues the progress of black American experience, from the rural folkways, religious practices, and exhausting labor of the South, through the cramped and confusing conditions of the northern urban centers, to what she hopes will be a racial awakening, blacks militantly rising up to take control of their own destinies.'' Collier relates, ''The final stanza is a reverberating cry for redress. It demands a new beginning. Our music then will be martial music; our peace will be hard-won, but it will be 'written in the sky.' And after the agony, the people whose misery spawned strength will control our world. This poem is the hallmark of Margaret Walker's works. It echoes in her subsequent poetry and even in her monumental novel *Jubilee.* It speaks to us, in our words and rhythms, of our history, and it radiates the promise of our future. It is the quintessential example of myth and ritual shaped by artistic genius.''

Reviewers especially praise Walker's control of poetic technique in the poem. Dudley Randall writes in Addison Gayle's *The Black Aesthetic,* ''The poem gains its force . . . by the sheer overpowering accumulation of a mass of details delivered in rhythmical parallel phrases.'' To cite Barksdale, ''it is magnificently wrought oral poetry. . . . In reading it aloud, one must be able to breathe and pause, pause and breathe preacher-style. One must be able to sense the ebb and flow of the intonations. . . . This is the kind of verbal music found in a well-delivered down-home folk sermon.'' By giving the poem a musical rhythm, Walker underscores the poem's message, observes Barksdale: ''The poet here is writing about the source of the Black peoples' blues, for out of their troubled past and turbulent present came the Black peoples' song.'' In this case, Walker steps forward to remind her people of the strength to be found in their cultural tradition as she calls for a new, hopeful literature that can inspire social action.

''If the test of a great poem is the universality of statement, then 'For My People' is a great poem,'' remarks Barksdale. The critic explains in Donald B. Gibson's *Modern Black Poets: A Collection of Critical Essays* that the poem was written when ''world-wide pain, sorrow, and affliction were tangibly evident, and few could isolate the Black man's dilemma from humanity's dilemma during the depression years or during the war years.'' Thus, the power of resilience presented in the poem is a hope Walker holds out not only to black people, but to all people, to ''all the adams and eves.'' As she once remarked, ''Writers should not write exclusively for black or white audiences, but most inclusively. After all, it is the business of all writers to write about the human condition, and all humanity must be involved in both the writing and in the reading.''

Jubilee, a historical novel, is the second book on which Walker's literary reputation rests. It is the story of a slave family during and after the civil war, and took her thirty years to write. During these years, she married a disabled veteran, raised four children, taught full time at Jackson State College in Mississippi, and earned a Ph.D. from the University of Iowa. The lengthy gestation, she believes, partly accounts for the book's quality. As she told Claudia Tate in *Black Women Writers at Work,* ''Living with the book over a long period of time was agonizing. Despite all of that, *Jubilee* is the product of a mature person,'' one whose own difficult pregnancies and economic struggles could lend authenticity to the lives of her characters. ''There's a difference between writing about something and living through it,'' she said in the interview; ''I did both.''

The story of *Jubilee*'s main characters Vyry and Randall Ware was an important part of Walker's life even before she began to write it down. As she explains in *How I Wrote ''Jubilee,''* she first heard about the ''slavery time'' in bedtime stories told by her maternal grandmother. When old enough to recognize the value of her family history, Walker took initiative, ''prodding'' her grandmother for more details, and promising to set down on paper the story that had taken shape in her mind. Later on, she completed extensive research on every aspect of the black experience touching the Civil War, from obscure birth records to information on the history of tin cans. ''Most of my life I have been involved with writing this story about my great-grandmother, and even if *Jubilee* were never considered an artistic or commercial success I would still be happy just to have finished it,'' she claims.

Soon after *Jubilee* was published in 1966, Walker was given a Fellowship award from Houghton-Mifflin, and a mixed reception from critics. Granting that the novel is ''ambitious,'' *New York Times Book Review* contributor Wilma Dykeman deemed it ''uneven.'' Arthur P. Davis, writing in *From the Dark Tower: Afro-American Writers, 1900-1960,* suggests that the author ''has crowded too much into her novel.'' Even so, say reviewers, the novel merits praise. Abraham Chapman of the *Saturday Review* appreciates the author's ''fidelity to fact and detail'' as she ''presents the little-known everyday life of the slaves,'' their music, and their folkways. In the *Christian Science Monitor,* Henrietta Buckmaster comments, ''In Vyry, Miss Walker has found a remarkable woman who suffered one outrage after the other and yet emerged with a humility and a mortal fortitude that reflected a spiritual wholeness.'' Dykeman concurs, ''In its best episodes, and in Vyry, 'Jubilee' chronicles the triumph of a free spirit over many kinds of bondages.'' Later critical studies of the book emphasize the importance of its themes and its position as the prototype for novels that present black history from a black perspective. Claims Whitlow, ''It serves especially well as a response to white 'nostalgia' fiction about the antebellum and Reconstruction South.''

Walker's next book to be highly acclaimed was *Prophets for a New Day,* a slim volume of poems. Unlike the poems in *For My People,* which, in a Marxist fashion, names religion an enemy of revolution, says Collier, *Prophets for a New Day* ''reflects a profound religious faith. The heroes of the sixties are named for the prophets of the Bible: Martin Luther King is Amos, Medgar Evars is Micah, and so on. The people and events of the sixties are paralleled with Biblical characters and occurrences. . . . The religious references are important. Whether one espouses the Christianity in which they are couched is not the issue. For the fact is that Black people from ancient Africa to now have always been a spiritual people, believing in an existence beyond the flesh.'' One poem in *Prophets* that harks back to African spiritism is ''Ballad of Hoppy Toad'' with its hexes that turn a murderous conjurer into a toad. Though Collier feels that Walker's ''vision of the African past is fairly dim and romantic,'' the critic goes on to say that this poetry ''emanates from a deeper area of the psyche, one which touches the mythic area of a collective being and reenacts the rituals which define a Black collective self.'' Perhaps more importantly, in all the poems, says Collier, Walker depicts ''a people striking back at oppression and emerging triumphant.''

Walker disclosed in *A Poetic Equation: Conversations between Nikki Giovanni and Margaret Walker* that the poem ''Ballad of the Free'' in *Prophets* articulates ''better than even 'For My People' so much of what I [feel] about black people and the whole movement toward freedom." Davis calls the book "the best poetical comment to come from the civil rights movement—the movement which came to a climax with the march on Washington and which began thereafter to change into a more militant type of liberation effort." Barksdale shares this view; as he comments in *Black American Poets between Worlds*, "Because of her experience, background, and training—her familial gift of word power, her intensive apprenticeship in Chicago's literary workshop in the 1930s, and her mastery of Black orature—her *Prophets* . . . stands out as the premier poetic statement of the death-riddled decade of the 1960s. The poems of this small volume reflect the full range of the Black protest during the time—the sit-ins, the jailings, the snarling dogs, the . . . lynching of the three Civil Rights workers in Mississippi. All of the poems in the volume touch the sensitive nerve of racial memory and bring back, in sharply etched detail, the trauma and tension and triumphs of that period."

In the same essay, Barksdale relates that Walker's books owe little to her academic life and much to a rich cultural sensibility gained in her youth. "There was . . . New Orleans with its . . . folk mythology, its music, . . . and its assortment of racial experiences to be remembered and recalled." And there was the shaping influence of Walker's parents. Born in Jamaica but educated at Atlanta's Gammon Theological Institute, her father Sigismond was a Methodist preacher. Her mother, Marion (nee Dozier), was a musician. "So [the poet] grew up in a household ruled by the power of the word, for undoubtedly few have a greater gift for articulate word power than an educated Jamaican trained to preach the doctrine of salvation in the Black South," Barksdale remarks. In such a home, survival "without mastery of words and language was impossible," he adds, citing Walker's comment. And, given her family background, Walker felt destined for an academic career.

That career was characterized by opposition and difficulty. In the interview with Tate, Walker reflects, "I'm a third-generation college graduate. Society doesn't want to recognize that there's this kind of black writer. I'm the Ph.D. black woman. That's horrible. That is to be despised. I didn't know how bad it was until I went back to school [to teaching] and found out." With her older children nearing college age, Walker had taken leave from her position at Jackson State University to earn an advanced degree in hope that afterward she would be given more pay. She returned only to be slighted by the administration. Eventually, she developed the school's black studies program, attaining personal fulfillment only during the last years of her career as an educator.

Discouragements of many kinds have not kept Walker from producing works that have encouraged many. *For My People, Jubilee,* and *Prophets for a New Day* are valued for their relation to social movements of twentieth century America. In 1937, the poem "For My People" called for a new generation to gather strength from a militant literature, and the black literature of the 1960s—including the autobiographies of Malcolm X, Eldridge Cleaver, Huey Newton, and Angela Davis, to name just a few—answered that challenge, suggests C.W.E. Bigsby in *The Second Black Renaissance: Essays in Black Literature*. Her example over the years has also proved to be instructive. This summary of Walker's achievement closes the epilogue of *How I Wrote "Jubilee"*: "She has revealed the creative ways in which methods and materials of the social science scholar may be joined with the craft and viewpoint of the poet/novelist to create authentic black literature. She has reaffirmed for us the critical importance of oral tradition in the

creation of our history. . . . Finally, she has made awesomely clear to us the tremendous costs which must be paid in stubborn, persistent work and commitment if we are indeed to write our own history and create our own literature."

BIOGRAPHICAL/CRITICAL SOURCES:

BOOKS

Bankier, Joanna and Dierdre Lashgari, editors, *Women Poets of the World,* Macmillan, 1983.

Baraka, Amiri, *The Black Nation,* Getting Together Publications, 1982.

Bigsby, C.W.E., editor, *The Second Black Renaissance: Essays in Black Literature,* Greenwood Press, 1980.

Contemporary Literary Criticism, Gale, Volume 1, 1973, Volume 2, 1976.

Davis, Arthur P., *From the Dark Tower: Afro-American Writers, 1900 to 1960,* Howard University Press, 1974.

Emanuel, James A., and Theodore L. Gross, editors, *Dark Symphony: Negro Literature in America,* Free Press, 1968.

Evans, Mari, editor, *Black Women Writers (1950-1980): A Critical Evaluation,* Anchor/Doubleday, 1982.

Gayle, Addison, editor, *The Black Aesthetic,* Doubleday, 1971.

Gibson, Donald B., editor, *Modern Black Poets: A Collection of Critical Essays,* Prentice-Hall, 1983.

Jackson, Blyden and Louis D. Rubin, Jr., *Black Poetry in America: Two Essays in Historical Interpretation,* Louisiana State University Press, 1974.

Jones, John Griffith, in *Mississippi Writers Talking,* Volume II, University of Mississippi Press, 1983.

Kent, George E., *Blackness and the Adventure of Western Culture,* Third World Press, 1972.

Lee, Don L., *Dynamite Voices I: Black Poets of the 1960s,* Broadside Press, 1971.

Miller, R. Baxter, editor, *Black American Poets between Worlds, 1940-1960,* University of Tennessee Press, 1986.

Redmond, Eugene B., *Drumvoices: The Mission of Afro-American Poetry—A Critical Evaluation,* Doubleday, 1976.

Tate, Claudia, editor, *Black Women Writers at Work,* Continuum, 1983.

Walker, Margaret, *For My People,* Yale University Press, 1942, reprinted, Ayer Co., 1969.

Walker, Margaret, *How I Wrote "Jubilee,"* Third World Press, 1972.

Walker, Margaret, and Nikki Giovanni, *A Poetic Equation: Conversations between Nikki Giovanni and Margaret Walker,* Howard University Press, 1974, reprinted with a new postscript, 1983.

Walker, Margaret, *Prophets for a New Day,* Broadside Press, 1970.

Whitlow, Roger, *Black American Literature: A Critical History,* NelsonHall, 1973.

PERIODICALS

Atlantic, December, 1942.

Best Sellers, October 1, 1966.

Black World, December, 1971, December, 1975.

Books, January 3, 1973.

Book Week, October 2, 1966.

Callaloo, May, 1979.

Christian Science Monitor, November 14, 1942, September 29, 1966, June 19, 1974.

Common Ground, autumn, 1943.

Ebony, February, 1949.

Freedomways, Volume 2, number 3, summer, 1967.

National Review, October 4, 1966.

Negro Digest, February, 1967, January, 1968.
New Republic, November 23, 1942.
New York Times, November 4, 1942.
New York Times Book Review, August 2, 1942, September 25, 1966.
Opportunity, December, 1942.
Publishers Weekly, April 15, 1944, March 24, 1945.
Saturday Review, September 24, 1966.
Times Literary Supplement, June 29, 1967.
Washington Post, February 9, 1983.
Yale Review, winter, 1943.

—*Sketch by Marilyn K. Basel*

*   *   *

WALLACE, Ruby Ann   1923(?)-
(Ruby Dee)

PERSONAL: Professionally known as Ruby Dee; born October 27, 1923 (some sources say 1924), in Cleveland, Ohio; daughter of Marshall Edward (a railroad porter and waiter) and Emma (a teacher; maiden name, Benson) Wallace; married Ossie Davis (an actor, writer, director, and producer of stage and motion picture productions), December 9, 1948; children: Nora, Guy, La Verne. *Education:* Hunter College (now of the City University of New York), B.A., 1945; also attended Actors Workshop during 1950s, Fairfield University, Iona College, and Virginia State University.

ADDRESSES: Agent—Artists Agency, 10000 Santa Monica Blvd., Suite 305, Los Angeles, Calif. 90067.

CAREER: Actress and writer. American Negro Theatre, apprentice, 1941-44. Actress in numerous Broadway productions, including "South Pacific," 1943, "Jeb," 1946, "A Raisin in the Sun," 1959, "Purlie Victorious," 1961, and "Boesman and Lena," 1970. Actress in motion pictures, including "No Way Out," 1950, "The Jackie Robinson Story," 1950, "Edge of the City," 1957, "St. Louis Blues," 1958, "A Raisin in the Sun," 1961, and "Gone Are the Days" (also released as "Purlie Victorious" and "The Man from C.O.T.T.O.N."), 1963. Actress in television productions, including "Black Monday," 1961. Co-host of radio program "Ossie Davis and Ruby Dee Story Hour," 1974-78, and of television series "With Ossie and Ruby," Public Broadcasting System (PBS-TV), 1981. Performer on recordings for Caedmon, Folkways Records, and Newbery Award Records. Civil rights activist.

MEMBER: American Federation of Television and Radio Artists, Screen Actors Guild, Actors Equity Association, National Association for the Advancement of Colored People, Negro American Labor Council, Southern Christian Leadership Conference, Students for Non-Violence (member of coordinating committee).

AWARDS, HONORS: Emmy Award nomination for outstanding single performance by an actress in a leading role, Academy of Television Arts and Sciences, 1964, for "Express Stop from Lenox Avenue"; with husband Ossie Davis, Frederick Douglass Award from New York Urban League, 1970; Obie Award, 1971, for "Boseman and Lena"; Martin Luther King, Jr., Award from Operation PUSH, 1972; Drama Desk Award, 1974.

WRITINGS—Under name Ruby Dee:

(With Jules Dassin and Julian Mayfield) "Up Tight" (screenplay; adapted from Liam O'Flaherty's novel *The Informer*), Paramount, 1968.
(Editor) *Glowchild, and Other Poems,* Third Press, 1972.
(And director) "Take It from the Top" (stage musical), first produced Off-Broadway at New Federal Theatre, January 19, 1979 (revised as "Twin Bit Gardens," 1979).
My One Good Nerve: Rhythms, Rhymes, Reasons (stories, poems, and essays), Third World Press, 1987.
Two Ways to Count to Ten, Holt, 1988.

Former columnist for *New York Amsterdam News;* associate editor, *Freedomways.*

SIDELIGHTS: Ruby Dee is among America's most prominent black performers. While studying at Hunter College in the early 1940s, Dee became involved with the American Negro Theatre. With fellow artists such as Sidney Poitier and Harry Belafonte, Dee contributed to all facets of the group's productions, mopping floors and selling tickets when not appearing in works such as "Natural Man" and "Starlight." She also participated in radio plays and acted in the Broadway production "South Pacific" (not the musical by Rodger and Hammerstein). In 1946 she appeared in Robert Ardrey's "Jeb," the drama of a black veteran's efforts to secure employment in the South, and eventually married the work's principal performer, Ossie Davis.

In the 1950s Dee continued working on the stage while expanding into television and film. Among her most acclaimed roles in this period were stirring performances as the wife of a young black working on the docks of New York in the film "Edge of the City" and as the daughter-in-law in Lorraine Hansberry's heralded play "A Raisin in the Sun." Dee repeated her performance in the film adaptation of the play in 1961, then worked in husband Davis's satirical play "Purlie Victorious." Dee played Lutiebelle Gussie Mae Jenkins, a young woman who helps Purlie, an eloquent itinerant preacher, bilk five hundred dollars from a bigoted plantation owner in order to establish an integrated church.

Throughout her career, Dee has appeared in a wide range of works, from Shakespearean productions to television series. She also co-authored the screenplay for the motion picture "Up Tight," which details the dilemma of a black man who betrays his friends after one of them murders a guard during a robbery. Vincent Canby, writing in the *New York Times,* called "Up Tight" "such an intense and furious movie that it's impossible not to take it seriously" and credited the screenplay by Dee, director Jules Dassin, and Julian Mayfield as possessing "the sound of authenticity." In addition to the musical stage production "Take It from the Top," in which she played the leading role of an angel who returns to earth to recruit good people to thwart an evil capitalist, Dee's other writing ventures include collections of poetry, stories, and essays.

BIOGRAPHICAL/CRITICAL SOURCES:

PERIODICALS

Book World, March 8, 1987.
Ebony, December, 1979.
Essence, May, 1987.
New Yorker, April 8, 1961.
New York Times, December 19, 1968, January 20, 1979.
New York Times Book Review, November 5, 1972.

WALROND, Eric (Derwent) 1898-1966

PERSONAL: Born in 1898 in Georgetown, British Guiana (now Guyana); immigrated to Barbados, 1906, to Panama Canal Zone, c. 1910, to United States, 1918, to Europe, c. 1928; died in 1966 in London, England; married twice; children: Jean, Dorothy, Lucille. *Education:* Attended City College of New York (now of the City University of New York), 1922-24, Columbia University, 1924-26, and University of Wisconsin, 1928.

ADDRESSES: Home—London, England.

CAREER: Worked in the Panama Canal Zone, c. 1916-18, as a clerk for the Health Department of the Canal Commission and as a reporter and sportswriter for *Panama Star and Herald* and aided in the publication of *Workman;* held various secretarial and stenographer positions in New York, N.Y., c. 1918-21; *Brooklyn and Long Island Informer,* New York City, co-owner, editor, and reporter, 1921-23; *Weekly Review,* New York City, associate editor, 1921-23; associate editor of *Negro World,* 1923-25; *Opportunity: Journal of Negro Life,* New York City, business manager, 1925-27.

MEMBER: Eclectic Club, Universal Negro Improvement Association.

AWARDS, HONORS: Received a John Simon Guggenheim Memorial Foundation Award and became a Zona Gale scholar at University of Wisconsin, both in 1928.

WRITINGS:

Tropic Death (short story collection), Boni & Liveright, 1926, Macmillan, 1972.
(Contributor) Van Wyck Brooks and others, editors, *The American Caravan* (anthology), Macaulay, 1927.
(Editor with Rosey E. Pool) *Black and Unknown Bards: A Collection of Negro Poetry,* Hand & Flower Press, 1958.
(Contributor) Richard Bardsdale and Kenneth Kinnaman, editors, *Black Writers of America* (anthology), Macmillan, 1972.

Work represented in anthologies, including *Anthology of American Negro Literature, Dark Symphony, Best Short Stories by Negro Writers, From the Roots,* and *Best Short Stories.* Contributor to periodicals such as *All Star Weekly, Black Man, Crisis, Current History, Dearborn Independent, Independent, Messenger, Negro World, New Age, New Republic, Opportunity, Saturday Review, Saturday Review of Literature, Smart Set, Success,* and *Vanity Fair.*

WORK IN PROGRESS: At the time of his death, Walrond was working on a book about the Panama Canal.

SIDELIGHTS: Eric Walrond migrated to New York City in 1918 at the age of twenty and within a few years established himself as one of the more important young writers associated with the black artistic movement known as the Harlem Renaissance. Initially Walrond concentrated on the subject of racial bigotry, which he personally experienced after arriving in the United States, and his writings reflect both his indignation and disillusionment. *Tropic Death,* his most significant work, however, focuses on and illuminates the multitudinal problems faced by migratory blacks of the Caribbean. A collection of short stories, the book was regarded as an outstanding example of avant-garde writing and drew high praise from contemporary critics.

BIOGRAPHICAL/CRITICAL SOURCES:

BOOKS

Dictionary of Literary Biography, Volume 51: *Afro-American Writers From the Harlem Renaissance to 1940,* Gale, 1987.

PERIODICALS

Savacou 2, September, 1970.

* * *

WARD, Douglas Turner 1930-

PERSONAL: Born May 5, 1930, in Burnside, La.; son of Roosevelt (co-owner of a tailoring business) and Dorothy (seamstress and co-owner of a tailoring business; maiden name, Short) Ward; married Diana Hoyt Powell (an editor), 1966; children: two. *Education:* Attended Wilberforce University, 1946-47, University of Michigan, 1947-48, and Paul Mann's Actors' Workshop, 1955-58.

ADDRESSES: Home—222 East 11th St., New York, N.Y. 10003. *Office*—Negro Ensemble Co., 424 West 55th St., New York, N.Y. 10019. *Agent*—Gilbert Parker, Curtis Brown Ltd., 575 Madison Ave., New York, N.Y. 10022.

CAREER: Playwright, actor, producer, and director; worked as a journalist in New York City, 1948-51; Negro Ensemble Company (NEC), New York City, co-founder, 1965, artistic director, 1967—. Appeared in productions of "The Iceman Cometh," 1956, 1959, and 1960-61, "Lost in the Stars," 1958, "A Raisin in the Sun," 1959, 1960-61, "The Blacks," 1961, "Pullman Car Hiawatha," 1962, "The Blood Knot," 1963, "Rich Little Rich Girl" and "One Flew Over the Cuckoo's Nest," 1964, "Coriolanus," "Happy Ending," and "Day of Absence," 1965, "Kongi's Harvest" and "Summer of the Seventeenth Doll," 1968, "The Reckoning" and "Ceremonies in Dark Old Men," 1969, and "Frederick Douglass in His Own Words," 1972; appeared as actor on television, including "Ceremonies in Dark Old Men," January 6, 1975, "Studio One," and "The Edge of Night"; appeared in film "Man and Boy," 1971. Producer or director of and actor in plays, including "Daddy Goodness," 1968, "Man Better Man," 1969, "Ododo," 1970, "The River Niger," 1972, and "First Breeze of Summer," 1975. Director of plays, including "Contribution," 1969, "Brotherhood" and "Day of Absence," 1970, "Ride a Black Horse," 1971, "Perry's Mission," 1971, "A Ballet Behind the Bridge," 1972, "The Great MacDaddy," "Black Sunlight," "Nowhere to Run, Nowhere to Hide," 1974, "Waiting for Mongo," 1975, "Livin' Fat," 1976, and "A Soldier's Play," 1982-83.

AWARDS, HONORS: Vernon Rice Drama Desk Award, 1966, Obie Award, 1966, Lambda Kappa Nu citation, 1968, special Tony award, League of American Theatres and Producers, Inc., 1969, Brandeis University creative arts award, 1969, all for "Happy Ending" and "Day of Absence"; Vernon Rice Drama Desk Award, 1969, for role in "Ceremonies in Dark Old Men"; Obie Award, *Village Voice,* 1970, for role in "The Reckoning"; Margo Jones Award, 1973, to Ward and NEC for producing new plays; Tony award nomination, 1974, best supporting actor.

WRITINGS:

Happy Ending and Day of Absence: Two Plays (comedies; first produced Off-Broadway at St. Mark's Playhouse, November 15, 1965), published with introduction by Sheila

A. Rush, Dramatists Play Service, 1966, published as *Two Plays,* Third Press, 1971.

(Contributor) William Couch, Jr., editor, *New Black Playwrights,* Louisiana State University Press, 1968.

(Contributor) William Brasmer and Dominick Consolo, editors, *Black Drama,* Merrill, 1970.

The Reckoning: A Surreal Southern Fable (first produced Off-Broadway at St. Mark's Playhouse, September 2, 1969), Dramatists Play Service, 1970.

Brotherhood (first produced Off-Broadway with "Day of Absence" at St. Mark's Playhouse, April 26, 1970), Dramatists Play Service, 1970.

(Contributor) Clinton Oliver and Stephanie Sills, editors, *Contemporary Black Drama,* Scribner, 1971.

(Contributor) Robert Hayden, David Burrows, and Frederick Lapides, editors, *Afro-American Literature,* Harcourt, 1971.

(Contributor) Ruth Miller, editor, *Blackamerican Literature,* Free Press, 1971.

"The Redeemer," first produced in Louisville at Actors' Theatre, January 26, 1979.

SIDELIGHTS: Throughout his theatrical career, playwright and actor Douglas Turner Ward has shown great versatility both on and off the stage. "Whatever role the versatile Mr. Ward plays—as actor, playwright, journalist, director, artistic director of the Negro Ensemble Company—he is a man of great force, dedication, and verbosity," writes Mel Gussow in the *New York Times.* Through the Negro Ensemble Company, or NEC, which he co-founded in 1965 with Robert Hooks and Off-Broadway producer Gerald A. Krone, Ward has helped shape contemporary black theatre. "Ward was one of the first writers to approach theater from a modern black perspective using humor," points out Stephen M. Vallillo in the *Dictionary of Literary Biography.* "Comic, not militant or angry, his plays tend to be extended jokes, ironic situations that he develops into short dramatic pieces. Underneath the humor, however, is a biting satire that examines the relations and interdependence between blacks and whites." Vallillo adds that Ward's "work, and that of his theater, explores the wide range of black experience—its politics, its home life, its humor, and its drama. Ward's contribution to black theater is immense."

An article Ward wrote for the *New York Times* gave birth to the NEC. Entitled "American Theatre: For Whites Only?" the article defined American theater, from off-off-Broadway to Broadway, as "a Theater of Diversion—a diversionary theater, whose main problem is not that it's too safe, but that it is surpassingly irrelevant." Ward emphasized the need for "the development of a permanent Negro repertory company of at least off-Broadway size and dimension. . . . A theater concentrating primarily on themes of Negro life, but also resilient enough to incorporate and interpret the best of world drama—whatever the source." He continued that "this is not a plea for either a segregated theater, or a separatist one. Negroes constitute a numerical minority, but Negro experience, from slavery to civil rights, has always been of crucial importance to America's existence." Shortly after the article was published, Ward received a Ford foundation grant to start his theater. Two years after the founding of the NEC, John G. O'Connor noted in the *Wall Street Journal* that "from the beginning, the NEC's productions have been notable for their excellent acting, intelligent direction, and imaginative presentation." He also felt that the company was "already perhaps the finest acting-producing company in the United States."

While the NEC produces the work of many playwrights, it has served Ward well as a vehicle for his own writing and acting skills. Two of Ward's early plays, "Happy Ending" and "Day of Absence" ran on a double bill at the NEC, and Ward took major roles in both productions. Critics have praised the two works' originality. "Both plays are comedy satires, with sharp, jagged teeth, drawing their substance and their thrust from the bitter-sweet reality of race relations as seen from the bottom side of the coin," notes William Barrow in *Negro Digest.* "Happy Ending" relates the plight of two black servants who despairingly face their employers' imminent divorce. When the women's proud nephew upbraids them for weeping, his aunts reveal that everything he owns, including his suits, have come from the white couple. The breakup of their home will mean the destruction of his lifestyle. At hearing this, the nephew starts to cry himself; part of the play's ironic humor comes from his change in attitude regarding his social status. According to Howard Taubman in the *New York Times,* "increasingly the Negro is using sardonic laughter to express his resentment at years of forced inferiority and to articulate his passion for change." Wilfrid Sheed in *Commonweal* comments on Ward's ability to portray the situation without racism: "Mr. Ward's message that the servant is finally corrupted as much as the master might not come so gracefully from a white playwright. But these are not raceplays in the usual sense; race is treated mainly as a local aspect of universal institution."

In "Day of Absence," white residents of a Southern town panic when the black labor force disappears for one day. Whites find themselves completely unable to function, and the Mayor ends up begging Washington to ship in more "Nigras." The play shows the dependence of all whites, but especially the middle and upper-classes, on blacks. "Day of Absence" was performed as a "reverse minstrel show." "The comedy is broad and heavy," writes Barrow. "The Negro actors wear white faces, and a few of them are wildly ingenuous." Writing in *Negro Digest,* Helen Armstead Johnson brings up the play's more serious aspects: "As funny as the images and memories are, the bitter truths and ironies are all too apparent. . . . It dramatizes a secret wish, which, no doubt, every Black person has had at one time or another." Barrow agrees, saying that both "Happy Ending" and "Day of Absence" "speak to black people with the resonance of experience."

In a discussion between playwrights and critics sponsored by the Modern Language Association, *New York Times* contributor Michael T. Kaufman reports that George Wellwarth objected to "outdated" relationships in "Happy Ending" and "Day of Absence." According to Wellwarth, Ward "writes about the master-servant relationship as if it still existed and presents us with the ironic paradox of the servant superior to the master." To this, Ward responded: "Stereotypes have changed—from Stepin Fetchit to a menacing black militant hiding behind every lamppost—but they are still stereotypes. As for the servant-master relationship, it exists, you can see it on the street corners in the Bronx where women shape up for jobs as domestics." Gail Stewart in the *Dictionary of Literary Biography* notes that Ward modified the cunning servant character found in Greek and Roman comedy to create his own servants; yet despite its association with the classical theater, Stewart finds that "'Day of Absence' is one of the most revolutionary plays written by an American black, for Ward depicts the enormity of the contribution of blacks to American life and in the same stroke the enormity of the exploitation that blacks have historically suffered."

Ward subsequently wrote a play called "The Reckoning." On a grimmer note than his two previous works, this picture of a Southern governor blackmailed by a pimp and his girlfriend still falls withn the realm of comedy. But critics have responded to "The Reckoning" with more ambivalence, partially because the black pimp who forces the governor to publicly welcome a black march on the state capitol becomes the hero. According to Theophilus Lewis in *America*, "the author substitutes social justice for moral principle." A *Variety* contributor claims that the conflict bewteen the governor and Scar, the pimp, "is resolved not on the basis of right and wrong, or logic, but as a test of unscrupulous force." However, Edith Oliver states in the *New Yorker* that Ward was probably not concerned over whether audiences feel comfortable with his play: "Liking or not liking the play does not seem especially pertinent.... Mr. Ward is not out to attract or enchant or lightly amuse us, but his play's passion is alive."

Despite critics' feelings about Ward's presentation of justice and morality in "The Reckoning," they continue to praise his writing. The *Variety* essayist also states that "as a playwright, Ward has admirable capacities. He has an instinct for provocative situation, and dramatic conflict." And in *Cue*, Lawrence Wunderlich writes that "Ward's concept and language soar well beyond the keyhole-and-tape-recorder school of playwriting into careening flights of blank verse, simile, metaphor, alliteration, and, in the final analysis, a perfectly viable poetry for the theatre."

In "Brotherhood," which ran on a double bill with a restaging of "Day of Absence," Ward mocks the idea of facile relationships between blacks and whites. The plot concerns a white man and woman who invite a black couple into their home for the evening. The living room set appears strange from the beginning, as objects are draped with sheets and left covered through the play. When the black man and woman arrive, they are well-dressed and polite, which seems to disconcert their hosts. The white couple behaves oddly throughout the visit, and when the guests leave, the coverings are removed, and the objects revealed represent the couple's true feelings. But the black couple has also been hiding hatred behind smiles. "'Brotherhood' is probably more of a dramatic metaphor than a play," writes Clive Barnes in the *New York Times*. "It is a stark and startling accusation of racism against white and black alike." While some critics dislike the play, finding it less satisfying than earlier works, Barnes praises Ward's objectivity. He continues, "Ward plays no sides. He looks at our two nations with an unvarying yet compassionate eye."

BIOGRAPHICAL/CRITICAL SOURCES:

BOOKS

Contemporary Literary Criticism, Volume 19, Gale, 1981.
Dictionary of Literary Biography, Volume 7: *Twentieth-Century American Dramatists*, 1981, Volume 38: *Afro-American Writers after 1955*, 1984.
Mitchell, Loften, *Black Drama: The Story of the American Negro Theatre*, Hawthorn, 1967.

PERIODICALS

Cue, April 5, 1969, September 13, 1969, March 28, 1970.
Negro Digest, March, 1967, December, 1967, April, 1970.
New Leader, September 29, 1969.
New Yorker, September 13, 1969, March 28, 1970.
New York Times, November 16, 1965, August 14, 1966, September 5, 1969, September 14, 1969, March 18, 1970, December 30, 1970.

Show Business, September 20, 1969, November 29, 1969.
Variety, September 10, 1969.
Village Voice, September 11, 1969, January 22, 1970, March 26, 1970.
Wall Street Journal, February 19, 1969.
Washington Post, January 31, 1970.

—*Sketch by Jani Prescott*

*   · *   *

WARD, Theodore (James)   1902-1983

PERSONAL: Born September 15, 1902, in Thibodeaux, La.; died of a heart attack, May 8, 1983, in Chicago, Ill.; son of Everett (a schoolteacher and book salesman) and Mary Louise (Pierre) Ward; married Mary Sangigian (an office manager), June 15, 1940; children: Elsie Virginia, Laura Louise. *Education:* Attended University of Utah, 1930, and University of Wisconsin, 1931-33.

CAREER: Playwright. Traveled around the United States and worked at various odd jobs, including elevator operator and barbershop porter. WIBA-Radio, Madison, Wis., staff artist, 1931-32; Works Progress Administration (WPA; renamed Work Projects Administration, 1939), Chicago, Ill., recreational director, 1934-38, instructor of dramatics at Lincoln Center, 1937, actor with Federal Theatre Project, 1937-39; Negro Playwrights Co. of Harlem, New York, N.Y., co-founding president, 1940-41; factory laborer and bootblack during early 1940s; writer for Office of War Information, c. 1944; taught adult writing seminars in Chicago and New Orleans, La., after 1960s, and drama classes for children in Chicago, 1963; South Side Center for the Performing Arts, Chicago, founding executive director, 1967-68; playwright-in-residence at Free Southern Theatre, New Orleans, during 1970s.

MEMBER: Dramatists Guild.

AWARDS, HONORS: "Sick and Tiahd" won second prize in Chicago Repertory Company theatre contest, 1937; National Theatre Conference fellowship, 1945-47; Theatre Guild Award, 1947, for play "Our Lan'"; named Negro of the Year, 1947; Guggenheim fellowship, 1947-48, for play "John Brown"; named Outstanding Pioneer of Black Theatre, 1975; DuSable Writers' Seminar and Poetry Festival Award for excellence in drama, 1982.

WRITINGS:

PLAYS

Big White Fog: A Negro Tragedy (first produced at Great Northern Theatre, Chicago, 1983; produced Off-Broadway at Lincoln Theatre, Harlem, 1940), privately printed, c. 1973.
"Our Lan'" (first produced at Henry Street Playhouse in New York, 1947; produced on Broadway, 1947), published in *A Theater in Your Head*, edited by Kenneth Thorpe Rowe, Funk, 1960.

Author of perhaps twenty or thirty other plays, including "Sick and Tiahd" (also as "Sick and Tired"), 1937; "The Daubers," 1953; "Candle in the Wind," 1967; "The Creole"; "John Brown"; "Whole Hog or Nothing"; "Challenge"; "Skin Deep"; "Even the Dead Arise and Shout Hallelujah"; "Falcon of Adowa"; "Throwback"; "Charity"; "The Life of Harriet Tubman"; "Deliver the Goods"; and "John de Conqueror."

Work represented in anthologies, including *Black Drama in America: An Anthology*, edited by Darwin T. Turner, Fawcett, 1971.

OTHER

Contributor of articles to periodicals, including *Current Opinion*, *Mainstream*, and *Black Theatre*.

Associate editor of *Mainstream*.

SIDELIGHTS: Regarded as "the dean of black dramatists" during his day, Theodore Ward contributed to the advancement of black theatre in the United States and was officially named Outstanding Pioneer of Black Theatre in 1975. His plays, which focus on themes of Negro life, were roundly acclaimed for their innovative depiction of the black experience and for avoiding the use of spirituals and feverish dancing that typically distinguished theatricals about Negro people. According to C. Gerald Fraser in the *New York Times,* former critic Brooks Atkinson once wrote that Ward "'made no concessions to the white man's taste.'" Similarly, Fraser reported that in Errol Hill's opinion Ward consistently endeavored through his work "'to establish heroes for the black race.'"

Between 1934 and 1939 Ward found employment with the Works Progress Administration (WPA), a U.S. Government agency designed to counter rising unemployment during the Great Depression by engaging the jobless in diverse projects. In particular, the program's Federal Theatre Project, which Ward joined in 1937, induced theatrical production and experimentation by impoverished writers. In 1938 it staged Ward's first major work, "Big White Fog." The play's success with Chicago audiences precipitated Ward's joining the newly formed Negro Playwrights Company in New York, where he and fellow members, such as Langston Hughes and Richard Wright, launched their fledgling company with an Off-Broadway production of Ward's "Big White Fog" in 1940. While critics and Ward's contemporaries applauded the play's seriousness and realism, New York theatergoers disapproved of its unrestrained leftist political tone. Consequently, "Big White Fog" closed after sixty-four performances, and the Negro Playwrights Company folded.

Undaunted but wary due to his experience in New York, Ward returned to Chicago for his next play, "Our Lan'." Circumstances including the outbreak of World War II, however, prevented the work from being staged until 1947, when it premiered at a New York playhouse. That same year "Our Lan'" opened on Broadway and ran forty-two shows before closing. Though short-lived, the play's appearance on Broadway distinguished Ward as one of the few black writers to have their work produced there following the end of the Harlem Renaissance of the late 1920s and early 1930s and earned him a 1947 Theatre Guild Award. Variously described as Ward's "best" and "best-known" play, "Our Lan'" was revised by Ward and restaged around 1967 at the Louis Theater in Chicago.

Factors such as a lack of support for the development of black theatre contributed to Ward's limited success as a playwright. In particular, the 1950s proved an increasingly difficult time for him to have his work produced. As a result, most of Ward's ensuing twenty or thirty plays were either short-term runs or not produced at all. Additionally, as some observers pointed out, much of Ward's work proved too radical for audiences of the time and thereby sacrificed popular appeal. In retrospect, critics have since deemed his work a major contribution to the early development of American black theatre, thus judging Ward an undeservedly neglected playwright.

BIOGRAPHICAL/CRITICAL SOURCES:

BOOKS

Abramson, Doris E., *Negro Playwrights in the American Theatre, 1925-1959*, Columbia University Press, 1969.
Flanagan, Hallie, *Arena: The History of the Federal Theatre*, Duell, Sloane & Pierce, 1940.
Nathan, George Jean, editor, *Theatre Book of the Year, 1948-1949*, Knopf, 1949.

OBITUARIES:

BOOKS

The Annual Obituary 1983, St. James Press, 1984.

PERIODICALS

Chicago Tribune, May 12, 1983.
Los Angeles Times, May 14, 1983.
Newsweek, May 23, 1983.
New York Times, May 11, 1983.
Time, May 23, 1983.
Washington Post, May 13, 1983.

*   *   *

WARUK, Kona
See HARRIS, (Theodore) Wilson

*   *   *

WASHINGTON, Booker T(aliaferro)   1856-1915

PERSONAL: Original name, Booker Taliaferro; later added surname Washington; born into slavery, April 5, 1856, on a plantation near Hale's Ford, Franklin County, Va.; died of arteriosclerosis and extreme exhaustion, November 14, 1915, in Tuskegee, Ala.; buried in a brick tomb, made by students, on a hill overlooking Tuskegee Institute; son of Jane Ferguson (a slave); married Fannie Norton Smith, 1882 (deceased, 1884); married Olivia A. Davidson (an educator), 1885 (deceased, 1889); married Margaret J. Murray (an educator), October 12, 1893; children: (first marriage) Portia Washington Pittman; (second marriage) Booker Taliaferro, Jr., Ernest Davidson. *Education:* Hampton Institute, B.A. (with honors), 1875; Wayland Seminary, M.A., 1879.

CAREER: Worked in the salt furnaces and coal mines of West Virginia as a child, and as a houseboy for General Lewis Ruffner, 1870-72; teacher at a rural school for blacks, Malden, W.Va., 1875-78; Hampton Institute, Hampton, Va., teacher and director of experimental educational program for Indians, 1879-81; Tuskegee Normal and Industrial Institute, Tuskegee, Ala., co-founder, principal, and professor of mental and moral sciences, 1881-1915; writer. Founder of National Negro Business League, 1900, and National Negro Health Week, 1914; adviser to several U.S. presidents, including Theodore Roosevelt and William Howard Taft, on racial and social matters; lecturer on racial and educational subjects.

AWARDS, HONORS: A.M., Harvard University, 1897; LL.D., Dartmouth College, 1901; first black elected to Hall of Fame, New York University, 1945.

WRITINGS:

Black-Belt Diamonds: Gems From the Speeches, Addresses, and Talks to Students of Booker T. Washington, compiled by Victoria Earle Matthews, introduction by Thomas Fortune, Fortune & Scott, 1898, reprinted, Negro Universities Press, 1969.

The Future of the American Negro (essays and speeches), Small, Maynard, 1899, reprinted, Negro Universities Press, 1969.

(With N. B. Wood and Fannie Barrier Williams) *A New Negro for a New Century,* American Publishing House, 1900, reprinted, AMS Press, 1973.

Sowing and Reaping, L. C. Page, 1900, reprinted, Books for Libraries, 1971.

(With Edgar Webber) *The Story of My Life and Work* (autobiography), illustrations by Frank Beard, J. L. Nichols, 1900, revised edition published as *An Autobiography by Booker T. Washington: The Story of My Life and Work,* introduction by J.L.M. Curry, J. L. Nichols, 1901, another revised edition published as *Booker T. Washington's Own Story of His Life and Work,* supplement by Albon L. Holsey, 1915, reprint of original edition, Negro Universities Press, 1969.

(With Max Bennett Thrasher) *Up From Slavery: An Autobiography,* A. L. Burt, 1901, reprinted, with an introduction by Langston Hughes, Dodd, 1965, reprinted, with an introduction by Booker T. Washington III and illustrations by Denver Gillen, Heritage Press, 1970, reprinted, with illustrations by Bart Forbes, Franklin Library, 1977, abridged edition, Harrap, 1929.

Character Building: Being Addresses Delivered on Sunday Evenings to the Students of Tuskegee Institute by Booker T. Washington, Doubleday, Page, 1902, reprinted, Haskell House, 1972.

(Contributor) *The Negro Problem* (articles), James Pott, 1903, reprinted, AMS Press, 1970.

Working With the Hands (autobiography), illustrations by Frances Benjamin Johnston, Doubleday, Page, 1904, reprinted, Arno, 1970.

(Editor with Emmett J. Scott) *Tuskegee and Its People: Their Ideals and Achievements,* Appleton, 1905, reprinted, Books for Libraries, 1971.

Putting the Most Into Life (addresses), Crowell, 1906.

(With S. Laing Williams) *Frederick Douglass* (biography), G. W. Jacobs, 1907, reprinted, edited by Ellis Paxson Oberholtzer, Argosy-Antiquarian, 1969.

The Negro in Business, Hertel, Jenkins, 1907, reprinted, AMS Press, 1971.

(With W.E.B. Du Bois) *The Negro in the South: His Economic Progress in Relation to His Moral and Religious Development* (addresses), G. W. Jacobs, 1907, reprinted, AMS Press, 1973.

The Story of the Negro: The Rise of the Race From Slavery, two volumes, Doubleday, Page, 1909, reprinted, Negro Universities Press, 1969.

(With Robert E. Park and Emmett J. Scott) *My Larger Education: Being Chapters From My Experience* (autobiography), illustrated with photographs, Doubleday, Page, 1911, reprinted, Mnemosyne Publishing, 1969.

(With Robert E. Park) *The Man Farthest Down: A Record of Observation and Study in Europe,* Doubleday, Page, 1912, reprinted, with an introduction by St. Clair Drake, Transaction Books, 1984.

The Story of Slavery, Hall & McCreary, 1913, reprinted, with biographical sketch by Emmett J. Scott and photographs from Tuskegee Institute, Owen Publishing, 1940.

One Hundred Selected Sayings of Booker T. Washington, compiled by Julia Skinner, Wilson Printing, 1923.

Selected Speeches of Booker T. Washington, edited by son, E. Davidson Washington, Doubleday, Doran, 1932, reprinted, Kraus Reprint, 1976.

Quotations of Booker T. Washington, compiled by E. Davidson Washington, Tuskegee Institute Press, 1938.

The Booker T. Washington Papers, thirteen volumes, University of Illinois Press, 1972-84, Volume I: *The Autobiographical Writings,* Volume II: *1860-1889,* Volume III: *1889-1895,* Volume IV: *1895-1898,* Volume V: *1899-1900,* Volume VI: *1901-1902,* Volume VII: *1903-1904,* all edited by Louis R. Harlan; Volume VIII: *1904-1906,* Volume IX: *1906-1908,* Volume X: *1909-1912,* Volume XI: *1911-1912, Volume XII: 1912-1914,* Volume XIII: *1914-1915,* all edited by Louis R. Harlan and Raymond W. Smock.

Author of numerous monographs, including *Education of the Negro,* J. B. Lyon, 1900.

SIDELIGHTS: Booker T. Washington was born near Roanoke, Virginia, at Hale's Farm, where his mother was the slave cook of James Burroughs, a small planter. His father was white and possibly a member of the Burroughs family. As a child Booker swept yards and brought water to slaves working in the fields. Freed after the Civil War, he and his mother went to Malden, West Virginia, to join Washington Ferguson, whom his mother had married during the war. There young Washington helped support the family by working in salt furnaces and coal mines. He taught himself the alphabet, then studied nights with the teacher of a local school for blacks. In 1870 he started doing housework for the owner of the coal mine where he worked at the time. The owner's wife, an austere New Englander, encouraged his studies and instilled in Washington a great regard for education. In 1872 he set out for the Hampton Institute, a school set up by the Virginia legislature for blacks. He walked much of the way and worked menial jobs to earn the fare to complete the five-hundred-mile journey.

Washington spent three years at Hampton, paying for his room and board by working as a janitor. After graduating with honors in 1875, he taught for two years in Malden, then returned to Hampton to teach in a program for American Indians. In 1881, General Samuel Chapman Armstrong, the principal at Hampton, recommended Washington to the Alabama legislature for the job of principal of a new normal school for black students at Tuskegee. Washington was accepted for the position, but when he arrived in Tuskegee he discovered that neither land nor buildings had been acquired for the projected school, nor were there any funds for these purposes. Consequently, Washington began classes with thirty students in a shanty donated by a black church. Soon, however, he was able to borrow money to buy an abandoned plantation nearby and moved the school there.

Convinced that economic strength was the best route to political and social equality for blacks, Washington encouraged Tuskegee students to learn industrial skills. Carpentry, cabinetmaking, printing, shoemaking, and tinsmithing were among the first courses the school offered. Boys also studied farming and dairying, while girls learned cooking and sewing and other skills related to homemaking. Strong empahsis was placed on personal hygiene, manners, and character building. Students followed a rigid schedule of study and work and were required to attend chapel daily and a series of religious services on Sunday. Washington usually conducted the Sunday evening program himself. During his thirty-four-year principalship of Tuskegee, the school's curriculum expanded to include instruction in professions as well as trades. At the time of Washington's death in 1915 Tuskegee had an endowment of $2 million and a staff of 200 members. Nearly 2,000 students were enrolled in the regular courses and about the same number in special courses and the extension division. Among its all-black faculty was the renowned agricultural scientist George Washington Carver.

Although his administration of Tuskegee was Washington's best-known achievement, his work as an educator was only one aspect of his multifaceted career. Washington spent much time raising money for Tuskegee and publicizing the school and its philosophy. His success in securing the praise and financial support of northern philanthropists was remarkable. One of his admirers was industrialist Andrew Carnegie, who thought Washington "one of the most wonderful men . . . who ever has lived." Many other political, intellectual, and religious leaders were almost as laudatory. Washington was also in demand as a speaker, winning national fame on the lecture circuit. His most famous speech was his address at the opening of the Cotton States and International Exposition in Atlanta in September, 1895.

Later known as the Atlanta Compromise, the speech contained the essence of Washington's educational and racial views and was, according to C. Vann Woodward in his review of Louis R. Harlan's biography *Booker T. Washington: The Making of a Black Leader, 1865-1901* for *New Republic*, "his stock speech for the rest of his life." Emphasizing to black members of the audience the imporance of economic power, Washington contended that "the opportunity to earn a dollar in a factory just now is worth infinitely more than the opportunity to spend a dollar in an opera house." Consequently he urged blacks not to strain relations in the South by demanding social equality with whites. To the white members of the audience he promised that "in all things that are purely social we can be as separate as fingers, yet one as the hand in all things essential to mutual progress."

The Atlanta speech, Woodward noted, "contained nothing [Washington] had not said many times before. . . . But in the midst of racial crisis, black disenfranchisement and Populist rebellion in the '90s, the brown orator electrified conservative hopes." Washington was hailed in the white press as leader and spokesman for all American blacks and successor to the prominent abolitionist Frederick Douglass, who had died a few months earlier. His position, however, was denounced by many black leaders, including civil rights activist W.E.B. Du Bois, who objected to Washington's emphasis on vocational training and economic advancement and argued that higher education and political agitation would win equality for blacks. According to August Meier, writing in the *Journal of Negro History*, those blacks who accepted Washington's "accommodation" doctrines "understood that through tact and indirection [Washington] hoped to secure the good will of the white man and the eventual recognition of the constitutional rights of American Negroes."

The contents of Washington's recently released private papers reinforce the latter interpretation of the educator's motives. These documents offer evidence that in spite of the cautious stance that he maintained publicly, Washington was covertly engaged in challenging racial injustices and in improving social and economic conditions for blacks. The prominence he gained by his placating demeanor enabled him to work surreptitiously against segregation and disenfranchisement and to win political appointments that helped advance the cause of racial equality. "In other words," Woodward posited, "he secretly attacked the racial settlement that he publicly sanctioned."

Among Washington's many published works is his autobiography *Up From Slavery*, a rousing account of his life from slave to eminent educator. Often referred to by critics as a classic, its style is simple, direct, and anecdotal. Like his numerous essays and speeches, *Up From Slavery* promotes his racial philosophy and, in Woodward's opinion, "presents [Washington's] experience mythically, teaches 'lessons' and reflects a sunny optimism about black life in America." Woodward added, "It was the classic American success story, 'the Horatio Alger myth in black.'" Praised lavishly and compared to Benjamin Franklin's *Autobiography*, *Up From Slavery* became a best-seller in the United States and was eventually translated into more than a dozen languages.

MEDIA ADAPTATIONS: Recordings—"Up From Slavery," read by Ossie Davis, Caedmon Records, 1976.

BIOGRAPHICAL/CRITICAL SOURCES:

BOOKS

Bontemps, Arna Wendell, *Young Booker: Booker T. Washington's Early Days*, Dodd, 1972.

Drinker, Frederick E., *Booker T. Washington: The Master Mind of a Child of Slavery*, National Publishing, 1915, reprinted, Negro Universities Press, 1970.

Harlan, Louis R., *Booker T. Washington: The Making of a Black Leader, 1856-1901*, Oxford University Press, 1972.

Harlan, Louis R., *Booker T. Washington: The Wizard of Tuskegee, 1901-1915*, Oxford University Press, 1983.

Hawkins, Hugh, editor, *Booker T. Washington and His Critics: The Problem of Negro Leadership*, Heath, 1962, 2nd edition, 1974.

Matthews, Basil Joseph, *Booker T. Washington, Educator and Interracial Interpreter*, 1948, reprinted, McGrath, 1969.

Meier, August, *Negro Thought in America, 1880-1915: Racial Ideologies in the Age of Booker T. Washington*, University of Michigan Press, 1963.

Scott, Emmett J. and Lyman Beecher Stowe, *Booker T. Washington, Builder of Civilization*, Doubleday, Page, 1916, reprinted, Kraus Reprint, 1972.

Spencer, Samuel R., Jr., *Booker T. Washington and the Negro's Place in American Life*, edited by Oscar Handlin, Little, Brown, 1955, reprinted, 1965.

Thornbrough, Emma Lou, editor, *Booker T. Washington*, Prentice-Hall, 1969.

Weisberger, Bernard A., *Booker T. Washington*, New American Library, 1972.

PERIODICALS

American Heritage, August, 1968.
American Historical Review, January, 1966, December, 1985.
Crisis, August, 1978, February, 1983.
Journal of American History, December, 1985.
Journal of Negro Education, fall, 1977.
Journal of Negro History, January, 1953, October, 1955, January, 1958, April, 1960, April, 1968, July, 1969.
Journal of Southern History, August, 1971, February, 1979, February, 1986.
Nation, November 18, 1915.
Negro History Bulletin, April, 1958.
New Republic, November 11, 1972, July 18, 1983.
New York Review of Books, August 9, 1973.
New York Times Book Review, March 4, 1973, May 22, 1983.
North American Review, August, 1901.
Phylon, September, 1976.
Social Education, May, 1968.

South Atlantic Quarterly, autumn, 1978.
Times Literary Supplement, April 13, 1973, November 15, 1974.

—*Sketch by Joanne M. Peters*

*   *   *

WASHINGTON, Mary Helen   1941-

PERSONAL: Born January 21, 1941, in Cleveland, Ohio; daughter of David C. and Mary Catherine (Dalton) Washington. *Education:* Notre Dame College, B.A., 1962; University of Detroit, M.A., 1966, Ph.D., 1976.

ADDRESSES: Office—Department of English, Boston Harbor College, University of Massachusetts, Boston, Mass. 02125.

CAREER: High school teacher of English in the public schools of Cleveland, Ohio, 1962-64; St. John College, Cleveland, instructor in English, 1966-68; University of Detroit, Detroit, Mich., assistant professor of English, 1972-75, director of Center for Black Studies, beginning 1975; currently associate professor of English, Boston Harbor College, University of Massachusetts, Boston. Bunting fellow, Radcliffe College.

MEMBER: National Council of Teachers of English, College Language Association, Michigan Black Studies Association.

AWARDS, HONORS: Richard Wright Award for Literary Criticism from *Black World,* 1974.

WRITINGS:

(Editor and author of introduction) *Black-Eyed Susans: Classic Stories By and About Black Women,* Doubleday, 1975.
(Editor and author of introduction and critical notes) *Midnight Birds: Stories by Contemporary Black Women Writers,* Doubleday, 1980 (published in England as *Any Woman's Blues: Stories by Black Women Writers,* Virago Press, 1980).
(Editor and author of introduction and critical notes) *Invented Lives: Narratives of Black Women, 1860-1960,* Doubleday, 1987.

Contributor of articles and reviews to *Negro Digest* and *Black World.*

SIDELIGHTS: Mary Helen Washington is the editor and author of introduction and critical notes of three valued anthologies containing the work of some of the best black women writers. In reviews of all three books, *Black-Eyed Susans: Classic Stories By and About Black Women, Midnight Birds: Stories by Contemporary Black Women Writers,* and *Invented Lives: Narratives of Black Women, 1860-1960,* reviewers have praised Washington for expertly assembling unique and sensitive stories describing the life and plight of black women.

Black-Eyed Susans, Washington's first anthology, presents the writing of such authors as Toni Cade Bambara, Gwendolyn Brooks, Louise Meriwether, Toni Morrison, Jean Wheeler Smith, and Alice Walker. Joyce Carol Oates writes in *Ms.* that *Black-Eyed Susans* "constitutes an indictment of stereotyped thinking." Oates goes on to state that "no one has been so misunderstood, perhaps, as the black woman: she has been defined by others, whether white writers or black men writers, always seen from the outside, ringed in by convenient stereotypes. . . . What strikes the reader who comes to most of these stories for the first time is the wide range of their humanity. All the protagonists are black women: they are *black* women, black *women,* and fiercely individualistic *persons.* And the

fiction that presents them is of a high order, the product of painstaking craftsmanship. There is much anger, and no little despair and heartbreak, but emotion has been kept under control; each of the stories is a work of art, moving and convincing."

Marlene Veach writes in *Best Sellers* that Washington's second book, *Midnight Birds,* "is a collection of stories that revolt against ideologies and attitudes that impress women into servitude. It deals with the real lives and actual experiences of black women, in the hope of demolishing racial and sexual stereotypes." And Margaret Atwood writes in a *Harvard Review* of *Midnight Birds* that "this is American writing at its finest, by turns earthy, sinuous, thoughtful, and full of power." Atwood continues to explain that the writers included in this collection, Toni Cade Bambara, Alexis De Veaux, Gayl Jones, Toni Morrison, Ntozake Shange, Alice Walker, and others, "know exactly whom they are writing for. They are writing for other black American women, and they believe in the power of their words. They see themselves as giving a voice to the voiceless. They perceive writing as the forging of saving myths, the naming of forgotten pasts, the telling of truths."

According to publicity material released by the publisher, Anchor Press, each contribution to *Midnight Birds* was "chosen to reflect the efforts of black women to liberate themselves from the structures and constraints of the past. These are not stories about victims but positive stories of and by those women who have provided models of how to live."

In *Invented Lives* Washington chose to highlight the work of ten women, including Harriet Jacobs, Frances E.W. Harper, Zora Neale Hurston, and Dorothy West, who wrote between the years of 1860 and 1960. Washington stated in a *New York Times Book Review* interview conducted by Rosemary L. Bray that "a lot of people think the tradition of black women writing began in the last 20 years. In fact, black women have been writing about their experiences in America for more than 200 years. . . . I found black women working as domestics, writers, migrant farmers, artists, secretaries—and having economic and personal problems centering around these jobs."

Henry Louis Gates, Jr. comments in the *New York Times Book Review* that in each author's selection "we hear a black woman *testifying* about what the twin scourges of sexism and racism, merged into one oppressive entity, actually *do* to a human being, how the combination confines the imagination, puzzles the will and delimits free choice. What unites these essays, short stories and novel excerpts is their common themes: 'Their literature is about black women; it takes the trouble to record the thoughts, words, feelings, and deeds of black women, experiences that make the realities of being black in America look very different from what men have written.'"

Although the contributors to Washington's anthologies are all of black heritage, their tales can be understood and felt by all women. For example, calling Washington's second book, *Midnight Birds,* "a book that is difficult to fault," Buchi Emecheta remarks in the *Washington Post* that this book "speaks through its admirable selection of stories to black women in particular and to all women in general. The message is clear: it is about time we women start to talking to each other, the white to the black, the black American to her African sister, ironing out our differences. For as Toni Morrison said, 'Because when you don't have a woman to really talk to, whether it be an aunt or a sister or a friend, that is the real loneliness.'"

BIOGRAPHICAL/CRITICAL SOURCES:

PERIODICALS

America, January 31, 1981.
Best Sellers, August, 1980.
Harvard Review, February, 1981.
Library Journal, January 15, 1980.
Ms., March, 1976, July, 1980.
New York Times Book Review, October 4, 1987.
Publishers Weekly, December 3, 1979.
Times Literary Supplement, October 30, 1981.
Washington Post, June 3, 1980.

*   *   *

WATKINS, Frances Ellen
See HARPER, Frances Ellen Watkins

*   *   *

WEATHERLY, Tom   1942-

PERSONAL: Born November 3, 1942, in Scottsboro, Ala.; son of Thomas Elias (a teacher) and Lucy Belle (Golson) Weatherly; divorced; children: Regina, Thomas Elias III. *Education:* Attended Morehouse College, 1958-61, Alabama Agricultural and Mechanical College (now University), 1961. *Politics:* "Oxymoronic conservative." *Religion:* Jewish.

ADDRESSES: Home—286 East Second Ave., Apt. A, New York, N.Y. 10009.

CAREER: Poet. Rutgers University, Newark, N.J., adjunct instructor in art, 1969-70, instructor in creative writing, summer, 1970; Bishop College, Dallas, Tex., poet-in-residence, 1970-71; Morgan State College, Baltimore, Md., poet-in-residence, 1971-72; E. S. Webb School, Westchester, N.Y., teacher of poetry, 1972; St. Mark's Church, New York, N.Y., teacher of creative writing, beginning 1972. Conductor of several poetry workshops, including Afro-Hispanic Poets' Workshop, 1967-68, Natural Process Workshop, and East Harlem for Teachers' and Writers' Collaborative, 1968-69. *Military service:* U.S. Marine Corps, 1961.

MEMBER: Guild of Order (poetry association; governor-general, 1988-89).

AWARDS, HONORS: Three grants from National Endowment for the Arts to support poetry workshops.

WRITINGS:

POETRY

Maumau American Cantos, Corinth Books, 1970.
Thumbprint, Telegraph (Philadelphia), 1971.
(Editor with Ted Wilentz, and contributor) *Natural Process: An Anthology of New Black Poetry,* Hill & Wang, 1971.
Climate (bound with *Stream,* by Ken Bluford), Middle Earth Books, 1972.

CONTRIBUTOR TO ANTHOLOGIES

The Poetry of Black America: An Anthology of the Twentieth Century, edited by Arnold Adoff, Harper, 1973.
America: A Prophecy, edited by George Quasha and Jerome Rothenberg, Vintage Books, 1973.

OTHER

Contributor to *Village Voice, For Now,* and *Phoenix* (Boston-area newspaper).

SIDELIGHTS: Besides in his books of poetry and contributions to anthologies and periodicals, Tom Weatherly also spreads his message representing the black experience in poetic form through his teaching in elementary and secondary schools and in his poetry workshops. Evelyn Hoard Roberts writes in the *Dictionary of Literary Biography:* "Seeking to interpret the human condition by particularizing the black experience, [Weatherly] has recognized African culture as the heritage of American blacks who have been brought to the Western world via the indentured servants and slaves who struggled through emancipation, reconstruction, and the American industrial revolution, and who are now engaged in social revolution. Weatherly, like poets Countee Cullen, Langston Hughes, and Amiri Baraka (LeRoi Jones), has made a dynamic contribution to Afro-American literature."

BIOGRAPHICAL/CRITICAL SOURCES:

BOOKS

Dictionary of Literary Biography, Volume 41: *Afro-American Poets since 1955,* Gale, 1986.

*   *   *

WELBURN, Ron(ald Garfield)   1944-

PERSONAL: Born April 30, 1944, in Berwyn, Pa.; stepson of Howard (a welder) and Jessie W. Watson; married Eileen D. Millett, August 21, 1971. *Education:* Lincoln University, Lincoln University, Pa., B.A., 1968; University of Arizona, M.A., 1970; New York University, Ph.D., 1983.

ADDRESSES: Home—Box 692, Guilderland, N.Y. 12084. *Office*—Poets & Writers, New York, N.Y.; and Institute of Jazz Studies, Rutgers University, Newark, N.J. 08903.

CAREER: File clerk in New York, N.Y., and Philadelphia, Pa., 1962-64; Lincoln University, Lincoln University, Pa., instructor in humanities, summer, 1968; Syracuse University, Syracuse, N.Y., assistant professor of Afro-American studies, 1970-75; Rutgers University, New Brunswick, N.J., formerly affiliated with Institute for Jazz Studies, assistant professor of English, fall, 1983. Visiting lecturer, Auburn Correctional Facility, 1972; adjunct teacher at Onondaga Community College, 1972-73, State University College at Oneonta, fall, 1973, City College of the City University of New York, summers, 1977-79, LaGuardia Community College, 1978, Hofstra University, 1978, Center for Labor Studies, 1978-79, Rutgers University, 1978-80, Bloomfield College, 1982-83, and Russell Sage-Junior College at Albany, 1984-85. Writer-in-residence at Lincoln University, 1973-74, Hartley House, 1982, and Schenectady County Public Library, 1985.

AWARDS, HONORS: Silvera Award for poetry from Lincoln University, 1967 and 1968; fellow, Smithsonian Institute and Music Critics Association, 1975; Langston Hughes Legacy Certificate from Lincoln University, 1981.

WRITINGS:

Peripheries: Selected Poems, 1966-1968, Greenfield Review Press, 1972.
Brownup: Selected Poems, Greenfield Review Press, 1977.
The Look in the Night Sky: Poems, BkMk Press, 1978.
Heartland: Selected Poems, Lotus Press, 1981.

Contributor of poetry, fiction, book reviews, and music reviews to *Giant Talk, Groundswell, Abraxas, Nickel Review, Coda, Jazz Times, Down Beat, Black World, Black Fire,*

Greenfield Review, Intro, and other periodicals. Co-founding editor, *Grackle,* 1976.

WORK IN PROGRESS: Stories of the Indian-Black color line; several poetry and short fiction manuscripts.

SIDELIGHTS: Ron Welburn commented: "Important to my career and development are a Pennsylvania oral tradition of several generations, a semi-rural sensibility and love of nature, a love of music, and a love-hate regard for urban life. I began writing as an undergraduate in the midst of an Afro-American sense of being; however, I believe my writing has always been subtly informed and shaped by a strong childhood awareness of an American Indian heritage and therefore a mixed-blood sense of self. Since the mid-1970s my creative writings increasingly probe the facets of life on the Indian-Black color line. And while I wear glasses, I am proud of my ability to see long distances. Most prominent influences have been Twain, Cicero, Levertov, the *Anthology of Negro Poets* on Folkways, Aiken, Eliot, William Carlos Williams's school, U'Tamsi, Faulkner. I am not very political. The current literary scene has some fine people as well as various levels of sharecroppers, brokers, martyrs, henchmen and women, hit men and women, left- and right-wing secret societies, and meetings and cliques. Small presses continue to salvage the works of this country's better writers. I'm partial to the *Greenfield Review.*

"I write to confront questions of the inner self and the world at large. Perversely I enjoy the special selfishness of artistic creation; I hope someone will gain insights about the self and the world in what I do. Everywhere I've traveled, in this country and abroad, I've met someone who's expressed appreciation for something of mine they've read. That's something to show for an 'obscure' career, something that money can't buy."

AVOCATIONAL INTERESTS: Musical composition, chess, bird watching, squash, hiking.

*   *   *

WESLEY, Richard (Errol) 1945-

PERSONAL: Born July 11, 1945, in Newark, N.J.; son of George Richard (a laborer) and Gertrude (Thomas) Wesley; married Valerie Wilson, May 22, 1972; children: Thembi, Nandi (daughters). *Education:* Howard University, B.F.A., 1967.

ADDRESSES: Office—Elegba Productions, P.O. Box 43091, Upper Montclair, N.J. 07043; and Jay D. Kramer, 36 East 61st St., New York, N.Y. 10021. *Agent*—Phil Gersh Agency, 130 West 42nd St., New York, N.Y. 10036.

CAREER: Playwright and screenwriter. United Airlines, Newark, N.J., passenger service agent, 1967-69; currently president of Elegba Productions, Upper Montclair, N.J. Member and playwright in residence with Ed Bullins and J. E. Gaines, New Lafayette Theatre, 1969-73. Guest lecturer in black theatre and film, Manhattanville College, 1975; guest lecturer in black art and creative writing, Manhattan Community College, 1980-81 and 1982-83. Member of board of directors, Theatre of Universal Images (Newark), and of Frank Silvera Writer's Workshop (New York), 1974-82. Member of selection committee for Black Film Festival, Newark, 1982—.

MEMBER: Writers Guild of America East.

AWARDS, HONORS: Outstanding Playwright Award, Samuel French, 1965, for "Put My Dignity on 307"; Drama Desk Award for Outstanding Playwrighting, 1972, for "The Black Terror"; Rockefeller grant, 1973; Image Award, NAACP, 1974,

for *The Sirens,* "The Past Is the Past," and "Goin' thru Changes," and 1977, for *The Mighty Gents.*

WRITINGS:

PLAYS

"Put My Dignity on 307," first produced in Washington, D.C., at Howard University, 1967.

"The Streetcorner," first produced in Seattle, Wash., at Black Arts/West, 1970, produced in New York at Lincoln Center Plaza, summer, 1972.

"Headline News," first produced in New York at the Black Theatre Workshop, 1970.

"Knock Knock, Who Dat," first produced in New York at Theatre Black, University of the Streets, October 1, 1970.

"The Black Terror," (first produced at Howard University, February, 1971; produced in New York at the Public Theatre, November, 1971), published in *New Lafayette Theatre Presents the Complete Plays and Aesthetic Comments by Six Black Playwrights,* edited by Ed Bullins, Doubleday, 1974.

"Gettin' It Together" (one act; also see below; first produced in Roxbury, Mass., at the Elma Lewis School of Fine Arts, May 13, 1971; produced in New York at the Public Theatre, 1972), published in *The Best Short Plays 1980,* edited by Stanley Richards, Chilton, 1980.

"Strike Heaven on the Face," first produced in New York at the Lyceum Theatre, January 15, 1973.

"Goin' thru Changes" (one-act), first produced in Waterford, Conn., at the Eugene O'Neill Memorial Theatre Center, 1974; produced in New York at the Billie Holliday Theatre, 1974.

The Sirens (first produced in New York at the Manhattan Theatre Club, 1974), Dramatists Play Service, 1975.

"The Past Is the Past" (one-act; also see below; first produced in Waterford, Conn. at the Eugene O'Neill Memorial Theatre Center, August 1, 1974; produced in New York at the Billie Holliday Theatre, 1974), published in *The Best Short Plays of 1975,* edited by Stanley Richards, Chilton, 1975.

The Mighty Gents (first produced in Waterford, Conn., at the Eugene O'Neill Memorial Theatre Center, 1974; produced as "The Last Street Play" in New York at the Urban Art Corps and the Manhattan Theatre Club, 1977; restaged under original title on Broadway at the Ambassador Theatre, April 16, 1978), Dramatists Play Service, 1979.

"The Past Is the Past" and "Gettin' It Together": Two Plays, Dramatists Play Service, 1979.

"The Dream Team," first produced in Chester, Ct., at the Goodspeed Opera House, 1984.

Also author of unproduced plays, "Springtime High," 1968, and "Another Way," 1969.

SCREENPLAYS AND TELEPLAYS

"Uptown Saturday Night," First Artists Corp., 1974.

"Let's Do it Again" (sequel to "Uptown Saturday Night"), First Artists Corp., 1975.

"The House of Digs Drear" (teleplay), Public Broadcasting Service, 1984.

"Fast Forward" (based on story by Timothy March), Columbia Pictures, 1985.

"Native Son" (based on novel of same title by Richard Wright), Cinecom, 1986.

OTHER

(Author of book) "On the Road to Babylon" (musical), first produced in Milwaukee, Wis., at the Todd Wehr Theatre, December 14, 1979.

Contributor to *Black World* and *Black Creation*. Managing editor, *Black Theatre Magazine*, 1969-73.

SIDELIGHTS: Richard Wesley once remarked that his writings are "inspired primarily by social and political conditions in the United States." Steven R. Carter observes in the *Dictionary of Literary Biography* that Wesley bridges "the two forms of black theater in the 1960s and 1970s, the militant theater and the theater of experience," adding that he "has made significant contributions to both." Recognizing most of Wesley's plays to be "sensitive, emphatic depictions of blacks who have either escaped from or remained fixed in various self-imprisoning and self-mutilating patterns of behavior arising from oppression," Carter notes that Wesley also expresses his talent in screenwriting. "All in all," says Carter, "Wesley is among the most versatile and perceptive Afro-American dramatists and scriptwriters."

"The Black Terror," first produced in 1971, brought Wesley recognition and earned him a Drama Desk Award. The play is about a black revolutionary group committed to violence. The protagonist, who has been trained in guerrilla warfare in Vietnam by the army, joins the group and becomes its assassin, but "begins to question their eagerness to die to demonstrate their revolutionary fervor," writes Carter. Troubled by the necessity of violence, his conflict is compounded when he is ordered to kill a black political moderate. Carter considers it "a powerful political statement urging black revolutionaries to abandon the rhetoric and practice of revolutionary suicide and to pay more attention to the concrete realities of black life in the United States in shaping their tactics." Calling it "grim and gripping" and "a thoughtful play that will annoy many people," Clive Barnes praises its objectivity and continues in the *New York Times:* "This is a remarkable and provocative play—the kind of political play that needs to be written and demands to be seen by black and white alike." Carter finds that the play "amply demonstrated Wesley's skill in dramatizing ideas, giving them an urgency, appeal, and impact that audiences cannot easily leave behind."

Wesley's "The Past Is the Past," which Carter deems his "finest short play," is about a father who coincidentally meets the illegitimate son he had abandoned twenty years earlier. He is "acutely aware of his son's identity and provides painful, honest answers to the boy's questions while striving to keep an emotional distance from him," says Carter. The critic adds that it is apparent that the answers reveal that the father "has reflected a great deal about the past without being able to overcome its effects and that he regards his own experience as typical of black men of his generation." In *Nation*, Harold Clurman states that "without recrimination there is a fiber of understanding between the two." And Edith Oliver, who feels the play may become a classic on the theme of mutual recognition and acceptance between father and son, declares that "the play is entirely about feelings, and it is written with a combination of strength and delicacy and craftsmanship that adds up to perfection."

Wesley's *The Mighty Gents* is about "the adult, drifting survivors of a youth gang in Newark's black ghetto," writes Richard Eder in the *New York Times*, adding that "ten years later they are trapped in poverty and lethargy; they spend their time sitting around aimlessly, drinking and engaging in ritualized horseplay." Carter observes that "they are all losers with only the memory of past 'wins' in gang fights to sustain their self-respect." And the protagonist, says Carter, believes that he and the other gang members can regain their past glory by "beating up and robbing a small-time gangster . . . who had once belonged to a rival gang." Although Eder thinks that the play "has some diffuseness and some uninspired and commonplace passages," he nonetheless finds it "moving and impressive." And Carter, who considers it "Wesley's finest work," explains that it is "filled with complex, intriguing characterizations, intricate, haunting symbolism, powerful poetic language, and searing, unforgettable insights." Describing the play as "poignant" and "truthful," Mel Gussow maintains in the *New York Times* that "Wesley is a natural playwright, with a great gift for creating character, evoking atmosphere and using dialogue and gestures as motifs."

Wesley debuted as a screenwriter with the comedy "Uptown Saturday Night" featuring Sidney Poitier, Bill Cosby, Harry Belafonte, Flip Wilson, and Richard Pryor. The film follows the adventures of two men who "sneak off from their wives for the first time and, during their one and only visit to an after-hours gambling club, are robbed of a $50,000 winning lottery ticket," writes Carter. The film's success led to a sequel, "Let's Do It Again," which Wesley also wrote. More recently, Wesley has written the screenplay for Richard Wright's classic novel, *Native Son*, about a poor black youth who accidentally murders the daughter of his white employer. Some critics believe that the film version, which features Victor Love and Oprah Winfrey, does not capture the novel's moral complexity. Richard Harrington, for instance, suggests in the *Washington Post* that Wesley fails to overcome "the central challenge posed by Wright's book, in which Bigger's complexity—and the context for the controversy raging around him—is contained outside the dialogue." According to Harrington, "Wesley's script is simply too literal." On the other hand, critics also acknowledge the difficulties inherent in the task of distilling such a classic into a two-hour film. While calling it a "magnanimous, modestly budgeted, morally medicinal adaptation," Rita Kempley concludes in the *Washington Post* that the film "is as worthy as it is self-righteous."

In addition to his screenwork, says Megan Rosenfeld in the *Washington Post*, Wesley "continues to work on several plays exploring his generation of middle-class black college graduates." Wesley refers to this generation, says Rosenfeld, as "the most spoiled of the 20th century." The deprivation and upheaval endured by the parents of this generation during the Great Depression and the war that followed resulted in a material wealth provided the children that had been denied the parents. Calling him a "thoughtful and serious man, always curious about how people think," Rosenfeld observes that Wesley "wants his plays to lead audiences to make their own choices, and believes that art must have a purpose to justify itself." Wesley strives to project in his work the idea that success is achieved through discipline: "Sometimes I meet people who are still stuck in 'black is beautiful.' The thing is, like, so what? So we're beautiful, now what? You can't use racism as an excuse any more for not doing anything. It's been like that for 400 years, so what? It's a racist society, and you have two alternatives: You can move ahead or you die."

BIOGRAPHICAL/CRITICAL SOURCES:

BOOKS

Contemporary Literary Criticism, Volume 7, Gale, 1977.

Dictionary of Literary Biography, Volume 38: *Afro-American Writers after 1955: Dramatists and Prose Writers,* Gale, 1985.

Fabre, Genevieve, *Drumbeats, Masks and Metaphor: Contemporary Afro-American Theater,* Harvard University Press, 1983.

Hughes, Catherine, *Plays, Politics and Polemics,* Drama Book Specialists, 1973.

PERIODICALS

Black Creation, winter, 1973.
Black World, April, 1972, July, 1973.
Los Angeles Times, November 13, 1978, January 26, 1983.
Nation, May 17, 1975.
New Yorker, January 28, 1974.
New York Times, November 11, 1971, November 21, 1971, April 25, 1977, April 18, 1978, February 15, 1985, December 23, 1986.
Show Business, May 23, 1974.
Variety, April 26, 1972.
Washington Post, November 16, 1982, November 19, 1982, January 16, 1987.

—Sketch by Sharon Malinowski

*   *   *

WHITE, Edgar (B.) 1947-

PERSONAL: Born April 4, 1947, in Montserrat, British West Indies; came to United States, 1952; son of Charles and Phyllis White. *Education:* Attended City College of the City University of New York, 1964-65; New York University, B.A., 1968; additional study at Yale University, 1971-73. *Politics:* "Rastafarian." *Religion:* "Rastafarian."

ADDRESSES: Home—6 Baalbee Rd., London N.5, England. *Office*—24 Bond St., New York, N.Y. 10003.

CAREER: Musician, playwright, and novelist. Playwright-in-residence at Yale University Drama School, 1971-72, and at New York Shakespeare Festival Public Theatre. Artistic director of acting company, Yardbird Players Co., 1974-77; member of Black Theatre Alliance.

MEMBER: Authors Guild.

AWARDS, HONORS: O'Neill playwright award; grants from Rockefeller Foundation, 1974, New York State Council on the Arts, 1975, Creative Artists Public Service, and National Endowment for the Arts.

WRITINGS:

PLAYS

"The Figures at Chartres," first produced Off-Broadway at the New York Shakespeare Festival Public Theatre, January 24, 1969.

Underground: Four Plays (contains "The Burghers of Calais" [first produced in Boston at Theatre Company of Boston, March 24, 1971; produced in Brooklyn at Billie Holiday Theatre, 1972], "Fun in Lethe; or, The Feast of Misrule," "The Mummer's Play" [first produced Off-Broadway at the New York Shakespeare Festival Public Theatre, 1965], and "The Wonderful Yeare" [first produced in New York at Other Stage Theatre, October 24, 1969]), Morrow, 1970.

"Seigismundo's Tricycle: A Dialogue of Self and Soul," first produced Off-Broadway at the New York Shakespeare Festival Public Theatre, April, 1971.

"Transformations: A Church Ritual," first produced Off-Broadway at the New York Shakespeare Festival Public Theatre, April 23, 1972.

The Crucificado: Two Plays (contains "The Crucificado" [first produced in New Haven, Conn. at Yale Repertory Theatre, January, 1972; produced in New York City at Vinnette Carroll's Urban Art Corps, June 13, 1972], and "The Life and Times of J. Walter Smintheus" [first produced Off-Broadway at Theatre DeLys, December 7, 1970]), Morrow, 1973.

"La Gente," first produced at the New York Shakespeare Festival, July 18, 1973.

"Ode to Charlie Parker," first produced in New York City at Studio Rivbea, September, 1973.

"Offering for Nightworld," first produced in Brooklyn at Brooklyn Academy of Music, 1973.

"Les Femmes Noires," first produced Off-Broadway at the New York Shakespeare Festival Public Theatre, February 21, 1974.

"The Pygmies and the Pyramid," first produced in New York City at Yardbird Theatre Co., August, 1976.

"The Defense," first produced in New York City at New Federal Theatre, November 11, 1976.

Lament for Rastafari and Other Plays (contains "Lament for Rastafari" [first produced in Brooklyn at Billie Holiday Theatre, 1971], "Trinity—The Long and Cheerful Road to Slavery" [first produced in London at Riverside Studio, February 25, 1982; produced Off-Broadway at Henry Street Playhouse, 1987], and "Like Them That Dream" [first produced in Albany, N.Y. at Market Theater, 1987; produced Off-Broadway at Theater Four, 1988]), Marion Boyars, 1983.

Nine Night and Ritual by Water, Methuen, 1984.

Redemption Song, Marion Boyars, 1985.

NOVELS

Sati, the Rastifarian, Lothrop, 1973.
Omar at Christmas, Lothrop, 1973.
Children of Night, Lothrop, 1974.
The Rising, Marion Boyars, 1988.

CONTRIBUTOR TO ANTHOLOGIES

What We Must See: Young Black Storytellers, edited by Orde Coombs, Dodd, 1971.
Black Review No. 1, edited by Mel Watkins, Morrow, 1971.
Black Short Story Anthology, edited by Woodie King, Jr., Columbia University Press, 1972.
Yardbird Lives!, edited by Ishmael Reed and Al Young, Grove, 1978.

OTHER

The Yardbird Reader, privately printed, 1973.

Also contributor to journals, including *Liberator* and *Scripts.*

SIDELIGHTS: Edgar White began his writing career at an early age. At sixteen White wrote his first drama, "The Mummer's Play." This work was produced at the Shakespeare Festival Public Theatre in 1965 when White was just eighteen. Since that time White has written numerous books and many plays. Over sixteen of these plays have been produced.

Steven Carter writes in the *Dictionary of Literary Biography* that White's work "abounds in irony, literary allusions, wit, and techniques inspired by an impressive knowledge of European, Oriental, African, and American drama. [White] has come to stress, coolly and symbolically, the importance of his black roots and the need to strike down white supremacy, even if it is only one absurdity in an absurd world.''

BIOGRAPHICAL/CRITICAL SOURCES:

BOOKS

Dictionary of Literary Biography, Gale, Volume 38: *Afro-American Writers after 1955: Dramatists and Prose Writers*, 1985.

Fabre, Genevieve, *Drumbeats, Masks and Metaphors: Contemporary Afro-American Theatre*, Harvard University Press, 1983.

Harrison, Paul Carter, *The Drama of Nommo*, Grove, 1972.

PERIODICALS

New York Times, December 3, 1986, April 6, 1988.
Times (London), April 15, 1983, October 16, 1985.

* * *

WHITE, Walter
 See WHITE, Walter F(rancis)

* * *

WHITE, Walter F(rancis)   1893-1955
 (Walter White)

PERSONAL: Born July 1, 1893, in Atlanta, Ga.; died of a heart attack, March 21, 1955, in New York, N.Y.; son of George (a postal worker) and Madeline (a teacher; maiden name, Harrison) White; married Leah Gladys Powell (a secretary), February 15, 1922 (divorced in 1949); married Poppy Cannon, July 6, 1949; children: (first marriage) Jane, Walter Carl Darrow. *Education:* Atlanta University, B.A., 1916; graduate study at College of the City of New York (now City College of the City University of New York). *Politics:* Democrat. *Religion:* Congregational.

CAREER: Insurance salesman in Atlanta, Ga., 1916-18; National Association for the Advancement of Colored People (NAACP), New York City, assistant secretary, 1918-29, acting secretary, 1929-30, secretary, 1931-55. War correspondent for *New York Post* in European, Mediterranean, Middle East, and Pacific theaters, 1943-45; columnist for newspapers, including *Chicago Defender* and Sunday *Herald Tribune*. Delegate to Second Pan-African Congress, 1921; member of advisory council for the Government of the Virgin Islands, 1934-35; member of governor's committee on the constitutional convention in New York state, 1938; member of executive committee of National Committee for Prevention and Control of Juvenile Delinquency, 1947, and of National Health Assembly, 1948; member of New York mayor's advisory committee on atomic education and committee for commemoration of the golden anniversary of New York, both 1948; member of American Committee on Economic Policy. Consultant to U.S. presidents, including Franklin D. Roosevelt and Harry S. Truman, to United Nations (U.N.) Conference on International Organizations, 1945, and to U.S. delegation to U.N. General Assembly, Paris, France, 1948. Member of board of visitors of New York State Training School for Boys, 1933.

MEMBER: P.E.N. (American Center).

AWARDS, HONORS: Guggenheim fellowship, 1927-28; award for literature from Harmon Foundation, 1929; Spingarn Medal from NAACP, 1937; Sir James Jeans Award from New Lon-

don Junior College, 1943; Order of Honor and Merit (Haiti), 1950; Star of Ethiopia, 1953; LL.D. from Howard University, 1939, and Atlanta University, 1943.

WRITINGS:

The Fire in the Flint (novel), Knopf, 1924, reprinted, Negro Universities Press, 1969.
(Under name Walter White) *Flight* (novel), Knopf, 1926, reprinted, Negro Universities Press, 1969.
(Under name Walter White) *Rope and Faggot: A Biography of Judge Lynch*, Knopf, 1929, reprinted, Arno Press, 1969.
(Under name Walter White, with Thurgood Marshall) *What Caused the Detroit Riot?* National Association for the Advancement of Colored People, 1943.
(Under name Walter White) *A Rising Wind* (essays), Doubleday, Doran & Co., 1945, reprinted, Negro Universities Press, 1971.
(Under name Walter White) *A Man Called White: The Autobiography of Walter White*, Viking, 1948.
How Far the Promised Land? Viking, 1955.

Contributor to periodicals.

SIDELIGHTS: Walter F. White, who worked for the National Association for the Advancement of Colored People (NAACP) for more than thirty years, was ''probably the most stentorian advocate of the Negro's rights'' in the United States, commented E. J. Kahn, Jr., in a 1948 *New Yorker* profile. Less than one-quarter Negro by blood, White had light skin, blue eyes, and blond hair but chose to remain in black society, in which he had grown up. He was able to cross the color line at will and frequently posed as a white to gather information in his fight against lynching, segregation, and other discrimination. ''The ranking Negro diplomat,'' according to Kahn, White was ''one of the ablest lobbyists in the Capital.'' His findings and achievements became the basis of several fiction and nonfiction books.

In his first ten years with the NAACP White investigated lynchings in the guise of a white reporter, gathering eyewitness accounts of more than forty incidents of mob violence and putting the information to use in his books. Observed Kahn: White ''could gain the confidence of Southern Negroes because he had been conditioned by a boyhood in the colored section of Atlanta [Georgia]. He could hobnob with Southern whites because of his outward resemblance to them and because of a genuine Georgia accent that precluded their suspecting him of being a prying agitator from up North.'' The evidence he uncovered suggested, as he wrote in *Rope and Faggot: A Biography of Judge Lynch*, that such violence had become ''an almost integral part of our national folkways.'' White traced the origins of lynching to economics—a Southern attempt to put blacks back in their place as industrialization began to make slavery unnecessary—and to intolerance by religious fundamentalists. Writing for the *New York Times Book Review*, Florence Finch Kelly deemed *Rope and Faggot* ''a challenge to national self-complacency'' and commended its ''searching analysis'' of the causes of mob violence. In his novel *The Fire in the Flint* White presented another aspect of the subject, showing how the lynching of his brother rouses a complacent black doctor to active opposition of racism. A *New York Times Book Review* critic called it ''an inevitable novel [that] deserves serious consideration.''

Later in his career, especially after he became secretary of the NAACP, White addressed other concerns in his work and writings, notably discrimination in the armed forces, education, employment, and the arts. His book *A Rising Wind* discusses the conditions of black soldiers abroad during World War II, including their limited participation in active combat. White points out that dangerous combat situations cause race barriers to drop and that black soldiers returning home "will not be content to return to the old way of life in the post-war era," noted *New York Times Book Review* writer John Desmond. White's "reasoned and reserved contribution" to the challenge of improving race relations "deserves to be read," asserted Desmond.

A Man Called White and *How Far the Promised Land?* describe many of the efforts by White and the NAACP to improve conditions for blacks. White spoke personally with congressmen, senators, and presidents, urging them to promote legislation that would uphold and extend black rights, became involved in legal cases addressing discrimination, and lectured extensively to raise public awareness. In his autobiography, *A Man Called White,* he revealed the atrocities against blacks that he witnessed while growing up in black society as well as the progress that has been made. Remarked a *Times Literary Supplement* reviewer, White's autobiography "gains a great deal from being the story of a man who has seen both sides of the fence that separates the two 'races' in America, and who has been able to use his physical characteristics to further his work for the coming of a day when the passions, hatred, crimes and follies associated with 'race' will seem like a morbid memory." Morroe Berger, writing for the *New York Times Book Review,* deemed it "more than personal history" also. "It is part of the history of twentieth century America, a vivid account of the efforts to save democracy by widening its scope and securing its benefits to an increasing number of Americans." Summing up the posthumously published *How Far the Promised Land?,* Gerald W. Johnson wrote in the *New York Times Book Review:* "If there were no other reason this book would command attention as the last word of a man who was cast in the truly heroic mold. But there is another and even better reason—the book is a careful account by a close observer of one of the most remarkable achievements in human history, the rise of the American Negro."

White's accomplishments reflected what Kahn termed his "penchant for taking resolute action," his belief in making a "frontal attack" on discrimination of all kinds. Using lectures, political pressure, and his writings as weapons, he oversaw part of the fight in which "former chattels have climbed almost to the rank of first-class citizens, as far as the law is concerned," wrote Johnson. White's life stands as testimony to what can be achieved "in the tradition of militant democracy, seeking to enforce existing laws which promise equality and to secure further legislation in protection of the civil rights of all," affirmed Berger.

BIOGRAPHICAL/CRITICAL SOURCES:

BOOKS

Cannon, Poppy, *A Gentle Knight: My Husband, Walter White,* Rinehart, 1956.
Twentieth-Century Literary Criticism, Volume 15, Gale, 1985.
Waldron, Edward E., *Walter White and the Harlem Renaissance,* Kennikat Press, 1978.
White, Walter, *Rope and Faggot: A Biography of Judge Lynch,* Knopf, 1929, reprinted, Arno Press, 1969.
White, Walter, *A Man Called White: The Autobiography of Walter White,* Viking, 1948.

PERIODICALS

Commonweal, November 5, 1948.
New Yorker, September 4, 1948, September 11, 1948.
New York Times Book Review, September 14, 1924, April 11, 1926, May 12, 1929, March 4, 1945, September 26, 1948, November 6, 1955.
Times Literary Supplement, December 9, 1926, October 17, 1929, May 27, 1949.

—*Sketch by Polly A. Vedder*

*   *   *

WIDEMAN, John Edgar   1941-

PERSONAL: Born June 14, 1941, in Washington, D.C.; son of Edgar and Betty (French) Wideman; married Judith Ann Goldman, 1965; children: Daniel Jerome, Jacob Edgar, Jamila Ann. *Education:* University of Pennsylvania, B.A., 1963; New College, Oxford, B.Phil., 1966.

ADDRESSES: Office—Department of English, University of Wyoming, Laramie, Wyo. 82070.

CAREER: Howard University, Washington, D.C., teacher of American literature, summer, 1965; University of Pennsylvania, Philadelphia, 1966-74, began as instructor, professor of English, 1974, director of Afro-American studies program, 1971-73; University of Wyoming, Laramie, professor of English, 1975—. Made state department lecture tour of Europe and the Near East, 1976; Phi Beta Kappa lecturer, 1976; visiting writer and lecturer at numerous colleges and universities; has also served as administrator/teacher in a curriculum planning, teacher-training institute sponsored by National Defense Education Act. Assistant basketball coach, University of Pennsylvania, 1968-72. National Humanities Faculty consultant in numerous states; consultant to secondary schools across the country, 1968—.

MEMBER: National Humanities Faculty, Association of American Rhodes Scholars (member of board of directors and of state and national selection committees), Phi Beta Kappa.

AWARDS, HONORS: Received creative writing prize, University of Pennsylvania; Rhodes Scholar, Oxford University, 1963; Thouron fellow, Oxford University, 1963-66; Kent fellow, University of Iowa, 1966, to attend creative writing workshop; named member of Philadelphia Big Five Basketball Hall of Fame, 1974; Young Humanist fellow, 1975—; P.E.N./ Faulkner Award for fiction, 1984, for *Sent for You Yesterday;* John Dos Passos Prize for Literature from Longwood College, 1986.

WRITINGS:

A Glance Away (novel), Harcourt, 1967, reprinted, H. Holt, 1985.
Hurry Home (novel), Harcourt, 1970, reprinted, H. Holt, 1986.
The Lynchers (novel), Harcourt, 1973.
Damballah (also see below; short stories), Avon, 1981.
Hiding Place (also see below; novel), Avon, 1981.
Sent for You Yesterday (also see below; novel), Avon, 1983.
Brothers and Keepers (memoirs), H. Holt, 1984.
The Homewood Trilogy (includes *Damballah, Hiding Place,* and *Sent For You Yesterday*), Avon, 1985.
Reuben (novel), H. Holt, 1987.

Contributor of articles, short stories, book reviews, and poetry to periodicals, including *American Poetry Review, Negro Di-*

gest, Black American Literature Forum, Black World, American Scholar, Gentleman's Quarterly, New York Times Book Review, North American Review, and *Washington Post Book World.*

SIDELIGHTS: John Edgar Wideman has been hailed by Don Strachen in the *Los Angeles Times Book Review* as "the black Faulkner, the softcover Shakespeare." Such praise is not uncommon for this author, whose novel *Sent for You Yesterday* was selected as the 1984 P.E.N./Faulkner Award winner over works by Bernard Malamud, Cynthia Ozick, and William Kennedy. Wideman attended Oxford University in 1963 on a Rhodes scholarship, earned a degree in eighteenth-century literature, and later accepted a fellowship at the prestigious University of Iowa Writers' Workshop. Yet this "artist with whom any reader who admires ambitious fiction must sooner or later reckon," as the *New York Times* calls him, began his college career not as a writer, but as a basketball star. "I always wanted to play pro basketball—ever since I saw a ball and learned you could make money at it," he told Curt Suplee in the *Washington Post.* Recruited by the University of Pennsylvania for its team, Wideman first attended that school as a psychology major, attracted by the "mystical insight" he told Suplee that he thought the study would yield. When "it turned out to be rats" and clinical experiments, Wideman changed his major to English, while continuing to be mainly concerned with basketball. He played well enough to earn a place in the Philadelphia Big Five Basketball Hall of Fame, but, he told Suplee, as his time at the university drew to a close, "I knew I wasn't going to be able to get into the NBA [National Basketball Association]. What was left?" The Rhodes scholarship answered that question. Wideman began to concentrate on his writing rather than sports and did so with such success that his first novel, *A Glance Away,* was published just a year after he earned his degree from Oxford.

The story of a day in the life of a drug addict, *A Glance Away* reflects the harsh realities that Wideman saw and experienced during his youth in Pittsburgh's ghetto, Homewood. And, though the author has lived in Laramie, Wyoming, since 1975, later novels also described black urban experiences. He explained to Suplee, "My particular imagination has always worked well in a kind of exile. It fits the insider-outside view I've always had. It helps to write away from the center of the action."

Wideman's highly literate style is in sharp contrast to his gritty subject matter, and while reviews of his books have been generally favorable from the start of his writing career, some critics initially expressed the opinion that such a formal style was not appropriate for his stories of street life. For example, Anatole Broyard praises *The Lynchers* in his *New York Times* review, stating: "Though we have heard the themes and variations of violence before in black writing, 'The Lynchers' touches us in a more personal way, for John Edgar Wideman has a weapon more powerful than any knife or gun. His weapon is art. Eloquence is his arsenal, his arms cache. His prose, at its best, is a black panther, coiled to spring." But Broyard goes on to say that the book is not flawless: "Far from it. Mr. Wideman ripples too many muscles in his writing, often cannot seem to decide whether to show or snow us.... [He] is wordy, and 'The Lynchers' is as shaky in its structure as some of the buildings his characters inhabit. But he can *write,* and you come away from his book with the feeling that he is, as they say, very close to getting it all together." In the *New York Times,* John Leonard comments on the extensive use of literary devices in *The Lynchers:* "Flashback, flashforward, first person, third person, journals, identity exchange, interior

monologue, dreams (historical and personal), puns, epiphanies [are all used]. At times the devices seem a thicket through which one must hack one's weary way toward meanings arbitrarily obscure, a vegetable indulgence. But John Edgar Wideman is up to much more than storytelling.... He is capable of moving from ghetto language to Joyce with a flip of the page."

Saturday Review critic David Littlejohn agrees that Wideman's novels are very complex, and in his review of *Hurry Home* he criticizes those who would judge this author as a storyteller: "Reviewers ... are probably more responsible than anyone else for the common delusion that a novel is somehow contained in its discernible, realistic plot.... *Hurry Home* is primarily an experience, not a plot: an experience of words, dense, private, exploratory, and non-progressive." Littlejohn describes *Hurry Home* as a retelling of an American myth, that of "the lonely search through the Old World" for a sense of cultural heritage, which "has been the pattern of a hundred thousand young Americans' lives and novels." According to Littlejohn, Wideman's version is "spare and eccentric, highly stylized, circling, allusive, antichronological, far more consciously symbolic than most versions, than the usual self-indulgent and romantic works of this genre—and hence both more rewarding and more difficult of access." Reviewing the same book in the *New York Times Book Review,* Joseph Goodman states: "Many of its pages are packed with psychological insight, and nearly all reveal Mr. Wideman's formidable command of the techniques of fiction. Moreover, the theme is a profound one—the quest for a substantive sense of self.... The prose, paratactic and rich with puns, flows as freely as thought itself, giving us ... Joycean echoes.... It is a dazzling display.... We can have nothing but admiration for Mr. Wideman's talent."

Enthusiastic reviews such as these established Wideman's reputation in the literary world as a major talent. When his fourth and fifth books—*Damballah,* a collection of short stories, and *Hiding Place,* a novel—were issued originally as paperbacks, some critics, such as John Leonard and Mel Watkins, reacted with indignation. Leonard's *New York Times* review uses extensive quotes from the books to demonstrate Wideman's virtuosity, and states, "That [these] two new books will fall apart after a second reading is a scandal." Watkins's *New York Times Book Review* article on the two books, which were published simultaneously, has special praise for the short-story volume, and ends with a sentiment much like Leonard's on the books' binding. He writes: "In freeing his voice from the confines of the novel form, [Wideman] has written what is possibly his most impressive work.... Each story moves far beyond the primary event on which it is focused. The prose is labyrinthine—events and details merge and overlap.... Like [Jean] Toomer, Mr. Wideman has used a narrative laced with myth, superstition and dream sequences to create an elaborate poetic portrait of the lives of ordinary black people. And also like Toomer, he has written tales that can stand on their own, but that assume much greater impact collectively. The individual 'parts' or stories, as disparate as they may initially seem, form a vivid and coherent montage of black life over a period of five generations.... These books once again demonstrate that John Wideman is one of America's premier writers of fiction. That they were published originally in paperback perhaps suggests that he is also one of our most underrated writers." Actually, it was the author himself who had decided to bring the books out as original paperbacks. His reasons were philosophical and pragmatic. "I spend an enormous amount of time and energy writing and I want to write good books, but I also want people to read them,'' he explained to Edwin McDowell in the *New York Times*. Wideman's first three novels had been slow sellers ''in spite of enormously positive reviews,'' he told Suplee, and it was his hope that the affordability of paperbacks would help give him a wider readership, particularly among ''the people and the world I was writing about. A $15.95 novel had nothing to do with that world.''

Damballah and *Hiding Place* had both been set in Homewood, Wideman's early home, and in 1983 he published a third book with the same setting, *Sent for You Yesterday*. Critics were enthusiastic. ''In this hypnotic and deeply lyrical novel, Mr. Wideman again returns to the ghetto where he was raised and transforms it into a magical location infused with poetry and pathos,'' writes Alan Cheuse in the *New York Times Book Review*. ''The narration here makes it clear that both as a molder of language and a builder of plots, Mr. Wideman has come into his full powers,'' he continues. ''He has the gift of making 'ordinary' folks memorable. . . . Mr. Wideman establishes a mythological and symbolic link between character and landscape, language and plot, that in the hands of a less visionary writer might be little more than stale sociology.'' States Garett Epps in the *Washington Post Book World*, ''Wideman has a fluent command of the American language, written and spoken, and a fierce, loving vision of the people he writes about. Like Faulkner's, Wideman's prose fiction is vivid and demanding—shuttling unpredictably between places, narrators and times, dwelling for a paragraph on the surface of things, then sneaking a key event into a clause that springs on the reader like a booby trap. . . . *Sent for You Yesterday* is a book to be savored, read slowly again and again.''

When he ventured into nonfiction for the first time with his book *Brothers and Keepers,* Wideman continued to draw inspiration from the same source, Homewood. In this book, Wideman comes to terms with his brother Robby, younger by ten years, whose life was influenced by the street, its drugs, and its crime. The author writes, ''Even as I manufactured fiction from the events of my brother's life, from the history of the family that had nurtured us both, I knew something of a different order remained to be extricated. The fiction writer was a man with a real brother behind real bars [serving a life sentence in a Pennsylvania penitentiary].'' In his review in the *Washington Post Book World,* Jonathan Yardley calls *Brothers and Keepers* ''the elder Wideman's effort to understand what happened, to confess and examine his own sense of guilt about his brother's fate (and his own).'' The result, according to the reviewer, is ''a depiction of the inexorably widening chasm that divides middle-class black Americans from the black underclass.'' Wideman's personal experience, adds Yardley, also reveals that for the black person ''moving out of the ghetto into the white world is a process that requires excruciating compromises, sacrifices and denials, that leaves the person who makes the journey truly at home in neither the world he has entered nor the world he has left.''

Wideman has, however, made a home for himself in literary circles, and at the same time has learned from his experience to handle his success. When *Sent for You Yesterday* won the P.E.N./Faulkner Award—the only major literary award in this country to be judged, administered, and largely funded by writers—Wideman told Suplee he felt ''warmth. That's what I felt. Starting at the toes and filling up. A gradual recognition that it could be real.'' Still, the author maintained that if such an honor ''doesn't happen again for a long time—or never happens again—it really doesn't matter,'' because he ''learned

more and more that the process itself was important, learned to take my satisfaction from the writing'' during the years of comparative obscurity. ''I'm an old jock,'' he explained. ''So I've kind of trained myself to be low-key. Sometimes the crowd screams, sometimes the crowd doesn't scream.''

BIOGRAPHICAL/CRITICAL SOURCES:

BOOKS

Contemporary Literary Criticism, Volume 5, Gale, 1976.
Dictionary of Literary Biography, Volume 33: *Afro-American Fiction Writers After 1955*, Gale, 1984.
O'Brien, John, editor, *Interviews with Black Writers*, Liveright, 1973.

PERIODICALS

American Scholar, autumn, 1967.
Chicago Tribune Book World, December 23, 1984.
Journal of Negro History, January, 1963.
Los Angeles Times, November 11, 1987.
Los Angeles Times Book Review, April 17, 1983, December 23, 1984, December 29, 1985.
Michigan Quarterly Review, winter, 1975.
Negro Digest, May, 1963.
Newsweek, May 7, 1970.
New York Times, April 2, 1970, May 15, 1973, November 27, 1981, May 16, 1984, October 29, 1984, September 4, 1986.
New York Times Book Review, September 10, 1967, April 19, 1970, April 29, 1973, April 11, 1982, May 15, 1983, November 4, 1984, January 13, 1985, November 8, 1987.
Saturday Review, October 21, 1967, May 2, 1970.
Shenandoah, winter, 1974.
Times (London), December 6, 1984.
Times Literary Supplement, December 21, 1984, January 16, 1987.
Washington Post, May 10, 1984, May 12, 1984.
Washington Post Book World, July 3, 1983, October 21, 1984, November 15, 1987.

*   *   *

WILKINS, Roger (Wood) 1932-

PERSONAL: Born March 25, 1932, in Kansas City, Mo.; son of Earl Williams (a journalist) and Helen Natalie (a national board member of the Young Women's Christian Association [YWCA]; maiden name, Jackson) Wilkins; married Eve Estelle Tyler (a public service executive), June 16, 1956 (divorced, 1976); married May Meyers (a stained glass artist), April 4, 1977 (divorced, 1978); married Patricia King (a teacher of law), February 21, 1981; children: (first marriage) Amy T., David E.; (third marriage) Elizabeth W. C. *Education:* University of Michigan, A.B., 1953, LL.B., 1956. *Politics:* Democrat. *Religion:* Christian.

ADDRESSES: Office—c/o Institute for Policy Studies, 1901 Q St. N.W., Washington, D.C. 20009.

CAREER: Welfare worker in Cleveland, Ohio, 1957; admitted to the Bar of the State of New York, 1958; Delson & Gordon (law firm), New York City, attorney, 1958-62; Agency for International Development (AID), Washington, D.C., special assistant administrator, 1962-64; U.S. Department of Commerce, Washington, D.C., director of community relations, 1964-66; U.S. Department of Justice, Washington, D.C., assistant attorney general, 1966-69; Ford Foundation, New York City, program director and adviser to foundation president,

1969-72; *Washington Post,* Washington, D.C., member of editorial page staff, 1972-74; *New York Times,* New York City, member of editorial board, 1974-77, urban affairs columnist, 1977-79; *Nation,* New York City, member of editorial board, 1979—; *Washington Star,* Washington, D.C., associate editor, 1980-81; CBS-Radio, New York City, commentator for "Spectrum" program, 1980-83; Institute for Policy Studies, Washington, D.C., senior fellow, 1982—.

Member of board of directors of Washington, D.C., Family and Child Service, Arena Stage, New York City Cultural Council, National Association for the Advancement of Colored People (NAACP), and Legal Defense and Educational Fund, Inc.; member of board of visitors of University of Michigan Law School; member of board of trustees of African-American Institute, 1979—, and Fund for Investigative Journalism, 1981—; senior adviser to Jesse Jackson's presidential campaign, 1983-84; member of steering committee of Free South Africa Movement, 1984—; member of visiting committee of Afro-American Studies Program, Harvard University, 1984—.

MEMBER: American Academy of Public Administration, National Association for the Advancement of Colored People (NAACP), National Urban League, American Democratic Action, Committee on Policy for Racial Justice, Council on Foreign Relations.

AWARDS, HONORS: Marc Corporation senior fellow, 1971; cited by Pulitzer Prize committee, 1972, for editorial writing on the Watergate scandal; LL.D. from Central Michigan University, 1974; named to the Pulitzer Prize board, 1979; D.H.L. from Wilberforce University, 1982; Regents' Lectureship, University of California, 1985; Otis Lecturer, Wheaton College, 1985; Commonwealth Professor, George Mason University, 1985-86.

WRITINGS:

A Man's Life: An Autobiography, Simon & Schuster, 1982.

Contributor of articles to periodicals, including *Esquire, Foreign Policy, Fortune, Mother Jones, Nation, New Yorker,* and *Village Voice,* and to newspapers, including *Los Angeles Times, New York Times, Washington Post,* and *Washington Star.*

WORK IN PROGRESS: "A book assessing the strengths and weaknesses of Great Society programs, based primarily on the experiences and the insights of poor, black, inner-city residents who were the objects of those programs."

SIDELIGHTS: The only son of college-educated, middle-class black parents and nephew of former National Association for the Advancement of Colored People (NAACP) director Roy Wilkins, Roger Wilkins spent the early years of his childhood in Kansas City, Missouri, until his father died of tuberculosis when Wilkins was only eight years old. He and his mother then moved to New York City, where they lived with relatives in the Sugar Hill section of Harlem that was, according to Wilkins, "where blacks who had it made were said to have lived the sweet life." In 1943 his mother remarried and Wilkins became the stepson of a successful Grand Rapids, Michigan, doctor, living in an all-white neighborhood and attending an all-white school.

Wilkins "came from the genteel Negro middle class at a time when the popular image of blackness was raw, poverty-stricken, angry," wrote Joseph Sobran in a *National Review* assessment of Wilkins's book *A Man's Life: An Autobiography.* Painfully aware of the differences between him and his Grand Rapids

schoolmates, Wilkins relates that "with my friends in the north, race was never mentioned. Ever. I carried my race around with me like an open basket of rotten eggs. I knew I could drop one at any moment and it would explode with a stench over everything." He excelled in after-school football games with the neighborhood boys only because members of the opposing team would avoid him, afraid that he might be carrying a knife.

His efforts to gain acceptance as a black adolescent in a predominantly white setting also created cultural gaps between Wilkins and other blacks his age. By trying to demonstrate to the white world—socially and academically—that he was not inferior (a term the young Wilkins associated with blackness), he grew increasingly disdainful of and uncomfortable with his black peers: "One day I was standing outside the church trying, probably at my mother's urging, to make contact," Wilkins recalls in his book. "Conversational sallies flew around me while I stood there stiff and mute, unable to participate. Because the language was so foreign to me, I understood little of what was being said, but I did know that the word used for a white was *paddy.* Then a boy named Nickerson, the one whom my mother particularly wanted me to be friends with, inclined his head slightly toward me and said, to whoops of laughter, 'technicolor paddy.' My feet felt rooted in stone, and my head was aflame, I never forgot that phrase."

Despite the obstacles he encountered and the conflicts he felt growing up in a white environment, Wilkins was elected president of his high school's student council in his senior year. "It was a breakthrough of sorts," he remarked in *A Man's Life.* After graduation he attended the University of Michigan, where he earned a degree in law in 1956. He then practiced international law in New York City for several years before joining the Agency for International Development (AID) in Washington, D.C. Sensitive to the demands of being successful in a field traditionally occupied by whites, Wilkins adapted to what he called "white power." Recalling those early years of his career in his autobiography, Wilkins wrote: "I had begun to know how white people operated in the world and had begun to emulate them. I had no aspirations that would have seemed foreign to my white contemporaries. I had abdicated my birthright and had become an ersatz white man." Even during the civil rights movements of the sixties and with the emergence of what he terms "the new black thought," Wilkins still felt a "sense of exclusion" and a degree of envy toward his white counterparts who, he assumed, were secure in "the absolute knowledge that America was their country."

From AID, Wilkins went on to serve as assistant attorney general with the U.S. Department of Justice from 1966 to 1969. He then left government work to accept a position with the Ford Foundation in New York City. As director of the foundation's domestic program that provided funds for job training, drug rehabilitation, education for the poor, and other such minority-related projects, Wilkins had a "daily connection with blackness." It was, however, a connection that only seemed to underscore the ambivalence he felt as a black man operating within a predominantly white institution.

During his years with the Ford Foundation, Wilkins socialized with many of Manhattan's cultural elite, including writers Norman Mailer, Gore Vidal, and Arthur Miller, as well as conductor-composer Leonard Bernstein and his wife. His circle of eminent friends "seemed as devoid of racism as any group of whites I had ever encountered," Wilkins explained in his book. Given such acceptance, he nevertheless felt out of place:

"Because my work was not individualistic, creative, or as celebrated as that of most of the people I saw around me, I didn't believe I belonged." He further reflected that he "was enjoying a kind of life that was far beyond the actual or even imaginative grasp of the poor blacks to whom the serious efforts of my life were supposed to be committed. . . . It was as if, by entering that world at night, I was betraying everything I told myself I stood for during the day."

What happened—according to *New York Times Book Review* critic Joel Dreyfuss—was that Wilkins "gradually abandoned the desperate search for white approval and took on a role as an advocate for all blacks." Realizing his mistake in joining the Ford Foundation (he viewed it as "another way station in the white establishment"), he left his post there in 1972 to serve on the editorial staff of the *Washington Post,* where his editorials, along with the contributions of other staff members, earned the paper a special Pulitzer Prize nomination for its coverage of the Watergate scandal. Wilkins also held editorial posts with the *New York Times* before joining *Nation* in 1979 as a member of the publication's editorial board.

When *A Man's Life* was published in 1982 it attracted national critical attention. Writing in the *Washington Post Book World,* award-winning author James Baldwin hailed the autobiography as "so unprecedented a performance . . . that I consider it to be indispensable reading." Baldwin added that "Wilkins has written a most beautiful book, has delivered an impeccable testimony out of that implacable private place where a man either lives or dies." Dreyfuss, who called *A Man's Life* "an important, ground-breaking work," reflected that in the book Wilkins "asks for the acceptance—if not approval—of his own people, abandons his efforts to please white America and takes an important first step toward his personal liberation as an American." Such liberation, as suggested by John Leonard in his *New York Times* critique, is the result of the author's having been "for most of his life, underground, a fabrication." In the autobiography, Leonard continued, Wilkins "emerges to scream. All those false identities gag and choke. He spits them out. There is an excess Dostoyevsky would have understood." Richard Rodriguez, who praised *A Man's Life* in the *Los Angeles Times Book Review,* wrote: "Struggling to learn what it means to be black and middle class, Wilkins compels attention."

Wilkins commented: "Your request for a comment arrived on a day when I had read a fine essay by Arthur Miller and the obituary of E. B. White. Those readings reminded me of how many miles short I had fallen of achieving my youthful dream of becoming a true professional writer. Whether for lack of urgent inclination or because of other pressures, whatever natural talent I may have had has not been shaped and honed by the hard year-by-year toil required to make me an artist or even a fine craftsman. Rather, the sentences, the paragraphs, and even the book have been forged as weapons and hurled into the struggle for justice, which has been my real lifelong occupation. That way of working has made a rich life, but it has not made out."

BIOGRAPHICAL/CRITICAL SOURCES:

BOOKS

Wilkins, Roger, *A Man's Life: An Autobiography,* Simon & Schuster, 1982.

PERIODICALS

Los Angeles Times Book Review, August 1, 1982.

National Review, August 20, 1982.
Newsweek, August 2, 1982.
New York Times, June 14, 1982.
New York Times Book Review, June 20, 1982.
Washington Post Book World, June 6, 1982.

*   *   *

WILKINS, Roy   1901-1981

PERSONAL: Born August 30, 1901, in St. Louis, Mo.; died of kidney failure, September 8, 1981, in New York, N.Y.; son of William D. (a minister) and Mayfield (Edmondson) Wilkins; married Aminda Ann Badeau (a social worker), September 15, 1929. *Education:* University of Minnesota, A.B., 1923. *Religion:* Protestant.

ADDRESSES: Home—147-15 Village Rd., Jamaica, N.Y. 11435. *Office*—National Association for the Advancement of Colored People, 1790 Broadway, New York, N.Y. 10019.

CAREER: Kansas City Call, Kansas City, Mo., managing editor, 1923-31; National Association for the Advancement of Colored People (NAACP), New York, N.Y., assistant executive secretary 1931-49, editor of *Crisis* magazine, 1939-49, acting executive secretary, 1949-50, administrator of internal affairs, 1950-55, executive secretary, 1955-64, executive director, 1965-77, director emeritus, 1978-81. Chairman of National Emergency Civil Rights Mobilization, 1949-50; chairman of American delegation to International Conference on Human Rights, Teheran, Iran, 1968; member of Presidential Leadership Conference on Civil Rights, 1968-78; affiliated with Freedom House, Muscular Dystrophy Association, and Friends of LBJ (Johnson Library).

AWARDS, HONORS: Outstanding achievement award from University of Minnesota, 1960; Spingarn Medal from NAACP, 1964; Freedom Award from Freedom House, 1967; Theodore Roosevelt Distinguished Service Medal, 1968; Presidential Medal of Freedom, 1969; honorary fellow of Hebrew University, 1972; Zale Award, 1973; Books Across the Sea Ambassador Book Award from English-Speaking Union of the United States for *Standing Fast: The Autobiography of Roy Wilkins;* Joseph Prize for Human Rights. Honorary degrees from numerous colleges and universities, including Lincoln University, 1958; Morgan State College, 1963; Manhattan College, Iona College, Howard University, Swarthmore College, Notre Dame University, and Middlebury College, all 1965; Fordham University and Tuskegee Institute, both 1966; Bucknell University and University of California, both 1968; Columbia University, 1969; Yeshiva University, 1972; Drake University and St. John's University, both 1975; Temple University, Villanova University, and Indiana State University, all 1977.

WRITINGS:

(Contributor) Rayford W. Logan, editor, *What the Negro Wants,* University of North Carolina Press, 1944.
Talking It Over with Roy Wilkins: Selected Speeches and Writings, compiled by wife, Aminda Wilkins, and Helen Solomon, M & B Publishing, 1977.
(With Tom Mathews) *Standing Fast: The Autobiography of Roy Wilkins,* Viking, 1982.

Author of a weekly column in *Amsterdam News,* New York, N.Y., until 1970, and a column syndicated by the Register and Tribune Syndicate, 1969-80.

SIDELIGHTS: The grandson of a Mississippi slave, Wilkins served for more than sixty years as a speaker for racial equality. He grew up in an integrated neighborhood in St. Paul, Minnesota, and later attended the University of Minnesota. While in college he won an oratory contest for his speech protesting a lynching in Duluth, but it was not until he became a newspaper reporter in Kansas City, Missouri, that he experienced racial prejudice firsthand. Working for a black weekly, the *Kansas City Call,* Wilkins realized "the magnitude of racial bias in the U.S. . . . It was a slow accumulation of humiliations and grievances," Wilkins remembered. "Kansas City ate my heart out. It was a Jim Crow town through and through." At the *Call,* Wilkins urged an end to police brutality and encouraged blacks to exercise their strength at the polls to defeat white supremacist politicians.

In 1931 Wilkins began working for the organization that had made the abolition of lynching its primary goal, the National Association for the Advancement of Colored People (NAACP). In one of his first assignments he directed an investigation of blacks working on the southern Mississippi River levees, and his ensuing report, "Mississippi Slave Labor," brought about congressional action to improve wages and working conditions. Several years later Wilkins succeeded W. E. B. Dubois as editor of the NAACP's *Crisis* magazine, where he led crusades against the poll tax and other forms of segregation. When NAACP Executive Secretary Walter White died in 1955, Wilkins was elected unanimously to the organization's top post. (The title was later changed to executive director.) He held the position for twenty-two years, during a time when forced integration of schools, protest marches, boycotts, sit-ins, and urban riots brought America's attention to its racial problems.

Wilkins's "crowning glory" in his career-long struggle for civil rights was the 1954 Supreme Court decision *Brown v. Board of Education* that declared segregation in public schools unconstitutional. The case had been argued before the Court by NAACP general counsel Thurgood Marshall, with Wilkins planning the case behind the scenes. Wilkins was also among the organizers of the celebrated March on Washington (August 28, 1963), and he worked personally with Presidents Kennedy and Johnson toward the passage of civil rights legislation. "Quiet confrontation," said Paul Delaney in the *New York Times,* was Wilkins's tactic.

As racial protests grew more militant during the 1960's, other groups stole attention from the NAACP. The Southern Christian Leadership Conference (SCLC) and Congress on Racial Equality (CORE) "furnish the noise," Wilkins explained at the time. The NAACP "pays the bills." The group's lawyers were particularly active, representing many of those arrested in the demonstrations and civil disturbances of the era. Later in the decade, when blacks rioted in the streets and called for separation from whites, Wilkins condemned the violence and warned of the dangers of a separate society. "Black power," he said, is "the father of hatred and the mother of violence. . . . In the quick, uncritical and highly emotional adoption it has received from some segments of a beleaguered people, [black power] can only mean black death. Even if it should be enthroned briefly, the human spirit would die a little." Due to his nonmilitant approach, Wilkins was sometimes called an Uncle Tom. But, as Delaney noted, "Keeping his cool was one virtue that made Mr. Wilkins the pre-eminent civil rights leader of his day. . . . He kept his head when all about him were losing theirs."

Wilkins once explained the reasons for his approach: "The Negro has to be a superb diplomat and a great strategist. He has to parlay what actual power he has along with the good will of the white majority. He has to devise and pursue those philosophies and activities which will least alienate the white majority opinion. And that doesn't mean that the Negro has to indulge in bootlicking. But he must gain the sympathy of the large majority of the American public. He must also seek to make an identification with the American tradition."

Wilkins's last years with the NAACP were difficult ones. The link he shared with the nation's presidency was broken: he accused President Nixon of turning "back the clock" on "racial progress" and criticized President Ford's efforts to reduce the courts' power in school busing decisions as a "craven, cowardly, despicable retreat." Wilkins also battled within the NAACP, presiding over internal conflicts and resisting charges that he was incapable of leading the group in a rapidly changing world. In 1977, at the age of seventy-six, Wilkins retired and Benjamin Hooks was named the new executive director. After Wilkins's death in 1981, Hooks remembered his predecessor as "a towering figure in American history and during the time he headed the NAACP. It was during this crucial period that the association was faced with some of its most serious challenges and the whole landscape of the black condition in America was changed, radically, for the better."

AVOCATIONAL INTERESTS: Sports cars.

BIOGRAPHICAL/CRITICAL SOURCES:

BOOKS

Fax, Elton C., *Contemporary Black Leaders,* Dodd, 1970.
Metcalf, George R., *Black Profiles,* McGraw, 1968.
Wilkins, Roy, *Talking It Over with Roy Wilkins: Selected Speeches and Writings,* compiled by wife, Aminda Wilkins, and Helen Solomon, M & B Publishing, 1977.
Wilkins, Roy, and Tom Mathews, *Standing Fast: The Autobiography of Roy Wilkins,* Viking, 1982.

PERIODICALS

American Teacher, October, 1977.
Chicago Tribune Book World, August 8, 1982.
Ebony, April, 1974.
Los Angeles Times Book Review, August 29, 1982.
Newsweek, June 24, 1949, July 14, 1975, June 12, 1978, August 2, 1982.
New York Times, September 28, 1969.
New York Times Book Review, August 1, 1982.
Reader's Digest, January, 1968.
Time, August 30, 1963, July 12, 1976.
Washington Post Book World, August 29, 1982.

OBITUARIES:

PERIODICALS

Detroit Free Press, September 9, 1981.
Newsweek, September 21, 1981.
New York Times, September 9, 1981.
Time, September 21, 1981.
Washington Post, September 9, 1981.

*   *   *

WILKINSON, Brenda 1946-

PERSONAL: Born January 1, 1946, in Moultrie, Ga.; daughter of Malcolm (in construction) and Ethel (a nurse; maiden name, Anderson) Scott; separated; children: Kim, Lori. *Education:* Attended Hunter College of the City University of New York.

ADDRESSES: Home—210 West 230th St., Bronx, N.Y. 10463. *Office*—Board of Global Ministries, 475 Riverside Dr., New York, N.Y.

CAREER: Poet and author of books for children. Conducts poetry readings.

MEMBER: Authors Guild of Authors League of America.

AWARDS, HONORS: National Book Award nominee, 1976, for *Ludell; Ludell and Willie* was named one of the outstanding children's books of the year by the *New York Times* and a best book for young adults by the American Library Association, both 1977.

WRITINGS:

BOOKS FOR CHILDREN

Ludell (first book in trilogy), Harper, 1975.
Ludell and Willie (second book in trilogy), Harper, 1976.
Ludell's New York Time (third book in trilogy), Harper, 1980.
Not Separate, Not Equal, Harper, 1987.

OTHER

Also author of poetry and short stories.

SIDELIGHTS: Brenda Wilkinson's Ludell trilogy has been praised for its accurate, yet sensitive and compassionate portrayal of rural black life. These books, *Ludell, Ludell and Willie,* and *Ludell's New York Time* follow the life of a poor, young, black child growing up in Waycross, Georgia, in the mid-fifties to early sixties.

In the first volume of this trilogy, Ludell Wilson is left in the care of her grandmother after her mother moves to New York City in search of a better life. L. W. Lindsay writes in the *Christian Science Monitor* that *Ludell* is a "beautiful little novel about a sensitive young girl whose individuality and talent blossom in spite of the abyssmal circumstances under which she has to live and go to school." Addison Gayle notes in *Nation* that "the universe of this novel is alive with innocence, which emanates from the community . . . and it is highlighted by the love and care that each black person exhibits toward the other—characteristics of black life from the days of slavery until the present time."

"Unlike many novels of the South, 'Ludell' is not a tragedy in any sense, not any angry book, nor is it soft-centered," remarks Cynthia King in the *New York Times Book Review.* "By the end of the book I liked Ludell. I was glad to have known her and her friends."

Wilkinson's second book, *Ludell and Willie,* tells the story of Ludell's teenage years when she falls in love, starts to plan for the future, and experiences the death of her grandmother. Ludell must leave her love, Willie, and her home in Georgia and live with her mother in New York City. *Publishers Weekly* calls *Ludell and Willie* "a brilliant novel." In the *New York Times Book Review* Georgess McHargue comments that "we should be grateful to Ludell and Willie, their families and friends, for living and talking like themselves, thus transcending weighty generalizations about black teen-agers, Southern mores or social justice. I'm looking forward to the next book about Ludell."

Ludell's New York Time, the last book in Wilkinson's trilogy, finds Ludell unhappily trying to cope with her separation from her love, while getting reacquainted with her mother, and adjusting to her vastly different life in New York City. "Wil-

kinson has crafted a special kind of love story with wide-ranging appeal," believes Jerrie Norris. Writing in the *Christian Science Monitor* Norris comments that "the clash of Ludell's Waycross background with the Harlem of the '60s reveals the social fabric of both places. [Wilkinson writes] with a keen eye for detail and a carefully paced presentation of events to totally involve us with Ludell and her life."

BIOGRAPHICAL/CRITICAL SOURCES:

PERIODICALS

Christian Science Monitor, November 5, 1975, April 14, 1980.
Ms., August, 1980.
Nation, April 17, 1976.
New York Times Book Review, February 22, 1976, August 3, 1980.
Publishers Weekly, February 7, 1977.

*   *   *

WILLIAMS, Eric (Eustace)   1911-1981

PERSONAL: Born September 25, 1911, in Port of Spain, Trinidad; died of a heart attack, March 29 (one source says March 31), 1981, in St. Anne, Trinidad; son of Thomas Henry (a postal clerk) and Eliza (Boissiere) Williams; married Elsie Ribeiro c. 1939 (divorced, 1951); married Soy Moyeau c. 1951 (divorced, 1953); married Mayleen Mook-Soong (a dentist), 1957 (divorced c. 1958); children: Alistair, Pamela (first marriage), Erica (second marriage). *Education:* Attended Queen's Royal College, 1922-31; St. Catherine's College, Oxford, B.A. (first class honors), 1935, D.Phil. (first class honors), 1938. *Religion:* Roman Catholic.

CAREER: Queen's Royal College, Port of Spain, Trinidad, acting master, and acting lecturer for the Government Training College for Teachers, 1931; Howard University, Washington, D.C., assistant professor, 1939-44, associate professor, 1944-47, professor of social and political science, 1947-1955; adviser to Trinidad Government, 1954-55; founded People's National Movement (PNM) in Trinidad, 1956; chief minister and minister of finance, planning, and development of Trinidad and Tobago, 1956-61; first prime minister of independent state of Trinidad and Tobago, 1962-81, also minister of external affairs, 1961-64, 1973-74, minister of community development, 1964-67, minister of Tobago affairs, minister of finance, planning, and development, and minister of national security, 1967-71, minister for finance beginning in 1975. Worked for the Anglo-American Caribbean Commission, consultant to the British, 1943-44, secretary of the Agricultural Committee, 1944-46, consultant, 1946-48, deputy chairman of the Caribbean Research Council and member of commission, 1948-55.

MEMBER: Historical Society of Trinidad and Tobago (past president).

AWARDS, HONORS: Julius Rosenwald fellowship, 1940, 1942; D.C.L. from Oxford University, and LL.D. from University of New Brunswick, both 1965.

WRITINGS:

The Negro in the Carribbean, Associates in Negro Folk Education, 1942, Negro Universities Press, 1969.
Capitalism and Slavery, University of North Carolina Press, 1944, Putnam, 1980.
Education in the British West Indies, foreword by John Dewey, Guardian Commercial Printery, 1950.

(Editor) *Documents on British West Indian History*, Trinidad, 1952.

History of the People of Trinidad and Tobago, People's National Movement Publishing, 1962, Praeger, 1964.

Documents of West Indian History, People's National Movement Publishing, 1963.

British Historians and the West Indies, People's National Movement Publishing, 1964, published with preface by Alan Bullock, Scribner, 1967.

Inward Hunger: The Education of a Prime Minister (autobiography), Deutsch, 1969, published with an introduction by Denis Brogan, University of Chicago Press, 1971.

From Columbus to Castro: The History of the Caribbean, 1492-1969, Deutsch, 1970, Harper, 1971.

(Contributor) Roy Boyke, editor, *Patterns of Progress: Trinidad and Tobago; Ten Years of Independence*, Key Caribbean Publications, 1972.

Forged From the Love of Liberty: Selected Speeches of Dr. Eric Williams, compiled by Paul K. Sutton, Longman Caribbean, 1981.

Also author of published political addresses, including *Federation: Two Public Lectures*, 1956; *Perspectives for Our Party*, 1958; *Revision of the Federal Constitution*, 1959; *From Slavery to Chaguaramas*, 1959; *Ghandi: A Broadcast on the 90th Anniversary of the Birth of Mahatma Ghandi*, 1959; *The Approach of Independence: An Address to the Fourth Annual Convention of the People's National Movement*, 1960; *Perspectives for the West Indies*, 1960; *Our Fourth Anniversary: The Last Lap*, 1960; *Responsibilities of the Party Member*, 1960; *Massa Day Done: A Masterpiece of Political and Sociological Analysis*, 1961; *Tagore: Centenary Celebration Address*, 1961; *Reports on the Inter-Governmental Conference: Two Broadcasts by the Premier of Trinidad and Tobago*, 1961; *Message to the Youth of the Nation*, 1962; *Some Thoughts on Economic Aid to Developing Countries*, 1963; *The Future of the West Indies and Guyana*, 1963; *The University: Symbol of Freedom*, 1963; *Trinidad and Tobago and the British Guiana Question*, 1963; *The Developing Nation in the Modern World*, 1965; *Reorganization of the Public Service: Three Speeches*, 1966; *A Review of the Political Scene*, 1966; *Prime Minister's Broadcast to the Nation on the Unemployment Situation in Trinidad and Tobago*, 1967; *Devaluation Speeches*, 1967; *People's National Movement's Perspectives in the World of the Seventies*, 1970; *Some Historical Reflections on the Church in the Caribbean*, 1973; and *The Energy Crisis, 1973-1974*, 1974. Author of pamphlets, including *Economic Problems of Trinidad and Tobago, Constitution Reform in Trinidad and Tobago, The Historical Background of Race Relations in the Caribbean*, and *The Case for Party Politics in Trinidad and Tobago*, all 1955.

SIDELIGHTS: Eric Williams became the first prime minister of Trinidad and Tobago when that two-island nation gained its independence from Great Britain in 1962. Also a respected historian, he taught at Howard University in Washington, D.C., and had published several well-received books on the history of the Caribbean before returning to his native Trinidad to become involved in its politics in 1955. There he founded colonial Trinidad and Tobago's first stable political party, the democratic, socialist People's National Movement (PNM). As the PNM gained in power and popularity, so did Williams. Under his leadership, in 1956 the PNM won a majority of the seats in the colony's legislative council by calling for reforms that included universal and secular education and wider availability of birth control. In accordance with the colonial con-

stitution, the British territorial governor named Williams, as leader of the majority party, chief minister of Trinidad and Tobago. He became prime minister when the colony was made an independent member of the British Commonwealth, and remained his nation's highest official until his death in 1981.

Williams's most famed historical work, *Capitalism and Slavery*, began as his Ph.D. thesis at Oxford University. Labeled "a classic in [its] field" by C. Gerald Fraser in Williams's *New York Times* obituary, the work explored the ways in which slavery contributed to the growth of British capitalism. Williams's scholarship carried over to his political life as well; his public addresses as prime minister given in Port of Spain's Woodford Square, many of which were published, were so full of factual information that the site was nicknamed the "University of Woodford Square."

From Columbus to Castro: The History of the Caribbean, published by Williams in 1970, is "less a history than an interesting and well-written essay on slavery and sugar-cane cultivation and the effects of their interaction on the peoples of the Caribbean," according to a *Times Literary Supplement* reviewer. The work covers the time span beginning when Columbus brought sugar cane from the Canary Islands to the region on his second voyage to the New World and ending with Fidel Castro's rule of Cuba. The *Times Literary Supplement* had particular praise for Williams's handling of "present conditions in the West Indies," and for his "suggestions for the future."

BIOGRAPHICAL/CRITICAL SOURCES:

PERIODICALS

Times Literary Supplement, September 11, 1970.

OBITUARIES:

PERIODICALS

Newsweek, April 13, 1981.
New York Times, March 31, 1981.
Time, April 13, 1981.

*   *   *

WILLIAMS, John A(lfred) 1925-
(J. Dennis Gregory)

PERSONAL: Born December 5, 1925, in Jackson, Miss.; son of John Henry (a laborer) and Ola Mae Williams; married Carolyn Clopton, 1947 (divorced); married Lorrain Isaac, October 5, 1965; children: (first marriage) Gregory D., Dennis A.; (second marriage) Adam J. *Education:* Syracuse University, A.B., 1950, graduate study, 1950-51.

ADDRESSES: Home—Teaneck, N.J. *Office*—Department of English, Rutgers University, Newark, N.J. 07102.

CAREER: Writer. Case worker for county welfare department, Syracuse, N.Y.; public relations man with Doug Johnson Associates, Syracuse, N.Y., 1952-54, and later with Arthur P. Jacobs Co.; Columbia Broadcasting System (CBS), Hollywood, Calif. and New York City, staff member for radio and television special events programs, 1954-55; Comet Press Books, New York City, publicity director, 1955-56; *Negro Market Newsletter*, New York City, publisher and editor, 1956-57; Abelard-Schuman Ltd., New York City, assistant to the publisher, 1957-58; American Committee on Africa, New York City, director of information, 1958; European correspondent for *Ebony* and *Jet* (magazines), New York City, 1958-59; Station WOV, New York, special events announcer, 1959; *Newsweek,* New York City, correspondent in Africa, 1964-65. Lecturer in writing, City College of the City University of New York, 1968; lecturer in Afro-American literature, College of the Virgin Islands, summer, 1968; guest writer at Sarah Lawrence College, Bronxville, N.Y., 1972; regents lecturer, University of California, Santa Barbara, 1972; distinguished professor of English, La Guardia Community College, 1973-74, 1974-75; visiting professor, University of Hawaii, summer, 1974, and Boston University, 1978-79; professor of English, Rutgers University, 1979—; Exxon Professor of English, New York University, 1986-87. National Education Television, narrator and co-producer of programs, 1965-66, interviewer on "Newsfront" program, 1968. Special assignments writer and stringer for about fifteen American newspapers. Has given lectures or readings at more than twenty major colleges and universities in the United States. *Military service:* U.S. Naval Reserve, pharmacist's mate, active duty, 1943-46; served in the Pacific.

MEMBER: Authors Guild, Authors League of America, New York State Council on the Arts (member of board of directors), Rabinowitz Foundation (member of board of directors), Coordinating Council of Literary Magazines (chair, 1984).

AWARDS, HONORS: Award from National Institute of Arts and Letters, 1962; centennial medal for outstanding achievement from Syracuse University, 1970; LL.D. from Southeastern Massachusetts University, 1978, Lindback Award, Rutgers University 1982, for distinguished teaching; American Book Award, Before Columbus Foundation, 1983, for *!Click Song.*

WRITINGS:

NOVELS

The Angry Ones, Ace Books, 1960, published as *One for New York,* Chatham Bookseller, 1975.
Night Song, Farrar, Straus, 1961.
Sissie, Farrar, Straus, 1963 (published in England as *Journey out of Anger,* Eyre & Spottiswoode, 1965).
The Man Who Cried I Am, Little, Brown, 1967.
Sons of Darkness, Sons of Light: A Novel of Some Probability, Little, Brown, 1969.
Captain Blackman, Doubleday, 1972.
Mothersill and the Foxes, Doubleday, 1975.
The Junior Bachelor Society, Doubleday, 1976.
!Click Song, Houghton, 1982.
The Berhama Account, New Horizon Press, 1985.
Jacob's Ladder, Thunder's Mouth, 1987.

NONFICTION

Africa: Her History, Lands, and People, Cooper Square, 1962, 3rd edition, 1969.
(Under pseudonym J. Dennis Gregory, with Harry J. Anslinger) *The Protectors: The Heroic Story of the Narcotics Agents, Citizens and Officials in Their Unending, Unsung Battles against Organized Crime in America and Abroad,* Farrar, Straus, 1964.
This Is My Country Too, New American Library, 1965.
The Most Native of Sons: A Biography of Richard Wright, Doubleday, 1970.
The King God Didn't Save: Reflections on the Life and Death of Martin Luther King, Jr., Coward, 1970.
Flashbacks: A Twenty-Year Diary of Article Writing, Doubleday, 1973.
(Author of introduction) *Romare Bearden,* Abrams, 1973.

Minorities in the City, Harper, 1975.

EDITOR

The Angry Black (anthology), Lancer Books, 1962, 2nd edition published as *Beyond the Angry Black,* Cooper Square, 1966.
(With Charles F. Harris) *Amistad I,* Knopf, 1970.
(With Harris) *Amistad II,* Knopf, 1971.
Yardbird No. 1, Reed & Young, 1979.
The McGraw-Hill Introduction to Literature, McGraw-Hill, 1985.

CONTRIBUTOR TO ANTHOLOGIES

Harlem: A Community in Transition, Citadel, 1964.
Best Short Stories of Negro Writers, Little, Brown, 1967.
Black on Black, Macmillan, 1968.
Thirty-four by Schwartze Lieb, Barmier & Nickel, 1968.
How We Live, Macmillan, 1968.
Dark Symphony, Free Press, 1968.
John Henrik Clarke, editor, *Nat Turner: Ten Black Writers Respond,* Beacon Press, 1968.
The Now Reader, Scott, Foresman, 1969.
The New Black Poetry, International, 1969.
Black Literature in America, Crowell, 1970.
The Black Novelist, C. E. Merrill, 1970.
Black Identity, Holt, 1970.
A Native Sons Reader, Lippincott, 1970.
The New Lively Rhetoric, Holt, 1970.
Brothers and Sisters, Macmillan, 1970.
Nineteen Necromancers from Now, Doubleday, 1970.
Black Insights, Ginn, 1971.
The Immigrant Experience, Dial, 1971.
Cavalcade, Houghton, 1971.
Racism, Crowell, 1971.
An Introduction to Poetry, St. Martin's, 1972.
Different Drummers, Random House, 1973.

OTHER

"The History of the Negro People: Omwale—The Child Returns Home" (for television; filmed in Nigeria), National Education Television, 1965.
"The Creative Person: Henry Roth" (for television; filmed in Spain), National Education Television, 1966.
"Sweet Love, Bitter" (screenplay), Film 2 Associates, 1967.
Last Flight from Ambo Ber (play; first produced in Boston, 1981), American Association of Ethiopian Jews, 1984.

Contributor of numerous stories and articles to newspapers and magazines, including *Negro Digest, Yardbird, Holiday, Saturday Review, Ebony,* and *New York.* Member of editorial board, *Audience,* 1970-72; contributing editor, *American Journal,* 1972—.

SIDELIGHTS: John A. Williams, says *Dictionary of Literary Biography* contributor James L. de Jongh, is "arguably the finest Afro-American novelist of his generation," although he "has been denied the full degree of support and acceptance some critics think his work deserves." Part of the reason for this, Williams believes, may be because of racial discrimination. In 1961, for instance, he was awarded a grant to the American Academy in Rome based on the quality of his novel *Night Song,* but the grant was rescinded by the awarding panel. Williams felt that this happened because he was black and because of rumors that he was about to marry a white woman, which he later did. However, Alan Dugan, "the poet who eventually was awarded the prize, courageously made public the issue at the presentation ceremony,'' explains Jeffrey Helterman, another *Dictionary of Literary Biography* commentator, and the resulting scandal caused the American Academy to discontinue its prize for literature for a time.

Williams's first three novels trace the problems facing blacks in a white society. The books *The Angry Ones, Night Song,* and *Sissie* relate attempts of black men and women to come to terms with a nation that discriminates against them. In *The Angry Ones,* for instance, the protagonist Steve Hill ''struggles with various kinds of racial prejudice in housing and employment, but the focus [of the novel] is on his growing realization of the way his employers at Rocket Press destroy the dreams of would-be authors,'' explains Helterman. Like Williams himself, Hill perceives that he is being exploited by a white-dominated industry in which a black artist has no place. Williams has said that ''the plain, unspoken fact is that the Negro is superfluous in American society as it is now constructed. Society must undergo a restructuring to make a place for him, or it will be called upon to get rid of him.''

The Man Who Cried I Am, a novel that brought Williams international recognition, further explores the exploitation of blacks by a white society. The protagonist, Max Reddick, is a black writer living in Europe, as did Williams for a time. Max is married to a Dutch woman, and he is dying of colon cancer. His chief literary rival and mentor is one Harry Ames, a fellow black author, but one who ''packages racial anger and sells it in his books,'' according to Helterman. While in Paris to attend Harry's funeral Max learns that Harry has in fact been murdered because he had uncovered a plot by the Western nations to prevent the unification of black Africa. Max himself unearths another conspiracy: America's genocidal solution to the race problem—code-named ''King Alfred''—which closely resembles Hitler's ''Final Solution.'' Finally Max, and a Malcolm X-like figure called Minister Q, are captured by the opposing forces and put to death.

The Man Who Cried I Am escapes the protest novel format of most black literature by putting the situation on an epic scale. Jerry H. Bryant describes the book in *Critique: Studies in Modern Fiction* as ''Williams's adaptation of the rhetoric of black power to his own needs as a novelist,'' calling it ''in a sense Williams's *Huckleberry Finn.* It reflects his deep skepticism over the capacity of America to live up to its professed ideals, and a development of deep pessimism about whites in particular and man in general.'' ''What purpose does the King Alfred portion of the novel serve?'' asks Robert E. Fleming in *Contemporary Literature.* ''In one sense, black people have been systematically killed off in the United States since their first introduction to its shores. Malnutrition, disease, poverty, psychological conditioning, and spiritual starvation have been the tools, rather than military operations and gas chambers, but the result has often been the same. King Alfred is not only a prophetic warning of what might happen here but a fictional metaphor for what has been happening and is happening still,'' he concludes.

Williams states in his *Contemporary Authors Autobiography Series* entry that he considers *!Click Song* to be his ''very best novel.'' Like *The Man Who Cried I Am,* the book details the careers of two writers, in this case Paul Cummings and Cato Caldwell Douglass, friends who attended school on the GI Bill after World War II. Cummings is Jewish; it is his reaffirmation of his Jewishness that provides the theme for his novels, and his suicide opens the book. Douglass, on the other hand, is black; his problem, as Jervis Anderson in the *New York Times*

Book Review indicates, is to overcome racism in the publishing industry. *Chicago Tribune Book World* contributor Seymour Krim compares the two characters: Cummings ''was a more successful competitor, a novelist who had won a National Book Award and all the attention that goes with it, while Cato was forced to lecture for peanuts before Black Studies groups. A further irony is the fact that Cummings was a 'passed' Jew who had only recently declared his real name, Kaminsky, in an effort to purge himself. Purge or not, his writing has gone downhill since his born-again declaration, while his earnings have gone up.'' Roy Hoffman, writing for the *Washington Post Book World* points out, however, that ''as Paul's career skyrockets, his private life goes to shambles. As Cato's career runs into brick walls, his personal life grows ever more fulfilled, ever more radiant.''

''*!Click Song* is at least the equal of Williams's other masterpiece, *The Man Who Cried I Am,*'' states de Jongh. ''The emotional power, the fluid structuring of time, the resonant synthesis of fiction and history are similar. But the novelist's mastery is greater, for Williams's technique here is seamless and invisible,'' the reviewer concludes. Other critics also celebrate Williams's work; says Krim, ''Unlike a James Baldwin or an Amiri Baraka, Williams is primarily a storyteller, which is what makes the reality of Black Rage become something other than a polemic in his hands. . . . Before [Cato Douglass's] odyssey is ended, we know in our bones what it is like to be a gifted black survivor in America today; we change skins as we read, so to speak, and the journey of living inside another is so intense that no white reader will ever again be able to plead ignorance.''

MEDIA ADAPTATIONS: The Junior Bachelor Society was filmed for television and broadcast by NBC as ''Sophisticated Gents'' in 1981.

AVOCATIONAL INTERESTS: Travel (has visited Belgium, Cameroon, the Caribbean, Congo, Cyprus, Denmark, Egypt, Ethiopia, France, Germany, Ghana, Great Britain, Greece, Israel, Italy, Mexico, the Netherlands, Nigeria, Portugal, Senegal, Spain, the Sudan, Sweden).

BIOGRAPHICAL/CRITICAL SOURCES:

BOOKS

Cash, Earl A., *Evolution of a Black Writer,* Third Press, 1975.
Contemporary Authors Autobiography Series, Volume 3, Gale, 1986.
Contemporary Literary Criticism, Gale, Volume 5, 1976, Volume 13, 1980.
Dictionary of Literary Biography, Gale, Volume 2: *American Novelists since World War II,* 1978, Volume 23: *Afro-American Fiction Writers after 1955,* 1984.
Muller, Gilbert H., *John A. Williams,* Twayne, 1984.

PERIODICALS

Black World, June, 1975.
Chicago Tribune Book World, April 18, 1982, November 17, 1985.
Contemporary Literature, spring, 1973.
Critic, April, 1963.
Critique: Studies in Modern Fiction, Volume 16, number 3, 1975.
Detroit News, June 6, 1982.
Library Journal, November 1, 1961, September 15, 1967.
Los Angeles Times Book Review, May 9, 1982, November 29, 1987.

Nation, September 18, 1976.
New Yorker, August 16, 1976.
New York Times Book Review, July 11, 1976, April 4, 1982,
    October 18, 1987, November 15, 1987.
Prairie Schooner, spring, 1976.
Publishers Weekly, November 11, 1974.
Time, April 12, 1982.
Washington Post Book World, March 23, 1982, October 4,
    1987.

—*Sketch by Kenneth R. Shepherd*

*   *   *

WILLIAMS, Samm-Art
See WILLIAMS, Samuel Arthur

*   *   *

WILLIAMS, Samuel Arthur   1946-
(Samm-Art Williams)

PERSONAL: Professionally known as Samm-Art Williams; born
January 20, 1946, in Burgaw, N.C.; son of Samuel and Val-
dosia (an English teacher) Williams. *Education:* Morgan State
College, B.S., 1968.

ADDRESSES: Home—Los Angeles, Calif.

CAREER: Worked as a salesman in Philadelphia, Pa., beginning in 1968; Freedom Theater, Philadelphia, Pa., actor, 1968-
73; worked intermittently as a gasoline station mechanic and
bartender, New York, N.Y., beginning in 1973; Negro Ensemble Company, New York, N.Y., actor and member of
Playwrights Workshop, beginning in 1974; independent playwright, New York, N.Y., and Los Angeles, Calif., beginning
in 1974; actor in stage, television, and film productions, 1974—.

AWARDS, HONORS: John Gassner Playwriting Award from
Critics Outer Circle, 1979-80, Audelio Recognition Award,
1980, and nomination for Antoinette Perry Award (''Tony''),
1981, all for ''Home''; North Carolina Governor's Award,
1980; Guggenheim fellow in playwriting, 1981-82.

WRITINGS—Under name Samm-Art Williams:

PLAYS

''Welcome to Black River,'' first produced in New York City
    at St. Mark's Playhouse, May 20, 1975.
''A Love Play,'' first produced in New York City at St. Mark's
    Playhouse, April, 1976.
''The Coming [and] Do Unto Others,'' first produced in New
    York City at the Billie Holiday Theatre, April 11, 1976.
''Brass Birds Don't Sing,'' first produced Off-Broadway at
    Stage Seventy-three, October 24, 1978.
Home (first produced in New York City at St. Mark's Play-
    house, December 19, 1979; produced on Broadway at
    Cort Theatre, May 7, 1980), Dramatists Play Service,
    1980.
''The Sixteenth Round,'' first produced Off-Broadway at The-
    atre Four, October 19, 1980.
''Friends,'' first produced in New York City at the Billie Hol-
    iday Theatre, 1983.
''Bojangles,'' produced on Broadway in 1985.
''Eyes of the American,'' first produced Off-Broadway at The-
    atre Four, 1985.
(Contributor) ''Orchards'' (seven-play anthology), first pro-
    duced in New York City at the Lucille Lortel Theatre,
    1985.

''Cork,'' first produced in New York City at Courtyard The-
    atre, 1986.

Also author of ''The Frost of Renaissance,'' first produced in
New York City at the Theatre of Riverside Church, and of
plays as yet neither published nor produced, including ''Ka-
milla,'' ''Sometime From Now,'' ''Break of Day Arising,''
and ''The Last Caravan.''

TELEPLAYS

(Co-author) ''Solomon Northup's Odyssey,'' Public Broad-
    casting Service, 1985.
''Charlotte Forten's Mission: Experiment in Freedom,'' Public
    Broadcasting Service, 1985.

OTHER

Scriptwriter for television series and specials, including ''Motown Returns to the Apollo,'' a National Broadcasting Company (NBC-TV) musical variety special broadcast in May,
1985. Contributing writer to musical stage productions, including ''Sophisticated Ladies'' in Philadelphia in 1980.

SIDELIGHTS: Playwright Samm-Art Williams is known for
creating humanistic characters whose sincere and positive attitudes help them transcend adversity. This vision was effectively realized in Williams's buoyant 1978 comedy-drama,
''Home,'' which was first produced by New York's Negro
Ensemble Company and later became a Broadway hit. The
play chronicles twenty years in the life of North Carolina farmer
Cephus Miles, whose simple, bucolic world falls apart when
he is jailed for refusing military service in the Vietnam war.
Released from prison five years later, Miles finds that his land
has been taken away for nonpayment of taxes, so he migrates
to a large northern city to seek a new life. His convict past
dogs him, however, costing him several well-paying jobs and
helping to push him into dependence on welfare, drugs, and
alcohol. But in the end, Cephus succeeds in redeeming himself
by sheer strength of character, and he makes his way home to
North Carolina to reclaim his land and marry his childhood
sweetheart.

Critics praised the ingenious dramatic structure and narrative
style Williams developed for ''Home.'' The story unfolds as
Cephus reminisces, relaxing in a splintered-back rocking chair
on his front porch, acting out the narrative as he goes along.
The dozens of characters he recalls are played by just two
actresses who manage lightning-quick role changes by adding
a cap or scarf to their costumes. With his penchant for tall
tales and pungent, down-home wit, Williams sets a warmly
humorous tone to the narrative that evokes inevitable comparisons with Mark Twain. Observed *New York Times* critic Mel
Gussow: ''If Twain were black and from North Carolina, he
might have written like Samm-Art Williams.'' Gussow also
commended Williams for his sensitivity to the musical qualities of language, as when the playwright mixes rhyming in-
terludes or ''talking blues'' into the dialogue. ''Mr. Williams
is clearly in love with words, which in his hands become a
rolling caravan of images,'' the critic remarked. And he deemed
the play ''a freshet of good will, a celebration of the indom-
itability of man, a call to return to the earth.'' ''Home'' received a Tony Award nomination for best Broadway play in
1980.

Williams's other plays, many of which were also originally
produced by the Negro Ensemble Company, range from epic
tragedies and political dramas to domestic farces and musicals.
''The Sixteenth Round,'' for example, is the playwright's

somber drama about a has-been Philadelphia prizefighter who is hunted down by mobsters for throwing a fight. And "Welcome to Black River" is an epic-styled psychological drama about the relations between two families, one black and one white, in rural North Carolina at the dawn of the civil rights era. Linked together by servitude, and secretly by blood, the families confront their shared pasts and futures when they are forced to join forces and battle flood tides. In a review of the New Federal Theater's 1984 revival of "Welcome to Black River," *New York Times* critic Stephen Holden commented that the play offers "tremendous dramatic possibilities" but "sadly fails to deliver the punches it sets up."

"Friends," Williams's 1980 domestic farce, revolves around an unusual love triangle made up of a Philadelphia boutique owner and two blind men. "Though most of the humor centers on the incapacities of the two men," wrote Gussow in a *New York Times* review, "the show avoids bad taste through the playwright's conviviality and evident sympathy for all of his characters." Also in a lighthearted vein, Williams wrote the book to the 1985 Broadway musical "Bojangles," based on the career of the renowned tap dancer Bill "Bojangles" Robinson. Williams shifted to the theme of political intrigue and the conflict between power and friendship for his 1985 drama, "Eyes of the American," which he set in an unnamed Caribbean nation. The playwright also contributed a sketch that year to a New York production of "Orchards," an anthology of seven Chekhov stories adapted for the stage by seven leading dramatists, including David Mamet, John Guare, and Wendy Wasserstein.

In addition to his theater projects, Williams has worked extensively in television as both a writer and an actor. His acting roles have included appearances on the soap operas "All My Children" and "Search for Tomorrow," and the part of Matthew Henson in a critically acclaimed 1983 Columbia Broadcasting System (CBS) drama about Arctic exploration, "Cook and Peary: The Race to the Pole." Williams also played the title role of a slave rebel in the 1985 American Playhouse documentary-drama "Denmark Vesey" for public television. And in February, 1986, Williams won critical praise for his portrayal of the fugitive slave Jim in the American Playhouse production of "The Adventures of Huckleberry Finn."

Among Williams's television writing credits are two American Playhouse historical dramas about American slavery, both broadcast in early 1985, "Solomon Northup's Odyssey" and "Charlotte Forten's Mission: Experiment in Freedom." The second play describes the experience of a black woman teacher from Philadelphia who traveled to the Sea Islands off the coast of Georgia and South Carolina during the Civil War years to educate the former slaves there. Charlotte Forten, the teleplay reveals, taught not only reading and writing but economic empowerment, striving to help the Sea Islanders become independent farmers. "At its core," noted Steve Lawson in a *New York Times* critique of Williams's drama, "the saga traces an immense event—the transition from working land to owning it, from oppressed dependency to liberty and self-esteem."

Williams discussed his writing influences and philosophy in an interview with Clarke Taylor of the *Los Angeles Times*. The playwright's mother, an English teacher, "made me read everything from Langston Hughes to Edgar Allan Poe," Williams recalled. "Actually I think [Poe's poem] 'The Raven' was my greatest influence—in *seeing* this bird, I saw what a great thing it was to be able to work on a person's mind with words." Williams added, "My whole life and my work is based on hope. It might be a desperate situation, and seemingly hopeless, but you have got to have tried." This is a message Williams wants to make accessible to both black and white audiences; although much of his work has a black focus, the playwright resists being categorized as a racial writer. "If it's in the English language, it's for everybody. This may not be everybody's truth—producers, directors, audiences—but it is Samm-Art Williams's truth."

BIOGRAPHICAL/CRITICAL SOURCES:

BOOKS

Dictionary of Literary Biography, Volume 38; *Afro-American Writers After 1955: Dramatists and Prose Writers*, Gale, 1985.

PERIODICALS

Christian Science Monitor, December 12, 1983.
Los Angeles Times, May 19, 1983, March 8, 1985.
New York, February 24, 1986.
New Yorker, November 3, 1980.
New York Times, December 20, 1979, January 4, 1980, March 16, 1980, May 8, 1980, January 10, 1982, May 29, 1983, August 12, 1983, September 29, 1983, November 20, 1984, February 24, 1985, August 25, 1985, October 29, 1985, December 9, 1986, December 27, 1986.
People, February 10, 1986.
Wall Street Journal, April 26, 1986.
Washington Post, October 29, 1982.

—*Sketch by Curtis Skinner*

*   *   *

WILLIAMS, Sherley Anne 1944-
(Shirley Williams)

PERSONAL: Born August 25, 1944, in Bakersfield, Calif.; daughter of Jessee Winson (a laborer) and Lelia Marie (Siler) Williams; children: John Malcolm. *Education:* Fresno State College (now California State University, Fresno), B.A., 1966; Howard University, graduate study, 1966-67; Brown University, M.A., 1972.

ADDRESSES: Office—Department of Literature, University of California, San Diego, La Jolla, Calif. 92093.

CAREER: Fresno State College (now California State University, Fresno), co-director of tutorial program, 1965-66, lecturer in ethnic studies, 1969-70; Miles College, Atlanta, Ga., administrative internal assistant to president, 1967-68; affiliated with Systems Development Corporation, Santa Monica, Calif., 1968-69; Federal City College, Washington, D.C., consultant in curriculum development and community educator, 1970-72; California State University, Fresno, associate professor of English, 1972-73; University of California, San Diego, La Jolla, assistant professor, 1973-76, associate professor, 1976-82, professor of Afro-American literature, 1982—, department chairman, 1976-82.

MEMBER: Poetry Society of America, Modern Language Association.

AWARDS, HONORS: National Book Award nomination, 1976, for *The Peacock Poems;* Fulbright lecturer, University of Ghana, 1984; *Dessa Rose* was named a notable book in 1986 by the *New York Times.*

WRITINGS:

Give Birth to Brightness: A Thematic Study in Neo-Black Literature, Dial, 1972.
(Under name, Shirley Williams) *The Peacock Poems*, Wesleyan University Press, 1975.
Some One Sweet Angel Chile (poems), Morrow, 1982.
Dessa Rose, Morrow, 1986.

Also author of "Letters from a New England Negro," a full-length drama produced in 1982, "Ours to Make," 1973, and "The Sherley Williams Special," 1977, both for television, and "Traveling Sunshine Good Time Show and Celebration," 1973, a stageshow.

WORK IN PROGRESS: "Dessa Rose," a screenplay based on the novel *Dessa Rose; Meanwhile, in Another Part of the City,* a collection of short fiction.

SIDELIGHTS: American critic, poet, novelist and educator Sherley Anne Williams during her early years may have seemed an unlikely candidate for fame. As a girl, she lived in a Fresno, California housing project, and worked with her parents in fruit and cotton fields. Her father died of tuberculosis before her eighth birthday, and her mother, a practical woman from rural Texas who had tried to discourage Williams's early interest in reading, died when Williams was sixteen. "My friends were what you would call juvenile delinquents. Most of them didn't finish school," and her future, she told Mona Gable in a *Los Angeles Times Magazine* interview, amounted to having children. But a series of events including guidance from a science teacher and the discovery of Richard Wright's *Black Boy*, Ertha Kitt's *Thursday's Child*, and other books by black authors about their lives stimulated her desire to write. "It was largely through these autobiographies I was able to take heart in my life," she told Gable. Williams studied at Fresno State, Fisk, Howard, and Brown Universities before deciding to become a writer and to support herself by teaching. Now a professor of Afro-American literature at the University of California, San Diego, Williams has become well-known for her books of criticism, poetry, and fiction, and is "living an extraordinary life," remarked poet Philip Levine, who had been her mentor at Fresno State.

The publication of *Give Birth to Brightness: A Thematic Study in Neo-Black Literature* in 1972 encouraged Williams to pursue a writing career. The essays are, she says in the book's dedication, "a public statement of how I feel about and treasure one small aspect of Blackness in America," and the collection is dedicated to her son Malcolm. *Give Birth to Brightness* claims that "a shared racial memory and a common future" are the foundations of the new black literature," reports Lillie P. Howard in the *Dictionary of Literary Biography: Afro-American Poets since 1955*. The author's aim, says Howard, "is to recreate 'a new tradition built on a synthesis of black oral traditions [such as the blues] and Western literate forms.'" Different from both the Harlem Renaissance (in which black writers spoke to white audiences) and from the literary protests of the 1960s, the new writers "speak directly *to* Black people *about themselves* in order to move them toward self-knowledge and collective freedom;" Williams states that this is achieved in art that presents a "liberating vision" of black life, past and future, that goes beyond protest.

Reviewers found some fault with *Give Birth to Brightness*, but it was generally well-received. Writing in the *New York Times*, Mel Watkins notes, "Miss Williams persuasively demonstrates the commonality of viewpoint that she asserts charac-

terizes neo-black fiction. Moreover, she evokes a real sense of what the street life is about." He takes issue with her portrayal of the street rebel as a symbolic hero, calling it a "dangerous and highly romantic idea" which may not be shared by all blacks, since they, too, may be victimized by streetmen. "Criticisms such as this notwithstanding," he adds, "Miss Williams has written a readable and informative survey of black literature. In using both her knowledge of Western literature and her understanding of black life, she provides insight into the sadly neglected area of reversed values that plays such a significant role in much black literature." Howard comments, "As a first major publication, *Give Birth to Brightness* is impressive."

The Peacock Poems, her second published book, was also well-received. The volume of autobiographical poems, some about her early family life, and the balance about her feelings as a single mother, drew a National Book Award nomination for poetry in 1976. Expressing herself in blues poetry, "Williams fingers the 'jagged' edges of a pain that is both hers and ours," Howard observes. She says the poems also assert and demonstrate "the therapeutic regenerative powers" of the traditional black music. Blues also shapes the poems in *Some One Sweet Angel Chile*. One of its sections looks at the life of blues singer Bessie Smith. "Singing the blues gave Smith a temporary lifeline which sustained her through all her sufferings," Howard relates. Other sections depict experiences of black women after the Civil War and in more recent times. Williams explains the focus of her early work in an interview with Claudia Tate, published in *Black Women Writers at Work*: "I wanted specifically to write about lower-income black women. . . . We were missing these stories of black women's struggles and their real triumphs. . . . I wanted to write about them because they had in a very real sense educated me and given me what it was going to take to get me through the world."

Two economically disadvantaged women tell their stories in Williams's first novel and most highly acclaimed book, *Dessa Rose*. The book begins with the memories of its title character, a whip-scarred, pregnant slave woman in jail for violent crimes against white men. Dessa recalls her life on the plantation with her lover, a life that ended when he was killed by their master. In turn, Dessa had killed the master, was arrested and chained to other slaves in a coffle, from which she escaped, again by violence to her white captors. Tracked down and sentenced to die after the birth of her child, who would be valuable property to the whites, Dessa is interviewed by Adam Nehemiah, a white author who expects to become famous when he publishes the analysis of her crimes. When asked why she kills white men, Dessa replies evenly, "Cause I can."

After Dessa escapes again, Rufel Sutton, a white woman in economic distress, provides refuge for her and other runaway slaves simply because she can. Marcia Gillespie, contributing editor to *Ms.* magazine, notes that Rufel breastfeeds Dessa's newborn infant for the same reason, and because the alternative is too severe for her to consider. "As a result of this extraordinary bond, the two women achieve one of the most intricate and ambivalent relationships in contemporary fiction," Elaine Kendall remarks in the *Los Angeles Times*. In a scam designed by the runaways, Rufel earns money for a new life, selling them as slaves, waiting for them to escape, and selling them again. All goes well until the end, when Dessa is arrested by the enraged Nehemiah, but the two women elude his grasp with the aid of a female officer who is sent to verify Dessa's identity by examining her scars. When the group disbands, Rufel goes off to prosperity in the East; the blacks go west to the hardships of prejudice on the frontier. "Thus has Sherley Anne Williams breathed wonderful life into the bare bones of the past," believes *New York Times* reviewer Christopher Lehmann-Haupt. "And thus does she resolve more issues than are dreamed of in most history textbooks."

Dessa Rose, Gable writes, "was an instant critical success. There were favorable reviews in the Washington Post, the Boston Globe, Ms. and a number of other publications. Writing in the New York Times, David Bradley called it 'artistically brilliant, emotionally affecting and totally unforgettable.'" Also "one of the biggest hits of the literary season," the book commanded a third printing only months after its debut and six figure amounts for paperback and film rights—unusual for a first novel, Gable reports. "What makes 'Dessa Rose' such an unlikely commercial hit—and what prompted the New York Times to give it two glowing reviews and place it for two weeks on its influential recommended reading list—is the book's unflinchingly realistic portrayal of American slavery," Gable suggests. For instance, the sexual exploitation of black men and women that was common to the condition of slavery is fully drawn here, say reviewers, in "a plot dealing with all the [sadism and lust] that Harriet Beecher Stowe [author of *Uncle Tom's Cabin*] did not dare to mention," as London *Times* reviewer Andrew Sinclair phrases it. Furthermore, notes Jane Perliz in the *New York Times Book Review*, Williams intends Dessa's rebellion, based on an actual uprising led by a pregnant slave in 1829, to refute the myth that black women were the passive collaborators of abusive masters under the system.

These realities, not apparent in *Gone with the Wind*, were also absent from William Styron's *Confessions of Nat Turner*, a novel about a slave revolt leader that enraged Williams because it suggested that Turner's rebellion was motivated by his lust for a white woman. With *Dessa Rose*, "Williams not only wanted to challenge Styron's . . . view of slavery, which she believes dismissed the brutal social and political conditions that led to Turner's revolt, but to show up the 'hypocrisy of the literary tradition' by detailing the strengths of black culture," Gable relates. That resilience, Williams told her, was the ability to build strong family relationships despite slavery's attack on the black family.

Williams told Gable she also hoped the novel would "heal some wounds" made by racism left in the wake of slavery. In her view, she explained, fiction is one way to conceive of "the impossible, . . . and putting these women together, I could come to understand something not only about their experience of slavery but about them as women, and imagine the basis for some kind of honest rapprochement between black and white women." Michele Wallace, writing in the *Women's Review of Books*, notes, for example, the change in Dessa's feelings for Rufel when she realizes that white women, too, are raped by white men. Wallace adds, "*Dessa Rose* reveals both the uniformities and the idiosyncracies of 'woman's place,' while making imaginative and unprecedented use of its male characters as well. Sherley Anne Williams's accomplishment is that she takes the reader someplace we're not accustomed to going, someplace historical scholarship may never take us—into the world that black and white women shared in the antebellum South. But what excites me the most, finally, about this novel is its definition of friendship as the collective struggle that ultimately transcends the stumbling-blocks of race and class."

BIOGRAPHICAL/CRITICAL SOURCES:

BOOKS

Dictionary of Literary Biography, Volume 41: *Afro-American Poets since 1955*, Gale, 1985.
Fisher, Dexter and Robert B. Stepto, editors, *Afro-American Literature: The Reconstruction of Instruction*, Modern Language Association of America, 1979.
Henderson, Stephen, *Understanding the New Black Poetry*, Morrow, 1973.
Tate, Claudia, editor, *Black Women Writers at Work*, Continuum, 1983.
Williams, Sherley Anne, *Give Birth to Brightness: A Thematic Study in Neo-Black Literature*, Dial, 1972.
Williams, Sherley Anne, *Dessa Rose*, Morrow, 1986.

PERIODICALS

Black American Literature Forum, fall, 1986.
Black Scholar, March, 1981.
Black World, June, 1976.
Commonweal, December 3, 1982.
Essence, August, 1986, December, 1986.
Los Angeles Times, July 23, 1986, August 8, 1986.
Los Angeles Times Book Review, July 4, 1982.
Los Angeles Times Magazine, December 7, 1986.
Ms., September, 1986.
New Yorker, September 8, 1986.
New York Times, July 8, 1982, July 12, 1986.
New York Times Book Review, August 3, 1986.
Publishers Weekly, February 19, 1982, May 30, 1986, October 3, 1986.
Times (London), March 19, 1987.
Virginia Quarterly Review, spring, 1976.
Washington Post Book World, August 3, 1986.
Women's Review of Books, Volume IV, number 1, October, 1986.

—*Sketch by Marilyn K. Basel*

*   *   *

WILLIAMS, Shirley
See WILLIAMS, Sherley Anne

*   *   *

WILSON, August   1945-

PERSONAL: Born in 1945 in Pittsburgh, Pa.

ADDRESSES: Home—St. Paul, Minn.

CAREER: Writer. Worked as founder and director of Black Horizons Theatre Company in St. Paul, Minn., beginning in 1968; scriptwriter for Science Museum of Minnesota.

AWARDS, HONORS: Award for best play of 1984-85 from New York Drama Critics Circle, 1985, Antoinette Perry ("Tony") Award nomination from League of New York Theatres and Producers, 1985, and Whiting Writers' Award from the Whiting Foundation, 1986, all for "Ma Rainey's Black Bottom"; Outstanding Play Award from American Theatre Critics, 1986, Pulitzer Prize for drama, Tony Award for best play, and award for best Broadway play from Outer Critics Circle, all 1987, all for "Fences"; John Gassner Award for best American playwright from Outer Critics Circle, 1987; named Artist of the Year by *Chicago Tribune*, 1987; award for best play of 1987-88 from New York Drama Critics Circle and Tony Award nomination, both 1988, both for "Joe Turner's Come and Gone."

WRITINGS:

"Jitney" (two-act play), first produced in Pittsburgh, Pa., at the Allegheny Repertory Theatre, 1982.

Ma Rainey's Black Bottom (play; first produced in New Haven, Conn., at the Yale Repertory Theatre, 1984; produced on Broadway at the Cort Theatre, October, 1984), New American Library, 1985.

Fences (play; first produced in New Haven at the Yale Repertory Theatre, 1985; produced on Broadway at 46th Street Theatre, March, 1987), New American Library, 1986.

Joe Turner's Come and Gone (play; first produced in New Haven at the Yale Repertory Theatre, 1986; produced on Broadway, March, 1988), New American Library, 1988.

"The Piano Lesson" (play), first produced in New Haven at the Yale Repertory Theatre, 1987.

Also author of play "Fullerton Street" and the book for a stage musical about jazz musician Jelly Roll Morton.

Poetry anthologized in *The Poetry of Blackamerica*, Adoff. Contributor to periodicals, including *Black Lines* and *Connection*.

WORK IN PROGRESS: "Two Trains Running," a play set in 1968; a screenplay adaptation of "Fences."

SIDELIGHTS: August Wilson has been hailed since the mid-1980s as an important talent in the American theatre. He spent his childhood in poverty in Pittsburgh, Pennsylvania, where he lived with his parents and five siblings. Though he grew up in a poor family, Wilson felt that his parents withheld knowledge of even greater hardships they had endured. "My generation of blacks knew very little about the past of our parents," he told the *New York Times* in 1984. "They shielded us from the indignities they suffered."

At age sixteen Wilson, who had already flunked ninth grade, quit school and began working at menial jobs. But he also pursued a literary career and successfully submitted poems to black publications at the University of Pittsburgh. In 1968 he became active in the theatre by founding—despite lacking prior experience—the Black Horizons Theatre Company in St. Paul, Minnesota. Recalling his early theatre involvement, Wilson described himself to the *New York Times* as "a cultural nationalist . . . trying to raise consciousness through theater."

In St. Paul Wilson wrote his first play, "Jitney," a realistic drama set in a Pittsburgh taxi station. "Jitney" was accepted for workshop production at the O'Neill Theatre Center's National Playwrights Conference in 1982. This brought Wilson into contact with other playwrights. Inspired, he wrote another play, "Fullerton Street," but this work failed to strengthen his reputation.

Wilson then resumed work on an earlier unfinished project, "Ma Rainey's Black Bottom," a play about a black blues singer's exploitation of her fellow musicians. This work, whose title role is named after an actual blues singer from the 1920s, is set in a recording studio in 1927. In the studio, temperamental Ma Rainey verbally abuses the other musicians and presents herself—without justification—as an important musical figure. But much of the play is also set in a rehearsal room, where Ma Rainey's musicians discuss their abusive employer and the hardships of life in racist America.

Eventually, the musicians are all revealed to have experienced, in varying degrees, racist treatment. The most resigned member is the group's leader, a trombonist who has learned to accept racial discrimination and merely negotiates around it. The bassist's response is to wallow in hedonism and ignore his nation's treatment of blacks, while the pianist takes an intellectual approach to solving racial problems. The group's trumpeter, however, is bitter and cynical. He is haunted by the memory of his mother's rape by four white men. Tensions mount in the play when the sullen trumpeter clashes with Ma Rainey and is fired. The manager of the recording studio then swindles him in a recording rights agreement, and a subsequent and seemingly insignificant incident precipitates a violent act from the trumpeter, who has simply endured too much abuse. The London *Times*'s Holly Hill called the play's climactic moment "a melodramatically violent act."

"Ma Rainey's Black Bottom" earned Wilson a return to the O'Neill Center's playwriting conference in 1983. There Wilson's play impressed director Lloyd Richards from the Yale Repertory Theatre. Richards worked with Wilson to refine the play, and when it was presented at Yale in 1984 it was hailed as the work of an important new playwright. Frank Rich, who reviewed the Yale production in the *New York Times*, acclaimed Wilson as "a major find for the American theater" and cited his ability to write "with compassion, raucous humor and penetrating wisdom."

Wilson enjoyed further success with "Ma Rainey's Black Bottom" after the play came to Broadway later in 1984. The *Chicago Tribune*'s Richard Christiansen reviewed the Broadway production as "a work of intermittent but immense power" and commended the "striking beauty" of the play's "literary and theatrical poetry." Christiansen added that "Wilson's power of language is sensational" and that "Ma Rainey's Black Bottom" was "the work of an impressive writer." The London *Times*'s Hill agreed, calling Wilson "a promising new playwright" and hailing his work as "a remarkable first play."

Wilson's subsequent plays include the Pulitzer Prize-winning "Fences," which is about a former athlete who forbids his son to accept an athletic scholarship, and "Joe Turner's Come and Gone," which concerns an ex-convict's efforts to find his wife. Like "Ma Rainey's Black Bottom," these plays underwent extensive rewriting. Guiding Wilson in this process was Lloyd Richards, dean of Yale's drama school and director of the school's productions of Wilson's plays. "August is a wonderful poet," Richards told the *New York Times* in 1986. "A wonderful poet turning into a playwright." Richards added that his work with Wilson involved "clarifying" each work's main theme and "arranging the material in a dynamic way."

Both "Fences" and "Joe Turner's Come and Gone" were praised when they played on American stages. The *New York Times*'s Frank Rich, in his review of "Fences," wrote that the play "leaves no doubt that Mr. Wilson is a major writer, combining a poet's ear for vernacular with a robust sense of humor (political and sexual), a sure instinct for cracking dramatic incident and passionate commitment to a great subject." And in his critique of "Joe Turner's Come and Gone," Rich speculated that the play "will give a lasting voice to a generation of uprooted black Americans." Rich contended that the work was "potentially its author's finest achievement yet" and described it as "a teeming canvas of black America . . . and a spiritual allegory."

Throughout his career Wilson has stressed that his first objective is in getting his work produced. "All I want is for the most people to get to see this play," he told the *New York Times* while discussing "Joe Turner's Come and Gone." Wilson added, however, that he was not opposed to having his works performed on Broadway. He told the *New York Times* that Broadway "still has the connotation of Mecca" and asked, "Who doesn't want to go to Mecca?"

BIOGRAPHICAL/CRITICAL SOURCES:

BOOKS

Contemporary Literary Criticism, Volume 39, Gale, 1986.

PERIODICALS

Chicago Tribune, October 15, 1984, June 8, 1987, December 17, 1987, December 27, 1987.
Chicago Tribune Book World, February 9, 1986.
Ebony, January, 1985.
Los Angeles Times, November 24, 1984, November 7, 1986, April 17, 1987, June 7, 1987, June 8, 1987, June 9, 1987, February 6, 1988.
Newsweek, April 6, 1987.
New York Times, April 11, 1984, April 13, 1984, October 12, 1984, October 22, 1984, May 6, 1986, May 14, 1986, June 20, 1986, March 27, 1987, April 5, 1987, April 9, 1987, April 17, 1987, May 7, 1987, December 10, 1987, December 11, 1987.
Saturday Review, January/February, 1985.
Time, April 27, 1987.
Times (London), November 6, 1984, April 18, 1987, April 24, 1987.
Washington Post, May 20, 1986, April 15, 1987, June 9, 1987, October 4, 1987, October 9, 1987.

*   *   *

WITHERSPOON, Naomi Long
See MADGETT, Naomi Long

*   *   *

WRIGHT, Charles Stevenson 1932-

PERSONAL: Born June 4, 1932, in New Franklin, Mo.; son of Stevenson (a laborer) and Dorthey (Hughes) Wright. *Education:* Attended public schools in New Franklin and Sedalia, Mo., left high school in his junior year; studied writing intermittently at Lowney Handy's Writers Colony in Marshall, Ill. *Religion:* Protestant.

ADDRESSES: c/o Farrar, Straus & Giroux, 19 Union Square W., New York, N.Y. 10003.

CAREER: Free-lance writer. Began his writing career as a teenager with a regular column in *Kansas City Call,* a weekly Negro paper in Kansas City, Mo., and received one dollar from this paper for his first published short story; has worked as a messenger and at various other jobs in New York City. *Military service:* U.S. Army, 1952-54; served in Korea.

WRITINGS:

The Messenger, Farrar, Straus, 1963.
The Wig: A Mirror Image, Farrar, Straus, 1966.
(Contributor) Langston Hughes, editor, *Best Short Stories by Negro Writers,* Little, Brown, 1967.
Absolutely Nothing to Get Alarmed About, Farrar, Straus, 1973.

Also author of short story collection, *Erotic Landslide;* author of "Madam on the Veranda," a play as yet neither published nor produced. Author of column "Wright's World," in *Village Voice.*

WORK IN PROGRESS: A novel based on the life of Jean Rhys.

SIDELIGHTS: Charles Stevenson Wright "has, with some justification, been called a satirist, a black humorist, a surrealist, an experimentalist—even a phenomenologist," remarks Joe Weixlmann in a *Dictionary of Literary Biography* essay. "By virtue of [his] probing examinations of contemporary America . . . Wright has earned an intense literary following." Jerome Klinkowitz, in *Literary Disruptions: The Making of a Post-Contemporary American Fiction,* says that "of young black fictionists, Charles Wright was one of the first to shatter the old conventions, presenting the usual 'search for meaning' theme in a radical new form: imaginative literature, and ultimately fantasy." *The Messenger,* his first novel, draws so heavily on Wright's own experiences as a messenger in New York City that some critics find it difficult to distinguish divisions between fact and fiction. The novel is a portrait of a young black New Yorker whose increasing awareness of the futility of his situation "individualizes issues of general, not just personal, significance—most saliently, the isolation and alienation produced in persons who fall prey to America's social, economic, and racial caste systems," relates Weixlmann.

Similar to Wright's first novel, *The Wig: A Mirror Image* is a "farcical novel blending reality and fantasy in the story of a young Harlemite's vain attempt at economic and personal self-realization during the Johnson era," says Eberhard Kreutzer in *The Afro-American Novel Since 1960.* The novel follows the attempts of another black New Yorker, Lester Jefferson, to gain financial and social success in the world of the "Great Society." In order to facilitate his entry into "mainstream" society, Lester uses a hair relaxer to make his "wig" straight and silky. He then "sets out on a series of picaresque adventures," summarizes a *Times Literary Supplement* reviewer, in which he meets some of "the most messed-up people imaginable—the fear-ridden products of the Great Society." Victor Navasky, writing in the *New York Times Book Review,* finds most of these characters "pass by . . . without really engaging the reader or each other"; nevertheless, the critic observes that "the varying guises adopted by his people suggest the ambiguous relationship man's social masks bear to his true identity."

Wright's sharply satiric style has led some critics to characterize him as a "black black humorist"; in *The Wig,* this element of satire accentuates the bleak situation facing many young blacks. The novel "is a tale of bitterness told with malice, alleviated only by satiric relief," comments Navasky. "[It] is a disturbing book by a man with a vicious, significant talent." Conrad Knickerbocker remarks in the *New York Times* that "Mr. Wright's style, as mean and vicious a weapon as a rusty hacksaw, is the perfect vehicle for his zany pessimism." Wright's satire incorporates elements of horror and comedy which are both bitter and realistic, leading the *Times Literary Supplement* critic to observe that the work "rings sickeningly true." "Like all good satirists, he sees no hope," notes Knickerbocker. "His jibes confirm the wounds no Great Society will ever salve, and his laughter has no healing powers. 'The Wig' is a brutal, exciting, and necessary book."

In *Absolutely Nothing to Get Alarmed About,* Wright breaks down "the artificial barriers between the personal essay and fiction," says Clarence Major in the *American Poetry Review.* As in his previous works, Wright weaves his own experiences into the fabric of the novel. Remarks David Freeman in the *New York Times Book Review,* "one of the pleasures of this book . . . is that one is never certain what is fact and what is fiction.'' As reflected in Wright's original title, *Black Studies: A Journal,* the work is a ''journal-novel, an act of self-definition [which] appears at first to be more an act of the will than of the imagination,'' according to Freeman. ''But at its best, the two worlds—private imagination and harsh reality—merge and hover between gentle evocation of the sad eccentricity of street life and canny social and political views.''

''There is plenty to get alarmed about in Charles Wright's literary world,'' says Weixlmann. ''On the one hand, it records, in excruciating detail, the result of deferred and destroyed black dreams. On the other hand, it warns of the consequences that await the destroyers.'' *Absolutely Nothing to Get Alarmed About* is perhaps more pessimistic than Wright's first two novels, for it relates all the disillusionment and none of the hope that Wright's previous characters had for the ''Great Society.'' Freeman describes the work as ''about a lost passion, and a weariness that envelops. . . . [It] feels like the rough draft of a suicide note.'' In assessing Wright's work, however, Major emphasizes its quality rather than its content: ''[Wright's] language has the power to suddenly illuminate the dullest moment. . . . He has worked out a language and a landscape that is a kaleidoscope of mystery and simplicity, filled with miracles and puzzles.'' Although there may be despair and disillusionment in Wright's work, Major also notes that ''there is humor and a kind of unholy wisdom.''

MEDIA ADAPTATIONS: The U.S. Information Agency broadcast *The Messenger* overseas.

AVOCATIONAL INTERESTS: Jazz, good books, good people, travel.

BIOGRAPHICAL/CRITICAL SOURCES:

BOOKS

Bruck, Peter, and Wolfgang Kaarer, editors, *The Afro-American Novel Since 1960,* Gruener, 1982.
Dictionary of Literary Biography, Volume 33: *Afro-American Fiction Writers after 1955,* Gale, 1984.
Klinkowitz, Jerome, *Literary Disruptions: The Making of a Post-Contemporary American Fiction,* University of Illinois Press, 1975.
O'Brien, John, *Interviews with Black Writers,* Liveright, 1973.
Black Humor Fiction of the Sixties: A Pluralistic Definition of Man and His World, Ohio University Press, 1973.

PERIODICALS

American Poetry Review, May, 1976.
Books and Bookmen, May, 1967.
New York Times, March 5, 1966.
New York Times Book Review, February 27, 1966, March 11, 1973.
Times Literary Supplement, March 9, 1967.

*   *   *

WRIGHT, Richard (Nathaniel)   1908-1960

PERSONAL: Born September 4, 1908, near Natchez, Miss.; died of a heart attack, November 28, 1960, in Paris, France; buried in Pere Lachaise, Paris, France; son of Nathan (a mill worker) and Ellen (a teacher) Wright; married Rose Dhima Meadman, 1938 (marriage ended); married Ellen Poplar, 1941; children: two daughters. *Education:* Attended school in Jackson, Miss.

CAREER: Novelist, short story writer, poet, and essayist. Worked at odd jobs in Memphis, Tenn., and other cities; clerk

at U.S. Post Office in Chicago, Ill., during 1920s; associated with Works Progress Administration Federal Writers' Project, Chicago, and New York, N.Y., 1935-37.

AWARDS, HONORS: Prize from *Story* magazine, 1938, for *Uncle Tom's Children;* Guggenheim fellowship, 1939; Spingarn Medal from National Association for the Advancement of Colored People, 1940, for *Native Son.*

WRITINGS:

Uncle Tom's Children: Four Novellas, Harper, 1938, expanded edition published as *Uncle Tom's Children: Five Long Stories,* 1938, reprinted, 1965.
Native Son (novel; also see below), Harper, 1940, reprinted, 1986.
Twelve Million Black Voices: A Folk History of the Negro in the U.S., Viking, 1941, reprinted, Thunder's Mouth, 1988.
(With Paul Green) *Native Son* (play; adapted from own novel; first produced on Broadway at the St. James Theatre, March 24, 1941), Harper, 1941, revised edition, Samuel French, 1980.
Black Boy: A Record of Childhood and Youth (autobiography), Harper, 1945, reprinted, 1969.
''Native Son'' (screenplay; adapted from own novel), Classic Films, 1951.
The Outsider (novel), Harper, 1953.
Savage Holiday (novel), Avon, 1954, reprinted, Chatham Bookseller, 1975.
Black Power: A Record of Reactions in a Land of Pathos, Harper, 1954, reprinted, Greenwood Press, 1974.
The Color Curtain (nonfiction), World, 1956.
Pagan Spain (nonfiction), Harper, 1957.
White Man, Listen! (nonfiction), Doubleday, 1957, reprinted, Greenwood Press, 1978.
The Long Dream (novel), Doubleday, 1958, reprinted, Harper, 1987.
(Editor and contributor) *Quintet* (short stories), Pyramid Books, 1961.
Eight Men (short stories), World, 1961, reprinted, Thunder's Mouth, 1987.
Lawd Today (novel), Avon, 1963, reprinted, Northeastern University Press, 1986.
(With Louis Sapin) ''Daddy Goodness'' (play), first produced Off-Broadway at St. Mark's Playhouse, June 4, 1968.
The Man Who Lived Underground (novella), Aubier-Flammarion, 1971.
(Contributor) Hiroshi Nagase and Tsutomu Kanashiki, editors, *What the Negro Wants,* Kaitakusha, 1972.
Farthing's Fortunes, Atheneum, 1976.
American Hunger (autobiography), Harper, 1977.
Ellen Wright and Michel Fabre, editors, *The Richard Wright Reader,* Harper, 1978.
David Ray and Robert M. Farnsworth, editors, *The Life and Works of Richard Wright,* University of Missouri, 1979.

Contributor of articles, essays, short stories, and poems to magazines and newspapers, including *Atlantic Monthly, Saturday Review, New Republic, Negro Digest, Daily Worker, New York World Telegram,* and *New Masses.*

SIDELIGHTS: One of the most influential black American authors of the twentieth century, Wright was ''the first American Negro writer of large ambitions to win a major reputation in [American] literary life.'' The Southern-born Wright was the first black novelist to write of life in the ghettos of northern cities and of the rage felt by blacks at the white society that excluded them. As James A. Page observed in *English Jour-*

nal, Wright was "powerful enough to break out of the narrow compartment previously occupied by Black writers. . . . He made sense, he handled his themes with authority, expressed himself with power and eloquence, and was entitled to the place he had won in the literary firmament of the Depression years. . . . That Wright was the most impressive literary talent yet produced by negro America was rarely disputed in his time. . . . His name was bracketed with the small handful of America's foremost writers."

Wright was largely self-educated. His formal schooling, frequently interrupted as he moved from town to town, ended when he was fifteen. Thereafter, he read widely, beginning with H. L. Mencken, whose books he obtained from Memphis's "whites only" public library by forging a note from a white patron: "Dear Madam: Will you please let this nigger boy have some books by H. L. Mencken?" Wright was strongly affected by the naturalistic fiction of Stephen Crane, Sinclair Lewis, and Theodore Dreiser, and, after he moved to Chicago in the late 1920s, by the Chicago school of sociologists, including Robert Redfield, Louis Wirth, and Robert Park. Wright also read, and was strongly impressed with, Marcel Proust and Gertrude Stein.

His concern with the social roots of racial oppression led Wright to join the Communist party in 1932. He was a party activist in Chicago and New York, and worked at developing a Marxist perspective in the poems and short stories he was writing at that time. But his individualism brought him into conflict with other party members, who labeled him an intellectual and regarded his writing with suspicion. Wright, in turn, found himself repelled by the narrowness and rigidity of his fellow Communists, whose minds he found "sealed against new ideas, new facts, new feelings, new attitudes, new hints at ways to live. They denounced books they could never understand, and doctrines they could not pronounce." In 1944, after witnessing the trial of a party member for ideological "deviationism," Wright resigned from the party.

Until 1938, Wright's work appeared only in left-wing publications such as *New Masses* and *Left Front.* In that year, *Story* magazine offered a $500 prize for the best book-length manuscript by a writer connected with the Federal Writers' Project. Wright's collection of four long stories inspired by the life of a black Communist he had known in Chicago won the contest and was published as *Uncle Tom's Children.* Malcolm Cowley, in the *New Republic,* found the book "heartening, as evidence of a vigorous new talent, and terrifying as the expression of a racial hatred that has never ceased to grow and gets no chance to die." All of the stories (a fifth, "Bright and Morning Star," was added to subsequent editions) deal with the oppression of black people in the South, of the violence of whites against blacks, and the violence to which the black characters are driven by their victimization. Some critics have found the stories in *Uncle Tom's Children* too melodramatic and marred by the infusion of Communist ideology. But Houston A. Baker, in his *Black Literature in America,* wrote: "Wright showed a mastery of style and a dramatic sense far superior to that of most of black contemporaries and predecessors and on a par with that of his most talented white contemporaries. The violence and the terrible effects of prejudice are perhaps nowhere more skillfully set forth."

Though *Uncle Tom's Children* was well received, Wright was dissatisfied with the response to it. He realized, he wrote later, "that I had written a book which even bankers' daughters could read and weep over and feel good. I swore to myself that if I ever wrote another book, no one would weep over it; that it would be so hard and deep that they would have to face it without the consolation of tears." The book he wrote was *Native Son,* the story of Bigger Thomas, a young black man in Chicago who murders two women and is condemned to death. To depict the dehumanization of blacks in the "hard and deep" manner he wished, Wright avoided making his protagonist a sympathetic character. As reviewer Margaret Marshall wrote in the *Nation,* "Mr. Wright has chosen for his 'hero,' not a sophisticated Negro who at least understands his predicament and can adapt himself to it, but a 'bad nigger,' a 'black ape,' who is only dimly aware of his extra-human status and therefore completely at the mercy of the impulses it generates. . . . One gets a picture of a dark world enclosed by a living white wall. . . . Bigger and his friends are resentful; all feel powerless and afraid of the white world, which exploits, condescends to, and in turn fears the race it has segregated. . . . Mr. Wright has laid bare, with a ruthlessness that spares neither race, the lower depths of the human and social relationship of blacks and whites; and his ruthlessness . . . clearly springs not from a vindictive desire to shock but from a passionate—and compassionate—concern with a problem obviously lying at the core of his own personal reality. . . . It is not pleasant to feel at the end that one is an accessory to the crimes of Bigger Thomas; but that feeling is impressive evidence of the power of Mr. Wright's indictment with its cutting and accurate title of 'Native Son.'"

Bigger Thomas is a young tough and a petty thief who is hired as a chauffeur by a rich white man. He drives his employer's daughter, Mary, to a political lecture, where he is confused and frightened by the white Communists' insistence on treating him as an equal, something he can only interpret as mockery. Mary gets drunk, and Bigger, after driving her home, carries her to her room. When Mary's mother, who is blind, enters the room, Bigger accidentally smothers Mary while trying to keep her from speaking and revealing his presence. He burns Mary's body in a furnace, then conceives a scheme to extort money from her parents by pretending to have kidnapped her and demanding ransom. When Mary's charred bones are discovered, Bigger kills his girlfriend, Bessie, who was his accomplice in the kidnap plot. He is captured by the police and, despite an eloquent defense by his Communist lawyer, convicted and condemned. The lawyer, Max, argues that Bigger cannot be held responsible for his crimes, that the greater guilt lies with the society that would not accept him as a full human being, and so drove him to his brutal acts. Bigger feels that he has found a measure of freedom in the act of murder—the only act in his life that seems to him to have been truly creative, to have involved genuine self-assertion.

Some critics have seen in the ending of *Native Son* a clash between two literary and philosophical visions. Much of the book is in the tradition of naturalism, especially of Theodore Dreiser's novel *An American Tragedy.* This deterministic philosophy is made explicit when Max argues, in Marxist terms, that Bigger, as a product of his environment, is not truly guilty of the murders he committed. But Bigger's final sense of violence as a vital act of self-definition is drawn from Dostoyevsky's *Crime and Punishment,* and prefigures the existentialist position Wright adopted in his later work. Edward Margolies found the two attitudes incompatible, and their conflict a weakness in the novel: "Wright was probing larger issues than racial injustice and social inequality. He was asking questions regarding the ultimate nature of man. What indeed are man's responsibilities in a world devoid of meaning and purpose? . . . The contradiction is never resolved, and it is precisely for this reason that the novel fails to fulfill itself. For the plot, the structure, even the portrayal of Bigger himself are often at odds with Wright's official determinism. . . . The chief philosophical weakness of *Native Son* is not that Bigger does not surrender his freedom to Max's determinism or that Bigger's Zarathustrian principles do not jibe with Max's socialist visions; it is that Wright himself does not seem able to make up his mind. . . . Wright, though intellectually committed to Max's views, is more emotionally akin to Bigger's. . . . There is an inconsistency of ideologies, an irresolution of philosophical attitudes which prevent Bigger and the other characters from developing properly, which adulterate the structure of the novel, and which occasionally cloud up an otherwise lucid prose style."

Sheldon Brivic, in *Novel: A Forum on Fiction,* defended the apparent contradiction, insisting that the "ambivalence which critics have attacked in *Native Son* is really a complexity that adds to its validity, comprehension and prophetic power." Brivic found that "a conflict of values is skillfully developed and organized throughout. This conflict is embodied in the plot, in American society as Wright sees it, and most centrally in Bigger's mind. . . . Bigger is both the helpless victim of social oppression and the purposeful hero of a racial war. . . . Wright has balanced both sides in a dialectic, and it is because he keeps the book open ended that *Native Son* has the depth of perspective of a major work of modern literature rather than mere propaganda."

James Baldwin, who began his writing career as Wright's protege, called *Native Son* "the most powerful and celebrated statement we have yet had of what it means to be a Negro in America." But for Baldwin, the novel is marred by Wright's use of Bigger as a social symbol. Baldwin noted: "Bigger has no discernible relationship to himself, to his own life, to his own people, nor to any other people—in this respect, perhaps, he is most American—and his force comes not from his significance as a social (or anti-social) unit, but from his significance as the incarnation of a myth. It is remarkable that, though we follow him step by step from the tenement room to the death cells, we know as little about him when this journey is ended as we did when it began; and, what is even more remarkable, we know almost as little about the social dynamic which we are to believe created him. . . . What is missing in this situation and in the representation of his psychology—which makes his situation false and his psychology incapable of development—is any revelatory apprehension of Bigger as one of the Negro's realities or as one of the Negro's roles. This failure is part of the . . . failure to convey any sense of Negro life as a continuing and complex group reality."

Darryl Pinckney, in the *Village Voice,* argued: "*Native Son* is unmatched in its power. The rage, the human misery, seizes the mind and there is no relief. It is not true, as Baldwin claims, that Bigger Thomas, the doomed, frustrated black boy, is just another stereotype. . . . Baldwin criticizes Wright for not giving us black life, black community, the sense of shared experience. But Bigger Thomas is not a social symbol, exactly, and it is precisely his isolation that causes his fury. What Bigger must combat is circumstance, and we know he cannot win. . . . Bigger's black skin is the real object of his scorn and he hates those who make him aware of it—whites. . . . Baldwin feels we do not get any understanding of Bigger's psychology, that we do not know him better in the end any more than we did in the beginning. But Bigger did not know himself. . . . To understand Bigger, the meaning in his crimes,

perhaps we should not view them as merely a desire to get revenge on white society. . . . It is wrong to read this novel as a matter of group reality, a matter of race. Bigger had no real relations with other blacks. Everyone was an enemy. . . . [Wright] claimed he valued the 'state of abandonment, aloneness.' In this he was, finally, a true product of Western culture. . . . In *Native Son* he gave us a lasting record of the howl of modern man."

Wright's autobiography, *Black Boy,* published in 1945, is considered by many critics to be his most important work. In it he told of his Southern childhood, up to the time when he left Memphis for Chicago. Ralph Ellison, in his essay "Richard Wright's Blues," wrote: "In *Black Boy* Wright has used his own life to probe what qualities of will, imagination, and intellect are required of a Southern Negro in order to possess the meaning of his life in the United States. . . . Imagine Bigger Thomas projecting his own life in lucid prose, guided, say, by the insights of Marx and Freud, and you have an idea of this autobiography. . . . Along with the themes, equivalent descriptions of milieu and the perspectives to be found in Joyce, Nehru, Dostoievsky, George Moore and Rousseau, *Black Boy* is filled with blues-tempered echoes of railroad trains, the names of Southern towns and cities, estrangements, fights and flights, deaths and disappointments, charged with physical and spiritual hungers and pain. And like a blues sung by such an artist as Bessie Smith, its lyrical prose evokes the paradoxical, almost surreal image of a black boy singing lustily as he probes his own grievous wound. . . . And while it is true that *Black Boy* presents an almost unrelieved picture of a personality corrupted by brutal environment, it also presents those fresh, human responses brought to its world by the sensitive child."

Along with his accounts of mistreatment by whites, Wright describes the complicity of Southern blacks in their own oppression. Wright's family strove to make him conform to the submissive, servile behavior expected of black people, often beating him when he asserted himself too strongly. "In scene after scene," noted Morris Dickstein in *Gates of Eden,* "Wright represents his younger self as a rebellious misfit, incapable of adapting to the modes of deference that obtain in his coarse and brutal family and in Southern life. . . . He makes an intense effort of self-restraint, but try as he will there is always a provocative hint of pride and self-respect, a touch of the uppity nigger about him. A latecomer to the white world, he is unable to quite master the shuffling, degraded, but apparently contented manner that will tell whites he not only knows his place but loves it." Christianity is portrayed as an instrument of white oppression, by which blacks are convinced of their inferiority and convinced to passively accept their position; Wright, like many of his fictional characters, bitterly rejects the black church. *Black Boy* was attacked by some for its one-sided picture of Southern life, but David Littlejohn, in *Black on White: A Critical Survey of Writing by American Negroes,* praised it for revealing "the inside dimension of the Negro's experience of prejudice in America: what it feels like to live in the mad prison house of sadistic white obsessions."

Howard Mumford Jones, writing in the *Saturday Review of Literature,* found *Black Boy* a powerful social document and indictment of racism, but a weak literary work. "The total effect of the volume is an effect of passive suffering, punctuated by outbursts of blind emotional rebellion. . . . [Wright] emphasizes an endless array of wrongs, but he minimizes the development of his own personality. . . . In contrast to the passivity of virtue in these pages, the acts of the boy's persecutors, white and black, are presented in dramatic scenes of vivid and even violent writing. . . . In some degree this verbal violence may conceal the central failure of the story, which is the failure to chronicle the growth of a personality under suffering. . . . This either-or formula of passive virtue . . . and active evil is the formula of melodrama; and just as an easy recourse to melodrama was the structural weakness of 'Native Son,' so it is the structural weakness of 'Black Boy.'''

Some critics have seemed unsure whether to consider *Black Boy* as a sociological statement, a true autobiography, or an autobiographical novel. Wright uses many of the techniques of fiction, and it has been suggested that some of the incidents may have been invented. At the time of its publication, *Black Boy* was seen primarily as an attack on Southern white supremacist society; critics in the 1960s came to view it as the story of the development of a young writer's sensibility, in which race was only one factor, albeit a central one. As Warren French pointed out in *The Black American Writer: Fiction,* "What few noticed in the hubbub over Wright's powerful apologia is that: (1) a great many Negroes and members of other minority groups had suffered as he had without ever being able to find an adequate vehicle for the articulation of their personal grievances; (2) Wright's account had many similarities to other non-Negro portraits of the artist as a young man, including Joyce's famous novel [*Portrait of the Artist as a Young Man*]. . . . *Black Boy* is an outstanding account of a particularly sensitive type of artistic personality striving for identity, but it is as erroneous to read it as an account of the representative Negro experience as it would be to read Winston Churchill's memoirs as an account of the representative British schoolboy's 'making his way.'''

In 1946, the government of France invited Wright to visit that country. He spent six months in Paris and returned to France in 1947, to live there until his death. In Paris, Wright became acquainted with the circle of existentialist writers of whom the most prominent were Jean-Paul Sartre and Simone de Beauvoir. Existentialism appealed to Wright's deeply felt sense of alienation and rootlessness, and his later work combined racial themes with existentialist metaphysics. Wright's existentialism was as much instinctive as adopted, and similar ideas inform his work as early as *Native Son,* but the first novel he wrote after moving to France, *The Outsider,* was more overtly motivated by philosophical concerns. Granville Hicks, in the *New York Times Book Review,* noted that *The Outsider* was "one of the first consciously existentialist novels to be written by an American."

Cross Damon, the hero of *The Outsider,* is black, but his central problems have nothing to do with race. Harassed by his wife, his mother, and his mistress, he finds an escape from his encumbered life when he is believed killed in a subway accident. Seeking a new identity, Damon joins the Communist party, not out of sympathy with its political goals but out of a fascination with the party's "conviction that it had mastered the art of living; its will that it could define the ends of existence." Damon kills two Communists and a Fascist, but the district attorney who solves the crimes understands Damon's nihilistic creed and chooses to let him go free: "You are your own law, so you'll be your own judge," the lawyer tells him. Left alone, more an outsider than ever, Damon is executed by the Communist party's hired gunmen.

Hicks concluded: "'The Outsider' is both melodrama and novel of ideas. . . . If the ideas are sometimes incoherent, that does not detract from the substance and power of the book. . . . [*The Outsider*] is only incidentally a book about Negroes. Being a

Negro helps Cross Damon to understand that he is an outsider, . . . but there are . . . many outsiders. 'The Outsider' is, as it was intended to be, a book about modern man, and, because of Mr. Wright's driving force, it challenges the modern mind as it has rarely been challenged in fiction." But *The Outsider* was not generally well received; a number of critics found the melodramatic aspects of the plot too lurid, the philosophy poorly integrated with the story (especially a fourteen-page speech in which Cross Damon explains his philosophy of history), and the style clumsy. Phoebe Adams of the *Atlantic Monthly* called *The Outsider* "a very disappointing novel, for the qualities of sympathy, directness, effective detail, and mordant humor which distinguished Mr. Wright's earlier books seem to operate at cross-purposes in *The Outsider*. . . . Whether Mr. Wright nailed his grim thesis to a plot already in his mind, or concocted his plot, which is full of coincidence, accident, and blind luck, to fit his thesis, the book shows a hiatus between means and ends."

Stanley Edgar Hyman, in his 1970 article "Richard Wright Reappraised," dismissed *The Outsider* as "wretched. . . . A kind of spurious display of French existentialism . . . , a mechanical and rigid parallel to *Crime and Punishment,* with Damon as Raskolnikov and Houston as Porfiry, all frozen in stiff postures by cold drafts of theory from Wright's friend Sartre." But Nathan A. Scott, Jr., in *Graduate Comment,* wrote: "For all its melodramatic sensationalism, [*The Outsider*] is an impressive book. Indeed, it is one of the very few American novels of our time that, in admitting into itself a large body of systematic ideas, makes us think that it wants seriously to compete with the major philosophic intelligence of the contemporary period. . . . [*The Outsider*], though it is a very imperfect work, is yet (after *Black Boy*) [Wright's] finest achievement and, as the one emphatically existentialist novel in contemporary American literature, a book that deserves to have commanded a great deal more attention than it has."

Many critics have felt that Wright made more effective use of existentialist ideas in his novella *The Man Who Lived Underground,* a surreal fable about a black man named Fred Daniels, a fugitive who takes refuge from the police in a sewer system. From his underground hiding place he spies on and robs the society from which he is excluded; he comes to understand the absurdity of that society and finds a new identity in his very anonymity and invisibility. When he emerges from his sewer, even though he has been cleared of the crime for which he was originally wanted, he is shot in cold blood by the police. Edward Margolies wrote: "Fred Daniels . . . is not merely the victim of a racist society, . . . he has become by the very nature of his experiences a symbol of all men in that society. . . . The underground man is the essential nature of all men—and is composed of dread, terror, and guilt. . . . Fred Daniels is then Everyman, and his story is very nearly a perfect modern allegory. The Negro who lives in the underground of the city amidst its sewage and slime is not unlike the creature who dwells amidst the sewage of the human heart. And Fred Daniels knows that all of the ways men attempt to persuade themselves that their lives are meaningful and rational are delusions." Hyman declared, "'The Man Who Lived Underground' is a pioneering work in going beyond realism and naturalism to symbolism and fantasy, and is thus perhaps the single most revolutionary work in American Negro literature."

Much of Wright's energy during his years in Paris was devoted to writing nonfiction and to supporting national independence movements in Africa. In 1953 he traveled to the Gold Coast (now Ghana), one of the first British colonies in Africa to be granted self-government. In *Black Power* Wright describes his experiences in Africa and sets forth his ideas for the political future of the continent under black rule. While critics praised Wright's reporting, his political recommendations sparked controversy, especially his advocacy of a militarized and regimented social structure to provide the coherence that tribal traditions, he believed, could not. Joyce Cary, in the *Nation*, remarked: "The author has rejected the party, but his political thinking still belongs to communism. He imagines that violence, cruelty, injustice, and some clever lying can achieve a new civilization. But this is false. They can only produce new forms of oppression." But Cary found that *Black Power*, as reporting, "is a first-class job and gives the best picture I've seen of an extraordinary situation. . . . Wright . . . writes so honestly, so directly as he feels, that he gives material for another book contradicting his own arguments. . . . There are no easy answers in politics. . . . We are still groping our way, and need, above all, the facts. . . . That is why books like this of Wright's are so valuable—so far, that is, as they give facts, and so far as the facts can be distinguished from the bias. Wright is so honest a reporter, so vivid a writer, that this is easily done."

Wright continued to deal with African and Asian nationalism in *The Color Curtain*, a book about the 1955 Bandung conference of Third World nations. Tillman Durdin of the *New York Times Book Review* found *The Color Curtain* "a vivid and illuminating job of reportage," though he thought the book unbalanced in some respects, especially in what he saw as Wright's overemphasis on race as a source of conflict between the new nations and the former colonial powers. Wright wrote on the same theme in the essays in *White Man, Listen!*, linking colonialism and imperialism to racism in Western civilization. Oscar Handlin, in the *New York Times Book Review*, wrote: "This is an indignant book. It is argumentative, belligerent, and often wrong-headed. But it deserves to be read with the utmost seriousness."

In his last novel (*Lawd Today*, which was written in the 1930s and posthumously published), Wright returned to his earliest subject matter, racial conflict in the South. *The Long Dream* is about Fishbelly, the son of a black vice lord in a Southern town. When his father, who was proud of the independence he had won through his illegal enterprises, is destroyed by the equally corrupt white leaders of the town, Fishbelly attempts to take his father's place. He is defeated and framed for a crime he did not commit, and when he is finally released he leaves for France. Charles Shapiro of the *New Republic* called *The Long Dream* "a powerful novel reminiscent of *Native Son*, one that smashes into experience treating it directly, not by analogy. . . . The imperfections are carried away by the power of the story, for the writing sins are of excess and not of cowardice."

Other critics were less pleased, pointing to the same faults that had been found in Wright's earlier work: a tendency toward melodrama and stylistic clumsiness. Granville Hicks of *Saturday Review* noted: "[Wright] displays a preoccupation with scenes of violence that can be understood but cannot be fully defended on literary grounds. His material constantly seems to be getting out of hand, as if he were driven—as I believe he is—by forces beyond his control. I am also troubled by the characterization of Fish Tucker. . . . One ought to feel, as I do not, that the ideas Fish expresses are his ideas and not Richard Wright's. . . . Finally, there is the question of style. Wright has never been a master of polished prose, and 'The Long

Dream' is marred by frequent lapses. . . . The characters are likely to talk in a fashion that is hard to accept . . . [and] the prose [sometimes] becomes pretentious." But Hicks acknowledged the novel's power, observing that "alienation is what Wright has from the first been able to render. He is not basically a realist, although he probably thinks that he is; he is a man who uses, and perhaps is used by, certain powerful symbols. . . . There are few signs of development in his work, but if he has not grown, he has never lost his ability to touch both the emotions and the consciences of his readers."

Wright's reputation ebbed during the 1950s as younger black writers such as James Baldwin and Ralph Ellison rejected his naturalistic approach and the ideological preoccupations of his fiction. But in the 1960s, with the growth of the militant black consciousness movement, there was a resurgence of interest in Wright's work. Wright's place in American literature remains controversial: some contend that his writing is of sociological and historical, rather than literary, interest; his defenders believe that his books of the early 1940s are as important in the American naturalist tradition as they are in the history of black literature, and that Wright is properly ranked with such writers as Theodore Dreiser, James T. Farrell, and John Steinbeck. Warren French wrote that Wright was "a man praised too soon for the wrong reasons and too soon dismissed for more wrong reasons. . . . In death as in life, Wright has been forced to win as a Negro who happened to be a writer the recognition that he desired as a *writer* who happened to be a Negro."

MEDIA ADAPTATIONS: Native Son was adapted again for a film of the same title by Richard Wesley for Cinecom, 1986.

BIOGRAPHICAL/CRITICAL SOURCES:

BOOKS

Baker, Houston A., Jr., *Black Literature in America*, McGraw, 1971.
Baldwin, James, *Notes of a Native Son*, Beacon Press, 1955.
Baldwin, James, *Nobody Knows My Name*, Dial, 1961.
Bigsby, C. W. E., editor, *The Black American Writer*, Volume 1: *Fiction*, Everett/Edwards, 1969.
Contemporary Literary Criticism, Gale, Volume 1, 1973, Volume 3, 1975, Volume 4, 1975, Volume 9, 1978, Volume 14, 1980, Volume 21, 1982.
Dickstein, Morris, *Gates of Eden*, Basic Books, 1977.
Dictionary of Literary Biography Documentary Series, Volume 2, Gale, 1982.
Ellison, Ralph, *Shadow and Act*, Random House, 1945.
Fabre, Michel, *The Unfinished Quest of Richard Wright*, Morrow, 1973.
Fabre, Michel, and Charles Davis, *Richard Wright: The Primary Sources*, G. K. Hall, 1982.
Gayle, Addison, Jr., *Richard Wright: Ordeal of a Native Son*, Anchor Press, 1980.
Littlejohn, David, *Black on White: A Critical Survey of Writing by American Negroes*, Viking, 1966.
Margolies, Edward, *The Art of Richard Wright*, Southern Illinois University Press, 1969.
Webb, Constance, *Richard Wright: A Biography*, Putnam, 1968.
Wright, Richard, *Black Boy: A Record of Childhood and Youth*, Harper, 1945.
Wright, Richard, *American Hunger*, Harper, 1977.

PERIODICALS

Atlantic Monthly, May, 1940, June, 1940, March, 1945, May, 1953, March, 1970.

Ebony, March, 1987.
English Journal, May, 1973.
Graduate Comment, 1964.
Los Angeles Times, December 24, 1986.
Nation, March 16, 1940, April 5, 1941, April 7, 1945, October 16, 1954, October 25, 1958.
National Review, February 3, 1978.
New Republic, April 6, 1938, April 7, 1941, March 12, 1945, February 18, 1957, November 24, 1958, February 13, 1961.
New York Times, December 23, 1986, December 24, 1986, December 26, 1986.
New York Times Book Review, March 3, 1940, March 4, 1945, March 22, 1953, September 26, 1954, March 18, 1956, February 24, 1957, October 26, 1958.
Novel: A Forum on Fiction, spring, 1974.
Saturday Review, March 28, 1953, October 23, 1954, October 18, 1958, March 30, 1963, January 21, 1978.
Saturday Review of Literature, March 2, 1940, March 3, 1945.
Village Voice, July 4, 1977.
Washington Post, January 16, 1987.

*　　*　　*

WRIGHT, Sarah E. 1928-

PERSONAL: Born December 9, 1928, in Wetipquin, Md.; daughter of Willis Charles (an oysterman, barber, farmer, and musician) and Mary Amelia (a homemaker, barber, farmer, and factory worker; maiden name, Moore) Wright; married Joseph G. Kaye (a composer); children: Michael, Shelley. *Education:* Attended Howard University, 1945-49, and Cheyney State Teachers College (now Cheyney State College), 1950-52; also attended writers' workshops at University of Pennsylvania and New School for Social Research.

ADDRESSES: Home—780 West End Ave., Apt. 1-D, New York, N.Y. 10025. *Agent*—Roberta Pryor, International Famous Agency, 1301 Avenue of the Americas, New York, N.Y. 10019.

CAREER: Writer. Worked as teacher, bookkeeper, and office manager.

MEMBER: Authors Guild, Authors League of America, International P.E.N., Harlem Writers Guild (past vice-president).

AWARDS, HONORS: Baltimore Sun Readability Award, 1969, for *This Child's Gonna Live;* McDowell Colony fellowships, 1972 and 1973; New York State Creative Artists Public Service Award for Fiction, and Novelist-Poet Award from Howard University's Institute for the Arts and Humanities' Second National Conference of Afro-American Writers, both 1976.

WRITINGS:

(With Lucy Smith) *Give Me a Child* (poetry; includes Wright's "To Some Millions Who Survive Joseph Mander, Sr."), Kraft Publishing, 1955.
This Child's Gonna Live (novel), Delacorte, 1969.

Work represented in anthologies, including *The Poetry of Black America; The Poetry of the Negro, 1946-1970; Beyond the Blues;* and *Poets of Today.* Contributor of essays, reviews, and poetry to journals.

WORK IN PROGRESS: A sequel to *This Child's Gonna Live;* a collection of verse, tentatively entitled *Why Do I Have Corns on My Feet?;* a screenplay adaptation of *This Child's Gonna Live.*

SIDELIGHTS: Sarah E. Wright distinguished herself as an important writer with her 1955 verse collection *Give Me a Child,* which she wrote with Lucy Smith, and her 1969 novel *This Child's Gonna Live.* Her contributions to *Give Me a Child* reveal a humanist perspective on life. Direct and dramatically charged, Wright's verses address both the despair of the black American and the faith in humanity that oppressed blacks must nonetheless maintain to continue living in a biased society. Wright's best-known poem is probably "To Some Millions Who Survive Joseph Mander, Sr.," which embodies many of her themes. The poem was inspired by the death of a black man who drowned while attempting to save a white person. Wright uses the death to dramatic advantage, asserting that it serves as an inspiring indication of humanism and compassion and urging readers to adopt Mander's compassion.

Two years after publishing *Give Me a Child,* Wright moved to New York City and became involved with various organizations concerning black writers. Among those groups was the Harlem Writers' Guild, in which she was particularly active from 1957 to 1972. Late in that period she wrote *This Child's Gonna Live,* a stylistically daring novel about a black couple's struggle to overcome poverty and strife in a destitute community. Using flashbacks and stream of consciousness, Wright fashions a moving account of desperate lives. Among the most memorable characters in the work is Mariah, the mother who tends three children—all in various stages of malnutrition—while also contending with oppressive economic conditions, a sexist husband, and pious, hypocritical neighbors. For its ambitious techniques and compelling drama, *Give Me a Child* was deemed by critics to be a major literary achievement.

BIOGRAPHICAL/CRITICAL SOURCES:

BOOKS

Dictionary of Literary Biography, Volume 33: *Afro-American Fiction Writers After 1955,* Gale, 1984.
Redmond, Eugene, *Drumvoices: The Mission of Afro-American Poetry,* Doubleday, 1976.
Schraufnagel, Noel, *From Apology to Protest: The Black American Novel,* Everett/Edwards, 1973.

PERIODICALS

Best Sellers, August 1, 1969.
Harper's, December, 1969.
Negro Digest, August, 1969.
New York Times Book Review, June 29, 1969.
Times Literary Supplement, October 16, 1969.

X-Y

XAVIER I
See HORNE, Frank (Smith)

* * *

YARBROUGH, Camille 1938-

PERSONAL: Born in 1938 in Chicago, Ill. *Education:* Studied acting and voice in United States and Australia; attended Roosevelt University.

CAREER: Employed in dance company of Katherine Dunham; dance instructor at Performing Arts Training center at Southern Illinois University, East St. Louis; provided drama workshops at high schools in New York; drama teacher. Actress in plays, including "To Be Young, Gifted, and Black," "Trumpets of the Lord," "Cities in Bezique," and "Sambo"; in films, including "Shaft," 1973; and in television. Singer on tour in United States, Canada, and South America.

WRITINGS:

Cornrows (poems for children), illustrations by Carole Byard, Coward, McCann & Geoghegan, 1979.

Also author of poetry and songs.

MEDIA ADAPTATIONS: A program of Yarbrough's songs and poetry was presented by Nina Simone at Philharmonic Hall, New York City, in 1972.

* * *

YERBY, Frank G(arvin) 1916-

PERSONAL: Born September 5, 1916, in Augusta, Ga.; son of Rufus Garvin (a postal clerk) and Wilhelmina (Smythe) Yerby; married Flora Helen Claire Williams, March 1, 1941 (divorced); married Blanca Call-Perez (now her husband's secretary, translator, researcher, and "general manager"), July 27, 1956; children: (first marriage) Jacques Loring, Nikki Ethlyn, Faune Ellena, Jan Keith. *Education:* Paine College, A.B., 1937; Fisk University, M.A., 1938; graduate study, University of Chicago, 1939. *Politics:* Independent. *Religion:* Agnostic.

ADDRESSES: Home and office—Edificio Torres Blancas, Apt. 710, Avenida de America, 37, Madrid 2, Spain. *Agent*—Owen Laster, William Morris Agency, 1350 Avenue of the Americas, New York, N.Y. 10019.

CAREER: Novelist. Florida Agricultural and Mechanical College (now University), Tallahassee, instructor in English, 1939-40; Southern University and Agricultural and Mechanical College, Baton Rouge, La., instructor in English, 1940-41; Ford Motor Co., Dearborn, Mich., laboratory technician, 1941-44; Ranger (Fairchild) Aircraft, Jamaica, N.Y., chief inspector, Magnaflux, 1944-45; resident of Madrid, Spain, since 1955; also lived in France for an extended period earlier in the fifties.

MEMBER: Authors Guild (New York), Authors League of America, Real Sociedad Hipica Espanola (Madrid), Madrid Country Club.

AWARDS, HONORS: O. Henry Memorial Award, 1944, for best first short story, "Health Card"; Doctor of Letters, Fisk University, 1976, and Doctor of Humane Letters, Paine College, 1977; named honorary citizen of State of Tennessee by Governor's Proclamation, 1977.

WRITINGS:

NOVELS; ORIGINALLY PUBLISHED BY DIAL

The Foxes of Harrow, 1946, reprinted, Dell, 1986.
The Vixens, 1947, reprinted, Dell, 1976.
The Golden Hawk, 1948.
Pride's Castle, 1949.
Floodtide, 1950.
A Woman Called Fancy, 1951.
The Saracen Blade, 1952.
The Devil's Laughter, 1953.
Benton's Row, 1954.
The Treasure of Pleasant Valley, 1955.
Captain Rebel, 1956.
Fairoaks, 1957.
The Serpent and the Staff, 1958.
Jarrett's Jade, 1959.
Gillian, 1960.
The Garfield Honor, 1961.
Griffin's Way, 1962.
The Old Gods Laugh: A Modern Romance, 1964.
An Odor of Sanctity: A Novel of Medieval Moorish Spain, 1965.
Goat Song: A Novel of Ancient Greece, 1968.
Judas My Brother: The Story of the Thirteenth Disciple, 1968.
Speak Now: A Modern Novel, 1969.

The Dahomean: An Historical Novel, 1971 (published in England as *The Man From Dahomey,* Heinemann, 1972).
The Girl from Storyville: A Victorian Novel, 1972.
The Voyage Unplanned, 1974.
Tobias and the Angel, 1975.
A Rose for Ana Maria, 1976.
Hail the Conquering Hero, 1977.
A Darkness at Ingraham's Crest: A Tale of the Slaveholding South, 1979.
Western: A Saga of the Great Plains, 1982.

NOVELS; PUBLISHED BY DOUBLEDAY

Bride of Liberty, 1954.
Devilseed, 1984.
McKenzie's Hundred, 1985.

CONTRIBUTOR

John Fischer and Robert B. Silvers, editors, *Writing in America,* Rutgers University Press, 1960.
Langston Hughes, editor, *The Best Short Stories by Negro Writers: An Anthology from 1899 to the Present,* Little, Brown, 1967.
Darwin T. Turner, editor, *Black American Literature,* C. E. Merrill. 1969.
Gerald Goff, editor, *Voices of Man/This Is Just to Say,* Addison-Wesley, 1969.
Arna Bontemps and Hughes, editors, *The Poetry of the Negro, 1746-1970,* Doubleday, 1970.
Stewart H. Benedict, editor, *Blacklash,* Popular Library, 1970.
Elizabeth White, Joan Wofford, and Edward J. Gordon, editors, *Understanding Literature,* Ginn, 1970.
Ramay K. Singh and Peter Fellowes, editors, *Black Literature in America: A Casebook,* Crowell, 1970.
Conn McAuliffe, editor, *Re-Action,* Boyd & Fraser, 1971.

OTHER

Contributor to *Harper's, Liberty, Collier's France Soir, Le Meuse, La Laterne, Berlin Zeitung,* and numerous other periodicals.

SIDELIGHTS: A prolific novelist who has published thirty-two tales of adventure, Frank G. Yerby has sold over fifty-five million hardback and paperback books in the last forty years. While many of these novels have been best-sellers, their popularity has had little effect on Yerby's critical stature. Since the appearance of his first novel, *The Foxes of Harrow,* in 1946, the author has been routinely—and some say unfairly—slighted by critics. Early in his career, for instance, when Yerby was producing mainstream fiction, black reviewers attacked him for abandoning his race. Those who knew his work, but not his color, accused him of squandering his writing talent on cardboard characters and hackneyed plots. Still others objected to his "over-blown" prose and the way he sensationalized his material. Writing in *The Negro Novel in America,* Robert A. Bone dubbed him "the prince of the pulpsters."

In the face of such criticism, Yerby has steadfastly maintained his integrity: "The only excuse for writing is that you love it beyond measure and beyond reason," he once commented, adding that "to make any compromise whatsoever for the sake of sales or popularity is to join the world's oldest profession. I believe that a writer should have the guts to starve; and that if he doesn't come close to it most of the time, he'd better take a long, hard look at what he's doing. . . . I write only because I have to. What I get out of it financially doesn't come under consideration at all. I write exactly what I feel and think . . . but within that framework I try to give pleasure to the reading public."

Yerby's novels are characterized by colorful language, complex plot lines, and a multiplicity of characters. Hugh M. Gloster calls Yerby's formula "the recipe of Southern historical romance," listing the following ingredients in *Crisis* magazine: "a bold, handsome, rakish, but withal somewhat honorable hero; a frigid, respectable wife; a torrid unrespectable mistress; and usually a crafty, fiendish villain." According to the *Washington Post Book World,* "a typical Yerby plot seems to involve a strong man who has to choose between two women and . . . more-than-generous helpings of revenge, madness, suffering and violence." *Time* sums up his writing as "a crude, shrewd combination of sex, violence, sadism, costuming and cliche."

A common criticism of Yerby's fiction is that he habitually solves apparently insoluble problems through a *deus ex machina,* or stroke of fate. "Despite his skillful tangling and untangling of exciting narratives which mesmerize even many sophisticated readers, Yerby too often depends on contrived endings," writes Darwin T. Turner in *The Black Novelist.* Nick Aaron Ford echoes this sentiment in *Phylon,* writing that in all Yerby's books "there are scenes of great literary power, followed by episodes of incredible adventure, with too little preparation for the miraculous results. . . . This is not to say that Yerby is an inferior writer. He has rich imagination, a talent for vivid expression, ability to create pity and terror, and an understanding of the suffering of the poor and the oppressed. In short, he possesses the qualifications that could make of him a great novelist. But it appears that Yerby is satisfied with popularity and greatness. He says emphatically, 'I think the novelist has a professional obligation to please his reading public.'"

A more sensitive arena is Yerby's treatment of racial issues. The second of four children of a racially mixed couple, Yerby encountered his share of discrimination as a boy. "When I was young," he told *People* magazine, "a bunch of us black kids would get in a fight with white kids and then I'd have to fight with a black kid who got on me for being so light." Though he was an excellent student and, after graduation, secured teaching positions at a number of black universities, Yerby became dissatisfied with what he regarded as the "stifling" atmosphere of these "Uncle Tom factories" and abandoned academia for a wartime factory job in Detroit. His first published fiction, which earned him an O. Henry Memorial Award in 1944, was a bitter story of racial injustice called "Health Card." It was the last black theme he would directly address in his fiction for almost thirty years.

Following "Health Card," Yerby published a string of historical novels with Anglo-Saxon protagonists, leading Hugh M. Gloster to surmise that Yerby "gained his laurels by focusing upon white rather than Negro characters. Peformance—and not pigmentation—has been the basis of his success." Yerby staunchly defends his focus, explaining that "the novelist hasn't any right to inflict on the public his private ideas on politics, religion or race. If he wants to preach he should go on the pulpit." Later he stated: "My mother was Scotch-Irish, a grandparent was an Indian; I've far more Irish blood than Negro. I simply insist on remaining a member of the human race. I don't think a writer's output should be dictated by a biological accident. It happens there are many things I know far better than the race problem." Yerby's personal solution to problems of discrimination was to leave the country.

He moved from the United States to Spain in 1955 and has remained there ever since.

Despite his contempt for didactic fiction, Yerby does address racial issues indirectly in several novels, some critics say. "In his earliest novels, the racial problems are employed peripherally, almost perfunctorily, and occupy little space or overt interest in the novel," writes Jack B. Moore in the *Journal of Popular Culture*. "None the less Yerby's racial attitudes pervade these early novels of the South, sometimes in obvious and sometimes in disguised fashion." Darwin T. Turner sees Yerby's position manifested in "the theme of the outcast who, as in existentialist literature, pits his will against a hostile universe. By intelligence and courage, he proves himself superior to a society which rejects him because of his alien, inferior, or illegitimate birth."

This theme surfaces in his first novel, *The Foxes of Harrow*, a lush southern romance which traces the fortunes of the dashing young Stephen Fox in his rise from poverty to great wealth. It is "a good, old-fashioned obese historical novel of the Old South that seems, more than once, to be haunted by the affluent ghost of Scarlett O'Hara." according to the *New York Times*. While acknowledging Yerby's ability to hold the reader captive with his fast-paced plotting and vivid prose, many critics dismiss the book as socially insignificant melodrama. *New Yorker* contributor Edmund Wilson, for instance, notes that Yerby "has packed everything in—passion, politics, creole society, sex, the clash of races, and war—but he never captures the faintest flutter of the breath of life." In N. L. Rothman's view, "the book rings throughout with colorful passions and the words to match. It is not a historical novel— for that must have some reality in it," he continues in the *Saturday Review of Literature*, "but it is a good example of the technicolored fantasies that have been passing as such of late." In recent years, Yerby himself has belittled the work, telling *People* magazine that *The Foxes of Harrow* comprises "every romantic cliche in history."

The novel's literary shortcomings had no effect on its enormous popularity. With sales of over two million copies, *The Foxes of Harrow* became one of the hottest titles of the decade. It was translated into at least twelve languages, reprinted in several national magazines, and made into a lucrative movie starring Rex Harrison and Maureen O'Hara.

Though Yerby despised the film adaptation, he was pleased with his novel's popular acceptance, and he continued to work the vein of historical fiction in future books. His next novel, *The Vixens*, utilized research material he hadn't been able to incorporate into his first book. And he followed *The Vixens* with a string of other southern romances, set for the most part in the nineteenth century. With *The Golden Hawk*, in 1948, Yerby turned to picaresque adventure in other lands and earlier centuries. And his research, which had been admittedly careless in his first novels, became meticulous.

While Yerby's novels of the 1950s and 1960s qualify as popular fiction, they also reflect some serious concerns. In addition to escapism, they "exhibit another dimension, disregarded by the readers who lament Yerby's failure to write an historical novel and by the others who condemn his refusal to write an overtly polemical treatise on the plight of the American Negro," according to Darwin T. Turner in *The Black Novelist*. "Ideas—bitter ironies, caustic debunkings, painful gropings for meaning—writhe behind the soap-facade of his fiction." And, in 1971, after protesting his indifference to racial issues for many, many years, Yerby addressed the matter directly in *The Dahomean*, his novel of Black Africa.

Set in the nineteenth century, *The Dahomean* traces the life of Nyasanu/Hwesu as he advances in position from a chief's son to governor of an entire province, only to be sold into American slavery by two jealous relatives. "At the same time, his rise and fall illustrates the customs and folkways of his country: the rites of manhood and marriage; the feudal system; war," according to the *New York Times Book Review*. "Virtues of the book," says Turner, writing in *Black World*, "are the presentation of an exciting and illuminating history of Black people and a determined focus of the story on a single Black hero. But there is more. In *The Dahomean*, Yerby's strength reveals itself to best advantage and even his former weaknesses become strengths.... Yerby is at his best when he envelops his plot with a history he has unearthed painstakingly and with a serious or satirical but always devastating debunking of historical legends and myths. That achievement is superior in *The Dahomean*, not so much in the presentation of historical facts as in the presentation of a people and a culture."

In a prefatory note to the novel, Yerby explains that part of his reason for writing the book was "to correct, so far as possible, the Anglo-Saxon reader's historical perspective" on black history. By portraying the Dahomean culture in all its rich complexity, Yerby dispells the myth of a totally primitive Africa, even hinting at times that the tribal cultures "sometimes surpassed in their subtlety, their complexity, their dignity the ones to which the slaves were brought," in the *Best Sellers* critic's words. But in depicting the cruelties that certain tribesmen perpetrated on their black brothers, including selling them into slavery, Yerby also shatters the illusion that blacks are inherently superior morally. What Yerby seems to be suggesting, Turner maintains, is that "the differences between people do not stem from a difference of blood, but from a difference of opportunity and power."

Hailed by several reviewers as Yerby's masterpiece, *The Dahomean* also settled an old score for the author, as he explained: "I am much more relaxed about racial matters, that increased tranquility being due in part to the fact that *The Dahomean* received (with one lone exception) rave notices from the critics. Thereafter, reviewers seemed to have waked up to what I was actually writing as distinct from and opposed to 1) what I used to write; and 2) what they thought I was writing. In short, I seem to have succeeded in changing many critics' minds. Pleasantly surprising was the high praise bestowed upon this novel by the critics of the South African papers. Needless to say, black critics immediately removed me from the list of 'non-conductors' and welcomed me back into the fold like a sinner redeemed by faith."

Yerby postulates that critical reaction to his books reflects the reviewers' biases: "Those who confuse literature with sexual morality damn them; those wise enough, emotionally mature enough to realize that the two things have practically nothing to do with each other, generally like them very much indeed." Since the publication of *The Dahomean*, Yerby admits, "two things have been of considerable comfort to me. First is the fact that I am no longer accused of colorful, purplish overwriting. And the second is the dawning realization that fifty-five million readers in eighty-two countries and twenty-three languages (who have bought and paid for my novels) are not necessarily all idiots. Strangely enough (or perhaps not so strangely after all) the degree of appreciation for a novel of mine is directly increased by the degree of knowledge the reader has of the subject. In other words, people who know the themes I've written about either by reason of having lived through them, or deeply and professionally studied them, find no fault with my novels. I am praised by experts, attacked by—well, let's be kind and call them amateurs.''

Ultimately, however, critical reaction is incidental. Yerby, who in recent years has turned increasingly to subjects he finds personally—rather than commercially—appealing, works from compulsion. As he told *People* magazine, ''I won't stop writing as long as there's breath in me.''

MEDIA ADAPTATIONS: The Foxes of Harrow was filmed by Twentieth Century-Fox in 1947.

BIOGRAPHICAL/CRITICAL SOURCES:

BOOKS

Bone, Robert A., *The Negro Novel in America,* Yale University Press, revised edition, 1965.
Breit, Harvey, *The Writer Observed,* World Publishing, 1956.
Contemporary Literary Criticism, Gale, Volume I, 1973, Volume VII, 1977, Volume XXII, 1982.
Hemenway, Robert, *The Black Novelist,* C. E. Merrill, 1970.
Yerby, Frank G., *The Dahomean: An Historical Novel,* Dial, 1971.

PERIODICALS

Best Sellers, February 15, 1968, January 1, 1969, September 1, 1971, November 1982.
Black World, February, 1972.
Book Week, February 10, 1946, April 27, 1947.
Crisis, January, 1948.
Journal of Popular Culture, spring, 1975.
Los Angeles Times Book Review, November 7, 1982.
Negro Digest, July, 1968, April, 1969.
Newsweek, November 30, 1959.
New Yorker, February 9, 1946, April 24, 1948.
New York Herald Tribune Book Review, May 4, 1947, June 12, 1949, October 22, 1950, July 15, 1951, September 21, 1952, October 4, 1953, November 14, 1954, December 19, 1954, October 14, 1956, September 22, 1957.
New York Times, February 10, 1946, May 2, 1948, May 15, 1949, September 10, 1950, May 6, 1951, April 6, 1952, November 15, 1953, December 5, 1954, September 23, 1956, September 8, 1957, October 12, 1958.
New York Times Book Review, November 10, 1968, October 17, 1971, September 17, 1972.
People, March 30, 1981.
Phylon: The Atlanta University Review of Race and Culture, Volume XXV, number 1, 1954.
Publishers Weekly, May 10, 1971, June 4, 1982.
Saturday Review, May 10, 1952, October 27, 1956, August 24, 1957.
Saturday Review of Literature, February 23, 1946, May 8, 1948, June 18, 1949, September 30, 1950, June 23, 1951.
Time, May 5, 1947, September 4, 1950, April 7, 1952, November 23, 1953, November 29, 1954.
Times Literary Supplement, March 27, 1959.
Washington Post Book World, August 15, 1982.

*   *   *

YOUNG, Al(bert James)   1939-

PERSONAL: Born May 31, 1939, in Ocean Springs, Miss.; son of Albert James (a professional musician and auto worker) and Mary (Campbell) Young; married Arline June Belch (a free-lance artist), October 8, 1963; children: Michael James. *Education:* Attended University of Michigan, 1957-61; University of California, Berkeley, B.A., 1969. *Politics:* Independent. *Religion:* ''Free Thinker.''

ADDRESSES: Home—514 Bryant St., Palo Alto, Calif. 94301. *Agent*—Lynn Nesbit, International Creative Management, 40 West 57th St., New York, N.Y. 10019.

CAREER: Free-lance musician playing guitar and flute, and singing professionally throughout the United States, 1957-64; KJAZ-FM, Alameda, Calif., disc jockey, 1961-65; San Francisco Museum of Art, San Francisco, Calif., writing instructor, 1967-69; Berkeley Neighborhood Youth Corps, Berkeley, Calif., writing instructor and language consultant, 1968-69; Stanford University, Stanford, Calif., Edward H. Jones Lecturer in creative writing, 1969-74; screenwriter for Laser Films, New York City, 1972, Stigwood Corporation, London, England, and New York City, 1972, Verdon Productions, Hollywood, Calif., 1976, First Artists Ltd., Burbank, Calif., 1976-77, and Universal Studios, Hollywood, Calif., 1979; director, Associated Writing Programs, 1979—. Writer in residence, University of Washington, Seattle, 1981-82. Vice-president, Yardbird Publishing Cooperative. Lecturer and speaker at numerous universities throughout the country.

MEMBER: American Association of University Professors, Authors League of America, Authors Guild, Writers Guild of America, Committee of Small Magazine Editors and Publishers, Sigma Delta Pi.

AWARDS, HONORS: Wallace E. Stegner fellowship in creative writing, Stanford University, 1966-67; National Endowment for the Arts grants, 1968, 1969, 1975; Joseph Henry Jackson Award, San Francisco Foundation, 1969, for *Dancing: Poems;* National Arts Council awards for poetry and editing, 1968-70; California Association of Teachers of English special award, 1973; Guggenheim fellowship, 1974; Outstanding Book of the Year citation, *New York Times,* 1980, for *Ask Me Now;* Pushcart Prize, Pushcart Press, 1980; Before Columbus Foundation award, 1982.

WRITINGS:

NOVELS

Snakes: A Novel, Holt, 1970.
Who Is Angelina?, Holt, 1975.
Sitting Pretty, Holt, 1976.
Ask Me Now, McGraw-Hill, 1980.

POETRY

Dancing: Poems, Corinth Books, 1969.
The Song Turning Back into Itself, Holt, 1971.
Some Recent Fiction, San Francisco Book Company, 1974.
Geography of the Near Past, Holt, 1976.
The Blues Don't Change: New and Selected Poems, Louisiana State University Press, 1982.

EDITOR

James P. Girard, *Changing All Those Changes,* Yardbird Wing, 1976.
William Lawson, *Zeppelin Coming Down,* Yardbird Wing, 1976.
(With Ishmael Reed) *Yardbird Lives!,* Grove Press, 1978.
(And contributor) Ishmael Reed, editor, *Calafia: The California Poetry,* Y'Bird Books, 1979.

CONTRIBUTOR

Wallace Stegner and Richard Scowcroft, editors, *Stanford Short Stories 1968*, Stanford University Press, 1968.
The Heath Introduction to Poetry, Heath, 1975.
John Ciardi and Miller Williams, editors, *How Does a Poem Mean?*, Houghton, 1976.

OTHER

Bodies and Soul: Musical Memoirs, Creative Arts Book Co., 1981.
Kinds of Blue: Musical Memoirs, Creative Arts Book Co., 1984.
Things Ain't What They Used to Be: Musical Memoirs, Creative Arts Book Co., 1987.

Also author of screenplays, *Nigger,* and *Sparkle,* both 1972. Contributor of articles, short stories, and reviews to *Audience, California Living, New Times, Rolling Stone, Evergreen Review, Encore, Journal of Black Poetry,* and others. Founding editor, *Loveletter,* 1966-68; co-editor, *Yardbird Reader,* 1972-76; contributing editor, *Changes,* 1972—, and *Umoja,* 1973—; co-editor and co-publisher, *Quilt,* 1981—.

SIDELIGHTS: American poet and novelist Al Young's art destroys "glib stereotypes of black Americans," states William J. Harris in the *Dictionary of Literary Biography,* presenting an image of the black person in "the American tradition of the singular individual." "Not surprisingly," the contributor continues, "his work illustrates the complexity and richness of contemporary Afro-American life through a cast of highly individualized black characters. Since he is a gifted stylist and a keen observer of the human comedy, he manages to be both a serious and an entertaining author." In his oeuvre, says Harris, Young explores themes of "the beauty of black music and speech, the importance of family love, the dignity and romance of vocation, the quest for identity and the need to come to terms with one's life."

Snakes, Young's first novel, is the story of MC, a young musician whose successful jazz single, called "Snakes," meets with a modest success in Detroit, his home town. Eventually, he leaves home for New York in order to start a career as a jazz musician. Like many of Young's characters MC is black, but the author's interest in him lies not only in his blackness, but also in his humanity; as Harris declares, "although it is important that MC . . . is undeniably black, it is equally important that he is young and trying to come to terms with who he is." MC faces, among other problems, the bleakness of his Detroit environment, but, as L. E. Sissman points out in the *New Yorker, Snakes* "offers some alternative to hopelessness." Sissman suggests that MC's pursuit of jazz as a vocation "gives his life purpose; it palliates the terrors and disjunctures of the ghetto; it restores his adolescence to a semblance of normal adolescent joy and hope." And Douglass Bolling of *Negro American Literature Forum* concludes that "*Snakes* is clearly a work which seeks to reach out for the universals of human experience rather than to restrict itself to Black protest or Black aesthetic considerations."

Similar statements are made about the main characters of *Who Is Angelina?* and *Sitting Pretty;* according to Jacqueline Adams in the *Christian Science Monitor,* Angelina "represents that classical Everyman figure struggling against conformity, commercialized sentiments, crime, life's insanities and riddles to find peace, happiness, security, honesty, love, beauty, soul." Sidney J. Prettymon, the philosophical janitor and protagonist of *Sitting Pretty,* is, in the opinion of Mel Watkins in the *New York Times Book Review,* "the natural man, with no pretenses, just trying to live with as little chaos as possible and to enjoy the simple pleasures of growing old." Even Durwood Knight, the ex-basketball player hero of *Ask Me Now,* says James A. Steck in the *San Francisco Review of Books,* discovers "how 'you learn everything there is to know about life no matter what line of endeavour you take up.'"

In his early career Young performed as a jazz musician, and his fascination with these musical rhythms permeates his writing. Harris states that "dancing and music figure as central metaphors in [Young's] poetry," and his novels, which are also "rich in black language." Not only is music the subject of *Snakes,* notes *Paunch*'s Neil Schmitz, but "the music heard in [the novel] is the music of voices speaking." "It is this elusive sound," he continues, "which hangs Grail-like before MC's imagination throughout *Snakes,* which figures finally as the novel's unifying theme." He concludes,"MC's quest for the right language in his music is a reflection of Young's discovery of the music in his language." Dean Flower remarks in the *Hudson Review,* "I don't know of any other black novel where the vernacular is used so well [as in *Sitting Pretty*], unless it be in Young's own *Snakes* and *Who Is Angelina?*" He is persuaded that "the beauty of Young's vernacular method is that it brings alive a thoroughly engaging human being"; and Sheldon Frank of the *National Observer* notices that *Sitting Pretty* "talks music all the time." "In sum," concludes Harris, "Al Young has captured much of the beauty and complexity of black life and black speech in his impressive and extensive oeuvre."

BIOGRAPHICAL/CRITICAL SOURCES:

BOOKS

Chapman, Abraham, editor, *New Black Voices,* New American Library, 1972.
Contemporary Literary Criticism, Volume 19, Gale, 1981.
Dictionary of Literary Biography, Volume 33: *Afro-American Fiction Writers after 1955,* Gale, 1984.
O'Brien, John, editor, *Interviews with Black Writers,* Liveright, 1973.
Rush, Theresa Gunnels, Carol Fairbanks Myers, and Esther Spring Arata, *Black American Writers Past and Present: A Biographical and Bibliographical Dictionary,* Scarecrow Press, 1975.

PERIODICALS

California Living (Sunday Supplement of *San Francisco Chronicle/Examiner*), May 3, 1970.
Christian Science Monitor, March 6, 1975, December 7, 1984.
Greenfield Review, summer/fall, 1982.
Hudson Review, summer, 1976.
Kite, June 9, 1976.
MELUS, winter, 1978.
National Observer, July 24, 1976.
Negro American Literature Forum, summer, 1974.
New Yorker, July 11, 1970, August 4, 1980.
New York Times, January 23, 1975.
New York Times Book Review, May 17, 1970, February 9, 1975, May 23, 1976, July 6, 1980, January 24, 1987.
Paunch, February, 1972.
Peninsula Magazine, June, 1976.
Poetry, May, 1977.
San Francisco Review of Books, August, 1979, September, 1980.
Saturday Review, August 22, 1970, March 20, 1976.

Stanford Observer, March, 1970.
Time, June 29, 1970.
Times Literary Supplement, July 30, 1971.
Washington Post Book World, May 17, 1970.
Yale Review, June, 1970.

*   *   *

YOUNG, Whitney M(oore), Jr.   1921-1971

PERSONAL: Born July 31, 1921, in Lincoln Ridge, Ky.; died March 11, 1971, of a heart attack while swimming, in Lagos, Nigeria; buried in Ferncliff Cemetery, Hartsdale, N.Y.; son of Whitney Moore (a headmaster of a preparatory school) and Laura (a teacher; maiden name, Ray) Young; married Margaret Buckner, January 2, 1944; children: Marcia Elaine, Lauren Lee. *Education:* Kentucky State College, B.S., 1941; Massachusetts Institute of Technology, graduate student, 1942-44; University of Minnesota, M.A. in Social Work, 1947. *Religion:* Unitarian.

CAREER: Rosenwald High School, Madisonville, Ky., instructor, coach, and assistant principal, 1941-42; Urban League, St. Paul, Minn., director of industrial relations and vocational guidance, 1947-50; College of St. Catherine, St. Paul, Minn., lecturer, 1949; Urban League, Omaha, Neb., executive secretary, 1950-53; University of Nebraska, Lincoln, School of Social Work, instructor, 1950-54; Creighton University, Omaha, Neb., instructor, 1951-53; Atlanta University, Atlanta, Ga., School of Social Work, dean, 1954-61; National Urban League, New York, N.Y., executive director, 1961-71.

Co-sponsor of the August, 1963, March on Washington. Co-founder and co-chairman of the Council for United Civil Rights Leadership; co-founder of the Urban Coalition. Former director of Federal Reserve Bank of New York. Member of national planning committee, White House Conference on Children and Youth, 1960. Member of President's Committee on Youth Employment, President's Committee on Equal Opportunity in the Armed Forces, President's Committee on Law Enforcement and Administration of Justice, Advisory Committee on Juvenile Delinquency, U.S. Department of Justice, Advisory Committee, Bureau of Public Assistance and Children's Bureau, U.S. Department of Health, Education, and Welfare, national advisory council, U.S. Office of Economic Opportunity. Member of national advisory council on Community Service Activities, AFL-CIO, and of advisory boards of the Rockefeller Foundation, Urban Coalition, Urban Institute, and Columbia University School of Social Work. Trustee, Eleanor Roosevelt Memorial Foundation and John F. Kennedy Library Corporation. *Military service:* U.S. Army, 1941-45; Army Specialist Training Program, 1941-44; served in England and France with Anti-Aircraft Artillery Group, 369th Regiment, 1944-45; became first sergeant.

MEMBER: National Association of Social Workers (former second vice-president), National Social Welfare Assembly (member, executive committee), National Conference of Social Welfare (NAACP; former president), National Association for the Advancement of Colored People (NAACP; former president of Georgia state branch), National Association of Practical Nurse Education (former director), Alpha Phi Alpha.

AWARDS, HONORS: Florina Lasker Award for outstanding achievement in field of social work, 1959; Outstanding Alumni Award, University of Minnesota, 1960; grant from Rockefeller Foundation, 1960-61; LL.D. from Agriculture and Technical College of North Carolina, 1961, Tuskegee Institute, 1963,

Princeton University, 1967, Harvard University, 1968, University of San Francisco, 1968, and Washington University, 1970; Charles Spurgeon Johnson Award, Fisk University, 1967; Golden Key Award, National Education Association, 1968; Outstanding Service Award, U.S. Jaycees, 1969; Medal of Freedom, 1969; Four Freedoms Award, Four Freedoms Foundation, 1970; Christopher Book Award, Christophers, 1970, for *Beyond Racism: Building an Open Society*.

WRITINGS:

To Be Equal, McGraw, 1964.
Beyond Racism: Building an Open Society, McGraw, 1969.

Also author of *Status of the Negro Community*, 1959, *Integration: The Role of Labor Education*, 1959, and *Intergroup Relations as a Challenge to Social Work Practice*, 1960. Co-author of *A Second Look: The Negro Citizen in Atlanta*, 1958. Writer of column "To Be Equal," which was carried in thirty-five daily and weekly newspapers.

SIDELIGHTS: As director of the National Urban League and member of several Presidential Commissions, Whitney M. Young, Jr., worked to increase civil rights for blacks through more traditional Establishment channels, a method which often brought criticism from other blacks in the civil rights movement. A personal acquaintance of such influential business figures as Henry Ford II, chairman of the Ford Motor Company, and an advisor with direct access to President Lyndon Johnson, Young used his contacts to increase the budget and effectiveness of the Urban League and secure agreements from business to open up the industrial job market to blacks. But despite his success in working with business and government, Young worried "about his reputation in the black community," as Tom Buckley remarked in a 1970 *New York Times Magazine* article. "The white media do in fact usually describe Young as a moderate, responsible black leader, and it listens to what he says with respect. Young is certainly responsible and moderate . . . but he leads few blacks."

Although during his tenure at the Urban League Young opened thirty-five new chapters, moved it into the urban slums where it was needed, and increased the annual budget from $300,000 in 1961 to almost $35 million in 1971, blacks often accused Young and the league of catering to the white Establishment. As Buckley related, "the Urban League's benefactors are almost entirely white, and this puts Young in a difficult position with his own race." Despite all his work to help blacks economically, many civil rights leaders felt Young's Urban League was not political enough, even though with its tax-exempt status the league was required to stay out of the political arena. Because "angry and cynical blacks, the young in particular, . . . tend to believe that the league is the prisoner of its benefactors," commented Buckley, ". . . and because he is widely regarded as incorrigibly middle class in outlook," Young was often the target of personal attacks accusing him of abandoning the principles of the black movement.

Young responded to these charges in Buckley's article: "Nobody who's working for black people is a moderate. . . . We're *all* militants in different ways. I can't afford the luxury of a completely dogmatic position that says, 'I won't make any compromises,' because I'm dealing with the real world. . . . Somebody's got to deal in a very practical way with the issues that are before them, and there's nobody else who's got the entree with the decision makers." Young's practical way was to work with the people who could most directly affect the economic fortune of blacks—the leaders of government and industry.

From the beginning of his career, Young liked to describe himself as "a mediator between blacks and whites, a power broker, a social engineer, a man with a foot in both caps, as it were," related Buckley. Young first discovered his mediating abilities during World War II, in an all-black engineering company that was officered by whites. "The young blacks weren't reconciled to second-class status," Young told Buckley, and subsequently refused to obey the officers. "Anyhow, the officers could see their lieutenant's bars, captain's bars, going down the drain. So they set down with me to try to straighten things out. That was the beginning of my work in that field—being an intermediary between whites and blacks." Even at that time, Young's fellows accused him of being overly accommodating to white authority, but since no one else would negotiate with the officers, Young stuck it out in order to benefit both sides.

At the time of his death, Young had hoped to join the Nixon administration as an "intermediary between the White House and black America, if he could be guaranteed direct access to the President and the Cabinet, and could consult with other black leaders in drawing up an agenda for action," described Buckley. Failing in this attempt, he began openly criticizing the administration as "consistent only in its inconsistency" toward blacks, and spoke out for ending the war in Vietnam, claiming it siphoned away money needed for social reforms.

Nevertheless, Young still had hopes for his "domestic Marshall plan," designed to help blacks recover from the economic inequalities perpetrated by white America over the course of three centuries. "I haven't lost the hope that right will win out," Buckley quoted him as saying, "but will it happen soon enough?" As *Time* reported in his obituary, Young once said of his place in the civil rights movement: "I'm not anxious to be the loudest voice, or the most popular. But I would like to think that, at a crucial moment, I was an effective voice of the voiceless, an effective hope of the hopeless."

BIOGRAPHICAL/CRITICAL SOURCES:

PERIODICALS

New York Times Book Review, June 15, 1969.
New York Times Magazine, September 20, 1970.
Saturday Review, January 24, 1970.

SOUND RECORDINGS

Black Americans: Whitney M. Young, Jr., Encyclopedia Americana/CBS News Audio Resource Library, 1973.
Race Relations and Community, Jeffrey Norton, 1974.

OBITUARIES:

PERIODICALS

Newsweek, March 22, 1971.
New York Times, March 12, 1971.
Time, March 22, 1971.